# 2001 Formula One Annual

Edited by Nigel Mansell

E·PRESS

# 2001 Formula One Annual

2001 Formula One Annual
First published in Great Britain in 2001
by European Press Limited

©Text: European Press Limited
©Photographs: Rainer Schlegelmilch,
Sutton Motorsport Images, Phipps/Sutton Library,
European Press Library, Cahier Archive

Printed in Germany and the United Kingdom
by Godfrey Lang Limited and Vertec Printing Limited

Colour reproduction by:
Graphic Facilities Limited

European Press Limited
8-16 Great New Street
Holborn, London
England  EC4A 3BN

A CIP catalogue record for this book is
available from the British Library
ISBN 0-9541368

Distributed by:
Virgin Publishing
Thames Wharf Studios,
Rainville Road, London

©European Press Limited

Editor-in-Chief: Nigel Mansell
Contributing Editors: Gerald Donaldson,
David Tremayne, Peter Collins, Jane Nottage,
Caroline Reid, Nick Hall
Technical Editors: John Barnard, Giorgio Piola
Art Editors: Jo Wardle, Stewart Wheeler, Cassandra Lear
Text Editors: Alan Rodney, Shelley White, Paul Jones
Publishing Executives: Tom Rubython,
Clive Greaves, Alex Wooff
Logistics: David Peett, Raj Dhawan
Production Editor: Aaron Guiney
Publishing Assistants: Ania Grzesik, Rowena Cremer-Price
Picture Editor: Simon Galloway
Photographers: Graham Fudger, Paul Sutton,
James Bearne, Mark Sutton, Clement Marin,
Russell Batchelor, Boris Schlegelmilch

2001 WORLD CHAMPION
**Michael Schumacher**

# Formula 1™

**SECTION ONE**

6  Publisher's Acknowledgements

9  Editor-in-Chief's Foreword

10  2001 Formula One Scoreboard

12  News Review of 2001

**SECTION TWO**
**2001 DRIVERS**

32  2001 Drivers' Record

34  Michael Schumacher

40  David Coulthard

44  Rubens Barrichello

48  Ralf Schumacher

52  Mika Häkkinen

56  Juan Pablo Montoya

60  Jacques Villeneuve

62  Nick Heidfeld

64  Jarno Trulli

66  Kimi Räikkönen

68  Giancarlo Fisichella

70  Eddie Irvine

74  Heinz-Harald Frentzen

76  Olivier Panis

78  Jean Alesi

80  Pedro de la Rosa

82  Jenson Button

84  Jos Verstappen

86  Ricardo Zonta

88  Luciano Burti

90  Enrique Bernoldi

91  Tarso Marques

92  Fernando Alonso

93  Gaston Mazzacane

94  Tomas Enge

95  Alex Yoong

# CONTENTS

## SECTION THREE
## 2001 TEAM REVIEWS

| | | | |
|---|---|---|---|
| 99 | Ferrari | 253 | Benetton |
| 125 | McLaren | 281 | Jaguar |
| 151 | Williams | 307 | Prost |
| 177 | Sauber | 333 | Arrows |
| 203 | Jordan | 359 | Minardi |
| 229 | BAR | | |

## SECTION FOUR
## 2001 RACE REVIEWS

| | | | |
|---|---|---|---|
| 386 | Australian Grand Prix | 458 | French Grand Prix |
| 394 | Malaysian Grand Prix | 466 | British Grand Prix |
| 402 | Brazilian Grand Prix | 474 | German Grand Prix |
| 410 | San Marino Grand Prix | 482 | Hungarian Grand Prix |
| 418 | Spanish Grand Prix | 490 | Belgian Grand Prix |
| 426 | Austrian Grand Prix | 498 | Italian Grand Prix |
| 434 | Monoco Grand Prix | 506 | United States Grand Prix |
| 442 | Canadian Grand Prix | 514 | Japanese Grand Prix |
| 450 | European Grand Prix | | |

## SECTION FIVE
## 2001 TECHNICAL REVIEWS

| | | | |
|---|---|---|---|
| 524 | 2001 Rules and Regulations | 544 | European Grand Prix |
| 528 | Australian Grand Prix | 546 | French Grand Prix |
| 531 | Malaysian Grand Prix | 548 | British Grand Prix |
| 532 | Brazilian Grand Prix | 550 | German Grand Prix |
| 534 | San Marino Grand Prix | 554 | Hungarian Grand Prix |
| 536 | Spanish Grand Prix | 556 | Belgian Grand Prix |
| 538 | Austrian Grand Prix | 558 | Italian Grand Prix |
| 540 | Monoco Grand Prix | 560 | United States Grand Prix |
| 542 | Canadian Grand Prix | 562 | Japanese Grand Prix |

## SECTION SIX

| | |
|---|---|
| 571 | Statistics 1950-2000 |

## SECTION SEVEN

| | |
|---|---|
| 668 | Index |

# Acknowledgements

## By Tom Rubython
## Publisher

However, he was in for a shock. He took the book to WH Smith and came away with an order for 8,000. Another 12,000 were quickly sold to bookshops in the UK. America came in for 10,000 and pre-publication readers ordered another 1,000 direct. Then the big markets of Canada and Australia took another 8,000 and suddenly it was in profit. Then India ordered 1,000 copies and we knew we were there. Add in the hundreds of orders for anything between 100 and 600 from the various countries that follow Formula One and 45,000 copies were soon sold.

On that basis it was a huge commercial success and, including a modest amount of advertising, it was soon a profitable publication despite the high production costs and freight charges to ship annuals by airfreight all over the world.

In the end, every one of the 45,000 was pre-sold and it is likely there will be none left by July 2002.

From the final green light at the end of July it has been a huge amount of work for a team of two-dozen people. Firstly the art team led by Jo Wardle and Stewart Wheeler spent many hours designing the publication from scratch and along with their colleague Cassandra Lear turning the concept into reality. Simon Galloway researched far and wide to secure the photographs that would perfectly illustrate the articles and reports.

Clive Greaves and David Peett went to work on the sales and Raj Dhawan sorted the logistics of shipping 45,000 books from Munich to 60 countries by 15th November to be on sale well in time for Christmas.

The writers and researchers went to work led by Caroline Reid. The sub editors Alan Rodney, Shelley White and Paul Jones forgot about any life they had planned for September and October and simply got down to it.

My thanks go out to them, without whom this book would not have been possible. My thanks also to Bernie Ecclestone for allowing it to happen and to Max Mosley for authorising the use of the FIA's statistics. And to all the advertisers who have supported us which enables us to get the price per copy down to a reasonable value.

And finally to Michael Schumacher and Jean Todt, the world championship winners, plus all the teams and drivers for providing the spectacle each year that we call Formula One.

The 2001 Formula One Annual was conceived six months ago. It was too good an opportunity to miss to use properly all the material that had been collected in a season and the knowledge of the contributors to our sister magazine.

But its conception was not a smooth ride. When all the information was added up that needed to be included to make a proper season review, it came to 700 pages. Then someone said no annual would be complete without a proper statistical section. That was another 100 pages.

The chairman of European Press Ltd – the publishers– Clive Greaves put his foot down and said that it was uncommercial. By clever packaging of the material it was reduced down to 672 pages and the chairman still ruled it uncommercial.

I can tell you there were many late-night rows between publishing director, Alex Wooff, and the chairman, with the chairman insisting on a profit and the publishing director arguing for a top quality product for readers.

It's the classic dilemma in any publishing company between commerce and creation.

Finally there was a compromise. The chairman agreed we could absorb a loss for the first year and peace reigned, but not before he got some firm promises of sales numbers for the 2002 Annual.

Tom Rubython
19th October 2001
Holborn
London

# TOBACCO SERIOUSLY DAMAGES HEALTH

**Source: EC Council Directive (89-622-EEC)**

THIRST

# TOBACCO SERIOUSLY DAMAGES HEALTH
**Source: EC Council Directive (89-622-EEC)**

# Foreword

## By Nigel Mansell OBE
## Editor-in-Chief

The year 2001 has been a significant one in the history of Formula One. It has been a season of uplifting highs and troubling lows.

In 2001 Michael Schumacher was confirmed as one of the all-time greats. The Ferrari star has been the most dominant world champion since I took my own title back in 1992. The records have crumbled beneath his feet. The achievement of retaining both world titles is incredible, for the driver and his team.

Ferrari has had a fantastic year. Schumacher is a prime motivator and the combination of him, Ross Brawn, Rory Byrne, Nigel Stepney and Jean Todt – the man who keeps it all together – is one of the most fantastic comings-together of skill and management in the history of Formula One. Schumacher and Ferrari are worthy champions.

There have been some great races and spectacular drives. It was phenomenal the way the Ferraris battled back to take the top two positions in Malaysia, after spinning into the gravel trap together and suffering an atrocious mixed-up double pitstop. Mika Häkkinen's two victories showed that there is still life in the Finn yet, although David Coulthard has proved with a series of neat drives in the first half of the season that, given the opportunity, he too can be a championship challenger. His taking of pole position in the dying moments of Saturday afternoon in Monte Carlo was one of the highlights of the season for me and for him. And wasn't it great to see Jaguar getting its first podium finish in Monte Carlo.

On a technical level, 2001 saw the return of legalised electronic driver aids. I'm no fan of electronic driver aids. There is now a general lack of overtaking, which I feel traction control has made worse. I am not sure what the FIA's strategy is in allowing two-way telemetry in 2002, unless it believes some teams are already using it now and it is impossible to police. The subsequent disappearance of power-steering will hurt some of the younger drivers, like Jenson Button, who have come to rely on it.

There have been too many big crashes this season: Michael Schumacher's barrel roll at Melbourne, on the first day of the season, demonstrated that Formula One safety has come a long way. That was followed by Jacques Villeneuve's extraordinary flying BAR Honda, which came close to going over that fence. Luciano Burti's crashes in Hungary and Belgium demonstrated the same, even though the Brazilian was injured: 10 years ago, the accident would have been a great deal worse. There is, however, still a long way to go to protect those outside the cars as well as their occupants.

But above all, 2001 has been the year of the rookie, in a season like no other I can remember. Juan Pablo Montoya and Kimi Räikkönen especially have changed the scene of Formula One. Montoya is my kind of driver, a real racer. His perfectly executed move on Michael Schumacher in Brazil was the best of the season. But the same race also demonstrated how cruel Formula One can be at times, when he lost the chance of victory in his first race after he was hit from behind by Jos Verstappen's lapped Arrows. Similarly, in Barcelona, Häkkinen could do nothing when his clutch gave out with only a few corners to go.

The season has also seen a departure or change of scenery for several old faces. The goings-on at Jaguar, McLaren Mercedes and Jordan Honda have been some of the biggest news stories of the season. The high-profile struggle between Jaguar and McLaren for the services of Adrian Newey, a super designer, highlighted how important technology is for a modern team. The sacking of Bobby Rahal, which came later, showed just how much pressure there is on the large car companies such as Ford to generate racing success. Heinz-Harald Frentzen was briefly another casualty when he was ousted from Jordan, but in the end it was his replacement Jean Alesi who lost out, as more young talent came through. Häkkinen leaves McLaren to be replaced by Kimi Räikkönen, and who knows whether he will choose to turn his back on retirement and return to racing – as I did myself. It is a decision only he can make. We also see the departure of Benetton – which becomes Renault in 2002 – and of my good friend Murray Walker. Murray is an icon, and I don't think anyone in the world has a bad word to say about him. Sadly, we have also lost a number of faces forever – Michele Alboreto and Ken Tyrrell, to mention just two.

From the evidence of 2001, 2002 has the makings of a great season and should be an all-out battle for the top between the new stars and the established icons. I can hardly wait for March.

Nigel Mansell
19th October 2001
Woodbury Park
Devon

## DRIVERS' CHAMPIONSHIP

| NO | ENTRANT | CAR | AUS | MAL | BRA | RSM | SPA | AUT | MON | CAN | EUR | FRA | GBR | GER | HUN | BEL | ITA | USA | JPN | POINTS |
|---|---|---|---|---|---|---|---|---|---|---|---|---|---|---|---|---|---|---|---|---|
| 1 | Michael Schumacher | Ferrari | 10 | 10 | 6 | DNF | 10 | 6 | 10 | 6 | 10 | 10 | 6 | DNF | 10 | 10 | 3 | 6 | 10 | 123 |
| 2 | David Coulthard | McLaren Mercedes | 6 | 4 | 10 | 6 | 2 | 10 | 2 | DNF | 4 | 3 | DNF | DNF | 4 | 6 | DNF | 4 | 4 | 65 |
| 3 | Rubens Barrichello | Ferrari | 4 | 6 | DNF | 4 | DNF | 4 | 6 | DNF | 2 | 4 | 4 | 6 | 6 | 2 | 6 | 0 | 2 | 56 |
| 4 | Ralf Schumacher | Williams BMW | DNF | 2 | DNF | 10 | DNF | DNF | DNF | 10 | 3 | 6 | DNF | 10 | 3 | 0 | 4 | DNF | 1 | 49 |
| 5 | Mika Häkkinen | McLaren Mercedes | DNF | 1 | DNF | 3 | 0 | DNF | DNF | 4 | 1 | DNS | 10 | DNF | 2 | 3 | DNF | 10 | 3 | 37 |
| 6 | Juan Pablo Montoya | Williams BMW | DNF | DNF | DNF | DNF | 6 | DNF | DNF | DNF | 6 | DNF | 3 | DNF | 0 | DNF | 10 | DNF | 6 | 31 |
| 7 | Jacques Villeneuve | BAR Honda | DNF | DNF | 0 | DNF | 4 | 0 | 3 | DNF | 0 | DNF | 0 | 4 | 0 | 0 | 1 | DNF | 0 | 12 |
| 8 | Nick Heidfeld | Sauber Petronas | 3 | DNF | 4 | 0 | 1 | 0 | DNF | DNF | DNF | 1 | 1 | DNF | 1 | DNF | 0 | 1 | 0 | 12 |
| 9 | Jarno Trulli | Jordan Honda | DNF | 0 | 2 | 2 | 3 | DSQ | DNF | 0 | DNF | 2 | DNF | DNF | DNF | DNF | DNF | 3 | 0 | 12 |
| 10 | Kimi Räikkönen | Sauber Petronas | 1 | DNF | DNF | DNF | 0 | 3 | 0 | 3 | 0 | 0 | 2 | DNF | 0 | DNS | 0 | DNF | DNF | 9 |
| 11 | Giancarlo Fisichella | Benetton Renault | 0 | DNF | 1 | DNF | 0 | DNF | DNF | DNF | 0 | 0 | 0 | 3 | DNF | 4 | 0 | 0 | 0 | 8 |
| 12 | Eddie Irvine | Jaguar Cosworth | 0 | DNF | DNF | DNF | DNF | 0 | 4 | DNF | 0 | DNF | 0 | DNF | DNF | DNS | DNF | 2 | DNF | 6 |
| 13 | Heinz-Harald Frentzen | Jordan/Prost | 2 | 3 | 0 | 1 | DNF | DNF | DNF | - | DNF | 0 | 0 | - | DNF | 0 | DNF | 0 | 0 | 6 |
| 14 | Olivier Panis | BAR Honda | 0 | DNF | 3 | 0 | 0 | 2 | DNF | 0 | DNF | 0 | DNF | 0 | DNF | 0 | 0 | 0 | 0 | 5 |
| 15 | Jean Alesi | Prost/Jordan | 0 | 0 | 0 | 0 | 0 | 0 | 1 | 2 | 0 | 0 | 0 | 1 | 0 | 1 | 0 | 0 | DNF | 5 |
| 16 | Pedro de la Rosa | Jaguar Cosworth | - | - | - | - | DNF | DNF | DNF | 1 | 0 | 0 | 0 | DNF | 0 | DNF | 2 | 0 | DNF | 3 |
| 17 | Jenson Button | Benetton Renault | 0 | 0 | 0 | 0 | DNF | 0 | DNF | 0 | 0 | 0 | 0 | 2 | DNF | DNF | DNF | 0 | 0 | 2 |
| 18 | Jos Verstappen | Arrows Asiatech | 0 | 0 | DNF | DNF | 0 | 1 | 0 | 0 | DNF | 0 | 0 | 0 | 0 | 0 | DNF | DNF | 0 | 1 |
| 19 | Ricardo Zonta | Jordan Honda | - | - | - | - | - | - | 0 | - | - | - | DNF | - | - | - | - | - | - | 0 |
| 20 | Luciano Burti | Jaguar/Prost | 0 | 0 | DNF | 0 | 0 | 0 | DNF | 0 | 0 | 0 | DNF | DNF | DNF | DNS | - | - | - | 0 |
| 21 | Enrique Bernoldi | Arrows Asiatech | DNF | DNF | DNF | 0 | DNF | DNF | 0 | DNF | DNF | DNF | 0 | 0 | DNF | 0 | DNF | 0 | 0 | 0 |
| 22 | Tarso Marques | Minardi European | DNF | 0 | 0 | DNF | 0 | DNF | DNF | 0 | DNF | 0 | DNQ | DNF | DNF | 0 | - | - | - | 0 |
| 23 | Fernando Alonso | Minardi European | 0 | 0 | DNF | DNF | 0 | DNF | DNF | 0 | 0 | 0 | 0 | 0 | DNF | DNS | 0 | DNF | 0 | 0 |
| 24 | Gaston Mazzacane | Prost Acer | DNF | 0 | 0 | DNF | - | - | - | - | - | - | - | - | - | - | - | - | - | 0 |
| 25 | Tomas Enge | Prost Acer | - | - | - | - | - | - | - | - | - | - | - | - | - | - | 0 | 0 | DNF | 0 |
| 26 | Alex Yoong | Minardi European | - | - | - | - | - | - | - | - | - | - | - | - | - | - | DNF | DNF | 0 | 0 |

## CONSTRUCTORS' CHAMPIONSHIP

| NO | ENTRANT | AUS | MAL | BRA | RSM | SPA | AUT | MON | CAN | EUR | FRA | GBR | GER | HUN | BEL | ITA | USA | JPN | POINTS |
|---|---|---|---|---|---|---|---|---|---|---|---|---|---|---|---|---|---|---|---|
| 1 | Scuderia Ferrari Marlboro | 14 | 16 | 6 | 4 | 10 | 10 | 16 | 6 | 12 | 14 | 10 | 6 | 16 | 12 | 9 | 6 | 12 | 179 |
| 2 | West McLaren Mercedes | 6 | 5 | 10 | 9 | 2 | 10 | 2 | 4 | 5 | 3 | 10 | - | 6 | 9 | - | 14 | 7 | 102 |
| 3 | BMW Williams F1 | - | 2 | - | 10 | 6 | - | - | 10 | 9 | 6 | 3 | 10 | 3 | 0 | 14 | - | 7 | 80 |
| 4 | Red Bull Sauber Petronas | 4 | - | 4 | 0 | 1 | 3 | 0 | 3 | 0 | 1 | 3 | - | 1 | - | 0 | 1 | 0 | 21 |
| 5 | B&H Jordan Honda | 2 | 3 | 2 | 3 | 3 | - | 0 | - | 2 | 0 | - | 0 | 1 | 0 | 3 | 0 | 0 | 19 |
| 6 | Lucky Strike BAR Honda | 0 | - | 3 | 0 | 4 | 2 | 3 | - | 0 | 0 | 0 | 4 | - | 0 | 1 | 0 | 0 | 17 |
| 7 | Mild Seven Benetton Renault | 0 | 0 | 1 | 0 | 0 | - | 0 | - | 0 | 0 | 0 | 5 | - | 4 | 0 | 0 | 0 | 10 |
| 8 | Jaguar Racing | 0 | 0 | - | 0 | - | 0 | 4 | 1 | 0 | 0 | 0 | - | 0 | - | 2 | 2 | - | 9 |
| 9 | Prost Acer | 0 | 0 | 0 | 0 | 0 | 0 | 1 | 2 | 0 | 0 | 0 | 1 | - | 0 | 0 | 0 | 0 | 4 |
| 10 | Orange Arrows Asiatech | 0 | 0 | 0 | 0 | 0 | 1 | 0 | 0 | - | 0 | 0 | 0 | 0 | 0 | - | 0 | 0 | 1 |
| 11 | European Minardi F1 | 0 | 0 | 0 | - | 0 | - | - | 0 | 0 | 0 | 0 | 0 | - | 0 | 0 | - | 0 | 0 |

## DRIVERS' RELIABILITY

| | DRIVER | RACES ENTERED* | MAXIMUM LAPS | LAPS COMPLETED | % OF LAPS RACED |
|---|---|---|---|---|---|
| 1 | Michael Schumacher | 17 | 1065 | 1005 | 94.4% |
| 2 | Jean Alesi | 17 | 1065 | 998 | 93.7% |
| 3 | Tomas Enge | 3 | 179 | 166 | 92.7% |
| 4 | Rubens Barrichello | 17 | 1065 | 928 | 87.1% |
| 5 | David Coulthard | 17 | 1065 | 926 | 86.9% |
| 6 | Jos Verstappen | 17 | 1065 | 889 | 83.5% |
| 7 | Jenson Button | 17 | 1065 | 861 | 80.8% |
| 8 | Giancarlo Fisichella | 17 | 1065 | 810 | 76.1% |
| 9 | HH Frentzen | 15 | 951 | 719 | 75.7% |
| 10 | Ralf Schumacher | 17 | 1065 | 806 | 75.7% |
| 11 | Jacques Villeneuve | 17 | 1065 | 790 | 74.2% |
| 12 | Alex Yoong | 3 | 179 | 132 | 73.7% |
| 13 | Olivier Panis | 17 | 1065 | 784 | 73.6% |
| 14 | Nick Heidfeld | 17 | 1065 | 764 | 71.7% |
| 15 | Kimi Räikkönen | 17 | 1065 | 756 | 71.0% |
| 16 | Jarno Trulli | 17 | 1065 | 755 | 70.9% |
| 17 | Pedro de la Rosa | 13 | 819 | 579 | 70.7% |
| 18 | Tarso Marques | 13 | 826 | 578 | 70.0% |
| 19 | Luciano Burti | 14 | 886 | 599 | 67.6% |
| 20 | Fernando Alonso | 17 | 1065 | 707 | 66.4% |
| 21 | Ricardo Zonta | 2 | 114 | 75 | 65.8% |
| 22 | Mika Häkkinen | 17 | 1065 | 689 | 64.7% |
| 23 | Juan Pablo Montoya | 17 | 1065 | 680 | 63.8% |
| 24 | Eddie Irvine | 17 | 1065 | 658 | 61.7% |
| 25 | Gaston Mazzacane | 4 | 246 | 135 | 54.9% |
| 26 | Enrique Bernoldi | 17 | 1065 | 568 | 53.3% |

*Includes non-starts but not non-qualifications.*

## CONSTRUCTORS' RELIABILITY

| | TEAM | RACES ENTERED* | MAXIMUM LAPS | LAPS COMPLETED | % OF LAPS RACED |
|---|---|---|---|---|---|
| 1 | Ferrari | 34 | 2130 | 1933 | 90.8% |
| 2 | Prost Acer | 34 | 2130 | 1707 | 80.1% |
| 3 | Benetton Renault | 34 | 2130 | 1671 | 78.4% |
| 4 | McLaren Mercedes | 34 | 2130 | 1615 | 75.8% |
| 5 | BAR Honda | 34 | 2130 | 1574 | 73.9% |
| 6 | Jordan Honda | 34 | 2130 | 1539 | 72.3% |
| 7 | Sauber Petronas | 34 | 2130 | 1520 | 71.4% |
| 8 | BMW Williams | 34 | 2130 | 1486 | 69.8% |
| 9 | European Minardi | 33 | 2070 | 1417 | 68.5% |
| 10 | Arrows Asiatech | 34 | 2130 | 1457 | 68.4% |
| 11 | Jaguar Racing | 34 | 2130 | 1438 | 67.5% |

*Includes non-starts but not non-qualifications.*

Jean Alesi could have been the only driver ever to be classified in all 17 races of a season but he failed in one.

## DRIVER CAREER RECORD

| | DRIVER | GP STARTS | TITLES | WINS | POLES | FAST LAPS | PODIUMS | POINTS |
|---|---|---|---|---|---|---|---|---|
| 1 | Jean Alesi | 201 | 0 | 1 | 2 | 4 | 32 | 241 |
| 2 | Fernando Alonso | 16 | 0 | 0 | 0 | 0 | 0 | 0 |
| 3 | Rubens Barrichello | 147 | 0 | 1 | 3 | 3 | 25 | 195 |
| 4 | Enrique Bernoldi | 17 | 0 | 0 | 0 | 0 | 0 | 0 |
| 5 | Luciano Burti | 14 | 0 | 0 | 0 | 0 | 0 | 0 |
| 6 | Jenson Button | 34 | 0 | 0 | 0 | 0 | 0 | 14 |
| 7 | David Coulthard | 124 | 0 | 11 | 12 | 17 | 51 | 359 |
| 8 | Tomas Enge | 3 | 0 | 0 | 0 | 0 | 0 | 0 |
| 9 | Giancarlo Fisichella | 91 | 0 | 0 | 1 | 1 | 9 | 75 |
| 10 | HH Frentzen | 129 | 0 | 3 | 2 | 6 | 17 | 159 |
| 11 | Mika Häkkinen | 161 | 2 | 20 | 26 | 25 | 51 | 420 |
| 12 | Nick Heidfeld | 33 | 0 | 0 | 0 | 0 | 1 | 12 |
| 13 | Eddie Irvine | 129 | 0 | 4 | 0 | 1 | 25 | 183 |
| 14 | Tarso Marques | 23 | 0 | 0 | 0 | 0 | 0 | 0 |
| 15 | Gaston Mazzacane | 21 | 0 | 0 | 0 | 0 | 0 | 0 |
| 16 | Juan Pablo Montoya | 17 | 0 | 1 | 3 | 3 | 4 | 31 |
| 17 | Olivier Panis | 108 | 0 | 1 | 0 | 0 | 5 | 61 |
| 18 | Kimi Räikkönen | 16 | 0 | 0 | 0 | 0 | 0 | 9 |
| 19 | Pedro de la Rosa | 45 | 0 | 0 | 0 | 0 | 0 | 6 |
| 20 | M Schumacher | 160 | 4 | 53 | 43 | 44 | 97 | 801 |
| 21 | Ralf Schumacher | 83 | 0 | 3 | 1 | 6 | 14 | 135 |
| 22 | Jarno Trulli | 79 | 0 | 0 | 0 | 0 | 1 | 29 |
| 23 | Jos Verstappen | 90 | 0 | 0 | 0 | 0 | 2 | 17 |
| 24 | Jacques Villeneuve | 99 | 1 | 11 | 13 | 9 | 23 | 209 |
| 24 | Alex Yoong | 3 | 0 | 0 | 0 | 0 | 0 | 0 |
| 26 | Ricardo Zonta | 31 | 0 | 0 | 0 | 0 | 0 | 3 |

## TEAM CAREER RECORD

| | DRIVER | GP STARTS | TITLES | WINS | POLES | FAST LAPS | PODIUMS | POINTS |
|---|---|---|---|---|---|---|---|---|
| 1 | Arrows | 700 | 0 | 0 | 1 | 0 | 9 | 165 |
| 2 | BAR | 99 | 0 | 0 | 0 | 0 | 2 | 37 |
| 3 | Benetton | 519 | 1 | 27 | 15 | 36 | 102 | 865 |
| 4 | Ferrari | 1501 | 11 | 144 | 148 | 147 | 485 | 3675 |
| 5 | Jaguar | 68 | 0 | 0 | 0 | 0 | 1 | 13 |
| 6 | Jordan | 360 | 0 | 3 | 2 | 2 | 17 | 252 |
| 7 | McLaren | 1104 | 8 | 134 | 112 | 107 | 339 | 2779 |
| 8 | Minardi | 499 | 0 | 0 | 0 | 0 | 0 | 28 |
| 9 | Prost | 162 | 0 | 0 | 0 | 0 | 3 | 35 |
| 10 | Sauber | 288 | 0 | 0 | 0 | 0 | 5 | 111 |
| 11 | Williams | 906 | 9 | 107 | 112 | 119 | 262 | 2184 |

The record for Arrows includes the results of Footwork. Benetton does not include Toleman, Jaguar does not include Stewart, BAR does not include Tyrrell and Prost does not include Ligier.

Ferrari were top in the reliability stakes.

## QUALIFYING PERFORMANCE OF TEAM-MATES

| TEAM | DRIVERS | RATIO | PERCENTAGE | COMBINED GAP |
|---|---|---|---|---|
| Ferrari | M Schumacher:Barrichello | 16:1 | 94% | 10.200secs (to MS) |
| European Minardi | Alonso:Marques/Yoong | 15:2 | 88% | 18.404secs (to FA) |
| Jordan Honda | Trulli:Frentzen/Zonta/Alesi | 15:2 | 88% | 6.434secs (to JT) |
| Prost Acer | Alesi/Frentzen: Mazzacane/Burti/Enge | 14:3 | 82% | 19.323secs (to JA/HHF) |
| Benetton Renault | Fisichella:Button | 13:4 | 76% | 8.574secs (to GF) |
| Jaguar Racing | Irvine:Burti/de la Rosa | 11:6 | 65% | 7.051secs (to EI) |
| BMW Williams | R Schumacher:Montoya | 11:6 | 65% | 4.938secs (to RS) |
| BAR Honda | Villeneuve:Panis | 11:6 | 65% | 1.334secs (to JV) |
| Sauber Petronas | Heidfeld:Räikkönen | 10:7 | 59% | 1.774secs (to NH) |
| Arrows Asiatech | Bernoldi:Verstappen | 10:7 | 59% | 2.190secs (to JV) |
| McLaren Mercedes | Häkkinen:Coulthard | 9:8 | 53% | 1.850secs (to MH) |

Häkkinen and Coulthard were the closest team-mates in qualifying

## MASTER GRID

**1 Michael Schumacher**
Average grid position 1.7
Average percentage of pole time 100.286%

**2 Ralf Schumacher**
Average grid position 3.4
Average percentage of pole time 100.681%

**3 Rubens Barrichello**
Average grid position 4.5
Average percentage of pole time 100.998%

**4 Mika Häkkinen**
Average grid position 4.5
Average percentage of pole time 101.033%

**5 David Coulthard**
Average grid position 4.8
Average percentage of pole time 101.124%

**6 Juan Pablo Montoya**
Average grid position 5.4
Average percentage of pole time 101.075%

**7 Jarno Trulli**
Average grid position 6.8
Average percentage of pole time 101.582%

**8 Heinz-Harald Frentzen**
Average grid position 9.6
Average percentage of pole time 101.983%

**9 Nick Heidfeld**
Average grid position 9.7
Average percentage of pole time 102.119%

**10 Kimi Räikkönen**
Average grid position 10.4
Average percentage of pole time 102.249%

**11 Jacques Villeneuve**
Average grid position 10.8
Average percentage of pole time 102.281%

**12 Olivier Panis**
Average grid position 11.4
Average percentage of pole time 102.397%

**13 Eddie Irvine**
Average grid position 12.8
Average percentage of pole time 102.724%

**14 Ricardo Zonta**
Average grid position 13.5
Average percentage of pole time 102.578%

**15 Pedro de la Rosa**
Average grid position 13.8
Average percentage of pole time 103.275%

**16 Jean Alesi**
Average grid position 14.1
Average percentage of pole time 103.079%

**17 Giancarlo Fisichella**
Average grid position 15.2
Average percentage of pole time 103.373%

**18 Luciano Burti**
Average grid position 15.8
Average percentage of pole time 104.011%

**19 Jenson Button**
Average grid position 16.9
Average percentage of pole time 103.934%

**20 Jos Verstappen**
Average grid position 18.0
Average percentage of pole time 104.166%

**21 Enrique Bernoldi**
Average grid position 18.5
Average percentage of pole time 104.359%

**22 Fernando Alonso**
Average grid position 19.5
Average percentage of pole time 104.653%

**23 Gaston Mazzacane**
Average grid position 20.0
Average percentage of pole time 104.460%

**24 Tomas Enge**
Average grid position 20.0
Average percentage of pole time 104.129%

**25 Tarso Marques**
Average grid position 21.8
Average percentage of pole time 106.144%

**26 Alex Yoong**
Average grid position 22.0
Average percentage of pole time 105.849%

## November 2000

When the 2000 season ended in Malaysia on Sunday 22nd October of that year, the 2001 season effectively began. It is always like that. Save for some mule testing, the seven or so cars built for the season just ended were sent off on promotional tours, put away in museums, sold or bubble-wrapped.

**Michael Schumacher** took the opportunity to go into hospital for removal of the pins that had

With the 2000 season just ended Jurgen Hubbert said it was more important in Germany for Mercedes-Benz to beat Michael Schumacher than to win with him. Hence Michael would never get an offer to drive for McLaren.

been inserted when he broke his leg during the 1999 British Grand Prix. Whilst he was there he read a story telling him he would never drive for **Mercedes**. **Jurgen Hubbert**, Mercedes' chairman, said: "In Germany Schumacher is more important than anything else. It is undoubtedly more crucial for us to win against him rather than with him." That was one way of putting it, and the world champion was doubtless amused. Meanwhile **Juan Pablo Montoya** and **Ralf Schumacher**, the **BMW Williams** drivers already announced for 2001, had begun their arguments. But in Dubai, Schumacher said they were overblown. Not as it would turn out.

Meanwhile, **Mercedes** motorsport chief **Norbert Haug** got it badly wrong when he predicted **BMW** would not be a force in the coming season, saying: "Even another 50hp will not be enough to make a difference." It turned out rather different: it was 80hp.

Experienced team manager **Joan Villadelprat** signed with **Prost** and couldn't have known what he had let himself in for. **Henri**

**Durand**, ex-**McLaren** aerodynamicist, also signed up. Both excellent choices, unbeknown to them the team had little money to go racing in 2001.

There was much speculation that **Kimi Räikkönen** was about to sign for Sauber. The 21-year-old Finn had only driven 23 car races and there was speculation, ill-informed, that he would not be granted a superlicence. **Keke Rosberg**, who would later have good reason to fear Räikkönen's arrival, said: "It will turn the whole driver market on its head." It did.

The **Minardi** team was in an end-of-season mess with no money for 2001, its leader Gabriele Rumi ill with cancer, and no engine to race with. Somehow it would all come good.

No one was ready for the bombshell announcement in the second week of November: the **Formula One Technical Working Group**, made up of the team's technical directors, voted for a return to traction control, banned since 1993. **BMW's Mario Theissen** welcomed it. Ratification was up to the **Formula One Commission** due to meet in early December.

Peace broke out at **British American Racing** as the owners and directors came to an accord to leave each other alone. Basically the **Adrian Reynard** camp said it would let the **Craig Pollock** camp get on with it and stand back. They were as good as their word.

**Fernando Alonso** landed a drive with **Minardi**, provided there was a Minardi team to drive for. He also visited **Jean Todt** at the **Ferrari** factory for evaluation. **Flavio Briatore** took over as his manager after buying up his contract.

**Renault** accused rivals of stealing the secrets of its new wide, vee-angle engine and stepped up security at its British base. If the story was true, the secrets would be of no use as the team started with the least powerful engine.

**Mark Webber** was confirmed as **Benetton's** official test driver for 2001 and **Mika Salo**

Gary Anderson, a hugely talented man with some demons to resolve, was sacked from Jaguar but found a new life in America working for Reynard in CART. He looked a new man as well when he returned to the Formula One paddock a year later at Indianapolis.

blasted his old team boss **Peter Sauber**, saying the team was no good. How wrong was he?

**Gary Anderson**, **Jaguar's** technical director, paid the price of failure and was on his way, later to re-emerge in champ cars in America. **Alain Prost** said he had no regrets about becoming a team principal after quitting as a driver. No one believed him but he appeared to believe it himself.

**Gaston Mazzacane** was rumoured to be the new **Prost** number two after introducing Brazilian sponsor **PSN** to the team. The rumours were true.

The car manufacturers

Pierre Dupasquier, Michelin's competition boss, was back for 2001 and proved what a great character he was. And how Formula One had missed him. The sport has no finer ambassador.

were kicking up a fuss over the future control of Formula One after **Bernie Ecclestone** retired, following the sale of part of **SLEC**, the commercial rights holding company of Formula One. He said he would stay on and run it for another five years, until the end of 2005.

There was strife at **Sauber** as **Red Bull** boss **Dietrich Mateschitz** put his majority share in the team up for sale. There was a stand-off between him and Peter Sauber over **Enrique Bernoldi**, whom Mateschitz wanted to be number two. But Peter Sauber didn't, and won.

Away from Formula One, **Niki Lauda** lost control of his airline **Lauda Air** and resigned as chairman. That was to have ramifications later for the **Jaguar** team.

It was rumoured that **Pedro Diniz** would retire

After a season of warring, peace was declared between Craig Pollock and Adrian Reynard of BAR. Designer Malcolm Oastler hoped it would hold. He had loyalties to both men. It did hold because Reynard withdrew from his involvement.

as a driver, take a stake in the **Prost** team and help manage it. The rumour was true, even if the idea was bad.

The **Hockenheim** circuit announced it had draft plans to upgrade and change the circuit. By the end of the year the plans would be finalised, along with a new contract to run the German Grand Prix.

It was announced that **Pedro de la Rosa** would stay at **Arrows** for the 2001 season by his manager, **Raimon Duran**. But the 29-year-old had yet to sign his new deal which was to prove a problem. Duran said: "**Tom Walkinshaw** told Pedro he would stay with the team in the summer and we stopped talking to other teams about a possible move from then on." **Paul Stewart** announced his resignation as executive director of **Jaguar Racing**. Stewart had been diagnosed with cancer of the colon in April.

**Toyota** bought a majority share in Japan's Fuji racing circuit and said it will develop the venue to secure a Grand Prix. Toyota spent $48.72 million for a 67 per cent stake in the circuit.

**Michael Schumacher** lost a court case in Stuttgart, Germany, after filing a multi-million pound damages claim against a lookalike called **Frank Sassen**. Schumacher launched the court action after Dutchman Sassen gave up his job as a horse food salesman to concentrate entirely on being the world champion's full-time double.

# December 2000

The **BRDC** and **Octagon**, owners of Brands Hatch, and **Bernie Ecclestone** surprised everyone when they announced an unusual tripartite deal to pump £15 million each into a new company to run Silverstone circuit and the British Grand Prix. The arrangements suited everyone. BRDC secured the event for Silverstone, Octagon got itself out of the embarrassing position of having signed a deal for 2002 but having no track to race on. The new consortium also announced a revamped Silverstone to host the Grand Prix for many years ahead.

With **Gary Anderson** booted out of **Jaguar**, ex-**McLaren** staffer **Steve Nichols** was shoehorned in. **David Coulthard** was already worrying about the tyre war between **Bridgestone** and **Michelin** set to begin in 2001. He clearly thought it wouldn't benefit him.

**Pedro Diniz** finally quit and became a Prost manager. **Alain Prost** said: "I am delighted because I have found in Pedro and his family not only a solid business partner for my team but also a great group of people and friends." He was to seriously regret that statement within weeks, as the two found themselves totally incompatible and resorted to communicating via their lawyers.

**Bobby Rahal** arrived to take up the reins as team principal of **Jaguar**. He was quoted as describing his first day in the job as 'interesting to say the least'. He was in for some shocks come February.

**Kirch Gruppe**, the big German TV broadcaster, rescued **EM.TV**, owner of 75 per cent of **SLEC**, the Formula One commercial rights holder. Kirch effectively agreed to buy out, in stages, all but 16 per cent of its 75 per cent share. In a first step it bought 25 per cent and took an option on a further 25 per cent.

Former **Williams** driver **Alex Zanardi** announced he was returning to racing in the American CART series after a year sabbatical. It would prove an ill-fated decision. Zanardi also warned **Juan Pablo Montoya** how difficult he would find Formula One at Williams. In the end Montoya coped admirably.

The **Formula One Commission** decided to re-introduce traction control and other electronic gizmos at the Spanish Grand Prix in 2001. It was a strange delay. But it emerged that **Ferrari**,

John Cooper was a legendary constructor in the days when Formula One was very different. In truth he couldn't live with the technical developments but he did enough to become a legend and get his name on a famous road car that endures today. He died on 24th December 2000.

**Sauber**, **Prost** and **Minardi** had tried to block it and as a compromise a delay was announced. Strange but true.

The **FIA** was involved in controversy over tyre treads and what constituted acceptable wear. It worried **Michelin's** competition boss **Pierre Dupasquier**, who believed it would be an important issue in 2001. So it proved, although no one ran foul.

**Kimi Räikkönen** was granted an FIA superlicence to drive for **Sauber**, but with a four-race probation. That proved a joke.

**Olivier Panis** drove a **BAR** for the first time, and showed he was as good as it gets. He looked set to give team leader **Jacques Villeneuve** a run for his money, and he did so. Meanwhile, **Mika Häkkinen** was unhappy that Panis had been replaced as McLaren test driver by **Alex Wurz**, and said so publicly.

Without Walter Hayes, Formula One would have been very different indeed. He created the Ford DFV and made it available to British teams for 14 years at a subsidised price. People like Frank Williams and Bernie Ecclestone had a lot to thank him for. He died on 26th December 2000.

**Takuma Sato** was given his first Formula One test in a **Jordan Honda**. It was a portent of things to come in 2002.

**Alain Prost** finally persuaded **Michelin** to supply tyres for his team in 2001. He would have to pay for the privilege, however. **Michael Schumacher** added his two penn'th to the tyre war debate, saying he expected it to shake up the grid in 2001. He was wrong about that, but got to throw his crutches away before Christmas after his successful operation to remove pins from the leg he injured in 1999.

It was announced that 2001 would be **Murray Walker's** last as ITV's principal Formula One commentator. It would bring an end to a 52-year career. Walker also said he would only commentate at 12 races in 2001.

In December 2000 it was announced that Murray Walker would retire as ITV's principal Formula One commentator after a 52-year career in broadcasting.

**BMW's Mario Theissen** said he didn't think **Renault's** new wide vee-angle engine, being introduced for 2001, would be any good. He knew what he was talking about.

The end of December was tinged with sadness as two Formula One legends departed. **John Cooper**, the famous 1960s constructor and **Walter Hayes**, who was responsible for the Ford DVF engine, died within 48 hours of each other.

Finally it was announced that a new Formula One magazine would be launched in March 2001, in time for the new season. Its title? **Formula 1 Magazine**. Some welcomed it but some were less enthusiastic.

# January 2001

Tobacco advertising was in the news, with pressure on Formula One to get rid of tobacco adverts before the 2006 voluntary ban. Most of the pressure came from the British government. But Formula One was in no mood to listen, having already made its decision. **Norbert Haug**, the **Mercedes** motorsport chief, said he thought **David Coulthard** could beat **Mika Häkkinen** and **Michael Schumacher** to the world title in 2001. No one took him particularly seriously, although he was right about ▷

Coulthard's new determination. **Rubens Barrichello** was also making noises about his chance of being world champ in 2001. Someone should have told him he had to win a race to do that. But no one did.

**Tom Walkinshaw**, the **Arrows** team principal, showed a computer-generated drawing of a three-seat F1 demonstration car. Everyone thought it was a joke, but it turned out to be deadly serious and was ready to run by the end of 2001. **Autosport** magazine carried the story on its front cover, labelling it a 'world exclusive'.

**Jaguar Racing** was the first team to

Tom Walkinshaw went one better than McLaren when he produced an Arrows three-seater Formula One car to enable sponsors to get the feel of a 130mph lap of a Grand Prix circuit.

announce its new 2001 car in the second week in January at its road car engineering base in Coventry. **Bobby Rahal** admitted the car was conventional and would not be earth-shatteringly fast. He was right about that. Meanwhile Rahal was negotiating to build the team a new factory at Silverstone circuit to encompass **Cosworth** as well. That plan was destined for the scrapheap.

**Honda** said it expected to challenge for the world championship in 2002. But that aspiration was soon to be dashed. Meanwhile **Benetton's** new technical director, **Mike Gascoyne**, suddenly realised that the 2001 car he had inherited was going to be a dog and the new **Renault** revolutionary engine was a little too revolutionary. He realised that he would earn his salary in 2001, and so he did.

**Rick Gorne**, general manager of **British American Racing**, quit the team. Gorne was a **Reynard** man and his departure was part of the smoking of the peace pipe between **Adrian Reynard** and **Craig Pollock**.

**PSN**, the South American TV network, announced it would sponsor **Prost**. There was less substance in the announcement than it appeared. Its contribution would only be a fraction of what Prost needed to go racing in 2001.

**Jordan Honda** announced its new car, dubbed the EJ11. At the factory there was immense enthusiasm for the works **Honda** engine, although **Heinz-Harald Frentzen** ominously played down the prospects. The car certainly looked the part.

It was also announced that **Eghbal Hamidy**, the former **Arrows** and **Stewart** designer, would soon join **Jordan** as technical director when Arrows released him from gardening leave. It was announced that **Niki Lauda** would be editor-in-chief of the new **Formula 1 Magazine**. But Lauda had other ideas and would last barely four issues before moving to **Jaguar Racing**.

**Jackie Stewart** began a crusade to attract government funding for the redevelopment of Silverstone circuit. Few reckoned much to his chances as he was asking for £40 million.

Meanwhile **Bernie Ecclestone** predicted that the EU's competition directorate would shortly approve the commercial arrangements of Formula One. He was right. **Eddie Irvine** predicted that **Michael Schumacher** would win the 2001 world championship. He was right as well.

**Jacques Villeneuve** dropped a bombshell on the **BAR** team, telling it the new 2001 car was too slow. **Olivier Panis** and **Adrian Reynard** disagreed with the assessment.

**Ferrari** suffered the first of what would be three serious accidents in testing in 2001 when its test driver **Luca Badoer** ended up dazed after a suspension failure in Barcelona pitched him into the air and onto the wrong side of a tyre barrier, but thankfully the right way up. He was lucky to survive. At other circuits in Spain – Jerez and Valencia – **Eddie Irvine** and **Jacques Villeneuve** also had serious accidents in their new cars. Villeneuve effectively wrote off the 2001 BAR Honda; only one example existed. Embarrassingly, **BAR** had to show its old 2000 car in new colours at the launch of its 2001 car. The cock-ups didn't come any bigger than that, although BAR boss **Craig Pollock** seemed unconcerned as he left journalists baffled by the cabaret in a cellar in London's East End.

In January 2001 Max Mosley was able to announce that the FIA had settled its six-year dispute with the European Commission. There were changes to be made as a result but none that anyone would notice.

At an emotional press conference in Venice in February 2001, Luciano Benetton bid an emotional goodbye to Formula One as he officially handed over leadership of his team after 17 years to Patrick Faure of Renault.

Aviation entrepreneur **Paul Stoddart** emerged as the most likely buyer for the distressed Italian **Minardi** team. It emerged that its owner **Gabriele Rumi** was dying of cancer, making a rescue more urgent. By the end of the month the deal was sealed, with Stoddart making some outrageous predictions about the team's new car. It proved as slow as the old ones.

In an effort to prevent **Nigel Stepney** moving to **Jaguar**, **Ferrari** promoted him and by all accounts doubled his salary to a whacking $700,000 a year. Ferrari launched its 2001 car by arranging hordes of fans to attend in a makeshift indoor grandstand inside a giant tent. The effect was magical and the confidence mesmerising.

**Peter Sauber** launched his 2001 challenge, the Sauber C20, without any paying spectators and no reindeer. Thanks to a new sponsorship package from **Credit Suisse** he was in the money. Soon he would be in the points as well.

If any doubts persisted that the **BMW Williams** team was going to win races in 2001, they were dispelled by the highly confident launch at Silverstone of the new car, the FW23. It was also the public debut of new engineer **Sam Michael**. Everyone had very high hopes for him.

At the close of the month, **FIA** president **Max Mosley** announced that it had indeed settled its six-year battle with the **European Commission**. Competition commissioner **Mario Monti**, Mosley and **Bernie Ecclestone** settled things at a meeting in Brussels.

# February 2001

Astonishingly, veteran – well, 33-year-old – driver **Gianni Morbidelli** was dreaming of a Formula One comeback with **Minardi**. It was not to be. **Paul Stoddart**, new owner of Minardi, had been busy signing up for Michelin tyres and confirming 19-year-old hotshot **Fernando Alonso** to drive. He also said he would continue using the lash-up four-year-old Cosworth engine for want of a better, or any, alternative.

Meanwhile the **BMW Williams** and **BAR**

**Honda** teams were out in Kyalami for their now annual winter hot-weather test session.

**Pedro de la Rosa** signed as **Prost's** test driver. Well, everyone thought he signed. He actually didn't and soon scooted off to **Jaguar** as its test driver, at least for the moment.

**Pedro Diniz** won a £500,000 settlement from **Tom Walkinshaw's Arrows** team over his time there as a driver.

Mid-month, there came an extraordinary announcement from **Jaguar Racing** when **Premier Automotive Group**, Jaguar's parent company, announced the appointment of **Niki Lauda** as chairman of a new division called **Premier Performance Group**, consisting of the team, **Cosworth** and electronics company **Pi**. At a press conference **Bobby Rahal**, who thought he was boss, looked put-out but said nothing. Predictably it would end in tears.

**Benetton Renault** and **McLaren Mercedes** simultaneously launched their new cars. Benetton's occasion in Venice was emotional as it marked a goodbye to Formula One from **Luciano Benetton**. At McLaren's launch in Valencia, morale was high. **David Coulthard**

One of the most bizarre events of the year occurred on 6th February 2001 in London at a press conference called by Wolfgang Reitzle, chairman of Jaguar Cars. He announced that Niki Lauda would join Jaguar as chief. It was a job that Bobby Rahal already thought he had. Turned out he didn't. Soon he had no job at all.

had been out testing the new 2001 McLaren and proclaimed it 'the best new car I have ever driven at the team'. He wasn't to be so enthusiastic by the first race, when the car was off the pace. It was later discovered the aero-calculations were wrong due to miscalibration of the windtunnel. Red faces all round, but experts realised it was all too easy to happen. The team were oblivious and McLaren's managing director, **Martin Whitmarsh**, voiced most concern about reliability. Meanwhile the **Ferrari** looked very strong and was breaking lap records wherever it went. But astonishingly not as strong as the new **Prost** which, with its **Ferrari** engine driven by **Jean Alesi**, set best time at Barcelona and Magny-Cours tests and the winter's best time at Estoril. Everyone suspected that **Alain Prost** was running a lighter car simply to attract sponsors. **Ron Dennis** famously said that Prost had won the winter world championship. No one

expected the team to be anywhere but at the rear of the grid come Melbourne in early March.

**Johnny Herbert** popped up again as test driver for **Arrows** after failing to land a drive in the American CART series.

**Toyota**, the new Formula One team scheduled to debut in 2002, made its first appearance and launched the team at the Paul Ricard circuit in France. It had rented space at the Ricard track to conduct a test programme. Toyota Motorsport president **Ove Andersson** presided.

**Kenneth Clarke**, former Chancellor of the Exchequer and top Conservative politician, was appointed chairman of **British American Racing** with a brief to beef up the management. The team had overspent its first season's budget by 115 per cent.

Sadly it was revealed that **Ken Tyrrell** was suffering from cancer and did not have long to live. He was however leading an active life in his last months.

**Ferrari** was estimated to have the biggest workforce in Formula One: 681 people. **Toyota** was second with 590.

**Michael Schumacher** was reportedly thinking about a $36 million offer to drive for **Ferrari** after his current contract expired at the end of 2002. And Ferrari was revealed as having the biggest budget in Formula One, with $284.35 million to spend. **McLaren** was second, $10 million behind. **Williams** got by on a relatively meagre $192 million.

## March 2001

**M**ichael Schumacher opened March as he was to carry on for the rest of 2001 by winning in Australia, but not before a nasty practice accident pitched him into a somersault on the Melbourne gravel. A marshal lost his life after **Jacques Villeneuve** ran into the back of **Ralf Schumacher** and barrel-rolled to a halt in a frightening accident so reminiscent of his father's on 8th May 1982.

The newly-named **European Minardi** team made it to Melbourne with just two cars. Australian native **Paul Stoddart** was fêted in his own country for his audacious bid. Minardi showed an advanced cast-titanium gearbox that it intended to run later in the year. It was the work of **Gustav Brunner** and featured new manufacturing techniques.

Schumacher also lost a legal battle with the **Bell** helmet company. He wanted to wear a **Schubert** helmet. **Benetton Renault** was demoralised by a poor start to the season but had not yet realised how bad it would get.

**Red Bull** decals appeared on the side of the **Arrows** car in Melbourne after the late signing of **Enrique Bernoldi** as second driver. **Dietrich Mateschitz**, Red Bull's boss, negotiated the rumoured $8 million deal after failing to

Craig Pollock appointed Kenneth Clarke, hopeful Tory leader and former chancellor, chairman of British American Racing on 1st February 2001. Clarke was a close friend of BAR co-founder, Adrian Reynard.

persuade **Peter Sauber** to take Bernoldi as a driver.

The big news of March was the row between the teams, car manufacturers and **Formula One Management**, the operating subsidiary of Formula One, over TV money. The teams who are car-makers wanted more money from the television revenues. The call for more was led by **BAR** boss **Craig Pollock**, who said: "We want more. The teams have made the true investment in the sport. As a businessman I know what the outgoings and the incomings are, and they just don't add up."

A minor – though at the time seemingly major – face-off came after **Jordan Honda** driver **Heinz-Harald Frentzen** accused the **Sauber** team of using traction control at the Australian Grand Prix. In one of a few dramatic announcements in 2001 on his own website, Frentzen said the cars had been difficult to keep up with coming out of corners. Sauber denied the claim and it was soon forgotten.

There was great discussion amongst everybody after lap speeds in Australia ▷

At Minardi Gustav Brunner developed a process that enabled a cast-titanium gearbox to be manufactured. A few months later he got his reward by moving to the new Toyota team for $4 million a year.

proved as much as three seconds quicker than the previous year – and especially after **Jacques Villeneuve's** accident. Everyone blamed the increased speeds on the tyre wars between **Michelin** and **Bridgestone**. But it was another problem that really wasn't one, and it was never discussed again. **FIA** president **Max Mosley** said he was irritated by the rise after his work over the winter to cut speeds.

There was also a proposal to fit wheel guards to F1 cars to stop front tyres riding over rear tyres and causing cars to take off. That was also quickly forgotten and was entirely impractical, although some people took it seriously.

Interestingly, one safety device widely used in American racing, the **HANS** head restraint, was rejected by F1 drivers as too uncomfortable.

There was much discussion about **Ferrari's** legal traction control device fitted to the cars for 2001. It involved pressure in the airbox being measured to control wheelspin. It was a remarkable achievement that needed hordes of software engineers to programme it. Hence the 30 or so Ferrari had in Australia. **Ron Dennis**

In March 2001 Allan McNish got Toyota's new Formula One car running for the first time. It was an interim test car that would never race. Just as well as it was at least 10 seconds a lap too slow.

magnanimously said he thought it legal. He had his own problems as **McLaren** team members confirmed the windtunnel had been miscalibrated, causing the front wing to work badly.

**Allan McNish** was all but confirmed as **Toyota's** number two driver for 2002. But there were continuing rumours surrounding **Prost** driver **Gaston Mazzacane** and **Jaguar** driver **Luciano Burti.** Both were poised for the sack.

**Bernie Ecclestone** pulled off a coup, as a by-product of the **European Commission** competition probe. **SLEC**, the holding company, bought the commercial rights to Formula One for around £240 million in a one-off deal for a period of 100 years from 2011. The **FIA** got an immediate cash windfall and the EC was satisfied.

The **British Grand Prix** was under threat from the foot-and-mouth epidemic, which was causing sporting events to be cancelled

wholesale. But the race looked fairly secure.

As **Michael Schumacher** walked the second race of March in Malaysia, people already predicted he would be champion. It was to be **Ferrari's** year again.

**Jaguar's** plans to build its new grand headquarters at Silverstone fell apart after several millions had been spent on evaluation.

There was much upset at Silverstone circuit, where huge redundancies were made following the takeover by **Octagon**, owner of **Brands Hatch**.

Meanwhile **McLaren's** new headquarters, called The Paragon, were taking shape and there were rumours that it might cost £225 million.

Many rumours were surrounding **Volkswagen** and a possible entry into Formula One. It surrounded the arrival of **Bernd Pischetsrieder** as chairman elect. He had brought **BMW** into Formula One.

**Bernie Ecclestone** unveiled a new electronic marshalling system he had developed at **FOM**. It would enable flag marshals to be done away with and make marshalling safer.

## April 2001

**D**avid Coulthard opened April in fine style by winning the Brazilian Grand Prix. He was set to go head-to-head with **Michael Schumacher** for the championship. He was the coming man – confident, all-conquering and dominating **Mika Häkkinen**. **McLaren** seemed to have the aerodynamic problems surrounding the front wing sorted out, following intense windtunnel work. There was also much news about Coulthard's sexual prowess in British tabloid newspapers. Split from his girlfriend, he was having a wonderful time.

**Benetton Renault** was in serious trouble with its new, 11-degree-wide vee engine.

For the first time car-makers began to rattle the cage, suggesting they would set up a Formula One series to rival the current **FIA/FOM** series. **ACEA**, a grouping of European companies –

A popular man departed the world on 25th April 2001. Michele Alboreto lost his life in an Audi sportscar in Germany after the limitations of a new circuit's safety measures were tragically tested.

**BMW, Fiat, Ford, DaimlerChrysler** and **Renault** – was seeking to establish its own series when the current **Concorde** agreement ended in 2007. Fiat chairman **Paolo Cantarella** was behind the move. It was all down to the arrival of the German **Kirch Gruppe** as majority owner of the commercial rights. ACEA eventually said it was happy with the status quo as long as **Bernie Ecclestone** was in control of the company.

There was much German joy when **Ralf Schumacher** scooped the San Marino Grand Prix. His first win – **Williams's** first in four years – came after an unprecedented drought for the team.

The predicted driver upheaval at **Jaguar** and **Prost** happened. **Gaston Mazzacane** was out altogether and **Luciano Burti** joined Prost from Jaguar after **Bobby Rahal** paid **Alain Prost** a rumoured $2 million sweetener to take him. **Pedro de la Rosa** was promoted to the race team from Barcelona onwards. The only surprise was that it had taken so long.

There were many rumours that **British American Tobacco** wished to dispose of its

After four years without a win BMW Williams took the honours at the San Marino Grand Prix in April 2001. The scene of much unhappiness in 1994 was so different in 2001 as Ralf Schumacher also took his maiden victory. He made history as the Schumachers became the first brothers to both have won Formula One races.

equity stake in the **BAR Honda** team and remain only as a sponsor. **Craig Pollock** admitted it had unsettled him.

Elsewhere there was increasing tension between **Niki Lauda** and **Bobby Rahal** over the management of the **Jaguar** team. That was to erupt later.

**Tom Walkinshaw**, team principal of **Arrows**, was pressing for a new rule to compel engine makers to supply more than one team. To no one's surprise, the call was rejected.

There was some discussion during the month about wheel tethers not working. **FIA** expert **Peter Wright** suggested stronger versions and decreed they had to stay.

**Michele Alboreto**, a Formula One driver until 1994, lost his life testing an **Audi** sportscar at the new Lausitzring circuit. The testing had been at high speed in preparation for the Le Mans 24-hours. Alboreto's car took off after a tyre failure and jumped an Armco barrier, bounced back off a bank and hit the rear of the barrier, flattening the top of the car.

**Mika Häkkinen** lost the Spanish Grand Prix on the very last lap after his car stopped in a cloud of smoke. He handed victory to **Michael Schumacher's Ferrari**.

The return of traction control provided no surprises at all and the grid stayed exactly the same as it might have been without.

**Jaguar** poached a new race engineer called **Mark Ellis** from **BAR**. He was to be paid £250,000 a year.

# May 2001

**G**ustav Brunner caused all the fuss in May when he dramatically left **Minardi** and took a rumoured $4 million-a-year cheque to join the **Toyota** programme. Simultaneously it was announced that Toyota's existing technical director, the highly regarded **André de Cortanze**, was resigning after refusing to work under Brunner. He took a lot of his team with him. The cause of the upheaval was clear. The test car designed by de Cortanze and his team was painfully slow in its first test against the other teams. As much as 10 seconds a lap too slow.

**Goodyear**, which had withdrawn from Formula One three years previously, was sniffing around for a comeback. The tyre giant admitted it had made a mistake getting out and now faced a long fight back. Its problem was that the best teams had the longest contracts and only **McLaren** was available. The soonest it

On 12th May 2001, Paul Morgan, managing director of Ilmor Engineering and one of Formula One's highest achievers, lost his life flying one of his personal collection of war planes at an aerodrome in Northamptonshire.

could be back would be 2003 – leaving the team high and dry for 2002. There was no solution.

**Paul Stoddart** proposed a new system to limit the poaching of employees within teams. This would become a big issue mid-year.

There was a minor row as **Michael Schumacher** took second in the Austrian Grand Prix, but not before his team-mate **Rubens Barrichello** had been ordered to move over.

Launch control failures were becoming an epidemic as drivers kept getting left on the grid. Four drivers had been left behind in Austria and the **McLaren** system had twice let **David Coulthard** down.

There was tragic news at the Austrian Grand Prix: 52-year-old **Paul Morgan**, one of the founders of **Ilmor Engineering**, the builder of the Mercedes Formula One engine, had lost his life in an aeroplane accident. The news reached the Formula One paddock late on Saturday afternoon.

Ferrari boss **Luca di Montezemolo** was offered a job as a minister in the cabinet of new Italian prime minister **Silvio Berlusconi**. He turned it down, saying he already had a better job.

**Sylvester Stallone's** new movie, Driven, originally to have been about Formula One, opened in America and topped the box-office charts, taking $13 million. It then dived

Gabriele Rumi, the Minardi team owner until the end of 2000, died on 21st May 2001 after a long illness. He was involved as a sponsor and team owner for 20 years.

and was dubbed an awful production by the critics. It wasn't as bad as that and most thought it entertaining. But they also thought **Bernie Ecclestone's** decision to reject Stallone's overtures to make the film about Formula One was the correct one.

**Tom Walkinshaw** appeared to have finally pulled off his dream to get a Grand Prix in Russia. **Bernie Ecclestone** and he travelled to Moscow before the Austrian Grand Prix to conduct negotiations.

**Patrick McNally**, the president of **Allsport**, owner of the Paddock Club, received an offer for his company from venture capitalists.

**Roger Silman**, long-time managing director of the **Arrows** team, retired at the age of 55 for a quieter life.

After it emerged that there would be a testing ban in 2001 for November and December, **Williams** said it would design a sportscar body to put Formula One components into so that it could legitimately go testing. The testing ban was to be revoked for 2002. No one knew if **Patrick Head** was serious or not.

The month ended at the Monaco Grand Prix

Luca de Montezemolo didn't have to think long when he was offered a job in Silvio Berlusconi's new Italian government. He already had the best job in the world.

as **David Coulthard** swept to pole position and then the team bungled his race again, letting **Michael Schumacher** in. It was the second race in succession that **McLaren** had handed **Ferrari** an easy race win. Team principal **Ron Dennis** also opened negotiations with his drivers for 2002. **Häkkinen** was offered a pay cut, Coulthard a big rise.

Meanwhile the big car-makers presented their demands to **Kirch Gruppe** for more participation in the sport. They wanted to buy 65 per cent of the equity in the rights holding company **SLEC**, for a reasonable price. They were, however, unprepared to pay the $2.4 billion being asked for the stake. There was an impasse. A threat to ▷

organise a rival series before the Concorde agreement ran out in 2007 was withdrawn as impractical.

At the end of the month **Michael Schumacher** finally signed a new contract to keep him at **Ferrari** until the end of 2004, and **Rubens Barrichello** was confirmed for 2002 as well: Schumacher for a rumoured $36 million a year, Barrichello at considerably less.

As the month ended it became clear that **McLaren's** technical director **Adrian Newey** was on the verge of signing a contract for **Jaguar Racing** and that he would be leaving

Alain Prost and Pedro Diniz started out as firm friends in 2001 and ended up the year as firm enemies.

**McLaren**. It was just the start of a saga that would get very messy in June.

The former owner of the **Minardi** team until this season, 61-year-old **Gabriele Rumi** died on Monday 21st May after a fight against cancer. The illness had forced Rumi to sell the team. He was a long-standing Formula One entrant through his **Fondmetal** company and had been involved in the sport for 20 years.

**Nigel Mansell** was appointed as the new editor-in-chief of **Formula 1 Magazine** after **Niki Lauda** resigned when he joined Jaguar. Lauda had been appointed last September before his involvement with Jaguar Racing became known.

## June 2001

The month was dominated by the **Adrian Newey** saga. It was an astonishing affair, as the **McLaren** man signed for **Jaguar** and then changed his mind within hours. It left his friend and Jaguar team principal, **Bobby Rahal**, highly bemused, as **Ron Dennis** persuaded Newey his best interests were in staying at McLaren. Jaguar

boss **Niki Lauda** instigated legal action and got a rumoured $1 million in compensation from McLaren. No one in Formula One could quite believe it, especially Ron Dennis, whose life had been ripped apart, as his mother **Evelyn Dennis** died the same day as Newey agreed his Jaguar deal. It was a treble blow for Dennis after the death of **Ilmor's Paul Morgan**.

**Vodafone** announced it was to sponsor the **Ferrari** team from 2002 for three years – a big-money deal arranged by title sponsor **Philip Morris** that was rumoured to be worth $150 million for second billing. Other small sponsors were being removed to give **Marlboro**, Vodafone and **Shell** almost a three-way exclusive.

**Vittorio Brambilla**, the Italian driver who raced Formula One in the 1970s, died of a heart attack at the age of 64.

The **Minardi** and **Arrows** teams were searching for engine suppliers for 2002. A supply of **Asiatech** and **Cosworth** engines was available.

**Ralf Schumacher** swept to victory in Montreal to win the Canadian Grand Prix. But the highlight for many was a weekend-long scuffle between drivers **Jacques Villeneuve** and **Juan Pablo Montoya** after they brake tested each other in Friday practice. A fracas in the garages and then in a driver briefing was defused by **Charlie Whiting** and **Bernie Ecclestone**.

Poor old **Heinz-Harald Frentzen** was forced to miss the Canadian Grand Prix due to headaches and dizziness suffered after a practice crash. He also announced he had taken up his option to drive for **Jordan Honda** in 2002. **Eddie Jordan** was not happy about that, as later developments would reveal.

**Michael Schumacher** scored his 49th Grand Prix victory and his fifth of the season when he led the European Grand Prix almost from start to finish to open up a 24-point lead over **David Coulthard** at the top of the world championship table.

**Mike Gascoyne**, **Benetton's** technical director, was furious with some Formula One websites after they started rumours that he and team principal **Flavio Briatore** had been fired

The month of June was dominated by the Adrian Newey saga. Everyone thought Newey had left McLaren for Jaguar. Then it turned out he hadn't. Bobby Rahal was bemused by the turn of events.

Vittorio Brambilla, an Italian legend of the 1970s, only one won race but he will always be remembered as one half of a brotherly act. He died of natural causes on 27th May 2001.

from the Benetton Renault team. There was no basis for the rumours and Gascoyne called the journalists involved 'pathetic'.

By then it was an open secret that **Mika Häkkinen** was considering retirement. He had rejected **McLaren's** offer of a reduced retainer for 2002 and would either move teams, retire altogether or take a sabbatical. All would become clear later in the year, or clearer.

**Craig Pollock** put his foot down and told **Adrian Reynard** that his company couldn't build a new windtunnel for **Jaguar** on the same trading estate as Reynard and **BAR** were based.

American driving star **Dario Franchitti**, the Scot with the Italian name, said he wanted to drive Formula One in 2002. The trouble was no one would offer him a drive. **Bridgestone** said it would stay as a Formula One tyre supplier indefinitely. There had been rumours it would withdraw.

Huge rumours also surrounded the **Prost** team as it became clear it had run out of cash. It owed suppliers millions and desperately needed money. The problem was that principal shareholders **Alain Prost** and **Abilio Diniz** had fallen out and a sponsorship deal with **Bertelsmann** offshoot **UFA Sports** had ground to a halt. It was desperate.

**Ron Dennis** and the publisher of the new **Formula 1 Magazine**, **Tom Rubython**, fell out after a huge public row at the European Grand Prix over the reporting of the **Adrian Newey** affair. The two agreed to disagree but not after some unseemly wrangling that benefited no one.

**Patrick Head** threw himself headlong into some 24-hour days and seven-day weeks as he sought to solve the **BMW Williams** team's reliability problems.

**Derek Wright**, the editor of an obscure but resilient magazine called **F1 News**, passed away after a long illness. He died of a heart attack. Having started his journalistic career writing ▷

Passion

ONE
AIM

"It's impossible," says Reason.  "It's reckless," says Experience.
"It's painful," says Pride.  "Try!" says Dream.
The challenge... to bring a dream to life.

2002 Formula 1 Competitor
www.toyota-f1.com

TOYOTA

manuals for fire extinguishers he progressed to mainstream journalism and confounded sceptics by keeping his magazine going year after year in the face of overwhelming competition.

**Craig Pollock** complained about the rising cost of employing staff for Formula One teams. Many **BAR** team members had been poached in 2001 to join **Jaguar** and **Toyota** with big offers.

It was finally Sir Jackie Stewart. Stewart celebrated by diving headfirst into a campaign to get £40 million of government money to help Silverstone redevelop.

Pollock had conveniently forgotten that he himself had started the trend when he set up BAR in 1998.

Silverstone owners **Octagon** announced big plans to redevelop the circuit. If fully implemented they could cost £100 million. Half the money had been found and **Jackie Stewart** wanted the government to fund the rest.

As for **Jackie Stewart** he finally got his long-deserved knighthood from the **Queen**. He thought himself far too grand to attend any more Grand Prix events, although he did go to two races, escorting **Lady Helen Windsor** at Silverstone and **Jacques Nasser** at Indianapolis.

**Dietrich Mateschitz** took an option out with **Morgan Grenfell Private Equity**, owner of 70 per cent of the **Arrows** team, to buy it.

Finally there was a proposal to introduce brake lights into Formula One after drivers had run into the back of each other at a few races. The idea appeared ridiculous and eventually it was proven so.

## July 2001

The first day of July started a hectic schedule that would see the month host three races as the teams cleared the decks to give themselves a three-week break in August. In France, at Magny-Cours, **Michael Schumacher** brought up his half century of victories with a comfortable win and a championship-winning 31-point advantage over **David Coulthard.** Tyres proved the crucial factor.

**Ferrari** also revealed it was building a

specially powerful qualifying engine to run at Silverstone for the British Grand Prix and the rest of the year.

There was a daft idea proposed for a Grand Prix to be held at night by **Philippe Gurdjian**, who promotes the Malaysian Grand Prix. Naturally the idea, if serious, didn't progress very far and was quickly filed with various other absurd notions such as brake lights.

Rumours began to circulate that **Minardi** driver **Tarso Marques** was not long for Formula One as the team prepared to bring on the first Malaysian driver, a young man called **Alex Yoong**. He would be bringing a fortune in sponsorship from the Malaysian national lottery called **Magnum**. It all came to pass.

**Arrows** boss **Tom Walkinshaw** finally got himself a decent engine when he signed a deal with **Niki Lauda** to secure **Cosworth** engines for 2002. Some people said it was costing $25 million, but others said it was very little in exchange for a lot of windtunnel time **Jaguar** desperately needed. Meanwhile **HSBC**, the bank, signed up as title sponsor for **Jaguar** for another four years.

The British Grand Prix in the middle of the month saw a welcome return to the winner's podium for **Mika Häkkinen**. He ended a barren spell dating right back to Spa in 2000. It was also the Finn's first ever win in the British Grand Prix. Surprisingly **McLaren** won by outthinking a clumsy **Ferrari** on strategy. Häkkinen adopted a two-stop approach that saw him open a 33-second advantage over **Michael Schumacher** by the end of the race. Fans were not so pleased, however, as huge traffic jams made getting in and out of Silverstone as difficult as ever. Park-and-ride schemes were marred by the fact that the coaches used also got caught in the jams and were delayed or late.

A big row broke out over the new **Toyota** team and testing. Toyota intended to test as much as it liked between the end of the season and 15th November, the date by which teams had to register for the 2002 championship. Other teams, notably **Craig Pollock**'s **BAR**, thought it

The Formula One world was shocked in late July when Eddie Jordan summarily fired his contracted number one driver in a terse fax and replaced him with Jean Alesi. Heinz-Harald Frentzen (above) found a drive with Prost in August and liked the French team.

Sid Watkins, the Formula One doctor, brought out a new book criticising the Monza chicanes. Surprisingly, nothing was done about them.

should abide by the testing ban that applied to competing teams. Toyota argued it was not a competing team until 15th November.

**Michael Schumacher** had yet another bad accident testing at Monza at the second chicane. Apparently the underbody broke. The Monza chicanes were to cause immense trouble later in the year. **Sid Watkins**, Formula One's doctor, also criticised the Monza chicanes in his new book called **Beyond The Limit**.

High drama was played out in the weeks after the British Grand Prix. **Heinz-Harald Frentzen** was sacked as **Jordan's** number one and replaced with test driver **Ricardo Zonta** for the German Grand Prix. Frentzen sat out his home race at home. When the dust settled for Hungary, **Jean Alesi** was out of **Prost** and into Jordan and Frentzen took Alesi's place at Prost, threatening to sue Jordan for millions.

At the end of the month **Ralf Schumacher** scored a comfortable third win of the season at the German Grand Prix from maiden pole-sitter **Juan Pablo Montoya**, whose **BMW** engine blew up on lap 25 heading for a big win. The race was enlivened by a flying start from **Prost** driver **Luciano Burti**, whose car took off over the wheel of **Michael Schumacher's** slowing Ferrari at the start of the race. Burti was unhurt as the teams headed for their holidays.

## August 2001

Formula One had a three-week rest in August and most protagonists went off on holiday. Early in the month it was confirmed that **Jean Alesi** would step into a **Jordan** in Hungary and his photograph appeared everywhere in yellow overalls. The biggest shock was **Heinz-Harald Frentzen** taking his place at **Prost**.

As all this was going on **Bobby Rahal** approached **Eddie Jordan** and offered him a $5 million sweetener to take **Eddie Irvine** off **Jaguar's** hands for the 2002 season. When a furious **Niki Lauda** heard about it, he told

**BRIDGESTONE**
A GRIP ON THE FUTURE

POTENZA S-03 *Pole Position*

*We Can't Promise The Same Thrills,*
*But We Guarantee The Same Technology.*

**BRIDGESTONE**
**POTENZA**
**S-03** *Pole Position*

# Beirut Grand Prix

## BEIRUT is ready to host
## FORMULA 1 GRAND PRIX

Traditionally a regional centre for business and leisure, Beirut is forging ahead as a unique venue for international events.

It is an exciting destination for Formula **1** fans, as one of the few places that can offer an ideal track, within the city and near the waterfront.

Endowed with a mild climate, Mediterranean panoramas, six thousand years of history, and a vibrant city centre, Beirut offers the visitor a cosmopolitan environment, world-class accommodation, fabulous shopping and a variety of entertainment.

**Let's make it happen in Beirut!**

Beirut Grand Prix

# the right Formula for 2004

The planned track winds through Beirut city centre and along its new waterfront

  **SOLIDERE** Developing the *finest* city centre in the Middle East.

Tel: (961-1) 980650 to 660 • e-mail. info@solidere.com.lb

Eddie Jordan it wasn't feasible. Rahal later claimed it was a joke. But a joke Lauda did not find funny.

Meanwhile **Peter Sauber's** Swiss team had made everybody take notice of its performance, as it looked as though it would hang on to fourth place in the constructors' championship. It was a wake-up call for a lot of other fancied teams, which were being beaten by a team that some in the paddock regard as Swiss hicks.

**Adrian Newey**, back in full harness after the **Jaguar** debacle, said **Mika Häkkinen** would

Ken Tyrrell, the great team entrant of the 1970s and winner of three world championships, finally succumbed to cancer at the end of August.

stay with the **McLaren Mercedes** team for 2002. Clearly he was not being kept up-to-date, as by early August his boss **Ron Dennis** had **Kimi Räikkönen's** signature on a provisional contract.

After a three-week rest **Michael Schumacher** sealed his fourth world championship and equalled **Alain Prost's** all-time record 51 Grand Prix wins with a dominant victory, his seventh of the season, in the Hungarian Grand Prix.

**Schumacher** repeated his back-to-back championships with **Benetton** in 1994-5 and then set his sights on **Juan Manuel Fangio's** record five titles. **David Coulthard** was 43 points behind with just four races remaining. Remarkably **Ferrari's** one-two with **Rubens Barrichello** also sealed the constructors' title – an incredible achievement with four races left.

**Jarno Trulli** was considering his future for the whole of August, wondering whether he should stay at Jordan for 2002 or go to **Benetton**, which will become **Renault** next year. Both teams wanted him but in the end he went to Renault, which meant current Benetton number one **Giancarlo Fisichella** went to **Jordan Honda**.

In the last days of August **Ken Tyrrell**, the great stalwart whose **Tyrrell** team competed for 30 years in Formula One and won three world championships, died. He had been suffering from cancer and it was no surprise. He was

mourned at the **Silverstone Historic Festival**, which lowered its flags for the great team entrant.

**Thomas Haffa**, the man who had steered **EM.TV** into Formula One and seen it own half of the sport's commercial rights, resigned and his place was taken by **Werner Klatten**, a member of the **BMW** founding family. EM.TV was left with a stake in Formula One of around 16 per cent but wanted to sell it. Haffa was preceded out of EM.TV by his brother **Florian**. The pair had entered Formula One triumphantly barely a year earlier but their company fell apart as technology shares bombed on Wall Street. It was generally perceived they had overpaid for these acquisitions.

**Charlie Whiting**, the **FIA's** technical supremo, was close to agreeing the teams could use electric fans to cool brakes in 2002. Teams had complained about the problems of cooling brakes properly without fan assistance. Any fans in Formula One cars had been banned since 1978 when the **Brabham** fan car was outlawed.

There was doubt over whether **McLaren Mercedes'** test driver **Alex Wurz** would be retained for 2003. He hoped to be. **Peter Sauber** was still hoping to retain the sponsorship of **Red Bull** despite an earlier fall-out with owner **Dietrich Mateschitz**.

Hockenheim finally announced plans that will see the circuit shortened and revamped. It will drop from 4.5 miles to 2.7 miles and increase seating capacity from 83,000 to 120,000. The Formula One contract was extended to 2008.

In the last week of the month the news broke that **Jaguar** team principal **Bobby Rahal** had been fired and **Niki Lauda** would take over as team principal. Rahal had been in the job for less than nine months but the tension between him and Lauda had been clear since Lauda's appointment in February. Rahal had made many friends and most were sorry to see him go.

Ove Andersson, Toyota's team principal got in a testing row with other teams. He stood his ground and criticised Formula One's coldness to his new team.

Mika Häkkinen ran his last race for McLaren in Japan and was adamant he was coming back to race again. The big question would be whether it was at McLaren. Ron Dennis was keeping all his options open.

## September 2001

Heinz-Harald Frentzen opened the month by serving a high court writ on the **Jordan** team demanding $9.35 million in compensation for his sacking mid-season. It was made up of $5.5 million in wages and the rest from lost personal sponsorship and race bonuses.

Three races were being shoehorned into September before the end of the season in early October. It was to be **Michael Schumacher's** month. On the 10th anniversary of his Grand Prix debut at Spa, he became the most successful driver in the history of Formula One by scoring his 52nd victory in the Belgian Grand Prix.

His record was overshadowed by the two starts that were necessary, first when **Frentzen's Prost** stalled from fourth on the grid and then when **Luciano Burti** had the worst accident of the year. It was a mishap that effectively ended his Formula One race career and he was not to appear for Prost again. It was a dreadful time for **Alain Prost**, who was also in the middle of a huge cash crunch that was threatening the team's survival. Saudi Arabian entrepreneur **Prince Khaled Al Waleed** wanted to ride to the rescue but due diligence was proving tricky.

It takes a very big news event to overshadow Formula One, but that is exactly what happened with the terrorist attacks in America on Tuesday 11th September. The Italian Grand Prix defied other sporting cancellations and went ahead, Formula One supremo **Bernie Ecclestone** firmly believing in the credo that business as usual is the best way to fight terrorism.

As a tribute to America, a very important market for **Ferrari** road cars, **Jean Todt** ordered the cars stripped of logos and added a black nose. It appeared to spook **Michael Schumacher**, who did not want to race and tried to lobby other drivers into race sanctions, concerned about the safety of the first two chicanes. He also refused to do any commercial work all weekend, which didn't please Ferrari's marketing team trying to keep sponsors and guests happy. **Ron Dennis** said he would support his drivers in whatever they wanted to do, but he didn't think half-an-hour before the race was the right time to be contemplating the safety of chicanes at Monza. **Flavio Briatore**, meanwhile, was much more vociferous. "If my drivers don't want to overtake on the first lap

## :: THE MICHELIN TEAM.
### COMMITTED FOR THE PERFORMANCE.
### FOR ITS DRIVERS, FOR YOU. ::

All the Michelin team, passionately fond of innovation, is committed
to always create the best tyre.
Today, researchers, engineers, technicians share their experiences to win
the race and take this advantage to let you benefit from their successes.
Today looks like yesterday and like tomorrow.
And you, do you have tyres or Michelin?

www.michelinf1.com

On 30th September 2001 Murray Walker and Martin Brundle spent their last day in the commentary box together, at Indianapolis. It was a highly emotional time for both men.

they can look for another team next year," he stormed.

**Michael Schumacher**, personally furious about drivers being pressured into a situation against their will, took it upon himself to go on a grid walk advocating first lap caution among his colleagues. It didn't work after it was revealed that most of the drivers had only reluctantly gone along with it and **Jacques Villeneuve** wanted nothing to do with it at all.

On Saturday, after qualifying, came dreadful news that **Alex Zanardi**, the former **Lotus** and **Williams** driver, had been badly injured in the first CART race in Europe at Germany's oval Lausitzring. Both his legs were later amputated. Zanardi's life was saved by **Dr Steve Olvey**, one of the superb CART medical team. Zanardi would soon be on his way to a full recovery apart from his disabilities. There was even talk of him being able to race again in specially-modified cars, such are the advances made by electronics.

The following day **Juan Pablo Montoya** won his first Grand Prix at Monza on a day when **BMW Williams** opted for a one-stop strategy and **Ferrari** went with two. Montoya was only the seventh rookie to win in the history of Formula One.

The race was also notable for an announcement on the Friday that **Mika Häkkinen** would take a year's sabbatical and be replaced in the **McLaren Mercedes** team by **Sauber's Kimi Räikkönen**. Räikkönen had an unusual one-year firm and three years at McLaren's option. He would be paid $8 million a year and Sauber would also get $5 million a year if he stayed the four years. Häkkinen seemed determined to return in 2003, which rather worried **David Coulthard**, who had a three-year driving contract in his pocket. Three into two doesn't go and **Ron Dennis** added to the concern when he appeared to offer hope for **Nick Heidfeld** in 2003 as well.

**Paul Stoddart**, the aviation entrepreneur, was reeling from the effects of 11th September on his airline business. But he joyfully announced a deal to get **Asiatech** engines for

2002. At least he didn't have to pay for them.

It was a time of emotion, when **Mika Häkkinen** scored a win in the United States Grand Prix after a superbly judged race of strategy. He was also lucky when **Juan Pablo Montoya** retired from certain victory. But the race was marked by the very last appearance of **Murray Walker** as **ITV's** commentator. It was an emotional time and **Martin Brundle** was close to tears in the commentary box. As for Walker, he had to endure more farewell parties than he could probably cope with. His passing was also marked by appearing simultaneously on the covers of the sport's two leading magazines – **F1 Racing** and **Formula 1 Magazine**. Not many people get to do that.

**Jean Alesi** ended the month having a go at **Flavio Briatore** over his ordering of drivers to race in Italy. He said: "He is a bully and this is a disgrace." No one took much notice or agreed with him. Most pundits reckoned that, as Briatore paid his drivers some $12 million a year, or $250,000 a week to race, he was entitled to ask them to do just that. Many journalists were, in any case, unhappy with **Alesi**, who had recently been spinning some big yarns regarding his contractual arrangements for 2001 and 2002.

Britain held its first CART race for some time at the new Rockingham oval track a few miles from Silverstone. Afterwards **David Grace**, the chief executive, said the annual event could come to rival Formula One. It was a great day of racing but not on the scale of Formula One. At the time the event had less atmosphere than a Brands Hatch club day, although when the race was getting started it all warmed up.

**Eddie Irvine** criticised the **Jaguar** team for recruiting inexperienced engineers. He said Jaguar was the least experienced team in Formula One.

There was massive competition for the one

A young man who was racing in go-karts two years before found himself a McLaren Mercedes driver. Kimi Räikkönen was also being paid $8 million a year.

top drive left in Formula One in 2002, at the **Jordan Honda** team. **Jean Alesi**, **Takuma Sato** and **Justin Wilson** all wanted it. But Sato, purely by reason of nationality, had it in the bag. **Eddie Jordan** saw what **Craig Pollock** apparently couldn't.

The provisional race calendar for 2002 revealed in mid-September was pronounced a hoax. Three weeks later the exact same schedule was released and this wasn't a hoax. It was more of the same on slightly different dates with the three-week holiday experiment in August repeated.

By the end of the month **Michael Schumacher** was up for breaking three season records: most points ever, most wins ever and most constructors' points ever. He managed to break the most points ever but the other two remained.

German entrepreneur Leo Kirch became the master of Formula One's commercial future when he finally ended up in control of 75 per cent of SLEC, the Formula One holding company. Bernie Ecclestone kept 25 per cent.

## October 2001

The month opened with the news that **Max Mosley** had been re-elected president of the **Fédération Internationale de l'Automobile** (FIA) for the next four years until 2005. After that he said he would retire at the age of 65. The FIA's general assembly in Cologne also announced a few other rule changes and new members. Britain lost its place on the council.

The **FIA** confirmed that power-steering would be banned for 2002 along with relaxing the restrictions on telemetry. Now teams will be able to reprogramme cars' electronics on the move from the pits. **Mosley** also said he wanted to see more races held outside Europe, including two in the United States and one in the Middle East. He said there was room on the calendar for 20 races and less testing.

Mosley said the FIA would be relocating to Paris from Geneva in 2002. It originally moved to Geneva from Paris a few years ago for tax and legal reasons. When it returns to France it will share office space with the **Automobile Club de France** on the Place de la Concorde.

With the news that **Takuma Sato** had signed for **Jordan Honda** and young Brazilian ▷

newcomer **Felipe Massa** for **Sauber**, the team line-up for 2002 was virtually complete, although inevitably the tail-end **Arrows**, **Prost** and **Minardi** drivers were all up for grabs, the teams scurrying around for the best rent-a-drive deals they could get. **Heinz-Harald Frentzen** looked set to lead either the **Prost** or **Arrows** teams for 2002. He has an advantage in that he does not require a large salary as he is likely to be paid by Jordan for 2002.

At the final general press conference of the year in Japan, team principals Craig Pollock, Ron Dennis and Eddie Jordan shared the platform with drivers Alex Yoong, Mika Häkkinen and Heinz-Harald Frentzen. The team principals all agreed that Formula One was about to enter a period of financial doom and gloom as far as sponsorship was concerned. The events of Tuesday 11th September had changed the economic landscape of Formula One.

By season's end a wealthy young man called Prince Khaled Al Waleed, the son of one of the wealthiest men in the world, was bidding to buy the Prost team.

**Mika Häkkinen** told the German magazine **Auto Moto und Sport** that he thought **Michael Schumacher** would retire imminently. Schumacher replied that Häkkinen didn't know what he would do in the future. But Häkkinen persisted: "I see certain signs that lead me to doubt whether he will continue driving for a long time."

In a small ceremony at home in Salzburg, **Ralf Schumacher** married **Cora Brinkmann**. She is expecting the couple's first child in November. Simultaneously **Jacques Villeneuve** got engaged again, this time to **Ellie Green**, a 19-year-old New York ballerina.

It was revealed that **Ron Dennis**, **Mario Illien**, **Jurgen Hubbert** and **Roger Penske** were in discussions about the future of **Mercedes** Formula One engine builder **Ilmor Engineering**. The likely result was that Penske would bail out and Ilmor would become part of **Tag McLaren**. It was also known that McLaren, **Ferrari** and **BMW Williams** would have cast-titanium gearboxes for 2002.

Barely was the maestro's seat cold than **James Allen**, as expected, was announced as **Murray Walker's** permanent successor as ITV's lead commentator.

**Dietrich Mateschitz** was on his way to forming a **Red Bull**-sponsored Formula One team out of the existing **Arrows** team run by **Tom Walkinshaw**. Mateschitz has an option to buy 70 per cent from venture capitalists **Morgan Grenfell Private Equity**. The future of Walkinshaw in that scenario was unknown.

The **Kirch Gruppe** was making all sorts of moves to consolidate its ownership of Formula One's commercial rights, which had been mixed up in a rag-bag of structures. By month end it was in a process that would see it own 75 per cent of holding company **SLEC** at an approximate cost of some $2.2 billion, valuing the whole at roughly $3 billion against a peak valuation of $4 billion two years before.

**Jean Alesi** announced he was retiring from the sport moments after **Takuma Sato** was revealed as his **Jordan** replacement. Alesi's announcement at a **Bridgestone** press conference in Tokyo surprised everyone including **Eddie Jordan**, and appears to have been made on the spur of the moment.

The season wound up with a resounding win for **Michael Schumacher** in the Japanese Grand Prix, equalling his own and **Nigel Mansell's** record for nine victories in a season. He also broke the all-time points scoring record, making 801 career points, beating **Alain Prost's** record of 798.5 career points. **Jean Alesi** threw away the opportunity to become the first driver for 37 years to finish every race in a season by running into a spinning **Kimi Räikkönen** at Suzuka.

There was speculation surrounding the future of **British American Racing**. It was known principal shareholder BAT wished to sell its shares and **Craig Pollock** was trying to put together a consortium to buy them, this time with **David Hunt**, an entrepreneur and brother of the late **James Hunt**.

**Ferrari** was apparently testing a new system developed by the **FOM** that detects cars on the

Tom Walkinshaw found his position uncertain at the end of the season as Austrian soft drinks entrepreneur, Dietrich Mateschitz, announced he was selling his share in the Sauber team to buy a share in Arrows and turn the team into a promotional vehicle in order to help sell Red Bull in America.

track in poor visibility and shows them to the driver in the cockpit by way of a radar system.

The season ended on a sombre note as four team principals – **Paul Stoddart**, **Ron Dennis**, **Eddie Jordan** and **Craig Pollock**, at the last general press conference of the race season – warned how the events of Tuesday 11th September were affecting teams' finances. The sport was already reeling at having lost all three telecoms sponsors: **Lucent**, **Marconi** and **Nortel**, at a cost of around $15 million. Worse was to come. New sponsorship deals had been lost and others delayed as it was revealed that some existing sponsors had tried to withdraw from long-standing signed contracts. **Paul Stoddart's Minardi** team was thought to be particularly vulnerable because of its links to the aviation industry.

Jean Alesi departed Formula One after a 12-year career and 201 races. He had earned plenty of money but achieved little success, winning only one race. He had also provided race fans with entertainment and enjoyment during his years in the sport.

Red Bull
SAUBER PETRONAS

RACE
TEST
HOME

# TEAM
# WORK

Thank you all **4** your dedication!

Red Bull · PETRONAS MALAYSIA · CREDIT SUISSE · BRIDGESTONE · BABCOCK BORSIG · walter meier oag · MAGNETI MARELLI · Emil Frey AG · Microsoft · BBS GIUGIARO · TOSHIBA · comROAD · MAN · sparco · CATIA SOLUTIONS · MSC SOFTWARE · TEMENOS · ERICSSON · MCM

# Formula 1 ™

# THE DRIVERS 2001

p56

7th p60

8th p62

9th p64

10th p66

11th p68

p82

18th p84

19th p86

20th p88

21st p90

22nd p91

23rd p92

24th p93

25th p94

26th p95

# 2001 Season Record

The drivers at the first race in Melbourne. Left to right, back row: Jean Alesi, Gaston Mazzacane, Jos Verstappen, Enrique Bernoldi, Jacques Villeneuve, Olivier Panis, Fernando Alonso, Tarso Marques. Middle row: Heinz-Harald Frentzen, Jarno Trulli, Nick Heidfeld, Kimi Räikkönen, Eddie Irvine, Luciano Burti. Front row: Giancarlo Fisichella, Jenson Button, David Coulthard, Mika Häkkinen, Michael Schumacher, Rubens Barrichello, Juan Pablo Montoya, Ralf Schumacher.

The drivers at the last race in Suzuka. Left to right, back row: Jos Verstappen, Enrique Bernoldi, Heinz-Harald Frentzen, Tomas Enge, Giancarlo Fisichella, Jenson Button, Alex Yoong, Fernando Alonso. Middle row: Juan Pablo Montoya, Ralf Schumacher, Michael Schumacher, Rubens Barrichello, David Coulthard, Mika Häkkinen. Front row: Olivier Panis, Jacques Villeneuve, Nick Heidfeld, Kimi Räikkönen, Jarno Trulli, Jean Alesi, Eddie Irvine, Pedro de la Rosa.

Note: classified places are not included in the retirement totals. Mechanical retirements are listed when the retirement is due to the car, driver error retirements due to the driver and accident retirements due to another driver.

## Rubens Barrichello

2001 Grand Prix entered: 17
Wins: 0
Pole positions: 0
Front row: 3 — 3rd
Points scored: 56
Qual against team mate: 1:16
Retirements: 3
Mechanical retirements: 1
Accident retirements: 1
Driving error retirements: 1
Reliability record: 87.1%

## Ralf Schumacher

2001 Grand Prix entered: 17
Wins: 3
Pole positions: 1 — 4th
Front row: 7
Points scored: 49
Qual against team mate: 11:6
Retirements: 7
Mechanical retirements: 4
Accident retirements: 2
Driving error retirements: 1
Reliability record: 75.7%

## Mika Häkkinen

2001 Grand Prix entered: 17
Wins: 2
Pole positions: 0 — 5th
Front row: 3
Points scored: 37
Qual against team mate: 9:8
Retirements: 7
Mechanical retirements: 7
Accident retirements: 0
Driving error retirements: 0
Reliability record: 64.7%

## Juan Pablo Montoya

2001 Grand Prix entered: 17
Wins: 1
Pole positions: 3 — 6th
Front row: 5
Points scored: 31
Qual against team mate: 6:11
Retirements: 11
Mechanical retirements: 7
Accident retirements: 1
Driving error retirements: 3
Reliability record: 63.8%

## Jacques Villeneuve

2001 Grand Prix entered: 17
Wins: 0
Pole positions: 0 — 7th
Front row: 0
Points scored: 12
Qual against team mate: 11:6
Retirements: 6
Mechanical retirements: 3
Accident retirements: 1
Driving error retirements: 2
Reliability record: 74.2%

## Nick Heidfeld

2001 Grand Prix entered: 17
Wins: 0
Pole positions: 0 — 8th
Front row: 0
Points scored: 12
Qual against team mate: 10:7
Retirements: 6
Mechanical retirements: 1
Accident retirements: 3
Driving error retirements: 2
Reliability record: 71.7%

## Michael Schumacher

2001 Grand Prix entered: 17
Wins: 9
Pole positions: 11 — 1st
Front row: 13
Points scored: 123
Qual against team mate: 16:1
Retirements: 2
Mechanical retirements: 2
Accident retirements: 0
Driving error retirements: 0
Reliability record: 94.4%

## David Coulthard

2001 Grand Prix entered: 17
Wins: 2
Pole positions: 2 — 2nd
Front row: 3
Points scored: 65
Qual against team mate: 8:9
Retirements: 4
Mechanical retirements: 3
Accident retirements: 0
Driving error retirements: 1
Reliability record: 86.9%

## Jarno Trulli

2001 Grand Prix entered: 17
Wins: 0
Pole positions: 0 — 9th
Front row: 0
Points scored: 12
Qual against team mate: 15:2
Retirements: 9
Mechanical retirements: 6
Accident retirements: 1
Driving error retirements: 2
Reliability record: 70.9%

## Kimi Räikkönen

2001 Grand Prix entered: 17
Wins: 0
Pole positions: 0 — 10th
Front row: 0
Points scored: 9
Qual against team mate: 7:10
Retirements: 7
Mechanical retirements: 5
Accident retirements: 0
Driving error retirements: 2
Reliability record: 71.0%

Illustrations: Emeric de Baré

## Giancarlo Fisichella

2001 Grand Prix entered: 17
Wins: 0
Pole positions: 0
Front row: 0
Points scored: 8
Qual against team mate: 13:4
Retirements: 6
Mechanical retirements: 5
Accident retirements: 0
Driving error retirements: 1
Reliability record: 76.1%

**11th**

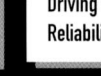

## Eddie Irvine

2001 Grand Prix entered: 17
Wins: 0
Pole positions: 0
Front row: 0
Points scored: 6
Qual against team mate: 11:6
Retirements: 11
Mechanical retirements: 7
Accident retirements: 0
Driving error retirements: 4
Reliability record: 62.3%

**12th**

 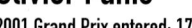

## Heinz-Harald Frentzen

2001 Grand Prix entered: 15
Wins: 0
Pole positions: 0
Front row: 0
Points scored: 6
Qual against team mate: 6:9
Retirements: 6
Mechanical retirements: 2
Accident retirements: 0
Driving error retirements: 4
Reliability record: 75.7%

**13th**

## Olivier Panis

2001 Grand Prix entered: 17
Wins: 0
Pole positions: 0
Front row: 0
Points scored: 5
Qual against team mate: 6:11
Retirements: 6
Mechanical retirements: 5
Accident retirements: 1
Driving error retirements: 0
Reliability record: 73.6%

**14th**

## Jean Alesi

2001 Grand Prix entered: 17
Wins: 0
Pole positions: 0
Front row: 0
Points scored: 5
Qual against team mate: 10:7
Retirements: 1
Mechanical retirements: 0
Accident retirements: 1
Driving error retirements: 0
Reliability record: 93.7%

**15th**

## Pedro de la Rosa

2001 Grand Prix entered: 13
Wins: 0
Pole positions: 0
Front row: 0
Points scored: 3
Qual against team mate: 6:7
Retirements: 6
Mechanical retirements: 3
Accident retirements: 2
Driving error retirements: 1
Reliability record: 70.7%

**16th**

## Jenson Button

2001 Grand Prix entered: 17
Wins: 0
Pole positions: 0
Front row: 0
Points scored: 2
Qual against team mate: 4:13
Retirements: 5
Mechanical retirements: 3
Accident retirements: 0
Driving error retirements: 2
Reliability record: 80.8%

**17th**

## Jos Verstappen

2001 Grand Prix entered: 17
Wins: 0
Pole positions: 0
Front row: 0
Points scored: 1
Qual against team mate: 7:10
Retirements: 5
Mechanical retirements: 4
Accident retirements: 0
Driving error retirements: 1
Reliability record: 83.5%

**18th**

## Ricardo Zonta

2001 Grand Prix entered: 2
Wins: 0
Pole positions: 0
Front row: 0
Points scored: 0
Qual against team mate: 0:2
Retirements: 1
Mechanical retirements: 0
Accident retirements: 0
Driving error retirements: 1
Reliability record: 65.8%

**19th**

## Luciano Burti

2001 Grand Prix entered: 14
Wins: 0
Pole positions: 0
Front row: 0
Points scored: 0
Qual against team mate: 3:11
Retirements: 6
Mechanical retirements: 3
Accident retirements: 1
Driving error retirements: 2
Reliability record: 67.6%

**20th**

## Enrique Bernoldi

2001 Grand Prix entered: 17
Wins: 0
Pole positions: 0
Front row: 0
Points scored: 0
Qual against team mate: 10:7
Retirements: 10
Mechanical retirements: 7
Accident retirements: 0
Driving error retirements: 3
Reliability record: 53.3%

**21st**

## Tarso Marques

2001 Grand Prix entered: 14 (incl.1 DNQ)
Wins: 0
Pole positions: 0
Front row: 0
Points scored: 0
Qual against team mate: 2:12
Retirements: 7
Mechanical retirements: 7
Accident retirements: 0
Driving error retirements: 0
Reliability record: 70.0%

**22nd**

## Fernando Alonso

2001 Grand Prix entered: 17
Wins: 0
Pole positions: 0
Front row: 0
Points scored: 0
Qual against team mate: 15:2
Retirements: 8
Mechanical retirements: 7
Accident retirements: 0
Driving error retirements: 1
Reliability record: 66.4%

**23rd**

## Gaston Mazzacane

2001 Grand Prix entered: 4
Wins: 0
Pole positions: 0
Front row: 0
Points scored: 0
Qual against team mate: 0:4
Retirements: 3
Mechanical retirements: 3
Accident retirements: 0
Driving error retirements: 0
Reliability record: 54.9%

**24th**

## Tomas Enge

2001 Grand Prix entered: 3
Wins: 0
Pole positions: 0
Front row: 0
Points scored: 0
Qual against team mate: 0:3
Retirements: 1
Mechanical retirements: 1
Accident retirements: 0
Driving error retirements: 0
Reliability record: 92.7%

**25th**

## Alex Yoong

2001 Grand Prix entered: 3
Wins: 0
Pole positions: 0
Front row: 0
Points scored: 0
Qual against team mate: 0:3
Retirements: 2
Mechanical retirements: 1
Accident retirements: 0
Driving error retirements: 1
Reliability record: 73.7%

**26th**

# World champion makes it all

**Is Michael Schumacher the best Formula One driver ever? The jury's still out, but after winning his fourth drivers' world championship with four races in hand — and confirming he intends to race for Ferrari until at least 2004 — observers who question his all-time primacy are becoming somewhat thinner on the ground. But behind the image of a ruthlessly perfectionist racer lies a surprisingly sensitive and vulnerable human being. The events in America of 11th September affected him greatly. But he won't rest until he has beaten Ayrton Senna's record of 65 pole positions and Juan Fangio's five world championships. The world is going to see a lot more of Michael Schumacher.**

Michael Schumacher is like a polar ice cap. At first, there is an icy blast of cool politeness, which gradually melts to reveal an intriguing personality. Behind the ice is a surprisingly warm human being, an interesting person with an unquenchable curiosity about life and the people he meets. His approach to life is ruled by the rational, but his feelings are ruled by his heart. His loyalty to his family, friends and colleagues is intense. After 11 seasons of Formula One, he has effectively driven for only two teams and it is likely to stay that way until the end of his career. He still has the same manager and support team that he started with. Michael Schumacher doesn't like change. When terrorists attacked America on 11th September he feared for the future, which led to his actions at the Italian Grand Prix that many disapproved of and he may come to regret.

But no one could take away his mesmerising season. After nearest challenger David Coulthard failed to press home his pole position at the Monaco Grand Prix in May and Schumacher raced unchallenged to the flag, his fourth world championship was never really in doubt.

That Michael Schumacher is a very special man is not in doubt either. Of the six billion people on earth, none can drive as fast as he can. But the cost of that unsurpassed talent is high: as he says: "Attention is always on me. I feel constantly watched whenever I go outside and that's not a comfortable feeling." Sometimes it is even dangerous. At the annual Marlboro ski trip to Madonna di Campiglio in January before the season started, hundreds of fans rushed onto the ice as he appeared on a sledge. As his personal security men also moved in to protect him, the ice cracked and there was a real fear they might all go under. The hysteria that Schumacher causes among fans – especially Germans and Italians – is akin to the attention pop stars like Michael Jackson and Madonna receive.

He admits it 'frightens' him. As a result, he keeps his distance from people. That is evident as he walks through the paddock. But at least in the relative privacy of the paddock, he can wander around without his personal security staff. Outside, it is impossible.

Inside the Ferrari motorhome, as he looks out at the people waiting for him, he says wistfully: "I'd love to go out there and meet them, talk to them and find out something about what they think. But it just isn't possible. I think there is far too much media attention on this sport. I'd rather have less money and more freedom to enjoy the racing."

Schumacher may be a superstar but his adoring fans would be astonished at the very ordinary life he leads outside racing at his home in the tranquil Swiss countryside near Lake Geneva. A prisoner of his famous face, he has found refuge in his family. And while the champion's mental focus and raw ingredients are heaven-sent, the credit for the making of the man goes to Corinna Schumacher, the biggest single influence on Schumacher.

They met when Michael and Heinz-Harald Frentzen were team-mates and Corinna was Frentzen's girlfriend. When that relationship faded, Schumacher pounced. Their first date was in 1990, before he entered Formula One, and they were married five years later. Theirs is not a glamorous relationship in the Hollywood mould; it is suburban and down-to-earth. On the slowing-down lap when he won his third world championship in Japan, he radioed his team and emotionally asked them to give Corinna a big kiss for him. Viewers of digital TV across Europe heard it live.

After being absent for a few races, she reappeared in late 1999 when Schumacher came back after his recovery from a broken leg, and she has been around ever since. Schumacher's race performances went up another notch.

All champions need to feel invincible, but Schumacher's unshakeable self-belief is accompanied by a sensitivity that he keeps well hidden. He agrees it needs to be tempered occasionally with a dose of reality, but reality is a rare commodity in the world of Formula One. It is the same problem that Ayrton Senna faced throughout his career and it may be the reason Schumacher feels a curious affinity with Senna, over seven years after he has gone.

That self-belief has caused Schumacher problems in the past and lay behind the incident with Jacques Villeneuve at the 1997 championship-deciding race at Jerez. When Villeneuve dived up the inside and Schumacher turned into him he was criticised around the world. A couple of months later, he freely admitted that, at the time, he had been convinced it was Jacques' fault. "I got out of the car in disbelief," he said. "I was convinced I had been on my line and Jacques had shut the door. I went straight up to Jean Todt to ask him to protest about Jacques' driving. It was only afterwards when I saw the video and my friends talked to me that I realised it had been my mistake."

In Formula One, where every move is analysed, dissected and then multiplied, this sense of invincibility has been translated into meaning that Schumacher is fallible under pressure. Invincibility and fallibility are not the same thing and he finds the accusation irritating: "I remember when I finished 1995 and won the world championship, and then left to join Ferrari, there were two other drivers who arrived at Benetton to drive my car, Jean Alesi and Gerhard Berger, and all they did was complain about the car, as it was difficult to drive. A lot of people don't know under what kind of circumstances you do your job. Maybe it's not fair, but I'd like to see what would happen if Damon Hill and I had swapped cars and how many mistakes he would have made, and how many I would have made. Sure I made a mistake, but I'm human. In all honesty I

# look so easy

don't feel I've made that many mistakes. I feel I've maximised my opportunities."

Schumacher has been heavily criticised for maximising his opportunities. In 2000 the finger was pointed at him for his controversial starting tactics – the zigzag across the grid. He sighs and looks perplexed: "This is just one point which is called aggressive, but the rule allows you to do this, so if I can win a position with this, then I will do it. I always play within the rules, but I'm hardly the type of guy to say 'oh sorry no, no I don't want to do this, please overtake me'."

Schumacher has a surprising supporter in British driver Jenson Button, who says: "I don't think Michael's tactics on the grid are bad at all and I don't think it is dangerous. It happens all the way down the grid. If you watch a race, the movement that goes on halfway down the grid at the start is horrendous. It's just that he's at the front and it gets noticed more."

Schumacher knows that his annual income of over $50 million a year breeds jealousy and that most of the other drivers feel he is overpaid, as he says: ""If you're fighting at the top then this will happen. A lot of people write that I'm the best, something I never say, but then whenever they have the opportunity to write bad things about me and criticise me, they do. I guess people are more forgiving of your mistakes if you are the underdog. They try and make you look better, but that is human nature. If I see a small team in football then I wish the small team better luck than the big team as it is something special if the small team beats the big team. That's the way life is."

But he says he is tired of his money always being mentioned, and he simply says: "I'm paid well but not as much as people think."

Schumacher is the biggest star Formula One has had since Ayrton Senna. If Senna had lived, their battles would have been great. But Schumacher will not be drawn on whether he would have beaten Senna in the battle to be the best. It was just hotting up in 1994 when Senna was killed, robbing motor racing of the immense spectacle that might have unfolded in the next five years or so before Senna would have finally retired.

Schumacher first came up against Senna in 1980, when at the age of 11 his travels took him to Nivelles in Belgium for the world kart championship. He was used to competing against and beating older boys, but this time one driver in particular caught his eye. "I saw this guy. ▶

He was so crazy and yet so impressive in the way he drove," he recalls. "I didn't know who he was, but the next day I looked in the newspaper to find out. It was Ayrton. After this I followed his career and he became my one idol in motor racing."

Fast-forward 14 years: Schumacher was trailing behind his idol, when Senna had his fatal crash at the Tamburello curve at Imola. It was a loss that affected him greatly and which he still acutely feels. That evening, he sobbed his heart out in private with Di Spires, who together with her husband Stuart then ran the Benetton motorhome. Six years later, after his 41st victory in the 2000 Italian Grand Prix at Monza, Schumacher broke down at the post-race TV conference and wept, to the acute embarrassment of his third-placed brother Ralf. He says now: "Emotions have no space in racing, unless something exceptional happens which causes them

should have just taken his batteries out and made him stop." The accident saw his batteries forcibly removed. As he rested at home, he realised he needed to reassess his work-load. He was not under pressure to return, as the insurers were paying his $2 million-a-race salary and anyway the world championship, which he undoubtedly would have won that year, gradually slipped out of his grasp. Back home in Switzerland, he had an opportunity to reflect, for the first time in many years: "I think my accident gave the team lessons in that if you want to fight for the world championship you have to pace yourself so you don't arrive burnt out at the end. Sometimes I get so heavily into it I don't realise I need to take a break." Valuable lessons were learnt. But Schumacher was ordered to return for the last two races of the season by Ferrari boss Luca di Montezemolo, after his young daughter famously landed him in it. When di

The moment Michael Schumacher's fourth world championship was secured in Hungary.

to come out. I don't think he's [Ralf] ever seen me cry before. It was Ayrton, I was remembering Ayrton. I still have very strong emotions towards him."

The next time Schumacher had time to reflect on life was when he broke his leg in two places at the start of the 1999 British Grand Prix at Silverstone. He ploughed into a tyre wall and made it through to the concrete at 100-plus mph. The live feed to the media room was heavily edited and viewers on terrestrial TV saw far more than insiders that day. Many in the press room thought Schumacher had perished, until an official announcement 30 minutes later said he had a broken leg and was conscious.

The injuries may have been clean and relatively light, but for him it was another life-changing experience. Suddenly finding himself with plenty of time to spend with his family, for the first time he discovered how pressured his life had become.

Nigel Stepney, Ferrari's racing manager, explains: "Michael never gives up, never knows when to stop. He is always 100 per cent committed and sometimes he gives too much. He is like one of those long-life battery-powered toys. You can see it beginning to slow down and you know it should stop and have a rest, recharge its batteries, but still it goes on and on and just won't give up. We

Montezemolo called to speak to Schumacher, Gina Maria told him her father couldn't come to the phone because he was in the garden, playing soccer.

The accident delayed Ferrari's inevitable world championship by a year and it duly collected both crowns in 2000. But the winning season was not without its moments of high drama. Schumacher cites the Suzuka win as the most perfect race of his career: "I think it was a perfect race for me. I think it was the best quality race I have ever done. It was precise and every lap was on the spot. I've never seen myself drive like that. The stakes were high and I was able to deliver." It was a championship he won as a man, not a boy: "With Benetton, I was a young boy and I was developing within the team. When I arrived at Ferrari I was already an experienced driver so I was able to work with the team to develop something special, which finally resulted in the championship. At Ferrari we have been through some very difficult times together and that makes it all the more special."

Schumacher is happy to discuss his relationship with his team-mates. He clearly enjoyed working with Eddie Irvine and gets on less well with Brazilian Rubens Barrichello. But he admits it is not easy to be Michael Schumacher's team-mate. He tends to chew them up and spit them out, suffering from a crisis of confidence

and a heap of insecurities. As Eddie Irvine says: "You look at Michael's times and think 'shit, how can I compete with that?' The answer, of course, is that you don't, you have to find your own way and do the best you can."

Whatever the platitudes paraded around at the beginning of the season, there is only one star at Ferrari and he is made in Germany not Brazil. The team revolves around Schumacher and it always will. The only way a team-mate is going to win more than one race in a season or the world championship is if Schumacher is injured and not competing – as happened with Irvine in 1999. Barrichello's confidence was shattered in 2000 by not taking this fact on board when he signed his Ferrari contract. He believed he could seriously contend for the championship.

Just like Alain Prost and Ayrton Senna, Michael Schumacher has the ruthless streak necessary to be world champion. He simply wills the best engines, chassis, gearboxes, chief engineers and even hotel rooms, as he says: "I know what I want and I fight very hard for it, and to some degree I am aggressive, but not as much as people think. But it is true to say the people at the track do not see the real Michael Schumacher. I am a different person professionally and in my personal life. I can't be as open or free at work. If you speak freely then you'll get into trouble, so I always have to concentrate and be careful what I say. At home, I talk freely, I am free and I don't have to worry about things being misinterpreted or exaggerated." The sight of Michael Schumacher thundering down the pit-lane ready for a mighty showdown with a chastened David Coulthard, after their *contretemps* at Spa during the 1998 race, was frightening to behold. Schumacher insists he wasn't up for any physical confrontation, he was simply annoyed at his championship chances being dented by a rival who was not in contention for leadership of the race. His will to win, and commitment to bringing the world championship to Ferrari, are all-consuming.

Away from the track, he is as startlingly ordinary as he is extraordinary behind the wheel. When he returned, jet-lagged, from the first race of the 1997 season in Australia, he took over the night feeds of newborn daughter Gina Maria, while Corinna caught up with her sleep. "To me it's natural that we share looking after the children. When I'm home, Corinna and I take it in turns to get up in the morning to deal with the kids. Our life is family-orientated."

He admits he is very vulnerable emotionally where his family are concerned. He remembers how worried he was, as he flew home from testing, about the way he might react at the birth of Gina Maria. He says: "I was worried I would feel ill or pass out during the birth and let Corinna down." In the event, being present at the birth of his children, Gina Maria on 20th February 1997 and Mick on 22nd March 1999, proved to be among the most memorable experiences of his life. It has also made him reflective about his own childhood: "My memories of childhood are of being free, of taking my own decisions about activities I wanted to do. At the time I was doing all sorts of things, football, judo, go-kart, badminton, and my over-riding memory is of having the freedom to decide which way to go in life and having my parents' support."

He is giving his own children that same sense of security and support, coupled with a strong sense of responsibility. "I want them to have the freedom to move around as they wish, and grow up with animals and do what they want, but they also have to be aware of their responsibilities. If they want a horse they'll have to look after it."

He is a father who devotes as much time as possible to his children. "The most important thing you can give your children is your time, especially when they need you. I hope I will always feel open to discuss everything with them. I don't try and hide anything."

There are no naughty boy stories of Schumacher from childhood. The naughtiest thing he can remember doing is creeping off to the disco when he should have been at home. Principles are important to Schumacher and that is why accusations of cheating have hurt so much. "These accusations bother me very much. Going back to 1994, I am 100 per cent sure I didn't have traction control, but people still accuse us of having one. If you do a good job they try and criticise you. I had a very long discussion about this with a good friend of mine who has a karting business and is winning everything in Germany. He won the European championship, and people immediately say, 'ah, he's cheating, he's doing this or that'. It's a shame it's like this."

His old friends are an important part of Schumacher's life. He has known his best friend, Heribert Fungeling, since he was 15 and the two are still very close. "I was in Germany recently and we saw each other. He asked me what I was doing the following weekend and I was at home, so he came over with his twins who are two years older than Gina, and we spent a very happy, normal weekend together. That's how it goes, not every moment of my life is programmed and when it's not I lead a very normal life with my family and friends."

Fortunately, Schumacher's mother Elisabeth and his in-laws are at hand to help with the children, so Michael and Corinna can spend some time together. Holidays are always spent with the children, except between races, when the two of them slip away and enjoy some freedom. Inevitably, bearing in mind the pressure he lives under, Schumacher chooses to spend his holidays in wide-open spaces, surrounded by beautiful scenery. He went to Utah to experience the freedom of free-falling ▶

and rock-climbing, experiences he'll never forget. "The thought of free-falling frightened me until I tried free-climbing, then I thought 'yes, I'd like to try free-falling' and I did and it was great."

Playing soccer is something Schumacher does for pure enjoyment. He has supported German team Cologne since childhood, and plays for his local Swiss team FC Aubonne. Playing football – he says he is good but not brilliant – allows him to be just one of the boys, unfettered by unwanted attention. After the launch of the 2001 Ferrari car at Maranello, he disappeared to Emilia Romagna in the evening to play with some locals. Soccer is clearly a source of great pleasure and relaxation for a man who carries so much weight on his shoulders in his chosen sport.

The moment of the launch was also a chance to look forward to the 2001 season. The pressure may have been off, but the motivation was as high as ever and resulted in Schumacher's fourth world championship. It also resulted in Schumacher becoming the all-time most winning driver, having surpassed Alain Prost's record at the Belgian Grand Prix.

But notwithstanding his incredible success, the flame of ambition burns just as great as ever in Schumacher's heart. Only a few days after sealing the 2001 world championship in Budapest, he was back at work mode testing at Mugello and effectively beginning his assault on the 2002 title.

Ferrari heads into 2002 stronger than ever. In 2001 contracts were renewed for Ross Brawn, Rory Byrne, Jean Todt and Rubens Barrichello. Which means that Brawn, Byrne and Schumacher will stay together for at least four years, a triumvirate that Schumacher is pleased to see continue.

As he says: "As long as people are happy I see no reason to change." In reality they had got nowhere else to go that would pay the same wages or offer the same freedom and resources. But there is more to it than that. The inner sanctum is like a very close Italian family. Witness the closing of ranks when key player Nigel Stepney was about to sign for Jaguar. He didn't – despite having been personally interviewed by Ford president Jacques Nasser.

Jean Todt and Schumacher are exceptionally close, more like father and son than employer and employee. As long as that relationship remains in place, stability and serenity will rule at Ferrari.

He says: "Sometimes people ask me what my wishes are, and I have to say, what could they be? Corinna and I love each other deeply, we have two wonderful kids, we are well looked after financially, we have a nice house, I have won the championship twice with Ferrari. Now I just want to continue to have professional and personal happiness."

Having his dreams come true does not mean that Michael Schumacher is going to be a softer touch on the racetrack. Racing drivers are born, not made. The will to win does not diminish with victory. Although he has won more Grands Prix than any other driver there are still a few records to be broken, legends to be beaten, notably equalling and then breaking Juan Manuel Fangio's record of five championships. It is something he badly wants. As Schumacher says, "I was born to race. As soon as I'm in the car I want to be driving on the limit, going as fast as I can. I can't see that desire getting any less in the next few years."

Despite constant talk of retirement most believe Michael Schumacher will race on into his late 30s. He loves Formula One and although he wobbles occasionally, as at Monza in 2001, few doubt he will race on as long as he can. And he is the absolute favourite for the 2002 world championship even though most feel the BMW Williams will be the car to beat.

State Government
# Victoria
The Place To Be

# *You thought the Sydney Olympics were good. Try the world according to Formula 1.*

AUSTRALIA MELBOURNE

*"We have the equivalent of the Sydney Olympics every year here in Melbourne."*

The Foster's Australian Formula 1 Grand Prix is Australia's largest annual sporting event.

Check out **www.grandprix.com.au** for more information.

*Steve Bracks MP*
*Premier of Victoria*

**Foster's Australian Grand Prix 28 February - 3 March 2002***

* Subjet to FIA confirmation. GPZ 0009

# Continuing quest for honours

**David Coulthard is one of Formula One's nearly men. For three of the last six years he has sat in the most competitive car on the F1 grid, yet failed to mount a challenge for the world championship. Only in 2001 did he finally make the grade, and then saw it fade away mid-season through no fault of his own. But for the first eight races of 2001 he was a real superstar, second only to Michael Schumacher. Then the team let him down, especially at Monte Carlo, as he was poised to give them a great victory.**

David Coulthard started 2001 a new man. He had shed his long-time girlfriend and was foot-loose and fancy-free. He exuded a powerful presence, apparent evidence of a powerful new intent. It started to have an effect, and by mid-season he was trading blow for blow with Michael Schumacher and there was nothing between them, even though Schumacher clearly had the superior car. But could the Scot keep it up?

At the 2001 Monaco Grand Prix, David Coulthard was on peak form. Placed second in the world championship, he was only four points behind Michael Schumacher. It was the closest he had ever been to the top berth since winning the Austrian Grand Prix a fortnight before.

Pole at Monaco was vital, as the pole-man stands an excellent chance of winning the race. Coulthard wanted it desperately – more desperately than anyone else, as it turned out.

On Saturday 26th May, in the closing seconds of qualifying, he pulled out a sensational lap to scorch faster round Monte Carlo than anyone else, and push Michael Schumacher into second place. It was a fantastic shoot-out and his last effort stopped the clock on 1m 17.631secs – 0.11secs quicker than Michael Schumacher had managed in his Ferrari.

But Coulthard, far from whooping it up, already had his mind on the race the next day. Describing his fantastic lap, he said it could have been better: "I made a mistake on Thursday at Tabac and lost time, so after that I was playing catch-up a bit. I was not really confident about the limits through the Swimming Pool and Rascasse sections, so when I saw the split on the last run, I knew that the pole was on. I just did what I knew through the last sector and didn't over-push. Thankfully, it was good enough."

Everyone else was extremely excited, but he stayed true to type: "I'm pleasantly surprised," he said. "Of course, there's still a lot of work to be done to turn it into 10 points."

He was right about that. But as everyone relaxed that evening, sipping drinks on yacht decks, Coulthard's reputation glowed brighter than it had ever done, and he was the toast of Monte Carlo. As he sat on the top deck of a yacht by the paddock gates, sipping a non-alcoholic cocktail before going off for sponsor commitments and an early night, fans chanted his name and he flashed his trademark smile.

He was only four points off the championship lead and there was everything to play for. Everyone expected him to win. It would never be that good again. It was also the perfect launch pad for his 2002 contract negotiations with team principal Ron Dennis. For the past five seasons, Dennis had had Coulthard where he wanted him. He knew the Scot wanted to drive the McLaren, so paid him as little as he could and made him feel grateful. This time Coulthard was hot and Dennis was on the back foot. For the first time he paid him what he was worth and the Scot agreed a three-year contract.

The Dennis deal in his pocket was likely to involve a wage hike to $6 million from the derisory few million Dennis had been paying him.

Race day, however, cut Coulthard cruelly down to size. On the formation lap his car failed to get off the line, for the second time in three races. He was forced to go to the back of the grid. Then he was trapped behind Enrique Bernoldi's Arrows all the way to its pitstop on lap 44 of 78. He was losing 3.5 seconds a lap and was lapped by rival Schumacher before 30 laps were up. When Coulthard finally managed to cut loose, he set a new lap record of 1m 19.42secs, fully two seconds quicker than Mika Häkkinen's lap record of 2000. In a race-winning drive, he got fifth and two points. Schumacher went 12 points ahead and it was all over. Coulthard would not win again. McLaren's cars, competitive up to that point, went downhill as team morale was shattered by the breaking Adrian Newey story. It affected the whole team and the championship was irrevocably lost. The points gap to Schumacher got bigger and bigger and it was a season lost. What is more, Coulthard reverted to type. He went steady with a new girl and reverted to his less-

than-powerful, morose persona. The championship was lost and so, it seemed for a time, was he.

But Monte Carlo had shown, to the surprise of many, that Coulthard had what it took. He had also pocketed a contract that ostensibly gave him security for the first time in his Formula One career, which had started when he took Ayrton Senna's vacant seat at Williams after his death in 1994.

It was final validation along a pathway that had begun in 1983. He hailed from a wealthy Scottish family which ran a trucking business. He was karting from the age of eight and was a Scottish champion before he moved into Formula Ford racing at the end of 1988. He won his very first race, at Thruxton, and went on to drive his Van Diemen RF89 to 18 more victories from 26 starts in the two junior championships.

He dominated both junior championships in 1989 and finished third in the Formula Ford Festival. He lucked in by securing a drive with the fledgling Paul Stewart Racing, run by Jackie and Paul Stewart. It didn't hurt that he was Scottish. Stewart was running the most professional team in Formula Vauxhall Lotus and in the GM Lotus Euro series. But in 1990, when set for the championship, he crashed in Belgium and broke a leg. He moved into Formula Three in 1991 with Stewart and fought Rubens Barrichello, who was driving for West Surrey Racing, but lost the title by a few points despite winning five races to the Brazilian's four. However, he won both the Marlboro Masters and Macau GP.

He graduated to Formula 3000 in 1992 with Stewart, finishing ninth. Somehow it was enough to get him a test with Benetton.

Stewart wasn't competitive in Formula 3000, so he switched to Pacific and came third in the championship. He got a test drive with Williams and also raced a Jaguar in the Le Mans 24-hours. He was named Williams' test driver in 1994.

After Senna died he shared the seat with former world champion Nigel Mansell. He raced eight times, scoring points in five of them, but was dominated by Damon Hill. Although Mansell won the last race of the season, he was surprised when for 1995 Williams decided on Coulthard. He claimed his first win in his first full season at the Portuguese Grand Prix at Estoril, after claiming pole position. He was lucky to be using an old-specification car as the number two driver, which turned out to be quicker than the newer car of his team-mate Damon Hill.

The rest of the season was relatively disappointing considering he was in the ▶

most competitive car on the grid, so at the end of the year he left Williams to join McLaren.

He found he was evenly matched with his new team-mate Mika Häkkinen, although neither won anything. But 1997 was the beginning of McLaren's renaissance and he convincingly won the opening race of the season in Australia. He also won at Monza that year, trouncing Häkkinen in the championship.

But in 1998 Häkkinen won the world title, completely eclipsing Coulthard, who looked pedestrian. It was a complete turnaround. Coulthard, driving easily the most competitive car, could only win in San Marino. It was a similar story in 1999: he had the best car but only won the British and Belgian races. He almost lost his McLaren drive. In 2000 Coulthard won the British GP and Monaco but was still outclassed by Häkkinen, in their third year with the best car.

Until 2001 that is: in the first half of the season, he won two races and gave Michael Schumacher a close run in the championship. But as Williams came on strong, so he faded away again, holding onto second place in the championship, but only just.

In six years he has 10 victories to his name for McLaren, and with Häkkinen gone has his chance in 2002. But if he can't beat Kimi Räikkönen it may be his last year at McLaren, whatever his contract may say. And it will be his last with a really top-line team. But most rule that out, instead expecting Coulthard to grab team leadership with both hands and make it his own. Then it's up to the car – and, as Monte Carlo 2001 showed, there is very little a driver can do about that.

While 2001 may have turned into a disaster on the track, Coulthard's love-life proved him Formula One's premier playboy. He split with long-term love Heidi Wichlinski and took up with a succession of girls including Ruth Taylor, Heidi Klum and Lady Victoria Hervey, before finally going steady with Simone Adbelnour, a Brazilian model, who debuted in Monaco.

Whether this had any effect on his performance, which deteriorated after Monaco, no one knows. But 2002 beckons and, with Häkkinen out of the way, his seventh season with McLaren may prove to be his last chance.

# Construction of Motorsport Centre with Formula 1 racetrack in Moscow

The project stipulates development of Nagatino Island, located in the flood plain of Moscow-river, very close to the city's centre. Its geographical location, isolation of the island, surrounded by water, well-developed transport and engineer infrastructure provide vast opportunities to turn this place into a modern sports, entertainment and leisure centre.

The racetrack will be 3,6 km long. Nagatino Island will host a TV centre for international broadcasting, movie theatres, video-clubs, casinos, hotels, convention-centres, trade space, office space, several restaurants, bars, cafes, discotheques, yacht-clubs with a harbour for water motor sports.

The master-plan of the racetrack has been

G. Antioufeev and B. Ecclestone

made by English and German racetrack architects – «Ridge» and «Tilke Gmbh», under the management of «TWR Group» – the proxy foreign partner of the Moscow City Government in this project. The racetrack plan stipulates three points for overtaking! Racetrack construction in Nagatino has been approved by FIA (M. Mosley), FIM (F. Zerby), FOA (B. Ecclestone) and a consortium of foreign investors. The Mayor of Moscow Yuri Lyzhkov is at the head of the project's board of guardians.

The Russian manager of the project is Gregory Antioufeev, Chief of Russian Automobile Federation, Chairman of the Committee for tourism of the Moscow City Government.

**G. Antioufeev (Boss of Russian F1 Project)** told the FINANCIAL RUSSIA: "The Nagatino racetrack will be unique in a way. We hope that the best pilots of the world would be able to appreciate its advantages if copared to other raceracks that traditionally host the "Formula" championships.

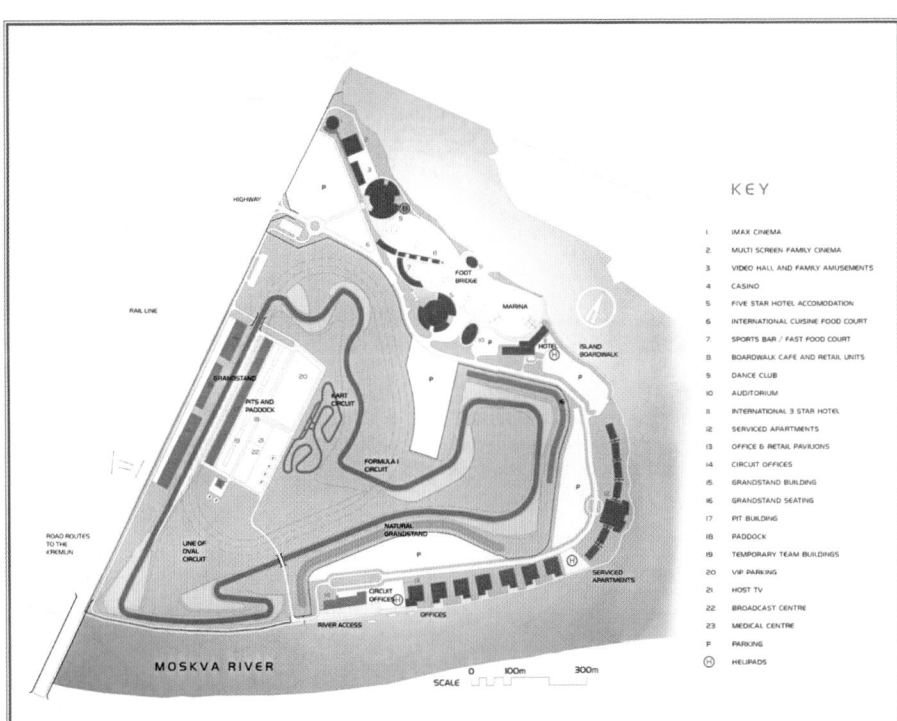

KEY

1. IMAX CINEMA
2. MULTI SCREEN FAMILY CINEMA
3. VIDEO HALL AND FAMILY AMUSEMENTS
4. CASINO
5. FIVE STAR HOTEL ACCOMODATION
6. INTERNATIONAL CUISINE FOOD COURT
7. SPORTS BAR / FAST FOOD COURT
8. BOARDWALK CAFE AND RETAIL UNITS
9. DANCE CLUB
10. AUDITORIUM
11. INTERNATIONAL 3 STAR HOTEL
12. SERVICED APARTMENTS
13. OFFICE & RETAIL PAVILIONS
14. CIRCUIT OFFICES
15. GRANDSTAND BUILDING
16. GRANDSTAND SEATING
17. PIT BUILDING
18. PADDOCK
19. TEMPORARY TEAM BUILDINGS
20. VIP PARKING
21. HOST TV
22. BROADCAST CENTRE
23. MEDICAL CENTRE
P. PARKING
H. HELIPADS

**B. Ecclestone (FOA, FOM)** told the NACIONAL newspaper: "Moscow is ready now for Formula 1. I am convinced that the first race there will be held within the next two years. My last visit to Moscow was 10 years ago, now I barely recognise the city – the changes are enormous. This, of course, is good for Russia, and even better for the Formula 1 organisation. It will be a great show."

# The perfect number

Early in the 2001 season, Rubens Barrichello was a troubled, frustrated man continually in Michael Schumacher's shadow. He is still under the shadow but as the season progressed he calmed down and accepted his lot. The Brazilian has come to terms with being team-mate to Michael Schumacher, the world's best driver. But his failure to win a race in 2001 has been noticed and when he leaves Ferrari his future is uncertain. Everything depends on 2002 but it is clear now he cannot beat Schumacher.

**A**t the start of 2001, Rubens Barrichello's future with the Italian Ferrari team seemed hazy and many observers did not expect his contract to be renewed when it expired at the end of the year. The Brazilian had already been racing for seven full seasons, and with fast youngsters emerging every minute, he could feel the pressure to perform. Barrichello was not a happy man. In fact, some said 'handle with care' was written all over him.

Everything came to a head in Austria. In the closing stages, Barrichello was running in second behind David Coulthard, with Michael Schumacher in third. The inevitable call from the pits came through on the radio, asking the Brazilian to move over and let Schumacher by. For a long time, he made no move. Then, on the very last corner of the very last lap, he slowed, allowing the German to sweep past to an extra two championship points – which, in retrospect, would have been far more useful to Barrichello than to Schumacher.

Paddock insiders said the team had been furious with Barrichello's public display of defiance. It was therefore a surprise when just nine days later, on the eve of the Monaco Grand Prix, Ferrari announced its driver line-up for 2002: no changes, and Barrichello's contract had been extended until the end of that year.

After that, his consistency in obtaining podium places became monotonous, although a win was elusive. As Schumacher eased away at the top of the standings, it became clear that Barrichello would be the Ferrari challenging Coulthard in 2001 in a battle for second place. Once the drivers' title had been wrapped up for Schumacher he came into scintillating form: the perfect number two who no longer complained about his predicament and was willing to accept a podium place when Schumacher was on top, and go for the wins once the championship was given the all-clear.

Barrichello had acquired a somewhat difficult reputation at the beginning of his second year at Ferrari. The reasons were clear: he had Michael Schumacher as his team-mate and he was still suffering from his first season in the pressure cooker. World champion Michael Schumacher takes no prisoners and has made a career out of tasting team-mates for dinner, swilling them around in his mouth during the season, then spitting them out when they don't pass muster. He terrifies them not by words but by his actions on the track, and in spite of the 'I'm going to be equal, and if I win and am ahead I'll go for the championship' pre-season talk in 2000, Barrichello soon found the reality very different.

He admitted it was all true: "If I made a mistake in 2000 it was this: at the start of the year I was very concerned about beating Michael. I only realised later that it wasn't the best thing to do, for me or the team. When, after Monaco, I stopped trying to beat him, things were better both for me and Ferrari."

So honesty is not one of Barrichello's problems and it is this that has endeared him to journalists – if not to his own team. He had irritated a few members of the team with his demands, but was given a quiet talking-to by Ferrari team supremo Jean Todt and the message was received loud and clear. He admitted it had been a difficult start.

The Schumacher Barrichello relation-

# two

ship has come a long way in two seasons, and no longer does Schumacher seem to miss Eddie Irvine, the ebullient, easy-going Irishman who was happy to play second fiddle to his superior talent. Barrichello said that things were so much better after he claimed his first race win at Hockenheim in his 124th Grand Prix. The year before, 1999, he had suffered the indignity of team-mate and number two Johnny Herbert winning the European Grand Prix for the Stewart team. After Barrichello's three years as Stewart team leader, that was not in the script at all. Barrichello had been labouring for three seasons without a win, and his grins on the podium for third place belied a deep frustration.

But Hockenheim in 2000 made up for the frustrations of the year before. It was a strange race. Schumacher had been booted off at the first corner again, this time after a collision with Benetton driver Giancarlo Fisichella. A protesting ex-Mercedes employee had crossed over the track, bringing out the safety car, and Barrichello won after starting 18th on the grid – a feat only rarely achieved. The abiding memory of the podium is of Barrichello sobbing his heart out, clutching the Brazilian flag and using it as a makeshift handkerchief. But the tears and tantrums were an integral part of his life in his first year with the scarlet team. "My victory at Hockenheim taught me a lot. I woke up on the Saturday and thought I'd have a great day. It was awful and I qualified 18th, so on Sunday I woke up with absolutely no expectations at all. I just went out, did my job well and won. Then up there on the podium I just couldn't stop crying. I was thinking of God, my father and Ayrton Senna and thanking them for helping me to be there.

"I learnt a valuable lesson at Hockenheim and that was you have to live life by the moment. You can make endless plans and they come to nothing, then unexpectedly it all comes together in the best possible way. Sometimes you just have to leave things to destiny. If it's meant to be, it will happen." But despite the win, relaxing is something Barrichello, even though he has been happily married to Sylvana for over four years, finds hard – especially with Schumacher continually pressuring him to perform. The birth of his first child, Eduardo, in September, may help him in this respect.

He still dreams the impossible – as does every Ferrari number two – that he too will be world champion. The team is completely geared towards Schumacher but that doesn't stop Barrichello from dreaming. He hopes fortune will shine on him and he'll finally get the chance to prove he has the makings of greatness. He truly believes it: "I think I was born to be a racing driver. I feel capable of winning a world championship in Formula One; it will become easier as I have experience with Ferrari, so we know each other."

Entering 2001, Barrichello said he had returned a different, more mature man with a retuned mindset: "I had time to think, get stronger both in mind management and physically, and time to recover. Going into 2001 I felt much more relaxed and at peace with myself."

He knew 2001 was a crunch year. He needed to put in a stunning performance to stand a chance of securing his future with Ferrari. If he didn't it could be the end of his career with a big team. After all, what was the alternative after Ferrari? A return to the wilderness of the mid- and lower-grid teams. In early 2001, it was the last thing Barrichello wanted or, indeed, what he deserved – if he could find a way of untapping his considerable talent to the full.

Under that immense pressure, he proved he was just the man Ferrari needed at Schumacher's side. ▶

He worked hard to put the experiences of his first year with Ferrari, positive and negative, to good use. "It's like changing school and seeing new friends, new teachers and learning your way around. The second year is much better. I like Ferrari and the way it works. Obviously things revolve around Michael so I have to slowly create my own space."

By Melbourne he was a changed man from the temper tantrums he had shown in pre-season testing at Barcelona. Gone was the irritable, uptight behaviour, to be replaced by a calmer, happier individual who seemed to feel that, after his baptism of fire, things were finally under control. More importantly, he had a better understanding with his race engineer, Carlo Cantoni. "After a year together we have that instinctive understanding that you need with your race engineer. He understands how I like the car and I understand him and how he likes to work. I have a good rapport with all my mechanics."

However, Senna's presence continues to hang over Barrichello like a death's head at the feast. A whole nation still expects – and

the time has come for him to take on the mantle of greatness or win the prize for best supporting act. The future is in his own hands.

Whatever form that takes it's a long way from his roots. He grew up in the Interlagos neighbourhood of São Paulo and started out racing go-karts. He won five national titles before he was 16 and in 1989 tried his hand at Formula Ford. He then went to Europe to compete in the GM Lotus Euroseries. He had backing from the supermarket chain Arisco which wanted to take him all the way to Formula One. He took the title at his first attempt. Barrichello then won the British Formula Three championship at first attempt. In 1992 he went to Formula 3000 and took third place in the championship, despite not winning a race. By 1993 he was in Formula One with the Jordan team. Then it was a short leap to Ferrari via three years at the Stewart team. After two seasons with Ferrari, 2002 is make or break. He is still a relatively young man but no longer a young charger. At Ferrari he has run into the Schumacher buffers. There is no longer any mystery to his talent or his capability.

# Transition year to greatness

**Ralf Schumacher is a world champion in waiting. After spending the winter of 2000/2001 reinventing himself he scored three victories to make himself the second biggest-winning driver after his brother. He is many people's favourite to be world champion in 2002, which will also feature a fascinating battle for supremacy between two brothers in the most dynamic sport in the world.**

Twenty-six-year-old Ralf Schumacher has a different racing life to that of the other drivers. His older brother just happens to be the best driver in the world, and he has lived the five years of his Formula One life being continually compared to the 32-year-old quadruple world champion. It is a burden that the other drivers don't have. But it is also an advantage psychologically, as Ralf enjoys the benefits of the Schumacher support system built up around Formula One over the last 10 years.

From humble beginnings operating a go-kart track the Schumacher family, led by father Rolf, aided by commercial supremo Willi Weber, is now the most powerful dynasty in motor racing. For sure this will endure long after they retire and perhaps the family will one day become team owners and tackle that field of endeavour.

In 2001 Ralf Schumacher won races. Next year it is his destiny to seriously challenge for the world championship. That is certain. With his first pole position and three race wins secured, he ended the season with honours.

The high point of the season was when he won his first pole at Magny-Cours, on 30th June 2001 – his 26th birthday. At first nearly a second, and ultimately one-100th, parted the Schumacher brothers. But Ralf won pole from his brother in the white heat of competition. The milestone was important: he knew pole position was the ultimate measure of sheer speed and skill over one lap.

In the past he has been accused of lacking focus and drive, but in 2001 that charge could no longer be heard. Another factor in 2001 that made a difference to Ralf and the whole BMW Williams team was the arrival of 30-year-old Sam Michael, who was Schumacher's race engineer at Jordan and does the same job for him now.

It was an important development because the maturing of Schumacher junior started at Jordan, as Sam Michael relates: "The biggest change I've seen in Ralf was in the last half of the year at Jordan in 1998. He started to drive more maturely. This year he started the season in a great frame of mind. Ralf always makes steps over the winter, and he always comes back more mature and more focused than before."

Schumacher did change over the 2000/2001 winter – he knew he had to. The breakthrough from journeyman to Grand Prix winner is a difficult psychological barrier. It took Ralf three times as long as his famous brother to win a race. So what happened last winter to boost his form so radically in 2001?

The answer was several things. First, his rapport with BMW motorsport boss Gerhard Berger. Schumacher made sure he was seen often at the BMW HQ in Munich. He also cultivated his ties with Michelin. Then his fitness regime was upped a few notches, including a special fitness programme with his personal trainer Daniel Dobringer.

He also made some far-reaching changes in his personal life. His apparent lack of lady friends prompted some British journalists to spread rumours he was gay. The rumours were fanned by a kiss 'n' tell story in a British tabloid newspaper by the model known as Jordan, who revealed she and Ralf had shared a bed but he refused to make love to her.

The rumours may have had no substance, but it was an anxiety he didn't need. Reflecting on his brother's perfect domestic situation, he thought about marriage and children. When he entered Formula One he as good as admitted he envied the stability of his brother's life. Ralf told friends that his ideal girlfriend and eventual wife 'would be just like Corinna'. "She is the ideal woman," he waxed. "I wish she had a sister and then my life would be settled." Corinna, wife of Michael and mother to Gina Maria and Mick, is a role model for domestic bliss.

The solution was at hand. Seven years ago, Ralf used to hang around with a group of friends in Kerpen. Among them was a girl called Cora Brinkmann, who at 17 was just a year younger than Ralf. Initially their lives went separate ways when Ralf went to the Far East to race in Formula Nippon and Cora moved to Cologne, where she worked as an administrator. A couple of years ago the two met again and started dating, but they split up and Cora started dating someone else. When that relationship ended, the two started dating again last year.

During the winter the relationship got very serious, to the point where he proposed. By the time they made their relationship public at the Australian Grand Prix in March, Cora was pregnant with their first child.

In fact, Ralf couldn't have chosen a woman more like his brother's wife, Corinna. Like her Cora has an understated presence in the Formula One paddock, offering quiet support rather than the showy publicity that other wives sometimes attract. She is a strong person and keeps her own counsel, a vital attribute in the gossip-fuelled world of Formula One.

She also delights in an uncluttered, down-to-earth lifestyle. In spite of their millions, neither brother seeks the jet-set lifestyle or glamorous parties. Between races they are at home with their families. They enjoy their toys, particularly the planes that make their lives easier. In 2001 Ralf took delivery of a new Hawker 800, which cost $9 million.

He has also made radical lifestyle changes. Like his brother, he used to live in tax-free Monaco, but also like his brother, he hated it, as he says: "I grew up in a rural area, surrounded by animals and open spaces where I could roam free. Suddenly I was stuck in this concrete desert, a kind of rich man's ghetto and all I wanted was wide open spaces, and a few dogs and horses."

So in the winter of 2000/2001 he took the decision to uproot, agree to fork out income tax and move to Austria. The Austrian government has a special negotiable tax rate for foreign nationals of around 15 per cent, and although even this low rate meant a $2 million tax bill, he decided it was well worth the peace of mind he has gained from the move.

He has renovated a large five-bedroom house in Hall-wang near Salzburg. The house has a big garden, indoor swimming pool and fitness centre, and enough space for his American western horse. Cora loves it and it is a family home. They finally tied the knot in October 2001.

All in all, life is good for Ralf Schumacher. He is happy, as evidenced by the way he fusses around Cora, carefully shepherding her around and making sure she is looked after while he is busy working.

BMW Williams technical director Patrick Head agrees that in 2001 there has been a sea change for the better: "Ralf seems more relaxed this year so he contributes more to team morale and atmosphere. You could share a joke with him much more easily than last year."

Ralf admits that he has never had the easiest of relationships with the other drivers in the paddock. He has always been only too aware of the pluses and minuses of having a name like Schumacher: "In terms of opening doors it is an advantage having the name Schumacher, as everyone is curious to know if the younger brother is as quick as the older one, but it is more difficult to keep the doors open as you are ▶

4th

judged against Michael. And for the other drivers, it is always a pleasure to beat a Schumacher."

For the past three seasons he has had to suffer different rookie team-mates. In the first, Alex Zanardi, although not a complete rookie, played out a poor season. Last year Jenson Button had the part of rookie team-mate, In 2001 it was Juan Pablo Montoya, an altogether different character.

Whereas Button and Zanardi were polite and diplomatic, Montoya is abrasive and opinionated and not at all frightened of showing his true feelings. It is clear they are not the happiest team-mates although they agreed to get along.

Ralf also has to cope with the increasing competition with his brother. Close competitors for the world championship are usually not friends. He realises much of the rest of his career will be spent duelling with his own brother and even any minor incidents that might flare up between them will be given the 'splash' treatment by the small pack of British journalists who inwardly dislike any driver with the name Schumacher.

There are many people who feel the rivalry between the two brothers could be detrimental to Ralf's challenge for the championship. There is no doubt that the two brothers are very close but

the big question is, would Ralf have the courage to threaten that rapport by going all out for victory irrespective of the cost to the sibling relationship?

Remember that it is big brother Michael who has always exercised a protective influence over Ralf. Schumacher junior climbed into a go-kart when he was two-and-a-half years old. Michael was then nine and already proving to be a champion in go-karts. And when little Ralf needed a mechanic, it was big brother Michael who volunteered.

It was also Michael who helped smooth the way for Ralf's move to BMW Williams from Jordan – a move that many observers considered unwise, especially as it was at the time Williams was sailing into the doldrums and Jordan was looking quite good.

Maybe Ralf Schumacher has the answer when he says: "A battle? I don't think so. One day he's going to retire and I guess that will be before me." Maybe we'll only see the real Ralf when Michael is no longer driving.

Whatever happens, the one certainty is that Ralf Schumacher is in transition stage en route to attaining the world championship. Only fate can intervene along the way – or a certain Colombian by the name of Juan Pablo Montoya.

# Indecision all the way

**Mika Häkkinen is gone for 2002 but Keke Rosberg, Ron Dennis and Häkkinen himself all insist that he will be back for 2003. If that does happen, then either David Coulthard or Kimi Räikkönen is going to be very disappointed. Although it seems unlikely, Häkkinen probably will be back. For a few races in 2001 he showed he has still got what it takes.**

Mika Häkkinen had a mostly poor 2001 for all sorts of reasons. But that did not tell the whole story. For three races he was the class of the field, and if he had driven everywhere like he drove at Silverstone, Barcelona and Indianapolis, then he would have been world champion again. But for the other 14 races he was lacklustre and showed all the signs of a man on the way out. As Peter Collins, his former mentor, says: "When they got the car to work in 2001, the bloke was sensational. When they put the right car under him he just rolled off the bloody quick laps you need to win. He is like a clock and that's what makes him so competitive. In a race he just rolls off the laps and that is what a lot of them can't do. In race trim he can produce qualifying speed just like Schumacher and Montoya can. They are the only three currently on the scene who can do that."

So why is Häkkinen unloved and unwanted for 2001 by his boss and friend, McLaren team principal Ron Dennis? Dennis and the 1998-99 world champion was the most enduring partnership in Formula One history. The 2001 season was his ninth in a row with McLaren. He and Dennis have enjoyed 20 wins, 14 second places and 17 thirds from a total of 162 Grands Prix contested, with 26 pole positions and 25 fastest laps.

Some say Häkkinen's decline has come with the birth of his first child, Hugo, in December 2000. They say his wife Erja has changed his life and made him relax more. For sure his fitness regime is not what it once was, and friends say he now enjoys a few more drinks in the evenings than perhaps a Formula One driver should in the 21st century. Others dismiss this and say the Scandinavian drivers have traditionally enjoyed a drink. They say Erja has been a good influence on his life.

Häkkinen first started winning at the age of six. A five-times Finnish kart champion by the time he was 18, he was close to unbeatable in his first season of car racing. In Formula Ford 1600, he took nine wins from 15 starts on the way to the Finnish, Nordic and Swedish titles in 1987.

In 1988 he became a Marlboro-sponsored driver and won the Formula Vauxhall Lotus Euroseries, racking up four victories.

In 1989, he entered the British Formula Three championship and won the 1990 British title with 11 poles, nine victories and five second places.

It was enough for him to attract the attention of Peter Collins, a well-known talent spotter who had just taken over the Lotus team. He offered Häkkinen's manager, former world champion Keke Rosberg, a three-year deal.

So Häkkinen started in Formula One as a rent-a-driver with team Lotus. Collins was looking for a driver to grow with the team and Häkkinen fitted the bill. He knew Häkkinen from Formula Vauxhall and had watched him in Formula Three. Collins rang Häkkinen's manager Keke Rosberg at the end of 1990 and said he wanted to put him in Formula One for 1991. Rosberg was surprised. Collins asked him to get together the $2 million it would cost from sponsors. Rosberg duly delivered him and a two-year contract was signed, with an option for 1993. The second year called for $1 million to be paid and the third year would have seen Häkkinen earn his first salary. Right from the moment he stepped aboard the uncompetitive Lotus Ford 102B in Phoenix in March 1991, it was clear that Mika Häkkinen possessed the sort of talent to progress to the very top. Over the next two years Häkkinen justified Collins' expectations, scoring 13 points from 30 starts over two seasons in the less-than-competitive car.

By the end of 1992 he had attracted the attention of McLaren team principal Ron Dennis and Williams' Frank Williams. Lotus took up its option and at the end of the season Williams made an approach to Lotus; Collins refused to release Häkkinen.

But Ron Dennis was not so easily defeated, and had made a direct approach to Häkkinen's manager Rosberg. Rosberg then informed Collins that Häkkinen was going to join McLaren. There was a dispute, which was taken to the Formula One Contracts Recognition Board in Switzerland. It decided that Häkkinen could join McLaren on a generous $1.5 million salary. In the end he was signed as test driver, to support Michael Andretti and Ayrton Senna. But two-thirds of the way through the season, Andretti returned to America under a cloud and Häkkinen got his chance.

Häkkinen celebrated by giving Senna a wake-up call in Portugal, out-qualifying the Brazilian. Although Häkkinen never beat Senna again, the performance was an indication of his potential. After Senna left for Williams at the end of 1993, he took over as McLaren team leader for 1994. But these were lean years for the McLaren team, with uncompetitive cars powered first by Peugeot and then Mercedes engines. His 1995 team-mate Nigel Mansell quit the team in disgust half-way through the season and repaid his retainer to Ron Dennis, so bad was the car. For Häkkinen it got worse at the end of the 1995 season: he crashed heavily in Adelaide after a tyre burst, and was near to death. Only an emergency tracheotomy, performed trackside by local doctors, saved his life.

Ron Dennis rushed into Adelaide's Victoria Hospital to be told by Formula One doctor Sid Watkins that he could not predict whether Mika Häkkinen would survive following the 120mph accident in practice.

In the weeks that followed, a deep personal bond was forged between Dennis and Häkkinen which defined the relationship between the two men. It was something that transcended an employer-employee relationship. Dennis says: "There is a perception that I have a closer relationship with Mika than with David [Coulthard]. There is that emotional value between us, but you've got to understand where it comes from. Walking into that Adelaide hospital, being sucked into the trauma of the whole thing.

Seeing the guy going through the medical stages that were predicted by the specialists. I am a guy who, if he ends up in a situation in which he doesn't want to be, then I've got to be able to look back and ask whether I did everything in my power. I got involved mentally in the milestones of his recovery through to the point where he was up and running again."

With Dennis's help Häkkinen recuperated during the winter of 1995, and came back as if nothing had happened. The 1996 season was more of the same, but by 1997 McLaren had developed a car capable of winning, as the Finn's new team-mate David Coulthard proved by bagging the season's Australian opener. Häkkinen's first victory came in Jerez in 1997 after he was let through to win. To look at the points table, it seemed David Coulthard had overshadowed him that season, but Häkkinen had had all the bad luck while running up front. Next season was a different story. He won his first world championship in style in 1998, winning eight of the 16 races, but although 1999 was a far tougher year, in which he twice made mistakes in Italy that cost him race wins, he came back strongly when it really mattered to retain his crown in the final race.

In 2000 he fought Michael Schumacher all the way for the title, but this time he lost out.

After three years at the very top he flunked 2001 despite the three shows of brilliance. By mid-season, out-driven and out-qualified by David Coulthard, Ron Dennis perceived that Häkkinen had peaked and was on the way down. His contract was up and there was nowhere else for him to go. Instead of the $9-$11 million he had paid him for the previous two years Dennis offered him and his manager, Keke Rosberg, $3 million basic plus $800,000 a win or thereabouts. It was effectively a 50 per cent pay cut. To add insult to injury Dennis told him it would only be a one-year contract, with a team option for a second. This was not what Häkkinen wanted to hear. He wanted a two-year deal at the same rate as before and after that would retire. He then told Dennis he was thinking of retiring and couldn't give him an answer. This took Dennis aback, but over the next few weeks his offer remained the same; so did Häkkinen's reply. He would not drive for ▶

less; Dennis would not pay more. And so it came to pass that Häkkinen decided to take Dennis's offer, but not to drive and take a season's sabbatical. Still it was indecision all the way, until Dennis settled it by signing new young Finnish star Kimi Räikkönen. Whether Häkkinen wanted to quit or not, the die was now cast. Dennis had made the decision for him.

Häkkinen and Dennis finally agreed he would stay on the McLaren payroll and get paid for his sabbatical season. McLaren would then have first option on him for the following season. Häkkinen liked the idea of a year off and being paid for it, and accepted. In mid-July, however, Niki Lauda approached his manager Rosberg about Häkkinen driving for Jaguar in 2002. Rosberg turned it down even though $12 million was on the table.

Instead Häkkinen, as a compromise, has accepted the $3 million flat retainer Dennis offered him for 2002 in order to stay as a contracted driver and not drive for another team. Dennis is also thought to have first option on him for 2003. Häkkinen will carry out some promotional work for McLaren during the year. Dennis simply said: "Mika has always done an incredible job for us and now is not the time to be bidding him farewell." Few actually believed him, but for a change Ron Dennis was probably speaking the 100 per cent truth. Häkkinen said: "I have been involved in racing since I was six years old. I have been doing many years of racing in many different categories and in F1 for 11 years. It's a really tough busi-

ness, which is why I came to the decision with the team and Ron that I needed to have a break and recharge my batteries and spend time with Erja and Hugo – that's it really. It's not that there is something I want to do instead. I simply just want to enjoy a break. If you look at other drivers in F1 history who have had a break, they have come back stronger – Alain [Prost] is a good example. There's also Niki Lauda, who had a break for other reasons, just like myself. It's good to just take time off and recharge the batteries."

Whether he will come back is unknown, but Keke Rosberg said: "He is honestly on sabbatical. He is not going to be looking for another team. He is very happy with his team and has no desire to change teams or anything like that. Absolutely not. He can come back after a year, but nobody knows what lies ahead. It's too difficult, too hypothetical. It is not in my agenda. Anyone can change their mind at any time. Ron Dennis (McLaren team principal) may retire. Who knows? People make their plans for the moment, that is all I know."

Häkkinen says of his future: "I just want to take time off. The team and Ron have been great. It's fantastic to have a friend like Ron, who understands the situation and has given me the opportunity, which is extremely unusual. You never know, I might enjoy something else, but at the moment I still love driving racing cars. Racing cars is my passion, so maybe after four or five months I will realise that I miss it too much."

# The rookie wins

**Juan Pablo Montoya was on a mission in 2001, and that mission was to win as many races as he could in his first season to become Formula One's most successful rookie. He could have won half a dozen but ended up with just one. He finished 2001 well behind his team-mate Ralf Schumacher in the points, and for the early part of the season seemed to be struggling to get everything together. But he is still the man most likely to beat Michael Schumacher — and he knows it. 2002 could easily be his year.**

That Juan Pablo Montoya is one of the most highly-rated rookies in Formula One history is not in doubt. That his debut is the most hyped since that of Jacques Villeneuve is also not in doubt. What is in doubt is whether he is one of the world's top three drivers (Michael Schumacher and Jacques Villeneuve being the other two), as his old champ car team boss Chip Ganassi insists.

On paper, the 25-year-old Colombian is certainly one of the best driving talents to emerge in the last 15 years. That is the estimation of retired CART and Formula One world champion Emerson Fittipaldi. Former Jaguar team boss Bobby Rahal goes a step further: "Montoya is the best driver I have ever seen."

"People talk too much," Montoya says of all the accolades heaped upon him. "It's good to hear, but the real stuff is what you do on the track, not what people say." Yet the hype has been generated by his trackwork. At the Italian Grand Prix he became only the seventh rookie in history to take a Formula One win, and in his debut season he has overtaken Michael Schumacher on track four times. He won the Indy 500 first time out in 2000. He took the US-based champ car series by storm in 1999. He'd done the same in Formula 3000 in 1997 and 1998. Now, after his messy early-season antics he has gained the upper hand on Ralf Schumacher and money is being placed on him ending 2002 as Formula One world champion.

His manager David Sears is convinced that the superstardom and storming performances will continue. "Montoya is a breath of fresh air in F1," predicts Sears. "He takes no prisoners and cuts through all the bullshit. There are going to be a lot of fireworks."

It all started in Brazil. With 10 laps of the Grand Prix still to run, most of the attention had shifted to the Williams motorhome. Montoya had just crashed out of the race when he was hit from behind by Jos Verstappen, after earlier performing a breathtaking manoeuvre on Michael Schumacher.

"So Juan, tell us how it felt overtaking the world champion. That must have been the most incredible feeling of your career," shouted an overzealous journalist. Montoya looked puzzled. "It was OK. The guy's good, but he ain't no Senna," he said. The scrum turned to silence. "Any more questions?" There were none. In one sentence Montoya had announced his arrival in Formula One. The new kid on the block, ready to race to the top, with no time for hero-worship or hierarchy. Montoya has charisma with a capital 'C', summed up by the fact that within the Williams team he has not just one nickname but four. While Ralf is just Ralf, Montoya is variously 'Juancho' to his Colombian pals, 'Monty' to Frank Williams and Patrick Head, 'Wayne' to his mechanics and, tellingly, 'Monster' to the PR people.

When he first appeared in champ cars, Montoya was branded a dangerous madman by the likes of Al Unser Jr and Michael Andretti after he dared to duel wheel-to-wheel with the champ car establishment at well over 200mph on the giant ovals. In last year's Michigan 500, in which there were 52 lead changes, he beat Andretti by 0.04 seconds after a breathtaking last-lap, wheel-banging battle with the veteran American. That had been preceded by a split-second slingshotting manoeuvre past back-marker Tarso Marques in the final turn. "There was this guy [Marques] in front of me and I wasn't gonna lift," Montoya vowed. "I was gonna hit him if I had to." Yet when Montoya left the US series for Formula One, he claims that many of his peers, including Paul Tracy, Dario Franchitti and the 2000 champ car champion Gil de Ferran, were sad to see him go. "That's one good thing about champ cars," says Montoya, whose vocabulary is spiced with colourful terms he has learned from Anglo-Saxon race personnel. "Most of the guys are quite friendly. If you're racing against someone on the track it doesn't mean you have to be a prick off the track, does it?"

In his off-track relationship with the American press, Montoya was not a media darling. He had a reputation for being hard to interview, a man of few words who answered questions with short sentences, flashed a quick grin or a dark frown then turned away. Some found him downright rude, even a spoiled brat; others more charitably thought him perhaps inter-personally challenged. His personality resembles that of extravagant lightweight boxer Prince Naseem, although the Colombian has never declared 'I am the greatest' as the boastful yet brilliant Muhammed Ali did. The assured arrogance of knowing he can be the best is out there and on display. There is never the slightest doubt in Montoya's mind that he can give BMW Williams team-mate Ralf Schumacher a sound thrashing, and then take on the other big fish as well.

With all this powerful self-confidence it was predicted Montoya could become the next great villain of Formula One, where anti-hero, superstar and clown are essential ingredients to provide maximum entertainment in the circus. He arrived at a time when Michael Schumacher had left the door slightly ajar for aspiring villains. The ice-cool German was swerving dangerously into 'decent bloke' territory with a heart-warming public display of weeping after winning for Ferrari at Monza in 2000.

But Montoya has instead become Formula One's new hero. Independent, politically incorrect and more than a little crazy on track, he has proved himself a good old-fashioned racer to fans around the world. Back in Bogotá, Montoya is a hero of the highest order, a position that fills him with immense pride. "I am a pretty big thing at home and I always try to bring good news to the country. I'm really happiest when I go there and see the faces of the little kids that look up to me. That's really cool." Montoya has a big heart and his very first move after signing with Williams was to introduce his parents and Spanish law-student girlfriend Connie to the team. They became engaged at Indianapolis.

Prior to Schumacher it was the late, great Ayrton Senna the

media loved to hate. But Senna was Montoya's idol, so he is fully aware that a negative reputation can go with the territory when a driver reaches the top. "It's part of the deal and you have to put up with it," shrugs Montoya. "The journalists in champ cars can be quite aggressive. And already some in F1 are trying to find weak points and whip me."

Montoya seems to have become media-savvy. In his first press conference he endeared himself to many scribblers – whether by accident or design – by simply pandering to their vanity, remembering familiar faces and calling some by name. Branded the decent bloke from Bogotá, he has had mainly favourable reviews since he returned to Europe.

However, in the heat of the cockpit, Montoya will still have to clear the 'Latin temperament' hurdle, a handy term of denigration greatly favoured by Anglo-ethnic critics. Drivers whose country of origin qualifies them for the label are deemed to be impulsive, short on self-control, hot-headed, short-fused and prone to road rage. While British world champions James Hunt and Nigel Mansell quite often fitted the bill, they were never accused of having a Latin temperament.

Although David Sears said Montoya had to 'retune his Latin brain', he thought the Colombian's Spanish South American heritage gave him an advantage in adapting to life at the zenith of motorsport. Montoya agrees: "Europeans think differently from Latins. For us life is less complicated. We don't make such a big deal about anything. I know my job here is difficult, but you shouldn't psyche yourself out over it. If you start thinking how hard it is, you put a lot more pressure on yourself, which is stupid." The champ car series is dominated by Latin American drivers. As Montoya says: "Maybe we try harder. Maybe it's the atmosphere in which we grow up. The culture and the way of life are different. Maybe the way we live makes us eager to prove that we can do it. I know I want to prove I can win, that I'm as quick as anyone else."

Brazilian Gil de Ferran, who succeeded Montoya as champ car champion in 2000, is wary of stereotyping drivers according to their country of origin. "Colombia is not a country that traditionally produces good racing drivers. But in Montoya you have a remarkable guy. Is it Colombia or is it Montoya? I rather believe it is him. He has certain traits that are not due to his nationality, but rather to his personality."  ▶

Montoya is reputed to have a very highly developed state of self-belief. His character traits satisfy the team requirements of what it takes to be a winner. Sir Frank's definition of the ideal Williams driver is based on his first world champion, rugged Australian Alan Jones. He says: "In a way Alan spoiled my relationships and attitude towards subsequent drivers, because he was a man's man and great fun to be with. He never needed propping up mentally, because he was a very determined and bullish character. He didn't need babysitting or hand-holding and that's the way it should be. It shouldn't be necessary for me to ask a driver if he is happy, or if he needs his underwear changed."

And no one can knock Williams' taste in drivers. All told, Williams drivers have won 103 races out of the 411 Grand Prix rounds it has contested. Seven drivers – Alan Jones, Keke Rosberg, Nelson Piquet, Nigel Mansell, Alain Prost, Damon Hill and Jacques Villeneuve – have won world championships in Williams cars.

Sir Frank says: "All the top drivers are difficult people with complex personalities. I wouldn't go so far as to say that nice guys finish last, but the best Grand Prix drivers are driven, motivated, pushy, won't-accept-second-best, immensely competitive people. That is what makes them good, because they're bastards." Montoya

isn't intimidated by his new employer's uncompromising attitude – indeed, he relishes the opportunity to work for like-minded men. He says: "Frank Williams and Patrick Head are real racers. You can see their spirit and you know that they just want to win. That's why the Williams team has been so successful."

Patrick Head, the team's technical director, makes it sound like a mutual love affair. He positively beams with goodwill when describing the most attractive quality he sees in his latest recruit. "Juan Pablo loves racing and is the sort of driver both Frank and I like having in the team. In fact, Juan Pablo really loves it! He loves racing other people. He doesn't just like doing a quick lap time, he likes being close to other people on the track, out-fumbling them and out-foxing them. That is the sort of driver we like."

It will be a tall order for Montoya to match Nigel Mansell's achievements, but he has already matched Mansell as a rookie US champ car winner, and he sounds quite capable of making tough, Mansell-style demands: "If someone is doing something wrong you gotta speak out. If I see something that's not going the way I want, I'll just go straight to Frank and say 'Look Frank, this is what's going on.' Winning is not about one thing, it's everything. You put it all together and you are gonna to win, if you don't you're not. So you've gotta know where you wanna go." In the 2001 Williams team, the potential for conflict was high. First Montoya and then Ralf Schumacher became frustrated with each other's superior performances, and as one star rose to the occasion the other began to make silly mistakes.

Things came to a head mid-season: twice Schumacher was asked to give way to Montoya for strategic reasons, and twice he refused. As with all teams, the personal competition between team-mates is used to spur progress, but at Williams a dominated driver tends to be doomed – as was Frentzen. As soon as one driver gets the upper hand, mainly by going faster, more moral support inevitably drifts his way and the other driver wanes – both in the team's estimation and on the track.

Montoya has ruffled a few feathers in his first season and is aiming even higher for 2002. He does not beat around the bush. "There's a hierarchy system where everyone wants to toe the line. It's been nearly 10 years now that everyone's been saying how good Schumacher is. Ten fucking years! Sure the guy is good but there is a bit of hype there. I treat him like anyone else. If I can pass him I will. So what if he is the champ. All the better.

"Ayrton was different. Maybe some kids will look at Michael the way I looked at Ayrton, but I don't look at him that way. I had respect for Ayrton – he was my hero. Michael is different. He's the best, but he's not unbeatable. When I passed him in Brazil I started pulling away. I thought ha ha ha, I'm quicker than you."

Montoya has arrived, but racing is much more important to him than superstardom. "Let's be clear. I don't care about glamour and fame. That's for other people, and they are usually people outside Formula One," he says. "I'm here to drive cars and win races. I really couldn't give a fuck about anything else. Some people might like to have their picture in the paper. That's OK but I'm only here to do a job. And I don't mean this bullshit that I just want to do well. It's about winning. Winning is everything."

That is the mentality Montoya needs if he is to become world champion one day. Those that say that 2002 will actually be his year and not Ralf Schumacher's already assume that the championship will be fought out by the two BMW Williams drivers. That may be so, but at the very least Montoya is poised to reverse his 2001 luck and pile up a load of victories. It is already written

# There are two kinds of fuel checks: the dashboard and the scoreboard.

*Four wins, four pole positions, placed eight times and eight fastest laps. From the first starting grid through to the final chequered flag of the season, the BMW WilliamsF1 Team has been backed by the fuel technology of Petrobras: one of the world's leading oil and energy companies.*

**PETROBRAS**

**BMW.WilliamsF1** Team
Technical Sponsor

# Formula One's daredevil

**Jacques Villeneuve is Formula One's biggest star – and the most intriguing personality in a paddock full of exceptional people. He is the daredevil, the man who races for the thrill of competing as much as winning. After a season that has been even more controversial than usual for him, he must sit back and take stock of some turbulent times.**

J acques Villeneuve hasn't won a Grand Prix since 1997 but is still ranked by the cognoscenti along with Michael Schumacher and Mika Häkkinen as one of the world's top three drivers. He is undoubtedly Formula One's biggest star, with a huge international following. On the track he is mesmerising, a daredevil whose lust for speed and passion for pure racing is a throwback to a different age of motorsport. For fighting spirit and attempted overtaking manoeuvres he is in a league of his own.

He may be a daredevil, but he vehemently denies he has a death wish, as some critics suggest: "I definitely don't have a death wish. If I did, I would be dead by now. I love life. But I believe that to be fully alive you have to push the envelope – the closer you are to it, the more alive you are. It doesn't only mean taking a risk physically, it can also mean pushing the envelope mentally. In a race car it means going fast, taking corners flat out, being sideways, overtaking – and feeling it is something that others might not have been able to do. It gives your pride a little boost and makes you feel more alive."

Villeneuve may well feel alive but the pure joy he gets from racing exposes him more than most to the dangers awaiting those who tempt fate too far. His accident in Australia was a harsh reminder of the sad consequences of speed gone wrong. No one was more shocked than Villeneuve and no one more distressed that a track marshal died. He knows what it means when a life is lost at a Formula One Grand Prix and the sympathy he expressed for the marshal's bereaved family was deeply felt. But the repercussions didn't stop there. After a couple of on-track brushes with Juan Pablo Montoya, the pair met in the drivers' meeting of the Canadian Grand Prix. When Villeneuve accused Montoya of being the 'most dangerous driver out there', the Colombian retorted he would 'put him into the wall' if he ever brake tested him again. Villeneuve replied that next time he would put Montoya 'into the trees'. Montoya shot back: "You've already killed someone this year." Villeneuve snapped and grabbed Montoya by the throat until the two men were separated by race director Charlie Whiting.

Then at Monza, when all the other drivers had agreed they would not race through the first two chicanes of the track after the events in America and the death of a marshal at the second chicane last

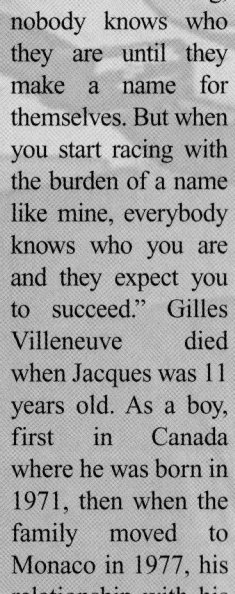

year, Villeneuve was the lone dissenting voice. He declared: "I disagreed and felt we should be racing – that's what we're paid for. The other thing we have to think about is that there are a lot of people in the grandstands who saved money for six months just to come and see a race. I am a professional racing driver. I signed a contract to race and that is what I want to do. That's our job and that's what we are here to do."

Gilles Villeneuve's son is in many ways a chip off the old block. Gilles, who said he only really felt alive in a race car, wanted to be the fastest driver on every lap, even in practice. Jacques has inherited the family traits of indomitable derring-do and shares the press-on-regardless mentality. But his father's precedent also set obstacles in his path. "My father's reputation certainly helped get my racing career started, but it also put a lot more pressure on me because people compared us all the time," he says. "When most drivers start racing, nobody knows who they are until they make a name for themselves. But when you start racing with the burden of a name like mine, everybody knows who you are and they expect you to succeed." Gilles Villeneuve died when Jacques was 11 years old. As a boy, first in Canada where he was born in 1971, then when the family moved to Monaco in 1977, his relationship with his father was uneasy. No matter how hard he tried it was never good enough for Gilles. It meant he was always a nervous child in his father's presence. But in a perverse way this negative influence in his formative years contributed to a greater strength of character and set him on course to becoming the fiercely independent man he is today.

After her husband was killed in 1982, Joann Villeneuve sent Jacques to a private school in Switzerland. It was there that Craig Pollock, who was one of the teachers, came into his life. Pollock went on to become Villeneuve's manager and is now his boss at BAR, as well as one of his closest friends. Pollock reveals: "There is no question that his father's unrealistically high expectations did have a lot to do with forming the Jacques Villeneuve we have today. As a kid he became totally independent and extremely hard-headed. He has tremendous determination and when he is motivated he will just keep going and going. He is extremely intelligent and also

has a tendency to be quite reclusive. He likes his own company and needs his own time and space." Villeneuve agrees that he can be reclusive. But despite his need for solitude, he has a colourful social life. He is also a poet and songwriter, writing since childhood, although he has shown his work to very few people.

It was a shared interest in music that helped him forge his relationship with former fiancée Dannii Minogue, the Australian singer/actress. Together for 18 months, they went their separate ways in January, citing the need to pursue their respective careers as the reason for growing apart. Since then Villeneuve has been dating 19-year-old Ellie Green. After just three months together he proposed and they became officially engaged.

With his steel-rimmed glasses he looks like a bookish student – and he is. Apart from writing, his other greatest pleasure is reading. His preferred genres are satirical humour, science fiction and the world of fantasy – another major theme in his life.

Many observers believe his dream world took him on a foolish flight of fancy when he decided to leave Williams after the 1998 season and join the new BAR team. People claimed it was a disastrous career move and that he was only doing it for the money, or else he was blindly following the lead of his misguided manager Pollock. Such opinions filled Villeneuve with even more resolve to prove his critics wrong. In reality he risked little, as he was destined for a few years in the wilderness with Williams while it sorted out its future with BMW, although if he had managed to stick with the team until this season, he would have added more race victories to his tally. When the BAR dream became a nightmare in its first, pointless season of 1999, Villeneuve tried harder than ever, flying in the face of adversity and gradually bringing BAR to competitiveness and respectability. Last year, which Jacques felt was his best ever season, he led BAR to a fifth place finish in the championship. Villeneuve's 2001 goals – and BAR's – were to win a race and finish third in the championship. But their ambitions fell short. Villeneuve had some great races – his podiums at Barcelona and Hockenheim and well-earned point at Monza where he started 15th spring to mind – but

also some disastrous ones, such as the accident at Melbourne and qualifying behind a Minardi in 18th at Indianapolis. It has left Villeneuve wondering whether he will ever beat his old adversary Michael Schumacher, or even win a race again. Jacques has been a constant critic of what he sees as Schumacher's overly aggressive driving. Several times in 2000 he condemned Schumacher for 'stupidly dangerous' driving, questioning his 'ethics and principles'. Nevertheless, his own driving style is rather worrying for some Villeneuve-watchers – including, no doubt, the insurance company with which he is personally insured for $60 million. His career has been punctuated by several heavy accidents, mostly occasioned by his relentless urge to probe the limits of what he calls 'the edge' – the outer confines of adhesion and, for him, the ultimate experience in racing. After six seasons in Formula One, how many more attempts will Villeneuve make before he decides to leave? "The day I think I've reached the limit in racing, that'll be it," he says. "I don't want people pointing at me and saying: 'Look at that guy – he used to be a racing driver'."

# Surviving in a tough school

Formula One is a notoriously impatient sport: flunk once and you may not survive to flunk again. Nick Heidfeld was lucky to come through his harrowing debut season with Prost. But survive he did, and he has gone on to rebuild his career with a string of impressive drives for Sauber Petronas. So is he just a bland techno-driver whose way has been smoothed by Mercedes-Benz, or will he prove to be one of the new breed of tough racers who will take over from the Schumachers and the Häkkinens in years ahead?

Twelve months ago Jenson Button was the rookie in the spotlight. If anyone paid any attention to Nick Heidfeld, it was usually just to make a disparaging remark and dismiss him as a no-hoper who would not see a second season in the big league. In 2001 the tables were reversed: Button got the flak, Heidfeld lapped up the attention.

When Heidfeld stepped onto the podium in Brazil this year, after driving his Red Bull Sauber Petronas C20 to a worthy third place in only his third outing for the team, he felt a sense of relief and, more importantly, vindication. The Sauber team mechanics, almost in tears, mobbed him as he returned to the garage in the gathering dusk.

"The chequered flag was a wonderful sight at the end of that race, so was the climb to the podium," Heidfeld recalls. "At the beginning of the season I wanted to get into the points and I managed to do that at the first race. Then I thought it would take a long time to get on the podium and instead it came so quickly. It was only 18 months since I'd last been there, in Formula 3000, but it seemed like 10 years.

"I could see and hear the guys in the team. They were below me and it was great, they were shouting the most! I was soaked in champagne

by the time I got back to the garage and that was bad enough, but then they squirted me with beer."

A year earlier, Heidfeld could only have dreamed of such a day. Throughout his tribulations at Prost, Heidfeld was quick to make the point that other drivers have had bad first seasons, yet still gone on to win a world title – Alain Prost and Nigel Mansell being just two. "But, yeah," he concedes, "a second season like that would have been difficult, for sure. It was so tough going to the next race knowing you probably weren't going to finish, that points would be very difficult if not impossible and that the car was not nice to drive. It took away some of the fun of driving and that's the most important thing for me, the physical enjoyment." Despite that first season, if you looked

beyond the surface, much was impressive about this quiet German with his schoolboy looks, perfect English and a slight tendency to mix his r's and w's. And he has to drive better than the rest, as his boyish looks count against him in the promotional activities modern-day racing drivers have to undertake. But that will improve with age.

His stroke of bad fortune – being signed by Prost, on an unexpected downturn – has been more than offset by signing for Sauber on an unexpected upturn.

Heidfeld's father, Wolfgang, was a motorsport fan who did some karting, then took courses driving round the infamous Nordschlieffe, the 'old' Nürburgring. "He just liked the sport," says Nick, one of three sons. "When I was three I learned to cycle at the Nürburgring. Then I wanted to drive a go-kart but there was a height restriction and if you were beneath it, as I was, you weren't allowed to drive. Then when I was eight we went to the Nürburgring and a new kart circuit had just opened. Finally I was allowed to drive. They stuck two tyres behind my back and some soft cushioning. My father told me to follow him and he would show me the line, but after one lap I overtook him because he was too slow."

By 1996 Heidfeld was well on the fast track. He'd claimed two German Formula Ford titles and that year won three German Formula Three races before taking pole for the prestigious Macau Grand Prix and winning the first leg. That was when Mercedes-Benz took an interest in the 19-year-old from Heinz-Harald Frentzen's home town of Mönchengladbach. The motor giant slotted him into McLaren's Formula 3000 junior team and three smooth victories left him runner-up to another upcomer making a lot of noise, Juan Pablo Montoya. Some felt that Heidfeld was ready for Formula One in 1999, but despite amassing many thousands of miles testing McLaren's Formula One challenger, he was advised to stay in Formula 3000. With six victories in eight races he was the runaway champion. Ron Dennis says: "He is still the driver who made the most of the opportunity we gave him."

Heidfeld's subsequent rollercoaster ride in Formula One is a parable of the times. Few drivers have graduated with such a strong CV, but that one duff season could have destroyed all his promise and condemned him to obscurity. "For me it was not an easy or calm year," he admits. "We had so many problems and had to talk to the press about what was wrong, then I had to go home and think about it all the time."

Talk to Heidfeld and you soon appreciate how well-mannered and well-presented he is. The schoolboy looks deceive: he knows what he wants. The media spotlight no longer seems to trouble him, although that may be because he now has something positive to say. His inter-

views tend to be focused and serious, but that is his racetrack persona. He has been case-hardened by the lessons of 2000 and is picking up the threads of a career that had delivered right up until the moment he encountered the 2000 Peugeot-engined Prost AP03.

Last year Jean Alesi forced his 'ugly partner' (as the car was nick-named) to dance whenever he could, wresting out of it speed it did not want to surrender. Alesi can do that; Heidfeld doesn't want to. Bully-ing a car is anathema to him. His old Formula 3000 engineer David Brown says he can drag a time from a car in qualifying, but Heidfeld really wants to do things the way he was brought up to. He has a Lauda-like capacity to assimilate and analyse data. He could drive round the problems if he really had to, but prefers to find solutions.

To some that makes for boring blandness, but today's racing drivers are test pilots who need a cold, acquisitive and inquisitive mentality and the calm, unflappable patience to mull over data during endless debriefs in pursuit of set-up perfection. His engineer René Decorzent loves that aspect of him. Heidfeld's spell with McLaren Mercedes made him a diplomat, too. Ask him how Sauber differs from Prost and he says: "I think there is not a big difference between any of the teams in Formula One. They are all quite professional. There were definitely things that were not good at Prost last season, and obvious-ly there have to be reasons why the team is not so successful. I did criticise them, but that was internally, and I don't want to do that to people outside the team." Of Sauber, he says: "The team is very open and the people are very, very nice. The structure seems quite good and the people are very motivated. Obviously there are no negatives yet!"

Heidfeld the technocrat is a thinker. Ask him whether any car will ultimately be difficult to drive right on the limit and he does not snap back with a conventional positive response that of course it will be. He pauses, then admits: "I'm not sure about that. To be on the limit is always difficult, but some cars are easier to drive there. The Prost from two years ago, when I first tested it, was a car that would go quite quick at 95 per cent, but when you pushed harder to get the last five per cent the lap time was almost the same. Last year's Prost was a difficult car to drive and it was slow. It was the worst thing."

He continues: "The Sauber is quite easy to drive and also quite quick. It's driver-friendly. Maybe it would be a little more difficult to drive if it was quicker, but at the moment we cannot complain because the car is really good. Even the McLaren was not an easy car to drive but it was very quick. If you tried to push a bit more, you got a lot of lap time out of it. I'm sure as well that there are some cars that are easy to drive and quick at the same time."

Heidfeld is effectively the team leader at Sauber, despite being in only his second season of Formula One, but he doesn't see things that way, nor acknowledge any special pressure from having had such an obvious future star as Kimi Räikkönen as his team-mate. "I may be team leader on experience, but there is no number one here," he says. "I had three years' testing with McLaren and obviously I learned a lot. Now I have a full season of racing behind me. I like to work with the engineers and spend a lot of time thinking about my work in Formula One."

Having seen McLaren from the inside, he should be able to bring Sauber some of that culture and discipline. Again the reply is careful. "I'm trying to do that, but you have to try to do these things slowly. You cannot simply jump into a team and start saying, 'Oh, this is completely wrong!' But you also have to be careful not to go round saying, 'They do this a lot better than you'. You have to be sub-

tle and prove yourself to the team before you can even think of saying anything constructive about how another team runs its operation."

But it was Räikkönen who snatched Häkkinen's McLaren seat, much to Heidfeld's chagrin. "Of course I would like to be there too but it's a Mercedes decision," he said. "They should know what they're doing but I don't think I've done a lot wrong. And they didn't even tell me they'd signed him. I think I've proved enough already. But the hype about Kimi is normal for a newcomer, similar to But-ton's last year. For me, it's a bit over the top." After the outburst, Ron Dennis was quick to calm Heidfeld's worries: "We will use the best drivers available to us. It may be a difficult decision but we'll take it. Nick has more than a chance of driving for us in the future. His con-tractual position was different. We're looking at developing the best future series of options. We have several drivers contracted to this team. It's a very nice problem to have." With Räikkönen, Häkkinen and David Coulthard on hand at the team though, it will take a monu-mental performance from Heidfeld to earn himself a drive.

Heidfeld has certainly proved himself so far, and although Räikkö-nen kept him on his toes from the outset in 2001, latterly Heidfeld was more consistently the better performer. At the end of the season he finished eighth behind the Ferrari, McLaren and Williams drivers and Jacques Villeneuve, three points ahead of Räikkönen. In 2000 the German outqualified Alesi seven times out of 17.

At the start of this season he was frequently asked what advice he had given to Räikkönen, but he would say: "It's most important for everyone to make their own experience. It's very difficult to explain something, especially about driving style. Learning by doing is the best way. But Kimi has already done a very good job, coming from only 180bhp in Formula Renault. He was very good in the way he behaved, he's very cool, very relaxed and didn't get over-excit-ed. He didn't make too many mistakes in the beginning and the lap times were OK."

Clearly Nick Heidfeld thinks about many things in his life, over and above his job as a racing driver. So he is not so much a computer-like technocrat, then, but rather a pretty shrewd, well-rounded cook-ie dressed up in schoolboy guise, who's on the fast track to a long career in Formu-la One.

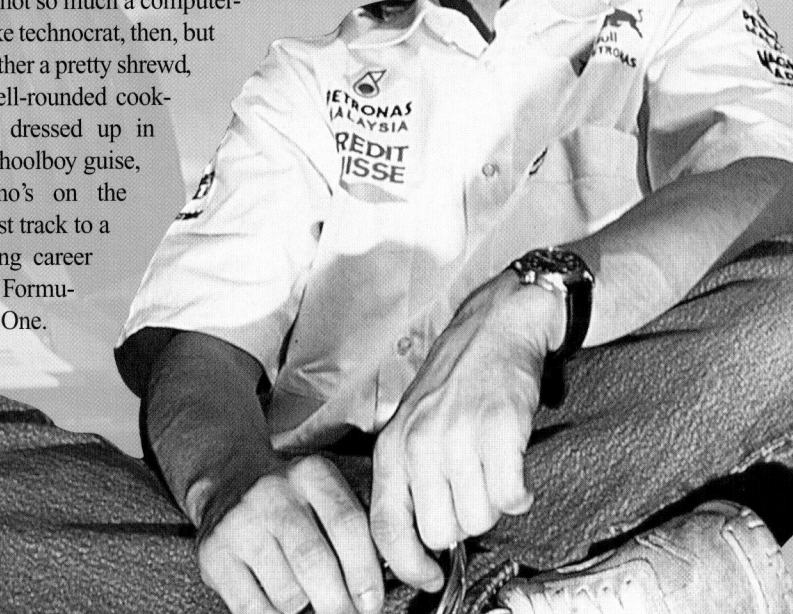

# The qualifier must learn to race

Jarno Trulli is the fastest man in Formula One who can't race. Such is his reputation. In five seasons of top-line car racing he has finished on the podium just once. And in his two years with Jordan Honda he hasn't managed it at all. What does the future hold for Renault's new number one, who has a serious credibility problem to overcome in 2002?

**9th**

If the world championship was decided on qualifying prowess, Jarno Trulli would be right up there in the top six. But it isn't, and in five years of top-line racing he has only ever once climbed onto the podium.

After 79 races he has scored just 29 points. It is a dismal performance. But in qualifying he has made the front row twice and the top six on countless occasions.

Trulli's problem is clear and not that difficult to analyse. His style is ragged and always on the edge. He doesn't have a structured technique for driving lap after lap. Nobody drives a Grand Prix at anywhere near qualifying pace, but Trulli is proportionally much further away from it than other drivers. Experts say his whole technique is wrong, and he clearly finds it difficult to get a race car set-up that suits him. One of Formula One's recognised driver experts, Peter Collins, says: "The skill is there, the problem is how it is used."

Indeed that was part of the problem for Heinz-Harald Frentzen, his partner at Jordan for the 2000 season and much of 2001. Frentzen was under-performing, and claimed the Jordan team was continually setting the car up for Trulli's on-the-edge style – which was useless for him and completely useless in the race. Hence the huge friction within the Jordan team prompted by Frentzen demanding changes in the car's set-up and design. Far from Frentzen being a troublemaker, his supporters say he was right and it was the team that was wrong.

Experts believe Trulli needs to radically overhaul his style and could do with some basic coaching from a man like John Stevens. Stevens is a driver coach who worked with John Watson in the

1980s, dramatically improving his driving after he suffered from a technique problem. Nigel Mansell, Alex Wurz and Ukyo Katayama have also benefited from Stevens' tuition in the past. Stevens is regarded by many as a brilliant driver coach, who specialises in changing basic technique and racing lines.

But racing drivers historically don't take well to outsiders telling them what to do. And Trulli's detractors say he displays touches of arrogance and doesn't easily take advice. He would be unlikely to accept coaching from a man like Stevens. But the problem remains, and will have to be addressed if Trulli is to develop a stellar career and ditch his 'great qualifier, poor racer' tag.

Trulli's career was always unusual in that he spent 12 years in go-kart racing before taking up car racing full-time in 1996 at the age of 22, old for a newcomer with big hopes to arrive in single-seaters. His performances in karting had marked him out to many as a future superstar. In 1994 he had eventually become the 125cc kart world champion and the dominant force in international karting. He continued in karts at first in 1995, before jumping straight to the German Formula Three championship for a short season of six races. He astonished his rivals when he dominated both races in the series finale at Hockenheim. The double victory there elevated him to fourth in the championship. In 1996, in his first full year, he won the German Formula Three championship outright with six wins in a notoriously competitive series. Trulli also contested the end-of-season showpiece Macau Formula Three Grand Prix, coming second. He should have won – he actually crossed the line before winner Ralph Firman – but a red flag meant the laps were counted back and he had to settle for only second best.

Trulli had caught the eye of Flavio Briatore, who arranged a series of test drives with Benetton at the end of 1996. He then bought him a drive at Minardi with Mild Seven tobacco money for 1997. Despite the obvious handicap of racing in a back-of-the-grid car and having just a season-and-a-half of car racing under his belt, Trulli impressed straight away with his obvious speed.

His opportunity came when Olivier Panis, Prost's number one driver, broke both his legs in a huge accident in the Canadian Grand Prix that year. Panis's bad luck was Trulli's good fortune, and Briatore quickly steered him into Panis's car. Trulli's luck was in and he grabbed it with both hands. The Mugen-Honda-engined Prost was an excellent car still bearing many of the hallmarks of a Ligier, and could even have won a Grand Prix but for better luck and reliability in the right race.

It was the perfect chance for a fast young driver like Trulli: the

opportunity to test his skills in good equipment, without the crushing pressures of being in an absolutely top team. He qualified a creditable sixth on his first outing with the team in France, and two races later picked up a fourth place at the German Grand Prix. His final race that season came in Austria. Panis was returning and Minardi was no longer the break it had been for Trulli at the beginning of the season. Austria was his big race. After qualifying in third he led for most of the race, only to be denied a good result when his Mugen-Honda blew. For many observers it was the sign of great things to come.

The following season was miserable for Trulli. He remained with Prost, but the influence of Ligier was fading further from the memory and the team had begun to lose the plot. He took just one point, and that was when only eight cars finished in that year's chaos at Spa. The 1999 season looked as if he might finish with a similar score, until he snatched second place at the topsy-turvy rain-affected European Grand Prix at the Nürburgring, which was won by Johnny Herbert in a Stewart Ford. The circumstances were reminiscent of the Belgian Grand Prix the previous year, but Trulli had worked hard for his six points and had held off a charging Rubens Barrichello in the closing stages. Although at the time it looked like it would be the beginning of a new era for the Italian, it has been his only career visit to the podium to date.

That wasn't enough to keep him at Prost, and in 2000 he went to Jordan as number two to Heinz-Harald Frentzen. He was fast at Jordan but couldn't race successfully – the same scenario as 2001.

In some races his qualifying was stupendous: he put his Jordan on the front row twice and was regularly a top-six qualifier, putting Frentzen in the shade.

But his two front-row opportunities had ended miserably. At Monte Carlo he was running ahead of eventual winner David Coulthard when his gearbox broke, and at Spa he was taken out by a moment of irrational exuberance from Jenson Button.

His 2001 season has proved equally trying. He has failed to finish more often than not and was disqualified at the A1 Ring and was lucky to escape disqualification at Indianapolis. His reputation for being involved in accidents at the start has grown, even though not all the misdemeanours have been his own fault. The highlight of his season was leading the race at Malaysia, again in the wet, conditions in which he comes into his own. However, he put himself out of contention with a spin and could crawl home in eighth place only.

Trulli's speed remains an enigma. Regularly sensational in qualifying, he has rarely shone come the race. His lack of race craft has been obvious at times. He has easily upstaged Frentzen, Jean Alesi and Ricardo Zonta on Saturday, but on Sunday afternoons his team-mates have matched or bettered him.

Next season he will be reunited with Briatore, as number one driver for the Renault team, a move he was loath to make after having an enjoyable time at Jordan. The spotlight will be shining on the rebadged Benetton team and it will be Trulli's big chance to prove he can race. The heat will really be on.

# Another Finn ready to fly

Kimi Räikkönen's sixth place in his Formula One debut at the 2001 Australian Grand Prix marked the beginning of a phenomenally successful year for the 21-year-old rookie. He is already being talked about as a future world champion. And with his move to McLaren Mercedes to replace fellow Finn, Mika Häkkinen for 2002, that prediction is a quantum leap nearer to coming true.

**K**imi Räikkönen, the rookie star of Formula One in 2001, may look like a pussycat but the 21-year-old Finn hides a steely determination behind a baby face that utterly belies an intention to succeed. His meek-and-mild image is the biggest con job in Formula One. If his new boss Ron Dennis thinks he will be able to manipulate his new driver in 2002, then he will have to rethink. Räikkönen knows what he wants and is no one's patsy. Peter Sauber confirms that Räikkönen is not the patsy he appears to be and says he was demanding to the point of arrogance to get his own way. At Sauber he told the team what he wanted, which at times didn't go down well and Peter Sauber criticised him for 'not wanting to listen'.

As recently as three years ago, Räikkönen was still karting. One year ago he had just taken his first run in a Sauber Petronas Formula One car. Now he is ready to drive for a top-three team – McLaren Mercedes – and will reputedly earn an $8 million annual salary, plus the $5- to $10-million-a-year that is having to be paid to Peter Sauber for releasing him. His limits seem astral.

Never has a sportsman achieved so little and got paid so much. But Räikkönen appears completely unaware of the sensation he has created. He has pretty much taken everything that Formula One has thrown at him without even noticing, let alone flinching. He lives a quiet life, couldn't care less about being famous and puts all his money into a savings account. He certainly has no intention of spending any yet.

As the rest of the world speculated about his future Räikkönen knew as far back as June 2001 that in 2002 he would be driving for McLaren Mercedes, after Ron Dennis had decided that a bold move to replace Finn with Finn was in the team's best interests. A week after Dennis approached Räikkönen's manager Steve Robertson, the die was effectively cast. All it would then take was for Peter Sauber to decide how much money he wanted to release Räikkönen from his contract two years early.

And what a debt Räikkönen owes the Swiss team principal of Sauber. Peter Sauber chose 2001 to make his best car ever – a non-works car that turned out to be fourth fastest on the grid after the Ferraris, McLarens and BMW Williams.

As a result of having a good car and fine talent, Räikkönen admits he found it all too easy. "I didn't really know anything about what to expect before season began," he says. "So many people were watching me, and the first race was quite easy for me. Then I had three races not so good. Some pressure came off." But the problems in Malaysia, Brazil, and at Imola were not of his making, and it wasn't long before speculation had him replacing Rubens Barrichello at Ferrari for 2002.

Räikkönen was surprised by the flattery: "I've had some good

races, but for sure it's been a surprise. I'm very happy with what I have done this year, but for sure there were a couple of races where I had good speed but the thing broke down. That's racing."

He wasn't the only one not surprised by his performances this year. Go-kart manufacturer Tim Gillard, whose kart Räikkönen used in 1998, says: "Kimi is exceptional. He makes things seem as if they are happening in slow motion. All the champions have had that." Gillard is making direct comparisons with Senna, and Räikkönen has certainly done as much as, if not more than, Senna did in his first year. When Räikkönen graduated from go-karts he spent two amazing years in Formula Renault, in 1999 and 2000. He won two championships, taking 11 wins and seven fastest laps plus six poles. It was an early indication that his

racing was better than his qualifying. On that basis he looks set to turn out to be an Alain Prost: not the fastest, but the best strategic thinker.

Räikkönen likes a car with a good front end. If it oversteers, he can cope. "It's not the quickest way," he concedes, "neutral is always better. But for me, is better a bit of oversteer than understeer. I can cope with understeer, but it isn't so nice. For sure the oversteer isn't always so nice either, but it's better for me if it's a bit oversteer. If a car is too pointy I can handle it, but for sure mistakes come easier."

It's Michael Schumacher's philosophy all over again. Enough said. In a few sentences, the comparison with Senna, Prost and Schumacher is made. The boy appears to have it all. No wonder Ron Dennis got his chequebook out.

He says he has never tried to analyse why his switch to Formula One has been so successful after only 23 junior formula car races. But he adds that it did not happen by accident: "It helped because I had so much testing in the winter time." He can rattle off the testing kilometres: 1,034kms at Mugello last September; 549 at

Jerez; 270 at Fiorano; another 1,300 at Jerez and Barcelona; more still at Vairano, Valencia and Mugello again. "That was when I learned loads of things, and I am learning all the time more and more."

His initial inexperience was one reason why the FIA put Räikkönen on probation when he first came into Formula One. When the probation was up there was no announcement; there was no need. Räikkönen had proved it ridiculous. He finished sixth in his first race, in Melbourne, and has been a regular top 10 qualifier; he added fourths in Austria and Canada and a fifth at Silverstone.

Räikkönen is not surprised he was put on probation: "Everything is at a higher level in Formula One. The engine is much better and there is a 600 horsepower difference between Formula One and anything I have driven before, and the aerodynamics and brakes are better. Everything happens a lot faster in F1 than Formula Renault. It takes a while for your eyes and brain to adjust, but it hasn't been too bad. If I had to single out the main difference it would be the brakes, because you approach a corner much faster and you brake unbelievably late."

After the first race Räikkönen didn't give it another thought. Nor has he worried about the physical side of the job, coping with 3.5G cornering forces and 5G under braking, despite graduating from 20-lap races to two-hour Grands Prix. " I trained pretty hard during the winter months with our physio, Josef Leberer, and we had a mock-up cockpit with steering wheel and a helmet with weights and he would be pulling with a big rubber band on my neck. That helped with the neck muscles."

Räikkönen is a rare driver in that he enjoys contact with journalists, who want to take up all his time, and has a simple way of dealing with awkward situations. "I just try to do it my way, and if somebody doesn't like it, I don't care."

Kimi Räikkönen might be only 21, but he's an upfront, what-you-see-is-what-you-get individual who isn't going to keep quiet if things aren't going the way he wants. He is very much his own man and likes to do things his own way or no way.

Supporters say Ron Dennis will end up loving him the way he did Senna. But it won't be as cosy a relationship as Dennis enjoyed with Häkkinen. Both sides will have to work hard at it before the relationship finds its level.

The man who originally spotted that Räikkönen was an exceptional talent and recommended him to Steve Robertson was former Lotus team manager Peter Collins, who also discovered Mika Häkkinen. "He is more his own man than Mika is," says Collins, who brought Häkkinen to Formula One with Team Lotus back in 1991, and who was closely involved with Räikkönen during his de Bruijn/Gillard days.

"Mika was a more pliable character. Kimi knows what he wants. More importantly, he knows what he doesn't want. That may not mesh with McLaren's professional requirements. In some ways another year at Sauber would have been very beneficial for him, in terms of all the things a driver has to take in outside the car. I have no doubt of his capabilities in the car, even though the things that he will have to learn there will have to be learned at a

greater rate than anything he experienced this season at Sauber. It's not just one step up when you go from the lower end of the top 10 to one of the three best teams in the world. It's a quantum leap. I'm sure that Kimi will drive the McLaren MP4-17 as quick as it will go, and he will do it neatly, but it may be a while before the light goes on about how to win races and how to deal with all of McLaren's other requirements."

The occasions Räikkönen's patience was used up in 2001 were when he either failed to set up his car to his satisfaction, or to pull off the performance he expected from himself. Even so, he was remarkably consistent. "Yeah," he agrees. "But there are some races where you have a better feeling, where you get the car working better. It was just small things that were making a difference on the grids this year because it was always so close in qualifying. But it's been a good year for me. I've had some races where I've made mistakes, but I just need to learn from them."

On the technical side, although he knows he has a lot more to learn, he usually knows what he wants in this arena, too, as his manager David Robertson says: "He would come in and say, please will you do something about this because I'm telling you that is the problem and we need to do something about it. That's Kimi's way. That's him losing it. That's as far as he gets to spitting the dummy."

So be warned. Kimi Räikkönen may look like a kid but he is no pushover. He knows exactly what he wants, and that's to win races. By jumping ship to McLaren he's already over halfway there.

67

# Worst of times, best of times

**When Giancarlo Fisichella stormed into Formula One in 1996, he was hyped as a future world champion. His $8 million-a-year salary justifies the talent, but his fourth season with Benetton Renault teetered on the brink of disaster until the second half of the season when he finally convinced everyone he was the superstar they always thought he was. But it was touch and go early on.**

11th

The Benetton driver is slumped back on a chair in the corner of his motorhome hours before the British Grand Prix, pondering a journalist's question about whether this is the worst season of his career. His team-mate Jenson Button, sitting a few yards away reading a newspaper, overhears the question and comes over. "Don't ask him that. Ask me that question. This season's been much worse for me than him," says Button. Fisichella is having none of it, explaining to the young British superstar: "No Jenson, I think I'm having a worse time. I've been driving longer than you. This is definitely worse for me."

Later on in the day, after Button finishes in 15th place, two positions behind Fisichella, he makes a point of telling me: "See, I was crap! Worse than him."

But that was then. If both had been asked the same question just a few months later, at the United States Grand Prix, the same journalists would have got an entirely different answer.

It sums up Benetton Renault this season: the challenge has been to avoid coming last. In the later stages of the season it was almost challenging for the lead. But early on the two millionaire drivers, both once tipped as future world champions, were reduced to laughing at their own predicaments. Morale was rock bottom, motivation factor zero and any hope of success a distant dream turned to dust.

But while Button still has at least the comfort of 2001 being only his second season in Formula One, the pain of the early part of Benetton's season was far greater for Fisichella. This has been his fifth year at the top level, having broken into Formula One with the Minardi team in 1996. Over the course of 90 races for Minardi, Jordan and Benetton, the Italian has scored 75 points, taken one pole and nine podiums. Not a bad record – until 2001 with Benetton, when his world crumbled around him.

That was before Spa-Francorchamps, however. Benetton's turnaround in form was so sudden it seemed miraculous. When the team scooped points at Hockenheim many observers dismissed it as a fluke. Two races later Fisichella was on the podium in Belgium after qualifying in eighth and spending his race battling with the McLarens. He even led the race, albeit for less than a lap. The team even emerged from the race in the unthinkable position of being ahead of Jaguar in the constructors' championship. One thing the team certainly had got right was the launch

control, as both drivers were making sensational starts. Although widely regarded as one of the nicest guys in the paddock, Fisichella is rarely seen venturing out of the Benetton motorhome during race weekends, preferring to bury his head in magazines at a corner table by the television. Many passing visitors don't even realise that one half of the Benetton driver line-up is in the same room as them during guided tours of the paddock.

He has done nothing to hide his frustration at being in a second-rate car with a team that promised much and delivered nothing. At his lowest point of the season he complained: "I'm so far at the back of the grid sometimes I can't even see the starting lights. It's difficult. This is the worst time of my career. It makes me angry sometimes. Not so much now as at the start of the season. Now I just want to go home and forget about racing. I can't say I actually enjoy coming to work every day, but I still try my best. I have to stay confident.

"It's very hard to give your best all the time when the car doesn't give its best. I just have to keep pushing. This season has been harder than I expected – much harder. Too tough to put into words. I expected the car to be much more competitive, especially on high-speed corners, where it hasn't really performed at all."

For Benetton, the season was always billed as a 'year of transition'. From next season Renault will completely take over the chassis and engine – and the Benetton name will disappear altogether. But that is of little matter to Fisichella, who has been swapped with Jarno Trulli for 2002, and will make a return to his old team Jordan. It is a good time for him to escape to a fresh environment.

Of the need to get away from a struggling team, he said: "I know that I am very lucky because I have a seat in F1 and so many people want that. It is something very special and I never forget that. But as a racing driver, my goal is to win races, not just make up the numbers. Most of this season all I have done is make up the numbers and I don't like that situation very much."

Fisichella started the season by coming 13th in Melbourne, then failed to finish in Malaysia. An impressive sixth place in Brazil gave the team some hope – although wet races are never the clearest indication of form – but Fisichella then managed only one finish in the next five races, coming a poor 14th in Barcelona.

He says: "Brazil was a very good result but I never thought for a moment that we would do the same the next

race. The car had so many problems there was no way I was going to reach that level again. I didn't leave the race with much confidence because I knew what was coming next. When you have a lot of problems, whatever position you finish in, it is impossible to say 'yes, I'm back, I'm back', because you are not back. You have to be realistic. And being realistic means it is difficult to be in the top 14."

Until Belgium, 10th on the grid in Monaco had been his only foray into the top 10 in qualifying, and for most of the season the goal had been to get in as many laps as possible so Benetton's engineers could work out how to make the car faster. At times the pain on Fisichella's face was very clear for all to see. It was compounded by the fact that this was his first season of disappointment after years of success in the junior formulas and then consistently being hailed the next star of Formula One. The 28-year-old Italian started karting at the age of eight after persuading his father to buy him a kart following a day out at a racing circuit near Rome. At 11, he went on to win the Italian minikart championship. Through karting he went to Formula Three in 1992 and in 1994 was crowned Italian Formula Three champion. After test driving for Minardi in 1996 he finally got a seat in the race car, before getting a seat at Jordan alongside Ralf Schumacher. His first full season was impressive, with third place in Canada and second in Belgium. Flavio Briatore had seen enough and personally engineered a move to Benetton the following year, where he grabbed second place in Monte Carlo and Canada plus a pole in Austria.

Suddenly the young Italian was being hyped as a future world champion. "It was a great time but I don't think it was too much too soon. I know some people think that because I was being described as a future champion I couldn't handle all the pressure but I never actually felt any pressure. I just felt a great buzz when I got on the podium, and real excitement when I had a pole position. I miss all that. That's what racing is for. That's what I'm paid to do and it's what I want to do, but I need the right car. I also think I've been very unlucky with the number of retirements I've had, but that's the way it goes sometimes. I want those days to come back but I still sleep well at night because I know that at the moment I couldn't try any harder."

You get the sense that for Fisichella, winning really is everything. Unlike many drivers, he has no interest in the hype that surrounds Formula One. He prefers to let team-mate Jenson Button take all the limelight, and even the $8 million-a-year salary – the fifth highest in the sport – appears little consolation for the fact that he is not winning races. He insists that despite the problems with the car, his relationship with Briatore is still strong. As for his team-mate, he says: "I get on with Jenson. He's a very nice guy and a very good driver. He just needs a little more experience."

The remark – and the scrap over who has had a worse season – points to a deeper tension between the two. Fisichella-Button was billed as the best team-mate battle on the grid at the start of the season, although it was soon resoundingly won by Fisichella. Both men's futures depended on the outcome. Fisichella had got the better of Button and was rewarded with the move to Jordan, while Button could only look on while his replacement at Williams, Juan Pablo Montoya, made his future at the team all the more secure. In a sense, the pressure is off the young Italian, who can arguably claim to have proved himself in the team. But that doesn't really mean much to him.

"I have no doubt in my own ability," he says. "I am good enough to win races, and good enough to go for the world championship. I just need a good car man, just give me a good car."

Coming from most drivers, these words would be dismissed as cheap talk from a man who is unable to deliver. Coming from Fisichella, they are probably true. He certainly deserves better. But will he get it?

# Swinging with the punches

Eddie Irvine is the cat who got the cream but didn't like the taste — at least so far. A Formula One driver since 1993, he is an unlikely veteran of a sport that is his passion. In spite of never having won a world championship, he is one of the highest-paid drivers in Formula One, earning a reputed $12 million a year. But this man's participation is important to Formula One — and to Jaguar.

There is a favourite story told in the Formula One paddock by a technical director who really should know better. He says if Eddie Irvine hadn't made it as a racing driver, he would have become a dustman. It sums up his image for most people – people who don't know him and don't want to try. But reality is very different, as Irvine is a person with an opinion about everything and a man who suggests the solution before he outlines the problem. He is also a cautious thinker who has an image he doesn't deserve because he doesn't care to bother to change the view that he is a fearless, carefree buccaneer with half a brain.

There is a childhood story about Eddie Irvine that sums up the dichotomy. His father Edmund tells it: "When Eddie was about six, his mother Kathleen and I were watching him at Bangor swimming pool. He could have been a champion swimmer, and this day he'd climbed to the top of the dive board and looked over the end to see if he was going to dive off. He must have been up there about three-quarters of an hour trying to make up his mind whether he was going to go or not. We were watching Eddie and shouting at him to dive, but he wouldn't do it. Finally, after thinking about it for ages, he dived off. That's Eddie – he weighs things up, he's not a natural risk taker. He likes to know the odds are stacked in his favour."

Irvine grew up in Newtownards, Northern Ireland, in the 1960s and 1970s, where taking risks could cost you your life. As he remembers: "I was certainly aware of the Troubles. You didn't want to go into certain areas of the city. I have a vivid memory of an occasion when dad had to drop one of our relatives back to the Falls Road area of Belfast. I was terrified he wouldn't come back. I also remember going to the shops and routinely getting searched. I thought it was a way of life for everyone. Then I went to England, walked into a shop, waited to be searched and nothing happened. It was only then I realised that the way we'd been living in Northern Ireland wasn't normal at all." Irvine's career has been like his life – one minute down, and the next flying high. He has gone from small outfit Jordan to the most famous team in the paddock, Ferrari, then on to Jaguar in a move that has made him very rich but killed the chance of winning races, let alone a championship.

His career is on hold and that doesn't sit easily on the outspoken Irishman's shoulders. He admits: "It is far worse than expected, far worse than Ferrari was when I joined the team. It is my hurricane." When he joined Jaguar, Irvine believed he would be challenging at the top by 2002. The original plan had him retiring at the end of 2002, but retirement is not scheduled for at least three years; 35-year-old Irvine believes he can drive on until he is 40. Certainly he believes he is driving as fast as he ever has.

His parents had pushed him to the top and took out a loan for a 'kitchen' that turned out to be a Formula Ford car. Irvine worked his way up and became a Formula One driver in 1993 with Jordan for the last two races, in Japan and Australia. He earned one point and came 20th in the championship. The following year he gained six points and finished 14th, and in 1995 he got 10 points and was 12th. For some of the time at Jordan he was a faster driver than teammate Rubens Barrichello.

His seminal year was 1995. Halfway through he got the break of his life when Jean Todt, Ferrari's new team principal, decided to hire Michael Schumacher and build a team that would bring the championship back to Ferrari. Both existing Ferrari drivers decided to leave in fits of pique, and after David Coulthard turned the offer down, Todt decided Irvine was the ideal number two. Philip Morris, Ferrari's main sponsor, was also hot for Irvine. He was photogenic, charismatic and fitted the image. Even more importantly, he was perceived as not being a threat to Schumacher. There was only one hitch – he was contracted to Jordan.

Eddie Jordan remembers: "Eddie and I were in Switzerland waiting for Ferrari to decide if it was going to buy him out of my contract, then the call came. I called Bernie and said: 'We've just tucked Ferrari up for another few mill'. In those days, Ferrari was our biggest sponsor." The deal solved both Eddies' problems: Jordan was desperate for cash, Irvine for the drive.

Irvine admits now it was to be the making of him. But at the time he confesses he wasn't that keen: "I'd been hot for Williams, but Ferrari was the way out of Jordan. Jordan didn't have the money to make a winning team, and I wanted to win."

It would be a long time before Irvine would achieve his first win.

"That first year was a nightmare. When I went to Ferrari I didn't realise quite how geared the whole thing was to Schumacher. I don't criticise him for that, but I totally underestimated how much the whole team was going to be focused on him." What he didn't do was moan, which is what has caused a great deal of friction between the team and Irvine's replacement, Rubens Barrichello – Irvine knew how to play the game.

Irvine says the German's dominance can take away the confidence of even the most secure individual. As he explains: "You climb out of your car having done what you think is a decent lap, then you look at Michael's times and you think: 'Shit, how do I compete with that?' Of course the answer is you don't – you find your own level and stick to it."

It was this attitude that saw him succeed as Schumacher's team-mate where others have failed. Instead of complaining he bided his time, and the team realised he had strengths where Michael had weaknesses. The best driver in the world is not necessarily the best tester; Schumacher can drive his way through problems that others have to confront and solve. He cites one instance where the engineers had fitted a new floor to the car and there was an immediate gain of half a second. But only when Irvine got in the car and said 'this is a real improvement' was it used.

Irvine says now: "There are advantages and disadvantages to having a one-man band. Ron Dennis of McLaren operates a different set-up. He lets his drivers have equal status until it becomes apparent one is going for the championship, then he'll concentrate on that driver. I think that is the right way to go. If you put all your eggs in one basket, the basket can crack under the strain." The basket did crack when in 1999 Schumacher broke his leg at Silverstone. The official mechanical explanation was brake failure, which there is no reason to doubt, but it also had something to do with the intense frustration and

rivalry that had built up between the drivers. Irvine was ahead of Schumacher when the German came to overtake him. There had been discord over comments Schumacher had made about overtaking Irvine fair and square rather than Irvine having to let him past, which had happened more than a few times.

Irvine says: "I made a really good start and Michael made a really bad one so I was ahead of him. My impression was that Michael tried to outbrake me and locked up the brakes; he then came off the brakes to unlock them as the car wasn't slowing down. We hadn't been told about the red flag – there was no red flag on the Hangar Straight – so Michael hit ▶

**12th**

the brakes again and that's when the rear brake nipple failed. He probably thought he'd go off and come back on again. I saw him coming up and thought, 'this time he ain't coming through – he ain't coming through until the team tell me to let him through'. He couldn't just presume I was going to pull over.

"I didn't know what had happened to him, I just thought he'd taken too long to get back to the pits. The team's objective was to concentrate on the race and try to win it. But I overshot the pitstop and that cost me victory. It was the first time I'd come into the pits when the McLaren guys were waiting for their driver. Once I'd passed them I realised how close my guys were and it was obvious I wasn't going to stop in time. As I'd overshot, they weren't immediately able to get the fuel hose on the nozzle."

Jean Todt criticised his number two driver for the error – out of frustration and probably shock at the accident his star driver had suffered – and received a short, sharp riposte in reply. "Michael goes into the wall in Canada and it's, 'oh well, just one of those things'. I go two feet wrong in a pitstop and I'm a tosser."

It was immediately obvious that Schumacher would be out for several races, if not the season. But on the Tuesday after Silverstone, Irvine and his manager met Ferrari president Luca di Montezemolo and Jean Todt and told them they didn't want to renew Irvine's contract. It was strange timing considering Irvine was now their only hope for the championship, although the team still dithered about making him the number one driver.

Meanwhile, Irvine was being criticised for not visiting his team-mate in hospital, but most people didn't understand Irvine's no-bullshit attitude. As he says: "First, I do not like hospitals, I try and avoid them. And second, the bottom line was that after I had established Michael was not badly injured, I was happy at the situation – this was my big chance to go for the championship. If I'd turned up with a long face, clutching a bunch of grapes, it would have been very hypocritical."

The truth is, Irvine doesn't like wasting time. He opted out of the Grand Prix Drivers' Association because "we couldn't even agree on group insurance, so what hope was there for agreeing on really big issues?" He doesn't have much time for the drivers' briefing, either. Every race weekend the drivers meet FIA technical director Charlie Whiting to discuss race issues. "The briefing is another example of hot air being blown about," says Irvine. "Some drivers are following their own agenda and not doing things for the good of the sport. Some want to change things for the good of the sport and some are asleep." He won't elaborate on which drivers fall into which category.

The one thing every driver does have in common is the dream of winning the world championship. For Irvine, 1999 was his chance and it didn't happen. There were lost opportunities, such as Silverstone, there were screw-ups like the pitstop chaos at the Nürburgring, and there was the question mark over Irvine's leadership qualities. Nearly two years down the line, he is philosophical about the outcome. "I made mistakes and the team made mistakes. In the end it just didn't happen – a lost opportunity. But you have to move on or it would affect your whole life."

Jaguar was not Irvine's first choice after Ferrari. He had struck a

very lucrative deal with Honda and agreed a contract. But when the man in charge of the new team project, Harvey Postlethwaite, died, the project was shelved and Jaguar came in for the man it thought could lead the team into a new era. So far Jaguar has not given him an easy time. In fact, as Irvine says: "We need to improve our infrastructure and strengthen every department. Each year should be a step forward but this year has been a step backwards. As 90 per cent of the car is aero, we need a windtunnel. Jaguar Racing is further away than Ferrari was when I joined it. When I signed with Jaguar I didn't realise how far away it was, just as I'm sure Michael didn't realise what an uphill struggle he would have at Ferrari."

The constant personnel changes at Jaguar have not helped an already fraught situation. As Irvine says: "For a while it seemed as if every time I came to work there had been some changes. We need a solid and stable infrastructure. That's what there is now at Ferrari and it's what is needed at Jaguar Racing. Stability brings confidence and trust and you need that to build a strong team. I am very encouraged by the arrival of chief race engineer Mark Ellis, who is a very good technical man. He is much more than a chief race engineer,

he is almost a technical director and so far he has done a fantastic job." Changes during the 2001 season included Niki Lauda's arrival and the departure of Bobby Rahal. After an initially rocky relationship, Irvine and Lauda are now firm friends: "He understands racing and what we need to win. He is a doer like me and he doesn't put up with bullshit."

Another change was Pedro de la Rosa taking over from Luciano Burti. Irvine had reservations. "Luciano was good, one of the best newcomers, and we worked very well together. He is sensible and clever and was coming on well, then suddenly it all changed. Now with Pedro we have to start again." But de la Rosa would soon prove a match for Irvine in qualifying and often in the race and in the latter half of the season the Spaniard more often had the upper hand in the team. Also, Irvine's friendship with Burti had been severely tested when the pair came together at Spa, resulting in the massive accident which ended Burti's season. Irvine was commended for rushing to his aid and helping the marshals to drag tyres off the stricken Prost car.

As he enters the twilight of his career, Irvine could reflect on what might have been. The big one is undoubtedly the championship and it's unlikely there will be another crack. The big question is, when will he give up? John Watson said he decided it was time to retire when a young Ayrton Senna blew him off the circuit: he knew he would never be able to compete. Irvine simply says: "I've had an Ayrton Senna to live up to all my racing life – his name is Michael Schumacher – but it doesn't make me want to give up."

Irvine's millions have made him unrealistic about the material side of life. He used to get a buzz out of wheeling and dealing. But no more: "The only thing that gives me a buzz is motor racing."

But for how much longer is debatable. Jaguar is still in trouble. Surprisingly, Irvine is a corporate player – he fulfils his media and sponsorship obligations and he is quick and experienced. If he sees light at the end of the tunnel he would like a fourth and maybe fifth year at Jaguar to get the job finished. It could happen.

RACING DRIVER

# Nearly man of Formula One

**Heinz-Harald Frentzen was being tipped for the world championship in 1999, and came within 10 points of winning it. But in 2001 his career fell apart, as he was humiliatingly fired by Eddie Jordan before the German Grand Prix.**

**13th**

Watching Heinz-Harald Frentzen wander around the Formula One paddock in late 2001 upset his many fans. He is one of the nearly men of Formula One – he was destined to be champion, he should have been champion, and many thought he deserved to be champion.

The 2001 season promised so much for Frentzen, who has long been tipped for great things. But the season proved to be a roller-coaster ride for the German star, and the rollercoaster went one way – down. His sacking from the Jordan Honda team just before the German Grand Prix was one of the year's big news stories.

But whatever the inner turmoil, Frentzen kept his smile, his cool and his charm. "It's been difficult for me, you can say that again. But this is life. I am very lucky to have the life I do, regardless of what else has gone on. I am old enough now to learn to be grateful rather than bitter," he says.

In his five races for Prost in 2001, Frentzen performed well enough to make many observers question the performance reasons Eddie Jordan had cited for sacking him. The highlight was a highly impressive fourth place in qualifying at Spa. It shows that the hunger and ability are still there. Frentzen qualified the car better than anyone before him, and was quicker than the man who replaced him at Jordan in a car acknowledged to be inferior. The irony is lost on him, as he says: "When Eddie Jordan fired me it would have been very easy to feel sorry for myself and probably even start thinking that maybe I wasn't really good enough at this level. But I'm a professional and I will never stop believing in myself. I know a lot of people are comparing the performances of myself and Jean Alesi, who took my seat at Jordan, but to be honest I don't even know how well he's been doing. I have to measure myself against myself before anyone else.

"I am paid to get into a car and drive it as fast as possible around a race circuit. That is one thing that has never changed, and it is something that I will never stop doing to the best of my ability. You have to keep believing in yourself in this business."

When he came into Formula One seven years ago, he was said to be the only one of the new crop of young drivers who could beat Michael Schumacher on the track. Without doubt, Sauber had obtained the services of a German who was one of Formula One's hottest new properties.

In 1994 he grabbed a fifth position in only his second race, in the Pacific Grand Prix at Aida in Japan, and went on to record points in three further races that season. Then he showed his mettle and sense of honour when he stayed hitched to Sauber.

It is a mark of the German's character that he turned down a move to Williams following the death of Ayrton Senna, opting through loyalty to see out his contractual obligations with Sauber for two more seasons. With the Swiss team's other driver, Austrian Karl Wendlinger, in a coma after his crash at Monte Carlo, the departure of Frentzen might have finished Sauber off.

Towards the end of the 1996 season, Frentzen eventually secured a drive with the Williams team to race in 1997, replacing the man who would become world champion that year, Damon Hill. It was an unpopular move amongst race fans. The pressure was on the German and his two years with Williams were a disaster.

Although he recorded a powerful debut drive for the team at Melbourne, some encouraging qualifying sessions and his first Grand Prix victory at Imola in 1997, Frentzen struggled for much of the season, his problems highlighted by Jacques Villeneuve's world championship. Despite the pitlane rumours, Williams honoured his contract and Frentzen retained the drive for 1998, though it proved to be a very disappointing time for both driver and team, with only one podium finish. It looked as though his career was over.

For 1999 he was rescued and moved to Jordan for a low salary of $1.5 million. It was to be the making of the man. He was transformed and from the outset it was clear the German had finally found a team that would bring out the best in him. In the opinion of many, he was the star of the 1999 season, and following fine victories in France and Italy he came within 10 points of taking the championship down to the wire in Japan. "That was a great time. I really felt at my best then, but to be honest I don't think I am a worse or better driver these days. It's a funny game, Formula One. The smallest thing can change everything, but

that year everything fell into place. I hope people who look back on it realise that it showed I can do the business," he says.

The following year, 2000, came as a nasty shock for the German. In a season of total domination by Ferrari and McLaren Mercedes, Jordan was nothing like the team it had been in 1999 and mechanical failures continually wrecked Frentzen's chances of building on his previous season. He did take two podiums, but was bitterly disappointed with the team's performance.

"That year proved how quickly everything can change. I had a lot of problems with the car. I just never felt I was getting all the support from the team I should have, and then when results stop going your way it gets even harder. There is so much money involved in Formula One that the smallest failure cannot be tolerated. I don't personally think I was a failure, but other people – I guess some of them in Jordan – appeared to have judged me in that way."

For the 2001 season, Jordan had access to Honda engines but it was set to be a long difficult season, with the yellow-and-black cars regularly failing to impress.

Frentzen outqualified his team-mate Jarno Trulli in the first race at Melbourne but he would not repeat the feat until he had switched to Prost. Following a massive accident when he crashed exiting the tunnel at Monte Carlo, Frentzen pulled out of the Canadian Grand Prix after he found he was suffering from severe headaches after the opening practice sessions, and was replaced by Ricardo Zonta.

Soon after the British Grand Prix, he was sensationally fired by Eddie Jordan; the dispute now promises a lengthy court battle. Frentzen has issued a writ claiming $9.35 million in salary and damages. He says: "I just want what's right, and I want history to record what really happened, not what people might think happened. It's nothing personal between me and Eddie Jordan. It's strictly business."

It is still unclear where Frentzen will be in 2002, but he will definitely be somewhere. His record in Formula One is impressive: 159 points from 128 races, including three wins and 17 podiums.

It was the passion for fast cars of his undertaker father Harald that first gave the young German the racing bug. For Harald Frentzen, the temptation to introduce his son to racing cars was a little too much to resist. He says: "Originally, dad just wanted to buy a car. It was meant to be a present for my stepmother. Yet dad suddenly changed his mind: he indeed bought something. Not a car, but a racing kart. So I made a start in karting!"

At Kerpen racetrack, Frentzen found himself racing alongside another promising youngster – Michael Schumacher. From there he stepped up to Formula Ford and Formula Opel Lotus Challenge.

By 1989 he was contesting the German Formula Three championship, and finished on equal points with Michael Schumacher and a place ahead in the standings. After a spell in Japan, four years later the Formula One doors opened at last. But for how long?

Frentzen has career earnings of approximately $35 million, and has no financial worries at the age of 34. But ambition still burns inside. "If I wanted

to retire tomorrow I could because I don't have the financial worries," he says. "The financial worry comes when you reach Formula Three because it is suddenly so much more expensive and you need wealthy backers to carry on. I have been through all that. I decided then that this was more than an expensive hobby for me – motor racing is a career. It is still a career and I still have a lot to prove."

Does he still have dreams of being world champion? "Well, I came within 10 points a couple of years ago, and I really think that with the right car I am good enough to come even closer. But that's the problem in F1. First you need to be a good driver. Then you need a good car."

# No one doubts him now

**After having struggled back to race fitness following a big crash in which he both broke his legs, Olivier Panis's reward was later to be dropped from the struggling Prost team. Many believed that was the end of his Formula One career. But the determined Frenchman took stock of his position and opted for a season as a test driver for McLaren rather than a racing role with a lesser team. It was a brave move – but it worked. Panis has proved he has the ability to mix it with the best and his determination has been rewarded for all to see.**

14th

Olivier Panis isn't like most Formula One drivers. He doesn't suffer from charisma overload, isn't ever difficult and always drives a race car fast. He has arguably been the revelation of the 2001 season, when he proved he is every bit as quick in a race car as BAR Honda team leader Jacques Villeneuve.

When Alain Prost effectively sacked him at the end of 1999, he threw the baby out with the bath water – there was nothing wrong with Panis's driving and plenty wrong with Prost's car. His career looked finished and the only drive Panis could secure for 2000 was as test driver for McLaren Mercedes. Little did he know he was starting a new trend when he became the first test driver to earn over a million dollars a year.

Panis's performance, which was very close to those of works drivers Mika Häkkinen and David Coulthard, started a fashion for hiring big names to be the test driver or, in team speak, the third driver. The Frenchman also started a trend that has been followed by Ricardo Zonta and Alex Wurz – instead of accepting poor drives, they have opted to take highly paid jobs as test drivers for Jordan Honda and McLaren Mercedes respectively, hoping to bounce back in the following year.

This situation worked like a dream for Panis. A year after his drubbing and, some would say, public humiliation at the hands of Alain Prost, he was back in a big way in 2001. He proved himself against Jacques Villeneuve at BAR, and comparing his performance with Villeneuve's indicates how under-rated Panis has been. While Villeneuve has been the BAR driver running well when the podium places have been up for grabs, Panis has been the Canadian's match in qualifying, especially in the first half of the season, and has out-raced his team-mate on several occasions. BAR had one of the strongest driver pairings in 2001.

Panis's situation today is a far cry from 1999, when he was effectively out of work. When he was dropped from Prost he didn't make a fuss and refused to get involved in mud-slinging. Today he is also a rare beast on the Formula One grid in that he is a Grand Prix winner, an accolade not yet achieved by such notables as Jarno Trulli and Giancarlo Fisichella who are more highly regarded and earn far more money than he does. In fact, of the 26 drivers who raced in

2001, fewer than half have actually won a Grand Prix. He is one of that elite group courtesy of winning the 1996 Monaco Grand Prix in a Ligier. But his career record does not tell his story. It is likely that Panis would be one of the big-name Grand Prix drivers by now if not for two slices of bad luck. One was not leaving the old Ligier team when Alain Prost took it over at the beginning of 1997, the other was an unlucky accident at the 1997 Canadian Grand Prix when he badly broke both his legs.

But he is now France's most famous and most successful driver. But the 35-year-old is not in the mould of Jean Alesi and certainly not in that of past French stars such as René Arnoux, Didier Pironi, François Cevert, even Alain Prost. He says: "Lots of people think I'm a nice guy. That is not true. When people are good and straight with me, I respect them. When they are not good with me, I am not a nice guy at all. When people" – and he lapses into French – "tread on my toes, I get angry. But if all the drivers are talking I stay out of it. If someone starts a fight with me I am not at all quiet." Few would agree with his self-analysis. Finding anyone who has had a run-in with Panis and who has a bad word against him is difficult, if not impossible.

In 1999, at the lowest point of his career, it proved a new beginning. Panis's renaissance was sparked by tragedy. In May 1999 his lawyer Peter Poelie-Zeewald, a Dutchman who had been acting as his manager, died suddenly at the age of 52. Poelie-Zeewald was a wily old bird who knew the ways of the world. His fatherly instincts had served Panis well. He admits it was a huge loss and he is still not over it: "It was very complicated after that to make a good decision about my career.

"One day I picked up the phone and called Didier Coton. I had talked to him and Keke Rosberg after I won the Formula 3000 title in 1993 but they were looking after Mika Häkkinen and I was a little bit afraid of that, so I went my own way. Maybe I was wrong. Maybe I stayed too long in a French team. Anyway, I told Didier that I needed help and explained that I was still hungry for success and still wanted to win in Formula One. Didier said he would talk to Keke. He called me back straight away and said: 'OK, we believe in you. We know you can be a winner'. And so I started

working with them and I am very happy about that because it completely changed my philosophy and together we took the right decision for my future. At the time I was tired and disillusioned. I knew I was quick but I did not know how quick. I needed to answer the question. I wanted to know where I was.

"We decided that the best thing would be to be the third driver with McLaren. I was going up against the fastest guys. When we started to talk to Ron Dennis and Martin Whitmarsh of McLaren I was quite excited about the programme. It was very clear when I spoke to them that they needed a driver with experience to help Mika and David." Rosberg had all the right connections as Häkkinen's manager and at the European races he always hung out in the McLaren Mercedes motorhome.

Just as that deal was being signed at the end of 1999, Panis got an urgent message to call Frank Williams. It could only have meant one thing. He was offered a drive in the second BMW Williams alongside Ralf Schumacher. Amazingly, Panis turned it down: "He proposed a one-year deal and that was too much of a risk. I did not know if the BMW engine would be good. I decided McLaren was the right decision.

"When I arrived I was a little bit afraid because I don't speak English very well and when I looked at McLaren from the outside I thought it was quite a cold team. But once I was inside it was a completely different world. The people were so good with me. They trusted me very quickly, we had a very good relationship and I started to get to know the big bosses: Ron Dennis, Martin Whitmarsh, Norbert Haug and Adrian Newey. For me, Adrian is the best engineer in the world. I was so happy with these people you cannot imagine. And I learned a lot. They are so human. McLaren is an unbelievable team and I am very happy to have worked with them.

"I pushed very hard whenever I drove the car and did the best I possibly could to improve the car for Mika and David. I had a good relationship with both of them, but particularly with Mika."

Panis still feels a great debt of gratitude to McLaren Mercedes: "They gave me the chance to prove my performance in comparison to Mika and David. I proved something to the team and I proved something to myself. Now I am very strong in the head. Some of the other teams saw the job I had done and asked me to join them this year. I discussed quite quickly with BAR and agreed to join the team this year. I decided to join BAR because it had made a big improvement in 2000 and had big potential. It was also because Jacques decided to stay there. I needed that challenge. For me, Jacques is a very quick driver – particularly in qualifying – and that made the challenge interesting. I have known him since my Formula Three days – we always had a good relationship and the thing I like about Jacques is that he respects the job others do. When you do a good job, or the team does a good job, he respects that. He's a good guy and I am happy

to work with him. I pushed him in winter testing and he has been pushing me and I think this is good for the team."

Panis brushed aside worries that the team would favour Villeneuve and he has been proved right. "That was before I spoke with Craig Pollock and Jacques. Craig told me the team needed two quick drivers with experience to score as many points as possible and I trusted that. From that moment on everything was very clear. We have done a good job together and we are going to go on pushing to get the best possible results for BAR and Honda. I was very pleased to be back with Honda because I was with them when I won in Monaco in 1996. I know it is a long time ago but we always had a good relationship." He is getting on surprisingly well with Jacques Villeneuve, helped by the fact they share a common language. Villeneuve is confident enough of his ability not to be fazed when Panis is faster than him, as happened in Brazil.

Although the quiet man of Formula One, Panis is a big star in France. In Paris he is recognised and mobbed where ever he goes. He says: "I have earned a lot of money and I am happy about that but the most important thing is that my family will be as they are now. Money is one thing but it is not the only thing. I don't live exactly a normal life but the French people respect me and leave me alone. Maybe it would be different if I lived in Paris. When I am there I have more difficulties but that is part of the job and if people are happy to see me I am happy to accept that." He has had a good year in 2001 even if the record books don't show it. He is capable of plenty more wins but age is against him. He only has a few years left to make his mark.

# Total passion to the end

Nigel Mansell tried 72 times before he finally won a Grand Prix. For Jean Alesi it was 91st time lucky when he won in Canada back in 1995. But though he had finally seduced Lady Luck she obviously regarded that great moment in Montreal as nothing more than a one-night stand. Since then she has resolutely spurned him. But rejection and the failure of his career to deliver on its initial promise have not been enough to quell the passion that continued to drive the mercurial racer from Avignon right to the very end of his career.

Even in 1995 Jean Alesi was regarded as a man owed some sort of payback from a sport that seemed oblivious to his emotional investment. He had burst onto the Formula One stage at Paul Ricard at the French Grand Prix in the middle of 1989, replacing Michele Alboreto. His luck was that Alboreto was irrevocably contracted to Marlboro and Tyrrell suddenly gained sponsorship from Camel.

He made the most of his luck that day and at one stage looked as if he might even win on his debut as he briefly ran second only to eventual victor Alain Prost. He finished an impressive fourth. Any driver that gets fourth on his debut in modern F1 can look forward to a long career. And true to form, 12 years later Alesi was still in the game.

But what really marked him as a man to watch was the United States Grand Prix at Phoenix a year later. By then he had won the F3000 championship for Eddie Jordan's team and was number one at the Tyrrell team then in its declining years. From the start he took command, fully exploiting his Tyrrell Ford's superior Pirelli tyres. As expected the inevitable happened and Ayrton Senna in his more powerful McLaren Honda took the lead. But at the very next corner he found Alesi edging alongside and snatching back the initiative. The crowd went mad. A man yet to complete a full season in Formula One had just outwitted the sport's master. Senna subsequently came back to win but for Alesi it was a defining moment. In the parc fermé afterwards Senna good-naturedly waved a reproving finger at him, as if to say, 'Don't make a habit of doing that!'

At Monaco later that year Alesi was at it again. This time Senna came to him on the grid and warned him not to do anything rash. Alesi, a proud man, was incensed and drove the race determined to prove he was no liability. He finished second, once again separated from victory only by the Brazilian. "I was so angry, especially after the way we had driven together in Phoenix!" he admits.

The world was at his feet. It seemed inconceivable that many victories would not follow. Both Ferrari and Williams Renault wanted him to drive for 1991. Typically Alesi signed both contracts. It personified his spontaneous nature. After committing himself to both teams he should have plumped for Williams but his heart overruled his head and the Italian blood in him opted for Ferrari. It was a life changing decision. He would become rich but not a superstar. Williams with its Renault engine was poised for a spell of seven seasons of greatness. Alesi could have feasibly picked up three world championships had he opted for the British team. In a Williams FW14B with which Mansell, who ultimately took Alesi's car, so decimated his opposition in 1992, he would undoubtedly have done the same. Instead he lost his way as Ferrari blundered along. "But I never looked back and regretted my choice," he says. "I enjoyed being at Ferrari. It was my passion." If any of today's drivers were put on earth to drive for the Scuderia, it was

Alesi. Sunday 11th June 1995 marked Alesi's 31st birthday. It was also the date of his maiden triumph. When Michael Schumacher's Benetton stopped with an electronic problem in the Canadian Grand Prix, all past disappointments were forgotten. Montreal finally yielded the greatest gift. Until then virtually no other winning driver had waited so long for his first win. "It was not so much seeing P1 on the pit board, because I have seen that many times before," he says. "But I had never seen P1 on my last lap! Suddenly, at the hairpin, I saw Schumacher's car on the big television screen and he was taking out the steering wheel. So I said in my mind, 'Maybe this is the right moment, Jean'. It was very difficult for me. I started to cry in the car and I couldn't see the road because when I braked for the corners the tears were going onto my visor. I was very bad at the time. I was a bit angry with myself and I had to tell myself to concentrate." Alesi was not the only one to feel emotional. When the Ferrari crossed the line fans flooded onto the track not

only in a celebration of his first success but also to salute the victory of the car bearing number 27, once worn by their legendary hero Gilles Villeneuve, who died in 1982. Back in 1992, when Alain Prost had left Ferrari, Alesi, Villeneuve's heir apparent, asked specifically to wear the special number in his predecessor's honour. Villeneuve had won his first Grand Prix in Montreal, and history repeated itself. "I waited a long time to get this," Alesi said, savouring his moment. And indeed he had. More than once Ferrari victory had beckoned. At Monza in particular, it had cruelly slipped away. "I've had moments in my career," he said, "when I've said to myself 'I don't know what I did to God because I have had so many opportunities to win'. Finally I won, so maybe now my life will be easier." Nobody could know at that moment of exhilaration it would be the only time Alesi would visit the top spot of a podium. Instead of getting easier, his life got progressively harder.

Even more painful than the dearth of wins in his five-year spell

at Ferrari was the parting. Walking out of Maranello for the last time he admits was one of the worst moments of his life. "It was terrible. I never imagined it was possible that I would not be there any more." Leaving Ferrari was also the start of a gentle decline for Alesi. As Schumacher and Irvine moved to Maranello, he and Gerhard Berger switched to Benetton. But Alesi and Flavio Briatore proved an explosive mix. There were some strong performances, but there was also the time in Melbourne in 1997 when he forgot to make his scheduled pitstop and ran out of fuel. He is perceived as a driver who needs a family atmosphere in a team, as if, like Mansell, he needs to feel loved and wanted. He certainly didn't get that at Benetton, but in any case disagrees with the perception. "It isn't that, really," he insists. "What I do need is respect."

Alesi has never been one of those lily-livered characters that Formula One seemed to turn out by the dozen in the 1990s. What would in other drivers be deemed unacceptable behaviour is somehow tolerated in him because he is that rarest of things in racing, a sentimental, honourable, honest man. His face, with its blue eyes and heavy brows, is the complete mirror of whatever emotions he is feeling. He is stocky, and has the dark good looks of a dashing brigand, yet something of the boy is still visible in the man. His occasional tantrums make you want to rebuke him as you would a fractious child. But he has no side. What you see is what you get.

In Hungary in 1999 Sauber personnel listened in utter bemusement as Alesi, having retired from the race, launched into a vocal explanation for the benefit of millions of television viewers of why he had decided not to stay with the team. Eventually somebody interrupted and asked if he had communicated this to team owner Peter Sauber, who was in the audience. Only then did a sheepish expression cross Alesi's face; again his heart had ruled his head. But fans adore him as a driver who doesn't give a damn for political correctness, and who wears his heart on his sleeve.

At Monza in 1995 he retired from the lead in the pits, then hurled his helmet at the far wall of Ferrari's garage. With his brother Jose he stormed off to his Alfa Romeo. But instead of heading for the airport, as originally intended, he flat-footed it all the way back to Avignon. Even Jose, who has seen his brother in a variety of moods over the years, admits that he would never forget that trip.

In a sport populated by the grim-faced and the colourless, Alesi has been a charismatic fellow whose strengths and weaknesses are all too visible. For some he epitomises the passion that drives men to race cars; to others he is superannuated, a man whose great achievement in re-passing Ayrton Senna in Phoenix is now ancient history. But those who have seen him make cars dance in the rain, who witnessed him take his chance in the ungainly Prost at Spa last year, and propel it against its will into a point-scoring position until, inevitably, it broke, know the real truth. 2000 was a season on the rack. Watching him at Magny-Cours struggling against a Minardi was a poignant waste. "It was very difficult, but I didn't give up. Sometimes I was just laughing. I didn't believe it!"

Such things made it all the more crucial to him that 2001's new AP04 should work. In pre-season testing it did. By Australia Alesi was still very excited. But the Prost flattered only to deceive. There were suggestions he mutinied when he realised the early runs were made with the car in qualifying trim, or even running under weight.

Prost was moved by Alesi's loyalty in sticking with the struggling team it was said. Few other drivers could have done what Alesi did with the team, taking points away from Monte Carlo and his special Montreal. At the Canadian race he once again threw his helmet – containing expensive radio equipment the team could ill-afford to pay for – into the crowd and performed 'doughnuts' on the track for his fans. Soon, however, a terrible weekend at his home race in Magny-Cours, rumours that he had been driving for free all year and the prospect of getting back in a real racing car with Jordan got the better of him. Prost's loyal star jumped ship.

The reactions to his behaviour varied. Some criticised him for standing by Prost only until a better offer came along. Some questioned the mind-set of Eddie Jordan in signing a driver who was clearly 'past it'. Others smiled at the prospect of Jean sitting back up at the front of the grid and said 'wait and see'. Alesi did not disgrace himself. Although falling below new team-mate Jarno Trulli's standard in qualifying, he was phenomenal in the race. In his first race back in the Jordan fold at the Hungaroring, a circuit where everyone knows overtaking is impossible, he performed the only real overtaking move of the race, wresting 12th place from Pedro de la Rosa's Jaguar. Then in the next race at Spa, a track which offers some of the best chances of overtaking in Formula One, he successfully held off Ralf Schumacher's BMW-powered Williams for lap after lap for sixth place, even though the Jordan team believed that the race would be judged on aggregate and Ralf must have got the point anyway.

It was still the same old Alesi. Not long into his Jordan term he announced that he would be staying with the team for 2002 as well. He was wrong. By the final race of the season he had heard the news that young Japanese hotshot Takuma Sato would be joining the team next year and he announced his retirement in true Alesi style – at a Bridgestone press event with no warning even to Eddie Jordan who was sitting by his side.

Life never became easier after Alesi's maiden victory in Montreal. But with all that Alesi passion still aflame it is even more poignant that Formula One's last reminder of a bygone age will never race a Grand Prix again.

# Coming of age at Jaguar

**At the age of 30, Pedro de la Rosa is older than most drivers in the sport, though he is fairly inexperienced by top-flight standards. But in an otherwise difficult season for Jaguar, the Spaniard has provided a ray of sunshine for his team.**

**16th**

The end of the 1997 Formula 3000 series in Japan should have been a cause for celebration for Pedro de la Rosa. The Spanish driver had just bagged the championship for Team Shionogi-Nova with a stunning six wins from 10 races. A career in Formula One was all but assured, with Eddie Jordan offering him a test drive the following season. Then the youngster was being described as Spain's greatest ever racing driver, even though, at that point, he had yet to sit in a Formula One car.

But de la Rosa knew better than to let himself be taken in by all the hype. "I stood on the podium clutching my championship trophy. Everyone around me was going crazy, cheering and taking photos. They were playing the Spanish national anthem. But you know what was really going through my mind? I knew I was heading to Formula One, and I thought, I wonder just how hard it will be to ever get on a podium again? I know now. Damn hard!"

He was right. Four years on, de la Rosa has come to the end of his third season at the top level, a season full of surprises for him. He expected to start the year again with Orange Arrows, but the team dumped him just before the season got underway. Then the Prost team signed him up as a test driver and most people believed this would become a race drive when Gaston Mazzacane was inevitably fired. But before he could do any testing, Jaguar swooped and got him to sign a contract as its test driver. Finally, after legal wranglings between the two teams, he got the second drive at Jaguar after Luciano Burti was pushed off to Prost at the

inevitable expense of Mazzacane. By the time the Spanish Grand Prix came round, de la Rosa was on the starting grid. He had a slow start to his Jaguar career, but when he settled in was regularly beating number one driver Eddie Irvine in qualifying, something Luciano Burti had been unable to do. In their 13 qualifying sessions together, de la Rosa had the upper hand on six occasions, recovering from his early struggles tremendously to out-qualify Irvine four times in a row between Germany and Italy.

De la Rosa came into an unsettled team, observing Jaguar's continuing management reshuffles and a car that looked great until the engine was turned on. "This season couldn't have started worse for me," he says. "I was upset when Arrows fired me. Not so much because they fired me but because of the timing, it was going to be very difficult to get another drive. It happened so early in the season there were no other seats available to me, even though I knew I would eventually get a drive again. It was just the worry of how long I would have to wait. It was a very depressing time for me because I felt I was at my best. But that's life. You learn in Formula One that you have to take care of yourself. It's a hard business to be in. You know the rules, so there is no point in complaining."

Despite all this, he has managed to finish in the points twice – at Monza and Montreal – and, more importantly, has often looked more accomplished than high-profile team-mate Irvine.

He says: "I've got more and more confident and I know the car much better. I know how to make the car go quicker and I think I'm better at doing that now. I wouldn't say I'm a better driver, even though the results have been improving. I haven't had a problem being focused. I know a lot of things have gone on this season but my approach to the race weekends has always been the same – to try and be as scientific as possible. There have been a lot of changes at Jaguar but from a driver's point of view things don't really change. You get into the car, you test and you race, and that's about it."

What has been impressive about de la Rosa has been his constant willingness to learn. While Jaguar was seen as being unreliable at one stage of the season, the Spaniard's finishing record in his last nine races was in the region of 70 per cent. Others in the team put that down to his sheer professionalism. He has little interest in the fame and glamour side of the sport, and throughout race weekends can be seen in intense discussions with his race engineers.

He explains: "I like to take a very scientific approach to races. I always believe there is a lot you can do to improve both your and the car's performance during the race weekend. There is enough time to do all this, if you put your mind to it. I take the view I'm being paid a lot of money to work during the weekend, not hang around to get my photograph in newspapers and my face on every television screen," he says.

The big question for de la Rosa and the Jaguar team is whether they are now ready to push for the top in 2002. The Spaniard is under no illusions. He says: "People often ask me how long before Jaguar can be a winning team? Is it going to be next year? I could

give them the answer they want to hear, which is that of course we will win races. But my honest opinion? We won't win. Absolutely no way. We are looking at three years. I am a realistic person. To get to where Williams, Ferrari and McLaren are will take a lot of investment and effort, whatever anyone else pretends. It will also require a lot more restructuring of the team. We have to grow but it's very difficult to grow when we are organised in this way."

He adds: "Niki Lauda has now taken over from Bobby Rahal, and we can already see that he is very hands-on. I think the difference is he will insist on progress every year in this three-year plan. To get to that winning stage, which like I said is three years away, there needs to be considerable progress every year. There is no point thinking that, oh yes, we'll have a new car next year so we are bound to win races. It doesn't work like that. How long has it taken Ferrari to win again? A long, very long time. What possible reason do we have for thinking we can do it in less time – absolutely none whatsoever. I know that might not go down well with some people, but there are many unrealistic people in Formula One."

So if winning isn't on the agenda, what does he have to look forward to? "I think when you are not winning is the time when you really have to test yourself. Even though I know that the car is not going to be good enough to win a race, I try and adjust my own targets accordingly. Some races I will judge that it is good enough to maybe only come in the top 10, and I will do everything I can to achieve that. If I do, in some ways I can say it was a winning weekend for me. You need a lot of self-discipline in this sport, so that there are always targets by which you can measure yourself."

Jaguar insiders openly admit they have been highly impressed with de la Rosa's attitude throughout the season, and the odds are he has a drive with the team for some years to come – assuming he still wants it. He looks a highly accomplished driver, even though this is only his third full season in the top flight. The only problem could come if Jaguar tries to lure the higher-profile stars away from other teams; then the Spaniard might find himself out in the cold.

De la Rosa had an unusual route into motor racing. While his contemporaries were out bagging the junior karting honours, he was conquering the world in the radio-controlled off-road cars championship. He tried karting seriously at the age of 16 at a local level, and the Spanish Automobile Federation offered him a scholarship. He entered the Spanish Formula Fiat Uno Series and won that championship in his first year, before turning to Spanish single-seater series. In 1992, aged 20, he moved to more recognised series – Formula Renault at British and European levels – and won both. The performance was easily good enough for him to step up into British Formula Three with West Surrey Racing: he finished sixth in the championship in his rookie season. The following year was a disappointment due to the dominance of Paul Stewart Racing, and for 1995 he turned to the Japanese equivalent with TOMs.

It was the right decision. He took the title with eight poles and eight wins from only nine races. In 1996 he competed in both Formula Nippon and the All-Japan GT Championship, and in 1997 took both

series titles. He had arrived on the international scene, and was snapped up for the Jordan test role.

By the sport's standards, he is relatively old at 30, but his ambition and determination to succeed are as strong as ever. "My goal has always been to win the world championship," he says. "That is what every driver wants. But to do that you have to go in stages. The first step for me is to become more complete as a driver. Some people just say well, if I had Michael's car I would win. I think they are kidding themselves. You have to look at your own performances, regardless of the car, and always look to improve."

But he admits that even after three years, the pressure at Formula One only grows. "There is a lot more pressure in F1 than most people can ever imagine. When you have a bad result there are many more eyes than you realise watching you and waiting to pounce on you. Everybody is suddenly asking questions – inside and outside the team. They question your ability, your motivation – everything is under scrutiny when you make the slightest mistake. You have to learn to keep your head level. That's even more important when you are not winning."

If he keeps a level head, don't bet against him grabbing a few victories when Jaguar finally makes it to the top level – whatever he says.

# A trying time in 2001

**Jenson Button had a very different year in 2001. From pacesetter hero with BMW Williams in 2000, he became a backmarker with Benetton Renault. But he has gone all out to treat failure in the same way as he treated success. That is what marks greatness, and it could well be that the advance of his Formula One career is merely delayed, rather than over. At the end his season came back, but the next is crucial.**

The 24th of January 2000 will forever be 'the day that changed my life' in the eyes of 21-year old Jenson Button. On 23rd January he was just another young racing driver, waiting for the big break, just as 20 or 30 other talented hopefuls waited. He was waiting to see whether he would get the vacant number-two drive at BMW Williams for the 2000 season and with it a five-year BMW Williams contract. When the decision was made, it was an intensely emotional moment between Jenson and his father, who had sacrificed much for his son's racing career. John Button recalls: "Jenson looked at me and said, 'Dad, I'm a Formula One driver.' Then we put our arms round each other and cried."

At the 2000 Australian Grand Prix he started a lowly 21st on the grid, moving to 15th on the first lap, then up to fourth in a stunning performance which nearly caused Murray Walker's trousers to proverbially catch fire. Eleven laps from the end he retired from sixth place.

One year on, at the 2001 Australian Grand Prix, things were a little different. He qualified better, in 16th ahead of his team-mate Giancarlo Fisichella, but on this occasion it was the best that could be eked out of the car. In the race he found himself battling with Minardi and Arrows and losing. He was classified 14th after electrical problems put him out, but had he finished he would only have been one place higher.

That would be his highest grid position until the team's turnaround in Belgium, when he qualified 15th. The race would prove to be the standard for most of the rest of the season. Even worse for Button, he would lose the battle against Fisichella and fall out of favour with the team when compared with the Italian, who outqualified Button on all but a handful of occasions. As the car and engine were tweaked and developed, it was Fisichella who reaped the benefits, leaving last year's new star wondering where his dazzling career had gone in so little time.

Worse, for Button as he struggled, his replacement at BMW Williams, Juan Pablo Montoya, was driving like a superstar. That Button would be invited back to Williams in 2003 was looking increasingly unlikely, with two top drivers in place at the team and plenty of new young hotshots straining to fill the seat should it become vacant – ironically the knock-on effect of Button's own meteoric rise. But from Hockenheim things started to get better. In Germany he managed to take fifth place, but even this was negated

by the fact that his team-mate Fisichella had trumped him, coming home in fourth.

After Germany Benetton Renault produced a better car until by the last race in Japan it was challenging in the top 10. In Japan Button qualified 10th – easily his best of the year. But his team-mate proved better again, in sixth place. Only four times out of 17 did Button manage to outqualify Fisichella.

It was so very different last year when Button had been closer and closer to Ralf Schumacher.

Last year was a terrific rookie year, highlighted by a stunning performance to qualify third at Spa and fifth at Suzuka, and to give team-mate Ralf Schumacher a persistent challenge. The failure has been just as dramatic. Saddled with a car that for much of the season was one of the worst on the grid, in the eyes of the public he had gone from rising star to loser in the space of just a few months.

Button has maturely settled down and accepted his lot, learning it is better to treat the imposters that are success and failure in the same way. As he says jokingly: "Being at the back is good for practising your starts, as you have to make good ones to get past the backmarkers and earn a decent place for the race." It is a sign of his determined mentality that he still views the cars around him as the backmarkers, not including himself in the group. John Button believed he was even better this year: "I noticed a difference with Jenson between 20 and 21. He became much more focused and determined." The father and son go everywhere together – testing, racing, even living together. It has been like that since John and his mother, Simone, got divorced when Jenson was eight. Racing karts was the substitute for father and son and it eventually led to Formula One. Since meeting his girlfriend Louise Griffiths last year at a film premiere, Jenson has become even more serene. It is this stable platform in a hugely volatile form of existence that has carried him onwards as he lives through arguably his biggest character test – going from Formula One frontrunner to backmarker.

One improvement he has made regards his fitness, which he admits to not taking seriously before. He has started a three-year programme with a top fitness expert, Norwegian Hogie Rorvik. The relationship began in Kyalami during testing in 2000. Rorvik says: "It will take three years to get him in the state where his body automatically responds to the demands of the training programme."

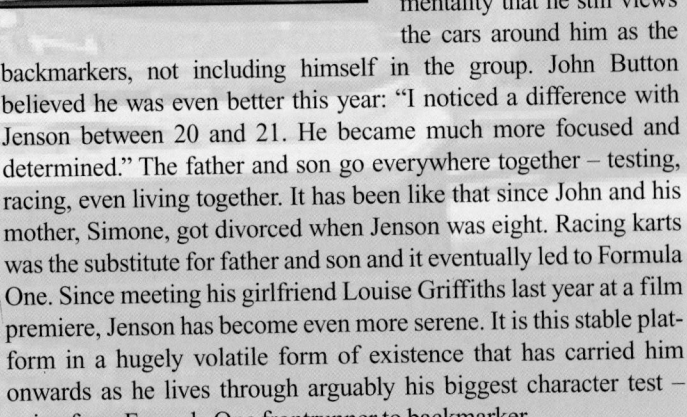

His 2001 season was not helped by a persistent, niggling shoulder injury, picked up before Brazil, and which kept him away from testing pre-Barcelona. The lack of power-steering in the car for over half of the season didn't help the injury. Button admits adjusting to Formula One's rigorous training schedule has been difficult. But he dropped three kilos over the 2000/2001 winter and now enjoys his training.

But for all the preparation, 2001 has been a wasted year and he knows it. The best he can do is look upon it as 'character building' and hope 2002 might bring better things. In Malaysia, somebody asked him how it felt to know he might have been on pole position had he still been driving a BMW Williams. He replied: "It would have been close, qualifying third or fourth there would have been a good possibility. But I'm not there and I can't think like that because there's no use."

Ironically, the removal made him much richer. He would have earned only $1 million as a BMW driver in 2001. He says: "I have a great lifestyle. It's terrific to have a great family and a great girl-friend and everything, but I'm still not completely happy. I need to win races. If you gave me the choice, to swap all that for race wins in Formula One, I'd do it straightaway."

He continues: "I pretty much knew at the start of the year it was only going to be a one-year deal, whatever I did. I wasn't too upset. Of the choices I had, I think I took the best option. It might not look it at the moment, but I'm sure I did the right thing. We spoke to quite a few teams, but thought Benetton was the best option long-term."

In the short term, though, it has proved to be an unmitigated disaster and he could not have foreseen the car's lack of pace. Some Benetton insiders suggest Renault's 111-degree engine may at its worst have produced a mere 745bhp; and that Button's engines even had 50bhp less than that. He says: "You are going to push harder and harder and it can sometimes be a bit too much. I haven't had many chances to take risks this year, but I am pushing harder than I did last year. It's just that no one can see it because I'm at the other end."

Button is careful when discussing the differences between the BMW Williams and Benetton Renault teams: "It's difficult to do that because I have had a lot more experience now, so I see things differently. A lot of Benetton's working practices are the same as BMW Williams, but everyone is going to have different ideas in every team. It was easier with Benetton when I first came into the team because they knew that I could drive an F1 car, whereas Williams had never heard of me and there was the risk because they'd taken a huge gamble."

Button is heartened by Ralf Schumacher's performances in 2000. Last year he proved himself as quick. He says, grinning: "I think people have seen this year that Ralf is unbelievably quick, but I really don't care because I'm confident that I'm going to be world champion whatever anyone thinks, so it's not going to change anything at all."

Giancarlo Fisichella comprehensively beat Button in 2001 and he is clearly a lot better driver than anyone previously imagined. Button doesn't mind that comparison: "Obviously I want to win races because that's my goal and I wouldn't be here if it wasn't." He is uneasy when someone tries to get under his skin or analyse his psyche. He continues: "I think if I was with a team where I knew things couldn't improve, I wouldn't even bother. At the circuit I don't tend to get angry, because racing is what I want to be doing. I'm a bit more impatient with people now than I was."

His drive with Renault for 2002 seems secure after numerous problems between himself and Flavio Briatore. Now he must beat Jarno Trulli in 2002.

# The struggle goes on and on

Jos Verstappen made his Formula One debut in 1993, starting a career that has been aided by the abundant sponsorship available in Holland for its star driver. He may not be the most amiable man in the Formula One paddock, but on his day, he is as good a driver as most. He is also the most insecure man in Formula One continually struggling for recognition. But each time he believes he has made it a knock back arrives. In 2001 it was in the shape of team-mate rookie Enrique Bernoldi who outqualified him more often than not.

**18th**

On several occasions in 2001 Jos Verstappen reminded his Dutch fans of the talent they have enthused about for the past eight years. In the right car and under the right circumstances he is a very quick driver. His Arrows team points out he overtook more cars than anyone else in 2001. In Malaysia he made a sensational start, storming from 18th on the grid to seventh at the finish and fighting for fourth along the way. In Austria he ran as high as second and finished sixth, and in Monte Carlo he did more overtaking than the rest of the field put together, passing five cars on his way from 19th to eighth. But putting performances like this aside, for the rest of the time he is an indistinguishable backmarker.

It is this wildly erratic form that has dogged Verstappen's career and meant that, in eight years, he has been dropped from teams four times. But things could have been so different. In the middle of 1996, after flashes of form and brilliant driving in the first half of the season, his manager was striding up and down the paddock asking teams for $4-$6 million a year for his driver's services next year. As it was Verstappen flopped in the remaining races and was lucky to get any drive. In the end Ken Tyrrell signed him – but for a lot less than the asking price.

It was his talent for flashes of brilliance that got Verstappen into Formula One, in 1994. Everyone was interested in the 21-year-old Formula Three star because of his performance in a test at Estoril after the 1993 Portuguese Grand Prix. He tested for the Footwork Arrows team and his performance started a fight for his services between McLaren and Benetton. McLaren looked favourite to secure the driver but Flavio Briatore seduced him to come to Benetton with one of his escalating six-year contracts, initially as a test driver but with racing promised. And his chance came sooner than he could have dreamed. When regular driver JJ Lehto injured his neck in a testing crash at Silverstone, Verstappen was called up to do his first race, in Brazil. But the dream turned into a nightmare. In the race Verstappen got caught up in a tangle with Eddie Irvine's Jordan and Martin Brundle's McLaren and barrel-rolled into the gravel. It was an almighty shunt. Despite the inauspicious start, he scored 10 points from the 10 races he drove, sharing the car with JJ Lehto and Johnny Herbert. He even got a couple of podiums. But it was not good enough as he was in the best car on the grid which won the championship for team-mate Michael Schumacher.

His high spot came, ironically, when his Benetton was engulfed in

flames during a pitstop in Germany in 1994. It made him famous throughout the world as more or less every newspaper carried the dramatic picture. He says now: "I had time to notice drops of fuel on my visor, then everything went yellow and orange." However, that season he was outperformed by Schumacher, Lehto and Herbert, and not surprisingly Briatore tore up the six-year contract. It damaged his career, some thought beyond repair. As he recalls: "It's a very difficult question, whether I regret joining Benetton. Ron [Dennis] offered me a testing contract with no guarantees to go racing, whereas Benetton gave me a testing contract but did guarantee me races." And he fluffed a test with McLaren when he shouldn't have driven at all. He admits: "McLaren offered me a test at Silverstone, but it was cold and there was ice on the circuit so we didn't do that many laps. But I think we did a reasonable test."

In 1995 he secured a rent-a-drive with the Simtek team, which was desperate for money. Again it was all about the flashes of brilliance when he climbed from 14th to sixth during the Argentine GP in the worst car on the grid. "It took Gerhard Berger in the Ferrari four laps to overtake me," he recalls with relish. When the team publicly went under he sat out the rest of 1995 but he was lucky in 1996 to join Footwork Arrows, a team in steep decline. In Argentina he humbled the McLarens of David Coulthard and Mika Häkkinen and ran as high as fifth, an impressive giant-slaying act. It was enough to get him a drive as team-mate to Mika Salo at Tyrrell in 1997, but he scored no points. Tyrrell had seen enough to want to keep him for 1998, but new owner BAR chose a fee-paying driver for 1998 and dropped him. It was a decision that caused team founder Ken Tyrrell to resign. Verstappen appreciated his old boss's loyalty, as he says: "It was good to know Ken was behind me – I think a lot of people were. Just one guy decided to take Ricardo Rosset instead of me, but what can I say? Ken pulled out because he wanted a good season with good results, then he wanted to retire. He said he didn't think we would get the results he wanted without me, so he walked away."

Verstappen steeled himself to sit out 1998. He remembers watching the 1998 Monaco Grand Prix in bed, pondering what might have been as he watched Häkkinen and Coulthard racing their McLarens. But all was not lost. Jan Magnussen was underperforming at the Stewart team and Verstappen was the choice to replace the Dane mid-season. Verstappen ploughed in as Stewart's saviour – but performed no better than Magnussen and was quietly

dropped at the end of the year. He did not get into a Formula One car the following year. But again it was not all over. At the start of 2000 Tom Walkinshaw had no sponsors for his Arrows team other than the $8 million brought with Pedro de la Rosa from Repsol. Verstappen's managers brought some Dutch sponsors in – and got their man the drive. Luckily the team attracted backing at the last minute and Verstappen had a good season. It continued for 2001. Verstappen says: "Sometimes it frustrates you when you think about it, but I'm here with Arrows trying to make the best out of it and perform as well as I can. You have to show the world you can still do it and maybe someone will pick it up and you will get the chance to drive in a better car. You never know. That's why you try." He continues: "I like Tom Walkinshaw very much and I think what he's doing is good. We are doing a lot more developing than ever and they are being very professional."

Apart from the high spots, Verstappen was also in the headlines for running into the back of race leader Juan Pablo Montoya while being lapped during the 2001 Brazilian Grand Prix. "The telemetry shows I was slower at that point than on the previous lap," he claims, and while he may be a hard racer, deliberate contact has never been his forte. "But the FIA said Montoya braked at the same point he had before. I don't know the reason why I was fined $15,000 and Rubens Barrichello was not fined at all for doing something similar to Ralf. I didn't do it on purpose and I think it looked very stupid and not very professional. The last thing I want to do is things like that. My career is very important to me. But the only thing I can say is that I was about 60kph slower than the lap before, I braked around 25, 30 metres earlier and I was surprised he was braking at that time. That's not just how I see it, but all the engineers who looked at the data. What can you say? Montoya is the upcoming star and whatever he says is more interesting than whatever I say…Why did I go to the left? To let him past, not to take him off.

"I must be honest," Verstappen adds, "if that happened to me I would be very pissed off. I would kill him! But he was very relaxed and professional. I know how difficult that is. I feel very sorry that it happened."

His performance in Malaysia was extraordinary as he battled with Ralf Schumacher, Heinz-Harald Frentzen and Häkkinen: "I really enjoyed that! Of course, you finish seventh and you think, 'Shit, I don't have a point!' But at the end of the day I think it was fantastic, playing with the big boys. They are normal human beings, they just drive a better car – that's why they are quicker. As long as you know that for yourself it's OK, otherwise you get crazy. I believe in my abilities and if I get the chance to show it I will do, like Malaysia, like Austria, like Monaco." But the hard reality is that Verstappen is lucky to still have a Formula One seat with so many youngsters snapping at his heels. He is fortunate in having aggressive managers and Dutch national support. He has also survived the reputation of being a bit of a bruiser. Last year he was fined for brawling at a go-kart race and he and his father could have gone to prison over the incident in which someone was badly injured.

He conceals his frustrations well. A few in the paddock still rate him, although most dismiss him as a journeyman capable of the odd strong showing. He hasn't won a race for eight years – since his Formula Three days – but he genuinely believes he could be a race winner in the right car. The truth is he had the right car in 1994 – and was left wanting. It is the difference between winners and losers. "I still believe in my abilities. But you need the chance. As a driver, I don't believe I have one reason why I shouldn't win. And I'm very committed. Last year I enjoyed Formula One more than ever. I don't know why. But we had to work together in the team. You had people around who liked you and were doing things for you, and we had some very good races in a reasonable car so you always went to a race feeling positive. This year I trained very hard to be fit and we are working to improve. It's hard for people outside F1 to understand the difference between the cars. They don't reckon Verstappen is as good as Coulthard, for example. But I do."

# Testing times ahead

**Brazilian Ricardo Zonta is faced with a stark reality: he hasn't got the pace to cut it in Formula One. After two unhappy years racing for BAR, he spent 2001 as Jordan Honda's test driver. He still hankers for a regular drive but in his heart knows that this may not happen. A test driver is where his role lies and for this role he is likely to be in demand.**

**19th**

Ricardo Zonta is one of the five Brazilian drivers who have raced in Formula One this year, and he is well aware of his status. He is number five in the public recognition stakes behind Luciano Burti, Rubens Barrichello, Enrique Bernoldi and Tarso Marques, and often even wonders if his own countrymen know he is Brazilian.

Even at the 2001 Brazilian Grand Prix, Zonta went unnoticed. He loves Brazil but not its racing capital São Paulo, where the Grand Prix is held.

Zonta has had a miserable 2001 as Jordan Honda's test driver, save for two races when he replaced a sick Heinz-Harald Frentzen and then a sacked Heinz-Harald Frentzen. If he needed any indication of how he is rated in Formula One, then he got it when Frentzen was fired and he didn't take over the drive. He has had his chance in Formula One and he knows it. He simply isn't fast enough. And the Brazilian fans know it too.

The 26-year-old Brazilian has never been given a chance to be a hero in his homeland. The two disastrous years at British American Racing dispelled any gladiator status Zonta had. In 1998 Craig Pollock plucked him from test-driver status and put him alongside the 1997 world champion in the brand spanking new, Lucky Strike-sponsored team. Against Villeneuve, Zonta never really stood a chance. Not only was he a Formula One race rookie, he says his mild-mannered and quiet exterior made him an easy doormat for Villeneuve and Pollock to wipe their feet on. Strong stuff, but the fact was even acknowledged by the team principal's wife, Barbara Pollock. She says Zonta was bullied and given secondary equipment. She says: "Jacques is a very strong character. It meant that Ricardo never stood a chance. Jacques walked all over him."

At a press conference in 2000, Pollock let slip his feelings, commenting: "It would be a mistake for a brand new team to hire a brand new driver." Realising what he had said, he backtracked furiously: "I mean it wasn't a mistake to hire Ricardo," he stuttered. "But maybe it was not the wisest decision to have a new, inexperienced driver in a new, inexperienced team."

That summed it up. Zonta said: "It was a difficult year for me. We had so many problems in the middle of the season, where I was crashing out alone and involving others and it was very bad for my career. But it was a good year for learning, and I think that to get three points is quite good. I think it is just bad luck. It has been a bad year for me in terms of luck, everything went wrong all at once, in the space of three or four months. But you have to learn to accept good and bad with dignity." He admits freely that he had 'problems' with the management, and his naivety was taken advantage of. "I liked the mechanics and the engineers, but I have had some problems with the directors. But it is business and I have certainly learned a lot about business – how to trust people. Before I trusted everybody, and now I know I cannot do that.

"I get a lot of satisfaction when Jordan beats BAR, but I want to beat other teams as well." Zonta's only

way back to Formula One now looks to be a rent-a-drive. But those are now fiercely contested, and few exist for 2002. He is managed by Brazilian Geraldo Rodrigues, and his father Joanir Zonta is a wealthy food-retailing entrepreneur. Both men shepherded his career when he turned out to be a karting star.

His father told him he would only let him race if he made good grades at school. There was a heritage, as his father was an amateur racing driver. Zonta says: "I spent a lot of time watching my father compete. I guess the bug bit me then, when I was about six."

He got good grades and his father let him race. At 11 years old, he won his first go-kart race from pole. By the time he was 18, in 1994, he had won virtually everything there was to win in karting in Brazil, and graduated to Formula Three. He says: "Formula Three is the best school for Formula One. You learn about racing on slick tyres, how to change suspension setting and the effects of aerodynamics by altering the wings on the front and back of the car." He won the Brazilian and South American F3 championships in 1995 and moved to Italy, where he settled in Florence. In 1996 he ran in Formula 3000 and won two races in his debut season. The following year he won three races and took the championship. He spent 1998 in sports cars for Mercedes and carried on winning. And then he landed the BAR drive for 1999 and 2000 where he was also paid $3 million a year to drive. It yielded just three points. In 2001 he was out, and was rescued by becoming Jordan's test driver and getting two lucky drives.

His racing career may be over now, but for testing assignments he will be in demand.

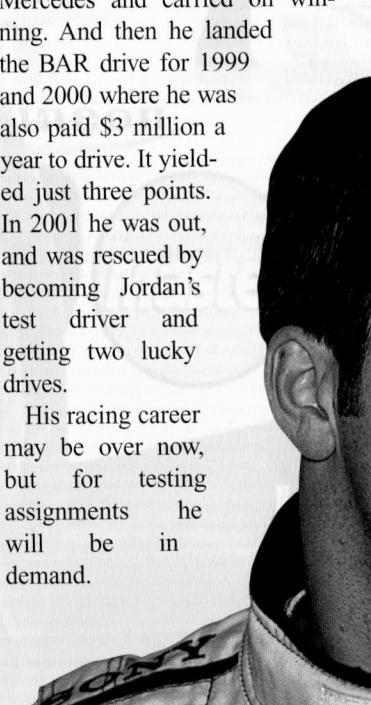

vision.
DESIGNED WITH A DIFFERENT PERSPECTIVE

FLYBRIDGE
25M
23M
20M
65
56
50
45
40
38

V CLASS
SPORTS
V65
V58
V50
V46
V42

Princess V65

POWER, PRECISION, PASSION.

PRINCESS
www.princess-yachts.com

# An unfortunate year

**Luciano Burti hit the headlines for all the wrong reasons in 2001. It was a season punctuated by spectacular accidents at Hockenheim and Spa and a series of smaller ones. In his first year in the big league he drove for two teams and scored points with neither. He has proved himself a neat driver, but will that turn out to be enough? With so many talented youngsters knocking on the door, he is struggling to stay in Formula One and may turn out to be a classic one-season wonder.**

20th

The world outside of Formula One probably first became aware of Luciano Burti as he flew in the air at the start of the German Grand Prix at Hockenheim. His aviating antics were beamed into millions of homes worldwide and then made the front page of most of the newspapers around the world as well.

Fortunately for him, apart from a bruised arm, he was unhurt after his Prost took off over the back wheel of Michael Schumacher's faltering Ferrari on the start-line. Burti says: "I think the accident looked worse on television than what I experienced in the car but I was lucky not to be hurt." At least he was around to give the interview. Not so five weeks later.

Two races later, at the Belgian Grand Prix, he was luckier still when his Prost slammed head-on into a tyre wall at the fast Blanchimont corner. The speed was estimated at 160mph. This time he was helicoptered to hospital suffering from concussion and severe facial

bruising as once again in the space of a few weeks he caused a Grand Prix to be stopped – no small thing when 300 million people are watching and millions of dollars of TV time are at stake. So he is a man who has been noticed for his misfortunes, not his racing. But that afternoon in Belgium the young Brazilian could count himself extremely lucky to have survived.

Although both accidents were just that – accidents – Burti has had more than his fair share of damaged cars in 2001. He has now had eight prangs at race weekends this year and on that basis alone there must be some doubt whether he will get a Formula One drive for 2002. In In addition, he must now struggle with a reputation for being 'accident prone'.

He has not had an easy entry into Formula One. He made his debut with Jaguar Racing at the Austrian Grand Prix in 2000 when Eddie Irvine was forced to stand down because of stomach pains. He qualified 21st out of 22 on the grid – between two Minardis. On race day he suffered a water leak and had to race the spare car, as well as start from the pitlane. His finished in 11th place, not a dis-

tinguished showing but it proved good enough to earn him the number two drive at Jaguar for the 2001 season.

He was replacing no less a figure than Johnny Herbert and it looked like Burti had made it. But he hadn't. Crucially, and shrewdly, his managers had signed a one-year pay-and-play contract that meant Jaguar legally had to provide him with a drive only for the 2001 season. Two weeks after the announcement, the Ford Motor Company put Bobby Rahal in charge of the team and then in February Niki Lauda was appointed head of a newly-created umbrella organisation called the Premier Performance Division. Within days of his appointment, Jaguar had snatched Pedro de la Rosa to be its test driver in 2001 and to race in 2002. As Eddie Irvine had a year to run on his contract, Burti went to Melbourne knowing that he would be out of work at the end of the year – even if he did well. Even worse, despite Jaguar's public pronouncements of support, he knew he could be out much sooner, although Jaguar is not a company or a team to break contracts. If it signed to provide Burti with a car, it would.

"It was supposed to be a normal year for me," says Burti. "I was a rookie driver in a car which was OK, but not great. And then one week before the first race I found out that Pedro had been signed for 2002. It really surprised me because I thought they would look at my performance before deciding if I would stay or not."

For most of the winter tests Burti struggled to match the pace of Irvine. But he claims the story is not as simple as that. "Michelin did not have enough development tyres to give to all the drivers so I was always running on the hard compounds," he says. "The only test when I got good tyres was at Valencia, the very last test before Melbourne, and during the five days I was quicker than Eddie on four of them. To find out a week later that I did not have a job for 2002 was tough. If I was struggling all the time and they had hired someone to replace me then I would have said 'OK, I did not do a good enough job – I am not good enough to be here'. But I took the only chance I had to prove myself and I thought I was doing OK. I felt they should have waited a bit longer. It is not easy to race when that happens to you."

Burti admits that the news was a big shock. "To be honest I was very confused," he says. "In Australia and Malaysia I lost my confidence totally. I did not know if the team was happy with what I was doing. They seemed quite happy but I never understood what was happening and that became very difficult. Then after Malaysia I decided to stop thinking about the future and just concentrate on doing my job. In Brazil I had quite a good run. I was unlucky because they had a new development engine which had about 20 extra horsepower but unfortunately there was only one of them and that went to Eddie. I qualified only a 10th behind him with less power so I was quite happy with my performance. It was the same at Imola. After that I had enough confidence to say to myself, 'if they are not happy with me, maybe I am not happy with them'. So

after the race in Brazil I spoke to Pedro Diniz of Prost. We talked about next year and he said that they were interested. Then suddenly the conversation became about this year."

Burti is managed by Rick Gorne, former commercial director of British American Racing, now head of Reynard and a driver manager. Gorne spoke to Prost – the two being old acquaintances – and it rapidly emerged that Prost wanted to replace Gaston Mazzacane, who was clearly out of his depth. A deal was done very quickly, with Burti leaving Jaguar for Prost and de la Rosa taking over his drive.

Burti says it was his choice to leave Jaguar. Others say it was a deal engineered by Bobby Rahal to both honour Burti's contract and get him out of the car and de la Rosa in. What is not in doubt is that some Jaguar dollars were transferred into Prost's coffers, making Burti's version of the story unlikely to be the whole truth and nothing but the truth. Whatever the scenario, as Burti says: "It was the best choice for me."

The difference between Jaguar Racing and Prost was a big one – even if the world championship points at the time did not reflect it. "Jaguar is a big team with lots of people and a big budget," says Burti. "It is the Ford Motor Company factory team. Prost is just a racing team. It is a lot smaller and there is a lot less money. But I was surprised to see how much motivation there is at Prost to do well." Burti did himself no end of favours on his debut and immediately out-qualified number one driver Jean Alesi. It was a clear signal for Alesi to pull his socks up and Burti spurred him to some fine performances. Since his arrival there is no doubt that Prost has improved. The now retired Alesi is famously quick as a racer but he has never been known for his skills as a development driver. Mazzacane had no experience to develop the car and so Burti was the first driver to make much of an impact on the car itself.

"I would like to think that I have helped," he says modestly. "Jean knows what he is doing. A driver who has driven 201 races is important for the team – even if he is not technical. And I am not saying Jean is not technically-minded. It is good for me because if I do well against a driver like Jean it is very good for my career. For my image. Everyone knows that Jean is a very good driver who is driving on the limit all the time, getting the most out of any kind of car, with any kind of set-up and in any conditions. He is pretty good at that! And to keep up with him is not an easy job. To show I can do as well and sometimes even better brings a lot of respect, which to be honest was something I needed after Jaguar."

Burti admits he has learned important lessons from Alesi. "He is pushing all the time," he explains. "When people say Jean is not motivated it is bullshit – he is flat out all the time. He has taught me that you always have to give 100 per cent – you have to keep pushing for more. Even at Monaco, when the track had no grip at all, Jean was the first guy out there and he was on it!"

By coincidence, Alesi was the first Formula One driver Burti ever saw race. "He was the first guy to go out and I was so excited I almost cried," he recalls. "There was the noise of the Ferrari V12 and Alesi at the wheel and now here I am with him. It is quite special to remember that day and also to remember that you can achieve so much in such a short time."

Burti is not a man who is overawed by famous names. It is not because of arrogance or ignorance – it is an element of his character. As he says: "I am a very simple person. I like to see people in a simple way. It never had a huge impact on me to be talk-

ing to or working with famous people. Guys who are very successful like Jackie Stewart and Alain Prost are not untouchable. I don't see them like that. I respect them but they are just people."

From an unimpressive performance with Jaguar, Burti shone at Prost. He out-qualified Jean Alesi a few times but did not improve his reputation for denting cars. He admits that it 'feels pretty good' to have come from Brazil to Formula One in such a short space of time, but adds: "Of course as a racing driver it is not enough. I want to do more than that. Then again, if I stop and think that a few years back I was in Brazil studying and not even thinking about Formula One, I am happy with what I have achieved. Now I want to be a success. I am starting out and I think I have been doing enough to show that I deserve to be in F1. Now I must make the next step to become a better driver in a better team and then start to think about winning races. It is not an easy thing."

Many doubt that a drive will materialise for 2002. But it won't be for any lack of trying on Burti's part. If it doesn't, then he will be highly sought after as a test driver. That is for sure.

89

# Go forward, go fast

**Enrique Bernoldi has had a rough ride in his rookie season in Formula One. But he has impressed against his Arrows team-mate Jos Verstappen and proved himself every bit as fast. Much to Verstappen's chagrin, he has outqualified his team-mate more often than not.**

**21st**

David Coulthard had grumbled in Monte Carlo: "A few years ago, in similar circumstances, I would have pushed him so far in the harbour he might not have come back."

The Monaco Grand Prix brought Enrique Bernoldi to the attention of the racing world. Rarely is a McLaren Mercedes held up behind an Arrows for 35 laps. Opinion was firmly divided on the episode, between those who would have been glad if Coulthard had put Bernoldi in the harbour, and those who saw the Brazilian as the architect of a flawless drive at the most unforgiving of circuits. McLaren Mercedes top brass Ron Dennis and Norbert Haug reportedly threatened to ruin Bernoldi's career, and the insults grew sillier until Coulthard began to question the Arrows driver's fashion sense. Bernoldi emerged as the more dignified party and won himself a few fans along the way.

Then in Italy, Bernoldi sat at the head of a long trail of cars for lap after lap. Olivier Panis in the superior BAR Honda could not pass him, even though Monza, unlike Monte Carlo, is a circuit suited to faster cars.

Bernoldi remains defiant about Monte Carlo. "I was not blocking," he said. "I was in a racing situation, and I was just concentrating on my own speed. My own speed was much slower than David's but Monaco is a difficult circuit on which to overtake. I was not there to be on television. I was there to race and do my job."

Like many of the Brazilian stars of his generation, Bernoldi was inspired to race by Nelson Piquet and Ayrton Senna. He had a successful record in karting, beating off rivals such as Helio Castro-Neves and Tony Kanaan, before moving to Europe where he became European Formula Renault champion first time out in 1996. The next step was British Formula Three. He signed with the respected Promatecme team, but a pre-season road accident in which he was a passenger left him out of sorts, and when he began to find his form his team-mate Nicolas Minassian had become championship favourite. Even so, a dominating win at the international invitation at Spa meant the team was keen to keep him on for the 1998 season.

That year would be remembered for Brazilian domination of the series. Between them Bernoldi, Luciano Burti and Mario Haberfeld

took all but two of the wins. Bernoldi dominated early on and took six wins, but an erratic Renault engine handed the title to Haberfeld.

It had been an eventful season for Bernoldi. At Brands Hatch in April he had been involved in a fight with Burti: his compatriot was fined £500 and had his licence endorsed as a result. What had driven Burti to punch Bernoldi? He thought he had been deliberately blocked in practice.

In 1999 Bernoldi progressed to Formula 3000 with the Red Bull Junior Team. In two years with the outfit he came close but never won a race. He was labelled fast but accident-prone. It was widely believed that he would make the transition to Sauber for 2001, as he had tested for them through his Red Bull connections, but it then dropped the bombshell that inexperienced Kimi Räikkönen was to drive for the team. Bernoldi was furious.

He soon discovered that sponsorship could get him a long way. With the prospect of luring Red Bull as a sponsor, Tom Walkinshaw's Arrows team itself dumped Pedro de la Rosa and leapt to sign the Brazilian. "I do feel bad for Pedro," Bernoldi admitted later. "It's not a very nice thing for him and it's a shame, but I guess that's the way it is. Formula One is a strange sport."

His season got off to a rocky start. His reputation as a crasher seemed well founded when he completed just five laps of the first two races, spinning off on both occasions. However, he persevered and since then has spun out of a race on only one occasion, in Hungary – a reasonable record for a rookie. His real achievement has been to outqualify Jos Verstappen more often than not. Rattled, the Dutchman retorted: "I think he is a talented driver in qualifying but he is not so strong in the race and I think he's struggling. He behaves confidently, but I think he is under pressure. I don't get on with him very well. We talk to each other very little and I must say, he is the worst team-mate I have had in Formula One."

The jury is still out on Bernoldi's efforts. Out of favour at Arrows and with a steady style rather than the spectacular stuff of Verstappen, he would probably benefit enormously from a second year in Formula One. The problem is, he doesn't look likely to get it.

# Bye bye Tarso

For a driver who has never scored a point and whose highest qualifying position has been 14th, it is rather strange that Tarso Marques keeps being asked back to the party. Until the Belgian Grand Prix, that is, when his gravy train finally hit the buffers. And for a man without a drive, he is astonishingly confident about his future.

Tarso Anibal Sant'Anna Marques debuted in Formula One when he was barely 20 years old. And from that time on, when he was shoehorned into the Minardi team for 1996 Brazilian and Argentinian Grand Prix races, he has known what it is to be in and out of Formula One like no other driver. He was first parachuted in to replace Giancarlo Fisichella after the Italian had signed for Minardi but couldn't provide the necessary cash to buy him a race seat for every Grand Prix. Brazilian Marques, backed by a wealthy family and local sponsors, could.

Team boss Giancarlo Minardi knew having a native in the car during the South American races would attract sponsors. But Marques's performance did nothing to help persuade them to stay around, and Fisichella was reinstated for the European Grand Prix.

In 1997 Minardi called on Marques again, to replace Jarno Trulli who had been called to Prost to replace the out-of-action Olivier Panis after his crash in Canada. Marques completed the remaining 10 races, finishing only four.

Marques believes 1997 could have been a turning-point in his career, had Minardi released him from their contract. "I had an offer from a better team – one that is doing well now – and we almost had a contract, but Minardi wouldn't let me go," he says.

Harsh reality hit again in 1998 when Minardi, always desperate for money, pushed Marques aside in favour of Esteban Tuero and Shinji Nakano and the sponsorship that accompanied them. "Not only had I lost the deal with another team, I had lost my Formula One drive altogether," rues Marques. After test-driving for Arrows Marques searched for a drive in the American CART series, and says he had lined up a deal when he got a call from Paul Stoddart who invited him to drive for European Minardi in 2001. "I changed my plans completely so I could drive in Formula One again," Marques says. He even bought a house in Faenza, Italy, where the team is based.

Marques thought Minardi was in a better position financially, with more equipment of a better standard and more testing to improve performance. But he soon realised it was the same old cash-starved team. "I knew it would be a hard season, but not as hard as it turned out to be. Minardi doesn't have enough good equipment for the car and doesn't have a hope of getting close to the performance levels of other teams." Minardi's lack of money meant Marques never received a salary for driving, relying on his wealthy Brazilian family for an income.

People in Formula One dispute Paul Stoddart's logic of his number one driver paying his way and his obviously less talented number two getting a free ride. The Brazilian didn't bring any sponsorship with him. It was 20-year-old rookie Spaniard, Fernando Alonso, whose career is masterminded by Flavio Briatore, who paid some of the bills.

Their on-track fortunes, too, were in stark contrast. As Alonso impressed with his speed in 2001, Marques started and finished races from the last row of the grid, and only twice in 14 races did he escape the last slot. At Silverstone, Melbourne and Spa, he didn't even make the 107 per cent mark. Luckily, the stewards allowed him to race in Australia and Belgium. "It was so frustrating," he admits. "I really wanted to come back to Formula One, but not to be in last place and never finish races."

Marques's dissatisfaction with Minardi finally came to a head after the European Grand Prix: 22nd on the grid, he promptly retired on lap seven with electrical problems. "It was ridiculous, it was the limit. It was then that Paul and I discussed my future with the team."

Keen to quash rumours of being fired because he didn't fulfil a performance clause in his contract (he asserts there was no performance clause), Marques says he approached Stoddart about quitting. "I was the one unhappy with the situation," he stresses. "Paul wanted to keep me, and he apologised for not providing competitive equipment, but he knew the car was getting worse and I wasn't even racing. He asked me to stay on until the end of the season, but there was no point. We came to an agreement that if the team could find someone to drive who had more money, I would be happy to leave. And I am happy to leave. I was not happy finishing last all the time." That someone is Alex Yoong.

But Marques is an eternal optimist and is confident he can get a race drive in Formula One next year. If he manages it, his ambition for the season is simple: "I don't want to be in last place anymore."

The reality, however, is more of the same if he ever gets himself on the entry lists again.

22nd

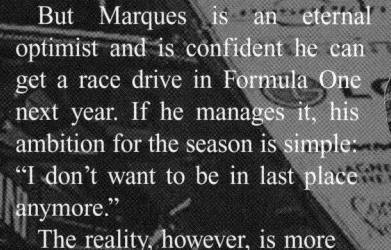

# Star in waiting

**Fernando Alonso has caught many people's eyes in 2001. When he qualified an inferior car 17th on the grid at Indianapolis, his talent was confirmed. But what will happen in 2002 is anyone's guess. He is a star in Spain and his country has great hopes.**

Few people expected that Fernando Alonso would qualify for the 2001 Australian Grand Prix, the first race of his Formula One career. Minardi had done minimal testing before the season began and one of the two cars wasn't even finished until the team arrived in Melbourne. At 19 years and seven months, Alonso was the third-youngest driver in the history of the sport, and he had only 26 car races under his belt, just three more than Kimi Räikkönen. When he qualified his car 19th on the grid, not just within the 107 per cent time but off the back row, and then steered his car home to a 12th place classification, people began to take notice.

After Australia, the young Spaniard did big things in qualifying for his team. Frequently qualifying as high as 18th — an achievement he likened to 'getting pole' for the minnow Minardi — at the US Grand Prix he went one better and made it 17th on the grid, ahead of Jacques Villeneuve's BAR Honda and within touching distance of the Jaguar of his compatriot Pedro de la Rosa. His races were more difficult: he finished only half of them, hampered mainly by mechanical failures, and suffered a car not up to challenging the rest of the field.

Alonso's name has been linked with almost half the grid over the silly season for 2002. Sauber, Jordan, Arrows, Renault and Minardi have all reportedly been battling to obtain his services at some stage. He was taken under the wing of veteran driver manager, Flavio Briatore as early as November 2000, buying out the five-year contract Alonso had signed with Minardi when he began testing for them earlier that year.

However, teams are cautious about taking on the Spaniard long-term. The only real yardstick to measure a driver against is the performance of his team-mate. Neither Tarso Marques nor Alex Yoong is a force to be reckoned with in international motor racing, so Alonso's ability remains an unknown quantity. He has proved much faster than his team-mates, certainly, but Marques and Yoong are unproven and until he drives against a fast team-mate the jury will still be out.

Life at the back of the grid is far from easy. Alonso has faced the same problem experienced by the majority of new Formula One drivers. When he arrived in the series, for the first time in his career he was not challenging for victories or podiums. He admitted at the beginning of the season that he knew what he was letting himself in for. He revealed: "I know it will be very difficult to achieve anything notable next season. I hope people will have patience with me because I will be starting from the back of the grid." Not everybody did. Ralf Schumacher was particularly disparaging about the hyped youngster. He complained: "I wouldn't even recognise him because I

haven't really seen him yet and I haven't really watched what he is doing. I saw he was always quicker than Tarso Marques but then, not to be unfair to Tarso, you wouldn't consider him as one of the best options to learn from or to be looked at."

Alonso picked up the racing bug at the tender age of three, when his father built him a kart. He was only seven years of age when he began karting in his local championship but he won all eight races that year. Over the two years that followed, Fernando was virtually unbeatable in his regional kart events, and he moved on to the national Cadet division in 1991, to finish runner-up.

In 1993, aged 12, he was ready for a crack at the Spanish national kart championship in the Junior division, which he duly won. He then repeated that success both in 1994 and in 1995, when he was disappointed to finish only third in the world championship. In 1996, however, having clinched his fourth consecutive national title, he put that right by becoming the junior world champion.

Two highly successful seasons followed in the Formula A class, yielding yet another national title, the Italian title, and the runner-up placing in the European championship in 1998. Graduating to cars he decided to skip Formula Three, instead choosing the Open Telefónica championship based in Spain.

Even stepping straight to this level of competition, Alonso was immediately the class of the field. During this debut season, he drove nine pole positions and eight fastest laps, winning six races – and romping to the championship.

It was Alonso's ticket to Formula 3000. The first half of the season was disastrous but the second half of the season was very different and he won the last race of the season. It was enough to secure a role with Minardi, as a test driver. 2001 saw him graduate to a race drive.

At barely 19, Alonso has the opportunity for a long career and could easily spend his next 19 years racing at the very pinnacle of the sport. That is his opportunity.

# Down and out in Formula One

**Gaston Mazzacane had four races to prove himself in 2001 and didn't make it. Before he was sacked to make way for Luciano Burti, he caused plenty of strife within the Prost team. His Formula One career was always destined to be brief. He simply didn't have what it takes to compete with the 22 best drivers in the world.**

When Gaston Mazzacane was sacked from Prost Acer following the San Marino Grand Prix, no one was surprised to see him go. In just over a year of Formula One he had established himself as one of the great also-rans of recent times. Without the steadiness of a Pedro Diniz that can sometimes lead to points, or the flamboyance of a Tora Takagi, he was for most of his short career unnoticed in the races he contested, clocking at his best an eighth place finish at the 2000 European Grand Prix. He gave his all, but he was never in the same league as most of the rest of the grid.

The Argentine driver had been a surprise addition to the Formula One grid when he signed for Minardi at the beginning of 2000. New sponsor Telefónica had wanted a South American driver in the car and Mazzacane was the unlikely choice. His progress up the lower echelons of motorsport had hardly set the world alight.

After leaving the obscure Italian Formula 2000 series in 1994 he had won just one race in any category, the Magny-Cours round of the 1999 Sports Racing World Cup championship in which he shared his GLV Brums Ferrari with another perpetual backmarker, Giovanni Lavaggi. In the intervening years he had tried his hand with an assortment of single-seater teams to no avail. Italian Formula Three was uninspiring. In over three seasons of International Formula 3000 he scraped just two points and could not blame the situation entirely on his teams: Auto Sport Racing, Astromega and GP Racing -- his some-time team-mates Tom Kristensen and the late Gonzalo Rodriguez performed admirably in the same equipment.

All the same, he began to test for Minardi in 1999 and made the race team the following year. To give him his due, he did not perform as badly as expected. He qualified for each of his 21 Grands Prix, albeit never higher than 19th, and usually did not crash the car. More often than not he was the last of the finishers, but he did finish. He even became a cult figure on some internet sites, due to his persistence and his awkward grasp of the English language.

Mazzacane's big moment came at the 2000 US Grand Prix.

The aerodynamics of the tidy Gustav Brunner-designed Minardis worked well on the fast straights and banked curves of Indianapolis. The track started wet, but within a few laps it had dried and the cars began to pit for dry tyres. As the order was shuffled, Mazzacane ended up in fourth place, just ahead of the McLaren Mercedes of Mika Häkkinen. Still wearing wet tyres, Mazzacane kept the Finn behind him for five laps. The battle spoils then became third when Pedro Diniz stopped for new tyres. Häkkinen only made it past when the Argentine himself pitted on lap 14. The Minardi team was delighted.

Mazzacane was proud of his moment in the limelight. He said: "At that moment I was defending my position. He could have passed me if he was really that fast, but that just wasn't the case. He was slightly faster than me at the first split, but I was quicker in the second and third sectors and he couldn't even slipstream me despite his engine having more power. So I said to myself, you might be world champion, but you can stay behind me!"

At the end of 2000 it looked like it might all be over for Mazzacane in Formula One, but he found his way into the Prost team for much the same reason he had found his way to Minardi. Prost's main sponsor, PSN, wanted a South American or Spanish-speaking driver and Mazzacane was available. The team played up his chances but no one was optimistic about his hopes, and almost immediately he was signed the rumours began that he would be replaced before the season was out. The team refused to confirm that his contract had a performance clause.

When Prost's Spanish test-driver Pedro de la Rosa was snatched away to Jaguar before the start of the season, it looked as if Mazzacane might have gained a reprieve, for a short while at least. Soon, however, Prost had done a deal with Jaguar and got Luciano Burti, another South American, in return. After just four races, Mazzacane was out.

Despite mid-season rumours that he would be the man to take Tarso Marques's seat at Minardi, Mazzacane's name has not been mentioned in connection with a drive for 2002. With many other well-supported young drivers flooding the market, he has had his glory days.

24th

# Check out the new Czech

**A big fuss has been made of Tomas Enge, the new Czech driver competing in Formula One for Prost. Enge has a big sponsorship deal with the eastern European bottling interests of Coca-Cola. But will it be enough to take him to the top? The experts say no, he simply isn't talented enough. But he has confounded the experts before.**

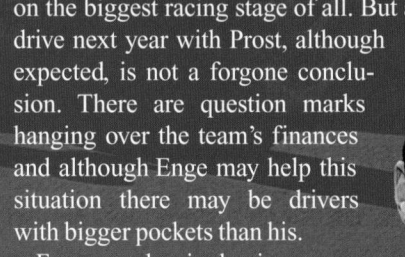

**25th**

At the Italian Grand Prix in Monza on 16th September 2001, two pieces of history were made. Alex Yoong became the first Malaysian driver to compete in a Grand Prix, and 25-year-old Tomas Enge became the first Czech driver to compete.

But while they have made sporting history, neither driver has set the world of Formula One alight with their performances. And although nothing was expected of Yoong, not so the Czech. But he was almost as unimpressive.

So much more had been expected from the winner of two Formula 3000 races in 2001. Enge benefited from personal sponsorship from Coca-Cola which got him a place with Prost when Luciano Burti's accident sidelined him for the last three races. But his Formula One debut lacked lustre, and he qualified and raced at the back of the field.

Tomas Enge comes from a touring car racing family. His father, Bretislav Enge, was a successful driver in Czechoslovakia 15 years ago, with backing from Skoda. He then ventured into the European arena, landing drives with BMW, Jaguar and Mercedes before his career petered out in hill climbs.

Tomas Enge never saw his father race and initially wasn't interested in cars. But in 1991, aged 14, following the fall of the Berlin Wall and liberalisation of eastern Europe, he went karting for a year and his world changed. "I was quick but I was really crazy. I either won or I crashed. It was everything or nothing," he recalls. After that he raced in Ford Fiestas, until the end of 1994 when he decided to try a single-seater. "I was able to go to Germany. It was much easier to do things after the revolution. I could not have done it before because I could not get out of the Czech Republic without leaving for ever," he says.

His luck took a positive turn when Czech entrepreneur Antonin Charouz became his manager. This got him into the German Formula Ford series in 1995, where Nick Heidfeld was his team-mate. At the end of the year, Enge was third as Heidfeld took the championship, moving on to better things and leaving Enge behind for another year of the same. But in 1996 Enge won the championship and the following year moved up to German Formula Three himself, once again teamed with Heidfeld. "Formula Three cars did not suit my driving style so I was not successful," says Enge. But he was lucky. Halfway through the 1998 season his manager decided to play double or quits and nailed Enge a drive with the Auto Sport Racing Formula 3000 team from Italy. In his first race he finished 15th. In his second race at the Hungaroring he qualified fifth, two weeks later he ran second at Spa for a time, and in his fourth race he took his first points in the season's finale at the Nürburgring.

That winter he was asked to drive for several Formula 3000 teams – including Supernova Racing. He decided in the end (largely down to money) to join forces with a new team being run by Gabriele Rafanelli for 1999. But he had a disappointing start to the season and initially found himself failing to qualify for races. The World Racing Team had sponsorship from Elf, but the team was a shambles and nearly wrecked Enge's career. Enge stuck to the task,

however, and was rewarded with a second place at the French Grand Prix support race. A fortnight after Magny-Cours, against all the odds, Enge got a Formula One test drive, completing 13 laps of Silverstone in a Jordan Mugen-Honda. The following day he did another 38. The test went well and Jordan asked Enge to be its test driver in 2000. In Formula 3000 he moved to the McLaren junior team to hone his race skills. The team had a dreadful year, but on one weekend everything went right and Enge led home his team-mate Tomas Scheckter to score a surprise one-two at Hockenheim.

In 2001, he signed for the Nordic Racing F3000 team run by Derek Mower, bringing the team Coca-Cola sponsorship, courtesy of Charouz. He scored a couple of wins but was outshone by his team-mate, British star Justin Wilson. But destiny beckoned: backed by Coca-Cola's money and Charouz's ambition, he rushed in to fill Luciano Burti's vacant seat in Italy for the season's last three races. At Prost, Enge has proved he is not a liability, and the added Coca-Cola support should net him a Formula One drive in 2002. The soft drinks giant is keen to break into Formula One and keen to promote itself in the Czech Republic, where Enge is a star.

Enge has been remarkably lucky to have a man like Charouz providing backing and management skills. He has succeeded where drivers with better CVs have failed, and is now out to prove himself on the biggest racing stage of all. But a drive next year with Prost, although expected, is not a forgone conclusion. There are question marks hanging over the team's finances and although Enge may help this situation there may be drivers with bigger pockets than his.

For now he is hoping the drive is his. So much is depending on it.

# Malaysian man up to speed?

Malaysia has at last found itself a motor racing hero in 25-year-old rookie Alex Yoong. But can the Minardi hotshot prove himself on the big stage? To qualify for a Formula One Grand Prix is a task beyond most but Yoong has proved he can do that. The rest may be more difficult. Luckily for Minardi he comes with a rumoured $20 million of Malaysian lottery money to spend.

At first sight, there were few clues that the fresh-faced man in the European Minardi motorhome was Formula One's newest star. Twenty-five-year-old Alex Yoong had an air of normality about him that is rare in the Formula One circus.

For his debut race Yoong was accompanied by his father Hanifah, sister Philipa and girlfriend Arianna Teoh, who was excitedly snapping Michael Schumacher outside the Ferrari garage.

A few hours later, Yoong lined up on the same grid as Schumacher at Monza; back home, almost the entire nation sat glued to the TV, watching the country's first-ever Formula One driver make his debut.

It didn't matter that Yoong retired after 44 laps, or that he failed to finish again two weeks later in Indianapolis. Make no mistake: not only does Yoong now have god-like status back home, he already looks like a driver with the attitude and ability to cut it in the big league. "It's kinda strange," he says, in his curious Malaysian-American accent. "All my life I have watched F1 on television, and wondered about the glamour, the media, and all the famous people in the paddock. I used to dream about just walking down the paddock one day, taking photos of these people. So I came here at the start of the race weekend, and I even brought my camera in case I got to meet some of these guys. Then I realised everyone was taking photos of me. It's great for me, and it's even better for my mum and dad. They're having a really cool weekend!"

There should be plenty more such weekends for the Yoong family, with Alex's seat at Minardi all but assured for 2002, especially with team principal Paul Stoddart keen to cement sponsorship money from Magnum, the Malaysian lottery. Stoddart was impressed with his young driver's performances, and many in the team were already raving about Yoong's technical knowledge. While some drivers focus on mental and physical preparation, Yoong is if anything a frustrated chief engineer, virtually taking over team briefings but, more importantly, willing to learn every step of the way.

He says one of the hardest challenges for him has not been the power and pace of the cars, but entering a new world where everyone outside Minardi is expecting him to fail. "Being from this part of the world means I have a lot to prove," he says.

Although new to F1, Yoong is no stranger to motor racing. At the age of eight, he started his career with motorcross bikes and turned to four-wheel racing at the age of 15, driving a Proton Saga in a regional championship. That was in 1992. After a successful spell in several variants of the Formula Asia series, in 1996 he decided to make the move to face the real competition in Europe and took part in the British Formula Renault Sport Championship, where he did not cut a dash.

In 1998 he took the step up to British Formula Three, but after a season-and-a-half in the series he had taken just one podium place. Halfway through 1999, after some attempts at Italian Formula 3000, he took the leap into International Formula 3000. He was entered for five races, failed to qualify for the first three, had a

massive crash at Eau Rouge at Spa in the fourth and didn't make it past the first lap in the fifth. He raced to seventh at the Macao F3 Grand Prix at the end of the year, but did not race again until 2001 when he returned to Asia and the Formula Nippon championship: in five rounds, he didn't make the top six. Then came the quantum leap to Formula One after a series of tests for Minardi at Mugello.

"That was quite something. I went out and did 1m34 on my first lap and thought I had done well. Then they told me on the radio that Schumacher does under 1m25 on that circuit. I realised this wasn't going to be easy," he says. Two laps later though, Yoong was clocking under 1m30 in his Minardi – comparatively a huge achievement – and a Minardi contract was soon on the way. The F1 drive was a culmination of Yoong's efforts but also his family's constant backing.

His father had started racing himself in 1978. Later, his wife Joanna joined him in rallying and racing. With their youngest son showing his own racing potential, they invested their life savings to back him – and then tapped their relatives. Yoong says: "They were tough times, but it's helped take the pressure off. I don't get that worried by the media in the paddock, or by all the attention in Malaysia, because there's nothing harder than your family putting their life savings behind you. That's what I call pressure."

Yoong admits he has made few friends among the other drivers. It would be awkward anyway – until recently many were his heroes. But 'cool cucumber' Yoong, as the Malaysian press has dubbed him, isn't here to make friends: "The other drivers pretty much keep to themselves. They haven't really spoken to me. Until I prove I'm worth my seat in Formula One, there's no reason for them to speak to me. If they're still not speaking to me next year, then I guess I have a problem."

He won't.

26th

95

# Team by Team
# REVIEWS

p253

p281

p307

p333

p359

# MAHLE MAKES
# WINNERS

Nowhere else are engines put to a tougher test than in big international races. Engine speeds of up to 18000 rpm and piston head temperatures of more than 300° C call for supreme skill in development and the highest standard of perfection in technology.

MAHLE has been a leading system supplier for decades to the World Champions in Formula 1, to the winners of the 24 Hours of Le Mans, and to the winners of all categories in touring car, sports and racing car events.

And when the favourites set out on the next races, MAHLE pistons and engine components will once again be there on the road to victory.

So that millions of motorists the world over benefit every day from MAHLE top technology proven time and again in motor racing.

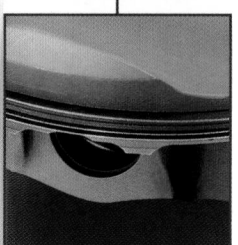

# MAHLE

MAHLE GmbH
Pragstraße 26–46
D-70376 Stuttgart
www.mahle.com

Team Review    Race by Race

# FERRARI

2001

## Contents

| | | | | | | |
|---|---|---|---|---|---|---|
| Team Review | - | The season | p100 | European Grand Prix | - | Nürburgring | p114 |
| Australian Grand Prix | - | Melbourne | p106 | French Grand Prix | - | Magny-Cours | p115 |
| Malaysian Grand Prix | - | Sepang | p107 | British Grand Prix | - | Silverstone | p116 |
| Brazilian Grand Prix | - | Interlagos | p108 | German Grand Prix | - | Hockenheim | p117 |
| San Marino Grand Prix | - | Imola | p109 | Hungarian Grand Prix | - | Hungaroring | p118 |
| Spanish Grand Prix | - | Barcelona | p110 | Belgian Grand Prix | - | Spa-Francorchamps | p119 |
| Austrian Grand Prix | - | A1 Ring | p111 | Italian Grand Prix | - | Monza | p120 |
| Monaco Grand Prix | - | Monte Carlo | p112 | USA Grand Prix | - | Indianapolis | p121 |
| Canadian Grand Prix | - | Montreal | p113 | Japanese Grand Prix | - | Suzuka | p122 |

Michael Schumacher

Jean Todt

Rubens Barrichello

Michael Schumacher

# The world champions

Ferrari had the advantage of finishing off 2000 on top and therefore coming into 2001 in a style it was not accustomed to: on top. It made the most of it. The 2001 car was, as Ferrari car designer Rory Byrne said, "quick out of the box". This had not happened before. And not only was it quick, it was supremely quick. The look of the car differed substantially from that of previous Ferraris, in part due to the modifications required by the new FIA technical regulations to improve safety, but mostly from discoveries in the windtunnel. Gone was the high needle nose; in was a drooping Concorde nose, with the front wing positioned, higher and longer sidepods. It was a balanced, fast car, and it handled well from the beginning. Ferrari clearly had the revised aerodynamics sorted out; the other teams had come up with a less-than-optimal solution, as time would prove.

The new 050 engine, from the technical team led by engine director Paolo Martinelli and his deputy Pino D'Agostino, was also quick out of the box. It was smaller, lighter, with a lower centre of gravity, and deadly reliable. It did not have as many horses as the BMW or arguably the Cosworth, but eclipsed the rest. The special Ferrari qualifying engines were a major contribution to the 11 pole positions achieved by Michael Schumacher in Australia, Malaysia, Brazil, Spain, Austria, Canada, Germany (Nürburgring), Britain, Hungary, USA and Japan.

But most of all, the team had the

benefit of stability. The principal players – Jean Todt, Ross Brawn, Rory Byrne and Michael Schumacher – were all in the process of negotiating longer-term contracts through to the end of the 2004 season. They had already been together for five years, and the extensions would see them through to 10. The rest of the Formula One grid shuddered.

## The Ferrari F2001 car

FERRARI had its windtunnel working 20 hours a day, seven days a week, for a total of 520 hours a month, purely on Formula One work. The 2001 car effectively had 4,000 hours' more windtunnel development than any of its Formula One counterparts. As a result the car was balanced, stable and less pitch sensitive than in the past, and also extremely easy on its tyres, especially the rear set.

The first chassis (206) out of the autoclave in 2001 was only five kilos heavier than its predecessor. This was a surprise, as the new regulations had added a minimum of 15kg, and an achievement, bearing in mind the new safety regulations and reinforcement of the chassis. A lot of teams were 15kg heavier.

Ferrari built a total of nine chassis in 2001: 206, 207, 208, 209, 210, 211, 212, 213 and 214. Rubens Barrichello's favourite was the 206, which he raced in Australia – in fact he would use it at almost every race, and was only torn away from his beloved chassis briefly in Canada, when he raced in chassis 212.

Schumacher raced chassis 208 in Australia and this was rebuilt for the race in Brazil after he shunted it during Friday practice. He also raced chassis number 208 in Imola, then planned to switch to 211 for Barcelona, but a total electronics shutdown during testing at Fiorano prior to race week prompted his switch to chassis 210. He then stuck to chassis number 210 for Austria, Monaco, Canada, the Nürburgring, France, Britain, Hockenheim and Hungary. At Spa, probably one of his best races of the year along with Japan, he switched to chassis 211, which had been his spare car for the previous eight races. At Monza and Indianapolis he had chassis number 213. In Japan a brand new chassis made its appearance: chassis 214, which in spite of the stringent safety ▷

Rubens Barrichello

regulations was five kilos lighter still; the design team had managed to make the sides stiffer and lighter to withstand the side impact safety tests. It also had longer sidepods and a different weight distribution, with the radiators moved forward.

Chassis number 207 was not used for races but was the chassis that underwent the FIA safety tests; these chassis, due to the large loads to which they are subjected, are not, generally speaking, used as race cars.

In Australia, Malaysia and Brazil, the spare car was chassis 209. At Imola it was chassis 210, in Barcelona chassis 208; then came chassis number 211's long run as the spare car. Chassis 213 was the spare car at Spa, before becoming the race car at Monza. At Monza and in the USA the spare car was once again 211, with 213 as the spare car in Japan.

The F2001 was a strong car and in spite of Schumacher's spectacular shunt in Australia, chassis 208 was rebuilt. No chassis was written off, but chassis numbers 210 and once again 208 suffered the big accidents at the hands of Schumacher – at the Monza test before Hockenheim, and at the Mugello test after he had clinched the world championship in Hungary. At Monza the floor broke and Schumacher went off at over 300kph; at Mugello he suffered another high-speed accident when his suspension broke. He was lucky to escape unscathed, especially as test driver Luca Badoer had suffered a suspension failure at the beginning of the season in Barcelona, and appeared at the launch of the new car a week later with his neck in a brace.

The reliability record of the Ferrari was extraordinary and there were few race failures. Schumacher suffered a suspension failure at Imola and a fuel pressure failure at Hockenheim: two non-finishes in 17 races was a phenomenal testament to the Ferrari's reliability –

a change from a few years ago when it was fast and fragile and prone to not finishing.

Barrichello only suffered two car failures: one in Spain when his suspension broke; and one at Indianapolis, when his engine blew just two laps from the end when he relinquished a certain second place, if not a win, although he was classified in 14th place in the latter race. Overall, the reliability score was 90.8 per cent. Of a maximum 2,130 laps, the Ferraris completed 1,933. Only five starts out of 34 resulted in unclassified positions. Over the 17 races, with 1,065 laps available per car, Schumacher covered 1,005, while Barrichello covered 928. That is an incredible figure, showing that Ferrari was the most reliable car out of all the teams, and that reliability counts. It wasn't necessarily the fastest, as BMW Williams and McLaren were both potentially much faster, but they were also unreliable and it's no good having a fast car if it doesn't finish races.

Michael Schumacher scored 11 poles, a season's best for him. He has never been a fast qualifier and much of it was down to the dominance of the car. That said, the car was a better qualifier than race car, as chief engineer Nigel Stepney explained: "The characteristics of this car were that we had to change the balance for the races to keep the tyres working at their best. After five laps we found that if you stayed with the qualifying set-up then you screwed up the race, so you had to compromise a bit on performance to have a more consistent race."

Ferrari had the ideal combination: almost the fastest, and the most reliable. After the first couple of races, the team managed to achieve the same level of downforce as in 2000, which was impressive considering the FIA's objectives and the constraints imposed by the rule changes.

Luca di Montezemolo

Ross Brawn

Rory Byrne

## Technical developments

SHELL developed a special fuel for the Ferrari engine to start the season, and this gave it an early-season edge in economy. Mobil came on strong at the end of the year to negate the advantage and move the process on. Shell fought back. There was, as ever, serious competition between the fuel companies throughout, and it went much further than just putting up cash sponsorship. Ian Gaillard, Shell's fuels expert, was an important figure in the Ferrari set-up with his sophisticated mobile fuel and oil analysis equipment, which gave Ferrari a real edge on reliability.

Ferrari built about 150 engines for testing and racing throughout the year. Starting with about 830bhp at the beginning of the year, against BMW Williams' 850bhp, they were up to 850bhp by season end. All year long, Ferrari tried to figure out where BMW was getting its extra horsepower from, and by Indianapolis it finally believed it had the answer. BMW's clever design had taken the revs

up to 20,000. Ferrari redesigned its inlet designs on the heads, to increase combustion. This has the advantage of producing more power, but the drawback of making the engine potentially more prone to blowing up – the likely cause of Barrichello's engine blow during the US race.

The single biggest technical development resulted from the tyre war between Bridgestone and new guys Michelin, making their return to Formula One. This significantly increased tyre testing. Ferrari reckoned its tyre test activity increased by a quarter in 2001.

Hirohide Hamashima, the head of Bridgestone's development, declared: "We made 120 different specifications in 2001 against four specifications a month in 2000."

As Ferrari had made such a good car, the technical developments throughout the year were microsteps rather than large strides forward. Its cooling system was much more efficient, as demonstrated by the fact the team didn't need the cooling chimneys it had fitted to the car in 2000's two hottest races, in Hungary and Malaysia. ▷

## FERRARI SEASON STATISTICS

### RELIABILITY PERFORMANCE

| Driver | Races | Max laps | Laps completed | Reliability rating |
|---|---|---|---|---|
| Michael Schumacher | 17 | 1,065 | 1,005 | 94.4% |
| Rubens Barrichello | 17 | 1,065 | 928 | 87.1% |
| Constructor | Races | Max laps | Laps completed | Reliability rating |
| Ferrari | 34 | 2,130 | 1,933 | 90.8% |

### CHAMPIONSHIP PERFORMANCE

| Driver | 2001 points | 2000 points | 12 month change |
|---|---|---|---|
| Michael Schumacher | 123 | 108 | +13.9% |
| Rubens Barrichello | 56 | 62 | -9.7% |
| Constructor | 2001 points | 2000 points | 12 month change |
| Ferrari | 179 | 170 | +5.3% |

Rubens Barrichello

### CHASSIS LOG

**F2001-206** Race car for Rubens Barrichello at Melbourne, Sepang, Interlagos (not used for the race after it failed on the installation lap), Imola, Barcelona, A1 Ring, Monte Carlo, the Nürburgring, Magny-Cours, Silverstone, Hockenheim, the Hungaroring, Spa-Francorchamps, Monza, Indianapolis and Suzuka. Spare car at Montreal (used in qualifying by Barrichello).

**F2001-207** Test car only.

**F2001-208** Race car for Michael Schumacher at Melbourne, Sepang (abandoned for the race when Schumacher preferred the spare), Interlagos and Imola. Spare car at Barcelona and the A1 Ring. Spare monocoque at Monte Carlo.

**F2001-209** Spare car at Melbourne, Sepang (raced there by Michael Schumacher) and Interlagos (raced by Barrichello when 206 failed on the installation lap). Spare monocoque at Imola.

**F2001-210** Spare car at Imola. Race car for Schumacher at Barcelona, A1 Ring, Monte Carlo, Montreal, the Nürburgring, Magny-Cours, Silverstone, Hockenheim (not used in the race after hit by Luciano Burti at the first start) and the Hungaroring.

**F2001-211** Race car for Schumacher at Spa-Francorchamps. Spare car at Monte Carlo, Montreal, the Nürburgring, Magny-Cours, Silverstone, Hockenheim (used by Schumacher in the race after the Burti incident), Hungaroring, Monza and Indianapolis. Spare monocoque at Suzuka.

**F2001-212** Race car for Barrichello at Montreal. Spare car at Monte Carlo. Spare monocoque at the Nürburgring, Magny-Cours, Silverstone, Hockenheim, the Hungaroring, Spa-Francorchamps, Monza, Indianapolis and Suzuka.

**F2001-213** Race car for Schumacher at Monza and Indianapolis. Spare car at Spa-Francorchamps and Suzuka.

**F2001-214** Race car for Schumacher at Suzuka.

Rubens Barrichello

In terms of aerodynamic development it had four new wings and 10 different flaps on the wings, to achieve the best downforce with the least drag.

Last but not least was the pseudo traction control system the team was using before conventional traction control was legalised. The team was controlling wheelspin not by wheelspin sensors, which were illegal, but by air pressure measurements in the airbox, which helped gauge the power fed to the rear wheels. It gave a system that required thousands of hours of software programming for each circuit, but had effects similar to those of traction control without actually being traction control.

Ferrari's conventional traction control, introduced in Spain, was very efficient from the start, as was its launch control. The launch control system works in a very specific way. To activate it, the drivers has to push a button on the left hand side of the steering wheel with his right hand; at the same time, he has to have his left hand on the clutch. When he pushes the button and releases the clutch the system will be activated. This was to stop the system being activated accidentally.

## The drivers

IT IS not easy being Michael Schumacher's team-mate, and Rubens Barrichello was no exception to the rule. In 2000 he struggled to fit into the team to the extent that, by the beginning of 2001, he and Schumacher were hardly speaking to each other, especially after Malaysia. They were far from friendly, but amid the frozen smiles the pairing proved to be the most successful.

It led to Jean Todt's decision to extend the Brazilian's contract by a year. When, after the early races, Barrichello finally realised he was not going to beat Schumacher (having previously believed he

could), he settled down and undoubtedly made a valuable contribution to the 2001 championship win.

At the post-race press conference in Malaysia, Barrichello criticised his team-mate for passing him in the deluge of rain, rather than waiting. This annoyed Schumacher, who had a heated discussion with the Brazilian during the press conference, with third-placed David Coulthard briefly halting his interview declaring that he couldn't make himself heard due to the conversation raging beside him.

The next time tensions spilled over into words was after the Austrian race, when Barrichello had almost refused to relinquish his second place to the number one driver, only doing so on the last lap at the last corner. He made his displeasure known. The team was clearly embarrassed at having to explain its actions, and it didn't sit well with many people that the leading team was making the drivers respond to team orders so early in the season.

The season was a complete triumph for Schumacher and on occasion for Barrichello: had his team leader not benefited from such a reliable car, he could have expected to pick up a couple of race wins to add to the one he claimed in 2000. For the first two races Ferrari was unbeatable, even in Malaysia, where it completely messed up the pitstop, bringing both drivers in at the same time. They still came first and second, but this was the moment when the tension between the two drivers really boiled over for the first time. But there is only one Schumacher, and Barrichello accepted this and got on with what he does best – driving. He was rewarded with a one-year extension to his two-year contract and will remain at Ferrari for 2002. Schumacher also signed an extension to his contract from 2002 to 2004, and many people feel he will end his career with the Italian team.

Schumacher outqualified Barrichello 16 times out of 17; the

only time Barrichello outqualified his team-mate was at Monza, when Schumacher was having a mini-crisis due to world events. But this figure is an unfair reflection of the Brazilian's achievements. He finished on the podium 10 times to Schumacher's 14, and he helped Ferrari achieve three one-twos, in Malaysia, Monaco and Hungary.

It became crystal clear during 2001 that the rest of Michael Schumacher's career will be spent at Ferrari. Mercedes has given up hope of signing him. He will almost certainly go on to break another record – that of the longest-serving driver with one team in Formula One.

He gave his all in every race except one: Monza, after the terrorist atrocities in the US on 11th September. At Monza, he was definitely out of sorts and frankly did his reputation with the fans no good at all. As his race engineer said: "Monza was the worst race of the year as Michael's head just wasn't there and we can't evaluate that weekend."

Given that he is the driving force of the team, there was definitely something lacking that weekend, as the world champion drifted around in fourth place, seemingly not really pushing for the podium. It was left to Rubens Barrichello to take on the lead driver's mantle, which he did admirably, finishing second.

Schumacher probably has more to lose than most in a less-than-ordered world, and he was fearful for his family's future. For a short period, his inner calm was destroyed by 11th September.

Schumacher's malaise did not last for long, as Nigel Stepney revealed: "Michael was testing at Fiorano before going to Japan and he was as committed as he had been at the first test. He is very focused and committed and he works carefully through all aspects of the test programme."

## Commercial

FERRARI is generally recognised as having the biggest budget in Formula One, partly because it is the only team that builds its own engine in the same budget. In truth no one really knows, because the car manufacturing and the race department are not separated financially. Ross Brawn admits the budget is big, and that 2001's

Michael Schumacher

was the biggest yet for the team: "Although winning the world championship makes life a lot easier financially, we have worked to a budget more than ever in 2001. We are now making sure that the money is channelled into the right places like research and development and the windtunnel and engine development. It is very easy to waste money."

At the beginning of the 2001 season, *EuroBusiness* magazine estimated Ferrari's overall budget at just over $284 million.

But Ferrari is different because it also attracts the most sponsorship, thanks to the allure of its famous name. Staggeringly it does not have to paint the car to suit. The sponsors fit in with its red. Philip Morris, owner of the Marlboro brand, pays the most of any sponsor in Formula One: around $65 million. Vodafone will bring an estimated $30 million next year as secondary sponsor, and Shell's contribution is believed to be $30 million, with technical support added in. In 2002 Tommy Hilfiger will be replaced by clothing company Fila. Other sponsors are likely to disappear to keep the car clean.

Merchandise sales bring in huge licensing revenues to the company. From an estimated $400 million of retail sales, the income is in excess of $50 million. Ferrari makes a good profit on its Formula One team in the 21st century.

Ferrari motorhome

# The perfect beginning

Ferrari arrived in Australia bent on continuing its dominant late-2000 form. It didn't disappoint. Most of the weekend the red team was a whole half-second ahead of the silver team. Ron Dennis, McLaren's uncompromising team boss, could only sit back and quietly fume.

In the past Ferrari had often arrived on a wing and a prayer that showed in the team's disappointing first few races. Until 2000, Ferrari inevitably came second in the first part of the season, caught up mid-season and lost by a hair's breadth in the final race. Racing manager Nigel Stepney said: "Since winning the championship, there is a new confidence in the senior management and this translates all the way down the team."

FRIDAY PRACTICE Ferrari brought three F2001 cars to Australia – chassis 208 for Michael Schumacher, 206 for Rubens Barrichello and 209 as Schumacher's spare. Barrichello completed 40 laps with 1m 28.965secs. Schumacher did 28 laps for third fastest, but his day was dominated by his dramatic accident. At Turn 6 the car tripped over the step that marked the transition from grass to gravel and went into a double somersault, bodywork flying. Schumacher said calmly afterwards: "That was a new experience. I was sitting waiting for the big bump, but fortunately it never came."

SATURDAY QUALIFYING Barrichello had an engine failure on Saturday morning and, unable to use the spare, had to sit out most of the second practice session. Schumacher pulled off in the first session with a front wheel-bearing problem. However, he still achieved pole with 1m 26.892secs. Barrichello was forced to abort his third run with a gear-selection problem. He was then called to the weigh-in, and so ran out of time. He felt he could have pipped his team-mate and claimed pole, but he had to settle for second on the grid with a 1m 27.263secs.

SUNDAY RACE Schumacher led the race almost from start to finish, relinquishing the lead only during pitstops and recording a new lap record, 1m 28.214secs. He made his one and only pitstop on lap 37.

During the last eight laps, his lead over Coulthard was cut from over eight seconds to 1.7secs, though he insisted the car was fine: "I was just managing the event. It worked out very well. I tried to split the race in rhythm and be fast when I had to but not overdrive the car." The other teams could only marvel.

The Brazilian slipped to fifth at the start. On lap three he charged inside Heinz-Harald Frentzen, and the two cars touched; Barrichello slipped by, but damaged a tyre. "Frentzen never gives up," he complained. "He was forced on the grass, I went inside, but he touched my front left tyre."

When the pace car came out he was third, but inherited second when Häkkinen crashed on lap 26. Then, on lap 34, he lost second spot to Coulthard in traffic. Barrichello said: "Alonso is a new boy and obviously didn't see the blue flag. I had to go on the grass and Coulthard got past me. There was nothing I could do, as I couldn't risk hitting Coulthard and taking us both out of the race."

Barrichello made his only pitstop on lap 39. Oil pressure problems slowed him near the end and he had to settle for third. He could have been second.

Above left: David Coulthard catches Rubens Barrichello during his charge. Above: The second part of Michael Schumacher's roll in practice. Right: The two Ferraris prepare for battle.

Right: Michael Schumacher got a clean start, chased by the McLarens. Below: Ferrari's mechanics went wild when Schumacher took the chequered flag, waved by former world champion Alan Jones.

## MALAYSIAN GRAND PRIX SEPANG
# Easy in the rain

Ferrari arrived in Malaysia with a confidence gained by winning 14 points out of 16. The machine seemed relentless. Shell brought a new oil to Malaysia as an option in the elevated temperatures, but in the event didn't need to use it. Fuel was a potential problem, as the lighter components evaporate in high temperatures, so the fuel analysis equipment was busy all weekend. Ferrari brought 10 units of its 050 engine to Malaysia, three of which were assigned to the Friday practice sessions, three for qualifying and three for the race, with one spare.

**FRIDAY PRACTICE** Michael Schumacher used his repaired chassis from Australia, and the spare chassis 209 was set up for him. He completed 34 laps on Friday and was second with a time of 1m 38.929secs, while Rubens Barrichello did 32 laps and was third with a time of 1m 38.931secs. Barrichello was running with a high downforce set-up and Schumacher with low downforce for more top speed. Schumacher was feeling the heat and admitted to sweating, which he never normally does.

**SATURDAY QUALIFYING** For qualifying, both cars were fitted with brake discs that were 22mm thick instead of the maximum 28mm.

With 37 minutes' qualifying left, Barrichello set the fastest time of 1m 36.365secs – good enough for pole, or so he thought. He was hardly out of his car when his team-mate clocked a 1m 36.282secs. Things looked set to stay that way until Ralf Schumacher blasted both Ferraris away with a 1m 36.036secs. Barrichello then put in a 1m 36.271secs, to put the elder Schumacher third. This did not sit well with him and he promptly set a 1m 35.597secs. A few seconds later, Ralf did a 1m 35.511secs.

This was the ultimate challenge the Ferraris needed and, with just over three minutes'

qualifying time to go, Michael Schumacher reclaimed pole in 1m 35.220secs, demoting Ralf to second – until Barrichello snatched that away with a lap of 1m 35.319secs.

**SUNDAY RACE** Schumacher opted for his spare car when he spotted oil at the back of his race car. After a perfect start to take the lead, Schumacher's race looked to be over almost before it had begun when he went off on oil dropped by Olivier Panis's BAR Honda at Turn 6 on lap three. He was joined by his team-mate: the two cars bounced across the gravel beds in perfectly choreographed unison. Luckily, both were able to rejoin the race. Afterwards, Schumacher was moved to comment: "I thought it was the end of the race. I saw the barrier and thought, here is my partner."

After his first pitstop Michael Schumacher was 11th, but as the pace car came out in the rain and the field bunched up, Schumacher was on the right tyres and cleaning up was easy. In only five laps he scythed his way through from 11th to the lead in a series of astonishing overtaking moves. By lap 25 Schumacher was 40 seconds ahead of Coulthard in second. Schumacher pitted again on lap 30 and retained the lead. It was an extraordinary victory – his sixth consecutive win.

Barrichello was not happy. His lap four stop was botched and the Brazilian made two more pitstops, losing his bargeboards along the way. But he kept on going, to secure second place.

The day ended sourly, though, when Schumacher and Barrichello had an altercation in the press conference about Schumacher's overtaking move. Barrichello thought his team-mate was ungentlemanly to pass him in such bad conditions; Schumacher thought he was racing. The two Ferrari drivers exchanged frank views, as Coulthard tried to continue summarising his race. In the end he gave up, remarking: "I can't continue with the discussion going on next to me."

**Top and above: Situation normal, Schumacher heads Ferrari team-mate Barrichello. Schumacher was untouchable.**

**Left: To the victor, the spoils, but the pantomime pitstop (below) nearly threw everything into jeopardy. Below right: Ross Brawn celebrates with Schumacher.**

## BRAZILIAN GRAND PRIX INTERLAGOS
# A blip in the winning sequence

Ferrari arrived in Brazil looking as if nothing could stop it. The red team looked set once again to blow everyone else away.

The only irritant was the simmering row between Michael Schumacher and Rubens Barrichello about the German's overtaking manoeuvre in the monsoon of Sepang. Publicly they kissed and made up. Schumacher said: "We have three identical cars and it's up to Rubens to beat me fair and square. It's racing. If you race for Ferrari you have a very good car and the opportunity to be in front, so we're all under pressure."

**FRIDAY PRACTICE** Ferrari brought three F2001 cars to Brazil and one extra chassis. Schumacher had 208, Barrichello 206, and 209 was set up for Schumacher as the spare.

Schumacher completed 37 laps with a best of 1m 16.598secs, making him third fastest. Barrichello completed 22 laps with a quickest of 1m 16.994secs for seventh. He was affected by low oil pressure which caused him to spin. Schumacher had a puncture and lost a set of tyres. Tellingly, he said: "Looking at the times it would seem the opposition is closer than in the past two races."

**SATURDAY QUALIFYING** Neither Ferrari shone in unofficial practice. Schumacher languished in fifth place on a 1m 14.652secs and Barrichello in seventh with a 1m 14.895secs. The team played around with a new rear wing which had a biplane configuration with one main profile and one flap. There was also a new Gurney flap on the front wing, smaller front brake ducts and the cars had more efficient radiator exit ducts.

Qualifying went smoothly for the world champion – but horribly wrong for the Brazilian in front of his home crowd. Schumacher earned his seventh consecutive pole

for Ferrari, giving him a total of 35 and Ferrari 140. Barrichello could only manage 1m 14.191secs for sixth in front of his home crowd.

**SUNDAY RACE** Schumacher left the pits at 1.42pm, only three minutes before the pitlane closed, and led easily off the line with Montoya second. When the safety car withdrew Montoya dived up the inside of Schumacher, forced him to one side and took the lead.

After Montoya was shunted out of the race and Coulthard had pitted a first time, Schumacher was ahead for two laps before the Scot overtook for the lead permanently, after Schumacher did a half-spin in the rain. After the race he was subdued: "The car wasn't working quite the way I like it, which is why I had a couple of offs, which isn't normal for me in these conditions."

Barrichello was in trouble before the race even started, coming to a halt with oil pressure problems. He ran back to the pits to get the spare, which the mechanics were frantically trying to change from Schumacher's set-up. This takes 20 minutes, but they only had 15 before the pitlane would close; they would finish the changes on the grid. It didn't matter anyway, as on lap three Barrichello ran into Ralf Schumacher. As he described it: "This was definitely not my lucky day."

Above left: Mechanics struggle to complete the changes on Rubens Barrichello's spare car after he spun on his way to the grid (above) and just made it back (right).

Above: Michael Schumacher felt the pressure and had two spins in the rain. Right: It's unlikely Ross Brawn's dry-race strategy would have produced a win.

## SAN MARINO GRAND PRIX IMOLA
# Outshone by little brother

Ferrari came to Imola with the cries of the tifosi ringing in its ears. The Italian fans expected victory. Jean Todt said: "People have such high expectations. We finish second after six victories in a row and they're disappointed."

Ferrari emerged from the weekend with a few problems to mull over. Michael Schumacher's retirement was an unusual blip, his first for nine races, and the team did not know it would be another seven before he would be put out again. Also, BMW's winning form, spearheaded by the other Schumacher, looked ominous, and McLaren Mercedes was no longer the only threat.

**FRIDAY PRACTICE** Ferrari couldn't complain about Bridgestone, which introduced a softer dry compound and a new, harder wet tyre. Ferrari brought three cars and a spare: 208 for Schumacher, 206 for Rubens, 210 as the T-car and 209 as the spare.

The team tried out a Sauber-like front wing and a revised rear wing. It also had new brake calipers made by Brembo – harder, stiffer and more powerful – with brake discs exclusive to Ferrari, using elliptical cooling holes instead of the usual circular ones. Engine maestro Paolo Martinelli was paying his first visit to a race to watch his new-generation 050 engine perform. It was revving 300rpm higher than the previous year.

Schumacher was fastest in the second practice, clocking up 1m 25.096secs. Barrichello was second with 1m 25.372secs. It looked as if Schumacher was set to take pole position.

**SATURDAY QUALIFYING** Ferrari made a bad decision that would effectively cost it the race. It decided the soft Bridgestones would wear too quickly and opted instead for the harder choice of tyres, thinking it would still be cold and wet on race day. But the Ferrari weather forecasters had got it wrong. Qualifying was frantic and Schumacher was pushed off the front row by the McLarens. He ended up fourth with a 1m 23.593secs. Barrichello qualified sixth on 1m 23.786secs. Jean Todt said ruefully: "It's the first time since last year's Belgian GP there has not been a Ferrari on the front row." Schumacher said: "I'm happier starting on the second row of the grid on the right tyres, than on pole with the wrong ones."

**SUNDAY RACE** Schumacher made a poor start, slipping from fourth to fifth. On lap three Montoya swept past him when he ran wide at the last corner. By lap four he had slipped to eighth. Something was wrong. On lap 23 Schumacher limped back to the pits with a front left puncture. After picking his way round the midfield runners for an exploratory lap, he retired. His only joy was celebrating his brother's maiden win, marking the first time two brothers had won a Grand Prix in 51 years. Ross Brawn said: "Michael had a problem on the left front corner that damaged the wheel, which broke, letting the air out of the tyre. It was not safe to continue so we had to retire him. At the start Michael had a problem with the gearbox and missed a gear."

Barrichello drove a solid race, slipping to eighth before moving into fourth. On lap 32 he made his first pitstop, and rejoined in third. His second stop, on lap 47, kept him in third, where he finished. He said: "Our strategy involved going late for the first stop and we had to gamble because of my grid position. This was one of my best races in terms of being consistent and overtaking." He qualified seventh, he raced well and – following Schumacher's retirement – saved some face for Ferrari.

Above: Rubens Barrichello turned in a strong drive for third. Left: Michael Schumacher's only joy was in seeing his brother Ralf's first win. Below: For a second race running, Ferrari was the only team forced to run the harder compound Bridgestone tyres.

Left: The Ferraris ran in formation until Michael Schumacher retired with a puncture. Below: Barrichello won praise from team boss Jean Todt for his feisty race performance.

# SPANISH GRAND PRIX BARCELONA

# A lucky day

Ferrari came to Barcelona after losing the early-season wind from its sails. David Coulthard was now on equal points at the top of the drivers' table. Engine guru Paolo Martinelli was on hand, as the team countered a perceived Mercedes advantage. The death of Michele Alboreto on the eve of the race also hit the team hard – he had been a Ferrari driver from 1984 to 1988.

Ferrari and the other Bridgestone teams were involved in intensive testing before Barcelona, believing the relaxed electronic-aid regulations would ease stresses on tyres.

**FRIDAY PRACTICE** Schumacher's new chassis, 211, suffered an electronic shutdown during a shakedown at Fiorano so he switched to chassis 210. Barrichello had chassis 206 and the spare was 208; the Brazilian completed 27 laps with a best time of 1m 20.823secs – third fastest. Schumacher did 41 laps with a best of 1m 20.880secs, for fifth. He said: "We are one of the few teams which has worked intensively on traction control and electronic aids, so we are pretty sorted, but I don't believe anyone has the perfect system."

**SATURDAY QUALIFYING** Schumacher dialled in more downforce to snatch his fourth pole position of the season. It was Ferrari's 141st pole, its eighth in Spain, and Schumacher's 36th. The world champion had a couple of runs and completed only eight laps out of an allowable 12 to take pole with a lap of 1m 18.201secs. Barrichello completed 11 laps to record a lap of 1m 18.674secs, but it was only good enough for fourth place. Schumacher said: "I am confident about the new electronics and I see no reason not to use all of it in the race."

Ferrari was using a new Shell fuel said to be giving 10 per cent better economy. The team introduced a new Shell race lubricant, better suited to the new 050 engine.

**SUNDAY RACE** Ferrari was up early, practising pitstops at 7.30am. In the warm-up, Schumacher was beaten to the fastest time by his team-mate. At the off, Schumacher made a superb start and got into the first corner ahead of Häkkinen. By the second lap he had built up a lead of just over a second and by lap 16 was two seconds ahead. On lap 23 he made his first pit-stop, in 8.7secs, rejoining in third place. Häkkinen made his stop on lap 27 and Schumacher was ahead of him when he came out of the pits. By lap 42 it seemed as though the race was in the bag as he was four seconds ahead of Häkkinen. But after his second pitstop, on lap 43 in 9.3secs, his lap times started to wane and Häkkinen was firm leader even after going in for his second stop on lap 50. On the last lap Häkkinen's exploding clutch handed victory to Schumacher.

The German driver was the first to go over and commiserate with the Finn. He said: "Sometimes luck is on your side and sometimes it isn't. I'm sure it will even out over the season."

Barrichello made a poor start but recovered into the first corner, overtaking Trulli and Ralf Schumacher to claim third place. Even after two pitstops, Rubens was still in third. On lap 48, however, he ran wide and went over the gravel trap. He called into the pits at the end of the lap, and when he rejoined the track dropped back to seventh. On the following lap he came into the pits again and retired, crippled by a broken suspension.

Barrichello was not a happy man. Ross Brawn said: "Rubens was unlucky; he had a broken suspension." But Barrichello was heard muttering that "it was more than that".

Above left: Michael Schumacher eyes his 36th pole. Above: Schumacher and Häkkinen scrapped right from the first corner. Right: The world champion worked hard all weekend for victory.

Right: Broken suspension gave Barrichello a rough ride and ended his race early. Below: Michael Schumacher locks a wheel en route to victory. He won despite suspension worries.

F1TVIMAGES

## AUSTRIAN GRAND PRIX A1 RING
# Following team orders

As the Grand Prix circus gathered in Austria, Ferrari test driver Luca Badoer took to the track at Fiorano for a short test of new aerodynamic solutions. He clocked up a total of 20 laps, carefully remaining within the 50km limit outlined in the Sporting Regulations covering testing in the week when a Grand Prix takes place. His best time was 1m 00.846secs. The results were wired to the Austrian paddock as part of Ferrari's meticulous preparation.

Michael Schumacher had experienced problems with his third set of tyres at Barcelona, but Bridgestone announced they were undamaged and correctly balanced on the day before the race, though out of balance at the end of the race. At least there was an explanation of sorts. Everyone was happy.

**FRIDAY PRACTICE** Schumacher went off the track briefly due to a brake problem and did 32 laps with a best of 1m 11.647secs, fifth fastest. He was not happy, saying: "The difficulty at this track is finding a good set-up, which is essential here." Barrichello had a better day, running 44 laps for 1m 11.401secs to claim third.

Jean Todt said: "Our programme for Friday centred on set-up and aerodynamic work, and gaining a clear picture of which tyre we should use."

**SATURDAY QUALIFYING** Schumacher took pole with a time of 1m 09.562secs just over halfway through the session. He would probably have improved on his last quick lap but for a spinning Jos Verstappen, who nearly took him off the circuit. Schumacher said afterwards: "The start will be crucial. With launch

control, the front-runners should get away at the same time and it will be vital to be first in the first corner."

Barrichello ended up fourth on the grid, behind the two BMW Williams, after 11 laps on 1m 09.786secs. Afterwards, he said: "My session was affected by traffic and it was very hard for me to get a clean lap." Ross Brawn said: "Today, the most important factor was to get the best out of the tyres. We went for a mix of old fronts and new rears which gave us the best balance."

**SUNDAY RACE** Schumacher's race car stopped with an electronic failure at the end of the pitlane in warm-up, but he was back in his race car for the start. After the lights went out, Montoya beat him into the first corner, as did his brother, and he found himself third. After the safety car went in he retained the position until lap 10, when his brother retired. He stayed in second until lap 16 when he challenged a struggling Montoya for the lead. The Colombian was having none of it and both drivers slid off the track, Schumacher rejoining in sixth place. This did not put Schumacher in a good mood, especially as his team-mate was leading until David Coulthard stayed out longer before his pitstop and came out ahead of the pack.

Barrichello was instructed to let Schumacher through for second place and six points. At the post-race press conference, an embarrassed Schumacher squirmed in his seat as he came under media fire. Replying to accusations of unsportsmanlike behaviour, he said: "We have to work for the team, not ourselves." He also promised to 'have a few words' with Montoya.

Barrichello was stony-faced and close to tears in the press conference, refusing to elaborate on his feelings. "I am not happy but I don't want to say anything further."

A Ferrari insider, tellingly and strictly confidentially, said: "When we told Rubens to give way to Schumacher he put in his fastest laps of the race. I wish we'd pissed him off on the first corner, he might have put his foot down."

**Top and above: Michael Schumacher celebrates second place, gifted by Rubens Barrichello. Left: Barrichello's hard drive deserved better than a stand-aside order. Below: Schumacher took six points from an eventful race.**

**Right: Juan Pablo Montoya and Michael Schumacher head for the gravel trap.**

## MONACO GRAND PRIX MONTE CARLO

# Almost perfect weekend

Ferrari's weekend was boosted when chairman Luca di Montezemolo announced that Vodafone would sponsor the team for three years for a reputed $125 million. The secondary sponsorship deal shocked the other teams with its scale.

It was also announced that Michael Schumacher and Rubens Barrichello had both re-signed for 2002. They were favourites to dominate Monaco – and they did. The only prize they didn't carry off was pole position.

**THURSDAY PRACTICE** Ferrari brought five chassis to Monaco: 210 as Schumacher's race car and 211 his T-car; 206 as Barrichello's race car and 212 his T-car. Chassis 208 was another spare.

Schumacher did 47 laps in practice and and was second fastest, concentrating on tyres and race set-up. Barrichello clocked 45 laps and the fourth best time. The main goal of the day was to establish the correct tyre choice for later in the weekend.

**SATURDAY QUALIFYING** The Ferraris and the McLarens were swapping pole until the end, and Schumacher was left second after a brush with the barrier at Portier on his last lap, which would have netted him pole. He said: "They must have moved it [the barrier]; I never got a perfect lap. I had to abort my first run as both Arrows weren't using their mirrors. But I am looking forward to the race because I think it will be very open."

Brawn remarked: "Michael had two laps available on his last run, so we used worn tyres on the front as they were more consistent over two laps. We used various combinations of new and used tyres and it was hard to work out which was best." Barrichello took fourth.

**SUNDAY RACE** Michael Schumacher ended up with pole position when Coulthard went to the back of the grid, denying fans a great race.

At the start Schumacher sped away to lead and didn't relinquish the place until he pitted, when Barrichello took over. Schumacher went on to take his fourth victory of the season, his 48th career win and his fifth at Monaco. "It's always special to win at Monaco," he said. 'I had no problem with concentration, but when I asked Ross about other drivers he told me to shut up and concentrate!"

Barrichello slipped one place at the start behind Häkkinen, where he stayed until lap 13 when the Finn started to lose speed before pitting then retiring. Rubens took over second, remaining there until lap 55 when his team-mate pitted; he then led until his stop.

Apart from cramp in his right foot it was an uneventful yet perfect drive to second – which would have been fourth but for the McLarens' problems. He said afterwards: "The team advised me on the radio to move my toes and drink more water. After the pitstop I pushed hard on the heel rest and the situation improved. I have to say that my car was brilliant, I've never had such a good car."

Above and right: Ferrari's dream race at Monaco was only interrupted briefly when Coulthard took pole position. At the moment, Ferrari can do no wrong and has a finely honed edge that virtually guarantees success.

Above and right: Schumacher, Häkkinen and Barrichello lead the field at the Grand Hairpin on the opening lap. Rubens Barrichello played the perfect supporting role, pleasing Jean Todt and Schumacher.

## CANADIAN GRAND PRIX MONTREAL
# Fuel economy poses a problem

The main topic of discussion in the paddock was the size of Ferrari's fuel tank. The consensus opinion was that Mercedes and BMW had overtaken Ferrari in the economy stakes.

Michael Schumacher admitted after the race that the team needed to work on fuel consumption – a clear indication that tank capacity was probably not the problem. Pitstop timing would prove crucial, though having sensed he could not match the BMW, Schumacher drove maturely for second. He knew he could polish off the championship by coming in second or third for the rest of the season.

The other vital ingredient was tyres. Bridgestone had the advantage as Michelin's softs were too soft – and Williams would start on hard compound tyres. Bridgestone's were better tuned, simply from knowledge of Montreal. Hisao Suganuma, technical manager at Bridgestone Motorsport, said: "With such hard braking, performance under braking will be a crucial issue. Wear should be good enough for a one-stop strategy."

Montreal highlighted the different tyre performances needed for qualifying and the race: Bridgestone took pole, but Michelin the victory.

**FRIDAY PRACTICE** Ferrari brought four chassis: 210 for Schumacher, 212 for Barrichello, 211 as the T-car and 206 as the spare tub.

Schumacher did 33 laps; Barrichello 42. Schumacher tinkered with the front suspension, camber and geometry, focusing purely on race set-up. He said: "We got through our programme, and worked a lot on the brakes, which are put under a lot of stress here." He was feeling confident.

**SATURDAY QUALIFYING** Michael took a devastatingly easy pole on Bridgestone's soft rubber. He took just six laps to clock his pole time and sat out the manic last one-and-a-half minutes of qualifying when the session restarted. Jean Todt declared: "Michael had a great session." It was the understatement of Montreal. But Schumacher knew his soft Bridgestones would deteriorate in the race.

Barrichello brought the red flag out when he crashed at the final chicane. He then ran back to the pits where the mechanics worked frantically to prepare the T-car. Then the team miscalculated the re-opening of the pitlane and Barrichello was sitting at the head of the line with his engine off and the tyre warmers on when the pitlane re-opened. He held up everyone else and, although Ferrari insisted it was not deliberate, the FIA fined the team $10,000. No one thought this unfair but all admitted it was probably a genuine mistake.

**SUNDAY RACE** Michael Schumacher made a good start and Ralf also got away well, the two going into the first corner side by side, but the Ferrari man maintained his position.

For 46 laps Michael held his patently faster brother back in second. When he pitted, Ralf reeled off successive record laps to give him four seconds on Michael. Ferrari's uncompetitive fuel economy compared to BMW cost it the race. When Ralf finally made his pitstop on lap 51 he emerged in the lead and stayed there, forcing Michael to settle for second.

It was the first time in the history of Formula One that brothers have finished one-two. For once Michael seemed almost pleased to be second: "If I had to be beaten by someone, my brother is the best person. I am sure our parents will be very proud."

Barrichello had a good first few laps, moving up to third by lap three, but on lap six he spun at the hairpin exit and dropped to 14th. On lap 12 he overtook Pedro de la Rosa for 11th. But by lap 20 it was curtains for the Brazilian when he went off into the barriers, avoiding Montoya's accident exiting the fast Esses at Turns 3 and 4.

Barrichello blamed his spin on the lack of traction control: "Right from the start, I had problems with the traction control. On lap three I had to switch it off as it was causing a misfire. I was very close to Ralf at the exit to the hairpin so I tried to push, but the car just went round. I tried to avoid him [Montoya] but there was no room to get by and I ended up in the wall."

Michael Schumacher's Montreal weekend started perfectly with a superb pole, but he was forced to cede to brother Ralf (below) in the race. He was still able to finish an easy second, well clear of third-placed Häkkinen.

Left and below: Rubens Barrichello's weekend produced various contacts with the scenery, including a major one in qualifying. He retired from the race after another crash.

113

## EUROPEAN GRAND PRIX NÜRBURGRING
# Unchallenged supremacy

Ferrari came to the Nürburgring with something to prove having been beaten fair and square in Canada by BMW Williams. Michael Schumacher had given way to little brother Ralf, so it was vital for Ferrari to recapture its winning ways. But it was destined to be Michael's weekend.

**FRIDAY PRACTICE** Ferrari brought three cars and a spare chassis: 210 for Schumacher, 206 for Rubens Barrichello and 211 as the spare. The extra chassis was 212.

Schumacher completed 49 laps in a best of 1m 17.507secs for fourth, while Barrichello did 41 laps and a 1m 17.665secs for fifth. It did not dent Ferrari's enthusiasm, as team principal Jean Todt said: "This was a classic Friday in which we worked mainly on race set-up. I think we can improve our performance at various points. The qualifying battle will be between three teams." He was right.

Schumacher was equally sanguine: "Everything went according to our plan and tomorrow I expect to be challenging for pole position. I'm not concerned that there are cars faster than us, as we had a similar situation in Canada."

**SATURDAY QUALIFYING** Schumacher pulled out all the stops to do a sensational lap and claim pole. He was the only driver to go below 1m 15secs with a fastest lap of 1m 14.960secs and in only eight laps. Teammate Barrichello completed 11 laps with a best of 1m 15.622secs for fourth.

Schumacher said: "After losing half the morning with a hydraulic problem we were not sure what to expect, as I did not have time to run new tyres this morning. Our tyres are very consistent here so I do not expect to see a repeat of Canada tomorrow." Barrichello was clearly disappointed to continue to be the only driver who has been out-qualified by his team-mate 9-0 in 2001. He said: "Things did not go smoothly." That was the long explanation. The short one is that he was not as quick as his team-mate for the ninth consecutive time in 2001. No disgrace when your team-mate is Michael Schumacher.

**SUNDAY RACE** When the pitlane opened, Schumacher first took out the spare car, which stopped with a fuel pump problem. His problem was getting back to the pits in time to pick up the race car. He said later: "The car stopped far away from the pits. I found a scooter but it didn't have a key in it. Luckily, someone came along with the key." Schumacher got back to the pits in time and picked up his race car.

Neither Ferrari's launch control worked as planned and Schumacher protected his first place by swerving across his brother's faster start. He built up a 2.4-second gap before Ralf fought back and whittled it down to 0.4 seconds. The race looked set to be decided on pitstops. This view was confirmed when both Michael and Ralf came in on lap 28. Michael's crew executed a perfect stop in 8.4secs, while Ralf pulled up 50cm over the line, causing a delay in refuelling and resulting in a 9.7secs stop. Michael's victory was assured by Ralf's 10-second stop-go penalty.

On lap 50 Schumacher made his second pitstop in 7.7secs, then sped to victory. He said later: "Ralf managed to push me hard in the early part of the race as my first set of tyres was slower. The second set was much faster. It now looks like BMW Williams is our main rival."

Due to his problems with launch control, Barrichello dropped three places at the start. He was on a one-stop strategy and stopped on lap 44 for 10.3secs. After a heart-stopping spin on lap 60 he finished fifth. Later he said: "I made a bad start and the launch control didn't help. I had a lot of fuel on board and am not sure this was the ideal choice, although starting with used front tyres was the right decision."

Jean Todt summed up the weekend: "We must continue to concentrate and keep our feet on the ground."

# The 50th win for the team leader

**Left and below:
Ferrari and Michael
Schumacher turned
in a great team
performance. It
needed all their
strategic brilliance
and a classic drive by
Michael Schumacher
to defeat the BMW
Williams challenge.
It was a thoroughly
deserved victory
and another step
towards the title.**

Michael Schumacher was still under the weather after encountering a bout of flu the previous weekend. His rivals despaired: even with that handicap he could still dominate the race effortlessly.

Schumacher came to Magny-Cours with the possibility of notching up his 50th victory, edging closer to Alain Prost's record of 51 wins. He said: "When I was young I didn't know Alain was driving races. I just drove go-karts and that was my world."

It was also Jean Todt's eighth anniversary as Ferrari team principal. He was already looking to the future: "It is decided in my head that somebody will take over my position after 2004. That is one reason we are so strong, as we are not worried about somebody taking over our positions."

On the Thursday before the race, Luca Badoer covered 45km testing at Fiorano, mainly doing practice starts, so a modified launch control system was in place for the race.

**FRIDAY PRACTICE** Ferrari brought three chassis to the race and a spare tub: 210 for Schumacher, 206 for Rubens Barrichello, 211 as the spare and 212 as the spare chassis. Both drivers suffered minor problems with gearbox electronics but they successfully concentrated on assessing the latest Bridgestones.

Schumacher said: "The circuit conditions are pretty much the same as they were for the test before Canada. Then the temperature was around 30°C, with a very high track temperature, and that's pretty much what we have had today. We are pretty confident."

**SATURDAY QUALIFYING** Schumacher was quickest in the morning, with his brother right behind him. In qualifying the situation was reversed, birthday boy Ralf snatching pole from his brother by a mere 100th of a second, with Michael clocking a 1m 12.999secs. This time after qualifying there was nothing but joviality from the brothers. Michael said: "My present to Ralf? His pole position!"

Ferrari technical director Ross Brawn said: "We were disappointed at the end because pole was within our grasp. We could not get the car handling well through every section of a lap. If you put the section times together Michael was a lot quicker, but of course that doesn't count. The tyres seem consistent and it looks set to be an interesting race."

**SUNDAY RACE** Schumacher got away adequately and maintained his second position behind his brother Ralf. He said later he had a clutch problem so was fortunate to maintain second.

By lap six Ralf's lead had grown to one second and it was still growing. Then Ralf made his pitstop and a problem changing his right rear wheel cost him time. Michael retook the lead and remained there. His only challenger was David Coulthard, and that ended when he got a penalty for speeding in the pitlane.

After winning his 50th Grand Prix, Schumacher said: "I had a problem with the clutch at the start and nearly lost position to David. I had the inside line and he was on the outside but it was still close up to Turn 3. I knew I had to be ahead of him or it would compromise our strategy. My second set of tyres was very good and I was flying, but I had some problems with the third ones. There are seven races to go and 70 points available, so we will fight until it is mathematically impossible for me to lose."

Barrichello made a good start, moving from eighth to fifth. He was the first front-runner to pit and Ross Brawn asked if he would like to change to a three-stop race. He did so, and finished third. Barrichello said: "I must admit I am surprised to be on the podium. I was going very well and saving fuel. Then the team suggested I switch to a three-stop strategy. I agreed to try. I must thank the team very much because it was a hell of a race. My only problem came on my last set of tyres, which blistered very early."

**Left and right: Rubens
Barrichello could not
match his team-
mate's pace over
the Magny-Cours
weekend, but drove
determinedly to fend
off David Coulthard
and take the final
podium position
and four valuable
points towards the
constructors' title.**

# Only second best

It was a real measure of Ferrari's superiority that it completely messed up its race strategy but still walked into second and third – although for Ferrari this was considered a failure. But it effectively wrapped up both world titles; even if Michael Schumacher failed to score another point, there was little danger of David Coulthard being able to haul him in.

At this point of the season Ferrari was running at 95 per cent reliability, excluding accidents. It was a record unheard of in modern Grand Prix racing.

The main topic in the Ferrari pit was the weather. Conditions were so unsettling that the team brought in its own weatherman for the weekend.

Intense testing took place before Silverstone, with Schumacher and Luca Badoer at Mugello. Then Alfa Romeo ETCC star Fabrizio Giovanardi tested a brand new chassis, 213, at Fiorano, while Badoer completed a shakedown of the three cars for Silverstone.

**FRIDAY PRACTICE** Ferrari brought three cars and a spare chassis to Silverstone: 210 for Schumacher, 206 for Rubens Barrichello, 211 as the spare car and 212 as the spare chassis. Ferrari concentrated on tyre assessment as rain was forecast, and worked on preparing the car for the race. Schumacher completed 22 laps with a fastest of 1m 23.619secs which was the best of the day. Barrichello did 19 laps with a 1m 24.405secs for second.

Schumacher said: "It was the usual Friday job list. The car was handling well and to be honest I'd have preferred a longer run in the rain at the end of the session to evaluate the rain tyres. I think we can expect variable weather conditions through the weekend, which will make life tough, especially as McLaren looks strong. I am not thinking about the 51 wins, but certainly I feel on top form at the moment."

Schumacher celebrated his 50 wins by going for a spin in the 1951 British Grand Prix winning Ferrari. It was also Ferrari's first Grand Prix victory.

**SATURDAY QUALIFYING** Ross Brawn was looking at the skies: "If it rains, track times slow so you need to get out early. But if it stays dry, track times will get

faster throughout qualifying. It's difficult to know what to do; you need nerves of steel at times like this."

Schumacher spent his first two qualifying runs sorting out set-up. Using all his 12 laps, he sealed his eighth pole of the season with a time of 1m 20.447secs. Barrichello managed sixth fastest with a time of 1m 21.715secs.

Schumacher said: "This was a difficult and interesting session as everyone waited before leaving the pits. For the race I don't really mind what conditions we have, but I'd prefer a dry race which is more consistent and safer. I hope it is entertaining for the spectators."

Ross Brawn said: "The balance of the car is still not perfect, but we can work on that. Rubens hit traffic, which was a shame as he was happy with the car. I am not worried if it rains because the Bridgestone tyres have an advantage in these conditions. The race should be between us, McLaren and Jordan."

**SUNDAY RACE** Schumacher took the lead at the start. However, Häkkinen was right on his tail and on lap five managed to get past when the German ran wide going into Copse. Häkkinen quickly pulled away from Schumacher, which indicated he could be on a lighter fuel load. For once Ferrari got just about everything wrong: set-up, tyres and strategy. Schumacher came in for his sole pitstop on lap 39 and finished the race second.

Barrichello made a very good start and was fourth at the end of the first lap. On lap 25 he inherited third when Montoya pitted. He stopped on lap 42 and went on to finish third. He said: "That's two podiums in two races, so I have to be reasonably happy." Jean Todt said: "We opted for a one-stop strategy and this turned out to be less effective than a two-stopper." Quite so.

Above: Michael Schumacher and Ross Brawn got qualifying right but the race wrong. Right: The pit board tells his story: no threat to Häkkinen and no challenge from behind.

Right: Barrichello finished a distant third. Below: Michael Schumacher's one stop was the wrong strategy. Below left: He drove a 375 to celebrate Ferrari's first win 50 years ago.

## GERMAN GRAND PRIX HOCKENHEIM
# Faltering on the way to glory

**Left and above:** Barrichello was in great form, out-performing team-mate Michael Schumacher. He took second after a spirited drive from sixth on the grid. Hockenheim's passing potential, which Barrichello exploited, will be lost on the new shorter track.

The Ferrari garage was still talking about Michael Schumacher's big accident in testing at Monza when the floor of the car broke between the Curva Grande and the second chicane, launching him off the track. Racing accidents seem to get more spectacular, and the drivers seem less fazed by them. Schumacher said: "I had a stiff neck and my bum was a bit sore but it's recovered and I played football yesterday." More worrying to the world champion was that Hockenheim didn't suit his car. He had neither won nor poled here with a Ferrari. He said: "In previous years it's been the characteristics of the circuit that didn't suit the car. I did win with Benetton. We simply need the car to deliver the performance. We are competitive at other circuits, except perhaps Monza, but this car is more competitive." With fast, hot circuits coming up it had dawned on everyone that Ferrari had lost its edge and was lucky to have effectively won the championship by the Nürburgring race.

**FRIDAY PRACTICE** Ferrari brought three chassis and one spare tub – 210 for Schumacher, 206 for Barrichello, 211 as the spare and 212 as the spare tub. There were a new front and rear wing and underfloor for Hockenheim and a qualifying engine.

Schumacher completed 35 laps with a best time of 1m 42.255secs to finish in fifth place, and Barrichello completed 22 laps with a best time of 1m 41.953secs to finish fourth. Schumacher said "We have to see where McLaren is and we seem to be matching it, so everything is in order. As usual the crowd here is a motivating factor."

**Left and below:** Michael Schumacher's German Grand Prix, abandoning his wreck in the first race and retiring in the second, bothered him little: his fourth title looked secure.

**SATURDAY QUALIFYING** Schumacher complet-

ed 22 laps in the morning's free practice, finishing in third place, while Barrichello completed 20 laps and finished in sixth. In qualifying Schumacher did a best time of 1m 38.941secs to finish in fourth and Barrichello managed a best of 1m 39.682secs to finish sixth. Ross Brawn said: "It will be tough for the tyres in the race in this heat, as we have seen some degradation on the rears. But it's not an abnormal situation. There is not a lot you can do here in terms of clever strategy, as there are only 45 laps."

Schumacher said: "I prefer to have the Williams eight-10ths in front of me as opposed to Coulthard. I have to look at the situation in terms of the championship. This is one of two tracks that are pretty much tailor-made for our rival's tyre company."

**SUNDAY RACE** The Ferraris were among the last out on the grid, leaving the pits just three minutes before the pitlane closed. After the start, Michael Schumacher's car suddenly slowed with a gear selection problem and he was left in the middle of the grid with Luciano Burti's Prost behind him, which had nowhere to go except over the top of him.

The resulting crash spread debris all over the first corner, and eventually the safety car was sent out. Schumacher started to trudge back to the pits, when suddenly he got the message that the red flags were out. He did a starting sprint down the pitlane to switch to the spare, rejoining the grid in his original fourth position.

This time Schumacher got away in fourth. On lap 23 he made a pitstop and then retired almost immediately, pulling off in the forest with a fuel pressure problem.

Barrichello remained in sixth place into the first corner of the restart, but quickly moved up into fifth when he passed Coulthard in a stunning overtaking move. On lap three he overtook Häkkinen at the Ostkurve. Three laps later he passed his team-mate for third place. Barrichello made his first pitstop on lap 16 in 8.9secs, rejoining in fifth place behind Coulthard. On lap 20 he pulled of another spectacular overtaking move, passing Coulthard on the outside of the fast right-hander into the stadium.

He remained in second place for the remainder of the race, in spite of having a problem with the refuelling machine during his second pitstop on lap 32, which dragged on for 19.5secs.

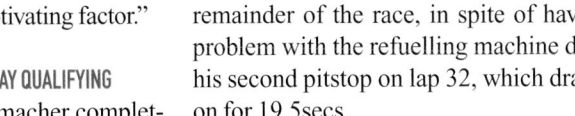

# HUNGARIAN GRAND PRIX HUNGARORING
# Championships confirmed

At the beginning of the weekend Michael Schumacher was not feeling optimistic about his chances of sealing the drivers' championship in Hungary, let alone the constructors' as well. But despite that, all the Ferrari factory department heads had turned up in case of eventual success. Chief aerodynamicist Nic Tombazis and engine supremo Paolo Martinelli had chosen to be in Budapest rather than with their families on the beach. Ferrari chairman Luca di Montezemolo, taking his vacation in Portofino, had his plane fired up ready to collect car designer Rory Byrne to join the celebrations. Byrne was hard at work at the Ferrari factory on the new 2002 car.

FRIDAY PRACTICE Ferrari brought three cars and one spare tub. Chassis 210 was for Michael Schumacher, 206 for Rubens Barrichello and 211 as the T-car. Number 212 was the spare. There was also a revised aerodynamic high downforce set-up for this race, an evolution of the Monte Carlo configuration.

Schumacher dominated the practice, completing 38 laps and recording a best of 1m 16.651secs with Barrichello doing 33 laps for a best of 1m 16.734secs for second.

SATURDAY QUALIFYING Although it was not in doubt, Schumacher got pole with a time of 1m 14.059secs. His complete dominance was highlighted by the fact that he was eight-10ths of a second faster than second-placed David Coulthard. He recorded the fastest time in all three sectors while completing his fast lap, and was so dominant that he used only six of his 12 allocated laps in order to conserve tyres for the race. It was a magnificent performance.

Rubens Barrichello qualified third with 1m 14.953secs, completing 10 of his 12 laps.

SUNDAY RACE Schumacher had a manic moment during the formation lap, running wide across a gravel trap. The Ferrari mechanics were luckily able to remove most of the stones from the car and change the bargeboards.

He went on to make a perfect start and led from beginning to end allowing for pitstops. He made his first pitstop on lap 28 in 8.4secs. He rejoined the race in third after handing the lead to Rubens Barrichello, who made his pitstop on lap 31. On lap 32, when Coulthard went into the pits, Schumacher regained the lead. He made his second pitstop on lap 52 in 8.6secs. He then led to the finish of the race.

Barrichello had made a good start, nipping ahead of Coulthard to take second. He held on to this until the first pitstop, which he made on lap 31 in 9.1secs. Coulthard made his pitstop on lap 32 and came out ahead of Barrichello, splitting the two Ferraris so that Schumacher was leading and Barrichello was in third.

This changed on lap 53 when Barrichello came in for his second pitstop, which was perfectly executed by the Ferrari team in 8.5secs. When Coulthard came in for his pitstop a lap later he couldn't get out on the track before the Brazilian, so it was Schumacher first and Barrichello second. And that was how it finished. Both championships were in the bag.

Schumacher also equalled Alain Prost's record of 51 wins and now only had to beat Juan Manuel Fangio's record five world championships and Ayrton Senna's record 65 pole positions. If he keeps racing, as he says he will, for another seven seasons, both records could tumble. And that will be that. Six world championships and 66 poles will be hard to beat. Michael Schumacher will have made himself statistically the greatest of all time.

Above: A perfect weekend for Michael Schumacher and Ferrari saw the German take pole, an unchallenged win and his fourth world championship title. Right: Schumacher celebrates his achievements with wife Corinna and the Ferrari team.

Right: Schumacher's only mistake was on his lap to the grid. Hurried repairs were necessary but caused no problems. Below: Jean Todt guided Ferrari to a third constructors' world championship. Far left: Michael Schumacher takes Jean Todt for another ride.

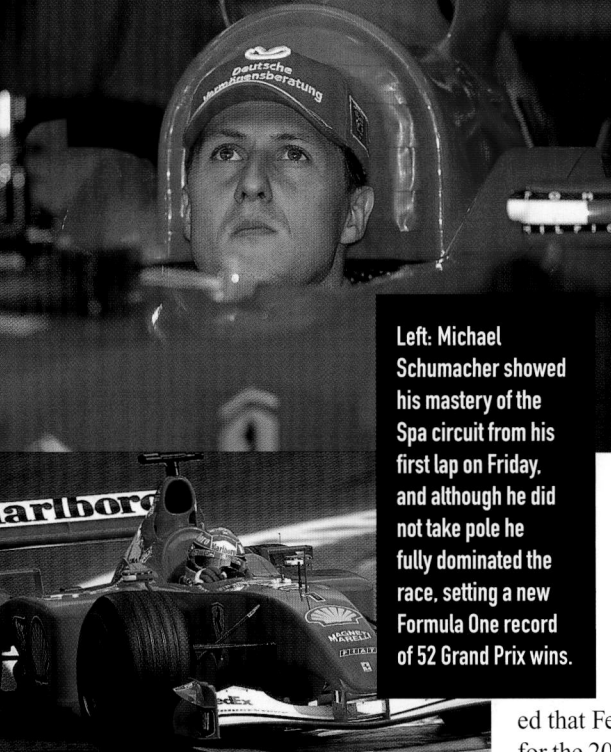

### BELGIAN GRAND PRIX SPA-FRANCORCHAMPS
# Carry on winning

Left: Michael Schumacher showed his mastery of the Spa circuit from his first lap on Friday, and although he did not take pole he fully dominated the race, setting a new Formula One record of 52 Grand Prix wins.

It was the 10th anniversary of Michael Schumacher's 1991 Formula One debut at Spa, and he was determined to make it a winning weekend. Ferrari tested at the Mugello track between Hungary and Spa, with focus on the new aerodynamic package and the tyres. The level of secrecy at Mugello, with photographers banned from trackside, suggested that Ferrari was also testing components for the 2002 car.

Ferrari's battle was now to get Rubens Barrichello second in the drivers' championship. Schumacher said he would help, but in a competitive sport like Formula One aiding a team-mate is not a high priority, unless contractual obligations demand it.

FRIDAY PRACTICE Ferrari brought three cars and a spare chassis to Spa. Chassis number 211 was Schumacher's, 206 Barrichello's, 213 the spare car and 212 the spare tub. There was a revised aerodynamic package including new front and rear wings.

Schumacher set the fastest time, 1m 48.655secs, completing 22 laps in the first dry session and six in the second session. In a re-enactment of his crash with David Coulthard at Spa in 1998, he went into the back of Pedro de la Rosa. Both drivers called it a "racing accident".

Above: Schumacher leads out of La Source at the second start following Burti's accident. It was a dominant win despite a lap that saw him on the grass at Stavelot. Below: Rubens Barrichello ruined his own race when he knocked his front wing off on the entry to the Bus Stop.

Barrichello set the third fastest time, 1m 49.456secs. He completed 19 laps in the first session and 16 more in the second.

Ferrari technical director Ross Brawn said: "We have a reasonable idea what tyres we want to use, although the incident with Michael and de la Rosa meant that we did not get as much done as we would have liked."

SATURDAY QUALIFYING Schumacher had one car set up for the dry and one for the wet. His practice session was stopped after seven laps, leaving him in 19th place on 1m 57.257secs. He sat unhappily as his mechanics made a lengthy front suspension camber change. Barrichello fared better, completing 10 laps and finishing fifth place with a best time of 1m 49.071secs.

Qualifying was chaotic as the track dried out. Schumacher was third fastest behind the Williams cars, completing eight laps with a best of 1m 54.685secs. Barrichello finished in fifth with 1m 56.116secs. Schumacher said: "I am not upset at being third. We timed the runs right and I have the 'Bridgestone pole'. It was tight for us to run the dry tyres at the end. When I went out for the final run, I was not sure that it would be all right, but luckily it had dried enough."

SUNDAY RACE After Frentzen's stall, Schumacher claimed second behind brother Ralf, with Barrichello third. Schumacher quickly overtook Ralf to claim the lead.

At the restart, Schumacher again went into the lead, with Barrichello third behind Fisichella. Schumacher then built up a big lead as Fisichella's Benetton slowed the field down. Schumacher came in for his first stop on lap 10.

On lap 18 Schumacher suffered a momentary lapse at Stavelot: "I was playing with too many buttons on the steering wheel, when I ran wide and almost hit the barrier." But that apart there was never any doubt he would achieve his 52nd victory, breaking Alain Prost's record.

Schumacher made his second pitstop on lap 24 and took the chequered flag 12 laps later to take his place in the record books.

Barrichello, meanwhile, was not having a good race. He made his first pit stop on lap nine of the restarted race, rejoining in fifth place before he too had a manic moment on lap 18, losing his front wing to the Bus Stop bollard, and making an enforced second stop. This dropped him to sixth, where he stayed until lap 32 when he managed to overtake Alesi and finish with two points.

Team principal Jean Todt was ecstatic about the unexpected victory: "Our will to win is as strong as ever. This is the 40th win for Ferrari since I joined the team, and the 200th Formula One victory for our partner Shell, which is such a vital part of our success."

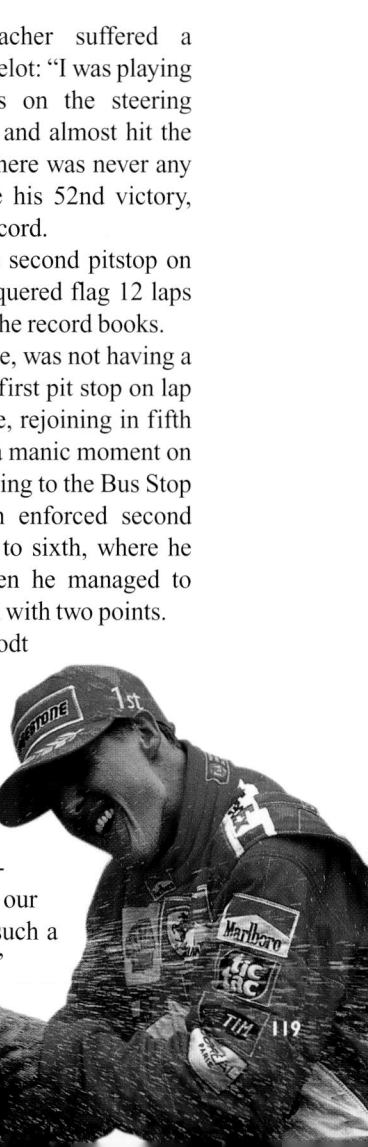

# An emotional weekend

Monza is a tough track: the cars are at full throttle for over 76 per cent of the lap, and use a low-downforce set-up that makes them sensitive to aerodynamic disruption and reliant on mechanical grip. Ferrari had continued developing the F2001 and arrived at Monza with a revised engine spec and further improved aerodynamics.

In deference to the victims of the World Trade Centre disaster, Ferrari elected to run plain red cars with a black nose. Team principal Jean Todt said: "With the agreement of our partners, we wanted to show our solidarity with the victims."

Michael Schumacher was visibly shaken. "It's pretty difficult to find the right expression for what happened and what we feel," he said. "We will support the victims as much as we can." Like quite a few drivers, he felt the race should not have gone ahead, and was out of sorts all weekend.

FRIDAY PRACTICE Ferrari brought three cars and a spare tub: 213 for Schumacher, 206 for Barrichello, plus 211 (spare) and 212 (spare tub).

The practice session started early, at 10.50am, so Formula One could join the minute's silence at midday. It was 25 minutes into the session before Schumacher tossed down the gauntlet, clocking the fastest time.

In the second session he ended third. Barrichello was in good shape and fifth. Technical director Ross Brawn said: "The cars are handling quite well. Grip and traction are obviously important coming out of the chicanes. There's not much difference between the two types of tyre."

SATURDAY QUALIFYING Michael Schumacher was fastest in practice; Barrichello took fourth.

Barrichello out-qualified Schumacher for the first time in 2001 to claim second; Schumacher was third. Both used special qualifying engines. Schumacher said: "I made a mistake in the first sector on what should have been my best lap." Barrichello said: "The team did a good job to find the best set-up. The engine side was very good. It's very special to be here in Monza, in front of all the tifosi, on what is a dark weekend, so it's good to be on the front row."

SUNDAY RACE Michael Schumacher was fastest in warm-up. He tried two runs each in his race car and the spare. Barrichello was fourth fastest. The front wing settings were altered.

Before the race Schumacher had tried to obtain all the drivers' agreement not to race through the first two chicanes, to make the race as safe as possible in light of last year's accident. But Jacques Villeneuve disagreed, and Flavio Briatore and Craig Pollock instructed their drivers to race. Schumacher walked down the grid talking to the other drivers before the race to lobby them not to make any dangerous race moves.

During the race Schumacher was a shadow of his aggressive self. He went wheel-to-wheel with brother Ralf on lap one and edged ahead to claim third, but otherwise was unusually anonymous.

It was soon obvious the Ferraris were on a two-stop race, and the BMW Williams on a one-stop. Schumacher made his first stop on lap 18. He rejoined in fourth, briefly claiming third when brother Ralf pitted on lap 35, before returning to fourth after his second pitstop on lap 40.

He finished in fourth, and said afterwards: "I'm glad the weekend is over. It was a pity Rubens was not able to win this race. But the most important thing is that nothing bad happened." Schumacher headed for his Norwegian retreat to mull over 11th September.

Barrichello had an excellent race and if a faulty fuel rig hadn't ruined his first pitstop would probably have won. He held second at the start, overtook Montoya on lap eight for the lead, and was looking good until his first pitstop on lap 19.

In fact, the tyres were changed before the fuel rig was taken to the car. Barrichello re-entered the race in third, moved to second when Montoya made his only pitstop on lap 28, led the race when Ralf made his only pitstop on lap 35, then lost the lead when he pitted again on lap 41. Barrichello claimed second when he out-braked Ralf Schumacher at Turn 1 on lap 47 and passed him.

Right: Ferrari paid its respects to the US attack victims in a typically unique manner. Below right: On this occasion Rubens Barrichello led the Ferrari victory push, while Michael Schumacher, who had been troubled by recent events, finished fourth.

Above and right: Michael lobbied all the drivers, including his brother, to be cautious on the first lap. It did not stop him elbowing Ralf out of the way on the first lap, but he then drove a restrained race.

Above: Rubens Barrichello came to the US with one mission in mind, but engine failure robbed him of a result. Left: Ross Brawn had some test components in the Ferraris. Below: Red #1 leads the field on the first lap.

## UNITED STATES GRAND PRIX INDIANAPOLIS
# Back to business as usual

After the rather sombre atmosphere and the cars' unbranded appearance at Monza, the Ferraris made a grand entrance at Indianapolis with the Stars and Stripes blazing on the cars and the drivers' helmets. The gesture was fully appreciated by the 200,000-strong crowd.

With Michael Schumacher now having already clinched the drivers' title, the emphasis had switched to Rubens Barrichello in an attempt to help the Brazilian secure the runner-up spot.

The cars were little changed from recent races but there were rumours of significant engine modifications for evaluation. Ferrari was effectively using the season's closing races for testing and development.

FRIDAY PRACTICE Ferrari brought four chassis: F2001/213 for Schumacher, F2001/206 for Barrichello, F2001/211 as the spare for Schumacher and F2001/212 as the tub.

Friday was spent evaluating the available dry tyre options and adapting the cars to the long straights and slow twisting infield.

Schumacher finished the session second quickest with a 1m 13.552secs; Barrichello was third on 1m 13.584secs. Schumacher reckoned the softer compound gave excellent grip but was concerned about tyre wear rates. "We just have to work a little more on our detailed set-up," he said.

SATURDAY QUALIFYING Saturday morning saw more race tyre evaluation. Schumacher's fastest time of the morning improved on his Friday time, putting him 0.252secs ahead of Häkkinen's McLaren, despite an oil pump failure which required installation of a fresh V10 for qualifying. Barrichello's fifth fastest time was not fully representative. His pace through the speed trap suggested he may have had use of a development engine.

Schumacher ended qualifying with his 42nd pole and Ferrari's 10th of the season, with a 1m 11.708secs, using nine of his 12 laps. He even sat out the final blast, sure that a quicker lap was not humanly possible. He just said: "I think the run to the first corner after the start tomorrow will be fun."

For Barrichello, qualifying was less satisfying, despite trying slipstreaming tactics to improve his time. His final runs on new tyres did not bring the expected return as track conditions had deteriorated. His first runs on old tyres gave better balance and brought his best time of 1m 12.327secs for fifth on the grid. He was not too concerned: "Overtaking is possible here, so I reckon I can have a good race," he said – with good reason, after being fastest through the speed trap in 335.7kph.

SUNDAY RACE From pole, Schumacher made a storming start to lead into the first turn, closely shadowed by a fast-starting Montoya. Barrichello was in third by the end of lap one, and by lap five had snatched the lead from Schumacher with an assertive move at the end of the infield straight. He then edged away from the field, and set a new fastest lap on lap 19 before pitting for the first of two stops on lap 27.

Meanwhile Schumacher, on a one-stop strategy, was defending his second place from Montoya's Williams. He led again on laps 27-33 following Barrichello's stop, until Montoya passed him. When Montoya retired Schumacher regained the lead until lap 39 when he pitted, rejoining in fourth, where he stayed until Coulthard pitted on lap 43.

Barrichello retook the lead on lap 46 when Häkkinen pitted and led through to his second fuel stop on lap 50. He rejoined in second with Schumacher third and proceeded to close the gap to Häkkinen to just over 2.5secs before clouds of smoke started to appear and Barrichello began to slow. He drove on with the smoke bellowing, dropping to fourth before the engine seized, locking the tyres on lap 71, with just two laps to go. He was lucky to avoid a serious accident. Schumacher rolled off the remaining laps to finish second, shadowed by a fast-closing Coulthard. Barrichello's retirement left the Brazilian seven points behind Coulthard – to finish second in the drivers' title he had to win at Suzuka.

Ferrari technical director Ross Brawn admitted tyre choice had hindered the team: "We probably made the wrong tyre choice, as the rise in temperature over the weekend meant there was better grip on the track because more rubber was laid down." Brawn also hinted that Ferrari had been running a few new components directed towards the 2002 car. "At this point in the championship, with the title already decided, we can try out some new things," he said with a wry smile.

Above and left: Michael Schumacher surveys his stranded Ferrari after suffering an oil pump failure in free practice. The 2001 champ added another six points to his tally for the season.

# Tyres hand it to the champions

This was BMW Williams' race but Bridgestone had other ideas – the tyre company focused on Michael Schumacher, McLaren's move to Michelin for 2002 being common knowledge.

Ferrari arrived in Japan with a completely new, slightly wider chassis for Michael Schumacher. For Ferrari, Suzuka was the first test session for 2002, with a test ban until 1st January 2002 taking effect right after the race. The team was also experimenting with engines.

FRIDAY PRACTICE Ferrari had three running chassis and two spare tubs: F2001/214 for Schumacher, F2001/206 for Rubens Barrichello and F2001/213 as the spare, with chassis 211 and 212 in reserve.

Schumacher dominated the first session, completing 12 laps with a best of 1m 37.443secs, three-10ths of a second faster than Mika Häkkinen. Schumacher completed 34 laps for the day, and finished eighth. Barrichello, who had some brake problems that the team managed to fix, completed 33 laps and finished in 10th place .

Bridgestone had developed two new compounds for its home Grand Prix, which gave Ferrari superiority over BMW Williams' faster cars. Technical director Ross Brawn said: "We did enough laps to get a tyre comparison done and we have enough information to have a good idea of what we need to run. This track is hypersensitive to fuel load, which is why you see a big gap between cars running a low load and those running more."

SATURDAY QUALIFYING It was a tale of tyres as the Michelin-shod BMW Williams cars dominated the first practice session. However, Schumacher put new Bridgestone boots on his car for qualifying and took a magnificent pole of 1m 32.484secs over nine laps, with a perfect one-lap display round the technically challenging Suzuka circuit. His time was a whole 1.065mph faster than the second-placed car, a differential virtually unheard of in Formula One.

Barrichello managed fourth over 11 laps with a best of 1m 33.323secs.

Schumacher said: "Bridgestone has produced a great tyre, which was particularly good through the Esses. I must say this section is very tough physically now. In the past, the cars used to slide around, but today

we had so much grip that it's quite a challenge. I think the Bridgestones were the best in the faster sections, whereas the other tyres might have an advantage here under braking and in terms of traction." The new wider chassis worked straight away and Ferrari was scaring other teams with stories of huge technical breakthroughs on next year's car.

SUNDAY RACE Michael Schumacher was fastest in warm-up and proceeded to dominate the race. He led at the start, moving all over the track to block Montoya. The idea was to help three-stopping Barrichello, who was running light to get past both the BMW Williams in front of him on the grid. It seemed to be working, as he overtook Ralf Schumacher on lap one, and then in a daring move on lap two overtook Montoya on the last corner. Montoya then reclaimed second place at the first corner of lap three and kept it as he used Barrichello's gameplan. Barrichello remained third until his first pitstop on lap 15, returning to the race in sixth. Schumacher made his first pitstop on lap 18, returning to the race in fourth. When the two BMW Williams and Häkkinen had all made their first pitstops, Schumacher returned to the lead, with Barrichello third. On lap 29 Barrichello made his second pitstop and could have kept third if he hadn't made a third stop on lap 41, returning to the race in fifth place, where he stayed.

Schumacher made his second stop on lap 36. After the second round of pitstops had ended he was in the lead and won the race, making his career score 801 points and breaking Alain Prost's record of 798.5. He also equalled his own and Nigel Mansell's record of nine wins in a season. He said: "This was the perfect end to the season, because winning the final race is just what you need before the long winter break. Today we had a good package and perfect tyres."

Right: Michael Schumacher wrapped up a triumphant year in style at Suzuka with an impressive win with a new development chassis.

Above: Rubens Barrichello and David Coulthard compare notes after the race. Right: Juan Pablo Montoya crowds Barrichello nearing the chicane.

駆けぬける歓び

Team Review      Race by Race

# McLAREN

2001

## Contents

| | | | | | | |
|---|---|---|---|---|---|---|
| Team Review | – | The season | p126 | European Grand Prix | – | Nürburgring | p140 |
| Australian Grand Prix | – | Melbourne | p132 | French Grand Prix | – | Magny-Cours | p141 |
| Malaysian Grand Prix | – | Sepang | p133 | British Grand Prix | – | Silverstone | p142 |
| Brazilian Grand Prix | – | Interlagos | p134 | German Grand Prix | – | Hockenheim | p143 |
| San Marino Grand Prix | – | Imola | p135 | Hungarian Grand Prix | – | Hungaroring | p144 |
| Spanish Grand Prix | – | Barcelona | p136 | Belgian Grand Prix | – | Spa-Francorchamps | p145 |
| Austrian Grand Prix | – | A1 Ring | p137 | Italian Grand Prix | – | Monza | p146 |
| Monaco Grand Prix | – | Monte Carlo | p138 | USA Grand Prix | – | Indianapolis | p147 |
| Canadian Grand Prix | – | Montreal | p139 | Japanese Grand Prix | – | Suzuka | p148 |

Ron Dennis

Mika Häkkinen

Mika Häkkinen

David Coulthard

# A season of shortfalls

It was a season of shortfalls, as McLaren's team principal Ron Dennis readily admitted: "We had a shortfall in reliability and performance this year." Dennis may be sometimes a little economical with the truth in his team press releases, but where the performance of the car is concerned he is brutally honest.

The years in the wilderness, 1994 to 1996, have long been forgotten and the team can only remember the winning years again. Having claimed the championship in 1998 and 1999 and finished second to Ferrari in the next season, McLaren ended 2001 again in second place, but far behind Ferrari and with BMW Williams breathing down its neck. On the positive side, David Coulthard finished second in the drivers' standings, his best-ever result in the championship. Coulthard might have been capable of more, had he not suffered from the shortfalls so succinctly summed up by his boss. Equally disadvantaged was Mika Häkkinen, who finished fifth overall in a season that he had preceded with two driving titles and one runner-up

result. It was thus his worst showing in four years, a reflection not only of his car's inadequacies but also of a waning motivation that culminated in his decision to take a sabbatical next season – a break that most believe will turn into his permanent retirement from the sport. Though McLaren's problems were mostly technical, the team's forward progress was also undermined by difficulties of a human nature. The near-defection of technical director Adrian Newey to Jaguar in mid-season could not be blamed for McLaren's drop-off in performance, since his chassis was designed before the season began. However the Newey saga did to a certain extent destabilise the team, and morale suffered somewhat. In a team where loyalty is paramount, Newey's behaviour is likely to adversely affect his future with McLaren.

In the short term, in 2001, his confused state of mind might have prevented him giving maximum effort at a time when the chassis needed vast improvement. A more significant blow to the team was the tragic death of Ilmor Engineering's Paul Morgan in a plane crash mid-season, which left his partner and Mercedes engine

designer Mario Illien with more work than he could handle in a season when the engines needed a great deal of attention. To stand still in this sport is to go backwards, goes a favourite saying of Ron Dennis, yet his team did just that. This year McLaren's total of 102 points was 77 fewer than Ferrari. Last year the gap was a mere 18 points. After 17 races this year, McLaren's advantage over BMW Williams was just 22 points, a deficit that would surely have been closed if the season had been longer. Dennis also famously claims that he feels physical pain after not winning, a state of affairs that must have left him in considerable discomfort on the 13 occasions when McLaren failed to win in 2001. Adding to his distress is the painful knowledge that a large amount of work must be done to restore McLaren's respectability.

At the end of the year Dennis suggested the solution lay in forming a closer relationship with the team's engine partner and engine builder. "The season has been a catalyst for change," Dennis said, "and we have gone way beyond just the engineering issues and looked at the relationships between Ilmor, Mercedes and McLaren." Whatever form the corporate overhaul takes, the team's needs are obvious: it simply has to come up with a much better car.

## The McLaren MP4-16 car

TECHNICAL director Adrian Newey and his design team spent nine months on the MP4-16 concept, placing particular emphasis on revised aerodynamics and the structural strengthening necessary to comply with the regulatory changes for 2001. The car, Newey said, was not an evolution of the MP4-15, which won seven races in 2000, but a completely new car for the new rules. However, the new car fell far short of perfection. Its sleek bodywork concealed a built-in handling imbalance that caused the cars to alternate between oversteer and understeer. Both drivers suffered from the team's inability to get its handling act together, particularly in qualifying, and as a consequence they had to play catch-up ▷

David Coulthard

in the races, where their progress was all too often halted by their woefully unreliable cars. Although the team went through seven versions of the chassis there were no major changes to their overall specifications. Instead, they were steadily refined in the search for performance improvements that were never really found.

Mario Illien took a more conservative approach for the Mercedes-Benz FO 110K engine, which had a lower centre of gravity but was otherwise structurally unchanged from 2000. Unlike last year's model, however, it was built without beryllium, the very hard, very light metal the use of which Ilmor pioneered but which the FIA banned in this year to cut costs. Some felt the ban would cost Mercedes most in terms of performance and reliability, which proved to be the case, despite a vigorous pre-season testing campaign. In search of greater reliability the 2001 engines, some 75 of which would be built during the season, completed over 16,000 miles on transient dynamometers and 7,000 miles in the cars before the first race.

Nevertheless, engine failures accounted for four of the team's mechanical retirements, most memorably and embarrassingly at Hockenheim in Germany, Mercedes' home race, where Häkkinen and Coulthard suffered spectacular engine blow-ups within a few laps of each other. Coulthard's engine also failed him in Canada and Italy. The fact that Ferrari had only one engine-related retirement all season underlined the Mercedes V10's disadvantage, while the consistent extra pace shown by both Ferrari and BMW pointed out their advantage in the horsepower department. Some even reckoned that Jaguar's Cosworth engine had more power than the Mercedes in 2001.

Coulthard started the season with MP4-16/01, while Häkkinen had 03. The T-car, which would alternate between the drivers all year, was 02 in Australia, where it was set up for Coulthard. In this first race of the season, Häkkinen's chassis had a worrying failure of its right front suspension that pitched the Finn headlong into a tyre barrier, where his helmet hit the tyres with considerable force. The heavy accident, Häkkinen later revealed, was a primary factor in his decision to take a sabbatical in 2002. Mindful of his near-fatal accident in Australia in 1995, his crash in Melbourne might also have contributed to the performance drop-off that was a feature of the first half of Häkkinen's troubled season.

Häkkinen also experienced the team's next equipment failure, in Brazil, where a malfunctioning clutch ended his race a few yards beyond the startline. Left cowering in his car while the rest of the field made frantic avoidance manoeuvres, Häkkinen said: "It was the scariest moment of my life." Coulthard, meanwhile, went on to claim his first win of the season, outperforming Michael Schumacher and establishing himself as a championship contender.

Häkkinen's chances of continuing as McLaren's main threat were effectively ended by yet another mechanical failure in Spain, where the team fielded two new cars armed with the now-legal launch control systems. Häkkinen had chassis 04, and first call on 03 – formerly his race car – while Coulthard had 05. Both race cars, as it transpired, had serious deficiencies, with Häkkinen's failing him at the worst possible time. In complete command of the race, and with a 40-second lead over Michael Schumacher, Häkkinen's clutch exploded on the final lap. In this race his team-mate staged a stirring comeback to finish fifth, having stalled on the formation lap because of an electronic glitch in 05's launch control system. But Ron Dennis at first blamed the Scot for the setback and the two exchanged harsh words. Dennis later apologised and said Coulthard was a champion in the making.

Mario Illien

Adrian Newey

Martin Whitmarsh

Coulthard's momentum and Häkkinen's misfortune continued in Austria, where the Scot won after the Finn's 04 car stalled on the grid with a launch control glitch of the same kind that had afflicted Coulthard in Spain, though Häkkinen was in this case unable to continue. McLaren's mechanical disasters further blighted both drivers in the showcase race of the season. At Monaco, Coulthard's brilliant pole position was negated by yet another launch control failure on the formation lap. While Coulthard went on to salvage fifth place Häkkinen failed to finish, dropping out of a seemingly secure second place with a suspension problem.

In Canada, where Häkkinen finished third, his team-mate fell victim to a potentially dangerous oversight in his new chassis, 06. On the starting grid Coulthard discovered an unwelcome presence in the cockpit: a nut that should have been affixed to the front suspension. Informed of this, the team offered the Scot the option of not racing, but he refused, instead throwing the offending nut over the pit wall. With its left front wheel not properly attached the car was dangerously askew, but braveheart Coulthard drove it heroically, only to have its engine explode 15 laps from the finish when he was in fourth place.

Häkkinen was provided with a new chassis, 07, for the European Grand Prix, where it ran reliably, if slowly, to a sixth place finish, in a race from which Coulthard salvaged third in a car that was also afflicted by serious oversteer. But in the next race, in France, Häkkinen was halted at the start by an improperly assembled gearbox, while Coulthard finished fourth, having missed the podium because of a stop-go penalty incurred for speeding in the pitlane. Coulthard's home race at Silverstone was ruined by a first-lap collision with Trulli's Jordan that damaged the McLaren's suspension, and the Scot spun out. Häkkinen emerged impressively from his slump, taking full advantage of a car that was finally on form and winning the race, his first victory since August of 2000.

This triumph for the Finn and McLaren was followed immediately by the twin engine failures in Germany. Thereafter both cars ran reliably until the Italian Grand Prix, where Coulthard's engine blew itself to smithereens and Häkkinen's gearbox gave up the ghost before the halfway mark in the race. Reliability returned in the USA, where Coulthard finished a steady third and Häkkinen, taking full advantage of less reliable frontrunners, won his second race of the season, and probably the last of his career. Finally, in ▷

## McLAREN SEASON STATISTICS

### RELIABILITY PERFORMANCE

| Driver | Races | Max laps | Laps completed | Reliability rating |
|---|---|---|---|---|
| David Coulthard | 17 | 1,065 | 926 | 86.9% |
| Mika Häkkinen | 17 | 1,065 | 689 | 64.7% |
| Constructor | Races | Max laps | Laps completed | Reliability rating |
| Team | 34 | 2,130 | 1,615 | 75.8% |

### CHAMPIONSHIP PERFORMANCE

| Driver | 2001 points | 2000 points | 12 month change |
|---|---|---|---|
| David Coulthard | 65 | 73 | -10.9% |
| Mika Häkkinen | 37 | 89 | -58.4% |
| Constructor | 2001 points | 2000 points | 12 month change |
| Team | 102 | 152 | -32.9% |

Mika Häkkinen

### CHASSIS LOG

**MP4-16/01** Race car for David Coulthard at Melbourne, Sepang, Interlagos and Imola. Spare car at Monte Carlo.
**MP4-16/02** Spare car at Melbourne, Sepang, Interlagos and Imola.
**MP4-16/03** Race car for Häkkinen at Melbourne, Sepang, Interlagos and Imola. Spare car at Barcelona, A1 Ring and Monte Carlo.
**MP4-16/04** Race car for Häkkinen at Barcelona, A1 Ring, Monte Carlo, Indianapolis and Suzuka. Spare car at Montreal (used in qualifying by Häkkinen), the Nürburgring (raced by Häkkinen), Magny-Cours, Hockenheim and the Hungaroring. Spare monocoque at Monza, built up for Häkkinen to race after his qualifying smash.
**MP4-16/05** Race car for Coulthard at Barcelona, A1 Ring, Monte Carlo and the Hungaroring (used in practice only when it was torn apart on a kerb); and for Häkkinen at Montreal. Spare car at Silverstone, Spa-Francorchamps, Monza, Indianapolis and Suzuka.
**MP4-16/06** Race car for Coulthard at Montreal, the Nürburgring, Magny-Cours, Silverstone, Hockenheim, the Hungaroring, Spa-Francorchamps, Monza, Indianapolis and Suzuka.
**MP4-16/07** Race car for Häkkinen at the Nürburgring (not used in the race due to an electronic sensor failure), Magny-Cours, Silverstone, Hockenheim, the Hungaroring, Spa-Francorchamps and Monza. Spare monocoque at Indianapolis and Suzuka.

Japan, the McLarens finished third and fourth, with Häkkinen donating the podium to Coulthard as a farewell gesture of appreciation for the Scot's loyal support over their six years as team-mates.

## Technical developments

McLAREN MERCEDES did not set the technical pace in 2001. This was the big difference from 2000. The team seemed technically frozen for reasons not obvious. The problems with the front wing in the early races were put down to miscalibration of the windtunnel, and were quickly resolved by Brazil.

A glaring example of the technical malaise was the team's failure to adopt the Ferrari-inspired drum brake duct innovation. That was the single biggest technical advance of the year in Formula One and McLaren was the only team not to mimic it in some manner, despite the obvious advantages.

The team also had an obsession during the year with minimising pitch sensitivity in the aerodynamics. It is believed that compromises were made in suspension geometry to achieve this objective, and the end result may have contributed to a lack of feel in the steering.

Much of this apparent lack of technical direction was put down to the unsettling effect of Adrian Newey's musings about leaving the team. It is clear that for a third of the season his mind was not fully on the job, and, as everyone knows, to succeed in Formula One requires total focus.

## The drivers

FOR THE first time in their lengthy tenure as team-mates, David Coulthard outperformed Mika Häkkinen. In qualifying, formerly the Flying Finn's forte, the Scot reduced the deficit, giving the advantage to the Finn just nine times in 17 races. In points scored,

Coulthard beat Häkkinen 65 to 37, and while they each had two wins, Coulthard was much the more consistent performer, mainly because he was more highly motivated more often. Once the prospect of emerging from his team-mate's long shadow became clear, and it did so early in the season, Coulthard's resolve deepened and his upward mobility quickened accordingly. Conversely, though he showed occasional glimpses of his old form and drove outstandingly when he had a sniff of victory, Häkkinen was too often uninspired. Undoubtedly, Hakkinen's desire was blunted by him suffering most from the team's appalling unreliability. Of McLaren's 10 mechanically-related race retirements, Häkkinen had seven, plus a classified finish when his clutch gave up in Spain. His most significant retirement was the suspension failure that pitched him into the barriers in Melbourne. There, Häkkinen would admit at the end of the season, he began to question the wisdom of continuing in his dangerous profession, especially now that he was a family man. His thoughts turned to his wife Erja and their baby Hugo.

"I have a new priority in life," Häkkinen told us in Japan. "Before, for 12 years, my priority was Formula One, but when I became a father things changed. I don't think it affected me in a speed sense but this is a dangerous sport and once you've got something so special you don't want to lose it. You think about it a lot more and when you cross the road you look twice each way. What happened in Melbourne did not help. I knew then I had to do something about the feeling and to understand what was best for my future."

If Häkkinen's domestic concerns were a factor in his faltering form this season, the reverse was true for his team-mate, according to no less an authority than Ron Dennis. Before the season began, when Coulthard ended his long-term relationship with fiancée Heidi Wichlinski, Dennis interpreted the split as proof of Coulthard's increased commitment to his profession. Coulthard later teamed up with another stunning model, Simone Abdelnour, though his relationship with his McLaren boss remained uneasy in comparison to the much closer bond between Häkkinen and Dennis. Though Häkkinen's car stalled at the start on two occasions with no comment from Dennis, he singled out Coulthard for being responsible for his failure to get off the line in Spain. The Scot was enraged by the unjust accusation of 'brain fade'; Dennis later apologised profusely and did some elaborate fence-mending with his disgruntled driver. Having reassured Coulthard that he would have the team's full support in McLaren's chase for the championship, Dennis gave his interpretation of the character transformation he felt was responsible for Coulthard's becoming McLaren's main man. According to Dennis, Coulthard had matured as a driver and was now a driven man, aggressively determined to fight everyone and take no prisoners en route to showing the world he's a winner. Dennis also admitted that his closer personal affinity with Häkkinen stemmed from seeing the Finn close to death after his dreadful accident in Australia in 1995. That said, Dennis insisted he doesn't care which of his drivers wins, and that 'I will be absolutely cheering if David wins the world championship, as I would for Mika'. Ultimately, of course, there was no cheering for a McLaren champion: Coulthard's year in the ascendancy was cruelly undermined by the team's failure to provide him with equipment capable of winning the championship, which Ferrari's Michael Schumacher clinched in Hungary with four races to go. Nevertheless, Coulthard's boss claimed that he has what it takes to beat Schumacher in 2002, providing McLaren gives him a better car. Dennis said: "David has beaten Michael in the past and he can do it again. We've just got to provide him with the best equipment, and we could make it easier for him by giving even better equipment. We will just have to try harder." Speaking of 2002, when he will have Kimi Räikkönen as his partner, the team's new leader looked forward to the improved car promised by Dennis. Coulthard said: "I see no reason why, with the same group of people who were able to design a car in 1998 that was dominant, it's not possible to do it again. I just hope it's next year." At the team's elaborate launch in Valencia in February, there was no hint that Adrian Newey's latest creation would be so inadequate. Sleek and purposeful in its familiar grey-on-grey livery, it looked every inch a winner and quite capable of battling wheel-to-wheel with the bright red Ferraris. "Even a brick looks beautiful if it wins," Ron Dennis said at the launch, adding a prophetic proviso that a winning season would require not only a significant performance improvement but also an absence of the reliability problems that had checked success in the previous two seasons.

Nine months later, after his reservations about the car were proven correct, Dennis said: "As always we win as a team and we lose as a team."

## Commercial

McLAREN'S budget for 2001 was just over $274 million, a shade less than Ferrari's. Once again, Ron Dennis found that not winning comes as expensive as winning in Formula One.

DaimlerChrysler, which owns 40 per cent of the McLaren team, did not have its customary successful year. But

Mika Häkkinen

Mercedes motorsport boss Norbert Haug has always said that it was not necessary for Mercedes to always win to achieve its marketing objectives. Even to be seen competing with the likes of Ferrari, the most celebrated of all racing teams, has added lustre to the Mercedes image. Haug says: "Formula One is really about overall image. It's a very tough playing field but for an automobile manufacturer probably the best playingfield to show competence in terms of sport, in terms of comparisons with your rivals, and in this way you can communicate to your customers and to your future customers. We have a strategic approach and use the sport as a marketing tool, and we communicate to much younger people now." Haug noted that since Mercedes began the partnership with McLaren in 1995, the average age of those who buy the company's road cars has dropped significantly, and that a winning or losing season doesn't seem to make much difference to Mercedes customers.

Though West McLaren Mercedes has a budget second only to Ferrari's, like the Italian team it will undoubtedly have to watch its belt in 2002. Dennis has the awkward job of completing his showcase Paragon headquarters, now due for occupation in 2003, at a time when funding is scarcer. The project is, by all accounts, well behind schedule and well over budget. And whether it gives the team any more competitive advantage over BMW Williams in the years to come remains very much to be seen.

McLaren motorhome

# Half a second adrift

McLaren Mercedes breezed into Melbourne for more of the same; only BMW Williams seemed an obvious threat to the top two status quo. But taken aback by Ferrari's form and its own non-response, the team lagged the Ferraris by a half-second throughout the weekend despite running on identical tyres. It was a reversal of the situation with Ferrari a year before, though the differential then had been below a quarter-second. The team was shocked, in particular Ron Dennis, who had expected his customary early-season dominance.

The new Mercedes engine was revving higher than in 2000 and had a note notably different from last year's engine – and from the other cars'.

FRIDAY PRACTICE McLaren Mercedes brought MP4-16 chassis 03 for Häkkinen, MP4-16 chassis 01 for Coulthard and MP4-16 chassis number 02 as the spare for Häkkinen. Häkkinen ran 31 laps for a best of 1m 29.799secs, good enough for fifth fastest.

Coulthard's 37 laps were spent fighting understeer for fourth on 1m 29.324secs. He was pleased with the mechanical grip, especially at the front. Ron Dennis said: "As always on a Friday, the lap times merely reflect the different fuel loads." But the sessions proved indicative of the weekend.

SATURDAY QUALIFYING Coulthard qualified a full 1.118secs off Michael Schumacher's pole pace for sixth on the grid, in 1m 28.010secs. Häkkinen managed third in 1m 27.461secs. The team admitted to balance problems with the car. The drivers shouldered the blame. Häkkinen conceded: "I didn't manage to get the best out of the car." Coulthard said: "It was a really messy session for me. I never got the rhythm." The general view was that McLaren had started 2001 with the second-fastest car and plenty to do.

SUNDAY RACE The team defined a predictable one-stop strategy, with a twist; they would run a long first stint and stop after the other leaders had pitted. Häkkinen ran second only to Michael Schumacher but his race ended on lap 26: he hit the brakes at over 170mph coming into the right-hander at Stewart corner and the car pitched forward to the right, pivoted around the left front wheel and spun and hurtled sideways into the tyre wall at around 45mph. Analysis would show the lower wishbone on the right front suspension had broken. The Finn got straight out of the car, unsteady on his feet with slight concussion after being hit on his helmet by a piece of bodywork. He went to hospital with concerns for any head injury after his terrible accident in Adelaide six years ago. Given his superior strategy he might even have won.

David Coulthard almost found himself out on the first lap as he disputed the same piece of road with Frentzen's Jordan Honda and Ralf Schumacher's BMW Williams. The wheels of all three cars briefly became intertwined as they banged sidepods.

He was squeezed down to seventh but took his revenge, passing both Frentzen and Schumacher with identical moves, out-braking them around the outside in Turn 4 on successive laps. When the safety car came out on lap five Coulthard was fourth, just behind Barrichello. When Häkkinen crashed he inherited third and started to pressure Barrichello, who was having problems. He stalked him until lap 32, and then he pounced as the Ferrari was baulked by rookie Fernando Alonso's Minardi. He pitted on lap 41, the last of the front-runners to do so. From then it was an easy run to the finish and second place.

Above: David Coulthard drove well enough to win the race, but the car just wasn't up to it. Häkkinen was on his way to a certain second place (below) when a wishbone failed and sent him into the barriers (bottom) leaving him with nothing but a long walk back to the pits (right).

## MALAYSIAN GRAND PRIX SEPANG
# Understanding the problem

Ferrari's obvious car advantage in the opener and McLaren Mercedes' aerodynamic problem with the front wing demanded improvisational solutions. The team was resigned to being second best until the circus reached Europe.

FRIDAY PRACTICE McLaren brought the same three MP4-16 cars to Malaysia as they did to Australia and logged 57 laps as the team tried to solve the worrying lack of balance caused by insufficient grip at the front end.

Both drivers complained of understeer, usually followed by snap oversteer, giving viciously twitching cars that required much application of opposite lock. In posting fourth and sixth fastest times respectively, Coulthard (1m 39.300secs) slid wide several times and kicked up clouds of dust, while Häkkinen (1m 39.861secs) had a spectacular tyre-smoking spin.

**Left and below: Coulthard continued to build his world championship bid with third place at Sepang and another four points.**

SATURDAY QUALIFYING It was a supreme effort that put Häkkinen fourth on the grid with a lap of 1m 36.040secs (0.820secs behind Michael Schumacher's pole pace). Meanwhile Coulthard clocked 1m 36.417secs – 1.197secs off pole, in eighth.

SUNDAY RACE In the warm-up, Mika Häkkinen ran on rain tyres to prepare for the bad weather foretold by the team's forecasters.

Coulthard made an excellent start, from eighth on the grid to fourth in the first few hundred metres. Häkkinen, having been delayed by Ralf Schu-

**Below: Häkkinen had anticipated a tough race, but finishing sixth was a major disappointment.**

macher's spin at the first corner, effectively exchanged places with his team-mate, dropping from fourth to eighth. Thus the Finn was forced into an unfamiliar supporting role. When the cloudburst began soaking the circuit near the end of lap two and chaos ensued, Coulthard stayed sure-footed longer than most and was in second place behind Jarno Trulli on lap three. He then survived a quick spin into the grass and gravel en route to the pits for the tyre change that was now required to stay afloat in the deluge. Häkkinen also pitted on lap four and both cars' tyres were changed efficiently: in 41.086secs for Coulthard and 44.016secs for Häkkinen. But the team's choice of full wets was wrong – Schumacher raced away on intermediates.

Coulthard, emerged as the race leader following the massed pitstops and led the field while the safety car circulated, managed to stay in front for four laps after racing resumed on lap 11. But on lap 16, hampered by full wets on a rapidly drying track, he was inevitably demoted to third place by the intermediate-shod Ferraris.

Coulthard's scheduled pitstop on lap 25 was for 8.8secs and afterwards made a relatively uneventful journey to the third step on the podium. Häkkinen had seldom had to work so hard to claim a single point. Hobbled by an ill-handling car and the wrong tyres in the early going, for much of the race even sixth place seemed out of reach. He was in unfamiliar territory, scrambling for a foothold among an ever-changing pack of cars desperate to finish in the points.

In all, Häkkinen stopped three times. His third stop was for the racing tyres that salvaged some honour for himself and McLaren. In a failed attempt to garner the fifth place held firmly by Ralf Schumacher, Häkkinen reeled off a succession of fast laps, clocking a 1m 40.962secs on lap 48 that was to prove the quickest of the day by more than half a second.

Technical director Adrian Newey summed up the team's day: "With hindsight we should have gone for the intermediates at the first stop. We took the conservative approach because we did not want to risk an accident ." McLaren consoled itself by pointing out that after the two races in 2000 it was trailing Ferrari by 26 points, so their deficit of 'only' 19 points this time left them with plenty of chances. No one believed it.

133

# Coulthard electrifies Brazil

David Coulthard's electrifying performance at Interlagos was unexpected and it sent sparks flying in all directions. It short-circuited Ferrari and kick-started McLaren's season. Technical director Adrian Newey stayed in the UK to concentrate on wind tunnel developments to help sort out the problems, so the team's expectations were limited by whatever makeshift solutions might be found to improve the handling problem that had inhibited the cars in the first two races.

FRIDAY PRACTICE Always a hive of activity, the McLaren garage was even busier than usual and the day amounted to a full-fledged test session as the team experimented with aerodynamic and suspension modifications intended to eliminate the chronic lack of front-end grip that was afflicting the MP4-16.

The three chassis were 01 for Häkkinen and 03 for Coulthard, who also had first claim on 02, the spare. The improvisations, including moving ballast around to find better balance, were plain to see. The pace was furious: Coulthard slid off the circuit twice and Häkkinen spun wildly during their respective 37 and 39 laps of practice as the ballast was shifted.

For Coulthard's last run the team dropped its traditionally methodical approach to Friday, fitting his car with fresh tyres, putting it in full qualifying trim and assigning the Scot a maximum mission. He recorded the fastest time by a full second. It served its purpose, proving the MP4-16 was well on the way to getting back on track, and also boosting morale.

SATURDAY QUALIFYING Modified components were flown in overnight from the UK and the understeer was reduced – as testified by the cars' second and third places. Both drivers were caught speeding in the pitlane, but a $500 fine for Häkkinen's 61.71kph misdemeanour and $1,500 for Coulthard's 66.0kph infraction failed to wipe the broad grins off their faces. Häkkinen dominated the team's qualifying session, taking third. Coulthard was fifth fastest, and said the latest Mercedes was a higher-revving, more powerful qualifying version of the FO 110K V10. DC noted that less than a second separated the first eight cars.

SUNDAY RACE At the start, Häkkinen's car lurched forward, then stopped with its engine stalled. Victim of a clutch malfunction, the Finn was left frantically gesticulating to warn those behind of his predicament. "It was one of the scariest moments of my life," he said, "and I could only hope for the best." All the avoidance manoeuvres mercifully succeeded, though in his scramble to safety Häkkinen forgot to replace his steering wheel, which subsequently earned him a $5,000 fine.

Coulthard inherited third before the first corner and then played a waiting game, watching for rain. He was fighting with a heavy car set up for the wet and 'praying for it'. On lap 25 Schumacher peeled off for the first of his two stops, leaving Coulthard second behind Montoya. On lap 39 Verstappen eliminated Montoya, promoting Coulthard to race leader. His stop was perfect, the McLaren crew servicing his car in 9.8secs – fast enough for him to rejoin ahead of Schumacher. Finally the rain came on lap 45: while Schumacher pitted for intermediates on lap 46 (8secs stop), Coulthard stayed out for another lap before stopping for only 5.9secs. Though now second to Schumacher, the Scot was poised to pounce.

Coulthard decisively out-drove Schumacher on lap 50. As the pair came to lap Marques, Schumacher stayed on the outside while DC dived inside, edging past the Ferrari into the first corner to assume a lead he never lost.

Above left: David Coulthard used a backmarker to pass Michael Schumacher and climb on the top of the podium. Right: Mika Häkkinen's car is pushed aside.

Above: Coulthard shows off the spoils of Brazil. Right: Team-mate Mika Häkkinen was first with the praise.

# Accepting second best

McLaren Mercedes' technical chief Adrian Newey summarised the situation as the weekend started: "We have struggled a bit with the car this year. We haven't quite got on top of the regulations fully. While the car worked well in Brazil, we haven't yet got the consistency out of it that we would like. It's a combination of several factors: partly aerodynamics, partly set-up, partly engine driveability characteristics. It's difficult to break down into one thing. We really haven't had a decent test since the start of the year, so in terms of set-up we're having to experiment at the races, which isn't ideal." Say no more.

**FRIDAY PRACTICE** Häkkinen had MP4-16/03 as his race car and Coulthard had MP4-16/01. The Scot had first call on the T-car, chassis 02. Experiments included minor front aerodynamic modifications and bargeboard rejigs.

Coulthard made several off-course excursions and sat out the last half hour, dropping to 11th; Häkkinen set an uneventful fourth. The crew worked until 4am on Saturday on Coulthard's monocoque, and perfecting major set-up changes that would pay off handsomely in qualifying.

**SATURDAY QUALIFYING** Having chosen the softer Bridgestone compound (as had all the relevant teams save Ferrari), the McLaren drivers made full use of their extra grip. At the end of a thrilling shoot-out, Coulthard emerged as top gun with the 11th pole position of his career. His time of 1m 23.054secs was a new Imola qualifying track record.

Häkkinen's qualifying lap, 1m 23.282secs, would have been good enough for pole on an ordinary day. But this was no ordinary day, as Coulthard said: "I knew I had to push on the last run. But I felt I was already at the limit of the car so it really was a journey into the unknown. In this situation you're either going to look great or you're going to look silly and with each corner I was thinking, 'I'm getting away with it, I'm getting away with it.' It was a great feeling to keep it together."

Häkkinen seemed remarkably comfortable in the unfamiliar role of second fiddle to Coulthard, whose 20 points in the first three races, versus one for Häkkinen, made him the unofficial team leader.

**SUNDAY RACE** Except for the few seconds after the start, Coulthard sat in second all afternoon and was happy to collect the six points. "I moved a little bit just before the start," he said, "and had to stop the car, just when the lights changed. Then I got too much wheelspin and Ralf managed to get past me on the inside. After that it was the most uneventful race I've had this season, but also the most difficult because my tyres were inconsistent and the handling was unpredictable." Coulthard stopped on laps 28 and 45.

Häkkinen's slow getaway determined the outcome of his race. On the first lap he was passed by Montoya and Trulli, the latter's Jordan damaging the McLaren's nose on the way by. Thereafter the front end of his McLaren was loose and he merely had to concentrate on keeping people behind him to protect fourth place. Häkkinen made each of his pitstops a lap later than Coulthard. Newey said: "We have a lot of work to do. BMW Williams is a serious contender for the championship, which is good for F1, but it means dealing with them is going to make our year tougher than ever."

Top: David Coulthard was delighted to take pole, but his lead was short-lived, as Ralf Schumacher squeezed by at the first corner.

Above: Severe disappointment for Häkkinen, who had a quiet race. Left: On the grid, Coulthard focuses on the run to the first corner. Right: Coulthard's joy at pole was not repeated in the race.

# Back to reality

McLaren Mercedes was a prime beneficiary of the return of traction control, having thrown vast software resources at the technology since its reintroduction was announced. It built two new cars for Barcelona with refined aerodynamics.

With three one-two finishes in its three previous Spanish races, McLaren should have been a firm favourite for a reprise. But for two glitches – a pesky clutch exploding and some equally pesky electronics – it would have come to pass. But such is F1.

McLaren's aero problem was forgotten. The deficiencies had been long solved and the wind tunnel engineers were back on top form. The cars were back at the front, if not as dominant as they had been over the last three years. Mika Häkkinen was back on form but now only fractionally faster than his team-mate. The Barcelona speed trap times indicated the new Mercedes engine was as powerful as the BMW that weekend.

FRIDAY PRACTICE With the facility for fully automatic gearchanges in their seven-speed boxes, two new cars arrived, MP4-16/05 for Coulthard, while Häkkinen had MP4-16/04 along with MP4-16/03, formerly his race car. The new cars were quick right out of the box. Coulthard, fastest by half a second, undercut Michael Schumacher's 2000 pole time on only his fourth lap and stayed atop the timesheets with a best of 1m 20.107secs. Häkkinen's sixth best time, a 1m 20.894secs, was the result of automatic gearchange problems which on occasion forced Häkkinen to shift for himself.

SATURDAY QUALIFYING Coulthard's first run of 1m 18.635secs, which gave him temporary pole, proved his best; traffic and mistakes restricted him to third on the grid.

Häkkinen expressed doubts about the superiority of driver aids over the seat-of-the-pants factor that had served him so well. He shut off his traction control to curb understeer, pulled out all the stops for his final run: with the chequered flag having fallen, he flew across the line to stop the clock at 1m 18.286secs, a mere 0.069secs short of Michael Schumacher's pole. It wasn't simply a time and a grid position, it was a message that Häkkinen was back on track.

SUNDAY RACE On the formation lap Coulthard's McLaren stayed where it was thanks to an electronic glitch in his launch control, and the Scot was forced to start from last. Häkkinen slotted into second to begin shadowing Schumacher. Coulthard, in the meantime, was rammed from behind and pushed into the back of Giancarlo Fisichella's Benetton and forced to pit for 15.4secs for a new nose cone. He rejoined last.

Häkkinen held second until lap 23 when Schumacher made his first pitstop. Thus handed the lead, Häkkinen stayed at the front until his own stop on lap 27. Schumacher's second pitstop, on lap 43, was the turning point. With Schumacher's fuel-laden Ferrari now second, Häkkinen was given the 'Push' message, and duly reeled off a succession of seven very quick laps that built up a cushion. On lap 50, and in a total time of 30.433secs (versus the 31.194secs it took Schumacher to get in and out of the pits), the McLaren pit crew got Häkkinen back out in front of Schumacher, who was struggling with his car.

Häkkinen was in complete command of the race and started the last lap with a 40-second lead when his McLaren's clutch exploded. A hydraulic leak triggered the problem; it coasting around a few corners, and stopped.

He finally rode back to the pits on the sidepod of Coulthard's car. The Scot had clawed his way back from 22nd to claim his fifth points-scoring finish in as many races. On lap 60 Coulthard had overtaken Heidfeld's Sauber for sixth, which five laps later became fifth, following the expiration of his team-mate. A shocked Häkkinen took it all very well and his McLaren Mercedes was classified ninth. He said: "It's difficult to describe how I feel and I don't think the outcome will sink in until later."

After the race, Coulthard had a brief but entertaining slanging-match with team boss Ron Dennis on live television, with each accusing the other of 'brain fade'. It was an extraordinary un-McLaren-like show of disunity and reflected some of the behind-the-scenes machinations currently going on at McLaren. "We have to take responsibility for our actions," Dennis said. "David's problem was that he didn't perform properly. He was a bit concerned about running into Schumacher ahead of him on the grid and didn't go through the launch sequence correctly."

A candid Coulthard said: "At the first corner, I was so pissed off I wanted to throw the car in the gravel and go home. I was beside myself with frustration. I did everything as I had in practice. At the start the theory is the engine can't stall. Was it my mistake? No. Was it a systems mistake? Yes." Subsequently Dennis amended his comments, although he stopped well short of apologising.

Above: Häkkinen out-raced Schumacher. Right: Newey and McLaren had a plan to beat Ferrari. Below: Coulthard was forced to start from the back, was delayed by an accident but still finished fifth. Bottom: Hydraulic fluid fire confirmed the end of Häkkinen's race.

# Championship comes alive

Team leader Ron Dennis did some fence-mending with David Coulthard, apologising again for wrongly accusing him of stalling at the start in Spain. He reassured the Scot that he would have the team's full support in McLaren's chase for the championship. Dennis then went public to spell out just why Coulthard had become McLaren's main man. According to Dennis, Coulthard was now aggressively determined to fight everyone and take no prisoners en route to showing the world he's a winner. "I will cheer if David wins the world championship, as I would for Mika," said Dennis.

**Below left: Hard work by David Coulthard and McLaren on race day rescued them from a disastrous qualifying session, which had left them seventh and eighth on the grid, and resulted in victory for the Scot.**

FRIDAY PRACTICE The MP4-16 chassis were allocated 03 (the spare) and 04 for Häkkinen and 05 for Coulthard. Both complained of a loose front end on the slippery track, but otherwise trouble-free runs left them fastest in opening practice. Coulthard was the quicker, while Häkkinen summoned up a surge of adrenaline to subdue a heavy dose of flu and set a time only 0.027secs slower.

SATURDAY QUALIFYING Coulthard maintained the McLaren momentum during practice while Häkkinen, split by the Ferraris, was fourth fastest. But in qualifying the team went backwards, with Coulthard's best of 1m 10.331secs good enough for only seventh on the grid. Häkkinen was eighth, 0.780secs away from Michael Schumacher's pole, but McLaren was miles from where it should have been.

A post-mortem held by the baffled engineers and bothered drivers revealed what had gone wrong. During practice, there was lots of time to dial out the oversteer. But McLaren's decision to keep its cars garaged until the last 25 minutes of qualifying did not leave time to find the right chassis balance. A strong headwind complicated the delicate business of adjusting the wings and the dreaded oversteer prevailed. The debriefing continued late into the night as heads were scratched, data pored over and calculations made to arrive at a race strategy to salvage a respectable result from this setback.

SUNDAY RACE Both cars were back in front in the warm-up, using the set-up that had worked well in practice. Häkkinen also did some laps in the T-car – and would later discover that it might have been a better choice than his race car.

When the race started, Häkkinen went nowhere. The field circulated behind the safety car for three laps as the Finn's launch control-free McLaren, and three other cars that had suffered similar problems, were removed. Coulthard was able to conserve fuel that would be put to excellent use in his late-race refuelling strategy. When action resumed he played a waiting game in fifth. The coming together between Montoya and Schumacher served only to help the Scot get to the head of the field.

The rest of the race unfolded perfectly for Coulthard: he saved fuel, short-shifted and waited to pounce. When the Ferrari stopped, Schumacher on lap 46 (for 8.7secs) and Barrichello a lap later (9.2secs), Coulthard sped up, setting the fastest lap of the race on lap 48 and building a cushion to protect his lead when he pitted. This came on lap 50: with the McLaren pit crew fuelling and re-tyring his car in a scant 8.0secs, DC came out ahead of Barrichello. Game, set and match to McLaren.

While Ferrari's 'arranged' finish gave Schumacher two extra points, DC showed he had the mettle to make a season-long assault on the driving title. "A sensational, disciplined and aggressive drive from David was a vital ingredient in the outcome," enthused Dennis, who was doubly pleased as McLaren had again outwitted Ferrari.

"It was great," said Coulthard with relish. "That's what Grand Prix racing should be like. I had a great view of what was happening in front and I thought this must make good TV. There's nothing better for a driver than to feel like you're battling in close quarters with your competitors. It's much better than just running around on an empty track, and it's even better if you're fortunate enough to win."

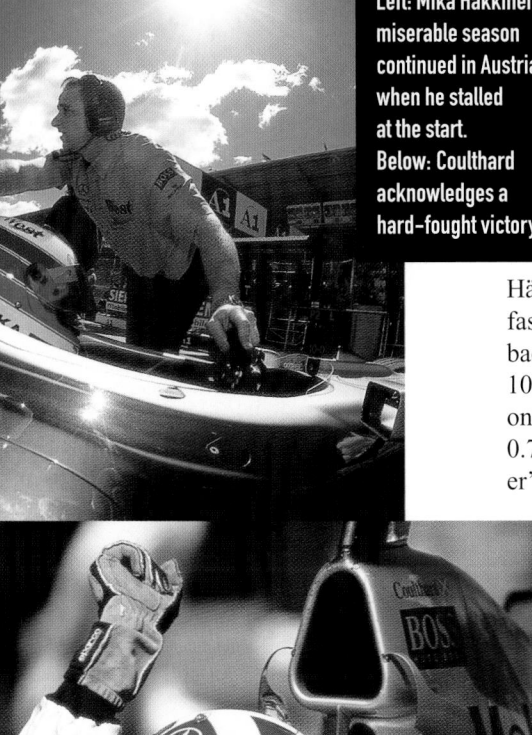

**Left: Mika Häkkinen's miserable season continued in Austria when he stalled at the start. Below: Coulthard acknowledges a hard-fought victory.**

# Problems again

Above and below right: After taking a superb pole, David Coulthard spent much of the race stuck behind Enrique Bernoldi's Arrows. His late pitstop gave Coulthard a clear track and points.

I n Monaco, qualifying was a triumph but the race was a disaster. Of the team's six starts in the three races since electronic driving aids became legal again, only one had been glitch-free. After seven races, McLaren Mercedes thus had a 32-point deficit to Ferrari in the constructors' championship.

THURSDAY PRACTICE Four McLaren MP4-16s, all in high-downforce trim and sporting subtle aerodynamic refinements made for Monaco, lined up – 16/04 for Häkkinen and 16/05 for Coulthard, with T-cars 16/03 and 16/01 respectively. Coulthard had a confrontation with the wall at Tabac and was sixth fastest; Häkkinen twice brushed the barriers but was still quickest of the day.

Technical director Adrian Newey said the extra day to work on the cars had upped the anxiety factor. "The difference here is that we have one-and-a-half days to worry about where we stand, instead of half a day."

Although both cars performed perfectly in practice, some team members still feared a reoccurrence of the dreaded launch control glitches. Not so Ron Dennis. The team principal asserted: "The nature of the problem, which I would rather not share with you, does not create any difficulties for using it here."

SATURDAY QUALIFYING Coulthard confessed that his confidence had taken a knock along with his car on Thursday. But any doubts were dispelled on his final run that deposed Monaco master Michael Schumacher from pole. He clocked a sensational time eight-10ths of a second faster than anyone had ever lapped Monaco before. The key was an inspired charge through the final sector with scrubbed Bridgestones on the front and new tyres on the rear to combat understeer. Coulthard, battling a chest infection, said: "It has to be the most satisfying pole of my career. Getting pole at Monaco is great on your CV. I've managed to keep the momentum going."

Häkkinen chose new tyres all around, which left him with understeer and restricted him to third position on the grid.

SUNDAY RACE As the field set off on the formation lap, Coulthard was left pounding his steering wheel in frustration at his stalled Mercedes engine. Schumacher assumed the vacated pole and Häkkinen slotted into second. The Scot started last and, in a single moment, lost a race he probably would have won. Häkkinen's comfortable hold on second began to loosen on lap 12 when he reported his car pulling alarmingly to the right. A quick pitstop on lap 14 failed to pinpoint the source (a suspension-related problem) and he returned to the track with the same problem, before retiring on lap 16.

Coulthard was stuck behind Bernoldi's Arrows, a humiliating position which continued until lap 43 when Bernoldi pitted. Then in 12th place, his way now clear, Coulthard reeled off a succession of fastest laps nearly three seconds quicker than Bernoldi was lapping. His patience, and the fastest turnaround time of the day by his pit crew, yielded fifth place.

After the race, Ron Dennis admonished Bernoldi for deliberately holding up his driver to glorify himself – and get more TV exposure for Arrows. Arrows team principal Tom Walkinshaw accused Dennis of unseemly behaviour in frightening his driver and suggested

Below: Mika Häkkinen watches forlornly as his McLaren is pushed away after a few laps.

Coulthard was too timid to overtake. Coulthard responded: "Two years ago I would probably have put him very deep into the harbour, but I'm a bit older and wiser now. I was afraid that if I took a dive he might cut across me and we would both end up in the barriers, so I had to be very patient."

That night, Coulthard forsook the invitation to attend Prince Rainier's traditional party and went to bed early instead.

Above: Mika Häkkinen celebrates his return to the podium with a hard-fought third from eighth on the grid. But his race was not smooth. A severe vibration following his sole pitstop hampered progress.

Above: Coulthard's unhappy race ended in the pits after a major Mercedes engine failure. Left: Both Mercedes' Norbert Haug and McLaren had other things on their minds. Below: David Coulthard's race handling was badly affected by the absence of a crucial nut.

FI TV IMAGES

## CANADIAN GRAND PRIX MONTREAL
# Down and depressed

Adrian Newey, McLaren said, was not in Canada because it had previously been arranged he would stay away to concentrate on development programmes. David Coulthard said he doubted the tug-of-war between McLaren and Jaguar for Newey's affections would adversely affect McLaren in Montreal, although he admitted he would find entertainment value in it: "I'm going to sit back and enjoy the soap opera, and we'll see what the outcome is."

At the end of the weekend Coulthard would find himself a reluctant star in what was indeed something of a soap opera, created not by the media but by his own team. His task was to deliver a performance that would keep him within shouting distance of Michael Schumacher in the championship. The Scot proved himself up to the task, but his team wasn't.

Häkkinen needed to salvage something from a dismal first half of the season in which he had scored a mere four points. Could the Finn fly again? McLaren had huge problems but Ron Dennis was predicted to pull them back on course. Häkkinen's podium was a happier end to a troubled fortnight.

FRIDAY PRACTICE With their cars sporting bigger brake ducts and revised rear wings to cope with the circuit's heavy braking and low downforce characteristics, the drivers set the fastest practice times. But both Häkkinen and Coulthard also sent their respective MP4-16/05 and MP4-16/06 machines skittering through gravel traps. There was no damage, and no doubting their resolve.

Both drivers threw their cars around with gusto, pressing home the advantage of what appeared wonderfully controlled traction. In and out of each corner, once the boom, blast, bang and crash of engine management systems controlling wheelspin was finished, the hullabaloo was succeeded by the shriek, wail, howl and scream of the Mercedes motors.

Häkkinen and Coulthard were on a mission, and in going for broke became the only drivers to break the previous lap record of 1m 18.095secs, set by Ferrari's Michael Schumacher in the 1997 season.

SATURDAY QUALIFYING Coulthard and Häkkinen were second and third to Michael Schumacher in morning practice, although Häkkinen seemed to struggle keeping up, twice floundering in gravel traps. In qualifying he was similarly ragged and had another off-course excursion. With his car in need of repair, Häkkinen had to commandeer the spare, which was set up for Coulthard's preference for neutral handling, compared to Häkkinen's ideal of a car that can be thrown around. The spare also misfired, so Häkkinen could not better his time.

Coulthard fared rather better, but admitted the MP4-16/06 was capable of doing more: "I under-performed. I didn't get the balance right and explore the limits of the car. We were fortunate to get third at the end, mainly because I happened to be at the head of the traffic queue on the last run. I made mistakes and the session was generally messy."

SUNDAY RACE Häkkinen went off-road yet again in the warm-up, but then stayed on-track and mobile – unlike his team-mate who, through no fault of his own, could do neither.

On the grid, moments before the formation lap, Coulthard found a loose nut in his cockpit that should have been fixed to the front roll bar. He chucked the nut over the pitwall but did not throw a tantrum, as he would have been entitled to do given this potentially dangerous oversight. The team gave him the option of not continuing, but he chose to race, albeit at a reduced pace, with the left front roll bar not attached on the cockpit side, meaning the whole car was askew and handling oddly.

Coulthard pushed as hard as he dared, holding third behind the Schumachers for three-quarters of the race, until his engine began to seriously overheat. His stop cost him two places and $5,000 for speeding in the pitlane. On lap 54, when he was in fourth place, his engine finally exploded in a cloud of smoke, right by the pits entrance.

Coulthard's retirement elevated Häkkinen to third – reward for a strong drive not without problems. The Finn's late-stop strategy had won him places with a lighter car, but on resuming his pace was hampered by an increasingly severe vibration. As he juddered across the finish line, Häkkinen was gripping the wheel so hard he could scarcely acknowledge the team's congratulations on securing his first podium of the season.

McLaren

**139**

# Best of the rest

Slow and steady may win the race in a fairy tale, but not in Formula One. Combining reliability and sufficient pace in the same race had been McLaren Mercedes' principal problem through the season. This time both cars had what it took to go the distance, but not to keep up with Ferrari and BMW Williams.

Considering their fight with ill-handling cars, third and sixth place results for David Coulthard and Mika Häkkinen were just rewards. But McLaren's mechanical shortcomings left it even further behind Ferrari in the constructors' championship and under increasing pressure from a surging BMW Williams team. Most agreed Ron Dennis had been distracted. Three hammer blows had sapped the team: the death of Paul Morgan; the death of Evelyn Dennis, Ron's mother and the team's matriarch; and the Adrian Newey saga, which instead of being put to bed, rumbled on under its own momentum, unfortunately fuelled on occasion by the team boss himself.

FRIDAY PRACTICE Sporting no major technical changes, the cars started the weekend in well-balanced form. Häkkinen's MP4-16/07 (he also had the spare /04) and Coulthard's MP4-16/06 were first and second fastest in opening practice. But it was not a true indicator – the times reflected McLaren Mercedes' experiments with qualifying set-ups, while most people were working on race set-ups.

SATURDAY QUALIFYING With everyone in qualifying trim in morning practice, Häkkinen and Coulthard placed fourth and fifth fastest, which did not bode well for the hour when grid positions would be set. Still, the first half hour of qualifying went Coulthard's way with a best time that gave him temporary pole. But that was only because the Schumachers had not yet started the sibling shoot-out that would send the McLaren men tumbling down the timesheets.

The McLarens looked increasingly desperate as they vainly tried to keep pace with both Schumachers and their respective Ferrari and Williams team-mates. Häkkinen's all-singing, all-dancing, dust-kicking effort was only good enough for sixth. Coulthard's last-gasp, last-lap attempt to improve only got him off the circuit where he slid to a stop on the last corner, leaving him stuck with fifth best time. Both complained of severe handling imbalance on new tyres.

SUNDAY RACE In the warm-up, with cooling ducts opened up for the warmer temperatures, Coulthard secured fifth place, with Häkkinen in eighth. After a problem cropped up with an electronic sensor, Häkkinen switched to the T-car, which he would use for the race. Ron Dennis said he was 'confident about our race pace and our potential strategy'. The strategy was obvious; stop once and hope for the best. As for the pace, McLaren was off it and that was that.

Coulthard and Häkkinen made good starts, overtaking Barrichello's faltering Ferrari and running fourth and fifth for the first third of the race. But both full-laden McLarens suffered ever more oversteer, due to rapidly wearing rear tyres caused by the handling imbalance. Häkkinen was further hampered by flat-spotting his right front tyre, which caused a severe vibration until the offending rubber was replaced in his pitstop on lap 33, for 36.581secs. Thereafter Häkkinen sped up, though only in relative terms – his quickest lap (65) was nearly a second slower than Montoya's fastest race lap. Coulthard, who pitted for 34.890secs on lap 38, also went faster thereafter, though his best lap (63) was still half a second down on the frontrunners.

After the race Coulthard conceded that half a second was about how far McLaren was adrift in this race. He also admitted his podium visit was a result of Ralf Schumacher's 10-second penalty: without it, Coulthard would have been fourth. Together with Mika Häkkinen's sixth, this is about what the team was worth over the weekend.

**Above and right: Lack of technical progress left McLaren struggling. Four points for third weren't enough to make David Coulthard smile, as his McLaren was worryingly off the winner's pace.**

**Right and below: Mika Häkkinen had to make do with sixth after he was unable to pass the Ferrari of Rubens Barrichello. It was another sparkle-free weekend for the Finn, amid rumours he would retire at the end of the season.**

FRENCH GRAND PRIX MAGNY-COURS

# Much head-scratching

F ollowing the previous weekend's mysterious performance drop-off at the Nürburgring, there had been much high-level head-scratching in the search for a solution. Happily the detective work was productive, and in France the team was closer to the pace it required to remain a serious championship contender.

But it all went wrong on race day when yet another mechanical failure kept Mika Häkkinen's car off the starting grid, while an error by David Coulthard prevented the other McLaren from collecting the points it was capable of.

"At times like this it is important to remember that through thick and thin we are a team and we all make mistakes," said team principal Ron Dennis in a statement no doubt intended to serve the dual purposes of comforting his embattled and embarrassed personnel while also reassuring a bewildered public that wondered where in the world McLaren was going.

FRIDAY PRACTICE The three cars – chassis 07 for Häkkinen and 06 (plus 04) for Coulthard – had only minor aerodynamic changes from the Nürburgring. While Häkkinen was a steady fourth best in practice, his teammate featured more prominently in the day's proceedings. Fastest in practice, Coulthard was also fastest in the pitlane where he was nabbed for speeding and forced by the FIA to part with $1,750.

Officially, the team declared the Friday session 'productive', run mostly in race trim. However, unlike Sunday when the team would have to race with what it started with, the opening practice session featured constant tinkering with chassis balance to regain the handling ground lost at the Nürburgring.

SATURDAY QUALIFYING In morning practice Coulthard and Häkkinen were third and fourth fastest, which is exactly where they stood again at the end of qualifying – on 1m 13.186secs and 1m 13.268 respectively – although they both gave their all. Other than a slight engine vibration that didn't interfere with his performance, the ever-optimistic Häkkinen said his car felt fine on an all-out lap and that it would surely maintain such form for 72 laps around Magny-Cours on Sunday.

Coulthard looked spectacular on a couple of his runs and said he might have been even faster had he not been waylaid by gravel strewn in his path, hence the sideways moments. Given that his car was potentially quicker than his main rivals', that the margin to the front row was closer than it was at the Nürburgring and that McLaren had recently raced better than it had qualified, DC concluded the team could only be encouraged.

SUNDAY RACE Häkkinen was quickest in warm-up – albeit only one-1000th of a second ahead of Michael Schumacher – and claimed that a quick spin at the end of the session was no cause for alarm. Coulthard was fourth, having had to switch briefly to the spare when his race car developed a power-steering problem. That was soon rectified – but there was a terminal problem waiting to afflict Häkkinen.

"It's pretty hard to race when your engine won't start," Mika quipped, trying to be lighthearted about a predicament that left him in shocked disbelief. His car had stalled on the grid again as the field took off on the formation lap. The McLaren men worked frantically to sort out what proved to be an irreparable problem caused by the faulty assembly of its gearbox, but Häkkinen's MP4-16/07 was *hors de combat* before the French Grand Prix began.

From the start Coulthard gamely set out as the team's sole representative, holding third behind the Schumachers and leading a lap when they pitted, then making a routine pit-stop of his own on lap 26. But he started racing again too soon, switching off his speed limiter a fraction before he left the 50mph zone, and earned his second penalty of the weekend. He served his 10-second sentence, rejoining in fifth. After that he raced hard, powered by frustration at his own mistake. Promoted to fourth when Montoya dropped out, he made his third pitstop a lap later and then took firm aim at the final podium place.

In his spirited pursuit of Rubens Barrichello's third place, Coulthard set the fastest lap of the race, a 1m 16.088secs. But it was not enough and he was only able to collect three points for himself and the team.

Above and left: The French Grand Prix looked like a return to form for McLaren, but David Coulthard's race was destroyed by a stop-go penalty. Fastest race lap demonstrated the team's potential. Below: Coulthard acknowledges the assistance as Panis keeps out of the way while being lapped.

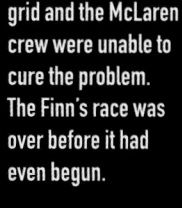

Left and below: Mika Häkkinen's car failed to start on the dummy grid and the McLaren crew were unable to cure the problem. The Finn's race was over before it had even begun.

141

# Winning the battle of Britain

Ron Dennis had cause to celebrate at last after the blackest two months of his F1 career. Mika Häkkinen's commanding victory was momentous – his first since August 2000 in Belgium, and a fillip for the flagging Finn. Häkkinen was emphatically back on track.

The team's 133rd win in its 520th Grand Prix was also a milestone for McLaren and it ended a serious slump that had prompted some observers to write the team off for 2001. While this view was short-sighted at the time, and certainly not shared by chief rivals Ferrari and BMW Williams, a win was sorely needed to restore respectability.

David Coulthard's disastrous race, however, left his championship chances remote, while an on-form Häkkinen looked as if at least another win in the season was just a matter of course.

FRIDAY PRACTICE The team made small aerodynamic alterations and added new front brake ducts to MP14-16/07 for Coulthard, 06 for Häkkinen and 05 the spare. All the cars had revised V10 FO 110K units fresh from Ilmor Engineering.

Again the team looked strong in practice, with the McLaren drivers comfortably quickest and pleased with their well balanced set-ups. But the prevailing mood was one of only cautious optimism: being fast on Friday has often been the highlight of the team's race weekends.

SATURDAY QUALIFYING After taking third and fourth in practice, Häkkinen and Coulthard praised cars that handled wet and drying conditions with aplomb. By the end of qualifying only Michael Schumacher stood between the team and perfection, with Häkkinen's best lap of 1m 20.529secs leaving him a mere 0.083secs short of his first pole of 2001. Coulthard was third with a 1m 20.927secs, saying time had run out before he found optimum balance. The Finn felt a slow Benetton on his last run might have cost him pole.

Häkkinen looked and sounded like the Flying Finn of old, showing scintillating speed then relating it with relish. "I'm delighted to be back at the front," he said. "What makes it even better is that the car is extremely enjoyable to drive. I was able to drive flat out, the front end worked really well and I could push hard."

SUNDAY RACE Coulthard was quickest in warm-up; Häkkinen was third. "I'm fascinated to see how all this is going to work out," Coulthard said just before what proved to be his shortest afternoon of the season.

At the start, as Häkkinen slotted into second behind Michael Schumacher, David Coulthard and Jarno Trulli carried their dispute for third into the first corner, where the Jordan hit the McLaren in a 'racing incident'; the drivers traded blame. Both spun, Trulli terminally into the gravel, while Coulthard gyrated to the inside of the corner, then rejoined at the back. But on lap three the McLaren's damaged rear suspension gave out, spinning the Scot out of a race he was convinced he could have won.

Meanwhile, Häkkinen was after Schumacher. On lap five, the way he sped by the German at Copse suggested flaws in Ferrari's two-stop strategy. But Häkkinen could also sniff a much-needed victory.

By lap 20 he was leading by over 25 seconds – enough time to pit. He rejoined in second behind Montoya, who then pitted, allowing a resumption of Häkkinen vs Schumacher. By his second stop, Häkkinen had built a lead-preserving gap with a succession of fastest race laps. The best, on lap 34, was 1m 23.045secs, a full 1.430secs faster than the 1997 record set by Schumacher's Ferrari.

As he took the flag, Mika swerved over to the pit-wall to acknowledge the victory salutes from the ecstatic McLaren Mercedes personnel.

Left: Mika Häkkinen and Adrian Newey produced a terrific result. Above: Michael Schumacher had no answer to the Finn. Right: The victory spoils were particularly sweet.

Above: An excellent pitstop completed Häkkinen's day. Below: Coulthard was quick but his race was very short. Left: McLaren's team co-ordinator Jo Ramirez and winner Häkkinen celebrate.

Left: Coulthard strongly resisted Barrichello's attacks in the less fuel-laden Ferrari. His efforts were in vain with a sudden engine failure after his pitstop. A lot of effort for little reward.

Left: Although unable to match the Williams on their Michelins, Häkkinen showed clear superiority over Schumacher's Ferrari in qualifying, and with a heavy fuel load was looking good, until robbed by a sudden engine failure.

# Speed, yes – reliability, no

Following the big win in Britain by Mika Häkkinen, the team approached its German weekend with a view to continuing the momentum at the home race of engine supplier Mercedes.

Imagine the embarrassment, then, when both engines failed – on a day when German rival BMW won. With Ferrari also racking up yet more points, McLaren Mercedes left Germany in a statistical squeeze: Ferrari running away at the front, with BMW Williams closing in.

Mercedes motorsport boss Norbert Haug admitted the team's championship chances were now minimal, while team principal Ron Dennis called on the team to regroup, focus on its problems and start fighting back.

FRIDAY PRACTICE The cars had only minor chassis changes, in the form of a few low-downforce aero components that had worked well in testing at Monza, where Coulthard was laid low by a food allergy problem.

In opening practice Coulthard was seventh quickest in chassis MP4-16/06, with the spare 04 to fall back on. He set a time of 1m 42.304secs while working methodically to dial out the oversteer that particularly manifested itself during the twisty stadium section of the track.

Mika Häkkinen, third fastest in opening practice with his 07 car on 1m 41.949secs, said that moving this quickly on a Friday while running with a heavy fuel load and testing the race set-up bode well for the rest of the weekend.

SATURDAY QUALIFYING In the first timed session of the day Häkkinen was caught at 40.33mph in the pitlane, for which he was fined $1,250. In the second session the timing devices calculated that the Finn averaged 152.56mph on a best lap, putting him fourth fastest on the timesheets. In that same session Coulthard was caught out by the contrary rear end of his car, which fought off his efforts to control a mid-corner twitch and sent the Scot spinning into a gravel trap at the Sachs-Kurve after only 14 laps.

Forbidden by the rules to use the spare until qualifying, the stranded Scot watched his best time being pushed down the order, where it ended up ninth overall.

His qualifying progress was also hindered by persistent oversteer, and though qualifying fifth with a time of 1m 39.574secs seemed respectable, it came at a cost. The loose rear end caused his back tyres to blister to such an extent that he abandoned a final run to conserve his fourth set for the race. He said only a miracle could keep his championship chances alive.

Häkkinen, meanwhile, was delighted with a best time of 1m 38.811secs that put him third on the grid. Like Coulthard he only used three sets of tyres, though unlike his team-mate he was happy with ever-improving handling. The fastest of the Bridgestone-shod runners, Häkkinen was also clocked by the speedtraps at 226.3mph, the fastest by far on the straight.

SUNDAY RACE Coulthard was third fastest in the warm-up, behind the Williams duo. Häkkinen was sixth, behind the Ferraris, so McLaren seemed well-placed to salvage something from Williams' leftovers.

Both drivers got away reasonably on the restart; on the first lap, though, Häkkinen was overtaken by Michael Schumacher and Coulthard by Barrichello. A lap later Barrichello took Häkkinen, yet there was no alarm because the cars – laden with fuel for a one-stop strategy – were running like clockwork. Suddenly, on lap 13, Häkkinen, who was still running in fifth, felt a strong vibration at his backside, saw smoke in his mirrors, heard an ominous silence and pulled off the track.

Meanwhile, Coulthard was in a tussle with Barrichello. On lap 16, having made the first of his two stops, Barrichello began bothering Coulthard with the intention of relieving him of fourth place. Coulthard mounted a stern defence but on lap 19 their wheel-to-wheel test of wills was finally resolved in favour of Barrichello's lighter Ferrari.

Coulthard stayed fifth to lap 27, then went into the pits for his scheduled stop, which was accomplished in a useful 8.6 seconds. He rejoined without losing position – albeit briefly. Moments after exiting the pits he had an identical experience to Häkkinen – the vibration, the smoke and the silence – and he coasted to a halt.

143

# The quest is over

Faced with the harsh reality of its title chances diminished to tiny mathematic possibility, the team's goal this weekend was nevertheless the same as always, according to Ron Dennis. "We are here to win," he said. But as the weekend progressed, and the likelihood of winning became ever more remote, Dennis became more stoical. And by Sunday he had little choice but to acknowledge Ferrari's dominance and congratulate his competitor.

FRIDAY QUALIFYING The trio of MP4-16s was trimmed in high-downforce configuration. Häkkinen had chassis 07 (and the spare 04), with which he clocked the third fastest time of 1m 16.789secs behind the two Ferraris. Coulthard drove 05, though only for nine practice laps before rendering it distinctly second-hand in a contretemps with a kerb that caused the session to be red-flagged. He was classified 10th on 1m 18.182secs. Meanwhile the team built up a new monocoque, designated 06, for him to use for the rest of the weekend while 05 was repaired to serve as a back-up.

SATURDAY PRACTICE Mika Häkkinen was fifth in the morning, while Coulthard got himself truly hooked up with his cobbled car to set the fastest time of all. His pace rose in qualifying, where his best lap of 1m 14.860secs was second only to championship rival Schumacher. Häkkinen was sixth with 1m 15.411secs, a tardy time he blamed on a serious lack of front end grip that left him with little hope of repeating last year's win.

As for the race, Coulthard thought his main chance lay in starting better than pole-sitter Schumacher, though with human reflexes now replaced by launch control systems a Ferrari computer glitch would have helped.

SUNDAY RACE Coulthard warmed up by setting the quickest time. Häkkinen was fifth fastest after changing his race car's spring rates in pursuit of improved handling.

Coulthard's launch control system did its best to cope with the sand and grit, but it wasn't enough and by the first corner he was third, behind Schumacher and Barrichello. In effect, the race was over. Schumacher emphatically drove home his advantage at the front. The Coulthard versus Barrichello contest to be best of the rest was more equal, though it was eventually resolved in the pits.

Coulthard, on a two-stop strategy, stayed close to Barrichello until the Ferrari pulled into the pits on lap 31; the McLaren came through and usurped second, albeit well behind Schumacher. Coulthard pitted a lap later, rejoining the circuit just ahead of the second Ferrari. He stayed there until the second round of stops, which ended with their positions reversed.

Stopping on lap 54, again a lap later than Barrichello, Coulthard was delayed when the fuel nozzle stuck momentarily. His car was stationary for just 9.9 seconds, only 1.4 seconds longer than Barrichello's, but it was enough for the Ferrari to reclaim second position, where it stayed to the finish.

With Coulthard stuck firmly in third, McLaren tried to improve Häkkinen's lot with a late-race switch in strategy that forced the Finn to make an unscheduled pit stop, in addition to those he made on laps 38 and 56. Having been held back in sixth place for the first 29 laps by Trulli's hopelessly slow Jordan, Häkkinen was finally able to overtake it during the first round of pit stops, by which time he was half-a-minute behind Ralf Schumacher in fourth place. In his spirited pursuit of this objective Häkkinen notched up the fastest lap of the race (1m 16.723secs on lap 51) but the team decided he was in need some extra help – a lighter fuel load which he received on his second stop. In fact, the calculations proved deficient: he had to come in again on lap 71 for a splash and go, though he still succeeded in holding onto his fifth place.

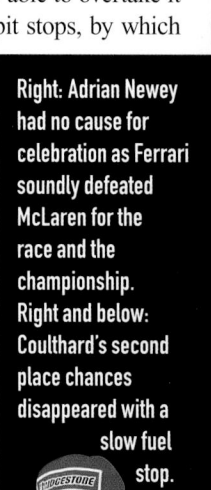

Right: McLaren's men get to pass Ferrari as David Coulthard's car is retrieved from the parc fermé after the race. Below right: Mika Häkkinen's race was destroyed by a very slow Jordan, which held the Finn up for many laps. Once clear, he set very quick times to finish fifth.

Right: Adrian Newey had no cause for celebration as Ferrari soundly defeated McLaren for the race and the championship. Right and below: Coulthard's second place chances disappeared with a slow fuel stop.

**Above and left:** After his crash on Friday, David Coulthard toiled after the restart and made amends for his indiscretion with a strong drive for second, once he had put paid to Fisichella's on-form Benetton Renault (below).

**Below and left:** Mika Häkkinen could not reproduce his 2000 Spa form and was forced to settle for fourth after a poor restart. It was a race McLaren will prefer to forget after a strategic disaster in qualifying that left them seventh and ninth on the grid.

## BELGIAN GRAND PRIX SPA-FRANCORCHAMPS

# Second tasted good

Years ago, when Formula One was less competitive, Ron Dennis made a statement that has dogged him ever since: second is just first of the losers. Nowadays second is a good result in F1. But instead of changing tack and welcoming any podium place, Dennis insisted seconds and thirds were useless to McLaren.

Dennis said the second places still up for grabs were irrelevant – McLaren's philosophy left no room for being second best. "We are not driving the team on the basis of finishing second in either championship," he said.

Later, Dennis tailored his philosophy to results: "In the circumstances our second and fourth places at least achieve consolidation in our championship positions. But as always we are here to win, so that will be our focus between now and Monza."

**FRIDAY PRACTICE** The team brought four cars, unchanged save for an aerodynamic package suitable for Spa. MP4-16/07 was for Häkkinen, while Coulthard had MP4-16/06, the chassis fixed up for him to race in Hungary after he had wrecked his regular car, MP4-16/05. Insurance was provided by the fourth chassis, Coulthard's rebuilt 05.

On his first flying lap, six minutes into the opening session, Coulthard crashed heavily, damaging the suspension, barge boards and bodywork. Blaming too much oversteer, he slid wide, dropped a wheel over a kerb and was thrown across the track into the barriers.

The damaged car was returned to the McLaren garage where Coulthard's crew quickly began to effect repairs. Frustratingly, their labours ended as the second session closed, leaving Coulthard with the slowest time of the day and with only three laps to his credit. In terms of mastering Spa he was in a deep hole, especially in the wet.

Häkkinen started the first session with a touch of understeer, but still set the fifth fastest time. When the second session was at its wettest and Spa at its worst, the Finn made short work of the treacherous track and set the fastest time.

**SATURDAY QUALIFYING** In the morning Häkkinen and Coulthard placed third and fourth fastest, the latter using his team-mate's data as a foundation. At this point both drivers looked capable of turning their practice slots into similar places in qualifying, though Häkkinen's chances of reprising last year's pole position looked remote.

Unfortunately, McLaren screwed up its chances of scooping the lottery that qualifying turned out to be. Häkkinen tried the full spectrum of tyres, starting on wets, then switching to intermediates and then dries for his final run. But the timing of the tyre changes – called by the team – was out of sync with the improving track conditions.

Coulthard went all the way on intermediates: his pleas to change to dries near the end were refused – no time, said the team. Häkkinen's best lap of 1m 57.043secs left him seventh on the grid and Coulthard's 1m 58.008secs set him back to ninth.

"The decisions were made with all the relevant factors being taken into consideration," was Ron Dennis's explanation. "In the circumstances we were wrong, but as always there is the race tomorrow."

**SUNDAY RACE** After having progressed to fourth and fifth in the ill-fated first race, after the restart Coulthard and Häkkinen immediately engaged in close-quarters combat – with each other. At the exit of La Source, Häkkinen edged ahead but by the time they got to Les Combes Coulthard had powered past his team-mate to regain fourth. From there he resolutely set about pursuing a podium position.

Given the surprising pace of Fisichella, Coulthard resigned himself to tucking in behind the Benetton, poised to overtake during one of the two pit stops. But Coulthard's first stop on lap 10 failed to accomplish the desired result, nor – when a back-marker impeded his progress on his in-lap – did his second on lap 24.

Overtaking was made more difficult by Fisichella's engine losing oil. "That was a bit of a distraction," Coulthard admitted. "I soon ran out of tear-off strips and had to wipe the visor with my glove on the straights. But I held on, stayed close, and when we caught up with a back-marker on lap 27 it upset Fisichella's rhythm and I was finally able to pass him at Eau Rouge."

In comparison to Coulthard's hard-earned second place, his team-mate had an uneventful run to fourth, behind Fisichella.

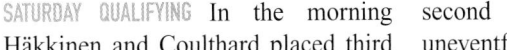

McLaren

# Simply off the pace

With cars demonstrably well off the pace compared to BMW Williams and Ferrari, McLaren Mercedes was only ever going to be fighting for third, as long as the cars remained reliable – which they didn't.

The Saturday announcement of its 2002 driver line-up was more newsworthy than McLaren's race. David Coulthard was confirmed as new team leader which, given Mika Häkkinen's faltering form, he had in fact been all this season.

Coulthard's upwardly mobile progress, negated by a drop-off in McLaren's competitiveness, continued at Monza. Early in the race his engine blew to smithereens, creating a huge smokescreen behind which the team was unable to hide.

"We definitely have to raise our game in terms of speed and reliability," said Mercedes motorsport boss Norbert Haug.

FRIDAY PRACTICE After a four-day test at Valencia the team brought four MP4-16s to Monza. Friday was also treated as a major test session, with chassis featuring low-downforce aerodynamic set-ups.

Häkkinen in chassis 07 and Coulthard in 06 (with first claim on the T-car 05) between them logged 76 trouble-free laps, amassing much data in search of a basic balance. They also did brake wear tests and evaluated the two Bridgestone tyre compounds, which were very close in both durability and grip levels. Häkkinen complained of excessive bouncing on his second set of tyres while Coulthard lost time in traffic going for a quick lap, but both were satisfied with their respective sixth and seventh fastest times, Häkkinen on 1m 25.343secs and Coulthard with a 1m 25.544secs.

SATURDAY QUALIFYING After being fifth and eighth in practice, both drivers worked hard to achieve their sixth and seventh grid positions, the team's third worst qualifying result of the season. The problem, 'a handling imbalance', manifested itself in either oversteer or understeer in the corners, sometimes both. Coulthard said after setting his 1m 23.148secs time that this unpredictability meant that corners could not be attacked wholeheartedly.

Häkkinen's best time of 1m 23.394secs was followed by a heavy accident at the second Lesmo corner, when his car crashed into a steel barrier and gyrated to a halt, by then missing its left front corner.

"I'm fine, but a bit shaken," Häkkinen said. "On my last timed lap I ran wide and the rear tyre went onto the gravel. The car went sideways and I thought if I lifted it would be worse, so I kept my foot down but the car snapped away and I went into the barrier." His car's tub was damaged beyond immediate repair, and rebuilding Häkkinen's car around a replacement monocoque, chassis 04, went on late into the night.

SUNDAY RACE Coulthard was second fastest in the warm-up while Häkkinen was ninth. Häkkinen experienced a setback at the race start when the Jenson Button versus Jarno Trulli *contretemps* forced him into straight-lining the chicane, coming out the other side in 13th place.

"This was extremely disappointing as the drivers had discussed that we should be particularly careful at the start because the chicane is so tight," said Häkkinen later.

The infamous chicane also became the scene of his demise – on lap 19. After fighting his way back to ninth, delayed for several laps by Bernoldi's hard-to-overtake Arrows, Häkkinen began to have a drivetrain problem. As he entered the chicane his car stuck in fifth gear and before he got to the exit there were no gears at all. Häkkinen clambered out of his gearless car and walked back to the pits.

Coulthard's race ended shortly after it started. Having been promoted to fifth by the chicanery that claimed Trulli on lap one, Coulthard hung on to that position – though trailing further and further behind the far faster foursome of Williams and Ferraris – until lap seven, when his engine blew up so spectacularly.

Right and below: Having announced his sabbatical and qualified seventh, Häkkinen's Monza weekend included a large accident on Saturday and retirement from the race with gearbox problems.

Above and right: Both McLaren drivers found the cars difficult to handle with unpredictable balance, and did well to qualify sixth and seventh. David Coulthard tried hard but had little to smile about when his Mercedes engine exploded after only seven race laps.

# Häkkinen's swansong

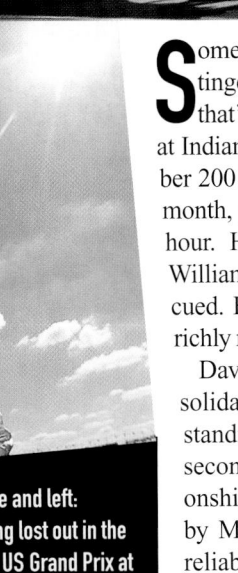

**Above and left:**
**Having lost out in the**
**2000 US Grand Prix at**
**Indianapolis, Mika**
**Häkkinen's luck held**
**for once and his**
**McLaren went like**
**a train to take the**
**2001 race.**
**Left: Häkkinen**
**receives the**
**applause of the US**
**fans before mounting**
**the rostrum.**

**Left: David Coulthard**
**made a late charge**
**after Schumacher**
**was delayed by**
**lapped cars, which**
**lost him momentum.**
**Below: The Scot's**
**determined drive**
**to third strengthened**
**his hold on second**
**in the championship.**

Sometimes victory is pure luck tinged with genuine skill – and that's how it was for Mika Häkkinen at Indianapolis. The last day of September 2001, America's most dreadful ever month, proved to be Häkkinen's finest hour. He was lucky, as both BMW Williams cars retired and Ferrari miscued. But his 20th career victory was richly merited and roundly applauded.

David Coulthard's third place, consolidating second spot in the drivers' standings, enabled the team to clinch second in the constructors' championship behind Ferrari, bested here by McLaren's superior strategy and reliability. Whatever the team principal thinks, second does matter and McLaren was mighty glad to have it.

The day belonged to Häkkinen, in what was surely the penultimate race of his illustrious F1 career. Informed observers believed he would not return from his 2002 sabbatical, making his performance all the more poignant. "It was a fantastic day," he said. "I can tell you I had a big smile on my face over the last few laps. This is very special indeed – one of my most important victories."

FRIDAY PRACTICE McLaren brought four cars (unchanged from Monza except for aerodynamic tweaks), with Häkkinen and Coulthard respectively allotted MP4-16/04 and MP4-16/06 chassis, the T-car 05 set up for Coulthard and the spare, 07, available for emergencies.

Häkkinen began his 33rd birthday twiddling his thumbs, while the team's mechanics completed an engine swap after a pneumatic valve gear failure halted Häkkinen's car on his installation lap. The McLaren men effected the changeover in only 45 minutes. In the final session Häkkinen extracted the fastest time of the day, a 1m 13.387secs.

Coulthard, complaining of persistent oversteer, was fourth fastest with 1m 13.656secs and in playful mood. He presented his team-mate with a cake complete with lighted candles, and joked that letting Häkkinen be quickest was part of his birthday gift.

SATURDAY QUALIFYING Häkkinen maintained his practice form, setting a time second only to Michael Schumacher. Coulthard was eighth, blaming a continuing oversteer problem.

In qualifying Coulthard's best time of 1m 12.500secs was worthy of only seventh on the grid. Häkkinen was on the front row thanks to an all-out 1m 11.945secs that put him alongside pole-sitter Michael Schumacher. The Flying Finn insisted: "I'm here to win this race. For me this one is as big as Silverstone and Monaco to have on your CV." Häkkinen's boss had no doubts of the source of his favourite driver's renewed motivation: "Mika is very comfortable with the knowledge that he is taking a year off, so he's been driving with that weight off his shoulders. He's really enjoying himself now," said Ron Dennis.

SUNDAY RACE Coulthard was an untroubled second in warm-up and Häkkinen third, despite a session shortened by an abrupt confrontation with the barriers after he out-braked himself at Turn 8, one of the infield kinks. The damage to the right front corner of Häkkinen's car was easily repaired, but an earlier warm-up error was a worse setback.

When the warm-up was stopped to clean up the track after Montoya's engine blew up, Häkkinen failed to see the red light at the pitlane exit and went back out. Despite claiming five other cars had blocked his vision, the race stewards decreed that Häkkinen's fastest qualifying time would be deleted. This meant he would start fourth and left the frustrated Häkkinen 'very pissed off, really upset' and more determined than ever to 'go flat out'. Pivotal to the Finn's chances was McLaren's decision to use the softer Bridgestone compound and make one stop, deciding it was the quicker way to go against Ferrari and Williams.

Both McLaren drivers had straightforward races. Coulthard admitted he didn't pass anybody en route from seventh on the grid to third at the finish. Häkkinen benefited from the self-destruction of the Williams challenge, the demise of Barrichello's Ferrari and Michael Schumacher's harder, and for him, slower tyre compound.

McLaren's reliability and pit work was faultless. Coulthard stopped on lap 43, Häkkinen on lap 46; and when Barrichello dropped out on lap 50, he took command. Michael Schumacher also stopped only once, but it was clearly Häkkinen's day.

# Third best on the day

Unable to match the pace set by Ferrari and Williams, McLaren managed third- and fourth-place finishes, mainly as two of the front-running foursome had problems. The results were probably a fair reflection of McLaren's current position.

Despite finishing second in the constructors' championship, 77 points behind Ferrari, 22 ahead of Williams, the team was only third best at the last event of 2001.

Yet McLaren scored points another way in Japan, thanks to a magnanimous move by the departing Mika Häkkinen. In the final race before his sabbatical, Häkkinen sacrificed third place to David Coulthard, who didn't really need it to secure second place in the drivers' championship.

He said: "I'm happy that David finished on the podium. I wanted to give him something back for the occasions when he has helped me." Coulthard added: "I had no idea he was going to do it and I must thank him for it. There's no doubt I have enjoyed working with him for the past six years and I will miss him next year."

Häkkinen's goodwill – and quite likely farewell – gesture was appreciated by all, especially Coulthard, and the team-mates' warm exchange gave McLaren full marks in the human-interest stakes, if not in the race.

FRIDAY PRACTICE The chassis showed no major specification changes: 04 (and the T-car, 05) was allotted to Häkkinen and 06 to Coulthard, with 07 on stand-by.

Häkkinen, fourth fastest in opening practice with a 1m 36.430secs, said that his car felt well-balanced, inspiring confidence. Coulthard, seventh best with a 1m 36.638secs, had a busier session that centred on his hard-working brakes. In the first instance DC toured down the pitlane with his right front brake assembly in flames, caused by a small piece of tape stuck in the brake-cooling duct which ignited in the 1000°C heat from the brake disc. The conflagration was quickly doused, and DC resumed running, only to fly off into the gravel trap at the first corner: the chastened Scot admitted he had braked too late.

SATURDAY QUALIFYING Coulthard was third and Häkkinen eighth in morning practice, as the team tried to improve front-end grip. That tack continued in qualifying, but even lowering the ride height and modifying the tyre pressures failed to dial out the understeer that Häkkinen said contributed to the 1.178secs that eventually separated him from Michael Schumacher, whose pole lap left all at McLaren shaking their heads in admiring disbelief.

Häkkinen's best lap of 1m 33.662secs put him fifth on the grid, two places ahead of Coulthard, who was 1.432secs slower than the pace-setting Schumacher. Race operations manager Steve Hallam admitted the team wasn't sure why the McLarens weren't further up the grid: "We are disappointed, but the situation tomorrow will depend on how the drivers and cars around us use their tyres. The race will be tough on tyres and we feel we have some scope for improvement."

SUNDAY RACE Coulthard was second and Häkkinen (who also tried the T-car) sixth in warm-up, by which time the team had resigned itself to results mostly dependent on better reliability – the speed to match Ferrari and Williams just wasn't there.

In the race, McLaren mostly played a waiting game – waiting to pounce on Ferrari's and Williams's leftovers. Both drivers had uneventful races. Coulthard later revealed he worked mainly on ways to improve his performance next year at a track where he has never really shone. Häkkinen thought about ways to enhance what was probably his Suzuka swansong.

The team's four pitstops were executed to perfection – Coulthard's on laps 23 and 39, Häkkinen's on laps 24 and 38. The cars ran like clockwork, although the clock – which gave Häkkinen and Coulthard the fifth and sixth fastest race laps – also showed that McLaren was sure to make the podium only if the four frontrunners stumbled. When this happened and two obstacles were removed (Barrichello and Ralf Schumacher), the chief beneficiary was Häkkinen, who had led his team-mate throughout. However, on lap 47, six from the finish, the Finn moved aside to fourth, handing Coulthard his podium on a plate.

Right: David Coulthard secured second in the drivers' championship with third place. Below: Mika Häkkinen let Coulthard through for a podium finish.

Above: Häkkinen drove a strong race which could have seen him on the podium.
Right: Häkkinen leads Schumacher's Ferrari before the Finn's pitstop.

148

WANT TO SEE

HOW WE HELP

COMPANIES

TO SUCCEED?

# IF YOU FOLLOW F1 YOU ALREADY KNOW.

If you've been following the Grand Prix, you'll have seen the successes the BMW WilliamsF1 Team has had this year with our help. We work with the race team at every level, from the design and testing of the car at the factory to the monitoring and maintenance of the car at the track. Millions of F1 enthusiasts worldwide have seen what we can do for the BMW WilliamsF1 Team. Contact us to find out what we could do for you.

INNOVATIVE PRODUCTS,
INTEGRATED INTO SOLUTIONS &
DELIVERED GLOBALLY

to find out more go to compaq.com/IT

COMPAQ
Inspiration Technology

Team Review    Race by Race

# WILLIAMS

## 2001

## Contents

| | | | | | | |
|---|---|---|---|---|---|---|
| Team Review | – | The season | p152 | European Grand Prix | – Nürburgring | p166 |
| Australian Grand Prix | – | Melbourne | p158 | French Grand Prix | – Magny-Cours | p167 |
| Malaysian Grand Prix | – | Sepang | p159 | British Grand Prix | – Silverstone | p168 |
| Brazilian Grand Prix | – | Interlagos | p160 | German Grand Prix | – Hockenheim | p169 |
| San Marino Grand Prix | – | Imola | p161 | Hungarian Grand Prix | – Hungaroring | p170 |
| Spanish Grand Prix | – | Barcelona | p162 | Belgian Grand Prix | – Spa-Francorchamps | p171 |
| Austrian Grand Prix | – | A1 Ring | p163 | Italian Grand Prix | – Monza | p172 |
| Monaco Grand Prix | – | Monte Carlo | p164 | USA Grand Prix | – Indianapolis | p173 |
| Canadian Grand Prix | – | Montreal | p165 | Japanese Grand Prix | – Suzuka | p174 |

**Frank Williams**

Ralf Schumacher

Juan Pablo Montoya

Ralf Schumacher

# BMW.WilliamsF1 Team

# Everything seemed possible

In 2000, after four years in the wilderness, many felt Williams was once again on the verge of great things. The signs were there for all to see – mainly the increasing confidence of Patrick Head, its technical director, who is an exact barometer of the speed of the car. When the car is slow Head is morose, even unpleasant. When the car is fast he is transformed into charm personified, with a cheery word for everyone. At the 2001 BMW Williams launch at

Silverstone, Head could not have been on better form, even strolling up to the media centre to give more impromptu journalists' briefings after the official ones were over.

And so it proved. The team took its first win in three years and then stormed to three more. If the car had not been so pathetically unreliable, and the drivers not got themselves into so many accidents, BMW Williams could have challenged Ferrari for the championship. With luck and reliability akin to Michael Schumacher's, it could have hap-

pened. Threatening McLaren in the constructors' championship was an impressive feat, considering the relatively young nature of the partnerships, human and mechanical, within the team. The technical team gelled with the arrival of Sam Michael. There was already a powerful threesome of Head, Gavin Fisher and Geoff Willis. Michael sealed the team and gave it the strong engineering presence it needed at the track. By mid-season, Head was publicly acknowledging Michael's massive contribution to the turnaround.

The BMW engine proved the class of the field on power. The car-maker pioneered a new breed of throwaway engine, where every part was designed to run a few hundred miles – exactly the requirement to finish a race with little margin. Insiders say BMW gained 80 horsepower between Melbourne and Suzuka, taking engine revs to a maximum 20,000. Towards the end it detuned the engines for reliability after the engine proved to have a glass jaw.

The team's relationship with Michelin can also take some of the credit: as the most competitive team on the French tyre manufacturer's books, it was almost certainly favoured when it came to development work. The team suffered for much of the season from understeer, like the other Michelin-shod teams, as well as the tyres 'going off' midway through their cycle, but the increasing use of

scrubbed tyres and a wider front introduced at Monza proved helpful. In addition, at the beginning of the season Michelin's tyres were extremely temperature sensitive, causing problems on cooler tracks, but the situation improved over the course of the year.

The team's partnership with Michelin was also behind some of the more public disasters. The understeer led the drivers to brake earlier than Bridgestone runners, and this undoubtedly contributed to the lapped Jos Verstappen punting Montoya out of the lead in Brazil, and to his team-mate being rear-ended by Rubens Barrichello in the same race. Schumacher's early braking had already been proffered as a reason for Jacques Villeneuve running into the back of him in the season opener, initiating an accident from which Villeneuve was very lucky to walk away; a marshal was not so lucky. The BMW Williams team turned up in San Marino with a 'Keep Your Distance!' sign on its rear wing, a mark of its growing frustration with rival drivers' braking skills.

The BMW Williams garage was enlivened in 2001 by the appearance of Juan Pablo Montoya, who displaced Jenson Button, farmed out to Benetton Renault. Patrick Head hinted that Ralf Schumacher had had an easy time with rookie Button, and that he could expect to be pushed hard by Montoya. For the first half of the season Schumacher easily saw off Montoya. The second half saw a reversal: Montoya grew dominant as he began to master the art of set-up and qualifying. All in all it was a potent combination of people and machines, which could have cleaned up in slightly different circumstances. As a result lots of money is going on the team at the bookies' for the 2002 championship.

## The BMW Williams FW23 car

THE BMW Williams FW23 chassis was Williams' best for years. But the new regulations contributed to a chronic lack of downforce that could not be dialled out. Maybe the team didn't expect such power from the motor, but the problem dogged the team all season: the unit was quickest almost everywhere through the speed traps, and showed dominant raw pace at fast circuits. But the cars struggled, hopelessly off the pace, on tight tracks such as in Monaco and ▷

Ralf Schumacher

## Technical developments

Hungary. One neat design trick, taking advantage of one of the few loopholes in Formula One's increasingly stringent laws, was the rear diffuser. By opening up the sidewalls of the diffuser and incorporating the vee structure of the component ahead of the axle line, the team effectively lengthened the diffuser and so increased its effectiveness in sucking the car to the track. Other teams noticed this in Spain, and the team was forced by the intervention of Charlie Whiting to close off the gearbox sidewalls. Sam Michael said they were happy to have 'got away with it for so long'.

In all the team built eight chassis in 2001. Montoya used chassis FW23-02 in Melbourne and right through until the Canadian Grand Prix, when he switched to FW23-06. That chassis lasted him until Italy, when he first got his hands on the heavily revised 'B' spec chassis, the FW23-08, which will form the basis of the 2002 car. Montoya then took charge of that car for the remainder of the year. Montoya used the spare car on numerous occasions: he first reverted to FW23-01 when his BMW engine refused to fire at the Malaysian Grand Prix. He had to qualify in the spare car (FW23-01) in Brazil, when he overstretched himself on the first run in qualifying and crashed heavily; luckily it was set up for him, the race being in South America.

Ralf Schumacher started the season with chassis FW23-03, which he used until San Marino when the newer 05 chassis became available to him. This tub served him well until the Belgian Grand Prix, when the German was the first recipient of the new interim 'B' spec chassis that was so new Montoya could not have one too. This was the basis of the 2002 car, and Schumacher made use of its lighter weight and narrower frame for the rest of the year.

BMW WILLIAMS was revising the car all season. In Malaysia it tried exhaust emission just under the top edge of the diffuser, and adopted the Ferrari-style chimneys on top of the car for extra cooling. It also used mini-diffusers around the rear tyre, a modified undertray for Imola and other mods. It also brought in qualifying bodywork.

The downforce problem was so acute that the team wanted to solve it well in advance of 2002. That led to a 'B' spec chassis being introduced from Spa onwards. It allowed the team to run the 2002 chassis at several races before the end-of-season testing ban, and also provided a more useful end-of-season weapon than would have been the case. The chassis was 10kg lighter, with a newer floor, narrower bodywork and smaller radiators. New top-exit exhausts also came in for Indianapolis.

Before Spa, the team resorted to all kinds of winglets and small tricks to generate more downforce, but designers Gavin Fisher and Geoff Willis worked frantically to prepare the 'B' spec car. Tensions were reported between Williams and BMW. The Germans believed their engines were so superior that the team should have been walking the races. The radical chassis work showed Williams' engineering strength in depth, and the remainder of 2001 turned into a dress rehearsal for 2002, a year that really matters for the team.

While the car itself could have been better, the engine was nothing short of phenomenal. Having exceeded all expectations in 2000, Gerhard Berger and Mario Theissen revealed it was prepared to blow up in 2001 in order to push the performance envelope. The engine was smaller, lighter and more powerful than that used in

Dickie Stanford

Sam Michael

Mario Theissen

BMW.WilliamsF1 Team

Patrick Head

Gavin Fisher

2000, and by mid-season it was revving to more than 20,000rpm while Ferrari was stuck on 18,000. The team started with a strong V10 and gained more than 50 extra horses before the Hungarian Grand Prix, such was the quest for power. The team was believed to be much more focused on 2002, and was prepared to take an aggressive and casualty-ridden approach to the 2001 season in order to be ready to fight for the title.

Ferrari's desperate bid for more horsepower in the closing stages of the season revealed its concern about the power of the BMW.

BMW's performance from scratch has been astounding and while motorsport boss Gerhard Berger had played down its prospects, the group had been secretly investing hundreds of millions of dollars to create a state-of-the-art engine facility. BMW is regarded as a small auto maker, but its sales are fast approaching $40 billion a year and its margins are the best in the business.

The power plant may have been fast but it was fragile by design. This led to problems. Engine traumas struck Montoya six times during races in Australia, Austria, France, Germany, Belgium and the United States. Schumacher's driving style was more sympathetic to engines. His engine held together in all of the races apart from the British Grand Prix. The number of failures in races do not tell the whole story, however. Montoya lost numerous V10s on ▷

## WILLIAMS SEASON STATISTICS

### RELIABILITY PERFORMANCE

| Driver | Races | Max laps | Laps completed | Reliability rating |
|---|---|---|---|---|
| Ralf Schumacher | 17 | 1,065 | 806 | 75.7% |
| Juan Pablo Montoya | 17 | 1,065 | 680 | 63.8% |
| Constructor | Races | Max laps | Laps completed | Reliability rating |
| Team | 34 | 2,130 | 1,486 | 69.8% |

Ralf Schumacher

### CHAMPIONSHIP PERFORMANCE

| Driver | 2001 points | 2000 points | 12 month change |
|---|---|---|---|
| Ralf Schumacher | 49 | 24 | +104.2% |
| Juan Pablo Montoya | 31 | - | Did not compete |
| Constructor | 2001 points | 2000 points | 12 month change |
| Team | 80 | 36 | +122.2% |

### CHASSIS LOG

**FW23-01** Spare car at Melbourne, Sepang (raced by Juan Pablo Montoya after 02 failed at the first start), Interlagos (used by Montoya in qualifying), Imola, Barcelona, A1 Ring and Monte Carlo.

**FW23-02** Race car for Montoya at Melbourne, Sepang (not used for the race after it failed on the original grid), Interlagos, Imola, Barcelona, A1 Ring and Monte Carlo. Spare car at Montreal, the Nürburgring, Magny-Cours, Silverstone (used in qualifying by Montoya), Hockenheim, the Hungaroring, Spa-Francorchamps, Monza, Indianapolis and Suzuka.

**FW23-03** Race car for Ralf Schumacher at Melbourne, Sepang, Interlagos and Imola. Spare car at Monte Carlo.

**FW23-05** Race car for Schumacher at Barcelona, A1 Ring, Monte Carlo, Montreal, the Nürburgring, Magny-Cours, Silverstone, Hockenheim and the Hungaroring.

**FW23-06** Race car for Montoya at Montreal, the Nürburgring, Magny-Cours, Silverstone, Hockenheim, the Hungaroring and Spa-Francorchamps.

**FW23-07** 'B' spec chassis. Race car for Schumacher at Spa-Francorchamps, Monza, Indianapolis and Suzuka.

**FW23-08** 'B' spec chassis. Race car for Montoya at Monza, Indianapolis and Suzuka.

Note: The 'B' spec chassis FW23-07 and -08 are sometimes referred to as FR23B-07 and B-08. The team itself does not list them as such.

the Friday and Saturday of race weekends, as did his team-mate, as they went for fast times. This cut short running time and often meant the team and drivers were playing continuous catch-up during race weekends.

Surprisingly, with such a huge budget to play with and BMW's development skills, the return of traction control proved a real problem for the team, although this may have been because it attempted to over-refine the system too early. It paid the price: having blown several engines in testing, the traction control system lay unused at the Spanish Grand Prix. The launch control system was superb, however, and stunning starts by the team drivers in the following races became the norm. And a testament to the engine and package is that, despite not having traction control, Montoya still finished second in Spain. Traction control did make it for the next race in Austria, so the German marque quickly rectified its expensive mistakes.

When on song, though, the BMW engine was unstoppable. The record of the team in the first five races – seven DNFs, three finishes, one win and a second place – said a lot for the temperamental nature yet blinding potential of both car and drivers. The BMW/Williams/Michelin package crushed the opposition in San Marino, Canada, Germany and Italy and also showed the way at Spa, Interlagos and Indianapolis before various problems put them out of contention at those Grands Prix. With reliability will come a return to the very top.

## The drivers

JUAN Pablo Montoya came to F1 with an awesome reputation. He had won the FIA F3000 championship while testing for Williams in 1998, before moving over to the US to win both the CART FedEx championship and the Indianapolis 500.

Ralf Schumacher was the established force and his talent was about to come alight. Neither driver likes the other. Schumacher is a relatively quiet, home-loving fellow with a silently ruthless outlook, while Montoya is a noisy, hard-charging enthusiast whose emotions are on full view all the time. The two were chalk and cheese, but surprisingly managed to tolerate each other all season long. Montoya was out of order on occasion, openly baiting his team-mate, who admirably refused to be drawn.

When he did comment, Schumacher wrote off his new team-mate as overhyped and big-mouthed before the two even tested together. Schumacher claimed his radio was not working at Magny-Cours and Silverstone, when he was asked to move over for his team-mate. Mind games henceforth became part of the scenery at Williams, with Montoya apparently cutting it fine on occasion as he waged the mental war.

The two never socialised together, though they recognised that each pushed the other further than they had thought possible at the start of the year. Ralf Schumacher knew he had a fight on his hands right from the outset. Montoya proved instantly popular with the media, even if his outspoken nature, ability to criticise the team and his speech littered with profanities did not go down well on occasion. The team loves him, and his trip to the fairground with the mechanics at Suzuka was an example of how willing he is to muck in. Ralf seems somewhat distant by comparison, and so faces losing the support of his own team.

At the start of the season Montoya tried a little too hard. He was generally at least 0.3secs a lap off the German in pre-season testing, and admitted he got a little lost trying to make up the deficit. In Australia, one local commentator noted that his style was 'rough as a badger's backside'. It summed him up. There is little doubt he would have won in Brazil, however, had Verstappen not slammed into his car from the back, but when he was not flying he suffered problems. He spun in wet conditions in Malaysia and crashed in Canada and Monaco. A nervous mid-season time attracted some criticism from Patrick Head, but in truth the speed of his team-mate, the failures accruing by the race and the pressure he had put on himself led to a certain note of desperation.

Montoya then took three pole positions in four races, in a scintillating run from Germany to Italy. After a number of calamities, including retiring from a winning position in Germany and losing his pole position to a starter motor problem in Belgium, Montoya finally claimed his first win at Monza – Michael Schumacher's 'home turf'. Once the millstone had been lifted from his neck and Montoya had won his first race, he began to look even more cocky and assured in the paddock. Many expect him to challenge for major honours in 2002, and insiders believe he has already won the intra-team war and rattled Schumacher to the point of no return.

Not content to needle his own team-mate, Montoya also turned his attention to the 'great' Michael Schumacher, Ralf's brother and four-time world champion. The mind games that Montoya uses so often have come out again: in dismissively stating that 'he ain't no Senna', Montoya has launched himself after Michael. He passed him four times, in Brazil, San Marino, Britain and the US. Each time it was an authoritative manoeuvre that Schumacher dared not resist. The two locked wheels the first time; since then Schumacher has given him noticeably more room.

In Austria, Montoya's dedication to taking Schumacher's mantle as the king of F1 went slightly too far. His tyres had clearly gone off and Schumacher was the faster man, when the German pulled out to go past and take the lead, and Montoya drove them both off the circuit. He has fast established himself, though, perhaps thanks to his moves on Schumacher; and the Colombian lists Monza, Indy and Brazil as his highlights of the season. On two of those occasions he did not finish, but he showed the world that he could take on and beat the best. Hungary and Monaco were his low points, as the car simply did not give him a fighting chance. Montoya's inimitable summary of the situation was: "If you start out competitive and something goes wrong, it's easier to accept. If everything starts out shit, turns shit and ends shit, it's tough."

Schumacher took the lion's share of Williams F1's wins, though, and this must count for something within the team. Schumacher suffered significantly fewer failures than Montoya, leading to idle speculation by the German that his counterpart was placing too much stress on the engine – something swiftly stamped on by Patrick Head.

Schumacher made his own share of careless errors too. He spun in Brazil, after he had soldiered on after being struck by Barrichello on lap two, and again in Spain. He lost the chance to challenge his brother for the win in the European Grand Prix, when he crossed the line on the pitlane exit and earned a 10-second stop-go penalty. He also spun in the US and collected another stop-go penalty in Suzuka for persistently cutting the chicane. He went on to repeat the offence while fending off Barrichello; some would say he was lucky not to be excluded from that race.

The team also had a nightmare in Spa. After the warm-up lap before the restart, the team decided to repair a strut that was broken on Schumacher's FW23. To this day it claims there was no five-minute warning, but when the cars roared off again Schumacher was left

standing on jacks and was put to the back of the grid. Montoya also stalled on pole in that race, showing that BMW Williams often did not capitalise on its dominance.

Ralf Schumacher started the season 0.8 seconds off his bother and ended it almost the same. Montoya started nearly two seconds off and ended 0.8 seconds off.

In all, Montoya completed 680 race laps out of a possible 1,065, giving a race reliability score of 63.8 per cent. His record – a win and three seconds out of six finishes – highlights the potential strength of the BMW Williams F1 package if reliability is thrown into the mix.

Ralf Schumacher and his car proved far more reliable, finishing 806 race laps for a far more acceptable record of 75.7 per cent completion. It is the difference in Formula One that may make Schumacher, and not Montoya, a champion. The problem for Williams is that a repeat of the 1986 season might be coming, when both its drivers dominated proceedings but saw Alain Prost nip in to claim the championship.

BMW.WilliamsF1 Team

## Commercial

AT THE highly confident 2001 car launch in February, Frank Williams, Patrick Head, Sam Michael, Gavin Fisher and Geoff Willis, Mario Theissen and Gerhard Berger were all lined up at a top table on the stage. Coyly, they all promised wins, 'only when the red and silver cars drop out'. But nobody was buying it and it was clear that the 2001 season would be a genuine three-horse race for the first time in many years.

Pre-season, BMW Williams was named as the team to beat. The Michelin tyres were the only doubt. The master plan from the very beginning was not to go for the championship in 2001, instead turning the season into an extended and successful test session.

The budget as always was a workmanlike one, and it is clear that Williams spent nothing like McLaren to achieve exactly the same end result. BMW is said to have spent $400 million on Formula One so far, and is set to reap the value. The Williams marketing department, led by Jim Wright, is much envied and second only to McLaren's, run by Ekrem Sami. It has a settled bunch of sponsors, the only blip coming when Compaq announced its intention to merge with Hewlett Packard during the season; but the team has a long-term contract that was not affected. Compaq, under the leadership of Andrew Collis, is one of the most diligent and serious sponsors in Formula One.

All in all, around $250 million (some $60 million above forecast) was spent during the year. A similar amount will be spent in 2002.

BMW Williams motorhome

## AUSTRALIAN GRAND PRIX MELBOURNE
# A statement of intent

The look on Patrick Head's face during the month before Melbourne said it all. BMW Williams had produced a championship-winning car that would mix it with McLaren and Ferrari. It was now all down to the tyres. It was clear that Michelin had done a good job – but not good enough. The French tyre company went to Australia guessing on a compound and, without any previous data about the track, the Michelin men had to do what they could; Williams engineers were then working through the night to fit the cars around the tyres. It was all about compromise. The ferocious development programme started by a reinvigorated Patrick Head continued in the week of the race with new parts being shipped in daily from the Grove factory.

The new BMW was clearly the most powerful on the grid. The two Williams BMWs were the fastest cars through the speed traps during the weekend, with new boy Juan Pablo Montoya recording 194mph in the race. At fast tracks with sticky Michelins, the cars were going to dominate. BMW had delivered.

**FRIDAY PRACTICE** BMW Williams brought three cars to Melbourne – FW23 chassis 03 for Ralf Schumacher, chassis 02 for Montoya and chassis 01 as the spare car, set up for Schumacher. Friday's sessions were dominated by Michelin-induced understeer and Patrick Head was surprised at how much quicker the Bridgestone-shod McLarens and Ferraris were. Soon it became clear that the Michelins were not soft enough. Consequently, Ralf Schumacher finished sixth on 1m 30.277secs. Montoya had two excursions off the track and struggled to 15th with an off-the-pace 1m 31.721secs. He was learning the circuit, getting used to new tyres, a new team, car and engine all at the same time. He was surprised at how quick Ralf was.

**SATURDAY QUALIFYING** Schumacher had a well-ordered session with four qualifying runs and, unlike almost everyone else, did not waste a run – luckily, he was only on the out-lap of his third run when the session was red-flagged. He found more grip and dialled out the understeer.

On his final attempt he pulled out everything. If he had been on Bridgestones he may well have taken pole, but he clocked up a best of 1m 27.719secs, which was good enough for fifth. The Michelins were very sensitive to very small changes in track conditions – the more rubber put down on the track by other cars, the better the Michelins gripped. Michelin runners were more than a second slower on Friday, but by Saturday they were catching up.

As Schumacher revelled in more grip, Montoya was a full second slower on 1m 28.738secs, back in 11th on the grid.

**SUNDAY RACE** After a great start, Schumacher's race was spoiled on the second lap when he went wide at the first corner. Running in fourth place behind his brother Michael, Mika Häkkinen and Heinz-Harald Frentzen, he rode the BMW Williams across the grass at Turn 1 and slipped behind Rubens Barrichello, David Coulthard and Jarno Trulli – then immediately came under pressure from Jacques Villeneuve. Three laps later Villeneuve ran into the back of him at Turn 3 in an accident that would lead to the tragic death of a marshal. As Villeneuve's BAR tumbled down the road on its side against the fence, Schumacher's car spun to a stop in a cloud of dust and debris, leaving him fuming with Villeneuve and shocked by the marshal's death.

Montoya made a good start then ruined it by spinning off at the first corner and found himself back in eighth place. Next he had a moment at Turn 3 with Eddie Irvine's Jaguar and tipped the Ulsterman into a spin. Montoya was running eighth when the pace car came out, and retirements promoted him to sixth. He fought his way up to fifth, but a faulty oil pipe fitting caused the engine to give way on lap 40, just before he was about to stop for tyres and fuel, denying him a points-scoring debut that he would have undoubtedly earned.

Above, right and below: BMW Williams' potential was already apparent at Melbourne, with Michelin's tyres appearing to be the weakest link. Juan Pablo Montoya battled through the field until retiring on lap 40.

Ralf Schumacher (left) and Juan Pablo Montoya (right) both had long walks home after retiring.

## MALAYSIAN GRAND PRIX SEPANG
# Waiting to win

BMW Williams came to Malaysia with confirmation it had a very fast car on its hands. Only bad luck had halted progress in Australia when Ralf Schumacher was unwittingly involved in the Villeneuve crash. Sepang was predicted to be a very hot race and BMW was one of two teams that had done hot-weather testing on its 2001 car, having spent a week at Kyalami in mid-February with Michelin, and the team went to Sepang with an advantage. But it also came knowing that its car lacked downforce and was not fully exploiting all the power from the new BMW engine – a unit that was generally regarded as the most powerful of 2001.

Ralf Schumacher had consistently been fastest through the speed traps and in quick sections of track. This was no different in Sepang. However Patrick Head was furiously denying it meant anything, saying the car had maximum downforce dialled in. ITV hit the nail on the head in its qualifying broadcast, as Louise Goodman told viewers the BMW Williams was really going to star when the teams moved to Europe.

Team principal Frank Williams was also playing the car down, saying it was not yet good enough to win the world championship. But in reality Head and Williams knew they had a winning car on their hands and targeted San Marino for their first victory in three years.

**FRIDAY PRACTICE** The drivers had the same cars they used in Melbourne, with the spare FW23-01 set up for Montoya. Schumacher was troubled by oversteer and could do no better than 10th, but he did complete 33 laps doing set-up work. His best time was a 1m 40.617secs. Juan Pablo Montoya got in only five laps all day – a disaster for him as he knew nothing about the complicated Sepang circuit. His day started with a leaking fuel pump, followed by an electrical system shutdown traced to the alternator.

**SATURDAY QUALIFYING** The biggest surprise of the day was the pace of the Williams BMWs. Overnight set-up had pro-

duced a car Schumacher could drive to the limit and, after 23 laps in the morning, he was second quickest to Rubens Barrichello with a time of 1m 36.475secs. Montoya did 25 laps, learning about the car and the track, and was 13th fastest with a 1m 37.502secs.

In qualifying Schumacher battled his brother for pole, but in the end was beaten by both Ferraris and had to settle for third on the grid. It was still a great effort. Montoya was very impressive, too, claiming fifth with a 1m 36.218secs. He reckoned he would have gone even quicker had he not been too conservative at the end of the lap. "He recovered remarkably from his lost first day," said Patrick Head, a man who is not easily impressed.

**SUNDAY RACE** Unaccustomed to being on the second row, Ralf Schumacher's BMW Williams nonetheless got the jump on Barrichello – but the pair tangled as he tried to turn in across the front of the Ferrari and spun. He rejoined at the back of the field. From 20th at the end of the first lap, the German was 16th at the end of the second and 12th by the start of lap four. He gained another four places during the rainstorm as other cars flew off and took advantage of the bunching to leap three more places on the lap after the safety car went in. But the incredible pace of the recovering Ferraris pushed him down to sixth, where he stayed until his pitstop on lap 18. When the other stops were over he was still charging, overtaking Jos Verstappen and Mika Häkkinen before stopping again on lap 38 while running fourth. Again he dropped to sixth, but managed to use the power of the BMW engine to hold off Häkkinen in the final laps. "It was a good feeling to be able to keep him behind me," he said later.

The aborted start proved to be Montoya's downfall as the BMW wouldn't fire up for the restart. He was left on the grid and, as attempts to start the car failed, there was a mad rush to get him into the spare before the first red light came on for the start. A new rule allowing this was agreed last year. Montoya started from the pitlane and was making progress – he was up from 21st to 17th – when the rain came. "I radioed the pitlane to say I did not need wets," he explained, "and we decided to stay out for one more lap. But I could not make it to the pit because there was so much aquaplaning." He went off into a gravel trap and retired.

BMW.WilliamsF1 Team

Above and below: Potent new combination at Williams of new chief racing engineer Sam Michael, Patrick Head and Ralf Schumacher.

Above left: Sibling rivalry: Ralf gave big brother something to think about in Malaysia. Left: Montoya was out early and watched the race with the team principal.

Left: Ralf Schumacher set fastest lap despite damaged rear tracking after the incident with Barrichello. Right: Juan Pablo Montoya gets some exercise as he runs for his spare in qualifying. Below: Montoya takes Michael Schumacher on lap three. It was a very close pass as the two cars rubbed wheels.

Right: Montoya brushes Schumacher aside. Below: Montoya, with Sam Michael, exudes pre-start confidence and deserved victory, but was rammed from behind by Jos Verstappen.

## BRAZILIAN GRAND PRIX INTERLAGOS
# Robbed of victory

BMW Williams was the moral victor in Brazil. But for Jos Verstappen and Rubens Barrichello, Juan Pablo Montoya and Ralf Schumacher could have finished one-two.

It was not the first time. In six starts this year, Williams cars had been rammed from the rear four times. Admittedly, braking distances had shortened, and they had shortened more than most for the Williams, shod on sticky Michelins.

After Malaysia, Patrick Head demanded more downforce – the result being a new front-end aerodynamic package, gaining several crucial pounds of downforce. The Michelins might not yet be as good as Bridgestones, but they were closing the gap. The real test, it was thought, would be at slightly slower tracks such as Imola.

FRIDAY PRACTICE The team used the same cars as in Melbourne, with Schumacher driving FW23-03, Montoya FW23-02 and FW23-01 as the spare, set up for the Colombian. Montoya had a trouble-free session and was reasonably happy with his car. Schumacher had gearbox trouble in the first session and was late starting in the afternoon. He then ran off the road and damaged the aerodynamic devices at the front end. He completed only 22 laps, but was still sixth fastest. Montoya did 43 laps and was a 10th of a second quicker than his team-mate.

SATURDAY QUALIFYING Montoya continued his solid preparation for the race on Saturday morning, completing 30 laps and setting the fastest time with 1m 13.963secs. Schumacher was fourth fastest, three-10ths behind Montoya, after 33 laps. In qualifying Montoya blew his chance of pole when he went off, so he hurried back to the pits, took the spare car and claimed fourth, just a few hundredths of a second slower than Ralf Schumacher's best, which had him on the front row with his brother – a historic moment.

SUNDAY RACE Only eighth fastest in the warm-up, Montoya made the most of the slow start by his team-mate and of Mika Häkkinen's stall, and arrived at the first corner in second place. After two laps behind the safety car, when racing resumed he got alongside Michael Schumacher and emerged from the first corner ahead and, as the German's tyres began to fade, pulled away. After Schumacher disappeared to the pits, Montoya continued to pull away from David Coulthard until lap 39 when Jos Verstappen rammed the Williams, ending its race. Montoya was six seconds clear of eventual winner Coulthard.

Ralf Schumacher was fourth fastest in warm-up but at the start of the race a brief engine problem lost him places to Montoya, Coulthard and Trulli and he found himself battling with Frentzen, Villeneuve and Barrichello as they exited the second corner. The dogfight on the straight saw a lot of manoeuvring and, as they braked for the double left, Barrichello misjudged his braking point and ran into the rear of the Williams. Both cars spun off, Schumacher's minus its rear wing. The German managed to recover and in just four minutes had a new rear wing and rejoined. He set the fastest lap of the race but threw away any chance of a result when he spun off on lap 55.

### SAN MARINO GRAND PRIX IMOLA
# The breakthrough arrives

Imola was a day of great joy for BMW Williams. Yet the race was decided in a moment when polesitter David Coulthard's McLaren Mercedes suffered too much wheelspin and Ralf Schumacher got the power down to the first corner for a start-to-finish victory.

However, Montoya became the only driver to fail to finish in the first four races of the year. It was a sign that the period of dominance predicted for Williams would be quashed by a reliability crisis.

**FRIDAY PRACTICE** BMW Williams arrived at Imola with the same three cars it used in Brazil allocated to the same drivers. The team had developed a new set-up for high-downforce circuits and this was very effective with Schumacher third fastest, seven-10ths slower than his brother's Ferrari. He managed to complete 43 laps on Friday. However, Montoya's progress was handicapped by an engine problem after only one lap in the second session. He was dead last on 1m 39.812secs.

**SATURDAY QUALIFYING** Schumacher qualified in third on 1m 23.357secs and never looked like challenging for pole. He out-qualified his brother for the first time ever, at the 70th attempt. Montoya was not very happy with his set-up: he pushed too hard, conceding around seven-10ths after putting a wheel on the grass at one of the chicanes. This dropped him to seventh on the grid on 1m 24.141secs.

*Above: Ralf Schumacher gets ready to drive to his maiden win.*
*Left: On the podium, celebrating a special moment, winning his first Grand Prix.*
*Below left: Into the first corner Ralf Schumacher is alongside pole man David Coulthard.*
*Below: The spoils of victory for Michelin and BMW Williams. Gerhard Berger nervously watches as BMW's first win since Mexico in 1986 unfolds.*

BMW Williams looked slightly off the pace. How wrong an assumption that was.

**SUNDAY RACE** At the start of the race Schumacher overtook Coulthard on the inside on the run down to the first turn, sneaking into the lead by just managing to avoid contact. He was fortunate that Coulthard gave him the space for the manoeuvre. With overtaking being so difficult at Imola Schumacher was never under any real threat of being overtaken, although the McLaren man was never far behind. The German was ahead all the way to his first pitstop on lap 29. Coulthard had pitted a lap earlier. He stopped again on lap 46, a lap after Coulthard, and remained in the lead again. The gap came down a little towards the end of the race but that was irrelevant.

Schumacher said afterwards: "I think I was lucky to get David right there. Luckily David gave me the space. I couldn't believe I could stay ahead. I pulled the gap out, but after a few laps I thought he was going to go quicker so I had to push again. From there on it was a pretty long race, I must say. It took ages."

Montoya started race day with a difficult car and was only 13th in the warm-up, complaining of understeer, bottoming out and poor traction. But despite his problems Montoya showed his ability with three spectacular overtaking manoeuvres in the race: one on Olivier Panis in the course of the first lap; the second on Michael Schumacher early in the race and the third on Jarno Trulli after the two men had both been in the pits for their first stops. At Montoya's second stop the mechanics couldn't get the refuelling nozzle off his car and he simultaneously stalled the engine. He had been having problems selecting gears before the stop. After he stalled, he could not get the car out of first gear. The only way to restart the engine was on the jacks, drop-starting the car. After two attempts, Montoya rejoined the race but as he was unable to change out of first, his race was over.

In yet another non-finish post-mortem, he simply observed: "We've been quite unlucky all weekend, but these things happen. I am very pleased for Ralf." So he said.

BMW.WilliamsF1 Team

# Caught out and off the pace

The cars were nowhere near the pace of the McLaren Mercedes and Ferraris. Williams and BMW had been caught short by the new electronics rules; they had not started early enough nor invested the money in software that McLaren and Ferrari had. And the team was on a continuing search for downforce.

Traction control affects the engine a lot more than BMW had assessed. The manufacturer was struggling to keep up with the engine supply needed and it was decided the team would run without traction control. That's how bad it was.

The only bright spot was the launch control, which catapulted Montoya from 12th on the grid to sixth in the first corner.

**FRIDAY PRACTICE** Williams arrived with a new chassis, FW23-05, for Ralf Schumacher. Juan Pablo Montoya retained FW23-02 and the spare was still FW23-01. Schumacher had use of the spare for the weekend.

Both drivers complained the cars did not suit the track and struggled to find a decent balance. Schumacher was eighth fastest on 1m 21.259secs and Montoya, who suffered an engine failure and lost a lot of time, was down in 13th on 1m 22.020secs. Michelin reported little difference in performance between its hard and soft tyres, and it was trying to decide which to use.

**SATURDAY QUALIFYING** Schumacher and Montoya strove for a better set-up, and to some extent succeeded. Ralf was fifth fastest but was quick to point out that he was eight-10ths of a second off pole, with a 1m 19.016secs, due to the team's choice of the harder tyre compound.

He did not think traction control would make that much difference in qualifying trim.

Montoya ended the day frustrated at being 12th on the grid with 1m 19.660secs, 0.6secs and seven places behind Ralf.

**SUNDAY RACE** Ralf was able to get to the first corner in fourth place. He stayed there, unable to match the pace of his brother, Häkkinen or Barrichello, until lap 21 when he spun off after locking up his rear brakes. "I don't know what happened," he said. "The car felt fine, but suddenly the rear came round and I spun off."

Montoya made a spectacularly good start and drove down the middle of the grid, avoiding the Saubers as they tried to miss one another and overtaking Frentzen. By the time Montoya reached the first corner he was alongside Villeneuve, who braked early, and he went ahead. The Colombian then shadowed Jarno Trulli until both men pitted. Williams had Montoya on his way first and that, with Ralf's retirement, promoted Montoya to fourth. In the second stint he was too far back to make an impression on the three cars ahead of him. But when Barrichello ran into trouble and Häkkinen disappeared on the last lap he moved into second. A great result for the Colombian. "The car was quite tricky to drive," he said. "Michael and the McLarens were in a different league. I wasn't expecting a podium, but I had a good start and kept pushing."

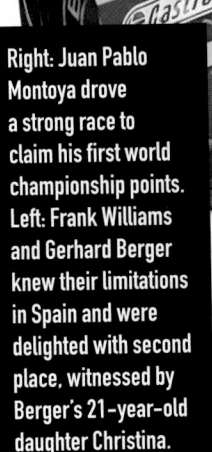

Above and right: Ralf Schumacher again looked like a contender for the top spots, qualifying and racing well, but after a strong start a spin put him out and he was forced to walk home.

Right: Juan Pablo Montoya drove a strong race to claim his first world championship points. Left: Frank Williams and Gerhard Berger knew their limitations in Spain and were delighted with second place, witnessed by Berger's 21-year-old daughter Christina.

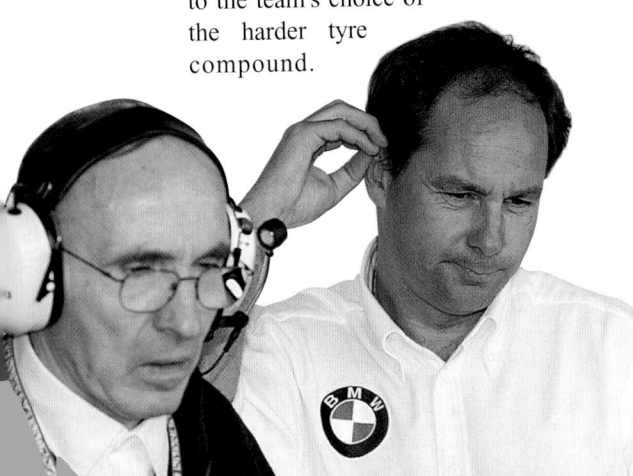

BMW.WilliamsF1 Team

## AUSTRIAN GRAND PRIX A1 RING
# What might have been

**B**MW Williams was running one-two at the end of lap one of the Austrian Grand Prix. A dream result seemed possible, until Ralf Schumacher retired with brake problems and Juan Pablo Montoya clashed with Michael Schumacher – the pair sliding off when the Ferrari driver tried to take the lead on lap 16. This dropped Montoya to seventh and, although he recovered some ground, his challenge was snuffed out on lap 42 by a hydraulic failure.

Despite the disappointment, it was the first time both Williams cars had run together at the front, hinting that the team could expect results later in the year.

**FRIDAY PRACTICE** Williams used the same chassis as in Barcelona, with Schumacher in FW23-05, Montoya in FW23-02 and FW23-01 as the spare. There were no major changes from Spain, but there was a completely new package of settings for the A1 Ring. Both Williams drivers had off-track moments as they worked to find the right balance and ended up setting the fourth (Schumacher) and 11th fastest (Montoya) times of the day.

"We have done a useful day of homework for the race," said technical director Patrick Head, "and we now understand the car set-up we have to achieve for the tyres in both new and used conditions." The team went into Saturday with quiet confidence.

**SATURDAY QUALIFYING** The team decided to go with softer tyres and during qualifying Montoya and Schumacher battled for second spot on the grid. Schumacher hit traffic on one run and committed an error on another, so Montoya took his first front row on a Formula One grid. Ralf was third.

The drivers were confident the cars would be quick off the line and were hoping to get ahead of Michael Schumacher at the start. After that they reckoned it was going to be difficult until there was plenty of rubber down on the circuit. However, as track position is important in Austria, there was still hope for a victory.

**SUNDAY RACE** In the cool conditions on Sunday morning, the Michelin soft compound would not heat up enough, with the result that Schumacher and Montoya were 15th and 16th on the timesheets. But by the race start the temperature had risen and the Williams drivers showed the team's launch control was the best by arriving at the first corner almost side by side. Following Montoya, Schumacher found he had problems with his brakes – they faded quickly and after 10 laps there was nothing left. Schumacher headed for the pits to retire. Montoya looked comfortable in the lead until just after Schumacher retired – when he found both Ferraris closing up quickly. On lap 16 Michael Schumacher tried to pass him on the run-up to turn two, choosing the outside line for his bid. The two cars arrived side by side but Schumacher braked late and could not turn in because Montoya was there. Juan Pablo braked even later and could not make the corner and both men slid off line and Montoya could only rejoin by driving across the gravel trap. His tyres needed several laps to be effective again.

He fought back from seventh and after Jos Verstappen disappeared from the front-running group, Montoya was sixth. He overtook Olivier Panis for fifth on lap 38, but as he was getting ready for his pitstop on lap 42 he suffered a hydraulic leak that resulted in the system shutting down. "I got an alarm two corners before it happened and I knew that was going to be it," he said.

Above: The two BMW Williams swamped pole-sitter Michael Schumacher at the start. Left: Juan Pablo Montoya paid for his robust defence of the lead with a trip through the gravel. Below: Williams again showed great pace, to take second and third on the grid.

Left: Having out-qualified Ralf Schumacher for the first time, Juan Pablo Montoya again led a Grand Prix. Below right: Words of advice from Patrick Head. Below: Montoya recovered from his excursion, but retired with hydraulic failure.

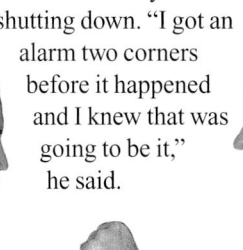

## MONACO GRAND PRIX MONTE CARLO

# A bad day in the streets

It might have been the dominant force in Brazil and at Imola, but at Monte Carlo the BMW Williams FW23 couldn't challenge the McLarens or Ferraris. Both cars retired and that immediately prompted technical director Patrick Head to instigate an emergency reliability programme; he and the engineers would get no time off between Monaco and Montreal. It is one of the reasons why Williams has been one of the most successful teams of the last 20 years.

Reliability was on everyone's mind: "It has cost us important points today," remarked BMW's Gerhard Berger.

**THURSDAY PRACTICE** Ralf Schumacher had his usual FW23-05 and the team's regular spare car FW23-01. Montoya stuck with FW23-02 and used FW23-03 as his spare. Both were going well until the last few minutes of the second qualifying session. Montoya dropped the ball at Rascasse while on a quick lap and crashed heavily into the barriers. It looked spectacular but the damage to his car was only slight. A few moments later Schumacher had an even bigger crash at the entry to the Swimming Pool, which damaged his car considerably. Both cars were repaired for qualifying.

**SATURDAY QUALIFYING** In the morning things looked good with Ralf Schumacher within 0.4secs of Mika Häkkinen and Montoya up to seventh. So the team went into qualifying in a confident frame of mind, hoping to get at least one car on the first two rows of the grid. But things did not work out like that: Ralf made a mistake on his best lap, then on his final run he found Jenson Button's Benetton in his way. This meant he was fifth on the grid, two-10ths of a second off the front row. Schumacher was disappointed, but Patrick Head did not seem to think it made much of a difference. "Ralf was held up on his last lap," he said, "but whether he would have improved or not is a different matter."

Montoya was seventh, which he felt 'wasn't such a bad qualifying' since he continued to complain of understeer and, during the

day, twice clipped walls, damaging tie-in rods.

**SUNDAY RACE** Ralf Schumacher was sixth fastest in the warm-up and confident things would go well in the race. At the start he held onto his position, despite a determined challenge from Eddie Irvine at the first corner. He then came under considerable pressure from team-mate Montoya until the Colombian made a mistake on the third lap and put himself out of the race. After that Schumacher was able to run without much pressure. His fourth place became third when Häkkinen hit trouble and he stayed there, unable to match the Ferraris but unchallenged by Irvine's Jaguar, until his retirement on lap 58, just before he was due to pit. The retirement was blamed on electronic problems, which deprived him of his power-steering and gear-change.

"A warning light came on," Ralf said. "Shortly after that, the power-steering failed and as I came into the pits I could no longer change gear."

Montoya's weekend had been less than settled, with handling problems and friction with the team. At the start he showed his usual aggression by trying to challenge his team-mate as they went into Ste Devote. As Schumacher was coping with Irvine, Montoya tucked in behind and, when Irvine went wide, made up a place. He then set about passing Ralf. At the end of the first lap the Williams drivers were separated by only half a second, and at the end of the second they were even closer. At the Swimming Pool on lap three, however, Montoya slid wide and hit the barrier on the outside. The car lurched down the wall and slid into the tyre barriers in the second part of the complex. "I made a mistake and I paid for it," he later admitted.

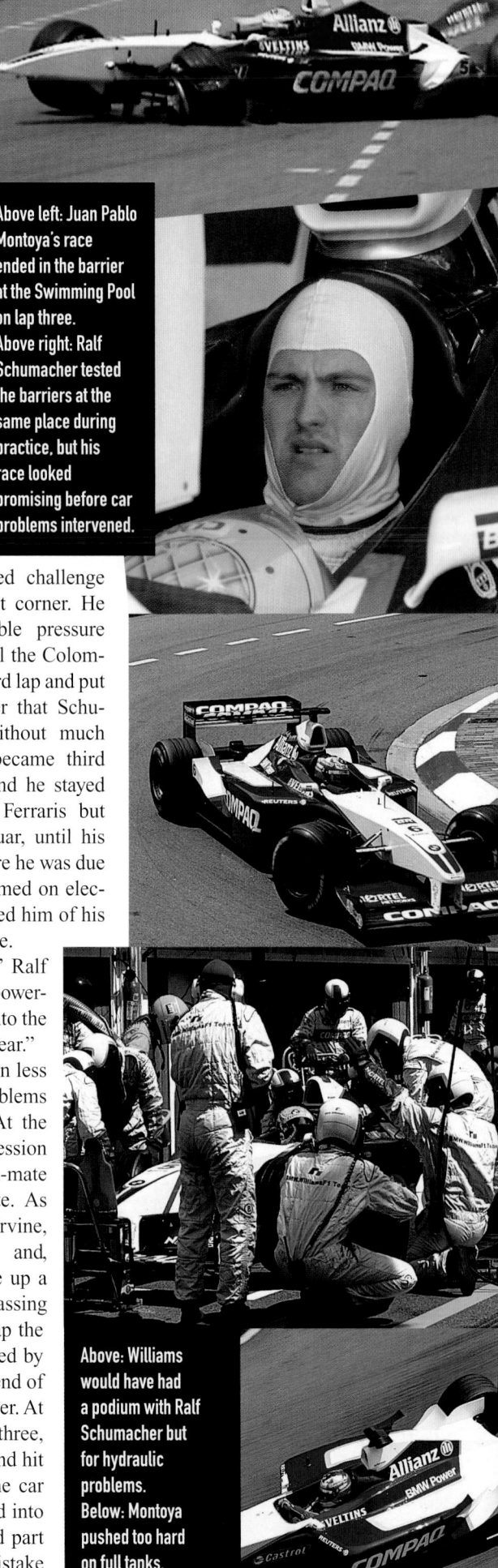

Above left: Juan Pablo Montoya's race ended in the barrier at the Swimming Pool on lap three.
Above right: Ralf Schumacher tested the barriers at the same place during practice, but his race looked promising before car problems intervened.

Above: Williams would have had a podium with Ralf Schumacher but for hydraulic problems.
Below: Montoya pushed too hard on full tanks.

## CANADIAN GRAND PRIX MONTREAL
# Unbeatable on race day

BMW.WilliamsF1 Team

With the startline statistic of only three finishes in 14 starts, BMW Williams technical director Patrick Head went into crisis mode and cancelled all the engineers' weekends off until the problem had been solved.

Even after 10 days' hard development labour, the team went to Montreal expecting a tough time. Michelin had no experience of the Canadian circuit and there were worries about whether the brakes would go the distance.

But by the end of the weekend the team had proved again that, although it was not really a championship challenger, there would be races this year at which the package was going to be more effective than anything Ferrari, McLaren Mercedes or Bridgestone could come up with.

From early in the race it was clear Ralf Schumacher had the advantage; in the end it was the BMW powerplant's impressive fuel consumption which triumphed.

But Williams' victory was tinged with frustration: Juan Pablo Montoya continued to struggle and made more mistakes than the team would have liked. In Montreal he became embroiled in a verbal spat with Jacques Villeneuve, the two nearly coming to blows during the drivers' briefing on Friday after an on-track incident earlier in the day, when Montoya ran into the BAR driver's back.

Montoya was in trouble and his performance and relationship with his team was far from perfect, despite the brave face put on by management.

**FRIDAY PRACTICE** Williams had a brand new chassis, FW23-06, for Montoya. Schumacher had FW23-05 as usual, with FW23-02, the spare, allocated to Montoya.

Montoya had a brush with Villeneuve but otherwise the day passed without drama. BMW had a new camshaft and there were worries the extra revs might cause problems, so the team ran with extra wing to keep the revs down. It was established that Michelin's soft rubber was too marginal to race, so both drivers used the harder compound. The brakes, featuring new ducts, proved effective.

**SATURDAY QUALIFYING** The day started badly with Montoya losing laps due to a gearbox problem. Schumacher completed his planned work and his sudden burst of performance in qualifying came as a surprise to most – although there was a suspicion it had been planned that way. "The car felt perfect," said Ralf, "and the increase in temperature helped us as well."

Montoya did his best but at the crucial moment was trapped behind a Benetton so ended up 10th on the grid. He remained less than happy with his car's handling. "The car was getting better and better with each run, but in the end it was just not enough," he said.

**SUNDAY RACE** Schumacher had a spin during warm-up but as the temperature rose, so did the team's chances of a competitive showing. In the race Ralf got alongside Michael in the run down to the first corner at the start, but he was on the outside and did not have enough of an advantage to drive around his brother, so had to settle for second to avoid losing the inside line to David Coulthard. For the first few laps Ralf struggled, then the Michelin performance kicked in and he was able to close the gap and press his brother. Neither man made a mistake. After the safety car went back in Ralf dropped away again, his tyres having picked up too much rubber, but once they had cleaned themselves off, Ralf was back on Michael's tail. However, overtaking at Montreal is not easy and he could not find a way past until Michael pitted for the second time on lap 46. Ralf put in a succession of fast laps and emerged from his own pitstop five laps later with a five-second lead. The race was won.

Montoya's race, however, was another disappointment. He was running 10th, chased by Rubens Barrichello, when he lost control of the car in the fast right-left sweeper at the back of the track. There was no time to recover and the car hit the wall hard. Behind Montoya, Barrichello also went off the track as he tried to avoid hitting the Williams.

Montoya discreetly suggested something in the car may have broken, but the team could find no trace of a breakage that might have been to blame.

Top: Ralf Schumacher celebrates a decisive BMW Williams victory. Above and left: Juan Pablo Montoya had a miserable weekend, including some physical confrontations – one with Villeneuve and one with the Armco, which ended his day. Below: Ralf Schumacher made his intentions clear from the start.

## EUROPEAN GRAND PRIX NÜRBURGRING
# A pleasant surprise

**B**MW Williams did not expect great things at the Nürburgring, so it came as a surprise when its cars proved so competitive. But the team was on a roll after the hard work put in by Patrick Head and his team at the three-day Monza test, and some weekend working was still delivering huge dividends. The cars showed well on the medium-speed circuit and most believed BMW Williams would dominate on the high-speed tracks later in the summer. Although challenging Ferrari for the 2001 constructors' title was hopeless, the team was emerging as favourite for 2002.

**FRIDAY PRACTICE** BMW Williams had the same three chassis as in Montreal, with Ralf Schumacher using FW23-05, Juan Pablo Montoya FW23-06 and FW23-02 remaining as the spare. Despite lower than expected temperatures the cars were competitive. They were also reliable, allowing Schumacher to complete 43 laps and Montoya 45. This gave the Colombian a much-needed boost in confidence and he worked with his engineers to develop the car. By the end of the day he was close to matching Schumacher, although that did not show in the final times as he had to lift when someone spun in front of him.

**SATURDAY QUALIFYING** The choice of tyre compound was not difficult but there were some fears that the tyre chosen would not be competitive in the race because there was not much rubber down. As the temperatures rose on Saturday morning the team became more confident. Schumacher battled for pole with brother Michael, and although he was beaten he ended up just behind his brother on a 1m 15.226secs. He was delighted. "I hope to get my first pole position soon," he said after setting the second fastest time. Montoya continued to make progress despite a wrong move in set-up between runs. In the end the car felt 'pretty good' although he complained of a shade too much oversteer. But he was happy with his 1m 15.490secs, which gave him third on the grid.

**SUNDAY RACE** Schumacher was third fastest in the cool conditions of the warm-up, behind both Ferraris, and as the temperatures rose the Williams team grew more confident the Michelin tyres would be able to do the job.

It was Ralf who managed the better start but his brother squeezed him towards the pitwall and in the end he had to give way, so allowing Michael to take the lead. As usual it took the Michelins around 12 laps to reach their maximum performance – and as soon as that happened Ralf was back on the Ferrari's tail. The Ferrari nearly went off on lap 18 when Michael locked his brakes going into Turn 5 and Ralf dived for the inside line, only to have the door slammed firmly in his face. The two men remained locked together until lap 28 when both went into the pits. Michael was slightly faster away and as Ralf came out he was worried about getting stuck behind David Coulthard's McLaren (which was running on a one-stop strategy). As a result, he moved too quickly across the track and in doing so crossed the white line. He was given a 10-second stop-go penalty, which dropped him a full half-minute behind his brother. "I was concentrating more on the traffic behind me than on the line," he said. "I have to accept the penalty." He ended the day in fourth place, collecting more points but wondering what might have been.

Montoya took it easy in the early part of the race to avoid any incidents and then gradually began to pick up the pace. He set the fastest lap of the race just before his pit-stop. And when his team-mate received a penalty he moved to second and chased Michael Schumacher through to the line. "The car was very positive," he enthused. "There was room to go quicker when I needed to."

**Ralf Schumacher's race might have been better had he not been edged out by his brother at the start (below) and then received a 10-second penalty for crossing the pit exit line.**

**Juan Pablo Montoya proved his critics wrong, taking his second piece of silverware of the year with a second place.**

## FRENCH GRAND PRIX MAGNY-COURS
# Another near miss

Above and left: Ralf Schumacher gave himself the perfect birthday present: his first pole for a Grand Prix. Below: Chief operations engineer Sam Michael and Ralf continued to make progress.

Ralf Schumacher looked a good bet for victory in France and BMW Williams was clearly on a roll. The German duly delivered with his first-ever pole position to confirm that BMW Williams was the team of the moment and had pushed McLaren down to third in the pecking order. Now all that remained was to continue putting points on the board and grab second place in the drivers' and constructors' championships. The stage was set for the second half of the season to be a tight fight between BMW Williams and McLaren Mercedes, which started with the upper hand from its superior performance earlier in the season. At this stage BMW Williams was favourite to take second, especially with Ralf Schumacher and Juan Montoya proving much better racers than qualifiers.

**FRIDAY PRACTICE** The Williams team used the same three chassis as in recent races, with Schumacher driving FW23-05, Montoya at the wheel of FW23-06 and FW23-02 as the spare.

Schumacher had a frustrating time when his car stopped on the circuit; he did only five morning laps. In the afternoon he fared better and ended the day with 27, despite losing more time to piping repairs after running over some wreckage. This left him fifth fastest on 1m 15.537secs.

Montoya ran without any technical problems and completed 52 trouble-free laps for the sixth fastest time, a 1m 15.582secs.

**SATURDAY QUALIFYING** The drivers opted for different tyre strategies: Schumacher went for the softer Michelin compounds while Montoya decided to sacrifice pace in qualifying for performance in the race (if the weather stayed hot).

Schumacher tussled for pole position with his brother and won the day, recording the first pole of his career with a stunning 1m 12.989secs which simply blew the rest of the field away. It was a nice present for him on his 26th birthday, and the first pole position for BMW and Michelin since the compa-

Above and left: Juan Pablo Montoya compromised his qualifying session by choosing tyres he felt would be better for the race. His strategy could have worked had he not been held up by team-mate Ralf Schumacher.

nies made their return to Formula One. Montoya lined up sixth on 1m 13.625secs and was annoyed that Jean Alesi's Prost had baulked him at a vital moment on his last lap. Interestingly, despite their different tyres, both men reckoned they had made the right choice.

**SUNDAY RACE** In the morning warm-up Schumacher did not try setting a quick time, leaving the opposition guessing how fast he could race. At the start he took advantage of pole to stay ahead of his brother and for the whole of the first stint he easily held off Michael. However, when he pitted there was a two-second delay with his right rear tyre, and Schumacher Senior got ahead as Ralf put in an extraordinarily slow out-lap. The problem was that Ralf's second set of tyres were not working well. "I was sliding everywhere," he said.

He may not have been able to mount a challenge to his brother but he was still quick enough to finish second, although he would almost certainly have been beaten by Montoya if the Colombian had not broken down.

At the start, Montoya jumped from sixth to fourth immediately. His plan had been to go for a long first stint and make up places during the pitstops, but gaining two places off the grid meant that the strategy was not really necessary. With a heavy fuel load he was unable to do much to challenge the two Schumachers early on, but as the fuel burned off Montoya went faster and faster.

As the race unfolded, so the second Williams driver emerged as the only real challenge to Michael Schumacher's dominance; but in order to attack the Ferrari, he needed a clear run and his quest was not helped when his team-mate failed to move over for him when he was running at his fastest. This cost Montoya at least 12 seconds and, while this might not have won the race, it would certainly have got him much closer to Michael. In the end it was all irrelevant, as his engine failed with 20 laps to go.

He said afterwards: "It started losing power on the lap before it stopped. The main thing was being on a different strategy to Ralf to try to beat him – and I was ahead." Unreliability again denied the Colombian a strong finish.

BMW.WilliamsF1 Team

167

## BRITISH GRAND PRIX SILVERSTONE
# Cold-weather blues

BMW Williams was not competitive; the best it could have hoped for was a podium for Juan Pablo Montoya had he not been held up by team-mate Ralf Schumacher for a crucial period mid-race. The team requested that Schumacher let Montoya through, but Schumacher reckoned he was in a position to overtake Rubens Barrichello and so stayed where he was. Neither man was very happy after the race, although strategy was the real problem.

The big question was why the stars of the last half-dozen races had suddenly become also-rans. It had to be the Michelin tyres, which simply did not work well at the lower temperatures in Britain. But at least the cars were fairly reliable, even if Schumacher's car did not last the race distance.

**FRIDAY PRACTICE** Schumacher had chassis FW23-05, Montoya had FW23-06, and FW23-02 was the spare. Schumacher did 42 laps and set the eighth fastest time, a 1m 24.222secs. Montoya clocked up 38 laps but was only 17th fastest on 1m 25.267secs – terrible for him, and he made his excuses.

**SATURDAY QUALIFYING** Michelin runners have traditionally struggled in the wet this season so it was little surprise on Saturday morning that the cars were off the pace on the sodden track. As it dried, though, things improved and by the end of the day the Williams drivers were 10th and 11th on the timesheets.

In the afternoon Montoya ran over a kerb at Becketts, damaged a pushrod and had to switch to the spare, which was set up for Schumacher. But it worked well and he was able to qualify eighth on a 1m 22.219secs. Schumacher complained about traffic after qualifying, reckoning other cars ruined all his fastest runs. He had to settle for 10th on the grid with a best time of 1m 22.283secs.

**SUNDAY RACE** Ralf Schumacher made a strong start in far warmer conditions which immediately made the tyres run better. He went from 10th to fifth on the first lap, helped by Williams' launch control being far superior to the team's rivals' systems and by three cars ahead going off.

Schumacher had decided on a one-stop strategy so he came under pressure from Kimi Räikkönen, who was running with light tanks. He managed to hold the Finn off and moved up to fourth when Montoya pitted. He was then pushing Barrichello hard for third, with Montoya behind him.

Dickie Stanford, Williams' team manager, asked Ralf to let Montoya through, but Schumacher decided he was as well placed to overtake the Ferrari driver as the Colombian, so stayed out until told to pit on lap 35. Angry at the decision (and slightly delayed because the fuel hose stuck on for a few extra seconds), he rejoined in sixth place, but two laps later he stopped when the engine lost power and switched itself off.

Montoya made a good start and moved from eighth to third in the first corner, aided when David Coulthard and Jarno Trulli took each other off. The Colombian was on a two-stop strategy but in the early laps he was unable to keep up with the pace of Mika Häkkinen and Michael Schumacher. As his fuel load lightened, however, he became more competitive and by lap 14 he was challenging Schumacher for second position. On lap 18 he got ahead on the run down to Copse. He took the lead when Häkkinen pitted four laps later and for four laps led the race before pitting himself. He rejoined in fifth just behind Barrichello and Ralf Schumacher, and was then stuck behind the pair until Ralf pitted on the orders of the team on lap 35. Montoya was unable to pass Barrichello and in the end had to settle for fourth. "I was aiming for one point so getting three is not bad," was his verdict.

Above: Sam Michael and Patrick Head discuss grip problems and the race. Right and below: Juan Pablo Montoya had a great start and a storming race. Held up briefly by team-mate Ralf, he finished fourth.

Right and below: Ralf Schumacher struggled with grip and handling at Silverstone. His one-stop strategy meant he could not keep pace with Montoya, but he also lost time during his pitstop before retiring.

## GERMAN GRAND PRIX HOCKENHEIM
# Complete domination

The BMW Williams was unbeatable at Hockenheim. It is unusual for the outcome of qualifying and a race to be so clear cut and expected. Conditions conspired in a rare fashion to favour cars and tyres. BMW engines work better when it's hot and Michelin tyres only function well in the heat.

BMW was also the engine builder of the moment and knocked Ilmor Engineering off the top spot – which was also totally unexpected. Insiders were telling people BMW had found an extra 60-80 horsepower since the first race of the season. Horsepower figures are closely guarded but speculation was rife that the Mercedes and Ferrari had around 800 horses and that BMW had 850.

BMW has got ahead by building an engine with lower tolerances and so finely machined that it is designed purely to last a little more than one race distance. Whatever the case, BMW had stolen a march and now had a state-of-the-art engine that matched the state-of-the-art chassis Patrick Head and his three engineers – Gavin Fisher, Geoff Willis and Sam Michael – had produced. Mid-season, this was without doubt the most feared team combination.

**FRIDAY PRACTICE** The team used the same cars as in all recent races with Juan Pablo Montoya at the wheel of FW23-06, Ralf Schumacher driving FW23-05 and FW23-02 acting as the spare. The cars featured a low-drag aerodynamic package developed for high-speed tracks. On Friday the team gave little away. Montoya was second quickest having completed a total of 43 laps for 1m 41.487secs. Ralf Schumacher struggled after a spin in the opening moments of the second session.

As a result he did only 18 laps and set only the 10th fastest lap for 1m 42.987secs.

**SATURDAY QUALIFYING** The true picture of the team's competitiveness emerged on Saturday morning when Schumacher did 25 laps and Montoya 23. The two were first and second on the timesheets and nearly half a second ahead of the nearest challenger.

For a long time it looked as though it was Ralf Schumacher's pole, but times were dropping with later runs and Montoya sneaked one in. Schumacher would probably have beaten it but his last runs were stuffed by slow runners and Burti's crash.

Schumacher was still comfortably second quickest while Montoya took his first F1 pole position for 1m 38.117secs. He was only one-100th of a second faster than Ralf but the pair were nearly seven-10ths faster than Mika Häkkinen.

**SUNDAY RACE** On Sunday morning Schumacher was fastest in the warm-up despite spending most of his time in the spare car in order to save his engine for the race. He was three-100ths faster than Montoya, who completed only seven laps as he tried to find a set-up with slightly less understeer.

In the race Schumacher immediately ran second to Montoya in both the first start and the restart as the drivers moved off in formation. But he was unable to keep on the pace and gradually dropped to 10 seconds behind, when Montoya pitted on lap 22 and encountered a severe delay. The BMW Williams refueller saw the indicator lights on the rig were not working and thought that no fuel had gone into the car. So he switched to the second refuelling rig. This lost 20 seconds because the original rig had in fact pumped fuel into the car, Montoya rejoined with a lot more than he needed for the rest of the race.

This put Ralf into an easy lead until his stop on lap 24. With Montoya delayed, Schumacher was able to retake the lead and there he stayed to win by 45 seconds, made easy when Montoya retired three laps after his pitstop when his BMW engine failed; he was left with just the fastest lap of the race. Schumacher said: "I have to admit that at the beginning my team-mate was faster than I was. But from early in the race I started to save fuel and be easy on the engine, as I knew it would be a race of attrition."

BMW Williams and Michelin were the class of the field in Germany in both qualifying and the race. Left: Ralf Schumacher made it a great day for BMW and Germany with an easy win after team-mate Juan Pablo Montoya retired.

Left and above: Montoya dominated qualifying and the race until a disastrous pitstop led to a BMW engine failure. Below: Ralf savours his first GP victory on home soil.

BMW.WilliamsF1 Team

## HUNGARIAN GRAND PRIX HUNGARORING
# Not quite there

BMW Williams could not make its cars go fast on slower circuits – a problem exacerbated when the weather was cold. The cold weather problem was down to Michelin and did not apply to the hot Hungaroring. But the slow circuit problem did and it appeared to be a lack of downforce. Williams simply couldn't dial in the downforce required for perfect balance. If BMW had not produced at least an extra 50 horsepower from its engine since Melbourne the team would have been in serious trouble and well down the grid.

The Hungary problem was further exacerbated by the fact that Michelin had no experience of the track conditions – a far cry from Bridgestone, which is very familiar with the vagaries of the Hungaroring. "Technically our compounds are quite different," explained Pierre Dupasquier of Michelin. "But paradoxically they are fairly similar as far as performance is concerned." Not similar enough, unfortunately.

**FRIDAY PRACTICE** Ralf Schumacher was running chassis FW23-05 and Montoya FW23-06. The spare remained FW23-02. The cars featured small secondary rear wings above the gearbox, designed to produce more downforce. The team also had air ducts on the sidepods to help engine cooling. These had not been seen since Malaysia in March.

Ralf Schumacher completed 40 laps with a couple of minor dramas and Montoya did 36, which included two harmless spins. The problem was that the cars were not that quick on a track where power was less relevant, ending the day with Ralf fourth, six-10th off his brother's pace with 1m 17.308secs and Montoya 1.2 seconds slower and down in 13th on 1m 18.524secs.

**SATURDAY QUALIFYING** The BMW Williams engineers had worked hard to cure Montoya's problems and on Saturday morning he was much happier with his car, improving to eighth fastest on 1m 15.881secs but still complaining of oversteer, which sent him

into a spin at one point. Team-mate Ralf Schumacher was seventh. In the afternoon, however, he qualified in fourth with a 1m 15.095secs, although a second off his brother's pole position. Montoya lined up eighth, having closed the gap to Ralf to just eight-10ths of a second.

**SUNDAY RACE** Ralf Schumacher was only fourth fastest in the warm-up and six-10ths down on the fastest time so it was clear he was not going to be a factor in the race. At the start he held on to fourth place but was never a threat to the three frontrunners and in the end finished exactly where he started. Although he had a quiet race in terms of battles, he was fighting the car all the way. "This was the toughest race of the year," he said. "I was constantly fighting both oversteer and understeer."

Juan Montoya was 12th quickest in the warm-up, trying both his race car and the spare. At the race start he held on to eighth and stayed there for the duration, except for the pitstop cycles. "This was a weekend when nothing worked for us," he said.

A rare non-event weekend for BMW Williams, but what the team expected.

## BELGIAN GRAND PRIX SPA-FRANCORCHAMPS
# Creative tension

**Above and left: Juan Pablo Montoya stamped his authority on qualifying despite not having the latest Williams. It proved the high point of his weekend: he stalled before the parade lap and retired when his engine failed in the second race.**

The Belgian Grand Prix was the wrong weekend for BMW Williams to cock it up. Making second place in the world championship was looking difficult – McLaren was 22 points ahead with three races left. Before Spa BMW was clear favourite to take second, and Ralf Schumacher was tipped as the drivers' runner-up. Before this race, at least.

BMW should have won in Belgium, but traded reliability for horsepower; Montoya's spectacular blow-up would probably not be the season's last.

Insiders said there was 'creative tension' between BMW and Williams at present, and that BMW had told technical director Patrick Head to find more downforce, to take the strain off the engine. BMW felt the car's speed was solely down to its efforts and that the chassis lacked the downforce to leverage its engine best. But insiders said Head's next car would address all these problems and be stunning. The interim chassis introduced at Spa had basically turned the remaining races into test sessions for the 2002 car.

**Left and below: Ralf Schumacher made it an all-BMW Williams front row but could not join the field for the formation lap of the second race and was forced to start from the back row. He charged through the field and caught Jean Alesi's Jordan. The pair then engaged in a spirited duel, with Ralf just missing out on the points.**

**FRIDAY PRACTICE** At Spa, BMW Williams had a new car for Schumacher. FW23-07, with a lighter and also stiffer chassis, replaced FW23-05; Juan Pablo Montoya kept FW23-06; the spare FW23-02 was unchanged. Insiders said FW23-07 was an 'A' version of 2002's chassis, not a 'B' version of 2001's. Patrick Head said little.

On Friday morning Schumacher lost time to a gearbox problem while Montoya blotted his copybook with a late-session crash. Schumacher ended seventh, on 1m 50.801secs, Montoya a lowly 16th on 1m 52.829secs.

**SATURDAY QUALIFYING** Both drivers went into qualifying with dry set-ups, hoping for the best of changing conditions. It was the right decision and in the final stages both drivers switched to dry tyres. Montoya took pole on 1m 52.072secs; Schumacher was second on 1m 52.959s. "It was a typical Spa gamble," said Gerhard Berger, head of BMW Motorsport. "The team's timing was perfect. We knew we had a good chance in the dry and both drivers gave top performances in the limited time available to them."

**SUNDAY RACE** At the start of the first race, Schumacher took the lead but only held off brother Michael until the top of the hill.

After the race was stopped, Ralf Schumacher was left sitting on his jacks when the parade lap began for the restart: the team decided late to change the rear wing of his car after Montoya's was found to have broken a strut, rather than attempting major alterations. Patrick Head said: "We had a failure of a wing beam on Juan Pablo's car in the first part of the race, and we judged we should change the beam on Ralf's car." Head also claimed that there was no five-minute board informing them of the restart.

Schumacher restarted at the back and stayed out of trouble to finish seventh, behind Jean Alesi and out of the points.

For Montoya, things went seriously wrong from the second start of the first race, his car stalling as he tried to set off for the parade lap. The problem was attributed to the starter motor failing to turn the engine over fast enough, so that although it fired up it was not running properly. All the effort that went into pole was instantly wiped out – starting from the back Montoya was up to 17th by the end of the first lap and started the second race from 15th.

He made a great start and was climbing up the race order when he fell victim to a chain reaction, started by Jos Verstappen's collision with Nick Heidfeld. Heidfeld hit Pedro de la Rosa who then hit Montoya. Montoya took it easy after that, worried about his suspension, but as he began to recover his engine failed spectacularly, rounding off a dismal day.

171

## ITALIAN GRAND PRIX MONZA
# Rookie winner

It was Juan Pablo Montoya's destiny to win a race in his rookie season and he duly delivered. The Williams team and engine partner BMW were always quietly confident about their chances of a win in Monza. Warm weather, low downforce levels and high-speed straights make it a dream come true for the team. The track is similar to Hockenheim where Ralf Schumacher won, and by dominating the front row of the grid in Spa, they knew that when things went together, they went together well. They prepared for Monza by testing in Magny-Cours and the BMW engineers developed the engine for yet more of that spine-tingling speed it is capable of. This weekend was theirs from the beginning.

FRIDAY PRACTICE Having given Schumacher a 'B' spec lighter and stiffer chassis in Belgium, BMW Williams came to Monza with a 'B' spec for Montoya, chassis FW23-08, while Schumacher had FW23-07 and the spare was FW23-02.

Montoya described his new chassis as 'floppy' but he and team-mate Schumacher still had a perfect start to the race weekend, finishing second and first respectively in the first practice session. Schumacher complained of understeer while Montoya reported oversteer in the faster sections. Montoya reckoned he could have won the top timesheet spot if he hadn't been stuck in traffic, unable to scrub his second set of tyres. Schumacher did 43 laps, Montoya 37. The German's best lap was 1m 24.667secs while Montoya managed 1m 25.067secs. "I think the potential is there to go a lot quicker," said the Colombian.

SATURDAY QUALIFYING On the Saturday morning Montoya did 1m 23.477secs, quicker than Friday but still only sixth fastest, while Schumacher recorded a 1m 23.917secs. As the air and track temperatures rose, the Michelins produced quicker and quicker lap times, and in the afternoon Montoya built on his improvement and took his third pole position for the team with a best lap of 1m 22.216secs. A buoyant Montoya suggested the car was capable of even more. "It is nice to beat Ferrari on their home ground," the Colombian said.

Schumacher's best time only managed fourth place on the grid next to brother Michael. "We just did not find the right set-up," explained Ralf, complaining of oversteer and understeer; his fastest run of 1m 22.841secs was also slowed by yellow flags.

SUNDAY RACE Montoya took the lead under constant pressure from Rubens Barrichello's and Michael Schumacher's Ferraris, both on two-stop strategies with lighter fuel and able to push their tyres. Ralf Schumacher overtook his brother at the first chicane to grab third place, only to be passed by Michael in the first Lesmo corner.

Eventually Barrichello got past but Montoya kept in front of Michael Schumacher. And once both Ferraris had pitted he was alone at the front until his own stop on lap 28, after which he ran third behind his team-mate and Barrichello. Montoya regained the lead on lap 42 and went on to win, but he failed to beat the record for the highest average speed ever. He needed a 150.755mph average and only got 148.571mph, backing off at the end and preferring to guarantee a win rather than a rather meaningless record.

Ralf Schumacher's strategy was to run as long as possible with a heavy fuel load and it worked, temporarily giving him the lead. But he was unable to hold Barrichello and settled for third, with the race's fastest lap: 1m 25.657secs for 152.322mph.

Right: Monza gave Juan Pablo Montoya and his engineers the reward they've been chasing with a first GP victory.
Below right: Having soundly beaten the Ferraris, Montoya celebrates his win.

Above and right: Ralf Schumacher ran a different strategy from Montoya's, and had to fight hard for third, though he set fastest lap. Left: Montoya and trophy, the first of many.

## UNITED STATES GRAND PRIX INDIANAPOLIS
# Throwing it all away

Indianapolis promised great things for BMW and delivered nothing after a brace of retirements, and the team came away from the weekend mathematically unable to take second in the constructors' championship. Juan Pablo Montoya was dazzling, although poor reliability let him down again; his star was shining brighter and brighter at Williams. Ralf Schumacher, on the other hand, was slipping into Montoya's shadow. Although he out-performed the Colombian in qualifying, he was slower in the race despite carrying less fuel, and compounded his misery by spinning himself into retirement. He was one of the drivers to question the wisdom of racing in the US so soon after the terrorist attacks, and at times looked as if he wished he'd stayed at home.

**FRIDAY PRACTICE** BMW Williams brought three cars to Indy: FW23-07 for Schumacher, 08 for Montoya and 02 set up as the Colombian's spare. Schumacher completed 42 laps for a best of 1m 13.919secs for ninth, while Montoya completed 45 laps for 1m 13.983secs and 10th – one place behind Schumacher. Both drivers struggled to find the right set-up.

**SATURDAY PRACTICE** In practice Schumacher took fourth after 26 laps with a 1m 12.454secs; Montoya was sixth after 23 laps with a best of 1m 12.668secs.

At the crucial hour Schumacher took second on the grid in 1m 11.986secs, with Montoya third on 1m 12.252secs. A fair showing, but it left the team a little downbeat.

Schumacher said realistically: "Maybe we're a bit lucky as the two team-mates of the guys in front of us maybe didn't get the optimum out of their cars. Apart from that, we've had a difficult weekend. We started a bit slowly on the tyre side, but we're hoping for better as the track and weather are due to improve tomorrow."

Patrick Head said: "I think we can say they are reasonably solid grid positions for the team rather than anything startling." Translation: he had been hoping for another pole position.

**SUNDAY RACE** In warm-up the Williams duo were first (Schumacher) and sixth (Montoya). Montoya's session was cut short when his engine died and he came to rest by the pitwall.

Pre-race, the pair found they had each moved up a place on the grid due to Häkkinen's relegation to fourth. Schumacher was thus next to his brother, with Montoya third.

When the lights went out, Montoya started best, blasting past Ralf but then failing to pass Michael into the first corner. Ralf was stuck in fourth behind Rubens Barrichello, who on lap three passed Montoya and sped into the distance. Ralf was soon on Montoya's tail as the Ferraris pulled away.

Suddenly the team came good. Montoya caught Michael Schumacher and Barrichello's lead over the Williams before his first stop wasn't enough to keep him ahead. But Ralf was also on a two-stopper. He came in on lap 24 but was slow back out after a problem with his left rear wheel.

Montoya was still following Michael Schumacher, so when Barrichello pitted on lap 27 it became a battle for the lead. On lap 34 Montoya made his move, slipstreaming the Ferrari down the straight and diving through at the first corner – a move he later described as 'good fun'. A lap later he set a new lap record of 1m 14.448secs; the lap after that he pitted for his only stop and, looking favourite to win, rejoined in fourth.

As quickly as Williams' race had turned around, it all went horribly wrong. On lap 37 Ralf Schumacher spun out, and admitted it was his own fault. Two laps later Montoya was out too, with faulty hydraulics, and parked his car in the same spot as in the warm-up. McLaren took home 14 points and an unassailable second place in the constructors' championship.

**Above and left:**
Juan Pablo Montoya again showed skill and self-belief with a supremely assertive move on Michael Schumacher for the lead. But a hydraulic fault again curtailed his race, after only 38 laps.

**Left and below:**
Ralf Schumacher out-qualified Montoya but was out-raced by his team-mate. He admitted his spin on lap 37, which left him stuck in the gravel trap, was his own mistake.

## JAPANESE GRAND PRIX SUZUKA
# Montoya a better bet for 2002

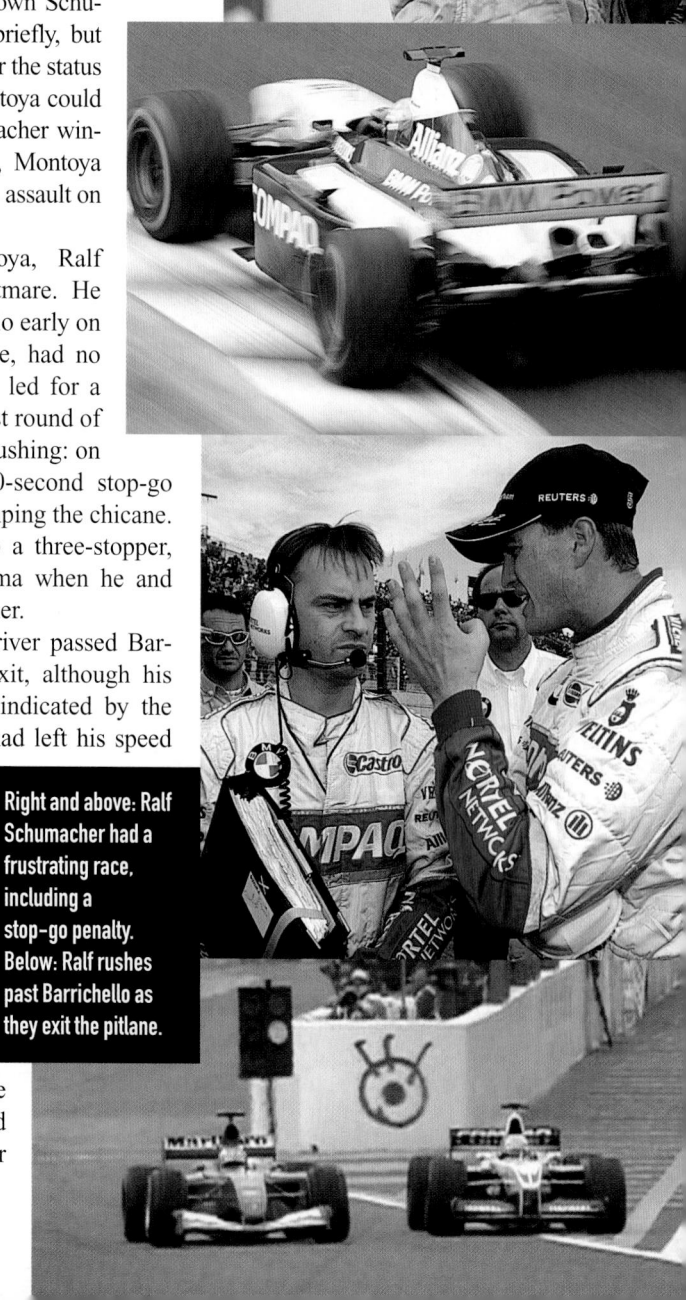

Right: Juan Pablo
Montoya leads
Barrichello into
the Suzuka hairpin.
Below: Montoya
celebrates another
fine result on
another new track.

The BMW Williams team came to Suzuka looking for a fifth-victory finale. It could have had many more, but reliability issues caused the team repeatedly to lose out when victory was at hand.

Just as tantalising as the potential of the BMW/Williams/Michelin package was the infighting between Juan Pablo Montoya and Ralf Schumacher and the growing grudge match between Montoya and Schumacher's brother Michael.

This was Montoya's first visit to Suzuka, but new playgrounds don't bother him. Even the BMW Williams team was beginning to admit that Montoya had rattled Ralf, and hoped the German could strike back and the two could raise their game yet further to pile pressure on Ferrari in 2002. But Ralf Schumacher did not hit back at Suzuka.

The FW23B featured new aerodynamic components, to gain valuable data before the test ban that would run until New Year's Day.

FRIDAY PRACTICE BMW Williams brought three cars, and it was Ralf Schumacher's turn to get the spare. Montoya drove 08; Schumacher had 07 to race and 02 on standby.

Montoya focused on learning the circuit and scrubbing tyres, something that Michelin runners had found increasingly important in trying to get past the window where the rubber grains and 'goes off'. He also worked on set-ups during his 44 laps, and finished second in 1m 35.977secs to Jean Alesi; he was clearly fastest, though, save for one banzai Alesi lap in a car with no fuel.

Schumacher, meanwhile, was unhappy with his FW23's balance and the fact that he only did 32 tours of the circuit. An electrical problem curtailed the German's day; he had to settle for a disgruntled ninth with a 1m 36.874secs.

SATURDAY QUALIFYING The BMW Williams cars seemed to have the edge in the last two sectors, but were roundly beaten by the Bridgestone-shod Ferraris and others in Sector One – where the Esses are crucial. Montoya opined in a derogatory manner that even Rubens Barrichello was faster through that section, giving him little chance to challenge the dominant Michael Schumacher. Having lost the balance slightly on low fuel loads, but exploiting the BMW engine's awesome grunt on the quicker sections, Montoya managed second on the grid with a 1m 33.184secs.

Schumacher fought back well after his Friday problems, but had to settle for third on the grid in 1m 33.297secs. In outqualifying him again, the Colombian had struck a psychological blow.

SUNDAY RACE Neither BMW Williams driver could touch Michael Schumacher, who was peerless in the race proper, but Montoya gave it the better shot. A titanic dice with Barrichello was first on the agenda, though. The Brazilian overtook him at th e chicane on lap two, only to see the BMW Williams man riposte a lap later. Clear of Barrichello, Montoya began chasing down Schumacher's Ferrari. He led briefly, but when the pitstops were over the status quo was restored and Montoya could do nothing to stop Schumacher winning. Happy with second, Montoya looked forward to a serious assault on the title-holder in 2002.

In contrast to Montoya, Ralf Schumacher had a nightmare. He dropped behind Barrichello early on and, unlike his team-mate, had no answers, although he too led for a two-lap window at the first round of pitstops. Clearly he was pushing: on lap 26 he received a 10-second stop-go penalty for repeatedly jumping the chicane. This turned his race into a three-stopper, and there was more drama when he and Barrichello stopped together.

The BMW Williams driver passed Barrichello on the pitlane exit, although his decision seemed to be vindicated by the claim that the Brazilian had left his speed limiter on as he ran out of the pits. Schumacher was lucky to avoid another stop-go penalty later, though: he appeared to repel Barrichello by again cutting the chicane as they battled for fifth. In the end Schumacher could not match the faster Ferrari, though, and yielded before settling for sixth place and one point.

Right and above: Ralf
Schumacher had a
frustrating race,
including a
stop-go penalty.
Below: Ralf rushes
past Barrichello as
they exit the pitlane.

# TEMENOS & Team RED BULL SAUBER PETRONAS
## A World Class Combination

With 4th place secured in this year's Formula One Constructors' Championship, and both drivers top 10 in the Drivers' Championship, Team RED BULL SAUBER PETRONAS' results speak for themselves.

TEMENOS is a global leader in providing financial institutions with integrated banking systems and are proud to be part of this world class partnership.

TEMENOS HEADQUARTERS SA
18 Place des Philosophes
CH-1205 Geneva
Switzerland
Tel:   +41 22 708 1150
Fax:  + 41 22 708 1160

**TEMENOS**
www.temenos.com

Team Review    Race by Race

# SAUBER

2001

## Contents

| | | | | | | |
|---|---|---|---|---|---|---|
| Team Review | – | The season | p178 | European Grand Prix | – | Nürburgring | p192 |
| Australian Grand Prix | – | Melbourne | p184 | French Grand Prix | – | Magny-Cours | p193 |
| Malaysian Grand Prix | – | Sepang | p185 | British Grand Prix | – | Silverstone | p194 |
| Brazilian Grand Prix | – | Interlagos | p186 | German Grand Prix | – | Hockenheim | p195 |
| San Marino Grand Prix | – | Imola | p187 | Hungarian Grand Prix | – | Hungaroring | p196 |
| Spanish Grand Prix | – | Barcelona | p188 | Belgian Grand Prix | – | Spa-Francorchamps | p197 |
| Austrian Grand Prix | – | A1 Ring | p189 | Italian Grand Prix | – | Monza | p198 |
| Monaco Grand Prix | – | Monte Carlo | p190 | USA Grand Prix | – | Indianapolis | p199 |
| Canadian Grand Prix | – | Montreal | p191 | Japanese Grand Prix | – | Suzuka | p200 |

Peter Sauber

Kimi Räikkönen

Nick Heidfeld

Kimi Räikkönen

**Red Bull**
SAUBER PETRONAS

# The surprise of the season

Without question, Peter Sauber's team sprung the surprise of the season, eclipsing the BAR Honda and Jordan Honda teams – not to mention Benetton Renault and Jaguar – to grab fourth place in the constructors' world championship after holding the position for most of the year.

The initial level of competitiveness from Sauber was one surprise; sustaining the effort throughout a season was an even bigger one. The Sauber C20s were as good in Suzuka as they had been in Melbourne, relative to the opposition.

There were a number of elements in Sauber's success. Effectively the best young drivers, chassis and engines came together in the same season. The C20 was obviously a very neat car penned by Argentinian Sergio Rinland, with input from long-time Sauber designer Leo Ress and other members of the technical team now led by Willy Rampf.

It was considerably lighter than its predecessor, and was driver-friendly, a valuable point as Sauber had deliberately opted for two inexperienced young drivers. It walked a neat aerodynamic line between outright efficiency and driveability.

And there was another change in the engine department. Sauber was contracted to get last year's Ferrari engine, but with a difference. Instead of being serviced and rebuilt after each race by Petronas Engineering, a Sauber offshoot, the Ferrari factory took responsibility and as a result – however it was achieved – Sauber got better engines. Towards the end of the season it was likely the engines were 2001 spec, and there were certainly special qualifying engines available, putting Sauber on the same level as works teams. It was a very strong technical package.

This success was despite all the ingredients of failure being apparent. Peter Sauber had fallen out with his main sponsor and majority shareholder, Dietrich Mateschitz. Chief designer Sergio Rinland was shown the door, for reasons never fully to be explained, before the season began. And the team thrived nonetheless.

By luck or judgement, Sauber also ended up with an extremely strong driver pairing. Nick Heidfeld, a refugee from an awful year at Prost, did a superb job in his second season. He was consistently the fastest driver under intense pressure from rookie Kimi Räikkönen. Räikkönen may have been number two, but it didn't feel like it. He gave Heidfeld a hard time all season, although by the end Heidfeld had the edge.

In selecting Nick Heidfeld and Kimi Räikkönen, Peter Sauber was taking the most successful gamble of his life. The team principal ended the year with lots of points and a hefty transfer fee from McLaren, which could top $20 million if Räikkönen stays at McLaren for four years. Heidfeld's contribution was overshadowed undeservedly, for he demonstrated his talent in forceful fashion.

It has been many years since the modern equivalent of a privateer team – one without an alliance with a major engine manufacturer – has shone the way Sauber did in 2001, as it comprehensively bloodied the noses of teams endowed with significantly greater funding.

## The Sauber C20 car

THE Sauber Petronas C20 was all designed and running when Sergio Rinland was summarily dismissed as chief designer before the season began. It was his bad luck, as just a few months later he would have been fêted. Strangely, he couldn't get another job until Arrows took him on at the end of the season.

According to the Argentinian Rinland, his peers lost faith in him

Nick Heidfeld

and questioned whether the new car would be ready on time (it was), whether he would spend too much on it (he didn't) and whether it would be overweight (it wasn't). Peter Sauber, team principal, took a view and got it wrong and thereby let slip through his fingers the most promising designer he has ever employed. Just as he called his drivers right for 2001, he sacked his designer; that call was the wrong one.

The Sauber C20 proved ▷

Nick Heidfeld

to be the best car that the Swiss team has ever made. It came in significantly lighter than last year's C19. That was crucial because the new side-impact regulations added 15kg to the cars' weights. The slimming-down of the C20 enabled Sauber to employ more ballast and move it around to improve the balance of the car. The latest Ferrari-spec engine was the first of the new-breed lightweights and that also helped. The engineers now had maximum flexibility with the weight distribution in order to optimise the car in qualifying.

The previous years' cars, the C18 and C19, had always qualified poorly although they raced well. The C20 was a strong qualifier throughout the year. It had good aerodynamics. In particular, by using two lower front suspension mounting points, one either side of the chassis, Rinland cleverly avoided the aerodynamic blockage that the more usual single mounting creates. That gave the C20 a great front end because the wing was so efficient. By opting to make a minimally pitch-sensitive car, the designer also created a driver-friendly machine that was proved competitive everywhere that it went.

Sauber built seven chassis in 2001. Räikkönen raced 01 in Malaysia, Brazil, San Marino and Spain; otherwise it was the spare in Australia, Austria, Monte Carlo, Canada, Germany (Nürburgring), France, Britain, Germany (Hockenheim), Hungary, Belgium, Italy, America and Japan. Chassis 02 was Räikkönen's race car in Australia, the spare in Malaysia; 03 was Heidfeld's race car in Australia, Malaysia, Brazil and San Marino and should have been in Spain before he had to switch to 05 when 03 developed drivetrain problems on the Saturday. Chassis 04 was only used for testing and as the spare in Brazil and San Marino. Chassis 05

became Heidfeld's race car from Spain through to France, having first appeared as the spare in Spain. It was also the spare tub in Canada, and was built up into his race car after he damaged 03 in qualifying. It also qualified in Italy after Heidfeld crunched 07 in practice. Chassis 06 became Räikkönen's car from Austria onwards, right through to America, where he took over 05 for the final two races. Chassis 07 was Heidfeld's race car from Britain onwards, having been the chassis in the box in France. It was sent back to the Sauber factory at Hinwil for repairs after his Monza shunt, where 05 deputised, and later survived his big crash in practice in Japan.

The C20 was also a very strong car. During the season there were a few major prangs, notably Heidfeld's in Canada where he shunted in qualifying, and again in the race when he was attacked by Irvine; Räikkönen's during testing at Magny-Cours in late August; both drivers' shunts in Friday free practice at Monza; Heidfeld's during Friday practice in Suzuka; and Räikkönen's during the Japanese Grand Prix itself.

Räikkönen's shunt in 06 on the Friday morning in Monza was significant, but the car was ready again on Saturday. Likewise, Heidfeld's accident in Japan was sizeable, his car shedding bits all over the Esses when he put a wheel over the kerb and spun, yet the team had C20-07 back in full working order for Saturday and the German continued to use it in the race.

Chassis 05 was also badly knocked about in Räikkönen's race shunt with Jean Alesi in Japan – three wheels were torn off and the right front was only hanging by a single tether, but once again the chassis survived intact.

Sergio Rinland

Willy Rampf

Leo Ress

Red Bull
SAUBER PETRONAS

## Technical developments

RIGHT out of the box the Sauber C20 was a good car, and Heidfeld and Räikkönen qualified strongly in Melbourne for the first race of the season. It took Sauber a long time to sort out its traction control system, and even longer to get its electronic differential working properly. This was one of the reasons the team's performance dropped momentarily in Monte Carlo. Power-steering was also a long time coming, which suggested that the team's budget was perhaps more limited than it let on. It was finally race-ready by Silverstone in mid-July.

The big difference from past seasons was that Sauber remained competitive right to the end. Willy Rampf took charge of development of the car after Rinland left. Aerodynamic work continued all season, with the team using two basic front wings and otherwise focusing on minor modifications to suit specific circuits. One wing was a normal spoon-shaped device, the other more Jordan-like, with a lower centre section.

At the beginning of the season the gap between Schumacher's pole-winning Ferrari and Heidfeld's 10th-fastest C20 in Melbourne was 1.723secs. At Suzuka at the end of the year Schumacher was again on pole and Heidfeld again 10th fastest, and this time the gap between them was 1.902secs over a slightly longer lap. This indicates that, comparatively, Sauber had kept up with Ferrari throughout the season, which was the real achievement.

The C20s used the 2000 version of the Ferrari V10 engine, in Monza specification, until receiving Melbourne 2001-spec units halfway through the new season. The team had 50 basic engines from Ferrari, badged as Petronas, and took 10 to each race. Altogether, including rebuilds, the team made 130 engine usages during the season, including racing and testing. ▷

## SAUBER PETRONAS SEASON STATISTICS

### RELIABILITY PERFORMANCE

| Driver | Races | Max laps | Laps completed | Reliability rating |
|---|---|---|---|---|
| Nick Heidfeld | 17 | 1,065 | 764 | 71.7% |
| Kimi Räikkönen | 17 | 1,065 | 756 | 71.0% |
| Constructor | Races | Max laps | Laps completed | Reliability rating |
| Team | 34 | 2,130 | 1,520 | 71.4% |

### CHAMPIONSHIP PERFORMANCE

| Driver | 2001 points | 2000 points | 12 month change |
|---|---|---|---|
| Nick Heidfeld | 12 | 0 | +1,200% |
| Kimi Räikkönen | 9 | - | Did not compete |
| Constructor | 2001 points | 2000 points | 12 month change |
| Team | 21 | 6 | +250% |

### CHASSIS LOG

**C20-01** Race car for Kimi Räikkönen at Sepang, Interlagos, Imola and Barcelona; and for Nick Heidfeld at Monza. Spare car at Melbourne, the A1 Ring, Monte Carlo (used by Heidfeld in qualifying), Montreal, Nürburgring, Magny-Cours, Silverstone, Hockenheim, Hungaroring, Spa-Francorchamps, Monza (eventually raced by Heidfeld after 05 failed with hydraulic problems before the start), Indianapolis and Suzuka.

**C20-02** Race car for Räikkönen at Melbourne. Spare car at Sepang.

**C20-03** Race car for Heidfeld at Melbourne, Sepang, Interlagos and Imola. Practised by Heidfeld at Barcelona as his race car but ditched in favour of the spare 05. Used by Heidfeld in practice and qualifying at Montreal before it was written off when he crashed in qualifying.

**C20-04** Spare car at Interlagos and Imola.

**C20-05** Race car for Heidfeld at the A1 Ring, Monte Carlo, Nürburgring and Magny-Cours; and for Räikkönen at Indianapolis and Suzuka. Spare car at Barcelona (used by Heidfeld in qualifying and the race) and at Montreal (raced by Heidfeld after he crashed 03). Qualified by Heidfeld in Monza after he damaged 07 on Friday but abandoned in favour of 01 for the race when it suffered hydraulic problems.

**C20-06** Race car for Räikkönen at the A1 Ring, Monte Carlo, Montreal, Nürburgring, Magny-Cours, Silverstone, Hockenheim, Hungaroring, Spa-Francorchamps and Monza.

**C20-07** Race car for Heidfeld at Silverstone, Hockenheim, Hungaroring, Spa-Francorchamps, Indianapolis and Suzuka. Spare monocoque at Magny-Cours. Crashed by Heidfeld in practice at Monza where it was intended for use as his race car.

Nick Heidfeld

The Ferrari engine was light, compact and had around 820bhp at the beginning of the year and 835bhp towards the end. It was reliable too, neither driver suffering a single failure in racing or testing. Rampf said: "The great thing about using the engine is that we can draw on Ferrari's experience with it to determine the cooling capacity and aerodynamic configuration that the sidepods require and, of course, we know the horsepower figures and reliability that we can expect. This makes the design side very much simpler that it would otherwise be."

Sauber's Achilles heel was its gearbox and drivetrain. Unlike Prost, which used a Ferrari gearbox as well as engine, Sauber had its own seven-speed transmission. Why the team chose to make its own, when it could have had the superbly reliable Italian system, is a mystery. Ferrari's package was immaculately reliable, as Prost proved.

Driveshaft failures undoubtedly stopped the team scoring more than 22 points. There were four known failures: Räikkönen didn't get off the line in Malaysia because one broke, Heidfeld sheared one at the Nürburgring, Räikkönen had another one go when well placed at Hockenheim, and lost another after the collision with Jarno Trulli at Indianapolis.

The gearbox was the other problem. The weakness in the transmission showed at Spa. Both drivers were in all sorts of trouble with fifth and sixth gears refusing to remain in engagement. The team was deliberately vague as to whether that problem stopped Räikkönen on the fourth lap of the aborted race, or whether it was another driveshaft. Whatever, the problem was still evident at Monza. There were suggestions that it caused Räikkönen's Friday morning shunt. Eventually, the team spotted blueing marks on the gear shafts and was able to have a new batch properly machined in time for free practice at qualifying for the Italian race, and finally

the problem went away as quickly as it had arrived. But for a while it had left the team dreadfully exposed.

Sauber's worst qualifying performance came at Monaco with 15th and 16th places as the team struggled to sort out its electronic diff. Belgium was also pretty dire, with 12th and 14th. When Heidfeld crashed into Pedro de la Rosa on the opening lap of the restart at Spa, that easily put the Belgian Grand Prix on a par with Malaysia and Hockenheim as the team's worst races. In Malaysia, Räikkönen failed to get off the line, while Heidfeld spun. At Hockenheim, the German was rammed out of the race, while Räikkönen broke a driveshaft.

## The drivers

THREE drivers drove a C20 during the course of the season. Nick Heidfeld and Kimi Räikkönen also drove the old C19 before the new car was ready. Both performed better than the 2000 drivers Mika Salo and Pedro Diniz. Peter Sauber had long believed that the outgoing drivers had not always been giving their best.

By contrast, neither Räikkönen nor Heidfeld had a weekend in 2001 where they could be accused of giving less than their best. That was a significant factor in Sauber's overall success. Both men made a strong contribution to the team's fourth place in the championship, not just because they drove hard but because by doing so they kept everyone else's motivation at maximum pitch.

In the final analysis, Heidfeld outqualified Räikkönen nine to eight, and scored more points: 13 to nine. But that disguises a number of things: the Finn was well placed on many occasions when his car let him down. In total the C20s qualified in the top 10 on 22 occasions out of 34, and both cars were in the top 10 on the grid eight times.

In the opening race in Melbourne, Heidfeld wiped away all trace of his disappointing 2000 rookie season with a strong fourth place, as Räikkönen made his mark by finishing sixth. Malaysia was a disaster in front of title sponsor Petronas, with Heidfeld spinning and Räikkönen's transmission breaking at the start. In Brazil, Heidfeld raced hard against Trulli and deserved the podium position for third place that would be the highlight of his season. Räikkönen spun there, possibly dropping it in the wet, possibly as a result of a tyre deflation.

Heidfeld went on to finish sixth five times, in Spain, France, Britain, Hungary and America, and was unlucky that an excellent sixth on the grid in Austria was wasted by the car's refusal to move off the grid. He staged a strong recovery to ninth. Räikkönen took fourth place twice, in Austria and Canada, and a fifth in Britain, and had been running a solid ninth in Imola when, of all things, the steering wheel came loose. It was a problem with the design that was quickly rectified.

Räikkönen might also have scored points in Germany, Belgium and America, but hitting Heidfeld and then being walloped by Trulli finished his chances at the United States Grand Prix. Heidfeld should also have taken points in Germany but was taken out on the first lap by de la Rosa; at Spa, Heidfeld returned the favour.

For the most part, Heidfeld and Räikkönen got on well together. At the end of the season Heidfeld said of his prospective team-mate for 2002: "I hope I get another one who will push me as hard as Kimi did. It's good for you."

Neither driver was particularly outgoing. Räikkönen was for the most part dour at best, sullen at worst, making little effort to ingratiate himself with anyone on the team socially. Driving the car was all he cared about. Heidfeld, meanwhile, was quiet and self-contained, and for the most part extremely serious.

There was evidence at the end of the year that the two drivers were getting tetchy with one another. At Indianapolis, Räikkönen blamed Heidfeld for their Turn 1 clash that ruined the Finn's race (though video evidence revealed Jarno Trulli as the prime culprit). In Suzuka, Heidfeld accused Räikkönen of pushing him onto the grass in the first corner on the opening lap, thereby ruining his race. The German was also miffed – understandably, given his past association with the team – that he was passed over at McLaren in favour of Räikkönen.

It was inevitable that the big teams would try to woo Räikkönen, even though Sauber held a three-year contract with its young star. Ferrari was the popular favourite and rumours abounded mid-season that he would replace Rubens Barrichello in 2002. Instead it was Ron Dennis at McLaren who first approached Räikkönen's management as early as the Canadian Grand Prix. And as Mika Häkkinen moved ever closer to his sabbatical decision, an accommodation was reached – a chunk of money changed hands – and Sauber yielded to the inevitable. It was announced at Monza in

September that Räikkönen would partner David Coulthard in 2002. In keeping with its aim of minimising costs, Sauber made do without a test driver throughout 2001. In previous years Red Bull protégé Enrique Bernoldi had been used in that role. But when it became clear that Räikkönen would not be staying, the team gave two runs to Euro Formula 3000 series champion Felipe Massa. The 20-year-old Brazilian ran both times at Mugello in September, just as Räikkönen had the previous year.

It is always difficult to quantify with absolute accuracy a driver's performance during testing, since so many factors can differ not just from team to team but from one of a team's cars to the other. But Massa appeared to acquit himself well and at Suzuka it was announced, as expected, that he would partner Heidfeld in 2002. Peter Sauber thinks he has found another impressive young talent, or else he has yielded to Ferrari's blandishments to run a driver who is highly rated by the Scuderia. Perhaps it is a combination of both. But one thing that Massa's performance hints at is that the C20 was indeed an extremely easy car to get the best from; that, after all, is the name of the game, and it excelled in that respect.

## Commercial

SAUBER launched its 2001 campaign in a relatively low-key manner at its factory in Hinwil, when Credit Suisse was announced as a primary sponsor in conjunction with Petronas, which continued as the title sponsor. Red Bull's space on the car was notably reduced after the disagreement between Peter Sauber and Dietrich Mateschitz over hiring Räikkönen instead of Red Bull's protégé Enrique Bernoldi. Red Bull's money instead went to Arrows. Nonetheless, the team had a total budget of only $87.15 million, which also had to pay for the engine.

Sauber motorhome

At the 2001 launch, Peter Sauber was being realistic and expressed the hope that his team might climb from eighth to seventh, or perhaps even sixth place in the constructors' championship. As it transpired he had the sort of season team principals dream of, exceeding his forecast. Any team will tell you it rarely happens that way.

The C20s were always immaculately presented, in their metallic dark blue and Petronas turquoise colours, the only significant change from 2000 being the white Credit Suisse nose after years of Red Bull's familiar yellow and red.

Over the course of the season's 17 races, with 1,065 laps available per car, Sauber Petronas covered a total of 1,520, 764 laps with Heidfeld and 756 with Räikkönen. It indicates that Sauber provides both drivers with equal equipment, and that reliability and driver capability were both at a high level, although not high enough. Sauber was the seventh most reliable team out of 11. The average reliability was 71.4 per cent against Prost's 78.3 per cent and Ferrari's 90.8 per cent with the same engine.

# Surprise turn of speed

Peter Sauber, team principal, left Melbourne with a smile the size of his trademark cigar, as his new car, designated C20, scored fourth and sixth places. Both Nick Heidfeld and Kimi Räikkönen were fast all weekend, the German shaking off the ghost of his awful 2000 season and the Finn replying to those who doubted his ability and qualification for an FIA super-licence. With 16 races to go, the points haul nearly matched the tally from 2000 and set Sauber Petronas up perfectly for its home race in Malaysia.

**FRIDAY PRACTICE** Sauber arrived with three cars: Nick Heidfeld in chassis C20-03, Kimi Räikkönen in chassis C20-02 and the spare C20-01 set up for Heidfeld. The German had a good first day, posting seventh fastest time. He was happy with his early running even though his second session was cut short when the brake pedal momentarily seized up, causing him to spin and accept 1m 30.345secs as his best for the day. He then narrowly escaped involvement in Michael Schumacher's dramatic accident. The Sauber pilot had just evacuated the cockpit and replaced the steering wheel after sliding off the road in Turn 6 when the Ferrari barrel-rolled behind his back.

Rookie Kimi Räikkönen was happy to achieve decent running on his first visit to Albert Park. He concentrated on learning the circuit and eliminating understeer in the final sector. He was a brilliant 11th on a time of 1m 31.453secs, just over a second adrift after running on the harder Bridgestones, driving smoothly and with none of the way-ward tendencies of some of his more experienced rivals.

**SATURDAY QUALIFYING** Nick Heidfeld spun during the morning free practice session but achieved the team's goal of qualifying in the top 10, although he felt that he could have gone faster than his 1m 28.615secs. He set his best first two sectors but then ran into traffic on the final sector. For the second day running he was lucky to avoid involvement in an accident – this time when a wheel from Burti's shunted Jaguar rolled towards his car.

He was similarly frustrated in his final attempt when he had to come to a stop as Fisichella slid into and out of the gravel just ahead of him.

Kimi Räikkönen lost half the morning with an engine sensor problem and the gearbox had to be removed to cure it. He was disappointed with 13th on the grid and complained of traffic during his good laps, and said that the C20 started with understeer and ended with oversteer. His time was nevertheless an impressive 1m 28.993secs. That the team was disappointed with 10th and 13th places on the grid spoke volumes.

**SUNDAY RACE** Nick Heidfeld avoided trouble at the start, didn't try to offer pointless resistance when Olivier Panis and Jos Verstappen slipped by under yellow flags on the third lap, and settled down in eighth, then seventh place to await developments. Häkkinen's demise put him into points-scoring contention and despite real pressure from Heinz-Harald Frentzen in the closing stages he held on for fifth. When Sauber's protest against Panis was subsequently upheld, he gained a place and some points, as did his team-mate.

Kimi Räikkönen didn't start brilliantly, but soon began to make amends for losing three places in the opening lap. Frentzen's problem with Barrichello gave him one back, then Villeneuve erased himself and Ralf Schumacher. Verstappen's fuel stop helped him again during the safety car period. First he caught and overtook Alesi – no mean feat in itself – then Jenson Button with insouciant ease on lap 17. By then he had Frentzen breathing down his collar, but he kept cool and took Fisichella eight laps later. Räikkönen's lap times were usually within a couple of 10ths of Heidfeld's. Frentzen finally made it through when Räikkönen pitted on lap 36, but even that went well. After standing still for 10.5secs, he accelerated back into the race like a veteran to his eventual sixth place.

Above and right: Kimi Räikkönen's stunning debut performance came as a surprise to many who argued that the Formula Renault racer shouldn't even have a super-licence.

Above and below: Nick Heidfeld put memories of his disastrous 2000 Prost season behind him. Qualifying 10th, he raced through to fourth place.

## MALAYSIAN GRAND PRIX SEPANG
# Fast but zero achievement

**M**alaysia was a bad race for Sauber. It was doubly important to perform well in front of its major Malaysian sponsor, Petronas. But it was all over for the team after four laps as both cars went out. Kimi Räikkönen never got to the first corner when his transmission failed leaving the start line, while Nick Heidfeld went off from ninth place four laps later. Luckily for the team it was a blip in what was to prove an outstanding season.

FRIDAY PRACTICE Heidfeld and Räikkönen had the same cars as in Melbourne, with the spare to the faster qualifier. Heidfeld finished the day 12th with a best of 1m 41.027secs. Räikkönen, by contrast, seemed rattled with his 14th fastest time. Most rookies would have been happy with that, but his anger was an indication of what he expected of his potential. He clocked a 1m 41.592secs but reported too much understeer and said the car generally felt nervous.

SATURDAY QUALIFYING Nick Heidfeld qualified strongly in 11th place and was happy with his C20, although he felt the scrubbed front Bridgestone tyres he had used for his first two runs in qualifying on Saturday afternoon were better suited to the car than the unscrubbed fronts he had used on his third.

Räikkönen admitted he was frustrated to line up 'only' 14th. After running strongly in the morning, when he was 10th fastest, he had entertained hopes of a top 10 qualifying slot, but changes to his C20 between sessions to dial out understeer were only partially successful. He set his best time on his second run, and had to abort the third after running wide in traffic just as his sector times looked promising. Just to ensure the pill had no sugar coating, he was then waved on to the FIA scales as he came into the pits and the time he lost there compromised his final run.

SUNDAY RACE Räikkönen's transmission let go as he left the start line and he was lucky not to be struck from behind as he crept towards the end of the pitlane. Heidfeld, however, made a good start and had moved up a place to ninth when Olivier Panis slid off on his own oil. "When it was just drizzling everything was OK," Heidfeld said. "But on the fourth lap I hit the standing water on the back of the circuit and just aquaplaned into the gravel." He was bogged down and left helplessly spinning his wheels. As others also failed to perform the Swiss team retained fourth place in the constructors' championship. But better was to come.

Red Bull
SAUBER PETRONAS

**Above and left:** Despite qualifying in a strong 10th place and starting well, Heidfeld ended his race in the gravel on lap four when he aquaplaned off.

**Left: Young rookie Kimi Räikkönen had less to smile about in Malaysia following his brilliant debut in Melbourne. Below: Despite promising performances on Friday and Saturday, Räikkönen's race ended almost as soon as it started when his transmission failed as he left the grid.**

## BRAZILIAN GRAND PRIX INTERLAGOS
# Podium finish

**N**obody admitted as much until it was all over – although the chances of a repeat were ultra-slim to zero – but Sauber Petronas ran all weekend under the shadow of last year's rear wing failures that put both cars out of the weekend. Thus it was a delighted Peter Sauber who saw both his cars qualify in the top 10, and then watched Nick Heidfeld put in the drive of his life to bring his C20 home in third place in the race. It was the team's first podium since Jean Alesi's at Spa back in 1998.

**FRIDAY PRACTICE** Heidfeld and Kimi Räikkönen stayed with the chassis they had used in Melbourne and Malaysia: C20-03 for the German and C20-01 for the Finn, with C20-04 as the spare. Heidfeld hit his stride early, despite losing time with a sensor problem, and set the ninth best lap of the day with 1m 17.102secs. Räikkönen, on the toughest of the three tracks he had raced so far, was initially unhappy when the steering wheel was on skew-whiff, and when a minor brake problem arose, but he settled in with the 15th fastest time of 1m 17.712secs.

**SATURDAY QUALIFYING** Sauber was overjoyed when both drivers made the top 10 in qualifying. The message from Interlagos was that, far from predictably sliding down the grid, the C20 was getting better.

Heidfeld worked steadily, making small adjustments all day. There was a minor glitch when this did not bring improvements on his third run, but the alteration for the final run was the most effective of all and he set the ninth fastest time – 1m 14.810secs.

Räikkönen was on the boil, too, setting eighth fastest time in the morning and running ahead of Heidfeld for most of qualifying. He improved further to 1m 14.924secs, good enough for 10th on the grid. "I'm very pleased because this is the result I have been aiming for since Melbourne," he said.

**SUNDAY RACE** Sauber set up both cars expecting a dry race, despite a gloomy forecast. The plan was, if it did rain, to let the drivers make the final decision on tyres. Both dri-

vers made great starts and by the third lap Heidfeld was up to seventh with Räikkönen in his wheeltracks. Both were soon demoted by a two-stopping Olivier Panis, but regained the places as Jacques Villeneuve stopped on his 12th lap. Points were always on the cards.

Heidfeld rose to sixth when Panis stopped on lap 28, but the BAR regained ground when the C20s pitted on laps 37 and 38. Räikkönen was briefly promoted to sixth as Heidfeld stopped in the rain on lap 45, crucially deciding on intermediates.

Räikkönen stopped on lap 46, vacating what had become fifth, and resumed sixth, separated from his team-mate by Trulli. But the Finn spun on the 52nd lap, dropping back to 10th, then repeated the error for good three laps later. "The first time I couldn't get enough traction on the grass to move uphill so I lost time rolling downhill before I could get going again," he said. "The second time it was just my fault, too."

Heidfeld lost fourth place to Trulli on the 50th lap but as conditions improved the under-rated German counter-attacked successfully on his intermediates, regaining the place 10 laps later. When Frentzen dropped out on the 64th lap, he inherited third place.

"I'm so happy for the team, they have really worked for this result," Heidfeld said after a finely judged race. "And for me it is just amazing! It's a lot more fun this year to be in the points, especially to finish on the podium."

Initial prospects looked promising for Kimi Räikkönen (above and right) as he continued to show pace and maturity, but no result this time.

Nick Heidfeld (below and celebrating) scored Sauber's first podium in three years, while Kimi Räikkönen (right) ended his race with a spin and a walk home.

## SAN MARINO GRAND PRIX IMOLA
# Smiles all round

Red Bull
SAUBER PETRONAS

**Above: Nick Heidfeld just missed out on a championship point . Left: Räikkönen's race ended in the wall with a steering wheel failure.**

The performance of the Swiss Sauber team underlined the competitiveness of the C20 car, which had put other well-financed works teams to shame. 2001 was shaping up to be Sauber's best ever season: a good car, good drivers and a reasonable engine, plus enough money in the bank even for the frugal Peter Sauber to make a good fist of things. Which he duly proceeded to do. Smiles all round in the Sauber motorhome. The drivers had also been a revelation with Heidfeld having a slight edge on Räikkönen, who had also proved a sensation.

FRIDAY PRACTICE Sauber brought the same cars to Imola, with Nick Heidfeld in C20-03, Kimi Räikkönen in C20-01 and C20-04 as the spare. The Finn gave notice of his potential by setting the sixth fastest time, despite the changeable conditions, with 1m 26.552secs and he had no problems learning another new circuit. He reported nonchalantly that his quick lap was nothing special.

Heidfeld was 12th on 1m 27.142secs, his final run on new tyres spoiled by yellow flags. Neither had any problems.

**Above and left: Kimi Räikkönen's weekend promised much, but after chasing the Ferraris he was left to walk home when his car failed with a steering fault. The Saubers were a match for the Ferraris on their home circuit but problems denied them points.**

SATURDAY QUALIFYING For the first time, Räikkönen out-qualified his team-mate. He set the fourth fastest time, a 1m 31.726secs, during damp free practice and his performance all day drew universal praise.

In the afternoon his best was a strong 1m 24.671secs, but it would have been quicker still had he not braked too late for the final corner, run across the grass on the entry and lost three or four 10ths. Without that mistake, he would have lined up eighth or ninth.

Räikkönen was annoyed with himself, but said: "These things happen. The car is very good here and it's doing everything I want it to." Heidfeld's was not. In the morning he was sixth quickest on 1m 32.392secs, but the best he could manage in qualifying was 1m 25.007secs for 12th. Understeer was his main problem. Both drivers used Bridgestone's softer compound rubber.

SUNDAY RACE The morning warm-up went well for Sauber, with Räikkönen eighth and Heidfeld fourth. In the race, Räikkönen jumped straight up to ninth place ahead of Heinz-Harald Frentzen and latched on to the group fighting for sixth place with Panis's BAR Honda and the two Ferraris. He looked perfectly comfortable, biding his time, but was unfortunate to lose a huge amount of time when he was unable to follow the red cars through as they passed Panis.

He was figuring a way past the Frenchman when his C20 turned sharp left as it climbed the hill after Tosa on lap 18 and hit the retaining wall at relatively slow speed. The steering wheel had come off its spline, making Räikkönen a passenger. Back in 1991 this happened to Mika Häkkinen at Phoenix and Monza when he was driving for Lotus, when bumps in the track knocked his knees against the quick-release mechanism. But Räikkönen's engineer, Jacky Eeckelaert, was adamant that was not possible on the C20. The Finn may not have refitted the wheel properly after climbing into the car on the grid and the error took 18 laps to manifest itself, or there may have been a mechanical failure. Investigations revealed nothing.

Heidfeld made an indifferent start when the long hold for the red lights to go out made the bite point of his clutch start to vary, but he soon re-passed Eddie Irvine for 12th and settled onto the tail end of the Räikkönen group. Unable quite to match Frentzen as his balance problem persisted, Heidfeld stopped for fuel on laps 25 and 45, and finished in seventh place – just outside the points.

## SPANISH GRAND PRIX BARCELONA
# Best of the rest

It was proving to be Sauber's year. Each race the pundits expected the Swiss team to slip back to second-division status and struggle at the back of the grid. But it was establishing 'best of the rest' status behind Ferrari, McLaren Mercedes and BMW Williams, with teams such as Benetton Renault and Jaguar well behind it. Sauber finished in the points yet again in Spain. It marked a milestone of 99 world championship points since it entered Formula One in 1993. One hundred beckoned.

FRIDAY PRACTICE The usual trio of C20s was on hand: 03 for Nick Heidfeld, 01 for Kimi Räikkönen, and the spare 05 set up for the Finn. All three were fitted with traction control and automatic gearshift, although the launch control and power-steering were not yet raceworthy.

Räikkönen, who assumed super-licence status despite apparently having no FIA confirmation, maintained the upper hand over Heidfeld as they worked through throttle mapping and tyre evaluation to finish in 11th and 12th respectively, on 1m 21.786secs and 1m 21.808secs. The traction control needed fine-tuning and Räikkönen complained of wheelspin and nervous handling.

SATURDAY QUALIFYING Overnight, technical director Willy Rampf and his crew got on top of the traction control problems and both drivers were pleased with the balance and grip on the soft Bridgestones, which they chose to use in qualifying and the race. In the afternoon Räikkönen regretted leaving his car as it had been in the morning as changing conditions prevented him from repeating his time. His best was 1m 19.229secs, and ninth, but if he could have repeated his early morning time he would have been fifth.

Heidfeld, too, was frustrated. A drive train problem on his race car forced him to switch to the spare after the installation lap of his first run, and he inevitably lost time while C20-05 was converted from Räikkönen's seat and pedals settings. He didn't get out until 45 minutes had elapsed, but quickly secured 10th slot with a lap of 1m 19.232secs. He said: "I'm happy to be in the top 10 in the circumstances, but not when I consider where I could have been without losing that time." He, too, felt he could have been fifth, as his performance in the time he had available showed the potential.

SUNDAY RACE Heidfeld opted to stay with chassis 05 and made a better start than Räikkönen. Going into the first corner the German was ahead of Jacques Villeneuve, but the Canadian edged the Sauber onto the grass. "I don't think we quite touched, but it was close!" Heidfeld said. "It was just normal racing. I would have done the same thing."

Heidfeld still maintained eighth place, then moved up to as high as fourth during the first pitstops. He made his own on lap 24, dropping back to seventh once the order had settled. He caught Jarno Trulli in sixth place, but after his second stop on lap 39 the German found his final set of Bridgestones wasn't as good as the others. He was running sixth on lap 49 after the second round of stops, but David Coulthard was gaining. For three laps Heidfeld gamely held him off, but a 10kph straight line speed advantage finally told on lap 60. If one McLaren had forced Sauber out of the points, however, the other would restore its position when Häkkinen's clutch failed on the final lap.

Räikkönen dropped to 10th on the first lap and was demoted again by Olivier Panis on lap three. He stayed in touch with the Frenchman as they chased after Irvine, but was bothered all by understeer and finished an unobtrusive eighth. Peter Sauber said: "The reality is that neither car was fast enough today to challenge BAR and Jordan."

Top: Heidfeld fought hard for sixth. Above: Kimi Räikkönen discusses race strategy before the start. Right and below: Heidfeld and Räikkönen were contenders for points all weekend and benefited from the retirements of Mika Häkkinen and Rubens Barrichello.

Red Bull
SAUBER PETRONAS

### AUSTRIAN GRAND PRIX A1 RING
# Running again with the hares

From the start the C20s looked quick but the team had a disaster when Nick Heidfeld's car failed to move off the grid. However, Kimi Räikkönen's charge from eighth to sixth in the opening laps proved yet again that the C20 was a very good car. Sauber was maturing with the resources and drivers to capitalise on its potential and turn it into points. In scoring another three the rookie Finn matched compatriot Mika Häkkinen's 2001 tally. Those who expected the team's form to fade were beginning to wipe egg off their faces.

**Above and Left:** Räikkönen scored the best finish of his very short Grand Prix career, with a fine fourth, here lapping Eddie Irvine's Jaguar during his pursuit of the Ferraris.

FRIDAY PRACTICE Heidfeld stuck with C20-05, the former T-car he had to race in Spain, and Räikkönen used the latest chassis, 06, which he had tested the previous week at Silverstone. Still no power-steering, but some small aero changes, and launch control was fitted for the first time at a race.

Both drivers had a trouble-free day, amassing 89 laps. Heidfeld was sixth fastest with 1m 11.776secs, pleased that the Bridgestone tyres performed with a consistency that helped dampen any confusion arising from the fluctuation in track condition.

Räikkönen adjusted to another new track with the speed that had become his hallmark, and having achieved a satisfactory set-up early on spent the rest of the day fine-tuning. Both drivers were happy that the software for their traction control was significantly better than it had been in Spain.

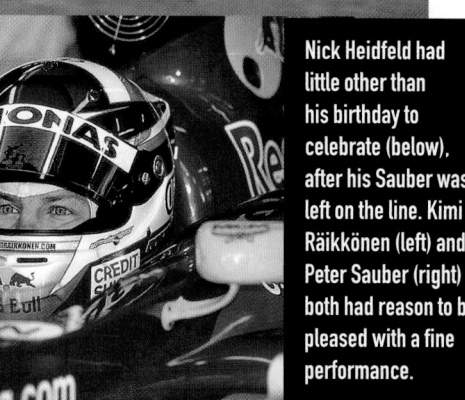

Nick Heidfeld had little other than his birthday to celebrate (below), after his Sauber was left on the line. Kimi Räikkönen (left) and Peter Sauber (right) both had reason to be pleased with a fine performance.

SATURDAY QUALIFYING Both the drivers were quick in the morning (9th and 12th) as they opted for the soft Bridgestones, but Heidfeld pulled a lap out of the bag to grab sixth in qualifying with 1m 10.211secs. It was a personal best and Sauber's best grid placing of the season so far.

Heidfeld got a good set-up early on, then played with tyre pressures. He was also one of the few to time things perfectly as far as the wind direction was concerned.

Räikkönen felt he'd have been quicker than his team-mate and was riled to have Jacques Villeneuve ruin his best qualifying effort. The French-Canadian let a Minardi past then speeded up and baulked the Finn, most likely because he simply didn't see him. Räikkönen had to be content with 1m 10.396secs when a subsequent attempt was thwarted by more traffic and a recurrence of a gearshift software problem that had bothered him in the morning. Prior to qualifying the team changed the internals of both gearboxes after discovering traction control wears the dog-rings faster.

SUNDAY RACE Disaster struck immediately. Heidfeld made a manual start on the formation lap to lay down some rubber ahead of his grid slot, but come the race start his launch control failed to trigger, leaving him sitting haplessly with Häkkinen and the Jordans.

Meanwhile, Räikkönen got away eighth and moved to sixth by lap 10. He had no problems, outrunning the BARs of Panis and Villeneuve, and initially hung on to Coulthard's McLaren. He was promoted to fourth by the Montoya/Schumacher fracas, and temporarily took third on Verstappen's stop on lap 22. The Finn didn't make life difficult for Schumacher as he recovered (Sauber relies on Ferrari engines, of course), and even a delay on his pitstop on lap 46 didn't upset his rhythm. The left rear wheel was reluctant to go on, but such was his advantage that he got going before Panis went past, and pulled away from him as he rejoined. Fourth emphasised his potential.

Heidfeld charged back up to ninth, never losing heart even when a clutch problem at his pitstop on lap 46 cost him 20 seconds and he had to be dropped off the rear jack to get going. After qualifying so well, this was a cruel blow.

# Brief hiatus from the scoreboard

Sauber's dream run encountered a nasty hiatus in Monte Carlo. A first-lap retirement for Nick Heidfeld and only a 10th-place finish for Kimi Räikkönen was all the team took home. But it was thankful to leave the principality still fifth in the constructors' championship.

Right from the start of the meeting it was clear the C20 did not suit the street circuit, despite running well the previous week at similarly low-grip Valencia. The cars lacked traction and grip, features that might have been improved had the new hydraulic differential been available.

THURSDAY PRACTICE Sauber had the same three cars on hand that it used in Austria – C20-05 for Heidfeld, C20-06 for Räikkönen and the spare (C20-01), but there was still no sign of power-steering or hydraulic differential. When Räikkönen finished the day 13th on 1m 22.800secs and Heidfeld 14th on 1m 22.807secs it was clear something was wrong, for the C20s had been well up in the timesheets all year – even in free practice. Both lost better runs when Ralf Schumacher crashed and brought out the yellow flags at the end of the afternoon session, and the pair found their cars hard to drive, with poor traction and understeer. Heidfeld, previously a Formula Three and F3000 winner here (in 1997 and 1998 respectively), had three visits to the Ste Devote escape road.

SATURDAY QUALIFYING In the morning Räikkönen went off at the Swimming Pool, damaging the left-hand side of his C20, and was only 15th fastest on 1m 21.621secs. Heidfeld trailed him in 19th place on 1m 22.207secs, although that was mainly due to persistent traffic problems. Like all the other Bridgestone runners both drivers opted for the softer compound tyres for qualifying, but for the first time all season the team failed to get its act together and the cars remained a handful.

Räikkönen complained about traffic and a yellow flag, but believed he would not have gone much faster than 1m 20.081secs for 15th place anyway.

Heidfeld's race car developed a throttle potentiometer problem on his second qualifying run and attempts to cure it proved fruitless. He used up another set of new tyres during an exploratory third outing then switched to the T-car, did one flying lap and ran into traffic again. He reckoned the T-car had better brakes than his race car, but a yellow flag on his last run, when his final set of tyres was past its best, left him to fall back on his previous best lap of 1m 20.261secs for 16th on the grid. It was the team's worst performance of the year so far and couldn't have come at a worse place.

SUNDAY RACE Heidfeld made a bad start and his unhappy weekend was halted before Portier when he was attacked by Verstappen and thrown into the air and the unyielding wall. After Austria, it was tough.

Räikkönen made up two places from his grid position at the expense of Heinz-Harald Frentzen and Pedro de la Rosa. He made up two more when Juan Pablo Montoya and Olivier Panis quit and another as Mika Häkkinen dropped back, putting him ninth by lap 15. Then a wheel-speed sensor problem forced him into the pits, where initially it seemed the Finn had retired. But the team switched the C20's electronic system to emergency mode and he rejoined the race five laps behind and without traction control. Despite the handicap Räikkönen drove strongly, setting the sixth fastest lap in a car he said felt much better after changes made in the morning warm-up. He was too far behind to catch anyone, but finished in 10th place.

Right: Kimi Räikkönen again displayed a rare natural talent.

Right: Nick Heidfeld's race ended just before Portier on the first lap. Below: Räikkönen set the sixth fastest lap after a nightmare pitstop dashed his chances.

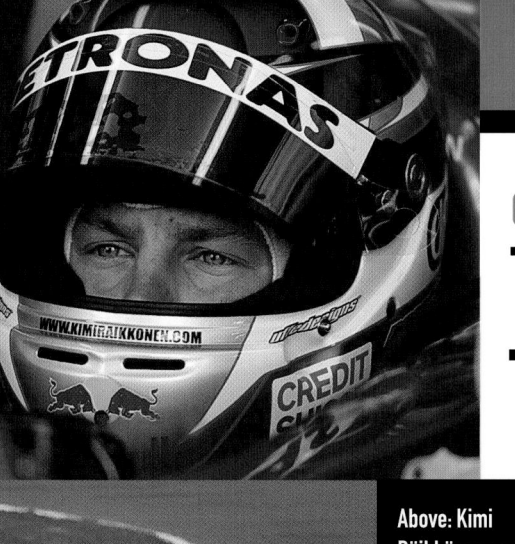

## CANADIAN GRAND PRIX MONTREAL

# The show gets back on the road

The blues of Monaco were dispelled in style as the Sauber team got its show well and truly back on the road in Canada. And what an impressive show it was, earning the admiration of everyone in the paddock.

From the start of the weekend the C20 looked comfortable on the demanding Montreal circuit, and with only slightly better luck Kimi Räikkönen could have qualified as high as fifth. As it was he scored the team's best grid position of the season so far and raced home fourth.

Räikkönen was proving himself the find of the season and Peter Sauber optimistically kept his hopes up of holding onto him for 2002.

**Above: Kimi Räikkönen again performed exceptionally, qualifying seventh and taking points for the third time in his very short Grand Prix career. Left: The Finn is trailed by Ricardo Zonta's Jordan and countryman Mika Häkkinen.**

FRIDAY PRACTICE Sauber brought three cars to Montreal, with a spare monocoque on hand. Nick Heidfeld started his weekend in C20-03, with Räikkönen in C20-06 and C20-01 as the spare. C20-05 would be built up as a complete car for Heidfeld to use in the race.

Although there was still no sign of power-steering, the electro-hydraulic differential made an appearance at last and transformed the car.

Just as it had been obvious from the start in Monte Carlo that the team was in trouble, so in Montreal it was clear the C20 was again performing as it had in previous races. Heidfeld had a very good day: he set the seventh quickest time of 1m 18.967secs in the course of 40 trouble-free laps and expressed the view that the new differential worked well and in particular improved traction and facilitated much faster adjustments than the old mechanical unit. After the disaster at Monaco, the German was significantly relieved, particularly as traction is also crucial in Montreal.

By contrast Räikkönen's 32 laps left the Finn irritable as he struggled with set-up problems on his differential and traction control systems, and with braking shortcomings. He learned yet another new circuit very quickly, but his best time was only 1m 19.427secs for 13th fastest. Once again underlining the talent.

**Left and above: Nick Heidfeld had another frustrating weekend, out-qualified by his team-mate. While trying to improve his grid position, he made a mistake which launched the Sauber into the wall.**

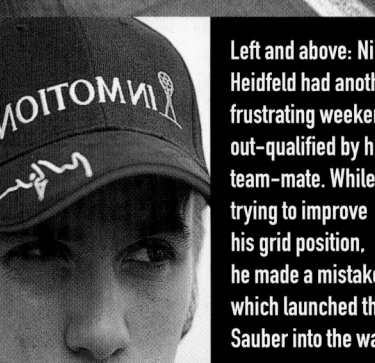

SATURDAY QUALIFYING The roles were reversed on Saturday as Räikkönen once more became voluble about the performance of his car. Heidfeld was chastened, however, after a heavy shunt in qualifying.

It was clear that Sauber had emphatically discovered its way again after Monaco, as Heidfeld and Räikkönen set fifth and sixth fastest times of 1m 17.103secs and 1m 17.144secs respectively in free practice. As a result, both opted to run Bridgestone's soft tyre option for qualifying and the race.

However, where Räikkönen was able to translate that promise into a brilliant seventh fastest qualifying run, with 1m 16.875secs, Heidfeld failed to better his early time of 1m 17.165secs after walloping the wall on the exit to the last corner on his final try.

The kerb on the inside had launched several people, including Rubens Barrichello, who had been caught out earlier and also clobbered the wall. Räikkönen admitted he'd had two close calls there the previous day, on one occasion missing the concrete by a millimetre, and it boiled down to how the car landed. In Heidfeld's case it was not good and the C20 crunched into the wall hard enough to remove its right-hand wheels. Heidfeld was unhurt.

Räikkönen admitted he had also lost time there on his best lap, and also at the hairpin, otherwise he believed he could have been sixth or even fifth.

SUNDAY RACE Within two laps of the start Sauber had only one car to worry about. Anxious to exploit a light fuel load, Jaguar's Eddie Irvine shoved Heidfeld into retirement going into Turn 3 on the second lap, taking off the C20's rear wing.

Räikkönen kept his grid position off the line, but was overtaken on the opening lap by the light-tanked Arrows of Jos Verstappen. Unfazed, he settled into a rhythm that was only upset when his rear tyres began to blister and go off. Shortly afterwards, on the 33rd lap, he was hit in the back by Ricardo Zonta, sustaining some rear wing damage.

The Finn made his stop on the 39th lap, finding that a new set of tyres made the C20 much better to drive. In the closing stages he hunted down Jarno Trulli for fourth place on lap 62, and kept hold of that position despite pressure from Jean Alesi. It was another highly impressive performance.

Red Bull
SAUBER PETRONAS

# Transmission dramas

All weekend Sauber seemed well placed to challenge for further championship points, especially as Nick Heidfeld and Kimi Räikkönen ran eighth and ninth early in the race. But a curious loss of pace allied to badly blistered Bridgestones left both C20s slipping back in the pack. As the post-race investigation began nobody would admit to anything, but adjustment problems with the electro-hydraulic differential seemed a possible culprit. With Jordan, BAR and Jaguar all failing to score points, at least Sauber remained fourth in the points table.

**FRIDAY PRACTICE** Following his hefty shunt on the first lap of the Canadian Grand Prix, Heidfeld had sufficiently recuperated to take his seat once more in C20-05, while Räikkönen had his usual 06; 01 was the spare.

The young German set the eighth fastest time of 1m 18.196secs after 38 laps. Räikkönen was less than three-10ths of a second slower but three places further back after his 37 laps for a best of 1m 18.413secs on his first visit to the track. Heidfeld was disappointed to find his car nervous on the limit and changes failed to have the desired effect, while Räikkönen muttered about traffic on his quick lap and failure to get the best out of his tyres. Otherwise, the Finn was happy.

**SATURDAY QUALIFYING** Both race C20s had Ferrari B+ specification V10s and Räikkönen was 10th to Heidfeld's 11th in practice. Subtle set-up changes improved both cars for qualifying, during which they used the soft Bridgestones. Räikkönen fractionally out-qualified his team-mate with 1m 16.402secs to the German's 1m 16.438secs, but both felt they could have done better. Heidfeld lost a good final run when he pushed too much in the first chicane and ran wide, while Räikkönen's last attempt was thwarted by David Coulthard's excursion into the gravel in the last corner. The rookie wasn't too bothered, however, having already lost time when a Benetton went off the road in front of him. The mood was optimistic.

**SUNDAY RACE** Heidfeld made a great start to go inside Frentzen off the line, while Räikkönen gathered pace and eventually swooped past the Jordan on the outside at the entry to the first corner. Both Saubers then pincered the yellow car, coming perilously close to one another, before Heidfeld had to back off a fraction to avoid over-running into the back of Jarno Trulli. That let Räikkönen get back in front of his team-mate, although Heidfeld passed the Finn on the exit to the last corner at the end of the lap to grab eighth place.

The C20s then ran nose-to-tail for 29 laps, with Frentzen and a pushy Eddie Irvine tailing them closely. On lap 30 Irvine successfully attacked Räikkönen, whose tyres were now blistered, and Heidfeld succumbed for a similar reason two laps later. For whatever reason the C20 was being unkind to its tyres; Räikkönen thought his second set was better than his first, Heidfeld that his first set had been better. The upshot was that both struggled and, after their pit-stops, they slipped off the pace.

When everyone had completed their stops the Saubers were 11th and 13th, separated by Jean Alesi. Heidfeld had slipped behind Räikkönen and succumbed to Alesi's attack on lap 45. During their duel they made contact and a few laps later Heidfeld felt the car beginning to handle oddly. A pitstop on lap 54 revealed that the knock had damaged a driveshaft, so the car was withdrawn on safety grounds.

Räikkönen then faced a challenge from Alesi and the two ran nose-to-tail to the end, but the Finn was closing the inside line into each corner and had Alesi under control when the Frenchman resolved the deadlock by spinning off at the hairpin on the last lap to his obvious frustration. But it was another cool showing from Räikkönen, the find of the season. But as Peter Sauber said, 10th place just wasn't good enough for a team enjoying its best-ever season.

Above and below: After the joy of points in Canada, Kimi Räikkönen had tyre problems and ended the race in a disappointing 10th place. Right: Nick Heidfeld was just out-qualified by his team-mate and his Sauber failed to go the full distance in the race.

Above and right: Having shared the fifth row of the grid, the Sauber drivers' battled with each other for much of the race providing some midfield excitement. Right: Nick Heidfeld headed his team-mate until the first pitstops, before a clash with Jean Alesi forced the German to retire.

Red Bull
SAUBER PETRONAS

## FRENCH GRAND PRIX MAGNY-COURS
# Heidfeld makes a point

It had been four races since he had scored any points, so when Nick Heidfeld qualified his Red Bull Sauber Petronas ninth on the grid he was determined to make the most of it. A controlled performance kept his tyres as close to their peak as possible throughout the race and minimised the late-race effect of blisters which began to develop. His tempered approach paid off with his ninth point of the season. It was timely, for without it Jordan's fifth place would have moved the British team into fourth place in the constructors' championship chase and that would have been disappointing.

**FRIDAY PRACTICE** Sauber had its usual trio of C20s in France: Heidfeld running chassis 05, Kimi Räikkönen chassis 06 and 01 as spare. A new chassis, 07, was a spare tub.

After the first day of free practice Räikkönen was 14th quickest and Heidfeld was 15th, having run 25 and 46 laps respectively. Heidfeld was pleased to cover so many laps to check out tyre degradation and, since his practice focused exclusively on race set-up, the team was not bothered about its relatively lowly positions on the timesheets. However, he voiced the need for a significant improvement the following day.

For only the third time in 2001, Räikkönen damaged his car after getting out of shape going into the first corner shortly after the session resumed after lunch. He autocrossed his way from the infield back onto the track, then off into the gravel on the outside. In so doing the nose wing was removed and the car was knocked around a bit, which spelt the end of his practice session.

**SATURDAY QUALIFYING** Eighth and 10th fastest for Heidfeld and Räikkönen respectively in the morning proved a better barometer of Sauber's performance. In the afternoon Heidfeld continued that form, clocking the ninth best time with a 1m 14.095secs on the harder Bridgestone compound that both Saubers used. He worked steadily through a number of minor changes as the session progressed, each yielding an improvement. His third run looked good until he encountered gravel thrown on to the track at the second chicane, and his fourth was better still, clear and clean. He went into the race in a more optimistic frame of mind. Räikkönen was not quite so happy, ending the day 13th on 1m 14.536secs and complaining he did not like the balance of his car as it moved around too much in corners. He said: "We struggled with set-up yesterday, but now I think we're in very good shape for the race."

**SUNDAY RACE** Heidfeld started his race on a two-stop strategy but, because Räikkönen lined up only 13th, Sauber decided to start him with a relatively light fuel load so it could be flexible on adopting a two or three-stop strategy. With his lighter car the Finn sprinted up to ninth place on the opening lap, lapping within half a second of the leaders, and was running eighth when he made the race's first pitstop on the 15th lap. Because of his progress, Sauber decided to put him on the same two-stop plan as Heidfeld.

The German had settled into ninth place behind his team-mate and benefited as Räikkönen did when Jacques Villeneuve's BAR expired on the sixth lap. He chased after Heinz-Harald Frentzen for seventh before coming in for his own stop six laps later. This proved to be the better alternative, for he regained the track comfortably ahead of his Finnish team-mate.

Both the Sauber C20s had a much better set-up than in Germany and perhaps Heidfeld had developed his slightly better, as it took a little less out of his tyres. Certainly he was the happier driver in the closing stages, as Räikkönen's car was troubled by poor traction in the slow corners and oversteer in the high-speed curves as his third set of Bridgestone tyres started to blister. Nevertheless, he was able to resist Frentzen's challenge and finished 13secs adrift of his team-mate.

# It keeps getting better

Sauber's season just kept getting better and the cool, detached Peter Sauber was clearly enjoying himself as his team lagged only fractions of a second behind the big three of Ferrari, McLaren and Williams. Silverstone has traditionally been a tough circuit for the Swiss cars, but a new aerodynamic package allied to typically strong driving performances from Kimi Räikkönen and Nick Heidfeld saw both cars finish in the points: three points in the bag, on a day when neither Jordan nor BAR could get a car home, was a stupendous, prediction-defying outcome.

FRIDAY PRACTICE Ending up sixth fastest after 42 laps, Heidfeld's weekend got off to a good start. He had a new car, C20-07, to play with, while Räikkönen stayed with 06 and 01 remained the spare. Heidfeld's crew made a lot of progress on set-up between the sessions and these were reflected as he moved up six places from 12th.

Räikkönen felt that, in a small way, it was helpful to be on the first circuit of the season that he knew really well, but his manner suggested learning tracks was no big deal. Although he was 10th in both sessions, he was a lot closer to the fastest time in the afternoon with 1m 24.387secs from 39 laps.

Both cars ran the revised brake ducts from Canada and Räikkönen's car had new barge boards. Each also had power-steering at last, but Heidfeld switched his off later in the day.

SATURDAY QUALIFYING Yet again both C20s qualified comfortably in the top 10, Heidfeld and Räikkönen opting for Bridgestone's soft tyres. The Finn was happy with the balance of his car and was content to make only small changes, having been first to emerge from the pitlane, some 24 minutes into the session. His 1m 22.023secs was good enough for seventh.

Heidfeld was disgruntled. All weekend he had the edge on his team-mate and the flow was running his way in qualifying, too. He had worked down to 1m 22.223secs on his third run and his fourth was better by two or three-10ths, until he came across Ralf Schumacher and the two

McLaren drivers all running very slowly through the Luffield complex. They were all on their out laps, slowing down deliberately to let other cars move away before starting their qualifying attempts, but Heidfeld had to brake hard and got his car sideways at Luffield to avoid running into Schumacher. The lap was ruined and he had to rely on his former time for ninth in the starting line-up. His disappointment was palpable.

SUNDAY RACE Heidfeld's chances of beating Räikkönen probably ended the moment he spun into the gravel 10 minutes into the warm-up and lost valuable set-up time.

Räikkönen made an indifferent race start, losing places to both Williams drivers. But Heinz-Harald Frentzen made an even worse start, then David Coulthard and Jarno Trulli eliminated themselves, so the Finn ended the first lap in sixth place.

Heidfeld was right on his team-mate's tail and they hounded Ralf Schumacher as Frentzen chased them. Sauber had chosen a two-stop strategy: when the pair refuelled they dropped behind Jacques Villeneuve and lost time behind the slower BAR. Otherwise, Räikkönen's race went to plan. He stopped again on lap 40, losing what had become fifth place upon Ralf Schumacher's demise but regaining it when Heidfeld and Frentzen pitted on lap 41. He later described his race as 'perfect'.

After losing time in the warm-up Heidfeld had used the grid formation lap as a test, and then made small electronic adjustments all through the race. Frentzen challenged him as Montoya came out of the pits ahead of them on lap 26, costing Heidfeld momentum. Frentzen managed to slip ahead, but as he ran wide, Heidfeld ducked back in front and thereafter pulled away.

Above: Celebrations for Sauber with both cars finishing in the points. Right: Kimi Räikkönen continued to drive like a real veteran, never putting a foot out of place to lead home team-mate Nick Heidfeld. Below right: Räikkönen prepares for what proved to be 'a perfect race'.

Above and right: Nick Heidfeld made a great start to his weekend, but was baulked in qualifying and went off in the warm-up. He fought hard to recover and take a worthy sixth place.

## GERMAN GRAND PRIX HOCKENHEIM
# The luck runs out

Sauber had had all the luck up to Hockenheim. But it suddenly ran out. A top three finish was on the cards until both cars went out of the race. However, the team still looked strong enough to take fourth place in the constructors' championship – an impossible thought at the beginning of the season.

FRIDAY PRACTICE Sauber brought the same trio of C20s it used at Silverstone, Nick Heidfeld having 07, Kimi Räikkönen 06 and 01 acting as spare. For this low downforce track there was a new front wing and two configurations of rear wing, one intended for qualifying, one for the race.

Heidfeld did 37 laps and set 12th fastest time, commenting that his car felt reasonably good but not as good as it had in low downforce trim at Monza during recent testing. He thought minor set-up changes would bring it to a similar level after the data analysis. The team was concerned that the Jaguars had made a giant step, however.

Räikkönen did only 26 laps, yet was only three-10ths off Heidfeld's time with 1m 43.528secs, leaving him 16th. The Finn's car developed an engine speed sensor problem in the morning session, which resulted in a random tendency to shift gears without Räikkönen's control. Since the gearbox had to be removed to gain access to the sensor, he lost the rest of the day's running when the problem became more acute in the second hour of practice.

SATURDAY QUALIFYING Heidfeld was delighted in Saturday morning free practice to find his hopes realised that analysis of Friday's data would lead to a low downforce qualifying set-up as good as achieved at Monza. He was fifth quickest on 1m 40.263secs, but Räikkönen struggled to improve his car's nervousness as he hammered it across the chicane kerbs. Every time he did that it jumped away from him, whereas Heidfeld's was much more composed.

Like the other Bridgestone runners, both drivers opted for the harder compound tyres due to the searing temperatures. Heidfeld honed the 07 with small changes between each run, and his final lap would have been even quicker than 1m 39.921secs had he not had to slow in the final sector, after Ralf Schumacher went off at the last corner and brought out yellow flags. Räikkönen had a tougher time but finally got a more comfortable set-up on his car and joined Heidfeld on the fourth row of the grid in eighth.

SUNDAY RACE Heidfeld got a really good run at David Coulthard in the first attempt to start the race, but only edged alongside the McLaren after missing the entrance to the first chicane. As he let the Scot re-pass, de la Rosa also took advantage. Then the race was red-flagged. Second time around Heidfeld was a little further behind Coulthard, in a comfortable seventh, and closed up significantly as he left his braking very late. Then de la Rosa came tanking up behind in the Jaguar, left his braking far too late and locked up before sliding into the back of the Sauber. Heidfeld spun as his rear wing added to the Jag's aerodynamics, to the not inconsiderable chagrin of Peter Sauber.

Räikkönen was the main beneficiary of the Spaniard's misjudgement and ended the opening lap in seventh. Despite running a single-stop strategy he kept ahead of Irvine's Jaguar, which was on two stops. The Finn got a breather when Irvine stopped to refuel after 12 laps, but four laps later the Sauber retired. A driveshaft had broken, and on a day when a podium finish beckoned, the Swiss team's race was over.

Red Bull
SAUBER PETRONAS

**Above and left:** After a difficult two days of practice Räikkönen came good in the race and looked like a possible podium contender. His race came to an end with driveshaft failure. With Heidfeld out early it ended Sauber's points run.

**Left:** Heidfeld's car after the de la Rosa attack and leading Irvine's Jaguar through the second chicane during practice. **Below:** The German Grand Prix brought an end to Peter Sauber's charmed season.

## HUNGARIAN GRAND PRIX HUNGARORING

# Right on target again

Right and above: Nick Heidfeld and Sauber came away from Hungary with a very hard-earned point. With few retirements ahead of him, Heidfeld deserved his point and on this occasion outshone team-mate Kimi Räikkönen (below), who finished seventh.

Above and right: Räikkönen again showed maturity to finish seventh on one of the season's most difficult tracks. He lost a rear brake duct following a pit-stop, but the young Finn dealt with the change to the handling with consummate ease.

Hungary was an acid test for Sauber following its disappointing performance in May in Monaco, the only other track on the calendar that demands maximum downforce. It came through with flying colours – an achievement that spoke volumes for the progress the team had made in the intervening months, not only with its aerodynamic package but also the traction. Observers in the paddock realised that the performance of the car was down to the prowess of the engineering team, which was performing with the best. And there is no doubt that Ferrari is supplying almost latest spec engines now it is looking after the team direct. Small wonder that Peter Sauber was momentarily seen juggling two cigars after the race as he celebrated yet another superb performance.

**FRIDAY PRACTICE** Though his expression didn't always confirm it, Nick Heidfeld was happy with his set-up right from the start of free practice, and was delighted to find that the Sauber's mechanical traction was so much better on a high downforce track. In the course of 33 laps he set eighth fastest time with a high fuel load, in 1m 17.928secs, using his regular chassis C20-07. He had a couple of minor moments with oversteer on the entry to corners, but managed to hone that tendency out with some small adjustments.

Learning a circuit never poses any problem for Räikkönen, especially one as simple as the Hungaroring, but the Finn lost valuable set-up time when a rear spring mounting became damaged on chassis C20-06, losing him three-quarters of an hour. He managed 20 laps in the morning before the problem struck, and as the track was still so dirty he and engineer Jacky Eeckelaert decided to do some experiments with the car prior to doing set-up work later in the day. The spring problem put paid to that plan and Räikkönen managed only nine more laps once his car was fixed, for 15th fastest time of 1m 18.834secs. He complained that the handling yawed from understeer to oversteer between the high- and medium-speed corners.

**SATURDAY QUALIFYING** Räikkönen had a corner weight problem in the morning, while the Heidfeld had a better platform to work from after his previous day's efforts and built on it throughout practice and qualifying. Like all Bridgestone runners bar Ferrari, McLaren and Jacques Villeneuve, the Sauber drivers opted for the soft rubber tyres. Having been a very satisfied fourth fastest in the morning on 1m 15.821secs, Heidfeld kept up his momentum to take seventh place on the grid in the afternoon with a best lap of 1m 15.739secs.

Räikkönen found his car much better than it had been on Friday, until understeer set in on his last two runs as track conditions changed. His second run was thus his quickest, in 1m15.906secs for ninth in the line-up, but he felt he could have shaved at least three-10ths off that had he not encountered one Jordan at the beginning of the lap and the other at the end.

**SUNDAY RACE** Sauber's plan was to bring at least one car to the finish ahead of Jarno Trulli's Jordan, but in the event it did this easily with both cars. However, it nearly went wrong when Heidfeld and Trulli brushed in the first corner. The German had intended to go for the inside but found himself making such a quick getaway that he was obliged to seek clear road rather than back off and had to try to turn into the corner from the dirty outer edge of the track. He just retained seventh place, but worried for a while about understeer resulting from minor front suspension realignment in the incident. At times his engine would also momentarily cut out exiting that corner, but the problem did not get any worse. His pit stops on laps 27 and 51 went perfectly, and sixth place was just reward for a solid performance.

Clever strategy gave Räikkönen a short middle stint to help him get up with Heidfeld and ahead of Montoya. After his fast stop on lap 26 the Finn rose to sixth place by lap 32, before dropping back behind his team-mate after his second stop on lap 46. He had a minor comfort problem when his drink bottle pipe became detached, and then he lost a rear brake duct as he left the pitlane after his second stop, but the latter did not affect his lap times even though it made the car oversteer a little more.

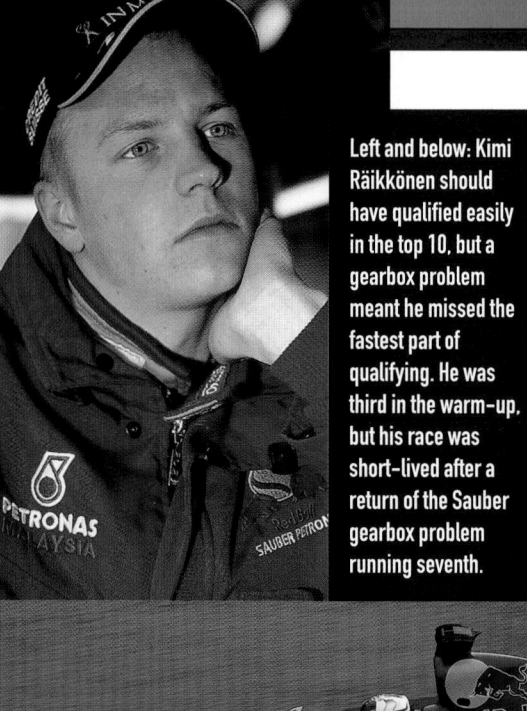

Left and below: Kimi Räikkönen should have qualified easily in the top 10, but a gearbox problem meant he missed the fastest part of qualifying. He was third in the warm-up, but his race was short-lived after a return of the Sauber gearbox problem running seventh.

Above left: Räikkönen's long run back to the pits was in vain, as he was not allowed to take the re-start. Below: Team-mate Nick Heidfeld left his braking too late into La Source and collided with Pedro de la Rosa. With front wing and suspension damage his race was immediately over.

## BELGIAN GRAND PRIX SPA-FRANCORCHAMPS
# Success builds pressure

For much of the season the Ferrari-engined Sauber cars were paragons of reliability, but after a double failure to finish at Hockenheim came another double retirement in Belgium. The Swiss team was plagued by an unusual transmission problem that dogged both drivers on the Saturday, and ended up depriving Kimi Räikkönen of seventh place.

There was still a very real likelihood that Sauber would finish fourth in the constructors' championship. But from no expectation there was now every expectation and for the first time real pressure was on. Unfortunately, the team cracked under pressure and it could count itself lucky to leave Spa with 20 points to BAR Honda's and Jordan Honda's 16. It would now have to fight for a possible maximum of 24 points available to the second division teams. But it was still favourite to capture the coveted fourth place and gain the title of best of the rest.

FRIDAY PRACTICE With a new qualifying gearbox to try and some aerodynamic modifications, Sauber came to Belgium brimful of confidence in a car that always goes well on fast tracks. Nick Heidfeld had his usual C20-07, Kimi Räikkönen his 06 and 01 was again on hand as the spare.

On the first day Räikkönen showed his talent yet again by blasting through Eau Rouge without the slightest qualm, drawing on his Formula Renault experience on the track to set the sixth fastest time of 1m 50.495secs in his 34 laps. He managed to get going well before the rain came, whereas Heidfeld was on his out-lap ready for his first really quick flier when the rain started. That left him in 14th with 1m 52.436secs, with three fewer laps.

Both drivers had the opportunity to try both wet and intermediate Bridgestones. There was little to choose between

them, with both in the 2m 02secs bracket, beaten only by Barrichello and Häkkinen.

SATURDAY QUALIFYING Saturday started badly for the team. First of all Räikkönen had a minor brake problem which was quickly solved, but then both cars developed a problem jumping out of fifth gear. At the time it was put down to the qualifying transmissions, which were changed for standard units in time for qualifying. The cars were bottom of the times when the morning's 45-minute session ended, and the team was concerned that it would not have the luxury of installation laps to check that everything was working smoothly when qualifying began.

Qualifying initially went well. Late in the session, Räikkönen was sixth fastest on 1m 59.050secs, while Heidfeld took eighth on 1m 59.302secs; both had their final runs to go on softer Bridgestone dries. But the gearbox gremlin put paid to that. Räikkönen reached the pits, but Heidfeld stopped at Stavelot, bringing out the yellow flags. In the final seconds, the Finn and the German dropped to 12th and 14th places respectively.

The transmission problem was baffling. Technical director Willy Rampf suspected it must be the dog-rings and the manner in which Spa places unusual loadings on the transmission. A machining problem was thought to be the root cause, and a major investigation was launched.

SUNDAY RACE Despite its problems, Sauber was full of optimism prior to the start, as Räikkönen had been a superb third fastest in the warm-up, only 1.3secs slower than Michael Schumacher. On the first start, the Finn got away strongly and had moved into seventh place, right behind Fisichella, when Burti's accident brought out the red flag. On that initial fifth lap, while the field ran behind the safety car, the Finn suddenly stopped just past the accident scene with a return of the gearbox problem. He ran back to the pits, hoping to take over the spare car, but the rules don't allow it and he was through.

At the second start Heidfeld got into a tight squeeze at La Source and the consensus of opinion was that on this occasion, in another Heidfeld/de la Rosa clash, he was the culprit as he went for a gap that closed. The result was front wing and suspension damage that brought his day to a close. Sauber's nightmare weekend was complete.

## ITALIAN GRAND PRIX MONZA
# Pressure on

Kimi Räikkönen's transfer to McLaren Mercedes was the talk of the race. Weeks of rumours gave way to the announcements. McLaren would pay Sauber a $20 million transfer fee over four years and Räikkönen $8 million a year. Ex-world champion Mika Häkkinen would be no more.

On the track, a distracted team let points slip just as its season-long fourth place faced a growing threat from BAR Honda and Jordan Honda.

After both drivers crashed on Friday, the team recovered remarkably to qualify them eighth and ninth. But Nick Heidfeld had to start from the pitlane and Räikkönen messed up his start, spoiling the team's fuelling strategy. The Finn eventually finished seventh: Jacques Villeneuve edged him at the line to bring the Brackley team within three points with two races left. The pressure was on.

FRIDAY PRACTICE Sauber Petronas began with Heidfeld in his regular C20-07 and Räikkönen in C20-06. But having set a best lap that was fleetingly fourth quickest, Räikkönen lost control under braking for the first chicane and crunched the retaining wall.

Then Heidfeld slithered into the tyre wall at the second Lesmo, shortly after setting a best of 1m 25.740secs. That was worth fourth throughout the afternoon session, which both drivers sat out while their cars were repaired. Räikkönen finally placed 16th.

Technical director Willy Rampf initially put the problems down to brake-locking given the low grip level of the track, but was encouraged by Heidfeld, who was fastest through the traps.

SATURDAY QUALIFYING Sauber faced a tough morning, having covered only 13 laps the previous day. Heidfeld had now switched to chassis 05 while 07 returned to Hinwil for further repairs; Räikkönen's car, to the surprise of observers, was ready to run.

Both drivers did far more race set-up running than usual, after the disastrous Friday, thus hampering their set-up work for qualifying. But Heidfeld was still seventh fastest and Räikkönen 10th, both good efforts in the circumstances. Like all the other Bridgestone runners they used the softer compound, after widespread initial worries about potential blistering proved unfounded.

They stayed on these tyres for qualifying, and though Heidfeld was still seeking the fine balance the C20 had displayed when last tested at the track, he was relatively satisfied with eighth, just ahead of Räikkönen. For the eighth time in 2001, the team had qualified both cars in the top 10.

SUNDAY RACE Sauber's prospects looked even rosier after the warm-up: Räikkönen was fifth fastest. But later Heidfeld's car developed a hydraulic pressure problem, and was wheeled off the grid. He started from the pitlane in the spare 01.

Räikkönen muffed his start, losing two places, and when Button hit Trulli in the first chicane the Finn lost more ground. That left him stuck behind the heavily fuel-laden Jaguars of de la Rosa and Irvine. Sauber had the opposite plan: Räikkönen was to get clear of the pack on a light load, then make his single stop. Trapped in traffic, he couldn't execute. It didn't help that fast-starting Verstappen was also ahead of him, in eighth.

Irvine fell back almost at once, but Räikkönen couldn't pass Verstappen and soon had Alesi breathing down his neck. The Frenchman overtook him on lap 12, and Räikkönen finally passed Verstappen four laps later to move back in the points. He and Alesi both stopped on lap 22: the Jordan driver rejoined ahead, in seventh. The Finn, who had taken on more fuel, fell back to 13th, behind Heidfeld.

The German had quickly caught the tailenders after his pitlane start, but despite being second quickest through the straightline speed trap he couldn't hold off Fisichella, who overtook on lap 23. The German pitted just once, on the 28th lap, and said afterwards his car had felt good on some laps, bad on others, as the tyres' efficiency varied. He finished a disappointed 11th.

Other drivers' stops took Räikkönen back up the order, but Villeneuve didn't stop for fuel until lap 33, and de la Rosa left it as late as lap 36. They rejoined in fifth and sixth, the Jaguar ahead, before Räikkönen passed the pits. As the Sauber strengthened in the closing stages, he slashed Villeneuve's lead to just over a half-second on the final lap, but it was too late.

*Above and right: Despite Friday's trauma, Sauber recovered well to qualify both cars in the top 10. Kimi Räikkönen's light-tank race strategy was negated when he muffed the start and was forced to settle for seventh.*

*Right and below: After a strong show in qualifying, Heidfeld took eighth ahead of team-mate Räikkönen, but finished a dejected 11th. Sauber's failure to turn qualifying speed into points meant BAR was now only three points behind.*

## UNITED STATES GRAND PRIX INDIANAPOLIS

# Holding on to fourth

Finishing fourth in the constructors' championship was everything to Peter Sauber. The team had gone to America needing a result, and thanks to Nick Heidfeld got one. It ended the weekend with a cushion of five points, meaning Sauber had fourth virtually in the bag. But it still had to be sealed, with BAR and Jordan still challengers at the last race in Japan.

Heidfeld took the limelight as Kimi Räikkönen disappointed again, outshone by the German. The Swiss team had been the star performer on the 2001 grid and Peter Sauber was revelling in it. His twin passions of ice cream and cigars were to the fore and he savoured every moment. Few believed he could hold that form into 2002.

**FRIDAY PRACTICE** Sauber's campaign to safeguard its fourth position in the constructors' championship got off to a promising start: Nick Heidfeld set the sixth fastest time of 1m 13.827secs over 48 laps in chassis C20-07 (01 was again the spare). The German was very happy with his car's balance, unlike team-mate Kimi Räikkönen, who found 05 understeering too much. The Finn's best was only 1m 14.027secs, for 11th fastest time over 45 laps.

**SATURDAY QUALIFYING** Heidfeld kept up his momentum with a forceful third fastest time of 1m 12.407secs on Saturday morning, and again praised his car's balance on the soft compound Bridgestone tyres. In qualifying that form continued: he took sixth on the grid with 1m 12.434secs, but felt he would have been at least fifth, or even fourth, had he not needed to brake early in sector two on his best lap.

Tomas Enge had crashed his Prost and yellow flags were out.

Räikkönen was struggling in comparison: his 1m 12.881secs was 1.3kph slower, for only 11th on the grid. He was again unhappy with the chassis balance, after small set-up changes throughout the session had no effect.

**SUNDAY RACE** Given Heidfeld's form all weekend, Sauber went into the race with high expectations, but it all so nearly ended in tears at the start of lap two. At the end of the first lap Heidfeld was eighth and Räikkönen ninth, both behind Jarno Trulli, but the Italian made an error that let both of them get ahead on the run to Turn 1 on lap two. As Räikkönen contemplated a move on Heidfeld, Trulli tried unsuccessfully to take the Finn on the outside. As Trulli cut across to the right to line up for the corner, Räikkönen found himself pincered. He locked up as he tried unsuccessfully to avoid damaging his nose on Heidfeld's left rear wheel, and was also clobbered by Trulli. At the end of the lap he pitted for a new nose, but no sooner had he rejoined at the back of the field that the left rear driveshaft broke, as a result of the impact from the Jordan.

That left Heidfeld flying the flag, and he did so superbly as he kept on the back of the Ferrari-Williams-McLaren train leading the field. David Coulthard actually held him up before his first fuel stop on lap 27. Shortly after, however, Heidfeld lost first, second and seventh gears, and suddenly his race turned from attack to survival mode. He lost ground on the infield, and a crucial 20kph off his top speed on the straight, and having pitted again on lap 48 he found himself powerless to resist Irvine as the Ulsterman came back at him after his own refuelling stop. All seemed lost as the Sauber dropped to seventh and a heroic late lunge by the German brought him up half a second shy of a point. But when Trulli was e x c l u d e d, Sauber jumped from two points ahead of Jordan to five, and Peter Sauber began to smile again.

**Above: A tight moment for Kimi Räikkönen as Nick Heidfeld and Jarno Trulli pincer him at the start of lap two. Left: Räikkönen pitted and continued, but retired with drive shaft failure after another lap.**

**Above and left: Nick Heidfeld qualified an excellent sixth for Sauber and drove a determined race to finish sixth, which then became fifth. Räikkönen (right) never got to grips with Indianapolis, qualifying in 11th.**

Red Bull
SAUBER PETRONAS

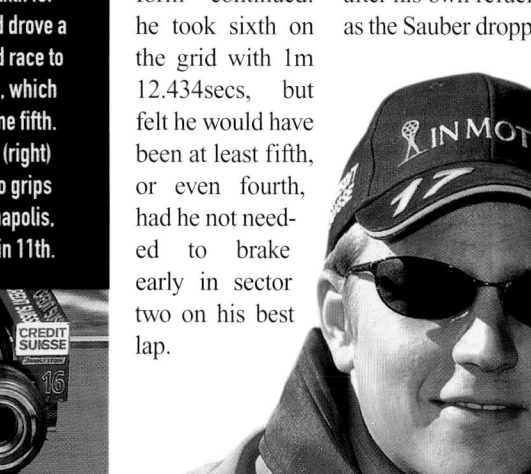

## JAPANESE GRAND PRIX SUZUKA
# Tears for souvenirs

In the end Sauber had to do nothing to retain fourth place in the constructors' championship. Only teams above it managed to score points, so with five points in hand the Swiss team could finally relax and celebrate its superb achievement. As team members whipped the appreciative Japanese fans into a post-race, horn-blowing frenzy, Peter Sauber surreptitiously wiped away a tear, lit another cigar and savoured his favourite ice cream. The man deserved it. But a disastrous start for Nick Heidfeld and a massive shunt for Kimi Räikkönen muted the occasion and sent a sharp warning that 2002 may not be so easy.

FRIDAY PRACTICE Half an hour into Friday afternoon's free practice at Suzuka, Sauber Petronas was looking in decent shape. Nick Heidfeld had the ninth best time of 1m 37.665secs from his 20 laps and had just begun a flyer to try Bridgestone's harder tyre compound for the first time. But as he turned C20-07 into the last right-hander in the Esses he got a front wheel over the kerb: in an instant the car spun and walloped the inside tyre wall very hard, backwards, before scattering itself all the way up to the final left-hand curve. This was a big accident, but the little German hopped out and, apart from a fleeting headache, was none the worse for his experience. The basic monocoque was intact, and the team had it running again on Saturday.

Räikkönen, meanwhile, seemed not to learn the circuit as quickly as usual, and ended his first day at Suzuka in only 15th after covering 31 laps in C20-05. The Finn was as silent as ever; engineer Jacky Eeckelaert looked pensive. Räikkönen completed a hitch-free programme with a best of 1m 38.315secs, but the Belgian's expression suggested expectations had not been met.

SATURDAY QUALIFYING As Peter Sauber celebrated his 58th birthday, Heidfeld gave him the present of a top 10 qualifying position, while Räikkönen was much closer with 12th place in the line-up.

In free practice Heidfeld showed no ill effects from his shunt, claiming seventh fastest in 1m 35.037secs; Räikkönen gathered pace with 1m 35.672secs for 12th. With both men following the Bridgestone trend and taking the softer tyre option, the team anticipated a tough tussle with closest rival Jordan in the climax to the constructors' championship.

Heidfeld was happy enough with his subsequent best of 1m 34.386secs, but was surprised to make the top 10. The C20 had not felt as strong as it had in qualifying for the previous two races, and he'd run into traffic on his last run and lost downforce. Nevertheless, he was able to shade Räikkönen by 0.4kph as the Finn found his rhythm to lap in 1m 34.581secs, without ever dialling out the understeer that hurt his times through the all-important sweeps of the Esses.

SUNDAY RACE The level of grip caught Heidfeld out at the start: from 10th he fell to 14th, losing time trying to skirt outside of Jarno Trulli and Jenson Button in the first corner and then being eased wide, and onto the grass, by Räikkönen.

The Finn clawed up to ninth, but going into lap six was under intense pressure from Jean Alesi. The Frenchman reported that the Finn almost lost control of his car in the last part of the Esses, and as they negotiated the two very quick left-handers behind the pits the C20 suddenly snapped sideways into a spin. It nearly went 360 degrees, but then Alesi, with nowhere to go, hit its right rear: the two cars tangled as they slid off to the right of the track. It was a massive accident, and Räikkönen was clearly winded as he climbed from his wheel-less machine. Both men had extremely lucky escapes, as did others who had to drive through as the sky rained wheels. Television evidence showed the Sauber's left rear suspension had broken.

With Heidfeld down in 12th, things looked bleak. Stuck behind Jacques Villeneuve's slower BAR, the German lost downforce and dug in for the long haul. His refuelling stops on laps 19 and 33 were OK, but only when Villeneuve spun on lap 49 did the understeering Sauber moved up to its eventual ninth. It was one of the team's worst performances of the season, but in the final analysis it didn't matter.

**Above and right:** Nick Heidfeld worked hard and drove a clean race to take seventh. **Right:** Heidfeld made a comprehensive job of wrecking his Sauber when he crashed very heavily in practice.

**Above right:** Kimi Räikkönen locks a brake in practice. **Above:** The remains of Räikkönen's Sauber rest behind the barrier. **Right:** Jean Alesi checks that the young Finn is OK.

200

Team Review    Race by Race

# JORDAN

**2001**

## Contents

| | | | | | | |
|---|---|---|---|---|---|---|
| Team Review | - | The season | p204 | European Grand Prix | - Nürburgring | p218 |
| Australian Grand Prix | - | Melbourne | p210 | French Grand Prix | - Magny-Cours | p219 |
| Malaysian Grand Prix | - | Sepang | p211 | British Grand Prix | - Silverstone | p220 |
| Brazilian Grand Prix | - | Interlagos | p212 | German Grand Prix | - Hockenheim | p221 |
| San Marino Grand Prix | - | Imola | p213 | Hungarian Grand Prix | - Hungaroring | p222 |
| Spanish Grand Prix | - | Barcelona | p214 | Belgian Grand Prix | - Spa-Francorchamps | p223 |
| Austrian Grand Prix | - | A1 Ring | p215 | Italian Grand Prix | - Monza | p224 |
| Monaco Grand Prix | - | Monte Carlo | p216 | USA Grand Prix | - Indianapolis | p225 |
| Canadian Grand Prix | - | Montreal | p217 | Japanese Grand Prix | - Suzuka | p226 |

Heinz-Harald Frentzen

Jarno Trulli

Ricardo Zonta

Eddie Jordan

Jean Alesi

# A season to forget

Heinz-Harald Frentzen claimed before the start of the 2001 season, after testing the new Jordan Honda EJ11, that it was the best Formula One car he had ever driven. But from that point on, it was all downhill. The year started out with the high hopes for which Eddie Jordan is renowned, and ended as a major disappointment.

The year 2001 was deemed crucially important for Jordan. It was the team's first year with works Honda engines and it went head-to-head with BAR in a separate Honda-powered race within the Grand Prix. That took on more importance as mid-season rumours swept the paddock that, when the existing contracts ended, Honda would choose to supply only one team from 2003 onwards.

For Jordan it was seen as vital to improve on its sixth place in 2000, a sharp downturn from third in 1999. It eventually managed to do so, courtesy of the FIA's stewards getting themselves mixed up at Indianapolis. But for that it would have been sixth, rather than fifth.

There was clearly something wrong in the chemistry of the team – so much so that Eddie Jordan caused the most enormous upset by sacking his number one driver Heinz-Harald Frentzen mid-season in an attempt to address the malaise. He failed; Jean Alesi may have brought a new spirit for a few races, but when he realised he would not be retained for 2002, that effect evaporated. Frentzen's departure also put a financial millstone around Jordan's neck, as he sued for damages. It became a bitterly demoralising season that made 2000 look like a cakewalk. The season ended with plans for a dramatic revamp of a team that had become disillusioned as results proved elusive. Even BAR achieved two podium finishes, something Jordan could only dream of in 2001.

Against this background was a stark reality that the Jordan Honda was actually the fourth-fastest car on the grid. It simply couldn't achieve any meaningful results. The team's ambience was wrong: not badly 'wrong' but nonetheless 'wrong'.

Given its budget and works Honda V10 engine, there was sufficient money to do the job properly. The alliance with Honda promised far more than it ever delivered.

As the team packed up in Suzuka, where Jarno Trulli finished eighth, well behind a Benetton Renault, the talk was all about restructuring and massive change was in the air.

So what went wrong? Why did the fourth-fastest car prove a lemon and why did its drivers fail so consistently to deliver the car into the top six, when its overall qualifying and reliability record was much better than the fourth-placed Sauber? Sauber also had less money, no works engine, two novice drivers and the disadvantage of being situated in Switzerland. If not beating BAR was bad, not beating Sauber was even worse. And yet the EJ11 was a fast car, driven by two superstar drivers and backed by a relatively big budget.

Finding the answers was not easy. For a start, the team was in a period of transition, recovering from the departures of technical director Mike Gascoyne to Benetton and engineer Sam Michael to BMW Williams. There were also other minor defections. When the dust had settled, the experienced Tim Holloway was chief designer and incoming Eghbal Hamidy was technical director with responsibility for aerodynamics. Then there was the disappointing performance of Honda's engine, which appeared to lack the horsepower of the frontrunners and was a second-division engine. Honda didn't expect this, especially as its budget was the biggest of all the engine makers.

Finally, there was the trauma, and then elation, of Jarno Trulli's exclusion, and then restoration, to and from and back again to fourth place in America, the penultimate race. Ultimately the team came within two points of Sauber for a fourth place in the constructors' standings, which gave it a measure of 11th-hour respectability.

With the resources at its disposal, Jordan should have done a lot better. And it will need to in 2002, the year in which Honda will ▷

205

Heinz-Harald Frentzen

make a decision about engine supply for the future. Either it will drop a team and focus on just one, or it will give works engines to another team. In 2002, the pressure to perform is on as never before. If Jordan genuinely aspires to become a leading player – as Honda expects – it has a mountain to climb over the winter. In 2001 it barely ascended past base camp.

## The Jordan EJ11 car

AFTER Heinz-Harald Frentzen's pre-season pronouncement about the new EJ11, great things were expected. Everyone was buoyed with the fresh enthusiasm that is inevitable at the start of a new season, when anything and everything seems possible. The promise of the works Honda V10, two seemingly motivated star drivers and the new car had everyone determined to do their best to erase the bad memories of 2000.

The EJ11 was a relatively simple car, devoid of sophisticated trickery in the interests of creating a reliable, raceworthy machine. It followed the high nose aerodynamic route, and built on the lessons learned with the EJ10.

The different external architecture of the Honda V10, compared to its Mugen-Honda predecessor, made installation a much easier business and enabled the team to make significant reductions in drag because smaller radiators were needed. Then there was the extra bonus of Honda's own technical input. In the early days of the relationship, Eddie Jordan could scarcely believe his good fortune.

The Jordan factory built seven EJ11s, and at Monte Carlo and Silverstone took as many as four complete cars to the races.

Chassis 01 was kept back for testing, and 02 was the spare for the first three races before reverting to test duties, but was called up as Frentzen's spare at Monaco and Trulli's at the British Grand Prix.

Chassis 03 was Trulli's race car in Australia, Malaysia and Brazil, before becoming the spare in San Marino and Spain. Later in the year it was used again as the spare in Britain, Hungary, Belgium, Italy, America and Japan. Chassis 04 was Frentzen's race car in the first five Grands Prix, before becoming the spare in Austria. It fulfilled that role for Trulli in Monte Carlo before becoming general spare again in Canada, Europe and France. The German then elected to race it again in Britain, and following his dismissal it became Ricardo Zonta's race car in the German Grand Prix at Hockenheim. It saw further race duty in Jean Alesi's hands in Belgium, Italy, America and Japan, where it ended its career getting badly knocked about when the retiring Frenchman got caught up in Kimi Räikkönen's spin on the sixth lap.

Chassis 05 was introduced at Imola as Trulli's new race mount, and he remained faithful to it right the way through to Silverstone, where he had 06 as his spare. The latter appeared first in Frentzen's hands in Austria, and he used it again in Monte Carlo where he inflicted damage by clobbering the wall exiting the tunnel. It was repaired in time for Frentzen to practise it in Canada, before he withdrew complaining of headaches after the Monaco incident. It was thus taken over by Zonta, and was used again by Frentzen upon his return to active duty at the Nürburgring. It was the spare in France, then briefly became Trulli's race chassis in Hockenheim. Alesi then took it as his race car in Hungary, whereafter it was assigned to test duties. Chassis 07 arrived at the Hungaroring for Trulli, but was only raced once.

Like all other teams, Jordan indulged in aerodynamic modification aimed at optimising its cars for each individual circuit, but the rate of development did not match that, say, of BAR, its main rival. A very significant update would only arrive in Hungary, when a new package of aerodynamics and bodywork finally appeared. It was Eghbal Hamidy's revamp of the concept that had been used all season. In a

Ian Phillips

John Putt

Tim Holloway

Eghbal Hamidy

very telling development, the cars went no better with the new bodywork in Hungary, and thereafter it was dumped and never seen again. Much money and effort had been expended, and led down a blind alley. It unsettled the Jordan team's fragile confidence ever further.

As in 2000, the team was losing its momentum, and didn't seem to have an awful lot of ideas on how to regain it. The problem was that, while the car was a good qualifier, it rarely went well in the races. Indeed, Trulli earned a reputation – perhaps not deserved – for becoming a mobile roadblock once a race started. It was a sort of reversal of what happened to Sauber in 2000. It was, most likely, a shortcoming in the car rather than in either of the drivers; Frentzen thought differently but nobody took any notice. Equally, no one seemed to know what to do to identify and rectify the problem.

The other problem was that although the drivers could usually extract what the car had to offer, that usually proved more than a second shy of what was needed. Again, the finger pointed at aerodynamics, and horsepower.         ▷

## JORDAN SEASON STATISTICS

### RELIABILITY PERFORMANCE

| Driver | Races | Max laps | Laps completed | Reliability rating |
|---|---|---|---|---|
| Jarno Trulli | 17 | 1065 | 755 | 70.9% |
| Heinz-Harald Frentzen | 10 | 659 | 469 | 71.2% |
| Jean Alesi | 5 | 292 | 240 | 82.2% |
| Ricardo Zonta | 2 | 114 | 75 | 65.8% |
| Constructor | Races | Max laps | Laps completed | Reliability rating |
| Team | 34 | 2130 | 1539 | 72.3% |

### CHAMPIONSHIP PERFORMANCE

| Driver | 2001 points | 2000 points | 12 month change |
|---|---|---|---|
| Jarno Trulli | 12 | 6 | +100% |
| Heinz-Harald Frentzen | 6 | 11 | -45.5% |
| Jean Alesi | 5 | 0 | +500% |
| Ricardo Zonta | 0 | 3 | -300% |
| Constructor | 2001 points | 2000 points | 12 month change |
| Team | 19 | 17 | +11.8% |

### CHASSIS LOG

**EJ11/01** Test car only.

**EJ11/02** Spare car at Melbourne, Sepang, Interlagos, Monte Carlo and Silverstone

**EJ11/03** Race car for Jarno Trulli at Melbourne, Sepang and Interlagos. Spare car at Imola, Barcelona, Silverstone, Hungaroring, Spa-Francorchamps, Monza, Indianapolis and Suzuka.

**EJ11/04** Race car for Heinz-Harald Frentzen at Melbourne, Sepang, Interlagos, Imola, Barcelona, and Silverstone. Spare car at the A1 Ring, Monte Carlo, Montreal, the Nürburgring and Magny-Cours. Race car for Ricardo Zonta at Hockenheim. Race car for Jean Alesi at Spa-Francorchamps, Monza, Indianapolis and Suzuka.

**EJ11/05** Race car for Trulli at Imola, Barcelona, A1 Ring, Monte Carlo, Montreal, Nürburgring, Magny-Cours, Silverstone, Spa-Francorchamps, Monza and Suzuka. Spare car at Hockenheim, Hungaroring and Indianapolis.

**EJ11/06** Race car for Frentzen at the A1 Ring, Monte Carlo, Montreal (taken over by Zonta for Saturday and Sunday when Frentzen felt ill following his Monte Carlo shunt) and the Nürburgring; for Trulli at Hockenheim; and for Alesi at the Hungaroring. Spare car at Magny-Cours and Silverstone.

**EJ11/07** Race car for Trulli at Hungaroring.

**Jarno Trulli**

## Technical developments

IT ALL looked very good but once the test team got the car on the track it was often woefully unreliable. At the races this continued. Hydraulics was the main bugbear, bringing Trulli to a premature stop in Germany and Hungary. There were two engine failures, again for Trulli, in Australia and Belgium, and at Monaco an unusual problem in the electronics jammed all the fuel injectors open and set the car on fire as the Italian lay sixth. In the previous year's race he had been a contender for the win.

The silliest reason for retirement was Frentzen's problem in Spain to do with the electronics and his understanding of them, or the lack of it. He was stranded on the grid, and when he finally did get away a subsequent collision with Pedro de la Rosa soon left him on the sidelines. Trulli's demise in Austria wasn't great either. He too was left on the grid, with electronic gremlins associated with the traction-control system, then had an off while trying to recover some of the lost lap; finally he exited the pits against the red light and was disqualified. With Frentzen's car suffering a gearbox failure at the start, the Austrian Grand Prix was undoubtedly the worst of Jordan's unhappy season. The high point, such as it was, came when Trulli briefly led the third lap in Malaysia. It was the only time that looked remotely like happening.

There were 2,130 racing laps during the season for each two-car team. Jordan completed 1,539 (including the Austrian Grand Prix at which Trulli was disqualified). That worked out as 755 laps for Trulli, 469 for Frentzen, 75 for Zonta and 240 for Alesi.

## The drivers

INITIALLY things looked reasonable for the driving duo of Heinz-Harald Frentzen and Jarno Trulli as they entered their second season together. They liked one another and their relationship was cordial and positive. The German finished fifth in Melbourne after a brush with Rubens Barrichello, and Trulli was headed for third in Brazil before dropping back to fifth. Frentzen was fourth there. Trulli finished fifth at Imola too, having initially fended off Mika Häkkinen. But after that the Italian did not score any more points except for two for fifth place in France and three in America, where he was excluded after the race for an infringement of the undercar plank regulations.

Frentzen, meanwhile, finished fourth in Malaysia after a fine battle in the rain with Ralf Schumacher and Häkkinen, then sixth at Imola. Then things really started going wrong.

First there was the electronic problem on the line in Spain followed by the collision with de la Rosa. Then the gearbox broke on the line in Austria. Then there was the crash in Monaco, which left the German sufficiently concussed to stop practising in Canada; he was temporarily replaced by test driver Ricardo Zonta. With Trulli struggling too, all the alarm bells were ringing at Jordan's headquarters. The sole consolation was that BAR was in even greater trouble.

At the Nürburgring, Frentzen spun off and Trulli's transmission broke, then France brought two points for the Italian's fifth place while the German only took eighth. Eddie Jordan was getting restless. The view was building within the team that the time was fast approaching for a long talk with Frentzen, who did not seem to be getting as much as Trulli out of the package. As far as Eddie himself was concerned, the crunch came when Trulli fell off on the opening lap of the British Grand Prix in July and Frentzen brought his car

## The Honda engine

HONDA built 120 brand-new V10 engines for 2001 and Jordan got 60 of them. It was lavish attention compared with the much smaller Mugen-Honda effort the season before. Jordan did not have to pay for the engines either, and got incredible technical back-up from Honda. But right from the beginning the horsepower figures were disappointing. At a time when BMW was nudging 840bhp with its brand-new V10, Honda had only 795bhp. Later, BMW topped 850bhp for qualifying, whereas Honda's effort at a more powerful engine had to wait until Suzuka and even then did not set pulses racing. Estimates suggested no more than 805bhp – leaving Honda, once the dominant engine manufacturer, struggling in the wake not just of BMW but also of Ferrari, Cosworth and Mercedes-Benz. The unit only seemed to have the legs of the new Renault V10.

Compared to 2000, when Jordan had to package the heavy and cumbersome Mugen-Honda V10, 2001 was an infinitely better situation. But others had moved on and Jordan and Honda together failed to do enough to help one another to follow suit.

home a lacklustre seventh, beaten by both Saubers after a momentary wheel-to-wheel fight with Nick Heidfeld.

It was breaking point. Frentzen's smooth driving method was totally different from Trulli's always-on-the-edge raggedness. Frentzen isn't as quick as Trulli but has a proper, structured driving style. Trulli doesn't have a structured technique for driving lap after lap – and Frentzen believed that, rather than himself, to be the problem.

Frentzen had a point. Nobody drives a Grand Prix at anywhere near qualifying pace, but Trulli is proportionally much further away from his qualifying pace than other drivers. Frentzen was consequently underperforming, claiming the Jordan team was continually setting the car up for Trulli, which was useless for him and completely useless in the race. It was Frentzen's demands for changes in the car set-up and design from the Jordan team that caused so much friction within the team.

Eddie Jordan and the team sided with Trulli. Jordan told Frentzen the day after the British Grand Prix that his services were no longer required. The decision caused morale to plummet, and Frentzen to rush to his lawyers. In Frentzen's place, Zonta again stood in at Hockenheim, before being supplanted by Jean Alesi. The French veteran and Eddie Jordan were old friends from their Formula 3000 championship-winning days in 1989, but even he faced an uphill struggle. Trulli would qualify well, then fade in the race; Alesi would struggle in qualifying, but would race his heart out. He made a hesitant start in Hungary as he learned about the EJ11, but then matched Trulli's speed in Belgium before driving a brilliant race to beat Ralf Schumacher to sixth place. He was as fast as Trulli at Monza, too, then thought he had inherited sixth place in Indianapolis when Trulli was initially booted out of fourth. Moving from Prost to Jordan was a gamble, and it failed to pay off. Before the Japanese Grand Prix, Alesi knew that his Formula One career was over, as Jordan opted for British Formula Three champion Takuma Sato to partner Giancarlo Fisichella in 2002. As Trulli took a lacklustre eighth at Suzuka, Alesi bowed out in spectacular fashion after his no-fault tangle with a spinning Räikkönen ruining his 100 per cent finishing record in the process.

Towards the end of the season Jordan also tested F3000 champion Justin Wilson and F3 upcomer Narain Karthikeyan.

While Sauber maintained its level of competitiveness as the season progressed, Jordan Honda went backwards. At the start of the season, Trulli in the lead car was 1.485secs slower than Michael Schumacher's pole, while against Michael Schumacher's pole time in Melbourne, Frentzen, fourth fastest, looked strong: only 0.766secs behind the world champion. At that stage of the season such a relatively small deficit gave Jordan great encouragement, but while Ferrari continued to develop its car, Jordan didn't. By Suzuka the deficit from pole (Schumacher again) to the best Jordan had doubled: Jarno Trulli, who was eighth quickest, was 1.518secs adrift.

## Commercial

STUNG by his team's failure to repeat in 2000 its third place in the 1999 constructors' championship, which he regarded as outright failure, Eddie Jordan did something calculated to convey the message to the workforce, even if it was unlikely to boost motivation. He cancelled the 2000 Christmas party, on the grounds that nobody deserved to do any celebrating. It was the first time he had ever really got tough with his workforce in his career. But it signalled a new Jordan – a Jordan that expected to win after so many years of just being grateful to qualify and make up the numbers. But he found there is much more to staff motivation than that. And the bigger an organisation gets, the more different the techniques needed.

Jordan brought in John Putt as chief executive and everyone expected incumbent managing director Trevor Foster to leave, but he didn't. Ian Phillips was a rock as commercial director and Eddie Jordan's right-hand man. It all worked well apart from the search for the missing ingredient called winning races and points that was there in 1999, when conditions were not so favourable, and went missing in 200 and 2001, when conditions were perfect.

The year started promisingly enough. Jordan's 2001 launch in February took place not at a plush London venue such as The London Palladium, as in previous years, but in a marquee set up at the Silverstone headquarters. Behind this perfectly sensible and practical choice was another message. By not requiring the test team to decamp to London, the team was able to continue testing almost without interruption.

Jordan's state-of-the-art motorhome

During the launch Eddie Jordan spoke tersely of the previous year's failure, and of his determination that Jordan would reward Honda's faith in his team's ability to get the job done. He sounded convincing, but then he usually does. And he announced that his significant funding from Benson & Hedges would be supplemented by sponsorship from Deutsche Post, Mastercard and Infineon. Money seemed to be no object to the team's future progress. The whole occasion was typically upbeat.

The 2001 budget was estimated by *EuroBusiness* magazine at $172.9 million; including the benefit of the free engine, it was well over twice what Sauber had.

As usual, the new car's turn-out was superb, for there is not a team in Formula One that does not appreciate the value of image and presentation. Jordan also had a brand-new state-of-the-art motorhome. But the car and the team failed on the track. Jordan's Christmas party in 2001 looks vulnerable again.

## AUSTRALIAN GRAND PRIX MELBOURNE
# False dawn of optimism

Heinz-Harald Frentzen described the new EJ11 as 'the best Jordan I have ever driven' after qualifying, and added that Melbourne was the first time in more than a year that he had really enjoyed driving an F1 car. Unable to challenge Ferrari and McLaren, Jordan nevertheless won the only race that mattered to it over the weekend – the one pitting it against the similarly Honda-powered BAR team. Managing director Trevor Foster said: "I think we were the third best package here this weekend. We're really pleased with the pace of the car and, while it's going to take a bit to catch McLaren and Ferrari, we have a good platform. I think we could say we got 90 per cent out of the car, so there's more to come." For once there was no bullshit, just honest assessment.

FRIDAY PRACTICE Jordan Honda had three cars on hand out of the four built. Frentzen had EJ11-04, Jarno Trulli had EJ11-03; and EJ11-02 was available for either driver.

Frentzen's Friday was highlighted by a minor slip into the gravel, which damaged his barge board and front wing, but he returned to the track and managed significant running. He finished the first day of the 2001 season in eighth place with a time of 1m 30.802secs.

Trulli lost half-an-hour of running due to an electronics problem on the steering wheel, but he came back strongly to split the Ferraris and take second place on the timesheets. It was a truly remarkable first day, which saw him record a best time of 1m 29.267secs.

SATURDAY QUALIFYING Frentzen continued to look strong and finished in the top five in morning practice, despite a harmless spin that caused the engine to stall. In qualifying he continued his strong form, set the fourth fastest time of 1m 27.658secs, and was able to save a set of unscrubbed Bridgestones for the race. Trulli shone again in the morning with the fifth-fastest time, but things went awry for him in the afternoon. He lost the EJ11's balance, as set-up changes turned initial mild understeer into oversteer. "He never really got it back together," said Trevor Foster. "I think he got a bit anxious in the circumstances, and maybe over-drove

as he saw things slipping away." Trulli placed seventh fastest with 1m 28.377secs, more than half-a-second adrift of Frentzen.

Both drivers used Bridgestone's soft-compound tyres. Trulli reported that the car felt different in qualifying and he could not reproduce the front-running performance of the day before.

SUNDAY RACE Frentzen quickly made his mark and at the start he had to get round Barrichello before clobbering Coulthard not once but twice with his left-hand wheels, as the field squeezed together on the run to the first corner. His EJ11 nonetheless held third place, hard on the heels of Michael Schumacher and Mika Häkkinen. Barrichello on the third lap made a rash stab at overtaking that ended in tears: his left front wheel hit Frentzen's right rear, taking a chunk out of its rim. Frentzen spun on to the gravel, then again, before pointing in the right direction.

Meanwhile Trulli was pounding along in fifth place and when racing resumed the Italian was comfortably ahead of Olivier Panis in the BAR.

Further back Frentzen launched a mighty climb back from 16th.

Trulli began to lose ground on lap 31. Suddenly Panis had gone by. Clearly Jordan number 12 was in trouble. "Trulli was unlucky," Trevor Foster said. "There was an electrical problem which affected the engine's response and lost it a cylinder. He kept going, then we smelled oil burning so we called him in to retire on the 39th lap rather than risk the engine."

Frentzen fought his way back from 16th place to sixth by the flag but was unable to find a way past Nick Heidfeld. Jordan might have been the moral victor of the Honda race, but it didn't have the points to consolidate that status. Until, that is, Panis was given a time penalty for passing Heidfeld under a yellow flag. Fifth place was still not what the team was looking for but, in the circumstances, Frentzen's terrific performance salvaged something worth having.

Above left: Frentzen visited the gravel trap on Friday, but came back with a well-deserved eighth place on the grid and finished fifth in the race (above). Trulli was squeezed early in the race (below) and then electrical failure ended his day.

Left and below: Frentzen scored a brilliant fourth place. Below: Despite leading early on, Trulli finished eighth.

Below: Frentzen damaged his Jordan slightly during qualifying.

# Fast but disappointing

Eddie Jordan's team thought they had stuffed the pre-season naysayers who wrote the yellow racers off after the design department rushed for the door. To most minds, Jordan had already won the Honda battle; BAR was simply not as fast.

In Malaysia a brilliant, fuel-conserving drive by Heinz-Harald Frentzen netted fourth and another three points to elevate Jordan to third in the constructors' championship. Furthermore, both cars continually featured in qualifying and the race. Jarno Trulli led the race briefly, before spinning in the monsoon. "It's quite encouraging," said managing director Trevor Foster in his understated way. Eddie Jordan added: "Fortune favours the brave is a philosophy I have had since I was young, and this was a great call." Eddie Jordan was back – with two fingers up to the doubters.

FRIDAY PRACTICE Jordan Honda again brought three EJ11s to the race, the chassis line-up duplicating Melbourne's and the spare left for whoever proved the quicker in qualifying. Friday was a great day for the team, with Trulli topping the times after a late burst of speed. He had been particularly delighted with his first trouble-free session in months. Right at the end of the second half of the practice, he aced Michael Schumacher with a lap of 1m 38.846secs – a fair bit slower than the German's 2000 pole position time, but good enough. "I am now confident that every time I step into the car I can push to 100 per cent," the Italian said. Frentzen, still smarting from the fallout of his controversial remarks about Ferrari engines and traction control the previous week, kept his head down to conduct the routine work of tyre assessment and set-up analysis to place seventh with a best lap of 1m 40.197secs.

SATURDAY QUALIFYING Neither driver could get on terms with the Ferraris but they were encouragingly close to the troubled McLarens. Trulli set the fifth-fastest time but was upstaged by Ralf Schumacher in the Michelin-shod BMW Williams and a relieved Mika Häkkinen. The Italian reported: "There were some corners where the car just didn't respond as well as it had, and fifth is not so bad." Frentzen was a disgruntled ninth. He admitted to a mistake on his third run, which prompted the team to change the set-up slightly and made the EJ11 understeer. He went off on his third run and damaged the floor and there wasn't enough time to change it – he got out too late to do a decent fourth run.

SUNDAY RACE Jarno Trulli made a great start and it was partly his attempt to slide down the inside of Rubens Barrichello at the first corner that distracted the Brazilian sufficiently for him to tap Ralf Schumacher into the spin that triggered mayhem. He ended the lap in third and when the Ferraris spun in unison on lap three, Trulli found himself leading a GP for the first time since Austria 1997. He lost it under braking for the final corner on the fourth lap, followed by David Coulthard who did likewise. The trip into the gravel broke Trulli's bargeboards and front wing. Fighting a recalcitrant car for the rest of the race, he finished eighth.

Frentzen owed his finish to Giancarlo Fisichella. On the original formation lap he discovered his car would not rev beyond 4,000rpm due to an electronic control fault. He was about to head into the pits when he realised the race was being aborted. Jordan was able to reboot the control system and, at the start, Heinz made up four places to run fifth. During the safety car period he moved up to second when Jos Verstappen spun through a couple of 360s, but then gave best to the Dutchman when racing resumed.

All afternoon Frentzen struggled with a difficult downchange due to a clutch fault – locking its rear wheels. As a result he see-sawed between second early on and seventh, which he fell to after pitting on lap 21. He was also in the thick of the Verstappen-Häkkinen-Schumacher spat for fourth. Frentzen had to wait for his rivals to make their second stops – Schumacher on lap 30, Häkkinen on lap 40 and Verstappen on lap 43 – to take fourth. With eight laps to go his Honda's computer said he would run dry with a lap left. But engineer David Brown calculated it would be OK. It was, just, and Frentzen was awarded with fourth place. "It's bloody impressive," Trevor Foster mused afterwards, "the way Heinz can do the same lap times while using 10 per cent less fuel."

## BRAZILIAN GRAND PRIX INTERLAGOS
# Down but not out

Right: Trulli beat his team-mate in qualifying. Below right: the team was kept busy with niggling engine problems.

Jordan Honda saw a weekend of promise evaporate as Heinz-Harald Frentzen dropped from third in the closing stages when Honda's mysterious 'misfire' problem again stymied the team. Jordan had to be satisfied with meagre points from Jarno Trulli's unimpressive fifth.

The team's main success of the weekend was to dupe the more gullible into believing it was relocating its HQ to a 120,000sq ft site close to the Leopardstown horse racing track near Dublin, to be codenamed Virtue (in an oblique swipe at McLaren and its Paragon facility). The date, of course, was 1st April…

FRIDAY PRACTICE Frentzen and Trulli had the brace of EJ11s from the first two races, with the spare again allocated to the faster qualifier. Friday was a good day, Trulli's lap of 1m 16.224secs being bettered only by David Coulthard, who was running with a light fuel load. He was pleased, having overcome a brake fault earlier on. Frentzen was less happy, stopping with an electrical fault and having to make do with eighth fastest time on 1m 17.072secs.

SATURDAY QUALIFYING Problems came early as Trulli's car developed the misfire that was becoming a Honda signature. The Japanese manufacturer dismissed it, but it was a significant problem to do with the timing trigger on the front of the engine. When it went awry it upset the ignition timing and created the misfire or cut the engine. Then Frentzen's V10 broke and the team opted to change both power units. Unfortunately these were the only qualifying engines available, so chances of good grid berths were compromised.

Qualifying showed how evenly matched the two drivers were, as Trulli set seventh best on 1m 14.630secs, with Frentzen alongside him with a time only three-1,000ths of a second slower. But although the team put on a brave face, the rise of Williams was a blow, as was the half-second gap between the Jordans and five of the six drivers ahead (Michael Schumacher's pace was something else.) Worse, Frentzen seemed to get stuck in the mid 1m 14secs band, merely chipping away fractions over his three runs. Both drivers felt they'd squeezed out everything their EJ11s had to offer.

SUNDAY RACE Jordan set both cars up for a single-stop race. Both managed to avoid the stalled Häkkinen, and Trulli was lucky to avoid the Rubens Barrichello vs. Ralf Schumacher brouhaha on lap three. Trulli settled into fourth behind Montoya, Michael Schumacher and Coulthard, unable to keep in touch but clear of Frentzen and the BARs. Advantage in the Honda race was a consolation.

Frentzen was overtaken by Panis on lap 15 and he caught and passed Trulli six laps later. But Panis was on a two-stop strategy, so the team was not too worried. Frentzen stopped on schedule on the 43rd lap, Trulli on the 44th, but both had to come in again for wet tyres on the 45th lap. As they were 20secs apart on the road, the team was able to service them both without either suffering too much. Frentzen switched to the intermediates he had requested and, behind him, Trulli arrived and lost a lot less time waiting to switch to full wets than he would have lost if he had done another lap on dry tyres.

Frentzen soon made third place his clear preserve; but Trulli, although he caught and passed Nick Heidfeld when the track was at its wettest on lap 50, fell back behind the intermediate-shod C20 10 laps later. With eight laps to go the most bitter blow came as Frentzen rolled to a halt with a repeat of Friday's electrical problem. That elevated Heidfeld to the podium, a position the Jordan team believed that Trulli should have occupied.

The Italian's wets were less suitable as the conditions improved, but now there was no mistaking the signs Jordan was losing patience with the Italian's weak wet-road form.

Above right: Heinz-Harald Frentzen was superb in the wet. Right: Eddie Jordan and Frank Williams compare notes on life with Honda. Below: Frentzen retires, giving up a certain and well-deserved third place.

## SAN MARINO GRAND PRIX IMOLA
# A long road ahead

For the fourth race in succession, Jordan won the Honda race and fifth and sixth places overall were the reward. The team, which had started the season with everyone writing them off after an exodus of engineering staff, was starting to look like the fourth-fastest team. Not bad, but not quite good enough when it had a Honda engine in the back.

Both drivers squeezed everything they could from the Jordan Honda EJ11s – and that was the problem: finding more speed from what was a good but wooden chassis. Managing director Trevor Foster said sanguinely: "Where we finished is where we are; the race was a good indication of where we stand. We are about a second off, and we need to find half of that from the chassis and half from the engine. There's a long, hard season ahead." It was gloomy talk, but now Jordan had taken it for granted that it could beat BAR, it wanted more – but was not destined to get it.

**FRIDAY PRACTICE** Jarno Trulli had a new car, EJ11-05, with his former race car EJ11-03 reverting to the spare role. Heinz-Harald Frentzen continued with 04. The cars were to the same spec as Interlagos, apart from brake revisions.

Both drivers did a lot of laps without drama. Honda has identified its recent misfire cum cutting-out problem as a faulty batch of engine sensors. It also reprogrammed its software to ensure the problem could not recur, even if the sensors malfunctioned. Clever stuff. Trulli was ninth fastest on 1m 26.923secs, Frentzen 13th on 1m 27.406secs.

**SATURDAY QUALIFYING** In the morning's changeable conditions Frentzen was fifth quickest on 1m 32.164secs and Trulli 16th on 1m 36.046secs. In qualifying, Trulli redeemed himself for his weak wet-weather showing in Brazil with a stunning 1m 23.658secs, which for a moment put him second fastest to David Coulthard and left Frentzen outpsyched. The time eventually translated into fifth.

Frentzen got himself wound up from the start of qualifying, following a run-in with Tarso Marques who spoiled his second run; as track conditions improved the German suffered understeer and overdrove the car for a disappointing ninth on 1m 24.436secs on soft compound tyres. There was tension building between him and his engineers, suggesting it was not the happiest of ships.

**SUNDAY RACE** Trulli completely upstaged Frentzen in the race, too, making a strong start. He was alongside Mika Häkkinen on the run down to Tamburello and out-braked him for third place. Then he held up a queue including the Finn, Juan Pablo Montoya, Olivier Panis and the two Ferraris. This let Ralf Schumacher and David Coulthard pull away and set the tone of the race.

His second set of tyres, fitted on lap 24, was not equal to the first, so he slipped back and lost touch with Rubens Barrichello and Häkkinen. Montoya also passed him, but Trulli was lucky when the Colombian hit trouble. By the time Trulli got a third set of Bridgestones on lap 43, he'd lost too much ground to do more than drive home for fifth and two points.

Frentzen was unsighted when Panis almost jumped the start and lifted off just as the lights went out. He then reacted with too much wheelspin and lost places to Kimi Räikkönen and Jacques Villeneuve. Like Trulli, Frentzen drove hard in his two-stop race (he came in for pitstops on laps 26 and 44) and struggled to finish in sixth place, which itself was down to all the retirements ahead of him.

*Left and below: Jarno Trulli got the most from the Jordan Honda to take fifth, despite a sub-standard second tyre set.*

*Left and below: Trulli and the Jordan crew did their best, but need to find another second per lap to get to the front. Right: Team principal Eddie Jordan ponders the future with Honda.*

213

## SPANISH GRAND PRIX BARCELONA
# Failing to make the podium

Jordan Honda's worst fears were realised in Barcelona as for the first time in 2001 the yellow cars were unable finish ahead of their Honda counterparts. Jarno Trulli once again scored, but the pleasure of three points for fourth place was tempered by BAR's superior podium finish.

Qualifying proved no problem, but there was a real fear that the maximum was being wrung out of the car, while it was clear there was much more to come from BAR. Both teams were waiting for Honda to push its V10 over the 800bhp mark required for serious F1 in 2001. Once again, everyone at Jordan was conscious that the Honda race was the race worth winning.

FRIDAY PRACTICE The trio of EJ11s was unchanged for this race, Jarno Trulli using 05, Heinz-Harald Frentzen 04, and 03 ready as spare for the faster qualifier. This first day of practice was initially a disaster. Trulli suffered from clutch slip after five laps and Frentzen went off-track and damaged his car after only six. Both recovered, although Trulli complained that his car lacked balance on his way to the 10th fastest time of 1m 21.647secs, and Frentzen had another spin and problems with his gears shifting abruptly and making the car nervous under braking and on turn-in. He was only 14th quickest on 1m 22.221secs, once again upstaged by his team-mate.

SATURDAY QUALIFYING Both Jordan drivers chose the soft Bridgestone tyres. This time neither had any problems, and sixth and eighth on the grid reflected current form. Trulli again out-psyched Frentzen with a lap of 1m 19.093secs to the German's 1m 19.150secs, neither believing he could have wrung more speed from his car.

SUNDAY RACE Jordan opted to use launch control for the start and Trulli benefited from Coulthard's misfortune and seized fifth place off the line. Frentzen's race immediately went to hell. The team suggested that at the 11th hour Frentzen had done the wrong thing and aborted an automatic launch to go to manual. "It was all primed

ready for him to lift off and press the go button," a source said. "But he let out the clutch instead and it all went awry. It was as if he tried to abort but did it all wrong. After he fiddled around he got started, in second gear." Frentzen's version was that the system went into neutral when he pressed the go button, obliging him to reselect the system and start in second.

Meanwhile, Trulli took Barrichello on the run to the first turn, but when Ralf Schumacher ran wide there the Italian got caught behind the BMW Williams and the Ferrari re-passed him. He then held fifth until his first stop on lap 21, but it was a slow stop. A chasing Montoya pitted at the same time and rejoined the race ahead, while Jacques Villeneuve also had a quicker stop and moved ahead. Trulli's second stop, on lap 40, did nothing to reverse this situation, and he settled for sixth as his brakes began fading intermittently from mid-distance. In the final three laps the clutch played up and he was lucky to hold off Coulthard at the flag – and luckier still that Mika Häkkinen retired.

Frentzen's unhappy race ended when he dived inside Pedro de la Rosa for 16th place on the sixth lap. The Jordan was partly on the kerb as de la Rosa lost the corner but refused to surrender it, and as the Jaguar driver squeezed the German, Frentzen slid off the kerb and over-steered into the green car. Both spun inelegantly out of the race. It was a stupid bit of driving by the Spaniard, and cost both the chance of a good result.

Top left: Jarno Trulli and Jordan put in a good performance, but just lacked the pace to beat Villeneuve and BAR to the podium. Jarno Trulli and the Jordan engineers (top right) discuss the car's handling.

Heinz-Harald Frentzen and engineer David Brown had a weekend they would rather forget.

## AUSTRIAN GRAND PRIX A1 RING
# Speed but not sustenance

After being beaten by arch-rival BAR in Spain, Jordan rallied in Austria and had the speed to reassert itself in the Honda contest. But what it crucially lacked was mechanical and electronic reliability.

Trulli qualified in fifth and Frentzen 11th, but both performances were rendered academic when neither car left the starting grid. In Trulli's case, launch control failed. In Frentzen's, it was the second time in a row that disaster has struck him at the start; this time it was a seized gearbox. Trulli eventually started the race a lap down, but was subsequently black-flagged for leaving the pitlane against the red light. It was one of the lowest days in the team's history.

FRIDAY PRACTICE Trulli stuck with his regular car, chassis EJ11-05, but Frentzen had a new chassis, 06, and his former race car, 04, became the spare, set up for Trulli.

In only 28 laps in the morning's free practice, Frentzen eclipsed Trulli with 1m 11.977secs for seventh fastest. The German did only five laps before a nagging problem with his car's hydraulics affected his steering, forcing him into the pits. Repairs were completed in time for him to resume running 10 minutes into the afternoon session, when he did a good job of making up for lost time.

Trulli ended the day 13th, on 1m 12.555secs, having clocked 45 laps. He complained of a dirty track surface and poor handling balance. He also damaged both his car's bargeboards after leaving the track in the afternoon.

SATURDAY QUALIFYING After five laps on Saturday morning Trulli's car suffered engine failure. Although the mechanics changed the engine in 50 minutes, he lost a lot of time. He managed another 10 laps and did well to set the eighth-fastest time: 1m 10.751secs, right behind Frentzen. The German managed 1m 10.434secs and covered 33 laps.

Trulli rose to the occasion in qualifying, achieving the fifth-fastest time during his first run on the soft Bridgestone tyres both drivers had chosen. After that he was mystified why he could not beat his 1m 10.202secs lap, but he wasn't alone in being stymied by varying conditions. The main problem was changing wind direction in the third sector.

Frentzen was again unable to match his team-mate, admitting that he had mistakenly activated the pitlane speed limiter button and was forced to abandon his first run. Subsequent runs were affected by track conditions, but he also complained of excessive understeer and was half-a-second off his practice time with a best of 1m 10.923secs, leaving him 11th. From the team's point of view, though, Trulli had socked it to Honda rival BAR, and at least Frentzen had split team-mates Olivier Panis and Jacques Villeneuve.

SUNDAY RACE The start dealt a devastating blow to Jordan. Trulli's electronics betrayed him and by the time he got going he was a lap down. He then had an off-track excursion, but none of it mattered: he had left the pits to rejoin the race on a red light. He finally retired on lap 14 and was promptly excluded from the results. "We think the revs were too low for launch control to activate," said Trevor Foster.

The origin of Frentzen's gearbox failure was still mysterious long after the race had finished, but initial investigation pointed to an internal breakage. "I've had some bad races," Eddie Jordan said, "and this was one of them!"

Above: The closest Heinz–Harald Frentzen got to the Austrian Grand Prix was his grid position. Left: Trulli again put in a strong qualifying performance for fifth on the grid. Below: The Jordan 'prat perch' was deserted after lap 14, when Jarno Trulli had been disqualified.

## MONACO GRAND PRIX MONTE CARLO
# Simply a pointless exercise

The Jordan Hondas were not as competitive in the principality as they had been in the previous year, but Jarno Trulli and Heinz-Harald Frentzen were both in the hunt for points before disaster struck. The Jordan-BAR became more urgent as paddock talk indicated that Honda would only supply engines to one team in 2002. In that respect, although it had the faster car, Jordan was gradually losing the race performance battle. Honda rival BAR's ongoing development had put its cars on the same plane as the once-superior yellow machines. To its chagrin, Jordan left Monte Carlo only one point ahead of its rival in the Japanese power race.

THURSDAY PRACTICE Frentzen had chassis 06 with 02 as his spare; Trulli had 05 with 02 to be reset for him as a spare; 04 was on hand as a spare, set for Frentzen on Saturday/Sunday.

Trulli opted to run an unusual scuttle-mounted front wing and completed 47 laps. Frentzen didn't think it was worth setting the car up differently to cater for the wing, so did 46 laps without it.

Trulli found it took a lot of work to get his car balanced properly, but Frentzen was happy until the end of the morning session when teams were allowed to do practice starts. For the third time in a row his car failed to get going because the engine's idle settings were too low, allowing it to stall.

SATURDAY QUALIFYING Eighth and 13th places on the grid for Trulli and Frentzen were disappointing after free practice. The Italian ran without his banned wing and still complained about the soft Bridgestones he and Frentzen had chosen for qualifying, claiming they were not suited to his car. It lacked slow-speed grip and felt nervous at high speed, while his final run was thwarted when he came across Rubens Barrichello's Ferrari crawling through the tunnel.

Frentzen's problems came early in the morning when his car ground to a halt with a hydraulic pressure failure. That cost him his chance to hone the car on new rubber, so

he had to do it during qualifying. He complained of understeer in the slow corners, but it was oversteer that caught him out at Portier on his best lap. He spun, kept the car off the wall by slowing its backward trajectory with violent wheelspin, but then stalled as he manoeuvered to restart.

SUNDAY RACE Trulli held seventh place from the grid (he was elevated from eighth by Coulthard's demise), and this became sixth as Juan Pablo Montoya crashed on the third lap. Thereafter the Italian ran ahead of Villeneuve and Giancarlo Fisichella, keeping out of their reach but without making serious inroads into Eddie Irvine's fifth place as he tried to conserve his tyres.

However, from lap 26 the rear of the Jordan began sliding and on the 31st lap the EJ11 came to an inglorious halt at Rascasse, its rear bodywork engulfed in flames. Leaking hydraulic fluid or lubricant were the prime suspects, but it transpired an electronic problem had jammed the fuel injectors wide open.

Frentzen opted for a manual start, and after 48 laps he was challenging Jean Alesi for sixth after momentarily setting the race's fastest lap on his 28th lap. But on lap 50 his car understeered into the wall in the tunnel. It was a hefty impact and the wreckage slid as far as the chicane before stopping. Frentzen admitted he clipped the kerb going into the tunnel, got onto the marbles and then slid out into the wall. He hit his head in the impact – but was in good enough shape to sign autographs, and made his own way back to the paddock. Only later did he start to suffer the full crash effects.

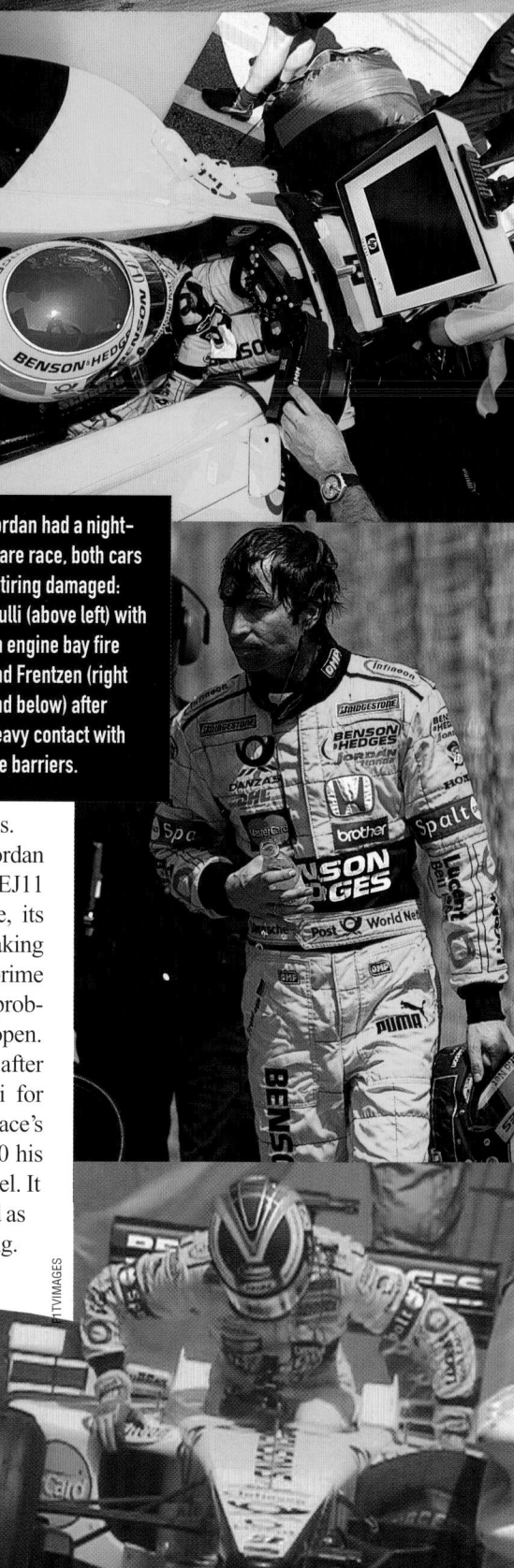

Jordan had a nightmare race, both cars retiring damaged: Trulli (above left) with an engine bay fire and Frentzen (right and below) after heavy contact with the barriers.

Left: Jordan test driver Ricardo Zonta was drafted in to replace Frentzen on the Saturday. Below: The Brazilian did an excellent job to qualify 12th and but for a misunderstanding with Kimi Räikkönen could have finished in the points on his return to racing.

## CANADIAN GRAND PRIX MONTREAL
# Low points, high stakes

If any reminder were needed of the heat in the Honda battle between Jordan and BAR, it was evident this weekend. Amid daft rumours that Honda would ditch one team at the end of 2002, both needed to perform well and score points. But fate was against Jordan; first Heinz-Harald Frentzen was unwell and had to be replaced by Ricardo Zonta, then Jarno Trulli's fine qualifying was wasted in the race by brake problems. Eddie Jordan admitted he had rarely felt so low.

FRIDAY PRACTICE Jordan was back to just three cars for this flyaway race, Frentzen and Trulli using the same two race cars they had in Monaco (EJ11 06 and 05 respectively), and 04 acting as the spare, set prior to the race for Trulli.

The Italian had a reasonable day, covering 48 laps while gathering data for qualifying and the race. He was happy with his car's balance and traction, but felt that the brakes required further work. The team was running new ducts, which needed some fine-tuning.

Frentzen was ninth after 39 laps, but had two spins. The first was on the short drag down to the Esses, the second at the same point a few laps later. He actually hit the same section of barrier which he crashed into and thus out of the 1999 race when one of his brake discs exploded. This time the German felt dirt on the track had caused his downfall.

He got away with the first spin, but on the second occasion he backed the car into the wall, damaging the rear suspension and bodywork. Worse still, the impact was recorded by the FIA at 17G and aggravated the headaches and dizziness he had suffered in the week after his Monaco

Left: Jarno Trulli again showed excellent qualifying form but his good race was destroyed by master cylinder problems and a long brake pedal. Below: On the Friday, Heinz-Harald Frentzen again suffered a heavy impact and decided, in the interests of safety, not to race.

shunt which had obliged him to stand down from the intervening test at Magny-Cours.

Overnight Frentzen felt worse, so the decision was taken to rest him for the remainder of the weekend. Test driver Ricardo Zonta was on hand, so the Brazilian took over.

SATURDAY QUALIFYING Under the circumstances, fourth and 12th places on the grid was a solid result for Jordan, although Trulli had a little trouble seeing the positive side after being bumped from third on the grid by Coulthard's McLaren in the dying moments of qualifying. Coulthard was among those who beat the chequered flag to commence a last flying lap with nine seconds to spare, while Trulli did not get out until the clock showed only 40secs of qualifying to go. As Coulthard improved, the Italian threw his helmet down in despair.

On Bridgestone's soft tyres Trulli had driven extremely well to record 1m 16.459secs, but when the red flag came out the marshals mistakenly thought the session was finished and waved him into parc fermé. By the time he extricated himself it was too late, but although dropping one place was hardly the end of the world, it was hard not to sympathise. Zonta did a fine job on his return to active Formula One duty, even though he lost much of the free practice having his car fixed after tail-ending Enrique Bernoldi's Arrows, then spinning into a gravel trap when he went out again. As his confidence improved he got faster, and 12th place was sound enough.

SUNDAY RACE Trulli made a strong start to run fourth, but wisely ceded a place to a pushy Barrichello on the first lap. Once the Ferrari driver spun Trulli was back in fourth and spent the time up until his pitstop on the 37th lap pushing Coulthard. They were only half a second apart when the Italian swept pitward.

As the order settled down he was back in fourth by lap 55, even though Häkkinen had passed him during his stop, for Coulthard's engine had blown up. But over the last 10 laps the brake pedal travel was getting longer; in the end an angry Trulli quit on lap 64 due to a problem with the master cylinder.

Zonta drove well to hold eighth ahead of Häkkinen, who finally got by on lap 34. The Brazilian lost time the lap before when he ran into the back of Räikkönen – he claimed the Finn brake-tested him. He lost ground – even though a fast stop let him rejoin ahead of Panis – and finished seventh.

217

## EUROPEAN GRAND PRIX NÜRBURGRING
# Pointless weekend

Once more the Jordan Hondas looked competitive enough to score points, but Eddie Jordan's team again went home empty-handed. It was small consolation that rival Honda-powered team BAR also failed to up its score. The opportunity had been there, but the Bitten Heroes (as they were called in cigarette advertising-conscious Germany) couldn't grab it due to minor but ultimately critical problems.

**FRIDAY PRACTICE** Heinz-Harald Frentzen had little to celebrate on his return to cockpit duty on Friday. The German pronounced himself fit and free of the headaches that had bothered him in Canada. He was quick, too – but then a trip over the kerb at the final chicane damaged a bargeboard and required repairs. When running resumed after lunch he got a little bit too enthusiastic under braking for the last corner and backed his EJ11 chassis 06 into the gravel bed. That lost him the rest of the session and left him only 19th fastest on 1m 19.988secs from his 17 laps. It was frustrating to know EJ11-04 was waiting in the pits but the rules precluded use of it until qualifying.

Jarno Trulli wound EJ11-05 up to 1m 18.133secs to record the seventh fastest time during the course of his 39 laps, and he did a lot of preparation work in the process. He appreciated the car's consistency and balance, but was less happy with the fact that he found no improvement.

**SATURDAY QUALIFYING** Jarno Trulli predicted that the yellow cars would qualify seventh and eighth, as they'd finished in those positions in free practice. He was proved correct, achieving 1m 16.138secs himself to claim the inside slot on row four, with his team-mate alongside him on a 1m 16.376secs.

Trulli felt there was a little more to come from the car, while Frentzen was happier with his performance than he had been for some time as he shadowed his team-mate. Trulli was reckoned to be the better qualifier but he was nowhere near as forceful a racer as Frentzen.

The team made an engine change at lightning pace after Frentzen's car suffered a major failure towards the end of free practice. It was a feat worthy of the Guinness Book of Records.

**SUNDAY RACE** Sunday began well when Jordan Honda announced that Frentzen had taken up his option to stay with the team in 2002. It was obvious, too, that Honda would also keep the engine supply going in 2002, despite rumours to the contrary.

But the good mood evaporated when Frentzen botched his start. Trulli, however, got ahead of fuel-heavy Rubens Barrichello leaving the line to run sixth in Mika Häkkinen's wake. They remained in those positions for the first 27 laps until a persistent Eddie Irvine found a way by Frentzen on lap 28; then the German pitted for fuel a lap later. Initially he found he could push again on fresh rubber, but as the rear quickly lost effectiveness he fell away and lost touch with the Jaguar.

Points had long ceased to be a realistic possibility when Frentzen's traction control stopped working at a critical moment and spun him terminally off the track at the hairpin on the 49th lap. He had been running in eighth.

Trulli, meanwhile, had been looking set for sixth ahead of Häkkinen. In the first part of the race he had pressured the Finn strongly, chasing the leading pack, despite some glitches with downshifting. Having stopped for fuel on lap 30 he then moved ahead of the McLaren and was well placed to resist any counter-attack.

But the telemetry began to show a gearbox oil pressure fault; after 44 laps the transmission seized. With Barrichello subsequently going autocrossing on lap 60, fifth place might have been feasible, but once again a Grand Prix left Jordan with potential unfulfilled.

## FRENCH GRAND PRIX MAGNY-COURS
# Moving up the table

For a team with the reliability inherent in a Honda engine, Jordan was creeping only slowly up the constructors' table. But fifth meant two points, and anyone who scored in the heat of Magny-Cours could feel a sense of achievement.

Jarno Trulli's result moved the team three points clear of arch-rival BAR Honda and within one of Sauber's fourth place. Heinz-Harald Frentzen would have finished sixth had the refuelling equipment not malfunctioned momentarily during his first pitstop. After four pointless outings – the team had not scored since the Italian's fourth place in Spain back in May– this was welcome progress.

**FRIDAY PRACTICE** With only a week between races, Jordan had the same three chassis on hand in France for Trulli (EJ11-05, with 06 as the spare) and Frentzen (EJ11-04). Trulli got straight in the groove with a best of 1m 16.187secs, the ninth fastest time on the 52-lap course, and pronounced himself very satisfied with his car's balance and grip.

Frentzen did 45 laps and ended 13th on 1m 16.868secs, hampered in the morning by a problem with brake balance. This was sorted during the lunch break: he was relieved to cover some distance in the second session, as his post-Monte Carlo headaches had stopped him testing at the French circuit.

**SATURDAY QUALIFYING** With Trulli placing fifth on 1m 13.310secs and Frentzen seventh with 1m 13.815secs, the Jordan team received a timely tonic. The practice runnings on Friday and Saturday led Jordan to the same conclusion as the other Bridgestone runners: the degradational effects of the high track and ambient temperatures here meant that the harder compound was the only option. Trulli improved steadily

all through qualifying, but vaulted ahead of Montoya in the closing stages of the session, much to Eddie Jordan's undisguised delight. It was the sixth time in 10 races that he had qualified in the top six. Although he had lost time in free practice with a faulty front suspension sensor, the Italian's sole concern in qualifying was that he might inadvertently have hampered Michael Schumacher during one run.

Frentzen, too, was pretty pleased to end his own run of bad luck with a strong showing, the more so because he had lost time in free practice because of a misfire caused, it was thought, by an electronics glitch. He had run out of time to complete his set-up for qualifying and had to rely on a 'guestimate' which proved near to the mark. He was relieved to find that the balance was pretty good and was philosophical when he met traffic on one run. He was less forgiving when blocked by Olivier Panis on an in-lap. The sector times revealed that he had been two-10ths of a second up on his previous best time, which could have moved him ahead of Montoya on the grid.

**SUNDAY RACE** Just getting both cars home was a big boost for Jordan, and Trulli always looked likely to take points away from Magny-Cours. The Italian lost a place to fast-starting Rubens Barrichello (on a light fuel load) during the opening lap, then settled down smoothly in sixth, with Frentzen dogging him.

Barrichello's stop on lap 21 moved both Jordan drivers up a place, but when Frentzen pitted on lap 24 the refuelling hose did not initially attach properly to his car. What should have been a nine-second stop at worst lasted an agonising 16.3secs, dropping the German behind both Saubers and ruining his hopes of taking the final point.

Trulli's stop a lap later went smoothly, as did both of their subsequent calls. Frentzen had an aggressive Eddie Irvine to contend with, but he held him off resolutely until the 43rd lap. Then, when the Jaguar got alongside him at the last chicane, Heinz vaulted across it but, having maintained his place in such a manner, he knew he would be penalised unless he surrendered to Irvine so he gave way as they approached the Adelaide hairpin. Later he had a quick spin exiting the final corner, while chasing Kimi Räikkönen for seventh.

Above and left: Jarno Trulli gave Jordan its first points since the Spanish Grand Prix with a solid fifth place finish. The Italian had improved steadily in qualifying for fifth grid spot, ahead of his team-mate, and he looked strong throughout the race to claim two well-earned points.

Above: Frustration for Heinz-Harald Frentzen and Eddie Jordan as the German finished out of the points. Left: The Jordans ran closely early in the race, but a refuelling problem dropped Heinz-Harald down the field.

Left and right: Heinz-Harald Frentzen qualified strongly to take fifth on the grid behind his team-mate Jarno Trulli, but could only race to a disappointing seventh place for Jordan.

## BRITISH GRAND PRIX SILVERSTONE
# Fast, but down and out

Was it David Coulthard's fault, or Jarno Trulli's? Opinion remained divided after the pair came to grief on the first lap at Copse. The collision finally killed off Coulthard's world championship aspirations for 2001 and destroyed Trulli's chances of a podium finish and Jordan's likelihood of points. It was the bitterest blow for Eddie Jordan, made all the tougher after the team's best qualifying performance of the season – Ferrari's Ross Brawn had even hinted at a yellow win.

Meanwhile, the real trouble was happening behind closed doors. After the race Eddie Jordan gave Heinz-Harald Frentzen a serious talking-to in the team's motorhome, which would have the knock-on effect of the German's surprise eviction from the team before the next race.

FRIDAY PRACTICE Jordan Honda brought four cars from its factory across the road. Trulli had EJ11-05 to race with 06 as back-up; Heinz-Harald Frentzen had EJ11-04 with 02 as his spare. The Bridgestone runners had another tyre to evaluate and things went well for Frentzen, his best of 1m 23.877secs leaving him fifth. He was happy with the work the team got through, though his session ended prematurely with the discovery of an oil leak on his car. Birthday boy Trulli was satisfied with ninth in 1m 24.343secs. Both drivers felt good about qualifying.

SATURDAY QUALIFYING Fourth and fifth on the grid for Trulli and Frentzen respectively shouldn't have raised eyebrows, although Frentzen had been second to Michael Schumacher during free practice. It was by far Jordan's most convincing performance of the year. What made their positions all the more creditable was that rain had affected the morning session, so everyone had to guess the ideal set-up for qualifying. A glitch in the timing system also meant no split times were available.

Trulli worked diligently and banged in a 1m 20.930secs, only 0.483secs off pole. His fourth run was looking faster still, but he had to pull off when a front suspension pushrod broke after he ran over the new kerb on the exit to Becketts. He was two-10ths below his previous time and described his car as 'brilliant'. Frentzen was also having a strong run. His best of 1m 21.217secs was good enough for fifth and he was happy with the EJ11.

Eddie Jordan said: "We were hopeful after practice but I think everybody was expecting us to perform better in the wet than in the dry, so it's good to show we are competitive in both." It was a much-needed tonic for Jordan morale.

SUNDAY RACE By the first corner Jordan's best hope for a podium place had gone. Trulli made a great start and was running third into Copse, but as Coulthard attempted to brave it out on the outside they touched. Coulthard spun and Trulli went into the gravel. Each driver blamed the other, but it was a typical racing incident.

Frentzen made a terrible start and lost four places heading into Copse. That put him behind the Saubers and although he never got near Kimi Räikkönen, he did get a stab at Nick Heidfeld as Montoya came out of the pits on lap 26. Frentzen sneaked by at the Complex, then ran wide on the exit, letting the Sauber driver re-pass. Frentzen then said he felt something break at the back of the car and for the remainder of the race was hampered by serious understeer. Seventh place was a massive disappointment.

Above and below: A great fourth in qualifying came to nothing for Jarno Trulli and Eddie Jordan when the Italian clashed with David Coulthard at the first corner.

## GERMAN GRAND PRIX HOCKENHEIM
# Tough at the top for Eddie

A Jordan team member remarked after the race: "It's good to see Benetton's luck changing, isn't it?" And then he added: "Do you suppose ours is going to turn soon?"

In fact Jordan's on-track performance was secondary. Having ousted Heinz-Harald Frentzen, Eddie Jordan had to endure a nightmare weekend of his own making. He had few friends in the paddock – the crowd and even his own team were against him.

From his point of view he felt he had to do something – the team had a fast car and that speed wasn't being delivered in the races. But he soon found out what the phrase 'tough at the top' really means.

The timing of his decision on the eve of the German Grand Prix was strange. German sponsors are immensely important in F1 and Jordan had a big one.

Lady Luck rubbed it in when Jacques Villeneuve took BAR Honda's second podium of the season, emphasising Jordan Honda had yet to achieve that feat in 2001.

FRIDAY PRACTICE Jordan Honda had the same three cars it had at Silverstone but there was, of course, a change on the driver front after Frentzen was replaced by reserve driver Ricardo Zonta, who had chassis EJ11-04. Jarno Trulli had EJ11-06 to race and EJ11/05 as back-up. He covered 34 laps, setting ninth fastest lap with 1m 42.941secs, but the Italian was unhappy with the brakes.

Zonta dropped back to 13th in the afternoon, racking up 36 laps and a best time of 1m 43.461secs.

SATURDAY QUALIFYING Zonta stopped with a clutch problem during the first half of the morning's free practice session, which required an engine and gearbox change. The switch took just 43 minutes, allowing the Brazilian out for the last 10 minutes.

Trulli ended his day only 10th fastest in qualifying, on 1m 40.322secs, after being stranded out on the circuit with engine failure after eight laps. He was on a faster run when the problem occurred but failed to reach the pits in the time needed to make it count.

Zonta battled initially with understeer but improved things with some set-up changes before losing time behind Panis in the stadium. His second run was good, his third spoiled when he whacked a chicane kerb too hard, and his final effort was too gentle after that mistake. It left him a disappointing 15th on 1m 41.174secs on the basis of his second run.

SUNDAY RACE After the drama of the initial start, Trulli lost a place to Irvine but made up two with the demise of Heidfeld and de la Rosa. That left him ninth at the end of the first lap, on the same one-stop refuelling strategy as Villeneuve, who had quickly closed in on him.

Panis was two-stopping, however, and after overtaking his team-mate on lap 10 he closed in on the Jordan, slipping ahead at the first chicane. But the Frenchman had run outside the kerbs, which meant he ought to surrender the place. As they sped down to the second chicane Panis appeared to lift off. Thinking the BAR driver was letting him by, Trulli dived down the inside, braking hard on the entry to the chicane, only to find Panis cutting in on his usual line as he drew level. On the tight inside line the Italian spun, dropping down to 17th place. His race now ruined, Trulli ironically soon found himself running just ahead of Panis after the Frenchman stopped on his 16th lap.

After his own stop on lap 27, Trulli was back in ninth, with little prospect of points. It was a moot point – he rolled to a halt by the side of the track on lap 35, when his Honda engine suffered a hydraulic pump failure.

Zonta repeated his Canadian trick, running into the back of another car on the straight. This time it was Verstappen and the Brazilian had been running 13th prior to the incident on the sixth lap. The ensuing pit-stop for a new nose killed his already slim race chances, which were not enhanced by damage also inflicted on a brake duct, the front suspension and a bargeboard. He did one more lap before calling it a day.

Left and above: Jarno Trulli defended his position rather too energetically against the BARs, and he eventually spun back to 17th. He later retired from ninth when the Honda's hydraulic pump failed.

Left and right: Ricardo Zonta made a return to racing following Eddie Jordan's sacking of Heinz–Harald Frentzen. It was an uncomfortable weekend for Jordan on and off the track, the Brazilian retiring after running into the back of Verstappen's Arrows.

# New face, same story

It was the same old story at Jordan Honda, adequately summarised one dispirited Jordan team member after a high-pressure weekend yielded only a 10th place finish for new boy Jean Alesi. What made the disappointment harder to bear was that Trulli's superb qualifying performance to place his EJ11 fifth on the grid could not be sustained in the race. Yet again the Italian and his car flopped, and having held up a pack of followers with indescribably slow pace, he fell back to become a backmarker before retiring with a hydraulic problem. Inevitably it would take Alesi time to acclimatise, but the team's failure to change its fortunes hit morale hard.

FRIDAY PRACTICE Jordan Honda played musical chassis as Alesi took over EJ11-06 and had 03 as his spare, while Trulli took over EJ11-07 and kept chassis 05 as back-up. In his excitement at joining the team the mercurial Alesi hit the headlines almost at once. First he stopped at the Prost area, then misread his braking at the penultimate corner and parked in the gravel. He stayed there until Coulthard's kerbing problem prompted the red flag. Having calmed down a bit he clocked 23 laps and placed sixth in 1m 17.862secs – well ahead of Trulli, whose 41 laps left him 12th on 1m 18.277secs. But Eddie Jordan had ordered Alesi's tank to be drained so he could go for a time.

SATURDAY QUALIFYING Trulli reasserted himself in qualifying, rising to the occasion with a superb lap of 1m 15.394secs which not only upstaged Alesi but also left Mika Häkkinen on the outside of the third row. It was confirmation of both the Italian's pace in such circumstances, and the EJ11's.

Alesi, meanwhile, was happier with his car after minor adjustments greatly improved the balance, which had gone awry during the morning's free practice as track conditions changed. But he paid the price for his lack of drive-time and had to make do with 12th in the line-up on 1m 16.471secs.

SUNDAY RACE Jarno Trulli's race went according to the expectations of his critics, who had deemed him something of a mobile chicane on race day. The Italian made a reasonable start, then survived a brush with Nick Heidfeld's Sauber Petronas going through the first corner. He slipped ahead, and managed to block Mika Häkkinen's fuel-heavy McLaren at the same time. While running on a clear road Trulli's lap times were up to six-10ths of a second slower than Alesi's further down the pack, and having initially had Häkkinen right on his tail, the Jordan driver found he had a queue as his first pitstop became due on lap 29. By then Häkkinen had the pack of Heidfeld, Montoya and Räikkönen running nose-to-tail behind him, and even the BAR Hondas were beginning to close in as the yellow car held everyone up.

Trulli's stop dropped him way back, partly because he lost about three seconds when the refuelling hose did not detach initially, and partly because others were able to go much faster without him blocking them. By the time everyone bar Häkkinen had pitted, Räikkönen, Heidfeld, Montoya and Panis had all overtaken Trulli. After that he struggled along until a hydraulic problem brought him to a halt on the 54th lap when he was running 10th ahead of Villeneuve but behind Panis.

Alesi distinguished himself not only by lapping quicker than his team-mate, but also by pulling off the only real overtaking move of the race, passing Pedro de la Rosa's Jaguar for 12th place on lap 10. He then set about a race-long pursuit of Villeneuve, vying for ninth place. He closed the gap to a fraction over two seconds by lap 62, before a combination of aerodynamic effects, traffic and the need to let the leaders by opened it up again.

Above: Eddie Jordan presents his new pairing of Alesi and Trulli to the press. Right: Trulli's race again ends in retirement. Below: Alesi and his manager compare notes with Trulli on life at Jordan. Alesi drove hard and made it to the finish.

Right and below: Jean Alesi gave a good account of himself on a difficult circuit on his Jordan debut. His pitstop went without problem and the finish provided him with valuable experience for the remaining races. Left: Trulli again had little to be happy about.

## BELGIAN GRAND PRIX SPA-FRANCORCHAMPS
# Alesi makes a point

The knives might have been out for Jean Alesi among the sceptics who said he was enjoying a five-race Formula One swansong with the Jordan Honda team, but the veteran Frenchman drove like a star at Spa to fend off a determined Ralf Schumacher and score Jordan Honda a much-needed point to bring the team back to level-pegging with BAR Honda.

In this war every point counted, and the victor would win the battle for Honda's favour. The only cloud looming on the horizon was the resurgence of Benetton Renault. That was grounds for serious concern.

**FRIDAY PRACTICE** Jarno Trulli likes Spa, as his second place in free practice – with a 1m 49.404secs – attested. Driving EJ11-05 with chassis 03 as back-up, the Italian was very pleased with the car's balance and declared it a productive day.

Alesi, who had matched Trulli's times during pre-event testing at Mugello as he became more familiar with EJ11-04, was also happy enough even though his 30 laps yielded only the ninth fastest time, a 1m 51.631secs. But Alesi was grateful for the chance to try the car for the first time in wet conditions, and it gave him a favourable impression.

**SATURDAY QUALIFYING** By Saturday evening, the mood in the Jordan camp could not have been more starkly contrasted to that of the previous day. Alesi

qualified in 13th place on 1m 59.128secs; Trulli managed 16th on 1m 59.647secs. Neither driver was put on dry tyres as qualifying drew to an end, and the intermediates were past their best by then. Managing director Trevor Foster admitted the team was caught out in its belief that the track wasn't dry enough for dry rubber, and that was that.

**SUNDAY RACE** Eddie Jordan's heart was well and truly in his mouth as his two drivers ran side by side up Raidillon after the restart, with Jacques Villeneuve's BAR making it a threesome of Honda-powered machines. Two into one doesn't go at Les Combes, let alone three: Trulli got the nod from Alesi. Villeneuve, meanwhile, got on the dirt and nearly lost it as he swept across team-mate Olivier Panis's bows exiting the corner.

Jenson Button's Benetton became Trulli's first victim, losing his sixth place on the third lap. Alesi followed him through a lap later, lapping slightly faster than the Italian. They stopped to refuel on laps six and seven respectively, then quickly worked back to sixth and seventh as others followed suit. Then Barrichello screwed up the Bus Stop chicane, dropping behind as he slowed and pitted for a new nose and wing.

The Jordans stopped again on laps 19 and 20. Now Alesi had reduced a 4.4secs gap to 2.5secs as he hounded Trulli, but as Barrichello began to close in, the Frenchman had to watch his mirrors rather than what lay ahead. Ralf Schumacher's belated fuel stop on lap 25 promoted Trulli to fifth, Alesi to sixth and Barrichello to seventh, but on the 32nd lap Barrichello vaulted to fifth as Trulli's engine blew up spectacularly, and the Brazilian eased by the other Jordan going up to Les Combes.

Now Alesi had Ralf Schumacher to worry about, as the BMW Williams driver harried him. For the last eight laps Ralf was right on his tailpipes, but Alesi was up to the challenge and never put a wheel wrong.

Eddie Jordan believed Alesi's performance fully justified taking him on. But never one to miss an opportunity he was quick to point out the stellar job his 2002 signing had done for Benetton.

*Above and left: Jean Alesi gave a brilliant display of driving at Spa to score a point in his second race for Jordan, exactly what Eddie expected. His successful defence of sixth place from Ralf Schumacher was a great example of racing skills without resorting to any type of bullying or intimidating tactics.*

*Left and below: Jarno Trulli again qualified and raced hard, but was once again let down by unreliability when the Honda imploded as he was on his way to fifth place. Eddie Jordan at first thought Alesi had missed a point, assuming it was an aggregate race. He'd forgotten the rules had changed some time ago.*

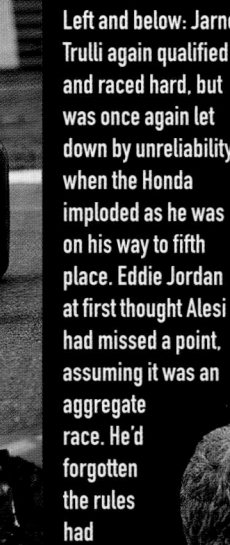

## ITALIAN GRAND PRIX MONZA
# Uncertain times

Jean Alesi may have raced brilliantly and rescued Jordan with a point in Belgium, but in qualifying – against the man he replaced, Heinz-Harald Frentzen – Alesi had not impressed. Before they changed teams, Alesi had only once out-qualified Frentzen, But Frentzen out-qualified Alesi twice in the three races since the switch. Some were muttering that Eddie Jordan had swapped a pig for a poke, whatever that meant.

Jean Alesi knew he had to impress the team to earn a Jordan Honda drive for 2002. As it turned out the die was already cast and Alesi faced retirement, his gamble of swapping teams having failed him miserably.

**FRIDAY PRACTICE** Despite this background Friday was Jean Alesi's day, the French veteran taking his Jordan Honda EJ11/04 to ninth best time in 37 laps. Team-mate Jarno Trulli in the EJ11/05 was only fractions behind, but over 39 laps he claimed only 12th place as the midfield times were so close.

The main task was the usual brake and tyre tests, Monza being very hard on them, so both drivers ran with high fuel loads.

Alesi slightly damaged his chassis and undertray, after a trip over the kerb as he got used to the car in its lowest-downforce trim. Trulli, who had call on the spare car (03), said he had a tough day but was ultimately satisfied with his performance.

**SATURDAY QUALIFYING** Saturday saw Trulli reassert himself. His speed in qualifying had generally shown Jean Alesi up, and whereas Frentzen could often hold his own, Alesi was more usually way off. In the morning session the Italian was third fastest, beaten only by Michael Schumacher and Montoya, and even then was only just over a half-second shy of the world champion. Alesi suffered gearbox bearing failure 20 minutes before the session ended, which stopped him from setting the car up fully for qualifying.

Both chose the softer Bridgestone compound, and the Italian really turned it on, for an inside third-row slot that left him beaming from ear to ear. The EJ11 was well balanced, braked consistently and had good straight-line speed – all he could wish for.

Alesi paid the price for his morning problem, struggling to 16th, 3.4kph off his team-mate's pace. He had problems under braking, the balance wasn't perfect, and the traffic was bad. At a time when he was sup-posedly 'on probation' before Eddie Jordan decided whether to give him a ride next year, the result was bitterly disappointing for him.

**SUNDAY RACE** Off the line Trulli made a strong start and comfortably retained his fifth place from the grid – until Jenson Button came tanking down the inside and sailed into the back of him. "He is a complete idiot," managing director Trevor Foster declared. "After all the aggravation between the drivers about whether to overtake or not in the first two chicanes, everyone had seemed to work it out in their heads. Then this happens…"

Trulli wasn't impressed either, accusing Button (who apologised and who may or may not be Trulli's team-mate at Renault next season) of badly misjudging his braking.

Cue Alesi, who rose to the occasion with a great start to move from an effective 14th on the grid to 10th by the end of lap one, ahead of Villeneuve in the dreaded BAR. Alesi quickly passed the white car – he was carrying less fuel – and chased Räikkönen and Verstappen as Irvine quickly fell back from his initial seventh. By lap five the Jordan had overtaken the de la Rosa in the other Jaguar, and Alesi then squeezed past Räikkönen on lap 12. Next up was Verstappen, but he lost time and momentum, cramped behind the Arrows, until he was able to outbrake it into the first chicane on the 16th lap.

Alesi's first pitstop went well on lap 22, dropping him only from fifth to seventh, but then things began to unravel. Five or six laps after his stop, Alesi locked up the left front tyre going into the first chicane, flat-spotting it but also blistering it badly. He stood the severe vibrations for another few laps before deciding to pit early as he believed he had a puncture. Despite the short notice his crew turned him round in 10.1secs, but the refuelling strategy was out of sync – he now had to take on enough to last him until the finish.

This time he fell behind Villeneuve and Räikkönen, and could not recover the ground on heavy tanks. He finished eighth.

*Right: Although disappointing in qualifying, Jean Alesi continued to prove he's a great racer, when he charged from 16th to fifth, and finished eighth. Below: Jarno Trulli's race was short-lived after he collided with Jenson Button at the first corner.*

*Right and below: Trulli's joy at qualifying fifth for his home race quickly evaporated on race day when Button's Benetton rammed him at the first corner. The incident is unlikely to have helped Button's position with team chief Flavio Briatore.*

## UNITED STATES GRAND PRIX INDIANAPOLIS
# Bitten and hissed

Jean Alesi came to Indianapolis with a thing or two to prove. Outshone by Heinz-Harald Frentzen in his old car, he needed to show Eddie Jordan he had not made a big mistake. He duly did so, qualifying well and scoring a point after his team-mate Jarno Trulli was excluded from fourth.

Jordan's weekend was ruined when a post-race check revealed the thickness of a rear skid block on the undercar plank to be 1.5mm less than regulation. The inference was that the car had gained a performance benefit by running too low a ride height, which had resulted in the block being worn away by the track – so Trulli lost fourth, Alesi gained sixth, and Jordan lost a net two points.

It was bad timing just as Jordan thought it had pulled ahead of BAR Honda in the points race. It was also a let-off for BAR chief Craig Pollock, who would lose serious face with Honda if Jordan beat his outfit. Now, with 17 points each, all was to play for in Japan, although both teams looked to have ceded championship fourth to Sauber, which had a far smaller budget and no works engine.

It was also Alesi's 200th Grand Prix: the 37-year-old's debut was 13 years ago. He was destined to get to 201 but no further.

FRIDAY PRACTICE Practice was tame. Twelfth and 14th places respectively for Jean Alesi and Jarno Trulli did not reflect Jordan Honda's potential, as they worked through their race-prep routine. Alesi, in his usual EJ11/04 (with 03 as his spare), covered 33 laps for a best of 1m 14.057secs. The Frenchman lost some running time with an electronics software glitch and was unhappy with his chassis balance. Trulli, in EJ11/05, did five more laps but was a trifle slower at 1m 14.215secs; his car was reliable, but blistering tyres sent him spinning twice in the first session.

SATURDAY QUALIFYING Eight and ninth on the grid, though respectable, were a downer for Eddie Jordan, especially as both drivers felt that they had maximised their equipment. Both were happy with the EJ11s' balance,

having chosen the softer Bridgestone tyre compound, but Jordan had hoped for more as the fight with BAR and Sauber intensified. Trulli set his 1m 12.605secs best on his third outing, as he encountered traffic on his final run. That left him two-1000ths of a second faster than Alesi, who really had the bit between his teeth on his way to a 1m 12.607secs close to the end of the session.

It was Alesi's best yet for Jordan, as he was really fired up to keep his place for 2002, though that looked more and more unlikely.

SUNDAY RACE Considering he had been so vocal about Jenson Button's start tactics at Monza, Jarno Trulli weaved sharply to the left off the line, then cut back hard to the right as he spied Button's Benetton Renault moving quickly up the inside. Only hard braking by Button prevented a collision. A lap later, having lost some ground to both Saubers in traffic, Trulli tried to squeeze by on the outside of Räikkönen going into the first turn. The Finn was just aborting a passing move on his team-mate, and as the Jordan tried to cut across it hit one Sauber, pushing it into the other.

The Jordan escaped unscathed, and Trulli settled down in ninth behind Button for the next seven laps before passing on sheer grunt down the pit straight. At this stage the Italian was unable to make any inroads into the deficit to Heidfeld in seventh – the Sauber driver was on a two-stop strategy and the Jordan on one. By the time Trulli pitted on lap 39 he was still behind the Sauber, but the Swiss car's gearbox problems made it easy meat. The retirements of both BMW Williams promoted Trulli further, as did Heidfeld's second stop and then Irvine's first. Thus he could bring his car to fifth, which became fourth when Barrichello fell back.

Alesi, meanwhile, passed five cars in a strong 200th GP showing, the French veteran stopping only once, on lap 37. He lapped at similar speed to his team-mate, but had to be content with seventh place – until the stewards dropped their bombshell and excluded Trulli. Alesi thus took the final point, but that was scant consolation for his despondent team, which gave immediate notice of its intention to appeal.

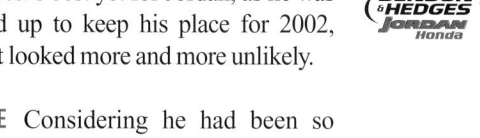

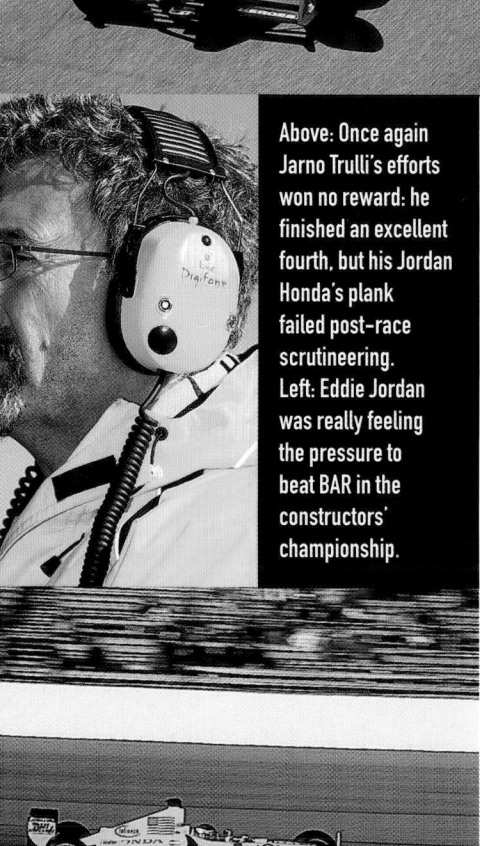

Above: Once again Jarno Trulli's efforts won no reward: he finished an excellent fourth, but his Jordan Honda's plank failed post-race scrutineering.
Left: Eddie Jordan was really feeling the pressure to beat BAR in the constructors' championship.

## JAPANESE GRAND PRIX SUZUKA
# Pipe dreams

Right and below:
Jarno Trulli's farewell
race with Jordan
Honda typified their
time together.
A disappointing end
to an association that
never quite lived up
to expectations.

**M**uch of 2001's misfortune went Eddie Jordan's way, and Suzuka proved the rule. The promise of Jarno Trulli's initial pace evaporated into a feeble finish in eighth position, while Jean Alesi's last hurrah ended in a spectacular shunt that destroyed his 100 per cent finishing record. Subject to its ultimately successful appeal to the FIA, Jordan Honda went away from Japan believing it had failed to get fourth in the championship, and also believing it had finished behind BAR Honda. As one team member succinctly summed up, it was now time to restructure before a new season of higher expectations – and, what's more, under a financial cloud. It appeared Jordan would have less money to do the job, given the events of 11th September and a likely sizeable pay-off to Heinz-Harald Frentzen.

**FRIDAY PRACTICE** Eddie Jordan was buoyant, and Jean Alesi's swansong Friday saw Jordan top the timesheets. Artificial maybe, but it cheered the team. The veteran Frenchman was in his element on a track where a driver can display his art. His best of 1m 35.454secs, over 32 laps, was half a second faster than Juan Pablo Montoya and more than two seconds ahead of team-mate Jarno Trulli. Alesi ran with minimal fuel; Trulli focused more on race work.

Using EJ11/04, Alesi pushed hard from the start and did work that would be valuable come Saturday afternoon. His sole problem, apart from some heavy bounces over the chicane, was a spin at the end of the afternoon session. No damage was done, and the yellow flags momentarily slowed down rivals.

Trulli had the spare for the weekend (EJ11/03) but set his 1m 37.564secs in 05, covering 34 laps. His eye on Sunday afternoon, he was quite satisfied with his day's smooth work, besides needing more traction.

**SATURDAY QUALIFYING** As expected, Trulli led the Jordan challenge in qualifying. The Italian carried on from his sixth fastest time in free practice, and felt his eighth fastest time of 1m 34.002secs was the EJ11's best offer. But he admitted he had been baulked slightly during the lap in sector two, which he felt cost him a possible sixth.

In his last Formula One qualifying session Alesi clocked a 1m 34.420secs, 1kph shy of Trulli, whom he hugged affectionately as they stepped from their cars. Despite working throughout the session with engineer David Brown, he was unable to close the 0.4-second gap on Trulli.

Both Jordan cars ran reliably, still with the latest specification Honda engine, and both drivers chose the softer Bridgestone tyre. But eighth and 11th fastest times caused tangible disappointment, and concern at the speed of the Benetton Renaults.

**SUNDAY RACE** When Trulli got away eighth things looked promising for Jordan, especially as Alesi soon found a way past Kimi Räikkönen's Sauber. But after six laps things began to go seriously awry. When Räikkönen's left rear suspension broke as he negotiated the quick double left-hander behind the pits, Alesi fell victim to high-speed circumstance, ploughing into the spinning C20. The two cars speared off to the right of the track, and Alesi was very fortunate not to be hit by flying debris as his car inadvertently pinned Räikkönen's up against the wall. Neither driver was injured, though Räikkönen complained of a headache, and both counted themselves very lucky. It was a mighty accident, and a sad end to a charismatic racer's F1 career.

Hopes then rested on Trulli, but it was immediately clear that he lacked the pace to challenge the three leading teams. He settled into seventh until his first stop on lap 16. After everyone else had refuelled he resumed the position until his second stop on lap 33, but better pit strategy by Benetton got both of its cars ahead, leaving Trulli to plug along in ninth under a growing threat from Villeneuve.

On lap 49 the Italian was lucky to escape when Villeneuve found himself short-braked at the chicane and the BAR just avoided the Jordan as Villeneuve spun. That let Heidfeld through for a crack at eighth, but Trulli signed off for Jordan by holding on.

Right and below:
Jean Alesi's 201st
and final Grand Prix
appearance ended
when Kimi Räikkönen
crashed and the
popular Frenchman
was unable to
avoid him.

Team Review    Race by Race

# BAR

| | | | | | |
|---|---|---|---|---|---|
| Team Review | - | The season | p230 | European Grand Prix | - Nürburgring | p244 |
| Australian Grand Prix | - | Melbourne | p236 | French Grand Prix | - Magny-Cours | p245 |
| Malaysian Grand Prix | - | Sepang | p237 | British Grand Prix | - Silverstone | p246 |
| Brazilian Grand Prix | - | Interlagos | p238 | German Grand Prix | - Hockenheim | p247 |
| San Marino Grand Prix | - | Imola | p239 | Hungarian Grand Prix | - Hungaroring | p248 |
| Spanish Grand Prix | - | Barcelona | p240 | Belgian Grand Prix | - Spa-Francorchamps | p249 |
| Austrian Grand Prix | - | A1 Ring | p241 | Italian Grand Prix | - Monza | p250 |
| Monaco Grand Prix | - | Monte Carlo | p242 | USA Grand Prix | - Indianapolis | p251 |
| Canadian Grand Prix | - | Montreal | p243 | Japanese Grand Prix | - Suzuka | p252 |

LUCKY STRIKE B.A.R Honda

2001

Jacques Villeneuve

Craig Pollock

Olivier Panis

Olivier Panis

## LUCKY STRIKE B.A.R Honda

# Dreams are not reality

**B**AR Honda team principal Craig Pollock said at the beginning of the 2001 season: "Our aim is to have at least a third place finish in the standings and win some races." It was a dream.

Pollock has come a long way with his steely stare and firm handshake, but he has found that neither attribute can make his car go faster. In reality, British American Racing never came remotely close to winning a race and scored even less points than it did last year. It finished Japan with a precarious hold on fifth place in the standings, which then became sixth when the FIA ruled in favour of an appeal by Jordan over points it lost in the United States Grand Prix.

For BAR's ambitions to be realised, there would need to be a dramatic improvement on the erratic progress made during the team's short history. Its disastrous debut in 1999, in which it was the only team not to score any points – after Pollock and company had pre-

dicted it would win its first race – was followed by a modicum of respectability achieved in 2000, when BAR finished fifth, equal on points with Benetton and ahead of Jordan. That both those teams also performed poorly this year, together with Sauber's sensational season, only magnified the embarrassing reality that BAR went backwards in 2001.

## The BAR Honda 003 car

THE TEAM'S problems centred on the deficiencies of the BAR 003 chassis, which the ever-forthright Jacques Villeneuve said was 'born bad'. His pre-season prognostication, widely ignored, that it was even slower than the 2000 car remained valid throughout the year; indeed it got worse as the season wore on. Villeneuve was right and the team should have listened, scrapping the design and

starting again to ensure a competitive 'B' spec car by mid season.

At least the car was moderately reliable, unlike in 1999. There were bouts of unreliability, however, but even when it ran perfectly the ill-fated car was simply too slow. Any complaints that part of the problem was Honda – and Villeneuve implied as much – were belied by Jordan's consistently better pace with identical engines. The exact nature of the chassis design faults was never fully understood, and in fact was only pinpointed towards the end of the season. The basic problem was a lack of grip that no amount of suspension fiddling, aerodynamic tweaking or ballast redistribution was able to solve. As a result, the team's on-going test programme suffered and developmental progress was impeded. BAR had no idea what to expect on race weekends, many of which deteriorated into little more than panic-stricken test sessions in pursuit of improvements that most often were never found.

It was only at the end of the season that technical director Malcolm Oastler and his design team were able to pinpoint the cause of the chronic lack of grip that had plagued the cars from the beginning. A fundamental design flaw – perhaps related to weight-saving measures in chassis that were 66lbs lighter than in 2000 – resulted in the chassis flexing, particularly in the rear end, so that the cars felt loose to the drivers and often lurched and yawed alarmingly between oversteer and understeer in the same corner. Worse still, and even more mystifying, the problem varied from car to car and from weekend to weekend. And only sometimes would the culprit chassis respond favourably to set-up changes, so that the team never knew what to expect next.

In fact during the season the car appeared to slide backwards relative to the competition. BAR was in worst shape at the last race, relatively speaking, than at the first. This was borne out by the ▷

**Olivier Panis**

numbers: Villeneuve was 1.543 seconds off polesitter Michael Schumacher at the Melbourne curtain-raiser, and by Japan he was 2.625 seconds off.

The car's only saving grace was that it tended to perform better in race trim, when a heavier fuel load helped mask the evil handling and provided more grip. But by then, having qualified poorly, the pursuit of points required extra pace that the car was incapable of delivering. The majority of the team's points were a result of faster cars failing to finish.

The chassis limitations meant BAR was never going to be the team that would enable its engine supplier to achieve pre-season objectives. "Our target is to have a Honda-powered team in the top three in the constructors' championship and have a Honda-powered driver win," declared Honda's Formula One project leader Takefumi Hosaki.

Villeneuve complained that the engine reached its performance zenith by about mid-season and, with very little room for improvement, Honda then began concentrating on next year's power plants. Honda denied this – though it admitted that development did not take place as fast as had been planned – mostly because of a spate of mid-season unreliability in testing. According to Honda, while work on the 2002 engines was ongoing in a parallel programme which began early this year, the 60-70 engines supplied to BAR – as was also the case with Jordan – were developed continually, with upgraded specifications for nearly every race in 2001.

Only three of the team's eight race retirements for mechanical reasons were attributable to the engines: two for Villeneuve (in San Marino and France) and one for Panis (in Malaysia), though Panis suffered more from overall unreliability. While Villeneuve stopped in Canada with a driveshaft problem, Panis was halted in Monaco,

Canada and Europe by electrical, brake and gearbox problems respectively, then failed to finish in Hungary because of another electrical fault. Beyond those retirements, both drivers lost valuable track time on several race weekends while hydraulic and electronic systems problems were repaired. The team went through eight versions of the BAR 003 chassis, usually bringing three to the races, where Villeneuve's contract stipulated that he had first call on the T-car. Villeneuve began the season with chassis 001, with 002 designated as the T-car and Panis using 003. But 001 went only as far as the fifth lap of the first race, in Australia, where it was destroyed in the huge accident caused by Villeneuve's ramming of Ralf Schumacher's Williams from behind. In Malaysia, Villeneuve had a new car, 004, which he also raced in Brazil, before getting yet another new chassis for San Marino, where his 005 chassis featured a revised aerodynamic package and a new exhaust system designed by Honda. Panis stayed with 003 until Spain, where it became the T-car and the Frenchman was given 006, a new chassis that incorporated the upgrades on 005, which in Spain transported Villeneuve to the podium – BAR's best-ever result.

Throughout the season those race chassis that became obsolete were flogged around in test sessions by a series of test drivers. By the end of the year these included Formula Three rookies Takuma Sato and Anthony Davidson, along with BAR's development driver (and Villeneuve's friend) Patrick Lemarie and BAR's regular test driver Darren Manning. Panis did much more testing than Villeneuve, who said: "I love racing but testing is very annoying. I'd rather have 30 races and no testing."

In Canada, after crashing his race car in practice, Villeneuve commandeered chassis 006, which had become the T-car, following the introduction of 007 for Panis at the previous race in Monaco.

Malcolm Oastler

Andy Green

For the next race, the European Grand Prix, the cars were upgraded with aerodynamic improvements in the form of new nosecones, bargeboards and rear diffusers. The chassis, now 007 for Villeneuve and 006 for Panis, also sported new front suspensions designed by the Honda engineers in residence at Brackley. Their rear suspension efforts appeared at the next race, the French Grand Prix. There, Panis was also given his own T-car, 005, for his home race, while Villeneuve's back-up was the veteran chassis 004 that was brought along in the vain hope that it might be better than the newer versions. Still, the cars were gradually becoming more reliable and it was mainly this factor, together with a useful one-stop strategy, that enabled Villeneuve to take his second podium of the season, at Hockenheim.

The next chassis revisions were low downforce modifications introduced in Hungary, where a new floor, front wing and rear diffuser made such little impression – in fact the handling was worse

– that Villeneuve raced with the unmodified T-car, 004.

The last 2001 chassis, 008, was used by Villeneuve in the final two races, both of which Panis contested in the now-upgraded 004 in a desperate move prompted by hopes that it might be an improvement over the newer models, which it wasn't. In Japan (where the T-car was still the venerable 005) Panis was further off the pace than he had been all year. Villeneuve's 008, which included some components intended for 2002, was also designed to be easier to work on – and there was plenty of that to be done.

## The drivers

THE DIRE situation in the team particularly vexed Villeneuve – winner of the 1997 driving title with Williams – around whom the team was built, but whose subsequent setbacks with BAR may have set a record for a former champion's fall from grace. Becoming increasingly exasperated as the season wore on, Villeneuve intensified his public criticism of the team. He might have intended this as a motivational exercise but it also threatened to undermine the morale of the race team personnel, who in fact performed reasonably well throughout a year in which Villeneuve's personal performance was decidedly uneven.

Though he provided the team with its best results, including ▷

---

## BAR SEASON STATISTICS

### RELIABILITY PERFORMANCE

| Driver | Races | Max laps | Laps completed | Reliability rating |
|---|---|---|---|---|
| Jacques Villeneuve | 17 | 1065 | 790 | 74.2% |
| Olivier Panis | 17 | 1065 | 784 | 73.6% |
| Constructor | Races | Max laps | Laps completed | Reliability rating |
| BAR Honda | 34 | 2130 | 1574 | 73.9% |

### CHAMPIONSHIP PERFORMANCE

| Driver | 2001 points | 2000 points | 12 month change |
|---|---|---|---|
| Jacques Villeneuve | 12 | 17 | -29.4% |
| Olivier Panis | 5 | - | Did not compete |
| Constructor | 2001 points | 2000 points | 12 month change |
| BAR Honda | 17 | 20 | -15% |

Olivier Panis

### CHASSIS LOG

**003/001** Race car for Jacques Villeneuve at Melbourne.

**003/002** Spare car at Melbourne, Sepang, Interlagos and Imola.

**003/003** Race car for Olivier Panis at Melbourne, Sepang, Interlagos and Imola; and for Villeneuve at Monte Carlo. Spare car at Barcelona and the A1 Ring (raced by Villeneuve after 005 suffered an engine failure).

**003/004** Race car for Villeneuve at Sepang, Interlagos, Montreal (badly damaged in practice and replaced by 006 for the rest of the weekend) and Spa-Francorchamps; and for Panis at Indianapolis and Suzuka. Spare car at Monte Carlo, Nürburgring, Magny-Cours, Silverstone (used in qualifying by Villeneuve), Hockenheim, Hungaroring (raced by Villeneuve instead of 007) and Monza (raced after 008 developed bad handling).

**003/005** Race car for Villeneuve at Imola, Barcelona and the A1 Ring (discarded in favour of 003 after an engine blow-out). Spare car at Monte Carlo, Magny-Cours, Spa-Francorchamps, Indianapolis (used briefly by Villeneuve in qualifying) and Suzuka.

**003/006** Race car for Panis at Barcelona, A1 Ring, Monte Carlo, Nürburgring, Magny-Cours, Silverstone, Hockenheim, Hungaroring, Spa-Francorchamps and Monza. Spare car at Montreal commandeered by Villeneuve after his Friday crash.

**003/007** Race car for Panis at Montreal; and for Villeneuve at the Nürburgring, Magny-Cours, Silverstone, Hockenheim and the Hungaroring (not raced after it was slow in warm-up). Taken to Montreal as the spare car but raced by Villeneuve after he crashed 004.

**003/008** Race car for Villeneuve at Monza (not raced due to poor handling), Indianapolis and Suzuka.

Note: the BAR Honda chassis designation is sometimes given as '030', and the chassis numbers are sometimes written in '02' rather than '002' format.

Jacques Villeneuve

two somewhat fortuitous podiums, Villeneuve only scored points in four races. His 12 points, five fewer than in 2000, left him seventh overall in the standings. Olivier Panis, 14th among the drivers with only five points, was usually much closer to Villeneuve than his results might suggest. Panis had more than his share of BAR's mechanical misfortunes, about which he complained a lot less than his celebrated team-mate.

In qualifying Villeneuve outperformed Panis 11 to six, but then he should have done, given his career record of 13 poles and 11 races wins versus zero poles and one victory for Panis. Not to mention the many millions more dollars BAR was paying its more celebrated driver in the belief he had so much more to offer than the French journeyman. Yet Panis played much more than a mere supporting role, racing as well as at any time in his career, and exerting valuable pressure on a team-mate whose motivation might otherwise have waned even more than it did. Panis, unlucky to have a fourth place in Australia erased by a dubious yellow flag infraction, finished fourth in Brazil and fifth in Austria, and failed to score anywhere else. Villeneuve's points-scoring races included his third place in Spain, a fourth in Monaco, another third at Hockenheim and a sixth in Italy.

In fact, the BAR team-mates got along quite well, united by their common French language and a shared misery in having hopeless cars to work with. Even when Villeneuve rammed him out at the start of the British Grand Prix – for which he apologised profusely – Panis refused to condemn his team-mate.

Where the veteran Panis outshone his Canadian counterpart was in matters of diplomacy. Unlike Panis, who was always tactful when discussing the team's problems and remained positive in his public comments, Villeneuve was a very sore loser and became increasingly outspoken about BAR's inadequacies. Over the season

he rubbished his car for being useless, its Honda engine for lacking power and his team for being amateurish. All of this was true to varying degrees, and the truth hurt, but within the team Villeneuve was sometimes seen as a demotivating force and not often enough the team leader he was hired to be.

Though he could rightly blame his car for much of the shortfall that amounted to his worst-ever season since his debut in 1996, Villeneuve also contributed to his own demise, with some inferior race performances in which his renowned fighting spirit and aggression, if not his judgement, seemed lacking. He got off to a bad start with the serious accident in Australia in which a track worker was killed by a flying wheel from his crashing car. The fact that he was shaken by this – though he refused to use it as an excuse – might help explain his spinning out of the next race, in Malaysia, on the fifth lap. Villeneuve later admitted that a sore back, a legacy of the crash, bothered him until mid-season.

By that time Villeneuve was BAR's hero, having hauled the team up by its bootstraps with the Spanish triumph of sorts that brought BAR its first-ever podium. But his see-saw season persisted. In his home race in Canada, Villeneuve made headlines by brake testing Juan Pablo Montoya in practice and later grabbing the Williams driver by the throat after an exchange of insults. A few races later, when an engine failure stopped him in France, Villeneuve stalked off in a huff and refused to speak to anyone on the team. In truth, he was an angry young man for most of the year.

As his results veered between bad and worse, with occasional excursions into mediocrity, Villeneuve's despair deepened. There were temper tantrums and shouting matches, not always behind closed doors. The team's PR department went into overdrive trying to put a positive spin on Villeneuve's constant complaining, which was also causing internal strife. Shut up and drive, said the team.

234

Give me a good car and I'll let it do the talking, retorted Villeneuve.

The improved car wasn't forthcoming, however, so he got himself a girl instead. His performance sagged because his mind was on romance and not on racing – or so said Villeneuve's critics at the penultimate race, the US Grand Prix in Indianapolis.

There, after Villeneuve took time out to become engaged to the American ballerina Ellie Green, he pulled out of the race and parked his car in the garage. At first Villeneuve claimed that accident damage had made it too dangerous to continue.

Meanwhile, at Indy, the hard-working Olivier Panis soldiered on to finish 11th, having also outqualified Villeneuve by five places on the grid. Asked to explain the difference between the drivers, one team insider said it was about a second a lap and twelve million dollars, a facetious remark referring to the imbalance between the drivers' salaries and their relative contributions to the team.

Villeneuve later admitted that his car's shortcomings – hopelessly slow on the straights and seriously gripless in the corners – caused frustration for which the only solution, he felt, was to exchange the cold comfort of his car for Miss Green's warm embrace. That night at Indy, Craig Pollock was incensed, singling out Villeneuve as the villain who dragged the team down in what Pollock described as BAR's 'worst-ever race'.

In a one-sided lecture, delivered to the embarrassed driver by his former schoolteacher and manager, Pollock told Villeneuve to get his head in gear immediately and start carrying his weight. Pollock said Villeneuve had to lead by example, especially in times of adversity, and he had to start showing the type of leadership typified by Michael Schumacher, who spearheaded Ferrari's return to supremacy. Pollock also pointed out that Villeneuve's salary was second only to Schumacher and that it was high time he started earning it. Granted, even superstar Schumacher could not be victorious in a 2001 BAR Honda, but nor would he rubbish the team in public, or give up on it as Villeneuve had apparently done. Pollock finished by demanding a return to form from Villeneuve in the season's finale, as a prelude to what was expected of him next year.

Pollock's pep-talk seemed to have worked. Villeneuve certainly worked hard at Suzuka, a weekend at which Panis had the misfortune to have the dreaded chassis deficiencies descend on his car, and he finished an unlucky 13th. Villeneuve fought as hard as he had all season, for which he was rewarded with 10th place, a lowly result that typified the team's season. It also showed just how far BAR Honda has to go in 2002.

## Commercial

FOR a team that was founded as a marketing exercise, 2001 was particularly disturbing, as was its mounting debt, reported to be $40 million more after a season in which British American Racing failed to pay dividends from any point of view. As unlikely as it seems, BAR's misfortunes have not affected the rise of the Lucky

Strike cigarette brand globally. Formula One has been very good for Lucky Strike, hence British American Tobacco – the cigarette brand's owner – continually guaranteeing a bigger and bigger overdraft for the team. The exercise has led to dramatically improved brand recognition of Lucky Strike cigarettes. Whether the team's performance accelerated the movement of Honda road cars out of showrooms around the world is much more debatable. So far Honda has received poor value for an investment in engines that is now thought to be in the region of $400 million.

In hindsight, BAR's ultimate failure might have been predicted at a highly hyped, yet chaotically disorganised London launch in January. Amidst the humourless comedy sketches, absurd fanfares and smoke and mirrors, the team's new livery was revealed without the new car which had been damaged in testing.

When both Craig Pollock and his technical director Malcolm Oastler talked about the new car they were surprisingly prophetic. Pollock unwittingly offered a prophesy: "There's no question that we've gone with a more aggressive design, so maybe we're expecting a few extra chassis-related problems." Oastler said that while its first tests showed the car was slower than its predecessor, this was only because "we haven't found the right set-up yet to unleash the speed we know is trapped in there. We'll check the suspension stiffness and the various dynamic properties in the chassis, because there is something on the car that wasn't there last year and we've got to put it right."

It was never put right and, as a result, BAR paid the painful price. The team has taken a long time to learn the awful truth: Formula One success is achieved not through marketing but through engi-

BAR Honda motorhome

neering prowess.

BAR's sad showing took a particular toll on Craig Pollock, who aged visibly during the year. By season's end the team's youthful founder looked much older than BAR's 50 Formula One races, and his forecast for the future sounded rather forced and forlorn. "I will not accept anything less than a race-winning package next year," Pollock said. With protective shareholder covenants expiring at the beginning of 2003, his whole career in Formula One depends on it.

## AUSTRALIAN GRAND PRIX MELBOURNE
# The Honda battle begins

Australia was more disastrous than it appeared for British American Racing. It allowed Jordan to establish itself as the faster Honda team, in a battle BAR had to win to remain the team favoured by the Japanese engine manufacturer.

Round one definitely went to Jordan, as its Jordan chassis was clearly set up better than its BAR counterpart. This was obvious from the speed trap results – the BARs were significantly quicker but they lost much more time in the corners. As simple as that.

FRIDAY PRACTICE BAR brought three cars to Australia – the B003/001 for Jacques Villeneuve, 002 as spare and 003 for Olivier Panis. Villeneuve elected to wear the number 10 and Panis nine. This was a superstition of the Frenchman who had been driving with the number when he scored his sole Formula One victory, for Ligier Mugen-Honda at Monaco back in 1996.

In the race that really mattered for BAR, Jordan's Jarno Trulli was second quickest and his team-mate Heinz-Harald Frentzen was eighth, whereas Villeneuve and Panis were 10th and 12th fastest. Villeneuve's car lost time in the garage, having a baulky gearbox attended to. "It was a frustrating day," he said. "I couldn't do all the work I hoped to." It was Panis's first race weekend with BAR. "It was a very good day," he said. "The car felt consistently well balanced."

SATURDAY QUALIFYING Villeneuve and Panis qualified eighth and ninth respectively, although Frentzen and Trulli managed to put their Jordan Hondas fourth and seventh on the grid. Both Villeneuve and Panis did 11 qualifying laps and BAR engineers pored over data sheets looking for reasons why Jordan had gained the upper hand.

While Panis and Villeneuve clocked 303.9kph and 303.8kph respectively in the speed trap, Trulli clocked 308.3kph and Frentzen 305.2kph. An analysis of the balance of power on the qualifying best-sector times showed the Jordans had overall advantage on all three sectors, which also suggested a chassis advantage over BAR. Honda personnel at BAR went over to their Jordan

counterparts and embraced them whole-heartedly in a symbolic display of congratulations. Senior Honda personnel then started applying acupressure to the BAR team's delicate feelings.

Villeneuve's car bore scratches from a close encounter with Montoya and he said: "Maybe in champ cars he was used to being in front and never looked in his mirrors. But he will have to look in them here. I am definitely upset about it because he ruined a good lap. I will be talking to him about it." It was the start of a feud that would have dramatic consequences later in the season.

SUNDAY RACE In the warm-up Panis was fifth and Villeneuve 14th and both were happy with their cars in race trim, which included 80kgs of fuel for their one-stop strategy.

Villeneuve's race lasted precisely five laps, until he launched himself on the back of Ralf Schumacher's BMW Williams. The crash had tragic consequences when a wheel from the BAR flew through a small gap in the fence, killing a spectator marshal.

Panis made a circumspect start, completing the first lap in 10th place then making up two places by lap three before being promoted to sixth after the accident involving Villeneuve and Schumacher; this put Panis behind Trulli's Jordan. He held that position, which was second place in the Honda race, until lap 33 when Trulli's Honda started misfiring and he had to stop.

Then in fourth place, which he maintained until the chequered flag, Panis took time out on lap 40 to stop for fresh tyres and fuel, which his pit crew accomplished in an impressive 10.3secs. Less respectable was the 25-second penalty he received for passing Nick Heidfeld under a yellow flag that, when added to his race time, completely ruined what was left of BAR's already bad day in Australia. BAR's appeal was rejected and Panis ultimately found himself unplaced and pointless.

Above: Olivier Panis leads an Arrows and a Sauber. Right: Jacques Villeneuve's season got off to a tragic start when he hit Ralf Schumacher's BMW Williams early in the race, which resulted in the death of a marshal.

Above and right: Panis drove well but was deprived of fourth place for overtaking Heidfeld's Sauber under yellow flags.

Above and below: Jacques Villeneuve qualified seventh but completed just three laps in the race before he aquaplaned off in the downpour.

Bottom: That was one more than team-mate Olivier Panis, who retired a lap earlier when an oil fitting failed, spreading oil, which nearly put both Ferraris out of the race as well.

# A tortuous Asian weekend

After the shock of its sad foray to Australia, BAR needed a good weekend to boost morale. Especially needy was Jacques Villeneuve. On his arrival at Sepang, he answered questions about his physical and mental state of mind. He had spent some time in seclusion, part of it with David Coulthard, at a resort in northern Australia.

He said: "The holiday was planned anyway and after the crash it was important to have some quiet time. Physically there is no problem now, and mentally you just have to come to terms with this kind of thing. It was bad luck. It's a very sad thing, but it's like walking on the street and a pot of flowers falls on your head. It was a freak accident and, apart from not having a race, there is not much you can do to avoid it." He added: "The lap times aren't making it more dangerous. I think the cars and the tracks now are, in general, plenty safe enough. There are just a few tracks and a few corners that are maybe too dangerous. But overall, safety is quite high. And you can't stop freak accidents like we had in Australia. Whatever speed you do, it will always be dangerous."

BAR was still suffering from a lack of downforce and insiders whispered that there was a good one-and-a-half seconds to come out of the chassis once proper testing resumed in Europe.

FRIDAY PRACTICE Three cars were brought to Malaysia, including a completely new chassis, number 004, for Villeneuve, shipped over from the UK. It had been built from scratch around a new monocoque to replace the 001 destroyed in the accident and impounded by the investigating authorities. Olivier Panis had number 003, while 002 was the spare, on which Villeneuve had first call.

Panis was ninth in practice and Villeneuve 11th, but their eyes were on the performance of the Jordans, especially Jarno Trulli's fastest time of the session, rather than on the rest of the field.

SATURDAY QUALIFYING In morning practice the team experimented with changes to the front wing. Panis

lost some time because of a cracked oil cooler, while Villeneuve ran trouble-free.

Villeneuve qualified a good seventh with a 1m 36.397secs, 0.284secs quicker than Panis who would start 10th. The honesty of both drivers and the obvious personal rivalry that gave them extra inspiration was noted and appreciated by BAR's Honda engineers; "What is important for Honda," said the team's chief engine engineer Tadasu Takahashi, "is that the level of performance is very close between Jacques' and Olivier's cars." His satisfaction with a qualifying performance that put the BAR on a par with the pace set by the team's chief rivals, the Honda-powered Jordans, was left unstated. With Jarno Trulli fifth and Heinz-Harald Frentzen ninth on the grid in their Jordans, the fiercely competitive Japanese personnel on both teams were looking forward to a private race for Honda supremacy; the first round had gone to Jordan. Everybody looked forward to round two on Sunday.

SUNDAY RACE Half of BAR's challenge went up in smoke and flames on lap two when an oil fitting burst on Panis's car. As it hit the hot engine it ignited spectacularly, gushing oil sprayed onto the car's rear tyres, sending the helpless Frenchman gyrating wildly off the circuit and looking like a fireball before the car changed direction and the breeze put the fire out in the gravel trap.

A few moments later, a trial by water terminated his Canadian team-mate's Grand Prix. Villeneuve was running sixth on lap three when the cloudburst that so suddenly soaked the Sepang circuit immediately made it imperative for everyone to stop for wet-weather tyres – providing they made it to the pits. Four cars didn't, among them Villeneuve's BAR which aquaplaned off the track and buried itself in the gravel. Afterwards, Villeneuve said he couldn't see where he was going and when the car started to slide there was nothing he could do to stop it.

Compounding BAR's misery was the fourth place Frentzen got for Jordan. After two races, the Honda score was Jordan five, BAR nil. Even worse for Villeneuve was his non-finishing record that put his name at the bottom of the list of 22 drivers. Having completed only three laps in Malaysia and four before his crash in Australia, Villeneuve had stayed on the track for only seven of the 103 racing laps to date.

# Some points at last

The team achieved one goal by scoring its first points of the season. But the real story of the race was Olivier Panis, who overshadowed his number one, Jacques Villeneuve, throughout the weekend, a sign of things to come later in the season. Villeneuve never cracked the Frenchman, who was faster in practice, qualifying and the race, scoring three points for fourth. Panis decisively won his private battle with Villeneuve, as BAR did with Jordan in the Honda war. BAR personnel were increasingly optimistic for the rest of the season as they believed there was more room for improvement in their car than there was in the Jordan.

FRIDAY PRACTICE Olivier Panis piloted chassis 003 and Jacques Villeneuve 004, with 002 the spare, this time reserved for Panis. Both drivers pronounced themselves relatively pleased with respective practice times of 1m 17.432secs (12th) and 1m 17.455secs (13th). A small brake balance problem in both cars was soon rectified and the session was devoted to testing shock absorbers, springs and race set-ups. The Honda engines, using a modified control system, didn't skip a beat.

SATURDAY QUALIFYING While Panis managed ninth quickest in morning practice, Villeneuve was 16th – and very unhappy about it. It started with a gearbox problem and the unit was changed. Then a gearbox hydraulic problem left him stranded on the circuit. As a result he logged 16 laps against Panis's 29, leaving a disgruntled Canadian with much to do in qualifying. He had predicted he could be as high as sixth.

In qualifying, both drivers complained of poor grip. Panis took 11th on 1m 15.046secs and Villeneuve 12th on 1m 15.182secs. He eloquently described it as 'a shit weekend so far'. He chose soft tyres but couldn't find a set-up to suit them. He said: "Now we have to race with them and I'm not sure they are the best way to go. So we lost out in two ways and that is why I am so angry. We're only going to get points if people drop out in front of us. I am not a happy man." The clouds were out for the normally sunny Canadian.

SUNDAY RACE In warm-up a similar situation continued, with Panis a happy seventh and Villeneuve a troubled 12th.

After the start, Panis made rapid progress. His speed was helped by his decision to stop twice so, with a lighter car, he impressively overtook several cars to go from 11th to fourth before the first stop.

Villeneuve was a miserable seventh after an impressive charge from 12th to sixth by lap 12. Then he unexpectedly pitted to rectify what he thought was a puncture. Instead, the problem proved to be a broken differential that left him struggling with a loose handling car for the rest of the race. His weekend was also marred by a communications mix-up.

Having completed their two planned stops without hitch, Villeneuve and Panis arrived in the pits at the same time on lap 45 to change to intermediate tyres. Ironically, their Honda-powered rivals Jordan made a similar miscue. Villeneuve was delayed for 1m 17.408secs, Panis for 1m 47.355secs. Panis diplomatically blamed a garbled radio message for the pitlane shambles; the always forthright Villeneuve called it a big mess. He said: "Even with my handling problems I could have got some points. OK, the team got fourth thanks to Olivier, but he should have been on the podium." Panis certainly would have been, had it not been for the long pitstop.

At least BAR had the consolation of being the only team to have both cars still running at the finish, but there was still need for further improvement.

Left: Olivier Panis outdrove Jacques Villeneuve in Brazil despite getting the worst of a pitstop for intermediate tyres.

Top: Race engineer Jock Clear and Villeneuve were in the dumps all weekend, out-qualified again by Panis. Above: The race might have been brighter had both cars not arrived together for their switch to intermediate tyres. Both still made the finish.

Left: Craig Pollock and Malcolm Oastler saw both cars finish the race, but speed was lacking.

## SAN MARINO GRAND PRIX IMOLA
# Playing second fiddle

**B**AR Honda brought to Imola a brand new aerodynamic package – with new winglets on each side of the nose, a new floor, sidepods, diffuser and rear wing – and a revised exhaust system. There was renewed optimism among BAR personnel and, while the victory promised prior to the season was no longer mentioned, the team felt podiums were possible.

But reality dictated that BAR's new equipment, while a step forward, fell far short of podium potential. The possibility of points was realistic, but even those failed to materialise when the equipment proved incapable of the sustained competitive effort needed to chalk them up.

The real story in the team, which had temporarily played second fiddle to Jordan in the Honda race, was the internal driver battle. After being close, Olivier Panis had now out-qualified Jacques Villeneuve twice to make it two-two. Astonishing as it was, Panis was currently on top.

Although neither of them mentioned it, the head-to-head between the BAR drivers was taking on split-second proportions. Panis increased his psychological advantage by 0.204secs on Friday and was never topped after that. Team principal Craig Pollock said they were sparking nicely off each other, to the betterment of all at BAR. But the fact that both drivers were a second-and-a-half from the front put the limitations of the team's revised equipment into thought-provoking perspective.

**FRIDAY PRACTICE** Panis and Villeneuve were fairly pleased with their revised aerodynamic package's performance in both the wet and dry conditions that prevailed. The Frenchman's BAR 003/003 chassis was an encouraging fifth fastest overall, three places ahead of his Canadian team-mate's BAR 003/005. This was a completely new chassis for Villeneuve, whose previous 004 model had been put out to pasture as the test car.

**SATURDAY QUALIFYING** Their respective eighth and 13th positions after morning practice were a forecast of what was to come in qualifying for Panis and Villeneuve. Running with their new aero package in low-downforce trim and using the softer Bridgestone compound, the BARs posted the eighth and 11th fastest times, Panis again beating his teammate. Their comments were a reflection of where they found themselves, especially in relation to each other. "I am very happy with the best qualifying position I have achieved this year," said Panis after posting 1m 24.213secs. "The team did a great job. I feel very positive about the race ."

"I am very disappointed," Villeneuve said of his time of 1m 24.769secs (the 0.555secs difference to Panis doubtless looming large in his mind). "I didn't get a good lap in at the start, then there was traffic at the end of the session. It is very frustrating."

**SUNDAY RACE** Panis finished eighth after 61 laps of hard racing. He deserved much more, after the best start in his F1 career when he leapt from eighth to fifth in the first half of the opening lap. Niggling problems, including too much oversteer and a gearbox electronic malfunction, saw him fall back and threatened to end his race. The gearbox problem was partly solved by replacing the steering wheel during his first pitstop. Both of his pitstops were accomplished with speedy efficiency, on lap 27 in 27.719secs and on lap 48 in 25.958secs.

"I am very disappointed for the team," said the ever-gracious Panis, whose three points in Brazil were all BAR had to show for the first quarter of the season. "I am sure that we will soon be rewarded with a good result." Villeneuve's race ended at the halfway mark when the dense cloud of smoke emitted from his revised exhaust system announced the spectacular demise of his Honda engine on lap 31. He had been as high as fifth (before pitting for 25.550secs on lap 29) and was convinced he could have finished there, or higher. "It was a huge disappointment that I could not finish," said a disgruntled Villeneuve. "It was looking as if I was finally going to get some points this year. It has been a very frustrating season."

Above: Olivier Panis, with his race engineer David Lloyd, again set the pace for BAR Honda, but his race was ruined by gearbox troubles. Left: Jacques Villeneuve, shaded by Jules Kulpinski, qualified 11th behind Panis, and was again frustrated in the race and forced to retire with a rare Honda failure.

LUCKY STRIKE B.A.R Honda

## SPANISH GRAND PRIX BARCELONA
# A real lucky strike

Above : A dogged third place for BAR and Villeneuve after a long battle with Trulli's Jordan. Right: Villeneuve visited the podium again after a long dry spell of 42 races.

Above: Olivier Panis had a disappointing race after a a slow pitstop with electrical problems. Right: Villeneuve's podium gave Craig Pollock and Malcolm Oastler reason to smile.

I f Craig Pollock and Adrian Reynard had thought it would take two-and-a-half years and 38 races for their new team to achieve one third place, they would not have taken up the cudgels. In those terms, they had been complete and utter failures. So the first podium in BAR's short history was a major milestone. It was also a timely boost in the power struggle with Jordan. The fickle affections of Honda's hierarchy now rested firmly with the team that had provided its first modern podium finish.

Jacques Villeneuve also re-established himself as team leader. It was hard to believe that it was his first podium for 42 races. The comeback was the immediate result of some harsh words spoken – sometimes shouted – behind closed doors between Villeneuve and his bothered boss, Craig Pollock. Pollock told Villeneuve he had to start earning his keep. Villeneuve retaliated by telling his employers to smarten up, saying that his reputation was on the line and if BAR gave him the car, he would show them what he could do.

FRIDAY PRACTICE Olivier Panis had a new chassis, 006, while Jacques Villeneuve had his usual 005 and first call on the spare 003, formerly raced by Panis. Teething troubles with traction and launch control befell both drivers. Panis at first switched off his traction control, then reactivated it to set the fourth fastest time.

Villeneuve, refusing launch control in preference to his own reflexes, quickly discovered the shortcomings of his traction control when an engine spectacularly blew itself to bits at the exit of the pitlane. BAR was careful not to apportion blame and Honda said the fiery blow-up might have something to do with the new systems. Honda discussed the difficulties with traction control and explained: "In extreme cases it is not unknown for engines, exhausts and drive trains to crack," which sounded suspiciously like what happened to Villeneuve's car.

After an engine and gearbox change Villeneuve set ninth fastest although he was obviously having difficulty containing what was a quite high dudgeon.

SATURDAY QUALIFYING In morning practice Panis was seventh fastest, while Villeneuve, delayed by an electrical problem, was 10th and still voicing his displeasure regarding the continuing unreliability of his equipment.

In qualifying Panis went backwards, blaming heavy traffic for restricting his time to 1m 19.479secs – slower than he had been in the morning and leaving him 11th. Although Villeneuve's 1m 19.122secs was good enough for seventh, it was not fast enough to prevent him from questioning the competence of his team, although restricting his comments to a terse summation of the facts. On his first run Villeneuve spun off because, he explained: "The rear brakes were not attached. And on the second run we discovered we were 10kg overweight." It was later discovered the FIA weigh scales were at fault – but forgetting to hook up the rear brakes was embarrassing. Craig Pollock was moved to call his own mechanics' toiling as 'the work of amateurs'.

SUNDAY RACE Villeneuve blamed himself for being asleep at the switch at the start and braking too early going into Turn 1, where he was overtaken by Juan Pablo Montoya's BMW Williams. Following this 'wake-up call' he pushed as hard as his car's lack of grip allowed and stayed behind Montoya for the rest of the afternoon. "We couldn't have gone any quicker and we were a bit lucky that a few cars dropped out," Villeneuve admitted. He paid special tribute to BAR's slick work on his first pitstop, which was accomplished half-a-second quicker than it took Jordan to turn around Jarno Trulli. This enabled Villeneuve to pass the Jordan and win the Honda battle.

A tardy first stop (an electrical glitch stalled his car) effectively prevented Panis, who finished the race in seventh position, from making a further contribution to the BAR cause.

Villeneuve said: "For sure we'll party tonight – big time." For him, however, it was very different from 1996 and 1997.

240

## AUSTRIAN GRAND PRIX A1 RING
# Confidence misplaced

Following Jacques Villeneuve's first-ever podium for BAR in Spain, the team was confident of building on that success. With Villeneuve seemingly back on form and the quick and consistent Olivier Panis proving capable of delivering whatever BAR had to offer, the team's main goal was to beat Jordan in the Honda engine battle.

There was, however, a cloud on Villeneuve's horizon, in the form of persistent back pain that was a legacy of his violent accident in Australia. Villeneuve said the problem was less pronounced in the cockpit, where adrenaline kicked in as a painkiller, and that it was not interfering with his driving. As it turned out he had a miserable weekend, driving poorly for whatever reason, and it was Panis who provided the points, albeit only two. It was some consolation for BAR that Jordan had a pointless weekend.

FRIDAY PRACTICE While the BAR chassis were unchanged from Spain (030/05 for Villeneuve, who also had the spare, 030/03; and 030/06 for Panis), Honda had modified the exhaust systems to produce more power. Making the most of this and, for once, a mechanically problem-free opening practice, Panis and Villeneuve clocked the ninth and 10th quickest times. Since neither was trying particularly hard (although Panis push hard enough to have a quick spin) and both were carrying heavy fuel loads, they were optimistic there was much more to come.

SATURDAY QUALIFYING Steady progress in the morning, when Villeneuve and Panis were 10th and 11th, left BAR feeling even more optimistic about moving forward in qualifying. But the afternoon session proved a shambles that left the team – and especially Villeneuve – with a lot of work to do in the race.

Panis, having initially been all over the place thanks to a poor tyre choice, never really got to grips with his car. Pushing hard on his last run he managed a lap of 1m 10.435secs that put him 10th on the grid. Villeneuve, having gone the wrong way with set-up changes and without time to sort things out, tried to overcome the problem by juggling weight distribution. However, he only managed a 12th best time of 1m 11.058secs. But Villeneuve's biggest problem, as he readily admitted, was himself: frustrated by his ill-handling car, he had over-driven it: "I did not drive very well at all. I tried too hard and made too many mistakes."

SUNDAY RACE Villeneuve's race day began with more problems in the warm-up, although this time it was 'Honda-related', as the team put it; he stopped out on the circuit in a cloud of smoke. He then commandeered BAR 030/03 for the race, in which he was out-driven by his team-mate.

Panis started the race well, impressively overtaking Irvine's Jaguar on lap seven. With the help of a retirement or two, by lap 16 he was up to the fifth place he held until the finish, by driving hard and not making any mistakes.

Meanwhile, Villeneuve floundered around out of the points all afternoon. After what he called a reasonable start he was overtaken by Irvine on lap nine, then spun a lap later while trying to defend his 11th place from Pedro de la Rosa in the other Jaguar. Although his BAR was not that fast on the track – he complained of 'a huge amount of push' – Villeneuve was nabbed for speeding in the pitlane on lap 47. Four laps later he pitted again to serve his penalty, although the delay did not cost him the eighth place that was all he had to show for another frustrating race.

LUCKY STRIKE B.A.R Honda

Left: Olivier Panis and engineer David Lloyd worked hard to salvage fifth place for BAR. Bottom: Jacques Villeneuve's over-exuberance cost him a possible points finish when he spun while trying to displace Eddie Irvine's Jaguar at the first corner.

Right: Again Olivier Panis had the upper hand over team-mate Jacques Villeneuve in both qualifying and the race.

## MONACO GRAND PRIX MONTE CARLO

# Three big points

It was only fourth place, but Jacques Villeneuve's hard-earned points were crucial both for his and BAR's credibility. Villeneuve single-handedly brought BAR to within a point of Jordan's similarly Honda-powered cars.

Olivier Panis is a Monaco star, having won in the principality in 1996. But Villeneuve's Monaco record was miserable, his best a fifth in 1998. In the event this race showed a change of fortunes, with Villeneuve out-performing Panis and driving his best race of the season so far.

Villeneuve's contribution came as a relief to BAR as paddock gossip wrongly murmured that Honda would shortly decide to supply its engine to only one team in 2002.

**THURSDAY PRACTICE** Other than high-downforce trim necessary for Monaco there was nothing new in the technical department from either BAR or Honda. Villeneuve's 030/03 race chassis was backed up by his spare, 030/05, while Panis had 030/06 to race and 030/04 for back-up in case disaster struck, although the rules stopped him from using it in practice following the incident that left 030/06 stranded after only 26 practice laps.

Early in the afternoon Panis had out-braked himself going into Ste Devote, where a misguided marshal manhandled his otherwise undamaged car. This breached the rules and the loss of track time left Panis a frustrated 16th fastest and having to play catch-up for the rest of the weekend. Thus Villeneuve got a head start on his team-mate, recovering from a harmless spin at Mirabeau in the morning to log 43 laps.

**SATURDAY QUALIFYING** Villeneuve's advantage over Panis was eroded in morning practice when his time was only a 10th better than his team-mate's, although Villeneuve claimed he was mostly running on full tanks and there was more to come in qualifying. Indeed there was, the Canadian securing ninth on the grid and Panis 12th – a reasonable comeback from his setback on Thursday and, he pointed out, in a time very

close to his team-mate's. Villeneuve was delighted with this (no doubt partly because his qualifying contest with Panis now stood at four-three), saying the car felt particularly strong and precise and he had extracted all its potential. Therefore, Villeneuve reasoned, having started 17th here last year and finished seventh among the mere nine survivors, he was optimistic that a mistake-free yet aggressive run in a reliable BAR Honda could result in his second points-scoring finish of the season.

**SUNDAY RACE** Their cars laden with fuel (100 litres), the warm-up times of Panis (who tried his spare while minor gear-change problems were fixed on his race car) and Villeneuve indicated the team's strategy to stop as late as possible in the race. Panis, however, had to pit after only 12 laps, hit by a steering problem that preliminary investigation showed to be 'somewhere between the steering wheel and the front wheels'. After one more slow, exploratory lap he trundled back to the pits and parked.

Villeneuve pressed on and, driving to his plan of controlled aggression augmented by the failure of cars in front, by mid-race he was in fifth frustratingly behind Irvine's suddenly respectable Jaguar. Following his pitstop and having been promoted to fourth by the retirement of Ralf Schumacher from third, Villeneuve decided to pull out all the stops and pressure Irvine for a place on the podium – a chase that enlivened the final stages of an otherwise boring and uneventful race. Although he reduced the Jaguar's 10-second advantage (on lap 75 of 78, Villeneuve set the fourth fastest lap), Villeneuve fell 1.756secs short of his goal and remained fourth at the finish.

It was Villeneuve's best-ever Monaco result – even more satisfying, he said, than the podium he inherited a month previously in Spain. He said: "We had to work for this, and to finish fourth in a car that is a bit slower than the others is great. The car was good and precise and I could push with it all weekend. It's been fun."

Above left: A Monaco huddle for Jacques Villeneuve and BAR engineers. Above and right: BAR reliability allowed Villeneuve to again score points with a fourth place, despite being slower than arch-rival Jordan in qualifying and in the race. Bottom: Jacques Villeneuve laps Jos Verstappen.

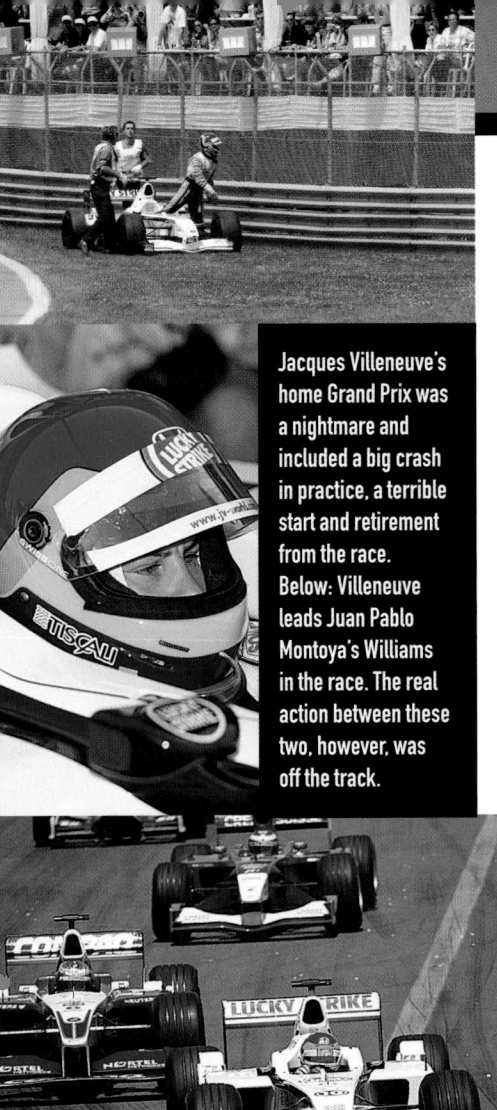

Jacques Villeneuve's home Grand Prix was a nightmare and included a big crash in practice, a terrible start and retirement from the race. Below: Villeneuve leads Juan Pablo Montoya's Williams in the race. The real action between these two, however, was off the track.

Left and above: Panis qualified an excellent sixth and was fastest in the warm-up, but his race efforts were wasted as BAR could not achieve brake-cooling efficiency. He was running in a strong fifth when deteriorating brakes forced him to pit and ultimately retire.

## CANADIAN GRAND PRIX MONTREAL
# Trouble on and off the track

Having scored points in three consecutive races, the BAR Honda team was reasonably confident about reliability. Momentum, however, would depend on its drivers avoiding the troubled Canadian races both had had in the past. Jacques Villeneuve had not fared well at the track since finishing second in his first appearance in 1996 with Williams. Assorted mechanical woes and a few fights with BMW Williams driver Juan Pablo Montoya meant that his weekend in Canada was, in his own words, the worst of his entire career.

Canada has not been very kind to Olivier Panis, either. The Frenchman crashed here in 1997 in a Prost, badly breaking both his legs. In 2001 Panis fought well but was also beset by car failure, making the sum total of BAR's effort in Canada two DNFs.

FRIDAY PRACTICE The local hero's bad luck began on lap 13 of opening practice, when Villeneuve's BAR 030/04 crashed into a barrier, rendering it a write-off. Since the use of spare cars is not allowed on Friday, Villeneuve was unable to commandeer the BAR 030/06, which was set up for him and which he would have to use for the rest of the weekend. As BAR set about organising a new spare tub to be flown in from Brackley overnight, Villeneuve blamed Montoya.

He said: "I am upset with him [Montoya] because it must be the fifth or sixth time this season he's been blocking me. Normally you try to get out of the way if you know you're blocking somebody, but it seems that every time he sees someone in his mirror he slows down and deliberately stays on the line. I don't know what kind of game he's trying to play."

Montoya replied: "He got pissed off and thought I should move earlier. I let him by, got to the next chicane and he stood on the brakes at a place where you're accelerating hard, and I hit him. He brake tested me and paid for it." Thus Panis was left to do all BAR's work, completing 47 laps and gathering valuable information for the race.

SATURDAY QUALIFYING In practice, electrical and hydraulic problems restricted Villeneuve to 20 laps. Panis later enjoyed his best qualifying session of the season with a time only a 10th slower than pole, while Villeneuve was back in ninth place.

Villeneuve's grid position was only newsworthy because it would position him on the grid next to new arch-enemy, Montoya.

The conflict between the Colombian and the Canadian had erupted in the drivers' meeting, Montoya telling Villeneuve he would 'put him into the wall' if he ever brake-tested him again. Villeneuve said that next time he would put Montoya 'into the trees'. Montoya shot back: "You've already killed somebody this year."

At this point, irate at the reference to his accident in Australia in which a marshal died, Villeneuve grabbed Montoya by the throat. The scuffle was short-lived but race director Charlie Whiting warned both combatants that the slightest hint of road-rage on the track would result in race bans – a warning endorsed by Bernie Ecclestone.

Craig Pollock followed up with a few well aimed threats at Montoya and Sir Frank Williams took the side of his former driver Villeneuve, and warned Montoya to watch his mouth. This Montoya did, concluding: "I have nothing to say." Villeneuve confined comment to: "He doesn't exist."

But Montoya did exist, alongside Villeneuve on the grid. The prospects for a resumption of road-rage loomed large.

SUNDAY RACE Panis topped the timesheets in warm-up, although his performance owed much to the 40 litres of fuel he carried. Similarly, Villeneuve's 11th fastest time was a reflection of his 90 litre fuel load.

But it was launch control failure, not a heavy fuel load, that caused Villeneuve to lose six places at the start. Montoya's subsequent retirement was of little consolation when Villeneuve himself retired on lap 34.

"The car was not running too badly after the anti-stall glitch," Villeneuve said, "but then the brakes started to go and finally a driveshaft failed. It was a very hard weekend. Every day something went wrong. I think – I hope – we used up all our bad luck for the year."

Luck also ran out for Panis, whose strong run in fifth belied steadily deteriorating brakes. His pitstop was followed by a couple of exploratory laps before he trundled brakeless back into the garage on lap 38.

LUCKY STRIKE B.A.R Honda

# Urgent quest for power

Jacques Villeneuve drove hard and talked tough. As usual Olivier Panis also drove well – while he lasted – and was more politically correct than his outspoken team-mate. For starters, Villeneuve said Honda's engines weren't up to the power standards set by BMW, Mercedes and Ferrari. He also claimed that the 2001 Hondas sometimes appeared inferior even to the 2000 Ferrari powerplants used by Sauber and Prost. Villeneuve also suggested that, instead of achieving only minor boosts to its current powerplants, Honda had decided to concentrate on next year's engines.

Prior to Villeneuve's revelations, Katzutoshi Nishizawa, technical director of Honda Racing Development, announced that Honda would continue supplying both BAR and Jordan in 2002: it never planned to drop either team, he said, and didn't understand how such a rumour had started.

Post-race, Villeneuve spoke of BAR's second handicap at the Nürburgring: having to use tyres developed for Bridgestone's top teams. He said: "Either our tyres weren't good enough or the others were too good. If the other ones were better, that means ours can be better and Bridgestone has to work hard. At the start and coming out of slow speed corners we couldn't keep up."

FRIDAY PRACTICE The team was buoyed by a session at Silverstone where Takuma Sato and Patrick Lemarie joined Panis and Villeneuve for three trouble-free days, testing developments including revised aerodynamics featuring a new nose, bargeboards and diffuser, plus a front suspension designed by the Honda engineers at team HQ. A Honda-designed rear suspension unit would be ready for testing soon.

The revised items, on Villeneuve's 003/07 and spare 003/04 and Panis's 003/06, were said to be worthwhile. Both Panis, 10th quickest, and Villeneuve, 12th, went off course searching for the right set-up. Their respective times, 1m 18.410secs and 1m 19.640secs, were, according to the Canadian, a by-product of engines not keeping pace with chassis developments.

SATURDAY QUALIFYING In the morning Panis was ninth and Villeneuve 12th after spinning twice, latterly to a halt. In qualifying Villeneuve improved only enough to claim 11th in 1m 16.439secs; Panis fell back to 13th with a lap of 1m 16.872secs.

Villeneuve, blaming traffic for ruining his best lap, said the car felt well balanced but was simply too slow. Panis was mystified as to why he couldn't match practice times set on full tanks. Technical director Malcolm Oastler also wondered where the time went. He said: "We believed we had much more potential and now we have to find out what we're missing on new tyres. The chassis balance isn't that bad but we're lacking grip. We're going to have to pull something out of the bag tomorrow for sure."

SUNDAY RACE Panis was 12th and Villeneuve 17th in a warm-up session that revealed their race prospects were grim. Team boss Craig Pollock hit the nail on the head: "It looks as though there is not much hope for us today. Scoring points will be a miracle."

No miracle materialised for Panis, whose car suffered a gearbox electrical glitch, causing him to spin out on lap 23.

Villeneuve's car ran like a top – albeit a slow one – and he finished one lap down in ninth. He said the best the team could have expected was to finish seventh behind Ferrari, Williams and McLaren. This didn't happen, in Villeneuve's view, because of the BAR's inferior tyres. He commented: "The car was quite driveable, but the tyres couldn't keep up with the opposition. The team worked well, the one-stop strategy was good and I pushed as hard as possible. But I just couldn't have gone any faster."

Right: A spin on Saturday robbed Villeneuve of track time. Below: The Canadian blamed inferior tyres and lack of power for his ninth place finish.

Right: A gearbox glitch caused Panis to spin out on lap 23. Below: Craig Pollock: was fed up.

**FRENCH GRAND PRIX** MAGNY-COURS

# Team leader speaks out

At the end of a troubled weekend, Jacques Villeneuve said the time was nigh to 'kick ass' in the team and even his normally placid team-mate, Olivier Panis, was heard muttering the word 'unprofessional'. Craig Pollock might have had to find some persuasive words for his disaffected Canadian driver.

Having assured everyone he was staying put in 2002, Villeneuve let it be known over the weekend that he was looking into other options, just in case. Paddock gossip had it that he had been in contact with McLaren (in case Mika Häkkinen retired) and Jaguar and Benetton (were they to become more competitive). Such rumours were normal at this time of year, Villeneuve maintained, and he would surely stay at BAR unless something happened to make him look hard. Many felt *that* something might have happened in France.

**FRIDAY PRACTICE** The team brought four cars: 003/07 (and the spare 003/04) for Villeneuve, along with 003/06 for Panis. These were unchanged from the Nürburgring, where the new aero package had been introduced to good effect. The fourth car, the spare 003/05 for Panis in his home race, featured rear suspension developed by the Honda chassis engineers who worked in tandem with the BAR designers to match the new front suspension that had performed well on its debut at the European Grand Prix.

Panis buried his BAR in the gravel trap after only 20 laps of practice because of a miscue triggered by locking rear brakes. He would have to rely on the set-up work of his Canadian team-mate, who logged 39 trouble-free, fast and confidence-inspiring laps.

Villeneuve admitted his impressive time – third quickest of the day – was the product of running with a qualifying set-up and low fuel, but he explained that was the point of the exercise. The concept was put into play for the first time this season to get a head start on qualifying, in which the team had had a persistent lack of pace. Villeneuve said the car was working especially well on Bridgestone's new tyre compounds and that much had been learned, although he admitted that tomorrow's times were likely to provide a reality check.

**SATURDAY QUALIFYING** Villeneuve and Panis finished practice buried back in 12th and 13th places and the team became worried that Friday's preparations would not suffice to haul the cars further up the qualifying grid. Their fears were realised as the timesheets revealed the harsh truth at the end of qualifying: Villeneuve placed 10th with 1m 14.096secs; Panis 11th on 1m 14.181secs.

While the team put on a brave PR face, issuing a press release full of hopeful proclamations, Villeneuve told it like it was – or at least the way he saw it. He remarked: "We are just not quick enough. It is disappointing. If we had the improvements the other teams have had, we'd be four positions higher on the grid and that would make a big difference for the result of the race."

**SUNDAY RACE** The drivers played musical chairs with their race and spare cars in the warm-up, before each settling on their race cars. Panis finished warm-up in seventh, while Villeneuve was 14th fastest yet still voiced confidence about climbing into the points in the race.

Unfortunately for Villeneuve, his race was 67 laps shorter than the 72-lap Grand Prix. From the way he angrily leapt out of his stranded BAR (it had stalled with an electrical problem) and stomped off purposefully towards the paddock, he looked like he was indeed searching for another team. Now his car had become unreliable as well as sluggish, and it appeared that enough was enough.

While Villeneuve was quickly put out of his misery, Panis had to endure his BAR Honda for the full race distance, puttering around ineffectually with a hopelessly gripless car that was flattered by the ninth place finish the plucky Frenchman wrung from it.

"I had a very difficult race today," Panis understated. "I did the best job I could and so did the team. Everyone worked very hard and both pitstops (lap 23 for 24.669secs and lap 45 for 26.294secs) were very good. I am sorry to disappoint my home crowd."

LUCKY STRIKE B.A.R Honda

**Above and left:** Olivier Panis lost a lot of practice time after a mistake, but he still qualified just behind his team-mate in 11th. His BAR kept going in the race, but lack of grip meant the Frenchman could only take a demoralising ninth in his home Grand Prix.

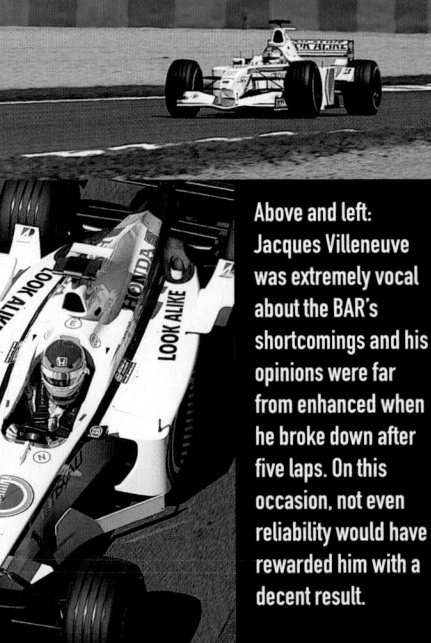

**Above and left:** Jacques Villeneuve was extremely vocal about the BAR's shortcomings and his opinions were far from enhanced when he broke down after five laps. On this occasion, not even reliability would have rewarded him with a decent result.

# Team principal faces his critics

At the start of the season Craig Pollock put his detractors behind him and was left to get on with the job. Adrian Reynard was vanquished. Mid-season the charm was still there but the performance was not, and Pollock was beginning to become irrational for a man whose talent was keeping his head while those all around were losing theirs. For the first time he started to lose staunch supporters.

The team had a weekend that was far from perfection, a sad state of affairs that hit home for the factory personnel, all 400 of whom were there to watch the team in action. It was made all the worse by the fact BAR had put all its resources into preparing for its home race, running two test teams at Mugello and Monza, then practising pit-stops and race starts at Santa Pod. The preparations had been positive according to technical director Malcolm Oastler, who said: "From now on all the circuits should suit the car for the rest of the season. There are no excuses for being slow anywhere."

Qualifying was a comedy of errors and the race a disaster, when Olivier Panis was taken out by team-mate Jacques Villeneuve at the first corner. Villeneuve managed to nurse his crippled car home to salvage eighth, then apologised for the incident.

Ways had to be found to turn the tide: "We're going backwards," said Villeneuve.

FRIDAY PRACTICE Panis had chassis 003/06 and Villeneuve had 003/07 plus first call on 003/04. In the first practice both drivers struggled with understeer. Although the problem was eventually dialled out, both BAR drivers remained in the midfield, Villeneuve ending the day 11th and Panis 12th. Villeneuve also had what he termed 'a little problem', damaging the front wing endplates in a spin at Woodcote. The reason he gave for the problem – 'a front suspension failure' – would prove to be an ill omen.

SATURDAY QUALIFYING Panis had 20 practice laps that left him ninth fastest, but 12 qualifying laps only produced a best time of 1m 22.316secs that put him 11th. He said the car felt OK but wasn't fast enough.

His disgruntled team-mate said much more. In the day's first practice session, Villeneuve had sat in the garage while a faulty gearbox was repaired. In the second session he spun off, having logged only six laps and clocked the 16th best time – meagre preparation.

He said: "We had engine problems in the race car, so I jumped in the spare, which was too slow. Then the race car was repaired so I jumped back into that, but it was very slow, so I got back in the spare. Because we didn't do any set-up work, we had terminal understeer. I did two runs in both cars and jumping between the two cost us time." So why, after qualifying 12th, was Jumping Jacques still smiling? He explained: "I'm smiling so I won't blow up."

SUNDAY RACE Overnight, in a desperate search for race pace, the team decided to start Sunday with the set-up used in the French Grand Prix. Panis found this worked quite well, and Villeneuve said the combination of the Magny-Cours set-up and heavier fuel load occasioned by the team's one-stop strategy had given a car capable of generating points.

In the event, Villeneuve staggered around the circuit in an aerodynamic wreck, suffering from a deranged front wing, mangled sidepod and rumpled floor, the consequence of a collision with his team-mate moments after the start. After the race he said: "When we got to the first corner I hit the brakes hard, which locked the front wheels, and I wasn't able to turn. Olivier was on my outside and when he turned I couldn't avoid him, so we banged wheels, which put him off and cost him his race. Things like that happen at the start, but it's not good for the team or Olivier, so I am very sorry." Panis replied: "What can I say? It was a real pity."

Above: BAR had a poor race at Silverstone. It started when Villeneuve bumped his team-mate into the gravel and ended with eighth place.

Above: Craig Pollock had to watch disaster unfold for BAR. Olivier Panis had a very short British Grand Prix, courtesy of Jacques Villeneuve. Left: Villeneuve had little to be pleased about and apologised to Panis. Right: Panis had little better fortune in qualifying.

# Back to prominence

BAR Honda came to Germany with low expectations and left sky-high, with Jacques Villeneuve's third place hauling the beleaguered team back into prominence.

The weekend began with the unexpected announcement that Olivier Panis and Villeneuve would continue with BAR in 2002. The Panis re-signing was confirmation of a happy marriage of convenience: BAR rescued his race career and the veteran Frenchman had performed yeoman duty in extracting the most from difficult cars and pushing his famous team-mate. But the news that Villeneuve would be continuing with BAR for a fourth term was something of a U-turn, given his scathing condemnation of the team for not giving him a competitive car and putting all its resources into developing next year's equipment. His rumoured $20 million-plus salary obviously helped his decision.

Villeneuve's public criticism had embarrassed BAR Honda, spurring it to produce a heavily revised chassis and an upgraded engine for the last four races.

**FRIDAY PRACTICE** Nothing new on the cars in practice – chassis 07 and the spare 04 for Villeneuve, 06 for Panis. They performed even worse than the team's usual Friday standard, leaving Panis 14th with a 1m 43.487secs and Villeneuve 17th on 1m 43.815 secs.

The Monza test proved that the Honda engines wouldn't be competitive on the Hockenheimring's high-speed straights, and that the fundamentally flawed chassis would not provide enough grip in the stadium.

**SATURDAY QUALIFYING** In the morning Panis and Villeneuve struggled with gripless chassis and horsepower deficiencies, leaving them glum about their chances. But in Villeneuve's case at least, the car exceeded his lowly expectations.

His time of 1m 40.437secs secured him 12th place. It was his fourth such starting spot this season – the product of much chassis-tweaking. Villeneuve admitted getting any worthwhile result would be largely a matter of luck.

Panis was more pleased than a 13th place might suggest – even a $3,000 fine for travelling at 42mph in the pitlane didn't trouble him. He squeezed everything possible out of the car. "This is the limit of our potential with the technical package we have at the moment," he said.

**SUNDAY RACE** Villeneuve and Panis could scarcely believe the transformation in their cars during morning warm-up. Even the engineers weren't exactly sure how they stumbled on a set-up that found much of the grip that was missing in the chicanes.

The team decided to cover both sides of the strategy spectrum, putting Panis on a two-stopper and filling Villeneuve's car with enough fuel to make a single stop.

Soon after the start BAR's strategy began to pay dividends, particularly for Villeneuve, who employed the slipstreaming techniques he learned in champ car racing.

Allowing Panis past, Villeneuve tucked in behind his team-mate and was towed down the straights to great effect, improving his own rate of progress while also conserving fuel. Panis inadvertently also performed battering ram duty on Villeneuve's behalf, engaging other cars in combat, stressing their components and their drivers, notably Jarno Trulli, who threw his Jordan momentarily off course, enabling both BARs to speed by.

It soon became clear Villeneuve's one-stopper was the way to go and poor Panis (who stopped on lap 16 for 31.247secs and lap 31 for 31.030secs) was unfortunately unable to collect the reward he deserved. He fought hard but finished seventh.

Villeneuve also came close to having fuel-related problems. His pitstop on lap 24 stretched on for a worryingly long 36.138secs – 14.8secs of which his car was stationary for because the refuelling rig warning light system wasn't working and the nozzleman overcompensated. He finished with very little fuel, but was remarkably on the podium for only the second time for the team.

LUCKY STRIKE B.A.R Honda

247

# Euphoria to despair

From the euphoria of Villeneuve's surprise podium in Germany the team rode into Hungary on a high, only to be plunged into despair by another reversal of fortune in what had been a roller-coaster ride of a season.

Off the pace in qualifying and, more worryingly, similarly disadvantaged in race trim, the team was also unable to benefit from the unreliability of others and instead suffered a retirement of its own. Olivier Panis, who had scored points here on three occasions in the past with Ligier, failed to finish in his BAR. And Villeneuve, who won here in 1996 and 1997, came home in a hopeless ninth place.

The only consolation for BAR was that Jordan had an even worse time of it in the Honda-powered division. But the fact that tiny little Sauber had a better race than either Honda team hammered home the reality of just how much work BAR faced to salvage some semblance of respectability from what remained of the season.

FRIDAY PRACTICE For the Hungaroring the team fielded a new aerodynamic package that had been developed at Valencia prior to the German Grand Prix. Featuring a new floor, rear diffuser and front wing, it worked well for Panis, who extracted a ninth fastest time from his 003/06 chassis and finished the day on 1m 17.970secs. Villeneuve's 003/07 race car proved worthy of only the 16th best time for 1m 19.238secs – not because the new modifications did not work but because, as Villeneuve said: "We got lost on the set-up and went the wrong way." Indeed, having a car that veered between oversteer and understeer about four times in each of the circuit's 14 corners was clearly the wrong way to go around the Hungaroring. Not for the first time during the season, the independently-minded Jacques Villeneuve would be forced to turn to his team-mate's set-up the following day.

SATURDAY QUALIFYING Panis was 12th and Villeneuve 14th in early practice, with the latter making several set-up changes that progressively improved the handling through the session. The fine-tuning continued in qualifying, with Villeneuve's best lap of 1m 16.212secs putting him 10th while Panis placed 11th with a 1m 16.382secs. Both drivers pronounced themselves pleased and felt there was more to come on Sunday.

SUNDAY RACE In the warm-up Panis sped smoothly to the eighth best time, while Villeneuve's car reluctantly managed only the 13th fastest time. A hurried inspection failed to reveal the source of the problem, so Villeneuve decided to race with the spare. Since 003/07 was not fitted with the new aero-dynamic package, the Canadian was rendered downforceless and doomed to an ignominious back-marking role.

In the race, with his BAR lurching and yawing, Villeneuve did well to steer clear of the frontrunners. He hung on grimly to finish ninth, one place higher than he started, but two laps down on the leaders.

Panis fared even worse, failing to finish with a car that was in any case very hard to drive and never going to bag points unless it held together while others didn't. After his second stop, on lap 53 while running ninth, Panis began to fall back with a worsening misfire that forced him to pit again on lap 57. Hasty repairs were attempted to fix what was identified as an engine-related electrical malfunction. Having ventured out again, he returned a lap later, his car sputtering and smoking. The BAR and Honda engineers got the car mobile once again: on lap 64 Panis made one more exploratory tour of the Hungaroring, before trundling terminally into the BAR garage.

Far left: Jacques Villeneuve and Jock Clear before the start of the race. They failed to get the BAR working well enough to be competitive. Right: Villeneuve prepares for a long, unrewarding afternoon that saw him start 10th and finish ninth.

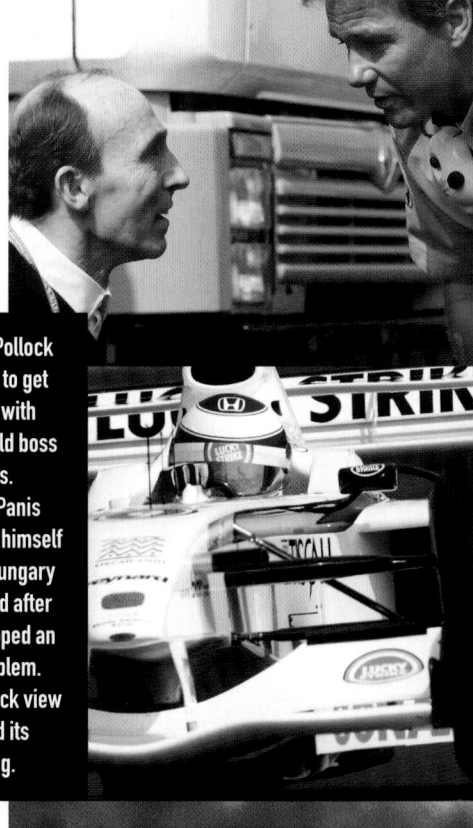

Above: Craig Pollock has a lot to do to get BAR on terms with Villeneuve's old boss Frank Williams. Right: Olivier Panis again applied himself well but left Hungary with no reward after his car developed an electrical problem. Below: The back view of the BAR and its extra rear wing.

## BELGIAN GRAND PRIX SPA-FRANCORCHAMPS
# Going nowhere slowly

**B**AR Honda was in a hurry to get its rapidly deteriorating season over with as quickly as possible after a weekend beset by equipment deficiencies. Jacques Villeneuve was left floundering helplessly around in eighth at the finish, three places better than his equally disadvantaged team-mate Olivier Panis. "We weren't quick enough and the car was difficult to drive," Villeneuve complained. "I fought as best I could but to get anywhere here you need to have enough power to do the job and a car that handles well. Our engine is not great and the chassis is not good, so we are going nowhere fast." Both the Honda teams had now compiled 16 points, four points behind Sauber, which had faltered.

**Above and left: Jacques Villeneuve put in plenty of effort to lift BAR's spirits but to no avail. World championship success is now a distant memory for the French-Canadian, and there was little sign of real competitiveness. His energetic race produced only eighth, two places behind Honda rival Jordan.**

**FRIDAY PRACTICE** After testing at both Mugello and Vairano, the team came to Belgium with the usual three cars – chassis 003/04 and the T-car 003/05 for Villeneuve, and 003/06 for Panis.

Panis was 11th in practice, despite completing only one lap in the dry first session before a gearbox problem began causing his car to jump out of sixth gear. The problem was rectified and in the second session Panis found that the car performed rather well, even in the wet conditions. Having run mostly in the wet, Villeneuve was 15th when frustrated by a stupid mistake: he did only three laps in the first session before spinning his car into a gravel trap.

Villeneuve was particularly irked at being unable to conduct his personal bravery test: taking Eau Rouge flat out. The daredevil Canadian driver was adamant Eau Rouge must be conquered again. "If we get enough running time tomorrow morning and it's dry," Villeneuve said, "I will definitely try it. You can't leave Spa not having tried it flat."

**Left and below: Despite his application to the job and contribution to testing and development, Olivier Panis was again disappointed after a troubled race with three pitstops. He struggled home in 11th place.**

**SATURDAY QUALIFYING** Eighth and 12th in practice respectively, Villeneuve and Panis were both optimistic about improving in qualifying. While the track was never dry enough for Villeneuve to test himself at Eau Rouge, his shrewdness in timing his change to dry tyres, coupled with a brave charge around Spa's twists and turns, resulted in a fastest lap of 1m 57.038secs that put him sixth on the grid – the best qualifying position he had achieved all year.

"The call was his," team technical director Malcolm Oastler revealed later. "He is the one driving round the track and he made a very confident call that proved to be exactly right."

Starting 11th was not so good for Panis, whose best lap of 1m 58.838secs was salvaged from a fraught session interrupted by an electrical problem that adversely affected his car's steering. A change of steering wheel failed to improve the situation and, faced with a potentially dangerous handicap on the treacherous track, Panis did well to maintain control.

**SUNDAY RACE** In the warm-up the 16th and 17th fastest times posted by Panis and Villeneuve were the products of heavy fuel loads for the planned one-stop strategy.

But Villeneuve was rendered helpless by a car that was simply too slow. His team-mate fared even worse: a first-lap incident with Villeneuve put both BARs briefly off the track and left Panis in 14th, six places behind his faltering team-mate. That embarrassment was wiped out when the first race was declared null and void.

For the restarted race, a switch to a two-stop strategy made little difference to what was a lost cause. In fact Panis was forced to make three stops, the unscheduled one coming after he was sentenced to a 10 second stop-go penalty for another pit lane infringement. His third stop, though scheduled, kept Panis out of action for nearly a minute, when a problem with the fuel nozzle forced a switch to Villeneuve's fuel rig. Panis soldiered on and finished an unhappy 11th, three places behind his even unhappier team-mate, who left one of the most exciting circuits in the world complaining that he had had "a boring day".

**LUCKY STRIKE B.A.R Honda**

# A stirring drive

Jacques Villeneuve was in fighting mood at Monza: "I'm a racing driver and I'm going to race," he said in defiance of Michael Schumacher's attempt to get everyone to agree to take it easy at the start. His mutiny led to a normal race start and his delivery on his promise 'to race' brought the team a precious point that had seemed way out of reach after BAR's worst qualifying performance of the season so far.

After his fighting drive, Villeneuve was still unrepentant about his earlier dissenting voice. "It is our job as professional racing drivers to go out and race, without acting stupidly," he said. "Yes, accidents will unfortunately happen from time to time, but if you are not prepared to take the risk, then you shouldn't race at all. You cannot make all the money we do and tell the fans you are not willing to compete from the very start.

"Michael was the one behind the no-over-taking start and if he felt that strongly about safety and really wanted to make a point, then he shouldn't have started at all.

"I don't want to get into a fight with him but it was a question of principles I've had since I was a boy dreaming of being a racing driver. I believe you have to go flat out from the start and give 100 per cent to the chequered flag."

Villeneuve's 100 per cent produced a precious point that broke the tie with Jordan and boosted BAR into fifth place among the teams. Villeneuve was seventh in the drivers' standings but in this race he was as good as any of them.

FRIDAY PRACTICE Following a three-day test at Mugello, where 2002 developments were tried out and a low downforce aerodynamic package for this race was fine-tuned, the team brought three cars to Monza. While Olivier Panis had his usual chassis, 003/06, Villeneuve (who had first choice of the T-car, 003/04) had a new model, 003/08, featuring a few components intended for 2002. Villeneuve said it was much easier to work on, which was important as it was still far too slow. Panis agreed – "It's been quite a struggle, to be honest" – so did the timesheets. The Frenchman and the Canadian were mired back in 14th and 15th, Panis on a 1m 26.354secs and Villeneuve a 1m 26.521secs.

For the first time since his Formula One debut with Williams in 1996, Villeneuve was without his race engineer Jock Clear, who had gone to America and was unable to get a return flight. But Villeneuve said his car was probably too far gone for it to matter.

SATURDAY QUALIFYING Panis's 14th and Villeneuve's 16th in practice were a good indication of what became BAR's worst qualifying session of the season. Villeneuve was 15th on the grid with a 1m 24.164secs, Panis 17th with a 1m 24.677secs. Both drove to their absolute maximum in cars handicapped by hopeless aerodynamics on a track where the long straights highlight such problems. "It's a struggle," repeated Panis, in what became BAR's byword for the weekend.

SUNDAY RACE Villeneuve was 10th in the warm-up, saying the car felt better with a set-up change made with the help of Jock Clear, who had finally returned from America. Panis was 15th, complaining of poor handling balance. For the race, he turned to the quickly adapted T-car, 003/04, and drove as hard as he has all season, fighting his way from 17th on the grid to ninth at the finish.

Villeneuve was even more impressive, moving from 15th to sixth, albeit aided by retirements. The last part of his race was handicapped when a problem with his fuel rig during his pitstop on lap 33 meant he had to temper his tendency to race flat out with the need to conduct something of an economy run to the finish.

"This meant I couldn't race de la Rosa for fifth, which was very annoying," Villeneuve said. "But at least we got a point out of it, which was pretty valuable to the team at this stage of the season."

Right and below: Olivier Panis had an unrewarding weekend despite a great effort which saw him qualify 15th, two places ahead of team-leader Jacques Villeneuve. His ninth place finish was a poor reward for his struggle with BAR off the pace.

Right and below: Villeneuve showed his racing skills with an aggressive drive to sixth place from 17th on the grid. A refuelling rig problem blunted his pursuit of de la Rosa as he had to conserve fuel.

Left and below: After his stirring performance at Monza, Jacques Villeneuve had another North American nightmare race. He did not mince his words: "We knew we wouldn't be competitive, but this is embarrassing."

## UNITED STATES GRAND PRIX INDIANAPOLIS
# Embarrassing weekend

The penultimate race of the season was one of BAR Honda's worst, its cars hopelessly off the pace. Reduced to humiliating back-marker status by equal shortages of straight-line speed and grip, the drivers had to fight despair as well as their grossly slow cars. Olivier Panis fared better in the mental battle and the results, though he finished well out of the points. Jacques Villeneuve was a despondent DNF at a venue where he was once a star, but that was in champ cars and a long time ago.

In 1994, his first visit to the super speedway, Villeneuve was an impressive second. In 1995, en route to the champ car championship, he conquered the oval brilliantly, coming from two laps down to win the Indy 500. But the 2001 US Grand Prix on the Indy road course in an uncompetitive BAR Honda was a huge comedown. "Yes, I have very, very good memories from the past," he said, "though I don't think that they will be replaced very soon. This year we knew we wouldn't be competitive here, but this is embarrassing."

FRIDAY PRACTICE The team's troubles started as soon as practice began: Villeneuve, in chassis 003/08 (with first call on the T-car 003/05) and Panis, in 003/04, both reported a twofold handicap: lack of straight-line speed and of grip in the corners. Thus hamstrung, Panis managed 15th in 1m 14.386secs; Villeneuve's 1m 14.999secs left him a despairing 18th.

"It can only go up from here, but that is what we say every race weekend," he sighed, his mood not improved by a power-steering problem that restricted his practice running. "It is going to be another tough weekend. But we were very uncompetitive in Italy and we managed to get a point, so why not here?"

SATURDAY QUALIFYING Panis improved to 12th in practice but Villeneuve dropped to 19th. In qualifying their fortunes were slightly reversed, with Panis dropping back to 13th and Villeneuve moving up to 18th.

And while the Frenchman continued his diplomatic policy of not publicly slating his car, Villeneuve, who also briefly tried the T-car in a fruitless search for improved performance, pulled out all the verbal stops, after what was the second worse qualifying position of his career.

"The car is sick and we can't cure it," he fumed. "It doesn't really have any grip and at the same time we aren't quick down the straights, so it is just undriveable. I don't know what's wrong. We couldn't pinpoint it. It could be two things: either we're carrying too much downforce or we just don't have the horsepower. Most likely it's both. It's not a winning combination."

SUNDAY RACE In the warm-up, with both drivers reporting their cars no better on full tanks, Panis was 15th and Villeneuve 19th.

Only minute scrutiny of a lap chart revealed a BAR in the race, though Villeneuve headed the list of DNFs because he was the last runner to drop out.

Panis had an uneventful race with a car whose only virtue was its reliability. He finished 11th, a lap down, though the later exclusion of Trulli's Jordan promoted Panis to 10th.

The team was on a one-stop strategy but Villeneuve actually made three, the last one to park his car in the garage. His first stop, on lap 43 was routine, as was that of Panis a lap later, but moments after Panis went back out Villeneuve trundled down the pitlane pointing to his car's left rear suspension.

Predictably, Villeneuve and de la Rosa had differing views about their coming-together on lap 44. The Spaniard said the Canadian made a mistake and opened the door for him, then unexpectedly shut it in his face. Villeneuve said de la Rosa was too optimistic in his attempted overtaking manoeuvre and their cars banged wheels and spun.

After a cursory examination in the BAR pit, Villeneuve went out again to complete lap 45, but immediately returned and pulled into the garage.

"The left rear of the car could have been damaged and it would have been dangerous to continue," Villeneuve said. "It was a very bad weekend. At least we're beating the traffic home tonight."

Left and below: Olivier Panis applied himself with dignity and commitment to the job of trying to make the BAR work around Indianapolis. His reward was a dissatisfying 10th place.

# Down and out

It was the 50th race in BAR's history, a milestone few felt like celebrating. BAR wasn't having a bad year by its standards, with two podiums. But the last few races had seen it collapse: Benetton and BAR had apparently swapped places in the performance leagues. And hopes of salvaging something from the season's finale were dashed by uncompetitive cars undeserving of points.

In a reversal of form from Indianapolis, where he admitted giving up on a hopeless car, Jacques Villeneuve fought hard to finish 10th. Olivier Panis, whose turn it was to suffer the indignity of having the poorer car, finished a frustrated 13th.

The team left Japan thinking it had beaten Jordan in the Honda-powered division to finish fifth in the standings. It depended on the FIA upholding Trulli's exclusion (for non-compliance of his Jordan's skid block) in the United States Grand Prix. It didn't know whether it would finally be classified fifth or sixth in the constructors' championship (depending on the outcome of Jordan's appeal), but the fact was that BAR fell far short of its pre-season goal of winning a race in 2001.

FRIDAY PRACTICE The fickleness of the flawed BAR003s favoured Villeneuve, whose 08 version responded well to changes. Panis, in 04, suffered from the lack of grip that had afflicted his team-mate's car in the US race and which no amount of set-up variations or ballast redistribution could eradicate. With a more balanced car, Villeneuve posted a 1m 38.312secs for 14th fastest in practice. Panis, with a 1m 39.108secs, was 18th.

While Honda's new 'Suzuka Special' spec engine was delivering an estimated 10bhp more, chassis limitations kept the BAR drivers shy of the Jordans' times. Nevertheless, Villeneuve was more cheerful than usual, mainly because his awful season was ending.

"This should be one of our good races," Villeneuve said, "which means hopefully qualifying on the right side of midfield and finishing in the points. I am looking forward to getting it over with because it has definitely not been a fun year."

SATURDAY QUALIFYING Tenth and 14th in morning practice, Villeneuve and Panis fell back to 14th and 17th in qualifying. Villeneuve said that his best lap of 1m 35.109secs was the absolute maximum he could extract from a fairly functional car.

"The good news is that I won't have to qualify this car again," Villeneuve said. "The car felt good, but the bad news is that it will not go any faster. It should be better in the race, but a slow car remains a slow car."

Panis, despondent about his 1m 35.766secs, could no longer contain the frustration he had been careful to manage this season: "I have nothing to say, except that we are just too bloody slow."

SUNDAY RACE The warm-up saw Villeneuve 13th and Panis 16th. The Canadian also tried the T-car (05), just in case; the Frenchman was resigned to the certainty of a slow afternoon.

Villeneuve, in fighting mood and bent on enjoying himself, attacked from the off, muscling his way past several cars in the early laps and benefiting from the accidental retirements of Alesi and Räikkönen, reaching ninth by his first stop on lap 19. Panis, who had stopped lengthily on lap 16 (ultimately futile chassis adjustments were to blame), was already being lapped by the frontrunners and having trouble holding his own against the backmarkers.

After second stops – Panis on lap 32, Villeneuve on 34 – they were in 17th and eighth respectively, and for the rest of the race drove as their equipment allowed. Panis clung on to finish 13th, two laps down.

Villeneuve soldiered on, enlivening the late laps with determined attacks on Trulli's eighth-placed Jordan. On lap 46 his pursuit of Trulli took Villeneuve briefly into the pit-lane entry, from where he botched the chicane and was overtaken by Trulli on the exit. Three laps later a similar move in the same spot caused a wild spin that dropped Villeneuve back to 10th, where he stayed to the chequered flag.

"That was a fun race," said Villeneuve, for whom being able to race hard was some compensation for being lapped by seven cars in the season's last race.

Right and below: Jacques Villeneuve showed some of his old fighting spirit to bring the difficult BAR Honda home in 10th. He also recovered some of the spirit lost at Indianapolis.

Right and below: Olivier Panis had a frustrating end to his season, qualifying 17th and finishing a disillusioned 13th, two laps down on the leaders.

Benetton
Formula 1
RACING TEAM

Team Review    Race by Race

# BENETTON

## 2001

### Contents

| | | | | | | |
|---|---|---|---|---|---|---|
| Team Review | – | The season | p256 | European Grand Prix | – | Nürburgring | p270 |
| Australian Grand Prix | – | Melbourne | p262 | French Grand Prix | – | Magny-Cours | p271 |
| Malaysian Grand Prix | – | Sepang | p263 | British Grand Prix | – | Silverstone | p272 |
| Brazilian Grand Prix | – | Interlagos | p264 | German Grand Prix | – | Hockenheim | p273 |
| San Marino Grand Prix | – | Imola | p265 | Hungarian Grand Prix | – | Hungaroring | p274 |
| Spanish Grand Prix | – | Barcelona | p266 | Belgian Grand Prix | – | Spa-Francorchamps | p275 |
| Austrian Grand Prix | – | A1 Ring | p267 | Italian Grand Prix | – | Monza | p276 |
| Monaco Grand Prix | – | Monte Carlo | p268 | USA Grand Prix | – | Indianapolis | p277 |
| Canadian Grand Prix | – | Montreal | p269 | Japanese Grand Prix | – | Suzuka | p278 |

8 October 2001

Dear Luciano

I am sure that Formula One followers throughout the world will miss the name Benetton in association with a Formula One team.

Since your involvement in Formula One, the team has conducted itself in the highest possible order, having won two World Championships. I know that you have been a real supporter, not only of your team, but of Formula One and we are really going to miss you.

I hope you won't forget us and, when possible, you will visit Formula One races as you have done in the past.

Thanks again for all your support.

Warmest personal regards

Bernie

# STOP & GO

THERE IS ALWAYS A NEW STARTING GRID BEHIND A FINISH LINE. THANKS BERNIE.

**BENETTON FORMULA 1986-2001** 2 WORLD CHAMPIONSHIP PILOTS CUPS (1994, 1995) 1 WORLD CHAMPIONSHIP CONSTRUCTORS CUP (1995) 27 GRAND PRIX 100 WORLD CHAMPIONSHIP PLACEMENTS 15 POLE POSITIONS

**UNITED COLORS OF BENETTON.**

Jenson Button

Flavio Briatore

Giancarlo Fisichella

Jenson Button

# A chameleon season

P at Symonds, one of the most experienced engineers in Formula One, was always going to have his work cut out in 2001: he had to co-ordinate a technical programme with a new engine supplier, a new tyre supplier and a new chassis that had to be constructed within the bounds of a whole new set of rules and regulations.

The biggest nightmare was the wide-vee engine, created by Renault engine guru Jean-Jacques His. It had a 111-degree V-cylinder bank slant, whereas most other teams had opted for a 90-degree. The idea was to provide a better aerodynamic package at the rear of the car, but the problems far outweighed the advantages: the team was severely limited in its testing programme due to the shortage of usable engines available, and the new engine developments to help it compete with the top teams would not be available until 2002. So 2001 was clearly a development year.

With Flavio Briatore and Mike Gascoyne effectively running the team, a solid performance was expected. No one was quite ready for the disaster the first race turned out to be, or for the next nine. There was a glimmer of a revival at Hockenheim, and it was in full swing by the time Spa came round as Fisichella qualified eighth and was unlucky not to be second, finally finishing third. He drove a remarkable race and it signalled that Benetton was back. It was arguably the single most impressive drive of the season. From then on it was plainer sailing, as both drivers qualified in or around the top 10 and Jenson Button regained form. As the car improved, Button began to match Fisichella blow for blow. He proved a man motivated only by success, not failure. Rivals and pundits put the turnaround down to an ingenious traction control system. In the opinion of the paddock pundits, Benetton had the finest software engineers.

Whilst little was expected from the car,

great things were expected from the drivers to compensate. Jenson Button, 21, arrived after a great first season with BMW Williams during which he had made his mark as the year's top rookie – good enough to get a $3.8 million retainer from Flavio Briatore. Here was a star in the making. Whereas Giancarlo Fisichella had been at Benetton since 1998, and though acknowledged as a talented driver, his promise had not converted talent to results. He easily outqualified Jenson Button and in the latter half of 2001 proved to be one of the top five, whereas Button struggled all year. Fisichella outqualified Button in 13 of the 17 races.

At the beginning of the season it looked as if Benetton would be fighting Minardi for last place in the constructors' championship; but, spurred by the sensational launch control system, the team pulled 10 points out of thin air and gave Jaguar a huge wake-up call.

## The Benetton Renault B201 car

THE Benetton Renault B201 was a totally new car, with nothing held over from the previous year. Mike Gascoyne arrived too late from Jordan to influence it; he got down to reorganising the structure, leaving Mark Wilson to complete the car. It had a new engine, gearbox and suspension. The wide-angled engine allowed Benetton to build a car with a low centre of gravity, with the optimal exhaust layout. But it started the year at 790bhp, some 30 horsepower down on everyone else. Pat Symonds believed that BMW Williams had 860bhp.

Renault manufactured a staggering 250 engines during the year. It confirmed that it also intended to introduce valve actuation solenoids instead of camshafts at the beginning of the year, but shelved them for the sake of reliability. ▷

Giancarlo Fisichella

Mercedes-Benz came to the same conclusion. Benetton built seven chassis in 2001. Fisichella raced 03 in Australia, Malaysia, Brazil, Imola, Spain and Austria and 06 in Monaco, Canada, Germany (Nürburgring), France, Britain, Germany (Hockenheim), Hungary, Belgium, Italy, the USA and Japan.

Chassis 01 was Button's car in Australia, Malaysia and Brazil; he had 05 for Imola, Spain, Austria, Monaco, Canada, Germany (Nürburgring), France, Britain, Germany (Hockenheim), Hungary, Belgium, Italy, the USA and Japan. Chassis 02 was the spare car a handful of times, once in Australia for Button and in Malaysia and Brazil for Fisichella. But generally, after appearing as the spare tub, it was used as the rig car: it was the chassis submitted to the FIA for crash tests, and due to the exceptional loads placed on it during these tests, the chassis was kept as a rig car, and not raced.

The 04 was used as a test car. Fisichella used 03 as his race car on all weekends up to and including Austria. The 02 was the spare car in Brazil, but for Spain and Austria this duty reverted to the 01, Button's old race chassis. From Monaco onwards Fisichella used 06 as a race car, with 03 appearing as the spare car in Monaco, Canada, France, Germany, Hungary, Belgium and Italy.

Button kept to chassis 01 for the first three races in Australia, Malaysia and Brazil. For the remainder of the year he used 05, with certain exceptions. He used the spare 03 for qualifying at the Hungaroring, when he suffered two engine failures during the morning practice sessions.

Neither driver suffered any major race accidents during the year. Fisichella crunched into the barrier at Ste Devote in Monaco, and managed to crash into his team-mate in Canada, but neither crash caused major chassis damage. Button spun out of the race in Malaysia when the monsoon was tipping down; and he crashed out

of Spa after hitting a bollard at the Bus Stop, which broke the front wing, then hit the wall, but again with no major chassis damage.

As far as team attitude was concerned, it was difficult to compare 2001 with 2000, as Mike Gascoyne said: "This year was very much a development year before our entry as a Renault works team in 2002. Everything was geared to putting the team in the right place for 2002. We made sacrifices at the start of the season to put the programmes in place that we said we would deliver at the end of the year. At the beginning of the year we were qualifying and racing at the back of the grid. At the last race of the year in Japan we qualified sixth and ninth and ran with the top three teams, so I think that demonstrates the progress we made this year."

## Technical developments

IN THE beginning the engine was a problem, the chassis was a problem and the electronics were a problem. Benetton did not even have power-steering early in the season, much to Jenson Button's disgust.

Renault's engine supremo Jean-Jacques His never lost confidence in his engineers' ability to get it right, but at the beginning it was a nightmare. Equally, Mike Gascoyne knew it was only a matter of time before he got his technical department in order. It was a case of when the going gets tough, the tough get going. His, Gascoyne and Symonds proved to be tough cookies.

Lack of reliability in the first few races meant very little data was recorded, and ample data is vital for a valid test programme.

In Melbourne both cars suffered from exhaust problems with the resultant loss of power, and in Malaysia Fisichella suffered a fuel pressure problem; but at least Button finished, thereby giving the

Pat Symonds

Mike Gascoyne

Patrick Faure

team valuable data. This was obviously useful, as Fisichella finished sixth in Brazil.

Pat Symonds named the points finish in Brazil as a high point of the season: "This was one of the highlights as the team was in such deep trouble at the time. We really needed that sixth place."

The leading highlight, however, was Fisichella's appearance on the podium at Spa in third place. It was a clever strategy to only change rear tyres, as the team found that new Michelins didn't work as well as used Michelins – which, combined with a determined Fisichella, produced an excellent result. In fact, for the rest of the season, both drivers made sure they scrubbed the tyres during Sunday warm-up.

Spa was a good example of how everything came together. The engine added a few horsepower more to about 830bhp, and the new aero package (new front wing and floor) worked well, as did the launch control system. The launch control system introduced in Hungary was one of the year's great success stories. As Symonds said: "We were one of the last teams to use launch control, as at Benetton we have always had absolute engineering integrity and there was no way we were going to introduce it before we knew we could make it work. In fact, during the time we spent analysing and working on it, we learnt a lot more about manual starts so we could

map the manual starts better, so it benefited us all round." It certainly did. At Spa, Fisichella set off like a rocket from eighth on the grid to slip in behind Michael Schumacher in second.

Power-steering was implemented at Silverstone, and not before time. Button had suffered severe shoulder problems through trying to haul the car, down on power and therefore heavier than usual, round the circuit. Fisichella also suffered to a lesser degree, although he didn't need pain-killing injections like the more delicate Button.

The introduction of traction control at Barcelona was also something that Benetton, and in particular Pat Symonds, relished. As he said: "I love electronics, the more the better, if I had my way I'd have it all electronically controlled like a Scalextric car, so we'd just press all the buttons in the garage. I love messing around with electronics, the more complex the better." In fact, compared to all its other chassis and engine problems, Benetton had little trouble with the traction control system.

The major aerodynamic changes throughout the year started in Brazil, with the introduction of new sidepods and undertray. At Magny-Cours a rear wing package was introduced. The major aero changes introduced in Hungary are mentioned above; at Monza there was a new front wing.  ▷

Benetton
Formula 1

## BENETTON SEASON STATISTICS

### RELIABILITY PERFORMANCE

Jenson Button

| Driver | Races | Max laps | Laps completed | Reliability rating |
|---|---|---|---|---|
| Jenson Button | 17 | 1065 | 861 | 80.8% |
| Giancarlo Fisichella | 17 | 1065 | 810 | 76.1% |
| Constructor | Races | Max laps | Laps completed | Reliability rating |
| Team | 34 | 2130 | 1671 | 78.4% |

### CHAMPIONSHIP PERFORMANCE

| Driver | 2001 points | 2000 points | 12 month change |
|---|---|---|---|
| Giancarlo Fisichella | 8 | 18 | -55.6% |
| Jenson Button | 2 | 12 | -83.3% |
| Constructor | 2001 points | 2000 points | 12 month change |
| Team | 10 | 20 | -50% |

### CHASSIS LOG

**B201-01** Jenson Button's race car at Melbourne, Sepang, and Interlagos. Spare car at Imola, A1 Ring and Monte Carlo.

**B201-02** Spare car at Melbourne, Sepang and Interlagos.

**B201-03** Giancarlo Fisichella's race car at Melbourne, Sepang, Interlagos, Imola, Barcelona and the A1 Ring. Spare car at Monte Carlo, Montreal, Magny-Cours, Silverstone, Hockenheim, Hungaroring, Spa-Francorchamps, Monza, Indianapolis and Suzuka.

**B201-04** Test car only.

**B201-05** Button's race car at Imola, Barcelona, A1 Ring, Monte Carlo, Montreal, Magny-Cours, Silverstone, Hockenheim, Hungaroring, Spa-Francorchamps, Monza, Indianapolis and Suzuka.

**B201-06** Fisichella's race car at Monte Carlo, Montreal, Magny-Cours, Silverstone, Hockenheim, Hungaroring, Spa-Francorchamps, Monza, Indianapolis and Suzuka.

Benetton plumbed the depths in 2001. But the worst qualifying performances of 19th and 21st at Imola, Spain and Austria were forgotten by the time of Japan, where they placed sixth and ninth. Over the course of the season's 17 races, with 1,065 laps available per car, Benetton covered a total of 1,671: 810 with Fisichella, 861 with Button. Reliability was third best on the grid, the team's score of 78.4 per cent bested only by Prost and Ferrari with their extraordinarily reliable power plant.

## The drivers

THREE drivers drove a B201 during the season. Giancarlo Fisichella and Jenson Button were the race team drivers, and Mark Webber the test driver. There was a lot of frustration at the beginning of the season, when testing was very limited due to the lack of engines for testing. Testing was thought to be 30 per cent down on last year, even though there was a tyre war raging.

This was very negative for new boy Jenson Button, who found out how you can go from hero to zero simply by stepping into a new car. Last year the new boy on the block was a phenomenon; this year he was not only struggling, but coming under pressure within the team. In spite of public declarations to the contrary, both Flavio Briatore and Mike Gascoyne were critical of Button. It is true that he had been through a very difficult time while settling in: he had only acquired a year's experience, and he was entering a team where the senior driver had a lot more experience but did not earn a lot more money.

Button was rumoured to be on a $9 million two-year deal, where-

as Fisichella was on about $8 million a year. As an insider said: "For $4.5 million, we can have a more experienced driver or for a couple of million dollars we can have a novice, but there's no point in paying an inexperienced driver $4.5 million dollars a year."

But by Canada, Button was fighting back and at a showdown meeting with his engineers in Nürburgring he was finally sorting the car out. It was a question of set-up. Button brakes in a certain way and the car didn't like it, so a compromise was found: he learnt to brake differently and the car responded. He also insisted on equal engines and equal equipment. He found a new race engineer in Rod Nelson and finally there was communication.

Fisichella outqualified his team-mate 13 times, meaning Button outqualified Fisichella just four times: in Australia, Britain, Italy and the USA. A driver is always compared with his team-mate, and it didn't look good for Button. In Monaco it seemed as if they were driving different cars: Fisichella was 10th on the grid, with Button a second off his team-mate, languishing in 17th. It was a crisis of confidence. Fisichella loves Monaco: he was on the limit straight out of the box, whereas Button wasn't.

But things turned around, and after Nürburgring there was a new, steely edge to Button. He said: "Things will be different by the end of the year, I'll be kicking arse." They were and he was. In Italy he outqualified his team-mate – 11th to Fisichella's 14th – and after a storming start to sixth place he squandered it, punting his 2002 team-mate, Jarno Trulli, out of the race. After that his engine blew, otherwise he could have been looking at a points finish.

In spite, or maybe because of, the dire technical situation, the drivers got on very well together. As Fisichella said: "We have to fight the car before we fight each other." Both drivers have easy temperaments. Fisichella is a laid-back Roman and Button has a very attractive and open personality. In many ways, 2001 was the making of Fisichella. His talent had never been in doubt but in the past his commitment was questioned. When the going got tough he used to apparently fade away, but this year he was fully committed and fully with the team at every race. Mike Gascoyne said: "Giancarlo performed fantastically for the team, he is one of the fastest drivers out there and has been committed all season. He really helped to carry the team in the early part of the year. His third place at Spa was fantastic. The whole team is sad to see him go."

Of Button he said: "Having to change teams and not having much experience in Formula One, he had to settle into a new team, which is never easy. We encouraged Jenson to work harder throughout the year and his performance improved through the year. We were able to give him more testing towards the end of the season, when we were running two car tests. I am sure next year he will perform at a higher level."

Next year is almost certainly Button's last at Benetton/Renault, and with Ralf Schumacher and Juan Pablo Montoya settled at BMW Williams he is unlikely to return there. He has to perform in 2002 or he'll be struggling to get a drive for 2003.

The team was very pleased with test driver Mark Webber, who did the brunt of the tyre testing on the B200 car when Benetton couldn't run the B201, because of the engine shortage.

But at the end of the year Button stayed, due more to contractual obligations than to free will. Flavio Briatore made it clear who was his favourite driver, and Fisichella swapped with Jordan driver Jarno Trulli: Fisichella got a three-year contract at Jordan, and Trulli arrived at Benetton when the option Briatore held on his contract was called in.

## Commercial

RENAULT was back in Formula One in 2001 after a three-year absence. When it left, chairman Louis Schweitzer said it was bored with winning. The chairman had no such problem in 2001.

At the launch of the new car in Venice, the entire technical team failed to show up. Symonds and Gascoyne appeared on a big TV screen, far removed from difficult technical questions. They had obviously realised that 2001 would be a nightmare, and didn't want to be caught making optimistic noises or being over-negative either. So they withdrew from the fray.

Having amassed 95 victories in Formula One as a team and an engine manufacturer, Renault is back to win. But like Honda, it is finding that Formula One in the 21st century has moved on a long way and winning is no longer as effortless as it once seemed. But failure on a scale seen in 2001 is unthinkable in 2002. Renault's competitions head, Patrick Faure, said at the beginning of 2001: "We are one of the top five car manufacturers in the world. We are in Formula One to increase our market share."

The new car's launch was emotional for Flavio Briatore: he said goodbye to Benetton chief Luciano Benetton, who in May 2000 had sold the team to Renault for a $82.4 million profit. The deal marked the end of the company's 17-year involvement in Formula One.

In 2001 Benetton spent around $180 million; in 2002 it will spend more. With sponsorship difficult, Renault will have to cover the shortfall.

Benetton seems to have spent a lot of the year groping in the dark for a cure to a car that was, as Benetton director of engineering Pat Symonds admitted, 'far worse than we thought'. That it found the cure, administered it and then advanced is a very good sign of what's to come. Renault is a dark horse for 2002.

Benetton motorhome

## AUSTRALIAN GRAND PRIX MELBOURNE
# An unexpected decline

It was always going to be a long, hard weekend for the Benetton team, as chief engineer Pat Symonds said: "We are at the start of an ambitious programme that we know will bring heartache – but it is the only way to go forward. We have a lot of new elements in the tyres and engine and we have to learn to optimise them."

If anything, this morose declaration was an understatement. Benetton had got it badly wrong. Technical director Mike Gascoyne was left to sum up a terrible weekend, and blamed the engine for all the problems: "Renault's Jean-Jacques His is an innovative leader and has the courage of his convictions, so once the problems are solved, we will become leaders."

Team principal Flavio Briatore said: "I am not confident this year. It's no different to the 1980s, when we first entered Formula One. Then we had six or seven teams in front of us and today is just the same." But it wasn't the same. This time there were eight or nine teams in front, and only 10 rival manufacturers as opposed to the 15 or 20 teams in the late eighties. It certainly seemed a wise decision by Renault not to have put its name to the team in the transition year.

FRIDAY PRACTICE Benetton brought three cars to Australia – B201/01 for Jenson Button, B201/03 for Giancarlo Fisichella and B201/02 as the spare. Benetton had a policy of assigning the spare to whichever driver qualified fastest. The only time it would be assigned specifically to one driver was at their home races, Silverstone for Button and Monza for Fisichella. The team brought 12 new Renault RS21 engines, based on a radically new design with a 111-degree 'V' angle as opposed to the usual 90 degrees.

Fisichella ran 32 laps, ending 16th with a 1m 32.475secs. Working mainly on race set-up, he progressed well with the balance and identified the best tyre for the car – the softer of the two Michelin options available. Jenson Button did a mere 26 laps, scoring only 21st fastest with a 1m 33.403secs. He had a problem with the engine and then got a puncture.

SATURDAY QUALIFYING Both drivers had problems in the morning practice sessions – Button experienced a gearbox failure, which meant very few laps were completed by either teammate. Fisichella managed 27 laps with a best of 1m 30.549secs; Button completed just 12 laps with a best of 1m 30.893secs.

Qualifying only bore out the morning pessimism. Button qualified 16th with a 1m 30.035secs and Fisichella was 17th in 1m 30.209secs. Fisichella's car had developed a water leak after the first two runs of qualifying, so he used the spare car for his final run. But that then developed a brake problem and he had to abort his last run.

Pat Symonds was despondent: "We have to regard it as part of a longer-term plan. Melbourne is a hard circuit and the first turn is slippery and bumpy. I'm not confident with the race set-up and would be happier if we'd done more miles, but we still hope to finish." Mike Gascoyne was more upbeat: "We knew we'd be about 14th or 15th so it was no big surprise. Renault is pushing back the barriers of design, which in the long-term will be successful, but we have to put up with short-term pain for long-term gain. We have taken a decision to look at the long term and we won't be distracted from that objective."

SUNDAY RACE Button's race began badly when he was given a 10-second stop-go penalty because his mechanics did not clear the grid within regulation time. But he made a good start, pulling up to 11th before having a battle with Jos Verstappen that cost him several places. The safety car came out on the fifth lap after Villeneuve's accident and went in again on lap 16. Button had to come in on lap 18 for his 10-second stop-go penalty. He pitted on lap 32 but the car developed exhaust problems resulting in a loss of power. An electrical fault from overheating caused by the exhaust problem forced his retirement on lap 53. He was classified 14th and last.

Fisichella also had exhaust problems with the same power loss. He made his first pitstop on lap 26, had to pit again on lap 50 and finished the race on lap 55. He was classified 13th. Fisichella said: "The car was running well and it felt good, but then it developed a problem that we're looking into. As a result I lost power and so could only cruise to the end of the race."

Above: It was a bad weekend for both Giancarlo Fisichella and Jenson Button when their season opened with a battle to keep off the back of the grid – a far cry from the points-worthy performances of 2000. Right: Flavio Briatore had nothing to smile about.

Right and below: Button had a terrible weekend which included a dramatic puncture on Friday.

FF TV IMAGES

# Season turns into nightmare

The Benetton team had talked itself down to such an extent that expectations were precisely nil. It came to Malaysia with the same problems it encountered in Australia. If anything it had gone backwards, though the flyaway races were always going to be hard – serious aerodynamic work was needed.

It would be a long, hard, tough job to develop the new Renault engine – as Benetton was finding. But Benetton was a top team and Renault a top car manufacturer. Few expected the development phase to last for long, although there was always the chance it could last all season. Already there was talk of a new car at mid-season. The team focus in Malaysia was on achieving race reliability, with the aim of getting the two cars to the finish and in a competitive state. Technical director Mike Gascoyne said: "We hope to achieve more reliability with the car here, as the more reliability we get, the more development work we can do with the engine." Benetton brought no fewer than 12 RS21 engines to Malaysia, so was clearly ready for plenty of changes if necessary.

FRIDAY PRACTICE Benetton brought its three Melbourne cars to the Penang circuit, with the spare this time set up for Jenson Button following the decision to alternate it between drivers for each race except their home Grand Prix events at Silverstone and Monza.

The expected rivalry between the two drivers had yet to flare up, although Giancarlo Fisichella stressed: "Before we can compete with each other we need a competitive car, so it's important that we work together to overcome the problems. We have to keep positive and not get down. There's a long way to go and things will get a lot better." They certainly needed to.

Button completed few timed laps in the first session due to a gearbox problem. In the afternoon he managed 23 laps, with a best time of 1m 42.214secs which placed him 17th. Fisichella also lost time due to a battery change. His afternoon went much better as he worked on the balance of the car and, in 21 laps, clocked a best time of 1m 41.375secs – 13th fastest.

SATURDAY QUALIFYING The team ran 53 laps in the morning session but qualifying inevitably disappointed. Fisichella ended up 16th on the grid with 1m 38.086secs; Button qualified 17th in 1m 38.258secs. Fisichella only got one run in at the beginning of the session; Button managed two.

The team's mood was general disappointment. Engineering director Pat Symonds explained: "I feel we could have got a bit higher, particularly with Giancarlo who unfortunately had a minor problem with his car. That meant a very late change to the T-car, which was set up for Jenson. Although the mechanics tried to change it, we were just a few seconds too late for the final run. Jenson had problems perfecting the balance, so was just a little off the pace."

SUNDAY RACE The race began badly when the first start had to be aborted due to Fisichella's clutch malfunctioning and causing him to creep. He had to stall the car to stop it, although everyone else thought he had missed his slot. As it happened he didn't incur a 10-second penalty, but did get sent to the back of the grid for his trouble as the start was aborted – serious stuff when 300 million people are watching. After the restart, by lap two, he had overtaken his team-mate for 11th place.

As it began to rain both Benettons pitted to change tyres, with Button echoing the situation at Ferrari – having to wait for Fisichella to leave the pit before receiving attention. The rain became a monsoon and even behind the safety car conditions were difficult. As Fisichella said: "Even behind the safety car it was almost impossible to drive, as the track was so wet and the rain so intense." After the safety car went in on lap 11 Fisichella had a good race, moving up to ninth at one point before a fuel pressure problem curtailed his afternoon on lap 32.

Button had a good start, quickly moving up to 12th. After he made his pitstop for wet-weather tyres on lap three the safety car came out and Button got caught behind it. On lap 21 while running 12th, he made a mistake and dropped to 14th. He made his scheduled pitstop on lap 23, then ran a steady race, finishing 11th.

Giancarlo Fisichella (top and below) and Jenson Button (above) once again had to endure an uncompetitive car. Bottom: How the mighty had fallen. Benetton was relegated to tussling with seasoned backmarkers Arrows, Prost and Minardi.

Benetton
Formula 1
RACING TEAM

# Amazing run to sixth

A single point was almost as good as a win, but the despondent team (top) and Flavio Briatore (bottom left) had memories of better times. Bottom: Button spent his race fighting Prosts and Minardis, although Fisichella struggled on for a point.

Long faces greeted the friendly Brazilian smiles as Flavio Briatore and his team rode into town; playing a bit part has never suited the flamboyant Italian. "We are making progress, we need time; the engine is going to be good," Briatore said. "We are breaking the technical boundaries in F1 and there has to be some pain before we have any gain. When Renault started the turbo, everybody laughed. When Renault started the V10, everyone said it was a compromise; now everyone has a V10." But the 111-degree V engine was a different proposition. As far as could be seen, no engine maker had rushed to the drawing board to copy it.

Renault arrived with nine RS21 engines and the team wondered whether that would be enough. A new aerodynamic package turned out to be slower than the old one. Technical chief Mike Gascoyne managed to spin the situation positively: "Pioneers have arrows shot at them and Renault is certainly going through that phase, but if you look at Renault's history it gets it right, and when it gets it right, it dominates."

However, against all expectations, the race turned out well for Benetton, with Fisichella taking a miraculous and well-earned point. After the race, accusations started flying. Insiders believed Jenson Button's engine was at least 50bhp down on Giancarlo Fisichella's. After only three races the drivers' gloves were off and the fight was on – each had to beat the other for his career. Button, on loan from Williams, seemed to be regarded as number two.

FRIDAY PRACTICE Benetton brought three cars to Brazil – 01 for Button, 03 for Fisichella and 02 as the spare for Fisichella. The Italian was 17th on 1m 18.096secs; Button was 22nd and last with 1m 19.585secs, four seconds off the pace. He said: "We had engine problems so were limited with improvements of the set-up and tyre developments. We have a lot of work to do to get where we need to be." An imperfect situation.

SATURDAY QUALIFYING Fisichella qualified 18th in 1m 16.175secs; Button languished at 20th in the penultimate row with 1m 16.467secs, slugging it out with the Minardis.

Button admitted it was a character-building year. Last year he was feted by the media; this year hardly more than a handful of hacks bothered to enquire. Happily Button was made of stern stuff, never complained, just got on with the job while occasionally gazing longingly at the Williams car that might have been his. The new aero package was quietly dropped from Fisichella's car and he qualified with the previous aero set-up on the car.

Pat Symonds looked gloomy as he struggled to find positive words: "The only consolation is to see everyone – drivers, engineers, mechanics and factory personnel – still pushing to the maximum."

SUNDAY RACE After starting 18th the Roman had a spectacular race. He moved steadily up the field to be reach 11th by lap 25, 10th by lap 30 and on lap 64 he overtook Jean Alesi to get in the points in sixth place, where he finished. The whole team was euphoric – it was as though Benetton had won the race.

Fisichella said: "I did not expect such a good result, and especially not to score a point, which is unbelievable. I would have been pleased to finish in the top 10. One point is perfect and I am happy for the team and myself." Symonds expressed his delight too: "It's an amazing result. Normally I wouldn't be happy, but in the circumstances..."

There were no celebrations for Button. After moving up to 16th from 20th by lap four, he started losing power and languished in 17th before being called in on lap 28 to repair an oil leak. The problem turned out to be the scavenge pump, which was not evacuating the required oil from the sump, resulting in a loss of power. Button then floated around at the back, advancing as cars dropped out, to finish 10th and last. He found his car very hard to handle in the wet.

Left: Jenson Button endured another weekend at the back of the grid. Below: Flavio Briatore's body language is the clearest in Formula One and in Imola it was not lost on Mike Gascoyne.

Above: Giancarlo Fisichella had a very disappointing time, retiring his Benetton Renault B201 in the race.

Benetton Formula 1 RACING TEAM

## SAN MARINO GRAND PRIX IMOLA
# An extended test session

Being a test team for Renault's new engine was always going to be difficult, if not downright embarrassing. And Benetton's situation was indeed becoming embarrassing. The team was up to four seconds slower – and a Formula One car goes a long way in four seconds.

The Benetton motor home was joyfully dispensing top hospitality but the mood among team members within was more akin to a funeral. Within the team the driver battle was not really raging, as it had been all but won by Giancarlo Fisichella. The Jenson Button-Fisichella fight had the big prize for the victor of a bright future Formula One career.

It was clear the package was lacking, being slowest in the speed traps and unable to use higher levels of downforce. It was beginning to dawn on some that Renault might be going down a blind alley – and, possibly, that the chassis designers were in the dark, too.

FRIDAY PRACTICE Benetton brought three cars to the race – chassis 05 for Jenson Button, 03 for Giancarlo Fisichella and 01 as the spare car, set up for Fisichella at his home race. The team brought nine RS21 engines to Imola, clearly expecting trouble, and it was rumoured they were all to different specs. Tyre choice was set to be critical, but as the team was at the bottom end of the grid the option was always going to be for the soft compound. It was a wet morning session and the Michelins were not competitive. Fisichella was 15th on 1m 28.322secs; Button 17th on 1m 28.902secs.

In the afternoon, when the circuit dried, the team worked on normal race set-up. After the practice session Giancarlo Fisichella said: "We have improved in the slow corners where I had too much understeer before."

SATURDAY QUALIFYING Benetton had an awful day, as dire as the weather. Fisichella qualified 19th with a best time of 1m 26.902secs and

Button in 21st, on the last row of the grid, with a best time of 1m 27.758secs – four seconds off pole. Renault had a development engine, which was 10kg lighter. The drivers tossed a coin for it and Button lost.

Technical director Mike Gascoyne said: "We said it would get worse before it got better and today we proved it. But we shouldn't have been as slow as we were, and we need to discover why. Neither driver improved on their last set of new tyres and they should have found seven or eight 10ths, as the cars were quicker at the end of the session as more rubber was laid down as the track dried out."

Gascoyne believed there was nothing wrong with the chassis: "It's easy to panic, but we have to keep our head down and keep moving in the right direction. Once the engine is right we have to make sure we are ready on the chassis side to match the engine, which we know will be competitive." The most disappointing thing was that in Brazil, we were only 1.2secs off Coulthard." The only saving grace was that the engine was proving reliable.

The slow pace had started to cause dissent and the engineers were blaming the drivers for some of the shortcomings, simply because they didn't believe the car could be that slow. Being four seconds off the pace didn't mean there was not worse to come.

SUNDAY RACE Fisichella had a great start, moving from 19th on the grid to 15th by the end of the first lap. He made his first pitstop on lap 21. But his race was over exactly halfway through the race, on lap 31, when he had to retire due to an engine misfire. Rather than risk a blown engine, the team decided to bring him in.

Button moved up two places at the start from 19th to 17th. On lap 19 he made his pitstop, but the fuel rig didn't work and no fuel was loaded, so he went round for another lap before coming in again on lap 20. He then drove a quiet but consistent race to finish last of the 12 remaining drivers, two laps behind the leaders.

Mike Gascoyne was philosophical. "Now it's back to the windtunnel. It is depressing for the team as we're all racers and we just want to race. The main thing is not to panic and keep to the plan, things will get better eventually." It was hard to imagine Flavio Briatore being so philosophical, as he was far better known for his impatience.

## SPANISH GRAND PRIX BARCELONA
# Absolute disaster

For a team such as Benetton Renault to be groping around the bottom of the grid was unseemly – even if it was a development year. It was rumoured there would be a totally new car sometime in July, though most people were sure it was probably only a rumour. For Spain there was no news and no new aero package. There were to be new bits for the car from Monaco, and from Magny-Cours a big step forward was expected. For a top team, some basic items – such as power-steering – were missing, which was inexplicable to some. Nine RS21 engines were brought to the race, all rumoured to be of a different specification.

Jenson Button had continuing shoulder problems, caused by heavy steering, and had to rest from testing.

With each race, the team's protestations of nil expectation and a development year fell on increasingly deaf ears. Everyone's confidence was draining, and talented, competent people were beginning to question their own self-worth. It was a keg of dynamite waiting to explode. Amazingly they held together.

FRIDAY PRACTICE Three B201 cars were brought to Barcelona, with chassis 03 for Giancarlo Fisichella, 05 for Button and 01 as the spare. The team made alterations to the car to protect Button's shoulder. Mike Gascoyne said: "We lightened the steering geometry to reduce the steering loads. We will have power-steering for Austria." Gascoyne had also made peace with the English driver following his contention at Imola that Button should raise his game. He said: "There is no doubt about Jenson Button's ability or speed."

Fisichella did 38 laps and recorded a 1m 22.971secs for 18th. Button did 33 laps, with his best a time of 1m 23.201secs for 19th.

SATURDAY QUALIFYING The day went much as expected. Fisichella recorded a time of 1m 21.065secs to secure 19th on the grid, while Button's best was a 1m 21.916secs for 21st. Last minute set-up changes to Button's car meant he missed his final run, while Fisichel-

la's later runs were hampered by traffic.

Benetton's director of engineering, Pat Symonds, said: "It was very difficult to get a competitive lap time today. We opted to use the harder tyres because we felt the difference in qualifying time would be relatively small. This gives us some hope for tomorrow's race."

SUNDAY RACE Button had a wake-up call in the morning when Michael Schumacher came out of the pits as he was coming in and they nearly collided. The Briton then swept into 15th during warm-up – a good sign for the race, it was thought. In fact it meant nothing.

Fisichella switched to his spare car before the start and was running 15th in the race. He made his first pitstop on lap 23 and changed the nose of his Benetton after damaging his front wing in a dust-up at the first corner. The stop took 14.6secs. He pitted for the second time on lap 40, this time being stationary for 9.2secs. He finished the race in 15th position.

On lap 17 Button made his first pitstop in 18.1secs with a puncture. He made his second pitstop on lap 41. The liveliest part of the race was on lap 52 when Button overtook Marques for last place. He finished 15th.

Gascoyne remained upbeat after the race: "Treating this race as a test session we would like to have done more laps than we managed, but one very positive note is that we had perfect engine reliability for the whole weekend, which is a very significant step forward. We struggled to get the tyres to work in the race and, on reflection, we chose the wrong tyre. For the hard tyre, the cool conditions on race day didn't suit. We have to work very hard on development to make sure that we are competitive when we get the engine improvements that are coming."

Above left: Jenson Button struggled with a sore shoulder and no power-steering. Above: The Benetton Renault garage has seen much happier times than 2001. Right: The high point of the weekend for Flavio Briatore and Giancarlo Fisichella was meeting King Juan Carlos.

Fisichella battled with and lost out to Alonso's Minardi.

## AUSTRIAN GRAND PRIX A1 RING
# Waiting for change

Benetton was treading water and no new aerodynamics were planned until the British Grand Prix or later. It was another weekend wallowing at the back of the grid and acting as a test team for Renault.

The team kept morale high by playing loud rock music in the garage. The drivers were finding it tough at the back. As Jenson Button said: "Giancarlo and I are on the back row behind the Minardis this year. They are our fighting companions. It's been an interesting battle at the back there, but I think I'd rather have it nearer the front. Now we've just got to keep pushing and pushing and making improvements and hopefully we will get some performance gains later on in the season."

The difficult thing with Benetton was to know exactly what the problem was – engine, chassis or both. Various chassis developments had been introduced since the first race and, similarly, Renault had definitely made progress with reliability, but the only gauge for improvement could be against Minardi, which had consistently matched Benetton. It was known that Minardi had made minimal improvements, and yet the under-funded Faenza-based team with its private Cosworth V10 continued to match the well-funded, Renault-backed Benetton team.

FRIDAY PRACTICE Benetton brought three chassis to the race, chassis 05 was for Button, 03 for Fisichella and 01 available as the spare car. It was an awful day, with Fisichella running for 37 laps and recording the 21st fastest time of 1m 14.833secs. Button ran for only 20 laps and recorded 22nd and slowest time of the day with a 1m 15.570secs. However, an engine problem forced Button to stop with 50 minutes of the practice still remaining. The team concentrated on doing set-up work in race trim.

SATURDAY QUALIFYING The softer of the tyre options was chosen. Fisichella qualified 19th with a time of 1m 12.644 secs, having completed only eight of his 12 allowable laps. Jenson Button qualified 21st in 1m 13.459secs and used up 11 laps.

An engine problem forced Fisichella to abandon his third run, leaving him unable to improve on a good second run. As the T-car was set up for Button, the Italian just missed being able to get out again as it takes about 10 minutes to change the settings and there were only 10 minutes of the qualifying session left.

SUNDAY RACE Fisichella had a very short race, despite having made progress through the field off the grid, moving from 19th to 12th. However, the team called him in after four laps as the information on the telemetry indicated that the engine was about to blow.

Fisichella said: "I had no option but to pull in and retire. It was disappointing, as I had made a very good start."

Button sped from 21st to 16th at the start. His goal was to finish but this was denied him as the same engine problem that had beset Fisichella suddenly occurred in Button's car, causing a failure. He made his pitstop on lap 39 in 10.6secs, but the second set of tyres did not work as well as the first set, and he retired at Turn 3 on lap 61.

Director of engineering Pat Symonds said: "One positive thing that came out of this was the good performance of our launch control. As for the other parts of the car, we just have to keep working to get it right. We are making small steps and progress is being made. We hope to make a good step forward at either Magny-Cours or Silverstone."

Left: Jenson Button was left to spectate from the side of the track after running at the tail of the field. Bottom right: His race came to an abrupt end when the rear of his Benetton locked up mid-corner. Below: Giancarlo Fisichella chases Enrique Bernoldi's Arrows, prior to retirement.

Left: The rear of the Benetton was becoming a familiar sight for 2001's pace-setters at each race. Below left: Giancarlo Fisichella qualified 19th, but his race was short-lived when he suffered an engine failure after only three laps. Team-mate Button qualified a lowly 21st.

Benetton Formula 1 RACING TEAM

## MONACO GRAND PRIX MONTE CARLO
# A ray of hope in the streets

When Mike Gascoyne, the technical director, said "we should be more competitive this weekend as we have some aerodynamic modifications that should suit this circuit," he was right. The peculiarities of Monaco enabled Benetton to look like a proper team again. The talk at Benetton was the form of Jenson Button, who was thrashed in qualifying by his team-mate. Team principal Flavio Briatore said some unprintable things about Button's form, although Gascoyne took a pragmatic approach: "Jenson hasn't done many laps here and this is one track where you need experience. Everyone expects him to be a wonderkid but he needs laps in the car. Giancarlo loves this track. He is naturally quick and on the pace as soon as he comes out of the pits."

Technically the team was also behind. So far it hadn't used launch control and was only just getting to grips with its power-steering system. Gerhard Berger, an ex-Benetton team driver, said: "Someone should have been hung and beheaded by now."

THURSDAY PRACTICE Benetton brought three chassis to Monaco: B201/05 for Button, B201/06 for Giancarlo Fisichella and the T-car B201/01 set up for Giancarlo Fisichella.

Fisichella settled easily into the Monaco rhythm and found his quickest laps immediately; Button did not. Fisichella completed 28 laps to finish 11th, a great improvement on his performance so far this season. Button completed 24 laps with a best time of 1m 24.026secs and 17th place.

SATURDAY QUALIFYING In the morning Fisichella spun off at Rascasse, knocking off his rear wing. Although he was happy with his car's handling,

he also had a straight-on moment at Ste Devote. The Button-Fisichella gap widened even further in qualifying – Fisichella took a highly credible 10th while Button, hampered by understeer and brake problems, only achieved 17th.

He said after qualifying: "I didn't get the right set-up and lost most of my time on the brakes. I didn't feel comfortable with the car. I thought I'd be closer to Giancarlo, even though he is always quick here. We're down on power so it's more difficult to balance the car. There are a lot of new things to test; we'll have to try a different set-up so I can drive more smoothly. The main objective is to feel comfortable with the car." The team took the soft tyre option from Michelin.

SUNDAY RACE Fisichella started well and he was in the points by lap 31. But then he bumped the barrier at Ste Devote for the second time. Previously he had brushed the barrier due to a brake problem but this time, on lap 44, he tore a front wheel as his car stuck in gear. That was the end of his race.

Button had a steady race, making his way up to 11th by lap 19. On lap 49 he did his pit-stop and went on to finish seventh.

He said: "Things felt quite good. In the first stint the car had a bit of understeer in the high-speed corners. In the low-speed corners we had a bit of oversteer. It was a little frustrating to be just outside the points but it was good fun and I hope we can sort out the problems we have had recently and chase points at every race."

Right: Before his crash, Fisichella had completely worn away the left rear tyre grooves. Bottom left: Some hope, but also disappointment, for Benetton technical director Mike Gascoyne.

268

## CANADIAN GRAND PRIX MONTREAL
# How much worse could it get

After a relatively good showing at Monaco, no one expected success to continue for Benetton in Montreal – and sure enough it didn't. On fast circuits the Renault engine was just not competitive. It was small, incredibly light (insiders talked of it being several kilos lighter than any competitor's) and mounted very low, but it was still slow and unreliable.

The team was trying to put on a brave face. Pat Symonds, director of engineering, said: "A number of compromises have to be made. It is a very fast circuit with speeds of up to 330kph, but with high fuel consumption and slow chicanes. The circuit suits a very soft tyre and this year, with both Bridgestone and Michelin participating, we can expect both tyre companies to be pushing their compounds to the limit."

The team was destined to be pushed to the limit in a comedy of errors that marked a disastrous qualifying session. Then at the start of the race the cars crashed into each other, one received a stop-go penalty for a jump start and neither driver finished the race. Just how much worse could it get?

FRIDAY PRACTICE The team brought three chassis: B201/06 for Giancarlo Fisichella, B201/05 for Jenson Button and B201/03 as the T-car set up for Button. Fisichella had a good day with 44 laps. He said: "By the end of the session the car felt quite a bit better when we put new tyres on. It is going to be difficult tomorrow, but we were running with a lot of fuel and I am confident we can get a better result than this in qualifying."

Button ran for 26 laps, clocking a best time of 1m 22.766secs for 17th place. He said: "During the second session we had some problems. I had much less straight-line speed than I was supposed to have, but hopefully tomorrow we can improve that. During the second session there wasn't time to work on set-up or balance of the car, so there is a lot still to do. Things have not been fantastic – but tomorrow is another day."

SATURDAY QUALIFYING
Tomorrow was indeed another day. Things got worse. Button completed 12 laps with a best time of 1m 19.033secs, beating only the Minardis. Fisichella also did 12 laps, with his fastest time leaving him 18th.

Technical director Mike Gascoyne said: "For some reason our tyres worked well on Friday but not Saturday. Normally, when it is hot Michelins work very well, but not today. Yesterday I thought we might be 14th and 15th, but we are 18th and 20th. Now it is down to who drops out of the race and whether we can make up a few places. Our objective is to finish. We are half a second off Jaguar. Jenson did a better job today – he was only four-10ths off Giancarlo. It's just frustrating when you don't get it right."

SUNDAY RACE On the first lap the Benettons tangled as Fisichella ran into the back of Button. Fisichella retired with his front right suspension broken, but Button carried on. However, the Brit was judged to have jumped the start and had to come in for a 10-second penalty on lap seven, dropping to the back of the field. His rear wing had been damaged by his team-mate, so on lap nine he was back in for a 20-second pitstop for a tyre change and safety check. He retired on lap 18.

Fisichella said: "On the first lap I was coming out of the hairpin and Enrique Bernoldi, who was ahead, appeared to have some kind of engine problem. He slowed as we accelerated and I couldn't avoid hitting him, which damaged my front wing. Then, as we were coming into the final corner, I touched Jenson's car, which broke my front right suspension and forced me out of the race."

Button said: "My car started to creep at the start, despite the clutch being right at the biting point, and that led to me picking up a stop-go penalty for moving too soon. After the incident with Bernoldi and Giancarlo, which damaged my rear wing, I had to come in for two pitstops, one for the stop-go penalty and one to change the tyres and have a safety check on the car. It wasn't too bad so we decided to carry on and I don't think the lap times were too bad in the circumstances. Unfortunately, the car developed an oil leak, so I had to stop." So that was that: nil points and a lot of work to do at the Silverstone test coming up the following week.

Top and above: Back to reality for Jenson Button. The Brit qualified 20th, ahead of the two Minardis, but his race finished early after collisions with team-mate Fisichella and Enrique Bernoldi on the first lap.
Left and below: Fisichella qualified 18th and retired on the opening lap.
Right: Flavio Briatore saw another poor qualifying performance and the team's worst result since Benetton bought the team in 1985.

# Difficult days

It was more of the same depressing story. Little had changed since the season's first race at Melbourne. An underpowered and unreliable engine and various chassis problems continued to try the whole team. What was different were the constant rumblings that Renault was unhappy with the top pairing of Flavio Briatore and Mike Gascoyne. But both men said they were determined to sort out the problems. A new engine package was due at Magny-Cours and the team was always going to struggle at Nürburgring.

Fisichella's continuing superior form was now causing much discussion about Button's future, with rumours flying that the Brit would not be with the team next year. A senior member said: "This is make or break time for Jenson."

Jenson was more optimistic and had the support of Briatore, who went on record recently backing his driver. Button said: "We have a new engine package coming at the next race and that should make a difference so I am optimistic for the rest of the season." But his managers did not appear, for the first race of the season, and he was particularly glum during TV interviews.

FRIDAY PRACTICE The team brought three chassis: B201/05 for Button, B201/06 for Fisichella and B201/03 as the spare, set up for the Italian. Fisichella completed 34 laps, finishing the day 14th, while Button did 32 laps for 18th. Benetton director of engineering Pat Symonds said: "We lost some time with Giancarlo during the morning part of the session because of a problem with his gearbox's oil system and we need to find a better balance for Jenson and to improve the chassis so that both drivers can attack the kerbs a little more. We suffered a general lack of grip today, but we don't appear to be the only ones. Watching on the TV screens, it looked more like there was a rally going on than a Formula One race."

SATURDAY QUALIFYING It was showdown time as Fisichella qualified 15th and Button could only manage 20th, over a second behind his team-mate. A discussion followed between Button and the engineers on why his car was still a long way off the pace. Button's car had continued, unexplained problems with understeer. He said: "This morning the car didn't feel too bad. There were a few things we had to change – and we thought we had done it,

but when qualifying came we had a bit too much understeer and that stopped me getting a good time. The grip level at the track is quite low, but that's the same for every driver. Unfortunately, this has been one of those days when the car got worse rather than better."

Pat Symonds said: "Giancarlo achieved as much if not more than we expected. The car is evolving very slowly but we can see we are making small steps of improvement and that is important in the overall development of the car. Jenson's qualifying session was disappointing. The team and Jenson are not understanding each other as much as we could. But you don't suddenly forget how to drive and we know how fast Jenson can go and we are still learning about each other. The human interaction between driver and car is important."

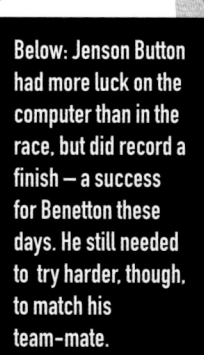

SUNDAY RACE An uneventful race for both Benetton drivers. At the start Fisichella moved up from 15th to 13th and hung onto Villeneuve. He went straight over the chicane and filled his rad ducts with dirt so had to come in for a pitstop on lap 21 which lasted 8.1secs. The second pitstop was on lap 42 and lasted 8.3secs. Both drivers struggled with their rear tyres and as the front tyres still felt pretty good the team only changed the rear tyres on the second pitstop. The team chose the soft Michelin compound which, in hindsight, was not perhaps the best choice. Button managed to make up two places at the start to move to 18th. Like his team-mate he also struggled with rear tyre problems. He first pitted on lap 23, for 8.0secs, and again on lap 43 (7.5secs), and eventually placed 16th, five behind Fisichella.

Pat Symonds said: "The tyre problems caused oversteer so we were losing some performance, but there was little we could do. We just have to work through our current problems and keep to our planned programme of testing and development."

Above, right and below: Giancarlo Fisichella put in a dependable performance, wrapping up qualifying five places ahead of Jenson Button, in 15th. He eventually finished just one place behind Kimi Räikkönen, in 11th.

Below: Jenson Button had more luck on the computer than in the race, but did record a finish – a success for Benetton these days. He still needed to try harder, though, to match his team-mate.

Left and below:
For Benetton,
Magny-Cours was
something of a
disappointment as
Renault's upgraded
engine package failed
to deliver enough
improvement to make
a real difference.

## FRENCH GRAND PRIX MAGNY-COURS
# Upgrading everything

Benetton came to France with its new upgraded engine package. It was an important weekend for the team, on Renault's home turf, and Renault Sport boss Patrick Faure put in an appearance to see how his team was faring.

The answer was, not very well. The team was still struggling with lack of testing due to unavailable engines, which in turn halted vital chassis work. The team was targeting the top 10 in France, but was still a long way off the pace.

FRIDAY PRACTICE Benetton brought along three chassis and a spare, B201/06 for Giancarlo Fisichella, B201/05 for Jenson Button, with B201/03 as the spare set up for Fisichella, and B201/02 as second spare.

The new rear wing and revised engine were not used on Friday. Button completed 34 laps with a best time of 1m 17.172secs to finish 17th and Fisichella completed 35 laps with a best of 1m 17.566secs to lurk in 20th place.

Both drivers struggled as they worked on race set-up. Fisichella said: "I have not had a fantastic day. On the positive side we did some work with the tyres and made some improvements. But at the end of the session, the car began to oversteer a lot." Benetton director of engineering Pat Symonds said: "Both drivers felt the car was quite nervous in the high-speed corners and that we needed to improve our exit speed in slow-speed corners. Other than that, it has been a straightforward, productive day's work."

SATURDAY QUALIFYING The long-awaited engine upgrade did not succeed in propelling the team into the top 10, although both drivers said that the new aerodynamic package and the engine upgrade both generated improvements. In the morning practice session Giancarlo Fisichella completed 28 laps to finish 18th;

Button 25 laps to finish 19th. Qualifying did not go as well as expected, Fisichella achieving 16th place with a time of 1m 15.220secs, more than two seconds off pole man Ralf Schumacher. Button was in 17th place with a best time of 1m 15.420secs, and said later: "My first run was spoiled because Eddie Irvine spun off in front of me. My second run was better, but I'm afraid I mucked up the next two because I was supposed to adjust the differential setting after turn 2."

Technical director Mike Gascoyne said: "This morning during the free practice session we introduced a new aerodynamic package and it took us a bit of time to find a reasonable balance. The sector one times show we still have to do a bit of fine tuning in the high-speed corners, but overall this has been a small step forward that, hopefully, marks the beginning of many steps forward. Both drivers did a good job today, especially Jenson who matched his team-mate's pace."

SUNDAY RACE Due to Häkkinen's non-start on the formation lap, and Pedro de la Rosa's electronic problem, both Benettons moved up two places on the grid to 14th and 15th.

Fisichella's race did not have a good start as he touched Jos Verstappen's Arrows on the first lap. He made his first pitstop on lap 20 in 7.4secs when the team changed the rear tyres. By lap 26, Fisichella was up to 13th. He made his second pitstop on lap 44 and the team changed the rear tyres. Unfortunately, both Benettons went into the pits at the same time with Button suffering the most. Fisichella finished 11th.

Button had a lot of wheelspin at the start but got past his team-mate and also Jean Alesi at the hairpin. He pitted for the first time on lap 19 and changed all the tyres in 9.5secs. He had engine problems before his second stop, got into the pits on lap 44 and found Fisichella occupying that all-important place in front of the tyres and fuel rig. But as Button had a fuel pressure problem he had to come in.

Button spun on lap 61 but remained in 12th place before retiring on lap 69 with a mechanical problem. He was classified 16th.

Mike Gascoyne said: "We qualified lower than expected, dropped a couple of places at the start, and spent the race trying to overtake drivers we should have been in front of. The middle of the race, when we were running 10th and 12th, was the best part of the race. Things should be a lot better at Silverstone."

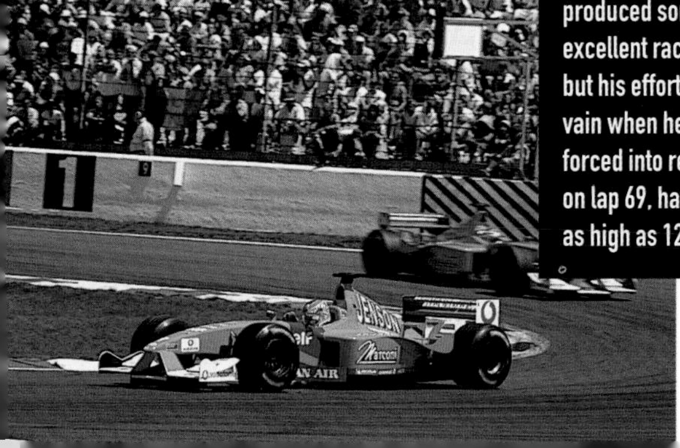

Benetton
Formula 1
RACING TEAM

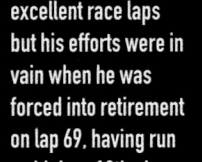

Above and left:
Jenson Button
produced some
excellent race laps
but his efforts were in
vain when he was
forced into retirement
on lap 69, having run
as high as 12th place.

271

## BRITISH GRAND PRIX SILVERSTONE
# A step forward, a step back

Renault Sport's engine guru, Jean-Jacques His, was at Silverstone; but in spite of the proclamations that it would be all right on the night, the performance of the car was still way off the pace. The aerodynamic and engine upgrades effected in France made little difference to the car, and morale was low.

It was Jenson Button's home race and he could only think about the difference a year makes: at last year's British Grand Prix he had been a talented rookie Formula One driver with BMW Williams, with a nation's expectations on his shoulders and the object of fan hysteria. This year it was very different. However Button was cheered by the fact he finally had power-steering; with it he was able to out-qualify Giancarlo Fisichella for only the second time this year.

FRIDAY PRACTICE Benetton brought B201/06 for Fisichella, B201/05 for Button and B201/03 as the spare, set up for Button. B201/02 was also in reserve.

Fisichella had an awful day, completing 26 laps with a best time of only 1m 26.730secs to finish in 21st place. Button did 35 laps with a best of 1m 25.673secs for 19th place. Fisichella needed an engine change and ended up with one of the older spec units.

The Michelins were struggling in the cool, rainy weather and looked uncompetitive against the Bridgestones.
Button said: "The car feels absolutely fine in slow corners but we could do with more grip in the faster stuff – even on new tyres." Power-steering and launch control were both being used for the first time.

SATURDAY QUALIFYING The morning practice was better for Fisichella, who completed 19 laps with a best of 1m 35.624secs – 15th fastest. Button did 23 laps with a best of 1m 35.974secs for 17th. The Brit finally out-qualified his team-mate – even if it was by only just over a 10th of a second and one place. He was to line up 18th with a best time of 1m 24.123secs; Fisichella's best was a 1m 24.275secs for 19th.

Button said: "We switched tyre compounds this morning,

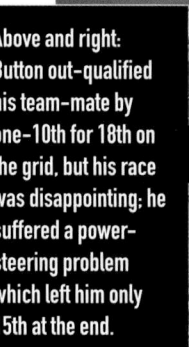

which improved the car considerably, but we were unable to put a time together in the end. During my first run I had understeer in high-speed corners and we need to look hard to identify why. We have to look to make improvements."

SUNDAY RACE The drivers swapped positions during warm-up, but with Fisichella 18th and Button 19th it was hardly a good start to the day.

Fisichella made up two places at the start. On lap four he left the track, bounced over a sandtrap and rejoined the race last behind Fernando Alonso. He was on a two-stop strategy, making his first pitstop on lap 24 and his second on lap 42. His second left him ahead of Button, and he finished 13th.

Button moved from 18th to 13th on the first lap and held this slot until he made his first pitstop on lap 22. He then fell back to 17th. By lap 25 he was back up to 14th, in front of Fisichella, but he lost out on his second stop on lap 39 and fell behind his team-mate to finish 15th. He had a problem with his power-steering, which had shut down on lap 15. At least both cars finished.

After the race, Pat Symonds said: "We found the Michelin tyres were not as competitive this weekend and we suffered from that. We found the hard compound was better suited to the car on Friday but we couldn't check this on Saturday due to the rain. We chose the hard tyre and I think it was the wrong choice. Benetton and Williams chose the hard tyre while Jaguar and Prost chose the soft tyre and in comparison, Jaguar and Prost's performance was better than ours and Williams'. The one good point was the launch control: both cars made stunning starts but were blocked by cars in front."

**Above and right: Button out-qualified his team-mate by one-10th for 18th on the grid, but his race was disappointing; he suffered a power-steering problem which left him only 15th at the end.**

**Above and right: Giancarlo Fisichella had a trip through the sand trap but struggled on to 13th. Left: For Jenson Button, the 2001 British GP was a stark contrast to 2000.**

## GERMAN GRAND PRIX HOCKENHEIM

# An unexpected relief

Benetton Renault arrived at Hockenheim with nothing to report. The much lauded engine and aero-package for Magny-Cours and Silverstone had not made a notable difference and the general feeling among the team was that 2001 was over. But the weekend was to bring unexpected fresh air.

Paddock gossip had both Benetton drivers Giancarlo Fisichella and Jenson Button moving to Jordan in a switch with Jarno Trulli. It was all speculative of course but nonetheless avidly discussed.

FRIDAY PRACTICE Benetton Renault brought four chassis: B201/06 for Fisichella, B201/05 for Button, B201/03 as the spare car set up for Button, and B201/02 as the spare tub.

The team made mild aerodynamic and mechanical changes and Fisichella completed 33 laps with a best time of 1m 43.014secs for 11th place. Button completed 30 laps with a best time of 1m 43.496secs to finish 15th.

Fisichella said: "It was quite a good day and we are pleased with the way things have gone. We had a small gearbox problem during the first session, but the car has been well balanced from the start and I think we can be consistently quick here."

Button said: "The biggest problem this morning was oversteer. I was quite a long way off Giancarlo but we were running different kinds of tyres. Generally the car has worked well, and Michelin has come up with a very effective tyre." It was the tyres that made the difference – not the car or engine.

SATURDAY QUALIFYING In the morning Fisichella encountered both engine and fuel pressure problems and had to have an engine change. Meanwhile Button's car had to undergo a gearbox change. Fisichella completed just five laps and finished in 20th place, while Button completed 10 laps to finish 16th. Qualifying did not hold out the great promise evident in Friday's performance. Fisichella completed all 12 laps with a best time of 1m 41.299secs to finish 17th. Button managed 10 laps with a best time of 1m 41.438secs for 18th.

Button said: "Everything looked so much better yesterday. I stopped on my first lap this morning with gearbox trouble and that set the scene for a tough day."

Fisichella said: "I had an engine change after this morning's practice and had to go straight into qualifying with a race engine. On my fourth and final qualifying lap I was a couple of 10ths up, but one of the Saubers was going slowly and held me up."

SUNDAY RACE Fisichella moved up two places at the start from 17th to 15th but dropped back to 16th when he was overtaken by Enrique Bernoldi. Then he moved progressively up the field, passing Bernoldi, Jean Alesi and his team-mate to be in the points as early as lap 24. After their pitstops Fisichella was in fourth, which he held for the rest of the race. He made his one and only pitstop on lap 26 in 9.9 seconds. Near the end of the race he nearly gave his team a heart-attack as he ran wide and lost a bit of time, but recovered to grab a sensational three points for fourth place.

Button's race was no less impressive. Starting in 18th he moved up five slots to 13th. He slipped back briefly to 14th before overtaking Bernoldi and then his team-mate to move into seventh before his pitstop on lap 24, which he completed in 11.2 seconds. He overtook Alesi and also Jos Verstappen when the latter driver was in for his pitstop to achieve fifth place, which he retained to the finish.

Button said: "We genuinely had good pace. This is the biggest boost the team has had all year. I had one slight problem – I pulled my water bottle tube out of my mouth, so it was spraying all over my face whenever I braked. It wasn't an easy race, especially with Alesi right behind, but it was good fun."

Fisichella added: "The whole result is a great one for the team and I would like to thank everyone who has helped to make it possible, especially Michelin, whose tyres were excellent."

Astonishingly Benetton Renault ended the day ahead of Jaguar in the constructors' table. That was bad news for Jaguar, astonishing news for Benetton. Could a podium now be in sight before the end of the season? Maybe.

**Above, left and below:** Giancarlo Fisichella again showed his Hockenheim form, making the most of Michelin's excellent tyres and a one-stop tyre strategy, coming home in fourth place for Benetton.

**Left: Button finally** had things work for him and backed up Fisichella's fourth place with a fine run for fifth. **Below:** Button leads Fernando Alonso in practice. **Right:** Flavio Briatore left Hockenheim happier.

Benetton
Formula 1
RACING TEAM

## HUNGARIAN GRAND PRIX HUNGARORING
# Start of something better

The Benetton Renault team was in better spirits – the engine had developed greater power and the team had moved up to eighth best from 10th. It now had the legs of Minardi, Prost and Arrows, and was hard on the heels of Jaguar, which it had actually overtaken in the constructors' championship, so the season was not the write-off it once looked like. Jarno Trulli and Jenson Button had been named as the driver line-up for 2002 and the team was more settled. Even team principal Flavio Briatore, the man with the longest face in the paddock for much of 2001, was looking brighter. The Benettons had gone well on the tighter tracks in 2001 so had high hopes for Hungary, and to some extent those hopes were justified.

FRIDAY PRACTICE Benetton Renault brought three chassis to the race – B201/06 for Giancarlo Fisichella, B201/05 for Button and B201/03 as the spare, set up for Fisichella.

Fisichella recorded a best of 1m 17.896secs, completing 33 laps and finishing in seventh, a truly remarkable feat given that the usual Benetton position in 2001 had been between 15th and 19th place. The cars had a new front wing, bargeboards, undertray and diffuser.

This revival was not reflected in Button's performance as he completed 31 laps with a best time of 1m 19.263secs to finish in 17th, 10 slots below his team-mate and one-and-a-half seconds off his pace. He was just a few places better than normal.

SATURDAY QUALIFYING At this stage things still looked good, with Fisichella 10th in free practice and Button 13th, despite the fact that Button suffered no fewer than two engine failures during the morning session.

In qualifying it was down the snakes rather than up the ladders as Button took the spare car, which had poor balance and grip as well as an older specification engine. It guaranteed that the session, which had held so much promise, was a waste of time and he qualified in 17th place on 1m 17.535secs. Once again he had the worse of the luck shared out to the two Benettons.

Fisichella qualified 15th with a 1m

16.632secs. It was all disappointing and the team appeared to have been knocked off its stride by the engine failures, indicating that increased horsepower had been gained at the expense of reliability.

Benetton technical director Mike Gascoyne said: "We certainly felt we could have qualified in the top 10 – especially as the car had been performing well in every previous session. Then Jenson had two engine failures. At the last race we scored points from worse grid positions so we have to look for a strong race performance tomorrow."

That the new engine was better was indicated by the speed traps and eighth fastest position.

SUNDAY RACE Fisichella warmed up in 15th place and Button last in 22nd. It was a sign of what was to come. Button said: "This is going to be one tough race." And it certainly was. He had to serve a 10-second stop-go penalty for a jump start. He made his first pitstop on lap 28 in 7.1secs. Out on the second stint the car was working well on new tyres, and he set his fastest lap and was holding his own in 17th place when he made a mistake and spun out of the race on lap 35.

Fisichella was in 14th place when he made his first pitstop on lap 22 in 6.4secs. This quick stop enabled him to move past Jaguar's Pedro de la Rosa and climb to 13th. Fisichella made his second pitstop on lap 45 in 9.4 seconds. After advancing to 12th and looking good for a race finish, he had engine problems and was obliged to retire on lap 70.

Nil points, no finishes and back to the drawing-board again.

Top: Jenson Button's race ended when he made a mistake with a spin as he exited the last corner.
Below right: Giancarlo Fisichella's disappointment was softened by the knowledge of a Jordan contract in his pocket.

Right: Fisichella's race ended with seven laps to go when the Renault engine blew, after modified pit strategy had moved him ahead of de la Rosa.
Below: Button was impatient at the start and copped a 10 second stop-go penalty which delayed him.

Left: Giancarlo Fisichella enjoys his return to the podium after a strong race. The Italian's Benetton Renault gave Rubens Barrichello, David Coulthard and Mika Häkkinen a lot to think about with its speed until it was slowed by loss of oil near the end of the race.

Left: It had been a long time since Flavio Briatore, Giancarlo Fisichella and Patrick Faure had cause to smile. Fisichella was rewarded with a fine third place for his efforts, while team-mate Jenson Button crashed at the Bus Stop in ninth (below).

## BELGIAN GRAND PRIX SPA-FRANCORCHAMPS

# The hoped-for miracle happens

What had looked like a disaster was turning into something quite hopeful as Benetton found itself seventh in the constructors' championship with 10 points – well ahead of Jaguar, Prost, Arrows and Minardi, and only six points behind BAR and Jordan. It could even displace them for fifth if its current form could be sustained.

Benetton undertook an extensive test programme at Barcelona, fine-tuning the new aerodynamic package that was introduced at Budapest. It clearly had some effect and restored Benetton to mid-grid.

At Spa, Giancarlo Fisichella found the right balance and set-up while Jenson Button found the car an uphill struggle. But within Benetton it was almost acknowledged that Fisichella was treated like the favoured son, while Button had to battle for what he wanted.

FRIDAY PRACTICE Benetton brought three cars and a spare chassis. B201/06 was Fisichella's, B201/05 Button's, B201/03 was the spare car set up for Button; B201/01 was the spare chassis.

The revised aerodynamics proved to be a winner. Fisichella posted a best time of 1m 50.192secs and was fourth fastest, just behind Rubens Barrichello's Ferrari and in front of both McLarens and both Williams.

For Button it was a different tale. His best time of 1m 51.673secs left him in 10th place after an engine problem cut short his time on the track.

That heralded a nightmare weekend for him as he languished behind his team-mate. As Benetton director of engineering Pat Symonds said: "Jenson got the short straw this weekend. He lost an engine so his running time was limited."

SATURDAY QUALIFYING Fisichella again figured among the leaders in the second practice session. He was sixth after completing 12 laps, with a best time of 1m 49.511secs. Button was ninth, completing 12 laps with a best time of 1m 50.130secs. Qualifying was chaotic with the track drying out. Fisichella qualified in eighth place with 1m 57.668secs. Button just got it wrong. The team tried to persuade him to put on dry tyres but he was adamant that the conditions weren't suitable, and as it was his call the team had no choice but to abide by that decision. Button ended up in 15th place with a best time of 1m 59.587secs.

Benetton technical director Mike Gascoyne said: "We're looking for a top six finish tomorrow. Weather conditions are forecast to be changeable, but we are confident with both wet and dry set-ups."

SUNDAY RACE Both drivers had great first starts, Fisichella moving up to sixth place and Button into eighth, although he had dropped back to 10th by the time the race was stopped.

At the restart Fisichella set off like a rocket, slipping into second place behind Schumacher. Button jumped into fifth place behind the McLaren of Häkkinen.

Pat Symonds commented: "It was great to see our launch control system working so well. We were the last to use it but that was because we made sure that it was working perfectly before using it on the cars."

Despite intense pressure from Barrichello and Coulthard, Fisichella hung onto second, and the new aerodynamics continued to work well in race trim.

On lap 10 Button made his first pitstop. Fisichella came in one lap later, changing his rear tyres only.

Button was in ninth position when he clipped a bollard at the Bus Stop, broke the front wing and hit the wall.

Fisichella made his second stop on lap 23, once again keeping his front tyres as the car was "better balanced that way". He held off Coulthard until lap 27, when the Scot slipped by to take second place, and managed to hang on to finish in third place ahead of Häkkinen.

A delighted Fisichella offered a highly upbeat verdict: "This was a brilliant result. Our new aerodynamic package has made the car much more competitive. It is easier to drive, easier to set up and it has much more grip than before.

"We are expecting a new engine development at Monza and hopefully that will take us forward."

275

# ITALIAN GRAND PRIX MONZA
# Refreshed and revitalised

The Benetton Renault team was reborn. No longer the runt of the litter of 11 Grand Prix teams, it was now running up with Jaguar. Mike Gascoyne and his team tested a new aerodynamic low-downforce package for Monza and it worked.

The only cloud concerned drivers. It lost the services of Giancarlo Fisichella for 2001 and got Jarno Trulli. That now looked a poor decision as Fisichella shined. There continued to be wars between Jenson Button and team principal Flavio Briatore. The two men do not gel but appeared stuck with each other for the 2002 season.

FRIDAY PRACTICE Benetton Renault brought chassis B201/06 for Fisichella, B201/05 for Button, B201/03 as the spare car set up for Fisichella, and B201/01 as the spare tub. Benetton ran a new front wing on both cars as part of its Monza aero package.

Button had one of his best Friday practice sessions, finishing sixth after the first session with 1m 26.197secs, just over 0.6secs slower than fastest man Michael Schumacher. Fisichella languished in 12th place with a best of 1m 27.276secs.

The second practice session changed things. Button ended 13th with 1m 26.197secs; Fisichella placed 11th with a 1m 25.911secs. Button said: "It was one of the best Fridays I have had this season."

SATURDAY QUALIFYING Fisichella continued to outdo Button, finishing in 12th position with his team-mate in 15th.

"I hope to get in the top seven," Fisichella said after practice. But his qualifying session was a nightmare. First his race car suffered a hydraulics failure after four laps, then the spare care suffered an engine problem. So he completed just nine laps with a best time of 1m 24.090secs for 14th on the grid. Button completed all 12 qualifying laps, clocking a best time of 1m 23.892secs for 11th. He said: "Everything's going my way for once this weekend. It's the best qualifying position of the year for me." Technical director Mike Gascoyne said: "Both drivers did an excellent job today and, if the team had handled it better, I am sure we could have got both cars in the top 10."

SUNDAY RACE Following Button's disastrous experience in Spa when the tyres were not scrubbed, both drivers spent most of the warm-up session scrubbing their tyres. Fisichella complained of poor grip and understeer. Button said he had a touch of high-speed understeer. Fisichella was 17th in warm-up, Button 18th.

Fisichella had a miserable start. A leaking fuel filler was discovered while his car was being prepared on the grid so he had to start from the pitlane in the spare car, which had been set up for Button due to his better qualifying position. Fisichella started immediately behind Heidfeld's Sauber, which had also been sent to the pits.

Fisichella lost traction control on lap one, but moved up to 13th position by lap 20. He made his only pitstop on lap 30 in ninth position, having overtaken Heidfeld, rejoining in 11th. He overtook Heidfeld again to finish in 10th.

After storming to sixth place from the start, Button squandered it by punting Trulli out of the race and losing his front wing when he found a dirty, oily track on the first corner and couldn't stop before sliding into the Italian. He made a pitstop and the team changed his nose/front wing. But Button's engine blew on the fifth lap, ending his race.

Mike Gascoyne said: "We chose the softest option tyres and were happy with the Michelin tyres. We should have got into the top eight but various problems prevented that. It is of course very frustrating but we are still improving and looking to improve our competitiveness in the last two races. We want to beat Jaguar in the constructors' championship and have a go at Jordan and BAR for fifth position." Bold talk, which would have been risible even a month ago. Now it is real.

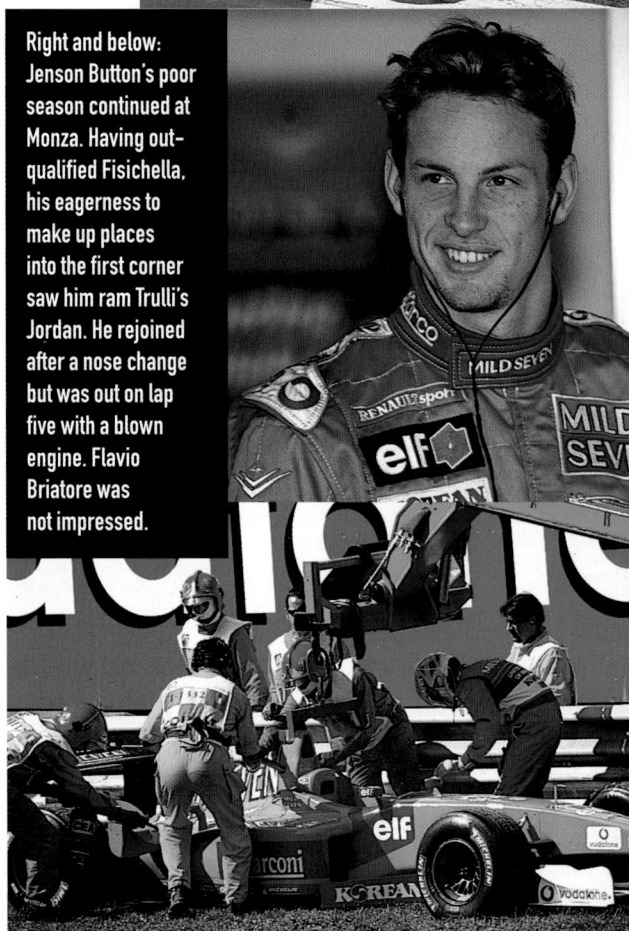

276

## UNITED STATES GRAND PRIX INDIANAPOLIS
# New spirit lifts hopes

Recent chassis and engine improvements had revived Benetton Renault to the point of respectability. It put daylight between itself and Prost, Arrows and Minardi, teams which it could barely match at the start of the season.

However, Benetton's engineering supremo Pat Symonds was more concerned with tyres. "Tyre choice will be important. Last year harder tyres were chosen, as teams were concerned about the loads that would be imposed on the cars by the high speed banking, but in fact loads were no higher than at any other circuit. We expect tyre companies to take a more aggressive attitude with softer, and hence quicker compounds. The circuit can be hard on engines – between the last and first corners the cars are on full throttle for 24 seconds, which is the longest single period experienced at Grand Prix tracks."

The rift between team principal Flavio Briatore and number two driver Jenson Button continued. Apparently Briatore had signed Button to a two-year pay-and-play deal which the chief couldn't get out of. He was therefore shopping him around, but Button was having none of it.

FRIDAY PRACTICE Benetton brought three cars: B201/06 for Giancarlo Fisichella; B201/05 and the spare B201/03 for Button.

In the morning session Fisichella clocked the fourth fastest time and was the last car in the 14-second bracket with a 1m 14.930secs. He reported good set-up and balance. Button was ninth fastest in 1m 15.537secs, still a fine show.

The afternoon proved to be less successful. Fisichella lost control of his car at Turn 6 and went into the gravel, ending up in 17th place overall with a best of 1m 14.911secs over 21 laps, just over one-and-a-half seconds behind fastest man Mika Häkkinen. Button was 13th with a 1m 14.186secs over 47 laps.

Michelin's new construction of tyre worked well with the revised traction control, which had caused problems for the team at the previous race.

SATURDAY QUALIFYING Fisichella was seventh fastest in the second practice session with 1m 12.672secs, just six-10ths of a second behind the fastest driver round the circuit, Michael Schumacher. Button was two places behind in ninth, clocking a best of 1m 12.955secs.

Both drivers expected to make the top 10 in qualifying, but it wasn't to be. Fisichella caught a yellow flag on his last run and also lost part of the engine cover, which flew off on the main straight. It left him in 12th on the grid in 1m 12.942secs. But Button had a year-best qualifying performance: 10th in 1m 12.805secs. He was third through the qualifying speed trap with 332.9kph; Fisichella managed seventh with 328.9kph.

SUNDAY RACE Fisichella made up a couple of places at the start of the race, moving from 12th position to 10th, with Button moving from 10th to 11th. Button then made progress in the early stages, overtaking his team-mate to move from 11th to ninth, then overtaking Trulli to move into eighth place. On lap nine Button was overtaken by Trulli and moved back to ninth place. As the rear tyres started to go on both cars they became quite difficult to drive and Button slipped back to 10th place with Fisichella in 11th.

Button made his one and only pitstop on lap 35 in 12.0secs, stopping a little earlier than scheduled because traffic was quite heavy and he was trying to gain track position for later in the race. Even though he locked his brakes when he came into the pits, the mechanics got him out without losing time.

Fisichella made his only pitstop on lap 41 in 10.0secs. It was then an uneventful race for both drivers: Fisichella finished eighth and Button ninth due to retirements.

Pat Symonds said: "I think the soft tyres were the right decision but they behaved in a manner we didn't expect. The fronts didn't grain as they usually do and the rears blistered. We go to Suzuka with the hope of achieving sixth place in the constructors' championship and overtaking BAR. It would be nice if Giancarlo could finish in the top 10 in the drivers' championship." Such talk would have been impossible a month previously.

Left: Reliable cars now give pitstop crews plenty of work. Below: Jenson Button put in his year's best performance to out-qualify, and for a while out-race, his team-mate Giancarlo Fisichella, who finished eighth with Button ninth.

Above: Fisichella remains focused as Button and Montoya swap pleasantries. Below left: Fisichella briefly leads an on-form Eddie Irvine. Rear tyre blistering hindered the Benettons' race.

Benetton Formula 1 RACING TEAM

277

## JAPANESE GRAND PRIX SUZUKA
# Astonishing turnaround

Benetton Renault arrived in Japan on a high, having regained the dignity lost earlier in the year. Its revival was largely down to an extremely sophisticated traction control system, a fact acknowledged by the other teams. Allied to other improvements, it had fully restored the team's confidence – to the extent that development for 2002 was in full swing during the practice sessions. Giancarlo Fisichella qualified with a special engine not used for the race.

The change since Italy had been astounding, as Fisichella made plain by qualifying sixth. The second half of the season proved him to be a very good driver, after one-and-a-half seasons during which poor equipment had masked his skill. Renault was beginning to regret his departure to Jordan, which was delighted at striking the deal.

Jenson Button also improved in the latter part of the season, matching his teammate's move up the grid in ratio terms.

Japan meant curtains for the Benetton team, which had been a Formula One entrant since 1986, a total of 16 years.

FRIDAY PRACTICE Benetton brought three chassis to the race and a spare tub: B201/06 for Fisichella; B201/05 for Button, who was also allotted the spare B201/03; and B201/01 as the spare tub.

It was a disappointing day, with both drivers encountering problems in the second session – Fisichella suffering an engine failure and Button a fuel leak. In the two sessions Fisichella completed 24 laps for a best of 1m 38.398secs to finish 16th. Button completed 34 laps for a best of 1m 37.645secs to finish 12th.

Fisichella said: "The chassis was a little bit nervous at first, but we managed to improve it and find a good balance. I had just gone out on my second set of tyres when the engine problem occurred and the session was over for me."

Jenson Button said: "We have made some major improvements with the brakes. This morning my car had a bit of understeer, but we sorted that out and afterwards the set-up was good."

SATURDAY QUALIFYING Button completed 21 laps for a best time of 1m 34.735secs, and looked like he might qualify in the top six. Fisichella did 32 laps with a best time of 1m 36.114secs to finish in 16th, having spent the morning scrubbing the tyres.

In the afternoon Fisichella qualified sixth with a best time of 1m 33.830secs, his best of the season but still 1.4 seconds off the pace of pole man Michael Schumacher. Button qualified ninth with 1m 34.375secs. He had first-sector problems with understeer and was very patchy through the sectors, whereas team-mate Fisichella was totally consistent through the sectors.

SUNDAY RACE In warm-up, tyre-scrubbing was both drivers' priority. Fisichella tried the spare car but encountered understeer – a difficulty mirrored by Button, who had too much understeer with his race car. Both were using standard spec engines.

Fisichella overtook Häkkinen at the start to move from sixth to fifth place. But he lost the advantage with a half-spin on lap three, falling to 12th. He moved back up to ninth by lap 11, passing Eddie Irvine, who had slowed to avoid the wreckage of the Räikkönen-Alesi accident. On lap 11 Fisichella overtook his team-mate to claim eighth.

Button moved from ninth to eighth in the opening laps. He came in for his first pitstop on lap 16, which he completed in 8.6 seconds. Fisichella pitted on lap 20 in 10.7 seconds. He made his second pitstop on lap 35 in 9.1 seconds and was in seventh place with a points finish in sight when he lost fourth gear and on lap 46 had to retire from his last race for the team.

Button was in seventh place by lap 36 and stayed there until his second pitstop on lap 38. When Fisichella retired Button took seventh again, which is where he finished. He summed it up: "Our target for this race was to make sure we kept seventh place in the constructors' championship, which we managed to do. Only this year's top three teams managed to beat us today, which was satisfying."

Above and right: Jenson Button showed some of his 2000 form with a clean run to seventh, after team-mate Giancarlo Fisichella retired from his last race with the team.

Image is everything

global

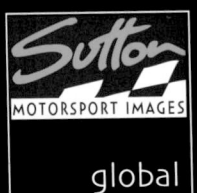

Team Review     Race by Race

# JAGUAR

2001

## Contents

| | | | | | | |
|---|---|---|---|---|---|---|
| Team Review | – | The season | p282 | European Grand Prix | – Nürburgring | p296 |
| Australian Grand Prix | – | Melbourne | p288 | French Grand Prix | – Magny-Cours | p297 |
| Malaysian Grand Prix | – | Sepang | p289 | British Grand Prix | – Silverstone | p298 |
| Brazilian Grand Prix | – | Interlagos | p290 | German Grand Prix | – Hockenheim | p299 |
| San Marino Grand Prix | – | Imola | p291 | Hungarian Grand Prix | – Hungaroring | p300 |
| Spanish Grand Prix | – | Barcelona | p292 | Belgian Grand Prix | – Spa-Francorchamps | p301 |
| Austrian Grand Prix | – | A1 Ring | p293 | Italian Grand Prix | – Monza | p302 |
| Monaco Grand Prix | – | Monte Carlo | p294 | USA Grand Prix | – Indianapolis | p303 |
| Canadian Grand Prix | – | Montreal | p295 | Japanese Grand Prix | – Suzuka | p304 |

Niki Lauda

Pedro de la Rosa

Luciano Burti

Eddie Irvine

# JAGUAR
### R A C I N G

# Leaping cat falls short

Jaguar Racing looked like a house approaching order at the start of 2001 after a wasted 2000 season. American legend Bobby Rahal had replaced Neil Ressler as team principal and was making friends and getting his arms around some obvious problems. But even insiders couldn't fathom whether he was solving the problems or becoming part of the problem.

Eddie Irvine and young Luciano Burti were set to drive a car that could not be worse than the 2000 offering. Or so they thought. Sacked technical director Gary Anderson had bungled in 2000 when he introduced a single-oiling system for engine and gearbox. Adopting an unproven concept, with no fallback plan, set Jaguar back months when the gearbox kept on eating cogs.

Anderson may have gone but his legacy remained, with the car he designed jointly with John Russell – designated R2 – being described as 'conservative' as a reaction to the unconservative R1.

Bobby Rahal consistently described a target of midfield respectability for 2001.

Anderson's replacement was American Steve Nichols, the man responsible for the McLaren MP4/4, the most successful Grand Prix car of all time. He would later be joined by champ car aerodynamicist Mark Handford, a Rahal import who was a big success. But he was not a magician and Handford was handicapped by the lack of a windtunnel, and Jaguar initially only had access to a less-than-perfect one in California. With some teams spending 24 hours a day in two windtunnels, a few hours a day in one 5,000 miles away was barely credible.

Things had not improved by the time the season began.

Rahal started in December 2000 and looked like he was making progress. But Wolfgang Reitzle, the man at the top, didn't care for his style and as insurance recruited Niki Lauda as overall boss.

Lauda didn't like Burti and recruited Pedro de la Rosa as insur-ance. Jaguar had solved its original problem, but here it was again: there was one boss too many. Burti was one of the final remnants of the Jackie Stewart regime.

In his bid to rebuild, Rahal attempted to lure Adrian Newey from McLaren to effectively replace Steve Nichols as technical director. This move descended into farce when both Jaguar and McLaren announced Newey had signed contracts with them. The evidence suggested he had signed for Jaguar, before going back on his word after blandishments from Ron Dennis.

Then Rahal decided Irvine's number was up and, without Lauda's knowledge, offered Jordan $5 million to take him in a swap for Heinz-Harald Frentzen. Instead, Irvine and Lauda sacked him mid-season.

The sacking of Rahal, together with the Adrian Newey débâcle and the attempted sale of Irvine, were the three biggest news stories of the year and Rahal was at the centre of all three. He exercised an astonishing impact on Formula One during his eight-month tenure.

With Rahal gone, it became Lauda's show. Things got worse, not better, as Jaguar was overtaken in the constructors' championship by Benetton, the really slow team of 2001.

Lauda hunkered down, securing a windtunnel by spending $30 million with Tom Walkinshaw to buy the DERA facility in Bedford and scrapping a move to a new HQ. It made perfect sense: after all, things often get worse before they get better.

## The Jaguar R2 car

AGAINST the backdrop of cloak-and-dagger intrigue, Jaguar's car paled into insignificance. After a rash of embarrassing failures in 2000, the ambition for 2001 was reliability. The sight of the leaping cat crawling to a smoking halt did nothing for Jaguar's image. ▷

Luciano Burti

The Cosworth CR3 engine and new gearbox had been running since before Christmas, and were based on the 2000 engine plus a much-revised double-oiling system, lighter and smaller. Trevor Crisp had opted for a safe design, and both the engine and gearbox were running in the back of a modified R1 in the winter. Following the Ferrari trend of 1999, of placing the exhaust exits atop the car, Jaguar also borrowed heavily from other designs, including the Minardi-pioneered semi-horizontal brake callipers for lower weight. But simple engineering would constantly bridle the search for pace.

The team also had to get used to another new element: Michelin. This was the French manufacturer's first year back in the sport and Jaguar was amongst the first to sign up. Sadly for the team, BMW Williams also put pen to paper and, though Michelin competition boss Pierre Dupasquier denied it, it was hard to imagine that the company did not give some preference to the team that was winning races, rather than those towards the rear. Jaguar struggled to find tyre balance on most circuits this season, and its own aerodynamic problems on high-downforce tracks only served to accentuate the problem.

Chassis R2-04 was Irvine's favoured weapon throughout the season. He started the year in the car and drove it until the Belgian Grand Prix, when he switched to the newer R2-06. The Ulsterman ran one race in the new car before switching to R2-05 in Italy, and then reverting to his preferred R2-04 for the final two races of the year. Burti started the year in R2-03, and de la Rosa inherited the chassis when he took over from Burti. He qualified in the spare car (R2-05) in Spain, after power-steering failure put him in the wall during Saturday's practice, but reverted to his race car as soon as possible. De la Rosa took R2-06 in Monaco, as R2-03 was pen-

sioned off, and kept that until Hungary, when he switched to R2-07, his steed for the rest of the year.

Despite the aim of reliability and little else, the team arguably failed to achieve it. For a top team, Jaguar's level of reliability was inexcusable. It took the wooden spoon in 2001, with a score of only 67.5 per cent.

The engine suffered just four real failures, but pulling the cars out of the race before the white smoke erupted was relatively common in the first half of the season. Fuel pick-up problems in Australia, and overheating after a first-corner off in Malaysia sent debris into the sidepods, combined with two genuine failures in San Marino and Spain to deny Irvine a finish in the first five races. A further engine failure in France; a terminal misfire in Germany after 16 laps when the team first tried a new engine; and a further unspecified engine problem after 14 laps in Italy meant Irvine suffered more than his fair share of engine-related retirements.

Burti retired with a water leak in Brazil, although he finished his other three races with the team despite losing half his gears in San Marino. De la Rosa retired with transmission failure in Austria, hydraulics failure in Monaco and an oil leak in Suzuka. In addition, Irvine and de la Rosa were forced to retire from one race each due to problems with the Intertechnic fuel rigs.

Irvine ran for 658 of a possible 1,065 race laps during the year, achieving 61.8 per cent reliability. Of a possible 819 race laps de la Rosa ran for 579, scoring 70.7 per cent reliability. Burti ran for 201 out of 246 possible race laps, making him Jaguar's most reliable driver (81.7 per cent).

Apart from an end-of-season blip at Suzuka, the team improved reliability during the season but still fell out of races 19 times. Reliability in the absence of speed is not what Formula One is about,

John Russell

Mark Handford

Steve Nichols

though. Two significant power hikes – at Melbourne and Hockenheim – undoubtedly gained the team significant horsepower. When the team introduced the second step, Irvine's race ended early with a misfire, however, proving the new engine still needed work.

While the engine proved strong enough mid-season to have Arrows and Minardi squabbling over customer supply, the R2's aerodynamics were truly awful. For 'conservative' read slow, although Russell and Handford made the best of a bad job with incremental improvements throughout the year and a major step in Monaco. The drivers, whoever they were at the time, told the same story: the car felt very stable on slow circuits but the speed was just not there. In his inimitable style, Lauda said: "I believe them. I have driven shit cars that felt well balanced too."

The R2 was exposed time and again when it mattered most – in qualifying. Simply put, it did not work in qualifying trim, especially on low-downforce circuits. Irvine consistently placed outside the top 10. After qualifying 12th or 13th in his first few outings, he could only say: "I've qualified in almost the same place for all the races so far this season and, quite simply put, this is where we are

right now as a team." He was right: 13th place would be his home on the grid for much of 2001.

Jaguar was also plagued in 2001 by an unusual problem; the power-steering system didn't work. Increasing kickback towards the end of the steering wheel's travel gave both drivers major headaches and de la Rosa suffered two failures (at Monaco and Barcelona), which both sent him into the wall.

## Technical developments

JAGUAR

BARCELONA heralded Jaguar's first real cause for celebration, though both drivers failed to finish. The team was delighted with the faultless running of the electronic driver aids – including traction and launch control – that had reappeared in Formula One for the first time since 1993, and claimed a victory for the Premier Performance Division's working method. New chief race engineer Mark Ellis, expensively hired from BAR Honda, made an immediate impact too and raised optimism.

There was the introduction of double-exit bargeboards in ▷

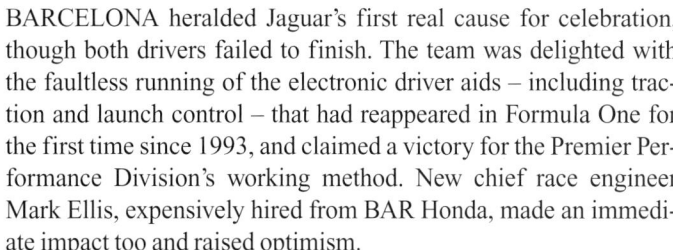

## JAGUAR SEASON STATISTICS

### RELIABILITY PERFORMANCE

| Driver | Races | Max laps | Laps completed | Reliability rating |
|---|---|---|---|---|
| Eddie Irvine | 17 | 1065 | 658 | 61.8% |
| Pedro de la Rosa | 13 | 819 | 579 | 70.7% |
| Luciano Burti | 4 | 246 | 201 | 81.7% |
| Constructor | Races | Max laps | Laps completed | Reliability rating |
| Team | 34 | 2130 | 1438 | 67.5% |

### CHAMPIONSHIP PERFORMANCE

| Driver | 2001 points | 2000 points | 12 month change |
|---|---|---|---|
| Eddie Irvine | 6 | 4 | +50% |
| Pedro de la Rosa | 3 | 2 | +50% |
| Luciano Burti | 0 | 0 | +0% |
| Constructor | 2001 points | 2000 points | 12 month change |
| Team | 9 | 4 | +125% |

Luciano Burti

### CHASSIS LOG

**R2-01** Test car only.

**R2-02** Test car only.

**R2-03** Race car for Burti at Melbourne, Sepang, Interlagos and Imola; and for De la Rosa at Barcelona and the A1 Ring. Spare car at Monte Carlo.

**R2-04** Race car for Eddie Irvine at Melbourne (dropped in favour of 05 for the race itself), Sepang, Interlagos, Imola, A1 Ring, Monte Carlo, Montreal, Nürburgring, Magny-Cours, Silverstone, Hockenheim, Hungaroring, Indianapolis and Suzuka. Spare car at Barcelona (used in qualifying by de la Rosa) and Spa-Francorchamps.

**R2-05** Race car for de la Rosa at Hockenheim; and for Irvine at Monza. Spare car at Melbourne (raced by Irvine in favour of 03), Sepang, Interlagos, Imola, Barcelona, A1 Ring, Monte Carlo, Montreal, Nürburgring, Magny-Cours, Silverstone and Suzuka.

**R2-06** Race car for de la Rosa at Monte Carlo, Montreal, Nürburgring, Magny-Cours and Silverstone; and for Irvine at Spa-Francorchamps. Spare car at Hockenheim, Hungaroring, Monza and Indianapolis.

**R2-07** Race car for de la Rosa at Hungaroring, Spa-Francorchamps, Monza, Indianapolis and Suzuka.

Eddie Irvine

France, but in truth the team marked time until the Monaco Grand Prix, when a completely revised aero package from John Russell *et al* put the team under the spotlight. Chassis 04 underwent a new crash test to the revised gearbox casing and the 'new' car appeared at a track that suited the R2's basic requirements. A stable car that struggled on high-speed circuits was perfect for the Principality, as the driver's inclination to hurl the car close to the wall round tight bends is far more important than outright speed.

With a new floor, rear end and several other major modifications, qualifying was a different story from the usual fare. Irvine stuck the R2 on sixth, while de la Rosa struggled due to a power-steering-induced crash on the Thursday. In the race, Irvine climbed the order through retirements ahead, but there was no doubting that the R2 felt at home at Monaco, and the team's elation was clear to see. In a season full of lows, the third place at Monaco was treated as a win. "Two Ferraris and a Jaguar on the podium at Monaco is what Formula One is all about," said Irvine, with the smile missing for so long returning in full effect. Rahal showed his corporate cunning, stating that 'a lot of Becks will be drunk tonight', hardly subtle but definitely effective – like the lager really.

The new aero package was hailed as a saviour, but it could do nothing to save the R2 on low-downforce circuits. Canada, Britain, Austria, Belgium, America and Japan all challenged the R2 in qualifying spec, although the race pace was much better and de la Rosa and Irvine collected vital points at Monza and Indianapolis respectively – circuits they might have expected to leave empty-handed. Monte Carlo, Monza and Indianapolis were the team's conspicuous highlights; the lows must have come at the start of the season, when the team realised just how far away it was from being competitive, and at Suzuka, when a fuel-pump problem cost the team the chance to beat Benetton Renault to seventh place in the constructors' championship.

## The drivers

MANY question-marks hung over Eddie Irvine as the year started – most of them put there by his team principal Bobby Rahal. The two spoke but did not get on. Rahal thought Irvine poor value on a retainer said to be $12 million a year. For his part, Irvine openly criticised the team. Irvine was also unpopular with some journalists, who continually tried to undermine him. He annoyed the scribes immensely by not caring.

Rahal's determination to rid himself of Irvine was hard to justify. Before Pedro de la Rosa, he had easily seen off his team-mates and was clearly fast in the car. He put in countless days of hard work in off-season testing.

But Rahal was even unhappier with Luciano Burti, whom he felt wasn't up to it and shouldn't have been in a top team earning $2 million a year. Burti was on his way out before the season began, despite stringent denials right up to departure time.

In reality Burti was a doomed man from the start, and was ousted after just a handful of races, after spending a year as Jaguar Racing's test driver and deputising for Irvine in the 2000 Austrian Grand Prix. The Brazilian rookie was actually not as bad as he was made out. But he gained a reputation as a crasher, shunting heavily on both Friday and Saturday in Melbourne, although a collapsed suspension caused the latter incident. He was sent to Prost after San Marino, and continued to crash.

When Niki Lauda arrived, everyone had predicted mayhem between Irvine and Lauda. They couldn't have been more wrong.

Irvine found a kindred spirit in Lauda, to the obvious displeasure of Rahal. The two hit it off and believed they could take the team forward together.

Irvine consistently qualified the car in 12th or 13th all season. Part of his process on understanding was complaining about it to anyone who would listen. He seemed to find it therapeutic. What was inexcusable was the number of times Irvine seemed to throw the car away in the early stages of a race. Part of Jaguar's woeful reliability record was down to driver errors from Irvine and Burti.

Five of Jaguar's retirements can be put down to Irvine, though, the first being a first-corner effort with Jos Verstappen in Malaysia. Irvine rejoined, but debris in his sidepods caused overheating and retirement. His second was a crucial mistake: having climbed through the field to a points-scoring position in Brazil, he spun and stalled. But perhaps his worst mistake came in Canada, when even he admitted his early pass on Nick Heidfeld was 'not one of the most intelligent moves ever'. That ended in tears, as did his coming-together with former team-mate Burti at Spa. Blame can hardly be placed on the Jaguar man, but the incident eliminated both men from the race.

The highlight was Irvine's faultless drive in Monaco. Third place was more than the team could have dreamed of, although Irvine did not do any overtaking, concentrating instead on keeping the car off the walls. Qualifying was the key, and proved Irvine's theory that if the team could sort out Saturday, Sunday would take care of itself. But a podium in the Principality was a great result for Irvine nonetheless.

After Burti was sent on his way, Pedro de la Rosa, stolen away from a test role at Prost, was proudly unveiled to the public as the new race driver, having tested since the start of the year. It was believed he would push Irvine harder than any other team-mate, but at first the Spaniard looked a duff investment. Outqualified by Irvine until Canada, when he just outpaced Irvine by spoiling his final run, de la Rosa finally felt he was finding his feet. In the British Grand Prix, he again held the upper hand in qualifying; this continued for a five-race stretch before Irvine redressed the balance in the USA. He also recorded a vital three points for the team.

Of the seven retirements de la Rosa recorded, four were of his own making. His crash in the German Grand Prix, when he simply outbraked himself at the chicane and slammed into Nick Heidfeld's Sauber, will probably go down as his worst gaffe; he also had two terminal accidents with Heinz-Harald Frentzen and with Jacques Villeneuve. In the latter two instances, both parties traded blame. The Spaniard has one year left to prove himself before his contract comes up for renewal. It will be interesting, for sure.

Mid-year, test driver Tomas Scheckter was also dismissed after his conviction for soliciting a prostitute in Milton Keynes was splashed all over the local newspapers. In reality, it was a good excuse to get rid of him.

## Commercial

THE commercial side of the team was dominated by the arrival of Niki Lauda and the newly formed umbrella division called Premier Performance Division. PPD was a division of Premier Automotive Group, itself a division of Ford. It gave PAG chairman Wolfgang Reitzle sole sway over the team, and he wanted his man in charge. The three-time world champion, who had helped rebuild Ferrari while running his airline in the mid-1990s, came in as chief executive of PPD: his job was vaguely described as getting the best from the PPD-owned Cosworth Racing, Pi Electronics and, most importantly, Jaguar Racing. At a London press conference to announce the deal in February, Bobby Rahal's bewilderment was plain to see. He was on borrowed time from that moment. Deep down he probably knew it, although he vowed to fight. He didn't like Lauda or what he stood for. To survive he knew he had to make the team his own. To do that, he sought to hire Adrian Newey as his technical partner.

If he had pulled that off, Rahal would have survived and ultimately Lauda would have been shown the door. Some conspiracy theorists believe that Lauda deliberately scuppered the Newey signing by tipping off the press and ultimately informing Ron Dennis before the deal was truly tight. That is unlikely, but nonetheless hints at the behind-the-scenes tension and infighting. Until Rahal left, Jaguar was not a team united.

**Jaguar Racing motorhome**

Jaguar started the year with plenty of money, compliments of Ford. With engines it had $175 million, a lot less than Ferrari and McLaren but enough to do a respectable job. That is was blown away by teams with cast-off engines and far less money told the whole story.

Now it will have an in-house competitor for 2002, as Arrows will get the same engine. That deal was Lauda's and he may come to regret it.

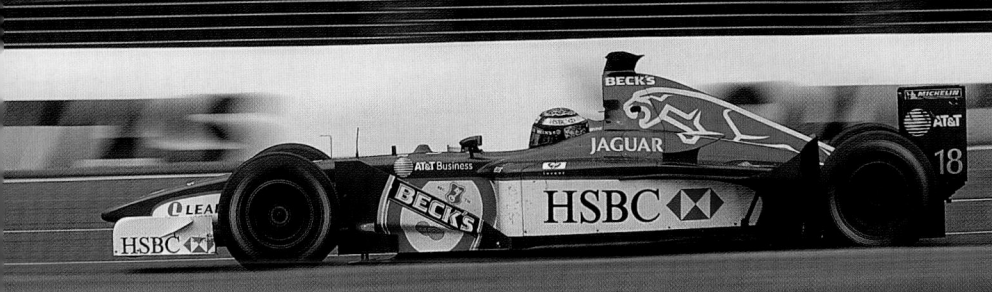

## AUSTRALIAN GRAND PRIX MELBOURNE
# An emotional mix of fortunes

The Jaguar team was a mixture of emotions with, once again, too many cooks spoiling the broth. The question was whether Niki Lauda would fix the problem or be part of it. He had already banned all non-essential personnel from the garage, including Eddie Irvine's manager Enrico Zanarini, and had removed Jackie Stewart from the pit wall. Team principal Bobby Rahal cut straight to the chase: "It is time to stop talking and go racing." Irvine summed it up perfectly: "This will be the weirdest first day we have ever known." What he meant was left to the imagination of everyone present.

**FRIDAY PRACTICE** Jaguar had three of the five new R2 cars it had built so far in Melbourne. Chassis 03 and 04 were the race cars and 05 the spare. In the first session Eddie Irvine and Luciano Burti completed 18 and 21 laps respectively, with 0.498 seconds separating them. They focused on the aerodynamic package and set-up. Irvine admitted: "We have to keep working away because we haven't done much set-up work with the car this year." Burti's morning session was interrupted by a minor trip off the track - but the afternoon was marred by something more serious. He lost the rear end of the car on the exit of the first turn when applying the power. The session was red flagged after he slammed the car into the wall. He admitted: "I was on new tyres and maybe I pushed a little bit too hard. I got my rear left wheel on the grass, which spun me around and into the wall. Unfortunately there is no room for mistakes on this circuit."

After posting the 13th and 18th fastest times respectively, Irvine and Burti were generally pleased with the R2's performance. "We have got to optimise what we have got," Irvine stated baldly.

**SATURDAY QUALIFYING** Saturday was dominated by a serious suspension failure on Burti's Jaguar R2. "There was absolutely no warning," he said. "I was spinning and just had to wait for the car to come to a halt, which it did in the barriers." Burti was on a slow lap when the accident occurred at Turn 10, along the Fittipaldi Curve. Jaguar admitted the left rear suspension broke due to a fault.

That was the end of Burti's qualifying and for some reason Jaguar refused to let him use the spare.

"If it were a running fault through all the cars, we would be risking another accident and the possibility of having to rebuild two cars overnight," said an anonymous spokesperson. But it didn't ring true, as Irvine carried on qualifying. He said that his 12th place was good, but not brilliant. He complained that yellow flags disrupted his session and halted his progress.

The R2s were running with a new Cosworth engine, the CR3, which had been described as a vast improvement. The cars ran with it for the first time on Saturday, and the straight-line speeds were notably faster than Friday's.

**SUNDAY RACE** Eddie Irvine's race was technically troubled before it had even begun. The power-steering failed in the garage and he had to abandon his R2 for the spare chassis, the R2-05. Fortunately it proved far better than his race car. He made a fantastic start, jumping from 12th to sixth only to have the bottle-neck effect caused by Juan Pablo Montoya push him to the back of the running order.

"It was a racing incident – there will be no repercussions," Irvine said. By lap 37, he had made his way up to seventh when he pitted and rejoined in ninth. He gained a place through a retirement and was skirting a finish in the points when an engine misfire brought him in for a late pitstop with a fuel pick-up problem on lap 50. Though inconvenient, he didn't lose his running and secured a final position of 11th.

Irvine's team-mate Burti kept the car on the track to finish just outside the points in eighth. He made a good start, overtaking a number of cars, and was up to 15th place by lap five. His car's lack of set-up gave no problems: he found a workable set-up that allowed the team to focus its attentions on increasing the pace of the car. He drove solidly but quietly to make up the rest of the places to eighth.

**Above and right:** Luciano Burti suffered three crashes of varying degrees over the Melbourne weekend. **Top left and below:** Eddie Irvine's troubles included a power-steering failure, some yellow flags and Juan Pablo Montoya.

Above: Jackie Stewart was on hand to advise the drivers, but he had less influence on the team than he probably would have liked.

Above and below: Irvine qualified 12th, but his race was over at the first corner after a clash with Verstappen.

## MALAYSIAN GRAND PRIX SEPANG
# Surprisingly reliable

Jaguar Racing surprised itself by bringing both cars home in Melbourne a fortnight earlier, and that had helped the team put its reliability inferiority complex to rest. Now the focus had switched to speed and set-up – because of the new R2's poor reliability in testing, very little set-up work had been done. At least Jaguar had the consolation of knowing that, further up the pitlane, Benetton Renault hadn't done a full race distance in testing and consequently was unable to relate adequate feedback to the team. It appeared that Luciano Burti had not yet got to grips with the car, a state of affairs not helped by the lack of chassis testing. With reliability improving, however, the team planned to spend the time between the Malaysian and Brazilian rounds testing the whole aerodynamic package of the car, specifically race set-up and balance.

Meanwhile, Jaguar was hindered by the car's susceptibility to the heat and only ran much faster relative to others when the temperature dropped. For the second race running, Eddie Irvine was plagued by power-steering failure all weekend.

**FRIDAY PRACTICE** Irvine spent the day working on chassis development but was beset by problems with the clutch, power-steering and handling. Some new aerodynamic components seemed to provide a startling improvement and he split the McLarens, emerging as comfortably the fastest man on Michelins and fifth overall. He said: "We were quicker than I expected but we need to understand why we're quick here and not elsewhere." Luciano Burti got in 37 laps familiarising himself with the circuit and set an impressive first session time of 1m 41.443secs. Team principal Bobby Rahal said: "There isn't any doubt that we have made progress since Mel-

bourne. The tyre wear rate here is also much better, which is encouraging."

**SATURDAY QUALIFYING** "The problem is that we can't take the same steps forward that others do after Friday's practice sessions," Irvine complained after qualifying. "At least we know tyres are not our problem, as Williams proved!" Irvine suffered more power-steering difficulties during the qualifying session, which ruined his final run. But he partly attributed his lowly 12th position on 1m 37.140secs to traffic: "Villeneuve held me up in my final run at the last corner and then he dived into the pits at the last minute. There is no excuse for this kind of behaviour; revenge is the only solution."

Burti was mystified as to his poor performance in the crucial afternoon session: "I thought I would improve even more for qualifying. The balance was better, but the car just reacted badly to the changes in track conditions." He said he kept losing control over the rear of his Jaguar because of the wind blowing in from behind and the blistering 41°C temperature of the track. He was, on average, 5.3 kilometres slower than his team-mate through the speed trap but finished a respectable 15th on 1m 38.035secs. Progress was obviously being made, however, as Rahal was expecting much better. He said: "I was hoping to see both cars in the top 10 – or at least better than this."

**SUNDAY RACE** Eddie Irvine was shunted off at Turn 1 of the very first lap by Jos Verstappen, who was on his way up the field from 18th. "Given the space available, I can't imagine what was going through Jos's head," stormed an angry Irvine. "And no sooner had I got back on the track, the heavens opened." Irvine ran wide at Turn 6, collected some debris in the sidepods which caused a water leak, and he retired on lap four. Burti soldiered on through the rain to secure 10th position. He made two pitstops – for wet tyres, then for dry tyres and fuel – losing a total of three minutes coming in and out of the pits.

Team boss Bobby Rahal summed the race up perfectly: "It is a damn shame we couldn't get Irvine through the first corner. We are still not in a position to threaten anybody, but we are developing reliability as a baseline." If Irvine had survived, he might have made the points.

JAGUAR RACING

## BRAZILIAN GRAND PRIX INTERLAGOS
# Going nowhere faster

Jaguar's mission so far had been reliability first, with speed coming later. Now that speed was back on the agenda, reliability could suffer. Neither Eddie Irvine nor Luciano Burti finished the Brazilian Grand Prix and Burti's retirement was the team's first real mechanical failure of the year. The one bright spot for Jaguar was that Burti set the fastest time through the speed traps in sector one, suggesting the Cosworth had the power or the chassis had been improved. The team had still not got its organisation right and had more people doing less work than any other team. The rumours of Burti's impending replacement by Pedro de la Rosa possibly helped to increase his speed. But most rightly reckoned de la Rosa in the second car was just a matter of time.

**FRIDAY PRACTICE** Irvine took control of chassis R2-04 and Burti the R2-03, with R2-05 as the spare set up for Irvine. The two spent the day tuning the modified front wing, dialling in a new set-up to optimise the revised endplates, and working on the R2's troublesome power-steering. The steering, with too much kickback towards the limits of its travel, had caused both drivers problems and Irvine welcomed the improvements. "We made big steps forward with the steering and that helped me a lot," he said. "It's good to see Luciano up there too – he's been giving me a hard time and that's great to see."

The two drivers were quick in the morning, but the afternoon session was faster and Irvine and Burti finished 10th and 11th respectively after running for 35 and 47 laps. The team could not balance the R2 on new rubber and the Michelins' characteristics change dramatically on rising temperatures. That set-up quandary suggested the R2's overall weight distribution might be wrong.

**SATURDAY QUALIFYING** There were problems balancing the car and dealing with Interlagos's legendary bumps, with Burti spinning in the early part of the session after placing his R2 on the kerb. Irvine, bizarrely, lost a wing-mirror and there were just six-100ths of a second between the two cars. Irvine felt his 13th berth on 1m 15.192secs a reliable yardstick. "I've qualified in almost the same place for all the races this season and, quite simply put, this is where we are right now as a team," he said. Irvine realised it could be a lot worse, glancing over his shoulder towards

Benetton Renault's pit. Burti, on home turf and under threat, finished under two-10ths of a second away from Irvine to take 14th grid slot on 1m 15.371secs. An unusually vocal Burti felt he could have gone faster, but that was his PR man speaking. For what it's worth: "I spoiled my last run losing two-10ths from the last corner to the finishing line. We were pretty close to the limit, but we probably could have squeezed an extra two or three-10ths from the car." To quell the rumours, he had to.

Both set their fastest times in the last 10 minutes of the session, when a dip in temperature brought some of the balance back to the Michelin-shod Jaguars.

**SUNDAY RACE** There were immediate problems before the start with the Cosworth engine in Irvine's Jaguar. By the time it burst into life, a 10-second stop-go penalty was imposed for not clearing the grid 15 seconds before the formation lap. Irvine served the penalty on lap six, sending him to the back. He battled to recover, despite blistered rear tyres that had to last until his second pitstop on lap 46. He gained places and by lap 30 had overtaken Jenson Button, both Prosts and both Minardis for 12th. A superb pitstop got him to seventh on wets and when the downpour came Irvine was even faster. Kimi Räikkönen's retirement gifted him sixth and possible points. In the excitement he lost the rear end almost immediately entering Turn 5 on lap 53, and stalled.

Burti suffered a poor getaway, losing places to Alesi and Verstappen. By lap 29 he was ninth, but on lap 30 a water-seal problem forced him into the pits, before the inevitable engine explosion.

Above: Ralf Schumacher inspects Burti's retired Jaguar. Right: Eddie Irvine's efforts and speed on a wet track ended with a DNF. Below right: Irvine and his manager Enrico Zanarini check things are as they should be in the latest issue. Below: Jaguar was beset by niggles. Burti and technical director Steve Nichols discuss set-up.

Left: Bobby Rahal ponders the team's performance and his future in F1. Below left: Luciano Burti's Jaguar ends its practice on the wrecker truck. Burti's future was also uncertain.

Left: Luciano Burti, still under pressure to perform, finished a lowly 11th. Below right: Jaguar bosses Bobby Rahal and Niki Lauda did not, by all accounts, have a harmonious weekend. Their future at Jaguar was fuelling much speculation.

## SAN MARINO GRAND PRIX IMOLA
# A team on the mend

Jaguar Racing arrived in Imola intent on holding its mid-grid position. It was a team in need of mend, but also in transition. Imola was a time for home truths. Jaguar had two bosses, Niki Lauda and Bobby Rahal, when only one was needed; and two second drivers, Pedro de la Rosa and Luciano Burti, a surplus of one. Few expected this still to be the case at de la Rosa's home race in Barcelona.

After an uncertain start, Eddie Irvine had forged a good relationship with Lauda – to the point where the parties were starting to talk about the possibility of Irvine staying for a fourth year after his three-year contract expires at the end of 2002. Burti owed his career to former Jaguar Racing boss Neil Ressler, now long departed. He was struggling and he knew it.

The R2 chassis continued to make life difficult for the drivers, and much of the instability was believed to stem from a shortage of overall downforce. This was a particular problem for the Michelin runners, as currently only BMW Williams seemed to be able to extract the maximum from the durable French rubber.

**FRIDAY PRACTICE** The drivers stuck to their Brazil cars and Irvine battled with understeer. To combat the problem he played with tyre pressures all session as he sampled wet, intermediate and dry tyres. He achieved seventh with 1m 26.599secs after 41 laps.

Burti concentrated on learning the track and tried a new front wing. This produced more front download, which allowed an improved overall balance and gave the driver more confidence in the car's nervous rear end. In the drier second session, Burti ran 10th on 1m 26.933secs in 43 laps.

**SATURDAY QUALIFYING** Eddie Irvine was setting his best sector times on his in-laps, not his qualifying flyer laps, due to the Jaguar's inability to sufficiently load its Michelin tyres. It was a problem that had no solution for the time being. New front wing endplates created more downforce and this was reflected in the speed trap times.

Irvine was unconvinced of the magnitude of these changes. He qualified in 13th with a 1m 25.392secs – some 2.338secs off the pole time. That sort of gap was devastating to Irvine, who could only shrug his shoulders and keep on banking his pay cheques. Burti's best effort was a time of 1m 25.572secs – good enough for 15th.

**SUNDAY RACE** Eddie Irvine's race was a non-event, ending on lap 43 when his engine erupted as he ran in ninth. Prior to the Cosworth's explosion, Irvine's one-stop strategy had still allowed him to resist all the efforts of Jean Alesi. Before the blow, he had been on course for seventh.

Burti suffered the loss of first, second and third gears. He could have finished in ninth but in the end was forced to settle for 11th place.

JAGUAR RACING

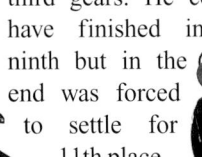

# SPANISH GRAND PRIX BARCELONA
# More of the same mediocre mix

Spaniard Pedro de la Rosa arrived to replace Luciano Burti, in whom no one had had any confidence. But over the weekend, judgement on the Brazilian was proved harsh as Prost-adopted Burti had a brilliant time, while de la Rosa failed miserably. It made Saturday a big day for number one Jaguar driver Eddie Irvine as he had to out-qualify new boy de la Rosa, from whom everyone expected great things.

In the event Irvine thrashed de la Rosa, proving he and Burti were far better drivers than most people took them for. A new chief race engineer, Mark Ellis, joined the team and immediately enamoured himself with Irvine. "We agreed instantly on the programme for the weekend and have made the first real progress this season," said an unusually upbeat Irvine.

The weekend was notable for the first doubts surfacing over Niki Lauda's leadership of the team. For once it was Lauda under pressure rather than team principal Bobby Rahal; he had temporarily seized the upper hand, but things were no better. The Formula One paddock can be a nasty, unforgiving place and Lauda was maybe starting to regret a few recent career decisions. Running Jaguar was no bed of roses and the champion was feeling the pressure of having too few good people behind him.

**FRIDAY PRACTICE** Jaguar brought three chassis to Barcelona: the R2-04 race chassis plus T-car 05 for Irvine, and R2-03 for de la Rosa.

Irvine stormed to a stunning second place on the timesheets due to precisely the right choice of Michelin tyre: compound B. 'B' was slightly softer and improved with track temperature, Irvine setting his best lap about 2pm. He completed 27 laps with a best of 1m 20.615secs on the 23rd. De la Rosa spent his session learning the set-up of the race car and settling his tyre choice. He achieved a time of 1m 21.184secs in 38 laps, winding up 0.569secs slower than his team-mate. He was classified a creditable seventh. There was a chink of light shining through the green on Friday evening, but Eddie Irvine was under no illusions that his time was a freak of the track.

**SATURDAY QUALIFYING** As Irvine predicted after his unexpected performance on Friday, things were back to normal in time for qualifying when the R2 lacked the essential downforce to cope with the track's crosswinds. With only two minutes of the qualifying hour left, Irvine had a scare when he found deposed team-mate Burti faster than him for the first time in 2001 – albeit in a different car. Irvine asked his old team-mate Michael Schumacher for a hand to reverse ease the embarrassment: towed by the Ferrari, he found a couple of tenths. Irvine ended 13th with 1m 20.326secs, 2.125secs off pole. His speed trap recording was more optimistic – seventh fastest on 313.8kph.

The power-steering on de la Rosa's car failed in the morning warm-up, causing him to drive into the wall. He had no choice but to qualify in the spare car set up for Irvine. Rear brake problems meant he only managed 20th in 1m 21.338secs. Irvine had met his goal: thrashing the highly rated de la Rosa.

**SUNDAY RACE** Neither driver reached the flag. Irvine made an excellent start, making up four places, and drove a steady race in eighth, despite his car's skittish rear end. After 48 laps the team alerted him to a loss of oil pressure: using fewer revs and short-shifting the gearbox, he tried to conserve the engine. But the strain was too much and the Cosworth unit croaked at loop three, denying Irvine a deserved finish. De la Rosa's race was short: he clashed with Heinz-Harald Frentzen as the German tried to pass him on the inside of Turn 8 on lap six. Frentzen overshot and hit the Spaniard's left front wing, sending both drivers into the gravel. Stewards declared it another racing incident.

Far left: Eddie Irvine and the Jaguar driver's favourite singer, Lisa Stansfield. Above left: Pedro de la Rosa's debut race with Jaguar was a disappointment. Above: Old masters Alain Prost and Jackie Stewart compare headaches. Below: Irvine's race came to an abrupt end with an engine failure right in front of the pits.

Right: Pedro de la Rosa put the Jaguar into the wall during practice and generally had a lacklustre weekend in Barcelona.

## AUSTRIAN GRAND PRIX A1 RING
# Waiting for better aero

The team reckoned it knew there was not much that could be done with the performance of the Jaguar Cosworth R2 until a new aerodynamic package arrived. This was due in Montreal mid-June, but had been rushed forward to be ready in time for Monaco.

So the Austrian Grand Prix was an event in which all the team could do was struggle on and hope for the best. As it turned out, the race gave Jaguar a good opportunity, with Eddie Irvine able to weave through the four stalled cars on the grid to move from 13th at the start to sixth position. Prospects looked good, but other cars were faster and Irvine had faded back to seventh by the finish, just missing out on a world championship point.

The team admitted that if it had scored, it would have been a lucky point, but a point is a point and how it is won is not important. "It is just a matter of waiting this period out," said team boss Bobby Rahal.

**FRIDAY PRACTICE** For Austria, Eddie Irvine used chassis R2-04 and Pedro de la Rosa was in R2-03, while the spare car was the newer R2-05. In the course of Friday there was not much to report apart from a persistent misfire for de la Rosa in the afternoon. The Spaniard completed 48 laps trying to cure the problem, while Irvine did 43. Irvine ended up 12th quickest with de la Rosa 15th. Most of the work done was on tyres, with the drivers trying the various Michelin compounds in different states of wear to find out which was the best combination. The duo both found what they felt was the best package but the lap times were still not that good. "Different circuit, same problems," concluded Irvine.

**SATURDAY QUALIFYING** Irvine and de la Rosa both had a scrappy qualifying with traffic problems. This was caused in part because everyone started the session late in an effort to take advantage of the improvement in the circuit in the final minutes. In the end Irvine was 13th and de la Rosa 14th, the pair split by only a 10th of a second. The day was trouble-free except for a driveshaft failure for de la Rosa in the morning. Both drivers admitted that, even without the other cars getting in the way, there was not much to be done. "I don't think I could have climbed much higher. I could have been a bit quicker but it would not have made that much difference," said Irvine.

Bobby Rahal reckoned the result was rather better than expected: "We are right up close with Villeneuve, Panis and Frentzen," he remarked optimistically.

**SUNDAY RACE** At the start of the race, four of the top 11 were left standing on the grid. Kimi Räikkönen and the two BARs were all trying to go through the same gap and stumbled over one another, which allowed Irvine to get ahead of them all. Having made up seven places Irvine was running sixth. De la Rosa was less fortunate and found himself only 13th.

Irvine could not sustain the pace, though, and in the early part of the race he was overtaken by Jos Verstappen (running his Arrows with a low fuel-load), Räikkönen, Olivier Panis and finally Enrique Bernoldi.

Irvine's 10th became eighth as Ralf Schumacher retired, then Bernoldi pitted, but he remained in that position until Juan Pablo Montoya disappeared on lap 42. Having started with a heavy fuel load Eddie was able to keep running until lap 48 and this took him up to sixth, but then he was dropped back behind Verstappen again and stayed in seventh all the way to the finish.

De la Rosa ran steadily early on, then diced with Jacques Villeneuve for 10th place. He then started suffering from rear tyre problems and encountered bad understeer, so pitted early on lap 35. This dropped him to the tail of the field. He retired on lap 48 with a transmission failure.

JAGUAR
RACING

Top: Eddie Irvine and Pedro de la Rosa were closely matched in qualifying and Irvine raced hard to bring the Jaguar home seventh, one lap down. De la Rosa's race came to an end on lap 48 with transmission failure (above). De la Rosa's qualifying push saw him just over a 10th slower than Irvine. The Jaguars were not quick enough.

## MONACO GRAND PRIX MONTE CARLO
# Big cat leaps to podium

Jaguar Racing had been waiting for a new aerodynamic package to enhance the recalcitrant chassis. It arrived in Monaco with a bang and everything was suddenly rosy again for Eddie Irvine. The Irishman's morale was also boosted by a flattering magazine profile and some independent analysis that said his race form was not his failing but the car's. His race result did not really reflect the team's actual level of competitiveness, given that both Williams and both Jordans retired and that McLaren was sidelined. But results were all that matter and Jaguar Racing was taking whatever fell its way.

Throughout the Monaco weekend talk centred around plans to move the team head- quarters. Ford Motor Company boss Jacques Nasser cancelled his planned trip to the race because of problems in America with Firestone tyres, and there was no whisper or sign of the events to follow when Adrian Newey would join, then resign from, Jaguar Racing in the space of a few hours.

**THURSDAY PRACTICE** For Monaco the team rolled out four cars. Eddie Irvine had his usual R2-04 and R2-05 as his spare, while Pedro de la Rosa had a new R2-06 and his old race car, R2-03, as his spare. The team had a heavily revised rear end package with a new undertray, diffuser, rear wing and rear crash structure, but as only two sets of the kit were available it was decided not to use them.

Irvine's 12th quickest time of the day was not a surprise, with one spin at the chicane and a trip up the escape road at Ste Devote. De la Rosa had his throttle stick open, which caused the car to go into the wall on the run downhill to Portier and the impact demolished his left front suspension. In the afternoon his progress was halted by another power-steering problem. While most of his rivals did around 45 laps, he did only nine and set the slowest time of the day.

**SATURDAY QUALIFYING** Both cars featured the new aerodynamic package and Irvine was fifth fastest in the morning and confirmed his pace by taking sixth berth on the grid. He managed to get four clear qualifying runs with no problems. Irvine described the new aero package as "by far the biggest development I have ever experienced in F1. To have the car on the third row is absolutely fantastic. It's a great morale booster!"

De la Rosa spent Saturday trying to catch up for the time that had been lost on Thursday, and ended the day with 14th place on the grid.

**SUNDAY RACE** Eddie Irvine was confident of points. However, it all nearly went wrong at the first corner as he was pushed wide by the two Williams drivers and brushed the outside wall at Ste Devote. This meant he lost some momentum, and was overtaken by Juan Pablo Montoya. With David Coulthard having disappeared to the back of the field, though, he was still sixth and that became fifth within a couple of laps after Montoya made his mistake in the Swimming Pool section. Fifth place became fourth on lap 15 when Mika Häkkinen disappeared into the pits and the departure of Ralf Schumacher on lap 58 promoted Eddie into third place.

He pitted two laps later but Jacques Villeneuve, his nearest challenger, was around 40 seconds adrift so Irvine was able to get out ahead. The gap between the two was about seven seconds and Villeneuve reduced this in the laps that followed, aided when Irvine slid wide and tapped the barriers at Ste Devote. The car was not damaged and the two men finished the race separated by 1.7secs. "I take great pride in having done our talking on the track today," concluded Irvine.

De la Rosa held on to his 14th place in the course of the first lap but since Coulthard was at the back and Nick Heidfeld's Sauber hit the wall just before Portier, de la Rosa had gained two places. He had made a good start and was ahead of Heinz-Harald Frentzen but the fast-starting Kimi Räikkönen forced the issue at the first corner and de la Rosa decided to let the Finn pass to avoid an accident. Further around the lap a desperate Frentzen dived for the inside line on the entry to Casino Square and de la Rosa again had to give way to avoid an accident.

Unfortunately de la Rosa's desire to finish was unfulfilled as the car suffered a hydraulic failure on lap 15 when he was running in 11th position. "I have never had any luck around Monaco," he said, "so I guess that is consistency for you!"

Right: Eddie Irvine was pushed wide at the first corner and lightly brushed the wall at Ste Devote after being elbowed out by the two Williams. He lost momentum and places until the Williams pair retired.

Right: Pedro de la Rosa could not match Irvine's speed; his star had waned a great deal since he joined Jaguar. Below: Jaguar's development of a new underbody at last allowed Irvine to display his full capability in a more competitive car.

## CANADIAN GRAND PRIX MONTREAL
# Getting back to normal

For Jaguar, the Monaco elation was quickly flattened by a lack of performance in Montreal. Above and left: Following Irvine's retirement, Pedro de la Rosa persevered to salvage something for the team with sixth place and one point.

Left and below: Eddie Irvine was quick to add to the criticism of Juan Pablo Montoya's driving qualities, but then clashed with Nick Heidfeld's Sauber on the opening lap of the race, bringing retirement for both. Jaguar's Monaco hero admitted that the accident was principally of his own making.

Jaguar Racing was in the spotlight – but for the wrong reasons. The weekend was dominated by speculation regarding whether McLaren technical director Adrian Newey would join the team. By the end of the weekend team boss Niki Lauda was wishing he'd never heard the name Newey. Bobby Rahal was alone in hoping the situation could be retrieved.

Then there were new technical challenges to overcome. The aerodynamic package that had proved so successful in Monaco did not work at all well in Canada and the team was confused as to why. Clearly more development was needed. In the circumstances, the fact that Pedro de la Rosa scored a point was a surprise bonus. The Spanish driver had not had much luck in 2001, so for him it was some reward.

FRIDAY PRACTICE For Canada, Jaguar had three chassis on hand. Eddie Irvine drove his R2-04, de la Rosa had a new chassis, R2-06; the spare was R2-05. The cars were little changed from Monaco, save for some additional aerodynamic devices.

On Friday morning Irvine ran with a heavy fuel load as he did tyre evaluation work, but in the afternoon the team took out the fuel, put on new tyres – and the Irishman ended up with the day's third fastest time. "The car did not feel as good as I expected it to," said Irvine. "There are some new bits but I don't know at this stage exactly what impact they are having."

De la Rosa struggled to get rid of understeer so did not have enough time to use new tyres, ending up 14th fastest.

SATURDAY QUALIFYING After opting for the softer of the two tyre compounds available, the team found that in the hot temperatures during qualifying, the rubber was blistering badly at the end of a fast lap. This meant the team did less well than it had hoped: Irvine and de la Rosa nearly came unstuck when the Spaniard had to lift off to avoid crashing at the final corner and Irvine had to swerve to avoid him. It ruined Irvine's best lap and meant that he lost his 100 per cent qualifying record of lining up in front of his team-mate, through no fault of his own.

With Irvine unable to get another run in, de la Rosa stayed ahead of him on the grid by 0.001secs, the two lining up in 14th and 15th.

"The new aero package is certainly an improvement but we are not quick enough," said de la Rosa. "There is still more work to be done. I am sorry about spoiling Eddie's last run but I had little choice but to lift off or hit the wall. I arrived too fast and unfortunately I spoiled it for myself and Eddie."

SUNDAY RACE The engineers worked on a new setting for Irvine's car in a bid to improve it for the race and during morning warm-up the car was suddenly transformed. According to Irvine the car 'felt great' and at the end of the session he had set the fourth fastest time.

He was still worried about tyre wear in the race, but did not have to worry for long: while going for quick progress on lap two, Irvine tried an overly optimistic move to pass Nick Heidfeld's Sauber. The two cars collided, and both men were out. Irvine later admitted he was largely to blame – all well and good, but Jaguar Racing bosses wanted points, so Irvine's early departure was not appreciated.

De la Rosa was rather more cautious than his team-mate and, despite having trouble with his rear tyres blistering, he had a good race, avoiding trouble and moving up the order as others ahead of him retired.

The choice of tyres was the wrong one given the temperature on Sunday, so the two-stop strategy did not work that well. However, de la Rosa was running seventh in the final laps when Jos Verstappen spun off, gifting Pedro his first point for Jaguar, which he took with glee.

"To score points in two consecutive races is great," said team boss Bobby Rahal. "But we were a little bit lucky today. Having said that we have given away points in recent races so we have to grab the chances that come along. Apart from Eddie's unfortunate exit, we have salvaged something positive from today."

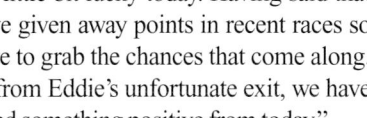

295

# EUROPEAN GRAND PRIX NÜRBURGRING
# Some light ahead

By the end of the weekend, team boss Bobby Rahal was calling the team's Nürburgring performance 'the best of the year', even though seventh and eighth places did not seem much. The key was that the cars had run reliably and the performance looked to be there waiting to emerge. Jaguar seemed to have turned the corner, as Eddie Irvine set the fifth fastest lap of the race behind the BMW Williams and the Ferraris. The problem was in qualifying but Jaguar knew if they could sort out that issue and keep up the pace of development, there was potential for some much better results in the second half of the year.

**FRIDAY PRACTICE** Jaguar had the same three chassis as in Canada, with Irvine using R2-04 and Pedro de la Rosa R2-06. The spare car was R2-05. The weekend did not get off to a good start as Irvine lost the whole of the morning session with a fuel pump problem. By the end of the day he had done only 23 laps compared to de la Rosa's 47, the pair finishing up 15th and 13th respectively with 1m 19.503secs and 1m 18.473secs. De la Rosa reported that his car was suffering from a lack of rear-end grip but the team seemed to think this was down to the tyres.

"It is a bit early to be critical of the tyres," said Rahal, "especially when you consider that the track temperature is much lower than everyone thought it would be. A hotter day tomorrow would not go amiss."

**SATURDAY QUALIFYING** Rahal's wish came true with temperatures much higher – but this seemed to make little difference to the Jaguars' performance in qualifying. But although 12th on a 1m 16.588secs for Irvine and 16th on a 1m 17.627secs for de la Rosa did not look very spectacular, the gap between Irvine and the fastest of his immediate rivals (seventh-placed Jarno Trulli) was only four-10ths and Irvine reckoned he lost half a second with yellow flags on his fastest lap. "The tyres are not the problem," Irvine admitted.

De la Rosa was still unhappy with his car – over a second behind Irvine, he complained of poor balance.

**SUNDAY RACE** Irvine's optimism on Saturday was underlined with the fourth fastest time in the warm-up. Eddie said he was keen to start well to offset the poor performance in qualifying. Irvine had a good start but made up only one place. He then spent a long time behind Heinz-Harald Frentzen and was surprised to discover he was quicker than the Jordan. "I was amazed at how easy it was to keep up with him," Irvine said. "I was even lifting off on the straights to conserve fuel and still managing to keep up with him."

Running a one-stop strategy, Irvine did not pit until lap 37, by which time he was running sixth, having overtaken both Frentzen and Kimi Räikkönen. The strategy proved good as Irvine ended the race seventh, the only man outside the points not to be lapped. He also set the fifth fastest lap of the race. "I could not have done any better today," he said. "It just shows how important it is for us to qualify better."

De la Rosa was still not completely happy with the handling of his car in the warm-up, although his 11th fastest lap despite mechanical problems was promising. He decided to make some changes for the race and these worked out well. De la Rosa chose to have a very long first stint – until lap 44 of 67 – and by the time he pitted he was up to seventh place. His stop dropped him only two places and after Frentzen retired he was eighth, although in the closing laps he had to hold off a serious challenge from Jacques Villeneuve. He finished the race a second-and-a-half clear of the BAR driver.

Top and above: Eddie Irvine just missed out on points, but Niki Lauda was overseeing changes to push the team back into the top six. Right: Irvine was surprised to find he was faster than Heinz-Harald Frentzen's Jordan and was unlucky not to score a point.

Right: Pedro de la Rosa was not happy with his car but finished eighth. Irvine was the last driver not to be lapped.

## FRENCH GRAND PRIX MAGNY-COURS
# Optimism abounds

Optimism was in plentiful supply at Jaguar Racing after its Monaco success and this was masking the difficulties that still needed to be overcome. The team now had some good people in place, including engineer Mark Ellis who was making his presence felt. But there was a desperate need for a strong team manager and Bobby Rahal was still searching for technical direction. Ellis had made a huge difference, but Jaguar needed to build a team above him.

Jaguar continued to suffer from poor qualifying which compromised its performances in the races. The cars were getting better as the aerodynamics were reworked, and reliability was improving. The problem was, every other team was had also progressed in these areas, so Jaguar had to pedal twice as hard to get ahead its rivals. But at least it had caught up.

**FRIDAY PRACTICE** Jaguar stuck with the same three chassis, Eddie Irvine at the wheel of R2-04 and Pedro de la Rosa driving R2-06. The spare car was again R2-05.

The team was surprised to discover that the track conditions were such that all the preparation done in pre-event testing at Magny-Cours served little purpose. The cars had scant grip and things were not helped when Irvine suffered an electrical failure and did only a handful of laps. In the second session he tried to catch up, but ended the day having completed only 27 laps. The fact he was second fastest was not really significant as he was running with a light fuel load. De la Rosa did 45 laps in all without finding a decent balance, but still ended up eighth fastest.

**SATURDAY QUALIFYING** There were some aerodynamic modifications for Irvine's car for qualifying, but while he looked good on his first run, he threw away his chances by spinning. He had to switch to the spare car, in which he did two more runs but could not improve, having another spin. He ended up 12th on 1m 14.441secs.

De la Rosa lost 20 minutes because of an electronic problem, then made a mistake on his fastest lap. But he managed to secure 14th on the grid with a 1m 15.020secs.

"Eddie started well with a great lap and it all looked good," said team principal Bobby Rahal, "but then he went off and lost time. I am pretty disappointed."

**SUNDAY RACE** Irvine decided to go for a long first stint and spent the early part of the race fighting with Olivier Panis for eighth place. On lap 21 he was finally able to outfox the Frenchman and get ahead. "I knew where I wanted to pass Olivier," Eddie explained later, "but after a while he began covering himself. I spent some time letting him think I wasn't going to take him at that point, then I pounced and made it through. It was great fun!"

Next Irvine caught and passed Heinz-Harald Frentzen, but the team then detected a pneumatic problem and during his second stop attempts were made to recharge the system. They failed and on lap 55 his engine also gave up.

De la Rosa had a bad time, his car stopping during the parade lap before the race started. He coasted downhill into the pits where the electronics were reset and he was able to start, but by the time that had been done he was a whole lap behind the rest of the field. It was then a question of chasing hard and it was not until near the end of the race that he was able to catch and finally pass Fernando Alonso's Minardi.

"It was very frustrating," he said. "And it was made worse by the fact that the car felt really good. It was well balanced and the tyres worked very well." But there was nothing more the Spaniard could do.

**Above: Pedro de la Rosa lost time in practice but qualified 14th.
Left: Bobby Rahal was pleased with his new staff, but now he needed to find performance improvements in the cars. Below: De la Rosa's car stopped on the parade lap but the team quickly solved the problem.**

**Left and below: Eddie Irvine had a couple of spins in qualifying which left him 12th on the grid. During the race he had a good battle with Olivier Panis, but his race was halted on lap 55, when engine failure struck.**

## BRITISH GRAND PRIX SILVERSTONE
# Promise but no results

Jaguar Racing continued to promise good results yet failed to deliver. The main reason was that the cars rarely ran without problems throughout a weekend and they did not work well in qualifying. In race trim the cars were much better, but poor qualifying performances meant the drivers spent too much time catching up to enable them to score points. That was again the story at Silverstone, this time coupled with the hindrance of a disastrous weekend for Michelin which was simply caught out by the colder weather that blew in.

**FRIDAY PRACTICE** Jaguar used the same three chassis as in recent races – Eddie Irvine had R2-04 and Pedro de la Rosa R2-06. The spare was R2-05. The team took another aerodynamic step forward which the drivers reported worked well.

Nevertheless, things got off to a bad start when de la Rosa's car stopped out on the circuit very early on in the first practice session. He missed pretty much the entire hour, but in the afternoon completed 22 laps and was able to set the seventh fastest time of the day on 1m 24.116secs. For his efforts he was given a giant, public, bear hug by Niki Lauda, which did wonders for his morale.

Irvine had a fairly good day and managed to complete 43 laps in all, but was only 13th fastest on 1m 24.733secs - his engine cut out while he was on his best flying lap.

**SATURDAY QUALIFYING** There were more problems for Irvine on Saturday morning and he completed only seven laps, while de la Rosa did 26 and wound up 12th fastest. In qualifying, Irvine was in all sorts of trouble when he was forced to switch to the spare car, which had been set up for de la Rosa, halfway through the session after a front left pushrod broke on his race car. The spare did not have all the latest aerodynamic enhancements: Irvine had to settle for 15th on the grid on 1m 23.439secs. De la Rosa was much happier and qualified 13th with a 1m 23.273secs. "The new aero package is

definitely a step forward," the Spaniard said as he celebrated out-qualifying Jaguar's number one driver for only the second time this year. He added: "We haven't even done a proper test, so I'm sure there's more pace to extract from it."

**SUNDAY RACE** Irvine decided to go for a two-stop strategy with a long first stint, so the car was fairly heavy at the start and he had failed to move up from his 15th place after completion of the first lap, despite the fact that four drivers were involved in incidents at the first corner.

His long first stint ended with a stop on lap 30 when he was running in 12th. He rejoined in the same position and rose to ninth before his second stop. Again he retained his position and ran in ninth all the way to the flag. "Without sounding like a stuck record, we have been reminded once again of the importance of qualifying better," he said.

De la Rosa also decided to go for a one-stop strategy, so he too was carrying a heavy fuel load at the start. He moved up to 12th on the opening lap (although in reality he had dropped two places after the incidents at the front of the field had been factored in). He moved up to ninth as others pitted, though when he stopped on lap 34 he dropped back to 12th. But the refuelling machine unfortunately malfunctioned and he was forced to stop again, dropping to 16th. He was able to make up places as the two-stop racers came a second time, but he ended up 12th. "That was a very boring race from my perspective," he concluded.

But both cars finished – crucial in an era where bosses are analysing reliability nearly as closely as overall speed. Both are needed to win, and 75 per cent reliability is now regarded as very low, whereas before 50 per cent was accepted as the norm.

Above: Eddie Irvine persevered with a heavy fuel load to take a well deserved ninth place. Right: Irvine qualified 15th after he was forced to use the spare R2, which had been set up for team-mate de la Rosa.

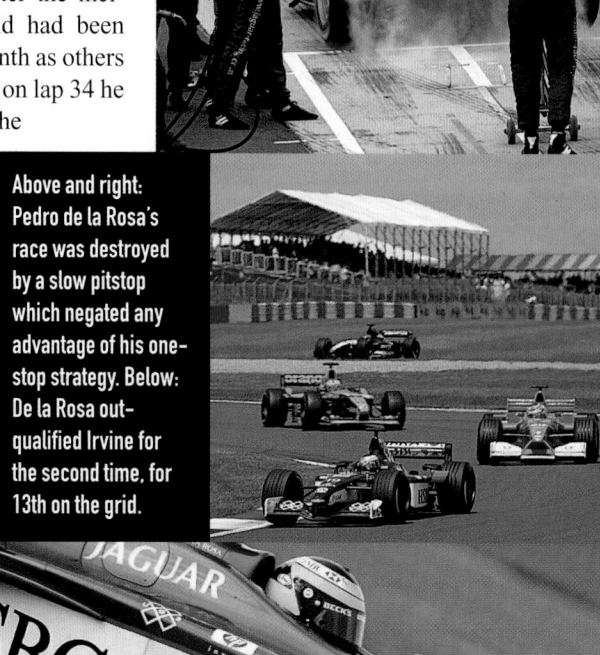

Above and right: Pedro de la Rosa's race was destroyed by a slow pitstop which negated any advantage of his one-stop strategy. Below: De la Rosa out-qualified Irvine for the second time, for 13th on the grid.

## GERMAN GRAND PRIX HOCKENHEIM
# Better times ahead?

In recent weeks Jaguar's drivers had stressed that they needed to improve their qualifying. At Hockenheim they did exactly that, with Pedro de la Rosa outshining Eddie Irvine for eighth place, leaving Irvine in 11th. Opting for softer Michelins, they expected a good race. But a double retirement spelt disaster. It was another blow for Bobby Rahal who, unbeknown to the rest of the world, spent some of his weekend trying to palm Irvine off to Eddie Jordan, setting in motion a sequence of events that would see him expelled from the team a few weeks later.

Commercially Niki Lauda did a deal to sell Tom Walkinshaw engines for his Arrows team in 2002 on the basis that development would be quicker with two teams. As Lauda said, in F1 two brains are probably better than one, and Jaguar needed all the help it could get.

**FRIDAY PRACTICE** Jaguar had the same three chassis as usual with Irvine in R2-04, de la Rosa in R2-05 and R2-06 acting as the spare. Mark Handford and his team worked hard to produce a new low-downforce aerodynamic package and it worked well on Friday as Irvine set the day's fastest time: 1m 41.424secs. He was using the softer Michelin tyres and carrying a light fuel load but it was progress nonetheless. De la Rosa was less happy with his car's handling and was sixth quickest on 1m 42.302secs. The only problem all day was a power-steering failure for Irvine at the end of the first session, which did not affect his running in the second.

"This is the best-handling car I have ever driven around Hockenheim," said Irvine. "We are not as quick as we look but we're not far away either. The Michelin tyres work very well here and the recent aerodynamic changes have made it a lot easier to drive. We won't be at the front tomorrow but we should certainly be setting our sights on P8 and above."

**SATURDAY QUALIFYING** Everything seemed to be going according to plan on Saturday morning when Irvine was seventh fastest, despite doing only 14 laps. De la Rosa was 11th quickest, having completed 27 laps. But in qualifying, things did not go well for Irvine. Both drivers complained of yellow-flag delays on their final runs but de la Rosa was still delighted to be ninth on the grid on 1m 40.265secs. However, Irvine was disappointed to be down in 11th on 1m 40.371secs. "The onboard readout in my car was saying that I was three-10ths up," said de la Rosa. "But I had little choice other than to lift completely and lose what should have been a much higher grid position. However, I am optimistic that I can score points in the race tomorrow."

**SUNDAY RACE** Irvine completed just one lap in his race car in the warm-up to save the engine for the race, in which he opted for a two-stop strategy because of the soft tyres. He ran eighth early on and remained there until his pitstop on lap 12. This dropped him back to 14th and he was beginning to charge when he suffered a misfire, which led to his retirement on lap 16. If he had stayed in the race he would have bagged points. It was a serious lost opportunity due to unreliability.

De la Rosa stopped out on the circuit during warm-up when a nut in the front suspension came undone. In the race he crashed out on the first lap after the restart. End of story.

He attempted to explain the incident: "As we approached the first chicane the cars ahead of me bunched up very quickly and before I knew it I was heading into the back of the bottleneck. I braked well before the 100-metre board but I underestimated how close Nick Heidfeld was and in the end there was little I could do. I locked up the brakes and hit him. I apologise for ruining his race. I have been the one on the receiving end many times and I sympathise with him."

JAGUAR
RACING

Left and above: Hockenheim looked to have promise for Eddie Irvine and Jaguar but qualifying was a disappointment with 11th position. Irvine's race saw him run as high as eighth in company with Trulli, until a misfire led to his retirement.

Left: Niki Lauda looks less than impressed as de la Rosa explains his crash. The Spaniard had a very short race after qualifying in ninth place. Below right: More disappointment for Bobby Rahal.

## HUNGARIAN GRAND PRIX HUNGARORING
# Showdown weekend

It was a funny old weekend for Jaguar Racing. Team principal Bobby Rahal held court with his trusted British journalists, while a few motor homes along Niki Lauda had breakfast with friends from Austria. It said it all. This was a team with two principals openly at war. Rahal knew he was sacked and he and his wife Debi were making their farewells to trusted friends and journalists. Rahal was resigned to the fact that although he had done his best and the team was improving, the Jaguar people no longer wanted him around. As a result the team's morale was rather low and its track performance suitably mediocre.

**FRIDAY PRACTICE** Jaguar had a brand new chassis for Pedro de la Rosa, replacing R2-05 with the new R2-07. Irvine stayed with his usual R2-04 while R2-06 continued to be the spare car. The team used an evolution of the successful high downforce aerodynamic set-up from Monaco, with a revised rear wing and engine cover. For Friday these were available only to Irvine. De la Rosa lost a few laps because of a fuel pressure problem but ended the day 11th fastest on 1m 18.195secs. Irvine was fifth fastest on 1m 17.409secs despite a power steering failure at the end of the first session. The team was optimistic that both men would be competitive on Saturday.

**SATURDAY QUALIFYING** De la Rosa's car was fitted with the new aerodynamic parts and he completed 30 laps in the morning session, while Irvine did 29. In the afternoon, however, things did not go according to plan. Irvine was happy with the set-up and reckoned there was not much more time in the car, but dur-ing the qualifying he pushed too hard and made mistakes. The result was that he ended up 14th on the grid with a time of 1m 16.607secs. De la Rosa was just ahead of him in 13th with 1m 16.543secs.

**SUNDAY RACE** Starting from so far back there was little hope for Irvine. He was 10th quickest in the warm-up but was not optimistic. "We will have our work cut out here to score points," he said. "It will depend on clever pit strategy." In fact it did not. Irvine went off at the first corner and retired. He admitted that the accident was his own fault, explaining that he had come into the corner too quickly.

De la Rosa, who came in 11th fastest in morning warm-up, made a sensible start and was running 12th, but was struggling with rear end grip until the 10th lap, when he was overtaken by Alesi. The second set of tyres proved to be a great deal better and shortly before his second pit stop the Spaniard set the eighth fastest lap of the race, showing once again that if the team can make a leap forward in qualifying, the results will be there. He finished 11th.

Above and left: Eddie Irvine spent more time talking than racing in Hungary after a basic error saw him slide off at the first corner. Right: Irvine qualified in 14th position behind team-mate Pedro de la Rosa, who at least had a longer race to finish 11th.

Right: Pedro de la Rosa drove a steady race to bring his Jaguar home in 11th place. Below: Turn 1 in Hungary is notorious for its lack of grip. This did not stop Eddie Irvine trying the outside line in an ill-conceived novice's move which put him on the grass.

## BELGIAN GRAND PRIX SPA-FRANCORCHAMPS
# A right mess to get into

Jaguar Racing made a right mess of Spa. Bobby Rahal's demise after the Hungarian Grand Prix hit morale; he was a popular figure. It later appeared that Rahal had been asked to leave before Hungary but stayed on for the final verdict from Jaguar Cars chairman Wolfgang Reitzle. If it was right to hire him, it wasn't right to fire was the general view.

Then everyone got on with racing and it didn't go well. "A terrible weekend for Jaguar Racing," said new team boss Niki Lauda. "Not the best first weekend in charge. There's nothing one can do about bad luck."

**FRIDAY PRACTICE** Amid lots of upheaval at the top level, Jaguar's engineers worked on normally, preparing chassis R2-06 for Eddie Irvine, R2-07 for Pedro de la Rosa and R2-04 as the spare. There was a bit of excitement when Michael Schumacher ran into the back of de la Rosa going into Eau Rouge, causing a left rear puncture which was soon repaired. When practice ended, Irvine was eighth on 1m 51.555secs having done 34 laps with de la Rosa 13th on 1m 52.119secs after 31. A solid start.

**SATURDAY QUALIFYING** Fog delays on Saturday morning meant very limited time to prepare for the qualifying session, and de la Rosa lost even more when he suffered a wishbone failure. So, while Irvine was seventh quickest in the session, Pedro was 14th. In the afternoon it all went wrong, with the team making the wrong tyre choices. Irvine's session was complicated by the fact that he switched to the spare car and was then baulked unintentionally by de la Rosa. He went on to intermediate tyres and ended up 17th on 1m 59.688secs. De la Rosa was 10th on 1m 58.519secs. His season was looking up. It was the fourth time in a row he had out-qualified his team-mate, the self-proclaimed second best driver in the world (although he meant to Michael Schumacher, not the Spaniard).

There was no excuse for not reading the conditions better, especially with Niki Lauda now in charge. Alain Prost used all his driving experience to call it right for Frentzen; with the same judgement, Jaguar could also have made the second row.

**SUNDAY RACE** The race started uneventfully as Eddie Irvine carefully made sure he got beyond the first corner. By the end of the first lap Irvine was 14th, ahead of Trulli. But he could not hold the position and on lap three Trulli went past him, and Juan-Pablo Montoya followed at the start of the fourth. Further around the lap Burti tried to overtake in the fast sweeper on the way up to Blanchimont. Irvine said he did not expect a challenge and took his line through the corner. But Burti was committed and the two cars made contact, Burti's front wing being torn off. They went off into the wall at high speed. Irvine was unharmed and went to try to help extricate Burti from the Prost, trapped beneath the tyre barrier.

De la Rosa lost out to Jenson Button and Kimi Räikkönen at the start but as Frentzen and Montoya were both at the back of the grid he remained in 10th on the road. On lap two he fell behind Jean Alesi and ran in 11th until the race was stopped after the Irvine-Burti crash. He lined up 11th on the grid for the second race but was taken out at the first corner when a tangle of cars ran into one another: Verstappen bumped Heidfeld who then ran into the Jaguar, knocking it into Montoya's path. De la Rosa retired with suspension damage. It was the end of a disastrous race.

Above: Eddie Irvine again ended his race in the dirt after colliding with Luciano Burti when he failed to see the Brazilian on the inside as they turned into Blanchimont. Left: Irvine and Jacques Villeneuve discuss how it used to be and life as also-rans.

Left: Pedro de la Rosa again out-qualified team-leader Irvine, the two Jaguars placing 10th and 17th respectively on the grid. Right: De la Rosa's race was destroyed at the re-start when he was hit by Heidfeld's Sauber and knocked into Montoya's Williams.

JAGUAR RACING

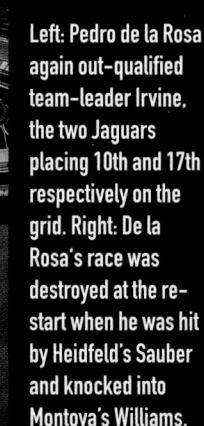

## ITALIAN GRAND PRIX MONZA
# Star of Italy

**W**hen Jaguar tested in Monza in July, it was the least competitive team. So there were no surprises when Jaguar admitted that Monza was not going to be an easy race: the car had been almost incompetent under low-downforce conditions such as at Monza. At least the team had the grace to admit it was not going to be at its best, which made Pedro de la Rosa's consistent performance, resulting in two points, a welcome surprise.

Jaguar had made no significant aerodynamic developments since Hungary and in a vain attempt to gain some performance took to Elvington airfield in Yorkshire, where sometime test driver Andre Lotterer focused on brake testing and aerodynamic set-up. The fact that Benetton rose above Jaguar in the constructors' championship after Spa was clearly playing on team principal Niki Lauda's mind. For him the stakes are very high and he was about to receive good news.

Equally high were the stakes for Eddie Irvine, who in the past three races had been completely overshadowed by his team-mate Pedro de la Rosa, a star of Monza.

**FRIDAY PRACTICE** Irvine ran in the R2-05, de la Rosa the R2-07, with the spare, R2-06, at his disposal. Both drivers complained of understeer, not helped by the slippery track. De la Rosa extracted a lot more pace out of his car than Irvine did, and wound up fourth in the practice times with a 1m 25.205secs after 43 laps. The rear brake bias was set incorrectly which caused him to spin under braking. This lost him a lot of time and he was only able to complete 23 laps with a best time of 1m 27.401secs. Both drivers were adamant that if they managed to balance their cars better they would go faster in qualifying.

**SATURDAY QUALIFYING** The team worked through the night to banish the understeer problems and Irvine's car was better than on Friday. In the morning session, Irvine was 11th with a best of 1m 24.642secs after 24 laps. De la Rosa was ninth quickest with a 1m 24.575secs. In qualifying de la Rosa's best time was 1m 23.693secs after 10 laps. Irvine was 13th, hampered by a persistent rear brake bias problem, which made his car twitchy under braking. Irvine was running two-10ths of a second faster on his last lap, which was aborted by the red flags. He had to make do with a best of 1m 24.031secs.

**SUNDAY RACE** At the start Irvine took advantage of the incident between Jenson Button and Jarno Trulli and made an astounding seventh place out of the first corner, just behind de la Rosa who had made an equally astounding sixth. Irvine then faded away with a loss of power, fell through the field and went into the pits on lap 14. The problem was deemed terminal even though it had failed to show on the telemetry. Irvine said: "It has been a bad weekend for me from the minute I arrived in Monza."

De la Rosa, meanwhile, sailed on to fifth and said: "Everything worked like clockwork." It was Michelin's victory as well as his superb one-stop strategy. He did not stop for fuel until lap 36, in fifth, was able to rejoin without losing a place and got home with two valuable points for his team.

Juan Pablo Montoya's first Grand Prix win stole the thunder from Jaguar at Monza. Above and right: Having qualified 10th, Pedro de la Rosa's strong run to fifth place captured two valuable constructors' points for the team.

Right: Pedro de la Rosa leads Jacques Villeneuve during their battle for fifth place. Below left and right: Eddie Irvine's weekend was less impressive. He qualified 13th and after an early charge to sixth retired on lap 14.

## UNITED STATES GRAND PRIX INDIANAPOLIS
# Chips are down

All it seemed Jaguar Racing needed was a goal. Now it had one: to overtake Benetton in the constructors' points rankings – by vastly improving its cars, Benetton had against the odds racked up 10 points. And Jaguar's goal had prompted a return to form and a new vigour. That's the problem with having the team run by an ex-racing driver – and, of course, the opportunity. Wave the flag and watch the charge. Jaguar Racing was elated to come away from Indianapolis level on points with Benetton, and one place ahead. The two teams – one backed by mighty Ford, the other by Renault – were slugging it out for seventh in the constructors' championship.

After being outraced and out-qualified by Pedro de la Rosa in recent races, Eddie Irvine regained the upper hand at Indianapolis, screaming round the famous banked track for fourth. A superb strategy with a single, very late stop and solid driving from Irvine turned it into a brilliant weekend for the team.

**FRIDAY PRACTICE** Jaguar brought three cars to Indy: chassis R2-04 for Irvine (with 06 as his spare) and 07 for de la Rosa. Irvine was fifth fastest over 52 laps with 1m 13.806secs; de la Rosa was just three places behind with 1m 13.917secs over 50. The drivers tested a range of tyre and set-up combinations. The team was under pressure to beat Benetton, but Niki Lauda was optimistic. "We had two trouble free sessions and we are in good shape for tomorrow," he said. "It's too early to make predictions about where we will end up."

**SATURDAY QUALIFYING** In morning practice, de la Rosa and Irvine finished in just 14th and 17th places respectively. This downturn in form was a small worry, but it became a big concern when it was repeated that afternoon.

Given Jaguar's great hopes, qualifying was a disaster. Irvine found his car suffered understeer and lost time on the fast, banked section of the track. He qualified in 14th with 1m 13.189secs. De la Rosa lagged behind for the first time since Magny-Cours, qualifying 16th with 1m 13.679secs.

Niki Lauda claimed 'it's no worse than we expected before we arrived' – a change of tune from the previous day. Worse, the team felt it had maximised the R2's performance. Jaguar's big hope was a hot raceday, to squeeze added performance from the Michelin tyres that the drivers had bitterly complained about, while conceding that the similarly-shod BMW Williams were not similarly afflicted.

**SUNDAY RACE** The warm-up brought de la Rosa and Irvine seventh and 11th; the slow session times offered few performance clues.

Irvine gained two places off the grid, then another on lap two as Kimi Räikkönen fell back, but he lost it almost immediately to a charging Jean Alesi. His next 31 laps were uneventful. As the rest peeled into the pits, Irvine stayed out an impossibly long time making up ground. He eventually pitted on lap 52, dropping back just two places to seventh. He overtook Heidfeld almost at once for sixth, then was promoted to fifth when Rubens Barrichello retired, which became fourth and three points after Jarno Trulli's exclusion.

It was a different matter for de la Rosa. He dropped three places at the start, gained one with the demise of Räikkönen and settled down into 18th until the one-stoppers started to pit on lap 35. Then he climbed gradually up the rankings until lap 42, when he finally decided to have a go at Jacques Villeneuve's BAR Honda, which he had been sitting behind since the start. The two cars collided, both drivers blaming the other. De la Rosa pitted from ninth two laps before Irvine, and emerged in 13th, where he would stay until Barrichello's disaster promoted him to his finishing position of only 12th, which later became 11th.

Irvine said: "That was excellent teamwork. It's a mystery why we seem to be so strong in race trim yet qualifying seems to elude us." Come Suzuka, the battle with Benetton could be close.

Above: Irvine earned his money with a strong drive to fourth. Left: Jaguar's 'Monday morning quarter back', Niki Lauda, was right whatever happened, good or bad.

Left and below: Pedro de la Rosa matched Irvine in qualifying, lining up two places behind him in 16th place. His race included a collision with Villeneuve, each driver blaming the other, but de la Rosa continued and finished 11th.

## JAPANESE GRAND PRIX SUZUKA
# Poor finish to a bad year

Jaguar Racing brought to Suzuka an R2 similar to the one that had raced in the US. Everyone else was still full on, and it showed Jaguar up.

It arrived eyeing a points finish to catch Benetton Renault. In driving terms it looked possible: Eddie Irvine and Pedro de la Rosa knew Suzuka well, having cut their teeth in Formula Nippon.

The car, however, just fell short of matching de la Rosa's potential. Irvine could have actually achieved the goal, but was robbed by yet another problem with the Intertechnic fuel rigs.

The Jaguar R2 had been a solid midfield runner at most of the season's events, and Suzuka's high-speed demands were never going to suit the Leaping Cat. In the end, though, recent improvements made by Steve Nichols and Mark Handford helped Irvine and de la Rosa to seventh and eighth before two unrelated problems struck.

The aero package had been the team's Achilles heel all year, with the team running back and forth between Milton Keynes and California for development. The purchase of the Orange Arrows windtunnel, which had been provisionally agreed, should be a major asset to handle this problem in the future.

**FRIDAY PRACTICE** Jaguar Racing arrived in Suzuka with three cars: Irvine used R2-04, which had been going strong since before Monaco; de la Rosa wielded the relatively new R2-07 and kept R2-05 in reserve.

Positions of third for de la Rosa and sixth for Irvine could not lift the team's despondency. The team said the R2 was suffering hugely from understeer through the high-speed corners, though both drivers reported it felt well balanced in the slower corners such as the Esses. Watching both drivers saw at the wheel through the daunting 130R, where Prost's Tomas Enge smashed off heavily, was enough to convince observers Jaguar's appraisal was honest.

De la Rosa suffered continuous understeer while scrubbing his tyres and maximising the aero package. Reliability was not a problem – typically for Jaguar Racing in 2001 – and he clocked up 39 laps on his way to third in 1m 36.225secs.

Irvine highlighted the problem when he complained the car felt 'twitchy' in the early stages. He did a 1m 36.589secs.

**SATURDAY QUALIFYING**
It was business as usual in qualifying, with Jaguar stuck in the lower midfield. The car's qualifying pace, or lack of it, had mystified Irvine all season – on most occasions, his race pace had been remarkably better. This time, though, the outspoken Ulsterman was stunned by his car's speed relative to the practice runs, but the end result was all too familiar: 13th, in 1m 25.132secs.

Spaniard de la Rosa was unsurprised to find himself down in 16th on 1m 35.639secs. He was still suffering from the problems that had plagued Jaguar all year. He also failed to find a suitable balance on the Michelins, which seem tailored increasingly to the specific requirements of the BMW Williams, despite vociferous denials from Michelin competition boss Pierre Dupasquier.

**SUNDAY RACE** Irvine got away cleanly, gaining a place courtesy of Nick Heidfeld's slow start and benefiting from the mammoth crash between Kimi Räikkönen and Alesi to take 10th. From there on, he waited behind the Benetton Renaults.

By his first stop Irvine had pushed up to seventh place, but a problem with the Intertechnic fuel pump's power source meant the R2 went back out on track without nourishment. Irvine came back in as the team hurriedly switched to his team-mate's power source, but that failed too and Irvine was forced to retire after scrapping his way through the order. The only consolation was that he could get in a taxi to Tokyo earlier than expected.

Irvine's team-mate also battled forward, exploiting carnage up ahead to occupy 13th by lap six. After his first pitstop on lap 26 the Spaniard came out just behind a battle raging between Jarno Trulli, Giancarlo Fisichella, Jacques Villeneuve, Jenson Button and Heidfeld. The Spaniard was running in 12th when an oil leak crippled the cat on lap 45, ending his race.

Right: Jaguar's unimpressive form, typical of its season, continued in Suzuka. A fuelling rig failed twice, ultimately spelling the end of Irvine's race and indicating the gap Jaguar needed to bridge to be a winner.

Right: Irvine's early charge saw him briefly lead Giancarlo Fisichella's Benetton Renault. Below right: On the parade lap Irvine flagged a taxi, a gesture which foretold his early departure from Suzuka.

304

305

Team Review    Race by Race
# PROST

## Contents

| | | | | | | |
|---|---|---|---|---|---|---|
| Team Review | – | The season | p308 | European Grand Prix | – Nürburgring | p322 |
| Australian Grand Prix | – | Melbourne | p314 | French Grand Prix | – Magny-Cours | p323 |
| Malaysian Grand Prix | – | Sepang | p315 | British Grand Prix | – Silverstone | p324 |
| Brazilian Grand Prix | – | Interlagos | p316 | German Grand Prix | – Hockenheim | p325 |
| San Marino Grand Prix | – | Imola | p317 | Hungarian Grand Prix | – Hungaroring | p326 |
| Spanish Grand Prix | – | Barcelona | p318 | Belgian Grand Prix | – Spa-Francorchamps | p327 |
| Austrian Grand Prix | – | A1 Ring | p319 | Italian Grand Prix | – Monza | p328 |
| Monaco Grand Prix | – | Monte Carlo | p320 | USA Grand Prix | – Indianapolis | p329 |
| Canadian Grand Prix | – | Montreal | p321 | Japanese Grand Prix | – Suzuka | p330 |

2001

Alain Prost

Tomas Enge

Gaston Mazzacane

Jean Alesi

Heinz-Harald Frentzen

Luciano Burti

# A fight for survival

Looking back, Alain Prost must wonder why he ever viewed the year 2001 with such optimism when the season opened in Melbourne. There was certainly no lack of action off the track.

It began with his old friend Jean Alesi faithfully striving to get the team on its feet, and bring in much-needed money from South American TV network PSN. PSN put Gaston Mazzacane into the seat vacated by the sacked Nick Heidfeld to partner Alesi. Pedro de la Rosa was waiting in the wings as test driver, should Mazzacane fail to make the grade. By the time he failed de la Rosa was gone.

There may have been little money but there was no shortage of activity, as retired driver Pedro Diniz and his father Abilio came on board as 40 per cent shareholders, helping guarantee the cost of the engines from Ferrari.

Alain Prost's frosty relations with the team's sponsors in 2000, including engine maker Peugeot, meant they had all decamped and left the team with no funds at all. The dreadful 2000 performance had also left it without TV money. The fact that it had to pay for its engines meant the finances were far from shipshape. In fact they were disastrous.

Alain Prost continued his winning ways by almost immediately falling out with Abilio and Pedro Diniz. The two parties started communicating via the lawyers. Relationships between them were strained to breaking-point.

So chaotic was it that the team started the season with two drivers and finished with two different ones, employing five in all. Jean Alesi and Gaston Mazzacane started and Heinz-Harald Frentzen and Tomas Enge finished off, with Luciano Burti in the middle.

Mazzacane was simply slow, Alesi showed an unbelievable ability to nurse a car to a finish and Burti the same ability to severely damage the team's cars. Drivers came and went as the team scrabbled for cash. It was that sort of season. By the end of the year a financial saviour had materialised, but there was no guarantee he would sign on the bottom line.

## The Prost AP04 car

PROST was saved by the acquisition of two top technical men for 2001, Joan Villadelprat and Henri Durand, who set to work on the Prost AP04. The job was made easier by the fact that the team elected to buy in the engine, gearbox and drivetrain as a complete unit from Ferrari. Ferrari also supplied plentiful data on installing its 2000 specification V10 engine. The third member of the team was John Barnard, whose company B3 Technologies supplied and developed various parts.

With Ferrari's data Durand thus knew the cooling parameters, centre of gravity and optimum geometry for the rear suspension that he would mount on the Ferrari gearbox. Certainly the AP04 was a big step over the AP03, but it was not big enough.

The team built six AP04s. AP04/01 appeared only fleetingly before being retired. AP04/02 was the race car for Mazzacane in

Melbourne and Sepang, but after that quickly became the spare and was used as such from Brazil through to France, and again in Hungary, Belgium and Italy. AP04/03 was Alesi's race car from Melbourne to Spain, and later appeared as the spare in America and Japan, after doing brief race duty for Tomas Enge in Italy. Chassis 04 was the spare in Melbourne and Sepang, afterwards becoming Mazzacane's race car in Brazil and San Marino, and was then taken over by Luciano Burti who used it until Monaco. Later it became the spare chassis in Britain and Germany before Burti went back to it for Hungary and Belgium. It was in this chassis that the young Brazilian had his horrific accident at Spa, and it says a great deal about the strength of the AP04 structure that he survived unharmed and that the chassis did likewise. Though heavily damaged, it was basically intact and was rebuilt as a test car.

AP04/05 appeared as Alesi's spare car in Monaco, then became Burti's regular race car from Canada until his massive accident ▷

Jean Alesi

in it at Hockenheim. After being rebuilt, it reappeared on active duty as Enge's race car in America and Japan. Finally, AP04/06 was Alesi's race car from Austria onwards, and was taken over by Heinz-Harald Frentzen from Hungary until the end of the season.

In its first tests the AP04 delighted Alesi, but he soon realised that the team was playing around – always running it in qualifying trim to try to attract desperately needed finance before the season began. Others believed the car was in non-regulation trim when it was topping test timesheets in Spain. Come Melbourne and the first race, the game was up and the Prost proved very average in speed, though exceptionally reliable. But this was no good to a racer like Alesi. Once he tried to run it in race trim, he came to realise that it lacked grip and had too much understeer. In fact there were serious aerodynamic deficiencies in Melbourne that hadn't come to light in testing, because the team was obsessed only with fast times to attract publicity. Alesi was duped like everyone else. McLaren's team principal, Ron Dennis, went as far as congratulating Prost for winning what he called the 'winter world championships'. Of course Dennis had seen it all before, and was not surprised when Alesi struggled to wrestle the car around Melbourne. Other experts were surprisingly taken in, and spent the first half of the year trying to tell everyone the Prost was a good car, but...

In Austria, Prost struggled vainly against the Saubers, which had the same engine but a slightly different transmission, and the car paled miserably in comparison. By the Nürburgring, however, it seemed to have made progress against the Swiss cars, until it transpired that they were having an off day with electronic differential maladies.

## Technical developments

DEVELOPMENT through the season was not outstanding, once two major aerodynamic revisions had been brought on stream for Monaco and Canada. Thereafter it was confined to minor aero work and playing around with revised suspension geometries.

However, Frentzen's arrival on the scene in Hungary, after Jordan had wooed Alesi away, proved a fillip. The German is a better chassis-sorter than the mercurial Frenchman, and he worked with the team to gradually massage the car into better shape. Frentzen reckoned that it was not a bad car, and that it would be hugely improved if its inherent understeer could be cured.

At the start of the season Alesi had been 3.001secs off Michael Schumacher's pole-position pace in Melbourne. By Suzuka, Frentzen had reduced that to 2.648secs, suggesting that progress had been made or, more likely, that Frentzen was a much better driver than Alesi.

Prost used 45 Ferrari engines during the season. They were very reliable, and up until Italy the only failure had been in Burti's car at Silverstone. However, during practice for the Italian Grand Prix, Tomas Enge encountered two engine problems, which the team put down to quality control at Ferrari. Like Sauber, Prost began the season with a Monza 2000 specification engine, which was updated subsequently to early 2001 spec. Thus its power rose from 820bhp to around 835bhp by the end of the year.

Jean Alesi in particular loved the engine, making a 'chalk and cheese' comparison with the Peugeot he had been saddled with in 2000. The Frenchman also revelled in his car's reliability. With Ferrari's own transmission Prost encountered none of the

John Barnard

Pedro Diniz

Joan Villadelprat

drama that blighted the second half of Sauber's season, and Alesi had the rare distinction of finishing every race that he started for the team.

Of the 2,130 racing laps available to the team in the 2001 season, Alesi finished 758. Frentzen managed 250 in his five races for Prost, Mazzacane 135 in his four, Burti 398 in his 10 and Enge 166 in his three outings. That gave a total of 1,707, a high figure. In fact the Prost team was the second most reliable team on the grid, with a score of 80.1 per cent, better than the mighty McLaren Mercedes.

## The drivers

JEAN Alesi was certain of a drive in 2001 and was full of the usual pre-season optimism and praise for the team principal, Alain Prost. Most thought it somewhat shallow and put it down to the fact that Alesi was unlikely to get a drive elsewhere – certainly not one that paid money (as opposed to him having to pay money). In the event Alesi was paid a $1.5 million retainer, which he never got because of the financial problems. It was that which enabled him to wriggle out of his contract after the German Grand Prix and move to ▷

# PROST SEASON STATISTICS

PROST

## RELIABILITY PERFORMANCE

| Driver | Races | Max laps | Laps completed | Reliability rating |
|---|---|---|---|---|
| Jean Alesi | 12 | 773 | 758 | 98.1% |
| Luciano Burti | 10 | 640 | 398 | 62.2% |
| Heinz-Harald Frentzen | 5 | 292 | 250 | 85.6% |
| Gaston Mazzacane | 4 | 246 | 135 | 54.9% |
| Tomas Enge | 3 | 179 | 166 | 92.7% |
| Constructor | Races | Max laps | Laps completed | Reliability rating |
| Team | 34 | 2130 | 1707 | 80.1% |

Gaston Mazzacane

## CHAMPIONSHIP PERFORMANCE

| Driver | 2001 points | 2000 points | 12 month change |
|---|---|---|---|
| Heinz-Harald Frentzen | 6 | 11 | -45.5% |
| Jean Alesi | 5 | 0 | +500% |
| Luciano Burti | 0 | 0 | +0% |
| Gaston Mazzacane | 0 | 0 | +0% |
| Tomas Enge | 0 | - | Did not compete |
| Constructor | 2001 points | 2000 points | 12 month change |
| Team | 4 | 0 | +400% |

## CHASSIS LOG

**AP04/01** Test car only.

**AP04/02** Race car for Gaston Mazzacane at Melbourne and Sepang. Spare car at Interlagos, Imola, Barcelona, A1 Ring, Monte Carlo, Montreal, Nürburgring (used by Luciano Burti in qualifying), Magny-Cours, Hungaroring, Spa-Francorchamps and Monza (used by Tomas Enge in qualifying).

**AP04/03** Race car for Jean Alesi at Melbourne, Sepang, Interlagos, Imola and Barcelona; and for Enge at Monza. Spare car at Indianapolis and Suzuka (qualified and raced by Enge after his practice shunt).

**AP04/04** Race car for Mazzacane at Interlagos and Imola; and for Burti at Barcelona, A1 Ring, Monte Carlo (not used after his practice crash), Hungaroring and Spa-Francorchamps where it was written off in his horrific collision with the tyre wall. Spare car at Melbourne, Sepang, Silverstone and Hockenheim (raced by Burti after his massive crash at the start).

**AP04/05** Race car for Burti at Montreal, Nürburgring, Magny-Cours, Silverstone and Hockenheim (not used for the race after it was almost destroyed in Burti's first start launch over Michael Schumacher); and for Enge at Indianapolis and Suzuka (only used in practice when he suffered a heavy shunt and had to switch to 03 for the rest of the weekend). Spare car at Monte Carlo (qualified and raced by Burti after he damaged 04 on Thursday).

**AP04/06** Race car for Alesi at the A1 Ring, Monte Carlo, Montreal, Nürburgring, Magny-Cours, Silverstone and Hockenheim; and for Heinz-Harald Frentzen at the Hungaroring, Spa-Francorchamps, Monza, Indianapolis and Suzuka.

Jordan Honda. Gaston Mazzacane was signed because the team attracted PSN to provide sponsorship, but hiring him was not a contractual obligation and Prost thought he would attract other South American sponsors. When he didn't he was ditched. Mazzacane simply wasn't good enough and there was much tension in the team over his employment.

Pedro de la Rosa was hired as a test driver after he was sacked from Arrows. But before he could get going he got a better offer as a test driver for Jaguar, much to Prost's chagrin. After four races de la Rosa got Burti's drive at Jaguar, and Prost took responsibility for providing Burti with a drive from Jaguar.

After that, things then settled down for a while, with Burti impressing as he outqualified Alesi in his first two races with the team, in Spain and Austria. But then came Monaco, where Alesi always shines. He took 11th place on the grid and finished sixth, and for the team that one point was as good as a victory. The tears flowed in the paddock afterwards, for that was a crucial psychological step.

Alesi helped the team to make another such step in Canada, a race later, when he took two more points after finishing fifth. At Hockenheim he chased Jacques Villeneuve and the Benetton duo home to score his final point for the team with sixth place. But there was no joy in Alesi's face as he was interviewed by ITV's Louise Goodman. From that moment it was clear he was going to Jordan and his loyalty to Prost was over.

But his contribution to the team had been critical. At the end of the season his four points lifted Prost from its 11th place in 2000 to ninth in 2001 and all the financial goodies that go with that.

When Frentzen was sacked he could have either sat out the season or taken up the offer to drive for Prost for nothing except his expenses, which he realised he was unlikely to be paid. He decided to go for it.

The highlight of the season came at Spa, when some smart think-ing got Frentzen onto the soft Michelin dry tyres at just the moment it mattered most in qualifying. He put the AP04 fourth on the grid there, and hearts beat faster as the start approached. That was when Alain Prost's day turned sour, however, for Frentzen could not engage a gear and stalled on the formation lap. It was a bitter blow, and had its roots in his lack of familiarity with the Prost's electronic system compared with that on the Jordan he had been driving earlier in the season. He finished ninth that day, and later made amends by taking a genuine 12th on the grid at Monza, which he felt was a fine indicator of the car's true potential. There he retired with gearbox failure.

Spa was a low point for another reason: Burti's accident.

The young Brazilian had shown flashes of promise after outqual-ifying Alesi initially, though usually he lacked the Frenchman's race pace. Then came the first blow to his career. At the start of the German Grand Prix at Hockenheim, Michael Schumacher's Ferrari broke its transmission and Burti's Prost was launched skyward as it ran into the back of the world champion's stricken car. The blue car barrel-rolled spectacularly before landing between the two Arrows and then slithering into the gravel bed in Turn 1. Burti was well enough to take the restart in the spare car after a miraculous escape, but retired after a short run complaining of pains in his arms.

He returned for Hungary, but then became involved in his huge accident with Eddie Irvine on the original fourth lap of the Belgian Grand Prix at Spa. The Ulsterman had clearly made an error on the exit to the right-hander before Blanchimont. As they approached the 190mph left-hander Burti had begun to draw alongside Irvine, who said that he had seen him. He kept moving over on Burti, who put two wheels on the grass in a belated attempt to avoid a colli-sion. As the two cars touched Irvine spun but Burti speared straight across the gravel trap and head-on into the tyre wall.

Initially observers feared the worst, but Burti escaped with bruising and a strong desire to discuss things with Irvine. As things stand, the accident probably ended his F1 career. With Burti advised by doctors to sit out the rest of the season, Prost turned to well-financed Tomas Enge, who did the final three races and paid handsomely for he privilege. The amiable Czech showed speed but also a propensity to damage cars, especially in Suzuka. There, he shunted heavily in the notorious 130R corner; another car was expensively rebuilt, doubtless to be immediately sold off to the highest bidder for as much as possible at the season ended for the wages to be paid.

## Commercial

THE commercial management of the Prost team in 2001 was a joke, and no one would disagree with that conclusion. But, on the other hand, how the team survived to the season end on the tiny amount of money it had is a tribute to the management. So it couldn't have been that much of a joke.

Joan Villadelprat's charm and skill was key, as he fended off creditors and made good so many times. He admits privately he used driveshafts and other items that were well past their sell-by dates. He had to use his eye to assess which parts would make it and which wouldn't. His skill was confirmed by the sheer reliability of the cars in such trying conditions.

The other big problem was Luciano Burti's ability to damage cars. Normally when a car is crashed, the parts bin is full and rebuilds cost nothing. Not so at Prost, where the parts bin was always empty.

At the beginning of the year there was no launch of the car and sponsors were few. PSN, the South American TV network, pitched in around $6 million; Adecco, the Franco-Swiss temping firm, another $4 million; and then Acer of Taiwan put in $8 million to have its name on the engine covers and the title of the car. The Diniz family effectively paid for the engine and the rest – some $18 million – was left for the team.

When the money ran out mid-season, it was left for Bernie

**Tomas Enge**

Ecclestone to advance some of 2002's TV money. The team scored points and looked certain to qualify for the 2002 payout – in sharp contrast to 2001, when it did not, and this was the only financial bright spot. Ecclestone was interested in keeping Alain Prost in Formula One, and he helped. The arrival of Luciano Burti with a dowry from Jaguar provided a $2 million cash injection.

Then a white knight turned up in the shape of Prince Khaled al Waleed, son of one of the world's richest men. Al Waleed wanted to buy into Prost and is said to have given the team a downpayment of $2 million before the Italian Grand Prix, before the deal was signed. It kept Prost going until the last race.

But many conflicts remained to be resolved, not least the matter of the team's other shareholders: LVMH, Bernard Arnault's luxury goods group; UFA Sports, a subsidiary of Bertelsmann; and the Diniz family. All were hostile and would take some placating.

The sole asset of the team is its qualification for next year's TV money, worth $16 million.

**The Prost motorhomes**

# Serious reality check

The Prost team spent all winter scrambling for sponsorship when, in unprecedented fashion, all its 2000 sponsors scarpered, even those under long-term contract. The team had topped the testing charts all winter with its new Ferrari-powered car, but Melbourne brought reality. Mid-grid was an achievement for them. Veteran Jean Alesi's skill was a big factor; he was driving as well as ever. "This is my 12th season in F1," he said, "so I know better than to try and predict what's going to happen. I don't know what I'm fighting for, but I know I'm fighting."

Prost, which only finished 13 times out of a possible 34 in 2000, was channelling all its energy into making sure it had reliable cars that could complete race distances. And then it would start work on increasing speed. Technical director Henri Durand was hopeful that the poor performance at Melbourne was not a precursor for the season. "We will have to act very rapidly in order to correct this," he said. "But we believe that once we get to fast circuits like Interlagos and Imola, we will be able to exploit the full potential of the car."

Prost's decision to hire Gaston Mazzacane on financial criteria did not go down well with the team, and his weekend performance changed no-one's view. Prost had regressed from points-challenger to back-of-grid no-hoper, and wasn't enjoying the experience.

**FRIDAY PRACTICE** Prost brought three cars to Melbourne: AP04-03 for Alesi, AP04-02 for Mazzacane, and AP04-04 as Alesi's spare. The Franco-Sicilian posted the ninth fastest time of the day – 1m 31.089secs. "Being in the first 10 is a great start for us," he said. Mazzacane was 10 places below his teammate in 19th with a time of 1m 33.153secs. This, he explained, was due to a full fuel load: "I did a lot of laps today with no mechanical problems, which was good as we were able to do a lot of work on set-up and brakes."

**SATURDAY QUALIFYING** Despite his hopes for a strong qualifying position, Alesi was only able to pedal his AP04 into 14th place with a time of 1m 29.893secs. He suffered from difficulties with set-up and balance. Starting from the seventh row, he was confident that he could still make an impression in the race and was positive about his condition for racing. "We had some difficulty finding the right set-up, as this circuit is very unusual," he said optimistically. "The car is very sensi-

tive, easily shifting from a good to a bad balance but it is basically a good car. I am sorry for not being higher on the grid, but I am in good spirits and in excellent physical and psychological condition." Mazzacane had a more difficult session, winding up in 20th position. He lost some valuable track time in the morning practice sessions due to an electrical problem. Alain Prost was disappointed with the performance of his cars and also blamed the AP04's incompatibility with the circuit.

**SUNDAY RACE** Prost's worries about reliability were confirmed almost immediately. Mazzacane didn't make it past the third lap before pulling out because of a loose brake pedal. It was almost farcical, as he said: "I had a good start and the car was going well, but I felt the brake pedal was totally loose and I had to pull out." Henri Durand vowed that the problem was a one-off. Prost was using new carbon fibre pedals in 2001 and there may have been confusion on the assembly. Alain Prost had a more elaborate reason after the race: "Gaston's retirement was caused by a failure in the brakes. The connector feeding the brake fluid broke down." But no one believed him.

Alesi came home in ninth place after an uneventful race. The team's race plan was a conventional one-stop strategy. Alesi was brought in on lap 35 from 12th position and was able to rejoin in the same place. With more fuel and new tyres, he took advantage of Jos Verstappen's pitstop on lap 38 to take 11th, and was elevated to 10th when Montoya retired from third place on lap 40. Verstappen retaliated in the closing stages of lap 47 and passed the Prost, which demoted him to 11th again, but Irvine's late stop on lap 50 gave Alesi the chance to grab 9th for the finish. It was far from what he had expected.

The Prost team had topped the testing tables in the winter and the drivers were expecting great things from their cars. But reality arrived in Melbourne when the French cars were unable to find their winter speed.

Above and right: Jean Alesi started a run of reliable classifications in Melbourne that was to last for the rest of his Prost career.

## MALAYSIAN GRAND PRIX SEPANG
# No respite in sight

Either Prost had suffered a huge reversal between the end of winter testing and the first race, or it was running an illegal car in testing to post good times and impress sponsors with unrealistic performance. There was nothing wrong with that, of course, as teams can do what they like in testing –- even bolt on a turbo if they so desire. Ron Dennis calls it 'winning the winter world championship'. Prost had done its credibility no favours but the tactics employed

**Top and above:** Jean Alesi was very disappointed with his car in Malaysia. He had expected more. Alesi was his usual feisty self, but although the Prost may have flown in winter testing it had failed to find that form in a race. Credibility had become an issue.

**Above and below:** Alesi began the race battling with the beleaguered Benetton Renaults, but when the rain came down he used his wet weather skill to creep up with the frontrunners. His chances of points were sadly ruined by oversteer problems.

had fooled some pretty wise people along the way.

It spoke volumes that technical director Henri Durand was not in Sepang but actually back at the factory in France, overseeing what was being hailed as a huge new technical programme. Basically, that meant he was trying to sort out the Prost's aerodynamics. Unlike last season, however, the cars were at least reliable.

**FRIDAY PRACTICE** Jean Alesi and Gaston Mazzacane kept their Australian chassis, with AP04-04 again the spare, again for Alesi, befitted Durand's aero reputation, significant modifications had been made to the front wing, which now sported a flip-up outside endplate. The new flap had a bigger cord in the middle section and ran higher in the middle. To improve airflow out of the car body, the chimney-style exhausts had been cut down to enhance the cooling systems – a feature first seen in Australia. Jean Alesi completed 40 laps, finishing the day 16th fastest with 1m 41.834secs – a time nearly a whopping three seconds off the pace. His team-mate Mazzacane clocked 1m 42.563secs after 33 laps to secure 19th place, but was beset with set-up problems.

**SATURDAY QUALIFYING** The aerodynamic modifications coupled with good work overnight saw Alesi qualify in 13th position with a time of 1m 37.406secs. He said his car felt more like the winter testing model in which he had performed so well. Mazzacane struggled and did not share his team-mate's optimism, ending up with a 1m 39.006secs – good enough for 19th. "The tyres are behaving very well," said team principal Alain Prost, "and we are some way to discovering why we have lost the good balance we had in testing."

**SUNDAY RACE** Prost had a relatively good day as both cars finished the race intact – Alesi crossed the line in 9th and Mazzacane was 12th. Alesi, starting in 13th, benefited from his low grid position as he missed the first-corner troubles. The rain then disposed of those separating him from the front-runners and by the time the safety car came out he was sixth. However, when the race re-started, he suffered badly with oversteer and had to yield several places. "When the track dried I was keeping up quite a good pace," he said, "but I could only stay where I was." In his second pit-stop he did not take on enough fuel and had to ease off to get to the finish. Alesi was disappointed. Mazzacane experienced huge trouble keeping the rear end of his Prost in check and had trouble with his pitstops: "On my first stop, the team had a problem with the fuel machine and could not refuel," he explained, "so I had to come in again."

# Alesi reads the riot act

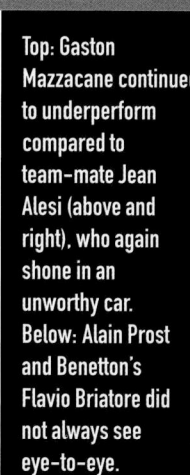

Jean Alesi was on the warpath, haunted by the fact that in Melbourne he had called the AP04 'one of best cars I have ever driven'. That was, of course, before driving the car in race form. In fact, so angry was Alesi that between Malaysia and Brazil he pulled out of a test session and refused to drive.

Many good things were in place at Prost, including sporting director Joan Villadelprat: experienced and determined, he had played a major role in Michael Schumacher's successful Benetton years. And technical director and former McLaren aerodynamicist Henri Durand knew what it took to win following his time with the Woking team. But despite the promise, nothing had yet been delivered.

FRIDAY PRACTICE Modifications included a new front wing with revised endplates and flaps – the first part of Durand's improvement programme – but only small interim steps were made for Interlagos. Slightly revised front suspension, a mildly revised floor and new brakes were also in evidence.

Alesi in chassis 03 (with 02 as his spare) and Mazzacane in 04 both suffered from separate handling problems. New brakes proved difficult to master and an aerodynamic imbalance dogged both drivers around the circuit. Alesi finished the day in 14th on a time of 1m 17.518secs, while Mazzacane could do no better than 20th after 40 laps. The Argentine recorded a time of 1m 18.269secs, some way off his team-mate.

Alesi said: "The car's balance is far from what I would like it to be and we have a problem adjusting the brakes, which is affecting our performance."

SATURDAY QUALIFYING In qualifying, Alesi's first flying lap proved his quickest and the Prost appeared to lose all balance as the track temperature increased. The Michelins' sensitivity to temperature change is well noted. But whereas the Williams found time as the track heated up, neither Prost driver could make the car work.

Alesi could only secure the 15th fastest time, on 1m 15.437secs, while Mazzacane limped to 21st place on the grid with a 1m 16.520secs. Alesi was fifth fastest through the speed trap, with Mazzacane 10th. Fellow Ferrari engine customer Sauber recorded the 18th and 19th fastest speeds, yet out-qualified the Prosts. This pointed to an incorrect set-up for Prost – which was unable to cope with the more technical sections of Interlagos – or serious chassis flaws.

SUNDAY RACE Jean Alesi jumped to 10th at the start of the race, aided by Olivier Panis's poor start and Mika Häkkinen's stall, and he gained another place on lap 12 when Jacques Villeneuve pitted. The Frenchman maintained his position until he made his first stop, on lap 24, which was to last an unusually long time. Prost stated afterwards that the stop took approximately 15 seconds longer than it should have done, due to the standardised refuelling rig 'jamming into alarm mode and refusing to deliver fuel'.

When Alesi came back out he overtook his team-mate, then got ahead of the Sauber pairing in the pitstop period. Alesi fared well in the second round of stops, when the teams reacted to the sudden rainfall, and he wound up sixth for two tantalising laps. He would lose out to the superior firepower of Olivier Panis and Giancarlo Fisichella in the closing stages, however, partially due to his severely damaged tyres. "The car became more and more difficult to drive and I could not stop the two cars behind me overtaking," admitted Alesi, who eventually came in eighth.

Mazzacane managed to overtake Jenson Button, but virtually nobody else. He moved up the order from his 21st place starting position, but only because of retirements and problems ahead. The Argentine ran as high as 12th prior to the first pitstop, before dropping back to fight with the Minardi of Tarso Marques over 14th and 15th places. He had to wait for the Brazilian to pit before taking the place, speaking volumes for his performance.

After the second stops Mazzacane found his way into 10th place, but couldn't prevent the recovering Jacques Villeneuve from firing past him in the BAR Honda – even though the French-Canadian was suffering with a broken differential. His clutch gave out on lap 54 and the Argentine limped off the track, to have the resulting fire extinguished into retirement.

Top: Gaston Mazzacane continued to underperform compared to team-mate Jean Alesi (above and right), who again shone in an unworthy car. Below: Alain Prost and Benetton's Flavio Briatore did not always see eye-to-eye.

## SAN MARINO GRAND PRIX IMOLA
# A light in the tunnel

Left and below: Gaston Mazzacane's days with the team were numbered and he knew it. He had got the drive through his ties with sponsor PSN but never looked likely to match the results of his illustrious team-mate Jean Alesi.

The first dramatic changes promised since Australia finally arrived. Technical director Henri Durand produced the initial batch of these, with a completely new brake system, including a heavily revised pedal assembly and improvements to the car's cooling system. Aerodynamic changes had also been made, including extended Gurney flaps on the front wing to create more downforce. The development of Michelin's dry tyres had helped with the car's balance, thus generating improved qualifying and race performances from Jean Alesi. With further developments promised, there was light at the end of the tunnel for the French team.

With rumours of further reinforcements to the technical department at Prost's HQ, more improvement could be expected. Though not yet able to repeat its winter testing performances, Prost had made considerable strides since its disastrous 2000 season and this progress was undoubtedly due largely to the availability of the Ferrari engine and gearbox package.

**FRIDAY PRACTICE** Prost brought three cars to Imola: AP04-

Below right: The first signs of improvement for Prost saw Jean Alesi race hard and finish ninth, despite being stuck behind Eddie Irvine's lighter one-fuel-stop Jaguar.

03 and spare chassis AP04-02 for Alesi, plus AP04-04 for Gaston Mazzacane. Alesi clocked up a satisfying fastest time of 1m 27.437secs that put him 14th position. He improved as the track dried – as did the Michelin tyres – and his lap time, set on a full fuel load, was very encouraging. Gaston Mazzacane's car also reacted well to the conditions and in his 38 laps he set a best time of 1m 28.586secs, which put him in 16th place in the day's listings.

**SATURDAY QUALIFYING** Alesi was unable to get the set-up to his liking and produce a more competitive package for the changeable conditions. After 12 laps he had set a best time of 1m 25.411secs, which put him 14th on the grid.

The performance of Mazzacane's car also deteriorated and he made no progress during the session, qualifying in his usual position of 20th with a time of 1m 27.750secs, using all his 12 laps. The drivers complained bitterly about the lack of grip and felt that the balance and set-up of the car did not suit the tyres. The one-hour session was not long enough to cure their problems.

**SUNDAY RACE** Mazzacane experienced an engine failure, when he was running in 16th place, that finally ended his race on lap 28. An oil leak led to a costly and damaging fire.

Alesi had an uneventful race, finishing one lap down in a disappointing ninth position. Shortly before his first stop, he had been setting more competitive lap times in the 1m 28secs bracket. But because he was racing to a two-stop strategy, the time conceded in the wake of Irvine's one-stopping Jaguar proved to be disastrous.

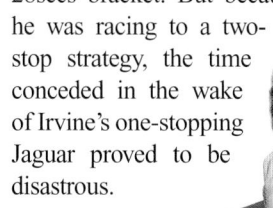

## SPANISH GRAND PRIX BARCELONA
# Moment of truth

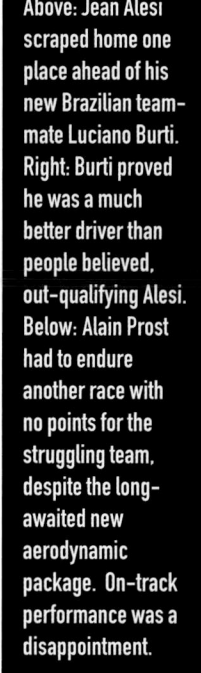

The Prost team was in a fine frame of mind, having sorted out its second-driver problem in a way that did not compromise its bank balance. Jaguar had contributed a driver and sponsor PSN seemed content with Brazilian replacement Luciano Burti. Burti's arrival put the wind up Jean Alesi and proved he wasn't the bad driver the Jaguar had made him look. He even out-qualified the Frenchman.

On the technical front, the long-awaited aerodynamic package had arrived and although the team was adamant it would make a difference, it did not produce the results. Now the team was promising another newer package in time for Monaco. Barcelona was the track at which Prost won the 'winter Grand Prix' and where it would all come good. It didn't.

**FRIDAY PRACTICE** Prost came to Spain with three cars: the new AP04-05 for Alesi, AP04-04 for new boy Burti and the spare, AP04-02, set up for Alesi.

Alesi completed 30 laps in all, setting a best of 1m 22.843secs – 2.736secs off the best time – for 15th. He failed to dial out the crippling, session-long understeer. Burti spent his sessions getting familiar with driving the Prost and ended up 21st with a time of 1m 23.885secs after 41 laps. More of the same, everyone thought. But Burti was getting used to a car with, inexplicably, no power-steering.

Both drivers set their times well into the session, with Alesi getting more out of the Michelin tyres as the track temperature increased.

**SATURDAY QUALIFYING** The crosswinds over the track severely affected the Prost,

despite the fact the team had tested extensively over the winter at the Circuit de Catalunya. Burti, although outpacing his team-mate in sector two, was slower by 1.6kph through the speed trap. The car's balance was thrown by the wind and the Brazilian took 14th on the grid with 1m 20.585secs. Outpacing his far more experienced team-mate in his first qualifying session was, though, encouraging.

Alesi struggled to find the balance and speed in his car and lined up 15th with a 1m 20.601secs, 0.016secs behind Burti. Both drivers completed their allotted 12 laps. Being out-qualified at the first attempt by his new team-mate was a colossal embarrassment for Alesi.

**SUNDAY RACE** It was to be another race without points for the French team. For Burti, however, the experience was useful and he was encouraged by the feel of the car, despite finishing in 11th having struggled with the unpowered-steering.

Jean Alesi ended up a place higher in 10th, but one lap behind the race winner. Both cars were on a two-stop strategy, with Alesi pitting on lap 23 and Burti one lap later for their first stops. Burti pitted for the second time on lap 47, followed three laps later by Alesi.

It was a humdrum race for a team struggling in every respect; but like everyone, Alain Prost was thanking his stars his team wasn't called Benetton.

Above: Jean Alesi scraped home one place ahead of his new Brazilian team-mate Luciano Burti. Right: Burti proved he was a much better driver than people believed, out-qualifying Alesi. Below: Alain Prost had to endure another race with no points for the struggling team, despite the long-awaited new aerodynamic package. On-track performance was a disappointment.

The team was very familiar with the Barcelona track but failed to reproduce old form.

## AUSTRIAN GRAND PRIX A1 RING
# No grip and no glory

It was a familiar story these days at Prost, and Austria did nothing to add a fresh chapter as Jean Alesi and Luciano Burti struggled home 10th and 11th in cars with less grip than a politician's handshake. Progress there was non-existent, and the serious aerodynamic revisions due by Monaco could not come soon enough.

**FRIDAY PRACTICE** Prost brought three AP04s to Austria – the new 06 was for Alesi's use, 04 for Burti's, with the spare 02 set up this weekend for the Brazilian.

Burti continued to settle well into his new team and ended the day in 17th place on 1m 13.169secs after covering 48 laps. Like everyone else, the Prost drivers found this low-grip track very slippery initially, a trait not helped by the AP04's inherent inability to use its Michelins as well as the Williams FW23 did. After struggling in the morning the Brazilian was slightly happier in the afternoon; Alesi, meanwhile, covered only 36 laps, letting others clean up the track surface initially before venturing out. Throughout, he was unhappy with his car's braking.

**SATURDAY QUALIFYING** Burti's form continued on Saturday morning as he set the 17th fastest time with 1m 12.714secs while Alesi struggled to 1m 13.485secs, a lowly 21st. Burti's gentler style was getting the best from a car with inherently poor grip, whereas Alesi only knows how to drive flat-out, which tended to exacerbate the AP04's shortcomings. Even on Michelin's softer tyres, it was a feeble showing.

Burti had an uneventful afternoon on his way to 17th place on the grid with 1m 12.206secs, but Alesi's first attempt at a flying lap saw the Prost get away from him in the penultimate corner. His lurid spin, in which he kept the power full on, compromised Eddie Irvine's run as the Jaguar driver narrowly missed the blue car.

Again Alesi's car was hampered by a brake problem, and he was very unhappy with 20th fastest time of 1m 12.910secs, three places behind Burti. Most worrying of all for Prost was that the AP04 demonstrated no discernible difference in lap time between light or full fuel loads, a sure sign of an inefficient chassis.

**SUNDAY RACE** Burti might have blown Alesi away in practice and qualifying, but the Frenchman was, as usual, at his best in the race. He shadowed his team-mate for the first 16 laps as they progressed to 12th and 13th places after the misfortunes of others, then pounced on lap 17 and thereafter pulled away. Burti was left to hold off Jenson Button, who was working wonders in the Benetton and pressured the Brazilian into a mistake just as they were lapped on lap 29. Burti regained the upper hand on the Englishman after their fuel stops on laps 39 (Button) and 44 (Burti).

Alesi drove his heart out as the AP04 slid all over the road, but even he was powerless to resist Nick Heidfeld's charge in the Sauber and he succumbed for ninth place on the 68th lap. The respective performances of these two cars, which used the same Ferrari engines, said it all.

**Top and above:** Luciano Burti again out-qualified Jean Alesi, but could not match his team-mate's race pace. **Left:** Austria produced another disappointing race for team chief Alain Prost. **Below:** Lack of downforce left the Prost AP04s off the pace – here Jean Alesi is passed by the swift Sauber of Nick Heidfeld.

## MONACO GRAND PRIX MONTE CARLO
# Into the points

Jean Alesi dispersed the French racing blues at Monaco and gave his beleaguered team a massive boost – albeit with only sixth place.

Emotions ran high at Prost afterwards: a huge psychological hurdle had been cleared. "Bravo Alain, c'est super!" Prost's countrymen cried as he walked back to the paddock. "But let's wait till Canada," counselled sporting director John Walton. "We'll have more aerodynamic parts there and further revised rear suspension. That will be the acid test."

**THURSDAY PRACTICE** Prost brought three cars to Monaco along with high hopes for a new aero package and rear suspension that had been tested with encouraging results the previous week in Valencia, Spain. Alesi had AP04-06, with AP04-05 set as his spare, while Luciano Burti had AP04-04. Chassis AP04-02 was on hand if required.

Since Alesi was fully familiar with the revisions, his car carried them well from the start. Burti initially had to make do with the old front wing as he set about learning the challenging Monte Carlo circuit; he had only raced there in the Porsche Supercup.

For the first time this year the Prost looked competent – at least in Alesi's hands. The veteran racer was delighted with eighth fastest time in his 40-lap run. But the team was careful to temper its optimism. Alesi loves Monaco and could be relied on to go well there, whatever he was driving. In contrast, Burti struggled badly. He completed 51 laps but his best left him 19th. The Brazilian offered no excuses, but conceded he was still seeking a set-up to suit his style.

**SATURDAY QUALIFYING** Alesi's strong form continued in free practice – he was again eighth fastest in a 23-lap run. But life got harder for Burti. He went off heavily at Ste Devote on his 14th lap when a brake problem caught him out and destroyed his car.

Both drivers decided on Michelin's softer rubber for qualifying. Buoyed by his morning speed, Alesi admitted that he was disappointed to miss out on Prost's first top 10 qualifying slot of the season, but a strong performance aced the Saubers, which used the same 2000-spec Ferrari V10. On his last run he made a small mistake in the tunnel and clipped the barriers. He was able to continue, but the tenths lost perhaps made the difference between ninth and 11th place.

Burti's horror weekend continued. Forced to switch to the spare car after his morning incident, he had more problems trying to set it up; and, to compound his misery, had to run the old aero package as his set of new parts had been so badly damaged.

**SUNDAY RACE** The warm-up proved Prost was right not to get overexcited as Alesi struggled with balance. Later he sketched tear tracks down his cheeks. But the race changed all that. Burti was a first-corner casualty as he took off his front wing against Jos Verstappen's Arrows and had to pit for a replacement. Later a brake problem sent him into the escape road at Ste Devote, but when he went for reverse gear it wasn't there. His race was over on lap 25.

The star was Alesi, whom Alain Prost later described as 'our superhero'. Never lower than 10th, he hung on for a long time to the trio of Jarno Trulli, Jacques Villeneuve and Giancarlo Fisichella then resisted Frentzen's persistent challenges for what had become eighth after 14 laps. By the time Alesi refuelled he was running sixth, free from the crashed Heinz-Harald Frentzen. But with 12 laps to run, the AP04 began to weave and he had to wind the brake balance forward to stop the left rear tyre locking. It had picked up a puncture and he screamed into the pits on lap 69. That was enough to let David Coulthard through to claim fifth, but Jean restarted and brought a result John Walton described as 'as good as a win'.

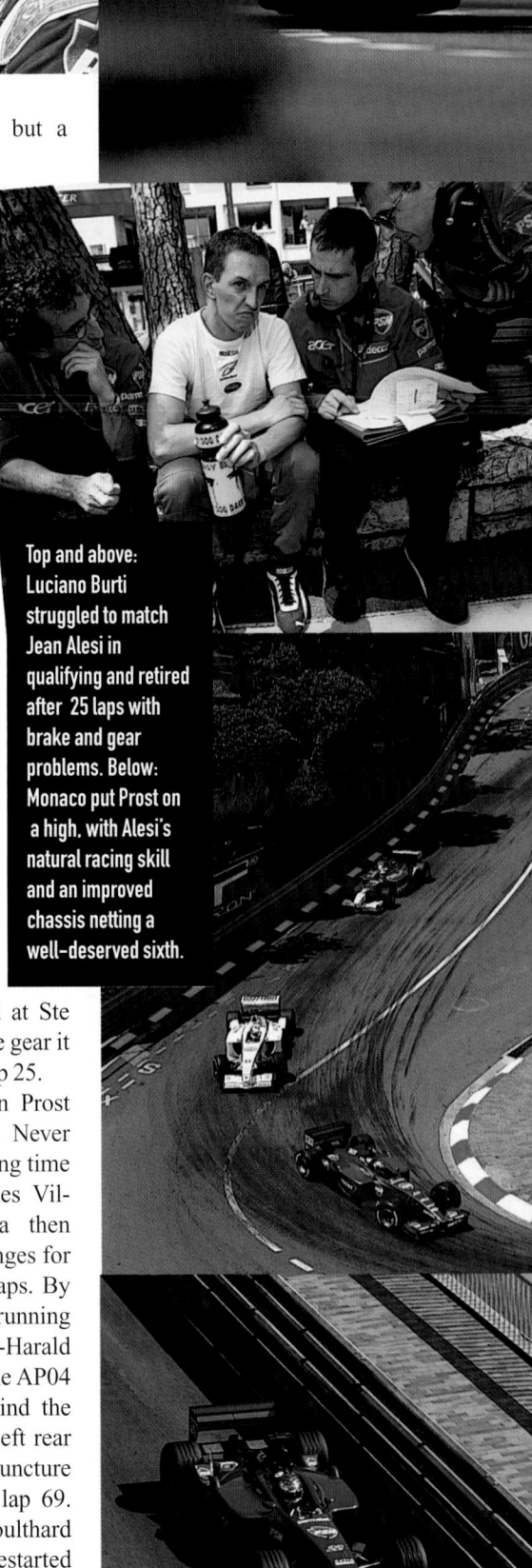

Top and above: Luciano Burti struggled to match Jean Alesi in qualifying and retired after 25 laps with brake and gear problems. Below: Monaco put Prost on a high, with Alesi's natural racing skill and an improved chassis netting a well-deserved sixth.

Left: Alesi's race performance was far more impressive than his celebratory post-race 'doughnuts'. Below: Prost again tried the double-mainplane front wing first used at Monaco but neither driver raced it.

## CANADIAN GRAND PRIX MONTREAL
# The acid test

In Monte Carlo, Jean Alesi and Prost deserved to finish fifth on merit, but had to be content with sixth. In Canada they went into the Grand Prix doubtful that they would even finish – and ended up taking the place they should have had a fortnight earlier. Despite recent modifications the Prost AP04 was still not a good car, but it was reliable and with a committed driver at the wheel it once more proved to be a points scorer. The arrival of Luciano Burti had galvanised Jean Alesi and he was a new man.

FRIDAY PRACTICE Prost had a new permutation of its chassis in Canada. Alesi had his Monaco car, AP04-06 but Burti had Alesi's spare from Monaco, 05, leaving 02 as the spare in Montreal.

Much was expected of a further revised rear suspension. At the end of the day the Frenchman was 12th fastest on 1m 19.209secs from 38 laps and the Brazilian 18th fastest in 1m 21.280secs from 46 laps as he learned the track. The team deliberately ran high downforce, which took the edge off top speed, but there was no mistaking the air of disappointment.

SATURDAY QUALIFYING Alesi again ran with the further modified rear suspension on Saturday morning, and ended the session by spinning and stalling. He reverted to the Monaco rear end for qualifying, as it was a little better, and chose the softer Michelin tyres. The AP04 was power-understeering, however, and Alesi reported that it felt unstable under braking and lacked traction.

He achieved 1m 18.178secs and was set to improve on that when his final qualifying attempt was thwarted when the red flag came out. That left him only 16th in the line-up.

Burti used the new rear suspension all day but never got to grips with the car or the circuit on his way to a disappointing best of 1m 18.753secs for only 19th fastest.

Privately, the team went into the race admitting that it would be surprised to finish.

SUNDAY RACE A terrible start for Alesi appeared to confirm the team's gloomy race prognosis, but within a few laps the Frenchman realised his brakes were standing up rather well to the treatment he was dishing out. Thus encouraged he was able to drive another of his flat-out races, pushing hard throughout.

From 19th place on the first lap he gradually advanced, mainly as others met ill fortune. By the time he made his single fuel stop on the 41st lap he was running fifth – a major surprise for those watching him on the pit wall. His stop dropped him back to ninth, but as he charged after Kimi Räikkönen they both benefited from the retirements of David Coulthard, Jarno Trulli and Jos Verstappen, along with Pedro de la Rosa's second stop.

Against all expectations the form from Monaco had been continued and fifth place proved every bit as great a reason for celebration as sixth had in the principality. Alain Prost concluded: "Today is an extraordinary encouragement."

Burti chased Alesi, having all but stalled at the start, but an off-course moment while he was pushing his team-mate had filled his radiator ducts with grass and obliged him to stop early to have the debris cleared out. Overdriving had also blistered his tyres and by the time he picked up his rhythm again there was only Ricardo Zonta's Jordan to chase to the finish. But eighth was progress for the Brazilian as he found his feet in his new team.

Below left: Luciano Burti leads Tarso Marques's Minardi during an eventful, disappointing race for the Prost driver. Right: Jean Alesi confirmed Prost's Monaco form with another stirring drive to fifth.

# Getting a grip on reality

It's not often nowadays that Jean Alesi spins out of races. He had put those days behind him to become the finest finisher on the grid. Even though a last-gasp error by the veteran Frenchman put an end to Prost's recent run of points-scoring finishes, there was an air of optimism in the team as the upturn in Michelin's performance had a knock-on benefit for the AP04.

With further aerodynamic and suspension modifications in the pipeline, the team remained on an upward swing, even though Luciano Burti was its sole finisher.

**FRIDAY PRACTICE** Ninth place for Alesi on Friday raised a few eyebrows, even though most agreed it was due to running on a relatively light fuel load. The team brought along its usual three AP04s (06 and 02 for Alesi, 05 for Burti) and was consolidating the spec around the modifications made at Monaco and Montreal.

Alesi was cheerful after his day's work, expressing satisfaction with the mechanical set-up in particular, and covered 47 laps for a best time of 1m 18.352secs. Burti, however, was once again in the wars. On another track that he had to learn, the Brazilian did only 30 laps and was 20th fastest on 1m 20.094secs after an engine problem brought his day to a premature halt.

**SATURDAY QUALIFYING** Like Sauber, Prost had the use of the specification B+ Ferrari engines for qualifying, with better power and economy. These were close to the specification Ferrari used in Australia. Burti and Alesi were 15th and 17th respectively in free practice, the Brazilian looking more convincing against his team-mate than he had since joining the team in Spain.

Both drivers were relatively satisfied with progress, but whereas Alesi subsequently went faster to qualify 14th on 1m 17.251secs on the softer Michelins that both men chose, Burti lost pace and had to be content with 1m 18.113secs for 17th fastest time.

Alesi was not happy, however, complaining that the rise in track temperature made his car oversteer far more than it had in the morning. Later he met traffic on his third run, and Coulthard's trip into the gravel spelled *finis* to the Frenchman's hopes of any further improvement.

Burti was similarly disappointed. A fuel pressure problem on his race car sent him into Alesi's spare, which had to be reset as best the mechanics could in the time available. Burti disliked its behaviour and found that he couldn't improve on his best lap from his first run. Nevertheless, Alain Prost expressed quiet optimism that at least one car could score further points in the race.

**SUNDAY RACE** Both drivers made awful starts to the race, Alesi dropping back from 14th to 19th and Burti from 17th to 20th at the end of the first lap. There they stayed until Burti pushed too hard in Alesi's wake on Michelins that were already starting to blister and momentarily speared off the road on lap 10. Two laps later he was in the pits to have the radiators cleaned out. The team had not understood his complaints over the radio about the state of his tyres, however, so once he had been sent back into the race on them he was condemned to struggle until his scheduled stop on the 49th lap. By then he was so far out of contention that it would probably have been worth a delay in his first stop while the crew rushed off to grab him a new set of Michelins.

Alesi, meanwhile, was pushing hard without taking so much out of his tyres, and was advancing steadily. From his initial 19th he had risen to 10th by lap 38 as others made their fuel stops. Finally he made his own stop on the 42nd lap, dropping back to 14th temporarily and then challenging Heidfeld hard for 12th place within a few laps. He passed his former team-mate, after a clash of wheels, and set out after Räikkönen's Sauber.

The Finn resisted him all the way, however, and when Alesi went too deep into the hairpin on his penultimate lap he spun into the gravel and was eventually classified 15th. It was the first time in the season that he had not actually finished a race. Burti's lonely run netted him 12th by the flag.

Right and below: Luciano Burti was invisible in the race, coming home in an unnoticed 12th. After showing initial promise on his Prost debut, he had since failed to match Jean Alesi's pace.

Above and right: The team was delighted with Jean Alesi's performance once again — until he spun into retirement with just two laps to go.

## FRENCH GRAND PRIX MAGNY-COURS
# Lack of testing shows

**Above and left:** Luciano Burti did well to qualify 15th, ahead of team-mate Jean Alesi. The Prost struggled for performance and grip, resulting in a very disappointing home race for the French team. **Below:** Pedro Diniz and Burti ponder their poor qualifying performance at Magny-Cours.

Buoyed by the progress its recent aerodynamic and mechanical set-up changes had provided and desperate for a big result on home turf, Prost was rashly tempted to race with further changes not tested prior to the French Grand Prix. The production ran late and performance inevitably marked a downturn. While the developments might have been effective – who could be sure in the circumstances? – they might have had some less beneficial side-effects.

After Jean Alesi's recent point-scoring performances it looked like his home Grand Prix and the 12th anniversary of his Formula One debut might give him something more to smile about. However, he was far from at his best and even the untested developments could not explain why team-mate Luciano Burti had the measure of him all weekend. The 10th and 12th places they came away with didn't do much to assuage the team's increasing need for further funding.

**FRIDAY PRACTICE** The Brazilian had AP04-05, the Frenchman 06, and 02 was set for Alesi as the spare. Right from the start Burti had the upper hand on Alesi and set 12th fastest time with a 1m 16.455secs to leave the veteran trailing four places behind on 1m 17.088secs. They stuck with high fuel loads, amassing 50 and 32 laps respectively.

Both cars were trying out new bargeboards, a slightly revised floor and a new engine cover, plus further revised rear suspension geometry. Alesi and Burti were adamant the new aero package was a step forward, but the engineers sounded less sure, even though the team had done back-to-back tests through the day.

**Left:** After his recent run of form, Jean Alesi's luck ran out in France with the AP04 lacking grip. Alesi again found it difficult to find a balance which suited his style. **Below:** For Alain Prost, the timing could not have been worse.

**SATURDAY QUALIFYING** The team struggled to set up the AP04s on a lighter fuel load in free practice, but while the recently effervescent Alesi neared despair, Burti opted to gamble with some major changes for qualifying and lucked into the right direction. The Brazilian's best time, 15th fastest on 1m 15.072secs, came on his second run and was, he felt, pretty close to the limit for the car in the conditions – which he proved by spinning in a later bid for more speed.

Alesi had a wild spin going into the first corner on his first qualifying run. He put it down to trying too hard in an ill-balanced car, but one team insider felt waving to the crowd on his out-lap 'like the Pope on tour' had not helped his concentration. When he got going properly, Jean had his worst Saturday of the season with 19th place in 1m 15.774secs. Both drivers had chosen Michelin's softer tyre, which would initially stand them in good stead in the race, but by now the drivers had come to realise that the previous day's enthusiasm for the new aero package might have been misplaced.

**SUNDAY RACE** Given what Michelin's tyres did for BMW Williams, Jaguar and even Benetton, Prost could feel deflated on race day.

Burti had a fine first stint as he battled up to 12th by the sixth lap, running behind Eddie Irvine and ahead of Jos Verstappen and believing himself quicker than Olivier Panis. But then serious oversteer set in and his second set of tyres didn't like the track conditions anything as much as the first.

From then on it was a matter of surviving until lap 48 when he got another set, which were a huge improvement. By then it was too late, but Burti did manage to claw his way back past Giancarlo Fisichella, who had passed him during the stops, for 10th.

Alesi's race followed on from his troubled practice and qualifying days as he struggled with his unloved set-up. Initially he trailed the Benettons in 17th, refuelled on lap 22, then ran as high as 14th before pitting again on lap 47. After that he chased Jenson Button until the Englishman's engine broke, thus inheriting a lacklustre 12th place. He performed some more 'doughnuts' for the home crowd anyway.

323

# BRITISH GRAND PRIX SILVERSTONE
# Backward to go forwards

Prost was riding relatively high, performance-wise, after scoring three points and making FOM TV money in 2002 a relative certainty. This would add $10 million to the team's 2002 budget – handy for a team desperately short of cash.

After the panic to make its cars competitive in France, Prost took a step backwards to make progress at Silverstone. It gave Jean Alesi a good car and he reaped 11th place, even if he did describe his afternoon as 'boring'.

Prost could be proud of its reliability – Alesi had been classified in all 11 rounds of the championship this year, failing to get to the chequered flag only once. The team's Ferrari engines, badged Acers, had been extraordinarily good too.

**FRIDAY PRACTICE** For the latest battle, the team brought chassis AP04-06 for Alesi with 04 as his spare and AP04-05 for Luciano Burti.

Since the last test outing at Silverstone had been less than successful, Friday was vital as the team tried to hone its cars. The plethora of new aerodynamic parts at Magny-Cours had left Prost confused, so the situation had been rationalised. "We took a step backwards on the aero package," admitted sporting director John Walton, although he did not divulge the details.

Alesi ended the day with a 1m 24.832secs for 14th fastest. But team-mate Burti had a traction control problem early on which caused him to spin and flat-spot his tyres. A later mistake accounted for another set and the third was lost to a gearbox problem, leaving him with a best lap of 1m 25.448secs and 18th position.

**SATURDAY QUALIFYING** Overnight test data from Prost's wind-tunnel helped to optimise the car's aerodynamics. The scale test model had been fitted with different size front wheels to reflect the wider front Michelins more accurately; the team found these significantly enhanced the performance of the bargeboards and undertray.

The Prosts were as hopeless as any car on Michelins in the rain, with Alesi and Burti 18th and 19th in the morning practice. Things looked up in dry qualifying, when both drivers used the soft tyre. Alesi advanced to 14th, confirming the basic set-up was better and each small change improved the AP04 further.

Burti was 16th on 1m 23.735secs to Alesi's 1m 23.392secs, so although he felt he could have done better, he was happier than the day before. But his set-up was not as good as Alesi's and he complained of serious understeer.

**SUNDAY RACE** Alesi made full use of the misfortune of others to vault from 14th to ninth at the end of the first lap, but four laps later lost a place to Jos Verstappen. He then fought to hold off Jacques Villeneuve before surrendering seven laps later. Alesi was left to fend off Pedro de la Rosa's Jaguar in a Prost that clearly lacked grip and did not appear to want to launch itself off the corners.

Alesi's sole fuel stop came on lap 30, when he lay 11th. He came out in the same position and retained held it to the end.

Burti's race was short. He held his grid position for five laps, then pulled off when he suffered a rare Ferrari engine failure.

Left: Alesi leads Burti as they chase the Benettons and points. Below: Another points finish should have been cause for rejoicing but Burti's explosive accident on the startline added further financial pressure for Alain Prost.

## GERMAN GRAND PRIX HOCKENHEIM
# Heroic efforts rewarded

The Prost team was in the news all weekend, but not for its racing. It raced successfully; financially the team was said to be on the edge. The cash shortage had been caused by the shareholder structure, which meant all four main shareholders had to agree to any refinancing. Alongside that, the team had barely any real commercial sponsorship. The lot probably added up to less than $14 million plus $14 million TV money, making a total of $28 million to service a budget of $60 million. That was supplemented by a complex deal that saw a further $4 million pumped in by UFA Sports, which owned 10 per cent of the team and had certain marketing rights.

All the shareholders were very rich but the shareholder structure was preventing any immediate rescue. A complex game of poker was going on: the predicted outcome was that three shareholders would lose their money while a fourth pumped in at least $30 million to save the day and take ownership of the team. But which one? The Diniz family was favourite. And their price was thought to be the departure of Alain Prost himself.

While all this was going on, Prost's loyal number one Jean Alesi, sighting a better offer, was preparing to jump ship. Some saw it as a replay of the scene at Sauber four years ago when Peter Sauber had Alesi's undivided loyalty only until a better offer surfaced. But as always, there was rather more to it.

**FRIDAY PRACTICE** Prost came to Hockenheim with its usual three cars: AP04-06 for Alesi and 05 for Burti, but this time it was the Brazilian's turn to have the spare 04 set for him. Jean Alesi enjoyed himself, carrying a light fuel load to bounce up into eighth in the afternoon. He did 35 laps for a best of 1m 42.828secs.

After a couple of strong outings, Burti was struggling on his first visit to Hockenheim and could only manage 19th fastest with 1m 44.162secs during his 39 laps.

**SATURDAY QUALIFYING** It said everything for the feeling he had for his AP04 that Alesi was disappointed to qualify only 14th, a position that in normal circumstances would have been cause for celebration in the beleaguered French team. He was delighted with the car's balance and power and with the way his hard Michelins handled the 41C track temperature. Burti was on the pace more than on Friday, getting down to 1m 41.213secs for 16th place on the grid. He too was disappointed, having gone the wrong way on set-up after his first run. Frustrated that his third run felt better without yielding any improvement, he then pushed too hard on the last one and spun.

**SUNDAY RACE** Burti began with a bang when he became the unwitting victim of Michael Schumacher's gearbox failure as the field left the start-line. Olivier Panis was the last man to avoid the stricken Ferrari, leaving Burti unsighted until it was too late. With a 100mph speed differential of 100mph, the Prost slammed into the back of the red car and leaped skywards, spiralling to the right before slamming back down on its rollover hoop. By sheer good fortune the Prost landed between the two Arrows, though its left front wheel hit Bernoldi's car. As it righted itself, the AP04 tobogganed into the gravel on the outside of the first corner.

Half-an-hour later the Brazilian was back on track in the spare. As Alesi made a terrible start, Burti was able to beat him for 17th place. Then the two blue cars ran together, chasing Giancarlo Fisichella's Benetton and moving up as others fell out. Alesi reversed their positions on the ninth lap, and then Burti lost places to Trulli and Panis on the 18th after a slight off-course moment. He'd hurt his left arm in the clash with Schumacher and was having trouble holding the wheel. He had to retire after 23 laps.

Alesi rose to fifth before his fuel stop on lap 25, then gave energetic chase to Villeneuve and the Benettons right up to the chequered flag and a point.

## HUNGARIAN GRAND PRIX HUNGARORING

# New face, new hope

Prost was in an even greater state of upheaval than normal following the defection of Jean Alesi to Jordan and his replacement by the deposed Heinz-Harald Frentzen. The German had only briefly been able to shake down his new mount at Magny-Cours prior to the race. Just to compound things, Michelin had problems making its tyres work on the Hungarian track. In Prost's case the AP04 was ill-balanced and wore its tyres out quickly. All the ingredients were there for a nightmare weekend. Meanwhile the team principal spent all weekend denying the team was running on empty money tanks. Few believed him.

**FRIDAY PRACTICE** Prost brought its familiar three AP04s to Hungary: 06 for Frentzen to race with 02 as his spare, and 04 for Burti, their aerodynamic package optimised for the track's high downforce requirements.

Frentzen was out early and completed 32 laps to achieve 14th fastest time of 1m 18.724secs. He had a lot to learn as he acclimatised to the car and, even more importantly, to its Michelin rubber. In the circumstances he put in a good performance, especially as team-mate Luciano Burti struggled to only 1m 20.615secs in his 36 laps for 21st.

**SATURDAY QUALIFYING** For Frentzen, qualifying was spoiled by an altercation with Coulthard, when the German appeared to block the Scot on his first flying run. The drivers have a history dating back to Spa last year, but on this occasion Frentzen was not doing anything deliberate. The team had changed the aero package on his car without adjusting the mirrors, and although it told him over the radio that Coulthard was approaching, he could not see the McLaren tucked right up behind him. He was quick to make a public apology afterwards. Both drivers fought

balance problems on their soft Michelins. In free practice Frentzen placed 15th on 1m 17.203secs and Burti 18th on 1m 17.992secs, but qualifying brought no improvement despite much juggling with settings. Frentzen lined up 16th on 1m 17.196secs and Burti 19th on 1m 18.238secs.

**SUNDAY RACE** Whatever aspirations Prost harboured for the race didn't look good after Frentzen and Burti were only 18th and 19th in the morning warm-up, and disappeared altogether right from the start. Frentzen's getaway was a disaster as he fell from his 16th grid slot to 20th, behind Burti and just ahead of Tarso Marques. The two blue cars ran in 19th and 20th positions for the first five laps before Button's stop-and-go penalty elevated them each a place, then Burti's race ended four laps later. The Brazilian slid off the track, later blaming poor grip from his Michelins.

Frentzen soldiered on in what had fast become a horrible baptism with his new team. Gradually he reeled in and passed Alonso for 16th place, after each had made their first stop. After that he was embroiled in a scrap for 13th with Fisichella, de la Rosa and Verstappen. Places see-sawed with pit stops, but after his second on the 52nd lap Frentzen resumed in 14th and had worked back up to 13th when he slewed off the road on the outside of the second corner on lap 64. Ostensibly he had given the AP04 too much throttle, but the traction control had failed mid-corner and thrown him off into the dirt.

"We learned a lot from Heinz this weekend," said sporting director John Walton. "He had an exceptional amount of work to do and he did an exceptional job for us even if the results don't reflect it."

Hungary marked the first time in 2001 that neither Prost made the finish, after both Luciano Burti (top left) and Heinz-Harald Frentzen (right) spun into retirement. It was a tough debut for Frentzen's first race taste of Prost and Michelin.

Right: Prost had big tyre wear problems in Hungary.
Below: Frentzen tried on his Prost debut but ended his race with a walk home after spinning on lap 64.

## BELGIAN GRAND PRIX SPA-FRANCORCHAMPS
# Impossible to believe

Alain Prost couldn't believe it when Heinz-Harald Frentzen stalled on the grid. Prost's one genuine bright spot of the year was ruined. But that was nothing compared with the moment when Luciano Burti went head-on into a tyre wall at Blanchimont. It was one of those times when things go quiet, and anxious faces watch TV screens.

**FRIDAY PRACTICE** The usual trio of Prost AP04s was on hand in Belgium: 06 for Frentzen, 04 for Burti and 02 as spare. Frentzen hit form quickly, taking 12th fastest time with 1m 52.073secs, but Burti could only manage 21st, with a lap of 2m 11.037secs.

The Brazilian spun after encountering the same traction control glitch that put Frentzen off the road in Hungary. He got back to the pits but the engine needed changing. After a strong effort from the team to ready the car for the afternoon session Burti just got going well before the rain came.

**SATURDAY QUALIFYING** Frentzen was the star of qualifying, the presence of a Prost on the second row taking observers back to the team's heyday in 1997.

Frentzen was already happy with the changes that had turned the Prost into a better-balanced car since Hungary. But even he was pleasantly surprised to see his boards giving him a lap in 1m 55.233secs, the fourth fastest time.

Burti was unlucky. He too had Michelin's softer dry tyres for his last run, but an error kept him in the pits another 30 seconds. That was the difference between one and two fast laps at the end, and a best of 1m 59.900secs brought him only 18th berth on the grid.

**SUNDAY RACE** Prost's race fell apart the moment Frentzen tried to engage a gear for the formation lap and encountered a "dog on dog" situation, where two gearbox dog-rings butted together and prevented him selecting the gear. The procedures for resolving the problem differed between Jordan and Prost. Frentzen was unfamiliar with the Prost drill, so off he went to the back of the grid. It was not a smart lapse from a professional driver, though Frentzen took it on the chin and admitted his error.

All that was put into perspective by Burti's accident. The Prost driver got alongside Irvine coming out of the right-hander and heading to the left at Blanchimont. As Irvine moved over to take his normal line, apparently unaware of the Prost's presence, Burti had nowhere to go. He put his left-hand wheels in the dirt, but still Irvine came across until they touched. The Jaguar spun; the Prost lost its front wing, skipped over the gravel bed and slammed very hard, at a sharp angle, into the tyre wall, which fortunately was built four tyres deep.

It looked like Irvine's fault but the stewards later ruled it a racing incident – which it was.

As the seriousness of the incident became apparent the race was red-flagged as rescuers pulled the tyre wall away from the Prost and discovered that Burti had not only survived, but was conscious. He was taken to the medical centre for inspection, and the good news was received as teams prepared for a restart.

Burti was flown to the University Hospital in Liège suffering from concussion.

On the restart, Frentzen was hit by Montoya at La Source and the Colombian's wheel damaged the Prost's undertray, significantly reducing downforce. That, combined with a high fuel load, condemned Frentzen to struggle with understeer for the rest of the race. He stopped once, on lap 16, and trudged round as best he could, for a dispiriting ninth place.

Left: Spa qualifying lifted the Prost team when Heinz-Harald Frentzen timed his qualifying run perfectly to take fourth place on the grid. A disappointing race followed as Frentzen stalled and then did not have the pace to race for points.

Below: Failure to get out on time for qualifying left Luciano Burti 18th on the grid. He was lucky to survive after he and Eddie Irvine clashed at the very fast Blanchimont corner. Burti was launched into the tyre wall at very high speed, but miraculously emerged with nothing more serious than bruising.

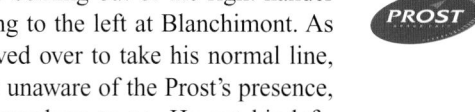

# New start beckons

The normal paddock gossips seemed oblivious to the fairly open secret that the Prost team was about to get new owners. Saudi Arabian Prince Khaled Al Waleed was set to take a 49 per cent stake and shore up the team's finances. Sources said the deal was all but done. Certainly Alain Prost looked a lot happier than of late.

He was also getting on well with Heinz-Harald Frentzen, a driver able to plant the Prost in the front half of the grid. The German was also driving for free – good for Prost's bank account and Frentzen's credibility. Prost was delighted when Frentzen out-qualified Jean Alesi in the Jordan Honda.

There was other news: Prost unveiled its fifth driver of the year: Formula 3000 star Tomas Enge, the first Czech to start and finish a Formula One race, and who brought Coca-Cola dollars to fund his drive.

**FRIDAY PRACTICE** Prost had its usual AP04/06 chassis for Frentzen, with 02 as spare. New boy Enge drove 03; 04 had been written off in Luciano Burti's Spa accident.

As Enge played himself in, an adventurous Frentzen missed numerous chicanes and had a seventh fastest time disallowed when he missed the second one altogether. Later he almost lost it in the second Lesmo, as Häkkinen would the next day, but just kept off the Armco. He was most irked by understeer, which was keeping the lid on the AP04's potential.

He still ended the day 10th after 37 laps. Enge, down the field, covered 29 laps. He damaged the floor of his car slightly over a kerb in the morning, and stopped with 10 minutes of the afternoon session left when the oil temperature warning light came on.

**SATURDAY QUALIFYING** Seventeenth and 20th in free practice did not bode well for Prost's qualifying chances, but the team was focusing on race set-up. In the afternoon, Frentzen clocked 12th on the grid. The delighted German said it was even better than his fourth on the grid at Spa, since it showed the car's inherent potential. But he still felt understeer was holding the AP04 back.

Enge had a less happy time. First his race car developed an engine problem – put down by the team to a quality control shortcoming at Ferrari. It re-occurred in qualifying, obliging him to run back for the spare, which was set up for Frentzen. That car then developed its own problem, leaving him stranded out on the circuit – a far-from-benign F1 baptism. His best lap left him 20th, but the team enthused about its new recruit.

**SUNDAY RACE** From his sixth-row slot, Frentzen got away quite well until the field reached the chicane. Button later complained that the inside line was slippery, but Frentzen felt the same about the outside: the Button-Trulli incident forced him into avoiding action that cost many places. He finished the lap 15th, with Enge 18th.

By lap 13 Frentzen had clawed up to 13th, but progress was slow. The team had run him on Michelin's hard-compound tyres so he could start with a heavy fuel load and top up near the finish. His first-corner problems did him no favours, but he rose to ninth by lap 28 before pulling off and retiring when a gearbox failure lost him all drive.

Enge plugged away, learning the rudiments of esoterica such as traction control and practicalities such as pitstops. Making no mistakes, he climbed steadily up the order as others retired, but the debris of Button's front wing in the first chicane had damaged one of his sidepods and affected the car's aerodynamic efficiency. He still brought it home a creditable 12th.

Right: Endorsing the standard of F3000, Tomas Enge made an impressive debut with the Prost team. He qualified 20th after a variety of problems but was a big hit with the team. He did a solid job to finish 12th.

Right and below: Heinz-Harald Frentzen qualified 12th, but after being delayed by the Trulli-Button clash, he made slow progress up to ninth by lap 28 before being forced to retire with gearbox failure. Prost's reliability fortunes have been reversed.

## UNITED STATES GRAND PRIX INDIANAPOLIS
# A new dignity

Prost had different drivers than at the start of the season, and while Jean Alesi's replacement Heinz-Harald Frentzen had arguably given the team a new dignity, new Czech recruit Tomas Enge did himself no favours with a somewhat lacklustre two races replacing Luciano Burti. But at Indianapolis the focus was on the team, not the drivers. Still struggling for cash, it was rumoured to be close to a deal with Saudi group Kingdom Holdings. Due diligence was under way and a complex takeover deal that would see Alain Prost remain as team principal being put in place. Until then no engine deal could be announced, but it would almost certainly be another year with Ferrari supplying the power plant provided the cash was there to pay for it.

**FRIDAY PRACTICE** Seventh fastest time, after 37 laps, of 1m 13.858secs was a fillip for the Prost team and Frentzen when practice began. The German had a good day with AP04-06 (03 was his spare) until the throttle link failed, and then a gearbox problem intervened and forced him to stop earlier than intended. While the experienced driver was working his way through his chassis set-up, partner Enge was learning the track in AP04-05. Enge got on quite well but had not optimised the degree of traction control when he pushed a little too hard, spun and stalled after 40 laps.

**SATURDAY QUALIFYING** All through Saturday Frentzen continued to make progress, honing the set-up but ultimately disappointed when his best lap of 1m 13.281secs earned him only 15th slot on the grid.

But the plan had been to play safe and run closer to race than qualifying trim on Michelin's softer tyre, even if it cost a couple of 10ths. Enge worked diligently to enhance his car's grip and balance in his first three qualifying runs, and it seemed to be paying off. On his last outing he set a first sector time that was very close to Frentzen's, but he lost it under braking for Turn 8, and as the Prost whipped round it smacked head-on into the tyre barrier at the end of the back straight. Enge was unharmed, but chagrined to have damaged the car. His 1m 14.185secs was a second – 2.5kph – slower than Frentzen and gave him 21st place on the grid.

**SUNDAY RACE** While drivers such as Eddie Irvine and Jos Verstappen forged forward at the start, Frentzen was one who lost out. From 15th on the grid he dropped a place at once, made it back when Kimi Räikkönen retired, and then spent 19 laps in 15th before moving up to 14th until lap 34, after a determined chase of Olivier Panis finally paid off. With a high fuel load he was able to stretch things out before making his single stop on lap 42, by when he had climbed to seventh.

That couldn't last, and he resumed in 13th, but soon he was on Jenson Button's tail and on lap 45 he squeaked ahead going down to Turn 1. Button returned the favour on the next lap, however, and they then circulated in close company, often within half a second of each other. Frentzen was unhappy with Prost's strategy: he believed staying out even longer before refuelling would have given him a chance of beating both Benettons.

Enge's clutch problem stranded him on the startline and obliged him to start the AP04 manually. He then got bottled up behind Alex Yoong until the Malaysian stopped for fuel on lap 26. After that he pushed as hard as he could, and though frustrated to finish only 14th he was relieved to have got to the chequered flag.

Top and left: Tomas Enge failed to match his Prost debut at Monza. After a glitchy start, the Czech finished 14th. Below: Frentzen and sporting director Joan Villadelprat exchange views. Frentzen was unhappy with his race strategy, which he felt cost him positions.

Below left: Prost needed all the advice he could get. Below: Heinz-Harald Frentzen leads Irvine's Jaguar in the race.

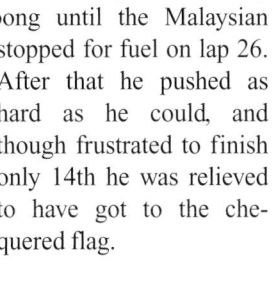

## JAPANESE GRAND PRIX SUZUKA
# Au revoir or à bientôt?

Alain Prost's team was in dire financial straits and getting to Japan was a feat in itself. Team members there were saying it faced closure within a fortnight.

In scintillating fashion, Heinz-Harald Frentzen clawed his way back to a 12th place finish from a pitstop that had dropped him to last place on lap three. Better news was that Frentzen wanted to stay for 2002, provided the team was still in business. Whatever Eddie Jordan thought of him, his five races at Prost had proved Frentzen to be a top Formula One driver.

**FRIDAY PRACTICE** Fifth fastest time for Frentzen boosted Alain Prost's team; nobody thought it a good predictor of Saturday form, but the German was enthused by his 1m 36.439secs lap. Describing his speed and consistency as his best ever round the circuit where he still held the lap record (with Williams Renault in 1997), Frentzen did 41 laps in AP04-06 (with 03 as his spare) and smoothly completed the Michelin tyre comparisons.

Team-mate Tomas Enge, meanwhile, once again did a destruction job on his car, AP04-05. While the track was still quite slippery in the morning, the Czech got off line with oversteer going into the 130R corner. He speared into the gravel bed on the outside, missing the apex by a country mile, and slammed heavily into the tyre wall. Another case of overdriving, which brought his day's running to an abrupt end and left him last in the line-up, with 1m 41.216secs from only 18 laps.

**SATURDAY QUALIFYING** After Frentzen's performance on Friday, and his 11th fastest time on Saturday morning (1m 35.483secs), Prost had high hopes for qualifying, which were soon dashed. Whatever he tried, the German could not better 1m 35.132secs in the afternoon, despite wringing the AP04 for all it was worth. His first run was the best; two further efforts yielded times within one-10th of it. Dogged by persistent understeer, the Prost could go no faster on its soft Michelin rubber.

Enge, in the spare 03, could not better 1m 36.446secs for 19th fastest time, three kilometres per hour slower than Frentzen. The Czech admitted taking things slightly easier than on the previous day, to keep his car in one piece; his best time was also on his first run. Unlike Frentzen, however, he found his chassis balance reasonable, but all kinds of tweaks couldn't make the blue car go faster. On his last run he spun and flat-spotted his tyres.

**SUNDAY RACE** Getting off the line Frentzen lost a place to de la Rosa, which proved to be his undoing. At the end of lap two the Spaniard locked his right front wheel braking for the chicane, and the German took avoiding action. This dislodged his front wing, which collapsed, and as debris was trapped under the car Frentzen lost a huge amount of time creeping round the full lap before he could pit for a new nose.

Exiting at the back, he embarked on a fabulous comeback. With his car reasonably balanced, Frentzen treated every lap like qualifying. On lap 14 he passed Yoong, made up another place on lap 17 after Panis's first pitstop, another when Bernoldi refuelled on lap 19, and yet another when he overtook Verstappen on lap 21.

His own fuel stop on lap 22 dropped him back again, but he caught and passed team-mate Enge on lap 33 for 14th. By his second stop on lap 38 he was up to 13th, and Fisichella's late retirement pushed him one place higher by the flag.

It was one of those performances that inevitably get overlooked, but seventh fastest lap showed how hard he pushed in what he described as the toughest race of his Formula One career. He deserved better than 12th place.

Enge, perturbed by the Prost's lack of power-steering, struggled all afternoon. He had nevertheless risen to 15th by his first fuel stop on lap 21. But later he mistakenly read a Minardi pit board and came in to refuel again a lap early; after pitting properly on lap 36, he dropped back to 16th. Still a bit detuned after his Friday shunt, he spent the rest of the race playing with differential and traction control settings until a brake problem stopped him for good on lap 43.

**Right:** After coming in for a pitstop on the second lap, Heinz-Harald Frentzen drove an inspired race to bring the Prost home in 12th place and to remind everyone of his latent ability.

**Right:** Tomas Enge and Nick Heidfeld compare notes on their respective accidents.
**Below:** A badly damaged Prost made a good job of protecting Enge in his high speed accident.

# global culture

over half a billion people can now
speak Orange, can you?

the future's bright, the future's Orange

orange™

Team Review    Race by Race

# ARROWS

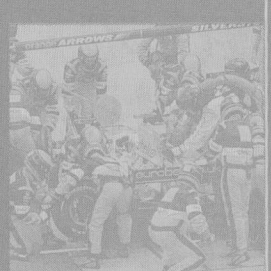

2001

## Contents

| Team Review | – | The season | p334 | European Grand Prix | – | Nürburgring | p348 |
| Australian Grand Prix | – | Melbourne | p340 | French Grand Prix | – | Magny-Cours | p349 |
| Malaysian Grand Prix | – | Sepang | p341 | British Grand Prix | – | Silverstone | p350 |
| Brazilian Grand Prix | – | Interlagos | p342 | German Grand Prix | – | Hockenheim | p351 |
| San Marino Grand Prix | – | Imola | p343 | Hungarian Grand Prix | – | Hungaroring | p352 |
| Spanish Grand Prix | – | Barcelona | p344 | Belgian Grand Prix | – | Spa-Francorchamps | p353 |
| Austrian Grand Prix | – | A1 Ring | p345 | Italian Grand Prix | – | Monza | p354 |
| Monaco Grand Prix | – | Monte Carlo | p346 | USA Grand Prix | – | Indianapolis | p355 |
| Canadian Grand Prix | – | Montreal | p347 | Japanese Grand Prix | – | Suzuka | p356 |

Tom Walkinshaw

Enrique Bernoldi

The Arrows Asiatech A22

Jos Verstappen

# orange™ **ARROWS** ///

# Another year at the back

O range Arrows had a bitterly disappointing season compared to 2000 – when Jos Verstappen and Pedro de la Rosa frequently showed up better-funded teams. The prime reason was the engine. Team principal Tom Walkinshaw elected to use the Asia-tech engine, in effect the 2000 Peugeot engine. He got the engines free, but were they as good in 2001 as they had been in 2000?

Walkinshaw has such a great reputation as an engineer, varnished by his 1994 and 1995 championships at Benetton, that it is hard to imagine him continually languishing at the back of the grid. But that has been the reality since he bought Arrows in 1996. His choice of engine consigned 2001 to be another year spent treading water.

In many ways the engine decision was forced upon him. When the Supertec Renault engine ceased to be available, Walkinshaw cast around for a stopgap to see him through while he sought something more potent for the longer term.

For 2002 he has solved the problem by buying Cosworth V10s. Walkinshaw worked very hard to secure the Cosworth, which is reckoned to be one of the best engines on the grid.

Poor reliability also hurt the team's slim chances in 2001: Arrows beat only Jaguar in the reliability league, and that by just 19 laps. Its reliability performance, 68.4 per cent, was worse than even Minardi's.

Walkinshaw may have an excuse for lack of speed, but an experienced racing engineer like him has no excuse for poor reliability. The uncompetitive nature of the package obliged the team to use some clever race strategies in order to get itself noticed. This worked well on several occasions, but it is not the way Walkinshaw has traditionally liked to go racing.

and were used as test cars only. Chassis number 04 was the spare in Melbourne, Malaysia and San Marino, and was raced by Enrique Bernoldi in Brazil, America and Japan; 08 was the spare in Italy and America; but for the most part the three chassis taken to races were 01, 03 and 06.

Verstappen began the year racing 01 in Australia, Malaysia and Brazil, with Bernoldi using 03 in the first two races. Thereafter 03 became the spare in Brazil, then Verstappen's race car at Imola, and from Spain onwards was Bernoldi's race car for the remainder of the season, except in America and Japan. From Spain until the end of the year, Verstappen used 06 as his race car, with 01 as the spare.

Development was confined to the introduction of power-steering

orange **ARROWS** /

## The Arrows A22 car

THE A22 was a logical evolution from the A21 design by aero-dynamicist Eghbal Hamidy and Mike Coughlan, Arrows' technical director. The A21 was regarded as a very good car and the new car closely followed its shape. It was a handsome machine, but it lacked both the ultimate downforce and ultimate horsepower of the previous year's design. The former may not have been helped by the departure of Hamidy for Jordan early in the season.

The aerodynamic problem meant that the A22 tended to perform better at some tracks than at others, where downforce was not at a premium, and its level of competitiveness therefore fluctuated. Arrows built eight A22s, but 02, 05 and 07 never appeared at races

and the usual fiddling around with aerodynamics to suit individual circuits, but one big step forward was the introduction of a spoon-shaped front wing in Hungary in place of the relatively flat wing used previously. This improved the car's behaviour by making it less pitch sensitive, and the drivers preferred it.

The one aerodynamic impact that Arrows did have came at Monaco, but it did not last long. This was the unusual high front wing that was quickly banned. The team also led the trend in small winglets atop the rear lights, and the use of two mini-wings on the trailing edge of the engine cover, which appeared in Monaco and Hungary, where maximum downforce was required. But they were still not enough.

That was the abiding problem with the A22, as it had been ▷

with the A21 the previous year. The team just couldn't generate sufficient downforce to make up for the lack of horsepower from the Asiatech V10. It was Arrows' flaw to expect that an engine which had failed to make the grade in 2000 would be any better in 2001, when most teams had brand-new power plants.

Asiatech used 50 engines during the course of the season, and brought 12 to each race to service the team. Based on the Peugeot V10 run by Prost in 2000, after Asiatech had bought the rights from the French manufacturer, the engine was already long in the tooth and lacked horsepower in comparison with its rivals. It had around 765bhp at the start of the season, and it's doubtful if it had more than 775bhp by the end, for Asiatech's focus after mid-year was on an all-new unit that would make its debut in 2002 and had nothing to do with the Peugeot inheritance.

Reliability was very poor at 68.4 per cent. The engine was notoriously unreliable in 2000 and that carried over, though not quite to the same extent. Engine failures stopped Bernoldi in Canada, France and Italy, and Verstappen in Germany (Nürburgring), Italy and America. The Dutchman finished in both France and Britain, but each time his engine was ailing in the closing laps. There were also several engine failures during practice for races. Verstappen in particular felt the Supertec Renault V10 that he used in 2000 was a much stronger unit. And it was less fragile, too. After all, it was a development of the unit that won world championships for Nigel Mansell, Michael Schumacher, Damon Hill and Jacques Villeneuve, whereas the Peugeot lacked such pedigree. In the reliability stakes Arrows didn't fare too well overall, as hydraulics problems and gearbox failures also took their toll. Of the 2,130

racing laps, its cars completed 1,457. At the start of the season, Verstappen in the lead car was 3.042secs slower than Michael Schumacher's pole. By season end at Suzuka this figure had risen to 4.401secs, a sure sign that whatever development there had been was on hold, as all of the team's effort was pumped into the A23 for 2002.

## The drivers

JOS VERSTAPPEN and Enrique Bernoldi were the only two drivers to handle race duties for Arrows Asiatech in 2002. Johnny Herbert and Johnny Kane carried out limited testing.

Bernoldi proved surprisingly quick and more than capable of matching veteran Verstappen's qualifying pace; by the end of the season the Brazilian had been the faster in 10 out of the 17 qualifying sessions. But he rarely matched Verstappen's race pace. Nobody started races better than the Dutchman. Time and again he made maximum use of relatively low initial fuel loads to sprint past rivals on the first lap, and nobody did more overtaking than he did during the season.

In fact, getaway and early-race form was the only thing that distinguished Arrows in 2001.

The first time Verstappen made a good getaway was in Malaysia, where he spurted up from 18th on the grid to race wheel-to-wheel with Heinz-Harald Frentzen, Mika Häkkinen and Ralf Schumacher throughout the wet race. Only a late fuel stop dropped him out of the points. In Austria he went from 16th on the grid to seventh at the end of the first lap, and this time the clever race strategy of run-

Mike Coughlan

Roger Silman

Johnny Herbert

ning low fuel initially, then a heavier load after the first stop, paid off as he scored a point for sixth place.

In Canada he went from 13th, his best qualifying position of the season and also Arrows' best, to seventh and was in the running for sixth place again when his brakes finally gave up the battle and he ended his day in a gravel trap. At Silverstone he flew from 17th to 11th, then overtook Panis and Alesi to run ninth, before finishing 10th. In Germany it was a similar story, as he speared from 20th to 11th on the opening lap; in Hungary from 21st to 15th (no mean feat on a circuit where overtaking is almost impossible); and in Belgium from 17th to 10th.

Light fuel loads undoubtedly helped, but Verstappen has a real racer's mentality once the lights go out.

Bernoldi usually got left behind. After a tentative start saw him spin out of his first two races, and then encounter hydraulic failure early in his home race, he began to find his feet at Imola, where he finished 10th. His qualifying pace picked up too, and he began to give Verstappen a run for his money. This led to some friction

between them, which developed into out-and-out irritation after Silverstone, where Verstappen claimed that Bernoldi had blocked him. At Hockenheim, Bernoldi drew great satisfaction from beating Verstappen for eighth place by mere fractions of a second, after the two of them had a gloves-off scrap right to the chequered flag that had team personnel hiding their eyes.

Verstappen will stay for 2002, but Bernoldi may have to look elsewhere as Walkinshaw courts Jean Alesi (despite his announced retirement) and Heinz-Harald Frentzen.

The Dutchman's season was not all good news and heroics: he messed up in Brazil, taking out leader Juan Pablo Montoya as his Arrows was being lapped. Verstappen was mortified, but Arrows' telemetry supported the Dutchman's view that the Colombian had braked earlier than usual for the corner in which he inadvertently rear-ended him.

The high point of Bernoldi's season was his performance in Monaco, when he kept David Coulthard's McLaren behind him for 43 laps, until his refuelling stop. Coulthard had taken pole ▷

orange **ARROWS**

## ARROWS SEASON STATISTICS

### RELIABILITY PERFORMANCE

| Driver | Races | Max laps | Laps completed | Reliability rating |
|---|---|---|---|---|
| Jos Verstappen | 17 | 1065 | 889 | 83.5% |
| Enrique Bernoldi | 17 | 1065 | 568 | 53.3% |
| Constructor | Races | Max laps | Laps completed | Reliability rating |
| Team | 34 | 2130 | 1457 | 68.4% |

### CHAMPIONSHIP PERFORMANCE

| Driver | 2001 points | 2000 points | 12 month change |
|---|---|---|---|
| Jos Verstappen | 1 | 5 | -80.0% |
| Enrique Bernoldi | 0 | - | Did not compete |
| Constructor | 2001 points | 2000 points | 12 month change |
| Team | 1 | 7 | -85.7% |

### CHASSIS LOG

**A22-01** Race car for Jos Verstappen at Melbourne, Sepang and Interlagos. Spare car at Barcelona, A1 Ring (used in qualifying by Verstappen), Monte Carlo, Montreal, Nürburgring, Magny-Cours, Silverstone, Hockenheim, Hungaroring and Suzuka (used by Verstappen in the race instead of 06).

**A22-02** Test car only

**A22-03** Race car for Enrique Bernoldi at Melbourne, Sepang (abandoned for 04 come the race), Barcelona, A1 Ring, Monte Carlo, Montreal, Nürburgring, Magny-Cours, Silverstone, Hockenheim, Hungaroring, Spa-Francorchamps and Monza; and for Verstappen at Imola. Spare car at Interlagos.

**A22-04** Race car for Bernoldi at Interlagos, Indianapolis and Suzuka. Spare car at Melbourne, Sepang (raced by Bernoldi) and Imola.

**A22-05** Test car only.

**A22-06** Race car for Bernoldi at Imola; and for Verstappen at Barcelona, A1 Ring, Monte Carlo, Montreal, Nürburgring, Magny-Cours, Silverstone, Hockenheim, Hungaroring, Spa-Francorchamps, Monza, Indianapolis and Suzuka.

**A22-07** Test car only.

**A22-08** Spare car at Monza and Indianapolis.

position but had stalled on the formation lap and been obliged to start from the back of the grid. After the race, in which he finished ninth, Bernoldi was lambasted by Ron Dennis, who accused him of deliberately holding up Coulthard just to get more television coverage for his sponsors. That was just sour grapes, born of frustration. The truth was that although he was lapping three seconds slower than Coulthard's potential, Bernoldi was racing legitimately for a place and had every right to defend against the Scot, who seemed to lack the resources to make a successful passing move. If nothing else, it showed that the occasionally impetuous Brazilian could keep his head under intense pressure when the mood was upon him.

## Commercial

ARROWS had only a low-key launch at its Leafield factory in late February, intended more to parade ex-Jaguar racer Johnny Herbert as its so-called test driver. The new car was not ready and the A22 appeared only days before being sent out to Melbourne for the first race. The Englishman did run the interim A21B (last year's car with the Asiatech engine) and did some running with an A22 early in the season.

In the distinctive orange-and-black livery the A22s looked good, but appearances were deceptive. Observers were surprised Chello, the telecoms company, appeared on the car in light of its problems, but not with the appearance of Eurobet, a company connected with Arrows' 70 per cent owner MGPE, the venture capital arm of Deutsche Bank. But Eurobet immediately asked Arrows to remove the logos from the cars and told the team it would not be sponsoring it in 2001. The 2000 deal, although successful, had been commission based. But Eurobet had suffered a minor disaster, losing $22 million after some Far Eastern syndicates made big bets that were not paid off. The managing director Trevor Beaumont was subsequently fired and the company hunkered down. Arrows refused to accept the cancellation and the logos remained on the cars all season, although Eurobet declined to participate or have anything to do with the team. It was all rather embarrassing because Eurobet and Arrows had a

Enrique Bernoldi

common owner. By season end, Arrows had issued a writ claiming over $20 million from Eurobet. One bit of good news for the team was the falling-out between Peter Sauber and Red Bull boss Dietrich Mateschitz. Some Red Bull money, thought to be as much as $12 million, transferred to Arrows. Bernoldi came as a driver as part of the deal.

Dietrich Mateschitz, from being a friendly sponsor at the beginning of the season, became a potential thorn in Walkinshaw's side by the end. Mateschitz revealed he had an option to buy MGPE's 70 per cent share in the team. Walkinshaw appeared to be unaware of this. There was much talk of an 'all-American' Formula One team sponsored by Red Bull. It appeared wide of the mark and there is no certainty that Mateschitz will take up his option, which is believed to be pitched at a price in excess of $50 million, a number most feel is more than the team is worth. Walkinshaw has also suffered from staff defections, possibly caused by the problems of running a team with a small budget. Roger Silman retired mid-season as managing director, aged 55. Technical director Eghbal Hamidy had already defected to Jordan and two commercial managers, put in by MGPE, resigned earlier in the year.

Next year will see the expunging of the two-year Eghbal Hamidy design era, and ex-Sauber designer Sergio Rinland will create a new A23 around the Cosworth CR4 engine. For once Walkinshaw has a proven designer and a proven engine in harness. It bodes for better times than of late.

Money talks at the team, however, and funds are limited. Last year's budget was $73.65 million including the benefit of the Asiatech engine. In 2002 Walkinshaw has to pay for his engines, and that will cost a minimum of $20 million, although he is set

Arrows motorhome

to receive a $30 million windfall from the sale of a windtunnel he bought in Bedford. There may even be less money in 2002 than there was in 2001. That is the true test for the team, and the reason why Tom Walkinshaw may not be the master of his own domain for very much longer, with a hungry and very wealthy Austrian on the prowl.

# Everything to race for

The Orange Arrows team's principal problem on arriving in Melbourne was a lack of mileage on its new A22 racers. Its shakedown test at Silverstone the week before the cars were shipped to Australia amounted to only a handful of laps before an 'electronic communications' problem arose.

Technical director Mike Coughlan admitted that Melbourne was the first time the team had run the A22 for more than 11 laps, so it was only just beginning to understand the optimum set-up. "It was always harder to set the car up for Jos Verstappen last year than it was for Pedro de la Rosa, because of their different driving styles," he said. "The A21 worked well straight out of the box, and generally the A22 should be similar, but we need to understand its electronics problems better." The reliability of the Asiatech engine was hugely encouraging, however: "Right now it's better than the car's," Coughlan admitted. A huge testing programme was planned back in England with Johnny Herbert driving.

FRIDAY PRACTICE Arrows may have arrived with only a few hours of testing under its belt but it had three cars ready – the A22-01 for Verstappen, the A22-03 for Enrique Bernoldi and the spare A22-04 set up for Verstappen. The Dutchman was very happy with the car, despite the lack of test mileage. He required a brake change at the end of the first session, then to get in the groove he carried out several long runs to assess tyres, ending up a very creditable 14th fastest on 1m 31.669secs. Meanwhile team-mate and F1 rookie Bernoldi concentrated on learning the circuit. He also experienced problems but completed 27 laps and came in 20th fastest with a best lap of 1m 33.203secs.

SATURDAY QUALIFYING Verstappen lost time on Saturday morning when a potentiometer failure left his car unable to figure out what gear it was in, and when it mattered in the afternoon he didn't get a clear lap. His best lap was hit by traffic but even so, in the circumstances, a brilliant 15th on 1m 29.934secs.

Bernoldi lapped almost half a second slower than his team-mate and blamed the lack of a clear track and a problem getting heat into the front tyres. He still qualified well in 18th, on 1m 30.52secs.

SUNDAY RACE Arrows was one of the few teams that planned a two-stop strategy in what is traditionally a one-stop race. This suggested the A22 had one of the smallest fuel tanks of the 2001 crop. The point was academic for rookie Bernoldi. He had already spun his A22 leaving the pits on a slightly damp track during the morning warm-up, and within three laps of the race he had backed it quite heavily into the wall after spinning out of 18th place. "He's the new kid in the big city, and I think he got a bit fazed by it," said Mike Coughlan.

Verstappen made the most of his light fuel load to scythe his way up the field in the early laps. Starting 15th, the Dutchman was up to ninth by the time Jacques Villeneuve hit Ralf Schumacher, his scalps including Jean Alesi, Jenson Button, Juan Pablo Montoya and Giancarlo Fisichella. Arrows then became the only team to make use of the safety car period to refuel, bringing Verstappen in on lap 14 just before the safety car was called in. "Given our two-stop strategy, it made perfect sense," said Coughlan. "A stop under the safety car is a free stop, so we brought Verstappen in a little earlier than planned." The Dutchman fell to 17th but worked his way back past Alesi, the Benetton duo, Eddie Irvine and Fernando Alonso by the flag. Unfortunately, he had passed Nick Heidfeld under a yellow flag on the third lap, so fell back to 10th place once a time penalty was imposed.

"Doing a race distance was a bonus to be honest," confessed Coughlan. "Verstappen went as fast as he did in qualifying, after we made some set-up changes, so we made good progress this weekend."

Above and right: Brazilian rookie Enrique Bernoldi's debut race was soon over as he backed the car into a wall after losing control on lap three.

Right and below: Jos Verstappen started 15th and showed superb overtaking skills to reach ninth by the time the safety car came out.

orange **ARROWS**

## MALAYSIAN GRAND PRIX SEPANG

# The future gets brighter

Orange Arrows Asiatech was one of the stars of Sepang – courtesy of Jos Verstappen. Only he knew how he stormed from 18th place on the grid to sixth by the end of the opening lap, or how he survived multiple spins in the rainstorm. But that fabulous early show meant his team and sponsors grabbed some prime TV time that may prove extremely valuable.

The Peugeot engine, so derided in 2000, made the Arrows the second fastest car through the speed traps – but only after the team backed off most of its downforce. Twice now the team had been on two-stop strategies when everyone else was on one, and this pointed to a very small fuel tank. Twice it had also proved the wrong decision.

FRIDAY PRACTICE Orange Arrows brought the same three cars to Malaysia that it had used in Melbourne. Both A22s embarrassingly ground to early halts with only six laps to their credit; Verstappen's car suffered a sensor glitch, while Enrique Bernoldi had clutch trouble. Verstappen was still struggling to set the car up to his liking as he worked through the various tyre permutations and had to make do with 15th slot on a 1m 41.794secs. Bernoldi did 16 laps in the afternoon and clocked the 18th fastest time on 1m 42.541secs.

SATURDAY QUALIFYING Bernoldi and Verstappen covered 26 and 28 laps respectively on Saturday morning, but the ongoing difficulty in achieving a satisfactory set-up spilled over into qualifying, when both drivers struggled. "We have yet to get the car sorted on low tanks," conceded technical director Mike

Coughlan. Verstappen was unhappy to qualify only 18th, with a best of 1m 38.509secs, blaming persistent understeer and a lack of power. "I just wasn't able to push the car any harder," he reported. Bernoldi looked more settled and lined up alongside his team-mate on the grid with a time only two-tenths of a second slower. "If it wasn't for being blocked by Räikkönen on my last run I would have gone quicker still," he claimed. After the session, however, Arrows was informed that Bernoldi's A22 did not comply with the regulations which require the middle section of the front wing to be five centimetres above the reference plane, and the outer edges to be 10cm above it.

"Enrique had been off the road and dinged the underside of the chassis," Coughlan explained. "That damaged a reference plane pick-up point, which accounted for the discrepancy." As a consequence, though, all Bernoldi's qualifying times were wiped. That put him at the back of the grid, behind Gaston Mazzacane's Prost and the Minardis of Tarso Marques and Fernando Alonso.

SUNDAY RACE Mike Coughlan reduced the downforce on Verstappen's car to give him a chance on Sepang's long straights and the Dutchman made a brilliant start, surviving a massive series of spins on the fateful fourth lap. A fast tyre change got him out in an amazing second place behind the McLaren of David Coulthard. Heinz-Harald Frentzen got by, but the Arrows driver did not make it easy when Michael Schumacher, his old Benetton team-leader, appeared in his mirrors. Verstappen repassed Frentzen on lap 11 as the safety car pulled in. By the time of his first stop he was still fourth, having been overtaken by Rubens Barrichello.

Stage two of Verstappen's race saw him battle superbly with Mika Häkkinen, Ralf Schumacher and Frentzen – he gave the former world champion short shrift every time the silver arrow got alongside. He was still hanging grimly on to fourth place when his second stop, on lap 43, dropped him out of the points; he finished seventh. By contrast, Arrows number two Bernoldi again looked shaky. He started the race in the spare after his race chassis developed an alternator problem. He climbed to 11th before falling off on the rain-soaked fourth lap.

**Above and left:** Good pitwork and wet weather skill meant Jos Verstappen was able to battle with the big boys. **Below:** Enrique Bernoldi could only add four more laps to the total of three he clocked in Melbourne.

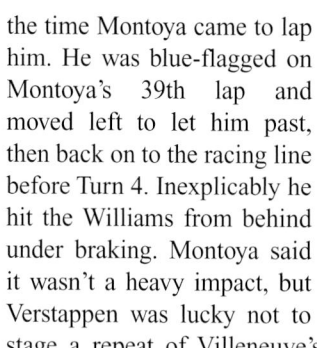

# More of the same

Orange Arrows continued to make head-lines despite scoring no points. Jos Verstappen may have been a hero in Malaysia but he was the villain of Brazil as he took out the race leader – an almost unforgivable sin in F1. The Dutchman was fined $15,000 for the lap 39 shunt, although Rubens Barrichello's similar shunt with Ralf Schumacher went unpunished.

FRIDAY PRACTICE Arrows brought the cars it had used in Melbourne and Malaysia. Jos Verstappen retained his race car as A22-01, but Enrique Bernoldi took over the former spare, A22-04, leaving his A22-03 as Ver-stappen's back-up.

Despite being Brazilian, Bernoldi had only previously raced a Formula Ford at Interlagos and that was seven years ago. But the local boy soon settled in, running a total of 38 laps for a disappointing 19th fastest on a 1m 18.233secs on a rare trou-ble-free day.

Verstappen's 32 laps were eventually worth 16th on 1m 17.792secs. He treated the session as a development test, trying a new power-steering system. In the after-noon a routine gear ratio change turned into a hydraulics problem, losing a little time.

SATURDAY QUALIFYING Technical director Mike Coughlan admitted the team was more comfortable running the car in low-downforce mode because of the Asiatech V10's lack of grunt. The speed trap on Saturday again saw Verstappen second fastest at 195.1mph, but downforce is everything at Interlagos and he could only make the 17th best time, one place behind his team-mate, following a good intra-team battle. After set-up changes intended to cure understeer in the morn-ing, he had too much oversteer in qualifying, recording a lap of 1m 15.704secs. Bernoldi was delighted to out-qualify Verstap-pen for the first time, securing 16th with 1m 15.657secs.

SUNDAY RACE Verstappen was up to ninth and planning to stop on his 39th lap, after battling Luciano Burti's Jaguar, by

the time Montoya came to lap him. He was blue-flagged on Montoya's 39th lap and moved left to let him past, then back on to the racing line before Turn 4. Inexplicably he hit the Williams from behind under braking. Montoya said it wasn't a heavy impact, but Verstappen was lucky not to stage a repeat of Villeneuve's Melbourne flight. "I saw I was given a blue flag and I saw Montoya coming, so I went to the left to let him past," he said. "Once he came past I moved back over on to the racing line and he then braked very early. I'm very sorry for him because I heard he was leading the race, but I couldn't avoid him. I hit him and that was it."

Arrows' telemetry suggested Verstappen was 30mph slower at the same point on the track than he had been on the previous lap, which seemed to support his claim. "He had already reacted because the data suggests he was already going slower," Coughlan said. "It's a shame, because I think we threw points away here."

Bernoldi's race was soon over. After 14 laps he began to have gear selection trouble due to a hydraulic fault and retired a lap later. He had only completed 20 racing laps so far all season.

Above: The Arrows showed pace through the speed traps, but lacked downforce in the corners. Right: After qualifying, Verstappen takes time to relax. He later had to explain why he hit the back of Juan Pablo Montoya's Williams.

## SAN MARINO GRAND PRIX IMOLA

# The quest for speed

Orange Arrows was a team making progress but, as technical director Mike Coughlan admitted, all the others were making more, and Arrows was a second off the pace. Increasingly the problem was the engine, which had started strongly but was not being developed anywhere near quick enough. The new Asiatech company had simply underestimated the development that goes on in-season.

**FRIDAY PRACTICE** Arrows arrived fresh from testing its new power-steering system and further electronic modifications at Magny-Cours the previous week, with a new A22 chassis and the hybrid A21B. It brought A22-03 to Imola for Jos Verstappen to use, with A22-04 as the spare and A22-06 for Enrique Bernoldi. None of the cars was fitted with power-steering for this race, since it is only required in really high-speed corners and there were none left at Imola following the 1995 revamp.

Top and left: Jos Verstappen's race was brief after an exhaust split. Below: Enrique Bernoldi was pleased to post his first Formula One finish in 10th place.

Verstappen's car was also fitted with slightly revised suspension. It improved feel and driver comfort, although the performance gain was negligible.

Friday was character-building: Verstappen managed only seven laps all day. On the wet track in the morning he didn't even complete one lap before stopping out on the track when the fuel pressure dropped.

The same thing happened in the afternoon, but at least this time it happened as he was leaving the pitlane. His seven laps yielded only 21st fastest time of 1m 29.750secs. The problem was finally traced to faulty fuel pumps, which engine maker Asiatech was able to rectify in time for Saturday.

Bernoldi fared better, covering 39 laps for a best time of 1m 29.273secs which left him 19th, before a minor electrical problem brought him to a halt.

**SATURDAY QUALIFYING** Jos Verstappen had to play catch-up after the loss of track time the previous day, but worked through his planned programme in a busy Saturday morning. In qualifying he set a best of 1m 26.062secs for 17th fastest as an engine-related electrical problem obliged him to switch to the T-car. "Although it had my settings," he said, "it is never quite the same as your race car, so I lost a lot of momentum and couldn't improve during my final run." The Dutchman was beaten for the second race running by his teammate. Bernoldi's ninth fastest time in practice was used as inspiration for 16th on the grid on the softer Bridgestone rubber.

**SUNDAY RACE** Jos Verstappen disappeared without trace after pushing up to 15th by the sixth lap, ahead of Bernoldi, and was sidelined by an exhaust pipe failure a lap later. "When something like that fails you have to remember how tightly packed everything is under the rear bodywork," said Mike Coughlan. "The underbody temperatures quickly go sky-high and the heat burns through all sorts of things…"

Bernoldi, chasing hard all afternoon after Burti's Jaguar, finally overtook him on lap 56 to score his first F1 career finish: 10th place.

# Nothing to get excited about

Formula One in 2001 had developed into two divisions. In the premier league was Ferrari, McLaren Mercedes, BMW Williams, Jordan Honda, BAR Honda and Sauber. The second division consisted of Jaguar, Benetton Renault, Arrows, Minardi and Prost. Jaguar currently headed division two, and was fighting for leadership with Arrows. Considering Jaguar had a budget three times as big, this was not bad going for the Arrows outfit, but it couldn't hide the fact that Arrows competed only to make up the numbers and had no realistic chance of winning – despite being owned by Tom Walkinshaw, a legend in motorsport circles. It showed just how competitive Formula One was – even a talented engineer such as Walkinshaw was no longer good enough.

Orange Arrows seemed content to play second fiddle to Jaguar in division two. But as Walkinshaw knew, glancing over his shoulder at his old team Benetton, things could be a lot worse.

**FRIDAY PRACTICE** Like everyone else, Orange Arrows had a lot of data acquisition to work through on Friday to set up its throttle mapping and traction control, and both cars ran reliably all day. Enrique Bernoldi worked mainly on traction and launch control in A22-03, covering 40 laps and setting the 16th fastest of 1m 22.888secs. Jos Verstappen also did a lot of miles, clocking up 37 laps in A22-06, his programme encompassing some traction control running then tyre evaluation and aero modifications. He was 17th fastest on 1m 22.962secs. A22-01 was Verstappen's spare chassis, but it would be allocated to the faster qualifier for the race.

**SATURDAY QUALIFYING** For the third race in succession Bernoldi and Verstappen qualified 16th and 17th, but there was a difference this time. Both drivers opted for Bridgestone's soft rubber and Bernoldi avoided making too many set-up changes, focusing instead on finding a good rhythm and building momentum. He believed he could have shaved something from his best lap of 1m 20.696secs on his last run, but a big slide put paid to that.

Verstappen was close behind, but Walkinshaw admitted: "We messed Jos up today by not giving him brakes that worked properly on his third run." The Dutchman was pleased with his second run, but spun when he encountered a long brake pedal on his third and ended up having to drive out of the gravel. The brakes were bled but the undertray had been damaged when he went off and he was subsequently unable to improve on that second-run result of 1m 20.737secs.

Arrows had expected a tough weekend on this power circuit, but technical director Mike Coughlan admitted he was disappointed. "We've certainly made improvements but are still half a second away from the top of the 'second division' and a full second from the bottom of the 'first division'."

**SUNDAY RACE** Arrows had early cause for celebration, when Verstappen made a perfect launch-control start. "It was better than the best of his manual getaways," said Mike Coughlan.

But things went wrong for Bernoldi: his start didn't work at all, as he immediately got wheelspin while trying to dodge the Jordan of Heinz-Harald Frentzen. Then in the first corner he hit part of David Coulthard's front wing. He pitted for repairs at the end of the first lap and, just as the Scot slipped ahead to steal 19th place on the ninth lap, Bernoldi pulled off with no fuel pressure.

Verstappen was in a scrap with Jean Alesi, just holding off the Prost and hanging on to 12th place until his first pit call on lap 19. When their fight resumed Alesi had moved ahead and on their 37th lap Verstappen lost ground after sliding into, and out of, the gravel in the last corner. He said later that the front end of the car lost its bite after the first pit-stop and it got to extract the same performance. He made another stop for fuel on lap 39, emerging in 13th place and regained 12th on lap 50 with Barrichello's retirement. It was nothing to get excited about.

Right and above: Bernoldi pulled off after only nine laps with no fuel pressure. The race weekend did little to encourage Arrows' hopes of eclipsing Jaguar at the top of the 'second division'. Bottom: Bernoldi was gradually getting on par with Verstappen.

## AUSTRIAN GRAND PRIX A1 RING
# Points are everything

Good strategy, good TV exposure and a world championship point – Orange Arrows could scarcely have asked for more in Austria. With its cars qualifying only 14th and 16th the team took a gamble that paid off and made monkeys out of others such as Jaguar, which should have finished ahead.

By making up ground hand over fist on this strategy, then switching Verstappen to a higher load after his first stop to align his second with rivals' first stops, the team snatched a well-deserved point. This was good progress. It masked other problems such as the engine, which was gradually falling down in power compared to others. Asiatech was now full at work on the 2002 engine – which was no help to Arrows.

**FRIDAY PRACTICE** Jos Verstappen and Enrique Bernoldi stayed with their regular A22s, the former with chassis 06, the latter with 03, and 01 as Verstappen's spare. Both drivers had an adventurous day with numerous spins on their way to 14th and 16th places respectively. Verstappen was just about able to complete his programme with a best of 1m 12.705secs over 40 laps. That was about what the team expected, but it hadn't figured on an oil supply problem that obliged Verstappen to stop on the circuit as a precaution at the end. Bernoldi also managed 40 laps, though an off in the afternoon cost him time. Like the other Bridgestone runners, both men opted for the softer tyres.

**SATURDAY QUALIFYING** Arrows had another trying day. Bernoldi's session was interrupted when he got a puncture after flat-spotting a tyre. Verstappen's work was also interrupted when a suspension failure threw him off the circuit after a rod-end broke, probably due to fatigue. The Dutchman was unharmed and set back on foot to the pits, where he took over A22-01 to resume running.

The two were in their usual cars for qualifying when the Brazilian again upstaged the Dutchman as the pair improved marginally on their usual placings with 15th and 16th respectively. Bernoldi used scrubbed front tyres because he felt they gave the A22 the best balance, and recorded 1m 11.823secs. Verstappen was very disappointed with his 1m 12.187secs, admitting that while the car was better on scrubbed front tyres, he had not been able to scrub in a sufficient number in the morning. Right at the end he gave himself and a following Michael Schumacher a bit of a shock when he spun on the exit to the last corner and nearly collected the Ferrari as his Arrows slid out of the run-off area and looped back on to the track. Subsequent inspection suggested that the right rear tyre had sustained a puncture.

**SUNDAY RACE** From 16th on the grid and with a light fuel load, Verstappen charged up to seventh at the end of the first lap. Then he picked off Eddie Irvine and David Coulthard to move to fifth after four laps. This became second after the tangle between Montoya and Schumacher on lap 16, and Verstappen stayed there comfortably until his first stop on lap 22. He was now far enough ahead of Irvine and Villeneuve to rejoin in seventh, then only dropped to eighth when he stopped again on lap 45. When Villeneuve and Irvine made their first stops on laps 47 and 48 respectively, he was home and dry for the final point. It was strategic thinking at its best.

"When you are so evenly matched with a lot of other people you have to think further," said technical director Mike Coughlan. "So we decided to start both cars with really light fuel loads. We were screaming to Jos on the radio, 'you've got to pass, you've got to pass!' And he did. He's good at that. Enrique did well, too, and the same strategy was working for him."

Bernoldi also moved early, running 11th on lap one, then overtaking both Villeneuve and Irvine in style to run ninth on lap nine. Ralf Schumacher's demise promoted the Brazilian to eighth, but on lap 17 he retired with a

*orange ARROWS*

**Above, left and below:** Jos Verstappen drove a storming race, using a two-stop, low fuel-load strategy to briefly lead both BAR Hondas and finish sixth. Below: Enrique Bernoldi out-qualified Verstappen for 15th on the grid, but retired after 17 laps.

**Left:** Verstappen lifted Arrows' hopes with a fine drive. In the early stages, he led the McLaren of ultimate winner David Coulthard.

# Wrong sort of exposure

Practice and qualifying were a disaster as Jos Verstappen and Enrique Bernoldi shared the penultimate row of the grid – the worst performance of the season. But sterling drives in the race pulled something out of the bag and the pair attracted much of the television airtime in what was a fundamentally dull race.

For a man who professes to detest racing in Monte Carlo, Verstappen provided fireworks by passing no fewer than five cars before a disastrous pitstop undid all his work. Bernoldi's resolute defence of his place, while harshly criticised by some, against David Coulthard did much to raise his stock.

THURSDAY PRACTICE Arrows brought its usual trio of A22s. Like Jordan, the team sought fresh solutions to the front-end grip problems posed by the circuit and Verstappen's car wore a high-mounted nose wing, which he believed added greater downforce. By the end of the day it had been removed at the behest of the stewards.

The Dutchman covered 41 laps of his 'home' track. Both he and technical director Mike Coughlan were delighted with a trouble-free day that enabled them to gather plenty of data. Bernoldi, who had raced here previously in F3000, completed two laps more than Verstappen.

SATURDAY QUALIFYING If Thursday had been good to the team, Saturday was a nightmare. It began when Verstappen's Asiatech V10 let go in a big way during free practice. Then Bernoldi's car developed a fuel leak. Sterling work by the team got both cars out just before the end of the second half, but Bernoldi did himself no favours by throwing his A22 into the wall at Rascasse in the closing stages.

With both cars shod with Bridgestone's soft rubber, Arrows ended a bruising and disappointing day with 19th and 20th on the grid. Verstappen out-qualified

his team-mate but complained of a rear damper problem on his final run. The cold fact is that when you have trouble of the sort Arrows had on Saturday morning, recovery in qualifying is always going to be difficult on such an unforgiving circuit.

SUNDAY RACE Verstappen made a terrible start and was tagged by Luciano Burti on the exit to Ste Devote as Bernoldi made up two places. When they got to Portier, Verstappen hit Nick Heidfeld, throwing the Sauber into the wall. Amazingly the Arrows was undamaged and Verstappen got his head down. Burti yielded on lap two, Tarso Marques a lap later, then Verstappen swept by Bernoldi on lap eight. Next he passed Fernando Alonso and Jenson Button, and the retirements of Juan Pablo Montoya, Olivier Panis, Mika Häkkinen, Pedro de la Rosa and Jarno Trulli promoted him to ninth as he made his stop. Unfortunately the engine stalled due to fluctuating fuel pressure, dropping him to 13th. Other drivers' stops raised him to ninth after 50 laps and Ralf Schumacher's demise moved him up a final place to eighth.

Bernoldi showed great poise in refusing to be intimidated by Coulthard's looming presence in his mirrors from the opening lap until his own stop. The Brazilian drove cleanly but rebuffed the few challenges the Scot made. He soldiered on to finish ninth.

The only other team to have both cars at the finish was Ferrari. Technical director Mike Coughlan admitted however that he was disappointed, considering the quality of Verstappen's drive, not to score a point.

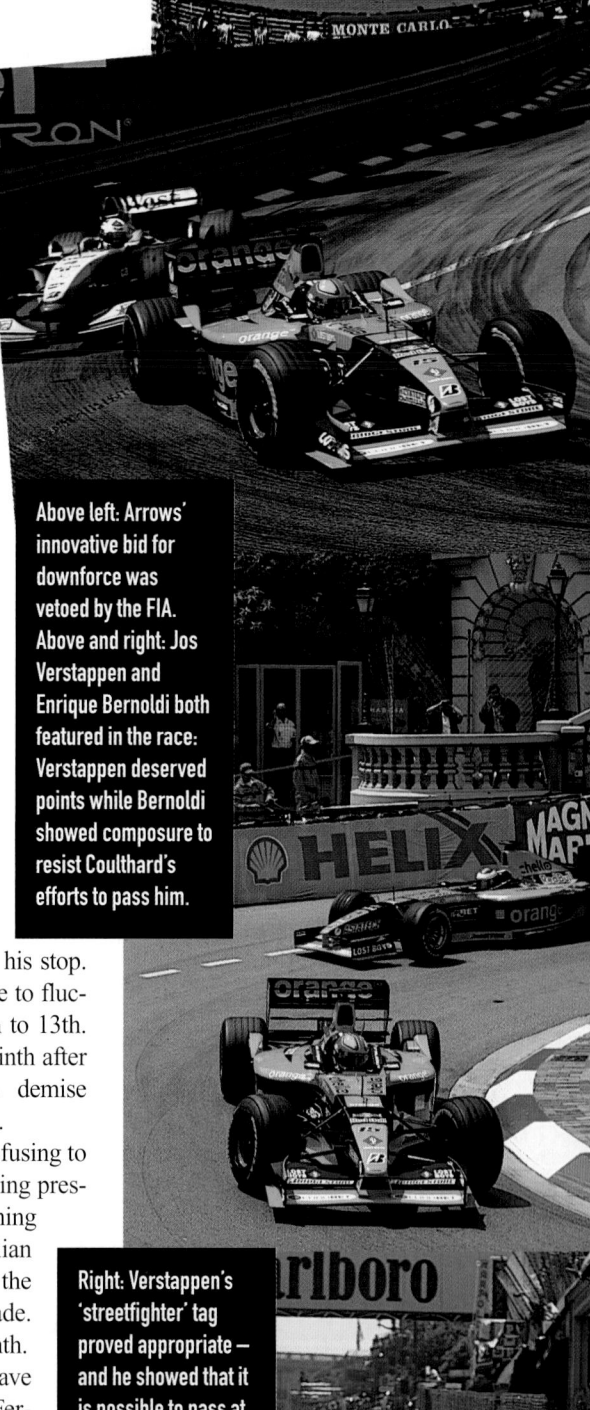

Above left: Arrows' innovative bid for downforce was vetoed by the FIA. Above and right: Jos Verstappen and Enrique Bernoldi both featured in the race: Verstappen deserved points while Bernoldi showed composure to resist Coulthard's efforts to pass him.

Right: Verstappen's 'streetfighter' tag proved appropriate – and he showed that it is possible to pass at Monaco.

# Bad breaks ruin race

It was a long time since a hamburger had caused a driver's retirement, but something as innocuous as a burger wrapper proved Enrique Bernoldi's undoing in a race in which he might have scored a point.

There was an unlucky break for Jos Verstappen, too, as he crashed out of the race just as Arrows' two-stop strategy was set to deliver a point. Team owner Tom Walkinshaw was focusing on finding an engine for next year. He was also eyeing up ex-Sauber designer Sergio Rinland.

**FRIDAY PRACTICE** Orange Arrows' chassis allocation was unchanged from Monaco: Verstappen used A22-06 as his race car and 01 as his spare, with Bernoldi relying on 03.

Friday was not one of the team's better days, as a gearbox oil leak delayed Verstappen for the majority of the morning session. But the Dutchman made up ground fast in the afternoon to set the 16th fastest time in the course of only 24 laps.

Bernoldi had never seen the Montreal track before, so spent much of his day learning it. He did 31 laps for a best time of 1m 21.259secs, which left him a place behind his team-mate. He lost one set from his tyre allocation after running over debris from Jacques Villeneuve's accident, which had the knock-on effect of delaying his start to the afternoon session.

**SATURDAY QUALIFYING** Verstappen boosted team morale with a strong performance in qualifying. Free practice had persuaded both Arrows drivers that Bridgestone's soft compound was the better: the Dutchman secured the 13th grid slot with a time of 1m 18.030secs then maintained that place with a two-10ths improvement in qualifying.

He was pleased with the handling of the A22 and in particular its consistency, and although he missed his final run because of the red flag he didn't feel he could have improved much further in any case.

Bernoldi had a less productive day, losing time in the morning after the assault by Ricardo Zonta and struggling slightly in the afternoon. He too improved on his morning time, to record 1m 18.575secs which left him 17th and disappointed he did not put a really good lap together.

**SUNDAY RACE** Both A22s went to the start line with light fuel loads and once again Verstappen made a dragster start. From 13th on the grid he was up to seventh at the end of the opening lap and in the points once Barrichello had spun.

There he stayed, sandwiched between Oliver Panis and Kimi Räikkönen, until his first stop on the 23rd lap. Unfortunately a radio glitch stopped him hearing the order to pit under the safety car, which came out on lap 20 and went back in on lap 23. That misunderstanding dropped him down to 15th place, but as others made their later stops he moved back up and was running ninth when he stopped again on lap 47. This time he resumed without losing a place.

He made up another when Pedro de la Rosa refuelled on lap 52 and yet another when David Coulthard blew up three laps later. When Jarno Trulli dropped back on lap 63 he moved up a further position. However, the brake pedal travel was getting longer by the lap, and eventually Verstappen ran out of stoppers on lap 66 and ended his race in the gravel.

Bernoldi was running 13th after eight laps, chasing Villeneuve, until rising temperatures prompted the team to call him in on his ninth lap. Investigation revealed a hamburger wrapper blocking the radiator – but by then the damage had been done.

**Above: Jos Verstappen put in a storming points-deserving drive, but was betrayed by failing brakes, which resulted in a crash. Left: Enrique Bernoldi leads Jenson Button and Luciano Burti.**

**Left: Enrique Bernoldi again showed promise but his race was destroyed by debris in the radiator intake. Bernoldi proved a thorn in the side for BAR team-leader Jacques Villeneuve. Below left: Verstappen gets set to dive inside Olivier Panis's BAR.**

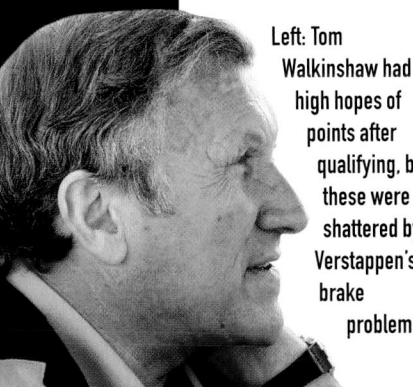

**Left: Tom Walkinshaw had high hopes of points after qualifying, but these were shattered by Verstappen's brake problems.**

orange *ARROWS*

## EUROPEAN GRAND PRIX NÜRBURGRING

# Zero weekend

The best that Orange Arrows could have hoped for at the Nürburgring was the 13th position in which Jos Verstappen was running when his A22's engine stopped on the 59th lap. The failure was perhaps symbolic for a difficult weekend that also saw Enrique Bernoldi retire from the race. But more positively, team principal Tom Walkinshaw announced that the agreement with French engine maker Asiatech would not be extended into 2002. This made it almost certain the team would be powered by versions of the light, powerful Cosworth from Jaguar.

This was good news beyond measure and pointed to Arrows having a competitive engine for the first time in recent memory. The engines would be expensive but Arrows would offset the cost by leasing a wind tunnel it has acquired to Jaguar. Another nifty deal by team principal Tom Walkinshaw.

FRIDAY PRACTICE Arrows brought three A22s to Germany: Verstappen using A22-06 as his race car and A22-01 as the back-up, and Bernoldi with A22-03. Bernoldi was able to get on with the usual set-up tasks and covered 39 laps for the 17th fastest time of 1m 19.822secs. Verstappen's day was a dead loss, however, when a power-steering hydraulics problem arose and repairs ran into the afternoon. He reckoned he barely left square one in terms of setting up his car, but 1m 19.640secs left him 16th.

SATURDAY QUALIFYING The two drivers reversed positions in qualifying. Bernoldi cut his time to 1m 18.151secs for 18th place, with Verstappen a shade behind on 1m 18.262secs. Both used Bridge-stone's soft tyres.

Technical director Mike Coughlan described the day as a disaster. The team had expected to be 13th or 14th on a circuit that should have favoured the nimble A22s. In the morning Bernoldi had managed a 1m 17.686secs lap and Verstappen a 1m 18.123secs, so the air of depression in the garage was understandable.

Both drivers clocked an identical time of 1m 18.369secs on their first runs, but after that it was downhill all the way. Bernoldi complained that the more the track temperature rose the less his car liked it, while Verstappen found he had lost straightline speed compared to the morning. The day's only good news for the team was the announcement that Verstappen would be staying another season.

SUNDAY RACE This time there was to be no lightning spurt into the top 10 by Verstappen, who Arrows calculated has overtaken 59 cars so far in 2001. But he did move from 19th on the grid to 14th to take that tally to 64. From then on he settled into the rhythm in Fisichella's wheeltracks, until the Italian pitted on the 21st lap. Verstappen then held 13th until his own first stop on lap 26 dropped him to 16th. There he remained until Fisichella's second stop on lap 42, and he was running 14th again when his own second stop came four laps later. As things settled down again he moved back up to 13th place before his engine stopped.

Bernoldi again failed to finish. He overtook slow-starting Olivier Panis and Luciano Burti on the opening lap and was running 15th just before his pitstop on the 23rd lap. The engine stalled when he tried to select neutral and after an 18.8secs stop he rejoined, only to quit seven laps later when the gearbox jammed in fifth.

"I think that was a fitting end to the kind of weekend we've had," Coughlan said after the race. "We just haven't been able to make the A22 work here."

**Above and right:** It was a quieter race than usual for newly re-signed Dutchman Jos Verstappen. He qualified 19th and never ran higher than 13th in the race before his engine gave up. **Below:** Enrique Bernoldi tried hard but a broken gearbox ended his race after only 30 laps.

**Enrique Bernoldi again got the better of Jos Verstappen in qualifying.**

## FRENCH GRAND PRIX MAGNY–COURS
# Dispiriting stuff

On a medium to high-downforce circuit, the Orange Arrows A22s were always likely to struggle, and the team's fears were realised when neither Jos Verstappen nor Enrique Bernoldi played a significant part in the French Grand Prix. They qualified 16th and 18th respectively, then fought for a lowly 13th place in the early going until Bernoldi's Asiatech engine broke. Not a weekend to remember for the orange and black cars, and a sign that Formula One never stays the same for long.

It was only two races ago that Arrows was full of optimism, pointing out that in an age of little over-taking Verstappen was cutting through fields like a hero of yesteryear. Since then the cars had been lucky to run in the top 10, let alone be real contenders for points.

FRIDAY PRACTICE The problems came early for Arrows when Bernoldi stopped his A22-03 on the circuit at the end of the morning session with a gearbox problem. Then no sooner had running resumed after lunch than Verstappen slid to a halt when the engine in his A22-06 broke. A22-01, the T-car, could not be pressed into service because of regulations that preclude such practice outside qualifying, so once Bernoldi had completed his running in his repaired chassis it was commandeered for the Dutchman – much to the chagrin of the Brazilian.

Verstappen ended his troubled day with 34 laps under his belt and the 18th fastest time of 1m 17.285secs set in lap three, while Bernoldi was, as usual, close behind with the 19th fastest time, a 1m 17.527secs. Considering that he did only 23 laps, it wasn't a bad effort. But the technical problems meant neither driver did any running on a light fuel load, so their times weren't a serious reflection of actual driving conditions.

Part of the reason for the chassis swap was that the team wanted Verstappen to complete the tyre evaluation, which simply resulted in both drivers doing what every other Bridgestone user did – they opted to run with the harder compound.

SATURDAY QUALIFYING Grid slots of 18th and 20th were pretty much what the team had feared as it went into qualifying, for the A22 was much happier on lower downforce tracks. Both drivers did a brace of runs early on in the one-hour session, before sitting back and waiting in the hope that the searing track temperature might abate slightly. When it didn't, they took to the track and did what they could, the Dutchman recording a 1m 15.707secs and his team-mate again close behind with 1m 15.828secs. Both men felt they had wrung out of the car the most that it could offer on a track that clearly did not suit its characteristics.

SUNDAY RACE This time Verstappen's 'getaway driver start' reaped only two places, at the expense of the admittedly inferior Benettons, and the Dutchman's progress was hampered when he came into contact with Giancarlo Fisichella somewhere on the first lap. Bernoldi shrewdly nailed himself to his team leader's tail and went through the gaps with him. Both had benefited from the parade lap problems of Mika Häkkinen and Pedro de la Rosa, so they ended the first lap 14th and 15th. That became 13th and 14th when Jacques Villeneuve stopped on the sixth lap, but that was as good as it got and as it ever looked likely to get.

On the 18th lap the same engine problem that had stopped Verstappen at the Nürburgring struck Bernoldi. Then there was a problem with the refuelling rig when Verstappen pitted on lap 25. That dropped him behind the Benetton duo and Jean Alesi and for the rest of the race he struggled with poor grip. His last set of Bridgestones was particularly lacking.

Then, to cap it all, Verstappen's Arrows failed to complete its slowing-down lap after he had taken the chequered flag, when rising engine temperatures prompted the team to signal him to stop as a precaution rather than damage equipment unnecessarily.

**Above left: With a small tank and light fuel load, Jos Verstappen was briefly able to run ahead of Kimi Räikkönen until his problematic pitstop. Left: Magny–Cours highlighted Arrows' shortage of downforce, with Verstappen finishing 13th.**

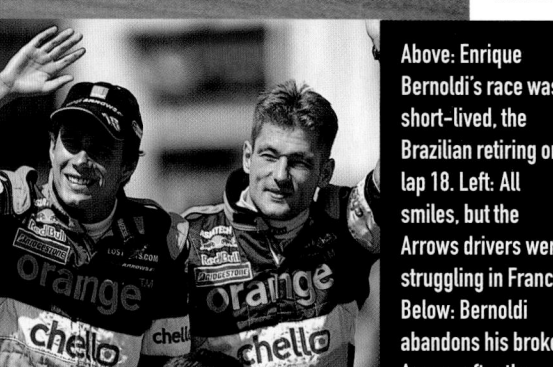

**Above: Enrique Bernoldi's race was short-lived, the Brazilian retiring on lap 18. Left: All smiles, but the Arrows drivers were struggling in France. Below: Bernoldi abandons his broken Arrows after the Asiatech V10 failed.**

*orange ARROWS*

# Light appears for 2002

Proof that Tom Walkinshaw can be a very charming man came at the British Grand Prix where he had smiles for everyone – even long-established adversaries. The reason was clear after he spent more of his time in the Jaguar motor home than he did in his own, ensconced in talks with Niki Lauda and Cosworth managing director Trevor Crisp about the finer points of him receiving top-spec Cosworth engines next year in return for $18 million and use of the Bedford windtunnel he cannily acquired for a snip. Jaguar badly needed the windtunnel, so had been forced to do a deal and make Ford chief executive Jacques Nasser bite his lip. It proved that Walkinshaw is one of the sharpest dealmakers in the paddock.

Arrows' Asiatech engine had less power than last year's Renault Supertec engines, according to Walkinshaw, and the team would do the best it could for the rest of the season. Team members knew if they could produce a half decent chassis, it would deliver in 2002 and make podiums a possibility.

FRIDAY PRACTICE Jos Verstappen again had A22-06 to race, with A22-01 as the spare, while Enrique Bernoldi had A22-03. Practice brought no surprises or dramas and both were happy. Verstappen covered 41 laps and his best of 1m 25.026secs was 15th quickest. Bernoldi, working with a new race engineer, recorded 1m 25.209secs for 16th, having done 36 laps.

SATURDAY QUALIFYING Rain or shine, it mattered little to the Arrows drivers. They were 13th and 14th in the morning's wet free practice and struggled on a dry track in the afternoon as they switched back to the new soft Bridgestone tyre in qualifying. Verstappen squeezed his car hard to lop a second off his Friday time, but 1m 24.067secs was still only good enough for 17th on the grid. The time was similar to the team's low-fuel running at the recent test but achieved on a track washed clean of rubber by the downpour so Arrows was heartened to be progressing.

Bernoldi's best lap was 1m 24.606secs, but despite being only six-10ths off Verstappen's time the gap was sufficient for both Benettons to slip between the Arrows. The Brazilian

lost his first run to a throttle problem and that threw an already tight programme into confusion. Like everyone else he had waited for the track to dry fully and now found himself having to cram three runs into an even tighter timescale. Ironically, he was then inadvertently blocked by Verstappen on his final run as they struggled in traffic.

SUNDAY RACE Taking full advantage of the Coulthard/Trulli debacle, Verstappen leapt from 17th on the grid to 11th by the end of the opening lap, then passed Jacques Villeneuve and Jean Alesi on successive laps to move into ninth by lap four. Although his A22 was oversteering a lot on its first set of Bridgestones, he held track position through to his first stop on lap 22. Unfortunately for Arrows, BAR's and Jaguar's tactics of keeping Villeneuve and Irvine out as long as possible saw both move ahead. Verstappen stopped again on lap 41 and his chances of coming back at them evaporated in the closing stages as he had to nurse a sick Asiatech V10.

Bernoldi had a good start, too, climbing to 14th by the end of lap one but then lacking downforce to make a move on Jenson Button. Eventually the Brazilian passed the Englishman as Arrows' race strategy won through, but Benetton did a better job with Fisichella and he passed both of them.

In the end Verstappen was 11th, Bernoldi 14th, but it says everything about Orange Arrows' British Grand Prix that it was more notable for the presence of the Gloucester Rugby Football Club squad courtesy of Tom Walkinshaw. The Cosworth CR3 engine couldn't come soon enough.

Above and right: Jos Verstappen had a great first lap, climbing to 11th, where he finished after his two-stop strategy. But he was beaten by the late-stopping Eddie Irvine and Jacques Villeneuve.

Above right: Bernoldi battled with Button to take 14th. Left: Tom Walkinshaw brightened up the pit by bringing his rugby team to the Grand Prix.

Left and above:
Bernoldi survived the
Burti accident to lead
Verstappen home in
eighth. Arrows
achieved reliability
on a circuit that
decimated the
opposition.

GERMAN GRAND PRIX HOCKENHEIM

# A very lucky day

Eighth and ninth places in a race of attrition were a lost opportunity for Orange Arrows. The team seemed to have written of the rest of the season and settled into last year's routine of fighting Minardi for the last four grid slots, but this time always winning.

The problem was the engine. Whilst every other engine had received heavy development, the Asiatech was exactly the same as in Australia. And that was another reason to look to 2002. Tom Walkinshaw has pulled it off again and secured a supply of 2002 specification Cosworth V10s for next year, which could see the team make a mid-grid position a reality.

With both cars finishing, Hockenheim was a win in the battle for reliability; midseason, Arrows had the worst record of all.

FRIDAY PRACTICE Arrows' three A22s were on hand in Germany, 06 for Verstappen to race, 01 as his spare, and 03 for Bernoldi.

Verstappen's day got off to a poor start when his A22 stopped with a fuel pressure problem. It was retrieved during the lunch break, and he covered another 20 laps. After the brake problem Arrows had in Canada it was on alert for similar problems, and to assess brake performance decided to run all sessions with a relatively high fuel load. The Dutchman did a good job of making up for lost time, setting the 18th quickest lap on 1m 44.143secs.

Bernoldi met trouble in the afternoon, when his Asiatech V10 developed an unidentified problem that prevented him running on new tyres, but as he had almost completed his intended programme for the day the team did not feel he had lost out too much. He was 20th, his 24 laps yielding a best of 1m 44.549secs.

SATURDAY QUALIFYING Securing 19th and 20th places was about as good as Arrows had expected, given the A22's lack of horsepower. Hockenheim's long straights place a premium on grunt and the orange and black cars simply couldn't aim for better.

Both Bernoldi (19th on 1m 41.668secs) and Verstappen (20th, on 1m 41.870secs) improved the handling of their cars as free practice and qualifying continued, but the Brazilian lost time when Button's Renault suffered a terminal failure in front of him during his last run of the afternoon. Verstappen also lost what should have been his best effort when he gambled too much and spun.

SUNDAY RACE Bernoldi was the luckiest man on the grid when the first attempt to start the race ended in drama. As Schumacher's Ferrari slowed suddenly with transmission failure, Luciano Burti's Prost ran into the back of it and took off. By sheer luck the blue car landed between the two Arrows, near the pit wall. Verstappen was ahead of Bernoldi, and the Brazilian did a fabulous avoidance job by hitting the brakes hard enough to lock all four wheels – no mean feat with carbon discs.

The left front wheel of the Prost was thrown into the air before crashing down on Bernoldi's car. He was lucky it landed on the left-hand sidepod and not the cockpit, and as the A22 slid into the gravel the wheel finally bounced away.

Amazingly, Arrows merely fitted a new rear wing and engine cover to Bernoldi's car, and with remarkable sang froid he re-entered the fray on the restart.

Verstappen made the better start, scooting up from 20th to 11th. He was deposed by Olivier Panis on lap six, and that was when Ricardo Zonta ran into the back of him, lacerating his left rear tyre. The subsequent pitstop put the Dutchman out of contention in what should have been a single-stop race.

Meanwhile, Bernoldi squeezed up to 13th on the fifth lap after straightlining a chicane to pass Button, but two laps later the Englishman outbraked him to regain what had become 12th. Bernoldi was on a two-stopper, and made his first refuelling call on lap 12 and his second on lap 28, bringing him back within Verstappen's reach. Over the remainder of the race the pair circulated nose-to-tail, crossing the finish line only three-10ths of a second apart.

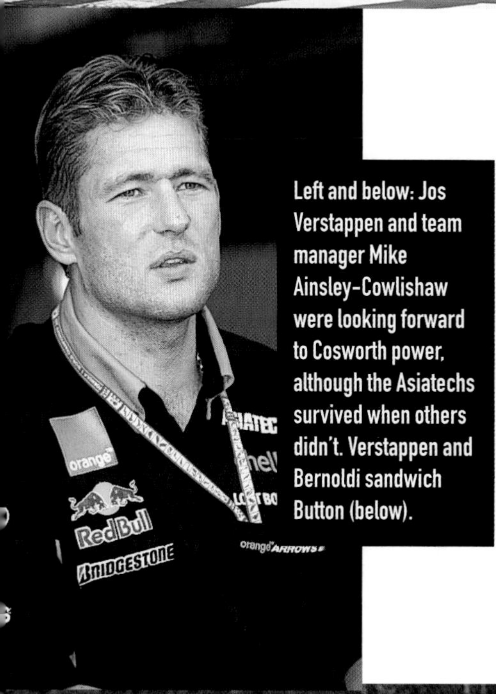

Left and below: Jos
Verstappen and team
manager Mike
Ainsley-Cowlishaw
were looking forward
to Cosworth power,
although the Asiatechs
survived when others
didn't. Verstappen and
Bernoldi sandwich
Button (below).

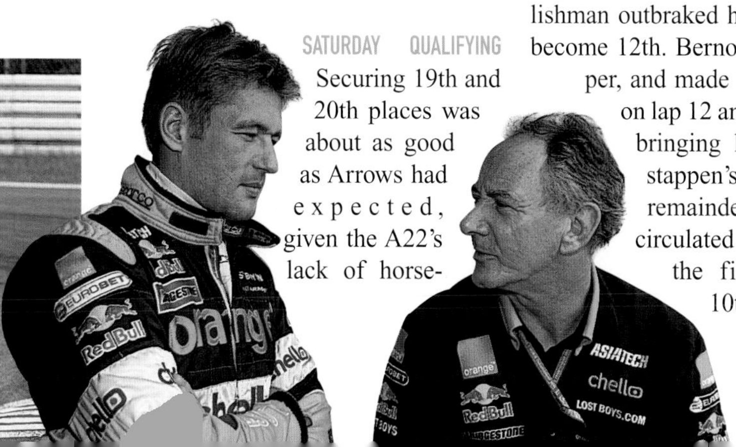

# Drivers have differences

High downforce and the Orange Arrows A22 have never been synonymous, so the team went to Hungary expecting the worst on a track where it was so crucial. And it got it. The Asiatech-engined cars ran at the tail of the field in the race, although hopefully 2002 should be different.

One other problem was vexing team principal Tom Walkinshaw – the unpleasantness that had developed between his two drivers. Jos Verstappen, annoyed at being outqualified a few times by team-mate Enrique Bernoldi, had commented widely on his driving ability. It was becoming increasingly unlikely that Bernoldi would be at Arrows next year.

FRIDAY PRACTICE Jos Verstappen had A22-06 to play with, and 01 as his spare. Bernoldi, who seemed a little bemused by the Dutchman's recent attack on him to journalists, had A22-03. Downforce aerodynamics aside, the cars were largely unchanged from Hockenheim.

Verstappen covered 39 laps in free practice, but having been 13th fastest by the lunch break he later dropped to 18th, setting a best of 1m 19.368secs. Bernoldi did one lap fewer and as usual was close behind, one place adrift on 1m 19.466secs. Neither of them encountered any problems, though both found it a difficult choice between Bridgestone's hard and soft rubber tyres.

SATURDAY QUALIFYING Saturday was an altogether tougher day for the team. Verstappen lost a lot of time in the morning after damaging his car when he hit a kerb. He blamed the dusty nature of the track for his scrape. Both drivers chose the soft Bridgestones, which featured a revised construction, but Bernoldi could only manage 20th fastest time with 1m 18.258secs and Verstappen 21st with 1m 18.389secs. The Brazilian was angry that the engine cut out on his final run, having been convinced he should have been ahead of Alonso and Burti on the grid. The Dutchman did what he could but was clearly bemused that the gap between Arrows and the front-runners was expanding rather than contracting. Maybe he was also peeved by the need to rely on his team-mate's settings after his morning altercation left him short of running time.

SUNDAY RACE There was yet another getaway driver start for Verstappen, this time with the Dutchman flying up from his 21st grid slot to 15th place by the end of the first lap. But that was as good as it got for Arrows. Behind him, Bernoldi trailed in 18th, though that too was an improvement on his 20th starting position.

The Brazilian's race lasted just 11 laps. He made another place when Button served his stop-go jump start penalty on the sixth lap, but then spun off on the uphill climb to the top chicane five laps later, after pushing too hard through the right-hander as he chased Verstappen and Fisichella.

Verstappen stopped for fuel on lap 24, dropping behind Fisichella and Frentzen in the fight for 14th place, and Frentzen's early-stop strategy kept him ahead of the Arrows when they made their second stops. The German came in on lap 52, the Dutchman on 53. But Frentzen's spin and Fisichella's engine failure, on laps 64 and 68 respectively, helped the Arrows move up to its final 12th place finish. It was a tough race for the team, with scant reward. But the fact that Verstappen brought his Asiatech-engined car home only 11 seconds shy of de la Rosa's Cosworth-engined Jaguar should sound alarm bells at Jaguar headquarters, while giving the Leafield team something to look forward to when both teams share the Cosworth engine next year.

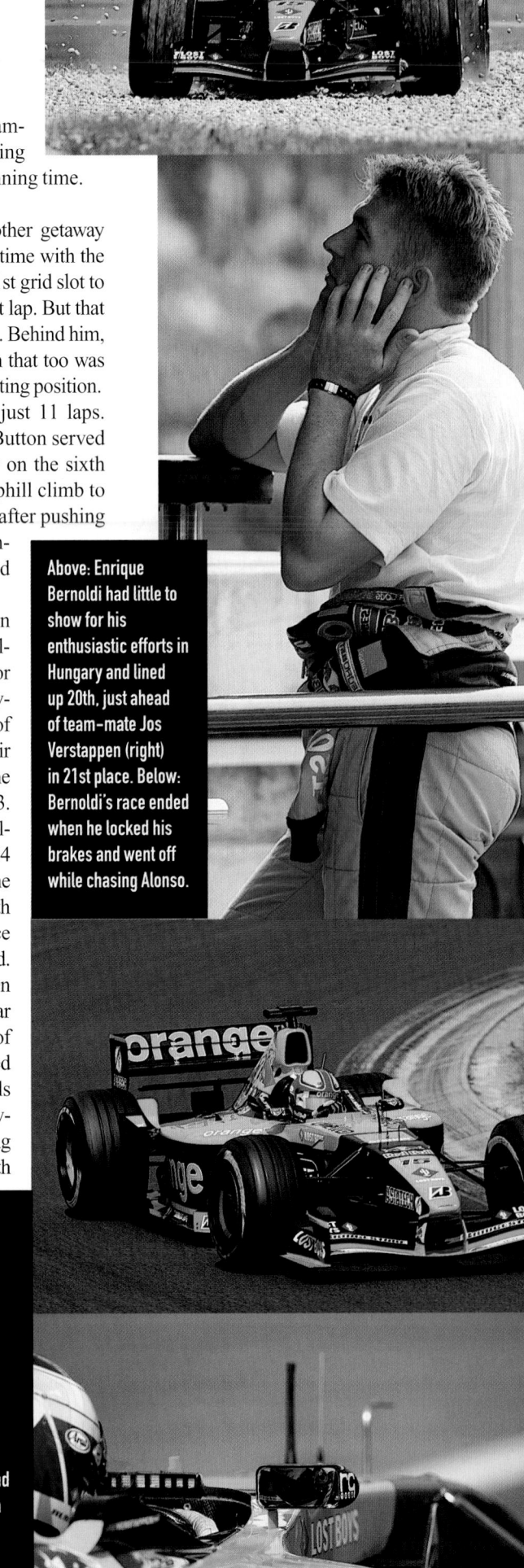

Above: Enrique Bernoldi had little to show for his enthusiastic efforts in Hungary and lined up 20th, just ahead of team-mate Jos Verstappen (right) in 21st place. Below: Bernoldi's race ended when he locked his brakes and went off while chasing Alonso.

Below right: Jos Verstappen's view of life from the Arrows cockpit. The Dutchman worked hard and finished, but again out of the points.
Left: Arrows boss Tom Walkinshaw and Jaguar's Niki Lauda no doubt had much to discuss.

## BELGIAN GRAND PRIX SPA-FRANCORCHAMPS
# Lucky to be at the start

In Hungary Arrows had lacked aerodynamic grunt. At Spa-Francorchamps it lacked grunt of a different kind: horsepower. Once again Jos Verstappen and Enrique Bernoldi were condemned to a struggle for speed on a circuit that takes no prisoners. And the nightmare that has condemned them to repeat their 2000 scenario of a four-car race with Minardi recurred as neither car qualified. Luckily wet qualifying sees the 107 per cent rule thrown out of the window. The race stewards decided that Arrows could start the race. Sponsors would have been most unimpressed if they hadn't. The 2002 deal to run Cosworth's new CR-4 engine had lulled the team into a feeling that 2001 didn't matter any more and, in a sense, it didn't. Roll on 2002.

**FRIDAY PRACTICE** Chassis A22-06 and 01 were on hand in Spa for Verstappen, with Bernoldi relying yet again on A22-03. The team had a new aerodynamic package, but there was an air of resignation. Asiatech has stood still during the season while everyone else has added at least 30hp.

Verstappen ended Friday in 17th place on 1m 52.955secs. Bernoldi was 20th with a best of 1m 55.491secs.

Like many teams, Arrows was caught out when the rain came part way through the day. Having achieved a reasonable balance, Verstappen was about to embark on a tyre-evaluation programme when the conditions changed. Bernoldi was less happy with his car's balance initially, but felt he was making progress when it rained.

**SATURDAY QUALIFYING** A tactical error saw both cars still running on intermediate tyres towards the end of qualifying, after other teams had already switched their drivers to dry rubber. Consequently, neither Verstappen nor Bernoldi qualified for the race under the 107 per cent rule. Conditions were improving by the lap, but their choice of rubber was wrong. Neither could make sufficiently great strides to lower their lap times as the BMW Williams duo switched from intermediate to dry tyres and suddenly knocked three seconds off their lap times to sew up the front row. Verstappen's best was 2m 02.039secs, for 19th place, with Bernoldi further adrift than usual on 2m 03.048secs for 21st.

Verstappen was blocked on his first flying lap by Eddie Irvine and elected to do another slow lap before making another attempt. That proved to be his undoing as he slowed too much and the chequered flag came out three seconds too soon for him to get one last chance. Bernoldi was plain unlucky. When he came in for a fuel top-up near the end he was ordered on to the weighbridge with only five minutes to go. By the time he got back to base he had acquired some new rubber but there was no time to refuel. He was sent back out and was on a quicker lap when the inevitable happened and he ran out of fuel at the Bus Stop chicane.

Appreciating the overall situation, the stewards took a look at the team's lap times throughout the weekend, took into account the conditions, and waived the rule. It was a relief for Tom Walkinshaw in particular, who was unable to understand why his orders for dry tyres were not implemented in time. His relief was tangible as he had more than a few high-profile corporate guests scheduled to arrive on Sunday.

Non-qualification is a terrible thing in 21st-century Formula One.

**SUNDAY RACE** Lining up on the grid on the softer Bridgestone tyres that they should have used at the end of qualifying, Verstappen and Bernoldi made reasonable starts before the first race was aborted. On the restart Verstappen took full advantage of the mayhem, sprinting from 17th to 10th by the end of the new first lap. His first fuel stop on lap eight undid that work and dropped him to 14th and penultimate place, but he fought back and regained as others (including his team-mate on the ninth lap) made their stops. He was back in 10th place when he pitted again for fuel on lap 22 (two laps before Bernoldi), dropped to 11th behind Heinz-Harald Frentzen who only stopped once, and was elevated to 10th again when Jarno Trulli retired on lap 32. Bernoldi was not able to match his partner, and trailed home in 12th.

353

# Treading water for now

As per usual Jos Verstappen made a great start, and as usual he drove a strong race. And, as was becoming more and more usual, he didn't finish the race. Nor did team-mate Enrique Bernoldi. The Arrows team was ignoring the old maxim that if you are not fast, at least be reliable. However, the team was full of good news for 2002. As well as Cosworth engines, it had secured the services of highly-regarded designer Sergio Rinland. But his talents would be wasted if the team principal couldn't finally sort out the long-running reliability problem that has shackled progress.

FRIDAY PRACTICE The team brought three of its A22s to Italy: 06 for Verstappen, 03 for Bernoldi, as usual, and a new chassis, 08, serving as the T-car.

Stability under braking is always a crucial factor at Monza, but early on Friday the team's plans to focus on setting the cars up for this backfired when Verstappen spun on the entrance to the Ascari chicane on his first flying lap and ended up in the gravel bed. That lost him a great deal of valuable track time, and left Bernoldi to shoulder much of the donkey-work.

The Brazilian recorded the 18th fastest time of 1m 27.217secs, covering 44 laps to Verstappen's 18. The Dutchman managed 21st fastest on 1m 27.900secs.

SATURDAY QUALIFYING With 18th and 19th places in free practice, neither Arrows driver had much cause to be cheerful as they worked on set-up. The Dutchman was resigned to fiddling with tyre pressures on a circuit that exposed the Asiatech V10's lack of horsepower, while the Brazilian complained of serious oversteer.

Bernoldi gradually felt better about his car's set-up during qualifying and was eventually 18th fastest on its soft compound Bridgestones, with a 1m 25.444secs,

which gave him the satisfaction of acing Verstappen, who recorded a 1m 25.511secs. Interestingly, both were slower than the times Arrows clocked at Monza in 2000 with Supertec power, despite the beneficial effects of the tyre war.

SUNDAY RACE True to the script, Verstappen made another 'flying Dutchman' start to grab an amazing eighth place by the end of the opening lap – from an effective 17th on the grid (taking into account the demise of Fisichella and Heidfeld). That became seventh as Eddie Irvine's Jaguar faded by lap three, then sixth as Verstappen overtook Pedro de la Rosa's fuel-laden Jag on the fifth lap. Things remained promising until Jean Alesi and Kimi Räikkönen demoted Verstappen two places in one hit on lap 16. Two laps later Verstappen made a pitstop and plummeted to 15th. Early on, even on light fuel, he'd been getting signs from the pits to preserve his brakes. But, long before his second fuel stop was due this became academic when he pulled off, on lap 26 in 14th place, with loss of power.

Bernoldi drove strongly, fending off Häkkinen from lap seven to lap 12 in a style reminiscent of his race with David Coulthard in Monaco. This was all the more praiseworthy given that he was on a single-stop plan. He wasn't in quite so much trouble with his brakes as Verstappen, but though he could defend against the likes of Villeneuve (who trailed him from the start until slipping by on lap seven) and Panis (who dogged him from lap 13 until lap 26, when Bernoldi refuelled), he couldn't really attack. In the end the team's disappointing weekend ended when the Brazilian's engine developed a problem on the 47th lap when he was running 13th.

**Above and right:** Enrique Bernoldi again out-qualified Jos Verstappen. They both struggled with a lack of power and straight-line speed, qualifying 18th and 19th. Once again Verstappen showed his racing skills with an early charge to sixth place before retiring.

**Above and right:** Both Verstappen and Bernoldi raced strongly, until engine failure ended their races, Verstappen's on lap 26 when 14th and Bernoldi's on lap 47 when 13th. The team was upbeat about 2002 after signing highly-rated designer Sergio Rinland.

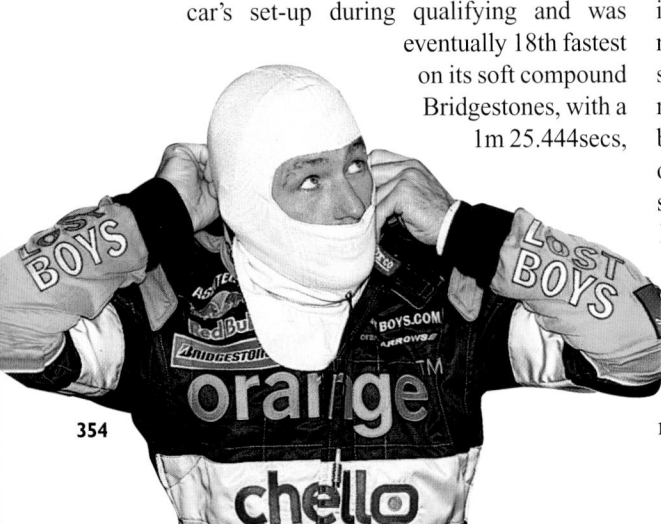

Above: Jos Verstappen was as anxious as Tom Walkinshaw to find some reliability. Lack of finishes had dogged the team all season.

# UNITED STATES GRAND PRIX INDIANAPOLIS
## Roll on 2002

While new designer Sergio Rinland continued work on a new car – the A23 – back at Arrows' headquarters in Leafield, Oxfordshire, and Cosworth Racing worked on creating a new Northampton-based racing department dedicated to engine supply, the team itself went through the motions at the US Grand Prix, which yielded no better than a 12th place finish for Enrique Bernoldi and saw Jos Verstappen retire with an engine problem. One hundred per cent failure was not what the team wanted at such a high-profile race. Team principal Tom Walkinshaw was thanking his lucky stars his men scored some lucky points early in the season to qualify for TV fees. Lacking grunt and grip, the drivers struggled all weekend, though Verstappen gave typically energetic chase to eventual fifth-place finisher Eddie Irvine as they ran 12th and 13th early on.

FRIDAY PRACTICE There was little new at Orange Arrows in Indianapolis beyond a new aero package to meet downforce needs. Enrique Bernoldi did a good job of learning the track on Friday as he used A22-04 to pip Jos Verstappen for 20th place. The Brazilian covered 48 laps for a best of 1m 15.449secs, and while he felt his crew had perhaps changed the car too much in the morning and that he didn't get the best from his tyres, he was fairly satisfied. Verstappen, in chassis 06, was not so cheerful after losing time with an electrical problem in the afternoon, which lost him a lot of running time. Just as he resumed, he suffered an Asiatech engine failure, so his best of 1m 15.547secs from only 26 laps left him 21st overall.

Left: Enrique Bernoldi continued to make progress with Arrows, performing well against team-mate Verstappen. He persevered to finish 12th despite overheating caused by debris damaging the radiators.
Below: Bernoldi leads Alonso.

SATURDAY QUALIFYING Overnight the Arrows mechanics had played musical chassis. Verstappen now had the original spare monocoque, 01, taken out of its travelling crate and built up into a race car. 06 became the spare car, while the original spare car, 08, was dismantled as the spare chassis.

Sadly, none of this made much difference to the team's qualifying position. Bernoldi maintained the upper hand with a best lap of 1m 14.129secs for 19th place on the grid, having had to dump his race car after its engine developed a chronic misfire and take over 08 for his best runs.

A major set-up change got Verstappen's car going a lot better than it had on Saturday morning, when he'd been 21st fastest, but his 1m 14.138secs qualifying best still left him only 20th. He made a small error on his first run, and was later baulked by Montoya on his last. Both he and Bernoldi went for the softer Bridgestones.

SUNDAY RACE If it's a race start, watch Verstappen fly. As usual, the Dutchman was on the move when the lights went out, sprinting up from 20th to 14th on the opening lap. He'd raised eyebrows with a remarkable fifth fastest time in the morning warm-up, and now felt his car was much better balanced.

Bernoldi, meanwhile, had switched to the T-car, which was set up for Verstappen, after his intended race car developed a problem with its mechanical fuel pump. He made places too, even though he couldn't use launch control, and came round 17th. Verstappen then chased after Eddie Irvine's Jaguar as Räikkönen's demise elevated them both a place, and when Jenson Button pitted on lap 35 he moved up again. By then his rear tyres were blistering badly, and he stopped for fuel and fresh rubber on lap 36, just before Ralf Schumacher's spin could be of help. Unfortunately he spun on his in-lap, and on lap 45 the engine cried 'enough' and he swept back into the pits with a small fire burning in his airbox.

Bernoldi soldiered on to an eventual 12th place finish, nursing his car in the final stages after debris from de la Rosa's Jaguar, lodged in his radiator, caused overheating.

# An unmitigated disaster

For the two races prior to Japan, 2001 had looked like a season that couldn't end fast enough for Orange Arrows, and Suzuka continued the trend. With Enrique Bernoldi being obliged to start from the pitlane, then later getting a stop-go penalty, and Jos Verstappen subsequently being penalised for overtaking on the formation lap, the Japanese Grand Prix brought precious little worth remembering for the team.

Many rumours concerned the team's future ownership. Dietrich Mateschitz, the owner of Red Bull, reportedly had an option to buy Morgan Grenfell Private Equity's 70 per cent share of the team. Its future was thrown into confusion: Tom Walkinshaw denied the option existed; Mateschitz insisted it did.

It was one of those situations where two men had conflicting opinions but both were telling the truth. In any case, it looked likely that Arrows would soon belong to Red Bull, a situation that could make Walkinshaw's position precarious.

FRIDAY PRACTICE Trouble-free runs for both drivers, and valuable tyre comparison work, made Friday a good day for Orange Arrows. The only thing lacking was fast lap times: it was difficult for the team to get overly excited as Jos Verstappen and Enrique Bernoldi set the 19th and 20th fastest times respectively.

The Dutchman knows Suzuka well: he did a 1m 39.511secs in 34 laps, driving A22-06; as usual his spare was 01. Against that, Bernoldi's 1m 39.744secs in 33 laps in 04 was highly respectable.

By the end of the day both drivers felt they had the direction to pursue on Saturday regarding tyre choice and chassis balance, but as usual lamented the lack of downforce from their machinery.

SATURDAY QUALIFYING Qualifying was as difficult as Arrows had anticipated, and after Saturday morning's free practice saw Bernoldi and Verstappen 20th and 21st with laps of 1m 37.514secs and 1m 37.805secs respectively,

nobody was expecting any miracles.

Bernoldi continued to outrun Verstappen, as he reduced his time to 1m 36.885secs to take 20th spot in the line-up, and was one of many drivers to complain about traffic on his fastest lap. Verstappen was disgruntled to be beaten by his team-mate, but had few excuses. His A22 was handling well enough, but both lacked sheer pace and that was that. His 1m 36.973secs was a couple of 10ths of a kilometre an hour off the Brazilian, but it was pride that mattered, not the speed difference.

SUNDAY RACE Things went wrong even before the start, when Bernoldi stalled on the formation lap and had to start in the pitlane. Then his power-steering failed on the second lap, condemning him to a tough race. When he first refuelled on lap 19, the system was reset but still only functioned intermittently, and two laps later he had to come back into the pits to serve a 10-second stop-go penalty for twice missing the chicane and setting fast laps as a result. That left him 19th, but he moved up a place at Verstappen's expense until his second stop on lap 37. On his 51st lap, the Brazilian had the small consolation of re-passing Verstappen to grab 14th, two laps down.

The Dutchman also got into trouble before the start, after overtaking Enge, whom he assumed was about to stop at the hairpin. As a result he lined up one place too high on the grid, and after he'd driven his heart out for 35 laps, officials finally got round to telling him of his sin and the 10-second stop-go penalty it warranted. Verstappen had stopped for fuel on lap 17 when he was running 16th, was still in that position when he refuelled again on lap 33, and then stopped a third time for his penalty on lap 35.

All in all, a day to forget.

Above and right: Enrique Bernoldi again outqualified Jos Verstappen to confirm the progress he had made since joining Arrows. His race was hampered by numerous troubles.

Above and right: Jos Verstappen had an eventful race, which included a stop-go penalty and ultimately offered little reward for a hard drive. He finished in 15th place.

Team Review    Race by Race

# MINARDI

## Contents

| | | | | | | |
|---|---|---|---|---|---|---|
| Team Review | – | The season | p360 | European Grand Prix | – | Nürburgring | p374 |
| Australian Grand Prix | – | Melbourne | p366 | French Grand Prix | – | Magny-Cours | p375 |
| Malaysian Grand Prix | – | Sepang | p367 | British Grand Prix | – | Silverstone | p376 |
| Brazilian Grand Prix | – | Interlagos | p368 | German Grand Prix | – | Hockenheim | p377 |
| San Marino Grand Prix | – | Imola | p369 | Hungarian Grand Prix | – | Hungaroring | p378 |
| Spanish Grand Prix | – | Barcelona | p370 | Belgian Grand Prix | – | Spa-Francorchamps | p379 |
| Austrian Grand Prix | – | A1 Ring | p371 | Italian Grand Prix | – | Monza | p380 |
| Monaco Grand Prix | – | Monte Carlo | p372 | USA Grand Prix | – | Indianapolis | p381 |
| Canadian Grand Prix | – | Montreal | p373 | Japanese Grand Prix | – | Suzuka | p382 |

2001

Fernando Alonso

Paul Stoddart

Tarso Marques

Alex Yoong

## EUROPEAN
### minardi F1

# A new beginning

Two months before the start of the 2001 season, Minardi was a team in desperate trouble. The team had no cash, no sponsor, no engine and little hope. Its owner, Italian businessman Gabriele Rumi, was dying of cancer. If the team wasn't sold it would be closed. Luckily the perfect buyer was at hand in Australian aviation entrepreneur Paul Stoddart. He bought the team lock, stock and barrel.

One of its few solid assets was $14 million of television money it had qualified for the year before by beating Prost in the constructors' championship.

Stoddart was a motor racing enthusiast with seemingly deep pockets. He also owned a mini airline, European Aviation. He had previously bought up the assets of the old Tyrrell team and installed it in a factory in Ledbury in the English Midlands. From there he ran a Formula 3000 team and historic cars. The base was equipped almost to Formula One standards when he bought Minardi. Now running from the team's traditional base at Faenza as well as from Ledbury, Minardi relies on Stoddart's entrepreneurial nous for its future. The team has facilities to match other teams'. In 2002 Stoddart plans to complete a windtunnel.

A test team was formed for the first time and a young driver development programme has spawned a raft of potential hopefuls.

But Stoddart elected to start the year with Fernando Alonso – who came complete with a few millions, compliments of his manager Flavio Briatore – and Tarso Marques, whom he hoped would attract some Brazilian money; but he didn't, and was dispatched later in the season.

Alex Yoong, the first Malaysian ever to race in Formula One, came in at Monza with many millions put up by Malaysian lottery operator Magnum. His three races this season were little more than test sessions, and he performed exactly as expected – bringing up the tail of the grid. Yoong's presence is more crucial than the Spaniard's, even though his results are unlikely to come close. He brings the weight, the money, the drive and the expectation of a country with him, and Stoddart looks likely to exploit this to devastating effect.

Minardi was, more than any other team, in transition in 2001. Effectively a new outfit, it looked to find its level.

The team was under no illusions as to its potential in 2001. The car was designed with two different engine mountings in mind, and the team got the worse option in the end. Just six weeks before the start of the year, the decision was made to stick with a four-year-old Cosworth-designed engine and rebadge it European.

One car was built in time to do a whole 50km of testing before the Australian Grand Prix, and the other chassis was finished in the pitlane on the week of the season-opener. Tarso Marques did not automatically qualify for the first race, but was allowed in thanks to the race stewards, who saw in his situation a kind of force majeure. The force majeure was that Paul Stoddart was Australian. It was a case of complete relief and amazing pride for Stoddart when he saw his cars roll out in Melbourne on Sunday. The result was irrelevant – European Minardi made it to the grid in time. And a bonus was that Alonso, effectively a rent-a-driver, looked like he was a star in the making. Now for a decent car.

## The Minardi PS01 car

LIKE most cars in recent years from the team's designer, Gustav Brunner, the PS01 was a neatly penned design despite the tight budget restraints imposed upon it. The smallest car in the field, it also boasted pullrod suspension to aid very low weight distribution, and transversely mounted dampers. Low sidepods, aggressively angled radiators and large exhausts showed the priorities: maximum aerodynamic efficiency to compensate for the engine's lack of power, and huge cooling for the Cosworth design that had been wound up as far as it would go.

This would be the highly-rated Brunner's last project for ▷

Fernando Alonso

Minardi, as he announced his move to Toyota in the days preceding the Austrian Grand Prix. He was under contract, but Stoddart couldn't hope to compete with the allure of Toyota's millions or the prospect of Brunner building a car on an unlimited budget. Brunner is believed to have paid Stoddart off personally with some of his signing-on fee. The loss of Brunner was an incalculable blow, ripping the guts out of the team in the short term. Gabriele Tredozi took over his responsibilities and Dr John Davis joined from Arrows as head of research and development and deputy technical director.

Stoddart's problem was the engine. The four-year-old Cosworth was outdated, overweight and underpowered, and Minardi would rarely get the chance to mix it with anyone – apart from the highly embarrassed Benetton Renault drivers earlier in the season, and Prost and Arrows on occasion.

The engines were built in Italian workshops of Fondmetal, Rumi's old firm. Around 700 horsepower was available, compared to the 850bhp of BMW. Paul Stoddart, braced for the worst, took a large number of engines to Melbourne.

While the team did manage various minor aerodynamic changes to the cars, which were readied just days before the first race, it was always playing catch-up and struggling for reliability. Although the team was remarkably consistent in the early races, thanks perhaps to a conservative rev limit and so on, the engine suffered numerous blow-ups and a plethora of minor problems cut deeply into the preparation time for each race. Brake problems, driveshaft failures, electronics woes and other detail problems caught the team out time and again, and the spare car was often needed. Minardi looked like a team struggling to recoup lost ground, and nobody at Ledbury or Faenza would treat that as criticism.

Splitting the team between two countries was also a problem. Stoddart couldn't make the decision to close the Italian factory, mainly because the design team and engine department were there.

There was a bit of an identity crisis as the Australian/Italian/English team got going.

The more alarming moments included Melbourne, when Marques suffered the first of many brake problems – which also caused Alonso to crash in Spain and spin in Hungary – and was forced to qualify in Alonso's car. Marques finished outside the 107 per cent qualifying threshold, one of only four occasions when a Minardi failed to qualify automatically, and was allowed to start by a sympathetic FIA. Both Minardis fell victim to the rule in Spa, when weather conditions caught them out, but again both were allowed to start. The only time the FIA rejected Minardi's appeals for leniency came in Britain, when Marques was forced to sit out and watch.

Marques was no stranger to his fire extinguisher during 2001. As well as a smoking departure from the Australian Grand Prix, Marques's car was also engulfed in flames in San Marino and Austria, while Alonso had to jump out on the grid in Germany.

Alonso enjoyed better reliability, and was also clearly the team's favourite. When his car caught fire in Germany he took the spare, and when that developed problems he took Marques's old race car. He also had full call on the spare in latter races; on several occasions he decided to ditch the faster but unreliable PS01B. He still suffered his fair share of reliability traumas, however, with brakes and electronics being the main culprits until the PS01B came in. When it did, the gearbox became the new reason for problems.

One thing the team had a headstart on – a rare occurrence this year – was traction control. The team made full use of its involvement in the Arrows two-seater programme, which it took full control of this year, to develop a system to increase the safety of the passenger car. Stoddart continued to use the two-seater as a test bed for the complex electronics that reappeared in Spain, and Minardi did not struggle as badly as some predicted it might when the major regulation changes came into effect.

Giancarlo Minardi

George Ryton

Rupert Manwaring

In Melbourne, Alonso used the very first chassis, which had only 50km on the proverbial clock, before switching to PS01/03 in Malaysia. He kept this chassis when the PS01B was introduced, but switched to PS01B/02 in Belgium after crashing his race car heavily in the warm-up. He was back in PS01B/03 in Italy, but ended up racing the spare with its older and more reliable gearbox, before finishing the season in 03.

Marques started the year in PS01/02, switched to PS01/01 in Melbourne and then took the new chassis, 04, when it arrived in San Marino. He used this tub until the German Grand Prix, when he ended up back in 01 for one race before reverting to his usual race car for his final two races with the team. With just three races left, Alex Yoong took over PS01B/04 and retained it for the remainder of the season.

It was run on Friday before Alonso abandoned it and it did not run reliably until the season-ending Japanese Grand Prix: it caused two retirements, even though Alonso rejected the car on two occasions and raced in the older speed machine with its more reliable fabricated titanium gearbox. With typical Minardi determination, the team designed and fabricated several new components in the period between the US and Japanese Grands Prix – a process that usually takes weeks. The PS01B ran faultlessly at Suzuka and proved the potential of Minardi. What it did not have this year was time; but with an entire off-season to prepare for next year, and having filled the void left by Brunner as best it can, Minardi may be a more potent force next season.

In all, out of 1,065 possible race laps, Alonso completed 707, which works out at a relatively poor 66.4 per cent reliability ▷

## MINARDI SEASON STATISTICS

EUROPEAN
minardiF1

### RELIABILITY PERFORMANCE

| Driver | Races | Max laps | Laps completed | Reliability rating |
|---|---|---|---|---|
| Fernando Alonso | 17 | 1,065 | 707 | 66.4% |
| Tarso Marques | 13 | 826 | 578 | 70.0% |
| Alex Yoong | 3 | 179 | 132 | 73.7% |
| Constructor | Races | Max laps | Laps completed | Reliability rating |
| Team | 33 | 2,070 | 1,417 | 68.5% |

### CHAMPIONSHIP PERFORMANCE

| Driver | 2001 points | 2000 points | 12 month change |
|---|---|---|---|
| Fernando Alonso | 0 | - | Did not compete |
| Tarso Marques | 0 | - | Did not compete |
| Alex Yoong | 0 | - | Did not compete |
| Constructor | 2001 points | 2000 points | 12 month change |
| Team | 0 | 0 | +0% |

Fernando Alonso

### CHASSIS LOG

**PS01/01** Race car for Fernando Alonso at Melbourne; and for Tarso Marques at Sepang and Interlagos. Spare car at Imola, Barcelona, A1 Ring (used in qualifying by Marques), Monte Carlo, Montreal, the Nürburgring, Magny-Cours (used in the race by Marques after the gearbox on 04 failed), Silverstone, Hockenheim (raced by Alonso at the first start but dismissed for the second), the Hungaroring, Monza (qualified by both drivers after gearbox problems developed on both race cars; raced by Alonso), Indianapolis and Suzuka (taken to the grid by Alex Yoong but not raced).

**PS01/02** (until Monte Carlo) **PS01B/02** (Spa-Francorchamps and after) Race car for Marques at Melbourne. Spare car at Sepang (used by Alonso in qualifying), Interlagos, Monte Carlo and Spa-Francorchamps (raced by Alonso after he crashed 03 in warm-up).

**PS01/03** (until Silverstone) **PS01B/03** (Hockenheim and after, but returned to PS01 spec for the Hungaroring race) Race car for Alonso at Sepang, Interlagos, Imola, Barcelona, A1 Ring, Monte Carlo, Montreal, the Nürburgring, Magny-Cours, Silverstone, Hockenheim (abandoned by Alonso after a fire on the grid, commandeered by Marques for the second start), Hungaroring, Spa-Francorchamps (not raced after Alonso's warm-up crash), Monza (not used in qualifying or the race after developing gearbox trouble), Indianapolis and Suzuka.

**PS01/04** (until Hockenheim) **PS01B/04** (Hungaroring and afterwards) Race car for Marques at Imola, Barcelona, A1 Ring, Monte Carlo, Montreal, the Nürburgring, Magny-Cours, Silverstone (made Alonso's spare for the race after Marques failed to qualify), Hockenheim (abandoned due to an oil leak on the grid, but raced by Alonso after the second start), the Hungaroring and Spa-Francorchamps; and for Yoong at Monza (not used in qualifying), Indianapolis and Suzuka.

**Note:** The PS01B cars were modifications of existing chassis, rather than new cars.

record. Marques achieved an even 578 laps out of a possible 826. His reliability record stood at 70.0 per cent. Alex Yoong had just three races and completed a relatively high ratio of laps, although he was far from pushing the machinery to the maximum and concentrated more on playing himself in. He completed 132 out of a possible 179 race laps and ended on a record of 73.7 per cent.

## Technical developments

AT THE German Grand Prix, however, the team made a major step with its new titanium gearbox and new rear end, which were the big changes in the PS01B chassis. This made the car even shorter, by 28mm, and used a heavily revised aerodynamic package. New rear suspension incorporated exhausts blowing to the middle of the car, in the McLaren style. The cast-titanium gearbox was the big one, though, weighing 25 per cent less than its predecessor thanks to production methods alone. While it was a major step forward, the new gearbox was unreliable.

Although Minardi's achievements have not been significant this year, the team definitely took steps in the right direction. And after the trauma of the pre-season, when Stoddart did not take a day off for six weeks and his mechanics worked through the night for just as long, Alonso's 12th place finish in the Australian Grand Prix was treated as a victory. As was the Japanese Grand Prix, when the team finally sorted out its gearbox gremlins, giving it a solid footing for next year. Quite right too: both were victories on a par with Ferrari's for the minnow of the Formula One paddock, which has much greater aspirations.

## The drivers

STODDART was a rookie team manager and certainly made a mistake gambling that the Brazilian would be able to bring money. But as soon as Fernando Alonso and Alex Yoong stood shoulder to shoulder at Minardi, Stoddart's strategic brilliance shone through. This was not just a driver line-up, it was the foundation for the team's future.

Alonso is very good. The young Spaniard gained less attention than Kimi Räikkönen when he graduated to Formula One at the tender age of 19, but this was because he had already won the Open Telefónica by Nissan championship and the final round of the 2000 FIA Formula 3000 championship. For such a young driver, Alonso's credentials were impeccable.

Minardi had a long-term deal with the youngster, but it needed money fast and Alonso was one of the few assets it could do anything with. After testing a Benetton just once in the off-season, and finishing second fastest on the day, his future was sold to Renault. With no seat to put him in immediately, Renault left him at Minardi. So not only did the team make a tidy profit from the youngster before he even raced in a Grand Prix, it also got his services for 2001. It's called having your cake and eating it.

It is difficult to judge a driver when his machinery is so far off the pace, but the team itself knew that Alonso was doing a mesmerising job. It was in qualifying that the young driver proved his ability most and, even though it was bizarre to hear cheers erupting from the garage as Minardi's driver nicked 18th on the grid in San Marino, the Spaniard's mistake-free runs and scintillating performances in an underperforming chassis garnered praise from all.

Many drivers believe Alonso was the third best rookie of the season, after Juan Pablo Montoya and Kimi Räikkönen grabbing the headlines. With similar machinery, Alonso could have probably run them close. It didn't help that the 19-year-old was forced to accept the role of team leader in his rookie year, something that may have caused others to wilt and wander into a technical wilderness.

Alonso had one or two bad moments, including his horrific accident in Sunday's warm-up at Spa, but the overall impression of the youngster at the end of the year was of a sensational talent who will challenge for top honours as soon as his machine allows.

Alonso suffered his fair share of reliability problems, including the gearbox and driveshaft failures that plagued the outfit. He also suffered the indignity of a wheel detaching from his car at Silverstone, not the most confidence-inspiring thing that could happen to a driver.

His qualifying performances and ability to make his team-mate look slow, whoever that team-mate may be, have attracted a great deal of attention, even though his 10th place finish in the German Grand Prix remains the best race result. Few expect Alonso to remain with Minardi for long, but Paul Stoddart is going to enjoy every minute he has one of Formula One's hottest properties on his books.

The youngest driver ever to win a Formula Three race in the dim and distant past, Tarso Marques was always destined to be replaced. The Brazilian was signed by virtue of his experience, which amounted to a handful of unsuccessful races with Minardi in its previous incarnation, and he was undoubtedly the team's number two.

He seemed to suffer the majority of problems in the build-up to the race, and got used to hopping into the spare car. He drove this in Malaysia without even a seat, as the car was set to Alonso's preferences and there simply was not room for protection. The fact that he finished and took the team's first top 10 finish, crossing the line in ninth, was a testament to his grit if not his speed. He made his mistakes too, including a spin in qualifying for the Austrian Grand Prix and his non-qualification for Silverstone, but for the most part he drove reliably until his replacement by Yoong at Monza.

Never has a pay driver's arrival been so keenly awaited as that of Alex Yoong – the first Malaysian to drive in Formula One. His home nation has pumped huge resources into motorsport in recent years, and Yoong's ascension to the highest ranks was vital if this trend was to continue. He arrived in Italy with a wave of publicity and he knew that Malaysia's hopes rested upon him.

Yoong brought in a huge chunk of money from four-digit betting specialist Magnum Corporation Berhad, and has enjoyed some government assistance in finding extra funds. Stoddart was among the first to recognise the true potential of Malaysia as a major backer, and is seeking to build on Yoong's first three races with the team and gain heavyweight investment from his driver's home nation. Rumours of a tie-up with Malaysian car manufacturer Proton and the renaming of the team to Team Malaysia show how far this deal may lead. And with a war chest of funds released by this developing country, Minardi could scamper its way up the grid in record time. Yoong is more than a driver, he is a ray of light.

This explains his presence in Formula One at once, for Yoong's curriculum vitae does not make impressive reading. Below-average performances in F3, F3000 and more recently Formula Nippon would not have led most drivers to world championship level.

His performances in F1 so far bear little analysis. The Malaysian youngster was thrown into the world championship with just three races left and minimal testing. The Italian, United States and Japanese Grands Prix were, therefore, a chance to acquaint himself with the team and sport in a competitive environment – invaluable experience with a view to 2002. In that time, Yoong has desperately tried to move away from Alonso's set-up, the antithesis of his own preference. Alonso drives with an unstable rear and a pointy front end, something Yoong has struggled with. He is looking forward to clocking winter mileage to tailor the next car, the PS02, to his liking.

Yoong has hardly set the world alight since entering Formula One, but he was never likely to. The 2002 season will be his chance to show what he can do, but if Alonso is there again, expect him to be overshadowed.

## Commercial

MINARDI'S financial mess was a very public affair in 2000. In relative terms 2000 was a well financed year, with $20 million from Spanish telecoms group Telefónica and Minardi's usual small sponsors chipping in another $10 million. It was still not enough for modern-day Formula One, and team owner Gabriele Rumi spoke of a sale mid-season. But several deals fell by the wayside before Paul Stoddart rescued the team just six weeks before Melbourne.

Stoddart has found debts, and Giancarlo Minardi was soon under investigation by the Italian authorities for tax irregularities during his time in charge of the team. There was never any doubt that the team's financial resurrection would be a complex process, but Stoddart has gone about the task with impressive verve. It seems he has had to spend around $20 million of his own money on running costs in 2001.

No one knows just how deep his pockets are, and since the 11th September terrorist attacks, he appeared worried for the first time. The aviation industry he depends on for his living is in a huge downturn and may affect Stoddart's ability to fund the team, but he is not a man who is easily daunted or likes to lose.

Having placed the name of his own airline on the engines, Stoddart has also brought a number of sponsors from his F3000 outfit into the Formula One fold. The team enjoyed very little new investment, though, until Yoong came to the fore with his Malaysian contacts. Now Stoddart is looking to the Far East as a financial foundation for his team, and the idea is a solid one. Stod-

**Minardi's twin double-deck motorhomes**

dart is looking to establish permanent links with a country increasingly interested in motorsport.

He is certainly not afraid of a fight and got himself noticed in the paddock when he bought two motorhomes previously owned by the Sultan of Brunei but basically unused. They replaced the two tatty buses used by the team for as long as anyone can remember. But, as many team principals have found to their chagrin, posh motorhomes do not make cars go fast.

## AUSTRALIAN GRAND PRIX MELBOURNE
# A race to get there

Arriving to compete at Melbourne was a triumph in itself. The fact that Australian-born entrepreneur Paul Stoddart had saved the team was evident from the almost complete lack of sponsorship on the black cars. Minardi was present, but only as a symbol of continuity.

On the Wednesday, as the mechanics finished the second car in the garage in the pitlane, the first car was unveiled on the steps of Victoria's Parliament House with Victoria Premier Steve Bracks in attendance and a large crowd cheering on Paul Stoddart's efforts. "When we came to Melbourne, just arriving felt like winning a Grand Prix," said Stoddart. In the end, the team performed creditably but predictably failed to qualify the car of Tarso Marques, although he was still let in to race.

FRIDAY PRACTICE European Minardi brought two cars to Melbourne: PS01-01 for Fernando Alonso and PS01-02 for Marques. Predictably there was no spare. But there was no shortage of engines, with 12 examples of the European V10, actually a four-year-old Cosworth design. Minardi was clearly expecting trouble but in the event only lost one engine, through a faulty water-cooling installation.

The second chassis had been fired up only the day before so when practice began on Friday the team could do little more than treat the day as a test session. Marques did not have an easy day as his engine blew up early in the second session. Friday was effectively a wasted day as the water hose blew off the engine and it failed after 19 laps. He finished the day last with a best of 1m 36.463secs.

Alonso, however, was 17th fastest, having overcome initial understeer problems. Alonso proved one of the star rookies, doing much better with an untried Minardi than anyone could have guessed. On Friday his big problem was eliminating excessive understeer, but he finished a resounding 17th with a best of 1m 32.587secs. As no one had expected him to be higher than 21st, this was a spectacular triumph for the team.

SATURDAY QUALIFYING Tarso Marques's woes continued with a major brake problem and a cooling system leak.

All this meant that in the final minutes of qualifying, Marques jumped into Alonso's car. He had his own seat but there was no time to change the pedal settings, so he had to drive the car as it was. He took six-10ths off his previous best but still found himself just outside the 107 per cent qualifying limit. As the gap was only a fraction (0.2 per cent), the team asked the FIA stewards if Marques could be allowed to start and good sense prevailed over the rulebook. Doubtless Marques was also helped by Paul Stoddart's Australian ancestry. But few disagreed with the decision. Marques thus lined up in 22nd place on 1m 33.228secs.

Alonso on Saturday had two tasks: to qualify and not to damage the car. He was 19th, although the Spanish youngster said that if he had not made a mistake on his fastest lap he would probably have been 15th. He said he was disappointed not to have qualified higher after missing a braking point on his fastest lap. He was 19th on the grid – beating Luciano Burti's Jaguar and Gaston Mazzacane's Prost with a 1m 30.657secs.

SUNDAY RACE Alonso ran reliably throughout the race and inadvertently helped David Coulthard overtake Rubens Barrichello. He had one close call when being lapped by Barrichello, but was able to finish 12th.

Tarso Marques's race lasted barely minutes and he was the first retirement, on lap four. The engine was misfiring and he was experiencing brake problems. Then the engine cut out altogether.

"When we qualified I felt it could not get any better," said Paul Stoddart. "I think this weekend we have earned the respect of our peers in the pitlane and to finish 12th first time out is more than I could ever have hoped for. Now I'm going to have some sleep."

Overall it was a fantastic weekend for the team and its new principal. Stoddart had bought Minardi and also the assets of the old Tyrrell team and combined them as effectively as he could. It was good enough to go racing.

Top: Designer Gustav Brunner, Marques and Alonso. Above: Tarso Marques's race lasted only minutes before his engine cut out.

Above: Fernando Alonso was one of the stars of qualifying and impressed many. Right: Gustav Brunner keeps an eye on progress.

## MALAYSIAN GRAND PRIX SEPANG
# The racing gets serious

Australia had been a case of battling through with untried cars. Happily the team was better prepared for Malaysia, although team principal Paul Stoddart said: "It is really an extended test session." Stoddart was planning major technical improvements in time for the Spanish Grand Prix, and he had secured sponsorship from Austrian computer manufacturer Gericom. "It may not have looked it, but the drivers were absolutely on the limit all weekend," said Stoddart. "I'm really pleased with the way they are going."

**Above and left: Tarso Marques qualified 20th, ahead of team-mate Fernando Alonso, but a puncture ruined his race.**

FRIDAY PRACTICE The team's third chassis – PS01-03 – arrived from Faenza as a bare monocoque on Tuesday; it was finished at 4am on Thursday. This meant a switch of cars, with Fernando Alonso taking the new one on Friday, Tarso Marques taking Alonso's car from Melbourne (PS01-01) and PS01-02 becoming the spare. However, the new car proved to have electronic gremlins and Alonso lost the whole morning session. In the afternoon he completed 18 laps before the gremlin returned and he was left second to last with a best lap of 1m 43.107secs. Marques was only 20th, turning in a fastest lap of 1m

**Left and below: Out-qualified by his team-mate, Fernando Alonso raced with Tarso Marques until gearbox problems slowed him.**

42.872secs, but he lost most of the second session with a gearbox problem resulting from an off-track excursion.

SATURDAY QUALIFYING Gearbox problems for Alonso forced him to use the spare car in qualifying. After two runs he went back to his own car, but it did not inspire confidence – he failed to improve his time and had a big spin. As a result he was at the back of the grid, but later promoted to 21st when Enrique Bernoldi's Arrows was dumped to the back for infringements. Marques had a more reliable car but its handling was not good, leaving him struggling with enormous oversteer which resulted in an off. A change of set-up helped Marques record a 1m 39.714secs – half a second faster than Alonso. "As we find out more about set-up we should move forward," said Stoddart. "We have a lot of developments coming. This car is still using the 2000 gearbox and we've only just started doing aerodynamic work."

SUNDAY RACE The race provided major problems for the drivers but both struggled through to the finish. Alonso quickly ran into problems with an overheating gearbox which, combined with the changing conditions, resulted in five pitstops, although the team decided to risk a gearbox failure to try to keep him going in the hope many of the other cars would fail. Marques did not have an easy time as the rain deprived the team of all telemetry and radio contact. Marques's progress was badly hit by a puncture in the middle of the race, which meant he had to do a slow lap to the pits. But he made it to the finish. "I learned a lot about my car today," he said, "and that is very important for the team."

**EUROPEAN** *minardiF1*

Left and right: Tarso Marques and Fernando Alonso showed remarkably well. The team was confident, hoping of more to come.

## BRAZILIAN GRAND PRIX INTERLAGOS
# Onward but not upward

The first two races were a question of hand-to-mouth survival for European Minardi, but in Brazil the emphasis moved from getting through to getting ahead. A deal had been struck for windtunnel time, a new aerodynamicist had been hired and there was to be a development package hopefully for the Spanish GP. Around the paddock everyone had to admit the sheer chutzpah of Australian entrepreneur Paul Stoddart. With no sponsors and all the other deprivations from being a back-runner, he was slugging it out with Benetton and Prost like a good 'un.

In Brazil the team wanted another finish and Tarso Marques delivered, with ninth in the race. This meant the team had four finishes from six starts and would be looking for a point to keep the TV money flowing.

The team was slowed in Brazil by the theft of some wheels and team manager Tony Lees' mugging in downtown São Paulo.

FRIDAY PRACTICE The team had the same three chassis as in Malaysia; a fourth was finished but not built up. As in Sepang, Fernando Alonso raced PS01-03 and Marques PS01-01, with PS01-02 the spare, prepared for local man Marques. As the team worked on set-ups, Alonso was 18th quickest on 1m 18.222secs and ran 40 laps with no problem. Marques was not happy with the deteriorating handling of the car and was 21st on 1m 19.005secs.

SATURDAY QUALIFYING Things initially ran smoothly but following an engine problem after 16 laps it was deemed necessary to change Marques's engine, so he went into qualifying without having done much set-up work in qualifying trim. The result was he ended up last on the grid on 1m 16.784secs. Alonso was much happier, six-10ths faster and good enough for 19th place. He felt he would have out-qualified Giancarlo Fisichella if he had not hit traffic on what was scheduled to be his final and best run.

SUNDAY RACE Marques had a fright before the start when the clutch failed and he had to switch to the spare. At the start Alonso had trouble with a potentiometer in the throttle mechanism and his engine began to misbehave. He kept going until the potentiometer actually failed on lap 25. Marques had it easier, ran a two-stop strategy and got to the finish in ninth. It was Stoddart's first top 10 finish. A triumph for him if not others.

The Minardi team was trying very hard after three successive away races had taxed its resources. Below: The weekend in Brazil was not without its upsets.

## SAN MARINO GRAND PRIX IMOLA
# A downbeat home race

Imola was Minardi's home Grand Prix and the team was hoping to make a good impression. The time to do any development had been very limited and problems with delays from suppliers meant Minardi had not been able to produce any new parts. So it was all about soldiering on with the same machinery. The team wanted to continue its record of finishing but both drivers – Fernando Alonso and Tarso Marques – retired. The result was a depressing end to a very difficult weekend, and meant that the team remained 11th and last in the constructors' championship standings.

FRIDAY PRACTICE Minardi had a brand new chassis, PS01-04, for Tarso Marques. Fernando Alonso retained PS01-03, while PS01-01 became the spare car and the previous spare, PS01-02, became the team's test car. Both drivers experienced mechanical problems in the course of Friday, with Marques suffering from a leaking radiator and Alonso from gearbox troubles. The result was that neither man had as much track time as he'd hoped. Despite this, Alonso ended up 18th with a 1m 28.931secs and Marques 20th on 1m 29.589secs, the two men separated by six-10ths of a second.

SATURDAY QUALIFYING The damp conditions of the morning sessions did not help Minardi catch up on time lost on Friday, but Alonso had no major problems and found a moderately good balance for qualifying. As a result he was able to take 18th on 1m 26.855secs – ahead of the two Benettons. Alonso reckoned there was not much more he could do to improve his times until the car underwent more development. Marques was less fortunate and again failed to find a decent set-up. Then, just as he was about to set off on his final run, he suffered a slow puncture so had to settle for 22nd on 1m 28.281secs and last place on the grid. He was happy just to qualify.

SUNDAY RACE Both drivers complained of brake problems in the race and Alonso decided to pit at the end of lap six. But at the Variante Alta corner, as he braked he found he had no brakes at all. As a result he was launched over a kerb onto the grass and ended up slamming into an Armco barrier, which wiped the left front suspension off his car.

It was later discovered that the problem had been caused by a leaking brake caliper. Marques struggled on despite his brakes and suffered increasing handling problems, later traced to a low pressure in the front right tyre. Marques's car retired on lap 54 with a fire in the airbox, probably occasioned by a leaking fuel line.

**Above: Tarso Marques qualified last and ended his race with engine failure (left).**
**Below left: Fernando Alonso's race ended in the tyre barriers after brake failure at a fast chicane.**

European Minardi was disappointed to lose its reliability record at its home race, with both cars uncharacteristically retiring.

EUROPEAN
minardiF1

## SPANISH GRAND PRIX BARCELONA
# Seeking a point

**Above and right: Fernando Alonso had a strong race to finish 13th.**

Regardless of the success European Minardi claimed in managing to qualify for every race, the team was still 11th and last in the constructors' championship. While merely surviving was the real scoreline for Paul Stoddart's team, he knew that being last would have serious financial implications when the television fees were divided for 2002. Stoddart knew Minardi had no realistic chance of scoring points in 2001. So it was racing for cash. Fernando Alonso's 13th place race finish was good enough to beat both Benetton Renaults, but Benetton was safe from financial oblivion as it had already scored a point.

Minardi was still waiting for a new rear-end package. After Imola the team did its first 2001 test at the Ferrari test track at Mugello, with Alonso and Tarso Marques joined by Dutchman Christijan Albers. The new traction control system was bedded in and worked well.

The biggest event for Minardi in Barcelona was the introduction of two giant rise-up motorhomes, bought second-hand from the Sultan of Brunei but with low mileage. These giant black palaces sent out the wrong message and were the last thing Minardi needed as its old buses were more than adequate. For some teams the battle to present the best motorhomes seems as important as the fight on the track. Doubtless Paul Stoddart had got himself a bargain.

**FRIDAY PRACTICE** Minardi arrived in Barcelona with the same cars as it had used in Imola, with Marques driving PS01-04, Alonso in PS01-03 and PS01-01 again the spare car. Alonso spent the day working his way through an electronic development programme but Marques lost a lot of track time when only 20 minutes into the second session he spun off after the brakes locked and he ended up with gravel everywhere. The two men ended the day in 20th and 22nd place on the timesheets.

**SATURDAY QUALIFYING** Alonso suffered an engine failure in the morning. The unit was rapidly changed and the team was able to try out several set-ups prior to qualifying. In the all-important one-hour session Alonso excelled himself and claimed 18th place on the grid on 1m 21.037secs, a result which was greeted with loud cheers in the Minardi garage. Marques was not able to emulate the Spanish teenager as he could not find a decent balance for his car. In the end he spun as he was going for a time and finished up 22nd and last on the grid with a 1m 22.522secs – but at least he qualified.

**SUNDAY RACE** With both drivers having opted for the softer Michelin tyres on Saturday the team was hoping for warm weather. But conditions were not great and both Alonso and Marques found that their cars did not handle well in the race. Despite this Alonso drove hard all afternoon to finish 13th of 16, commenting afterwards that he was delighted to see the team was not so far behind its major rivals in racing conditions.

Marques suffered from serious understeer in his Minardi all afternoon but enjoyed a lengthy battle with Jenson Button's Benetton Renault in the latter stages of the race. He was eventually overtaken by Button but ended the day in 16th place.

**Right: Tarso Marques had a troubled weekend and could not match his teenage team-mate, but he brought the second Minardi home 16th, behind Jenson Button. Left and right: Marques had a troubled weekend. Below: Fernando Alonso was the centre of Spanish attention.**

## AUSTRIAN GRAND PRIX A1 RING
# Hammer-blow defection

In the days before the Austrian Grand Prix, the European Minardi team suffered the indignity of having technical director Gustav Brunner poached by the new Toyota team. Brunner still had 19 months to run on his $1 million-a-year Minardi deal, but the lure of a rumoured $4 million a year convinced him to leave the team early. Brunner was a star and a furious Minardi team principal Paul Stoddart became even more incensed when Toyota refused even to discuss paying compensation.

Despite all this, the running of the team remained quite smooth and Brunner's position was filled by his deputy, Gabriele Tredozi.

But the race weekend was a disaster as Paul Stoddart confirmed: "This year's Austrian Grand Prix is not an event the European Minardi team will wish to remember. The week got off to a bad start with the technical director breaching his contract, and today's double retirement just added insult to injury." Stoddart was an unhappy man.

**Left:** Following the departure of Gustav Brunner, Minardi had a torrid race. Despite a quick spin (below) Fernando Alonso qualified 18th, ahead of both Benettons, but retired from the race on lap 39.

**Left and below:** Tarso Marques' Minardi is winched away after he was forced to retire on lap 26 when he could no longer select gears. His back-row grid slot gave him an exciting moment as he jinked between the stalled Sauber, McLaren and Jordans when the lights went out.

**FRIDAY PRACTICE** Minardi had the same cars as in Barcelona, with Marques driving PS01-04, Alonso PS01-03 and PS01-01 again the spare. The morning was not much use as the track was still very dirty, but in the afternoon both drivers were able to begin work on chassis set-up. Marques suffered a slight setback when he lost time because of a leaking radiator; he ended the day 19th fastest. Alonso was 20th after a programme of testing new settings failed to show any improvement, so he reverted to the original settings.

**SATURDAY QUALIFYING** Saturday was a difficult day for the team but Fernando Alonso again qualified 18th with Tarso Marques 22nd.

Marques began the day with a leaking oil seal in his gearbox, which meant he missed most of the first morning session. In the second session Marques lost still more time because of worries about his engine. On his first run in qualifying he spun off, so had to rush back to take the spare car. He did one (fairly cautious) run but then suffered a rear damper problem that resulted in the back end of the car catching fire. He qualified 22nd as a result. Alonso had an easier time and qualified in 18th place, although he too had a spin.

"We had a nervous moment when Fernando spun," admitted Stoddart, "because Tarso was already in the spare."

**SUNDAY RACE** All the Michelin runners were in trouble during the warm-up as temperatures were very low, but the Minardis did better than some, with Alonso 18th fastest and Marques right behind him in 19th.

The start of the race was exciting as the Minardis had to weave through the cars left standing on the grid. Both drivers had to jink past the four cars that stalled. They emerged in 16th and 17th, with Alonso ahead of Marques. They settled down into 13th and 15th positions.

It stayed that way until Marques retired on lap 26 when he was no longer able to select any gears. Alonso lost his clutch on lap 10 but battled on until lap 39 when he suffered a similar fate to Marques: a broken gearbox.

EUROPEAN
*minardiF1*

# A very poor time

**M**onaco was a disastrous race for European Minardi. It went into the weekend looking to get to the finish with a decent result to pull clear of the other two teams which had failed to score a point: Prost and Jaguar. Unfortunately, Prost and Jaguar both scored and Minardi was left as the only team still not to get any points, posing severe danger to its income. The last team would not get any TV money in 2002, and that could push Minardi over the edge.

With only one ninth place to its name, the team was now a long way behind. Arrows, Benetton and Prost had all collected seventh or eighth places in addition to their points, so Minardi needed a massive fifth place to get into the top 10. The team was still awaiting its new rear end package, including a revised gearbox. This had been delayed until the French Grand Prix because suppliers could not meet the deadlines. The mood was not helped by the death at the start of the week of Gabriele Rumi, former owner and a friend to many in the organisation. The team was also still in shock over the defection of designer Gustav Brunner to Toyota.

**THURSDAY PRACTICE** Minardi had all four cars at Monaco, with Marques driving PS01-04 as usual and team-mate Fernando Alonso in his habitual PS01-03. Chassis PS01-01 and PS01-02 were also on hand. Halfway through the first session Marques spun off and hit the barriers at Rascasse. The car was hurriedly rebuilt for the second session and by end of the day he had completed 36 laps and was not unhappy. Just as work was finishing on Marques's car Alonso hit the barriers and, as his Minardi could not be repaired in the time remaining, the young Spaniard ended up with only 30 laps on the board. The pair ended the day with the 20th and 21st fastest times; only Pedro de la Rosa was slower. "Both drivers sadly learned that the walls do bite around here," said team boss Paul Stoddart.

**SATURDAY QUALIFYING** Things calmed down a bit and by the end of qualifying Alonso had again qualified 18th. The youngster had just one small spin during the day, coming out of the hairpin, and the car was not damaged. The team reckoned things could not have been much

better and was pleased Alonso's time was a full three seconds faster than Minardi's best qualifying lap achieved by Marc Gené last year; the top teams had improved their lap times by only two seconds. It was an indication the team was becoming more competitive. Marques had an incident-free day but struggled with bad understeer and qualified 22nd and last. The Brazilian commented that his engine did not seem to be as powerful as the one being used by Alonso. "I really couldn't have gone any faster with the car as it was," said a disappointed Marques. "That was it!"

**SUNDAY RACE** Fernando Alonso made a better start than Jenson Button and the Spaniard found himself running in 16th place. In the early laps he ran well but eventually fell behind Jos Verstappen's lighter Arrows. As others retired he moved up to ninth place before being overtaken on lap 46 by Coulthard. Alonso then pitted and was running in 10th place when he retired with a gearbox failure.

Tarso Marques also made up some places at the start but was unable to hold off either Verstappen or Coulthard, so found himself running way down in 19th. He had risen up to as high as 11th place when his Minardi suffered a driveshaft failure on lap 57.

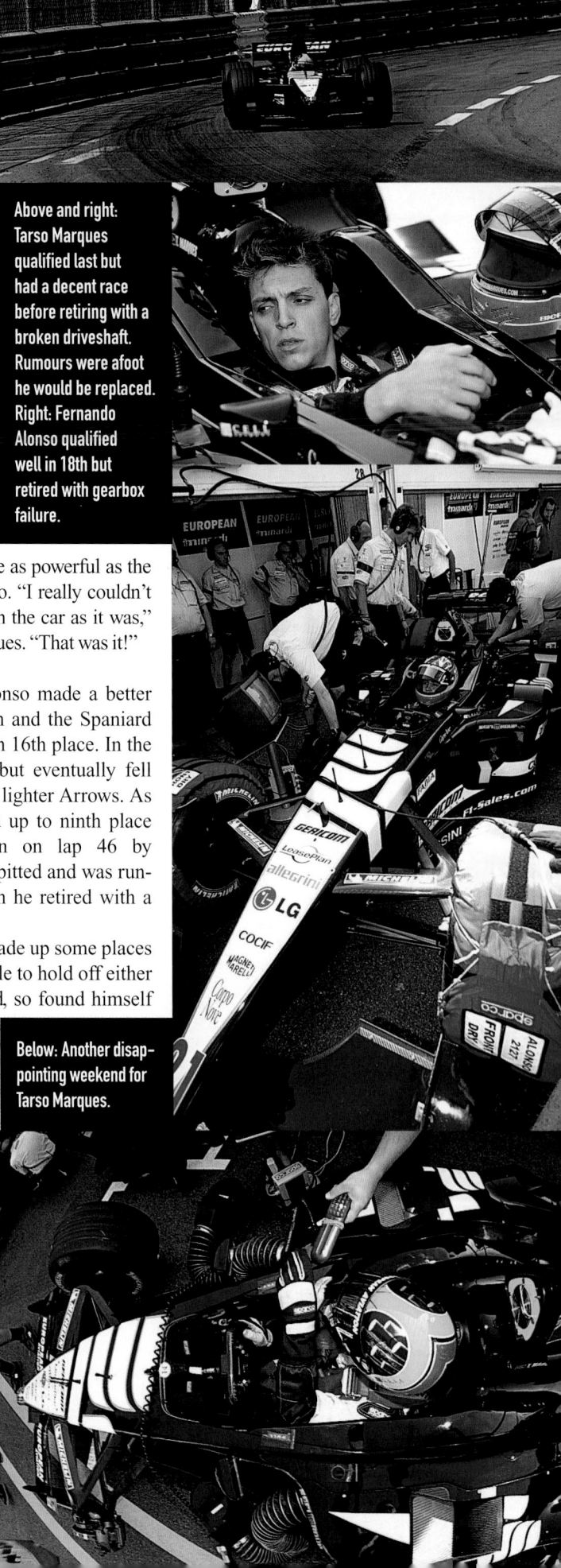

**Above and right:** Tarso Marques qualified last but had a decent race before retiring with a broken driveshaft. Rumours were afoot he would be replaced. **Right:** Fernando Alonso qualified well in 18th but retired with gearbox failure.

**Below:** Another disappointing weekend for Tarso Marques.

Above: Tarso Marques persevered to bring his Minardi home ninth after a difficult race. Left: Fernando Alonso was forced to start behind his team-mate when his best qualifying lap was scrubbed.

## CANADIAN GRAND PRIX MONTREAL
# A very bad weekend

The Canadian Grand Prix turned out to be another tough one. There was constant technical trouble during practice and qualifying, while in the race Fernando Alonso disappeared after only a few laps. Tarso Marques's ninth place finish equalled the team's best performance of the year. That was the best that the team could hope for. It was not, however, enough to get Minardi off the bottom of the constructors' table and the team was now facing up to the fact that it was going to finish 11th and last and lose $10 million of TV income in 2002. This was a frightening thought for team principal, Paul Stoddart. But no doubt, as a total realist, he had a plan up his sleeve. And so it ultimately proved.

The team was negotiating an engine deal for 2001 and had decided to finish off the year with a pay driver to prepare financially for next season. It would shortly introduce its new rear end package, but it was unlikely to make a huge difference as all the other teams were developing quickly.

FRIDAY PRACTICE There were no major changes with the cars used in Monaco, with Alonso driving PS01-03 and Marques using PS01-04. The spare on this occasion was the original PS01-01. Friday resulted in a string of problems which meant neither driver could complete the planned programme. Alonso did 21 laps but Marques did only six. This left the pair 20th and 22nd fastest. Both suffered engine failures, while Marques had a driveshaft failure and a fuel leak as well. "It was a very disappointing start to the weekend," said team boss Paul Stoddart. "Hopefully things will improve tomorrow."

SATURDAY QUALIFYING Saturday was another tale of woe, with Alonso losing a lot of time with brake caliper problems and more engine trouble. To add to the team's ever mounting problems, Alonso's best time was cancelled by the FIA stewards when his front wing was found to be set slightly too low. This meant the Spaniard had to start from 22nd on the grid, swapping places with his team-mate. "I know it doesn't make a big difference, but I have still lost a position," he said.

Marques was not very happy with his car. "It is acceptable," he said, "but there is not a great deal more we can do to it. All we can do is try."

SUNDAY RACE Marques had a good start in the race to make up a number of places, but in the laps that followed he was overtaken by all the cars he had been able to pass. In his second stint he struggled badly with blistered tyres but he battled on to the finish, despite a broken bargeboard which was dragging on the ground in the final laps.

Alonso's race was short and not very sweet, with a driveshaft failure after just a few laps. "Tarso's ninth place," said team principal Paul Stoddart, "was a positive result at the end of a weekend-long struggle."

Minardi's poor weekend was a reflection of the team's limited resources and development. Both drivers struggled during qualifying and occupied the last row of the grid. Left: Tarso Marques had several excursions. Below: Alonso's race ended with driveshaft failure.

EUROPEAN
minardiF1

373

## EUROPEAN GRAND PRIX NÜRBURGRING
# Not fast or reliable

Sitting in last place in the constructors' championship remained a worry for European Minardi, with the spectre of a significantly reduced income in 2002 still hanging over it. The two points needed to put them in with a chance of the TV money were looking all the more impossible, even though at the Nürburgring the team closed the gap on nearest rivals Arrows.

The only way to scrape the fifth place would be through reliability in a war of attrition, but the Minardis were not reliable. At the Nürburgring there were no improvements, but the team continued to plug away with developments in the vain hope it would somehow move forward.

FRIDAY PRACTICE There were no major changes to the cars used in Montreal, with Fernando Alonso driving PS01-03, Tarso Marques using PS01-04 and PS01-01 remaining the spare. Marques lost most of the morning session with an electrical problem which proved hard to find. As a result he ended the day having completed only 21 laps compared to Alonso's 45. The pair clocked 21st and 22nd fastest times, with Alonso complaining that the car was seriously lacking in grip.

SATURDAY QUALIFYING The cars were more reliable and Marques made rapid progress on set-up. In qualifying the Brazilian completed three good qualifying runs and was only a fraction slower than his Spanish teammate. Alonso, who usually is notably faster, lost his third run because of a mistake but

admitted he could not have done much better. "I feel sure we could have done more if we'd had more time at our disposal," said Marques. Team boss Paul Stoddart added: "We may be starting 21st and 22nd on the grid, but our lap times are less than a second off the pace of the midfield teams."

SUNDAY RACE Marques had an engine failure in the warm-up and there was further drama when his launch control failed at the beginning of the parade lap. As he was starting at the back of the grid anyway it made no difference, although he had to make a manual start.

At the first corner his enthusiasm got the better of him and he ran across the sand trap. Soon after that the car began to suffer from voltage fluctuations, a problem that caused damage to the electronics and led to a gearbox malfunction.

Alonso drove a steady race but in the latter stages struggled because of an engine problem. He held on to finish in 14th place. "I just concentrated on keeping going until the end," he said. "That was what really mattered today."

Above and right: Fernando Alonso continued to impress other teams as rumours persisted of a possible move to the Benetton team and a brighter future.

Above and right: Tarso Marques had another mistake-strewn weekend. Below: Minardi team personnel are desperate to see their cars score some championship points.

Above and left: Tarso Marques struggled with understeer during qualifying and ended up last on the grid. Below: Marques had to race the spare car and finished 15th despite gear selection trouble.

### FRENCH GRAND PRIX MAGNY-COURS

# Hope on the horizon

European Minardi continued to struggle along, waiting for subcontractors to finish and deliver the team's new gearbox. When this work was completed, the team would be able to introduce a whole new rear end, complete with some aerodynamic changes and a new rear suspension. It was hoping to have this for Silverstone, but further delays were expected. Until then Fernando Alonso and Tarso Marques were left to struggle with existing machinery that was simply inadequate. As a result, in France Minardi resumed its traditional position of 21st and 22nd on the grid.

FRIDAY PRACTICE There were no major changes to the chassis so Alonso continued to use PS01-03 and Marques ran with PS01-04, leaving PS01-01 as the spare car.

In the course of Friday the two drivers worked to assess the tyres and see if they could find a good balance. Alonso was able to complete his entire programme and did 45 laps with a best time of 1m 17.866secs, while Marques had a problem with his electronic upshift and downshift system and had to settle for 38 laps and a best of 1m 18.372secs. The pair ended the day 21st and 22nd.

SATURDAY QUALIFYING Minardi continued to develop the cars without too much trouble, though Marques struggled with too much understeer in qualifying. Alonso's best run was ruined by being baulked by the Arrows of Enrique Bernoldi. The team felt strongly that this had been done deliberately.

"What would have been a reasonably good qualifying session for us was marred by an intentional blocking manoeuvre," said team boss Paul Stoddart. "That undoubtedly lost Fernando what would have been his best run of the afternoon."

Stoddart's remarks led to a curious denial being issued by Arrows team boss Tom Walkinshaw, although his words failed to convince Stoddart or indeed most other observers in the paddock.

Whatever the details, Alonso and Marques ended up taking 21st and 22nd slots on the grid, with times of 1m 16.039secs and 1m 16.500secs respectively.

SUNDAY RACE In the morning warm-up session, Marques had a gearbox failure and had to switch to the team's spare car for the race. He had decided to go for a two-stop strategy, while Alonso took the decision to try to go right through with only one stop.

Both men ran at the rear of the field and although Marques began to suffer some gear selection trouble in the final laps of the race, he was able to finish 15th. Alonso was running behind him, battling with Pedro de la Rosa, when he was advised to pit to avoid an engine blow-up. As this happened within five laps of the finish the Spanish teenager was still classified a finisher, in 17th place.

"A bit more luck and both cars would have finished," said Stoddart. "But having two classified is not bad. Every result counts."

Left and below: Although an engine failure meant Alonso didn't take the flag, he was classified 17th. Far left: Minardi was just grateful to get two cars home.

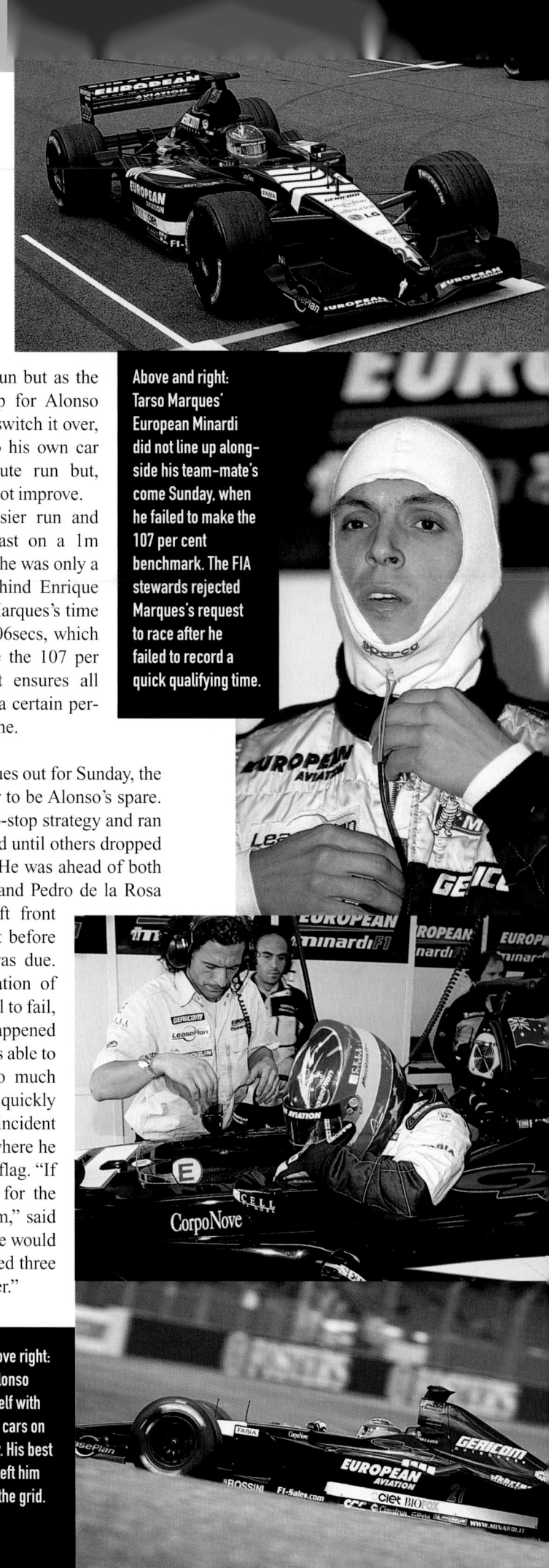

## BRITISH GRAND PRIX SILVERSTONE
# One down, one out

The European Minardi team suffered a big setback in qualifying at Silverstone when after many mechanical problems Tarso Marques failed to set a time within 107 per cent of the pole position benchmark. The team asked the FIA stewards for a waiver, but the request was rightly declined. Rules are rules, so come Sunday Minardi found itself down to one car.

Fernando Alonso did what he could in the race, but that was only 16th – although his cause was not helped when a wheel fell off his car as he was nearing his second pitstop.

Although team principal Paul Stoddart remained upbeat and easily won the tag of 'nicest' team principal, his team was fading. Non-qualification is a death knell in modern-day Formula One – and he knew it.

One of the most astute financial brains in the paddock, Stoddart said a $50 million budget was already in place for next year. He believed the system for allocating FOM TV fees would be revised to give all 12 teams, instead of only 10, a share of next year's cake. He had a point: the current system simply makes the weak weaker.

But for the moment, however, a more equitable share-out was wishful thinking and relied on the other team principals ceding some of their share, which seemed unrealistic. Small teams such as Stoddart's are needed in Formula One though, and, as Frank Williams amply demonstrates, they can eventually become big teams. Stoddart has the ambition to do that. Whether it can be achieved in modern day Formula One is unknown, but that hasn't stopped this supreme enthusiast trying his hardest.

**FRIDAY PRACTICE** Minardi had three cars as usual at Silverstone, with Alonso driving PS01-03 and Marques at the wheel of PS01-04. The spare was once again the original PS01-01.

Friday saw both men having spins but neither damaged his car. Marques once again seemed to have most of the problems, with rear suspension trouble in the morning and a gearbox malfunction in the afternoon. Despite this, both men did the same number of laps – but Alonso was a whole second quicker.

**SATURDAY QUALIFYING** Qualifying proved a big disappointment for the Minardi team. Marques found his car had throttle problems on his second run but as the spare car was set up for Alonso there was no time to switch it over, so he went back into his own car for a final last-minute run but, unfortunately, could not improve.

Alonso had an easier run and qualified 21st and last on a 1m 24.792secs, although he was only a 10th of a second behind Enrique Bernoldi's Arrows. Marques's time was a sorry 1m 26.506secs, which left him well outside the 107 per cent benchmark that ensures all qualifiers are within a certain percentage of the pole time.

**SUNDAY RACE** With Marques out for Sunday, the team prepared his car to be Alonso's spare. Fernando chose a two-stop strategy and ran at the back of the field until others dropped back with problems. He was ahead of both Giancarlo Fisichella and Pedro de la Rosa when he lost his left front wheel on lap 39, just before his second pitstop was due. There was no indication of what caused the wheel to fail, but fortunately it happened near the pits so he was able to get back without too much damage and get quickly underway again. The incident left Alonso in 16th, where he stayed through to the flag. "If it had not been for the wheel problem," said Stoddart, "he would have finished three places higher."

# A complex afternoon

It was a traumatic race day afternoon at Hockenheim for the European Minardi team. Watching both cars wheeled off the grid was soul-destroying for team principal Paul Stoddart, one of the nicest men in the paddock.

The truth was, Minardi was falling behind and the sheer pace of development over a season had hit Stoddart firmly in the face. The new launch and traction control demands had also been tough to master.

The team was also hit hard by the defection of Gustav Brunner to Toyota. He was the technical glue on which the under-funded team relied. Now his legacy was a clearly brilliant chassis let down by a poor engine and a serious absence of dollars.

Added to the problems was the cars' tendency to catch fire, embarrassingly on the starting grid itself. As it was, both cars started from the pitlane, not that it mattered. "Whoever says F1 is boring has to be crazy," observed Minardi team boss Stoddart at the end of a bizarre afternoon of racing.

**FRIDAY PRACTICE** Minardi had the usual three cars, with Fernando Alonso driving PS01-03, Tarso Marques in PS01-04 and the spare the original PS01-01. But on Friday Alonso's car was fitted with the long-awaited PS01B package, which included a new gearbox, rear suspension and aerodynamic set-up. In the afternoon Alonso reverted to the standard rear end, and he and Marques ended the day stuck in 21st and 22nd as usual.

**SATURDAY QUALIFYING** There were no changes to the chassis for Saturday but Alonso lost time during the morning sessions because of a sensor failure, which meant he did only 21 laps while Marques completed 28. Both men complained that the major problem was a simple lack of horsepower at a track where it is vital. The Ford-based European engine was the weakest out there, with maybe as little as 700 horsepower, which showed how good the chassis was.

Alonso still managed to get under the 1m 42secs barrier for 21st. Marques again had trouble and lost his first run because of a gear-selection problem. On his last run he encountered a spinning Arrows and so had to settle for 22nd on the grid, eight-10ths of a second slower than Alonso.

**SUNDAY RACE** Sunday was Alonso's 20th birthday but it got off to a ropey start when he spun into a tyre barrier in warm-up. Despite this he was 19th fastest. Marques also had a spin but did not hit anything.

As the cars were lining up on the dummy grid, the rear of Alonso's car suddenly caught fire. This was extinguished and investigations revealed that the refuelling valve was leaking. A further investigation revealed that Marques's car had a similar problem and they were both were pushed into the pits. Alonso took the spare car while Marques went into Alonso's PS01-03, which was hurriedly repaired. Both cars then started from the pitlane, which was probably not a bad idea given what happened with Luciano Burti.

In the course of the short first race Alonso suffered a driveshaft failure and so was fortunate there was a red flag. As a result he switched to Marques's car for the restart. The race saw the two men use different strategies, with Marques going for one stop and Alonso trying a two-stop race. Marques retired with a gearbox problem after 26 laps but Alonso made it to the finish in 10th place. "Tenth is my best result in Formula One and today is my birthday," he said. "What more could I ask for?" What indeed.

**Left and above:** The German Grand Prix held its share of trouble for Fernando Alonso, but brought the Spaniard a worthy reward with his best GP result when he guided the European Minardi home in 10th place.

**Left:** Both Minardis had problems on the grid, with both drivers forced to start from the pitlane.
**Below:** A disappointed Paul Stoddart could only watch the problems unfold.

*EUROPEAN minardi F1*

## HUNGARIAN GRAND PRIX HUNGARORING
# Promising better times

The European Minardi team went to Hungary keen to continue developing its new titanium gearbox and revised rear suspension and aerodynamics. The results were promising, if not reliable.

Minardi was a team in transition in every respect. New principal Paul Stoddart was struggling: every time he lifted a floorboard he discovered another debt. It was cramping the recovery and he was said to be seriously mulling the team's future in Italy, though no immediate decisions were expected.

There was much speculation about the arrival of Malaysian Alex Yoong and bundles of Malaysian money. But Yoong could not drive until he had an FIA superlicence and the Malaysian money was banked.

Meanwhile Giancarlo Minardi continued to appear to cheer the team on, even if Stoddart was tired of inheriting liabilities he knew nothing about. The new boss would have been justified in taking a sterner line, but is simply too nice to be a team principal and still has the burning ambition of youth. That mindset may not last forever.

FRIDAY PRACTICE Minardi had the same three cars as usual with Fernando Alonso driving PS01-03, Tarso Marques in PS01-04, and the original PS01-01 as the spare. However, the team has continued to develop its new gearbox and rear end and so chassis 03 and 04 were both modified to B-spec. On Friday only Alonso tried the new rear end. Both drivers had spins in the slippery conditions, which meant Alonso did 35 laps for 20th place on 1m 19.992secs and Marques came 22nd on 1m 20.981secs after 38 laps.

SATURDAY QUALIFYING On Saturday both drivers ran with B-spec cars but Marques's hopes took a dive in the morning session when he lost 25 minutes because of a faulty sensor, which had to be changed. This meant he did only 18 laps while Alonso managed 30. As a result Marques was struggling more with his car's handling, as well as the fact that the engine was down on power, and therefore qualified a poor 22nd on 1m 19.139secs. Alonso was a more promising 18th with 1m 17.624secs, ahead of both Arrows cars and Burti's Prost.

SUNDAY RACE The team decided to play it safe on race day and so Alonso's car was switched back to its original configuration. Marques, who knew his days at the team were numbered, agreed to race his car in B-spec. Both drivers completed 12 laps in the warm-up but in race trim they were not as fast as the Arrows or Prost entries. At the start the action was lively at the back of the grid, with Marques and Heinz-Harald Frentzen clashing at the second corner. Alonso ran 17th and Marques 20th in the early stages but as the race progressed both men had technical problems. Alonso had trouble with his brakes and spun off on lap 38. Marques lasted until lap 64, battling with an inconsistent throttle and gearbox trouble before being told to turn the engine off to avoid it blowing up.

Above: Hungary did not bring any results for Paul Stoddart and European Minardi but provided valuable mileage for their new gearbox.

Above: Fernando Alonso ended up in the gravel after brake problems sent him off. Right: Alonso was disappointed not to finish, while Tarso Marques was pushed off on lap one by Frentzen, then plagued by problems with the new Minardi gearbox and an inconsistent throttle, before falling oil pressure ended his race.

## BELGIAN GRAND PRIX SPA-FRANCORCHAMPS

# More money appears

It was the last race for Brazilian Tarso Marques before he was replaced by Malaysian Alex Yoong, who brought the team much-needed cash sponsorship for the final three races and rumoured for 2002 as well. The logo of new sponsor Magnum appeared on the black cars to show intent.

Amazingly, it transpired that Marques had been enjoying a free ride at Minardi and had brought no money. He told journalists during his farewell interviews that team-mate Fernando Alonso had brought all the cash, and that he was very grateful to team boss Paul Stoddart for the opportunity to race. He had no complaints at being bumped.

Paul Stoddart was a man apart, with a long-term mission to take his team to the top. It appeared that he had already spent $50 million of his own cash buying, sorting out and running the team. That was a huge outlay for a private individual and others in the paddock were shaking their heads in wonder at his commitment. In 2002, he was almost certain to lose the $10 million TV money the team enjoyed in 2001 – the price for last place in the constructors' championship. The year after will be even harder: Toyota's arrival will mean the team has to finish at least 10th of 12 to get any TV money.

**FRIDAY PRACTICE** Minardi's gradual switch to the B-spec PS01 chassis continued: Alonso drove PS01B-03, Marques PS01B-04. PS01B-02 was the spare car. Paddock pundits felt the team was heading up a technical blind alley, and the B chassis was not worth the time and money. The results supported that view. The original PS01-01 chassis, in its original configuration, was the spare car. On Friday morning both drivers enjoyed relatively untroubled runs, with Alonso completing 26 laps and setting the 18th quickest time with 1m 55.021secs despite an electronic problem. Marques was 19th, on 1m 55.099secs after 30 laps, despite two spins. The difference between the two drivers was a mere 0.092mph. "We now have a good baseline for what is certain to be an interesting weekend," said Stoddart. Translation: things couldn't get any worse. Wrong.

**SATURDAY QUALIFYING** The morning fog meant that there was no real chance to work on the qualifying set-up. The team decided to wait until the end of the qualifying session and use intermediate tyres. It would have been better off with dry tyres. The result was that neither car got within the required 107 per cent of Juan Pablo Montoya's pole time, and so they did not qualify. The FIA stewards, however, decided that all cars should start the race.

For the record, Alonso finished 20th on a time of 2m 02.594secs and Marques 22nd and last on 2m 04.204secs.

**SUNDAY RACE** Sunday started badly when Alonso crashed heavily at Stavelot in the final seconds of the warm-up. The mechanics worked flat out to build a new car around the PS01B-02 in time for the start. Alonso went out with gearbox failure after just three laps. Marques then hit debris from the Irvine-Burti crash, damaging a tyre, and went into the pits with a puncture. As the second race unfolded it was clear his suspension had been damaged, and he pitted six times to try and fix it. He was five laps down at the finish. "We sincerely thank Tarso for a fantastic effort in what has been a difficult year," said Stoddart. Minardi is such a polite team.

Spa was not a great weekend for European Minardi after Fernando Alonso destroyed his race car at Stavelot during warm-up, and then retired in the race. Left: Paul Stoddart was pleased to confirm that the team would use Asiatech V10 engines for 2002.

Alonso and Marques failed to make the 107 per cent cut in qualifying but were allowed to start given the constantly changing track conditions at the end of the session. Below: Tarso Marques had his last race for the team and finished five laps behind after six pitstops.

EUROPEAN
minardiF1

# Bring on the Malaysians

Minardi made history at Monza with the new pilot of car number 20, Alex Yoong, who was the first Malaysian to secure a Formula One drive. Although his performances on track weren't enough to impress, he did make and impression on journalists with his articulacy and beautiful girlfriend, his impeccable manners and his uncontained delight at becoming a Formula One driver.

Minardi was one of the few teams yet to announce its driver line-up for 2002 which wasn't particularly unusual. It hoped to retain Fernando Alonso, whose talent had shone through the inferiority of the PS01 car in 2001. But few observers expected him to stay with Minardi for another year.

It was being said that Yoong had not signed for 2002, but it was expected that he would remain with the team for a full season. Recently departed Tarso Marques claimed that Paul Stoddart was keen to have him back within the team. The future was, as always, uncertain at Minardi.

FRIDAY PRACTICE Both drivers had access to the new 'B' spec chassis for Monza, with Alonso once again in the PS01B/03 and newcomer Yoong in the PS01B/04. The spare car was the older PS01/01. The new chassis had yet to display any notable improvements from its predecessor, and the team was struggling.

Alonso did 34 laps and recorded the 17th fastest time on Friday, with a best of 1m 26.972secs. Yoong had an electrical problem and sat at the bottom of the timing sheets, having clocked a 1m 28.250secs, 3.6secs off the fastest time. Stoddart spoke of the progress the team had made, of which there was no evidence so far.

SATURDAY QUALIFYING Saturday was a nightmare day for Minardi. Both Yoong's and Alonso's cars developed gearbox gremlins during the morning session which, by qualifying, the engineers insisted had been solved. But lo and behold, on their respective out-laps, both drivers pulled off after exiting the pitlane, complaining that the gearboxes had given up. This left both drivers without cars, needing to qualify for the Italian Grand Prix.

The only solution was for both drivers to share the one spare car. The PS01 was set up in long-wheelbase configuration that allowed both drivers to miraculously qualify within 107 per cent of the pole time. Alonso completed nine laps and secured the 21st slot on the grid with a 1m 26.218secs. Yoong was last after 11 laps with a 1m 27.463secs, only 0.508secs inside the crucial 107 per cent time.

SUNDAY RACE Alonso decided to race in the spare car, which had an older gearbox fitted as a precautionary measure after the problems on Saturday. This, however, diminished the car in terms of performance, but Alonso drove a strong race, finishing 13th, eight places up on his starting position, albeit two laps down from winner Juan Pablo Montoya.

Yoong complained of a 'scare' when the wing of Jenson Button's Benetton flew by him on the opening lap. Sensibly, he took the next couple of laps steady to test the car, and when he found nothing was broken, he pressed on full power, promptly spinning in the Lesmos complex on lap 16. He complained of understeer throughout the race, and spun again in the same place eight laps from the finish, this time retiring from the race.

Above and right: European Minardi and Fernando Alonso had a busy Monza with a succession of gearbox problems through practice and qualifying. Both got it right for the race, with Alonso putting in a solid performance to take eighth, two laps behind Montoya.

Right and below: Malaysian Alex Yoong made history, but an unimpressive debut. Sharing the spare with Alonso, his qualifying was respectable but his race performance less so: he retired after two spins.

## UNITED STATES GRAND PRIX INDIANAPOLIS
# Uncertain times ahead

**Above and left:**
**Fernando Alonso did a great job to qualify the Minardi in 17th, three-10ths behind de la Rosa's Jaguar. His race was short-lived, with a driveshaft failure after his pitstop on lap 36.**

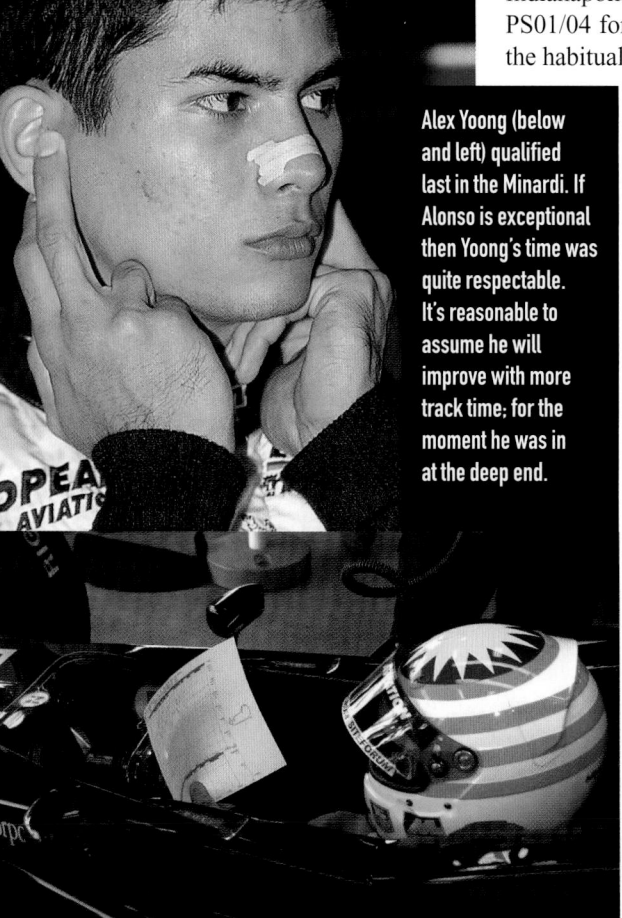

**Alex Yoong (below and left) qualified last in the Minardi. If Alonso is exceptional then Yoong's time was quite respectable. It's reasonable to assume he will improve with more track time; for the moment he was in at the deep end.**

European Minardi's season had been atrocious even by its own standards. And to compound the misery it looked even more certain to lose its biggest asset, Fernando Alonso. His driving was one of the team's key assets, but his future was rumoured to be elsewhere in 2002.

The young Spaniard was impressive in qualifying at Indianapolis, exceeding expectations with 17th spot on the grid – the team's highest qualifying spot since Marc Gené claimed 15th at the 1999 German Grand Prix. In doing so he beat the likes of Jacques Villeneuve. Sauber, Jordan and Arrows were said to be chasing his services for 2002, although team principal Paul Stoddart seemed determined not to let him go.

Stoddart signed a deal with the Motor Club of Argentina to promote the country's young talent. Unkind wags said this was really another way of relieving the country's young talent of their wallets. But that's the name of the game at the back of the grid and there was no dressing it up.

FRIDAY PRACTICE Minardi took three cars to Indianapolis: PS01B/03 for Alonso and PS01/04 for Alex Yoong, with 01 in tow as the habitual spare. The drivers concentrated on finding the right set-up to balance the high downforce needed for the banked section with the high grip needed for the twisty infield. Alonso set the 19th fastest time with 1m 15.131secs and Yoong was 22nd and last with 1m 16.318secs.

Stoddart said: "The team now looks forward to tomorrow's practice and qualifying sessions which, we trust, will be without the dramas encountered at Monza." He could breathe easy.

SATURDAY QUALIFYING In morning practice, Alonso completed 32 laps for 20th place and a 1m 14.867secs. Yoong was again last in 1m 15.604secs over 29 laps, and had a few spins.

Alonso's show in qualifying proved why teams had been courting him assiduously for 2002. He clocked a time on his second run of 1m 13.991secs, which gained him 17th place on the grid. Sensing a problem with the engine, he took his last run in the spare and felt he could have even taken 16th place away from Pedro de la Rosa's Jaguar if he had had another chance in his race car. Alonso once said taking 18th spot was like getting pole for him, so one could only guess what 17th meant. Paul Stoddart summed it up: "What a fantastic effort! It would be a major understatement to say we are looking forward to the race."

Meanwhile, Yoong set a time of 1m 15.247secs to qualify last, over one-and-a-quarter seconds behind Alonso.

SUNDAY RACE The Minardis finished the warm-up at the back: Alonso was 21st in 1m 16.332secs, Yoong 22nd in 1m 16.646secs.

The team's fantastic race never materialised. Alonso's launch control switched itself off on the formation lap and as a result he lost three places at the start. When Räikkönen retired he moved up to 19th position, a place behind the tussle between de la Rosa and Villeneuve. On lap 36 he came into the pits for his scheduled stop, but found himself unable to continue because of a driveshaft failure.

Yoong made up a place at the start thanks to Enge's poor getaway, then another with Räikkönen's retirement. He flat-spotted a tyre in the first few laps and suffered vibrations thereafter. He dropped to last after his stop on lap 26, and remained at the back until gearbox problems ended his race on the 38th lap.

Paul Stoddart said of the team's disappointing weekend: "Sadly today neither European Minardi driver was able to profit from what, up to that point, had been a constructive weekend. It's particularly frustrating for Fernando, after his brilliant performance in qualifying yesterday, that the gearbox let him down today. With Alex suffering similar problems, it's clear the team needs to work on drive train reliability before Suzuka in two weeks."

**EUROPEAN**
**minardiF1**

381

# Amazing to be here

It was an amazing season in many respects for European Minardi. A team fighting for its financial existence just six weeks before the Australian Grand Prix produced an amazing turnaround and qualified for 30 out of 34 starts. Only once did it actually fail to start a race. Fernando Alonso is a star in the making and the fact that he's Spanish does him no harm at all.

Being so far behind the competition at the outset spurred Minardi to keep developing its car until the end. Besides several aerodynamic tweaks, the team also achieved the near-impossible feat of both designing and manufacturing new components for the team's troublesome titanium gearbox in the 10 days between the US Grand Prix and the start of the race weekend at Suzuka. The box's reliability was seen as a major plus for a team building towards 2002, when its new Asiatech engine can't be any worse than the four-year-old engines it used this year.

**FRIDAY PRACTICE** European Minardi brought three cars to Japan: Alonso used PS01B/03, while the older and more basic chassis 01 was his designated spare – emphasising the team's unfounded fears concerning the reliability of the new gearbox. Yoong took control of 04.

The team did an hour's set-up and then concentrated on tyre comparisons, all the while keeping an eye on the gearbox modifications. Alonso was making his first visit to the circuit and so his 17th fastest time was all the more impressive. The young Spaniard, who is on a long-term contract with Renault and may even jump ship in 2002, had been one of the most impressive rookies of 2001, and again his ability outshone the car. Outpacing Olivier Panis was a scalp for the youngster.

Since coming in at Monza, Yoong had struggled to come to grips with a car tailored to Alonso's preferences, and noted that he likes the exact opposite to the Spaniard. Alonso, like Michael Schumacher and Kimi Räikkönen, likes a car with a knife-like front end and can live with an unstable rear. Yoong suffered from this and was looking forward to off-season testing so that he could change his Minardi's handling characteristics. Twenty-first was the best he could have hoped for, outpacing only the crashed Prost of Tomas Enge.

**SATURDAY QUALIFYING** European Minardi boss Paul Stoddart hailed Alonso's fastest qualifying lap as 'outstanding', and there was little more to say. The Spaniard arrived at what he described as a perfect balance in his car, and drove a blistering lap to finish 18th – not two events that normally go hand in hand, but Alonso outpaced Yoong by almost two seconds, putting things into perspective. Apart from one minor off in the morning session, Alonso just got better and better.

Yoong was planted firmly to the bottom of the timesheets once again, although that was not a surprise. The Malaysian was disappointed not to have registered a significant improvement between qualifying runs, though, and traffic on his third run may have robbed him of a more respectable time.

**SUNDAY RACE** Alonso's weekend struck perfection in the race. He managed to keep ahead of the Prost of Tomas Enge – who admitted to lifting through 130R after his Friday accident – among others. He gained the rest of the places through retirements, but an 11th place finish in a Minardi was as good as it would ever get this season.

Yoong's race soured before the pitlane even opened. An electrical fault on his car was discovered before he went out and the team switched the Malaysian to the spare car, set up for Alonso. Yoong put a brave face on it, but the seating position was alien and back cramps set on his out-lap. Luckily the team repaired his race car and elected to bring him in and start him in it from the pitlane. The cramps returned, though, and Yoong spent the majority of the race in severe pain. His fastest lap was some six seconds off that set by Ralf Schumacher, but Yoong managed to clinch his first finish and 16th and last place.

Above and right: Fernando Alonso finished his first Grand Prix season with a fine 11th place at Suzuka in the European Minardi. The Spaniard has a bright future.

Right and below: Despite severe pain from back cramps, Malaysian Alex Yoong brought his Minardi home for his first race finish in 16th place.

Australia
p386

Malaysia
p394

Brazil
p402

San Marino
p410

Spain
p418

Austria
p426

Monaco
p434

Canada
p442

# Race
# REVIEWS

Europe
p450

France
p458

Great Britain
p466

Germany
p474

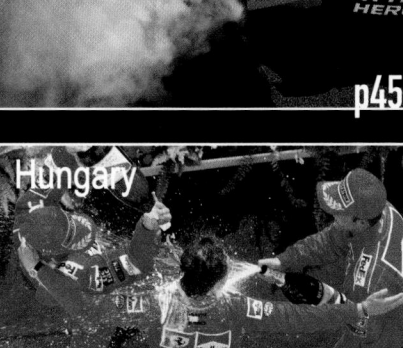
Hungary
p482

Belgium
p490

Italy
p498

USA
p506

Japan
p514

# Australian Grand Prix

## 2nd–4th March 2001  LAPS: 58  LENGTH OF LAP: 3.295 miles

STORY OF THE SEASON  Even in the season opener at Melbourne, the scarlet Ferrari of Michael Schumacher is already pulling away into the distance.  Mika Häkkinen, in the McLaren Mercedes, tries  vainly to make up the ground to first place.  PHOTOGRAPH BY CLEMENT MARIN

Heinz-Harald Frentzen's Jordan visits the gravel trap following a brush with Rubens Barrichello's Ferrari.

# A sad day down under

The start of the 2001 Grand Prix season seemed full of promise. But hopes were soon dashed when an incident of catastrophic proportions resulted in the death of a marshal.

It was a glorious start to the new season of Formula One. The host nation, as ever, provided a spectacular bill of supporting entertainment, seamless organisation and atmosphere. After the withdrawal symptoms of winter, the anticipation of car launches and the speculation of testing, everyone gathered in marvellous Melbourne to get down to the business of racing renewed and reinvigorated.

Sunday, however, dawned grey and insipid after the azure skies of practice and qualifying. By the time the cars lined up on the grid it was at least a little brighter. The carnival atmosphere born of an incessantly diverting line-up of support races and genuine excitement for the start of a new season reached a peak as the field lined up. It was almost as if they had never been away. The mantra

Racing at over 140mph Jacques Villeneuve's BAR Honda cannoned into the back of Ralf Schumacher's BMW Williams. The BAR is launched into a sickening flight to destruction. Villeneuve was lucky to survive a very heavy impact.

throughout the rounds of car launches and winter testing had been that nobody would really know where they stood until Melbourne, but that everybody would doubtless be playing catch-up to Ferrari and McLaren. This all-too-predictable phrase became all-too-predictable reality when Michael Schumacher and Rubens Barrichello lined up on the front row of the grid with Mika Häkkinen in third. It looked like 2000 all over again.

One of the main subjects of gossip was the three major crashes – two for Jaguar's almost rookie Luciano Burti and one for Michael Schumacher – that had occurred so far that weekend. Worryingly for the FIA, the new double tethers intended to keep the wheels attached to the wreck in the event of a big accident summarily failed, although they were pleased to discover that somehow neither driver had suffered injury. Formula One seemed safer than ever.

When the 2001 championship got underway for real, Schumacher's Ferrari gained almost half a car length on everyone else as the lights turned. There was a first-day-of-term mentality, with new-boy Juan Pablo Montoya clipping Eddie Irvine, and Rubens Barrichello clipping Heinz-Harald Frentzen.

All this was soon of little consequence, as the fifth lap brought an incident of catastrophic proportions. Riding on board with Jacques Villeneuve, digital TV viewers saw the rear of Ralf Schumacher's Williams swell hugely and rode through a gigantic impact. The BAR was launched upwards, pivoting over to the left and hitting the retaining wall almost backwards, debris flying past

David Coulthard smokes his rear tyres as the McLaren struggles for grip following his pitstop.

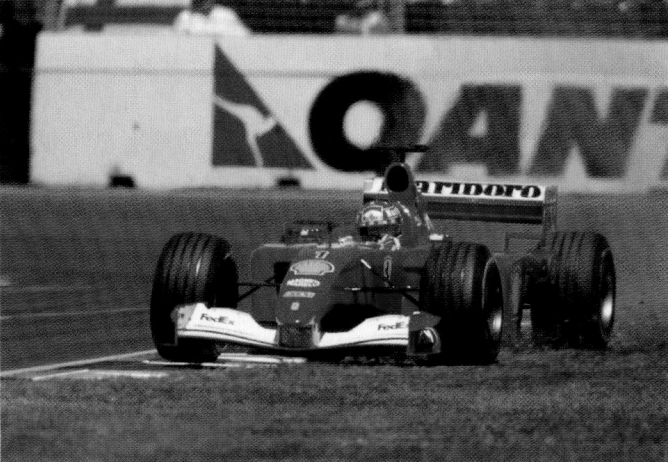

Ferrari team leader Michael Schumacher used every inch of the track.

Michael Schumacher celebrates his perfect start to the 2001 season, momentarily unaware that a marshall had been killed.

the camera and Villeneuve's exposed helmet until the signal from the camera was cut. However, the magnitude of the accident amid the high-walled confines of Albert Park was only really evident from outside: Villeneuve's front wing disappearing skyward at untold speed, the car spinning nose high through the air to destroy itself against the wall and spectator fence. As the dust settled both drivers emerged to great relief.

That relief was short-lived. It became apparent that bystanders had been caught up in the carnage. Word soon filtered back that a marshal was involved. The medical crews lingered at the scene for an uncomfortably long time, and when the ambulance finally pulled away it was with a solemn lack of urgency. Media workers discreetly began to work through the carefully structured crisis communications schedules that everybody in professional motor racing keeps and hopes never to use. It was reported that a wheel had entered the marshal's enclosure through a gap in the debris fence provided for photographers, hitting the marshal in the chest, while 11 spectators suffered cuts and bruises from debris. A second Grand Prix safety worker lay at the trackside undergoing cardiac massage in the space of six months.

Life went on, perhaps a little crassly. Motor racing can be like that. At the end of the 15th lap the safety car pulled off, the green flags waved and Michael Schumacher set about building himself a lead. Häkkinen was chasing hard when his left front suspension gave way at the end of the back straight, and the Finn suffered a very sizeable impact with the tyre wall, prompting a quick trip to the medical centre, where he was declared okay.

The incident put Schumacher in a commanding lead that was easily maintained to the flag. The top three drivers stood solemnly on the podium, having been informed of the death of a man who had volunteered to try to ensure their safety. "Unfortunately we've just been told that the marshal did die," Michael Schumacher announced at the post-race press conference. "Obviously we are all shocked about this and we have to look at what support we can give."

At the marshal's funeral the following week his widow summed it up: "He wasn't in the wrong place at the wrong time. He was in the right place at the wrong time."

These Australian fans were the most enthusiastic ever seen at a race outside Europe.

389

# Australian Grand Prix Race Statistics

## ALBERT PARK CIRCUIT DIAGRAM

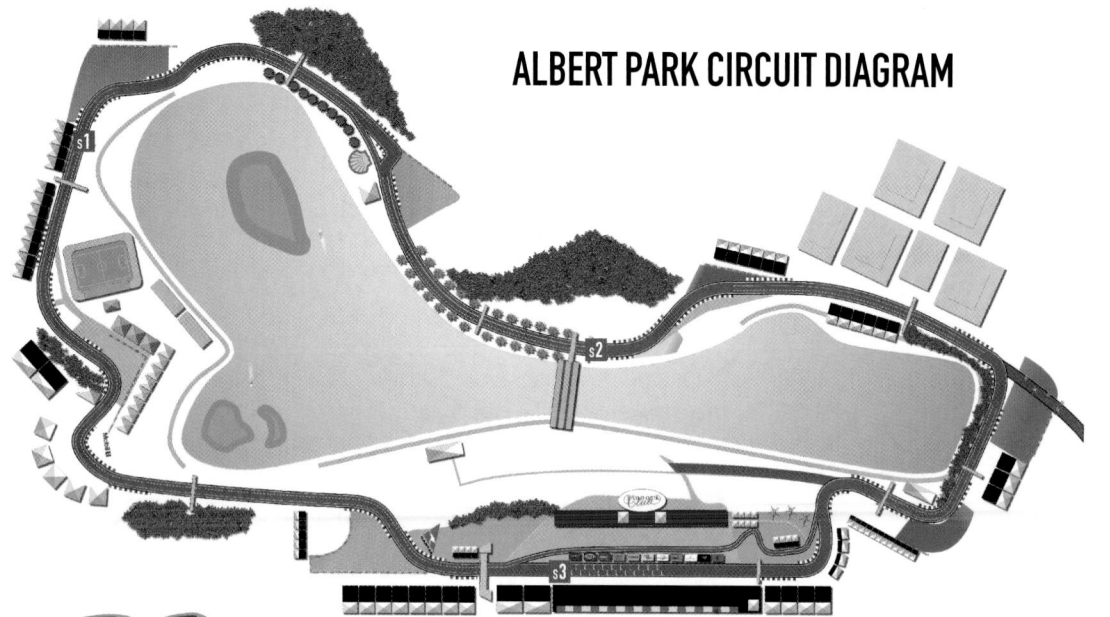

Illustration by Emeric de Baré

## FASTEST LAPS

| | DRIVER | TIME | LAP |
|---|---|---|---|
| 1 | M Schumacher | 1m 28.214s | 34 |
| 2 | Coulthard | 1m 28.838s | 40 |
| 3 | Barrichello | 1m 29.060s | 33 |
| 4 | Montoya | 1m 29.606s | 40 |
| 5 | Häkkinen | 1m 29.612s | 25 |
| 6 | Panis | 1m 30.199s | 36 |
| 7 | Räikkönen | 1m 30.229s | 35 |
| 8 | Frentzen | 1m 30.266s | 35 |
| 9 | Heidfeld | 1m 30.317s | 35 |
| 10 | Trulli | 1m 30.432s | 29 |
| 11 | Burti | 1m 30.903s | 31 |
| 12 | Alesi | 1m 31.030s | 31 |
| 13 | Irvine | 1m 31.267s | 29 |
| 14 | Verstappen | 1m 31.999s | 56 |
| 15 | Button | 1m 32.001s | 24 |
| 16 | Alonso | 1m 32.043s | 56 |
| 17 | Fisichella | 1m 32.407s | 23 |
| 18 | R Schumacher | 1m 34.406s | 3 |
| 19 | Villeneuve | 1m 34.432s | 3 |
| 20 | Bernoldi | 1m 36.689s | 2 |
| 21 | Marques | 1m 38.249s | 2 |
| | Mazzacane | No laps completed | |

## RACE: SUNDAY 4TH MARCH 2001, 2PM

| | DRIVER | CAR | TIME/RETIREMENT | LAPS | PITSTOP LAPS |
|---|---|---|---|---|---|
| 1 | Michael Schumacher | Ferrari | 1h 38m 26.533s | 58 | 37 |
| 2 | David Coulthard | McLaren Mercedes | +0m 01.717s | 58 | 41 |
| 3 | Rubens Barrichello | Ferrari | +0m 33.491s | 58 | 39 |
| 4 | Nick Heidfeld | Sauber Petronas | +1m 11.479s | 58 | 37 |
| 5 | Heinz-Harald Frentzen | Jordan Honda | +1m 12.807s | 58 | 37 |
| 6 | Kimi Räikkönen | Sauber Petronas | +1m 24.143s | 58 | 36 |
| 7 | Olivier Panis | BAR Honda | +1m 27.050s | 58 | 40 |
| 8 | Luciano Burti | Jaguar Racing | +1 lap | 57 | 36 |
| 9 | Jean Alesi | Prost Acer | +1 lap | 57 | 35 |
| 10 | Jos Verstappen | Arrows Asiatech | +1 lap | 57 | 14 38 |
| 11 | Eddie Irvine | Jaguar Racing | +1 lap | 57 | 39 50 |
| 12 | Fernando Alonso | European Minardi | +2 laps | 56 | 32 41 |
| 13 | Giancarlo Fisichella | Benetton Renault | +3 laps | 55 | 26 50 |
| 14 | Jenson Button | Benetton Renault | Electrical | 52 | 18 32 |
| Ret | Juan Pablo Montoya | BMW Williams | Engine | 40 | |
| Ret | Jarno Trulli | Jordan Honda | Engine | 38 | 33 |
| Ret | Mika Häkkinen | McLaren Mercedes | Front suspension | 25 | |
| Ret | Ralf Schumacher | BMW Williams | Collision | 4 | |
| Ret | Jacques Villeneuve | BAR Honda | Collision | 4 | |
| Ret | Tarso Marques | European Minardi | Battery | 3 | |
| Ret | Enrique Bernoldi | Arrows Asiatech | Spin | 2 | |
| Ret | Gaston Mazzacane | Prost Acer | Brakes | 0 | |

*Conditions: Dry and sunny.*

## RACE SPEED TRAP TIMES

| | | |
|---|---|---|
| 1 | Montoya | 194.3mph |
| 2 | Alesi | 193.1mph |
| 3 | Coulthard | 193.0mph |
| 4 | Frentzen | 192.0mph |
| 5 | Verstappen | 191.6mph |
| 6 | Häkkinen | 191.5mph |
| 7 | M Schumacher | 190.5mph |
| 8 | Irvine | 190.3mph |
| 9 | Heidfeld | 190.3mph |
| 10 | Räikkönen | 190.0mph |
| 11 | Trulli | 189.8mph |
| 12 | Barrichello | 189.6mph |
| 13 | R Schumacher | 189.5mph |
| 14 | Panis | 189.0mph |
| 15 | Burti | 188.3mph |
| 16 | Alonso | 187.3mph |
| 17 | Bernoldi | 186.0mph |
| 18 | Fisichella | 184.6mph |
| 19 | Button | 184.4mph |
| 20 | Villeneuve | 183.3mph |
| 21 | Marques | 178.3mph |
| 22 | Mazzacane | 137.3mph |

## DRIVER POINTS

| | | |
|---|---|---|
| 1 | Michael Schumacher | 10 |
| 2 | David Coulthard | 6 |
| 3 | Rubens Barrichello | 4 |
| 4 | Nick Heidfeld | 3 |
| 5 | Heinz-Harald Frentzen | 2 |
| 6 | Kimi Räikkönen | 1 |
| 7 | Olivier Panis | 0 |
| 8 | Luciano Burti | 0 |
| 9 | Jean Alesi | 0 |
| 10 | Jos Verstappen | 0 |
| 11 | Eddie Irvine | 0 |
| 12 | Fernando Alonso | 0 |
| 13 | Giancarlo Fisichella | 0 |
| 14 | Jenson Button | 0 |
| = | Juan Pablo Montoya | 0 |
| = | Jarno Trulli | 0 |
| = | Mika Häkkinen | 0 |
| = | Ralf Schumacher | 0 |
| = | Jacques Villeneuve | 0 |
| = | Tarso Marques | 0 |
| = | Enrique Bernoldi | 0 |
| = | Gaston Mazzacane | 0 |

## CONSTRUCTOR POINTS

| | | |
|---|---|---|
| 1 | Scuderia Ferrari-Marlboro | 14 |
| 2 | West McLaren Mercedes | 6 |
| 3 | Red Bull Sauber Petronas | 4 |
| 4 | Benson & Hedges Jordan Honda | 2 |
| 5 | Lucky Strike Reynard BAR Honda | 0 |
| 6 | Jaguar Racing | 0 |
| 7 | Prost Acer | 0 |
| 8 | Orange Arrows Asiatech | 0 |
| 9 | European Minardi F1 | 0 |
| 10 | Mild Seven Benetton Renault | 0 |
| 11 | BMW Williams F1 | 0 |

## PITSTOP TIMES (from pitlane entrance to exit)

| | | | | |
|---|---|---|---|---|
| Fastest pitstop: | Fisichella | Benetton Renault | 25.972s | Lap 50 |
| Slowest pitstop: | Irvine | Jaguar Racing | 32.568s | Lap 17 |
| Most pitstops: | Five drivers | Two stops | | |

## PENALTIES AND FINES

| DRIVER | WHEN | PENALTY | REASON |
|---|---|---|---|
| Jenson Button | Race | 10 seconds | Receiving assistance on the starting grid |
| Fernando Alonso | Race | 10 seconds | Speeding in the pitlane |
| Olivier Panis | Post-race | 25 seconds | Overtaking under yellow flags |
| Jos Verstappen | Post-race | 25 seconds | Overtaking under yellow flags |

## LAP LEADERS

| | |
|---|---|
| Michael Schumacher | 1-36: 41-58 |
| David Coulthard | 37-40 |
| Total laps led: M Schumacher 54; Coulthard 4 | |

## TEMPERATURES

| | | |
|---|---|---|
| Friday: | Air: 21-22°C | Track: 26-28°C |
| Saturday: | Air: 21°C | Track: 30-32°C |
| Sunday: | Air: 23°C | Track: 28°C |

## WARM-UP

### SUNDAY 4TH MARCH 2001, 9.30AM-10AM

| | | |
|---|---|---|
| 1 | Coulthard | 1m 30.099s |
| 2 | Häkkinen | 1m 30.152s |
| 3 | Verstappen | 1m 30.396s |
| 4 | Montoya | 1m 30.559s |
| 5 | Panis | 1m 30.584s |
| 6 | M.Schumacher | 1m 30.839s |
| 7 | Heidfeld | 1m 30.966s |
| 8 | Irvine | 1m 31.061s |
| 9 | Barrichello | 1m 31.450s |
| 10 | Frentzen | 1m 31.566s |
| 11 | Räikkönen | 1m 31.665s |
| 12 | Trulli | 1m 31.811s |
| 13 | Bernoldi | 1m 32.106s |
| 14 | Villeneuve | 1m 32.108s |
| 15 | R.Schumacher | 1m 32.687s |
| 16 | Alonso | 1m 33.717s |
| 17 | Mazzacane | 1m 33.747s |
| 18 | Burti | 1m 33.772s |
| 19 | Alesi | 1m 34.421s |
| 20 | Button | 1m 34.554s |
| 21 | Fisichella | 1m 34.572s |
| 22 | Marques | 1m 35.514s |

L Burti 21

F Alonso 19

G Fisichella 17

J Verstappen 15

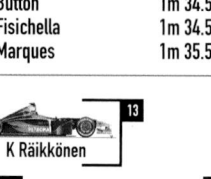
K Räikkönen 13

T Marques 22

G Mazzacane 20

E Bernoldi 18

J Button 16

J Alesi 14

E Irvine 12

## AUSTRALIAN GRAND PRIX RACE ENTRY

| | DRIVER | TEAM | CHASSIS/ENGINE |
|---|---|---|---|
| 1 | Michael Schumacher | Scuderia Ferrari Marlboro | Ferrari F2001 |
| 2 | Rubens Barrichello | Scuderia Ferrari Marlboro | Ferrari F2001 |
| 3 | Mika Häkkinen | West McLaren Mercedes | McLaren Mercedes MP4-16 |
| 4 | David Coulthard | West McLaren Mercedes | McLaren Mercedes MP4-16 |
| 5 | Ralf Schumacher | BMW Williams F1 Team | BMW Williams FW23 |
| 6 | Juan Pablo Montoya | BMW Williams F1 Team | BMW Williams FW23 |
| 7 | Giancarlo Fisichella | Mild Seven Benetton Renault | Benetton Renault B201 |
| 8 | Jenson Button | Mild Seven Benetton Renault | Benetton Renault B201 |
| 9 | Olivier Panis | Lucky Strike BAR Honda | BAR Honda B003 |
| 10 | Jacques Villeneuve | Lucky Strike BAR Honda | BAR Honda B003 |
| 11 | Heinz-Harald Frentzen | Benson & Hedges Jordan Honda | Jordan Honda EJ11 |
| 12 | Jarno Trulli | Benson & Hedges Jordan Honda | Jordan Honda EJ11 |
| 14 | Jos Verstappen | Orange Arrows Asiatech | Arrows Asiatech A22 |
| 15 | Enrique Bernoldi | Orange Arrows Asiatech | Arrows Asiatech A22 |
| 16 | Nick Heidfeld | Red Bull Sauber Petronas | Sauber Petronas C20 |
| 17 | Kimi Räikkönen | Red Bull Sauber Petronas | Sauber Petronas C20 |
| 18 | Eddie Irvine | Jaguar Racing | Jaguar Cosworth R2 |
| 19 | Luciano Burti | Jaguar Racing | Jaguar Cosworth R2 |
| 20 | Tarso Marques | European Minardi | Minardi European PS01 |
| 21 | Fernando Alonso | European Minardi | Minardi European PS01 |
| 22 | Jean Alesi | Prost Grand Prix | Prost ACER AP04 |
| 23 | Gaston Mazzacane | Prost Grand Prix | Prost ACER AP04 |

It was a sombre podium following the death of marshal Graham Beveridge during the race.

## FASTEST SECTOR TIMES IN QUALIFYING *Ideal lap time: 1m 26.729s (diff. from pole: 0.163s)*

| | SECTOR 1 | SECS | | SECTOR 2 | SECS | | SECTOR 3 | SECS |
|---|---|---|---|---|---|---|---|---|
| 1 | Barrichello | 28.914 | 1 | R Schumacher | 23.200 | 1 | M Schumacher | 34.615 |
| 2 | Häkkinen | 28.957 | 2 | Häkkinen | 23.244 | 2 | Barrichello | 34.782 |
| 3 | M Schumacher | 29.003 | 3 | M Schumacher | 23.274 | 3 | Häkkinen | 34.988 |
| 4 | Frentzen | 29.045 | 4 | Montoya | 23.353 | 4 | Frentzen | 35.174 |
| 5 | R Schumacher | 29.071 | 5 | Coulthard | 23.357 | 5 | Coulthard | 35.273 |
| 6 | Coulthard | 29.276 | 6 | Irvine | 23.405 | 6 | Trulli | 35.315 |
| 7 | Villeneuve | 29.300 | 7 | Frentzen | 23.439 | 7 | Alesi | 35.324 |
| 8 | Räikkönen | 29.309 | 8 | Barrichello | 23.508 | 8 | R Schumacher | 35.398 |
| 9 | Trulli | 29.338 | 9 | Trulli | 23.546 | 9 | Heidfeld | 35.425 |
| 10 | Heidfeld | 29.391 | 10 | Villeneuve | 23.585 | 10 | Panis | 35.516 |
| 11 | Panis | 29.409 | 11 | Panis | 23.593 | 11 | Villeneuve | 35.550 |
| 12 | Montoya | 29.503 | 12 | Räikkönen | 23.611 | 12 | Räikkönen | 35.657 |
| 13 | Irvine | 29.771 | 13 | Alesi | 23.634 | 13 | Irvine | 35.789 |
| 14 | Alesi | 29.798 | 14 | Heidfeld | 23.667 | 14 | Montoya | 35.796 |
| 15 | Verstappen | 29.924 | 15 | Verstappen | 23.867 | 15 | Verstappen | 36.076 |
| 16 | Button | 29.960 | 16 | Burti | 23.837 | 16 | Button | 36.095 |
| 17 | Fisichella | 29.978 | 17 | Mazzacane | 23.903 | 17 | Alonso | 36.147 |
| 18 | Alonso | 30.040 | 18 | Bernoldi | 23.957 | 18 | Fisichella | 36.172 |
| 19 | Marques | 30.125 | 19 | Button | 23.980 | 19 | Bernoldi | 36.339 |
| 20 | Bernoldi | 30.148 | 20 | Alonso | 23.981 | 20 | Mazzacane | 36.573 |
| 21 | Mazzacane | 30.251 | 21 | Fisichella | 24.063 | 21 | Marques | 36.460 |
| 22 | Burti | 30.509 | 22 | Marques | 24.643 | 22 | Burti | 36.632 |

## QUALIFYING: SATURDAY 3RD MARCH 2001, 1PM–2PM *107 per cent time: 1'm 32.974s

| | DRIVER | TEAM | TIME | GAP | LAPS |
|---|---|---|---|---|---|
| 1 | Michael Schumacher | Ferrari | 1m 26.892s | 0.000 | 10 |
| 2 | Rubens Barrichello | Ferrari | 1m 27.263s | +0'00.371s | 11 |
| 3 | Mika Häkkinen | McLaren Mercedes | 1m 27.461s | +0'00.569s | 12 |
| 4 | Heinz-Harald Frentzen | Jordan Honda | 1m 27.658s | +0'00.766s | 10 |
| 5 | Ralf Schumacher | BMW Williams | 1m 27.719s | +0'00.827s | 12 |
| 6 | David Coulthard | McLaren Mercedes | 1m 28.010s | +0'01.118s | 12 |
| 7 | Jarno Trulli | Jordan Honda | 1m 28.377s | +0'01.485s | 11 |
| 8 | Jacques Villeneuve | BAR Honda | 1m 28.435s | +0'01.543s | 11 |
| 9 | Olivier Panis | BAR Honda | 1m 28.518s | +0'01.626s | 11 |
| 10 | Nick Heidfeld | Sauber Petronas | 1m 28.615s | +0'01.723s | 11 |
| 11 | Juan Pablo Montoya | BMW Williams | 1m 28.738s | +0'01.846s | 11 |
| 12 | Eddie Irvine | Jaguar Racing | 1m 28.965s | +0'02.073s | 10 |
| 13 | Kimi Räikkönen | Sauber Petronas | 1m 28.993s | +0'02.101s | 12 |
| 14 | Jean Alesi | Prost Acer | 1m 29.893s | +0'03.001s | 11 |
| 15 | Jos Verstappen | Arrows Asiatech | 1m 29.934s | +0'03.042s | 11 |
| 16 | Jenson Button | Benetton Renault | 1m 30.035s | +0'03.143s | 10 |
| 17 | Giancarlo Fisichella | Benetton Renault | 1m 30.209s | +0'03.317s | 11 |
| 18 | Enrique Bernoldi | Arrows Asiatech | 1m 30.520s | +0'03.628s | 12 |
| 19 | Fernando Alonso | European Minardi | 1m 30.657s | +0'03.765s | 12 |
| 20 | Gaston Mazzacane | Prost Acer | 1m 30.798s | +0'03.906s | 12 |
| 21 | Luciano Burti | Jaguar Racing | 1m 30.978s | +0'04.086s | 7 |
| 22 | Tarso Marques | European Minardi | 1m 33.228s | +0'06.336s | 11 |

*Stewards' decision: Tarso Marques did not qualify to start the race under FIA rules. However, he was allowed to start the race at the discretion of the stewards.*

## PRACTICE SESSION ONE
### FRIDAY 2ND MARCH 2001, 11AM–12PM

| | | |
|---|---|---|
| 1 | Barrichello | 1m 29.056s |
| 2 | M Schumacher | 1m 29.368s |
| 3 | Häkkinen | 1m 30.037s |
| 4 | Coulthard | 1m 30.052s |
| 5 | R Schumacher | 1m 31.352s |
| 6 | Verstappen | 1m 31.830s |
| 7 | Frentzen | 1m 31.908s |
| 8 | Montoya | 1m 32.287s |
| 9 | Heidfeld | 1m 32.329s |
| 10 | Panis | 1m 32.330s |
| 11 | Trulli | 1m 32.347s |
| 12 | Räikkönen | 1m 33.369s |
| 13 | Burti | 1m 33.471s |
| 14 | Irvine | 1m 33.969s |
| 15 | Button | 1m 34.522s |
| 16 | Alonso | 1m 34.829s |
| 17 | Fisichella | 1m 34.892s |
| 18 | Mazzacane | 1m 34.941s |
| 19 | Bernoldi | 1m 35.752s |
| 20 | Marques | 1m 36.463s |
| 21 | Villeneuve | 1m 38.349s |
| 22 | Alesi | 1m 46.977s |

## PRACTICE SESSION TWO
### FRIDAY 2ND MARCH 2001, 1PM–2PM

| | | |
|---|---|---|
| 1 | Barrichello | 1m 28.965s |
| 2 | Trulli | 1m 29.267s |
| 3 | M Schumacher | 1m 29.284s |
| 4 | Coulthard | 1m 29.324s |
| 5 | Häkkinen | 1m 29.799s |
| 6 | R Schumacher | 1m 30.277s |
| 7 | Heidfeld | 1m 30.345s |
| 8 | Frentzen | 1m 30.802s |
| 9 | Alesi | 1m 31.089s |
| 10 | Panis | 1m 31.166s |
| 11 | Räikkönen | 1m 31.453s |
| 12 | Villeneuve | 1m 31.559s |
| 13 | Irvine | 1m 31.573s |
| 14 | Verstappen | 1m 31.669s |
| 15 | Montoya | 1m 31.721s |
| 16 | Fisichella | 1m 32.475s |
| 17 | Alonso | 1m 32.587s |
| 18 | Burti | 1m 33.011s |
| 19 | Mazzacane | 1m 33.153s |
| 20 | Bernoldi | 1m 33.203s |
| 21 | Button | 1m 33.403s |
| 22 | Marques | 1m 36.463s |

## PRACTICE SESSION THREE
### SATURDAY 3RD MARCH 2001, 9AM–9.45AM

| | | |
|---|---|---|
| 1 | M Schumacher | 1m 28.134s |
| 2 | Coulthard | 1m 28.852s |
| 3 | Häkkinen | 1m 29.231s |
| 4 | Trulli | 1m 29.459s |
| 5 | Villeneuve | 1m 29.465s |
| 6 | Panis | 1m 29.600s |
| 7 | Frentzen | 1m 29.868s |
| 8 | Barrichello | 1m 29.945s |
| 9 | Pablo Montoya | 1m 30.188s |
| 10 | Irvine | 1m 30.190s |
| 11 | R Schumacher | 1m 30.208s |
| 12 | Heidfeld | 1m 30.360s |
| 13 | Verstappen | 1m 31.590s |
| 14 | Bernoldi | 1m 31.599s |
| 15 | Alesi | 1m 32.113s |
| 16 | Fisichella | 1m 32.130s |
| 17 | Burti | 1m 32.274s |
| 18 | Alonso | 1m 32.350s |
| 19 | Mazzacane | 1m 34.431s |
| 20 | Marques | 1m 35.028s |
| 21 | Button | 1m 57.479s |
| 22 | Räikkönen | 13m 51.787s |

## PRACTICE SESSION FOUR
### SATURDAY 3RD MARCH 2001, 10.15AM–11AM

| | | |
|---|---|---|
| 1 | Coulthard | 1m 27.540s |
| 2 | M Schumacher | 1m 27.561s |
| 3 | Häkkinen | 1m 27.775s |
| 4 | Frentzen | 1m 27.940s |
| 5 | Trulli | 1m 28.193s |
| 6 | R Schumacher | 1m 28.666s |
| 7 | Panis | 1m 28.677s |
| 8 | Räikkönen | 1m 28.851s |
| 9 | Irvine | 1m 28.861s |
| 10 | Heidfeld | 1m 28.895s |
| 11 | Villeneuve | 1m 28.962s |
| 12 | Montoya | 1m 29.184s |
| 13 | Barrichello | 1m 29.945s |
| 14 | Alesi | 1m 29.981s |
| 15 | Alonso | 1m 30.360s |
| 16 | Fisichella | 1m 30.549s |
| 17 | Burti | 1m 30.578s |
| 18 | Bernoldi | 1m 30.782s |
| 19 | Button | 1m 30.893s |
| 20 | Verstappen | 1m 31.590s |
| 21 | Mazzacane | 1m 34.431s |
| 22 | Marques | 1m 34.491s |

JP Montoya 11

O Panis 9

J Trulli 7

R Schumacher 5

M Häkkinen 3

M Schumacher 1

N Heidfeld 10

J Villeneuve 8

D Coulthard 6

HH Frentzen 4

R Barrichello 2

## MELBOURNE LAP-BY-LAP REPORT

**PRE-START** In the run-up to the race there was trouble for two British drivers – Jenson Button and Eddie Irvine – with both having to switch to their spare cars. Button's exchange resulted in a penalty, as his mechanics were still working on his car within 15 seconds of the start of the parade lap.

**START** When the lights went out, Michael Schumacher made a good start but Rubens Barrichello was slower away and Mika Häkkinen was soon past the second Ferrari. Behind them, David Coulthard was very quick away and tried to pass Heinz-Harald Frentzen. The two touched wheels and Coulthard had to back off, as Ralf Schumacher was on his outside. Into the first corner Michael Schumacher led Häkkinen, Frentzen, Ralf Schumacher, Barrichello, Jarno Trulli and the delayed Coulthard. Juan Pablo Montoya was briefly among the leaders but arrived too quickly in Turn One and lost several places as he bounced across the grass. He rejoined but at Turn Three had another incident while trying to hold off Eddie Irvine. Irvine spun down to 21st position. At the back, Gaston Mazzacane retired with brake problems.

**LAP 2** Michael Schumacher and Mika Häkkinen duelled at the front while third-placed Frentzen was unable to keep up. At Turn One Ralf Schumacher ran wide and dropped behind Barrichello, Trulli and Coulthard. He then came under pressure from eighth-placed Jacques Villeneuve. Further around the lap Barrichello pulled off an aggressive pass on Trulli to snatch fifth. There was also action in the midfield when Enrique Bernoldi, benefiting from a light fuel load in his Arrows, overtook Luciano Burti for 17th place.

**LAP 3** Barrichello challenged Frentzen for third place but the move went wrong and the two cars collided. This sent Frentzen spinning off but he managed to rejoin, albeit annoyed, in 16th position. Barrichello's Ferrari began to handle badly afterwards. Ninth-placed Nick Heidfeld backed off for the yellow flags at the scene of the incident and was overtaken by Olivier Panis and Jos Verstappen. Both men were later penalised for the move. Bernoldi spun out of 17th position and retired.

**LAP 4** Tarso Marques retired, suffering from electrical gremlins.

**LAP 5** The battle at the front continued, Schumacher and Häkkinen fighting over hundredths of a second. Third-placed Barrichello fell to over four seconds behind Häkkinen with Coulthard, Trulli and then the duelling Ralf Schumacher and Villeneuve. At Turn Three Villeneuve missed his braking point, ran into the back of Schumacher and was launched into a horrific accident. Both drivers were unhurt but a marshal was hit by one of Villeneuve's wheels and killed. Several spectators also suffered minor injuries when hit by wreckage from the BAR Honda. The safety car was sent out and the race neutralised.

**LAPS 6-15** The field held station behind the safety car.

**LAP 14** The order was unchanged behind the safety car, Michael Schumacher leading Häkkinen, Barrichello, Coulthard, Trulli and Panis. Verstappen dived into the pits to minimise loss of time on his two-stop strategy. Heidfeld, Montoya, Giancarlo Fisichella and Button moved up to complete the top 10. Verstappen rejoined in last place.

**LAP 16** Schumacher controlled the restart neatly and left Häkkinen a second behind by the end of the lap. Further back, Montoya overtook Fisichella for eighth place while Jean Alesi made a mistake and dropped from 12th to 14th. At the back, Irvine overtook Fernando Alonso to move up to 15th. Only 17 cars were still running.

**LAP 17** Schumacher set the first of a string of fastest laps in an effort to get away from Häkkinen. Eleventh-placed Kimi Räikkönen overtook Button to move into the top 10 on his Formula One debut.

**LAP 18** Button went into the pits for his 10-second penalty imposed after the team's infringement of the rules before the start of the parade lap. He dropped to the back of the field.

**LAP 19** Schumacher's pressure began to pay off as Häkkinen lost three-10ths of a second on one lap.

**LAP 21** Having posted five consecutive fastest laps, Schumacher dropped Häkkinen and the gap stretched out to 2.4 seconds. The rest of the field remained static, although Räikkönen began to challenge Fisichella for ninth place.

**LAP 22** Schumacher carved a further seven-10ths' lead over Häkkinen.

**LAP 25** The gap between Schumacher and Häkkinen increased to nearly five seconds. Fisichella was no longer able to hold off Räikkönen and dropped behind the Finn and Frentzen.

**LAP 26** Häkkinen crashed heavily at the end of the back straight after a failure of his McLaren's right front suspension. He ran into a tyre barrier at high speed and later visited the medical centre for a check-up because he had received a bang on the head from the tyre barrier. Schumacher was left with a 10-second lead. Fisichella disappeared into the pits with a loss of power caused by a broken exhaust. He rejoined at the tail end of the field.

**LAP 32** Fourth-placed Trulli suffered a loss of power from his Honda V10 and dropped behind Panis. Alonso came in for his mid-race pitstop and Button also pitted with a rough-sounding engine.

**LAP 33** Trulli pitted. He rejoined but retired after five more laps.

**LAP 34** The gap between Schumacher and Barrichello remained at 10 seconds but Barrichello stumbled slightly while lapping Alonso and came under pressure from Coulthard, who passed the Ferrari with an elegant outside manoeuvre at Turn Three.

**LAP 35** Alesi stopped for fuel and tyres but retained his 12th place.

**LAP 36** Räikkönen and Burti both took to the pits for their mid-race stops. They retained ninth and 11th positions respectively.

**LAP 37** The leader, Michael Schumacher, dived into the pits, leaving Coulthard to take over the lead with Barrichello second. Schumacher rejoined in third place ahead of Panis. Further back, Heidfeld and Frentzen pitted from fifth and seventh positions. Heidfeld rejoined in sixth and Frentzen in eighth place.

**LAP 38** Verstappen called into the pits for a second time, dropping back from 10th place to 12th.

**LAP 39** Coulthard was pushing hard to widen the gap from Schumacher. Barrichello dived into the pits and emerged in fourth, allowing Panis to run briefly in third position. Eddie Irvine, running in seventh place, pitted and dropped to eighth.

**LAP 40** Panis pitted and dropped from third to fifth.

**LAP 41** Coulthard pitted, allowing Schumacher back into the lead. Coulthard rejoined in second, having shaved five seconds off Schumacher's lead. Halfway around the lap third-placed Montoya, who was due to stop, came to a smoky halt with an oil pipe failure. Barrichello was promoted back to third place with Panis fourth, Heidfeld fifth and Frentzen sixth. At the tail end of the field Alonso pitted to take a 10-second penalty given for speeding in the pitlane.

**LAP 48** Tenth-placed Alesi was overtaken by Verstappen.

**LAP 50** Irvine pitted unexpectedly because of a fuel feed problem that meant he needed extra fuel in order to be able to finish the race. He dropped from eighth position to 11th.

**LAP 53** Button retired when his Renault engine lost power.

**LAP 56** Schumacher was taking it easy and the gap behind him to Coulthard came down to five seconds. Further back, Heidfeld came under strong pressure from Frentzen for fifth place.

**LAP 58** Coulthard closed to within 1.7 seconds of Schumacher at the flag. Barrichello was third with Panis fourth, Heidfeld fifth and Frentzen sixth. Räikkönen was seventh, the last man on the same lap as the leaders. Burti, Verstappen, Alesi and Irvine finished a lap down with Alonso two laps down and Fisichella three laps behind.

**POST-RACE** Both Panis and Verstappen were penalised 25 seconds for overtaking under yellow flags. This dropped Panis from fourth to seventh, promoting Räikkönen to sixth and giving him a point on his Formula One debut. Verstappen dropped from ninth to 10th.

# Malaysian Grand Prix

**16th–18th March 2001**  LAPS: 55  LENGTH OF LAP: 3.344 miles

EASTERN PROMISE  Rubens Barrichello's Ferrari glides past Sepang's distinctive hibiscus flower grandstands as the Brazilian prepares and perfects the car that will take him to an impressive and well-earned second place in the Malaysian Grand Prix.  PHOTOGRAPH BY CLEMENT MARIN

# When chaos rained

Rain wreaked havoc at the start of the Malaysian Grand Prix – in the early stages the pitlane was busier than the track itself and at one point it looked like Ferrari might be out of the race. But less than two hours after both cars had been heading for the barriers, Schumacher and Barrichello worked their magic to make it a convincing one-two victory.

There were two distinct opinions in the aftermath of the 2001 Malaysian Grand Prix: either that it was one of the greatest drives by the greatest driver of his age, or that maybe where there was smoke over the issue of traction control there might be some fire. Whether or not Michael Schumacher's drive from disaster to crushing domination was one of the great drives of our time or a blatant fraud divided the paddock. For only this reason could the reintroduction of driver aids across the board be not only accepted but actively looked forward to. However, the rumours were swiftly muffled, as all conversation was cut to a minimum by the oppressive heat and humidity of Sepang in its late summer.

Sunday 18th March 2001 dawned in the last throes of a mini monsoon. It had cleared by the time the grid lined up but there were clouds on the horizon. Michael Schumacher sat on pole in his T-Car. At the green flag Heinz-Harald Frentzen fell back through the field as he struggled with a misfire. As the lights went on Giancarlo Fisichella was hopelessly out of position and took it upon himself to cross back to his original grid spot and sit perpendicular across the track. Frentzen arrived just in time to see the lights turn red. The second attempt saw Juan Pablo Montoya's Williams stranded and the Colombian was forced to run for the spare. Had Fisichella found last place on the grid straight away it would all have come to nought. As it was Montoya made it to the end of the pitlane before all the starting lights were on, and was cleared to go.

Michael Schumacher pounces on David Coulthard to snatch the lead on lap 16.

After as much excitement in a couple of warm-up laps as had been seen in many of last year's entire races, Ferrari's Michael Schumacher shot into the lead. Brother Ralf attempted to close the door on Schumacher senior's team-mate Rubens Barrichello and spun, causing a few wobbly moments when other drivers found themselves confronted with a Schumacher staring back at them.

Almost immediately the second lap had begun the first few drops of rain started to fall. The Ferraris were aware of the rain but not of the oil spilt by Olivier Panis's ailing BAR Honda and speared off the road in unison. Somehow they narrowly avoided each other and the barriers. Barrichello regained the track before Schumacher as the drizzle swelled into another mini monsoon that swamped the circuit.

Chaos reigned. Before the safety car was called out to lead the fifth lap, four cars had been accounted for and 11 hurtled off the circuit. The pitlane was a crowded place, nowhere more so than the Ferrari pit, where Barrichello arrived first and Schumacher sat impatiently behind for a full 72 seconds as detritus was cleared from every nook and cranny. They rejoined in 10th and 11th positions a long, long way behind the safety car. The Ferrari duo opted for intermediate tyres, although everyone else played safe with full wets and felt glad to have done so. Coulthard led Frentzen who in turn led Verstappen, who six laps and two starts before had been sitting on the grid in a lowly 18th.

They think it's all over – but despite this excursion and a subsequent lengthy pitstop, the Ferrari pair managed to recover and score a one-two victory.

Jacques Villeneuve again failed to score, his BAR Honda sliding off on lap four.

Follow my leader: Tarso Marques made a stronger showing against rookie Minardi team-mate Fernando Alonso, seen following him in the mist and spray.

Fast recovering from his painfully slow pitstop, Barrichello slips ahead of Frentzen.

Schumacher got the drop at the start, but within four laps the heavens opened and the safety car had to be deployed for the second consecutive Grand Prix.

The safety car stayed out until lap 10, allowing the 16 surviving cars to bunch up and a good deal of the standing water to be displaced. As David Coulthard set about establishing his lead, Jos Verstappen surprised Heinz-Harald Frentzen and accelerated into second place. The two Ferraris soon devoured Jean Alesi and were on unbelievable form. Michael Schumacher trailed Rubens Barrichello as they both charged up behind Jarno Trulli's Jordan. Barrichello made a go inside, was blocked and then suddenly found Schumacher barging past the two of them. As they crossed the line Schumacher's time was a second quicker than David Coulthard in the lead.

On the next lap Michael Schumacher passed Heinz-Harald Frentzen, his brother Ralf and McLaren's Mika Häkkinen. On the next he closed in on Jos Verstappen, but struggled to find a way by. Finally, on lap 15, the job was done – Schumacher crossed the line, then swept imperiously round the outside of David Coulthard at Turn One to assume the lead as Rubens Barrichello went through to second.

The race was effectively over from that point. The remainder failed to live up to the excitement of the earlier laps. Jos Verstappen pitted three times in his Arrows Asiatech to get to the end of the race in only seventh position. Ferrari took a convincing one-two less than two hours after both cars had been heading for the barriers. With his sixth win in a row Michael Schumacher looked ominously invincible.

# Malaysian Grand Prix Race Statistics

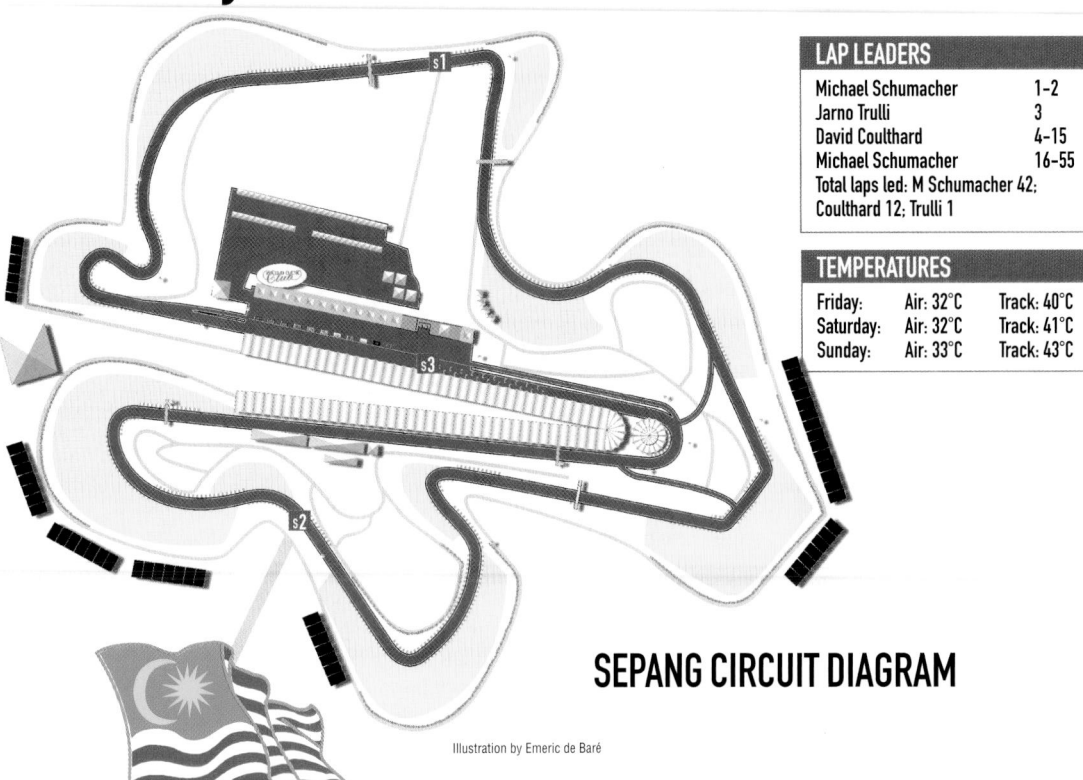

**SEPANG CIRCUIT DIAGRAM**

Illustration by Emeric de Baré

## LAP LEADERS

| Driver | Laps |
|---|---|
| Michael Schumacher | 1–2 |
| Jarno Trulli | 3 |
| David Coulthard | 4–15 |
| Michael Schumacher | 16–55 |

Total laps led: M Schumacher 42; Coulthard 12; Trulli 1

## TEMPERATURES

| | | |
|---|---|---|
| Friday: | Air: 32°C | Track: 40°C |
| Saturday: | Air: 32°C | Track: 41°C |
| Sunday: | Air: 33°C | Track: 43°C |

## FASTEST LAPS

| | DRIVER | TIME | LAP |
|---|---|---|---|
| 1 | Häkkinen | 1m 40.962s | 48 |
| 2 | R Schumacher | 1m 41.503s | 54 |
| 3 | M Schumacher | 1m 41.833s | 2 |
| 4 | Barrichello | 1m 42.037s | 2 |
| 5 | Frentzen | 1m 42.119s | 50 |
| 6 | Coulthard | 1m 42.839s | 47 |
| 7 | Verstappen | 1m 43.029s | 55 |
| 8 | Villeneuve | 1m 43.470s | 2 |
| 9 | Trulli | 1m 43.559s | 52 |
| 10 | Burti | 1m 43.697s | 52 |
| 11 | Alesi | 1m 43.853s | 53 |
| 12 | Montoya | 1m 43.926s | 2 |
| 13 | Mazzacane | 1m 43.991s | 53 |
| 14 | Button | 1m 44.891s | 52 |
| 15 | Heidfeld | 1m 45.328s | 2 |
| 16 | Alonso | 1m 45.585s | 50 |
| 17 | Marques | 1m 46.016s | 50 |
| 18 | Fisichella | 1m 46.982s | 2 |
| 19 | Bernoldi | 1m 47.294s | 2 |
| 20 | Irvine | 1m 51.532s | 2 |
| 21 | Panis | 1m 54.538s | 1 |
| | Räikkönen | No lap completed | |

## RACE SPEED TRAP TIMES

| | | |
|---|---|---|
| 1 | Verstappen | 194.9mph |
| 2 | R Schumacher | 194.6mph |
| 3 | Häkkinen | 193.4mph |
| 4 | Trulli | 191.8mph |
| 5 | Coulthard | 191.3mph |
| 6 | Frentzen | 190.1mph |
| 7 | Burti | 190.0mph |
| 8 | Barrichello | 189.9mph |
| 9 | Alonso | 189.8mph |
| 10 | M Schumacher | 189.3mph |
| 11 | Marques | 187.8mph |
| 12 | Heidfeld | 187.3mph |
| = | Alesi | 187.3mph |
| 14 | Mazzacane | 186.3mph |
| 15 | Montoya | 186.0mph |
| 16 | Button | 184.1mph |
| 17 | Villeneuve | 184.0mph |
| 18 | Fisichella | 183.2mph |
| 19 | Panis | 178.6mph |
| 20 | Irvine | 177.7mph |
| 21 | Bernoldi | 159.3mph |
| | Räikkönen | No lap completed |

## WARM-UP

SUNDAY 18TH MARCH 2001, 9.30AM–10AM

| | | |
|---|---|---|
| 1 | Barrichello | 1m 49.763s |
| 2 | Coulthard | 1m 50.846s |
| 3 | Trulli | 1m 51.046s |
| 4 | Räikkönen | 1m 51.265s |
| 5 | Verstappen | 1m 51.508s |
| 6 | Frentzen | 1m 52.061s |
| 7 | M Schumacher | 1m 52.316s |
| 8 | Heidfeld | 1m 53.352s |
| 9 | Panis | 1m 53.470s |
| 10 | Villeneuve | 1m 53.482s |
| 11 | R Schumacher | 1m 55.109s |
| 12 | Montoya | 1m 55.278s |
| 13 | Häkkinen | 1m 57.064s |
| 14 | Alesi | 1m 57.832s |
| 15 | Irvine | 1m 58.322s |
| 16 | Mazzacane | 1m 58.416s |
| 17 | Fisichella | 1m 58.656s |
| 18 | Burti | 2m 01.120s |
| 19 | Bernoldi | 2m 01.630s |
| 20 | Alonso | 2m 01.771s |
| 21 | Marques | 2m 04.349s |
| 22 | Button | 2m 07.047s |

## DRIVER POINTS

| | | |
|---|---|---|
| 1 | Michael Schumacher | 20 |
| 2 | Rubens Barrichello | 10 |
| = | David Coulthard | 10 |
| 4 | Heinz-Harald Frentzen | 5 |
| 5 | Nick Heidfeld | 3 |
| 6 | Ralf Schumacher | 2 |
| 7 | Mika Häkkinen | 1 |
| = | Kimi Räikkönen | 1 |
| 9 | Jos Verstappen | 0 |
| 10 | Olivier Panis | 0 |
| 11 | Luciano Burti | 0 |
| 12 | Jarno Trulli | 0 |
| 13 | Jean Alesi | 0 |
| 14 | Jenson Button | 0 |
| 15 | Eddie Irvine | 0 |
| 16 | Fernando Alonso | 0 |
| 17 | Gaston Mazzacane | 0 |
| 18 | Giancarlo Fisichella | 0 |
| 19 | Tarso Marques | 0 |
| 20 | Enrique Bernoldi | 0 |
| = | Juan Pablo Montoya | 0 |
| = | Jacques Villeneuve | 0 |

## RACE: SUNDAY 18TH MARCH 2001, 3PM

| | DRIVER | CAR | TIME/RETIREMENT | LAPS | PITSTOP LAPS |
|---|---|---|---|---|---|
| 1 | Michael Schumacher | Ferrari | 1h 47m 34.801s | 55 | 4 30 |
| 2 | Rubens Barrichello | Ferrari | +23.660s | 55 | 4 21 41 |
| 3 | David Coulthard | McLaren Mercedes | +28.555s | 55 | 4 25 |
| 4 | Heinz-Harald Frentzen | Jordan Honda | +46.543s | 55 | 4 21 |
| 5 | Ralf Schumacher | BMW Williams | +48.233s | 55 | 4 18 38 |
| 6 | Mika Häkkinen | McLaren Mercedes | +48.606s | 55 | 4 18 40 |
| 7 | Jos Verstappen | Arrows Asiatech | +1m 21.560s | 55 | 4 22 43 |
| 8 | Jarno Trulli | Jordan Honda | +1 lap | 54 | 4 23 39 |
| 9 | Jean Alesi | Prost Acer | +1 lap | 54 | 4 23 |
| 10 | Luciano Burti | Jaguar Racing | +1 lap | 54 | 3 23 |
| 11 | Jenson Button | Benetton Renault | +2 laps | 53 | 3 23 |
| 12 | Gaston Mazzacane | Prost Acer | +2 laps | 53 | 4 24 34 |
| 13 | Fernando Alonso | European Minardi | +3 laps | 52 | 2 3 18 31 40 |
| 14 | Tarso Marques | European Minardi | +4 laps | 51 | 3 28 |
| Ret | Giancarlo Fisichella | Benetton Renault | Fuel pressure | 31 | 3 20 |
| Ret | Jacques Villeneuve | BAR Honda | Spin | 3 | |
| Ret | Nick Heidfeld | Sauber Petronas | Spin | 3 | |
| Ret | Enrique Bernoldi | Arrows Asiatech | Spin | 3 | |
| Ret | Juan Pablo Montoya | BMW Williams | Spin | 3 | |
| Ret | Eddie Irvine | Jaguar Racing | Water leak | 3 | |
| Ret | Olivier Panis | BAR Honda | Oil leak | 1 | |
| Ret | Kimi Räikkönen | Sauber Petronas | Transmission | 0 | |

Conditions: Wet.

## CONSTRUCTOR POINTS

| | | |
|---|---|---|
| 1 | Scuderia Ferrari-Marlboro | 30 |
| 2 | West McLaren Mercedes | 11 |
| 3 | Benson & Hedges Jordan Honda | 5 |
| 4 | Red Bull Sauber Petronas | 4 |
| 5 | BMW Williams F1 | 2 |
| 6 | Orange Arrows Asiatech | 0 |
| 7 | Lucky Strike Reynard BAR Honda | 0 |
| 8 | Jaguar Racing | 0 |
| 9 | Prost Acer | 0 |
| 10 | Mild Seven Benetton Renault | 0 |
| 11 | European Minardi F1 | 0 |

## PITSTOP TIMES (from pitlane entrance to exit)

| | | | | |
|---|---|---|---|---|
| Fastest pitstop: | Verstappen | Arrows Asiatech | 33.263s | Lap 43 |
| Slowest pitstop: | M Schumacher | Ferrari | 1m 56.461s | Lap 4 |
| Most pitstops: | Alonso | European Minardi | Five stops | |

## PENALTIES AND FINES

| DRIVER | WHEN | PENALTY | REASON |
|---|---|---|---|
| Olivier Panis | Friday | $2,250 | Exceeding speed limit |
| Olivier Panis | Saturday practice | $1,250 | Exceeding speed limit |
| Enrique Bernoldi | Qualifying | All times disallowed | Illegal front wing |
| Giancarlo Fisichella | Start | Put to back of grid | Incorrectly parked |

F Alonso 21

G Mazzacane 19

J Button 17

L Burti 15

J Alesi 13

E Bernoldi 22

T Marques 20

J Verstappen 18

G Fisichella 16

K Räikkönen 14

E Irvine 12

## MALAYSIAN GRAND PRIX RACE ENTRY

| | DRIVER | TEAM | CHASSIS/ENGINE |
|---|---|---|---|
| 1 | Michael Schumacher | Scuderia Ferrari Marlboro | Ferrari F2001 |
| 2 | Rubens Barrichello | Scuderia Ferrari Marlboro | Ferrari F2001 |
| 3 | Mika Häkkinen | West McLaren Mercedes | McLaren Mercedes MP4-16 |
| 4 | David Coulthard | West McLaren Mercedes | McLaren Mercedes MP4-16 |
| 5 | Ralf Schumacher | BMW Williams F1 Team | BMW Williams FW23 |
| 6 | Juan Pablo Montoya | BMW Williams F1 Team | BMW Williams FW23 |
| 7 | Giancarlo Fisichella | Mild Seven Benetton Renault | Benetton Renault B201 |
| 8 | Jenson Button | Mild Seven Benetton Renault | Benetton Renault B201 |
| 9 | Olivier Panis | Lucky Strike BAR Honda | BAR Honda B003 |
| 10 | Jacques Villeneuve | Lucky Strike BAR Honda | BAR Honda B003 |
| 11 | Heinz-Harald Frentzen | Benson & Hedges Jordan Honda | Jordan Honda EJ11 |
| 12 | Jarno Trulli | Benson & Hedges Jordan Honda | Jordan Honda EJ11 |
| 14 | Jos Verstappen | Orange Arrows Asiatech | Arrows Asiatech A22 |
| 15 | Enrique Bernoldi | Orange Arrows Asiatech | Arrows Asiatech A22 |
| 16 | Nick Heidfeld | Red Bull Sauber Petronas | Sauber Petronas C20 |
| 17 | Kimi Räikkönen | Red Bull Sauber Petronas | Sauber Petronas C20 |
| 18 | Eddie Irvine | Jaguar Racing | Jaguar Cosworth R2 |
| 19 | Luciano Burti | Jaguar Racing | Jaguar Cosworth R2 |
| 20 | Tarso Marques | European Minardi | Minardi European PS01 |
| 21 | Fernando Alonso | European Minardi | Minardi European PS01 |
| 22 | Jean Alesi | Prost Grand Prix | Prost ACER AP04 |
| 23 | Gaston Mazzacane | Prost Grand Prix | Prost ACER AP04 |

A one–two victory for Ferrari – the sixth win in a row for Michael Schumacher.

## QUALIFYING: SATURDAY 17TH MARCH 2001, 1PM–2PM  107 per cent time: 1m 41.885s

| | DRIVER | TEAM | TIME | GAP | LAPS |
|---|---|---|---|---|---|
| 1 | Michael Schumacher | Ferrari | 1m 35.220s | 0.000 | 12 |
| 2 | Rubens Barrichello | Ferrari | 1m 35.319s | +0.099s | 12 |
| 3 | Ralf Schumacher | BMW Williams | 1m 35.511s | +0.291s | 12 |
| 4 | Mika Häkkinen | McLaren Mercedes | 1m 36.040s | +0.820s | 11 |
| 5 | Jarno Trulli | Jordan Honda | 1m 36.180s | +0.960s | 11 |
| 6 | Juan Pablo Montoya | BMW Williams | 1m 36.218s | +0.998s | 11 |
| 7 | Jacques Villeneuve | BAR Honda | 1m 36.397s | +1.177s | 12 |
| 8 | David Coulthard | McLaren Mercedes | 1m 36.417s | +1.197s | 12 |
| 9 | Heinz-Harald Frentzen | McLaren Mercedes | 1m 36.578s | +1.358s | 11 |
| 10 | Olivier Panis | BAR Honda | 1m 36.681s | +1.461s | 12 |
| 11 | Nick Heidfeld | Sauber Petronas | 1m 36.913s | +1.693s | 12 |
| 12 | Eddie Irvine | Jaguar Racing | 1m 37.140s | +1.920s | 12 |
| 13 | Jean Alesi | Prost Acer | 1m 37.406s | +2.186s | 12 |
| 14 | Kimi Räikkönen | Sauber Petronas | 1m 37.728s | +2.508s | 9 |
| 15 | Luciano Burti | Jaguar Racing | 1m 38.035s | +2.815s | 12 |
| 16 | Giancarlo Fisichella | Benetton Renault | 1m 38.086s | +2.866s | 7 |
| 17 | Jenson Button | Benetton Renault | 1m 38.258s | +3.038s | 12 |
| 18 | Jos Verstappen | Arrows Asiatech | 1m 38.509s | +3.289s | 12 |
| 19 | Gaston Mazzacane | Prost Acer | 1m 39.006s | +3.786s | 12 |
| 20 | Tarso Marques | European Minardi | 1m 39.714s | +4.494s | 12 |
| 21 | Fernando Alonso | European Minardi | 1m 40.249s | +5.029s | 11 |
| 22 | Enrique Bernoldi | Arrows Asiatech | Times disallowed | | |

## FASTEST SECTOR TIMES IN QUALIFYING  Ideal lap time: 1m 35.105s (diff. from pole: 0.115s)

| | SECTOR 1 | SECS | | SECTOR 2 | SECS | | SECTOR 3 | SECS |
|---|---|---|---|---|---|---|---|---|
| 1 | R Schumacher | 24.402 | 1 | M Schumacher | 31.804 | 1 | Barrichello | 38.899 |
| 2 | M Schumacher | 24.475 | 2 | Barrichello | 31.843 | 2 | R Schumacher | 38.932 |
| 3 | Barrichello | 24.577 | 3 | Häkkinen | 32.026 | 3 | M Schumacher | 38.941 |
| 4 | Trulli | 24.595 | 4 | R Schumacher | 32.036 | 4 | Montoya | 39.076 |
| 5 | Coulthard | 24.623 | 5 | Montoya | 32.254 | 5 | Trulli | 39.096 |
| 6 | Villeneuve | 24.637 | 6 | Villeneuve | 32.443 | 6 | Coulthard | 39.150 |
| 7 | Häkkinen | 24.673 | 7 | Panis | 32.446 | 7 | Panis | 39.166 |
| 8 | Montoya | 24.687 | 8 | Coulthard | 32.462 | 8 | Frentzen | 39.194 |
| 9 | Panis | 24.705 | 9 | Frentzen | 32.463 | 9 | Häkkinen | 39.243 |
| 10 | Frentzen | 24.769 | 10 | Trulli | 32.489 | 10 | Villeneuve | 39.276 |
| 11 | Irvine | 24.985 | 11 | Heidfeld | 32.568 | 11 | Irvine | 39.283 |
| 12 | Alesi | 24.993 | 12 | Irvine | 32.657 | 12 | Heidfeld | 39.304 |
| 13 | Heidfeld | 25.017 | 13 | Alesi | 32.903 | 13 | Alesi | 39.510 |
| 14 | Burti | 25.059 | 14 | Räikkönen | 32.959 | 14 | Fisichella | 39.603 |
| 15 | Verstappen | 25.097 | 15 | Button | 33.050 | 15 | Räikkönen | 39.668 |
| 16 | Räikkönen | 25.101 | 16 | Fisichella | 33.138 | 16 | Burti | 39.763 |
| 17 | Mazzacane | 25.109 | 17 | Burti | 33.190 | 17 | Button | 39.825 |
| 18 | Bernoldi | 25.191 | 18 | Bernoldi | 33.350 | 18 | Verstappen | 39.913 |
| 19 | Fisichella | 25.211 | 19 | Verstappen | 33.376 | 19 | Bernoldi | 40.028 |
| 20 | Button | 25.252 | 20 | Mazzacane | 33.633 | 20 | Mazzacane | 40.264 |
| 21 | Marques | 25.539 | 21 | Marques | 33.653 | 21 | Marques | 40.522 |
| 22 | Alonso | 25.586 | 22 | Alonso | 33.862 | 22 | Alonso | 40.616 |

## PRACTICE SESSION ONE

FRIDAY 16TH MARCH 2001, 11AM–12PM

| | | |
|---|---|---|
| 1 | Barrichello | 1m 39.502s |
| 2 | M Schumacher | 1m 40.123s |
| 3 | Trulli | 1m 40.135s |
| 4 | Coulthard | 1m 40.490s |
| 5 | Irvine | 1m 41.000s |
| 6 | Frentzen | 1m 41.007s |
| 7 | Häkkinen | 1m 41.008s |
| 8 | Panis | 1m 41.063s |
| 9 | Burti | 1m 41.443s |
| 10 | Heidfeld | 1m 41.866s |
| 11 | Räikkönen | 1m 42.221s |
| 12 | Alesi | 1m 42.299s |
| 13 | Villeneuve | 1m 42.309s |
| 14 | R Schumacher | 1m 42.718s |
| 15 | Fisichella | 1m 43.045s |
| 16 | Marques | 1m 43.177s |
| 17 | Mazzacane | 1m 44.380s |
| 18 | Verstappen | 1m 45.175s |
| 19 | Bernoldi | 1m 46.627s |
| 20 | Button | 1m 48.547s |
| 21 | Alonso | 12m 44.956s |
| 22 | Montoya | No laps |

## PRACTICE SESSION TWO

FRIDAY 16TH MARCH 2001, 1PM–2PM

| | | |
|---|---|---|
| 1 | Trulli | 1m 38.846s |
| 2 | M Schumacher | 1m 38.929s |
| 3 | Barrichello | 1m 38.931s |
| 4 | Coulthard | 1m 39.300s |
| 5 | Irvine | 1m 39.520s |
| 6 | Häkkinen | 1m 39.861s |
| 7 | Frentzen | 1m 40.197s |
| 8 | Burti | 1m 40.211s |
| 9 | Panis | 1m 40.229s |
| 10 | R Schumacher | 1m 40.617s |
| 11 | Villeneuve | 1m 41.003s |
| 12 | Heidfeld | 1m 41.027s |
| 13 | Fisichella | 1m 41.375s |
| 14 | Räikkönen | 1m 41.592s |
| 15 | Verstappen | 1m 41.794s |
| 16 | Alesi | 1m 41.834s |
| 17 | Button | 1m 42.214s |
| 18 | Bernoldi | 1m 42.541s |
| 19 | Mazzacane | 1m 42.563s |
| 20 | Marques | 1m 42.872s |
| 21 | Alonso | 1m 43.107s |
| 22 | Montoya | 2m 13.188s |

## PRACTICE SESSION THREE

SATURDAY 17TH MARCH 2001, 9AM–9.45AM

| | | |
|---|---|---|
| 1 | Coulthard | 1m 36.814s |
| 2 | Barrichello | 1m 37.004s |
| 3 | M Schumacher | 1m 37.320s |
| 4 | Häkkinen | 1m 37.456s |
| 5 | R Schumacher | 1m 37.458s |
| 6 | Heidfeld | 1m 37.823s |
| 7 | Frentzen | 1m 37.839s |
| 8 | Montoya | 1m 37.918s |
| 9 | Panis | 1m 37.940s |
| 10 | Irvine | 1m 38.064s |
| 11 | Villeneuve | 1m 38.254s |
| 12 | Trulli | 1m 38.286s |
| 13 | Räikkönen | 1m 39.237s |
| 14 | Burti | 1m 39.268s |
| 15 | Verstappen | 1m 39.401s |
| 16 | Fisichella | 1m 39.999s |
| 17 | Bernoldi | 1m 40.081s |
| 18 | Mazzacane | 1m 40.543s |
| 19 | Alonso | 1m 40.667s |
| 20 | Alesi | 1m 40.759s |
| 21 | Button | 1m 41.630s |
| 22 | Marques | 1m 42.042s |

## PRACTICE SESSION FOUR

SATURDAY 17TH MARCH 2001, 10.15–11.00AM

| | | |
|---|---|---|
| 1 | Barrichello | 1m 36.188s |
| 2 | R Schumacher | 1m 36.475s |
| 3 | Häkkinen | 1m 36.519s |
| 4 | M Schumacher | 1m 36.548s |
| 5 | Coulthard | 1m 36.814s |
| 6 | Frentzen | 1m 37.030s |
| 7 | Trulli | 1m 37.231s |
| 8 | Irvine | 1m 37.360s |
| 9 | Panis | 1m 37.391s |
| 10 | Räikkönen | 1m 37.428s |
| 11 | Heidfeld | 1m 37.459s |
| 12 | Villeneuve | 1m 37.463s |
| 13 | Montoya | 1m 37.502s |
| 14 | Burti | 1m 37.636s |
| 15 | Alesi | 1m 38.130s |
| 16 | Fisichella | 1m 38.548s |
| 17 | Button | 1m 38.712s |
| 18 | Bernoldi | 1m 38.958s |
| 19 | Verstappen | 1m 39.401s |
| 20 | Mazzacane | 1m 39.651s |
| 21 | Alonso | 1m 39.956s |
| 22 | Marques | 1m 40.171s |

N Heidfeld  11

HH Frentzen  9

J Villeneuve  7

J Trulli  5

R Schumacher  3

M Schumacher  1

O Panis  10

D Coulthard  8

JP Montoya  6

M Häkkinen  4

R Barrichello  2

## SEPANG LAP-BY-LAP REPORT

**PRE-START** Problems for Michael Schumacher and Enrique Bernoldi meant both had to switch to their spare cars for the race. The start had to be aborted when Fisichella's clutch began to drag, forcing him out of position until he ended up stuck at an angle, stalled, in the middle of the track. As a result, the Italian had to line up at the back of the field for the second start and the race was reduced to 55 laps. Montoya's Williams refused to start because of an overheating problem. His car was pushed off the grid but he was able to start from the pitlane as he got to the spare before the first red light went on for the starting procedure.

**LAP 1** Michael Schumacher made a good start, but Barrichello was challenged for second place by both Ralf Schumacher and Jarno Trulli. Going into the first corner, Ralf Schumacher and Barrichello collided and the Williams spun. This caused a lot of excitement in the midfield, where Verstappen punted Irvine into a spin. By the end of the first lap Michael Schumacher led Barrichello by 1.3secs with Trulli third and Coulthard fourth. Häkkinen had a terrible start and dropped back to eighth.

**LAP 2** Olivier Panis, ninth in his BAR Honda, suffered an oil pipe failure and spun off, spraying flaming oil from the car as it speared into the sand trap. Meanwhile, the recovering Ralf Schumacher blasted up the field, going from 20th to 16th in a single lap, while Fisichella overtook Button to claim 11th. At the tail end, Alonso pitted because of soaring gearbox temperatures. The team decided to send him out again and risk a failure.

**LAP 3** Schumacher and Barrichello both went off on the oil from Panis's BAR. Barrichello scrambled back onto the track first, taking third place behind Trulli and Coulthard, while Schumacher rejoined in seventh behind Frentzen, Verstappen and Villeneuve. Simultaneously it began to rain heavily. Several drivers went off as the track became slippery but the leaders had all gone past the pits before it was clear how serious the storm was. Some of the midfield runners dived into the pits for wet-weather tyres. Both Benettons arrived at their garage at the same moment and Button lost time as he was forced to wait for Fisichella. Irvine retired with radiator damage after an off.

**LAP 4** Both Trulli and Coulthard went off at the same corner. The McLaren rejoined first and, with Barrichello also going off again, David was left in the lead. There were a number of spinners in the midfield with Villeneuve, Bernoldi, Montoya and Heidfeld all retiring. The major runners all pitted. The two Ferraris came in together for new tyres, Barrichello arriving first, but his pitstop was chaotic and meant Schumacher was in the pitlane for almost two minutes waiting for attention. However, luck was on Ferrari's side, as the safety car was sent out to slow the cars on the sodden track. It meant both drivers were able to catch up, thus ending up only 12 seconds behind the leaders at the restart. They both rejoined with extra fuel and an intermediate tyre choice that would prove crucial – the masterstroke that was to win them the race.

**LAP 5** Verstappen overtook Frentzen to claim second place, having failed to see the safety car signals.

**LAP 6** Verstappen allowed Frentzen to re-pass him and so avoided a penalty. As the rain stopped, Coulthard was leading Frentzen, Verstappen, Häkkinen, Trulli and Alesi. Fisichella was next ahead of Ralf Schumacher, Mazzacane, Barrichello and Michael Schumacher. The only other remaining runners were Button, Burti, Alonso and Marques.

**LAP 11** The race restarted, with Verstappen overtaking Frentzen. Ralf Schumacher overtook Fisichella, Alesi and Trulli during the lap, while the two Ferraris both overtook Mazzacane.

**LAP 12** Although the track was still very wet, the Ferrari duo reduced their lap times by more than two seconds and overtook Trulli. Schumacher also pushed his way ahead of Barrichello, who was not amused.

**LAP 13** Schumacher drove around Frentzen, his brother Ralf and Häkkinen to move up to third. He was lapping three seconds quicker than his rivals. Barrichello was only able to pass Trulli. In the midfield, Button spun.

**LAP 14** Barrichello overtook Ralf Schumacher and Häkkinen to take fourth place and the Ferraris closed on the two leaders – Coulthard and Verstappen – at more than four seconds a lap.

**LAP 15** Verstappen could not hold off Schumacher for more than half a lap. The German then closed quickly on Coulthard.

**LAP 16** Schumacher passed Coulthard with dismissive ease to take the lead, then built a five-and-a-half second lead in the course of one lap. Barrichello overtook Verstappen and Coulthard to make it a Ferrari one-two.

**LAP 17** Schumacher added another five seconds to his advantage over Coulthard, while Barrichello struggled to get within half a second of his team-mate.

**LAP 18** Häkkinen and Ralf Schumacher both stopped to switch from wet tyres. Häkkinen rejoined in sixth and Ralf in 11th.

**LAP 19** In four laps Schumacher had made up 20 seconds over Coulthard, while Barrichello had dropped to nearly 10 seconds behind his team-mate.

**LAP 21** Barrichello pitted to have gravel removed from his sidepods, dropping to fourth. Frentzen stopped to change his tyres and fell back to seventh. Ralf Schumacher benefited from his change of tyres and began to lap quickly, passing Burti for eighth, but he was still five seconds off his brother's pace.

**LAP 22** Michael Schumacher passed three backmarkers in the course of the lap and still posted a lap time a second-and-a-half faster than the next quickest car – his brother Ralf. Verstappen pitted to get rid of his wet tyres. This promoted Barrichello to third.

**LAP 23** Trulli stopped to switch from wets, dropping to eighth place.

**LAP 24** The leader had increased his advantage over Coulthard to 38 seconds after only eight laps. After racing side-by-side for four corners, Ralf Schumacher overtook Frentzen to claim fifth position.

**LAP 25** Coulthard stopped to change tyres and refuel. He rejoined in third, 15 seconds behind Barrichello and 75 seconds down on Michael Schumacher.

**LAP 26** Schumacher took another four seconds off Barrichello and six seconds off Coulthard.

**LAP 28** Häkkinen was overtaken by Ralf Schumacher for fifth; the world champion continued to lap incredibly quickly, recording a 1m 46.223secs compared to his brother's best of 1m 49.641secs.

**LAP 30** With an advantage over Barrichello of more than a minute, Michael Schumacher finally stopped for new tyres and fuel. He re-emerged on the track still half a minute in the lead.

**LAP 31** The flying Ralf Schumacher overtook Verstappen for fourth place. Häkkinen was now lapping quickly as well and closed on Verstappen's low-drag Arrows, although he wasn't able to overtake. The battling pair were later joined by a flying Frentzen.

**LAP 38** With a full fuel load, Schumacher could no longer pull away and those behind could close up. But with such a huge advantage he was under no threat. The Verstappen-Häkkinen-Frentzen battle ended up with Häkkinen being pushed wide by Verstappen and losing out to Frentzen. Ralf Schumacher stopped for more fuel and tyres.

**LAP 40** Häkkinen pitted again and dropped behind Ralf Schumacher.

**LAP 41** Barrichello pitted again but retained second place.

**LAP 43** Verstappen pitted for more fuel and fell from fourth to seventh. Häkkinen started to lap very quickly, setting times four-and-a-half seconds quicker than Michael Schumacher.

**LAP 48** Häkkinen closed on Ralf Schumacher and set the fastest lap of the race with a 1m 40. 962secs – three-and-a-half seconds faster than Michael Schumacher's pace at the front.

**LAP 50** Häkkinen caught Ralf Schumacher but could not pass the Williams, which was proving very fast in a straight line.

**LAP 55** The race ended with Michael Schumacher backing off in the final laps to let Barrichello close to within 23 seconds. Coulthard was third, five seconds behind the second Ferrari but still nearly 20 seconds ahead of Frentzen, Ralf Schumacher and team-mate Häkkinen who were all covered by less than two seconds. After his earlier heroics, Verstappen finished a disappointed seventh.

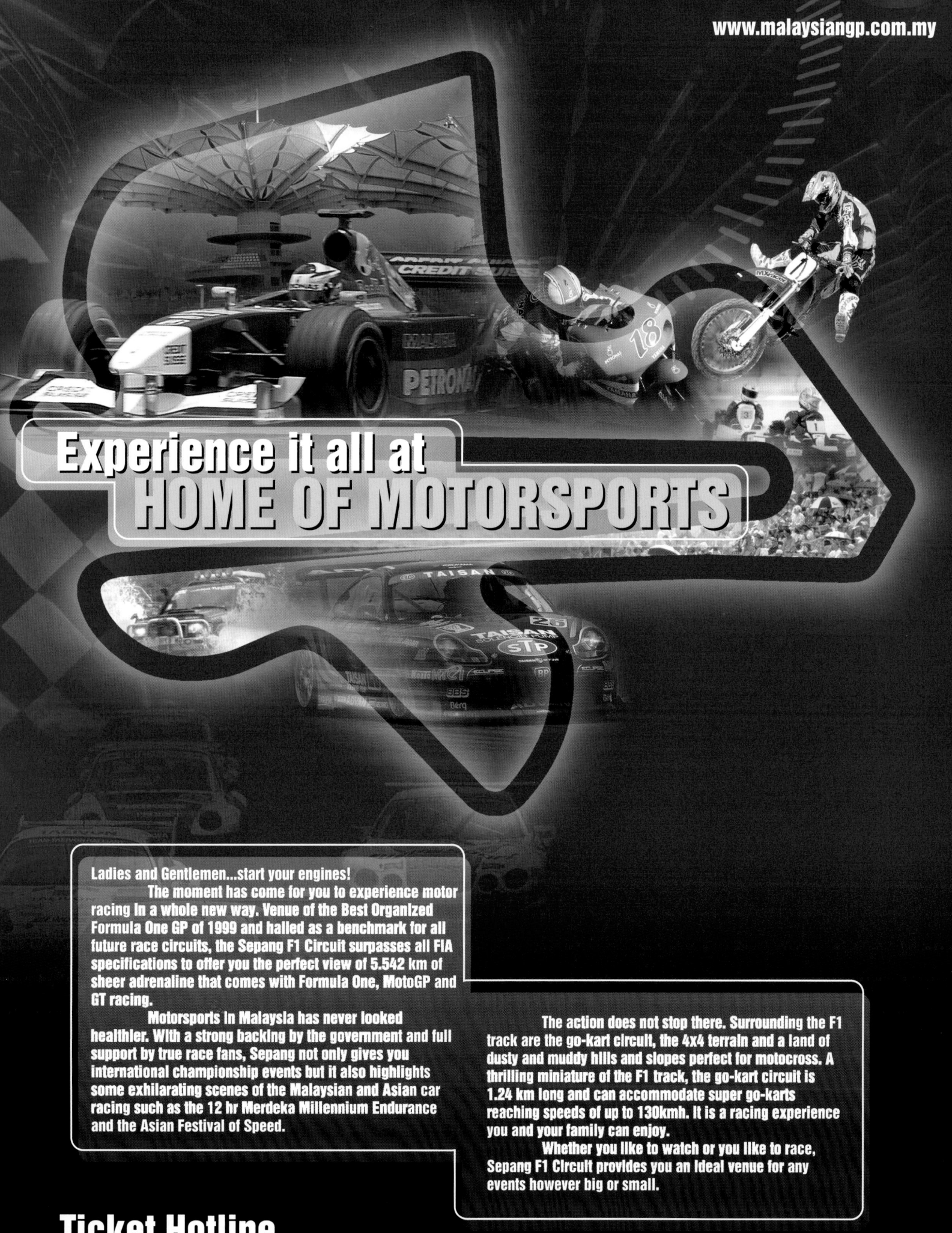

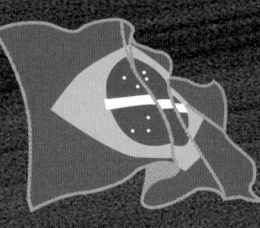

# Brazilian Grand Prix

30th March–1st April 2001    LAPS: 71  LENGTH OF LAP: 2.667 miles

JORDAN HONDA ON THE EDGE Searching for those elusive 10ths in qualifying for the Brazilian Grand Prix, Jarno Trulli's Jordan Honda locks its left front wheel on Turn Nine. The weight transfer to the outside of the car causes the left front to become lightly loaded, making it the limiting factor in the equation and ultimately costing the Italian time instead of saving it. PHOTOGRAPH BY RAINER SCHLEGELMILCH

## A new hero

**A fabulous overtaking manoeuvre by Juan Pablo Montoya on Michael Schumacher, the loss of the Colombian's maiden victory through intervention of a backmarker and a brilliant win for David Coulthard helped make the Brazilian Grand Prix a gripping race.**

A light aircraft buzzed over the Interlagos circuit, spraying out the colours of the Brazilian flag for the last time. The green and yellow smoke broke the strict colour code followed by 200,000 racing fans: at the Brazilian Grand Prix, you either wore the red of Ferrari or the blue and white of Ferrari's parent company Fiat. And nothing else.

With 40 minutes to go before the race, the frenzy began. The grid girls took their positions as the roar of the engines drowned out the Mexican wave competition between the grandstand and the Paddock Club. At last, at 1.28pm, local hero Rubens Barrichello stepped out of the Ferrari garage to the biggest cheer of the afternoon. He was so busy milking the applause that he forgot to kiss his wife Sylvana goodbye, much to her disgust. At least she wouldn't have to wait long before seeing him again. Moments later, the 22 cars that would line up for the race left the garages for their out-laps and the last-minute check before they joined the grid.

For Barrichello, the nightmare began. At 1.37pm, the giant television screens dotted around the circuit showed pictures of his red Ferrari parked on the grass. He had either spun off on his reconnaissance lap or had a failure. There was an outbreak of silence among the 'Mexican-waving' fans. Formula One rules dictate that the pitlane closes at 1.45pm – Ferrari had eight minutes to get Barrichello back to the garage, convert the spare car from Schumacher's settings and get him out again – or his race was over before it began.

Barrichello hitched a lift from an Iveco van to the start of the pitlane and began a 150-metre sprint to the Ferrari garage, egged on by 10,000 fans in the grandstand. Even the Brazilian television crew ditched their cameras to chase behind him, shouting encouragement. Forget Ferrari. Forget Formula One. Right now, this looked more like Monty Python. After frantic activity and with exactly 38 seconds to spare before the pitlane closed, Barrichello was on his way to the grid. Visibly upset and emotional, it looked like the occasion had already got the better of him. As soon as Barrichello settled into position on the third row of the grid, Ferrari technical director Ross Brawn ordered him out of the car to sit on the wall by the grid. "Just relax," he said. That was very hard to do – the air temperature had soared to 30°C, the Brazilian national anthem was playing, the world was waiting to see if the local boy could deliver. But with only 12 minutes to go his Ferrari was still having some serious work done to it, while the driver looked close to a breakdown.

The uncharitable buzz in the media centre was that Jean Todt wanted to pull Barrichello out of the race altogether, given his mental state.

He came, he saw, and he nearly conquered. In the end, Juan Pablo Montoya left Brazil without scoring any points. But the manner in which he passed Michael Schumacher made it clear it was only a matter of time before he won.

He knew no good would come of the situation. The chaos within Ferrari (which brought a smile to Ron Dennis's face for the first time all weekend) took the limelight away from the ritual parade of celebrities on the starting grid.

Of the 22 cars and drivers on the grid, only one was free of mechanics, engineers, team bosses and celebrities fussing over it. Juan Pablo Montoya was standing by the side of his BMW Williams, staring at the first corner. He preferred concentration to chaos. The grid suddenly cleared. It was 2pm and the cars were off for the 2.667-mile parade lap. At 2.02pm, as the cars were back in their grid slots, the last of the red lights flashed on and the race proper began. Now the smile was wiped from Ron Dennis's face. Mika Häkkinen, third on the grid, stalled his engine and desperately threw his hands in the air to warn the 19 cars behind him of the danger.

It was a serious situation, but this was still Monty Python. The race director didn't see the funny side and dispatched the safety car. Two laps later, after the safety car pulled in, Montoya made his move at the first corner with an audacious manoeuvre to overtake Michael Schumacher and steal first place – from fourth on the grid minutes earlier.

The moment of truth for McLaren's stranded Mika Häkkinen as the field departs.

Even Barrichello's army of fans stood to applaud the move. In the media centre, an unprecedented standing ovation broke out. Somebody dared to do a Schuey to Schuey – and got away with it. We had a race on our hands.

Unless your name was Rubens Barrichello. The hapless Brazilian crashed into the back of Ralf Schumacher, taking both the Ferrari and Williams out of contention. Martin Brundle explained to TV viewers at home how it would take an hour to fix the Williams. Somehow, though, Patrick Head turned the job around in five minutes. Ralf Schumacher rejoined four laps down and started setting fastest laps.

The despondent Brazilian made his way back to the Ferrari garage, where Sylvana was waiting. The fickle crowd barely acknowledged his return, quickly switching allegiances to their new Latino hero, Juan Pablo Montoya. It was a bizarre scene: 80,000 Brazilian racing fans dressed in Ferrari red cheering on a man born in Colombia driving a blue and white BMW Williams.

Only 24 laps into the race and most of Brazil was going mad for the Colombian – as was everyone in the Paddock Club. Schumacher couldn't get closer than 0.716secs to the leader after Montoya notched two of the fastest laps of the day in succession.

Ross Brawn and Schumacher's race engineer Luca Baldisserri were in deep discussion over when to bring their man in. On lap 25, Schumacher's Ferrari pulled in to the pits and was stationary for 9.6secs.

The relatively lengthy stop sent the former Ferrari-loving crowd even wilder. Juan Pablo could just do it. Now 34 laps into the race, Williams technical boss Patrick Head walked across to the pit wall, deciding whether to bring Montoya in. Spots of rain suggested a downpour was on the way. If he could wait, he should. Montoya was 35 seconds ahead of Schumacher as the drizzle strengthened. He could be in and out, and fit wet tyres, while Schumacher needed an additional pitstop for tyres and fuel. The first Williams victory in four years would be all but guaranteed.

Moments later, on lap 38, the dream was shattered as Jos Verstappen cannoned into the back of Montoya. Rarely had one crash provoked such anger among so many. Not for the first time this afternoon, Ferrari shirts were drenched in tears – this time because the Williams driver had been taken out. It made no sense, but then little had this weekend. Montoya calmly walked out of his mangled machine and waved to his new-found fans. Back in the Williams garage, where most of the crew held their heads in despair, Frank Williams was smiling broadly. Whatever else happened, he knew his man was the best today. But what he couldn't understand was that out of six starts in 2001, his cars had been run into four times.

Eight laps later, second-placed Schumacher made his move on Coulthard's McLaren to take the lead. The fickle Brazilian crowd, back supporting Ferrari, had something to shout about again. But this frenzy lasted only for two laps as Coulthard effortlessly overtook Schumacher to regain – and this time keep – the lead. It was a strange feeling in 2001, a McLaren Mercedes leading a Grand Prix. McLaren is one of those rare teams that provokes little emotion – neither the manufacturer nor the drivers. And they seem to like it that way.

There was no such lack of emotion at Sauber, where Nick Heidfeld was on course to record the team's first podium finish for years. By the time the chequered flag appeared the entire Sauber team were doing the conga in the pitlane. Ron Dennis led a more restrained celebration for Coulthard's victory. The only place where silence prevailed was the Ferrari garage, as boss Jean Todt forced a brave smile for Schumacher's second place. Coming second in a Formula One race was an achievement most teams would give anything for. But that afternoon Ferrari learnt the merit of Ron Dennis's favourite expression, that second place is 'first of the losers'. To observe Sauber celebrating third as if it had won the world championship, and Ferrari lamenting second, said everything about Formula One.

Away from the bedlam, in the Williams canteen, a solitary figure sat unnoticed by everyone – Juan Pablo Montoya. "You OK?" I asked. "Yeah." "Don't you want to punch Jos Verstappen in the face?" Montoya smiled. "Punch him? No. That's life. That's racing."

**405**

# Brazilian Grand Prix Race Statistics

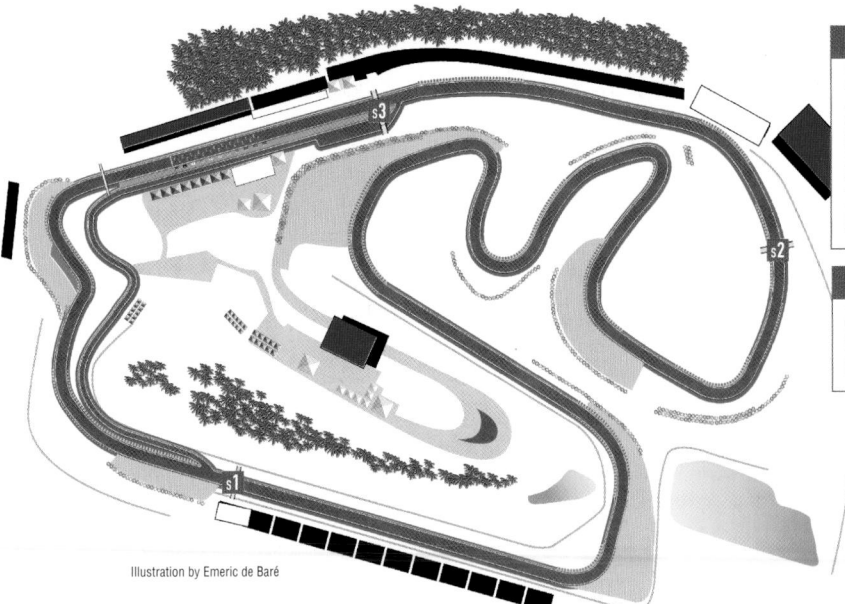

Illustration by Emeric de Baré

## FASTEST LAPS

|   | DRIVER | TIME | LAP |
|---|---|---|---|
| 1 | R Schumacher | 1m 15.692s | 38 |
| 2 | Coulthard | 1m 16.498s | 44 |
| 3 | M Schumacher | 1m 16.545s | 44 |
| 4 | Montoya | 1m 16.593s | 31 |
| 5 | Panis | 1m 16.732s | 44 |
| 6 | Villeneuve | 1m 17.106s | 44 |
| 7 | Irvine | 1m 17.132s | 43 |
| 8 | Frentzen | 1m 17.522s | 41 |
| 9 | Alesi | 1m 17.609s | 43 |
| 10 | Trulli | 1m 17.632s | 41 |
| 11 | Räikkönen | 1m 17.816s | 33 |
| 12 | Fisichella | 1m 17.830s | 41 |
| 13 | Heidfeld | 1m 18.064s | 42 |
| 14 | Mazzacane | 1m 18.176s | 23 |
| 15 | Burti | 1m 18.759s | 29 |
| 16 | Verstappen | 1m 18.875s | 26 |
| 17 | Bernoldi | 1m 19.449s | 12 |
| 18 | Marques | 1m 19.734s | 34 |
| 19 | Alonso | 1m 19.765s | 16 |
| 20 | Button | 1m 19.846s | 38 |
| 21 | Barrichello | 1m 58.705s | 2 |
|  | Häkkinen | No lap completed | |

## LAP LEADERS

| | |
|---|---|
| Michael Schumacher | 1–2 |
| Juan Pablo Montoya | 3–38 |
| David Coulthard | 39–46 |
| Michael Schumacher | 47–48 |
| David Coulthard | 49–71 |

Total laps led: Montoya 36; Coulthard 31; M Schumacher 4

## TEMPERATURES

| | | |
|---|---|---|
| Friday: | Air: 32°C | Track: 40°C |
| Saturday: | Air: 38°C | Track: 37–40°C |
| Sunday: | Air: 30°C | Track: 39°C |

## AUTODROMO CARLOS PACE CIRCUIT DIAGRAM

### RACE: SUNDAY 1ST APRIL 2001, 2PM

|   | DRIVER | CAR | TIME/RETIREMENT | LAPS | PITSTOP LAPS |
|---|---|---|---|---|---|
| 1 | David Coulthard | McLaren Mercedes | 1h 39m 00.834s | 71 | 40 47 |
| 2 | Michael Schumacher | Ferrari | + 16.164s | 71 | 25 46 |
| 3 | Nick Heidfeld | Sauber Petronas | +1 lap | 70 | 38 45 |
| 4 | Olivier Panis | BAR Honda | +1 lap | 70 | 28 45 |
| 5 | Jarno Trulli | Jordan Honda | +1 lap | 70 | 44 45 |
| 6 | Giancarlo Fisichella | Benetton Renault | +1 lap | 70 | 42 44 |
| 7 | Jacques Villeneuve | BAR Honda | +1 lap | 70 | 12 42 44 |
| 8 | Jean Alesi | Prost Acer | +1 lap | 70 | 24 44 |
| 9 | Tarso Marques | European Minardi | +3 laps | 68 | 38 44 |
| 10 | Jenson Button | Benetton Renault | +7 laps | 64 | 28 39 |
| 11 | Heinz-Harald Frentzen | Jordan Honda | +8 laps (electrical) | 63 | 43 45 |
| Ret | Kimi Räikkönen | Sauber Petronas | Spin | 55 | 37 46 |
| Ret | Ralf Schumacher | BMW Williams | Spin | 54 | 3 41 42 48 |
| Ret | Gaston Mazzacane | Prost Acer | Clutch | 54 | 25 45 |
| Ret | Eddie Irvine | Jaguar Racing | Spin | 52 | 6 46 |
| Ret | Juan Pablo Montoya | BMW Williams | Collision | 38 | |
| Ret | Jos Verstappen | Arrows Asiatech | Collision | 37 | |
| Ret | Luciano Burti | Jaguar Racing | Engine | 30 | |
| Ret | Fernando Alonso | European Minardi | Electrical | 25 | |
| Ret | Enrique Bernoldi | Arrows Asiatech | Hydraulics | 15 | |
| Ret | Rubens Barrichello | Ferrari | Collision | 2 | |
| Ret | Mika Häkkinen | McLaren Mercedes | Stalled on grid | 0 | |

Conditions: Sunny at first, rain from lap 34.

## RACE SPEED TRAP TIMES

|   |   |   |
|---|---|---|
| 1 | M Schumacher | 194.9mph |
| 2 | Coulthard | 194.2mph |
| 3 | Mazzacane | 194.1mph |
| 4 | R Schumacher | 193.7mph |
| 5 | Panis | 192.3mph |
| 6 | Heidfeld | 191.9mph |
| 7 | Montoya | 191.7mph |
| 8 | Räikkönen | 191.1mph |
| 9 | Alesi | 191.0mph |
| 10 | Barrichello | 190.7mph |
| 11 | Frentzen | 189.5mph |
| 12 | Trulli | 189.1mph |
| 13 | Verstappen | 188.3mph |
| 14 | Irvine | 188.2mph |
| 15 | Villeneuve | 188.1mph |
| 16 | Button | 186.2mph |
| 17 | Fisichella | 185.9mph |
| 18 | Burti | 185.5mph |
| 19 | Alonso | 185.4mph |
| 20 | Marques | 184.2mph |
| 21 | Bernoldi | 177.2mph |
|  | Häkkinen | No speed set |

## DRIVER POINTS

|   |   |   |
|---|---|---|
| 1 | M Schumacher | 26 |
| 2 | Coulthard | 20 |
| 3 | Barrichello | 10 |
| 4 | Heidfeld | 7 |
| 5 | Frentzen | 5 |
| 6 | Panis | 3 |
| 7 | Trulli | 2 |
| 8 | R Schumacher | 2 |
| 9 | Fisichella | 1 |
| 10 | Häkkinen | 1 |
| = | Räikkönen | 1 |
| 12 | Verstappen | 0 |
| 13 | Alesi | 0 |
| 14 | Burti | 0 |
| 15 | Marques | 0 |
| 16 | Button | 0 |
| 17 | Irvine | 0 |
| 18 | Alonso | 0 |
| 19 | Mazzacane | 0 |
| 20 | Bernoldi | 0 |
| = | Montoya | 0 |
| = | Villeneuve | 0 |

## WARM-UP

SUNDAY 1ST APRIL 2001, 9.30AM–10AM

|   |   |   |
|---|---|---|
| 1 | M Schumacher | 1m 15.971s |
| 2 | Barrichello | 1m 16.145s |
| 3 | Häkkinen | 1m 16.308s |
| 4 | R Schumacher | 1m 16.375s |
| 5 | Trulli | 1m 16.449s |
| 6 | Coulthard | 1m 16.679s |
| 7 | Panis | 1m 16.711s |
| 8 | Montoya | 1m 17.008s |
| 9 | Heidfeld | 1m 17.135s |
| 10 | Frentzen | 1m 17.138s |
| 11 | Räikkönen | 1m 17.213s |
| 12 | Villeneuve | 1m 17.405s |
| 13 | Irvine | 1m 17.420s |
| 14 | Burti | 1m 17.674s |
| 15 | Mazzacane | 1m 17.681s |
| 16 | Alesi | 1m 17.728s |
| 17 | Alonso | 1m 18.016s |
| 18 | Verstappen | 1m 18.074s |
| 19 | Bernoldi | 1m 18.460s |
| 20 | Fisichella | 1m 18.773s |
| 21 | Marques | 1m 19.126s |
| 22 | Button | 1m 20.008s |

## PITSTOP TIMES (from pitlane entrance to exit)

| | | | | |
|---|---|---|---|---|
| Fastest pitstop: | Coulthard | McLaren Mercedes | 33.037s | Lap 46 |
| Slowest pitstop: | Button | Benetton Renault | 6m 42.403s | Lap 28 |
| Most pitstops: | R Schumacher | Four stops | | |

## CONSTRUCTOR POINTS

|   |   |   |
|---|---|---|
| 1 | Ferrari | 36 |
| 2 | McLaren | 21 |
| 3 | Sauber | 8 |
| 4 | Jordan | 7 |
| 5 | BAR | 3 |
| 6 | Williams | 2 |
| 7 | Benetton | 1 |
| 8 | Arrows | 0 |
| 9 | Prost | 0 |
| 10 | Jaguar | 0 |
| 11 | Minardi | 0 |

## PENALTIES AND FINES

| DRIVER | WHEN | PENALTY | REASON |
|---|---|---|---|
| Jos Verstappen | Saturday morning | $1,750 | Speeding in the pitlane |
| Mika Häkkinen | Qualifying | $500 | Speeding in the pitlane |
| David Coulthard | Qualifying | $1,500 | Speeding in the pitlane |
| Eddie Irvine | Race | 10 seconds | Receiving assistance on grid |
| Mika Häkkinen | Race | $5,000 | Failure to replace steering wheel |
| Jos Verstappen | Race | $15,000 | Colliding with Montoya |
| Ralf Schumacher | Race | Warning | Colliding with Barrichello |
| Rubens Barrichello | Race | Warning | Colliding with Ralf Schumacher |

T Marques 22

G Mazzacane 21

J Button 20

F Alonso 19

G Fisichella 18

J Verstappen 17

E Bernoldi 16

J Alesi 15

L Burti 14

E Irvine 13

J Villeneuve 12

## BRAZILIAN GRAND PRIX RACE ENTRY

| | DRIVER | TEAM | CHASSIS/ENGINE |
|---|---|---|---|
| 1 | Michael Schumacher | Scuderia Ferrari Marlboro | Ferrari F2001 |
| 2 | Rubens Barrichello | Scuderia Ferrari Marlboro | Ferrari F2001 |
| 3 | Mika Häkkinen | West McLaren Mercedes | McLaren Mercedes MP4-16 |
| 4 | David Coulthard | West McLaren Mercedes | McLaren Mercedes MP4-16 |
| 5 | Ralf Schumacher | BMW Williams F1 Team | BMW Williams FW23 |
| 6 | Juan Pablo Montoya | BMW Williams F1 Team | BMW Williams FW23 |
| 7 | Giancarlo Fisichella | Mild Seven Benetton Renault | Benetton Renault B201 |
| 8 | Jenson Button | Mild Seven Benetton Renault | Benetton Renault B201 |
| 9 | Olivier Panis | Lucky Strike BAR Honda | BAR Honda B003 |
| 10 | Jacques Villeneuve | Lucky Strike BAR Honda | BAR Honda B003 |
| 11 | Heinz-Harald Frentzen | Benson & Hedges Jordan Honda | Jordan Honda EJ11 |
| 12 | Jarno Trulli | Benson & Hedges Jordan Honda | Jordan Honda EJ11 |
| 14 | Jos Verstappen | Orange Arrows Asiatech | Arrows Asiatech A22 |
| 15 | Enrique Bernoldi | Orange Arrows Asiatech | Arrows Asiatech A22 |
| 16 | Nick Heidfeld | Red Bull Sauber Petronas | Sauber Petronas C20 |
| 17 | Kimi Räikkönen | Red Bull Sauber Petronas | Sauber Petronas C20 |
| 18 | Eddie Irvine | Jaguar Racing | Jaguar Cosworth R2 |
| 19 | Luciano Burti | Jaguar Racing | Jaguar Cosworth R2 |
| 20 | Tarso Marques | European Minardi | Minardi European PS01 |
| 21 | Fernando Alonso | European Minardi | Minardi European PS01 |
| 22 | Jean Alesi | Prost Grand Prix | Prost ACER AP04 |
| 23 | Gaston Mazzacane | Prost Grand Prix | Prost ACER AP04 |

David Coulthard was pleasantly surprised to find himself on the top step of the podium.

## QUALIFYING: SATURDAY 31ST MARCH 2001, 1PM-2PM  107 per cent time: 1m 18.944s

| | DRIVER | TEAM | TIME | GAP | LAP |
|---|---|---|---|---|---|
| 1 | Michael Schumacher | Ferrari | 1m 13.780s | 0.000 | 11 |
| 2 | Ralf Schumacher | BMW Williams | 1m 14.090s | +00.310s | 12 |
| 3 | Mika Häkkinen | McLaren Mercedes | 1m 14.122s | +00.342s | 10 |
| 4 | Juan Pablo Montoya | BMW Williams | 1m 14.165s | +00.385s | 11 |
| 5 | David Coulthard | McLaren Mercedes | 1m 14.178s | +00.398s | 11 |
| 6 | Rubens Barrichello | Ferrari | 1m 14.191s | +00.411s | 11 |
| 7 | Jarno Trulli | Jordan Honda | 1m 14.630s | +00.850s | 11 |
| 8 | Heinz-Harald Frentzen | Jordan Honda | 1m 14.633s | +00.853s | 11 |
| 9 | Nick Heidfeld | Sauber Petronas | 1m 14.810s | +01.030s | 12 |
| 10 | Kimi Räikkönen | Sauber Petronas | 1m 14.924s | +01.144s | 11 |
| 11 | Olivier Panis | BAR Honda | 1m 15.046s | +01.266s | 11 |
| 12 | Jacques Villeneuve | BAR Honda | 1m 15.182s | +01.402s | 12 |
| 13 | Eddie Irvine | Jaguar Racing | 1m 15.192s | +01.412s | 12 |
| 14 | Luciano Burti | Jaguar Racing | 1m 15.371s | +01.591s | 12 |
| 15 | Jean Alesi | Prost Acer | 1m 15.437s | +01.657s | 12 |
| 16 | Enrique Bernoldi | Arrows Asiatech | 1m 15.657s | +01.877s | 12 |
| 17 | Jos Verstappen | Arrows Asiatech | 1m 15.704s | +01.924s | 12 |
| 18 | Giancarlo Fisichella | Benetton Renault | 1m 16.175s | +02.395s | 12 |
| 19 | Fernando Alonso | European Minardi | 1m 16.184s | +02.404s | 12 |
| 20 | Jenson Button | Benetton Renault | 1m 16.229s | +02.449s | 12 |
| 21 | Gaston Mazzacane | Prost Acer | 1m 16.520s | +02.740s | 12 |
| 22 | Tarso Marques | European Minardi | 1m 16.784s | +03.004s | 12 |

## FASTEST SECTOR TIMES IN QUALIFYING  Ideal lap time: 1m 13.511s (diff. from pole: 0.269s)

| | SECTOR 1 | SECS | | SECTOR 2 | SECS | | SECTOR 3 | SECS |
|---|---|---|---|---|---|---|---|---|
| 1 | R Schumacher | 18.455 | 1 | M Schumacher | 37.779 | 1 | Montoya | 17.277 |
| 2 | M Schumacher | 18.582 | 2 | Barrichello | 38.005 | 2 | R Schumacher | 17.285 |
| 3 | Coulthard | 18.591 | 3 | Häkkinen | 38.011 | 3 | Barrichello | 17.238 |
| 4 | Häkkinen | 18.652 | 4 | R Schumacher | 38.082 | 4 | M Schumacher | 17.352 |
| 5 | Montoya | 18.719 | 5 | Frentzen | 38.154 | 5 | Coulthard | 17.408 |
| 6 | Barrichello | 18.735 | 6 | Montoya | 38.158 | 6 | Häkkinen | 17.439 |
| 7 | Trulli | 18.783 | 7 | Coulthard | 38.179 | 7 | Frentzen | 17.458 |
| 8 | Frentzen | 18.845 | 8 | Räikkönen | 38.195 | 8 | Panis | 17.501 |
| 9 | Heidfeld | 18.847 | 9 | Heidfeld | 38.208 | 9 | Verstappen | 17.511 |
| 10 | Panis | 18.889 | 10 | Trulli | 38.272 | 10 | Trulli | 17.536 |
| 11 | Alesi | 18.896 | 11 | Irvine | 38.518 | 11 | Räikkönen | 17.560 |
| 12 | Villeneuve | 18.941 | 12 | Panis | 38.543 | 12 | Irvine | 17.587 |
| 13 | Irvine | 18.944 | 13 | Villeneuve | 38.639 | 13 | Bernoldi | 17.591 |
| 14 | Burti | 18.976 | 14 | Burti | 38.723 | 14 | Villeneuve | 17.602 |
| 15 | Räikkönen | 18.979 | 15 | Alesi | 38.842 | 15 | Burti | 17.607 |
| 16 | Verstappen | 19.042 | 16 | Bernoldi | 38.870 | 16 | Alesi | 17.670 |
| 17 | Fisichella | 19.055 | 17 | Fisichella | 39.037 | 17 | Heidfeld | 17.682 |
| 18 | Mazzacane | 19.122 | 18 | Button | 39.042 | 18 | Alonso | 17.684 |
| 19 | Bernoldi | 19.143 | 19 | Verstappen | 39.052 | 19 | Mazzacane | 17.752 |
| 20 | Alonso | 19.266 | 20 | Alonso | 39.159 | 20 | Fisichella | 17.822 |
| 21 | Button | 19.267 | 21 | Marques | 39.449 | 21 | Marques | 17.849 |
| 22 | Marques | 19.363 | 22 | Mazzacane | 39.617 | 22 | Button | 17.920 |

## PRACTICE SESSION ONE

FRIDAY 30TH MARCH 2001, 11AM-12PM

| | | |
|---|---|---|
| 1 | M Schumacher | 1m 16.832s |
| 2 | Häkkinen | 1m 16.882s |
| 3 | Barrichello | 1m 16.994s |
| 4 | Coulthard | 1m 17.736s |
| 5 | Panis | 1m 17.759s |
| 6 | Irvine | 1m 17.840s |
| 7 | Burti | 1m 18.141s |
| 8 | Montoya | 1m 18.215s |
| 9 | Heidfeld | 1m 18.271s |
| 10 | Trulli | 1m 18.291s |
| 11 | Bernoldi | 1m 18.295s |
| 12 | Frentzen | 1m 18.410s |
| 13 | Räikkönen | 1m 18.601s |
| 14 | Alesi | 1m 18.731s |
| 15 | Villeneuve | 1m 18.892s |
| 16 | Marques | 1m 19.055s |
| 17 | Verstappen | 1m 19.182s |
| 18 | Fisichella | 1m 19.314s |
| 19 | Mazzacane | 1m 19.600s |
| 20 | Button | 1m 19.811s |
| 21 | Alonso | 1m 19.990s |
| 22 | R Schumacher | 1m 56.634s |

## PRACTICE SESSION TWO

FRIDAY 30TH MARCH 2001, 1PM-2PM

| | | |
|---|---|---|
| 1 | Coulthard | 1m 15.220s |
| 2 | Trulli | 1m 16.224s |
| 3 | M Schumacher | 1m 16.598s |
| 4 | Montoya | 1m 16.851s |
| 5 | Häkkinen | 1m 16.882s |
| 6 | R Schumacher | 1m 16.929s |
| 7 | Barrichello | 1m 16.994s |
| 8 | Frentzen | 1m 17.072s |
| 9 | Heidfeld | 1m 17.102s |
| 10 | Irvine | 1m 17.295s |
| 11 | Burti | 1m 17.430s |
| 12 | Panis | 1m 17.432s |
| 13 | Villeneuve | 1m 17.455s |
| 14 | Alesi | 1m 17.518s |
| 15 | Räikkönen | 1m 17.712s |
| 16 | Verstappen | 1m 17.792s |
| 17 | Fisichella | 1m 18.096s |
| 18 | Alonso | 1m 18.222s |
| 19 | Bernoldi | 1m 18.233s |
| 20 | Mazzacane | 1m 18.269s |
| 21 | Marques | 1m 19.005s |
| 22 | Button | 1m 19.585s |

## PRACTICE SESSION THREE

SATURDAY 31ST MARCH 2001, 9AM-9.45AM

| | | |
|---|---|---|
| 1 | Häkkinen | 1m 14.503s |
| 2 | Coulthard | 1m 14.656s |
| 3 | M Schumacher | 1m 14.707s |
| 4 | R Schumacher | 1m 15.024s |
| 5 | Barrichello | 1m 15.032s |
| 6 | Montoya | 1m 15.047s |
| 7 | Trulli | 1m 15.163s |
| 8 | Frentzen | 1m 15.275s |
| 9 | Heidfeld | 1m 15.633s |
| 10 | Räikkönen | 1m 15.833s |
| 11 | Panis | 1m 16.035s |
| 12 | Irvine | 1m 16.114s |
| 13 | Villeneuve | 1m 16.135s |
| 14 | Alesi | 1m 16.702s |
| 15 | Burti | 1m 16.773s |
| 16 | Bernoldi | 1m 16.828s |
| 17 | Verstappen | 1m 16.835s |
| 18 | Fisichella | 1m 17.192s |
| 19 | Mazzacane | 1m 17.209s |
| 20 | Alonso | 1m 17.433s |
| 21 | Button | 1m 17.860s |
| 22 | Marques | 1m 18.212s |

## PRACTICE SESSION FOUR

SATURDAY 31ST MARCH 2001, 10.15AM-11AM

| | | |
|---|---|---|
| 1 | Montoya | 1m 13.963s |
| 2 | Häkkinen | 1m 14.108s |
| 3 | Coulthard | 1m 14.182s |
| 4 | R Schumacher | 1m 14.282s |
| 5 | M Schumacher | 1m 14.652s |
| 6 | Frentzen | 1m 14.837s |
| 7 | Barrichello | 1m 14.895s |
| 8 | Räikkönen | 1m 15.031s |
| 9 | Panis | 1m 15.039s |
| 10 | Heidfeld | 1m 15.096s |
| 11 | Trulli | 1m 15.163s |
| 12 | Irvine | 1m 15.409s |
| 13 | Burti | 1m 15.470s |
| 14 | Alesi | 1m 15.735s |
| 15 | Verstappen | 1m 15.972s |
| 16 | Villeneuve | 1m 16.135s |
| 17 | Bernoldi | 1m 16.160s |
| 18 | Mazzacane | 1m 16.347s |
| 19 | Button | 1m 16.411s |
| 20 | Fisichella | 1m 16.439s |
| 21 | Alonso | 1m 16.602s |
| 22 | Marques | 1m 18.212s |

 1 M Schumacher
 3 M Häkkinen
 5 D Coulthard
 7 J Trulli
 9 N Heidfeld
 11 O Panis

 2 R Schumacher
 4 JP Montoya
 6 R Barrichello
 8 HH Frentzen
10 K Räikkonen

## INTERLAGOS LAP-BY-LAP REPORT

**PRE-START** Rubens Barrichello's Ferrari failed on the way to the start, leaving the irate Brazilian to run back to the garage to take Michael Schumacher's spare car. The Ferrari mechanics worked frantically to change the pedals in time. Barrichello got out of the pitlane 25 seconds before it closed. On the grid, the Jaguar mechanics were late getting Eddie Irvine's car fired up and were still working on the car 15 seconds before the start of the parade lap, an offence which carries a 10-second stop-go penalty. Irvine's race was screwed before the start.

**LAP 1** Michael Schumacher blasted away into the lead but his brother had a pick-up problem and was slow away from the grid. This was better than Mika Häkkinen's fortune as his McLaren stalled. Fortunately, everyone avoided the Finn's stranded car, although the shorter lap meant the safety car had to be brought out so the McLaren could be cleared.

**LAP 3** The safety car was withdrawn at the start of the previous lap and within a lap Juan Pablo Montoya challenged Michael Schumacher for the lead. He dived for the inside line, held his ground and, after a brief wheel-rubbing moment, the Colombian went ahead. The two then traded blows 10th for 10th. Meanwhile, on the run from Turns Three to Four, Ralf Schumacher charged hard to make up for lost time and overtook Rubens Barrichello. Barrichello was unsettled, misjudged his braking and ran into the back of the Williams. Barrichello was unsettled, misjudged his braking and ran into the back of the Williams. Barrichello was out of the race, while Ralf headed for the pits for repairs.

**LAP 6** Irvine paid his penalty and dropped to the tail of the field. At the back, Ralf Schumacher was lapping very quickly but had lost several laps so was too far back to make any impression.

**LAP 7** Olivier Panis took ninth place by overtaking Jean Alesi.

**LAP 8** Olivier Panis moved up to claim eighth position with a clean pass on Kimi Räikkönen.

**LAP 9** Panis made it three consecutive moves, demoting Nick Heidfeld to eighth. The BAR driver was clearly on a two-stop strategy.

**LAP 12** Sixth-placed Jacques Villeneuve went into the pits to report a differential problem. Heinz-Harald Frentzen moved up to fifth, but Olivier Panis was closing in.

**LAP 15** Panis overtook Frentzen. Enrique Bernoldi retired with a hydraulic problem, while at the tail of the field Jacques Villeneuve, having rejoined, passed Irvine for 17th.

**LAP 20** Villeneuve overtook Jenson Button for 16th position.

**LAP 21** Montoya finally had a second over Michael Schumacher while David Coulthard watched the pair from close behind. The gap to the rest of the pack was already huge. Olivier Panis moved ahead of Jarno Trulli to take fourth.

**LAP 23** Villeneuve continued his charge, taking 15th from Alonso.

**LAP 24** Jean Alesi's hopes of a good result were dashed when the Prost refuelling rig malfunctioned and he lost vital seconds during his first scheduled pitstop. The problem left Jean to work his way through the backmarkers.

**LAP 25** Michael Schumacher made an early pitstop, confirming his two-stop strategy. He dropped to fifth place. It was clear that Ferrari was in trouble.

**LAP 28** Olivier Panis, running third, pitted and at the same time Michael Schumacher overtook Jarno Trulli. The Ferrari driver was now back in a podium position.

**LAP 29** Montoya had built a gap over Coulthard as the McLaren/Bridgestone combination began to fade.

**LAP 30** Luciano Burti disappeared with an engine problem. Further back, the recovering Irvine overtook Tarso Marques for 13th.

**LAP 37** The status quo was unchanged for several laps as Juan Pablo Montoya built up his lead. Rain became more and more likely as the clouds closed in. The rain came at a critical point as the one-stop runners began to pit. The first of these was seventh-placed Kimi Räikkönen, followed a lap later by team-mate Nick Heidfeld, who had been running sixth.

**LAP 39** Montoya had no plans to pit early but as he lapped Jos Verstappen the Arrows driver made a mistake and rammed into the back of the Williams. Both cars were out. Coulthard found himself in the lead with Michael Schumacher second, Trulli third, Frentzen fourth and Panis fifth. The high rate of attrition meant that Giancarlo Fisichella was now sixth in his Benetton.

**LAP 40** Coulthard pitted but emerged still ahead of Michael Schumacher, who was now second.

**LAP 44** The mid-race pitstops shuffled the order, with Olivier Panis moving up to third place ahead of the Jordans. Then it began to rain heavily. The tailenders were the first to pit with Alesi, Fisichella and Villeneuve leading the way.

**LAP 45** The situation was perfect for Panis as he was now in a position to combine his final stop with a change to wet tyres. Unfortunately, when he arrived at the BAR garage, Jacques Villeneuve was still there. The team made a complete mess of the stop and Olivier Panis lost over a minute, throwing away a certain third place. The two Jordans were also delayed when both arrived at the same time. Kimi Räikkönen was ordered to stay out, so Nick Heidfeld gained time on his team-mate, who had to struggle round for an extra slow lap before gaining access to the pits.

**LAP 46** David Coulthard stayed out and surprised everyone by continuing to do so now. Michael Schumacher and Kimi Räikkönen pitted, as did Eddie Irvine, who had risen to fifth place in the confusion.

**LAP 47** David Coulthard finally pitted and rejoined behind Michael Schumacher. Heinz-Harald Frentzen was third but almost a minute behind with Nick Heidfeld, now fourth, and the delayed Jarno Trulli in fifth. Kimi Räikkönen was sixth.

**LAP 48** Schumacher dropped the ball and spun — but still managed to rejoin ahead of Coulthard. Back down the field a fired-up Panis overtook Fisichella to regain ninth place.

**LAP 50** Coulthard pulled off an exciting manoeuvre to grab the lead, diving inside Marques at the first corner. Schumacher had decided to go around the outside of the Minardi and ended up outfumbled by the McLaren. Trulli overtook Heidfeld for fourth.

**LAP 51** Coulthard quickly pulled away from Schumacher. Further back, Panis closed up on Alesi and Irvine.

**LAP 52** Räikkönen blew his hopes of a finish with a spin that dropped him to 10th place.

**LAP 53** Schumacher made another mistake and ran wide across a gravel trap. All hope of catching Coulthard disappeared. Irvine blew his chances of scoring points as the Jaguar spun and stalled.

**LAP 55** With Eddie Irvine out of the way, Olivier Panis moved up to sixth position by passing Jean Alesi. Kimi Räikkönen spun again, this time taking himself out of the race.

**LAP 58** Ralf Schumacher spun into retirement after a lonely afternoon at the tail of the field. His only consolation was to have set the fastest lap of the race.

**LAP 60** As the track dried, Nick Heidfeld hauled in Jarno Trulli in order to retake fourth place.

**LAP 64** Frentzen lost third when his Jordan stopped with an electrical problem, while the team's hopes for Trulli were under threat as Panis closed on him, intent on taking what had become fourth.

**LAP 65** Fisichella bundled his way past Alesi to take sixth place.

**LAP 67** Panis passed Trulli to take fourth but Heidfeld was too far ahead in third to be under threat from the BAR.

**LAP 71** Struggling Alesi was passed on the final lap by Villeneuve so ended the day in eighth position and out of the points.

# San Marino Grand Prix

## 13th–15th April 2001 LAPS: 62 LENGTH OF LAP: 3.064 miles

POWERED TO SUCCESS After 62 laps, Ralf Schumacher takes the chequered flag for his first Formula One victory. It is also the first win for Williams since 1997, the first for BMW since 1986 and the first for Michelin since 1984. PHOTOGRAPH BY KEITH SUTTON

# An old order restored

After the excitement of the first three races, the incident-free Grand Prix at Imola was almost disappointing. But it did produce one significant moment – a new winner. No longer did Ferrari and McLaren rule Formula One – BMW and Williams had worked their way back to the top.

The sun beat down on the expectant tifosi as the cars lined up on the grid for the race. Ferrari's fans were not present in their usual droves due to the clash with the Easter holidays, and those who had come to Imola were a little downbeat following Ferrari's qualifying performance – only fourth and sixth, with a McLaren front row to boot. Still, they beeped their air-horns for the cars, if with a little less enthusiasm than usual, and their banners invariably expressed support for their favourite scarlet team. Many had been waiting since dawn, and they were restless.

On the grid, many of the drivers felt the same agitation. Jean Alesi was having an animated conversation with his engineers, clearly unhappy with something on the car. They shrugged and walked away. After Ferrari's recent dominance, the order of a McLaren Mercedes front row had been restored and David Coulthard and Mika Häkkinen were under close scrutiny from the hostile fans, whose weekend highlight came when Coulthard's silver car returned to the pits after the Friday practice on the back of a pick-up truck.

Häkkinen had spent most of his weekend walking hand-in-hand around the paddock with his wife Erja, visiting her first Grand Prix of the year after the birth of baby Hugo. Häkkinen was busy denying the baby was named after one of his sponsors, Hugo Boss.

The McLaren team gave nothing away, showing neither anxiety nor excitement. There had been rumours that Ferrari suffered in qualifying due to its choice of a harder compound of Bridgestone tyre that it hoped would work better in the race. However, as with all Formula One rumours, it had a flipside and that flipside said Ferrari was being hard on tyre wear and would be in trouble come the race. Frank Williams reminded Patrick Head that in Formula One a rumour is simply a premature fact.

The parade lap passed smoothly and the cars lined up perfectly on the grid with no problems, an occurrence so rare these days that the

Tarso Marques's Minardi engine lets go in a flash of flame. Irvine, Fisichella, Villeneuve, Mazzacane and Verstappen all retired with engine-related problems.

lack of interest almost created its own excitement. The tifosi waved their flags, praying that Schumacher would have a good start and give them something to shout about. Schumacher did, but it was the wrong one. It was Ralf who shot into the lead after taking advantage of Coulthard's wheelspin, a hindrance about to become extinct when traction control returned at the next race in Barcelona.

Rubens Barrichello drove a determined race to salvage Ferrari's honour and was rewarded with third place.

All cars eased through the first corner safely and no driver changed position by more than a couple of places, except for Giancarlo Fisichella whose surge of four places up the field might have caused a stir had he not started a lowly 19th. Ralf's elder brother had dropped a place and Rubens Barrichello had lost two, hardly the scenario the impatient tifosi demanded.

Only a few weeks ago the tifosi had firmly believed this was Ferrari's year and that the team could easily win every race this season; now they were beginning to think it would have been better to stay at home for Mass and Easter eggs. Worst of all, Schumi was pursued by Juan Pablo Montoya (or Gianpaulo as he's called in Italy), the man who forcefully shattered their illusions in Brazil. For a couple of laps the race settled down without major incident. Then a whisper ran through the media centre and quickly crescendoed into a clamour. Unseen by television screens at the circuit or around the world, and noted only by the official timing monitor, somewhere out on the circuit new hero Juan Pablo Montoya had once again bludgeoned past Michael Schumacher to take fifth.

The noise in the media centre had reached a roar. Michael was not a popular man there – no one is after winning six races in a row – and Montoya was just the man needed to shake up any tedious accepted order of events. With Ralf out in front, it looked like Williams was back and any talk of the 'big two' had decisively become redundant.

Of course, it is impossible to overtake at Imola, as Barrichello explained later at the post-race press conference. But Montoya was having none of that. He immediately set off after Trulli, leaving his team-mate's brother more than a little rattled. In another lap Olivier Panis and Barrichello had also shot past the champion, leaving people to think Michael must have had a problem that even the presence of the priest from Ferrari's hometown of Maranello could not rectify. But nothing happened and Schumacher didn't lose any more ground.

The Ferraris eventually worked their way past Panis's BAR, but

Michael Schumacher was out of luck at Imola but was the first to congratulate his brother on his maiden Formula One victory.

Jarno Trulli took two points at the Grand Prix nearest to his hometown of Pescara.

Michelin's veteran racing chief Pierre Dupasquier and his team of tyre technicians celebrate a famous victory. It was the French tyre company's first win since it returned to Formula One this season – it last won in Portugal in 1984, prior to withdrawing.

this progress was far overshadowed by Montoya's tussle with Trulli, whom he couldn't pass but would not give up trying to demote. After both cars pitted and emerged in the same order, the Colombian finally got his chance and overtook the Jordan in style. All this time little Ralf, as he is affectionately known in the paddock, was pulling away at the front like a pro.

When his brother began to slow on lap 23 it was greeted with great surprise across the circuit – the man who seemed unstoppable only two races ago had barely been able to make an impression all weekend. He limped into the pits with a puncture but could only manage another lap before the real damage became apparent. As he wandered back to the Ferrari motorhome he was stopped by an Italian TV crew. "If I can't win, I at least hope my brother can," he muttered reluctantly. The fans expected more.

Michael proved to be a prophet and Ralf cruised round to the chequered flag and his first Formula One victory. His one scary moment was when Eddie Irvine's Jaguar pulled in a little too closely when being lapped, raising memories of Montoya's clash with Verstappen in Brazil. But today there were no Verstappens or Barrichellos poised to spoil BMW Williams' race.

Ralf stepped from the car, triumphant, to be met by a jubilant team, and the German was popular enough to be congratulated by the rest of the drivers too, an unusual occurrence in Formula One. Even old rival Barrichello gave him a hug, but the younger Schumacher's warmest welcome was reserved for his brother. The win made them the first siblings in Formula One history to both stand on the top step of the podium. Herr and Frau Schumacher were presumably jumping up and down in front of their television sets back home, being the first parents in history to have two children as Grand Prix winners. It confirmed there was indeed something special about the brothers.

There was a sense of relief that a car that was not red or silver had at last won a Grand Prix, and the white motorhome was surrounded. Williams last won at the Nürburgring towards the end of 1997, in a race that saw little Ralf heavily criticised as

an idiot who didn't deserve to be in Formula One, after shunting his brother off the track at the start. But things change in Formula One and new orders come along, no matter how long the old ones have lasted – just ask Jenson Button, who finished a miserable last only four races after he was a Williams driver, too. Or ask the last three world champions, Michael Schumacher, Mika Häkkinen and Jacques Villeneuve, who all put in lacklustre performances in Imola.

Formula One is as fickle as the tifosi, half of whom left when they realised their team was underperforming; the other half stayed to invade the track and celebrate a win that wasn't theirs. Equally unhappy were the race organisers. On Thursday the sounds of the German and Italian national anthems could be heard across the circuit as they practised the podium ceremony as a Ferrari one-two.

Williams has never been a team for big celebrations. It had won again and brought to prominence both a new order in Ralf Schumacher and an old one in the shape of Williams, a team so successful that now it had won again it seemed as if it had hardly been away. The team personnel were happy, but apart from Ralf, who wandered round the paddock wearing the biggest grin since Rubens Barrichello was victorious at Hockenheim last year, they took it all in their stride.

They had seen it all before and as Patrick Head met the press crowding around his motorhome, he merely smiled proudly, used passionless words like 'impressive' and played down the team's hopes for the rest of the season. Gerhard Berger went off for a quiet family meal in a Bologna restaurant, displaying none of the laddish excitement with which he celebrated after taking BMW's last victory for Benetton in Mexico 15 years ago. Only Michelin's Pierre Dupasquier was really getting into the spirit of things, larking about with Flavio Briatore, who kept soaking him in champagne.

Tucked away in quiet corners, the losers – the three ex-world champions, plus Jenson Button and Juan Pablo Montoya, who was robbed of this glory in Brazil – looked on. The old dynasty had been restored to the throne and they were not a part of the glory today.

# San Marino Grand Prix
# Race Statistics

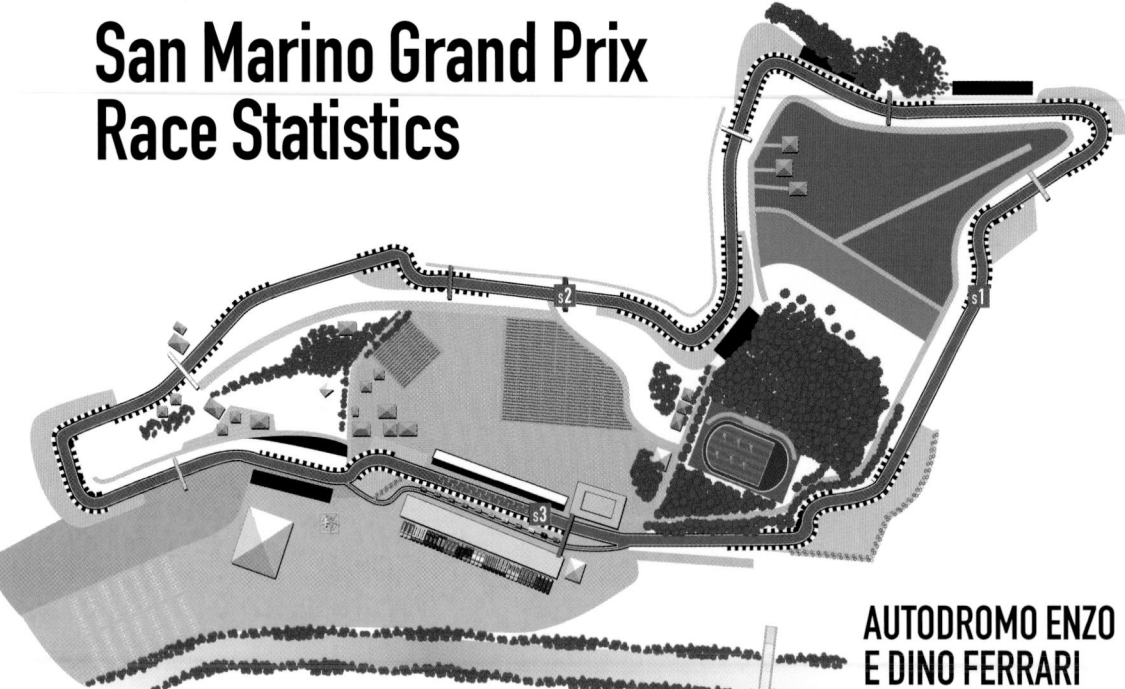

Illustration by Emeric de Baré

**AUTODROMO ENZO
E DINO FERRARI
CIRCUIT DIAGRAM**

## FASTEST LAPS

|    | DRIVER | TIME | LAP |
|----|--------|------|-----|
| 1  | R Schumacher | 1m 25.524s | 27 |
| 2  | Coulthard | 1m 25.569s | 44 |
| 3  | Barrichello | 1m 26.117s | 46 |
| 4  | Häkkinen | 1m 26.308s | 61 |
| 5  | Montoya | 1m 26.385s | 46 |
| 6  | M Schumacher | 1m 27.229s | 21 |
| 7  | Frentzen | 1m 27.243s | 36 |
| 8  | Heidfeld | 1m 27.350s | 57 |
| 9  | Trulli | 1m 27.358s | 20 |
| 10 | Panis | 1m 27.582s | 47 |
| 11 | Villeneuve | 1m 27.614s | 27 |
| 12 | Irvine | 1m 27.854s | 28 |
| 13 | Burti | 1m 27.932s | 29 |
| 14 | Alesi | 1m 28.369s | 44 |
| 15 | Räikkönen | 1m 28.604s | 17 |
| 16 | Mazzacane | 1m 28.954s | 21 |
| 17 | Bernoldi | 1m 28.956s | 37 |
| 18 | Button | 1m 29.096s | 38 |
| 19 | Fisichella | 1m 29.644s | 14 |
| 20 | Verstappen | 1m 30.403s | 4 |
| 21 | Alonso | 1m 31.671s | 4 |
| 22 | Marques | 1m 31.725s | 38 |

## RACE SPEED TRAP TIMES

| 1 | R Schumacher | 194.1mph |
|---|--------------|----------|
| 2 | Montoya | 193.5mph |
| 3 | Coulthard | 192.4mph |
| 4 | Panis | 191.6mph |
| 5 | Häkkinen | 191.6mph |
| 6 | Räikkönen | 191.5mph |
| 7 | Frentzen | 191.3mph |
| 8 | Bernoldi | 191.2mph |
| 9 | Heidfeld | 190.9mph |
| 10 | Villeneuve | 190.9mph |
| 11 | M Schumacher | 190.5mph |
| 12 | Alesi | 190.0mph |
| 13 | Barrichello | 189.9mph |
| 14 | Mazzacane | 189.6mph |
| 15 | Burti | 189.5mph |
| 16 | Irvine | 189.4mph |
| 17 | Trulli | 189.0mph |
| 18 | Verstappen | 188.9mph |
| 19 | Fisichella | 187.0mph |
| 20 | Button | 186.1mph |
| 21 | Marques | 185.7mph |
| 22 | Alonso | 185.0mph |

## DRIVER POINTS

| 1  | Michael Schumacher | 26 |
|----|--------------------|-----|
| 2  | David Coulthard | 26 |
| 3  | Rubens Barrichello | 14 |
| 4  | Ralf Schumacher | 12 |
| 5  | Nick Heidfeld | 7 |
| 6  | Heinz-Harald Frentzen | 6 |
| 7  | Mika Häkkinen | 4 |
| 8  | Jarno Trulli | 4 |
| 9  | Olivier Panis | 3 |
| 10 | Giancarlo Fisichella | 1 |
| 11 | Kimi Räikkönen | 1 |
| 12 | Jos Verstappen | 0 |
| 13 | Jacques Villeneuve | 0 |
| 14 | Jean Alesi | 0 |
| 15 | Luciano Burti | 0 |
| 16 | Tarso Marques | 0 |
| 17 | Jenson Button | 0 |
| 18 | Enrique Bernoldi | 0 |
| 19 | Eddie Irvine | 0 |
| 20 | Fernando Alonso | 0 |
| 21 | Gaston Mazzacane | 0 |
| 22 | Juan Pablo Montoya | 0 |

## RACE: SUNDAY 15TH APRIL 2001, 2PM

|     | DRIVER | CAR | TIME/RETIREMENT | LAPS | PITSTOP LAPS |
|-----|--------|-----|-----------------|------|--------------|
| 1   | Ralf Schumacher | BMW Williams | 1h 30m 44.817s | 62 | 29 46 |
| 2   | David Coulthard | McLaren Mercedes | +4.352s | 62 | 28 45 |
| 3   | Rubens Barrichello | Ferrari | +34.766s | 62 | 32 47 |
| 4   | Mika Häkkinen | McLaren Mercedes | + 36.315s | 62 | 29 46 |
| 5   | Jarno Trulli | Jordan Honda | +1m 25.558s | 62 | 24 43 |
| 6   | Heinz-Harald Frentzen | Jordan Honda | +1 lap | 61 | 26 44 |
| 7   | Nick Heidfeld | Sauber Petronas | +1 lap | 61 | 25 45 |
| 8   | Olivier Panis | BAR Honda | +1 lap | 61 | 27 48 |
| 9   | Jean Alesi | Prost Acer | +1 lap | 61 | 21 46 |
| 10  | Enrique Bernoldi | Arrows Asiatech | +2 laps | 60 | 21 41 |
| 11  | Luciano Burti | Jaguar Racing | +2 laps | 60 | 32 |
| 12  | Jenson Button | Benetton Renault | +2 laps | 60 | 19 20 39 |
| Ret | Tarso Marques | Minardi European | Engine | 50 | 21 40 |
| Ret | Juan Pablo Montoya | BMW Williams | Clutch | 48 | 27 47 |
| Ret | Eddie Irvine | Jaguar Racing | Engine | 42 | 31 |
| Ret | Giancarlo Fisichella | Benetton Renault | Engine | 31 | 21 |
| Ret | Jacques Villeneuve | BAR Honda | Engine | 30 | 29 |
| Ret | Gaston Mazzacane | Prost Acer | Engine | 28 | 25 |
| Ret | Michael Schumacher | Ferrari | Suspension | 24 | 23 |
| Ret | Kimi Räikkönen | Sauber Petronas | Steering | 17 | |
| Ret | Jos Verstappen | Arrows Asiatech | Exhaust | 6 | |
| Ret | Fernando Alonso | Minardi European | Spin | 5 | |

*Conditions: dry and sunny.*

## CONSTRUCTOR POINTS

| 1  | Scuderia Ferrari-Marlboro | 40 |
|----|---------------------------|-----|
| 2  | West McLaren Mercedes | 30 |
| 3  | BMW Williams F1 | 12 |
| 4  | Benson & Hedges Jordan Honda | 10 |
| 5  | Red Bull Sauber Petronas | 8 |
| 6  | Lucky Strike Reynard BAR Honda | 3 |
| 7  | Mild Seven Benetton Renault | 1 |
| 8  | Orange Arrows Asiatech | 0 |
| 9  | Prost Acer | 0 |
| 10 | Jaguar Racing | 0 |
| 11 | European Minardi F1 | 0 |

## PITSTOP TIMES *(from pitlane entrance to exit)*

| Fastest pitstop: | Coulthard | McLaren Mercedes | 24.324s | Lap 45 |
|------------------|-----------|------------------|---------|--------|
| Slowest pitstop: | Montoya | BMW Williams | 1m 25.595s | Lap 47 |
| Most pitstops: | Button | Benetton Renault | Three stops | |

## PENALTIES AND FINES

| DRIVER | WHEN | PENALTY | REASON |
|--------|------|---------|--------|
| Kimi Räikkönen | Friday Practice One | $1500 | Speeding in the pitlane |
| Giancarlo Fisichella | Friday | $500 | Late for press conference |

## LAP LEADERS

| Ralf Schumacher | 1-62 |
|-----------------|------|

Total laps led: R Schumacher 62

## TEMPERATURES

| Friday: | Air: 14°C | Track: 7-12°C |
|---------|-----------|---------------|
| Saturday: | Air: 6-10°C | Track: 4-22°C |
| Sunday: | Air: 14°C | Track: 25°C |

## WARM-UP

### SUNDAY 15TH APRIL 2001, 9.30AM-10AM

| 1 | Coulthard | 1m 26.440s |
|---|-----------|------------|
| 2 | R Schumacher | 1m 26.727s |
| 3 | Häkkinen | 1m 26.836s |
| 4 | Heidfeld | 1m 26.929s |
| 5 | Barrichello | 1m 26.941s |
| 6 | M.Schumacher | 1m 26.948s |
| 7 | Frentzen | 1m 26.954s |
| 8 | Räikkönen | 1m 27.492s |
| 9 | Olivier Panis | 1m 27.534s |
| 10 | Trulli | 1m 27.575s |
| 11 | Verstappen | 1m 27.728s |
| 12 | Villeneuve | 1m 28.035s |
| 13 | Montoya | 1m 28.142s |
| 14 | Mazzacane | 1m 28.404s |
| 15 | Bernoldi | 1m 28.639s |
| 16 | Irvine | 1m 28.655s |
| 17 | Alesi | 1m 29.347s |
| 18 | Marques | 1m 29.480s |
| 19 | Button | 1m 29.593s |
| 20 | Fisichella | 1m 29.623s |
| 21 | Burti | 1m 30.030s |
| 22 | Alonso | 1m 30.150s |

T Marques / J Button

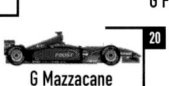
G Mazzacane / G Fisichella

F Alonso / J Verstappen

E Bernoldi / L Burti

J Alesi / E Irvine

N Heidfeld

## SAN MARINO GRAND PRIX RACE ENTRY

| | DRIVER | TEAM | CHASSIS/ENGINE |
|---|---|---|---|
| 1 | Michael Schumacher | Scuderia Ferrari Marlboro | Ferrari F2001 |
| 2 | Rubens Barrichello | Scuderia Ferrari Marlboro | Ferrari F2001 |
| 3 | Mika Häkkinen | West McLaren Mercedes | McLaren Mercedes MP4-16 |
| 4 | David Coulthard | West McLaren Mercedes | McLaren Mercedes MP4-16 |
| 5 | Ralf Schumacher | BMW Williams F1 Team | BMW Williams FW23 |
| 6 | Juan Pablo Montoya | BMW Williams F1 Team | BMW Williams FW23 |
| 7 | Giancarlo Fisichella | Mild Seven Benetton Renault | Benetton Renault B201 |
| 8 | Jenson Button | Mild Seven Benetton Renault | Benetton Renault B201 |
| 9 | Olivier Panis | Lucky Strike BAR Honda | BAR Honda B003 |
| 10 | Jacques Villeneuve | Lucky Strike BAR Honda | BAR Honda B003 |
| 11 | Heinz-Harald Frentzen | Benson & Hedges Jordan Honda | Jordan Honda EJ11 |
| 12 | Jarno Trulli | Benson & Hedges Jordan Honda | Jordan Honda EJ11 |
| 14 | Jos Verstappen | Orange Arrows Asiatech | Arrows Asiatech A22 |
| 15 | Enrique Bernoldi | Orange Arrows Asiatech | Arrows Asiatech A22 |
| 16 | Nick Heidfeld | Red Bull Sauber Petronas | Sauber Petronas C20 |
| 17 | Kimi Räikkönen | Red Bull Sauber Petronas | Sauber Petronas C20 |
| 18 | Eddie Irvine | Jaguar Racing | Jaguar Cosworth R2 |
| 19 | Luciano Burti | Jaguar Racing | Jaguar Cosworth R2 |
| 20 | Tarso Marques | European Minardi | Minardi European PS01 |
| 21 | Fernando Alonso | European Minardi | Minardi European PS01 |
| 22 | Jean Alesi | Prost Grand Prix | Prost ACER AP04 |
| 23 | Gaston Mazzacane | Prost Grand Prix | Prost ACER AP04 |

Ralf Schumacher was overjoyed to take his debut win in Imola.

## QUALIFYING: SATURDAY 14TH APRIL 2001, 1PM–2PM  *107 per cent time: 1m 28.867s*

| | DRIVER | TEAM | TIME | GAP | LAP |
|---|---|---|---|---|---|
| 1 | David Coulthard | McLaren Mercedes | 1m 23.054s | 0.000 | 12 |
| 2 | Mika Häkkinen | McLaren Mercedes | 1m 23.282s | +0.228s | 12 |
| 3 | Ralf Schumacher | BMW Williams | 1m 23.357s | +0.303s | 12 |
| 4 | Michael Schumacher | Ferrari | 1m 23.593s | +0.539s | 12 |
| 5 | Jarno Trulli | Jordan Honda | 1m 23.658s | +0.604s | 12 |
| 6 | Rubens Barrichello | Ferrari | 1m 23.786s | +0.732s | 10 |
| 7 | Juan Pablo Montoya | BMW Williams | 1m 24.141s | +1.087s | 12 |
| 8 | Olivier Panis | BAR Honda | 1m 24.213s | +1.159s | 12 |
| 9 | Heinz-Harald Frentzen | Jordan Honda | 1m 24.436s | +1.382s | 11 |
| 10 | Kimi Räikkönen | Sauber Petronas | 1m 24.671s | +1.617s | 12 |
| 11 | Jacques Villeneuve | BAR Honda | 1m 24.769s | +1.715s | 12 |
| 12 | Nick Heidfeld | Sauber Petronas | 1m 25.007s | +1.953s | 12 |
| 13 | Eddie Irvine | Jaguar Racing | 1m 25.392s | +2.338s | 12 |
| 14 | Jean Alesi | Prost Acer | 1m 25.411s | +2.357s | 12 |
| 15 | Luciano Burti | Jaguar Racing | 1m 25.572s | +2.518s | 12 |
| 16 | Enrique Bernoldi | Arrows Asiatech | 1m 25.872s | +2.818s | 12 |
| 17 | Jos Verstappen | Arrows Asiatech | 1m 26.062s | +3.008s | 12 |
| 18 | Fernando Alonso | European Minardi | 1m 26.855s | +3.801s | 12 |
| 19 | Giancarlo Fisichella | Benetton Renault | 1m 26.902s | +3.848s | 11 |
| 20 | Gaston Mazzacane | Prost Acer | 1m 27.750s | +4.696s | 12 |
| 21 | Jenson Button | Benetton Renault | 1m 27.758s | +4.704s | 11 |
| 22 | Tarso Marques | European Minardi | 1m 28.281s | +5.227s | 12 |

## FASTEST SECTOR TIMES IN QUALIFYING  *Ideal lap time: 1m 22.903s (diff. from pole: 0.151s)*

| | SECTOR 1 | SECS | | SECTOR 2 | SECS | | SECTOR 3 | SECS |
|---|---|---|---|---|---|---|---|---|
| 1 | M Schumacher | 17.971 | 1 | Häkkinen | 31.745 | 1 | Coulthard | 33.187 |
| 2 | Häkkinen | 18.033 | 2 | Coulthard | 31.789 | 2 | M Schumacher | 33.262 |
| 3 | Trulli | 18.061 | 3 | R Schumacher | 31.903 | 3 | R Schumacher | 33.340 |
| 4 | Barrichello | 18.075 | 4 | M Schumacher | 31.925 | 4 | Häkkinen | 33.454 |
| 5 | Coulthard | 18.078 | 5 | Trulli | 31.932 | 5 | Barrichello | 33.520 |
| 6 | R Schumacher | 18.114 | 6 | Montoya | 32.044 | 6 | Montoya | 33.549 |
| 7 | Villeneuve | 18.119 | 7 | Räikkönen | 32.117 | 7 | Panis | 33.625 |
| 8 | Montoya | 18.140 | 8 | Barrichello | 32.191 | 8 | Trulli | 33.665 |
| 9 | Frentzen | 18.239 | 9 | Frentzen | 32.286 | 9 | Villeneuve | 33.864 |
| 10 | Räikkönen | 18.259 | 10 | Panis | 32.323 | 10 | Frentzen | 33.889 |
| 11 | Panis | 18.265 | 11 | Irvine | 32.441 | 11 | Räikkönen | 33.923 |
| 12 | Heidfeld | 18.311 | 12 | Villeneuve | 32.471 | 12 | Heidfeld | 34.066 |
| 13 | Irvine | 18.324 | 13 | Heidfeld | 32.507 | 13 | Alesi | 34.136 |
| 14 | Bernoldi | 18.388 | 14 | Burti | 32.641 | 14 | Irvine | 34.142 |
| 15 | Verstappen | 18.443 | 15 | Alesi | 32.669 | 15 | Burti | 34.159 |
| 16 | Alesi | 18.606 | 16 | Bernoldi | 32.762 | 16 | Alonso | 34.551 |
| 17 | Burti | 18.747 | 17 | Verstappen | 32.921 | 17 | Fisichella | 34.685 |
| 18 | Fisichella | 18.818 | 18 | Fisichella | 33.093 | 18 | Verstappen | 34.698 |
| 19 | Alonso | 18.863 | 19 | Button | 33.400 | 19 | Bernoldi | 34.722 |
| 20 | Mazzacane | 18.887 | 20 | Alonso | 33.440 | 20 | Marques | 34.946 |
| 21 | Button | 19.035 | 21 | Mazzacane | 33.725 | 21 | Mazzacane | 34.963 |
| 22 | Marques | 19.252 | 22 | Marques | 33.792 | 22 | Button | 35.110 |

## PRACTICE SESSION ONE
### FRIDAY 13TH APRIL 2001, 11AM–12PM

| | | |
|---|---|---|
| 1 | Barrichello | 1m 31.998s |
| 2 | M Schumacher | 1m 33.998s |
| 3 | Häkkinen | 1m 33.911s |
| 4 | Coulthard | 1m 33.978s |
| 5 | Trulli | 1m 34.119s |
| 6 | Frentzen | 1m 34.549s |
| 7 | Räikkönen | 1m 35.153s |
| 8 | Panis | 1m 35.390s |
| 9 | Irvine | 1m 35.683s |
| 10 | Villeneuve | 1m 36.192s |
| 11 | Bernoldi | 1m 36.521s |
| 12 | Fisichella | 1m 37.231s |
| 13 | Heidfeld | 1m 37.727s |
| 14 | R Schumacher | 1m 37.837s |
| 15 | Button | 1m 38.256s |
| 16 | Mazzacane | 1m 38.382s |
| 17 | Montoya | 1m 39.812s |
| 18 | Alesi | 1m 39.961s |
| 19 | Marques | 1m 41.116s |
| 20 | Burti | 1m 41.867s |
| 21 | Alonso | 1m 41.763s |
| 22 | Verstappen | No time set |

## PRACTICE SESSION TWO
### FRIDAY 13TH APRIL 2001, 1PM–2PM

| | | |
|---|---|---|
| 1 | M Schumacher | 1m 25.096s |
| 2 | Barrichello | 1m 25.372s |
| 3 | R Schumacher | 1m 25.829s |
| 4 | Häkkinen | 1m 26.341s |
| 5 | Panis | 1m 26.535s |
| 6 | Räikkönen | 1m 26.552s |
| 7 | Irvine | 1m 26.599s |
| 8 | Villeneuve | 1m 26.739s |
| 9 | Trulli | 1m 26.923s |
| 10 | Burti | 1m 26.933s |
| 11 | Coulthard | 1m 27.132s |
| 12 | Heidfeld | 1m 27.142s |
| 13 | Frentzen | 1m 27.406s |
| 14 | Alesi | 1m 27.437s |
| 15 | Fisichella | 1m 28.322s |
| 16 | Mazzacane | 1m 28.586s |
| 17 | Button | 1m 28.902s |
| 18 | Alonso | 1m 28.931s |
| 19 | Bernoldi | 1m 29.273s |
| 20 | Marques | 1m 29.589s |
| 21 | Verstappen | 1m 29.750s |
| 22 | Montoya | 1m 39.812s |

## PRACTICE SESSION THREE
### SATURDAY 14TH APRIL 2001, 9AM–9.45AM

| | | |
|---|---|---|
| 1 | M Schumacher | 1m 35.633s |
| 2 | Barrichello | 1m 35.688s |
| 3 | Häkkinen | 1m 36.019s |
| 4 | Coulthard | 1m 36.443s |
| 5 | Trulli | 1m 37.422s |
| 6 | Frentzen | 1m 38.091s |
| 7 | Räikkönen | 1m 38.731s |
| 8 | Heidfeld | 1m 39.328s |
| 9 | Villeneuve | 1m 39.417s |
| 10 | Montoya | 1m 39.813s |
| 11 | Panis | 1m 40.264s |
| 12 | Verstappen | 1m 40.595s |
| 13 | Bernoldi | 1m 41.347s |
| 14 | Irvine | 1m 41.771s |
| 15 | Fisichella | 1m 42.056s |
| 16 | R Schumacher | 1m 42.620s |
| 17 | Alonso | 1m 44.002s |
| 18 | Button | 1m 44.752s |
| 19 | Marques | 1m 45.509s |
| 20 | Alesi | 1m 45.533s |
| 21 | Mazzacane | 1m 47.794s |
| 22 | Burti | No time set |

## PRACTICE SESSION FOUR
### SATURDAY 14TH APRIL 2001, 10.15AM–11AM

| | | |
|---|---|---|
| 1 | M Schumacher | 1m 30.737s |
| 2 | Barrichello | 1m 31.003s |
| 3 | Coulthard | 1m 31.536s |
| 4 | Räikkönen | 1m 31.726s |
| 5 | Frentzen | 1m 32.164s |
| 6 | Heidfeld | 1m 32.392s |
| 7 | R Schumacher | 1m 33.025s |
| 8 | Panis | 1m 33.071s |
| 9 | Bernoldi | 1m 33.884s |
| 10 | Häkkinen | 1m 34.036s |
| 11 | Alesi | 1m 34.531s |
| 12 | Montoya | 1m 34.036s |
| 13 | Villeneuve | 1m 34.789s |
| 14 | Verstappen | 1m 34.948s |
| 15 | Mazzacane | 1m 35.056s |
| 16 | Trulli | 1m 36.046s |
| 17 | Alonso | 1m 36.058s |
| 18 | Marques | 1m 36.671s |
| 19 | Button | 1m 38.306s |
| 20 | Fisichella | 1m 39.214s |
| 21 | Irvine | 1m 41.771s |
| 22 | Burti | No time set |

J Villeneuve — 11

HH Frentzen — 9

JP Montoya — 7

J Trulli — 5

R Schumacher — 3

D Coulthard — 1

K Räikkönen — 10

O Panis — 8

R Barrichello — 6

M Schumacher — 4

M Häkkinen — 2

## IMOLA LAP-BY-LAP REPORT

**LAP 1** David Coulthard and Mika Häkkinen made poor starts. This allowed third-placed Ralf Schumacher to get the momentum necessary to challenge for the lead as he and Coulthard went into the fast left-hander on the way down to Tamburello. Schumacher junior went between Coulthard's McLaren and the grass and was fortunate that the pole man left him enough room to get through.

Behind Ralf and Coulthard, Jarno Trulli forced his way past McLaren Mercedes' Mika Häkkinen to take third as they braked for the Tamburello chicane. Michael Schumacher was fifth ahead of Olivier Panis, Juan Pablo Montoya and Rubens Barrichello. Later in the lap, Montoya overtook Olivier Panis. Giancarlo Fisichella made a remarkable start to move up four slots from 19th position to 15th.

**LAP 2** Ralf Schumacher was a second ahead of David Coulthard by the second lap of the race and both men were quickly pulling away from Jarno Trulli and Mika Häkkinen, who were fighting over third position. Eddie Irvine lost 12th position to a charging Nick Heidfeld in his Sauber Petronas while Arrows Asiatech's Jos Verstappen passed Luciano Burti to take 16th place.

**LAP 3** Ralf Schumacher extended his lead to 2.2secs. Brother Michael was obviously struggling in fifth place; he missed a gear exiting the final corner and was overtaken by Montoya.

**LAP 4** Michael Schumacher was overtaken by both Panis and Barrichello in the course of the lap.

**LAP 5** Running with a light fuel load (as usual), Jos Verstappen moved ahead of Giancarlo Fisichella to take 15th.

**LAP 6** Fernando Alonso was the first retirement of the race when he suffered a brake failure at the Variante Alta and was launched over a kerb. This threw him off the track and he was unable to avoid hitting a tyre barrier, tearing off his right front suspension.

**LAP 7** Jos Verstappen's race ended with a number of overheating problems caused by a broken exhaust.

**LAP 8** Rubens Barrichello passed a struggling Olivier Panis in order to take sixth place.

**LAP 9** Michael Schumacher followed Ferrari team-mate Rubens Barrichello through, leaving BAR Honda's Olivier Panis to drop back into eighth position.

**LAP 14** The two leaders were well ahead of the chasing pack but Jarno Trulli and Mika Häkkinen had been joined in the battle for third place by Juan Pablo Montoya and the two Ferraris of Michael Schumacher and Rubens Barrichello. Meanwhile, Olivier Panis was left holding off Kimi Räikkönen's Sauber.

**LAP 18** Kimi Räikkönen retired when his steering wheel came off in his hands after Tosa and he crashed out of ninth place.

**LAP 19** Jenson Button's frustrating Formula One race season continued. Running in 17th place, he pitted for fuel and tyres. However, the Benetton refuelling machine malfunctioned, which meant that Button had to be sent back into the race without fuel – a move that cost him precious seconds.

**LAP 20** Button pitted again – this time successfully managing to refuel and change tyres. But as a result of the extra stop he was now a long way behind the rest of the field.

**LAP 22** Olivier Panis's BAR selected the wrong gear and he dropped from eighth to 12th place.

**LAP 23** Michael Schumacher suffered a puncture on his left front wheel rim and was forced to complete the best part of a lap before he was able to pit. He rejoined down in the midfield but retired after a further exploratory lap. The team decided that it would have been dangerous for him to continue.

**LAP 24** Jordan Honda's Jarno Trulli was the first of the front-running cars to stop. He rejoined the race in eighth place. Mika Häkkinen began to charge in his McLaren Mercedes, hoping to pass Trulli during the pitstop sequence.

**LAP 27** Juan Pablo Montoya pitted. He rejoined the race behind Jarno Trulli but quickly forced his way ahead of the Jordan driver. This meant that Rubens Barrichello was up to fourth and likely to gain additional places with what looked like being a one-stop strategy in his Ferrari.

**LAP 28** David Coulthard pitted to refuel but he had established a big enough lead over third-placed Mika Häkkinen in order to remain in second position.

**LAP 29** Ralf Schumacher pitted but he was able to get out again ahead of David Coulthard's McLaren. Mika Häkkinen also pitted and emerged ahead of Jarno Trulli's Jordan Honda but behind the Ferrari of Rubens Barrichello. BAR Honda's Jacques Villeneuve went into the pits as well. Meanwhile, at the back of the field, Gaston Mazzacane retired when his Prost Acer's engine caught fire.

**LAP 31** Jacques Villeneuve's engine blew up with a huge cloud of oil smoke on the 31st lap of the race. Benetton Renault's Giancarlo Fisichella also retired from the race with a persistent misfire. Jaguar Racing's Eddie Irvine, who was on a one-stop strategy, went into the pits and dropped from seventh place to 10th.

**LAP 32** Rubens Barrichello finally pitted and had built a sufficient advantage over Mika Häkkinen to rejoin the race in third position. For the next few laps the order at the front remained stable with Ralf Schumacher's BMW Williams ahead of the McLaren Mercedes of David Coulthard, Rubens Barrichello's Ferrari, Mika Häkkinen's McLaren, Juan Pablo Montoya's BMW Williams and Jarno Trulli's Jordan Honda.

**LAP 43** Jarno Trulli became the first man at this year's San Marino Grand Prix to stop for a second time. He lost a place to Jordan Honda's Heinz-Harald Frentzen. Meanwhile Eddie Irvine's Jaguar retired with a blown engine.

**LAP 44** Heinz-Harald Frentzen pitted, allowing Jordan Honda's Jarno Trulli to pass him again.

**LAP 45** David Coulthard came in for his second pitstop of the race. Once again he was able to hold on to his second position. Eighth-placed Nick Heidfeld also brought his Sauber Petronas in for its second pitstop of the Grand Prix.

**LAP 46** Ralf Schumacher pitted for his second stop but managed to hold on to the race lead. Mika Häkkinen also stopped but was able to maintain his fourth place. Juan Pablo Montoya pitted but stalled his BMW Williams, which was jammed in first gear. He lost almost a minute before the car was restarted and back in the race – but not for long. He completed just one more lap before retiring from the race altogether, unable to select gears. His early departure moved Jordan Honda's Jarno Trulli into fifth place and the lapped Heinz-Harald Frentzen up to sixth position. Of the other survivors, Nick Heidfeld of Sauber Petronas was seventh, Olivier Panis of BAR Honda eighth and Jean Alesi's Prost Acer ninth.

**LAP 47** Ferrari's Rubens Barrichello pitted for a second time and resumed the race in third place. Juan Pablo Montoya pitted, rejoined, then retired, stuck in gear.

**LAP 62** The order remained unchanged all the way to the chequered flag, although Mika Häkkinen charged hard in an effort to catch the Ferrari of Rubens Barrichello. In the final laps of the race David Coulthard closed the gap a little bit on Ralf Schumacher but the BMW Williams driver was under no threat. It was Schumacher junior's first Grand Prix victory. Michelin and BMW also celebrated their first wins in recent times and the Williams team was able to enjoy its first triumph since the Luxembourg Grand Prix in 1997.

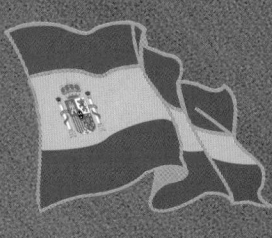

# Spanish Grand Prix

**27th–29th April 2001**    LAPS: 65  LENGTH OF LAP: 2.937 miles

**THE PERFECT LINE AND BALANCE** Michael Schumacher's Ferrari hugs the kerb in Turn Two at the Circuit de Catalunya, as the world champion races towards another victory. The perfect posture of the Ferrari shows no understeer or drift angle, the car's traction control ensuring maximum grip from its rear tyres. PHOTOGRAPH BY CLEMENT MARIN

## Fate is sealed by a kiss

**The Formula One fraternity are a suspicious bunch of people and when Catherine Zeta Jones blew Mika Häkkinen's McLaren Mercedes a long, red kiss the team knew it was in for some adverse fortune. It was right.**

It all started with a kiss. Catherine Zeta Jones placed her hands over her deep red lipstick, then wiped it across Mika Häkkinen's McLaren. Husband Michael Douglas offered the Finn a handshake while King Juan Carlos looked on, hoping to join in the photo shoot. Only five minutes before the start of the Spanish Grand Prix, the new laid-back Häkkinen was enjoying all the attention. No more did the ex-world champion carry the world's problems on his shoulders, no more did he display suspicion towards all around. That attitude had brought him zero points so far, so he had ditched it for Barcelona and the change was so far working wonders. Even the night before, in Barcelona's Port Olympic district, the hundreds of normally subdued Finnish fans had a feeling their hero would deliver, as they drowned the Catalonian street guitar players with chants of 'Mika! Mika! Mika!'

As the parade lap began, David Coulthard's McLaren's launch control failed, sending him to the back of the grid. You got the feeling this really was Mika's day at last. Back in the McLaren garage, Ron Dennis looked angrier than usual as the inquiry into who to blame over the Coulthard fiasco began. Michael Douglas, Dennis's personal guest for the afternoon, looked embarrassed. Moments later, the lights went out and Michael Schumacher and Häkkinen began the chase. Schumacher led, but laid-back Mika didn't look worried. With Catherine Zeta Jones's lipstick still drying on his front wing, wife Erja smiling in the garage and baby Hugo plonked in front of a TV in a Barcelona hotel, life was good right now.

Life was also good for Juan Pablo 'Mr Cool' Montoya, who raced from 12th to sixth in one lap. Even beleaguered Jenson Button was

David Coulthard risked a fine to give his beleaguered team-mate Häkkinen first-class transport back to the parc ferme.

Mika Häkkinen is consoled by his biggest rival and gifted race winner, Michael Schumacher, when he finally made it back to the pitlane.

enjoying lap one: thanks to Coulthard's disaster, the British hope was already up to 20th; this could be his best race of the season.

After lap one the crowd settled down to their paellas, safe in the knowledge they wouldn't miss much. The Spanish Grand Prix has a reputation for being the dullest on the calendar: the drivers know the circuit too well from testing. Overtaking is as hard as it is in Monaco, but the circuit lacks the glamour of that location. Apart

from Douglas and Zeta Jones, a blurry-eyed Mick Hucknall in the paddock and fellow pop star Sonique in a skirt too short even for baby Hugo, there was little to excite fans – for now.

Oh, there was the small matter of Pedro de la Rosa making his debut for Jaguar, in front of his home crowd. De la Rosa had looked grumpy all weekend and was probably even grumpier after realising there was not a single banner with his name on it. Thankfully Pedro was put out of his misery on lap five when Heinz-Harald Frentzen's Jordan piled into him. The incident had no effect on the crowd. 'Pedro who?' stepped out of his tangled car and looked to throw his gloves into the arms of adoring fans – except there weren't any. Come back Luciano Burti, all is forgiven.

By lap 18 the best of the action was still at the back, with Coulthard fighting Button for the coveted 20th spot. With Frentzen and de la Rosa long gone, the winner of this engrossing duel could hit the dizzy heights of 18th place. The thought clearly didn't impress Ron Dennis, who by now had lost interest in his new best pal Michael Douglas. The Hollywood superstar was confined to the back of the garage with a set of headphones and a TV screen; who knows what he was watching. A lap later Button spoiled the party by pitting, leaving Coulthard free to drive his way right up the field.

With Schumacher and Häkkinen still duelling at the front, the only excitement came on lap 21 as Imola's hero, Ralf Schumacher, span off in his BMW Williams. Wife-to-be Cora wasn't impressed

Mika Häkkinen can't quite believe the bad luck that saw his McLaren Mercedes retire with clutch failure almost within sight of the chequered flag.

Rubens Barrichello's Ferrari runs wide on lap 48 with suspension failure that ended his race.

The Barcelona flag girls practise their moves.

and Montoya's partner, Connie, flashed a wry smile. This could be her man's day yet, with the Colombian now promoted to fifth place.

By lap 27 the action switched to the front for the first time. Schumacher had pitted – Häkkinen followed soon after but couldn't get out ahead of the Ferrari. There was always the next pitstop. That came on lap 40 of 65, with Häkkinen this time having built a 25-second lead over Schumacher by staying out longer – just enough to get in and get out ahead. The flying Finn did just that and, within two laps, was roaring away 5.67secs in front of the Ferrari. Joy at last for the Finnish contingent, and joy for Ron Dennis, who decided it was time to be pals with Michael Douglas again.

With four laps remaining, Häkkinen was a storming 25 seconds clear of Schumacher, who had problems. Whatever they were, no one at McLaren cared. Michael Douglas got ready to congratulate his friend, while team personnel made their way to the McLaren motorhome to uncork the champagne. Then disaster – with only half a lap to go, Häkkinen's clutch failed. Schumacher swept past him to take the flag. With Barrichello managing to spin off earlier, Montoya and Villeneuve were more surprised than anyone to find themselves in second and third places. Villeneuve's boss Craig Pollock, who never stops smiling, couldn't believe it. He had a genuine reason to be cheerful for the first time in his F1 career.

Häkkinen accepted the disaster well; Ron Dennis less so, as he took his disappointment out on Coulthard, accusing him of 'brain fade' at the start of the parade lap. Michael Douglas made his excuses and left. As for Catherine Zeta Jones – well, it proved to be a kiss of the wrong sort.

# Spanish Grand Prix Race Statistics

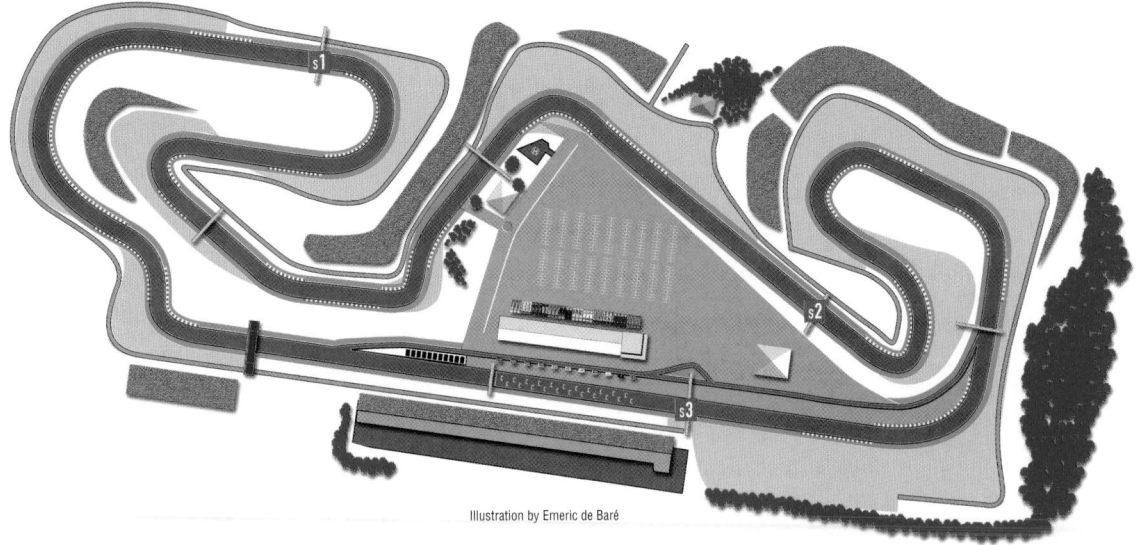

Illustration by Emeric de Baré

## CATALUNYA CIRCUIT DIAGRAM

### FASTEST LAPS

| | DRIVER | TIME | LAP |
|---|---|---|---|
| 1 | M Schumacher | 1m 21.151s | 25 |
| 2 | Häkkinen | 1m 21.368s | 49 |
| 3 | Barrichello | 1m 21.720s | 27 |
| 4 | Coulthard | 1m 22.091s | 41 |
| 5 | R Schumacher | 1m 22.362s | 19 |
| 6 | Panis | 1m 22.475s | 26 |
| 7 | Villeneuve | 1m 22.513s | 22 |
| 8 | Irvine | 1m 22.568s | 23 |
| 9 | Heidfeld | 1m 22.738s | 26 |
| 10 | Montoya | 1m 22.841s | 39 |
| 11 | Räikkönen | 1m 23.049s | 40 |
| 12 | Trulli | 1m 23.087s | 24 |
| 13 | Alesi | 1m 23.668s | 20 |
| 14 | Burti | 1m 23.794s | 23 |
| 15 | Verstappen | 1m 23.965s | 17 |
| 16 | Alonso | 1m 24.423s | 37 |
| 17 | Bernoldi | 1m 24.740s | 4 |
| 18 | Fisichella | 1m 25.298s | 14 |
| 19 | Button | 1m 25.406s | 57 |
| 20 | Marques | 1m 25.791s | 16 |
| 21 | de la Rosa | 1m 25.932s | 3 |
| 22 | Frentzen | 1m 26.158s | 3 |

### RACE SPEED TRAP TIMES

| | | |
|---|---|---|
| 1 | Häkkinen | 199.3mph |
| 2 | Coulthard | 198.0mph |
| 3 | Verstappen | 197.8mph |
| 4 | Montoya | 197.7mph |
| 5 | R Schumacher | 197.0mph |
| 6 | Panis | 196.9mph |
| 7 | de la Rosa | 195.7mph |
| 8 | Villeneuve | 194.7mph |
| 9 | Frentzen | 194.7mph |
| 10 | Trulli | 194.2mph |
| 11 | Heidfeld | 194.0mph |
| 12 | Burti | 193.9mph |
| 13 | Räikkönen | 193.6mph |
| 14 | M Schumacher | 193.2mph |
| 15 | Irvine | 192.6mph |
| 16 | Alesi | 192.1mph |
| 17 | Alonso | 192.1mph |
| 18 | Bernoldi | 191.6mph |
| 19 | Barrichello | 191.1mph |
| 20 | Fisichella | 189.6mph |
| 21 | Button | 189.4mph |
| 22 | Marques | 188.4mph |

### WARM-UP

SUNDAY 29TH APRIL 2001, 9.30AM-10AM

| | | |
|---|---|---|
| 1 | Barrichello | 1m 20.680s |
| 2 | Häkkinen | 1m 20.901s |
| 3 | Coulthard | 1m 21.148s |
| 4 | M Schumacher | 1m 21.211s |
| 5 | Panis | 1m 21.558s |
| 6 | Frentzen | 1m 21.558s |
| 7 | R Schumacher | 1m 21.886s |
| 8 | Trulli | 1m 21.929s |
| 9 | Villeneuve | 1m 22.120s |
| 10 | Heidfeld | 1m 22.343s |
| 11 | Montoya | 1m 22.558s |
| 12 | Räikkönen | 1m 22.864s |
| 13 | Verstappen | 1m 23.240s |
| 14 | Irvine | 1m 23.294s |
| 15 | Button | 1m 23.754s |
| 16 | Alesi | 1m 23.794s |
| 17 | de la Rosa | 1m 23.847s |
| 18 | Bernoldi | 1m 24.138s |
| 19 | Alonso | 1m 24.361s |
| 20 | Fisichella | 1m 24.468s |
| 21 | Burti | 1m 24.633s |
| 22 | Marques | 1m 24.924s |

### DRIVER POINTS

| | | |
|---|---|---|
| 1 | Michael Schumacher | 36 |
| 2 | David Coulthard | 28 |
| 3 | Rubens Barrichello | 14 |
| 4 | Ralf Schumacher | 12 |
| 5 | Nick Heidfeld | 8 |
| 6 | Jarno Trulli | 7 |
| 7 | Juan Pablo Montoya | 6 |
| 8 | Heinz-Harald Frentzen | 6 |
| 9 | Jacques Villeneuve | 4 |
| 10 | Mika Häkkinen | 4 |
| 11 | Olivier Panis | 3 |
| 12 | Kimi Räikkönen | 1 |
| 13 | Giancarlo Fisichella | 1 |
| 14 | Jos Verstappen | 0 |
| 15 | Jean Alesi | 0 |
| 16 | Luciano Burti | 0 |
| 17 | Tarso Marques | 0 |
| 18 | Jenson Button | 0 |
| 19 | Enrique Bernoldi | 0 |
| 20 | Eddie Irvine | 0 |
| 21 | Fernando Alonso | 0 |
| 22 | Gaston Mazzacane | 0 |
| 23 | Pedro de la Rosa | 0 |

### RACE: SUNDAY 29TH APRIL 2001, 2PM

| | DRIVER | CAR | TIME/RETIREMENT | LAPS | PITSTOP LAPS |
|---|---|---|---|---|---|
| 1 | Michael Schumacher | Ferrari | 1h 31m 03.305s | 65 | 23 43 |
| 2 | Juan Pablo Montoya | BMW Williams | +40.738s | 65 | 21 41 |
| 3 | Jacques Villeneuve | BAR Honda | +49.626s | 65 | 23 41 |
| 4 | Jarno Trulli | Jordan Honda | +51.253s | 65 | 21 40 |
| 5 | David Coulthard | McLaren Mercedes | +51.616s | 65 | 1 28 44 |
| 6 | Nick Heidfeld | Sauber Petronas | +1m 01.893s | 65 | 24 39 |
| 7 | Olivier Panis | BAR Honda | +1m 04.977s | 65 | 24 43 |
| 8 | Kimi Räikkönen | Sauber Petronas | +1m 19.808s | 65 | 23 38 |
| 9 | Mika Häkkinen | McLaren Mercedes | Clutch | 64 | 27 50 |
| 10 | Jean Alesi | Prost Acer | +1 lap | 64 | 23 50 |
| 11 | Luciano Burti | Prost Acer | +1 lap | 64 | 24 47 |
| 12 | Jos Verstappen | Arrows Asiatech | +2 laps | 63 | 19 39 |
| 13 | Fernando Alonso | European Minardi | +2 laps | 63 | 16 39 |
| 14 | Giancarlo Fisichella | Benetton Renault | +2 laps | 63 | 23 40 |
| 15 | Jenson Button | Benetton Renault | +3 laps | 62 | 17 41 |
| 16 | Tarso Marques | European Minardi | +3 laps | 62 | 18 41 |
| Ret | Rubens Barrichello | Ferrari | Suspension | 49 | 25 44 48 |
| Ret | Eddie Irvine | Jaguar Racing | Engine | 48 | 24 45 |
| Ret | Ralf Schumacher | BMW Williams | Brakes | 20 | |
| Ret | Enrique Bernoldi | Arrows Asiatech | Fuel pressure | 8 | 1 |
| Ret | Pedro de la Rosa | Jaguar Racing | Collision | 5 | |
| Ret | Heinz-Harald Frentzen | Jordan Honda | Collision | 5 | |

*Conditions: overcast.*

### PITSTOP TIMES (from pitlane entrance to exit)

| | | | | |
|---|---|---|---|---|
| Fastest pitstop: | Barrichello | Ferrari | 29.205s | Lap 48 |
| Slowest pitstop: | Button | Benetton Renault | 44.060s | Lap 17 |
| Most pitstops: | Coulthard, Button | Three stops | | |

### PENALTIES AND FINES

| DRIVER | WHEN | PENALTY | REASON |
|---|---|---|---|
| Rubens Barrichello | Friday Practice | $5,250 | Speeding in the pitlane |
| Olivier Panis | Friday Practice | $500 | Speeding in the pitlane |

### LAP LEADERS

| | |
|---|---|
| Michael Schumacher | 1-22; 28-43; 65 |
| Mika Häkkinen | 23-27; 44-64 |
| Total laps led: M Schumacher 39; Häkkinen 26 | |

### TEMPERATURES

| | | |
|---|---|---|
| Friday: | Air: 27-28°C | Track: 17-19°C |
| Saturday: | Air: 29-30°C | Track: 18-20°C |
| Sunday: | Air: 17°C | Track: 18°C |

### CONSTRUCTOR POINTS

| | | |
|---|---|---|
| 1 | Scuderia Ferrari-Marlboro | 50 |
| 2 | West McLaren Mercedes | 32 |
| 3 | BMW Williams F1 | 18 |
| 4 | Benson & Hedges Jordan Honda | 13 |
| 5 | Red Bull Sauber Petronas | 9 |
| 6 | Lucky Strike Reynard BAR Honda | 7 |
| 7 | Mild Seven Benetton Renault | 1 |
| 8 | Orange Arrows Asiatech | 0 |
| 9 | Prost Acer | 0 |
| 10 | Jaguar Racing | 0 |
| 11 | European Minardi F1 | 0 |

T Marques  22

P de la Rosa  20
J Button  21

F Alonso  18
G Fisichella  19

E Bernoldi  16
J Verstappen  17

L Burti  14
J Alesi  15

JP Montoya  12
E Irvine  13

## SPANISH GRAND PRIX RACE ENTRY

| | DRIVER | TEAM | CHASSIS/ENGINE |
|---|---|---|---|
| 1 | Michael Schumacher | Scuderia Ferrari Marlboro | Ferrari F2001 |
| 2 | Rubens Barrichello | Scuderia Ferrari Marlboro | Ferrari F2001 |
| 3 | Mika Häkkinen | West McLaren Mercedes | McLaren Mercedes MP4-16 |
| 4 | David Coulthard | West McLaren Mercedes | McLaren Mercedes MP4-16 |
| 5 | Ralf Schumacher | BMW Williams F1 Team | BMW Williams FW23 |
| 6 | Juan Pablo Montoya | BMW Williams F1 Team | BMW Williams FW23 |
| 7 | Giancarlo Fisichella | Mild Seven Benetton Renault | Benetton Renault B201 |
| 8 | Jenson Button | Mild Seven Benetton Renault | Benetton Renault B201 |
| 9 | Olivier Panis | Lucky Strike BAR Honda | BAR Honda B003 |
| 10 | Jacques Villeneuve | Lucky Strike BAR Honda | BAR Honda B003 |
| 11 | Heinz-Harald Frentzen | Benson & Hedges Jordan Honda | Jordan Honda EJ11 |
| 12 | Jarno Trulli | Benson & Hedges Jordan Honda | Jordan Honda EJ11 |
| 14 | Jos Verstappen | Orange Arrows Asiatech | Arrows Asiatech A22 |
| 15 | Enrique Bernoldi | Orange Arrows Asiatech | Arrows Asiatech A22 |
| 16 | Nick Heidfeld | Red Bull Sauber Petronas | Sauber Petronas C20 |
| 17 | Kimi Räikkönen | Red Bull Sauber Petronas | Sauber Petronas C20 |
| 18 | Eddie Irvine | Jaguar Racing | Jaguar Cosworth R2 |
| 19 | Pedro de la Rosa | Jaguar Racing | Jaguar Cosworth R2 |
| 20 | Tarso Marques | European Minardi | Minardi European PS01 |
| 21 | Fernando Alonso | European Minardi | Minardi European PS01 |
| 22 | Jean Alesi | Prost Grand Prix | Prost ACER AP04 |
| 23 | Luciano Burti | Prost Grand Prix | Prost ACER AP04 |

Michael Schumacher sprays Juan Pablo Montoya on his first trip to the podium.

## QUALIFYING: SATURDAY 28TH APRIL, 1PM–2PM *107 per cent time: 1m 23.675s*

| | DRIVER | TEAM | TIME | GAP | LAPS |
|---|---|---|---|---|---|
| 1 | Michael Schumacher | Ferrari | 1m 18.201s | 0.000 | 8 |
| 2 | Mika Häkkinen | McLaren Mercedes | 1m 18.286s | +0.085s | 12 |
| 3 | David Coulthard | McLaren Mercedes | 1m 18.635s | +0.434s | 12 |
| 4 | Rubens Barrichello | Ferrari | 1m 18.674s | +0.473s | 11 |
| 5 | Ralf Schumacher | BMW Williams | 1m 19.016s | +0.815s | 12 |
| 6 | Jarno Trulli | Jordan Honda | 1m 19.093s | +0.892s | 12 |
| 7 | Jacques Villeneuve | BAR Honda | 1m 19.122s | +0.921s | 10 |
| 8 | Heinz-Harald Frentzen | Jordan Honda | 1m 19.150s | +0.949s | 12 |
| 9 | Kimi Räikkönen | Sauber Petronas | 1m 19.229s | +1.028s | 12 |
| 10 | Nick Heidfeld | Sauber Petronas | 1m 19.232s | +1.031s | 11 |
| 11 | Olivier Panis | BAR Honda | 1m 19.479s | +1.278s | 11 |
| 12 | Juan Pablo Montoya | BMW Williams | 1m 19.660s | +1.459s | 11 |
| 13 | Eddie Irvine | Jaguar Racing | 1m 20.326s | +2.125s | 12 |
| 14 | Luciano Burti | Prost Acer | 1m 20.585s | +2.384s | 12 |
| 15 | Jean Alesi | Prost Acer | 1m 20.601s | +2.400s | 12 |
| 16 | Enrique Bernoldi | Arrows Asiatech | 1m 20.696s | +2.495s | 12 |
| 17 | Jos Verstappen | Arrows Asiatech | 1m 20.737s | +2.536s | 11 |
| 18 | Fernando Alonso | European Minardi | 1m 21.037s | +2.836s | 12 |
| 19 | Giancarlo Fisichella | Benetton Renault | 1m 21.065s | +2.864s | 12 |
| 20 | Pedro de la Rosa | Jaguar Racing | 1m 21.338s | +3.137s | 10 |
| 21 | Jenson Button | Benetton Renault | 1m 21.916s | +3.715s | 11 |
| 22 | Tarso Marques | European Minardi | 1m 22.522s | +4.321s | 12 |

## FASTEST SECTOR TIMES IN QUALIFYING *Ideal lap time: 1m 17.973s (diff. from pole: 0.228s)*

| | SECTOR 1 | SECS | | SECTOR 2 | SECS | | SECTOR 3 | SECS |
|---|---|---|---|---|---|---|---|---|
| 1 | M Schumacher | 22.679 | 1 | M Schumacher | 31.070 | 1 | Häkkinen | 24.224 |
| 2 | Barrichello | 22.710 | 2 | Häkkinen | 31.199 | 2 | M Schumacher | 24.332 |
| 3 | Häkkinen | 22.727 | 3 | Barrichello | 31.203 | 3 | Coulthard | 24.346 |
| 4 | Coulthard | 22.851 | 4 | R. Schumacher | 31.293 | 4 | Frentzen | 24.493 |
| 5 | R Schumacher | 22.930 | 5 | Coulthard | 31.349 | 5 | Heidfeld | 24.531 |
| 6 | Trulli | 22.933 | 6 | Villeneuve | 31.379 | 6 | Räikkönen | 24.560 |
| 7 | Heidfeld | 23.006 | 7 | Trulli | 31.421 | 7 | Barrichello | 24.585 |
| 8 | Frentzen | 23.018 | 8 | Frentzen | 31.435 | 8 | Villeneuve | 24.600 |
| 9 | Montoya | 23.028 | 9 | Räikkönen | 31.445 | 9 | Trulli | 24.608 |
| 10 | Panis | 23.034 | 10 | Heidfeld | 31.456 | 10 | R Schumacher | 24.644 |
| 11 | Räikkönen | 23.064 | 11 | Montoya | 31.542 | 11 | Panis | 24.742 |
| 12 | Villeneuve | 23.143 | 12 | Panis | 31.566 | 12 | Irvine | 24.944 |
| 13 | Verstappen | 23.296 | 13 | Irvine | 31.944 | 13 | Alesi | 24.989 |
| 14 | Bernoldi | 23.350 | 14 | Burti | 31.980 | 14 | Montoya | 25.003 |
| 15 | Irvine | 23.435 | 15 | Bernoldi | 31.992 | 15 | Burti | 25.011 |
| 16 | Alesi | 23.478 | 16 | Alesi | 32.060 | 16 | Fisichella | 25.126 |
| 17 | Fisichella | 23.554 | 17 | Verstappen | 32.192 | 17 | Alonso | 25.142 |
| 18 | Burti | 23.594 | 18 | Fisichella | 32.271 | 18 | Bernoldi | 25.246 |
| 19 | Alonso | 23.601 | 19 | Alonso | 32.291 | 19 | Verstappen | 25.249 |
| 20 | de la Rosa | 23.684 | 20 | de la Rosa | 32.313 | 20 | de la Rosa | 25.341 |
| 21 | Button | 23.773 | 21 | Button | 32.529 | 21 | Button | 25.498 |
| 22 | Marques | 24.044 | 22 | Marques | 32.768 | 22 | Marques | 25.530 |

## PRACTICE SESSION ONE

FRIDAY 27TH APRIL 2001, 11AM–12PM

| | | |
|---|---|---|
| 1 | Coulthard | 1m 20.388s |
| 2 | Barrichello | 1m 20.823s |
| 3 | M Schumacher | 1m 20.992s |
| 4 | R Schumacher | 1m 21.259s |
| 5 | Häkkinen | 1m 21.265s |
| 6 | Panis | 1m 21.815s |
| 7 | Montoya | 1m 22.020s |
| 8 | Trulli | 1m 22.194s |
| 9 | Frentzen | 1m 22.221s |
| 10 | Heidfeld | 1m 22.561s |
| 11 | Räikkönen | 1m 23.042s |
| 12 | Irvine | 1m 23.213s |
| 13 | de la Rosa | 1m 23.395s |
| 14 | Villeneuve | 1m 23.704s |
| 15 | Bernoldi | 1m 23.784s |
| 16 | Alesi | 1m 23.979s |
| 17 | Burti | 1m 24.361s |
| 18 | Fisichella | 1m 24.370s |
| 19 | Verstappen | 1m 24.873s |
| 20 | Alonso | 1m 25.199s |
| 21 | Button | 1m 25.336s |
| 22 | Marques | 1m 25.540s |

## PRACTICE SESSION TWO

FRIDAY 27TH APRIL 2001, 1PM–2PM

| | | |
|---|---|---|
| 1 | Coulthard | 1m 20.107s |
| 2 | Irvine | 1m 20.615s |
| 3 | Barrichello | 1m 20.823s |
| 4 | Panis | 1m 20.826s |
| 5 | M Schumacher | 1m 20.880s |
| 6 | Häkkinen | 1m 20.894s |
| 7 | de la Rosa | 1m 21.184s |
| 8 | R Schumacher | 1m 21.259s |
| 9 | Villeneuve | 1m 21.401s |
| 10 | Trulli | 1m 21.647s |
| 11 | Räikkönen | 1m 21.786s |
| 12 | Heidfeld | 1m 21.808s |
| 13 | Montoya | 1m 22.020s |
| 14 | Frentzen | 1m 22.221s |
| 15 | Alesi | 1m 22.843s |
| 16 | Bernoldi | 1m 22.888s |
| 17 | Verstappen | 1m 22.962s |
| 18 | Fisichella | 1m 22.971s |
| 19 | Button | 1m 23.201s |
| 20 | Alonso | 1m 23.801s |
| 21 | Burti | 1m 23.885s |
| 22 | Marques | 1m 25.540s |

## PRACTICE SESSION THREE

SATURDAY 28TH APRIL 2001, 9AM–9.45AM

| | | |
|---|---|---|
| 1 | M Schumacher | 1m 18.634s |
| 2 | Häkkinen | 1m 19.281s |
| 3 | Coulthard | 1m 19.363s |
| 4 | Barrichello | 1m 19.363s |
| 5 | Trulli | 1m 19.827s |
| 6 | Frentzen | 1m 19.903s |
| 7 | Heidfeld | 1m 20.042s |
| 8 | Räikkönen | 1m 20.469s |
| 9 | R Schumacher | 1m 20.527s |
| 10 | Panis | 1m 20.689s |
| 11 | Villeneuve | 1m 20.855s |
| 12 | Irvine | 1m 21.289s |
| 13 | Montoya | 1m 21.328s |
| 14 | Verstappen | 1m 22.136s |
| 15 | Alesi | 1m 22.264s |
| 16 | de la Rosa | 1m 22.296s |
| 17 | Bernoldi | 1m 22.384s |
| 18 | Burti | 1m 23.042s |
| 19 | Fisichella | 1m 23.147s |
| 20 | Button | 1m 23.506s |
| 21 | Alonso | 1m 23.956s |
| 22 | Marques | 1m 24.469s |

## PRACTICE SESSION FOUR

SATURDAY 28TH APRIL 2001, 10.15AM–11AM

| | | |
|---|---|---|
| 1 | M Schumacher | 1m 18.634s |
| 2 | Barrichello | 1m 18.674s |
| 3 | Coulthard | 1m 18.686s |
| 4 | Räikkönen | 1m 18.765s |
| 5 | Heidfeld | 1m 19.010s |
| 6 | Trulli | 1m 19.186s |
| 7 | Panis | 1m 19.253s |
| 8 | Häkkinen | 1m 19.281s |
| 9 | R Schumacher | 1m 19.406s |
| 10 | Villeneuve | 1m 19.577s |
| 11 | Frentzen | 1m 19.903s |
| 12 | Montoya | 1m 20.202s |
| 13 | Alesi | 1m 20.741s |
| 14 | Burti | 1m 20.801s |
| 15 | Bernoldi | 1m 20.997s |
| 16 | Verstappen | 1m 21.069s |
| 17 | Irvine | 1m 21.289s |
| 18 | Fisichella | 1m 21.404s |
| 19 | Alonso | 1m 21.493s |
| 20 | Button | 1m 21.804s |
| 21 | de la Rosa | 1m 22.296s |
| 22 | Marques | 1m 24.371s |

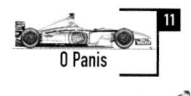
O Panis — 11

K Räikkönen — 9

J Villeneuve — 7

R Schumacher — 5

D Coulthard — 3

M Schumacher — 1

N Heidfeld — 10

HH Frentzen — 8

J Trulli — 6

R Barrichello — 4

M Häkkinen — 2

## BARCELONA LAP-BY-LAP REPORT

**PRE-START** At the start of the parade lap, David Coulthard's McLaren failed to leave the grid. The McLaren mechanics restarted the engine but Coulthard was forced to start from the back of the grid — a major setback at a track where overtaking is very difficult.

**LAP 1** Despite all the new electronic systems, the only man to suffer at the start was Heinz-Harald Frentzen, who somehow managed to de-activate his launch-control system and was left sitting on the grid. This caused a few anxious moments as cars jinked to avoid the Jordan. The Saubers had to be careful to avoid hitting each other and this allowed Juan Pablo Montoya to get ahead of both of them. At the first corner Montoya was alongside Jacques Villeneuve. The BAR driver braked earlier so Montoya took sixth place behind Michael Schumacher, Mika Häkkinen, Rubens Barrichello, Ralf Schumacher and Jarno Trulli. Coulthard had further problems when he was hit from behind by Giancarlo Fisichella's Benetton and punted into Enrique Bernoldi's Arrows Asiatech. This meant both Coulthard and Bernoldi had to pit at the end of the first lap.

**LAP 2** Michael Schumacher tried to break away from Mika Häkkinen but the Finn held on grimly as the two leaders began to pull away from Rubens Barrichello.

**LAP 3** Olivier Panis tried to make up for a slow start and passed Kimi Räikkönen to take 10th. Further back, Alonso made a mistake and dropped behind Pedro de la Rosa's Jaguar and Frentzen's recovering Jordan. At the very back of the field Coulthard set the fastest lap of the race as he tried to recover from his early problems.

**LAP 4** Olivier Panis tried to take ninth place away from Eddie Irvine but the move at the first corner was not successful. The Frenchman thus found himself stuck behind the Jaguar. At the back, David Coulthard set another fastest lap.

**LAP 6** Frentzen and de la Rosa collided as the Jordan driver tried to force his way past the local hero in his first race for Jaguar. Both men retired from the race, Frentzen feeling particularly aggrieved that de la Rosa had taken him out.

**LAP 9** Bernoldi, who was running at the tail of the field, retired with a fuel pressure problem.

**LAP 13** Coulthard caught and overtook the Minardi of Tarso Marques, which was running in 18th.

**LAP 15** David Coulthard overtook Jenson Button in order to move into 17th place.

**LAP 16** Sixteenth-placed Fernando Alonso pitted for the first time and fell to the back of the field.

**LAP 17** Button went into the pits for his scheduled stop. Coulthard, in the meantime, overtook Button's team-mate, Giancarlo Fisichella, to move up to 15th position.

**LAP 19** Jos Verstappen fell from 12th to 16th position when he pitted.

**LAP 21** Ralf Schumacher went off into the sand with a brake problem. The BMW Williams driver was not able to rejoin after his spin. At the same time Jarno Trulli and Juan Pablo Montoya, who were suddenly fighting for fourth position, both screamed into the pits. BAR Honda's Jacques Villeneuve moved up to fourth place. Montoya got ahead of Trulli at the stop.

**LAP 23** Michael Schumacher pitted and handed over the lead to Häkkinen. Barrichello was promoted to second place. Villeneuve pitted and rejoined in eighth. Räikkönen, Jean Alesi and Fisichella each also called in to the pits for fuel and tyres.

**LAP 24** As Häkkinen worked hard to give himself an advantage, he set the fastest lap of the race. While this was happening, the pitstops continued with Nick Heidfeld, Eddie Irvine, Olivier Panis and Luciano Burti all stopping for fuel and tyres.

**LAP 25** Second-placed Rubens Barrichello pitted and fell back behind Schumacher. Michael then set the fastest lap as he tried to maintain his advantage over Mika Häkkinen.

**LAP 27** Crunch time! Mika Häkkinen pitted, but Michael Schumacher had done enough to keep the lead when the Finn came hurrying out to rejoin the track. Rubens Barrichello was back to third, with BMW Williams' Juan Pablo Montoya fourth and Jacques Villeneuve fifth, having got the better of Jarno Trulli during the pitstop sequence. By then, Nick Heidfeld was seventh. David Coulthard had not pitted and so had moved up to eighth place.

**LAP 28** David Coulthard pitted and rejoined the race in 11th place. His next target was Olivier Panis, who was behind the duelling duo of Eddie Irvine and Kimi Räikkönen. The race then settled down, with no one able to overtake.

**LAP 38** Räikkönen, running ninth, pitted for a second time, hoping to get ahead of Irvine who was slowing him down. The Finn rejoined in 11th place, behind Coulthard.

**LAP 39** Heidfeld dived into the pits from seventh position. He emerged ahead of Räikkönen in 10th. At the back of the field, Verstappen and Alonso came in for their second stops.

**LAP 40** Sixth-placed Jarno Trulli came into the pits and fell behind Eddie Irvine, Olivier Panis and David Coulthard. But all three would have to stop again. Further back down the field, Giancarlo Fisichella had his second pitstop and fell behind Fernando Alonso.

**LAP 41** Montoya and Villeneuve stopped at the same time. Montoya was not under threat, but when Villeneuve rejoined he found himself behind Coulthard. At the tail of the field Marques and Button both pitted. They re-emerged nose-to-tail.

**LAP 43** The leader, Michael Schumacher, pitted, letting Mika Häkkinen head the field again. Olivier Panis, running fifth for a moment, also stopped and dropped back to 10th.

**LAP 44** Rubens Barrichello and David Coulthard stopped. The former rejoined in third position while Coulthard got out in 10th, ahead of Olivier Panis. Mika Häkkinen was now lapping much faster than Michael Schumacher, who had encountered a vibration problem with his new set of tyres.

**LAP 45** Eddie Irvine's decision to run for longer than his rivals had lifted the Jaguar driver to fourth place, but his pitstop dropped him back to eighth position.

**LAP 48** Barrichello had a suspension problem and ran off the track into a sandtrap. The Ferrari driver pitted, thinking that he had a puncture, and rejoined in seventh place.

**LAP 49** Rubens Barrichello retired from the race, having realised his Ferrari's problem was not tyre-related. Eddie Irvine also disappeared with engine failure.

**LAP 50** Mika Häkkinen pitted and rejoined in the lead, ahead of the troubled Schumacher. Montoya was third with Villeneuve fourth and Trulli running in fifth place.

**LAP 52** Button finally overtook Marques to take 15th place.

**LAP 60** Coulthard caught Heidfeld and overtook him as they ran to the first corner, claiming sixth place — and now in the points.

**LAP 65** Mika Häkkinen began the last lap but, as he did, his clutch exploded. The McLaren coasted down the main straight and up the hill after the first corner. It was then able to trickle down through the next few corners but, with no drive, Häkkinen was forced to pull off just after Turn Seven. The struggling Michael Schumacher — around 40 seconds behind — caught the Finn and took the lead. Juan Pablo Montoya moved into second place with Jacques Villeneuve third. Häkkinen dropped to ninth. Jarno Trulli took three points for fourth place and David Coulthard picked up two well-deserved points after a strong drive. The final point went to Nick Heidfeld and Sauber.

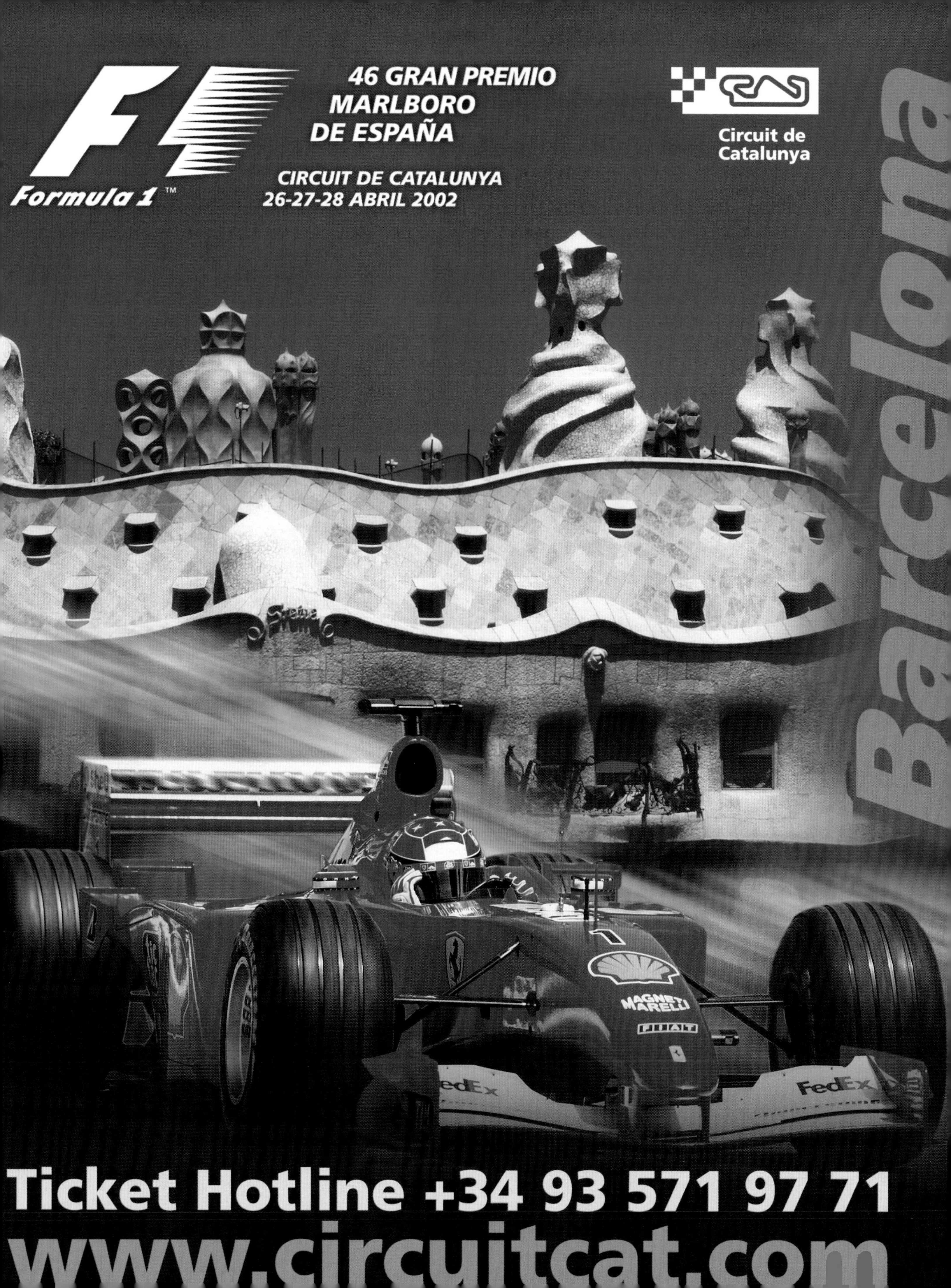

**Formula 1** ™

**46 GRAN PREMIO
MARLBORO
DE ESPAÑA**

CIRCUIT DE CATALUNYA
26-27-28 ABRIL 2002

Circuit de
Catalunya

Barcelona

# Ticket Hotline +34 93 571 97 71
# www.circuitcat.com

# Austrian Grand Prix

## 11th–13th May 2001    LAPS: 71   LENGTH OF LAP: 2.685 miles

THE OFF-ROAD RACER  A momentary concentration lapse from 1997 world champion Jacques Villeneuve sees him run
wide and take to the grass on the exit of Turn One at the A1 Ring during the Austrian Grand Prix. The French-Canadian
managed to avoid the gravel by hugging the grass verge between track and gravel trap. Pressure from the performance
of team-mate Olivier Panis has provoked maximum effort from the BAR team leader.  PHOTOGRAPH BY RAINER SCHLEGELMILCH

Juan Pablo Montoya and Ralf Schumacher demonstrated that BMW Williams had the best launch control in Formula One as they swamped the opposition at the start.

# Seventh to heaven

The Austrian Grand Prix saw an unusual phenomenon – a fight for the lead between at least three cars, from start to finish. It was the most consistently entertaining race for years and any one of the leaders could have won.

On Saturday morning, Williams' technical director Patrick Head pondered: "You know, the thing I really hope Juan Pablo doesn't come to believe is that old chestnut that overtaking is not possible in Formula One. If you look back at Jacques Villeneuve when he came into Formula One in 1996, he didn't believe it either. Remember how he passed Michael round the outside in Estoril? He was the same in 1997, too. But then we had a bad car in 1998 and he got into that old F1 habit of running with maximum downforce, and started finding it hard to pass people."

That bold pro-passing attitude is clearly one of the things Head likes most about Montoya. The last time the Colombian was at the sharp end of a Formula One grid – the last time he had a relatively trouble-free practice and qualifying – was in Brazil, where he handed Michael Schumacher the same sort of warning that Schumacher had himself delivered to the likes of Ayrton Senna, Alain Prost and Nigel Mansell in 1991: 'Watch me, I'm the next star'.

Qualifying in Austria went all Schumacher's way, giving him his 37th pole position with insouciant ease. He could barely suppress a smirk when McLaren outfumbled itself with some uncharacteristically ham-fisted set-up decisions. The two teams had been virtually inseparable all weekend, but when it mattered the red cars had an easy ride. But Barrichello was separated from his team-mate by the two BMW Williams of Montoya and Ralf Schumacher; Michael's antenna pricked up as he saw the Colombian's speed. So did Head's. "Juan Pablo is very like Nigel [Mansell]. He catches people, but you know he isn't going to be satisfied just sitting behind them," Head enthused. "Alan Jones was just like that, too. He'd sit behind a guy, placing himself one side then the other, always in the other guy's mirrors. He'd send that message that you could expect a tap pretty soon if you didn't get out of the way. The wonderful thing about Nigel was that he would come from a long way back, arc into the apex of a corner far too early and grab a place. It shouldn't have worked, but once he was alongside someone, how could they turn in? They had to give way. It's what Juan Pablo did to Michael in Brazil. I really do hope he doesn't get brainwashed by the Formula One non-overtaking syn-

drome…" Ironically, on this occasion overtaking was the least of

Set in the Tyrol mountains, the A1 Ring is a challenging and picturesque circuit.

Montoya's worries. It was Schumacher's problem. Electronics ruled the start of this race. Schumacher didn't like the feel of his launch control system on the formation lap and reverted to manual. It said everything for the champion's acumen that he made the switch flawlessly; knowing your machinery intimately is all part of the game. But here it was no match for the drag-race starts of both BMW Williams. Montoya blasted away and, as Michael lagged, Ralf stormed past him. Only a little robust positioning by Montoya kept the younger German out of the lead. His race was already doomed, however, damned by tape inadvertently left blocking part of the right rear brake duct. Within 10 laps, Ralf would be a spectator.

Chaos reigned on the grid after the start when two Jordan Hondas, a Sauber and Mika Häkkinen's McLaren were stranded on the line.

Irresistible force meets immovable object. Michael Schumacher's will to pass Juan Pablo Montoya met with an equal will on the part of the Colombian to resist the challenge. The result was that both ran wide and handed the lead to Barrichello.

Mika Häkkinen already was. And so was Heinz-Harald Frentzen. The new electronic dawn proved a false one for both men as their systems, or their understanding of their systems, let them down. They were not alone. Nick Heidfeld's excellent sixth place on the grid for Sauber was similarly wasted, as was Jarno Trulli's fifth for Jordan. It was a miracle nobody hit the four stranded cars. So much for progress.

Six laps into the race, Head's greatest fears were realised: Michelin's tyres were degrading faster than Bridgestone's. Montoya's initial spurt abated. By the time Ralf wobbled towards retirement, Michael smelled blood. For the next five laps it was cut-and-thrust, the champion trying unsuccessfully to unseat the rookie. But whatever Schumacher did, Montoya had an answer, even when the Ferrari momentarily drew alongside on the inside at the Remus right-hander on lap 12. BMW power saw Montoya through the crisis. It was only a matter of time, but he wouldn't concede the lead. Four laps later Schumacher had better grip exiting the first corner and towed along behind the Williams going down to Remus.

Montoya had been inside Schumacher's head ever since his passing move in Brazil. Now the champion became increasingly rattled at his inability to pass the Colombian. Ego was at stake here. But going down to Remus he made the sort of elementary mistake for which eight-year-old cadet karters might be forgiven, not

world champions. Montoya would not yield the inside line, so Schumacher tried a fruitless lunge down the outside, desperate to assert himself. He would not have been able to turn in cleanly even if he had outbraked Montoya but, as it was, Montoya outbraked Schumacher. In doing so he ran wide, across Schumacher's bow. They missed by a hair and neither won the battle of wills or the corner. Montoya ran wide into the gravel. Schumacher held a tighter line and got going on the grass, but not before dropping to sixth. It was no consolation for him that Montoya subsequently retired; the damage to his race prospects had been done. Had he watched how F3000 racer Justin Wilson handled a similar situation with Bas Leinders at Remus the previous day, braking harder and ducking up the inside on turn-in, he might have learned something.

After their pitstops Barrichello and Coulthard resumed what had become a race for the lead, but now the Scot had taken the initiative and resisted persistent pressure from the two Ferraris. He took a superbly judged win to maintain the championship-contending form his critics said would never last.

In defeat, Schumacher reacted angrily to questions about the ethics of Barrichello being obliged to surrender second place in the last corner. But his mind was on Montoya, whom he accused of trying to force him off the track. Recalling Schumacher's incidents with Damon Hill at Adelaide in 1994, or with Jacques Villeneuve at Jerez three years later, his audience subsided into disbelieving laughter.

Schumacher might still have been leading the world championship, but in Austria he lost on and off the track. Watch out for Schumacher v Montoya III, coming soon to a race track near you.

David Coulthard was jubilant after taking victory from way back in seventh on the grid.

# Austrian Grand Prix Race Statistics

## A1 RING CIRCUIT DIAGRAM

Illustration by Emeric de Baré

## FASTEST LAPS

|  | DRIVER | TIME | LAP |
|---|---|---|---|
| 1 | Coulthard | 1m 10.843s | 48 |
| 2 | Barrichello | 1m 11.009s | 68 |
| 3 | M Schumacher | 1m 11.030s | 69 |
| 4 | Montoya | 1m 11.140s | 40 |
| 5 | Räikkönen | 1m 11.284s | 69 |
| 6 | Heidfeld | 1m 11.388s | 69 |
| 7 | Villeneuve | 1m 11.718s | 70 |
| 8 | Irvine | 1m 12.088s | 69 |
| 9 | Panis | 1m 12.204s | 39 |
| 10 | Verstappen | 1m 12.423s | 36 |
| 11 | Burti | 1m 12.642s | 69 |
| 12 | Alesi | 1m 13.130s | 41 |
| 13 | Button | 1m 13.498s | 38 |
| 14 | Bernoldi | 1m 13.587s | 15 |
| 15 | R Schumacher | 1m 13.888s | 7 |
| 16 | de la Rosa | 1m 13.978s | 35 |
| 17 | Alonso | 1m 14.432s | 36 |
| 18 | Marques | 1m 15.212s | 25 |
| 19 | Fisichella | 1m 58.438s | 2 |
| 20 | Häkkinen | 7m 26.036s | 1 |
|  | Frentzen | No lap completed | |
|  | Trulli | Disqualified | |

## RACE SPEED TRAP TIMES

| 1 | Montoya | 191.6mph |
|---|---|---|
| 2 | M Schumacher | 190.7mph |
| 3 | Villeneuve | 190.2mph |
| 4 | Heidfeld | 189.7mph |
| 5 | Barrichello | 189.5mph |
| 6 | Räikkönen | 189.0mph |
| 7 | Verstappen | 188.8mph |
| 8 | Coulthard | 188.6mph |
| 9 | Irvine | 187.9mph |
| 10 | Burti | 187.8mph |
| 11 | de la Rosa | 187.0mph |
| 12 | Panis | 186.5mph |
| 13 | Alesi | 186.1mph |
| 14 | Bernoldi | 185.4mph |
| 15 | Trulli | 185.4mph |
| 16 | Button | 184.4mph |
| 17 | R Schumacher | 184.3mph |
| 18 | Marques | 182.1mph |
| 19 | Alonso | 181.9mph |
| 20 | Fisichella | 170.0mph |
| 21 | Häkkinen | 114.9mph |
|  | Frentzen | No speed recorded |

## RACE: SUNDAY 13TH MAY 2001, 2PM

|  | DRIVER | CAR | TIME/RETIREMENT | LAPS | PITSTOP LAPS |
|---|---|---|---|---|---|
| 1 | David Coulthard | McLaren Mercedes | 1h 27m 45.927s | 71 | 50 |
| 2 | Michael Schumacher | Ferrari | +2.190s | 71 | 46 |
| 3 | Rubens Barrichello | Ferrari | +2.527s | 71 | 47 |
| 4 | Kimi Räikkönen | Sauber Petronas | +41.593s | 71 | 46 |
| 5 | Olivier Panis | BAR Honda | +53.775s | 71 | 44 |
| 6 | Jos Verstappen | Arrows Asiatech | +1 lap | 70 | 22 45 |
| 7 | Eddie Irvine | Jaguar Racing | +1 lap | 70 | 48 |
| 8 | Jacques Villeneuve | BAR Honda | +1 lap | 70 | 47 51 |
| 9 | Nick Heidfeld | Sauber Petronas | +2 laps | 69 | 46 |
| 10 | Jean Alesi | Prost Acer | +2 laps | 69 | 43 |
| 11 | Luciano Burti | Prost Acer | +2 laps | 69 | 44 |
| Ret | Jenson Button | Benetton Renault | Engine | 60 | 38 |
| Ret | Pedro de la Rosa | Jaguar Racing | Transmission | 48 | 35 |
| Ret | Juan Pablo Montoya | BMW Williams | Hydraulics | 41 | |
| Ret | Fernando Alonso | European Minardi | Gearbox | 38 | |
| Ret | Tarso Marques | European Minardi | Gearbox | 25 | |
| Ret | Enrique Bernoldi | Arrows Asiatech | Hydraulics | 17 | |
| DSQ | Jarno Trulli | Jordan Honda | Ignoring lights | 14 | |
| Ret | Ralf Schumacher | BMW Williams | Brakes | 10 | |
| Ret | Giancarlo Fisichella | Benetton Renault | Engine | 3 | |
| Ret | Mika Häkkinen | McLaren Mercedes | Transmission | 1 | |
| Ret | Heinz-Harald Frentzen | Jordan Honda | Stalled on grid | 0 | |

Conditions: sunny.

## DRIVER POINTS

| 1 | Michael Schumacher | 42 |
|---|---|---|
| 2 | David Coulthard | 38 |
| 3 | Rubens Barrichello | 18 |
| 4 | Ralf Schumacher | 12 |
| 5 | Nick Heidfeld | 8 |
| 6 | Jarno Trulli | 7 |
| 7 | Juan Pablo Montoya | 6 |
| 8 | Heinz-Harald Frentzen | 6 |
| 9 | Olivier Panis | 5 |
| 10 | Jacques Villeneuve | 4 |
| 11 | Kimi Räikkönen | 4 |
| 12 | Mika Häkkinen | 4 |
| 13 | Jos Verstappen | 1 |
| 14 | Giancarlo Fisichella | 1 |
| 15 | Eddie Irvine | 0 |
| 16 | Jean Alesi | 0 |
| 17 | Luciano Burti | 0 |
| 18 | Tarso Marques | 0 |
| 19 | Jenson Button | 0 |
| 20 | Enrique Bernoldi | 0 |
| 21 | Fernando Alonso | 0 |
| 22 | Gaston Mazzacane | 0 |
| 23 | Pedro de la Rosa | 0 |

## CONSTRUCTOR POINTS

| 1 | Scuderia Ferrari-Marlboro | 60 |
|---|---|---|
| 2 | West McLaren Mercedes | 42 |
| 3 | BMW Williams F1 | 18 |
| 4 | Benson & Hedges Jordan Honda | 13 |
| 5 | Red Bull Sauber Petronas | 12 |
| 6 | Lucky Strike Reynard BAR Honda | 9 |
| 7 | Orange Arrows Asiatech | 1 |
| 8 | Mild Seven Benetton Renault | 1 |
| 9 | Jaguar Racing | 0 |
| 10 | Prost Acer | 0 |
| 11 | European Minardi F1 | 0 |

## PITSTOP TIMES (from pitlane entrance to exit)

Due to a technical fault pitstop times for the Austrian Grand Prix are unavailable

Most pitstops:     Verstappen, Villeneuve     Two stops

## PENALTIES AND FINES

| DRIVER | WHEN | PENALTY | REASON |
|---|---|---|---|
| Olivier Panis | Friday Practice One | $500 | Speeding in the pitlane |
| Olivier Panis | Warm-up | $2,500 | Speeding in the pitlane |
| Jarno Trulli | Race | Disqualified | Ignoring safety lights |
| Jacques Villeneuve | Race | 10 seconds | Speeding in the pitlane |

## LAP LEADERS

| Juan Pablo Montoya | 1–15 |
|---|---|
| Rubens Barrichello | 16–46 |
| David Coulthard | 47–71 |

Total laps led: Barrichello 31, Coulthard 25, Montoya 15

## TEMPERATURES

| Friday: | Air: 12–14°C | Track: 19–21°C |
|---|---|---|
| Saturday: | Air: 25–26°C | Track: 17–18°C |
| Sunday: | Air: 26°C | Track: 19°C |

## WARM-UP

### SUNDAY 13TH MAY 2001, 9.30AM–10AM

| 1 | Häkkinen | 1m 11.647s |
|---|---|---|
| 2 | Coulthard | 1m 11.765s |
| 3 | Frentzen | 1m 11.800s |
| 4 | Barrichello | 1m 12.331s |
| 5 | M Schumacher | 1m 12.790s |
| 6 | Trulli | 1m 12.993s |
| 7 | Räikkönen | 1m 13.005s |
| 8 | Villeneuve | 1m 13.012s |
| 9 | de la Rosa | 1m 13.149s |
| 10 | Heidfeld | 1m 13.201s |
| 11 | Panis | 1m 13.221s |
| 12 | Irvine | 1m 13.406s |
| 13 | Bernoldi | 1m 13.543s |
| 14 | Verstappen | 1m 13.548s |
| 15 | R Schumacher | 1m 13.549s |
| 16 | Montoya | 1m 13.558s |
| 17 | Alesi | 1m 14.611s |
| 18 | Alonso | 1m 14.745s |
| 19 | Marques | 1m 15.265s |
| 20 | Burti | 1m 15.487s |
| 21 | Fisichella | 1m 15.662s |
| 22 | Button | 1m 15.692s |

J Button — 21
G Fisichella — 19
L Burti — 17
E Bernoldi — 15
E Irvine — 13
T Marques — 22
J Alesi — 20
F Alonso — 18
J Verstappen — 16
P de la Rosa — 14
J Villeneuve — 12

## AUSTRIAN GRAND PRIX RACE ENTRY

| | DRIVER | TEAM | CHASSIS/ENGINE |
|---|---|---|---|
| 1 | Michael Schumacher | Scuderia Ferrari Marlboro | Ferrari F2001 |
| 2 | Rubens Barrichello | Scuderia Ferrari Marlboro | Ferrari F2001 |
| 3 | Mika Häkkinen | West McLaren Mercedes | McLaren Mercedes MP4-16 |
| 4 | David Coulthard | West McLaren Mercedes | McLaren Mercedes MP4-16 |
| 5 | Ralf Schumacher | BMW Williams F1 Team | BMW Williams FW23 |
| 6 | Juan Pablo Montoya | BMW Williams F1 Team | BMW Williams FW23 |
| 7 | Giancarlo Fisichella | Mild Seven Benetton Renault | Benetton Renault B201 |
| 8 | Jenson Button | Mild Seven Benetton Renault | Benetton Renault B201 |
| 9 | Olivier Panis | Lucky Strike BAR Honda | BAR Honda B003 |
| 10 | Jacques Villeneuve | Lucky Strike BAR Honda | BAR Honda B003 |
| 11 | Heinz-Harald Frentzen | Benson & Hedges Jordan Honda | Jordan Honda EJ11 |
| 12 | Jarno Trulli | Benson & Hedges Jordan Honda | Jordan Honda EJ11 |
| 14 | Jos Verstappen | Orange Arrows Asiatech | Arrows Asiatech A22 |
| 15 | Enrique Bernoldi | Orange Arrows Asiatech | Arrows Asiatech A22 |
| 16 | Nick Heidfeld | Red Bull Sauber Petronas | Sauber Petronas C20 |
| 17 | Kimi Räikkönen | Red Bull Sauber Petronas | Sauber Petronas C20 |
| 18 | Eddie Irvine | Jaguar Racing | Jaguar Cosworth R2 |
| 19 | Pedro de la Rosa | Jaguar Racing | Jaguar Cosworth R2 |
| 20 | Tarso Marques | European Minardi | Minardi European PS01 |
| 21 | Fernando Alonso | European Minardi | Minardi European PS01 |
| 22 | Jean Alesi | Prost Grand Prix | Prost ACER AP04 |
| 23 | Luciano Burti | Prost Grand Prix | Prost ACER AP04 |

David Coulthard fortunately separated Ferrari team-mates Michael Schumacher and Rubens Barrichello on the A1 podium — Ferrari tension was high.

## QUALIFYING: SATURDAY 12TH MAY 2001, 1PM-2PM 107 per cent time: 1m 14.431s.

| | DRIVER | TEAM | TIME | GAP | LAPS |
|---|---|---|---|---|---|
| 1 | Michael Schumacher | Ferrari | 1m 09.562s | 0.000 | 12 |
| 2 | Juan Pablo Montoya | BMW Williams | 1m 09.686s | +0.124s | 12 |
| 3 | Ralf Schumacher | BMW Williams | 1m 09.769s | +0.207s | 11 |
| 4 | Rubens Barrichello | Ferrari | 1m 09.786s | +0.224s | 11 |
| 5 | Jarno Trulli | Jordan Honda | 1m 10.202s | +0.640s | 11 |
| 6 | Nick Heidfeld | Sauber Petronas | 1m 10.211s | +0.649s | 12 |
| 7 | David Coulthard | McLaren Mercedes | 1m 10.331s | +0.769s | 12 |
| 8 | Mika Häkkinen | McLaren Mercedes | 1m 10.342s | +0.780s | 11 |
| 9 | Kimi Räikkönen | Sauber Petronas | 1m 10.396s | +0.834s | 12 |
| 10 | Olivier Panis | BAR Honda | 1m 10.435s | +0.873s | 12 |
| 11 | Heinz-Harald Frentzen | Jordan Honda | 1m 10.923s | +1.361s | 11 |
| 12 | Jacques Villeneuve | BAR Honda | 1m 11.058s | +1.496s | 11 |
| 13 | Eddie Irvine | Jaguar Racing | 1m 11.632s | +2.070s | 12 |
| 14 | Pedro de la Rosa | Jaguar Racing | 1m 11.752s | +2.190s | 12 |
| 15 | Enrique Bernoldi | Arrows Asiatech | 1m 11.823s | +2.261s | 12 |
| 16 | Jos Verstappen | Arrows Asiatech | 1m 12.187s | +2.625s | 11 |
| 17 | Luciano Burti | Prost Acer | 1m 12.206s | +2.644s | 12 |
| 18 | Fernando Alonso | European Minardi | 1m 12.640s | +3.078s | 12 |
| 19 | Giancarlo Fisichella | Benetton Renault | 1m 12.644s | +3.082s | 8 |
| 20 | Jean Alesi | Prost Acer | 1m 12.910s | +3.348s | 10 |
| 21 | Jenson Button | Benetton Renault | 1m 13.459s | +3.897s | 11 |
| 22 | Tarso Marques | European Minardi | 1m 13.585s | +4.023s | 5 |

## FASTEST SECTOR TIMES IN QUALIFYING Ideal lap time: 1m 09.149s (diff. from pole: 0.413s)

| | SECTOR 1 | SECS | | SECTOR 2 | SECS | | SECTOR 3 | SECS |
|---|---|---|---|---|---|---|---|---|
| 1 | Montoya | 17.411 | 1 | M Schumacher | 29.509 | 1 | M Schumacher | 22.229 |
| 2 | R Schumacher | 17.451 | 2 | Trulli | 29.606 | 2 | Barrichello | 22.478 |
| 3 | Barrichello | 17.453 | 3 | Montoya | 29.647 | 3 | Heidfeld | 22.504 |
| 4 | Trulli | 17.556 | 4 | R Schumacher | 29.708 | 4 | Montoya | 22.513 |
| 5 | Panis | 17.585 | 5 | Barrichello | 29.809 | 5 | R Schumacher | 22.589 |
| 6 | M Schumacher | 17.587 | 6 | Coulthard | 29.842 | 6 | Häkkinen | 22.610 |
| 7 | Frentzen | 17.637 | 7 | Räikkönen | 29.843 | 7 | Räikkönen | 22.683 |
| 8 | Coulthard | 17.646 | 8 | Panis | 29.878 | 8 | Coulthard | 22.761 |
| 9 | Häkkinen | 17.670 | 9 | Heidfeld | 29.881 | 9 | Trulli | 22.880 |
| 10 | Heidfeld | 17.715 | 10 | Häkkinen | 29.924 | 10 | Panis | 22.906 |
| 11 | Räikkönen | 17.731 | 11 | Frentzen | 29.948 | 11 | Villeneuve | 22.974 |
| 12 | Villeneuve | 17.783 | 12 | Villeneuve | 30.220 | 12 | Frentzen | 23.109 |
| 13 | Verstappen | 17.839 | 13 | Irvine | 30.334 | 13 | Verstappen | 23.121 |
| 14 | Irvine | 17.846 | 14 | de la Rosa | 30.453 | 14 | Irvine | 23.201 |
| 15 | Bernoldi | 17.854 | 15 | Bernoldi | 30.613 | 15 | de la Rosa | 23.227 |
| 16 | Burti | 17.974 | 16 | Fisichella | 30.617 | 16 | Bernoldi | 23.356 |
| 17 | Alonso | 18.017 | 17 | Burti | 30.698 | 17 | Burti | 23.482 |
| 18 | de la Rosa | 18.029 | 18 | Verstappen | 30.726 | 18 | Alesi | 23.526 |
| 19 | Alesi | 18.078 | 19 | Alonso | 30.788 | 19 | Alonso | 23.653 |
| 20 | Fisichella | 18.219 | 20 | Button | 31.029 | 20 | Fisichella | 23.808 |
| 21 | Button | 18.288 | 21 | Marques | 31.069 | 21 | Marques | 23.855 |
| 22 | Marques | 18.661 | 22 | Alesi | 31.091 | 22 | Button | 23.973 |

## PRACTICE SESSION ONE

FRIDAY 11TH MAY 2001, 11AM-12PM

| | | |
|---|---|---|
| 1 | Häkkinen | 1m 11.751s |
| 2 | Coulthard | 1m 12.036s |
| 3 | Barrichello | 1m 12.222s |
| 4 | Räikkönen | 1m 12.617s |
| 5 | R Schumacher | 1m 12.668s |
| 6 | M Schumacher | 1m 12.851s |
| 7 | Bernoldi | 1m 12.853s |
| 8 | Panis | 1m 12.954s |
| 9 | Verstappen | 1m 13.024s |
| 10 | Heidfeld | 1m 13.259s |
| 11 | Trulli | 1m 13.315s |
| 12 | Montoya | 1m 13.366s |
| 13 | Villeneuve | 1m 13.492s |
| 14 | Irvine | 1m 14.027s |
| 15 | de la Rosa | 1m 14.636s |
| 16 | Alesi | 1m 14.742s |
| 17 | Burti | 1m 15.086s |
| 18 | Fisichella | 1m 15.256s |
| 19 | Button | 1m 15.570s |
| 20 | Alonso | 1m 15.945s |
| 21 | Marques | 1m 15.965s |
| 22 | Frentzen | 1m 21.728s |

## PRACTICE SESSION TWO

FRIDAY 11TH MAY 2001, 1PM-2PM

| | | |
|---|---|---|
| 1 | Coulthard | 1m 11.245s |
| 2 | Häkkinen | 1m 11.272s |
| 3 | Barrichello | 1m 11.401s |
| 4 | R Schumacher | 1m 11.555s |
| 5 | M Schumacher | 1m 11.647s |
| 6 | Heidfeld | 1m 11.776s |
| 7 | Frentzen | 1m 11.977s |
| 8 | Räikkönen | 1m 12.189s |
| 9 | Panis | 1m 12.259s |
| 10 | Villeneuve | 1m 12.290s |
| 11 | Montoya | 1m 12.299s |
| 12 | Irvine | 1m 12.346s |
| 13 | Trulli | 1m 12.555s |
| 14 | Verstappen | 1m 12.705s |
| 15 | de la Rosa | 1m 12.847s |
| 16 | Bernoldi | 1m 12.853s |
| 17 | Burti | 1m 13.169s |
| 18 | Alesi | 1m 13.288s |
| 19 | Marques | 1m 14.314s |
| 20 | Alonso | 1m 14.523s |
| 21 | Fisichella | 1m 14.833s |
| 22 | Button | 1m 15.570s |

## PRACTICE SESSION THREE

SATURDAY 12TH MAY 2001, 9AM-9.45AM

| | | |
|---|---|---|
| 1 | M Schumacher | 1m 10.094s |
| 2 | Montoya | 1m 10.391s |
| 3 | Häkkinen | 1m 10.548s |
| 4 | Barrichello | 1m 10.821s |
| 5 | Coulthard | 1m 10.966s |
| 6 | Frentzen | 1m 11.052s |
| 7 | Panis | 1m 11.351s |
| 8 | Villeneuve | 1m 11.367s |
| 9 | Räikkönen | 1m 11.784s |
| 10 | Heidfeld | 1m 11.795s |
| 11 | Verstappen | 1m 11.831s |
| 12 | R Schumacher | 1m 11.937s |
| 13 | Irvine | 1m 12.197s |
| 14 | Trulli | 1m 12.283s |
| 15 | Bernoldi | 1m 12.418s |
| 16 | de la Rosa | 1m 13.313s |
| 17 | Alesi | 1m 13.485s |
| 18 | Fisichella | 1m 13.928s |
| 19 | Burti | 1m 14.056s |
| 20 | Alonso | 1m 14.132s |
| 21 | Button | 1m 14.638s |
| | Marques | No time set |

## PRACTICE SESSION FOUR

SATURDAY 12TH MAY 2001, 10.15AM-11AM

| | | |
|---|---|---|
| 1 | Coulthard | 1m 10.010s |
| 2 | M Schumacher | 1m 10.039s |
| 3 | Barrichello | 1m 10.103s |
| 4 | Häkkinen | 1m 10.148s |
| 5 | Montoya | 1m 10.391s |
| 6 | R Schumacher | 1m 10.397s |
| 7 | Frentzen | 1m 10.434s |
| 8 | Trulli | 1m 10.751s |
| 9 | Heidfeld | 1m 10.863s |
| 10 | Villeneuve | 1m 10.935s |
| 11 | Panis | 1m 11.351s |
| 12 | Räikkönen | 1m 11.382s |
| 13 | Irvine | 1m 11.543s |
| 14 | Verstappen | 1m 11.831s |
| 15 | de la Rosa | 1m 11.994s |
| 16 | Bernoldi | 1m 12.029s |
| 17 | Burti | 1m 12.714s |
| 18 | Alonso | 1m 13.333s |
| 19 | Fisichella | 1m 13.345s |
| 20 | Marques | 1m 13.368s |
| 21 | Alesi | 1m 13.485s |
| 22 | Button | 1m 13.969s |

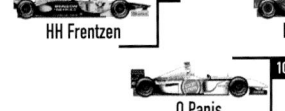
HH Frentzen

K Räikkönen

D Coulthard

J Trulli

R Schumacher

M Schumacher

O Panis

M Häkkinen

N Heidfeld

R Barrichello

JP Montoya

## A1 RING LAP-BY-LAP REPORT

**LAP 1** The start was a muddled business with no fewer than four cars left standing on the grid when the lights went out: fifth-placed Jarno Trulli, sixth-placed Nick Heidfeld, eighth-placed Mika Häkkinen and 11th-placed Heinz-Harald Frentzen. There were several near-misses as those behind weaved through the car park, with drivers at the very back able to gain the most as they had more time to react. Eddie Irvine came from 13th to sixth, Jos Verstappen from 16th to seventh and Giancarlo Fisichella from 19th to 12th. At the front of the grid everyone got away without a problem, but the Williams' launch control was the best and Juan Pablo Montoya took the lead, fending off Ralf Schumacher under braking for the first corner. Michael Schumacher was third with Rubens Barrichello behind him followed by David Coulthard and Eddie Irvine, although the Jaguar driver soon dropped behind Kimi Räikkönen's Sauber. Mika Häkkinen's car refused to be moved so the race director sent out the safety car. Jarno Trulli and Nick Heidfeld were able to get going, Jarno rejoining at high speed and ignoring the red light as he did so. Mika Häkkinen also rejoined later but retired after one exploratory lap.

**LAP 4** As the race restarted Juan Pablo Montoya maintained his advantage as the two Williams BMWs went into the first corner. The man on the move was Jos Verstappen, who was able to pass Eddie Irvine and Kimi Räikkönen with ease, suggesting the Arrows team (as usual) was running with a light fuel load. Giancarlo Fisichella went out with an engine failure.

**LAP 5** Jos Verstappen continued to make dramatic progress and swept ahead of David Coulthard with such ease, it was clear the Arrows was on a two-stop strategy and Coulthard's McLaren had a heavy fuel load. At the tail of the field Jarno Trulli went off and lost a place to Nick Heidfeld.

**LAP 7** Juan Pablo Montoya and Ralf Schumacher were not able to pull away from the Ferraris or Jos Verstappen because of their heavy fuel loads. Ralf began to struggle as his brakes faded. BAR Honda's Olivier Panis, who lost out at the start, was beginning to charge and overtook Eddie Irvine for eighth.

**LAP 9** Enrique Bernoldi began to make progress and passed Jacques Villeneuve and Eddie Irvine in order to move up to ninth position. Villeneuve then found himself under attack from Pedro de la Rosa in the second Jaguar.

**LAP 10** Ralf Schumacher disappeared into the pits with no brakes at all and retired immediately. Jacques Villeneuve, suffering from bad understeer, was challenged for 11th place by de la Rosa and ended up spinning at Turn One.

**LAP 11** Juan Pablo Montoya appeared to be in trouble as the gap to the Ferraris of Schumacher and Barrichello disappeared. The Colombian was struggling with a heavy fuel load.

**LAP 14** Pedro de la Rosa was overtaken by Jacques Villeneuve, who repassed him for what had by then become 10th place. The field was thinned out further when Jarno Trulli was black-flagged for having ignored the red light at the pitlane exit.

**LAP 16** After two laps of running nose-to-tail, Michael Schumacher challenged Juan Pablo Montoya for the lead on the outside on the run-up to Turn Two. Schumacher braked late but Montoya braked even later and both slid off the racing line. Schumacher later complained that Montoya took him off deliberately, but neither was fully in control as they tried to out-do one another. The move let Rubens Barrichello take the lead, chased by Jos Verstappen, David Coulthard, Kimi Räikkönen and Olivier Panis. Schumacher rejoined in sixth, with Montoya slower to rejoin as he had to drive across the sandtrap, causing his tyres to lose grip. He was running seventh.

**LAP 17** Enrique Bernoldi stopped with hydraulic failure, allowing Jaguar's Eddie Irvine to move up to eighth position. Further back the two Prosts swapped places, Jean Alesi overtaking team-mate Luciano Burti to run in 12th place.

**LAP 23** Everyone knew Verstappen's position was a temporary one and the Arrows driver pitted. He dropped to seventh.

**LAP 25** Michael Schumacher was now the man on the move. He overtook Panis to claim fourth position.

**LAP 26** Tarso Marques went out with a gearbox problem.

**LAP 28** Michael Schumacher passed Kimi Räikkönen to move up to third place. Also on the move was Jean Alesi, who overtook Jaguar's Pedro de la Rosa for 10th.

**LAP 29** Burti was passed for 12th place by Jenson Button.

**LAP 36** Pedro de la Rosa pitted with a transmission problem, which dropped him to the back of the field.

**LAP 38** Juan Pablo Montoya overtook Olivier Panis to take fifth place. Further back, European Minardi's Fernando Alonso retired from 13th position with a gearbox problem.

**LAP 39** Button was the first one-stopper to come into the pits.

**LAP 41** Michael Schumacher's charge had taken him up to David Coulthard and the pair started to reel in Rubens Barrichello to make it a three-man fight for the lead.

**LAP 42** Fifth-placed Montoya suffered a hydraulic failure and retired, promoting Panis to fifth and Verstappen to sixth.

**LAP 44** Panis stopped and dropped behind Verstappen.

**LAP 45** As expected Verstappen stopped again and lost more ground, dropping from fifth to eighth position.

**LAP 46** Schumacher and Räikkönen both pitted but were able to retain their positions in the race.

**LAP 47** Rubens Barrichello had to stop to refuel his Ferrari so David Coulthard took the lead and immediately began to charge hard to build a big gap before his pitstop. Jacques Villeneuve also stopped but drove too quickly in the pitlane and was later given a 10-second stop-go speeding penalty.

**LAP 48** Coulthard set the fastest lap of the race. Irvine, running in sixth place, pitted and fell back to seventh position.

**LAP 50** Coulthard pitted for his critical stop. His extra fast laps had made the difference and he rejoined still in the lead.

**LAP 51** Villeneuve paid his penalty but had a big enough advantage in eighth position to retain the place.

**LAP 55** After driving hard all day at the back of the field, Heidfeld finally caught up with Button and was able to take 11th.

**LAP 62** Jenson Button went out with engine failure, which set the rear end of the car on fire and caused the Benetton driver to spin on his own oil. Nick Heidfeld passed Luciano Burti to take 10th, while Kimi Räikkönen lapped Burti near to the scene of the Button incident. BAR later protested that Räikkönen should have been penalised for overtaking under a yellow flag. The protest was rejected, but BAR announced that it would appeal the decision.

**LAP 68** Nick Heidfeld continued to make progress and overtook Jean Alesi to claim ninth place.

**LAP 71** On the last lap Ferrari team boss Jean Todt radioed Rubens Barrichello to tell him to allow Schumacher to overtake him. Barrichello did not respond to several radio calls. Todt became increasingly agitated, reminding Barrichello that it was 'for the championship'. Barrichello decided at the last corner to lift off and let Schumacher go ahead but was very unhappy after the race, barely acknowledging Todt before the podium ceremony and refusing to discuss his feelings about Todt's instructions. Behind Coulthard, Michael Schumacher and Barrichello was a delighted Räikkönen in fourth. Panis was fifth with Verstappen sixth, a lap behind. Irvine was only four seconds behind. Villeneuve finished a lacklustre eighth.

# Monaco Grand Prix

24th–27th May 2001  LAPS: 78  LENGTH OF LAP: 2.094 miles

MAGICAL MONACO  Eddie Irvine swings the Jaguar R2 into Portier between the confines of Armco and advertising hoardings. The Monaco circuit demands total concentration and discipline. Irvine's efforts brought Jaguar its first podium and its best result of the year.  PHOTOGRAPH BY RAINER SCHLEGELMILCH

## Formula One's fabulous weekend

The Monaco Grand Prix is the most important motor race in the world — and the most difficult for drivers. Guiding 220mph cars through narrow roads with only inches to spare is a true test of driver ability. Michael Schumacher is the acknowledged master of Monaco — and so it proved again in 2001. He now only needs one more victory to beat the late Ayrton Senna's record of six wins. But until 2pm it seemed as though another driver might carry off the spoils and challenge Monaco's master. That David Coulthard didn't win his second Monaco Grand Prix in a row was pure bad luck; that he didn't challenge for a podium was down to his own caution and his eye being firmly on the championship table. But Monaco is more than just racing — it is also about 150,000 people enjoying themselves. For the lucky few it is the ultimate in hedonism and a weekend to remember.

T he Monaco Grand Prix is actually two races: the small matter of a Formula One battle for two hours on the Sunday afternoon and the huge matter of having the swankiest yacht on the swankiest mooring with the swankiest celebrities on board. This year was no different. The big battle actually took place three hours before the race, as Jacques Villeneuve and Eddie Irvine fought it out for pole position in the harbour. Their battle would resume on track later in the afternoon.

Jenson Button qualified third in the harbour, with an impressive new £1 million Princess yacht bedecked with beautiful girls who seemed to have packed only bikinis. McLaren's Ron Dennis made an impressive bid to steal the limelight, but could only manage fourth after his gigantic yacht was mistaken for a Club 18-30 cruise ship.

By midday, with two hours to go before the Grand Prix, gentlemen think about starting their engines and ladies think about starting their hairdryers ready for a grid appearance that must be perfect for the TV cameras. Rachel Hunter was on parade for Jaguar, which thought she was an important role model for selling the new X-Type to indepen-

Sainte Devote on the first lap requires great precision and skill in the jockeying for position at the first corner and sets the running order.

Jenson Button battled on to a surprise Benetton finish in seventh place.

dent ladies of independent means. The notion that a Jaguar is a man's car is being well and truly buried.

Fleet Street's best had forgotten about the race — all they wanted to know was whether rap singer Sean 'Puff Daddy' Coombs was dating Naomi Campbell. They were certainly an item on the starting grid and in the paddock, which probably explained why Benetton boss Flavio Briatore had been looking so miserable lately. Elsewhere Pelé, the Duchess of York, Prince Albert of Monaco and reportedly Julia Roberts were lapping up the atmosphere, as were 150,000 other people.

Monaco's notorious street circuit does little for overtaking and race excitement. The question was this: would David Coulthard, in pole position, stall his car? If so Michael Schumacher, second on the grid, would win. If not, Coulthard would win.

We didn't have to wait long to find out. Once Puff Daddy's cigar ash had been cleared, the parade lap got underway. Except for — yes, you guessed it — David Coulthard. The Scot's McLaren Mercedes stalled: traction control, brain fade, whatever. Who cared? The race was over. Schumacher had won. The red lights hadn't even gone out yet, but some of the crowd were on their way home.

To be fair to the drivers there is no harder circuit than Monaco. But then there is no better driver than Michael Schumacher who, unsurprisingly, roared away at the start. By the end of the first corner, Nick Heidfeld's Sauber found the barrier. The rest of the pack got away cleanly and from then on most of the excitement was confined to what happened behind Schumacher — right at the back of the grid, in fact, where Coulthard started after stalling. Would he claw his way up into the points by the end of 78 laps? Time would tell — if you were still watching the race, that is.

Further up, Schumacher was pursued by Mika Häkkinen, Rubens Barrichello, Ralf Schumacher and Juan Pablo Montoya. But not for long. On lap two Montoya crashed into the barrier. It was a shame for the likeable Colombian; and an even bigger shame for the thousands who had placed a wager on this being his first-ever victory.

The talking point of Monaco: Enrique Bernoldi holds up David Coulthard.

Coulthard started working his way up the field but was held back by an inferior Arrows car and the less experienced Enrique Bernoldi. Surely the Scot would pass him soon? His McLaren team-mate Mika Häkkinen looked like keeping up with Schumacher at the front – until lap 15, when he headed for the pits. Unfortunately, his race was over.

With Häkkinen gone and Barrichello in second place, Ralf Schumacher looked set for his first-ever podium finish in Monaco. The German had one victory to his name and, deep down, was probably spurred on by the fact that his team-mate had made such a hash of the race. The two men reputedly don't get on. When Montoya performed, as in Barcelona, Schumacher usually drew a blank. And vice versa. But his hydraulic system had other ideas and on lap 58, BMW Williams' weekend was over. Meanwhile, Ron Dennis's planned party looked like being shelved. Coulthard bizarrely needed 40 laps to get past Bernoldi – and only did so when the Arrows car pitted. Monaco was hard to overtake at, but surely Coulthard could manage it? Not so.

Later, Ron Dennis informed Bernoldi that he had no future in Formula One because he wouldn't let Coulthard pass. Coulthard himself added: "He's [Bernoldi] an idiot." Nobody outside the world of McLaren could understand what either man was going on about. Surely this was a motor race, and the idea is to stay ahead of the driver behind you unless you're being lapped? Not in the McLaren textbook of racing, which states that all drivers must quickly move aside at the sight of a grey Mercedes in the rear-view mirror.

Ironically, after getting past Bernoldi, Coulthard posted the fastest lap of the afternoon. By the late stages of the race, his pace had taken him up to fifth place. A few more laps and he might well have caught up with Villeneuve. But overtake him? Forget it.

In front and bored, Schumacher varied in pace. Only Barrichello could have caught up, but overtaking his Ferrari team-mate would have earned the Brazilian the sack.

As the streets of Monaco took their toll on the engines, only 10 cars were left by lap 78. Kimi Räikkönen took care of the back with an impressive 10th in his Sauber. It was a fine afternoon for the Arrows team, too, with Bernoldi and Verstappen in ninth and eighth respectively. Britain's Jenson Button delivered his best drive of the season to take seventh place – or third from last, depending which way you look at it. And at long last Jean Alesi had something to smile about, scoring a point to finish just behind Coulthard.

Schumacher roared to victory. No surprise. Barrichello was second. No surprise. In fact, the only real battle of the day on the track was between Eddie Irvine, who managed a brilliant third, and Jacques Villeneuve, who finished less than two seconds behind him. This was Eddie's day and Jaguar's day – the team's first-ever podium finish.

Schumacher and Häkkinen lead the field on the very steep climb to Casino Square.

# Monaco Grand Prix Race Statistics

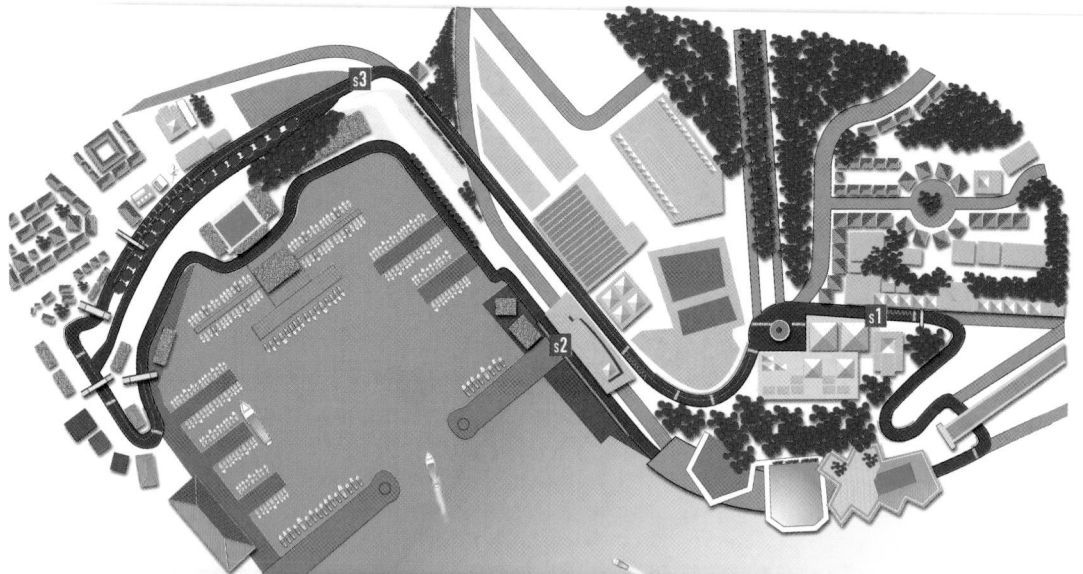

## MONACO CIRCUIT DIAGRAM

Illustration by Emeric de Baré

### FASTEST LAPS

| | DRIVER | TIME | LAP |
|---|---|---|---|
| 1 | Coulthard | 1m 19.424s | 68 |
| 2 | M Schumacher | 1m 19.770s | 50 |
| 3 | Barrichello | 1m 20.329s | 57 |
| 4 | Villeneuve | 1m 20.417s | 75 |
| 5 | Irvine | 1m 20.681s | 76 |
| 6 | Räikkönen | 1m 20.705s | 60 |
| 7 | Frentzen | 1m 20.810s | 46 |
| 8 | R Schumacher | 1m 20.975s | 47 |
| 9 | Alesi | 1m 21.151s | 73 |
| 10 | Button | 1m 21.580s | 65 |
| 11 | Fisichella | 1m 21.646s | 37 |
| 12 | Häkkinen | 1m 21.682s | 12 |
| 13 | Verstappen | 1m 21.732s | 74 |
| 14 | Bernoldi | 1m 22.053s | 75 |
| 15 | Trulli | 1m 22.345s | 30 |
| 16 | Alonso | 1m 22.956s | 28 |
| 17 | de la Rosa | 1m 23.483s | 18 |
| 18 | Burti | 1m 24.206s | 18 |
| 19 | Marques | 1m 24.570s | 33 |
| 20 | Panis | 1m 24.719s | 10 |
| 21 | Montoya | 1m 25.773s | 2 |
| | Heidfeld | No lap completed | |

### RACE SPEED TRAP TIMES

| | | |
|---|---|---|
| 1 | R Schumacher | 182.7mph |
| 2 | Coulthard | 181.1mph |
| 3 | Irvine | 180.8mph |
| 4 | Alesi | 180.4mph |
| 5 | Villeneuve | 179.6mph |
| 6 | Button | 179.5mph |
| 7 | M Schumacher | 179.1mph |
| 8 | Bernoldi | 178.9mph |
| 9 | Frentzen | 178.8mph |
| 10 | Barrichello | 178.8mph |
| 11 | Verstappen | 178.7mph |
| 12 | Räikkönen | 178.7mph |
| 13 | de la Rosa | 178.3mph |
| 14 | Fisichella | 177.8mph |
| 15 | Burti | 177.0mph |
| 16 | Häkkinen | 176.5mph |
| 17 | Trulli | 176.1mph |
| 18 | Alonso | 176.0mph |
| 19 | Marques | 173.8mph |
| 20 | Montoya | 172.6mph |
| 21 | Panis | 170.2mph |
| | Heidfeld | No speed recorded |

### WARM-UP

SUNDAY 27TH MAY 2001, 9.30AM–10AM

| | | |
|---|---|---|
| 1 | Coulthard | 1m 20.944s |
| 2 | Häkkinen | 1m 21.017s |
| 3 | M Schumacher | 1m 21.650s |
| 4 | Barrichello | 1m 22.502s |
| 5 | Frentzen | 1m 22.566s |
| 6 | R Schumacher | 1m 22.650s |
| 7 | Irvine | 1m 22.816s |
| 8 | Verstappen | 1m 23.066s |
| 9 | de la Rosa | 1m 23.200s |
| 10 | Fisichella | 1m 23.407s |
| 11 | Trulli | 1m 23.574s |
| 12 | Montoya | 1m 23.590s |
| 13 | Panis | 1m 23.595s |
| 14 | Villeneuve | 1m 23.747s |
| 15 | Heidfeld | 1m 23.842s |
| 16 | Räikkönen | 1m 24.042s |
| 17 | Alesi | 1m 24.046s |
| 18 | Button | 1m 24.137s |
| 19 | Alonso | 1m 24.941s |
| 20 | Bernoldi | 1m 25.328s |
| 21 | Burti | 1m 25.938s |
| 22 | Marques | 1m 26.365s |

### DRIVER POINTS

| | | |
|---|---|---|
| 1 | Michael Schumacher | 52 |
| 2 | David Coulthard | 40 |
| 3 | Rubens Barrichello | 24 |
| 4 | Ralf Schumacher | 12 |
| 5 | Nick Heidfeld | 8 |
| 6 | Jacques Villeneuve | 7 |
| 7 | Jarno Trulli | 7 |
| 8 | Juan Pablo Montoya | 6 |
| 9 | Heinz-Harald Frentzen | 6 |
| 10 | Olivier Panis | 5 |
| 11 | Eddie Irvine | 4 |
| 12 | Kimi Räikkönen | 4 |
| 13 | Mika Häkkinen | 4 |
| 14 | Jos Verstappen | 1 |
| 15 | Jean Alesi | 1 |
| 16 | Giancarlo Fisichella | 1 |
| 17 | Jenson Button | 0 |
| 18 | Luciano Burti | 0 |
| 19 | Enrique Bernoldi | 0 |
| 20 | Tarso Marques | 0 |
| 21 | Fernando Alonso | 0 |
| 22 | Gaston Mazzacane | 0 |
| 23 | Pedro de la Rosa | 0 |

### RACE: SUNDAY 27TH MAY 2001, 2PM

| | DRIVER | CAR | TIME/RETIREMENT | LAPS | PITSTOP LAPS |
|---|---|---|---|---|---|
| 1 | Michael Schumacher | Ferrari | 1h 47m 22.561s | 78 | 55 |
| 2 | Rubens Barrichello | Ferrari | +0.431s | 78 | 60 |
| 3 | Eddie Irvine | Jaguar Racing | +30.698s | 78 | 60 |
| 4 | Jacques Villeneuve | BAR Honda | +32.454s | 78 | 56 |
| 5 | David Coulthard | McLaren Mercedes | +1 lap | 77 | 65 |
| 6 | Jean Alesi | Prost Acer | +1 lap | 77 | 51 69 |
| 7 | Jenson Button | Benetton Renault | +1 lap | 77 | 49 |
| 8 | Jos Verstappen | Arrows Asiatech | +1 lap | 77 | 42 |
| 9 | Enrique Bernoldi | Arrows Asiatech | +2 laps | 76 | 43 |
| 10 | Kimi Räikkönen | Sauber Petronas | +5 laps | 73 | 15 58 |
| Ret | Ralf Schumacher | BMW Williams | Electrical | 57 | |
| Ret | Tarso Marques | European Minardi | Transmission | 56 | 44 |
| Ret | Fernando Alonso | European Minardi | Gearbox | 54 | 47 |
| Ret | Heinz-Harald Frentzen | Jordan Honda | Accident | 49 | |
| Ret | Giancarlo Fisichella | Benetton Renault | Gearbox | 43 | |
| Ret | Jarno Trulli | Jordan Honda | Hydraulics | 30 | |
| Ret | Luciano Burti | Prost Acer | Gearbox | 24 | 3 |
| Ret | Pedro de la Rosa | Jaguar Racing | Hydraulics | 18 | |
| Ret | Mika Häkkinen | McLaren Mercedes | Steering | 15 | 14 |
| Ret | Olivier Panis | BAR Honda | Steering | 13 | 12 13 |
| Ret | Juan Pablo Montoya | BMW Williams | Spin | 2 | |
| Ret | Nick Heidfeld | Sauber Petronas | Accident | 0 | |

*Conditions: sunny.*

### PITSTOP TIMES (from pitlane entrance to exit)

| | | | |
|---|---|---|---|
| Fastest pitstop: | David Coulthard, McLaren Mercedes | 26.954s | Lap 65 |
| Slowest pitstop: | Kimi Räikkönen, Sauber Petronas | 5m 05.935s | Lap 15 |
| Most pitstops: | Panis, Räikkönen, Alesi | Two stops | |

### PENALTIES AND FINES

| TEAM | WHEN | PENALTY | REASON |
|---|---|---|---|
| Arrows Asiatech | Friday | Warning | Dangerous bodywork |
| Jordan Honda | Friday | Warning | Dangerous bodywork |

### LAP LEADERS

| | |
|---|---|
| Michael Schumacher | 1–54 |
| Rubens Barrichello | 55–59 |
| Michael Schumacher | 60–78 |

Total laps led: M Schumacher 73; Barrichello 5.

### TEMPERATURES

| | | |
|---|---|---|
| Thursday: | Air: 21–23°C | Track: 37–38°C |
| Saturday: | Air: 36–42°C | Track: 22–23°C |
| Sunday: | Air: 23°C | Track: 38°C |

### CONSTRUCTOR POINTS

| | | |
|---|---|---|
| 1 | Scuderia Ferrari-Marlboro | 76 |
| 2 | West McLaren Mercedes | 44 |
| 3 | BMW Williams F1 | 18 |
| 4 | Benson & Hedges Jordan Honda | 13 |
| 5 | Red Bull Sauber Petronas | 12 |
| 6 | Lucky Strike Reynard BAR Honda | 12 |
| 7 | Jaguar Racing | 4 |
| 8 | Orange Arrows Asiatech | 1 |
| 9 | Mild Seven Benetton Renault | 1 |
| 10 | Prost Acer | 1 |
| 11 | European Minardi F1 | 0 |

L Burti 21

J Verstappen 19

J Button 17

K Räikkönen 15

HH Frentzen 13

T Marques 22

E Bernoldi 20

F Alonso 18

N Heidfeld 16

P de la Rosa 14

O Panis 12

## MONACO GRAND PRIX RACE ENTRY

| | DRIVER | TEAM | CHASSIS/ENGINE |
|---|---|---|---|
| 1 | Michael Schumacher | Scuderia Ferrari Marlboro | Ferrari F2001 |
| 2 | Rubens Barrichello | Scuderia Ferrari Marlboro | Ferrari F2001 |
| 3 | Mika Häkkinen | West McLaren Mercedes | McLaren Mercedes MP4-16 |
| 4 | David Coulthard | West McLaren Mercedes | McLaren Mercedes MP4-16 |
| 5 | Ralf Schumacher | BMW Williams F1 Team | BMW Williams FW23 |
| 6 | Juan Pablo Montoya | BMW Williams F1 Team | BMW Williams FW23 |
| 7 | Giancarlo Fisichella | Mild Seven Benetton Renault | Benetton Renault B201 |
| 8 | Jenson Button | Mild Seven Benetton Renault | Benetton Renault B201 |
| 9 | Olivier Panis | Lucky Strike BAR Honda | BAR Honda B003 |
| 10 | Jacques Villeneuve | Lucky Strike BAR Honda | BAR Honda B003 |
| 11 | Heinz-Harald Frentzen | Benson & Hedges Jordan Honda | Jordan Honda EJ11 |
| 12 | Jarno Trulli | Benson & Hedges Jordan Honda | Jordan Honda EJ11 |
| 14 | Jos Verstappen | Orange Arrows Asiatech | Arrows Asiatech A22 |
| 15 | Enrique Bernoldi | Orange Arrows Asiatech | Arrows Asiatech A22 |
| 16 | Nick Heidfeld | Red Bull Sauber Petronas | Sauber Petronas C20 |
| 17 | Kimi Räikkönen | Red Bull Sauber Petronas | Sauber Petronas C20 |
| 18 | Eddie Irvine | Jaguar Racing | Jaguar Cosworth R2 |
| 19 | Pedro de la Rosa | Jaguar Racing | Jaguar Cosworth R2 |
| 20 | Tarso Marques | European Minardi | Minardi European PS01 |
| 21 | Fernando Alonso | European Minardi | Minardi European PS01 |
| 22 | Jean Alesi | Prost Grand Prix | Prost ACER AP04 |
| 23 | Luciano Burti | Prost Grand Prix | Prost ACER AP04 |

Michael Schumacher, in the royal box, acknowledges another victory at Monaco.

## QUALIFYING: SATURDAY 26TH MAY 2001, 1PM-2PM *107 per cent time: 1m 22.850s.*

| | DRIVER | TEAM | TIME | GAP | LAPS |
|---|---|---|---|---|---|
| 1 | David Coulthard | McLaren Mercedes | 1m 17.430s | 0.000 | 12 |
| 2 | Michael Schumacher | Ferrari | 1m 17.631s | +0.201s | 11 |
| 3 | Mika Häkkinen | McLaren Mercedes | 1m 17.749s | +0.319s | 12 |
| 4 | Rubens Barrichello | Ferrari | 1m 17.856s | +0.426s | 11 |
| 5 | Ralf Schumacher | BMW Williams | 1m 18.029s | +0.599s | 11 |
| 6 | Eddie Irvine | Jaguar Racing | 1m 18.432s | +1.002s | 12 |
| 7 | Juan Pablo Montoya | BMW Williams | 1m 18.751s | +1.321s | 12 |
| 8 | Jarno Trulli | Jordan Honda | 1m 18.921s | +1.491s | 12 |
| 9 | Jacques Villeneuve | BAR Honda | 1m 19.086s | +1.656s | 12 |
| 10 | Giancarlo Fisichella | Benetton Renault | 1m 19.220s | +1.790s | 11 |
| 11 | Jean Alesi | Prost Acer | 1m 19.245s | +1.815s | 12 |
| 12 | Olivier Panis | BAR Honda | 1m 19.294s | +1.864s | 12 |
| 13 | Heinz-Harald Frentzen | Jordan Honda | 1m 19.316s | +1.886s | 11 |
| 14 | Pedro de la Rosa | Arrows Asiatech | 1m 20.033s | +2.603s | 12 |
| 15 | Kimi Räikkönen | Sauber Petronas | 1m 20.081s | +2.651s | 12 |
| 16 | Nick Heidfeld | Sauber Petronas | 1m 20.261s | +2.831s | 12 |
| 17 | Jenson Button | Benetton Renault | 1m 20.342s | +2.912s | 12 |
| 18 | Fernando Alonso | European Minardi | 1m 20.788s | +3.358s | 12 |
| 19 | Jos Verstappen | Arrows Asiatech | 1m 20.823s | +3.393s | 12 |
| 20 | Enrique Bernoldi | Arrows Asiatech | 1m 21.336s | +3.906s | 11 |
| 21 | Luciano Burti | Prost Acer | 1m 21.771s | +4.341s | 10 |
| 22 | Tarso Marques | European Minardi | 1m 22.201s | +4.771s | 12 |

## FASTEST SECTOR TIMES IN QUALIFYING *Ideal lap time: 1m 20.788s (diff. from pole: 0.186s)*

| | SECTOR 1 | SECS | | SECTOR 2 | SECS | | SECTOR 3 | SECS |
|---|---|---|---|---|---|---|---|---|
| 1 | Häkkinen | 19.756s | 1 | Coulthard | 35.145s | 1 | R Schumacher | 22.337s |
| 2 | Coulthard | 19.778s | 2 | M Schumacher | 35.200s | 2 | M Schumacher | 22.366s |
| 3 | M Schumacher | 19.844s | 3 | Barrichello | 35.316s | 3 | Irvine | 22.422s |
| 4 | Barrichello | 20.005s | 4 | Trulli | 35.434s | 4 | Barrichello | 22.455s |
| 5 | R Schumacher | 20.055s | 5 | Häkkinen | 35.447s | 5 | Coulthard | 22.463s |
| 6 | Trulli | 20.178s | 6 | R Schumacher | 35.465s | 6 | Häkkinen | 22.472s |
| 7 | Räikkönen | 20.180s | 7 | Irvine | 35.631s | 7 | Montoya | 22.515s |
| 8 | Panis | 20.226s | 8 | Frentzen | 35.678s | 8 | Villeneuve | 22.783s |
| 9 | Frentzen | 20.256s | 9 | Montoya | 35.730s | 9 | Alesi | 22.783s |
| 10 | Alesi | 20.360s | 10 | Fisichella | 35.819s | 10 | Trulli | 22.809s |
| 11 | Villeneuve | 20.371s | 11 | Panis | 35.836s | 11 | Fisichella | 22.857s |
| 12 | Irvine | 20.379s | 12 | Villeneuve | 35.892s | 12 | de la Rosa | 22.928s |
| 13 | Fisichella | 20.390s | 13 | Alesi | 35.996s | 13 | Heidfeld | 22.938s |
| 14 | Montoya | 20.416s | 14 | de la Rosa | 36.149s | 14 | Panis | 22.968s |
| 15 | Verstappen | 20.611s | 15 | Räikkönen | 36.271s | 15 | Räikkönen | 22.988s |
| 16 | Heidfeld | 20.651s | 16 | Button | 36.291s | 16 | Frentzen | 22.996s |
| 17 | Alonso | 20.772s | 17 | Heidfeld | 36.366s | 17 | Button | 23.005s |
| 18 | Bernoldi | 20.791s | 18 | Alonso | 36.469s | 18 | Alonso | 23.313s |
| 19 | de la Rosa | 20.818s | 19 | Verstappen | 36.540s | 19 | Burti | 23.481s |
| 20 | Button | 20.909s | 20 | Bernoldi | 36.721s | 20 | Marques | 23.604s |
| 21 | Marques | 21.050s | 21 | Burti | 36.982s | 21 | Verstappen | 23.639s |
| 22 | Burti | 21.218s | 22 | Marques | 37.237s | 22 | Bernoldi | 23.824s |

## PRACTICE SESSION ONE

### THURSDAY 24TH MAY 2001, 11AM-12PM

| | | |
|---|---|---|
| 1 | M Schumacher | 1m 21.577s |
| 2 | Coulthard | 1m 22.404s |
| 3 | Trulli | 1m 22.667s |
| 4 | Frentzen | 1m 23.024s |
| 5 | Barrichello | 1m 23.337s |
| 6 | Häkkinen | 1m 23.347s |
| 7 | Panis | 1m 23.662s |
| 8 | R Schumacher | 1m 23.678s |
| 9 | Irvine | 1m 23.930s |
| 10 | Alesi | 1m 24.019s |
| 11 | Räikkönen | 1m 24.441s |
| 12 | Heidfeld | 1m 24.762s |
| 13 | Fisichella | 1m 24.871s |
| 14 | Villeneuve | 1m 24.918s |
| 15 | Verstappen | 1m 24.931s |
| 16 | Montoya | 1m 25.838s |
| 17 | Bernoldi | 1m 25.952s |
| 18 | Button | 1m 26.702s |
| 19 | Alonso | 1m 26.759s |
| 20 | Burti | 1m 26.905s |
| 21 | de la Rosa | 1m 27.316s |
| 22 | Marques | 1m 30.230s |

## PRACTICE SESSION TWO

### THURSDAY 24TH MAY 2001, 1PM-2PM

| | | |
|---|---|---|
| 1 | Häkkinen | 1m 19.853s |
| 2 | M Schumacher | 1m 20.316s |
| 3 | R Schumacher | 1m 20.938s |
| 4 | Barrichello | 1m 20.959s |
| 5 | Trulli | 1m 21.048s |
| 6 | Coulthard | 1m 21.091s |
| 7 | Frentzen | 1m 21.505s |
| 8 | Alesi | 1m 21.935s |
| 9 | Villeneuve | 1m 22.010s |
| 10 | Montoya | 1m 22.035s |
| 11 | Fisichella | 1m 22.214s |
| 12 | Irvine | 1m 22.302s |
| 13 | Räikkönen | 1m 22.800s |
| 14 | Heidfeld | 1m 22.807s |
| 15 | Verstappen | 1m 23.409s |
| 16 | Panis | 1m 23.662s |
| 17 | Button | 1m 24.026s |
| 18 | Bernoldi | 1m 24.105s |
| 19 | Burti | 1m 24.857s |
| 20 | Marques | 1m 25.920s |
| 21 | Alonso | 1m 26.393s |
| 22 | de la Rosa | 1m 27.316s |

## PRACTICE SESSION THREE

### SATURDAY 26TH MAY 2001, 9AM-9.45AM

| | | |
|---|---|---|
| 1 | R Schumacher | 1m 21.036s |
| 2 | Villeneuve | 1m 21.200s |
| 3 | Coulthard | 1m 21.288s |
| 4 | M Schumacher | 1m 21.377s |
| 5 | Räikkönen | 1m 22.053s |
| 6 | Irvine | 1m 22.131s |
| 7 | Alesi | 1m 22.141s |
| 8 | Frentzen | 1m 22.373s |
| 9 | Panis | 1m 22.514s |
| 10 | Trulli | 1m 22.562s |
| 11 | Barrichello | 1m 22.678s |
| 12 | Fisichella | 1m 22.834s |
| 13 | Montoya | 1m 23.111s |
| 14 | Button | 1m 23.756s |
| 15 | Heidfeld | 1m 24.067s |
| 16 | de la Rosa | 1m 24.135s |
| 17 | Alonso | 1m 24.460s |
| 18 | Burti | 1m 25.795s |
| 19 | Marques | 1m 26.558s |
| 20 | Verstappen | 1m 27.829s |
| | Häkkinen | - |
| | Bernoldi | - |

## PRACTICE SESSION FOUR

### SATURDAY 26TH MAY 2001, 10.15AM-11AM

| | | |
|---|---|---|
| 1 | Häkkinen | 1m 18.282s |
| 2 | M Schumacher | 1m 18.456s |
| 3 | R Schumacher | 1m 18.725s |
| 4 | Coulthard | 1m 19.031s |
| 5 | Irvine | 1m 19.031s |
| 6 | Trulli | 1m 19.307s |
| 7 | Montoya | 1m 19.603s |
| 8 | Barrichello | 1m 19.651s |
| 9 | Alesi | 1m 20.020s |
| 10 | Frentzen | 1m 20.064s |
| 11 | Villeneuve | 1m 20.397s |
| 12 | Panis | 1m 20.528s |
| 13 | Fisichella | 1m 20.591s |
| 14 | Button | 1m 21.316s |
| 15 | Räikkönen | 1m 21.621s |
| 16 | Alonso | 1m 21.670s |
| 17 | Verstappen | 1m 21.827s |
| 18 | Bernoldi | 1m 22.024s |
| 19 | Heidfeld | 1m 22.207s |
| 20 | de la Rosa | 1m 22.316s |
| 21 | Marques | 1m 23.313s |
| 22 | Burti | 1m 25.795s |

J Alesi — 11

J Villeneuve — 9

JP Montoya — 7

R Schumacher — 5

M Häkkinen — 3

D Coulthard — 1

G Fisichella — 10 | J Trulli — 8 | E Irvine — 6

R Barrichello — 4 | M Schumacher — 2

## MONTE CARLO LAP-BY-LAP REPORT

**PRE-START** Disaster struck pole man David Coulthard when the cars set off on the parade lap. The McLaren's launch control malfunctioned and the Scot was left sitting on the grid. For a moment Mika Häkkinen was stuck behind him but was able to get around his team-mate before the last car on the grid passed him, so he was able to take his grid position. Coulthard's car was fired up by McLaren mechanics and he chased after the rest of the field, driving straight across the chicane as he went, to start from the back of the grid.

**LAP 1** With most of the frontrunners now using launch-control, the majority of the cars got away well in Monaco and held station as they filed into Ste Devote. Juan Pablo Montoya positioned himself neatly behind Ralf Schumacher, who was being challenged on the outside by Eddie Irvine. The Jaguar ran wide as a result, brushing the barrier and losing momentum, and Montoya was able to nip ahead into fifth behind Michael Schumacher, Mika Häkkinen, Rubens Barrichello and Ralf Schumacher. There was no major accident at Ste Devote, although Jos Verstappen tried hard at the tail of the field by nearly losing control as he attempted to pass Luciano Burti's Prost on the outside. The Arrows slewed wildly across the road, damaging Burti's front wing as it went, but Verstappen caught the car before it hit the wall. Further around the lap Verstappen struck again, this time punting Nick Heidfeld into the barriers on the run down to Portier. Jos lost several places as a result and Heidfeld was eliminated.

**LAP 2** Montoya set the fastest lap of the race as he harried his team-mate. Burti, struggling with his damaged front wing, dropped to the tail of the field, being overtaken by Verstappen and Coulthard.

**LAP 3** Montoya slid wide in the Swimming Pool section and glanced the wall which deranged the rear suspension, causing the Williams to slide into the tyres at the end of the short straight and retire. This promoted Eddie Irvine to fifth, with Jarno Trulli sixth for Jordan. Verstappen overtook Tarso Marques to move up to 17th. As usual the two Arrows were running with a much lighter fuel load than their rivals. At the back Burti went into the pits to get a new nose for his Prost. He rejoined a long way behind the rest of the field.

**LAP 4** Coulthard also overtook 18th-placed Tarso Marques.

**LAP 8** Mika Häkkinen began to reduce Michael Schumacher's lead. Jos Verstappen overtook Arrows team-mate Enrique Bernoldi to move into 16th place.

**LAP 12** Mika Häkkinen moved to within a second of Michael Schumacher but Rubens Barrichello dropped away from the two leaders, suffering from serious cramp in his foot. BAR Honda's Olivier Panis, who was running in 10th position, dropped out with power-steering failure. He rejoined the race after a long pitstop but having completed a couple of exploratory laps he retired. Jos Verstappen moved to 15th, ahead of Fernando Alonso's Minardi. But behind this pair Coulthard found it impossible to overtake Enrique Bernoldi.

**LAP 13** Häkkinen suffered a steering problem and dropped to third.

**LAP 14** Mika Häkkinen came into the pits to have the steering problem on his McLaren investigated, but nothing was found and he was sent back out again. However the problem remained, so it was decided the Finn should retire. His disappearance moved Ralf Schumacher to third behind the Ferraris of Michael Schumacher and Rubens Barrichello, with Eddie Irvine in fourth, Jarno Trulli in fifth and Jacques Villeneuve promoted to sixth place.

**LAP 15** Kimi Räikkönen pitted, leaving his 11th place to Verstappen, who overtook Jenson Button on the same lap. Räikkönen had suffered a wheel sensor failure. The team botched a repair for the car and sent the rookie on his way, five laps down.

**LAP 19** Pedro de la Rosa retired with a hydraulic failure.

**LAP 26** Luciano Burti spun off at Ste Devote. He avoided hitting anything but was unable to rejoin the race as the reverse gear on his Prost Acer would not engage.

**LAP 31** Trulli disappeared in a sheet of flame from the back of the Jordan. He pulled off at Rascasse and fire marshals extinguished the blaze, which the team said was caused by a hydraulic leak.

**LAP 34** Benetton's joy turned to horror when Giancarlo Fisichella hit the barriers quite heavily at Ste Devote. However, he managed to keep the car going without being overtaken by Jean Alesi.

**LAP 42** Jos Verstappen pitted and dropped from ninth to 12th position. Without a weight advantage, he made little impression from then on.

**LAP 43** Bernoldi pitted, dropping behind Verstappen. With the Arrows out of the way Coulthard was finally able to reduce his times by four seconds a lap and he set a series of fastest laps.

**LAP 44** Tarso Marques pitted for fuel and tyres. He rejoined the race at the back of the field with only Kimi Räikkönen behind him. Giancarlo Fisichella ran wide at Ste Devote a second time and on this occasion there was no escape. He tried to swerve to avoid the crash but the left rear of the Benetton hit the wall heavily – the car slewed around and the left front was torn off. Fisichella could not drive that one home. Jean Alesi moved up to take his sixth place.

**LAP 46** Coulthard's charge began to pay off. He caught and overtook Alonso for ninth. Soon afterwards Alonso pitted.

**LAP 49** Button pitted, so Coulthard moved up to eighth place.

**LAP 50** Coulthard gained another place as Heinz-Harald Frentzen had a big crash in the tunnel. The Jordan was running seventh when it suddenly veered into the barriers at around 175mph. The car was seriously damaged but fortunately did not bounce off the barriers, instead sliding along the guardrail before finally coming to rest just before the chicane. A shaken Frentzen climbed out.

**LAP 51** Alesi pitted and was able to rejoin ahead of Coulthard.

**LAP 55** The leader came in for fuel and tyres. This meant Barrichello took the lead. Alonso retired with a gearbox failure.

**LAP 56** Jacques Villeneuve pitted but rejoined the race without losing his fifth place.

**LAP 58** Ralf Schumacher's hopes of a podium evaporated when his Williams suffered electronic failure. He coasted into the pits. This put Irvine third, Villeneuve fourth, Alesi fifth and Coulthard sixth. Marques retired with a driveshaft failure.

**LAP 60** Rubens Barrichello's moment of glory came to an end as he pitted and Michael Schumacher went back into the lead. Eddie Irvine also pitted but was far enough ahead of Jacques Villeneuve not to lose his place. Further back David Coulthard was charging in an effort to build up a big enough advantage to be able to pit without losing his place to Jenson Button, who was also charging.

**LAP 65** It was a close thing. David Coulthard pitted and emerged with a couple of seconds in hand over Jenson Button. He then set his sights on Jean Alesi, more than half a minute ahead. With 13 laps to go it looked as though the Scot had a chance of catching him.

**LAP 66** Irvine nearly dropped the ball, brushing a wall at Ste Devote but escaping the incident without any major damage.

**LAP 69** Jean Alesi had a puncture and had to head for the pits. The Prost team was slightly slower changing the tyres than it could have been, but Alesi was quickly on his way. However, the delay was enough to allow David Coulthard to take fifth position. The French team was gutted to have lost the extra point – the only consolation was that Alesi was still in sixth place.

**LAP 78** The Ferraris staged a one-two finish. Eddie Irvine was half a minute down in third place, a second-and-a-half ahead of Jacques Villeneuve. David Coulthard was a lap down in fifth, with Jean Alesi taking one point for sixth position.

# Canadian Grand Prix

**8th–10th June 2001**    LAPS: 69   LENGTH OF LAP: 2.747 miles

442

SIBLING BATTLE Around the distinctive landscape of the Circuit Villeneuve in Montreal, Ralf Schumacher and Michael Schumacher fought a tough duel which saw Ralf chase and catch Michael. The balance moved in Ralf's favour when Michael pitted his Ferrari whilst the BMW Williams raced on to give Ralf his second GP victory. PHOTOGRAPH BY MARK SUTTON

# But for a few litres more

The first law of motor racing is that ifs don't count. If Michael Schumacher's Ferrari had been able to carry a few litres more fuel he might have been able to go further and lead longer in Canada. But he couldn't. Instead, the larger fuel tank and more frugal engine of younger brother Ralf's BMW Williams proved critical. After stalking his sibling until the pitstops, he swept ahead and stayed there comfortably even after refuelling, as the pair of them left everyone else behind to score the first fraternal one-two in Formula One history.

C anada was not the first occasion on which Mr and Mrs Schumacher's boys had shared the front row for a Grand Prix. They'd already made that little piece of history back in March in Interlagos. But while Michael was always confident of keeping his little brother in check in Brazil, he knew from the moment the BMW Williams popped on to the front row on Saturday afternoon that the race in Montreal was going to be no cakewalk.

Qualifying saw a lot of hotshoes temporarily grabbing the lime-light: Fernando Alonso set the ball rolling (beating only himself as the first car out of the pits on a balmy afternoon), but then Giancarlo Fisichella, local hero Jacques Villeneuve, Juan Pablo Montoya, Kimi Räikkönen, Nick Heidfeld, David Coulthard and Jarno Trulli each had their moments before Michael Schumacher redefined the speed limit. Though quick, the German was only limbering up with a 1m 16.145secs – as he demonstrated soon afterwards with a nonchalant best of 1m 15.782secs on his second run. Take that!

McLaren made the running all through Friday and again on Saturday morning, but it's never over until the fat lady sings, and this time

On the run to the first corner the Schumacher brothers took control.

Ralf Schumacher makes his pitstop — and rejoins still in the lead.

her aria was in Italian. As the McLaren drivers wondered what happened to their practice speed, Michael had it made. So much so that when Heidfeld creamed his Sauber into the wall on the exit to the final corner – necessitating a red flag which then left the world champion's rivals with a mere 90 seconds to complete a single warm-up lap before commencing their final attempts to unseat him – Michael merely stood serenely in the pits. He'd done in only two runs what nobody else would achieve in four, so why should he worry?

When Mika Häkkinen and Coulthard indulged in a Grand Prix of their own, trying to beat Rubens Barrichello and an unimpressed Villeneuve out of the pits in this slice of Formula One vaudeville, Schumacher's face broke into a broad grin. And when only Coulthard improved – a fine effort when the chips were down after the Scot had,

by his own admission, underperformed on previous runs – it was nothing to get excited about.

But there was one little itch Michael knew had the potential to become a full-blown scratchfest: the speed of his baby brother.

Ralf did not look much of a threat on Friday, posting the sixth fastest time. But a lot of changes to his BMW Williams made a big difference on Saturday – a fact not lost on Michael who, like all the Bridgestone runners, opted for the softer available compound. Ralf had done his qualifying on Michelin's harder tyres. It was one of those hot weekends when some runners had been marginal on soft rubber, as blisters attested. With more hot weather promised for the race, Ralf could have been in the pound seats. Michael was thoughtful that night. "I need to build a margin in the race tomorrow," he said, alluding to the one-stop strategy Ferrari would undoubtedly adopt. He didn't say that if he failed to, his chances of beating Ralf were nil.

Twenty laps into the race the next day, the best Michael could do was eke out six-10ths of a second. But that damn blue-and-white car was still hovering in his mirrors. When the safety car came out, as Ralf's team-mate Montoya once again creased a Williams into something solid, Michael knew it was over.

Within three laps the mess had been cleared and he did what he did at Monza last year, slowing the field down so much that by the time the safety car moved into the pit entry the race cars were barely in sight down the last straight. Michael, who makes it his business to know everyone else's, knew Ralf's hard tyres would have lost temperature cruising for three laps, and got the hammer down. On lap 24 the gap to his brother was 2.6secs, the biggest it had been all race.

But Ralf wasn't worried – even when David Coulthard and Jarno Trulli momentarily closed in. He soon dumped them and set out again

The safety car led the pack between laps 20 and 22 after Montoya's crash.

after Michael. Ten laps later he had restored the status quo; they were six-10ths apart again. But after another lap the gap was only a 10th. Ralf began to think about having a go at his brother. Thank the Lord he did; without him the Canadian Grand Prix would have been a tedious Ferrari/Schumacher demonstration.

Now it was all down to who stopped first. And it was Michael, on lap 46. He was serviced in 8.4secs and went on his way. But now Ralf had a clear road and was mentally tearing pages out of the Michael Schumacher Race Book like there was no tomorrow. How did it go? Oh yes, page 15: give it large when your leading rival makes his pit-stop and open as big a gap as you possibly can. Ralf showed he could think and drive at the same time as he set a string of fastest laps, culminating in a new record of 1m 17.205secs on lap 50. It was an impressive showing.

The BMW Williams has the tankage of a fuel bowser, and he didn't need to stop until lap 51. Things went smoother than a Cirque du Soleil production – no stalling, none of the occasional Williams Fred Karno loose wheels – and he was already at the first corner before Michael crossed the start/finish line. Game over.

It remained only for him to reel off the remaining 18 laps – and he did so in style, never putting a wheel wrong. It might be fanciful when some speak of him donning his brother's mantle, but it was a damn good drive however you cared to slice it.

Häkkinen survived a vibro-massaging McLaren run to double his season's points score with third place. He was so outclassed, however, that all the alarm bells in the world must have been tolling right then in Woking, especially as Coulthard's Mercedes engine had puked out its innards in an unseemly plume of smoke and fire after 55 laps. Nil points for the Scot for the first time this year. He must have felt thankful to Ralf for beating Michael.

Williams' technical director Patrick Head beamed in the afterglow, cheerfully discussing all the aspects of another well-won triumph for the re-emergent team. Then someone asked him about Montoya. "Yeees…" Head replied in the sort of tone teachers use to terrify you at school, then said nothing more. Enough said, on this occasion.

British Airways flight BA94 prepared to board later that evening at Dorval and Head was now in full flow, extolling the virtues of his forthcoming 'boys only' motorbike trek to Magny-Cours and regaling his audience with his inimitable blend of anecdotes. He was interrupted frequently by rivals, such as Tom Walkinshaw and Jackie Stewart, all of whom wanted to say 'well done, Patrick'. Their sentiments were genuine. Everyone loved a BMW Williams victory. Even Michael Schumacher.

Ralf and Michael embrace post-race despite their on-track differences.

# Canadian Grand Prix Race Statistics

## MONTREAL CIRCUIT DIAGRAM

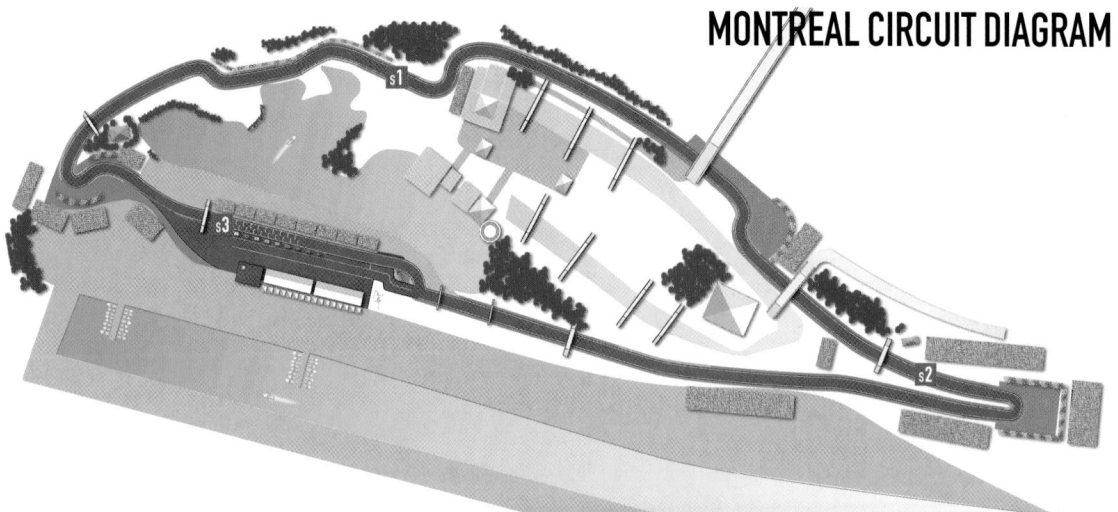

Illustration by Emeric de Baré

### FASTEST LAPS

| | DRIVER | TIME | LAP |
|---|---|---|---|
| 1 | R Schumacher | 1m 17.205s | 50 |
| 2 | Häkkinen | 1m 18.148s | 45 |
| 3 | M Schumacher | 1m 18.176s | 48 |
| 4 | de la Rosa | 1m 19.006s | 50 |
| 5 | Verstappen | 1m 19.257s | 59 |
| 6 | Räikkönen | 1m 19.309s | 63 |
| 7 | Alesi | 1m 19.328s | 59 |
| 8 | Trulli | 1m 19.414s | 29 |
| 9 | Barrichello | 1m 19.722s | 13 |
| 10 | Coulthard | 1m 19.745s | 32 |
| 11 | Villeneuve | 1m 19.782s | 30 |
| 12 | Burti | 1m 19.841s | 60 |
| 13 | Panis | 1m 19.856s | 30 |
| 14 | Zonta | 1m 20.078s | 38 |
| 15 | Montoya | 1m 20.159s | 18 |
| 16 | Bernoldi | 1m 20.767s | 11 |
| 17 | Button | 1m 21.124s | 11 |
| 18 | Marques | 1m 22.312s | 19 |
| 19 | Alonso | 1m 22.413s | 4 |
| 20 | Nick Heidfeld | 1m 31.894s | 1 |
| 21 | Eddie Irvine | 1m 32.210s | 1 |
| | Fisichella | No lap completed | |

### RACE SPEED TRAP TIMES

| 1 | R Schumacher | 207.5mph |
|---|---|---|
| 2 | Montoya | 207.4mph |
| 3 | Bernoldi | 205.4mph |
| 4 | Häkkinen | 205.4mph |
| 5 | de la Rosa | 205.1mph |
| 6 | Barrichello | 205.0mph |
| 7 | Alonso | 204.6mph |
| 8 | Villeneuve | 204.0mph |
| 9 | Zonta | 204.0mph |
| 10 | Räikkönen | 203.9mph |
| 11 | Alesi | 203.6mph |
| 12 | Verstappen | 203.3mph |
| 13 | M Schumacher | 202.9mph |
| 14 | Burti | 202.8mph |
| 15 | Panis | 202.1mph |
| 16 | Trulli | 202.1mph |
| 17 | Heidfeld | 202.0mph |
| 18 | Irvine | 201.5mph |
| 19 | Coulthard | 198.8mph |
| 20 | Marques | 198.5mph |
| 21 | Button | 198.4mph |
| 22 | Fisichella | 194.3mph |

### RACE: SUNDAY 10TH JUNE 2001, 1PM

| | DRIVER | CAR | TIME/RETIREMENT | LAPS | PITSTOP LAPS |
|---|---|---|---|---|---|
| 1 | Ralf Schumacher | BMW Williams | 1h 34m 31.522s | 69 | 51 |
| 2 | Michael Schumacher | Ferrari | +20.235s | 69 | 46 |
| 3 | Mika Häkkinen | McLaren Mercedes | +40.672s | 69 | 49 |
| 4 | Kimi Räikkönen | Sauber Petronas | +1m 08.116s | 69 | 39 |
| 5 | Jean Alesi | Prost Acer | +1m 10.435s | 69 | 41 |
| 6 | Pedro de la Rosa | Jaguar Racing | +1 lap | 68 | 30 52 |
| 7 | Ricardo Zonta | Jordan Honda | +1 lap | 68 | 36 |
| 8 | Luciano Burti | Prost Acer | +1 lap | 68 | 33 |
| 9 | Tarso Marques | European Minardi | +3 laps | 66 | 21 47 |
| 10 | Jos Verstappen | Arrows Asiatech | Brakes | 65 | 23 47 |
| 11 | Jarno Trulli | Jordan Honda | Brakes | 63 | 38 |
| Ret | David Coulthard | McLaren Mercedes | Engine | 54 | 42 |
| Ret | Olivier Panis | BAR Honda | Brakes | 38 | 36 37 |
| Ret | Jacques Villeneuve | BAR Honda | Halfshaft | 34 | |
| Ret | Enrique Bernoldi | Arrows Asiatech | Engine | 24 | 9 |
| Ret | Juan Pablo Montoya | BMW Williams | Accident | 19 | |
| Ret | Rubens Barrichello | Ferrari | Spin | 19 | |
| Ret | Jenson Button | Benetton Renault | Oil leak | 17 | 7 9 |
| Ret | Fernando Alonso | European Minardi | Transmission | 7 | |
| Ret | Nick Heidfeld | Sauber Petronas | Collision | 1 | |
| Ret | Eddie Irvine | Jaguar Racing | Collision | 1 | |
| Ret | Giancarlo Fisichella | Benetton Renault | Collision | 0 | |

*Conditions: sunny.*

### DRIVER POINTS

| 1 | Michael Schumacher | 58 |
|---|---|---|
| 2 | David Coulthard | 40 |
| 3 | Rubens Barrichello | 24 |
| 4 | Ralf Schumacher | 22 |
| 5 | Nick Heidfeld | 8 |
| 6 | Mika Häkkinen | 8 |
| 7 | Jacques Villeneuve | 7 |
| 8 | Kimi Räikkönen | 7 |
| 9 | Jarno Trulli | 7 |
| 10 | Juan Pablo Montoya | 6 |
| 11 | Heinz-Harald Frentzen | 6 |
| 12 | Olivier Panis | 5 |
| 13 | Eddie Irvine | 4 |
| 14 | Jean Alesi | 3 |
| 15 | Jos Verstappen | 1 |
| 16 | Giancarlo Fisichella | 1 |
| 17 | Pedro de la Rosa | 1 |
| 18 | Jenson Button | 0 |
| 19 | Ricardo Zonta | 0 |
| 20 | Luciano Burti | 0 |
| 21 | Tarso Marques | 0 |
| 22 | Enrique Bernoldi | 0 |
| 23 | Fernando Alonso | 0 |
| 24 | Gaston Mazzacane | 0 |

### CONSTRUCTOR POINTS

| 1 | Scuderia Ferrari-Marlboro | 82 |
|---|---|---|
| 2 | West McLaren Mercedes | 48 |
| 3 | BMW Williams F1 | 28 |
| 4 | Red Bull Sauber Petronas | 15 |
| 5 | Benson & Hedges Jordan Honda | 13 |
| 6 | Lucky Strike Reynard BAR Honda | 12 |
| 7 | Jaguar Racing | 5 |
| 8 | Prost Acer | 3 |
| 9 | Orange Arrows Asiatech | 1 |
| 10 | Mild Seven Benetton Renault | 1 |
| 11 | European Minardi F1 | 0 |

### PITSTOP TIMES (from pitlane entrance to exit)

| Fastest pitstop: | Ralf Schumacher | BMW Williams | 29.038s | Lap 51 |
|---|---|---|---|---|
| Slowest pitstop: | Jenson Button | Benetton Renault | 45.431s | Lap 9 |
| Most pitstops: | Five drivers | | | Two stops |

### PENALTIES AND FINES

| DRIVER/TEAM | WHEN | PENALTY | REASON |
|---|---|---|---|
| Ferrari | Qualifying | $10,000 | Working on Barrichello's car in pitlane |
| Fernando Alonso | Post-qualifying | Times disallowed | Illegal front wing |
| Jenson Button | Race | 10 seconds | Jump start |
| David Coulthard | Race | $5,000 | 39.8kph over pitlane speed limit |

### LAP LEADERS

| Michael Schumacher | 1-45 |
|---|---|
| Ralf Schumacher | 46-69 |

Total laps led:
M Schumacher 45; R Schumacher 24

### TEMPERATURES

| Friday: | Air: 21-26°C | Track: 27°C |
|---|---|---|
| Saturday: | Air: 21-26°C | Track: 27°C |
| Sunday: | Air: 24°C | Track: 26°C |

### WARM-UP

SUNDAY 10TH JUNE 2001, 8.30AM-9AM

| 1 | Panis | 1m 18.512s |
|---|---|---|
| 2 | Coulthard | 1m 18.540s |
| 3 | Zonta | 1m 18.545s |
| 4 | Irvine | 1m 18.594s |
| 5 | Häkkinen | 1m 18.650s |
| 6 | M Schumacher | 1m 18.663s |
| 7 | Trulli | 1m 18.875s |
| 8 | Barrichello | 1m 19.201s |
| 9 | Montoya | 1m 19.372s |
| 10 | R Schumacher | 1m 19.536s |
| 11 | Villeneuve | 1m 19.572s |
| 12 | Verstappen | 1m 19.775s |
| 13 | Räikkönen | 1m 19.876s |
| 14 | de la Rosa | 1m 20.012s |
| 15 | Bernoldi | 1m 20.059s |
| 16 | Heidfeld | 1m 20.062s |
| 17 | Alesi | 1m 20.943s |
| 18 | Alonso | 1m 21.071s |
| 19 | Button | 1m 21.114s |
| 20 | Fisichella | 1m 21.344s |
| 21 | Marques | 1m 21.415s |
| 22 | Burti | 1m 21.563s |

F Alonso 22

T Marques 21

J Button 20

L Burti 19

G Fisichella 18

E Bernoldi 17

J Alesi 16

E Irvine 15

P de la Rosa 14

J Verstappen 13

R Zonta 12

## CANADIAN GRAND PRIX RACE ENTRY

| | DRIVER | TEAM | CHASSIS/ENGINE |
|---|---|---|---|
| 1 | Michael Schumacher | Scuderia Ferrari Marlboro | Ferrari F2001 |
| 2 | Rubens Barrichello | Scuderia Ferrari Marlboro | Ferrari F2001 |
| 3 | Mika Häkkinen | West McLaren Mercedes | McLaren Mercedes MP4-16 |
| 4 | David Coulthard | West McLaren Mercedes | McLaren Mercedes MP4-16 |
| 5 | Ralf Schumacher | BMW Williams F1 Team | BMW Williams FW23 |
| 6 | Juan Pablo Montoya | BMW Williams F1 Team | BMW Williams FW23 |
| 7 | Giancarlo Fisichella | Mild Seven Benetton Renault | Benetton Renault B201 |
| 8 | Jenson Button | Mild Seven Benetton Renault | Benetton Renault B201 |
| 9 | Olivier Panis | Lucky Strike BAR Honda | BAR Honda B003 |
| 10 | Jacques Villeneuve | Lucky Strike BAR Honda | BAR Honda B003 |
| 11 | Ricardo Zonta | Benson & Hedges Jordan Honda | Jordan Honda EJ11 |
| 12 | Jarno Trulli | Benson & Hedges Jordan Honda | Jordan Honda EJ11 |
| 14 | Jos Verstappen | Orange Arrows Asiatech | Arrows Asiatech A22 |
| 15 | Enrique Bernoldi | Orange Arrows Asiatech | Arrows Asiatech A22 |
| 16 | Nick Heidfeld | Red Bull Sauber Petronas | Sauber Petronas C20 |
| 17 | Kimi Räikkönen | Red Bull Sauber Petronas | Sauber Petronas C20 |
| 18 | Eddie Irvine | Jaguar Racing | Jaguar Cosworth R2 |
| 19 | Pedro de la Rosa | Jaguar Racing | Jaguar Cosworth R2 |
| 20 | Tarso Marques | European Minardi | Minardi European PS01 |
| 21 | Fernando Alonso | European Minardi | Minardi European PS01 |
| 22 | Jean Alesi | Prost Grand Prix | Prost ACER AP04 |
| 23 | Luciano Burti | Prost Grand Prix | Prost ACER AP04 |

Ralf Schumacher uses the top step of the podium to his advantage.

## QUALIFYING: SATURDAY 9TH JUNE 2001, 1PM–2PM *107 per cent time: 1m 21.086s*

| | DRIVER | TEAM | TIME | GAP | LAPS |
|---|---|---|---|---|---|
| 1 | Michael Schumacher | Ferrari | 1m 15.782s | 0.000 | 6 |
| 2 | Ralf Schumacher | BMW Williams | 1m 16.297s | +0.515s | 8 |
| 3 | David Coulthard | McLaren Mercedes | 1m 16.423s | +0.641s | 12 |
| 4 | Jarno Trulli | Jordan Honda | 1m 16.459s | +0.677s | 10 |
| 5 | Rubens Barrichello | Ferrari | 1m 16.760s | +0.978s | 11 |
| 6 | Olivier Panis | BAR Honda | 1m 16.771s | +0.989s | 10 |
| 7 | Kimi Räikkönen | Sauber Petronas | 1m 16.875s | +1.093s | 11 |
| 8 | Mika Häkkinen | McLaren Mercedes | 1m 16.979s | +1.197s | 12 |
| 9 | Jacques Villeneuve | BAR Honda | 1m 17.035s | +1.253s | 11 |
| 10 | Juan Pablo Montoya | BMW Williams | 1m 17.123s | +1.341s | 12 |
| 11 | Nick Heidfeld | Sauber Petronas | 1m 17.165s | +1.383s | 11 |
| 12 | Ricardo Zonta | Jordan Honda | 1m 17.328s | +1.546s | 11 |
| 13 | Jos Verstappen | Arrows Asiatech | 1m 17.903s | +2.121s | 10 |
| 14 | Pedro de la Rosa | Jaguar Racing | 1m 18.015s | +2.233s | 12 |
| 15 | Eddie Irvine | Jaguar Racing | 1m 18.016s | +2.234s | 12 |
| 16 | Jean Alesi | Prost Acer | 1m 18.178s | +2.396s | 10 |
| 17 | Enrique Bernoldi | Arrows Asiatech | 1m 18.575s | +2.793s | 11 |
| 18 | Giancarlo Fisichella | Benetton Renault | 1m 18.622s | +2.840s | 11 |
| 19 | Luciano Burti | Prost Acer | 1m 18.753s | +2.971s | 11 |
| 20 | Jenson Button | Benetton Renault | 1m 19.033s | +3.251s | 12 |
| 21 | Tarso Marques | European Minardi | 1m 20.690s | +4.908s | 12 |
| 22 | Fernando Alonso | European Minardi | Times disallowed | | |

## FASTEST SECTOR TIMES IN QUALIFYING *Ideal lap time: 1m 15.782s (diff. from pole: 0.000s)*

| | SECTOR 1 | SECS | | SECTOR 2 | SECS | | SECTOR 3 | SECS |
|---|---|---|---|---|---|---|---|---|
| 1 | M Schumacher | 21.225s | 1 | M Schumacher | 24.050s | 1 | M Schumacher | 30.507s |
| 2 | Barrichello | 21.344s | 2 | R Schumacher | 24.086s | 2 | Coulthard | 30.599s |
| 3 | Trulli | 21.405s | 3 | Coulthard | 24.128s | 3 | Barrichello | 30.651s |
| 4 | Häkkinen | 21.406s | 4 | Trulli | 24.148s | 4 | Trulli | 30.733s |
| 5 | Coulthard | 21.406s | 5 | Panis | 24.195s | 5 | R Schumacher | 30.764s |
| 6 | R Schumacher | 21.447s | 6 | Häkkinen | 24.197s | 6 | Räikkönen | 30.787s |
| 7 | Panis | 21.537s | 7 | Räikkönen | 24.254s | 7 | Häkkinen | 30.798s |
| 8 | Räikkönen | 21.547s | 8 | Barrichello | 24.422s | 8 | Villeneuve | 30.801s |
| 9 | Montoya | 21.622s | 9 | Heidfeld | 24.488s | 9 | Montoya | 30.898s |
| 10 | Villeneuve | 21.622s | 10 | Zonta | 24.531s | 10 | Panis | 30.968s |
| 11 | Heidfeld | 21.628s | 11 | Villeneuve | 24.546s | 11 | Heidfeld | 31.009s |
| 12 | Zonta | 21.678s | 12 | Montoya | 24.603s | 12 | Irvine | 31.019s |
| 13 | Verstappen | 21.844s | 13 | de la Rosa | 24.679s | 13 | Zonta | 31.029s |
| 14 | Alesi | 22.002s | 14 | Alesi | 24.785s | 14 | Verstappen | 31.139s |
| 15 | Irvine | 22.065s | 15 | Irvine | 24.807s | 15 | de la Rosa | 31.201s |
| 16 | de la Rosa | 22.084s | 16 | Fisichella | 24.841s | 16 | Alesi | 31.364s |
| 17 | Bernoldi | 22.107s | 17 | Verstappen | 24.851s | 17 | Fisichella | 31.395s |
| 18 | Burti | 22.231s | 18 | Burti | 24.933s | 18 | Bernoldi | 31.411s |
| 19 | Fisichella | 22.263s | 19 | Burti | 25.002s | 19 | Burti | 31.459s |
| 20 | Button | 22.354s | 20 | Button | 25.032s | 20 | Button | 31.647s |
| 21 | Alonso | 22.409s | 21 | Alonso | 25.281s | 21 | Alonso | 31.692s |
| 22 | Marques | 22.721s | 22 | Marques | 25.391s | 22 | Marques | 32.210s |

## PRACTICE SESSION ONE

FRIDAY 8TH JUNE 2001, 11AM–12PM

| | | |
|---|---|---|
| 1 | Coulthard | 1m 18.763s |
| 2 | Barrichello | 1m 19.140s |
| 3 | M Schumacher | 1m 19.166s |
| 4 | Häkkinen | 1m 19.569s |
| 5 | Panis | 1m 20.119s |
| 6 | Heidfeld | 1m 20.378s |
| 7 | Trulli | 1m 20.513s |
| 8 | Räikkönen | 1m 20.515s |
| 9 | R Schumacher | 1m 20.665s |
| 10 | Montoya | 1m 20.822s |
| 11 | Frentzen | 1m 20.909s |
| 12 | de la Rosa | 1m 21.046s |
| 13 | Alesi | 1m 21.412s |
| 14 | Irvine | 1m 21.622s |
| 15 | Villeneuve | 1m 21.916s |
| 16 | Fisichella | 1m 22.016s |
| 17 | Bernoldi | 1m 22.337s |
| 18 | Burti | 1m 22.696s |
| 19 | Button | 1m 22.816s |
| 20 | Alonso | 1m 32.967s |
| 21 | Marques | 1m 35.472s |
| | Verstappen | No lap completed |

## PRACTICE SESSION TWO

FRIDAY 8TH JUNE 2001, 1PM–2PM

| | | |
|---|---|---|
| 1 | Häkkinen | 1m 17.672s |
| 2 | Coulthard | 1m 18.086s |
| 3 | Irvine | 1m 18.508s |
| 4 | Barrichello | 1m 18.570s |
| 5 | Montoya | 1m 18.639s |
| 6 | R Schumacher | 1m 18.641s |
| 7 | Heidfeld | 1m 18.967s |
| 8 | Trulli | 1m 18.990s |
| 9 | Frentzen | 1m 19.057s |
| 10 | Panis | 1m 19.102s |
| 11 | M Schumacher | 1m 19.166s |
| 12 | Alesi | 1m 19.209s |
| 13 | Räikkönen | 1m 19.427s |
| 14 | de la Rosa | 1m 19.707s |
| 15 | Fisichella | 1m 20.561s |
| 16 | Verstappen | 1m 20.561s |
| 17 | Bernoldi | 1m 21.259s |
| 18 | Burti | 1m 21.280s |
| 19 | Villeneuve | 1m 21.916s |
| 20 | Alonso | 1m 22.206s |
| 21 | Button | 1m 22.766s |
| 22 | Marques | 1m 25.415s |

## PRACTICE SESSION THREE

SATURDAY 9TH JUNE 2001, 9AM–9.45AM

| | | |
|---|---|---|
| 1 | Häkkinen | 1m 16.828s |
| 2 | Coulthard | 1m 16.875s |
| 3 | M Schumacher | 1m 16.913s |
| 4 | Barrichello | 1m 17.441s |
| 5 | R Schumacher | 1m 17.777s |
| 6 | Irvine | 1m 18.019s |
| 7 | Heidfeld | 1m 18.268s |
| 8 | de la Rosa | 1m 18.359s |
| 9 | Räikkönen | 1m 18.393s |
| 10 | Panis | 1m 18.407s |
| 11 | Trulli | 1m 18.575s |
| 12 | Alesi | 1m 18.935s |
| 13 | Zonta | 1m 19.141s |
| 14 | Fisichella | 1m 19.347s |
| 15 | Bernoldi | 1m 19.561s |
| 16 | Verstappen | 1m 19.757s |
| 17 | Montoya | 1m 19.811s |
| 18 | Burti | 1m 19.903s |
| 19 | Button | 1m 20.403s |
| 20 | Alonso | 1m 20.549s |
| 21 | Marques | 1m 21.067s |
| | Villeneuve | No lap completed |

## PRACTICE SESSION FOUR

SATURDAY 9TH JUNE 2001, 10.15AM–11AM

| | | |
|---|---|---|
| 1 | M Schumacher | 1m 16.200s |
| 2 | Coulthard | 1m 16.707s |
| 3 | Häkkinen | 1m 16.828s |
| 4 | Barrichello | 1m 16.986s |
| 5 | Heidfeld | 1m 17.103s |
| 6 | Räikkönen | 1m 17.144s |
| 7 | Panis | 1m 17.284s |
| 8 | R Schumacher | 1m 17.521s |
| 9 | Trulli | 1m 17.618s |
| 10 | de la Rosa | 1m 17.774s |
| 11 | Villeneuve | 1m 17.937s |
| 12 | Irvine | 1m 17.982s |
| 13 | Verstappen | 1m 18.030s |
| 14 | Montoya | 1m 18.216s |
| 15 | Zonta | 1m 18.595s |
| 16 | Bernoldi | 1m 18.649s |
| 17 | Alesi | 1m 18.935s |
| 18 | Button | 1m 19.213s |
| 19 | Fisichella | 1m 19.347s |
| 20 | Burti | 1m 19.693s |
| 21 | Alonso | 1m 20.549s |
| 22 | Marques | 1m 21.013s |

**11** N Heidfeld

**9** J Villeneuve

**7** K Räikkönen

**5** R Barrichello

**3** D Coulthard

**1** M Schumacher

**10** JP Montoya

**8** M Häkkinen

**6** O Panis

**4** J Trulli

**2** R Schumacher

## MONTREAL LAP-BY-LAP REPORT

**PRE-START** David Coulthard found a nut in his cockpit. He threw it over the pitwall, hoping it was nothing important.

**LAP 1** Jacques Villeneuve got away very slowly as his anti-stall system cut in. Williams still had the best start system and as the cars went into the first corner, Ralf Schumacher was looking for a way to pass his brother Michael. But the Ferrari driver had the better line and Ralf had to settle for second with David Coulthard third, having beaten Jarno Trulli off the line. The Italian was under attack from Rubens Barrichello and the Brazilian slipped ahead as the field went through the fast sweepers at the back of the circuit. Olivier Panis was sixth but under pressure from Jos Verstappen, who again made a great start in his lightweight Arrows, jumping from 13th on the grid to seventh. Also making a good start was Ricardo Zonta in the second Jordan, up from 12th to ninth position. Predictions of mayhem in the first corner proved wide of the mark but at the tail of the field Jenson Button bumped his nose against another car, albeit without doing too much damage. At the hairpin Giancarlo Fisichella ran into the back of Enrique Bernoldi's Arrows and damaged his front wing, which meant at the end of the main straight, as Bernoldi went to pass both Benettons and Button moved to avoid an impact, Fisichella braked but did not have enough front downforce so drove into the back of Button. This broke Fisichella's right front suspension and he went into the pits on three wheels, which surprised the team as it was ready in case Button needed a new nose. Fisichella was out; Button's car was damaged front and rear and behaved oddly from then on.

**LAP 2** Eddie Irvine, running with a low fuel load, made a bid to grab 12th from Nick Heidfeld. Irvine's move was over-optimistic and the two collided. Both were out of the race. At the back of the field Jenson Button overtook Tarso Marques for what had become 15th place.

**LAP 3** The Schumacher brothers started to pull away from Coulthard, who realised the nut must have been important as his car was handling very oddly. It turned out that one part of the front suspension linkage was not attached as it should be. This had the effect of disrupting the cross-weighting of the car and Coulthard found his McLaren difficult to drive, although he soon ascertained that the problem was consistent and there were no nasty surprises. As a result of all this, Rubens Barrichello was able to overtake Coulthard to grab third. Down at the back of the field the fast-starting Marques was being put back in his place by Jean Alesi and Fernando Alonso.

**LAP 5** At the front of the pack Ralf Schumacher came under attack from his brother's Ferrari team-mate Rubens Barrichello, as the Williams' Michelin tyres took time to come good.

**LAP 6** Barrichello spun at the exit of the hairpin. He later blamed a faulty sensor on the traction control system, which was causing it to switch on and off. Rubens dropped to 14th place. Benetton's terrible day continued when the FIA stewards announced Button had to serve a 10-second stop-go penalty for jumping the start. At the back of the field Marques was overtaken by Luciano Burti.

**LAP 7** Jenson Button came in for his penalty, dropping way behind the rest of the field.

**LAP 8** Alonso's afternoon came to a premature close when he pulled off with a driveshaft failure. This let Burti move onto Alesi's tail.

**LAP 9** Bernoldi and Button pitted to have their cars repaired.

**LAP 11** Rubens Barrichello overtook Jacques Villeneuve in order to move up to 12th position.

**LAP 12** Barrichello made short work of Pedro de la Rosa for 11th.

**LAP 13** Ralf Schumacher's Michelins began to work more effectively and he quickly closed the gap to his brother.

**LAP 18** Button pitted to retire with an oil leak.

**LAP 20** The safety car was deployed after Juan Pablo Montoya crashed while defending his 10th place against Barrichello. The Ferrari driver spun as he tried to avoid the accident and had an accident of his own on the other side of the road. Montoya pitted, saying he thought something might have broken.

**LAP 21** Marques tried to take advantage of the safety car and was the first driver to pit for fuel and new tyres.

**LAP 23** Verstappen pitted just as the safety car was pulling off. This curious strategic decision was blamed on a malfunctioning radio. The stop dropped the Dutchman from sixth to 15th.

**LAP 24** Michael Schumacher pulled out a lead of two-and-a-half seconds as his brother Ralf was struggling after his tyres had picked up rubber behind the safety car and were not at full efficiency.

**LAP 25** Bernoldi retired because of his Arrows overheating. Later, a hamburger wrapper was found to have blocked his radiator.

**LAP 26** Jos Verstappen began to recover, passing Tarso Marques for 13th position.

**LAP 28** Burti nearly ran into the back of his team-mate Alesi and had to take to the grass to avoid impact. He rejoined without losing a place but with debris in his sidepods.

**LAP 30** Ralf Schumacher's tyres were finally effective again and he closed up on Michael. Two-stop racer de la Rosa, who was running 10th, came in for fuel and tyres. He rejoined 13th.

**LAP 32** Zonta ran into Kimi Räikkönen on the back straight when the Finn braked unexpectedly. Neither car was badly damaged but both lost aerodynamic parts. This enabled Mika Häkkinen to close up and prepare to challenge the pair for sixth place.

**LAP 33** Burti came in to have his sidepods cleaned out.

**LAP 35** Villeneuve retired from 10th with a driveshaft failure. Häkkinen passed Zonta for seventh and Ralf Schumacher made his first real attempt to pass Michael for the lead.

**LAP 36** Olivier Panis pitted with brake problems. The team tried to fix it but after a couple of exploratory laps Panis retired. Mika Häkkinen overtook Kimi Räikkönen while Jordan Honda's Ricardo Zonta headed for the pits for his stop.

**LAP 38** Jarno Trulli pitted and fell back from fourth place to eighth.

**LAP 39** Räikkönen headed for the pits so Alesi moved up to fifth with Verstappen sixth, although both were still to stop again.

**LAP 41** Alesi dropped back to ninth at his stop.

**LAP 42** Third-placed Coulthard came in for his stop. This allowed Häkkinen to move up to third and Verstappen to fourth.

**LAP 46** Michael Schumacher pitted, allowing brother Ralf to take the lead and set a string of fastest laps. Pedro de la Rosa took sixth from Jordan Honda's Jarno Trulli.

**LAP 47** Verstappen pitted and fell back from fourth to ninth, while Marques had his second scheduled stop.

**LAP 49** Häkkinen pitted but stayed in third ahead of Coulthard.

**LAP 51** The leader Ralf came into the pits and emerged with a five-second advantage over his brother. The race was won.

**LAP 52** Pedro de la Rosa pitted for the second time.

**LAP 55** Coulthard's race ended with a major engine failure.

**LAP 62** Trulli hit trouble with his brakes. He was passed by Räikkönen. The next lap he was passed by Alesi and Verstappen.

**LAP 64** Trulli retired with a brake cylinder failure.

**LAP 66** Verstappen spun into the gravel with brake trouble.

**LAP 69** Ralf Schumacher won the Canadian Grand Prix by 20 seconds. Brother Michael was second, with Mika Häkkinen 20 seconds behind him. Another half a minute behind Häkkinen was Räikkönen, only a couple of seconds ahead of an ecstatic Jean Alesi, who picked up another two points for Prost. The other surviving runners, de la Rosa, Zonta, Burti and Marques, were all lapped.

# pity!

"It's a shame there aren't 17 races a year in Montréal."

*Jonathan Noble,*
*Autosport*
*June 14 2001*

Air Canada Grand Prix
**M O N T R É A L**
7-9th June 2002

# European Grand Prix

## 22nd–24th June 2001     LAPS: 67  LENGTH OF LAP: 2.831 miles

**EDDIE IRVINE'S JAGUAR BITES BACK** Having pushed his Jaguar R2 beyond the limits of balance and grip, Eddie Irvine's cat bites back and is launched over the kerb in a wild, dusty ride that brings its on-track activity to an end. With the right-side tyres devoid of contact with anything and the monocoque straddling the kerb, the left-side tyres have little hope of arresting the car's wayward progress. PHOTOGRAPH BY MICHAEL STIRNDENG

## Water is thicker than blood

A great race was in the offing and it seemed that Ralf and Michael Schumacher would fight the European Grand Prix out to the finish line. But then a little white line, a highly observant Ross Brawn and Jean Todt intervened. Brawn and Todt sent race director Charlie Whiting an e-mail pointing out that Ralf Schumacher had infringed the rules by crossing the line at the exit from the pits. In a move that was presumably approved by his brother, it showed that, where Grand Prix racing is concerned, water is thicker than blood and although each brother is genuinely pleased to see the other succeed, that only applies after the chequered flag has dropped. Before then, it's war as usual.

Twenty-seven minutes to go before the start of the European Grand Prix at the Nürburgring, and there was high drama. On his lap out of the garage before positioning his car on the grid, the red Ferrari of Michael Schumacher suddenly stopped in the middle of the track. The 150,000-strong crowd were silent. In the ITV studio, Jim Rosenthal was in the middle of his pre-race preamble when the camera showed the stranded German. Rosenthal wasn't used to action before the race had even started and he was befuddled. He got through it, just as the driver did.

Schumacher made a hasty return to the garage on a politically incorrect BMW motorcycle. It should have been a Piaggio – and James Allen made sure everyone knew it. Two minutes later, the German crowd was back doing its subdued version of the Mexican wave. False alarm. Michael was only trying out the spare car, which was the one that broke down.

Michael Schumacher was straight into the lead but brother Ralf gave him no rest.

As the field descends on the first corner of the European Grand Prix, Michael and Ralf Schumacher have already fought their first battle.

The excitement gave false hope that this would be a day of surprises and action. The circuit has a history of producing high drama but the feeling throughout the weekend was that such drama was just that – history. Many teams appeared jaded at the season's halfway mark, and were already talking about the trip to Magny-Cours the following week for the back-to-back race. Most betting inside the paddock was on how long the post-race drive to Cologne airport would take rather than who would actually win the Grand Prix. Even the normally stunning Warsteiner grid girls were below par, dressed in funereal black skirts that were not really appropriate for a Formula One race.

As the red lights went out, Michael Schumacher on pole did a bit of brotherly blocking and put an early end to his brother's dreams of a home victory. Both had decided on a two-stop rather than one-

stop strategy and the plan meant they had to pit together. As Ferrari's stops are the best in the business, it was obvious who had the advantage. Schumacher senior was on the pace immediately and by lap four was 2.2secs ahead of his brother. Montoya kept his concentration by staying third and out of trouble, followed by David Coulthard, Mika Häkkinen and Jarno Trulli.

By now, even the subdued Mexican wave was struggling to maintain momentum. Seven laps into the race, though, there was some excitement as a car spun off – but it only turned out to be Tarso Marques's Minardi. Nevertheless, some of the crowd cheered the fact that he had even made it this far.

Soon after, the focus shifted to lap times: so far, there was no sign of the BMW Williams cars using their supposed greater speed to better effect. On lap 10 Michael Schumacher set the fastest lap for the third time with a 1m 19.415secs. The following lap he opened up a gap of 3.7secs to his brother, who in turn was leading his team-mate Juan Pablo Montoya by 7.1secs. Just as an afternoon nap beckoned, those Michelin tyres on the Williams started warming up nicely and suddenly it looked like the crowd might have a race on its hands after all. On lap 13, Ralf Schumacher clocked the fastest lap at 1m 19.205secs. The gap to his brother's Ferrari was down to 2.3secs, with both Montoya and Ralf circulating half-a-second quicker than anyone else. By lap 16 Ralf clocked the fastest lap of 1m 18.770secs, bringing the gap down to a mere second.

By now Montoya was joining in the lap-record game too, setting a new benchmark of 1m 18.354secs. Once again, this race could and should have come down to pitstop strategy.

On lap 29, Ralf Schumacher committed his BMW Williams to the pitlane. At the last minute Michael came in as well, cutting across the front of his brother in dramatic style as he took to the pitlane. There

Michael pretends he can't hear Ralf's comments about the incident at the start.

The moment the race was lost: Ralf Schumacher just crosses the white pix exit line.

are no rules about running over lines at the entrance to the pits. The Ferrari and BMW garages were both ready and waiting and the Schumacher brothers entered the pits together. Michael had a 0.4sec lead coming in and extended it coming out. BMW Williams had run to form but at least managed to equal Ferrari's pitstop performance.

But then disaster struck and the race was over. In the heat of competition, Ralf rejoined the racetrack prematurely by crossing the white exit line, forbidden in the rules but missed by everybody including, it seemed, race director Charlie Whiting.

However, the young German's actions were not overlooked by the eagle-eyed Ross Brawn, who told Ferrari team principal Jean Todt to e-mail Whiting about the infringement. When Whiting got the e-mail, he had no choice but to order Schumacher junior in for a 10-second stop-and-go penalty. End of race. Brother Michael later described the penalty as 'harsh' but, in truth, he was over the moon. Odds on this was baby brother's race – and he knew it.

It was left to Montoya, now in second place, to take up the chase, but for once the Colombian kept his cool. Hanging on to his job was the name of the game today and he happily stayed 10secs behind the Ferrari, never once trying to catch Schumacher senior.

Ralf's penalty relegated him to fourth place, while McLaren's one-stop strategy for Coulthard paid dividends, moving him into third.

With 20 laps still to go, the only uncertainty now was who would take the points behind Schumacher, Montoya and Coulthard.

Down the grid, the midfielders' ritual mechanical woes kicked in. First off was Jarno Trulli's Jordan on lap 46 with gearbox failure. Then team-mate Heinz-Harald Frentzen spun off. They had company in the early-bath queue: Nick Heidfeld spun his Sauber out on lap 53 and Jos Verstappen's Arrows packed up on lap 58.

Cars made their stops but nothing changed. The only debate was

Montoya had the best views of the brotherly warfare ahead of him.

whether Ralf Schumacher could catch Coulthard's McLaren and steal third place. But his pace late in the race had mysteriously gone and even with plenty of time in hand he made no impression. As the cars approach the last lap there were no surprises: Schumacher took the chequered flag, followed by Montoya and Coulthard. A dejected Ralf came in fourth, ahead of Barrichello and Häkkinen.

As the podium-placed drivers headed for the champagne celebrations, Ralf and Michael traded seemingly strong words over that brotherly block on lap one. At least Ralf would only have to wait a week to exact revenge.

Later, when he found that it was Ferrari who told the FIA about his line infringement, he realised that in Formula One water is thicker than blood and that he and his team must give Ferrari and its number one no quarter.

# European Grand Prix Race Statistics

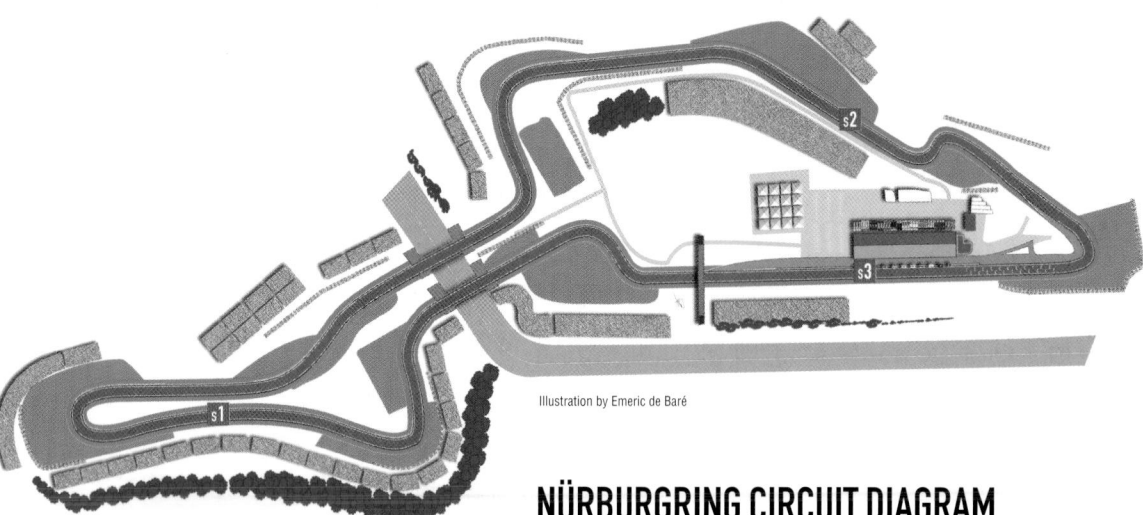

**NÜRBURGRING CIRCUIT DIAGRAM**

Illustration by Emeric de Baré

## FASTEST LAPS

| | DRIVER | TIME | LAP |
|---|---|---|---|
| 1 | Montoya | 1m 18.354s | 27 |
| 2 | R Schumacher | 1m 18.498s | 54 |
| 3 | Barrichello | 1m 18.537s | 59 |
| 4 | M Schumacher | 1m 18.612s | 49 |
| 5 | Irvine | 1m 18.674s | 34 |
| 6 | Coulthard | 1m 18.883s | 63 |
| 7 | Burti | 1m 19.105s | 57 |
| 8 | Häkkinen | 1m 19.273s | 65 |
| 9 | Trulli | 1m 19.484s | 32 |
| 10 | de la Rosa | 1m 19.737s | 65 |
| 11 | Villeneuve | 1m 19.797s | 65 |
| 12 | Frentzen | 1m 19.892s | 31 |
| 13 | Alesi | 1m 20.049s | 48 |
| 14 | Button | 1m 20.069s | 25 |
| 15 | Räikkönen | 1m 20.498s | 34 |
| 16 | Fisichella | 1m 20.729s | 26 |
| 17 | Alonso | 1m 20.937s | 29 |
| 18 | Heidfeld | 1m 20.976s | 53 |
| 19 | Verstappen | 1m 21.154s | 23 |
| 20 | Bernoldi | 1m 21.188s | 25 |
| 21 | Panis | 1m 21.314s | 23 |
| 22 | Marques | 1m 23.778s | 4 |

## RACE SPEED TRAP

| | | |
|---|---|---|
| 1 | R Schumacher | 192.1mph |
| 2 | de la Rosa | 192.1mph |
| 3 | Montoya | 191.4mph |
| 4 | Alesi | 190.5mph |
| 5 | Burti | 190.3mph |
| 6 | Irvine | 190.1mph |
| 7 | Villeneuve | 189.8mph |
| 8 | Bernoldi | 189.4mph |
| 9 | M Schumacher | 189.0mph |
| 10 | Verstappen | 188.7mph |
| 11 | Räikkönen | 188.6mph |
| 12 | Frentzen | 188.4mph |
| 13 | Trulli | 188.2mph |
| 14 | Heidfeld | 187.9mph |
| 15 | Barrichello | 187.7mph |
| 16 | Coulthard | 187.4mph |
| 17 | Häkkinen | 187.2mph |
| 18 | Alonso | 187.2mph |
| 19 | Button | 185.8mph |
| 20 | Panis | 185.3mph |
| 21 | Marques | 185.2mph |
| 22 | Fisichella | 184.9mph |

## WARM-UP

SUNDAY 24TH JUNE 2001, 9.30AM–10AM

| | | |
|---|---|---|
| 1 | Barrichello | 1m 18.209s |
| 2 | M Schumacher | 1m 18.371s |
| 3 | R Schumacher | 1m 18.392s |
| 4 | Irvine | 1m 18.466s |
| 5 | Coulthard | 1m 18.674s |
| 6 | Montoya | 1m 18.843s |
| 7 | Trulli | 1m 19.002s |
| 8 | Häkkinen | 1m 19.164s |
| 9 | Heidfeld | 1m 19.732s |
| 10 | Räikkönen | 1m 19.787s |
| 11 | de la Rosa | 1m 19.796s |
| 12 | Panis | 1m 19.808s |
| 13 | Alesi | 1m 19.854s |
| 14 | Frentzen | 1m 19.917s |
| 15 | Bernoldi | 1m 20.098s |
| 16 | Verstappen | 1m 20.115s |
| 17 | Villeneuve | 1m 20.320s |
| 18 | Burti | 1m 20.608s |
| 19 | Marques | 1m 20.988s |
| 20 | Alonso | 1m 21.367s |
| 21 | Button | 1m 21.423s |
| 22 | Fisichella | 1m 21.766s |

## DRIVER POINTS

| | | |
|---|---|---|
| 1 | Michael Schumacher | 68 |
| 2 | David Coulthard | 44 |
| 3 | Rubens Barrichello | 26 |
| 4 | Ralf Schumacher | 25 |
| 5 | Juan Pablo Montoya | 12 |
| 6 | Mika Häkkinen | 9 |
| 7 | Nick Heidfeld | 8 |
| 8 | Jacques Villeneuve | 7 |
| 9 | Kimi Räikkönen | 7 |
| 10 | Jarno Trulli | 7 |
| 11 | Heinz-Harald Frentzen | 6 |
| 12 | Olivier Panis | 5 |
| 13 | Eddie Irvine | 4 |
| 14 | Jean Alesi | 3 |
| 15 | Jos Verstappen | 1 |
| 16 | Pedro de la Rosa | 1 |
| 17 | Giancarlo Fisichella | 1 |
| 18 | Jenson Button | 0 |
| 19 | Ricardo Zonta | 0 |
| 20 | Luciano Burti | 0 |
| 21 | Tarso Marques | 0 |
| 22 | Enrique Bernoldi | 0 |
| 23 | Fernando Alonso | 0 |
| 24 | Gaston Mazzacane | 0 |

## EUROPEAN GRAND PRIX RACE RESULTS: SUNDAY 24TH JUNE 2001, 2PM

| | DRIVER | CAR | TIME/RETIREMENT | LAPS | PITSTOP LAPS |
|---|---|---|---|---|---|
| 1 | Michael Schumacher | Ferrari | 1h 29m 42.724s | 67 | 28 50 |
| 2 | Juan Pablo Montoya | BMW Williams | +4.217s | 67 | 29 50 |
| 3 | David Coulthard | McLaren Mercedes | +24.993s | 67 | 38 |
| 4 | Ralf Schumacher | BMW Williams | +33.345s | 67 | 28 39 52 |
| 5 | Rubens Barrichello | Ferrari | +45.495s | 67 | 44 |
| 6 | Mika Häkkinen | McLaren Mercedes | +1m 04.868s | 67 | 33 |
| 7 | Eddie Irvine | Jaguar Racing | +1m 06.198s | 67 | 37 |
| 8 | Pedro de la Rosa | Jaguar Racing | +1 lap | 66 | 44 |
| 9 | Jacques Villeneuve | BAR Honda | +1 lap | 66 | 43 |
| 10 | Kimi Räikkönen | Sauber Petronas | +1 lap | 66 | 32 |
| 11 | Giancarlo Fisichella | Benetton Renault | +1 lap | 66 | 21 42 |
| 12 | Luciano Burti | Prost Acer | +2 laps | 65 | 12 49 |
| 13 | Jenson Button | Benetton Renault | +2 laps | 65 | 23 43 |
| 14 | Fernando Alonso | European Minardi | +2 laps | 65 | 25 46 |
| 15 | Jean Alesi | Prost Acer | Spin | 64 | 42 |
| Ret | Jos Verstappen | Arrows Asiatech | Engine | 58 | 26 46 |
| Ret | Nick Heidfeld | Sauber Petronas | Driveshaft | 54 | 33 |
| Ret | Heinz-Harald Frentzen | Jordan Honda | Spin | 48 | 29 |
| Ret | Jarno Trulli | Jordan Honda | Transmission | 44 | 30 |
| Ret | Enrique Bernoldi | Arrows Asiatech | Gearbox | 29 | 23 |
| Ret | Olivier Panis | BAR Honda | Electrics | 23 | |
| Ret | Tarso Marques | European Minardi | Electrics | 7 | |

*Conditions: sunny.*

## PITSTOP TIMES (from pitlane entrance to exit)

| | | | | |
|---|---|---|---|---|
| Fastest pitstop: | Michael Schumacher | Ferrari | 31.983s | Lap 50 |
| Slowest pitstop: | Enrique Bernoldi | Arrows Asiatech | 43.799s | Lap 23 |
| Most pitstops: | Ralf Schumacher | BMW Williams | Three stops | |

## PENALTIES AND FINES

| DRIVER | WHEN | PENALTY | REASON |
|---|---|---|---|
| Ralf Schumacher | Race | 10 seconds | Crossing line on pitlane exit |

## CONSTRUCTOR POINTS

| | | |
|---|---|---|
| 1 | Scuderia Ferrari-Marlboro | 94 |
| 2 | West McLaren Mercedes | 53 |
| 3 | BMW Williams F1 | 37 |
| 4 | Red Bull Sauber Petronas | 15 |
| 5 | Benson & Hedges Jordan Honda | 13 |
| 6 | Lucky Strike Reynard BAR Honda | 12 |
| 7 | Jaguar Racing | 5 |
| 8 | Prost Acer | 3 |
| 9 | Orange Arrows Asiatech | 1 |
| 10 | Mild Seven Benetton Renault | 1 |
| 11 | European Minardi F1 | 0 |

## LAP LEADERS

| | |
|---|---|
| Michael Schumacher | 1–28 |
| Juan Pablo Montoya | 29 |
| Michael Schumacher | 30–67 |

Total laps led:
M Schumacher 66: Montoya 1.

## TEMPERATURES

| | | |
|---|---|---|
| Friday: | Air: 18–26°C | Track: 21°C |
| Saturday: | Air: 14–15°C | Track: 25–27°C |
| Sunday: | Air: 23°C | Track: 34°C |

 F Alonso **21**

 J Verstappen **19**

 L Burti **17**

 G Fisichella **15**

 O Panis **13**

 T Marques **22**

 J Button **20**

 E Bernoldi **18**

 P de la Rosa **16**

 J Alesi **14**

 E Irvine **12**

## SPANISH GRAND PRIX RACE ENTRY

| | DRIVER | TEAM | CHASSIS/ENGINE |
|---|---|---|---|
| 1 | Michael Schumacher | Scuderia Ferrari Marlboro | Ferrari F2001 |
| 2 | Rubens Barrichello | Scuderia Ferrari Marlboro | Ferrari F2001 |
| 3 | Mika Häkkinen | West McLaren Mercedes | McLaren Mercedes MP4-16 |
| 4 | David Coulthard | West McLaren Mercedes | McLaren Mercedes MP4-16 |
| 5 | Ralf Schumacher | BMW Williams F1 Team | BMW Williams FW23 |
| 6 | Juan Pablo Montoya | BMW Williams F1 Team | BMW Williams FW23 |
| 7 | Giancarlo Fisichella | Mild Seven Benetton Renault | Benetton Renault B201 |
| 8 | Jenson Button | Mild Seven Benetton Renault | Benetton Renault B201 |
| 9 | Olivier Panis | Lucky Strike BAR Honda | BAR Honda B003 |
| 10 | Jacques Villeneuve | Lucky Strike BAR Honda | BAR Honda B003 |
| 11 | Heinz-Harald Frentzen | Benson & Hedges Jordan Honda | Jordan Honda EJ11 |
| 12 | Jarno Trulli | Benson & Hedges Jordan Honda | Jordan Honda EJ11 |
| 14 | Jos Verstappen | Orange Arrows Asiatech | Arrows Asiatech A22 |
| 15 | Enrique Bernoldi | Orange Arrows Asiatech | Arrows Asiatech A22 |
| 16 | Nick Heidfeld | Red Bull Sauber Petronas | Sauber Petronas C20 |
| 17 | Kimi Räikkönen | Red Bull Sauber Petronas | Sauber Petronas C20 |
| 18 | Eddie Irvine | Jaguar Racing | Jaguar Cosworth R2 |
| 19 | Pedro de la Rosa | Jaguar Racing | Jaguar Cosworth R2 |
| 20 | Tarso Marques | European Minardi | Minardi European PS01 |
| 21 | Fernando Alonso | European Minardi | Minardi European PS01 |
| 22 | Jean Alesi | Prost Grand Prix | Prost ACER AP04 |
| 23 | Luciano Burti | Prost Grand Prix | Prost ACER AP04 |

Michael Schumacher celebrates another victory on home soil.

## QUALIFYING: SATURDAY 23RD JUNE 2001, 1PM–2PM  *107 per cent time: 1m 20.207s*

| | DRIVER | TEAM | TIME | GAP | LAPS |
|---|---|---|---|---|---|
| 1 | Michael Schumacher | Ferrari | 1m 14.960s | 0.000 | 8 |
| 2 | Ralf Schumacher | BMW Williams | 1m 15.226s | +0.266s | 12 |
| 3 | Juan Pablo Montoya | BMW Williams | 1m 15.490s | +0.530s | 11 |
| 4 | Rubens Barrichello | Ferrari | 1m 15.622s | +0.662s | 11 |
| 5 | David Coulthard | McLaren Mercedes | 1m 15.717s | +0.757s | 12 |
| 6 | Mika Häkkinen | McLaren Mercedes | 1m 15.776s | +0.816s | 12 |
| 7 | Jarno Trulli | Jordan Honda | 1m 16.138s | +1.178s | 10 |
| 8 | Heinz-Harald Frentzen | Jordan Honda | 1m 16.376s | +1.416s | 11 |
| 9 | Kimi Räikkönen | Sauber Petronas | 1m 16.402s | +1.442s | 11 |
| 10 | Nick Heidfeld | Sauber Petronas | 1m 16.438s | +1.478s | 11 |
| 11 | Jacques Villeneuve | BAR Honda | 1m 16.439s | +1.479s | 12 |
| 12 | Eddie Irvine | Jaguar Racing | 1m 16.588s | +1.628s | 11 |
| 13 | Olivier Panis | BAR Honda | 1m 16.872s | +1.912s | 11 |
| 14 | Jean Alesi | Prost Acer | 1m 17.251s | +2.291s | 11 |
| 15 | Giancarlo Fisichella | Benetton Renault | 1m 17.378s | +2.418s | 11 |
| 16 | Pedro de la Rosa | Jaguar Racing | 1m 17.627s | +2.667s | 12 |
| 17 | Luciano Burti | Prost Acer | 1m 18.113s | +3.153s | 11 |
| 18 | Enrique Bernoldi | Arrows Asiatech | 1m 18.151s | +3.191s | 12 |
| 19 | Jos Verstappen | Arrows Asiatech | 1m 18.262s | +3.302s | 11 |
| 20 | Jenson Button | Benetton Renault | 1m 18.626s | +3.666s | 11 |
| 21 | Fernando Alonso | European Minardi | 1m 18.630s | +3.670s | 11 |
| 22 | Tarso Marques | European Minardi | 1m 18.689s | +3.729s | 12 |

## FASTEST SECTOR TIMES IN QUALIFYING  *Ideal lap time: 1m 14.907s (diff. from pole: 0.053s)*

| | SECTOR 1 | SECS | | SECTOR 2 | SECS | | SECTOR 3 | SECS |
|---|---|---|---|---|---|---|---|---|
| 1 | M Schumacher | 27.071s | 1 | M Schumacher | 25.179s | 1 | R Schumacher | 22.657s |
| 2 | R Schumacher | 27.117s | 2 | R Schumacher | 25.327s | 2 | M Schumacher | 22.697s |
| 3 | Barrichello | 27.246s | 3 | Montoya | 25.418s | 3 | Montoya | 22.700s |
| 4 | Montoya | 27.342s | 4 | Barrichello | 25.341s | 4 | Häkkinen | 22.781s |
| 5 | Coulthard | 27.425s | 5 | Häkkinen | 25.444s | 5 | Coulthard | 22.791s |
| 6 | Häkkinen | 27.437s | 6 | Coulthard | 25.489s | 6 | Barrichello | 22.848s |
| 7 | Villeneuve | 27.469s | 7 | Frentzen | 25.601s | 7 | Trulli | 22.980s |
| 8 | Frentzen | 27.472s | 8 | Trulli | 25.621s | 8 | Frentzen | 23.019s |
| 9 | Trulli | 27.498s | 9 | Heidfeld | 25.632s | 9 | Räikkönen | 23.066s |
| 10 | Räikkönen | 27.563s | 10 | Villeneuve | 25.716s | 10 | Heidfeld | 23.068s |
| 11 | Panis | 27.696s | 11 | Irvine | 25.768s | 11 | Fisichella | 23.074s |
| 12 | Irvine | 27.701s | 12 | Räikkönen | 25.773s | 12 | Irvine | 23.119s |
| 13 | Heidfeld | 27.712s | 13 | Panis | 25.812s | 13 | de la Rosa | 23.126s |
| 14 | Alesi | 27.906s | 14 | Fisichella | 25.949s | 14 | Villeneuve | 23.128s |
| 15 | Bernoldi | 28.124s | 15 | Alesi | 26.056s | 15 | Panis | 23.193s |
| 16 | de la Rosa | 28.156s | 16 | de la Rosa | 26.221s | 16 | Alesi | 23.233s |
| 17 | Fisichella | 28.194s | 17 | Burti | 26.232s | 17 | Verstappen | 23.527s |
| 18 | Verstappen | 28.238s | 18 | Bernoldi | 26.262s | 18 | Marques | 23.594s |
| 19 | Burti | 28.258s | 19 | Alonso | 26.393s | 19 | Bernoldi | 23.600s |
| 20 | Alonso | 28.329s | 20 | Verstappen | 26.398s | 20 | Burti | 23.623s |
| 21 | Marques | 28.377s | 21 | Button | 26.401s | 21 | Button | 23.627s |
| 22 | Button | 28.598s | 22 | Marques | 26.537s | 22 | Alonso | 23.642s |

## PRACTICE SESSION ONE

FRIDAY 22ND JUNE 2001, 11AM–12PM

| | | |
|---|---|---|
| 1 | Coulthard | 1m 16.888s |
| 2 | Häkkinen | 1m 17.022s |
| 3 | M Schumacher | 1m 17.797s |
| 4 | Barrichello | 1m 17.912s |
| 5 | Trulli | 1m 18.755s |
| 6 | Räikkönen | 1m 19.072s |
| 7 | Panis | 1m 19.086s |
| 8 | Villeneuve | 1m 19.154s |
| 9 | Heidfeld | 1m 19.399s |
| 10 | R Schumacher | 1m 19.500s |
| 11 | Alesi | 1m 19.650s |
| 12 | Montoya | 1m 19.940s |
| 13 | Frentzen | 1m 19.988s |
| 14 | de la Rosa | 1m 20.267s |
| 15 | Verstappen | 1m 20.553s |
| 16 | Bernoldi | 1m 21.079s |
| 17 | Fisichella | 1m 21.233s |
| 18 | Burti | 1m 21.370s |
| 19 | Button | 1m 21.615s |
| 20 | Alonso | 1m 21.644s |
| | Irvine | No lap completed |
| | Marques | No lap completed |

## PRACTICE SESSION TWO

FRIDAY 22ND JUNE 2001, 1PM–2PM

| | | |
|---|---|---|
| 1 | Häkkinen | 1m 16.408s |
| 2 | Coulthard | 1m 16.579s |
| 3 | R Schumacher | 1m 17.355s |
| 4 | M Schumacher | 1m 17.507s |
| 5 | Barrichello | 1m 17.665s |
| 6 | Montoya | 1m 17.737s |
| 7 | Trulli | 1m 18.133s |
| 8 | Heidfeld | 1m 18.196s |
| 9 | Alesi | 1m 18.352s |
| 10 | Panis | 1m 18.410s |
| 11 | Räikkönen | 1m 18.413s |
| 12 | Villeneuve | 1m 18.434s |
| 13 | de la Rosa | 1m 18.473s |
| 14 | Fisichella | 1m 19.339s |
| 15 | Irvine | 1m 19.503s |
| 16 | Verstappen | 1m 19.640s |
| 17 | Bernoldi | 1m 19.822s |
| 18 | Button | 1m 19.978s |
| 19 | Frentzen | 1m 19.988s |
| 20 | Burti | 1m 20.094s |
| 21 | Alonso | 1m 20.183s |
| 22 | Marques | 1m 21.129s |

## PRACTICE SESSION THREE

SATURDAY 23RD JUNE 2001, 9.00AM–9.45AM

| | | |
|---|---|---|
| 1 | M Schumacher | 1m 16.308s |
| 2 | R Schumacher | 1m 16.574s |
| 3 | Häkkinen | 1m 16.631s |
| 4 | Coulthard | 1m 16.733s |
| 5 | Barrichello | 1m 16.769s |
| 6 | Montoya | 1m 17.021s |
| 7 | Villeneuve | 1m 17.061s |
| 8 | Frentzen | 1m 17.374s |
| 9 | Panis | 1m 17.446s |
| 10 | Heidfeld | 1m 17.642s |
| 11 | Räikkönen | 1m 17.693s |
| 12 | Trulli | 1m 17.978s |
| 13 | de la Rosa | 1m 18.522s |
| 14 | Irvine | 1m 18.630s |
| 15 | Alesi | 1m 18.979s |
| 16 | Verstappen | 1m 19.006s |
| 17 | Burti | 1m 19.107s |
| 18 | Bernoldi | 1m 19.394s |
| 19 | Fisichella | 1m 19.575s |
| 20 | Alonso | 1m 20.079s |
| 21 | Marques | 1m 20.208s |
| 22 | Button | 1m 20.256s |

## PRACTICE SESSION FOUR

SATURDAY 23RD JUNE 2001, 10.15AM–11AM

| | | |
|---|---|---|
| 1 | R Schumacher | 1m 15.355s |
| 2 | Montoya | 1m 15.749s |
| 3 | Barrichello | 1m 15.855s |
| 4 | Häkkinen | 1m 16.038s |
| 5 | Coulthard | 1m 16.237s |
| 6 | M Schumacher | 1m 16.308s |
| 7 | Trulli | 1m 16.385s |
| 8 | Frentzen | 1m 16.407s |
| 9 | Panis | 1m 16.625s |
| 10 | Räikkönen | 1m 16.852s |
| 11 | Heidfeld | 1m 16.941s |
| 12 | Villeneuve | 1m 17.006s |
| 13 | Irvine | 1m 17.609s |
| 14 | Bernoldi | 1m 17.686s |
| 15 | Burti | 1m 17.688s |
| 16 | Fisichella | 1m 17.785s |
| 17 | Alesi | 1m 17.839s |
| 18 | de la Rosa | 1m 18.048s |
| 19 | Verstappen | 1m 18.123s |
| 20 | Button | 1m 18.674s |
| 21 | Alonso | 1m 19.164s |
| 22 | Marques | 1m 20.208s |

J Villeneuve — 11

K Räikkönen — 9

J Trulli — 7

D Coulthard — 5

JP Montoya — 3

M Schumacher — 1

N Heidfeld — 10

HH Frentzen — 8

M Häkkinen — 6

R Barrichello — 4

R Schumacher — 2

## NÜRBURGRING LAP-BY-LAP REPORT

**PRE-START** There was drama before the cars had even lined up on the grid when Michael Schumacher's Ferrari broke down at the far side of the track. He commandeered a BMW motor scooter and, not worrying about brand issues, raced back to the pits. Fortunately the failed car was his spare and his race chassis was ready. As the cars headed off on the parade lap Tarso Marques was left behind on the grid. The Minardi was fired up and chased after the rest of the field. This meant he would have to start at the back of the grid — an irrelevant punishment, as he'd qualified last anyway.

**LAP 1** Ralf Schumacher's Williams had a slight advantage over his brother's Ferrari so Michael edged his brother towards the pitwall to prevent him getting ahead. This was successful, although Ralf was none too happy. Michael took the lead, followed by Ralf and Juan Pablo Montoya. Rubens Barrichello was overtaken by David Coulthard, Mika Häkkinen and Jarno Trulli. Nick Heidfeld got away well and jumped from 10th to eighth, ahead of Kimi Räikkönen and Heinz-Harald Frentzen. Olivier Panis was the big loser in the midfield, dropping from 13th to 17th as he tried to avoid being hit. At the tail of the field Marques went for a trip across the sandtrap.

**LAP 7** Michael Schumacher had built up a small advantage as brother Ralf waited for his Michelin tyres to become fully competitive. Tarso Marques became the first retirement, with a gearbox failure traced to an electrical problem.

**LAP 10** Michael Schumacher's Ferrari was 3.5secs ahead. Ralf was still second, over six seconds ahead of Juan Pablo Montoya. Luciano Burti went off because his tyres had blistered. He bounced over the dirt but held on to his 20th place.

**LAP 12** As usual the Michelin tyres began to work after 12 laps and quickly Ralf Schumacher began to catch his brother. Luciano Burti rushed into the pits to have his radiators cleaned out, but a radio problem meant the Prost team was not ready to change tyres, so he went out again on blistered rubber.

**LAP 18** Under pressure from Ralf, Michael Schumacher locked his brakes going into Turn Five and slid wide. Ralf went for the inside but his brother cut back onto the racing line and held the position.

**LAP 21** As the Schumacher brothers continued their battle for dominance, Giancarlo Fisichella pitted for fuel and tyres. The Italian was struggling with blistered tyres. He dropped to 20th, with only Burti behind him.

**LAP 23** Montoya began to charge and closed the gap on the Schumachers. Enrique Bernoldi stopped for tyres, but the Arrows pitstop went wrong and the Brazilian lost 10secs and five places. Jenson Button also pitted.

**LAP 24** Olivier Panis, who was running in 16th, suffered an electronically-linked gearshift problem which caused him to spin off into a gravel trap.

**LAP 25** Fernando Alonso stopped in his Minardi and dropped to 19th. He had been struggling along in 16th with a gearbox problem.

**LAP 26** Jos Verstappen pitted from 13th position. The stop was slightly longer than normal and he rejoined in 17th position.

**LAP 27** Montoya set the fastest lap as he closed in on the Schumachers.

**LAP 28** Michael and Ralf Schumacher revealed their strategies as both headed for the pitlane. The Ferrari stop was 1.3secs quicker than the Williams', so Michael remained ahead. As Ralf left the pitlane he found himself rejoining the track behind Coulthard. Concentrating on this, he crossed the white line at the pitlane exit — an illegal move. At the front, Montoya briefly enjoyed leading a Grand Prix. In the midfield Eddie Irvine nabbed 10th place from Frentzen.

**LAP 29** Montoya went into the pits and was quickly on his way again, but the stop let Michael Schumacher back into the lead. Ralf remained stuck behind Coulthard and Montoya rejoined behind them all. Heinz-Harald Frentzen became the first one-stopper to pit, falling back to 14th.

**LAP 30** As the mid-race stage approached, one-stopper Trulli pitted and dropped from sixth to 11th behind Barrichello, Nick Heidfeld, Kimi Räikkönen, Irvine and Jacques Villeneuve. Irvine overtook Räikkönen for ninth while Bernoldi's race ended with his car stuck in fifth gear.

**LAP 32** Barrichello passed Häkkinen for fifth place, the McLaren driver suffering from tyre troubles. Räikkönen dived in and out of the pits, the time taken to pump in extra fuel dropping him from ninth to 14th.

**LAP 33** Montoya nearly blew it. The Colombian got too close to Coulthard's McLaren and went off across the chicane. Happily, he rejoined without losing a place. Häkkinen pitted and dropped from sixth to 10th. Heidfeld also stopped and fell from eighth to 14th.

**LAP 34** A flying Irvine set the fifth fastest lap of the race, the Jaguar lapping faster than all but the Williams and Ferrari cars.

**LAP 37** The FIA announced that Ralf Schumacher had to serve a 10-second stop-go penalty for crossing the white line while exiting the pits. Irvine came in for his pitstop, dropping from sixth to 11th.

**LAP 38** Third-placed Coulthard stopped for his refuelling. He fell behind Montoya and Barrichello, who was still to pit for the first time.

**LAP 39** Ralf came in for his penalty. He lost half a minute and emerged in fourth place, ahead of Coulthard but needing to pit again.

**LAP 42** One-stopper Jean Alesi pitted and Fisichella came in again.

**LAP 43** Villeneuve had his pitstop and dropped from sixth to 11th. Button pitted for his second stop and rejoined at the tail of the field.

**LAP 44** The last men to choose a one-stop strategy came into the pits. Ralf Schumacher and David Coulthard overtook Rubens Barrichello while he was in the pits. He rejoined in fifth. Pedro de la Rosa was the final man to stop, slipping from seventh to ninth behind Eddie Irvine and Heinz-Harald Frentzen.

**LAP 45** Trulli ground to a halt when his gearbox ran out of oil because of a leak. Häkkinen moved up to sixth place.

**LAP 46** Two-stopping Verstappen pitted and fell behind Fisichella and Burti. Alonso stopped again and dropped from 16th to 18th place.

**LAP 47** Alesi was flying and overtook Heidfeld to grab 12th position. The two cars had touched prior to the overtaking manoeuvre and Heidfeld later reported that the handling of his Sauber seemed odd.

**LAP 49** Jordan's day ended in depressing fashion as Frentzen spun off, the victim of a traction-control failure. Fourteenth-placed Burti stopped for new tyres and fuel. He rejoined and began lapping very quickly.

**LAP 50** The leaders dived into the pits. Michael Schumacher was eight seconds ahead and held the gap; Montoya rejoined, still in second.

**LAP 52** Ralf Schumacher fell behind Coulthard as he pitted for fuel and tyres. Coulthard was thus up to third.

**LAP 54** Heidfeld, who had been running 12th, came in to retire. The handling problem was diagnosed as a damaged driveshaft.

**LAP 56** Burti caught and passed 14th-placed Button.

**LAP 57** Burti set the seventh fastest lap of the race, quicker than both Häkkinen and Trulli.

**LAP 59** Barrichello spun but managed to hold onto fifth despite the incident. Arrows' miserable day ended when Verstappen pulled off with an engine problem. He'd been running 13th — unlucky for some.

**LAP 65** Alesi challenged Räikkönen for 10th place but the Prost driver made a mistake and spun off.

**LAP 67** Michael Schumacher took the chequered flag for his fifth win of the year and increased his lead in the world championship. Juan Pablo Montoya was 4.2secs behind but happy to have a solid result after a series of poor races. David Coulthard was happy to be third on a day when McLaren was not competitive. A frustrated Ralf Schumacher came home fourth, ahead of Rubens Barrichello and Mika Häkkinen. The only other runner who was not lapped was Eddie Irvine in seventh place, while the battle for eighth saw Pedro de la Rosa get home just ahead of Jacques Villeneuve.

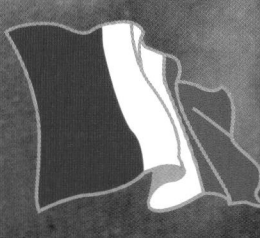

# French Grand Prix

**29th June–1st July 2001**   LAPS: 72  LENGTH OF LAP: 2.638 miles

NO BITE FOR HEROES Heinz-Harald Frentzen's Jordan is engulfed in smoke as the German tries to mate Honda's 795 brake horsepower with the road through its relatively narrow grooved Bridgestone tyres. Clearly on this occasion the Jordan's traction control system has not been activated. PHOTOGRAPH BY RAINER SCHLEGELMILCH

## Ferrari's steamroller

Practice and qualifying suggested that Ralf Schumacher and Michelin would dominate the race on the tyre manufacturer's home turf, as the young German finally upstaged big brother Michael to take the first pole position of his Formula One career. But one should never discount world champion Michael Schumacher, who was only 100th of a second slower in qualifying. In the event he, Ferrari and Bridgestone ran away with the race as, once again, all the luck went their way. It was Michael's 50th Formula One victory.

It was getting to be the norm, the Schumacher boys annexing the front row of a Grand Prix grid. But here was a change: Ralf had finally succeeded in out-running Michael, after a gripping (literally and figuratively) qualifying hour. In previous sessions Ralf had looked promising, only to fall foul of his brother's extraordinary speed. This time he set the pace before Michael redefined it, but then Ralf went faster still, smashing Michael's best with a dramatic lap of 1m 12.989secs. This weekend marked the first time anyone had managed to get below Nigel Mansell's fastest-ever lap of Magny-Cours, 1m 13.8secs, which had dated back to 1992 and the days of electronic aids such as active ride, traction control and anti-lock braking, as well as slick tyres and 3.5-litre engines. It was further endorsement of the strength of the BMW Williams package and Ralf Schumacher's growing ability to shine.

In qualifying, Michael Schumacher's subsequent efforts all fell short, despite his brio. His last run was the best of all, the stuff of Formula One folklore, as the watches tracked him round the broiling tarmac. He was tantalisingly close, but there would be no cigar for him this time: 1m 12.999secs was just short. Ralf was inadvertently handed a sparkling 26th birthday present by big brother.

The McLaren Mercedes of David Coulthard and Mika Häkkinen showed better form than of late and neither was a long way behind on the second row of the grid. Nor was Juan Pablo Montoya out of touch, having opted for the harder Michelin compound in prefer-

BMW Williams looked good for a win all weekend but it was Michael Schumacher's Ferrari that took the chequered flag as the BMW Williams challenge faded.

Ralf Schumacher's early race pace could not be repeated on his second set of tyres, which blunted his charge after brother Michael.

ence to the soft rubber his team-mate favoured. It gave BMW Williams a good split bet for the race. But it came at a price in the closing stages, as Jarno Trulli put his Jordan-Honda into fifth place at the Colombian's expense.

Come race day Ralf was still inwardly celebrating his break-through moment, although you wouldn't have know it from his expression. But for a guy used to living life in his sibling's shadow, it

was a nice feeling and the perfect fodder for a hungry media that sent his image all round the globe and described his achievement in thousands of warm words. Nothing energises people more than an emergent new star and there was sufficient left unknown about Ralf to keep interest in him at a high level. And, of course, the press was still buzzing about the way Michael tried to drive him into the pitwall the previous week in Germany. On that occasion Michael had the advantage of pole. Now the boot was on Ralf's foot, would he put it in? Was Michael about to get his comeuppance?

The air of tension on the grid in Magny-Cours was thicker than Los Angeles smog as the ambient temperature sidled up to 27°C. Michael's move at the Nürburgring was legal, by the clarification he himself sought after using it to good effect on drivers who aren't his relatives. But Ralf still wasn't amused. The two of them were reunited in parc fermé in Germany, when the atmosphere was frosty but polite. Ralf had been in no mood to congratulate his brother on his 49th Grand Prix victory, especially after finishing an unhappy fourth in a race he might have won. However, they kept their feelings bottled up for public consumption, aware of many lenses trained on them, but later Ralf spent hours cooling down in the BMW Williams motor home. Brotherly love is a wonderful thing.

So now everyone wanted to know how little brother would behave at the start. Patrick Head, technical director of BMW Williams, was pleased with the way his young driver had come on this year and, as usual, he analysed what had happened in Germany: "Michael just

Once again Mika Häkkinen's only involvement was his trip to the dummy grid.

Jean Alesi's home race proved a great disappointment to the Frenchman and his fans.

David Coulthard's race was ruined by a 10-second speeding penalty.

moved across until Ralf had nowhere to go," he said. "The only thing he could do not to have an accident was to lift off. By the rule, Michael was precisely correct. But we have got to run our game accordingly now that they are first and second on the grid." Then Head said something else interesting: "Ralf needs to work out in his mind how he is going to sort out certain things, because his brother is a very tough competitor. Ralf will work out how to deal with that and I don't think that necessarily driving into the side of Michael is the way he will deal with it."

Beating Michael to pole was a form of revenge for Ralf, but he was not vengeful as they left the startline. Already Mika Häkkinen was out. As Ron Dennis tells everyone, McLaren makes history – but not much on this day as the Finn's gearbox broke on the parade lap. Pedro de la Rosa also went a lap down when his electronics glitched momentarily, obliging the team to reboot the system.

Ralf resisted the temptation to do unto his brother what was done to him a week earlier and charged into the lead. But Schumacher senior and David Coulthard ran him close enough in the early laps to suggest this would be no walkover for the Williams driver.

For 24 laps it was Ralf's race to lose, and when he made his first refuelling stop that's just what he did. The right rear wheel was troublesome and a 10.3secs stop was not what he needed. Michael pitted a lap later, and was turned round in 7.7secs. He dropped to third, behind David Coulthard and Juan Pablo Montoya but, crucially, ahead of Ralf. Coulthard stopped on lap 26, Montoya on 30. The Colombian rejoined in fifth, separated from Michael, Ralf and Coulthard by Rubens Barrichello, who started on a light fuel load and had stopped on lap 21. It was looking good for Ferrari.

McLaren wasn't really a threat, even before Coulthard got a stop-and-go penalty for speeding during his pitstop; he served it on lap 32 and out of the window went his chance of a podium place.

The rest of the race was classic Michael. Hammer down hard, he upset all the predictions of a Michelin grand slam and hardly broke sweat heading for his half-century of Formula One victories. Behind him, Ralf was beaten and Coulthard failed to do anything about Barrichello, who had driven a strong race after a poor qualifying performance. Montoya didn't make the finish, retiring with an electronic problem three laps after his stop. Trulli drove well for fifth, with the Saubers sixth and seventh, Nick Heidfeld ahead.

It wasn't a great race after Ralf's problem. But great race, dull race, it was all the same to his brother as he did his victory leap on the podium and later squirmed as Ralf poured a magnum of Mumm's finest down his neck. Doubtless Rolf and Elisabeth Schumacher were relieved to see that their boys were mates again – at least until the next time their wheels nearly interlock going into the first corner.

**461**

# French Grand Prix Race Statistics

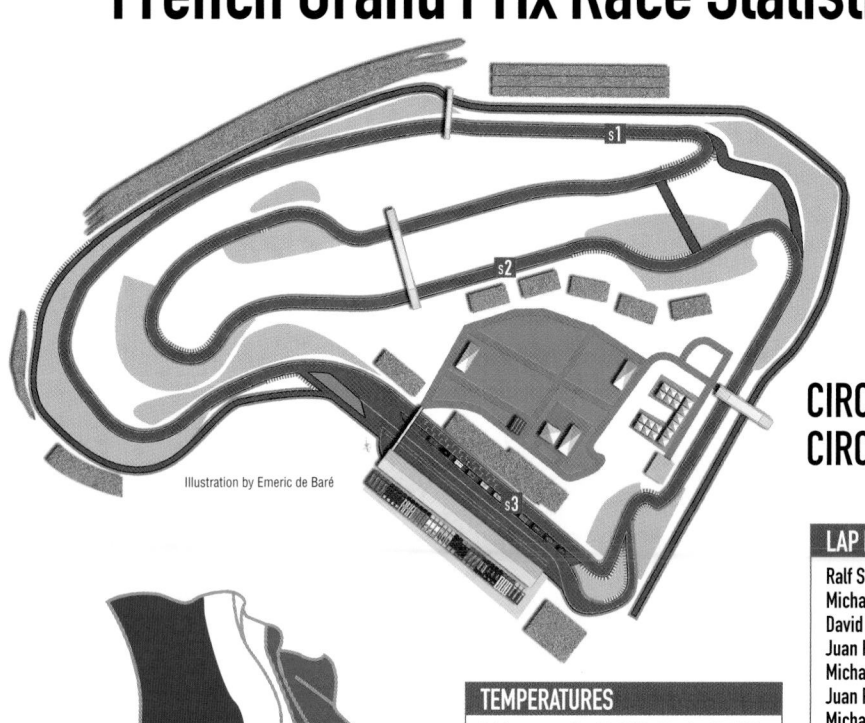

Illustration by Emeric de Baré

## CIRCUIT DE NEVERS CIRCUIT DIAGRAM

### FASTEST LAPS

| | DRIVER | TIME | LAP |
|---|---|---|---|
| 1 | Coulthard | 1m 16.088s | 53 |
| 2 | Barrichello | 1m 16.181s | 23 |
| 3 | M Schumacher | 1m 16.286s | 27 |
| 4 | Montoya | 1m 16.355s | 34 |
| 5 | R Schumacher | 1m 16.585s | 18 |
| 6 | Irvine | 1m 17.304s | 23 |
| 7 | Räikkönen | 1m 17.311s | 8 |
| 8 | Trulli | 1m 17.369s | 29 |
| 9 | de la Rosa | 1m 17.508s | 67 |
| 10 | Heidfeld | 1m 17.538s | 23 |
| 11 | Frentzen | 1m 17.540s | 20 |
| 12 | Fisichella | 1m 17.968s | 26 |
| 13 | Villeneuve | 1m 18.181s | 4 |
| 14 | Panis | 1m 18.250s | 68 |
| 15 | Burti | 1m 18.253s | 50 |
| 16 | Button | 1m 18.359s | 25 |
| 17 | Verstappen | 1m 18.662s | 47 |
| 18 | Alesi | 1m 18.817s | 14 |
| 19 | Bernoldi | 1m 19.181s | 13 |
| 20 | Alonso | 1m 19.199s | 62 |
| 21 | Marques | 1m 19.608s | 54 |
| | Häkkinen | DNS | |

### LAP LEADERS

| | |
|---|---|
| Ralf Schumacher | 1–23 |
| Michael Schumacher | 24–25 |
| David Coulthard | 26 |
| Juan Pablo Montoya | 27–30 |
| Michael Schumacher | 31–45 |
| Juan Pablo Montoya | 46–50 |
| Michael Schumacher | 51–72 |

Total laps led: M Schumacher 39;
R Schumacher 23; Montoya 9; Coulthard 1

### TEMPERATURES

| | | |
|---|---|---|
| Friday: | Air: 24–27°C | Track: 40–46°C |
| Saturday: | Air: 23–25°C | Track: 43–45°C |
| Sunday: | Air: 26°C | Track: 43°C |

### RACE SPEED TRAP TIMES

| | | |
|---|---|---|
| 1 | de la Rosa | 84.32mph |
| 2 | Burti | 84.13mph |
| 3 | Button | 83.82mph |
| 4 | Irvine | 83.57mph |
| 5 | Barrichello | 83.08mph |
| 6 | Montoya | 82.27mph |
| 7 | Fisichella | 82.27mph |
| 8 | Coulthard | 82.02mph |
| 9 | Panis | 81.83mph |
| 10 | Heidfeld | 81.83mph |
| 11 | R Schumacher | 81.65mph |
| 12 | M Schumacher | 81.59mph |
| 13 | Verstappen | 81.59mph |
| 14 | Bernoldi | 80.28mph |
| 15 | Räikkönen | 80.16mph |
| 16 | Alesi | 80.16mph |
| 17 | Trulli | 79.54mph |
| 18 | Villeneuve | 78.73mph |
| 19 | Alonso | 78.73mph |
| 20 | Frentzen | 78.67mph |
| 21 | Marques | 78.23mph |
| | Häkkinen | DNS |

### DRIVER POINTS

| | | |
|---|---|---|
| 1 | Michael Schumacher | 78 |
| 2 | David Coulthard | 47 |
| 3 | Ralf Schumacher | 31 |
| 4 | Rubens Barrichello | 30 |
| 5 | Juan Pablo Montoya | 12 |
| 6 | Nick Heidfeld | 9 |
| 7 | Mika Häkkinen | 9 |
| 8 | Jarno Trulli | 9 |
| 9 | Jacques Villeneuve | 7 |
| 10 | Kimi Räikkönen | 7 |
| 11 | Heinz-Harald Frentzen | 6 |
| 12 | Olivier Panis | 5 |
| 13 | Eddie Irvine | 4 |
| 14 | Jean Alesi | 3 |
| 15 | Jos Verstappen | 1 |
| 16 | Pedro de la Rosa | 1 |
| 17 | Giancarlo Fisichella | 1 |
| 18 | Jenson Button | 0 |
| 19 | Ricardo Zonta | 0 |
| 20 | Luciano Burti | 0 |
| 21 | Tarso Marques | 0 |
| 22 | Enrique Bernoldi | 0 |
| 23 | Fernando Alonso | 0 |
| 24 | Gaston Mazzacane | 0 |

### RACE: SUNDAY 1ST JULY 2001, 2PM

| | DRIVER | CAR | TIME/RETIREMENT | LAPS | PITSTOP LAPS |
|---|---|---|---|---|---|
| 1 | Michael Schumacher | Ferrari | 1h 33m 35.636s | 72 | 25 45 |
| 2 | Ralf Schumacher | BMW Williams | +10.399s | 72 | 24 44 |
| 3 | Rubens Barrichello | Ferrari | +16.381s | 72 | 21 36 54 |
| 4 | David Coulthard | McLaren Mercedes | +17.106s | 72 | 26 32 51 |
| 5 | Jarno Trulli | Jordan Honda | +1m 08.285s | 72 | 25 47 |
| 6 | Nick Heidfeld | Sauber Petronas | +1 lap | 71 | 21 42 |
| 7 | Kimi Räikkönen | Sauber Petronas | +1 lap | 71 | 15 40 |
| 8 | Heinz-Harald Frentzen | Jordan Honda | +1 lap | 71 | 24 46 |
| 9 | Olivier Panis | BAR Honda | +1 lap | 71 | 23 45 |
| 10 | Luciano Burti | Prost Acer | +1 lap | 71 | 25 48 |
| 11 | Giancarlo Fisichella | Benetton Renault | +1 lap | 71 | 20 44 |
| 12 | Jean Alesi | Prost Acer | +2 laps | 70 | 22 47 |
| 13 | Jos Verstappen | Arrows Asiatech | +2 laps | 70 | 25 45 |
| 14 | Pedro de la Rosa | Jaguar Racing | +2 laps | 70 | 28 43 |
| 15 | Tarso Marques | European Minardi | +3 laps | 69 | 26 50 |
| 16 | Jenson Button | Benetton Renault | Fuel pressure | 68 | 19 44 |
| 17 | Fernando Alonso | European Minardi | Engine | 65 | 36 |
| Ret | Eddie Irvine | Jaguar Racing | Engine | 54 | 27 48 |
| Ret | Juan Pablo Montoya | BMW Williams | Engine | 52 | 30 50 |
| Ret | Enrique Bernoldi | Arrows Asiatech | Engine | 17 | |
| Ret | Jacques Villeneuve | BAR Honda | Engine | 5 | |
| DNS | Mika Häkkinen | McLaren Mercedes | Gearbox | 0 | |

*Conditions: hot and sunny.*

### CONSTRUCTOR POINTS

| | | |
|---|---|---|
| 1 | Scuderia Ferrari-Marlboro | 108 |
| 2 | West McLaren Mercedes | 56 |
| 3 | BMW Williams F1 | 43 |
| 4 | Red Bull Sauber Petronas | 16 |
| 5 | Benson & Hedges Jordan Honda | 15 |
| 6 | Lucky Strike Reynard BAR Honda | 12 |
| 7 | Jaguar Racing | 5 |
| 8 | Prost Acer | 3 |
| 9 | Orange Arrows Asiatech | 1 |
| 10 | Mild Seven Benetton Renault | 1 |
| 11 | European Minardi F1 | 0 |

### PITSTOP TIMES (from pitlane entrance to exit)

| | | | | |
|---|---|---|---|---|
| Fastest pitstop: | Barrichello | Ferrari | 23.585s | Lap 21 |
| Slowest pitstop: | Verstappen | Arrows Asiatech | 47.249s | Lap 25 |
| Most pitstops: | Coulthard, Barrichello | Three stops | | |

### PENALTIES AND FINES

| DRIVER/TEAM | WHEN | PENALTY | REASON |
|---|---|---|---|
| David Coulthard | Friday practice | $1,750 | Speeding in the pitlane |
| Nick Heidfeld | Saturday practice | $1,250 | Speeding in the pitlane |
| David Coulthard | Race | 10 seconds | Speeding in the pitlane |

### WARM-UP

SUNDAY 1ST JULY 2001, 9.30AM–10AM

| | | |
|---|---|---|
| 1 | Häkkinen | 1m 15.428s |
| 2 | M Schumacher | 1m 15.429s |
| 3 | Barrichello | 1m 15.676s |
| 4 | Coulthard | 1m 15.780s |
| 5 | Trulli | 1m 15.980s |
| 6 | Räikkönen | 1m 16.136s |
| 7 | Panis | 1m 16.184s |
| 8 | de la Rosa | 1m 16.426s |
| 9 | Heidfeld | 1m 16.559s |
| 10 | Irvine | 1m 16.567s |
| 11 | Montoya | 1m 16.735s |
| 12 | Bernoldi | 1m 16.777s |
| 13 | Frentzen | 1m 16.952s |
| 14 | Villeneuve | 1m 17.073s |
| 15 | Verstappen | 1m 17.120s |
| 16 | Burti | 1m 17.443s |
| 17 | R Schumacher | 1m 17.605s |
| 18 | Alesi | 1m 17.945s |
| 19 | Fisichella | 1m 18.084s |
| 20 | Button | 1m 18.431s |
| 21 | Alonso | 1m 19.986s |
| 22 | Marques | 1m 21.295s |

21 F Alonso

19 J Alesi

17 J Button

15 L Burti

13 K Räikkönen

22 T Marques

20 E Bernoldi

18 J Verstappen

16 G Fisichella

14 P de la Rosa

12 E Irvine

## FRENCH GRAND PRIX RACE ENTRY

| | DRIVER | TEAM | CHASSIS/ENGINE |
|---|---|---|---|
| 1 | Michael Schumacher | Scuderia Ferrari Marlboro | Ferrari F2001 |
| 2 | Rubens Barrichello | Scuderia Ferrari Marlboro | Ferrari F2001 |
| 3 | Mika Häkkinen | West McLaren Mercedes | McLaren Mercedes MP4-16 |
| 4 | David Coulthard | West McLaren Mercedes | McLaren Mercedes MP4-16 |
| 5 | Ralf Schumacher | BMW Williams F1 Team | BMW Williams FW23 |
| 6 | Juan Pablo Montoya | BMW Williams F1 Team | BMW Williams FW23 |
| 7 | Giancarlo Fisichella | Mild Seven Benetton Renault | Benetton Renault B201 |
| 8 | Jenson Button | Mild Seven Benetton Renault | Benetton Renault B201 |
| 9 | Olivier Panis | Lucky Strike BAR Honda | BAR Honda B003 |
| 10 | Jacques Villeneuve | Lucky Strike BAR Honda | BAR Honda B003 |
| 11 | Heinz-Harald Frentzen | Benson & Hedges Jordan Honda | Jordan Honda EJ11 |
| 12 | Jarno Trulli | Benson & Hedges Jordan Honda | Jordan Honda EJ11 |
| 14 | Jos Verstappen | Orange Arrows Asiatech | Arrows Asiatech A22 |
| 15 | Enrique Bernoldi | Orange Arrows Asiatech | Arrows Asiatech A22 |
| 16 | Nick Heidfeld | Red Bull Sauber Petronas | Sauber Petronas C20 |
| 17 | Kimi Räikkönen | Red Bull Sauber Petronas | Sauber Petronas C20 |
| 18 | Eddie Irvine | Jaguar Racing | Jaguar Cosworth R2 |
| 19 | Pedro de la Rosa | Jaguar Racing | Jaguar Cosworth R2 |
| 20 | Tarso Marques | European Minardi | Minardi European PS01 |
| 21 | Fernando Alonso | European Minardi | Minardi European PS01 |
| 22 | Jean Alesi | Prost Grand Prix | Prost ACER AP04 |
| 23 | Luciano Burti | Prost Grand Prix | Prost ACER AP04 |

Michael Schumacher again takes the top spot on the podium.

## QUALIFYING: SATURDAY 30TH JUNE 2001, 1PM–2PM *107 per cent time: 1m 18.098s*

| | DRIVER | TEAM | TIME | GAP | LAPS |
|---|---|---|---|---|---|
| 1 | Ralf Schumacher | BMW Williams | 1m 12.989s | +0.000s | 10 |
| 2 | Michael Schumacher | Ferrari | 1m 12.999s | +0.010s | 12 |
| 3 | David Coulthard | McLaren Mercedes | 1m 13.186s | +0.197s | 12 |
| 4 | Mika Häkkinen | McLaren Mercedes | 1m 13.268s | +0.279s | 12 |
| 5 | Jarno Trulli | Jordan Honda | 1m 13.310s | +0.321s | 12 |
| 6 | Juan Pablo Montoya | BMW Williams | 1m 13.625s | +0.636s | 12 |
| 7 | Heinz-Harald Frentzen | Jordan Honda | 1m 13.815s | +0.826s | 11 |
| 8 | Rubens Barrichello | Ferrari | 1m 13.867s | +0.878s | 11 |
| 9 | Nick Heidfeld | Sauber Petronas | 1m 14.095s | +1.106s | 12 |
| 10 | Jacques Villeneuve | BAR Honda | 1m 14.096s | +1.107s | 12 |
| 11 | Olivier Panis | BAR Honda | 1m 14.181s | +1.192s | 12 |
| 12 | Eddie Irvine | Jaguar Racing | 1m 14.441s | +1.452s | 10 |
| 13 | Kimi Räikkönen | Sauber Petronas | 1m 14.536s | +1.547s | 12 |
| 14 | Pedro de la Rosa | Jaguar Racing | 1m 15.020s | +2.031s | 11 |
| 15 | Luciano Burti | Prost Acer | 1m 15.072s | +2.083s | 11 |
| 16 | Giancarlo Fisichella | Benetton Renault | 1m 15.220s | +2.231s | 11 |
| 17 | Jenson Button | Benetton Renault | 1m 15.420s | +2.431s | 12 |
| 18 | Jos Verstappen | Arrows Asiatech | 1m 15.707s | +2.718s | 12 |
| 19 | Jean Alesi | Prost Acer | 1m 15.774s | +2.785s | 11 |
| 20 | Enrique Bernoldi | Arrows Asiatech | 1m 15.828s | +2.839s | 12 |
| 21 | Fernando Alonso | European Minardi | 1m 16.039s | +3.050s | 12 |
| 22 | Tarso Marques | European Minardi | 1m 16.500s | +3.511s | 11 |

## FASTEST SECTOR TIMES IN QUALIFYING *Ideal lap time: 1m 12.696s (diff. from pole: 0.293s)*

| | SECTOR 1 | SECS | | SECTOR 2 | SECS | | SECTOR 3 | SECS |
|---|---|---|---|---|---|---|---|---|
| 1 | M Schumacher | 22.368s | 1 | R Schumacher | 29.281s | 1 | Häkkinen | 21.047s |
| 2 | R Schumacher | 22.555s | 2 | M Schumacher | 29.312s | 2 | Coulthard | 21.077s |
| 3 | Häkkinen | 22.578s | 3 | Coulthard | 29.435s | 3 | M Schumacher | 21.078s |
| 4 | Coulthard | 22.607s | 4 | Häkkinen | 29.449s | 4 | R Schumacher | 21.153s |
| 5 | Montoya | 22.618s | 5 | Trulli | 29.449s | 5 | Trulli | 21.163s |
| 6 | Trulli | 22.668s | 6 | Montoya | 29.460s | 6 | Frentzen | 21.303s |
| 7 | Heidfeld | 22.766s | 7 | Frentzen | 29.560s | 7 | Montoya | 21.375s |
| 8 | Barrichello | 22.767s | 8 | Barrichello | 29.572s | 8 | Heidfeld | 21.478s |
| 9 | Panis | 22.789s | 9 | Villeneuve | 29.641s | 9 | Barrichello | 21.480s |
| 10 | Villeneuve | 22.886s | 10 | Panis | 29.768s | 10 | Villeneuve | 21.498s |
| 11 | Frentzen | 22.892s | 11 | Irvine | 29.780s | 11 | Irvine | 21.555s |
| 12 | Räikkönen | 22.947s | 12 | Heidfeld | 29.830s | 12 | Panis | 21.567s |
| 13 | Burti | 23.056s | 13 | de la Rosa | 29.865s | 13 | Räikkönen | 21.579s |
| 14 | Irvine | 23.081s | 14 | Burti | 29.946s | 14 | Fisichella | 21.692s |
| 15 | Bernoldi | 23.219s | 15 | Fisichella | 29.992s | 15 | de la Rosa | 21.722s |
| 16 | de la Rosa | 23.238s | 16 | Räikkönen | 29.999s | 16 | Button | 21.844s |
| 17 | Verstappen | 23.317s | 17 | Alesi | 30.072s | 17 | Burti | 21.916s |
| 18 | Alesi | 23.362s | 18 | Button | 30.141s | 18 | Alonso | 21.916s |
| 19 | Button | 23.435s | 19 | Verstappen | 30.161s | 19 | Alesi | 22.069s |
| 20 | Fisichella | 23.487s | 20 | Bernoldi | 30.423s | 20 | Bernoldi | 22.071s |
| 21 | Alonso | 23.516s | 21 | Alonso | 30.467s | 21 | Verstappen | 22.119s |
| 22 | Marques | 23.578s | 22 | Marques | 30.640s | 22 | Marques | 22.282s |

## PRACTICE SESSION ONE
### FRIDAY 29TH JUNE 2001, 11AM–12PM

| | | |
|---|---|---|
| 1 | Häkkinen | 1m 15.889s |
| 2 | M Schumacher | 1m 16.044s |
| 3 | Coulthard | 1m 16.364s |
| 4 | Barrichello | 1m 16.398s |
| 5 | R Schumacher | 1m 16.438s |
| 6 | Montoya | 1m 16.553s |
| 7 | Trulli | 1m 16.570s |
| 8 | Panis | 1m 16.842s |
| 9 | Frentzen | 1m 16.868s |
| 10 | Villeneuve | 1m 16.973s |
| 11 | Räikkönen | 1m 17.180s |
| 12 | Heidfeld | 1m 17.365s |
| 13 | Verstappen | 1m 17.495s |
| 14 | Bernoldi | 1m 17.527s |
| 15 | Alonso | 1m 18.036s |
| 16 | de la Rosa | 1m 18.059s |
| 17 | Button | 1m 18.443s |
| 18 | Burti | 1m 18.599s |
| 19 | Fisichella | 1m 18.736s |
| 20 | Alesi | 1m 19.132s |
| 21 | Marques | 1m 19.984s |
| 22 | Irvine | 7m 15.769s |

## PRACTICE SESSION TWO
### FRIDAY 29TH JUNE 2001, 1PM–2PM

| | | |
|---|---|---|
| 1 | Coulthard | 1m 14.935s |
| 2 | Irvine | 1m 15.133s |
| 3 | Villeneuve | 1m 15.224s |
| 4 | Häkkinen | 1m 15.372s |
| 5 | R Schumacher | 1m 15.537s |
| 6 | Montoya | 1m 15.582s |
| 7 | M Schumacher | 1m 15.810s |
| 8 | de la Rosa | 1m 16.140s |
| 9 | Trulli | 1m 16.187s |
| 10 | Barrichello | 1m 16.325s |
| 11 | Panis | 1m 16.364s |
| 12 | Burti | 1m 16.455s |
| 13 | Frentzen | 1m 16.868s |
| 14 | Räikkönen | 1m 16.906s |
| 15 | Heidfeld | 1m 17.011s |
| 16 | Alesi | 1m 17.088s |
| 17 | Button | 1m 17.172s |
| 18 | Verstappen | 1m 17.285s |
| 19 | Bernoldi | 1m 17.527s |
| 20 | Fisichella | 1m 17.566s |
| 21 | Alonso | 1m 17.866s |
| 22 | Marques | 1m 18.372s |

## PRACTICE SESSION THREE
### SATURDAY 30TH JUNE 2001, 9.AM–9.45AM

| | | |
|---|---|---|
| 1 | M Schumacher | 1m 13.729s |
| 2 | Coulthard | 1m 14.135s |
| 3 | R Schumacher | 1m 14.932s |
| 4 | Barrichello | 1m 15.044s |
| 5 | Montoya | 1m 15.712s |
| 6 | Trulli | 1m 15.787s |
| 7 | Frentzen | 1m 15.866s |
| 8 | Panis | 1m 15.868s |
| 9 | Villeneuve | 1m 15.931s |
| 10 | Räikkönen | 1m 16.053s |
| 11 | Heidfeld | 1m 16.195s |
| 12 | Verstappen | 1m 16.463s |
| 13 | Bernoldi | 1m 16.897s |
| 14 | de la Rosa | 1m 16.949s |
| 15 | Alesi | 1m 16.958s |
| 16 | Irvine | 1m 17.140s |
| 17 | Fisichella | 1m 17.313s |
| 18 | Burti | 1m 17.341s |
| 19 | Button | 1m 17.445s |
| 20 | Alonso | 1m 17.940s |
| 21 | Marques | 1m 18.107s |
| | Häkkinen | No lap recorded |

## PRACTICE SESSION FOUR
### SATURDAY 30TH JUNE 2001, 10.15AM–11AM

| | | |
|---|---|---|
| 1 | M Schumacher | 1m 13.729s |
| 2 | R Schumacher | 1m 13.953s |
| 3 | Coulthard | 1m 13.972s |
| 4 | Häkkinen | 1m 14.295s |
| 5 | Trulli | 1m 14.482s |
| 6 | Barrichello | 1m 14.515s |
| 7 | Montoya | 1m 14.652s |
| 8 | Heidfeld | 1m 14.652s |
| 9 | Irvine | 1m 14.824s |
| 10 | Räikkönen | 1m 14.872s |
| 11 | Frentzen | 1m 14.992s |
| 12 | Villeneuve | 1m 15.061s |
| 13 | Panis | 1m 15.122s |
| 14 | de la Rosa | 1m 15.602s |
| 15 | Alesi | 1m 15.750s |
| 16 | Verstappen | 1m 15.829s |
| 17 | Burti | 1m 15.846s |
| 18 | Fisichella | 1m 15.873s |
| 19 | Button | 1m 16.129s |
| 20 | Bernoldi | 1m 16.177s |
| 21 | Alonso | 1m 17.135s |
| 22 | Marques | 1m 17.156s |

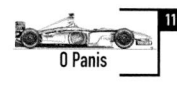 O Panis — 11
 N Heidfeld — 9
 HH Frentzen — 7
 J Trulli — 5
 D Coulthard — 3
 R Schumacher — 1
 J Villeneuve — 10
 R Barrichello — 8
 JP Montoya — 6
 M Häkkinen — 4
M Schumacher — 2

## MAGNY-COURS LAP-BY-LAP REPORT

**PRE-START** Disaster struck Mika Häkkinen as the field set off on the final parade lap before the start of the French Grand Prix. The Finn's McLaren refused to budge because of what the team called 'an incorrectly assembled component in the gearbox'. Häkkinen was pushed into the pitlane but the car could not be fixed and he was out of the race. At the end of the parade lap disaster also struck Pedro de la Rosa when the throttle on his Jaguar failed and he was forced to drive into the pits.

**LAP 1** The start of the race saw the two Schumacher brothers head-to-head again, but this time it was Ralf who emerged in front after the Adelaide hairpin. Coulthard was third while Montoya jumped up from sixth, taking advantage of the disappearance of Häkkinen to overtake Trulli. Also making a great start was Barrichello, who jumped from eighth to fifth. Drivers running with light fuel loads also made progress: Räikkönen leapt up from 13th to ninth and Verstappen rose from 18th to 14th, despite a brush with Fisichella's Benetton. Pedro de la Rosa's Jaguar had its electronics reset and the Spaniard started the race almost a lap down. At the end of the lap Ralf Schumacher led brother Michael by 3/10ths of a second.

**LAP 2** Ralf Schumacher tried to pull away. Olivier Panis grabbed 11th position from Eddie Irvine, who was running with a heavy fuel load. Button also made an impression by getting ahead of Fisichella to claim 16th place.

**LAP 6** Ralf was still trying to build his lead but Michael stayed less than a second behind him. BAR's day took a turn for the worse when Villeneuve's engine stopped and he pulled off, allowing Räikkönen to take eighth place.

**LAP 15** After the early action the race calmed down and nothing much happened until Räikkönen went into the pits and dropped back to 16th position. The Finn had been stuck behind Heinz-Harald Frentzen's Jordan Honda and Räikkönen was hoping to get ahead with an early pitstop.

**LAP 18** Bernoldi's Arrows was running in 14th when it ground to a halt with the same engine problem that had ended Verstappen's European Grand Prix.

**LAP 19** Button was running 13th but was stuck behind Verstappen, so Benetton opted to pull him in early. He dropped behind Fisichella, Räikkönen and Alesi.

**LAP 20** Benetton decided to do the same with Fisichella and he then fell behind Räikkönen and Alesi but was ahead of Button thanks to a quicker stop.

**LAP 21** Barrichello was the first of the top six to pit, having decided to go for a three-stop strategy. He lost fifth place to Trulli, while Frentzen took sixth and Barrichello rejoined in seventh. Behind this Nick Heidfeld also pitted. He was overtaken by Irvine, Panis and Burti.

**LAP 22** The switcharound in the midfield continued as Alesi stopped and Fisichella moved into 14th, with Button 15th then Alesi rejoining behind them.

**LAP 23** Having lost out to Irvine for eighth, Panis decided to pit. He rejoined in 13th behind Ricardo Zonta, Heidfeld, Verstappen and Räikkönen.

**LAP 24** Michael Schumacher took the lead as Ralf pitted. The Williams pitstop went slightly wrong, the right rear wheel change taking a couple of seconds longer than normal. Ralf rejoined in fourth place. Frentzen also stopped and dropped from sixth to ninth, having been overtaken by Barrichello, Irvine and Heidfeld.

**LAP 25** Coulthard went into the lead as Michael Schumacher pitted. He emerged ahead of his brother, who had driven a rather slow out-lap. Trulli also stopped and fell from fifth to seventh, rejoining behind Barrichello and Irvine. Burti and Verstappen both pitted. The Arrows pitstop went wrong and Verstappen lost 20 seconds as the team fiddled with the refuelling machine. This meant he tumbled down the order to 17th position. The Prost crew was rather more effective and Burti rejoined in 12th behind Heidfeld, Frentzen, Räikkönen and Panis.

**LAP 26** Montoya took the lead as Coulthard pitted and rejoined in fourth behind the two Schumachers. However, in his haste to get back into action he was clocked speeding in the pitlane. At the back of the field 18th-placed Tarso Marques pitted and was overtaken by his team-mate, Fernando Alonso.

**LAP 27** Irvine went into the pits and fell behind Trulli, Heidfeld and Frentzen.

**LAP 28** Pedro de la Rosa completed his first pitstop.

**LAP 30** Michael Schumacher went into the lead as Montoya came into the pits. This put Ralf up to second with Coulthard third and Barrichello fourth. McLaren was notified that Coulthard had been given a 10-second speeding penalty.

**LAP 32** Coulthard paid his penalty and in doing so lost any chance of challenging for a podium finish. He rejoined behind Barrichello and Montoya.

**LAP 33** A frustrated Verstappen overtook Alonso to move up to 16th place.

**LAP 36** As Michael Schumacher pulled away from Ralf, who was struggling with tyres, Montoya closed fast on Barrichello. The Brazilian came into the pits for the second of his three planned stops, dropping behind Montoya but staying ahead of Trulli. Alonso, the only man on a one-stop strategy, pitted and held on to his 17th position.

**LAP 40** Räikkönen began the second round of stops for those on a two-stop strategy. He lost only one place to Panis to rejoin in 11th position.

**LAP 41** Montoya's burst of speed had taken him on to Ralf Schumacher's tail. The Williams team tried to get Ralf to move over but he did not hear the radio calls and in the course of the next six laps Montoya lost around 12 seconds.

**LAP 42** Heidfeld had his second pitstop and was passed by the battling duo of Frentzen and Irvine.

**LAP 43** Irvine overtook Frentzen to move to seventh. Jaguar called in de la Rosa after a short middle stint and he rejoined still in pursuit of Alonso.

**LAP 44** The Williams team called Ralf Schumacher into the pits early, to clear the way for Montoya. Once out of traffic, Montoya's lap times dropped dramatically but by then Michael Schumacher was 20 seconds ahead, so Montoya's hopes of catching him were reduced. There was a disaster in the Benetton pit when Fisichella and Button arrived at the same moment because of a fuel-feed problem. Jenson was the one to lose time behind his team-mate and he rejoined in 15th.

**LAP 45** Montoya went back into the lead when Michael Schumacher pitted but the Ferrari rejoined only 3.6secs behind the Williams. Although Montoya was faster, he was not able to build a big enough gap before his second pitstop. The midfield stops continued with Panis dropping behind Räikkönen and Burti. Verstappen also stopped again.

**LAP 46** Frentzen pitted, dropping from eighth to 10th behind Heidfeld and Räikkönen.

**LAP 47** Next to stop was Trulli, who lost sixth place to Irvine as a result. Frentzen had a spin but did not lose a place while, behind him, Panis overtook Burti for 11th. Alesi also pitted and dropped behind Button.

**LAP 48** Trulli climbed back to sixth when Irvine pitted. The Irishman rejoined just behind seventh-placed Heidfeld.

**LAP 50** Michael Schumacher went back into the lead when Montoya stopped. The Colombian rejoined behind Barrichello and Coulthard but ahead of Ralf Schumacher. Ferrari was running one-two.

**LAP 51** Montoya's BMW Williams began to suffer with an engine problem and the Colombian was overtaken by Ralf Schumacher.

**LAP 52** Montoya nursed his car around but retired just after crossing the line to commence his 53rd lap. This promoted Coulthard to fourth place, Trulli to fifth and put Heidfeld into the points in sixth.

**LAP 54** Barrichello went in for his third stop. He dropped behind Ralf Schumacher and found himself under pressure from Coulthard.

**LAP 55** Seventh-placed Irvine pulled off with a pneumatic problem on his Cosworth engine. Räikkönen moved up to seventh place.

**LAP 60** Burti overtook a fading Fisichella to snatch 10th place.

**LAP 61** Button spun but rejoined without losing his 12th position.

**LAP 64** After a 10-lap battle, de la Rosa finally overtook Alonso to claim 15th place.

**LAP 65** Alonso pitted and retired with an engine problem.

**LAP 69** Button's race came to an end with engine failure.

**LAP 72** Michael Schumacher completed his 50th Grand Prix victory with brother Ralf in second and Ferrari team-mate Rubens Barrichello third. His title rival Coulthard was fourth and at this point trailed Michael in the world championship by 31 points with seven races to go. Michael's title victory was all but assured.

# British Grand Prix

**13th–15th July 2001**   LAPS: 60  LENGTH OF LAP: 3.194 miles

**HÄKK IS BACK** McLaren Mercedes' Flying Finn Mika Häkkinen ended his drought with a seemingly effortless, commanding victory at Silverstone. PHOTOGRAPH BY BORIS SCHLEGELMILCH

## Faultless Finnish

Mika Häkkinen returned to the podium in style while David Coulthard saw chances of a third successive British Grand Prix win disappear thanks to a first-corner crash with Jarno Trulli's Jordan. But fate had seemed to be on Coulthard's side all weekend, as thousands of fellow Scots descended on the circuit. They came in droves, wearing kilts, singing songs and downing pints of lager. By Friday night, with qualifying still to come, any visitor would have thought Coulthard had already won the race.

Like his thousands of fans, the McLaren Mercedes ace looked confident, focusing on the job at hand. While Jacques Villeneuve entertained Kylie Minogue and Eddie Irvine rubbed shoulders with Sir Jackie Stewart (who no longer appears attached to Jaguar and acts as a celebrity himself in the paddock following his knighthood), Coulthard played with his own mind. And as race time approached, Schumacher – a motor home away and two places on the grid ahead in pole – played his own Ferrari mind games. Let the battle commence. Or so it looked.

Everyone had forgotten about Mika Häkkinen. This was after all the same Finn who had won two of the last three drivers' world titles, and but for some incredibly bad luck would probably have been ahead of Coulthard in this year's championship. By lap four, everyone at Silverstone got a sharp reminder that on his day, Häkkinen is the closest thing to Michael Schumacher in Formula One – certainly closer than Coulthard. With his team-mate taking an early bath, the Finn did a Schuey on the man himself to take the lead. A lighter fuel load probably helped, but an 18.7-second lead after just 14 laps wasn't all down to strategy.

Jarno Trulli qualified brilliantly, then crashed with David Coulthard at the first corner.

As the field streams through Copse on the first lap, team-mates Panis and Villeneuve get too close for comfort and the Frenchman ends his race in the gravel trap.

Juan Pablo Montoya squeezes past Michael Schumacher into Copse. Montoya could have been on the podium with a little help from team-mate Ralf.

Two laps later Schumacher's weekend got even worse as Montoya outraced him into second. The Colombian, starting from eighth on the grid, was proving to be one of the fastest starters in the business.

Sadly for Silverstone's 120,000 fans, that was about as much of a race as they got. Schumacher's strange one-stop strategy (strange when it fails, brilliant when it works) effectively put him out of contention. Montoya could have hung on for a podium had he not been held up by team-mate Ralf Schumacher (who wouldn't let Montoya pass despite being a pitstop behind him in the race).

Ralf had been running well until a technical problem forced him to retire with just 23 laps to go. He showed his disappointment by nearly punching a cameraman in the paddock. The BMW Williams simply did not go well in cold conditions. Luckily all the upcoming races, bar Indianapolis, were forecast to be scorchers.

Sauber continued to demonstrate renewed competitiveness at Silverstone, and Räikkönen and Heidfeld crossed the line in fifth and sixth respectively.

Despite a strong qualifying performance, it was a disappointing day for Jordan Honda. Jarno Trulli's race was over before it really began, after an incident with Coulthard at the start, while Heinz-Harald Frentzen just missed out on points, crossing the line in seventh in what turned out to be his last race for Jordan.

BAR Honda was another team experiencing mixed fortunes. Olivier Panis appeared to clip the side of team-mate Villeneuve's car at the start, and spun out into the gravel. Jacques continued, and managed to keep Eddie Irvine behind despite a strong charge from

the Ulsterman, finally finishing in eighth. Jenson Button was disappointed to finish 15th in front of his home fans, while Benetton team-mate Fisichella crossed the line in 13th. Button summed his day up perfectly, telling journalists: "I was crap." That was of course code for something else. There was some drama further down the grid. Fernando Alonso's Minardi suddenly found itself with just three wheels. The Spaniard managed to get the car back to the pits and continued in the race, but was last of the 16 cars to make it home.

This was Mika Häkkinen's day. As speculation over his possible retirement continued, he demonstrated that he had lost none of his desire to win, and the Finn was clearly delighted as he stepped out of the car. "It feels really good," he said. "Obviously after all the trouble that's been going on this year it was good to win, particularly at Silverstone. We've made a great show. Hopefully there will be more before the end of the season."

Although Michael Schumacher was not his usual aggressive self, the German refuted claims that he simply let Mika Häkkinen pass him early on, and put his lack of pace down to a far from perfect car. "I parked the car and waved him by," he joked. But no one saw the funny side. Least of all him.

The end of David Coulthard's race after his first-corner clash with Trulli's Jordan.

# British Grand Prix Race Statistics

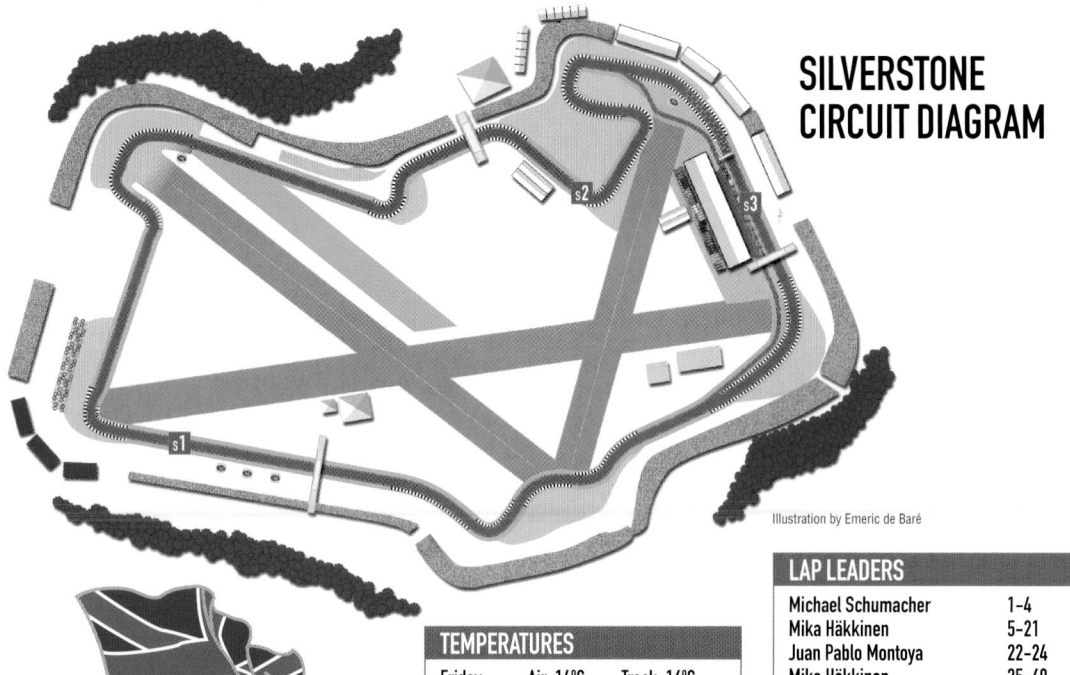

**SILVERSTONE CIRCUIT DIAGRAM**

Illustration by Emeric de Baré

## FASTEST LAPS

| | DRIVER | TIME | LAP |
|---|---|---|---|
| 1 | Häkkinen | 1m 23.405s | 34 |
| 2 | M Schumacher | 1m 23.928s | 42 |
| 3 | Montoya | 1m 24.437s | 23 |
| 4 | Barrichello | 1m 24.445s | 44 |
| 5 | Irvine | 1m 24.544s | 59 |
| 6 | Räikkönen | 1m 24.563s | 34 |
| 7 | Heidfeld | 1m 24.765s | 46 |
| 8 | Frentzen | 1m 25.029s | 23 |
| 9 | R Schumacher | 1m 25.188s | 33 |
| 10 | de la Rosa | 1m 25.739s | 33 |
| 11 | Villeneuve | 1m 25.809s | 27 |
| 12 | Verstappen | 1m 26.394s | 40 |
| 13 | Alesi | 1m 26.497s | 29 |
| 14 | Bernoldi | 1m 26.695s | 25 |
| 15 | Fisichella | 1m 26.798s | 41 |
| 16 | Button | 1m 26.963s | 24 |
| 17 | Alonso | 1m 27.091s | 30 |
| 18 | Coulthard | 1m 28.908s | 2 |
| 19 | Burti | 1m 29.252s | 4 |
| | Trulli | No lap completed | |
| | Panis | No lap completed | |

## LAP LEADERS

| | |
|---|---|
| Michael Schumacher | 1–4 |
| Mika Häkkinen | 5–21 |
| Juan Pablo Montoya | 22–24 |
| Mika Häkkinen | 25–60 |

Total laps led: Häkkinen 53;
M Schumacher 4; Montoya 3

## RACE SPEED TRAP TIMES

| | | |
|---|---|---|
| 1 | Montoya | 189.5mph |
| 2 | R Schumacher | 187.5mph |
| 3 | Räikkönen | 186.8mph |
| 4 | Irvine | 186.7mph |
| 5 | Barrichello | 186.5mph |
| 6 | Villeneuve | 186.3mph |
| 7 | M Schumacher | 186.2mph |
| 8 | Heidfeld | 186.1mph |
| 9 | Häkkinen | 186.0mph |
| 10 | Bernoldi | 185.8mph |
| 11 | Frentzen | 185.7mph |
| 12 | Alesi | 185.2mph |
| 13 | de la Rosa | 184.9mph |
| 14 | Verstappen | 183.8mph |
| 15 | Burti | 183.6mph |
| 16 | Alonso | 183.3mph |
| 17 | Button | 182.4mph |
| 18 | Coulthard | 182.2mph |
| 19 | Fisichella | 181.9mph |
| | Trulli | No speed recorded |
| | Panis | No speed recorded |

## TEMPERATURES

| | | |
|---|---|---|
| Friday: | Air: 14°C | Track: 16°C |
| Saturday: | Air: 14°C | Track: 22°C |
| Sunday: | Air: 16°C | Track: 28°C |

## RACE: SUNDAY 15TH JULY 2001, 1PM

| | DRIVER | CAR | TIME/RETIREMENT | LAPS | PITSTOP LAPS |
|---|---|---|---|---|---|
| 1 | Mika Häkkinen | McLaren Mercedes | 1h 25m 33.770s | 60 | 21 39 |
| 2 | Michael Schumacher | Ferrari | +33.646s | 60 | 39 |
| 3 | Rubens Barrichello | Ferrari | +59.281s | 60 | 42 |
| 4 | Juan Pablo Montoya | BMW Williams | +1m 08.772s | 60 | 25 41 |
| 5 | Kimi Räikkönen | Sauber Petronas | +1 lap | 59 | 20 40 |
| 6 | Nick Heidfeld | Sauber Petronas | +1 lap | 59 | 21 41 |
| 7 | Heinz-Harald Frentzen | Jordan Honda | +1 lap | 59 | 24 41 |
| 8 | Jacques Villeneuve | BAR Honda | +1 lap | 59 | 32 |
| 9 | Eddie Irvine | Jaguar Racing | +1 lap | 59 | 30 45 |
| 10 | Jos Verstappen | Arrows Asiatech | +2 laps | 58 | 22 41 |
| 11 | Jean Alesi | Prost Acer | +2 laps | 58 | 30 |
| 12 | Pedro de la Rosa | Jaguar Racing | +2 laps | 58 | 34 35 |
| 13 | Giancarlo Fisichella | Benetton Renault | +2 laps | 58 | 24 42 |
| 14 | Enrique Bernoldi | Arrows Asiatech | +2 laps | 58 | 23 42 |
| 15 | Jenson Button | Benetton Renault | +2 laps | 58 | 22 39 |
| 16 | Fernando Alonso | European Minardi | +3 laps | 57 | 23 39 |
| Ret | Ralf Schumacher | BMW Williams | Engine | 36 | 35 |
| Ret | Luciano Burti | Prost Acer | Engine | 6 | |
| Ret | David Coulthard | McLaren Mercedes | Suspension | 2 | |
| Ret | Jarno Trulli | Jordan Honda | Collision | 0 | |
| Ret | Olivier Panis | BAR Honda | Collision | 0 | |

*Conditions: bright.*

## DRIVER POINTS

| | | |
|---|---|---|
| 1 | Michael Schumacher | 84 |
| 2 | David Coulthard | 47 |
| 3 | Rubens Barrichello | 34 |
| 4 | Ralf Schumacher | 31 |
| 5 | Mika Häkkinen | 19 |
| 6 | Juan Pablo Montoya | 15 |
| 7 | Nick Heidfeld | 10 |
| 8 | Kimi Räikkönen | 9 |
| 9 | Jarno Trulli | 9 |
| 10 | Jacques Villeneuve | 7 |
| 11 | Heinz-Harald Frentzen | 6 |
| 12 | Olivier Panis | 5 |
| 13 | Eddie Irvine | 4 |
| 14 | Jean Alesi | 3 |
| 15 | Jos Verstappen | 1 |
| 16 | Pedro de la Rosa | 1 |
| 17 | Giancarlo Fisichella | 1 |
| 18 | Jenson Button | 0 |
| 19 | Ricardo Zonta | 0 |
| 20 | Luciano Burti | 0 |
| 21 | Tarso Marques | 0 |
| 22 | Enrique Bernoldi | 0 |
| 23 | Fernando Alonso | 0 |
| 24 | Gaston Mazzacane | 0 |

## CONSTRUCTOR POINTS

| | | |
|---|---|---|
| 1 | Scuderia Ferrari-Marlboro | 118 |
| 2 | West McLaren Mercedes | 66 |
| 3 | BMW Williams F1 | 46 |
| 4 | Red Bull Sauber Petronas | 19 |
| 5 | Benson & Hedges Jordan Honda | 15 |
| 6 | Lucky Strike Reynard BAR Honda | 12 |
| 7 | Jaguar Racing | 5 |
| 8 | Prost Acer | 3 |
| 9 | Orange Arrows Asiatech | 1 |
| 10 | Mild Seven Benetton Renault | 1 |
| 11 | European Minardi F1 | 0 |

## PITSTOP TIMES (from pitlane entrance to exit)

| | | | | |
|---|---|---|---|---|
| Fastest pitstop: | Eddie Irvine | Jaguar Racing | 30.727s | Lap 30 |
| Slowest pitstop: | Fernando Alonso | European Minardi | 51.879s | Lap 39 |
| Most pitstops: | 12 cars | | 2 stops | |

## PENALTIES AND FINES

| DRIVER/TEAM | WHEN | PENALTY | REASON |
|---|---|---|---|
| Michael Schumacher | Friday | $2,500 | Using wet tyres before the track was declared wet |
| Olivier Panis | Friday | $2,500 | Using wet tyres before the track was declared wet |
| Jarno Trulli | Friday | $2,500 | Using wet tyres before the track was declared wet |
| Tarso Marques | Qualifying | Exclusion | Failing to qualify within 107% of pole |

## WARM-UP

SUNDAY 15TH JULY 2001, 8.30AM-9AM

| | | |
|---|---|---|
| 1 | Coulthard | 1m 22.994s |
| 2 | Trulli | 1m 23.182s |
| 3 | Häkkinen | 1m 23.416s |
| 4 | Frentzen | 1m 24.052s |
| 5 | M Schumacher | 1m 24.407s |
| 6 | Panis | 1m 24.598s |
| 7 | Räikkönen | 1m 24.609s |
| 8 | R Schumacher | 1m 24.631s |
| 9 | Barrichello | 1m 24.657s |
| 10 | Irvine | 1m 25.147s |
| 11 | Villeneuve | 1m 25.217s |
| 12 | Montoya | 1m 25.260s |
| 13 | Verstappen | 1m 25.581s |
| 14 | Bernoldi | 1m 25.658s |
| 15 | Heidfeld | 1m 25.734s |
| 16 | de la Rosa | 1m 26.463s |
| 17 | Alonso | 1m 26.988s |
| 18 | Fisichella | 1m 27.198s |
| 19 | Button | 1m 27.987s |
| 20 | Alesi | 1m 28.060s |
| 21 | Burti | 1m 28.240s |

F Alonso 21

G Fisichella 19

J Verstappen 17

E Irvine 15

P de la Rosa 13

E Bernoldi 20

J Button 18

L Burti 16

J Alesi 14

J Villeneuve 12

## BRITISH GRAND PRIX RACE ENTRY

| | DRIVER | TEAM | CHASSIS/ENGINE |
|---|---|---|---|
| 1 | Michael Schumacher | Scuderia Ferrari Marlboro | Ferrari F2001 |
| 2 | Rubens Barrichello | Scuderia Ferrari Marlboro | Ferrari F2001 |
| 3 | Mika Häkkinen | West McLaren Mercedes | McLaren Mercedes MP4-16 |
| 4 | David Coulthard | West McLaren Mercedes | McLaren Mercedes MP4-16 |
| 5 | Ralf Schumacher | BMW Williams F1 Team | BMW Williams FW23 |
| 6 | Juan Pablo Montoya | BMW Williams F1 Team | BMW Williams FW23 |
| 7 | Giancarlo Fisichella | Mild Seven Benetton Renault | Benetton Renault B201 |
| 8 | Jenson Button | Mild Seven Benetton Renault | Benetton Renault B201 |
| 9 | Olivier Panis | Lucky Strike BAR Honda | BAR Honda B003 |
| 10 | Jacques Villeneuve | Lucky Strike BAR Honda | BAR Honda B003 |
| 11 | Heinz-Harald Frentzen | Benson & Hedges Jordan Honda | Jordan Honda EJ11 |
| 12 | Jarno Trulli | Benson & Hedges Jordan Honda | Jordan Honda EJ11 |
| 14 | Jos Verstappen | Orange Arrows Asiatech | Arrows Asiatech A22 |
| 15 | Enrique Bernoldi | Orange Arrows Asiatech | Arrows Asiatech A22 |
| 16 | Nick Heidfeld | Red Bull Sauber Petronas | Sauber Petronas C20 |
| 17 | Kimi Räikkönen | Red Bull Sauber Petronas | Sauber Petronas C20 |
| 18 | Eddie Irvine | Jaguar Racing | Jaguar Cosworth R2 |
| 19 | Pedro de la Rosa | Jaguar Racing | Jaguar Cosworth R2 |
| 20 | Tarso Marques | European Minardi | Minardi European PS01 |
| 21 | Fernando Alonso | European Minardi | Minardi European PS01 |
| 22 | Jean Alesi | Prost Grand Prix | Prost ACER AP04 |
| 23 | Luciano Burti | Prost Grand Prix | Prost ACER AP04 |

Mika Häkkinen revelled in the new construction Bridgestone, turning in a sensational performance to take a dominant first win in the British Grand Prix.

## QUALIFYING: SATURDAY 14TH JULY 2001, 1PM–2PM  *107 per cent time: 1m 26.078s*

| | DRIVER | TEAM | TIME | GAP | LAPS |
|---|---|---|---|---|---|
| 1 | Michael Schumacher | Ferrari | 1m 20.447s | 0.000 | 12 |
| 2 | Mika Häkkinen | McLaren Mercedes | 1m 20.529s | +0.082s | 12 |
| 3 | David Coulthard | McLaren Mercedes | 1m 20.927s | +0.480s | 12 |
| 4 | Jarno Trulli | Jordan Honda | 1m 20.930s | +0.483s | 10 |
| 5 | Heinz-Harald Frentzen | Jordan Honda | 1m 21.217s | +0.770s | 12 |
| 6 | Rubens Barrichello | Ferrari | 1m 21.715s | +1.268s | 12 |
| 7 | Kimi Räikkönen | Sauber Petronas | 1m 22.023s | +1.576s | 12 |
| 8 | Juan Pablo Montoya | BMW Williams | 1m 22.219s | +1.772s | 9 |
| 9 | Nick Heidfeld | Sauber Petronas | 1m 22.223s | +1.776s | 11 |
| 10 | Ralf Schumacher | BMW Williams | 1m 22.283s | +1.836s | 9 |
| 11 | Olivier Panis | BAR Honda | 1m 22.316s | +1.869s | 12 |
| 12 | Jacques Villeneuve | BAR Honda | 1m 22.916s | +2.469s | 11 |
| 13 | Pedro de la Rosa | Jaguar Racing | 1m 23.273s | +2.826s | 12 |
| 14 | Jean Alesi | Prost Acer | 1m 23.392s | +2.945s | 12 |
| 15 | Eddie Irvine | Jaguar Racing | 1m 23.439s | +2.992s | 11 |
| 16 | Luciano Burti | Prost Acer | 1m 23.735s | +3.288s | 12 |
| 17 | Jos Verstappen | Arrows Asiatech | 1m 24.067s | +3.620s | 12 |
| 18 | Jenson Button | Benetton Renault | 1m 24.123s | +3.676s | 12 |
| 19 | Giancarlo Fisichella | Benetton Renault | 1m 24.275s | +3.828s | 12 |
| 20 | Enrique Bernoldi | Arrows Asiatech | 1m 24.606s | +4.159s | 10 |
| 21 | Fernando Alonso | European Minardi | 1m 24.792s | +4.345s | 12 |
| DNQ | Tarso Marques | European Minardi | 1m 26.506s | +6.059s | 12 |

## FASTEST SECTOR TIMES IN QUALIFYING  *Ideal lap time: 1m 20.332s (diff. from pole: 0.115s)*

| | SECTOR 1 | SECS | | SECTOR 2 | SECS | | SECTOR 3 | SECS |
|---|---|---|---|---|---|---|---|---|
| 1 | M Schumacher | 26.315s | 1 | Häkkinen | 33.676s | 1 | M Schumacher | 20.341s |
| 2 | Häkkinen | 26.414s | 2 | Coulthard | 33.723s | 2 | Häkkinen | 20.390s |
| 3 | Coulthard | 26.619s | 3 | M Schumacher | 33.754s | 3 | Frentzen | 20.475s |
| 4 | Barrichello | 26.748s | 4 | Frentzen | 33.968s | 4 | Coulthard | 20.483s |
| 5 | Frentzen | 26.774s | 5 | Barrichello | 34.014s | 5 | Barrichello | 20.600s |
| 6 | Heidfeld | 26.861s | 6 | Räikkönen | 34.166s | 6 | Räikkönen | 20.641s |
| 7 | Räikkönen | 26.957s | 7 | Montoya | 34.190s | 7 | Heidfeld | 20.682s |
| 8 | R Schumacher | 27.049s | 8 | Panis | 34.255s | 8 | Panis | 20.812s |
| 9 | Montoya | 27.135s | 9 | Heidfeld | 34.297s | 9 | Montoya | 20.894s |
| 10 | Alesi | 27.152s | 10 | R Schumacher | 34.334s | 10 | R Schumacher | 20.900s |
| 11 | Panis | 27.209s | 11 | de la Rosa | 34.576s | 11 | Villeneuve | 20.926s |
| 12 | Burti | 27.244s | 12 | Villeneuve | 34.616s | 12 | de la Rosa | 21.043s |
| 13 | Villeneuve | 27.251s | 13 | Irvine | 34.812s | 13 | Irvine | 21.047s |
| 14 | de la Rosa | 27.446s | 14 | Alesi | 34.861s | 14 | Alonso | 21.160s |
| 15 | Verstappen | 27.504s | 15 | Fisichella | 34.983s | 15 | Button | 21.190s |
| 16 | Irvine | 27.527s | 16 | Burti | 35.073s | 16 | Verstappen | 21.221s |
| 17 | Fisichella | 27.632s | 17 | Button | 35.074s | 17 | Burti | 21.298s |
| 18 | Bernoldi | 27.670s | 18 | Verstappen | 35.093s | 18 | Fisichella | 21.346s |
| 19 | Button | 27.779s | 19 | Alonso | 35.455s | 19 | Alesi | 21.379s |
| 20 | Alonso | 28.112s | 20 | Bernoldi | 35.468s | 20 | Bernoldi | 21.404s |
| 21 | Marques | 28.644s | 21 | Marques | 36.065s | 21 | Marques | 21.797s |

*Sector times for Jarno Trulli were not available due to a technical fault.*

## PRACTICE SESSION ONE
FRIDAY 13TH JULY 2001, 11AM–12PM

| | | |
|---|---|---|
| 1 | M Schumacher | 1m 23.619s |
| 2 | Barrichello | 1m 24.405s |
| 3 | Häkkinen | 1m 24.413s |
| 4 | Coulthard | 1m 24.430s |
| 5 | Frentzen | 1m 25.234s |
| 6 | Irvine | 1m 25.572s |
| 7 | Panis | 1m 25.617s |
| 8 | Villeneuve | 1m 25.627s |
| 9 | Trulli | 1m 25.908s |
| 10 | Räikkönen | 1m 25.923s |
| 11 | R Schumacher | 1m 26.168s |
| 12 | Heidfeld | 1m 26.324s |
| 13 | Montoya | 1m 26.663s |
| 14 | Verstappen | 1m 26.809s |
| 15 | Alesi | 1m 26.814s |
| 16 | Bernoldi | 1m 27.212s |
| 17 | Burti | 1m 27.311s |
| 18 | Button | 1m 27.857s |
| 19 | Fisichella | 1m 28.213s |
| 20 | Alonso | 1m 28.541s |
| 21 | Marques | 1m 29.850s |
| | de la Rosa | No laps |

## PRACTICE SESSION TWO
FRIDAY 13TH JULY 2001, 1PM–2PM

| | | |
|---|---|---|
| 1 | Häkkinen | 1m 22.827s |
| 2 | Coulthard | 1m 22.894s |
| 3 | Barrichello | 1m 23.578s |
| 4 | M Schumacher | 1m 23.619s |
| 5 | Frentzen | 1m 23.877s |
| 6 | Heidfeld | 1m 24.096s |
| 7 | de la Rosa | 1m 24.116s |
| 8 | R Schumacher | 1m 24.222s |
| 9 | Trulli | 1m 24.343s |
| 10 | Räikkönen | 1m 24.387s |
| 11 | Villeneuve | 1m 24.436s |
| 12 | Panis | 1m 24.562s |
| 13 | Irvine | 1m 24.733s |
| 14 | Alesi | 1m 24.832s |
| 15 | Verstappen | 1m 25.026s |
| 16 | Bernoldi | 1m 25.209s |
| 17 | Montoya | 1m 25.267s |
| 18 | Burti | 1m 25.448s |
| 19 | Button | 1m 25.673s |
| 20 | Alonso | 1m 26.695s |
| 21 | Fisichella | 1m 26.730s |
| 22 | Marques | 1m 27.203s |

## PRACTICE SESSION THREE
SATURDAY 14TH JULY 2001, 9AM–9.45AM

| | | |
|---|---|---|
| 1 | M Schumacher | 1m 31.430s |
| 2 | Frentzen | 1m 31.803s |
| 3 | Häkkinen | 1m 31.849s |
| 4 | Coulthard | 1m 32.014s |
| 5 | Barrichello | 1m 32.128s |
| 6 | Heidfeld | 1m 33.837s |
| 7 | Trulli | 1m 33.879s |
| 8 | R Schumacher | 1m 34.248s |
| 9 | Panis | 1m 34.350s |
| 10 | Montoya | 1m 34.674s |
| 11 | de la Rosa | 1m 35.157s |
| 12 | Verstappen | 1m 35.173s |
| 13 | Bernoldi | 1m 35.402s |
| 14 | Räikkönen | 1m 35.490s |
| 15 | Fisichella | 1m 35.882s |
| 16 | Alesi | 1m 36.193s |
| 17 | Button | 1m 37.374s |
| 18 | Alonso | 1m 38.748s |
| 19 | Burti | 1m 39.935s |
| 20 | Marques | 1m 40.199s |
| 21 | Irvine | 1m 43.227s |
| | Villeneuve | No laps |

## PRACTICE SESSION FOUR
SATURDAY 14TH JULY 2001, 10.15AM–11AM

| | | |
|---|---|---|
| 1 | M Schumacher | 1m 31.430s |
| 2 | Frentzen | 1m 31.803s |
| 3 | Häkkinen | 1m 31.849s |
| 4 | Coulthard | 1m 32.014s |
| 5 | Barrichello | 1m 32.128s |
| 6 | Heidfeld | 1m 33.837s |
| 7 | Trulli | 1m 33.879s |
| 8 | Räikkönen | 1m 34.069s |
| 9 | Panis | 1m 34.097s |
| 10 | R Schumacher | 1m 34.248s |
| 11 | Montoya | 1m 34.674s |
| 12 | de la Rosa | 1m 35.157s |
| 13 | Verstappen | 1m 35.173s |
| 14 | Bernoldi | 1m 35.402s |
| 15 | Fisichella | 1m 35.624s |
| 16 | Villeneuve | 1m 35.690s |
| 17 | Button | 1m 35.974s |
| 18 | Alesi | 1m 36.193s |
| 19 | Burti | 1m 37.203s |
| 20 | Alonso | 1m 38.748s |
| 21 | Marques | 1m 40.199s |
| 22 | Irvine | 1m 43.227s |

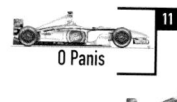
R Schumacher — 10

O Panis — 11

JP Montoya — 8

N Heidfeld — 9

R Barrichello — 6

K Räikkönen — 7

HH Frentzen — 5

J Trulli — 4

D Coulthard — 3

M Häkkinen — 2

M Schumacher — 1

## SILVERSTONE LAP-BY-LAP REPORT

**LAP 1** Michael Schumacher and Mika Häkkinen both got off the line well at Silverstone. David Coulthard and Jarno Trulli followed but behind them the two BMW Williams made their usual good starts: Juan Pablo Montoya was fifth going into the first corner from eighth on the grid while team-mate Ralf Schumacher was seventh from 11th. In the first corner Coulthard was hit from behind by Jarno Trulli and both spun: Trulli to the outside of the circuit and Coulthard towards the infield. Coulthard was able to rejoin at the back of the field but Trulli was out. At the same time, BAR Honda's Olivier Panis was forced off the road by his team-mate Jacques Villeneuve and the Frenchman ended up in the sandtrap not far from Trulli's car. So two Honda-powered cars were out at the first corner. This meant Montoya was third with Rubens Barrichello fourth, Ralf Schumacher fifth, then the two Saubers: Kimi Räikkönen leading Nick Heidfeld. The big loser was Heinz-Harald Frentzen, who dropped from fifth on the grid to eighth. At the end of the first lap Michael Schumacher was only a couple of 10ths ahead of Mika Häkkinen; Juan Pablo Montoya was already nearly two seconds behind.

**LAP 3** Mika Häkkinen closed the gap to Ferrari's Michael Schumacher to a 10th and looked threatening. The rear suspension failed on David Coulthard's McLaren Mercedes, as a result of the assault from Jarno Trulli, and he went off at Priory.

**LAP 4** Jos Verstappen's Arrows Asiatech moved up to ninth place by overtaking both BAR Honda's Jacques Villeneuve and Prost Acer's Jean Alesi on the same lap. Further back, Giancarlo Fisichella ran wide in his Benetton Renault and bounced over a sandtrap, losing a place to Fernando Alonso's Minardi.

**LAP 5** At Copse, Michael Schumacher ran wide and Mika Häkkinen was able to get alongside him and take the lead. It was an important moment as Häkkinen was running with a much lighter fuel load than his Ferrari counterpart. The Finn then quickly pulled away from Schumacher.

**LAP 6** Luciano Burti's Prost Acer was running in 16th position when he retired with engine failure.

**LAP 11** At Stowe Corner Jacques Villeneuve overtook Jean Alesi in order to claim 10th place.

**LAP 14** Michael Schumacher was clearly struggling, which enabled Mika Häkkinen to build up a lead of 20 seconds while his rival came under attack from Juan Pablo Montoya.

**LAP 18** Going into Copse, Juan Pablo Montoya was able to use the power of his BMW engine to overtake Michael Schumacher and move into second place.

**LAP 20** The first man to pit was Kimi Räikkönen. The stop was fast but the Sauber driver still dropped from sixth to 10th.

**LAP 21** Mika Häkkinen went into the pit, confirming suspicions that he was planning a two-stop strategy. He rejoined in third place, just behind Juan Pablo Montoya. Nick Heidfeld stopped as well and fell from sixth to 10th, behind Heinz-Harald Frentzen, Jos Verstappen, Jacques Villeneuve and Kimi Räikkönen.

**LAP 22** Jos Verstappen went into the pits and dropped from seventh to 13th position. Benetton Renault's Jenson Button also stopped and rejoined in 17th. At the front, Mika Häkkinen began to put pressure on new leader Juan Pablo Montoya.

**LAP 23** The two-stop pitstops continued with midfielders Enrique Bernoldi of Arrows Asiatech and Fernando Alonso of European Minardi dropping to the back of the field.

**LAP 24** Heinz-Harald Frentzen stopped and BAR Honda's Jacques Villeneuve moved into sixth ahead of the two Saubers of Kimi Räikkönen and Nick Heidfeld.

**LAP 25** Mika Häkkinen went back into the lead when Juan Pablo Montoya pitted. The Colombian rejoined in fourth behind Rubens Barrichello and Ralf Schumacher.

**LAP 27** Mika Häkkinen continued to push hard and built his lead over Ferrari's Michael Schumacher to 10 seconds. Behind them Schumacher's team-mate Rubens Barrichello and BMW Williams driver Ralf Schumacher began to hold up Juan Pablo Montoya. Ralf was asked by the Williams team to move over in order to let his team-mate past, but he replied that he felt he could overtake the Ferrari.

**LAP 30** As Juan Pablo Montoya sat behind Rubens Barrichello and Ralf Schumacher, his hopes of a podium finish in Britain were fast disappearing. In the midfield, 10th-placed Jean Alesi became the first of the one-stop runners to pit and dropped three places as a result. Jaguar's Eddie Irvine also pitted but he had a big enough gap to retain his 12th position.

**LAP 32** Jacques Villeneuve finally pitted, releasing the two Saubers driven by Kimi Räikkönen and Nick Heidfeld, which had been stuck behind him for several laps. Villeneuve's strategy meant that he dropped from sixth to 11th position.

**LAP 34** Ralf Schumacher was given the order to 'switch' by the Williams team. Further back up the field Pedro de la Rosa dropped from ninth to 12th position when he completed his stop. Unfortunately the refuelling machine failed to work properly and de la Rosa was sent out again while Jaguar team-mate Eddie Irvine's machine was made ready.

**LAP 35** An angry Ralf Schumacher pitted, allowing Juan Pablo Montoya to take up the attack on Rubens Barrichello. The Colombian's tyres were already past their best. Ralf Schumacher was slightly delayed by a rear wheel problem during his tyre change and as a result dropped back to sixth position. Jaguar's Pedro de la Rosa pitted again and ended up in 16th place.

**LAP 37** Ralf Schumacher's race ended with an engine problem on the 37th lap. His retirement promoted Nick Heidfeld's Sauber Petronas to sixth place.

**LAP 39** Race leaders Mika Häkkinen and Michael Schumacher both pitted, the McLaren driver for the second time and Michael for the first. Häkkinen remained in the lead while Schumacher's odd strategy saw him drop behind Rubens Barrichello and Juan Pablo Montoya. At the back of the field, Jenson Button and Fernando Alonso both pitted for a second time.

**LAP 40** Fifth-placed Kimi Räikkönen stopped for the second time and fell behind Nick Heidfeld and Heinz-Harald Frentzen. At the back of the field Fernando Alonso lost a wheel and had to go back to the pits with only three wheels.

**LAP 41** There was a rush of activity in the pits as Juan Pablo Montoya, Nick Heidfeld, Heinz-Harald Frentzen and Jos Verstappen all stopped for a second time.

**LAP 42** Rubens Barrichello finally stopped for the first and only time. The Brazilian had driven hard enough to keep hold of his third place. Also stopping were Enrique Bernoldi and Giancarlo Fisichella, who were fighting for 12th place. The two were side-by-side as they went down the pitlane but Fisichella was in the high-speed lane and Bernoldi in the acceleration lane, so the Brazilian had to back off in order to avoid a penalty.

**LAP 45** Ninth-placed Jaguar Racing driver Eddie Irvine stopped for a second time but was able to retain his position when he rejoined the race.

**LAP 60** For the last 15 laps of the British Grand Prix very little happened and Mika Häkkinen duly won his first victory in nearly a year. Michael Schumacher was second with Ferrari team-mate Rubens Barrichello taking third.

Be there to soak up the atmosphere...
It'll be Buzzin!

The Fosters British Grand Prix returns to Silverstone on the

5, 6 and 7th July 2002 *(provisional)*

Don't miss out on the top sporting event in the motorsport calendar,
book your tickets now on-line at **www.octagonmotorsports.com**

For more information call +44 (0)1327 850 211

SILVERSTONE
**BRANDS HATCH
OULTON PARK
SNETTERTON
CADWELL PARK**

# German Grand Prix

**27th–29th July 2001**  LAPS: 45  LENGTH OF LAP: 4,239 miles

CARBON FIBRE SHOWER AT HOCKENHEIM  The cameras did not record Jacques Villeneuve's spectacular crash after riding over the wheel of Ralf Schumacher's BMW Williams in Melbourne. But there was no such problem when Luciano Burti's Prost did the same thing over Michael Schumacher's Ferrari rear wheel. The impact launched the blue machine into a sickening somersault as it dispersed energy and carbon fibre. That no one was even injured was a miracle. But it destroyed a $500,000 chassis for the Prost team, a loss it can ill afford.  PHOTOGRAPH BY MARK SUTTON

Ralf Schumacher takes his third Grand Prix victory, this time on home soil. With an all-BMW Williams Michelin front row, the only disappointment was Juan Pablo Montoya's retirement.

## BMW's horse for the course

A fast track with long straights and high ambient temperature provided ideal conditions for Michelin, BMW and WIlliams to display their prowess. Michelin's exceptional product helped both Benettons to score.

The hare ran off into the distance but the tortoise romped home, as the grandprix.com website put it. Neither were apt descriptions of the dominant drivers and although the BMW Williams team looked dominant, it was lucky to get even one car home so fragile were the engines in the white heat of Hockenheim. But as well as fragile, they were also mighty fast, maybe 50 horsepower quicker than the competition. On paper, Juan Pablo Montoya was the stronger of the two drivers all weekend, just a few 100ths of a second a lap faster than team-mate Ralf Schumacher. But the BMW duo could lap 7/10ths ahead of their nearest challenger – a huge amount in the world of Formula One. So the race was a foregone conclusion. For some reason Ralf Schumacher always looked more of a winner than Montoya and so it turned out.

Minardi was in a mess, as the two black cars were pushed off to start from the pitlane amid smoke and flames. The start itself was a nightmare in which Luciano Burti and Enrique Bernoldi were lucky not to have been killed. Burti went head-over-heels after running into the back of Schumacher, falling down the grid after losing his gears. The accident was his luck as Burti had not been able to see the slow Ferrari because Panis was in his way. The

Frenchman swerved at the last moment, having only seen Schumacher at the last minute because his view had been obscured by Zonta's Jordan. The chain reaction left Burti with no time to do anything, as he said afterwards: "It happened so fast – when I saw him it was too late to avoid the crash."

Burti braked but the Prost ran slam into the back of the Ferrari and was launched skyward, shedding carbon fibre as it did so. The entire car went over the top of Enrique Bernoldi's Arrows and almost landed on top of the other Arrows car being driven by Jos Verstappen. Both were showered with wreckage. Understating the situation Bernoldi said: "I think I was pretty lucky. A wheel landed on my car and broke the engine cover and the rear wing. It was a pretty big hit." This was the second shunt for Burti, who was due another before the day was out. He has had more accidents than any other driver this season. Luckily Burti's car came to a halt the right way up, having bounced across the gravel and hit the barrier. Schumacher was unscathed and the race should have been stopped. It wasn't until a lap later.

The entire field started again after a further 20 minutes. The stoppage was completely justified and later David Coulthard, with renewed brain fade, risked being hauled up before the FIA on a charge of bringing the sport into disrepute by openly alleging that the race stewards had corruptly favoured Ferrari by red flagging the race. There were some who argued that such an incident did not warrant a red flag but, in truth, that would have been an unnecessary risk. Carbon fibre can cause disastrous tyre deflations and the red flag was the only course of action. Some people's memories went straight back to the F2 race at the track in 1968 when a tyre

Montoya, Ralf Schumacher and Barrichello pass the debris of the first start.

Juan Pablo Montoya leads Williams team-mate Ralf Schumacher into the Ostkurve chicane on lap one as Häkkinen dives down the inside of Barrichello's Ferrari.

At the first chicane of the second start, Pedro de la Rosa assaulted Nick Heidfeld with an absurd, ill-judged move which ended the German's race.

deflation caused the death of Jim Clark. Charlie Whiting would have remembered that and no way was he risking anything similar.

"The track looked a bit like a battlefield," said Michelin's Pierre Dupasquier. "It would have been dangerous not to stop it – you do not want tyres picking up pieces of carbon shrapnel when the cars are travelling at 350kph. Debris like that tends to be razor-sharp and works its way slowly into a tyre before causing it to puncture. The race director did the sensible thing."

And so the race start process began again, this time with a full grid. Once again Montoya beat Ralf Schumacher away. Ralf was comfortable in second, while the battle for third place was lively indeed in those wild early moments of the race. Häkkinen, Michael Schumacher, Coulthard and Barrichello was the order going out of the stadium, but by the time the cars reached the exit of the Ostkurve, Schumacher had sliced ahead of Häkkinen. On the run down to the stadium Barrichello pulled off an audacious outside overtaking manoeuvre on Coulthard to steal fifth. It was fine action.

Barrichello clearly had an advantage and it was pretty safe to assume that he had decided to run a light fuel load and go for a two-stop race. On the third lap he overtook Häkkinen at the Ostkurve and on lap six he overtook Michael Schumacher. "The two BMW Williams cars were on another level," he said. "I think that the best I was hoping for or could achieve was third because they were really fast. I was the only one at their pace to start with."

At the front it became very clear that Ralf Schumacher either had no answer for Montoya's pace or didn't want to have an answer. It turned out the latter was the case. He was waiting for the impulsive

Montoya's engine to blow, as indeed it did. He said afterwards: "When Juan Pablo pulled away I thought 'OK, you do whatever you want to'. I had already started to save the engine because I know how long and how hard this race is."

Montoya built himself a 10-second lead and his team-mate was nearly 20 seconds ahead of his nearest challenger. The advantage was a second-and-a-half a lap. But Montoya ran out of luck after trouble with refuelling, a subsequent overheated engine and a blow-up.

Ralf Schumacher drove smoothly on for a German victory in a half German car at the German race. Near perfection.

Barrichello tied up second, as has become his expertise, and Jacques Villeneuve was a surprising third after his car miraculously transformed itself overnight. The team hadn't got a clue what it had done to make it right. Says it all really.

Third place was a much bigger surprise because no one would have bet on Villeneuve getting onto the podium — least of all Villeneuve himself. "We haven't been competitive in the last few months and this was probably the race we expected to be least competitive in," he said. "It's great that we got another podium but we still need to be more competitive."

Even more astonishing were the Benetton Renaults arriving in formation harried by a muddled Jean Alesi – driving a Prost for the last time, his loyalties as ever sorely tested by a better offer – for the last three points scoring places.

The final amazing act of the afternoon was the announcement that Benetton had actually moved ahead of Jaguar on the constructors' scoreboard.

# German Grand Prix Race Statistics

## HOCKENHEIM CIRCUIT DIAGRAM

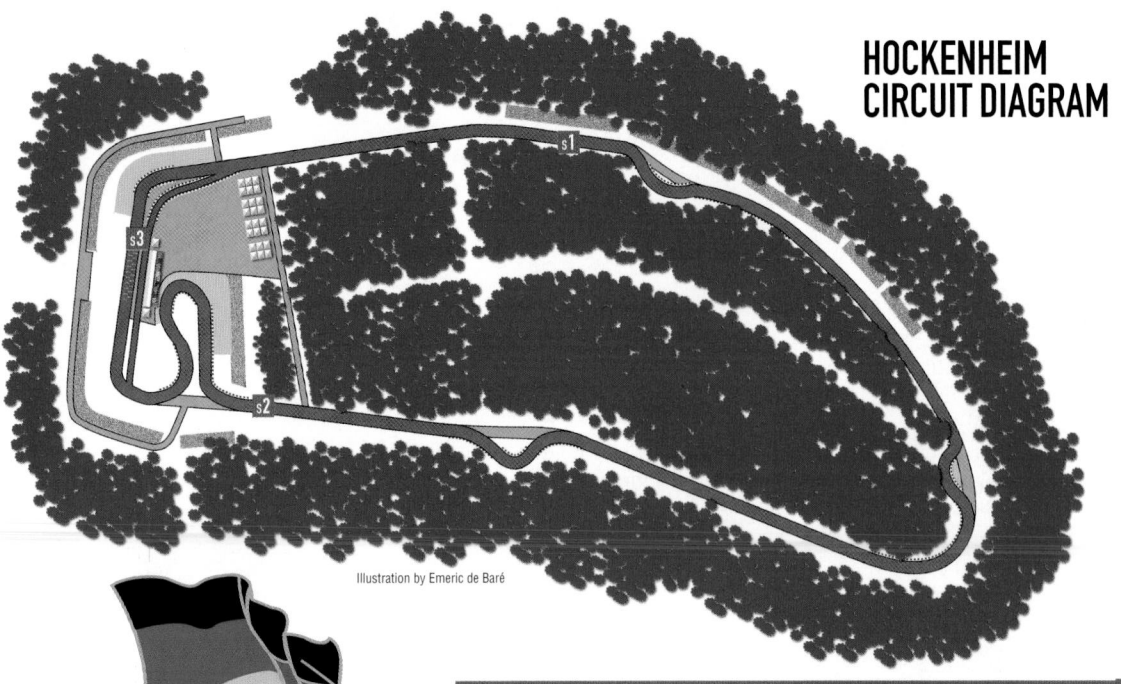

Illustration by Emeric de Baré

### FASTEST LAPS

| | DRIVER | TIME | LAP |
|---|---|---|---|
| 1 | Montoya | 1m 41.808s | 20 |
| 2 | R Schumacher | 1m 42.048s | 17 |
| 3 | Barrichello | 1m 42.638s | 10 |
| 4 | M Schumacher | 1m 42.853s | 21 |
| 5 | Panis | 1m 43.329s | 30 |
| 6 | Villeneuve | 1m 43.448s | 21 |
| 7 | Häkkinen | 1m 43.516s | 4 |
| 8 | Coulthard | 1m 43.571s | 26 |
| 9 | Trulli | 1m 43.740s | 33 |
| 10 | Fisichella | 1m 43.999s | 34 |
| 11 | Button | 1m 44.051s | 31 |
| 12 | Alesi | 1m 44.135s | 42 |
| 13 | Räikkönen | 1m 44.365s | 10 |
| 14 | Irvine | 1m 44.415s | 11 |
| 15 | Verstappen | 1m 44.681s | 35 |
| 16 | Burti | 1m 44.683s | 17 |
| 17 | Bernoldi | 1m 44.785s | 31 |
| 18 | Zonta | 1m 45.591s | 4 |
| 19 | Alonso | 1m 45.908s | 4 |
| 20 | Marques | 1m 46.013s | 12 |
| | Heidfeld | No lap completed | |
| | de la Rosa | No lap completed | |

### RACE SPEED TRAP TIMES

| | | |
|---|---|---|
| 1 | Zonta | 222.0mph |
| 2 | Irvine | 221.0mph |
| 3 | Bernoldi | 220.8mph |
| 4 | Montoya | 220.7mph |
| 5 | Panis | 220.3mph |
| 6 | Villeneuve | 220.2mph |
| = | Fisichella | 220.2mph |
| 8 | Verstappen | 220.1mph |
| 9 | Barrichello | 219.5mph |
| 10 | R Schumacher | 219.2mph |
| 11 | Trulli | 218.5mph |
| 12 | Alonso | 218.3mph |
| 13 | M Schumacher | 218.0mph |
| 14 | Coulthard | 217.7mph |
| 15 | Button | 217.5mph |
| 16 | Heidfeld | 217.3mph |
| 17 | Burti | 217.2mph |
| 18 | Häkkinen | 217.1mph |
| 19 | Räikkönen | 216.2mph |
| = | Alesi | 216.2mph |
| 21 | de la Rosa | 215.7mph |
| 22 | Marques | 215.6mph |

### WARM-UP

SUNDAY 29TH JULY 2001, 9.30AM–10AM

| | | |
|---|---|---|
| 1 | R Schumacher | 1m 42.621s |
| 2 | Montoya | 1m 42.651s |
| 3 | Coulthard | 1m 42.743s |
| 4 | M Schumacher | 1m 42.747s |
| 5 | Barrichello | 1m 42.989s |
| 6 | Häkkinen | 1m 43.129s |
| 7 | Heidfeld | 1m 43.479s |
| 8 | Bernoldi | 1m 43.512s |
| 9 | Villeneuve | 1m 43.570s |
| 10 | Panis | 1m 43.615s |
| 11 | Verstappen | 1m 43.704s |
| 12 | de la Rosa | 1m 43.706s |
| 13 | Irvine | 1m 43.851s |
| 14 | Trulli | 1m 43.856s |
| 15 | Räikkönen | 1m 43.986s |
| 16 | Alesi | 1m 44.300s |
| 17 | Fisichella | 1m 44.601s |
| 18 | Burti | 1m 45.004s |
| 19 | Alonso | 1m 45.263s |
| 20 | Button | 1m 45.653s |
| 21 | Marques | 1m 45.981s |
| 22 | Zonta | 6m 35.247s |

### DRIVER POINTS

| | | |
|---|---|---|
| 1 | Michael Schumacher | 84 |
| 2 | David Coulthard | 47 |
| 3 | Ralf Schumacher | 41 |
| 4 | Rubens Barrichello | 40 |
| 5 | Mika Häkkinen | 19 |
| 6 | Juan Pablo Montoya | 15 |
| 7 | Jacques Villeneuve | 11 |
| 8 | Nick Heidfeld | 10 |
| 9 | Kimi Räikkönen | 9 |
| 10 | Jarno Trulli | 9 |
| 11 | Heinz-Harald Frentzen | 6 |
| 12 | Olivier Panis | 5 |
| 13 | Eddie Irvine | 4 |
| 14 | Giancarlo Fisichella | 4 |
| 15 | Jean Alesi | 4 |
| 16 | Jenson Button | 2 |
| 17 | Jos Verstappen | 1 |
| 18 | Pedro de la Rosa | 1 |
| 19 | Ricardo Zonta | 0 |
| 20 | Luciano Burti | 0 |
| 21 | Tarso Marques | 0 |
| 22 | Enrique Bernoldi | 0 |
| 23 | Fernando Alonso | 0 |
| 24 | Gaston Mazzacane | 0 |

### RACE: SUNDAY 29TH JULY 2001, 2PM

| | DRIVER | CAR | TIME/RETIREMENT | LAPS | PITSTOP LAPS |
|---|---|---|---|---|---|
| 1 | Ralf Schumacher | BMW Williams | 1h 18m 17.873s | 45 | 24 |
| 2 | Rubens Barrichello | Ferrari | +46.117s | 45 | 16 32 |
| 3 | Jacques Villeneuve | BAR Honda | +1m 02.806s | 45 | 24 |
| 4 | Giancarlo Fisichella | Benetton Renault | +1m 03.477s | 45 | 26 |
| 5 | Jenson Button | Benetton Renault | +1m 05.454s | 45 | 24 |
| 6 | Jean Alesi | Prost Acer | +1m 05.950s | 45 | 25 |
| 7 | Olivier Panis | BAR Honda | +1m 17.527s | 45 | 16 31 |
| 8 | Enrique Bernoldi | Arrows Asiatech | +1 lap | 44 | 12 28 |
| 9 | Jos Verstappen | Arrows Asiatech | +1 lap | 44 | 7 27 |
| 10 | Fernando Alonso | European Minardi | +1 lap | 44 | 13 25 |
| Ret | Jarno Trulli | Jordan Honda | Hydraulics | 34 | 27 |
| Ret | David Coulthard | McLaren Mercedes | Engine | 27 | 27 |
| Ret | Tarso Marques | European Minardi | Gearbox | 26 | 20 |
| Ret | Juan Pablo Montoya | BMW Williams | Engine | 24 | 22 |
| Ret | Michael Schumacher | Ferrari | Fuel pressure | 23 | 23 |
| Ret | Luciano Burti | Prost Acer | Injury/spin | 23 | |
| Ret | Kimi Räikkönen | Sauber Petronas | Halfshaft | 16 | |
| Ret | Eddie Irvine | Jaguar Racing | Fuel pressure | 16 | 12 |
| Ret | Mika Häkkinen | McLaren Mercedes | Engine | 13 | |
| Ret | Ricardo Zonta | Jordan Honda | Collision | 7 | 6 |
| Ret | Nick Heidfeld | Sauber Petronas | Collision | 0 | |
| Ret | Pedro de la Rosa | Jaguar Racing | Collision | 0 | |

*Conditions: sunny and hot.*

### PITSTOP TIMES (from pitlane entrance to exit)

| | | | | |
|---|---|---|---|---|
| Fastest pitstop: | Rubens Barrichello | Ferrari | 28.910s | Lap 16 |
| Slowest pitstop: | Juan Pablo Montoya | BMW Williams | 50.808s | Lap 22 |
| Most pitstops: | Five drivers | Two stops | | |

### CONSTRUCTOR POINTS

| | | |
|---|---|---|
| 1 | Scuderia Ferrari-Marlboro | 124 |
| 2 | West McLaren Mercedes | 66 |
| 3 | BMW Williams F1 | 56 |
| 4 | Red Bull Sauber Petronas | 19 |
| 5 | Lucky Strike Reynard BAR Honda | 16 |
| 6 | Benson & Hedges Jordan Honda | 15 |
| 7 | Mild Seven Benetton Renault | 6 |
| 8 | Jaguar Racing | 5 |
| 9 | Prost Acer | 4 |
| 10 | Orange Arrows Asiatech | 1 |
| 11 | European Minardi F1 | 0 |

### PENALTIES AND FINES

| DRIVER | WHEN | PENALTY | REASON |
|---|---|---|---|
| Jenson Button | Friday | $3,000 | Speeding in the pitlane |
| Mika Häkkinen | Friday | $1,250 | Speeding in the pitlane |
| Olivier Panis | Qualifying | $3,000 | Speeding in the pitlane |

### LAP LEADERS

| | |
|---|---|
| Juan Pablo Montoya | 1–22 |
| Ralf Schumacher | 23–45 |
| Total laps led: R Schumacher 23; Montoya 22 | |

### TEMPERATURES

| | | |
|---|---|---|
| Friday: | Air: 34–42°C | Track: 34–42°C |
| Saturday: | Air: 30–33°C | Track: 37–41°C |
| Sunday: | Air: 29°C | Track: 34°C |

F Alonso 21

E Bernoldi 19

G Fisichella 17

R Zonta 15

O Panis 13

T Marques 22

J Verstappen 20

J Button 18

L Burti 16

J Alesi 14

J Villeneuve 12

## GERMAN GRAND PRIX RACE ENTRY

| | DRIVER | TEAM | CHASSIS/ENGINE |
|---|---|---|---|
| 1 | Michael Schumacher | Scuderia Ferrari Marlboro | Ferrari F2001 |
| 2 | Rubens Barrichello | Scuderia Ferrari Marlboro | Ferrari F2001 |
| 3 | Mika Häkkinen | West McLaren Mercedes | McLaren Mercedes MP4-16 |
| 4 | David Coulthard | West McLaren Mercedes | McLaren Mercedes MP4-16 |
| 5 | Ralf Schumacher | BMW Williams F1 Team | BMW Williams FW23 |
| 6 | Juan Pablo Montoya | BMW Williams F1 Team | BMW Williams FW23 |
| 7 | Giancarlo Fisichella | Mild Seven Benetton Renault | Benetton Renault B201 |
| 8 | Jenson Button | Mild Seven Benetton Renault | Benetton Renault B201 |
| 9 | Olivier Panis | Lucky Strike BAR Honda | BAR Honda B003 |
| 10 | Jacques Villeneuve | Lucky Strike BAR Honda | BAR Honda B003 |
| 11 | Ricardo Zonta | Benson & Hedges Jordan Honda | Jordan Honda EJ11 |
| 12 | Jarno Trulli | Benson & Hedges Jordan Honda | Jordan Honda EJ11 |
| 14 | Jos Verstappen | Orange Arrows Asiatech | Arrows Asiatech A22 |
| 15 | Enrique Bernoldi | Orange Arrows Asiatech | Arrows Asiatech A22 |
| 16 | Nick Heidfeld | Red Bull Sauber Petronas | Sauber Petronas C20 |
| 17 | Kimi Räikkönen | Red Bull Sauber Petronas | Sauber Petronas C20 |
| 18 | Eddie Irvine | Jaguar Racing | Jaguar Cosworth R2 |
| 19 | Pedro de la Rosa | Jaguar Racing | Jaguar Cosworth R2 |
| 20 | Tarso Marques | European Minardi | Minardi European PS01 |
| 21 | Fernando Alonso | European Minardi | Minardi European PS01 |
| 22 | Jean Alesi | Prost Grand Prix | Prost ACER AP04 |
| 23 | Luciano Burti | Prost Grand Prix | Prost ACER AP04 |

Ralf Schumacher scored a sweet victory in front of thousands of his countrymen.

## QUALIFYING: SATURDAY 28TH JULY 2001, 1PM  *107 per cent time: 1m 44.985s*

| | DRIVER | TEAM | TIME | GAP | LAPS |
|---|---|---|---|---|---|
| 1 | Juan Pablo Montoya | BMW Williams | 1m 38.117s | 0.000 | 8 |
| 2 | Ralf Schumacher | BMW Williams | 1m 38.136s | +0.019s | 12 |
| 3 | Mika Häkkinen | McLaren Mercedes | 1m 38.811s | +0.694s | 10 |
| 4 | Michael Schumacher | Ferrari | 1m 38.941s | +0.824s | 11 |
| 5 | David Coulthard | McLaren Mercedes | 1m 39.574s | +1.457s | 9 |
| 6 | Rubens Barrichello | Ferrari | 1m 39.682s | +1.565s | 11 |
| 7 | Nick Heidfeld | Sauber Petronas | 1m 39.921s | +1.804s | 12 |
| 8 | Kimi Räikkönen | Sauber Petronas | 1m 40.072s | +1.955s | 12 |
| 9 | Pedro de la Rosa | Jaguar Racing | 1m 40.265s | +2.148s | 12 |
| 10 | Jarno Trulli | Jordan Honda | 1m 40.322s | +2.205s | 8 |
| 11 | Eddie Irvine | Jaguar Racing | 1m 40.371s | +2.254s | 12 |
| 12 | Jacques Villeneuve | BAR Honda | 1m 40.437s | +2.320s | 12 |
| 13 | Olivier Panis | BAR Honda | 1m 40.610s | +2.493s | 12 |
| 14 | Jean Alesi | Prost Acer | 1m 40.724s | +2.607s | 12 |
| 15 | Ricardo Zonta | Jordan Honda | 1m 41.174s | +3.057s | 12 |
| 16 | Luciano Burti | Prost Acer | 1m 41.213s | +3.096s | 11 |
| 17 | Giancarlo Fisichella | Benetton Renault | 1m 41.299s | +3.182s | 12 |
| 18 | Jenson Button | Benetton Renault | 1m 41.438s | +3.321s | 10 |
| 19 | Enrique Bernoldi | Arrows Asiatech | 1m 41.668s | +3.551s | 11 |
| 20 | Jos Verstappen | Arrows Asiatech | 1m 41.870s | +3.753s | 11 |
| 21 | Fernando Alonso | European Minardi | 1m 41.913s | +3.796s | 12 |
| 22 | Tarso Marques | European Minardi | 1m 42.716s | +4.599s | 11 |

## FASTEST SECTOR TIMES IN QUALIFYING  *Ideal lap time: 1m 37.865s (diff. from pole: 0.252s)*

| | SECTOR 1 | SECS | | SECTOR 2 | SECS | | SECTOR 3 | SECS |
|---|---|---|---|---|---|---|---|---|
| 1 | R Schumacher | 30.883 | 1 | R Schumacher | 40.727 | 1 | Montoya | 26.255 |
| 2 | Montoya | 30.900 | 2 | Montoya | 40.743 | 2 | M Schumacher | 26.281 |
| 3 | Häkkinen | 30.979 | 3 | Häkkinen | 41.276 | 3 | R Schumacher | 26.447 |
| 4 | M Schumacher | 31.208 | 4 | M Schumacher | 41.390 | 4 | Häkkinen | 26.530 |
| 5 | Trulli | 31.304 | 5 | Coulthard | 41.452 | 5 | Barrichello | 26.594 |
| 6 | Coulthard | 31.326 | 6 | Barrichello | 41.540 | 6 | Coulthard | 26.600 |
| 7 | Heidfeld | 31.376 | 7 | de la Rosa | 41.541 | 7 | Heidfeld | 26.615 |
| 8 | Barrichello | 31.459 | 8 | Räikkönen | 41.744 | 8 | Räikkönen | 26.649 |
| 9 | Panis | 31.561 | 9 | Villeneuve | 41.752 | 9 | de la Rosa | 26.854 |
| 10 | Zonta | 31.615 | 10 | Irvine | 41.764 | 10 | Irvine | 26.860 |
| 11 | Irvine | 31.632 | 11 | Trulli | 41.772 | 11 | Fisichella | 26.893 |
| 12 | Villeneuve | 31.636 | 12 | Panis | 41.815 | 12 | Trulli | 26.948 |
| 13 | Räikkönen | 31.638 | 13 | Heidfeld | 41.827 | 13 | Villeneuve | 26.963 |
| 14 | Alesi | 31.712 | 14 | Alesi | 41.939 | 14 | Alesi | 26.980 |
| 15 | de la Rosa | 31.731 | 15 | Zonta | 41.961 | 15 | Burti | 27.038 |
| 16 | Burti | 31.866 | 16 | Verstappen | 41.984 | 16 | Panis | 27.100 |
| 17 | Verstappen | 31.897 | 17 | Bernoldi | 42.040 | 17 | Button | 27.181 |
| 18 | Fisichella | 31.924 | 18 | Button | 42.113 | 18 | Zonta | 27.326 |
| 19 | Bernoldi | 31.941 | 19 | Burti | 42.138 | 19 | Alonso | 27.372 |
| 20 | Alonso | 31.953 | 20 | Fisichella | 42.357 | 20 | Bernoldi | 27.552 |
| 21 | Button | 32.063 | 21 | Alonso | 42.362 | 21 | Verstappen | 27.601 |
| 22 | Marques | 32.199 | 22 | Marques | 42.680 | 22 | Marques | 27.715 |

## PRACTICE SESSION ONE

FRIDAY 27TH JULY 2001, 11AM–12PM

| | | |
|---|---|---|
| 1 | Barrichello | 1m 41.953s |
| 2 | de la Rosa | 1m 42.302s |
| 3 | Coulthard | 1m 42.621s |
| 4 | M Schumacher | 1m 42.826s |
| 5 | R Schumacher | 1m 42.987s |
| 6 | Häkkinen | 1m 42.994s |
| 7 | Montoya | 1m 43.212s |
| 8 | Irvine | 1m 43.275s |
| 9 | Fisichella | 1m 43.894s |
| 10 | Trulli | 1m 43.970s |
| 11 | Zonta | 1m 44.333s |
| 12 | Heidfeld | 1m 44.351s |
| 13 | Räikkönen | 1m 44.372s |
| 14 | Villeneuve | 1m 44.532s |
| 15 | Panis | 1m 44.616s |
| 16 | Alesi | 1m 45.151s |
| 17 | Bernoldi | 1m 45.469s |
| 18 | Burti | 1m 45.767s |
| 19 | Button | 1m 45.798s |
| 20 | Alonso | 1m 45.627s |
| 21 | Marques | 1m 47.292s |
| | Verstappen | No laps |

## PRACTICE SESSION TWO

FRIDAY 27TH JULY 2001, 1PM–2PM

| | | |
|---|---|---|
| 1 | Irvine | 1m 41.424s |
| 2 | Montoya | 1m 41.487s |
| 3 | Häkkinen | 1m 41.949s |
| 4 | Barrichello | 1m 41.953s |
| 5 | M Schumacher | 1m 42.255s |
| 6 | de la Rosa | 1m 42.302s |
| 7 | Coulthard | 1m 42.304s |
| 8 | Alesi | 1m 42.828s |
| 9 | Trulli | 1m 42.941s |
| 10 | R Schumacher | 1m 42.987s |
| 11 | Fisichella | 1m 43.014s |
| 12 | Heidfeld | 1m 43.211s |
| 13 | Zonta | 1m 43.461s |
| 14 | Panis | 1m 43.487s |
| 15 | Button | 1m 43.496s |
| 16 | Räikkönen | 1m 43.528s |
| 17 | Villeneuve | 1m 43.815s |
| 18 | Verstappen | 1m 44.143s |
| 19 | Burti | 1m 44.162s |
| 20 | Bernoldi | 1m 44.549s |
| 21 | Alonso | 1m 44.730s |
| 22 | Marques | 1m 45.005s |

## PRACTICE SESSION THREE

SATURDAY 28TH JULY 2001, 9AM–9.45AM

| | | |
|---|---|---|
| 1 | M Schumacher | 1m 39.937s |
| 2 | Barrichello | 1m 40.436s |
| 3 | R Schumacher | 1m 40.457s |
| 4 | Montoya | 1m 40.661s |
| 5 | Coulthard | 1m 40.697s |
| 6 | Häkkinen | 1m 40.905s |
| 7 | Heidfeld | 1m 41.520s |
| 8 | Villeneuve | 1m 41.683s |
| 9 | Irvine | 1m 41.693s |
| 10 | Räikkönen | 1m 41.833s |
| 11 | de la Rosa | 1m 41.839s |
| 12 | Trulli | 1m 41.887s |
| 13 | Panis | 1m 42.417s |
| 14 | Zonta | 1m 42.424s |
| 15 | Bernoldi | 1m 42.492s |
| 16 | Verstappen | 1m 42.580s |
| 17 | Alesi | 1m 42.964s |
| 18 | Fisichella | 1m 43.256s |
| 19 | Burti | 1m 43.356s |
| 20 | Alonso | 1m 44.574s |
| 21 | Marques | 1m 45.406s |
| | Button | No laps |

## PRACTICE SESSION FOUR

SATURDAY 28TH JULY 2001, 10.15AM–11AM

| | | |
|---|---|---|
| 1 | R Schumacher | 1m 39.188s |
| 2 | Montoya | 1m 39.469s |
| 3 | M Schumacher | 1m 39.937s |
| 4 | Häkkinen | 1m 40.069s |
| 5 | Heidfeld | 1m 40.263s |
| 6 | Barrichello | 1m 40.436s |
| 7 | Irvine | 1m 40.443s |
| 8 | Panis | 1m 40.575s |
| 9 | Coulthard | 1m 40.697s |
| 10 | Trulli | 1m 40.894s |
| 11 | de la Rosa | 1m 40.905s |
| 12 | Räikkönen | 1m 41.153s |
| 13 | Alesi | 1m 41.428s |
| 14 | Zonta | 1m 41.534s |
| 15 | Villeneuve | 1m 41.683s |
| 16 | Button | 1m 41.771s |
| 17 | Burti | 1m 42.136s |
| 18 | Bernoldi | 1m 42.223s |
| 19 | Verstappen | 1m 42.580s |
| 20 | Fisichella | 1m 43.256s |
| 21 | Alonso | 1m 43.512s |
| 22 | Marques | 1m 43.909s |

| 11 | 9 | 7 | 5 | 3 | 1 |
|---|---|---|---|---|---|
| E Irvine | P de la Rosa | N Heidfeld | D Coulthard | M Häkkinen | JP Montoya |

| 10 | 8 | 6 | 4 | 2 |
|---|---|---|---|---|
| J Trulli | K Räikkönen | R Barrichello | M Schumacher | R Schumacher |

## HOCKENHEIM LAP-BY-LAP REPORT

**PRE-START** As the cars formed up on the dummy grid before the start of the final parade lap, there were major problems for the European Minardi team when Fernando Alonso's car caught fire because of fuel leaking from the refuelling valve. The fire was quickly doused but the problem needed fixing and so Alonso ran to the pit to take over the spare car. Soon after there was a similar problem with Tarso Marques's car (although it did not catch fire) and he too went running back to the pit garage. There was no spare available so the team worked frantically to fix Alonso's car and Marques took that. However, both men had to start the race from the pitlane because their cars did not get out before the pit was closed.

**START** At the start Montoya took the lead from pole with Ralf Schumacher behind him. Michael Schumacher made a normal start but then the Ferrari suddenly slowed. The cars behind took avoiding action with near-misses for both Panis and Zonta but Burti was unable to avoid smashing into the back of Schumacher's car. The Prost was launched into the air, showering wreckage on cars around it. Burti flew over Bernoldi's Arrows, the car turning in the air and narrowly missing landing on Verstappen's Arrows. It then hit the ground and rolled, ending up the right way up, but bouncing off the road and into the outside barriers of the first corner. Schumacher's car came to a halt with a deranged right rear suspension. Everyone else got through without stopping but Bernoldi's car was damaged when one of Burti's wheels landed on it. At the first chicane Häkkinen ran into the back of Barrichello (for which he later apologised) but both continued without a problem while at the Ostkurve Heidfeld tried to pass Coulthard for sixth place but overshot and had to let the McLaren ahead again. Also in trouble at the back of the field was Alonso, who suffered a driveshaft problem and went straight to the pits. The safety car was dispatched but the cars still had to thread through the wreckage at the end of the first lap. Soon afterwards, race director Charlie Whiting decided to red-flag because he felt it was too dangerous to allow cars to run through so much wreckage. The grid reformed with Schumacher and Burti in their spares. Bernoldi's Arrows was repaired and Alonso switched to Tarso Marques's car (which had been repaired). This meant that the two Minardi drivers found themselves driving each other's cars.

**LAP 1** Montoya took the lead at the second start and was chased into the first corner by Ralf Schumacher. Then came Häkkinen, Michael Schumacher, Coulthard and Barrichello, all quibbling over third. Behind them de la Rosa misjudged his braking point at the first chicane and smashed into Heidfeld's Sauber. On the run down to the Ostkurve, Michael Schumacher was able to pass Häkkinen for third place while Barrichello overtook Coulthard for fifth, passing the McLaren on the outside in the fast corner going into the stadium area. By the end of the first lap it was clear that the BMW Williams cars were dominant, with Montoya a second-and-a-half ahead of Ralf Schumacher, who in turn was a second clear of his brother Michael. Häkkinen was fourth, coming under pressure from Barrichello and then Coulthard. There was then a gap back to Räikkönen, Irvine and Trulli with Villeneuve completing the top 10.

**LAP 2** Montoya increased his advantage over Schumacher to more than two seconds and the gap between Ralf and Michael grew to a similar amount. Back in the midfield Bernoldi overtook 15th-placed Giancarlo Fisichella.

**LAP 3** Barrichello outbraked Häkkinen going into the Ostkurve to move into fourth. Further back 13th-placed Panis was able to pass Button, who had overtaken the BAR driver at the start. Panis then chased after 12th-placed Zonta.

**LAP 5** Panis overtook Zonta for 12th position and Bernoldi passed Button for 14th.

**LAP 6** As Montoya drove away from Ralf Schumacher, taking his lead up to more than four seconds, Barrichello closed on Michael Schumacher and moved to third place. Eleventh-placed Verstappen made a mistake at the Ostkurve and was slow out of the corner. Zonta tried to pass him and the two cars collided. Zonta lost his front wing and had to pit for repairs while Verstappen lost momentum and was overtaken by Panis.

**LAP 7** Verstappen had to pit because of a punctured rear tyre and fell from 12th to the tail of the field. Zonta checked out his car after repairs but pitted at the end of the lap to retire as there was too much damage.

**LAP 9** Burti began to struggle because of a bruised arm and was overtaken for 15th by team-mate Jean Alesi.

**LAP 10** Villeneuve (on a one-stop strategy) allowed Panis to pass him for 10th.

**LAP 12** The battle between the Honda teams came to a head as Panis overtook Trulli to move to ninth. Panis ran over the kerb to achieve this and Trulli assumed Olivier would then allow him to retake the position. Panis seemed under the impression that Trulli was trying to overtake him. The result was that Trulli spun, avoiding a collision. This meant he dropped back from 10th to 17th. On the same lap, eighth-placed Irvine and 13th-placed Bernoldi both stopped for the first time. Irvine rejoined in 16th with Bernoldi 18th.

**LAP 14** Coulthard moved up to fifth position when Häkkinen pulled off with an engine failure. This meant Räikkönen was sixth and Panis seventh.

**LAP 15** The recovering Verstappen overtook Marques to take 15th place.

**LAP 16** Barrichello went into the pits for his first stop and fell to fifth behind Michael Schumacher and Coulthard. Barrichello and Coulthard began to scrap over fourth. At the same time sixth-placed Räikkönen slowed with driveshaft failure and Panis went into the pits, so Villeneuve was suddenly sixth. Panis dropped to 12th while Irvine retired with a terminal misfire.

**LAP 18** Burti was up to 10th but was struggling badly with his arm and was overtaken by both Trulli and Panis.

**LAP 20** Barrichello finally managed to get ahead of Coulthard and take fourth place with another brave move around the outside in the fast left-hander going into the stadium area.

**LAP 22** Montoya was the first of the one-stop runners to pit. This put Ralf Schumacher into the lead. A problem with the indicator light on the Williams refuelling hose led the refueller to switch rigs. In fact the fuel had flowed into the car without a problem. This not only lost Montoya around 20 seconds (he rejoined in fourth), it also meant he went out with too much fuel.

**LAP 23** Second-placed Michael Schumacher pitted. His stop went without a hitch but as he accelerated off into the forests he developed a fuel pressure problem and the Ferrari stopped. This put Barrichello in second with Montoya third.

**LAP 24** Ralf Schumacher pitted but rejoined in the lead. On the same lap, fifth-placed Villeneuve and sixth-placed Button stopped. Villeneuve dropped behind Fisichella and Alesi, while Button was less fortunate and lost four places. At the back of the field Burti spun off, unable to drive any further, while Alonso had a dramatic pitstop, as the Minardi refuelling valve was leaking when he left the pits and the rear of the car was engulfed in flames. The fire extinguished itself as he accelerated out of the pits.

**LAP 25** Montoya's race ended with an engine failure. Coulthard inherited third place with Fisichella fourth after Alesi pitted and slipped back to eighth.

**LAP 27** Coulthard and Trulli were the last one-stop racers to pit. Coulthard rejoined still in third but retired with an engine failure on the first lap out of the pits. This promoted Villeneuve to third, Fisichella to fourth with Panis fifth and Button sixth. Alesi was seventh ahead of Trulli.

**LAP 31** Panis pitted for his second stop and fell to seventh, behind Button and Alesi.

**LAP 32** Second-placed Barrichello came in for his second stop. The refuelling machine malfunctioned but he was still able to rejoin in the same position.

**LAP 35** Trulli's race came to an end with a hydraulic pump failure. This promoted Bernoldi and Verstappen to eighth and ninth.

**LAP 43** As the two Arrows drivers battled for eighth, Fisichella tried to catch Villeneuve. The Benetton driver was able to rejoin ahead of his team-mate Button, under pressure from Alesi.

**LAP 45** Schumacher took the chequered flag to win by 46 seconds. Barrichello was second with Villeneuve third, a minute behind the Ferrari. Fisichella, Button and Alesi were all within a couple of seconds of the BAR driver while Panis was seventh, the last man not lapped. The only other cars to reach the finish were the two Arrows Asiatechs and Alonso's battle-scarred Minardi.

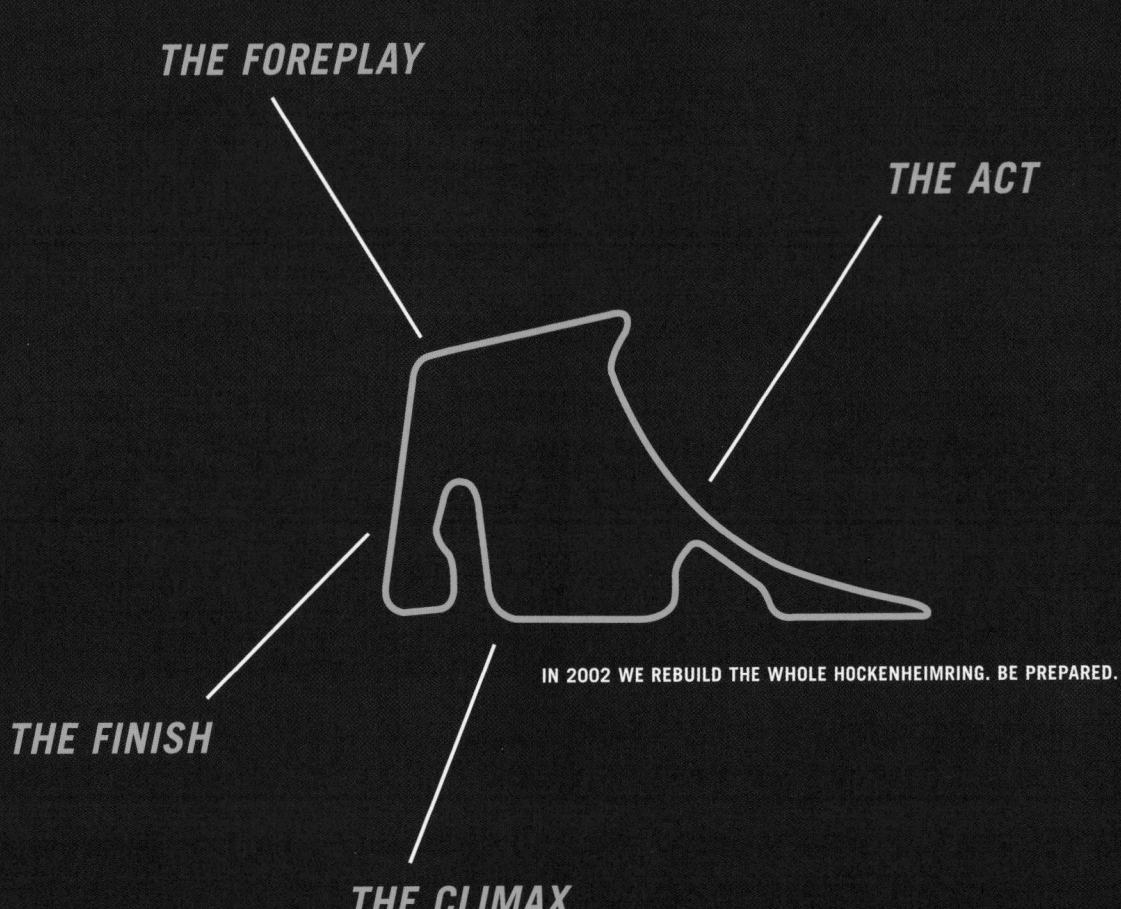

# Hungarian Grand Prix

**17th–19th August 2001**    LAPS: 77  LENGTH OF LAP: 2.465 miles

SCARLET CELEBRATION The champagne flows as Michael Schumacher, Jean Todt and Rubens Barrichello celebrate a historic day for Ferrari. One-two in the race, an 11th drivers' championship, an 11th constructors' championship, and a record-equalling 51st win for Schumacher — things couldn't be any better. PHOTOGRAPH BY KEITH SUTTON

The Hungaroring's 180-degree final corner is bumpy and plays a significant role in lap time and generating passing opportunities.

Schumacher's pursuers scrabble for position on the run to Turn 2.

# They came and they conquered

**Another drivers' title. Another constructors' title. Another day at the office for Ferrari. History was made at the Hungaroring as Ferrari and Michael Schumacher swept the board.**

Three hours before show time, something strange was going on in the Ferrari motorhome. Ann Bradshaw, the charming BMW Williams media manager, was seen hovering outside the red temple, waiting to be greeted by Ferrari's Ross Brawn. "There you go Ann," said Ross, as he proudly handed out three Ferrari baseball caps. "They're for the party tonight."

It seemed most Formula One teams had given up the fight long before the red lights went off at the Hungaroring circuit. The race was billed as another epic Coulthard/Schumacher battle, with the McLaren driver supposedly doing his best to scupper Schumacher's hopes of securing the world title on the outskirts of Budapest. Unfortunately, someone forgot to tell Coulthard, BMW Williams and just about every other Formula One team that there was the small matter of the race before the coronation.

At least some racing fans had faith in the race. An hour before the start, more than 50 Union Jack-clad Jenson Button supporters were in position at the second corner, chanting 'come on Jenson, you can win it'. Oh dear.

With a track temperature of 39 degrees Celsius, the race proper got under way at 2pm as usual. At precisely seven seconds past the hour, Jaguar's Eddie Irvine was preparing for the journey back to his yacht in the Mediterranean, after disastrously spinning off at the first corner. His American girlfriend Katheryn, watching from the Jaguar motorhome, was at first confused. "Is it Pedro or Eddie? Please tell me it's Pedro," she screamed. "Erm, no. It's Eddie. Again," replied one of the Jaguar hostesses. "Oh shit," said Katheryn, as she tucked back into her pasta.

The start was unspectacular for everyone else. Schumacher stormed in front as expected, with team-mate Rubens Barrichello edging ahead of Coulthard for second place. The grand David and Goliath battle we were promised didn't even get as far as the first corner.

Two laps into the race, and by the second corner the British racing fans were wondering where their hero Jenson Button was. Having started near the back, he disappeared altogether. Their hopes of a top 15 finish dashed already? Jenson was forced to pit for a 10-second penalty, having jumped the start.

And so the order of the day was set: the Ferraris in front, Coulthard in third, with Ralf Schumacher just ahead of Mika Häkkinen.

Racing action of any kind didn't come until lap eight, when Luciano Burti's Prost spun off – a feat matched by Bernoldi's Arrows three laps later. By then, up at the front, Schumacher was pushing away 7.39 seconds ahead of third-placed Coulthard, and managing to set a number of new records along the way.

Then, 32 laps in, the hint of drama. Coulthard pitstopped behind Barrichello and after some lightning pit work managed to get out

Pedro de la Rosa's Jaguar again explores the kitty litter after leaving the racing line. The Spaniard has not given up the fight for control, as evidenced by the amount of steering lock and the direction in which he is looking. The Jaguar's attempt to find grip off the track is shown clearly by the caked dirt on the front tyre.

just one second ahead of the Ferrari. Suddenly the race was on. Three laps later Coulthard had shaved three seconds off the leader and was 11 seconds behind. The normally subdued Ron Dennis punched his fist in the air at this achievement (forgetting his own words that coming second is simply being first of the losers).

Two laps later, on lap 34, poor Jenson Button's miserable weekend was over when he spun by the start-finish line. Luckily for him, the British fans had left the track long before. Elsewhere, the failures continued. Alonso's Minardi's brakes failed on lap 37; Trulli's Jordan Honda pulled off on lap 53 with hydraulic failure; Panis's BAR Honda had electrical failure on lap 58; Frentzen's new Prost had old engine problems on lap 63; Marques's Minardi had an electrical failure on lap 63; and Fisichella's Renault engine failed on lap 67.

Back in the race, a miserable afternoon for the off-pace BMW Williams was completed on lap 48 when Michael Schumacher lapped Juan Pablo Montoya. The memories of Brazil, when Montoya brilliantly stormed into the lead from fourth on the grid, leaving Schumacher in shock, were just that: distant memories.

At least Ron Dennis still had something to smile about, with Coulthard remaining within 'hoping' distance of Schumacher. Maybe the champ would make a silly mistake and leave the world title open. Or maybe Coulthard would blow it again. Unfortunately for Coulthard it was the latter of the two. With 23 laps to go, his second pitstop wasn't so lightning and saw him emerge behind Rubens Barrichello. That meant no more smiles from Ron Dennis.

Twenty-three more laps of this, and not only was Schumacher world champion, but Ferrari had secured the constructors' title too, a race earlier than expected. The whitewash was humiliating for McLaren Mercedes after a season of anguish and tragedy it would rather forget. It was fighting for second place as hard as it could, indicating that second is rather more important than Ron Dennis believes.

As the chequered flag approached, attention first turned to the rest. Nick Heidfeld scored another point for Sauber, after a strong drive, and the German's team-mate Räikkönen finished just behind in seventh, concluding a positive weekend for the Swiss team. It was an unusual race as none of the frontrunners retired, leaving only a few meagre crumbs for the supporting cast.

As usual Jos Verstappen managed to move himself up from a poor grid position, gaining six places before the end of the second lap, to eventually finish in 12th. Alesi's strong debut for Jordan got him 10th place, just behind Villeneuve and Montoya. And Häkkinen settled for fifth, behind Ralf Schumacher, Coulthard and Barrichello.

Again it was Schumacher's day. As expected by everyone including all the other teams, Ferrari came and conquered. And minutes after crossing the finish, Schumacher, Todt and Barrichello were on the podium singing 'we are the champions', with an embarrassed Coulthard looking on. Most drivers would give anything for third place. Coulthard would have given anything for fourth place that afternoon.

So what did Schumacher make of all this? "I was talking to the team trying to find the right words," he said. "In such a moment it is quite hard to find the right words. I can't say much more than it's been a beautiful weekend. It's such a good feeling. We got pole position, the victory, I equalised with Alain and took the championship. It's a bit too much for me at the moment. It's just such a great achievement. I feel so fantastic. I can't believe how wonderful the guys are. We have a great crew – I'm really in love with all of them and it's so much fun to work for them. It's their achievement and I'm more than thankful to all of them."

Technical director Ross Brawn summed up the team's feelings. "The dream continues," he smiled. "It is unbelievable. We never imagined this could happen. It's a great group of people, Michael, Jean and everybody. I'm lost for words. We knew we had a few opportunities, but to win it here today. The drivers have been superb. We can always improve, but I can't think how at the moment."

For the sake of some competitive motor racing, rivals are hoping he doesn't figure out how.

David Coulthard straddles the kerb which destroyed one McLaren.

# Hungarian Grand Prix Race Statistics

## HUNGARORING CIRCUIT DIAGRAM

Illustration by Emeric de Baré

486

## FASTEST LAPS

| | DRIVER | TIME | LAP |
|---|---|---|---|
| 1 | Häkkinen | 1m 16.723s | 51 |
| 2 | Coulthard | 1m 17.054s | 53 |
| 3 | R Schumacher | 1m 17.233s | 54 |
| 4 | Barrichello | 1m 17.274s | 51 |
| 5 | M Schumacher | 1m 17.436s | 23 |
| 6 | Montoya | 1m 18.030s | 34 |
| 7 | Heidfeld | 1m 18.165s | 50 |
| 8 | de la Rosa | 1m 18.186s | 51 |
| 9 | Räikkönen | 1m 18.216s | 28 |
| 10 | Trulli | 1m 18.536s | 50 |
| 11 | Alesi | 1m 19.134s | 32 |
| 12 | Panis | 1m 19.222s | 29 |
| 13 | Fisichella | 1m 19.471s | 24 |
| 14 | Button | 1m 19.475s | 29 |
| 15 | Villeneuve | 1m 19.494s | 75 |
| 16 | Frentzen | 1m 20.046s | 50 |
| 17 | Verstappen | 1m 20.401s | 51 |
| 18 | Marques | 1m 21.379s | 51 |
| 19 | Alonso | 1m 21.533s | 18 |
| 20 | Burti | 1m 21.912s | 8 |
| 21 | Bernoldi | 1m 22.045s | 7 |
| | Irvine | No lap completed | |

## RACE SPEED TRAP TIMES

| | DRIVER | SPEED |
|---|---|---|
| 1 | Montoya | 189.3mph |
| 2 | R Schumacher | 188.4mph |
| 3 | Coulthard | 186.2mph |
| 4 | Häkkinen | 185.0mph |
| 5 | Verstappen | 184.9mph |
| = | de la Rosa | 184.9mph |
| 7 | Frentzen | 184.6mph |
| = | M Schumacher | 184.6mph |
| 9 | Panis | 184.3mph |
| 10 | Trulli | 184.1mph |
| 11 | Räikkönen | 183.7mph |
| = | Heidfeld | 183.7mph |
| 13 | Burti | 183.6mph |
| 14 | Barrichello | 183.4mph |
| 15 | Button | 183.3mph |
| 16 | Fisichella | 182.7mph |
| 17 | Villeneuve | 182.6mph |
| 18 | Alonso | 182.1mph |
| = | Bernoldi | 182.1mph |
| 20 | Marques | 181.6mph |
| 21 | Irvine | 158.1mph |

*Speeds for Alesi are unavailable as the relevant transponder fell off his car.*

## RACE: SUNDAY 19TH AUGUST 2001, 2PM

| | DRIVER | CAR | TIME/RETIREMENT | LAPS | PITSTOP LAPS |
|---|---|---|---|---|---|
| 1 | Michael Schumacher | Ferrari | 1h 41m 49.675s | 77 | 28 52 |
| 2 | Rubens Barrichello | Ferrari | +3.363s | 77 | 31 53 |
| 3 | David Coulthard | McLaren Mercedes | +3.940s | 77 | 32 54 |
| 4 | Ralf Schumacher | BMW Williams | +49.687s | 77 | 30 52 |
| 5 | Mika Häkkinen | McLaren Mercedes | +1m 10.293s | 77 | 38 56 71 |
| 6 | Nick Heidfeld | Sauber Petronas | +1 lap | 76 | 27 51 |
| 7 | Kimi Räikkönen | Sauber Petronas | +1 lap | 76 | 26 46 |
| 8 | Juan Pablo Montoya | BMW Williams | +1 lap | 76 | 32 49 |
| 9 | Jacques Villeneuve | BAR Honda | +2 laps | 75 | 30 49 |
| 10 | Jean Alesi | Jordan Honda | +2 laps | 75 | 30 51 |
| 11 | Pedro de la Rosa | Jaguar Racing | +2 laps | 75 | 53 |
| 12 | Jos Verstappen | Arrows Asiatech | +3 laps | 74 | 24 53 |
| Ret | Giancarlo Fisichella | Benetton Renault | Engine | 67 | 21 45 |
| Ret | Heinz-Harald Frentzen | Prost Acer | Spin | 63 | 18 52 |
| Ret | Tarso Marques | European Minardi | Oil pressure | 63 | 26 52 |
| Ret | Olivier Panis | BAR Honda | Electrical | 58 | 27 53 57 |
| Ret | Jarno Trulli | Jordan Honda | Hydraulics | 53 | 29 48 |
| Ret | Fernando Alonso | European Minardi | Brakes | 37 | 20 |
| Ret | Jenson Button | Benetton Renault | Spin | 34 | 6 27 |
| Ret | Enrique Bernoldi | Arrows Asiatech | Spin | 11 | |
| Ret | Luciano Burti | Prost Acer | Spin/tyres | 8 | |
| Ret | Eddie Irvine | Jaguar Racing | Spin | 0 | |

*Conditions: very hot*

## PITSTOP TIMES (from pitlane entrance to exit)

| | | | | |
|---|---|---|---|---|
| Fastest pitstop | Mika Häkkinen | McLaren Mercedes | 26.245s | Lap 22 |
| Slowest pitstop | Jarno Trulli | Jordan Honda | 34.780s | Lap 29 |
| Most pitstops | Mika Häkkinen | Three stops | | |

## PENALTIES AND FINES

| DRIVER/TEAM | WHEN | PENALTY | REASON |
|---|---|---|---|
| Jenson Button | Race | 10 seconds | Jumped the start |

## LAP LEADERS

| | |
|---|---|
| M Schumacher | 1-28, 33-52, 55-77 |
| Barrichello | 29-30 |
| Coulthard | 31-32, 53-54 |

Total laps led: M Schumacher 71; Coulthard 4; Barrichello 2

## TEMPERATURES

| | | |
|---|---|---|
| Friday | Air: 28-29°C | Track: 36-49°C |
| Saturday | Air: 29-31°C | Track: 33-41°C |
| Sunday | Air: 33°C | Track: 40-41°C |

## DRIVER POINTS

| | | |
|---|---|---|
| 1 | Michael Schumacher | 94 |
| 2 | David Coulthard | 51 |
| 3 | Rubens Barrichello | 46 |
| 4 | Ralf Schumacher | 44 |
| 5 | Mika Häkkinen | 21 |
| 6 | Juan Pablo Montoya | 15 |
| 7 | Jacques Villeneuve | 11 |
| 8 | Nick Heidfeld | 11 |
| 9 | Kimi Räikkönen | 9 |
| 10 | Jarno Trulli | 9 |
| 11 | Heinz-Harald Frentzen | 6 |
| 12 | Olivier Panis | 5 |
| 13 | Eddie Irvine | 4 |
| 14 | Giancarlo Fisichella | 4 |
| 15 | Jean Alesi | 4 |
| 16 | Jenson Button | 2 |
| 17 | Jos Verstappen | 1 |
| 18 | Pedro de la Rosa | 1 |
| 19 | Ricardo Zonta | 0 |
| 20 | Luciano Burti | 0 |
| 21 | Enrique Bernoldi | 0 |
| 22 | Tarso Marques | 0 |
| 23 | Fernando Alonso | 0 |
| 24 | Gaston Mazzacane | 0 |

## CONSTRUCTOR POINTS

| | | |
|---|---|---|
| 1 | Scuderia Ferrari-Marlboro | 140 |
| 2 | West McLaren Mercedes | 72 |
| 3 | BMW Williams F1 | 59 |
| 4 | Red Bull Sauber Petronas | 20 |
| 5 | Lucky Strike Reynard BAR Honda | 16 |
| 6 | Benson & Hedges Jordan Honda | 15 |
| 7 | Mild Seven Benetton Renault | 6 |
| 8 | Jaguar Racing | 5 |
| 9 | Prost Acer | 4 |
| 10 | Orange Arrows Asiatech | 1 |
| 11 | European Minardi F1 | 0 |

## WARM-UP

### SUNDAY 19TH AUGUST 2001, 9.30AM-10AM

| | DRIVER | TIME |
|---|---|---|
| 1 | Coulthard | 1m 16.915s |
| 2 | M Schumacher | 1m 17.338s |
| 3 | Barrichello | 1m 17.360s |
| 4 | R Schumacher | 1m 17.608s |
| 5 | Häkkinen | 1m 17.704s |
| 6 | Trulli | 1m 18.433s |
| 7 | Heidfeld | 1m 18.851s |
| 8 | Panis | 1m 18.881s |
| 9 | Räikkönen | 1m 19.068s |
| 10 | Irvine | 1m 19.148s |
| 11 | de la Rosa | 1m 19.393s |
| 12 | Montoya | 1m 19.465s |
| 13 | Villeneuve | 1m 19.554s |
| 14 | Alesi | 1m 19.581s |
| 15 | Fisichella | 1m 19.704s |
| 16 | Verstappen | 1m 19.887s |
| 17 | Bernoldi | 1m 20.500s |
| 18 | Frentzen | 1m 20.546s |
| 19 | Burti | 1m 20.895s |
| 20 | Alonso | 1m 20.965s |
| 21 | Marques | 1m 21.354s |
| 22 | Button | 1m 21.397s |

T Marques — 22

J Verstappen — 21

E Bernoldi — 20

L Burti — 19

F Alonso — 18

J Button — 17

HH Frentzen — 16

G Fisichella — 15

E Irvine — 14

P de la Rosa — 13

J Alesi — 12

## HUNGARIAN GRAND PRIX RACE ENTRY

| | DRIVER | TEAM | CHASSIS/ENGINE |
|---|---|---|---|
| 1 | Michael Schumacher | Scuderia Ferrari Marlboro | Ferrari F2001 |
| 2 | Rubens Barrichello | Scuderia Ferrari Marlboro | Ferrari F2001 |
| 3 | Mika Häkkinen | West McLaren Mercedes | McLaren Mercedes MP4-16 |
| 4 | David Coulthard | West McLaren Mercedes | McLaren Mercedes MP4-16 |
| 5 | Ralf Schumacher | BMW Williams F1 Team | BMW Williams FW23 |
| 6 | Juan Pablo Montoya | BMW Williams F1 Team | BMW Williams FW23 |
| 7 | Giancarlo Fisichella | Mild Seven Benetton Renault | Benetton Renault B201 |
| 8 | Jenson Button | Mild Seven Benetton Renault | Benetton Renault B201 |
| 9 | Olivier Panis | Lucky Strike BAR Honda | BAR Honda B003 |
| 10 | Jacques Villeneuve | Lucky Strike BAR Honda | BAR Honda B003 |
| 11 | Jarno Trulli | Benson & Hedges Jordan Honda | Jordan Honda EJ11 |
| 12 | Jean Alesi | Benson & Hedges Jordan Honda | Jordan Honda EJ11 |
| 14 | Jos Verstappen | Orange Arrows Asiatech | Arrows Asiatech A22 |
| 15 | Enrique Bernoldi | Orange Arrows Asiatech | Arrows Asiatech A22 |
| 16 | Nick Heidfeld | Red Bull Sauber Petronas | Sauber Petronas C20 |
| 17 | Kimi Räikkönen | Red Bull Sauber Petronas | Sauber Petronas C20 |
| 18 | Eddie Irvine | Jaguar Racing | Jaguar Cosworth R2 |
| 19 | Pedro de la Rosa | Jaguar Racing | Jaguar Cosworth R2 |
| 20 | Tarso Marques | European Minardi | Minardi European PS01B |
| 21 | Fernando Alonso | European Minardi | Minardi European PS01 |
| 22 | Heinz-Harald Frentzen | Prost Grand Prix | Prost ACER AP04 |
| 23 | Luciano Burti | Prost Grand Prix | Prost ACER AP04 |

The assembled crowd salutes Schumacher's record-equalling Hungarian race victory and his fourth drivers' world championship.

## QUALIFYING: SATURDAY 18TH AUGUST 2001, 1PM–2PM *107% time: 1m 19.243s*

| | DRIVER | TEAM | TIME | GAP | LAPS |
|---|---|---|---|---|---|
| 1 | Michael Schumacher | Ferrari | 1m 14.059s | 0.000 | 6 |
| 2 | David Coulthard | McLaren Mercedes | 1m 14.860s | +0.801s | 11 |
| 3 | Rubens Barrichello | Ferrari | 1m 14.953s | +0.894s | 11 |
| 4 | Ralf Schumacher | BMW Williams | 1m 15.095s | +1.036s | 12 |
| 5 | Jarno Trulli | Jordan Honda | 1m 15.394s | +1.335s | 10 |
| 6 | Mika Häkkinen | McLaren Mercedes | 1m 15.411s | +1.352s | 11 |
| 7 | Nick Heidfeld | Sauber Petronas | 1m 15.739s | +1.680s | 9 |
| 8 | Juan Pablo Montoya | BMW Williams | 1m 15.881s | +1.822s | 11 |
| 9 | Kimi Räikkönen | Sauber Petronas | 1m 15.906s | +1.847s | 12 |
| 10 | Jacques Villeneuve | BAR Honda | 1m 16.212s | +2.153s | 11 |
| 11 | Olivier Panis | BAR Honda | 1m 16.382s | +2.323s | 8 |
| 12 | Jean Alesi | Jordan Honda | 1m 16.471s | +2.412s | 12 |
| 13 | Pedro de la Rosa | Jaguar Racing | 1m 16.543s | +2.484s | 10 |
| 14 | Eddie Irvine | Jaguar Racing | 1m 16.607s | +2.548s | 11 |
| 15 | Giancarlo Fisichella | Benetton Renault | 1m 16.632s | +2.573s | 11 |
| 16 | Heinz-Harald Frentzen | Prost Acer | 1m 17.196s | +3.137s | 12 |
| 17 | Jenson Button | Benetton Renault | 1m 17.535s | +3.476s | 12 |
| 18 | Fernando Alonso | European Minardi | 1m 17.624s | +3.565s | 11 |
| 19 | Luciano Burti | Prost Acer | 1m 18.238s | +4.179s | 12 |
| 20 | Enrique Bernoldi | Arrows Asiatech | 1m 18.258s | +4.199s | 11 |
| 21 | Jos Verstappen | Arrows Asiatech | 1m 18.389s | +4.330s | 12 |
| 22 | Tarso Marques | European Minardi | 1m 19.139s | +5.080s | 11 |

## FASTEST SECTOR TIMES IN QUALIFYING *Ideal lap time: 1m 14.059s (diff. from pole: 0.000s)*

| | SECTOR 1 | SECS | | SECTOR 2 | SECS | | SECTOR 3 | SECS |
|---|---|---|---|---|---|---|---|---|
| 1 | M Schumacher | 24.173s | 1 | M Schumacher | 29.441s | 1 | M Schumacher | 20.445s |
| 2 | Coulthard | 24.292s | 2 | Barrichello | 29.750s | 2 | Coulthard | 20.475s |
| 3 | Häkkinen | 24.409s | 3 | Coulthard | 29.830s | 3 | R Schumacher | 20.498s |
| 4 | R Schumacher | 24.429s | 4 | Räikkönen | 29.966s | 4 | Barrichello | 20.553s |
| 5 | Barrichello | 24.488s | 5 | Häkkinen | 29.969s | 5 | Häkkinen | 20.616s |
| 6 | Trulli | 24.555s | 6 | Heidfeld | 29.980s | 6 | Trulli | 20.714s |
| 7 | Heidfeld | 24.597s | 7 | R Schumacher | 30.056s | 7 | Montoya | 20.878s |
| 8 | Montoya | 24.689s | 8 | Trulli | 30.073s | 8 | Heidfeld | 20.899s |
| 9 | Villeneuve | 24.797s | 9 | Montoya | 30.234s | 9 | Panis | 20.970s |
| 10 | Fisichella | 24.824s | 10 | Villeneuve | 30.320s | 10 | Räikkönen | 20.975s |
| 11 | Räikkönen | 24.889s | 11 | Panis | 30.405s | 11 | Irvine | 20.986s |
| 12 | de la Rosa | 24.901s | 12 | Irvine | 30.414s | 12 | de la Rosa | 21.024s |
| 13 | Alesi | 24.921s | 13 | Alesi | 30.474s | 13 | Villeneuve | 21.064s |
| 14 | Irvine | 24.938s | 14 | Fisichella | 30.504s | 14 | Alesi | 21.076s |
| 15 | Frentzen | 24.961s | 15 | de la Rosa | 30.618s | 15 | Fisichella | 21.098s |
| 16 | Button | 24.998s | 16 | Alonso | 30.968s | 16 | Frentzen | 21.224s |
| 17 | Panis | 25.007s | 17 | Button | 30.971s | 17 | Alonso | 21.276s |
| 18 | Burti | 25.258s | 18 | Frentzen | 31.011s | 18 | Button | 21.393s |
| 19 | Alonso | 25.260s | 19 | Bernoldi | 31.097s | 19 | Verstappen | 21.415s |
| 20 | Bernoldi | 25.334s | 20 | Verstappen | 31.400s | 20 | Burti | 21.457s |
| 21 | Verstappen | 25.477s | 21 | Burti | 31.484s | 21 | Marques | 21.624s |
| 22 | Marques | 25.532s | 22 | Marques | 31.855s | 22 | Bernoldi | 21.640s |

## PRACTICE SESSION ONE

FRIDAY 17TH AUGUST 2001, 11AM–12PM

| | | |
|---|---|---|
| 1 | M Schumacher | 1m 16.995s |
| 2 | Barrichello | 1m 17.290s |
| 3 | Häkkinen | 1m 17.606s |
| 4 | Coulthard | 1m 18.182s |
| 5 | R Schumacher | 1m 18.456s |
| 6 | Heidfeld | 1m 18.851s |
| 7 | Trulli | 1m 19.430s |
| 8 | Panis | 1m 19.460s |
| 9 | Villeneuve | 1m 19.707s |
| 10 | Räikkönen | 1m 19.971s |
| 11 | Irvine | 1m 19.996s |
| 12 | Fisichella | 1m 20.308s |
| 13 | Verstappen | 1m 20.706s |
| 14 | Button | 1m 20.935s |
| 15 | de la Rosa | 1m 21.204s |
| 16 | Montoya | 1m 21.211s |
| 17 | Bernoldi | 1m 21.324s |
| 18 | Frentzen | 1m 21.540s |
| 19 | Alesi | 1m 21.590s |
| 20 | Burti | 1m 21.986s |
| 21 | Alonso | 1m 22.215s |
| 22 | Marques | 1m 22.748s |

## PRACTICE SESSION TWO

FRIDAY 17TH AUGUST 2001, 1PM–2PM

| | | |
|---|---|---|
| 1 | M Schumacher | 1m 16.651s |
| 2 | Barrichello | 1m 16.734s |
| 3 | Häkkinen | 1m 16.789s |
| 4 | R Schumacher | 1m 17.308s |
| 5 | Irvine | 1m 17.409s |
| 6 | Alesi | 1m 17.862s |
| 7 | Fisichella | 1m 17.896s |
| 8 | Heidfeld | 1m 17.928s |
| 9 | Panis | 1m 17.970s |
| 10 | Coulthard | 1m 18.182s |
| 11 | de la Rosa | 1m 18.195s |
| 12 | Trulli | 1m 18.277s |
| 13 | Montoya | 1m 18.524s |
| 14 | Frentzen | 1m 18.724s |
| 15 | Räikkönen | 1m 18.834s |
| 16 | Villeneuve | 1m 19.238s |
| 17 | Button | 1m 19.263s |
| 18 | Verstappen | 1m 19.368s |
| 19 | Bernoldi | 1m 19.466s |
| 20 | Alonso | 1m 19.992s |
| 21 | Burti | 1m 20.615s |
| 22 | Marques | 1m 20.981s |

## PRACTICE SESSION THREE

SATURDAY 18TH AUGUST 2001, 9AM–9.45AM

| | | |
|---|---|---|
| 1 | M Schumacher | 1m 15.466s |
| 2 | Barrichello | 1m 15.730s |
| 3 | Häkkinen | 1m 15.839s |
| 4 | Coulthard | 1m 16.204s |
| 5 | Heidfeld | 1m 16.755s |
| 6 | R Schumacher | 1m 16.784s |
| 7 | Panis | 1m 16.941s |
| 8 | Trulli | 1m 17.106s |
| 9 | Montoya | 1m 17.191s |
| 10 | Räikkönen | 1m 17.293s |
| 11 | de la Rosa | 1m 17.549s |
| 12 | Fisichella | 1m 17.551s |
| 13 | Alesi | 1m 17.726s |
| 14 | Villeneuve | 1m 17.837s |
| 15 | Irvine | 1m 17.975s |
| 16 | Button | 1m 18.532s |
| 17 | Frentzen | 1m 18.786s |
| 18 | Verstappen | 1m 18.954s |
| 19 | Bernoldi | 1m 19.281s |
| 20 | Alonso | 1m 20.324s |
| 21 | Burti | 1m 20.617s |
| 22 | Marques | 1m 21.627s |

## PRACTICE SESSION FOUR

SATURDAY 18TH AUGUST 2001, 10.15AM–11AM

| | | |
|---|---|---|
| 1 | Coulthard | 1m 15.263s |
| 2 | M Schumacher | 1m 15.466s |
| 3 | Barrichello | 1m 15.650s |
| 4 | Heidfeld | 1m 15.821s |
| 5 | Häkkinen | 1m 15.839s |
| 6 | Trulli | 1m 16.021s |
| 7 | R Schumacher | 1m 16.033s |
| 8 | Montoya | 1m 16.098s |
| 9 | Irvine | 1m 16.471s |
| 10 | Fisichella | 1m 16.513s |
| 11 | Räikkönen | 1m 16.578s |
| 12 | Panis | 1m 16.581s |
| 13 | Button | 1m 16.619s |
| 14 | Villeneuve | 1m 17.087s |
| 15 | Frentzen | 1m 17.203s |
| 16 | Alesi | 1m 17.334s |
| 17 | de la Rosa | 1m 17.549s |
| 18 | Burti | 1m 17.992s |
| 19 | Alonso | 1m 18.234s |
| 20 | Bernoldi | 1m 18.533s |
| 21 | Verstappen | 1m 18.054s |
| 22 | Marques | 1m 19.153s |

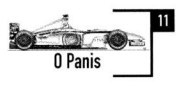
O Panis — 11

K Räikkönen — 9

N Heidfeld — 7

J Trulli — 5

R Barrichello — 3

M Schumacher — 1

J Villeneuve — 10

JP Montoya — 8

M Häkkinen — 6

R Schumacher — 4

D Coulthard — 2

## HUNGARORING LAP-BY-LAP REPORT

**PRE-START** There was big drama during the recognition laps when Michael Schumacher was caught out and went for a ride across a gravel bed. It meant that the Ferrari mechanics were working until the last possible moment to make sure everything was in order. The bargeboards were changed but there was nothing that could be done about the stones that were hidden away in every corner of the sidepods. The only way to get rid of them was for Schumacher to brake hard on the parade lap, which he did, leaving stones bouncing all over the track at the first corner.

**LAP 1** Traditionally in Hungary those on the left side of the grid get better starts, as this is the side of the track that is cleanest because of the constant passage of cars in qualifying and support races. It was no surprise to see Michael Schumacher and Rubens Barrichello get ahead of David Coulthard on the run down to the first corner. Ralf Schumacher was able to hang on to his fourth place, as behind him Jarno Trulli and Nick Heidfeld touched. Both managed to keep going but Heidfeld dropped behind Mika Häkkinen as a result. Further back Eddie Irvine made a mistake and went off into the sandtrap to retire. Jenson Button made a quick start and made up two places but this was later judged to have been too quick and he was given a 10-second stop-go penalty. Jos Verstappen made a very good start to move from 21st on the grid to 15th at the end of the first lap. Tarso Marques was not so lucky – he had a brush with Heinz-Harald Frentzen's Prost on the second corner. At the end of the lap Schumacher was over a second ahead of Rubens Barrichello, with David Coulthard trying to pass the Brazilian. Ralf Schumacher dropped back quickly, unable to keep up with the pace of the three leaders.

**LAP 6** Schumacher's lead remained much the same for the first few laps while Coulthard continued to pressure Barrichello. There was then a big gap back to Ralf Schumacher and a gap from him to Trulli and Häkkinen. The order was unchanged. Button stopped for his penalty, which ruined his afternoon.

**LAP 9** The order was still not changed at the front, although a queue of cars had built up behind Trulli with Häkkinen, Heidfeld, Juan Pablo Montoya and Kimi Räikkönen all being slowed down by the Jordan. At the back of the field Luciano Burti spun off and retired.

**LAP 10** Barrichello's lap time increased by half a second for no apparent reason. This enabled Michael Schumacher to begin to pull away while Coulthard remained trapped behind Barrichello. Frustration got the better of Montoya and he went for a bumpy ride across the grass but managed to rejoin without being overtaken by Räikkönen. At the second corner Jean Alesi pulled off the only real overtaking manoeuvre of the race, snatching 12th position from Pedro de la Rosa.

**LAP 12** Seventeenth-placed Enrique Bernoldi spun his Arrows into retirement.

**LAP 13** Button, trying to make up for his penalty, caught and overtook Marques. He then began chasing after Frentzen's Prost.

**LAP 15** The gap between Michael Schumacher and Rubens Barrichello was up to five seconds.

**LAP 16** Barrichello suddenly dropped his lap time by half a second and was soon matching Schumacher's lap times. But the gap remained the same and Coulthard remained stuck behind Barrichello.

**LAP 18** Heinz-Harald Frentzen was the first man to pit for fuel and tyres. He stayed in 17th place.

**LAP 20** Next to pit was Fernando Alonso, who dropped behind Heinz-Harald Frentzen and Jenson Button.

**LAP 21** Fisichella lost only one place when he pitted, dropping to 15th behind Jos Verstappen.

**LAP 24** Verstappen stopped and fell behind Giancarlo Fisichella and Heinz-Harald Frentzen. At the front traffic had helped Schumacher increase his lead to nearly 10 seconds.

**LAP 26** The first major runner stopped for fuel and tyres. Räikkönen fell behind the two BARs of Olivier Panis and Jacques Villeneuve as well as Jean Alesi's Jordan.

**LAP 27** There was a lot of pit action with Nick Heidfeld, Olivier Panis and Jenson Button all stopping. Heidfeld dropped from eighth to 11th behind Jacques Villeneuve, Jean Alesi and Kimi Räikkönen.

**LAP 28** Rubens Barrichello went into the lead when Michael Schumacher pitted. He rejoined in third place behind David Coulthard but ahead of his brother Ralf.

**LAP 29** Trulli went into the pits and lost five places because of a problem with the nozzle on the refuelling hose.

**LAP 30** Ralf Schumacher held on to fourth place when he pitted. Villeneuve, Alesi and de la Rosa also stopped and shuffled the order in the midfield.

**LAP 31** Coulthard went into the lead when Barrichello stopped. Rubens rejoined in third. Räikkönen made a mistake and ran over a kerb but he did not lose much time and managed to stay ahead of Heidfeld.

**LAP 32** Coulthard pitted and managed to get out ahead of Barrichello to take second place. Montoya also stopped, falling from sixth place to eighth behind the two Saubers. Button continued his catching up by overtaking Alonso to move up to 17th place. The only man who had not stopped was Häkkinen, who was running in fifth.

**LAP 35** Button made a mistake and spun out of the race in the final corner.

**LAP 37** Coulthard's charge to catch Michael Schumacher ended after just five laps, during which he had taken a couple of seconds off the leader.

**LAP 38** Mika Häkkinen pitted and was able to rejoin still ahead of Kimi Räikkönen. At the back of the field Fernando Alonso went out, spinning into a sandtrap.

**LAP 45** The second pitstops began, with Fisichella dropping from 13th to 14th behind de la Rosa.

**LAP 46** Räikkönen stopped again and was overtaken by Heidfeld and Montoya.

**LAP 48** Jarno Trulli stopped and fell from 10th to 12th behind Jacques Villeneuve and Jean Alesi.

**LAP 52** David Coulthard went into the lead again when Michael Schumacher pitted. Ralf Schumacher also stopped and in doing so fell behind Mika Häkkinen.

**LAP 53** Barrichello pitted again, dropping to third behind Michael Schumacher but hoping that Coulthard would have a slow stop so he could reclaim second place.

**LAP 54** Coulthard went into the pits but had a slower stop than he had hoped for and emerged behind Barrichello again. Trulli disappeared with a hydraulic problem.

**LAP 56** McLaren decided to try to keep Häkkinen ahead of Ralf Schumacher and brought in the Finn for a very quick pitstop. But the gamble failed and Häkkinen found himself still behind the Williams and without enough fuel to make it to the finish.

**LAP 57** Panis went into the pits with an electrical problem. The engineers conducted some searches to try to pinpoint the difficulty and 10 laps later sent Panis out again for another exploratory lap. The problem was not solved and Olivier then retired.

**LAP 64** Thirteenth-placed Frentzen spun his Prost into retirement.

**LAP 67** Marques's race ended with an engine problem, which caused the team to order him to switch off the V10 before it blew up.

**LAP 68** Fisichella's race ended with an engine failure. He had been running 12th.

**LAP 71** Häkkinen's strategy was revealed when he rushed into the pits for a splash-and-dash pitstop. He had enough time in hand to stay ahead of Nick Heidfeld.

**LAP 77** Schumacher won his 51st victory to take his fourth world championship title and equal Alain Prost's all-time record of Formula One victories. Barrichello's second place guaranteed Ferrari another constructors' championship. The remaining points went to Coulthard, Ralf Schumacher, Häkkinen and the lapped Heidfeld.

# Belgian Grand Prix

**31st August–2nd September 2001**   LAPS: 36   LENGTH OF LAP: 4.329 miles

MASTER OF SPA–FRANCORCHAMPS  Michael Schumacher's Ferrari is already ahead of the field as the drivers emerge from La Source after the race's third start. The tricky hairpin is one of the most difficult first corners to negotiate in Formula One.  PHOTOGRAPH BY RAINER SCHLEGELMILCH  **491**

There was little opposition to Michael Schumacher winning the Belgian Grand Prix and setting a new record of 52 Grand Prix wins.

The first corner at the Spa-Francorchamps circuit always produces plenty of action and physical contact between cars, as can be seen here when the rear of Jos Verstappen's Arrows is elevated by side wall contact with Nick Heidfeld's Sauber.

## Comedy of errors

**Juan Pablo Montoya, Ralf Schumacher and Heinz-Harald Frentzen performed heroics in qualifying only to blow it completely on the startline and head for the back row – leaving Michael Schumacher with a clear run to a record 52nd victory.**

One start was aborted as fourth man Heinz-Harald Frentzen stalled on the grid. As he went to select first gear he encountered a 'dog-to-dog' situation in the gearbox, which prevented the gear engaging properly. He did not know how to overcome the problem so his engine stalled. Exit one frontrunner, to the back of the grid.

They lined up again, and this time it was Juan Pablo Montoya – who had taken pole position from team-mate Ralf Schumacher after some brilliant pit work by Williams – whose engine stopped. Exit another leading light to the murk of the back row.

Third time around, the race finally got started, but Ralf Schumacher's sprint into the lead was short-lived. On the climb to Les Combes his brother blew him into the weeds. Already the BMW Williams team was wondering what had prompted it to go for a high-drag wet set-up. Barrichello was third, with Fisichella flying to fourth ahead of the McLaren duo, running in numerical order. They were chased in turn by Villeneuve, Räikkönen and Button.

But on lap four came a reminder that, no matter how much thought goes into modern motor racing, the unthinkable can still happen. Luciano Burti was edging alongside Eddie Irvine as they headed for Blanchimont. Irvine cut the Brazilian no slack, leaving him nowhere

to go but half onto the grass on the inside of the curve. The Jaguar was so close that it took off the Prost's front wing. Irvine's race was finished as he spun and lost a wheel.

Meanwhile, Burti was now a passenger as his Prost speared at almost unabated speed into a tyre wall at Blanchimont.

That was when those teams who had benefited from the chaotic start stopped smiling, and those who thought they were anguished when their cars lost places found themselves reconsidering their definition of the word.

Spa-Francorchamps is rarely kind to Grand Prix drivers, although the circuit is more benign than it was in the old days, when it extended over eight dramatic miles of the Ardennes forest.

The sight of Burti's car skimming across the gravel bed and head-on into the tyre wall made those with long memories fear that Spa had reverted to its bad old ways. Few believed he could have survived that sort of accident even two years ago. But cars in 2001 were far stronger. Burti was conscious, though pretty banged about.

The incident was chilling, but its outcome was uplifting: Burti survived his second big crash inside four weeks and his eighth of the season. Better still, his Prost provided a ringing endorsement of all the safety legislation of recent years, emerging with its basic structure intact. What had looked like another tragic chapter turned into a reason for celebration.

The race was stopped, which was the cue for more farce. First Kimi Räikkönen ran back to the pits, hoping to take over the spare Sauber after his had bitten the dust. Somebody eventually told him that the rules precluded that.

After a tussle with Eddie Irvine, Luciano Burti's Prost ended up sickeningly buried in the tyre wall at Blanchimont.

At the restart Ralf Schumacher was left high and dry on the warm-up lap, his BMW Williams still sitting on its low work stands on the grid.

Then Ralf Schumacher's Williams was still up on jacks when the rest of the field set off on the grid formation lap for the new race. Exit yet another star to the back row. It was getting monotonous, though Michael Schumacher wasn't bothered – he was at the front.

The previous four laps were scrubbed, so Burti had crashed out of a race the history books will say he never started.

When the field finally got away it was Michael Schumacher who screamed off into the distance, followed by Giancarlo Fisichella. If you find it hard to believe that Fisichella was running in second, you'll find it even harder to believe that team-mate Jenson Button, courtesy of a great start, was fifth at the time.

For poor Montoya, a day that had promised so much delivered absolutely nothing. After just two laps of the 'new' race his engine gave up the ghost, and his day's work was done.

The first round of pitstops came early, as the new race was to be 36 laps against the original 44, leaving the tacticians a lot of work to do.

David Coulthard spent much of the race shadowing Fisichella but was seemingly unable to find a way past the Benetton. This was particularly strange when you consider how easily the Scot had passed his Italian rival in the first race.

Finally, as the two drivers lapped Jos Verstappen towards the end of the race, Coulthard was able to get it together at Eau Rouge, mustering enough speed to sweep past Fisichella on the approach to Les Combes.

It looked like Eddie Jordan was set to see both of his cars finish in the points with both Jarno Trulli and Jean Alesi looking reasonably good. However, agonisingly close to the end Trulli's engine expired, leaving the Benetton-bound driver to reflect on what might have been.

Alesi, who finished sixth, had his own problem to deal with: Ralf Schumacher. The German had fought his way back through the field, and was all over the Jordan. It was a titanic battle but at the flag it was Alesi who took the point. No surprise there.

Despite finishing in the points, Häkkinen and Barrichello were disappointed with their performances. Häkkinen never seemed to figure in the race, and Barrichello lost time when he hit a bollard, removing his front wing.

Jacques Villeneuve was also disappointed with eighth, while Frentzen reflected on what might have been. It was a disappointing day for Sauber too, with both cars retiring early on, while de la Rosa's retirement, and Irvine's crash, merely added to Jaguar's woes.

Of course there was one event that went according to the script. You guessed it: amid all the mayhem, Michael Schumacher collected the 52nd victory of his career, a new all-time record.

So Häkkinen had another lacklustre race, in stark contrast to last year's blinder. Barrichello blotted his copybook, as did Button, by taking his front wing off on the same Bus Stop chicane entry marker. And Trulli blew up in sight of fifth place. Once Coulthard had passed Fisichella the excitement centred on Ralf Schumacher's fruitless chase of a rejuvenated Jean Alesi for the final point.

And Michael Schumacher? He ran away and hid, of course. It was as if he was driving in a different race. The route to a record 52nd Grand Prix triumph was marred only by a moment's lapse of concentration that nearly put him in the wall at Stavelot. It proved that he's not infallible. But when you're as quick as he is, have his reactions, a car as good as the Ferrari beneath you, and can make Spa your own, what does it matter?

**493**

# Belgian Grand Prix Race Statistics

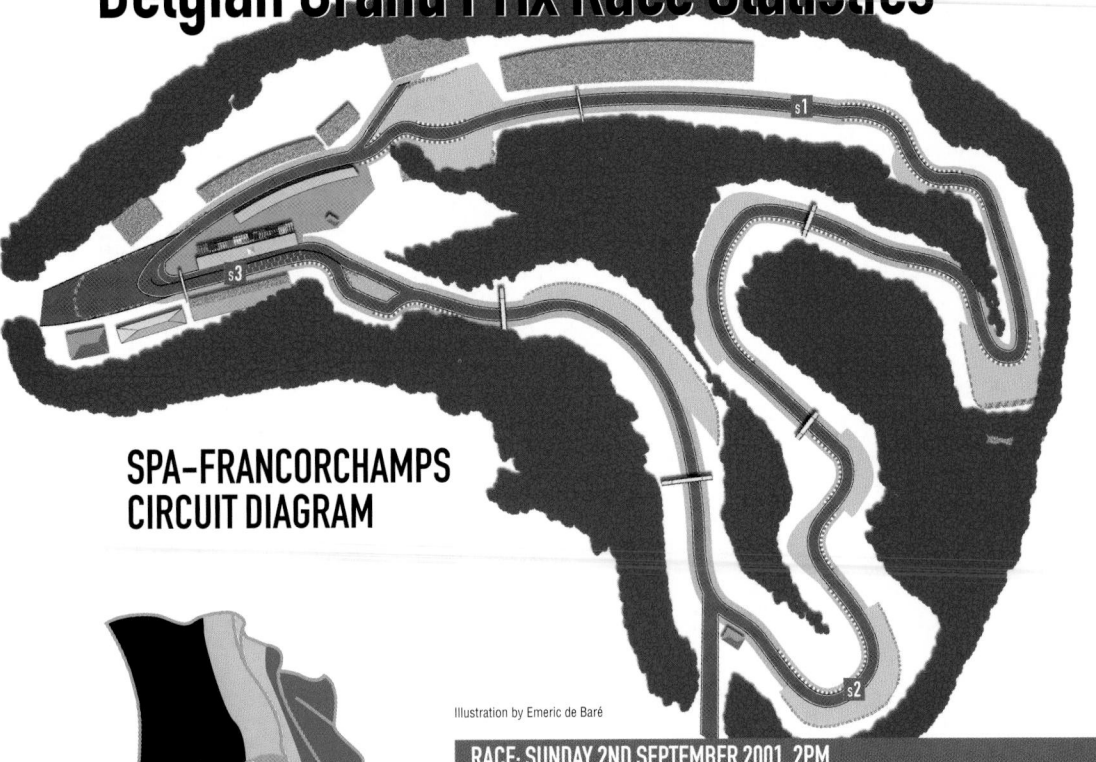

### SPA-FRANCORCHAMPS CIRCUIT DIAGRAM

Illustration by Emeric de Baré

## FASTEST LAPS

| | DRIVER | TIME | LAP |
|---|---|---|---|
| 1 | M Schumacher | 1m 49.758s | 3 |
| 2 | R Schumacher | 1m 51.058s | 21 |
| 3 | Coulthard | 1m 51.608s | 31 |
| 4 | Fisichella | 1m 51.725s | 10 |
| 5 | Häkkinen | 1m 51.741s | 9 |
| 6 | Barrichello | 1m 51.776s | 20 |
| 7 | Trulli | 1m 51.828s | 4 |
| 8 | Alesi | 1m 51.996s | 5 |
| 9 | Villeneuve | 1m 52.372s | 11 |
| 10 | Panis | 1m 52.533s | 24 |
| 11 | Button | 1m 53.409s | 17 |
| 12 | Frentzen | 1m 54.051s | 15 |
| 13 | Verstappen | 1m 54.095s | 4 |
| 14 | Bernoldi | 1m 55.196s | 4 |
| 15 | Marques | 1m 56.484s | 8 |
| 16 | Montoya | 2m 05.821s | 1 |
| 17 | de la Rosa | 3m 49.381s | 1 |
| | Heidfeld | No lap completed | |
| | Räikkönen | Did not take restart | |
| | Irvine | Did not take restart | |
| | Burti | Did not take restart | |
| | Alonso | Did not take restart | |

## RACE SPEED TRAP

| | | |
|---|---|---|
| 1 | Häkkinen | 189.8mph |
| 2 | M Schumacher | 189.3mph |
| 3 | Coulthard | 187.8mph |
| 4 | Alesi | 186.5mph |
| 5 | R Schumacher | 184.9mph |
| = | Barrichello | 184.9mph |
| 7 | Fisichella | 183.6mph |
| 8 | Panis | 183.3mph |
| 9 | Montoya | 182.5mph |
| = | Trulli | 182.5mph |
| 11 | Button | 181.4mph |
| 12 | Frentzen | 179.8mph |
| 13 | Villeneuve | 179.3mph |
| 14 | Verstappen | 178.0mph |
| 15 | de la Rosa | 175.4mph |
| 16 | Bernoldi | 175.1mph |
| 17 | Heidfeld | 173.5mph |
| 18 | Marques | 167.8mph |
| | Räikkönen | Did not take restart |
| | Irvine | Did not take restart |
| | Burti | Did not take restart |
| | Alonso | Did not take restart |

## WARM-UP

SUNDAY 2ND SEPTEMBER 2001, 9.30AM–10AM

| | | |
|---|---|---|
| 1 | M Schumacher | 1m 49.495s |
| 2 | Häkkinen | 1m 50.694s |
| 3 | Räikkönen | 1m 50.738s |
| 4 | R Schumacher | 1m 50.776s |
| 5 | Irvine | 1m 50.818s |
| 6 | Frentzen | 1m 50.908s |
| 7 | Montoya | 1m 50.993s |
| 8 | Trulli | 1m 51.062s |
| 9 | Heidfeld | 1m 51.317s |
| 10 | Barrichello | 1m 51.394s |
| 11 | de la Rosa | 1m 51.418s |
| 12 | Coulthard | 1m 51.750s |
| 13 | Alesi | 1m 52.338s |
| 14 | Fisichella | 1m 52.436s |
| 15 | Alonso | 1m 52.479s |
| 16 | Panis | 1m 52.519s |
| 17 | Villeneuve | 1m 52.903s |
| 18 | Marques | 1m 52.908s |
| 19 | Burti | 1m 53.083s |
| 20 | Verstappen | 1m 53.737s |
| 21 | Bernoldi | 1m 54.472s |
| 22 | Button | 2m 34.526s |

## DRIVER POINTS

| | | |
|---|---|---|
| 1 | Michael Schumacher | 104 |
| 2 | David Coulthard | 57 |
| 3 | Rubens Barrichello | 48 |
| 4 | Ralf Schumacher | 44 |
| 5 | Mika Häkkinen | 24 |
| 6 | Juan Pablo Montoya | 15 |
| 7 | Jacques Villeneuve | 11 |
| 8 | Nick Heidfeld | 11 |
| 9 | Kimi Räikkönen | 9 |
| 10 | Jarno Trulli | 9 |
| 11 | Giancarlo Fisichella | 8 |
| 12 | Heinz-Harald Frentzen | 6 |
| 13 | Olivier Panis | 5 |
| 14 | Jean Alesi | 5 |
| 15 | Eddie Irvine | 4 |
| 16 | Jenson Button | 2 |
| 17 | Jos Verstappen | 1 |
| 18 | Pedro de la Rosa | 1 |
| 19 | Ricardo Zonta | 0 |
| 20 | Luciano Burti | 0 |
| 21 | Enrique Bernoldi | 0 |
| 22 | Tarso Marques | 0 |
| 23 | Fernando Alonso | 0 |
| 24 | Gaston Mazzacane | 0 |

## RACE: SUNDAY 2ND SEPTEMBER 2001, 2PM

| | DRIVER | CAR | TIME/RETIREMENT | LAPS | PITSTOP LAPS |
|---|---|---|---|---|---|
| 1 | Michael Schumacher | Ferrari | 1h 08m 05.002s | 36 | 10 25 |
| 2 | David Coulthard | McLaren Mercedes | +10.098s | 36 | 10 24 |
| 3 | Giancarlo Fisichella | Benetton Renault | +27.742s | 36 | 11 23 |
| 4 | Mika Häkkinen | McLaren Mercedes | +36.087s | 36 | 7 23 |
| 5 | Rubens Barrichello | Ferrari | +54.521s | 36 | 9 18 |
| 6 | Jean Alesi | Jordan Honda | +59.684s | 36 | 7 20 |
| 7 | Ralf Schumacher | BMW Williams | +59.986s | 36 | 9 25 |
| 8 | Jacques Villeneuve | BAR Honda | +1m 04.970s | 36 | 9 21 |
| 9 | Heinz-Harald Frentzen | Prost Acer | +1 lap | 35 | 16 |
| 10 | Jos Verstappen | Arrows Asiatech | +1 lap | 35 | 8 22 |
| 11 | Olivier Panis | BAR Honda | +1 lap | 35 | 7 12 21 |
| 12 | Enrique Bernoldi | Arrows Asiatech | +1 lap | 35 | 9 24 |
| 13 | Tarso Marques | European Minardi | +5 laps | 31 | 9 15 16 17 |
| Ret | Jarno Trulli | Jordan Honda | Engine | 31 | 6 19 |
| Ret | Jenson Button | Benetton Renault | Spin | 17 | 10 |
| Ret | Juan Pablo Montoya | BMW Williams | Engine | 1 | |
| Ret | Pedro de la Rosa | Jaguar Racing | Collision/suspension | 1 | |
| Ret | Nick Heidfeld | Sauber Petronas | Collision/suspension | 0 | |
| DNS | Kimi Räikkönen | Sauber Petronas | Transmission | 0 (5) | |
| DNS | Eddie Irvine | Jaguar Racing | Collision | 0 (4) | |
| DNS | Luciano Burti | Prost Acer | Collision | 0 (4) | |
| DNS | Fernando Alonso | European Minardi | Gearbox | 0 (3) | |

*Conditions: overcast*

## PITSTOP TIMES (from pitlane entrance to exit)

| | | | | |
|---|---|---|---|---|
| Fastest pitstop: | David Coulthard | McLaren Mercedes | 28.483s | Lap 10 |
| Slowest pitstop: | Tarso Marques | European Minardi | 4m 23.621s | Lap 17 |
| Most pitstops: | Tarso Marques | Four stops | | |

## PENALTIES AND FINES

| DRIVER/TEAM | WHEN | PENALTY | REASON |
|---|---|---|---|
| Olivier Panis | Race | 10 seconds | Crossing white line in pitlane |

## LAP LEADERS

| | |
|---|---|
| Michael Schumacher | 36 |
| Total laps led: M Schumacher | 36 |

## TEMPERATURES

| | | |
|---|---|---|
| Friday: | Air: 14°C | Track: 13°C |
| Saturday: | Air: 14°C | Track: 13°C |
| Sunday: | Air: 17°C | Track: 21°C |

## CONSTRUCTOR POINTS

| | | |
|---|---|---|
| 1 | Scuderia Ferrari-Marlboro | 152 |
| 2 | West McLaren Mercedes | 81 |
| 3 | BMW Williams F1 | 59 |
| 4 | Red Bull Sauber Petronas | 20 |
| 5 | Lucky Strike Reynard BAR Honda | 16 |
| 6 | Benson & Hedges Jordan Honda | 16 |
| 7 | Mild Seven Benetton Renault | 10 |
| 8 | Jaguar Racing | 5 |
| 9 | Prost Acer | 4 |
| 10 | Orange Arrows Asiatech | 1 |
| 11 | European Minardi F1 | 0 |

E Bernoldi 21

J Verstappen 19

E Irvine 17

J Button 15

J Alesi 13

T Marques 22

F Alonso 20

L Burti 18

J Trulli 16

N Heidfeld 14

K Räikkönen 12

## BELGIAN GRAND PRIX RACE ENTRY

| | DRIVER | TEAM | CHASSIS/ENGINE |
|---|---|---|---|
| 1 | Michael Schumacher | Scuderia Ferrari Marlboro | Ferrari F2001 |
| 2 | Rubens Barrichello | Scuderia Ferrari Marlboro | Ferrari F2001 |
| 3 | Mika Häkkinen | West McLaren Mercedes | McLaren Mercedes MP4-16 |
| 4 | David Coulthard | West McLaren Mercedes | McLaren Mercedes MP4-16 |
| 5 | Ralf Schumacher | BMW Williams F1 Team | BMW Williams FW23 |
| 6 | Juan Pablo Montoya | BMW Williams F1 Team | BMW Williams FW23 |
| 7 | Giancarlo Fisichella | Mild Seven Benetton Renault | Benetton Renault B201 |
| 8 | Jenson Button | Mild Seven Benetton Renault | Benetton Renault B201 |
| 9 | Olivier Panis | Lucky Strike BAR Honda | BAR Honda B003 |
| 10 | Jacques Villeneuve | Lucky Strike BAR Honda | BAR Honda B003 |
| 11 | Jarno Trulli | Benson & Hedges Jordan Honda | Jordan Honda EJ11 |
| 12 | Jean Alesi | Benson & Hedges Jordan Honda | Jordan Honda EJ11 |
| 14 | Jos Verstappen | Orange Arrows Asiatech | Arrows Asiatech A22 |
| 15 | Enrique Bernoldi | Orange Arrows Asiatech | Arrows Asiatech A22 |
| 16 | Nick Heidfeld | Red Bull Sauber Petronas | Sauber Petronas C20 |
| 17 | Kimi Räikkönen | Red Bull Sauber Petronas | Sauber Petronas C20 |
| 18 | Eddie Irvine | Jaguar Racing | Jaguar Cosworth R2 |
| 19 | Pedro de la Rosa | Jaguar Racing | Jaguar Cosworth R2 |
| 20 | Tarso Marques | European Minardi | Minardi European PS01B |
| 21 | Fernando Alonso | European Minardi | Minardi European PS01B |
| 22 | Heinz-Harald Frentzen | Prost Grand Prix | Prost ACER AP04 |
| 23 | Luciano Burti | Prost Grand Prix | Prost ACER AP04 |

David Coulthard celebrates with Michael Schumacher on the podium.

## FASTEST SECTOR TIMES IN QUALIFYING
Ideal lap time: 1m 52.072s (diff. from pole: 0.000s)

| | SECTOR 1 | SECS | | SECTOR 2 | SECS | | SECTOR 3 | SECS |
|---|---|---|---|---|---|---|---|---|
| 1 | Montoya | 30.952s | 1 | Montoya | 50.890s | 1 | Montoya | 30.230s |
| 2 | R Schumacher | 31.370s | 2 | R Schumacher | 50.919s | 2 | R Schumacher | 30.670s |
| 3 | Frentzen | 31.436s | 3 | M Schumacher | 52.391s | 3 | M Schumacher | 30.839s |
| 4 | M Schumacher | 31.455s | 4 | Frentzen | 52.571s | 4 | Frentzen | 31.226s |
| 5 | Barrichello | 31.505s | 5 | Häkkinen | 52.959s | 5 | Barrichello | 31.239s |
| 6 | Coulthard | 31.707s | 6 | Villeneuve | 53.028s | 6 | Villeneuve | 31.254s |
| 7 | Häkkinen | 31.889s | 7 | Barrichello | 53.372s | 7 | Häkkinen | 31.702s |
| 8 | Alesi | 31.905s | 8 | Fisichella | 53.621s | 8 | Fisichella | 31.739s |
| 9 | de la Rosa | 32.027s | 9 | Coulthard | 54.086s | 9 | Coulthard | 31.823s |
| 10 | Räikkönen | 32.143s | 10 | Panis | 54.123s | 10 | Alesi | 31.874s |
| 11 | Verstappen | 32.184s | 11 | de la Rosa | 54.403s | 11 | Burti | 31.932s |
| 12 | Irvine | 32.250s | 12 | Räikkönen | 54.482s | 12 | Button | 32.025s |
| 13 | Fisichella | 32.308s | 13 | Trulli | 54.704s | 13 | Irvine | 32.069s |
| 14 | Burti | 32.336s | 14 | Heidfeld | 54.728s | 14 | de la Rosa | 32.089s |
| 15 | Bernoldi | 32.344s | 15 | Button | 54.798s | 15 | Heidfeld | 32.101s |
| 16 | Trulli | 32.398s | 16 | Bernoldi | 54.826s | 16 | Räikkönen | 32.172s |
| 17 | Heidfeld | 32.447s | 17 | Irvine | 54.990s | 17 | Panis | 32.228s |
| 18 | Panis | 32.487s | 18 | Alesi | 55.349s | 18 | Trulli | 32.235s |
| 19 | Villeneuve | 32.756s | 19 | Burti | 55.632s | 19 | Verstappen | 32.871s |
| 20 | Button | 32.764s | 20 | Alonso | 55.869s | 20 | Bernoldi | 33.184s |
| 21 | Alonso | 32.845s | 21 | Marques | 56.269s | 21 | Marques | 33.243s |
| 22 | Marques | 33.116s | 22 | Verstappen | 56.421s | 22 | Alonso | 33.277s |

## QUALIFYING: SATURDAY 1ST SEPTEMBER 2001, 1PM
107 per cent time: 1m 59.917s

| | DRIVER | TEAM | TIME | GAP | LAPS |
|---|---|---|---|---|---|
| 1 | Juan Pablo Montoya | BMW Williams | 1m 52.072s | 0.000 | 7 |
| 2 | Ralf Schumacher | BMW Williams | 1m 52.959s | +0.887s | 10 |
| 3 | Michael Schumacher | Ferrari | 1m 54.685s | +2.613s | 8 |
| 4 | Heinz-Harald Frentzen | Prost Acer | 1m 55.233s | +3.161s | 10 |
| 5 | Rubens Barrichello | Ferrari | 1m 56.116s | +4.044s | 7 |
| 6 | Jacques Villeneuve | BAR Honda | 1m 57.038s | +4.966s | 11 |
| 7 | Mika Häkkinen | McLaren Mercedes | 1m 57.043s | +4.971s | 12 |
| 8 | Giancarlo Fisichella | Benetton Renault | 1m 57.668s | +5.596s | 7 |
| 9 | David Coulthard | McLaren Mercedes | 1m 58.008s | +5.936s | 10 |
| 10 | Pedro de la Rosa | Jaguar Racing | 1m 58.519s | +6.447s | 11 |
| 11 | Olivier Panis | BAR Honda | 1m 58.838s | +6.766s | 8 |
| 12 | Kimi Räikkönen | Sauber Petronas | 1m 59.050s | +6.978s | 8 |
| 13 | Jean Alesi | Jordan Honda | 1m 59.128s | +7.056s | 10 |
| 14 | Nick Heidfeld | Sauber Petronas | 1m 59.302s | +7.230s | 9 |
| 15 | Jenson Button | Benetton Renault | 1m 59.587s | +7.515s | 7 |
| 16 | Jarno Trulli | Jordan Honda | 1m 59.647s | +7.575s | 10 |
| 17 | Eddie Irvine | Jaguar Racing | 1m 59.689s | +7.617s | 9 |
| 18 | Luciano Burti | Prost Acer | 1m 59.900s | +7.828s | 7 |
| 19 | Jos Verstappen | Arrows Asiatech | 2m 02.039s | +9.967s | 10 |
| 20 | Fernando Alonso | European Minardi | 2m 02.594s | +10.522s | 8 |
| 21 | Enrique Bernoldi | Arrows Asiatech | 2m 03.048s | +10.976s | 10 |
| 22 | Tarso Marques | European Minardi | 2m 04.204s | +12.132s | 10 |

*Conditions: wet then drying later on. The Arrows Asiatech and European Minardi drivers did not make the 107% time but were allowed to race due to 'exceptional circumstances'.*

## PRACTICE SESSION ONE
FRIDAY 31ST AUGUST 2001, 11AM-12PM

| | | |
|---|---|---|
| 1 | M Schumacher | 1m 48.655s |
| 2 | Trulli | 1m 49.404s |
| 3 | Barrichello | 1m 49.456s |
| 4 | Häkkinen | 1m 50.239s |
| 5 | R Schumacher | 1m 50.801s |
| 6 | Alesi | 1m 51.631s |
| 7 | Räikkönen | 1m 51.645s |
| 8 | Heidfeld | 1m 52.436s |
| 9 | Montoya | 1m 52.829s |
| 10 | Fisichella | 1m 52.943s |
| 11 | Verstappen | 1m 52.955s |
| 12 | Irvine | 1m 53.087s |
| 13 | Frentzen | 1m 53.320s |
| 14 | Panis | 1m 53.807s |
| 15 | de la Rosa | 1m 54.352s |
| 16 | Button | 1m 54.711s |
| 17 | Alonso | 1m 55.329s |
| 18 | Bernoldi | 1m 55.491s |
| 19 | Marques | 1m 56.194s |
| 20 | Villeneuve | 1m 57.639s |
| 21 | Burti | 10m 43.872s |
| 22 | Coulthard | 12m 37.913s |

## PRACTICE SESSION TWO
FRIDAY 31ST AUGUST 2001, 12PM-1PM

| | | |
|---|---|---|
| 1 | M Schumacher | 1m 48.655s |
| 2 | Trulli | 1m 49.404s |
| 3 | Barrichello | 1m 49.456s |
| 4 | Fisichella | 1m 50.192s |
| 5 | Häkkinen | 1m 50.239s |
| 6 | Räikkönen | 1m 50.495s |
| 7 | R Schumacher | 1m 50.801s |
| 8 | Irvine | 1m 51.555s |
| 9 | Alesi | 1m 51.631s |
| 10 | Button | 1m 51.673s |
| 11 | Panis | 1m 52.071s |
| 12 | Frentzen | 1m 52.073s |
| 13 | de la Rosa | 1m 52.119s |
| 14 | Heidfeld | 1m 52.436s |
| 15 | Villeneuve | 1m 52.804s |
| 16 | Montoya | 1m 52.829s |
| 17 | Verstappen | 1m 52.955s |
| 18 | Alonso | 1m 55.021s |
| 19 | Marques | 1m 55.099s |
| 20 | Bernoldi | 1m 55.491s |
| 21 | Burti | 2m 11.037s |
| 22 | Coulthard | 12m 37.913s |

## PRACTICE SESSION THREE
SATURDAY 1ST SEPT. 2001, 11AM-11.45AM

| | | |
|---|---|---|
| 1 | Montoya | 1m 47.494s |
| 2 | R Schumacher | 1m 47.768s |
| 3 | Häkkinen | 1m 48.465s |
| 4 | Coulthard | 1m 48.698s |
| 5 | Barrichello | 1m 49.071s |
| 6 | Fisichella | 1m 49.511s |
| 7 | Irvine | 1m 49.857s |
| 8 | Villeneuve | 1m 49.953s |
| 9 | Button | 1m 50.130s |
| 10 | Alesi | 1m 50.485s |
| 11 | Trulli | 1m 50.494s |
| 12 | Panis | 1m 50.501s |
| 13 | Frentzen | 1m 50.765s |
| 14 | de la Rosa | 1m 52.267s |
| 15 | Burti | 1m 52.740s |
| 16 | Bernoldi | 1m 52.906s |
| 17 | Alonso | 1m 53.546s |
| 18 | Marques | 1m 53.861s |
| 19 | M Schumacher | 1m 57.257s |
| 20 | Verstappen | 1m 57.477s |
| 21 | Räikkönen | 1m 58.547s |
| 22 | Heidfeld | 2m 55.816s |

## PRACTICE SESSION FOUR
SATURDAY 1ST SEPTEMBER 2001

Only one practice session was held on Saturday due to heavy fog preventing medical helicopters flying in.

O Panis — 11

D Coulthard — 9

M Häkkinen — 7

R Barrichello — 5

M Schumacher — 3

JP Montoya — 1

P de la Rosa — 10

G Fisichella — 8

J Villeneuve — 6

HH Frentzen — 4

R Schumacher — 2

## SPA-FRANCORCHAMPS LAP-BY-LAP REPORT

**PRE-START** Alain Prost's hopes of a good result evaporated even before the start when Heinz-Harald Frentzen, who was fourth on the grid, stalled. At the back the same happened to Tarso Marques so the start was aborted and both drivers sent to the back of the grid. As the field went off on its second parade lap, pole man Juan Pablo Montoya was left behind, his engine dead, and was forced to start at the back as well. This left the Schumacher brothers with no real rivals for the top two slots at the start.

**LAP 1** Ralf Schumacher took the lead but brother Michael soon overtook him for first place. Barrichello was third and Fisichella fourth (from eighth). Initially Villeneuve was fifth but then both Häkkinen and Coulthard overtook him. The fast-starting Button was up to eighth (from 15th) before being re-passed by Räikkönen. Pedro de la Rosa completed the top 10. By the end of the lap Michael Schumacher had built a lead of over two seconds on his brother.

**LAP 2** Schumacher added another 1.3 seconds to his lead. Barrichello tried to challenge Ralf for second place but then there was a big gap back to Fisichella, who was under pressure from both McLarens. Alesi moved into the top 10 by overtaking Panis and de la Rosa. Montoya passed Verstappen for 16th place, having gone through the other backmarkers on the first lap.

**LAP 3** Schumacher added another 1.9 seconds to his lead. Fisichella ran out of steam going up the hill and both McLarens went ahead, leaving Giancarlo in sixth. At the same time Räikkönen overtook Villeneuve to take seventh, and Trulli overtook Irvine for 14th. Alonso, last, retired with gearbox failure.

**LAP 4** Schumacher added another second to his lead while Alesi overtook Button for ninth. Panis also dropped a couple of places being overtaken for 12th by Heidfeld and then Trulli. Montoya made quick work of Irvine, who was left holding off Burti until they arrived at the fast left-hander before Blanchimont. Burti challenged Irvine on the inside and was nearly level when Irvine pulled across to take his line. Burti had nowhere to go and the Prost careered off the track and into a barrier. Irvine's car also crashed but the Jaguar driver was unhurt. Burti's car, however, was barely visible beneath the tyre barrier it had hit. A safety car was dispatched and the medical cars raced to the scene. Meanwhile Frentzen took advantage of the safety car, heading for the pits to take on fuel and allow for a one-stop race. Marques also pitted with a puncture caused by wreckage at the scene. As the cars slowed down behind the safety car Räikkönen suffered a transmission failure and stopped. When it became clear that extracting Burti was going to be difficult the race was red-flagged. It was not until a course car arrived and attached a rope to the Prost that it was pulled out from under the tyres. Burti was conscious and after an initial inspection was flown to the University Hospital in Liege, where he was given a brain scan to check that he had no damage beyond concussion. On the grid there was confusion, as not everyone knew the rules about race stoppages. The grid for the new race was established by the finishing order of the first but the gaps between the racers were discounted to avoid aggregate results. Several teams had damage to repair, notably Williams. Montoya's car had a broken rear wing support. This was changed and the team then decided to do the same to Ralf Schumacher's car. This was done but the team ran out of time before the start of the new parade lap and Ralf was left sitting on jacks as the field headed off. Bernoldi was also late away as the Arrows mechanics were still working on the car.

**RESTART** With Ralf Schumacher gone, the two Ferraris were one-two on the grid with the two McLarens next up, but Fisichella once again made a sensational start and almost took the lead. Button too made a great start, moving into fourth behind Michael, Fisichella and Barrichello. Häkkinen was briefly ahead of Coulthard before the Scotsman passed him and Button. Behind Häkkinen a number of cars made contact with one another. Verstappen knocked into Heidfeld who hit de la Rosa who in turn hit Montoya. The man who gained the biggest advantage from this was Panis but at Les Combes his team-mate Villeneuve went off and in rejoining cut across in front of Panis, causing him to go off. At the end of the lap

Schumacher was nearly four seconds ahead of Fisichella with Barrichello and Coulthard stuck behind him. Button was still ahead of Häkkinen and then came Trulli, Alesi, Villeneuve, Verstappen and Panis. The two Williams-BMWs were next with the field being completed by Frentzen, Bernoldi and Marques. Heidfeld was out with suspension damage, and so was de la Rosa.

**LAP 2** Schumacher's lead increased to nearly six seconds while behind him the pattern remained the same, although Häkkinen got the better of Button and moved to fifth place. Montoya's engine broke.

**LAP 3** Schumacher's lead went up to eight seconds while Trulli passed Button.

**LAP 4** Button was pushed back to eighth place by Alesi in the second Jordan.

**LAP 6** Schumacher's lead increased to 14 seconds as Fisichella continued to hold up Barrichello. Trulli made a pitstop and was overtaken by Alesi, Villeneuve, Button, Verstappen, Ralf Schumacher and Panis.

**LAP 7** Häkkinen, Alesi and Panis all stopped. Häkkinen rejoined behind Ralf Schumacher, while Alesi found himself behind Verstappen. Panis crossed the white line while accelerating out of the pits and was later given a 10-second stop-go penalty for his misdemeanour.

**LAP 8** Verstappen, who was in 10th, stopped and fell back to second-to-last place.

**LAP 9** The pits were again busy with Barrichello, Villeneuve, Ralf Schumacher, Bernoldi and Marques all stopping. The order at the front was Michael Schumacher, Fisichella, Coulthard, Button, Häkkinen, Barrichello and Trulli.

**LAP 10** Michael Schumacher stopped and Fisichella took the lead. Coulthard and Button also pitted. Schumacher rejoined in second with Coulthard third, Häkkinen fourth, Barrichello fifth and Trulli sixth. There was then a gap to Alesi. Villeneuve was eighth with Frentzen and Button behind him. Then came Ralf Schumacher, Panis and Verstappen. Bernoldi and Marques were a long way behind but still running.

**LAP 11** Fisichella pitted and Michael Schumacher went back into a lead of 20 seconds. Fisichella exited the pits ahead of the rest and stayed in second.

**LAP 12** Panis's miserable race continued as he stopped for his 10-second penalty.

**LAP 15** Marques went into the pits to have his suspension checked as the car was handling oddly. He subsequently pitted three times trying to cure the problem.

**LAP 16** Frentzen pitted and dropped behind Button, Ralf Schumacher and Verstappen.

**LAP 17** Michael Schumacher, in the lead by 25 seconds, lost concentration and ran wide at Stavelot but managed to avoid having an accident. At the end of the lap Barrichello ran into a marker cone at the entry to the chicane and lost the front wing. He had to do a full lap before stopping.

**LAP 18** Barrichello pitted and rejoined in ninth. At the chicane, Button made the same mistake as Barrichello and his front wing came off. The car ran into the wall.

**LAP 19** Trulli made a second stop, falling behind Alesi, Villeneuve and Ralf Schumacher.

**LAP 20** Alesi pitted and was passed by Villeneuve, Ralf Schumacher and Trulli.

**LAP 21** Villeneuve took his turn in the pitlane but had a problem with the nozzle on the refuelling hose and dropped behind Ralf Schumacher, Trulli, Alesi and even the recovering Barrichello. Panis also stopped and lost yet more time.

**LAP 22** Verstappen had his second stop and was overtaken by Frentzen.

**LAP 23** Fisichella and Häkkinen both stopped again, rejoining in third and fourth.

**LAP 24** Coulthard pitted and fell behind Fisichella again.

**LAP 25** Michael Schumacher came into the pits and departed without drama. His lead was still half a minute. Fisichella was second with Coulthard right on his tail. There was then a 10-second gap back to Häkkinen. Ralf Schumacher pitted and dropped behind Trulli, Alesi, Barrichello and Villeneuve.

**LAP 28** As they lapped Bernoldi, Fisichella lost a little momentum and Coulthard managed to get ahead of the Benetton at Les Combes.

**LAP 29** Ralf made short work of Villeneuve and began chasing Barrichello.

**LAP 32** Trulli retired with engine failure, leaving Barrichello free to overtake Alesi for fifth. Ralf and Alesi then began a desperate fight for the final point.

**LAP 36** Michael Schumacher won his 52nd Grand Prix to become the most successful driver in the championship's history. In the final laps he let his lead dwindle to 15 seconds. Coulthard was second, 15 seconds clear of Fisichella, with Häkkinen 10 seconds behind the Benetton. There was a 20 second gap back to Barrichello and a five second gap from him to Alesi and Ralf.

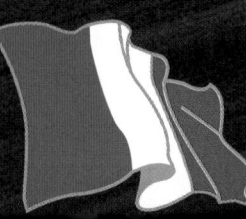

# Italian Grand Prix

**14th–16th September 2001**   LAPS: 53   LENGTH OF LAP: 3.6 miles

POWERING TO VICTORY On the fast Monza circuit the BMW–Williams–Michelin package was the class of the field. Juan Pablo Montoya finally took his first Grand Prix victory, at one of racing's most famous tracks. He is only the seventh driver to do so in a debut season. PHOTOGRAPH BY RAINER SCHLEGELMILCH

Montoya celebrates his first Formula One victory.

Barrichello was a potential winner but his pitstop ruined his chances.

Mayhem at the first corner as Trulli spins after being rammed by an impetuous Button's Benetton.

# A question of balance

Michael Schumacher's go-slow policy heralds a much-anticipated first Grand Prix victory for Juan Pablo Montoya.

Michael Schumacher looked very second-rate all weekend as the events in New York threw him, as well as a lot of other people, off-balance.

Both Schumacher brothers looked uninspired. They did not appear to want to be at Monza at all, and on Sunday Michael tried to organise that the drivers would not overtake one another in the first two chicanes and go slowly at the start. Jacques Villeneuve refused and the plan crumbled.

The memories of what happened here 12 months ago when a marshal was killed were still fresh in the mind, but Monza was passed as safe by the FIA. Schumacher's lobbying was an odd thing for a racing driver to do.

McLaren boss Ron Dennis said he would support his drivers in whatever they wanted to do, but he didn't think that half an hour before the race was the right time to be contemplating the safety or otherwise of chicanes at Monza.

Flavio Briatore, meanwhile, was much more vociferous. "If my drivers don't want to overtake on the first lap they can look for another team next year," he stormed.

Bernie Ecclestone put immense pressure on the drivers to fulfil their contracts and race. His view prevailed. Michael Schumacher,

personally furious about drivers being pressured into a situation against their will, took it upon himself to go on a grid walk advocating first lap caution among his colleagues. But the driver's move to start the race with no overtaking in the first two chicanes was abandoned after team bosses pressured their drivers not to conform and it was agreed that, without unanimity, it couldn't go ahead. They all duly went wheel-to-wheel through the high-speed Lesmo corners and came out the other side intact.

At the race start, there was no evidence of any lack of commitment among the drivers, and noticeably perhaps one of Briatore's. A fast-starting Jenson Button was up to sixth at the first chicane, but took his nose off against the back of Jarno Trulli's Jordan, which spun the B&H car into retirement.

Ralf Schumacher never looked like beating Juan Pablo Montoya. And Mika Häkkinen had a good reason not to perform as his career was over. It was left to Montoya and Rubens Barrichello to supply the drama. Montoya on pole and Barrichello second chose different strategies: Montoya won his first Grand Prix at Monza on a day when BMW Williams F1 opted for a one-stop strategy and Ferrari went with two.

Montoya led early on but then Barrichello overtook him and pulled quickly away with a much lighter fuel load. In 10 laps he built a lead of 10 seconds and dived for the pits. There was a problem with the refuelling rig and six or seven precious seconds were lost in the pit-lane. If that had not happened he would have been ahead of Montoya.

In the laps that followed, the gap between the two men widened from 23.4 seconds on lap 20 to 25.8 seconds on lap 27. It was not a

Kimi Räikkönen has a big off during Friday's practice, narrowly missing Alex Yoong's parked Minardi.

Trulli's Jordan and Häkkinen's McLaren sit out the race behind the barriers after both drivers retired.

massive leap, but then Montoya by that time knew he did not have to worry too much; in addition, he was struggling a bit with oversteer. At the pitstop he had the front wing tweaked by the mechanics which meant that at the end of the race he had way too much understeer.

Barrichello, meanwhile, settled for second place and was disappointed with that. Michael Schumacher ended up fourth – which is a rare thing indeed – and his post-race comments were short and not very sweet.

Behind these three there was not much left. McLaren went boom. David Coulthard was gone in a cloud of smoke on lap seven. Häkkinen drove across the first chicane to avoid hitting anyone, which dropped him from seventh on the grid to 13th place and he never really recovered. He did 20 laps and then the car lost all its gears.

Some 50 seconds behind Schumacher, Pedro de la Rosa turned in a fine drive to claim two points for Jaguar, and Jacques Villeneuve grabbed a point for British American Racing, moving the team into lone fifth place in the constructors' championship, a point ahead of Jordan and three behind fourth-placed Sauber.

Kimi Räikkönen finished seventh, right on Villeneuve's gearbox, for the Swiss team. Olivier Panis made little impression all afternoon and finished ninth. It was another poor day for the Honda teams with Jarno Trulli, who had done a good job to qualify fifth, being punted off at the first corner by a rather over-enthusiastic Jenson Button – his future team-mate.

Jean Alesi was a good 10th at the end of the first lap and was sixth by lap 12. He was fifth when he made his pitstop on lap 22 and dropped back to seventh, but during his second stint he flat-spotted a tyre massively at one point and so had to pit earlier than he wanted to, worried that the tyre might even go bang. And so he lost out and ended up eighth.

Räikkönen had looked set for points, but an early pitstop (with a one-stop strategy) left him stuck behind a bunch of cars: he could only crawl back up to seventh. Nick Heidfeld had even less to write home about. He lost hydraulic pressure on the grid, so had to take the spare and start from the pitlane. He finished 11th as a result.

Between Alesi and Heidfeld at the finish was Giancarlo Fisichella, who had also started from the pits because of a fuel leak. He then had traction-control trouble and had to struggle through the race.

The only Prost to finish belonged to debutant Tomas Enge. His was a good effort to make it home in 12th place.

Heinz-Harald Frentzen had a bad first lap and lost a lot of places, and so found himself 15th (from 12th on the grid). He retired on lap 29 when the gearbox failed while he was running ninth.

Minardi managed to get Fernando Alonso home in 13th place but debutant Alex Yoong had a rather more exciting race. He had a hair-raising spin in the Lesmos on lap 16 and then did it again with eight laps to go and this time retired.

Arrows ran light fuel loads as always and so made an impression early on with Jos Verstappen going from 19th on the grid to fifth in the course of seven laps. But then, of course, he had to stop early and that sent him tumbling all the way back to 15th. He was in the process of doing it all over again when his engine stopped working. Enrique Bernoldi went for a one-stop strategy (which must have been marginal) and was running in 13th when his engine stopped as well.

# Italian Grand Prix Race Statistics

## MONZA CIRCUIT DIAGRAM

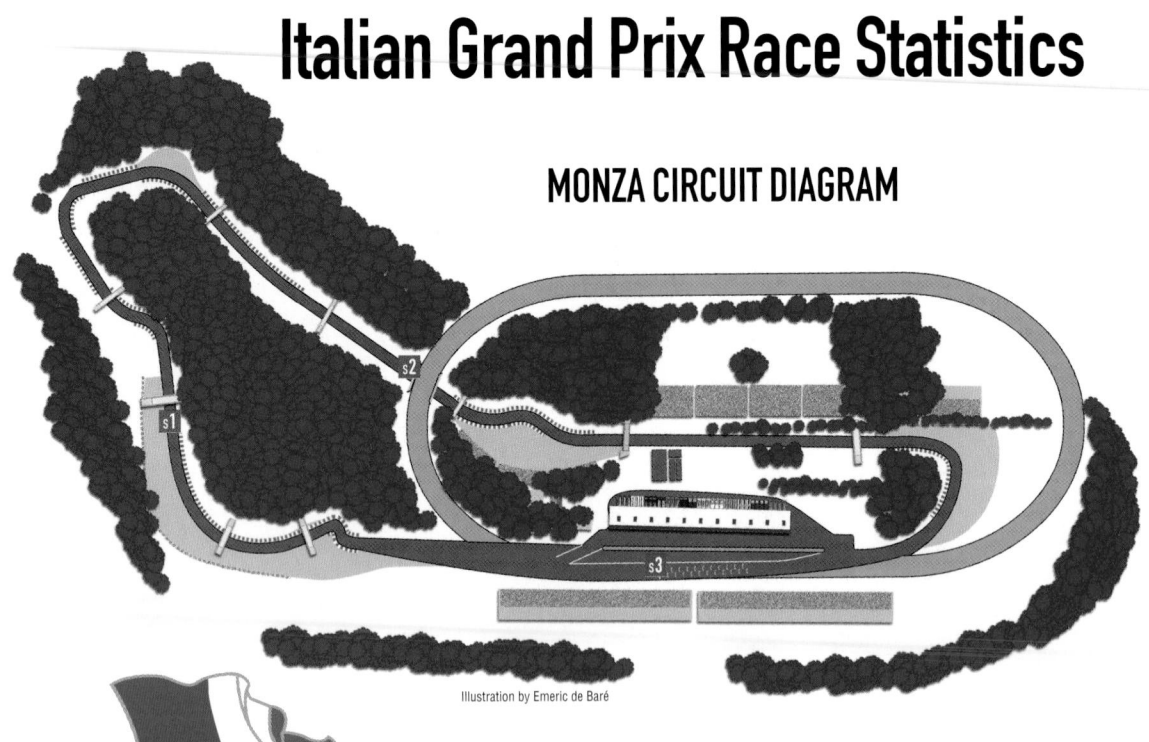

Illustration by Emeric de Baré

## FASTEST LAPS

| | DRIVER | TIME | LAP |
|---|---|---|---|
| 1 | R Schumacher | 1m 25.073s | 39 |
| 2 | Barrichello | 1m 25.221s | 39 |
| 3 | M Schumacher | 1m 25.525s | 52 |
| 4 | Montoya | 1m 25.657s | 52 |
| 5 | Alesi | 1m 26.365s | 28 |
| 6 | de la Rosa | 1m 26.381s | 34 |
| 7 | Panis | 1m 26.386s | 31 |
| 8 | Räikkönen | 1m 26.656s | 51 |
| 9 | Villeneuve | 1m 26.657s | 31 |
| 10 | Heidfeld | 1m 26.825s | 52 |
| 11 | Fisichella | 1m 27.283s | 29 |
| 12 | Coulthard | 1m 27.323s | 4 |
| 13 | Frentzen | 1m 27.394s | 28 |
| 14 | Häkkinen | 1m 27.627s | 15 |
| 15 | Enge | 1m 27.643s | 52 |
| 16 | Alonso | 1m 27.709s | 50 |
| 17 | Verstappen | 1m 27.945s | 22 |
| 18 | Button | 1m 28.268s | 4 |
| 19 | Bernoldi | 1m 28.578s | 24 |
| 20 | Irvine | 1m 29.262s | 5 |
| 21 | Yoong | 1m 30.605s | 21 |
| | de la Rosa | No lap completed | |

## RACE SPEED TRAP TIMES

| | | |
|---|---|---|
| 1 | Alesi | 225.7mph |
| 2 | Heidfeld | 224.8mph |
| 3 | Räikkönen | 223.9mph |
| 4 | R Schumacher | 222.7mph |
| 5 | Fisichella | 221.6mph |
| 6 | Bernoldi | 221.3mph |
| 7 | M Schumacher | 221.2mph |
| 8 | Verstappen | 221.1mph |
| 9 | Montoya | 221.0mph |
| 10 | Barrichello | 220.5mph |
| 11 | Villeneuve | 219.2mph |
| = | Alonso | 219.2mph |
| 13 | Panis | 219.1mph |
| 14 | Häkkinen | 217.4mph |
| 15 | de la Rosa | 217.2mph |
| 16 | Enge | 216.4mph |
| 17 | Frentzen | 216.3mph |
| 18 | Coulthard | 215.6mph |
| 19 | Irvine | 215.3mph |
| 20 | Button | 214.0mph |
| 21 | Yoong | 213.3mph |
| 22 | Trulli | 161.2mph |

## DRIVER POINTS

| | | |
|---|---|---|
| 1 | Michael Schumacher | 107 |
| 2 | David Coulthard | 57 |
| 3 | Rubens Barrichello | 54 |
| 4 | Ralf Schumacher | 48 |
| 5 | Juan Pablo Montoya | 25 |
| 6 | Mika Häkkinen | 24 |
| 7 | Jacques Villeneuve | 12 |
| 8 | Nick Heidfeld | 11 |
| 9 | Kimi Räikkönen | 9 |
| 10 | Jarno Trulli | 9 |
| 11 | Giancarlo Fisichella | 8 |
| 12 | Heinz-Harald Frentzen | 6 |
| 13 | Olivier Panis | 5 |
| 14 | Jean Alesi | 5 |
| 15 | Eddie Irvine | 4 |
| 16 | Pedro de la Rosa | 3 |
| 17 | Jenson Button | 2 |
| 18 | Jos Verstappen | 1 |
| 19 | Ricardo Zonta | 0 |
| 20 | Luciano Burti | 0 |
| 21 | Enrique Bernoldi | 0 |
| 22 | Tarso Marques | 0 |
| 23 | Fernando Alonso | 0 |
| 24 | Gaston Mazzacane | 0 |

## ITALIAN GRAND PRIX RACE RESULTS: SUNDAY 16TH SEPTEMBER 2001, 2PM

| | DRIVER | CAR | TIME/RETIREMENT | LAPS | PITSTOP LAPS |
|---|---|---|---|---|---|
| 1 | Juan Pablo Montoya | BMW Williams | 1h 16m 58.493s | 53 | 28 |
| 2 | Rubens Barrichello | Ferrari | +5.175s | 53 | 19 41 |
| 3 | Ralf Schumacher | BMW Williams | +17.335s | 53 | 35 |
| 4 | Michael Schumacher | Ferrari | +24.991s | 53 | 18 40 |
| 5 | Pedro de la Rosa | Jaguar Racing | +1m 14.984s | 53 | 36 |
| 6 | Jacques Villeneuve | BAR Honda | +1m 22.469s | 53 | 33 |
| 7 | Kimi Räikkönen | Sauber Petronas | +1m 23.107s | 53 | 22 |
| 8 | Jean Alesi | Jordan Honda | +1 lap | 52 | 22 32 |
| 9 | Olivier Panis | BAR Honda | +1 lap | 52 | 32 |
| 10 | Giancarlo Fisichella | Benetton Renault | +1 lap | 52 | 30 |
| 11 | Nick Heidfeld | Sauber Petronas | +1 lap | 52 | 28 |
| 12 | Tomas Enge | Prost Acer | +1 lap | 52 | 32 |
| 13 | Fernando Alonso | European Minardi | +2 laps | 51 | 17 33 |
| Ret | Enrique Bernoldi | Arrows Asiatech | Crankshaft sensor | 46 | 27 |
| Ret | Alex Yoong | European Minardi | Spin | 44 | 27 |
| Ret | Heinz-Harald Frentzen | Prost Acer | Gearbox | 28 | |
| Ret | Jos Verstappen | Arrows Asiatech | Fuel pressure | 25 | 18 |
| Ret | Mika Häkkinen | McLaren Mercedes | Gearbox | 19 | |
| Ret | Eddie Irvine | Jaguar Racing | Engine | 14 | |
| Ret | David Coulthard | McLaren Mercedes | Engine | 6 | |
| Ret | Jenson Button | Benetton Renault | Engine | 4 | 1 |
| Ret | Jarno Trulli | Jordan Honda | Collision | 0 | |

*Conditions: warm and sunny.*

## CONSTRUCTOR POINTS

| | | |
|---|---|---|
| 1 | Scuderia Ferrari-Marlboro | 161 |
| 2 | West McLaren Mercedes | 81 |
| 3 | BMW Williams F1 | 73 |
| 4 | Red Bull Sauber Petronas | 20 |
| 5 | Lucky Strike Reynard BAR Honda | 17 |
| 6 | Benson & Hedges Jordan Honda | 16 |
| 7 | Mild Seven Benetton Renault | 10 |
| 8 | Jaguar Racing | 7 |
| 9 | Prost Acer | 4 |
| 10 | Orange Arrows Asiatech | 1 |
| 11 | European Minardi F1 | 0 |

## PITSTOP TIMES (from pitlane entrance to exit)

| | | | | |
|---|---|---|---|---|
| Fastest pitstop | Rubens Barrichello | Ferrari | 20.754s | Lap 41 |
| Slowest pitstop | Fernando Alonso | Minardi | 1m 10.931s | Lap 33 |
| Most pitstops | Four drivers | Two stops | | |

## LAP LEADERS

| | |
|---|---|
| Montoya | 1–8 |
| Barrichello | 9–19 |
| Montoya | 20–28 |
| R Schumacher | 29–35 |
| Barrichello | 36–41 |
| Montoya | 42–53 |

Total laps led: Montoya 29; Barrichello 17; R Schumacher 7.

## TEMPERATURES

| | | |
|---|---|---|
| Friday: | Air: 19°C | Track: 20°C |
| Saturday: | Air: 20°C | Track: 26°C |
| Sunday: | Air: 20°C | Track: 28°C |

## WARM-UP

### SUNDAY 16TH SEPT. 2001. 9.30AM–10AM

| | | |
|---|---|---|
| 1 | M Schumacher | 1m 26.029s |
| 2 | Coulthard | 1m 26.086s |
| 3 | Montoya | 1m 26.247s |
| 4 | Barrichello | 1m 26.296s |
| 5 | Räikkönen | 1m 26.389s |
| 6 | Trulli | 1m 26.446s |
| 7 | Alesi | 1m 26.778s |
| 8 | R Schumacher | 1m 26.778s |
| 9 | Häkkinen | 1m 26.793s |
| 10 | Villeneuve | 1m 27.161s |
| 11 | Heidfeld | 1m 27.218s |
| 12 | de la Rosa | 1m 27.351s |
| 13 | Irvine | 1m 27.458s |
| 14 | Verstappen | 1m 27.548s |
| 15 | Panis | 1m 27.708s |
| 16 | Bernoldi | 1m 27.766s |
| 17 | Fisichella | 1m 28.137s |
| 18 | Button | 1m 28.633s |
| 19 | Frentzen | 1m 28.752s |
| 20 | Alonso | 1m 29.027s |
| 21 | Yoong | 1m 29.826s |
| 22 | Enge | 1m 30.445s |

F Alonso 21

J Verstappen 19

O Panis 17

J Villeneuve 15

E Irvine 13

A Yoong 22

T Enge 20

E Bernoldi 18

J Alesi 16

G Fisichella 14

HH Frentzen 12

## ITALIAN GRAND PRIX RACE ENTRY

| | DRIVER | TEAM | CHASSIS/ENGINE |
|---|---|---|---|
| 1 | Michael Schumacher | Scuderia Ferrari Marlboro | Ferrari F2001 |
| 2 | Rubens Barrichello | Scuderia Ferrari Marlboro | Ferrari F2001 |
| 3 | Mika Häkkinen | West McLaren Mercedes | McLaren Mercedes MP4-16 |
| 4 | David Coulthard | West McLaren Mercedes | McLaren Mercedes MP4-16 |
| 5 | Ralf Schumacher | BMW Williams F1 Team | BMW Williams FW23 |
| 6 | Juan Pablo Montoya | BMW Williams F1 Team | BMW Williams FW23 |
| 7 | Giancarlo Fisichella | Mild Seven Benetton Renault | Benetton Renault B201 |
| 8 | Jenson Button | Mild Seven Benetton Renault | Benetton Renault B201 |
| 9 | Olivier Panis | Lucky Strike BAR Honda | BAR Honda B003 |
| 10 | Jacques Villeneuve | Lucky Strike BAR Honda | BAR Honda B003 |
| 11 | Jarno Trulli | Benson & Hedges Jordan Honda | Jordan Honda EJ11 |
| 12 | Jean Alesi | Benson & Hedges Jordan Honda | Jordan Honda EJ11 |
| 14 | Jos Verstappen | Orange Arrows Asiatech | Arrows Asiatech A22 |
| 15 | Enrique Bernoldi | Orange Arrows Asiatech | Arrows Asiatech A22 |
| 16 | Nick Heidfeld | Red Bull Sauber Petronas | Sauber Petronas C20 |
| 17 | Kimi Räikkönen | Red Bull Sauber Petronas | Sauber Petronas C20 |
| 18 | Eddie Irvine | Jaguar Racing | Jaguar Cosworth R2 |
| 19 | Pedro de la Rosa | Jaguar Racing | Jaguar Cosworth R2 |
| 20 | Alex Yoong | European Minardi | Minardi European PS01B |
| 21 | Fernando Alonso | European Minardi | Minardi European PS01 |
| 22 | Heinz-Harald Frentzen | Prost Grand Prix | Prost ACER AP04 |
| 23 | Tomas Enge | Prost Grand Prix | Prost ACER AP04 |

Winner Juan Pablo Montoya and the Williams team with the spoils of victory.

## FASTEST SECTOR TIMES IN QUALIFYING *Ideal lap time: 1m 22.032s (diff. from pole: 0.184s).*

| | SECTOR 1 | SECS | | SECTOR 2 | SECS | | SECTOR 3 | SECS |
|---|---|---|---|---|---|---|---|---|
| 1 | R Schumacher | 26.272s | 1 | Montoya | 27.862s | 1 | Montoya | 27.898s |
| 2 | Montoya | 26.333s | 2 | M Schumacher | 27.870s | 2 | M Schumacher | 27.921s |
| 3 | Trulli | 26.385s | 3 | Barrichello | 28.044s | 3 | Barrichello | 28.067s |
| 4 | Barrichello | 26.417s | 4 | R Schumacher | 28.050s | 4 | R Schumacher | 28.191s |
| 5 | M Schumacher | 26.432s | 5 | Häkkinen | 28.134s | 5 | Coulthard | 28.251s |
| 6 | Button | 26.593s | 6 | Coulthard | 28.227s | 6 | Häkkinen | 28.252s |
| 7 | Frentzen | 26.597s | 7 | Trulli | 28.233s | 7 | Trulli | 28.316s |
| 8 | Heidfeld | 26.628s | 8 | Räikkönen | 28.293s | 8 | de la Rosa | 28.372s |
| 9 | Coulthard | 26.630s | 9 | Heidfeld | 28.393s | 9 | Heidfeld | 28.373s |
| 10 | Alesi | 26.634s | 10 | Irvine | 28.411s | 10 | Fisichella | 28.518s |
| 11 | Räikkönen | 26.646s | 11 | Fisichella | 28.501s | 11 | Räikkönen | 28.523s |
| 12 | de la Rosa | 26.676s | 12 | de la Rosa | 28.503s | 12 | Villeneuve | 28.525s |
| 13 | Häkkinen | 26.821s | 13 | Alesi | 28.535s | 13 | Irvine | 28.576s |
| 14 | Fisichella | 26.822s | 14 | Frentzen | 28.576s | 14 | Alesi | 28.648s |
| 15 | Irvine | 26.877s | 15 | Button | 28.644s | 15 | Button | 28.655s |
| 16 | Villeneuve | 26.898s | 16 | Villeneuve | 28.723s | 16 | Frentzen | 28.711s |
| 17 | Verstappen | 26.927s | 17 | Panis | 28.732s | 17 | Panis | 28.731s |
| 18 | Panis | 26.979s | 18 | Bernoldi | 28.934s | 18 | Verstappen | 29.195s |
| 19 | Enge | 27.027s | 19 | Verstappen | 29.251s | 19 | Bernoldi | 29.232s |
| 20 | Bernoldi | 27.084s | 20 | Alonso | 29.439s | 20 | Enge | 29.323s |
| 21 | Alonso | 27.185s | 21 | Enge | 29.608s | 21 | Alonso | 29.510s |
| 22 | Yoong | 27.556s | 22 | Yoong | 29.720s | 22 | Yoong | 30.067s |

## QUALIFYING: SATURDAY 15TH SEPTEMBER 2001, 1PM-2PM *107% time: 1m27.971s.*

| | DRIVER | TEAM | TIME | GAP | LAPS |
|---|---|---|---|---|---|
| 1 | Juan Pablo Montoya | BMW Williams | 1m 22.216s | 0.000 | 12 |
| 2 | Rubens Barrichello | Ferrari | 1m 22.528s | +0.312s | 11 |
| 3 | Michael Schumacher | Ferrari | 1m 22.624s | +0.408s | 11 |
| 4 | Ralf Schumacher | BMW Williams | 1m 22.841s | +0.625s | 12 |
| 5 | Jarno Trulli | Jordan Honda | 1m 23.126s | +0.910s | 13 |
| 6 | David Coulthard | McLaren Mercedes | 1m 23.148s | +0.932s | 12 |
| 7 | Mika Häkkinen | McLaren Mercedes | 1m 23.394s | +1.178s | 11 |
| 8 | Nick Heidfeld | Sauber Petronas | 1m 23.417s | +1.201s | 12 |
| 9 | Kimi Räikkönen | Sauber Petronas | 1m 23.595s | +1.379s | 12 |
| 10 | Pedro de la Rosa | Jaguar Racing | 1m 23.693s | +1.477s | 12 |
| 11 | Jenson Button | Benetton Renault | 1m 23.892s | +1.676s | 12 |
| 12 | Heinz-Harald Frentzen | Prost Acer | 1m 23.943s | +1.727s | 12 |
| 13 | Eddie Irvine | Jaguar Racing | 1m 24.031s | +1.815s | 11 |
| 14 | Giancarlo Fisichella | Benetton Renault | 1m 24.090s | +1.874s | 9 |
| 15 | Jacques Villeneuve | BAR Honda | 1m 24.164s | +1.948s | 12 |
| 16 | Jean Alesi | Jordan Honda | 1m 24.198s | +1.982s | 13 |
| 17 | Olivier Panis | BAR Honda | 1m 24.677s | +2.461s | 12 |
| 18 | Enrique Bernoldi | Arrows Asiatech | 1m 25.444s | +3.228s | 13 |
| 19 | Jos Verstappen | Arrows Asiatech | 1m 25.511s | +3.295s | 13 |
| 20 | Tomas Enge | Prost Acer | 1m 26.039s | +3.823s | 9 |
| 21 | Fernando Alonso | European Minardi | 1m 26.218s | +4.002s | 10 |
| 22 | Alex Yoong | European Minardi | 1m 27.463s | +5.247s | 11 |

*Drivers on the track when the red flags were brought out due to Häkkinen's accident were credited with an extra lap.*

## PRACTICE SESSION ONE
### FRIDAY 14TH SEPT. 2001 10.50AM-11.50AM

| | | |
|---|---|---|
| 1 | M Schumacher | 1m 25.524s |
| 2 | Coulthard | 1m 25.592s |
| 3 | Barrichello | 1m 25.728s |
| 4 | Heidfeld | 1m 25.740s |
| 5 | Häkkinen | 1m 26.053s |
| 6 | Button | 1m 26.197s |
| 7 | Räikkönen | 1m 26.701s |
| 8 | R Schumacher | 1m 26.843s |
| 9 | Trulli | 1m 27.001s |
| 10 | de la Rosa | 1m 27.066s |
| 11 | Panis | 1m 27.259s |
| 12 | Fisichella | 1m 27.276s |
| 13 | Irvine | 1m 27.401s |
| 14 | Villeneuve | 1m 27.502s |
| 15 | Frentzen | 1m 27.644s |
| 16 | Montoya | 1m 27.667s |
| 17 | Alesi | 1m 28.148s |
| 18 | Bernoldi | 1m 28.866s |
| 19 | Alonso | 1m 29.184s |
| 20 | Enge | 1m 29.948s |
| 21 | Yoong | 1m 31.192s |
| 22 | Verstappen | 5m 43.120s |

## PRACTICE SESSION TWO
### FRIDAY 14TH SEPTEMBER 2001 1PM-2PM

| | | |
|---|---|---|
| 1 | R Schumacher | 1m 24.667s |
| 2 | Montoya | 1m 25.067s |
| 3 | M Schumacher | 1m 25.131s |
| 4 | de la Rosa | 1m 25.205s |
| 5 | Barrichello | 1m 25.311s |
| 6 | Häkkinen | 1m 25.343s |
| 7 | Coulthard | 1m 25.544s |
| 8 | Heidfeld | 1m 25.740s |
| 9 | Alesi | 1m 25.849s |
| 10 | Frentzen | 1m 25.860s |
| 11 | Fisichella | 1m 25.911s |
| 12 | Trulli | 1m 25.987s |
| 13 | Button | 1m 26.197s |
| 14 | Panis | 1m 26.354s |
| 15 | Villeneuve | 1m 26.521s |
| 16 | Räikkönen | 1m 26.701s |
| 17 | Alonso | 1m 26.972s |
| 18 | Bernoldi | 1m 27.217s |
| 19 | Irvine | 1m 27.401s |
| 20 | Enge | 1m 27.662s |
| 21 | Verstappen | 1m 27.900s |
| 22 | Yoong | 1m 28.250s |

## PRACTICE SESSION THREE
### SATURDAY 15TH SEPT. 2001 9AM-9.45AM

| | | |
|---|---|---|
| 1 | Montoya | 1m 25.558s |
| 2 | Barrichello | 1m 25.894s |
| 3 | de la Rosa | 1m 26.542s |
| 4 | Villeneuve | 1m 26.622s |
| 5 | Panis | 1m 26.729s |
| 6 | Räikkönen | 1m 27.535s |
| 7 | Irvine | 1m 27.625s |
| 8 | Verstappen | 1m 27.853s |
| 9 | Bernoldi | 1m 27.944s |
| 10 | Heidfeld | 1m 28.066s |
| 11 | Enge | 1m 28.791s |
| 12 | Trulli | 1m 30.536s |
| 13 | Frentzen | 1m 32.214s |
| 14 | R Schumacher | 1m 47.742s |
| | Yoong | No laps |
| | Button | No laps |
| | Alesi | No laps |
| | Alonso | No laps |
| | Coulthard | No laps |
| | Häkkinen | No laps |
| | M Schumacher | No laps |

## PRACTICE SESSION FOUR
### SATURDAY 15TH SEPT. 2001 10.15AM-11AM

| | | |
|---|---|---|
| 1 | M Schumacher | 1m 23.178s |
| 2 | Montoya | 1m 23.477s |
| 3 | Trulli | 1m 23.762s |
| 4 | Barrichello | 1m 23.828s |
| 5 | Coulthard | 1m 23.873s |
| 6 | R Schumacher | 1m 23.917s |
| 7 | Heidfeld | 1m 24.251s |
| 8 | Häkkinen | 1m 24.263s |
| 9 | de la Rosa | 1m 24.575s |
| 10 | Räikkönen | 1m 24.586s |
| 11 | Irvine | 1m 24.642s |
| 12 | Fisichella | 1m 24.683s |
| 13 | Alesi | 1m 24.928s |
| 14 | Panis | 1m 24.990s |
| 15 | Button | 1m 25.062s |
| 16 | Villeneuve | 1m 25.258s |
| 17 | Frentzen | 1m 25.600s |
| 18 | Verstappen | 1m 26.285s |
| 19 | Bernoldi | 1m 27.309s |
| 20 | Enge | 1m 28.064s |
| | Yoong | No laps |
| | Alonso | No laps |

J Button — 11

K Räikkönen — 9

M Häkkinen — 7

J Trulli — 5

M Schumacher — 3

JP Montoya — 1

P de la Rosa — 10

N Heidfeld — 8

D Coulthard — 6

R Schumacher — 4

R Barrichello — 2

## MONZA LAP-BY-LAP REPORT

**PRE-START:** The pre-race mood at Monza was gloomy indeed, overshadowed by three tragic events: the death of marshal Paolo Ghislimberti on the first lap last year, the terrorist attacks in the United States and the horrific crash in the CART race in Germany on the Saturday afternoon, from which popular Italian driver Alex Zanardi was lucky to escape with 'only' the amputation of both his legs. At the drivers' meeting that morning, all of them except Jacques Villeneuve agreed not to race until through the dangerous first two chicanes. Villeneuve pointed out just how much the drivers were paid to entertain the fans who had saved up for months to get a ticket. Michael Schumacher was particularly distracted by the situation and on the grid was still talking to each driver in turn, in a bid to reach some sort of compromise. He was hindered not only by Villeneuve but also by some of the team bosses, including Flavio Briatore of launch control masters Benetton Renault, which had ordered their drivers to race, threatening them with the loss of their drives should they disobey. When the drivers set off on the parade lap it was still unclear to observers whether a consensus had been reached. Giancarlo Fisichella and Nick Heidfeld would both start from the pitlane, the Italian in the spare car after suffering a fuel leak; the German a hydraulic failure while sitting on the grid.

**LAP 1** When the lights went out it was racing as usual. Juan Pablo Montoya held his pole position from Rubens Barrichello and Ralf Schumacher in the other BMW Williams got ahead of his brother Michael. Jenson Button made the best of his launch control to make up five places from his 11th place grid spot by the first corner, but then cancelled his performance out by failing to brake in time and pushing future team-mate Jarno Trulli out of the race at the first corner. Consequently Mika Häkkinen had to run down the escape road to avoid the stricken Jordan and the bunching cars, and dropped right back down the order. Button's front wing was ripped off in the accident and he was forced to pit for a new nose at the end of the lap. Yellow flags were waved at the first chicane as a result of the Button-Trulli fracas.

Meanwhile, Michael Schumacher pushed past his brother into third place at the first Lesmo, the corner where the race would have begun in earnest had Michael got his way on the grid. By the end of the first lap, the Williams and Ferraris had already started to visibly pull away from David Coulthard's McLaren in fifth and the fast-starting Pedro de la Rosa a place behind, having made up four places. Further top starters were the other Jaguar of Eddie Irvine, who had made up six places to end the first lap in seventh, and Jos Verstappen in eighth who had started a lowly 19th. Jean Alesi was up to 10th from 16th.

**LAP 2** Barrichello closed on Montoya while his team-mate Michael Schumacher closed on him. Enrique Bernoldi passed Jacques Villeneuve for 11th.

**LAP 3** Irvine lost two places, to Verstappen and Kimi Räikkönen.

**LAP 4** Nick Heidfeld retired from 21st position. Irvine lost out to Alesi, Bernoldi and Villeneuve.

**LAP 5** Jenson Button retired from 21st and last position after his Renault engine failed. After five laps the running order was Montoya, Barrichello, Michael Schumacher, Ralf Schumacher, Coulthard, Verstappen, Räikkönen, Alesi, de la Rosa, Bernoldi. Häkkinen languished in 13th.

**LAP 7** David Coulthard retired from fifth place after his Ilmor engine expired. Irvine had now lost so much ground he was overtaken by the Minardi of Fernando Alonso.

**LAP 8** Irvine hit penultimate place ahead only of rookie Alex Yoong.

**LAP 9** At the second chicane, Barrichello took the lead from Montoya, whose Michelin tyres were badly blistered, and immediately began to pull away. The crowd went wild.

**LAP 12** Schumacher was running very close to the struggling Montoya but could not find a way past. Alesi snatched sixth place from Kimi Räikkönen.

**LAP 14** Still hit by a mysterious power loss, Irvine pitted from 18th and retired.

**LAP 16** Barrichello's lead was almost nine seconds, fuelling talk that he was on a two-stop strategy to Montoya's one. Michael Schumacher was still on the Colombian's tail. At the other end of the grid, Yoong spun at the Lesmos but rejoined. Verstappen dropped to seventh, promoting Alesi to fifth and Räikkönen to sixth.

**LAP 17** The first scheduled stop took place when Alonso came in.

**LAP 18** Michael Schumacher pitted, as did Verstappen, revealing that Ferrari must have been planning a two-stop strategy. He rejoined in fourth.

**LAP 19** Barrichello made his first stop, but was stationary for 16.3secs as the team switched to Schumacher's fuel rig when Barrichello's own proved faulty. The Brazilian rejoined in third as Montoya regained the lead.

**LAP 20** Mika Häkkinen, who had worked his way up to ninth, retired with a transmission failure.

**LAP 22** Jean Alesi and Kimi Räikkönen made pitstops, rejoining out of the points in seventh and 13th respectively.

**LAP 26** Jos Verstappen retired from 14th position, reporting a loss of brake power and fading fuel pressure. The order after the first round of pitstops read Montoya, Ralf Schumacher, Barrichello, Michael Schumacher, de la Rosa, Villeneuve, Alesi, Bernoldi, Panis, Frentzen.

**LAP 27** Bernoldi, the first of the one-stoppers, and Yoong pitted.

**LAP 28** Montoya came in early for his one and only pitstop to avoid the traffic that had built up behind the slow but unpassable Bernoldi. Ralf Schumacher took the lead as Montoya rejoined behind Barrichello in third.

**LAP 29** Frentzen retired from ninth with a transmission failure.

**LAP 30** Fisichella pitted.

**LAP 32** Jean Alesi pitted for his second time. A flat-spotted front tyre mistaken for a puncture forced him into the pits early. A tardy stop and the mix-up of his strategy ruined his chances of scoring points. Olivier Panis and Tomas Enge made their single stops.

**LAP 33** Alonso and Villeneuve pitted, the BAR team doing a good job for the Canadian and allowing him to retain sixth place. Alonso's stop went badly wrong when his right rear tyre could not be fitted. It took him 1m 10.931secs from pitlane entrance to exit, though he did not lose his 14th and penultimate place as his team-mate Yoong was not in the same race.

**LAP 35** Ralf Schumacher took his sole pitstop very late. Barrichello regained the lead, albeit only 15secs ahead of Montoya, with one pitstop for the Brazilian remaining.

**LAP 36** De la Rosa became the last of the one-stoppers to pit and he managed to hold onto his fifth place. Following this round of stops the order went Barrichello, Montoya, Michael Schumacher, Ralf Schumacher, de la Rosa, Villeneuve, Räikkönen, Alesi, Panis, Fisichella, Heidfeld.

**LAP 40** Michael Schumacher pitted a second time, and dropped to fourth behind his brother.

**LAP 41** Barrichello pitted a second time. Although this stop was much better than the last, he rejoined in third behind both Williams cars. Montoya was in the lead again and looked likely to take his debut Grand Prix victory. Barrichello emerged from the pits very close behind Ralf.

**LAP 47** Ralf Schumacher, suffering from blistered tyres and braking difficulties, was unable to put up much resistance to Barrichello and the Ferrari driver overtook him for second place at the first chicane. Yoong again spun his car at the Lesmos, although this time he retired as a result, and Enrique Bernoldi also retired when his Asiatech engine let go.

**LAP 53** Juan Pablo Montoya took his first Formula One victory in his rookie season, which was also the first victory for a Colombian in Formula One. Rubens Barrichello came in second, 5.175secs behind, followed by Ralf Schumacher, who had lost almost 12secs to the Ferrari in the last six laps, and Michael Schumacher in a lacklustre fourth. A stunning drive from Pedro de la Rosa netted Jaguar two points and Jacques Villeneuve rounded off the points-scorers in sixth. There was no champagne on the podium, as a mark of respect to the victims of the American tragedy.

**WINNING WAYS:** The Indianapolis Motor Speedway joined the Grand Prix calendar in 2000. The Formula One fraternity returned in September 2001 to entertain a downcast population keen for relief and a fast return to normal life. Here, soon-to-retire Mika Häkkinen's McLaren Mercedes crosses Indy's legendary yard of brick track for the 73rd time to take the chequered flag. It was the 20th victory of his Formula One career. PHOTOGRAPH BY KEITH SUTTON

# United States Grand Prix

## 28th-30th September 2001     LAPS: 73    LENGTH OF LAP: 2.604 miles

## Rip-roaring show

**The United States Grand Prix was a huge success despite all the nay-sayers who didn't want it to take place at all. But when it did, everyone was delighted – not least Mika Häkkinen, who was coming to the end of his career in a brilliant blaze of glory. It was a fine day for international sport, a fine day for motor racing and a very fine day for Formula One.**

It's a sign of the times when a Grand Prix promoter is not pleased at a race day turn-out of between 180,000 and 200,000 and a weekend attendance of 300,000. But this is the USA and the event was deemed less than a success simply because the Indianapolis stadium can hold 400,000. Well, it wasn't any less: 200,000 people packed in to watch a Formula One Grand Prix create an amazing atmosphere. If the paddock was dead, the race wasn't. Mika Häkkinen sparkled and, as both BMW Williams retired, he netted a win instead of third. But that's what motor racing is – the chance of the day – and Häkkinen took his chance for an incredibly popular win.

It didn't look that way earlier in the day as Häkkinen fluffed his pit exit, leaving when the track was red-lighted and overtaking stationary cars to do so. It was inexplicable and Häkkinen was lucky to get away with a grid demotion – joining the circuit under a red light is very serious, especially when it involves passing a queue of stationary cars. Leniency left Häkkinen ungrateful. "I was pissed off," he said. "Rules are rules, but there has to be some common sense."

Americans understand drama – the tragedy of 11th September enabled the organisers to drum up a real atmosphere: the Indianapolis Children's Choir performed the national anthem and soul diva Patti LaBelle sang *God Bless America*, a sentiment shared by all.

BAR team principal Craig Pollock's prophecy that holding the US Grand Prix was like 'painting a bull's eye over Indianapolis' was not fulfilled: spectators and TV viewers enjoyed a fantastic day's racing.

All-American ra-ra girls led the celebrations on the grid, and America was so glad the Formula One circus had crossed the Atlantic. So glad. It wouldn't have happened without the firm resolve of Bernie Ecclestone and USGP promoter Tony George. The consensus amongst F1 people was not to go. Once again Bernie prevailed and by the end of it everyone could see what a terrible mistake it would have been not to go.

Michael Schumacher out-powered Ralf off the line as Juan Pablo Montoya shot off the second row to become the lead Williams, while the Rubens Barrichello's Ferrari moved into third. Mika Häkkinen held onto fourth with team-mate David Coulthard fifth, while the two Benettons behind them didn't manage their usual pace off the line. Trulli's Jordan bobbed and weaved to maintain position as team-mate Jean Alesi shot back three places in the mêlée, leaving the McLarens to carry on their pursuit of the top four. The two Arrows, towards the rear of the field, made storming starts. With just one lap completed Kimi Räikkönen's race turned to disaster: his Sauber clashed with Jarno Trulli's Jordan, leaving his nosecone in need of replacement; soon after, he was the first to quit the race.

The order up front took shape: Barrichello sliced down the outside of Montoya into Turn One the second time around, and made off after his fast-disappearing team-mate. The Ferraris' pace – over 1.2 seconds a lap better than anyone else – signalled a light fuel load and a two-stop plan.

Barrichello wasn't finished yet, however, and on lap five raced through into the lead at the end of the back straight, with Michael Schumacher happily letting him scamper away in pursuit of the one-two championship finish, and ready to hold off the Williams boys as

required. The Jordan Hondas and Benetton Renaults diced on the early laps, and Alesi slipstreamed both Giancarlo Fisichella and Jenson Button in two laps to get ninth, one behind his team-mate. By one-fifth distance, Barrichello led Schumacher by nine seconds, with Montoya four seconds back and staving off Ralf, and the McLarens keeping a watching brief at three-second intervals. On lap 25 Ralf Schumacher's BMW Williams shot into the pits from fourth and disaster struck. A faulty air gun lost on the left rear tyre meant a quick swap and four seconds lost. Exiting the pits after 12.5 seconds, a potential win was squandered and the frustrated German threw it away on lap 38, when a spin left beached the car in the gravel trap.

At the end of lap 27, race leader Barrichello pitted for the first of two stops, and 8.6 seconds later returned to the track in fifth, leaving Montoya chasing his team-mate's Ferrari for the lead.

Montoya's tyres seemed suspect – the car was all over the place until he spectacularly stole the lead on lap 34 and the crowd went wild. It was a typical Montoya move and the highlight of the race: as he got an extremely good run onto the main straight and approached the braking area at the turn after the pits, he was under Schumacher's rear wing; as they both braked, he darted out from behind the Ferrari in an assertive spurt that sent the crowd to its feet. Schumacher knew full well Montoya was coming through, and did not try to resist. "I don't know where he was coming from, he was quite far back through Turn 11 and then suddenly he was flying at me down the straight," said a bewildered Schumacher afterwards. "He got me, I accept that."

Montoya immediately drove away from Schumacher and, clock-

Jacques Villeneuve's BAR Honda flashes past the grandstands on the main straight as a patriotic fan enthusiastically waves the star-spangled banner of support.

Despite being relegated to fourth on the grid Mika Häkkinen drove a superb race just as he had in Barcelona, but this time he received the victory rewards he so richly deserved, not to mention hiking his market value if and when he returns in 2003. It was a faultless display.

The end of the road for Rubens Barrichello as the Ferrari engine finally lets go on the last-but-one lap, after four smokey, painful laps.

ing a new lap record, began to assert his authority. But it was not to last long; he pulled into the pits soon after. A 13-second stop did not help his cause, and Schumacher assumed the lead once again with Häkkinen and David Coulthard chasing, but all were yet to stop.

Then in a matter of one lap Williams' American misery was complete: Montoya was looking good for a victory battle, but at the end of lap 39 he came to a halt at the end of the pit counter. Jinxed, Montoya accepted the applause of the crowd, and said afterwards: "It just died. The engine was running but something broke in the gearbox I guess when I came off the banking and that was it." The very lap Montoya went out, Schumacher came in and pitted to leave Häkkinen a surprise leader of the race, with Coulthard in second, just five seconds behind, and Schumacher coming out one place behind team-mate Barrichello in fourth.

Alex Yoong hit trouble, cruising slowly around the track before pulling in to retire. Fernando Alonso was already back in the garage. Coulthard made a 10.2-second stop, but could not get out ahead of either Ferrari and ended up back in fourth with 29 laps remaining. A battle between Pedro de la Rosa and Jacques Villeneuve ended in contact, when the Jaguar driver clipped Villeneuve at Turn Nine and the pair were sent into a slow spin before both getting back.

Häkkinen was charging and gained three seconds on Schumacher. He pitted on lap 45 and got out in second, sensing victory. Barrichello was 21 seconds ahead, but had yet to stop. The race was Häkkinen's.

Barrichello was aided as Häkkinen got caught up in traffic, letting Barrichello extend his lead. He slotted in just ahead of Schumacher in second place and waited for either to make a mistake or retire.

Despite dropping back after a pitstop, Eddie Irvine fought back to pass Sauber's Nick Heidfeld and move into the top six, brightening Jaguar's hopes as he brought it into a points-scoring position.

Enrique Bernoldi's Arrows ran over some debris from de la Rosa's Jaguar in the middle of the main straight and left shards of carbon fibre over the track. But it didn't bother anyone.

Meanwhile Barrichello's engine was slowly expiring over three laps, as puffs of smoke but thankfully no oil smeared the track. With a few laps left, Barrichello foolishly thought he could make it home; the engine slowly began to seize, and Barrichello pulled off. Then it suddenly locked, fortunately after he had slowed to a crawl. He was a lucky man or unlucky, depending on which way you looked at it.

Jarno Trulli capitalised on Barrichello's problems to complete a lonely race and claim fourth place, with Irvine fifth for Jaguar and the final point going to Nick Heidfeld and the Sauber team.

Häkkinen said ahead pre-race that Indy meant something special and that not having won in America would be like a 'missing feather in the cap'. As he said: "That was one of the highlights of this season for me, definitely. I damaged the race car in the morning, the mechanics did a great job, then I had the problem with the red light, which pissed me off. So I have gone from a lot of frustration to a feeling of elation. Indianapolis means a lot to me and I will always remember this as a career highlight."

After the race the stewards found a technical infringement on Trulli's undertray and everyone moved up a position from fourth downwards, including Trulli's team-mate, Alesi, into sixth. A bitter-sweet end for the yellow cars in a bitter season.

# United States Grand Prix Race Statistics

## INDIANAPOLIS CIRCUIT DIAGRAM

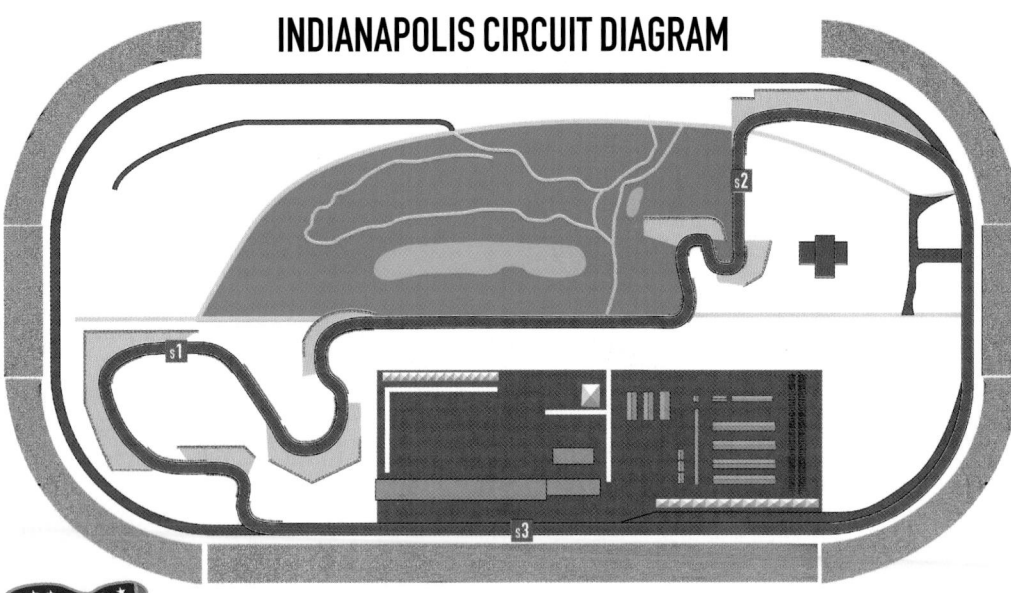

Illustration by Emeric de Baré

## FASTEST LAPS

| | DRIVER | TIME | LAP |
|---|---|---|---|
| 1 | Montoya | 1m 14.448s | 35 |
| 2 | Häkkinen | 1m 14.481s | 45 |
| 3 | Barrichello | 1m 14.629s | 47 |
| 4 | Coulthard | 1m 14.641s | 39 |
| 5 | R Schumacher | 1m 14.706s | 22 |
| 6 | M Schumacher | 1m 14.841s | 32 |
| 7 | Irvine | 1m 15.139s | 58 |
| 8 | Heidfeld | 1m 15.169s | 29 |
| 9 | Trulli | 1m 15.199s | 63 |
| 10 | Button | 1m 15.252s | 71 |
| 11 | Frentzen | 1m 15.296s | 38 |
| 12 | Fisichella | 1m 15.457s | 40 |
| 13 | Alesi | 1m 15.659s | 67 |
| 14 | de la Rosa | 1m 15.758s | 68 |
| 15 | Panis | 1m 15.919s | 67 |
| 16 | Bernoldi | 1m 16.068s | 68 |
| 17 | Enge | 1m 16.155s | 71 |
| 18 | Verstappen | 1m 16.342s | 35 |
| 19 | Villeneuve | 1m 16.680s | 40 |
| 20 | Alonso | 1m 16.694s | 30 |
| 21 | Yoong | 1m 17.079s | 25 |
| 22 | Räikkönen | 1m 51.518s | 2 |

## RACE SPEED TRAP

| 1 | Montoya | 216.3mph |
|---|---|---|
| 2 | Alesi | 212.5mph |
| 3 | R Schumacher | 211.6mph |
| 4 | Barrichello | 211.0mph |
| 5 | Button | 210.4mph |
| 6 | Häkkinen | 210.0mph |
| 7 | Fisichella | 209.7mph |
| 8 | Coulthard | 209.5mph |
| 9 | M Schumacher | 209.3mph |
| 10 | Heidfeld | 209.2mph |
| 11 | Trulli | 208.8mph |
| 12 | Panis | 208.5mph |
| 13 | Villeneuve | 207.2mph |
| 14 | Alonso | 207.0mph |
| 15 | Yoong | 206.6mph |
| 16 | Frentzen | 206.3mph |
| 17 | de la Rosa | 206.1mph |
| 18 | Bernoldi | 205.5mph |
| 19 | Verstappen | 205.2mph |
| 20 | Enge | 204.5mph |
| 21 | Irvine | 204.3mph |
| 22 | Räikkönen | 202.8mph |

## US GRAND PRIX RACE RESULTS: SUNDAY 30TH SEPTEMBER 2001, 1PM

| | DRIVER | CAR | TIME/RETIREMENT | LAPS | PITSTOP LAPS |
|---|---|---|---|---|---|
| 1 | Mika Häkkinen | McLaren Mercedes | 1h 32m 42.840s | 73 | 46 |
| 2 | Michael Schumacher | Ferrari | +11.046s | 73 | 39 |
| 3 | David Coulthard | McLaren Mercedes | +12.043s | 73 | 43 |
| 4 | Jarno Trulli | Jordan Honda | +57.423s | 73 | 39 |
| 5 | Eddie Irvine | Jaguar Racing | +1m 12.434s | 73 | 52 |
| 6 | Nick Heidfeld | Sauber Petronas | +1m 12.996s | 73 | 27 48 |
| 7 | Jean Alesi | Jordan Honda | +1 lap | 72 | 37 |
| 8 | Giancarlo Fisichella | Benetton Renault | +1 lap | 72 | 41 |
| 9 | Jenson Button | Benetton Renault | +1 lap | 72 | 35 |
| 10 | Heinz-Harald Frentzen | Prost Acer | +1 lap | 72 | 42 |
| 11 | Olivier Panis | BAR Honda | +1 lap | 72 | 44 |
| 12 | Pedro de la Rosa | Jaguar Racing | +1 lap | 72 | 50 |
| 13 | Enrique Bernoldi | Arrows Asiatech | +1 lap | 72 | 37 |
| 14 | Tomas Enge | Prost Acer | +1 lap | 72 | 37 |
| 15 | Rubens Barrichello | Ferrari | Engine | 71 | 27 50 |
| Ret | Jacques Villeneuve | BAR Honda | Suspension | 45 | 44 |
| Ret | Jos Verstappen | Arrows Asiatech | Engine | 44 | 36 |
| Ret | Juan Pablo Montoya | BMW Williams | Hydraulics | 38 | 36 |
| Ret | Alex Yoong | European Minardi | Gearbox | 38 | 26 38 |
| Ret | Ralf Schumacher | BMW Williams | Spin | 36 | 24 |
| Ret | Fernando Alonso | European Minardi | Driveshaft | 36 | |
| Ret | Kimi Räikkönen | Sauber Petronas | Driveshaft | 2 | 2 |

Conditions: hot and sunny.

## DRIVER POINTS

| 1 | Michael Schumacher | 113 |
|---|---|---|
| 2 | David Coulthard | 61 |
| 3 | Rubens Barrichello | 54 |
| 4 | Ralf Schumacher | 48 |
| 5 | Mika Häkkinen | 34 |
| 6 | Juan Pablo Montoya | 25 |
| 7 | Jacques Villeneuve | 12 |
| 8 | Nick Heidfeld | 12 |
| 9 | Jarno Trulli | 12 |
| 10 | Kimi Räikkönen | 9 |
| 11 | Giancarlo Fisichella | 8 |
| 12 | Eddie Irvine | 6 |
| 13 | Heinz-Harald Frentzen | 6 |
| 14 | Olivier Panis | 5 |
| 15 | Jean Alesi | 5 |
| 16 | Pedro de la Rosa | 3 |
| 17 | Jenson Button | 2 |
| 18 | Jos Verstappen | 1 |
| 19 | Ricardo Zonta | 0 |
| 20 | Luciano Burti | 0 |
| 21 | Enrique Bernoldi | 0 |
| 22 | Tarso Marques | 0 |
| 23 | Fernando Alonso | 0 |
| 24 | Gaston Mazzacane | 0 |

## CONSTRUCTOR POINTS

| 1 | Scuderia Ferrari-Marlboro | 167 |
|---|---|---|
| 2 | West McLaren Mercedes | 95 |
| 3 | BMW Williams F1 | 73 |
| 4 | Red Bull Sauber Petronas | 21 |
| 5 | Benson & Hedges Jordan Honda | 19 |
| 6 | Lucky Strike Reynard BAR Honda | 17 |
| 7 | Mild Seven Benetton Renault | 10 |
| 8 | Jaguar Racing | 9 |
| 9 | Prost Acer | 4 |
| 10 | Orange Arrows Asiatech | 1 |
| 11 | European Minardi F1 | 0 |

## PITSTOP TIMES (from pitlane entrance to exit)

| Fastest pitstop: | Rubens Barrichello | Ferrari | 22.214s | Lap 50 |
|---|---|---|---|---|
| Slowest pitstop: | Alex Yoong | European Minardi | 58.200s | Lap 38 |
| Most pitstops: | Four drivers | Two stops | | |

## PENALTIES AND FINES

| DRIVER/TEAM | WHEN | PENALTY | REASON |
|---|---|---|---|
| Mika Häkkinen | Warm-up | Loss of best qualifying time | Ignoring red light |

## LAP LEADERS

| M Schumacher | 1-4, 27-33, 36-38 |
|---|---|
| Barrichello | 5-26, 46-49 |
| Montoya | 34-35 |
| Häkkinen | 39-45, 50-73 |

Total laps led: Häkkinen 31; Barrichello 26; M Schumacher 14; Montoya 2.

## TEMPERATURES

| Friday: | Air: 14°C | Track: 15°C |
|---|---|---|
| Saturday: | Air: 18°C | Track: 25°C |
| Sunday: | Air: 22°C | Track: 34°C |

## WARM-UP

SUNDAY 30TH SEPT. 2001, 8.30AM-9.00AM

| 1 | R Schumacher | 1m 13.912s |
|---|---|---|
| 2 | Coulthard | 1m 13.982s |
| 3 | Häkkinen | 1m 14.025s |
| 4 | M Schumacher | 1m 14.029s |
| 5 | Verstappen | 1m 14.036s |
| 6 | Montoya | 1m 14.063s |
| 7 | de la Rosa | 1m 14.083s |
| 8 | Räikkönen | 1m 14.145s |
| 9 | Barrichello | 1m 14.220s |
| 10 | Heidfeld | 1m 14.528s |
| 11 | Irvine | 1m 14.597s |
| 12 | Trulli | 1m 14.778s |
| 13 | Fisichella | 1m 14.979s |
| 14 | Button | 1m 15.122s |
| 15 | Panis | 1m 15.201s |
| 16 | Alesi | 1m 15.344s |
| 17 | Enge | 1m 15.437s |
| 18 | Bernoldi | 1m 15.649s |
| 19 | Villeneuve | 1m 15.958s |
| 20 | Frentzen | 1m 16.037s |
| 21 | Alonso | 1m 16.332s |
| 22 | Yoong | 1m 16.646s |

21 T Enge

19 E Bernoldi

17 F Alonso

15 HH Frentzen

13 O Panis

22 A Yoong

20 J Verstappen

18 J Villeneuve

16 P de la Rosa

14 E Irvine

12 G Fisichella

### UNITED STATES GRAND PRIX RACE ENTRY

| | DRIVER | TEAM | CHASSIS/ENGINE |
|---|---|---|---|
| 1 | Michael Schumacher | Scuderia Ferrari Marlboro | Ferrari F2001 |
| 2 | Rubens Barrichello | Scuderia Ferrari Marlboro | Ferrari F2001 |
| 3 | Mika Häkkinen | West McLaren Mercedes | McLaren Mercedes MP4-16 |
| 4 | David Coulthard | West McLaren Mercedes | McLaren Mercedes MP4-16 |
| 5 | Ralf Schumacher | BMW Williams F1 Team | BMW Williams FW23 |
| 6 | Juan Pablo Montoya | BMW Williams F1 Team | BMW Williams FW23 |
| 7 | Giancarlo Fisichella | Mild Seven Benetton Renault | Benetton Renault B201 |
| 8 | Jenson Button | Mild Seven Benetton Renault | Benetton Renault B201 |
| 9 | Olivier Panis | Lucky Strike BAR Honda | BAR Honda B003 |
| 10 | Jacques Villeneuve | Lucky Strike BAR Honda | BAR Honda B003 |
| 11 | Jarno Trulli | Benson & Hedges Jordan Honda | Jordan Honda EJ11 |
| 12 | Jean Alesi | Benson & Hedges Jordan Honda | Jordan Honda EJ11 |
| 14 | Jos Verstappen | Orange Arrows Asiatech | Arrows Asiatech A22 |
| 15 | Enrique Bernoldi | Orange Arrows Asiatech | Arrows Asiatech A22 |
| 16 | Nick Heidfeld | Red Bull Sauber Petronas | Sauber Petronas C20 |
| 17 | Kimi Räikkönen | Red Bull Sauber Petronas | Sauber Petronas C20 |
| 18 | Eddie Irvine | Jaguar Racing | Jaguar Cosworth R2 |
| 19 | Pedro de la Rosa | Jaguar Racing | Jaguar Cosworth R2 |
| 20 | Alex Yoong | European Minardi | Minardi European PS01B |
| 21 | Fernando Alonso | European Minardi | Minardi European PS01B |
| 22 | Heinz-Harald Frentzen | Prost Grand Prix | Prost ACER AP04 |
| 23 | Tomas Enge | Prost Grand Prix | Prost ACER AP04 |

Häkkinen back on top. His US GP victory was his 20th Grand Prix success.

### FASTEST SECTOR TIMES IN QUALIFYING
Ideal lap time: 1m 11.642s (diff. from pole: 0.066s).

| | SECTOR 1 | SECS | | SECTOR 2 | SECS | | SECTOR 3 | SECS |
|---|---|---|---|---|---|---|---|---|
| 1 | M Schumacher | 22.107s | 1 | Häkkinen | 29.729s | 1 | M Schumacher | 19.806s |
| 2 | R Schumacher | 22.137s | 2 | M Schumacher | 29.795s | 2 | Barrichello | 19.906s |
| 3 | Häkkinen | 22.213s | 3 | Heidfeld | 29.806s | 3 | Montoya | 19.939s |
| 4 | Barrichello | 22.292s | 4 | Coulthard | 29.830s | 4 | R Schumacher | 19.994s |
| 5 | Montoya | 22.301s | 5 | R Schumacher | 29.836s | 5 | Häkkinen | 20.003s |
| 6 | Coulthard | 22.306s | 6 | Trulli | 29.851s | 6 | Coulthard | 20.056s |
| 7 | Heidfeld | 22.352s | 7 | Räikkönen | 29.861s | 7 | Heidfeld | 20.116s |
| 8 | Alesi | 22.381s | 8 | Barrichello | 29.884s | 8 | Fisichella | 20.134s |
| 9 | Fisichella | 22.486s | 9 | Fisichella | 29.945s | 9 | Button | 20.140s |
| 10 | Trulli | 22.489s | 10 | Montoya | 29.963s | 10 | Alesi | 20.171s |
| 11 | Irvine | 22.632s | 11 | Panis | 29.971s | 11 | Frentzen | 20.228s |
| 12 | Panis | 22.649s | 12 | Button | 29.989s | 12 | Räikkönen | 20.252s |
| 13 | Räikkönen | 22.660s | 13 | Alesi | 30.055s | 13 | Trulli | 20.265s |
| 14 | Enge | 22.673s | 14 | Frentzen | 30.179s | 14 | Verstappen | 20.319s |
| 15 | Frentzen | 22.674s | 15 | Irvine | 30.218s | 15 | Irvine | 20.325s |
| 16 | Button | 22.788s | 16 | de la Rosa | 30.391s | 16 | de la Rosa | 20.333s |
| 17 | de la Rosa | 22.848s | 17 | Enge | 30.424s | 17 | Panis | 20.434s |
| 18 | Alonso | 22.911s | 18 | Villeneuve | 30.447s | 18 | Enge | 20.447s |
| 19 | Bernoldi | 22.914s | 19 | Alonso | 30.467s | 19 | Yoong | 20.491s |
| 20 | Verstappen | 22.918s | 20 | Verstappen | 30.588s | 20 | Alonso | 20.509s |
| 21 | Villeneuve | 22.950s | 21 | Bernoldi | 30.605s | 21 | Bernoldi | 20.549s |
| 22 | Yoong | 23.375s | 22 | Yoong | 31.060s | 22 | Villeneuve | 20.565s |

### QUALIFYING: SATURDAY 29TH SEPTEMBER 2001, 1PM-2PM
107% time: 1m 16.727s.

| | DRIVER | TEAM | TIME | GAP | LAPS |
|---|---|---|---|---|---|
| 1 | Michael Schumacher | Ferrari | 1m 11.708s | 0.000 | 9 |
| 2 | Ralf Schumacher | BMW Williams | 1m 11.986s | +0.278s | 11 |
| 3 | Juan Pablo Montoya | BMW Williams | 1m 12.252s | +0.544s | 11 |
| 4 | Mika Häkkinen | McLaren Mercedes | 1m 12.309s | +0.601s | 11 |
| 5 | Rubens Barrichello | Ferrari | 1m 12.327s | +0.617s | 12 |
| 6 | Nick Heidfeld | Sauber Petronas | 1m 12.434s | +0.726s | 11 |
| 7 | David Coulthard | McLaren Mercedes | 1m 12.500s | +0.792s | 12 |
| 8 | Jarno Trulli | Jordan Honda | 1m 12.605s | +0.897s | 11 |
| 9 | Jean Alesi | Jordan Honda | 1m 12.607 | +0.899s | 12 |
| 10 | Jenson Button | Benetton Renault | 1m 12.805s | +1.097s | 12 |
| 11 | Kimi Räikkönen | Sauber Petronas | 1m 12.881s | +1.173s | 12 |
| 12 | Giancarlo Fisichella | Benetton Renault | 1m 12.942s | +1.234s | 12 |
| 13 | Olivier Panis | BAR Honda | 1m 13.122s | +1.414s | 12 |
| 14 | Eddie Irvine | Jaguar Racing | 1m 13.189s | +1.481s | 12 |
| 15 | Heinz-Harald Frentzen | Prost Acer | 1m 13.281s | +1.573s | 11 |
| 16 | Pedro de la Rosa | Jaguar Racing | 1m 13.679s | +1.971s | 12 |
| 17 | Fernando Alonso | European Minardi | 1m 13.991s | +2.283s | 12 |
| 18 | Jacques Villeneuve | BAR Honda | 1m 14.012s | +2.304s | 12 |
| 19 | Enrique Bernoldi | Arrows Asiatech | 1m 14.129s | +2.421s | 10 |
| 20 | Jos Verstappen | Arrows Asiatech | 1m 14.138s | +2.430s | 12 |
| 21 | Tomas Enge | Prost Acer | 1m 14.185s | +2.477s | 11 |
| 22 | Alex Yoong | European Minardi | 1m 15.247s | +3.539s | 12 |

Mika Häkkinen originally qualified in second position but his best time was disallowed after a red light infringement in warm-up. Conditions: fine.

### PRACTICE SESSION ONE
FRIDAY 28TH SEPT. 2001 11AM-12PM

| | | |
|---|---|---|
| 1 | M Schumacher | 1m 14.085s |
| 2 | Coulthard | 1m 14.130s |
| 3 | Barrichello | 1m 14.141s |
| 4 | Fisichella | 1m 14.930s |
| 5 | Räikkönen | 1m 15.156s |
| 6 | Heidfeld | 1m 15.367s |
| 7 | Trulli | 1m 15.507s |
| 8 | Frentzen | 1m 15.523s |
| 9 | Button | 1m 15.537s |
| 10 | Verstappen | 1m 15.547s |
| 11 | Irvine | 1m 15.764s |
| 12 | Montoya | 1m 15.836s |
| 13 | Panis | 1m 15.850s |
| 14 | Häkkinen | 1m 15.860s |
| 15 | R Schumacher | 1m 16.031s |
| 16 | de la Rosa | 1m 16.241s |
| 17 | Bernoldi | 1m 16.368s |
| 18 | Alonso | 1m 16.498s |
| 19 | Alesi | 1m 16.543s |
| 20 | Enge | 1m 16.681s |
| 21 | Villeneuve | 1m 16.955s |
| 22 | Yoong | 1m 17.508s |

### PRACTICE SESSION TWO
FRIDAY 28TH SEPT. 2001 1PM-2PM

| | | |
|---|---|---|
| 1 | Häkkinen | 1m 13.387s |
| 2 | M Schumacher | 1m 13.552s |
| 3 | Barrichello | 1m 13.584s |
| 4 | Coulthard | 1m 13.656s |
| 5 | Irvine | 1m 13.806s |
| 6 | Heidfeld | 1m 13.827s |
| 7 | Frentzen | 1m 13.858s |
| 8 | de la Rosa | 1m 13.917s |
| 9 | R Schumacher | 1m 13.919s |
| 10 | Montoya | 1m 13.983s |
| 11 | Räikkönen | 1m 14.027s |
| 12 | Alesi | 1m 14.057s |
| 13 | Button | 1m 14.186s |
| 14 | Trulli | 1m 14.215s |
| 15 | Panis | 1m 14.386s |
| 16 | Enge | 1m 14.767s |
| 17 | Fisichella | 1m 14.911s |
| 18 | Villeneuve | 1m 14.999s |
| 19 | Alonso | 1m 15.131s |
| 20 | Bernoldi | 1m 15.449s |
| 21 | Verstappen | 1m 15.547s |
| 22 | Yoong | 1m 16.318s |

### PRACTICE SESSION THREE
SATURDAY 29TH SEPT. 2001 9AM-9.45AM

| | | |
|---|---|---|
| 1 | M Schumacher | 1m 12.078s |
| 2 | R Schumacher | 1m 12.454s |
| 3 | Barrichello | 1m 12.463s |
| 4 | Häkkinen | 1m 12.617s |
| 5 | Coulthard | 1m 12.724s |
| 6 | Montoya | 1m 12.787s |
| 7 | Button | 1m 12.955s |
| 8 | Heidfeld | 1m 13.079s |
| 9 | Fisichella | 1m 13.283s |
| 10 | Trulli | 1m 13.429s |
| 11 | Räikkönen | 1m 13.520s |
| 12 | Panis | 1m 13.521s |
| 13 | Alesi | 1m 13.931s |
| 14 | Frentzen | 1m 14.122s |
| 15 | de la Rosa | 1m 14.126s |
| 16 | Irvine | 1m 14.212s |
| 17 | Bernoldi | 1m 14.390s |
| 18 | Villeneuve | 1m 14.460s |
| 19 | Enge | 1m 14.675s |
| 20 | Verstappen | 1m 15.005s |
| 21 | Alonso | 1m 15.271s |
| | Yoong | No laps |

### PRACTICE SESSION FOUR
SATURDAY 29TH SEPT. 2001 10.15AM-11AM

| | | |
|---|---|---|
| 1 | M Schumacher | 1m 12.078s |
| 2 | Häkkinen | 1m 12.330s |
| 3 | Heidfeld | 1m 12.407s |
| 4 | R Schumacher | 1m 12.454s |
| 5 | Barrichello | 1m 12.463s |
| 6 | Montoya | 1m 12.668s |
| 7 | Fisichella | 1m 12.672s |
| 8 | Coulthard | 1m 12.724s |
| 9 | Button | 1m 12.955s |
| 10 | Räikkönen | 1m 13.186s |
| 11 | Trulli | 1m 13.205s |
| 12 | Panis | 1m 13.521s |
| 13 | Alesi | 1m 13.675s |
| 14 | de la Rosa | 1m 13.753s |
| 15 | Frentzen | 1m 13.870s |
| 16 | Bernoldi | 1m 13.978s |
| 17 | Irvine | 1m 14.052s |
| 18 | Enge | 1m 14.205s |
| 19 | Villeneuve | 1m 14.346s |
| 20 | Alonso | 1m 14.867s |
| 21 | Verstappen | 1m 14.902s |
| 22 | Yoong | 1m 15.604s |

 **11** K Räikkönen
 **9** J Alesi
 **7** D Coulthard
 **5** R Barrichello
 **3** JP Montoya
 **1** M Schumacher

 **10** J Button
 **8** J Trulli
 **6** N Heidfeld
**4** M Häkkinen
**2** R Schumacher

## INDIANAPOLIS LAP-BY-LAP REPORT

PRE-START Mika Häkkinen was harshly relegated to fourth on the grid after ignoring a red light in the pitlane during warm-up — usually a fineable offence. Behind the all-Schumacher front row: ex-Indy racer Juan Pablo Montoya.

LAP 1 The lights went out and Michael Schumacher got away well from pole. Fast-starting Juan Pablo Montoya made a bold outside manoeuvre into the first corner but could not get past. Rubens Barrichello also started well to grab third, with Ralf Schumacher in a bad fourth, Häkkinen fifth and David Coulthard up to sixth. At the end of the first lap Jarno Trulli and Nick Heidfeld rounded up the top eight. Jos Verstappen had jumped six places to 14th, with Tomas Enge dead last after an atrocious getaway.

LAP 2 Kimi Räikkönen ran into the back of his Sauber team-mate Heidfeld while battling for eighth, and broke his front wing. Heidfeld sneaked past Trulli in the confusion. Barrichello was challenging Montoya for second.

LAP 3 Barrichello charged past Montoya for second at Turn 1 and began to pull away, prompting talk he was on a light fuel load. Ralf Schumacher closed on his team-mate. Räikkönen stopped for a new nosecone. Räikkönen finished returning his car to the Sauber garage. Indicating Benetton's stronger late-season form, Jenson Button passed Jarno Trulli for eighth.

LAP 5 On the infield section, Schumacher moved over to allow his Ferrari team-mate Barrichello into the lead. Michael Schumacher was already 3.4secs up on the leading Williams of Montoya, who appeared to be struggling.

LAP 6 Barrichello clocked the fastest lap in 1m 15.355secs.

LAP 9 Montoya was trailing Barrichello by over seven seconds. Coulthard was being pestered by Heidfeld for sixth.

LAP 10 Button seemed to have a problem and Trulli regained his eighth place.

LAP 12 Barrichello clocked a fastest lap of 1m 15.179secs.

LAP 13 Jean Alesi overtook Giancarlo Fisichella at Turn 1, and set off after Button.

LAP 14 Alesi repeated his Fisichella move on Button, moving him up into ninth.

LAP 16 The gap between leader Barrichello and Michael Schumacher in second was already 8.5 seconds, with Montoya a further four seconds behind that. Heidfeld eyed Coulthard going into Turn 1 but nothing came of it.

LAP 17 In just one lap Barrichello had increased his lead over Schumacher by six-10ths of a second.

LAP 20 Eddie Irvine, coming from nowhere, was now only just over a second behind Fisichella in 11th.

LAP 21 Montoya had also sneaked up on Michael Schumacher: the gap between them was a mere 2.263secs. Barrichello's lead was now 10.483secs.

LAP 24 Barrichello's lead topped 13secs but Montoya was less than 1.5secs behind Schumacher. Ralf Schumacher came in: a problem with the left rear tyre meant his stop lasted 12.5secs and he emerged in only 10th.

LAP 26 The race was suddenly perking up for Häkkinen, who had fumed at his demotion and struggled early on. He was 23.055secs shy of Barrichello and his lack of pace suggested he was on a one-stopper. If Michael Schumacher and Montoya followed their team-mates' strategy, he would be in with a chance of victory. Montoya meanwhile had closed the gap on Michael to 0.608secs. In the meantime, Alex Yoong pitted.

LAP 27 Barrichello, just 12.574secs ahead of his team-mate, pitted in 8.6secs to emerge in fifth. Michael Schumacher, the new race leader, was still harassed by Montoya. Heidfeld also stopped, dropping out of the top six.

LAP 29 The race order was Michael Schumacher, Montoya, Häkkinen, Coulthard, Barrichello, Trulli, Alesi, Ralf Schumacher. The temperature was now 30°C.

LAP 34 Montoya snatched the lead from Michael Schumacher at Turn 1 after the Ferrari towed him down the straight. The Colombians in the crowd and his friends and colleagues in the Williams garage went wild. It was the fourth time the Colombian had overtaken the four-time world champion all year (previously at Interlagos, Imola and Silverstone) — no mean feat. By the end of the lap his lead was already 1.208secs. Nine laps after his team-mate pitted, it looked certain Montoya was running a different, one-stop strategy and victory was clearly possible. The other Williams was doing less

gloriously: Heidfeld had just overtaken Ralf Schumacher for eighth.

LAP 35 Montoya recorded a new lap record of 1m 14.448secs.

LAP 36 Montoya pitted in 13.2secs, emerging in fourth as Michael Schumacher retook the lead. Ralf Schumacher reclaimed eighth from Heidfeld.

LAP 37 Worse, with team-mate Montoya much faster on a heavier fuel load, Ralf Schumacher spun out of the race at Turn 6. Alesi, Bernoldi and Enge pitted.

LAP 38 Both Minardis pitted, Alonso to retire with mechanical problems.

LAP 39 A double disaster for Williams. Montoya's BMW engine let go on the straight and he had to park near the pitwall, in a replay of the warm-up. Cool as ever, he remembered to wish Murray Walker a happy retirement as he was swamped by TV crews on his way back to the garage. Second place in the constructors' championship was looking very difficult for Williams now. The yellow flags were brought out as marshals wheeled away his car. Michael Schumacher came in, handing the lead to Häkkinen. His stop lasted 11.4secs and he returned to the track in fourth. Trulli also pitted.

LAP 41 The order was Häkkinen, Coulthard, Barrichello, Michael Schumacher, Fisichella, Heidfeld, Irvine, Fisichella pitted, elevating Heidfeld to sixth.

LAP 42 Häkkinen was 26 seconds ahead of Michael Schumacher in fourth and flying, with both drivers inbetween also needing to pit. Frentzen pitted.

LAP 43 Coulthard pitted and regained the track in fourth, seven seconds behind Michael Schumacher. Pedro de la Rosa moved ambitiously on Villeneuve for 11th and both cars spun across the track. Villeneuve pitted at the end of his lap, but was waved out again to make way for Olivier Panis.

LAP 44 Panis pitted shortly followed by the troubled Villeneuve, who soon retired.

LAP 45 The top 10 was now Häkkinen, Barrichello, Schumacher, Coulthard, Heidfeld, Irvine, Trulli, Panis and Alesi. Verstappen retired.

LAP 46 Häkkinen pitted handing the lead back to Barrichello. The stop went well, lasting 9.6secs and he emerged fractionally in front of Schumacher's scarlet car with only two-stopping Barrichello in front of him.

LAP 48 Heidfeld made his second stop.

LAP 50 Barrichello pitted with a 22-second lead. His stop was 8.2secs and Häkkinen took the lead with time to spare. Barrichello just took second from Schumacher. De la Rosa also pitted. Yoong retired.

LAP 52 Irvine made his second stop.

LAP 53 The race order was Häkkinen, Barrichello, Schumacher, Coulthard, Trulli, Heidfeld, Irvine, Alesi.

LAP 54 Barrichello slashed Häkkinen's lead to 4.6secs.

LAP 56 Häkkinen's lead was now just 3.4secs. Irvine overtook Heidfeld for sixth at the popular spot of Turn 1.

LAP 63 Häkkinen's lead had stabilised at around 2.8secs as Barrichello worked his way through traffic.

LAP 69 After running consistently behind Häkkinen at just under three seconds, Barrichello's engine started to sound rough and he began to slow. Smoke was squirting from the Ferrari but instead of pitting at the end of the lap, he pressed on, probably hoping to snaffle a point or two and boost his chances of second place in the championship.

LAP 71 Barrichello was still trailing round the track. He let team-mate Michael Schumacher past, but was weaving in front of Coulthard a little selfishly. Coulthard broke through at the end of the lap for a podium place.

LAP 72 Barrichello, after driving brilliantly, came to a smoky halt on the straight. Back in the pitlane he sat head on knees, mulling over lost chances.

LAP 73 Soon-on-sabbatical Mika Häkkinen took the chequered flag for the 20th time, the second win of his disastrous season. The team handed the Finn a mysterious black bag. He had secured the team second in the constructors' championship, capping BMW Williams' bad day. He was joined on the podium by Michael Schumacher and David Coulthard. Trulli was fourth, Eddie Irvine a well-deserved fifth and Heidfeld sixth. Poor Barrichello was classified 15th and last.

POST-RACE Jarno Trulli was disqualified from fourth after stewards found illegal wear to his plank. This promoted Irvine to fourth, Heidfeld to fifth and Alesi to sixth. It was scant consolation for the Jordan team.

# Japanese Grand Prix

**12th–14th October 2001**   LAPS: **53**  LENGTH OF LAP: **3.644** miles

WHEEL-TO-WHEEL: The giant ferris wheel at Suzuka Playland complex dwarfs Michael Schumacher's Ferrari during the Japanese Grand Prix. The twisting and challenging Suzuka circuit in Honda's backyard perfectly suited the latest specification Ferrari chassis, which was racing for the first time. PHOTOGRAPH BY CLEMENT MARIN

At Suzuka, Mika Häkkinen had his last ride with McLaren Mercedes before taking what he says will be a year-long sabbatical.

# Perfect ending for a storybook season

In a fitting finale to the 2001 season at Suzuka, Michael Schumacher and Ferrari again ruled supreme with an emphatically easy victory; second place went to the Williams of Juan Pablo Montoya, arguably the most credible challenger for 2002.

After the extraordinary drama of some races in 2001, the Japanese Grand Prix went off gracefully and ended the season perfectly. The Japanese track, the only one with a Scalextric crosser, provides superb entertainment and if anyone doubted that Michael Schumacher is the best driver in the world he proved he was in Suzuka, crushing everyone in qualifying. He was 1.065mph faster than second best. And Schumacher turned domination in qualifying into true domination of the race.

It was a ninth victory from 17 races and 11 pole positions. It was also career victory number 53, making him the first driver to pass the 800 career points mark, with 801, overtaking Alain Prost's previous best of 798.5. Schumacher's ninth win equalled his own previous achievement and that of Nigel Mansell in 1992. One record he failed to lift was Mansell's all-time record of 14 pole positions in a season.

But the race also showed how the reliability of cars is changing the face of Grand Prix racing. For the second time this season the top six cars finished in the top six places – albeit not in championship order. The last time that occurred, before Nürburgring this year, was the 1996 Belgian Grand Prix.

From pole at Suzuka, Schumacher perfectly controlled the start and was only headed while he pitted for fuel and tyres. He had Bridgestone behind him all weekend, as he will in 2002. Over the first three laps, Schumacher built an embarrassing lead of 8.2 seconds and made the rest of the field look like old grannies. He said: "Today we had a great package and perfect tyres. Despite the records, to finish the season in first place is what you want to do. We have had two races that were a bit difficult for us but now we are back to normality and it's a great result for the team."

Apart from Schumacher, the other driver chasing records was Jean Alesi, with his bid to become the first driver for 37 years to finish every race in a season.

Rubens Barrichello had a forlorn hope of coming second. David Coulthard was rightly dismissive of the Brazilian's efforts: the Scot said it didn't even matter to him. It did, of course, but Barrichello had no chance. And in stark contrast to his team-mate's nine victories and 11 poles, not managing to take one of either was highly disappointing.

As the season progressed, Barrichello cast away dreams of challenging Schumacher and changed from petulant, hard-done-by team-mate to best driver in a supporting role. He realised just how valuable the drive is and how badly he wants it.

On the day, Barrichello was given a driving lesson by Juan Pablo Montoya, who showed him who the better driver is.

Barrichello needed to win the race to take second place, and after getting through the first corner in fourth he rapidly passed Ralf Schumacher's BMW Williams and attacked Montoya in the sister car. Barrichello dived inside the Colombian at the chicane at the end of the second lap, but was re-passed by a determined Montoya into the first corner. That was it: the race was settled. Montoya explained it simply: "Rubens was on new tyres and I was on old ones." Ferrari then switched Barrichello onto an adventurous three-stop strategy, but any hopes he had went out of the window when they lost the engine at the second stop.

Schumacher paced himself to Montoya and ran out a comfortable winner. Brother Ralf's chances were ruined when he received a 10-second stop-go penalty for missing out the chicane, which had allowed him a best sector time. Montoya actually appeared to do the same thing on lap 29, but got away with it. Unofficially, it

Michael Schumacher and Ferrari had a perfect end to their 2001 championship season, with pole and another victory.

The end of the 2001 season for Kimi Räikkönen and Jean Alesi.

seems that the stewards' discretion might have been applied the first time, but Ralf actually committed the offence twice. Mika Häkkinen, in his last Grand Prix before a year-long sabbatical, was running a solid third in the closing stages, although he was never able to repeat his scintillating Suzuka form of last year, which had generated such a tense battle with Schumacher's Ferrari. Suddenly though, with five laps to go, he moved over and let team-mate David Coulthard claim the final place on the podium. Perhaps it was a rather tepid, belated payback for Coulthard's help in 1998-99, or perhaps he just couldn't face another press conference of questions about his impending sabbatical. "I was helped a bit by Mika at the end," Coulthard smiled. "I didn't really know what that was about. He's a very quiet chap and he doesn't give much away!"

Barrichello salvaged fifth place from his busy afternoon, fending off a late challenge from Schumacher junior, each of them having made three pitstops.

Alesi's Grand Prix career ended in the barriers when Kimi Räikkönen lost his Sauber right in front of the Jordan Honda. Räikkönen's Sauber suddenly went out of control and spun. Alesi tried to avoid him but ended up sliding into the barrier with the Sauber. The resulting accident was a huge one, and both drivers were fortunate not to have been hit by debris. Alesi said: "There was no way I could avoid him. Kimi and I were lucky to get away without any injuries." So were the following drivers: the energy

unleashed in the accident exceeded the design capability of the wheel tethers, as all four wheels and tyres pounded across the track in the face of oncoming cars and drivers. Alesi was fortunate not to be hit by an errant wheel. He unbuckled himself, went over to check on the Finn, shook his hand and then walked in, acknowledging the applause for his last race and cursing to himself that the reliability record had been lost. His wife Kumiko hugged him, and he shook hands with every member of the team as he walked around the garage saying goodbye.

Meanwhile Jacques Villeneuve spent the whole afternoon fighting assorted Jordans and Saubers. The Arrows team finished 14th and 15th, and even some of the personnel were wondering why they had bothered: both drivers suffered stop-go penalties and power-steering failures.

When Häkkinen stepped from his car in fourth place, after waving Coulthard through for third, it became obvious that wife Erja was the driving force behind his sabbatical. She was delighted he had driven a racing car for the last time, for a while. There was no emotion à la Alesi. This was sheer joy. Erja had the broadest smile in Suzuka, as she wandered up and down the pitlane saying her goodbyes before taking her husband away.

Ron Dennis was still working extraordinarily hard to convince anyone listening that Häkkinen would soon be back at McLaren Mercedes in harness with David Coulthard. Did he expect Kimi Räikkönen to fail? That's how it sounded to some. Or maybe he was having second thoughts about the extraordinarily generous financial terms he had settled with his new Finn. Far more than he offered the old Finn for 2002.

Coulthard and Häkkinen met the media late on Saturday for a knockabout Q&A session, which threw up memories and jokes and plenty of laughs. Everyone was reminded that Häkkinen and Coulthard had enjoyed the longest and most successful team-driver relationship in Formula One history. The Japanese race marked their 99th Grand Prix together since the Australian Grand Prix in Melbourne in 1996. In that time they had racked up 30 Grands Prix and claimed 33 pole positions. On paper, the combination of Häkkinen and Coulthard outperformed McLaren's all-time-great pairing of Ayrton Senna and Alain Prost; together they recorded 28 wins and 30 poles, although they did take only two seasons to do it.

It was a fitting end to a partnership that Ron Dennis may have tinkered with at his peril. Belatedly he had come to realise it.

# Japanese Grand Prix Race Statistics

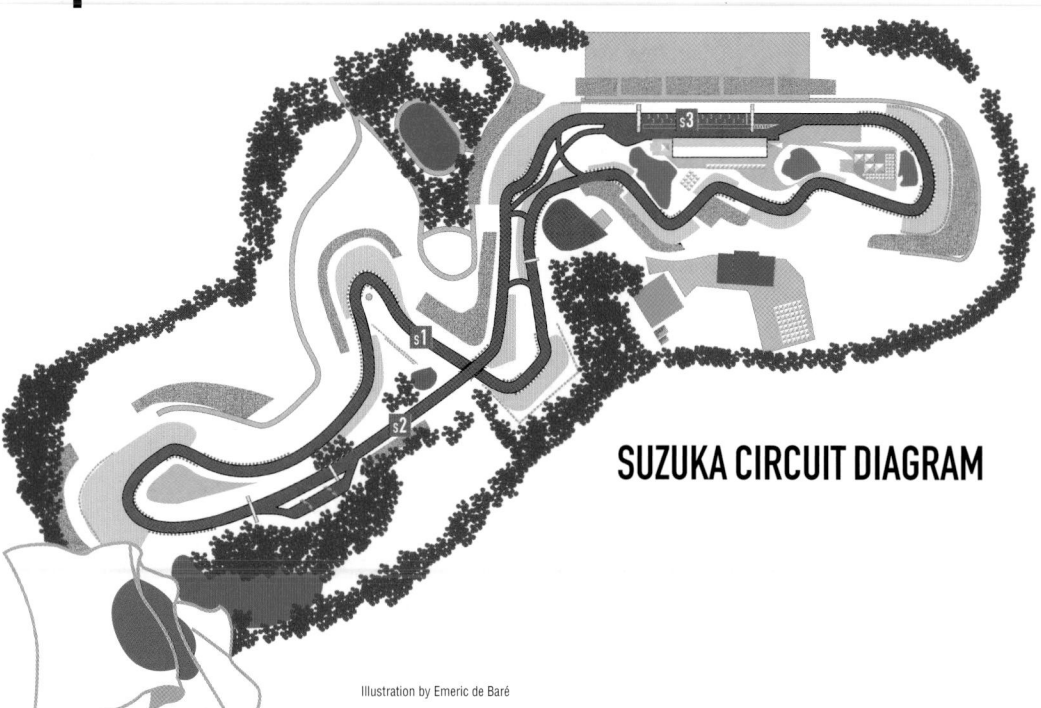

SUZUKA CIRCUIT DIAGRAM

Illustration by Emeric de Baré

## FASTEST LAPS

| | DRIVER | TIME | LAP |
|---|---|---|---|
| 1 | R Schumacher | 1m 36.944s | 46 |
| 2 | Barrichello | 1m 36.970s | 17 |
| 3 | Montoya | 1m 37.017s | 20 |
| 4 | M Schumacher | 1m 37.133s | 29 |
| 5 | Häkkinen | 1m 37.298s | 40 |
| 6 | Coulthard | 1m 37.313s | 51 |
| 7 | Frentzen | 1m 38.240s | 48 |
| 8 | Fisichella | 1m 38.361s | 13 |
| 9 | Button | 1m 38.526s | 36 |
| 10 | Irvine | 1m 38.620s | 22 |
| 11 | Heidfeld | 1m 38.647s | 21 |
| 12 | Trulli | 1m 38.857s | 28 |
| 13 | Villeneuve | 1m 38.887s | 22 |
| 14 | Alonso | 1m 39.153s | 36 |
| 15 | de la Rosa | 1m 39.182s | 40 |
| 16 | Panis | 1m 39.299s | 44 |
| 17 | Enge | 1m 39.827s | 27 |
| 18 | Räikkönen | 1m 39.991s | 4 |
| 19 | Alesi | 1m 40.225s | 4 |
| 20 | Bernoldi | 1m 40.940s | 46 |
| 21 | Verstappen | 1m 41.383s | 16 |
| 22 | Yoong | 1m 42.915s | 42 |

## RACE SPEED TRAP TIMES

| | | |
|---|---|---|
| 1 | Häkkinen | 182.6mph |
| 2 | M Schumacher | 182.1mph |
| 3 | Coulthard | 178.6mph |
| 4 | Montoya | 178.0mph |
| 5 | R Schumacher | 176.5mph |
| 6 | Villeneuve | 176.0mph |
| 7 | Barrichello | 175.9mph |
| 8 | Frentzen | 175.0mph |
| 9 | Alonso | 173.0mph |
| 10 | Alesi | 171.6mph |
| 11 | Button | 171.0mph |
| 12 | Trulli | 171.0mph |
| 13 | Panis | 170.6mph |
| 14 | Fisichella | 170.3mph |
| 15 | Irvine | 170.0mph |
| 16 | Heidfeld | 169.3mph |
| 17 | Verstappen | 168.4mph |
| 18 | Räikkönen | 168.1mph |
| 19 | Enge | 167.6mph |
| 20 | Bernoldi | 166.3mph |
| 21 | de la Rosa | 164.7mph |
| 22 | Yoong | 157.3mph |

## DRIVER POINTS

| | | |
|---|---|---|
| 1 | Michael Schumacher | 123 |
| 2 | David Coulthard | 65 |
| 3 | Rubens Barrichello | 56 |
| 4 | Ralf Schumacher | 49 |
| 5 | Mika Häkkinen | 37 |
| 6 | Juan Pablo Montoya | 31 |
| 7 | Jacques Villeneuve | 12 |
| 8 | Nick Heidfeld | 12 |
| 9 | Jarno Trulli | 12 |
| 10 | Kimi Räikkönen | 9 |
| 11 | Giancarlo Fisichella | 8 |
| 12 | Eddie Irvine | 6 |
| 13 | Heinz-Harald Frentzen | 6 |
| 14 | Olivier Panis | 5 |
| 15 | Jean Alesi | 5 |
| 16 | Pedro de la Rosa | 3 |
| 17 | Jenson Button | 2 |
| 18 | Jos Verstappen | 1 |
| 19 | Ricardo Zonta | 0 |
| 20 | Luciano Burti | 0 |
| 21 | Enrique Bernoldi | 0 |
| 22 | Tarso Marques | 0 |
| 23 | Fernando Alonso | 0 |
| 24 | Gaston Mazzacane | 0 |
| 25 | Tomas Enge | 0 |
| 26 | Alex Yoong | 0 |

## JAPANESE GRAND PRIX RACE RESULTS: SUNDAY 14TH OCTOBER 2001, 2.30PM

| | DRIVER | CAR | TIME/RETIREMENT | LAPS | PITSTOP LAPS |
|---|---|---|---|---|---|
| 1 | Michael Schumacher | Ferrari | 1h 27m 33.298s | 53 | 18 36 |
| 2 | Juan Pablo Montoya | BMW Williams | +3.154s | 53 | 21 38 |
| 3 | David Coulthard | McLaren Mercedes | +23.262s | 53 | 23 39 |
| 4 | Mika Häkkinen | McLaren Mercedes | +35.539s | 53 | 24 38 |
| 5 | Rubens Barrichello | Ferrari | +36.544s | 53 | 15 29 41 |
| 6 | Ralf Schumacher | BMW Williams | +37.122s | 53 | 23 29 39 |
| 7 | Jenson Button | Benetton Renault | +1m 37.102s | 53 | 20 38 |
| 8 | Jarno Trulli | Jordan Honda | +1 lap | 52 | 33 |
| 9 | Nick Heidfeld | Sauber Petronas | +1 lap | 52 | 19 33 |
| 10 | Jacques Villeneuve | BAR Honda | +1 lap | 52 | 19 34 |
| 11 | Fernando Alonso | European Minardi | +1 lap | 52 | 21 37 |
| 12 | Heinz-Harald Frentzen | Prost Acer | +1 lap | 52 | 3 22 38 |
| 13 | Olivier Panis | BAR Honda | +2 laps | 51 | 16 32 |
| 14 | Enrique Bernoldi | Arrows Asiatech | +2 laps | 51 | 19 21 37 |
| 15 | Jos Verstappen | Arrows Asiatech | +2 laps | 51 | 17 33 35 |
| 16 | Alex Yoong | European Minardi | +3 laps | 50 | 18 34 |
| 17 | Giancarlo Fisichella | Benetton Renault | Gearbox | 47 | 16 35 |
| Ret | Pedro de la Rosa | Jaguar Racing | Oil leak | 45 | 26 41 |
| Ret | Tomas Enge | Prost Acer | Brakes | 42 | 21 35 36 41 |
| Ret | Eddie Irvine | Jaguar Racing | Fuel rig | 24 | 23 |
| Ret | Kimi Räikkönen | Sauber Petronas | Collision | 5 | |
| Ret | Jean Alesi | Jordan Honda | Collision | 5 | |

Conditions: fine.

## CONSTRUCTOR POINTS

| | | |
|---|---|---|
| 1 | Scuderia Ferrari Marlboro | 179 |
| 2 | West McLaren Mercedes | 102 |
| 3 | BMW Williams F1 | 80 |
| 4 | Red Bull Sauber Petronas | 21 |
| 5 | Benson & Hedges Jordan Honda | 19 |
| 6 | Lucky Strike Reynard BAR Honda | 17 |
| 7 | Mild Seven Benetton Renault | 10 |
| 8 | Jaguar Racing | 9 |
| 9 | Prost Acer | 4 |
| 10 | Orange Arrows Asiatech | 1 |
| 11 | European Minardi F1 | 0 |

## PITSTOP TIMES (from pitlane entrance to exit)

| | | | | |
|---|---|---|---|---|
| Fastest pitstop: | Tomas Enge | Prost Acer | 25.302s | 35 |
| Slowest pitstop: | Tomas Enge | Prost Acer | 1m 09.393s | 41 |
| Most pitstops: | Tomas Enge | Four stops | | |

## LAP LEADERS

| | |
|---|---|
| M Schumacher | 1-18 |
| Montoya | 19-21 |
| R Schumacher | 22-23 |
| M Schumacher | 24-36 |
| Montoya | 37-38 |
| M Schumacher | 39-53 |

Total laps led: M Schumacher 46; Montoya 5; R Schumacher 2.

## TEMPERATURES

| | | |
|---|---|---|
| Friday: | Air: 25°C | Track: 30°C |
| Saturday: | Air: 21-23°C | Track: 22-27°C |
| Sunday: | Air: 24°C | Track: 27°C |

## WARM-UP

SUNDAY 14TH OCTOBER 2001, 10AM–10.30AM

| | | |
|---|---|---|
| 1 | M Schumacher | 1m 36.231s |
| 2 | Coulthard | 1m 36.685s |
| 3 | Heidfeld | 1m 36.966s |
| 4 | Trulli | 1m 37.140s |
| 5 | Alesi | 1m 37.361s |
| 6 | Häkkinen | 1m 37.584s |
| 7 | Barrichello | 1m 37.813s |
| 8 | Frentzen | 1m 37.891s |
| 9 | Räikkönen | 1m 37.942s |
| 10 | de la Rosa | 1m 37.970s |
| 11 | R Schumacher | 1m 38.183s |
| 12 | Irvine | 1m 38.263s |
| 13 | Villeneuve | 1m 38.604s |
| 14 | Fisichella | 1m 38.641s |
| 15 | Button | 1m 38.740s |
| 16 | Panis | 1m 39.091s |
| 17 | Montoya | 1m 39.182s |
| 18 | Bernoldi | 1m 39.295s |
| 19 | Enge | 1m 40.324s |
| 20 | Verstappen | 1m 40.482s |
| 21 | Yoong | 1m 41.104s |
| 22 | Alonso | 1m 42.142s |

J Verstappen 21

T Enge 19

O Panis 17

HH Frentzen 15

E Irvine 13

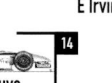

A Yoong 22

E Bernoldi 20

F Alonso 18

P de la Rosa 16

J Villeneuve 14

K Räikkönen 12

## JAPANESE GRAND PRIX RACE ENTRY

| | DRIVER | TEAM | CHASSIS/ENGINE |
|---|---|---|---|
| 1 | Michael Schumacher | Scuderia Ferrari Marlboro | Ferrari F2001 |
| 2 | Rubens Barrichello | Scuderia Ferrari Marlboro | Ferrari F2001 |
| 3 | Mika Häkkinen | West McLaren Mercedes | McLaren Mercedes MP4-16 |
| 4 | David Coulthard | West McLaren Mercedes | McLaren Mercedes MP4-16 |
| 5 | Ralf Schumacher | BMW Williams F1 Team | BMW Williams FW23 |
| 6 | Juan Pablo Montoya | BMW Williams F1 Team | BMW Williams FW23 |
| 7 | Giancarlo Fisichella | Mild Seven Benetton Renault | Benetton Renault B201 |
| 8 | Jenson Button | Mild Seven Benetton Renault | Benetton Renault B201 |
| 9 | Olivier Panis | Lucky Strike BAR Honda | BAR Honda B003 |
| 10 | Jacques Villeneuve | Lucky Strike BAR Honda | BAR Honda B003 |
| 11 | Jean Alesi | Benson & Hedges Jordan Honda | Jordan Honda EJ11 |
| 12 | Jarno Trulli | Benson & Hedges Jordan Honda | Jordan Honda EJ11 |
| 14 | Jos Verstappen | Orange Arrows Asiatech | Arrows Asiatech A22 |
| 15 | Enrique Bernoldi | Orange Arrows Asiatech | Arrows Asiatech A22 |
| 16 | Nick Heidfeld | Red Bull Sauber Petronas | Sauber Petronas C20 |
| 17 | Kimi Räikkönen | Red Bull Sauber Petronas | Sauber Petronas C20 |
| 18 | Eddie Irvine | Jaguar Racing | Jaguar Cosworth R2 |
| 19 | Pedro de la Rosa | Jaguar Racing | Jaguar Cosworth R2 |
| 20 | Alex Yoong | European Minardi | Minardi European PS01B |
| 21 | Fernando Alonso | European Minardi | Minardi European PS01B |
| 22 | Heinz-Harald Frentzen | Prost Grand Prix | Prost ACER AP04 |
| 23 | Tomas Enge | Prost Grand Prix | Prost ACER AP04 |

Suzuka's podium trio wave goodbye to the 2001 season.

## QUALIFYING: SATURDAY 15TH SEPTEMBER 2001, 1PM-2PM 107% time: 1m 38.957s.

| | DRIVER | TEAM | TIME | GAP | LAPS |
|---|---|---|---|---|---|
| 1 | Michael Schumacher | Ferrari | 1m 32.484s | 0.000 | 9 |
| 2 | Juan Pablo Montoya | BMW Williams | 1m 33.184s | +0.700s | 12 |
| 3 | Ralf Schumacher | BMW Williams | 1m 33.297s | +0.813s | 12 |
| 4 | Rubens Barrichello | Ferrari | 1m 33.323s | +0.839s | 11 |
| 5 | Mika Häkkinen | McLaren Mercedes | 1m 33.662s | +1.178s | 11 |
| 6 | Giancarlo Fisichella | Benetton Renault | 1m 33.830s | +1.346s | 11 |
| 7 | David Coulthard | McLaren Mercedes | 1m 33.916s | +1.432s | 11 |
| 8 | Jarno Trulli | Jordan Honda | 1m 34.002s | +1.518s | 12 |
| 9 | Jenson Button | Benetton Renault | 1m 34.375s | +1.891s | 12 |
| 10 | Nick Heidfeld | Sauber Petronas | 1m 34.386s | +1.902s | 12 |
| 11 | Jean Alesi | Jordan Honda | 1m 34.420s | +1.936s | 12 |
| 12 | Kimi Räikkönen | Sauber Petronas | 1m 34.581s | +2.097s | 11 |
| 13 | Eddie Irvine | Jaguar Racing | 1m 34.851s | +2.367s | 11 |
| 14 | Jacques Villeneuve | BAR Honda | 1m 35.109s | +2.625s | 12 |
| 15 | Heinz-Harald Frentzen | Prost Acer | 1m 35.132s | +2.648s | 11 |
| 16 | Pedro de la Rosa | Jaguar Racing | 1m 35.639s | +3.155s | 12 |
| 17 | Olivier Panis | BAR Honda | 1m 35.766s | +3.282s | 12 |
| 18 | Fernando Alonso | European Minardi | 1m 36.410s | +3.926s | 11 |
| 19 | Tomas Enge | Prost Acer | 1m 36.446s | +3.962s | 10 |
| 20 | Enrique Bernoldi | Arrows Asiatech | 1m 36.885s | +4.401s | 12 |
| 21 | Jos Verstappen | Arrows Asiatech | 1m 36.973s | +4.489s | 11 |
| 22 | Alex Yoong | European Minardi | 1m 38.246s | +5.762s | 11 |

## FASTEST SECTOR TIMES IN QUALIFYING Ideal lap time: 1m 32.330s (diff. from pole: 0.154s).

| | SECTOR 1 | SECS | | SECTOR 2 | SECS | | SECTOR 3 | SECS |
|---|---|---|---|---|---|---|---|---|
| 1 | M Schumacher | 30.655s | 1 | M Schumacher | 41.633s | 1 | R Schumacher | 20.042s |
| 2 | Barrichello | 31.055s | 2 | Montoya | 41.737s | 2 | Montoya | 20.048s |
| 3 | Trulli | 31.132s | 3 | R Schumacher | 41.809s | 3 | M Schumacher | 20.196s |
| 4 | Montoya | 31.197s | 4 | Barrichello | 41.924s | 4 | Häkkinen | 20.204s |
| 5 | R Schumacher | 31.310s | 5 | Häkkinen | 41.960s | 5 | Barrichello | 20.254s |
| 6 | Fisichella | 31.331s | 6 | Coulthard | 42.149s | 6 | Button | 20.265s |
| 7 | Häkkinen | 31.345s | 7 | Fisichella | 42.152s | 7 | Fisichella | 20.297s |
| 8 | Coulthard | 31.390s | 8 | Button | 42.183s | 8 | Alesi | 20.331s |
| 9 | Heidfeld | 31.413s | 9 | Trulli | 42.249s | 9 | Trulli | 20.343s |
| 10 | Alesi | 31.448s | 10 | Heidfeld | 42.309s | 10 | Coulthard | 20.351s |
| 11 | Räikkönen | 31.569s | 11 | Irvine | 42.366s | 11 | Frentzen | 20.420s |
| 12 | Villeneuve | 31.787s | 12 | Frentzen | 42.467s | 12 | Irvine | 20.470s |
| 13 | Button | 31.835s | 13 | Alesi | 42.472s | 13 | Villeneuve | 20.498s |
| 14 | Panis | 31.917s | 14 | Räikkönen | 42.506s | 14 | Räikkönen | 20.506s |
| 15 | Irvine | 31.936s | 15 | de la Rosa | 42.614s | 15 | Heidfeld | 20.529s |
| 16 | Frentzen | 31.990s | 16 | Villeneuve | 42.679s | 16 | de la Rosa | 20.597s |
| 17 | Alonso | 32.107s | 17 | Panis | 42.959s | 17 | Panis | 20.697s |
| 18 | Enge | 32.250s | 18 | Enge | 43.176s | 18 | Verstappen | 20.787s |
| 19 | de la Rosa | 32.258s | 19 | Alonso | 43.230s | 19 | Alonso | 20.956s |
| 20 | Bernoldi | 32.505s | 20 | Bernoldi | 43.263s | 20 | Bernoldi | 20.992s |
| 21 | Verstappen | 32.601s | 21 | Verstappen | 43.428s | 21 | Enge | 21.020s |
| 22 | Yoong | 33.248s | 22 | Yoong | 43.708s | 22 | Yoong | 21.129s |

## PRACTICE SESSION ONE
FRIDAY 12TH OCTOBER 2001, 11AM-12PM

| | | |
|---|---|---|
| 1 | M Schumacher | 1m 37.443s |
| 2 | Häkkinen | 1m 37.798s |
| 3 | Montoya | 1m 37.947s |
| 4 | Barrichello | 1m 38.032s |
| 5 | Alesi | 1m 38.157s |
| 6 | Coulthard | 1m 38.160s |
| 7 | R Schumacher | 1m 38.276s |
| 8 | Frentzen | 1m 38.445s |
| 9 | de la Rosa | 1m 38.555s |
| 10 | Heidfeld | 1m 38.937s |
| 11 | Irvine | 1m 38.953s |
| 12 | Fisichella | 1m 39.000s |
| 13 | Trulli | 1m 39.361s |
| 14 | Villeneuve | 1m 39.532s |
| 15 | Button | 1m 40.018s |
| 16 | Räikkönen | 1m 40.197s |
| 17 | Verstappen | 1m 40.381s |
| 18 | Panis | 1m 40.652s |
| 19 | Alonso | 1m 41.097s |
| 20 | Enge | 1m 41.216s |
| 21 | Bernoldi | 1m 41.376s |
| 22 | Yoong | 1m 43.800s |

## PRACTICE SESSION TWO
FRIDAY 12TH OCTOBER 2001, 1PM-2PM

| | | |
|---|---|---|
| 1 | Alesi | 1m 35.454s |
| 2 | Montoya | 1m 35.977s |
| 3 | de la Rosa | 1m 36.225s |
| 4 | Häkkinen | 1m 36.430s |
| 5 | Frentzen | 1m 36.439s |
| 6 | Irvine | 1m 36.589s |
| 7 | Coulthard | 1m 36.638s |
| 8 | M Schumacher | 1m 36.727s |
| 9 | R Schumacher | 1m 36.874s |
| 10 | Barrichello | 1m 36.994s |
| 11 | Trulli | 1m 37.564s |
| 12 | Button | 1m 37.645s |
| 13 | Heidfeld | 1m 37.665s |
| 14 | Villeneuve | 1m 38.312s |
| 15 | Räikkönen | 1m 38.315s |
| 16 | Fisichella | 1m 38.398s |
| 17 | Alonso | 1m 38.961s |
| 18 | Panis | 1m 39.108s |
| 19 | Verstappen | 1m 39.511s |
| 20 | Bernoldi | 1m 39.744s |
| 21 | Yoong | 1m 39.952s |
| 22 | Enge | 1m 41.216s |

## PRACTICE SESSION THREE
SATURDAY 13TH OCTOBER 2001, 9AM-9.45AM

| | | |
|---|---|---|
| 1 | M Schumacher | 1m 34.711s |
| 2 | Häkkinen | 1m 35.043s |
| 3 | Barrichello | 1m 35.222s |
| 4 | Coulthard | 1m 35.424s |
| 5 | R Schumacher | 1m 35.651s |
| 6 | Montoya | 1m 35.742s |
| 7 | Räikkönen | 1m 36.597s |
| 8 | Trulli | 1m 36.710s |
| 9 | Button | 1m 36.819s |
| 10 | Frentzen | 1m 36.820s |
| 11 | Heidfeld | 1m 36.899s |
| 12 | Villeneuve | 1m 36.964s |
| 13 | Alesi | 1m 36.987s |
| 14 | Irvine | 1m 37.028s |
| 15 | Fisichella | 1m 37.035s |
| 16 | Panis | 1m 37.493s |
| 17 | de la Rosa | 1m 38.049s |
| 18 | Bernoldi | 1m 38.416s |
| 19 | Enge | 1m 38.868s |
| 20 | Verstappen | 1m 39.050s |
| 21 | Alonso | 1m 39.172s |
| 22 | Yoong | 1m 40.678s |

## PRACTICE SESSION FOUR
SATURDAY 13TH OCT. 2001, 10.15AM-11AM

| | | |
|---|---|---|
| 1 | R Schumacher | 1m 33.969s |
| 2 | Montoya | 1m 34.301s |
| 3 | Coulthard | 1m 34.562s |
| 4 | M Schumacher | 1m 34.711s |
| 5 | Button | 1m 34.735s |
| 6 | Trulli | 1m 34.909s |
| 7 | Heidfeld | 1m 35.037s |
| 8 | Häkkinen | 1m 35.043s |
| 9 | Barrichello | 1m 35.222s |
| 10 | Villeneuve | 1m 35.457s |
| 11 | Frentzen | 1m 35.483s |
| 12 | Räikkönen | 1m 35.672s |
| 13 | Panis | 1m 35.719s |
| 14 | Alesi | 1m 36.051s |
| 15 | Irvine | 1m 36.060s |
| 16 | Fisichella | 1m 36.114s |
| 17 | de la Rosa | 1m 36.144s |
| 18 | Enge | 1m 37.246s |
| 19 | Alonso | 1m 37.429s |
| 20 | Bernoldi | 1m 37.514s |
| 21 | Verstappen | 1m 37.805s |
| 22 | Yoong | 1m 38.839s |

 **11** J Alesi
 **9** J Button
 **7** D Coulthard
 **5** M Häkkinen
 **3** R Schumacher
 **1** M Schumacher

**10** N Heidfeld
**8** J Trulli
**6** G Fisichella
**4** R Barrichello
**2** JP Montoya

## SUZUKA LAP-BY-LAP REPORT

PRE-START Alex Yoong started from the pitlane due to an electrical fault. He was joined by Enrique Bernoldi, who failed to get away for the formation lap.

LAP 1 Michael Schumacher had a brilliant start, cutting across the track from pole; the two BMW Williams of Juan Pablo Montoya and Ralf Schumacher, then Michael Schumacher's team-mate Rubens Barrichello, followed in grid order. Giancarlo Fisichella used his Benetton Renault's superior launch control, in the team's last race under the Benetton name, to jump the McLarens for fifth. Halfway through the first lap, Michael Schumacher was already pulling away massively. Nick Heidfeld almost clashed with Jacques Villeneuve and dropped back to 14th. At 130R, Barrichello passed Ralf Schumacher into third. Mika Häkkinen tried to pass Fisichella, but failed. After lap one, the order was: Michael Schumacher, Montoya, Barrichello, Ralf Schumacher, Fisichella, Häkkinen, David Coulthard, Jarno Trulli, Jenson Button and Kimi Räikkönen.

LAP 2 In a single lap Michael Schumacher had built a huge 3.6secs lead over Montoya. Heinz-Harald Frentzen shunted Eddie Irvine's Jaguar, damaging his Prost's front wing. At the chicane Barrichello passed Montoya.

LAP 3 The gap between race leader Schumacher and Barrichello was already 6.3secs. Montoya riposted, retaking second at the first corner. Fisichella spun as Häkkinen chased him, and rejoined behind Irvine in 12th. Frentzen pitted for a new nosecone and rejoined at the back of the field.

LAP 4 The Schumacher-Montoya gap again stretched dramatically, to 8.2secs.

LAP 6 Schumacher was leading by 9.7secs, causing speculation that both Ferraris might be running on a one-stop strategy. Montoya was still followed closely by Barrichello for second, then by Ralf Schumacher, Häkkinen, Coulthard, Trulli and Button. Räikkönen and Jean Alesi scrapped for ninth. As they entered the Esses, the Finn hit a bump and spun. With nowhere to go, Alesi T-boned the Sauber. Both cars crashed into the tyre wall. Despite much flying debris and a wheel bouncing across the track, both drivers were OK. After being classified in every race this season, it was a cruel blow for Alesi in his swansong. Räikkönen was a little shaken, and Alesi comforted him before trudging back to the pits. The Finn was declared fit and well. In the chaos of the accident, Fisichella passed Irvine for what had become ninth.

LAP 9 His lead now 11.6secs, Michael Schumacher seemed to be trying too hard. After a scrappy lap he ran wide at the chicane, the likely reason being he was on a three-stopper and desperate to up his lead to Montoya.

LAP 10 In response, Montoya set the fastest lap of the race at 1m 37.551secs.

LAP 11 Fisichella passed his team-mate Button for eighth.

LAP 15 Montoya had cut Schumacher's lead to 10.3secs when the Ferrari crew were sighted in the pitlane. It looked a disaster for Schumacher, until he passed the entrance at the end of the lap and Barrichello was brought in. The Brazilian was clearly on a three-stop strategy, ruined by Montoya's bold take-back, and emerged in seventh behind Fisichella.

LAP 16 The Brazilian took the Italian at the chicane, but seconds later Fisichella and sixth-placed Trulli pitted; Trulli stayed ahead. Panis pitted from 17th.

LAP 17 The Schumacher-Montoya gap had stabilised at around 10.7secs. Michael Schumacher set the fastest lap of 1m 37.509secs, but right away it was bettered by Barrichello with 1m 36.952secs. Jos Verstappen pitted.

LAP 18 With it still unclear whether he was on a two- or three-stop strategy, Michael Schumacher pitted and Montoya took the lead. An 8.8secs stop suggested the former. Schumacher returned in fourth, behind Montoya, Ralf Schumacher and Häkkinen and ahead of Coulthard, Barrichello, Button and Irvine. Alex Yoong made his first stop.

LAP 19 Villeneuve, Heidfeld and Bernoldi came into the pits.

LAP 20 Villeneuve pitted. Michael Schumacher was right on Häkkinen's tail. He had a go at the Finn at the chicane and kept trying right up to the first corner, but Häkkinen somehow kept ahead. Button made his first stop.

LAP 21 Häkkinen ran wide but stayed ahead. Bernoldi got a stop-go penalty for

cutting the chicane. Montoya pitted. His team-mate Ralf Schumacher took the lead and Montoya emerged amid the Coulthard-Barrichello battle. Alonso and Enge also stopped.

LAP 22 Frentzen made his second stop.

LAP 23 The running order was Ralf Schumacher, Häkkinen, Michael Schumacher, Coulthard, Montoya, Barrichello, Irvine, and Pedro de la Rosa. Ralf Schumacher and Coulthard pitted, handing Häkkinen the lead. Ralf rejoined in fifth, Coulthard in sixth. A failed rig caused Irvine to abort his fuel stop.

LAP 24 Häkkinen pitted from the lead and Michael Schumacher again took over at the front. The stop lasted 7.6secs and the Finn came out in fifth. Irvine retired in the pits when he still could not take on fuel.

LAP 27 Pedro de la Rosa pitted from seventh.

LAP 28 The running order was Michael Schumacher with 6.7secs to Montoya, then Barrichello, Ralf Schumacher, Häkkinen, Coulthard, Trulli and Fisichella. Ralf Schumacher got a 10-second stop-go penalty for 'cutting the chicane with an advantage'.

LAP 29 Rubens Barrichello pitted a second time as Ralf Schumacher came in for his penalty. The Brazilian took on 12.6secs of fuel, rejoining just ahead of the German, but as they exited the pitlane Schumacher ducked a wheel over the white line and got in front.

LAP 30 That move put Ralf Schumacher under scrutiny again. The Williams team successfully argued it was the only way to avoid Barrichello, whose speed limiter had stayed on. Jos Verstappen was also under investigation.

LAP 32 Panis stopped again, still in 17th place.

LAP 33 Trying to stay ahead of Barrichello, Ralf Schumacher ran over the chicane, raising speculation he might be investigated a third time, but the Brazilian immediately made a stunning move to vanquish the Williams driver. Trulli, Heidfeld and Verstappen pitted.

LAP 34 Villeneuve pitted.

LAP 35 Fisichella and Enge pitted.

LAP 36 Verstappen served his 10-second penalty for overtaking on the formation lap. Fisichella and Michael Schumacher pitted, giving Montoya the lead. The German was 6.6secs ahead: if Montoya could avoid pitting soon and put in some hot laps, he might win. Schumacher pitted for 9.0secs, rejoining in third behind Häkkinen. Enge pitted again with a mechanical problem.

LAP 38 Thwarted by traffic, Montoya was brought in. A 7.6secs stop could not get him out ahead of Schumacher. Häkkinen pitted, as did Button and Frentzen.

LAP 39 Coulthard pitted in 6.8sec, Ralf Schumacher in 9.2secs.

LAP 41 Barrichello pitted in 7.2secs. When he emerged the running order, with none of the frontrunners still to stop, was Michael Schumacher, Montoya, Häkkinen, Coulthard, Barrichello, Ralf Schumacher, Fisichella and Button. Schumacher's lead was over eight seconds. Pedro de la Rosa pitted, as did Enge for the fourth time.

LAP 42 Enge retired with brake problems.

LAP 45 Pedro de la Rosa retired with a fuel pressure problem.

LAP 47 As Michael Schumacher struggled in traffic, Montoya slashed his lead to 5.6secs. Fisichella retired with a mechanical fault.

LAP 48 Schumacher's lead was reduced to 5.2secs.

LAP 49 Häkkinen allowed Coulthard past into third. He remembered that he had always promised to pay the Scot back for the victories he gained at the 1997 European Grand Prix and the 1998 Australian Grand Prix. A nice gesture, but with the championship positions all but tied up, the Finn clearly got the better part of the deal. Villeneuve spun at the chicane. The Schumacher-Montoya gap had increased to 5.6secs.

LAP 53 Michael Schumacher took his record-equalling ninth win of the season, with Montoya and a bemused Coulthard joining him on the podium. Häkkinen, Barrichello and Ralf Schumacher made up the points-scoring positions. Button finished a creditable 'best of the rest' in seventh to put Benetton ahead of Jaguar in the constructors' championship. The remaining classified runners were Trulli, Heidfeld, Villeneuve, Alonso in an impressive 11th, Frentzen, Panis, Verstappen, Bernoldi and Yoong.

p530

AUSTRALIA

p533

MALAYSIA

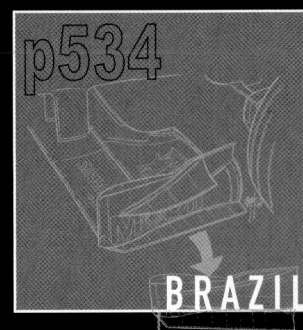

p534

BRAZIL

p540

AUSTRIA

p542

MONACO

p546

CANADA

p548

EUROPE

p550

FRANCE

p558

HUNGARY

p560

BELGIUM

p562

ITALY

6

MARINO

p538

SPAIN

Technical
# REVIEW

2001

p552

BRITAIN

p554

GERMANY

p564

USA

p566

JAPAN

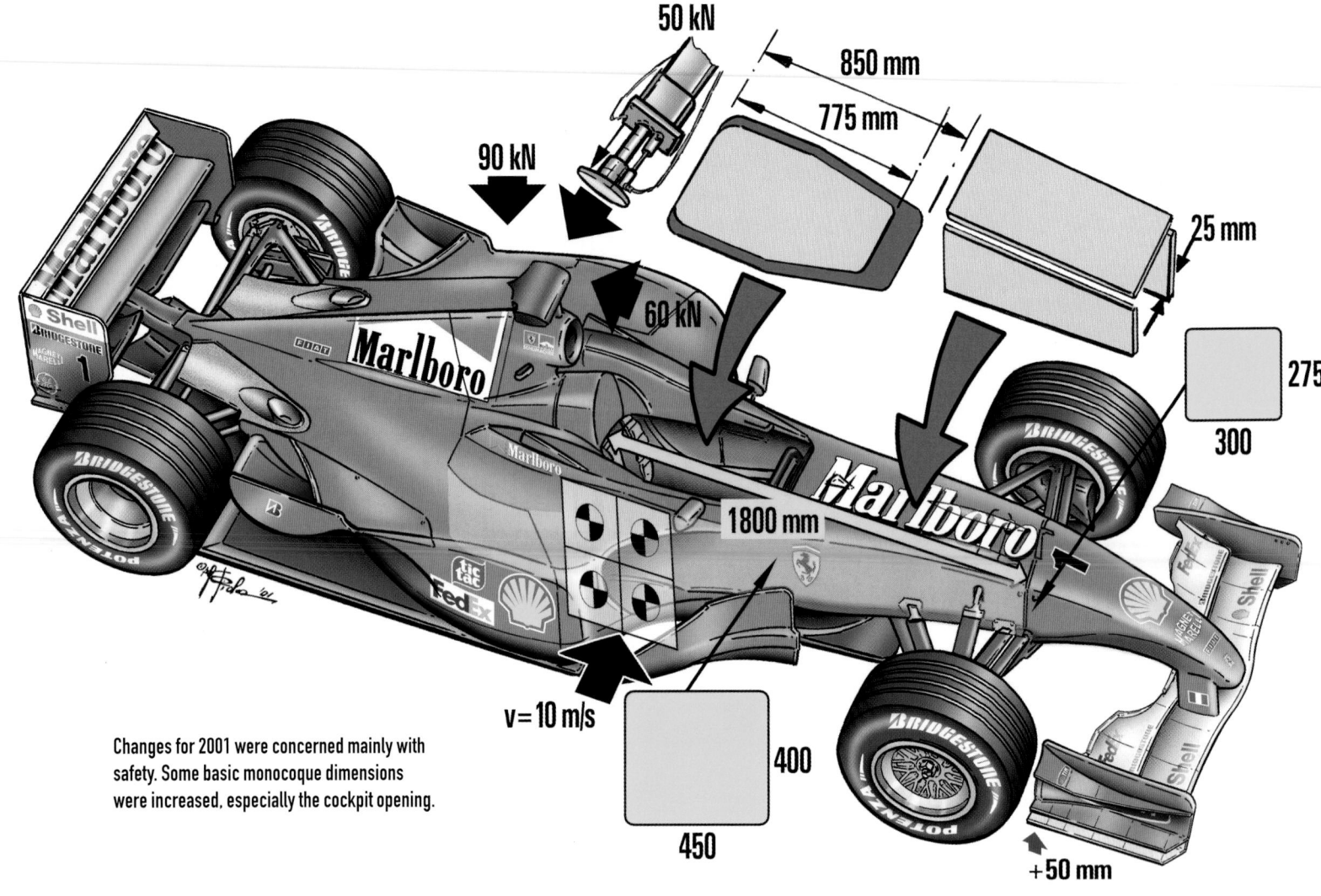

Changes for 2001 were concerned mainly with safety. Some basic monocoque dimensions were increased, especially the cockpit opening.

# Technology – governed by rules

## Formula One's rules and regulations were changed in 2001 in a number of important areas, with improved safety as the primary motivation. Renowned Formula One car designer John Barnard explains the major changes and their significance.

Everyone knows that Formula One is run to a pretty rigid set of rules and regulations. But break it down and it becomes much more understandable and not the technical abyss most think. There are two forms of regulations: one set called the Technical Regulations and another set called the Sporting Regulations. The Sporting Regulations deal with such things as how the race is started, when the pace car should be used, what conditions require the race to be stopped and so on. However, it is the Technical Regulations that are important to designers.

Since my first involvement at McLaren in the early 1970s the Technical Regulations have become increasingly complicated. When cars are deemed illegal today, for a couple of millimetres, it is nothing new. I clearly remember when James Hunt's McLaren car was thrown out for being 15mm too wide across the rear tyres.

The regulations are issued and policed by the FIA (Fédération Internationale de l'Automobile) under the auspices of the president Max Mosley who takes an active, hands-on role in the framing of

the rules. The FIA's technical department is headed by Charlie Whiting and oversees the implementation of the regulations. The manner in which regulations are formulated and instigated is something not too many people outside Formula One understand. Back in the early 1980s it wasn't even that obvious to those of us involved. At this time, Formula One was effectively run by a triumvirate that consisted of Jean-Marie Balestre, president of the FIA, then Brabham owner and FOCA (Formula One Constructors Association) president Bernie Ecclestone, representing the British teams, and Enzo Ferrari, represented by his deputy Marco Piccinini. This triumvirate brought with it an interesting division of teams, as Enzo Ferrari referred rather disparagingly to the English teams as the 'garagisti', basically meaning a bunch of ragamuffins who bolted other peoples' engines to their chassis!

Whatever their cultural differences, that power base seemed to be able to effect rules and regulations without any intervention from teams, unlike today. I remember towards the end of 1982 suddenly receiving a new regulation that banned what we then knew as a ground effect car. The upstart 'garagisti' had managed to gain a significant advantage over people like Ferrari through some innovative thinking on aerodynamics by Colin Chapman of Lotus.

It is true to say that those cars were capable of cornering at astonishing speeds and those speeds would have continued to increase if left unchecked. I remember distinctly being told of the regulation that 'from now' (ie from the 1983 season onwards) all cars would be required to have a flat bottom. I was absolutely dumbstruck. We had just spent 18 months working with Porsche to design and build an engine specifically optimised for a ground effect car. We already had a windtunnel model running which was producing some truly astonishing downforce numbers. The engine configuration, which I had defined for Porsche, had been integrated carefully for a ground effect car. All that work suddenly lost about 50 per cent of its performance advantage. The new regulations shifted the emphasis back to engine performance and thereby satisfied Ferrari.

The benefit of a beautifully crafted, slick, slim engine was lost. But as history has shown, it didn't turn out too badly for McLaren and that engine.

Many of us were most upset by the way these sudden changes were applied. Slowly, the system changed and the technical people became more involved in discussing and framing new rules and regulations. Today, there is a pretty well defined procedure for changing rules or instigating new ones. Charlie Whiting normally drafts new regulations or redrafts old regulations following discussion with Max Mosley. Whiting will then take this proposal to the Technical Working Group, which includes the teams' senior technical people such as Patrick Head of Williams and Ross Brawn of Ferrari. This Group meets approximately every three months, more often when necessary, to discuss the proposed regulations or changes and on most occasions reaches some kind of agreement or compromise acceptable to all the teams. Any regulation change must then be rubber-stamped by the FIA. Sometimes a rule change proposal is rejected or altered by a meeting of the team principals and Mosley. Many times this is to do with the politics of Formula One rather than technical practicalities.

Theoretically, the rules must be decided one year in advance of the season they are to apply, but this doesn't happen often. Sometimes rules are still being discussed a few months before the start of the season. This is possible because any changes at this point may only take place with the agreement of all teams.

The case of deregulation of electronic controls being approved by the Technical Working Group, and then being vetoed by the team principals' meeting is rare enough to demand comment. Delaying the introduction of the new regulations until after Barcelona was an unusual arrangement, but again nothing new.

One very significant year, was 1985 when the first safety regulation requiring a physical test on the car was introduced. This was the nosebox crash test. Amazingly, before this, just about the only safety regulation was the requirement of a roll-hoop behind the driver. My reaction was to build a drop test tower and see what happened to our existing nosebox. At that time the McLaren nosebox was made from aluminium. I remember getting some of the guys to build a huge block of concrete with tall posts set into it, in the backyard of McLaren, so that we could drop this nosebox with something like 700kg of weight behind it onto the concrete block. The rig stood as high as the factory roof and the first time we dropped it I couldn't believe my eyes. What started off as a nice smart aluminium nosebox about 50cm long ended up resembling a pancake. It was a real eye opener and we had to get to work to design a new nosebox in aluminium, which would absorb the energy involved in the drop test, not transmit it to the chassis. Since then F1 safety regulations have gradually increased in number and become more severe. It is easy to see why the frequency of fatalities has tailed off.

There is one overriding proviso to the system of devising and introducing new regulations. The FIA retains the absolute right to change the rules at a moment's notice if it believes safety conditions require it. This happened in 1994 after the deaths of Roland Ratzenberger and Ayrton Senna at Imola. At the next race in Monaco, only two weeks later, the FIA required the teams to shorten the cars diffuser, (part of the aerodynamic surface at the back of the car) to reduce downforce and immediately slow the cars. That kind of sudden intervention doesn't happen very often and usually it's because of a tragic event.

From 1994 to 1995, the regulations changed again. For 1995, completely flat-bottomed cars were banned, and what we call the step-bottom was introduced. The step-bottom regulation basically increased the distance from the ground to the sidepods, thereby reducing downforce further but at the same time making the cars slightly less sensitive and slightly less dependent on maintaining ride height. At the time of the introduction of the step-bottom regulation, Mosley sought a schedule of changes to take place virtually year on year, in an attempt to peg lap times to the 1995 level. Since that time, there have been regulation changes for each new ▷

The new 2001 front wing regulation stipulates that the outside two thirds of the front wing must be raised by 5cm. The middle dimension of the wing structure is unchanged.

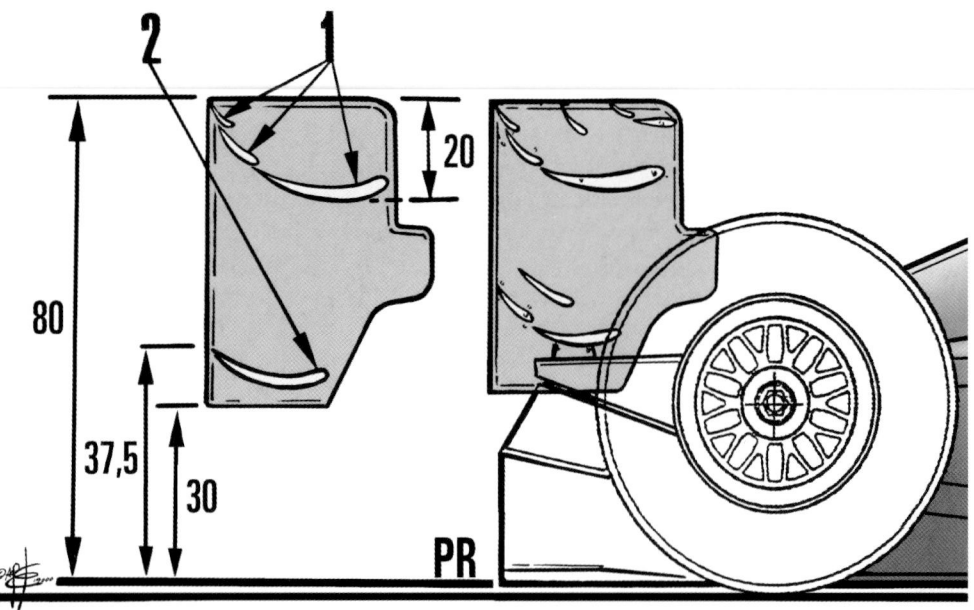

A view of the 2000 wing (right) through the endplates. For 2001 (left) the rear wing sizes were further limited. There may only be three elements in the upper plane and one in the lower.

that's the theory. Designers had been coming up with completely different front wings, in which the middle part of the front wing was dropped right down, near the ground, thus creating ground effects from the underside of the front wing.

Along with the raised front wing, there was a new rear wing regulation which defines the size of a box to contain the rear wing. If you look at photos of older cars on high downforce circuits you will see rear wings with three, four, five or more individual elements. These were now limited to three.

## MONOCOQUE

First of all, the monocoque dimensions were altered. The internal size of the monocoque as well as the external are both regulated. There was now effectively a minimum internal length, which is a new regulation. In the past, if a team hired a smaller driver they benefited with a packaging advantage as the space could be used for extra fuel or a smaller cockpit opening.

The minimum internal height of the monocoque was increased to allow leg padding to be added to the forward part of the cockpit, thus offering protection for the driver's legs in an accident – it's quite common for a driver's legs to be thrown around inside the car and damaged during an accident. Along with the padding a new so-called cockpit template was introduced – a minimum size for the opening in the monocoque through which the driver enters the car. The cockpit template is now positioned at a minimum length dimension, which is tied to dimensions at the front of the monocoque, thereby ensuring cars cannot be built specifically for very small drivers. Cars now have to be made suitable in size to take even the tallest drivers in F1 and the smaller drivers will simply end up having to move their pedals back. Another reason for defining a bigger cockpit template is that the smaller the cockpit opening, the stiffer the monocoque becomes, and also the better aerodynamically, thereby giving a performance advantage. However, this had led

season. The following changes made for the 2001 season were significant:

### NEW RAISED FRONT WING AND SMALLER REAR WING

The increase in the height from the ground of the front wing was a direct attempt to reduce efficiency of the aerodynamics and therefore the speed of the car. For 2001 the outer two-thirds of the front wing were raised by another 50mm, making them 100mm above the bottom of the car. The desire to decrease overall downforce comes from the simple expedient that if you can't create enough downforce at the front it becomes the limiting factor. You are therefore forced to lose downforce from the back of the car, thereby overall downforce, thus reducing cornering speeds. At least

The diagram below shows the methods for the side impact test. The four bulls-eyes on the side of the car indicate the division of the impact plate is divided into four sections to ensure that the resisting structure is more evenly spread along the side of the monocoque.

The datum point for the impact plate is determined by a measurement from the back of the cockpit opening, thereby ensuring it is optimally placed for driver protection.

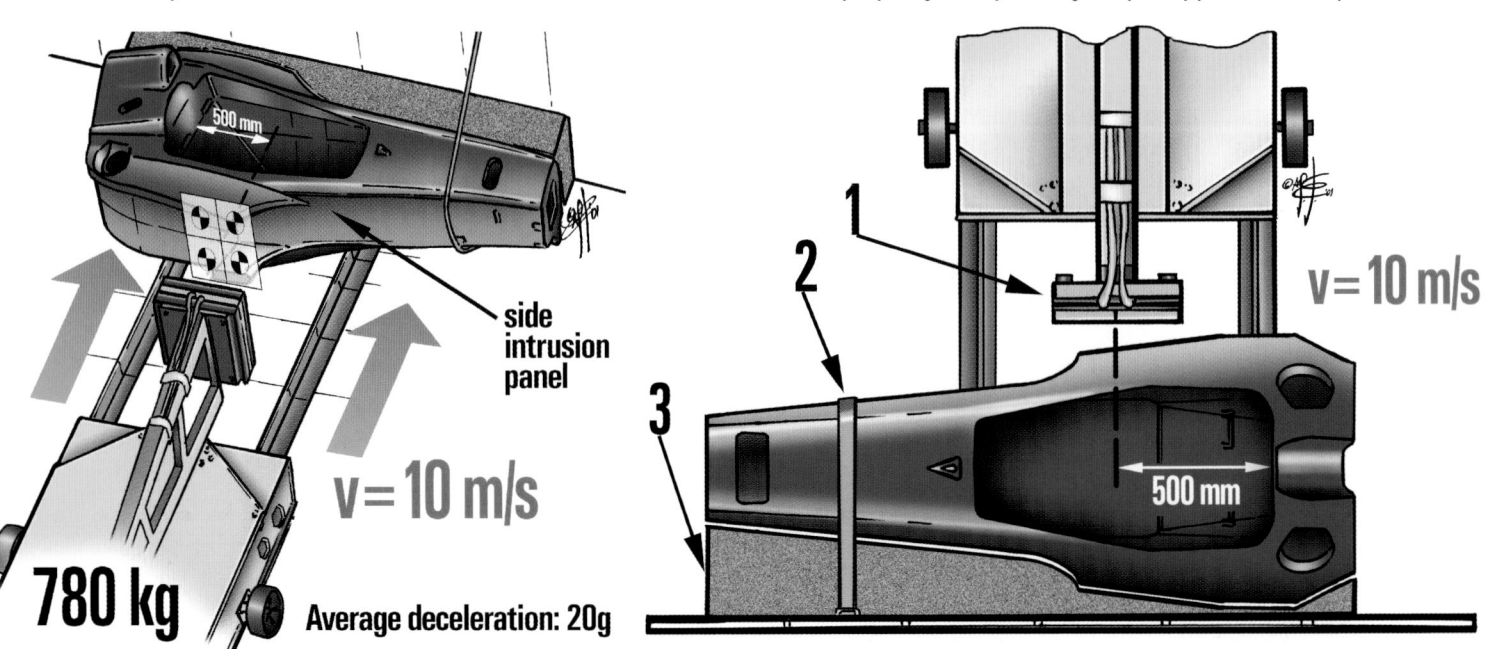

to drivers being seated in very awkward and tight situations, where there has been only just enough clearance between the steering wheel and cockpit surround, resulting in the driver's knuckles rubbing on the monocoque as he turned the wheel. Some years ago this problem was dealt with by increasing the cockpit opening size. This year it increased again, in principle, to go along with the minimum inside dimension to accommodate tall drivers. A precise template is used by the FIA to check that all cars comply with the minimum cockpit dimensions.

## NEW SIDE IMPACT REGULATIONS

Since 1995 the teams have had to pass a side impact test aimed at improving driver protection through increased resistance to side penetration. This is a static test on the monocoque safety cell, involving a mass of 780kg, driven into the side of the monocoque at a prescribed speed. Last year's speed was seven metres per second (7m/sec), and it increased this year to 10 metres a second (10m/sec). Although this does not appear a big increase, in reality, it nearly doubles the energy to be absorbed. To resist these side impacts, the monocoques are specially strengthened locally in the area ahead of the sidepods. Since 1995, the teams have developed this crash resistant section to the point that it is now more efficient and smaller than when the tests first started. The impact plate is non-pivoting, therefore the impact resisting part of the sidepod could be concentrated in the rear lowest corner of the plate, leaving the sidepods to be as short as possible and the weight as low as possible. The end result was that although the regulation was intended to protect the driver from side impacts in the event of an accident, much of the side of the cockpit where the driver sits was left exposed because of the inadequacy of the test.

This year the test changed and the impact plate has been divided into four sections. Each section must take a certain proportion of the impact energy, ensuring that instead of having one impact resisting area of the sidepod you have at least four spread around the area of the impact plate. This test is now much more useful in defining a structure that will protect the driver from side impact. Another problem with the chassis is the possibility of penetration by small objects. It had been seen in some Formula 3000 accidents that even a nosecone of another car, fairly rounded and relatively soft, (and built to Formula One regulations) could penetrate the side of the monocoque in a T-bone accident. Last year's F1 regulations required monocoques to be built with an external two millimetre thick Kevlar skin. This was a big step forward in reducing penetration, but this year's regulation for side penetration was even

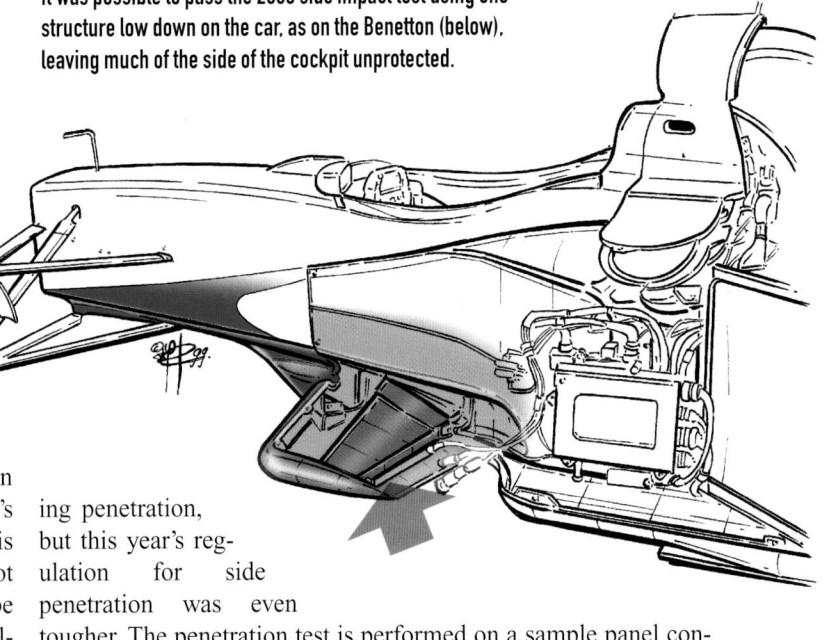

It was possible to pass the 2000 side impact test using one structure low down on the car, as on the Benetton (below), leaving much of the side of the cockpit unprotected.

tougher. The penetration test is performed on a sample panel constructed to the exact same specification as the final monocoque. This panel is tested by attempting to force through a cone of a particular size and shape. A minimum force of 150kNs must be applied to push the cone through the test panel for 100mm, together with a minimum energy requirement of 6,000 joules.

These tests are conducted at recognised test centres in the presence of an FIA inspector. Usually the basic monocoque is undamaged during these tests. It is the bolt-on structures that are thrown away. The teams make many private tests on these structures before taking the official FIA test. As a result of these changes the monocoques were much heavier this year, by some 15 per cent to 25 per cent. An average bare monocoque for 2000 was approximately 44 kilos to 48 kilos, and this year it was around 54 kilos to 60 kilos.

## STRONGER ROLLOVER BARS

When in 1999 Pedro Diniz's Sauber flipped onto its back and skidded sideways across the track and over the kerb on the roll-hoop at the Nürburgring, everyone in F1 was shocked to see how easily the car's roll-hoop was detached by the kerb. New regulations were formulated and drafted which dramatically increased the test loads for Formula One roll-hoops. This new roll-hoop regulation took effect in 2001. It has taken quite a lot of work for most teams to achieve the structural integrity to resist these loads and has added more weight to the roll-hoop. This is something designers do not want, as if the weight is very high up it raises the centre of gravity which affects performance. However, it is certainly an area where there is universal agreement on the need for strength in order to avoid a repetition of Diniz's Sauber failure.

## WHEEL TETHERS

In 1999 a new regulation was introduced requiring so-called 'wheel tethers'. Usually the first thing that happens in an accident is that wheels are detached and bounce around the race track. In a few instances these loose wheels have bounced over quite high fences, injuring spectators, or worse. To limit this problem wheel tethers were introduced. In 1999 and 2000 single tethers were used which reduced the problem, although not ▷

The ram, fixed to the trolley, travels at 10 metres per second and impacts on the rigidly fixed monocoque. No damage to the basic monocoque structure is tolerated.

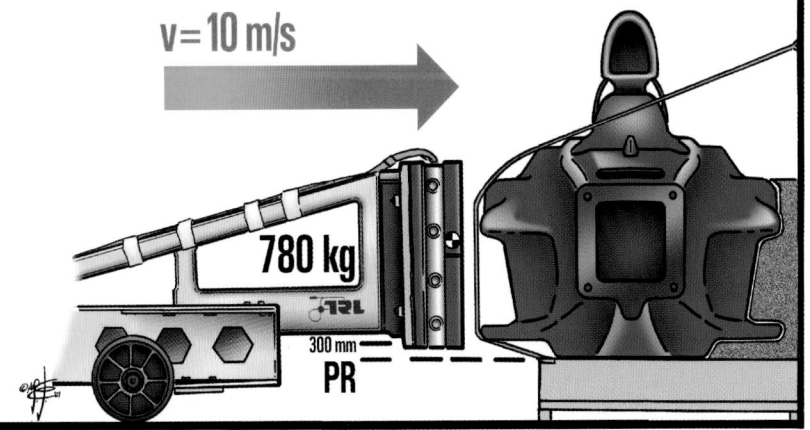

v = 10 m/s

780 kg

TRL

300 mm

PR

entirely. Therefore, for 2001 double wheel tethers were attached between each wheel and the monocoque. The tethers are made from high tensile manmade fibre called zylon, originally developed for racing yachts. They are contained within the hollow suspension links and are attached at one end to the wheel upright (hub) and at the other end to the monocoque. Regulations require these cables to have a minimum load capacity of five tons and to attach the wheel assembly to the monocoque separately from the wishbones or suspension components.

Double tethers substantially decrease the chances of a wheel detaching. In reality, when a car hits a barrier at over 150mph nothing can contain the wheels, but the tethers take out some energy from the wheel as it is separated from the car and this means it is detached with lower energy, more safely.

## WET TYRE DIAMETER CHANGES

Some regulation changes are made simply for the convenience of the teams. An example is the change to the maximum tyre diameter. For 2001 the teams were allowed to run wet tyres that have a slightly larger diameter than dry tyres. The aim has been to prevent aquaplaning, not of the tyres but of the bottom of the chassis.

Today's F1 cars run very close to the ground. At speed on the straights, the regulation 10mm thick plank on the bottom of the chassis can touch the ground, whereas in a slow corner it may be 40mm or 50mm above the ground. In some of the faster corners the flat bottom of the chassis may be only 10mm to 15mm above the track surface. If it rains, this low ride height can cause a kind of

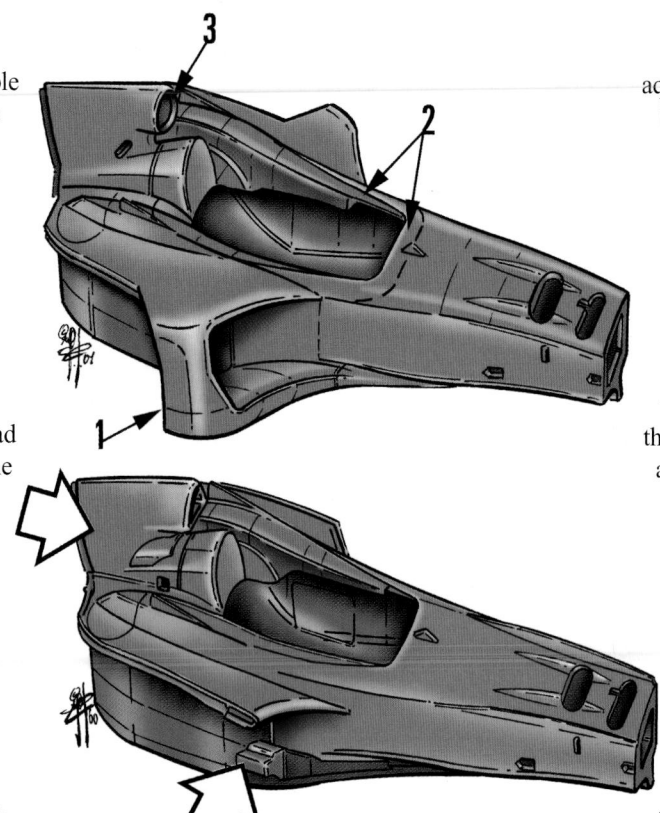

The 2001 rollover structure regulations effectively require each car to be capable of withstanding the weight of the entire 22 car grid on its roll-hoop. The top illustration shows Ferrari's 2001 solution compared with its 2000 contender below.

aquaplaning of the chassis, thereby minimising the grip of the tyres. In such circumstances, to avoid aquaplaning, it may be necessary to actually raise the car. Of course, this depends on the amount of water lying on the the track surface. In the event that you have a race that starts dry and then becomes wet, changing to the larger diameter wet tyre will automatically raise the car a few millimetres, reducing the potential for aquaplaning. Obviously, the opposite can happen as well, when the race starts wet and then dries. Providing the car's ride height on wet tyres has been correctly set, changing to dry tyres should compensate and lower the chassis to its optimum dry weather ride height. The new regulation allows for a 10mm difference of diameter. Wet tyres therefore have a maximum of 670mm in diameter, and dry tyres a maximum 660mm diameter, changing the ride height of the car by five millimetres!

## POLITICAL CHANGES

Some regulations do not come under the safety heading, but more to do with keeping Formula One as a driver's formula, and not computer controlled, ie 'political' regulations. When active suspension was banned in 1993, the FIA's technical arm was responsible for inspecting and verifying the software legality of the teams' electronic systems. However, since that time a great deal of effort has been spent by the teams on circumventing parts of the regulations.

Traction control is an example of the difficulties faced by the FIA. In theory, traction control was not allowed, but by clever configuration and measurement of other inputs, engine software can be configured to achieve a form of traction control. Software to operate these systems had become so complicated and sophisticated, that it was impossible for the FIA electronics 'police' to know exactly what teams were doing. To resolve this, it was proposed for 2001 that all the regulations be removed concerning electronic control of the engine, gearbox, clutch and differential. This removed the concern that some people were successfully circumventing the regulations.

The relevant electronic regulations, with the agreement of the Technical Working Group, were duly removed. Later, however, at a team principals' meeting, it was felt by some that it was too short notice or not in their interest to introduce these regulations at the beginning of the season. Consequently, the old electronic regulations stayed in force until Barcelona 2001, after which the new regulation became effective. It was not the first time this had happened, as previously when teams were unable to comply with new regulations for the start of the season, because of manufacturing difficulties, introduction had also been delayed.

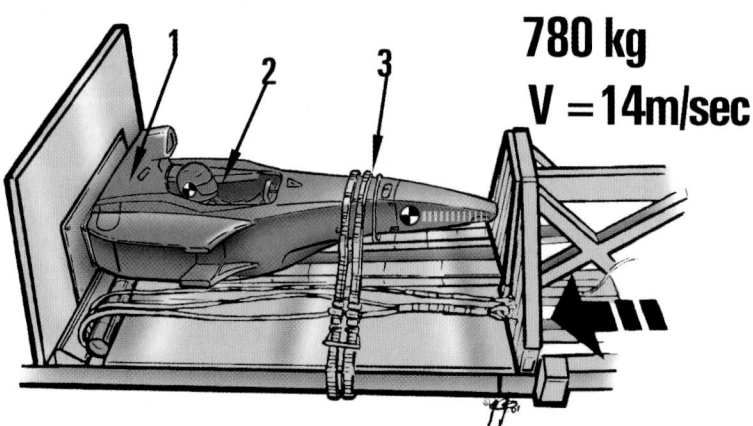

# 780 kg
# V = 14m/sec

The nosebox impact test is unchanged for 2001. The nosebox must withstand an impact from a trolley weighing 780kg that strikes the nose at a velocity of 14 metres per second. The basic monocoque must remain intact and the nose must provide an average deceleration not exceeding 40g. During the test the 600mm nose is crushed to 100mm.

# The search for downforce

It has always been interesting technically to stand back and take a general look at what teams have been doing since the teams' official launches in January and February, and how the cars have changed by the opening races of the year. By Australia there had been a plethora of little bits and pieces already added to the cars to an extent not seen for 20 years. Generally speaking, these were part of a desperate search for more downforce, particularly at the front of the car. It seemed that the new front wing regulation had certainly limited the ability to generate downforce at the front and it was very early in the season to be seeing so many little fins, flick ups, winglets, fences, etc, being added to the cars. Normally these pieces are reserved for races such as Hungary and Monaco, which require maximum downforce even at the sacrifice of efficiency. Lap times at tracks such as Hungary can be improved by adding downforce even when the efficiency of this downforce may only be in the order of say 1.2:1. Certain teams, such as McLaren, Prost, etc, seemed intent on not adding too many of these bits and pieces for fear of sacrificing efficiency. However, it was was surprising with these two cars in particular not to have seen fences tried under the middle part of the wing, as BMW Williams did in Melbourne.

These fences introduce an amount of ground effect in the middle part of the wing and are a relatively simply fix. The downside to that is probably an increase in the car's pitch and ride height (height from the ground to the bottom of the car) sensitivity.

There has always been a tremendously important interaction between the front wing flap, front wing endplate and the brake duct area around the front wing. Teams had been investigating this in great detail and Ferrari had seemingly done a particularly good job, judging by the size of its front brake inlet, which was very small. However, this may have also been due to the fact that it was running a different brake disc and pad material, allowing it to run less cooling air. By contrast, the McLaren was running, especially in Melbourne, particularly large brake inlet ducts. It is not the first time this area has been investigated. In fact, fully enclosing brake ducts were run on the 1984 and 1985 McLarens (diagram A). At that time they were called 'elephant ears' and they led to the introduction of a regulation that limited the size of front brake ducts. Unfortunately at that time, the next step was not taken to start to tailor the front wing endplate to achieve maximum flow around the

inside of the wheel. There is, as they say, nothing new under the sun. Even Ferrari – which appeared by now to have had the best overall compromise of downforce, aerodynamic efficiency and sensitivity – tried an unusual forward top flap between its front wing endplates. As mentioned before, it was very early in the year to be trying such add-ons. Considering that tyre development was going to run apace, and that teams were already playing with such little bits and pieces to gain every point of downforce, it would be interesting to see just how quick these cars were by the end of the season. It was already thought that the two to three seconds reduction in lap times already seen may have generated to four or five seconds. A big step in one year.

**A**

Nothing is new under the F1 sun. In 1984 and 1985 McLaren used this special front brake duct until the FIA outlawed ducts that partially covered a wheel rim or part of a tyre. Then brake ducts had a serious aerodynamic influence, just as they have today.

## EXHAUST SYSTEMS

Six of the 11 teams followed the trend of the top-exit exhaust arrangement that Ferrari introduced in 1999, Benetton joining the group of five from 2000 that comprised Ferrari, Jordan Honda, Sauber, Jaguar and Prost. Three teams – BMW Williams, BAR and Arrows – retained the more conventional layout with the exhaust exit on the top of the side channel of the diffuser. Minardi blew its exhaust into the side channel of the diffuser, closer to the top edge of the channel, while McLaren retained the unique solution of blowing low in the central diffuser that was introduced by Williams in 1999, but which it dropped in 2000. McLaren used it last year on the MP4/15 and retained it for the MP4/16.

## LOW-MOUNTED BRAKE CALLIPERS

Seven teams had adapted the semi-horizontal position of the rear brake callipers used in 2000 by Ferrari, Arrows and Minardi. The solution was introduced by Gustav Brunner at Minardi in 1999 and copied by the others in 2000; its advantage lies in keeping the centre of gravity as low as possible. Ferrari, Jordan, Jaguar, Arrows, Sauber, Minardi and Prost followed suit.

McLaren used the rear callipers in the standard vertical position at the front of the disc, but was the only team to use the horizontal low position for its front callipers (B). This obliged AP to design a new calliper because it required a new system for bleeding and hydraulic oil circulation. A low centre of gravity is always important and the new calliper position was another step towards improving the centre of gravity position. Two brake calliper manufacturers supply the field: Brembo and AP. Brembo had Ferrari, Jordan, Prost, Minardi and Sauber; AP McLaren, Williams, Benetton, Jaguar, Arrows and BAR. Brembo discs were used by Ferrari,

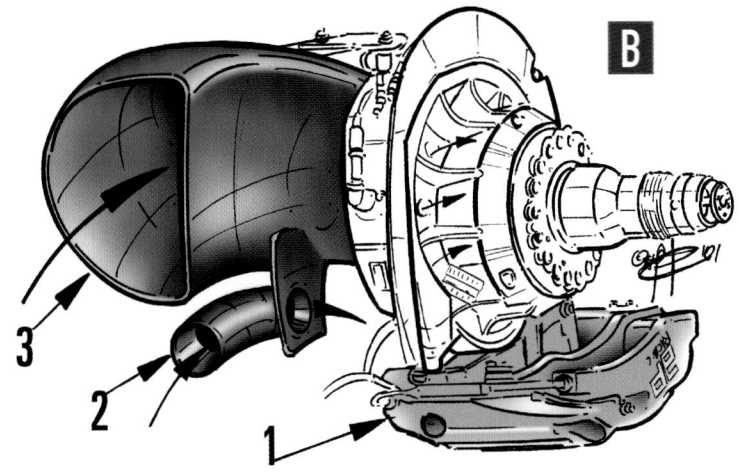

This is the special 'laydown' AP calliper (1) on the McLaren MP4/16. McLaren had a larger duct (3) for the race (Coulthard favoured bigger ducts than Mika). It cools the disc and middle of the upright. These ducts were smaller for qualifying than for the race. (2) shows a separate duct used to cool the calliper. For clarity the drawing is shown minus the brake disc .

Sauber, BAR, Irvine and Mazzacane. Hitco discs were used by McLaren Mercedes, Jordan Honda, Benetton Renault, Arrows and Minardi. The French Carbon Industrie discs were used by BMW Williams, Jean Alesi and Luciano Burti.

## SUPER-CLEAN BRAKE DUCTS

Last year Ferrari introduced special brake ducts at the rear. In 2001, with the new front wing regulations, it was even more

Ferrari's new cylindrical front brake duct was a mirror image of the inside of the wheel rim. To maximise smooth airflow over the front wing and front suspension, it works like a centrifugal fan, facilitating much better extraction of hot air and carbon brake dust to the outside of the wheel.

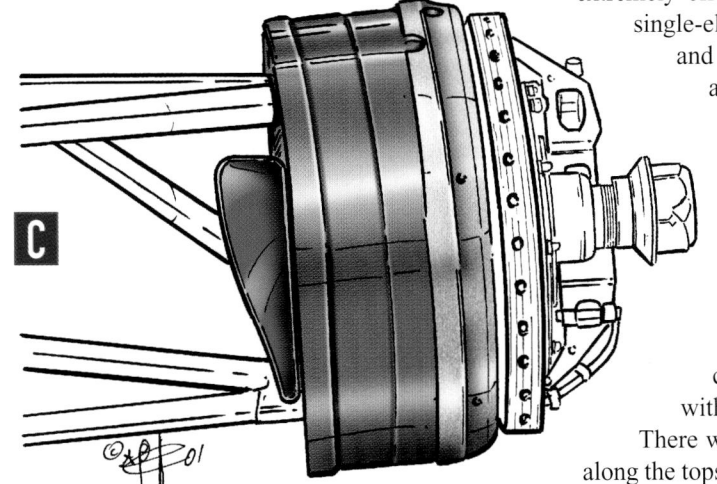

important to have minimal air blockage behind the front wing and to smooth the airflow for the rest of the car, therefore brake ducts had become more and more important. Ferrari had a duct in Melbourne that was cylindrical and completely closed to smooth airflow as much as possible (C). Effectively it was a mirror image of the inside of the wheel rim. The duct is divided into three sections internally, and there are several versions of the middle intake section to suit different circumstances. The duct works like a centrifugal fan facilitating much better extraction of hot air from the brakes. All of this hot air and the carbon dust from the brakes is drawn from outside of the wheel rim and flows out over the top of the bodywork. At the end of the race the flow pattern was clearly visible on the Ferrari's flanks. The downside of the new design was that changing the camber plate in the front suspension now took 10 minutes, where last year it was only two.

## FERRARI

In Melbourne, Ferrari had a revised version of the F2001 car shown at the Maranello launch. It had added the 'ears' at the base of the roll-hoop structure, which were simply a means of respecting rules governing roll-hoop area. Most team's rear wings had two upper plane wing elements towards the rear of the endplates, and the other high at the front edge, but Ferrari had one huge top element, with two standard ones beneath it. For Saturday qualifying in Melbourne, Ferrari introduced something new, following McLaren's practice in 2000. This was to integrate in a long chord profile the driveshaft and the rear suspension toe-in link. It was similar to the idea pioneered by Williams FW16 back in 1994, where the driveshaft was shrouded together with the top link. Ferrari's chord profile was nearly 30cm long. McLaren and Jaguar use something similar, albeit with chords no longer than 18-20cm.

This system confers an aerodynamic advantage, as the rotating driveshaft induces drag and disturbs airflow; enclosing the driveshaft makes the system more efficient.

## McLAREN MERCEDES

The team used new brake ducts at the front in Melbourne with different size options for qualifying and the race (when greater cooling capacity was needed). The MP4/16 demonstrated McLaren's total commitment to reducing mass in all parts of the car. There was a large sculptured area beneath the seat, and the bottom section of the chassis was also very sculptured and narrow to increase the quality of airflow around the lower section of the car. The engine cover was also very low at its trailing edge, to the point where the rear wishbones stick out from the bodywork where previously they lay flush with it on the MP4/15. This promotes extremely efficient airflow over the rear wing. The single-element lower plane position is very low and is fixed by the rules, hence the need for a low engine cover. McLaren also tested three different types of chimneys on the sidepods, to improve the extraction of hot air from the radiators.

## BAR HONDA

BAR in Australia had revised versions of the car tested in Kyalami. It came to Melbourne with its 03 festooned with little wings to increase downforce. There was an unusual mounting for a small fin along the topside of the nose; it was located the opposite way round to similar appendages tried in the past by Arrows, Minardi and Tyrrell.

Tests showed that the fin worked better in this 'reversed' position; according to one source mechanics fitted them the other way round during testing at Kyalami but were told by aero man Willem Toet to fit them properly. The top wishbone and steering arm were covered with wing-profile sections, while the lower wishbone cover had a longer chord. There was another triangular horizontal fin, for further airflow efficiency, just inside the front suspension. The front wing endplate featured the standard sort of triangular fin used by other teams, but had an unusual small vertical finlet to improve the efficiency of the front wing. The 03 also used the cutaway rear wing endplate profile seen last year in Monaco, plus distinctive upswept leading edge profile to the main upper plane element.

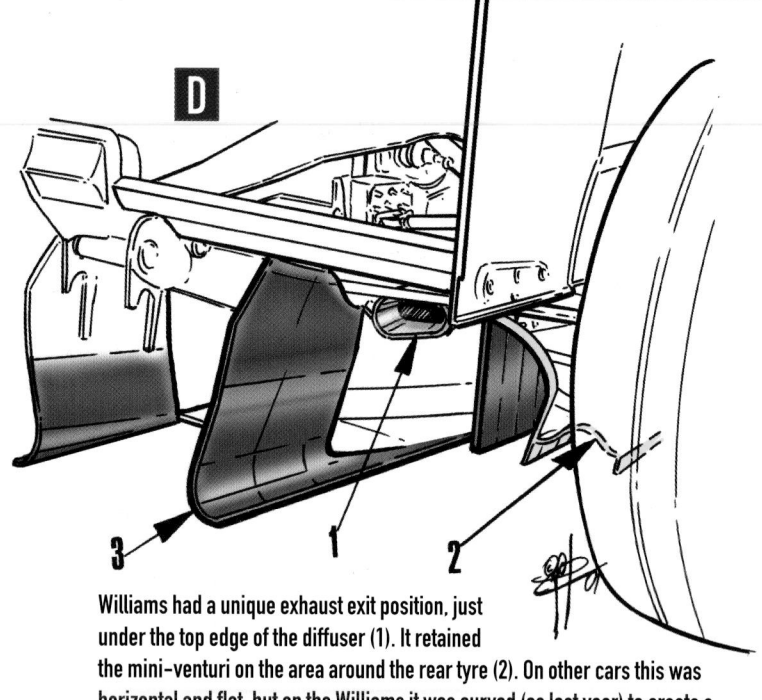

**D**

Williams had a unique exhaust exit position, just under the top edge of the diffuser (1). It retained the mini-venturi on the area around the rear tyre (2). On other cars this was horizontal and flat, but on the Williams it was curved (as last year) to create a mini-diffuser. The lower section of the central tunnel (3) curves outwards on its lower edge.

## BMW WILLIAMS

In Melbourne BMW Williams had revised versions of the cars shown at the Silverstone launch. Williams used winglets ahead of the rear tyres à la BAR, Jaguar and Prost, to maximise downforce. Williams was one of teams using the new solution for the rear wing profile, and on Saturday added two vertical turning vanes under the front wing, either side of the 50cm-wide section where you can go to the reference plane level. They had a divergent shape to clean up the airflow in this critical area. For the race the team cut away a small area at the leading edge of the vanes to avoid damage where excessive understeer in qualifying had caused them to touch the track because of the necessity to run very stiff rear suspension and a relatively soft front suspension set-up.

## BENETTON RENAULT

Benetton is the only team to use long radius arms to connect the gearbox to the chassis to stiffen the rear end, and this is facilitated by the very low and wide angle of the engine. In Melbourne there was also a new rear wing (one large element, two smaller). For optimum cooling, the sidepods had larger openings for the race.

## PROST ACER

The Prost AP04 is very similar to McLaren's MP4/15. Of those teams using exhaust exits on the top of the bodywork, Prost is the one that exits nearest to the back of the car. The front brake ducts are the closest to Ferrari's, albeit not such an extreme solution. The AP04 uses the low brake calliper position at the back, but is the only car to have vertically mounted front callipers ahead of the discs to aid airflow through the disc. Like Sauber, Prost used a Monza 2000 specification Ferrari V10.

## JORDAN HONDA

Compared to launch specification, the EJ11 in Melbourne boasted new front brake ducts and a new rear wing. Last year Jordan was the only team to use four-piston brake callipers instead of six. Now it uses six-piston callipers like everyone else, a new lighter and smaller design from Brembo.

## ARROWS ASIATECH

Mike Coughlan's new A22 had pushrod front suspension, in common with everyone else apart from Minardi. The car had the lowest front wing profile in the field, without any hint of spoon shape, and a conventional configuration rear wing. The diffuser was very similar to the A21's.

## SAUBER PETRONAS

Sauber had a new rear wing and new sidepod chimneys in Melbourne, which were used only in the warm-up and the race. The chimneys were longer and lower than McLaren's and had a divergent shape when viewed from the front, probably to help the air extraction.

## JAGUAR RACING

Jaguar added a new flap to the front wing in Melbourne, very similar to Sauber's, which rises almost to touch the underside of chassis. Like McLaren, the R2 had the covered driveshaft and toe link, and also featured new bargeboards.

## EUROPEAN MINARDI

The Minardi PS01 was the smallest car in the field in Melbourne and was full of very clever ideas from designer Gustav Brunner.

The front suspension was unique in using pullrods, and all of its elements are very cleverly packaged and mounted very low in the chassis. The dampers are mounted transversely and are very short.

The chassis and nose are very low, and taper in plan view. The sidepods are also very low, the radiators are angled downwards, and there is a large exhaust exit for hot air in front of the rear tyres.

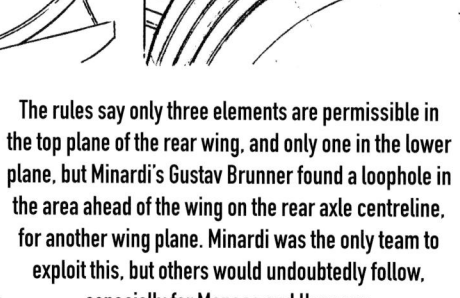

The rules say only three elements are permissible in the top plane of the rear wing, and only one in the lower plane, but Minardi's Gustav Brunner found a loophole in the area ahead of the wing on the rear axle centreline, for another wing plane. Minardi was the only team to exploit this, but others would undoubtedly follow, especially for Monaco and Hungary.

Brunner had also exploited a loophole in the regulations (E). The rules allow only three elements in the upper plane of the rear wing and only one in the lower plane, but Brunner found a loophole in the area ahead of the wing, on the rear axle centreline.

The trend towards lower engine covers had exposed a new area, hitherto covered by bodywork, where an additional wing was permissible under the new rules. So far Minardi was the only team to exploit this, but others would undoubtedly follow, especially for Monaco and Hungary. The PS01 used the suspension and gearbox from last year's car, but hoped to have a new rear end ready for Imola.

# Something to compare

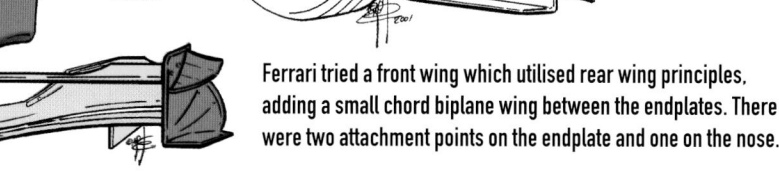

In Malaysia many of the teams arrived with hurried developments to correct problems experienced in the first Grand Prix in Melbourne, as this race had provided the first real opportunity to compare performances. The developments evident on many cars in Malaysia highlighted deficiencies the teams perceived in their own designs, as well as cooling modifications specifically required by the high ambient temperatures at Sepang.

**A** Ferrari tried a front wing which utilised rear wing principles, adding a small chord biplane wing between the endplates. There were two attachment points on the endplate and one on the nose.

## FERRARI

Ferrari decided against top exit exhaust chimneys and instead opened up the air extraction panels on the sidepods to the point where the radiators were visible. It also tried the biplane front wing (diagram A), but ultimately set up the F1-2001 with less rear wing than in Australia, using only two planes at the rear instead of three. New Brembo callipers were used, and for qualifying they used 22mm-thick brake discs instead of the usual 28mm.

## McLAREN MERCEDES

McLaren Mercedes had stiffened the front suspension where the lower wishbone broke on Häkkinen's car in Melbourne. On Saturday

**B** McLaren ran these extremely long winglets on the nose of David Coulthard's car on Saturday morning. They were bigger than any seen previously, but disappeared after that session.

McLaren also produced the fourth version of its sidepod air exhaust chimneys in Malaysia, based on the one seen in Australia, but cut down at a slant on the outer edge further to improve hot air extraction.

Coulthard tried a nose with large winglets (B), then McLaren also tried two of its chimney options (C). In qualifying the smaller brake ducts were used, in the race, with a heavier fuel load, the larger ones.

## BMW WILLIAMS

BMW Williams retained its unique exhaust blowing position, just under the diffuser's top edge, with a mini-diffuser around the rear tyre. It also had two versions of its air-extracting chimneys. The race version was similar to McLaren and Ferrari's 2000 versions, but in qualifying it used one with a winglet integrated on the outside.

## BENETTON RENAULT

Benetton opened up the cooling holes in the sidepods for better cooling, as cooling was a major problem. Significantly, Benetton also announced that it would build a completely new car for debut around the time of the British Grand Prix, following the disappointing form of the B201 to date. It meant that the team would be waiting for the new car while trying to race the

original design, meaning limited interim development.

## BAR HONDA

Olivier Panis tried a narrow winglet atop the airbox on Friday and Saturday in the search for more downforce, and he and Villeneuve used it in the race morning warm-up but not in the race.

## JORDAN HONDA

Jordan reintroduced its relatively wide airbox winglet, but it was not used for qualifying or the race. For the race the Jordans used very long and open brake ducts, of rectangular section.

## ARROWS ASIATECH

Attempting to reduce the understeer that plagued the cars in Melbourne, Arrows used 12.5-inch wide front rims instead of the usual 12-inch. Bernoldi had his qualifying times disallowed after his front wing infringed height regulations.

## JAGUAR RACING

Before Malaysia, Jaguar sent Burti's damaged Melbourne chassis back to the factory for repair. All of the R2s featured a large opening on top of the engine cover, to improve cooling.

## EUROPEAN MINARDI

In common with many other teams in Malaysia the Minardi tried large openings on the top of the sidepods, for better cooling.

## PROST ACER

In an effort to overcome its Melbourne problems and reduce the performance deficiency Prost had a new front wing to try with endplates similar to McLaren's, and with the flap rising in the mid-section to create a spoon.

## SAUBER PETRONAS

Sauber used a modified winglet ahead of the rear wheels, which incorporated an endplate to improve downforce (D).

**D** Sauber's chimneys were unusual in that they were narrow but long, and mounted at an angle on the outside of the sidepod to deflect the air away from the centreline of the car. They were used all weekend in Malaysia. There was also a modified winglet ahead of the rear tyre, which incorporated a vertical endplate.

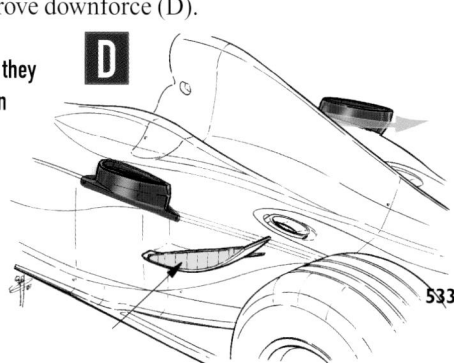

# Weighty concerns

The third round of the 2001 FIA Formula One world championship saw no let-up in the intensive search for greater performance and, as usual, aerodynamics was the prime area of development for technical directors and chief designers. Plenty of downforce is required for qualifying at the Brazilian Grand Prix at Interlagos to cope with the tricky infield section, but in the race teams back off the downforce to reduce drag and give the drivers a better chance of using superior top speed to pass rivals. This usually happens either on the front straight after the long climb from the last corner (which is where Montoya gained the momentum to pass Michael Schumacher), or down the long back straight.

It is not a tough race on brakes because speeds are quite consistently fast, so in qualifying Ferrari, Sauber, Minardi's Alonso and Prost's Mazzacane all tried much thinner brake discs – 23mm-thick instead of the maximum allowable 28mm – in an effort to reduce unsprung weight and improve the handling over the circuit's notorious bumps.

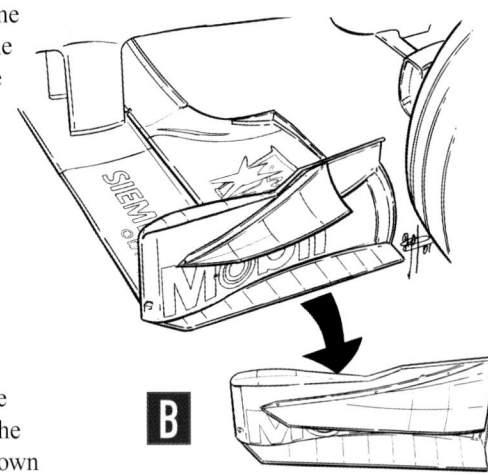

B

McLaren tried two types of large winglet on the outer face of the endplate.

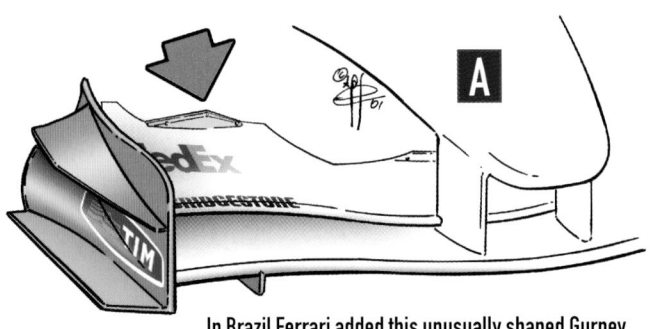

A

In Brazil Ferrari added this unusually shaped Gurney lip on the front wing to generate extra downforce.

## FERRARI

Ferrari was the only team in Brazil to have a spare chassis on hand as well as a spare race car. Ferrari had no completely new bits except for some components on the rear wing. It had used a biplane top element and a large-chord third element in Malaysia, but this time it went for the biplane with the option of two different third elements with a much smaller chord than used previously. The bi-plane was ultimately used for qualifying and the race.

On the front wing, a small, unusually shaped Gurney lip (diagram A) was used in qualifying and the race, to generate more frontal downforce. As less braking effort is required at Interlagos, the smaller centre section inlet was used on the front brake ducts.

McLaren also had modified barge-boards, which curved inwards and were thinner towards the bottom (2, 3 and 4). On Saturday some aerodynamically shaped ballast (1) was mounted on the front of the shadow plate beneath the chassis, to improve weight distribution.

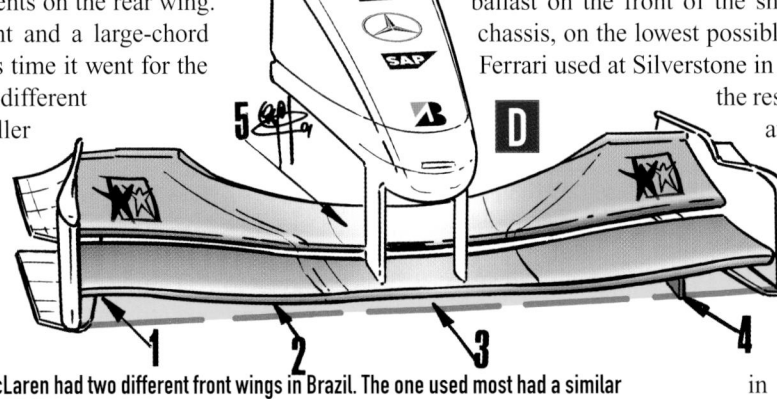

D

McLaren had two different front wings in Brazil. The one used most had a similar spoon shape to Ferrari's, but with the external sides running higher and the centre incorporating a flattened W shape. Part of the profile was slightly twisted (1) and lower (2). The wing flap had a smoother curve (5) and was cup-shaped in the centre (3). McLaren also briefly tried two middle endplates (4).

## McLAREN MERCEDES

After disappointing races in Melbourne and Malaysia, much change was evident at McLaren. On Friday Coulthard tried a new front wing endplate with an outer fin similar to Ferrari's but more steeply angled and not running the full length of the endplate (B). It was an experiment not repeated. McLaren also had two different front wings. The one used most in practice, and in the race, had a spoon shape similar in concept to Ferrari's, but with the external sides running higher (D). Part of the profile was slightly twisted, and lower, and where Ferrari's wing was spoon shaped in the middle, the McLaren's rose up slightly, again like a very flat W shape. The shape of this front wing's flap was also different, with a smoother curve, and cup-shaped in the centre. On Saturday McLaren tried this wing with two middle endplates like Ferrari, the first time this sort of endplate was employed on an Adrian Newey front wing. These vanes were not used for the race. The front wing package was intended to create less pitch sensitivity and give better stability and generate more downforce.

McLaren also modified its large bargeboards, which had a new front section which curved inwards, and were thinner towards the bottom (C).

On Saturday, it placed some aerodynamically shaped ballast on the front of the shadow plate beneath the chassis, on the lowest possible points, copying a idea Ferrari used at Silverstone in 2000. This was used for the rest of the weekend, generating more heat and grip in the front tyres by placing more weight on them.

In qualifying McLaren used the same sidepod air extraction chimneys as in qualifying in Malaysia, albeit with more exhaust area, but in the race it reverted to pure Malaysian exhaust chimneys.

## BMW WILLIAMS

BMW Williams had some interesting aerodynamic modifications at Interlagos. It continued not to use large bargeboards, preferring a combination of smaller boards inside the front wheels (F) to separate drag from the wheels and bodywork. A horizontal fin worked to increase the speed of air under the bottom of the car, just ahead of the sidepods. The fin had a thinner outer section and the turning vanes by the front wheels curved outwards more

**In Brazil, Williams modified the combination of smaller bargeboards inside the front wheels (2) and these featured greater outward curvature. A thin-section horizontal fin (1) was used to increase the speed of air under the bottom of the car, just ahead of the sidepods.**

sharply to deflect air further around the wheels. There was also a new rear wing, similar to Ferrari's biplane with the additional profile on top. because the team opted to be conservative in case cooling in the race became an issue as the ambient temperature was in the 30-degree region.

**In Brazil, Arrows exploited a loophole to mount two small additional 15cm-wide wings in the section of the lower rear wing where the rear-facing red warning light is mounted.**

## ARROWS ASIATECH

This team cunningly exploited a loophole in the regulations (G) to mount two small additional 15cm-wide wings in the section of the lower rear wing where the rear-facing red warning light is mounted. These were used all weekend.

## BENETTON RENAULT

At Interlagos, like BMW Williams, Benetton-Renault had a new rear wing which aped Ferrari's biplane with an additional profile on top. On Friday it also tried new bodywork on both cars, although only Jenson Button used it for qualifying. Both drivers used the old bodywork for the race because the new one was creating more drag to go with the extra downforce it generated. The top speed of the B201s was low enough, without adding to the problem.

The bodywork had an additional winglet (H) atop the sidepod, similar to Ferrari's in Australia, and again used two small-profile winglets in front of the rear tyre. The section of that second winglet was more steeply curved downward.

## BAR HONDA

BAR tried two different front wings and again had the little reverse fin on the side of the nose. There was also a modified upswept exhaust to increase the engine's revs and to avoid a problem with the old system tending to overheat the gearbox.

**Williams' interpretation of the Sauber winglets saw them added to the outside of the front wing endplates (E).**

**E**

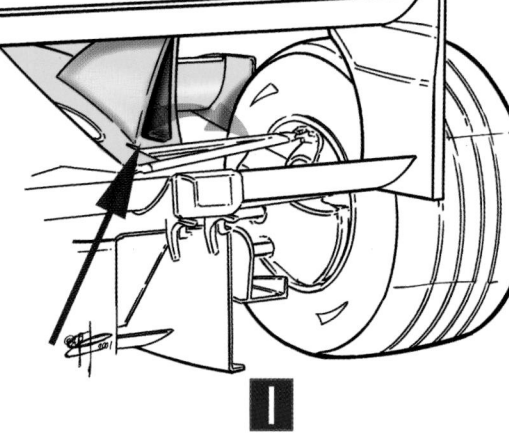

**I**

**Jordan's version of the McLaren style exhaust chimneys were hidden inside the vertical fin ahead of the rear wheels directing the exhaust gases to the rear of the car.**

**F**

**G**

## JORDAN HONDA

Heinz-Harald Frentzen qualified with 25mm-thick Hitco discs and no front brake ducts, while Jarno Trulli used standard ducts and standard 28mm discs. The Jordan Honda EJ11s also sported new versions of McLaren's chimneys (I) hidden inside the vertical fin ahead of rear wheels, with the extracted air exiting towards the rear.

## SAUBER PETRONAS

Sauber introduced two small winglets on the sidepods, in front of the air extractor chimneys, to improve downforce at Interlagos.

## JAGUAR RACING

The bargeboards on the Jaguar R2s had been cut down, with at least 30cm removed from the top in an effort to improve efficiency. The front wing endplates were now wider, out to the full 140cm permitted, but narrowed sharply towards the rear to deflect air inside the front tyres.

## EUROPEAN MINARDI

There was nothing new on these cars, which were the only ones to race with Brembo's 25mm discs at Interlagos.

## PROST ACER

There were new aerodynamic profiles bonded to the front upper wishbones. There were also minor geometry changes in the rear suspension at Interlagos.

**H**

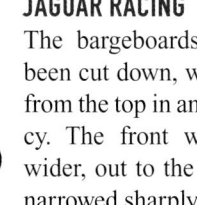

**Benetton tried new bodywork in Brazil. It featured an additional winglet (1), similar to Ferrari's in Australia, and also again used two small-profile winglets in front of rear tyre (2). The section of the second winglet was more steeply curved downward.**

# Development hots up

After the intercontinental races, the fourth round of the 2001 FIA Formula One world championship saw the teams arrive at Imola for the San Marino Grand Prix with further development modifications in their quest for performance.

The San Marino Grand Prix is traditionally very hard on brakes, so there was much evidence of experimentation with brake ducts, to ensure that hot discs and callipers received the right amount of cooling air, and with aerodynamic packages to maximise downforce.

### FERRARI

On its home ground, Ferrari had a version of its 050 V10 engine that revved 300-500rpm higher. The red cars also had a revised aerodynamic package. There were new front and rear wings for both wet and dry conditions, with a single profile at the leading edge of the rear wings. The new dry road front wing was used in both the practice and race. It was similar to the unit Ferrari ran in Brazil, but had two Sauber-like winglets fitted on the inside edge of the endplates to improve airflow away from the front tyres (diagram A). Ferrari also used special specification brakes for Imola, which utilised a new Brembo calliper which was a bit heavier but stiffer and more powerful. Prost and Jordan also used them. These callipers were used in conjunction with new Brembo discs manufactured in CCR material. Normal discs have circular ventilation holes, but these had elongated holes made specially for Ferrari.

Ferrari had a new front wing at Imola, similar to the one used in Brazil, but with these two Sauber-like winglets fitted on the inside edge of the endplates.

### McLAREN MERCEDES

McLaren's mechanics worked a lot of hours during the Imola race weekend – up until three and four o'clock in the morning – with new components arriving daily from England. The aerodynamic ballast on the leading edge of the underbody as used in Brazil was retained, while the bargeboards had been further modified (B) with an outer air extraction channel which extended down further and had a lower extension to conform with the shadow plate regulations. The two outer channels behave the same way as the underwing strakes on the Williams front wing, to enhance its efficiency. There was also a new three-element rear wing, which featured a fresh main profile since Brazil. More new qualifying chimneys were in evidence, slimmer and shorter than those used in Brazil.

David Coulthard's Friday accident was caused by another front suspension failure, so overnight the team stiffened all the front and

At Imola the McLaren bargeboards featured a new outer air extraction channel (1) which extended down further (2) and had a lower extension (3) to conform with the shadow plate regulations.

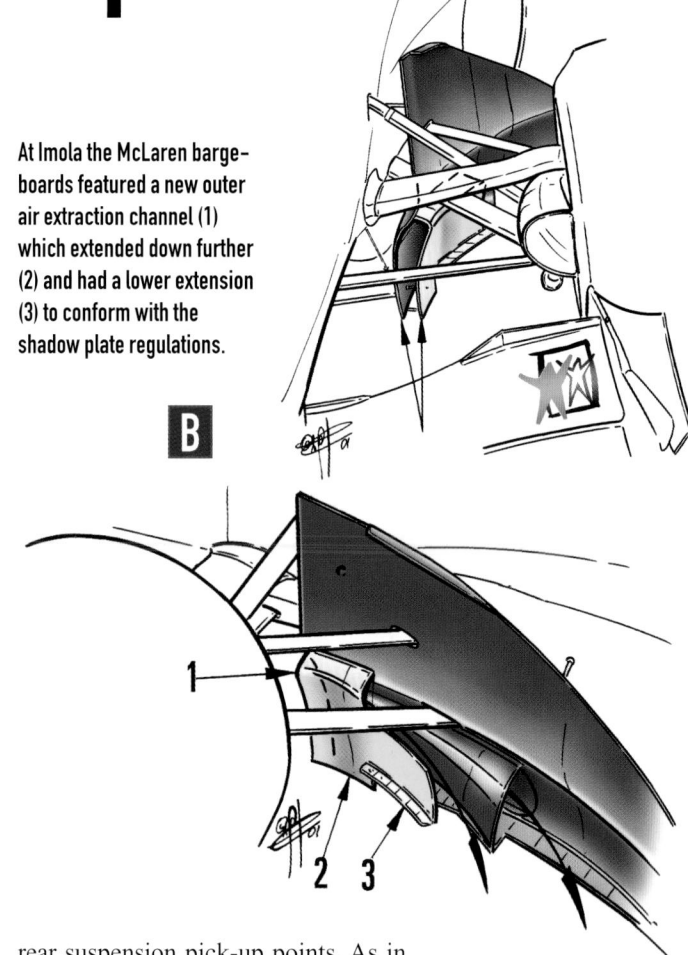

rear suspension pick-up points. As in Brazil, Häkkinen opted to qualify with Brembo discs but raced with Hitco products, where as Coulthard stuck with Hitco throughout. Once again the smaller front brake ducts were used in qualifying.

### BMW WILLIAMS

Williams focused on brake performance at Imola with only small aerodynamic changes. The Williams FW23s had modified undertrays and like other teams experimented with bigger brake ducts.

### BENETTON RENAULT

Downforce is important at Imola, and following its early disappointing performances, the B201s used the new bodywork first tried in Brazil for the whole weekend, together with modified brake ducts. Giancarlo Fisichella used Brembo discs in qualifying, but both cars ran Hitco products for the race. In qualifying the Italian driver also had an engine that was 8kg lighter; there was only one, so the drivers tossed a coin to see who would get it.

### BAR HONDA

Disappointed with early season race performance, the team had a large programme of aerodynamic improvements for Imola, as well as the revised exhaust system run in Brazil. The latter facilitated narrower bodywork at the rear with a more pronounced coke-bottle shape (E). The side flip-ups ahead of the rear wheels were noticeably wider as a result. A new engine cover, sidepods and undertray completed the package. At the front some of the area of the reverse fins on the nose were removed to generate vortices that helped to improve airflow over the rear of the car (C). The BAR 003 retained the new front wing from Brazil, but the underwing strakes had been moved further outboard (D) to improve efficiency. The bargeboards had also been modified. In the wet sessions BAR also tried a new aero package which had a curved wing in the most rear position, exploited first by Minardi. This drooped at either end, like the aerofoils on road cars, to improve efficiency of airflow to the rear wing. There was also an Arrows-like mini-wing where the rear light is mounted.

BAR also tried the middle wing, seen but not used in

**D**

BAR retained the new front wing from Brazil, but the underwing strakes had been moved further outboard (1) to improve efficiency. A small winglet tip had also been added (2).

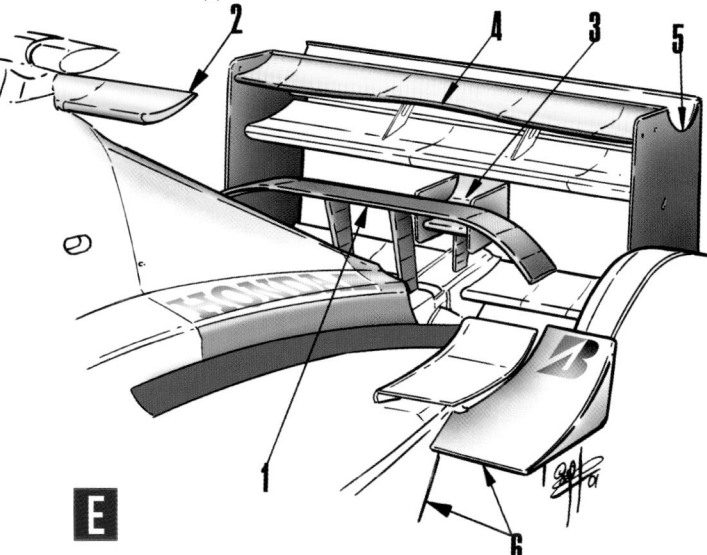

**E**

BAR had very different rear bodywork in Imola, with a more pronounced coke-bottle shape inside the rear wheels. The side flip-ups ahead of the rear wheels were noticeably wider as a result (6). In the wet the team tried a new aero package using a drooping curved wing (1) in the position at the rear exploited first by Minardi. There was also an Arrows-like mini-wing where the rear light is mounted (3). BAR also used the middle wing on the engine cover (2) and high downforce-generating rear wing endplates (5). Only the distinctive spoon-shaped upper rear wing element (4) was used in the race.

*Some of the surface area of the reverse fins on the new BAR nose was cut away deliberately to generate vortices that helped to improve airflow over the rear of the car.*

Malaysia, and the downforce-generating rear wing endplates used in Spain, Monaco and Hungary in 2000. From this package the team selected the distinctive spoon-shaped upper rear wing element for use in the race. For Spain it was planned that the exhausts would blow upwards through the top skin of the bodywork, as on the Ferrari, Benetton, Jordan, Sauber, Jaguar and Prost.

**C**

### JORDAN HONDA

For Imola, Jordan had new brake ducts and Brembo's new callipers, while on the aero side the fins ahead of the rear wheels had their exits closed off for qualifying to improve airflow.

*At Imola, Jordan added an engine cover mounted middle wing in the search for downforce (F).*

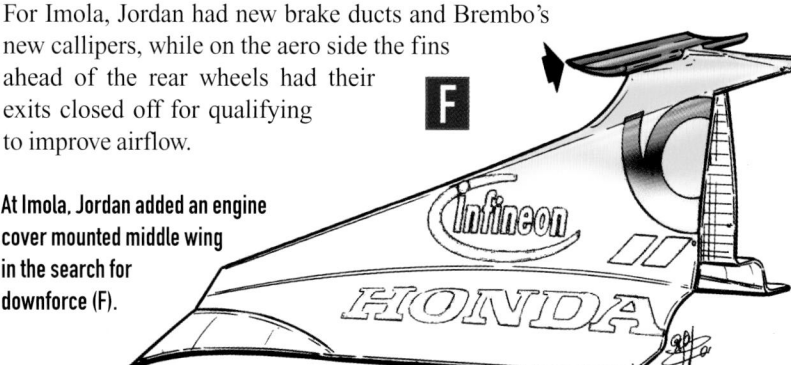

**F**

### ARROWS ASIATECH

In Imola the team retained the mini rear wings seen in Brazil and had a new front wing with a wider flap to generate more downforce. Jos Verstappen's car also featured mildly revised front suspension, produced at his suggestion, which had been fabricated in steel because of the lack of time to make it in carbon fibre.

### SAUBER PETRONAS

The Sauber C20s were the same at Imola as they had been in Brazil. The team did not use the new Brembo calliper because it had not tested the component enough, and its new power-steering system was absent for similar reasons.

### JAGUAR RACING

Eddie Irvine experimented a lot with brakes at Imola and there was a new front wing, which was less spoon-shaped and more like a subtle version of Jordan's.

### EUROPEAN MINARDI

At Imola there was a fourth chassis, for Tarso Marques, and some new front brake ducts. The aero package that had been anticipated was not ready, as the cars had been late coming back from Brazil.

### PROST ACER

The flip-ups which featured ahead of the rear tyres had vertical endplates, while the front wing endplate flip-ups had been modified, although this was for purely practical reasons. They had been cut back because it had been found that they damaged the tyres when the cars were being manoeuvred on full lock in the garage.

# Aerodynamically challenged

It is tempting to think that there are no secrets in Formula One, such is the pace at which teams discover what their rivals are up to. But in Spain an unusual diffuser that BMW Williams had been using since the middle of the 2000 season was finally detected and competitors were quick to launch protests to the FIA. However, technical delegate Charlie Whiting had already declared that the component was

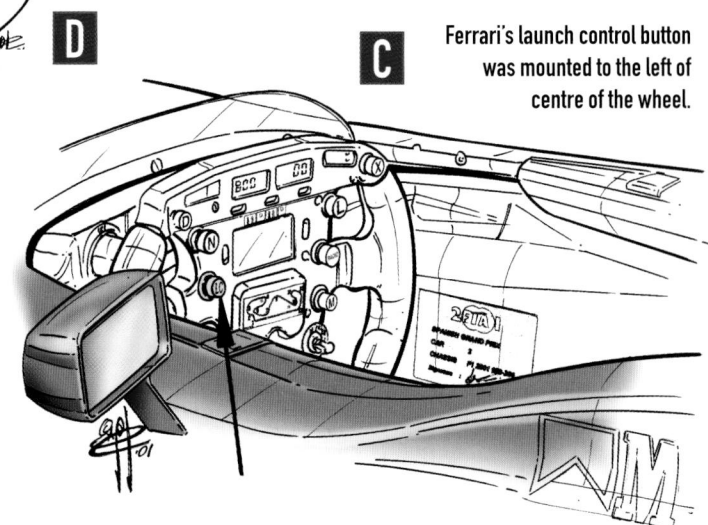

Diagram A shows two types of Williams diffusers used since the 2000 San Marino Grand Prix to the end of the season, both of which incorporated the imaginative interpretation arrowed.

legal last year. On all cars, the step in the flat bottom tapers to a vee in plan view, then becomes an aerodynamic diffuser, but this happens after the rear axle line. Williams had come up with a novel means of incorporating this vee ahead of the axle line. Either side of the gearbox Williams used a small opening (arrowed red, diagram A) so that air flowed more efficiently around the transmission. Most teams use closed sections at this this point.

In Barcelona, McLaren Mercedes used a button situated on the top right of the steering wheel to activate its launch control.

Articles 3.12.2 and 3.12.5 in the technical regulations define this area and the rules state that the stepped bottom on each car must be a minimum of 30cm and a maximum of 50cm wide. But there is no specific point at which this transformation from 50 to 30 must occur; the rules only say that beyond the rear axle line, the step may not be any wider than 30cm. BMW Williams' technical director, Patrick Head, was adamant at the Spanish Grand Prix that the design complied fully with the regulations and the FIA allowed it to be raced, pending further investigation. Other teams argued that opening up the sidewalls by the gearbox effectively lengthened the diffuser and therefore enhanced airflow and made the aerodynamics more efficient. That, of course, was the idea, but rivals were annoyed they had not thought of it first and demanded one of the FIA's famous 'clarifications'. In other words,

Jean Alesi preferred a foot-operated clutch. A button on the left of his steering wheel initiated the launch control system. Alesi still engaged gears via the normal paddles.

they wanted majority rule to overturn Whiting's original ruling.

Ferrari, McLaren, Jordan and Jaguar had traction control, launch control and automatic gear shifting, but Benetton Renault would not have traction control until Magny-Cours at the earliest, when the new version of Renault's V10 engine was due to arrive. Unkind critics suggested that until then, the unit did not develop sufficient power to justify the system.

Sauber had traction control in Spain but did not have launch control, while there were doubts that British American Racing used traction control after having a Honda engine in Jacques Villeneuve's car blow up while testing the system.

Williams used launch control and automatic shifting, but did not use traction control in the race after also blowing an engine while testing it. Minardi's traction control system would not be ready until Austria.

Teams used different solutions to control their electronics. McLaren employed a button on the top right of the steering wheel (B), while Ferrari's button was located on the left (C). Jean Alesi still preferred a foot-operated clutch and a button on the left of his steering wheel to initiate the system before engaging gears via the normal paddles (D). Minardi had no special buttons but used a clutch for its automatic start system.

In tests Jordan discovered that by starting with the automatic starting system, Jarno Trulli could repeatedly accelerate from rest to 160kph in 3.5secs. With manual control his best was 3.4secs, but that was a one-off time.

On the brake front the Circuit de Catalunya presented few problems, so there was less need to focus on cooling them. The Ferrari, Sauber, Minardi and Jaguar teams, plus drivers Luciano Burti, Enrique Bernoldi, Mika Häkkinen, Giancarlo Fisichella, Olivier Panis and Villeneuve all opted for Brembo discs, while Williams and Alesi went

Ferrari's launch control button was mounted to the left of centre of the wheel.

for Carbon Industrie. Panis tried its product in qualifying before reverting to Brembo for the race. The Jordan team and David Coulthard used Hitco.

## FERRARI

Ferrari brought a new chassis, 211, to use as the T-car in Barcelona and had incorporated temperature sensors inside the wheel rims to monitor temperatures around them and avoid a repeat of the problem that struck Michael Schumacher at Imola.

Aerodynamically the team used the same front wing as at Imola, but on Saturday morning it fitted a windscreen that resembled the clear fairing on a motorcycle. It was never tried, however. Ferrari's traction control had at least 12 different set-up positions, with a control similar to a rheostat.

## McLAREN MERCEDES

The team had a new front brake duct for qualifying and the race in Barcelona. It was smaller and cleaner than before. In diagram E, (1) indicates the cooling intake for the brake disc and (2) the smaller opening to cool the calliper. Also visible are the unusual serrated-edge Gurney flaps (3) to create a vortex and speed airflow over the wing. These were used from Saturday onwards.

There was also a new chassis for Coulthard, after chassis 01 was damaged in testing at Santa Pod. Häkkinen qualified and raced with Brembo discs, which he tried in qualifying in Brazil and Imola while Coulthard stayed with Hitco.

## BMW WILLIAMS

In Barcelona there was nothing new on the FW23s, but Williams had enough on its hands with the controversy over its long-used 'mystery' diffuser. The new traction control system had three set-up positions.

## BENETTON RENAULT

There was nothing new for the team in Barcelona, even in the electronics department, as it was awaiting a heavily revised version of the Renault V10 engine before introducing its new traction control system.

## BAR HONDA

On Saturday morning in Barcelona, BAR used exhausts with an upward exit on Olivier Panis's car; they were fitted to Villeneuve's later, in free practice. There were only two sets of them, however, after one broke in testing. BAR also had small aerodynamic modifications, including a triangular fin behind the front tyres and small triangular Gurney flaps on the front wing.

## JORDAN HONDA

Jordan introduced a new rear wing in Barcelona with revised profile, and used the rear-exit chimneys just inside the rear tyres. Trulli used small brake ducts in qualifying and Heinz-Harald Frentzen the larger ones.

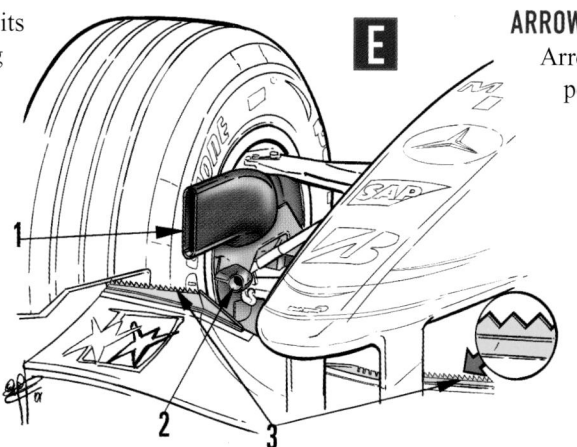

McLaren Mercedes had a smaller, neater front brake duct for qualifying and the race in Spain. (1) indicates the cooling intake for the brake disc and (2) the smaller opening to cool the calliper. Also visible are the unusual serrated-edge Gurney flaps (3).

## ARROWS ASIATECH

Arrows' T-car was fitted with new front suspension that had been conceived by Jos Verstappen. It offered different steering positions to improve the geometry and make the steering lighter. The steering arms were lower than the upper wishbone rather than at the same level. There were also new front wing endplates with horizontal flip-up winglets, à la McLaren.

## SAUBER PETRONAS

Yet again in Barcelona, Sauber ran without power-steering after the team deemed it had insufficient reliability testing. However, the Saubers did have traction control. Launch control was due to be tested the following week at Silverstone.

One of the advantages of the increasingly impressive C20 was that with the new aerodynamic rules introduced for 2001, the use of individual pick-up points (F) conceived by designer Sergio Rinland had been instrumental in the development of the spoon-shaped front wings. As the performance of the front wing is influenced greatly by the level of obstruction behind it, the removal of the central pick-up point for the front suspension was an innovative and significant concept, as it reduced the blockage that a single point created. It also enhanced the total aerodynamic efficiency of the aerodynamic package.

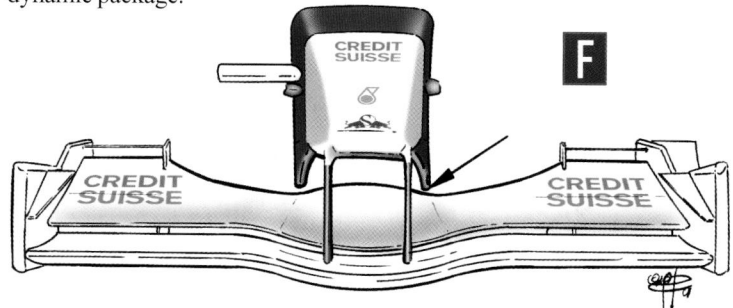

The two front suspension pick-up points (arrowed) are one of the secrets of the Sauber C20's performance. They allow better airflow than a bulky central single pick-up, as they significantly reduce the blockage in a crucial area behind the wing.

## JAGUAR RACING

Chief designer John Russell was absent from Barcelona, chained to his drawing board penning a heavily revised version of the R2 for the Canadian Grand Prix. The team again used the new front wing introduced at Imola.

## EUROPEAN MINARDI

In Barcelona, Minardi used the typical array of new electronics gadgets, but had nothing else new on its cars. This was not surprising as the team's technical director, Gustav Brunner, was about to decamp to Toyota from an unsuspecting Minardi.

## PROST ACER

Jean Alesi had a new AP04 chassis, number 06, in Spain but apart from traction control Prost had nothing else visibly different on its cars. This was a surprise as Prost was debuting a new, long-awaited aerodynamic package, which suggested the changes were rather subtle.

# Technical legality dominates

The BMW Williams controversy in Spain had overshadowed the return of traction and launch control and automatic gear shifting, which was quite a feat given how much fuss had been made in the weeks prior to the Spanish Grand Prix about the return of electronic control.

All this interest in aerodynamic interpretation meant there was ever greater scrutiny on the technical front in Austria. The FIA had made a swift clarification on the Williams diffuser issue (diagram A) and declared that, while the step in the floor could legally taper to 30cm ahead of the rear axle line, the sidewall openings had to be closed off. Williams duly complied (B). At the same time, however, both Ferrari and McLaren Mercedes had been obliged to change aspects of their cars, in particular aerodynamically shaped shrouding of some rear suspension components. Both teams had used aerofoil-section shrouds over multiple rear suspension components to enhance air-

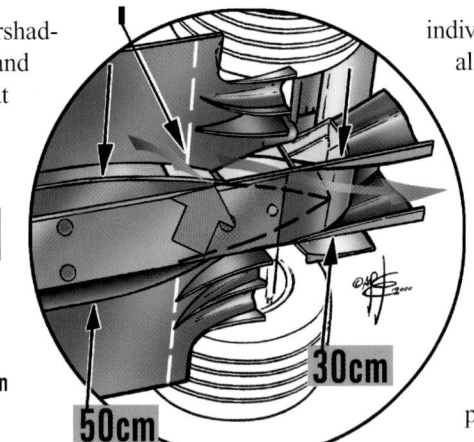

**Diagram B shows the solution required by the FIA from the Austrian Grand Prix onwards.**

50cm 30cm

**Diagram A shows the Williams diffuser as it ran up to and including the Spanish Grand Prix. The yellow sections either side of the gearbox encourage the air to flow around this crucial area of the car through to the centre rear diffuser. The white dotted line running across the underbody indicates the forward most point at which the 50mm step may be opened.**

individual drivers Fisichella and Burti all used Brembo products; McLaren stayed with Hitco, as did Arrows, Jaguar and Jenson Button, while Williams and Alesi stuck with Carbon Industrie.

## FERRARI

In Austria, Ferrari's development continued relentlessly with a new aero package. This included a new front wing end-plate (E) which retained the inside edge flip-ups used at Imola but changed to banana shape and aerofoil section, similar to those on the McLaren, to speed up airflow on the outer edge and therefore enhance efficiency. The outer edge winglets were narrower and longer. There was also a revised system to adjust the incidence of the winglets. The access hole was no longer in the endplate, but on the inside wall. Ferrari also had new bargeboards. The lower edge was deeper than the old ones and the attachments were strengthened.

In qualifying the team tried two different rear wings. Rubens Barrichello used one with two top elements, while Schumacher's had three, the extra one being on top at the leading edge. To improve straightline speed in the race, however, the twin-element wings were used. Ferrari again used the Brembo discs with elongated cooling holes first tried in Imola, while Schumacher used the largest available brake duct

flow. The relevant rules stipulated that the chord length of these aerodynamic (wing) sections cannot be any larger than three-and-a-half times the thickness of the section. Because Ferrari had two wishbones closely spaced together, Ferrari had argued since their introduction in Melbourne that it could justifiably have shrouds 7cm long; the FIA clarification ruled this to be illegal. Similarly, it decreed that aspects of McLaren's interpretation of the regulations as applied to the set-up of wings and underbodies infringed the five per cent tolerance that is permissible. As a result McLaren Mercedes had to tighten up some component dimensions. The A1 Ring is quite hard on brakes, so again there was experimentation with cooling ducts. The Ferrari, BAR, Sauber, Jordan and Minardi teams plus

**The questionable Williams diffuser last used in Spain.**

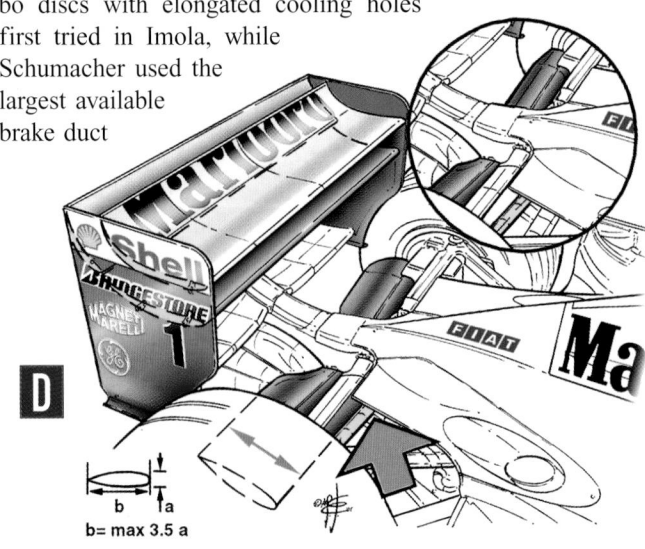

$b = max\ 3.5\ a$

For Austria, Ferrari was forced to modify its rear suspension shroudings after an FIA rule clarification (inset) – the shroudings may not be any bigger than three-and-a-half times the thickness of the section. Because it has two wishbones close together, Ferrari argued that it could have a shroud 7cm long.

in the Sunday morning warm-up and in the race. Barrichello stayed with the standard duct. All of the F2001s also had revised rear dampers.

## McLAREN MERCEDES

There was nothing visibly new on the McLarens in Austria, the cars retaining the revised aero package that had been introduced in Spain. It also used two different kinds of extractor chimneys, racing the one that had outside wall cutaway.

Diagram F shows the rear suspension of the MP4/16, which required a bit of modification to comply with new rule clarifications. The rear suspension is virtually a multi-link system and instead of an upper wishbone there are two arms which each connect separately to the upright (F3). The wing profile shroud covers the toe-in link (F1) and the driveshaft (F2).

Häkkinen qualified and raced with new Hitco discs replacing the Brembo products he tried in Brazil, Imola and Spain. Two different brake ducts were available in qualifying. Häkkinen had always used the small one, but both he and Coulthard raced with the larger option.

Technical director Adrian Newey promised a wing 'in an unusual position' in Monaco, but anticipated that others would have something similar to maximise downforce.

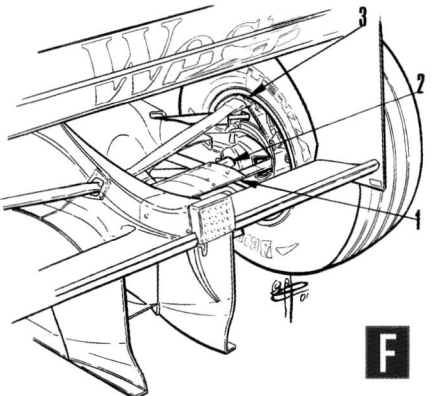

In Austria, Ferrari used this new aerofoil section front wing endplate. The outer edge winglets were now narrower and longer, with a revised system to adjust the incidence of the winglets. The access hole had been moved to the inside wall.

In Austria, McLaren Mercedes had to modify its rear suspension shrouding to comply with the FIA rule clarifications. The rear suspension of the MP4/16 is essentially a multi-link system and, instead of an upper wishbone, there are two arms which each connect separately to the upright (3). The wing profile shroud covers the toe adjustment link (1) and the driveshaft (2).

## BMW WILLIAMS

Following the diffuser issue, rivals in Austria watched the team closely, but apart from closure of the windows in the outlawed area of the diffuser, there was nothing visibly new. The team tried traction control in practice and qualifying, and raced with it for the first time.

## BENETTON RENAULT

Benetton had finalised its launch control and auto shifting software for the drivers to use. Technical director Mike Gascoyne was absent

from Austria, and the B201's featured nothing new. However a revised package was expected for Monaco, including a new front suspension and power-steering.

## BAR HONDA

In Austria there was nothing visibly new on the B003s, hardly surprising following the big aero packages introduced at Imola and Spain, but the drivers had qualifying engines available. Panis raced with a B specification engine, Villeneuve with a C spec. The team retained the top exit exhaust arrangement introduced in Spain (G).

## JORDAN HONDA

In Austria the EJ11s had new flick-ups in front of rear tyres (H) and the closed extractor chimneys again for qualifying. Jordan was the only team to use 23mm qualifying discs from Hitco and used Honda's new qualifying engines. Its launch control was suspected to have been the root cause of Trulli's failed start at the A1-Ring, as it had Frentzen's in Spain.

## ARROWS ASIATECH

In Austria, all three Arrows featured the modified front suspension that had appeared on Verstappen's race car in Spain, but there was nothing else new in evidence.

## SAUBER PETRONAS

In Austria Sauber had launch control to go with its traction control, but still no hydraulic differential or power-steering. These were expected for Monaco. The team used a new front wing flap in qualifying, with a slightly squarer spoon section.

## JAGUAR RACING

In Austria there was nothing visibly new apart from further modified bargeboards. But a heavy revised R2 was promised for Monaco with a completely new rear suspension, engine cover, bodywork and diffuser. The work was thought significant enough for the gearbox protection to require a new FIA crash test.

## EUROPEAN MINARDI

At Spielberg, the team, sans Gustav Brunner, briefly tried a double profile rear wing ahead of the axle line with Fernando Alonso, similar to the single wing used in Melbourne. Although it disappeared quickly it was thought likely to reappear in Monaco. The second version of the team's titanium gearbox was anticipated to be ready for the French Grand Prix at Magny-Cours.

## PROST ACER

In Austria the car was similar, but significant modifications were due for Monaco. These would include new front suspension plus other undisclosed changes.

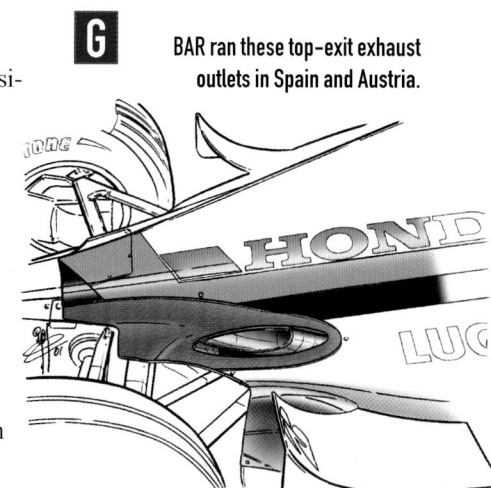

BAR ran these top-exit exhaust outlets in Spain and Austria.

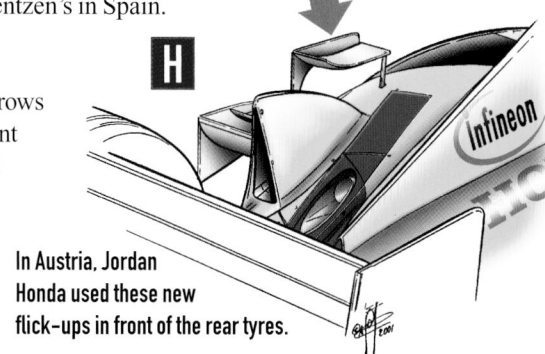

In Austria, Jordan Honda used these new flick-ups in front of the rear tyres.

# Focus shifts to downforce and brake

Set-up for Monaco was all about maximising downforce and improving brake efficiency. Brake wear at Monaco is not a problem because the range of temperatures is lower than at other circuits due to the fact that speeds are generally much lower. Temperature peaks at around 70 per cent of what is reached at other high braking tracks.

Due to the ever continuing search for maximum downforce, some unusual aerodynamic solutions were expected in an effort to claw back what the new regulations had taken away.

Surprisingly only Arrows and Jordan decided to push the envelope – and both got their knuckles rapped for what were actually legal interpretations of the rules.

Arrows created a front wing that mimicked in miniature the old high-mounted units last used in the 1960s when teams first began to exploit the aerodynamic phenomenon. Ironically, these were banned at Monaco in 1969. This time round Arrows employed a wing 50cm wide, mounted at the maximum permissible height of 95cm from the reference plane (diagram A). The wing was supported by thick, ugly endplates and came complete with its own hood in case rivals felt inclined to copy it.

Jos Verstappen ran with it on Thursday and said that it improved the front-end downforce, but that evening FIA Formula One technical delegate Jo Bauer took a dim view of the

— 95cm

**A**

Arrows tried this innovative mini-wing mounted high above the nose of the car. Although it showed some potential, it was banned from use by the FIA.

Nothing is ever completely new (B). The 1972 Eiffelland F1 car had aerodynamics by colourful industrial designer Luigi Colani, and a central scuttle-mounted rear view mirror.

**B**

**C**

Jordan's pillar-mounted scuttle mini-wing showed some promise, but was also banned by the FIA.

component. After further examination he expressed the view that it constituted a dangerous construction, as described in Article 2.3 of the 2001 Formula One technical regulations. Race stewards Paul Gutjahr, Katsutoshi Tamura and Christian Calmes agreed, so it came off for good long before Saturday's sessions. The team appealed, but the stewards refused to let the wing be used while the appeal was pending.

Jordan's solution was slightly more elegant (B). The team took the wing that had been mounted behind the rollover hoop in Malaysia, and relocated it on a central pillar on the scuttle, just ahead of the aeroscreen, at a height of 80cm. Once again Bauer took a dislike to it, as did the stewards, so it went the same way as Arrows' wing. Jordan did not bother to appeal.

There was much focus in Monte Carlo on the braking system that BMW Williams was using. The regulations state that the front brakes may only have a single calliper with a maximum of six pots (or pistons) and two pads per wheel. Use of the exotic material beryllium is no longer allowed and the maximum permitted thickness of the pads is 28mm. Williams is the only team to use pads supplied by Carbon Industrie and those the firm supplies are effectively cut into two sections (D1).

The smaller section of the two-part pad is activated by the top piston (D2) in each calliper half. The larger section of the two-part pad is activated by the remaining two pistons in the lower half of each calliper. The objective is to enhance braking efficiency by reducing tapered wear on the pads which can cause pad knock-off and a soft brake pedal. But the question arose as to whether this interpretation was legal because, although there are nominally only two pads, they actually work like four, which would contravene the rules. This was another grey area, similar to the innovative underbody Williams introduced in the middle of 2000 and which was finally banned in Austria 2001. Williams continued using this

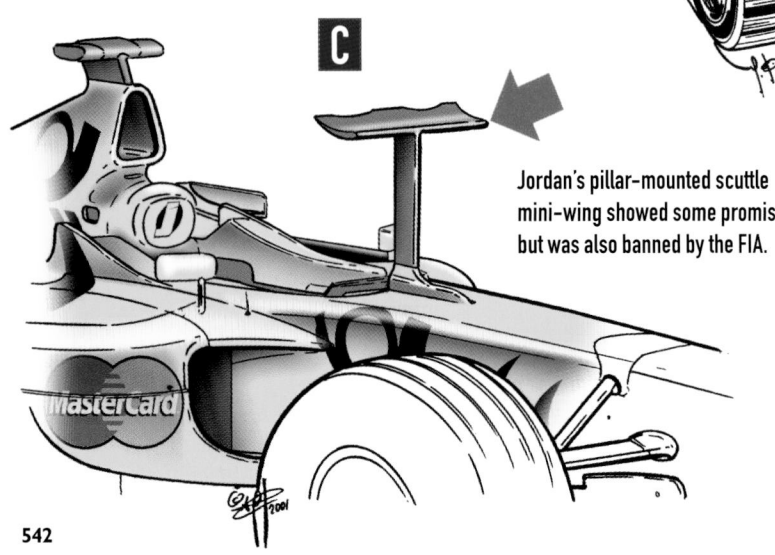

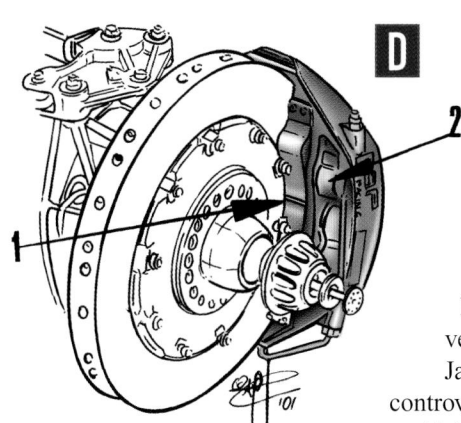

Williams' split brake pads (1) with one calliper piston (2) operating the top section and two pistons operating the bottom section.

braking system, but its long-term acceptance was very much in question.

Jaguar, too, had something controversial in its braking system, which raised question marks amongst other teams. The callipers were mounted at the base of the rear upright, lower than any other team's and almost horizontal. The new rear brake duct was thought to extend beneath the horizontal plane outside the permitted 140mm distance from the car's centreline. Some other designers were unhappy about its legality and sought clarification from the FIA.

## FERRARI

The championship leader had five chassis and four complete cars in Monte Carlo (the only teams that did not bring four cars were Arrows, Benetton and Sauber).

Michael Schumacher tested a new front wing (E) in the first half of Saturday morning free practice. Instead of a large secondary element it had two separate elements, similar to the solution that had been introduced on the F310B way back in 1997.

Ferrari's three element front wing introduced in Monaco by both Schumacher and Barrichello.

Rubens Barrichello tried this configuration during the second half of the session, and both used it in qualifying. For the race, Schumacher used the oval cooling slot brake discs that had been introduced in Imola, but Barrichello retained the conventional design. Both cars also ran with larger openings in front of the rear tyres to maximise hot air extraction and assist with cooling.

## McLAREN MERCEDES

In Monaco, McLaren ha a totally new rear wing (F). This had an additional element (F2) beneath the two main plane elements (F1). Mika Häkkinen tried completely new-shape air exit chimneys in the morning warm-up, but both he and David Coulthard used the standard design to achieve maximum cooling in the race.

At Monaco, McLaren tried a third rear wing element mounted just below the main upper assembly.

## BMW WILLIAMS

Besides it's new brakes, Williams had a revised front wing in Monaco with a completely straight main plane and no intermediate turning vanes beneath it. Both drivers tried the old set-up on Saturday but quickly reverted to the new one for qualifying and the race. There was also a new type brake duct (G2). The top and bottom front wishbone legs were modified (G1) to allow greater steering lock for Monaco's hairpins.

In front of the rear tyres, the flat section of the bodywork had a plastic insert to create a better air seal around the tyres and had been used all season. Benetton used this system two years ago and Ferrari tested it in Austria.

Williams modified the outer rear legs of the top and bottom front wishbones (1) to allow the drivers greater steering lock at the hairpins.

## BENETTON RENAULT

There was evidence of a lot of experimentation by Benetton who had new bodywork in Monaco, with some extensions added between the rear wing and the engine cover. There should also have been an additional Minardi-type wing ahead of the rear axle line, but this was not used. For the race the B201s reverted to the original bodywork from the beginning of season, albeit with very large (high-drag) cooling holes which suggested the car was marginal on cooling.

## BAR HONDA

As at Imola, BAR Honda had a plethora of new parts in Monte Carlo. The Imola configuration wing above the rear axle made a reappearance (H) while the size of the middle wing mounted behind the rollover hoop had been dramatically reduced (H2) to half the size of the original. There were different front wings and a completely new diffuser with a fresh centre section that featured very square sidewalls.

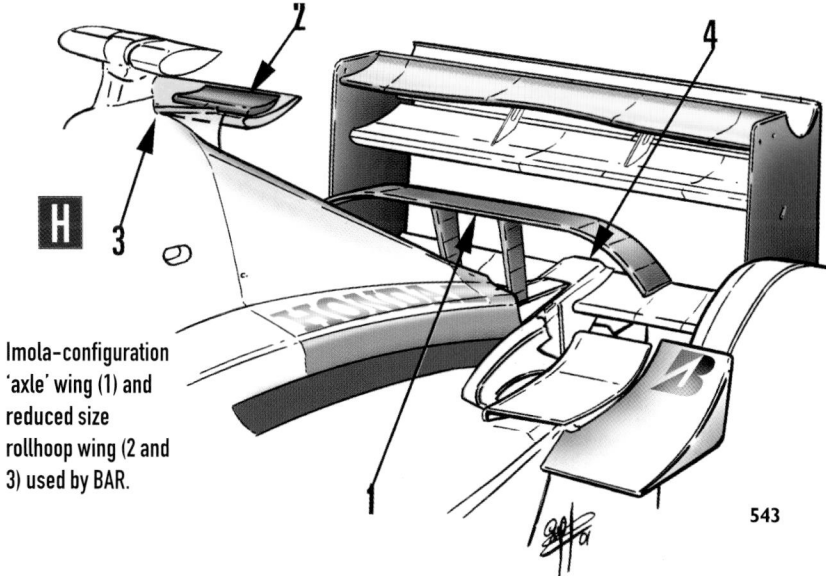

Imola-configuration 'axle' wing (1) and reduced size rollhoop wing (2 and 3) used by BAR.

## JORDAN HONDA

After its scuttle-mounted central pillar mini-wing was banned, Jordan was left with two Arrows-like mini-wings over the rear axle (I) to generate more downforce for the tight MonteCarlo track. Jarno Trulli used the middle wing behind the rollover hoop, seen in Malaysia, for his race car and the spare. In qualifying he had Hitco's 22mm discs, while Heinz-Harald Frentzen chose the 25mm version. Trulli used new bargeboards with a small horizontal upper lip.

**Jordan's rollover bar-mounted middle wing used at Monaco.**

## ARROWS ASIATECH

Besides the 'silly' wing (A, previous page), Arrows had new brake ducts (K) on Jos Verstappen's car – similar to Ferrari's but fabricated in aluminium since they were only prototypes.

A double rear wing arrangement was also used (J). One 100cm

**The search for downforce explored every conceivable area on the car not limited by regulations, however small that may have been, as evidenced by the staggered wings over the rear axle line of the Arrows.**

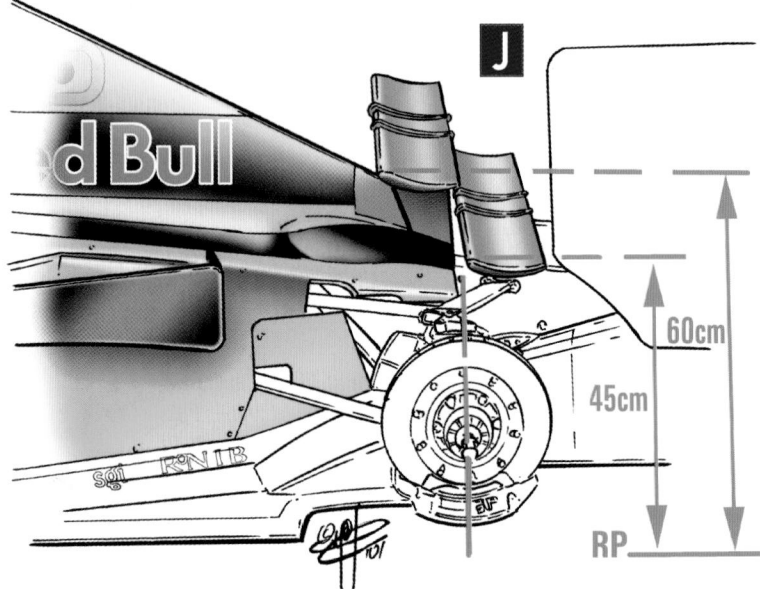

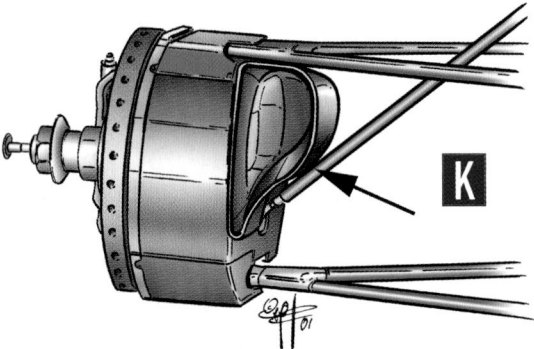

**Arrows' drum-type brake duct with the intake nestled in the triangle outside the pushrod.**

wide plane was mounted behind the rear axle, where a maximum height of 45cm is permissible; the other was mounted at 60cm, ahead of the axle line. On Thursday only one car had the low-exit exhaust, the other two had new top-exit exhausts. These were saved for the race and used on both cars.

## SAUBER PETRONAS

The only 'new' thing Sauber had in Monaco was the front wing flap it had introduced in Austria. There was no sign of power-steering or the hydraulic differential. This showed in the performance, as Monte Carlo marked the team's worst showing of the year.

## JAGUAR RACING

In Monaco Jaguar made use of its long-anticipated modifications, which comprised a completely revised rear end: a new diffuser and, of necessity, a deformable structure that is very large and runs on to the top of the lower element of the lower rear wing. The changes made to the R2 required certification by the FIA. It had to go through crash tests again, which it passed with flying colours. There were also some new rear brake ducts, very similar to Ferrari's, but they gave rise to legality questions from other teams.

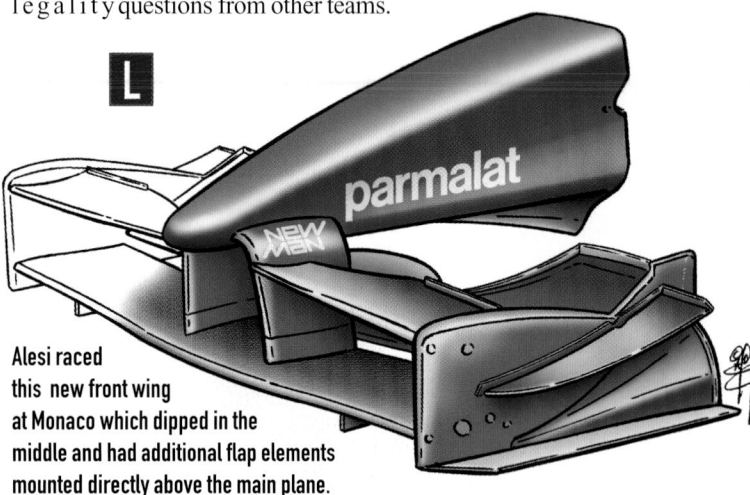

**Alesi raced this new front wing at Monaco which dipped in the middle and had additional flap elements mounted directly above the main plane.**

## PROST ACER

In Monaco, Prost had more technical novelties than anyone. There were three different front wings – the standard one plus two with secondary flap elements mounted above the main plane, similar to the system tried by Ferrari in Malaysia. The latter pair differed in the shape of their main profile. On Saturday, Jean Alesi tried the one with the middle of the central main plane raised, but in the race he used the version with the main plane which dipped in the centre (L).

There was a new deformable structure of symmetrical shape at the rear, together with a new diffuser which featured a revised central section and rear suspension. The rearmost arm of the top link had hitherto been attached to the titanium gearbox, but now it was wider based and mounted on the deformable structure. These new parts were only fitted to Alesi's two AP04s. Prost also had some interesting brake ducts, which had a ducted section on the outside of the disc rather than just on the inside, to direct airflow. Rear suspension modifications were promised for Canada.

## EUROPEAN MINARDI

The team only boasted qualifying discs in Monaco, as it was still working on a new rear end that would use the latest incarnation of the cast-titanium box. Following Gustav Brunner's defection to Toyota, it's introduction was re-scheduled for Magny-Cours.

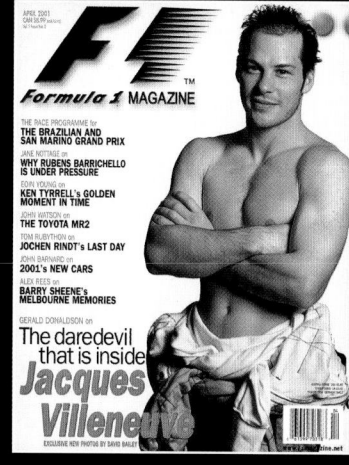

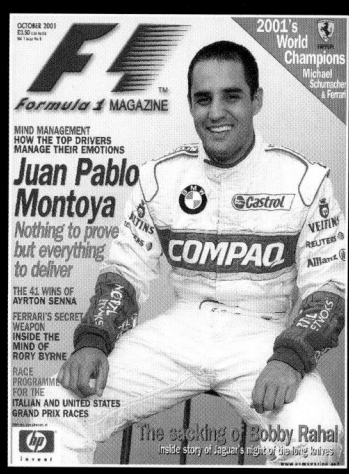
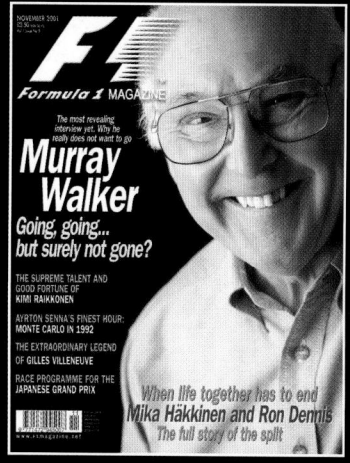

# Getting to grips with brakes

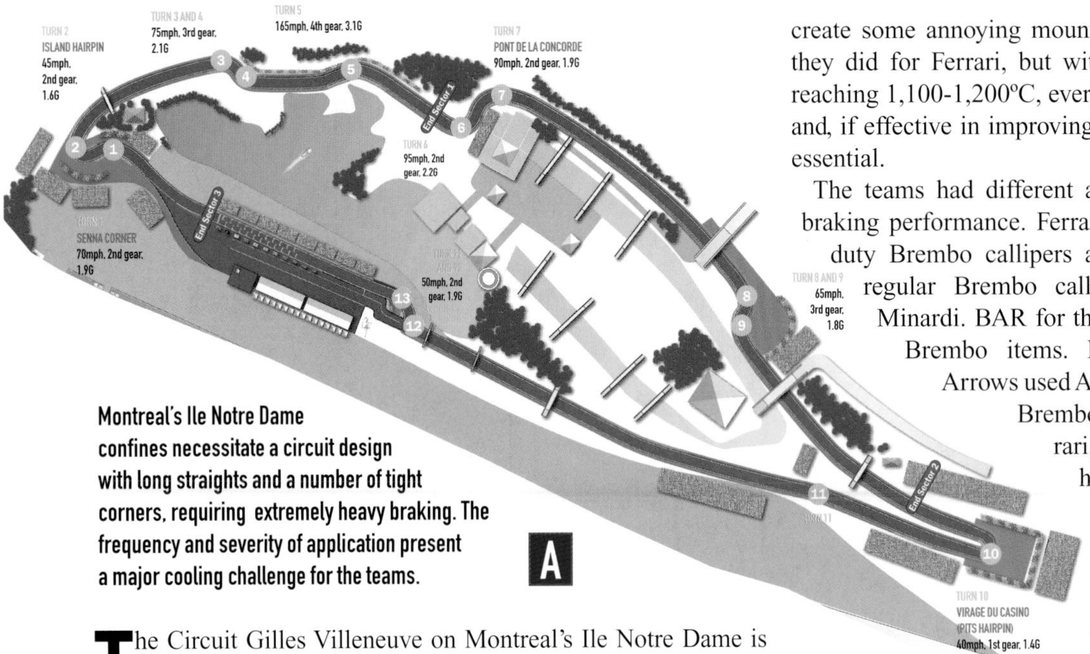

TURN 2
ISLAND HAIRPIN
45mph,
2nd gear,
1.6G

TURN 3 AND 4
75mph, 3rd gear,
2.1G

TURN 5
165mph, 4th gear, 3.1G

TURN 7
PONT DE LA CONCORDE
90mph, 2nd gear, 1.9G

TURN 6
95mph, 2nd
gear, 2.2G

SENNA CORNER
70mph, 2nd gear,
1.9G

50mph, 2nd
gear, 1.9G

TURN 8 AND 9
65mph,
3rd gear,
1.8G

TURN 10
VIRAGE DU CASINO
(PITS HAIRPIN)
40mph, 1st gear, 1.4G

**Montreal's Ile Notre Dame confines necessitate a circuit design with long straights and a number of tight corners, requiring extremely heavy braking. The frequency and severity of application present a major cooling challenge for the teams.**

**A**

The Circuit Gilles Villeneuve on Montreal's Ile Notre Dame is one of the toughest tracks of the season – perhaps even the toughest. It places a massive premium on braking efficiency, although that is not surprising when you consider the geography: there are six corners that require massive deceleration and this season's tyre war, resulting in higher grip levels, only exacerbated the problem. The 2000 season saw deceleration peaks of 4G; now they regularly reach 5G. Strong, consistent brake performance almost guarantees a strong race for those who get it right.

To give some perspective, from the start-finish line the first hard braking application from 198+ mph occurs after only three seconds for Turns 1 and 2 (see circuit map (A) above); the second after another 12secs at the entry to Turns 3 and 4, the third 13secs later for Turn 6, another 7secs later, the fourth application for Turns 8 and 9, the fifth after 12secs more for Turn 10, the pits hairpin, and the sixth after a further 20secs at the end of the long straight for the final chicane, Turn 12/13 which leads onto the pit straight. Speeds reach 155mph before the second and third braking points and a maximum of 202mph before the fourth application at Turns 8 and 9. But the hardest and most severe application of all is the fifth braking application, the Turn 10 hairpin, where cars brake from 186mph+ to only 35mph in four seconds – a reduction in braking time for deceleration of 0.6secs over those seen at the 2000 race. Naturally this led to a huge concentration by all teams on braking performance and efficiency – some with considerably more success than others.

Three teams copied Ferrari's enclosed brake duct system which aims to exit the brake cooling airflow to the outside of the wheel, the objective being to leave an undisturbed air path for the underbody aerodynamics: Arrows appeared with the prototype used in Monaco, now manufactured in carbon, while Jordan and Sauber had their own versions of the solution. The new barrel-type ducts

create some annoying mounting problems for the mechanics, as they did for Ferrari, but with peak braking temperatures easily reaching 1,100-1,200ºC, everything that might help is investigated and, if effective in improving performance, immediately becomes essential.

The teams had different approaches to achieving the desired braking performance. Ferrari and Prost used the special heavy-duty Brembo callipers as employed in Imola. Jordan used regular Brembo callipers, as did Sauber, Jaguar and Minardi. BAR for the first time this year, was also using Brembo items. McLaren, Williams, Benetton and Arrows used AP callipers.

Brembo had CCR discs exclusively for Ferrari, featuring the unique elongated holes; the Jordan, Sauber and Jaguar teams, plus drivers Luciano Burti and Fernando Alonso, used the regular Brembos. McLaren, Benetton and Arrows, plus Minardi driver Tarso Marques, decided on Hitco discs. Williams and the Prost of Jean Alesi opted for those made by Carbon Industrie. The French company had a new carbon material in Canada to provide two different choices for disc and pads.

## FERRARI

In Montreal, Ferrari had a new upright (B), shown here for clarity, without the brake disc. The new upright (B1) was cast for the first time in titanium, using the same technique employed by CPR, which also makes the titanium uprights and gearbox for Minardi.

The brake duct has two sections, one a heat-dissipating material and the other the carbon fibre duct itself. (B2) is the sensor in the calliper that monitors brake pad thickness. For qualifying Schumacher used standard discs, but both drivers raced with Ferrari's unique elongated slot discs.

Ferrari used four configurations of front wing in practice in Montreal, based on three different flaps – one completely new, utilising three different profile elements. Combinations of these provided four different options. The team also tried two rear wings, one with two elements and one with three. It settled on the triple-element version for qualifying and the race. There were modified air exits ahead of rear tyres with the aperture on the right-hand side being longer than the one on the left.

**The upright is the heart of the front suspension. Ferrari's new cast titanium upright (1) is lighter and stronger (2) indicates location of brake pad wear sensor**

**B**

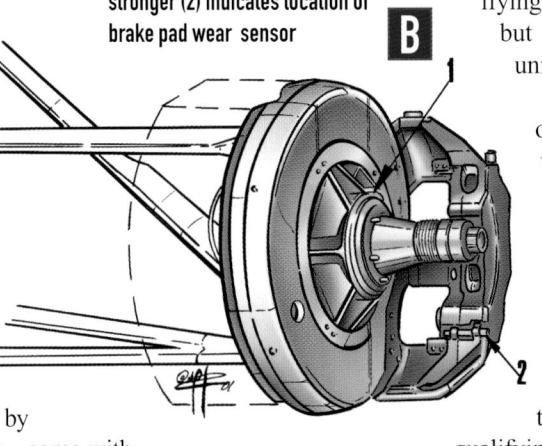

## McLAREN MERCEDES

In Montreal McLaren had new wings, with two secondary elements and different Gurney lip options. The permutations differed between drivers who qualified and raced, with various combinations. A new triple element rear wing was used throughout. McLaren also had bigger brake ducts. Häkkinen raced with Hitco discs after using Brembos in qualifying; Coulthard used Hitco products all weekend.

## BMW WILLIAMS

Williams arrived in Montreal with new front brake ducts and Carbon Industrie discs. In qualifying for the Canadian Grand Prix Williams used a rear wing with two main elements and a third at the leading edge. In the race only the double element wing was used, probably for less drag. In practice Williams tried the front wing it had used in Monaco and the standard version, and used the latter for qualifying and the race.

## BENETTON RENAULT

In Montreal the team had a new two-element rear wing with, a new front wing flap whose outer edges had Gurney lips and whose centre section was more curved. The drivers used this new bodywork all the way through the weekend.

## BAR HONDA

In Canada, BAR had two different noses to try. On Friday, Olivier Panis used Brembo callipers with Brembo discs. Jacques Villeneuve followed suit on Saturday.

## JORDAN HONDA

There were lots of new bits for Jordan in Canada, including drum type front brake ducts. Diagram C shows the clever triangular rear ducts; like all such designs, the hot air and dust are encouraged to exit to the outside of the wheel so the 'dirty' air doesn't interfere with the critical airflow between the main body and wheel and the flow over the diffuser, but the cooling volume needs to be precise to avoid over-cooling or overheating the disc and calliper. When a car is stationary, extractors are needed to expel hot air from the drum/wheel centre and prevent damage to the wheel bearings.

Jarno Trulli again used the bargeboard inside the front wheel, as seen in Monaco, albeit with a revised, longer

Jordan 'drum' rear brake duct used a triangular entry which utilised the space available between the top link, the push rod and the vertical wall of the brake drum.

**C**

shape. For the race, the team opened up the exhaust and radiator exits, and even in practice and qualifying used the manual start system, not launch control. Manual starts were also used in the race – and will be for the foreseeable future until the launch control system is fully sorted.

## ARROWS ASIATECH

Arrows' new – or Monaco – brake ducts were produced in carbon fibre in time for Montreal. There were two options, a large one as

Sauber's narrow 'drum' type front brake duct assembly used a sculptured NACA style intake.

used in Monaco and a very thin one for qualifying. There was also a new rear wing and this time all three cars had the top-exit exhaust fitted. Arrows was the only team not to have a spare monocoque available in Canada.

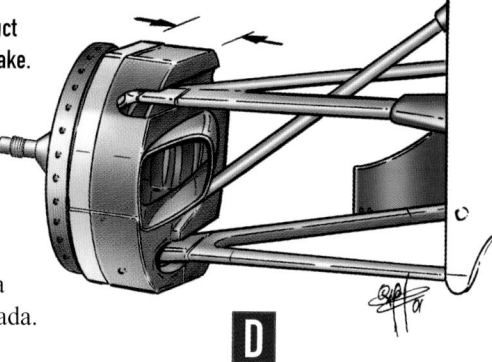

**D**

## SAUBER PETRONAS

Sauber used a narrow-section version of the Ferrari brake duct in Canada (D), but only in qualifying as the team reverted to its standard configuration for the race. The new design was not a completely round one-piece unit, but flexible carbon that is effectively wrapped around the discs. Sauber also ran its electro-hydraulic differential for the first time, in both practice and the race.

**E**

Jaguar tried these warped, asymmetrically shaped winglets mounted on the rear bodywork in practice in Montreal, but did not race them.

## JAGUAR RACING

In Montreal, complementing the new rear end introduced in Monaco, Jaguar introduced an unusually-shaped small winglet atop the sidepods (E). It had a curved shape unlike any other. However, the team decided not to use it in the race.

## EUROPEAN MINARDI

Minardi had new brake ducts front and rear in Montreal, and was scheduled to test its latest titanium gearbox and rear suspension the week after the Canadian race.

## PROST ACER

For Montreal Prost had some new brake ducts (F). These incorporated the flat section on the outside (F2) that acts as a blanking disc to close off the inside of the wheel rim. The steering arm (F3) of the AP04 is unusual in that it attaches to the middle rear of the upright, unlike any other team's design. Prost is also the only team to have the calliper mounted ahead of the front axle. The suspension pushrod (4F) is also unusual as it tapers in thickness from the top to the bottom where it picks up on the upright.

The team used the new front wing from Monaco in practice and qualifying for the Canadian Grand Prix, but raced with the standard design. It also used the stiffer Brembo callipers seen at Imola.

There was a further iteration of the new rear suspension seen in Monaco, but although Luciano Burti used it all day on Saturday, Jean Alesi ran it only in the morning before reverting to the Monaco set-up he preferred for qualifying. Both cars raced with the rear suspension first employed at Monaco.

**F**

(1) shows the cooling duct passage between the disc and wheel, and the closing disc (2) which helps seal the assembly. (3) shows the rear pick-up of the tie rod on the upright and (4) the tapered push rod.

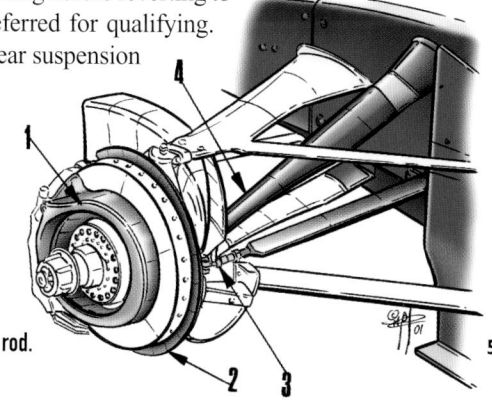

# Aerodynamic tweaking

The new Nürburgring is a medium to high-downforce circuit, but most teams opted to try similar aerodynamic configurations to those they had employed at Monaco, albeit without the sort of imaginative approaches Jordan and Arrows had conceived. Ferrari, for example, used its Monaco rear wing and the same front wing with a slightly revised second flap profile. McLaren again used its unique rear wing with the third element behind the two principal elements, and Arrows briefly tried the double wing situated above the rear axle, first seen in Monte Carlo.

The German track used to be quite light on brakes, but the tyre war has led to dramatically increased grip levels – witness Michael Schumacher's pole speed this year of 1m 14.960secs compared to David Coulthard's 2000 mark of 1m 17.526secs – and that in turn requires greater retardation. Thus the Nürburgring has become tougher and is now a medium-wear circuit for brakes. Cooling arrangements reflected this.

On the engine front, the three top companies – Ferrari, BMW and Mercedes – used special qualifying engines, while Sauber and Prost had later specification Ferrari V10s (badged as Petronas and Acer respectively) available for qualifying only.

## FERRARI

The Italian team used the same rear wing it had in Monaco, together with a subtly revised version of the front wing used in the principality (see diagrams A and B). It used the revised bodywork with larger air exits, as introduced in Canada, but the exits were no longer asymmetric. In qualifying, both drivers used lightweight brake callipers and thinner discs. For the race both had standard, thicker discs but Rubens Barrichello retained the lightweight callipers, indicating there may have been a disc wear problem but not a temperature problem.

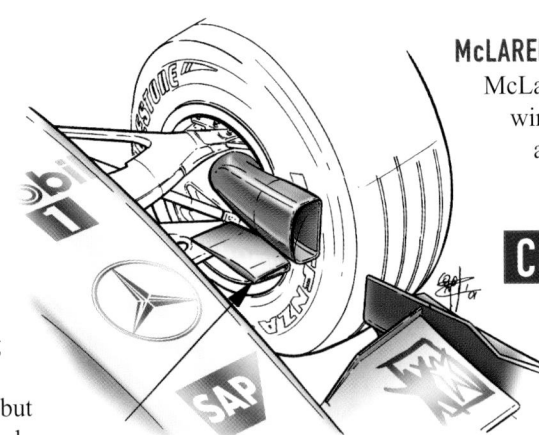

**A**

On Ferrari's Monaco front wing, the front wing endplate tapered in towards the centre line of the car as it neared the tyre.

**B**

In the search for downforce, Ferrari's Monaco rear wing had an additional element mounted directly above the main plane of the two-element top wing section.

McLaren's latest flat front brake duct allowed it to achieve the desired air volume without undue disruption to airflow to the radiators and underbody.

## McLAREN MERCEDES

McLaren used its Monaco rear wing, but at the front employed a bigger flap in conjunction with the unusual, serrated Gurney flaps introduced in Spain. There was also a new front brake duct (C). The lower section was no longer a small round pipe but had a flat wing-profile duct. This was used in qualifying, while the race version used the same new duct in conjunction with a larger upper duct.

In qualifying and the race Mika Häkkinen used Brembo discs, while David Coulthard stayed faithful to Hitco. This was only the second time Häkkinen has raced the Brembos (Spain was the first), although he used them in qualifying in Brazil and at Imola.

## BMW WILLIAMS

There were some important modifications for the Nürburgring. The most obvious was a revised fin ahead of the air intakes in the sidepods (E). Instead of the previous gold ingot-shaped fin, it now had a sharp profile that was wider at the end, so much so that its outer edge was protected when the cars were not running, to safeguard the mechanics. Juan Pablo Montoya used the fin on Friday and Schumacher followed suit on Saturday. All three cars were equipped with it on race day.

The BMW Williams FW23s used the Monaco front wing and, in qualifying, revised rear bodywork (D) with a lower profile. This was not used in the race because the

Williams had a new engine cover which lowered the deck height of the bodywork over the rear axle to encourage better airflow to the rear wing.

**D**

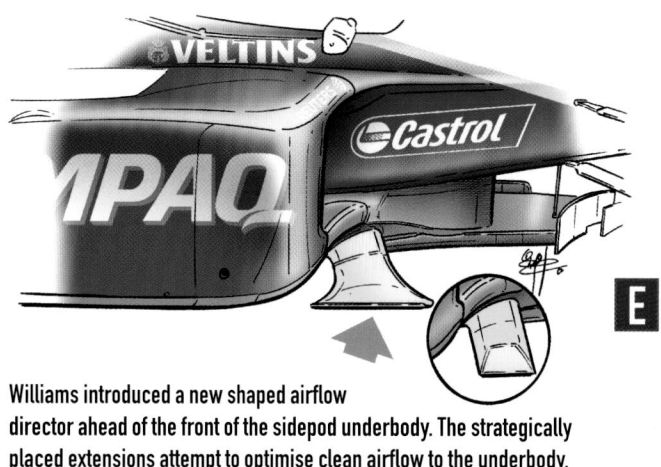

Williams introduced a new shaped airflow director ahead of the front of the sidepod underbody. The strategically placed extensions attempt to optimise clean airflow to the underbody.

team opted to be conservative just in case cooling in the race became an issue as the ambient temperature was in the 30-degree region.

## BENETTON RENAULT

Benetton was supposed to have a new rear wing but it wasn't ready. Instead the team used the bodywork with the extended front wing that was introduced in Monaco. The much-vaunted big step on Renault's lacklustre RS21 engine was scheduled to appear at Magny-Cours, with a significant aerodynamic update from the team for Silverstone.

## BAR HONDA

Once again the team had lots of new aerodynamic bits to try. The most visible was the shaped section which was bonded beneath the nose (F) like a pelican's gullet, and which the team claimed increased frontal downforce by two per cent. There was also a new front wing flap and curved bargeboards, while the shape of the small fins in front of the sidepods was also modified. The front suspension was slightly revised and the diffuser that was changed in Monaco had further detailed changes to its centre section. The small airbox wing used in Monaco reappeared, but not the smaller wing atop the rear axle.

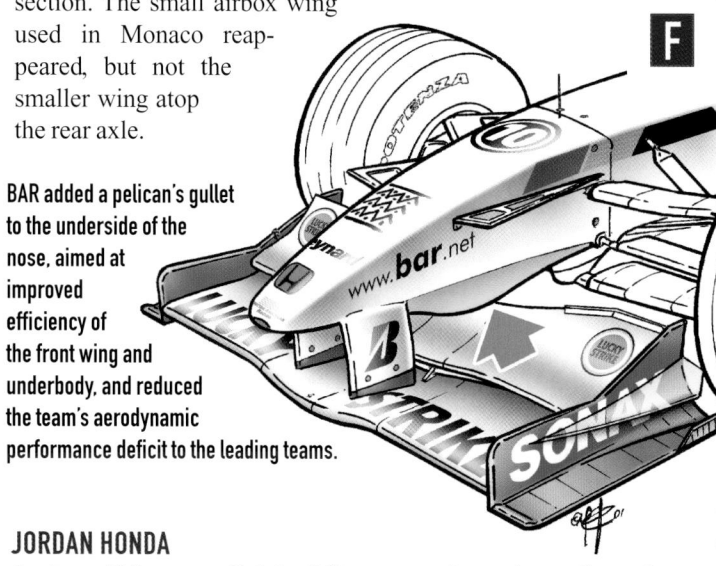

BAR added a pelican's gullet to the underside of the nose, aimed at improved efficiency of the front wing and underbody, and reduced the team's aerodynamic performance deficit to the leading teams.

## JORDAN HONDA

Jordan still has two slightly different aerodynamic configurations for Jarno Trulli and Heinz-Harald Frentzen: the Italian prefers the longer bargeboards, the German the shorter ones. Trulli also used the small-profile winglets atop the rear light, although Frentzen didn't. There was another new front brake duct, similar to the Ferrari copy introduced in Canada, but with a choice of two duct sizes. Although it had similar external appearance, it lacked the efficien-

cy of the Ferrari system. It was used by both drivers with a small duct in qualifying and Frentzen opted to race it with a larger duct. Trulli raced the conventional ducts.

Together with Prost and Ferrari, Jordan used the lightweight Brembo callipers throughout. There were also revised hot air exits for the radiators, which were used by both Jordan drivers through qualifying and the race.

## ARROWS ASIATECH

There was nothing new technically on the Arrows A22s, which were the same as they had been in Montreal, except that they ran with Monaco wings. Jos Verstappen briefly tried the twin wings over the rear axle on Friday, but they were not used further.

Sauber tried a straight edge at the top of the front wing endplate, following wind tunnel tests, but the tunnel improvements did not translate into lap time on the track.

## SAUBER PETRONAS

On Saturday, the Sauber C20s appeared with a revised front wing endplate on which the sculpted upper edge was filled in with a carbon insert (G), but the team reverted to its standard design for the race.

## JAGUAR RACING

The R2s appeared with their Monaco wings and used the curved sidepod winglets that appeared in Canada, in both qualifying and the race.

## EUROPEAN MINARDI

Minardi had modified the pedals to suit Tarso Marques, who has large feet. The new gearbox casing should have been tested just prior to the European Grand Prix but was late and scheduled to test either just before or after Magny-Cours.

## PROST ACER

The French team had nothing new to try apart from the lightweight Brembo callipers and its double-flap front wing which was used briefly on Friday, before the team reverted to its standard configuration. Further significant aerodynamic and suspension modifications were expected for Magny-Cours.

# Refining airflow control

Magny-Cours is a medium to high-downforce circuit so most teams ran similar wings to those they had used in Germany. Because it is the smoothest track in the calendar, they were able to run the cars lower and stiffer than anywhere else. The circuit's smooth surface makes it a low dynamic grip and can highlight a shortage in downforce and a difficulty in achieving a balance.

Ferrari's modified bargeboards had 3-4cm shaved off the top edge in the interests of increased cooling.

### FERRARI

Ferrari further modified its barge-boards (see diagram A) by cutting down the top edge by 3-4cm. It used the same wings as at the Nürburgring, albeit with slightly less incidence. In qualifying both drivers used smaller discs and the lighter Brembo callipers, and for the race additional ducts were fitted atop the chassis to cool the cockpits.

### McLAREN MERCEDES

McLaren used different Gurney flaps in the middle and outer edges of the trailing edge of its front wing. They were still of distinctive serrated shape, but had a curved profile rather than the usual straight edge.

The team used the front brake ducts seen in Germany, but for the first time Häkkinen qualified and raced with the Hitco discs that Coulthard habitually uses.

The shadow plate had two attachment cables rather than one, and on Saturday the team changed the position of the ballast on the plate. It transpired that the reason one of Häkkinen's side-pods was punctured when he ran over the final kerb in Canada was that the ballast was punched through it by the impact, and in general there are moves afoot to consider banning the fitting of ballast on the shadow plate from 2002 onwards. The location of balance is used as a tool in trimming the balance of the car by modifying its weight distribution to suit a particular circuit.

### BMW WILLIAMS

Williams again used two sets of bodywork, as it had in Germany. The lowline engine cover first seen at the Nürburgring was again used for qualifying and the original one for the race. In France, ambient temperature was again to be a reliability issue and required additional cooling margin.

In the Sunday morning warm-up Montoya used the original front wing with its two distinctive underside strakes, while Schumacher used the Monaco wing. Montoya retained the set-up for the race.

### BENETTON RENAULT

Renault's much-vaunted upgrade of its RS21 engine proved very disappointing when it was introduced for qualifying. Fisichella was the slowest on the straight and Button was beaten by one of the Minardis, which use Ford's 1998 chain-driven technology.

The latest engine features variable inlet trumpets and a new shape for the combustion chambers. A further evolution, with more revs, was due to appear in September.

On the Friday and Saturday mornings Button tried low barge-boards (B), and both drivers raced with them. While there was little difference in performance, the cooling was better.

On Saturday Benetton introduced a new rear wing whose lower main plane mount had a distinctive forward-angled delta profile (C). It had been due to appear at the Nürburgring but had collapsed on its initial test prior to the European GP, hence the delay. It was

Benetton had revised bargeboards in France (B) which were significantly lower, as indicated by the yellow shading which represents the height of the originals.

The yellow shading shows the difference between the original lower main plane and Benetton's new swept forward version, which droops at each end.

not used for the race. Further big aerodynamic changes were due for Silverstone as Benetton was still lagging behind the lead teams aerodynamically.

## BAR HONDA

BAR had virtually nothing new at Magny-Cours but by Sunday, the team had four cars for its drivers to try in the race morning warm-up. Panis's T-car was due to test in both Monza and Mugello in the week following the race. It featured completely new front and rear suspension designed and built with direct research input from Honda.

Further evolutions were scheduled to appear at Silverstone.

## JORDAN HONDA

Jordan had another iteration of its front brake duct. This had a modified middle section and was effectively an intermediate version of the big duct seen in Canada and the smaller one used in qualifying at the Nürburgring. The small duct was used again in qualifying together with the 22mm Brembo discs, and the cars raced with the standard long brake ducts. The Jordan drum duct lacks the complicated inner ducting that makes the Ferrari duct so effective.

## ARROWS ASIATECH

Arrows had nothing new, but raced with the brake ducts seen in Canada.

## SAUBER PETRONAS

On Saturday Sauber introduced a new front wing similar in shape to Jordan's, with a vee-shaped squared-off central support. It was also used in the race (D).

Prost's new bargeboards featured multi-section channelling in an effort to control airflow attachment around the side of the car.

## PROST ACER

Prost had three big aerodynamic changes. Like Jaguar, it had double-section bargeboards (F); there was also a revised engine cover with different shaped flick-ups ahead of the rear tyres. It also took a leaf from Williams' book: a new diffuser with an extra venturi on the outer section by the rear tyres.

The rear suspension had been modified further, allowing more anti-squat adjustment.

## EUROPEAN MINARDI

Minardi had nothing new but chief engineer Gabriele Tredozzi stayed back in Faenza supervising assembly of the new titanium gearbox, which was due to appear with new rear suspension at Silverstone.

Sauber's Jordan type front main plane attempted to make more use of the clean underside of the team's monocoque generated by its separate front forward wishbone mountings.

## JAGUAR RACING

On Saturday a new bargeboard with a double lower section similar to McLaren's appeared on Irvine's car (E). This was fitted to the car that stopped early on in qualifying, but the new boards were used on both cars in the race.

On Friday the drivers had a choice of front wing: both chose the one with the deeper and squarer central spoon section.

Jaguar had a new bargeboard with a double lower wall, in an attempt to control the airflow around the sidepods.

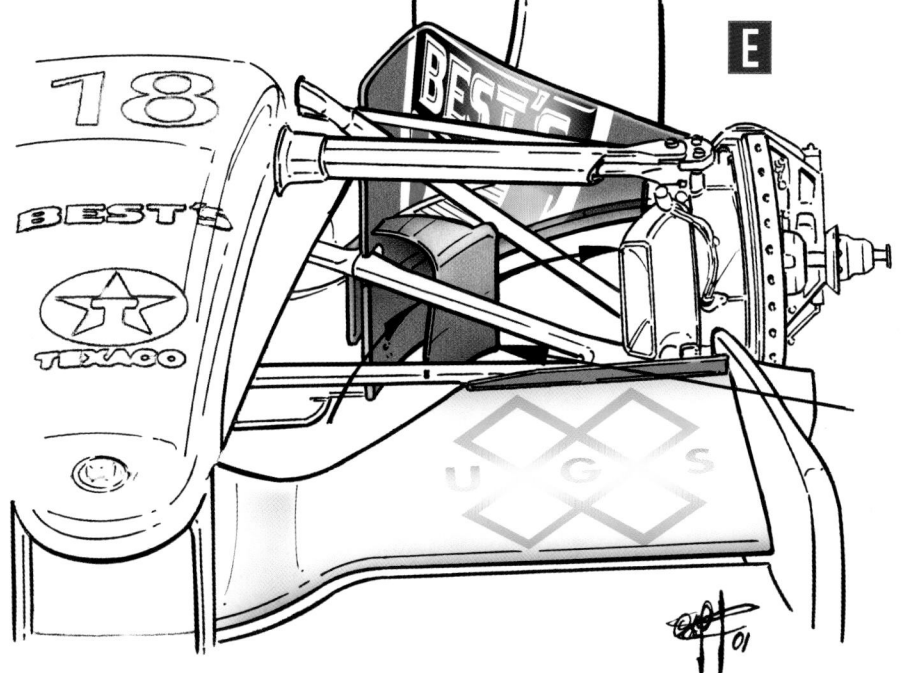

# Logistics slow down development

In some ways more had been expected in the way of technical development from the teams at Silverstone than they actually delivered. The reason for this apparent slowdown was the necessity to build parts and test them in readiness for the forthcoming races at the low-downforce circuits of Hockenheim and Monza (many teams having tested at the Italian track the week prior to the British GP). At the same time Hungary was lurking, where the same high downforce levels of Monte Carlo are required, so teams were also having to analyse any shortcomings their cars had revealed in the principality. Hence some developments expected to appear at Silverstone had to be postponed in order to address the extreme requirement of the next two races.

Silverstone these days is a medium downforce circuit, very similar to Magny-Cours. It was once a fast circuit, but has now been slowed down considerably. Since the cars were much quicker this season than they were in 2000, however, thanks largely to the tyre war, this created some suspension problems for some teams through a combination of much faster cornering speeds and the loadings inflicted by the high kerbs now employed at the British track.

Juan Pablo Montoya, Eddie Irvine and Jarno Trulli all damaged front pushrods when trying to drive too ambitiously over the latter.

The story of the Silverstone race was how McLaren ran its cars virtually in qualifying trim, with qualifying brake ducts and low fuel load, and in the case of Häkkinen no air-extraction chimneys, and that its gamble paid off handsomely as Häkkinen took his first win of the year in dominant manner.

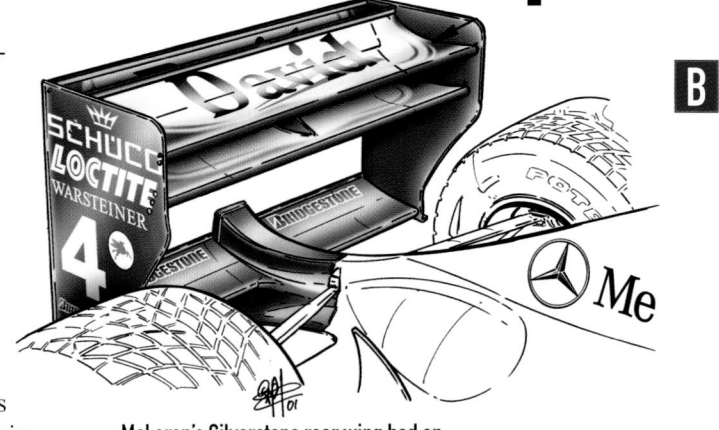

McLaren's Silverstone rear wing had an additional large flap mounted directly above the original main plane and flap.

## FERRARI

Ferrari again used its latest specification engine for qualifying, which revs 300rpm higher thanks to different camshafts. This was still only a qualifying engine although its race debut was scheduled for Hockenheim. Otherwise there was nothing new on the cars, which were in broadly similar configuration to Magny-Cours except for a minor modification to the lower part of the front wing endplates, which featured widened shaped sections on the inner edge of the endplate (see diagram A).

All day on Friday and in the race Michael Schumacher used the Imola brake discs with elongated radial cooling holes, and the spare car was similarly equipped, but Rubens Barrichello, who does not use the brakes as hard, stuck with the standard discs with circular radial cooling holes.

Ferrari's new front wing endplate featured a sculptured inner horizontal extension toward the leading edge.

## McLAREN MERCEDES

After a lot of recent testing the team found the complex MP4/16 slightly easier to set up. There was a new front brake duct for qualifying, which was also used in the race by both Häkkinen and Coulthard. Häkkinen also drove on Saturday and in the race without the air-extracting but drag-inducing chimneys on the sidepods.

McLaren also had a new rear wing. In Magny-Cours the team used a double profile rear wing, but at Silverstone it had one with a deeper element mounted at the leading edge of the endplates, above the main element. This larger element had a longer chord similar to the concept used in Melbourne, which echoed Ferrari's arrangement (B).

There were also some revisions to the rear suspension geometry, but no sign of a new set-up that had been tested at Monza. This rear suspension and a new gearbox were due to appear in Hungary, and the package was said to be smaller and 4kg lighter.

## BMW WILLIAMS

BMW Williams had some new bargeboards of a different profile and curvature, and as always in two pieces. The larger one was mounted just below the upper front wishbone on the monocoque and extended forward towards the front wing and featured a curve

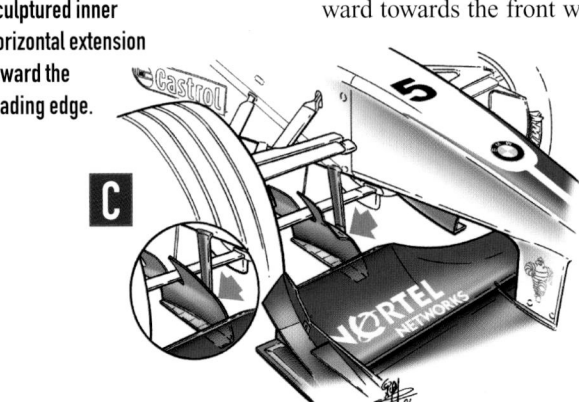

BMW Williams introduced modified bargeboards, the forward one mounted off the monocoque which stretched forward to the trailing edge of the front wing. The circled drawing shows the previous shape.

to its outer top section (C), while the smaller one behind it had a different profile with a step to its bottom section. The team had also cut away the rear edge of the engine cover above the rear suspension, to improve cooling.

A different front wing flap was tried in testing prior to the meeting, while in the wet on Saturday morning Montoya briefly tried the Melbourne front wing with its two vertical underwing strakes. Ralf Schumacher used the Monaco front wing throughout, in the 30-degree region.

## BAR HONDA

All three cars featured new front and rear suspension built in collaboration with Honda, with the rear suspension system featuring carbon fibre pushrods for the first time, which reduce weight over the standard steel versions (D). For the wet on Saturday, the rear wing end-plates with cut away sections from Monaco were used, and all weekend the team retained the small middle wing on the engine cover.

BAR ran its new carbon fibre rear pushrods for the first time.

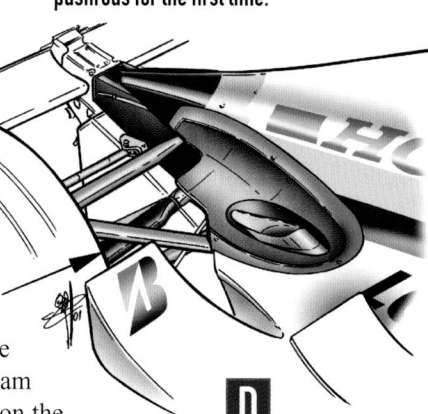

## BENETTON RENAULT

All weekend Benetton used the rear wing with the delta shaped lower section introduced in France, and for the first time had launch control. Giancarlo Fisichella qualified with Brembo discs, Jenson Button with Hitco.

## JORDAN HONDA

Jordan was the only team with four fully assembled cars in the paddock, hardly surprising since its factory is literally only across the road from the main entry gate.

The team introduced a new rear wing (E) whose lower element featured upward curvature where the outer edges met the endplates. The brake ducts had been modified yet again, in echo of Ferrari's, but both cars raced with the traditional long and square-shaped ducts. For the first time Frentzen used the same long bargeboards as Trulli has used since Austria. In the wet on Saturday both cars used the middle rear wing seen in Monaco.

Jordan had a new multi-curvature lower rear main plane of which the trailing edge swept upwards at the endplates. The yellow shading of the rear flap highlights its semi-delta shape.

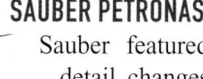

## ARROWS ASIATECH

Arrows used one of the two engine cover-mounted wing profiles at the rear axle line that were introduced in Monaco, and the A22s also featured new brake ducts with the middle sections extended forwards for enhanced cooling.

Arrows again ran one of its axle line rear wing elements in the search for downforce.

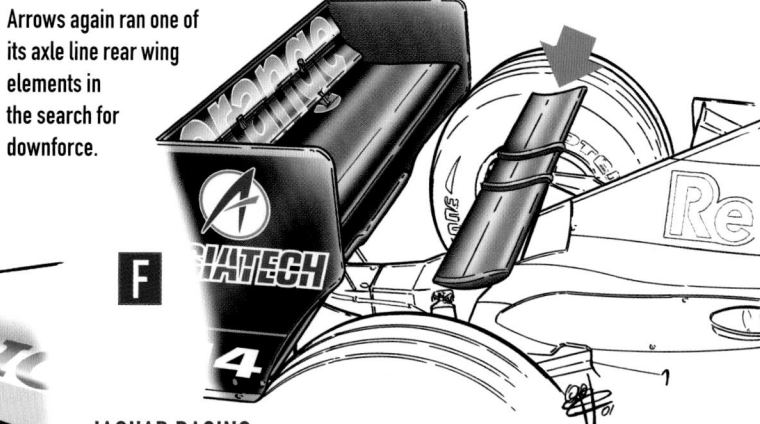

## JAGUAR RACING

Jaguar had modified the central section of the diffuser introduced at Monaco, and the trailing edge was now higher than before. The double-exit bargeboards introduced in France were retained.

## SAUBER PETRONAS

Sauber featured lots of small detail changes. The new Ferrari-style brake ducts were used, but rather than exhausting brake dust through the wheel as the Italian system does, these directed it downward onto the road. There were also slightly modified bargeboards (G) with greater inward curvature narrowing the gap to the monocoque at the leading edge. For the first time Sauber also had its much-tested power-steering system at a race.

Sauber had modified bargeboards which tapered in more aggressively towards the monocoque at the leading edge.

## EUROPEAN MINARDI

Minardi had nothing new because at Faenza it was working flat-out on its new titanium gearbox. There was also to be a new rear suspension and underbody with exhausts blowing to the middle of the car like McLaren: as the new transmission is very narrow, it allows larger air passage between gearbox and inner face of the wheel.

## PROST ACER

Having confused itself running new bargeboards, diffuser and bodywork in France, Prost arrived at Silverstone with only the new bodywork. All weekend the team experimented with the standard front wing and the double-flap version seen in Monaco and Canada. The latter was used for the race.

# Aerodynamically, drag is speed

Together with Monza, Hockenheim is the lowest-downforce circuit on the calendar. It demands efficient aerodynamics, because teams naturally want to run as much downforce as they can get away with for optimum performance in the tight stadium section without inducing excessive drag, which would be severely constraining for straight line performance on Hockenheim's long straights. Those teams with the best ratio of negative lift over drag find themselves at an advantage, the more so if they have good engine power.

Aerodynamic configurations thus tend to be very similar, because most teams find similar solutions. All the teams tested at Monza in preparation for Hockenheim, though several did not use the more extreme solutions they tried in Italy, even in qualifying in Germany, because their findings at Monza suggested the cars would not be sufficiently well balanced at Hockenheim. Examples were the very small rear wing McLaren tested at Monza, very similar to the one it used with two flaps (rather than a flap and profile) at Monza last year. BAR tried a single profile rear wing, but didn't use it at Hockenheim. Jordan had a single profile rear wing that collapsed at Monza. On Saturday Trulli briefly tried a strengthened version in qualifying (see inset on diagram J) before reverting to the standard low downforce Jordan rear wing.

Because of the long straights and slow chicanes Hockenheim is also very hard on engines and brakes. BMW's Dr Mario Thiessen calculated the flat-out, high-revs loading on the engine: "The first straight is about 16 seconds, the other three are between 10 and 15. So overall it comes close to 50 seconds at full throttle and quite a part of it in top gear and at high revs. I would say it comes between 60 and 70 per cent of the lap in the dry."

Michelin runners had the advantage of its slightly wider front tyres, which reduce understeer and give a larger tyre contact patch which helps under heavy braking. The toughest part of Hockenheim is braking for the first chicane – named after the great Jim Clark. Speeds here must be reduced from 350 to 110kph. All Brembo's runners used the heavy-duty calliper, introduced at Imola,

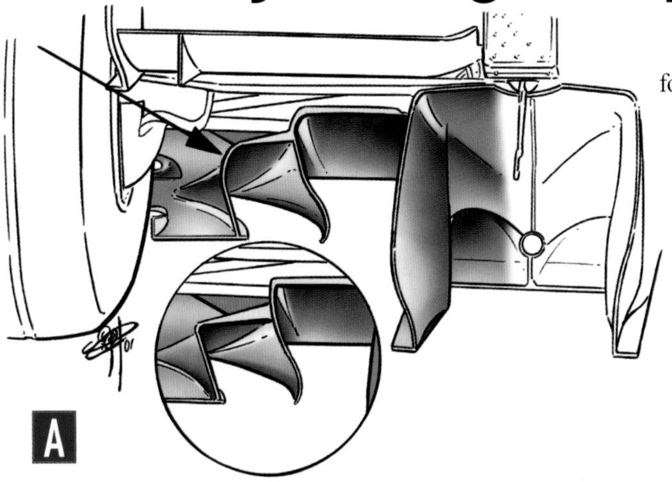

**A**

The most important new development at Hockenheim came from Ferrari which introduced a new diffuser with exit shapes that had a softer radius than the previous underbody (inset). The taller and more rounded side channels had a deeper angle.

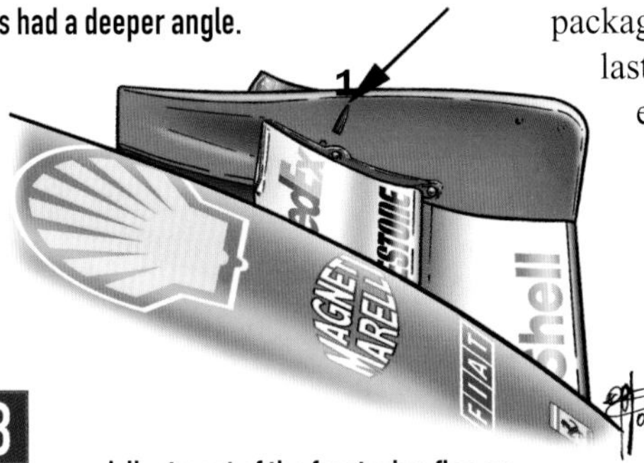

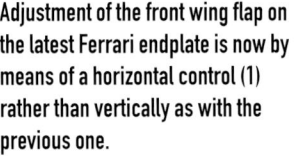

**B**

Adjustment of the front wing flap on the latest Ferrari endplate is now by means of a horizontal control (1) rather than vertically as with the previous one.

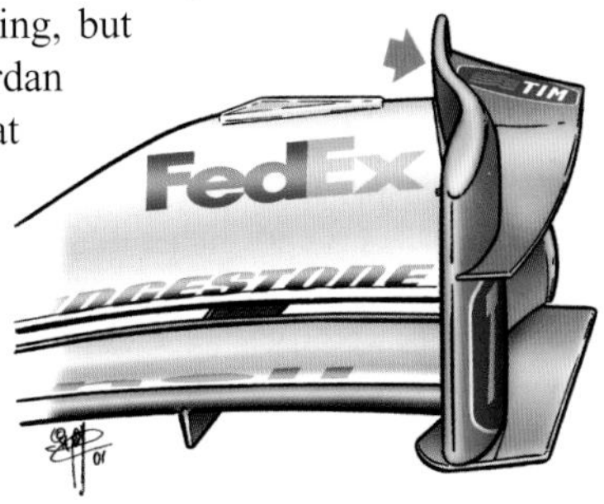

**C**

Ferrari's new front wing endplate did away with the horizontal inner fins near the upper edge.

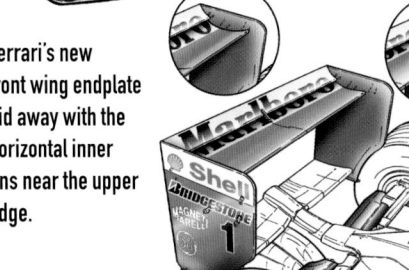

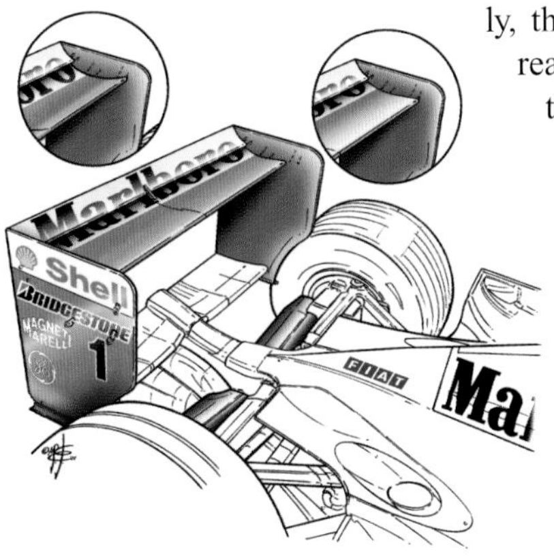

**D**

Ferrari ran three different rear wings at Hockenheim. Inset left: The qualifying wing using the banana chord used by both drivers. Inset right: A flatter, longer chord used in Friday practice. Main drawing: The short chord flatter profile used in the race.

for qualifying and the race, except for Jordan which did not use it on Saturday. Carbon Industries supplied one team more than usual, Jaguar, along with Williams and Prost, while Hitco supplied McLaren, Arrows, Benetton and Minardi and CCR Brembo had Ferrari, BAR, Jordan and Sauber. On Panis's car BAR also tried the larger brake pedal (see BAR section) and the Frenchman experimented with right-foot braking, which he preferred.

## FERRARI

Ferrari had a completely new aero package for fast circuits, as it did last year. There were three elements to this. First there was a new floor (A) with taller and more rounded side channels (arrowed) which also had a deeper angle. There was a new front wing, with smaller chord flaps (C) and the third design of endplate this season (B). The vertical section of the endplate now had an S-shaped wing section. The fins on the inside edge of the endplates had been deleted and the flap adjustment was done horizontally on the inside of the endplate rather than vertically (B). Finally, there were three different rear wings (D). One was tested at Monza, the other two were new. For qualifying both drivers used a wing with a banana-shaped main upper profile (D, inset left). In the warm-up and the race a wing similar to that tried at Monza (D), but with smaller chord, was used to reduce downforce and generate faster straightline speed. Both drivers used the bigger Brembo discs with elongated holes (the first time for Barrichello). Interestingly, these are manufactured specially for Brembo by a company called Oram, which is owned by the former 1960s and 1970s Ferrari technical director, Mauro Forghieri.

For the first time the team used its more powerful qualifying engine in the race. Previously it was used only in qualifying at Magny-Cours and Silverstone. Schumacher's fuel pump broke in the race, giving him his first retirement since Imola in April, but this was the third time this component has let Ferrari down. It happened to Barrichello in Brazil, necessitating his frantic sprint back to the garage on race day for the spare; and it happened to Schumacher on the warm-up lap to the grid at the Nürburgring.

## McLAREN MERCEDES

Mercedes-Benz had a more powerful engine for both qualifying and the race. And McLaren brought along a new front wing for use on faster circuits. The team had tested this wing at Monza with endplates that did not have fins on the outside, but the fins reappeared at Hockenheim. This wing was used in conjunction with a low-downforce rear wing (E), albeit not the one tested at Monza.

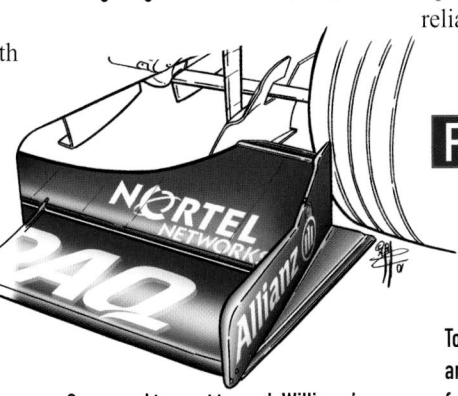

McLaren ran a low drag rear wing for Hockenheim which had a larger chord than the low drag wing tested at Monza (inset).

The air-extraction chimneys were back on all three cars at Hockenheim, having been deleted on Häkkinen's race car at Silverstone.

There were also bigger front brake ducts, but there was no sign of the new rear end with revised gearbox and suspension that was also tested at Monza. This would not be used until it had proved itself superior to the standard version.

## BMW WILLIAMS

Williams also had a new aero package. The front wing (F) was based on the main profile from Australia but without vertical strakes on the underside. It had a new flap and the endplate sides were straight as on the FW22, rather than curved. This was complemented by a double profile rear wing (G) which had a relatively large chord by Hockenheim standards. On Saturday Schumacher tried new front brake ducts similar to Ferrari's, but they were later removed.

For Belgium Williams was to introduce a completely new version of the chassis (FW23B) facilitating use of a superior aerodynamic package. In October it would also be able to accept the BMW's 2002 engine and a new gearbox in readiness for the pukka FW24's arrival in January/February. This interim chassis would enable the team to accumulate a significant amount of mileage directly applicable to the FW24 before the testing ban in November and December.

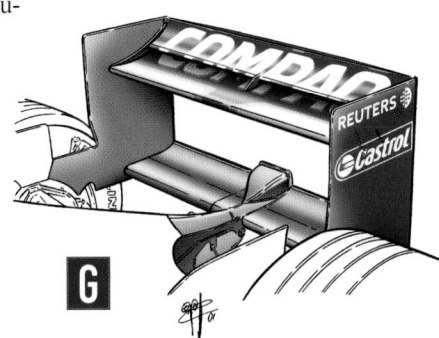

Compared to most teams', Williams' new front wing and endplate are simple and uncomplicated without any horizontal airflow strakes.

Williams introduced a new double profile rear wing to go with its new front wing. Although the chord of this new rear wing was quite long it was obviously efficient as evidenced by its lap times and speed on the straight.

## BENETTON RENAULT

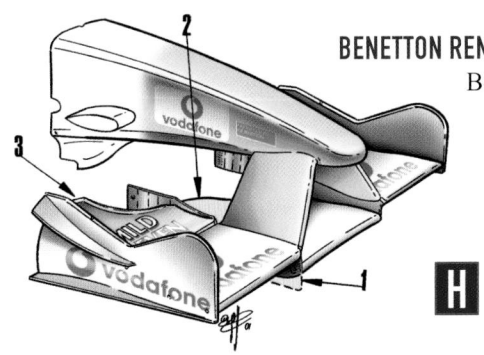

Benetton had a new front wing with the lower central skirts removed, extensions to the wing flaps, and new Gurney lips at the rear of the flaps.

Benetton ran the new bodywork from Magny-Cours with double flap ahead of the rear tyres, and a small rear wing with two small-chord profiles and narrow endplates. The nose was also revised (H) with deletion of the two low central skirts (H1). There was a small flap in the middle section (H2) for qualifying but this was deleted for the race. There were new flaps with Gurney lips (H3), which were used in qualifying and the race.

Fisichella had to qualify with the standard engine after his qualifying engine broke in the morning, and Button's qualifying engine broke during his final run on Saturday afternoon. But the engines used in the race proved surprisingly reliable.

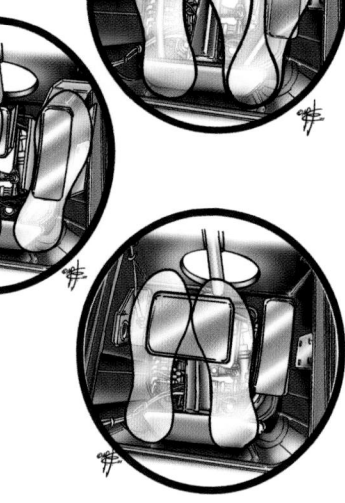

Top: The three pedal arrangement used by Prost for Jean Alesi. Middle: Typical standard left foot braking arrangement. Bottom: BAR's large brake pedal pad as used by Olivier Panis at Hockenheim.

## BAR HONDA

BAR had a lot of small detail changes. The wavy nose used in France and Britain had been changed back to the original unit. Behind the front suspension, however, the small horizontal plates had a more semi-circular shape to enhance airflow. The entry to the sidepods was also reduced, by raising the lower edges, to reduce cooling capacity and drag. The rear wing was a two-profile design, not the single profile tried at Monza. This rear wing had narrow endplates with scalloped leading edges. At the Monza test BAR tried a modified brake pedal arrangement (I) to ▷

Like McLaren, Jordan had a new low drag wing (inset) for Hockenheim which Trulli tried briefly, but he raced with the standard 2000 twin-profile small-chord version.

enable the driver to use both feet for heavy braking. At Hockenheim it was tried again but only Panis persevered with it. Villeneuve did not think the experiment was worthwhile and did not like the lack of feel. Panis had a particular need in this respect as the BAR has very short brake pedal travel, requiring up to 70kg of pedal pressure for very heavy braking. Although fully recovered from his 1998 Montreal accident, the Frenchman finds the system beneficial where such heavy pedal pressure is required, and when needed was able to use his left foot on the wide pedal. This larger size pedal may also allow the use of different size brake master cylinders.

## JAGUAR RACING

Jaguar brought new, quite neutral, front and two rear wings to Hockenheim. These had been tested successfully at Monza. Both drivers used Carbon Industries discs and a more powerful engine in both qualifying and the race.

## ARROWS ASIATECH

All three Arrows A22s featured modified power-steering. The team also had the smallest chord front and rear wings that were used in Hockenheim.

## SAUBER PETRONAS

Sauber had two options of front wing, one based on the Jordan-type nose introduced in Magny-Cours. This had two small flaps and no central curved section (K). The other was based on the original nose with a the gently curved central spoon section (L) that closely resembled the original small-chord flap front wing that McLaren launched on the MP4/16.

There were also two different rear wings, each with two profiles, and there was a modified diffuser with an additional flap in the central tunnel.

Above: Sauber had the Magny-Cours Jordan- type front wing. Below: Modified original Rinland designed spoon-shaped wing.

## EUROPEAN MINARDI

On Friday, Alonso did 90 laps with the long-awaited new gearbox, rear suspension and revised rear bodywork. This version of the car was 28mm shorter. He did not use the new exhaust which blows gases low down and centrally into the diffuser. Instead he ran the normal exhaust which blows into the top of the diffuser's side channels.

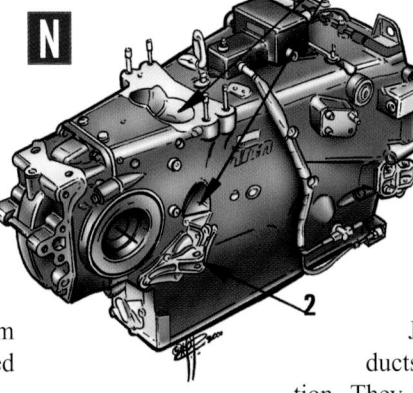

Above: Minardi debuted its new titanium gearbox at Hockenheim which achieved the anticipated advantages in weight and size over the magnesium version (below). Shock absorber/roll bar mountings (1), rear lower wishbone pickup (2).

Both drivers used the standard cars from Friday afternoon, with low-down-force front and rear wings. They also tried bargeboards similar to McLaren's, with a second channel mounted low down. The new cast titanium gearbox (M) represented a 25 per cent weight saving over its fabricated titanium predecessor which in itself was in the region of 25 per cent lighter than the magnesium casing (N). The advantages of the cast titanium system are significant and it was expected that Ferrari would have a cast titanium gear casing for the 2002 season.

## JORDAN HONDA

Jordan had new front brake ducts with a different centre section. They were tried in qualifying, but both drivers raced the standard ducts. Jordan was the only Brembo team to use the lighter callipers in qualifying, but ran the heavy-duty versions on the race.

The front wing endplates had small horizontal fins mounted on the top of their inside edge. There were also small angled fins on the outer edges.

In the main profile of the front wing the spoon section remained deep but there were only flaps on the outer channels, not in the spoon itself.

There were two rear wings (J), the single profile briefly tried by Trulli and the standard 2000 twin-profile small-chord version which was used in qualifying and the race. The team had also reverted to the original rear bodywork without the double flip-ups ahead of the rear wheels, to improve drag.

## PROST ACER

The new diffuser and bargeboards introduced at Magny-Cours had been deleted, and only the new bodywork was used for Hockenheim. The front and rear wings were from the 2000 AP03. Hockenheim marked engineer Andy Le Fleming's last race with the team.

# Never enough grip

The Hungaroring may not look like Monaco, but it demands the same maximum levels of downforce as the principality. Extra wings thus sprouted like crocuses in spring. With three weeks since the last race, most of the teams had made modifications to their cars. Ferrari, McLaren and Williams in particular had changes geared to the circuit's characteristics, but Benetton and Jordan had made significant modifications to their basic specification that were intended to give benefits elsewhere too.

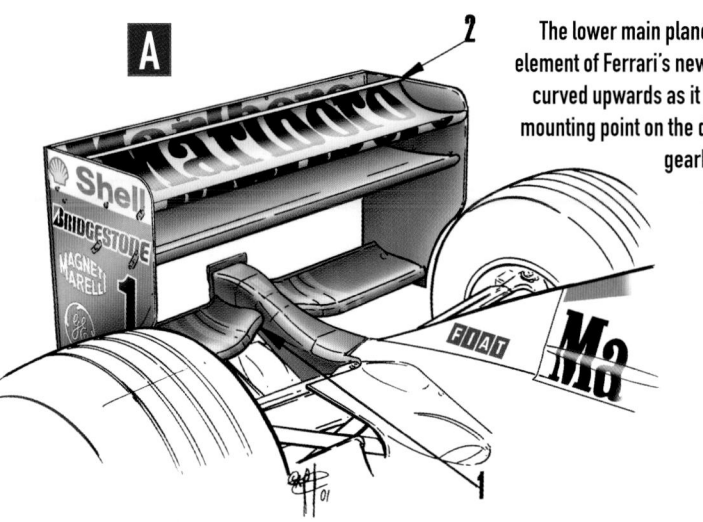

The lower main plane mounting element of Ferrari's new rear wing curved upwards as it neared the mounting point on the deformable gearbox central pylon.

Two views of McLaren's latest rear wing had endplates which tapered as they descended to the lower mounting plane. This wing was used in conjunction with a body mounted element just ahead of the main structure which directed the flow of air off the tail section.

## FERRARI

Ferrari's new aerodynamic package was based on its Monte Carlo set-up, with a very similar front wing, but this now incorporated the curved endplates first seen at Hockenheim. There was a new rear wing (see diagram A) which featured a lower element that curved up by the mounting pylon (1) and had three upper elements. The leading edge upper element incorporated a Gurney flap (2) for the first time and a longer chord than usual.

At Hockenheim last year Ferrari introduced a new diffuser that was not subsequently used in Hungary; this year there was another new diffuser at Hockenheim but this time it was carried over to the Hungarian race. In qualifying both drivers used lighter qualifying discs, and for the race both reverted to the Imola discs with elongated cooling holes. Neither used Ferrari's qualifying engine in the race, in the interests of reliability on a track that is notably hard on mechanical components. Interestingly, Ferrari did not appear to have any cooling issues; the team neither used air extractor chimneys nor opened up the sidepod cooling apertures any more than usual for what is historically a hot race.

## McLAREN MERCEDES

McLaren had a new front wing with a Rinland/Sauber style spoon shape and a Gurney flap contoured distinctively to its outline, in contrast to the straight Gurney used in Monaco. There was also a new rear wing (B) with a mini wing mounted behind the engine cover (B1 and also diagram C) and cutaway endplates (B2) similar to those tried previously by Minardi and Arrows. These were the most significant changes, but the larger of the two bargeboards had also been lengthened and the double channel ran 5-6cm further

forward than usual. Different air extractor chimneys were used in qualifying and the race, the larger units being employed for the latter.

## BMW WILLIAMS

Williams' new front wing featured a distinctive curved fin on the inside of the endplates (D) to enhance airflow, while at the rear the team had added what looked like a Rippspeed bolt-on rear spoiler (E2) at the rear of the engine cover. There was also the mini wing atop the airbox that had not been used in Monaco (E1). Williams' car was the most

Williams' new front wing employed a new fin aimed at controlling airflow around the front wing endplate and wing and the effect of tyre turbulence.

visually different from the version run in the principality.

Williams had so far used air extractor chimneys only in Malaysia; some were ready in the truck in Hungary, but never actually used.

Williams' rear bodywork had additions to virtually every location, evidence of the difficulty in finding downforce regardless of drag penalty.

## BENETTON RENAULT

Benetton had made some fundamental changes to the concept of the B201, which almost qualified it as a B201B. These included a move away from the distinctive low-centre front wing used previously which was designed to take advantage of the rules which allow the 50cm wide central section to run right down to the reference plane before the outer edges sweep sharply upwards. In its place was a more conventional spoon-shaped wing (F). The central supports were now vertical, and integrated more smoothly into the nose (1), while the wing had only a gentle curve (2). The endplates had a sophisticated bonded curve (3) and large fins (4), while the Gurney flap was of triangular shape where it followed the contour of the second wing element's trailing edge (5).

Benetton also tried drum style brake ducts similar to Ferrari's and found them to be a big advantage, and ran the shorter bargeboards first used in Magny-Cours. In France they had been used because of the high ambient temperatures, but in Hungary they were used not only for that purpose but also because they worked better in the windtunnel with the new front wing. The bodywork was similar to that used in Monaco, with the extension to the rear wing, and there was a new front suspension with modified upper wishbone.

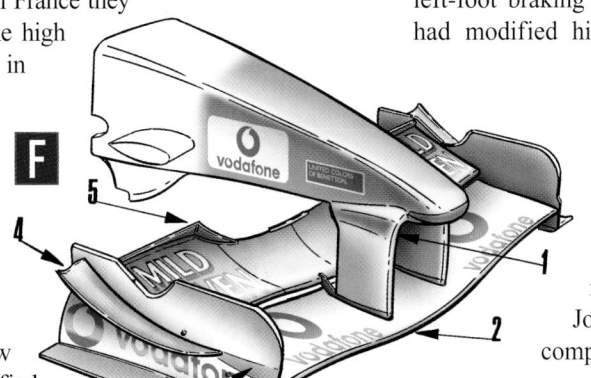

Benetton's new front wing very much mirrored the spoon-shaped design pioneered by Sergio Rinland on 2001's successful Sauber C20

## BAR HONDA

BAR had a new diffuser. Most teams use one vertical plate in their diffusers' side channels, but BAR uses two. Now these had been angled to the outside, in parallel, to enhance airflow. The bulbous Monaco front wing was not used in Hungary, but the mini wing and the engine cover wing from Monte Carlo reappeared.

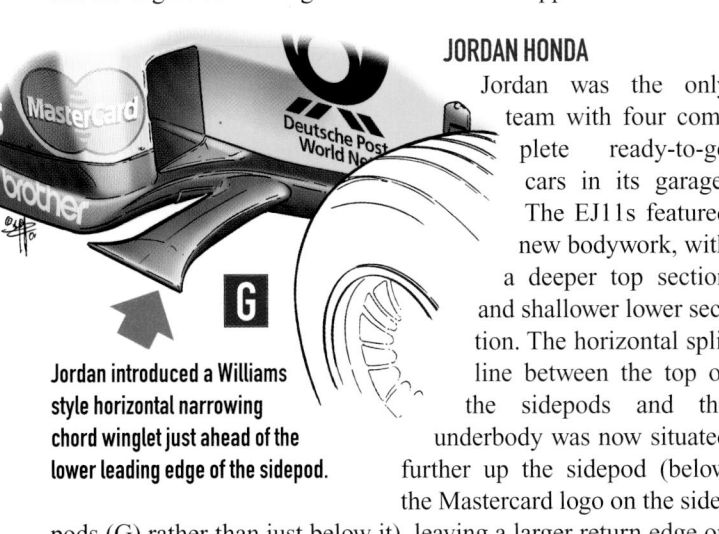

Jordan introduced a Williams style horizontal narrowing chord winglet just ahead of the lower leading edge of the sidepod.

## JORDAN HONDA

Jordan was the only team with four complete ready-to-go cars in its garage. The EJ11s featured new bodywork, with a deeper top section and shallower lower section. The horizontal split line between the top of the sidepods and the underbody was now situated further up the sidepod (below the Mastercard logo on the sidepods (G) rather than just below it), leaving a larger return edge on the underbody when the pod top was removed.

The shape of the bodywork was now more conventional on its upper section, and incorporated a revised coke bottle shape around the rear suspension. It was complemented by a new undertray and diffuser, and slightly modified flip-ups ahead of the rear wheels. The cars also featured an exact copy of the horizontal fin ahead of the sidepods introduced by Williams in Austria (G). There was also a mini wing atop the rear safety light.

At the front there were further changes to the wing (H). There was a full Gurney lip along the inner trailing edge of the flap as well as a small Gurney lip at the peak of the flap which formed the

end of a longitudinal strake to help define the air more efficiently over the upper flap surface. The small fins on the endplates (2 and 3) seen at Hockenheim were retained.

As Alesi does not like left-foot braking the team had modified his cars quite

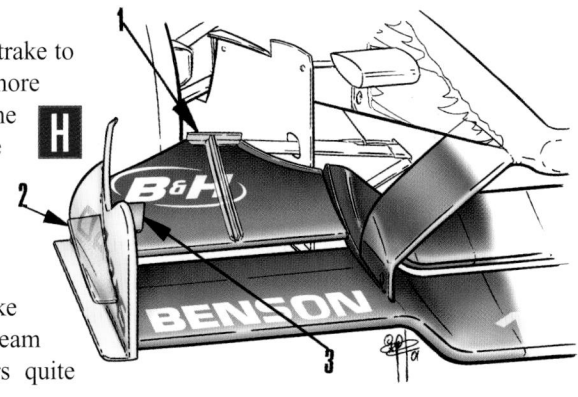

Jordan added a longitudinal strake the depth of the front wing flap, which culminated in a short Gurney flap at its tail.

significantly to give him a brake pedal that is closer to the throttle pedal, the pedal position being more like that of a three pedal arrangement. He now had to use Hitco discs because of Jordan's contract, rather than the Carbon Industrie components that he always specified at Prost.

## ARROWS ASIATECH

Arrows had some significant changes, including a new gentle spoon front wing, while the mini rear light wing and the small wing over the rear axle, both seen at Monaco, were reintroduced. The rear wing had one element and two vertical flaps, and was used on all three cars in both qualifying and the race.

## SAUBER PETRONAS

Sauber used the same front wing configuration as in Monaco, but tried a revised undertray and two sizes of air extractor chimney.

Rather than add a mini wing above the engine cover, Jaguar re-profiled the rear quarters of the upper sidepod with a more angular shape in an effort to improve air extraction.

## JAGUAR RACING

Jaguar had some new sidepods with a squarer section at the rear edge to improve hot air extraction and hence cooling. The team also tried three or four front wings, with revised endplates and a variety of outer fin configurations. The flip-ups seen in Canada were reintroduced ahead of the rear tyres, and there was also a mini wing over the rear light.

## EUROPEAN MINARDI

On Friday and Saturday both drivers used the new version of the titanium gearbox, but only Marques raced it. The cars had Jaguar-like flip-ups ahead of the rear tyres and modified front wings with fins outside the endplates, and revised rear wings. The team did not use the exhausts that blow into the diffuser's central tunnel, as these needed more development.

## PROST ACER

Prost used its Monaco front wing with the distinctive double element in the leading edge, and added a mini wing over the rear axle. Frentzen used Brembo discs, instead of the Carbon Industrie components previously preferred by Jean Alesi.

# A case of compromise

Spa-Francorchamps rates as a high-speed circuit, but also requires relatively high downforce because of its mixture of corners, even more so this year as power outputs continued to rise. Naturally the tight La Source hairpin requires plenty of both mechanical and aerodynamic grip, while aerodynamics dominate at Eau Rouge. Setting the car up for this challenging circuit is thus a difficult compromise between low drag for high speed on the run uphill from Eau Rouge, through Raidillon and up to Les Combes, and similarly from Blanchimont to the Bus Stop chicane as the circuit heads back to the start line, with high downforce needed for this late, slow interruption to the lap and then also for the La Source hairpin.

Eau Rouge is unique in that it induces compression loads that are not seen at any other track on the calendar, as the speed of the car and the inclination change of the road bottoms the car instantaneously as it also changes direction. It is thus an art to set up the ride height so that it is low enough to optimise underbody downforce, but not so low that the car bottoms out too heavily and is thus prone to tobogganing on its undertray in Eau Rouge. Running too low can be catastrophic as the driver will become a passenger as the car is flung out of control.

Teams also have to prepare their cars very carefully in the interests of reliability. In the past even Ferrari and McLaren have suffered suspension breakages because of the unusually high loadings imparted in Eau Rouge, so even if they don't always admit to it, many teams bring their strongest possible suspension components to Spa.

The main talking point in the Spa paddock was the heavily revamped version of the Williams FW23, unofficially referred to as the FW23 'B' (see below).

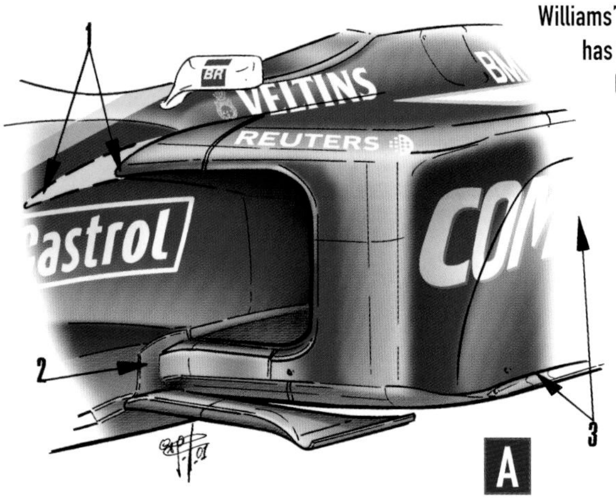

**Right:** The new FW23 'B' specification bodywork, which, by virtue of its concave sides, allowed a significantly wider side fin within overall width restriction.

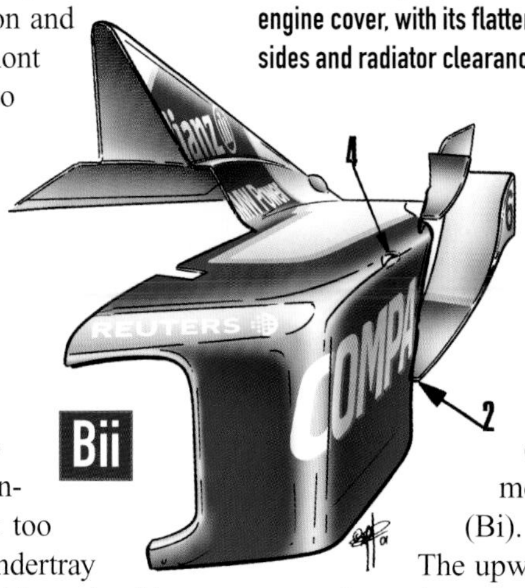

**Below:** The original FW23 sidepod and engine cover, with its flatter vertical sides and radiator clearance bump.

began further aft and had less lead-in on the monocoque.

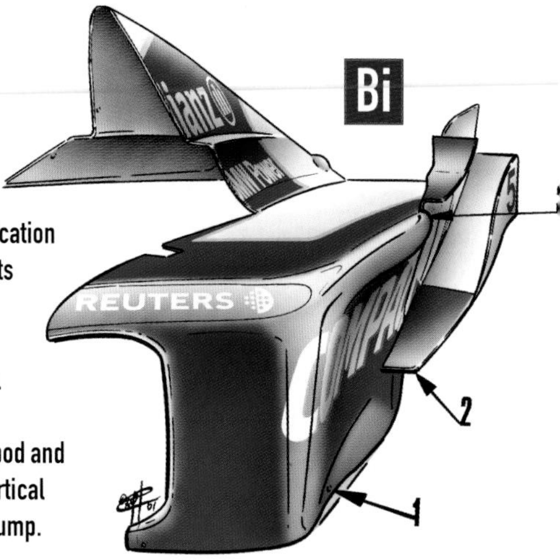

The shape of the sidepods was broadly similar, with the sides of the pods having a concave face and an S-shape curve in the lower section (A3).

However, diagrams Bi and Bii illustrate how the old bodywork had only a minor concavity (Bii), while this aspect was a much more pronounced concave curve on the new car (Bi). The bodywork was also markedly narrower.

The upward curving horizontal side fin at the rear of the pods on the old bodywork protruded only about one inch at its leading edge (Bii/2), but the same measurement on the new bodywork is about three inches (Bi/2). This new shape provides greater surface area of the side fin and promotes better airflow round the back of the car, allied to a deeper coke-bottle shape around the rear side fins (Bi/3).

The new car was able to use smaller radiators, which did away with the clearance bump on the old bodywork (Bii/4). The team was concerned about temperatures for the race, so reverted to the standard radiators and the standard bodywork package.

The new bodywork was complemented by a new underbody and diffuser (C). The shape of the side channels was more gently curved (C1) and more vertical (C2). The old shape is circled in the colour diagram.

Only one of these new 'B' specification cars was available at Spa and was entrusted to Schumacher, while Montoya was scheduled to get his new car at Monza, and BMW's Dr Mario Thiessen confirmed that the 2002 engine and gearbox would run in the new cars for the first time in the week after Indianapolis. The 2002 engine is said to be much smaller and lighter, and 'certainly no less powerful'.

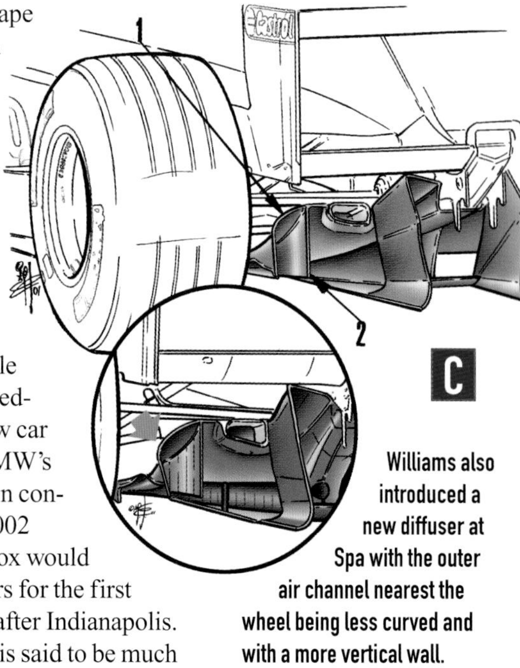

Williams' new monocoque has re-profiled upper and lower leading edges (1) to the sidepods, but utilised the same joint line for them as the original car, which allowed the team to swap back to the old sidepods for the race.

**A**

## BMW WILLIAMS

The new FW23 'B' was 10kg lighter than the original car, 3kg of the saving coming from revised chassis manufacturing techniques.

Diagrams A, Bi and Bii illustrate the differences between the two cars. On the new chassis as on the original (diagram A) the leading edge of the sidepods remained an integrated part of the chassis, but both the upper leading edge (A1) and the lower leading edge (A2),

Williams also introduced a new diffuser at Spa with the outer air channel nearest the wheel being less curved and with a more vertical wall.

**C**

## FERRARI

Ferrari introduced a new front wing (D). The curved wing profile endplates from Hockenheim were retained, with the small double horizontal fins on the inner face (D1). This was combined with a different Gurney lip (D2).

On Friday and Saturday the team used a biplane rear wing in the dry and a triplane in the wet, with the extra profile on the leading edge of the endplates. In the race both cars used a standard triplane with the elements in conventional steps.

Both drivers used the qualifying brake discs, and Schumacher missed running time at the end of Saturday morning's practice when a camber change was initiated. This is a difficult job at the best of times with the enclosed brake ducts, and when a mechanic dropped a bolt into the upright during the process the whole system on the left front corner had to be disassembled to recover the bolt. This only became apparent when the rebuild of the unit was almost complete.

Barrichello did not run much in the race morning warm-up as he had a new version of the V10 engine which was higher-revving and the team wanted to preserve it for the race.

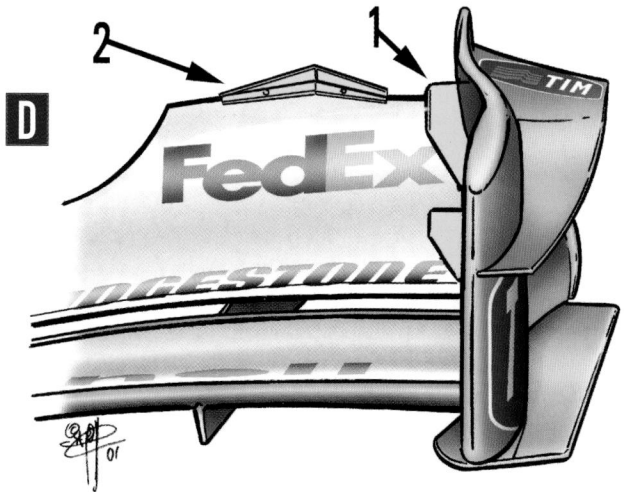

Ferrari's new front wing consisted of a combination of Gurney lips and double horizontal strakes attached to the inner upper face of the front wing endplate.

## McLAREN MERCEDES

McLaren tested its new rear suspension package again at Silverstone, prior to the Spa race, but did not take it to Belgium because there were insufficient parts. Neither did it bring along the lighter gearbox which is part of the package. This was scheduled to appear at Monza. The MP4–16s ran quite conventionally, with small brake ducts for qualifying, and a triplane rear wing in both qualifying and the race.

## BENETTON RENAULT

Benetton retained the new aero package tried for the first time in Hungary and all three cars had modified front suspension with new top wishbones. It kept the Ferrari-style brake ducts, but this time in conjunction with the high standard bargeboards rather than the lower boards used in Hungary, where temperature was of greater concern. The package had performed very well in testing in Barcelona the previous week, when Jenson Button went faster than Ralf Schumacher.

For the wet running Benetton reverted to its Monaco bodywork, and during the weekend tried a new front wing evolved from Hungary but with a different flap to generate less downforce. Yet another new aero package was scheduled for Monza.

## BAR HONDA

BAR ran the new front wing that first appeared in Hungary. This had a deep-chord main element, but this time not the bulbous section beneath the nose that would have generated too much front downforce as it was only really suited to Hungary.

Anticipated for Monza was a revised chassis, BAR 003-8, which would be stiffer but heavier as the necessary ballast had been incorporated low down as part of the tub itself. The revised monocoque was aimed at producing a belated cure for the suspension pick-up point flexure problem that has plagued the 003 all season, particularly on turn-in and under brakes.

## JORDAN HONDA

All of the new aero package that Jordan had introduced in Hungary, including the bodywork, was scrapped after Hungary, and in Belgium the team reverted to standard bodywork and diffuser. Jordan was the only team to run qualifying Brembo discs in the race.

## ARROWS ASIATECH

Arrows again ran its new spoon-shaped front wing that was introduced in Hungary (E). A triplane rear wing was used all weekend, but in the wet the team also added the winglet over the rear axle first seen at Silverstone and last used in Hungary. The ability to generate high downforce continued to be an issue for the team.

Arrows again ran its new spoon-shaped front wing in search of additional front downforce.

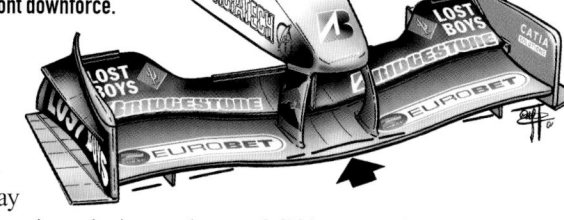

## SAUBER PETRONAS

Sauber had a special lightweight 'qualifying' gearbox, which proved problematic on Saturday morning as both units persistently jumped out of fifth gear. The team reverted to the standard transmissions for qualifying, and were disappointed and perplexed when the problem continued. Possible machining faults on the dog-rings was suspected, especially when Räikkönen was forced out of his seventh place in the race when the problem arose yet again.

Two different front wings were tried over the weekend, both drivers preferring the original Rinland-designed gentle spoon shape.

## JAGUAR RACING

All three cars had the new bodywork used on the race cars in Hungary. The hot air opening in the upper section was closed off as temperature was less of a concern in Belgium, and the team also experimented with different front wings in search of the desired balance.

## EUROPEAN MINARDI

Both race cars had the new titanium gearbox and there were some modifications to the lower section of the bargeboards. The triplane rear wing was a different arrangement, assembled from existing profiles but in a new combination of positions and angles.

## PROST ACER

Prost had a new rear suspension, and on Frentzen's car the driveshaft and trailing link were covered with a very long chord shroud similar to that previously employed by Ferrari, and aimed at improving airflow and rear downforce.

# Designed for speed

**M**onza is an extremely demanding track that requires very high top speed – the highest seen all season – and therefore a need for very little downforce and very low drag. This year top speeds exceeded 360kph in qualifying and the race. The autodrome in Monza's picturesque park allows drivers the second longest amount of full-throttle motoring of the season, some 76 per cent of the lap. They are flat-out all the way from the exit of the Ascari chicane down the back straight to the entry to the Parabolica, and then on the exit of that 180-degree corner they get back on the throttle to go flat-out past the pits and all the way down to the first chicane.

The high speed has to be pared off efficiently, however, which places a premium not only on outright braking performance but also on chassis stability that must accompany it. Due to the low downforce this can be difficult to achieve and cars are often sensitive to aerodynamic disruption and are heavily reliant on mechanical grip.

Most teams in 2001 simply refined the low downforce set-ups that they had employed at Hockenheim in July, but many played with brake configurations.

## FERRARI

The plain red bodywork and black noses were the most visible changes to the Ferraris at Monza (diagram A), but otherwise the F2001s were largely in the same specification that they had been at Hockenheim. They used the same front and rear wings and diffuser. The most significant difference, however, was the switch in brake supplier to Carbone Industrie in place of the customary Brembo. Ferrari first tested the French manufacturer's products in May, and took the decision to use them at Monza following a test with Luca Badoe the preceding week in Fiorano.

**The pure lines and detail of the Ferrari nose were clear to see when devoid of any advertising decals at Monza.**

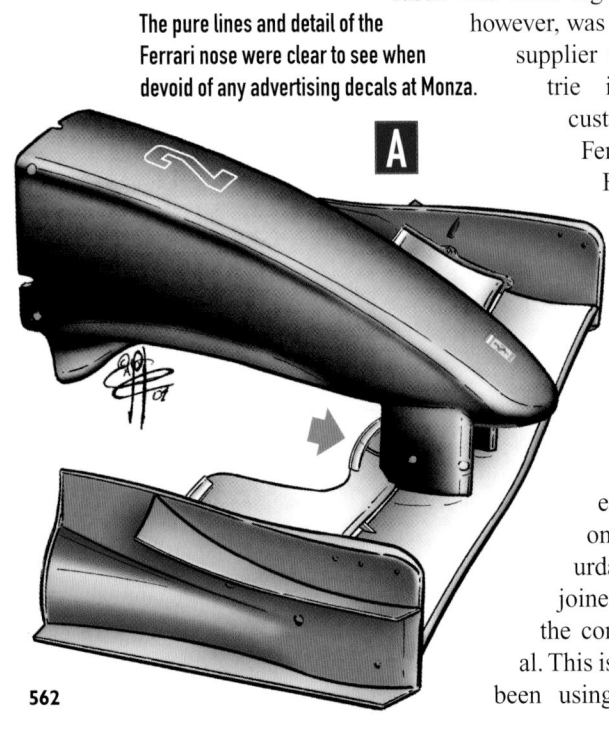

Only Schumacher used the CI brakes on Friday, but on Saturday Barrichello joined him as they used the company's P7 material. This is what Williams had been using all year, and is believed by Ferrari to be part of the reason for the Anglo-German cars' superiority on circuits such as Imola and Montreal, which are so hard on brakes. For the race they switched to the more durable P16 material.

Both drivers also had a new, more powerful specification 'qualifying' engine, which they used on Saturday afternoon and again in the race.

**Infra-red thermo sensors were placed laterally ahead of the McLaren's rear tyres monitor tyre temperature when running on Monza's long fast corners and straights.**

## MCLAREN MERCEDES

McLaren brought a modified rear suspension to Monza, but it was not the significantly different rear end that had been tested previously at the venue and was initially intended to make its debut there. Likewise, there was no sign of the new transmission. McLaren decided that further testing of the whole package was needed.

The aerodynamic set-up of the MP4-16s was the same as Hockenheim, with the medium-sized rear wing used.

In practice the team used five laterally placed sensors mounted in front of the rear tyres for the first time (B), similar to a system to monitor rear tyre temperatures, introduced by Ferrari in Austria two years ago. McLaren is very sensitive to such issues as it may have been a contributing factor to Mika Häkkinen's high-speed blow-out at Hockenheim in 1999.

The team used its large circular brake ducts in both qualifying and the race.

## BMW WILLIAMS

Williams had an interesting dichotomy on its intended race cars. Both drivers had new 23 'B' chassis, but while Juan Pablo Montoya went for the full 'B' specification with the lighter chassis, smaller radiators, narrower bodywork and new floor, Ralf Schumacher stayed all weekend with the configuration that he had raced at Spa: the new chassis with standard radiators and bodywork, and the standard underbody.

In qualifying they used different brake ducts and the P7 discs, but raced with the P16s. As at Hockenheim, the FW23Bs used relatively large wings in comparison with their opponents. The cars have won on all of the circuits where heavy braking is required – Imola, Montreal and Monza – and rivals perceive this to be due to a combination of the advantage conferred by the CI disc and from the wider Michelin front tyres which have a larger contact patch than the equivalent Bridgestones, which further helps stability under braking and braking performance.

## BENETTON RENAULT

Benetton had another new front wing (C). This used the new mounting seen in Hungary and the same curved spoon shape, but there was a smaller flap (C1) and the endplates from Hungary and Belgium had been modified with a distinctive filling in the vee cutouts on the top edge (C2).

In qualifying, the cars used the higher bargeboards, but they raced with the lower versions in the interests of better cooling.

Benetton produced another version of the front wing first seen in Hungary, this time with modified wing endplates.

## BAR HONDA

BAR had a new monocoque chassis which had strengthened suspension pick-up points and was predictably heavier as it incorporated ballast that would otherwise have to be mounted elsewhere in the car. Aerodynamically the 03s ran in the same configuration as Hockenheim, but with the new diffuser from Hungary. The biplane rear wing (D) featured clearly sculpted endplates. Olivier Panis again opted to use the wide brake pedal on a circuit that demands maximum muscle pressure on the pedal.

BAR's bi-plane Monza rear wing had the wing endplate leading edges sculpted, in an effort to reduce drag further on the long straights.

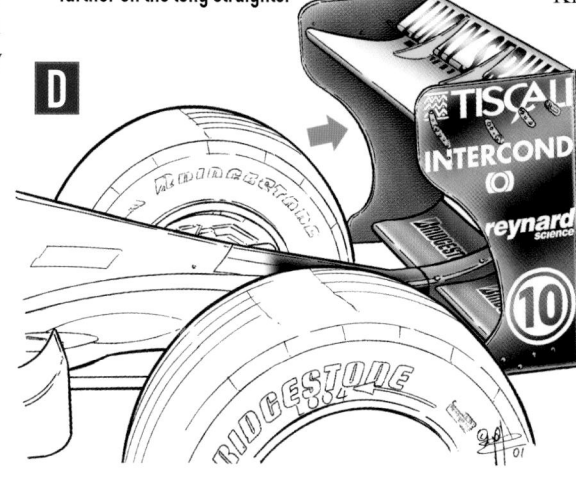

## JAGUAR RACING

The Jaguars were in Hockenheim configuration, with the addition of the new bodywork with the square air exit seen in Hungary. They tried two different biplane rear wings, where the main profile was very flat and had a long chord.

## ARROWS ASIATECH

Arrows was one of the teams with a smaller rear wing, and used this in conjunction with the old front wing used earlier in the season, in particular at Hockenheim. Jos Verstappen tried another new front suspension, and a new diffuser.

## SAUBER PETRONAS

The Sauber C20s were the same as at Hockenheim, and used only their spoon-shaped front wings. Kimi Räikkönen was supposed to test some new 25mm-thick Brembo discs, but after his testing shunt at Magny-Cours the previous week this idea was shelved due to lack of time to assess them prior to the meeting.

## EUROPEAN MINARDI

Minardi had a separate flap each side on the front wing (F). Fernando Alonso raced with the new titanium gearbox. The cars used the little winglets on top of the sidepods, which had been introduced in Budapest. The rear wings were small, and the team had abandoned its McLaren-style exhaust blowing.

Jordan produced a longer engine cover and single element rear wing for Monza. The Hockenheim bi-plane version is inset top right.

To reduce drag, yet still retain the necessary downforce at Monza, Minardi had a new front wing that employed separate flaps mounted independently either side of the nose.

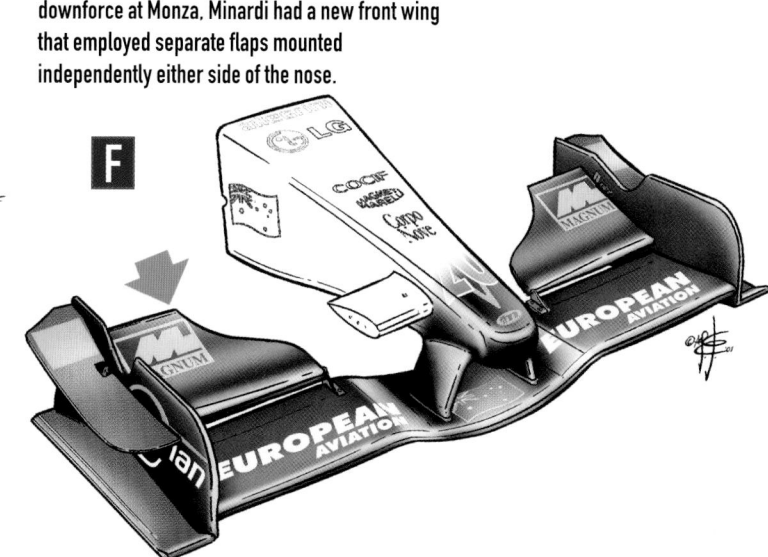

## JORDAN HONDA

At Hockenheim Jordan had briefly tried a single plane rear wing before going over to a biplane. At Monza it stayed all the time with the single plane (E).

There was a slightly longer engine cover to improve the airflow to the lower wing element and, like Minardi, Jordan used a front wing with two separate flaps

Standard brake ducts were used for the race.

## PROST ACER

Prost used its smallest rear wing, which was virtually a biplane element five inches wide. It also used new rear suspension, an aerofoil shroud for the driveshafts, and bigger brake callipers.

# Fast/tight compromise

Indianapolis is a medium to low downforce circuit that demands a tricky compromise on chassis and aerodynamic set-up from the teams. You need plenty of grip in the twisting infield section, but you don't want to have any more drag than absolutely necessary as part of your downforce setting for the very important run through the banked final corner, and all the way down the long pit straight to the first corner. That braking zone is where the best overtaking opportunities lie, together with the tight right, left, right flick that also demands very good stability under braking if a driver is to be in a position to make the most of whatever opportunities present themselves.

The banked final corner (Turn 1 on the famed anti-clockwise oval course) does not present any problems. The drivers like the sensation it gives them, with its 3.5G loading, but to a man they describe it as just part of the pit straight because it's too easily flat-out. The corner

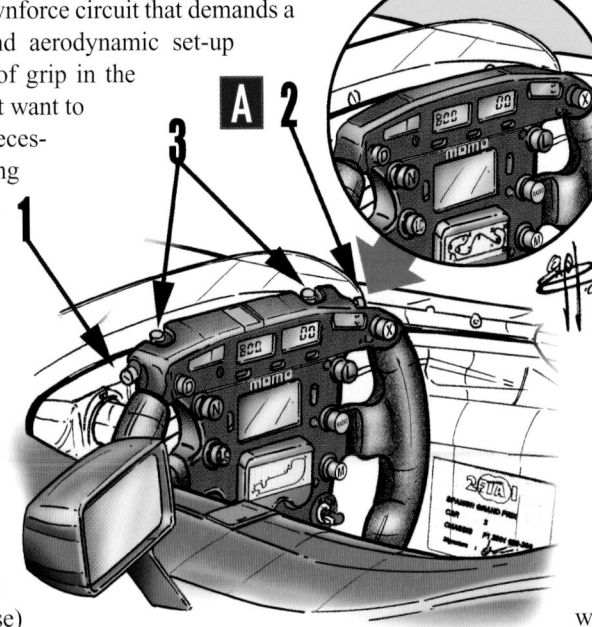

Ferrari's new steering wheel had a modified upper section which incorporated four new buttons (1) and (2) for adjusting traction control and two other new buttons (3) that are allocated for future applications.

Seven years after commencing fabricated titanium gearbox casing development, Ferrari completed its latest cast titanium gearbox casing intended to replace the existing composite and fabricated titanium gearbox. Minardi pioneered much of the development of titanium gearbox casting process.

## FERRARI F2001

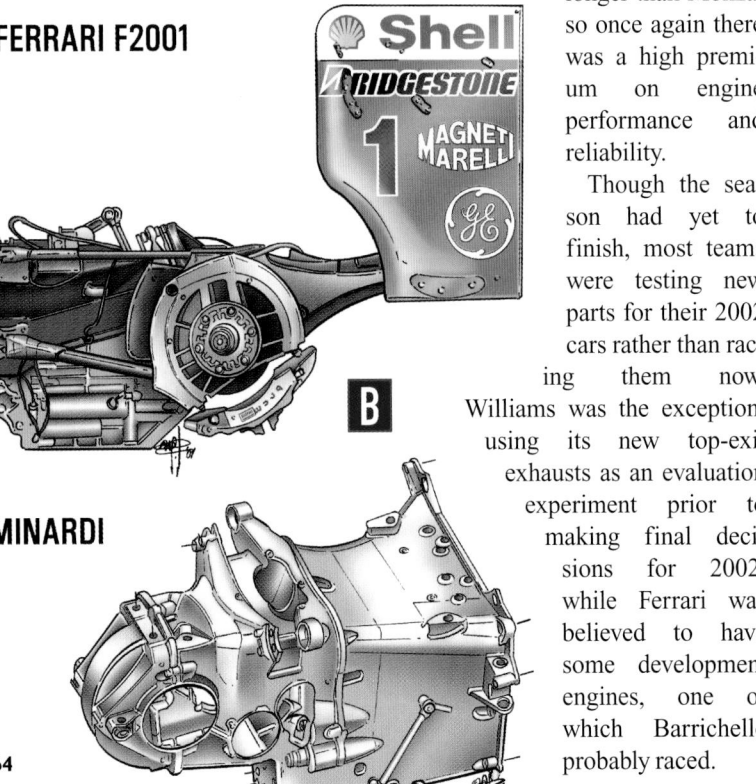

## MINARDI

lies in the middle of the longest full-throttle run of any circuit in the F1 calendar. It's even longer than Monza, so once again there was a high premium on engine performance and reliability.

Though the season had yet to finish, most teams were testing new parts for their 2002 cars rather than racing them now. Williams was the exception, using its new top-exit exhausts as an evaluation experiment prior to making final decisions for 2002, while Ferrari was believed to have some development engines, one of which Barrichello probably raced.

## FERRARI

Ferrari had a new steering wheel (diagram A) with a modified upper section that was notably thicker and contained four new buttons. Two at the side were for traction control, increased traction effect being controlled by the right button (A2), decreased on the left (A1). The inner two (A3) had no function but are there for future applications.

Aerodynamically, Ferrari used medium to high downforce wings. The rear wing was the one used in Canada, and there were two different front wing flap wings. Barrichello used one without any Gurneys, while Schumacher used one with them. The team had also slightly modified the central section of the diffuser. After the unique experiment with Carbon Industrie discs at Monza, the team reverted to Brembo discs and for the first time both drivers raced with the 22mm-thick qualifying discs.

On Saturday morning Ferrari was also the only team to test the proposed rear brake lights, which were activated by an accelerometer that measures peaks in deceleration, either under braking or when the driver lifts off the throttle.

At Mugello prior to Suzuka, Ferrari was due to again test the new cast titanium gearbox built in collaboration with Agusta (B). Luca Badoer tested this for the first time at Fiorano on the Saturday before Indianapolis.

## McLAREN MERCEDES

There was nothing new on the MP4-16s, for the new rear suspension was still on test. David Coulthard used bigger brake ducts all weekend, Mika Häkkinen preferring smaller units. Both cars had triplane rear wings.

## BMW WILLIAMS

Williams brought more new parts to the US race. On Friday Ralf Schumacher tried the new top-exit exhausts, and both drivers had them on Saturday and for the race (diagrams C and D). The lower planes of the rear wings featured heat-resistant material (C2) to protect the elements after a heat-associated failure during initial testing. Both drivers had FW23Bs, but with the standard bodywork and radiators as used by Schumacher at Monza. On Friday and Saturday the team experimented with different wings. At the rear there was a biplane with a third profile at the front similar to Monaco and Budapest. The front wings also changed as the weekend progressed. Schumacher tried a front plane that was similar to Monaco but with the endplates from Hockenheim. Juan Pablo Montoya had the Budapest front wing with the winglets inside the endplates. In qualifying they swapped round, all the time seeking maximum downforce. In the race both used a Monaco type front wing for medium downforce, and standard triplane rear wings to boost straightline speed. Prior to Suzuka, Marc Gene was due to test another variant of the 'new' chassis, effectively an FW23'C', with revised engine pick-up points. This was to enable the team to run the new 2002 BMW V10 for the first time, mated to a new cast titanium gearbox and new rear suspension as soon as it was available. Thus BMW Williams was able to test almost half of its 2002 car before the existing season has finished. Schumacher and Antonio Pizzonia were also due to test two standard FW23Bs.

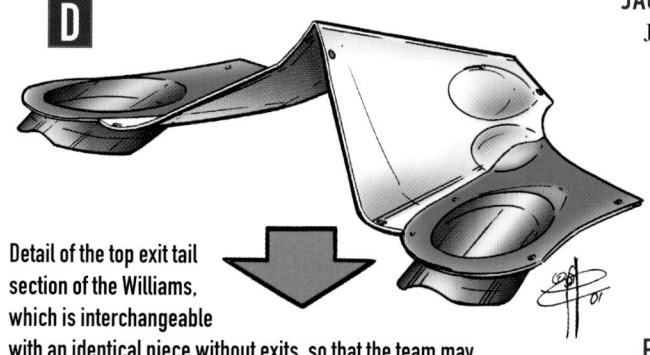

The new rear end of the Williams FW 23B showing the top exit exhaust and the location of heat shielding on the wing main beam following heat-related failures.

## BENETTON RENAULT

Benetton's only new parts were the new front wing from Budapest with the vertical pillar and big flaps, and the new 'filled in' endplates seen at Monza. Another new iteration of the Renault V10 was promised for Japan.

Detail of the top exit tail section of the Williams, which is interchangeable with an identical piece without exits, so that the team may alternate between top exit or rear exit configurations.

## JORDAN HONDA

Jordan had another version of its Ferrari-inspired brake ducts for qualifying. For qualifying and for the race the team opted for quite high levels of downforce due to handling problems with the car which led to the bottoming problem that later resulted in Jarno Trulli's exclusion.

## BAR HONDA

BAR tried high and low downforce on Friday and Saturday, with a biplane rear wing for the latter. It ran this set-up in the race, too. In Mugello prior to Suzuka the team was due to test new rear suspension and Ferrari-type front brake ducts.

## ARROWS ASIATECH

The Arrows boasted a large biplane rear wing, and Jos Verstappen as usual used different front suspension to Enrique Bernoldi. On Saturday the team built up the spare 01 chassis to replace Verstappen's intended 06 race car, which became the T-car. The original T-car, 08, was dismantled and put into the transport box from which 01 had come.

## JAGUAR RACING

Jaguar had nothing of note and always ran low downforce configuration, even in qualifying.

## SAUBER PETRONAS

On Friday Sauber started with the old Jordan-type front wing but quickly reverted to the new standard spoon shape for the remainder of the weekend.

## EUROPEAN MINARDI

Minardi's focus was on its titanium gearbox and both drivers raced the unit for the first time.

## PROST ACER

Both cars had Monaco configuration triplane rear wings and the double-decker profile front wings.

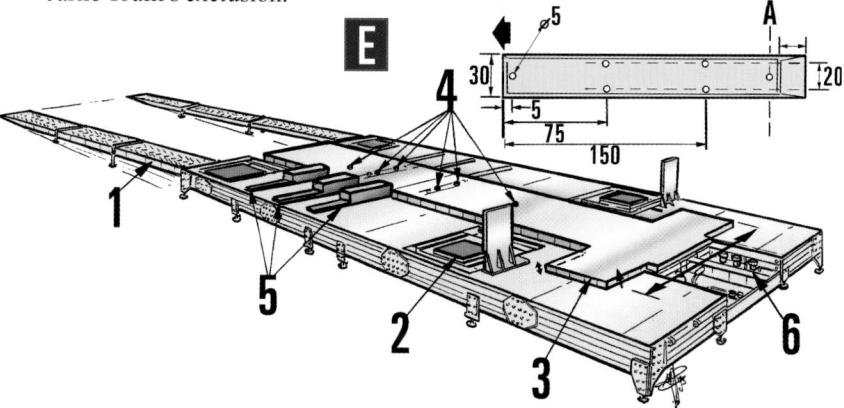

FIA Technical Verification platform, which quickly and accurately measures the compliance of each car with the stringent FIA Technical Regulations. (1) are access ramps for cars. Red pads (2) are Captel load cells for weight checks, which also locate the car in the correct position for determining other coachwork dimension compliance. (3) provides a shadow plate for checking front wing dimensions. (4) are machined bobbins that must locate in recesses of skid plank and determine legality of thickness. Raised elements at (5) check compliance with 50mm-step bottom regulation. (6) are hydraulic adjustment controls. At the top in yellow is a plan view of the plank showing the location of the six titanium bobbins specified by the FIA.

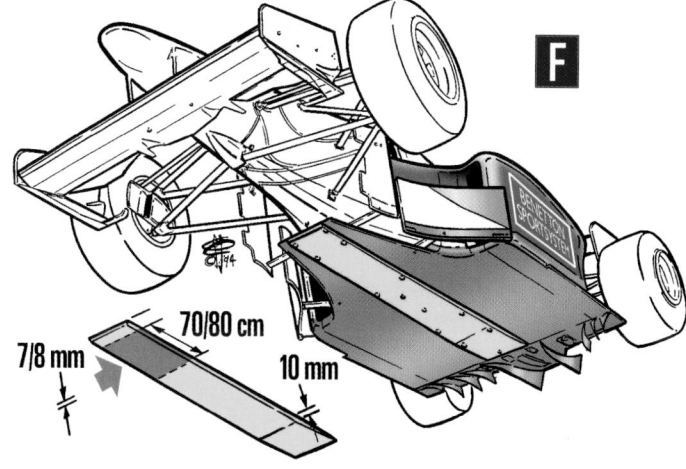

Diagram F shows Michael Schumacher's Benetton that was disqualified after the 1994 Belgian Grand Prix when the 'plank' was less than the designated 10mm thickness. The red section of the plank indicates the area of the plank that is subject to wear when the car runs too low and bottoms consistently, as Trulli's did in the US Grand Prix, resulting in Jordan's disqualification.

# Set-up is a compromise

At 3.644 miles the Suzuka circuit is one of the longer circuits in F1, and it has everything. Designed in the 1960s by the highly respected John Hugenholtz, the father of Zandvoort, it has a fast first corner followed by the twisting Esses, a series of fast sweeping curves, a hairpin, a flyover and a ridiculously tight chicane (an FIA addition to the original design for 1987 in order to host the Grand Prix), so set-up is inevitably a compromise. It demands good chassis balance, powerful and stable braking, good traction and good horsepower. It is a circuit that requires a chassis with all-round performance capabilities as a quick lap at Suzuka only comes from a driver and chassis with the full array of performance capability and skills.

## FERRARI

Ferrari had tested its new cast titanium gearbox and new rear suspension package at Mugello and Fiorano prior to Suzuka, and for the season finale brought along a new chassis – 214 – for Michael Schumacher. This used new

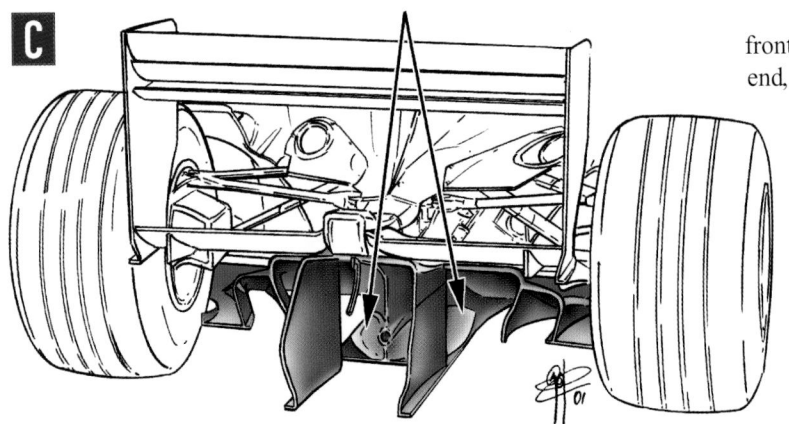

A

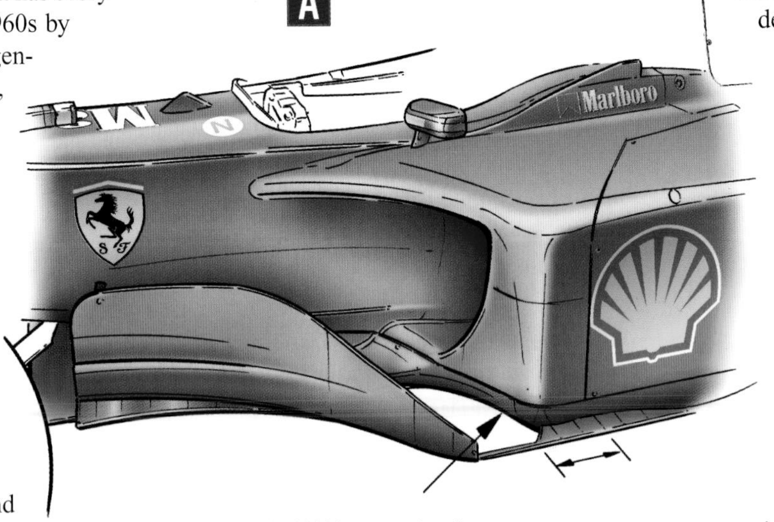

Ferrari's standard 2001 season chassis as used by both drivers up to Suzuka.

B

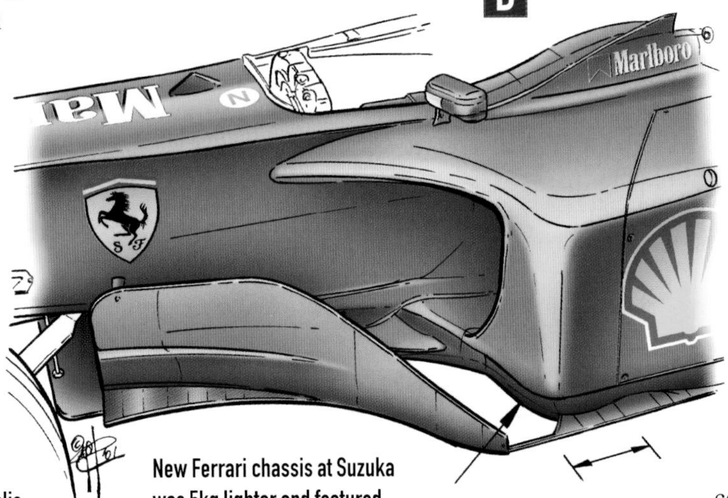

New Ferrari chassis at Suzuka was 5kg lighter and featured shorter, squarer sidepods.

Ferrari tested a new diffuser at Indianapolis from USA, featuring filleting that reduced the area and downforce.

C

technology to make the chassis lighter, while revised deformable structure made it stronger and more efficient. The difference was visible as the deformable structure at the leading edge of the sidepods is two centimetres longer and has a squarer profile (diagrams A and B). The team had also tried a new diffuser at Indianapolis (C), but this was not used in Japan.

On the aerodynamic front it used a Monaco front wing, and on Friday both drivers used a Budapest rear wing. In the warm-up and the race Rubens Barrichello used a biplane rear wing for greater straightline speed. He also used 22mm qualifying Brembo discs in the race, while Michael Schumacher used standard 28 mm discs with elongated cooling holes.

## McLAREN MERCEDES

McLaren's aero package centred on Budapest configuration, with triplane rear wings and large front flaps with the unusually shaped Gurney lips. The only other significant difference was the use of maximum width front track. There was still no sign of the new gearbox and rear end, which needs more testing.

## BMW WILLIAMS

Williams still showed signs of a high workload, in readiness for 2002. Marc Gene had tried the new BMW V10 engine in Barcelona the week before Japan. There the top-exit exhaust introduced in Indianapolis was used on both race cars, and also ready on the T-car in time for the race (D).

Williams had also followed Ferrari and McLaren by introducing rear tyre sensors. New turning vanes, with a double element on the leading edge, were also in evidence (E).

On Saturday, in practice and in qualifying, Ralf Schumacher used Ferrari-type brake ducts (F) with an upper opening to facilitate camber change. They were not used in the race, as they had only been tested the week before in Spain.

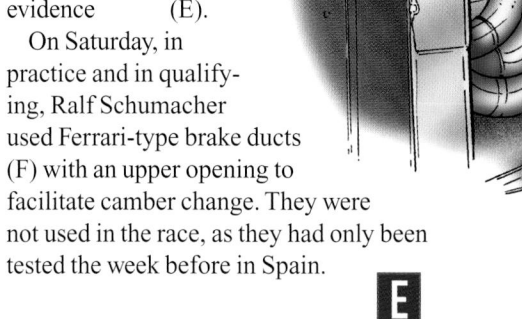

Williams's exhaust pipes and tail pipe are very neatly packaged.

**D**

## SAUBER PETRONAS

Sauber had little that was new, apart from new Brembo discs with 2002 specification material that Heidfeld used on Friday and Saturday. The team did a fine job to repair chassis 07 for the German to use again on Saturday, following his major accident on Friday.

## BAR HONDA

Honda introduced a new specification engine for use all weekend, and BAR also had Ferrari-type brake ducts tested previously in Mugello (G). Like those on the Williams, there was an opening for camber change. The aero package used the mini-wing behind the engine air intake.

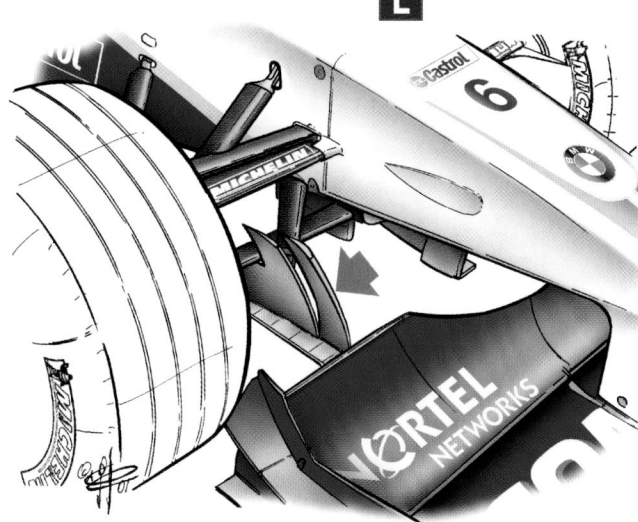

**E**

Williams had modified leading edge turning vanes.

BAR introduced a Ferrari-style brake duct at Suzuka, with a single entry above the steering arm.

**G**

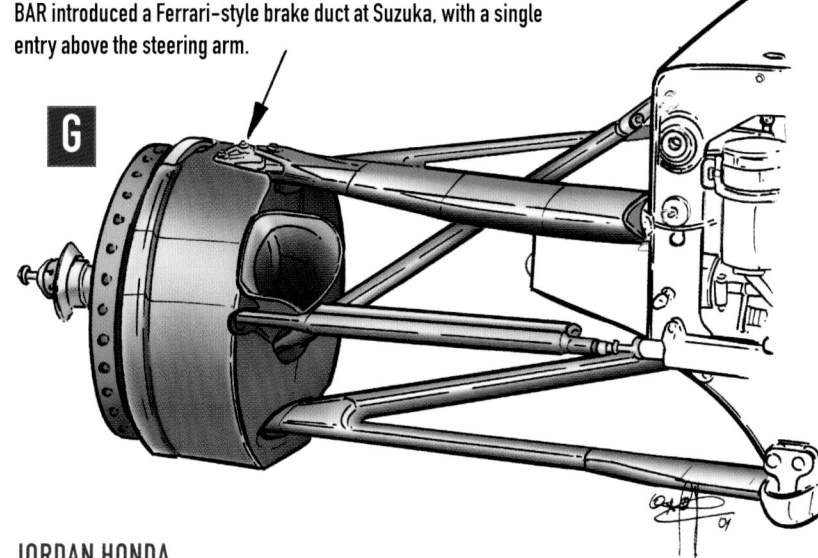

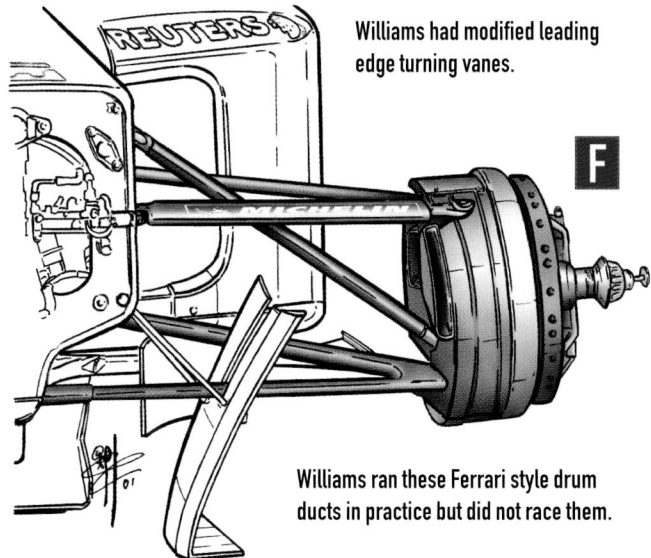

**F**

Williams ran these Ferrari style drum ducts in practice but did not race them.

## JORDAN HONDA

Jordan also had Honda's revised spec engine. Jarno Trulli used Brembo's 22mm discs in qualifying and in the race, while Jean Alesi relied on standard Brembos in the race.

## JAGUAR RACING

Cosworth brought along a revised specification engine, and ran Budapest aerodynamics.

## ARROWS ASIATECH

Development of the A22 had stopped as work focused on Sergio Rinland's forthcoming new car. The A22s used Budapest aerodynamics, but none featured the new front suspension used recently on Jos Verstappen's cars.

## PROST ACER

Prost relied on Monaco aerodynamics. After Enge destroyed AP04-05 on Friday, this being the chassis that was damaged by Luciano Burti in Germany and subsequently repaired, the T-car became his race car and the chassis from the freight transport box was built up as the new T-car. Like Heidfeld, Heinz-Harald Frentzen ran the new Brembo discs.

## BENETTON RENAULT

Renault introduced a new qualifying engine, which seemed effective, otherwise there was little new on Benetton's B201 going into the marque's final race. The team used its Budapest aero package. In qualifying it used its high bargeboards, but for the race reverted to the low vanes in the interests of temperature management.

## EUROPEAN MINARDI

Both cars raced with the new titanium gearbox, and Hitco discs were used in the race instead of the Brembos fitted for qualifying.

# Most development ever

The 2001 season produced an intensity of development from beginning to end that exceeded any previous season. Not surprisingly, leading the way were 2000 world champions Ferrari, who got off on the right foot with a car that was quick straight out of the box. Its testing performances and early season races quickly confirmed what an excellent car the F2001 was and this, coupled with a fast but measured development programme, left most of the opposition breathless. Ferrari's development programme never stopped, and if the opposition didn't feel properly battered and beaten before the last race, Ferrari made sure they were on their return from Suzuka, the Italian team having arrived there with a new specification car which left their rivals in no doubt.

The one team to rise to the occasion and compete with Ferrari in performance development was BMW Williams. The British chassis manufacturer and Bavarian engine manufacturer demonstrated their ability to strategically plan the season and to compete with Ferrari on track. Their achievements during 2001 are strong indication of the threat they will be to the world champions in the 2002 season.

## FERRARI BRAKE DUCT

The single most important technical development of the 2001 season was without doubt the enclosed 'drum' type brake duct which Ferrari pioneered (diagram A). Ferrari was the first to fully appreciate the importance of shielding the airflow, from behind the front wing to the entry to the underbody, from turbulence created by the rotating front wheel, and in this case specifically the air ejected

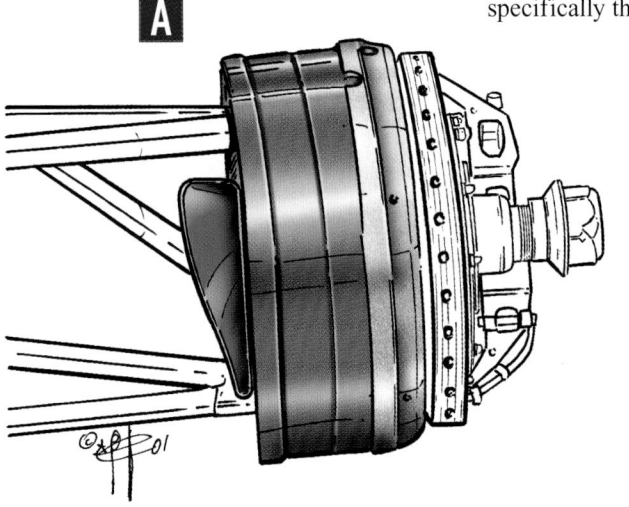

from the centre of the wheel. This was a very difficult challenge, as it required the utilisation of different pad and disc materials and dealing with higher operating temperatures, which were inevitably raised by enclosing the wheel centre. This was achieved by creating a combination carbon fibre sealing drum and brake duct in one, which was a mirror image of the inner face of the front wheel. To obtain the necessary airflow for the brakes the system operated as a centrifugal fan which drew air into the duct from the monocoque side of the wheel and ejected air and carbon brake dust to the outer side of the wheel. Once this had been perfected there were few problems for Ferrari, with the exception of the San Marino Grand Prix when a small stone was trapped between the duct and wheel, and machined its way through the wheel rim, causing Schumacher's retirement. The concept was copied by all the other teams apart from McLaren, Minardi and Prost, but not all with similar success. Jordan produced a lookalike quite early in the season, but this only really mimicked the appearance, not the performance. Sauber did get it right and was astonished at the aerodynamic performance gains to be had by improving the quality of airflow between the front wheel and the underbody. While Prost did not copy the 'drum', its front brake duct achieved virtually the same result in a different manner. Inevitably there was some drawback, and in Ferrari's case it was that it was not very user friendly for the mechanics, turning a front camber change from what had been a simple, quick job, into a difficult 10-minute operation. The penalty for dropping a single nut into the drum turned into loss of precious practice or qualifying minutes and a lot of extra work.

## AERODYNAMIC DEVELOPMENT

With the adoption of the new FIA regulations governing front wing dimensions, teams anticipated a serious loss in aerodynamic performance, but in typical F1 fashion the challenge to recover lost performance was soon defeated. Leading the way in this area was the Sergio Rinland-designed Sauber, which was the first to appear with what quickly became known as the spoon shaped front wing. Again with the immediate impressive performance and driveability of the C20 in testing, the concept was soon recognised and copied. But in all cases, by the time the Sauber appeared, it was too late for other teams to copy the innovative and adventurous bottom wishbone pick-ups the Argentine had created (arrowed, diagram B), and which played an important role. There is no doubt many of next year's chassis will adopt the pick-up system as it clears a major area of blockage in the crucial area behind the front wing. Front

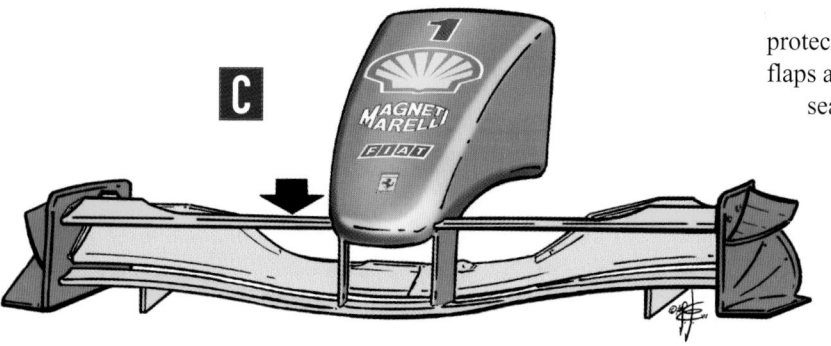

protected the main aerodynamic section of the front wing and/or flaps and reduced the negative effect of the tyre spillage. The 2001 season saw the appearance of a multi-height main plane configured front wing as introduced by Ferrari in Malaysia (C), and various combinations of main planes and multi-element trailing flaps continued to appear throughout the season depending on circuit requirement, ie low downforce and drag for Hockenheim, or high drag and downforce for Hungary.

downforce was going to be an issue all season as the level of downforce that could be generated by the front wing was the limiting factor in how much rear wing could be run. As a result the season produced an amazing array of front wings from all the teams in the search for elusive downforce. But it was not

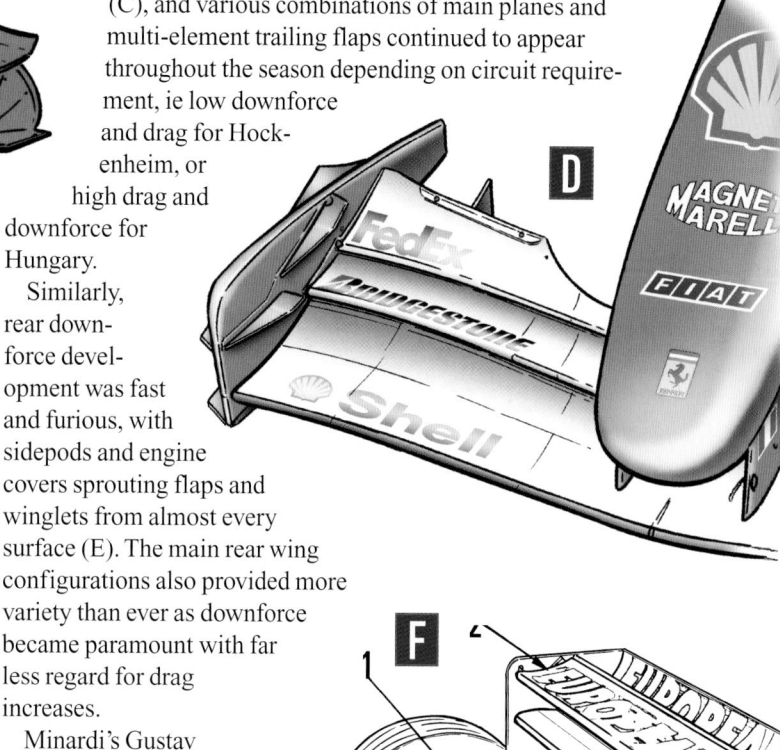

only the design of the wing itself, but also front wing endplate development that reached new heights of innovation and variety. Again Sauber's early design provided direction, with the introduction of small horizontal flaps on the front wing endplates (D). These contributed to front wing performance by their influence on the turbulent air spilling off the front tyre. Performance was improved because the small flaps to some degree

Similarly, rear downforce development was fast and furious, with sidepods and engine covers sprouting flaps and winglets from almost every surface (E). The main rear wing configurations also provided more variety than ever as downforce became paramount with far less regard for drag increases.

Minardi's Gustav Brunner spotted a loophole in the regulations which allowed the mounting of some decent size wing elements low down and ahead of the main rear wing (F).

## TITANIUM GEARBOX CASINGS

Almost a decade after Ferrari's first attempt at manufacturing a fabricated titanium gearbox casing, the Minardi team debuted a major technical development with its cast-titanium gear casing (G) which had been developed in conjunction with Agusta. Minardi is to be commended for its pursuit of such a lofty technical challenge

and deserves to be rewarded in the future with the ability to produce a significantly smaller, lighter package, which should be very beneficial in handling terms. To put this into perspective, Ferrari's optimised gearbox arrangement for the 2001 season (H) was a composite package comprising a fabricated titanium and carbon fibre combination. In pure engineering terms, this is a very high technology achievement, which will undoubtedly become the norm in Formula One in the coming season.

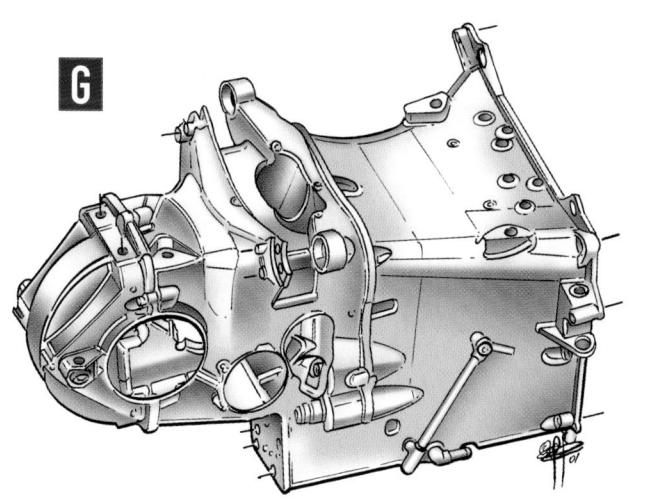

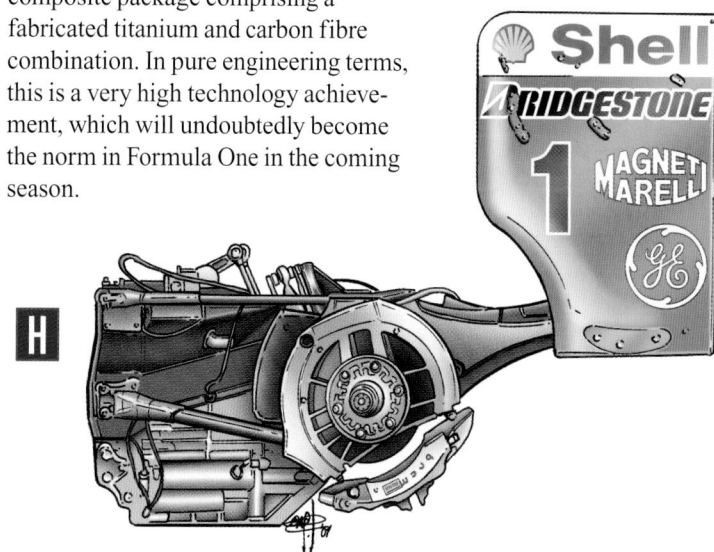

1950s
p572-583

1960s
p584-597

1970s
p597-617

# Season
# STATISTICS

1980s
p618–640

1990s
p641–664

2000
p664–667

| Key to Abbreviations | | | |
|---|---|---|---|
| DNPQ | Did not pre-qualify | NC | Not classified |
| DNQ | Did not qualify | Ret | Retired |
| DNS | Did not start | Wth | Withdrawn |
| DSQ | Disqualified | | |

# 1950

DRIVERS' CHAMPION: GIUSEPPE FARINA

## DRIVERS' CHAMPIONSHIP

| POS | DRIVER | COUNTRY | CAR | POINTS |
|---|---|---|---|---|
| 1 | Giuseppe Farina | Italy | Alfa Romeo | 30 |
| 2 | Juan Manuel Fangio | Argentina | Alfa Romeo | 27 |
| 3 | Luigi Fagioli | Italy | Alfa Romeo | 24(4) |
| 4 | Louis Rosier | France | Lago-Talbot | 13 |
| 5 | Alberto Ascari | Italy | Ferrari | 11 |
| 6 | Johnny Parsons | USA | Kurtis Kraft-Offenhauser | 8 |
| 7 | Bill Holland | USA | Deidt-Offenhauser | 6 |
| 8 | Prince Bira | Thailand | Maserati | 5 |
| 9 | Reg Parnell | GB | Alfa Romeo, Maserati | 4 |
| = | Louis Chiron | Monaco | Maserati | 4 |
| = | Mauri Rose | USA | Deidt-Offenhauser | 4 |
| = | Peter Whitehead | GB | Ferrari | 4 |
| 13 | Yves Giraud-Cabantous | France | Lago-Talbot | 3 |
| = | Raymond Sommer | France | Ferrari, Lago-Talbot | 3 |
| = | Cecil Green | USA | Kurtis –Offenhauser | 3 |
| = | Robert Manzon | France | Simca-Gordini | 3 |
| = | Dorino Serafini | Italy | Ferrari | 3 |
| = | Phillipe Étancelin | France | Lago-Talbot | 3 |
| 19 | Felice Bonetto | Italy | Maserati | 2 |
| 20 | Joie Chitwood | USA | Kurtis –Offenhauser | 1 |
| = | Tony Bettenhausen | USA | Kurtis-Offenhauser | 1 |
| = | Eugène Chaboud | France | Lago-Talbot | 1 |
| | Johnny Claes | Belgium | Lago-Talbot | |
| | Emmanuel de Graffenried | Switzerland | Maserati | |
| | Cuth Harrison | GB | ERA | |
| | Bob Gerard | GB | ERA | |
| | Eugène Martin | France | Lago-Talbot | |
| | Geoffrey Crossley | GB | Alta | |
| | David Hampshire | GB | Maserati | |
| | David Murray | GB | Maserati | |
| | Joe Kelly | GB | Alta | |
| | Joe Fry | GB | Maserati | |
| | Peter Walker | GB | ERA | |
| | Leslie Johnson | GB | ERA | |
| | Tony Rolt | GB | ERA | |
| | Brian Shawe-Taylor | GB | Maserati | |
| | Luigi Villoresi | Italy | Ferrari | |
| | Harry Schell | USA | Cooper, Lago-Talbot | |
| | Franco Rol | Italy | Maserati | |
| | José Froilan Gonzalez | Argentina | Maserati | |
| | Maurice Trintignant | France | Simca-Gordini | |
| | Alfredo Piàn | Argentina | Maserati | |
| | Antonio Branca | Italy | Maserati | |
| | Nello Pagani | Italy | Maserati | |
| | "Pierre Levegh" | France | Lago-Talbot | |
| | Charles Pozzi | France | Lago-Talbot | |
| | Clemente Biondetti | Italy | Ferrari | |
| | Gianfranco Comotti | Italy | Maserati | |
| | Consalvo Sanesi | Italy | Alfa Romeo | |
| | Henri Louveau | France | Lago-Talbot | |
| | Guy Mairesse | France | Lago-Talbot | |
| | Piero Taruffi | Italy | Alfa Romeo | |
| | Paul Pietsch | Germany | Maserati | |

**Points for top five finishers (8, 6, 4, 3, 2) plus a point for fastest lap. Only the best four scores counted towards the championship. Points for shared drives were divided equally between the drivers.**

## BRITISH GRAND PRIX: SILVERSTONE *13 May Round: 1 Race: 1 70 x 2.889 miles*

| POS. | NO. | DRIVER | CAR/ENGINE | LAPS | TIME/RETIRED | GRID |
|---|---|---|---|---|---|---|
| 1 | 2 | Giuseppe Farina | Alfa Romeo | 70 | 2:13'23.6 | 1 |
| 2 | 3 | Luigi Fagioli | Alfa Romeo | 70 | +2.6 | 2 |
| 3 | 4 | Reg Parnell | Alfa Romeo | 70 | +52.0 | 4 |
| 4 | 14 | Y.G.-Cabantous | Talbot-Lago-Talbot | 68 | +2 Laps | 6 |
| 5 | 15 | Louis Rosier | Talbot-Lago-Talbot | 68 | +2 Laps | 9 |
| 6 | 12 | Bob Gerard | ERA | 67 | +3 Laps | 13 |
| 7 | 11 | Cuth Harrison | ERA | 67 | +3 Laps | 15 |
| 8 | 16 | P.Etancelin | Talbot-Lago-Talbot | 65 | +5 Laps | 14 |
| 9 | 6 | David Hampshire | Maserati | 64 | +6 Laps | 16 |
| 10 | 10 | Fry/Shawe-Taylor | Maserati | 64 | +6 Laps | 20 |
| 11 | 18 | Johnny Claes | Talbot-Lago-Talbot | 64 | +6 Laps | 21 |
| Ret | 1 | Juan Manuel Fangio | Alfa Romeo | 62 | Oil leak | 3 |
| NC | 23 | Joe Kelly | Alta | 57 | Not classified | 19 |
| Ret | 21 | Prince Bira | Maserati | 49 | Out of fuel | 5 |
| Ret | 5 | David Murray | Maserati | 44 | Engine | 18 |
| NC | 24 | Geoff Crossley | Alta | 43 | Not classified | 17 |
| Ret | 20 | E.de Graffenried | Maserati | 36 | Engine | 8 |
| Ret | 19 | Louis Chiron | Maserati | 24 | Clutch | 11 |
| Ret | 17 | Eugene Martin | Talbot-Lago-Talbot | 8 | Oil pressure | 7 |
| Ret | 9 | Walker/Rolt | ERA | 5 | Gearbox | 10 |
| Ret | 8 | Leslie Johnson | ERA | 2 | Compressor | 12 |

Winning speed: 90.963mph
Lap leaders: Farina 1-9, 16-37, 39-70; Fagioli 10-14, 38; Fangio 15
Pole position: Farina, 1m 50.800s, 93.866mph
Fastest lap: Farina, 1m 50.600s, 94.036mph

## MONACO GRAND PRIX: MONTE CARLO *21 May Round: 2 Race: 2 100 x 1.760 miles*

| POS. | NO. | DRIVER | CAR/ENGINE | LAPS | TIME/RETIRED | GRID |
|---|---|---|---|---|---|---|
| 1 | 34 | Juan Manuel Fangio | Alfa Romeo | 100 | 3:13'18.7 | 1 |
| 2 | 40 | Alberto Ascari | Ferrari | 99 | +1 Lap | 7 |
| 3 | 48 | Louis Chiron | Maserati | 98 | +2 Laps | 8 |
| 4 | 42 | Raymond Sommer | Ferrari | 97 | +3 Laps | 9 |
| 5 | 50 | Prince Bira | Maserati | 95 | +5 Laps | 15 |
| 6 | 26 | Bob Gerard | ERA | 94 | +6 Laps | 16 |
| 7 | 6 | Johnny Claes | Talbot-Lago-Talbot | 94 | +6 Laps | 19 |
| Ret | 38 | Luigi Villoresi | Ferrari | 63 | Axle | 6 |
| Ret | 14 | P.Etancelin | Talbot-Lago-Talbot | 38 | Oil leak | 4 |
| Ret | 2 | J.F.Gonzalez | Maserati | 1 | Accident | 3 |
| Ret | 32 | Giuseppe Farina | Alfa Romeo | 0 | Accident | 2 |
| Ret | 36 | Luigi Fagioli | Alfa Romeo | 0 | Accident | 5 |
| Ret | 16 | Louis Rosier | Talbot-Lago-Talbot | 0 | Accident | 10 |
| Ret | 10 | Robert Manzon | Simca-Gordini | 0 | Accident | 11 |
| Ret | 52 | E.de Graffenried | Maserati | 0 | Accident | 12 |
| Ret | 12 | M.Trintignant | Simca-Gordini | 0 | Accident | 13 |
| Ret | 24 | Cuth Harrison | ERA | 0 | Accident | 14 |
| Ret | 44 | Franco Rol | Maserati | 0 | Accident | 17 |
| Ret | 8 | Harry Schell | Cooper-JAP | 0 | Collision | 20 |

Winning speed: 61.330mph Lap leaders: Fangio 1-100
Pole position: Fangio, 1m 50.200s, 64.550mph
Fastest lap: Fangio, 1m 51.000s, 64.085

## INDIANAPOLIS 500 *30 May Round: 3 Race: 3 138 x 2.500 miles*

| POS. | NO. | DRIVER | CAR/ENGINE | LAPS | TIME/RETIRED | GRID |
|---|---|---|---|---|---|---|
| 1 | 1 | Johnnie Parsons | Kurtis Kraft-Offenhauser | 138 | 2:46'55.97 | 5 |
| 2 | 3 | Bill Holland | Deidt-Offenhauser | 137 | +1 Lap | 10 |
| 3 | 31 | Mauri Rose | Deidt-Offenhauser | 137 | +1 Lap | 3 |
| 4 | 54 | Cecil Green | Kurtis Kraft-Offenhauser | 137 | +1 Lap | 12 |
| 5 | 17 | Chitwood/B'hausen | Kurtis Kraft-Offenhauser | 136 | +2 Laps | 9 |
| 6 | 8 | Lee Wallard | Moore-Offenhauser | 136 | +2 Laps | 23 |
| 7 | 98 | Walt Faulkner | Kurtis Kraft-Offenhauser | 135 | +3 Laps | 1 |
| 8 | 5 | George Connor | Lesovsky-Offenhauser | 135 | +3 Laps | 4 |
| 9 | 7 | Paul Russo | Nichels-Offenhauser | 135 | +3 Laps | 19 |
| 10 | 59 | Pat Flaherty | Kurtis Kraft-Offenhauser | 135 | +3 Laps | 11 |
| 11 | 2 | Myron Fohr | Marchese-Offenhauser | 133 | +5 Laps | 16 |
| 12 | 18 | Duane Carter | Stevens-Offenhauser | 133 | +5 Laps | 13 |
| 13 | 15 | Mack Hellings | Kurtis Kraft-Offenhauser | 132 | +6 Laps | 26 |
| 14 | 49 | Jack McGrath | Kurtis Kraft-Offenhauser | 131 | Spun off | 6 |
| 15 | 55 | Troy Ruttman | Lesovsky-Offenhauser | 130 | +8 Laps | 24 |
| 16 | 75 | Gene Hartley | Langley-Offenhauser | 128 | +10 Laps | 31 |
| 17 | 22 | Jimmy Davies | Ewing-Offenhauser | 128 | +10 Laps | 27 |
| 18 | 62 | Johnny McDowell | Kurtis Kraft-Offenhauser | 128 | +10 Laps | 33 |
| 19 | 4 | Walt Brown | Kurtis Kraft-Offenhauser | 127 | +11 Laps | 20 |
| 20 | 21 | Spider Webb | Maserati-Offenhauser | 126 | +12 Laps | 14 |
| 21 | 81 | Jerry Hoyt | Kurtis Kraft-Offenhauser | 125 | +13 Laps | 15 |
| 22 | 27 | Walt Ader | Rae-Offenhauser | 123 | +15 Laps | 29 |
| 23 | 77 | Jackie Holmes | Olson-Offenhauser | 123 | Spun off | 30 |
| 24 | 76 | Jim Rathmann | Wetteroth-Offenhauser | 122 | +16 Laps | 28 |
| Ret | 12 | Banks/Agabashian | Maserati-Offenhauser | 112 | Oil leak | 21 |
| Ret | 67 | Bill Schindler | Snowberger-Offenhauser | 111 | Transmission | 22 |
| Ret | 24 | Levrett/Cantrell | Adams-Offenhauser | 108 | Oil pressure | 17 |
| Ret | 28 | Fred Agabashian | Kurtis Kraft-Offenhauser | 64 | Oil leak | 2 |
| Ret | 61 | Jimmy Jackson | Kurtis Kraft-Cummins | 52 | Compressor | 32 |
| Ret | 23 | Sam Hanks | Kurtis Kraft-Offenhauser | 42 | Oil pressure | 25 |
| Ret | 14 | T.Bettenhausen | Deidt-Offenhauser | 30 | Wheel bearing | 8 |
| Ret | 45 | Dick Rathmann | Watson-Offenhauser | 25 | Retirement | 18 |
| Ret | 69 | Duke Dinsmore | Kurtis Kraft-Offenhauser | 10 | Oil leak | 7 |

Winning Speed: 124.002mph
Pole Position: Faulkner, 1m 6.992s, 134.344mph
Fastest Lap: Parsons, 1m 09.770s, 128.997mph
*Stopped early because of rain. Original distance 200 laps.*

## SWISS GRAND PRIX: BREMGARTEN *4 June Round: 4 Race: 4 42 x 4.524 miles*

| POS. | NO. | DRIVER | CAR/ENGINE | LAPS | TIME/RETIRED | GRID |
|---|---|---|---|---|---|---|
| 1 | 16 | Giuseppe Farina | Alfa Romeo | 42 | 2:02'53.7 | 2 |
| 2 | 12 | Luigi Fagioli | Alfa Romeo | 42 | +0.4 | 3 |
| 3 | 10 | Louis Rosier | Talbot-Lago-Talbot | 41 | +1 Lap | 10 |
| 4 | 30 | Prince Bira | Maserati | 40 | +2 Laps | 8 |
| 5 | 34 | Felice Bonetto | Maserati | 40 | +2 Laps | 12 |
| 6 | 32 | E.de Graffenried | Maserati | 40 | +2 Laps | 11 |
| 7 | 2 | Nello Pagani | Maserati | 39 | +3 Laps | 15 |
| 8 | 44 | Harry Schell | Talbot-Lago-Talbot | 39 | +3 Laps | 18 |
| 9 | 26 | Louis Chiron | Maserati | 39 | +3 Laps | 16 |
| 10 | 4 | Johnny Claes | Talbot-Lago-Talbot | 38 | +4 Laps | 14 |
| 11 | 40 | Toni Branca | Maserati | 35 | +7 Laps | 17 |
| Ret | 14 | Juan Manuel Fangio | Alfa Romeo | 32 | Engine | 1 |
| Ret | 42 | P.Etancelin | Talbot-Lago-Talbot | 25 | Gearbox | 6 |
| Ret | 8 | Eugene Martin | Talbot-Lago-Talbot | 19 | Accident | 9 |
| Ret | 20 | Raymond Sommer | Ferrari | 19 | Suspension | 13 |
| Ret | 22 | Luigi Villoresi | Ferrari | 9 | Engine | 4 |
| Ret | 18 | Alberto Ascari | Ferrari | 4 | Oil pump | 5 |
| Ret | 6 | Y.G.-Cabantous | Talbot-Lago-Talbot | 0 | Accident | 7 |

Winning speed: 92.757mph Lap leaders: Fangio 1-6, 21-22; Farina 7-20, 24-42; Fagioli 23
Pole position: Fangio, 2m 42.100s, 100.462mph
Fastest lap: Farina, 2m 41.600s,100.773mph

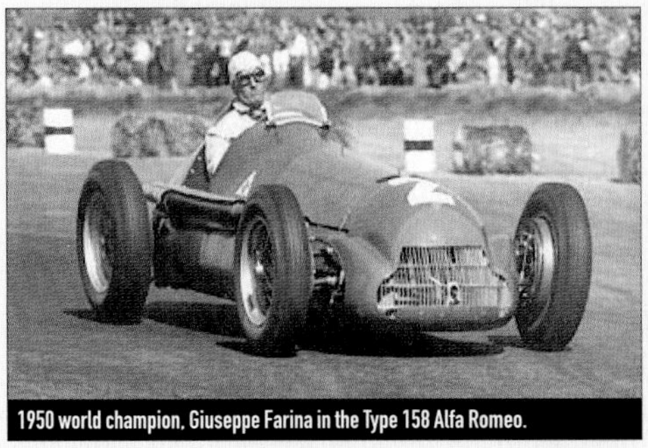

1950 world champion, Giuseppe Farina in the Type 158 Alfa Romeo.

## BELGIAN GRAND PRIX: SPA-FRANCORCHAMPS *18 June Round: 5 Race: 5 35 x 8.774 miles*

| POS. | NO. | DRIVER | CAR/ENGINE | LAPS | TIME/RETIRED | GRID |
|---|---|---|---|---|---|---|
| 1 | 10 | Juan Manuel Fangio | Alfa Romeo | 35 | 2:47'26. | 2 |
| 2 | 12 | Luigi Fagioli | Alfa Romeo | 35 | +14. | 3 |
| 3 | 14 | Louis Rosier | Talbot-Lago-Talbot | 35 | +2'19. | 8 |
| 4 | 8 | Giuseppe Farina | Alfa Romeo | 35 | +4'05. | 1 |
| 5 | 4 | Alberto Ascari | Ferrari | 34 | +1 Lap | 7 |
| 6 | 2 | Luigi Villoresi | Ferrari | 33 | +2 Laps | 4 |
| 7 | 22 | Pierre Levegh | Talbot-Lago-Talbot | 33 | +2 Laps | 10 |
| 8 | 24 | Johnny Claes | Talbot-Lago-Talbot | 32 | +3 Laps | 14 |
| 9 | 26 | Geoff Crossley | Alta | 30 | +5 Laps | 12 |
| 10 | 30 | Toni Branca | Maserati | 29 | +6 Laps | 11 |
| Ret | 20 | Eugene Chaboud | Talbot-Lago-Talbot | 22 | Oil pipe | 13 |
| Ret | 6 | Raymond Sommer | Talbot-Lago-Talbot | 20 | Oil pressure | 5 |
| Ret | 16 | P.Etancelin | Talbot-Lago-Talbot | 15 | Overheating | 6 |
| Ret | 18 | Y.G.-Cabantous | Talbot-Lago-Talbot | 2 | Oil pipe | 9 |

Winning speed: 110.043mph
Lap leaders: Fangio 1-6, 20-35; Farina 7-11, 18-19; Fagioli 12; Sommer 13-17
Pole position: Farina, 4m 37.000s, 114.027mph
Fastest lap: Farina, 4m 34.100s, 115.234mph

## FRENCH GRAND PRIX: REIMS-GUEUX *2 July Round: 6 Race: 6 64 x 4.857 miles*

| POS. | NO. | DRIVER | CAR/ENGINE | LAPS | TIME/RETIRED | GRID |
|---|---|---|---|---|---|---|
| 1 | 6 | Juan Manuel Fangio | Alfa Romeo | 64 | 2:57'52.8 | 1 |
| 2 | 4 | Luigi Fagioli | Alfa Romeo | 64 | +25.7 | 3 |
| 3 | 14 | Peter Whitehead | Ferrari | 61 | +3 Laps | 19 |
| 4 | 44 | Robert Manzon | Simca-Gordini | 61 | +3 Laps | 13 |
| 5 | 16 | Chaboud/Etancelin | Talbot-Lago-Talbot | 59 | +5 Laps | 4 |
| 6 | 26 | Rosier/Pozzi | Talbot-Lago-Talbot | 56 | +8 Laps | 16 |
| 7 | 2 | Giuseppe Farina | Alfa Romeo | 55 | Fuel pump | 2 |
| 8 | 18 | Y.G.-Cabantous | Talbot-Lago-Talbot | 52 | +12 Laps | 5 |
| Ret | 22 | Pierre Levegh | Talbot-Lago-Talbot | 36 | Engine | 9 |
| Ret | 40 | Felice Bonetto | Maserati-Milano | 14 | Engine | 11 |
| Ret | 42 | Johnny Claes | Talbot-Lago-Talbot | 11 | Overheating | 15 |
| Ret | 20 | Louis Rosier | Talbot-Lago-Talbot | 10 | Overheating | 6 |
| Ret | 32 | Reg Parnell | Maserati | 9 | Engine | 12 |
| Ret | 28 | Franco Rol | Maserati | 6 | Engine | 7 |
| Ret | 30 | Louis Chiron | Maserati | 6 | Engine | 14 |
| Ret | 34 | David Hampshire | Maserati | 5 | Engine | 18 |
| Ret | 12 | Raymond Sommer | Talbot-Lago-Talbot | 4 | Overheating | 17 |
| Ret | 36 | J.F.Gonzalez | Maserati | 3 | Engine | 8 |

Winning speed: 104.843mph Lap leaders: Farina 1-16; Fangio 17-64
Pole position: Fangio: 2m 30.600s, 116.095mph
Fastest lap: Fangio, 2m 35.600s, 112.364mph

## ITALIAN GRAND PRIX: MONZA *3 September Round: 7 Race: 7 80 x 3.915 miles*

| POS. | NO. | DRIVER | CAR/ENGINE | LAPS | TIME/RETIRED | GRID |
|---|---|---|---|---|---|---|
| 1 | 10 | Giuseppe Farina | Alfa Romeo | 80 | 2:51'17.4 | 3 |
| 2 | 48 | Serafini/Ascari | Ferrari | 80 | +1'18.6 | 6 |
| 3 | 36 | Luigi Fagioli | Alfa Romeo | 80 | +1'35.6 | 5 |
| 4 | 58 | Louis Rosier | Talbot-Lago-Talbot | 75 | +5 Laps | 13 |
| 5 | 24 | P.Etancelin | Talbot-Lago-Talbot | 75 | +5 Laps | 16 |
| 6 | 38 | E.de Graffenried | Maserati | 72 | +8 Laps | 17 |
| 7 | 8 | Peter Whitehead | Ferrari | 72 | +8 Laps | 18 |
| Ret | 50 | David Murray | Maserati | 56 | Gearbox | 24 |
| Ret | 32 | Cuth Harrison | ERA | 51 | Radiator | 21 |
| Ret | 12 | Raymond Sommer | Talbot-Lago-Talbot | 48 | Gearbox | 8 |
| Ret | 40 | Guy Mairesse | Talbot-Lago-Talbot | 42 | Oil pipe | 11 |
| Ret | 4 | Franco Rol | Maserati | 39 | Retirement | 9 |
| Ret | 60 | Taruffi/Fangio | Alfa Romeo | 34 | Engine | 7 |
| Ret | 56 | Pierre Levegh | Talbot-Lago-Talbot | 29 | Gearbox | 20 |
| Ret | 18 | Juan Manuel Fangio | Alfa Romeo | 23 | Gearbox | 1 |
| Ret | 2 | Johnny Claes | Talbot-Lago-Talbot | 22 | Overheating | 22 |
| Ret | 16 | Alberto Ascari | Ferrari | 21 | Engine | 2 |
| Ret | 22 | C.Biondetti | Ferrari-Jaguar | 17 | Engine | 25 |
| Ret | 64 | Henri Louveau | Talbot-Lago-Talbot | 16 | Brakes | 14 |
| Ret | 62 | Franco Comotti | Maserati-Milano | 15 | Retirement | 26 |
| Ret | 42 | M.Trintignant | Simca-Gordini | 13 | Water pipe | 12 |
| Ret | 6 | Louis Chiron | Maserati | 13 | Oil pressure | 19 |
| Ret | 46 | Consalvo Sanesi | Alfa Romeo | 11 | Engine | 4 |
| Ret | 44 | Robert Manzon | Simca-Gordini | 7 | Transmission | 10 |
| Ret | 30 | Prince Bira | Maserati | 1 | Engine | 15 |
| Ret | 28 | Paul Pietsch | Maserati | 0 | Engine | 27 |
| DNS | 52 | Felice Bonetto | Milano | 0 | Non starter | |

Winning speed: 109.699mph Lap leaders: Farina 1-13, 16-80; Ascari 14-15
Pole position: Fangio, 1m 58.600s, 118.825mph
Fastest lap: Fangio, 2m 0.000s, 117.439mph

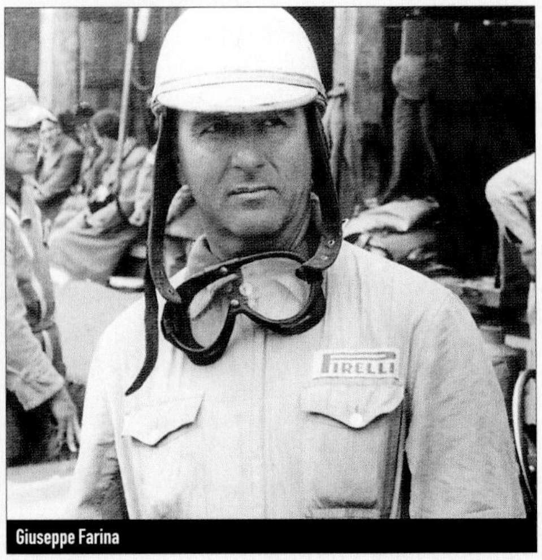

Giuseppe Farina

# 1951

## DRIVERS' CHAMPION: JUAN MANUEL FANGIO

### DRIVERS' CHAMPIONSHIP

| POS | DRIVER | COUNTRY | CAR | POINTS |
|---|---|---|---|---|
| 1 | Juan Manuel Fangio | Argentina | Alfa Romeo | 31(6) |
| 2 | Alberto Ascari | Italy | Ferrari | 25(3) |
| 3 | Jose Froilan Gonzalez | Argentina | Ferrari, Lago-Talbot | 24(3) |
| 4 | Giuseppe Farina | Italy | Alfa Romeo | 19(3) |
| 5 | Luigi Villoresi | Italy | Ferrari | 15(3) |
| 6 | Piero Taruffi | Italy | Ferrari | 10 |
| 7 | Lee Wallard | USA | Kurtis-Offenhauser | 8 |
| 8 | Felice Bonetto | Italy | Alfa Romeo | 7 |
| 9 | Mike Nazaruk | USA | Kurtis-Offenhauser | 6 |
| 10 | Reg Parnell | GB | Ferrari, BRM | 5 |
| 11 | Luigi Fagioli | Italy | Alfa Romeo | 4 |
| 12 | Consalvo Sanesi | Italy | Alfa Romeo | 3 |
| = | Louis Rosier | France | Lago-Talbot | 3 |
| = | Andy Linden | USA | Sherman-Offenhauser | 3 |
| 15 | Emmanuel de Graffenried | Switzerland | Alfa Romeo, Maserati | 2 |
| = | Yves Giraud-Cabantous | France | Lago-Talbot | 2 |
| = | Bobby Ball | USA | Schroeder-Offenhauser | 2 |
| = | Jack McGrath | USA | Kurtis-Offenhauser | 2 |
| = | Manuel Ayulo | USA | Kurtis -Offenhauser | 2 |
| | Rudi Fischer | Switzerland | Ferrari | |
| | Joe Kelly | Ireland | Alta GP | |
| | Peter Whitehead | GB | Ferrari | |
| | André Pilette | France | Lago-Talbot | |
| | Louis Chiron | Monaco | Maserati, Lago-Talbot | |
| | Stirling Moss | GB | HWM | |
| | Phillipe Étancelin | France | Lago-Talbot | |
| | Harry Schell | USA | Maserati | |
| | Johnny Claes | Belgium | Lago-Talbot | |
| | Guy Mairesse | France | Lago-Talbot | |
| | Peter Hirt | Switzerland | Veritas-Meteor | |
| | George Abecassis | GB | HMW 51-Alta | |
| | Henri Louveau | France | Lago-Talbot | |
| | "Pierre Levegh" | France | Lagot-Talbot | |
| | Eugene Chaboud | France | Lagot-Talbot | |
| | Onofre Marimon | Italy | Maserati | |
| | Robert Manzon | France | Simca-Gordini | |
| | Maurice Trintignant | France | Simca-Gordini | |
| | Aldo Gordini | France | Simca-Gordini | |
| | André Simon | France | Simca-Gordini | |
| | Peter Walker | GB | BRM | |
| | Brian Shawe-Taylor | GB | Ferrari, E.R.A | |
| | Bob Gerard | GB | E.R.A. | |
| | Duncan Hamilton | GB | Lago-Talbot | |
| | John James | GB | Maserati | |
| | David Murray | GB | Maserati | |
| | Philip Fotheringham-Parker | GB | Maserati | |
| | Jacques Swaters | Belgium | Lago-Talbot | |
| | Antonio Branca | Switzerland | Maserati | |
| | Paul Pietsch | Germany | Alfa Romeo | |
| | Chico Landi | Brazil | Ferrari | |
| | Franco Rol | Italy | Osca | |
| | Ken Richardson | GB | BRM | |
| | Francisco Godia-Sales | Italy | Maserati | |
| | Prince Bira | Thailand | Maserati | |
| | Georges Grignard | France | Lago-Talbot | |
| | Juan Jover | Spain | Maserati | |
| | Hans Stuck | Germany | BRM | |

**Points for top five finishers (8, 6, 4, 3, 2) plus a point for fastest lap. Only the best four scores counted towards the championship. Points for shared drives were divided equally between the drivers.**

### SWISS GRAND PRIX: BREMGARTEN *27 May Round: 1 Race: 8 42 x 4.524 miles*

| POS. | NO. | DRIVER | CAR/ENGINE | LAPS | TIME/RETIRED | GRID |
|---|---|---|---|---|---|---|
| 1 | 24 | Juan Manuel Fangio | Alfa Romeo | 42 | 2:07'53.64 | 1 |
| 2 | 44 | Piero Taruffi | Ferrari | 42 | +55.24 | 6 |
| 3 | 22 | Giuseppe Farina | Alfa Romeo | 42 | +1'19.31 | 2 |
| 4 | 28 | Consalvo Sanesi | Alfa Romeo | 41 | +1 Lap | 4 |
| 5 | 26 | E.de Graffenried | Alfa Romeo | 40 | +2 Laps | 5 |
| 6 | 20 | Alberto Ascari | Ferrari | 40 | +2 Laps | 7 |
| 7 | 30 | Louis Chiron | Maserati | 40 | +2 Laps | 19 |
| 8 | 14 | Stirling Moss | HWM-Alta | 40 | +2 Laps | 14 |
| 9 | 8 | Louis Rosier | Talbot-Lago-Talbot | 39 | +3 Laps | 8 |
| 10 | 4 | P.Etancelin | Talbot-Lago-Talbot | 39 | +3 Laps | 12 |
| 11 | 38 | Rudi Fischer | Ferrari | 39 | +3 Laps | 10 |
| 12 | 32 | Harry Schell | Maserati | 38 | +4 Laps | 17 |
| 13 | 2 | Johnny Claes | Talbot-Lago-Talbot | 35 | +7 Laps | 18 |
| 14 | 40 | Guy Mairesse | Talbot-Lago-Talbot | 31 | +11 Laps | 21 |
| Ret | 16 | Peter Whitehead | Ferrari | 36 | Accident | 9 |
| Ret | 10 | Henri Louveau | Talbot-Lago-Talbot | 30 | Accident | 11 |
| Ret | 12 | George Abecassis | HWM-Alta | 23 | Magneto | 20 |
| Ret | 6 | Y.G.-Cabantous | Talbot-Lago-Talbot | 14 | Ignition | 15 |
| Ret | 18 | Luigi Villoresi | Ferrari | 12 | Accident | 3 |
| Ret | 42 | J.F.Gonzalez | Talbot-Lago-Talbot | 10 | Oil pump | 13 |
| Ret | 52 | Peter Hirt | Veritas | 0 | Fuel system | 16 |

Winning speed: 89.132 mph Lap leaders: Fangio 1-23 29-42, Farina 24-28
Pole position: Fangio, 2 min 35.900s, 104.457mph
Fastest lap: Fangio, 2 min 51.100s, 95.178mph

### INDIANAPOLIS 500 *30 May Round: 2 Race: 9 200 x 2.500 miles*

| POS. | NO. | DRIVER | CAR/ENGINE | LAPS | TIME/RETIRED | GRID |
|---|---|---|---|---|---|---|
| 1 | 99 | Lee Wallard | Kurtis Kraft-Offenhauser | 200 | 3:57'38.05 | 2 |
| 2 | 83 | Mike Nazaruk | Kurtis Kraft-Offenhauser | 200 | +1'47.24 | 7 |
| 3 | 9 | Ayulo/McGrath | Kurtis Kraft-Offenhauser | 200 | +2'51.39 | 3 |
| 4 | 57 | Andy Linden | Sherman-Offenhauser | 200 | +4'40.12 | 31 |
| 5 | 52 | Bobby Ball | Schroeder-Offenhauser | 200 | +4'52.23 | 29 |
| 6 | 1 | Henry Banks | Moore-Offenhauser | 200 | +5'40.02 | 17 |
| 7 | 68 | Carl Forberg | Kurtis Kraft-Offenhauser | 193 | +7 Laps | 24 |
| 8 | 27 | Duane Carter | Deidt-Offenhauser | 180 | +20 Laps | 4 |
| Ret | 5 | T.Bettenhausen | Deidt-Offenhauser | 178 | Spun off | 9 |
| Ret | 18 | Duke Nalon | Kurtis Kraft-Novi | 151 | Retirement | 1 |
| Ret | 69 | Gene Force | Kurtis Kraft-Offenhauser | 142 | Engine | 22 |
| Ret | 25 | Sam Hanks | Kurtis Kraft-Offenhauser | 135 | Engine | 12 |
| Ret | 10 | Bill Schindler | Kurtis Kraft-Offenhauser | 129 | Engine | 16 |
| Ret | 16 | Mauri Rose | Deidt-Offenhauser | 126 | Accident | 5 |
| Ret | 2 | Walt Faulkner | Kuzma-Offenhauser | 123 | Engine | 14 |
| Ret | 76 | Jimmy Davies | Pawl-Offenhauser | 110 | Axle | 27 |
| Ret | 59 | Fred Agabashian | Kurtis Kraft-Offenhauser | 109 | Clutch | 11 |
| Ret | 73 | Carl Scarborough | Kurtis Kraft-Offenhauser | 100 | Axle | 15 |
| Ret | 71 | Bill Mackey | Hall-Offenhauser | 97 | Clutch | 33 |
| Ret | 8 | Chuck Stevenson | Marchese-Offenhauser | 93 | Fire | 19 |
| Ret | 3 | Johnnie Parsons | Kurtis Kraft-Offenhauser | 87 | Magneto | 8 |
| Ret | 4 | Cecil Green | Kurtis Kraft-Offenhauser | 80 | Engine | 10 |
| Ret | 98 | Troy Ruttman | Kurtis Kraft-Offenhauser | 78 | Engine | 6 |
| Ret | 6 | Duke Dinsmore | Schroeder-Offenhauser | 73 | Overheating | 32 |
| Ret | 32 | Chet Miller | Kurtis Kraft-Novi | 56 | Ignition | 28 |
| Ret | 44 | Walt Brown | Kurtis Kraft-Offenhauser | 55 | Magneto | 13 |
| Ret | 48 | Rodger Ward | Bromme-Offenhauser | 34 | Oil pipe | 25 |
| Ret | 23 | Cliff Griffith | Kurtis Kraft-Offenhauser | 30 | Axle | 18 |
| Ret | 81 | Bill Vukovich | Trevis-Offenhauser | 29 | Oil leak | 20 |
| Ret | 22 | George Connor | Lesovsky-Offenhauser | 29 | Transmission | 21 |
| Ret | 19 | Mack Hellings | Deidt-Offenhauser | 18 | Engine | 23 |
| Ret | 12 | Johnny McDowell | Maserati-Offenhauser | 15 | Fuel leak | 26 |
| Ret | 26 | Joe James | Watson-Offenhauser | 8 | Transmission | 30 |

Winning speed: 126.244mph
Pole position: Nalon, 1m 5.935s, 136.498mph
Fastest lap: Wallard, 1m 7.260s, 133.809mph

### BELGIAN GRAND PRIX: SPA-FRANCORCHAMPS *17 June Round: 3 Race: 10 36 x 8.774 miles*

| POS. | NO. | DRIVER | CAR/ENGINE | LAPS | TIME/RETIRED | GRID |
|---|---|---|---|---|---|---|
| 1 | 4 | Giuseppe Farina | Alfa Romeo | 36 | 2:45'46.2 | 2 |
| 2 | 8 | Alberto Ascari | Ferrari | 36 | +2'51.0 | 4 |
| 3 | 10 | Luigi Villoresi | Ferrari | 36 | +4'21.9 | 3 |
| 4 | 14 | Louis Rosier | Talbot-Lago-Talbot | 34 | +2 Lap | 7 |
| 5 | 22 | Y.G.-Cabantous | Talbot-Lago-Talbot | 34 | +2 Laps | 8 |
| 6 | 24 | Andre Pilette | Talbot-Lago-Talbot | 33 | +3 Laps | 12 |
| 7 | 16 | Johnny Claes | Talbot-Lago-Talbot | 33 | +3 Laps | 11 |
| 8 | 26 | Pierre Levegh | Talbot-Lago-Talbot | 32 | +4 Laps | 13 |
| 9 | 2 | Juan Manuel Fangio | Alfa Romeo | 32 | +4 Laps | 1 |
| Ret | 18 | Louis Chiron | Talbot-Lago-Talbot | 28 | Engine | 9 |
| Ret | 6 | Consalvo Sanesi | Alfa Romeo | 11 | Radiator | 6 |
| Ret | 12 | Piero Taruffi | Ferrari | 8 | Transmission | 5 |
| Ret | 20 | P.Etancelin | Talbot-Lago-Talbot | 1 | Transmission | 10 |

Winning speed: 114.323mph Lap leaders: Villoresi 1-2, Farina 3-14 16-36, Fangio 15
Pole position: Fangio, 4m 25.000s, 119.191mph
Fastest lap: Fangio, 4m 22.100s, 120.510mph

### FRENCH GRAND PRIX: REIMS-GUEUX *1 July Round: 4 Race: 11 77 x 4.857 miles*

| POS. | NO. | DRIVER | CAR/ENGINE | LAPS | TIME/RETIRED | GRID |
|---|---|---|---|---|---|---|
| 1 | 8 | Fangio/Fagioli | Alfa Romeo | 77 | 3:22'11.0 | 7 |
| 2 | 14 | Ascari/Gonzalez | Ferrari | 77 | +58.2 | 6 |
| 3 | 10 | Luigi Villoresi | Ferrari | 74 | +3 Laps | 4 |
| 4 | 26 | Reg Parnell | Ferrari | 73 | +4 Laps | 9 |
| 5 | 2 | Giuseppe Farina | Alfa Romeo | 73 | +4 Laps | 2 |
| 6 | 42 | Louis Chiron | Talbot-Lago-Talbot | 71 | +6 Laps | 8 |
| 7 | 46 | Y.G.-Cabantous | Talbot-Lago-Talbot | 71 | +6 Laps | 11 |
| 8 | 44 | Eugene Chaboud | Talbot-Lago-Talbot | 69 | +8 Laps | 14 |
| 9 | 48 | Guy Mairesse | Talbot-Lago-Talbot | 66 | +11 Laps | 19 |
| 10 | 6 | Consalvo Sanesi | Alfa Romeo | 58 | +19 Laps | 5 |
| 11 | 4 | Fagioli/Fangio | Alfa Romeo | 55 | +22 Laps | 1 |
| Ret | 28 | Johnny Claes | Talbot-Lago-Talbot | 54 | Accident | 12 |
| Ret | 40 | Louis Rosier | Talbot-Lago-Talbot | 43 | Transmission | 13 |
| Ret | 38 | P.Etancelin | Talbot-Lago-Talbot | 37 | Engine | 10 |
| Ret | 36 | Aldo Gordini | Simca-Gordini | 27 | Engine | 17 |
| Ret | 20 | Harry Schell | Maserati | 23 | Overheating | 22 |
| Ret | 32 | M.Trintignant | Simca-Gordini | 11 | Engine | 18 |
| Ret | 12 | Alberto Ascari | Ferrari | 10 | Gearbox | 3 |
| Ret | 34 | Andre Simon | Simca-Gordini | 7 | Engine | 21 |
| Ret | 30 | Robert Manzon | Simca-Gordini | 3 | Engine | 23 |
| Ret | 50 | Onofre Marimon | Maserati-Milano | 2 | Engine | 15 |
| Ret | 18 | E.de Graffenried | Maserati | 1 | Transmission | 16 |
| Ret | 24 | Peter Whitehead | Ferrari | 1 | Engine | 20 |

Winning speed: 110.977mph Lap leaders: Ascari 1-8, 45-50; Fangio 9, 51-77; Farina 10-44
Pole position: Fangio, 2m 25.700s, 119.999mph
Fastest lap: Fangio, 2m 27.800s, 118.294mph

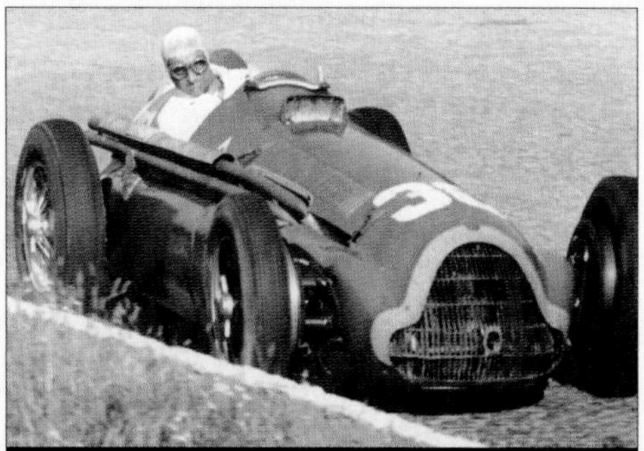

**1951 world champion, Juan Manuel Fangio in the Type 159 Alfa Romeo.**

### BRITISH GRAND PRIX: SILVERSTONE *14 July Round: 5 Race: 12 90 x 2.889 miles*

| POS. | NO. | DRIVER | CAR/ENGINE | LAPS | TIME/RETIRED | GRID |
|---|---|---|---|---|---|---|
| 1 | 12 | J.F.Gonzalez | Ferrari | 90 | 2:42'18.2 | 1 |
| 2 | 2 | Juan Manuel Fangio | Alfa Romeo | 90 | +51.0 | 2 |
| 3 | 10 | Luigi Villoresi | Ferrari | 88 | +2 Laps | 5 |
| 4 | 4 | Felice Bonetto | Alfa Romeo | 87 | +3 Laps | 7 |
| 5 | 6 | Reg Parnell | BRM | 85 | +5 Laps | 20 |
| 6 | 3 | Consalvo Sanesi | Alfa Romeo | 84 | +6 Laps | 6 |
| 7 | 7 | Peter Walker | BRM | 84 | +6 Laps | 19 |
| 8 | 9 | B.Shawe-Taylor | ERA | 84 | +6 Laps | 12 |
| 9 | 14 | Peter Whitehead | Ferrari | 83 | +7 Laps | 8 |
| 10 | 22 | Louis Rosier | Talbot-Lago-Talbot | 83 | +7 Laps | 9 |
| 11 | 8 | Bob Gerard | ERA | 82 | +8 Laps | 10 |
| 12 | 18 | Duncan Hamilton | Talbot-Lago-Talbot | 81 | +9 Laps | 11 |
| 13 | 25 | Johnny Claes | Talbot-Lago-Talbot | 80 | +10 Laps | 14 |
| Ret | 1 | Giuseppe Farina | Alfa Romeo | 75 | Clutch | 3 |
| NC | 5 | Joe Kelly | Alta | 75 | Not classified | 18 |
| Ret | 11 | Alberto Ascari | Ferrari | 56 | Gearbox | 4 |
| Ret | 17 | P.F.-Parker | Maserati | 46 | Oil leak | 16 |
| Ret | 15 | David Murray | Maserati | 45 | Engine | 15 |
| Ret | 23 | Louis Chiron | Talbot-Lago-Talbot | 41 | Brakes | 13 |
| Ret | 16 | John James | Maserati | 23 | Radiator | 17 |

Winning speed: 110.977mph
Lap leaders: Bonetto 1; Gonzalez 2-9, 39-47, 49-90; Fangio 10-38, 48
Pole position: Gonzalez, 1m 43.400s, 100.600mph
Fastest lap: Farina, 1m 44.000s, 100.004mph

### GERMAN GRAND PRIX: NURBURGRING *29 July Round: 6 Race: 13 20 x 14.173 miles*

| POS. | NO. | DRIVER | CAR/ENGINE | LAPS | TIME/RETIRED | GRID |
|---|---|---|---|---|---|---|
| 1 | 71 | Alberto Ascari | Ferrari | 20 | 3:23'03.3 | 1 |
| 2 | 75 | Juan Manuel Fangio | Alfa Romeo | 20 | +30.5 | 3 |
| 3 | 74 | J.F.Gonzalez | Ferrari | 20 | +4'39.0 | 2 |
| 4 | 72 | Luigi Villoresi | Ferrari | 20 | +5'50.2 | 5 |
| 5 | 73 | Piero Taruffi | Ferrari | 20 | +7'49.1 | 6 |
| 6 | 91 | Rudi Fischer | Ferrari | 19 | +1 Lap | 8 |
| 7 | 82 | Robert Manzon | Simca-Gordini | 19 | +1 Lap | 9 |
| 8 | 84 | Louis Rosier | Talbot-Lago-Talbot | 19 | +1 Lap | 15 |
| 9 | 90 | Pierre Levegh | Talbot-Lago-Talbot | 18 | +2 Laps | 19 |
| 10 | 93 | Jacques Swaters | Talbot-Lago-Talbot | 18 | +2 Laps | 22 |
| 11 | 94 | Johnny Claes | Talbot-Lago-Talbot | 17 | +3 Laps | 18 |
| Ret | 87 | Y.G.-Cabantous | Talbot-Lago-Talbot | 17 | Accident | 11 |
| Ret | 81 | M.Trintignant | Simca-Gordini | 13 | Engine | 14 |
| Ret | 77 | Felice Bonetto | Alfa Romeo | 12 | Magneto | 10 |
| Ret | 88 | Duncan Hamilton | Talbot-Lago-Talbot | 12 | Oil pressure | 20 |
| Ret | 78 | Paul Pietsch | Alfa Romeo | 11 | Accident | 7 |
| Ret | 83 | Andre Simon | Simca-Gordini | 11 | Engine | 12 |
| Ret | 76 | Giuseppe Farina | Alfa Romeo | 8 | Overheating | 4 |
| Ret | 86 | P.Etancelin | Talbot-Lago-Talbot | 4 | Gearbox | 21 |
| Ret | 85 | Louis Chiron | Talbot-Lago-Talbot | 3 | Ignition | 13 |
| Ret | 92 | Toni Branca | Maserati | 3 | Engine | 17 |
| Ret | 79 | E.de Graffenried | Maserati | 2 | Engine | 16 |

Winning speed: 83.761mph Lap leaders: Fangio 1-4, 11-14; Ascari 5-9, 15-20; Gonzalez 10
Pole position: Ascari, 9m 55.800s, 85.640mph
Fastest lap: Fangio, 9m 55.800s, 85.640mph

### ITALIAN GRAND PRIX: MONZA *16 September Round: 7 Race: 14 80 x 3.915 miles*

| POS. | NO. | DRIVER | CAR/ENGINE | LAPS | TIME/RETIRED | GRID |
|---|---|---|---|---|---|---|
| 1 | 2 | Alberto Ascari | Ferrari | 80 | 2:42'39.3 | 3 |
| 2 | 6 | J.F.Gonzalez | Ferrari | 80 | +44.6 | 4 |
| 3 | 40 | Farina/Bonetto | Alfa Romeo | 79 | +1 Lap | 7 |
| 4 | 4 | Luigi Villoresi | Ferrari | 79 | +1 Lap | 5 |
| 5 | 8 | Piero Taruffi | Ferrari | 78 | +2 Laps | 6 |
| 6 | 48 | Andre Simon | Simca-Gordini | 74 | +6 Laps | 11 |
| 7 | 18 | Louis Rosier | Talbot-Lago-Talbot | 73 | +7 Laps | 15 |
| 8 | 24 | Y.G.-Cabantous | Talbot-Lago-Talbot | 72 | +8 Laps | 14 |
| 9 | 44 | Franco Rol | Osca | 67 | +13 Laps | 18 |
| Ret | 38 | Juan Manuel Fangio | Alfa Romeo | 39 | Engine | 1 |
| Ret | 50 | M.Trintignant | Simca-Gordini | 29 | Engine | 12 |
| Ret | 46 | Robert Manzon | Simca-Gordini | 29 | Engine | 13 |
| Ret | 20 | Louis Chiron | Talbot-Lago-Talbot | 23 | Ignition | 17 |
| Ret | 22 | Pierre Levegh | Talbot-Lago-Talbot | 9 | Engine | 20 |
| Ret | 28 | Jacques Swaters | Talbot-Lago-Talbot | 7 | Overheating | 22 |
| Ret | 34 | Giuseppe Farina | Alfa Romeo | 6 | Engine | 2 |
| Ret | 26 | Johnny Claes | Talbot-Lago-Talbot | 4 | Oil pump | 21 |
| Ret | 36 | E.de Graffenried | Alfa Romeo | 1 | Compressor | 9 |
| Ret | 16 | Peter Whitehead | Ferrari | 1 | Magneto | 19 |
| Ret | 12 | Chico Landi | Ferrari | 0 | Transmission | 16 |
| DNS | 30 | Reg Parnell | BRM | 0 | Non starter | |
| DNS | 32 | Ken Richardson | BRM | 0 | Non starter | |

Winning speed: 115.522mph Lap leaders: Fangio 1-3, 8-13; Ascari 4-7, 14-80
Pole position: Fangio, 1m 53.200s, 124.494mph
Fastest lap: Farina, 1m 56.500s, 120.967mph

### SPANISH GRAND PRIX: PEDRALBES *28 October Round: 8 Race: 15 70 x 3.925 miles*

| POS. | NO. | DRIVER | CAR/ENGINE | LAPS | TIME/RETIRED | GRID |
|---|---|---|---|---|---|---|
| 1 | 22 | Juan Manuel Fangio | Alfa Romeo | 70 | 2:46'54.10 | 2 |
| 2 | 6 | J.F.Gonzalez | Ferrari | 70 | +54.28 | 3 |
| 3 | 20 | Giuseppe Farina | Alfa Romeo | 70 | +1'45.54 | 4 |
| 4 | 2 | Alberto Ascari | Ferrari | 68 | +2 Laps | 1 |
| 5 | 24 | Felice Bonetto | Alfa Romeo | 68 | +2 Laps | 8 |
| 6 | 26 | E.de Graffenried | Alfa Romeo | 66 | +4 Laps | 6 |
| 7 | 28 | Louis Rosier | Talbot-Lago-Talbot | 64 | +6 Laps | 20 |
| 8 | 34 | P.Etancelin | Talbot-Lago-Talbot | 63 | +7 Laps | 13 |
| 9 | 14 | Robert Manzon | Simca-Gordini | 63 | +7 Laps | 9 |
| 10 | 44 | Paco Godia | Maserati | 60 | +10 Laps | 17 |
| Ret | 4 | Luigi Villoresi | Ferrari | 48 | Ignition | 5 |
| Ret | 16 | Andre Simon | Simca-Gordini | 48 | Engine | 10 |
| Ret | 36 | Johnny Claes | Talbot-Lago-Talbot | 37 | Accident | 15 |
| Ret | 8 | Piero Taruffi | Ferrari | 30 | Wheel | 7 |
| Ret | 12 | M.Trintignant | Simca-Gordini | 25 | Engine | 11 |
| Ret | 38 | Georges Grignard | Talbot-Lago-Talbot | 23 | Engine | 16 |
| Ret | 32 | Y.G.-Cabantous | Talbot-Lago-Talbot | 7 | Accident | 14 |
| Ret | 30 | Louis Chiron | Talbot-Lago-Talbot | 4 | Ignition | 12 |
| Ret | 18 | Prince Bira | Maserati-Osca | 1 | Engine | 19 |

Winning speed: 98.760mph Lap leaders: Ascari 1-3; Fangio 4-70
Pole position: Ascari, 2m 10.590s, 108.190mph Fastest lap: Fangio, 2m 16.930s, 103.180mph

# 1952

## DRIVERS' CHAMPION: ALBERTO ASCARI

### DRIVERS' CHAMPIONSHIP

| POS | DRIVER | COUNTRY | CAR | POINTS |
|---|---|---|---|---|
| 1 | Alberto Ascari | Italy | Ferrari | 36(12.5) |
| 2 | Giuseppe Farina | Italy | Ferrari | 24(3) |
| 3 | Piero Taruffi | Italy | Ferrari | 22 |
| 4 | Rudi Fischer | Switzerland | Ferrari | 10 |
| = | Mike Hawthorn | GB | Cooper –Bristol | 10 |
| 6 | Robert Manzon | France | Gordini | 9 |
| 7 | Troy Ruttman | USA | Kuzma-Offenhauser | 8 |
| = | Luigi Villoresi | Italy | Ferrari | 8 |
| 9 | Jose Froilan Gonzalez | Argentina | Maserati | 6.5 |
| 10 | Jean Behra | France | Gordini | 6 |
| = | Jim Rathmann | USA | Kurtis-Offenhauser | 6 |
| 12 | Sam Hanks | USA | Kurtis-Offenhauser | 4 |
| 13 | Ken Wharton | GB | Frazer-Nash –Bristol | 3 |
| = | Dennis Poore | GB | Connaught -Lea-Francis | 3 |
| = | Duane Carter | USA | Levosky-Offenhauser | 3 |
| 16 | Alan Brown | GB | Cooper –Bristol | 2 |
| = | Art Cross | USA | Kurtis-Offenhauser | 2 |
| = | Paul Frere | Belgium | HMW-Alta, Simca-Gordini | 2 |
| = | Maurice Trintignant | France | Ferrari, Simca-Gordini | 2 |
| = | Eric Thompson | GB | Connaught -Lea-Francis | 2 |
| = | Felice Bonnetto | Italy | Maserati | 2 |
| 22 | Billy Vukovich | USA | Kurtis-Offenhauser | 1 |
| | Hans Stuck | West Germany | AFM-Kuechen | |
| | Emmanuel de Graffenried | Switzerland | Maserati | |
| | Robin Montague-Charrington | GB | Aston-Butterworth | |
| | Stirling Moss | GB | HMW-Alta, ERA-Bristol, Connaught -Lea-Francis | |
| | Peter Collins | GB | HMW-Alta | |
| | George Abecassis | GB | HMW-Alta | |
| | Lance Macklin | GB | HMW-Alta | |
| | Peter Hirt | Switzerland | Ferrari | |
| | Prince Bira | Thailand | Simca-Gordini, Gordini | |
| | Louis Rosier | France | Ferrari | |
| | Eric Brandon | GB | Cooper-Bristol | |
| | André Simon | France | Ferrari | |
| | Max de Terra | Switzerland | Simca-Gordini | |
| | Toni Ulmen | Germany | Veritas-Meteor | |
| | Harry Schell | USA | Maserati | |
| | Johnny Claes | Belgium | Simca-Gordini, HMW-Alta | |
| | Robert O'Brien | USA | Simca-Gordini | |
| | Roger Laurent | Belgium | HMW-Alta, Ferrari | |
| | Arthur Legat | Belgium | Veritas-Meteor | |
| | Charles de Tornaco | Belgium | Ferrari | |
| | Tony Gaze | Australia | HMW-Alta | |
| | Phillipe Etancelin | France | Maserati | |
| | Yves Giraud-Cabantous | France | HMW-Alta | |
| | Gianfranco Comotti | Italy | Ferrari | |
| | Piero Carini | Italy | Ferrari | |
| | Peter Whitehead | GB | Alta | |
| | Ken Downing | GB | Connaught -Lea-Francis | |
| | Kenneth McAlpine | GB | Connaught -Lea-Francis | |
| | Reg Parnell | GB | Cooper-Bristol | |
| | Roy Salvadori | GB | Ferrari | |
| | Graham Whitehead | GB | Alta | |
| | Gino Bianco | Italy | Maserati | |
| | Tony Crook | GB | Frazer-Nash-BMW | |
| | Heitel Cantoni | Italy | Maserati | |
| | David Murray | GB | Cooper -Bristol | |
| | Ernst Klodwig | East Germany | Heck-BMW | |
| | Duncan Hamilton | GB | HMW-Alta | |
| | Fritz Riess | West Germany | Veritas-BMW | |
| | Paul Pietsch | West Germany | Veritas-Meteor | |
| | Theo Helfrich | West Germany | Veritas-BMW | |
| | Josef Peters | West Germany | Veritas-BMW | |
| | Bill Aston | GB | Aston -Butterworth | |
| | Rudolf Schoeller | Switzerland | Ferrari | |
| | Rudolf Krause | East Germany | Greifzu-BMW | |
| | Bernd Nacke | West Germany | BMW Eigenbau | |
| | Adolf Brudes | West Germany | Verita RS-BMW | |
| | Marcel Balsa | France | BMW Special | |
| | Willi Heeks | West Germany | AFM -BMW | |
| | Hans Klenk | West Germany | Veritas-Meteor | |
| | Helmut Niedermayer | West Germany | AFM-BMW | |
| | Ludwig Fischer | West Germany | AFM-BMW | |
| | Willi Krakau | West Germany | AFM -BMW | |
| | Harry Merkel | West Germany | BMW Eigenbau | |
| | Chico Landi | Brazil | Maserati | |
| | Jan Flinterman | Netherlands | Maserati | |
| | Dries van der Lof | Netherlands | HMW-Alta | |
| | Elie Bayol | France | Osca | |
| | Franco Rol | Italy | Maserati | |
| | Alberto Crespo | Argentina | Maserati | |
| | Piero Dusio | Italy | Cisitalia -BPM | |

Points for top five finishers (8, 6, 4, 3, 2) plus a point for fastest lap. Only the best four scores counted towards the championship. Points for shared drives were divided equally between the drivers.

### SWISS GRAND PRIX: BREMGARTEN 18 May Round: 1 Race: 16 62 x 4.524 miles

| POS. | NO. | DRIVER | CAR/ENGINE | LAPS | TIME/RETIRED | GRID |
|---|---|---|---|---|---|---|
| 1 | 30 | Piero Taruffi | Ferrari | 62 | 3:01'46.1 | 2 |
| 2 | 42 | Rudi Fischer | Ferrari | 62 | +2'37.2 | 5 |
| 3 | 6 | Jean Behra | Gordini | 61 | +1 Lap | 7 |
| 4 | 22 | Ken Wharton | Frazer-Nash-Bristol | 60 | +2 Laps | 13 |
| 5 | 26 | Alan Brown | Cooper-Bristol | 59 | +3 Laps | 15 |
| 6 | 38 | E.de Graffenried | Maserati-Plate | 58 | +4 Laps | 8 |
| 7 | 44 | Peter Hirt | Ferrari | 56 | +6 Laps | 19 |
| 8 | 24 | Eric Brandon | Cooper-Bristol | 55 | +7 Laps | 17 |
| Ret | 10 | Prince Bira | Simca-Gordini-Gordini | 52 | Engine | 11 |
| Ret | 32 | Simon/Farina | Ferrari | 51 | Magneto | 4 |
| Ret | 40 | Harry Schell | Maserati-Plate | 31 | Engine | 18 |
| With | 46 | Stirling Moss | HWM-Alta | 24 | Withdrew | 9 |
| With | 20 | Lance Macklin | HWM-Alta | 24 | Withdrew | 12 |
| Ret | 8 | Robert Manzon | Gordini | 20 | Radiator | 3 |
| Ret | 28 | Giuseppe Farina | Ferrari | 16 | Magneto | 1 |
| Ret | 18 | Peter Collins | HWM-Alta | 12 | Halfshaft | 6 |
| Ret | 16 | George Abecassis | HWM-Alta | 12 | Halfshaft | 10 |
| Ret | 2 | Hans von Stuck | AFM-Kuchen | 4 | Engine | 14 |
| Ret | 4 | Toni Ulmen | Veritas | 4 | Fuel leak | 16 |
| Ret | 12 | Louis Rosier | Ferrari | 2 | Accident | 20 |
| Ret | 50 | Max de Terra | Simca-Gordini-Simca | 1 | Magneto | 21 |

Winning speed: 92.578mph Lap leaders: Farina 1-16; Taruffi 17-62
Pole position: Farina, 2m 47.500s, 97.223mph
Fastest lap: Taruffi, 2m 49.100s, 96.303mph

### INDIANAPOLIS 500 30 May Round: 2 Race: 17 200 x 2.500 miles

| POS. | NO. | DRIVER | CAR/ENGINE | LAPS | TIME/RETIRED | GRID |
|---|---|---|---|---|---|---|
| 1 | 98 | Troy Ruttman | Kuzma-Offenhauser | 200 | 3:52'41.88 | 7 |
| 2 | 59 | Jim Rathmann | Kurtis Kraft-Offenhauser | 200 | +4'02.33 | 10 |
| 3 | 18 | Sam Hanks | Kurtis Kraft-Offenhauser | 200 | +6'11.61 | 5 |
| 4 | 1 | Duane Carter | Lesovsky-Offenhauser | 200 | +6'48.34 | 6 |
| 5 | 33 | Art Cross | Kurtis Kraft-Offenhauser | 200 | +8'40.15 | 20 |
| 6 | 77 | Jimmy Bryan | Kurtis Kraft-Offenhauser | 200 | +9'24.32 | 21 |
| 7 | 37 | Jimmy Reece | Kurtis Kraft-Offenhauser | 200 | +10'35.24 | 23 |
| 8 | 54 | George Connor | Kurtis Kraft-Offenhauser | 200 | +12'00.61 | 14 |
| 9 | 22 | Cliff Griffith | Kurtis Kraft-Offenhauser | 200 | +12'23.76 | 9 |
| 10 | 5 | Johnnie Parsons | Kurtis Kraft-Offenhauser | 200 | +13'37.78 | 31 |
| 11 | 4 | Jack McGrath | Kurtis Kraft-Offenhauser | 200 | +14'21.72 | 3 |
| 12 | 29 | Jim Rigsby | Watson-Offenhauser | 200 | +16'05.10 | 26 |
| 13 | 14 | Joe James | Kurtis Kraft-Offenhauser | 200 | +16'55.65 | 16 |
| 14 | 7 | Bill Schindler | Stevens-Offenhauser | 200 | +18'48.66 | 15 |
| 15 | 65 | George Fonder | Sherman-Offenhauser | 197 | +3 Laps | 13 |
| 16 | 81 | Eddie Johnson | Trevis-Offenhauser | 193 | +7 Laps | 24 |
| 17 | 26 | Bill Vukovich | Kurtis Kraft-Offenhauser | 191 | Steering | 8 |
| 18 | 16 | Chuck Stevenson | Kurtis Kraft-Offenhauser | 187 | +13 Laps | 11 |
| 19 | 2 | Henry Banks | Lesovsky-Offenhauser | 184 | +16 Laps | 12 |
| 20 | 8 | Manny Ayulo | Lesovsky-Offenhauser | 184 | +16 Laps | 28 |
| 21 | 31 | Johnny McDowell | Kurtis Kraft-Offenhauser | 182 | +18 Laps | 33 |
| Ret | 48 | Spider Webb | Bromme-Offenhauser | 162 | Oil leak | 29 |
| Ret | 34 | Rodger Ward | Kurtis Kraft-Offenhauser | 130 | Oil pressure | 22 |
| Ret | 27 | Tony Bettenhausen | Deidt-Offenhauser | 93 | Oil pressure | 30 |
| Ret | 36 | Duke Nalon | Kurtis Kraft-Novi | 84 | Compressor | 4 |
| Ret | 73 | Bob Sweikert | Kurtis Kraft-Offenhauser | 77 | Differential | 32 |
| Ret | 28 | Fred Agabashian | Kurtis Kraft-Cummins | 71 | Compressor | 1 |
| Ret | 67 | Gene Hartley | Kurtis Kraft-Offenhauser | 65 | Exhaust | 18 |
| Ret | 93 | Bob Scott | Kurtis Kraft-Offenhauser | 49 | Transmission | 25 |
| Ret | 21 | Chet Miller | Kurtis Kraft-Novi | 41 | Compressor | 27 |
| Ret | 12 | Alberto Ascari | Ferrari | 40 | Wheel | 19 |
| Ret | 55 | Bobby Ball | Stevens-Offenhauser | 34 | Gearbox | 17 |
| Ret | 9 | Andy Linden | Kurtis Kraft-Offenhauser | 20 | Oil pump | 2 |

Winning speed: 128.922mph
Pole position: Agabashian, 1m 5.212s, 138.011mph
Fastest lap: Vukovich, 1m 06.600s, 135.135mph

### BELGIAN GRAND PRIX: SPA-FRANCORCHAMPS 22 June Round: 3 Race: 18 36 x 8 .774 miles

| POS. | NO. | DRIVER | CAR/ENGINE | LAPS | TIME/RETIRED | GRID |
|---|---|---|---|---|---|---|
| 1 | 4 | Alberto Ascari | Ferrari | 36 | 3:03'46.3 | 1 |
| 2 | 2 | Giuseppe Farina | Ferrari | 36 | +1'55.2 | 2 |
| 3 | 14 | Robert Manzon | Gordini | 36 | +4'28.4 | 4 |
| 4 | 8 | Mike Hawthorn | Cooper-Bristol | 35 | +1 Lap | 6 |
| 5 | 28 | Paul Frere | HWM-Alta | 34 | +2 Laps | 8 |
| 6 | 10 | Alan Brown | Cooper-Bristol | 34 | +2 Laps | 9 |
| 7 | 34 | Charles de Tornaco | Ferrari | 33 | +3 Laps | 13 |
| 8 | 18 | Johnny Claes | Gordini | 33 | +3 Laps | 19 |
| 9 | 12 | Eric Brandon | Cooper-Bristol | 33 | +3 Laps | 12 |
| 10 | 20 | Prince Bira | Simca-Gordini-Gordini | 32 | +4 Laps | 18 |
| 11 | 24 | Lance Macklin | HWM-Alta | 32 | +4 Laps | 14 |
| 12 | 30 | Roger Laurent | HWM-Alta | 32 | +4 Laps | 20 |
| 13 | 38 | Arthur Legat | Veritas | 31 | +5 Laps | 21 |
| 14 | 44 | Robert O'Brien | Simca-Gordini-Gordini | 30 | +6 Laps | 22 |
| 15 | 42 | Tony Gaze | HWM-Alta | 30 | +6 Laps | 16 |
| Ret | 40 | R.M.-Charrington | Aston-Butterworth | 17 | Engine | 15 |
| Ret | 6 | Piero Taruffi | Ferrari | 13 | Accident | 3 |
| Ret | 16 | Jean Behra | Gordini | 13 | Accident | 5 |
| Ret | 36 | Ken Wharton | Frazer-Nash-Bristol | 10 | Spun off | 7 |
| Ret | 22 | Louis Rosier | Ferrari | 6 | Transmission | 17 |
| Ret | 26 | Peter Collins | HWM-Alta | 3 | Halfshaft | 11 |
| Ret | 32 | Stirling Moss | ERA-Bristol | 0 | Engine | 10 |

Winning speed: 103.124mph Lap leaders: Behra 1; Ascari 2-36
Pole position: Ascari, 4m 37.000s, 114.027mph
Fastest lap: Ascari, 4m 55.000s, 107.070mph

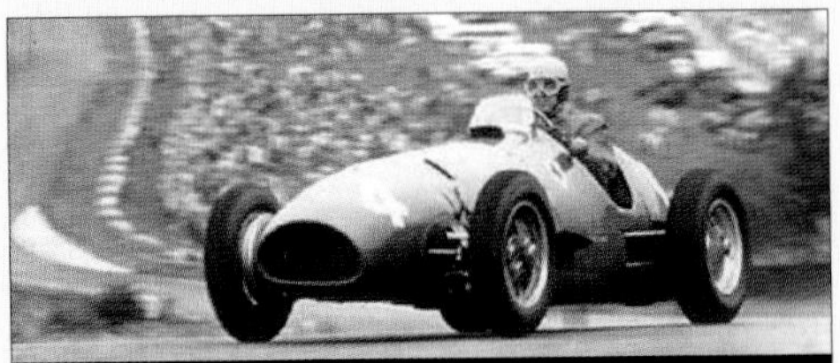
1952 world champion, Alberto Ascari in the type 500 Ferrari.

### FRENCH GRAND PRIX: ROUEN-LES-ESSARTS 6 July Round: 4 Race: 19 76 x 3.169 miles

| POS. | NO. | DRIVER | CAR/ENGINE | LAPS | TIME/RETIRED | GRID |
|---|---|---|---|---|---|---|
| 1 | 8 | Alberto Ascari | Ferrari | 77 | 3:00'00 | 1 |
| 2 | 10 | Giuseppe Farina | Ferrari | 76 | +1 Lap | 2 |
| 3 | 12 | Piero Taruffi | Ferrari | 75 | +2 Laps | 3 |
| 4 | 2 | Robert Manzon | Gordini | 74 | +3 Laps | 5 |
| 5 | 44 | M.Trintignant | Simca-Gordini-Gordini | 72 | +5 Laps | 6 |
| 6 | 22 | Peter Collins | HWM-Alta | 70 | +7 Laps | 8 |
| 7 | 4 | Jean Behra | Gordini | 70 | +7 Laps | 4 |
| 8 | 28 | P.Etancelin | Maserati | 70 | +7 Laps | 18 |
| 9 | 20 | Lance Macklin | HWM-Alta | 70 | +7 Laps | 14 |
| 10 | 24 | Y.G.-Cabantous | HWM-Alta | 68 | +9 Laps | 10 |
| 11 | 34 | Hirt-Fischer | Ferrari | 66 | +11 Laps | 17 |
| 12 | 38 | Franco Comotti | Ferrari | 63 | +14 Laps | 16 |
| Ret | 6 | Prince Bira | Gordini | 56 | Axle | 7 |
| Ret | 42 | Mike Hawthorn | Cooper-Bristol | 51 | Ignition | 15 |
| Ret | 16 | Graffenried-Schell | Maserati | 34 | Brakes | 12 |
| Ret | 26 | Peter Whitehead | Alta | 26 | Clutch | 13 |
| Ret | 14 | Louis Rosier | Ferrari | 17 | Engine | 9 |
| Ret | 32 | Johnny Claes | Simca-Gordini-Gordini | 15 | Engine | 20 |
| Ret | 18 | Harry Schell | Maserati | 7 | Gearbox | 11 |
| Ret | 40 | Piero Carini | Ferrari | 2 | Engine | 19 |

Winning speed: 80.131mph Lap leaders: Ascari 1-77
Pole position: Ascari, 2m 14.800s, 84.632mph
Fastest lap: Ascari, 2m 17.300s, 83.091mph

### BRITISH GRAND PRIX: SILVERSTONE 19 July Round: 5 Race: 20 85 x 2.927 miles

| POS. | NO. | DRIVER | CAR/ENGINE | LAPS | TIME/RETIRED | GRID |
|---|---|---|---|---|---|---|
| 1 | 15 | Alberto Ascari | Ferrari | 85 | 2:44'11 | 2 |
| 2 | 17 | Piero Taruffi | Ferrari | 84 | +1 Lap | 3 |
| 3 | 9 | Mike Hawthorn | Cooper-Bristol | 83 | +2 Laps | 7 |
| 4 | 6 | Dennis Poore | Connaught-Francis | 83 | +2 Laps | 8 |
| 5 | 5 | Eric Thompson | Connaught-Francis | 82 | +3 Laps | 9 |
| 6 | 16 | Giuseppe Farina | Ferrari | 82 | +3 Laps | 1 |
| 7 | 8 | Reg Parnell | Cooper-Bristol | 82 | +3 Laps | 6 |
| 8 | 14 | Roy Salvadori | Ferrari | 82 | +3 Laps | 19 |
| 9 | 4 | Ken Downing | Connaught-Francis | 82 | +3 Laps | 5 |
| 10 | 21 | Peter Whitehead | Ferrari | 81 | +4 Laps | 20 |
| 11 | 26 | Prince Bira | Gordini | 81 | +4 Laps | 10 |
| 12 | 1 | Graham Whitehead | Alta | 80 | +5 Laps | 12 |
| 13 | 19 | Rudi Fischer | Ferrari | 80 | +5 Laps | 15 |
| 14 | 27 | Johnny Claes | Simca-Gordini-Gordini | 79 | +6 Laps | 23 |
| 15 | 31 | Lance Macklin | HWM-Alta | 79 | +6 Laps | 29 |
| 16 | 3 | Ken McAlpine | Connaught-Francis | 79 | +6 Laps | 17 |
| 17 | 33 | Harry Schell | Maserati | 78 | +7 Laps | 32 |
| 18 | 34 | Gino Bianco | Maserati | 77 | +8 Laps | 28 |
| 19 | 32 | E.de Graffenried | Maserati | 76 | +9 Laps | 31 |
| 20 | 10 | Eric Brandon | Cooper-Bristol | 76 | +9 Laps | 18 |
| 21 | 23 | Tony Crook | Frazer-Nash-BMW | 75 | +10 Laps | 25 |
| 22 | 11 | Alan Brown | Cooper-Bristol | 69 | +16 Laps | 13 |
| Ret | 29 | Peter Collins | HWM-Alta | 73 | Ignition | 14 |
| Ret | 30 | Duncan Hamilton | HWM-Alta | 44 | Engine | 11 |
| Ret | 12 | Stirling Moss | ERA-Bristol | 36 | Engine | 16 |
| Ret | 25 | M.Trintignant | Gordini | 21 | Gearbox | 21 |
| Ret | 28 | Tony Gaze | HWM-Alta | 19 | Engine | 26 |
| Ret | 7 | David Murray | Cooper-Bristol | 14 | Engine | 22 |
| Ret | 24 | Robert Manzon | Gordini | 9 | Clutch | 4 |
| Ret | 20 | Peter Hirt | Ferrari | 3 | Brakes | 24 |
| Ret | 35 | Eitel Cantoni | Maserati | 0 | Brakes | 27 |
| DNS | 2 | Bill Aston | Aston-Butterworth | 0 | Non start | |

Winning speed: 90.921mph Lap leaders: Ascari 1-85
Pole position: Farina, 1m 50.000s, 95.793mph
Fastest lap: Ascari, 1m 52.000s, 94.082mph

### GERMAN GRAND PRIX: NÜRBURGRING 3 August Round: 6 Race: 21 18 x 14.173 miles

| POS. | NO. | DRIVER | CAR/ENGINE | LAPS | TIME/RETIRED | GRID |
|---|---|---|---|---|---|---|
| 1 | 101 | Alberto Ascari | Ferrari | 18 | 3:06'13.3 | 1 |
| 2 | 102 | Giuseppe Farina | Ferrari | 18 | +14.1 | 2 |
| 3 | 117 | Rudi Fischer | Ferrari | 18 | +7'10.1 | 6 |
| 4 | 103 | Piero Taruffi | Ferrari | 17 | +1 Lap | 5 |
| 5 | 108 | Jean Behra | Gordini | 17 | +1 Lap | 11 |
| 6 | 119 | Roger Laurent | Ferrari | 16 | +2 Laps | 17 |
| 7 | 121 | Fritz Riess | Veritas-BMW | 16 | +2 Laps | 12 |
| 8 | 125 | Toni Ulmen | Veritas-BMW | 16 | +2 Laps | 15 |
| 9 | 124 | H.Niedermayr | AFM-BMW | 15 | +3 Laps | 22 |
| 10 | 113 | Johnny Claes | HWM-Alta | 15 | +3 Laps | 32 |
| 11 | 128 | Hans Klenk | Veritas | 14 | +4 Laps | 8 |
| 12 | 135 | Ernst Klodwig | BMW | 14 | +4 Laps | 29 |
| Ret | 107 | Robert Manzon | Gordini | 8 | Accident | 4 |
| Ret | 123 | Willi Heeks | AFM-BMW | 7 | Retirement | 9 |
| Ret | 120 | Tony Gaze | HWM-Alta | 6 | Gearbox | 14 |
| Ret | 126 | Adolf Brudes | Veritas-BMW | 5 | Engine | 19 |
| Ret | 110 | Marcel Balsa | BMW | 5 | Retirement | 25 |
| Ret | 130 | Bernd Nacke | BMW | 5 | Ignition | 30 |
| Ret | 116 | Eitel Cantoni | Maserati | 4 | Axle | 26 |
| Ret | 136 | Rudolf Krause | BMW | 3 | Retirement | 23 |
| Ret | 118 | Rudolf Schoeller | Ferrari | 3 | Suspension | 24 |
| Ret | 114 | Bill Aston | Aston-Butterworth | 2 | Oil pressure | 21 |
| Ret | 109 | M.Trintignant | Gordini | 1 | Accident | 3 |
| Ret | 127 | Paul Pietsch | Veritas | 1 | Gearbox | 7 |
| DSQ | 105 | Felice Bonetto | Maserati | 1 | Disqualified | 10 |
| Ret | 112 | Paul Frere | HWM-Alta | 1 | Gearbox | 13 |
| Ret | 122 | Theo Helfrich | Veritas-BMW | 1 | Retirement | 18 |
| Ret | 129 | Josef Peters | Veritas-BMW | 1 | Retirement | 20 |
| Ret | 104 | Piero Carini | Ferrari | 1 | Brakes | 27 |
| Ret | 115 | Gino Bianco | Maserati | 0 | Retirement | 16 |

Winning speed: 82.200mph Lap leaders: Ascari 1-18
Pole position: Ascari, 10m 4.400s, 84.422mph
Fastest lap: Ascari, 10m 5.100s, 84.324mph

### DUTCH GRAND PRIX: ZANDVOORT 17 August Round: 7 Race: 22 90 x 2.605 miles

| POS. | NO. | DRIVER | CAR/ENGINE | LAPS | TIME/RETIRED | GRID |
|---|---|---|---|---|---|---|
| 1 | 2 | Alberto Ascari | Ferrari | 90 | 2:53'28.5 | 1 |
| 2 | 4 | Giuseppe Farina | Ferrari | 90 | +40.1 | 2 |
| 3 | 6 | Luigi Villoresi | Ferrari | 90 | +1'34.4 | 4 |
| 4 | 32 | Mike Hawthorn | Cooper-Bristol | 88 | +2 Laps | 3 |
| 5 | 10 | Robert Manzon | Gordini | 87 | +3 Laps | 6 |
| 6 | 12 | M.Trintignant | Gordini | 87 | +3 Laps | 5 |
| 7 | 28 | Duncan Hamilton | HWM-Alta | 85 | +5 Laps | 10 |
| 8 | 26 | Lance Macklin | HWM-Alta | 84 | +6 Laps | 9 |
| 9 | 16 | Landi/Flinterman | Maserati | 83 | +7 Laps | 16 |
| Ret | 34 | Ken Wharton | Frazer-Nash-Bristol | 76 | Wheel bearing | 7 |
| Ret | 36 | Stirling Moss | ERA | 73 | Engine | 18 |
| NC | 30 | D.van der Lof | HWM-Alta | 70 | Not classified | 14 |
| Ret | 22 | Ken Downing | Connaught-Francis | 27 | Oil pressure | 13 |
| Ret | 24 | Charles de Tornaco | Ferrari | 19 | Engine | 17 |
| Ret | 14 | Paul Frere | Simca-Gordini-Gordini | 15 | Clutch | 11 |
| Ret | 8 | Jean Behra | Gordini | 10 | Electrical | 6 |
| Ret | 20 | Jan Flinterman | Maserati | 7 | Differential | 15 |
| Ret | 18 | Gino Bianco | Maserati | 4 | Axle | 12 |

Winning speed: 81.102mph Lap leaders: Ascari 1-90
Pole position: Ascari, 1m 46.500s, 88.070mph
Fastest lap: Ascari, 1m 49.800s, 85.423mph

### ITALIAN GRAND PRIX: MONZA 7 September Round: 8 Race: 23 80 x 3.915 miles

| POS. | NO. | DRIVER | CAR/ENGINE | LAPS | TIME/RETIRED | GRID |
|---|---|---|---|---|---|---|
| 1 | 12 | Alberto Ascari | Ferrari | 80 | 2:50'45.6 | 1 |
| 2 | 26 | J.F.Gonzalez | Maserati | 80 | +1'01.8 | 5 |
| 3 | 16 | Luigi Villoresi | Ferrari | 80 | +2'04.2 | 2 |
| 4 | 10 | Giuseppe Farina | Ferrari | 80 | +2'11.4 | 3 |
| 5 | 22 | Felice Bonetto | Maserati | 79 | +1 Lap | 13 |
| 6 | 8 | Andre Simon | Ferrari | 79 | +1 Lap | 8 |
| 7 | 14 | Piero Taruffi | Ferrari | 77 | +3 Laps | 6 |
| 8 | 48 | Chico Landi | Maserati | 76 | +4 Laps | 18 |
| 9 | 40 | Ken Wharton | Cooper-Bristol | 76 | +4 Laps | 15 |
| 10 | 62 | Louis Rosier | Ferrari | 75 | +5 Laps | 17 |
| 11 | 50 | Eitel Cantoni | Maserati | 75 | +5 Laps | 23 |
| 12 | 30 | Dennis Poore | Connaught-Francis | 74 | +6 Laps | 19 |
| 13 | 36 | Eric Brandon | Cooper-Bristol | 73 | +7 Laps | 20 |
| 14 | 2 | Robert Manzon | Gordini | 71 | +9 Laps | 7 |
| 15 | 38 | Alan Brown | Cooper-Bristol | 68 | +12 Laps | 21 |
| Ret | 32 | Stirling Moss | Connaught-Francis | 60 | Suspension | 9 |
| Ret | 46 | Gino Bianco | Maserati | 46 | Engine | 25 |
| Ret | 6 | Jean Behra | Gordini | 42 | Engine | 11 |
| NC | 42 | Mike Hawthorn | Cooper-Bristol | 38 | Not classified | 12 |
| Ret | 24 | Franco Rol | Maserati | 24 | Engine | 16 |
| Ret | 4 | M.Trintignant | Gordini | 5 | Engine | 4 |
| Ret | 28 | Ken McAlpine | Connaught-Francis | 4 | Suspension | 2 |
| Ret | 18 | Rudi Fischer | Ferrari | 3 | Engine | 14 |
| Ret | 34 | Elie Bayol | Osca | 0 | Gearbox | 10 |
| DNQ | 70 | Charles de Tornaco | Ferrari | | | |
| DNQ | 58 | Alberto Crespo | Maserati | | | |
| DNQ | 60 | E.de Graffenried | Maserati | | | |
| DNQ | 54 | Peter Collins | HWM-Alta | | | |
| DNQ | 68 | Peter Whitehead | Ferrari | | | |
| DNQ | 56 | Tony Gaze | HWM-Alta | | | |
| DNQ | 64 | Bill Aston | Aston-Butterworth | | | |
| DNQ | 52 | Lance Macklin | HWM-Alta | | | |
| DNQ | 20 | Hans von Stuck | Ferrari | | | |
| DNQ | 44 | Piero Dusio | Cisitalia-BPM | | | |
| DNQ | 66 | Johnny Claes | Simca-Gordini-Gordini | | | |

Winning speed: 110.039mph Lap leaders: González 1-36; Ascari 37-80
Pole position: Ascari, 2m 5.700s, 112.114mph
Fastest lap: Ascari-González, 2m 6.100s, 111.758mph

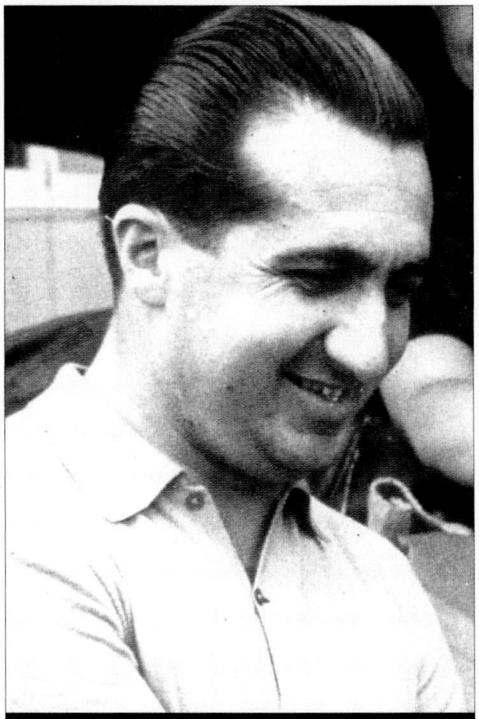
1952 world champion, Alberto Ascari

# 1953

## DRIVERS' CHAMPION: ALBERTO ASCARI

### DRIVERS' CHAMPIONSHIP

| POS | DRIVER | COUNTRY | CAR | POINTS |
|---|---|---|---|---|
| 1 | Alberto Ascari | Italy | Ferrari | 34.5 (12) |
| 2 | Juan Manuel Fangio | Argentina | Maserati | 27.5 (1.5) |
| 3 | Giuseppe Farina | Italy | Ferrari | 26 (6) |
| 4 | Mike Hawthorn | GB | Ferrari | 19 (8) |
| 5 | Luigi Villoresi | Italy | Ferrari | 17 |
| 6 | Jose Froilan Gonzalez | Argentina | Maserati | 13.5 (1) |
| 7 | Billy Vukovich | USA | Kurtis-Offenhauser | 8 |
| 8 | Emmanuel de Graffenried | Switzerland | Maserati | 7 |
| 9 | Felice Bonetto | Italy | Maserati | 6.5 |
| 10 | Art Cross | USA | Kurtis-Offenhauser | 6 |
| 11 | Maurice Trintignant | France | Gordini | 4 |
| = | Onofre Marimon | Argentina | Maserati | 4 |
| 13 | Oscar Galvez | Argentina | Maserati | 2 |
| = | Jack McGrath | USA | Kurtis-Offenhauser | 2 |
| = | Hermann Lang | West Germany | Maserati | 2 |
| = | Sam Hanks | USA | Kurtis-Offenhauser | 2 |
| = | Duane Carter | USA | Kurtis-Offenhauser | 2 |
| 18 | Fred Agabashian | USA | Kurtis-Offenhauser | 1.5 |
| = | Paul Russo | USA | Kurtis-Offenhauser | 1.5 |
| | Jean Behra | France | Gordini | |
| | Harry Schell | USA | Gordini | |
| | John Barber | GB | Cooper-Bristol | |
| | Alan Brown | GB | Cooper-Bristol | |
| | Adolfo Schwelm-Cruz | Argentina | Cooper-Bristol | |
| | Pablo Birger | Argentina | Simca-Gordini | |
| | Carlos Menditéguy | Argentina | Gordini | |
| | Robert Manzon | France | Gordini | |
| | Ken Wharton | GB | Cooper -Bristol | |
| | Stirling Moss | GB | Connaught-Lea-Francis, Cooper -Alta | |
| | Louis Rosier | France | Ferrari | |
| | Peter Collins | GB | HWM-Alta | |
| | Lance Macklin | GB | HWM-Alta | |
| | Roy Salvadori | GB | Connaught-Lea-Francis | |
| | Ken McAlpine | GB | Connaught-Lea-Francis | |
| | Roberto Mieres | Argentina | Gordini | |
| | Fred Wacker | USA | Gordini | |
| | Paul Frere | Belgium | HWM-Alta | |
| | Arthur Legat | Belgium | Veritas-Meteor | |
| | Georges Berger | Belgium | Simca-Gordini | |
| | André Pilette | Belgium | Connaught-Lea-Francis | |
| | Johnny Claes | Belgium | Maserati, Connaught-Lea-Francis | |
| | Charles de Tornaco | Belgium | Ferrari | |
| | Yves Giraud-Cabantous | France | HWM-Alta | |
| | Elie Bayol | France | Osca | |
| | Louis Chiron | Monaco | Osca | |
| | Birabongse Bhanuban | Thailand | Connaught-Lea-Francis, Maserati | |
| | Bob Gerard | GB | Cooper-Bristol | |
| | Tony Crook | GB | Cooper-Alta | |
| | Duncan Hamilton | GB | HWM-Alta | |
| | Ian Stewart | GB | Connaught-Lea-Francis | |
| | Tony Rolt | GB | Connaught-Lea-Francis | |
| | Jimmy Stewart | GB | Cooper-Bristol | |
| | Peter Walker | GB | Connaught-Lea-Francis | |
| | Peter Whitehead | GB | Cooper-Alta | |
| | Jack Fairman | GB | HWM-Alta, Connaught-Lea-Fancis | |
| | Jacques Swaters | Belgium | Ferrari | |
| | Rodney Nuckey | GB | Cooper-Bristol | |
| | Theo Helfrich | West Germany | Veritas | |
| | Wolfgan Seidel | West Germany | Veritas | |
| | Ernst Loof | West Germany | Veritas-Meteor | |
| | Hans Hermann | West Germany | Veritas-Meteor | |
| | Ernst Klodwig | East Germany | Heck-BMW | |
| | Rudolf Krause | West Germany | BMW-Eigenbau | |
| | Hans Stuck | West Germany | AFM-Kuechen | |
| | Erwin Bauer | West Germany | Veritas | |
| | Guenther Bechem | West Germany | AFM-BMW | |
| | Kurt Adolff | West Germany | Ferrari | |
| | Theo Fitzau | West Germany | AFM-BMW | |
| | Willi Heeks | West Germany | Veritas-Meteor | |
| | Oto Karch | West Germany | Veritas | |
| | Edgar Barth | East Germany | EMW-BMW | |
| | Helmut Glöckler | West Germany | EMW-BMW | |
| | Max de Terra | Switzerland | Ferrari | |
| | Albert Scherrer | Switzerland | HWM-Alta | |
| | Peter Hirt | Switzerland | Ferrari | |
| | Chico Landi | Brazil | Maserati | |
| | Sergio Mantovani | Italy | Maserati | |
| | Luigi Musso | Italy | Maserati | |
| | Umberto Maglioli | Italy | Ferrari | |
| | John Fitch | USA | HWM-Alta | |
| | Piero Carini | Italy | Ferrari | |

**Points for top five finishers (8, 6, 4, 3, 2) plus a point for fastest lap. Only the best four scores counted towards the championship. Points for shared drives were divided equally between the drivers.**



### ARGENTINE GRAND PRIX: BUENOS AIRES 18 January Round: 1 Race: 24 97 x 2.431 miles

| POS. | NO. | DRIVER | CAR/ENGINE | LAPS | TIME/RETIRED | GRID |
|---|---|---|---|---|---|---|
| 1 | 10 | Alberto Ascari | Ferrari | 97 | 3:01'04.6 | 1 |
| 2 | 14 | Luigi Villoresi | Ferrari | 96 | +1 Lap | 3 |
| 3 | 4 | J.F.Gonzalez | Maserati | 96 | +1 Lap | 5 |
| 4 | 16 | Mike Hawthorn | Ferrari | 96 | +1 Lap | 6 |
| 5 | 8 | Oscar Galvez | Maserati | 96 | +1 Lap | 9 |
| 6 | 30 | Jean Behra | Gordini | 94 | +3 Laps | 11 |
| 7 | 28 | Trintignant/Schell | Gordini | 91 | +6 Laps | 7 |
| 8 | 22 | John Barber | Cooper-Bristol | 90 | +7 Laps | 16 |
| 9 | 20 | Alan Brown | Cooper-Bristol | 87 | +10 Laps | 12 |
| Ret | 26 | Robert Manzon | Gordini | 67 | Wheel | 8 |
| Ret | 2 | Juan Manuel Fangio | Maserati | 36 | Transmission | 2 |
| Ret | 6 | Felice Bonetto | Maserati | 32 | Transmission | 15 |
| Ret | 12 | Giuseppe Farina | Ferrari | 31 | Accident | 4 |
| Ret | 32 | C.Menditeguy | Gordini | 24 | Gearbox | 10 |
| Ret | 34 | Pablo Birger | Simca-Gordini-Gordini | 21 | Differential | 14 |
| Ret | 24 | Adolfo S-Cruz | Cooper-Bristol | 20 | Wheel | 13 |

Winning speed: 78.129mph Lap leaders: Ascari 1-97
Pole position: Ascari, 1m 55.400s, 75.831mph
Fastest lap: Ascari, 1m 48.400s, 80.728mph

### INDIANAPOLIS 500 30 May Round: 2 Race: 25 200 x 2.500 miles

| POS. | NO. | DRIVER | CAR/ENGINE | LAPS | TIME/RETIRED | GRID |
|---|---|---|---|---|---|---|
| 1 | 14 | Bill Vukovich | Kurtis Kraft-Offenhauser | 200 | 3:53'01.69 | 1 |
| 2 | 16 | Art Cross | Kurtis Kraft-Offenhauser | 200 | +3'30.87 | 12 |
| 3 | 3 | Hanks/Carter | Kurtis Kraft-Offenhauser | 200 | +4'11.50 | 9 |
| 4 | 59 | Agabashian/Russo/McGrath | Kurtis Kraft-Offenhauser | 200 | +4'39.24 | 2 |
| 5 | 5 | Jack McGrath | Kurtis Kraft-Offenhauser | 200 | +7'49.64 | 3 |
| 6 | 48 | Jimmy Daywalt | Kurtis Kraft-Offenhauser | 200 | +8'10.21 | 21 |
| 7 | 2 | Rathmann/Johnson | Kurtis Kraft-Offenhauser | 200 | +8'46.02 | 25 |
| 8 | 12 | Ernie McCoy | Stevens-Offenhauser | 200 | +10'04.55 | 20 |
| 9 | 98 | B'hausen/Stevenson/Hartley | Kuzma-Offenhauser | 196 | Accident | 6 |
| 10 | 53 | Jimmy Davies | Kurtis Kraft-Offenhauser | 193 | +7 Laps | 32 |
| 11 | 9 | Duke Nalon | Kurtis Kraft-Novi | 191 | Accident | 26 |
| 12 | 73 | Scott/Scarborough | Kurtis Kraft-Offenhauser | 190 | +10 Laps | 19 |
| 13 | 88 | Manny Ayulo | Kuzma-Offenhauser | 184 | Engine | 4 |
| 14 | 8 | Jimmy Bryan | Schroeder-Offenhauser | 183 | +17 Laps | 31 |
| 15 | 49 | Holland/Rathmann | Kurtis Kraft-Offenhauser | 177 | Magneto | 28 |
| 16 | 92 | Ward/Linden/Dinsmore | Kurtis Kraft-Offenhauser | 177 | Axle | 10 |
| 17 | 23 | Faulkner/Mantz | Kurtis Kraft-Offenhauser | 176 | +24 Laps | 14 |
| Ret | 22 | Marshall Teague | Kurtis Kraft-Offenhauser | 169 | Oil leak | 22 |
| Ret | 62 | Webb/Thomson/Holmes | Kurtis Kraft-Offenhauser | 166 | Oil leak | 18 |
| Ret | 51 | Bob Sweikert | Kuzma-Offenhauser | 151 | Suspension | 29 |
| Ret | 83 | Mike Nazaruk | Turner-Offenhauser | 146 | Transmission | 23 |
| Ret | 77 | Pat Flaherty | Kurtis Kraft-Offenhauser | 115 | Accident | 24 |
| Ret | 55 | Hoyt/Stevenson/Linden | Kurtis Kraft-Offenhauser | 107 | Overheating | 7 |
| Ret | 4 | Duane Carter | Lesovsky-Offenhauser | 94 | Ignition | 27 |
| Ret | 7 | Paul Russo | Kurtis Kraft-Offenhauser | 89 | Magneto | 17 |
| Ret | 21 | Johnnie Parsons | Kurtis Kraft-Offenhauser | 86 | Engine | 8 |
| Ret | 38 | Don Freeland | Watson-Offenhauser | 76 | Accident | 15 |
| Ret | 41 | Gene Hartley | Kurtis Kraft-Offenhauser | 53 | Accident | 13 |
| Ret | 97 | Chuck Stevenson | Kuzma-Offenhauser | 42 | Fuel leak | 16 |
| Ret | 99 | Cal Niday | Kurtis Kraft-Offenhauser | 30 | Magneto | 30 |
| Ret | 29 | Bob Scott | Bromme-Offenhauser | 14 | Oil leak | 11 |
| Ret | 56 | Johnny Thomson | Del Roy-Offenhauser | 6 | Ignition | 33 |
| Ret | 32 | Andy Linden | Stevens-Offenhauser | 3 | Accident | 5 |

Winning speed: 128.740mph
Pole position: Vukovich, 1m 05.032s, 138.393mph
Fastest lap: Vukovich, 1m 06.240s, 135.870mph

### DUTCH GRAND PRIX: ZANDVOORT 7 June Round: 3 Race: 26 90 x 2.605 miles

| POS. | NO. | DRIVER | CAR/ENGINE | LAPS | TIME/RETIRED | GRID |
|---|---|---|---|---|---|---|
| 1 | 2 | Alberto Ascari | Ferrari | 90 | 2:53'35.8 | 1 |
| 2 | 6 | Giuseppe Farina | Ferrari | 90 | +10.4 | 3 |
| 3 | 16 | Gonzalez/Bonetto | Maserati | 89 | +1 Lap | 13 |
| 4 | 8 | Mike Hawthorn | Ferrari | 89 | +1 Lap | 6 |
| 5 | 18 | E.de Graffenried | Maserati | 88 | +2 Laps | 7 |
| 6 | 24 | M.Trintignant | Gordini | 87 | +3 Laps | 12 |
| 7 | 10 | Louis Rosier | Ferrari | 86 | +4 Laps | 8 |
| 8 | 36 | Peter Collins | HWM-Alta | 84 | +6 Laps | 16 |
| 9 | 34 | Stirling Moss | Connaught-Francis | 83 | +7 Laps | 9 |
| Ret | 4 | Luigi Villoresi | Ferrari | 67 | Throttle | 4 |
| Ret | 28 | Ken McAlpine | Connaught-Francis | 63 | Engine | 14 |
| Ret | 20 | Harry Schell | Gordini | 59 | Transmission | 10 |
| NC | 30 | Johnny Claes | Connaught-Francis | 52 | Not classified | 17 |
| Ret | 12 | Juan Manuel Fangio | Maserati | 36 | Axle | 2 |
| Ret | 22 | Roberto Mieres | Gordini | 28 | Transmission | 19 |
| Ret | 14 | J.F.Gonzalez | Maserati | 22 | Axle | 5 |
| Ret | 32 | Ken Wharton | Cooper-Bristol | 19 | Physical | 18 |
| Ret | 26 | Roy Salvadori | Connaught-Francis | 14 | Engine | 11 |
| Ret | 38 | Lance Macklin | HWM-Alta | 7 | Throttle | 15 |

Winning speed: 81.045mph Lap leaders: Ascari 1-90
Pole position: Ascari, 1m 51.100s, 84.424mph
Fastest lap: Villoresi, 1m 52.800s, 83.151mph

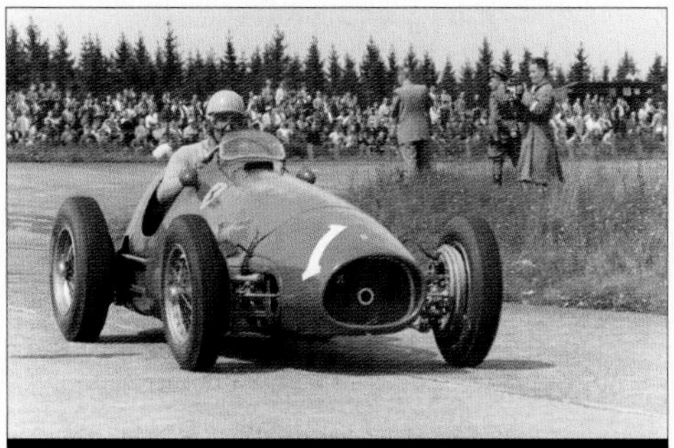
1953 world champion, Alberto Ascari in the type 500 Ferrari.

BELGIAN GRAND PRIX: SPA-FRANCORCHAMPS 21 June Round: 4 Race: 27 36 x 8.774 miles

| POS. | NO. | DRIVER | CAR/ENGINE | LAPS | TIME/RETIRED | GRID |
|---|---|---|---|---|---|---|
| 1 | 10 | Alberto Ascari | Ferrari | 36 | 2:48'30.3 | 2 |
| 2 | 8 | Luigi Villoresi | Ferrari | 36 | +2'48.2 | 5 |
| 3 | 28 | Onofre Marimon | Maserati | 35 | +1 Lap | 16 |
| 4 | 30 | E.de Graffenried | Maserati | 35 | +1 Lap | 9 |
| 5 | 18 | M.Trintignant | Gordini | 35 | +1 Lap | 8 |
| 6 | 14 | Mike Hawthorn | Ferrari | 35 | +1 Lap | 7 |
| 7 | 20 | Harry Schell | Gordini | 33 | +3 Laps | 12 |
| 8 | 32 | Louis Rosier | Ferrari | 33 | +3 Laps | 13 |
| 9 | 38 | Fred Wacker | Gordini | 32 | +4 Laps | 15 |
| 10 | 24 | Paul Frere | HWM-Alta | 30 | +6 Laps | 11 |
| 11 | 40 | Andre Pilette | Connaught-Francis | 29 | +7 Laps | 18 |
| Ret | 6 | Claes/Fangio | Maserati | 35 | Accident | 10 |
| Ret | 22 | Lance Macklin | HWM-Alta | 19 | Engine | 17 |
| Ret | 12 | Giuseppe Farina | Ferrari | 16 | Engine | 4 |
| Ret | 4 | Juan Manuel Fangio | Maserati | 13 | Engine | 1 |
| Ret | 2 | J.F.Gonzalez | Maserati | 11 | Throttle | 3 |
| Ret | 16 | Jean Behra | Gordini | 9 | Engine | 14 |
| Ret | 26 | Peter Collins | HWM-Alta | 4 | Clutch | 16 |
| Ret | 34 | Georges Berger | Simca-Gordini-Gordini | 3 | Engine | 20 |
| Ret | 36 | Arthur Legat | Veritas | 0 | Transmission | 19 |

Winning speed: 112.467mph Lap leaders: González 1-11; Fangio 12-13; Ascari 14-36
Pole position: Fangio, 4m 30.000s, 116.983mph
Fastest lap: González, 4m 34.000s, 115.276mph

FRENCH GRAND PRIX: REIMS 5 July Round: 5 Race: 28 60 x 5.18 miles

| POS. | NO. | DRIVER | CAR/ENGINE | LAPS | TIME/RETIRED | GRID |
|---|---|---|---|---|---|---|
| 1 | 16 | Mike Hawthorn | Ferrari | 60 | 2:44'18.6 | 7 |
| 2 | 18 | Juan Manuel Fangio | Maserati | 60 | +1.0 | 4 |
| 3 | 20 | J.F.Gonzalez | Maserati | 60 | +1.4 | 5 |
| 4 | 10 | Alberto Ascari | Ferrari | 60 | +4.6 | 1 |
| 5 | 14 | Giuseppe Farina | Ferrari | 60 | +1'07.6 | 6 |
| 6 | 12 | Luigi Villoresi | Ferrari | 60 | +1'15.9 | 3 |
| 7 | 46 | E.de Graffenried | Maserati | 58 | +2 Laps | 9 |
| 8 | 44 | Louis Rosier | Ferrari | 56 | +4 Laps | 10 |
| 9 | 22 | Onofre Marimon | Maserati | 55 | +5 Laps | 8 |
| 10 | 2 | Jean Behra | Gordini | 55 | +5 Laps | 22 |
| 11 | 38 | Bob Gerard | Cooper-Bristol | 55 | +5 Laps | 12 |
| 12 | 48 | Johnny Claes | Connaught-Francis | 53 | +7 Laps | 21 |
| 13 | 28 | Peter Collins | HWM-Alta | 52 | +8 Laps | 17 |
| 14 | 30 | Y.G.-Cabantous | HWM-Alta | 50 | +10 Laps | 18 |
| 15 | 32 | Louis Chiron | Osca | 43 | +17 Laps | 25 |
| Ret | 24 | Felice Bonetto | Maserati | 42 | Engine | 2 |
| Ret | 36 | Stirling Moss | Cooper-Alta | 38 | Clutch | 13 |
| Ret | 42 | Prince Bira | Connaught-Francis | 29 | Differential | 11 |
| Ret | 34 | Elie Bayol | Osca | 18 | Engine | 15 |
| Ret | 40 | Ken Wharton | Cooper-Bristol | 17 | Wheel bearing | 14 |
| Ret | 4 | M.Trintignant | Gordini | 14 | Transmission | 23 |
| Ret | 26 | Lance Macklin | HWM-Alta | 9 | Clutch | 16 |
| Ret | 6 | Harry Schell | Gordini | 4 | Engine | 20 |
| Ret | 8 | Roberto Mieres | Gordini | 4 | Axle | 24 |
| Ret | 50 | Roy Salvadori | Connaught-Francis | 2 | Ignition | 19 |

Winning speed: 113.637mph Lap leaders: González 1-29; Fangio 30-31, 35-36, 39-41, 45-47, 49-53, 55-56; Hawthorn 32-34, 37-38, 42-44, 48, 54, 57-60
Pole position: Ascari, 2m 41.200s, 115.829mph
Fastest lap:Fangio-Ascari, 2m 41.100s, 115.901mph

BRITISH GRAND PRIX: SILVERSTONE 18 July Round: 6 Race: 29 90 x 2.927 miles

| POS. | NO. | DRIVER | CAR/ENGINE | LAPS | TIME/RETIRED | GRID |
|---|---|---|---|---|---|---|
| 1 | 5 | Alberto Ascari | Ferrari | 90 | 2:50'00 | 1 |
| 2 | 23 | Juan Manuel Fangio | Maserati | 90 | +1'00 | 4 |
| 3 | 6 | Giuseppe Farina | Ferrari | 88 | +2 Laps | 5 |
| 4 | 24 | J.F.Gonzalez | Maserati | 88 | +2 Laps | 2 |
| 5 | 8 | Mike Hawthorn | Ferrari | 87 | +3 Laps | 3 |
| 6 | 25 | Felice Bonetto | Maserati | 82 | +8 Laps | 16 |
| 7 | 10 | Prince Bira | Connaught-Francis | 82 | +8 Laps | 19 |
| 8 | 16 | Ken Wharton | Cooper-Bristol | 80 | +10 Laps | 11 |
| 9 | 20 | Peter Whitehead | Cooper-Alta | 79 | +11 Laps | 14 |
| 10 | 9 | Louis Rosier | Ferrari | 78 | +12 Laps | 24 |
| Ret | 18 | Jimmy Stewart | Cooper-Bristol | 79 | Spun off | 15 |
| Ret | 14 | Tony Rolt | Connaught-Francis | 70 | Halfshaft | 10 |
| Ret | 7 | Luigi Villoresi | Ferrari | 65 | Axle | 6 |
| Ret | 26 | Onofre Marimon | Maserati | 65 | Engine | 7 |
| Ret | 19 | Alan Brown | Cooper-Bristol | 56 | Overheating | 21 |
| Ret | 2 | Peter Collins | HWM-Alta | 56 | Spun off | 23 |
| Ret | 4 | Jack Fairman | HWM-Alta | 54 | Clutch | 27 |
| Ret | 12 | Roy Salvadori | Connaught-Francis | 50 | Wheel | 28 |
| Ret | 31 | E.de Graffenried | Maserati | 34 | Clutch | 26 |
| Ret | 1 | Lance Macklin | HWM-Alta | 31 | Clutch | 12 |
| Ret | 30 | Jean Behra | Gordini | 30 | Fuel pump | 22 |
| Ret | 15 | Ian Stewart | Connaught-Francis | 24 | Ignition | 20 |
| Ret | 29 | M.Trintignant | Gordini | 14 | Axle | 8 |
| Ret | 3 | Duncan Hamilton | HWM-Alta | 14 | Clutch | 25 |
| Ret | 17 | Bob Gerard | Cooper-Bristol | 8 | Suspension | 18 |
| Ret | 28 | Harry Schell | Gordini | 5 | Electrical | 9 |
| Ret | 11 | Ken McAlpine | Connaught-Francis | 0 | Retirement | 13 |
| Ret | 22 | Tony Crook | Cooper-Bristol | 0 | Fuel system | 25 |

Winning speed: 92.975mph Lap leaders: Ascari 1-90
Pole position: Ascari, 1m 48.000s, 97.567mph
Fastest lap: Ascari-González, 1m 50.000s, 95.793mph

GERMAN GRAND PRIX: NÜRBURGRING 2 August Round: 7 Race: 30 18 x 14.173 miles

| POS. | NO. | DRIVER | CAR/ENGINE | LAPS | TIME/RETIRED | GRID |
|---|---|---|---|---|---|---|
| 1 | 2 | Giuseppe Farina | Ferrari | 18 | 3:02'25.0 | 3 |
| 2 | 5 | Juan Manuel Fangio | Maserati | 18 | 1'04.0 | 2 |
| 3 | 3 | Mike Hawthorn | Ferrari | 18 | 1'43.6 | 4 |
| 4 | 7 | Felice Bonetto | Maserati | 18 | 8'48.6 | 7 |
| 5 | 17 | E.de Graffenried | Maserati | 17 | +1 Lap | 11 |
| 6 | 19 | Stirling Moss | Cooper-Alta | 17 | +1 Lap | 12 |
| 7 | 18 | Jacques Swaters | Ferrari | 17 | +1 Lap | 19 |
| 8 | 1 | Ascari/Villoresi | Ferrari | 17 | +1 Lap | 1 |
| 9 | 31 | Hans Herrmann | Veritas | 17 | +1 Lap | 14 |
| 10 | 20 | Louis Rosier | Ferrari | 17 | +1 Lap | 22 |
| 11 | 40 | Rodney Nuckey | Cooper-Bristol | 16 | +2 Laps | 20 |
| 12 | 24 | Theo Helfrich | Veritas | 16 | +2 Laps | 28 |
| 13 | 16 | Ken McAlpine | Connaught-Francis | 16 | +2 Laps | 16 |
| 14 | 36 | Rudolf Krause | BMW | 16 | +2 Laps | 26 |
| 15 | 37 | Ernst Klodwig | BMW | 15 | +3 Laps | 32 |
| 16 | 22 | Wolfgang Seidel | Veritas | 14 | +4 Laps | 29 |
| Ret | 4 | Villoresi/Ascari | Ferrari | 15 | Engine | 6 |
| Ret | 38 | Alan Brown | Cooper-Bristol | 15 | Engine | 17 |
| Ret | 8 | Onofre Marimon | Maserati | 13 | Suspension | 8 |
| Ret | 35 | Edgar Barth | EMW-BMW | 12 | Retirement | 24 |
| Ret | 12 | Johnny Claes | Connaught-Francis | 12 | Retirement | 25 |
| Ret | 26 | Oswald Karch | Veritas | 10 | Retirement | 34 |
| Ret | 23 | Willi Heeks | Veritas | 8 | Retirement | 18 |
| Ret | 9 | Jean Behra | Gordini | 7 | Gearbox | 9 |
| Ret | 11 | Harry Schell | Gordini | 6 | Engine | 10 |
| Ret | 14 | Prince Bira | Connaught-Francis | 6 | Suspension | 15 |
| Ret | 28 | Theo Fitzau | AFM-BMW | 3 | Retirement | 21 |
| Ret | 34 | Kurt Adolff | Ferrari | 3 | Retirement | 27 |
| Ret | 41 | Guenther Bechem | AFM-BMW | 2 | Retirement | 30 |
| Ret | 10 | M.Trintignant | Gordini | 1 | Differential | 5 |
| Ret | 15 | Roy Salvadori | Connaught-Francis | 1 | Engine | 13 |
| Ret | 32 | Erwin Bauer | Veritas | 1 | Retirement | 33 |
| Ret | 21 | Hans von Stuck | AFM-Bristol | 0 | Retirement | 23 |
| Ret | 30 | Ernst Loof | Veritas | 0 | Fuel pump | 31 |

Winning speed: 83.914mph Lap Leaders: Ascari 1-4; Hawthorn 5-7; Farina 8-18
Pole position: Ascari, 9m 59.800s, 85.069mph
Fastest lap: Ascari, 9m 56.000s, 85.612mph

SWISS GRAND PRIX: BREMGARTEN 23 August Round: 8 Race: 31 65 x 4.524 miles

| POS. | NO. | DRIVER | CAR/ENGINE | LAPS | TIME/RETIRED | GRID |
|---|---|---|---|---|---|---|
| 1 | 46 | Alberto Ascari | Ferrari | 65 | 3:01'34.40 | 2 |
| 2 | 24 | Giuseppe Farina | Ferrari | 65 | +1'12.93 | 3 |
| 3 | 26 | Mike Hawthorn | Ferrari | 65 | +1'35.96 | 7 |
| 4 | 32 | Bonetto/Fangio | Maserati | 64 | +1 Lap | 1 |
| 5 | 34 | Hermann Lang | Maserati | 62 | +3 Laps | 11 |
| 6 | 28 | Luigi Villoresi | Ferrari | 62 | +3 Laps | 6 |
| 7 | 20 | Ken Wharton | Cooper-Bristol | 62 | +3 Laps | 9 |
| 8 | 40 | Max de Terra | Ferrari | 51 | +14 Laps | 19 |
| 9 | 18 | Albert Scherrer | HWM-Alta | 49 | +16 Laps | 18 |
| Ret | 4 | Chico Landi | Maserati | 54 | Gearbox | 20 |
| Ret | 42 | E.de Graffenried | Maserati | 49 | Transmission | 8 |
| Ret | 36 | Onofre Marimon | Maserati | 46 | Engine | 5 |
| Ret | 8 | M.Trintignant | Gordini | 43 | Axle | 4 |
| Ret | 6 | Jean Behra | Gordini | 37 | Oil pressure | 12 |
| Ret | 30 | Bonetto/Fangio | Maserati | 29 | Engine | 10 |
| Ret | 16 | Lance Macklin | HWM-Alta | 29 | Engine | 15 |
| Ret | 38 | Peter Hirt | Ferrari | 17 | Engine | 17 |
| Ret | 14 | Paul Frere | HWM-Alta | 1 | Engine | 16 |
| Ret | 2 | Jacques Swaters | Ferrari | 0 | Spun off | 13 |
| Ret | 10 | Louis Rosier | Ferrari | 0 | Spun off | 14 |

Winning speed: 97.162mph Lap leaders: Ascari 1-40, 54-65; Farina 41-53
Pole position: Fangio, 2m 40.100s, 101.717mph
Fastest lap: Ascari, 2m 41.300sec, 100.960mph

ITALIAN GRAND PRIX: MONZA 13 September Round: 9 Race: 32 80 x 3.915 miles

| POS. | NO. | DRIVER | CAR/ENGINE | LAPS | TIME/RETIRED | GRID |
|---|---|---|---|---|---|---|
| 1 | 50 | Juan Manuel Fangio | Maserati | 80 | 2:49'45.9 | 2 |
| 2 | 6 | Giuseppe Farina | Ferrari | 79 | +1 Lap | 3 |
| 3 | 2 | Luigi Villoresi | Ferrari | 79 | +1 Lap | 5 |
| 4 | 8 | Mike Hawthorn | Ferrari | 79 | +1 Lap | 6 |
| 5 | 36 | M.Trintignant | Gordini | 79 | +1 Lap | 8 |
| 6 | 40 | Roberto Mieres | Gordini | 77 | +3 Laps | 16 |
| 7 | 56 | Mantovani/Musso | Maserati | 76 | +4 Laps | 12 |
| 8 | 10 | Umberto Maglioli | Ferrari | 75 | +5 Laps | 11 |
| 9 | 38 | Harry Schell | Gordini | 75 | +5 Laps | 15 |
| 10 | 32 | Louis Chiron | Osca | 72 | +8 Laps | 25 |
| 11 | 44 | Prince Bira | Maserati | 72 | +8 Laps | 23 |
| 12 | 46 | Alan Brown | Cooper-Bristol | 70 | +10 Laps | 24 |
| 13 | 28 | Stirling Moss | Cooper-Alta | 70 | +10 Laps | 10 |
| 14 | 48 | Hans von Stuck | AFM-Bristol | 67 | +13 Laps | 29 |
| 15 | 16 | Y.G.-Cabantous | HWM-Alta | 67 | +13 Laps | 28 |
| 16 | 64 | Louis Rosier | Ferrari | 65 | +15 Laps | 17 |
| Ret | 4 | Alberto Ascari | Ferrari | 79 | Accident | 1 |
| Ret | 52 | Felice Bonetto | Maserati | 77 | Out of fuel | 7 |
| Ret | 54 | Onofre Marimon | Maserati | 75 | Accident | 4 |
| Ret | 58 | E.de Graffenried | Maserati | 70 | Engine | 9 |
| NC | 20 | Jack Fairman | Connaught-Francis | 61 | Not classified | 22 |
| NC | 30 | Ken Wharton | Cooper-Bristol | 57 | Not classified | 19 |
| NC | 24 | Ken McAlpine | Connaught-Francis | 56 | Not classified | 18 |
| Ret | 12 | Piero Carini | Ferrari | 40 | Engine | 20 |
| Ret | 22 | Roy Salvadori | Connaught-Francis | 33 | Throttle | 14 |
| Ret | 42 | Chico Landi | Maserati | 18 | Engine | 21 |
| Ret | 34 | Elie Bayol | Osca | 17 | Engine | 13 |
| Ret | 18 | John Fitch | HWM-Alta | 14 | Engine | 26 |
| Ret | 26 | Johnny Claes | Connaught-Francis | 7 | Fuel system | 30 |
| Ret | 14 | Lance Macklin | HWM-Alta | 6 | Engine | 27 |

Winning speed: 110.684mph Lap leaders: Ascari 1-6, 9, 14-24, 29-33, 36-40, 42-45, 47-49, 53-79; Fangio 7-8,11, 25, 27-28, 34-35, 41, 50-52, 80; Farina 10,12-13,26,46
Pole position: Ascari, 2m 2.700s, 114.855mph
Fastest lap: Fangio, 2m 4.500s, 113.194mph

# 1954

## DRIVERS' CHAMPION: JUAN MANUEL FANGIO

DRIVERS' CHAMPIONSHIP

| POS | DRIVER | COUNTRY | CAR | POINTS |
|---|---|---|---|---|
| 1 | Juan Manuel Fangio | Argentina | Maserati, Mercedes-Benz | 42 (15.14) |
| 2 | Jose Froilan Gonzalez | Argentina | Ferrari | 25.14 (1.5) |
| 3 | Mike Hawthorn | GB | Ferrari | 24.64 |
| 4 | Maurice Trintignant | France | Ferrari | 17 |
| 5 | Karl Kling | West Germany | Mercedes-Benz | 12 |
| 6 | Billy Vukovich | USA | Kurtis-Offenhauser | 8 |
| = | Hans Hermann | West Germany | Mercedes-Benz | 8 |
| 8 | Giuseppe Farina | Italy | Ferrari | 6 |
| = | Jimmy Bryan | USA | Kuzma-Offenhauser | 6 |
| = | Luigi Musso | Italy | Maserati | 6 |
| = | Roberto Mieres | Argentina | Maserati | 6 |
| 12 | Stirling Moss | GB | Maserati | 4.14 |
| = | Onofre Marimon | Argentina | Maserati | 4.14 |
| 14 | Jack McGrath | USA | Kurtis-Offenhauser | 4 |
| = | Robert Manzon | France | Ferrari | 4 |
| = | Sergio Mantovani | Italy | Maserati | 4 |
| 17 | Prince Bira | Thailand | Maserati | 3 |
| 18 | Elie Bayol | France | Gordini | 2 |
| = | Mike Nazurak | USA | Kurtis-Offenhauser | 2 |
| = | André Pilette | Belgium | Gordini | 2 |
| = | Luigi Villoresi | Italy | Maserati, Lancia | 2 |
| = | Umberto Maglioli | Italy | Ferrari | 2 |
| 22 | Troy Ruttman | USA | Kurtis-Offenhauser | 1.5 |
| = | Duane Carter | USA | Kurtis-Offenhauser | 1.5 |
| 24 | Alberto Ascari | Italy | Maserati, Ferrari, Lancia | 1.14 |
| 25 | Jean Behra | France | Gordini | 0.14 |
| | Harry Schell | USA | Maserati | |
| | Louis Rosier | France | Ferrari, Maserati | |
| | Emmanuel de Graffenried | Switzerland | Maserati | |
| | Jorge Daponte | Argentina | Maserati | |
| | Roger Loyer | France | Gordini | |
| | Carlos Menditéquy | Argentina | Maserati | |
| | Jacques Swaters | Belgium | Ferrari | |
| | Paul Frere | Belgium | Gordini | |
| | Ken Wharton | GB | Maserati | |
| | Jacques Pollet | France | Gordini | |
| | Georges Berger | Belgium | Gordini | |
| | Lance Macklin | GB | HWM-Alta | |
| | Roy Salvadori | GB | Maserati | |
| | Bob Gerard | GB | Cooper -Bristol | |
| | Don Beauman | GB | Connaught-Lea-Francis | |
| | Leslie Marr | GB | Connaught-Lea-Francis | |
| | Leslie Thorne | GB | Connaught-Lea-Francis | |
| | Horace Gould | GB | Cooper-Bristol | |
| | Eric Brandon | GB | Cooper-Bristol | |
| | Peter Whitehead | GB | Cooper-Alta | |
| | Peter Collins | GB | Vanwall Special | |
| | Clemar Bucci | Argentina | Gordini | |
| | Reg Parnell | GB | Ferrari | |
| | John Riseley-Pritchard | GB | Connaught-Lea-Francis | |
| | Ron Flockhart | GB | Maserati | |
| | Bill Whitehouse | GB | Connaught-Lea-Francis | |
| | Piero Taruffi | Italy | Ferrari | |
| | Theo Helfrich | West Germany | Klenk-Meteor BMW | |
| | Hermann Lang | West Germany | Mercedes-Benz | |
| | Fred Wacker | USA | Gordini | |
| | Giovanni de Riu | Italy | Maserati | |
| | Francesco Godia-Sales | Italy | Maserati | |
| | Ottorino Volonterio | Switzerland | Maserati | |

**Points for top five finishers (8, 6, 4, 3, 2) plus a point for fastest lap. Only the best five scores counted towards the championship. Points for shared drives (except where 'insufficient distance' was deemed to have been covered by one of the drivers) and shared fastest laps were divided equally between the drivers. Drivers sharing two cars in a race received points only for their highest finish.**

ARGENTINE GRAND PRIX: BUENOS AIRES 17 January Round: 1 Race: 33 87 x 2.431 miles

| POS. | NO. | DRIVER | CAR/ENGINE | LAPS | TIME/RETIRED | GRID |
|---|---|---|---|---|---|---|
| 1 | 2 | Juan Manuel Fangio | Maserati | 87 | 3:00'55.8 | 3 |
| 2 | 10 | Giuseppe Farina | Ferrari | 87 | +1'19.0 | 1 |
| 3 | 12 | J.F.Gonzalez | Ferrari | 87 | +2'01.0 | 2 |
| 4 | 26 | M.Trintignant | Ferrari | 86 | +1 Lap | 5 |
| 5 | 20 | Elie Bayol | Gordini | 85 | +2 Laps | 15 |
| 6 | 28 | Harry Schell | Maserati | 84 | +3 Laps | 11 |
| 7 | 8 | Prince Bira | Maserati | 83 | +4 Laps | 10 |
| 8 | 30 | E.de Graffenried | Maserati | 83 | +4 Laps | 13 |
| 9 | 16 | Umberto Maglioli | Ferrari | 82 | +5 Laps | 12 |
| DSQ | 18 | Jean Behra | Gordini | 61 | Disqualified | 17 |
| DSQ | 14 | Mike Hawthorn | Ferrari | 52 | Disqualified | 4 |
| Ret | 4 | Onofre Marimon | Maserati | 48 | Engine | 6 |
| Ret | 32 | Roberto Mieres | Maserati | 37 | Oil leak | 8 |
| Ret | 22 | Roger Loyer | Gordini | 19 | Oil pressure | 16 |
| Ret | 34 | Jorge Daponte | Maserati | 19 | Gearbox | 18 |
| Ret | 24 | Louis Rosier | Ferrari | 1 | Accident | 14 |
| DNS | 6 | Luigi Musso | Maserati | 0 | Non starter | 7 |

Winning speed: 70.131mph
Lap leaders: Farina 1-14, 63-64; González 15-32, 47-58, 61-62; Hawthorn 33-34; Fangio 35-46, 59-60, 65-87
Pole position: Farina, 1m 44.800s, 83.501mph
Fastest lap: González, 1m 48.200s, 80.877mph

### INDIANAPOLIS 500 31 May Round: 2 Race: 34 200 x 2.500 miles

| POS. | NO. | DRIVER | CAR/ENGINE | LAPS | TIME/RETIRED | GRID |
|---|---|---|---|---|---|---|
| 1 | 14 | Bill Vukovich | Kurtis Kraft-Offenhauser | 200 | 3:49'17.27 | 19 |
| 2 | 9 | Jimmy Bryan | Kuzma-Offenhauser | 200 | +1'09.95 | 3 |
| 3 | 2 | Jack McGrath | Kurtis Kraft-Offenhauser | 200 | +1'19.73 | 1 |
| 4 | 34 | Ruttman/Carter | Kurtis Kraft-Offenhauser | 200 | +2'52.68 | 11 |
| 5 | 73 | Mike Nazaruk | Kurtis Kraft-Offenhauser | 200 | +3'24.55 | 14 |
| 6 | 77 | Fred Agabashian | Kurtis Kraft-Offenhauser | 200 | +3'47.55 | 24 |
| 7 | 7 | Don Freeland | Phillips-Offenhauser | 200 | +4'13.35 | 6 |
| 8 | 5 | Russo/Hoyt | Kurtis Kraft-Offenhauser | 200 | +5'01.17 | 32 |
| 9 | 28 | Larry Crockett | Kurtis Kraft-Offenhauser | 200 | +7'07.24 | 25 |
| 10 | 24 | Cal Niday | Stevens-Offenhauser | 200 | +7'07.69 | 13 |
| 11 | 45 | Cross/Davies/Hanks/ Linden/Parsons | Kurtis Kraft-Offenhauser | 200 | +8'22.19 | 27 |
| 12 | 98 | Faulkner/Stevenson | Kuzma-Offenhauser | 199 | +1 Lap | 5 |
| 13 | 88 | Manny Ayulo | Kuzma-Offenhauser | 197 | +3 Laps | 22 |
| 14 | 17 | Bob Sweikert | Kurtis Kraft-Offenhauser | 197 | +3 Laps | 9 |
| 15 | 16 | Bettenhausen/ Carter/Jackson/Teague | Kurtis Kraft-Offenhauser | 196 | +4 Laps | 8 |
| 16 | 32 | Ernie McCoy | Kurtis Kraft-Offenhauser | 194 | +6 Laps | 20 |
| 17 | 25 | Jimmy Reece | Pankratz-Offenhauser | 194 | +6 Laps | 7 |
| 18 | 27 | Elisian/Scott | Stevens-Offenhauser | 193 | +7 Laps | 31 |
| 19 | 71 | Armi/Fonder | Kurtis Kraft-Offenhauser | 193 | +7 Laps | 33 |
| Ret | 1 | Hanks/Davies/ Rathmann | Kurtis Kraft-Offenhauser | 191 | Spun off | 10 |
| Ret | 35 | Pat O'Connor | Kurtis Kraft-Offenhauser | 181 | Spun off | 12 |
| Ret | 12 | Ward/Johnson | Pawl-Offenhauser | 172 | Retirement | 16 |
| Ret | 31 | Hartley/Teague | Kurtis Kraft-Offenhauser | 168 | Clutch | 17 |
| Ret | 74 | Linden/Scott | Schroeder-Offenhauser | 165 | Suspension | 23 |
| Ret | 43 | Thomson/Linden/ Homeier | Nichels-Offenhauser | 165 | Retirement | 4 |
| Ret | 99 | Jerry Hoyt | Kurtis Kraft-Offenhauser | 130 | Engine | 30 |
| Ret | 19 | Jimmy Daywalt | Kurtis Kraft-Offenhauser | 111 | Accident | 2 |
| Ret | 38 | Rathmann/Flaherty | Kurtis Kraft-Offenhauser | 110 | Accident | 28 |
| Ret | 10 | T.Bettenhausen | Kurtis Kraft-Offenhauser | 105 | Wheel bearing | 21 |
| Ret | 65 | Webb/Kladis | Bromme-Offenhauser | 104 | Fuel pump | 29 |
| Ret | 33 | Duncan/Fonder | Schroeder-Offenhauser | 101 | Brakes | 26 |
| Ret | 15 | Johnnie Parsons | Kurtis Kraft-Offenhauser | 79 | Engine | 15 |
| Ret | 51 | Bill Homeier | Kurtis Kraft-Offenhauser | 74 | Accident | 18 |

Winning Speed: 130.840mph
Pole position: McGrath, 1m 3.815s, 141.033mph
Fastest lap: McGrath, 1m 4.040s, 140.537mph

### BELGIAN GRAND PRIX: SPA-FRANCORCHAMPS 20 June Round: 3 Race: 35 36 x 8.774 miles

| POS. | NO. | DRIVER | CAR/ENGINE | LAPS | TIME/RETIRED | GRID |
|---|---|---|---|---|---|---|
| 1 | 26 | Juan Manuel Fangio | Maserati | 36 | 2:44'42.4 | 1 |
| 2 | 8 | M.Trintignant | Ferrari | 36 | +24.2 | 6 |
| 3 | 22 | Stirling Moss | Maserati | 35 | +1 Lap | 9 |
| 4 | 10 | Hawthorn/Gonzalez | Ferrari | 35 | +1 Lap | 5 |
| 5 | 18 | Andre Pilette | Gordini | 35 | +1 Lap | 8 |
| 6 | 20 | Prince Bira | Maserati | 35 | +1 Lap | 13 |
| 7 | 30 | Sergio Mantovani | Maserati | 34 | +2 Laps | 11 |
| Ret | 4 | Giuseppe Farina | Ferrari | 14 | Ignition | 3 |
| Ret | 16 | Paul Frere | Gordini | 14 | Engine | 10 |
| Ret | 12 | Jean Behra | Gordini | 12 | Suspension | 7 |
| Ret | 28 | Onofre Marimon | Maserati | 3 | Engine | 4 |
| Ret | 6 | J.F.Gonzalez | Ferrari | 1 | Engine | 2 |
| Ret | 2 | Jacques Swaters | Ferrari | 1 | Engine | 14 |
| Ret | 24 | Roberto Mieres | Maserati | 0 | Fire | 12 |

Winning speed: 115.061mph Lap leaders: Farina 1-2, 11-13; Fangio 3-10, 14-36
Pole position: Fangio, 4m 22.100s, 120.510mph
Fastest lap: Fangio, 4m 25.500s, 118.966mph

### FRENCH GRAND PRIX: REIMS 4 July Round: 4 Race: 36 61 x 5.159 miles

| POS. | NO. | DRIVER | CAR/ENGINE | LAPS | TIME/RETIRED | GRID |
|---|---|---|---|---|---|---|
| 1 | 18 | Juan Manuel Fangio | Mercedes | 61 | 2:42'47.9 | 1 |
| 2 | 20 | Karl Kling | Mercedes | 61 | +0.1 | 2 |
| 3 | 34 | Robert Manzon | Ferrari | 60 | +1 Lap | 12 |
| 4 | 46 | Prince Bira | Maserati | 60 | +1 Lap | 6 |
| 5 | 14 | Luigi Villoresi | Maserati | 58 | +3 Laps | 14 |
| 6 | 24 | Jean Behra | Gordini | 56 | +5 Laps | 17 |
| Ret | 28 | Paul Frere | Gordini | 50 | Axle | 19 |
| Ret | 4 | M.Trintignant | Ferrari | 36 | Engine | 9 |
| Ret | 12 | Onofre Marimon | Maserati | 27 | Gearbox | 5 |
| Ret | 36 | Louis Rosier | Ferrari | 27 | Engine | 13 |
| Ret | 16 | Roberto Mieres | Maserati | 24 | Engine | 11 |
| Ret | 42 | Ken Wharton | Maserati | 19 | Transmission | 16 |
| Ret | 48 | Harry Schell | Maserati | 19 | Fuel pump | 21 |
| Ret | 22 | Hans Herrmann | Mercedes | 16 | Engine | 7 |
| Ret | 44 | Roy Salvadori | Maserati | 15 | Halfshaft | 10 |
| Ret | 2 | J.F.Gonzalez | Ferrari | 13 | Engine | 4 |
| Ret | 32 | Lance Macklin | HWM-Alta | 10 | Engine | 15 |
| Ret | 6 | Mike Hawthorn | Ferrari | 9 | Engine | 8 |
| Ret | 30 | Georges Berger | Gordini | 9 | Engine | 20 |
| Ret | 26 | Jacques Pollet | Gordini | 8 | Engine | 18 |
| Ret | 10 | Alberto Ascari | Maserati | 1 | Transmission | 3 |

Winning speed: 115.975mph
Lap leaders: Kling 1-2, 29-33, 38, 54-57, 60; Fangio 3-28, 34-37, 39-53, 58-59, 61
Pole position: Fangio, 2m 29.400s, 124.304mph
Fastest lap: Herrmann, 2m 32.900s, 121.459mph

### BRITISH GRAND PRIX: SILVERSTONE 17 July Round: 5 Race: 37 90 x 2.927 miles

| POS. | NO. | DRIVER | CAR/ENGINE | LAPS | TIME/RETIRED | GRID |
|---|---|---|---|---|---|---|
| 1 | 9 | J.F.Gonzalez | Ferrari | 90 | 2:56'14 | 2 |
| 2 | 11 | Mike Hawthorn | Ferrari | 90 | +1 Lap | 3 |
| 3 | 33 | Onofre Marimon | Maserati | 89 | +1 Lap | 28 |
| 4 | 1 | Juan Manuel Fangio | Mercedes | 89 | +1 Lap | 1 |
| 5 | 10 | M.Trintignant | Ferrari | 87 | +3 Laps | 8 |
| 6 | 4 | Roberto Mieres | Maserati | 87 | +3 Laps | 32 |
| 7 | 2 | Karl Kling | Mercedes | 87 | +3 Laps | 6 |
| 8 | 8 | Ken Wharton | Maserati | 86 | +4 Laps | 9 |
| 9 | 19 | Andre Pilette | Gordini | 86 | +4 Laps | 12 |
| 10 | 29 | Bob Gerard | Cooper-Bristol | 85 | +5 Laps | 18 |
| 11 | 25 | Don Beauman | Connaught-Francis | 84 | +6 Laps | 17 |
| 12 | 3 | Harry Schell | Maserati | 83 | +7 Laps | 16 |
| 13 | 23 | Leslie Marr | Connaught-Francis | 82 | +8 Laps | 22 |
| 14 | 26 | Leslie Thorne | Connaught-Francis | 78 | +12 Laps | 23 |
| 15 | 28 | Horace Gould | Cooper-Bristol | 44 | +46 Laps | 20 |
| Ret | 7 | Stirling Moss | Maserati | 80 | Axle | 4 |
| Ret | 22 | Bill Whitehouse | Connaught-Francis | 63 | Fuel system | 19 |
| Ret | 17 | Jean Behra | Gordini | 54 | Suspension | 5 |
| Ret | 5 | Roy Salvadori | Maserati | 53 | Transmission | 7 |
| Ret | 6 | Bira/Flockhart | Maserati | 44 | Accident | 10 |
| Ret | 32 | Villoresi/Ascari | Maserati | 40 | Engine | 27 |
| Ret | 24 | J.R.-Prichard | Connaught-Francis | 40 | Accident | 21 |
| Ret | 12 | Reg Parnell | Ferrari | 25 | Engine | 14 |
| Ret | 31 | Alberto Ascari | Maserati | 21 | Engine | 30 |
| Ret | 18 | Clemar Bucci | Gordini | 18 | Accident | 13 |
| Ret | 20 | Peter Collins | Vanwall | 16 | Engine | 11 |
| Ret | 14 | Robert Manzon | Ferrari | 16 | Engine | 15 |
| Ret | 21 | Peter Whitehead | Cooper-Alta | 4 | Oil leak | 24 |
| Ret | 30 | Eric Brandon | Cooper-Bristol | 2 | Engine | 25 |
| Ret | 15 | Louis Rosier | Ferrari | 2 | Engine | 31 |
| DNS | 27 | Alan Brown | Cooper-Bristol | 0 | Non Starter | |

Winning speed: 89.687mph Lap leaders: Gonzalez 1-90
Pole position: Fangio, 1m 45.000s, 100.354mph
Fastest lap: Ascari, Behra, Fangio, Gonzalez, Hawthorn, Marimon, Moss, 1m 50.000s, 95.793mph

### GERMAN GRAND PRIX: NURBURGRING 1 August Round: 6 Race: 38 22 x 14.173 miles

| POS. | NO. | DRIVER | CAR/ENGINE | LAPS | TIME/RETIRED | GRID |
|---|---|---|---|---|---|---|
| 1 | 18 | Juan Manuel Fangio | Mercedes | 22 | 3:45'45.8 | 1 |
| 2 | 1 | Gonzalez/Hawthorn | Ferrari | 22 | +1'36.5 | 5 |
| 3 | 2 | M.Trintignant | Ferrari | 22 | +5'08.6 | 7 |
| 4 | 19 | Karl Kling | Mercedes | 22 | +6'06.5 | 23 |
| 5 | 7 | Sergio Mantovani | Maserati | 22 | +8'50.5 | 15 |
| 6 | 4 | Piero Taruffi | Ferrari | 21 | +1 Lap | 13 |
| 7 | 15 | Harry Schell | Maserati | 21 | +1 Lap | 14 |
| 8 | 25 | Louis Rosier | Ferrari | 21 | +1 Lap | 18 |
| 9 | 24 | Robert Manzon | Ferrari | 20 | +2 Laps | 12 |
| 10 | 9 | Jean Behra | Gordini | 20 | +2 Laps | 9 |
| Ret | 14 | Prince Bira | Maserati | 18 | Steering | 19 |
| Ret | 21 | Hermann Lang | Mercedes | 10 | Spun off | 11 |
| Ret | 11 | Clemar Bucci | Gordini | 8 | Wheel | 16 |
| Ret | 22 | Theo Helfrich | Klenk-Meteor-BMW | 8 | Engine | 21 |
| Ret | 20 | Hans Herrmann | Mercedes | 7 | Fuel leak | 4 |
| Ret | 10 | Paul Frere | Gordini | 4 | Wheel | 6 |
| Ret | 3 | Mike Hawthorn | Ferrari | 3 | Transmission | 2 |
| Ret | 8 | Roberto Mieres | Maserati | 2 | Fuel leak | 17 |
| Ret | 16 | Stirling Moss | Maserati | 1 | Wheel bearing | 3 |
| Ret | 12 | Andre Pilette | Gordini | 0 | Suspension | 20 |

Winning speed: 82.870mph Lap leaders: Fangio 1-14, 17-22; Kling 15-16
Pole position: Fangio, 9m 50.100s, 86.468mph
Fastest lap: Kling, 9m 55.100s, 85.741mph

### SWISS GRAND PRIX: BREMGARTEN 22 August Round: 7 Race: 39 66 x 4.524 miles

| POS. | NO. | DRIVER | CAR/ENGINE | LAPS | TIME/RETIRED | GRID |
|---|---|---|---|---|---|---|
| 1 | 4 | Juan Manuel Fangio | Mercedes | 66 | 3:00'34.5 | 2 |
| 2 | 20 | J.F.Gonzalez | Ferrari | 66 | +57.8 | 1 |
| 3 | 6 | Hans Herrmann | Mercedes | 65 | +1 Lap | 7 |
| 4 | 30 | Roberto Mieres | Maserati | 64 | +2 Laps | 12 |
| 5 | 28 | Sergio Mantovani | Maserati | 64 | +2 Laps | 9 |
| 6 | 18 | Ken Wharton | Maserati | 64 | +2 Laps | 8 |
| 7 | 24 | Umberto Maglioli | Ferrari | 61 | +5 Laps | 11 |
| 8 | 2 | Jacques Swaters | Ferrari | 58 | +8 Laps | 16 |
| Ret | 8 | Karl Kling | Mercedes | 38 | Fuel system | 5 |
| Ret | 26 | M.Trintignant | Ferrari | 33 | Engine | 4 |
| Ret | 22 | Mike Hawthorn | Ferrari | 30 | Oil pump | 6 |
| Ret | 34 | Harry Schell | Maserati | 23 | Oil pump | 13 |
| Ret | 32 | Stirling Moss | Maserati | 21 | Oil pump | 3 |
| Ret | 14 | Fred Wacker | Gordini | 10 | Transmission | 15 |
| Ret | 10 | Jean Behra | Gordini | 8 | Clutch | 14 |
| Ret | 12 | Clemar Bucci | Gordini | 0 | Fuel pump | 10 |

Winning speed: 99.202mph Lap leaders: Fangio 1-66
Pole position: Gonzalez, 2m 39.500s, 102.100mph
Fastest lap: Fangio, 2m 39.700s, 101.972 mph

### ITALIAN GRAND PRIX: MONZA 5 September Round: 8 Race: 40 80 x 3.195 miles

| POS. | NO. | DRIVER | CAR/ENGINE | LAPS | TIME/RETIRED | GRID |
|---|---|---|---|---|---|---|
| 1 | 16 | Juan Manuel Fangio | Mercedes | 80 | 2:47'47.9 | 1 |
| 2 | 40 | Mike Hawthorn | Ferrari | 79 | +1 Lap | 7 |
| 3 | 38 | Gonzalez/Maglioli | Ferrari | 78 | +2 Laps | 13 |
| 4 | 12 | Hans Herrmann | Mercedes | 77 | +3 Laps | 8 |
| 5 | 30 | M.Trintignant | Ferrari | 75 | +5 Laps | 11 |
| 6 | 42 | Fred Wacker | Gordini | 75 | +5 Laps | 18 |
| 7 | 10 | Peter Collins | Vanwall | 75 | +5 Laps | 16 |
| 8 | 26 | Louis Rosier | Maserati | 74 | +6 Laps | 20 |
| 9 | 18 | Sergio Mantovani | Maserati | 74 | +6 Laps | 9 |
| 10 | 28 | Stirling Moss | Maserati | 71 | +9 Laps | 3 |
| 11 | 8 | Jorge Daponte | Maserati | 70 | +10 Laps | 19 |
| Ret | 34 | Alberto Ascari | Ferrari | 48 | Engine | 2 |
| Ret | 22 | Luigi Villoresi | Maserati | 42 | Clutch | 6 |
| Ret | 14 | Karl Kling | Mercedes | 36 | Accident | 4 |
| Ret | 24 | Roberto Mieres | Maserati | 34 | Suspension | 10 |
| Ret | 20 | Luigi Musso | Maserati | 32 | Transmission | 14 |
| Ret | 32 | J.F.Gonzalez | Ferrari | 16 | Gearbox | 5 |
| Ret | 6 | Robert Manzon | Ferrari | 16 | Engine | 15 |
| Ret | 46 | Clemar Bucci | Gordini | 13 | Transmission | 17 |
| Ret | 44 | Jean Behra | Gordini | 2 | Engine | 12 |

Winning speed: 111.981mph
Lap leaders: Kling 1-3; Fangio 4-5, 23, 68-80; Ascari 6-22, 24-44, 46-48; Moss 45, 49-67
Pole position: Fangio, 1m 59.000s, 118.426mph
Fastest lap: Gonzalez, 2m 0.800s, 116.661mph

### SPANISH GRAND PRIX: PEDRALBES 24 October Round: 9 Race: 41 80 x 3.925 miles

| POS. | NO. | DRIVER | CAR/ENGINE | LAPS | TIME/RETIRED | GRID |
|---|---|---|---|---|---|---|
| 1 | 38 | Mike Hawthorn | Ferrari | 80 | 3:13'52.1 | 3 |
| 2 | 14 | Luigi Musso | Maserati | 80 | +1'13.2 | 7 |
| 3 | 2 | Juan Manuel Fangio | Mercedes | 79 | +1 Lap | 2 |
| 4 | 10 | Roberto Mieres | Maserati | 79 | +1 Lap | 11 |
| 5 | 4 | Karl Kling | Mercedes | 79 | +1 Lap | 12 |
| 6 | 16 | Paco Godia | Maserati | 76 | +4 Laps | 13 |
| 7 | 26 | Louis Rosier | Maserati | 74 | +6 Laps | 20 |
| 8 | 28 | Ken Wharton | Maserati | 74 | +6 Laps | 14 |
| 9 | 18 | Prince Bira | Maserati | 68 | +12 Laps | 15 |
| Ret | 12 | Sergio Mantovani | Maserati | 58 | Brakes | 10 |
| Ret | 22 | Graffenried/Volonterio | Maserati | 57 | Engine | 21 |
| Ret | 6 | Hans Herrmann | Mercedes | 50 | Injection | 9 |
| Ret | 40 | M.Trintignant | Ferrari | 47 | Gearbox | 8 |
| Ret | 48 | Jacques Pollet | Gordini | 37 | Engine | 16 |
| Ret | 24 | Harry Schell | Maserati | 29 | Transmission | 14 |
| Ret | 8 | Stirling Moss | Maserati | 20 | Oil pump | 6 |
| Ret | 46 | Jean Behra | Gordini | 17 | Brakes | 8 |
| Ret | 30 | Jacques Swaters | Ferrari | 16 | Engine | 19 |
| Ret | 34 | Alberto Ascari | Lancia | 10 | Clutch | 1 |
| Ret | 36 | Luigi Villoresi | Lancia | 2 | Brakes | 5 |
| Ret | 20 | Robert Manzon | Ferrari | 2 | Engine | 17 |

Winning speed: 97.169mph Lap leaders: Schell 1-2, 10, 13, 15-17, 19, 21, 23; Ascari 3-9; Trintignant 11-12, 14, 18, 20; Hawthorn 22, 24-80
Pole position: Ascari, 2 m 18.100s, 102.306mph
Fastest lap: Ascari, 2m 20.400s, 100.630mph

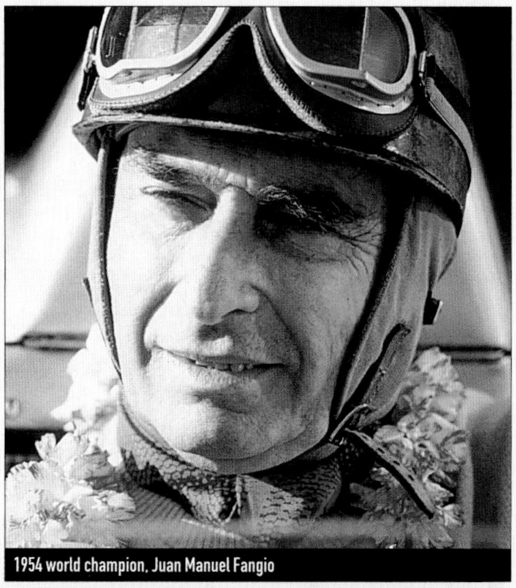

1954 world champion, Juan Manuel Fangio

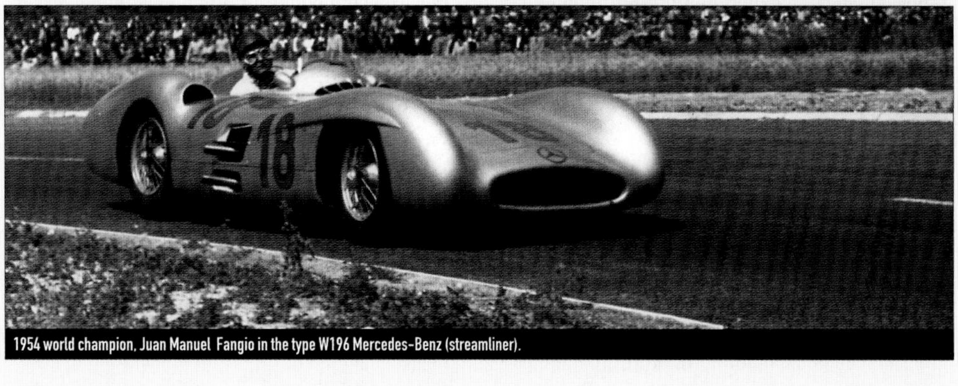

1954 world champion, Juan Manuel Fangio in the type W196 Mercedes-Benz (streamliner).

# 1955

## DRIVERS' CHAMPION: JUAN MANUEL FANGIO

### DRIVERS' CHAMPIONSHIP

| POS. | DRIVER | NATIONALITY | CAR | POINTS |
|---|---|---|---|---|
| 1 | Juan Manuel Fangio | Argentina | Mercedes-Benz | 40 (1) |
| 2 | Stirling Moss | GB | Mercedes-Benz | 23 |
| 3 | Eugenio Castellotti | Italy | Lancia, Ferrari | 12 |
| 4 | Maurice Trintignant | France | Ferrari | 11.33 |
| 5 | Giuseppe Farina | Italy | Ferrari, Lancia-Ferrari | 10.33 |
| 6 | Piero Taruffi | Italy | Ferrari, Mercedes-Benz | 9 |
| 7 | Bob Sweikert | USA | Kurtis-Offenhauser | 8 |
| 8 | Roberto Mieres | Argentina | Maserati | 7 |
| 9 | Luigi Musso | Italy | Maserati | 6 |
| = | Jean Behra | France | Maserati | 6 |
| 11 | Karl Kling | West Germany | Mercedes-Benz | 5 |
| 12 | Jimmy Davis | USA | Kurtis-Offenhauser | 4 |
| 13 | Tony Bettenhausen | USA | Kurtis-Offenhauser | 3 |
| = | Paul Russo | USA | Kurtis-Offenhauser | 3 |
| = | Johnny Thompson | USA | Kuzma-Offenhauser | 3 |
| = | Paul Frere | Belgium | Ferrari | 3 |
| 17 | Jose Froilan Gonzalez | Argentina | Ferrari | 2 |
| = | Cesare Perdisa | Italy | Maserati | 2 |
| = | Luigi Villoresi | Italy | Lancia | 2 |
| = | Carlos Menditéguy | Argentina | Maserati | 2 |
| 21 | Umberto Maglioli | Italy | Ferrari | 1.33 |
| 22 | Walt Faulkner | USA | Kurtis-Offenhauser | 1 |
| = | Bill Homeier | USA | Kurtis-Offenhauser | 1 |
| = | Hans Hermann | West Germany | Mercedes-Benz | 1 |
| = | Bill Vukovich | USA | Kurtis-Offenhauser | 1 |
| | Harry Schell | USA | Maserati, Ferrari | |
| | Alberto Ascari | Italy | Lancia | |
| | Robert Manzon | France | Gordini | |
| | Pablo Birger | Argentina | Gordini | |
| | Elie Bayol | France | Gordini | |
| | Alberto Uria | Italy | Maserati | |
| | Jesus Iglesias | Argentina | Gordini | |
| | Clemar Bucci | Argentina | Maserati | |
| | Sergio Mantovani | Italy | Maserati | |
| | Louis Chiron | Monaco | Lancia | |
| | Mike Hawthorn | GB | Vanwall, Ferrari | |
| | Jacques Pollet | France | Gordini | |
| | Louis Rosier | France | Maserati | |
| | Lance Macklin | GB | Maserati | |
| | André Simon | France | Mercedes-Benz, Maserati | |
| | Ted Whiteaway | GB | HWM-Alta | |
| | Johnny Claes | Belgium | Maserati, Ferrari | |
| | Peter Walker | GB | Maserati, Connaught-Alta | |
| | Horace Gould | GB | Maserati | |
| | Hermanos da Silva Ramos | Brazil | Gordini | |
| | Jack Brabham | Australia | Cooper-Bristol | |
| | Tony Rolt | GB | Connaught-Alta | |
| | Leslie Marr | GB | Connaught-Alta | |
| | Peter Collins | GB | Maserati | |
| | Jack Fairman | GB | Connaught–Alta | |
| | Kenneth McAlpine | GB | Connaught–Alta | |
| | Michel Poberejsky | USA | Gordini | |
| | Ken Wharton | GB | Vanwall | |
| | Jean Lucas | France | Gordini | |
| | John Fitch | USA | Maserati | |
| | Luigi Piotti | Italy | Arzani Volpini-Maserati | |

**Points for top five finishers (8, 6, 4, 3, 2) plus a point for fastest lap. Only the best five scores counted towards the championship. Points for shared drives (except where 'insufficient distance' was deemed to have been covered by one of the drivers) and shared fastest laps were divided equally between the drivers. Drivers sharing two cars in a race received points only for their highest finish.**

### ARGENTINE GRAND PRIX: BUENOS AIRES *16 January Round: 1 Race: 42 96 x 2.431 miles*

| POS. | NO. | DRIVER | CAR/ENGINE | LAPS | TIME/RETIRED | GRID |
|---|---|---|---|---|---|---|
| 1 | 2 | Juan Manuel Fangio | Mercedes | 96 | 3:00'38.6 | 3 |
| 2 | 12 | Gonzalez/Farina/Trintignant | Ferrari | 96 | +1'29.6 | 1 |
| 3 | 10 | Farina/Maglioli/Trintignant | Ferrari | 94 | +2 Laps | 5 |
| 4 | 8 | Moss/Kling/Herrmann | Mercedes | 94 | +2 Laps | 10 |
| 5 | 18 | Roberto Mieres | Maserati | 91 | +5 Laps | 16 |
| 6 | 28 | Schell/Behra/ | Maserati | 88 | +8 Laps | 7 |
| 7 | 22 | Musso/Mantovani/Schell | Maserati | 83 | +13 Laps | 18 |
| Ret | 20 | Mantovani/Behra/Musso | Maserati | 54 | Engine | 19 |
| Ret | 26 | Bucci/Schell/Menditeguy | Maserati | 54 | Fuel pressure | 20 |
| Ret | 42 | Jesus Iglesias | Gordini | 38 | Transmission | 17 |
| Ret | 14 | M.Trintignant | Ferrari | 36 | Engine | 19 |
| Ret | 36 | Castellotti/Villoresi | Lancia | 35 | Accident | 12 |
| Ret | 6 | Stirling Moss | Mercedes | 29 | Fuel system | 8 |
| Ret | 30 | Alberto Uria | Maserati | 22 | Out of fuel | 21 |
| Ret | 32 | Alberto Ascari | Lancia | 21 | Accident | 2 |
| Ret | 38 | Elie Bayol | Gordini | 7 | Transmission | 15 |
| Ret | 16 | Jean Behra | Maserati | 2 | Accident | 4 |
| Ret | 4 | Karl Kling | Mercedes | 2 | Accident | 6 |
| Ret | 34 | Luigi Villoresi | Lancia | 2 | Fuel leak | 11 |

Winning speed: 77.509mph
Lap leaders: Fangio 1-2, 26-34, 43-96; Ascari 3-4, 11-20; Gonzalez 5-10, 21-25; Schell 35-38; Mieres 39-42
Pole Position: Gonzalez, 1m 43.100s, 84.878mph
Fastest lap: Fangio, 1m 48.300s, 80.802mph

### MONACO GRAND PRIX: MONTE CARLO *22 May Round: 2 Race: 43 100 x 1.954 miles*

| POS. | NO. | DRIVER | CAR/ENGINE | LAPS | TIME/RETIRED | GRID |
|---|---|---|---|---|---|---|
| 1 | 44 | M.Trintignant | Ferrari | 100 | 2:58'09.8 | 9 |
| 2 | 30 | E.Castellotti | Lancia | 100 | +20.2 | 4 |
| 3 | 34 | Perdisa/Behra | Maserati | 99 | +1 Lap | 5 |
| 4 | 42 | Nino Farina | Ferrari | 99 | +1 Lap | 14 |
| 5 | 28 | Luigi Villoresi | Lancia | 99 | +1 Lap | 7 |
| 6 | 32 | Louis Chiron | Lancia | 95 | +5 Laps | 19 |
| 7 | 10 | Jacques Pollet | Gordini | 91 | +9 Laps | 20 |
| 8 | 48 | Taruffi/Frere | Ferrari | 86 | +14 Laps | 15 |
| 9 | 6 | Stirling Moss | Mercedes | 81 | +19 Laps | 3 |
| Ret | 40 | Perdisa/Behra | Maserati | 86 | Spun off | 11 |
| Ret | 26 | Alberto Ascari | Lancia | 80 | Accident | 2 |
| Ret | 46 | Harry Schell | Ferrari | 68 | Engine | 18 |
| Ret | 36 | Roberto Mieres | Maserati | 64 | Transmission | 6 |
| Ret | 12 | Elie Bayol | Gordini | 63 | Transmission | 16 |
| Ret | 2 | Juan Manuel Fangio | Mercedes | 49 | Transmission | 1 |
| Ret | 8 | Robert Manzon | Gordini | 38 | Gearbox | 13 |
| Ret | 4 | Andre Simon | Mercedes | 24 | Engine | 10 |
| Ret | 18 | Mike Hawthorn | Vanwall | 22 | Throttle | 12 |
| Ret | 14 | Louis Rosier | Maserati | 8 | Fuel leak | 17 |
| Ret | 38 | Luigi Musso | Maserati | 7 | Transmission | 8 |
| DNQ | 22 | Lance Macklin | Maserati | | | |
| DNQ | 24 | Ted Whiteaway | HWM-Alta | | | |

Winning speed: 65.813mph Lap leaders: Fangio 1-49; Moss 50-80; Trintignant 81-100
Pole position: Fangio, 1m 41.100s, 69.586mph Fastest lap: Fangio, 1m 42.400s, 68.703mph

### INDIANAPOLIS 500 *30 May Round: 3 Race: 44 200 x 2.500 miles*

| POS. | NO. | DRIVER | CAR/ENGINE | LAPS | TIME/RETIRED | GRID |
|---|---|---|---|---|---|---|
| 1 | 6 | Bob Sweikert | Kurtis Kraft-Offenhauser | 200 | 3:53'59.53 | 14 |
| 2 | 10 | Bettenhausen/Russo | Kurtis Kraft-Offenhauser | 200 | +2'43.56 | 2 |
| 3 | 15 | Jimmy Davies | Kurtis Kraft-Offenhauser | 200 | +3'32.36 | 10 |
| 4 | 44 | Johnny Thomson | Kuzma-Offenhauser | 200 | +3'38.91 | 33 |
| 5 | 77 | Faulkner/Homeier | Kurtis Kraft-Offenhauser | 200 | +5'17.17 | 7 |
| 6 | 19 | Andy Linden | Kurtis Kraft-Offenhauser | 200 | +5'57.94 | 8 |
| 7 | 71 | Al Herman | Kurtis Kraft-Offenhauser | 200 | +6'24.24 | 16 |
| 8 | 29 | Pat O'Connor | Kurtis Kraft-Offenhauser | 200 | +6'41.60 | 19 |
| 9 | 48 | Jimmy Daywalt | Kurtis Kraft-Offenhauser | 200 | +7'09.81 | 17 |
| 10 | 89 | Pat Flaherty | Kurtis Kraft-Offenhauser | 200 | +7'46.54 | 12 |
| 11 | 98 | Duane Carter | Kuzma-Offenhauser | 197 | +3 Laps | 18 |
| 12 | 41 | Chuck Weyant | Kurtis Kraft-Offenhauser | 196 | +4 Laps | 25 |
| 13 | 83 | Eddie Johnson | Trevis-Offenhauser | 196 | +4 Laps | 32 |
| 14 | 33 | Jim Rathmann | Epperly-Offenhauser | 191 | +9 Laps | 20 |
| Ret | 12 | Don Freeland | Phillips-Offenhauser | 178 | Transmission | 21 |
| Ret | 22 | Cal Niday | Kurtis Kraft-Offenhauser | 170 | Accident | 9 |
| Ret | 99 | Art Cross | Kurtis Kraft-Offenhauser | 168 | Engine | 24 |
| Ret | 81 | Shorty Templeman | Trevis-Offenhauser | 142 | Transmission | 31 |
| Ret | 8 | Sam Hanks | Kurtis Kraft-Offenhauser | 134 | Transmission | 6 |
| Ret | 31 | Keith Andrews | Schroeder-Offenhauser | 120 | Fuel pump | 28 |
| Ret | 16 | Johnnie Parsons | Kurtis Kraft-Offenhauser | 119 | Magneto | 27 |
| Ret | 37 | Eddie Russo | Pawl-Offenhauser | 112 | Ignition | 13 |
| Ret | 49 | Ray Crawford | Kurtis Kraft-Offenhauser | 111 | Engine | 23 |
| Ret | 1 | Jimmy Bryan | Kuzma-Offenhauser | 90 | Fuel pump | 11 |
| Ret | 4 | Bill Vukovich | Kurtis Kraft-Offenhauser | 56 | Accident | 5 |
| Ret | 3 | Jack McGrath | Kurtis Kraft-Offenhauser | 54 | Magneto | 3 |
| Ret | 42 | Al Keller | Kurtis Kraft-Offenhauser | 54 | Accident | 22 |
| Ret | 39 | Johnny Boyd | Kurtis Kraft-Offenhauser | 53 | Accident | 26 |
| Ret | 68 | Ed Elisian | Kurtis Kraft-Offenhauser | 53 | Retirement | 29 |
| Ret | 27 | Rodger Ward | Kuzma-Offenhauser | 53 | Accident | 30 |
| Ret | 23 | Jerry Hoyt | Stevens-Offenhauser | 40 | Oil leak | 1 |
| Ret | 14 | Fred Agabashian | Kurtis Kraft-Offenhauser | 39 | Spun off | 4 |
| Ret | 5 | Jimmy Reece | Pankratz-Offenhauser | 10 | Engine | 15 |

Winning speed: 128.209mph Pole Position: Hoyt, 1m 4.265s, 140.045mph
Fastest lap: Vukovich, 1m 3.670s, 141.354mph

### BELGIAN GRAND PRIX: SPA-FRANCORCHAMPS *5 June Round: 4 Race: 45 36 x 8.774 miles*

| POS. | NO. | DRIVER | CAR/ENGINE | LAPS | TIME/RETIRED | GRID |
|---|---|---|---|---|---|---|
| 1 | 10 | Juan Manuel Fangio | Mercedes | 36 | 2:39'29.0 | 2 |
| 2 | 14 | Stirling Moss | Mercedes | 36 | +8.1 | 3 |
| 3 | 2 | Giuseppe Farina | Ferrari | 36 | +1'40.5 | 4 |
| 4 | 6 | Paul Frere | Ferrari | 36 | +3'25.5 | 8 |
| 5 | 24 | Behra/Mieres | Maserati | 35 | +1 Lap | 13 |
| 6 | 4 | M.Trintignant | Ferrari | 35 | +1 Lap | 10 |
| 7 | 22 | Luigi Musso | Maserati | 34 | +2 Laps | 7 |
| 8 | 26 | Cesare Perdisa | Maserati | 33 | +3 Laps | 11 |
| 9 | 28 | Louis Rosier | Maserati | 33 | +3 Laps | 12 |
| Ret | 12 | Karl Kling | Mercedes | 21 | Oil leak | 6 |
| Ret | 30 | E.Castellotti | Lancia | 16 | Gearbox | 1 |
| Ret | 40 | Mike Hawthorn | Vanwall | 8 | Gearbox | 9 |
| Ret | 20 | Jean Behra | Maserati | 3 | Spun off | 5 |

Winning speed: 118.829mph Lap leaders: Fangio 1-36 Pole position: Castellotti, 4m 18.100s, 122.377mph. Fastest lap: Fangio, 4m 20.600s, 121.203mph

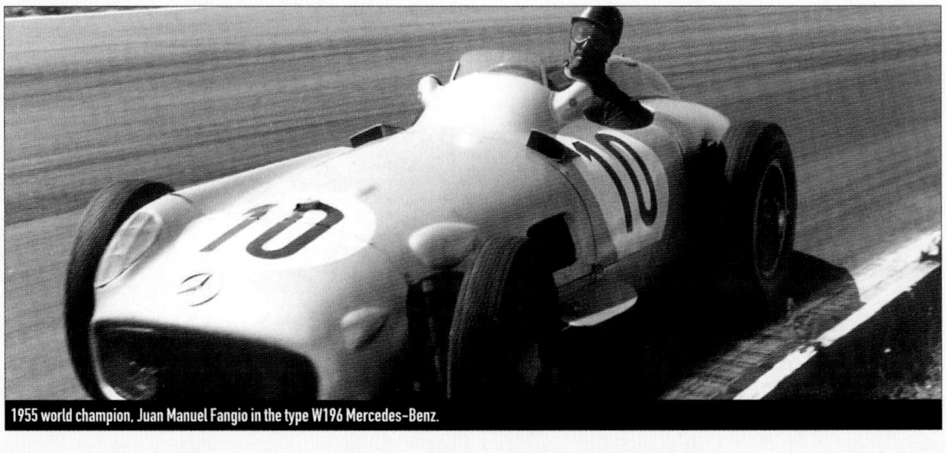

1955 world champion, Juan Manuel Fangio in the type W196 Mercedes-Benz.

### DUTCH GRAND PRIX: ZANDVOORT *19 June Round: 5 Race: 46 100 x 2.605 miles*

| POS. | NO. | DRIVER | CAR/ENGINE | LAPS | TIME/RETIRED | GRID |
|---|---|---|---|---|---|---|
| 1 | 8 | Juan Manuel Fangio | Mercedes | 100 | 2:54'23.8 | 1 |
| 2 | 10 | Stirling Moss | Mercedes | 100 | +0.3 | 2 |
| 3 | 18 | Luigi Musso | Maserati | 100 | +57.1 | 4 |
| 4 | 16 | Roberto Mieres | Maserati | 99 | +1 Lap | 7 |
| 5 | 6 | E.Castellotti | Ferrari | 97 | +3 Laps | 9 |
| 6 | 14 | Jean Behra | Maserati | 97 | +3 Laps | 6 |
| 7 | 2 | Mike Hawthorn | Ferrari | 95 | +5 Laps | 5 |
| 8 | 22 | H.da Silva-Ramos | Gordini | 92 | +8 Laps | 14 |
| 9 | 28 | Louis Rosier | Maserati | 92 | +8 Laps | 13 |
| 10 | 24 | Jacques Pollet | Gordini | 90 | +10 Laps | 12 |
| 11 | 30 | Johnny Claes | Ferrari | 88 | +12 Laps | 16 |
| Ret | 4 | M.Trintignant | Ferrari | 65 | Gearbox | 8 |
| Ret | 20 | Robert Manzon | Gordini | 44 | Transmission | 11 |
| Ret | 32 | Horace Gould | Maserati | 23 | Spun off | 15 |
| Ret | 12 | Karl Kling | Mercedes | 21 | Spun off | 3 |
| Ret | 26 | Peter Walker | Maserati | 2 | Wheel bearing | 10 |

Winning speed: 89.637mph Lap leaders: Fangio 1-100
Pole Position: Fangio, 1m 40.000s, 93.795mph
Fastest lap: Mieres, 1m 40.900s, 92.958mph.

### BRITISH GRAND PRIX: AINTREE *16 July Round: 6 Race: 47 90 x 3.000 miles*

| POS. | NO. | DRIVER | CAR/ENGINE | LAPS | TIME/RETIRED | GRID |
|---|---|---|---|---|---|---|
| 1 | 12 | Stirling Moss | Mercedes | 90 | 3:07'21.2 | 1 |
| 2 | 10 | Juan Manuel Fangio | Mercedes | 90 | +0.2 | 2 |
| 3 | 14 | Karl Kling | Mercedes | 90 | +1'11.8 | 4 |
| 4 | 50 | Piero Taruffi | Mercedes | 89 | +1 Lap | 5 |
| 5 | 4 | Luigi Musso | Maserati | 89 | +1 Lap | 9 |
| 6 | 16 | Hawthorn/Castellotti | Ferrari | 87 | +3 Laps | 12 |
| 7 | 26 | Mike Sparken | Gordini | 81 | +9 Laps | 23 |
| 8 | 46 | Lance Macklin | Maserati | 79 | +11 Laps | 16 |
| 9 | 28 | Wharton/Schell | Vanwall | 72 | +18 Laps | 15 |
| Ret | 18 | M.Trintignant | Ferrari | 59 | Overheating | 13 |
| Ret | 6 | Roberto Mieres | Maserati | 47 | Engine | 6 |
| Ret | 32 | Ken McAlpine | Connaught-Alta | 30 | Oil pressure | 17 |
| Ret | 40 | Jack Brabham | Cooper-Bristol | 30 | Engine | 25 |
| Ret | 42 | Peter Collins | Maserati | 29 | Clutch | 24 |
| Ret | 24 | H.da Silva-Ramos | Gordini | 26 | Oil pressure | 18 |
| Ret | 48 | Horace Gould | Maserati | 22 | Brakes | 22 |
| Ret | 44 | Roy Salvadori | Maserati | 19 | Gearbox | 20 |
| Ret | 36 | Rolt/Walker | Connaught-Alta | 18 | Transmission | 14 |
| Ret | 38 | Leslie Marr | Connaught-Alta | 18 | Brakes | 19 |
| Ret | 20 | E.Castellotti | Ferrari | 16 | Transmission | 10 |
| Ret | 8 | Andre Simon | Maserati | 15 | Gearbox | 8 |
| Ret | 30 | Harry Schell | Vanwall | 13 | Throttle | 7 |
| Ret | 2 | Jean Behra | Maserati | 9 | Oil leak | 3 |
| Ret | 22 | Robert Manzon | Gordini | 4 | Transmission | 11 |

Winning speed: 86.468mph Lap leaders: Fangio 1-2, 18-25; Moss 3-17, 26-90
Pole position: Moss, 2m 0.400s, 89.701mph
Fastest lap: Moss, 2m 0.400s, 89.701mph

### ITALIAN GRAND PRIX: MONZA *11 September Round: 7 Race: 48 50 x 6.214 miles*

| POS. | NO. | DRIVER | CAR/ENGINE | LAPS | TIME/RETIRED | GRID |
|---|---|---|---|---|---|---|
| 1 | 18 | Juan Manuel Fangio | Mercedes | 50 | 2:25'04.4 | 1 |
| 2 | 14 | Piero Taruffi | Mercedes | 50 | +0.7 | 9 |
| 3 | 4 | E.Castellotti | Ferrari | 50 | +46.2 | 4 |
| 4 | 36 | Jean Behra | Maserati | 50 | +3'57.5 | 6 |
| 5 | 34 | C.Menditeguy | Maserati | 49 | +1 Lap | 16 |
| 6 | 12 | Umberto Maglioli | Ferrari | 49 | +1 Lap | 12 |
| 7 | 28 | Roberto Mieres | Maserati | 48 | +2 Laps | 7 |
| 8 | 8 | M.Trintignant | Ferrari | 47 | +3 Laps | 15 |
| 9 | 40 | John Fitch | Maserati | 46 | +4 Laps | 20 |
| Ret | 6 | Mike Hawthorn | Ferrari | 38 | Gearbox | 14 |
| Ret | 20 | Karl Kling | Mercedes | 32 | Gearbox | 3 |
| Ret | 30 | Luigi Musso | Maserati | 31 | Gearbox | 10 |
| Ret | 38 | Horace Gould | Maserati | 31 | Suspension | 21 |
| Ret | 16 | Stirling Moss | Mercedes | 27 | Engine | 2 |
| Ret | 26 | Jacques Pollet | Gordini | 26 | Engine | 19 |
| Ret | 22 | H.da Silva-Ramos | Gordini | 23 | Fuel system | 18 |
| Ret | 32 | Peter Collins | Maserati | 22 | Suspension | 11 |
| Ret | 42 | Harry Schell | Vanwall | 7 | Suspension | 13 |
| Ret | 24 | Jean Lucas | Gordini | 7 | Engine | 22 |
| Ret | 44 | Ken Wharton | Vanwall | 0 | Injection | 17 |
| DNS | 2 | Nino Farina | Ferrari | 0 | Non Starter | |
| DNS | 10 | Luigi Villoresi | Ferrari | 0 | Non Starter | |

Winning speed: 128.495mph Lap leaders: Fangio 1-7, 9-50; Moss 8
Pole position: Fangio, 2m 46.500s, 134.351mph
Fastest lap: Moss, 2m 46.900s, 134.029mph

# 1956

## DRIVERS' CHAMPION: JUAN MANUEL FANGIO

### DRIVERS' CHAMPIONSHIP

| POS. | DRIVER | NATIONALITY | CAR | POINTS |
|---|---|---|---|---|
| 1 | Juan Manuel Fangio | Argentina | Lancia-Ferrari | 30(3) |
| 2 | Stirling Moss | GB | Maserati | 27(28) |
| 3 | Peter Collins | GB | Ferrari | 25 |
| 4 | Jean Behra | France | Maserati | 22 |
| 5 | Pat Flaherty | USA | Watson-Offenhauser | 8 |
| 6 | Eugenio Castellotti | Italy | Lancia-Ferrari | 7.5 |
| 7 | Paul Frere | Belgium | Lancia | 6 |
| = | Sam Hanks | USA | Kurtis-Offenhauser | 6 |
| = | Francesco Godia-Sales | Italy | Maserati | 6 |
| 10 | Jack Fairman | GB | Connaught-Alta | 5 |
| 11 | Luigi Musso | Italy | Lancia-Ferrari | 4 |
| = | Mike Hawthorn | GB | Maserati, BRM, Vanwall | 4 |
| = | Don Freeland | USA | Philips-Offenhauser | 4 |
| = | Ron Flockhart | GB | BRM, Connaught-Alta | 4 |
| 15 | Johnnie Parsons | USA | Kuzma-Offenhauser | 3 |
| = | Harry Schell | USA | Vanwall, Maserati | 3 |
| = | Alfonso de Portago | Spain | Lancia | 3 |
| = | Cesare Perdisa | Italy | Maserati | 3 |
| 19 | Olivier Gendebien | Belgium | Lancia | 2 |
| = | Hermanos da Silva Ramos | Belgium | Gordini | 2 |
| = | Luigi Villoresi | Italy | Maserati | 2 |
| = | Dick Rathmann | USA | Kurtis-Offenhauser | 2 |
| = | Horace Gould | GB | Maserati | 2 |
| = | Louis Rosier | France | Maserati | 2 |
| 25 | Chico Landi | Brazil | Maserati | 1.5 |
| = | Gerino Gerini | Italy | Maserati | 1.5 |
| 27 | Paul Russo | USA | Kurtis-Offenhauser | 1 |
| | Jose Froilan Gonzalez | Argentina | Vanwall | |
| | Alberto Uria | Italy | Maserati | |
| | Oscar Gonzalez | Uruguay | Maserati | |
| | Carlos Menditéguy | Argentina | Maserati | |
| | Luigi Piotti | Italy | Maserati | |
| | Robert Manzon | France | Gordini | |
| | Elie Bayol | France | Gordini | |
| | André Pilette | Belgium | Gordini, Ferrari | |
| | Louis Chiron | Monaco | Maserati | |
| | Piero Scotti | Italy | Connaught-Alta | |
| | Maurice Trintignant | France | Vanwall, Bugatti | |
| | Tony Brooks | GB | BRM | |
| | Piero Taruffi | Italy | Maserati, Vanwall | |
| | André Simon | France | Maserati | |
| | Archie Scott-Brown | GB | Connaught-Alta | |
| | Desmond Titterington | GB | Connaught-Alta | |
| | Colin Chapman | GB | Vanwall | |
| | Paul Emery | GB | Emeryson-Alta | |
| | Jack Brabham | Australia | Maserati | |
| | Umberto Maglioli | Italy | Maserati | |
| | Bruce Halford | GB | Maserati | |
| | Roy Salvadori | GB | Maserati | |
| | Bob Gerard | GB | Cooper-Bristol | |
| | Ottorino Volonterio | Italy | Maserati | |
| | Giorgio Scarletti | Italy | Ferrari | |
| | Emmanuel de Graffenried | Switzerland | Maserati | |
| | André Milhoux | Belgium | Gordini | |
| | Les Leston | GB | Connaught-Alta | |
| | Jo Bonnier | Sweden | Maserati | |
| | Wolfgang von Trips | West Germany | Ferrari | |

Points for top five finishers (8, 6, 4, 3, 2) plus a point for fastest lap. Only the best five scores counted towards the championship. Points for shared drives (except where 'insufficient distance' was deemed to have been covered by one of the drivers) and shared fastest laps were divided equally between the drivers. Drivers sharing two cars in a race received points only for their highest finish.

### ARGENTINE GRAND PRIX: BUENOS AIRES *11 January Round: 1 Race: 49 98 x 2.431 miles*

| POS. | NO. | DRIVER | CAR/ENGINE | LAPS | TIME/RETIRED | GRID |
|---|---|---|---|---|---|---|
| 1 | 34 | Fangio/Musso | Ferrari | 98 | 3:00'03.7 | 3 |
| 2 | 4 | Jean Behra | Maserati | 98 | +24.4 | 4 |
| 3 | 14 | Mike Hawthorn | Maserati | 96 | +2 Laps | 8 |
| 4 | 10 | Gerini/Landi | Maserati | 92 | +6 Laps | 11 |
| 5 | 38 | O.Gendebien | Ferrari | 91 | +7 Laps | 10 |
| 6 | 16 | Gonzalez/Uria | Maserati | 88 | +10 Laps | 13 |
| Ret | 2 | Stirling Moss | Maserati | 81 | Engine | 7 |
| Ret | 36 | Peter Collins | Ferrari | 58 | Accident | 9 |
| Ret | 8 | Luigi Piotti | Maserati | 57 | Accident | 12 |
| Ret | 6 | C.Menditeguy | Maserati | 42 | Halfshaft | 6 |
| Ret | 32 | E.Castellotti | Ferrari | 40 | Gearbox | 2 |
| Ret | 12 | J.F.Gonzalez | Maserati | 24 | Engine | 5 |
| Ret | 30 | Juan Manuel Fangio | Ferrari | 22 | Fuel pump | 1 |

Winning speed: 79.379mph
Lap leaders: Gonzalez 1-3; Medinteguy 4-42; Moss 43-66; Fangio 67-98
Pole position: Fangio, 1m 42.500s, 85.375mph
Fastest lap: Fangio, 1m 45.300s, 83.104mph

### MONACO GRAND PRIX: MONTE CARLO *13 May Round: 2 Race: 50 100 x 1.954 miles*

| POS. | NO. | DRIVER | CAR/ENGINE | LAPS | TIME/RETIRED | GRID |
|---|---|---|---|---|---|---|
| 1 | 28 | Stirling Moss | Maserati | 100 | 3:00'32.9 | 2 |
| 2 | 26 | Collins/Fangio | Ferrari | 100 | +6.1 | 9 |
| 3 | 30 | Jean Behra | Maserati | 99 | +1 Lap | 4 |
| 4 | 20 | Castellotti/Fangio | Ferrari | 94 | +6 Laps | 1 |
| 5 | 6 | H.da Silva-Ramos | Gordini | 93 | +7 Laps | 14 |
| 6 | 4 | Pilette/Bayol | Gordini | 88 | +12 Laps | 11 |
| 7 | 32 | Cesare Perdisa | Maserati | 86 | +14 Laps | 7 |
| 8 | 18 | Horace Gould | Maserati | 85 | +15 Laps | 16 |
| Ret | 2 | Robert Manzon | Gordini | 90 | Accident | 12 |
| Ret | 8 | Louis Rosier | Maserati | 72 | Engine | 15 |
| Ret | 22 | E.Castellotti | Ferrari | 14 | Clutch | 3 |
| Ret | 14 | M.Trintignant | Vanwall | 13 | Overheating | 6 |
| Ret | 16 | Harry Schell | Vanwall | 2 | Accident | 5 |
| Ret | 24 | Luigi Musso | Ferrari | 2 | Accident | 8 |
| DNQ | 36 | G.Scarlatti | Ferrari | | | |

Winning speed: 64.934mph Lap leaders: Moss 1-100
Pole position: Fangio, 1m 44.000s, 67.646mph
Fastest lap: Fangio, 1m 44.400s, 67.387mph

### INDIANAPOLIS 500 *30 May Round: 3 Race: 54 200 x 2.500 miles*

| POS. | NO. | DRIVER | CAR/ENGINE | LAPS | TIME/RETIRED | GRID |
|---|---|---|---|---|---|---|
| 1 | 8 | Pat Flaherty | Watson/Offenhauser | 200 | 3:53'28.84 | 1 |
| 2 | 4 | Sam Hanks | Kurtis Kraft/Offenhauser | 200 | +20.45 | 13 |
| 3 | 16 | Don Freeland | Phillips/Offenhauser | 200 | +1'30.23 | 26 |
| 4 | 98 | Johnnie Parsons | Kuzma/Offenhauser | 200 | +3'25.69 | 6 |
| 5 | 73 | Dick Rathmann | Kurtis Kraft/Offenhauser | 200 | +4'21.81 | 4 |
| 6 | 1 | Bob Sweikert | Kuzma/Offenhauser | 200 | +5'35.05 | 10 |
| 7 | 14 | Bob Veith | Kurtis Kraft/Offenhauser | 200 | + 6'25.63 | 23 |
| 8 | 19 | Rodger Ward | Kurtis Kraft/Offenhauser | 200 | +6'32.31 | 15 |
| 9 | 26 | Jimmy Reece | Lesovsky/Offenhauser | 200 | +6'38.31 | 21 |
| 10 | 27 | Cliff Griffith | Stevens/Offenhauser | 199 | +1 Lap | 30 |
| 11 | 82 | Gene Hartley | Kuzma/Offenhauser | 196 | +4 Laps | 22 |
| 12 | 42 | Fred Agabashian | Kurtis Kraft/Offenhauser | 196 | +4 Laps | 7 |
| 13 | 57 | Bob Christie | Kurtis Kraft/Offenhauser | 196 | +4 Laps | 25 |
| 14 | 55 | Al Keller | Kurtis Kraft/Offenhauser | 195 | +5 Laps | 28 |
| 15 | 81 | Eddie Johnson | Kuzma/Offenhauser | 195 | +5 Laps | 32 |
| 16 | 41 | Billy Garrett | Kuzma/Offenhauser | 194 | +6 Laps | 29 |
| 17 | 64 | Duke Dinsmore | Kurtis Kraft/Offenhauser | 191 | +9 Laps | 33 |
| 18 | 7 | Pat O'Connor | Kurtis Kraft/Offenhauser | 187 | +13 Laps | 3 |
| 19 | 2 | Jimmy Bryan | Kuzma/Offenhauser | 185 | +15 Laps | 19 |
| Ret | 24 | Jim Rathmann | Kurtis Kraft/Offenhauser | 175 | Engine | 2 |
| Ret | 34 | Johnnie Tolan | Kurtis Kraft/Offenhauser | 173 | Engine | 31 |
| Ret | 10 | Elisian/Russo | Kurtis Kraft/Offenhauser | 160 | Brakes | 14 |
| Ret | 99 | T.Bettenhausen | Kurtis Kraft/Offenhauser | 160 | Accident | 5 |
| Ret | 48 | Jimmy Daywalt | Kurtis Kraft/Offenhauser | 134 | Accident | 16 |
| Ret | 54 | Jack Turner | Kurtis Kraft/Offenhauser | 131 | Engine | 24 |
| Ret | 89 | Keith Andrews | Kurtis Kraft/Offenhauser | 94 | Transmission | 20 |
| Ret | 5 | Andy Linden | Kurtis Kraft/Offenhauser | 90 | Oil leak | 9 |
| Ret | 12 | Al Herman | Kurtis Kraft/Offenhauser | 74 | Accident | 27 |
| Ret | 49 | Ray Crawford | Kurtis Kraft/Offenhauser | 49 | Accident | 17 |
| Ret | 15 | Johnny Boyd | Kurtis Kraft/Offenhauser | 35 | Oil leak | 12 |
| Ret | 53 | Troy Ruttman | Kurtis Kraft/Offenhauser | 22 | Spun off | 11 |
| Ret | 88 | Johnny Thomson | Kuzma/Offenhauser | 22 | Spun off | 18 |
| Ret | 29 | Paul Russo | Kurtis Kraft/Novi | 21 | Accident | 8 |

Winning speed: 128.490mph
Pole position: Flaherty, 1m 1.815s, 145.596mph
Fastest lap: Russo, 1m 2.320s, 144.416mph

### BELGIAN GRAND PRIX: SPA-FRANCORCHAMPS *3 June Round: 4 Race: 52 36 x 14.120 miles*

| POS. | NO. | DRIVER | CAR/ENGINE | LAPS | TIME/RETIRED | GRID |
|---|---|---|---|---|---|---|
| 1 | 8 | Peter Collins | Ferrari | 36 | 2:40'00.3 | 3 |
| 2 | 6 | Paul Frere | Ferrari | 36 | +1'51.3 | 8 |
| 3 | 34 | Moss/Perdisa | Maserati | 36 | +3'16.6 | 9 |
| 4 | 10 | Harry Schell | Vanwall | 35 | +1 Lap | 6 |
| 5 | 22 | Luigi Villoresi | Maserati | 34 | +2 Laps | 11 |
| 6 | 20 | Andre Pilette | Ferrari | 33 | +3 Laps | 16 |
| 7 | 32 | Jean Behra | Maserati | 33 | +3 Laps | 4 |
| 8 | 24 | Louis Rosier | Maserati | 33 | +3 Laps | 10 |
| Ret | 2 | Juan Manuel Fangio | Ferrari | 23 | Transmission | 1 |
| Ret | 12 | M.Trintignant | Vanwall | 11 | Fuel system | 7 |
| Ret | 30 | Stirling Moss | Maserati | 10 | Wheel | 2 |
| Ret | 4 | E.Castellotti | Ferrari | 10 | Transmission | 5 |
| Ret | 28 | Piero Scotti | Connaught-Alta | 10 | Engine | 12 |
| Ret | 26 | Horace Gould | Maserati | 2 | Gearbox | 15 |
| Ret | 36 | Paco Godia | Maserati | 0 | Accident | 13 |

Winning speed: 118.443mph Lap leaders: Moss 1-4, Fangio 5-23, Collins 24-36
Pole Position: Fangio, 4m 9.800s, 126.443mph
Fastest lap: Moss, 4m 14.700s, 124.011mph

### FRENCH GRAND PRIX: REIMS *1 July Round: 5 Race: 53 61 x 5.159 miles*

| POS. | NO. | DRIVER | CAR/ENGINE | LAPS | TIME/RETIRED | GRID |
|---|---|---|---|---|---|---|
| 1 | 14 | Peter Collins | Ferrari | 61 | 2:34'23.4 | 3 |
| 2 | 12 | E.Castellotti | Ferrari | 61 | +0.3 | 2 |
| 3 | 4 | Jean Behra | Maserati | 61 | +1'29.9 | 7 |
| 4 | 10 | Juan Manuel Fangio | Ferrari | 61 | +1'35.1 | 1 |
| 5 | 6 | Moss/Perdisa | Maserati | 59 | +2 Laps | 13 |
| 6 | 36 | Louis Rosier | Maserati | 58 | +3 Laps | 12 |
| 7 | 40 | Paco Godia | Maserati | 57 | +4 Laps | 17 |
| 8 | 32 | H.da Silva-Ramos | Gordini | 57 | +4 Laps | 14 |
| 9 | 30 | Robert Manzon | Gordini | 56 | +5 Laps | 15 |
| 10 | 24 | Schell/Hawthorn | Vanwall | 56 | +5 Laps | 6 |
| 11 | 34 | Andre Pilette | Gordini | 55 | +6 Laps | 19 |
| Ret | 42 | Andre Simon | Maserati | 41 | Engine | 20 |
| Ret | 8 | Piero Taruffi | Maserati | 40 | Engine | 16 |
| Ret | 44 | O.Gendebien | Ferrari | 38 | Clutch | 11 |
| Ret | 38 | Luigi Villoresi | Maserati | 23 | Brakes | 10 |
| Ret | 16 | A.de Portago | Ferrari | 20 | Gearbox | 9 |
| Ret | 28 | M.Trintignant | Bugatti | 18 | Throttle | 18 |
| Ret | 2 | Stirling Moss | Maserati | 12 | Gearbox | 8 |
| Ret | 22 | Harry Schell | Vanwall | 5 | Engine | 4 |
| DNS | 26 | Colin Chapman | Vanwall | 0 | Non Starter | |

Winning speed: 122.291mph
Lap leaders: Collins 1, 47-48, 50-61; Castellotti 2-3, 39-46, 49; Fangio 4-38
Pole position: Fangio, 2m 23.300s, 129.596mph Fastest lap: Fangio, 2m 25.800s, 127.373mph

### BRITISH GRAND PRIX: SILVERSTONE *14 July Round: 6 Race: 54 101 x 2.927 miles*

| POS. | NO. | DRIVER | CAR/ENGINE | LAPS | TIME/RETIRED | GRID |
|---|---|---|---|---|---|---|
| 1 | 1 | Juan Manuel Fangio | Ferrari | 101 | 2:59'47.0 | 2 |
| 2 | 4 | Portago/Collins | Ferrari | 100 | +1 Lap | 12 |
| 3 | 8 | Jean Behra | Maserati | 99 | +2 Laps | 13 |
| 4 | 21 | Jack Fairman | Connaught-Alta | 98 | +3 Laps | 21 |
| 5 | 31 | Horace Gould | Maserati | 97 | +4 Laps | 14 |
| 6 | 11 | Luigi Villoresi | Maserati | 96 | +5 Laps | 19 |
| 7 | 9 | Cesare Perdisa | Maserati | 95 | +6 Laps | 15 |
| 8 | 10 | Paco Godia | Maserati | 94 | +7 Laps | 25 |
| 9 | 15 | Robert Manzon | Gordini | 94 | +7 Laps | 18 |
| 10 | 3 | Castellotti/Portago | Ferrari | 92 | +9 Laps | 8 |
| 11 | 26 | Bob Gerard | Cooper-Bristol | 88 | +13 Laps | 22 |
| Ret | 7 | Stirling Moss | Maserati | 94 | Axle | 1 |
| Ret | 16 | Harry Schell | Vanwall | 86 | Fuel system | 5 |
| Ret | 20 | D.Titterington | Connaught-Alta | 74 | Engine | 11 |
| Ret | 17 | M.Trintignant | Vanwall | 74 | Fuel system | 16 |
| Ret | 14 | H.da Silva-Ramos | Gordini | 71 | Axle | 26 |
| Ret | 2 | Peter Collins | Ferrari | 64 | Oil pressure | 4 |
| Ret | 28 | Roy Salvadori | Maserati | 59 | Fuel system | 7 |
| Ret | 24 | Tony Brooks | BRM | 39 | Accident | 9 |
| Ret | 23 | Mike Hawthorn | BRM | 24 | Transmission | 3 |
| Ret | 29 | Bruce Halford | Maserati | 23 | Engine | 20 |
| Ret | 27 | Louis Rosier | Maserati | 23 | Electrical | 27 |
| Ret | 12 | Umberto Maglioli | Maserati | 21 | Gearbox | 24 |
| Ret | 19 | A.Scott-Brown | Connaught-Alta | 16 | Transmission | 10 |
| Ret | 32 | Paul Emery | Emeryson-Alta | 12 | Ignition | 23 |
| Ret | 30 | Jack Brabham | Maserati | 4 | Engine | 28 |
| Ret | 25 | Ron Flockhart | BRM | 2 | Engine | 17 |
| Ret | 18 | J.F.Gonzalez | Vanwall | 0 | Transmission | 6 |

Winning speed: 158.780mph Lap leaders: Hawthorn 1-15; Moss 16-68; Fangio 69-101
Pole position: Moss, 1m 41.000s, 104.329mph
Fastest lap: Moss, 1m 43.200s, 102.105mph

### GERMAN GRAND PRIX: NÜRBURGRING *5 August Round: 7 Race: 55 22 x 14.173 miles*

| POS. | NO. | DRIVER | CAR/ENGINE | LAPS | TIME/RETIRED | GRID |
|---|---|---|---|---|---|---|
| 1 | 1 | Juan Manuel Fangio | Ferrari | 22 | 3:38'43.7 | 1 |
| 2 | 7 | Stirling Moss | Maserati | 22 | +46.4 | 4 |
| 3 | 6 | Jean Behra | Maserati | 22 | +7'38.3 | 8 |
| 4 | 20 | Paco Godia | Maserati | 20 | +2 Laps | 16 |
| 5 | 15 | Louis Rosier | Maserati | 19 | +3 Laps | 14 |
| DSQ | 21 | Bruce Halford | Maserati | 20 | Disqualified | 11 |
| NC | 22 | O.Volonterio | Maserati | 16 | Not classified | 19 |
| Ret | 11 | Andre Milhoux | Gordini | 15 | Engine | 21 |
| Ret | 5 | Portago/Collins | Ferrari | 14 | Accident | 10 |
| Ret | 12 | Harry Schell | Maserati | 13 | Overheating | 12 |
| Ret | 18 | Luigi Villoresi | Maserati | 13 | Engine | 20 |
| Ret | 4 | Musso/Castellotti | Ferrari | 11 | Accident | 5 |
| Ret | 2 | Peter Collins | Ferrari | 8 | Fuel leak | 2 |
| Ret | 3 | E.Castellotti | Ferrari | 5 | Electrical | 3 |
| Ret | 8 | Umberto Maglioli | Maserati | 3 | Steering | 7 |
| Ret | 19 | Horace Gould | Maserati | 3 | Oil pressure | 13 |
| Ret | 16 | Roy Salvadori | Maserati | 2 | Suspension | 9 |
| Ret | 10 | Robert Manzon | Gordini | 0 | Suspension | 15 |
| Ret | 14 | G.Scarlatti | Ferrari | 0 | Engine | 17 |
| Ret | 8 | Cesare Perdisa | Maserati | 0 | Accident | 6 |
| Ret | 11 | Andre Pilette | Gordini | 0 | Accident | 18 |

Winning speed: 85.535mph Lap leaders: Fangio 1-22
Pole position: Fangio, 9m 51.200s, 86.307mph
Fastest lap: Fangio, 9m 41.600s, 87.738mph

### ITALIAN GRAND PRIX: MONZA *2 September Round: 8 Race: 56 50 x 6.214 miles*

| POS. | NO. | DRIVER | CAR/ENGINE | LAPS | TIME/RETIRED | GRID |
|---|---|---|---|---|---|---|
| 1 | 36 | Stirling Moss | Maserati | 50 | 2:23'41.3 | 6 |
| 2 | 26 | Collins/Fangio | Ferrari | 50 | +5.7 | 7 |
| 3 | 4 | Ron Flockhart | Connaught-Alta | 49 | +1 Lap | 24 |
| 4 | 38 | Paco Godia | Maserati | 49 | +1 Lap | 18 |
| 5 | 6 | Jack Fairman | Connaught-Alta | 47 | +3 Laps | 16 |
| 6 | 40 | Luigi Piotti | Maserati | 47 | +3 Laps | 15 |
| 7 | 14 | E.de Graffenried | Maserati | 46 | +4 Laps | 19 |
| 8 | 22 | Fangio/Castellotti | Ferrari | 46 | +4 Laps | 1 |
| 9 | 12 | Andre Simon | Gordini | 45 | +5 Laps | 25 |
| 10 | 42 | Gerino Gerini | Maserati | 42 | +8 Laps | 17 |
| 11 | 44 | Roy Salvadori | Maserati | 41 | +9 Laps | 14 |
| Ret | 28 | Luigi Musso | Ferrari | 47 | Steering | 3 |
| Ret | 46 | Maglioli/Behra | Maserati | 42 | Steering | 13 |
| Ret | 18 | Harry Schell | Vanwall | 32 | Transmission | 10 |
| Ret | 32 | Jean Behra | Maserati | 23 | Magneto | 5 |
| Ret | 48 | Bruce Halford | Maserati | 16 | Engine | 22 |
| Ret | 20 | M.Trintignant | Vanwall | 13 | Transmission | 11 |
| Ret | 16 | Piero Taruffi | Vanwall | 12 | Oil leak | 4 |
| Ret | 24 | E.Castellotti | Ferrari | 9 | Tyre | 2 |
| Ret | 34 | Villoresi/Bonnier | Maserati | 7 | Engine | 8 |
| Ret | 10 | Robert Manzon | Gordini | 7 | Chassis | 23 |
| Ret | 30 | A.de Portago | Ferrari | 6 | Tyre | 9 |
| Ret | 2 | Les Leston | Connaught-Alta | 6 | Suspension | 20 |
| Ret | 8 | H.da Silva-Ramos | Gordini | 3 | Engine | 21 |

Winning speed: 129.733mph
Lap leaders: Castellotti 1-4; Moss 5-10, 12-45, 48-50; Schell 11; Musso 46-47
Pole position: Fangio, 2m 42.600s, 137.573mph
Fastest lap: Moss, 2m 45.500s, 135.162mph

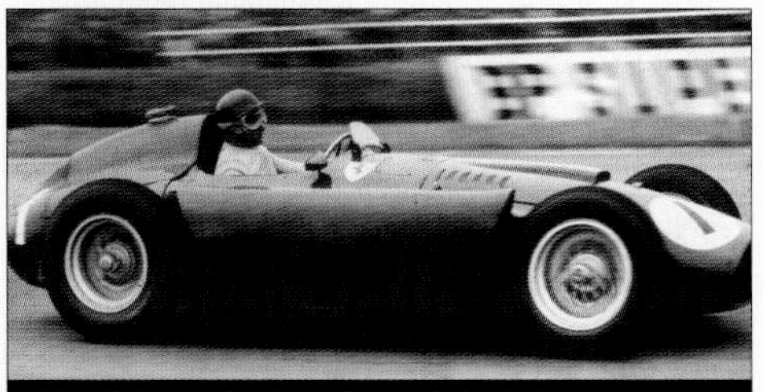

1956 world champion, Juan Manuel Fangio in the Lancia-Ferrari.

# 1957

## DRIVERS' CHAMPION: JUAN MANUEL FANGIO

### DRIVERS' CHAMPIONSHIP

| POS. | DRIVER | NATIONALITY | CAR | POINTS |
|---|---|---|---|---|
| 1 | Juan Manuel Fangio | Argentina | Maserati | 40 (6) |
| 2 | Stirling Moss | GB | Maserati, Vanwall | 25 |
| 3 | Luigi Musso | Italy | Lancia-Ferrari | 16 |
| 4 | Mike Hawthorn | GB | Lancia-Ferrari | 13 |
| 5 | Tony Brooks | GB | Vanwall | 11 |
| 6 | Masten Gregory | USA | Maserati | 10 |
| = | Harry Schell | USA | Maserati | 10 |
| 8 | Peter Collins | GB | Lancia-Ferrari | 8 |
| = | Sam Hanks | USA | Epperly-Offenhauser | 8 |
| 10 | Jim Rathmann | USA | Epperly-Offenhauser | 7 |
| 11 | Jean Behra | France | Maserati | 6 |
| 12 | Stuart Lewis-Evans | GB | Connaught-Alta, Vanwall | 5 |
| = | Maurice Trintignant | France | Lancia-Ferrari | 5 |
| 14 | Carlos Menditéguy | Argentina | Maserati | 4 |
| = | Wolfgang von Trips | West Germany | Lancia | 4 |
| = | Jimmy Bryan | USA | Kuzma-Offenhauser | 4 |
| = | Paul Russo | USA | Kurtis-Novi | 4 |
| 18 | Andy Linden | USA | Kurtis-Offenhauser | 3 |
| 19 | Roy Salvadori | GB | BRM, Vanwall, Cooper –Climax | 2 |
| = | Jose Froilan Gonzalez | Argentina | Lancia-Ferrari | 2 |
| 20 | Alfonso de Portago | Spain | Lancia-Ferrari | 1 |
| = | Giorgio Scarlatti | Italy | Maserati | 1 |
| | Cesare Perdisa | Italy | Lancia-Ferrari | |
| | Jo Bonnier | Sweden | Maserati | |
| | Liugi Piotti | Italy | Maserati | |
| | Alessandro de Tomaso | Italy | Ferrari | |
| | Eugenio Castellotti | Italy | Lancia-Ferrari | |
| | Jack Brabham | Australia | Cooper –Climax | |
| | Ron Flockhart | GB | BRM | |
| | Ivor Bueb | GB | Connaught-Alta, Maserati | |
| | Horace Gould | GB | Maserati | |
| | Les Leston | GB | Cooper –Climax, BRM | |
| | André Simon | France | Maserati | |
| | Herbert MacKay-Fraser | USA | BRM | |
| | Mike MacDowell | GB | Cooper –Climax | |
| | Bob Gerard | GB | Cooper –Bristol | |
| | Jack Fairman | GB | BRM | |
| | Francesco Godia-Sales | Spain | Maserati | |
| | Bruce Halford | GB | Maserati | |
| | Hans Hermann | West Germany | Maserati | |
| | Ottorino Volonterio | Italy | Maserati | |

Points for top five finishers (8, 6, 4, 3, 2) plus a point for fastest lap. Only the best five scores counted towards the championship. Points for shared drives (except where 'insufficient distance' was deemed to have been covered by one of the drivers) and shared fastest laps were divided equally between the drivers. Drivers sharing two cars in a race received points only for their highest finish. At the German Grand Prix Formula Two cars raced simultaneously with Formula One cars but were ineligible for points.

### ARGENTINE GRAND PRIX: BUENOS AIRES *13 January Round: 1 Race: 57 100 x 2.431 miles*

| POS. | NO. | DRIVER | CAR/ENGINE | LAPS | TIME/RETIRED | GRID |
|---|---|---|---|---|---|---|
| 1 | 2 | Juan Manuel Fangio | Maserati | 100 | 3:00'55.9 | 2 |
| 2 | 6 | Jean Behra | Maserati | 100 | +18.3 | 3 |
| 3 | 8 | C.Menditeguy | Maserati | 99 | +1 Lap | 8 |
| 4 | 22 | Harry Schell | Maserati | 98 | +2 Laps | 9 |
| 5 | 20 | Portago/Gonzalez | Ferrari | 98 | +2 Laps | 10 |
| 6 | 18 | Collins/Trips/Perdisa | Ferrari | 98 | +2 Laps | 11 |
| 7 | 24 | Jo Bonnier | Maserati | 95 | +5 Laps | 13 |
| 8 | 4 | Stirling Moss | Maserati | 93 | +7 Laps | 1 |
| 9 | 26 | A.de Tomaso | Ferrari | 91 | +9 Laps | 12 |
| 10 | 28 | Luigi Piotti | Maserati | 90 | +10 Laps | 14 |
| Ret | 14 | E.Castellotti | Ferrari | 75 | Wheel | 4 |
| Ret | 16 | Mike Hawthorn | Ferrari | 35 | Clutch | 7 |
| Ret | 12 | Luigi Musso | Ferrari | 31 | Clutch | 6 |
| Ret | 10 | Peter Collins | Ferrari | 26 | Clutch | 5 |

Winning speed: 80.610mph
Lap leaders: Behra 1-2, 9-12, 81,84; Castellotti 3-8; Collins 13-25; Fangio 26-80, 82-83, 85-100
Pole position: Moss, 1m 42.600s, 85.291mph
Fastest lap: Moss, 1m 44.700s, 83.581mph

### MONACO GRAND PRIX: MONTE CARLO *19 May Round: 2 Race: 58 105 x 3.145 miles*

| POS. | NO. | DRIVER | CAR/ENGINE | LAPS | TIME/RETIRED | GRID |
|---|---|---|---|---|---|---|
| 1 | 32 | Juan Manuel Fangio | Maserati | 105 | 3:10'12.8 | 1 |
| 2 | 20 | Tony Brooks | Vanwall | 105 | +25.2 | 4 |
| 3 | 2 | Masten Gregory | Maserati | 103 | +2 Laps | 10 |
| 4 | 10 | S.Lewis-Evans | Connaught-Alta | 102 | +3 Laps | 13 |
| 5 | 30 | M.Trintignant | Ferrari | 100 | +5 Laps | 6 |
| 6 | 14 | Jack Brabham | Cooper-Climax | 100 | +5 Laps | 15 |
| Ret | 24 | von Trips/Hawthorn | Ferrari | 95 | Engine | 9 |
| Ret | 34 | Scarlatti/ Schell | Maserati | 64 | Oil leak | 14 |
| Ret | 6 | Ron Flockhart | BRM | 60 | Engine | 11 |
| Ret | 36 | C.Menditeguy | Maserati | 51 | Spun off | 7 |
| Ret | 12 | Ivor Bueb | Connaught-Alta | 47 | Fuel leak | 16 |
| Ret | 38 | Harry Schell | Maserati | 23 | Suspension | 8 |
| Ret | 22 | Horace Gould | Maserati | 10 | Accident | 12 |
| Ret | 26 | Peter Collins | Ferrari | 4 | Accident | 2 |
| Ret | 18 | Stirling Moss | Vanwall | 4 | Accident | 3 |
| Ret | 28 | Mike Hawthorn | Ferrari | 4 | Accident | 5 |
| DNQ | 8 | Roy Salvadori | BRM | | | |
| DNQ | 40 | Hans Herrmann | Maserati | | | |
| DNQ | 4 | Andre Simon | Maserati | | | |
| DNQ | 42 | Luigi Piotti | Maserati | | | |
| DNQ | 16 | Les Leston | Cooper-Climax | | | |

Winning speed: 64.725mph Lap leaders: Moss 1-4; Fangio 5-105;
Pole position: Fangio, 1m 42.700s, 68.502mph
Fastest lap: Fangio, 1m 45.600s, 66.621mph

### INDIANAPOLIS 500 *30 May Round: 3 Race: 59 200 x 2.500 miles*

| POS. | NO. | DRIVER | CAR/ENGINE | LAPS | TIME/RETIRED | GRID |
|---|---|---|---|---|---|---|
| 1 | 9 | Sam Hanks | Epperly-Offenhauser | 200 | 3:41'14.25 | 13 |
| 2 | 26 | Jim Rathmann | Epperly-Offenhauser | 200 | +21.46 | 32 |
| 3 | 1 | Jimmy Bryan | Kuzma-Offenhauser | 200 | +2'13.97 | 15 |
| 4 | 54 | Paul Russo | Kurtis Kraft-Novi | 200 | +2'56.86 | 10 |
| 5 | 73 | Andy Linden | Kurtis Kraft-Offenhauser | 200 | +3'14.27 | 12 |
| 6 | 6 | Johnny Boyd | Kurtis Kraft-Offenhauser | 200 | +4'35.27 | 5 |
| 7 | 48 | Marshall Teague | Kurtis Kraft-Offenhauser | 200 | +4'45.58 | 28 |
| 8 | 12 | Pat O'Connor | Kurtis Kraft-Offenhauser | 200 | +5'33.15 | 1 |
| 9 | 7 | Bob Veith | Phillips-Offenhauser | 200 | +6'17.11 | 16 |
| 10 | 22 | Gene Hartley | Lesovsky-Offenhauser | 200 | +7'10.12 | 14 |
| 11 | 19 | Jack Turner | Kurtis Kraft-Offenhauser | 200 | +7'56.07 | 19 |
| 12 | 10 | Johnny Thomson | Kuzma-Offenhauser | 199 | +1 Lap | 11 |
| 13 | 95 | Bob Christie | Kurtis Kraft-Offenhauser | 197 | +3 Laps | 33 |
| 14 | 82 | Chuck Weyant | Kuzma-Offenhauser | 196 | +4 Laps | 25 |
| 15 | 27 | T.Bettenhausen | Kurtis Kraft-Novi | 195 | +5 Laps | 22 |
| 16 | 8 | Johnnie Parsons | Kurtis Kraft-Offenhauser | 195 | +5 Laps | 17 |
| 17 | 3 | Don Freeland | Kurtis Kraft-Offenhauser | 192 | +8 Laps | 21 |
| Ret | 5 | Jimmy Reece | Kurtis Kraft-Offenhauser | 182 | Throttle | 6 |
| Ret | 92 | Don Edmunds | Kurtis Kraft-Offenhauser | 170 | Spun off | 27 |
| Ret | 28 | Johnnie Tolan | Kuzma-Offenhauser | 138 | Clutch | 31 |
| Ret | 89 | Al Herman | Dunn-Offenhauser | 111 | Accident | 30 |
| Ret | 14 | Fred Agabashian | Kurtis Kraft-Offenhauser | 107 | Fuel leak | 4 |
| Ret | 88 | Eddie Sachs | Kuzma-Offenhauser | 105 | Fuel pump | 2 |
| Ret | 77 | Mike Magill | Kurtis Kraft-Offenhauser | 101 | Accident | 18 |
| Ret | 43 | Eddie Johnson | Kurtis Kraft-Offenhauser | 93 | Wheel bearing | 20 |
| Ret | 31 | Bill Cheesbourg | Kurtis Kraft-Offenhauser | 81 | Fuel leak | 23 |
| Ret | 16 | Al Keller | Kurtis Kraft-Offenhauser | 75 | Accident | 8 |
| Ret | 57 | Jimmy Daywalt | Kurtis Kraft-Offenhauser | 53 | Accident | 29 |
| Ret | 83 | Ed Elisian | Kurtis Kraft-Offenhauser | 51 | Retirement | 7 |
| Ret | 8 | Rodger Ward | Lesovsky-Offenhauser | 27 | Compressor | 24 |
| Ret | 52 | Troy Ruttman | Watson-Offenhauser | 13 | Engine | 3 |
| Ret | 23 | Elmer George | Kurtis Kraft-Offenhauser | 0 | Accident | 9 |
| Ret | 55 | Eddie Russo | Kurtis Kraft-Offenhauser | 0 | Accident | 26 |

Winning speed: 135.601mph
Pole position: O'Connor, 1m 02.522s, 143.949mph
Fastest lap: Rathmann, 1m 02.750s, 143.426mph

### FRENCH GRAND PRIX: ROUEN-LES-ESSARTS *7 July Round: 4 Race: 60 77 x 4.065 miles*

| POS. | NO. | DRIVER | CAR/ENGINE | LAPS | TIME-RETIRED | GRID |
|---|---|---|---|---|---|---|
| 1 | 2 | Juan Manuel Fangio | Maserati | 77 | 3:07'46.4 | 1 |
| 2 | 10 | Luigi Musso | Ferrari | 77 | +50.8 | 3 |
| 3 | 12 | Peter Collins | Ferrari | 77 | +2'06.0 | 5 |
| 4 | 14 | Mike Hawthorn | Ferrari | 76 | +1 Lap | 7 |
| 5 | 6 | Harry Schell | Maserati | 70 | +7 Laps | 4 |
| 6 | 4 | Jean Behra | Maserati | 69 | +8 Laps | 2 |
| 7 | 24 | Brabham/MacDowel | Cooper-Climax | 68 | +9 Laps | 15 |
| Ret | 8 | C.Menditeguy | Maserati | 30 | Engine | 9 |
| Ret | 18 | S.Lewis-Evans | Vanwall | 30 | Steering | 10 |
| Ret | 20 | Roy Salvadori | Vanwall | 25 | Engine | 6 |
| Ret | 28 | H.MacKay-Fraser | BRM | 24 | Transmission | 12 |
| Ret | 16 | M.Trintignant | Ferrari | 23 | Electrical | 8 |
| Ret | 22 | Jack Brabham | Cooper-Climax | 4 | Accident | 13 |
| Ret | 30 | Horace Gould | Maserati | 4 | Halfshaft | 14 |
| Ret | 26 | Ron Flockhart | BRM | 2 | Accident | 11 |

Winning speed: 100.016mph Lap leaders: Musso 1-3; Fangio 4-77
Pole position: Fangio, 2m 21.500s, 103.421mph
Fastest lap: Musso, 2m 22.400s, 102.767mph

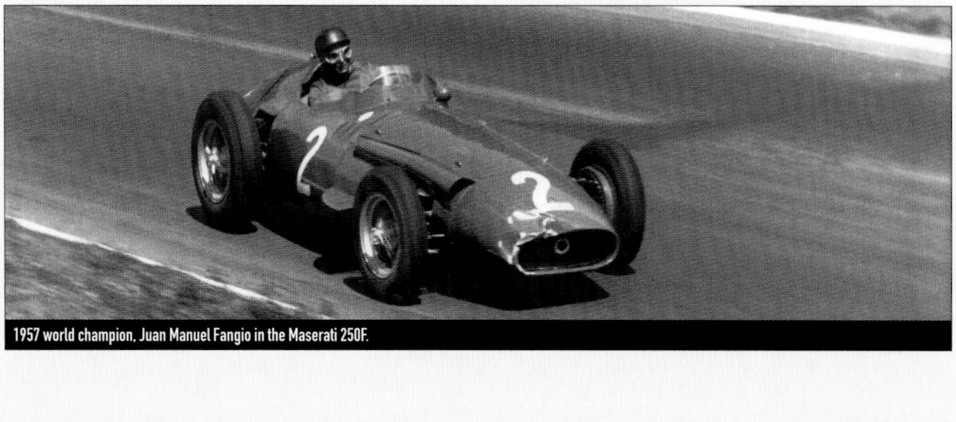

1957 world champion, Juan Manuel Fangio in the Maserati 250F.

### BRITISH GRAND PRIX: AINTREE *20 July Round: 5 Race: 61 90 x 3.000 miles*

| POS. | NO. | DRIVER | CAR/ENGINE | LAPS | TIME/RETIRED | GRID |
|---|---|---|---|---|---|---|
| 1 | 20 | Moss/Brooks | Vanwall | 90 | 3:06'37.8 | 3 |
| 2 | 14 | Luigi Musso | Ferrari | 90 | +25.6 | 10 |
| 3 | 10 | Mike Hawthorn | Ferrari | 90 | +42.8 | 5 |
| 4 | 16 | Trintignant/Collins | Ferrari | 88 | +2 Laps | 9 |
| 5 | 36 | Roy Salvadori | Cooper-Climax | 85 | +5 Laps | 15 |
| 6 | 38 | Bob Gerard | Cooper-Bristol | 82 | +8 Laps | 18 |
| 7 | 22 | S.Lewis-Evans | Vanwall | 82 | +8 Laps | 6 |
| 8 | 32 | Ivor Bueb | Maserati | 71 | +19 Laps | 19 |
| Ret | 34 | Jack Brabham | Cooper-Climax | 74 | Clutch | 13 |
| Ret | 4 | Jean Behra | Maserati | 69 | Clutch | 2 |
| Ret | 12 | Peter Collins | Ferrari | 53 | Water leak | 8 |
| Ret | 18 | Moss/ Brooks | Vanwall | 51 | Engine | 1 |
| Ret | 2 | Juan Manuel Fangio | Maserati | 49 | Engine | 4 |
| Ret | 24 | Jack Fairman | BRM | 46 | Engine | 16 |
| Ret | 26 | Les Leston | BRM | 44 | Engine | 12 |
| Ret | 6 | Harry Schell | Maserati | 39 | Water pump | 7 |
| Ret | 8 | C.Menditeguy | Maserati | 35 | Transmission | 11 |
| Ret | 28 | Jo Bonnier | Maserati | 18 | Gearbox | 17 |
| DNS | 30 | Horace Gould | Maserati | 0 | Non starter | |

Winning speed: 86.803mph Lap leaders: Moss 1-22, 70-90; Behra 23-69
Pole position: Moss, 2m 00.200s, 89.850mph
Fastest lap: Moss, 1m 59.200s, 90.600mph

### GERMAN GRAND PRIX: NÜRBURGRING *4 August Round: 7 Race: 55 22 x 14.173 miles*

| POS. | NO. | DRIVER | CAR/ENGINE | LAPS | TIME/RETIRED | GRID |
|---|---|---|---|---|---|---|
| 1 | 1 | Juan Manuel Fangio | Maserati | 22 | 3:30'38.3 | 1 |
| 2 | 8 | Mike Hawthorn | Ferrari | 22 | +3.6 | 2 |
| 3 | 7 | Peter Collins | Ferrari | 22 | +35.6 | 4 |
| 4 | 6 | Luigi Musso | Ferrari | 22 | + 3'37.6 | 8 |
| 5 | 10 | Stirling Moss | Vanwall | 22 | +4'37.5 | 7 |
| 6 | 2 | Jean Behra | Maserati | 22 | +4'38.5 | 3 |
| 7 | 3 | Harry Schell | Maserati | 22 | +6'47.5 | 6 |
| 8 | 16 | Masten Gregory | Maserati | 21 | +1 Lap | 10 |
| 9 | 11 | Tony Brooks | Vanwall | 21 | +1 Lap | 5 |
| 10 | 4 | G.Scarlatti | Maserati | 21 | +1 Lap | 13 |
| 11 | 15 | Bruce Halford | Maserati | 21 | +1 Lap | 16 |
| 12 | 21 | Edgar Barth | Porsche F2 | 21 | +1 Lap | 12 |
| 13 | 28 | Brian Naylor | Cooper-Climax F2 | 20 | +2 Laps | 17 |
| 14 | 27 | C.G.de Beaufort | Porsche F2 | 20 | +2 Laps | 20 |
| 15 | 25 | Tony Marsh | Cooper-Climax F2 | 17 | +5 Laps | 22 |
| Ret | 17 | Hans Herrmann | Maserati | 14 | Chassis | 11 |
| Ret | 20 | Umberto Maglioli | Porsche F2 | 13 | Engine | 15 |
| Ret | 23 | Roy Salvadori | Cooper-Climax F2 | 11 | Transmission | 14 |
| Ret | 18 | Francesco Godia-S | Maserati | 11 | Steering | 21 |
| Ret | 12 | S.Lewis-Evans | Vanwall | 10 | Gearbox | 9 |
| Ret | 24 | Jack Brabham | Cooper-Climax F2 | 6 | Transmission | 18 |
| Ret | 26 | Paul England | Cooper-Climax F2 | 4 | Distributor | 23 |
| Ret | 29 | Dick Gibson | Cooper-Climax F2 | 3 | Suspension | 24 |
| Ret | 19 | Horace Gould | Maserati | 1 | Axle | 19 |

Winning speed: 88.794mph
Lap leaders: Hawthorn 1-2, 15-20; Fangio 3-11, 21-22; Collins 12-14
Pole position: Fangio, 9m 25.600s, 910.223mph
Fastest lap: Fangio, 9m 17.400s, 91.528mph

### PESCARA GRAND PRIX: PESCARA *18 August Round: 7 Race: 63 18 x 15.894 miles*

| POS. | NO. | DRIVER | CAR/ENGINE | LAPS | TIME/RETIRED | GRID |
|---|---|---|---|---|---|---|
| 1 | 26 | Stirling Moss | Vanwall | 18 | 2:59'22.7 | 2 |
| 2 | 2 | Juan Manuel Fangio | Maserati | 18 | +3'13.9 | 1 |
| 3 | 6 | Harry Schell | Maserati | 18 | +6'46.8 | 5 |
| 4 | 14 | Masten Gregory | Maserati | 18 | +8'16.5 | 7 |
| 5 | 30 | S.Lewis-Evans | Vanwall | 17 | +1 Lap | 8 |
| 6 | 8 | G.Scarlatti | Maserati | 17 | +1 Lap | 10 |
| 7 | 24 | Jack Brabham | Cooper-Climax | 15 | +3 Laps | 16 |
| Ret | 34 | Luigi Musso | Ferrari | 9 | Oil leak | 3 |
| Ret | 10 | Francesco Godia-S | Maserati | 9 | Engine | 12 |
| Ret | 20 | Bruce Halford | Maserati | 9 | Transmission | 14 |
| Ret | 16 | Jo Bonnier | Maserati | 7 | Overheating | 9 |
| Ret | 4 | Jean Behra | Maserati | 3 | Oil leak | 4 |
| Ret | 22 | Roy Salvadori | Cooper-Climax | 3 | Accident | 15 |
| Ret | 28 | Tony Brooks | Vanwall | 1 | Engine | 6 |
| Ret | 18 | Horace Gould | Maserati | 0 | Accident | 11 |
| Ret | 12 | Luigi Piotti | Maserati | 0 | Engine | 13 |

Winning speed: 95.695mph Lap leaders: Musso 1; Moss 2-18
Pole position: Fangio, 9m 44.600s, 97.876mph
Fastest lap: Moss, 9m 44.600s, 97.876mph

### ITALIAN GRAND PRIX: MONZA *8 September Round: 8 Race: 64 87 x 3.573 miles*

| POS. | NO. | DRIVER | CAR/ENGINE | LAPS | TIME/RETIRED | GRID |
|---|---|---|---|---|---|---|
| 1 | 18 | Stirling Moss | Vanwall | 87 | 2:35'03.9 | 2 |
| 2 | 2 | Juan Manuel Fangio | Maserati | 87 | +41.2 | 4 |
| 3 | 36 | W.von Trips | Ferrari | 85 | +2 Laps | 8 |
| 4 | 26 | Masten Gregory | Maserati | 84 | +3 Laps | 11 |
| 5 | 8 | Scarlatti/Schell | Maserati | 84 | +3 Laps | 12 |
| 6 | 34 | Mike Hawthorn | Ferrari | 83 | +4 Laps | 10 |
| 7 | 22 | Tony Brooks | Vanwall | 82 | +5 Laps | 3 |
| 8 | 32 | Luigi Musso | Ferrari | 82 | +5 Laps | 9 |
| 9 | 10 | Francesco Godia-S | Maserati | 81 | +6 Laps | 15 |
| 10 | 14 | Horace Gould | Maserati | 78 | +9 Laps | 18 |
| 11 | 28 | Simon/Volonterio | Maserati | 72 | +15 Laps | 16 |
| Ret | 30 | Peter Collins | Ferrari | 62 | Engine | 7 |
| Ret | 20 | S.Lewis-Evans | Vanwall | 49 | Engine | 1 |
| Ret | 6 | Jean Behra | Maserati | 49 | Overheating | 5 |
| Ret | 16 | Bruce Halford | Maserati | 47 | Engine | 14 |
| Ret | 4 | Harry Schell | Maserati | 34 | Oil leak | 6 |
| Ret | 24 | Jo Bonnier | Maserati | 31 | Overheating | 13 |
| Ret | 12 | Luigi Piotti | Maserati | 3 | Engine | 17 |

Winning speed: 120.275mph Lap leaders: Moss 1-3, 5,11, 21-87; Behra 4, 6; Fangio 7-10; Brooks 12-15; Lewis-Evans 16-20
Pole position: Lewis-Evans, 1m 42.400s, 125.609mph
Fastest lap: Brooks, 1m 43.700s, 124.035mph

# 1958

## DRIVERS' CHAMPION: MIKE HAWTHORN
## CONSTRUCTORS' CHAMPION: VANWALL

### DRIVERS' CHAMPIONSHIP

| POS. | DRIVER | NATIONALITY | CAR | POINTS |
|---|---|---|---|---|
| 1 | Mike Hawthorn | GB | Ferrari | 42(49) |
| 2 | Stirling Moss | GB | Cooper-Climax, Vanwall | 41 |
| 3 | Tony Brooks | GB | Vanwall | 24 |
| 4 | Roy Salvadori | GB | Cooper-Climax | 15 |
| 5 | Peter Collins | GB | Ferrari | 14 |
| = | Harry Schell | USA | Maserati, BRM | 14 |
| 7 | Maurice Trintignant | France | Cooper-Climax, Maserati, BRM | 12 |
| = | Luigi Musso | Italy | Ferrari | 12 |
| 9 | Stuart Lewis-Evans | GB | Vanwall | 11 |
| 10 | Jean Behra | France | Maserati | 9 |
| = | Wolfgang von Trips | West Germany | Ferrari | 9 |
| = | Phil Hill | USA | Maserati, Ferrari | 9 |
| 13 | Jimmy Bryan | USA | Epperly-Offenhauser | 8 |
| 14 | Juan Manuel Fangio | Argentina | Maserati | 7 |
| 15 | George Amick | USA | Epperly-Offenhauser | 6 |
| 16 | Johnny Boyd | USA | Kurtis-Offenhauser | 4 |
| 17 | Tony Bettenhausen | USA | Epperly-Offenhauser | 3 |
| = | Jack Brabham | Australia | Cooper-Climax | 3 |
| = | Cliff Allison | GB | Lotus-Climax, Maserati | 3 |
| = | Jo Bonnier | Sweden | Maserati, BRM | 3 |
| 21 | Jim Rathmann | USA | Watson-Offenhauser | 2 |
| | Olivier Gendebien | Belgium | Ferrari | |
| | Masten Gregory | USA | Maserati | |
| | Caroll Shelby | USA | Maserati | |
| | Graham Hill | GB | Lotus –Climax | |
| | Ron Flockhart | GB | BRM | |
| | Carlos Menditéguy | Argentina | Maserati | |
| | Francesco Godia-Sales | Spain | Maserati | |
| | Horace Gould | GB | Maserati | |
| | Giorgio Scarlatti | Italy | Maserati | |
| | Liugi Piotti | Italy | Maserati | |
| | Gerino Gerini | Italy | Maserati | |
| | Maria Teresa de Fillippis | Italy | Maserati | |
| | André Testut | Monaco | Maserati | |
| | Louis Chiron | Monaco | Maserati | |
| | Liugi Tarmozzo | Italy | Maserati | |
| | Gulio Cabianca | Italy | Osca, Maserati | |
| | Paul Emery | GB | Connaught-Alta | |
| | Kevin Kavanaugh | Australia | Maserati | |
| | Bruce Kessler | USA | Connaught-Alta | |
| | Carel Godin de Beaufort | Netherlands | Porsche | |
| | Wolfgang Seidel | West Germany | Maserati | |
| | Troy Ruttman | USA | Maserati | |
| | Hans Herrmann | West Germany | Maserati | |
| | Ian Burgess | GB | Cooper-Climax | |
| | Jack Fairman | GB | Connaught-Alta, Cooper-Climax | |
| | Alan Stacey | GB | Lotus-Climax | |
| | Ivor Bueb | GB | Connaught-Alta | |
| | Bernie Ecclestone | GB | Connaught-Alta | |

Points for top five finishers (8, 6, 4, 3, 2) plus a point for fastest lap. Only the best six scores counted towards the championship. Points were no longer awarded to either driver for shared drives. Formula Two cars raced simultaneously with Formula One cars in Germany and Morocco but were ineligible for points.

### CONSTRUCTORS' CHAMPIONSHIP

| POS. | CONSTRUCTOR | POINTS |
|---|---|---|
| 1 | Vanwall | 48 |
| 2 | Ferrari | 40 |
| 3 | Cooper-Climax | 31 |
| 4 | BRM | 18 |
| 5 | Maserati | 6 |
| 6 | Lotus-Climax | 3 |

Points for top five finishers (8, 6, 4, 3, 2). Points only counted for top-placed car for each constructor. Only the best six scores counted towards the championship. Indianapolis excluded.

### ARGENTINE GRAND PRIX: BUENOS AIRES *19 January Round: 1 Race: 65 80 x 2.431 miles*

| POS. | NO. | DRIVER | CAR/ENGINE | LAPS | TIME/RETIRED | GRID |
|---|---|---|---|---|---|---|
| 1 | 14 | Stirling Moss | Cooper-Climax | 80 | 2:19'33.7 | 7 |
| 2 | 16 | Luigi Musso | Ferrari | 80 | +2.7 | 5 |
| 3 | 20 | Mike Hawthorn | Ferrari | 80 | +12.6 | 2 |
| 4 | 2 | Juan Manuel Fangio | Maserati | 80 | +53.0 | 1 |
| 5 | 4 | Jean Behra | Maserati | 78 | +2 Laps | 4 |
| 6 | 8 | Harry Schell | Maserati | 77 | +3 Laps | 8 |
| 7 | 6 | C.Menditeguy | Maserati | 76 | +4 Laps | 6 |
| 8 | 10 | Francesco Godia-S | Maserati | 75 | +5 Laps | 9 |
| 9 | 12 | Horace Gould | Maserati | 71 | +9 Laps | 10 |
| Ret | 18 | Peter Collins | Ferrari | 0 | Halfshaft | 3 |

Winning speed: 83.604mph Lap leaders: Behra 1; Hawthorn 2-9; Fangio 10-34; Moss 35-80
Pole position: Fangio, 1m 42.000s, 85.793mph
Fastest lap: Fangio, 1m 41.800s, 85.962mph

### MONACO GRAND PRIX: MONTE CARLO *18 May Round: 2 Race: 66 100 x 1.954 miles*

| POS. | NO. | DRIVER | CAR/ENGINE | LAPS | TIME/RETIRED | GRID |
|---|---|---|---|---|---|---|
| 1 | 20 | M.Trintignant | Cooper-Climax | 100 | 2:52'27.9 | 5 |
| 2 | 34 | Luigi Musso | Ferrari | 100 | +20.2 | 10 |
| 3 | 36 | Peter Collins | Ferrari | 100 | +38.8 | 9 |
| 4 | 16 | Jack Brabham | Cooper-Climax | 97 | +3 Laps | 3 |
| 5 | 8 | Harry Schell | BRM | 91 | +9 Laps | 12 |
| 6 | 24 | Cliff Allison | Lotus-Climax | 87 | +13 Laps | 13 |
| Ret | 40 | W.von Trips | Ferrari | 91 | Engine | 11 |
| Ret | 58 | Jo Bonnier | Maserati | 71 | Accident | 16 |
| Ret | 26 | Graham Hill | Lotus-Climax | 69 | Halfshaft | 15 |
| Ret | 18 | Roy Salvadori | Cooper-Climax | 56 | Gearbox | 4 |
| Ret | 38 | Mike Hawthorn | Ferrari | 47 | Fuel pump | 6 |
| Ret | 28 | Stirling Moss | Vanwall | 38 | Engine | 8 |
| Ret | 6 | Jean Behra | BRM | 29 | Brakes | 2 |
| Ret | 46 | G.Scarlatti | Maserati | 28 | Engine | 14 |
| Ret | 30 | Tony Brooks | Vanwall | 22 | Engine | 1 |
| Ret | 32 | S.Lewis-Evans | Vanwall | 11 | Overheating | 7 |
| DNQ | 22 | Ron Flockhart | Cooper-Climax | | | |
| DNQ | 50 | Ken Kavanagh | Maserati | | | |
| DNQ | 48 | Gerino Gerini | Maserati | | | |
| DNQ | 12 | Bruce Kessler | Connaught-Alta | | | |
| DNQ | 14 | Paul Emery | Connaught-Alta | | | |
| DNQ | 44 | M.T.de Filippis | Maserati | | | |
| DNQ | 56 | Andre Testut | Maserati | | | |
| DNQ | 52 | Giulio Cabianca | Osca | | | |
| DNQ | 54 | Luigi Piotti | Osca | | | |
| DNQ | 42 | Horace Gould | Maserati | | | |
| DNQ | 10 | Ron Flockhart | BRM | | | |
| DNQ | 12 | B.Ecclestone | Connaught-Alta | | | |
| DNQ | 50 | Luigi Taramazzo | Maserati | | | |
| DNQ | 56 | Louis Chiron | Maserati | | | |
| DNQ | 4 | Francesco Godia-S | Maserati | | | |

Winning speed: 67.986mph
Lap leaders: Behra 1-27; Hawthorn 28-32, 39-47; Moss 33-38; Trintignant 48-100
Pole position: Brooks, 1m 39.800s, 70.493mph
Fastest lap: Hawthorn, 1m 40.600s, 69.932mph

### DUTCH GRAND PRIX: ZANDVOORT *25 May Round: 3 Race: 67 75 x 2.605 miles*

| POS. | NO. | DRIVER | CAR/ENGINE | LAPS | TIME/RETIRED | GRID |
|---|---|---|---|---|---|---|
| 1 | 1 | Stirling Moss | Vanwall | 75 | 2:04'49.2 | 2 |
| 2 | 15 | Harry Schell | BRM | 75 | +47.9 | 7 |
| 3 | 14 | Jean Behra | BRM | 75 | +1'42.3 | 4 |
| 4 | 7 | Roy Salvadori | Cooper-Climax | 74 | +1 Lap | 9 |
| 5 | 5 | Mike Hawthorn | Ferrari | 74 | +1 Lap | 6 |
| 6 | 17 | Cliff Allison | Lotus-Climax | 73 | +2 Laps | 11 |
| 7 | 6 | Luigi Musso | Ferrari | 73 | +2 Laps | 12 |
| 8 | 8 | Jack Brabham | Cooper-Climax | 73 | +2 Laps | 5 |
| 9 | 9 | M.Trintignant | Cooper-Climax | 72 | +3 Laps | 8 |
| 10 | 11 | Jo Bonnier | Maserati | 71 | +4 Laps | 15 |
| 11 | 18 | C.G.de Beaufort | Porsche | 69 | +6 Laps | 17 |
| Ret | 10 | G.Scarlatti | Maserati | 52 | Halfshaft | 16 |
| Ret | 3 | S.Lewis-Evans | Vanwall | 46 | Engine | 1 |
| Ret | 16 | Graham Hill | Lotus-Climax | 40 | Overheating | 13 |
| Ret | 4 | Peter Collins | Ferrari | 32 | Gearbox | 10 |
| Ret | 12 | Masten Gregory | Maserati | 16 | Fuel pump | 14 |
| Ret | 2 | Tony Brooks | Vanwall | 13 | Halfshaft | 3 |

Winning speed: 93.930mph Lap leaders: Moss 1-75
Pole position: Lewis-Evans, 1m 37.100s, 96.596mph
Fastest lap: Moss, 1m 37.600s, 96.101mph

### INDIANAPOLIS 500 *30 May Round: 4 Race: 68 200 x 2.500 miles*

| POS. | NO. | DRIVER | CAR/ENGINE | LAPS | TIME/RETIRED | GRID |
|---|---|---|---|---|---|---|
| 1 | 1 | Jimmy Bryan | Epperly-Offenhauser | 200 | 3:44'13.80 | 7 |
| 2 | 99 | George Amick | Epperly-Offenhauser | 200 | +27.63 | 25 |
| 3 | 9 | Johnny Boyd | Kurtis Kraft-Offenhauser | 200 | +1'09.97 | 8 |
| 4 | 33 | Tony Bettenhausen | Epperly-Offenhauser | 200 | +1'34.81 | 9 |
| 5 | 2 | Jim Rathmann | Epperly-Offenhauser | 200 | +1'35.62 | 20 |
| 6 | 16 | Jimmy Reece | Watson-Offenhauser | 200 | +2'16.95 | 3 |
| 7 | 26 | Don Freeland | Phillips-Offenhauser | 200 | +2'21.06 | 13 |
| 8 | 44 | Jud Larson | Watson-Offenhauser | 200 | +5'34.02 | 19 |
| 9 | 61 | Eddie Johnson | Kurtis Kraft-Offenhauser | 200 | +6'15.76 | 26 |
| 10 | 54 | Bill Cheesbourg | Kurtis Kraft-Novi | 200 | +8'03.59 | 33 |
| 11 | 52 | Al Keller | Kurtis Kraft-Offenhauser | 200 | +9'14.20 | 21 |
| 12 | 45 | Johnnie Parsons | Kurtis Kraft-Offenhauser | 200 | +9'40.85 | 6 |
| 13 | 19 | Johnnie Tolan | Kuzma-Offenhauser | 200 | +9'52.24 | 3 |
| Ret | 65 | Bob Christie | Kurtis Kraft-Offenhauser | 189 | Spun off | 17 |
| Ret | 59 | Dempsey Wilson | Kuzma-Offenhauser | 151 | Fire | 32 |
| Ret | 29 | A J Foyt | Kuzma-Offenhauser | 148 | Spun off | 12 |
| DSQ | 77 | Mike Magill | Kurtis Kraft-Offenhauser | 136 | Disqualified | 31 |
| Ret | 15 | Paul Russo | Kurtis Kraft-Novi | 122 | Throttle | 14 |
| Ret | 83 | Shorty Templeman | Kurtis Kraft-Offenhauser | 116 | Brakes | 23 |
| Ret | 8 | Rodger Ward | Lesovsky-Offenhauser | 93 | Magneto | 11 |
| Ret | 43 | Billy Garrett | Kurtis Kraft-Offenhauser | 80 | Magneto | 15 |
| Ret | 88 | Eddie Sachs | Kuzma-Offenhauser | 68 | Transmission | 18 |
| Ret | 7 | Johnny Thomson | Kurtis Kraft-Offenhauser | 52 | Steering | 22 |
| Ret | 89 | Chuck Weyant | Dunn-Offenhauser | 38 | Accident | 29 |
| Ret | 25 | Jack Turner | Lesovsky-Offenhauser | 21 | Fuel pump | 10 |
| Ret | 14 | Bob Veith | Kurtis Kraft-Offenhauser | 1 | Accident | 4 |
| Ret | 97 | Dick Rathmann | Watson-Offenhauser | 0 | Accident | 1 |
| Ret | 5 | Ed Elisian | Watson-Offenhauser | 0 | Accident | 3 |
| Ret | 4 | Pat O'Connor | Kurtis Kraft-Offenhauser | 0 | Accident | 5 |
| Ret | 31 | Paul Goldsmith | Kurtis Kraft-Offenhauser | 0 | Accident | 16 |
| Ret | 92 | Jerry Unser | Kurtis Kraft-Offenhauser | 0 | Accident | 21 |
| Ret | 68 | Len Sutton | Kurtis Kraft-Offenhauser | 0 | Accident | 27 |
| Ret | 57 | Art Bisch | Kuzma-Offenhauser | 0 | Accident | 28 |

Winning speed: 133.791mph
Pole position: Rathmann, 1m 01.655s, 145.975mph
Fastest lap: Bettenhausen, 1m 02.370s, 144.300mph

### BELGIAN GRAND PRIX: SPA-FRANCORCHAMPS *15 June Round: 5 Race: 69 24 x 8.761 miles*

| POS. | NO. | DRIVER | CAR/ENGINE | LAPS | TIME/RETIRED | GRID |
|---|---|---|---|---|---|---|
| 1 | 4 | Tony Brooks | Vanwall | 24 | +1:37'06.3 | 5 |
| 2 | 16 | Mike Hawthorn | Ferrari | 24 | +20.7 | 1 |
| 3 | 6 | S.Lewis-Evans | Vanwall | 24 | +3'00.9 | 11 |
| 4 | 40 | Cliff Allison | Lotus-Climax | 24 | +4'15.5 | 12 |
| 5 | 10 | Harry Schell | BRM | 23 | +1 Lap | 7 |
| 6 | 20 | O.Gendebien | Ferrari | 23 | +1 Lap | 6 |
| 7 | 28 | M.Trintignant | Maserati | 23 | +1 Lap | 16 |
| 8 | 24 | Roy Salvadori | Cooper-Climax | 23 | +1 Lap | 13 |
| 9 | 36 | Jo Bonnier | Maserati | 22 | +2 Laps | 14 |
| 10 | 26 | M.T.de Filippis | Maserati | 22 | +2 Laps | 19 |
| Ret | 38 | Francesco Godia-S | Maserati | 22 | Engine | 18 |
| Ret | 22 | Jack Brabham | Cooper-Climax | 16 | Overheating | 8 |
| Ret | 42 | Graham Hill | Lotus-Climax | 12 | Engine | 15 |
| Ret | 18 | Luigi Musso | Ferrari | 5 | Accident | 2 |
| Ret | 14 | Peter Collins | Ferrari | 5 | Overheating | 4 |
| Ret | 8 | Jean Behra | BRM | 5 | Oil pressure | 10 |
| Ret | 32 | Wolfgang Seidel | Maserati | 4 | Halfshaft | 17 |
| Ret | 2 | Stirling Moss | Vanwall | 0 | Engine | 9 |
| Ret | 30 | Masten Gregory | Maserati | 0 | Engine | 3 |

Winning speed: 129.925mph Lap leaders: Brooks 1, 3, 5-24; Collins 2, 4
Pole position: Hawthorn, 3m 57.100s, 133.027mph
Fastest lap: Hawthorn, 3m 58.300s, 132.358mph

### FRENCH GRAND PRIX: REIMS *6 July Round: 6 Race: 70 50 x 5.159 miles*

| POS. | NO. | DRIVER | CAR/ENGINE | LAPS | TIME/RETIRED | GRID |
|---|---|---|---|---|---|---|
| 1 | 4 | Mike Hawthorn | Ferrari | 50 | 2:03'21.3 | 1 |
| 2 | 8 | Stirling Moss | Vanwall | 50 | +24.6 | 6 |
| 3 | 6 | W.von Trips | Ferrari | 50 | +59.7 | 21 |
| 4 | 34 | Juan Manuel Fangio | Maserati | 50 | +2'30.6 | 8 |
| 5 | 42 | Peter Collins | Ferrari | 50 | +5'24.9 | 4 |
| 6 | 22 | Jack Brabham | Cooper-Climax | 49 | +1 Lap | 12 |
| 7 | 36 | Phil Hill | Maserati | 49 | +1 Lap | 13 |
| 8 | 38 | Jo Bonnier | Maserati | 48 | +2 Laps | 16 |
| 9 | 32 | Gerino Gerini | Maserati | 47 | +3 Laps | 15 |
| 10 | 30 | Troy Ruttman | Maserati | 45 | +5 Laps | 18 |
| 11 | 20 | Roy Salvadori | Cooper-Climax | 37 | +13 Laps | 14 |
| Ret | 16 | Harry Schell | BRM | 41 | Overheating | 3 |
| Ret | 14 | Jean Behra | BRM | 41 | Fuel pump | 9 |
| Ret | 12 | Lewis-Evans/Brooks | Vanwall | 35 | Engine | 10 |
| Ret | 24 | Graham Hill | Lotus-Climax | 33 | Overheating | 19 |
| Ret | 40 | Francesco Godia-S | Maserati | 28 | Accident | 11 |
| Ret | 18 | M.Trintignant | BRM | 23 | Fuel pump | 7 |
| Ret | 10 | Tony Brooks | Vanwall | 16 | Engine | 5 |
| Ret | 2 | Luigi Musso | Ferrari | 9 | Accident | 2 |
| Ret | 28 | Carroll Shelby | Maserati | 9 | Engine | 17 |
| Ret | 26 | Cliff Allison | Lotus-Climax | 6 | Engine | 20 |

Winning speed: 125.458mph Lap leaders: Hawthorn 1-50
Pole position: Hawthorn, 2m 21.700s, 131.059mph
Fastest lap: Hawthorn, 2m 24.900s, 128.165mph

### BRITISH GRAND PRIX: SILVERSTONE *19 July Round: 7 Race: 71 75 x 2.927 miles*

| POS. | NO. | DRIVER | CAR/ENGINE | LAPS | TIME/RETIRED | GRID |
|---|---|---|---|---|---|---|
| 1 | 1 | Peter Collins | Ferrari | 75 | 2:09'04.2 | 6 |
| 2 | 2 | Mike Hawthorn | Ferrari | 75 | +24.2 | 4 |
| 3 | 10 | Roy Salvadori | Cooper-Climax | 75 | +50.6 | 3 |
| 4 | 9 | S.Lewis-Evans | Vanwall | 75 | +50.8 | 7 |
| 5 | 20 | Harry Schell | BRM | 75 | +1'14.8 | 2 |
| 6 | 11 | Jack Brabham | Cooper-Climax | 75 | +1'23.2 | 10 |
| 7 | 8 | Tony Brooks | Vanwall | 74 | +1 Lap | 9 |
| 8 | 4 | M.Trintignant | Cooper-Climax | 73 | +2 Laps | 12 |
| 9 | 5 | Carroll Shelby | Maserati | 72 | +3 Laps | 15 |
| Ret | 3 | W.von Trips | Ferrari | 59 | Engine | 11 |
| Ret | 22 | Jo Bonnier | Maserati | 49 | Gearbox | 13 |
| Ret | 6 | Gerino Gerini | Maserati | 44 | Gearbox | 18 |
| Ret | 12 | Ian Burgess | Cooper-Climax | 40 | Clutch | 16 |
| Ret | 7 | Stirling Moss | Vanwall | 25 | Engine | 1 |
| Ret | 17 | Cliff Allison | Lotus-Climax | 21 | Engine | 5 |
| Ret | 19 | Jean Behra | BRM | 19 | Suspension | 8 |
| Ret | 15 | Ivor Bueb | Connaught-Alta | 19 | Gearbox | 17 |
| Ret | 18 | Alan Stacey | Lotus-Climax | 19 | Overheating | 20 |
| Ret | 16 | Graham Hill | Lotus-Climax | 17 | Overheating | 14 |
| Ret | 14 | Jack Fairman | Connaught-Alta | 7 | Ignition | 19 |

Winning speed: 102.049mph Lap leaders: Collins 1-75
Pole position: Moss, 1m 39.400s, 106.008mph
Fastest lap: Hawthorn, 1m 40.800s, 104.536mph

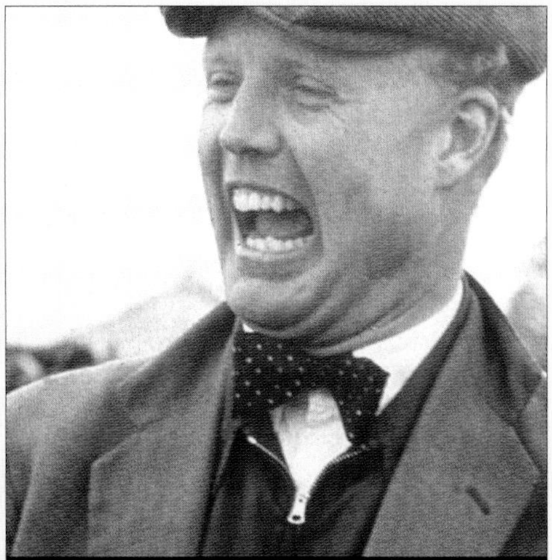
1958 world champion, Mike Hawthorn

## GERMAN GRAND PRIX: NÜRBURGRING *3 August Round: 8 Race: 72 15 x 14.173 miles*

| POS. | NO. | DRIVER | CAR/ENGINE | LAPS | TIME/RETIRED | GRID |
|------|-----|--------|------------|------|--------------|------|
| 1 | 8 | Tony Brooks | Vanwall | 15 | 2:21'15.0 | 2 |
| 2 | 10 | Roy Salvadori | Cooper-Climax | 15 | +3'29.7 | 6 |
| 3 | 11 | M.Trintignant | Cooper-Climax | 15 | +5'11.2 | 7 |
| 4 | 4 | W.von Trips | Ferrari | 15 | +6'16.3 | 5 |
| 5 | 20 | Bruce McLaren | Cooper-Climax F2 | 15 | +6'26.3 | 12 |
| 6 | 21 | Edgar Barth | Porsche F2 | 15 | +6'32.4 | 13 |
| 7 | 26 | Ian Burgess | Cooper-Climax F2 | 15 | +6'59.3 | 11 |
| 8 | 30 | Tony Marsh | Cooper-Climax F2 | 15 | +7'09.9 | 14 |
| 9 | 23 | Phil Hill | Ferrari F2 | 15 | +7'45.5 | 10 |
| 10 | 12 | Cliff Allison | Lotus-Climax | 13 | +Laps | 24 |
| 11 | 28 | Ivor Bueb | Lotus-Climax F2 | 13 | +2 Laps | 16 |
| Ret | 3 | Mike Hawthorn | Ferrari | 11 | Clutch | 1 |
| Ret | 2 | Peter Collins | Ferrari | 10 | Accident | 4 |
| Ret | 6 | Harry Schell | BRM | 9 | Brakes | 8 |
| Ret | 22 | Wolfgang Seidel | Cooper-Climax F2 | 9 | Suspension | 17 |
| Ret | 5 | Jean Behra | BRM | 4 | Suspension | 9 |
| Ret | 25 | Graham Hill | Lotus-Climax F2 | 4 | Oil pipe | 22 |
| Ret | 27 | C.Goethals | Cooper-Climax F2 | 4 | Fuel pump | 23 |
| Ret | 7 | Stirling Moss | Vanwall | 3 | Magneto | 3 |
| Ret | 18 | C.G.de Beaufort | Porsche F2 | 3 | Engine | 15 |
| Ret | 17 | Hans Herrmann | Maserati | 3 | Engine | 20 |
| Ret | 19 | Dick Gibson | Cooper-Climax F2 | 2 | Engine | 18 |
| Ret | 24 | Jack Brabham | Cooper-Climax F2 | 1 | Collision | 19 |
| Ret | 29 | Brian Naylor | Maserati | 1 | Fuel pump | 25 |
| Ret | 16 | Jo Bonnier | Maserati | 1 | Accident | 21 |

Winning speed: 90.309mph  Lap leaders: Moss 1-3; Hawthorn 4; Collins 5-10; Brooks 11-15
Pole Position: Hawthorn, 9m 14.00s, 92.102mph
Fastest lap: Moss, 9m 9.200s, 92.907mph

## PORTUGUESE GRAND PRIX: OPORTO *24 August Round: 9 Race: 73 50 x 4.602 miles*

| POS. | NO. | DRIVER | CAR/ENGINE | LAPS | TIME/RETIRED | GRID |
|------|-----|--------|------------|------|--------------|------|
| 1 | 2 | Stirling Moss | Vanwall | 50 | 2:11'27.80 | 1 |
| 2 | 24 | Mike Hawthorn | Ferrari | 50 | +5'12.75 | 2 |
| 3 | 6 | S.Lewis-Evans | Vanwall | 49 | +1 Lap | 3 |
| 4 | 8 | Jean Behra | BRM | 49 | +1 Lap | 4 |
| 5 | 22 | W.von Trips | Ferrari | 49 | +1 Lap | 6 |
| 6 | 10 | Harry Schell | BRM | 49 | +1 Lap | 7 |
| 7 | 14 | Jack Brabham | Cooper-Climax | 48 | +2 Laps | 8 |
| 8 | 12 | M.Trintignant | Cooper-Climax | 48 | +2 Laps | 9 |
| 9 | 16 | Roy Salvadori | Cooper-Climax | 46 | +4 Laps | 11 |
| Ret | 28 | Carroll Shelby | Maserati | 47 | Brakes | 10 |
| Ret | 4 | Tony Brooks | Vanwall | 37 | Spun off | 5 |
| Ret | 20 | Graham Hill | Lotus-Climax | 25 | Spun off | 12 |
| Ret | 18 | Cliff Allison | Maserati | 15 | Engine | 13 |
| Ret | 32 | Jo Bonnier | Maserati | 9 | Physical | 14 |
| Ret | 30 | M.T.de Filippis | Maserati | 6 | Engine | 15 |

Winning speed: 105.029mph  Lap leaders: Moss 1, 8-50; Hawthorn 2-7
Pole position: Moss, 2m 34.210s, 107.444mph
Fastest lap: Hawthorn, 2m 32.370s, 108.742mph

## ITALIAN GRAND PRIX: MONZA *7 September Round: 10 Race: 74 70 x 3.573 miles*

| POS. | NO. | DRIVER | CAR/ENGINE | LAPS | TIME/RETIRED | GRID |
|------|-----|--------|------------|------|--------------|------|
| 1 | 28 | Tony Brooks | Vanwall | 70 | 2:03'47.8 | 2 |
| 2 | 14 | Mike Hawthorn | Ferrari | 70 | +24.2 | 3 |
| 3 | 18 | Phil Hill | Ferrari | 70 | +28.3 | 7 |
| 4 | 32 | Gregory/Shelby | Maserati | 69 | +1 Lap | 11 |
| 5 | 6 | Roy Salvadori | Cooper-Climax | 62 | +8 Laps | 14 |
| 6 | 38 | Graham Hill | Lotus-Climax | 62 | +8 Laps | 12 |
| 7 | 36 | Cliff Allison | Lotus-Climax | 61 | +9 Laps | 16 |
| Ret | 42 | M.T.de Filippis | Maserati | 57 | Engine | 21 |
| Ret | 22 | Giulio Cabianca | Maserati | 51 | Engine | 20 |
| Ret | 8 | Jean Behra | BRM | 42 | Clutch | 8 |
| Ret | 24 | Hans Herrmann | Maserati | 32 | Engine | 18 |
| Ret | 30 | S.Lewis-Evans | Vanwall | 30 | Overheating | 4 |
| Ret | 2 | M.Trintignant | Cooper-Climax | 24 | Gearbox | 13 |
| Ret | 26 | Stirling Moss | Vanwall | 17 | Gearbox | 1 |
| Ret | 12 | Jo Bonnier | BRM | 14 | Transmission | 10 |
| Ret | 20 | O.Gendebien | Ferrari | 4 | Suspension | 5 |
| Ret | 40 | Gerino Gerini | Maserati | 2 | Accident | 19 |
| Ret | 34 | Carroll Shelby | Maserati | 1 | Handling | 17 |
| Ret | 16 | W.von Trips | Ferrari | 0 | Accident | 6 |
| Ret | 10 | Harry Schell | BRM | 0 | Accident | 9 |
| Ret | 4 | Jack Brabham | Cooper-Climax | 0 | Suspension | 15 |

Winning speed: 121.216mph
Lap leaders: Hill 1-4, 35-37; Hawthorn 5-6, 9, 15-34, 38-60; Moss 7-8, 10-14; Brooks 61-70
Pole position: Moss, 1m 40.500s, 127.984mph
Fastest lap: Hill, 1m 42.900s, 124.999mph

## MOROCCAN GRAND PRIX: AIN-DIAB *19 October Round: 11 Race: 75 53 x 4.734 miles*

| POS. | NO. | DRIVER | CAR/ENGINE | LAPS | TIME/RETIRED | GRID |
|------|-----|--------|------------|------|--------------|------|
| 1 | 8 | Stirling Moss | Vanwall | 53 | 2:09'15.1 | 2 |
| 2 | 6 | Mike Hawthorn | Ferrari | 53 | +1'24.7 | 1 |
| 3 | 4 | Phil Hill | Ferrari | 53 | +1'25.5 | 5 |
| 4 | 18 | Jo Bonnier | BRM | 53 | +1'46.7 | 8 |
| 5 | 16 | Harry Schell | BRM | 53 | +2'33.7 | 10 |
| 6 | 22 | Masten Gregory | Maserati | 52 | +1 Lap | 13 |
| 7 | 28 | Roy Salvadori | Cooper-Climax | 51 | +2 Laps | 14 |
| 8 | 30 | Jack Fairman | Cooper-Climax | 50 | +3 Laps | 11 |
| 9 | 38 | Hans Herrmann | Maserati | 50 | +3 Laps | 16 |
| 10 | 34 | Cliff Allison | Lotus-Climax | 49 | +4 Laps | 16 |
| 11 | 50 | Jack Brabham | Cooper-Climax F2 | 49 | +4 Laps | 19 |
| 12 | 26 | Gerino Gerini | Maserati | 48 | +5 Laps | 17 |
| 13 | 52 | Bruce McLaren | Cooper-Climax F2 | 48 | +5 Laps | 21 |
| 14 | 58 | Robert La Caze | Cooper-Climax F2 | 48 | +5 Laps | 23 |
| 15 | 48 | Andre Guelfi | Cooper-Climax F2 | 48 | +5 Laps | 25 |
| 16 | 32 | Graham Hill | Lotus-Climax | 46 | +7 Laps | 12 |
| Ret | 12 | S.Lewis-Evans | Vanwall | 41 | Engine | 3 |
| Ret | 54 | Francois Picard | Cooper-Climax F2 | 31 | Accident | 24 |
| Ret | 56 | Tom Bridger | Cooper-Climax F2 | 30 | Accident | 22 |
| Ret | 2 | O.Gendebien | Ferrari | 29 | Accident | 6 |
| Ret | 10 | Tony Brooks | Vanwall | 29 | Engine | 7 |
| Ret | 14 | Jean Behra | BRM | 26 | Engine | 4 |
| Ret | 20 | Ron Flockhart | BRM | 15 | Engine | 15 |
| Ret | 24 | Wolfgang Seidel | Maserati | 15 | Accident | 20 |
| Ret | 36 | M.Trintignant | Cooper-Climax | 9 | Engine | 9 |

Winning speed: 116.462mph  Lap leaders: Moss 1-53
Pole Position: Hawthorn, 2m 23.100s, 119.084mph
Fastest lap: Moss, 2m 22.500s, 119.586mph

# 1959

DRIVERS' CHAMPION: JACK BRABHAM
CONSTRUCTORS' CHAMPION: COOPER CLIMAX

## DRIVERS' CHAMPIONSHIP

| POS. | DRIVER | NATIONALITY | CAR | POINTS |
|------|--------|-------------|-----|--------|
| 1 | Jack Brabham | Australia | Cooper-Climax | 31(3) |
| 2 | Tony Brooks | GB | Ferrari, Vanwall | 27 |
| 3 | Stirling Moss | GB | Cooper-Climax | 25.5 |
| 4 | Phil Hill | USA | Ferrari | 20 |
| 5 | Maurice Trintignant | France | Cooper-Climax | 19 |
| 6 | Bruce McLaren | New Zealand | Cooper-Climax | 16.5 |
| 7 | Dan Gurney | USA | Ferrari | 13 |
| 8 | Jo Bonnier | Sweden | BRM | 10 |
| = | Masten Gregory | USA | Cooper-Climax | 10 |
| 10 | Roger Ward | USA | Watson-Offenhauser | 8 |
| 11 | Jim Rathmann | USA | Watson-Offenhauser | 6 |
| 12 | Innes Ireland | GB | Lotus-Climax | 5 |
| = | Harry Schell | USA | BRM, Cooper-Climax | 5 |
| = | Johnny Thomson | USA | Lesovsky-Offenhauser | 5 |
| 15 | Tony Bettenhausen | USA | Epperly-Offenhauser | 3 |
| = | Olivier Gendebien | Belgium | Ferrari | 3 |
| 17 | Jean Behra | France | Ferrari, Behra-Porsche | 2 |
| = | Cliff Allison | GB | Ferrari | 2 |
| = | Paul Goldsmith | USA | Epperly-Offenhauser | 2 |
| | Graham Hill | GB | Lotus-Climax | |
| | Roy Salvadori | GB | Cooper-Maserati, Aston Martin | |
| | Giorgio Scarlatti | Italy | Maserati, Cooper-Climax | |
| | Ron Flockhart | GB | BRM | |
| | Lucien Bianchi | Italy | Cooper-Climax | |
| | Ivor Bueb | GB | Cooper-Climax, Cooper-Borgward | |
| | Wolfgang von Trips | West Germany | Porsche, Ferrari | |
| | Alain de Chagny | Belgium | Cooper-Climax | |
| | Maria Teresa de Filippis | Italy | Behra-Porsche | |
| | Bruce Halford | GB | Lotus-Climax | |
| | Pete Lovely | USA | Lotus-Climax | |
| | Jean Lucienbonnet | France | Cooper-Climax | |
| | André Testut | Monaco | Maserati | |
| | Carel Godin de Beaufort | Netherlands | Porsche, Maserati | |
| | Carroll Shelby | USA | Aston Martin | |
| | Ian Burgess | GB | Cooper-Maserati | |
| | Astrubel Bayardo | Brazil | Maserati | |
| | Colin Davis | GB | Cooper-Maserati | |
| | Fritz d'Orey | Brazil | Maserati, Tec-Mec-Maserato | |
| | Peter Ashdown | GB | Cooper-Climax | |
| | Chris Bristow | GB | Cooper-Borgward | |
| | Hans Herrmann | Germany | Cooper-Maserati, BRM | |
| | Alessandro de Tomaso | Italy | Cooper-OSCA | |
| | Jack Fairman | GB | Cooper-Climax, Cooper-Maserati | |
| | Keith Greene | GB | Cooper-Climax | |
| | Brian Naylor | GB | JBW-Maserati | |
| | Micheal Parks | GB | Fry-Climax | |
| | Tim Parnell | GB | Cooper-Climax | |
| | David Piper | GB | Lotus-Climax | |
| | Alan Stacey | GB | Lotus-Climax | |
| | Henry Taylor | GB | Cooper-Climax | |
| | Mike Taylor | GB | Cooper-Climax | |
| | Trevor Taylor | GB | Cooper-Climax | |
| | Mario Araujo de Cabral | Portugal | Cooper-Maserati | |
| | Bob Said | USA | Connaught-Alta | |
| | Giulio Cabianca | Italy | Maserati | |
| | Harry Blanchard | USA | Porsche | |
| | Phil Cade | USA | Maserati | |
| | George Constantine | USA | Cooper-Climax | |
| | Roger Ward | USA | Kurtis-Offenhauser | |

Points for top five finishers (8, 6, 4, 3, 2) plus a point for fastest lap. Only the best five scores counted towards the championship. Points were not awarded for shared drives

## CONSTRUCTORS' CHAMPIONSHIP

| POS. | CONSTRUCTOR | POINTS |
|------|-------------|--------|
| 1 | Cooper-Climax | 40 |
| 2 | Ferrari | 32 |
| 3 | BRM | 18 |
| 4 | Lotus-Climax | 5 |

Points for top five finishers (8, 6, 4, 3, 2). Points only counted for top-placed car for each constructor. Only the best five scores counted towards the championship. Indianapolis excluded.

1958 world champion, Mike Hawthorn in the Type 246 Ferrari Dino.

### MONACO GRAND PRIX: MONTE CARLO *10 May Round: 1 Race: 76 100 x 1.954 miles*

| POS. | NO. | DRIVER | CAR/ENGINE | LAPS | TIME/RETIRED | GRID |
|---|---|---|---|---|---|---|
| 1 | 24 | Jack Brabham | Cooper-Climax | 100 | 2:55'51.3 | 3 |
| 2 | 50 | Tony Brooks | Ferrari | 100 | +20.4 | 4 |
| 3 | 32 | M.Trintignant | Cooper-Climax | 98 | +2 Laps | 6 |
| 4 | 48 | Phil Hill | Ferrari | 97 | +3 Laps | 5 |
| 5 | 22 | Bruce McLaren | Cooper-Climax | 96 | +4 Laps | 13 |
| 6 | 38 | Roy Salvadori | Cooper-Maserati | 83 | +17 Laps | 8 |
| Ret | 30 | Stirling Moss | Cooper-Climax | 81 | Transmission | 1 |
| Ret | 20 | Ron Flockhart | BRM | 64 | Spun off | 10 |
| Ret | 16 | Harry Schell | BRM | 48 | Accident | 9 |
| Ret | 18 | Jo Bonnier | BRM | 44 | Brakes | 7 |
| Ret | 46 | Jean Behra | Ferrari | 24 | Engine | 2 |
| Ret | 40 | Graham Hill | Lotus-Climax | 21 | Fire | 14 |
| Ret | 26 | Masten Gregory | Cooper-Climax | 6 | Gearbox | 11 |
| Ret | 6 | W.von Trips | Porsche | 1 | Collision | 12 |
| Ret | 52 | Cliff Allison | Ferrari | 1 | Collision | 15 |
| Ret | 44 | Bruce Halford | Lotus-Climax | 1 | Collision | 16 |
| DNQ | 34 | Ivor Bueb | Cooper-Climax | | | |
| DNQ | 54 | G.Scarlatti | Maserati | | | |
| DNQ | 12 | Alain de Changy | Cooper-Climax | | | |
| DNQ | 10 | Lucien Bianchi | Cooper-Climax | | | |
| DNQ | 4 | M.T.de Filippis | Porsche | | | |
| DNQ | 42 | Pete Lovely | Lotus-Climax | | | |
| DNQ | 14 | J.Lucienbonnet | Cooper-Climax | | | |
| DNQ | 56 | Andre Testut | Maserati | | | |

Winning speed: 66.676mph Lap leaders: Behra 1-21; Moss 22-81; Brabham 82-100
Pole position: Moss, 1m 39.600s, 70.634mph
Fastest lap: Brabham, 1m 40.400s, 70.071mph

### INDIANAPOLIS 500 *30 May Round: 2 Race: 77 200 x 2.500 miles*

| POS. | NO. | DRIVER | CAR/ENGINE | LAPS | TIME/RETIRED | GRID |
|---|---|---|---|---|---|---|
| 1 | 5 | Rodger Ward | Watson-Offenhauser | 200 | 3:40'49.20 | 6 |
| 2 | 16 | Jim Rathmann | Watson-Offenhauser | 200 | +23.28 | 3 |
| 3 | 3 | Johnny Thomson | Lesovsky-Offenhauser | 200 | +50.64 | 1 |
| 4 | 1 | Tony Bettenhausen | Epperly-Offenhauser | 200 | +1'47.09 | 15 |
| 5 | 99 | Paul Goldsmith | Epperly-Offenhauser | 200 | +2'06.44 | 16 |
| 6 | 33 | Johnny Boyd | Epperly-Offenhauser | 200 | +3'16.98 | 11 |
| 7 | 37 | Duane Carter | Kurtis Kraft-Offenhauser | 200 | +4'09.92 | 12 |
| 8 | 19 | Eddie Johnson | Kurtis Kraft-Offenhauser | 200 | +4'10.53 | 8 |
| 9 | 45 | Paul Russo | Kurtis Kraft-Offenhauser | 200 | +4'11.04 | 28 |
| 10 | 10 | A J Foyt | Kuzma-Offenhauser | 200 | +4'14.48 | 17 |
| 11 | 88 | Gene Hartley | Kuzma-Offenhauser | 200 | +5'42.48 | 9 |
| 12 | 74 | Bob Veith | Moore-Offenhauser | 200 | +6'09.73 | 7 |
| 13 | 89 | Al Herman | Dunn-Offenhauser | 200 | +6'40.40 | 23 |
| 14 | 66 | Jimmy Daywalt | Kurtis Kraft-Offenhauser | 200 | +6'41.54 | 13 |
| 15 | 71 | Chuck Arnold | Kurtis Kraft-Offenhauser | 200 | +8'19.86 | 31 |
| 16 | 58 | Jim McWithey | Kurtis Kraft-Offenhauser | 200 | +11'41.69 | 33 |
| Ret | 44 | Eddie Sachs | Kuzma-Offenhauser | 182 | Spun off | 2 |
| Ret | 57 | Al Keller | Kuzma-Offenhauser | 163 | Engine | 28 |
| Ret | 64 | Pat Flaherty | Watson-Offenhauser | 162 | Accident | 18 |
| Ret | 73 | Dick Rathmann | Watson-Offenhauser | 150 | Fire | 4 |
| Ret | 53 | Bill Cheesbourg | Kuzma-Offenhauser | 147 | Magneto | 12 |
| Ret | 15 | Don Freeland | Kurtis Kraft-Offenhauser | 136 | Magneto | 21 |
| Ret | 49 | Ray Crawford | Elder-Offenhauser | 115 | Accident | 32 |
| Ret | 9 | Don Branson | Phillips-Offenhauser | 112 | Suspension | 10 |
| Ret | 65 | Bob Christie | Kurtis Kraft-Offenhauser | 109 | Engine | 24 |
| Ret | 48 | Bobby Grim | Kurtis Kraft-Offenhauser | 85 | Magneto | 5 |
| Ret | 24 | Jack Turner | Christensen-Offenhauser | 47 | Fuel leak | 14 |
| Ret | 7 | Jud Larson | Kurtis Kraft-Offenhauser | 45 | Accident | 19 |
| Ret | 87 | Red Amick | Kurtis Kraft-Offenhauser | 45 | Accident | 26 |
| Ret | 47 | Chuck Weyant | Kurtis Kraft-Offenhauser | 45 | Accident | 29 |
| Ret | 77 | Mike Magill | Sutton-Offenhauser | 45 | Accident | 31 |
| Ret | 8 | Len Sutton | Lesovsky-Offenhauser | 34 | Accident | 22 |
| Ret | 6 | Jimmy Bryan | Epperly-Offenhauser | 1 | Engine | 20 |

Winning speed: 135.857mph
Pole position: Thomson, 1m 1.683s, 145.907mph
Fastest lap: Thomson, 1m 1.890s, 145.419mph

### DUTCH GRAND PRIX: ZANDVOORT *31 May Round: 3 Race: 78 75 x 2.605 miles*

| POS. | NO. | DRIVER | CAR/ENGINE | LAPS | TIME/RETIRED | GRID |
|---|---|---|---|---|---|---|
| 1 | 7 | Jo Bonnier | BRM | 75 | 2:05'26.8 | 1 |
| 2 | 8 | Jack Brabham | Cooper-Climax | 75 | +14.2 | 2 |
| 3 | 9 | Masten Gregory | Cooper-Climax | 75 | +1'23.0 | 7 |
| 4 | 12 | Innes Ireland | Lotus-Climax | 74 | +1 Lap | 9 |
| 5 | 1 | Jean Behra | Ferrari | 74 | +1 Lap | 4 |
| 6 | 3 | Phil Hill | Ferrari | 73 | +2 Laps | 12 |
| 7 | 14 | Graham Hill | Lotus-Climax | 73 | +2 Laps | 5 |
| 8 | 10 | M.Trintignant | Cooper-Climax | 73 | +2 Laps | 11 |
| 9 | 16 | Cliff Allison | Ferrari | 71 | +4 Laps | 15 |
| 10 | 15 | C.G.de Beaufort | Porsche | 68 | +7 Laps | 14 |
| Ret | 11 | Stirling Moss | Cooper-Climax | 62 | Gearbox | 3 |
| Ret | 6 | Harry Schell | BRM | 46 | Gearbox | 6 |
| Ret | 2 | Tony Brooks | Ferrari | 42 | Oil leak | 8 |
| Ret | 5 | Carroll Shelby | Aston Martin | 25 | Engine | 10 |
| Ret | 4 | Roy Salvadori | Aston Martin | 3 | Engine | 13 |

Winning speed: 93.461 mph Lap leaders: Bonnier 1, 12-29, 34-59, 63-75; Gregory 2-11; Brabham 30-33; Moss 60-62
Pole position: Bonnier, 1m 36.000s, 97.703mph
Fastest lap: Moss, 1m 36.700s, 96.996mph

### FRENCH GRAND PRIX: REIMS *5 July Round: 4 Race: 79 50 x 5.159 miles*

| POS. | NO. | DRIVER | CAR/ENGINE | LAPS | TIME/RETIRED | GRID |
|---|---|---|---|---|---|---|
| 1 | 24 | Tony Brooks | Ferrari | 50 | 2:01'26.5 | 1 |
| 2 | 26 | Phil Hill | Ferrari | 50 | +27.5 | 3 |
| 3 | 8 | Jack Brabham | Cooper-Climax | 50 | +1'37.7 | 2 |
| 4 | 22 | O.Gendebien | Ferrari | 50 | +1'47.5 | 11 |
| 5 | 12 | Bruce McLaren | Cooper-Climax | 50 | +1'47.7 | 10 |
| 6 | 44 | Ron Flockhart | BRM | 50 | +2'05.7 | 13 |
| 7 | 6 | Harry Schell | BRM | 47 | +3 Laps | 9 |
| 8 | 40 | G.Scarlatti | Maserati | 41 | +9 Laps | 21 |
| 9 | 42 | C.G.de Beaufort | Maserati | 40 | +10 Laps | 20 |
| 10 | 38 | Fritz d' Orey | Maserati | 40 | +10 Laps | 18 |
| 11 | 14 | M.Trintignant | Cooper-Climax | 36 | +14 Laps | 8 |
| DSQ | 2 | Stirling Moss | BRM | 42 | Disqualified | 4 |
| Ret | 30 | Jean Behra | Ferrari | 31 | Engine | 5 |
| Ret | 16 | Roy Salvadori | Cooper-Maserati | 20 | Engine | 16 |
| Ret | 28 | Dan Gurney | Ferrari | 19 | Radiator | 12 |
| Ret | 34 | Innes Ireland | Lotus-Climax | 14 | Wheel | 15 |
| Ret | 18 | Ian Burgess | Cooper-Maserati | 13 | Engine | 19 |
| Ret | 10 | Masten Gregory | Cooper-Climax | 8 | Physical | 7 |
| Ret | 32 | Graham Hill | Lotus-Climax | 7 | Radiator | 14 |
| Ret | 20 | Colin Davis | Cooper-Maserati | 7 | Oil leak | 17 |
| Ret | 4 | Jo Bonnier | BRM | 6 | Engine | 6 |

Winning speed: 127.435mph Lap leaders: Brooks 1-50
Pole position: Brooks, 2m 19.400s, 133.221mph
Fastest lap: Moss, 2m 22.800s, 130.049mph

### BRITISH GRAND PRIX: AINTREE *18 July Round: 5 Race: 80 75 x 3.000 miles*

| POS. | NO. | DRIVER | CAR/ENGINE | LAPS | TIME/RETIRED | GRID |
|---|---|---|---|---|---|---|
| 1 | 12 | Jack Brabham | Cooper-Climax | 75 | 2:30'11.6 | 1 |
| 2 | 6 | Stirling Moss | BRM | 75 | +22.2 | 7 |
| 3 | 16 | Bruce McLaren | Cooper-Climax | 75 | +22.4 | 8 |
| 4 | 8 | Harry Schell | BRM | 74 | +1 Lap | 3 |
| 5 | 18 | M.Trintignant | Cooper-Climax | 74 | +1 Lap | 4 |
| 6 | 2 | Roy Salvadori | Aston Martin | 74 | +1 Lap | 2 |
| 7 | 14 | Masten Gregory | Cooper-Climax | 73 | +2 Laps | 5 |
| 8 | 30 | Alan Stacey | Lotus-Climax | 71 | +5 Laps | |
| 9 | | Graham Hill | Lotus-Climax | 70 | +5 Laps | 9 |
| 10 | 48 | Chris Bristow | Cooper-Borgward | 70 | +5 Laps | 16 |
| 11 | 58 | Henry Taylor | Cooper-Climax | 69 | +6 Laps | 21 |
| 12 | 52 | Peter Ashdown | Cooper-Climax | 69 | +6 Laps | 23 |
| 13 | 46 | Ivor Bueb | Cooper-Borgward | 69 | +6 Laps | 18 |
| Ret | 4 | Carroll Shelby | Aston Martin | 69 | Ignition | 6 |
| Ret | 40 | Fritz d' Orey | Maserati | 57 | Accident | 20 |
| Ret | 42 | Ron Flockhart | BRM | 53 | Spun off | 11 |
| Ret | 38 | Jack Fairman | Cooper-Climax | 39 | Gearbox | 15 |
| Ret | 10 | Jo Bonnier | BRM | 37 | Brakes | 10 |
| Ret | 22 | Ian Burgess | Cooper-Maserati | 31 | Transmission | 13 |
| Ret | 24 | Hans Herrmann | Cooper-Maserati | 21 | Gearbox | 19 |
| Ret | 64 | David Piper | Lotus-Climax | 19 | Overheating | 22 |
| Ret | 36 | Brian Naylor | JBW-Maserati | 18 | Transmission | 14 |
| Ret | 50 | Mike Taylor | Cooper-Climax | 17 | Transmission | 24 |
| Ret | 20 | Tony Brooks | Vanwall | 13 | Ignition | 17 |
| DNQ | 54 | Keith Greene | Cooper-Climax | | | |
| DNQ | 56 | Bill Moss | Cooper-Climax | | | |
| DNQ | 60 | Mike Parkes | Fry-Climax | | | |
| DNQ | 62 | Dennis Taylor | Lotus-Climax | | | |
| DNQ | 44 | Trevor Taylor | Cooper-Climax | | | |
| DNQ | 66 | Tim Parnell | Cooper-Climax | | | |

Winning speed: 89.884mph Lap leaders: Brabham 1-75
Pole position: Brabham, 1m 58.000s, 91.525mph
Fastest lap: Moss/McLaren, 1m 57.000s, 92.308mph

### GERMAN GRAND PRIX: AVUS *2 August Round: 6 Race: 81 60 x 5.157 miles*

| POS. | NO. | DRIVER | CAR/ENGINE | LAPS | TIME/RETIRED | GRID |
|---|---|---|---|---|---|---|
| 1 | 4 | Tony Brooks | Ferrari | 60 | 2:09'31.6 | 1 |
| 2 | 6 | Dan Gurney | Ferrari | 60 | +2.9 | 3 |
| 3 | 5 | Phil Hill | Ferrari | 60 | +1'04.8 | 6 |
| 4 | 8 | M.Trintignant | Cooper-Climax | 59 | +1 Lap | 12 |
| 5 | 9 | Jo Bonnier | BRM | 58 | +2 Laps | 7 |
| 6 | 18 | Ian Burgess | Cooper-Maserati | 56 | +4 Laps | 15 |
| 7 | 10 | Harry Schell | BRM | 49 | +11 Laps | 8 |
| Ret | 2 | Bruce McLaren | Cooper-Climax | 36 | Transmission | 9 |
| Ret | 11 | Hans Herrmann | BRM | 36 | Accident | 11 |
| Ret | 3 | Masten Gregory | Cooper-Climax | 23 | Engine | 5 |
| Ret | 1 | Jack Brabham | Cooper-Climax | 15 | Transmission | 4 |
| Ret | 16 | Graham Hill | Lotus-Climax | 10 | Gearbox | 10 |
| Ret | 15 | Innes Ireland | Lotus-Climax | 7 | Differential | 13 |
| Ret | 17 | Cliff Allison | Ferrari | 2 | Clutch | 14 |
| Ret | 7 | Stirling Moss | Cooper-Climax | 1 | Transmission | 2 |

### PORTUGUESE GRAND PRIX: MONSANTO PARK *23 August Round: 7 Race: 82 62 x 3.380 miles*

| POS. | NO. | DRIVER | CAR/ENGINE | LAPS | TIME/RETIRED | GRID |
|---|---|---|---|---|---|---|
| 1 | 4 | Stirling Moss | Cooper-Climax | 62 | 2:11'55.41 | 1 |
| 2 | 2 | Masten Gregory | Cooper-Climax | 61 | +1 Lap | 3 |
| 3 | 16 | Dan Gurney | Ferrari | 61 | +1 Lap | 6 |
| 4 | 5 | M.Trintignant | Cooper-Climax | 60 | +2 Laps | 4 |
| 5 | 6 | Harry Schell | BRM | 59 | +3 Laps | 9 |
| 6 | 10 | Roy Salvadori | Aston Martin | 59 | +3 Laps | 12 |
| 7 | 8 | Ron Flockhart | BRM | 59 | +3 Laps | 11 |
| 8 | 9 | Carroll Shelby | Aston Martin | 58 | +4 Laps | 13 |
| 9 | 14 | Tony Brooks | Ferrari | 57 | +5 Laps | 10 |
| 10 | 18 | M.A.Cabral | Cooper-Maserati | 56 | +6 Laps | 14 |
| Ret | 3 | Bruce McLaren | Cooper-Climax | 38 | Transmission | 8 |
| Ret | 1 | Jack Brabham | Cooper-Climax | 23 | Transmission | 2 |
| Ret | 7 | Jo Bonnier | BRM | 10 | Engine | 5 |
| Ret | 15 | Phil Hill | Ferrari | 5 | Accident | 7 |
| Ret | 11 | Graham Hill | Lotus-Climax | 5 | Accident | 15 |
| Ret | 12 | Innes Ireland | Lotus-Climax | 3 | Gearbox | 16 |

Winning speed: 95.317 mph Lap leaders: Moss 1-62
Pole position: Moss, 2m 2.890s, 99.023mph
Fastest lap: Moss, 2m 5.070s, 97.297mph

### ITALIAN GRAND PRIX: MONZA *13 September Round: 8 Race: 83 72 x 3.573 miles*

| POS. | NO. | DRIVER | CAR/ENGINE | LAPS | TIME/RETIRED | GRID |
|---|---|---|---|---|---|---|
| 1 | 14 | Stirling Moss | Cooper-Climax | 72 | 2:04'05.4 | 1 |
| 2 | 32 | Phil Hill | Ferrari | 72 | +46.7 | 5 |
| 3 | 12 | Jack Brabham | Cooper-Climax | 72 | +1'12.5 | 3 |
| 4 | 36 | Dan Gurney | Ferrari | 72 | +1'19.6 | 4 |
| 5 | 34 | Cliff Allison | Ferrari | 71 | +1 Lap | 8 |
| 6 | 38 | O.Gendebien | Ferrari | 71 | +1 Lap | 6 |
| 7 | 2 | Harry Schell | BRM | 70 | +2 Laps | 7 |
| 8 | 6 | Jo Bonnier | BRM | 70 | +2 Laps | 11 |
| 9 | 16 | M.Trintignant | Cooper-Climax | 70 | +2 Laps | 13 |
| 10 | 26 | Carroll Shelby | Aston Martin | 70 | +2 Laps | 19 |
| 11 | 40 | Colin Davis | Cooper-Maserati | 68 | +4 Laps | 18 |
| 12 | 10 | G.Scarlatti | Cooper-Climax | 68 | +4 Laps | 12 |
| 13 | 4 | Ron Flockhart | BRM | 67 | +5 Laps | 15 |
| 14 | 42 | Ian Burgess | Cooper-Maserati | 67 | +5 Laps | 16 |
| 15 | 28 | Giulio Cabianca | Maserati | 64 | +8 Laps | 21 |
| Ret | 24 | Roy Salvadori | Aston Martin | 44 | Engine | 17 |
| Ret | 8 | Bruce McLaren | Cooper-Climax | 22 | Engine | 9 |
| Ret | 22 | Jack Fairman | Cooper-Maserati | 18 | Engine | 12 |
| Ret | 20 | Innes Ireland | Lotus-Climax | 14 | Brakes | 14 |
| Ret | 18 | Graham Hill | Lotus-Climax | 1 | Clutch | 10 |
| Ret | 30 | Tony Brooks | Ferrari | 0 | Clutch | 2 |

Winning speed: 124.384mph Lap leaders: Moss 1, 4, 15, 33-72; Hill 2-3, 5-14, 16-32
Pole position: Moss, 1m 39.700s, 129.011mph
Fastest lap: Hill, 1m 40.400s, 128.111mph

### UNITED STATES GRAND PRIX: SEBRING *12 December Round: 9 Race: 84 42 x 5.200 miles*

| POS. | NO. | DRIVER | CAR/ENGINE | LAPS | TIME/RETIRED | GRID |
|---|---|---|---|---|---|---|
| 1 | 9 | Bruce McLaren | Cooper-Climax | 42 | 2:12'35.7 | 10 |
| 2 | 6 | M.Trintignant | Cooper-Climax | 42 | +0.6 | 5 |
| 3 | 2 | Tony Brooks | Ferrari | 42 | +3'00.9 | 4 |
| 4 | 8 | Jack Brabham | Cooper-Climax | 42 | +4'57.3 | 2 |
| 5 | 10 | Innes Ireland | Lotus-Climax | 39 | +3 Laps | 9 |
| 6 | 4 | W.von Trips | Ferrari | 38 | +Engine | 6 |
| 7 | 17 | Harry Blanchard | Porsche | 38 | +4 Laps | 16 |
| Ret | 3 | Cliff Allison | Ferrari | 23 | Clutch | 7 |
| Ret | 12 | Roy Salvadori | Cooper-Maserati | 23 | Transmission | 11 |
| Ret | 1 | Rodger Ward | Kurtis Kraft-Offenhauser | 20 | Clutch | 19 |
| Ret | 14 | A.de Tomaso | Cooper-Osca | 13 | Brakes | 14 |
| Ret | 5 | Phil Hill | Ferrari | 8 | Clutch | 8 |
| Ret | 15 | Fritz d'Orey | Tec-Mec-Maserati | 6 | Oil leak | 17 |
| Ret | 7 | Stirling Moss | Cooper-Climax | 5 | Transmission | 1 |
| Ret | 19 | Harry Schell | Cooper-Climax | 5 | Clutch | 3 |
| Ret | 16 | G.Constantine | Cooper-Climax | 5 | Overheating | 15 |
| Ret | 11 | Alan Stacey | Lotus-Climax | 2 | Clutch | 12 |
| Ret | 18 | Bob Said | Connaught-Alta | 0 | Accident | 13 |
| DNS | 22 | Phil Cade | Maserati | 0 | Non starter | |

Winning speed: 98.827mph Lap leaders: Moss 1-5, Brabham 6-41, McLaren 42
Pole Position: Moss, 3m 0.000s, 104.000mph
Fastest lap: Trintignant, 3m 5.000s, 101.189mph

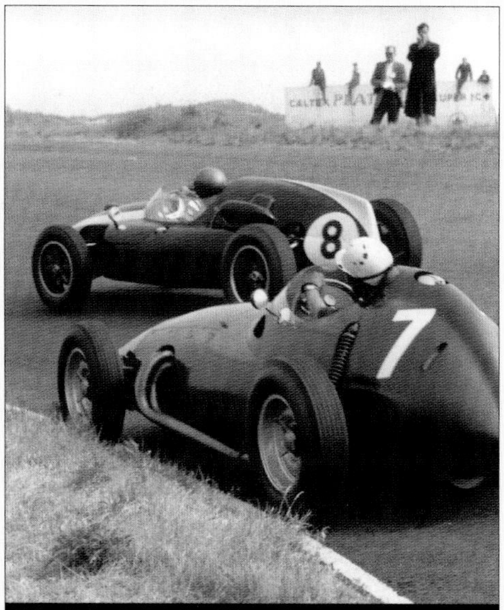

1959 world champion in the Type 53 Cooper Climax leads Jo Bonnier's BRM P.25.

# 1960

## DRIVERS' CHAMPION: JACK BRABHAM
## CONSTRUCTORS' CHAMPION: COOPER CLIMAX

### DRIVERS' CHAMPIONSHIP

| POS | DRIVER | COUNTRY | CAR | POINTS |
|---|---|---|---|---|
| 1 | Jack Brabham | Australia | Cooper-Climax | 43 |
| 2 | Bruce McLaren | New Zealand | Cooper-Climax | 34(3) |
| 3 | Stirling Moss | GB | Cooper-Climax, Lotus-Climax | 19 |
| 4 | Innes Ireland | GB | Lotus-Climax | 18 |
| 5 | Phil Hill | USA | Ferrari, Cooper-Climax | 16 |
| 6 | Olivier Gendebien | Belgium | Cooper-Climax | 10 |
| = | Wolfgang von Trips | West Germany | Ferrari, Cooper-Maserati | 10 |
| 8 | Richie Ginther | USA | Ferrari | 8 |
| = | Jim Rathmann | USA | Watson-Offenhauser | 8 |
| = | Jim Clark | GB | Lotus-Climax | 8 |
| 11 | Tony Brooks | GB | Cooper-Climax, Vanwall | 7 |
| 12 | Cliff Allison | GB | Ferrari | 6 |
| = | Roger Ward | USA | Watson-Offenhauser | 6 |
| = | John Surtees | GB | Lotus-Climax | 6 |
| 15 | Paul Goldsmith | USA | Epperly-Offenhauser | 4 |
| = | Graham Hill | GB | BRM | 4 |
| = | Willy Mairesse | Belgium | Ferrari | 4 |
| = | Jo Bonnier | Sweden | BRM | 4 |
| 19 | Carlos Menditéguy | Argentina | Cooper-Maserati | 3 |
| = | Don Branson | USA | Philips-Offenhauser | 3 |
| = | Henry Taylor | GB | Cooper-Climax | 3 |
| = | Guilio Cabianca | Italy | Cooper-Ferrari | 3 |
| 23 | Johnny Thomson | USA | Lesovsky-Offenhauser | 2 |
| 24 | Eddie Johnson | USA | Trevis-Offenhauser | 1 |
| = | Lucien Bianchi | Belgium | Cooper-Climax | 1 |
| = | Ron Flockhart | GB | Lotus-Climax, Cooper-Climax | 1 |
| = | Hans Herrmann | West Germany | Porsche | 1 |
| | Masten Gregory | USA | Behra-Porsche, Cooper-Maserati | |
| | Maurice Trintignant | France | Cooper-Climax, Cooper-Maserati, Aston Martin | |
| | Giorgio Scarlatti | Italy | Maseratl, Cooper-Ferrari Cooper-Maserati | |
| | Roberto Bonomi | Argentina | Cooper-Maserati | |
| | Ettore Chimeri | Venezuela | Maserati | |
| | Antonio Creus | Spain | Maserati | |
| | Estefano Nasif | Argentina | Maserati | |
| | Jose Froilan Gonzalez | Argentina | Ferrari | |
| | Alberto Rodriquez Larreta | Argentina | Lotus-Climax | |
| | Gino Munaron | Italy | Maserati, Cooper-Castellotti | |
| | Alan Stacey | GB | Lotus-Climax | |
| | Harry Schell | USA | Cooper-Climax | |
| | Dan Gurney | USA | BRM | |
| | Ian Burgess | GB | Cooper-Maserati | |
| | Chris Bristow | GB | Cooper-Climax | |
| | Chuck Daigh | USA | Scarab Cooper-Climax | |
| | Bruce Halford | GB | Cooper-Climax | |
| | Brian Naylor | GB | JBW-Maserati | |
| | Lance Reventlow | USA | Scarab Cooper-Climax | |
| | Roy Salvadori | GB | Cooper-Climax, Aston Martin | |
| | Carel Godin de Beufort | Netheralands | Cooper-Climax | |
| | Mike Taylor | GB | Lotus-Climax | |
| | David Piper | GB | Lotus-Climax | |
| | Jack Fairman | GB | Cooper-Climax | |

Points for top six finishers (8, 6, 4, 3, 2, 1). Only the best six scores counted towards the championship.

### CONSTRUCTORS' CHAMPIONSHIP

| POS. | CONSTRUCTOR | POINTS |
|---|---|---|
| 1 | Cooper-Climax | 48 |
| 2 | Lotus-Climax | 34 |
| 3 | Ferrari | 26 |
| 4 | BRM | 8 |
| 5 | Cooper-Maserati | 3 |
| 5 | Cooper-Castellotti | 3 |
| 7 | Porsche | 1 |

Points for top six finishers (8, 6, 4, 3, 2, 1). Points only counted for top-placed car for each constructor. Only the best six scores counted towards the championship. Indianapolis excluded.

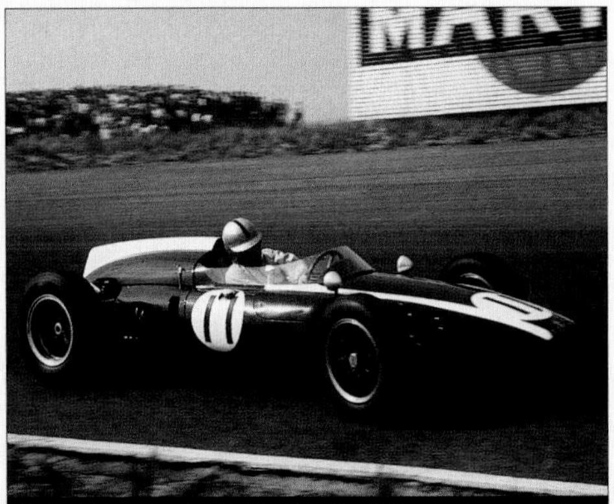

1960 world champion, Jack Brabham in the Type 53 Cooper-Climax (lowline).

### ARGENTINE GRAND PRIX: BUENOS AIRES *7 February Round: 1 Race: 85 80 x 2.431 miles*

| POS. | NO. | DRIVER | CAR/ENGINE | LAPS | TIME/RETIRED | GRID |
|---|---|---|---|---|---|---|
| 1 | 16 | Bruce McLaren | Cooper-Climax | 80 | 2:17'49.5 | 13 |
| 2 | 24 | Cliff Allison | Ferrari | 80 | +26.3 | 7 |
| 3 | 38 | Trintignant/Moss | Cooper-Climax | 80 | +36.9 | 8 |
| 4 | 6 | C.Menditeguy | Cooper-Maserati | 80 | +53.3 | 12 |
| 5 | 30 | W.von Trips | Ferrari | 79 | +1 Lap | 5 |
| 6 | 20 | Innes Ireland | Lotus-Climax | 79 | +1 Lap | 2 |
| 7 | 40 | Jo Bonnier | BRM | 79 | +1 Lap | 4 |
| 8 | 26 | Phil Hill | Ferrari | 77 | +3 Laps | 6 |
| 9 | 46 | A.R.Larreta | Lotus-Climax | 77 | +3 Laps | 15 |
| 10 | 32 | J.F.Gonzalez | Ferrari | 77 | +3 Laps | 11 |
| 11 | 4 | Roberto Bonomi | Cooper-Maserati | 76 | +4 Laps | 17 |
| 12 | 2 | Masten Gregory | Behra-Porsche-Porsche | 76 | +4 Laps | 16 |
| 13 | 14 | Gino Munaron | Maserati | 72 | +8 Laps | 19 |
| 14 | 10 | Nasif Estefano | Maserati | 70 | +10 Laps | 20 |
| Ret | 34 | Harry Schell | Cooper-Climax | 63 | Fuel pump | 9 |
| Ret | 18 | Jack Brabham | Cooper-Climax | 42 | Gearbox | 10 |
| Ret | 36 | Stirling Moss | Cooper-Climax | 40 | Suspension | 1 |
| Ret | 42 | Graham Hill | BRM | 37 | Overheating | 3 |
| Ret | 22 | Alan Stacey | Lotus-Climax | 24 | Physical | 14 |
| Ret | 44 | Ettore Chimeri | Maserati | 23 | Physical | 21 |
| Ret | 12 | Antonio Creus | Maserati | 16 | Physical | 22 |
| Ret | 8 | G.Scarlatti | Maserati | 11 | Overheating | 18 |

Winning speed: 84.657mph Lap leaders: Ireland 1; Bonnier 2-15, 21-36, 41-67; Moss 16-20, 37-40; McLaren 68-80
Pole position: Moss, 1m 36.900s, 90.309mph
Fastest lap: Moss, 1m 38.900s, 88.482mph

### MONACO GRAND PRIX: MONTE CARLO *29 May Round: 2 Race: 86 100 x 1.954 miles*

| POS. | NO. | DRIVER | CAR/ENGINE | LAPS | TIME/RETIRED | GRID |
|---|---|---|---|---|---|---|
| 1 | 28 | Stirling Moss | Lotus-Climax | 100 | 2:53'45.5 | |
| 2 | 10 | Bruce McLaren | Cooper-Climax | 100 | +52.1 | |
| 3 | 36 | Phil Hill | Ferrari | 100 | +1'01.9 | |
| 4 | 18 | Tony Brooks | Cooper-Climax | 99 | +1 Lap | |
| 5 | 2 | Jo Bonnier | BRM | 83 | +17 Laps | |
| 6 | 34 | Richie Ginther | Ferrari | 70 | +30 Laps | |
| 7 | 6 | Graham Hill | BRM | 66 | Spun off | |
| 8 | 38 | W.von Trips | Ferrari | 61 | Clutch | |
| 9 | 22 | Innes Ireland | Lotus-Climax | 56 | +44 Laps | |
| Ret | 4 | Dan Gurney | BRM | 44 | Suspension | |
| DSQ | 8 | Jack Brabham | Cooper-Climax | 40 | Disqualified | |
| Ret | 14 | Roy Salvadori | Cooper-Climax | 29 | Overheating | |
| Ret | 24 | Alan Stacey | Lotus-Climax | 23 | Chassis | |
| Ret | 16 | Chris Bristow | Cooper-Climax | 17 | Gearbox | |
| Ret | 26 | John Surtees | Lotus-Climax | 17 | Transmission | |
| Ret | 44 | M.Trintignant | Cooper-Maserati | 4 | Gearbox | |
| DNQ | 12 | Bruce Halford | Cooper-Climax | | | |
| DNQ | 32 | Cliff Allison | Ferrari | | | |
| DNQ | 20 | Brian Naylor | JBW-Maserati | | | |
| DNQ | 40 | Masten Gregory | Cooper-Maserati | | | |
| DNQ | 46 | Chuck Daigh | Scarab | | | |
| DNQ | 30 | G.Scarlatti | Cooper-Castellotti | | | |
| DNQ | 48 | Lance Reventlow | Scarab | | | |
| DNQ | 42 | Ian Burgess | Cooper-Maserati | | | |

Winning speed: 67.480mph
Lap leaders: Bonnier 1-16, 61-67; Moss 17-33, 41-60, 68-100; Brabham 34-40
Pole Position: Moss, 1m 36.300s, 73.055mph
Fastest lap: McLaren, 1m 36.200s, 73.131mph

### INDIANAPOLIS 500 *30 May Round: 3 Race: 87 200 x 2.500 miles*

| POS. | NO. | DRIVER | CAR/ENGINE | LAPS | TIME/RETIRED | GRID |
|---|---|---|---|---|---|---|
| 1 | 4 | Jim Rathmann | Watson-Offenhauser | 200 | 3:36'11.36 | 2 |
| 2 | 1 | Rodger Ward | Watson-Offenhauser | 200 | +12.75 | 3 |
| 3 | 99 | Paul Goldsmith | Epperly-Offenhauser | 200 | +3'07.30 | 26 |
| 4 | 7 | Don Branson | Phillips-Offenhauser | 200 | +3'07.98 | 8 |
| 5 | 3 | Johnny Thomson | Lesovsky-Offenhauser | 200 | +3'11.35 | 17 |
| 6 | 22 | Eddie Johnson | Trevis-Offenhauser | 200 | +4'10.61 | 7 |
| 7 | 98 | Lloyd Ruby | Watson-Offenhauser | 200 | +4'25.59 | 12 |
| 8 | 44 | Bob Veith | Meskowski-Offenhauser | 200 | +5'17.48 | 25 |
| 9 | 18 | Bud Tingelstad | Trevis-Offenhauser | 200 | +8'09.91 | 28 |
| 10 | 38 | Bob Christie | Kurtis Kraft-Offenhauser | 200 | +8'40.28 | 14 |
| 11 | 27 | Red Amick | Epperly-Offenhauser | 200 | +11'10.58 | 22 |
| 12 | 17 | Duane Carter | Kuzma-Offenhauser | 200 | +11'17.20 | 27 |
| 13 | 39 | Bill Homeier | Kuzma-Offenhauser | 200 | +12'10.71 | 31 |
| 14 | 48 | Gene Hartley | Kurtis Kraft-Offenhauser | 196 | +4 Laps | 24 |
| 15 | 65 | Chuck Stevenson | Watson-Offenhauser | 196 | +4 Laps | 9 |
| 16 | 14 | Bobby Grim | Meskowski-Offenhauser | 194 | +6 Laps | 21 |
| Ret | 26 | Shorty Templeman | Kurtis Kraft-Offenhauser | 191 | Clutch | 19 |
| Ret | 56 | Jim Hurtubise | Christensen-Offenhauser | 185 | Engine | 23 |
| Ret | 10 | Jimmy Bryan | Epperly-Offenhauser | 152 | Fuel pump | 10 |
| Ret | 28 | Troy Ruttman | Watson-Offenhauser | 134 | Axle | 6 |
| Ret | 6 | Eddie Sachs | Ewing-Offenhauser | 132 | Magneto | 1 |
| Ret | 73 | Don Freeland | Kurtis Kraft-Offenhauser | 129 | Magneto | 11 |
| Ret | 2 | T.Bettenhausen | Watson-Offenhauser | 125 | Engine | 18 |
| Ret | 32 | Wayne Weiler | Epperly-Offenhauser | 103 | Accident | 15 |
| Ret | 5 | A J Foyt | Kurtis Kraft-Offenhauser | 90 | Clutch | 16 |
| Ret | 46 | Eddie Russo | Kurtis Kraft-Offenhauser | 84 | Accident | 29 |
| Ret | 8 | Johnny Boyd | Epperly-Offenhauser | 77 | Engine | 13 |
| Ret | 37 | Gene Force | Kurtis Kraft-Offenhauser | 74 | Brakes | 20 |
| Ret | 16 | Jim McWithey | Epperly-Offenhauser | 60 | Brakes | 32 |
| Ret | 9 | Len Sutton | Watson-Offenhauser | 47 | Engine | 5 |
| Ret | 97 | Dick Rathmann | Watson-Offenhauser | 42 | Brakes | 4 |
| Ret | 76 | Al Herman | Ewing-Offenhauser | 34 | Clutch | 30 |
| Ret | 23 | Dempsey Wilson | Kurtis Kraft-Offenhauser | 11 | Magneto | 33 |

Winning speed: 138.767mph
Pole position: Sachs, 1m 01.395s, 146.592mph
Fastest lap: Rathmann, 1m 01.590s, 146.128mph

### DUTCH GRAND PRIX: ZANDVOORT *6 June Round: 4 Race: 88 75 x 2.605 miles*

| POS. | NO. | DRIVER | CAR/ENGINE | LAPS | TIME/RETIRED | GRID |
|---|---|---|---|---|---|---|
| 1 | 11 | Jack Brabham | Cooper-Climax | 75 | 2:01'47.2 | 2 |
| 2 | 4 | Innes Ireland | Lotus-Climax | 75 | +24.0 | 3 |
| 3 | 16 | Graham Hill | BRM | 75 | +56.6 | 5 |
| 4 | 7 | Stirling Moss | Lotus-Climax | 75 | +57.7 | 1 |
| 5 | 2 | W.von Trips | Ferrari | 74 | +1 Lap | 15 |
| 6 | 3 | Richie Ginther | Ferrari | 74 | +1 Lap | 12 |
| 7 | 10 | Henry Taylor | Cooper-Climax | 70 | +5 Laps | 14 |
| 8 | 20 | C.G.de Beaufort | Cooper-Climax | 69 | +6 Laps | 18 |
| Ret | 5 | Alan Stacey | Lotus-Climax | 57 | Transmission | 8 |
| Ret | 14 | Jo Bonnier | BRM | 54 | Engine | 4 |
| Ret | 1 | Phil Hill | Ferrari | 54 | Engine | 13 |
| Ret | 6 | Jim Clark | Lotus-Climax | 42 | Transmission | 11 |
| Ret | 18 | M.Trintignant | Cooper-Maserati | 39 | Gearbox | 17 |
| Ret | 15 | Dan Gurney | BRM | 11 | Accident | 6 |
| Ret | 8 | Chris Bristow | Cooper-Climax | 9 | Engine | 7 |
| Ret | 12 | Bruce McLaren | Cooper-Climax | 8 | Transmission | 9 |
| Ret | 9 | Tony Brooks | Cooper-Climax | 4 | Gearbox | 10 |
| DNS | 17 | Roy Salvadori | Aston Martin | 0 | Non starter | |
| DNS | 19 | Masten Gregory | Cooper-Maserati | 0 | Non starter | |
| DNS | 21 | Lance Reventlow | Scarab | 0 | Non starter | |
| DNS | 22 | Chuck Daigh | Scarab | 0 | Non starter | |

Winning speed: 96.270mph Lap leaders: Brabham 1-75
Pole Position: Moss, 1m 33.200s, 100.638mph
Fastest lap: Moss, 1m 33.800s, 99.994mph

### BELGIAN GRAND PRIX: SPA-FRANCORCHAMPS *19 June Round: 5 Race: 89 36 x 8.761 miles*

| POS. | NO. | DRIVER | CAR/ENGINE | LAPS | TIME/RETIRED | GRID |
|---|---|---|---|---|---|---|
| 1 | 2 | Jack Brabham | Cooper-Climax | 36 | 2:21'37.3 | 1 |
| 2 | 4 | Bruce McLaren | Cooper-Climax | 36 | +1'03.3 | 14 |
| 3 | 34 | O.Gendebien | Cooper-Climax | 35 | +1 Lap | 5 |
| 4 | 24 | Phil Hill | Ferrari | 35 | +1 Lap | 4 |
| 5 | 18 | Jim Clark | Lotus-Climax | 34 | +2 Laps | 10 |
| 6 | 32 | Lucien Bianchi | Cooper-Climax | 28 | +8 Laps | 15 |
| Ret | 10 | Graham Hill | BRM | 35 | Engine | 6 |
| Ret | 16 | Alan Stacey | Lotus-Climax | 24 | Accident | 17 |
| Ret | 22 | Willy Mairesse | Ferrari | 23 | Transmission | 13 |
| Ret | 26 | W.von Trips | Ferrari | 22 | Transmission | 11 |
| Ret | 36 | Chris Bristow | Cooper-Climax | 19 | Accident | 9 |
| Ret | 30 | Chuck Daigh | Scarab | 16 | Engine | 18 |
| Ret | 6 | Jo Bonnier | BRM | 14 | Engine | 7 |
| Ret | 14 | Innes Ireland | Lotus-Climax | 13 | Accident | 8 |
| Ret | 8 | Dan Gurney | BRM | 4 | Engine | 12 |
| Ret | 38 | Tony Brooks | Cooper-Climax | 2 | Gearbox | 2 |
| Ret | 28 | Lance Reventlow | Scarab | 1 | Engine | 16 |
| Ret | 12 | Stirling Moss | Lotus-Climax | 0 | Accident | 3 |
| Ret | 20 | Mike Taylor | Lotus-Climax | 0 | Accident | 19 |

Winning speed: 133.627 mph Lap leaders: Brabham 1-36
Pole position: Brabham, 3m 50.000s, 137.134mph
Fastest lap: Hill/Brabham/Ireland, 3m 51.900s, 136.010mph

### FRENCH GRAND PRIX: REIMS *3 July Round: 6 Race: 90 50 x 5.159 miles*

| POS. | NO. | DRIVER | CAR/ENGINE | LAPS | TIME/RETIRED | GRID |
|---|---|---|---|---|---|---|
| 1 | 16 | Jack Brabham | Cooper-Climax | 50 | 1:57'24.9 | 1 |
| 2 | 44 | O.Gendebien | Cooper-Climax | 50 | +48.3 | 9 |
| 3 | 18 | Bruce McLaren | Cooper-Climax | 50 | +51.9 | 7 |
| 4 | 46 | Henry Taylor | Cooper-Climax | 49 | +1 Lap | 12 |
| 5 | 24 | Jim Clark | Lotus-Climax | 49 | +1 Lap | 10 |
| 6 | 22 | Ron Flockhart | Lotus-Climax | 49 | +1 Lap | 14 |
| 7 | 20 | Innes Ireland | Lotus-Climax | 43 | +7 Laps | 4 |
| 8 | 48 | Bruce Halford | Cooper-Climax | 40 | Engine | 15 |
| 9 | 40 | Masten Gregory | Cooper-Maserati | 37 | +13 Laps | 17 |
| 10 | 42 | Ian Burgess | Cooper-Maserati | 36 | +14 Laps | 22 |
| 11 | 4 | W.von Trips | Ferrari | 30 | Transmission | 5 |
| 12 | 2 | Phil Hill | Ferrari | 29 | Transmission | 2 |
| Ret | 8 | Jo Bonnier | BRM | 22 | Engine | 8 |
| Ret | 36 | Lucien Bianchi | Cooper-Climax | 18 | Transmission | 15 |
| Ret | 10 | Dan Gurney | BRM | 17 | Engine | 6 |
| Ret | 30 | Gino Munaron | Cooper-Castellotti | 16 | Transmission | 19 |
| Ret | 6 | Willy Mairesse | Ferrari | 14 | Transmission | 11 |
| Ret | 14 | Tony Brooks | Vanwall | 7 | Vibrations | 13 |
| Ret | 12 | Graham Hill | BRM | 0 | Accident | 3 |
| Ret | 38 | M.Trintignant | Cooper-Maserati | 0 | Accident | 18 |
| Ret | 28 | Richie Ginther | Scarab | 0 | Engine | 20 |
| Ret | 34 | David Piper | Lotus-Climax | 0 | Engine | 21 |
| Ret | 26 | Chuck Daigh | Scarab | 0 | Engine | 23 |

Winning speed: 131.805mph
Lap leaders: Brabham 1-3, 5, 7, 9-10, 12, 14, 18-50; Hill 4, 6, 8, 11, 13, 15-17
Pole position: Brabham, 2m 16.800s, 135.753mph
Fastest lap: Brabham, 2m 17.500s, 135.062mph

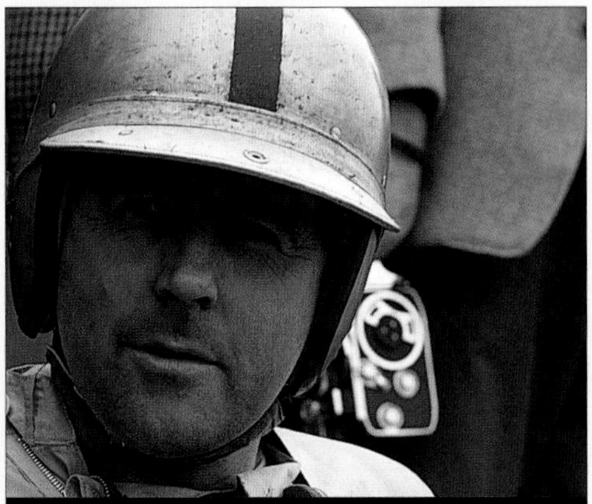
1960 world champion, Jack Brabham.

## BRITISH GRAND PRIX: SILVERSTONE *16 July Round: 7 Race: 91 77 x 2.927 miles*

| POS. | NO. | DRIVER | CAR/ENGINE | LAPS | TIME/RETIRED | GRID |
|---|---|---|---|---|---|---|
| 1 | 1 | Jack Brabham | Cooper-Climax | 77 | 2:04'24.6 | 1 |
| 2 | 9 | John Surtees | Lotus-Climax | 77 | +49.6 | 11 |
| 3 | 7 | Innes Ireland | Lotus-Climax | 77 | +1'29.6 | 5 |
| 4 | 2 | Bruce McLaren | Cooper-Climax | 76 | +1 Lap | 3 |
| 5 | 12 | Tony Brooks | Cooper-Climax | 76 | +1 Lap | 9 |
| 6 | 11 | W.von Trips | Ferrari | 75 | +2 Laps | 7 |
| 7 | 10 | Phil Hill | Ferrari | 75 | +2 Laps | 10 |
| 8 | 15 | Henry Taylor | Cooper-Climax | 74 | +3 Laps | 16 |
| 9 | 14 | O.Gendebien | Cooper-Climax | 74 | +3 Laps | 12 |
| 10 | 5 | Dan Gurney | BRM | 74 | +3 Laps | 6 |
| 11 | 19 | M.Trintignant | Aston Martin | 72 | +5 Laps | 21 |
| 12 | 26 | David Piper | Lotus-Climax | 72 | +5 Laps24 | |
| 13 | 25 | Brian Naylor | JBW-Maserati | 72 | +5 Laps | 18 |
| 14 | 16 | Masten Gregory | Cooper-Maserati | 71 | +6 Laps | 14 |
| 15 | 21 | Gino Munaron | Cooper-Castellotti | 70 | +7 Laps | 25 |
| 16 | 8 | Jim Clark | Lotus-Climax | 70 | +7 Laps | 8 |
| Ret | 4 | Graham Hill | BRM | 71 | Spun off | 2 |
| Ret | 24 | Lucien Bianchi | Cooper-Climax | 62 | Electrical | 17 |
| Ret | 6 | Jo Bonnier | BRM | 59 | Suspension | 4 |
| Ret | 3 | Chuck Daigh | Cooper-Climax | 58 | Overheating | 19 |
| Ret | 17 | Ian Burgess | Cooper-Maserati | 58 | Engine | 20 |
| Ret | 18 | Roy Salvadori | Aston Martin | 46 | Steering | 13 |
| Ret | 23 | Jack Fairman | Cooper-Climax | 46 | Fuel pump | 15 |
| Ret | 22 | Keith Greene | Cooper-Maserati | 12 | Overheating | 22 |

Winning speed: 108.695mph Lap leaders: Brabham 1-54, 72-77; G Hill 55-71
Pole Position: Brabham, 1m 34.600s, 111.387mph
Fastest lap: G Hill, 1m 34.400s, 111.623mph

## PORTUGUESE GRAND PRIX: PORTO *14 August Round: 8 Race: 92 55 x 4.602 miles*

| POS. | NO. | DRIVER | CAR/ENGINE | LAPS | TIME/RETIRED | GRID |
|---|---|---|---|---|---|---|
| 1 | 2 | Jack Brabham | Cooper-Climax | 55 | 2:19'00.03 | 3 |
| 2 | 4 | Bruce McLaren | Cooper-Climax | 55 | +57.97 | 6 |
| 3 | 14 | Jim Clark | Lotus-Climax | 55 | +1'53.23 | 8 |
| 4 | 28 | W.von Trips | Ferrari | 55 | +1'58.81 | 9 |
| 5 | 6 | Tony Brooks | Cooper-Climax | 49 | +6 Laps | 12 |
| 6 | 16 | Innes Ireland | Lotus-Climax | 48 | +7 Laps | 7 |
| 7 | 8 | O.Gendebien | Cooper-Climax | 46 | +9 Laps | 14 |
| DSQ | 12 | Stirling Moss | Lotus-Climax | 51 | Disqualified | 4 |
| Ret | 32 | M.A.Cabral | Cooper-Maserati | 38 | Accident | 15 |
| Ret | 18 | John Surtees | Lotus-Climax | 37 | Radiator | 1 |
| Ret | 26 | Phil Hill | Ferrari | 30 | Accident | 10 |
| Ret | 24 | Dan Gurney | BRM | 25 | Engine | 2 |
| Ret | 30 | Masten Gregory | Cooper-Maserati | 21 | Gearbox | 11 |
| Ret | 22 | Graham Hill | BRM | 9 | Gearbox | 5 |
| Ret | 20 | Jo Bonnier | BRM | 6 | Engine | 13 |

Winning speed: 109.268mph Lap leaders: Gurney 1-10; Surtees 11-35; Brabham 36-55
Pole position: Surtees, 2m 25.560s, 113.829mph
Fastest lap: Surtees, 2m 27.530s, 112.309mph

## ITALIAN GRAND PRIX: MONZA *4 September Round: 9 Race: 93 50 x 6.214 miles*

| POS. | NO. | DRIVER | CAR/ENGINE | LAPS | TIME/RETIRED | GRID |
|---|---|---|---|---|---|---|
| 1 | 20 | Phil Hill | Ferrari | 50 | 2:21'09.2 | 1 |
| 2 | 18 | Richie Ginther | Ferrari | 50 | +2'27.6 | 2 |
| 3 | 16 | Willy Mairesse | Ferrari | 49 | +1 Lap | 3 |
| 4 | 2 | Giulio Cabianca | Cooper-Castellotti | 48 | +2 Laps | 4 |
| 5 | 22 | W.von Trips | Ferrari | 48 | +2 Laps | 6 |
| 6 | 26 | Hans Herrmann | Porsche | 47 | +3 Laps | 10 |
| 7 | 24 | Edgar Barth | Porsche | 47 | +3 Laps | 12 |
| 8 | 12 | Piero Drogo | Cooper-Climax | 45 | +5 Laps | 15 |
| 9 | 10 | Wolfgang Seidel | Cooper-Climax | 44 | +6 Laps | 13 |
| 10 | 28 | Fred Gamble | Behra-Porsche-Porsche | 41 | +9 Laps | 14 |
| Ret | 6 | Brian Naylor | JBW-Maserati | 41 | Gearbox | 7 |
| Ret | 34 | Alfonso Thiele | Cooper-Maserati | 32 | Gearbox | 9 |
| Ret | 4 | Gino Munaron | Cooper-Castellotti | 27 | Engine | 8 |
| Ret | 36 | G.Scarlatti | Cooper-Maserati | 26 | Engine | 5 |
| Ret | 30 | Vic Wilson | Cooper-Climax | 23 | Engine | 16 |
| Ret | 8 | Arthur Owen | Cooper-Climax | 0 | Accident | 11 |

Winning speed: 132.063mph Lap leaders: Ginther 1-16, 18-25; P Hill 17, 26-50
Pole Position: P Hill, 2m 41.400s, 138.596mph
Fastest lap: P Hill, 2m 43.600s, 136.732mph

## UNITED STATES GRAND PRIX: RIVERSIDE *20 November Round: 10 Race: 94 75 x 3.275 miles*

| POS. | NO. | DRIVER | CAR/ENGINE | LAPS | TIME/RETIRED | GRID |
|---|---|---|---|---|---|---|
| 1 | 5 | Stirling Moss | Lotus-Climax | 75 | 2:28'52.2 | 1 |
| 2 | 10 | Innes Ireland | Lotus-Climax | 75 | +38.0 | 7 |
| 3 | 3 | Bruce McLaren | Cooper-Climax | 75 | +52.0 | 10 |
| 4 | 2 | Jack Brabham | Cooper-Climax | 74 | +1 Lap | 2 |
| 5 | 15 | Jo Bonnier | BRM | 74 | +1 Lap | 4 |
| 6 | 9 | Phil Hill | Cooper-Climax | 74 | +1 Lap | 13 |
| 7 | 24 | Jim Hall | Lotus-Climax | 73 | +2 Laps | 12 |
| 8 | 14 | Roy Salvadori | Cooper-Climax | 73 | +2 Laps | 15 |
| 9 | 26 | W.von Trips | Cooper-Maserati | 72 | +3 Laps | 16 |
| 10 | 23 | Chuck Daigh | Scarab | 70 | +5 Laps | 18 |
| 11 | 25 | Pete Lovely | Cooper-Ferrari | 69 | +6 Laps | 20 |
| 12 | 7 | O.Gendebien | Cooper-Climax | 69 | +6 Laps | 8 |
| 13 | 20 | Bob Drake | Maserati | 68 | +7 Laps | 22 |
| 14 | 8 | Henry Taylor | Cooper-Climax | 68 | +7 Laps | 14 |
| 15 | 18 | M.Trintignant | Cooper-Maserati | 66 | +9 Laps | 19 |
| 16 | 12 | Jim Clark | Lotus-Climax | 61 | +14 Laps | 5 |
| Ret | 17 | Graham Hill | BRM | 34 | Gearbox | 11 |
| Ret | 19 | Ian Burgess | Cooper-Maserati | 29 | Ignition | 23 |
| Ret | 21 | Brian Naylor | JBW-Maserati | 20 | Engine | 17 |
| Ret | 16 | Dan Gurney | BRM | 18 | Overheating | 3 |
| Ret | 4 | Ron Flockhart | Cooper-Climax | 11 | Transmission | 21 |
| Ret | 6 | Tony Brooks | Cooper-Climax | 6 | Spun off | 9 |
| Ret | 11 | John Surtees | Lotus-Climax | 3 | Accident | 6 |

Winning speed: 98.996mph Lap leaders: Brabham 1-4; Moss 5-75
Pole position: Moss, 1m 54.400s, 103.059mph
Fastest lap: Brabham, 1m 56.300s, 101.376mph

# 1961

## DRIVERS' CHAMPION: PHIL HILL
## CONSTRUCTORS' CHAMPION: FERRARI

### DRIVERS' CHAMPIONSHIP

| POS | DRIVER | COUNTRY | CAR | POINTS |
|---|---|---|---|---|
| 1 | Phil Hill | USA | Ferrari | 34(4) |
| 2 | Wolfgang von Trips | West Germany | Ferrari | 33 |
| 3 | Stirling Moss | GB | Lotus-Climax, Ferguson-Climax | 21 |
| = | Dan Gurney | USA | Porsche | 21 |
| 5 | Richie Ginther | USA | Ferrari | 16 |
| 6 | Innes Ireland | GB | Lotus-Climax | 12 |
| 7 | Jim Clark | GB | Lotus-Climax | 11 |
| = | Bruce McLaren | New Zealand | Cooper-Climax | 11 |
| 9 | Giancarlo Baghetti | Italy | Ferrari | 9 |
| 10 | Tony Brooks | GB | BRM-Climax | 6 |
| 11 | Jack Brabham | Australia | Cooper-Climax | 4 |
| = | John Surtees | GB | Cooper-Climax | 4 |
| 13 | Olivier Gendebien | Belgium | Emeryson-Maserati Ferrari, Lotus-Climax | 3 |
| = | Graham Hill | GB | BRM-Climax | 3 |
| = | Jo Bonnier | Sweden | Porsche | 3 |
| = | Jackie Lewis | GB | Cooper-Climax | 3 |
| 17 | Roy Salvadori | GB | Cooper-Climax | 2 |
| | Lucien Bianchi | Belgian | Emeryson-Maserati Lotus-Climax | |
| | Masten Gregory | USA | Cooper-Climax | |
| | Hans Herrmann | West Germany | Porsche | |
| | Michael May | Switzerland | Lotus-Climax | |
| | Henry Taylor | GB | Lotus-Climax | |
| | Maurice Trintignant | France | Cooper-Maserati | |
| | Cliff Allison | GB | Lotus-Climax | |
| | Carel Godin de Beaufort | Netherlands | Porsche | |
| | Ian Burgess | GB | Lotus-Climax, Cooper-Climax | |
| | Trevor Taylor | GB | Lotus-Climax | |
| | Willy Mairesse | Belgium | Lotus-Climax, Ferrari | |
| | Tony Marsh | GB | Lotus-Climax | |
| | Wolfgang Seidel | West Germany | Lotus-Climax | |
| | Lorenzo Bandini | Italy | Cooper-Maserati | |
| | Giorgio Scarlatti | Italy | de Tomaso-OSCA | |
| | Bernard Collomb | France | Cooper-Climax | |
| | Gerry Ashmore | GB | Lotus-Climax | |
| | Tony Maggs | South Africa | Lotus-Climax | |
| | Massimo Natali | Italy | Cooper-Climax | |
| | Tim Parnell | GB | Lotus-Climax | |
| | Jack Fairman | GB | Ferguson-Climax, Cooper-Climax | |
| | Keith Greene | GB | Gilby-Climax | |
| | Brian Naylor | GB | JBW-Climax | |
| | André Pilette | Belgium | Emeryson-Climax | |
| | Renato Pirocchi | Italy | Cooper-Climax | |
| | Gaetano Starrabba | Italy | Lotus-Maserati | |
| | Ricardo Rodriguez | Mexico | Ferrari | |
| | Nino Vacarella | Italy | de Tomaso-Alfa Romeo | |
| | Roberto Lippi | Italy | de Tomaso-OSCA | |
| | Roberto Bussinello | Italy | de Tomaso-Alfa Romeo | |
| | Jim Hall | USA | Lotus-Climax | |
| | Walt Hansgen | USA | Cooper-Climax | |
| | Roger Penske | USA | Cooper-Climax | |
| | Lloyd Ruby | USA | Lotus-Climax | |
| | Peter Ryan | Canada | Lotus-Climax | |
| | Hap Sharp | USA | Cooper-Climax | |

Points for the top six finishers (9, 6, 4, 3, 2, 1). Only the best five scores counted towards the championship.

### CONSTRUCTORS' CHAMPIONSHIP

| POS. | CONSTRUCTOR | POINTS |
|---|---|---|
| 1 | Ferrari | 40 |
| 2 | Lotus-Climax | 32 |
| 3 | Porsche | 22 |
| 4 | Cooper-Climax | 14 |
| 5 | BRM-Climax | 7 |

Points for top six finishers (8, 6, 4, 3, 2, 1). Points only counted for top-placed car for each constructor. Only the best five scores counted towards the championship.

## MONACO GRAND PRIX: MONTE CARLO *14 May Round: 1 Race: 95 100 x 1.954 miles*

| POS. | NO. | DRIVER | CAR/ENGINE | LAPS | TIME/RETIRED | GRID |
|---|---|---|---|---|---|---|
| 1 | 20 | Stirling Moss | Lotus-Climax | 100 | 2:45'50.1 | 1 |
| 2 | 36 | Richie Ginther | Ferrari | 100 | +3.6 | 2 |
| 3 | 38 | Phil Hill | Ferrari | 100 | +41.3 | 5 |
| 4 | 40 | W.von Trips | Ferrari | 98 | Accident | 6 |
| 5 | 4 | Dan Gurney | Porsche | 98 | +2 Laps | 11 |
| 6 | 26 | Bruce McLaren | Cooper-Climax | 95 | +5 Laps | 7 |
| 7 | 42 | M.Trintignant | Cooper-Maserati | 95 | +5 Laps | 16 |
| 8 | 32 | Cliff Allison | Lotus-Climax | 93 | +7 Laps | 15 |
| 9 | 6 | Hans Herrmann | Porsche | 91 | +9 Laps | 13 |
| 10 | 28 | Jim Clark | Lotus-Climax | 89 | +11 Laps | 3 |
| 11 | 22 | John Surtees | Cooper-Climax | 68 | Engine | 12 |
| 12 | 2 | Jo Bonnier | Porsche | 59 | Injection | 9 |
| 13 | 16 | Tony Brooks | BRM-Climax | 54 | Engine | 8 |
| Ret | 8 | Michel May | Lotus-Climax | 42 | Oil pipe | 14 |
| Ret | 24 | Jack Brabham | Cooper-Climax | 38 | Ignition | 21 |
| Ret | 18 | Graham Hill | BRM-Climax | 11 | Fuel pump | 4 |
| DNQ | 34 | Henry Taylor | Lotus-Climax | | | |
| DNQ | 14 | Masten Gregory | Cooper-Climax | | | |
| DNQ | 10 | Lucien Bianchi | Emeryson-Maserati | | | |
| DNQ | 12 | O.Gendebien | Emeryson-Maserati | | | |

Winning speed: 70.704mph Lap leaders: Ginther 1-13; Moss 14-100
Pole position: Moss, 1m 39.100s, 70.991mph
Fastest lap: Ginther/Moss, 1m 36.300s, 73.055mph

## DUTCH GRAND PRIX: ZANDVOORT *22 May Round: 2 Race: 96 75 x 2.605 miles*

| POS. | NO. | DRIVER | CAR/ENGINE | LAPS | TIME/RETIRED | GRID |
|---|---|---|---|---|---|---|
| 1 | 3 | W.von Trips | Ferrari | 75 | 2:01'52.1 | 2 |
| 2 | 1 | Phil Hill | Ferrari | 75 | +0.9 | 1 |
| 3 | 15 | Jim Clark | Lotus-Climax | 75 | +13.1 | 11 |
| 4 | 14 | Stirling Moss | Lotus-Climax | 75 | +22.2 | 4 |
| 5 | 2 | Richie Ginther | Ferrari | 75 | +22.3 | 3 |
| 6 | 10 | Jack Brabham | Cooper-Climax | 75 | +1'20.1 | 7 |
| 7 | 12 | John Surtees | Cooper-Climax | 75 | +1'26.7 | 9 |
| 8 | 4 | Graham Hill | BRM-Climax | 75 | +1'39.8 | 5 |
| 9 | 5 | Tony Brooks | BRM-Climax | 74 | +1 Lap | 8 |
| 10 | 7 | Dan Gurney | Porsche | 74 | +1 Lap | 6 |
| 11 | 6 | Jo Bonnier | Porsche | 73 | +2 Laps | 12 |
| 12 | 11 | Bruce McLaren | Cooper-Climax | 73 | +2 Laps | 14 |
| 13 | 16 | Trevor Taylor | Lotus-Climax | 73 | +2 Laps | 16 |
| 14 | 8 | C.G.de Beaufort | Porsche | 72 | +3 Laps | 17 |
| 15 | 9 | Hans Herrmann | Porsche | 72 | +3 Laps | 13 |

Winning speed: 96.205mph Lap leaders: von Trips 1-75
Pole position: P Hill, 1m 35.700s, 98.009mph
Fastest lap: Clark, 1m 35.500s, 98.214mph

## BELGIAN GRAND PRIX: SPA-FRANCORCHAMPS *18 June Round: 3 Race: 97 30 x 8.761 miles*

| POS. | NO. | DRIVER | CAR/ENGINE | LAPS | TIME/RETIRED | GRID |
|---|---|---|---|---|---|---|
| 1 | 4 | Phil Hill | Ferrari | 30 | 2:03'03.8 | 1 |
| 2 | 2 | W.von Trips | Ferrari | 30 | +0.7 | 2 |
| 3 | 6 | Richie Ginther | Ferrari | 30 | +19.5 | 5 |
| 4 | 8 | O.Gendebien | Ferrari | 30 | +45.6 | 3 |
| 5 | 24 | John Surtees | Cooper-Climax | 30 | +1'26.8 | 4 |
| 6 | 20 | Dan Gurney | Porsche | 30 | +1'31.0 | 10 |
| 7 | 18 | Jo Bonnier | Porsche | 30 | +2'47.1 | 9 |
| 8 | 14 | Stirling Moss | Lotus-Climax | 30 | +3'55.6 | 8 |
| 9 | 40 | Jackie Lewis | Cooper-Climax | 29 | +1 Lap | 13 |
| 10 | 44 | Masten Gregory | Cooper-Climax | 29 | +1 Lap | 12 |
| 11 | 22 | C.G.de Beaufort | Porsche | 28 | +2 Laps | 14 |
| 12 | 34 | Jim Clark | Lotus-Climax | 24 | +6 Laps | 16 |
| 13 | 38 | Tony Brooks | BRM-Climax | 24 | +6 Laps | 7 |
| Ret | 36 | Graham Hill | BRM-Climax | 24 | Ignition | 6 |
| Ret | 26 | M.Trintignant | Cooper-Maserati | 23 | Gearbox | 20 |
| Ret | 46 | Lorenzo Bandini | Cooper-Maserati | 20 | Wheel bearing | 17 |
| Ret | 28 | Jack Brabham | Cooper-Climax | 12 | Engine | 11 |
| Ret | 30 | Bruce McLaren | Cooper-Climax | 9 | Ignition | 15 |
| Ret | 32 | Innes Ireland | Lotus-Climax | 9 | Engine | 18 |
| Ret | 12 | Lucien Bianchi | Lotus-Climax | 9 | Oil leak | 23 |
| Ret | 10 | Willy Mairesse | Lotus-Climax | 7 | Ignition | 19 |
| DNQ | 42 | Tony Marsh | Lotus-Climax | | | |
| DNQ | 48 | Wolfgang Seidel | Lotus-Climax | | | |
| DNQ | 50 | Ian Burgess | Lotus-Climax | | | |

Winning speed: 128.149mph Lap leaders: P Hill 1, 3-5, 8, 11-13, 15, 17-18, 21-23, 25-30; Gendebien 2, 6-7; von Trips 9-10, 14, 16, 19-20, 24
Pole Position: P Hill, 3m 59.300s, 131.804mph
Fastest lap: Ginther, 3m 59.800s, 131.530 mph

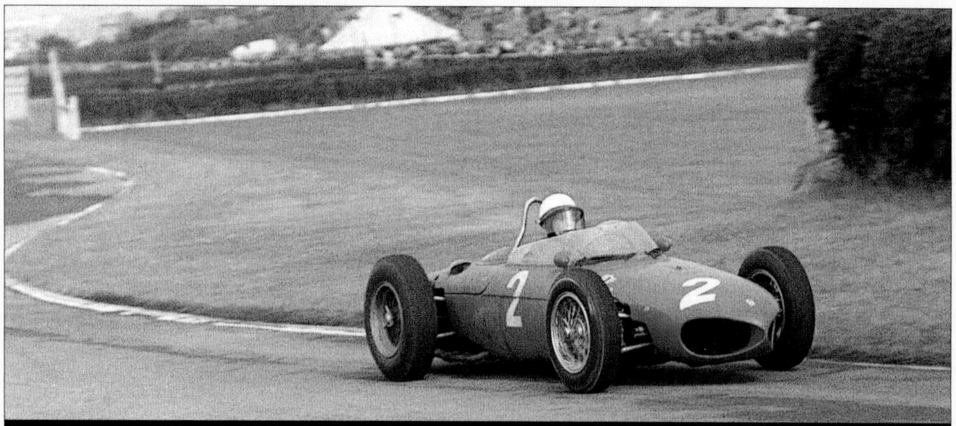

1961 world champion, Phil Hill in the Type 156 Ferrari Sharknose.

### FRENCH GRAND PRIX: REIMS *2 July Round: 4 Race: 98 52 x 5.159 miles*

| POS. | NO. | DRIVER | CAR/ENGINE | LAPS | TIME/RETIRED | GRID |
|---|---|---|---|---|---|---|
| 1 | 50 | Giancarlo Baghetti | Ferrari | 52 | 2:14'17.5 | 12 |
| 2 | 12 | Dan Gurney | Porsche | 52 | +0.1 | 5 |
| 3 | 8 | Jim Clark | Lotus-Climax | 52 | +1'01.1 | 9 |
| 4 | 6 | Innes Ireland | Lotus-Climax | 52 | +1'10.3 | 10 |
| 5 | 4 | Bruce McLaren | Cooper-Climax | 52 | +1'41.8 | 8 |
| 6 | 22 | Graham Hill | BRM-Climax | 52 | +1'41.9 | 6 |
| 7 | 10 | Jo Bonnier | Porsche | 52 | +3'15.4 | 13 |
| 8 | 42 | Roy Salvadori | Cooper-Climax | 51 | +1 Lap | 15 |
| 9 | 16 | Phil Hill | Ferrari | 50 | +2 Laps | 1 |
| 10 | 30 | Henry Taylor | Lotus-Climax | 49 | +3 Laps | 25 |
| 11 | 46 | Michel May | Lotus-Climax | 48 | +4 Laps | 22 |
| 12 | 36 | Masten Gregory | Cooper-Climax | 43 | +9 Laps | 16 |
| 13 | 32 | M.Trintignant | Cooper-Maserati | 42 | +10 Laps | 23 |
| 14 | 38 | Ian Burgess | Lotus-Climax | 42 | +10 Laps | 24 |
| 15 | 18 | Richie Ginther | Ferrari | 40 | Oil pressure | 3 |
| Ret | 26 | Stirling Moss | Lotus-Climax | 31 | Brakes | 4 |
| Ret | 38 | Willy Mairesse | Lotus-Climax | 27 | Engine | 20 |
| Ret | 14 | C.G.de Beaufort | Porsche | 23 | Overheating | 17 |
| Ret | 28 | Lucien Bianchi | Lotus-Climax | 21 | Overheating | 19 |
| Ret | 20 | W.von Trips | Ferrari | 18 | Engine | 2 |
| Ret | 34 | G.Scarlatti | De Tomaso-Osca | 15 | Engine | 26 |
| Ret | 2 | Jack Brabham | Cooper-Climax | 14 | Oil pressure | 14 |
| Ret | 52 | Bernard Collomb | Cooper-Climax | 6 | Engine | 21 |
| Ret | 40 | John Surtees | Cooper-Climax | 4 | Accident | 7 |
| Ret | 24 | Tony Brooks | BRM-Climax | 4 | Overheating | 11 |
| Ret | 44 | Jackie Lewis | Cooper-Climax | 4 | Overheating | 18 |

Winning speed: 119.850mph Lap leaders: P Hill 1-12, 18-37; von Trips 13-17; Ginther 38-40; Baghetti 41-43, 45, 47, 50, 52; Bonnier 44; Gurney 46, 48-49, 51
Pole Position: P Hill, 2m 24.900s, 128.165mph
Fastest lap: P Hill, 2m 27.100s, 126.248mph

### BRITISH GRAND PRIX: AINTREE *15 July Round: 5 Race: 99 75 x 3.000 miles*

| POS. | NO. | DRIVER | CAR/ENGINE | LAPS | TIME/RETIRED | GRID |
|---|---|---|---|---|---|---|
| 1 | 4 | W.von Trips | Ferrari | 75 | 2:40'53.6 | 4 |
| 2 | 2 | Phil Hill | Ferrari | 75 | +46.0 | 1 |
| 3 | 6 | Richie Ginther | Ferrari | 75 | +46.8 | 2 |
| 4 | 12 | Jack Brabham | Cooper-Climax | 75 | +1'08.6 | 9 |
| 5 | 8 | Jo Bonnier | Porsche | 75 | +1'16.2 | 3 |
| 6 | 36 | Roy Salvadori | Cooper-Climax | 75 | +1'26.2 | 13 |
| 7 | 10 | Dan Gurney | Porsche | 74 | +1 Lap | 12 |
| 8 | 14 | Bruce McLaren | Cooper-Climax | 74 | +1 Lap | 14 |
| 9 | 22 | Tony Brooks | BRM-Climax | 73 | +2 Laps | 6 |
| 10 | 16 | Innes Ireland | Lotus-Climax | 72 | +3 Laps | 7 |
| 11 | 42 | Masten Gregory | Cooper-Climax | 71 | +4 Laps | 16 |
| 12 | 60 | Lorenzo Bandini | Cooper-Maserati | 71 | +4 Laps | 21 |
| 13 | 50 | Tony Maggs | Lotus-Climax | 69 | +6 Laps | 24 |
| 14 | 44 | Ian Burgess | Lotus-Climax | 69 | +6 Laps | 25 |
| 15 | 54 | Keith Greene | Gilby-Climax | 69 | +6 Laps | 23 |
| 16 | 56 | C.G.de Beaufort | Porsche | 69 | +6 Laps | 18 |
| 17 | 52 | Wolfgang Seidel | Lotus-Climax | 58 | +17 Laps | 22 |
| Ret | 18 | Jim Clark | Lotus-Climax | 62 | Oil leak | 8 |
| DSQ | 26 | Fairman/Moss | Ferguson-Climax | 56 | Disqualified | 20 |
| Ret | 32 | Lucien Bianchi | Lotus-Climax | 45 | Gearbox | 30 |
| Ret | 28 | Stirling Moss | Lotus-Climax | 44 | Brakes | 5 |
| Ret | 20 | Graham Hill | BRM-Climax | 43 | Engine | 11 |
| Ret | 58 | Giancarlo Baghetti | Ferrari | 27 | Accident | 19 |
| Ret | 48 | Tony Marsh | Lotus-Climax | 25 | Ignition | 27 |
| Ret | 34 | John Surtees | Cooper-Climax | 23 | Differential | 10 |
| Ret | 38 | Tim Parnell | Lotus-Climax | 12 | Clutch | 29 |
| Ret | 46 | Jackie Lewis | Cooper-Climax | 7 | Handling | 15 |
| Ret | 40 | Gerry Ashmore | Lotus-Climax | 7 | Ignition | 26 |
| Ret | 30 | Henry Taylor | Lotus-Climax | 5 | Accident | 17 |
| Ret | 62 | Massimo Natili | Cooper-Maserati | 0 | Gearbox | 28 |

Winning speed: 83.907mph Lap leaders: P Hill 1-6; von Trips 7-75
Pole Position: P Hill, 1m 58.800s, 90.909mph
Fastest lap: Brooks, 1m 57.800s, 91.681mph

### GERMAN GRAND PRIX: NÜRBURGRING *6 August Round: 6 Race: 100 15 x 14.173 miles*

| POS. | NO. | DRIVER | CAR/ENGINE | LAPS | TIME/RETIRED | GRID |
|---|---|---|---|---|---|---|
| 1 | 7 | Stirling Moss | Lotus-Climax | 15 | 2:18'12.4 | 3 |
| 2 | 3 | W.von Trips | Ferrari | 15 | +21.4 | 5 |
| 3 | 4 | Phil Hill | Ferrari | 15 | +22.5 | 1 |
| 4 | 14 | Jim Clark | Lotus-Climax | 15 | +1'17.1 | 8 |
| 5 | 18 | John Surtees | Cooper-Climax | 15 | +1'53.1 | 10 |
| 6 | 2 | Bruce McLaren | Cooper-Climax | 15 | +2'41.4 | 12 |
| 7 | 9 | Dan Gurney | Porsche | 15 | +3'23.1 | 7 |
| 8 | 5 | Richie Ginther | Ferrari | 15 | +5'23.1 | 14 |
| 9 | 28 | Jackie Lewis | Cooper-Climax | 15 | +5'23.7 | 18 |
| 10 | 19 | Roy Salvadori | Cooper-Climax | 15 | +12'11.5 | 15 |
| 11 | 33 | Tony Maggs | Lotus-Climax | 14 | +1 Lap | 22 |
| 12 | 30 | Ian Burgess | Cooper-Climax | 14 | +1 Lap | 24 |
| 13 | 11 | Hans Herrmann | Porsche | 14 | +1 Lap | 11 |
| 14 | 31 | C.G.de Beaufort | Porsche | 14 | +1 Lap | 17 |
| 15 | 37 | Tony Marsh | Lotus-Climax | 13 | +2 Laps | 20 |
| 16 | 27 | Gerry Ashmore | Lotus-Climax | 13 | +2 Laps | 25 |
| Ret | 6 | Willy Mairesse | Ferrari | 13 | Accident | 13 |
| Ret | 20 | M.Trintignant | Cooper-Maserati | 12 | Engine | 21 |
| NC | 38 | Bernard Collomb | Cooper-Climax | 11 | Not classified | 26 |
| Ret | 32 | Lorenzo Bandini | Cooper-Maserati | 10 | Engine | 19 |
| Ret | 16 | Tony Brooks | BRM-Climax | 6 | Engine | 9 |
| Ret | 8 | Jo Bonnier | Porsche | 5 | Engine | 4 |
| Ret | 26 | Wolfgang Seidel | Lotus-Climax | 3 | Handling | 23 |
| Ret | 17 | Graham Hill | BRM-Climax | 1 | Accident | 16 |
| Ret | 15 | Innes Ireland | Lotus-Climax | 1 | Fire | 6 |
| Ret | 1 | Jack Brabham | Cooper-Climax | 0 | Accident | 2 |

Winning speed: 92.297mph Lap leaders: Moss 1-15
Pole Position: P Hill, 8m 55.200s, 95.337mph
Fastest lap: P Hill, 8m 57.800s, 94.876mph

### ITALIAN GRAND PRIX: MONZA *10 September Round: 7 Race: 101 43 x 6.214 miles*

| POS. | NO. | DRIVER | CAR/ENGINE | LAPS | TIME/RETIRED | GRID |
|---|---|---|---|---|---|---|
| 1 | 2 | Phil Hill | Ferrari | 43 | 2:03'13.0 | 4 |
| 2 | 46 | Dan Gurney | Porsche | 43 | +31.2 | 12 |
| 3 | 12 | Bruce McLaren | Cooper-Climax | 43 | +2'28.4 | 14 |
| 4 | 60 | Jackie Lewis | Cooper-Climax | 43 | +2'40.4 | 16 |
| 5 | 26 | Tony Brooks | BRM-Climax | 43 | +2'40.5 | 13 |
| 6 | 40 | Roy Salvadori | Cooper-Climax | 42 | +1 Lap | 18 |
| 7 | 74 | C.G.de Beaufort | Porsche | 41 | +2 Laps | 15 |
| 8 | 62 | Lorenzo Bandini | Cooper-Maserati | 41 | +2 Laps | 21 |
| 9 | 48 | M.Trintignant | Cooper-Maserati | 41 | +2 Laps | 22 |
| 10 | 16 | Tim Parnell | Lotus-Climax | 40 | +3 Laps | 27 |
| 11 | 20 | Henry Taylor | Lotus-Climax | 39 | +4 Laps | 23 |
| 12 | 58 | Renato Pirocchi | Cooper-Maserati | 38 | +5 Laps | 29 |
| Ret | 28 | Stirling Moss | Lotus-Climax | 36 | Wheel bearing | 11 |
| Ret | 6 | Richie Ginther | Ferrari | 23 | Engine | 3 |
| Ret | 72 | G.Starrabba | Lotus-Maserati | 19 | Engine | 30 |
| Ret | 44 | Jo Bonnier | Porsche | 14 | Suspension | 8 |
| Ret | 8 | R.Rodriguez | Ferrari | 13 | Fuel pump | 2 |
| Ret | 32 | Giancarlo Baghetti | Ferrari | 13 | Engine | 6 |
| Ret | 50 | Nino Vaccarella | De Tomaso-Alfa Romeo | 13 | Engine | 20 |
| Ret | 22 | Masten Gregory | Lotus-Climax | 11 | Suspension | 17 |
| Ret | 24 | Graham Hill | BRM-Climax | 10 | Engine | 5 |
| Ret | 10 | Jack Brabham | Cooper-Climax | 8 | Overheating | 10 |
| Ret | 14 | Brian Naylor | JBW-Climax | 6 | Engine | 31 |
| Ret | 38 | Innes Ireland | Lotus-Climax | 5 | Chassis | 9 |
| Ret | 30 | Jack Fairman | Cooper-Climax | 5 | Engine | 26 |
| Ret | 42 | John Surtees | Cooper-Climax | 2 | Accident | 19 |
| Ret | 4 | W.von Trips | Ferrari | 1 | Accident | 1 |
| Ret | 36 | Jim Clark | Lotus-Climax | 1 | Accident | 7 |
| Ret | 54 | R.Bussinello | De Tomaso-Alfa Romeo | 1 | Engine | 24 |
| Ret | 56 | Wolfgang Seidel | Lotus-Climax | 1 | Engine | 28 |
| Ret | 52 | Roberto Lippi | De Tomaso-Osca | 1 | Engine | 32 |
| Ret | 18 | Gerry Ashmore | Lotus-Climax | 0 | Accident | 25 |
| DNQ | 68 | Andre Pilette | Emeryson-Climax | | | |

Winning speed: 130.107mph Lap leaders: P Hill 1-3, 5, 7, 10, 14-43; Ginther 4, 6, 8-9, 11-13
Pole position: von Trips, 2m 46.300s, 134.512mph
Fastest lap: Baghetti, 2m 48.400s, 132.835mph

### UNITED STATES GRAND PRIX: WATKINS GLEN *8 October Round: 8 Race: 102 100 x 2.300 miles*

| POS. | NO. | DRIVER | CAR/ENGINE | LAPS | TIME/RETIRED | GRID |
|---|---|---|---|---|---|---|
| 1 | 15 | Innes Ireland | Lotus-Climax | 100 | 2:13'45.8 | 8 |
| 2 | 12 | Dan Gurney | Porsche | 100 | + 4.3 | 7 |
| 3 | 5 | Tony Brooks | BRM-Climax | 100 | +49.0 | 5 |
| 4 | 2 | Bruce McLaren | Cooper-Climax | 100 | +58.0 | 4 |
| 5 | 4 | Graham Hill | BRM-Climax | 99 | +1 Lap | 2 |
| 6 | 11 | Jo Bonnier | Porsche | 98 | +2 Laps | 10 |
| 7 | 14 | Jim Clark | Lotus-Climax | 96 | +4 Laps | 6 |
| 8 | 6 | Roger Penske | Cooper-Climax | 96 | +4 Laps | 16 |
| 9 | 16 | Peter Ryan | Lotus-Climax | 96 | +4 Laps | 13 |
| 10 | 3 | Hap Sharp | Cooper-Climax | 93 | +7 Laps | 17 |
| 11 | 21 | Gregory/Gendebien | Lotus-Climax | 92 | +8 Laps | 15 |
| Ret | 19 | Roy Salvadori | Cooper-Climax | 96 | Engine | 12 |
| Ret | 17 | Jim Hall | Lotus-Climax | 76 | Fuel leak | 18 |
| Ret | 26 | Lloyd Ruby | Lotus-Climax | 76 | Magneto | 19 |
| Ret | 7 | Stirling Moss | Lotus-Climax | 58 | Engine | 3 |
| Ret | 1 | Jack Brabham | Cooper-Climax | 57 | Overheating | 1 |
| Ret | 22 | Masten Gregory | Lotus-Climax | 23 | Gearbox | 11 |
| Ret | 60 | Walt Hansgen | Cooper-Climax | 14 | Accident | 14 |
| Ret | 18 | John Surtees | Cooper-Climax | 0 | Engine | 9 |

Winning speed: 103.167mph Lap leaders: Moss 1-5, 16, 24-25, 34-35, 39-58; Brabham 6-15, 17-23, 26-33, 36-38; Ireland 59-100
Pole position: Brabham, 1m 17.000s, 107.532mph
Fastest lap: Brabham, 1m 18.200s, 105.882mph

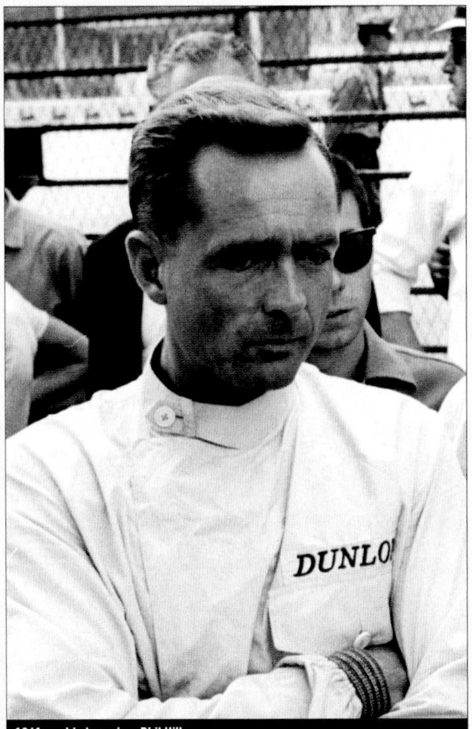


1961 world champion, Phil Hill.

# 1962

**DRIVERS' CHAMPION: GRAHAM HILL**
**CONSTRUCTORS' CHAMPION: BRM**

### DRIVERS' CHAMPIONSHIP

| POS | DRIVER | COUNTRY | CAR | POINTS |
|---|---|---|---|---|
| 1 | Graham Hill | GB | BRM | 42(10) |
| 2 | Jim Clark | GB | Lotus-Climax | 30 |
| 3 | Bruce McLaren | New Zealand | Cooper-Climax | 27(32) |
| 4 | John Surtees | GB | Lola-Climax | 19 |
| 5 | Dan Gurney | USA | Porsche, Lotus-BRM | 15 |
| 6 | Phil Hill | USA | Porsche | 14 |
| 7 | Tony Maggs | South Africa | Cooper-Climax | 13 |
| 8 | Richie Ginther | USA | BRM | 10 |
| 9 | Jack Brabham | Australia | Lotus-Climax, Brabham-Climax | 9 |
| 10 | Trevor Taylor | GB | Lotus-Climax | 6 |
| 11 | Giancarlo Baghetti | Italy | Ferrari | 5 |
| 12 | Lorenzo Bandini | Italy | Ferrari | 4 |
| = | Ricardo Rodriguez | Mexico | Ferrari | 4 |
| 14 | Willy Mairesse | Belgium | Ferrari | 3 |
| = | Jo Bonnier | Sweden | Porsche | 3 |
| 16 | Innes Ireland | GB | Lotus-Climax | 2 |
| = | Carel Godin de Beaufort | Netherlands | Porsche | 2 |
| 18 | Masten Gregory | USA | Lotus-Climax, Lotus-BRM | 1 |
| = | Neville Lederle | South Africa | Lotus-Climax | 1 |
| | Roy Salvadori | GB | Lola-Climax | |
| | Jackie Lewis | GB | Cooper –Climax, BRM | |
| | Ben Pon | Netherlands | Porsche | |
| | Wolfgang Seidel | West Germany | Emeryson-Climax, Lotus-BRM | |
| | Jo Siffert | Switzerland | Lotus-Climax, Lotus-BRM | |
| | Maurice Trintignant | France | Lotus-Climax | |
| | Nino Vacarella | Italy | Lotus-Climax, Porsche | |
| | John Campbell-Jones | GB | Lotus-Climax, Emeryson-Climax | |
| | Lucien Bianchi | Belgium | Lotus-Climax, ENB-Maserati | |
| | Tony Shelly | New Zealand | Lotus-Climax, Lotus-BRM | |
| | Jay Chamberlain | GB | Lotus-Climax | |
| | Ian Burgess | GB | Cooper-Climax | |
| | Tony Settember | USA | Emeryson-Climax | |
| | Keith Greene | GB | Lotus-Climax, Gilby-BRM | |
| | Bernard Collomb | France | Cooper-Climax | |
| | Heinz Schiller | Switzerland | Lotus-BRM | |
| | Günther Seifert | West Germany | Lotus-BRM | |
| | Hieni Walter | West Germany | Porsche | |
| | Estefano Nasif | Argentinia | de Tomaso | |
| | Roberto Lippi | Italy | de Tomaso –OSCA | |
| | Gerry Ashmore | GB | Lotus-Climax | |
| | Ernesto Prinoth | Italy | Lotus-Climax | |
| | Jim Hall | USA | Lotus-Climax | |
| | Timmy Mayer | USA | Cooper-Climax | |
| | Rob Schroeder | USA | Lotus-Climax | |
| | Roger Penske | USA | Lotus-Climax | |
| | Hap Sharp | USA | Cooper-Climax | |
| | Bruce Johnstone | South Africa | BRM | |
| | Ernst Pieterse | South Africa | Lotus-Climax | |
| | John Love | South Africa | Cooper-Climax | |
| | Mike Harris | Rhodesia | Cooper-Alfa Romeo | |
| | Doug Serrurier | South Africa | LDS-Alfa Romeo | |

Points for the top six finishers (9, 6, 4, 3, 2, 1). Only the best five scores counted towards the championship.

### CONSTRUCTORS' CHAMPIONSHIP

| POS. | CONSTRUCTOR | POINTS |
|---|---|---|
| 1 | BRM | 42 |
| 2 | Lotus-Climax | 36 |
| 3 | Cooper-Climax | 29 |
| 4 | Lola-Climax | 19 |
| 5 | Porsche | 18 |
| 6 | Ferrari | 18 |
| 7 | Brabham-Climax | 6 |
| 8 | Lotus-BRM | 1 |

Points for top six finishers (9, 6, 4, 3, 2, 1). Points only counted for top-placed car for each constructor. Only the best five scores counted towards the championship.

 

### DUTCH GRAND PRIX: ZANDVOORT *20 May Round: 1 Race: 103 80 x 2.605 miles*

| POS. | NO. | DRIVER | CAR/ENGINE | LAPS | TIME/RETIRED | GRID |
|---|---|---|---|---|---|---|
| 1 | 17 | Graham Hill | BRM | 80 | 2:11'02.1 | 2 |
| 2 | 5 | Trevor Taylor | Lotus-Climax | 80 | +27.2 | 10 |
| 3 | 1 | Phil Hill | Ferrari | 80 | +1'21.1 | 9 |
| 4 | 2 | Giancarlo Baghetti | Ferrari | 79 | +1 Lap | 12 |
| 5 | 7 | Tony Maggs | Cooper-Climax | 78 | +2 Laps | 15 |
| 6 | 14 | C.G.de Beaufort | Porsche | 76 | +4 Laps | 14 |
| 7 | 11 | Jo Bonnier | Porsche | 75 | +5 Laps | 13 |
| 8 | 21 | Jackie Lewis | Cooper-Climax | 70 | +10 Laps | 7 |
| 9 | 4 | Jim Clark | Lotus-Climax | 70 | +10 Laps | 3 |
| Ret | 3 | Ricardo Rodriguez | Ferrari | 73 | Accident | 11 |
| Ret | 18 | Richie Ginther | BRM | 71 | Accident | 7 |
| Ret | 9 | Innes Ireland | Lotus-Climax | 61 | Accident | 6 |
| Ret | 10 | Masten Gregory | Lotus-Climax | 54 | Halfshaft | 16 |
| NC | 16 | Wolfgang Seidel | Emeryson-Climax | 52 | Not classified | 20 |
| Ret | 12 | Dan Gurney | Porsche | 47 | Gearbox | 8 |
| Ret | 6 | Bruce McLaren | Cooper-Climax | 21 | Gearbox | 5 |
| Wth | 20 | Roy Salvadori | Lola-Climax | 12 | Withdrew | 17 |
| Ret | 19 | John Surtees | Lola-Climax | 8 | Accident | 1 |
| Ret | 8 | Jack Brabham | Lotus-Climax | 4 | Accident | 4 |
| Ret | 15 | Ben Pon | Porsche | 2 | Accident | 18 |

Winning speed: 95.440mph Lap leaders: Clark 1-11, G Hill 12-80
Pole position: Surtees, 1m 32.500s, 101.400mph
Fastest lap: McLaren, 1m 34.400s, 99.359mph

### MONACO GRAND PRIX: MONTE CARLO *3 June Round: 2 Race: 104 100 x 1.954 miles*

| POS. | NO. | DRIVER | CAR/ENGINE | LAPS | TIME/RETIRED | GRID |
|---|---|---|---|---|---|---|
| 1 | 14 | Bruce McLaren | Cooper-Climax | 100 | 2:46'29.7 | 3 |
| 2 | 36 | Phil Hill | Ferrari | 100 | +1.3 | 9 |
| 3 | 38 | Lorenzo Bandini | Ferrari | 100 | +1'24.1 | 10 |
| 4 | 28 | John Surtees | Lola-Climax | 99 | +1 Lap | 11 |
| 5 | 2 | Jo Bonnier | Porsche | 93 | +7 Laps | 18 |
| 6 | 10 | Graham Hill | BRM | 92 | Engine | 2 |
| 7 | 40 | Willy Mairesse | Ferrari | 90 | Oil pressure | 4 |
| 8 | 22 | Jack Brabham | Lotus-Climax | 77 | Accident | 6 |
| Ret | 34 | Innes Ireland | Lotus-Climax | 64 | Fuel pump | 8 |
| Ret | 18 | Jim Clark | Lotus-Climax | 55 | Clutch | 1 |
| Ret | 26 | Roy Salvadori | Lola-Climax | 44 | Suspension | 12 |
| Ret | 16 | Tony Maggs | Cooper-Climax | 43 | Gearbox | 19 |
| Ret | 20 | Trevor Taylor | Lotus-Climax | 24 | Oil leak | 17 |
| Ret | 4 | Dan Gurney | Porsche | 0 | Accident | 5 |
| Ret | 30 | M.Trintignant | Lotus-Climax | 0 | Accident | 7 |
| Ret | 8 | Richie Ginther | BRM | 0 | Accident | 14 |
| DNQ | 46 | Jo Siffert | Lotus-Climax | | | |
| DNQ | 24 | Jackie Lewis | BRM | | | |
| DNQ | 32 | Masten Gregory | Lotus-BRM | | | |
| DNQ | 44 | C.G.de Beaufort | Porsche | | | |
| DNQ | 42 | Nino Vaccarella | Lotus-Climax | | | |

Winning speed: 70.424mph Lap leaders: McLaren 1-6, 93-100; G Hill 7-92
Pole position: Clark, 1m 35.400s, 73.744 mph
Fastest lap: Clark, 1m 35.500s, 73.667mph

### BELGIAN GRAND PRIX: SPA-FRANCORCHAMPS *17 June Round: 3 Race: 105 32 x 8.761 miles*

| POS. | NO. | DRIVER | CAR/ENGINE | LAPS | TIME/RETIRED | GRID |
|---|---|---|---|---|---|---|
| 1 | 16 | Jim Clark | Lotus-Climax | 32 | 2:07'32.3 | 12 |
| 2 | 1 | Graham Hill | BRM | 32 | +44.1 | 1 |
| 3 | 9 | Phil Hill | Ferrari | 32 | +2'06.5 | 4 |
| 4 | 12 | Ricardo Rodriguez | Ferrari | 32 | +2'06.6 | 7 |
| 5 | 5 | John Surtees | Lola-Climax | 31 | +1 Lap | 11 |
| 6 | 15 | Jack Brabham | Lotus-Climax | 30 | +2 Laps | 15 |
| 7 | 7 | C.G.de Beaufort | Porsche | 30 | +2 Laps | 13 |
| 8 | 18 | M.Trintignant | Lotus-Climax | 30 | +2 Laps | 16 |
| 9 | 19 | Lucien Bianchi | Lotus-Climax | 29 | +3 Laps | 18 |
| 10 | 22 | Jo Siffert | Lotus-Climax | 29 | +3 Laps | 17 |
| 11 | 4 | J.C.-Jones | Lotus-Climax | 16 | +16 Laps | 19 |
| Ret | 17 | Trevor Taylor | Lotus-Climax | 25 | Accident | 3 |
| Ret | 10 | Willy Mairesse | Ferrari | 25 | Accident | 6 |
| Ret | 2 | Richie Ginther | BRM | 22 | Gearbox | 9 |
| Ret | 26 | Tony Maggs | Cooper-Climax | 22 | Gearbox | 10 |
| Ret | 25 | Bruce McLaren | Cooper-Climax | 19 | Wheel bearing | 2 |
| Wth | 21 | Masten Gregory | Lotus-BRM | 13 | Withdrew | 8 |
| Ret | 20 | Innes Ireland | Lotus-Climax | 8 | Suspension | 5 |
| Ret | 11 | Giancarlo Baghetti | Ferrari | 3 | Ignition | 14 |

Winning speed: 131.896mph Lap leaders: G Hill 1; Taylor 2-3, 5, 7-8; Mairesse 4, 6; Clark 9-32
Pole position: G Hill, 3m 57.000s, 133.084mph
Fastest lap: Clark, 3m 55.600s, 133.874mph

### FRENCH GRAND PRIX: ROUEN-LES-ESSARTS *8 July Round: 4 Race: 106 54 x 4.065*

| POS. | NO. | DRIVER | CAR/ENGINE | LAPS | TIME/RETIRED | GRID |
|---|---|---|---|---|---|---|
| 1 | 30 | Dan Gurney | Porsche | 54 | 2:07'35.5 | 6 |
| 2 | 24 | Tony Maggs | Cooper-Climax | 53 | +1 Lap | 11 |
| 3 | 10 | Richie Ginther | BRM | 52 | +2 Laps | 10 |
| 4 | 22 | Bruce McLaren | Cooper-Climax | 51 | +3 Laps | 3 |
| 5 | 18 | John Surtees | Lola-Climax | 51 | +3 Laps | 5 |
| 6 | 38 | C.G.de Beaufort | Porsche | 51 | +3 Laps | 17 |
| 7 | 28 | M.Trintignant | Lotus-Climax | 50 | +4 Laps | 13 |
| 8 | 14 | Trevor Taylor | Lotus-Climax | 48 | +6 Laps | 12 |
| 9 | 8 | Graham Hill | BRM | 44 | +10 Laps | 2 |
| Ret | 32 | Jo Bonnier | Porsche | 43 | Fuel system | 9 |
| Ret | 12 | Jim Clark | Lotus-Climax | 34 | Suspension | 1 |
| Ret | 42 | Jackie Lewis | Cooper-Climax | 28 | Accident | 16 |
| Ret | 20 | Roy Salvadori | Lola-Climax | 21 | Oil pressure | 14 |
| Ret | 34 | Masten Gregory | Lotus-BRM | 15 | Overheating | 7 |
| Ret | 26 | Jack Brabham | Lotus-Climax | 11 | Suspension | 4 |
| Ret | 40 | Jo Siffert | Lotus-BRM | 6 | Clutch | 15 |
| Ret | 36 | Innes Ireland | Lotus-Climax | 1 | Puncture | 8 |

Winning speed: 103.225mph Lap leaders: G Hill 1-29, 33-41; Clark 30-32; Gurney 42-54
Pole position: Clark, 2m 14.800s, 108.561mph
Fastest lap: G Hill, 2m 16.900s, 106.896mph

### BRITISH GRAND PRIX: AINTREE *21 July Round: 5 Race: 107 75 x 3.000 miles*

| POS. | NO. | DRIVER | CAR/ENGINE | LAPS | TIME/RETIRED | GRID |
|---|---|---|---|---|---|---|
| 1 | 20 | Jim Clark | Lotus-Climax | 75 | 2:26'20.8 | 1 |
| 2 | 24 | John Surtees | Lola-Climax | 75 | +49.2 | 2 |
| 3 | 16 | Bruce McLaren | Cooper-Climax | 75 | +1'44.8 | 4 |
| 4 | 12 | Graham Hill | BRM | 75 | +1'56.8 | 5 |
| 5 | 30 | Jack Brabham | Lotus-Climax | 74 | +1 Lap | 9 |
| 6 | 18 | Tony Maggs | Cooper-Climax | 74 | +1 Lap | 13 |
| 7 | 34 | Masten Gregory | Lotus-Climax | 74 | +1 Lap | 14 |
| 8 | 22 | Trevor Taylor | Lotus-Climax | 74 | +1 Lap | 10 |
| 9 | 8 | Dan Gurney | Porsche | 73 | +2 Laps | 6 |
| 10 | 42 | Jackie Lewis | Cooper-Climax | 72 | +3 Laps | 15 |
| 11 | 40 | Tony Settember | Emeryson-Climax | 71 | +4 Laps | 19 |
| 12 | 36 | Ian Burgess | Cooper-Climax | 71 | +4 Laps | 16 |
| 13 | 14 | Richie Ginther | BRM | 70 | +5 Laps | 8 |
| 14 | 54 | C.G.de Beaufort | Porsche | 69 | +6 Laps | 17 |
| 15 | 46 | Jay Chamberlain | Lotus-Climax | 64 | +11 Laps | 20 |
| 16 | 32 | Innes Ireland | Lotus-Climax | 61 | +14 Laps | 3 |
| Ret | 2 | Phil Hill | Ferrari | 47 | Engine | 12 |
| Ret | 26 | Roy Salvadori | Lola-Climax | 35 | Battery | 11 |
| Ret | 10 | Jo Bonnier | Porsche | 27 | Differential | 7 |
| Ret | 44 | Wolfgang Seidel | Lotus-BRM | 11 | Brakes | 21 |
| Ret | 48 | Tony Shelly | Lotus-Climax | 6 | Engine | 18 |

Winning speed: 92.247 mph Lap leaders: Clark 1-75
Pole position: Clark, 1m 53.600s, 95.070mph
Fastest lap: Clark, 1m 55.000s, 93.913mph

### GERMAN GRAND PRIX: NÜRBURGRING *5 August Round: 6 Race: 108 15 x 14.173 miles*

| POS. | NO. | DRIVER | CAR/ENGINE | LAPS | TIME/RETIRED | GRID |
|---|---|---|---|---|---|---|
| 1 | 11 | Graham Hill | BRM | 15 | 2:38'45.3 | 2 |
| 2 | 14 | John Surtees | Lola-Climax | 15 | +2.5 | 4 |
| 3 | 7 | Dan Gurney | Porsche | 15 | +4.4 | 1 |
| 4 | 5 | Jim Clark | Lotus-Climax | 15 | +42.1 | 3 |
| 5 | 9 | Bruce McLaren | Cooper-Climax | 15 | +1'19.6 | 5 |
| 6 | 3 | Ricardo Rodriguez | Ferrari | 15 | +1'23.8 | 10 |
| 7 | 8 | Jo Bonnier | Porsche | 15 | +4'37.3 | 6 |
| 8 | 12 | Richie Ginther | BRM | 15 | +5'00.1 | 7 |
| 9 | 10 | Tony Maggs | Cooper-Climax | 15 | +5'07.0 | 23 |
| 10 | 2 | Giancarlo Baghetti | Ferrari | 15 | +8'14.7 | 13 |
| 11 | 25 | Ian Burgess | Cooper-Climax | 15 | +8'15.3 | 16 |
| 12 | 19 | Jo Siffert | Lotus-Climax | 15 | +8'18.5 | 17 |
| 13 | 18 | C.G.de Beaufort | Porsche | 15 | +9'11.8 | 8 |
| 14 | 32 | Heini Walter | Porsche | 14 | +1 Lap | 14 |
| 15 | 26 | Nino Vaccarella | Porsche | 14 | +1 Lap | 15 |
| 16 | 21 | Lucien Bianchi | ENB-Maserati | 14 | +1 Lap | 25 |
| Ret | 20 | Jackie Lewis | Cooper-Climax | 10 | Suspension | 21 |
| Ret | 1 | Phil Hill | Ferrari | 9 | Suspension | 12 |
| Ret | 16 | Jack Brabham | Brabham-Climax | 9 | Throttle | 24 |
| Ret | 27 | Keith Greene | Gilby-BRM | 7 | Suspension | 19 |
| Ret | 15 | Roy Salvadori | Lola-Climax | 4 | Gearbox | 9 |
| Ret | 17 | M.Trintignant | Lotus-Climax | 4 | Gearbox | 11 |
| Ret | 4 | Lorenzo Bandini | Ferrari | 4 | Accident | 18 |
| Ret | 28 | Heinz Schiller | Lotus-BRM | 4 | Oil pressure | 20 |
| Ret | 31 | Bernard Collomb | Cooper-Climax | 2 | Gearbox | 22 |
| Ret | 6 | Trevor Taylor | Lotus-Climax | 0 | Accident | 26 |
| DNQ | 29 | Tony Shelly | Lotus-Climax | | | |
| DNQ | 34 | Wolfgang Seidel | Lotus-BRM | | | |
| DNQ | 30 | Jay Chamberlain | Lotus-Climax | | | |
| DNQ | 34 | Gunther Seiffert | Lotus-BRM | | | |

Winning speed: 80.351mph Lap leaders: Gurney 1-2; G Hill 3-15
Pole position: Gurney, 8m 47.200s, 96.784mph
Fastest lap: G Hill, 10m 12.200s, 83.346mph

### ITALIAN GRAND PRIX: MONZA *16 September Round: 7 Race: 109 86 x 3.573 miles*

| POS. | NO. | DRIVER | CAR/ENGINE | LAPS | TIME/RETIRED | GRID |
|---|---|---|---|---|---|---|
| 1 | 14 | Graham Hill | BRM | 86 | 2:29'08.4 | 2 |
| 2 | 12 | Richie Ginther | BRM | 86 | +29.8 | 3 |
| 3 | 28 | Bruce McLaren | Cooper-Climax | 86 | +57.8 | 4 |
| 4 | 8 | Willy Mairesse | Ferrari | 86 | +58.2 | 10 |
| 5 | 2 | Giancarlo Baghetti | Ferrari | 86 | +1'31.3 | 18 |
| 6 | 18 | Jo Bonnier | Porsche | 85 | +1 Lap | 9 |
| 7 | 30 | Tony Maggs | Cooper-Climax | 85 | +1 Lap | 12 |
| 8 | 6 | Lorenzo Bandini | Ferrari | 84 | +2 Laps | 17 |
| 9 | 24 | Nino Vaccarella | Lotus-Climax | 84 | +2 Laps | 14 |
| 10 | 32 | C.G.de Beaufort | Porsche | 81 | +5 Laps | 20 |
| 11 | 10 | Phil Hill | Ferrari | 81 | +5 Laps | 15 |
| 12 | 38 | Masten Gregory | Lotus-BRM | 77 | +9 Laps | 6 |
| 13 | 16 | Dan Gurney | Porsche | 66 | Differential | 7 |
| 14 | 4 | Ricardo Rodriguez | Ferrari | 63 | Ignition | 11 |
| Ret | 40 | Innes Ireland | Lotus-Climax | 45 | Suspension | 5 |
| Ret | 46 | John Surtees | Lola-Climax | 42 | Engine | 8 |
| Ret | 44 | Roy Salvadori | Lola-Climax | 41 | Engine | 13 |
| Ret | 22 | Trevor Taylor | Lotus-Climax | 25 | Gearbox | 16 |
| Ret | 48 | Tony Settember | Emeryson-Climax | 18 | Engine | 21 |
| Ret | 36 | M.Trintignant | Lotus-Climax | 17 | Electrical | 19 |
| Ret | 20 | Jim Clark | Lotus-Climax | 12 | Gearbox | 1 |
| DNQ | 60 | Tony Shelly | Lotus-BRM | | | |
| DNQ | 56 | Keith Greene | Gilby-BRM | | | |
| DNQ | 52 | Gerry Ashmore | Lotus-Climax | | | |
| DNQ | 62 | Ian Burgess | Cooper-Climax | | | |
| DNQ | 42 | Jo Siffert | Lotus-BRM | | | |
| DNQ | 54 | Ernesto Prinoth | Lotus-Climax | | | |
| DNQ | 50 | Roberto Lippi | De Tomaso-Osca | | | |
| DNQ | 26 | Jay Chamberlain | Lotus-Climax | | | |
| DNQ | 34 | Nasif Estefano | De Tomaso | | | |

Winning speed: 123.616mph Lap leaders: G Hill 1-86
Pole position: Clark, 1m 40.350s, 128.175mph
Fastest lap: G Hill, 1m 42.300s, 125.732mph

### UNITED STATES GRAND PRIX: WAKTINS GLEN *7 October Round: 8 Race: 110 100 x 2.300 miles*

| POS. | NO. | DRIVER | CAR/ENGINE | LAPS | TIME/RETIRED | GRID |
|---|---|---|---|---|---|---|
| 1 | 8 | Jim Clark | Lotus-Climax | 100 | 2:07'13.0 | 1 |
| 2 | 4 | Graham Hill | BRM | 100 | +9.2 | 3 |
| 3 | 21 | Bruce McLaren | Cooper-Climax | 99 | +1 Lap | 6 |
| 4 | 17 | Jack Brabham | Brabham-Climax | 99 | +1 Lap | 5 |
| 5 | 10 | Dan Gurney | Porsche | 99 | +1 Lap | 4 |
| 6 | 16 | Masten Gregory | Lotus-BRM | 99 | +1 Lap | 7 |
| 7 | 22 | Tony Maggs | Cooper-Climax | 97 | +3 Laps | 10 |
| 8 | 15 | Innes Ireland | Lotus-Climax | 96 | +4 Laps | 16 |
| 9 | 14 | Roger Penske | Lotus-Climax | 96 | +4 Laps | 13 |
| 10 | 26 | Rob Schroeder | Lotus-Climax | 93 | +7 Laps | 17 |
| 11 | 24 | Hap Sharp | Cooper-Climax | 91 | +9 Laps | 15 |
| 12 | 9 | Trevor Taylor | Lotus-Climax | 85 | +15 Laps | 8 |
| 13 | 11 | Jo Bonnier | Porsche | 79 | +21 Laps | 9 |
| Ret | 5 | Richie Ginther | BRM | 35 | Engine | 2 |
| Ret | 6 | M.Trintignant | Lotus-Climax | 32 | Brakes | 19 |
| Ret | 23 | Tim Mayer | Cooper-Climax | 31 | Ignition | 12 |
| Ret | 18 | John Surtees | Lola-Climax | 19 | Engine | 20 |
| Ret | 2 | C.G.de Beaufort | Porsche | 9 | Accident | 14 |

Winning speed: 108.476mph Lap leaders: Clark 1-11, 19-100; G Hill 12-18
Pole position: Clark, 1m 15.800s, 109.235mph
Fastest lap: Clark, 1m 15.000s, 110.400mph

### SOUTH AFRICAN GRAND PRIX: EAST LONDON *29 December Round: 9 Race: 111 82 x 2.436 miles*

| POS. | NO. | DRIVER | CAR/ENGINE | LAPS | TIME/RETIRED | GRID |
|---|---|---|---|---|---|---|
| 1 | 3 | Graham Hill | BRM | 82 | 2:08'03.3 | 2 |
| 2 | 8 | Bruce McLaren | Cooper-Climax | 82 | +49.8 | 8 |
| 3 | 9 | Tony Maggs | Cooper-Climax | 82 | +50.3 | 6 |
| 4 | 10 | Jack Brabham | Brabham-Climax | 82 | +53.8 | 3 |
| 5 | 11 | Innes Ireland | Lotus-Climax | 81 | +1 Lap | 4 |
| 6 | 20 | Neville Lederle | Lotus-Climax | 78 | +4 Laps | 10 |
| 7 | 4 | Richie Ginther | BRM | 78 | +4 Laps | 7 |
| 8 | 18 | John Love | Cooper-Climax | 78 | +4 Laps | 12 |
| 9 | 5 | Bruce Johnstone | BRM | 76 | +6 Laps | 17 |
| 10 | 14 | Ernie Pieterse | Lotus-Climax | 71 | +11 Laps | 13 |
| 11 | 15 | C.G.de Beaufort | Porsche | 70 | Fuel pump | 16 |
| Ret | 1 | Jim Clark | Lotus-Climax | 62 | Oil leak | 14 |
| Ret | 21 | Doug Serrurier | LDS-Alfa Romeo | 62 | Radiator | 1 |
| Ret | 7 | Roy Salvadori | Lola-Climax | 56 | Fuel leak | 11 |
| Ret | 22 | Mike Harris | Cooper-Alfa Romeo | 31 | Wheel bearing | 15 |
| Ret | 6 | John Surtees | Lola-Climax | 26 | Engine | 5 |
| Ret | 2 | Trevor Taylor | Lotus-Climax | 11 | Gearbox | 9 |

Winning speed: 93.594mph Lap leaders: Clark 1-61; G Hill 62-82
Pole position: Clark, 1m 29.300s, 98.204mph
Fastest lap: Clark, 1m 31.000s, 96.369mph

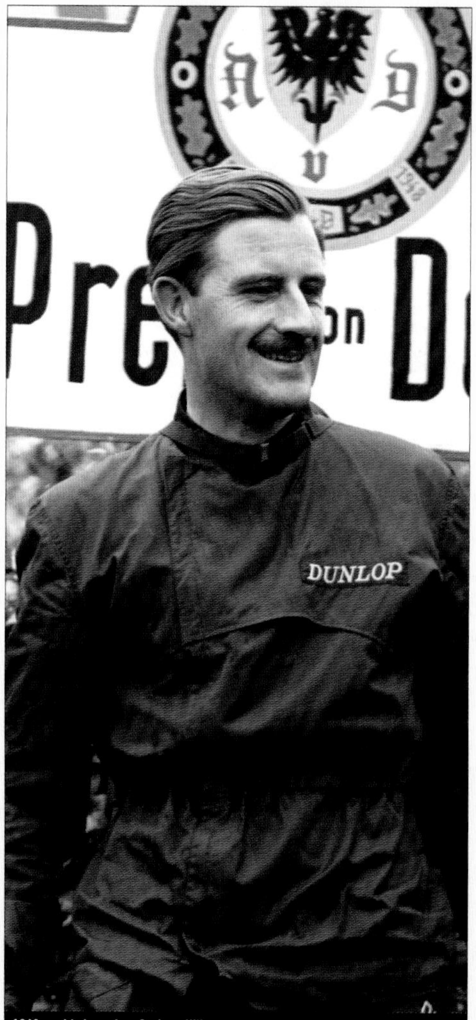

1962 world champion, Graham Hill.

# 1963

## DRIVERS' CHAMPION: JIM CLARK
## CONSTRUCTORS' CHAMPION: LOTUS CLIMAX

### DRIVERS' CHAMPIONSHIP

| POS. | DRIVER | NATIONALITY | CAR | POINTS |
|---|---|---|---|---|
| 1 | Jim Clark | GB | Lotus-Climax | 54 (19) |
| 2 | Graham Hill | GB | BRM | 29 |
| = | Richie Ginther | USA | BRM | 29 (5) |
| 4 | John Surtees | GB | Ferrari | 22 |
| 5 | Dan Gurney | USA | Brabham-Climax | 19 |
| 6 | Bruce McLaren | New Zealand | Cooper-Climax | 17 |
| 7 | Jack Brabham | Australia | Lotus-Climax, Brabham-Climax | 14 |
| 8 | Tony Maggs | South Africa | Cooper-Climax | 9 |
| 9 | Innes Ireland | GB | Lotus-Climax, BRP-BRM | 6 |
| = | Lorenzo Bandini | Italy | BRM, Ferrari | 6 |
| = | Jo Bonnier | Sweden | Cooper-Climax | 6 |
| 12 | Gerhard Mitter | West Germany | Porsche | 3 |
| = | Jim Hall | USA | Lotus-BRM | 3 |
| 14 | Carel Godin de Beaufort | Netherlands | Porsche | 2 |
| 15 | Trevor Taylor | GB | Lotus-Climax | 1 |
| = | Ludovico Scarfiotti | Italy | Ferrari | 1 |
| = | Jo Siffert | Switzerland | Lotus-BRM | 1 |
| | Willy Mairesse | Belgium | Ferrari | |
| | Chris Amon | New Zealand | Lola-Climax, Lotus-BRM | |
| | Maurice Trintignant | France | Lola-Climax, Lotus-Climax, BRM | |
| | Bernard Collomb | France | Lotus-Climax | |
| | Tony Settember | South Africa | Scirocco-BRM | |
| | Phil Hill | USA | ATS, Lotus-BRM | |
| | Giancarlo Baghetti | Italy | ATS | |
| | Lucien Bianchi | Belgium | Lola-Climax | |
| | Peter Arundell | GB | Lotus-Climax | |
| | Masten Gregory | USA | Lotus-BRM, Lola-Climax | |
| | Ian Raby | GB | Gilby-BRM | |
| | Bob Anderson | Rhodesia | Lola-Climax | |
| | Ian Burgess | GB | Scirocco-BRM | |
| | John Campbell-Jones | GB | Lola-Climax | |
| | Estefano Nasif | Argentinia | de Tomaso | |
| | Mike Hailwood | GB | Lotus-Climax, Lola-Climax | |
| | Mario Araujo de Cabral | Portugal | Cooper-Climax | |
| | Kurt Kuhnke | West Germany | Lotus-Borgward | |
| | Tim Parnell | GB | Lotus-Climax | |
| | André Pilette | GB | Lotus-Climax | |
| | Roberto Lippi | Italy | de Tomaso-Ferrari | |
| | Tino Brambilla | Italy | Cooper –Maserati | |
| | Mike Spence | GB | Lotus-Climax | |
| | Peter Broeker | Canada | Stebro-Ford | |
| | Pedro Rodriguez | Mexico | Lotus-Climax | |
| | Hap Sharp | USA | Lotus-BRM | |
| | Roger Ward | USA | Lotus-BRM | |
| | Frank Dochnal | USA | Cooper-Climax | |
| | Moisés Solana | Mexico | BRM | |
| | Trevor Blokdyk | South Africa | Cooper-Maserati | |
| | Paddy Driver | South Africa | Lotus-BRM | |
| | Piet de Klerk | South Africa | Alfa | |
| | John Love | South Africa | Cooper-Climax | |
| | Brausch Niemann | South Africa | Lotus-Ford | |
| | Ernest Pieterse | South Africa | Lotus-Climax | |
| | David Prophet | South Africa | Brabham-Ford | |
| | Doug Serrurier | South Africa | LDS-Alfa Romeo | |
| | Sam Tingle | Rhodesia | LDS-Alfa Romeo | |

Points for the top six finishers (9, 6, 4, 3, 2, 1). Only the best six scores counted towards the championship.

### CONSTRUCTORS' CHAMPIONSHIP

| POS. | CONSTRUCTOR | POINTS |
|---|---|---|
| 1 | Lotus-Climax | 54 |
| 2 | BRM | 36 |
| 3 | Brabham-Climax | 28 |
| 4 | Ferrari | 26 |
| 5 | Cooper-Climax | 25 |
| 6 | BRP-BRM | 6 |
| 7 | Porsche | 5 |
| 8 | Lotus-BRM | 4 |

Points for top six finishers (9, 6, 4, 3, 2, 1). Points only counted for top-placed car for each constructor. Only the best six scores counted towards the championship.

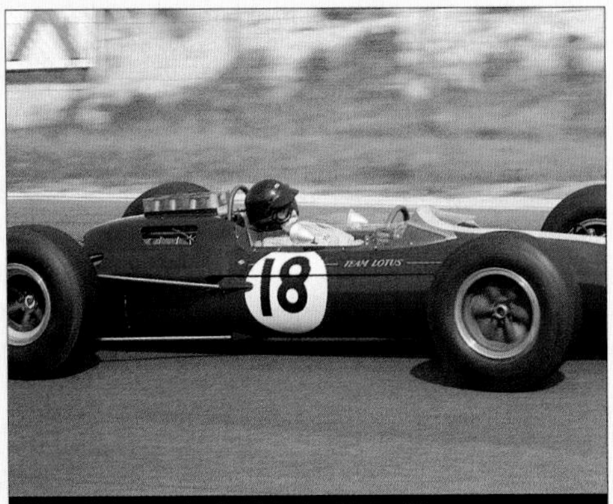


1963 world champion, Jim Clark in the Type 25 Lotus-Climax.

### MONACO GRAND PRIX: MONTE CARLO *26 May Round: 1 Race: 112 100 x 1.954 miles*

| POS. | NO. | DRIVER | CAR/ENGINE | LAPS | TIME/RETIRED | GRID |
|---|---|---|---|---|---|---|
| 1 | 6 | Graham Hill | BRM | 100 | 2:41'49.7 | 2 |
| 2 | 5 | Richie Ginther | BRM | 100 | +4.6 | 4 |
| 3 | 7 | Bruce McLaren | Cooper-Climax | 100 | +12.8 | 8 |
| 4 | 21 | John Surtees | Ferrari | 100 | +14.1 | 3 |
| 5 | 8 | Tony Maggs | Cooper-Climax | 98 | +2 Laps | 10 |
| 6 | 10 | Trevor Taylor | Lotus-Climax | 98 | +2 Laps | 9 |
| 7 | 11 | Jo Bonnier | Cooper-Climax | 94 | +6 Laps | 11 |
| 8 | 9 | Jim Clark | Lotus-Climax | 78 | Gearbox | 1 |
| 9 | 3 | Jack Brabham | Lotus-Climax | 77 | Gearbox | 16 |
| Ret | 14 | Innes Ireland | Lotus-BRM | 40 | Accident | 5 |
| Ret | 20 | Willy Mairesse | Ferrari | 37 | Gearbox | 7 |
| Ret | 17 | M.Trintignant | Lola-Climax | 34 | Clutch | 14 |
| Ret | 4 | Dan Gurney | Brabham-Climax | 25 | Differential | 6 |
| Ret | 12 | Jim Hall | Lotus-BRM | 20 | Gearbox | 13 |
| Ret | 25 | Jo Siffert | Lotus-BRM | 3 | Engine | 12 |
| DNQ | 24 | Bernard Collomb | Lotus-Climax | | | |

Winning speed: 72.455mph Lap leaders: G Hill 1-17, 79-100; Clark 18-78
Pole position: Clark, 1m 34.300s, 74.604mph
Fastest lap: Surtees, 1m 34.500s, 74.446mph

### BELGIAN GRAND PRIX: SPA-FRANCORCHAMPS *9 June Round: 2 Race: 113 32 x 8.761 miles*

| POS. | NO. | DRIVER | CAR/ENGINE | LAPS | TIME/RETIRED | GRID |
|---|---|---|---|---|---|---|
| 1 | 1 | Jim Clark | Lotus-Climax | 32 | 2:27'47.6 | 8 |
| 2 | 14 | Bruce McLaren | Cooper-Climax | 32 | +4'54.0 | 5 |
| 3 | 18 | Dan Gurney | Brabham-Climax | 31 | +1 Lap | 2 |
| 4 | 8 | Richie Ginther | BRM | 31 | +1 Lap | 9 |
| 5 | 12 | Jo Bonnier | Cooper-Climax | 30 | +2 Laps | 13 |
| 6 | 29 | C.G.de Beaufort | Porsche | 30 | +2 Laps | 18 |
| 7 | 15 | Tony Maggs | Cooper-Climax | 27 | Accident | 4 |
| 8 | 24 | Tony Settember | Scirocco-BRM | 25 | Accident | 19 |
| Ret | 9 | John Surtees | Ferrari | 19 | Injection | 10 |
| Ret | 7 | Graham Hill | BRM | 17 | Gearbox | 1 |
| Ret | 22 | Lucien Bianchi | Lola-Climax | 17 | Accident | 16 |
| Ret | 5 | Jim Hall | Lotus-BRM | 16 | Accident | 12 |
| Ret | 28 | Jo Siffert | Lotus-BRM | 16 | Accident | 14 |
| Ret | 26 | Phil Hill | A.T.S. | 13 | Gearbox | 17 |
| Ret | 17 | Jack Brabham | Brabham-Climax | 12 | Injection | 6 |
| Ret | 21 | Chris Amon | Lola-Climax | 10 | Oil leak | 15 |
| Ret | 4 | Innes Ireland | BRP-BRM | 9 | Gearbox | 7 |
| Ret | 10 | Willy Mairesse | Ferrari | 7 | Injection | 3 |
| Ret | 27 | Giancarlo Baghetti | A.T.S. | 7 | Gearbox | 20 |
| Ret | 2 | Trevor Taylor | Lotus-Climax | 5 | Physical | 11 |

Winning speed: 113.819mph Lap leader: Clark 1-32
Pole position: G Hill, 3m 54.100s, 134.732mph
Fastest lap: Clark, 3m 58.100s, 132.469mph

### DUTCH GRAND PRIX: ZANDVOORT *23 June Round: 3 Race: 114 80 x 2.605 miles*

| POS. | NO. | DRIVER | CAR/ENGINE | LAPS | TIME/RETIRED | GRID |
|---|---|---|---|---|---|---|
| 1 | 6 | Jim Clark | Lotus-Climax | 80 | 2:08'13.7 | 1 |
| 2 | 18 | Dan Gurney | Brabham-Climax | 79 | +1 Lap | 14 |
| 3 | 2 | John Surtees | Ferrari | 79 | +1 Lap | 5 |
| 4 | 30 | Innes Ireland | BRP-BRM | 79 | +1 Lap | 7 |
| 5 | 14 | Richie Ginther | BRM | 79 | +1 Lap | 6 |
| 6 | 4 | L.Scarfiotti | Ferrari | 78 | +2 Laps | 11 |
| 7 | 36 | Jo Siffert | Lotus-BRM | 77 | +3 Laps | 17 |
| 8 | 42 | Jim Hall | Lotus-BRM | 77 | +3 Laps | 18 |
| 9 | 32 | C.G.de Beaufort | Porsche | 75 | +5 Laps | 19 |
| 10 | 8 | Trevor Taylor | Lotus-Climax | 66 | +14 Laps | 10 |
| 11 | 28 | Jo Bonnier | Cooper-Climax | 56 | +24 Laps | 8 |
| Ret | 12 | Graham Hill | BRM | 69 | Overheating | 2 |
| Ret | 16 | Jack Brabham | Brabham-Climax | 68 | Accident | 4 |
| Ret | 10 | Chris Amon | Lola-Climax | 29 | Water pump | 12 |
| Ret | 26 | Giancarlo Baghetti | A.T.S. | 17 | Ignition | 15 |
| Ret | 24 | Phil Hill | A.T.S. | 15 | Suspension | 13 |
| Ret | 22 | Tony Maggs | Cooper-Climax | 14 | Overheating | 9 |
| Ret | 20 | Bruce McLaren | Cooper-Climax | 7 | Gearbox | 3 |
| Ret | 34 | Gerhard Mitter | Porsche | 2 | Clutch | 16 |

Winning speed: 97.529mph Lap leaders: Clark 1-80
Pole position: Clark, 1m 31.600s, 102.396mph
Fastest lap: Clark, 1m 33.700s, 100.101mph

### FRENCH GRAND PRIX: REIMS *30 June Round: 4 Race: 115 53 x 5.159 miles*

| POS. | NO. | DRIVER | CAR/ENGINE | LAPS | TIME/RETIRED | GRID |
|---|---|---|---|---|---|---|
| 1 | 18 | Jim Clark | Lotus-Climax | 53 | 2:10'54.3 | 1 |
| 2 | 12 | Tony Maggs | Cooper-Climax | 53 | +1'04.9 | 8 |
| 3 | 2 | Graham Hill | BRM | 53 | +1'13.9 | 2 |
| 4 | 6 | Jack Brabham | Brabham-Climax | 53 | +2'15.2 | 5 |
| 5 | 8 | Dan Gurney | Brabham-Climax | 53 | +2'33.4 | 3 |
| 6 | 36 | Jo Siffert | Lotus-BRM | 52 | +1 Lap | 10 |
| 7 | 30 | Chris Amon | Lola-Climax | 51 | +2 Laps | 17 |
| 8 | 28 | M.Trintignant | Lotus-Climax | 50 | +3 Laps | 15 |
| 9 | 32 | Innes Ireland | BRP-BRM | 49 | +4 Laps | 9 |
| 10 | 46 | Lorenzo Bandini | BRM | 45 | +8 Laps | 21 |
| 11 | 34 | Jim Hall | Lotus-BRM | 45 | +8 Laps | 18 |
| 12 | 10 | Bruce McLaren | Cooper-Climax | 42 | Ignition | 6 |
| 13 | 20 | Trevor Taylor | Lotus-Climax | 41 | Suspension | 7 |
| NC | 42 | Phil Hill | Lotus-BRM | 34 | Not classified | 13 |
| NC | 44 | Jo Bonnier | Cooper-Climax | 32 | Not classified | 11 |
| Ret | 48 | Masten Gregory | Lotus-BRM | 30 | Gearbox | 19 |
| Ret | 16 | John Surtees | Ferrari | 12 | Fuel pump | 4 |
| Ret | 38 | Tony Settember | Scirocco-BRM | 5 | Wheel bearing | 20 |
| Ret | 4 | Richie Ginther | BRM | 4 | Radiator | 12 |

Winning speed: 125.315mph Lap leaders: Clark 1-53
Pole position: Clark, 2m 20.200s, 132.461 mph
Fastest lap: Clark, 2m 21.600s, 131.151mph

### BRITISH GRAND PRIX: SILVERSTONE *20 July Round: 5 Race: 116 82 x 2.927 miles*

| POS. | NO. | DRIVER | CAR/ENGINE | LAPS | TIME/RETIRED | GRID |
|---|---|---|---|---|---|---|
| 1 | 4 | Jim Clark | Lotus-Climax | 82 | 2:14'09.6 | 1 |
| 2 | 10 | John Surtees | Ferrari | 82 | +25.8 | 5 |
| 3 | 1 | Graham Hill | BRM | 82 | +37.6 | 3 |
| 4 | 2 | Richie Ginther | BRM | 81 | +1 Lap | 9 |
| 5 | 3 | Lorenzo Bandini | BRM | 81 | +1 Lap | 8 |
| 6 | 12 | Jim Hall | Lotus-BRM | 80 | +2 Laps | 13 |
| 7 | 19 | Chris Amon | Lola-Climax | 80 | +2 Laps | 14 |
| 8 | 20 | Mike Hailwood | Lotus-Climax | 78 | +4 Laps | 17 |
| 9 | 7 | Tony Maggs | Cooper-Climax | 78 | +4 Laps | 7 |
| 10 | 23 | C.G.de Beaufort | Porsche | 76 | +6 Laps | 21 |
| 11 | 21 | Masten Gregory | Lotus-BRM | 75 | +7 Laps | 22 |
| 12 | 22 | Bob Anderson | Lola-Climax | 75 | +7 Laps | 16 |
| 13 | 24 | J.C.-Jones | Lola-Climax | 74 | +8 Laps | 23 |
| Ret | 25 | Jo Siffert | Lotus-BRM | 66 | Gearbox | 15 |
| Ret | 14 | Jo Bonnier | Cooper-Climax | 65 | Oil pressure | 12 |
| Ret | 9 | Dan Gurney | Brabham-Climax | 59 | Engine | 2 |
| Ret | 26 | Ian Raby | Gilby-BRM | 59 | Gearbox | 19 |
| Ret | 16 | Ian Burgess | Scirocco-BRM | 36 | Ignition | 20 |
| Ret | 8 | Jack Brabham | Brabham-Climax | 27 | Engine | 4 |
| Ret | 11 | Innes Ireland | BRP-BRM | 26 | Ignition | 11 |
| Ret | 5 | Trevor Taylor | Lotus-Climax | 23 | Fuel pump | 10 |
| Ret | 15 | Tony Settember | Scirocco-BRM | 20 | Ignition | 18 |
| Ret | 6 | Bruce McLaren | Cooper-Climax | 6 | Engine | 6 |

Winning speed: 107.341mph Lap leaders: Brabham 1-3; Clark 4-82
Pole position: Clark, 1m 34.400s, 111.623mph
Fastest lap: Surtees, 1m 36.000s, 109.763mph

### GERMAN GRAND PRIX: NÜRBURGRING *4 August Round: 6 Race: 117 15 x 14.173 miles*

| POS. | NO. | DRIVER | CAR/ENGINE | LAPS | TIME/RETIRED | GRID |
|---|---|---|---|---|---|---|
| 1 | 7 | John Surtees | Ferrari | 15 | 2:13'06.8 | 2 |
| 2 | 3 | Jim Clark | Lotus-Climax | 15 | +1'17.5 | 1 |
| 3 | 2 | Richie Ginther | BRM | 15 | +2'44.9 | 6 |
| 4 | 26 | Gerhard Mitter | Porsche | 15 | +8'11.5 | 15 |
| 5 | 20 | Jim Hall | Lotus-BRM | 14 | +1 Lap | 16 |
| 6 | 16 | Jo Bonnier | Cooper-Climax | 14 | +1 Lap | 12 |
| 7 | 9 | Jack Brabham | Brabham-Climax | 14 | +1 Lap | 8 |
| 8 | 4 | Trevor Taylor | Lotus-Climax | 14 | +1 Lap | 18 |
| 9 | 18 | Jo Siffert | Lotus-BRM | 10 | Differential | 9 |
| 10 | 28 | Bernard Collomb | Lotus-Climax | 10 | +5 Laps | 21 |
| Ret | 17 | C.G.de Beaufort | Porsche | 9 | Wheel | 17 |
| Ret | 6 | Tony Maggs | Cooper-Climax | 7 | Engine | 10 |
| Ret | 10 | Dan Gurney | Brabham-Climax | 6 | Gearbox | 13 |
| Ret | 22 | M.A.Cabral | Cooper-Climax | 6 | Gearbox | 20 |
| Ret | 24 | Ian Burgess | Scirocco-BRM | 5 | Steering | 19 |
| Ret | 23 | Tony Settember | Scirocco-BRM | 5 | Accident | 22 |
| Ret | 5 | Bruce McLaren | Cooper-Climax | 3 | Accident | 5 |
| Ret | 1 | Graham Hill | BRM | 2 | Gearbox | 4 |
| Ret | 21 | Chris Amon | Lola-Climax | 2 | Accident | 14 |
| Ret | 8 | Willy Mairesse | Ferrari | 1 | Accident | 7 |
| Ret | 14 | Innes Ireland | Lotus-BRM | 1 | Accident | 11 |
| Ret | 15 | Lorenzo Bandini | BRM | 0 | Accident | 3 |
| DNQ | 29 | Andre Pilette | Lotus-Climax | | | |
| DNQ | 25 | Ian Raby | Gilby-BRM | | | |
| DNQ | 30 | Tim Parnell | Lotus-Climax | | | |
| DNQ | 27 | Kurt Kuhnke | Lotus-Borgward | | | |

Winning speed: 95.829mph Lap leaders: Ginther 1; Surtees 2-3, 5-15; Clark 4
Pole position: Clark, 8m 45.800s, 97.042mph
Fastest lap: Surtees, 8m 47.000s, 96.821mph

### ITALIAN GRAND PRIX: MONZA *8 September Round: 7 Race: 118 86 x 3.573 miles*

| POS. | NO. | DRIVER | CAR/ENGINE | LAPS | TIME/RETIRED | GRID |
|---|---|---|---|---|---|---|
| 1 | 8 | Jim Clark | Lotus-Climax | 86 | 2:24'19.6 | 3 |
| 2 | 10 | Richie Ginther | BRM | 86 | +1'35.0 | 4 |
| 3 | 18 | Bruce McLaren | Cooper-Climax | 85 | +1 Lap | 8 |
| 4 | 32 | Innes Ireland | BRP-BRM | 84 | +Engine | 10 |
| 5 | 22 | Jack Brabham | Brabham-Climax | 84 | +2 Laps | 7 |
| 6 | 20 | Tony Maggs | Cooper-Climax | 84 | +2 Laps | 13 |
| 7 | 58 | Jo Bonnier | Cooper-Climax | 84 | +2 Laps | 11 |
| 8 | 30 | Jim Hall | Lotus-BRM | 84 | +2 Laps | 17 |
| 9 | 66 | M.Trintignant | BRM | 83 | +3 Laps | 20 |
| 10 | 40 | Mike Hailwood | Lola-Climax | 82 | +4 Laps | 18 |
| 11 | 16 | Phil Hill | A.T.S. | 79 | +7 Laps | 14 |
| 12 | 48 | Bob Anderson | Lola-Climax | 79 | +7 Laps | 19 |
| 13 | 6 | Mike Spence | Lotus-Climax | 73 | Oil pressure | 9 |
| 14 | 24 | Dan Gurney | Brabham-Climax | 64 | Fuel system | 5 |
| 15 | 14 | Giancarlo Baghetti | A.T.S. | 63 | +23 Laps | 25 |
| 16 | 12 | Graham Hill | BRM | 59 | Clutch | 2 |
| Ret | 54 | Jo Siffert | Lotus-BRM | 40 | Oil pressure | 16 |
| Ret | 2 | Lorenzo Bandini | Ferrari | 37 | Gearbox | 6 |
| Ret | 42 | Masten Gregory | Lotus-BRM | 26 | Engine | 12 |
| Ret | 4 | John Surtees | Ferrari | 16 | Engine | 1 |
| DNQ | 50 | Ian Raby | Gilby-BRM | | | |
| DNQ | 34 | Tony Settember | Scirocco-BRM | | | |
| DNQ | 28 | C.G.de Beaufort | Porsche | | | |
| DNQ | 62 | E.Brambilla | Cooper-Maserati | | | |
| DNQ | 46 | Andre Pilette | Lotus-Climax | | | |
| DNQ | 44 | Roberto Lippi | De Tomaso-Ferrari | | | |

Winning speed: 127.739mph Lap leaders: G Hill 1-3, 24-26, 29-30, 32, 34-35, 39, 41; Surtees 4-16; Clark 17-22, 28, 36, 40, 42-43, 45, 47-51, 53-54, 56-86; Gurney 23, 27, 31, 33, 37-38, 44, 46, 52, 55
Pole position: Surtees, 1m 37.300s, 132.193mph
Fastest lap: Clark, 1m 38.900s, 130.054mph

### UNITED STATES GRAND PRIX: WATKINS GLEN *6 October Round: 8 Race: 119 110 x 2.300 miles*

| POS. | NO. | DRIVER | CAR/ENGINE | LAPS | TIME/RETIRED | GRID |
|---|---|---|---|---|---|---|
| 1 | 1 | Graham Hill | BRM | 110 | 2:19'22.1 | 1 |
| 2 | 2 | Richie Ginther | BRM | 110 | +34.3 | 4 |
| 3 | 8 | Jim Clark | Lotus-Climax | 109 | +1 Lap | 2 |
| 4 | 5 | Jack Brabham | Brabham-Climax | 108 | +2 Laps | 5 |
| 5 | 24 | Lorenzo Bandini | Ferrari | 106 | +4 Laps | 9 |
| 6 | 12 | C.G.de Beaufort | Porsche | 99 | +11 Laps | 19 |
| 7 | 21 | Peter Broeker | Stebro-Ford | 88 | +22 Laps | 21 |
| 8 | 11 | Jo Bonnier | Cooper-Climax | 85 | +25 Laps | 12 |
| 9 | 23 | John Surtees | Ferrari | 82 | Engine | 3 |
| 10 | 16 | Jim Hall | Lotus-BRM | 76 | Gearbox | 16 |
| 11 | 3 | Bruce McLaren | Cooper-Climax | 74 | Fuel pump | 11 |
| Ret | 14 | Jo Siffert | Lotus-BRM | 56 | Gearbox | 14 |
| Ret | 4 | Tony Maggs | Cooper-Climax | 44 | Ignition | 10 |
| Ret | 18 | Rodger Ward | Lotus-BRM | 44 | Gearbox | 17 |
| Ret | 6 | Dan Gurney | Brabham-Climax | 42 | Chassis | 6 |
| Ret | 10 | Pedro Rodriguez | Lotus-Climax | 36 | Engine | 13 |
| Ret | 9 | Trevor Taylor | Lotus-Climax | 24 | Electrical | 7 |
| Ret | 17 | Masten Gregory | Lola-Climax | 14 | Engine | 8 |
| Ret | 22 | Hap Sharp | Lotus-BRM | 6 | Retirement | 18 |
| Ret | 25 | Phil Hill | A.T.S. | 4 | Oil pump | 15 |
| Ret | 26 | Giancarlo Baghetti | A.T.S. | 0 | Oil pump | 20 |

Winning speed: 108.920mph
Lap leaders: G Hill 1-6, 32, 35, 83-110; Surtees 7-31, 33-34, 36-82
Pole position: G Hill, 1m 13.400s, 112.807mph
Fastest lap: Clark, 1m 14.500s, 111.141mph

### MEXICAN GRAND PRIX: MEXICO CITY *27 October Round: 9 Race: 120 65 x 3.107 miles*

| POS. | NO. | DRIVER | CAR/ENGINE | LAPS | TIME/RETIRED | GRID |
|---|---|---|---|---|---|---|
| 1 | 8 | Jim Clark | Lotus-Climax | 65 | 2:09'52.1 | 1 |
| 2 | 5 | Jack Brabham | Brabham-Climax | 65 | +1'41.1 | 10 |
| 3 | 2 | Richie Ginther | BRM | 65 | +1'54.7 | 5 |
| 4 | 1 | Graham Hill | BRM | 64 | +1 Lap | 3 |
| 5 | 11 | Jo Bonnier | Cooper-Climax | 62 | +3 Laps | 8 |
| 6 | 6 | Dan Gurney | Brabham-Climax | 62 | +3 Laps | 4 |
| 7 | 22 | Hap Sharp | Lotus-BRM | 61 | +4 Laps | 16 |
| 8 | 16 | Jim Hall | Lotus-BRM | 61 | +4 Laps | 15 |
| 9 | 14 | Jo Siffert | Lotus-BRM | 59 | +6 Laps | 9 |
| 10 | 12 | C.G.de Beaufort | Porsche | 58 | +7 Laps | 18 |
| 11 | 13 | Moises Solana | BRM | 57 | Engine | 11 |
| Ret | 25 | Phil Hill | A.T.S. | 46 | Suspension | 17 |
| Ret | 24 | Lorenzo Bandini | Ferrari | 36 | Ignition | 7 |
| Ret | 3 | Bruce McLaren | Cooper-Climax | 30 | Engine | 6 |
| Ret | 10 | Pedro Rodriguez | Lotus-Climax | 26 | Suspension | 20 |
| Ret | 17 | Masten Gregory | Lola-Climax | 23 | Suspension | 14 |
| DSQ | 23 | John Surtees | Ferrari | 19 | Disqualified | 2 |
| Ret | 9 | Trevor Taylor | Lotus-Climax | 19 | Engine | 12 |
| Ret | 26 | Giancarlo Baghetti | A.T.S. | 12 | Engine | 21 |
| Ret | 18 | Chris Amon | Lotus-BRM | 9 | Gearbox | 19 |
| Ret | 4 | Tony Maggs | Cooper-Climax | 7 | Engine | 13 |
| DNQ | 20 | Frank Dochnal | Cooper-Climax | | | |

Winning speed: 93.300mph Lap leaders: Clark 1-65
Pole position: Clark, 1m 58.800s, 94.147mph
Fastest lap: Clark, 1m 58.100s, 94.705mph

### SOUTH AFRICAN GRAND PRIX: EAST LONDON *28 December Round: 10 Race: 121 85 x 2.436 miles*

| POS. | NO. | DRIVER | CAR/ENGINE | LAPS | TIME/RETIRED | GRID |
|---|---|---|---|---|---|---|
| 1 | 1 | Jim Clark | Lotus-Climax | 85 | 2:10'36.9 | 1 |
| 2 | 9 | Dan Gurney | Brabham-Climax | 85 | +1'06.8 | 3 |
| 3 | 5 | Graham Hill | BRM | 84 | +1 Lap | 6 |
| 4 | 10 | Bruce McLaren | Cooper-Climax | 84 | +1 Lap | 9 |
| 5 | 4 | Lorenzo Bandini | Ferrari | 84 | +1 Lap | 5 |
| 6 | 12 | Jo Bonnier | Cooper-Climax | 83 | +2 Laps | 11 |
| 7 | 11 | Tony Maggs | Cooper-Climax | 82 | +3 Laps | 10 |
| 8 | 2 | Trevor Taylor | Lotus-Climax | 81 | +4 Laps | 8 |
| 9 | 19 | John Love | Cooper-Climax | 80 | +5 Laps | 13 |
| 10 | 14 | C.G.de Beaufort | Porsche | 79 | +6 Laps | 20 |
| 11 | 16 | Doug Serrurier | LDS-Alfa Romeo | 78 | +7 Laps | 18 |
| 12 | 23 | Trevor Blokdyk | Cooper-Maserati | 77 | +8 Laps | 19 |
| 13 | 8 | Jack Brabham | Brabham-Climax | 70 | Accident | 2 |
| 14 | 21 | Brausch Niemann | Lotus-Ford | 66 | +19 Laps | 15 |
| Ret | 18 | Peter de Klerk | Alfa Romeo | 53 | Gearbox | 16 |
| Ret | 22 | David Prophet | Brabham-Ford | 49 | Oil pressure | 14 |
| Ret | 3 | John Surtees | Ferrari | 43 | Engine | 4 |
| Ret | 6 | Richie Ginther | BRM | 43 | Halfshaft | 7 |
| Ret | 7 | Ernie Pieterse | Lotus-Climax | 3 | Engine | 12 |
| Ret | 20 | Sam Tingle | LDS-Alfa Romeo | 2 | Halfshaft | 17 |

Winning speed: 95.116mph Lap leaders: Clark 1-85
Pole position: Clark, 1m 28.900s, 98.646mph
Fastest lap: Gurney, 1m 29.100s, 98.424mph

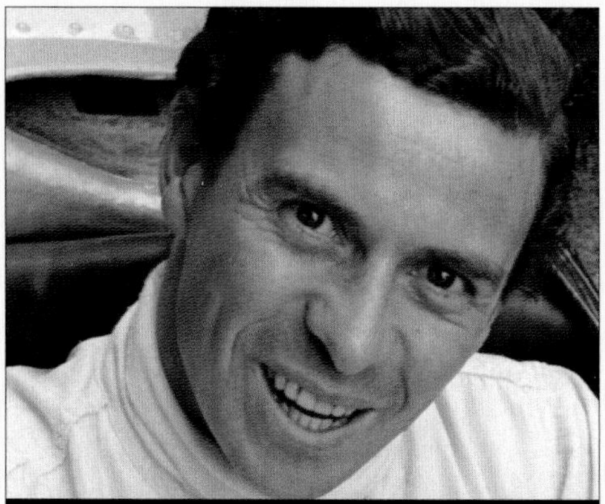

1963 world champion, Jim Clark.

# 1964

## DRIVERS' CHAMPION: JOHN SURTEES
## CONSTRUCTORS' CHAMPION: FERRARI

### DRIVERS' CHAMPIONSHIP

| POS. | DRIVER | NATIONALITY | CAR | POINTS |
|---|---|---|---|---|
| 1 | John Surtees | GB | Ferrari | 40 |
| 2 | Graham Hill | GB | BRM | 39(2) |
| 3 | Jim Clark | GB | Lotus-Climax | 32 |
| 4 | Lorenzo Bandini | Italy | Ferrari | 23 |
| = | Richie Ginther | USA | BRM | 23 |
| 6 | Dan Gurney | USA | Brabham-Climax | 19 |
| 7 | Bruce McLaren | New Zealand | Cooper-Climax | 13 |
| 8 | Peter Arundell | GB | Lotus-Climax | 11 |
| = | Jack Brabham | Australia | Brabham-Climax | 11 |
| 10 | Jo Siffert | Switzerland | Lotus-BRM, Brabham-BRM | 7 |
| 11 | Bob Anderson | GB | Brabham-Climax | 5 |
| 12 | Tony Maggs | South Africa | BRM | 4 |
| = | Mike Spence | GB | Lotus-Climax | 4 |
| = | Innes Ireland | GB | Lotus-BRM, BRP-BRM | 4 |
| 15 | Jo Bonnier | Sweden | Cooper-Climax Brabham-BRM, Brabham-Climax | 3 |
| 16 | Chris Amon | New Zealand | Lotus-BRM, Lotus-Climax | 2 |
| = | Maurice Trintignant | France | BRM | 2 |
| = | Walt Hansgen | USA | Lotus-Climax | 2 |
| 19 | Mike Hailwood | GB | Lotus-BRM | 1 |
| = | Phil Hill | USA | Cooper-Climax | 1 |
| = | Trevor Taylor | GB | BRP-BRM, Lotus-BRM | 1 |
| = | Pedro Rodriguez | Mexico | Ferrari | 1 |
| | Carel Godin de Beaufort | Netherlands | Porsche | |
| | André Pilette | Belgium | Scirocco-Climax | |
| | Ian Raby | GB | Brabham-BRM | |
| | Frank Gardner | Australia | Brabham-Ford | |
| | Mario Araujo de Cabral | Portugal | Derrington-Francis-ATS | |
| | Ludovico Scarfiotti | Italy | Ferrari | |
| | Bernard Collomb | France | Lotus-Climax | |
| | Peter Revson | USA | Lotus-BRM | |
| | Giancarlo Baghetti | Italy | BRM | |
| | John Taylor | GB | Cooper-Ford | |
| | Richard Atwood | GB | BRM | |
| | Edgar Barth | East Germany | Cooper-Climax | |
| | Ronnie Bucknum | USA | Honda | |
| | Gerhard Mitter | West Germany | Lotus-Climax | |
| | Jochen Rindt | Austria | Brabham-BRM | |
| | John Love | South Africa | Cooper-Climax | |
| | Jean-Claude Rudaz | Switzerland | Cooper-Climax | |
| | Giacomo Russo | Italy | Brabham-BRM | |
| | Hap Sharp | USA | Brabham-BRM | |
| | Moises Solana | Mexico | Lotus-Climax | |

Points for the top six finishers (9, 6, 4, 3, 2, 1). Only the best six scores counted towards the championship.

### CONSTRUCTORS' CHAMPIONSHIP

| POS. | CONSTRUCTOR | POINTS |
|---|---|---|
| 1 | Ferrari | 45 |
| 2 | BRM | 42 |
| 3 | Lotus-Climax | 37 |
| 4 | Brabham-Climax | 30 |
| 5 | Cooper-Climax | 16 |
| 6 | Brabham-BRM | 7 |
| 7 | BRP-BRM | 5 |
| 8 | Lotus-BRM | 3 |

Points for top six finishers (9, 6, 4, 3, 2, 1). Points only counted for top-placed car for each constructor. Only the best six scores counted towards the championship.

### MONACO GRAND PRIX: MONTE CARLO *10 May Round: 1 Race: 122 100 x 1.954 miles*

| POS. | NO. | DRIVER | CAR/ENGINE | LAPS | TIME/RETIRED | GRID |
|---|---|---|---|---|---|---|
| 1 | 8 | Graham Hill | BRM | 100 | 2:41'19.5 | 3 |
| 2 | 7 | Richie Ginther | BRM | 99 | +1 Lap | 8 |
| 3 | 11 | Peter Arundell | Lotus-Climax | 97 | +3 Laps | 6 |
| 4 | 12 | Jim Clark | Lotus-Climax | 96 | Engine | 1 |
| 5 | 19 | Jo Bonnier | Cooper-Climax | 96 | +4 Laps | 11 |
| 6 | 18 | Mike Hailwood | Lotus-BRM | 96 | +4 Laps | 15 |
| 7 | 16 | Bob Anderson | Brabham-Climax | 86 | Gearbox | 12 |
| 8 | 24 | Jo Siffert | Lotus-BRM | 78 | +22 Laps | 16 |
| 9 | 9 | Phil Hill | Cooper-Climax | 70 | Suspension | 9 |
| 10 | 20 | Lorenzo Bandini | Ferrari | 68 | Gearbox | 7 |
| Ret | 6 | Dan Gurney | Brabham-Climax | 62 | Gearbox | 5 |
| Ret | 4 | M.Trintignant | BRM | 53 | Overheating | 13 |
| Ret | 5 | Jack Brabham | Brabham-Climax | 29 | Injection | 2 |
| Ret | 10 | Bruce McLaren | Cooper-Climax | 17 | Wheel bearing | 10 |
| Ret | 21 | John Surtees | Ferrari | 15 | Gearbox | 4 |
| Ret | 15 | Trevor Taylor | BRP-BRM | 8 | Fuel leak | 14 |
| DNQ | 17 | Chris Amon | Lotus-BRM | | | |
| DNQ | 2 | Peter Revson | Lotus-BRM | | | |
| DNQ | 3 | Bernard Collomb | Lotus-BRM | | | |

Winning speed: 72.681mph Lap leaders: Clark 1-36; Gurney 37-52; G Hill 53-100
Pole position: Clark, 1m 34.000s, 74.842mph
Fastest lap: G Hill, 1m 33.900s, 74.922mph

### DUTCH GRAND PRIX: ZANDVOORT *24 May Round: 2 Race: 123 80 x 2.605 miles*

| POS. | NO. | DRIVER | CAR/ENGINE | LAPS | TIME/RETIRED | GRID |
|---|---|---|---|---|---|---|
| 1 | 18 | Jim Clark | Lotus-Climax | 80 | 2:07'35.4 | 2 |
| 2 | 2 | John Surtees | Ferrari | 80 | +53.6 | 4 |
| 3 | 20 | Peter Arundell | Lotus-Climax | 79 | +1 Lap | 6 |
| 4 | 6 | Graham Hill | BRM | 79 | +1 Lap | 3 |
| 5 | 10 | Chris Amon | Lotus-BRM | 79 | +1 Lap | 13 |
| 6 | 34 | Bob Anderson | Brabham-Climax | 78 | +2 Laps | 11 |
| 7 | 24 | Bruce McLaren | Cooper-Climax | 78 | +2 Laps | 5 |
| 8 | 22 | Phil Hill | Cooper-Climax | 76 | +4 Laps | 9 |
| 9 | 26 | Jo Bonnier | Brabham-BRM | 76 | +4 Laps | 12 |
| 10 | 32 | Giancarlo Baghetti | BRM | 74 | +6 Laps | 16 |
| 11 | 8 | Richie Ginther | BRM | 64 | +16 Laps | 8 |
| 12 | 12 | Mike Hailwood | Lotus-BRM | 57 | Differential | 14 |
| 13 | 36 | Jo Siffert | Brabham-BRM | 55 | +25 Laps | 18 |
| Ret | 14 | Jack Brabham | Brabham-Climax | 44 | Ignition | 7 |
| Ret | 16 | Dan Gurney | Brabham-Climax | 23 | Retirement | 1 |
| Ret | 4 | Lorenzo Bandini | Ferrari | 20 | Injection | 10 |
| Ret | 28 | C.G.de Beaufort | Porsche | 8 | Engine | 17 |
| Ret | 30 | Tony Maggs | BRM | 0 | Accident | 15 |

Winning speed: 98.017 mph Lap leaders: Clark 1-80
Pole position: Gurney, 1m 31.200s, 102.845mph
Fastest lap: Clark, 1m 32.800s, 101.072mph

### BELGIAN GRAND PRIX: SPA-FRANCORCHAMPS *14 June Round: 3 Race: 124 32 x 8.761 miles*

| POS. | NO. | DRIVER | CAR/ENGINE | LAPS | TIME/RETIRED | GRID |
|---|---|---|---|---|---|---|
| 1 | 23 | Jim Clark | Lotus-Climax | 32 | 2:06'40.5 | 6 |
| 2 | 20 | Bruce McLaren | Cooper-Climax | 32 | +3.4 | 7 |
| 3 | 14 | Jack Brabham | Brabham-Climax | 32 | +48.1 | 3 |
| 4 | 2 | Richie Ginther | BRM | 32 | +1'58.6 | 8 |
| 5 | 1 | Graham Hill | BRM | 31 | Fuel pump | 2 |
| 6 | 15 | Dan Gurney | Brabham-Climax | 31 | Out of fuel | 1 |
| 7 | 4 | Trevor Taylor | BRP-BRM | 31 | 1 Lap | 12 |
| 8 | 6 | Giancarlo Baghetti | BRM | 31 | 1 Lap | 17 |
| 9 | 24 | Peter Arundell | Lotus-Climax | 28 | Overheating | 4 |
| 10 | 3 | Innes Ireland | BRP-BRM | 28 | 4 Laps | 16 |
| DSQ | 29 | Peter Revson | Lotus-BRM | 28 | Disqualified | 10 |
| Ret | 17 | Jo Siffert | Brabham-Climax | 14 | Engine | 13 |
| Ret | 21 | Phil Hill | Cooper-Climax | 13 | Engine | 15 |
| Ret | 11 | Lorenzo Bandini | Ferrari | 12 | Engine | 9 |
| Ret | 28 | Andre Pilette | Scirocco-Climax | 11 | Engine | 20 |
| Ret | 16 | Jo Bonnier | Brabham-BRM | 8 | Unwell | 14 |
| Ret | 10 | John Surtees | Ferrari | 4 | Engine | 11 |
| Ret | 27 | Chris Amon | Lotus-BRM | 3 | Engine | 5 |

Winning speed: 132.795mph Lap leaders: Gurney 1-2, 4-29; Surtees 3; G Hill 30-31; Clark 32
Pole position: Gurney, 3m 50.900s, 136.599mph
Fastest lap: Gurney, 3m 49.200s, 137.613mph

### FRENCH GRAND PRIX: ROUEN-LES-ESSARTS *28 June Round: 4 Race: 125 57 x 4.065 miles*

| POS. | NO. | DRIVER | CAR/ENGINE | LAPS | TIME/RETIRED | GRID |
|---|---|---|---|---|---|---|
| 1 | 22 | Dan Gurney | Brabham-Climax | 57 | 2:07'49.1 | 2 |
| 2 | 8 | Graham Hill | BRM | 57 | +24.1 | 6 |
| 3 | 20 | Jack Brabham | Brabham-Climax | 57 | +24.9 | 5 |
| 4 | 4 | Peter Arundell | Lotus-Climax | 57 | +1'10.6 | 4 |
| 5 | 10 | Richie Ginther | BRM | 57 | +2'12.1 | 9 |
| 6 | 12 | Bruce McLaren | Cooper-Climax | 56 | +1 Lap | 7 |
| 7 | 14 | Phil Hill | Cooper-Climax | 56 | +1 Lap | 10 |
| 8 | 36 | Mike Hailwood | Lotus-BRM | 56 | +1 Lap | 13 |
| 9 | 26 | Lorenzo Bandini | Ferrari | 55 | +2 Laps | 8 |
| 10 | 34 | Chris Amon | Lotus-BRM | 53 | +4 Laps | 14 |
| 11 | 28 | M.Trintignant | BRM | 52 | +5 Laps | 16 |
| 12 | 32 | Bob Anderson | Brabham-Climax | 50 | +7 Laps | 15 |
| Ret | 16 | Innes Ireland | BRP-BRM | 32 | Accident | 11 |
| Ret | 2 | Jim Clark | Lotus-Climax | 31 | Engine | 1 |
| Ret | 24 | John Surtees | Ferrari | 6 | Engine | 3 |
| Ret | 18 | Trevor Taylor | BRP-BRM | 6 | Accident | 12 |
| Ret | 30 | Jo Siffert | Brabham-BRM | 4 | Clutch | 17 |

Winning speed: 108.766mph Lap leaders: Clark 1-30; Gurney 31-57
Pole position: Clark, 2m 9.600s, 112.917mph
Fastest lap: Brabham, 2m 11.400s, 111.370mph

### BRITISH GRAND PRIX: BRANDS HATCH *11 July Round: 5 Race: 126 80 x 2.650 miles*

| POS. | NO. | DRIVER | CAR/ENGINE | LAPS | TIME/RETIRED | GRID |
|---|---|---|---|---|---|---|
| 1 | 1 | Jim Clark | Lotus-Climax | 80 | 2:15'07.0 | 1 |
| 2 | 3 | Graham Hill | BRM | 80 | +2.8 | 2 |
| 3 | 7 | John Surtees | Ferrari | 80 | +1'20.6 | 5 |
| 4 | 5 | Jack Brabham | Brabham-Climax | 79 | +1 Lap | 4 |
| 5 | 8 | Lorenzo Bandini | Ferrari | 78 | +2 Laps | 8 |
| 6 | 10 | Phil Hill | Cooper-Climax | 78 | +2 Laps | 15 |
| 7 | 19 | Bob Anderson | Brabham-Climax | 78 | +2 Laps | 7 |
| 8 | 4 | Richie Ginther | BRM | 77 | +3 Laps | 14 |
| 9 | 2 | Mike Spence | Lotus-Climax | 77 | +3 Laps | 13 |
| 10 | 11 | Innes Ireland | BRP-BRM | 77 | +3 Laps | 10 |
| 11 | 20 | Jo Siffert | Brabham-BRM | 76 | +4 Laps | 16 |
| 12 | 18 | Giancarlo Baghetti | BRM | 76 | +4 Laps | 21 |
| 13 | 6 | Dan Gurney | Brabham-Climax | 75 | +5 Laps | 3 |
| 14 | 22 | John Taylor | Cooper-Ford | 56 | +24 Laps | 20 |
| Ret | 16 | Jo Bonnier | Brabham-BRM | 45 | Brakes | 9 |
| Ret | 24 | Peter Revson | Lotus-BRM | 43 | Differential | 22 |
| Ret | 17 | Tony Maggs | BRM | 38 | Gearbox | 17 |
| Ret | 23 | Ian Raby | Brabham-BRM | 37 | Accident | 23 |
| Ret | 12 | Trevor Taylor | Lotus-BRM | 23 | Unwell | 18 |
| Ret | 14 | Mike Hailwood | Lotus-BRM | 17 | Oil pipe | 12 |
| Ret | 15 | Chris Amon | Lotus-BRM | 9 | Clutch | 11 |
| Ret | 9 | Bruce McLaren | Cooper-Climax | 7 | Gearbox | 6 |
| Ret | 26 | Frank Gardner | Brabham-Ford | 0 | Accident | 19 |
| DNQ | 25 | M.Trintignant | BRM | | | |

Winning speed: 94.141mph Lap leaders: Clark 1-80
Pole position: Clark, 1m 38.100s, 97.248mph
Fastest lap: Clark, 1m 38.800s, 96.559mph

Photographs from Keith Sutton and David Phipps © 2001 The Sutton/ Phipps Library

## GERMAN GRAND PRIX: NURBURGRING *2 August Round: 6 Race: 127 15 x 14.173 miles*

| POS. | NO. | DRIVER | CAR/ENGINE | LAPS | TIME/RETIRED | GRID |
|---|---|---|---|---|---|---|
| 1 | 7 | John Surtees | Ferrari | 15 | 2:12'04.8 | 1 |
| 2 | 3 | Graham Hill | BRM | 15 | +1'15.6 | 5 |
| 3 | 8 | Lorenzo Bandini | Ferrari | 15 | +4'52.8 | 4 |
| 4 | 19 | Jo Siffert | Brabham-BRM | 15 | +5'23.1 | 10 |
| 5 | 22 | M.Trintignant | BRM | 14 | Battery | 14 |
| 6 | 26 | Tony Maggs | BRM | 14 | +1 Lap | 16 |
| 7 | 4 | Richie Ginther | BRM | 14 | +1 Lap | 11 |
| 8 | 2 | Mike Spence | Lotus-Climax | 14 | +1 Lap | 17 |
| 9 | 23 | Gerhard Mitter | Lotus-Climax | 14 | +1 Lap | 19 |
| 10 | 5 | Dan Gurney | Brabham-Climax | 14 | +1 Lap | 3 |
| 11 | 14 | Chris Amon | Lotus-Climax | 12 | Suspension | 9 |
| 12 | 6 | Jack Brabham | Brabham-Climax | 11 | Differential | 6 |
| 13 | 20 | Ronnie Bucknum | Honda | 11 | Accident | 22 |
| 14 | 27 | Peter Revson | Lotus-BRM | 10 | Accident | 18 |
| Ret | 1 | Jim Clark | Lotus-Climax | 7 | Engine | 2 |
| Ret | 9 | Bruce McLaren | Cooper-Climax | 4 | Engine | 7 |
| Ret | 16 | Bob Anderson | Brabham-Climax | 4 | Suspension | 15 |
| Ret | 12 | Edgar Barth | Cooper-Climax | 3 | Clutch | 20 |
| Ret | 18 | Giancarlo Baghetti | BRM | 2 | Throttle | 21 |
| Ret | 10 | Phil Hill | Cooper-Climax | 1 | Engine | 8 |
| Ret | 11 | Jo Bonnier | Brabham-BRM | 0 | Electrical | 12 |
| Ret | 15 | Mike Hailwood | Lotus-BRM | 0 | Engine | 13 |
| DNQ | 28 | Andre Pilette | Scirocco-Climax | | | |

Winning speed: 96.579mph  Lap leaders: Clark 1; Surtees 2-3, 5-15; Gurney 4
Pole position: Surtees, 8m 38.400s, 98.427mph
Fastest lap: Surtees, 8m 39.000s, 98.313mph

## AUSTRIAN GRAND PRIX: ZELTWEG *23 August Round: 7 Race: 128 105 x 1.988 miles*

| POS. | NO. | DRIVER | CAR/ENGINE | LAPS | TIME/RETIRED | GRID |
|---|---|---|---|---|---|---|
| 1 | 8 | Lorenzo Bandini | Ferrari | 105 | 2:06'18.23 | 7 |
| 2 | 4 | Richie Ginther | BRM | 105 | +6.18 | 5 |
| 3 | 22 | Bob Anderson | Brabham-Climax | 102 | +3 Laps | 14 |
| 4 | 19 | Tony Maggs | BRM | 102 | +3 Laps | 19 |
| 5 | 14 | Innes Ireland | BRP-BRM | 102 | +3 Laps | 11 |
| 6 | 11 | Jo Bonnier | Brabham-Climax | 101 | +4 Laps | 10 |
| 7 | 18 | Giancarlo Baghetti | BRM | 96 | +9 Laps | 15 |
| 8 | 17 | Mike Hailwood | Lotus-BRM | 95 | +10 Laps | 18 |
| 9 | 6 | Jack Brabham | Brabham-Climax | 76 | +29 Laps | 6 |
| Ret | 12 | Jochen Rindt | Brabham-BRM | 58 | Steering | 13 |
| Ret | 10 | Phil Hill | Cooper-Climax | 58 | Accident | 20 |
| Ret | 5 | Dan Gurney | Brabham-Climax | 47 | Suspension | 4 |
| Ret | 9 | Bruce McLaren | Cooper-Climax | 43 | Engine | 9 |
| Ret | 2 | Mike Spence | Lotus-Climax | 41 | Halfshaft | 8 |
| Ret | 1 | Jim Clark | Lotus-Climax | 40 | Halfshaft | 3 |
| Ret | 15 | Trevor Taylor | BRP-BRM | 21 | Suspension | 16 |
| Ret | 20 | Jo Siffert | Brabham-BRM | 18 | Accident | 12 |
| Ret | 7 | John Surtees | Ferrari | 9 | Suspension | 2 |
| Ret | 16 | Chris Amon | Lotus-Climax | 7 | Engine | 17 |
| Ret | 3 | Graham Hill | BRM | 5 | Distributor | 1 |

Winning speed: 99.180mph  Lap leaders: Gurney 1, 8-46; Surtees 2-7; Bandini 47-105
Pole position: G Hill, 1m 9.840s, 102.494mph
Fastest lap: Gurney, 1m 10.560s, 101.448mph

## ITALIAN GRAND PRIX: MONZA *6 September Round: 8 Race: 129 78 x 3.573 miles*

| POS. | NO. | DRIVER | CAR/ENGINE | LAPS | TIME/RETIRED | GRID |
|---|---|---|---|---|---|---|
| 1 | 2 | John Surtees | Ferrari | 78 | 2:10'51.8 | 1 |
| 2 | 26 | Bruce McLaren | Cooper-Climax | 78 | +1'06.0 | 5 |
| 3 | 4 | Lorenzo Bandini | Ferrari | 77 | +1 Lap | 9 |
| 4 | 20 | Richie Ginther | BRM | 77 | +1 Lap | 7 |
| 5 | 46 | Innes Ireland | BRP-BRM | 77 | +1 Lap | 13 |
| 6 | 10 | Mike Spence | Lotus-Climax | 77 | +1 Lap | 8 |
| 7 | 12 | Jo Siffert | Brabham-BRM | 77 | +1 Lap | 6 |
| 8 | 30 | Giancarlo Baghetti | BRM | 77 | +1 Lap | 15 |
| 9 | 6 | Ludovico Scarfiotti | Ferrari | 77 | +1 Lap | 16 |
| 10 | 16 | Dan Gurney | Brabham-Climax | 75 | +3 Laps | 2 |
| 11 | 22 | Bob Anderson | Brabham-Climax | 75 | +3 Laps | 14 |
| 12 | 34 | Jo Bonnier | Brabham-Climax | 74 | +4 Laps | 12 |
| 13 | 38 | Peter Revson | Lotus-BRM | 72 | +6 Laps | 18 |
| 14 | 14 | Jack Brabham | Brabham-Climax | 59 | Engine | 11 |
| Ret | 8 | Jim Clark | Lotus-Climax | 28 | Engine | 4 |
| Ret | 50 | M.A.Cabral | Derrington-Francis-A.T.S. | 25 | Ignition | 19 |
| Ret | 48 | M.Trintignant | BRM | 22 | Injection | 21 |
| Ret | 28 | Ronnie Bucknum | Honda | 13 | Brakes | 10 |
| Ret | 40 | Mike Hailwood | Lotus-BRM | 3 | Engine | 17 |
| Ret | 18 | Graham Hill | BRM | 0 | Clutch | 3 |
| DNQ | 44 | Trevor Taylor | BRP-BRM | | | |
| DNQ | 36 | Geki | Brabham-BRM | | | |
| DNQ | 24 | John Love | Cooper-Climax | | | |
| DNQ | 56 | Ian Raby | Brabham-BRM | | | |

Winning speed: 127.775mph  Lap leaders: Gurney 1, 6-7, 10, 12-14, 16, 22, 25-26, 29, 32, 37-38, 45, 47-48, 50-52, 55; Surtees 2-5, 8-9, 11, 15, 17-21, 23-24, 27-28, 30-31, 33-36, 39-44, 46, 49, 53-54, 56-78
Pole position: Surtees, 1m 37.400s, 132.057mph
Fastest lap: Surtees, 1m 38.800s, 130.186mph

## UNITED STATES GRAND PRIX: WATKINS GLEN *4 October Round: 9 Race: 130 110 x 2.300 miles*

| POS. | NO. | DRIVER | CAR/ENGINE | LAPS | TIME/RETIRED | GRID |
|---|---|---|---|---|---|---|
| 1 | 3 | Graham Hill | BRM | 110 | 2:16'38.0 | 4 |
| 2 | 7 | John Surtees | Ferrari | 110 | +30.5 | 2 |
| 3 | 22 | Jo Siffert | Brabham-BRM | 109 | +1 Lap | 13 |
| 4 | 4 | Richie Ginther | BRM | 107 | +3 Laps | 13 |
| 5 | 12 | Walt Hansgen | Lotus-Climax | 107 | +3 Laps | 17 |
| 6 | 17 | Trevor Taylor | BRP-BRM | 106 | +4 Laps | 15 |
| 7 | 2 | Clark/Spence | Lotus-Climax | 102 | Out of fuel | 1 |
| 8 | 14 | Mike Hailwood | Lotus-BRM | 101 | Oil pipe | 16 |
| Ret | 6 | Dan Gurney | Brabham-Climax | 69 | Oil pressure | 3 |
| NC | 23 | Hap Sharp | Brabham-BRM | 65 | Not classified | 18 |
| Ret | 8 | Lorenzo Bandini | Ferrari | 58 | Engine | 8 |
| Ret | 1 | Clark/Spence | Lotus-Climax | 54 | Injection | 1 |
| Ret | 25 | Ronnie Bucknum | Honda | 50 | Overheating | 14 |
| Ret | 15 | Chris Amon | Lotus-BRM | 47 | Engine | 11 |
| Ret | 16 | Jo Bonnier | Brabham-Climax | 37 | Wheel | 9 |
| Ret | 9 | Bruce McLaren | Cooper-Climax | 27 | Engine | 5 |
| Ret | 5 | Jack Brabham | Brabham-Climax | 14 | Engine | 7 |
| Ret | 10 | Phil Hill | Cooper-Climax | 4 | Ignition | 19 |
| Ret | 11 | Innes Ireland | BRP-BRM | 2 | Gearbox | 12 |

Winning speed: 111.100 mph  Lap leaders: Surtees 1-12, 44; Clark 13-43; G Hill 45-110
Pole position: Clark, 1m 12.650s, 113.971mph
Fastest lap: Clark, 1m 12.700s, 113.893mph

## MEXICAN GRAND PRIX: MEXICO CITY *25 October Round: 10 Race: 131 65 x 3.107 miles*

| POS. | NO. | DRIVER | CAR/ENGINE | LAPS | TIME/RETIRED | GRID |
|---|---|---|---|---|---|---|
| 1 | 6 | Dan Gurney | Brabham-Climax | 65 | 2:09'50.32 | 2 |
| 2 | 7 | John Surtees | Ferrari | 65 | +1'08.94 | 4 |
| 3 | 8 | Lorenzo Bandini | Ferrari | 65 | +1'09.63 | 3 |
| 4 | 2 | Mike Spence | Lotus-Climax | 65 | +1'21.86 | 5 |
| 5 | 1 | Jim Clark | Lotus-Climax | 64 | Engine | 1 |
| 6 | 18 | Pedro Rodriguez | Ferrari | 64 | +1 Lap | 9 |
| 7 | 9 | Bruce McLaren | Cooper-Climax | 64 | +1 Lap | 10 |
| 8 | 4 | Richie Ginther | BRM | 64 | +1 Lap | 11 |
| 9 | 10 | Phil Hill | Cooper-Climax | 63 | Engine | 15 |
| 10 | 17 | Moises Solana | Lotus-Climax | 63 | +2 Laps | 14 |
| 11 | 3 | Graham Hill | BRM | 63 | +2 Laps | 6 |
| 12 | 11 | Innes Ireland | BRP-BRM | 61 | +4 Laps | 16 |
| 13 | 23 | Hap Sharp | Brabham-BRM | 60 | +5 Laps | 19 |
| Ret | 15 | Chris Amon | Lotus-BRM | 46 | Gearbox | 12 |
| Ret | 5 | Jack Brabham | Brabham-Climax | 44 | Electrical | 7 |
| Ret | 14 | Mike Hailwood | Lotus-BRM | 12 | Overheating | 17 |
| Ret | 22 | Jo Siffert | Brabham-BRM | 11 | Fuel pump | 8 |
| Ret | 16 | Jo Bonnier | Brabham-Climax | 9 | Suspension | 8 |
| Ret | 12 | Trevor Taylor | BRP-BRM | 6 | Overheating | 18 |

Winning speed: 150.186mph  Lap leaders: Clark 1-63; Gurney 64-65
Pole position: Clark, 1m 57.240s, 95.400mph
Fastest lap: Clark, 1m 58.370s, 94.489mph

1964 world champion, John Surtees.

# 1965

**DRIVERS' CHAMPION: JIM CLARK**
**CONSTRUCTORS' CHAMPION: LOTUS CLIMAX**

## DRIVERS' CHAMPIONSHIP

| POS. | DRIVER | NATIONALITY | CAR | POINTS |
|---|---|---|---|---|
| 1 | Jimmy Clark | GB | Lotus-Climax | 54 |
| 2 | Graham Hill | GB | BRM | 40 (7) |
| 3 | Jackie Stewart | GB | BRM | 33 (1) |
| 4 | Dan Gurney | USA | Brabham-Climax | 25 |
| 5 | John Surtees | GB | Ferrari | 17 |
| 6 | Lorenzo Bandini | Italy | Ferrari | 13 |
| 7 | Richie Ginther | USA | Honda | 11 |
| 8 | Mike Spence | GB | Lotus-Climax | 10 |
| = | Bruce McLaren | New Zealand | Cooper-Climax | 10 |
| 10 | Jack Brabham | Australia | Brabham-Climax | 9 |
| 11 | Jo Siffert | Switzerland | Brabham-BRM | 5 |
| = | Denny Hulme | New Zealand | Brabham-Climax | 5 |
| 13 | Jochen Rindt | Austria | Cooper-Climax | 4 |
| 14 | Pedro Rodriguez | Mexico | Ferrari | 2 |
| = | Ronnie Bucknum | USA | Honda | 2 |
| = | Dick Attwood | GB | Lotus-Climax, Lotus-BRM | 2 |
| | Frank Gardner | Australia | Brabham-BRM | |
| | Bob Anderson | GB | Brabham-Climax | |
| | Jo Bonnier | Sweden | Brabham-Climax | |
| | Trevor Blokdyk | South Africa | Cooper-Ford | |
| | Neville Lederle | South Africa | Lotus-Climax | |
| | Doug Serruier | South Africa | LDS –Climax | |
| | Brausch Niemann | South Africa | Lotus-Ford | |
| | Ernest Pieterse | South Africa | Lotus-Climax | |
| | Paul Hawkins | GB | Brabham-Ford, Lotus-Climax | |
| | Tony Maggs | GB | Lotus-BRM | |
| | Piet de Klerk | South Africa | Alfa | |
| | Sam Tingle | South Africa | LDS-Alfa Romeo | |
| | David Prophet | GB | Brabham-Ford | |
| | John Love | South Africa | Cooper-Climax | |
| | Dave Charlton | South Africa | Lotus-Ford | |
| | Jackie Pretorius | South Africa | LDS-Alfa Romeo | |
| | Clive Puzey | South Africa | Lotus-Climax | |
| | Mike Hailwood | GB | Lotus-BRM | |
| | Lucien Bianchi | Belgium | BRM | |
| | Innes Ireland | GB | Lotus-BRM | |
| | Masten Gregory | USA | BRM | |
| | Willy Mairesse | France | BRM | |
| | Chris Amon | New Zealand | Lotus-BRM, Brabham-BRM | |
| | Alan Rollison | GB | Cooper-Ford | |
| | Brian Gubby | GB | Lotus-Climax | |
| | Ian Raby | GB | Brabham-BRM | |
| | John Rhodes | GB | Cooper-Climax | |
| | Roberto Bussinello | Italy | BRM | |
| | Gerhard Mitter | West Germany | Lotus-Climax | |
| | Giorgio Bassi | Italy | BRM | |
| | Giacomo Russo | Italy | Lotus-Climax | |
| | Giancarlo Baghetti | Italy | Brabham-Climax | |
| | Nino Vacarella | Italy | Ferrari | |
| | Bob Bondurant | USA | Ferrari, Lotus-BRM | |
| | Moises Solana | Mexico | Lotus-Climax | |
| | Ludovico Scarfotti | Italy | Ferrari | |

Points for the top six finishers (9, 6, 4, 3, 2, 1). Only the best six scores counted towards the championship.

## CONSTRUCTORS' CHAMPIONSHIP

| POS. | CONSTRUCTOR | POINTS |
|---|---|---|
| 1 | Lotus-Climax | 54 |
| 2 | BRM | 45 |
| 3 | Brabham-Climax | 27 |
| 4 | Ferrari | 26 |
| 5 | Cooper-Climax | 14 |
| 6 | Honda | 11 |
| 7 | Brabham-BRM | 5 |
| 8 | Lotus-BRM | 2 |

Points for top six finishers (9, 6, 4, 3, 2, 1). Points only counted for top-placed car for each constructor. Only the best six scores counted towards the championship.

1964 world champion, John Surtees in the Type 158 Ferrari.

## SOUTH AFRICAN GRAND PRIX: EAST LONDON *1 January Round: 1 Race: 132 85 x 2.436 miles*

| POS. | NO. | DRIVER | CAR/ENGINE | LAPS | TIME/RETIRED | GRID |
|---|---|---|---|---|---|---|
| 1 | 5 | Jim Clark | Lotus-Climax | 85 | 2:06'46.0 | 1 |
| 2 | 1 | John Surtees | Ferrari | 85 | +29.0 | 2 |
| 3 | 3 | Graham Hill | BRM | 85 | +31.8 | 5 |
| 4 | 6 | Mike Spence | Lotus-Climax | 85 | +54.4 | 4 |
| 5 | 9 | Bruce McLaren | Cooper-Climax | 84 | +1 Lap | 8 |
| 6 | 4 | Jackie Stewart | BRM | 83 | +2 Laps | 11 |
| 7 | 12 | Jo Siffert | Brabham-BRM | 83 | +2 Laps | 14 |
| 8 | 7 | Jack Brabham | Brabham-Climax | 81 | +4 Laps | 3 |
| 9 | 18 | Paul Hawkins | Brabham-Ford | 81 | +4 Laps | 16 |
| 10 | 20 | Peter de Klerk | Alfa Romeo | 79 | +6 Laps | 17 |
| 11 | 15 | Tony Maggs | Lotus-BRM | 77 | +8 Laps | 13 |
| 12 | 16 | Frank Gardner | Brabham-BRM | 75 | +10 Laps | 15 |
| 13 | 25 | Sam Tingle | LDS-Alfa Romeo | 73 | +12 Laps | 20 |
| 14 | 19 | David Prophet | Brabham-Ford | 71 | +14 Laps | 19 |
| 15 | 2 | Lorenzo Bandini | Ferrari | 66 | Ignition | 6 |
| NC | 14 | Bob Anderson | Brabham-Climax | 50 | Not classified | 12 |
| Ret | 11 | Jo Bonnier | Brabham-Climax | 42 | Clutch | 7 |
| Ret | 10 | Jochen Rindt | Cooper-Climax | 39 | Electrical | 10 |
| Ret | 17 | John Love | Cooper-Climax | 20 | Halfshaft | 18 |
| Ret | 8 | Dan Gurney | Brabham-Climax | 11 | Ignition | 9 |
| DNQ | 28 | Trevor Blokdyk | Cooper-Ford | | | |
| DNQ | 23 | Neville Lederle | Lotus-Climax | | | |
| DNQ | 21 | Doug Serrurier | LDS-Climax | | | |
| DNQ | 27 | Brausch Niemann | Lotus-Ford | | | |
| DNQ | 22 | Ernie Pieterse | Lotus-Climax | | | |
| DNPQ | 24 | Clive Puzey | Lotus-Climax | | | |
| DNPQ | 29 | Jackie Pretorius | LDS-Alfa Romeo | | | |
| DNPQ | 32 | Dave Charlton | Lotus-Ford | | | |

Winning speed: 98.004mph Lap leaders: Clark 1-85
Pole position: Clark, 1m 27.200s, 100.569mph
Fastest lap: Clark, 1m 27.600s, 100.110mph

## MONACO GRAND PRIX: MONTE CARLO *30 May Round: 2 Race: 133 100 x 1.954 miles*

| POS. | NO. | DRIVER | CAR/ENGINE | LAPS | TIME/RETIRED | GRID |
|---|---|---|---|---|---|---|
| 1 | 3 | Graham Hill | BRM | 100 | 2:37'39.6 | 1 |
| 2 | 17 | Lorenzo Bandini | Ferrari | 100 | +1'04.0 | 4 |
| 3 | 4 | Jackie Stewart | BRM | 100 | +1'41.9 | 3 |
| 4 | 18 | John Surtees | Ferrari | 99 | Out of fuel | 5 |
| 5 | 7 | Bruce McLaren | Cooper-Climax | 98 | +2 Laps | 7 |
| 6 | 14 | Jo Siffert | Brabham-BRM | 98 | +2 Laps | 10 |
| 7 | 12 | Jo Bonnier | Brabham-Climax | 97 | +3 Laps | 13 |
| 8 | 2 | Denny Hulme | Brabham-Climax | 92 | +8 Laps | 8 |
| 9 | 9 | Bob Anderson | Brabham-Climax | 85 | +15 Laps | 9 |
| 10 | 10 | Paul Hawkins | Lotus-Climax | 79 | Accident | 14 |
| Ret | 1 | Jack Brabham | Brabham-Climax | 43 | Engine | 2 |
| Ret | 15 | Richard Attwood | Lotus-BRM | 43 | Wheel | 6 |
| Ret | 19 | Ronnie Bucknum | Honda | 33 | Gearbox | 15 |
| Ret | 11 | Frank Gardner | Brabham-BRM | 29 | Engine | 11 |
| Ret | 16 | Mike Hailwood | Lotus-BRM | 12 | Gearbox | 12 |
| Ret | 20 | Richie Ginther | Honda | 0 | Halfshaft | 17 |
| DNQ | 8 | Jochen Rindt | Cooper-Climax | | | |

Winning speed: 74.371mph Lap leaders: G Hill 1-24, 65-100; Stewart 25-29; Bandini 30-33, 43-64; Brabham 34-42
Pole position: G Hill, 1m 32.500s, 76.056mph
Fastest lap: G Hill, 1m 31.700s, 76.719mph

## BELGIAN GRAND PRIX: SPA-FRANCORCHAMPS *13 June Round: 3 Race: 135 32 x 8.761 miles*

| POS. | NO. | DRIVER | CAR/ENGINE | LAPS | TIME/RETIRED | GRID |
|---|---|---|---|---|---|---|
| 1 | 17 | Jim Clark | Lotus-Climax | 32 | 2:23'34.8 | 2 |
| 2 | 8 | Jackie Stewart | BRM | 32 | +44.8 | 3 |
| 3 | 4 | Bruce McLaren | Cooper-Climax | 31 | +1 Lap | 9 |
| 4 | 14 | Jack Brabham | Brabham-Climax | 31 | +1 Lap | 10 |
| 5 | 7 | Graham Hill | BRM | 31 | +1 Lap | 1 |
| 6 | 10 | Richie Ginther | Honda | 31 | +1 Lap | 4 |
| 7 | 18 | Mike Spence | Lotus-Climax | 31 | +1 Lap | 12 |
| 8 | 21 | Jo Siffert | Brabham-BRM | 31 | +1 Lap | 8 |
| 9 | 2 | Lorenzo Bandini | Ferrari | 30 | +2 Laps | 15 |
| 10 | 15 | Dan Gurney | Brabham-Climax | 30 | +2 Laps | 5 |
| 11 | 5 | Jochen Rindt | Cooper-Climax | 29 | +3 Laps | 14 |
| 12 | 27 | Lucien Bianchi | BRM | 29 | +3 Laps | 17 |
| 13 | 22 | Innes Ireland | Lotus-BRM | 27 | +5 Laps | 16 |
| 14 | 23 | Richard Attwood | Lotus-BRM | 26 | Accident | 13 |
| Ret | 29 | Masten Gregory | BRM | 12 | Fuel pump | 20 |
| Ret | 20 | Jo Bonnier | Brabham-Climax | 9 | Ignition | 7 |
| Ret | 11 | Ronnie Bucknum | Honda | 9 | Gearbox | 11 |
| Ret | 1 | John Surtees | Ferrari | 5 | Engine | 6 |
| Ret | 26 | Frank Gardner | Brabham-BRM | 3 | Ignition | 19 |

Winning speed: 117.159mph Lap leaders: Clark 1-32
Pole position: G Hill, 3m 45.400s, 139.933mph
Fastest lap: Clark, 4m 12.900s, 124.716mph

## FRENCH GRAND PRIX: CLERMONT-FERRAND *27 June Round: 4 Race: 135 40 x 5.005 miles*

| POS. | NO. | DRIVER | CAR/ENGINE | LAPS | TIME/RETIRED | GRID |
|---|---|---|---|---|---|---|
| 1 | 6 | Jim Clark | Lotus-Climax | 40 | 2:14'38.4 | 1 |
| 2 | 12 | Jackie Stewart | BRM | 40 | +26.3 | 2 |
| 3 | 2 | John Surtees | Ferrari | 40 | +2'33.5 | 4 |
| 4 | 16 | Denny Hulme | Brabham-Climax | 40 | +2'53.1 | 6 |
| 5 | 10 | Graham Hill | BRM | 39 | +1 Lap | 13 |
| 6 | 36 | Jo Siffert | Brabham-BRM | 39 | +1 Lap | 14 |
| 7 | 8 | Mike Spence | Lotus-Climax | 39 | +1 Lap | 10 |
| 8 | 4 | Lorenzo Bandini | Ferrari | 36 | Accident | 3 |
| 9 | 30 | Bob Anderson | Brabham-Climax | 34 | Fuel system | 15 |
| Ret | 18 | Bruce McLaren | Cooper-Climax | 23 | Suspension | 9 |
| Ret | 34 | Jo Bonnier | Brabham-Climax | 21 | Alternator | 11 |
| Ret | 24 | Chris Amon | Lotus-BRM | 20 | Fuel system | 8 |
| Ret | 22 | Innes Ireland | Lotus-BRM | 18 | Gearbox | 17 |
| Ret | 14 | Dan Gurney | Brabham-Climax | 16 | Engine | 5 |
| Ret | 26 | Richie Ginther | Honda | 9 | Ignition | 7 |
| Ret | 28 | Ronnie Bucknum | Honda | 4 | Ignition | 16 |
| Ret | 20 | Jochen Rindt | Cooper-Climax | 3 | Accident | 12 |

Winning speed: 89.218 mph Lap leaders: Clark 1-40
Pole position: Clark, 3m 18.300s, 90.865mph
Fastest lap: Clark, 3m 18.900s, 90.591mph

## BRITISH GRAND PRIX: SILVERSTONE *10 July Round: 5 Race: 136 80 x 2.927 miles*

| POS. | NO. | DRIVER | CAR/ENGINE | LAPS | TIME/RETIRED | GRID |
|---|---|---|---|---|---|---|
| 1 | 5 | Jim Clark | Lotus-Climax | 80 | 2:05'25.4 | 1 |
| 2 | 3 | Graham Hill | BRM | 80 | +3.2 | 2 |
| 3 | 1 | John Surtees | Ferrari | 80 | +27.6 | 5 |
| 4 | 6 | Mike Spence | Lotus-Climax | 80 | +39.6 | 6 |
| 5 | 4 | Jackie Stewart | BRM | 80 | +1'14.6 | 4 |
| 6 | 7 | Dan Gurney | Brabham-Climax | 79 | +1 Lap | 7 |
| 7 | 15 | Jo Bonnier | Brabham-Climax | 79 | +1 Lap | 14 |
| 8 | 17 | Frank Gardner | Brabham-BRM | 78 | +2 Laps | 13 |
| 9 | 16 | Jo Siffert | Brabham-BRM | 78 | +2 Laps | 18 |
| 10 | 9 | Bruce McLaren | Cooper-Climax | 77 | +3 Laps | 11 |
| 11 | 24 | Ian Raby | Brabham-BRM | 73 | +7 Laps | 20 |
| 12 | 12 | Masten Gregory | BRM | 70 | +10 Laps | 19 |
| 13 | 22 | Richard Attwood | Lotus-BRM | 63 | +17 Laps | 16 |
| 14 | 10 | Jochen Rindt | Cooper-Climax | 62 | Engine | 12 |
| Ret | 23 | Innes Ireland | Lotus-BRM | 41 | Engine | 15 |
| Ret | 20 | John Rhodes | Cooper-Climax | 38 | Ignition | 21 |
| Ret | 18 | Bob Anderson | Brabham-Climax | 33 | Gearbox | 17 |
| Ret | 14 | Denny Hulme | Brabham-Climax | 29 | Alternator | 10 |
| Ret | 11 | Richie Ginther | Honda | 26 | Injection | 3 |
| Ret | 2 | Lorenzo Bandini | Ferrari | 2 | Engine | 9 |
| DNS | 8 | Jack Brabham | Brabham-Climax | 0 | Non starter | 8 |
| DNQ | 25 | Alan Rollinson | Cooper-Ford | | | |
| DNQ | 26 | Brian Gubby | Lotus-Climax | | | |

Winning speed: 112.017 mph Lap leaders: Clark 1-80
Pole position: Clark, 1m 30.800s, 116.048mph
Fastest lap: G Hill, 1m 32.200s, 114.286mph

## DUTCH GRAND PRIX: ZANDVOORT *18 July Round: 6 Race: 137 80 x 2.605 miles*

| POS. | NO. | DRIVER | CAR/ENGINE | LAPS | TIME/RETIRED | GRID |
|---|---|---|---|---|---|---|
| 1 | 6 | Jim Clark | Lotus-Climax | 80 | 2:03'59.1 | 2 |
| 2 | 12 | Jackie Stewart | BRM | 80 | +8.0 | 6 |
| 3 | 16 | Dan Gurney | Brabham-Climax | 80 | +13.0 | 5 |
| 4 | 10 | Graham Hill | BRM | 80 | +45.1 | 1 |
| 5 | 14 | Denny Hulme | Brabham-Climax | 79 | +1 Lap | 7 |
| 6 | 22 | Richie Ginther | Honda | 79 | +1 Lap | 3 |
| 7 | 2 | John Surtees | Ferrari | 79 | +1 Lap | 4 |
| 8 | 8 | Mike Spence | Lotus-Climax | 79 | +1 Lap | 8 |
| 9 | 4 | Lorenzo Bandini | Ferrari | 79 | +1 Lap | 12 |
| 10 | 38 | Innes Ireland | Lotus-BRM | 78 | +2 Laps | 13 |
| 11 | 30 | Frank Gardner | Brabham-BRM | 77 | +3 Laps | 11 |
| 12 | 34 | Richard Attwood | Lotus-BRM | 77 | +3 Laps | 17 |
| 13 | 28 | Jo Siffert | Brabham-BRM | 55 | +25 Laps | 10 |
| Ret | 20 | Jochen Rindt | Cooper-Climax | 48 | Oil pressure | 14 |
| Ret | 18 | Bruce McLaren | Cooper-Climax | 36 | Differential | 9 |
| Ret | 26 | Jo Bonnier | Brabham-Climax | 16 | Oil leak | 15 |
| Ret | 36 | Bob Anderson | Brabham-Climax | 11 | Engine | 16 |

Winning speed: 100.867 miles Lap leaders: Ginther 1-2; G Hill 3-5; Clark 6-80;
Pole position: G Hill, 1m 30.700s, 103.412mph
Fastest lap: Clark, 1m 30.600s, 103.526mph

## GERMAN GRAND PRIX: NURBURGRING *1 August Round: 7 Race: 138 15 x 14.173 miles*

| POS. | NO. | DRIVER | CAR/ENGINE | LAPS | TIME/RETIRED | GRID |
|---|---|---|---|---|---|---|
| 1 | 1 | Jim Clark | Lotus-Climax | 15 | 2:07'52.4 | 1 |
| 2 | 9 | Graham Hill | BRM | 15 | +15.9 | 3 |
| 3 | 5 | Dan Gurney | Brabham-Climax | 15 | +21.4 | 5 |
| 4 | 12 | Jochen Rindt | Cooper-Climax | 15 | +3'29.6 | 8 |
| 5 | 4 | Jack Brabham | Brabham-Climax | 15 | +4'41.2 | 14 |
| 6 | 8 | Lorenzo Bandini | Ferrari | 15 | +5'08.6 | 7 |
| 7 | 16 | Jo Bonnier | Brabham-Climax | 15 | +5'58.5 | 9 |
| 8 | 24 | Masten Gregory | BRM | 14 | +1 Lap | 19 |
| Ret | 7 | John Surtees | Ferrari | 11 | Gearbox | 4 |
| Ret | 17 | Jo Siffert | Brabham-BRM | 9 | Engine | 11 |
| Ret | 2 | Mike Spence | Lotus-Climax | 8 | Transmission | 6 |
| Ret | 3 | Gerhard Mitter | Lotus-Climax | 8 | Water leak | 12 |
| Ret | 20 | Richard Attwood | Lotus-BRM | 8 | Water leak | 17 |
| Ret | 11 | Bruce McLaren | Cooper-Climax | 7 | Gearbox | 10 |
| Ret | 6 | Denny Hulme | Brabham-Climax | 5 | Fuel leak | 13 |
| Ret | 19 | Chris Amon | Lotus-BRM | 3 | Electrical | 16 |
| Ret | 22 | Paul Hawkins | Lotus-Climax | 3 | Oil leak | 20 |
| Ret | 10 | Jackie Stewart | BRM | 2 | Suspension | 2 |
| Ret | 21 | Frank Gardner | Brabham-BRM | 0 | Gearbox | 18 |
| DNQ | 25 | R.Bussinello | BRM | | | |
| DNQ | 23 | Ian Raby | Brabham-Climax | | | |

Winning speed: 99.756mph Lap leaders: Clark 1-15
Pole position: Clark, 8m 22.700s, 101.501mph
Fastest lap: Clark, 8m 24.100s, 101.219mph

## ITALIAN GRAND PRIX: MONZA *12 September Round: 8 Race: 139 76 x 3.573 miles*

| POS. | NO. | DRIVER | CAR/ENGINE | LAPS | TIME/RETIRED | GRID |
|---|---|---|---|---|---|---|
| 1 | 32 | Jackie Stewart | BRM | 76 | 2:04'52.8 | 3 |
| 2 | 30 | Graham Hill | BRM | 76 | +3.3 | 4 |
| 3 | 12 | Dan Gurney | Brabham-Climax | 76 | +16.5 | 9 |
| 4 | 4 | Lorenzo Bandini | Ferrari | 76 | +1'15.9 | 5 |
| 5 | 16 | Bruce McLaren | Cooper-Climax | 75 | +1 Lap | 11 |
| 6 | 40 | Richard Attwood | Lotus-BRM | 75 | +1 Lap | 13 |
| 7 | 42 | Jo Bonnier | Brabham-Climax | 74 | +2 Laps | 14 |
| 8 | 18 | Jochen Rindt | Cooper-Climax | 74 | +2 Laps | 7 |
| 9 | 38 | Innes Ireland | Lotus-BRM | 74 | +2 Laps | 18 |
| 10 | 24 | Jim Clark | Lotus-Climax | 63 | Fuel pump | 1 |
| 11 | 26 | Mike Spence | Lotus-Climax | 62 | Alternator | 8 |
| 12 | 6 | Nino Vaccarella | Ferrari | 58 | Engine | 15 |
| 13 | 50 | R.Bussinello | BRM | 58 | Oil pressure | 21 |
| 14 | 20 | Richie Ginther | Honda | 56 | Ignition | 17 |
| Ret | 14 | Denny Hulme | Brabham-Climax | 46 | Suspension | 12 |
| Ret | 46 | Frank Gardner | Brabham-BRM | 45 | Engine | 16 |
| Ret | 44 | Jo Siffert | Brabham-BRM | 43 | Gearbox | 10 |
| Ret | 28 | Geki | Lotus-Climax | 37 | Gearbox | 20 |
| Ret | 8 | John Surtees | Ferrari | 34 | Clutch | 2 |
| Ret | 22 | Ronnie Bucknum | Honda | 27 | Ignition | 6 |
| Ret | 48 | Masten Gregory | BRM | 22 | Gearbox | 23 |
| Ret | 10 | Giancarlo Baghetti | Brabham-Climax | 12 | Engine | 19 |
| Ret | 52 | Giorgio Bassi | BRM | 8 | Engine | 22 |

Winning speed: 130.464mph Lap leaders: Clark 1-2, 4, 7, 10, 18, 21, 27, 33-36, 38, 44, 46, 51, 53-54, 57; G Hill 3, 5, 25-26, 28, 40-41, 43, 45, 50, 55-56, 64, 70-71, 73, 74; Stewart 6, 8-9, 11-17, 19-20, 22-24, 29-32, 37, 39, 42, 47-49, 52, 58-63, 65-69, 72, 75-76
Pole position: Clark, 1m 35.900s, 134.123mph
Fastest lap: Clark, 1m 36.400s, 133.427mph

## UNITED STATES GRAND PRIX: WATKINS GLEN *3 October Round: 9 Race: 140 110 x 2.300 miles*

| POS. | NO. | DRIVER | CAR/ENGINE | LAPS | TIME/RETIRED | GRID |
|---|---|---|---|---|---|---|
| 1 | 3 | Graham Hill | BRM | 110 | 2:20'36.1 | 1 |
| 2 | 8 | Dan Gurney | Brabham-Climax | 110 | +12.5 | 8 |
| 3 | 7 | Jack Brabham | Brabham-Climax | 110 | +57.5 | 7 |
| 4 | 2 | Lorenzo Bandini | Ferrari | 109 | +1 Lap | 5 |
| 5 | 14 | Pedro Rodriguez | Ferrari | 109 | +1 Lap | 15 |
| 6 | 10 | Jochen Rindt | Cooper-Climax | 108 | +2 Laps | 13 |
| 7 | 11 | Richie Ginther | Honda | 108 | +2 Laps | 3 |
| 8 | 15 | Jo Bonnier | Brabham-Climax | 107 | +3 Laps | 10 |
| 9 | 24 | Bob Bondurant | Ferrari | 106 | +4 Laps | 14 |
| 10 | 21 | Richard Attwood | Lotus-BRM | 101 | +9 Laps | 16 |
| 11 | 16 | Jo Siffert | Brabham-BRM | 99 | +11 Laps | 11 |
| 12 | 18 | Moises Solana | Lotus-Climax | 95 | +15 Laps | 17 |
| 13 | 12 | Ronnie Bucknum | Honda | 92 | +18 Laps | 12 |
| Ret | 4 | Jackie Stewart | BRM | 12 | Suspension | 6 |
| Ret | 5 | Jim Clark | Lotus-Climax | 11 | Engine | 9 |
| Ret | 9 | Bruce McLaren | Cooper-Climax | 11 | Oil pressure | 2 |
| Ret | 6 | Mike Spence | Lotus-Climax | 9 | Engine | 4 |
| Ret | 22 | Innes Ireland | Lotus-BRM | 9 | Unwell | 18 |

Winning speed: 107.965mph Lap leaders: G Hill 1, 5-110; Clark 2-4
Pole position: G Hill, 1m 11.250s, 116.211mph
Fastest lap: G Hill, 1m 11.900s, 115.160mph

## MEXICAN GRAND PRIX: MEXICO CITY *24 October Round: 10 Race: 14 65 x 3.107 miles*

| POS. | NO. | DRIVER | CAR/ENGINE | LAPS | TIME/RETIRED | GRID |
|---|---|---|---|---|---|---|
| 1 | 11 | Richie Ginther | Honda | 65 | 2:08'32.10 | 3 |
| 2 | 8 | Dan Gurney | Brabham-Climax | 65 | +2.89 | 2 |
| 3 | 6 | Mike Spence | Lotus-Climax | 65 | +1'00.15 | 6 |
| 4 | 16 | Jo Siffert | Brabham-BRM | 65 | +1'54.42 | 11 |
| 5 | 12 | Ronnie Bucknum | Honda | 64 | +1 Lap | 10 |
| 6 | 21 | Richard Attwood | Lotus-BRM | 64 | +1 Lap | 17 |
| 7 | 14 | Pedro Rodriguez | Ferrari | 62 | +3 Laps | 14 |
| 8 | 2 | Lorenzo Bandini | Ferrari | 62 | +3 Laps | 7 |
| Ret | 3 | Graham Hill | BRM | 56 | Engine | 5 |
| Ret | 18 | Moises Solana | Lotus-Climax | 55 | Ignition | 9 |
| Ret | 15 | Jo Bonnier | Brabham-Climax | 43 | Suspension | 12 |
| Ret | 10 | Jochen Rindt | Cooper-Climax | 39 | Ignition | 16 |
| Ret | 7 | Jack Brabham | Brabham-Climax | 38 | Oil leak | 14 |
| Ret | 4 | Jackie Stewart | BRM | 35 | Clutch | 8 |
| Ret | 22 | Bob Bondurant | Lotus-BRM | 29 | Suspension | 18 |
| Ret | 9 | Bruce McLaren | Cooper-Climax | 25 | Gearbox | 15 |
| Ret | 5 | Jim Clark | Lotus-Climax | 8 | Engine | 1 |

Winning speed: 94.268mph Lap leaders: Ginther 1-65
Pole position: Clark, 1m 56.170s, 96.279mph
Fastest lap: Gurney, 1m 55.840s, 96.553mph

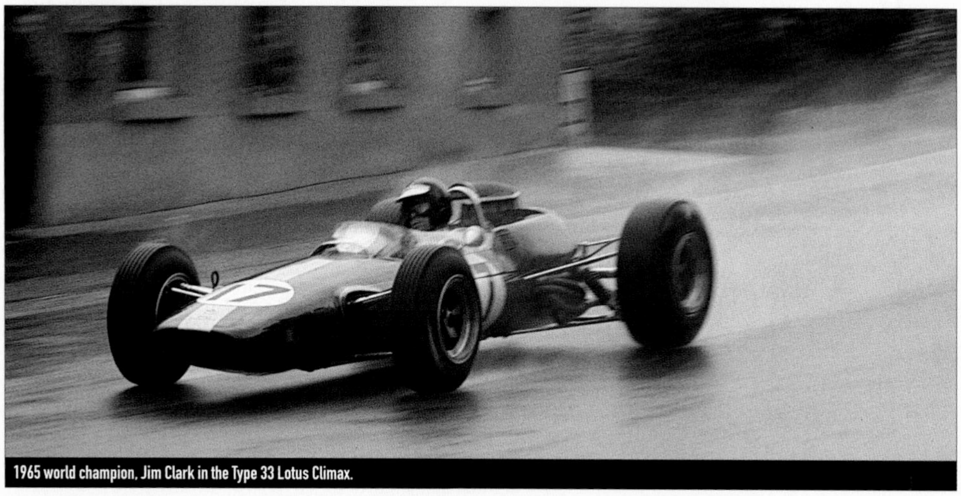

1965 world champion, Jim Clark in the Type 33 Lotus Climax.

# 1966

## DRIVERS' CHAMPION: JACK BRABHAM
## CONSTRUCTORS' CHAMPION: BRABHAM REPCO

### DRIVERS' CHAMPIONSHIP

| POS. | DRIVER | NATIONALITY | CAR | POINTS |
|---|---|---|---|---|
| 1 | Jack Brabham | Australia | Brabham-Repco | 42 (3) |
| 2 | John Surtees | GB | Ferrari, Cooper-Maserati | 28 |
| 3 | Jochen Rindt | Austria | Cooper-Maserati | 22 (2) |
| 4 | Denny Hulme | New Zealand | Brabham-Climax, Brabham-Repco | 18 |
| 5 | Graham Hill | GB | BRM | 17 |
| 6 | Jim Clark | GB | Lotus-Climax, Lotus-BRM | 16 |
| 7 | Jackie Stewart | GB | BRM | 14 |
| 8 | Mike Parks | GB | Ferrari | 12 |
| = | Lorenzo Bandini | Italy | Ferrari | 12 |
| 10 | Ludovico Scarfiotti | Italy | Ferrari | 9 |
| 11 | Richie Ginther | USA | Cooper-Maserati, Honda | 5 |
| 12 | Dan Gurney | USA | Eagle-Climax, Eagle-Weslake | 4 |
| = | Mike Spence | GB | Lotus-BRM | 4 |
| 14 | Bob Bondurant | USA | BRM, Eagle-Climax Eagle-Weslake | 3 |
| = | Jo Siffert | Switzerland | Brabham-BRM, Cooper-Maserati | 3 |
| = | Bruce McLaren | New Zealand | McLaren-Serenissima McLaren-Ford | 3 |
| 17 | John Taylor | GB | Brabham-BRM | 1 |
| = | Bob Anderson | GB | Brabham-Climax | 1 |
| = | Peter Arundell | GB | Lotus-Climax, Lotus-BRM | 1 |
| = | Jo Bonnier | Sweden | Cooper-Maserati, Brabham-Climax | 1 |
| | Phil Hill | USA | Lotus-Climax, McLaren-Ford Eagle-Climax | |
| | Guy Ligier | France | Cooper-Maserati | |
| | Vic Wilson | GB | BRM | |
| | Chris Amon | NZ | Cooper-Maserati, Brabham-BRM | |
| | Pedro Rodriguez | Mexico | Lotus-Climax, Lotus-BRM | |
| | Trevor Taylor | GB | Shannon-Climax | |
| | Chris Lawrence | GB | Cooper-Ferrari | |
| | Chris Irwin | GB | Brabham-Climax | |
| | Giacomo Russo | Italy | Lotus-Climax | |
| | Giancarlo Baghetti | Italy | Ferrari | |
| | Ronnie Bucknum | USA | Honda | |
| | Innes Ireland | GB | BRM | |
| | Moises Solana | Mexico | Cooper-Maserati | |

Points for the top six finishers (9, 6, 4, 3, 2, 1). Only the best five scores counted towards the championship. Drivers who were not classified did not get points. Formula Two cars raced simulataneously with Formula One cars at the German Grand Prix but were ineligible for points which were awarded to the top six Formula One finishers.

### CONSTRUCTORS' CHAMPIONSHIP

| POS. | CONSTRUCTOR | POINTS |
|---|---|---|
| 1 | Brabham-Repco | 42 |
| 2 | Ferrari | 31 |
| 3 | Cooper-Maserati | 30 |
| 4 | BRM | 22 |
| 5 | Lotus-BRM | 13 |
| 6 | Lotus-Climax | 8 |
| 7 | Eagle-Climax | 4 |
| 8 | Honda | 3 |
| 9 | McLaren-Ford | 2 |
| 10 | Brabham-BRM | 1 |
| = | McLaren-Serenissima | 1 |
| = | Brabham-Climax | 1 |

Points for top six finishers (9, 6, 4, 3, 2, 1). Points only counted for top-placed car for each constructor. Only the best five scores counted towards the championship.

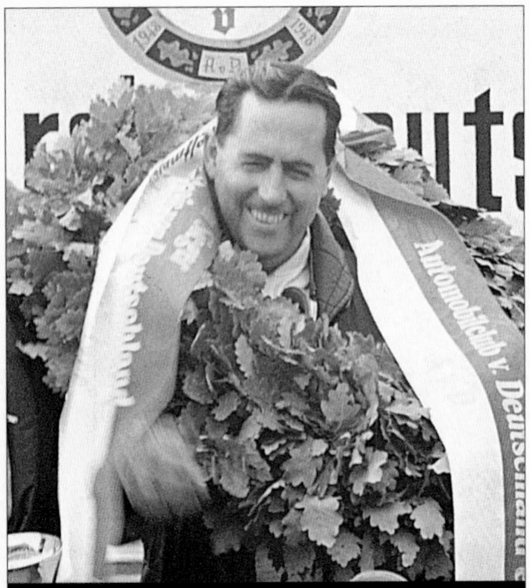

1966 world champion, Jack Brabham.

### MONACO GRAND PRIX: MONTE CARLO *22 May Round: 1 Race: 142 100 x 1.954 miles*

| POS. | NO. | DRIVER | CAR/ENGINE | LAPS | TIME/RETIRED | GRID |
|---|---|---|---|---|---|---|
| 1 | 12 | Jackie Stewart | BRM | 100 | 2:33'10.5 | 3 |
| 2 | 16 | Lorenzo Bandini | Ferrari | 100 | +40.2 | 5 |
| 3 | 11 | Graham Hill | BRM | 99 | +1 Lap | 4 |
| 4 | 19 | Bob Bondurant | BRM | 95 | +5 Laps | 16 |
| Ret | 9 | Richie Ginther | Cooper-Maserati | 80 | Transmission | 9 |
| NC | 21 | Guy Ligier | Cooper-Maserati | 75 | Not classified | 15 |
| NC | 18 | Jo Bonnier | Cooper-Maserati | 73 | Not classified | 14 |
| Ret | 4 | Jim Clark | Lotus-Climax | 60 | Suspension | 1 |
| Ret | 10 | Jochen Rindt | Cooper-Maserati | 56 | Engine | 7 |
| Ret | 14 | Jo Siffert | Brabham-BRM | 35 | Clutch | 13 |
| Ret | 6 | Mike Spence | Lotus-BRM | 34 | Suspension | 12 |
| Ret | 7 | Jack Brabham | Brabham-Repco | 17 | Gearbox | 11 |
| Ret | 17 | John Surtees | Ferrari | 16 | Transmission | 2 |
| Ret | 8 | Denny Hulme | Brabham-Climax | 15 | Transmission | 6 |
| Ret | 2 | Bruce McLaren | McLaren-Ford | 9 | Oil leak | 10 |
| Ret | 15 | Bob Anderson | Brabham-Climax | 3 | Engine | 8 |

Winning speed: 76.548mph Lap leaders: Surtees 1-14; Stewart 15-100
Pole position: Clark, 1m 29.900s, 78.255mph
Fastest lap: Bandini, 1m 29.800s, 78.343mph

### BELGIAN GRAND PRIX: SPA-FRANCORCHAMPS *12 June Round: 2 Race: 143 28 x 8.761 miles*

| POS. | NO. | DRIVER | CAR/ENGINE | LAPS | TIME/RETIRED | GRID |
|---|---|---|---|---|---|---|
| 1 | 6 | John Surtees | Ferrari | 28 | 2:09'11.3 | 1 |
| 2 | 19 | Jochen Rindt | Cooper-Maserati | 28 | +42.1 | 2 |
| 3 | 7 | Lorenzo Bandini | Ferrari | 27 | +1 Lap | 5 |
| 4 | 3 | Jack Brabham | Brabham-Repco | 26 | +2 Laps | 4 |
| 5 | 18 | Richie Ginther | Cooper-Maserati | 25 | +3 Laps | 8 |
| NC | 22 | Guy Ligier | Cooper-Maserati | 24 | Not classified | 12 |
| NC | 27 | Dan Gurney | Eagle-Climax | 23 | Not classified | 15 |
| Ret | 15 | Jackie Stewart | BRM | 0 | Accident | 3 |
| Ret | 20 | Jo Bonnier | Cooper-Maserati | 0 | Accident | 6 |
| Ret | 16 | Mike Spence | Lotus-BRM | 0 | Accident | 7 |
| Ret | 14 | Graham Hill | BRM | 0 | Accident | 9 |
| Ret | 10 | Jim Clark | Lotus-Climax | 0 | Engine | 10 |
| Ret | 8 | Bob Bondurant | BRM | 0 | Accident | 11 |
| Ret | 4 | Denny Hulme | Brabham-Climax | 0 | Accident | 13 |
| Ret | 21 | Jo Siffert | Cooper-Maserati | 0 | Accident | 14 |

Winning speed: 113.935mph Lap leaders: Surtees 1, 3, 24-28; Bandini 2; Rindt 4-23
Pole position: Surtees, 3m 38.000s, 144.683mph
Fastest lap: Surtees, 4m 18.700s, 121.920mph

### FRENCH GRAND PRIX: REIMS *3 July Round: 3 Race: 144 48 x 5.159 miles*

| POS. | NO. | DRIVER | CAR/ENGINE | LAPS | TIME/RETIRED | GRID |
|---|---|---|---|---|---|---|
| 1 | 12 | Jack Brabham | Brabham-Repco | 48 | 1:48'31.3 | 4 |
| 2 | 22 | Mike Parkes | Ferrari | 48 | +9.5 | 3 |
| 3 | 14 | Denny Hulme | Brabham-Repco | 46 | +2 Laps | 9 |
| 4 | 6 | Jochen Rindt | Cooper-Maserati | 46 | +2 Laps | 5 |
| 5 | 26 | Dan Gurney | Eagle-Climax | 45 | +3 Laps | 14 |
| 6 | 44 | John Taylor | Brabham-BRM | 45 | +3 Laps | 15 |
| 7 | 36 | Bob Anderson | Brabham-Climax | 44 | +4 Laps | 12 |
| 8 | 8 | Chris Amon | Cooper-Maserati | 44 | +4 Laps | 7 |
| NC | 42 | Guy Ligier | Cooper-Maserati | 42 | Not classified | 11 |
| Ret | 2 | Pedro Rodriguez | Lotus-Climax | 40 | Oil leak | 13 |
| NC | 20 | Lorenzo Bandini | Ferrari | 37 | Not classified | 1 |
| NC | 30 | Jo Bonnier | Brabham-Climax | 32 | Not classified | 17 |
| Ret | 16 | Graham Hill | BRM | 13 | Engine | 8 |
| Ret | 38 | Jo Siffert | Cooper-Maserati | 10 | Fuel system | 6 |
| Ret | 32 | Mike Spence | Lotus-BRM | 8 | Clutch | 10 |
| Ret | 10 | John Surtees | Cooper-Maserati | 5 | Fuel system | 2 |
| Ret | 4 | Peter Arundell | Lotus-BRM | 3 | Gearbox | 16 |

Winning speed: 136.902mph Lap leaders: Bandini 1-31; Brabham 32-48
Pole position: Bandini, 2m 7.800s, 145.313mph
Fastest lap: Bandini, 2m 11.300s, 141.440mph

### BRITISH GRAND PRIX: BRANDS HATCH *16 July Round: 4 Race: 145 80 x 2.650 miles*

| POS. | NO. | DRIVER | CAR/ENGINE | LAPS | TIME/RETIRED | GRID |
|---|---|---|---|---|---|---|
| 1 | 5 | Jack Brabham | Brabham-Repco | 80 | 2:13'13.4 | 1 |
| 2 | 6 | Denny Hulme | Brabham-Repco | 80 | +9.6 | 2 |
| 3 | 3 | Graham Hill | BRM | 79 | +1 Lap | 4 |
| 4 | 1 | Jim Clark | Lotus-Climax | 79 | +1 Lap | 5 |
| 5 | 11 | Jochen Rindt | Cooper-Maserati | 79 | +1 Lap | 7 |
| 6 | 14 | Bruce McLaren | McLaren-Serenissima | 78 | +2 Laps | 13 |
| 7 | 7 | Chris Irwin | Brabham-Climax | 78 | +2 Laps | 12 |
| 8 | 22 | John Taylor | Brabham-BRM | 76 | +4 Laps | 16 |
| 9 | 25 | Bob Bondurant | BRM | 76 | +4 Laps | 14 |
| 10 | 19 | Guy Ligier | Cooper-Maserati | 75 | +5 Laps | 17 |
| 11 | 24 | Chris Lawrence | Cooper-Ferrari | 73 | +7 Laps | 19 |
| NC | 21 | Bob Anderson | Brabham-Climax | 70 | Not classified | 10 |
| NC | 20 | Jo Siffert | Cooper-Maserati | 70 | Not classified | 11 |
| Ret | 12 | John Surtees | Cooper-Maserati | 67 | Transmission | 6 |
| Ret | 18 | Jo Bonnier | Brabham-Climax | 42 | Clutch | 15 |
| Ret | 2 | Peter Arundell | Lotus-BRM | 32 | Gearbox | 20 |
| Ret | 4 | Jackie Stewart | BRM | 17 | Engine | 8 |
| Ret | 17 | Mike Spence | Lotus-BRM | 15 | Oil leak | 9 |
| Ret | 16 | Dan Gurney | Eagle-Climax | 9 | Engine | 3 |
| Ret | 23 | Trevor Taylor | Shannon-Climax | 0 | Engine | 18 |

Winning speed: 95.479mph Lap leaders: Brabham 1-80
Pole position: Brabham, 1m 34.500s, 100.952mph
Fastest lap: Brabham, 1m 37.000s, 98.351mph

### DUTCH GRAND PRIX: ZANDVOORT *Round: 5 Race: 146 90 x 2.605 miles*

| POS. | NO. | DRIVER | CAR/ENGINE | LAPS | TIME/RETIRED | GRID |
|---|---|---|---|---|---|---|
| 1 | 16 | Jack Brabham | Brabham-Repco | 90 | 2:20'32.5 | 1 |
| 2 | 12 | Graham Hill | BRM | 89 | +1 Lap | 7 |
| 3 | 6 | Jim Clark | Lotus-Climax | 88 | +2 Laps | 3 |
| 4 | 14 | Jackie Stewart | BRM | 88 | +2 Laps | 8 |
| 5 | 32 | Mike Spence | Lotus-BRM | 87 | +3 Laps | 12 |
| 6 | 2 | Lorenzo Bandini | Ferrari | 87 | +3 Laps | 9 |
| 7 | 30 | Jo Bonnier | Cooper-Maserati | 84 | +6 Laps | 13 |
| 8 | 38 | John Taylor | Brabham-BRM | 84 | +6 Laps | 17 |
| 9 | 36 | Guy Ligier | Cooper-Maserati | 84 | +6 Laps | 16 |
| Ret | 28 | Jo Siffert | Cooper-Maserati | 79 | Engine | 11 |
| Ret | 34 | Bob Anderson | Brabham-Climax | 73 | Suspension | 14 |
| Ret | 24 | John Surtees | Cooper-Maserati | 44 | Electrical | 10 |
| Ret | 18 | Denny Hulme | Brabham-Repco | 37 | Ignition | 2 |
| Ret | 8 | Peter Arundell | Lotus-BRM | 28 | Ignition | 15 |
| Ret | 10 | Dan Gurney | Eagle-Climax | 26 | Oil leak | 4 |
| Ret | 4 | Mike Parkes | Ferrari | 10 | Accident | 5 |
| Ret | 26 | Jochen Rindt | Cooper-Maserati | 2 | Accident | 6 |

Winning speed: 100.107mph Lap leaders: Brabham 1-26, 76-90; Clark 27-75
Pole position: Brabham, 1m 28.100s, 106.464mph
Fastest lap: Hulme, 1m 30.600s, 103.526mph

### GERMAN GRAND PRIX: NURBURGRING *7 August Round: 6 Race: 147 15 x 14.173 miles*

| POS. | NO. | DRIVER | CAR/ENGINE | LAPS | TIME/RETIRED | GRID |
|---|---|---|---|---|---|---|
| 1 | 3 | Jack Brabham | Brabham-Repco | 15 | 2:27'03.0 | 5 |
| 2 | 7 | John Surtees | Cooper-Maserati | 15 | +44.4 | 2 |
| 3 | 8 | Jochen Rindt | Cooper-Maserati | 15 | +2'32.6 | 9 |
| 4 | 5 | Graham Hill | BRM | 15 | +6'41.4 | 10 |
| 5 | 6 | Jackie Stewart | BRM | 15 | +8'28.9 | 3 |
| 6 | 9 | Lorenzo Bandini | Ferrari | 15 | +10'56.4 | 6 |
| 7 | 12 | Dan Gurney | Eagle-Climax | 14 | Electrical | 8 |
| 8 | 34 | Jean Pierre Beltoise | Matra Ford F2 | 14 | + 1 Lap | 18 |
| 9 | 26 | Hubert Hahne | Matra BRM F2 | 14 | + 1 Lap | 27 |
| 10 | 33 | Jo Schlesser | Matra Ford F2 | 14 | + 1 Lap | 19 |
| 11 | 8 | Hans Herrmann | Brabham Ford | 14 | + 1 Lap | 22 |
| 12 | 2 | Peter Arundell | Lotus-BRM | 14 | +1 Lap | 17 |
| Ret | 15 | Mike Spence | Lotus-BRM | 12 | Alternator | 13 |
| Ret | 1 | Jim Clark | Lotus-Climax | 11 | Accident | 1 |
| Ret | 20 | Chris Lawrence | Cooper-Ferrari | 10 | Suspension | 26 |
| Ret | 11 | Ludovico Scarfiotti | Ferrari | 9 | Electrical | 4 |
| Ret | 10 | Mike Parkes | Ferrari | 9 | Accident | 7 |
| Ret | 4 | Denny Hulme | Brabham-Repco | 8 | Ignition | 15 |
| Ret | 31 | Pedro Rodriguez | Lotus Ford F2 | 7 | Engine | 20 |
| Ret | 29 | Alan Rees | Brabham Ford F2 | 4 | Engine | 24 |
| Ret | 17 | Jo Bonnier | Cooper-Maserati | 4 | Clutch | 12 |
| Ret | 14 | Bob Bondurant | BRM | 3 | Engine | 11 |
| Ret | 32 | Piers Courage | Lotus Ford F2 | 3 | Accident | 23 |
| Ret | 25 | Kurt Ahrens | Brabham Ford F2 | 3 | Gearbox | 21 |
| Ret | 19 | Bob Anderson | Brabham-Climax | 2 | Transmission | 14 |
| Ret | 27 | Jacky Ickx | Matra Ford F2 | 1 | Accident | 16 |
| Ret | 16 | John Taylor | Brabham-BRM | 0 | Fatal accident | 25 |
| DNS | 30 | Gerhard Mitter | Lotus Ford F2 | 0 | Injured | |
| DNS | 35 | Silvio Moser | Brabham Ford F2 | 0 | Engine | |
| DNS | 18 | Guy Ligier | Cooper Maserati | 0 | Injured | |

Winning speed: 86.747mph Lap leaders: Brabham 1-15
Pole position: Clark, 8m 16.500s, 102.768
Fastest lap: Surtees, 8m 49.000s, 96.455mph

### ITALIAN GRAND PRIX: MONZA *4 September Round: 7 Race: 148 68 x 3.573 miles*

| POS. | NO. | DRIVER | CAR/ENGINE | LAPS | TIME/RETIRED | GRID |
|---|---|---|---|---|---|---|
| 1 | 6 | Ludovico Scarfiotti | Ferrari | 68 | 1:47'14.8 | 2 |
| 2 | 4 | Mike Parkes | Ferrari | 68 | +5.8 | 1 |
| 3 | 12 | Denny Hulme | Brabham-Repco | 68 | + 6.1 | 10 |
| 4 | 16 | Jochen Rindt | Cooper-Maserati | 67 | +1 Lap | 8 |
| 5 | 42 | Mike Spence | Lotus-BRM | 67 | +1 Lap | 14 |
| 6 | 40 | Bob Anderson | Brabham-Climax | 66 | +2 Laps | 15 |
| 7 | 48 | Bob Bondurant | BRM | 65 | +3 Laps | 18 |
| 8 | 24 | Peter Arundell | Lotus-BRM | 63 | Engine | 13 |
| 9 | 20 | Geki | Lotus-Climax | 63 | +5 Laps | 20 |
| NC | 44 | Giancarlo Baghetti | Ferrari | 59 | Not classified | 16 |
| Ret | 22 | Jim Clark | Lotus-BRM | 58 | Gearbox | 3 |
| Ret | 36 | Jo Siffert | Cooper-Maserati | 46 | Engine | 17 |
| Ret | 2 | Lorenzo Bandini | Ferrari | 33 | Ignition | 5 |
| Ret | 14 | John Surtees | Cooper-Maserati | 31 | Fuel leak | 4 |
| Ret | 18 | Richie Ginther | Honda | 16 | Accident | 7 |
| Ret | 10 | Jack Brabham | Brabham-Repco | 7 | Oil leak | 6 |
| Ret | 30 | Dan Gurney | Eagle-Weslake | 7 | Engine | 19 |
| Ret | 28 | Jackie Stewart | BRM | 5 | Fuel leak | 9 |
| Ret | 38 | Jo Bonnier | Cooper-Maserati | 3 | Throttle | 12 |
| Ret | 26 | Graham Hill | BRM | 0 | Engine | 11 |
| DNQ | 34 | Phil Hill | Eagle-Climax | | | |
| DNQ | 32 | Chris Amon | Brabham-BRM | | | |

Winning speed: 135.924mph Lap leaders: Bandini 1, Parkes 2, 8-12, 27; Surtees 3; Brabham 4-7; Hulme 11; Scarfiotti 13-26, 28-68
Pole position: Parkes, 1m 31.300s, 140.880mph
Fastest lap: Scarfiotti, 1m 32.400s, 139.203mph

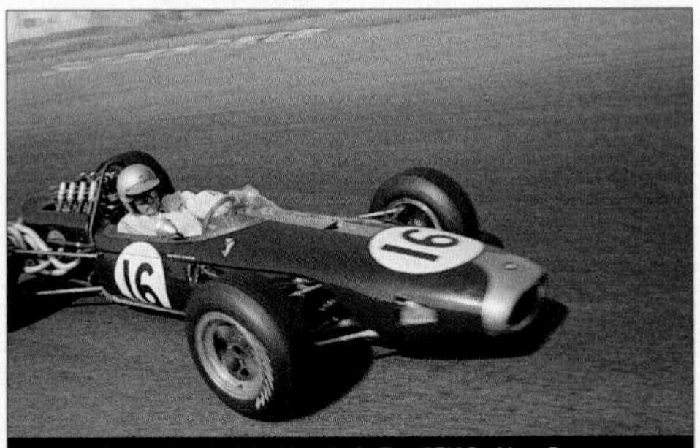

1966 world champion, Jack Brabham in the Type BT19 Brabham Repco.

**UNITED STATES GRAND PRIX: WATKINS GLEN** *Round: 8 Race: 149 108 x 2.300 miles*

| POS. | NO. | DRIVER | CAR/ENGINE | LAPS | TIME/RETIRED | GRID |
|---|---|---|---|---|---|---|
| 1 | 1 | Jim Clark | Lotus-BRM | 108 | 2:09'40.11 | 2 |
| 2 | 8 | Jochen Rindt | Cooper-Maserati | 107 | Out of fuel | 9 |
| 3 | 7 | John Surtees | Cooper-Maserati | 107 | +1 Lap | 4 |
| 4 | 19 | Jo Siffert | Cooper-Maserati | 105 | +3 Laps | 13 |
| 5 | 17 | Bruce McLaren | McLaren-Ford | 105 | +3 Laps | 11 |
| 6 | 2 | Peter Arundell | Lotus-Climax | 101 | +7 Laps | 19 |
| Ret | 10 | Innes Ireland | BRM | 96 | Alternator | 17 |
| NC | 12 | Richie Ginther | Honda | 81 | Not classified | 8 |
| Ret | 18 | Mike Spence | Lotus-BRM | 74 | Ignition | 12 |
| Ret | 14 | Ronnie Bucknum | Honda | 58 | Engine | 18 |
| NC | 22 | Jo Bonnier | Cooper-Maserati | 57 | Not classified | 15 |
| Ret | 5 | Jack Brabham | Brabham-Repco | 55 | Engine | 1 |
| Ret | 4 | Jackie Stewart | BRM | 53 | Engine | 6 |
| Ret | 3 | Graham Hill | BRM | 52 | Differential | 5 |
| Ret | 9 | Lorenzo Bandini | Ferrari | 34 | Engine | 3 |
| Ret | 6 | Denny Hulme | Brabham-Repco | 18 | Engine | 7 |
| Ret | 11 | Pedro Rodriguez | Lotus-BRM | 13 | Retirement | 10 |
| Ret | 15 | Dan Gurney | Eagle-Weslake | 13 | Clutch | 14 |
| DSQ | 16 | Bob Bondurant | Eagle-Climax | 5 | Disqualified | 16 |

Winning speed: 114.939mph Lap leaders: Bandini 1-9, 20-34; Brabham 10-19, 35-55; Clark 56-108
Pole position: Brabham, 1m 08.420s, 121.017mph
Fastest lap: Surtees, 1m 09.670s, 118.846mph

**MEXICAN GRAND PRIX: MEXICO CITY** *23 October Round: 9 Race: 150 65 x 3.107 miles*

| POS. | NO. | DRIVER | CAR/ENGINE | LAPS | TIME/RETIRED | GRID |
|---|---|---|---|---|---|---|
| 1 | 7 | John Surtees | Cooper-Maserati | 65 | 2:06'35.34 | 1 |
| 2 | 5 | Jack Brabham | Brabham-Repco | 65 | +7.88 | 4 |
| 3 | 6 | Denny Hulme | Brabham-Repco | 64 | +1 Lap | 6 |
| 4 | 12 | Richie Ginther | Honda | 64 | +1 Lap | 3 |
| 5 | 15 | Dan Gurney | Eagle-Climax | 64 | +1 Lap | 9 |
| 6 | 22 | Jo Bonnier | Cooper-Maserati | 63 | +2 Laps | 12 |
| 7 | 2 | Peter Arundell | Lotus-BRM | 61 | +4 Laps | 17 |
| 8 | 14 | Ronnie Bucknum | Honda | 60 | +5 Laps | 13 |
| Ret | 11 | Pedro Rodriguez | Lotus-BRM | 49 | Differential | 8 |
| Ret | 17 | Bruce McLaren | McLaren-Ford | 40 | Engine | 14 |
| Ret | 19 | Jo Siffert | Cooper-Maserati | 33 | Suspension | 11 |
| Ret | 8 | Jochen Rindt | Cooper-Maserati | 32 | Suspension | 5 |
| Ret | 10 | Innes Ireland | BRM | 28 | Transmission | 16 |
| Ret | 4 | Jackie Stewart | BRM | 26 | Oil leak | 10 |
| Ret | 16 | Bob Bondurant | Eagle-Weslake | 24 | Fuel system | 18 |
| Ret | 3 | Graham Hill | BRM | 18 | Engine | 7 |
| Ret | 1 | Jim Clark | Lotus-BRM | 9 | Gearbox | 2 |
| Ret | 9 | Moises Solana | Cooper-Maserati | 9 | Overheating | 15 |

Winning speed: 95.717mph Lap leaders: Ginther 1; Brabham 2-5; Surtees 6-65
Pole position: Surtees, 1m 53.180s, 98.822mph
Fastest lap: Ginther, 1m 53.750s, 98.327mph

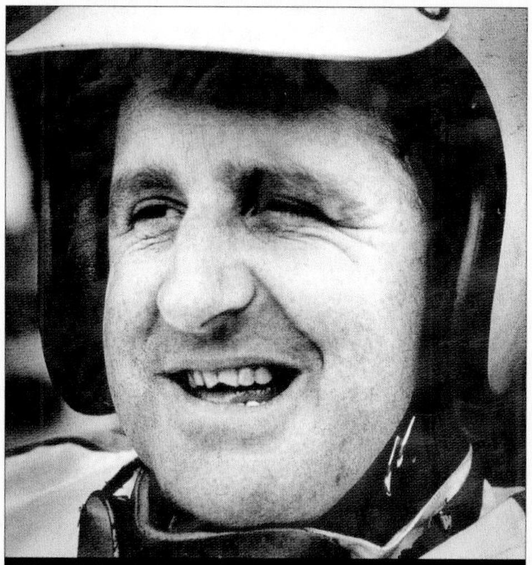
1967 world champion, Denny Hulme.

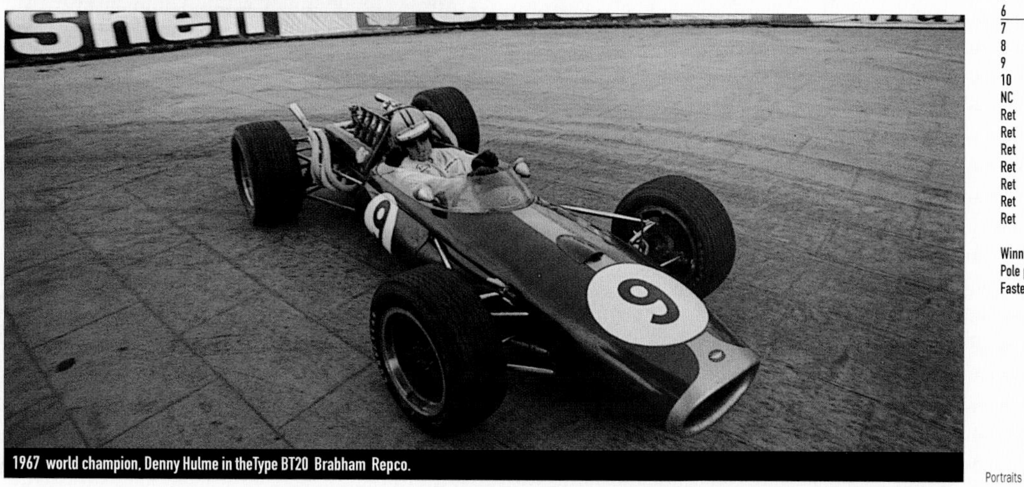
1967 world champion, Denny Hulme in theType BT20 Brabham Repco.

# 1967

## DRIVERS' CHAMPION: DENNY HULME
## CONSTRUCTORS' CHAMPION: BRABHAM REPCO

**DRIVERS' CHAMPIONSHIP**

| POS. | DRIVER | NATIONALITY | CAR | POINTS |
|---|---|---|---|---|
| 1 | Denny Hulme | New Zealand | Brabham-Repco | 51 |
| 2 | Jack Brabham | Australia | Brabham-Repco | 46 (2) |
| 3 | Jim Clark | GB | Lotus-BRM, Lotus-Climax, Lotus-Ford | 41 |
| 4 | John Surtees | GB | Honda | 20 |
| = | Chris Amon | New Zealand | Ferrari | 20 |
| 6 | Pedro Rodriquez | Mexico | Cooper-Maserati | 15 |
| = | Graham Hill | GB | Lotus-BRM, Lotus-Ford | 15 |
| 8 | Dan Gurney | USA | Eagle-Climax, Eagle-Weslake | 13 |
| 9 | Jackie Stewart | GB | BRM | 10 |
| 10 | Mike Spence | GB | BRM | 9 |
| 11 | John Love | South Africa | Cooper-Climax | 6 |
| = | Jochen Rindt | Austria | Cooper-Maserati | 6 |
| = | Jo Siffert | Switzerland | Cooper-Maserati | 6 |
| 14 | Bruce McLaren | New Zealand | McLaren-BRM, Eagle-Weslake | 3 |
| = | Jo Bonnier | Sweden | Cooper-Maserati | 3 |
| 16 | Bob Anderson | GB | Brabham-Climax | 2 |
| = | Mike Parkes | GB | Ferrari | 2 |
| = | Chris Irwin | GB | Lotus-BRM, BRM | 2 |
| 19 | Ludovico Scarfiotti | Italy | Ferrari, Eagle-Weslake | 1 |
| = | Guy Ligier | France | Brabham-Repco, Cooper-Maserati | 1 |
| = | Jacky Ickx | Belgium | Cooper-Maserati | 1 |
| | Jean-Pierre Beltoise | France | Matra-Ford, Matra-Cosworth | |
| | Richie Ginther | USA | Eagle-Weslake | |
| | David Hobbs | GB | BRM | |
| | Jonathan Williams | GB | Ferrari | |
| | Alan Rees | GB | Cooper-Maserati | |
| | Dick Atwood | GB | Cooper-Maserati | |
| | Mike Fisher | USA | Lotus-BRM | |
| | Dave Carlton | South Africa | Brabham-Climax | |
| | Luki Botha | South Africa | Brabham-Climax | |
| | Sam Tingle | South Africa | LDS-Climax | |
| | Piers Courage | GB | Lotus-BRM, BRM | |
| | Lorenzo Bandini | Italy | Ferrari | |
| | Johnny Servoz-Gavin | France | Matra-Ford | |
| | Silvio Moser | Switerland | Cooper-ATS | |
| | Hubert Hahne | West Germany | Lola-BMW | |
| | Al Pease | Canada | Eagle-Climax | |
| | Eppie Wietzes | Canada | Lotus-Ford | |
| | Tom Jones | Canada | Cooper-Climax | |
| | Giancarlo Baghetti | Italy | Lotus-Ford | |
| | Moises Solana | Mexico | Lotus-Ford | |

Points for top six finishers (9, 6, 4, 3, 2, 1). Only the best five scores from the first six races and the best four scores from the remaining five races counted towards the championship. Formula Two cars raced simulataneously with Formula One cars at the German Grand Prix but were ineligible for points which were awarded to the top six Formula One finishers.

**CONSTRUCTORS' CHAMPIONSHIP**

| POS. | CONSTRUCTOR | POINTS |
|---|---|---|
| 1 | Brabham-Repco | 63 |
| 2 | Lotus-Ford | 44 |
| 3 | Cooper-Maserati | 28 |
| 4 | Honda | 20 |
| 5 | Ferrari | 20 |
| 6 | BRM | 17 |
| 7 | Eagle-Weslake | 13 |
| 8 | Cooper-Climax | 6 |
| = | Lotus-BRM | 6 |
| 10 | McLaren-BRM | 3 |
| 11 | Brabham-Climax | 2 |

Points for top six finishers (9, 6, 4, 3, 2, 1). Points only counted for top-placed car for each constructor. Only the best five scores from the first six races and the best four scores from the remaining five races counted towards the championship.

**SOUTH AFRICAN GRAND PRIX: KYALAMI** *2 January Round: 1 Race: 151 80 x 2.544 miles*

| POS. | NO. | DRIVER | CAR/ENGINE | LAPS | TIME/RETIRED | GRID |
|---|---|---|---|---|---|---|
| 1 | 4 | Pedro Rodriguez | Cooper-Maserati | 80 | 2:05'45.9 | 4 |
| 2 | 17 | John Love | Cooper-Climax | 80 | +26.4 | 5 |
| 3 | 11 | John Surtees | Honda | 79 | +1 Lap | 6 |
| 4 | 2 | Denny Hulme | Brabham-Repco | 78 | +2 Laps | 2 |
| 5 | 14 | Bob Anderson | Brabham-Climax | 78 | +2 Laps | 10 |
| 6 | 1 | Jack Brabham | Brabham-Repco | 76 | +4 Laps | 1 |
| NC | 19 | Dave Charlton | Brabham-Climax | 63 | Not classified | 8 |
| NC | 20 | Luki Botha | Brabham-Climax | 60 | Not classified | 17 |
| Ret | 18 | Sam Tingle | LDS-Climax | 56 | Accident | 14 |
| Ret | 16 | Piers Courage | Lotus-BRM | 51 | Fuel system | 18 |
| Ret | 9 | Dan Gurney | Eagle-Climax | 44 | Suspension | 11 |
| Ret | 12 | Jo Siffert | Cooper-Maserati | 41 | Engine | 16 |
| Ret | 3 | Jochen Rindt | Cooper-Maserati | 38 | Engine | 7 |
| Ret | 6 | Mike Spence | BRM | 31 | Oil leak | 13 |
| Ret | 15 | Jo Bonnier | Cooper-Maserati | 30 | Engine | 12 |
| Ret | 7 | Jim Clark | Lotus-BRM | 22 | Engine | 3 |
| Ret | 8 | Graham Hill | Lotus-BRM | 6 | Accident | 15 |
| Ret | 5 | Jackie Stewart | BRM | 2 | Engine | 9 |

Winning speed: 97.095mph Lap leaders: Hulme 1-60; Love 61-73; Rodriguez 74-80
Pole position: Brabham, 1m 28.300s, 103.719mph
Fastest lap: Hulme, 1m 29.900s, 101.873mph

**MONACO GRAND PRIX: MONTE CARLO** *7 May Round: 2 Race: 152 100 x 1.954 miles*

| POS. | NO. | DRIVER | CAR/ENGINE | LAPS | TIME/RETIRED | GRID |
|---|---|---|---|---|---|---|
| 1 | 9 | Denny Hulme | Brabham-Repco | 100 | 2:34'34.3 | 4 |
| 2 | 14 | Graham Hill | Lotus-BRM | 99 | +1 Lap | 8 |
| 3 | 20 | Chris Amon | Ferrari | 98 | +2 Laps | 14 |
| 4 | 16 | Bruce McLaren | McLaren-BRM | 97 | +3 Laps | 10 |
| 5 | 11 | Pedro Rodriguez | Cooper-Maserati | 96 | +4 Laps | 16 |
| 6 | 5 | Mike Spence | BRM | 96 | +4 Laps | 12 |
| Ret | 18 | Lorenzo Bandini | Ferrari | 81 | Fatal accident | 2 |
| Ret | 6 | Piers Courage | BRM | 64 | Spun off | 13 |
| Ret | 12 | Jim Clark | Lotus-Climax | 42 | Suspension | 5 |
| Ret | 7 | John Surtees | Honda | 32 | Engine | 3 |
| Ret | 17 | Jo Siffert | Cooper-Maserati | 31 | Oil pressure | 9 |
| Ret | 4 | Jackie Stewart | BRM | 14 | Differential | 6 |
| Ret | 10 | Jochen Rindt | Cooper-Maserati | 14 | Gearbox | 15 |
| Ret | 23 | Dan Gurney | Eagle-Weslake | 4 | Fuel pump | 7 |
| Ret | 2 | J.Servoz-Gavin | Matra-Ford | 4 | Injection | 11 |
| Ret | 8 | Jack Brabham | Brabham-Repco | 0 | Engine | 1 |
| DNQ | 15 | Bob Anderson | Brabham-Climax | | | |
| DNQ | 1 | Jean Pierre Beltoise | Matra-Ford | | | |
| DNQ | 22 | Richie Ginther | Eagle-Weslake | | | |

Winning speed: 75.857mph Lap leaders: Bandini 1; Hulme 2-5, 15-100; Stewart 6-14
Pole position: Brabham, 1m 27.600s, 80.310mph
Fastest lap: Clark, 1m 29.500s, 78.605mph

**DUTCH GRAND PRIX: ZANDVOORT** *4 June Round: 3 Race: 153 90 x 2.605 miles*

| POS. | NO. | DRIVER | CAR/ENGINE | LAPS | TIME/RETIRED | GRID |
|---|---|---|---|---|---|---|
| 1 | 5 | Jim Clark | Lotus-Ford | 90 | 2:14'45.1 | 8 |
| 2 | 1 | Jack Brabham | Brabham-Repco | 90 | +23.6 | 3 |
| 3 | 2 | Denny Hulme | Brabham-Repco | 90 | +25.7 | 7 |
| 4 | 3 | Chris Amon | Ferrari | 90 | +27.3 | 9 |
| 5 | 4 | Mike Parkes | Ferrari | 89 | +1 Lap | 10 |
| 6 | 22 | Ludovico Scarfiotti | Ferrari | 89 | +1 Lap | 15 |
| 7 | 18 | Chris Irwin | Lotus-BRM | 88 | +2 Laps | 13 |
| 8 | 10 | Mike Spence | BRM | 87 | +3 Laps | 12 |
| 9 | 21 | Bob Anderson | Brabham-Climax | 86 | +4 Laps | 17 |
| 10 | 20 | Jo Siffert | Cooper-Maserati | 83 | +7 Laps | 16 |
| Ret | 7 | John Surtees | Honda | 73 | Throttle | 6 |
| Ret | 9 | Jackie Stewart | BRM | 51 | Brakes | 11 |
| Ret | 12 | Jochen Rindt | Cooper-Maserati | 41 | Suspension | 4 |
| Ret | 14 | Pedro Rodriguez | Cooper-Maserati | 39 | Gearbox | 5 |
| Ret | 6 | Graham Hill | Lotus-Ford | 11 | Engine | 1 |
| Ret | 15 | Dan Gurney | Eagle-Weslake | 8 | Injection | 2 |
| Ret | 17 | Bruce McLaren | McLaren-BRM | 1 | Accident | 14 |

Winning speed: 104.408mph Lap leaders: G Hill 1-10; Brabham 11-15; Clark 16-90
Pole position: G Hill, 1m 24.600s, 110.868mph
Fastest lap: Clark, 1m 28.080s, 106.488mph

**BELGIAN GRAND PRIX: SPA-FRANCORCHAMPS** *18 June Round: 4 Race: 154 28 x 8.761 miles*

| POS. | NO. | DRIVER | CAR/ENGINE | LAPS | TIME/RETIRED | GRID |
|---|---|---|---|---|---|---|
| 1 | 36 | Dan Gurney | Eagle-Weslake | 28 | 1:40'49.4 | 2 |
| 2 | 14 | Jackie Stewart | BRM | 28 | +1'03.0 | 6 |
| 3 | 1 | Chris Amon | Ferrari | 28 | +1'40.0 | 5 |
| 4 | 29 | Jochen Rindt | Cooper-Maserati | 28 | +2'13.9 | 4 |
| 5 | 12 | Mike Spence | BRM | 27 | +1 Lap | 11 |
| 6 | 21 | Jim Clark | Lotus-Ford | 27 | +1 Lap | 1 |
| 7 | 34 | Jo Siffert | Cooper-Maserati | 27 | +1 Lap | 16 |
| 8 | 19 | Bob Anderson | Brabham-Climax | 26 | +2 Laps | 17 |
| 9 | 30 | Pedro Rodriguez | Cooper-Maserati | 25 | Engine | 13 |
| 10 | 32 | Guy Ligier | Cooper-Maserati | 25 | +3 Laps | 18 |
| NC | 2 | Ludovico Scarfiotti | Ferrari | 24 | Not classified | 9 |
| Ret | 25 | Jack Brabham | Brabham-Repco | 15 | Engine | 7 |
| Ret | 26 | Denny Hulme | Brabham-Repco | 14 | Engine | 14 |
| Ret | 39 | Jo Bonnier | Cooper-Maserati | 10 | Engine | 12 |
| Ret | 22 | Graham Hill | Lotus-Ford | 3 | Clutch | 3 |
| Ret | 7 | John Surtees | Honda | 1 | Engine | 10 |
| Ret | 17 | Chris Irwin | BRM | 1 | Engine | 15 |
| Ret | 3 | Mike Parkes | Ferrari | 0 | Accident | 8 |

Winning speed: 145.987mph Lap leaders: Clark 1-12; Stewart 13-20; Gurney 21-28
Pole position: Clark, 3m 28.100s, 151.566mph
Fastest lap: Gurney, 3m 31.900s, 148.848mph

Portraits by Rainer Schlegelmilch © 2001 Schlegelmilch Archive

### FRENCH GRAND PRIX: BUGATTI AU MANS *2 July Round: 5 Race: 155 80 x 2.748 miles*

| POS. | NO. | DRIVER | CAR/ENGINE | LAPS | TIME/RETIRED | GRID |
|---|---|---|---|---|---|---|
| 1 | 3 | Jack Brabham | Brabham-Repco | 80 | 2:13'21.3 | 2 |
| 2 | 4 | Denny Hulme | Brabham-Repco | 80 | +49.5 | 6 |
| 3 | 10 | Jackie Stewart | BRM | 79 | +1 Lap | 10 |
| 4 | 18 | Jo Siffert | Cooper-Maserati | 77 | +3 Laps | 11 |
| 5 | 15 | Chris Irwin | BRM | 76 | Engine | 9 |
| 6 | 14 | Pedro Rodriguez | Cooper-Maserati | 76 | +4 Laps | 13 |
| NC | 16 | Guy Ligier | Cooper-Maserati | 68 | Not classified | 15 |
| Ret | 2 | Chris Amon | Ferrari | 47 | Throttle | 7 |
| Ret | 9 | Dan Gurney | Eagle-Weslake | 40 | Fuel leak | 3 |
| Ret | 12 | Jochen Rindt | Cooper-Maserati | 33 | Engine | 8 |
| Ret | 8 | Bruce McLaren | Eagle-Weslake | 26 | Ignition | 5 |
| Ret | 6 | Jim Clark | Lotus-Ford | 23 | Differential | 4 |
| Ret | 17 | Bob Anderson | Brabham-Climax | 16 | Ignition | 14 |
| Ret | 7 | Graham Hill | Lotus-Ford | 13 | Differential | 1 |
| Ret | 11 | Mike Spence | BRM | 9 | Halfshaft | 12 |

Winning speed: 98.901mph
Lap leaders: G Hill 1, 11-13; Brabham 2-4, 24-28; Clark 5-10, 14-23
Pole position: G Hill, 1m 36.200s, 102.825mph
Fastest lap: G Hill, 1m 36.700s, 102.293mph

### BRITISH GRAND PRIX: SILVERSTONE *15 July Round: 6 Race: 156 80 x 2.927 miles*

| POS. | NO. | DRIVER | CAR/ENGINE | LAPS | TIME/RETIRED | GRID |
|---|---|---|---|---|---|---|
| 1 | 5 | Jim Clark | Lotus-Ford | 80 | 1:59'25.6 | 1 |
| 2 | 2 | Denny Hulme | Brabham-Repco | 80 | +12.8 | 4 |
| 3 | 8 | Chris Amon | Ferrari | 80 | +16.6 | 6 |
| 4 | 1 | Jack Brabham | Brabham-Repco | 80 | +21.8 | 3 |
| 5 | 12 | Pedro Rodriguez | Cooper-Maserati | 79 | +1 Lap | 9 |
| 6 | 7 | John Surtees | Honda | 78 | +2 Laps | 7 |
| 7 | 15 | Chris Irwin | BRM | 77 | +3 Laps | 13 |
| 8 | 20 | David Hobbs | BRM | 77 | +3 Laps | 14 |
| 9 | 14 | Alan Rees | Cooper-Maserati | 76 | +4 Laps | 15 |
| 10 | 18 | Guy Ligier | Brabham-Repco | 76 | +4 Laps | 21 |
| Ret | 19 | Bob Anderson | Brabham-Climax | 67 | Engine | 17 |
| Ret | 6 | Graham Hill | Lotus-Ford | 64 | Engine | 2 |
| Ret | 4 | Mike Spence | BRM | 44 | Ignition | 11 |
| Ret | 9 | Dan Gurney | Eagle-Weslake | 34 | Clutch | 5 |
| Ret | 22 | Silvio Moser | Cooper-A.T.S. | 29 | Oil pressure | 20 |
| Ret | 11 | Jochen Rindt | Cooper-Maserati | 26 | Engine | 8 |
| Ret | 3 | Jackie Stewart | BRM | 20 | Transmission | 12 |
| Ret | 10 | Bruce McLaren | Eagle-Weslake | 14 | Engine | 10 |
| Ret | 17 | Jo Siffert | Cooper-Maserati | 10 | Engine | 18 |
| Ret | 23 | Jo Bonnier | Cooper-Maserati | 0 | Engine | 9 |
| DNS | 16 | Piers Courage | BRM | 0 | Non starter | |

Winning speed: 117.642mph Lap leaders: Clark 1-25, 55-80; Hill 26-54
Pole position: Clark, 1m 25.300s, 123.531mph
Fastest lap: Hulme, 1m 27.000s, 121.117mph

### GERMAN GRAND PRIX: NURBURGRING *6 August Round: 7 Race: 157 15 x 14.189 miles*

| POS. | NO. | DRIVER | CAR/ENGINE | LAPS | TIME/RETIRED | GRID |
|---|---|---|---|---|---|---|
| 1 | 2 | Denny Hulme | Brabham-Repco | 15 | 2:05'55.7 | 2 |
| 2 | 1 | Jack Brabham | Brabham-Repco | 15 | +38.5 | 7 |
| 3 | 8 | Chris Amon | Ferrari | 15 | +39.0 | 8 |
| 4 | 7 | John Surtees | Honda | 15 | +2'25.7 | 6 |
| 5 | 24 | Jackie Oliver | Lotus Ford F2 | 15 | +4'09.2 | 19 |
| 6 | 16 | Jo Bonnier | Cooper-Maserati | 15 | +8'42.1 | 16 |
| 7 | 22 | Alan Rees | Brabham Ford F2 | 15 | +8'47.96 | 20 |
| 8 | 15 | Guy Ligier | Brabham-Repco | 14 | +1 Lap | 17 |
| 9 | 18 | Chris Irwin | BRM | 13 | +2 Laps | 15 |
| 10 | 27 | David Hobbs | Lola BMW F2 | 13 | +2 Laps | 22 |
| 11 | 6 | Pedro Rodriguez | Cooper-Maserati | 13 | +2 Laps | 10 |
| Ret | 9 | Dan Gurney | Eagle-Weslake | 12 | Halfshaft | 4 |
| Ret | 29 | Jacky Ickx | Matra Ford F2 | 12 | Suspension | 18 |
| NC | 25 | Brian Hart | Protos Ford F2 | 12 | Not Classified | 25 |
| Ret | 14 | Jo Siffert | Cooper-Maserati | 12 | Fuel pump | 12 |
| Ret | 4 | Graham Hill | Lotus-Ford | 8 | Suspension | 13 |
| Ret | 17 | Hubert Hahne | Lola-BMW | 6 | Suspension | 14 |
| Ret | 11 | Jackie Stewart | BRM | 5 | Differential | 3 |
| Ret | 3 | Jim Clark | Lotus-Ford | 4 | Suspension | 1 |
| Ret | 26 | Kurt Ahrens | Protos Ford | 4 | Radiator | 23 |
| Ret | 5 | Jochen Rindt | Cooper-Maserati | 4 | Handling | 9 |
| Ret | 10 | Bruce McLaren | Eagle-Weslake | 3 | Oil leak | 5 |
| Ret | 12 | Mike Spence | BRM | 3 | Differential | 11 |
| Ret | 23 | Jo Schlesser | Matra Ford F2 | 2 | Clutch | 21 |
| Ret | 20 | Gerhard Mitter | Brabham Ford F2 | 0 | Engine | 24 |
| DNS | 28 | Brian Redman | Lola Ford | 0 | Non starter | |

Winning speed: 101.408mph Lap leaders: Clark 1-3; Gurney 4-12; Hulme 13-15
Pole position: Clark, 8m 4.100s, 105.516mph
Fastest lap: Gurney, 8m 15.100s, 103.455mph

### CANADIAN GRAND PRIX: MOSPORT PARK *27 August Round: 8 Race: 158 90 x 2.459 miles*

| POS. | NO. | DRIVER | CAR/ENGINE | LAPS | TIME/RETIRED | GRID |
|---|---|---|---|---|---|---|
| 1 | 1 | Jack Brabham | Brabham-Repco | 90 | 2:40'40.0 | 7 |
| 2 | 2 | Denny Hulme | Brabham-Repco | 90 | +1'01.9 | 3 |
| 3 | 10 | Dan Gurney | Eagle-Weslake | 89 | +1 Lap | 5 |
| 4 | 4 | Graham Hill | Lotus-Ford | 88 | +2 Laps | 2 |
| 5 | 16 | Mike Spence | BRM | 87 | +3 Laps | 10 |
| 6 | 20 | Chris Amon | Ferrari | 87 | +3 Laps | 4 |
| 7 | 19 | Bruce McLaren | McLaren-BRM | 86 | +4 Laps | 6 |
| 8 | 9 | Jo Bonnier | Cooper-Maserati | 85 | +5 Laps | 14 |
| 9 | 12 | David Hobbs | BRM | 85 | +5 Laps | 12 |
| 10 | 8 | Richard Attwood | Cooper-Maserati | 84 | +6 Laps | 13 |
| 11 | 6 | Mike Fisher | Lotus-BRM | 81 | +9 Laps | 17 |
| Ret | 3 | Jim Clark | Lotus-Ford | 69 | Ignition | 1 |
| DSQ | 5 | Eppie Wietzes | Lotus-Ford | 69 | Disqualified | 16 |
| Ret | 15 | Jackie Stewart | BRM | 65 | Throttle | 9 |
| NC | 11 | Al Pease | Eagle-Climax | 47 | Not classified | 15 |
| Ret | 17 | Chris Irwin | BRM | 18 | Spun off | 11 |
| Ret | 71 | Jochen Rindt | Cooper-Maserati | 4 | Ignition | 8 |
| DNQ | 41 | Tom Jones | Cooper-Climax | | | |

Winning speed: 82.647mph Lap leaders: Clark 1-3, 58-67; Hulme 4-57; Brabham 68-90
Pole position: Clark, 1m 22.400s, 107.432mph
Fastest lap: Clark, 1m 23.100s, 106.527mph

### ITALIAN GRAND PRIX: MONZA *10 September Round: 9 Race: 159 68 x 3.573 miles*

| POS. | NO. | DRIVER | CAR/ENGINE | LAPS | TIME/RETIRED | GRID |
|---|---|---|---|---|---|---|
| 1 | 14 | John Surtees | Honda | 68 | 1:43'45.0 | 9 |
| 2 | 16 | Jack Brabham | Brabham-Repco | 68 | +0.2 | 2 |
| 3 | 20 | Jim Clark | Lotus-Ford | 68 | +23.1 | 1 |
| 4 | 30 | Jochen Rindt | Cooper-Maserati | 68 | +56.6 | 11 |
| 5 | 36 | Mike Spence | BRM | 67 | +1 Lap | 12 |
| 6 | 32 | Jacky Ickx | Cooper-Maserati | 66 | +2 Laps | 15 |
| 7 | 2 | Chris Amon | Ferrari | 64 | +4 Laps | 4 |
| Ret | 22 | Graham Hill | Lotus-Ford | 58 | Engine | 8 |
| Ret | 6 | Jo Siffert | Cooper-Maserati | 50 | Accident | 13 |
| Ret | 24 | Giancarlo Baghetti | Lotus-Ford | 50 | Engine | 17 |
| Ret | 4 | Bruce McLaren | McLaren-BRM | 46 | Engine | 3 |
| Ret | 26 | Jo Bonnier | Cooper-Maserati | 46 | Overheating | 14 |
| Ret | 31 | Jackie Stewart | BRM | 45 | Engine | 7 |
| Ret | 18 | Denny Hulme | Brabham-Repco | 30 | Overheating | 6 |
| Ret | 12 | Guy Ligier | Brabham-Repco | 26 | Engine | 18 |
| Ret | 38 | Chris Irwin | BRM | 16 | Injection | 16 |
| Ret | 10 | Ludovico Scarfiotti | Eagle-Weslake | 5 | Engine | 10 |
| Ret | 8 | Dan Gurney | Eagle-Weslake | 4 | Engine | 5 |

Winning speed: 140.505mph Lap leaders: Gurney 1-2; Clark 3-9, 11-12, 61-67; Hulme 10, 13-15, 17, 24-27; Brabham 16, 59-60; Hill 18-23, 28-58; Surtees 68
Pole position: Clark, 1m 28.500s, 145.338mph
Fastest lap: Clark, 1m 28.500s, 145.338mph

### UNITED STATES GRAND PRIX: WATKINS GLEN *1 October Round: 10 Race: 160 108 x 2.300 miles*

| POS. | NO. | DRIVER | CAR/ENGINE | LAPS | TIME/RETIRED | GRID |
|---|---|---|---|---|---|---|
| 1 | 5 | Jim Clark | Lotus-Ford | 108 | 2:03'13.2 | 2 |
| 2 | 6 | Graham Hill | Lotus-Ford | 108 | +6.3 | 1 |
| 3 | 2 | Denny Hulme | Brabham-Repco | 107 | +1 Lap | 6 |
| 4 | 15 | Jo Siffert | Cooper-Maserati | 106 | +2 Laps | 12 |
| 5 | 1 | Jack Brabham | Brabham-Repco | 104 | +4 Laps | 5 |
| 6 | 16 | Jo Bonnier | Cooper-Maserati | 101 | +7 Laps | 15 |
| 7 | 22 | Jean Pierre Beltoise | Matra-Ford | 101 | +7 Laps | 18 |
| Ret | 3 | John Surtees | Honda | 96 | Alternator | 11 |
| Ret | 9 | Chris Amon | Ferrari | 95 | Engine | 4 |
| Ret | 7 | Jackie Stewart | BRM | 72 | Injection | 10 |
| Ret | 21 | Jacky Ickx | Cooper-Maserati | 45 | Overheating | 16 |
| Ret | 19 | Guy Ligier | Brabham-Repco | 43 | Engine | 17 |
| Ret | 17 | Chris Irwin | BRM | 41 | Engine | 14 |
| Ret | 8 | Mike Spence | BRM | 35 | Engine | 13 |
| Ret | 4 | Jochen Rindt | Cooper-Maserati | 33 | Engine | 8 |
| Ret | 11 | Dan Gurney | Eagle-Weslake | 24 | Suspension | 3 |
| Ret | 14 | Bruce McLaren | McLaren-BRM | 16 | Water leak | 9 |
| Ret | 18 | Moises Solana | Lotus-Ford | 7 | Ignition | 7 |

Winning speed: 120.954 miles Lap leaders: G Hill 1-40; Clark 41-108
Pole position: G Hill, 1m 05.480s, 126.451mph
Fastest lap: G Hill, 1m 06.000s, 125.455mph

### MEXICAN GRAND PRIX: MEXICO CITY *22 October Round: 11 Race: 161 65 x 3.107 miles*

| POS. | NO. | DRIVER | CAR/ENGINE | LAPS | TIME/RETIRED | GRID |
|---|---|---|---|---|---|---|
| 1 | 5 | Jim Clark | Lotus-Ford | 65 | 1:59'28.70 | 1 |
| 2 | 1 | Jack Brabham | Brabham-Repco | 65 | +1'25.36 | 5 |
| 3 | 2 | Denny Hulme | Brabham-Repco | 64 | +1 Lap | 6 |
| 4 | 3 | John Surtees | Honda | 64 | +1 Lap | 7 |
| 5 | 8 | Mike Spence | BRM | 63 | +2 Laps | 11 |
| 6 | 21 | Pedro Rodriguez | Cooper-Maserati | 63 | +2 Laps | 13 |
| 7 | 22 | Jean Pierre Beltoise | Matra-Ford | 63 | +2 Laps | 14 |
| 8 | 12 | J.Williams | Ferrari | 63 | +2 Laps | 16 |
| 9 | 9 | Chris Amon | Ferrari | 62 | Out of fuel | 2 |
| 10 | 16 | Jo Bonnier | Cooper-Maserati | 61 | +4 Laps | 17 |
| 11 | 19 | Guy Ligier | Brabham-Repco | 61 | +4 Laps | 19 |
| 12 | 15 | Jo Siffert | Cooper-Maserati | 59 | Overheating | 10 |
| Ret | 14 | Bruce McLaren | McLaren-BRM | 45 | Oil pressure | 8 |
| Ret | 17 | Chris Irwin | BRM | 33 | Oil leak | 15 |
| Ret | 7 | Jackie Stewart | BRM | 24 | Engine | 12 |
| Ret | 6 | Graham Hill | Lotus-Ford | 18 | Halfshaft | 4 |
| Ret | 18 | Moises Solana | Lotus-Ford | 12 | Suspension | 9 |
| Ret | 11 | Dan Gurney | Eagle-Weslake | 4 | Radiator | 3 |
| Ret | 10 | Mike Fisher | Lotus-BRM | 0 | Fuel system | 18 |

Winning speed: 101.414mph Lap leaders: G Hill 1-2; Clark 3-65
Pole position: Clark, 1m 47.560s, 103.986mph
Fastest lap: Clark, 1m 48.130s, 103.437mph

# 1968

## DRIVERS' CHAMPION: GRAHAM HILL
## CONSTRUCTORS' CHAMPION: LOTUS FORD

### DRIVERS' CHAMPIONSHIP

| POS. | DRIVER | NATIONALITY | CAR | POINTS |
|---|---|---|---|---|
| 1 | Graham Hill | GB | Lotus-Ford | 48 |
| 2 | Jackie Stewart | GB | Matra-Ford | 36 |
| 3 | Denny Hulme | New Zealand | McLaren-BRM, McLaren-Ford | 33 |
| 4 | Jacky Ickx | Belgium | Ferrari | 27 |
| 5 | Bruce McLaren | New Zealand | McLaren-Ford | 22 |
| 6 | Pedro Rodriguez | Mexico | BRM | 18 |
| 7 | Jo Siffert | Switerland | Cooper-Maserati, Lotus-Ford | 12 |
| = | John Surtees | GB | Honda | 12 |
| 9 | Jean-Pierre Beltoise | France | Matra-Ford | 11 |
| 10 | Chris Amon | New Zealand | Ferrari | 10 |
| 11 | Jim Clark | GB | Lotus-Ford | 9 |
| 12 | Jochen Rindt | Austria | Brabham-Repco | 8 |
| 13 | Dick Atwood | GB | BRM | 6 |
| = | Johnny Servoz-Gavin | France | Matra-Ford, Cooper-BRM | 6 |
| = | Jackie Oliver | GB | Lotus-Ford | 6 |
| = | Ludovico Scarfiotti | Italy | Cooper-Maserati, Cooper-BRM | 6 |
| 17 | Lucien Bianchi | Belgium | Cooper-BRM | 5 |
| = | Vic Elford | GB | Cooper-BRM | 5 |
| 19 | Brian Redman | GB | Cooper-Maserati Cooper-BRM | 4 |
| = | Piers Courage | GB | BRM | 4 |
| 21 | Dan Gurney | USA | Eagle-Weslake, Brabham-Repco, McLaren-Ford | 3 |
| = | Jo Bonnier | Sweden | Cooper-Maserati, McLaren-BRM, Honda | 3 |
| 23 | Silvio Moser | Switzerland | Brabham-Repco | 2 |
| = | Jack Brabham | Australia | Brabham-Repco | 2 |
| | John Love | South Africa | Brabham-Repco | |
| | Jackie Pretorius | South Africa | Brabham-Climax | |
| | Sam Tingle | South Africa | LDS-Repco | |
| | Basil van Rooyen | South Africa | Cooper-Climax | |
| | Andrea de Adamich | Italy | Ferrari | |
| | Mike Spence | GB | BRM | |
| | Dave Charlton | South Africa | Brabham-Repco | |
| | Jo Schlesser | France | Honda | |
| | Robin Widdows | GB | Cooper-BRM | |
| | Hubert Hahne | West Germany | Lola-BMW | |
| | Kurt Ahrens | West Germany | Brabham-Repco | |
| | David Hobbs | GB | Honda | |
| | Derek Bell | GB | Ferrari | |
| | Henri Pescarolo | France | Matra | |
| | Bill Brack | Canada | Lotus-Ford | |
| | Bobby Unser | USA | BRM | |
| | Mario Andretti | USA | Lotus-Ford | |
| | Moises Solana | Mexico | Lotus-Ford | |
| | Frank Gardner | GB | BRM | |
| | Al Pease | Canada | Eagle-Climax | |

Points for top six finishers (9, 6, 4, 3, 2, 1). Only the best five scores from the first six races and the best five scores from the remaining six races counted towards the championship.

### CONSTRUCTORS' CHAMPIONSHIP

| POS. | CONSTRUCTOR | POINTS |
|---|---|---|
| 1 | Lotus-Ford | 62 |
| 2 | McLaren-Ford | 49 |
| 3 | Matra-Ford | 45 |
| 4 | Ferrari | 32 |
| 5 | BRM | 28 |
| 6 | Honda | 14 |
| 7 | Cooper-BRM | 14 |
| 8 | Brabham-Repco | 10 |
| 9 | Matra | 8 |
| 10 | McLaren-BRM | 3 |

Points for top six finishers (9, 6, 4, 3, 2, 1). Points only counted for top-placed car for each constructor. Only the best five scores from the first six races and the best five scores from the remaining six races counted towards the championship.

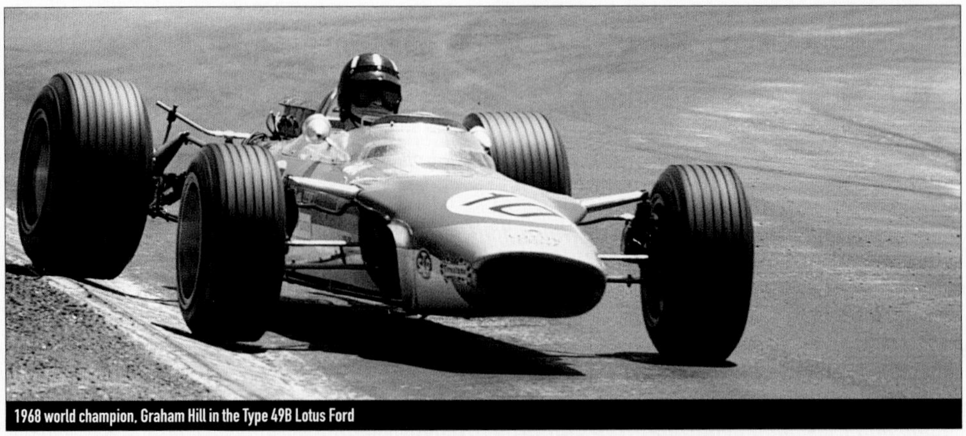

1968 world champion, Graham Hill in the Type 49B Lotus Ford

## SOUTH AFRICAN GRAND PRIX: KYALAMI *1 January Round: 1 Race: 162 80 x 2.550 miles*

| POS. | NO. | DRIVER | CAR/ENGINE | LAPS | TIME/RETIRED | GRID |
|---|---|---|---|---|---|---|
| 1 | 4 | Jim Clark | Lotus-Ford | 80 | 1:53'56.6 | 1 |
| 2 | 5 | Graham Hill | Lotus-Ford | 80 | +25.3 | 2 |
| 3 | 3 | Jochen Rindt | Brabham-Repco | 80 | +30.4 | 4 |
| 4 | 8 | Chris Amon | Ferrari | 78 | +2 Laps | 8 |
| 5 | 1 | Denny Hulme | McLaren-BRM | 78 | +2 Laps | 9 |
| 6 | 21 | Jean Pierre Beltoise | Matra-Ford | 77 | +3 Laps | 18 |
| 7 | 19 | Jo Siffert | Cooper-Maserati | 77 | +3 Laps | 16 |
| 8 | 7 | John Surtees | Honda | 75 | +5 Laps | 6 |
| 9 | 17 | John Love | Brabham-Repco | 75 | +5 Laps | 17 |
| NC | 23 | Jackie Pretorius | Brabham-Climax | 71 | Not classified | 23 |
| Ret | 6 | Dan Gurney | Eagle-Weslake | 58 | Oil leak | 12 |
| Ret | 9 | Jacky Ickx | Ferrari | 51 | Oil leak | 11 |
| Ret | 20 | Jo Bonnier | Cooper-Maserati | 46 | Overheating | 19 |
| Ret | 16 | Jackie Stewart | Matra-Ford | 43 | Engine | 3 |
| Ret | 18 | Sam Tingle | LDS-Repco | 35 | Overheating | 22 |
| Ret | 25 | Basil van Rooyen | Cooper-Climax | 22 | Engine | 20 |
| Ret | 11 | Pedro Rodriguez | BRM | 20 | Fuel system | 10 |
| Ret | 2 | Jack Brabham | Brabham-Repco | 16 | Engine | 5 |
| Ret | 10 | A.de Adamich | Ferrari | 13 | Accident | 7 |
| Ret | 12 | Mike Spence | BRM | 7 | Fuel system | 14 |
| Ret | 14 | Brian Redman | Cooper-Maserati | 4 | Oil leak | 21 |
| Ret | 22 | Dave Charlton | Brabham-Repco | 3 | Differential | 14 |
| Ret | 15 | Ludovico Scarfiotti | Cooper-Maserati | 2 | Water pipe | 15 |

Winning speed: 107.422mph Lap leaders: Stewart 1; Clark 2–80
Pole position: Clark, 1m 21.600s, 112.500mph
Fastest lap: Clark, 1m 23.700s, 109.677 mph

## SPANISH GRAND PRIX: JÁRAMA *12 May Round: 2 Race: 163 90 x 2.115 miles*

| POS. | NO. | DRIVER | CAR/ENGINE | LAPS | TIME/RETIRED | GRID |
|---|---|---|---|---|---|---|
| 1 | 10 | Graham Hill | Lotus-Ford | 90 | 2:15'20.1 | 6 |
| 2 | 1 | Denny Hulme | McLaren-Ford | 90 | +15.9 | 3 |
| 3 | 14 | Brian Redman | Cooper-BRM | 89 | +1 Lap | 13 |
| 4 | 15 | Ludovico Scarfiotti | Cooper-BRM | 89 | +1 Lap | 12 |
| 5 | 6 | Jean Pierre Beltoise | Matra-Ford | 81 | +9 Laps | 5 |
| Ret | 2 | Bruce McLaren | McLaren-Ford | 77 | Oil leak | 4 |
| Ret | 7 | John Surtees | Honda | 74 | Gearbox | 7 |
| Ret | 16 | Jo Siffert | Lotus-Ford | 62 | Transmission | 10 |
| Ret | 19 | Chris Amon | Ferrari | 57 | Fuel pump | 1 |
| Ret | 5 | Piers Courage | BRM | 52 | Fuel system | 11 |
| Ret | 9 | Pedro Rodriguez | BRM | 27 | Accident | 2 |
| Ret | 21 | Jacky Ickx | Ferrari | 13 | Ignition | 8 |
| Ret | 4 | Jochen Rindt | Brabham-Repco | 10 | Oil pressure | 9 |

Winning speed: 84.396mph Lap leaders: Rodriguez 1–11; Beltoise 12–15; Amon 16–57; G Hill 58–90
Pole position: Amon, 1m 27.900s, 86.627mph
Fastest lap: Beltoise, 1m 28.300s, 86.235mph

## MONACO GRAND PRIX: MONTE CARLO *26 May Round: 3 Race: 164 80 x 1.954 miles*

| POS. | NO. | DRIVER | CAR/ENGINE | LAPS | TIME/RETIRED | GRID |
|---|---|---|---|---|---|---|
| 1 | 9 | Graham Hill | Lotus-Ford | 80 | 2:00'32.3 | 1 |
| 2 | 15 | Richard Attwood | BRM | 80 | +2.2 | 6 |
| 3 | 7 | Lucien Bianchi | Cooper-BRM | 76 | +4 Laps | 14 |
| 4 | 6 | Ludovico Scarfiotti | Cooper-BRM | 76 | +4 Laps | 15 |
| 5 | 12 | Denny Hulme | McLaren-Ford | 73 | +7 Laps | 10 |
| Ret | 8 | John Surtees | Honda | 16 | Gearbox | 4 |
| Ret | 4 | Pedro Rodriguez | BRM | 16 | Accident | 9 |
| Ret | 17 | Jo Siffert | Lotus-Ford | 11 | Differential | 3 |
| Ret | 1 | Jean Pierre Beltoise | Matra | 11 | Accident | 8 |
| Ret | 16 | Piers Courage | BRM | 11 | Chassis | 11 |
| Ret | 19 | Dan Gurney | Eagle-Weslake | 9 | Engine | 16 |
| Ret | 3 | Jochen Rindt | Brabham-Repco | 8 | Accident | 5 |
| Ret | 2 | Jack Brabham | Brabham-Repco | 7 | Suspension | 12 |
| Ret | 11 | J.Servoz-Gavin | Matra-Ford | 3 | Halfshaft | 2 |
| Ret | 14 | Bruce McLaren | McLaren-Ford | 0 | Accident | 7 |
| Ret | 10 | Jackie Oliver | Lotus-Ford | 0 | Accident | 13 |
| DNQ | 18 | Jo Bonnier | McLaren-BRM | | | |
| DNQ | 21 | Silvio Moser | Brabham-Repco | | | |

Winning speed: 77.819mph Lap leaders: Servoz-Gavin 1–3; G Hill 4–80
Pole position: G Hill, 1m 28.200s, 79.764mph
Fastest Lap: Attwood 1m 28.100s, 79.854mph

## BELGIAN GRAND PRIX: SPA-FRANCORCHAMPS *9 June Round: 4 Race: 165 28 x 8.761 miles*

| POS. | NO. | DRIVER | CAR/ENGINE | LAPS | TIME/RETIRED | GRID |
|---|---|---|---|---|---|---|
| 1 | 5 | Bruce McLaren | McLaren-Ford | 28 | 1:40'02.1 | 6 |
| 2 | 11 | Pedro Rodriguez | BRM | 28 | +12.1 | 8 |
| 3 | 23 | Jacky Ickx | Ferrari | 28 | +39.6 | 3 |
| 4 | 7 | Jackie Stewart | Matra-Ford | 27 | Out of fuel | 2 |
| 5 | 2 | Jackie Oliver | Lotus-Ford | 26 | Transmission | 15 |
| 6 | 15 | Lucien Bianchi | Cooper-BRM | 26 | +2 Laps | 12 |
| 7 | 3 | Jo Siffert | Lotus-Ford | 25 | Oil pressure | 9 |
| 8 | 10 | Jean Pierre Beltoise | Matra | 25 | +3 Laps | 13 |
| Ret | 14 | Piers Courage | BRM | 22 | Engine | 7 |
| Ret | 6 | Denny Hulme | McLaren-Ford | 18 | Halfshaft | 5 |
| Ret | 20 | John Surtees | Honda | 11 | Suspension | 4 |
| Ret | 22 | Chris Amon | Ferrari | 8 | Radiator | 1 |
| Ret | 16 | Brian Redman | Cooper-BRM | 6 | Spun off | 11 |
| Ret | 12 | Richard Attwood | BRM | 6 | Oil pipe | 18 |
| Ret | 18 | Jack Brabham | Brabham-Repco | 6 | Throttle | 10 |
| Ret | 1 | Graham Hill | Lotus-Ford | 5 | Halfshaft | 14 |
| Ret | 19 | Jochen Rindt | Brabham-Repco | 5 | Engine | 17 |
| Ret | 17 | Jo Bonnier | McLaren-BRM | 1 | Wheel | 16 |

Winning speed: 147.139mph Lap leaders: Amon 1; Surtees 2–10; Hulme 11,15; Stewart 12–14,16–27; McLaren 28
Pole position: Amon, 3m 28.600s, 151.202mph
Fastest lap: Surtees, 3m 30.500s, 149.838mph

## DUTCH GRAND PRIX: ZANDVOORT *23 June Round: 5 Race: 166 90 x 2.605 miles*

| POS. | NO. | DRIVER | CAR/ENGINE | LAPS | TIME/RETIRED | GRID |
|---|---|---|---|---|---|---|
| 1 | 8 | Jackie Stewart | Matra-Ford | 90 | 2:46'11.26 | 5 |
| 2 | 17 | Jean Pierre Beltoise | Matra | 90 | +1'33.93 | 16 |
| 3 | 15 | Pedro Rodriguez | BRM | 89 | +1 Lap | 11 |
| 4 | 10 | Jacky Ickx | Ferrari | 88 | +2 Laps | 6 |
| 5 | 22 | Silvio Moser | Brabham-Repco | 87 | +3 Laps | 7 |
| 6 | 9 | Chris Amon | Ferrari | 85 | +5 Laps | 1 |
| 7 | 16 | Richard Attwood | BRM | 85 | +5 Laps | 15 |
| 8 | 19 | Jo Bonnier | McLaren-BRM | 82 | +8 Laps | 19 |
| 9 | 3 | Graham Hill | Lotus-Ford | 81 | Accident | 3 |
| NC | 4 | Jackie Oliver | Lotus-Ford | 80 | Not classified | 10 |
| Ret | 18 | Dan Gurney | Brabham-Repco | 63 | Throttle | 12 |
| Ret | 21 | Jo Siffert | Lotus-Ford | 55 | Gearbox | 13 |
| Ret | 7 | John Surtees | Honda | 50 | Alternator | 9 |
| Ret | 20 | Piers Courage | BRM | 50 | Spun off | 14 |
| Ret | 6 | Jochen Rindt | Brabham-Repco | 39 | Ignition | 2 |
| Ret | 5 | Jack Brabham | Brabham-Repco | 22 | Spun off | 4 |
| Ret | 2 | Bruce McLaren | McLaren-Ford | 19 | Accident | 8 |
| Ret | 1 | Denny Hulme | McLaren-Ford | 10 | Ignition | 7 |
| Ret | 14 | Lucien Bianchi | Cooper-BRM | 9 | Accident | 18 |

Winning speed: 84.659mph Lap leaders: G Hill 1–3; Stewart 4–90
Pole position: Amon 1m 23.540s, 112.275mph
Fastest lap: Beltoise 1m 45.910s, 88.561mph

## FRENCH GRAND PRIX: ROUEN-LES-ESSARTS *7 July Round: 6 Race: 167 80 x 2.650 miles*

| POS. | NO. | DRIVER | CAR/ENGINE | LAPS | TIME/RETIRED | GRID |
|---|---|---|---|---|---|---|
| 1 | 26 | Jacky Ickx | Ferrari | 60 | 2:25'40.9 | 3 |
| 2 | 16 | John Surtees | Honda | 60 | +1'58.6 | 7 |
| 3 | 28 | Jackie Stewart | Matra-Ford | 59 | +1 Lap | 2 |
| 4 | 30 | Vic Elford | Cooper-BRM | 58 | +2 Laps | 17 |
| 5 | 8 | Denny Hulme | McLaren-Ford | 58 | +2 Laps | 4 |
| 6 | 36 | Piers Courage | BRM | 57 | +3 Laps | 14 |
| 7 | 22 | Richard Attwood | BRM | 57 | +3 Laps | 12 |
| 8 | 10 | Bruce McLaren | McLaren-Ford | 56 | +4 Laps | 6 |
| 9 | 6 | Jean Pierre Beltoise | Matra | 56 | +4 Laps | 8 |
| 10 | 24 | Chris Amon | Ferrari | 55 | +5 Laps | 5 |
| 11 | 34 | Jo Siffert | Lotus-Ford | 54 | +6 Laps | 11 |
| NC | 20 | Pedro Rodriguez | BRM | 53 | Not classified | 10 |
| Ret | 2 | Jochen Rindt | Brabham-Repco | 45 | Fuel leak | 1 |
| Ret | 4 | Jack Brabham | Brabham-Repco | 15 | Fuel pump | 13 |
| Ret | 12 | Graham Hill | Lotus-Ford | 14 | Halfshaft | 9 |
| Ret | 32 | J.Servoz-Gavin | Cooper-BRM | 14 | Accident | 15 |
| Ret | 18 | Jo Schlesser | Honda | 2 | Accident | 16 |

Winning speed: 100.452mph Lap leaders: Ickx 1–18, 20–60; P Rodriguez 19
Pole position: Rindt, 1m 56.100s, 126.047mph
Fastest lap: P Rodriguez, 2m 11.500s, 111.285mph

## BRITISH GRAND PRIX: BRANDS HATCH *20 July Round: 7 Race: 168 80 x 2.650 miles*

| POS. | NO. | DRIVER | CAR/ENGINE | LAPS | TIME/RETIRED | GRID |
|---|---|---|---|---|---|---|
| 1 | 22 | Jo Siffert | Lotus-Ford | 80 | 2:01'20.3 | 4 |
| 2 | 5 | Chris Amon | Ferrari | 80 | +4.4 | 3 |
| 3 | 6 | Jacky Ickx | Ferrari | 79 | +1 Lap | 12 |
| 4 | 1 | Denny Hulme | McLaren-Ford | 79 | +1 Lap | 11 |
| 5 | 7 | John Surtees | Honda | 78 | +2 Laps | 9 |
| 6 | 14 | Jackie Stewart | Matra-Ford | 78 | +2 Laps | 7 |
| 7 | 2 | Bruce McLaren | McLaren-Ford | 77 | +3 Laps | 10 |
| 8 | 20 | Piers Courage | BRM | 72 | +8 Laps | 16 |
| Ret | 4 | Jochen Rindt | Brabham-Repco | 55 | Fuel leak | 5 |
| Ret | 10 | Pedro Rodriguez | BRM | 52 | Engine | 13 |
| NC | 19 | Silvio Moser | Brabham-Repco | 52 | Not classified | 19 |
| Ret | 9 | Jackie Oliver | Lotus-Ford | 43 | Transmission | 2 |
| Ret | 16 | Robin Widdows | Cooper-BRM | 34 | Ignition | 18 |
| Ret | 8 | Graham Hill | Lotus-Ford | 26 | Halfshaft | 1 |
| Ret | 15 | Vic Elford | Cooper-BRM | 26 | Engine | 7 |
| Ret | 18 | Jean Pierre Beltoise | Matra | 11 | Engine | 14 |
| Ret | 11 | Richard Attwood | BRM | 10 | Radiator | 15 |
| Ret | 24 | Dan Gurney | Eagle-Weslake | 8 | Fuel pump | 6 |
| Ret | 23 | Jo Bonnier | McLaren-BRM | 6 | Engine | 20 |
| Ret | 3 | Jack Brabham | Brabham-Repco | 0 | Engine | 8 |

Winning speed: 104.831mph Lap leaders: Oliver 1–3, 27–43; G Hill 4–26; Siffert 44–80
Pole position: G Hill, 1m 28.900s, 107.312mph
Fastest lap: Siffert, 1m 29.700s, 106 355mph

## GERMAN GRAND PRIX: NÜRBURGRING *4 August Round: 8 Race: 169 14 x 14.189 miles*

| POS. | NO. | DRIVER | CAR/ENGINE | LAPS | TIME/RETIRED | GRID |
|---|---|---|---|---|---|---|
| 1 | 6 | Jackie Stewart | Matra-Ford | 14 | 2:19'03.2 | 6 |
| 2 | 3 | Graham Hill | Lotus-Ford | 14 | +4'03.2 | 4 |
| 3 | 5 | Jochen Rindt | Brabham-Repco | 14 | +4'09.4 | 3 |
| 4 | 9 | Jacky Ickx | Ferrari | 14 | +5'55.2 | 1 |
| 5 | 4 | Jack Brabham | Brabham-Repco | 14 | +6'21.1 | 15 |
| 6 | 10 | Pedro Rodriguez | BRM | 14 | +6'25.0 | 14 |
| 7 | 1 | Denny Hulme | McLaren-Ford | 14 | +6'31.0 | 11 |
| 8 | 22 | Piers Courage | BRM | 14 | +7'56.4 | 8 |
| 9 | 14 | Dan Gurney | Eagle-Weslake | 14 | +8'13.7 | 10 |
| 10 | 18 | Hubert Hahne | Lola-BMW | 14 | +10'11.4 | 18 |
| 11 | 21 | Jackie Oliver | Lotus-Ford | 13 | +1 Lap | 13 |
| 12 | 17 | Kurt Ahrens | Brabham-Repco | 13 | +1 Lap | 17 |
| 13 | 2 | Bruce McLaren | McLaren-Ford | 13 | +1 Lap | 16 |
| 14 | 11 | Richard Attwood | BRM | 13 | +1 Lap | 20 |
| Ret | 8 | Chris Amon | Ferrari | 11 | Accident | 2 |
| Ret | 12 | Jean Pierre Beltoise | Matra | 8 | Accident | 12 |
| Ret | 16 | Jo Siffert | Lotus-Ford | 6 | Ignition | 9 |
| Ret | 19 | Lucien Bianchi | Cooper-BRM | 6 | Fuel leak | 19 |
| Ret | 7 | John Surtees | Honda | 3 | Ignition | 7 |
| Ret | 20 | Vic Elford | Cooper-BRM | 0 | Accident | 5 |

Winning speed: 85.714mph Lap leaders: Stewart 1–14
Pole position: Ickx, 9m 04.000s, 93.898mph
Fastest lap: Stewart, 9m 36.000s, 88.681mph

## ITALIAN GRAND PRIX: MONZA *8 September Round: 9 Race: 170 68 x 3.573 miles*

| POS. | NO. | DRIVER | CAR/ENGINE | LAPS | TIME/RETIRED | GRID |
|---|---|---|---|---|---|---|
| 1 | 1 | Denny Hulme | McLaren-Ford | 68 | 1:40'14.8 | 7 |
| 2 | 5 | J.Servoz-Gavin | Matra-Ford | 68 | +1'28.4 | 13 |
| 3 | 8 | Jacky Ickx | Ferrari | 68 | +1'28.6 | 4 |
| 4 | 27 | Piers Courage | BRM | 67 | +1 Lap | 17 |
| 5 | 6 | Jean Pierre Beltoise | Matra | 66 | +2 Laps | 18 |
| 6 | 3 | Jo Bonnier | McLaren-BRM | 64 | +4 Laps | 19 |
| Ret | 20 | Jo Siffert | Lotus-Ford | 58 | Suspension | 9 |
| Ret | 10 | Jack Brabham | Brabham-Repco | 56 | Oil pressure | 16 |
| Ret | 4 | Jackie Stewart | Matra-Ford | 42 | Engine | 6 |
| Ret | 15 | David Hobbs | Honda | 42 | Engine | 14 |
| Ret | 19 | Jackie Oliver | Lotus-Ford | 38 | Transmission | 11 |
| Ret | 2 | Bruce McLaren | McLaren-Ford | 34 | Oil leak | 2 |
| Ret | 11 | Jochen Rindt | Brabham-Repco | 33 | Engine | 10 |
| Ret | 26 | Pedro Rodriguez | BRM | 22 | Engine | 15 |
| Ret | 21 | Dan Gurney | Eagle-Weslake | 19 | Engine | 12 |
| Ret | 16 | Graham Hill | Lotus-Ford | 10 | Wheel | 5 |
| Ret | 14 | John Surtees | Honda | 8 | Accident | 1 |
| Ret | 9 | Chris Amon | Ferrari | 8 | Accident | 3 |
| Ret | 7 | Derek Bell | Ferrari | 4 | Fuel system | 8 |
| Ret | 23 | Vic Elford | Cooper-BRM | 2 | Accident | 20 |
| DNQ | 28 | Frank Gardner | BRM | | | |
| DNQ | 12 | Silvio Moser | Brabham-Repco | | | |

Winning speed: 145.415mph Lap leaders: McLaren 1–6, 8–12, 14; Surtees 7; Stewart 13, 17–18, 27, 30, 33, 40; Siffert 15–16; Hulme 19–26, 28–29, 31–32, 34–39, 41–68
Pole position: Surtees, 1m 26.070s, 149.441mph
Fastest lap: Oliver, 1m 26.500s, 148.698mph

## CANADIAN GRAND PRIX: MONT-TREMBLANT *22 September Round: 10 Race: 171 90 x 2.650 miles*

| POS. | NO. | DRIVER | CAR/ENGINE | LAPS | TIME/RETIRED | GRID |
|---|---|---|---|---|---|---|
| 1 | 1 | Denny Hulme | McLaren-Ford | 90 | 2:27'11.2 | 6 |
| 2 | 2 | Bruce McLaren | McLaren-Ford | 89 | +1 Lap | 8 |
| 3 | 16 | Pedro Rodriguez | BRM | 88 | +2 Laps | 12 |
| 4 | 3 | Graham Hill | Lotus-Ford | 86 | +4 Laps | 5 |
| 5 | 21 | Vic Elford | Cooper-BRM | 86 | +4 Laps | 16 |
| 6 | 14 | Jackie Stewart | Matra-Ford | 83 | +7 Laps | 11 |
| Ret | 18 | Jean Pierre Beltoise | Matra | 77 | Gearbox | 15 |
| Ret | 9 | Chris Amon | Ferrari | 72 | Transmission | 2 |
| Ret | 15 | J.Servoz-Gavin | Matra-Ford | 71 | Accident | 13 |
| NC | 20 | Lucien Bianchi | Cooper-BRM | 56 | Not classified | 18 |
| Ret | 19 | Henri Pescarolo | Matra | 54 | Oil pressure | 19 |
| Ret | 6 | Jochen Rindt | Brabham-Repco | 39 | Engine | 1 |
| Ret | 4 | Jackie Oliver | Lotus-Ford | 32 | Halfshaft | 19 |
| Ret | 5 | Jack Brabham | Brabham-Repco | 31 | Suspension | 10 |
| Ret | 12 | Jo Siffert | Lotus-Ford | 29 | Oil leak | 3 |
| Ret | 11 | Dan Gurney | McLaren-Ford | 29 | Radiator | 4 |
| Ret | 24 | Piers Courage | BRM | 22 | Gearbox | 14 |
| Ret | 27 | Bill Brack | Lotus-Ford | 18 | Halfshaft | 20 |
| Ret | 8 | John Surtees | Honda | 10 | Gearbox | 7 |
| Ret | 22 | Jo Bonnier | McLaren-BRM | 0 | Fuel system | 17 |

Winning speed: 97.223mph Lap leaders: Amon 1–72; Hulme 73–90
Pole position: Rindt, 1m 33.800s, 101.706mph
Fastest lap: Siffert, 1m 35.100s, 100.315mph

## UNITED STATES GRAND PRIX: WATKINS GLEN *6 October Round: 11 Race: 172 108 x 2.300 miles*

| POS. | NO. | DRIVER | CAR/ENGINE | LAPS | TIME/RETIRED | GRID |
|---|---|---|---|---|---|---|
| 1 | 15 | Jackie Stewart | Matra-Ford | 108 | 1:59'20.29 | 2 |
| 2 | 10 | Graham Hill | Lotus-Ford | 108 | +24.68 | 3 |
| 3 | 5 | John Surtees | Honda | 107 | +1 Lap | 9 |
| 4 | 14 | Dan Gurney | McLaren-Ford | 107 | +1 Lap | 7 |
| 5 | 16 | Jo Siffert | Lotus-Ford | 105 | +3 Laps | 12 |
| 6 | 2 | Bruce McLaren | McLaren-Ford | 103 | +5 Laps | 10 |
| Ret | 22 | Piers Courage | BRM | 93 | Out of fuel | 14 |
| Ret | 1 | Denny Hulme | McLaren-Ford | 92 | Accident | 5 |
| NC | 19 | Lucien Bianchi | Cooper-BRM | 88 | Not classified | 20 |
| Ret | 3 | Jack Brabham | Brabham-Repco | 77 | Engine | 8 |
| Ret | 4 | Jochen Rindt | Brabham-Repco | 73 | Engine | 6 |
| Ret | 18 | Vic Elford | Cooper-BRM | 71 | Engine | 17 |
| Ret | 8 | Pedro Rodriguez | BRM | 66 | Suspension | 11 |
| NC | 17 | Jo Bonnier | McLaren-BRM | 62 | Not classified | 18 |
| Ret | 6 | Chris Amon | Ferrari | 59 | Water pump | 4 |
| Ret | 21 | Jean Pierre Beltoise | Matra | 44 | Transmission | 13 |
| Ret | 9 | Bobby Unser | BRM | 35 | Engine | 19 |
| Ret | 12 | Mario Andretti | Lotus-Ford | 32 | Clutch | 1 |
| Ret | 7 | Derek Bell | Ferrari | 14 | Engine | 15 |
| DNS | 11 | Jackie Oliver | Lotus-Ford | 0 | Non starter | |

Winning speed: 124.889mph Lap Leaders: Stewart 1–108
Pole position: Andretti, 1m 04.200s, 128.972mph
Fastest lap: Stewart, 1m 05.220s, 126.955mph

## MEXICAN GRAND PRIX: MEXICO CITY *3 November Round: 12 Race: 173 65 x 3.107 miles*

| POS. | NO. | DRIVER | CAR/ENGINE | LAPS | TIME/RETIRED | GRID |
|---|---|---|---|---|---|---|
| 1 | 10 | Graham Hill | Lotus-Ford | 65 | 1:56'43.95 | 3 |
| 2 | 2 | Bruce McLaren | McLaren-Ford | 65 | +1'19.32 | 9 |
| 3 | 11 | Jackie Oliver | Lotus-Ford | 65 | +1'40.65 | 14 |
| 4 | 8 | Pedro Rodriguez | BRM | 65 | +1'41.09 | 12 |
| 5 | 17 | Jo Bonnier | Honda | 64 | +1 Lap | 18 |
| 6 | 16 | Jo Siffert | Lotus-Ford | 64 | +1 Lap | 1 |
| 7 | 15 | Jackie Stewart | Matra-Ford | 64 | +1 Lap | 7 |
| 8 | 18 | Vic Elford | Cooper-BRM | 63 | +2 Laps | 17 |
| 9 | 9 | Henri Pescarolo | Matra | 62 | +3 Laps | 20 |
| 10 | 3 | Jack Brabham | Brabham-Repco | 59 | Oil pressure | 8 |
| Ret | 23 | J.Servoz-Gavin | Matra-Ford | 57 | Ignition | 16 |
| Ret | 14 | Dan Gurney | McLaren-Ford | 28 | Suspension | 5 |
| Ret | 22 | Piers Courage | BRM | 25 | Engine | 19 |
| Ret | 19 | Lucien Bianchi | Cooper-BRM | 21 | Engine | 21 |
| Ret | 5 | John Surtees | Honda | 17 | Overheating | 6 |
| Ret | 6 | Chris Amon | Ferrari | 16 | Transmission | 2 |
| Ret | 12 | Moises Solana | Lotus-Ford | 14 | Broken wing | 11 |
| Ret | 1 | Denny Hulme | McLaren-Ford | 10 | Suspension | 4 |
| Ret | 21 | Jean Pierre Beltoise | Matra | 10 | Suspension | 13 |
| Ret | 7 | Jacky Ickx | Ferrari | 3 | Ignition | 15 |
| Ret | 4 | Jochen Rindt | Brabham-Repco | 2 | Ignition | 10 |

Winning speed: 103.049mph Lap leaders: Hill 1–4, 9–21, 25–65; Stewart 5–8; Siffert 22–24
Pole position: Siffert, 1m 45.220s, 106.298mph Fastest lap: Siffert, 1m 44.230s, 107.308mph

# 1969

## DRIVERS' CHAMPION: JACKIE STEWART
## CONSTRUCTORS' CHAMPION: MATRA FORD

### DRIVERS' CHAMPIONSHIP

| POS. | DRIVER | NATIONALITY | CAR | POINTS |
|---|---|---|---|---|
| 1 | Jackie Stewart | GB | Matra-Ford | 63 |
| 2 | Jacky Ickx | Belgium | Brabham-Ford | 37 |
| 3 | Bruce Mclaren | New Zealand | McLaren-Ford | 26 |
| 4 | Jochen Rindt | Austria | Lotus-Ford | 22 |
| 5 | Jean-Pierre Beltoise | France | Matra-Ford | 21 |
| 6 | Denny Hulme | New Zealand | McLaren-Ford | 20 |
| 7 | Graham Hill | GB | Lotus-Ford | 19 |
| 8 | Piers Courage | GB | Brabham-Ford | 16 |
| 9 | Jo Siffert | Switzerland | Lotus-Ford | 15 |
| 10 | Jack Brabham | Australia | Brabham-Ford | 14 |
| 11 | John Surtees | GB | B.R.M. | 6 |
| 12 | Chris Amon | New Zealand | Ferrari | 4 |
| 13 | Richard Attwood | GB | Lotus-Ford, Brabham-Cosworth | 3 |
| = | Vic Elford | GB | Cooper-Maserati McLaren-Ford | 3 |
| = | Pedro Rodriguez | Mexico | BRM, Ferrari | 3 |
| 16 | Johnny Servoz-Gavin | France | Matra-Cosworth Matra-Ford | 1 |
| = | Silvio Moser | Switzerland | Brabham-Ford | 1 |
| = | Jackie Oliver | GB | BRM | 1 |
| | Sam Tingle | South Africa | Brabham-Repco | |
| | Piet de Klerk | South Africa | Brabham-Repco | |
| | Mario Andretti | USA | Lotus-Ford | |
| | John Love | South Africa | Lotus-Ford | |
| | Basil van Rooyen | South Africa | McLaren-Ford | |
| | John Miles | GB | Lotus-Ford | |
| | Jo Bonnier | Sweden | Lotus-Ford | |
| | Derek Bell | GB | McLaren-Ford | |
| | Kurt Ahrens Jr | West Germany | Brabham-Cosworth | |
| | François Cevert | France | Tecno-Cosworth | |
| | Xavier Perrot | France | Brabham-Cosworth | |
| | Henri Pescarolo | France | Matra-Cosworth | |
| | Rolf Stommelen | West Germany | Lotus-Cosworth | |
| | Peter Westbury | GB | Brabham-Cosworth | |
| | Hubert Hahne | West Germany | BMW | |
| | Dieter Quester | West Germany | BMW | |
| | Gerhard Mitter | West Germany | BMW | |
| | Hans Herrmann | Germany | Lotus-Cosworth | |
| | Ernesto Brambilla | Italy | Ferrari | |
| | Pete Lovely | USA | Lotus-Ford | |
| | Bill Brack | Canada | BRM | |
| | Al Pease | Canada | Eagle-Climax | |
| | John Cordts | Canada | Brabham-Climax | |

Points for top six finishers (9, 6, 4, 3, 2, 1). Only the best five scores from the first six races and the best four scores from the remaining five races counted towards the championship. Formula Two cars raced simulataneously with Formula One cars at the German Grand Prix but were ineligible for points which were awarded to the top six Formula One finishers.

### CONSTRUCTORS' CHAMPIONSHIP

| POS. | CONSTRUCTOR | POINTS |
|---|---|---|
| 1 | Matra-Ford | 66 |
| 2 | Brabham-Ford | 49 |
| 3 | Lotus-Ford | 47 |
| 4 | McLaren-Ford | 38 |
| 5 | Ferrari | 7 |
| = | BRM | 7 |

Points for top six finishers (9, 6, 4, 3, 2, 1). Points only counted for top-placed car for each constructor. Only the best five scores from the first six races and the best four scores from the remaining five races counted towards the championship.

### SOUTH AFRICAN GRAND PRIX: KYALAMI *1 March Round: 1 Race: 174 80 x 2.550 miles*

| POS. | NO. | DRIVER | CAR-ENGINE | LAPS | TIME/RETIRED | GRID |
|---|---|---|---|---|---|---|
| 1 | 7 | Jackie Stewart | Matra-Ford | 80 | 1:50'39.1 | 4 |
| 2 | 1 | Graham Hill | Lotus-Ford | 80 | +18.8 | 7 |
| 3 | 5 | Denny Hulme | McLaren-Ford | 80 | +31.8 | 3 |
| 4 | 4 | Jo Siffert | Lotus-Ford | 80 | +49.2 | 12 |
| 5 | 6 | Bruce McLaren | McLaren-Ford | 79 | +1 Lap | 8 |
| 6 | 8 | Jean Pierre Beltoise | Matra-Ford | 78 | +2 Laps | 11 |
| 7 | 11 | Jackie Oliver | BRM | 77 | +3 Laps | 14 |
| 8 | 17 | Sam Tingle | Brabham-Repco | 73 | +7 Laps | 17 |
| NC | 19 | Peter de Klerk | Brabham-Repco | 67 | Not classified | 16 |
| Ret | 2 | Jochen Rindt | Lotus-Ford | 44 | Fuel pump | 2 |
| Ret | 10 | John Surtees | BRM | 40 | Engine | 18 |
| Ret | 12 | Pedro Rodriguez | BRM | 38 | Water leak | 15 |
| Ret | 9 | Chris Amon | Ferrari | 34 | Engine | 5 |
| Ret | 14 | Jack Brabham | Brabham-Ford | 32 | Handling | 1 |
| Ret | 3 | Mario Andretti | Lotus-Ford | 31 | Gearbox | 6 |
| Ret | 16 | John Love | Lotus-Ford | 31 | Ignition | 10 |
| Ret | 15 | Jacky Ickx | Brabham-Ford | 20 | Ignition | 13 |
| Ret | 18 | Basil van Rooyen | McLaren-Ford | 12 | Brakes | 9 |

Winning speed: 110.617mph Lap leaders: Stewart 1-80
Pole position: Brabham, 1m 20.000s, 114.750mph
Fastest lap: Stewart, 1m 21.600s, 112.500mph

### SPANISH GRAND PRIX: MONTJUICH PARK *4 May Round: 2 Race:175 90 x 2.356 miles*

| POS. | NO. | DRIVER | CAR-ENGINE | LAPS | TIME/RETIRED | GRID |
|---|---|---|---|---|---|---|
| 1 | 7 | Jackie Stewart | Matra-Ford | 90 | 2:16'54.0 | 4 |
| 2 | 6 | Bruce McLaren | McLaren-Ford | 88 | +2 Laps | 13 |
| 3 | 8 | Jean Pierre Beltoise | Matra-Ford | 87 | +3 Laps | 12 |
| 4 | 5 | Denny Hulme | McLaren-Ford | 87 | +3 Laps | 8 |
| 5 | 14 | John Surtees | BRM | 84 | +6 Laps | 9 |
| 6 | 4 | Jacky Ickx | Brabham-Ford | 83 | +7 Laps | 7 |
| Ret | 9 | Pedro Rodriguez | BRM | 73 | Engine | 14 |
| Ret | 15 | Chris Amon | Ferrari | 56 | Engine | 2 |
| Ret | 3 | Jack Brabham | Brabham-Ford | 51 | Engine | 5 |
| Ret | 10 | Jo Siffert | Lotus-Ford | 30 | Oil leak | 6 |
| Ret | 2 | Jochen Rindt | Lotus-Ford | 19 | Accident | 1 |
| Ret | 11 | Piers Courage | Brabham-Ford | 18 | Engine | 11 |
| Ret | 1 | Graham Hill | Lotus-Ford | 8 | Accident | 3 |
| Ret | 12 | Jackie Oliver | BRM | 1 | Oil pipe | 10 |

Winning speed: 92.917mph Lap leaders: Rindt 1-19; Amon 20-56; Stewart 57-90
Pole position: Rindt, 1m 25.700s, 98.952mph
Fastest lap: Rindt, 1m 28.300s, 96.039mph

### MONACO GRAND PRIX: MONTE CARLO *18 May Round: 3 Race: 176 80 x 1.954 miles*

| POS. | NO. | DRIVER | CAR-ENGINE | LAPS | TIME/RETIRED | GRID |
|---|---|---|---|---|---|---|
| 1 | 1 | Graham Hill | Lotus-Ford | 80 | 1:56'59.4 | 4 |
| 2 | 16 | Piers Courage | Brabham-Ford | 80 | +17.3 | 9 |
| 3 | 9 | Jo Siffert | Lotus-Ford | 80 | +34.6 | 5 |
| 4 | 2 | Richard Attwood | Lotus-Ford | 80 | +52.9 | 10 |
| 5 | 4 | Bruce McLaren | McLaren-Ford | 79 | +1 Lap | 11 |
| 6 | 3 | Denny Hulme | McLaren-Ford | 78 | +2 Laps | 12 |
| 7 | 12 | Vic Elford | Cooper-Maserati | 74 | +6 Laps | 16 |
| Ret | 6 | Jacky Ickx | Brabham-Ford | 48 | Suspension | 7 |
| Ret | 7 | Jackie Stewart | Matra-Ford | 22 | Halfshaft | 1 |
| Ret | 8 | Jean Pierre Beltoise | Matra-Ford | 20 | Halfshaft | 3 |
| Ret | 11 | Chris Amon | Ferrari | 16 | Differential | 2 |
| Ret | 10 | Pedro Rodriguez | BRM | 15 | Engine | 14 |
| Ret | 17 | Silvio Moser | Brabham-Ford | 15 | Halfshaft | 15 |
| Ret | 14 | John Surtees | BRM | 9 | Gearbox | 6 |
| Ret | 5 | Jack Brabham | Brabham-Ford | 9 | Accident | 8 |
| Ret | 15 | Jackie Oliver | BRM | 0 | Accident | 13 |

Winning speed: 80.180mph Lap leaders: Stewart 1-22; G Hill 23-80
Pole position: Stewart, 1m 24.600s, 83.158mph
Fastest lap: Stewart, 1m 25.100s, 82.669mph

### DUTCH GRAND PRIX: ZANDVOORT *21 June Round: 4 Race: 177 90 x 2.605 miles*

| POS. | NO. | DRIVER | CAR-ENGINE | LAPS | TIME/RETIRED | GRID |
|---|---|---|---|---|---|---|
| 1 | 4 | Jackie Stewart | Matra-Ford | 90 | 2:06'42.08 | 2 |
| 2 | 10 | Jo Siffert | Lotus-Ford | 90 | +24.52 | 10 |
| 3 | 8 | Chris Amon | Ferrari | 90 | +30.51 | 4 |
| 4 | 7 | Denny Hulme | McLaren-Ford | 90 | +37.16 | 7 |
| 5 | 12 | Jacky Ickx | Brabham-Ford | 90 | +37.67 | 5 |
| 6 | 11 | Jack Brabham | Brabham-Ford | 90 | +1'10.81 | 8 |
| 7 | 1 | Graham Hill | Lotus-Ford | 88 | +2 Laps | 3 |
| 8 | 5 | Jean Pierre Beltoise | Matra-Ford | 87 | +3 Laps | 11 |
| 9 | 14 | John Surtees | BRM | 87 | +3 Laps | 12 |
| 10 | 18 | Vic Elford | McLaren-Ford | 84 | +6 Laps | 15 |
| Ret | 17 | Silvio Moser | Brabham-Ford | 54 | Ignition | 14 |
| Ret | 6 | Bruce McLaren | McLaren-Ford | 24 | Suspension | 6 |
| Ret | 2 | Jochen Rindt | Lotus-Ford | 16 | Halfshaft | 1 |
| Ret | 16 | Piers Courage | Brabham-Ford | 12 | Clutch | 9 |
| Ret | 15 | Jackie Oliver | BRM | 9 | Gearbox | 13 |

Winning speed: 111.042 mph Lap leaders: G Hill 1-2; Rindt 3-16; Stewart 17-90
Pole position: Rindt, 1m 20.850s, 116.011mph
Fastest lap: Stewart, 1m 22.940s, 113.087mph

### FRENCH GRAND PRIX: CLERMONT-FERRAND *6 July Round: 5 Race: 178 38 x 5.005 miles*

| POS. | NO. | DRIVER | CAR-ENGINE | LAPS | TIME/RETIRED | GRID |
|---|---|---|---|---|---|---|
| 1 | 2 | Jackie Stewart | Matra-Ford | 38 | 1:56'47.4 | 1 |
| 2 | 7 | Jean Pierre Beltoise | Matra-Ford | 38 | +57.1 | 5 |
| 3 | 11 | Jacky Ickx | Brabham-Ford | 38 | +57.3 | 4 |
| 4 | 5 | Bruce McLaren | McLaren-Ford | 37 | +1 Lap | 7 |
| 5 | 10 | Vic Elford | McLaren-Ford | 37 | +1 Lap | 10 |
| 6 | 1 | Graham Hill | Lotus-Ford | 37 | +1 Lap | 8 |
| 7 | 12 | Silvio Moser | Brabham-Ford | 36 | +2 Laps | 13 |
| 8 | 4 | Denny Hulme | McLaren-Ford | 35 | +3 Laps | 2 |
| 9 | 3 | Jo Siffert | Lotus-Ford | 34 | +4 Laps | 9 |
| Ret | 6 | Chris Amon | Ferrari | 30 | Engine | 6 |
| Ret | 15 | Jochen Rindt | Lotus-Ford | 22 | Physical | 3 |
| Ret | 9 | Piers Courage | Brabham-Ford | 21 | Chassis | 11 |
| Ret | 14 | John Miles | Lotus-Ford | 1 | Fuel pump | 12 |

Winning speed: 97.712mph Lap leaders: Stewart 1-38
Pole position: Stewart, 3m 0.600s, 99.770mph
Fastest lap: Stewart, 3m 2.700s, 98.624mph

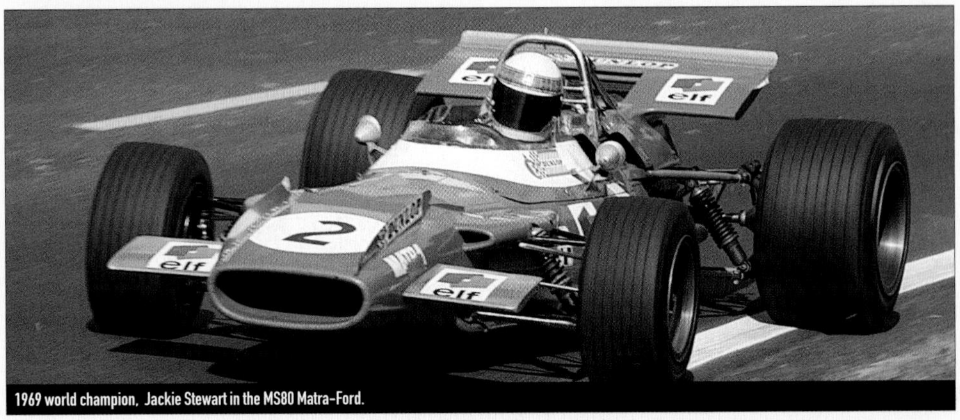

1969 world champion, Jackie Stewart in the MS80 Matra-Ford.

### BRITISH GRAND PRIX: SILVERSTONE *19 July Round: 6 Race: 179 84 x 2.927 miles*

| POS. | NO. | DRIVER | CAR-ENGINE | LAPS | TIME/RETIRED | GRID |
|---|---|---|---|---|---|---|
| 1 | 3 | Jackie Stewart | Matra-Ford | 84 | 1:55'55.6 | 2 |
| 2 | 7 | Jacky Ickx | Brabham-Ford | 83 | +1 Lap | 4 |
| 3 | 6 | Bruce McLaren | McLaren-Ford | 83 | +1 Lap | 7 |
| 4 | 2 | Jochen Rindt | Lotus-Ford | 83 | +1 Lap | 1 |
| 5 | 16 | Piers Courage | Brabham-Ford | 83 | +1 Lap | 10 |
| 6 | 19 | Vic Elford | McLaren-Ford | 82 | +2 Laps | 11 |
| 7 | 1 | Graham Hill | Lotus-Ford | 82 | +2 Laps | 12 |
| 8 | 10 | Jo Siffert | Lotus-Ford | 81 | +3 Laps | 9 |
| 9 | 4 | Jean Pierre Beltoise | Matra-Ford | 78 | +6 Laps | 17 |
| 10 | 9 | John Miles | Lotus-Ford | 75 | +9 Laps | 14 |
| Ret | 12 | Pedro Rodriguez | Ferrari | 61 | Engine | 8 |
| Ret | 11 | Chris Amon | Ferrari | 45 | Gearbox | 5 |
| Ret | 5 | Denny Hulme | McLaren-Ford | 27 | Ignition | 3 |
| Ret | 15 | Jackie Oliver | BRM | 19 | Transmission | 13 |
| Ret | 18 | Jo Bonnier | Lotus-Ford | 6 | Engine | 16 |
| Ret | 20 | Derek Bell | McLaren-Ford | 5 | Suspension | 15 |
| Ret | 14 | John Surtees | BRM | 1 | Suspension | 6 |

Winning speed: 127.254mph Lap leaders: Rindt 1-5, 16-61; Stewart 6-15, 62-84
Pole position: Rindt, 1m 20.800s, 130.411mph
Fastest lap: Stewart: 1m 21.300s, 129.609mph

### GERMAN GRAND PRIX: NÜRBURGRING *3 August Round: 7 Race: 180 14 x 14.189 miles*

| POS. | NO. | DRIVER | CAR-ENGINE | LAPS | TIME/RETIRED | GRID |
|---|---|---|---|---|---|---|
| 1 | 6 | Jacky Ickx | Brabham-Ford | 14 | 1:49'55.4 | 1 |
| 2 | 7 | Jackie Stewart | Matra-Ford | 14 | +57.7 | 2 |
| 3 | 10 | Bruce McLaren | McLaren-Ford | 14 | +3'21.6 | 8 |
| 4 | 1 | Graham Hill | Lotus-Ford | 14 | +3'58.8 | 9 |
| 5 | 26 | Henri Pescarolo | Matra Ford F2 | 14 | +8'11.0 | 17 |
| 6 | 29 | Dickie Attwood | Brabham Ford F2 | 13 | + 1 Lap | 20 |
| 7 | 20 | Kurt Ahrens | Brabham Ford F2 | 13 | + 1 Lap | 19 |
| 8 | 22 | Rolf Stommelen | Lotus Ford F2 | 13 | + 1 Lap | 21 |
| 9 | 31 | Peter Westbury | Brabham Ford F2 | 13 | + 1 Lap | 18 |
| 10 | 30 | Xavier Perrot | Brabham Ford F2 | 13 | + 1 Lap | 22 |
| 11 | 11 | Jo Siffert | Lotus-Ford | 12 | Suspension | 4 |
| 12 | 8 | Jean Pierre Beltoise | Matra-Ford | 12 | Suspension | 10 |
| Ret | 9 | Denny Hulme | McLaren-Ford | 11 | Transmission | 5 |
| Ret | 15 | Jackie Oliver | BRM | 11 | Oil leak | 13 |
| Ret | 2 | Jochen Rindt | Lotus-Ford | 10 | Ignition | 3 |
| Ret | 28 | François Cevert | Tecno Ford F2 | 9 | Crown Wheel | 16 |
| Ret | 27 | Johnny Servoz Gavin | Matra Ford F2 | 6 | Engine | 15 |
| Ret | 16 | Jo Bonnier | Lotus-Ford | 4 | Fuel leak | 14 |
| Ret | 17 | Piers Courage | Brabham-Ford | 1 | Accident | 7 |
| Ret | 12 | Vic Elford | McLaren-Ford | 0 | Accident | 6 |
| Ret | 3 | Mario Andretti | Lotus-Ford | 0 | Accident | 12 |
| DNS | 14 | John Surtees | BRM | 0 | Not started | |
| Wth | 23 | Hubert Hahne | BMW F2 | 0 | Withdrawn | |
| Wth | 25 | Dieter Quester | BMW | 0 | Withdrawn | |
| Wth | 21 | Hans Herrmann | Lotus Ford F2 | 0 | Withdrawn | |
| DNS | 24 | Gerhard Mitter | BMW F2 | 0 | Fatal Accident | |

Winning speed: 108.428mph Lap leaders: Stewart 1-6; Ickx 7-14
Pole position: Ickx, 7m 42.100s, 110.540mph
Fastest lap: Ickx, 7m 43.800s, 110.135mph

### ITALIAN GRAND PRIX: MONZA *7 September Round:8 Race: 181 68 x 3.573 miles*

| POS. | NO. | DRIVER | CAR-ENGINE | LAPS | TIME/RETIRED | GRID |
|---|---|---|---|---|---|---|
| 1 | 20 | Jackie Stewart | Matra-Ford | 68 | 1:39'11.26 | 3 |
| 2 | 4 | Jochen Rindt | Lotus-Ford | 68 | +0.08 | 1 |
| 3 | 22 | Jean Pierre Beltoise | Matra-Ford | 68 | +0.17 | 6 |
| 4 | 18 | Bruce McLaren | McLaren-Ford | 68 | +0.19 | 5 |
| 5 | 32 | Piers Courage | Brabham-Ford | 68 | +33.44 | 4 |
| 6 | 10 | Pedro Rodriguez | Ferrari | 66 | +2 Laps | 12 |
| 7 | 16 | Denny Hulme | McLaren-Ford | 66 | +2 Laps | 2 |
| 8 | 30 | Jo Siffert | Lotus-Ford | 64 | Engine | 8 |
| 9 | 2 | Graham Hill | Lotus-Ford | 63 | Halfshaft | 9 |
| 10 | 26 | Jacky Ickx | Brabham-Ford | 61 | Out of fuel | 15 |
| NC | 14 | John Surtees | BRM | 60 | Not classified | 10 |
| Ret | 12 | Jackie Oliver | BRM | 48 | Oil pressure | 11 |
| Ret | 36 | Silvio Moser | Brabham-Ford | 9 | Fuel leak | 13 |
| Ret | 28 | Jack Brabham | Brabham-Ford | 6 | Oil leak | 7 |
| Ret | 6 | John Miles | Lotus-Ford | 3 | Engine | 14 |

Winning speed: 146.968mph Lap leaders: Stewart 1-6, 9-17, 19-24, 28-30, 33, 35-36, 38-68; Rindt 7, 25-27,31, 34, 37; Hulme 8; Courage 18, 32
Pole position: Rindt, 1m 25.480s, 150.472mph
Fastest lap: Beltoise, 1m 25.200s, 150.472mph

## CANADIAN GRAND PRIX: MOSPORT PARK *20 September Round: 9 Race: 182 90 x 2.459 miles*

| POS. | NO. | DRIVER | CAR-ENGINE | LAPS | TIME/RETIRED | GRID |
|---|---|---|---|---|---|---|
| 1 | 11 | Jacky Ickx | Brabham-Ford | 90 | 1:59'25.7 | 1 |
| 2 | 12 | Jack Brabham | Brabham-Ford | 90 | +46.2 | 6 |
| 3 | 2 | Jochen Rindt | Lotus-Ford | 90 | +52.0 | 3 |
| 4 | 18 | Jean Pierre Beltoise | Matra-Ford | 89 | +1 Lap | 2 |
| 5 | 4 | Bruce McLaren | McLaren-Ford | 87 | +3 Laps | 9 |
| 6 | 19 | J.Servoz-Gavin | Matra-Ford | 84 | +6 Laps | 15 |
| 7 | 25 | Pete Lovely | Lotus-Ford | 81 | +9 Laps | 16 |
| NC | 16 | Bill Brack | BRM | 80 | Not classified | 18 |
| Ret | 1 | Graham Hill | Lotus-Ford | 42 | Engine | 7 |
| Ret | 9 | Jo Siffert | Lotus-Ford | 40 | Halfshaft | 8 |
| Ret | 3 | John Miles | Lotus-Ford | 40 | Gearbox | 11 |
| Ret | 6 | Pedro Rodriguez | Ferrari | 37 | Oil pressure | 13 |
| Ret | 17 | Jackie Stewart | Matra-Ford | 32 | Collision | 4 |
| DSQ | 69 | Al Pease | Eagle-Climax | 22 | Disqualified | 17 |
| Ret | 14 | John Surtees | BRM | 15 | Engine | 14 |
| Ret | 21 | Piers Courage | Brabham-Ford | 13 | Fuel leak | 10 |
| Ret | 26 | John Cordts | Brabham-Climax | 10 | Oil leak | 19 |
| Ret | 5 | Denny Hulme | McLaren-Ford | 9 | Distributor | 5 |
| Ret | 15 | Jackie Oliver | BRM | 2 | Engine | 12 |
| Ret | 20 | Silvio Moser | Brabham-Ford | 0 | Accident | 20 |

Winning speed: 111.185mph Lap leaders: Rindt 1-5; Stewart 6-32; Ickx 33-90
Pole position: Ickx, 1m 17.400s, 114.372mph
Fastest lap: Ickx-Brabham, 1m 18.100s, 113.347mph

## UNITED STATES GRAND PRIX: WATKINS GLEN *5 October Round: 10 Race: 183 108 x 2.300 miles*

| POS. | NO. | DRIVER | CAR-ENGINE | LAPS | TIME/RETIRED | GRID |
|---|---|---|---|---|---|---|
| 1 | 2 | Jochen Rindt | Lotus-Ford | 108 | 1:57'56.84 | 1 |
| 2 | 18 | Piers Courage | Brabham-Ford | 108 | +46.99 | 9 |
| 3 | 14 | John Surtees | BRM | 106 | +2 Laps | 11 |
| 4 | 8 | Jack Brabham | Brabham-Ford | 106 | +2 Laps | 10 |
| 5 | 12 | Pedro Rodriguez | Ferrari | 101 | +7 Laps | 12 |
| 6 | 19 | Silvio Moser | Brabham-Ford | 98 | +10 Laps | 17 |
| NC | 16 | J.Servoz-Gavin | Matra-Ford | 92 | Not classified | 15 |
| Ret | 1 | Graham Hill | Lotus-Ford | 90 | Accident | 4 |
| Ret | 7 | Jacky Ickx | Brabham-Ford | 77 | Engine | 8 |
| Ret | 22 | George Eaton | BRM | 76 | Engine | 9 |
| Ret | 4 | Jean Pierre Beltoise | Matra-Ford | 72 | Engine | 7 |
| Ret | 5 | Denny Hulme | McLaren-Ford | 52 | Gearbox | 2 |
| Ret | 3 | Jackie Stewart | Matra-Ford | 35 | Engine | 3 |
| Ret | 21 | Pete Lovely | Lotus-Ford | 25 | Halfshaft | 16 |
| Ret | 15 | Jackie Oliver | BRM | 23 | Engine | 14 |
| Ret | 10 | Jo Siffert | Lotus-Ford | 3 | Fuel system | 13 |
| Ret | 9 | Mario Andretti | Lotus-Ford | 3 | Suspension | 5 |
| Ret | 6 | Bruce McLaren | McLaren-Ford | 0 | Engine | 6 |

Winning speed: 126.361mph Lap leaders: Rindt 1-11, 21-108; Stewart 12-20
Pole position: Rindt, 1m 03.620s, 130.148mph
Fastest lap: Rindt, 1m 04.340s, 128.691mph

## MEXICAN GRAND PRIX: MEXICO CITY *19 October Round: 11 Race: 184 65 x 3.107 miles*

| POS. | NO. | DRIVER | CAR-ENGINE | LAPS | TIME/RETIRED | GRID |
|---|---|---|---|---|---|---|
| 1 | 5 | Denny Hulme | McLaren-Ford | 65 | 1:54'08.80 | 4 |
| 2 | 7 | Jacky Ickx | Brabham-Ford | 65 | +2.56 | 2 |
| 3 | 8 | Jack Brabham | Brabham-Ford | 65 | +38.48 | 1 |
| 4 | 3 | Jackie Stewart | Matra-Ford | 65 | +47.04 | 3 |
| 5 | 4 | Jean Pierre Beltoise | Matra-Ford | 65 | +1'38.52 | 8 |
| 6 | 15 | Jackie Oliver | BRM | 63 | +2 Laps | 12 |
| 7 | 12 | Pedro Rodriguez | Ferrari | 63 | +2 Laps | 15 |
| 8 | 16 | J.Servoz-Gavin | Matra-Ford | 63 | +2 Laps | 14 |
| 9 | 21 | Pete Lovely | Lotus-Ford | 62 | +3 Laps | 16 |
| 10 | 18 | Piers Courage | Brabham-Ford | 61 | +4 Laps | 9 |
| 11 | 19 | Silvio Moser | Brabham-Ford | 60 | Fuel leak | 13 |
| Ret | 14 | John Surtees | BRM | 53 | Gearbox | 10 |
| Ret | 2 | Jochen Rindt | Lotus-Ford | 21 | Suspension | 6 |
| Ret | 22 | George Eaton | BRM | 6 | Gearbox | 17 |
| Ret | 10 | Jo Siffert | Lotus-Ford | 4 | Accident | 5 |
| Ret | 9 | John Miles | Lotus-Ford | 3 | Fuel pump | 11 |
| DNS | 6 | Bruce McLaren | McLaren-Ford | 0 | Not started | 7 |

Winning speed: 106.151mph Lap leaders: Stewart 1-5; Ickx 6-9; Hulme 10-65
Pole position: Brabham, 1m 42.900s, 108.695 mph
Fastest lap: Ickx, 1m 43.050s, 108.536mph

# 1970

## DRIVERS' CHAMPION: JOCHEN RINDT
## CONSTRUCTORS' CHAMPION: LOTUS FORD

### DRIVERS' CHAMPIONSHIP

| POS | DRIVER | COUNTRY | CAR | POINTS |
|---|---|---|---|---|
| 1 | Jochen Rindt | Austria | Lotus-Ford | 45 |
| 2 | Jacky Ickx | Belgium | Ferrari | 40 |
| 3 | Clay Regazzoni | Switzerland | Ferrari | 33 |
| 4 | Denny Hulme | New Zealand | McLaren-Ford | 27 |
| 5 | Jack Brabham | Australia | Brabham-Ford | 25 |
| = | Jackie Stewart | GB | March-Ford, Tyrrell-Ford | 25 |
| 7 | Pedro Rodriguez | Mexico | BRM | 23 |
| = | Chris Amon | New Zealand | March-Ford | 23 |
| 9 | Jean Pierre Beltoise | France | Matra-Simca | 16 |
| 10 | Emerson Fittipaldi | Brazil | Lotus-Ford | 12 |
| 11 | Rolf Stommelen | West Germany | Brabham-Ford | 10 |
| 12 | Henri Pescarolo | France | Matra-Simca | 8 |
| 13 | Graham Hill | GB | Lotus-Ford | 7 |
| 14 | Bruce McLaren | New Zealand | McLaren-Ford | 6 |
| 15 | Mario Andretti | USA | March-Ford | 4 |
| = | Reine Wisell | Sweden | Lotus-Ford | 4 |
| 17 | Ignazio Giunti | Italy | Ferrari | 3 |
| = | John Surtees | GB | McLaren-Ford, Surtees-Ford | 3 |
| 19 | John Miles | GB | Lotus-Ford | 2 |
| = | Johnny Servoz-Gavin | France | March-Ford | 2 |
| = | Jackie Oliver | GB | BRM | 2 |
| 22 | Dan Gurney | USA | McLaren-Ford | 1 |
| = | Francois Cevert | France | March-Ford | 1 |
| = | Peter Gethin | GB | McLaren-Ford | 1 |
| = | Derek Bell | GB | Brabham-Ford, Surtees-Ford | 1 |
| | Piers Courage | GB | De Tomaso-Ford | |
| | John Love | South Africa | Lotus-Ford | |
| | Jo Siffert | Switzerland | March-Ford | |
| | Peter de Klerk | South Africa | Brabham-Ford | |
| | Dave Charlton | South Africa | Lotus-Ford | |
| | George Eaton | Canada | BRM | |
| | Ronnie Peterson | Sweden | March-Ford | |
| | Alex Soler-Roig | Spain | Lotus-Ford | |
| | Andrea de Adamich | Italy | McLaren-Alfa | |
| | Pete Lovely | USA | Lotus-Ford | |
| | Silvio Moser | Switzerland | Bellasi-Ford | |
| | Tim Schenken | Australia | De Tomaso-Ford | |
| | Gus Hutchison | USA | Brabham-Ford | |
| | Jo Bonnier | Sweden | McLaren-Ford | |
| | Brian Redman | GB | Lotus-Ford, De Tomaso-Ford | |
| | Hubert Hahne | West Germany | March-Ford | |
| | Nami Galli | Italy | McLaren-Alfa Romeo | |
| | Peter Westbury | GB | BRM | |

Points for top six finishers (9, 6, 4, 3, 2, 1). Only the best six scores from the first seven races and the best five scores from the remaining six races counted towards the championship.

### CONSTRUCTORS' CHAMPIONSHIP

| POS. | CONSTRUCTOR | POINTS |
|---|---|---|
| 1 | Lotus-Ford | 59 |
| 2 | Ferrari | 52 |
| 3 | March-Ford | 48 |
| 4 | Brabham-Ford | 35 |
| 5 | McLaren-Ford | 35 |
| 6 | BRM | 23 |
| 7 | Matra | 23 |
| 8 | Surtees-Ford | 3 |

Points for top six finishers (9, 6, 4, 3, 2, 1). Points only counted for top-placed car for each constructor. Only the best six scores from the first seven races and the best five scores from the remaining six races counted towards the championship

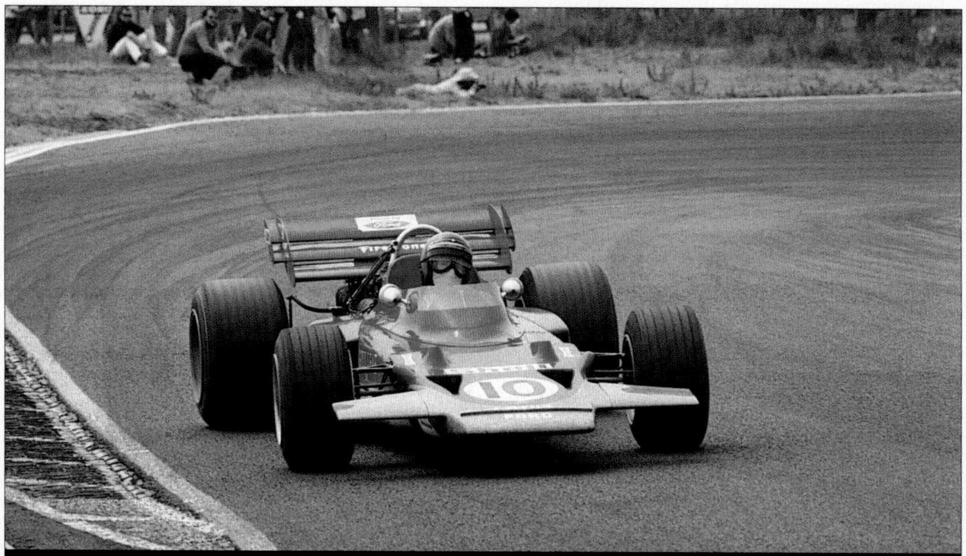
1970 world champion Jochen Rindt in the Type 72 Lotus Ford

## SOUTH AFRICAN GRAND PRIX: KYALAMI *7 March Round: 1 Race: 185 80 x 2.550 miles*

| POS. | NO. | DRIVER | CAR-ENGINE | LAPS | TIME/RETIRED | GRID |
|---|---|---|---|---|---|---|
| 1 | 12 | Jack Brabham | Brabham-Ford | 80 | 1:49'34.6 | 3 |
| 2 | 6 | Denny Hulme | McLaren-Ford | 80 | +8.1 | 6 |
| 3 | 1 | Jackie Stewart | March-Ford | 80 | +17.1 | 1 |
| 4 | 3 | Jean Pierre Beltoise | Matra | 80 | +1'13.1 | 8 |
| 5 | 10 | John Miles | Lotus-Ford | 79 | +1 Lap | 14 |
| 6 | 11 | Graham Hill | Lotus-Ford | 79 | +1 Lap | 19 |
| 7 | 4 | Henri Pescarolo | Matra | 78 | +2 Laps | 18 |
| 8 | 23 | John Love | Lotus-Ford | 78 | +2 Laps | 22 |
| 9 | 20 | Pedro Rodriguez | BRM | 76 | +4 Laps | 16 |
| 10 | 16 | Jo Siffert | March-Ford | 75 | +5 Laps | 9 |
| 11 | 24 | Peter de Klerk | Brabham-Ford | 75 | +5 Laps | 21 |
| 12 | 25 | Dave Charlton | Lotus-Ford | 73 | Engine | 13 |
| 13 | 9 | Jochen Rindt | Lotus-Ford | 72 | Engine | 4 |
| Ret | 17 | Jacky Ickx | Ferrari | 60 | Engine | 5 |
| Ret | 7 | John Surtees | McLaren-Ford | 60 | Engine | 7 |
| Ret | 21 | George Eaton | BRM | 58 | Engine | 23 |
| Ret | 2 | J.Servoz-Gavin | March-Ford | 57 | Engine | 17 |
| Ret | 5 | Bruce McLaren | McLaren-Ford | 39 | Engine | 10 |
| Ret | 22 | Piers Courage | De Tomaso-Ford | 39 | Accident | 20 |
| Ret | 8 | Mario Andretti | March-Ford | 26 | Overheating | 11 |
| Ret | 14 | Rolf Stommelen | Brabham-Ford | 23 | Engine | 15 |
| Ret | 19 | Jackie Oliver | BRM | 22 | Gearbox | 12 |
| Ret | 15 | Chris Amon | March-Ford | 14 | Overheating | 2 |

Winning speed: 111.173mph Lap leaders: Stewart 1-19; Brabham 20-80
Pole position: Stewart 1m 19.300s, 115.763mph
Fastest lap: Surtees-Brabham, 1m 20.800s, 113.614mph

## SPANISH GRAND PRIX: JARAMA *19 April Round: 2 Race: 186 90 x 2.115 miles*

| POS. | NO. | DRIVER | CAR-ENGINE | LAPS | TIME/RETIRED | GRID |
|---|---|---|---|---|---|---|
| 1 | 1 | Jackie Stewart | March-Ford | 90 | 2:10'58.2 | 3 |
| 2 | 11 | Bruce McLaren | McLaren-Ford | 89 | +1 Lap | 11 |
| 3 | 18 | Mario Andretti | March-Ford | 89 | +1 Lap | 16 |
| 4 | 6 | Graham Hill | Lotus-Ford | 89 | +1 Lap | 15 |
| 5 | 16 | J.Servoz-Gavin | March-Ford | 88 | +2 Laps | 14 |
| Ret | 8 | John Surtees | McLaren-Ford | 76 | Gearbox | 12 |
| Ret | 7 | Jack Brabham | Brabham-Ford | 61 | Engine | 1 |
| Ret | 24 | Rolf Stommelen | Brabham-Ford | 43 | Engine | 17 |
| Ret | 22 | Henri Pescarolo | Matra | 33 | Engine | 9 |
| Ret | 4 | Jean Pierre Beltoise | Matra | 31 | Engine | 4 |
| Ret | 5 | Denny Hulme | McLaren-Ford | 10 | Ignition | 2 |
| Ret | 9 | Chris Amon | March-Ford | 10 | Engine | 6 |
| Ret | 3 | Jochen Rindt | Lotus-Ford | 9 | Ignition | 8 |
| Wth | 10 | Pedro Rodriguez | BRM | 4 | Withdrew | 5 |
| Ret | 2 | Jacky Ickx | Ferrari | 0 | Accident | 7 |
| Ret | 15 | Jackie Oliver | BRM | 0 | Accident | 10 |
| DNS | 12 | Piers Courage | De Tomaso-Ford | 0 | Not started | 13 |
| DNQ | 20 | A.de Adamich | McLaren-Alfa Romeo | | | |
| DNQ | 19 | John Miles | Lotus-Ford | | | |
| DNQ | 14 | Jo Siffert | March-Ford | | | |
| DNQ | 21 | George Eaton | BRM | | | |
| DNQ | 23 | Alex Soler-Roig | Lotus-Ford | | | |

Winning speed: 87.209mph Lap leaders: Stewart 1-90
Pole position: Brabham, 1m 23.900s, 90.757mph
Fastest lap: Brabham, 1m 24.300s, 90.327mph

## MONACO GRAND PRIX: MONTE CARLO *10 May Round: 3 Race 187 80x1.954miles*

| POS. | NO. | DRIVER | CAR-ENGINE | LAPS | TIME/RETIRED | GRID |
|---|---|---|---|---|---|---|
| 1 | 3 | Jochen Rindt | Lotus-Ford | 80 | 1:54'36.6 | 8 |
| 2 | 5 | Jack Brabham | Brabham-Ford | 80 | +23.1 | 4 |
| 3 | 9 | Henri Pescarolo | Matra | 80 | +51.4 | 7 |
| 4 | 11 | Denny Hulme | McLaren-Ford | 80 | +1'28.3 | 3 |
| 5 | 1 | Graham Hill | Lotus-Ford | 79 | +1 Lap | 16 |
| 6 | 17 | Pedro Rodriguez | BRM | 78 | +2 Laps | 15 |
| 7 | 23 | Ronnie Peterson | March-Ford | 78 | +2 Laps | 12 |
| 8 | 19 | Jo Siffert | March-Ford | 76 | Out of fuel | 11 |
| Ret | 28 | Chris Amon | March-Ford | 60 | Suspension | 2 |
| NC | 24 | Piers Courage | De Tomaso-Ford | 58 | Not classified | 9 |
| Ret | 21 | Jackie Stewart | March-Ford | 57 | Engine | 1 |
| Ret | 16 | Jackie Oliver | BRM | 42 | Engine | 14 |
| Ret | 8 | Jean Pierre Beltoise | Matra | 21 | Differential | 6 |
| Ret | 12 | Bruce McLaren | McLaren-Ford | 19 | Suspension | 10 |
| Ret | 14 | John Surtees | McLaren-Ford | 14 | Oil pressure | 13 |
| Ret | 26 | Jacky Ickx | Ferrari | 11 | Halfshaft | 5 |
| DNQ | 10 | A.de Adamich | McLaren-Alfa Romeo | | | |
| DNQ | 6 | Rolf Stommelen | Brabham-Ford | | | |
| DNQ | 15 | George Eaton | BRM | | | |
| DNQ | 2 | John Miles | Lotus-Ford | | | |
| DNQ | 20 | J.Servoz-Gavin | March-Ford | | | |

Winning speed: 81.835mph Lap leaders: Stewart 1-27; Brabham 28-79, Rindt 80
Pole position: Stewart, 1m 24.000s, 83.761mph
Fastest lap: Rindt, 1m 23.200s, 84.569mph

## BELGIAN GRAND PRIX: SPA-FRANCORCHAMPS *7 June Round: 4 Race: 188 28 x 8.761 miles*

| POS. | NO. | DRIVER | CAR-ENGINE | LAPS | TIME/RETIRED | GRID |
|---|---|---|---|---|---|---|
| 1 | 1 | Pedro Rodriguez | BRM | 28 | 1:38'09.9 | 6 |
| 2 | 10 | Chris Amon | March-Ford | 28 | +1.1 | 3 |
| 3 | 25 | Jean Pierre Beltoise | Matra | 28 | +1'43.7 | 11 |
| 4 | 28 | Ignazio Giunti | Ferrari | 28 | +2'38.5 | 8 |
| 5 | 19 | Rolf Stommelen | Brabham-Ford | 28 | +3'31.8 | 7 |
| 6 | 26 | Henri Pescarolo | Matra | 27 | Electrical | 17 |
| 7 | 9 | Jo Siffert | March-Ford | 26 | Fuel pressure | 10 |
| 8 | 27 | Jacky Ickx | Ferrari | 26 | +2 Laps | 4 |
| NC | 14 | Ronnie Peterson | March-Ford | 20 | Not classified | 9 |
| Ret | 18 | Jack Brabham | Brabham-Ford | 19 | Clutch | 5 |
| Ret | 23 | Graham Hill | Lotus-Ford | 19 | Engine | 16 |
| Ret | 11 | Jackie Stewart | March-Ford | 14 | Engine | 1 |
| Ret | 21 | John Miles | Lotus-Ford | 13 | Gearbox | 13 |
| Ret | 20 | Jochen Rindt | Lotus-Ford | 10 | Engine | 2 |
| Ret | 2 | Jackie Oliver | BRM | 7 | Engine | 14 |
| Ret | 7 | Piers Courage | De Tomaso-Ford | 4 | Oil pressure | 12 |
| Ret | 8 | Derek Bell | Brabham-Ford | 1 | Gearbox | 15 |

Winning speed: 149.942mph Lap leaders: Amon 1, 3-4; Stewart 2; Rodriguez 5-28
Pole position: Stewart, 3m 28.000s, 151.638mph
Fastest lap: Amon, 3m 27.400s, 152.077mph

## DUTCH GRAND PRIX: ZANDVOORT 21 June Round: 5 Race: 189 80 x 2.605 miles

| POS. | NO. | DRIVER | CAR-ENGINE | LAPS | TIME/RETIRED | GRID |
|---|---|---|---|---|---|---|
| 1 | 10 | Jochen Rindt | Lotus-Ford | 80 | 1:50'43.41 | 1 |
| 2 | 5 | Jackie Stewart | March-Ford | 80 | +30.00 | 2 |
| 3 | 25 | Jacky Ickx | Ferrari | 79 | +1 Lap | 3 |
| 4 | 26 | Clay Regazzoni | Ferrari | 79 | +1 Lap | 6 |
| 5 | 23 | Jean Pierre Beltoise | Matra | 79 | +1 Lap | 10 |
| 6 | 16 | John Surtees | McLaren-Ford | 79 | +1 Lap | 14 |
| 7 | 12 | John Miles | Lotus-Ford | 78 | +2 Laps | 8 |
| 8 | 24 | Henri Pescarolo | Matra | 78 | +2 Laps | 13 |
| 9 | 22 | Ronnie Peterson | March-Ford | 78 | +2 Laps | 16 |
| 10 | 1 | Pedro Rodriguez | BRM | 77 | +3 Laps | 7 |
| 11 | 18 | Jack Brabham | Brabham-Ford | 76 | +4 Laps | 12 |
| NC | 15 | Graham Hill | Lotus-Ford | 71 | Not classified | 20 |
| Ret | 6 | Francois Cevert | March-Ford | 31 | Engine | 15 |
| Ret | 3 | George Eaton | BRM | 26 | Oil leak | 18 |
| Ret | 2 | Jackie Oliver | BRM | 23 | Engine | 5 |
| Ret | 4 | Piers Courage | De Tomaso-Ford | 22 | Fatal Accident | 9 |
| Ret | 9 | Jo Siffert | March-Ford | 22 | Engine | 17 |
| Ret | 20 | Peter Gethin | McLaren-Ford | 18 | Accident | 11 |
| Ret | 32 | Dan Gurney | McLaren-Ford | 2 | Engine | 19 |
| Ret | 8 | Chris Amon | March-Ford | 1 | Clutch | 4 |
| DNQ | 21 | A.de Adamich | McLaren-Alfa Romeo | | | |
| DNQ | 19 | Rolf Stommelen | Brabham-Ford | | | |
| DNQ | 31 | Pete Lovely | Lotus-Ford | | | |
| DNQ | 29 | Silvio Moser | Bellasi-Ford | | | |

Winning speed: 112.948mph Lap leaders: Ickx 1-2; Rindt 3-80
Pole position: Rindt, 1m 18.500s, 119.484mph
Fastest lap: Ickx, 1m 19.230s, 118.383mph

## FRENCH GRAND PRIX: CLERMONT-FERRAND 7 July Round: 6 Race: 190 38 x 5.005 miles

| POS. | NO. | DRIVER | CAR-ENGINE | LAPS | TIME/RETIRED | GRID |
|---|---|---|---|---|---|---|
| 1 | 6 | Jochen Rindt | Lotus-Ford | 38 | 1:55'57.00 | 6 |
| 2 | 14 | Chris Amon | March-Ford | 38 | +7.61 | 3 |
| 3 | 23 | Jack Brabham | Brabham-Ford | 38 | +44.83 | 5 |
| 4 | 19 | Denny Hulme | McLaren-Ford | 38 | +45.66 | 7 |
| 5 | 20 | Henri Pescarolo | Matra | 38 | +1'19.42 | 8 |
| 6 | 17 | Dan Gurney | McLaren-Ford | 38 | +1'19.65 | 17 |
| 7 | 22 | Rolf Stommelen | Brabham-Ford | 38 | +2'20.16 | 14 |
| 8 | 7 | John Miles | Lotus-Ford | 38 | +2'47.17 | 18 |
| 9 | 1 | Jackie Stewart | March-Ford | 38 | +3'09.61 | 4 |
| 10 | 8 | Graham Hill | Lotus-Ford | 37 | +1 Lap | 20 |
| 11 | 2 | Francois Cevert | March-Ford | 37 | +1 Lap | 13 |
| 12 | 4 | George Eaton | BRM | 36 | +2 Laps | 19 |
| 13 | 21 | Jean Pierre Beltoise | Matra | 35 | Out of fuel | 2 |
| 14 | 11 | Ignazio Giunti | Ferrari | 35 | +3 Laps | 11 |
| NC | 16 | A.de Adamich | McLaren-Alfa Romeo | 29 | Not classified | 15 |
| Ret | 12 | Jo Siffert | March-Ford | 23 | Accident | 16 |
| Ret | 18 | Ronnie Peterson | March-Ford | 17 | Differential | 9 |
| Ret | 10 | Jacky Ickx | Ferrari | 16 | Engine | 1 |
| Ret | 3 | Pedro Rodriguez | BRM | 6 | Gearbox | 10 |
| Ret | 5 | Jackie Oliver | BRM | 5 | Engine | 12 |
| DNQ | 24 | Silvio Moser | Bellasi-Ford | | | |
| DNQ | 9 | Alex Soler-Roig | Lotus-Ford | | | |
| DNQ | 25 | Pete Lovely | Lotus-Ford | | | |

Winning speed: 98.419mph Lap leaders: Ickx 1-14; Beltoise 15-25; Rindt 26-38
Pole position: Ickx, 2m 58.220s, 101.103mph
Fastest lap: Brabham, 3m 0.750s, 99.688mph

## BRITISH GRAND PRIX: BRANDS HATCH 18 July Round: 7 Race: 191 80 x 2.650 miles

| POS. | NO. | DRIVER | CAR-ENGINE | LAPS | TIME/RETIRED | GRID |
|---|---|---|---|---|---|---|
| 1 | 5 | Jochen Rindt | Lotus-Ford | 80 | 1:57'02.0 | 1 |
| 2 | 17 | Jack Brabham | Brabham-Ford | 80 | +32.9 | 2 |
| 3 | 9 | Denny Hulme | McLaren-Ford | 80 | +54.4 | 5 |
| 4 | 4 | Clay Regazzoni | Ferrari | 80 | +54.8 | 6 |
| 5 | 16 | Chris Amon | March-Ford | 79 | +1 Lap | 17 |
| 6 | 14 | Graham Hill | Lotus-Ford | 79 | +1 Lap | 22 |
| 7 | 2 | Francois Cevert | March-Ford | 79 | +1 Lap | 14 |
| 8 | 28 | E.Fittipaldi | Lotus-Ford | 78 | +2 Laps | 21 |
| 9 | 27 | Ronnie Peterson | March-Ford | 72 | +8 Laps | 13 |
| NC | 29 | Pete Lovely | Lotus-Ford | 69 | Not classified | 23 |
| Ret | 10 | Dan Gurney | McLaren-Ford | 60 | Oil pressure | 11 |
| Ret | 22 | Pedro Rodriguez | BRM | 58 | Accident | 15 |
| Ret | 23 | Jackie Oliver | BRM | 54 | Engine | 4 |
| Ret | 1 | Jackie Stewart | March-Ford | 52 | Clutch | 8 |
| Ret | 20 | John Surtees | Surtees-Ford | 51 | Oil pressure | 19 |
| Ret | 8 | Henri Pescarolo | Matra | 41 | Accident | 12 |
| Ret | 7 | Jean Pierre Beltoise | Matra | 24 | Wheel | 10 |
| Ret | 26 | Mario Andretti | March-Ford | 21 | Suspension | 9 |
| Ret | 15 | Jo Siffert | March-Ford | 19 | Suspension | 20 |
| Ret | 6 | John Miles | Lotus-Ford | 15 | Engine | 7 |
| Ret | 24 | George Eaton | BRM | 10 | Oil pressure | 16 |
| Ret | 3 | Jacky Ickx | Ferrari | 6 | Transmission | 3 |
| Ret | 11 | A.de Adamich | McLaren-Alfa Romeo | 0 | Fuel leak | 18 |

Winning speed: 108.687mph Lap leaders: Ickx 1-6; Rindt 7-68, 80; Brabham 69-79
Pole position: Rindt, 1m 24.800s, 112.500mph
Fastest lap: Brabham, 1m 25.900s, 111.059mph

## GERMAN GRAND PRIX: HOCKENHEIM 2 August Round: 8 Race: 192 50 x 4.218 miles

| POS. | NO. | DRIVER | CAR-ENGINE | LAPS | TIME/RETIRED | GRID |
|---|---|---|---|---|---|---|
| 1 | 2 | Jochen Rindt | Lotus-Ford | 50 | 1:42'00.3 | 2 |
| 2 | 10 | Jacky Ickx | Ferrari | 50 | +0.7 | 1 |
| 3 | 4 | Denny Hulme | McLaren-Ford | 50 | +1'21.8 | 16 |
| 4 | 17 | Emerson Fittipaldi | Lotus-Ford | 50 | +1'55.1 | 13 |
| 5 | 21 | Rolf Stommelen | Brabham-Ford | 49 | +1 Lap | 11 |
| 6 | 14 | Henri Pescarolo | Matra | 49 | +1 Lap | 5 |
| 7 | 23 | Francois Cevert | March-Ford | 49 | +1 Lap | 14 |
| 8 | 12 | Jo Siffert | March-Ford | 47 | Ignition | 4 |
| 9 | 7 | John Surtees | Surtees-Ford | 46 | Engine | 15 |
| Ret | 9 | Graham Hill | Lotus-Ford | 37 | Engine | 20 |
| Ret | 5 | Chris Amon | March-Ford | 34 | Engine | 6 |
| Ret | 15 | Clay Regazzoni | Ferrari | 30 | Engine | 3 |
| Ret | 16 | John Miles | Lotus-Ford | 24 | Engine | 10 |
| Ret | 1 | Jackie Stewart | March-Ford | 20 | Engine | 7 |
| Ret | 11 | Mario Andretti | March-Ford | 15 | Gearbox | 9 |
| Ret | 22 | Ronnie Peterson | March-Ford | 11 | Engine | 19 |
| Ret | 6 | Pedro Rodriguez | BRM | 7 | Ignition | 8 |
| Ret | 18 | Jackie Oliver | BRM | 5 | Engine | 18 |
| Ret | 3 | Jack Brabham | Brabham-Ford | 4 | Oil leak | 12 |
| Ret | 8 | Jean Pierre Beltoise | Matra | 4 | Suspension | 21 |
| Ret | 24 | Peter Gethin | McLaren-Ford | 3 | Throttle | 17 |
| DNQ | 25 | Brian Redman | De Tomaso-Ford | | | |
| DNQ | 20 | A.de Adamich | McLaren-Alfa Romeo | | | |
| DNQ | 27 | Silvio Moser | Bellasi-Ford | | | |
| DNQ | 26 | Hubert Hahne | March-Ford | | | |

Winning speed: 124.067mph Lap leaders: Ickx 1-6, 10-17, 26-31, 36-43, 45-46, 48; Rindt 7-9, 18-21, 24-25, 32-35, 44, 47, 49-50; Regazzoni 22-23
Pole position: Ickx, 1m 59.500s, 127.084mph
Fastest lap: Ickx, 2m 0.500s, 126.030mph

## AUSTRIAN GRAND PRIX: OSTERREICHRING 16 August Round: 9 Race: 193 50 x 4.218 miles

| POS. | NO. | DRIVER | CAR-ENGINE | LAPS | TIME/RETIRED | GRID |
|---|---|---|---|---|---|---|
| 1 | 12 | Jacky Ickx | Ferrari | 60 | 1:42'17.32 | 3 |
| 2 | 27 | Clay Regazzoni | Ferrari | 60 | + 0.61 | 2 |
| 3 | 11 | Rolf Stommelen | Brabham-Ford | 60 | +1'27.88 | 17 |
| 4 | 17 | Pedro Rodriguez | BRM | 59 | +1 Lap | 22 |
| 5 | 16 | Jackie Oliver | BRM | 59 | +1 Lap | 14 |
| 6 | 19 | Jean Pierre Beltoise | Matra | 59 | +1 Lap | 7 |
| 7 | 14 | Ignazio Giunti | Ferrari | 59 | +1 Lap | 5 |
| 8 | 4 | Chris Amon | March-Ford | 59 | +1 Lap | 6 |
| 9 | 3 | Jo Siffert | March-Ford | 59 | +1 Lap | 20 |
| 10 | 23 | Peter Gethin | McLaren-Ford | 59 | +1 Lap | 21 |
| 11 | 18 | George Eaton | BRM | 58 | +2 Laps | 23 |
| 12 | 22 | A.de Adamich | McLaren-Alfa Romeo | 57 | +3 Laps | 15 |
| 13 | 10 | Jack Brabham | Brabham-Ford | 56 | +4 Laps | 8 |
| 14 | 20 | Henri Pescarolo | Matra | 56 | +4 Laps | 13 |
| 15 | 8 | Emerson Fittipaldi | Lotus-Ford | 55 | +5 Laps | 16 |
| Ret | 21 | Denny Hulme | McLaren-Ford | 30 | Engine | 11 |
| Ret | 15 | John Surtees | Surtees-Ford | 27 | Engine | 12 |
| Ret | 26 | Tim Schenken | De Tomaso-Ford | 25 | Engine | 19 |
| Ret | 6 | Jochen Rindt | Lotus-Ford | 21 | Engine | 1 |
| Ret | 5 | Mario Andretti | March-Ford | 13 | Accident | 18 |
| Ret | 24 | Silvio Moser | Bellasi-Ford | 13 | Radiator | 24 |
| Ret | 1 | Jackie Stewart | March-Ford | 7 | Fuel pipe | 4 |
| Ret | 7 | John Miles | Lotus-Ford | 4 | Brakes | 10 |
| Ret | 2 | Francois Cevert | March-Ford | 0 | Engine | 9 |

Winning speed: 129.267mph Lap leaders: Regazzoni 1; Ickx 2-60
Pole position: Rindt, 1m 39.230s, 133.251mph
Fastest lap: Ickx Regazzoni, 1m 40.400s, 131.699mph

## ITALIAN GRAND PRIX: MONZA 6 September Round: 10 Race: 194 68 x 3.573 miles

| POS. | NO. | DRIVER | CAR-ENGINE | LAPS | TIME/RETIRED | GRID |
|---|---|---|---|---|---|---|
| 1 | 4 | Clay Regazzoni | Ferrari | 68 | 1:39'06.88 | 3 |
| 2 | 18 | Jackie Stewart | March-Ford | 68 | +5.73 | 4 |
| 3 | 40 | Jean Pierre Beltoise | Matra | 68 | +5.80 | 14 |
| 4 | 30 | Denny Hulme | McLaren-Ford | 68 | +6.15 | 9 |
| 5 | 46 | Rolf Stommelen | Brabham-Ford | 68 | +6.41 | 17 |
| 6 | 20 | Francois Cevert | March-Ford | 68 | +1'03.46 | 11 |
| 7 | 48 | Chris Amon | March-Ford | 67 | +1 Lap | 18 |
| 8 | 34 | A.de Adamich | McLaren-Alfa Romeo | 61 | +7 Laps | 12 |
| NC | 32 | Peter Gethin | McLaren-Ford | 60 | Not classified | 16 |
| Ret | 8 | Jackie Oliver | BRM | 36 | Engine | 6 |
| Ret | 52 | Ronnie Peterson | March-Ford | 35 | Engine | 13 |
| Ret | 44 | Jack Brabham | Brabham-Ford | 31 | Accident | 8 |
| Ret | 2 | Jacky Ickx | Ferrari | 25 | Clutch | 1 |
| Ret | 12 | George Eaton | BRM | 21 | Overheating | 20 |
| Ret | 54 | Tim Schenken | De Tomaso-Ford | 17 | Engine | 19 |
| Ret | 6 | Ignazio Giunti | Ferrari | 14 | Fuel system | 15 |
| Ret | 42 | Henri Pescarolo | Matra | 14 | Engine | 5 |
| Ret | 10 | Pedro Rodriguez | BRM | 12 | Engine | 2 |
| Ret | 50 | Jo Siffert | March-Ford | 3 | Engine | 7 |
| Ret | 14 | John Surtees | Surtees-Ford | 0 | Electrical | 10 |
| Wth | 28 | Graham Hill | Lotus-Ford | | Withdrawn | 7 |
| Wth | 24 | John Miles | Lotus-Ford | | Withdrawn | 7 |
| DNS | 22 | Jochen Rindt | Lotus-Ford | | Fatal accident | 7 |
| DNQ | 38 | Jo Bonnier | McLaren-Ford | | | |
| Wth | 26 | Emerson Fittipaldi | Lotus-Ford | | | |
| DNQ | 36 | Nanni Galli | McLaren-Alfa Romeo | | | |
| DNQ | 56 | Silvio Moser | Bellasi-Ford | | | |

Winning speed: 147.076mph Lap leaders: Ickx 1-3, 19-20; Rodriguez 4, 7-8; Stewart 5-6, 9, 11, 14-17, 26-27, 31, 35, 37, 42-43, 51, 53; Regazzoni 10, 12, 32-34, 36, 38-41, 44-50, 52, 54-68; Oliver 13, 18, 21-25, 28, 30; Hulme 29
Pole position: Ickx, 1m 24.140s, 152.869mph
Fastest lap: Regazzoni, 1m 25.200s, 150.967mph

## CANADIAN GRAND PRIX: MONT-TREMBLANT 20 September Round: 11 Race: 195 90 x 2.650 miles

| POS. | NO. | DRIVER | CAR-ENGINE | LAPS | TIME/RETIRED | GRID |
|---|---|---|---|---|---|---|
| 1 | 18 | Jacky Ickx | Ferrari | 90 | 2:21'18.4 | 2 |
| 2 | 19 | Clay Regazzoni | Ferrari | 90 | +14.8 | 3 |
| 3 | 20 | Chris Amon | March-Ford | 90 | +57.9 | 6 |
| 4 | 14 | Pedro Rodriguez | BRM | 89 | +1 Lap | 7 |
| 5 | 4 | John Surtees | Surtees-Ford | 89 | +1 Lap | 5 |
| 6 | 6 | Peter Gethin | McLaren-Ford | 88 | +2 Laps | 11 |
| 7 | 24 | Henri Pescarolo | Matra | 87 | +3 Laps | 8 |
| 8 | 23 | Jean Pierre Beltoise | Matra | 85 | Clutch | 13 |
| 9 | 2 | Francois Cevert | March-Ford | 85 | +5 Laps | 4 |
| 10 | 16 | George Eaton | BRM | 85 | +5 Laps | 9 |
| NC | 10 | Tim Schenken | De Tomaso-Ford | 79 | Not classified | 17 |
| NC | 9 | Graham Hill | Lotus-Ford | 77 | Not classified | 20 |
| Ret | 8 | A.de Adamich | McLaren-Alfa Romeo | 69 | Oil pressure | 12 |
| NC | 26 | Ronnie Peterson | March-Ford | 65 | Not classified | 16 |
| Ret | 5 | Denny Hulme | McLaren-Ford | 58 | Engine | 15 |
| Ret | 11 | Jack Brabham | Brabham-Ford | 57 | Oil leak | 19 |
| NC | 15 | Jackie Oliver | BRM | 52 | Not classified | 10 |
| Ret | 3 | Jackie Stewart | Tyrrell-Ford | 31 | Axle | 1 |
| Ret | 12 | Rolf Stommelen | Brabham-Ford | 22 | Handling | 18 |
| Ret | 21 | Jo Siffert | March-Ford | 21 | Engine | 14 |

Winning speed: 101.269mph Lap leaders: Stewart 1-31; Ickx 32-90
Pole position: Stewart, 1m 31.500s, 104.262mph
Fastest lap: Regazzoni, 1m 32.200s, 103.471mph

## UNITED STATES GRAND PRIX: WATKINS GLEN 4 October Round: 12 Race: 196 108 x 2.300 miles

| POS. | NO. | DRIVER | CAR-ENGINE | LAPS | TIME/RETIRED | GRID |
|---|---|---|---|---|---|---|
| 1 | 24 | Emerson Fittipaldi | Lotus-Ford | 108 | 1:57'32.79 | 3 |
| 2 | 19 | Pedro Rodriguez | BRM | 108 | +36.39 | 4 |
| 3 | 23 | Reine Wisell | Lotus-Ford | 108 | + 45.17 | 9 |
| 4 | 3 | Jacky Ickx | Ferrari | 107 | +1 Lap | 1 |
| 5 | 12 | Chris Amon | March-Ford | 107 | +1 Lap | 5 |
| 6 | 18 | Derek Bell | Surtees-Ford | 107 | +1 Lap | 13 |
| 7 | 8 | Denny Hulme | McLaren-Ford | 106 | +2 Laps | 11 |
| 8 | 7 | Henri Pescarolo | Matra | 105 | +3 Laps | 12 |
| 9 | 11 | Jo Siffert | March-Ford | 105 | +3 Laps | 23 |
| 10 | 15 | Jack Brabham | Brabham-Ford | 105 | +3 Laps | 16 |
| 11 | 29 | Ronnie Peterson | March-Ford | 104 | +4 Laps | 15 |
| 12 | 16 | Rolf Stommelen | Brabham-Ford | 104 | +4 Laps | 19 |
| 13 | 4 | Clay Regazzoni | Ferrari | 101 | +7 Laps | 6 |
| 14 | 9 | Peter Gethin | McLaren-Ford | 100 | +8 Laps | 21 |
| Ret | 1 | Jackie Stewart | Tyrrell-Ford | 82 | Oil leak | 2 |
| Ret | 14 | Graham Hill | Lotus-Ford | 72 | Clutch | 10 |
| Ret | 2 | Francois Cevert | March-Ford | 62 | Wheel | 17 |
| Ret | 30 | Tim Schenken | De Tomaso-Ford | 61 | Suspension | 20 |
| Ret | 27 | Jo Bonnier | McLaren-Ford | 50 | Water pipe | 24 |
| Ret | 6 | Jean Pierre Beltoise | Matra | 27 | Handling | 18 |
| Ret | 31 | Gus Hutchison | Brabham-Ford | 21 | Fuel leak | 22 |
| Ret | 20 | Jackie Oliver | BRM | 14 | Engine | 7 |
| Ret | 21 | George Eaton | BRM | 10 | Engine | 14 |
| Ret | 17 | John Surtees | Surtees-Ford | 6 | Engine | 8 |
| DNQ | 32 | Peter Westbury | BRM | | | |
| DNQ | 28 | Pete Lovely | Lotus-Ford | | | |
| DNQ | 10 | A.de Adamich | McLaren-Alfa Romeo | | | |

Winning speed: 126.792mph Lap leaders: Stewart 1-82; Rodriguez 83-100; Fittipaldi 101-108
Pole position: Ickx, 1m 3.070s, 131.283mph
Fastest lap: Ickx, 1m 2.740s, 131.973mph

## MEXICAN GRAND PRIX: MEXICO CITY 25 October Round: 13 Race: 197 65 x 3.107 miles

| POS. | NO. | DRIVER | CAR-ENGINE | LAPS | TIME/RETIRED | GRID |
|---|---|---|---|---|---|---|
| 1 | 3 | Jacky Ickx | Ferrari | 65 | 1:53'28.36 | 3 |
| 2 | 4 | Clay Regazzoni | Ferrari | 65 | +24.64 | 1 |
| 3 | 8 | Denny Hulme | McLaren-Ford | 65 | +45.97 | 14 |
| 4 | 12 | Chris Amon | March-Ford | 65 | +47.05 | 5 |
| 5 | 6 | Jean Pierre Beltoise | Matra | 65 | +50.11 | 6 |
| 6 | 19 | Pedro Rodriguez | BRM | 65 | +1'24.76 | 7 |
| 7 | 20 | Jackie Oliver | BRM | 64 | +1 Lap | 13 |
| 8 | 17 | John Surtees | Surtees-Ford | 64 | +1 Lap | 15 |
| 9 | 7 | Henri Pescarolo | Matra | 61 | +4 Laps | 11 |
| NC | 23 | Reine Wisell | Lotus-Ford | 56 | Not classified | 12 |
| Ret | 15 | Jack Brabham | Brabham-Ford | 52 | Engine | 4 |
| Ret | 1 | Jackie Stewart | Tyrrell-Ford | 33 | Suspension | 2 |
| Ret | 9 | Peter Gethin | McLaren-Ford | 27 | Engine | 10 |
| Ret | 16 | Rolf Stommelen | Brabham-Ford | 15 | Fuel system | 17 |
| Ret | 2 | Francois Cevert | March-Ford | 8 | Engine | 9 |
| Ret | 14 | Graham Hill | Lotus-Ford | 4 | Overheating | 8 |
| Ret | 11 | Jo Siffert | March-Ford | 3 | Engine | 16 |
| Ret | 24 | Emerson Fittipaldi | Lotus-Ford | 1 | Engine | 18 |

Winning speed: 106.781 Lap leaders: Regazzoni 1; Ickx 2-65
Pole position: Regazzoni, 1m 41.860s, 109.804mph
Fastest lap: Ickx, 1m 43.110s, 108.473mph

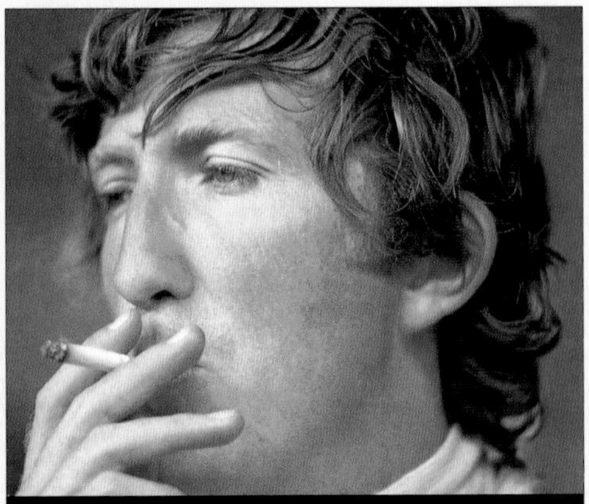

1970 world champion, Jochen Rindt

### Key to Abbreviations

| | | | |
|---|---|---|---|
| DNPQ | Did not pre-qualify | NC | Not classified |
| DNQ | Did not qualify | Ret | Retired |
| DNS | Did not start | Wth | Withdrawn |
| DSQ | Disqualified | | |

# 1971

## DRIVERS' CHAMPION: JACKIE STEWART
## CONSTRUCTORS' CHAMPION: TYRRELL FORD

### DRIVERS' CHAMPIONSHIP

| POS | DRIVER | COUNTRY | CAR | POINTS |
|---|---|---|---|---|
| 1 | Jackie Stewart | GB | Tyrrell-Ford | 62 |
| 2 | Ronnie Peterson | Sweden | March-Ford, March-Alfa Romeo | 33 |
| 3 | François Cevert | France | Tyrrell-Ford | 26 |
| 4 | Jacky Ickx | Belgium | Ferrari | 19 |
| = | Jo Siffert | Switzerland | BRM | 19 |
| 6 | Emerson Fittipaldi | Brazil | Lotus-Ford, Lotus-Pratt & Whitney | 16 |
| 7 | Clay Regazzoni | Switzerland | Ferrari | 13 |
| 8 | Mario Andretti | USA | Ferrari | 12 |
| 9 | Peter Gethin | GB | McLaren-Ford, BRM | 9 |
| = | Chris Amon | New Zealand | Matra-Simca | 9 |
| = | Reine Wisell | Sweden | Lotus-Ford, Lotus-Pratt & Whitney | 9 |
| = | Denny Hulme | New Zealand | McLaren-Ford | 9 |
| = | Pedro Rodriguez | Mexico | BRM | 9 |
| 14 | Tim Schenken | Australia | Brabham-Ford | 5 |
| = | Howden Ganley | New Zealand | BRM | 5 |
| 16 | Mark Donohue | USA | McLaren-Ford | 4 |
| = | Henri Pescarolo | France | March-Ford | 4 |
| 18 | Mike Hailwood | GB | Surtees-Ford | 3 |
| = | Rolf Stommelen | West Germany | Surtees-Ford | 3 |
| = | John Surtees | GB | Surtees-Ford | 3 |
| 21 | Graham Hill | GB | Brabham-Ford | 2 |
| 22 | Jean Pierre Beltoise | France | Matra-Simca | 1 |
| | John Love | South Africa | March-Ford | |
| | Jacky Pretorious | South Africa | Brabham-Ford | |
| | Jo Bonnier | Sweden | McLaren-Ford | |
| | Brian Redman | GB | Surtees-Ford | |
| | Andrea de Adamich | Italy | March-Alfa Romeo | |
| | Alex Soler-Roig | Spain | March-Ford, Brabham-Ford, Lotus-Ford | |
| | Nanni Galli | Italy | March-Alfa Romeo, March-Ford | |
| | Skip Barber | USA | March-Ford | |
| | Gijs van Lenep | Netherlands | Surtees-Ford | |
| | Dave Walker | GB | Lotus-Pratt & Whitney | |
| | François Mazet | France | March-Ford | |
| | Jean Max | France | March-Ford | |
| | Jackie Oliver | GB | McLaren-Ford | |
| | Derek Bell | GB | Surtees-Ford | |
| | Mike Beuttler | GB | March-Ford | |
| | Vic Elford | GB | BRM | |
| | Helmut Marko | Austria | McLaren-Ford, BRM | |
| | Niki Lauda | Austria | March-Ford | |
| | Jean-Pierre Jarier | France | March-Ford | |
| | Silvio Moser | Switzerland | Bellasi-Ford | |
| | George Eaton | Canada | BRM | |
| | Pete Lovely | USA | Lotus-Ford | |
| | Chris Craft | Canada | Brabham-Ford | |
| | David Hobbs | GB | McLaren-Ford | |
| | Peter Revson | USA | Tyrrell-Ford | |
| | Sam Posey | USA | Surtees-Ford | |
| | John Cannon | CDN | BRM | |

Points for top six finishers (9, 6, 4, 3, 2, 1). Only the best five scores from the first six races and the best four scores from the remaining five races counted towards the championship.

### CONSTRUCTORS' CHAMPIONSHIP

| POS. | CONSTRUCTOR | POINTS |
|---|---|---|
| 1 | Tyrrell-Ford | 73 |
| 2 | BRM | 36 |
| 3 | Ferrari | 33 |
| 4 | March-Ford | 33 |
| 5 | Lotus-Ford | 21 |
| 6 | McLaren-Ford | 10 |
| 7 | Matra | 9 |
| 8 | Surtees-Ford | 8 |
| 9 | Brabham-Ford | 5 |

Points for top six finishers (9, 6, 4, 3, 2, 1). Points only counted for top-placed car for each constructor. Only the best five scores from the first six races and the best four scores from the remaining five races counted towards the championship.

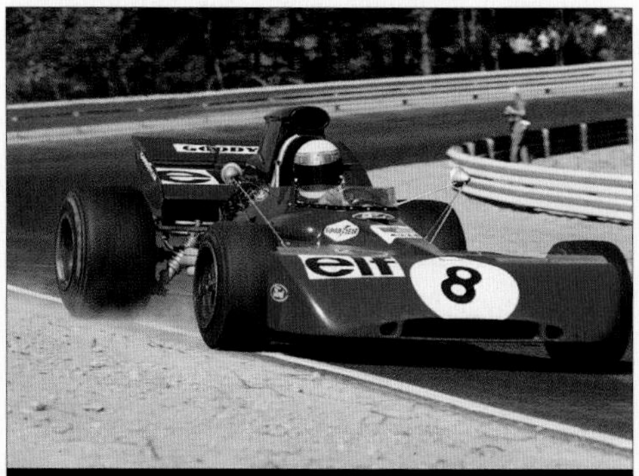

1971 world champion Jackie Stewart in the 003 Tyrrell Ford.

### SOUTH AFRICAN GRAND PRIX: KYALAMI 6 March Round: 1 Race: 198 79 x 2.550 miles

| POS. | NO. | DRIVER | CAR-ENGINE | LAPS | TIME/RETIRED | GRID |
|---|---|---|---|---|---|---|
| 1 | 6 | Mario Andretti | Ferrari | 79 | 1:47'35.5 | 4 |
| 2 | 9 | Jackie Stewart | Tyrrell-Ford | 79 | +20.9 | 1 |
| 3 | 5 | Clay Regazzoni | Ferrari | 79 | +31.4 | 3 |
| 4 | 3 | Reine Wisell | Lotus-Ford | 79 | +1'09.4 | 14 |
| 5 | 19 | Chris Amon | Matra | 78 | +1 Lap | 2 |
| 6 | 11 | Denny Hulme | McLaren-Ford | 78 | +1 Lap | 7 |
| 7 | 28 | Brian Redman | Surtees-Ford | 78 | +1 Lap | 17 |
| 8 | 4 | Jacky Ickx | Ferrari | 78 | +1 Lap | 8 |
| 9 | 14 | Graham Hill | Brabham-Ford | 77 | +2 Laps | 19 |
| 10 | 7 | Ronnie Peterson | March-Ford | 77 | +2 Laps | 13 |
| 11 | 22 | Henri Pescarolo | March-Ford | 77 | +2 Laps | 18 |
| 12 | 21 | Rolf Stommelen | Surtees-Ford | 77 | +2 Laps | 15 |
| 13 | 8 | A.de Adamich | March-Alfa Romeo | 75 | +4 Laps | 22 |
| Ret | 2 | Emerson Fittipaldi | Lotus-Ford | 58 | Engine | 5 |
| Ret | 20 | John Surtees | Surtees-Ford | 56 | Gearbox | 6 |
| Ret | 10 | Francois Cevert | Tyrrell-Ford | 45 | Accident | 9 |
| Ret | 27 | Howden Ganley | BRM | 42 | Physical | 24 |
| Ret | 16 | Pedro Rodriguez | BRM | 33 | Overheating | 10 |
| Ret | 15 | Dave Charlton | Brabham-Ford | 31 | Engine | 16 |
| Ret | 17 | Jo Siffert | BRM | 31 | Overheating | 12 |
| Ret | 24 | John Love | March-Ford | 30 | Differential | 21 |
| Ret | 25 | Jackie Pretorius | Brabham-Ford | 22 | Engine | 20 |
| Ret | 12 | Peter Gethin | McLaren-Ford | 7 | Fuel leak | 11 |
| Ret | 23 | Jo Bonnier | McLaren-Ford | 5 | Suspension | 23 |
| Ret | 26 | Alex Soler-Roig | March-Ford | 5 | Engine | 25 |

Winning speed: 112.346mph Lap leaders: Regazzoni 1-16; Hulme 17-75; Andretti 76-79
Pole position: Stewart, 1m 17.800s, 118.000mph
Fastest lap: Andretti, 1m 20.300s, 114.326mph

### SPANISH GRAND PRIX: MONTJUICH PARK 18 April Round: 2 Race: 199 75 x 2.356 miles

| POS. | NO. | DRIVER | CAR-ENGINE | LAPS | TIME/RETIRED | GRID |
|---|---|---|---|---|---|---|
| 1 | 11 | Jackie Stewart | Tyrrell-Ford | 75 | 1:49'03.4 | 4 |
| 2 | 4 | Jacky Ickx | Ferrari | 75 | +3.4 | 1 |
| 3 | 20 | Chris Amon | Matra | 75 | +58.1 | 3 |
| 4 | 14 | Pedro Rodriguez | BRM | 75 | +1'17.9 | 5 |
| 5 | 9 | Denny Hulme | McLaren-Ford | 75 | +1'27.0 | 9 |
| 6 | 21 | Jean Pierre Beltoise | Matra | 74 | +1 Lap | 6 |
| 7 | 12 | Francois Cevert | Tyrrell-Ford | 74 | +1 Lap | 12 |
| 8 | 10 | Peter Gethin | McLaren-Ford | 73 | +2 Laps | 7 |
| 9 | 8 | Tim Schenken | Brabham-Ford | 72 | +3 Laps | 21 |
| 10 | 16 | Howden Ganley | BRM | 71 | +4 Laps | 17 |
| 11 | 24 | John Surtees | Surtees-Ford | 67 | +8 Laps | 22 |
| NC | 3 | Reine Wisell | Lotus-Ford | 58 | Not classified | 16 |
| Ret | 2 | Emerson Fittipaldi | Lotus-Ford | 54 | Suspension | 14 |
| Ret | 27 | Henri Pescarolo | March-Ford | 53 | Engine | 11 |
| Ret | 6 | Mario Andretti | Ferrari | 50 | Engine | 8 |
| Ret | 19 | Alex Soler-Roig | March-Ford | 46 | Fuel pipe | 20 |
| Ret | 17 | A.de Adamich | March-Alfa Romeo | 26 | Transmission | 18 |
| Ret | 18 | Ronnie Peterson | March-Ford | 24 | Ignition | 13 |
| Ret | 5 | Clay Regazzoni | Ferrari | 13 | Engine | 2 |
| Ret | 25 | Rolf Stommelen | Surtees-Ford | 9 | Fuel pressure | 19 |
| Ret | 15 | Jo Siffert | BRM | 5 | Gearbox | 15 |
| Ret | 7 | Graham Hill | Brabham-Ford | 5 | Steering | 10 |

Winning speed: 97.200mph Lap leaders: Ickx 1-5; Stewart 6-75
Pole position: Ickx, 1m 25.900s, 98.722mph
Fastest lap: Ickx, 1m 25.100s, 99.650mph

### MONACO GRAND PRIX: MONTE CARLO 23 May Round: 3 Race: 200 80 x 1.954 miles

| POS. | NO. | DRIVER | CAR-ENGINE | LAPS | TIME/RETIRED | GRID |
|---|---|---|---|---|---|---|
| 1 | 11 | Jackie Stewart | Tyrrell-Ford | 80 | 1:52'21.3 | 1 |
| 2 | 17 | Ronnie Peterson | March-Ford | 80 | +25.6 | 8 |
| 3 | 4 | Jacky Ickx | Ferrari | 80 | +53.3 | 2 |
| 4 | 9 | Denny Hulme | McLaren-Ford | 80 | +1'06.7 | 6 |
| 5 | 1 | Emerson Fittipaldi | Lotus-Ford | 79 | +1 Lap | 17 |
| 6 | 24 | Rolf Stommelen | Surtees-Ford | 79 | +1 Lap | 16 |
| 7 | 22 | John Surtees | Surtees-Ford | 79 | +1 Lap | 10 |
| 8 | 27 | Henri Pescarolo | March-Ford | 77 | +3 Laps | 13 |
| 9 | 15 | Pedro Rodriguez | BRM | 76 | +4 Laps | 5 |
| 10 | 8 | Tim Schenken | Brabham-Ford | 76 | +4 Laps | 18 |
| Ret | 14 | Jo Siffert | BRM | 58 | Oil pipe | 3 |
| Ret | 21 | Jean Pierre Beltoise | Matra | 47 | Differential | 7 |
| Ret | 20 | Chris Amon | Matra | 45 | Differential | 4 |
| Ret | 5 | Clay Regazzoni | Ferrari | 24 | Accident | 11 |
| Ret | 10 | Peter Gethin | McLaren-Ford | 22 | Accident | 14 |
| Ret | 2 | Reine Wisell | Lotus-Ford | 21 | Wheel bearing | 12 |
| Ret | 12 | Francois Cevert | Tyrrell-Ford | 5 | Accident | 15 |
| Ret | 7 | Graham Hill | Brabham-Ford | 1 | Accident | 9 |
| DNQ | 16 | Howden Ganley | BRM | | | |
| DNQ | 6 | Mario Andretti | Ferrari | | | |
| DNQ | 19 | Nanni Galli | March-Alfa Romeo | | | |
| DNQ | 18 | Alex Soler-Roig | March-Ford | | | |
| DNQ | 28 | Skip Barber | March-Ford | | | |

Winning speed: 83.487mph Lap leaders: Stewart 1-80
Pole position: Stewart, 1m 23.200s, 84.557mph
Fastest lap: Stewart, 1m 22.200s, 85.586mph

### DUTCH GRAND PRIX: ZANDVOORT 20 June Round: 4 Race: 201 70x 2.605miles

| POS. | NO. | DRIVER | CAR-ENGINE | LAPS | TIME/RETIRED | GRID |
|---|---|---|---|---|---|---|
| 1 | 2 | Jacky Ickx | Ferrari | 70 | 1:56'20.09 | 1 |
| 2 | 8 | Pedro Rodriguez | BRM | 70 | +7.99 | 2 |
| 3 | 3 | Clay Regazzoni | Ferrari | 69 | +1 Lap | 4 |
| 4 | 16 | Ronnie Peterson | March-Ford | 68 | +2 Laps | 13 |
| 5 | 23 | John Surtees | Surtees-Ford | 68 | +2 Laps | 7 |
| 6 | 9 | Jo Siffert | BRM | 68 | +2 Laps | 8 |
| 7 | 10 | Howden Ganley | BRM | 66 | +4 Laps | 9 |
| 8 | 30 | Gijs van Lennep | Surtees-Ford | 65 | +5 Laps | 21 |
| 9 | 21 | Jean Pierre Beltoise | Matra | 65 | +5 Laps | 11 |
| 10 | 24 | Graham Hill | Brabham-Ford | 65 | +5 Laps | 16 |
| 11 | 5 | Jackie Stewart | Tyrrell-Ford | 65 | +5 Laps | 3 |
| 12 | 26 | Denny Hulme | McLaren-Ford | 63 | +7 Laps | 14 |
| NC | 31 | Henri Pescarolo | March-Ford | 62 | Not classified | 15 |
| NC | 22 | Skip Barber | March-Ford | 60 | Not classified | 24 |
| NC | 28 | Peter Gethin | McLaren-Ford | 60 | Not classified | 23 |
| Ret | 19 | Alex Soler-Roig | March-Ford | 57 | Engine | 17 |
| Ret | 25 | Tim Schenken | Brabham-Ford | 39 | Suspension | 19 |
| Ret | 6 | Francois Cevert | Tyrrell-Ford | 29 | Accident | 12 |
| DSQ | 29 | Rolf Stommelen | Surtees-Ford | 19 | Disqualified | 10 |
| DSQ | 14 | Reine Wisell | Lotus-Ford | 17 | Disqualified | 6 |
| Ret | 18 | Nanni Galli | March-Alfa Romeo | 7 | Accident | 20 |
| Ret | 4 | Mario Andretti | Ferrari | 5 | Fuel pump | 18 |
| Ret | 15 | Dave Walker | Lotus-Pratt & Whitney | 5 | Accident | 22 |
| Ret | 20 | Chris Amon | Matra | 2 | Spun off | 5 |

Winning speed: 94.062mph Lap leaders: Ickx 1-8, 30, 32-70; Rodriguez 9-29, 31
Pole position: Ickx, 1m 17.420s, 121.151mph
Fastest lap: Ickx, 1m 34.950s, 98.783mph

### FRENCH GRAND PRIX: PAUL RICARD 4 July Round: 5 Race: 202 55 x 3.610 miles

| POS. | NO. | DRIVER | CAR-ENGINE | LAPS | TIME/RETIRED | GRID |
|---|---|---|---|---|---|---|
| 1 | 11 | Jackie Stewart | Tyrrell-Ford | 55 | 1:46'41.68 | 1 |
| 2 | 12 | Francois Cevert | Tyrrell-Ford | 55 | +28.12 | 7 |
| 3 | 1 | Emerson Fittipaldi | Lotus-Ford | 55 | +34.07 | 17 |
| 4 | 14 | Jo Siffert | BRM | 55 | +37.17 | 6 |
| 5 | 20 | Chris Amon | Matra | 55 | +41.08 | 9 |
| 6 | 2 | Reine Wisell | Lotus-Ford | 55 | +1'16.02 | 15 |
| 7 | 21 | Jean Pierre Beltoise | Matra | 55 | +1'16.93 | 8 |
| 8 | 22 | John Surtees | Surtees-Ford | 55 | +1'24.91 | 13 |
| 9 | 10 | Peter Gethin | McLaren-Ford | 54 | +1 Lap | 19 |
| 10 | 16 | Howden Ganley | BRM | 54 | +1 Lap | 16 |
| 11 | 24 | Rolf Stommelen | Surtees-Ford | 53 | +2 Laps | 10 |
| 12 | 8 | Tim Schenken | Brabham-Ford | 50 | Oil pressure | 14 |
| 13 | 34 | Francois Mazet | March-Ford | 50 | +5 Laps | 23 |
| NC | 28 | Max Jean | March-Ford | 46 | Not classified | 22 |
| Ret | 27 | Henri Pescarolo | March-Ford | 45 | Gearbox | 18 |
| Ret | 7 | Graham Hill | Brabham-Ford | 34 | Oil pipe | 4 |
| Ret | 19 | A.de Adamich | March-Alfa Romeo | 31 | Engine | 20 |
| Ret | 15 | Pedro Rodriguez | BRM | 27 | Ignition | 5 |
| Ret | 5 | Clay Regazzoni | Ferrari | 20 | Accident | 2 |
| Ret | 17 | Ronnie Peterson | March-Alfa Romeo | 19 | Engine | 12 |
| Ret | 9 | Denny Hulme | McLaren-Ford | 16 | Ignition | 11 |
| Ret | 4 | Jacky Ickx | Ferrari | 4 | Engine | 3 |
| Ret | 18 | Alex Soler-Roig | March-Ford | 4 | Fuel pump | 21 |

Winning speed: 111.660mph Lap leaders: Stewart 1-55
Pole position: Stewart, 1m 50.710s, 117.393mph
Fastest lap: Stewart, 1m 54.090mph, 113.915mph

### BRITISH GRAND PRIX: SILVERSTONE 17 July Round: 6 Race: 203 68 x 2.927 miles

| POS. | NO. | DRIVER | CAR-ENGINE | LAPS | TIME/RETIRED | GRID |
|---|---|---|---|---|---|---|
| 1 | 12 | Jackie Stewart | Tyrrell-Ford | 68 | 1:31'31.5 | 2 |
| 2 | 18 | Ronnie Peterson | March-Ford | 68 | +36.1 | 5 |
| 3 | 1 | Emerson Fittipaldi | Lotus-Ford | 68 | +50.5 | 4 |
| 4 | 26 | Henri Pescarolo | March-Ford | 67 | +1 Lap | 17 |
| 5 | 24 | Rolf Stommelen | Surtees-Ford | 67 | +1 Lap | 12 |
| 6 | 23 | John Surtees | Surtees-Ford | 67 | +1 Lap | 18 |
| 7 | 22 | Jean Pierre Beltoise | Matra | 66 | +2 Laps | 15 |
| 8 | 17 | Howden Ganley | BRM | 66 | +2 Laps | 11 |
| 9 | 16 | Jo Siffert | BRM | 66 | +2 Laps | 3 |
| 10 | 14 | Francois Cevert | Tyrrell-Ford | 65 | +3 Laps | 10 |
| 11 | 20 | Nanni Galli | March-Ford | 65 | +3 Laps | 21 |
| 12 | 8 | Tim Schenken | Brabham-Ford | 63 | Gearbox | 7 |
| NC | 3 | Reine Wisell | Lotus-Pratt & Whitney | 57 | Not classified | 19 |
| NC | 19 | A.de Adamich | March-Alfa Romeo | 56 | Not classified | 24 |
| Ret | 10 | Peter Gethin | McLaren-Ford | 53 | Engine | 14 |
| Ret | 4 | Jacky Ickx | Ferrari | 51 | Engine | 6 |
| Ret | 5 | Clay Regazzoni | Ferrari | 48 | Oil pressure | 1 |
| Ret | 21 | Chris Amon | Matra | 35 | Engine | 9 |
| Ret | 9 | Denny Hulme | McLaren-Ford | 32 | Engine | 8 |
| Ret | 25 | Derek Bell | Surtees-Ford | 23 | Suspension | 23 |
| Ret | 6 | Mike Beuttler | March-Ford | 21 | Oil pressure | 20 |
| Ret | 2 | Dave Charlton | Lotus-Ford | 1 | Engine | 13 |
| Ret | 7 | Graham Hill | Brabham-Ford | 0 | Accident | 22 |
| Ret | 11 | Jackie Oliver | McLaren-Ford | 0 | Accident | 16 |

Winning speed: 130.480mph Lap leaders: Regazzoni 1-3; Stewart 4-68
Pole position: Regazzoni, 1m 18.100s, 134.919mph
Fastest lap: Stewart, 1m 19.900s, 131.880mph

## GERMAN GRAND PRIX: NURBURGRING *1 August Round: 7 Race: 204 12 x 14.189 miles*

| POS. | NO. | DRIVER | CAR-ENGINE | LAPS | TIME/RETIRED | GRID |
|---|---|---|---|---|---|---|
| 1 | 2 | Jackie Stewart | Tyrrell-Ford | 12 | 1:29'15.7 | 1 |
| 2 | 3 | Francois Cevert | Tyrrell-Ford | 12 | +30.1 | 5 |
| 3 | 6 | Clay Regazzoni | Ferrari | 12 | +37.1 | 4 |
| 4 | 5 | Mario Andretti | Ferrari | 12 | +2'05.0 | 11 |
| 5 | 15 | Ronnie Peterson | March-Ford | 12 | +2'29.1 | 3 |
| 6 | 25 | Tim Schenken | Brabham-Ford | 12 | +2'58.6 | 9 |
| 7 | 7 | John Surtees | Surtees-Ford | 12 | +3'19.0 | 15 |
| 8 | 9 | Reine Wisell | Lotus-Ford | 12 | +6'31.7 | 17 |
| 9 | 24 | Graham Hill | Brabham-Ford | 12 | +6'37.0 | 13 |
| 10 | 12 | Rolf Stommelen | Surtees-Ford | 11 | +1 Lap | 12 |
| 11 | 22 | Vic Elford | BRM | 11 | +1 Lap | 18 |
| 12 | 17 | Nanni Galli | March-Alfa Romeo | 10 | +2 Laps | 21 |
| Ret | 8 | Emerson Fittipaldi | Lotus-Ford | 8 | Oil leak | 8 |
| DSQ | 21 | Jo Siffert | BRM | 6 | Disqualified | 3 |
| Ret | 10 | Chris Amon | Matra | 6 | Accident | 16 |
| Ret | 14 | Henri Pescarolo | March-Ford | 5 | Suspension | 10 |
| Ret | 20 | Peter Gethin | McLaren-Ford | 5 | Accident | 19 |
| Ret | 18 | Denny Hulme | McLaren-Ford | 3 | Fuel leak | 6 |
| DSQ | 28 | Mike Beuttler | March-Ford | 3 | Disqualified | 22 |
| Ret | 23 | Howden Ganley | BRM | 2 | Engine | 14 |
| Ret | 16 | A.de Adamich | March-Alfa Romeo | 2 | Injection | 20 |
| Ret | 4 | Jacky Ickx | Ferrari | 1 | Accident | 2 |
| DNQ | 27 | Jo Bonnier | McLaren-Ford | | | |

Winning speed: 114.451mph Lap leaders: Stewart 1-12
Pole position: Stewart, 7m 19.000s, 116.356mph
Fastest lap: Cevert, 7m 20.100s, 116.066mph

## AUSTRIAN GRAND PRIX: OSTERREICHRING *15 August Round: 8 Race: 205 54 x 3.673 miles*

| POS. | NO. | DRIVER | CAR-ENGINE | LAPS | TIME/RETIRED | GRID |
|---|---|---|---|---|---|---|
| 1 | 14 | Jo Siffert | BRM | 54 | 1:30'23.91 | 1 |
| 2 | 2 | Emerson Fittipaldi | Lotus-Ford | 54 | +4.12 | 5 |
| 3 | 8 | Tim Schenken | Brabham-Ford | 54 | +19.77 | 7 |
| 4 | 3 | Reine Wisell | Lotus-Ford | 54 | +31.87 | 10 |
| 5 | 7 | Graham Hill | Brabham-Ford | 54 | +48.43 | 8 |
| 6 | 25 | Henri Pescarolo | March-Ford | 54 | +1'24.51 | 13 |
| 7 | 24 | Rolf Stommelen | Surtees-Ford | 54 | +1'37.42 | 12 |
| 8 | 17 | Ronnie Peterson | March-Ford | 53 | +1 Lap | 11 |
| 9 | 10 | Jackie Oliver | McLaren-Ford | 53 | +1 Lap | 22 |
| 10 | 23 | Peter Gethin | BRM | 52 | +2 Laps | 16 |
| 11 | 16 | Helmut Marko | BRM | 52 | +2 Laps | 17 |
| 12 | 19 | Nanni Galli | March-Alfa Romeo | 51 | +3 Laps | 15 |
| NC | 27 | Mike Beuttler | March-Ford | 47 | Not classified | 19 |
| Ret | 12 | Francois Cevert | Tyrrell-Ford | 42 | Engine | 3 |
| Ret | 11 | Jackie Stewart | Tyrrell-Ford | 35 | Halfshaft | 2 |
| Ret | 4 | Jacky Ickx | Ferrari | 31 | Engine | 6 |
| Ret | 26 | Niki Lauda | March-Ford | 20 | Handling | 21 |
| Ret | 22 | John Surtees | Surtees-Ford | 12 | Engine | 18 |
| Ret | 5 | Clay Regazzoni | Ferrari | 8 | Engine | 4 |
| Ret | 15 | Howden Ganley | BRM | 5 | Ignition | 14 |
| Ret | 9 | Denny Hulme | McLaren-Ford | 4 | Engine | 9 |
| Ret | 28 | Jo Bonnier | McLaren-Ford | 0 | Fuel leak | 20 |

Winning speed: 131.642mph Lap leaders: Siffert 1-54
Pole position: Siffert, 1m 37.440s, 135.699mph
Fastest lap: Siffert, 1m 38.470s, 134.280mph

## ITALIAN GRAND PRIX: MONZA *5 September Round: 9 Race: 206 55 x 3.573 miles*

| POS. | NO. | DRIVER | CAR-ENGINE | LAPS | TIME/RETIRED | GRID |
|---|---|---|---|---|---|---|
| 1 | 18 | Peter Gethin | BRM | 55 | 1:18'12.60 | 11 |
| 2 | 25 | Ronnie Peterson | March-Ford | 55 | +0.01 | 6 |
| 3 | 2 | Francois Cevert | Tyrrell-Ford | 55 | +0.09 | 5 |
| 4 | 9 | Mike Hailwood | Surtees-Ford | 55 | +0.18 | 17 |
| 5 | 19 | Howden Ganley | BRM | 55 | +0.61 | 4 |
| 6 | 12 | Chris Amon | Matra | 55 | +32.36 | 1 |
| 7 | 14 | Jackie Oliver | McLaren-Ford | 55 | +1'24.83 | 13 |
| 8 | 5 | Emerson Fittipaldi | Lotus-Pratt & Whitney | 54 | +1 Lap | 18 |
| 9 | 20 | Jo Siffert | BRM | 53 | +2 Laps | 3 |
| 10 | 28 | Jo Bonnier | McLaren-Ford | 51 | +4 Laps | 21 |
| Ret | 10 | Graham Hill | Brabham-Ford | 47 | Gearbox | 14 |
| NC | 26 | Jean-Pierre Jarier | March-Ford | 47 | Not classified | 24 |
| Ret | 24 | Mike Beuttler | March-Ford | 41 | Engine | 16 |
| Ret | 16 | Henri Pescarolo | March-Ford | 40 | Suspension | 10 |
| Ret | 23 | A.de Adamich | March-Alfa Romeo | 33 | Engine | 20 |
| Ret | 4 | Clay Regazzoni | Ferrari | 17 | Engine | 8 |
| Ret | 3 | Jacky Ickx | Ferrari | 15 | Engine | 2 |
| Ret | 30 | Jackie Stewart | Tyrrell-Ford | 15 | Engine | 7 |
| Ret | 22 | Nanni Galli | March-Ford | 11 | Electrical | 19 |
| Ret | 11 | Tim Schenken | Brabham-Ford | 5 | Suspension | 9 |
| Ret | 27 | Silvio Moser | Bellasi-Ford | 5 | Suspension | 22 |
| Ret | 21 | Helmut Marko | BRM | 3 | Engine | 12 |
| Ret | 7 | John Surtees | Surtees-Ford | 3 | Engine | 15 |
| Ret | 8 | Rolf Stommelen | Surtees-Ford | 0 | Accident | 23 |

Winning speed: 150.755mph Lap leaders: Regazzoni 1-3, 9; Peterson 4-7, 10-14, 17-22, 24, 26, 33, 47-50, 54; Stewart 8; Cevert 15-16, 23, 31-32, 34, 36; Hailwood 25, 27, 35, 42, 51; Siffert 28-30; Amon 37-41, 43-46; Gethin 52-53, 55
Pole position: Amon, 1m 22.400s, 156.097mph
Fastest lap: Pescarolo, 1m 23.800s, 153.489mph

## CANADIAN GRAND PRIX: MOSPORT PARK *16 September Round: 10 Race: 207 64 x 2.459 miles*

| POS. | NO. | DRIVER | CAR-ENGINE | LAPS | TIME/RETIRED | GRID |
|---|---|---|---|---|---|---|
| 1 | 11 | Jackie Stewart | Tyrrell-Ford | 64 | 1:55'12.9 | 1 |
| 2 | 17 | Ronnie Peterson | March-Ford | 64 | +38.3 | 6 |
| 3 | 10 | Mark Donohue | McLaren-Ford | 64 | +1'35.8 | 8 |
| 4 | 9 | Denny Hulme | McLaren-Ford | 63 | +1 Lap | 10 |
| 5 | 3 | Reine Wisell | Lotus-Ford | 63 | +1 Lap | 7 |
| 6 | 12 | Francois Cevert | Tyrrell-Ford | 62 | +2 Laps | 3 |
| 7 | 2 | Emerson Fittipaldi | Lotus-Ford | 62 | +2 Laps | 4 |
| 8 | 4 | Jacky Ickx | Ferrari | 62 | +2 Laps | 12 |
| 9 | 14 | Jo Siffert | BRM | 61 | +3 Laps | 2 |
| 10 | 20 | Chris Amon | Matra | 61 | +3 Laps | 5 |
| 11 | 22 | John Surtees | Surtees-Ford | 60 | +4 Laps | 14 |
| 12 | 31 | Helmut Marko | BRM | 60 | +4 Laps | 19 |
| 13 | 6 | Mario Andretti | Ferrari | 60 | +4 Laps | 13 |
| 14 | 15 | Peter Gethin | BRM | 59 | +5 Laps | 16 |
| 15 | 28 | George Eaton | BRM | 59 | +5 Laps | 21 |
| 16 | 18 | Nanni Galli | March-Ford | 57 | +7 Laps | 20 |
| NC | 19 | Mike Beuttler | March-Ford | 56 | Not classified | 22 |
| NC | 35 | Pete Lovely | Lotus-Ford | 55 | Not classified | 25 |
| Ret | 24 | Rolf Stommelen | Surtees-Ford | 26 | Overheating | 23 |
| Ret | 21 | Jean Pierre Beltoise | Matra | 15 | Accident | 11 |
| Ret | 33 | Skip Barber | March-Ford | 13 | Oil pressure | 24 |
| Ret | 5 | Clay Regazzoni | Ferrari | 7 | Accident | 18 |
| Ret | 37 | Graham Hill | Brabham-Ford | 2 | Accident | 15 |
| Ret | 8 | Tim Schenken | Brabham-Ford | 1 | Ignition | 17 |
| Ret | 16 | Howden Ganley | BRM | 0 | Accident | 9 |
| DNQ | 26 | Chris Craft | Brabham-Ford | | | |

Winning speed: 81.956mph Lap leaders: Stewart 1-17, 31-64; Peterson 18-30
Pole position: Stewart, 1m 15.300s, 117.562mph
Fastest lap: Hulme, 1m 43.500s, 85.530mph
Scheduled for 80 laps but stopped early because of rain.

## UNITED STATES GRAND PRIX: WATKINS GLEN *3 October Round: 11 Race: 208 59 x 3.377 miles*

| POS. | NO. | DRIVER | CAR-ENGINE | LAPS | TIME/RETIRED | GRID |
|---|---|---|---|---|---|---|
| 1 | 9 | Francois Cevert | Tyrrell-Ford | 59 | 1:43'51.991 | 5 |
| 2 | 14 | Jo Siffert | BRM | 59 | +40.062 | 6 |
| 3 | 25 | Ronnie Peterson | March-Ford | 59 | +44.070 | 11 |
| 4 | 16 | Howden Ganley | BRM | 59 | +56.749 | 12 |
| 5 | 8 | Jackie Stewart | Tyrrell-Ford | 59 | +1'00.003 | 1 |
| 6 | 5 | Clay Regazzoni | Ferrari | 59 | +1'16.426 | 4 |
| 7 | 22 | Graham Hill | Brabham-Ford | 58 | +1 Lap | 18 |
| 8 | 12 | Jean Pierre Beltoise | Matra | 58 | +1 Lap | 10 |
| 9 | 15 | Peter Gethin | BRM | 58 | +1 Lap | 21 |
| 10 | 31 | David Hobbs | McLaren-Ford | 58 | +1 Lap | 22 |
| 11 | 27 | A.de Adamich | March-Alfa Romeo | 57 | +2 Laps | 26 |
| 12 | 11 | Chris Amon | Matra | 57 | +2 Laps | 8 |
| 13 | 17 | Helmut Marko | BRM | 57 | +2 Laps | 16 |
| 14 | 28 | John Cannon | BRM | 56 | +3 Laps | 24 |
| 15 | 20 | Mike Hailwood | Surtees-Ford | 54 | Accident | 14 |
| 16 | 29 | Jo Bonnier | McLaren-Ford | 54 | Out of fuel | 28 |
| 17 | 18 | John Surtees | Surtees-Ford | 54 | +5 Laps | 13 |
| NC | 33 | Skip Barber | March-Ford | 52 | Not classified | 25 |
| Ret | 32 | Jacky Ickx | Ferrari | 49 | Alternator | 7 |
| NC | 2 | Emerson Fittipaldi | Lotus-Ford | 49 | Not classified | 2 |
| NC | 30 | Pete Lovely | Lotus-Ford | 49 | Not classified | 29 |
| Ret | 7 | Denny Hulme | McLaren-Ford | 47 | Accident | 3 |
| Ret | 23 | Tim Schenken | Brabham-Ford | 41 | Engine | 15 |
| Ret | 24 | Chris Craft | Brabham-Ford | 30 | Suspension | 27 |
| Ret | 21 | Henri Pescarolo | March-Ford | 23 | Engine | 20 |
| Ret | 19 | Sam Posey | Surtees-Ford | 15 | Engine | 17 |
| Ret | 26 | Nanni Galli | March-Ford | 11 | Wheel | 23 |
| Ret | 3 | Reine Wisell | Lotus-Ford | 5 | Brakes | 9 |
| Ret | 10 | Peter Revson | Tyrrell-Ford | 1 | Clutch | 19 |

Winning speed: 115.096mph Lap leaders: Stewart 1-13, Cevert, 14-59
Pole position: Stewart, 1m 42.642s, 118.443mph
Fastest lap: Ickx, 1m 43.474s, 117.490mph

# 1972

## DRIVERS' CHAMPION: EMERSON FITTIPALDI
## CONSTRUCTORS' CHAMPION: LOTUS FORD

### DRIVERS' CHAMPIONSHIP

| POS | DRIVER | COUNTRY | CAR | POINTS |
|---|---|---|---|---|
| 1 | Emerson Fittipaldi | Brazil | Lotus-Ford | 61 |
| 2 | Jackie Stewart | GB | Tyrrell-Ford | 45 |
| 3 | Denny Hulme | New Zealand | McLaren-Ford | 39 |
| 4 | Jacky Ickx | Belgium | Ferrari | 27 |
| 5 | Peter Revson | USA | McLaren-Ford | 23 |
| 6 | François Cevert | France | Tyrrell-Ford | 15 |
| = | Clay Regazzoni | Switzerland | Ferrari | 15 |
| 8 | Mike Hailwood | GB | Surtees –Ford | 13 |
| 9 | Chris Amon | New Zealand | Matra-Simca | 12 |
| = | Ronnie Peterson | Sweden | March-Ford | 12 |
| 11 | Jean-Pierre Beltoise | France | BRM | 9 |
| 12 | Mario Andretti | USA | Ferrari | 4 |
| = | Howden Ganley | New Zealand | BRM | 4 |
| = | Brian Redman | GB | McLaren-Ford, BRM | 4 |
| = | Graham Hill | GB | Brabham –Ford | 4 |
| 16 | Andrea de Adamich | Italy | Surtees-Ford | 3 |
| = | Carlos Reutemann | Argentina | Brabham-Ford | 3 |
| = | Carlos Pace | Brazil | March-Ford | 3 |
| 19 | Tim Schenken | Australia | Surtees-Ford | 2 |
| 20 | Arturo Merzario | Italy | Ferrari | 1 |
| = | Peter Gethin | GB | BRM | 1 |
| | Henri Pescarolo | France | March-Ford, Politoys-Ford | |
| | Helmut Marko | Austria | BRM | |
| | Niki Lauda | Austria | March-Ford | |
| | Reine Wisell | Sweden | BRM, Lotus-Ford | |
| | Dave Walker | GB | Lotus-Ford | |
| | Alex Soler-Roig | Spain | BRM | |
| | Rolf Stommelen | West Germany | Eifelland-Ford | |
| | John Love | South Africa | Surtees-Ford | |
| | Dave Charlton | South Africa | Lotus-Ford | |
| | William Ferguson | South Africa | Brabham-Ford | |
| | Wilson Fittipaldi | Brazil | Brabham-Ford | |
| | Mike Beuttler | GB | March-Ford | |
| | Nanni Galli | Italy | Tecno, Ferrari | |
| | Vern Schuppan | Australia | BRM | |
| | Patrick Depailler | France | Tyrrell-Ford | |
| | Jackie Oliver | GB | BRM | |
| | Derek Bell | GB | Tecno | |
| | François Migault | France | Connew-Ford | |
| | John Surtees | GB | Surtees-Ford | |
| | Skip Barber | USA | March-Ford | |
| | Bill Brack | Canada | BRM | |
| | Jody Scheckter | South Africa | McLaren-Ford | |
| | Sam Posey | USA | Surtees-Ford | |

Points for top six finishers (9, 6, 4, 3, 2, 1). Only the best five scores from the first six races and the best five scores from the remaining six races counted towards the championship.

### CONSTRUCTORS' CHAMPIONSHIP

| POS. | CONSTRUCTOR | POINTS |
|---|---|---|
| 1 | Lotus-Ford | 61 |
| 2 | Tyrrell-Ford | 51 |
| 3 | McLaren-Ford | 47 |
| 4 | Ferrari | 33 |
| 5 | Surtees-Ford | 18 |
| 6 | March-Ford | 15 |
| 7 | BRM | 14 |
| 8 | Matra | 12 |
| 9 | Brabham-Ford | 7 |

Points for top six finishers (9, 6, 4, 3, 2, 1). Points only counted for top-placed car for each constructor. Only the best five scores from the first six races and the best five scores from the remaining six races counted towards the championship

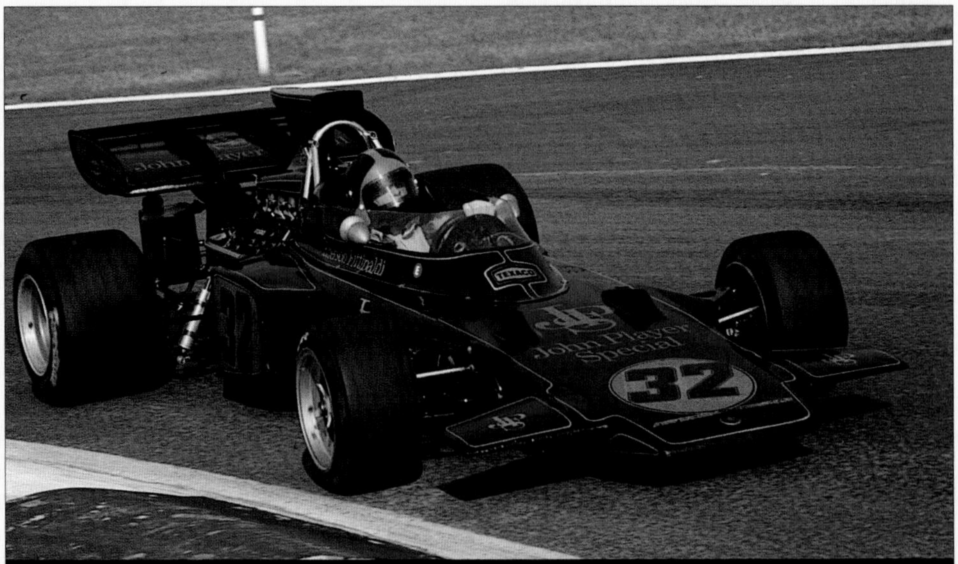


1972 world champion Emerson Fittipaldi in the Type 72 Lotus Ford

### ARGENTINE GRAND PRIX: BUENOS AIRES *23 January Round: 1 Race: 209 95 x 2.078 miles*

| POS. | NO. | DRIVER | CAR-ENGINE | LAPS | TIME/RETIRED | GRID |
|---|---|---|---|---|---|---|
| 1 | 21 | Jackie Stewart | Tyrrell-Ford | 95 | 1:57'58.82 | 2 |
| 2 | 17 | Denny Hulme | McLaren-Ford | 95 | +25.96 | 4 |
| 3 | 8 | Jacky Ickx | Ferrari | 95 | +59.39 | 8 |
| 4 | 9 | Clay Regazzoni | Ferrari | 95 | +1'06.72 | 6 |
| 5 | 19 | Tim Schenken | Surtees-Ford | 95 | +1'09.11 | 11 |
| 6 | 14 | Ronnie Peterson | March-Ford | 94 | +1 Lap | 10 |
| 7 | 2 | Carlos Reutemann | Brabham-Ford | 93 | +2 Laps | 1 |
| 8 | 23 | Henri Pescarolo | March-Ford | 93 | +2 Laps | 15 |
| 9 | 3 | Howden Ganley | BRM | 93 | +2 Laps | 13 |
| 10 | 7 | Helmut Marko | BRM | 93 | +2 Laps | 19 |
| 11 | 15 | Niki Lauda | March-Ford | 93 | +2 Laps | 22 |
| Ret | 11 | Emerson Fittipaldi | Lotus-Ford | 61 | Suspension | 5 |
| Ret | 22 | Francois Cevert | Tyrrell-Ford | 59 | Gearbox | 17 |
| Ret | 4 | Reine Wisell | BRM | 59 | Water leak | 7 |
| Ret | 18 | Peter Revson | McLaren-Ford | 49 | Engine | 3 |
| Ret | 10 | Mario Andretti | Ferrari | 20 | Engine | 9 |
| Ret | 20 | A.de Adamich | Surtees-Ford | 11 | Fuel system | 14 |
| Ret | 1 | Graham Hill | Brabham-Ford | 11 | Fuel pump | 16 |
| DSQ | 12 | Dave Walker | Lotus-Ford | 8 | Disqualified | 20 |
| Ret | 5 | Peter Gethin | BRM | 1 | Oil leak | 18 |
| Ret | 6 | Alex Soler-Roig | BRM | 1 | Accident | 21 |
| DNS | 16 | Chris Amon | Matra | 0 | Not started | 12 |

Winning speed: 100.418mph Lap leaders: Stewart 1-95
Pole position: Reutemann, 1m 12.460s, 103.265mph
Fastest lap: Stewart, 1m 13.660s, 101.582mph

### SOUTH AFRICAN GRAND PRIX: KYALAMI *4 March Round: 2 Race: 210 79 x 2.550 miles*

| POS. | NO. | DRIVER | CAR-ENGINE | LAPS | TIME/RETIRED | GRID |
|---|---|---|---|---|---|---|
| 1 | 12 | Denny Hulme | McLaren-Ford | 79 | 1:45'49.1 | 5 |
| 2 | 8 | Emerson Fittipaldi | Lotus-Ford | 79 | +14.1 | 3 |
| 3 | 14 | Peter Revson | McLaren-Ford | 79 | +25.8 | 12 |
| 4 | 7 | Mario Andretti | Ferrari | 79 | +38.5 | 6 |
| 5 | 3 | Ronnie Peterson | March-Ford | 79 | +49.0 | 9 |
| 6 | 19 | Graham Hill | Brabham-Ford | 78 | +1 Lap | 14 |
| 7 | 4 | Niki Lauda | March-Ford | 78 | +1 Lap | 21 |
| 8 | 5 | Jacky Ickx | Ferrari | 78 | +1 Lap | 7 |
| 9 | 2 | Francois Cevert | Tyrrell-Ford | 78 | +1 Lap | 8 |
| 10 | 9 | Dave Walker | Lotus-Ford | 78 | +1 Lap | 19 |
| 11 | 21 | Henri Pescarolo | March-Ford | 78 | +1 Lap | 22 |
| 12 | 6 | Clay Regazzoni | Ferrari | 77 | +2 Laps | 2 |
| 13 | 25 | Rolf Stommelen | March-Ford | 77 | +2 Laps | 25 |
| 14 | 24 | Helmut Marko | BRM | 76 | +3 Laps | 23 |
| 15 | 15 | Chris Amon | Matra | 76 | +3 Laps | 13 |
| 16 | 27 | John Love | Surtees-Ford | 73 | Spun off | 26 |
| 17 | 22 | Carlos Pace | March-Ford | 73 | +6 Laps | 24 |
| NC | 23 | Howden Ganley | BRM | 70 | Not classified | 16 |
| NC | 18 | A.de Adamich | Surtees-Ford | 69 | Not classified | 20 |
| NC | 11 | Peter Gethin | BRM | 65 | Not classified | 18 |
| Ret | 10 | Jean Pierre Beltoise | BRM | 61 | Engine | 11 |
| Ret | 1 | Jackie Stewart | Tyrrell-Ford | 45 | Gearbox | 1 |
| Ret | 17 | Mike Hailwood | Surtees-Ford | 28 | Suspension | 4 |
| Ret | 20 | Carlos Reutemann | Brabham-Ford | 27 | Fuel system | 15 |
| Ret | 16 | Tim Schenken | Surtees-Ford | 9 | Engine | 10 |
| Ret | 26 | Dave Charlton | Lotus-Ford | 2 | Fuel pump | 17 |

Winning speed: 114.229mph Lap leaders: Hulme 1, 57-79; Stewart 2-44; E Fittipaldi 45-56
Pole position: Stewart, 1m 17.000s, 119.226mph
Fastest lap: Hailwood, 1m 18.900s, 116.355mph

### SPANISH GRAND PRIX: JARAMA *1 May Round: 3 Race: 211 90 x 2.115 miles*

| POS. | NO. | DRIVER | CAR-ENGINE | LAPS | TIME/RETIRED | GRID |
|---|---|---|---|---|---|---|
| 1 | 5 | Emerson Fittipaldi | Lotus-Ford | 90 | 2:03'41.23 | 3 |
| 2 | 4 | Jacky Ickx | Ferrari | 90 | +18.92 | 1 |
| 3 | 6 | Clay Regazzoni | Ferrari | 89 | +1 Lap | 8 |
| 4 | 26 | A.de Adamich | Surtees-Ford | 89 | +1 Lap | 13 |
| 5 | 20 | Peter Revson | McLaren-Ford | 89 | +1 Lap | 11 |
| 6 | 29 | Carlos Pace | March-Ford | 89 | +1 Lap | 16 |
| 7 | 22 | Wilson Fittipaldi | Brabham-Ford | 88 | +2 Laps | 14 |
| 8 | 12 | Tim Schenken | Surtees-Ford | 88 | +2 Laps | 18 |
| 9 | 21 | Dave Walker | Lotus-Ford | 87 | +3 Laps | 24 |
| 10 | 18 | Graham Hill | Brabham-Ford | 86 | +4 Laps | 23 |
| 11 | 14 | Henri Pescarolo | March-Ford | 86 | +4 Laps | 19 |
| Ret | 1 | Jackie Stewart | Tyrrell-Ford | 69 | Accident | 4 |
| Ret | 9 | Chris Amon | Matra | 66 | Gearbox | 6 |
| Ret | 3 | Francois Cevert | Tyrrell-Ford | 65 | Ignition | 12 |
| Ret | 8 | Peter Gethin | BRM | 65 | Engine | 21 |
| Ret | 11 | Denny Hulme | McLaren-Ford | 48 | Gearbox | 2 |
| Ret | 25 | Howden Ganley | BRM | 38 | Engine | 20 |
| Ret | 10 | Reine Wisell | BRM | 24 | Accident | 10 |
| Ret | 7 | Mario Andretti | Ferrari | 23 | Oil pressure | 5 |
| Ret | 15 | Mike Hailwood | Surtees-Ford | 20 | Electrical | 15 |
| Ret | 2 | Ronnie Peterson | March-Ford | 16 | Fuel leak | 9 |
| Ret | 16 | Rolf Stommelen | March-Ford | 15 | Accident | 17 |
| Ret | 19 | Jean Pierre Beltoise | BRM | 9 | Gearbox | 7 |
| Ret | 24 | Niki Lauda | March-Ford | 6 | Differential | 25 |
| Ret | 28 | Alex Soler-Roig | BRM | 6 | Accident | 22 |
| DNQ | 23 | Mike Beuttler | March-Ford | | | |

Winning speed: 92.344mph Lap leaders: Hulme 1-4; Stewart 5-8; E Fittipaldi 9-90
Pole position: Ickx, 1m 18.430s, 97.087mph
Fastest lap: Ickx, 1m 21.010s, 93.995mph

### MONACO GRAND PRIX: MONTE CARLO *14 May Round: 4 Race: 212 80 x 1.954 miles*

| POS. | NO. | DRIVER | CAR-ENGINE | LAPS | TIME/RETIRED | GRID |
|---|---|---|---|---|---|---|
| 1 | 17 | Jean Pierre Beltoise | BRM | 80 | 2:26'54.7 | 4 |
| 2 | 6 | Jacky Ickx | Ferrari | 80 | +38.2 | 2 |
| 3 | 8 | Emerson Fittipaldi | Lotus-Ford | 79 | +1 Lap | 1 |
| 4 | 1 | Jackie Stewart | Tyrrell-Ford | 78 | +2 Laps | 8 |
| 5 | 15 | Brian Redman | McLaren-Ford | 77 | +3 Laps | 10 |
| 6 | 16 | Chris Amon | Matra | 77 | +3 Laps | 6 |
| 7 | 12 | A.de Adamich | Surtees-Ford | 77 | +3 Laps | 18 |
| 8 | 26 | Helmut Marko | BRM | 77 | +3 Laps | 17 |
| 9 | 21 | Wilson Fittipaldi | Brabham-Ford | 77 | +3 Laps | 21 |
| 10 | 27 | Rolf Stommelen | March-Ford | 77 | +3 Laps | 25 |
| 11 | 3 | Ronnie Peterson | March-Ford | 76 | +4 Laps | 15 |
| 12 | 20 | Graham Hill | Brabham-Ford | 76 | +4 Laps | 19 |
| 13 | 5 | Mike Beuttler | March-Ford | 76 | +4 Laps | 23 |
| 14 | 9 | Dave Walker | Lotus-Ford | 75 | +5 Laps | 14 |
| 15 | 14 | Denny Hulme | McLaren-Ford | 74 | +6 Laps | 7 |
| 16 | 4 | Niki Lauda | March-Ford | 74 | +6 Laps | 22 |
| 17 | 23 | Carlos Pace | March-Ford | 72 | +8 Laps | 24 |
| NC | 2 | Francois Cevert | Tyrrell-Ford | 70 | Not classified | 12 |
| Ret | 22 | Henri Pescarolo | March-Ford | 58 | Accident | 9 |
| Ret | 7 | Clay Regazzoni | Ferrari | 51 | Accident | 3 |
| Ret | 11 | Mike Hailwood | Surtees-Ford | 48 | Accident | 11 |
| Ret | 19 | Howden Ganley | BRM | 47 | Accident | 20 |
| Ret | 10 | Tim Schenken | Surtees-Ford | 31 | Accident | 13 |
| Ret | 18 | Peter Gethin | BRM | 27 | Accident | 5 |
| Ret | 28 | Reine Wisell | BRM | 16 | Engine | 16 |

Winning speed: 63.849mph Lap leaders: Beltoise 1-80
Pole position: E Fittipaldi, 1m 21.400s, 86.427mph
Fastest lap: Beltoise, 1m 40.000s, 70.352mph

### BELGIAN GRAND PRIX: NIVELLES *4 June Round: 5 Race: 213 85 x 2.314 miles*

| POS. | NO. | DRIVER | CAR-ENGINE | LAPS | TIME/RETIRED | GRID |
|---|---|---|---|---|---|---|
| 1 | 32 | Emerson Fittipaldi | Lotus-Ford | 85 | 1:44'06.7 | 1 |
| 2 | 8 | Francois Cevert | Tyrrell-Ford | 85 | +26.6 | 5 |
| 3 | 9 | Denny Hulme | McLaren-Ford | 85 | +58.1 | 3 |
| 4 | 34 | Mike Hailwood | Surtees-Ford | 85 | +1'12.0 | 8 |
| 5 | 16 | Carlos Pace | March-Ford | 84 | +1 Lap | 11 |
| 6 | 5 | Chris Amon | Matra | 84 | +1 Lap | 13 |
| 7 | 10 | Peter Revson | McLaren-Ford | 83 | +2 Laps | 7 |
| 8 | 25 | Howden Ganley | BRM | 83 | +2 Laps | 15 |
| 9 | 11 | Ronnie Peterson | March-Ford | 83 | +2 Laps | 14 |
| 10 | 27 | Helmut Marko | BRM | 83 | +2 Laps | 23 |
| 11 | 6 | Rolf Stommelen | March-Ford | 83 | +2 Laps | 20 |
| 12 | 12 | Niki Lauda | March-Ford | 82 | +3 Laps | 25 |
| 13 | 19 | Carlos Reutemann | Brabham-Ford | 81 | +4 Laps | 9 |
| 14 | 33 | Dave Walker | Lotus-Ford | 79 | +6 Laps | 12 |
| Ret | 17 | Graham Hill | Brabham-Ford | 73 | Suspension | 16 |
| NC | 15 | Henri Pescarolo | March-Ford | 59 | Not classified | 19 |
| Ret | 30 | Clay Regazzoni | Ferrari | 57 | Accident | 2 |
| Ret | 36 | A.de Adamich | Surtees-Ford | 55 | Engine | 10 |
| Ret | 22 | Nanni Galli | Tecno | 54 | Accident | 24 |
| Ret | 29 | Jacky Ickx | Ferrari | 47 | Injection | 4 |
| Ret | 14 | Mike Beuttler | March-Ford | 31 | Halfshaft | 22 |
| Ret | 18 | Wilson Fittipaldi | Brabham-Ford | 28 | Gearbox | 18 |
| Ret | 24 | Peter Gethin | BRM | 27 | Fuel pump | 17 |
| Ret | 23 | Jean Pierre Beltoise | BRM | 15 | Overheating | 6 |
| Ret | 35 | Tim Schenken | Surtees-Ford | 11 | Overheating | 21 |

Winning speed: 113.353mph Lap leaders: Regazzoni 1-8; Fittipaldi 9-85
Pole position: E Fittipaldi, 1m 11.430s, 116.623mph
Fastest lap: Amon, 1m 12.120s, 115.507mph

### FRENCH GRAND PRIX: CLERMONT-FERRAND *2 July Round: 6 Race: 214 38 x 5.005 miles*

| POS. | NO. | DRIVER | CAR-ENGINE | LAPS | TIME/RETIRED | GRID |
|---|---|---|---|---|---|---|
| 1 | 4 | Jackie Stewart | Tyrrell-Ford | 38 | 1:52'21.5 | 3 |
| 2 | 1 | Emerson Fittipaldi | Lotus-Ford | 38 | +27.7 | 8 |
| 3 | 9 | Chris Amon | Matra | 38 | +31.9 | 1 |
| 4 | 7 | Francois Cevert | Tyrrell-Ford | 38 | +49.3 | 7 |
| 5 | 12 | Ronnie Peterson | March-Ford | 38 | +56.8 | 9 |
| 6 | 26 | Mike Hailwood | Surtees-Ford | 38 | +1'36.1 | 10 |
| 7 | 2 | Denny Hulme | McLaren-Ford | 38 | +1'48.1 | 2 |
| 8 | 19 | Wilson Fittipaldi | Brabham-Ford | 38 | +2'25.1 | 14 |
| 9 | 11 | Brian Redman | McLaren-Ford | 38 | +2'55.5 | 13 |
| 10 | 18 | Graham Hill | Brabham-Ford | 38 | +2'59.5 | 20 |
| 11 | 3 | Jacky Ickx | Ferrari | 37 | +1 Lap | 4 |
| 12 | 20 | Carlos Reutemann | Brabham-Ford | 37 | +1 Lap | 17 |
| 13 | 30 | Nanni Galli | Ferrari | 37 | +1 Lap | 19 |
| 14 | 28 | A.de Adamich | Surtees-Ford | 37 | +1 Lap | 12 |
| 15 | 5 | Jean Pierre Beltoise | BRM | 37 | +1 Lap | 24 |
| 16 | 10 | Rolf Stommelen | March-Ford | 37 | +1 Lap | 15 |
| 17 | 27 | Tim Schenken | Surtees-Ford | 36 | +2 Laps | 5 |
| 18 | 6 | Dave Walker | Lotus-Ford | 34 | Halfshaft | 22 |
| 19 | 15 | Mike Beuttler | March-Ford | 33 | Out of fuel | 23 |
| NC | 8 | P.Depailler | Tyrrell-Ford | 33 | Not classified | 16 |
| Ret | 24 | Reine Wisell | BRM | 25 | Gearbox | 18 |
| Ret | 17 | Carlos Pace | March-Ford | 18 | Engine | 11 |
| Ret | 25 | Helmut Marko | BRM | 8 | Physical | 6 |
| Ret | 14 | Niki Lauda | March-Ford | 4 | Halfshaft | 21 |
| DNQ | 29 | Dave Charlton | Lotus-Ford | | | |

Winning speed: 101.566mph Lap leaders: Amon 1-19; Stewart 20-38
Pole position: Amon, 2m 53.400s, 103.913mph
Fastest lap: Amon, 2m 53.900s, 103.614mh

### BRITISH GRAND PRIX: BRANDS HATCH *15 July Round: 7 Race: 215 76 x 2.650 miles*

| POS. | NO. | DRIVER | CAR-ENGINE | LAPS | TIME/RETIRED | GRID |
|---|---|---|---|---|---|---|
| 1 | 8 | Emerson Fittipaldi | Lotus-Ford | 76 | 1:47'50.2 | 2 |
| 2 | 1 | Jackie Stewart | Tyrrell-Ford | 76 | +4.1 | 4 |
| 3 | 19 | Peter Revson | McLaren-Ford | 76 | +1'12.5 | 3 |
| 4 | 17 | Chris Amon | Matra | 75 | +1 Lap | 17 |
| 5 | 18 | Denny Hulme | McLaren-Ford | 75 | +1 Lap | 11 |
| 6 | 6 | Arturo Merzario | Ferrari | 75 | +1 Lap | 9 |
| 7 | 3 | Ronnie Peterson | March-Ford | 74 | Spun off | 8 |
| 8 | 27 | Carlos Reutemann | Brabham-Ford | 73 | +3 Laps | 10 |
| 9 | 4 | Niki Lauda | March-Ford | 73 | +3 Laps | 19 |
| 10 | 33 | Rolf Stommelen | March-Ford | 71 | +5 Laps | 25 |
| 11 | 11 | Jean Pierre Beltoise | BRM | 70 | +6 Laps | 6 |
| 12 | 28 | Wilson Fittipaldi | Brabham-Ford | 69 | Suspension | 22 |
| 13 | 31 | Mike Beuttler | March-Ford | 69 | +7 Laps | 23 |
| Ret | 22 | Tim Schenken | Surtees-Ford | 64 | Suspension | 5 |
| Ret | 2 | Francois Cevert | Tyrrell-Ford | 60 | Spun off | 12 |
| Ret | 9 | Dave Walker | Lotus-Ford | 59 | Suspension | 15 |
| Ret | 5 | Jacky Ickx | Ferrari | 49 | Oil pressure | 1 |
| Ret | 26 | Graham Hill | Brabham-Ford | 47 | Spun off | 21 |
| Ret | 25 | Carlos Pace | March-Ford | 39 | Differential | 13 |
| Ret | 14 | Jackie Oliver | BRM | 36 | Suspension | 14 |
| Ret | 21 | Mike Hailwood | Surtees-Ford | 31 | Gearbox | 7 |
| Ret | 29 | Dave Charlton | Lotus-Ford | 21 | Gearbox | 24 |
| Ret | 30 | Nanni Galli | Tecno | 9 | Spun off | 18 |
| Ret | 24 | Henri Pescarolo | Politoys-Ford | 7 | Accident | 26 |
| Ret | 12 | Peter Gethin | BRM | 5 | Engine | 16 |
| Ret | 23 | A.de Adamich | Surtees-Ford | 3 | Accident | 20 |

Winning speed: 112.058mph Lap leaders: Ickx 1-48; E Fittipaldi 49-76
Pole position: Ickx, 1m 22.200s, 116.058mph
Fastest lap: Stewart, 1m 24.000s, 113.571mph

### GERMAN GRAND PRIX: NURBURGRING *30 July Round: 8 Race: 216 14 x 14.189 miles*

| POS. | NO. | DRIVER | CAR-ENGINE | LAPS | TIME/RETIRED | GRID |
|---|---|---|---|---|---|---|
| 1 | 4 | Jacky Ickx | Ferrari | 14 | 1:42'12.3 | 1 |
| 2 | 9 | Clay Regazzoni | Ferrari | 14 | +48.3 | 7 |
| 3 | 10 | Ronnie Peterson | March-Ford | 14 | +1'06.7 | 4 |
| 4 | 17 | Howden Ganley | BRM | 14 | +2'20.2 | 18 |
| 5 | 5 | Brian Redman | McLaren-Ford | 14 | +2'35.7 | 19 |
| 6 | 11 | Graham Hill | Brabham-Ford | 14 | +2'59.6 | 15 |
| 7 | 26 | Wilson Fittipaldi | Brabham-Ford | 14 | +3'00.1 | 21 |
| 8 | 28 | Mike Beuttler | March-Ford | 14 | +5'10.7 | 27 |
| 9 | 6 | Jean Pierre Beltoise | BRM | 14 | +5'20.2 | 13 |
| 10 | 7 | Francois Cevert | Tyrrell-Ford | 14 | +5'43.7 | 5 |
| 11 | 1 | Jackie Stewart | Tyrrell-Ford | 13 | Collision | 2 |
| 12 | 19 | Arturo Merzario | Ferrari | 13 | +1 Lap | 22 |
| 13 | 16 | A.de Adamich | Surtees-Ford | 13 | +1 Lap | 20 |
| 14 | 15 | Tim Schenken | Surtees-Ford | 13 | +1 Lap | 12 |
| 15 | 8 | Chris Amon | Matra | 13 | +1 Lap | 8 |
| NC | 21 | Carlos Pace | March-Ford | 11 | Not classified | 11 |
| Ret | 2 | Emerson Fittipaldi | Lotus-Ford | 10 | Gearbox | 3 |
| Ret | 20 | Henri Pescarolo | March-Ford | 10 | Accident | 9 |
| Ret | 3 | Denny Hulme | McLaren-Ford | 8 | Engine | 10 |
| Ret | 14 | Mike Hailwood | Surtees-Ford | 8 | Suspension | 16 |
| Ret | 12 | Carlos Reutemann | Brabham-Ford | 6 | Differential | 6 |
| Ret | 22 | Rolf Stommelen | March-Ford | 6 | Electrical | 14 |
| Ret | 25 | Dave Walker | Lotus-Ford | 6 | Oil leak | 23 |
| Ret | 23 | Niki Lauda | March-Ford | 4 | Oil leak | 24 |
| Ret | 27 | Derek Bell | Tecno | 4 | Engine | 25 |
| Ret | 29 | Dave Charlton | Lotus-Ford | 4 | Physical | 26 |
| Ret | 18 | Reine Wisell | BRM | 3 | Engine | 17 |

Winning speed: 116.616mph Lap leaders: Ickx 1-14
Pole position: Ickx, 7m 7.000sec, 119.626mph
Fastest lap: Ickx, 7m 13.600s, 117.805mph

### AUSTRIAN GRAND PRIX: OSTERREICHRING *13 August Round: 9 Race 217 54 x 3.673 miles*

| POS. | NO. | DRIVER | CAR-ENGINE | LAPS | TIME/RETIRED | GRID |
|---|---|---|---|---|---|---|
| 1 | 31 | Emerson Fittipaldi | Lotus-Ford | 54 | 1:29'16.66 | 1 |
| 2 | 12 | Denny Hulme | McLaren-Ford | 54 | +1.18 | 7 |
| 3 | 14 | Peter Revson | McLaren-Ford | 54 | +36.53 | 4 |
| 4 | 25 | Mike Hailwood | Surtees-Ford | 54 | +44.76 | 12 |
| 5 | 10 | Chris Amon | Matra | 54 | +45.64 | 6 |
| 6 | 9 | Howden Ganley | BRM | 54 | +1'01.19 | 10 |
| 7 | 1 | Jackie Stewart | Tyrrell-Ford | 54 | +1'09.09 | 3 |
| 8 | 7 | Jean Pierre Beltoise | BRM | 54 | +1'21.45 | 21 |
| 9 | 2 | Francois Cevert | Tyrrell-Ford | 53 | +1 Lap | 20 |
| 10 | 4 | Niki Lauda | March-Ford | 53 | +1 Lap | 22 |
| 11 | 24 | Tim Schenken | Surtees-Ford | 52 | +2 Laps | 8 |
| 12 | 5 | Ronnie Peterson | March-Ford | 52 | +2 Laps | 11 |
| 13 | 6 | Peter Gethin | BRM | 51 | +3 Laps | 16 |
| 14 | 11 | A.de Adamich | Surtees-Ford | 51 | +3 Laps | 13 |
| Ret | 27 | Rolf Stommelen | March-Ford | 48 | Engine | 17 |
| NC | 23 | Carlos Pace | March-Ford | 46 | Not classified | 18 |
| Ret | 15 | Nanni Galli | Tecno | 45 | Oil leak | 23 |
| Ret | 16 | Graham Hill | Brabham-Ford | 36 | Injection | 14 |
| Ret | 28 | Wilson Fittipaldi | Brabham-Ford | 31 | Brakes | 15 |
| Ret | 3 | Mike Beuttler | March-Ford | 24 | Fuel system | 24 |
| Ret | 29 | Francois Migault | Connew-Ford | 22 | Suspension | 25 |
| Ret | 18 | Jacky Ickx | Ferrari | 20 | Fuel system | 9 |
| Ret | 17 | Carlos Reutemann | Brabham-Ford | 14 | Injection | 5 |
| Ret | 19 | Clay Regazzoni | Ferrari | 13 | Fuel system | 2 |
| Ret | 21 | Dave Walker | Lotus-Ford | 6 | Engine | 19 |

Winning speed: 133.295mph Lap leaders: Stewart 1-23; E Fittipaldi 24-54
Pole position: E Fittipaldi, 1m 35.970s, 137.778mph
Fastest lap: Hulme, 1m 38.320s, 134.485mph

### ITALIAN GRAND PRIX: MONZA *10 September Round: 10 Race: 218 55 x 3.588 miles*

| POS. | NO. | DRIVER | CAR-ENGINE | LAPS | TIME/RETIRED | GRID |
|---|---|---|---|---|---|---|
| 1 | 6 | Emerson Fittipaldi | Lotus-Ford | 55 | 1:29'58.4 | 6 |
| 2 | 10 | Mike Hailwood | Surtees-Ford | 55 | +14.5 | 9 |
| 3 | 14 | Denny Hulme | McLaren-Ford | 55 | +23.8 | 5 |
| 4 | 15 | Peter Revson | McLaren-Ford | 55 | +35.7 | 8 |
| 5 | 28 | Graham Hill | Brabham-Ford | 55 | +1'05.6 | 13 |
| 6 | 23 | Peter Gethin | BRM | 55 | +1'21.9 | 12 |
| 7 | 3 | Mario Andretti | Ferrari | 54 | +1 Lap | 7 |
| 8 | 21 | Jean Pierre Beltoise | BRM | 54 | +1 Lap | 16 |
| 9 | 19 | Ronnie Peterson | March-Ford | 54 | +1 Lap | 24 |
| 10 | 16 | Mike Beuttler | March-Ford | 54 | +1 Lap | 25 |
| 11 | 22 | Howden Ganley | BRM | 52 | +3 Laps | 17 |
| 12 | 24 | Reine Wisell | BRM | 51 | +4 Laps | 10 |
| 13 | 18 | Niki Lauda | March-Ford | 50 | +5 Laps | 20 |
| Ret | 4 | Jacky Ickx | Ferrari | 46 | Electrical | 1 |
| Ret | 20 | Chris Amon | Matra | 38 | Brakes | 2 |
| Ret | 9 | A.de Adamich | Surtees-Ford | 33 | Brakes | 21 |
| Ret | 29 | Wilson Fittipaldi | Brabham-Ford | 20 | Suspension | 19 |
| Ret | 7 | John Surtees | Surtees-Ford | 20 | Fuel system | 22 |
| Ret | 8 | Tim Schenken | Surtees-Ford | 20 | Spun off | 15 |
| Ret | 5 | Clay Regazzoni | Ferrari | 16 | Collision | 4 |
| Ret | 26 | Carlos Pace | March-Ford | 15 | Collision | 18 |
| Ret | 30 | Carlos Reutemann | Brabham-Ford | 14 | Suspension | 11 |
| Ret | 2 | Francois Cevert | Tyrrell-Ford | 14 | Engine | 14 |
| Ret | 11 | Nanni Galli | Tecno | 6 | Engine | 23 |
| Ret | 1 | Jackie Stewart | Tyrrell-Ford | 0 | Clutch | 3 |
| DNQ | 25 | Henri Pescarolo | March-Ford | | | |
| DNQ | 12 | Derek Bell | Tecno | | | |

Winning speed: 131.614mph
Lap leaders: Ickx 1-13, 17-45; Regazzoni 14-16; E fittipaldi 46-55
Pole position: Ickx, 1m 35.650s, 135.058mph
Fastest lap: Ickx, 1m 36.300s, 134.146mph

### CANADIAN GRAND PRIX: MOSPORT PARK *24 September Round: 11 Race: 219 80 x 2.459 miles*

| POS. | NO. | DRIVER | CAR-ENGINE | LAPS | TIME/RETIRED | GRID |
|---|---|---|---|---|---|---|
| 1 | 1 | Jackie Stewart | Tyrrell-Ford | 80 | 1:43'16.9 | 5 |
| 2 | 19 | Peter Revson | McLaren-Ford | 80 | +48.2 | 1 |
| 3 | 18 | Denny Hulme | McLaren-Ford | 80 | +54.6 | 2 |
| 4 | 8 | Carlos Reutemann | Brabham-Ford | 80 | +1'00.7 | 9 |
| 5 | 11 | Clay Regazzoni | Ferrari | 80 | +1'07.0 | 7 |
| 6 | 4 | Chris Amon | Matra | 79 | +1 Lap | 10 |
| 7 | 22 | Tim Schenken | Surtees-Ford | 79 | +1 Lap | 13 |
| 8 | 7 | Graham Hill | Brabham-Ford | 79 | +1 Lap | 17 |
| 9 | 29 | Carlos Pace | March-Ford | 78 | Out of fuel | 18 |
| 10 | 15 | Howden Ganley | BRM | 78 | +2 Laps | 14 |
| 11 | 5 | Emerson Fittipaldi | Lotus-Ford | 78 | +2 Laps | 4 |
| 12 | 10 | Jacky Ickx | Ferrari | 76 | +4 Laps | 8 |
| 13 | 28 | Henri Pescarolo | March-Ford | 73 | +7 Laps | 21 |
| Ret | 6 | Reine Wisell | Lotus-Ford | 65 | Engine | 16 |
| DSQ | 26 | Niki Lauda | March-Ford | 64 | Disqualified | 19 |
| DSQ | 25 | Ronnie Peterson | March-Ford | 61 | Disqualified | 3 |
| NC | 27 | Mike Beuttler | March-Ford | 59 | Not classified | 24 |
| Ret | 2 | Francois Cevert | Tyrrell-Ford | 51 | Gearbox | 6 |
| Ret | 16 | Peter Gethin | BRM | 25 | Suspension | 12 |
| NC | 33 | Skip Barber | March-Ford | 24 | Not classified | 22 |
| Ret | 14 | Jean Pierre Beltoise | BRM | 21 | Oil leak | 20 |
| Ret | 17 | Bill Brack | BRM | 20 | Spun off | 23 |
| Ret | 9 | Wilson Fittipaldi | Brabham-Ford | 5 | Gearbox | 11 |
| Ret | 23 | A.de Adamich | Surtees-Ford | 2 | Gearbox | 15 |

Winning speed: 114.282mph Lap leaders: Peterson 1-3; Stewart 4-80
Pole position: Revson, 1m 13.600s, 120.277mph
Fastest lap: Stewart, 1m 15.700s, 116.941mph

### UNITED STATES GRAND PRIX: WATKINS GLEN *8 October Round: 12 Race: 220 59 x 3.377 miles*

| POS. | NO. | DRIVER | CAR-ENGINE | LAPS | TIME/RETIRED | GRID |
|---|---|---|---|---|---|---|
| 1 | 1 | Jackie Stewart | Tyrrell-Ford | 59 | 1:41'45.354 | 1 |
| 2 | 2 | Francois Cevert | Tyrrell-Ford | 59 | +32.268 | 4 |
| 3 | 19 | Denny Hulme | McLaren-Ford | 59 | +37.528 | 3 |
| 4 | 4 | Ronnie Peterson | March-Ford | 59 | +1'22.516 | 26 |
| 5 | 7 | Jacky Ickx | Ferrari | 59 | +1'23.119 | 12 |
| 6 | 9 | Mario Andretti | Ferrari | 58 | +1 Lap | 10 |
| 7 | 3 | P.Depailler | Tyrrell-Ford | 58 | +1 Lap | 11 |
| 8 | 8 | Clay Regazzoni | Ferrari | 58 | +1 Lap | 6 |
| 9 | 21 | Jody Scheckter | McLaren-Ford | 58 | +1 Lap | 8 |
| 10 | 12 | Reine Wisell | Lotus-Ford | 57 | +2 Laps | 16 |
| 11 | 28 | Graham Hill | Brabham-Ford | 57 | +2 Laps | 27 |
| 12 | 34 | Sam Posey | Surtees-Ford | 57 | +2 Laps | 23 |
| 13 | 6 | Mike Beuttler | March-Ford | 57 | +2 Laps | 21 |
| 14 | 26 | Henri Pescarolo | March-Ford | 57 | +2 Laps | 22 |
| 15 | 18 | Chris Amon | Matra | 57 | +2 Laps | 7 |
| 16 | 33 | Skip Barber | March-Ford | 57 | +2 Laps | 20 |
| 17 | 23 | Mike Hailwood | Surtees-Ford | 56 | Collision | 14 |
| 18 | 20 | Peter Revson | McLaren-Ford | 54 | Electrical | 2 |
| NC | 5 | Niki Lauda | March-Ford | 49 | Not classified | 25 |
| Ret | 27 | Carlos Pace | March-Ford | 48 | Fuel system | 15 |
| Ret | 14 | Peter Gethin | BRM | 47 | Engine | 28 |
| Ret | 16 | Howden Ganley | BRM | 44 | Engine | 17 |
| Ret | 11 | Dave Walker | Lotus-Ford | 44 | Engine | 30 |
| Ret | 30 | Wilson Fittipaldi | Brabham-Ford | 43 | Engine | 13 |
| Ret | 17 | Jean Pierre Beltoise | BRM | 40 | Ignition | 18 |
| Ret | 15 | Brian Redman | BRM | 34 | Engine | 24 |
| Ret | 29 | Carlos Reutemann | Brabham-Ford | 31 | Engine | 5 |
| Ret | 25 | A.de Adamich | Surtees-Ford | 25 | Collision | 19 |
| Rett | 24 | Tim Schenken | Surtees-Ford | 22 | Suspension | 31 |
| Ret | 10 | Emerson Fittipaldi | Lotus-Ford | 17 | Suspension | 9 |
| Ret | 31 | Derek Bell | Tecno | 8 | Engine | 29 |

Winning speed: 117.483mph Lap leaders: Stewart 1-59
Pole position: Stewart, 1m 40.481s, 120.990mph
Fastest lap: Stewart, 1m 41.644s, 119.606mph

# 1973

## DRIVERS' CHAMPION: JACKIE STEWART
## CONSTRUCTORS' CHAMPION: LOTUS FORD

### DRIVERS' CHAMPIONSHIP

| POS | DRIVER | COUNTRY | CAR | POINTS |
|---|---|---|---|---|
| 1 | Jackie Stewart | GB | Tyrrell-Ford | 71 |
| 2 | Emerson Fittipaldi | Brazil | Lotus-Ford | 55 |
| 3 | Ronnie Peterson | Sweden | Lotus-Ford | 52 |
| 4 | François Cevert | France | Tyrrell-Ford | 47 |
| 5 | Peter Revson | USA | McLaren-Ford | 38 |
| 6 | Denny Hulme | New Zealand | McLaren-Ford | 26 |
| 7 | Carlos Reutemann | Argentina | Brabham-Ford | 16 |
| 8 | James Hunt | GB | March-Ford | 14 |
| 9 | Jacky Ickx | Belgium | Ferrari, McLaren, Williams-Ford | 12 |
| 10 | Jean Pierre Beltoise | France | BRM | 9 |
| 11 | Carlos Pace | Brazil | Surtees-Ford | 7 |
| 12 | Arturo Merzario | Italy | Ferrari | 6 |
| 13 | George Follmer | USA | Shadow-Ford | 5 |
| 14 | Jackie Oliver | GB | Shadow-Ford | 4 |
| 15 | Andrea de Adamich | Italy | Surtees-Ford, Brabham-Ford | 3 |
| 16 | Wilson Fittipaldi | Brazil | Brabham-Ford | 2 |
| = | Niki Lauda | Austria | BRM | 2 |
| 18 | Clay Regazzoni | Switzerland | BRM | 1 |
| = | Chris Amon | New Zealand | Tecno-Ford | 1 |
| = | Gijs van Lennep | Netherlands | Williams-Ford | 1 |
| = | Howden Ganley | New Zealand | Williams-Ford | 1 |
| | Roger Williamson | GB | March-Ford | |
| | Mike Beuttler | GB | March-Ford | |
| | Jean-Pierre Jarier | France | March-Ford | |
| | Nanni Galli | Italy | Williams-Ford | |
| | Mike Hailwood | GB | Surtees-Ford | |
| | Luis-Pereira Bueno | Brazil | Surtees-Ford | |
| | Jody Scheckter | South Africa | McLaren-Ford | |
| | Eddie Keizan | Brazil | Tyrrell-Ford | |
| | Dave Charlton | South Africa | Lotus-Ford | |
| | Jackie Pretorius | South Africa | Williams-Ford | |
| | Henri Pescarolo | France | March-Ford | |

Points for top six finishers (9, 6, 4, 3, 2, 1). Only the best seven scores from the first eight races and the best six scores from the remaining seven races counted towards the championship.

### CONSTRUCTORS' CHAMPIONSHIP

| POS. | CONSTRUCTOR | POINTS |
|---|---|---|
| 1 | Lotus-Ford | 92 |
| 2 | Tyrrell-Ford | 82 |
| 3 | McLaren-Ford | 58 |
| 4 | Brabham-Ford | 22 |
| 5 | March-Ford | 14 |
| 6 | Ferrari | 12 |
| 7 | BRM | 12 |
| 8 | Shadow-Ford | 9 |
| 9 | Surtees-Ford | 7 |
| 10 | Iso Marlboro-Ford | 2 |
| 11 | Tecno | 1 |

Points for top six finishers (9, 6, 4, 3, 2, 1). Points only counted for top-placed car for each constructor. Only the best seven scores from the first eight races and the best six scores from the remaining seven races counted towards the championship.

### ARGENTINE GRAND PRIX: BUENOS AIRES *28 January Round: 1 Race: 221 96 x 2.078 miles*

| POS. | NO. | DRIVER | CAR-ENGINE | LAPS | TIME/RETIRED | GRID |
|---|---|---|---|---|---|---|
| 1 | 2 | Emerson Fittipaldi | Lotus-Ford | 96 | 1:56'18.22 | 2 |
| 2 | 8 | Francois Cevert | Tyrrell-Ford | 96 | +4.69 | 6 |
| 3 | 6 | Jackie Stewart | Tyrrell-Ford | 96 | +33.19 | 4 |
| 4 | 18 | Jacky Ickx | Ferrari | 96 | +42.57 | 3 |
| 5 | 14 | Denny Hulme | McLaren-Ford | 95 | +1 Lap | 8 |
| 6 | 12 | Wilson Fittipaldi | Brabham-Ford | 95 | +1 Lap | 12 |
| 7 | 32 | Clay Regazzoni | BRM | 93 | +3 Laps | 1 |
| 8 | 16 | Peter Revson | McLaren-Ford | 92 | +4 Laps | 11 |
| 9 | 20 | Arturo Merzario | Ferrari | 92 | +4 Laps | 14 |
| 10 | 22 | Mike Beuttler | March-Ford | 90 | Suspension | 18 |
| Ret | 24 | Jean-Pierre Jarier | March-Ford | 84 | Radiator | 17 |
| Ret | 30 | Jean Pierre Beltoise | BRM | 79 | Engine | 7 |
| NC | 38 | Howden Ganley | Iso Marlboro-Ford | 79 | Not classified | 19 |
| Ret | 4 | Ronnie Peterson | Lotus-Ford | 67 | Oil pressure | 5 |
| Ret | 34 | Niki Lauda | BRM | 66 | Oil pressure | 13 |
| Ret | 10 | Carlos Reutemann | Brabham-Ford | 16 | Gearbox | 9 |
| Ret | 26 | Mike Hailwood | Surtees-Ford | 10 | Halfshaft | 10 |
| Ret | 28 | Carlos Pace | Surtees-Ford | 10 | Suspension | 15 |
| Ret | 36 | Nanni Galli | Iso Marlboro-Ford | 0 | Engine | 16 |

Winning speed: 102.938mph Lap leaders: Regazzoni 1-28; Cevert 29-85; E fittipaldi 86-96
Pole position: Regazzoni, 1m 10.540s, 106.075mph
Fastest lap: E fittipaldi, 1m 11.220s, 105.063mph

### BRAZILIAN GRAND PRIX: INTERLAGOS *11 February Round: 2 Race: 222 40 x 4.946 miles*

| POS. | NO. | DRIVER | CAR-ENGINE | LAPS | TIME/RETIRED | GRID |
|---|---|---|---|---|---|---|
| 1 | 1 | Emerson Fittipaldi | Lotus-Ford | 40 | 1:43'55.6 | 2 |
| 2 | 3 | Jackie Stewart | Tyrrell-Ford | 40 | +13.5 | 8 |
| 3 | 7 | Denny Hulme | McLaren-Ford | 40 | +1'46.4 | 5 |
| 4 | 10 | Arturo Merzario | Ferrari | 39 | +1 Lap | 17 |
| 5 | 9 | Jacky Ickx | Ferrari | 39 | +1 Lap | 3 |
| 6 | 14 | Clay Regazzoni | BRM | 39 | +1 Lap | 4 |
| 7 | 19 | Howden Ganley | Iso Marlboro-Ford | 39 | +1 Lap | 16 |
| 8 | 16 | Niki Lauda | BRM | 38 | +2 Laps | 13 |
| 9 | 20 | Nanni Galli | Iso Marlboro-Ford | 38 | +2 Laps | 18 |
| 10 | 4 | Francois Cevert | Tyrrell-Ford | 38 | +2 Laps | 9 |
| 11 | 17 | Carlos Reutemann | Brabham-Ford | 38 | +2 Laps | 7 |
| 12 | 23 | Luiz Bueno | Surtees-Ford | 36 | +4 Laps | 20 |
| Ret | 15 | Jean Pierre Beltoise | BRM | 23 | Electrical | 10 |
| Ret | 12 | Mike Beuttler | March-Ford | 18 | Overheating | 19 |
| Ret | 6 | Carlos Pace | Surtees-Ford | 9 | Suspension | 6 |
| Ret | 5 | Mike Hailwood | Surtees-Ford | 6 | Gearbox | 14 |
| Ret | 11 | Jean-Pierre Jarier | March-Ford | 6 | Gearbox | 15 |
| Ret | 2 | Ronnie Peterson | Lotus-Ford | 5 | Wheel | 1 |
| Ret | 18 | Wilson Fittipaldi | Brabham-Ford | 5 | Overheating | 11 |
| Ret | 8 | Peter Revson | McLaren-Ford | 3 | Gearbox | 12 |

Winning speed: 114.222mph Lap leaders: E fittipaldi 1-40
Pole position: Peterson, 2m 30.500s, 118.312mph
Fastest lap: E fittipaldi-Hulme, 2m 35.000s, 114.878mph

### SOUTH AFRICAN GRAND PRIX: KYALAMI *3 March Round: 3 Race: 223 79 x 2.550 miles*

| POS. | NO. | DRIVER | CAR-ENGINE | LAPS | TIME/RETIRED | GRID |
|---|---|---|---|---|---|---|
| 1 | 3 | Jackie Stewart | Tyrrell-Ford | 79 | 1:43'11.07 | 16 |
| 2 | 6 | Peter Revson | McLaren-Ford | 79 | +24.55 | 6 |
| 3 | 1 | Emerson Fittipaldi | Lotus-Ford | 79 | +25.06 | 2 |
| 4 | 9 | Arturo Merzario | Ferrari | 78 | +1 Lap | 15 |
| 5 | 5 | Denny Hulme | McLaren-Ford | 77 | +2 Laps | 1 |
| 6 | 23 | George Follmer | Shadow-Ford | 77 | +2 Laps | 21 |
| 7 | 18 | Carlos Reutemann | Brabham-Ford | 77 | +2 Laps | 8 |
| 8 | 12 | A.de Adamich | Surtees-Ford | 77 | +2 Laps | 20 |
| 9 | 7 | Jody Scheckter | McLaren-Ford | 75 | Engine | 3 |
| 10 | 21 | Howden Ganley | Iso Marlboro-Ford | 73 | +6 Laps | 19 |
| 11 | 2 | Ronnie Peterson | Lotus-Ford | 73 | +6 Laps | 4 |
| Ret | 11 | Carlos Pace | Surtees-Ford | 69 | Accident | 9 |
| NC | 26 | Eddie Keizan | Tyrrell-Ford | 67 | Not classified | 22 |
| NC | 14 | Jean-Pierre Jarier | March-Ford | 66 | Not classified | 18 |
| NC | 4 | Francois Cevert | Tyrrell-Ford | 66 | Not classified | 25 |
| NC | 24 | Mike Beuttler | March-Ford | 65 | Not classified | 23 |
| Ret | 19 | Wilson Fittipaldi | Brabham-Ford | 52 | Gearbox | 17 |
| Ret | 20 | Jackie Pretorius | Iso Marlboro-Ford | 35 | Overheating | 24 |
| Ret | 17 | Niki Lauda | BRM | 26 | Engine | 10 |
| Ret | 22 | Jackie Oliver | Shadow-Ford | 14 | Engine | 14 |
| Ret | 16 | Jean Pierre Beltoise | BRM | 4 | Clutch | 7 |
| Ret | 25 | Dave Charlton | Lotus-Ford | 3 | Accident | 13 |
| Ret | 15 | Clay Regazzoni | BRM | 2 | Accident | 5 |
| Ret | 8 | Jacky Ickx | Ferrari | 2 | Accident | 11 |
| Ret | 10 | Mike Hailwood | Surtees-Ford | 2 | Accident | 12 |

Winning speed: 117.145mph Lap leaders: Hulme 1-4; Scheckter 5-6; Stewart 7-79
Pole position: Hulme, 1m 16.280s, 120.351mph
Fastest lap: E Fittipaldi, 1m 17.100s, 119.071mph

### SPANISH GRAND PRIX: MONTJUICH PARK *29 April Round: 4 Race: 224 75 x 2.356 miles*

| POS. | NO. | DRIVER | CAR-ENGINE | LAPS | TIME/RETIRED | GRID |
|---|---|---|---|---|---|---|
| 1 | 1 | Emerson Fittipaldi | Lotus-Ford | 75 | 1:48'18.7 | 7 |
| 2 | 4 | Francois Cevert | Tyrrell-Ford | 75 | +42.7 | 3 |
| 3 | 20 | George Follmer | Shadow-Ford | 75 | +1'13.1 | 14 |
| 4 | 6 | Peter Revson | McLaren-Ford | 74 | +1 Lap | 5 |
| 5 | 15 | Jean Pierre Beltoise | BRM | 74 | +1 Lap | 10 |
| 6 | 5 | Denny Hulme | McLaren-Ford | 74 | +1 Lap | 2 |
| 7 | 12 | Mike Beuttler | March-Ford | 74 | +1 Lap | 19 |
| 8 | 11 | Henri Pescarolo | March-Ford | 73 | +2 Laps | 18 |
| 9 | 14 | Clay Regazzoni | BRM | 69 | +6 Laps | 8 |
| 10 | 17 | Wilson Fittipaldi | Brabham-Ford | 69 | +6 Laps | 12 |
| 11 | 24 | Nanni Galli | Iso Marlboro-Ford | 69 | +6 Laps | 20 |
| 12 | 7 | Jacky Ickx | Ferrari | 69 | +6 Laps | 6 |
| Ret | 18 | Carlos Reutemann | Brabham-Ford | 66 | Halfshaft | 15 |
| Ret | 23 | Howden Ganley | Iso Marlboro-Ford | 63 | Out of fuel | 21 |
| Ret | 2 | Ronnie Peterson | Lotus-Ford | 56 | Gearbox | 1 |
| Ret | 3 | Jackie Stewart | Tyrrell-Ford | 47 | Brakes | 4 |
| Ret | 16 | Niki Lauda | BRM | 28 | Tyre | 11 |
| Ret | 25 | Graham Hill | Shadow-Ford | 27 | Brakes | 22 |
| Ret | 9 | Mike Hailwood | Surtees-Ford | 25 | Oil leak | 9 |
| Ret | 19 | Jackie Oliver | Shadow-Ford | 23 | Engine | 13 |
| Ret | 21 | A.de Adamich | Brabham-Ford | 17 | Wheel | 17 |
| Ret | 10 | Carlos Pace | Surtees-Ford | 13 | Halfshaft | 16 |

Winning speed: 97.868mph Lap leaders: Peterson 1-56; E Fittipaldi 57-75
Pole position: Peterson, 1m 21.800s, 103.670mph
Fastest lap: Peterson, 1m 23.800s, 101.196mph

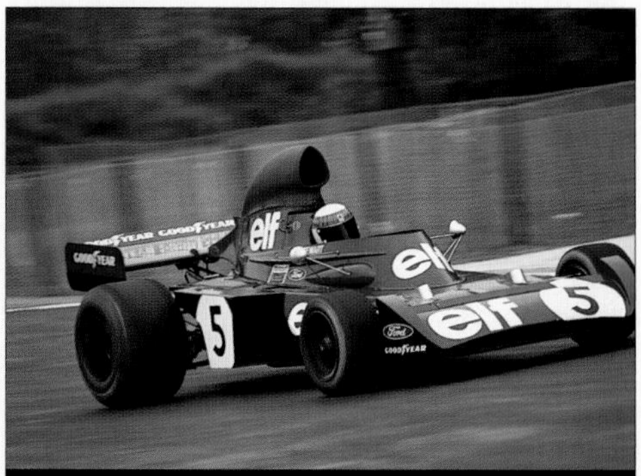

1973 world champion Jackie Stewart in the 005 Tyrrell Ford.

### BELGIAN GRAND PRIX: ZOLDER *29 May Round: 5 Race: 225 70 x 2.622 miles*

| POS. | NO. | DRIVER | CAR-ENGINE | LAPS | TIME/RETIRED | GRID |
|---|---|---|---|---|---|---|
| 1 | 5 | Jackie Stewart | Tyrrell-Ford | 70 | 1:42'13.43 | 6 |
| 2 | 6 | Francois Cevert | Tyrrell-Ford | 70 | +31.84 | 4 |
| 3 | 1 | Emerson Fittipaldi | Lotus-Ford | 70 | +2'02.79 | 9 |
| 4 | 9 | A.de Adamich | Brabham-Ford | 69 | +1 Lap | 18 |
| 5 | 21 | Niki Lauda | BRM | 69 | +1 Lap | 14 |
| 6 | 22 | Chris Amon | Tecno | 67 | +3 Laps | 15 |
| 7 | 7 | Denny Hulme | McLaren-Ford | 67 | +3 Laps | 2 |
| 8 | 24 | Carlos Pace | Surtees-Ford | 66 | +4 Laps | 8 |
| 9 | 12 | Graham Hill | Shadow-Ford | 65 | +5 Laps | 23 |
| 10 | 19 | Clay Regazzoni | BRM | 63 | Accident | 12 |
| 11 | 15 | Mike Beuttler | March-Ford | 63 | Accident | 20 |
| Ret | 14 | Jean-Pierre Jarier | March-Ford | 60 | Accident | 16 |
| Ret | 20 | Jean Pierre Beltoise | BRM | 56 | Not classified | 5 |
| Ret | 11 | Wilson Fittipaldi | Brabham-Ford | 46 | Engine | 19 |
| Ret | 2 | Ronnie Peterson | Lotus-Ford | 42 | Accident | 1 |
| Ret | 8 | Peter Revson | McLaren-Ford | 33 | Accident | 10 |
| Ret | 25 | Howden Ganley | Iso Marlboro-Ford | 16 | Accident | 21 |
| Ret | 10 | Carlos Reutemann | Brabham-Ford | 14 | Engine | 7 |
| Ret | 16 | George Follmer | Shadow-Ford | 13 | Throttle | 11 |
| Ret | 17 | Jackie Oliver | Shadow-Ford | 11 | Accident | 22 |
| Ret | 3 | Jacky Ickx | Ferrari | 6 | Oil pump | 3 |
| Ret | 26 | Nanni Galli | Iso Marlboro-Ford | 6 | Engine | 17 |
| Ret | 23 | Mike Hailwood | Surtees-Ford | 4 | Accident | 13 |

Winning speed: 107.736mph
Lap leaders: Peterson 1; Cevert 2-19; E Fittipaldi 20-24; Stewart 25-70
Pole position: Peterson, 1m 22.460s, 114.478mph
Fastest lap: Cevert, 1m 25.420s, 110.511mph

### MONACO GRAND PRIX: MONTE CARLO *3 June Round: 6 Race: 226 78 x 2.037 miles*

| POS. | NO. | DRIVER | CAR-ENGINE | LAPS | TIME/RETIRED | GRID |
|---|---|---|---|---|---|---|
| 1 | 5 | Jackie Stewart | Tyrrell-Ford | 78 | 1:57'44.3 | 1 |
| 2 | 1 | Emerson Fittipaldi | Lotus-Ford | 78 | +1.3 | 5 |
| 3 | 2 | Ronnie Peterson | Lotus-Ford | 77 | +1 Lap | 2 |
| 4 | 6 | Francois Cevert | Tyrrell-Ford | 77 | +1 Lap | 4 |
| 5 | 8 | Peter Revson | McLaren-Ford | 76 | +2 Laps | 15 |
| 6 | 7 | Denny Hulme | McLaren-Ford | 76 | +2 Laps | 3 |
| 7 | 9 | A.de Adamich | Brabham-Ford | 75 | +3 Laps | 25 |
| 8 | 23 | Mike Hailwood | Surtees-Ford | 75 | +3 Laps | 13 |
| 9 | 27 | James Hunt | March-Ford | 73 | Engine | 18 |
| 10 | 17 | Jackie Oliver | Shadow-Ford | 72 | +6 Laps | 22 |
| 11 | 11 | Wilson Fittipaldi | Brabham-Ford | 71 | Fuel system | 9 |
| Ret | 14 | Jean-Pierre Jarier | March-Ford | 67 | Gearbox | 14 |
| Ret | 12 | Graham Hill | Shadow-Ford | 62 | Suspension | 24 |
| Ret | 4 | Arturo Merzario | Ferrari | 58 | Oil pressure | 16 |
| Ret | 10 | Carlos Reutemann | Brabham-Ford | 46 | Gearbox | 19 |
| Ret | 3 | Jacky Ickx | Ferrari | 44 | Halfshaft | 7 |
| Ret | 25 | Howden Ganley | Iso Marlboro-Ford | 41 | Halfshaft | 10 |
| Ret | 20 | Jean Pierre Beltoise | BRM | 39 | Accident | 11 |
| Ret | 24 | Carlos Pace | Surtees-Ford | 31 | Halfshaft | 17 |
| Ret | 18 | David Purley | March-Ford | 31 | Fuel leak | 23 |
| Ret | 26 | Nanni Galli | Iso Marlboro-Ford | 30 | Halfshaft | 21 |
| Ret | 21 | Niki Lauda | BRM | 24 | Gearbox | 6 |
| Ret | 22 | Chris Amon | Tecno | 22 | Overheating | 12 |
| Ret | 19 | Clay Regazzoni | BRM | 15 | Brakes | 8 |
| Ret | 15 | Mike Beuttler | March-Ford | 3 | Engine | 20 |

Winning speed: 80.936mph Lap leaders: Cevert 1; Peterson 2-7; Stewart 8-78
Pole position: Stewart, 1m 27.500s, 83.802mph
Fastest lap: E Fittipaldi, 1m 28.100s, 83.231mph

### SWEDISH GRAND PRIX: ANDERSTORP *17 June Round: 7 Race: 227 80 x 2.497 miles*

| POS. | NO. | DRIVER | CAR-ENGINE | LAPS | TIME/RETIRED | GRID |
|---|---|---|---|---|---|---|
| 1 | 7 | Denny Hulme | McLaren-Ford | 80 | 1:56'46.049 | 6 |
| 2 | 2 | Ronnie Peterson | Lotus-Ford | 80 | +4.039 | 1 |
| 3 | 6 | Francois Cevert | Tyrrell-Ford | 80 | +14.667 | 2 |
| 4 | 10 | Carlos Reutemann | Brabham-Ford | 80 | +18.068 | 5 |
| 5 | 5 | Jackie Stewart | Tyrrell-Ford | 80 | +25.998 | 3 |
| 6 | 3 | Jacky Ickx | Ferrari | 79 | +1 Lap | 8 |
| 7 | 8 | Peter Revson | McLaren-Ford | 79 | +1 Lap | 7 |
| 8 | 15 | Mike Beuttler | March-Ford | 78 | +2 Laps | 21 |
| 9 | 19 | Clay Regazzoni | BRM | 77 | +3 Laps | 12 |
| 10 | 24 | Carlos Pace | Surtees-Ford | 77 | +3 Laps | 16 |
| 11 | 25 | Howden Ganley | Iso Marlboro-Ford | 77 | +3 Laps | 11 |
| 12 | 1 | Emerson Fittipaldi | Lotus-Ford | 76 | Gearbox | 4 |
| 13 | 21 | Niki Lauda | BRM | 75 | +5 Laps | 15 |
| 14 | 16 | George Follmer | Shadow-Ford | 74 | +6 Laps | 19 |
| Ret | 20 | Jean Pierre Beltoise | BRM | 57 | Engine | 9 |
| Ret | 17 | Jackie Oliver | Shadow-Ford | 50 | Suspension | 17 |
| Ret | 23 | Mike Hailwood | Surtees-Ford | 41 | Tyre | 10 |
| Ret | 14 | Jean-Pierre Jarier | March-Ford | 38 | Throttle | 20 |
| Ret | 12 | Graham Hill | Shadow-Ford | 16 | Ignition | 18 |
| Ret | 11 | Wilson Fittipaldi | Brabham-Ford | 0 | Accident | 12 |
| Ret | 27 | Reine Wisell | March-Ford | 0 | Suspension | 14 |

Winning speed: 102.631mph Lap leaders: Peterson 1-78; Hulme 79-80
Pole position: Peterson, 1m23.810s, 107.243mph
Fastest lap: Hulme, 1m26.146s, 104.335mph

### FRENCH GRAND PRIX: PAUL RICARD *1 July Round: 8 Race: 228 54 x 3.610 miles*

| POS. | NO. | DRIVER | CAR-ENGINE | LAPS | TIME/RETIRED | GRID |
|---|---|---|---|---|---|---|
| 1 | 2 | Ronnie Peterson | Lotus-Ford | 54 | 1:41'36.52 | 5 |
| 2 | 6 | Francois Cevert | Tyrrell-Ford | 54 | +40.92 | 4 |
| 3 | 10 | Carlos Reutemann | Brabham-Ford | 54 | +46.48 | 8 |
| 4 | 5 | Jackie Stewart | Tyrrell-Ford | 54 | +46.93 | 1 |
| 5 | 3 | Jacky Ickx | Ferrari | 54 | +48.90 | 12 |
| 6 | 27 | James Hunt | March-Ford | 54 | +1'22.54 | 14 |
| 7 | 4 | Arturo Merzario | Ferrari | 54 | +1'29.19 | 10 |
| 8 | 7 | Denny Hulme | McLaren-Ford | 54 | +1'29.53 | 6 |
| 9 | 21 | Niki Lauda | BRM | 54 | +1'45.76 | 17 |
| 10 | 12 | Graham Hill | Shadow-Ford | 53 | +1 Lap | 16 |
| 11 | 20 | Jean Pierre Beltoise | BRM | 53 | +1 Lap | 15 |
| 12 | 19 | Clay Regazzoni | BRM | 53 | +1 Lap | 9 |
| 13 | 24 | Carlos Pace | Surtees-Ford | 51 | +3 Laps | 18 |
| 14 | 25 | Howden Ganley | Iso Marlboro-Ford | 51 | +3 Laps | 24 |
| 15 | 29 | Rikky von Opel | Ensign-Ford | 51 | +3 Laps | 25 |
| 16 | 11 | Wilson Fittipaldi | Brabham-Ford | 50 | +4 Laps | 19 |
| Ret | 8 | Jody Scheckter | McLaren-Ford | 43 | Accident | 2 |
| Ret | 1 | Emerson Fittipaldi | Lotus-Ford | 41 | Accident | 3 |
| Ret | 23 | Mike Hailwood | Surtees-Ford | 29 | Oil leak | 11 |
| Ret | 9 | A.de Adamich | Brabham-Ford | 28 | Halfshaft | 13 |
| Ret | 15 | Reine Wisell | March-Ford | 20 | Overheating | 22 |
| Ret | 16 | George Follmer | Shadow-Ford | 16 | Fuel system | 20 |
| Ret | 26 | Henri Pescarolo | Iso Marlboro-Ford | 16 | Overheating | 23 |
| Ret | 14 | Jean-Pierre Jarier | March-Ford | 7 | Halfshaft | 7 |
| Ret | 17 | Jackie Oliver | Shadow-Ford | 0 | Clutch | 21 |

Winning speed: 115.118mph Lap leaders: Scheckter 1-41; Peterson 42-54
Pole position: Stewart, 1m48.370s, 119.928mph
Fastest lap: Hulme, 1m50.990s, 117.097mph

### BRITISH GRAND PRIX: SILVERSTONE *14 July Round 9 Race 229 67 x 2.927 miles*

| POS. | NO. | DRIVER | CAR-ENGINE | LAPS | TIME/RETIRED | GRID |
|---|---|---|---|---|---|---|
| 1 | 8 | Peter Revson | McLaren-Ford | 67 | 1:29'18.5 | 3 |
| 2 | 2 | Ronnie Peterson | Lotus-Ford | 67 | +2.8 | 1 |
| 3 | 7 | Denny Hulme | McLaren-Ford | 67 | +3.0 | 2 |
| 4 | 27 | James Hunt | March-Ford | 67 | +3.4 | 11 |
| 5 | 6 | Francois Cevert | Tyrrell-Ford | 67 | +36.6 | 7 |
| 6 | 10 | Carlos Reutemann | Brabham-Ford | 67 | +44.7 | 8 |
| 7 | 19 | Clay Regazzoni | BRM | 67 | +1'11.7 | 10 |
| 8 | 3 | Jacky Ickx | Ferrari | 67 | +1'17.4 | 19 |
| 9 | 25 | Howden Ganley | Iso Marlboro-Ford | 66 | +1 Lap | 18 |
| 10 | 5 | Jackie Stewart | Tyrrell-Ford | 66 | +1 Lap | 4 |
| 11 | 15 | Mike Beuttler | March-Ford | 65 | +2 Laps | 24 |
| 12 | 21 | Niki Lauda | BRM | 63 | +4 Laps | 9 |
| 13 | 28 | Rikky von Opel | Ensign-Ford | 61 | +6 Laps | 21 |
| Ret | 11 | Wilson Fittipaldi | Brabham-Ford | 44 | Oil leak | 13 |
| Ret | 1 | Emerson Fittipaldi | Lotus-Ford | 36 | Transmission | 5 |
| Ret | 29 | John Watson | Brabham-Ford | 36 | Fuel system | 23 |
| Ret | 12 | Graham Hill | Shadow-Ford | 24 | Chassis | 27 |
| Ret | 22 | Chris Amon | Tecno | 6 | Fuel system | 29 |
| Ret | 30 | Jody Scheckter | McLaren-Ford | 0 | Collision | 6 |
| Ret | 23 | Mike Hailwood | Surtees-Ford | 0 | Collision | 12 |
| Ret | 31 | Jochen Mass | Surtees-Ford | 0 | Collision | 14 |
| Ret | 24 | Carlos Pace | Surtees-Ford | 0 | Collision | 15 |
| Ret | 20 | Jean Pierre Beltoise | BRM | 0 | Collision | 17 |
| Ret | 9 | A.de Adamich | Brabham-Ford | 0 | Collision | 20 |
| Ret | 14 | Roger Williamson | March-Ford | 0 | Collision | 22 |
| Ret | 16 | George Follmer | Shadow-Ford | 0 | Collision | 25 |
| Ret | 17 | Jackie Oliver | Shadow-Ford | 0 | Collision | 26 |
| Ret | 26 | Graham McRae | Iso Marlboro-Ford | 0 | Throttle | 28 |
| Ret | 18 | David Purley | March-Ford | 0 | Spun off | 16 |

Winning speed: 131.752mph Lap leaders: Peterson 1-38; Revson 39-67
Pole position: Peterson, 1m16.300s, 138.102mph
Fastest lap: Hunt, 1m18.600s, 134.061mph

Interrupted after second lap, because of a pile-up. Restarted for original distance.

### DUTCH GRAND PRIX: ZANDVOORT *29 July Round 10 Race 230 72 x 2.626 miles*

| POS. | NO. | DRIVER | CAR-ENGINE | LAPS | TIME/RETIRED | GRID |
|---|---|---|---|---|---|---|
| 1 | 5 | Jackie Stewart | Tyrrell-Ford | 72 | 1:39'12.45 | 2 |
| 2 | 6 | Francois Cevert | Tyrrell-Ford | 72 | +15.83 | 3 |
| 3 | 27 | James Hunt | March-Ford | 72 | +1'03.01 | 7 |
| 4 | 8 | Peter Revson | McLaren-Ford | 72 | +1'09.13 | 6 |
| 5 | 20 | Jean Pierre Beltoise | BRM | 72 | +1'13.37 | 9 |
| 6 | 26 | Gijs van Lennep | Iso Marlboro-Ford | 70 | +2 Laps | 20 |
| 7 | 24 | Carlos Pace | Surtees-Ford | 69 | +3 Laps | 8 |
| 8 | 19 | Clay Regazzoni | BRM | 68 | +4 Laps | 12 |
| 9 | 25 | Howden Ganley | Iso Marlboro-Ford | 68 | +4 Laps12 | 15 |
| 10 | 16 | George Follmer | Shadow-Ford | 67 | +5 Laps | 22 |
| 11 | 2 | Ronnie Peterson | Lotus-Ford | 66 | Engine | 1 |
| NC | 12 | Graham Hill | Shadow-Ford | 56 | Not classified | 17 |
| Ret | 21 | Niki Lauda | BRM | 52 | Fuel pump | 11 |
| Ret | 23 | Mike Hailwood | Surtees-Ford | 52 | Electrical | 24 |
| Ret | 7 | Denny Hulme | McLaren-Ford | 31 | Engine | 4 |
| Ret | 11 | Wilson Fittipaldi | Brabham-Ford | 27 | Accident | 13 |
| Ret | 22 | Chris Amon | Tecno | 22 | Fuel system | 19 |
| Ret | 10 | Carlos Reutemann | Brabham-Ford | 9 | Tyre | 5 |
| Wth | 18 | David Purley | March-Ford | 8 | Withdrew | 21 |
| Ret | 14 | Roger Williamson | March-Ford | 7 | Fatal Accident | 18 |
| Ret | 1 | Emerson Fittipaldi | Lotus-Ford | 2 | Physical | 16 |
| Ret | 15 | Mike Beuttler | March-Ford | 2 | Electrical | 23 |
| Ret | 17 | Jackie Oliver | Shadow-Ford | 1 | Accident | 10 |
| DNS | 28 | Rikky von Opel | Ensign-Ford | 0 | Not started | 14 |

Winning speed: 114.346mph Lap leaders: Peterson 1-63, Stewart 64-72
Pole position: Peterson, 1m19.470s, 118.954mph
Fastest lap: Peterson, 1m20.310s, 117.710mph

### GERMAN GRAND PRIX: NURBURGRING *5 August Round 11 Race 231 14 x 14.189 miles*

| POS. | NO. | DRIVER | CAR-ENGINE | LAPS | TIME/RETIRED | GRID |
|---|---|---|---|---|---|---|
| 1 | 5 | Jackie Stewart | Tyrrell-Ford | 14 | 1:42'03.0 | 1 |
| 2 | 6 | Francois Cevert | Tyrrell-Ford | 14 | +1.6 | 3 |
| 3 | 30 | Jacky Ickx | McLaren-Ford | 14 | + 41.2 | 7 |
| 4 | 24 | Carlos Pace | Surtees-Ford | 14 | +53.8 | 11 |
| 5 | 11 | Wilson Fittipaldi | Brabham-Ford | 14 | +1'19.9 | 13 |
| 6 | 1 | Emerson Fittipaldi | Lotus-Ford | 14 | +1'24.3 | 14 |
| 7 | 31 | Jochen Mass | Surtees-Ford | 14 | +1'25.2 | 15 |
| 8 | 17 | Jackie Oliver | Shadow-Ford | 14 | +1'25.7 | 17 |
| 9 | 8 | Peter Revson | McLaren-Ford | 14 | +2'11.8 | 7 |
| 10 | 26 | Henri Pescarolo | Iso Marlboro-Ford | 14 | +2'22.5 | 12 |
| 11 | 9 | Rolf Stommelen | Brabham-Ford | 14 | +3'27.3 | 16 |
| 12 | 7 | Denny Hulme | McLaren-Ford | 14 | +3'38.7 | 8 |
| 13 | 12 | Graham Hill | Shadow-Ford | 14 | +3'49.0 | 20 |
| 14 | 23 | Mike Hailwood | Surtees-Ford | 13 | +1 Lap | 18 |
| 15 | 18 | David Purley | March-Ford | 13 | +1 Lap | 22 |
| 16 | 15 | Mike Beuttler | March-Ford | 13 | +1 Lap | 19 |
| Ret | 10 | Carlos Reutemann | Brabham-Ford | 7 | Engine | 6 |
| Ret | 19 | Clay Regazzoni | BRM | 7 | Engine | 10 |
| Ret | 16 | George Follmer | Shadow-Ford | 5 | Accident | 21 |
| Ret | 20 | Jean Pierre Beltoise | BRM | 4 | Gearbox | 9 |
| Ret | 21 | Niki Lauda | BRM | 1 | Accident | 5 |
| Ret | 2 | Ronnie Peterson | Lotus-Ford | 0 | Ignition | 2 |

Winning speed: 116.793mph Lap leaders: Stewart 1-14
Pole position: Stewart, 7m7.800s, 119.403mph
Fastest lap: Pace, 7m11.400s, 118.406mph

### AUSTRIAN GRAND PRIX: OSTERREICHRING *19 August Round 12 Race 232 54 x 3.673 miles*

| POS. | NO. | DRIVER | CAR-ENGINE | LAPS | TIME/RETIRED | GRID |
|---|---|---|---|---|---|---|
| 1 | 2 | Ronnie Peterson | Lotus-Ford | 54 | 1:28'48.78 | 2 |
| 2 | 5 | Jackie Stewart | Tyrrell-Ford | 54 | +9.01 | 7 |
| 3 | 24 | Carlos Pace | Surtees-Ford | 54 | +46.64 | 8 |
| 4 | 10 | Carlos Reutemann | Brabham-Ford | 54 | +47.91 | 5 |
| 5 | 20 | Jean Pierre Beltoise | BRM | 54 | +1'21.60 | 13 |
| 6 | 19 | Clay Regazzoni | BRM | 54 | +1'38.40 | 14 |
| 7 | 4 | Arturo Merzario | Ferrari | 53 | +1 Lap | 6 |
| 8 | 7 | Denny Hulme | McLaren-Ford | 53 | +1 Lap | 3 |
| 9 | 26 | Gijs van Lennep | Iso Marlboro-Ford | 52 | +2 Laps | 23 |
| 10 | 23 | Mike Hailwood | Surtees-Ford | 49 | +5 Laps | 15 |
| Ret | 1 | Emerson Fittipaldi | Lotus-Ford | 48 | Fuel system | 1 |
| NC | 25 | Howden Ganley | Iso Marlboro-Ford | 44 | Not classified | 21 |
| Ret | 18 | Jean-Pierre Jarier | March-Ford | 37 | Engine | 12 |
| Ret | 28 | Rikky von Opel | Ensign-Ford | 34 | Fuel system | 19 |
| Ret | 11 | Wilson Fittipaldi | Brabham-Ford | 31 | Fuel system | 16 |
| Ret | 12 | Graham Hill | Shadow-Ford | 28 | Suspension | 22 |
| Ret | 16 | George Follmer | Shadow-Ford | 23 | Differential | 20 |
| Ret | 9 | Rolf Stommelen | Brabham-Ford | 21 | Wheel | 17 |
| Ret | 17 | Jackie Oliver | Shadow-Ford | 9 | Fuel leak | 18 |
| Ret | 6 | Francois Cevert | Tyrrell-Ford | 6 | Suspension | 10 |
| Ret | 27 | James Hunt | March-Ford | 3 | Injection | 9 |
| Ret | 8 | Peter Revson | McLaren-Ford | 0 | Clutch | 4 |
| Ret | 15 | Mike Beuttler | March-Ford | 0 | Collision | 11 |

Winning speed: 133.993mph Lap leaders: Peterson 1-16, 49-54; E Fittipaldi 17-48
Pole position: E Fittipaldi, 1m34.980s, 139.214mph
Fastest lap: Pace, 1m37.290s, 135.908mph

### ITALIAN GRAND PRIX: MONZA *9 September Round: 13 Race: 233 55 x 3.588miles*

| POS. | NO. | DRIVER | CAR-ENGINE | LAPS | TIME/RETIRED | GRID |
|---|---|---|---|---|---|---|
| 1 | 2 | Ronnie Peterson | Lotus-Ford | 55 | 1:29'17.0 | 1 |
| 2 | 1 | Emerson Fittipaldi | Lotus-Ford | 55 | +0.8 | 4 |
| 3 | 8 | Peter Revson | McLaren-Ford | 55 | +28.8 | 2 |
| 4 | 5 | Jackie Stewart | Tyrrell-Ford | 55 | +33.2 | 6 |
| 5 | 6 | Francois Cevert | Tyrrell-Ford | 55 | +46.2 | 11 |
| 6 | 10 | Carlos Reutemann | Brabham-Ford | 55 | +59.8 | 10 |
| 7 | 23 | Mike Hailwood | Surtees-Ford | 55 | +1'28.7 | 8 |
| 8 | 3 | Jacky Ickx | Ferrari | 54 | +1 Lap | 14 |
| 9 | 29 | David Purley | March-Ford | 54 | +1 Lap | 24 |
| 10 | 16 | George Follmer | Shadow-Ford | 54 | +1 Lap | 21 |
| 11 | 17 | Jackie Oliver | Shadow-Ford | 54 | +1 Lap | 19 |
| 12 | 9 | Rolf Stommelen | Brabham-Ford | 54 | +1 Lap | 9 |
| 13 | 20 | Jean Pierre Beltoise | BRM | 54 | +1 Lap | 13 |
| 14 | 12 | Graham Hill | Shadow-Ford | 54 | +1 Lap | 22 |
| 15 | 7 | Denny Hulme | McLaren-Ford | 53 | +2 Laps | 3 |
| NC | 25 | Howden Ganley | Iso Marlboro-Ford | 44 | Not classified | 20 |
| Ret | 15 | Mike Beuttler | March-Ford | 34 | Gearbox | 12 |
| Ret | 21 | Niki Lauda | BRM | 33 | Accident | 15 |
| Ret | 19 | Clay Regazzoni | BRM | 30 | Ignition | 18 |
| Ret | 24 | Carlos Pace | Surtees-Ford | 17 | Tyre | 5 |
| Ret | 26 | Gijs van Lennep | Iso Marlboro-Ford | 14 | Overheating | 23 |
| Ret | 28 | Rikky von Opel | Ensign-Ford | 10 | Overheating | 17 |
| Ret | 11 | Wilson Fittipaldi | Brabham-Ford | 6 | Brakes | 16 |
| Ret | 4 | Arturo Merzario | Ferrari | 2 | Suspension | 7 |

Winning speed: 132.663mph Lap leaders: Peterson 1-55
Pole position: Peterson, 1m34.800s, 136.267mph
Fastest lap: Stewart, 1m35.300s, 135.583mph

### CANADA GRAND PRIX: MOSPORT *23 September Round: 13 Race: 234 80 x 2.458miles*

| POS. | NO. | DRIVER | CAR-ENGINE | LAPS | TIME/RETIRED | GRID |
|---|---|---|---|---|---|---|
| 1 | 8 | Peter Revson | McLaren-Ford | 80 | 1:59'04.083 | 2 |
| 2 | 1 | Emerson Fittipaldi | Lotus-Ford | 80 | +32.734 | 5 |
| 3 | 17 | Jackie Oliver | Shadow-Ford | 80 | +34.505 | 14 |
| 4 | 20 | Jean Pierre Beltoise | BRM | 80 | +36.514 | 16 |
| 5 | 5 | Jackie Stewart | Tyrrell-Ford | 79 | +1 Lap | 9 |
| 6 | 25 | Howden Ganley | Iso Marlboro-Ford | 79 | +1 Lap | 22 |
| 7 | 27 | James Hunt | March-Ford | 78 | +2 Laps | 15 |
| 8 | 10 | Carlos Reutemann | Brabham-Ford | 78 | +2 Laps | 4 |
| 9 | 23 | Mike Hailwood | Surtees-Ford | 78 | +2 Laps | 12 |
| 10 | 29 | Chris Amon | Tyrrell-Ford | 77 | +3 Laps | 11 |
| 11 | 11 | Wilson Fittipaldi | Brabham-Ford | 77 | +3 Laps | 10 |
| 12 | 9 | Rolf Stommelen | Brabham-Ford | 76 | +4 Laps | 18 |
| 13 | 7 | Denny Hulme | McLaren-Ford | 75 | +5 Laps | 7 |
| 14 | 26 | Tim Schenken | Iso Marlboro-Ford | 75 | +5 Laps | 24 |
| 15 | 4 | Arturo Merzario | Ferrari | 75 | +5 Laps | 20 |
| 16 | 12 | Graham Hill | Shadow-Ford | 73 | +7 Laps | 17 |
| 17 | 16 | George Follmer | Shadow-Ford | 73 | +7 Laps | 13 |
| 18 | 24 | Carlos Pace | Surtees-Ford | 72 | +8 Laps | 19 |
| NC | 18 | Jean-Pierre Jarier | March-Ford | 71 | Not classified | 23 |
| NC | 28 | Rikky von Opel | Ensign-Ford | 68 | Not classified | 26 |
| Ret | 21 | Niki Lauda | BRM | 62 | Transmission | 8 |
| Ret | 0 | Jody Scheckter | McLaren-Ford | 32 | Accident | 3 |
| Ret | 6 | Francois Cevert | Tyrrell-Ford | 32 | Accident | 6 |
| Ret | 15 | Mike Beuttler | March-Ford | 20 | Engine | 21 |
| Ret | 2 | Ronnie Peterson | Lotus-Ford | 16 | Suspension | 1 |
| Ret | 19 | Peter Gethin | BRM | 5 | Oil pump | 25 |

Winning speed: 99.121mph
Lap leaders: Peterson 1-2 Lauda 3-19; E Fittipalda 20-32; Stewart 33; Beltoise 34-39, Oliver 40-46; Reuson 47-80
Pole position: Peterson, 1m 13.697s, 120.107mph
Fastest lap: E Fittipaldi, 1m 15.496s, 117.245mph

### UNITED STATES GRAND PRIX: WATKINS GLEN *7 October Round: 14 Race 235 59 x 3.376 miles*

| POS. | NO. | DRIVER | CAR-ENGINE | LAPS | TIME/RETIRED | GRID |
|---|---|---|---|---|---|---|
| 1 | 2 | Ronnie Peterson | Lotus-Ford | 59 | 1:41'15.799 | 1 |
| 2 | 27 | James Hunt | March-Ford | 59 | +0.668 | 4 |
| 3 | 10 | Carlos Reutemann | Brabham-Ford | 59 | +22.930 | 2 |
| 4 | 7 | Denny Hulme | McLaren-Ford | 59 | +50.226 | 8 |
| 5 | 8 | Peter Revson | McLaren-Ford | 59 | +1'20.367 | 7 |
| 6 | 1 | Emerson Fittipaldi | Lotus-Ford | 59 | +1'47.945 | 3 |
| 7 | 26 | Jacky Ickx | Iso Marlboro-Ford | 58 | +1 Lap | 23 |
| 8 | 19 | Clay Regazzoni | BRM | 58 | +1 Lap | 15 |
| 9 | 20 | Jean Pierre Beltoise | BRM | 58 | +1 Lap | 14 |
| 10 | 15 | Mike Beuttler | March-Ford | 58 | +1 Lap | 26 |
| 11 | 18 | Jean-Pierre Jarier | March-Ford | 57 | Accident | 17 |
| 12 | 25 | Howden Ganley | Iso Marlboro-Ford | 57 | +2 Laps | 19 |
| 13 | 12 | Graham Hill | Shadow-Ford | 57 | +2 Laps | 18 |
| 14 | 16 | George Follmer | Shadow-Ford | 57 | +2 Laps | 20 |
| 15 | 17 | Jackie Oliver | Shadow-Ford | 55 | +4 Laps | 22 |
| 16 | 4 | Arturo Merzario | Ferrari | 55 | +4 Laps | 11 |
| NC | 11 | Wilson Fittipaldi | Brabham-Ford | 52 | Not classified | 25 |
| Ret | 0 | Jody Scheckter | McLaren-Ford | 39 | Suspension | 10 |
| Ret | 30 | Jochen Mass | Surtees-Ford | 35 | Engine | 16 |
| Ret | 21 | Niki Lauda | BRM | 35 | Fuel pump | 21 |
| Ret | 23 | Mike Hailwood | Surtees-Ford | 34 | Suspension | 6 |
| Ret | 24 | Carlos Pace | Surtees-Ford | 32 | Suspension | 9 |
| Ret | 9 | John Watson | Brabham-Ford | 7 | Engine | 24 |
| DSQ | 31 | Brian Redman | Shadow-Ford | 5 | Disqualified | 13 |
| Ret | 28 | Rikky von Opel | Ensign-Ford | 0 | Throttle | 27 |
| Wth | 5 | Jackie Stewart | Tyrrell-Ford | 0 | Withdrew | 5 |
| Wth | 29 | Chris Amon | Tyrrell-Ford | 0 | Withdrew | 12 |
| DNS | 6 | Francois Cevert | Tyrrell-Ford | | Fatal Accident | |

Winning speed: 118.060mph
Lap leaders: Peterson 1-59
Pole position: Peterson, 1m 39.657s, 121.996mph
Fastest lap: Hunt, 1m 41.652s, 110.602mph

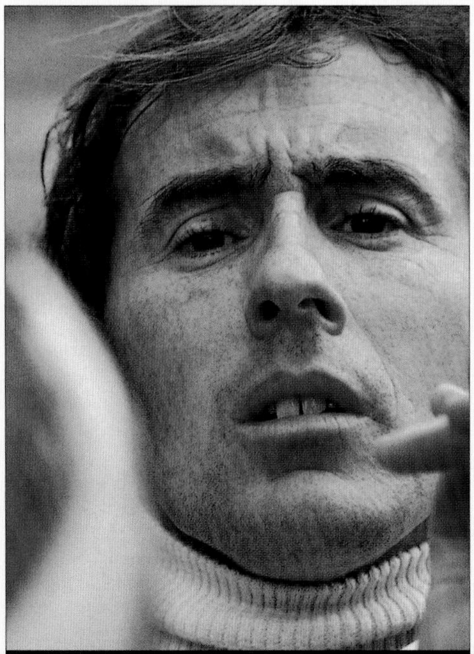

1973 world champion, Jackie Stewart

# 1974

## DRIVERS' CHAMPION: EMERSON FITTIPALDI
## CONSTRUCTORS' CHAMPION: McLAREN FORD

### DRIVERS' CHAMPIONSHIP

| POS | DRIVER | COUNTRY | CAR | POINTS |
|---|---|---|---|---|
| 1 | Emerson Fittipaldi | Brazil | McLaren-Ford | 55 |
| 2 | Clay Regazzoni | Switzerland | Ferrari | 52 |
| 3 | Jody Scheckter | South Africa | Tyrrell-Ford | 45 |
| 4 | Niki Lauda | Austria | Ferrari | 38 |
| 5 | Ronnie Peterson | Sweden | Lotus-Ford | 35 |
| 6 | Carlos Reutemann | Argentina | Brabham-Ford | 32 |
| 7 | Denny Hulme | New Zealand | McLaren-Ford | 20 |
| 8 | James Hunt | GB | March-Ford, Hesketh-Ford | 15 |
| 9 | Patrick Depailler | France | Tyrrell-Ford | 14 |
| 10 | Mike Hailwood | GB | McLaren-Ford | 12 |
| 11 | Jacky Ickx | B | Lotus-Ford | 12 |
| 12 | Carlos Pace | Brazil | Surtees-Ford, Brabham-Ford | 11 |
| 13 | Jean-Pierre Beltoise | France | BRM | 10 |
| 14 | Jean-Pierre Jarier | France | Shadow-Ford | 6 |
| = | John Watson | GB | Brabham-Ford | 6 |
| 16 | Hans-Joachim Stuck | West Germany | March-Ford | 5 |
| 17 | Arturo Merzario | Italy | Williams-Ford | 4 |
| 18 | Graham Hill | GB | Lola-Ford | 1 |
| = | Tom Pryce | GB | Token-Ford, Shadow-Ford | 1 |
| = | Vittorio Brambilla | Italy | March | 1 |
| | Peter Revson | USA | Shadow-Ford | |
| | Howden Ganley | New Zealand | March-Ford, Maki-Ford | |
| | Henri Pescarolo | France | BRM | |
| | Richard Robarts | GB | Brabham-Ford, Williams-Ford | |
| | Francois Migault | France | BRM | |
| | Jochen Mass | West Germany | Surtees-Ford, McLaren-Ford | |
| | Guy Edwards | GB | Lola-Ford | |
| | Dave Charlton | South Africa | McLaren-Ford | |
| | Tom Belso | Denmark | Williams-Ford | |
| | John McNicol | GB | Lotus-Ford | |
| | Ian Scheckter | South Africa | Lotus-Ford, Hesketh-Ford | |
| | Paddy Driver | South Africa | Lotus-Ford | |
| | Eddie Keizan | South Africa | Tyrrell-Ford | |
| | Rikky von Opel | West Germany | Ensign-Ford, Brabham-Ford | |
| | Brian Redman | GB | Shadow-Ford | |
| | Silvio Moser | Switzerland | Brabham-Ford | |
| | Chris Amon | New Zealand | Amon-Ford, BRM | |
| | Tim Schenken | Australia | Trojan-Ford, Lotus-Ford | |
| | Teddy Pilette | Belgium | Brabham-Ford | |
| | Gijs van Lennep | Netherlands | Williams-Ford | |
| | Vern Schuppan | Australia | Ensign-Ford | |
| | Leo Kinnunen | Finland | Surtees-Ford | |
| | Gerard Larrousse | France | Brabham-Ford | |
| | Reine Wisell | Sweden | March-Ford | |
| | Bertil Roos | Sewden | Shadow-Ford | |
| | Jose Dolhem | France | Surtees-Ford | |
| | Jean-Pierre Jabouille | France | Williams-Ford, Surtees-Ford | |
| | Jacques Laffite | France | Token-Ford, Williams-Ford | |
| | Derek Bell | GB | Surtees-Ford | |
| | Peter Gethin | GB | Lola-Ford | |
| | John Nicholson | GB | Lyncar-Ford | |
| | Dave Purley | GB | Token-Ford | |
| | Lella Lombardi | I | Brabham-Ford | |
| | Mike Wilds | GB | March-Ford, Ensign-Ford | |
| | Larry Perkins | GB | Amon-Ford | |
| | Ian Ashley | GB | Token-Ford, Brabham-Ford | |
| | Dieter Quester | West Germany | Surtees-Ford | |
| | Rolf Stommelen | West Germany | Lola-Ford | |
| | David Hobbs | GB | McLaren-Ford | |
| | Helmuth Koenigg | West Germany | Brabham-Ford, Surtees-Ford | |
| | Carlo Facetti | Italy | Brabha-Ford | |
| | Eppie Wietzes | Canada | Brabham-Ford | |
| | Mario Andretti | USA | Parnelli-Ford | |
| | Mark Donohue | USA | Penske-Ford | |

Points for top six finishers (9, 6, 4, 3, 2, 1). Only the best seven scores from the first eight races and the best six scores from the remaining seven races counted towards the championship.

### CONSTRUCTORS' CHAMPIONSHIP

| POS. | CONSTRUCTOR | POINTS |
|---|---|---|
| 1 | McLaren-Ford | 73 |
| 2 | Ferrari | 65 |
| 3 | Tyrrell-Ford | 52 |
| 4 | Lotus-Ford | 42 |
| 5 | Brabham-Ford | 35 |
| 6 | Hesketh-Ford | 15 |
| 7 | BRM | 10 |
| 8 | Shadow-Ford | 7 |
| 9 | March-Ford | 6 |
| 10 | Iso Marlboro-Ford | 4 |
| 11 | Surtees-Ford | 3 |
| 12 | Lola-Ford | 1 |

Points for top six finishers (9, 6, 4, 3, 2, 1). Points only counted for top-placed car for each constructor. Only the best seven scores from the first eight races and the best six scores from the remaining seven races counted towards the championship

### ARGENTINE GRAND PRIX: BUENOS AIRES *NO.15 13 January Round: 1 Race: 236 53x3.708 miles*

| POS. | NO. | DRIVER | CAR-ENGINE | LAPS | TIME/RETIRED | GRID |
|---|---|---|---|---|---|---|
| 1 | 6 | Denny Hulme | McLaren-Ford | 53 | 1:41'02.01 | 10 |
| 2 | 12 | Niki Lauda | Ferrari | 53 | +9.27 | 8 |
| 3 | 11 | Clay Regazzoni | Ferrari | 53 | +20.41 | 2 |
| 4 | 33 | Mike Hailwood | McLaren-Ford | 53 | +31.79 | 9 |
| 5 | 14 | Jean Pierre Beltoise | BRM | 53 | +51.84 | 14 |
| 6 | 4 | P.Depailler | Tyrrell-Ford | 53 | +1'52.48 | 15 |
| 7 | 7 | Carlos Reutemann | Brabham-Ford | 52 | Out of fuel | 6 |
| 8 | 10 | Howden Ganley | March-Ford | 52 | Out of fuel | 19 |
| 9 | 15 | Henri Pescarolo | BRM | 52 | +1 Lap | 21 |
| 10 | 5 | Emerson Fittipaldi | McLaren-Ford | 52 | +1 Lap | 3 |
| 11 | 27 | Guy Edwards | Lola-Ford | 51 | +2 Laps | 25 |
| 12 | 28 | John Watson | Brabham-Ford | 49 | +4 Laps | 20 |
| 13 | 1 | Ronnie Peterson | Lotus-Ford | 48 | +5 Laps | 1 |
| Ret | 26 | Graham Hill | Lola-Ford | 45 | Engine | 17 |
| Ret | 2 | Jacky Ickx | Lotus-Ford | 36 | Clutch | 7 |
| Ret | 8 | Richard Robarts | Brabham-Ford | 36 | Gearbox | 22 |
| Ret | 9 | H.J.Stuck | March-Ford | 31 | Clutch | 23 |
| Ret | 37 | Francois Migault | BRM | 31 | Water leak | 24 |
| Ret | 3 | Jody Scheckter | Tyrrell-Ford | 25 | Engine | 12 |
| Ret | 18 | Carlos Pace | Surtees-Ford | 21 | Suspension | 11 |
| Ret | 20 | Arturo Merzario | Iso Marlboro-Ford | 19 | Overheating | 13 |
| Ret | 24 | James Hunt | March-Ford | 11 | Overheating | 5 |
| Ret | 19 | Jochen Mass | Surtees-Ford | 10 | Engine | 18 |
| Ret | 16 | Peter Revson | Shadow-Ford | 1 | Accident | 4 |
| Ret | 17 | Jean-Pierre Jarier | Shadow-Ford | 0 | Accident | 16 |

Winning speed: 116.719mph Lap leaders; Peterson 1-2; Reutemann 3-51; Hulme 52-53
Pole position: Peterson, 1m 50.780s, 120.509mph
Fastest lap: Regazzoni, 1m 52.100s, 119.090mph

### BRAZILIAN GRAND PRIX: INTERLAGOS *27 January Round: 2 Race: 237 32 x 4.946 miles*

| POS. | NO. | DRIVER | CAR-ENGINE | LAPS | TIME/RETIRED | GRID |
|---|---|---|---|---|---|---|
| 1 | 5 | Emerson Fittipaldi | McLaren-Ford | 32 | 1:24'37.06 | 1 |
| 2 | 11 | Clay Regazzoni | Ferrari | 32 | +13.57 | 8 |
| 3 | 2 | Jacky Ickx | Lotus-Ford | 31 | +1 Lap | 5 |
| 4 | 18 | Carlos Pace | Surtees-Ford | 31 | +1 Lap | 12 |
| 5 | 33 | Mike Hailwood | McLaren-Ford | 31 | +1 Lap | 7 |
| 6 | 1 | Ronnie Peterson | Lotus-Ford | 31 | +1 Lap | 4 |
| 7 | 7 | Carlos Reutemann | Brabham-Ford | 31 | +1 Lap | 2 |
| 8 | 4 | P.Depailler | Tyrrell-Ford | 31 | +1 Lap | 16 |
| 9 | 24 | James Hunt | March-Ford | 31 | +1 Lap | 18 |
| 10 | 14 | Jean Pierre Beltoise | BRM | 31 | +1 Lap | 17 |
| 11 | 26 | Graham Hill | Lola-Ford | 31 | +1 Lap | 21 |
| 12 | 6 | Denny Hulme | McLaren-Ford | 31 | +1 Lap | 11 |
| 13 | 3 | Jody Scheckter | Tyrrell-Ford | 31 | +1 Lap | 14 |
| 14 | 15 | Henri Pescarolo | BRM | 30 | +2 Laps | 22 |
| 15 | 8 | Richard Robarts | Brabham-Ford | 30 | +2 Laps | 24 |
| 16 | 37 | Francois Migault | BRM | 30 | +2 Laps | 23 |
| 17 | 19 | Jochen Mass | Surtees-Ford | 30 | +2 Laps | 10 |
| Ret | 28 | John Watson | Brabham-Ford | 27 | Clutch | 15 |
| Ret | 9 | H.J.Stuck | March-Ford | 24 | Transmission | 13 |
| Ret | 17 | Jean-Pierre Jarier | Shadow-Ford | 21 | Brakes | 19 |
| Ret | 20 | Arturo Merzario | Iso Marlboro-Ford | 20 | Throttle | 9 |
| Ret | 16 | Peter Revson | Shadow-Ford | 10 | Overheating | 6 |
| Ret | 10 | Howden Ganley | March-Ford | 8 | Ignition | 20 |
| Ret | 12 | Niki Lauda | Ferrari | 2 | Engine | 25 |
| Ret | 27 | Guy Edwards | Lola-Ford | 2 | Chassis | 3 |

Winning speed: 112.229mph Lap leaders: Reutemann 1-3; Peterson 4-15; E Fittipaldi 16-32
Pole position: Fittipaldi, 2m 32.970s, 116.402mph
Fastest lap: Regazzoni, 2m 36.050s, 114.105mph
Scheduled for 40 laps, but stopped early because of rain.

### SOUTH AFRICAN GRAND PRIX: KYALAMI *30 March Round: 3 Race: 238 78 x 2.550 miles*

| POS. | NO. | DRIVER | CAR-ENGINE | LAPS | TIME/RETIRED | GRID |
|---|---|---|---|---|---|---|
| 1 | 7 | Carlos Reutemann | Brabham-Ford | 78 | 1:42'40.96 | 4 |
| 2 | 14 | Jean Pierre Beltoise | BRM | 78 | +33.94 | 11 |
| 3 | 33 | Mike Hailwood | McLaren-Ford | 78 | +42.16 | 12 |
| 4 | 4 | P.Depailler | Tyrrell-Ford | 78 | +44.19 | 15 |
| 5 | 9 | H.J.Stuck | March-Ford | 78 | +46.23 | 7 |
| 6 | 20 | Arturo Merzario | Iso Marlboro-Ford | 78 | +56.04 | 3 |
| 7 | 5 | Emerson Fittipaldi | McLaren-Ford | 78 | +1'08.39 | 5 |
| 8 | 3 | Jody Scheckter | Tyrrell-Ford | 78 | +1'10.54 | 8 |
| 9 | 6 | Denny Hulme | McLaren-Ford | 77 | +1 Lap | 9 |
| 10 | 10 | V.Brambilla | March-Ford | 77 | +1 Lap | 19 |
| 11 | 18 | Carlos Pace | Surtees-Ford | 77 | +1 Lap | 2 |
| 12 | 26 | Graham Hill | Lola-Ford | 77 | +1 Lap | 18 |
| 13 | 29 | Ian Scheckter | Lotus-Ford | 76 | +2 Laps | 22 |
| 14 | 32 | Eddie Keizan | Tyrrell-Ford | 76 | +2 Laps | 24 |
| 15 | 37 | Francois Migault | BRM | 75 | +3 Laps | 25 |
| 16 | 12 | Niki Lauda | Ferrari | 74 | Ignition | 1 |
| 17 | 8 | Richard Robarts | Brabham-Ford | 74 | +4 Laps | 23 |
| 18 | 15 | Henri Pescarolo | BRM | 72 | +6 Laps | 21 |
| 19 | 23 | Dave Charlton | McLaren-Ford | 71 | +7 Laps | 20 |
| Ret | 11 | Clay Regazzoni | Ferrari | 65 | Oil pressure | 6 |
| Ret | 28 | John Watson | Brabham-Ford | 54 | Fuel system | 13 |
| Ret | 2 | Jacky Ickx | Lotus-Ford | 31 | Brakes | 10 |
| Ret | 24 | James Hunt | Hesketh-Ford | 13 | Transmission | 14 |
| Ret | 19 | Jochen Mass | Surtees-Ford | 11 | Suspension | 17 |
| Ret | 30 | Paddy Driver | Lotus-Ford | 6 | Clutch | 26 |
| Ret | 1 | Ronnie Peterson | Lotus-Ford | 2 | Collision | 16 |
| Ret | 21 | Tom Belso | Iso Marlboro-Ford | 0 | Clutch | 27 |

Winning speed: 116.227mph Lap leaders: Lauda 1-8; Reutemann 9-78
Pole position: Lauda, 1m 16.580s, 119.880mph
Fastest lap: Reutemann, 1m 18.160s, 117.456mph

### SPANISH GRAND PRIX: JARAMA *28 April Round: 4 Race: 239 84 x 2.115 miles*

| POS. | NO. | DRIVER | CAR-ENGINE | LAPS | TIME/RETIRED | GRID |
|---|---|---|---|---|---|---|
| 1 | 12 | Niki Lauda | Ferrari | 84 | 2:00'29.56 | 1 |
| 2 | 11 | Clay Regazzoni | Ferrari | 84 | +35.61 | 3 |
| 3 | 5 | Emerson Fittipaldi | McLaren-Ford | 83 | +1 Lap | 4 |
| 4 | 9 | H.J.Stuck | March-Ford | 82 | +2 Laps | 13 |
| 5 | 3 | Jody Scheckter | Tyrrell-Ford | 82 | +2 Laps | 9 |
| 6 | 6 | Denny Hulme | McLaren-Ford | 82 | +2 Laps | 8 |
| 7 | 16 | Brian Redman | Shadow-Ford | 81 | +3 Laps | 21 |
| 8 | 4 | P.Depailler | Tyrrell-Ford | 81 | +3 Laps | 16 |
| 9 | 33 | Mike Hailwood | McLaren-Ford | 81 | +3 Laps | 17 |
| 10 | 24 | James Hunt | Hesketh-Ford | 81 | +3 Laps | 10 |
| 11 | 28 | John Watson | Brabham-Ford | 80 | +4 Laps | 15 |
| 12 | 15 | Henri Pescarolo | BRM | 80 | +4 Laps | 20 |
| 13 | 18 | Carlos Pace | Surtees-Ford | 78 | +6 Laps | 14 |
| 14 | 23 | Tim Schenken | Trojan-Ford | 76 | Spun off | 25 |
| Ret | 17 | Jean-Pierre Jarier | Shadow-Ford | 73 | Not classified | 12 |
| Ret | 26 | Graham Hill | Lola-Ford | 43 | Engine | 19 |
| Ret | 20 | Arturo Merzario | Iso Marlboro-Ford | 37 | Accident | 7 |
| Ret | 19 | Jochen Mass | Surtees-Ford | 35 | Gearbox | 18 |
| Ret | 37 | Francois Migault | BRM | 27 | Engine | 22 |
| Ret | 2 | Jacky Ickx | Lotus-Ford | 26 | Brakes | 5 |
| Ret | 1 | Ronnie Peterson | Lotus-Ford | 23 | Engine | 2 |
| Ret | 30 | Chris Amon | Amon-Ford | 22 | Brakes | 23 |
| Ret | 8 | Rikky von Opel | Brabham-Ford | 14 | Oil leak | 24 |
| Ret | 7 | Carlos Reutemann | Brabham-Ford | 12 | Spun off | 6 |
| Ret | 14 | Jean Pierre Beltoise | BRM | 2 | Engine | 11 |
| DNQ | 27 | Guy Edwards | Lola-Ford | | | |
| DNQ | 21 | Tom Belso | Iso Marlboro-Ford | | | |

Winning speed: 88.473mph Lap leaders: Peterson 1-20; Lauda 21-23, 25-84, Ickx 24
Pole position: Lauda, 1m 18.440s, 97.075mph
Fastest lap: Lauda, 1m 20.830s, 94.204mph
Scheduled for 90 laps, but stopped at 2 hours

### BELGIAN GRAND PRIX: NIVELLES *12 May Round: 5 Race: 240 85 x 2.314 miles*

| POS. | NO. | DRIVER | CAR-ENGINE | LAPS | TIME/RETIRED | GRID |
|---|---|---|---|---|---|---|
| 1 | 5 | Emerson Fittipaldi | McLaren-Ford | 85 | 1:44'20.57 | 4 |
| 2 | 12 | Niki Lauda | Ferrari | 85 | +0.35 | 3 |
| 3 | 3 | Jody Scheckter | Tyrrell-Ford | 85 | +45.61 | 2 |
| 4 | 11 | Clay Regazzoni | Ferrari | 85 | +52.02 | 1 |
| 5 | 14 | Jean Pierre Beltoise | BRM | 85 | +1'08.05 | 7 |
| 6 | 6 | Denny Hulme | McLaren-Ford | 85 | +1'10.54 | 12 |
| 7 | 33 | Mike Hailwood | McLaren-Ford | 84 | +1 Lap | 13 |
| 8 | 26 | Graham Hill | Lola-Ford | 83 | +2 Laps | 29 |
| 9 | 10 | V.Brambilla | March-Ford | 83 | +2 Laps | 31 |
| 10 | 41 | Tim Schenken | Trojan-Ford | 83 | +2 Laps | 23 |
| 11 | 28 | John Watson | Brabham-Ford | 83 | +2 Laps | 19 |
| 12 | 27 | Guy Edwards | Lola-Ford | 82 | +3 Laps | 21 |
| 13 | 17 | Jean-Pierre Jarier | Shadow-Ford | 82 | +3 Laps | 17 |
| 14 | 21 | Gijs van Lennep | Iso Marlboro-Ford | 82 | +3 Laps | 30 |
| 15 | 22 | Vern Schuppan | Ensign-Ford | 82 | +3 Laps | 14 |
| 16 | 37 | Francois Migault | BRM | 82 | +3 Laps | 25 |
| 17 | 34 | Teddy Pilette | Brabham-Ford | 81 | +4 Laps | 27 |
| 18 | 16 | Brian Redman | Shadow-Ford | 80 | Engine | 18 |
| Ret | 2 | Jacky Ickx | Lotus-Ford | 72 | Overheating | 16 |
| Ret | 42 | Tom Pryce | Token-Ford | 66 | Collision | 20 |
| Ret | 7 | Carlos Reutemann | Brabham-Ford | 62 | Engine | 24 |
| Ret | 1 | Ronnie Peterson | Lotus-Ford | 56 | Fuel leak | 5 |
| Ret | 4 | P.Depailler | Tyrrell-Ford | 53 | Brakes | 28 |
| Ret | 19 | Jochen Mass | Surtees-Ford | 53 | Suspension | 26 |
| Ret | 43 | Gerard Larrousse | Brabham-Ford | 53 | Tyre | 11 |
| Ret | 18 | Carlos Pace | Surtees-Ford | 50 | Handling | 8 |
| Ret | 8 | Rikky von Opel | Brabham-Ford | 49 | Engine | 22 |
| Ret | 24 | James Hunt | Hesketh-Ford | 45 | Accident | 9 |
| Ret | 20 | Arturo Merzario | Iso Marlboro-Ford | 29 | Transmission | 6 |
| Ret | 15 | Henri Pescarolo | BRM | 12 | Collision | 15 |
| Ret | 9 | H.J.Stuck | March-Ford | 6 | Clutch | 10 |
| DNQ | 44 | Leo Kinnunen | Surtees-Ford | | | |

Winning speed: 113.101mph Lap leaders: Regazzoni 1-38; Fittipaldi 39-85
Pole position: Regazzoni, 1m 9.820s, 119.312mph
Fastest lap: Hulme, 1m 11.310s, 116.819mph

### MONACO GRAND PRIX: MONTE CARLO *26 May Round: 6 Race: 241 78 x 2.037 miles*

| POS. | NO. | DRIVER | CAR-ENGINE | LAPS | TIME/RETIRED | GRID |
|---|---|---|---|---|---|---|
| 1 | 1 | Ronnie Peterson | Lotus-Ford | 78 | 1:58'03.7 | 3 |
| 2 | 3 | Jody Scheckter | Tyrrell-Ford | 78 | +28.8 | 5 |
| 3 | 17 | Jean-Pierre Jarier | Shadow-Ford | 78 | +48.9 | 6 |
| 4 | 11 | Clay Regazzoni | Ferrari | 78 | +1'03.1 | 2 |
| 5 | 5 | Emerson Fittipaldi | McLaren-Ford | 77 | +1 Lap | 13 |
| 6 | 28 | John Watson | Brabham-Ford | 77 | +1 Lap | 23 |
| 7 | 26 | Graham Hill | Lola-Ford | 76 | +2 Laps | 21 |
| 8 | 27 | Guy Edwards | Lola-Ford | 75 | +3 Laps | 26 |
| 9 | 4 | P.Depailler | Tyrrell-Ford | 74 | +4 Laps | 4 |
| Ret | 15 | Henri Pescarolo | BRM | 62 | Gearbox | 27 |
| Ret | 2 | Jacky Ickx | Lotus-Ford | 34 | Engine | 19 |
| Ret | 12 | Niki Lauda | Ferrari | 32 | Ignition | 1 |
| Ret | 24 | James Hunt | Hesketh-Ford | 27 | Halfshaft | 7 |
| Ret | 33 | Mike Hailwood | McLaren-Ford | 11 | Accident | 10 |
| Ret | 7 | Carlos Reutemann | Brabham-Ford | 5 | Suspension | 8 |
| Ret | 37 | Francois Migault | BRM | 4 | Accident | 22 |
| Ret | 22 | Vern Schuppan | Ensign-Ford | 4 | Accident | 25 |
| Ret | 9 | H.J.Stuck | March-Ford | 3 | Collision | 9 |
| Ret | 14 | Jean Pierre Beltoise | BRM | 0 | Collision | 11 |
| Ret | 6 | Denny Hulme | McLaren-Ford | 0 | Collision | 12 |
| Ret | 20 | Arturo Merzario | Iso Marlboro-Ford | 0 | Collision | 14 |
| Ret | 10 | V.Brambilla | March-Ford | 0 | Collision | 15 |
| Ret | 16 | Brian Redman | Shadow-Ford | 0 | Collision | 16 |
| Ret | 18 | Carlos Pace | Surtees-Ford | 0 | Collision | 18 |
| Ret | 23 | Tim Schenken | Trojan-Ford | 0 | Collision | 24 |
| DNQ | 8 | Rikky von Opel | Brabham-Ford | | | |

Winning speed: 80.742mph Lap leaders: Regazzoni 1-20; Lauda 21-32; Peterson 33-78
Pole position: Lauda, 1m 26.300s, 84.967mph
Fastest lap: Peterson, 1m 27.900s, 83.421mph

### SWEDISH GRAND PRIX: ANDERSTORP *9 June Round: 7 Race: 242 80 x 2.497 miles*

| POS. | NO. | DRIVER | CAR-ENGINE | LAPS | TIME/RETIRED | GRID |
|---|---|---|---|---|---|---|
| 1 | 3 | Jody Scheckter | Tyrrell-Ford | 80 | 1:58'31.391 | 2 |
| 2 | 4 | P.Depailler | Tyrrell-Ford | 80 | +0.380 | 1 |
| 3 | 24 | James Hunt | Hesketh-Ford | 80 | +3.325 | 6 |
| 4 | 5 | Emerson Fittipaldi | McLaren-Ford | 80 | +53.507 | 9 |
| 5 | 17 | Jean-Pierre Jarier | Shadow-Ford | 80 | +1'16.403 | 8 |
| 6 | 26 | Graham Hill | Lola-Ford | 79 | +1 Lap | 15 |
| 7 | 27 | Guy Edwards | Lola-Ford | 79 | +1 Lap | 18 |
| 8 | 21 | Tom Belso | Iso Marlboro-Ford | 79 | +1 Lap | 21 |
| 9 | 8 | Rikky von Opel | Brabham-Ford | 79 | +1 Lap | 20 |
| 10 | 10 | V.Brambilla | March-Ford | 78 | Engine | 17 |
| 11 | 28 | John Watson | Brabham-Ford | 77 | +3 Laps | 14 |
| Ret | 22 | Vern Schuppan | Ensign-Ford | 77 | Disqualified | 26 |
| Ret | 12 | Niki Lauda | Ferrari | 70 | Gearbox | 3 |
| Ret | 9 | Reine Wisell | March-Ford | 59 | Suspension | 16 |
| Ret | 6 | Denny Hulme | McLaren-Ford | 56 | Suspension | 12 |
| Ret | 19 | Jochen Mass | Surtees-Ford | 53 | Suspension | 22 |
| Ret | 7 | Carlos Reutemann | Brabham-Ford | 30 | Oil leak | 10 |
| Ret | 2 | Jacky Ickx | Lotus-Ford | 27 | Engine | 7 |
| Ret | 11 | Clay Regazzoni | Ferrari | 24 | Gearbox | 4 |
| Ret | 18 | Carlos Pace | Surtees-Ford | 15 | Handling | 24 |
| Ret | 1 | Ronnie Peterson | Lotus-Ford | 8 | Halfshaft | 5 |
| Ret | 23 | Leo Kinnunen | Surtees-Ford | 8 | Engine | 25 |
| Ret | 33 | Mike Hailwood | McLaren-Ford | 5 | Fuel leak | 11 |
| Ret | 14 | Jean Pierre Beltoise | BRM | 3 | Engine | 13 |
| Ret | 16 | Bertil Roos | Shadow-Ford | 2 | Gearbox | 23 |
| Ret | 15 | Henri Pescarolo | BRM | 0 | Fire | 19 |
| DNQ | 20 | Richard Robarts | Iso Marlboro-Ford | | | |

Winning speed: 101.111mph Lap leaders: Scheckter 1-80
Pole position: Depailler, 1m 24.758s, 106.043mph
Fastest lap: Depailler, 1m 27.262s, 103.000mph

### DUTCH GRAND PRIX: ZANDVOORT *23 June Round: 8 Race: 243 75 x 2.626 miles*

| POS. | NO. | DRIVER | CAR-ENGINE | LAPS | TIME/RETIRED | GRID |
|---|---|---|---|---|---|---|
| 1 | 12 | Niki Lauda | Ferrari | 75 | 1:43'00.35 | 1 |
| 2 | 11 | Clay Regazzoni | Ferrari | 75 | +8.25 | 2 |
| 3 | 5 | Emerson Fittipaldi | McLaren-Ford | 75 | +30.27 | 3 |
| 4 | 33 | Mike Hailwood | McLaren-Ford | 75 | +31.29 | 4 |
| 5 | 3 | Jody Scheckter | Tyrrell-Ford | 75 | +34.28 | 5 |
| 6 | 4 | P.Depailler | Tyrrell-Ford | 75 | +51.52 | 8 |
| 7 | 28 | John Watson | Brabham-Ford | 75 | +1'13.95 | 13 |
| 8 | 1 | Ronnie Peterson | Lotus-Ford | 73 | +2 Laps | 10 |
| 9 | 8 | Rikky von Opel | Brabham-Ford | 73 | +2 Laps | 23 |
| 10 | 10 | V.Brambilla | March-Ford | 72 | +3 Laps | 15 |
| 11 | 2 | Jacky Ickx | Lotus-Ford | 71 | +4 Laps | 18 |
| 12 | 7 | Carlos Reutemann | Brabham-Ford | 71 | +4 Laps | 12 |
| DSQ | 22 | Vern Schuppan | Ensign-Ford | 69 | Disqualified | 17 |
| Ret | 6 | Denny Hulme | McLaren-Ford | 65 | Ignition | 9 |
| Ret | 37 | Francois Migault | BRM | 60 | Gearbox | 25 |
| Ret | 20 | Arturo Merzario | Iso Marlboro-Ford | 54 | Gearbox | 21 |
| Ret | 27 | Guy Edwards | Lola-Ford | 36 | Fuel system | 14 |
| Ret | 17 | Jean-Pierre Jarier | Shadow-Ford | 28 | Clutch | 7 |
| Ret | 14 | Jean Pierre Beltoise | BRM | 18 | Gearbox | 16 |
| Ret | 26 | Graham Hill | Lola-Ford | 16 | Gearbox | 19 |
| Ret | 15 | Henri Pescarolo | BRM | 15 | Handling | 24 |
| Ret | 19 | Jochen Mass | Surtees-Ford | 8 | Transmission | 20 |
| Ret | 24 | James Hunt | Hesketh-Ford | 2 | Collision | 6 |
| Ret | 16 | Tom Pryce | Shadow-Ford | 0 | Collision | 11 |
| Ret | 9 | H.J.Stuck | March-Ford | 0 | Accident | 22 |
| DNQ | 23 | Tim Schenken | Trojan-Ford | | | |
| DNQ | 21 | Gijs van Lennep | Iso Marlboro-Ford | | | |

Winning speed: 114.718mph Lap leaders: Lauda 1-75
Pole position: 1m 18.310s, 120.716mph
Fastest lap: Peterson, 1m 21.440s, 116.077mph

### FRENCH GRAND PRIX: DIJON- PRENOIS *7 July Round: 9 Race: 244 80 x 2.044 miles*

| POS. | NO. | DRIVER | CAR-ENGINE | LAPS | TIME/RETIRED | GRID |
|---|---|---|---|---|---|---|
| 1 | 1 | Ronnie Peterson | Lotus-Ford | 80 | 1:21'55.02 | 2 |
| 2 | 12 | Niki Lauda | Ferrari | 80 | +20.36 | 1 |
| 3 | 11 | Clay Regazzoni | Ferrari | 80 | +27.84 | 4 |
| 4 | 3 | Jody Scheckter | Tyrrell-Ford | 80 | +28.11 | 7 |
| 5 | 2 | Jacky Ickx | Lotus-Ford | 80 | +37.54 | 13 |
| 6 | 6 | Denny Hulme | McLaren-Ford | 80 | +38.14 | 11 |
| 7 | 33 | Mike Hailwood | McLaren-Ford | 79 | +1 Lap | 6 |
| 8 | 4 | P.Depailler | Tyrrell-Ford | 79 | +1 Lap | 9 |
| 9 | 20 | Arturo Merzario | Iso Marlboro-Ford | 79 | +1 Lap | 15 |
| 10 | 14 | Jean Pierre Beltoise | BRM | 79 | +1 Lap | 17 |
| 11 | 10 | V.Brambilla | March-Ford | 79 | +1 Lap | 16 |
| 12 | 17 | Jean-Pierre Jarier | Shadow-Ford | 79 | +1 Lap | 12 |
| 13 | 26 | Graham Hill | Lola-Ford | 78 | +2 Laps | 21 |
| 14 | 37 | Francois Migault | BRM | 78 | +2 Laps | 22 |
| 15 | 27 | Guy Edwards | Lola-Ford | 77 | +3 Laps | 20 |
| 16 | 28 | John Watson | Brabham-Ford | 76 | +4 Laps | 14 |
| Ret | 5 | Emerson Fittipaldi | McLaren-Ford | 27 | Engine | 5 |
| Ret | 7 | Carlos Reutemann | Brabham-Ford | 24 | Handling | 8 |
| Ret | 19 | Jochen Mass | Surtees-Ford | 4 | Clutch | 18 |
| Ret | 16 | Tom Pryce | Shadow-Ford | 1 | Collision | 3 |
| Ret | 15 | Henri Pescarolo | BRM | 1 | Clutch | 19 |
| Ret | 24 | James Hunt | Hesketh-Ford | 0 | Collision | 10 |
| DNQ | 22 | Vern Schuppan | Ensign-Ford | | | |
| DNQ | 8 | Rikky von Opel | Brabham-Ford | | | |
| DNQ | 34 | Carlos Pace | Brabham-Ford | | | |
| DNQ | 21 | J.P.Jabouille | Iso Marlboro-Ford | | | |
| DNQ | 9 | H.J.Stuck | March-Ford | | | |
| DNQ | 18 | Jose Dolhem | Surtees-Ford | | | |
| DNQ | 23 | Leo Kinnunen | Surtees-Ford | | | |
| DNQ | 43 | Gerard Larrousse | Brabham-Ford | | | |

Winning speed: 119.752mph Lap leaders: Lauda 1-16, Peterson 17-80
Pole position : Lauda, 58.790s, 125.145mph
Fastest lap Scheckter, 1m 0.000s, 122.621 mph

### BRITISH GRAND PRIX: BRANDS HATCH *20 July Round: 10 Race: 245 75 x 2.650 miles*

| POS. | NO. | DRIVER | CAR-ENGINE | LAPS | TIME/RETIRED | GRID |
|---|---|---|---|---|---|---|
| 1 | 3 | Jody Scheckter | Tyrrell-Ford | 75 | 1:43'02.2 | 3 |
| 2 | 5 | Emerson Fittipaldi | McLaren-Ford | 75 | +15.3 | 8 |
| 3 | 2 | Jacky Ickx | Lotus-Ford | 75 | +1'01.5 | 12 |
| 4 | 11 | Clay Regazzoni | Ferrari | 75 | +1'07.2 | 7 |
| 5 | 12 | Niki Lauda | Ferrari | 74 | +1 Lap | 1 |
| 6 | 7 | Carlos Reutemann | Brabham-Ford | 74 | +1 Lap | 4 |
| 7 | 6 | Denny Hulme | McLaren-Ford | 74 | +1 Lap | 19 |
| 8 | 16 | Tom Pryce | Shadow-Ford | 74 | +1 Lap | 5 |
| 9 | 8 | Carlos Pace | Brabham-Ford | 74 | +1 Lap | 20 |
| 10 | 1 | Ronnie Peterson | Lotus-Ford | 73 | +2 Laps | 2 |
| 11 | 28 | John Watson | Brabham-Ford | 73 | +2 Laps | 13 |
| 12 | 14 | Jean Pierre Beltoise | BRM | 72 | +3 Laps | 23 |
| 13 | 26 | Graham Hill | Lola-Ford | 69 | +6 Laps | 22 |
| 14 | 19 | Jochen Mass | Surtees-Ford | 68 | +7 Laps | 17 |
| Ret | 15 | Henri Pescarolo | BRM | 64 | Engine | 24 |
| NC | 37 | Francois Migault | BRM | 62 | Not classified | 14 |
| Ret | 33 | Mike Hailwood | McLaren-Ford | 57 | Spun off | 11 |
| Ret | 17 | Jean-Pierre Jarier | Shadow-Ford | 45 | Suspension | 16 |
| Ret | 9 | H.J.Stuck | March-Ford | 36 | Accident | 9 |
| Ret | 4 | P.Depailler | Tyrrell-Ford | 35 | Engine | 10 |
| Ret | 20 | Arturo Merzario | Iso Marlboro-Ford | 25 | Engine | 15 |
| Ret | 10 | V.Brambilla | March-Ford | 17 | Fuel system | 18 |
| Ret | 23 | Tim Schenken | Trojan-Ford | 6 | Suspension | 25 |
| Ret | 24 | James Hunt | Hesketh-Ford | 2 | Suspension | 6 |
| Ret | 27 | Peter Gethin | Lola-Ford | 0 | Physical | 21 |
| DNQ | 42 | David Purley | Token-Ford | | | |
| DNQ | 18 | Derek Bell | Surtees-Ford | | | |
| DNQ | 21 | Tom Belso | Iso Marlboro-Ford | | | |
| DNQ | 208 | Lella Lombardi | Brabham-Ford | | | |
| DNQ | 22 | Vern Schuppan | Ensign-Ford | | | |
| DNQ | 29 | John Nicholson | Lyncar-Ford | | | |
| DNQ | 25 | Howden Ganley | Maki-Ford | | | |
| DNQ | 35 | Mike Wilds | March-Ford | | | |
| DNQ | 43 | Leo Kinnunen | Surtees-Ford | | | |

Winning speed: 115.735mph Lap leaders: Lauda 1-69; Scheckter 70-75
Pole position: Lauda, 1m 19.700s, 119.699mph
Fastest lap: Lauda, 1m 21.100s, 117.633mph
Lauda completed just 73 laps but was allowed an extra lap after the team protested his exit from the pitlane was blocked

### GERMAN GRAND PRIX: NURBURGRING *4 August Round:11 Race: 246 14 x 14.189 miles*

| POS. | NO. | DRIVER | CAR-ENGINE | LAPS | TIME/RETIRED | GRID |
|---|---|---|---|---|---|---|
| 1 | 11 | Clay Regazzoni | Ferrari | 14 | 1:41'35.0 | 2 |
| 2 | 3 | Jody Scheckter | Tyrrell-Ford | 14 | +50.7 | 4 |
| 3 | 7 | Carlos Reutemann | Brabham-Ford | 14 | +1'23.3 | 6 |
| 4 | 1 | Ronnie Peterson | Lotus-Ford | 14 | +1'24.2 | 8 |
| 5 | 2 | Jacky Ickx | Lotus-Ford | 14 | +1'25.0 | 9 |
| 6 | 16 | Tom Pryce | Shadow-Ford | 14 | +2'18.1 | 11 |
| 7 | 9 | H.J.Stuck | March-Ford | 14 | +2'58.7 | 20 |
| 8 | 17 | Jean-Pierre Jarier | Shadow-Ford | 14 | +3'25.9 | 18 |
| 9 | 26 | Graham Hill | Lola-Ford | 14 | +3'26.4 | 19 |
| 10 | 15 | Henri Pescarolo | BRM | 14 | +4'17.7 | 24 |
| 11 | 18 | Derek Bell | Surtees-Ford | 14 | +5'17.7 | 25 |
| 12 | 8 | Carlos Pace | Brabham-Ford | 14 | +6'26.3 | 17 |
| 13 | 10 | V.Brambilla | March-Ford | 14 | +8'43.1 | 23 |
| 14 | 32 | Ian Ashley | Token-Ford | 13 | +1 Lap | 20 |
| 15 | 33 | Mike Hailwood | McLaren-Ford | 12 | Accident | 12 |
| Ret | 19 | Jochen Mass | Surtees-Ford | 10 | Engine | 13 |
| Ret | 24 | James Hunt | Hesketh-Ford | 10 | Gearbox | 10 |
| Ret | 4 | P.Depailler | Tyrrell-Ford | 5 | Accident | 5 |
| Ret | 20 | Arturo Merzario | Iso Marlboro-Ford | 5 | Throttle | 16 |
| Ret | 14 | Jean Pierre Beltoise | BRM | 4 | Fuel system | 15 |
| Ret | 22 | Vern Schuppan | Ensign-Ford | 4 | Gearbox | 22 |
| Ret | 5 | Emerson Fittipaldi | McLaren-Ford | 2 | Suspension | 3 |
| Ret | 21 | Jacques Laffite | Iso Marlboro-Ford | 2 | Suspension | 21 |
| Ret | 28 | John Watson | Brabham-Ford | 1 | Suspension | 14 |
| Ret | 12 | Niki Lauda | Ferrari | 0 | Accident | 1 |
| Ret | 6 | Denny Hulme | McLaren-Ford | 0 | Accident | 7 |
| DNQ | 37 | Francois Migault | BRM | | | |
| DNQ | 23 | Tim Schenken | Trojan-Ford | | | |
| DNQ | 27 | Guy Edwards | Lola-Ford | | | |
| DNQ | 30 | Larry Perkins | Amon-Ford | | | |
| DNQ | 30 | Chris Amon | Amon-Ford | | | |
| DNQ | 25 | Howden Ganley | Maki-Ford | | | |

Winning speed: 117.330mph Lap leaders: Regazzoni 1-14
Pole position: Lauda, 7m 0.800s, 121.389mph
Fastest lap: Scheckter, 7m 11.100s, 118.489mph
Hulme took over the spare car after retiring, and was disqualified as a result.

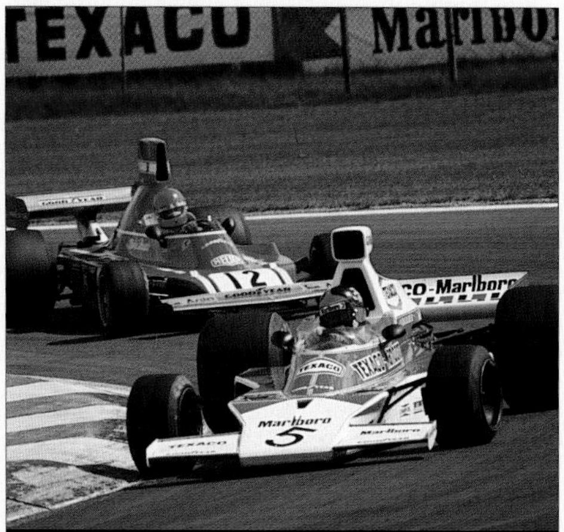

1974 world champion Emerson Fittipaldi in the M23 McLaren Ford.

### AUSTRIAN GRAND PRIX: OSTERREICHRING *18 August Round:12 Race: 247 54 x 3.673 miles*

| POS. | NO. | DRIVER | CAR-ENGINE | LAPS | TIME/RETIRED | GRID |
|---|---|---|---|---|---|---|
| 1 | 7 | Carlos Reutemann | Brabham-Ford | 54 | 1:28'44.72 | 2 |
| 2 | 6 | Denny Hulme | McLaren-Ford | 54 | +42.92 | 10 |
| 3 | 24 | James Hunt | Hesketh-Ford | 54 | +1'01.54 | 7 |
| 4 | 28 | John Watson | Brabham-Ford | 54 | +1'09.39 | 11 |
| 5 | 11 | Clay Regazzoni | Ferrari | 54 | +1'13.08 | 8 |
| 6 | 10 | V.Brambilla | March-Ford | 54 | +1'13.82 | 20 |
| 7 | 33 | David Hobbs | McLaren-Ford | 53 | +1 Lap | 17 |
| 8 | 17 | Jean-Pierre Jarier | Shadow-Ford | 52 | +2 Laps | 23 |
| 9 | 30 | Dieter Quester | Surtees-Ford | 51 | +3 Laps | 25 |
| 10 | 23 | Tim Schenken | Trojan-Ford | 50 | +4 Laps | 19 |
| 11 | 9 | H.J.Stuck | March-Ford | 48 | Suspension | 15 |
| 12 | 26 | Graham Hill | Lola-Ford | 48 | +6 Laps | 21 |
| NC | 35 | Ian Ashley | Token-Ford | 46 | Not classified | 24 |
| Ret | 1 | Ronnie Peterson | Lotus-Ford | 45 | Halfshaft | 6 |
| Ret | 2 | Jacky Ickx | Lotus-Ford | 43 | Collision | 22 |
| Ret | 4 | P.Depailler | Tyrrell-Ford | 42 | Collision | 14 |
| Ret | 8 | Carlos Pace | Brabham-Ford | 41 | Fuel leak | 4 |
| Ret | 5 | Emerson Fittipaldi | McLaren-Ford | 37 | Engine | 3 |
| NC | 21 | Jacques Laffite | Iso Marlboro-Ford | 37 | Not classified | 12 |
| Ret | 20 | Arturo Merzario | Iso Marlboro-Ford | 24 | Fuel system | 9 |
| Ret | 16 | Tom Pryce | Shadow-Ford | 22 | Spun off | 16 |
| Ret | 14 | Jean Pierre Beltoise | BRM | 22 | Engine | 18 |
| Ret | 12 | Niki Lauda | Ferrari | 17 | Engine | 1 |
| Ret | 27 | Rolf Stommelen | Lola-Ford | 14 | Accident | 13 |
| Ret | 3 | Jody Scheckter | Tyrrell-Ford | 8 | Engine | 5 |
| DNQ | 31 | Ian Scheckter | Hesketh-Ford | | | |
| DNQ | 43 | Leo Kinnunen | Surtees-Ford | | | |
| DNQ | 18 | Derek Bell | Surtees-Ford | | | |
| DNQ | 22 | Mike Wilds | Ensign-Ford | | | |
| DNQ | 19 | J.P.Jabouille | Surtees-Ford | | | |
| DNQ | 32 | Helmuth Koinigg | Brabham-Ford | | | |

Winning speed: 134.095mph Lap leaders: Reutemann 1-54
Pole position: Lauda, 1m 35.400s, 138.601mph
Fastest lap: Regazzoni, 1m 37.220s, 136.006mph

### ITALIAN GRAND PRIX: MONZA *6 September Round:13 Race: 248 52 x 3.592 miles*

| POS. | NO. | DRIVER | CAR-ENGINE | LAPS | TIME/RETIRED | GRID |
|---|---|---|---|---|---|---|
| 1 | 1 | Ronnie Peterson | Lotus-Ford | 52 | 1:22'56.6 | 7 |
| 2 | 5 | Emerson Fittipaldi | McLaren-Ford | 52 | +0.8 | 6 |
| 3 | 3 | Jody Scheckter | Tyrrell-Ford | 52 | +24.7 | 12 |
| 4 | 20 | Arturo Merzario | Iso Marlboro-Ford | 52 | +1'27.7 | 15 |
| 5 | 8 | Carlos Pace | Brabham-Ford | 51 | +1 Lap | 3 |
| 6 | 6 | Denny Hulme | McLaren-Ford | 51 | +1 Lap | 19 |
| 7 | 28 | John Watson | Brabham-Ford | 51 | +1 Lap | 4 |
| 8 | 26 | Graham Hill | Lola-Ford | 51 | +1 Lap | 21 |
| 9 | 33 | David Hobbs | McLaren-Ford | 51 | +1 Lap | 23 |
| 10 | 16 | Tom Pryce | Shadow-Ford | 50 | +2 Laps | 22 |
| 11 | 4 | P.Depailler | Tyrrell-Ford | 50 | +2 Laps | 10 |
| Ret | 11 | Clay Regazzoni | Ferrari | 40 | Engine | 5 |
| Ret | 12 | Niki Lauda | Ferrari | 32 | Engine | 1 |
| Ret | 2 | Jacky Ickx | Lotus-Ford | 30 | Throttle | 16 |
| Ret | 27 | Rolf Stommelen | Lola-Ford | 25 | Suspension | 14 |
| Ret | 21 | Jacques Laffite | Iso Marlboro-Ford | 22 | Engine | 17 |
| Ret | 17 | Jean-Pierre Jarier | Shadow-Ford | 19 | Engine | 9 |
| Ret | 10 | V.Brambilla | March-Ford | 16 | Accident | 13 |
| Ret | 29 | Tim Schenken | Trojan-Ford | 15 | Gearbox | 20 |
| Ret | 7 | Carlos Reutemann | Brabham-Ford | 12 | Gearbox | 2 |
| Ret | 9 | H.J.Stuck | March-Ford | 11 | Chassis | 18 |
| Ret | 15 | Henri Pescarolo | BRM | 3 | Engine | 25 |
| Ret | 24 | James Hunt | Hesketh-Ford | 2 | Engine | 8 |
| Ret | 37 | Francois Migault | BRM | 1 | Gearbox | 24 |
| Ret | 14 | Jean Pierre Beltoise | BRM | 0 | Electrical | 11 |
| DNQ | 19 | Jose Dolhem | Surtees-Ford | | | |
| DNQ | 31 | Carlo Facetti | Brabham-Ford | | | |
| DNQ | 18 | Derek Bell | Surtees-Ford | | | |
| DNQ | 25 | Mike Wilds | Ensign-Ford | | | |
| DNQ | 22 | Chris Amon | Amon-Ford | | | |
| DNQ | 23 | Leo Kinnunen | Surtees-Ford | | | |

Winning speed: 135.099mph Lap leaders: Lauda 1-29; Regazzoni 30-40; Peterson 41-52
Pole position: Lauda, 1m 33.160s, 138.788mph
Fastest lap: Pace, 1m 34.200s, 137.256mph

### CANADIAN GRAND PRIX: MOSPORT PARK *22 September Round: 14 Race: 249 80 x 2.459 miles*

| POS. | NO. | DRIVER | CAR-ENGINE | LAPS | TIME/RETIRED | GRID |
|---|---|---|---|---|---|---|
| 1 | 5 | Emerson Fittipaldi | McLaren-Ford | 80 | 1:40'26.136 | 1 |
| 2 | 11 | Clay Regazzoni | Ferrari | 80 | +13.034 | 6 |
| 3 | 1 | Ronnie Peterson | Lotus-Ford | 80 | +14.494 | 10 |
| 4 | 24 | James Hunt | Hesketh-Ford | 80 | +15.669 | 8 |
| 5 | 4 | P.Depailler | Tyrrell-Ford | 80 | +55.322 | 7 |
| 6 | 6 | Denny Hulme | McLaren-Ford | 79 | +1 Lap | 14 |
| 7 | 55 | Mario Andretti | Parnelli-Ford | 79 | +1 Lap | 16 |
| 8 | 8 | Carlos Pace | Brabham-Ford | 79 | +1 Lap | 9 |
| 9 | 7 | Carlos Reutemann | Brabham-Ford | 79 | +1 Lap | 4 |
| 10 | 19 | Helmuth Koinigg | Surtees-Ford | 78 | +2 Laps | 22 |
| 11 | 27 | Rolf Stommelen | Lola-Ford | 78 | +2 Laps | 11 |
| 12 | 66 | Mark Donohue | Penske-Ford | 78 | +2 Laps | 24 |
| 13 | 2 | Jacky Ickx | Lotus-Ford | 78 | +2 Laps | 21 |
| 14 | 26 | Graham Hill | Lola-Ford | 77 | +3 Laps | 20 |
| 15 | 21 | Jacques Laffite | Iso Marlboro-Ford | 74 | Puncture | 18 |
| 16 | 33 | Jochen Mass | McLaren-Ford | 72 | +8 Laps | 12 |
| NC | 15 | Chris Amon | BRM | 70 | Not classified | 25 |
| Ret | 12 | Niki Lauda | Ferrari | 67 | Accident | 2 |
| Ret | 16 | Tom Pryce | Shadow-Ford | 65 | Engine | 13 |
| Ret | 28 | John Watson | Brabham-Ford | 61 | Suspension | 15 |
| NC | 14 | Jean Pierre Beltoise | BRM | 60 | Not classified | 17 |
| Ret | 3 | Jody Scheckter | Tyrrell-Ford | 48 | Brakes | 3 |
| Ret | 17 | Jean-Pierre Jarier | Shadow-Ford | 46 | Halfshaft | 5 |
| Ret | 20 | Arturo Merzario | Iso Marlboro-Ford | 40 | Handling | 19 |
| Ret | 50 | Eppie Wietzes | Brabham-Ford | 33 | Engine | 26 |
| Ret | 9 | H.J.Stuck | March-Ford | 12 | Fuel system | 23 |
| DNQ | 18 | Derek Bell | Surtees-Ford | | | |
| DNQ | 22 | Mike Wilds | Ensign-Ford | | | |
| DNQ | 10 | V.Brambilla | March-Ford | | | |
| DNQ | 42 | Ian Ashley | Brabham-Ford | | | |

Winning speed: 117.520mph Lap leaders: Lauda 1-67; Fittipaldi 68-80
Pole position: Fittipaldi, 1m 13.188s, 120.954mph
Fastest lap: Lauda, 1m 13.659s, 120.181mph

### UNITED STATES GRAND PRIX: WATKINS GLEN *6 October Round: 15 Race: 250 59 x 3.377 miles*

| POS. | NO. | DRIVER | CAR-ENGINE | LAPS | TIME/RETIRED | GRID |
|---|---|---|---|---|---|---|
| 1 | 7 | Carlos Reutemann | Brabham-Ford | 59 | 1:40'21.439 | 1 |
| 2 | 8 | Carlos Pace | Brabham-Ford | 59 | +10.735 | 4 |
| 3 | 24 | James Hunt | Hesketh-Ford | 59 | +1'10.384 | 2 |
| 4 | 5 | Emerson Fittipaldi | McLaren-Ford | 59 | +1'17.753 | 8 |
| 5 | 28 | John Watson | Brabham-Ford | 59 | +1'25.804 | 7 |
| 6 | 4 | P.Depailler | Tyrrell-Ford | 59 | +1'27.506 | 13 |
| 7 | 33 | Jochen Mass | McLaren-Ford | 59 | +1'30.012 | 20 |
| 8 | 26 | Graham Hill | Lola-Ford | 58 | +1 Lap | 24 |
| 9 | 15 | Chris Amon | BRM | 57 | +2 Laps | 12 |
| 10 | 17 | Jean-Pierre Jarier | Shadow-Ford | 57 | +2 Laps | 10 |
| 11 | 11 | Clay Regazzoni | Ferrari | 55 | +4 Laps | 9 |
| 12 | 27 | Rolf Stommelen | Lola-Ford | 54 | +5 Laps | 21 |
| Ret | 1 | Ronnie Peterson | Lotus-Ford | 52 | Fuel system | 19 |
| NC | 22 | Mike Wilds | Ensign-Ford | 50 | Not classified | 22 |
| NC | 16 | Tom Pryce | Shadow-Ford | 47 | Not classified | 18 |
| Ret | 3 | Jody Scheckter | Tyrrell-Ford | 44 | Fuel system | 6 |
| Ret | 20 | Arturo Merzario | Iso Marlboro-Ford | 43 | Electrical | 15 |
| Ret | 12 | Niki Lauda | Ferrari | 38 | Suspension | 5 |
| Ret | 21 | Jacques Laffite | Iso Marlboro-Ford | 31 | Engine | 11 |
| Ret | 66 | Mark Donohue | Penske-Ford | 27 | Suspension | 14 |
| WH | 18 | Jose Dolhem | Surtees-Ford | 25 | Withdrew | 26 |
| Ret | 10 | V.Brambilla | March-Ford | 21 | Fuel system | 25 |
| Ret | 19 | Helmuth Koinigg | Surtees-Ford | 9 | Fatal accident | 23 |
| Ret | 2 | Jacky Ickx | Lotus-Ford | 7 | Suspension | 16 |
| DSQ | 31 | Tim Schenken | Lotus-Ford | 6 | Disqualified | 27 |
| DSQ | 55 | Mario Andretti | Parnelli-Ford | 4 | Disqualified | 13 |
| Ret | 6 | Denny Hulme | McLaren-Ford | 4 | Engine | 17 |
| DNQ | 9 | H.J.Stuck | March-Ford | | | |
| DNQ | 42 | Ian Ashley | Brabham-Ford | | | |
| DNQ | 14 | Jean Pierre Beltoise | BRM | | | |

Winning speed: 119.120mph Lap leaders: Reutemann 1-59
Pole position: Reutemann, 1m 38.978s, 122.827mph
Fastest lap: Pace, 1m 40.608s, 120.837mph

# 1975

## DRIVERS' CHAMPION: NIKI LAUDA
## CONSTRUCTORS' CHAMPION: FERRARI

### DRIVERS' CHAMPIONSHIP

| POS | DRIVER | COUNTRY | CAR | POINTS |
|---|---|---|---|---|
| 1 | Niki Lauda | Austria | Ferrari | 64.5 |
| 2 | Emerson Fittipaldi | Brazil | McLaren-Ford | 45 |
| 3 | Carlos Reutemann | Argentina | Brabham-Ford | 37 |
| 4 | James Hunt | GB | Hesketh-Ford | 33 |
| 5 | Clay Regazzoni | Switzerland | Ferrari | 25 |
| 6 | Carlos Pace | Brazil | Brabham-Ford | 24 |
| 7 | Jody Scheckter | South Africa | Tyrrell-Ford | 20 |
| = | Jochen Mass | West Germany | McLaren-Ford | 20 |
| 9 | Patrick Depailler | France | Tyrrell-Ford | 12 |
| 10 | Tom Pryce | GB | Shadow-Ford | 8 |
| 11 | Vittorio Brambilla | Italy | March-Ford | 6.5 |
| 12 | Jacques Laffite | France | Williams-Ford | 6 |
| = | Ronnie Peterson | Sweden | Lotus-Ford | 6 |
| 14 | Mario Andretti | USA | Parnelli-Ford | 5 |
| 15 | Mark Donohue | USA | Penske-Ford, March-Ford | 4 |
| 16 | Jacky Ickx | Belgium | Lotus-Ford | 3 |
| 17 | Alan Jones | Australia | Hesketh-Ford, Hill-Ford | 2 |
| 18 | Jean-Pierre Jarier | France | Shadow-Ford | 1.5 |
| 19 | Tony Brise | GB | Williams-Ford | 1 |
| = | Gijs van Lennep | Netherlands | Ensign-Ford | 1 |
| 21 | Lella Lombardi | Italy | March-Ford, Williams-Ford | 0.5 |
| | Rolf Stommelen | West Germany | Lola-Ford, Hill-Ford | |
| | John Nicholson | New Zealand | Lyncar-Ford | |
| | Graham Hill | GB | Lola-Ford, Hill-Ford | |
| | Arturo Merzario | Italy | Williams-Ford, Fittipaldi-Ford | |
| | John Watson | GB | Surtees-Ford, Lotus-Ford Penske-Ford | |
| | Wilson Fittipaldi | Brazil | Fittipaldi-Ford | |
| | Mike Wilds | GB | Stanley BRM | |
| | Guy Tunmer | South Africa | Lotus-Ford | |
| | Eddie Keizan | South Africa | Lotus-Ford | |
| | Dave Charlton | South Africa | McLaren-Ford | |
| | Bob Evans | GB | Stanley BRM | |
| | Ian Scheckter | South Africa | Tyrrell-Ford, Williams-Ford | |
| | François Migault | France | Hill-Ford, Williams-Ford | |
| | Roelof Wunderink | Netherlands | Ensign-Ford | |
| | Torsten Palm | Sweden | Hesketh-Ford | |
| | Damien Magee | Ireland | Williams-Ford | |
| | Vern Schuppan | Australia | Hill-Ford | |
| | Jean-Pierre Jabouille | France | Tyrrell-Ford | |
| | Hiroshi Fushida | Japan | Maki-Ford | |
| | Dave Morgan | GB | Surtees-Ford | |
| | Jim Crawford | GB | Lotus-Ford | |
| | Brian Henton | GB | Lotus-Ford | |
| | Hans-Joachim Stuck | West Germany | March-Ford | |
| | Tony Trimmer | GB | Maki-Ford | |
| | Ian Ashley | GB | Williams-Ford | |
| | Harald Ertl | Austria | Hesketh-Ford | |
| | Chris Amon | New Zealand | Ensign-Ford | |
| | Brett Lunger | USA | Hesketh-Ford | |
| | Joseph Vonlanthen | Switzerland | Williams-Ford | |
| | Renzo Zorzi | Italy | Williams-Ford | |
| | Michel Leclère | France | Tyrrell-Ford | |

Points for top six finishers (9, 6, 4, 3, 2, 1). Only the best seven scores from the first eight races and the best five scores from the remaining six races counted towards the championship.

### CONSTRUCTORS' CHAMPIONSHIP

| POS. | CONSTRUCTOR | POINTS |
|---|---|---|
| 1 | Ferrari | 72.5 |
| 2 | Brabham-Ford | 54 |
| 3 | McLaren-Ford | 53 |
| 4 | Hesketh-Ford | 33 |
| 5 | Tyrrell-Ford | 25 |
| 6 | Shadow-Ford | 9.5 |
| 7 | Lotus-Ford | 9 |
| 8 | March-Ford | 7.5 |
| 9 | Williams-Ford | 6 |
| 10 | Parnelli-Ford | 5 |
| 11 | Hill-Ford | 3 |
| 12 | Penske-Ford | 2 |
| 13 | Ensign-Ford | 1 |

Points for top six finishers (9, 6, 4, 3, 2, 1). Points only counted for top-placed car for each constructor. Only the best seven scores from the first eight races and the best five scores from the remaining six races counted towards the championship

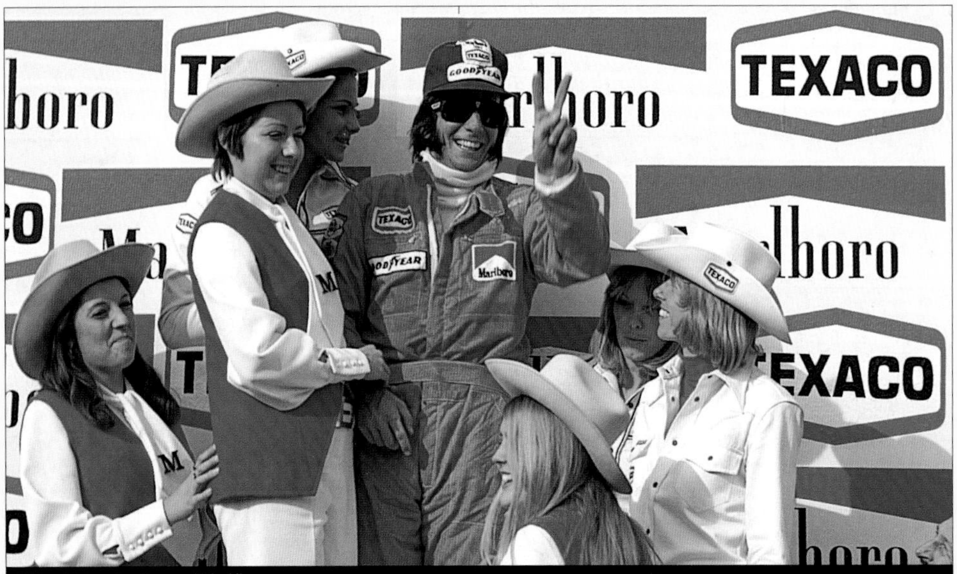

1974 world champion, Emerson Fittipaldi

### ARGENTINE GRAND PRIX: BUENOS AIRES *NO.15 12 January Round: 1 Race: 251 53 x 3.708 miles*

| POS. | NO. | DRIVER | CAR-ENGINE | LAPS | TIME/RETIRED | GRID |
|---|---|---|---|---|---|---|
| 1 | 1 | Emerson Fittipaldi | McLaren-Ford | 53 | 1:39'26.29 | 5 |
| 2 | 24 | James Hunt | Hesketh-Ford | 53 | +5.91 | 6 |
| 3 | 7 | Carlos Reutemann | Brabham-Ford | 53 | +17.06 | 3 |
| 4 | 11 | Clay Regazzoni | Ferrari | 53 | +35.79 | 7 |
| 5 | 4 | P.Depailler | Tyrrell-Ford | 53 | +54.25 | 8 |
| 6 | 12 | Niki Lauda | Ferrari | 53 | +1'19.65 | 4 |
| 7 | 28 | Mark Donohue | Penske-Ford | 52 | +1 Lap | 16 |
| 8 | 6 | Jacky Ickx | Lotus-Ford | 52 | +1 Lap | 18 |
| 9 | 9 | V.Brambilla | March-Ford | 52 | +1 Lap | 12 |
| 10 | 22 | Graham Hill | Lola-Ford | 52 | +1 Lap | 21 |
| 11 | 3 | Jody Scheckter | Tyrrell-Ford | 52 | +1 Lap | 9 |
| 12 | 16 | Tom Pryce | Shadow-Ford | 51 | Transmission | 14 |
| 13 | 23 | Rolf Stommelen | Lola-Ford | 51 | +2 Laps | 19 |
| 14 | 2 | Jochen Mass | McLaren-Ford | 50 | +3 Laps | 13 |
| Ret | 8 | Carlos Pace | Brabham-Ford | 46 | Engine | 2 |
| NC | 20 | Arturo Merzario | Williams-Ford | 44 | Not classified | 20 |
| Ret | 27 | Mario Andretti | Parnelli-Ford | 27 | Transmission | 10 |
| Ret | 14 | Mike Wilds | BRM | 24 | Engine | 22 |
| Ret | 5 | Ronnie Peterson | Lotus-Ford | 15 | Engine | 11 |
| Ret | 21 | Jacques Laffite | Williams-Ford | 15 | Gearbox | 17 |
| Ret | 30 | Wilson Fittipaldi | Fittipaldi-Ford | 12 | Accident | 23 |
| DSQ | 18 | John Watson | Surtees-Ford | 6 | Disqualified | 15 |
| DNS | 17 | Jean-Pierre Jarier | Shadow-Ford | 0 | Transmission | 1 |

Winning speed: 118.592mph Lap leaders: Reutemann 1-25; Hunt 26-34; Fittipaldi 35-53
Pole position: Jarier, 1m 49.210s, 122.242mph
Fastest lap: Hunt, 1m 50.910s, 120.368mph
Jarier qualified for pole position , but did not start due to car failure in warm-up. Pole position left vacant.

### BRAZILIAN GRAND PRIX: INTERLAGOS *26 January Round: 2 Race: 252 40 x 4.946 miles*

| POS. | NO. | DRIVER | CAR-ENGINE | LAPS | TIME/RETIRED | GRID |
|---|---|---|---|---|---|---|
| 1 | 8 | Carlos Pace | Brabham-Ford | 40 | 1:44'41.17 | 6 |
| 2 | 1 | Emerson Fittipaldi | McLaren-Ford | 40 | +5.79 | 2 |
| 3 | 2 | Jochen Mass | McLaren-Ford | 40 | +26.66 | 10 |
| 4 | 11 | Clay Regazzoni | Ferrari | 40 | +43.28 | 5 |
| 5 | 12 | Niki Lauda | Ferrari | 40 | +1'01.88 | 4 |
| 6 | 24 | James Hunt | Hesketh-Ford | 40 | +1'05.12 | 7 |
| 7 | 27 | Mario Andretti | Parnelli-Ford | 40 | +1'06.81 | 18 |
| 8 | 7 | Carlos Reutemann | Brabham-Ford | 40 | +1'39.62 | 3 |
| 9 | 6 | Jacky Ickx | Lotus-Ford | 40 | +1'51.84 | 12 |
| 10 | 18 | John Watson | Surtees-Ford | 40 | +2'29.60 | 13 |
| 11 | 21 | Jacques Laffite | Williams-Ford | 39 | +1 Lap | 19 |
| 12 | 22 | Graham Hill | Lola-Ford | 39 | +1 Lap | 20 |
| 13 | 30 | Wilson Fittipaldi | Fittipaldi-Ford | 39 | +1 Lap | 21 |
| 14 | 23 | Rolf Stommelen | Lola-Ford | 39 | +1 Lap | 23 |
| 15 | 5 | Ronnie Peterson | Lotus-Ford | 38 | +2 Laps | 16 |
| Ret | 17 | Jean-Pierre Jarier | Shadow-Ford | 32 | Fuel system | 1 |
| Ret | 4 | P.Depailler | Tyrrell-Ford | 31 | Suspension | 9 |
| Ret | 16 | Tom Pryce | Shadow-Ford | 31 | Accident | 14 |
| Ret | 20 | Arturo Merzario | Williams-Ford | 24 | Fuel system | 11 |
| Ret | 28 | Mark Donohue | Penske-Ford | 22 | Handling | 15 |
| Ret | 14 | Mike Wilds | BRM | 22 | Electrical | 22 |
| Ret | 3 | Jody Scheckter | Tyrrell-Ford | 18 | Oil leak | 8 |
| Ret | 9 | V.Brambilla | March-Ford | 1 | Engine | 17 |

Winning speed: 113.393mph Lap leaders: Reutemann 1-4; Jarier 5-32; Pace 33-40
Pole position: Jarier, 2m 29.880s, 118.802mph
Fastest Speed: Jarier, 2m 34.160s, 115.503mph

### SOUTH AFRICAN GRAND PRIX: KYALAMI *1 March Round: 3 Race: 253 78 x 2.550 miles*

| POS. | NO. | DRIVER | CAR-ENGINE | LAPS | TIME/RETIRED | GRID |
|---|---|---|---|---|---|---|
| 1 | 3 | Jody Scheckter | Tyrrell-Ford | 78 | 1:43'16.90 | 3 |
| 2 | 7 | Carlos Reutemann | Brabham-Ford | 78 | +3.74 | 2 |
| 3 | 4 | P.Depailler | Tyrrell-Ford | 78 | +16.92 | 5 |
| 4 | 8 | Carlos Pace | Brabham-Ford | 78 | +17.31 | 1 |
| 5 | 12 | Niki Lauda | Ferrari | 78 | +28.64 | 4 |
| 6 | 2 | Jochen Mass | McLaren-Ford | 78 | +1'03.34 | 16 |
| 7 | 23 | Rolf Stommelen | Hill-Ford | 78 | +1'12.91 | 14 |
| 8 | 28 | Mark Donohue | Penske-Ford | 77 | +1 Lap | 18 |
| 9 | 16 | Tom Pryce | Shadow-Ford | 77 | +1 Lap | 19 |
| 10 | 5 | Ronnie Peterson | Lotus-Ford | 77 | +1 Lap | 8 |
| 11 | 34 | Guy Tunmer | Lotus-Ford | 76 | +2 Laps | 25 |
| 12 | 6 | Jacky Ickx | Lotus-Ford | 76 | +2 Laps | 21 |
| 13 | 33 | Eddie Keizan | Lotus-Ford | 76 | +2 Laps | 22 |
| 14 | 31 | Dave Charlton | McLaren-Ford | 76 | +2 Laps | 20 |
| 15 | 14 | Bob Evans | BRM | 76 | +2 Laps | 24 |
| 16 | 11 | Clay Regazzoni | Ferrari | 71 | Throttle | 9 |
| 17 | 27 | Mario Andretti | Parnelli-Ford | 70 | Transmission | 6 |
| NC | 21 | Jacques Laffite | Williams-Ford | 69 | Not classified | 23 |
| NC | 1 | Emerson Fittipaldi | McLaren-Ford | 65 | Not classified | 11 |
| Ret | 32 | Ian Scheckter | Tyrrell-Ford | 55 | Accident | 17 |
| Ret | 24 | James Hunt | Hesketh-Ford | 53 | Fuel system | 12 |
| Ret | 17 | Jean-Pierre Jarier | Shadow-Ford | 37 | Overheating | 13 |
| Ret | 10 | Lella Lombardi | March-Ford | 23 | Fuel system | 26 |
| Ret | 20 | Arturo Merzario | Williams-Ford | 22 | Engine | 15 |
| Ret | 18 | John Watson | Surtees-Ford | 19 | Clutch | 10 |
| Ret | 9 | V.Brambilla | March-Ford | 16 | Radiator | 7 |
| DNQ | 30 | Wilson Fittipaldi | Fittipaldi-Ford | | | |
| DNQ | 22 | Graham Hill | Lola-Ford | | | |

Winning speed: 115.553mph Lap leaders: Pace 1-2; Scheckter 3-78
Pole position: Pace, 1m 16.410s, 120.146mph
Fastest Speed: Pace, 1m 17.200s, 118.917mph

### SPANISH GRAND PRIX: MONTJUICH PARK *27 April Round: 4 Race: 254 29 x 2.356 miles*

| POS. | NO. | DRIVER | CAR-ENGINE | LAPS | TIME/RETIRED | GRID |
|---|---|---|---|---|---|---|
| 1 | 2 | Jochen Mass | McLaren-Ford | 29 | 42'53.7 | 11 |
| 2 | 6 | Jacky Ickx | Lotus-Ford | 29 | +1.1 | 16 |
| 3 | 7 | Carlos Reutemann | Brabham-Ford | 28 | +1 Lap | 15 |
| 4 | 17 | Jean-Pierre Jarier | Shadow-Ford | 28 | +1 Lap | 10 |
| 5 | 9 | V.Brambilla | March-Ford | 28 | +1 Lap | 5 |
| 6 | 10 | Lella Lombardi | March-Ford | 27 | +2 Laps | 24 |
| 7 | 21 | Tony Brise | Williams-Ford | 27 | +2 Laps | 18 |
| 8 | 18 | John Watson | Surtees-Ford | 26 | +3 Laps | 6 |
| NC | 11 | Clay Regazzoni | Ferrari | 25 | Not classified | 2 |
| Ret | 22 | Rolf Stommelen | Hill-Ford | 25 | Accident | 9 |
| Ret | 8 | Carlos Pace | Brabham-Ford | 25 | Accident | 14 |
| Ret | 16 | Tom Pryce | Shadow-Ford | 23 | Accident | 8 |
| Ret | 5 | Ronnie Peterson | Lotus-Ford | 23 | Suspension | 12 |
| Ret | 31 | Roelof Wunderink | Ensign-Ford | 20 | Transmission | 19 |
| NC | 23 | Francois Migault | Hill-Ford | 18 | Not classified | 22 |
| Ret | 27 | Mario Andretti | Parnelli-Ford | 16 | Suspension | 4 |
| Ret | 14 | Bob Evans | BRM | 7 | Fuel system | 23 |
| Ret | 24 | James Hunt | Hesketh-Ford | 6 | Accident | 3 |
| Ret | 3 | Jody Scheckter | Tyrrell-Ford | 3 | Engine | 13 |
| Ret | 28 | Mark Donohue | Penske-Ford | 3 | Accident | 17 |
| Ret | 25 | Alan Jones | Hesketh-Ford | 3 | Accident | 20 |
| Ret | 4 | P.Depailler | Tyrrell-Ford | 1 | Accident | 7 |
| Wth | 30 | Wilson Fittipaldi | Fittipaldi-Ford | 1 | Withdrew | 21 |
| Wth | 20 | Arturo Merzario | Williams-Ford | 1 | Withdrew | 25 |
| Ret | 12 | Niki Lauda | Ferrari | 0 | Accident | 1 |
| DNS | 1 | Emerson Fittipaldi | McLaren-Ford | 0 | Non starter | 26 |

Winning speed: 95.554mph Lap leaders: Hunt1-6; Andretti 7-16; Stommelen 17-21, 23-25; Pace 22; Mass 26-27, 29; Ixkx 28
Pole position: Lauda, 1m 23.400s, 101.681mph
Fastest lap: Andretti, 1m 25.100s, 99.650mph
Race stopped before the scheduled 75 laps following Stommelen's accident which killed five spectators; half points were awarded.
Jarier was penalised a lap for ignoring a yellow flag.

### MONACO GRAND PRIX: MONTE CARLO *11 May Round: 5 Race: 255 75 x 2.037 miles*

| POS. | NO. | DRIVER | CAR-ENGINE | LAPS | TIME/RETIRED | GRID |
|---|---|---|---|---|---|---|
| 1 | 12 | Niki Lauda | Ferrari | 75 | 2:01'21.31 | 1 |
| 2 | 1 | Emerson Fittipaldi | McLaren-Ford | 75 | +2.78 | 9 |
| 3 | 8 | Carlos Pace | Brabham-Ford | 75 | +17.81 | 8 |
| 4 | 5 | Ronnie Peterson | Lotus-Ford | 75 | +38.45 | 4 |
| 5 | 4 | P.Depailler | Tyrrell-Ford | 75 | +40.86 | 12 |
| 6 | 2 | Jochen Mass | McLaren-Ford | 75 | +42.07 | 15 |
| 7 | 3 | Jody Scheckter | Tyrrell-Ford | 74 | +1 Lap | 7 |
| 8 | 6 | Jacky Ickx | Lotus-Ford | 74 | +1 Lap | 14 |
| 9 | 7 | Carlos Reutemann | Brabham-Ford | 73 | +2 Laps | 10 |
| Ret | 28 | Mark Donohue | Penske-Ford | 66 | Accident | 16 |
| Ret | 24 | James Hunt | Hesketh-Ford | 63 | Accident | 11 |
| Ret | 26 | Alan Jones | Hesketh-Ford | 61 | Wheel | 18 |
| Ret | 9 | V.Brambilla | March-Ford | 48 | Accident | 5 |
| Ret | 16 | Tom Pryce | Shadow-Ford | 39 | Accident | 2 |
| Ret | 11 | Clay Regazzoni | Ferrari | 36 | Accident | 17 |
| Ret | 18 | John Watson | Surtees-Ford | 36 | Spun off | 6 |
| Ret | 27 | Mario Andretti | Parnelli-Ford | 9 | Oil leak | 13 |
| Ret | 17 | Jean-Pierre Jarier | Shadow-Ford | 0 | Accident | 3 |
| DNQ | 21 | Jacques Laffite | Williams-Ford | | | |
| DNQ | 20 | Arturo Merzario | Williams-Ford | | | |
| DNQ | 23 | Graham Hill | Hill-Ford | | | |
| DNQ | 14 | Bob Evans | BRM | | | |
| DNQ | 31 | Roelof Wunderink | Ensign-Ford | | | |
| DNQ | 25 | Torsten Palm | Hesketh-Ford | | | |
| DNQ | 10 | Lella Lombardi | March-Ford | | | |
| DNQ | 30 | Wilson Fittipaldi | Fittipaldi-Ford | | | |

Winning speed: 75.529mph Lap leaders: Lauda 1-23, 25-75; Peterson 24
Pole position: Lauda, 1m 26.400s, 84.869mph
Fastest lap: Depailler, 1m 28.670s, 82.696mph
Scheduled for 78 laps, but stopped at 2 hours. Hill was also practiced in a Lola T370-Cosworth V8

### BELGIAN GRAND PRIX: ZOLDER *25 May Round: 6 Race: 256 70 x 2.648 miles*

| POS. | NO. | DRIVER | CAR-ENGINE | LAPS | TIME/RETIRED | GRID |
|---|---|---|---|---|---|---|
| 1 | 12 | Niki Lauda | Ferrari | 70 | 1:43'53.98 | 1 |
| 2 | 3 | Jody Scheckter | Tyrrell-Ford | 70 | +19.22 | 9 |
| 3 | 7 | Carlos Reutemann | Brabham-Ford | 70 | +41.82 | 6 |
| 4 | 4 | P.Depailler | Tyrrell-Ford | 70 | +1'00.08 | 12 |
| 5 | 11 | Clay Regazzoni | Ferrari | 70 | +1'03.86 | 4 |
| 6 | 16 | Tom Pryce | Shadow-Ford | 70 | +1'28.45 | 5 |
| 7 | 1 | Emerson Fittipaldi | McLaren-Ford | 69 | +1 Lap | 8 |
| 8 | 8 | Carlos Pace | Brabham-Ford | 69 | +1 Lap | 2 |
| 9 | 14 | Bob Evans | BRM | 68 | +2 Laps | 20 |
| 10 | 18 | John Watson | Surtees-Ford | 68 | +2 Laps | 18 |
| 11 | 28 | Mark Donohue | Penske-Ford | 67 | +3 Laps | 21 |
| 12 | 30 | Wilson Fittipaldi | Fittipaldi-Ford | 67 | +3 Laps | 24 |
| Ret | 22 | Francois Migault | Hill-Ford | 57 | Suspension | 22 |
| Ret | 9 | V.Brambilla | March-Ford | 54 | Brakes | 3 |
| Ret | 6 | Jacky Ickx | Lotus-Ford | 52 | Brakes | 16 |
| Ret | 5 | Ronnie Peterson | Lotus-Ford | 36 | Brakes | 14 |
| Ret | 21 | Jacques Laffite | Williams-Ford | 18 | Gearbox | 23 |
| Ret | 10 | Lella Lombardi | March-Ford | 18 | Engine | 17 |
| Ret | 23 | Tony Brise | Hill-Ford | 17 | Engine | 7 |
| Ret | 24 | James Hunt | Hesketh-Ford | 15 | Transmission | 11 |
| Ret | 17 | Jean-Pierre Jarier | Shadow-Ford | 13 | Spun off | 10 |
| Ret | 20 | Arturo Merzario | Williams-Ford | 2 | Clutch | 19 |
| Ret | 26 | Alan Jones | Hesketh-Ford | 1 | Accident | 13 |
| Ret | 2 | Jochen Mass | McLaren-Ford | 0 | Accident | 15 |

Winning speed: 107.053mph Lap leaders: Pace 1-3; Brambilla 4-5; Lauda 6-70
Pole position: Lauda, 1m 25.430s, 111.598mph
Fastest lap: Regazzoni, 1m 26. 760s, 109.887mph

### SWEDISH GRAND PRIX: ANDERSTORP *8 June Round: 7 Race: 257 80 x 2.497 miles*

| POS. | NO. | DRIVER | CAR-ENGINE | LAPS | TIME/RETIRED | GRID |
|---|---|---|---|---|---|---|
| 1 | 12 | Niki Lauda | Ferrari | 80 | 1:59'18.319 | 5 |
| 2 | 7 | Carlos Reutemann | Brabham-Ford | 80 | +6.288 | 4 |
| 3 | 11 | Clay Regazzoni | Ferrari | 80 | +29.095 | 12 |
| 4 | 27 | Mario Andretti | Parnelli-Ford | 80 | +44.380 | 15 |
| 5 | 28 | Mark Donohue | Penske-Ford | 80 | +1'30.763 | 16 |
| 6 | 23 | Tony Brise | Hill-Ford | 79 | +1 Lap | 17 |
| 7 | 3 | Jody Scheckter | Tyrrell-Ford | 79 | +1 Lap | 8 |
| 8 | 1 | Emerson Fittipaldi | McLaren-Ford | 79 | +1 Lap | 11 |
| 9 | 5 | Ronnie Peterson | Lotus-Ford | 79 | +1 Lap | 9 |
| 10 | 32 | Torsten Palm | Hesketh-Ford | 78 | Out of fuel | 21 |
| 11 | 26 | Alan Jones | Hesketh-Ford | 78 | +2 Laps | 19 |
| 12 | 4 | P.Depailler | Tyrrell-Ford | 78 | +2 Laps | 2 |
| 13 | 14 | Bob Evans | BRM | 78 | +2 Laps | 23 |
| 14 | 20 | Damien Magee | Williams-Ford | 78 | +2 Laps | 22 |
| 15 | 6 | Jacky Ickx | Lotus-Ford | 77 | +3 Laps | 18 |
| 16 | 18 | John Watson | Surtees-Ford | 77 | +3 Laps | 10 |
| 17 | 30 | Wilson Fittipaldi | Fittipaldi-Ford | 74 | +6 Laps | 25 |
| Ret | 16 | Tom Pryce | Shadow-Ford | 53 | Spun off | 7 |
| Ret | 21 | Ian Scheckter | Williams-Ford | 49 | Tyre | 20 |
| Ret | 22 | Vern Schuppan | Hill-Ford | 47 | Transmission | 26 |
| Ret | 8 | Carlos Pace | Brabham-Ford | 41 | Spun off | 6 |
| Ret | 17 | Jean-Pierre Jarier | Shadow-Ford | 38 | Engine | 3 |
| Ret | 9 | V.Brambilla | March-Ford | 36 | Transmission | 1 |
| Ret | 2 | Jochen Mass | McLaren-Ford | 34 | Overheating | 14 |
| Ret | 24 | James Hunt | Hesketh-Ford | 21 | Brakes | 13 |
| Ret | 10 | Lella Lombardi | March-Ford | 10 | Fuel system | 24 |

Winning speed: 100.448mph Lap leaders: Brambilla 1-15; Reutemann 16-69; Lauda 70-80
Pole position: Brambilla, 1m 24.630s, 106.204mph
Fastest lap: Lauda, 1m 28.267s, 101.828mph

### DUTCH GRAND PRIX: ZANDVOORT *22 June Round: 8 Race: 258 75 x 2.626 miles*

| POS. | NO. | DRIVER | CAR-ENGINE | LAPS | TIME/RETIRED | GRID |
|---|---|---|---|---|---|---|
| 1 | 24 | James Hunt | Hesketh-Ford | 75 | 1:46'57.40 | 3 |
| 2 | 12 | Niki Lauda | Ferrari | 75 | +1.06 | 1 |
| 3 | 11 | Clay Regazzoni | Ferrari | 75 | +55.06 | 2 |
| 4 | 7 | Carlos Reutemann | Brabham-Ford | 74 | +1 Lap | 5 |
| 5 | 8 | Carlos Pace | Brabham-Ford | 74 | +1 Lap | 9 |
| 6 | 16 | Tom Pryce | Shadow-Ford | 74 | +1 Lap | 12 |
| 7 | 23 | Tony Brise | Hill-Ford | 74 | +1 Lap | 7 |
| 8 | 28 | Mark Donohue | Penske-Ford | 74 | +1 Lap | 18 |
| 9 | 4 | P.Depailler | Tyrrell-Ford | 73 | +2 Laps | 13 |
| 10 | 31 | Gijs van Lennep | Ensign-Ford | 71 | +4 Laps | 22 |
| 11 | 30 | Wilson Fittipaldi | Fittipaldi-Ford | 71 | +4 Laps | 24 |
| 12 | 20 | Ian Scheckter | Williams-Ford | 70 | +5 Laps | 19 |
| 13 | 22 | Alan Jones | Hill-Ford | 70 | +5 Laps | 17 |
| 14 | 10 | Lella Lombardi | March-Ford | 70 | +5 Laps | 23 |
| 15 | 5 | Ronnie Peterson | Lotus-Ford | 69 | Out of fuel | 16 |
| 16 | 3 | Jody Scheckter | Tyrrell-Ford | 67 | Engine | 4 |
| Ret | 21 | Jacques Laffite | Williams-Ford | 64 | Engine | 15 |
| Ret | 2 | Jochen Mass | McLaren-Ford | 61 | Accident | 8 |
| Ret | 17 | Jean-Pierre Jarier | Shadow-Ford | 44 | Tyre | 10 |
| Ret | 18 | John Watson | Surtees-Ford | 43 | Vibrations | 14 |
| Ret | 1 | Emerson Fittipaldi | McLaren-Ford | 40 | Engine | 6 |
| Ret | 14 | Bob Evans | BRM | 23 | Differential | 20 |
| Ret | 6 | Jacky Ickx | Lotus-Ford | 6 | Engine | 21 |
| Ret | 9 | V.Brambilla | March-Ford | 0 | Suspension | 11 |
| DNQ | 35 | Hiroshi Fushida | Maki-Ford | | | |

Winning speed: 110.480mph Lap leaders: Lauda 1-12; Regazzoni 13-14; Hunt 15-75
Pole position: Lauda, 1m 20.290s, 117.739mph
Fastest lap: Lauda, 1m 21.540s, 115.934mph

### FRENCH GRAND PRIX: PAUL RICARD *6 July Round: 9 Race 259 54 x 3.610 miles*

| POS. | NO. | DRIVER | CAR-ENGINE | LAPS | TIME/RETIRED | GRID |
|---|---|---|---|---|---|---|
| 1 | 12 | Niki Lauda | Ferrari | 54 | 1:40'18.84 | 1 |
| 2 | 24 | James Hunt | Hesketh-Ford | 54 | +1.59 | 3 |
| 3 | 2 | Jochen Mass | McLaren-Ford | 54 | +2.31 | 7 |
| 4 | 1 | Emerson Fittipaldi | McLaren-Ford | 54 | +39.77 | 10 |
| 5 | 27 | Mario Andretti | Parnelli-Ford | 54 | +1'02.08 | 15 |
| 6 | 4 | P.Depailler | Tyrrell-Ford | 54 | +1'07.40 | 13 |
| 7 | 23 | Tony Brise | Hill-Ford | 54 | +1'09.61 | 12 |
| 8 | 17 | Jean-Pierre Jarier | Shadow-Ford | 54 | +1'19.78 | 4 |
| 9 | 3 | Jody Scheckter | Tyrrell-Ford | 54 | +1'31.68 | 2 |
| 10 | 5 | Ronnie Peterson | Lotus-Ford | 54 | +1'36.02 | 17 |
| 11 | 21 | Jacques Laffite | Williams-Ford | 54 | +1'36.77 | 16 |
| 12 | 15 | J.P.Jabouille | Tyrrell-Ford | 54 | +1'37.13 | 21 |
| 13 | 18 | John Watson | Surtees-Ford | 53 | +1 Lap | 14 |
| 14 | 7 | Carlos Reutemann | Brabham-Ford | 53 | +1 Lap | 11 |
| 15 | 31 | Gijs van Lennep | Ensign-Ford | 53 | +1 Lap | 22 |
| 16 | 22 | Alan Jones | Hill-Ford | 53 | +1 Lap | 20 |
| 17 | 14 | Bob Evans | BRM | 52 | +2 Laps | 25 |
| 18 | 10 | Lella Lombardi | March-Ford | 50 | +4 Laps | 26 |
| Ret | 8 | Carlos Pace | Brabham-Ford | 26 | Transmission | 5 |
| Ret | 6 | Jacky Ickx | Lotus-Ford | 17 | Brakes | 19 |
| Ret | 30 | Wilson Fittipaldi | Fittipaldi-Ford | 14 | Engine | 23 |
| Ret | 9 | V.Brambilla | March-Ford | 6 | Chassis | 8 |
| Ret | 11 | Clay Regazzoni | Ferrari | 6 | Engine | 9 |
| Ret | 28 | Mark Donohue | Penske-Ford | 6 | Transmission | 18 |
| Ret | 16 | Tom Pryce | Shadow-Ford | 2 | Transmission | 6 |
| DNS | 20 | Francois Migault | Williams-Ford | 0 | Not started | 24 |

Winning speed: 116.603mph Lap leaders: Lauda 1-54
Pole position: Lauda 1m 47.820s, 120.540mph
Fastest lap: Mass, 1m 50.600s, 117.510mph

## BRITISH GRAND PRIX: SILVERSTONE *19 July Round: 10 Race:260 56 x 2.932 miles*

| POS. | NO. | DRIVER | CAR-ENGINE | LAPS | TIME/RETIRED | GRID |
|---|---|---|---|---|---|---|
| 1 | 1 | Emerson Fittipaldi | McLaren-Ford | 56 | 1:22'05.0 | 1 |
| 2 | 8 | Carlos Pace | Brabham-Ford | 55 | Accident | 2 |
| 3 | 3 | Jody Scheckter | Tyrrell-Ford | 55 | Accident | 6 |
| 4 | 24 | James Hunt | Hesketh-Ford | 55 | Accident | 9 |
| 5 | 28 | Mark Donohue | March-Ford | 55 | Accident | 15 |
| 6 | 9 | V.Brambilla | March-Ford | 55 | +1 Lap | 5 |
| 7 | 2 | Jochen Mass | McLaren-Ford | 55 | Accident | 10 |
| 8 | 12 | Niki Lauda | Ferrari | 54 | +2 Laps | 3 |
| 9 | 4 | P.Depailler | Tyrrell-Ford | 54 | Accident | 17 |
| 10 | 22 | Alan Jones | Hill-Ford | 54 | +2 Laps | 20 |
| 11 | 18 | John Watson | Surtees-Ford | 54 | Accident | 18 |
| 12 | 27 | Mario Andretti | Parnelli-Ford | 54 | +2 Laps | 12 |
| 13 | 11 | Clay Regazzoni | Ferrari | 54 | +2 Laps | 4 |
| 14 | 17 | Jean-Pierre Jarier | Shadow-Ford | 53 | Accident | 11 |
| 15 | 23 | Tony Brise | Hill-Ford | 53 | Accident | 13 |
| 16 | 15 | Brian Henton | Lotus-Ford | 53 | Accident | 21 |
| 17 | 32 | John Nicholson | Lyncar-Ford | 51 | Accident | 26 |
| 18 | 19 | Dave Morgan | Surtees-Ford | 50 | Accident | 23 |
| 19 | 30 | Wilson Fittipaldi | Fittipaldi-Ford | 50 | Accident | 24 |
| Ret | 10 | H.J.Stuck | March-Ford | 45 | Accident | 14 |
| Ret | 6 | Jim Crawford | Lotus-Ford | 28 | Accident | 25 |
| Ret | 16 | Tom Pryce | Shadow-Ford | 20 | Accident | 1 |
| Ret | 29 | Lella Lombardi | March-Ford | 18 | Engine | 22 |
| Ret | 5 | Ronnie Peterson | Lotus-Ford | 7 | Engine | 16 |
| Ret | 21 | Jacques Laffite | Williams-Ford | 5 | Gearbox | 19 |
| Ret | 7 | Carlos Reutemann | Brabham-Ford | 4 | Engine | 8 |
| DNQ | 31 | Roelof Wunderink | Ensign-Ford | | | |
| DNQ | 35 | Hiroshi Fushida | Maki-Ford | | | |

Winning speed: 120.019mph Lap leaders: Pace 1-12, 22-26; Regazzoni 13-18; Pryce 19-20; Scheckter 21, 27-32; Jarier 33-34; Hunt 35-42; Fittipaldi 43-56
Pole position: Pryce 1m 19.360s, 133.004mph
Fastest lap: Regazzoni, 1m 20.900s, 130.472mph
Scheduled for 67 laps but stopped early because of rain.

## GERMAN GRAND PRIX: NURBURGRING *3 August Round: 11 Race: 261 14 x 14.189 miles*

| POS. | NO. | DRIVER | CAR-ENGINE | LAPS | TIME/RETIRED | GRID |
|---|---|---|---|---|---|---|
| 1 | 7 | Carlos Reutemann | Brabham-Ford | 14 | 1:41'14.1 | 10 |
| 2 | 21 | Jacques Laffite | Williams-Ford | 14 | +1'37.7 | 15 |
| 3 | 12 | Niki Lauda | Ferrari | 14 | +2'23.3 | 1 |
| 4 | 16 | Tom Pryce | Shadow-Ford | 14 | +3'31.4 | 16 |
| 5 | 22 | Alan Jones | Hill-Ford | 14 | +3'50.3 | 21 |
| 6 | 19 | Gijs van Lennep | Ensign-Ford | 14 | +5'05.5 | 24 |
| 7 | 29 | Lella Lombardi | March-Ford | 14 | +7'30.4 | 25 |
| 8 | 25 | Harald Ertl | Hesketh-Ford | 14 | +7'40.9 | 23 |
| 9 | 4 | P.Depailler | Tyrrell-Ford | 13 | +1 Lap | 4 |
| 10 | 27 | Mario Andretti | Parnelli-Ford | 12 | Out of fuel | 13 |
| Ret | 24 | James Hunt | Hesketh-Ford | 10 | Wheel | 9 |
| Ret | 11 | Clay Regazzoni | Ferrari | 9 | Engine | 5 |
| Ret | 23 | Tony Brise | Hill-Ford | 9 | Accident | 17 |
| Ret | 3 | Jody Scheckter | Tyrrell-Ford | 7 | Accident | 3 |
| Ret | 17 | Jean-Pierre Jarier | Shadow-Ford | 7 | Tyre | 12 |
| Ret | 8 | Carlos Pace | Brabham-Ford | 5 | Suspension | 2 |
| Ret | 30 | Wilson Fittipaldi | Fittipaldi-Ford | 4 | Engine | 22 |
| Ret | 10 | H.J.Stuck | March-Ford | 3 | Engine | 7 |
| Ret | 1 | Emerson Fittipaldi | McLaren-Ford | 3 | Suspension | 8 |
| Ret | 9 | V.Brambilla | March-Ford | 3 | Suspension | 11 |
| Ret | 6 | John Watson | Lotus-Ford | 2 | Suspension | 14 |
| Ret | 5 | Ronnie Peterson | Lotus-Ford | 1 | Clutch | 18 |
| Ret | 28 | Mark Donohue | March-Ford | 1 | Tyre | 19 |
| Ret | 2 | Jochen Mass | McLaren-Ford | 0 | Accident | 6 |
| Ret | 20 | Ian Ashley | Williams-Ford | 0 | Accident | 20 |
| DNQ | 35 | Tony Trimmer | Maki-Ford | | | |

Winning speed: 117.734mph Lap leaders: Lauda 1-9; Reutemann 10-14
Pole position: Lauda, 6 m 58.600s,122.027mph
Fastest lap: Regazzoni, 7m 6.400s, 119.795mph

## AUSTRIAN GRAND PRIX: OSTERREICHRING *17 August Round: 12 Race: 262 29 x 3.673 miles*

| POS. | NO. | DRIVER | CAR-ENGINE | LAPS | TIME/RETIRED | GRID |
|---|---|---|---|---|---|---|
| 1 | 9 | V.Brambilla | March-Ford | 29 | 57'56.69 | 8 |
| 2 | 24 | James Hunt | Hesketh-Ford | 29 | +27.03 | 2 |
| 3 | 16 | Tom Pryce | Shadow-Ford | 29 | +34.85 | 15 |
| 4 | 2 | Jochen Mass | McLaren-Ford | 29 | +1'12.66 | 9 |
| 5 | 5 | Ronnie Peterson | Lotus-Ford | 29 | +1'23.33 | 13 |
| 6 | 12 | Niki Lauda | Ferrari | 29 | +1'30.28 | 1 |
| 7 | 11 | Clay Regazzoni | Ferrari | 29 | +1'39.07 | 5 |
| 8 | 3 | Jody Scheckter | Tyrrell-Ford | 28 | +1 Lap | 10 |
| 9 | 1 | Emerson Fittipaldi | McLaren-Ford | 28 | +1 Lap | 3 |
| 10 | 18 | John Watson | Surtees-Ford | 28 | +1 Lap | 18 |
| 11 | 4 | P.Depailler | Tyrrell-Ford | 28 | +1 Lap | 7 |
| 12 | 31 | Chris Amon | Ensign-Ford | 28 | +1 Lap | 23 |
| 13 | 25 | Brett Lunger | Hesketh-Ford | 28 | +1 Lap | 17 |
| 14 | 7 | Carlos Reutemann | Brabham-Ford | 28 | +1 Lap | 11 |
| 15 | 23 | Tony Brise | Hill-Ford | 28 | +1 Lap | 16 |
| 16 | 22 | Rolf Stommelen | Hill-Ford | 27 | +2 Laps | 25 |
| 17 | 29 | Lella Lombardi | March-Ford | 26 | +3 Laps | 21 |
| NC | 33 | Roelof Wunderink | Ensign-Ford | 25 | Not classified | 27 |
| Ret | 32 | Harald Ertl | Hesketh-Ford | 23 | Electrical | 26 |
| Ret | 21 | Jacques Laffite | Williams-Ford | 21 | Handling | 12 |
| Ret | 8 | Carlos Pace | Brabham-Ford | 17 | Engine | 6 |
| Ret | 20 | Jo Vonlanthen | Williams-Ford | 14 | Engine | 28 |
| Ret | 10 | H.J.Stuck | March-Ford | 10 | Accident | 4 |
| Ret | 17 | Jean-Pierre Jarier | Shadow-Matra | 10 | Injection | 14 |
| Ret | 14 | Bob Evans | BRM | 2 | Engine | 24 |
| Ret | 27 | Mario Andretti | Parnelli-Ford | 1 | Accident | 19 |
| NC | 28 | Mark Donohue | March-Ford | 0 | Fatal accident | 20 |
| NC | 6 | Brian Henton | Lotus-Ford | 0 | Accident | 22 |
| DNQ | 35 | Tony Trimmer | Maki-Ford | | | |
| DNQ | 30 | Wilsin Fittipaldi | Fittipaldi-Ford | | | |

Winning speed: 110.293mph Lap leaders: Lauda 1-14; Hunt 15-18; Brambilla 19-29
Pole position: Lauda, 1m 34.850s, 139.405mph
Fastest lap: Brambilla, 1m 53.900s, 116.089mph
Scheduled for 54 laps, but stopped early because of rain. Half points were awarded. Also the Grand Prix of Europe.

## ITALIAN GRAND PRIX: MONZA *7 September Round: 13 Race: 263 52 x 3.592 miles*

| POS. | NO. | DRIVER | CAR-ENGINE | LAPS | TIME/RETIRED | GRID |
|---|---|---|---|---|---|---|
| 1 | 11 | Clay Regazzoni | Ferrari | 52 | 1:22'42.6 | 2 |
| 2 | 1 | Emerson Fittipaldi | McLaren-Ford | 52 | +16.6 | 3 |
| 3 | 12 | Niki Lauda | Ferrari | 52 | +23.2 | 1 |
| 4 | 7 | Carlos Reutemann | Brabham-Ford | 52 | +55.1 | 7 |
| 5 | 24 | James Hunt | Hesketh-Ford | 52 | +57.1 | 8 |
| 6 | 16 | Tom Pryce | Shadow-Ford | 52 | +1'15.9 | 14 |
| 7 | 4 | P.Depailler | Tyrrell-Ford | 51 | +1 Lap | 12 |
| 8 | 3 | Jody Scheckter | Tyrrell-Ford | 51 | +1 Lap | 4 |
| 9 | 34 | Harald Ertl | Hesketh-Ford | 51 | +1 Lap | 17 |
| 10 | 25 | Brett Lunger | Hesketh-Ford | 50 | +2 Laps | 21 |
| 11 | 30 | Arturo Merzario | Fittipaldi-Ford | 48 | +4 Laps | 26 |
| 12 | 32 | Chris Amon | Ensign-Ford | 48 | +4 Laps | 19 |
| 13 | 6 | Jim Crawford | Lotus-Ford | 46 | +6 Laps | 25 |
| 14 | 20 | Renzo Zorzi | Williams-Ford | 46 | +6 Laps | 22 |
| Ret | 17 | Jean-Pierre Jarier | Shadow-Matra | 32 | Fuel pump | 13 |
| Ret | 29 | Lella Lombardi | March-Ford | 21 | Accident | 24 |
| Ret | 10 | H.J.Stuck | March-Ford | 15 | Accident | 16 |
| Ret | 21 | Jacques Laffite | Williams-Ford | 7 | Gearbox | 18 |
| Ret | 8 | Carlos Pace | Brabham-Ford | 6 | Throttle | 10 |
| Ret | 22 | Rolf Stommelen | Hill-Ford | 3 | Accident | 23 |
| Ret | 2 | Jochen Mass | McLaren-Ford | 2 | Accident | 5 |
| Ret | 5 | Ronnie Peterson | Lotus-Ford | 1 | Engine | 11 |
| Ret | 23 | Tony Brise | Hill-Ford | 1 | Accident | 6 |
| Ret | 27 | Mario Andretti | Parnelli-Ford | 1 | Accident | 15 |
| Ret | 9 | V.Brambilla | March-Ford | 1 | Clutch | 9 |
| Ret | 14 | Bob Evans | BRM | 0 | Electrical | 20 |
| DNQ | 31 | Roelof Wunderink | Ensign-Ford | | | |
| DNQ | 35 | Tony Trimmer | Maki-Ford | | | |

Winning speed: 135.480mph Lap leaders: Regazzoni 1-52
Pole position: Lauda, 1m 32.240s, 140.172mph
Fastest lap: Regazzoni, 1m 33.100s, 138.877mph

## UNITED STATES GRAND PRIX: WATKINS GLEN *5 October Round: 14 Race: 264 59 x 3.377 miles*

| POS. | NO. | DRIVER | CAR-ENGINE | LAPS | TIME/RETIRED | GRID |
|---|---|---|---|---|---|---|
| 1 | 12 | Niki Lauda | Ferrari | 59 | 1:42'58.175 | 1 |
| 2 | 1 | Emerson Fittipaldi | McLaren-Ford | 59 | +4.943 | 2 |
| 3 | 2 | Jochen Mass | McLaren-Ford | 59 | +47.637 | 9 |
| 4 | 24 | James Hunt | Hesketh-Ford | 59 | +49.475 | 15 |
| 5 | 5 | Ronnie Peterson | Lotus-Ford | 59 | +49.986 | 14 |
| 6 | 3 | Jody Scheckter | Tyrrell-Ford | 59 | +50.321 | 10 |
| 7 | 9 | V.Brambilla | March-Ford | 59 | +1'44.031 | 6 |
| 8 | 10 | H.J.Stuck | March-Ford | 58 | +1 Lap | 13 |
| 9 | 28 | John Watson | Penske-Ford | 57 | +2 Laps | 12 |
| 10 | 30 | Wilson Fittipaldi | Fittipaldi-Ford | 55 | +4 Laps | 23 |
| NC | 16 | Tom Pryce | Shadow-Ford | 52 | Not classified | 7 |
| NC | 6 | Brian Henton | Lotus-Ford | 49 | Not classified | 19 |
| Ret | 25 | Brett Lunger | Hesketh-Ford | 46 | Accident | 18 |
| Ret | 31 | Roelof Wunderink | Ensign-Ford | 41 | Gearbox | 22 |
| Wth | 11 | Clay Regazzoni | Ferrari | 28 | Withdrew | 11 |
| Ret | 17 | Jean-Pierre Jarier | Shadow-Ford | 19 | Wheel bearing | 4 |
| Ret | 7 | Carlos Reutemann | Brabham-Ford | 9 | Engine | 3 |
| Ret | 27 | Mario Andretti | Parnelli-Ford | 9 | Suspension | 5 |
| Ret | 23 | Tony Brise | Hill-Ford | 5 | Accident | 17 |
| Ret | 15 | Michel Leclere | Tyrrell-Ford | 5 | Engine | 20 |
| Ret | 4 | P.Depailler | Tyrrell-Ford | 2 | Accident | 8 |
| Ret | 8 | Carlos Pace | Brabham-Ford | 2 | Accident | 16 |
| Ret | 21 | Jacques Laffite | Williams-Ford | 0 | Physical | 21 |
| Ret | 20 | Lella Lombardi | Williams-Ford | 0 | Ignition | 24 |

Winning speed: 116.098 mph Lap leaders: Lauda
Pole position: Lauda, 1m 42.003s, 119.185mph
Fastest lap: Fittipaldi, 1m 43.374s, 117.604mph

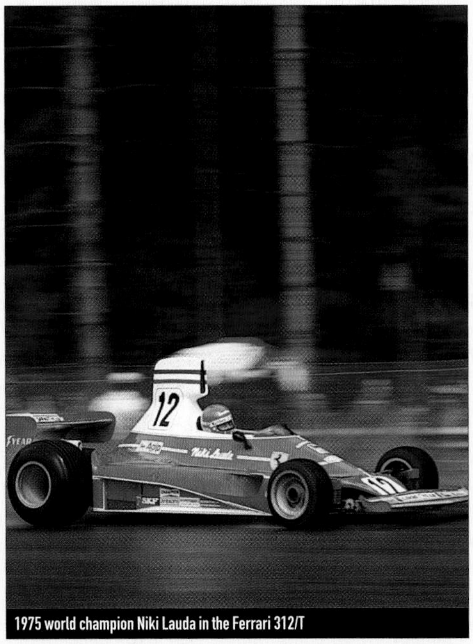

1975 world champion Niki Lauda in the Ferrari 312/T

# 1976

## DRIVERS' CHAMPION: JAMES HUNT
## CONSTRUCTORS' CHAMPION: FERRARI

### DRIVERS' CHAMPIONSHIP

| POS | DRIVER | COUNTRY | CAR | POINTS |
|---|---|---|---|---|
| 1 | James Hunt | GB | McLaren-Ford | 69 |
| 2 | Niki Lauda | Austria | Ferrari | 68 |
| 3 | Jody Scheckter | South Africa | Tyrrell-Ford | 49 |
| 4 | Patrick Depailler | France | Tyrrell-Ford | 39 |
| 5 | Gianclaudio Regazzoni | Switzerland | Ferrari | 31 |
| 6 | Mario Andretti | USA | Lotus-Ford, Parnelli-Ford | 22 |
| 7 | Jacques Laffite | France | Ligier-Matra | 20 |
| = | John Watson | GB | Penske-Ford | 20 |
| 9 | Jochen Mass | West Germany | McLaren-Ford | 19 |
| 10 | Gunnar Nilsson | Sweden | Lotus-Ford | 11 |
| 11 | Tom Pryce | GB | Shadow-Ford | 10 |
| = | Ronnie Peterson | Sweden | Lotus-Ford, March-Ford | 10 |
| 13 | Hans Stuck | West Germany | March-Ford | 8 |
| 14 | Carlos Pace | Brazil | Brabham-Alfa | 7 |
| 15 | Alan Jones | Australia | Surtees-Ford | 7 |
| 16 | Carlos Reutemann | Argentina | Brabham-Alfa, Ferrari | 3 |
| = | Emerson Fittipaldi | Brazil | Copersucar-Ford | 3 |
| 18 | Chris Amon | New Zealand | Ensign-Ford, Williams-Ford | 2 |
| 19 | Vittorio Brambilla | Italy | March-Ford | 1 |
| = | Rolf Stommelen | West Germany | Brabham-Alfa, Hesketh-Ford | 1 |
| | Jean-Pierre Jarier | France | Shadow-Ford | |
| | Jacky Ickx | Belgium | Williams-Ford, Ensign-Ford | |
| | Lella Lombardi | Italy | March-Ford, Brabham-Alfa | |
| | Ian Ashley | GB | BRM | |
| | Renzo Zorzi | Italy | Williams-Ford | |
| | Ingo Hoffman | Brazil | Copersucar-Ford | |
| | Harald Ertl | Austria | Hesketh-Ford | |
| | Brett Lunger | USA | Surtees-Ford | |
| | Michel Leclere | France | Williams-Ford | |
| | Bob Evans | GB | Lotus-Ford, Brabham-Ford | |
| | Ian Scheckter | South Africa | Tyrrell-Ford | |
| | Arturo Merzario | Italy | March-Ford, Williams-Ford | |
| | Larry Perkins | Australia | Boro-Ford, Brabham-Alfa | |
| | Loris Kessel | Switzerland | Brabham-Ford | |
| | Patrick Neve | Belgium | Brabham-Ford, March-Ford, Ensign-Ford | |
| | Henri Pescarolo | France | Surtees-Ford | |
| | Guy Edwards | GB | Hesketh-Ford | |
| | Sandro Presenti-Rossi | Italy | Tyrrell-Ford | |
| | Hans Binder | Austria | Ensign-Ford, Williams-Ford | |
| | Boy Hayje | Netherlands | Penske-Ford | |
| | Connie Andersson | Sweden | Surtees-Ford | |
| | Alex Ribeiro | Brazil | Hesketh-Ford | |
| | Warwick Brown | New Zealand | Williams-Ford | |
| | Noritake Takahara | Japan | Surtees-Ford | |
| | Masahiro Hasemi | Japan | Kojima-Ford | |
| | Kazuyoshi Hoshino | Japan | Tyrrell-Ford, Brabham-Ford | |
| | Emilio Zapico | Spain | Williams-Ford | |
| | Emilio Villota | Spain | March-Ford | |
| | Jac Nelleman | Denmark | March-Ford | |
| | Damien Magee | Australia | March-Ford | |
| | Otto Stuppacher | Austria | Tyrrell-Ford | |
| | Mazami Kuwashima | Japan | Williams-Ford | |
| | Tony Trimmer | GB | Maki-Ford | |
| | Mike Wilds | GB | Shadow-Ford | |
| | Divina Galica | GB | Surtees-Ford | |

Points for top six finishers (9, 6, 4, 3, 2, 1). Only the best seven scores from the first eight races and the best seven scores from the remaining eight races counted towards the championship.

### CONSTRUCTORS' CHAMPIONSHIP

| POS. | CONSTRUCTOR | POINTS |
|---|---|---|
| 1 | Ferrari | 83 |
| 2 | McLaren-Ford | 74 |
| 3 | Tyrrell-Ford | 71 |
| 4 | Lotus-Ford | 29 |
| 5 | Penske-Ford | 20 |
| 6 | Ligier-Matra | 20 |
| 7 | March-Ford | 19 |
| 8 | Shadow-Ford | 10 |
| 9 | Brabham-Alfa Romeo | 9 |
| 10 | Surtees-Ford | 7 |
| 11 | Fittipaldi-Ford | 3 |
| 12 | Ensign-Ford | 2 |
| 13 | Parnelli-Ford | 1 |

Points for top six finishers (9, 6, 4, 3, 2, 1). Points only counted for top-placed car for each constructor. Only the best seven scores from the first eight races and the best seven scores from the remaining eight races counted towards the championship

### BRAZILIAN GRAND PRIX: INTERLAGOS *25 January Round: 1 Race: 265 40 x 4.946miles*

| POS. | NO. | DRIVER | CAR-ENGINE | LAPS | TIME/RETIRED | GRID |
|---|---|---|---|---|---|---|
| 1 | 1 | Niki Lauda | Ferrari | 40 | 1:45'16.78 | 2 |
| 2 | 4 | P.Depailler | Tyrrell-Ford | 40 | +21.47 | 9 |
| 3 | 16 | Tom Pryce | Shadow-Ford | 40 | +23.84 | 12 |
| 4 | 34 | H.J.Stuck | March-Ford | 40 | +1'28.17 | 14 |
| 5 | 3 | Jody Scheckter | Tyrrell-Ford | 40 | +1'56.46 | 13 |
| 6 | 12 | Jochen Mass | McLaren-Ford | 40 | +1'58.27 | 6 |
| 7 | 2 | Clay Regazzoni | Ferrari | 40 | +2'15.24 | 4 |
| 8 | 20 | Jacky Ickx | Wolf-Williams-Ford | 39 | +1 Lap | 19 |
| 9 | 21 | Renzo Zorzi | Williams-Ford | 39 | +1 Lap | 17 |
| 10 | 8 | Carlos Pace | Brabham-Alfa Romeo | 39 | +1 Lap | 10 |
| 11 | 31 | Ingo Hoffman | Fittipaldi-Ford | 39 | +1 Lap | 20 |
| 12 | 7 | Carlos Reutemann | Brabham-Alfa Romeo | 37 | Out of fuel | 15 |
| 13 | 30 | Emerson Fittipaldi | Fittipaldi-Ford | 37 | +3 Laps | 5 |
| 14 | 10 | Lella Lombardi | March-Ford | 36 | +4 Laps | 22 |
| Ret | 17 | Jean-Pierre Jarier | Shadow-Ford | 33 | Accident | 3 |
| Ret | 11 | James Hunt | McLaren-Ford | 32 | Accident | 1 |
| Ret | 9 | V.Brambilla | March-Ford | 15 | Oil leak | 7 |
| Ret | 26 | Jacques Laffite | Ligier-Matra | 14 | Transmission | 11 |
| Ret | 5 | Ronnie Peterson | Lotus-Ford | 10 | Accident | 18 |
| Ret | 6 | Mario Andretti | Lotus-Ford | 6 | Accident | 16 |
| Ret | 28 | John Watson | Penske-Ford | 2 | Fuel system | 8 |
| Ret | 14 | Ian Ashley | BRM | 2 | Oil pump | 21 |

Winning speed: 112.754mph Lap leaders: Regazzoni 1-8, Lauda 9-40
Pole position: Hunt, 2m 32.500s, 116.761mph
Fastest lap: Jarier, 2m 35.070s, 114.826mph

### SOUTH AFRICAN GRAND PRIX: KYALAMI *6 March Round: 2 Race: 266 78 x 2.550miles*

| POS. | NO. | DRIVER | CAR-ENGINE | LAPS | TIME/RETIRED | GRID |
|---|---|---|---|---|---|---|
| 1 | 1 | Niki Lauda | Ferrari | 78 | 1:42'18.4 | 2 |
| 2 | 11 | James Hunt | McLaren-Ford | 78 | +1.3 | 1 |
| 3 | 12 | Jochen Mass | McLaren-Ford | 78 | +45.9 | 4 |
| 4 | 3 | Jody Scheckter | Tyrrell-Ford | 78 | +1'08.4 | 12 |
| 5 | 28 | John Watson | Penske-Ford | 77 | +1 Lap | 3 |
| 6 | 27 | Mario Andretti | Parnelli-Ford | 77 | +1 Lap | 13 |
| 7 | 16 | Tom Pryce | Shadow-Ford | 77 | +1 Lap | 7 |
| 8 | 9 | V.Brambilla | March-Ford | 77 | +1 Lap | 5 |
| 9 | 4 | P.Depailler | Tyrrell-Ford | 77 | +1 Lap | 6 |
| 10 | 5 | Bob Evans | Lotus-Ford | 77 | +1 Lap | 23 |
| 11 | 18 | Brett Lunger | Surtees-Ford | 77 | +1 Lap | 20 |
| 12 | 34 | H.J.Stuck | March-Ford | 76 | +2 Laps | 17 |
| 13 | 21 | Michel Leclere | Wolf-Williams-Ford | 76 | +2 Laps | 22 |
| 14 | 22 | Chris Amon | Ensign-Ford | 76 | +2 Laps | 18 |
| 15 | 24 | Harald Ertl | Hesketh-Ford | 74 | +4 Laps | 24 |
| 16 | 20 | Jacky Ickx | Wolf-Williams-Ford | 73 | +5 Laps | 19 |
| 17 | 30 | Emerson Fittipaldi | Fittipaldi-Ford | 70 | Engine | 21 |
| Ret | 2 | Clay Regazzoni | Ferrari | 52 | Engine | 9 |
| Ret | 26 | Jacques Laffite | Ligier-Matra | 49 | Engine | 8 |
| Ret | 17 | Jean-Pierre Jarier | Shadow-Ford | 28 | Radiator | 15 |
| Ret | 8 | Carlos Pace | Brabham-Alfa Romeo | 22 | Oil pressure | 14 |
| Ret | 6 | Gunnar Nilsson | Lotus-Ford | 18 | Clutch | 25 |
| Ret | 7 | Carlos Reutemann | Brabham-Alfa Romeo | 16 | Oil pressure | 11 |
| Ret | 10 | Ronnie Peterson | March-Ford | 15 | Accident | 10 |
| Ret | 15 | Ian Scheckter | Tyrrell-Ford | 0 | Accident | 16 |

Winning speed: 116.654mph Lap leaders: Lauda 1-78
Pole position: Hunt, 1m 16.100s, 120.636mph
Fastest lap: Lauda, 1m 17.970s, 117.743mph

### USA WEST GRAND PRIX: LONG BEACH *28 March Round: 3 Race: 267 80 x 2.020miles*

| POS. | NO. | DRIVER | CAR-ENGINE | LAPS | TIME/RETIRED | GRID |
|---|---|---|---|---|---|---|
| 1 | 2 | Clay Regazzoni | Ferrari | 80 | 1:53'18.471 | 1 |
| 2 | 1 | Niki Lauda | Ferrari | 80 | +42.414 | 4 |
| 3 | 4 | P.Depailler | Tyrrell-Ford | 80 | +49.972 | 2 |
| 4 | 26 | Jacques Laffite | Ligier-Matra | 80 | +1'12.828 | 12 |
| 5 | 12 | Jochen Mass | McLaren-Ford | 80 | +1'22.292 | 14 |
| 6 | 30 | Emerson Fittipaldi | Fittipaldi-Ford | 79 | +1 Lap | 16 |
| 7 | 17 | Jean-Pierre Jarier | Shadow-Ford | 79 | +1 Lap | 7 |
| 8 | 22 | Chris Amon | Ensign-Ford | 78 | +2 Laps | 17 |
| 9 | 8 | Carlos Pace | Brabham-Alfa Romeo | 77 | +3 Laps | 13 |
| 10 | 10 | Ronnie Peterson | March-Ford | 77 | +3 Laps | 6 |
| NC | 19 | Alan Jones | Surtees-Ford | 70 | Not classified | 19 |
| NC | 28 | John Watson | Penske-Ford | 69 | Not classified | 9 |
| Ret | 3 | Jody Scheckter | Tyrrell-Ford | 34 | Suspension | 11 |
| Ret | 16 | Tom Pryce | Shadow-Ford | 32 | Halfshaft | 5 |
| Ret | 27 | Mario Andretti | Parnelli-Ford | 15 | Water leak | 15 |
| Ret | 11 | James Hunt | McLaren-Ford | 3 | Accident | 3 |
| Ret | 34 | H.J.Stuck | March-Ford | 2 | Accident | 18 |
| Ret | 9 | V.Brambilla | March-Ford | 0 | Accident | 20 |
| Ret | 7 | Carlos Reutemann | Brabham-Alfa Romeo | 0 | Accident | 10 |
| Ret | 6 | Gunnar Nilsson | Lotus-Ford | 0 | Suspension | 8 |
| DNQ | 21 | Michel Leclere | Wolf-Williams-Ford | | | |
| DNQ | 31 | Ingo Hoffman | Fittipaldi-Ford | | | |
| DNQ | 35 | Arturo Merzario | March-Ford | | | |
| DNQ | 5 | Bob Evans | Lotus-Ford | | | |
| DNQ | 20 | Jacky Ickx | Wolf-Williams-Ford | | | |
| DNQ | 24 | Harald Ertl | Hesketh-Ford | | | |
| DNQ | 18 | Brett Lunger | Surtees-Ford | | | |

Winning speed: 85.582mph Lap leaders: Regazzoni 1-80
Pole position: Regazzoni, 1m 23.099s, 87.510mph
Fastest lap: Regazzoni, 1m 23.076s, 87.534mph

### SPANISH GRAND PRIX: JÁRAMA *2 May Round: 4 Race: 268 75 x 3.404miles*

| POS. | NO. | DRIVER | CAR-ENGINE | LAPS | TIME/RETIRED | GRID |
|---|---|---|---|---|---|---|
| 1 | 11 | James Hunt | McLaren-Ford | 75 | 1:42'20.43 | 1 |
| 2 | 1 | Niki Lauda | Ferrari | 75 | +30.97 | 2 |
| 3 | 6 | Gunnar Nilsson | Lotus-Ford | 75 | + 48.02 | 7 |
| 4 | 7 | Carlos Reutemann | Brabham-Alfa Romeo | 74 | +1 Lap | 12 |
| 5 | 22 | Chris Amon | Ensign-Ford | 74 | +1 Lap | 10 |
| 6 | 8 | Carlos Pace | Brabham-Alfa Romeo | 74 | +1 Lap | 11 |
| 7 | 20 | Jacky Ickx | Wolf-Williams-Ford | 74 | +1 Lap | 21 |
| 8 | 16 | Tom Pryce | Shadow-Ford | 74 | +1 Lap | 22 |
| 9 | 19 | Alan Jones | Surtees-Ford | 74 | +1 Lap | 20 |
| 10 | 21 | Michel Leclere | Wolf-Williams-Ford | 73 | +2 Laps | 23 |
| 11 | 2 | Clay Regazzoni | Ferrari | 72 | +3 Laps | 5 |
| 12 | 26 | Jacques Laffite | Ligier-Matra | 72 | +3 Laps | 8 |
| 13 | 37 | Larry Perkins | Boro-Ford | 72 | +3 Laps | 24 |
| Ret | 12 | Jochen Mass | McLaren-Ford | 65 | Engine | 4 |
| Ret | 17 | Jean-Pierre Jarier | Shadow-Ford | 61 | Electrical | 15 |
| Ret | 3 | Jody Scheckter | Tyrrell-Ford | 53 | Engine | 14 |
| Ret | 28 | John Watson | Penske-Ford | 51 | Engine | 13 |
| Ret | 35 | Arturo Merzario | March-Ford | 36 | Gearbox | 18 |
| Ret | 5 | Mario Andretti | Lotus-Ford | 34 | Gearbox | 9 |
| Ret | 4 | P.Depailler | Tyrrell-Ford | 25 | Accident | 3 |
| Ret | 9 | V.Brambilla | March-Ford | 21 | Suspension | 6 |
| Ret | 34 | H.J.Stuck | March-Ford | 16 | Gearbox | 17 |
| Ret | 10 | Ronnie Peterson | March-Ford | 11 | Transmission | 16 |
| Ret | 30 | Emerson Fittipaldi | Fittipaldi-Ford | 3 | Transmission | 19 |
| DNQ | 18 | Brett Lunger | Surtees-Ford | | | |
| DNQ | 32 | Loris Kessel | Brabham-Ford | | | |
| DNQ | 25 | Emilio Zapico | Williams-Ford | | | |
| DNQ | 33 | E.de Villota | Brabham-Ford | | | |
| DNQ | 24 | Harald Ertl | Hesketh-Ford | | | |
| DNQ | 31 | Ingo Hoffman | Fittipaldi-Ford | | | |

Winning speed: 93.005mph Lap leaders: Lauda 1-31, Hunt 32-75
Pole position: Hunt, 1m 18.520s, 96.976mph
Fastest lap: Mass, 1m 20.930s, 94.088mph

### BELGIAN GRAND PRIX: ZOLDER *16 May Round: 5 Race: 269 70 x 2.648miles*

| POS. | NO. | DRIVER | CAR-ENGINE | LAPS | TIME/RETIRED | GRID |
|---|---|---|---|---|---|---|
| 1 | 1 | Niki Lauda | Ferrari | 70 | 1:42'53.23 | 1 |
| 2 | 2 | Clay Regazzoni | Ferrari | 70 | +3.46 | 2 |
| 3 | 26 | Jacques Laffite | Ligier-Matra | 70 | +35.38 | 6 |
| 4 | 3 | Jody Scheckter | Tyrrell-Ford | 70 | +1'31.08 | 7 |
| 5 | 19 | Alan Jones | Surtees-Ford | 69 | +1 Lap | 16 |
| 6 | 12 | Jochen Mass | McLaren-Ford | 69 | +1 Lap | 18 |
| 7 | 28 | John Watson | Penske-Ford | 69 | +1 Lap | 17 |
| 8 | 37 | Larry Perkins | Boro-Ford | 69 | +1 Lap | 20 |
| 9 | 17 | Jean-Pierre Jarier | Shadow-Ford | 69 | +1 Lap | 14 |
| 10 | 16 | Tom Pryce | Shadow-Ford | 68 | +2 Laps | 13 |
| 11 | 21 | Michel Leclere | Wolf-Williams-Ford | 68 | +2 Laps | 25 |
| 12 | 32 | Loris Kessel | Brabham-Ford | 63 | +7 Laps | 23 |
| Ret | 18 | Brett Lunger | Surtees-Ford | 62 | Electrical | 26 |
| Ret | 8 | Carlos Pace | Brabham-Alfa Romeo | 58 | Electrical | 9 |
| Ret | 22 | Chris Amon | Ensign-Ford | 51 | Accident | 8 |
| Ret | 11 | James Hunt | McLaren-Ford | 35 | Gearbox | 3 |
| Ret | 34 | H.J.Stuck | March-Ford | 33 | Suspension | 15 |
| Ret | 24 | Harald Ertl | Hesketh-Ford | 31 | Engine | 24 |
| Ret | 4 | P.Depailler | Tyrrell-Ford | 29 | Engine | 4 |
| Ret | 5 | Mario Andretti | Lotus-Ford | 28 | Halfshaft | 11 |
| Ret | 33 | Patrick Neve | Brabham-Ford | 26 | Halfshaft | 19 |
| Ret | 35 | Arturo Merzario | March-Ford | 21 | Engine | 21 |
| Ret | 7 | Carlos Reutemann | Brabham-Alfa Romeo | 17 | Engine | 12 |
| Ret | 10 | Ronnie Peterson | March-Ford | 16 | Accident | 10 |
| Ret | 6 | Gunnar Nilsson | Lotus-Ford | 7 | Accident | 22 |
| Ret | 9 | V.Brambilla | March-Ford | 6 | Halfshaft | 5 |
| DNQ | 30 | Emerson Fittipaldi | Fittipaldi-Ford | | | |
| DNQ | 20 | Jacky Ickx | Wolf-Williams-Ford | | | |
| DNQ | 25 | Guy Edwards | Hesketh-Ford | | | |

Winning speed: 108.107mph Lap leaders: Lauda 1-70
Pole position: Lauda, 1m 26.550s, 110.154mph
Fastest lap: Lauda, 1m 25.980s, 110.884mph

### MONACO GRAND PRIX: MONTE CARLO *30 May Round: 6 Race: 270 78 x 2.058miles*

| POS. | NO. | DRIVER | CAR-ENGINE | LAPS | TIME/RETIRED | GRID |
|---|---|---|---|---|---|---|
| 1 | 1 | Niki Lauda | Ferrari | 78 | 1:59'51.47 | 1 |
| 2 | 3 | Jody Scheckter | Tyrrell-Ford | 78 | +11.13 | 5 |
| 3 | 4 | P.Depailler | Tyrrell-Ford | 78 | +1'04.84 | 4 |
| 4 | 34 | H.J.Stuck | March-Ford | 77 | +1 Lap | 6 |
| 5 | 12 | Jochen Mass | McLaren-Ford | 77 | +1 Lap | 11 |
| 6 | 30 | Emerson Fittipaldi | Fittipaldi-Ford | 77 | +1 Lap | 7 |
| 7 | 16 | Tom Pryce | Shadow-Ford | 77 | +1 Lap | 15 |
| 8 | 17 | Jean-Pierre Jarier | Shadow-Ford | 76 | +2 Laps | 10 |
| 9 | 8 | Carlos Pace | Brabham-Alfa Romeo | 76 | +2 Laps | 17 |
| 10 | 28 | John Watson | Penske-Ford | 76 | +2 Laps | 18 |
| 11 | 21 | Michel Leclere | Wolf-Williams-Ford | 76 | +2 Laps | 8 |
| 12 | 26 | Jacques Laffite | Ligier-Matra | 75 | Accident | 12 |
| 13 | 22 | Chris Amon | Ensign-Ford | 74 | +4 Laps | 2 |
| 14 | 2 | Clay Regazzoni | Ferrari | 73 | Accident | 16 |
| Ret | 6 | Gunnar Nilsson | Lotus-Ford | 39 | Engine | 3 |
| Ret | 10 | Ronnie Peterson | March-Ford | 26 | Accident | 14 |
| Ret | 11 | James Hunt | McLaren-Ford | 24 | Engine | 9 |
| Ret | 9 | V.Brambilla | March-Ford | 9 | Suspension | 19 |
| Ret | 19 | Alan Jones | Surtees-Ford | 1 | Collision | 20 |
| Ret | 7 | Carlos Reutemann | Brabham-Alfa Romeo | 0 | Accident | 21 |
| DNQ | 20 | Jacky Ickx | Wolf-Williams-Ford | | | |
| DNQ | 38 | Henri Pescarolo | Surtees-Ford | | | |
| DNQ | 37 | Larry Perkins | Boro-Ford | | | |
| DNQ | 24 | Harald Ertl | Hesketh-Ford | | | |
| DNQ | 35 | Arturo Merzario | March-Ford | | | |

Winning speed: 80.356mph Lap leaders: Lauda 1-78
Pole position: Lauda, 1m 29.650s, 82.641mph
Fastest lap: Regazzoni, 1m 30.280s, 82.064mph

### SWEDISH GRAND PRIX: ANDERSTORP *13 June Round: 7 Race: 271 72 x 2.497miles*

| POS. | NO. | DRIVER | CAR-ENGINE | LAPS | TIME/RETIRED | GRID |
|---|---|---|---|---|---|---|
| 1 | 3 | Jody Scheckter | Tyrrell-Ford | 72 | 1:46'53.729 | 1 |
| 2 | 4 | P.Depailler | Tyrrell-Ford | 72 | +19.766 | 4 |
| 3 | 1 | Niki Lauda | Ferrari | 72 | +33.866 | 5 |
| 4 | 26 | Jacques Laffite | Ligier-Matra | 72 | +55.819 | 7 |
| 5 | 11 | James Hunt | McLaren-Ford | 72 | +59.483 | 8 |
| 6 | 2 | Clay Regazzoni | Ferrari | 72 | +1'00.366 | 11 |
| 7 | 10 | Ronnie Peterson | March-Ford | 72 | +1'03.493 | 9 |
| 8 | 8 | Carlos Pace | Brabham-Alfa Romeo | 72 | +1'11.613 | 10 |
| 9 | 16 | Tom Pryce | Shadow-Ford | 71 | +1 Lap | 12 |
| 10 | 9 | V.Brambilla | March-Ford | 71 | +1 Lap | 15 |
| 11 | 12 | Jochen Mass | McLaren-Ford | 71 | +1 Lap | 13 |
| 12 | 17 | Jean-Pierre Jarier | Shadow-Ford | 71 | +1 Lap | 14 |
| 13 | 19 | Alan Jones | Surtees-Ford | 71 | +1 Lap | 18 |
| 14 | 35 | Arturo Merzario | March-Ford | 70 | Engine | 19 |
| 15 | 18 | Brett Lunger | Surtees-Ford | 70 | +2 Laps | 24 |
| Ret | 24 | Harald Ertl | Hesketh-Ford | 54 | Spun off | 23 |
| Ret | 34 | H.J.Stuck | March-Ford | 52 | Engine | 20 |
| Ret | 5 | Mario Andretti | Lotus-Ford | 45 | Engine | 2 |
| Ret | 22 | Chris Amon | Ensign-Ford | 38 | Accident | 3 |
| Ret | 21 | Michel Leclere | Wolf-Williams-Ford | 20 | Engine | 25 |
| Ret | 37 | Larry Perkins | Boro-Ford | 18 | Engine | 22 |
| Ret | 30 | Emerson Fittipaldi | Fittipaldi-Ford | 10 | Handling | 21 |
| Ret | 32 | Loris Kessel | Brabham-Ford | 5 | Accident | 26 |
| Ret | 6 | Gunnar Nilsson | Lotus-Ford | 2 | Accident | 6 |
| Ret | 7 | Carlos Reutemann | Brabham-Alfa Romeo | 2 | Engine | 16 |
| Ret | 28 | John Watson | Penske-Ford | 0 | Accident | 17 |
| DNQ | 33 | Jac Nelleman | Brabham-Ford | | | |

Winning speed: 100.899mph Lap leaders: Andretti 1-45, Scheckter 46-72
Pole position: Scheckter, 1m 25.659s, 104.928mph
Fastest lap: Andretti, 1m 28.002, 102.134mph

### FRENCH GRAND PRIX: PAUL RICARD *4 July Round: 8 Race: 272 54 x 3.610miles*

| POS. | NO. | DRIVER | CAR-ENGINE | LAPS | TIME/RETIRED | GRID |
|---|---|---|---|---|---|---|
| 1 | 11 | James Hunt | McLaren-Ford | 54 | 1:40'58.60 | 1 |
| 2 | 4 | P.Depailler | Tyrrell-Ford | 54 | +12.70 | 3 |
| 3 | 28 | John Watson | Penske-Ford | 54 | +23.55 | 8 |
| 4 | 8 | Carlos Pace | Brabham-Alfa Romeo | 54 | +24.82 | 5 |
| 5 | 5 | Mario Andretti | Lotus-Ford | 54 | +43.92 | 7 |
| 6 | 3 | Jody Scheckter | Tyrrell-Ford | 54 | +55.07 | 9 |
| 7 | 34 | H.J.Stuck | March-Ford | 54 | +1'21.55 | 17 |
| 8 | 16 | Tom Pryce | Shadow-Ford | 54 | +1'30.67 | 16 |
| 9 | 35 | Arturo Merzario | March-Ford | 54 | +1'53.57 | 20 |
| 10 | 20 | Jacky Ickx | Wolf-Williams-Ford | 53 | +1 Lap | 19 |
| 11 | 7 | Carlos Reutemann | Brabham-Alfa Romeo | 53 | +1 Lap | 10 |
| 12 | 17 | Jean-Pierre Jarier | Shadow-Ford | 53 | +1 Lap | 15 |
| 13 | 21 | Michel Leclere | Wolf-Williams-Ford | 53 | +1 Lap | 22 |
| 14 | 26 | Jacques Laffite | Ligier-Matra | 53 | +1 Lap | 13 |
| 15 | 12 | Jochen Mass | McLaren-Ford | 53 | +1 Lap | 14 |
| 16 | 18 | Brett Lunger | Surtees-Ford | 53 | +1 Lap | 23 |
| 17 | 25 | Guy Edwards | Hesketh-Ford | 53 | +1 Lap | 25 |
| 18 | 22 | Patrick Neve | Ensign-Ford | 53 | +1 Lap | 26 |
| 19 | 10 | Ronnie Peterson | March-Ford | 51 | Fuel system | 6 |
| Ret | 19 | Alan Jones | Surtees-Ford | 44 | Suspension | 18 |
| Ret | 9 | V.Brambilla | March-Ford | 28 | Oil pressure | 11 |
| Ret | 30 | Emerson Fittipaldi | Fittipaldi-Ford | 21 | Oil pressure | 21 |
| Ret | 38 | Henri Pescarolo | Surtees-Ford | 19 | Suspension | 24 |
| Ret | 2 | Clay Regazzoni | Ferrari | 17 | Engine | 4 |
| Ret | 1 | Niki Lauda | Ferrari | 8 | Engine | 2 |
| Ret | 6 | Gunnar Nilsson | Lotus-Ford | 8 | Gearbox | 12 |
| Ret | 24 | Harald Ertl | Hesketh-Ford | 4 | Differential | 29 |
| DNQ | 33 | Damien Magee | Brabham-Ford | | | |
| DNQ | 31 | Ingo Hoffman | Fittipaldi-Ford | | | |
| DNQ | 32 | Loris Kessel | Brabham-Ford | | | |

Winning speed: 115.838mph Lap leaders: Lauda 1-8, Hunt 9-54
Pole position: Hunt, 1m 47.890s, 120.462mph
Fastest lap: Lauda, 1m 51.000s, 117.086mph

### BRITISH GRAND PRIX: BRANDS HATCH *18 July Round: 9 Race: 273 76 x 2.614miles*

| POS. | NO. | DRIVER | CAR-ENGINE | LAPS | TIME/RETIRED | GRID |
|---|---|---|---|---|---|---|
| 1 | 1 | Niki Lauda | Ferrari | 76 | 1:44'19.66 | 2 |
| 2 | 3 | Jody Scheckter | Tyrrell-Ford | 76 | +16.18 | 1 |
| 3 | 28 | John Watson | Penske-Ford | 75 | +1 Lap | 8 |
| 4 | 16 | Tom Pryce | Shadow-Ford | 75 | +1 Lap | 11 |
| 5 | 19 | Alan Jones | Surtees-Ford | 75 | +1 Lap | 20 |
| 6 | 30 | Emerson Fittipaldi | Fittipaldi-Ford | 74 | +2 Laps | 19 |
| 7 | 24 | Harald Ertl | Hesketh-Ford | 73 | +3 Laps | 21 |
| 8 | 8 | Carlos Pace | Brabham-Alfa Romeo | 73 | +3 Laps | 24 |
| 9 | 17 | Jean-Pierre Jarier | Shadow-Ford | 70 | +6 Laps | 16 |
| DSQ | 11 | James Hunt | McLaren-Ford | 76 | Disqualified | 23 |
| Ret | 6 | Gunnar Nilsson | Lotus-Ford | 67 | Engine | 14 |
| Ret | 10 | Ronnie Peterson | March-Ford | 60 | Fuel system | 7 |
| Ret | 18 | Brett Lunger | Surtees-Ford | 55 | Gearbox | 18 |
| Ret | 4 | P.Depailler | Tyrrell-Ford | 47 | Engine | 5 |
| Ret | 7 | Carlos Reutemann | Brabham-Alfa Romeo | 46 | Oil pressure | 15 |
| Ret | 35 | Arturo Merzario | March-Ford | 39 | Engine | 9 |
| Ret | 2 | Clay Regazzoni | Ferrari | 36 | Oil pressure | 4 |
| Ret | 26 | Jacques Laffite | Ligier-Matra | 31 | Suspension | 13 |
| Ret | 32 | Bob Evans | Brabham-Ford | 24 | Gearbox | 22 |
| Ret | 9 | V.Brambilla | March-Ford | 22 | Accident | 10 |
| Ret | 38 | Henri Pescarolo | Surtees-Ford | 16 | Fuel system | 26 |
| Ret | 22 | Chris Amon | Ensign-Ford | 8 | Water leak | 6 |
| Ret | 5 | Mario Andretti | Lotus-Ford | 4 | Ignition | 3 |
| Ret | 12 | Jochen Mass | McLaren-Ford | 1 | Clutch | 12 |
| Ret | 34 | H.J.Stuck | March-Ford | 0 | Accident | 17 |
| Ret | 25 | Guy Edwards | Hesketh-Ford | 0 | Accident | 25 |
| Ret | 20 | Jacky Ickx | Wolf-Williams-Ford | | | |
| Ret | 13 | Divina Galica | Surtees-Ford | | | |
| Ret | 40 | Mike Wilds | Shadow-Ford | | | |
| Ret | 33 | Lella Lombardi | Brabham-Ford | | | |

Winning speed: 114.254mph Lap leaders: Lauda 1-44, Hunt 45-76
Pole position: Lauda, 1m 19.350s, 118.594mph
Fastest lap: Lauda, 1m 19.910s, 117.762mph
Restarted for original distance following first lap pile-up.

**GERMAN GRAND PRIX: NÜRBURGRING** *1 August Round: 10 Race: 274 14 x 14.189miles*

| POS. | NO. | DRIVER | CAR-ENGINE | LAPS | TIME/RETIRED | GRID |
|---|---|---|---|---|---|---|
| 1 | 11 | James Hunt | McLaren-Ford | 14 | 1:41'42.7 | 1 |
| 2 | 3 | Jody Scheckter | Tyrrell-Ford | 14 | +27.7 | 8 |
| 3 | 12 | Jochen Mass | McLaren-Ford | 14 | +52.4 | 9 |
| 4 | 8 | Carlos Pace | Brabham-Alfa Romeo | 14 | +54.2 | 7 |
| 5 | 6 | Gunnar Nilsson | Lotus-Ford | 14 | +1'57.3 | 16 |
| 6 | 77 | Rolf Stommelen | Brabham-Alfa Romeo | 14 | +2'30.3 | 15 |
| 7 | 28 | John Watson | Penske-Ford | 14 | + 2'33.9 | 19 |
| 8 | 16 | Tom Pryce | Shadow-Ford | 14 | + 2'48.2 | 18 |
| 9 | 2 | Clay Regazzoni | Ferrari | 14 | + 3'46.0 | 5 |
| 10 | 19 | Alan Jones | Surtees-Ford | 14 | +3'47.3 | 14 |
| 11 | 17 | Jean-Pierre Jarier | Shadow-Ford | 14 | +4'51.7 | 23 |
| 12 | 5 | Mario Andretti | Lotus-Ford | 14 | +4'58.1 | 12 |
| 13 | 30 | Emerson Fittipaldi | Fittipaldi-Ford | 14 | +5'25.2 | 20 |
| 14 | 40 | A.Pesenti-Rossi | Tyrrell-Ford | 13 | +1 Lap | 26 |
| 15 | 25 | Guy Edwards | Hesketh-Ford | 13 | +1 Lap | 25 |
| Ret | 20 | Arturo Merzario | Wolf-Williams-Ford | 3 | Brakes | 21 |
| Ret | 9 | V.Brambilla | March-Ford | 1 | Accident | 13 |
| Ret | 1 | Niki Lauda | Ferrari | 0 | Accident | 3 |
| Ret | 4 | P.Depailler | Tyrrell-Ford | 0 | Accident | 10 |
| Ret | 34 | H.J.Stuck | March-Ford | 0 | Clutch | 11 |
| Ret | 26 | Jacques Laffite | Ligier-Matra | 0 | Gearbox | 4 |
| Ret | 7 | Carlos Reutemann | Brabham-Alfa Romeo | 0 | Fuel system | 6 |
| Ret | 10 | Ronnie Peterson | March-Ford | 0 | Accident | 17 |
| Wth | 22 | Chris Amon | Ensign-Ford | 0 | Withdrew | 2 |
| Ret | 24 | Harald Ertl | Hesketh-Ford | 0 | Accident | 24 |
| Ret | 18 | Brett Lunger | Surtees-Ford | 0 | Accident | 22 |
| DNQ | 33 | Lella Lombardi | Brabham-Ford | | | |
| DNQ | 38 | Henri Pescarolo | Surtees-Ford | | | |

Winning speed: 117.182mph Lap leaders: Hunt 1-14
Pole position: Hunt, 7m 06.500s, 119.767mph
Fastest lap: Scheckter, 7m 10.800s, 118.571mph
Restarted for original distance following first lap accident.

**AUSTRIAN GRAND PRIX: ÖSTERREICHRING** *15 August Round: 11 Race: 275 54 x 3.672miles*

| POS. | NO. | DRIVER | CAR-ENGINE | LAPS | TIME/RETIRED | GRID |
|---|---|---|---|---|---|---|
| 1 | 28 | John Watson | Penske-Ford | 54 | 1:30'07.86 | 2 |
| 2 | 26 | Jacques Laffite | Ligier-Matra | 54 | +10.79 | 5 |
| 3 | 6 | Gunnar Nilsson | Lotus-Ford | 54 | +11.98 | 4 |
| 4 | 11 | James Hunt | McLaren-Ford | 54 | +12.44 | 1 |
| 5 | 5 | Mario Andretti | Lotus-Ford | 54 | +21.49 | 9 |
| 6 | 10 | Ronnie Peterson | March-Ford | 54 | +34.34 | 3 |
| 7 | 12 | Jochen Mass | McLaren-Ford | 54 | +59.45 | 12 |
| 8 | 24 | Harald Ertl | Hesketh-Ford | 53 | +1 Lap | 20 |
| 9 | 38 | Henri Pescarolo | Surtees-Ford | 52 | +2 Laps | 22 |
| 10 | 18 | Brett Lunger | Surtees-Ford | 51 | Accident | 16 |
| 11 | 39 | A.Pesenti-Rossi | Tyrrell-Ford | 51 | +3 Laps | 23 |
| 12 | 33 | Lella Lombardi | Brabham-Ford | 50 | +4 Laps | 24 |
| Ret | 22 | Hans Binder | Ensign-Ford | 47 | Throttle | 19 |
| NC | 32 | Loris Kessel | Brabham-Ford | 44 | Not classified | 25 |
| Ret | 9 | V.Brambilla | March-Ford | 43 | Accident | 7 |
| Ret | 30 | Emerson Fittipaldi | Fittipaldi-Ford | 43 | Accident | 17 |
| Ret | 8 | Carlos Pace | Brabham-Alfa Romeo | 40 | Accident | 18 |
| Ret | 17 | Jean-Pierre Jarier | Shadow-Ford | 40 | Fuel pump | 8 |
| Ret | 19 | Alan Jones | Surtees-Ford | 30 | Accident | 15 |
| Ret | 34 | H.J.Stuck | March-Ford | 26 | Fuel system | 11 |
| Ret | 4 | P.Depailler | Tyrrell-Ford | 24 | Suspension | 13 |
| Ret | 20 | Arturo Merzario | Wolf-Williams-Ford | 17 | Accident | 21 |
| Ret | 16 | Tom Pryce | Shadow-Ford | 14 | Brakes | 6 |
| Ret | 3 | Jody Scheckter | Tyrrell-Ford | 14 | Suspension | 10 |
| Ret | 7 | Carlos Reutemann | Brabham-Alfa Romeo | 1 | Clutch | 14 |

Winning speed: 132.011mph Lap leaders: Watson 1-2 12-54, Peterson 3-9 11, Scheckter 10
Pole position: Hunt, 1m 35.020s, 139.132mph
Fastest lap: Hunt, 1m 35.910s, 137.841mph

**DUTCH GRAND PRIX: ZANDVOORT** *29 August Round: 12 Race: 276 75 x 2.626miles*

| POS. | NO. | DRIVER | CAR-ENGINE | LAPS | TIME/RETIRED | GRID |
|---|---|---|---|---|---|---|
| 1 | 11 | James Hunt | McLaren-Ford | 75 | 1:44'52.09 | 2 |
| 2 | 2 | Clay Regazzoni | Ferrari | 75 | +0.92 | 5 |
| 3 | 5 | Mario Andretti | Lotus-Ford | 75 | +2.09 | 6 |
| 4 | 16 | Tom Pryce | Shadow-Ford | 75 | +6.94 | 3 |
| 5 | 3 | Jody Scheckter | Tyrrell-Ford | 75 | +22.46 | 8 |
| 6 | 9 | V.Brambilla | March-Ford | 75 | +45.03 | 7 |
| 7 | 4 | P.Depailler | Tyrrell-Ford | 75 | +56.28 | 14 |
| 8 | 19 | Alan Jones | Surtees-Ford | 74 | +1 Lap | 16 |
| 9 | 12 | Jochen Mass | McLaren-Ford | 74 | +1 Lap | 15 |
| 10 | 17 | Jean-Pierre Jarier | Shadow-Ford | 74 | +1 Lap | 20 |
| 11 | 38 | Henri Pescarolo | Surtees-Ford | 74 | +1 Lap | 22 |
| 12 | 35 | Rolf Stommelen | Hesketh-Ford | 72 | +3 Laps | 25 |
| Ret | 22 | Jacky Ickx | Ensign-Ford | 66 | Electrical | 11 |
| Ret | 39 | Boy Hayje | Penske-Ford | 63 | Halfshaft | 21 |
| Ret | 8 | Carlos Pace | Brabham-Alfa Romeo | 53 | Oil leak | 9 |
| Ret | 26 | Jacques Laffite | Ligier-Matra | 53 | Oil pressure | 10 |
| Ret | 10 | Ronnie Peterson | March-Ford | 52 | Oil pressure | 1 |
| Ret | 24 | Harald Ertl | Hesketh-Ford | 49 | Spun off | 24 |
| Ret | 28 | John Watson | Penske-Ford | 47 | Gearbox | 4 |
| Ret | 27 | Larry Perkins | Boro-Ford | 44 | Accident | 19 |
| Ret | 30 | Emerson Fittipaldi | Fittipaldi-Ford | 40 | Electrical | 17 |
| Ret | 7 | Carlos Reutemann | Brabham-Alfa Romeo | 11 | Clutch | 12 |
| Ret | 6 | Gunnar Nilsson | Lotus-Ford | 10 | Accident | 13 |
| Ret | 34 | H.J.Stuck | March-Ford | 9 | Engine | 26 |
| Ret | 18 | Conny Andersson | Surtees-Ford | 9 | Engine | 18 |
| Ret | 20 | Arturo Merzario | Wolf-Williams-Ford | 5 | Accident | 23 |
| DNQ | 40 | A.Pesenti-Rossi | Tyrrell-Ford | | | |

Winning speed: 112.342mph Lap leaders: Peterson 1-11, Hunt 12-75
Pole position: Peterson, 1m 21.310s, 116.262mph
Fastest lap: Regazzoni, 1m 22.590s, 114.461mph

**ITALIAN GRAND PRIX: MONZA** *12 September Round: 13 Race: 277 52 x 3.604miles*

| POS. | NO. | DRIVER | CAR-ENGINE | LAPS | TIME/RETIRED | GRID |
|---|---|---|---|---|---|---|
| 1 | 10 | Ronnie Peterson | March-Ford | 52 | 1:30'35.6 | 8 |
| 2 | 2 | Clay Regazzoni | Ferrari | 52 | +2.3 | 9 |
| 3 | 26 | Jacques Laffite | Ligier-Matra | 52 | +3.0 | 1 |
| 4 | 1 | Niki Lauda | Ferrari | 52 | +19.4 | 5 |
| 5 | 3 | Jody Scheckter | Tyrrell-Ford | 52 | +19.5 | 2 |
| 6 | 4 | P.Depailler | Tyrrell-Ford | 52 | +35.7 | 4 |
| 7 | 9 | V.Brambilla | March-Ford | 52 | +43.9 | 16 |
| 8 | 16 | Tom Pryce | Shadow-Ford | 52 | +52.9 | 15 |
| 9 | 35 | Carlos Reutemann | Ferrari | 52 | +57.5 | 7 |
| 10 | 22 | Jacky Ickx | Ensign-Ford | 52 | +1'12.4 | 10 |
| 11 | 28 | John Watson | Penske-Ford | 52 | +1'42.2 | 29 |
| 12 | 19 | Alan Jones | Surtees-Ford | 51 | +1 Lap | 18 |
| 13 | 6 | Gunnar Nilsson | Lotus-Ford | 51 | +1 Lap | 12 |
| 14 | 18 | Brett Lunger | Surtees-Ford | 50 | +2 Laps | 24 |
| 15 | 30 | Emerson Fittipaldi | Fittipaldi-Ford | 50 | +2 Laps | 20 |
| 16 | 24 | Harald Ertl | Hesketh-Ford | 49 | Halfshaft | 19 |
| 17 | 38 | Henri Pescarolo | Surtees-Ford | 49 | +3 Laps | 22 |
| 18 | 37 | A.Pesenti-Rossi | Tyrrell-Ford | 49 | +3 Laps | 21 |
| 19 | 17 | Jean-Pierre Jarier | Shadow-Ford | 47 | +5 Laps | 17 |
| Ret | 7 | Rolf Stommelen | Brabham-Alfa Romeo | 41 | Fuel system | 11 |
| Ret | 34 | H.J.Stuck | March-Ford | 23 | Accident | 6 |
| Ret | 5 | Mario Andretti | Lotus-Ford | 23 | Accident | 14 |
| Ret | 11 | James Hunt | McLaren-Ford | 11 | Spun off | 27 |
| Ret | 40 | Larry Perkins | Boro-Ford | 8 | Engine | 13 |
| Ret | 8 | Carlos Pace | Brabham-Alfa Romeo | 4 | Engine | 3 |
| Ret | 12 | Jochen Mass | McLaren-Ford | 2 | Ignition | 28 |
| DNS | 25 | Guy Edwards | Hesketh-Ford | 0 | Non starter | 23 |
| DNS | 20 | Arturo Merzario | Wolf-Williams-Ford | 0 | Non starter | |
| DNS | 39 | Otto Stuppacher | Tyrrell-Ford | 0 | Non starter | |

Winning speed: 124.119mph Lap leaders: Scheckter 1-10, Peterson 11-52
Pole position: Laffite, 1m 41.350s
Fastest lap: Peterson, 1m 41.300s

**CANADIAN GRAND PRIX: MOSPORT** *3 October Round: 14 Race: 278 80 x 2.459miles*

| POS. | NO. | DRIVER | CAR-ENGINE | LAPS | TIME/RETIRED | GRID |
|---|---|---|---|---|---|---|
| 1 | 11 | James Hunt | McLaren-Ford | 80 | 1:40'09.626 | 1 |
| 2 | 4 | P.Depailler | Tyrrell-Ford | 80 | +6.331 | 4 |
| 3 | 5 | Mario Andretti | Lotus-Ford | 80 | +10.366 | 5 |
| 4 | 3 | Jody Scheckter | Tyrrell-Ford | 80 | +19.745 | 7 |
| 5 | 12 | Jochen Mass | McLaren-Ford | 80 | +41.811 | 11 |
| 6 | 2 | Clay Regazzoni | Ferrari | 80 | +46.256 | 12 |
| 7 | 8 | Carlos Pace | Brabham-Alfa Romeo | 80 | +46.472 | 10 |
| 8 | 1 | Niki Lauda | Ferrari | 80 | +1'12.957 | 6 |
| 9 | 10 | Ronnie Peterson | March-Ford | 79 | +1 Lap | 2 |
| 10 | 28 | John Watson | Penske-Ford | 79 | +1 Lap | 14 |
| 11 | 16 | Tom Pryce | Shadow-Ford | 79 | +1 Lap | 13 |
| 12 | 6 | Gunnar Nilsson | Lotus-Ford | 79 | +1 Lap | 15 |
| 13 | 22 | Jacky Ickx | Ensign-Ford | 79 | +1 Lap | 16 |
| 14 | 9 | V.Brambilla | March-Ford | 79 | +1 Lap | 3 |
| 15 | 18 | Brett Lunger | Surtees-Ford | 78 | +2 Laps | 22 |
| 16 | 19 | Alan Jones | Surtees-Ford | 78 | +2 Laps | 20 |
| 17 | 7 | Larry Perkins | Brabham-Alfa Romeo | 78 | +2 Laps | 19 |
| 18 | 17 | Jean-Pierre Jarier | Shadow-Ford | 77 | +3 Laps | 18 |
| 19 | 38 | Henri Pescarolo | Surtees-Ford | 77 | +3 Laps | 21 |
| 20 | 25 | Guy Edwards | Hesketh-Ford | 75 | +5 Laps | 24 |
| Ret | 26 | Jacques Laffite | Ligier-Matra | 43 | Oil pressure | 9 |
| Ret | 30 | Emerson Fittipaldi | Fittipaldi-Ford | 41 | Exhaust | 17 |
| Ret | 34 | H.J.Stuck | March-Ford | 36 | Handling | 8 |
| Ret | 20 | Arturo Merzario | Wolf-Williams-Ford | 11 | Accident | 25 |
| DNQ | 39 | Otto Stuppacher | Tyrrell-Ford | | | |

Winning speed: 117.843mph Lap leaders: Peterson 1-8, Hunt 9-80
Pole position: Hunt, 1m 12.389s, 122.289mph
Fastest lap: Depailler, 1m 13.817s, 119.924mph

**USA EAST GRAND PRIX: WATKINS GLEN** *10 October Round: 15 Race: 279 59 x 5.435miles*

| POS. | NO. | DRIVER | CAR-ENGINE | LAPS | TIME/RETIRED | GRID |
|---|---|---|---|---|---|---|
| 1 | 11 | James Hunt | McLaren-Ford | 59 | 1:42'40.741 | 1 |
| 2 | 3 | Jody Scheckter | Tyrrell-Ford | 59 | +8.030 | 2 |
| 3 | 1 | Niki Lauda | Ferrari | 59 | +1'02.324 | 5 |
| 4 | 12 | Jochen Mass | McLaren-Ford | 59 | +1'02.458 | 17 |
| 5 | 34 | H.J.Stuck | March-Ford | 59 | +1'07.978 | 6 |
| 6 | 28 | John Watson | Penske-Ford | 59 | +1'08.190 | 8 |
| 7 | 2 | Clay Regazzoni | Ferrari | 58 | +1 Lap | 14 |
| 8 | 19 | Alan Jones | Surtees-Ford | 58 | +1 Lap | 18 |
| 9 | 30 | Emerson Fittipaldi | Fittipaldi-Ford | 57 | +2 Laps | 15 |
| 10 | 17 | Jean-Pierre Jarier | Shadow-Ford | 57 | +2 Laps | 16 |
| 11 | 18 | Brett Lunger | Surtees-Ford | 57 | +2 Laps | 24 |
| 12 | 25 | Alex Ribeiro | Hesketh-Ford | 57 | +2 Laps | 22 |
| 13 | 24 | Harald Ertl | Hesketh-Ford | 54 | +5 Laps | 21 |
| 14 | 21 | Warwick Brown | Wolf-Williams-Ford | 54 | +5 Laps | 23 |
| NC | 38 | Henri Pescarolo | Surtees-Ford | 48 | Not classified | 26 |
| Ret | 16 | Tom Pryce | Shadow-Ford | 45 | Engine | 9 |
| Ret | 9 | V.Brambilla | March-Ford | 34 | Tyre | 12 |
| Ret | 26 | Jacques Laffite | Ligier-Matra | 34 | Tyre | 4 |
| Ret | 8 | Carlos Pace | Brabham-Alfa Romeo | 31 | Collision | 10 |
| Ret | 7 | Larry Perkins | Brabham-Alfa Romeo | 30 | Suspension | 13 |
| Ret | 5 | Mario Andretti | Lotus-Ford | 23 | Suspension | 11 |
| Ret | 22 | Jacky Ickx | Ensign-Ford | 14 | Accident | 19 |
| Ret | 6 | Gunnar Nilsson | Lotus-Ford | 13 | Engine | 20 |
| Ret | 10 | Ronnie Peterson | March-Ford | 12 | Suspension | 3 |
| Ret | 20 | Arturo Merzario | Wolf-Williams-Ford | 9 | Accident | 25 |
| Ret | 4 | P.Depailler | Tyrrell-Ford | 7 | Fuel pipe | 7 |
| DNQ | 39 | Otto Stuppacher | Tyrrell-Ford | | | |

Winning speed: 116.427mph Lap leaders: Scheckter 1-36 41-45, Hunt 37-40 46-59
Pole position: Hunt, 1m 43.622s, 117.323mph
Fastest lap: Hunt, 1m 42.851s, 118.202mph

**JAPANESE GRAND PRIX: FUJI** *24 October Round: 16 Race: 280 73 x 2.709miles*

| POS. | NO. | DRIVER | CAR-ENGINE | LAPS | TIME/RETIRED | GRID |
|---|---|---|---|---|---|---|
| 1 | 5 | Mario Andretti | Lotus-Ford | 73 | 1:43'58.86 | 1 |
| 2 | 4 | P.Depailler | Tyrrell-Ford | 72 | +1 Lap | 13 |
| 3 | 11 | James Hunt | McLaren-Ford | 72 | +1 Lap | 2 |
| 4 | 19 | Alan Jones | Surtees-Ford | 72 | +1 Lap | 20 |
| 5 | 2 | Clay Regazzoni | Ferrari | 72 | +1 Lap | 7 |
| 6 | 6 | Gunnar Nilsson | Lotus-Ford | 72 | +1 Lap | 16 |
| 7 | 26 | Jacques Laffite | Ligier-Matra | 72 | +1 Lap | 11 |
| 8 | 24 | Harald Ertl | Hesketh-Ford | 72 | +1 Lap | 22 |
| 9 | 18 | N.Takahara | Surtees-Ford | 70 | +3 Laps | 24 |
| 10 | 17 | Jean-Pierre Jarier | Shadow-Ford | 69 | +4 Laps | 15 |
| 11 | 51 | Masahiro Hasemi | Kojima-Ford | 66 | +7 Laps | 10 |
| Ret | 3 | Jody Scheckter | Tyrrell-Ford | 58 | Overheating | 5 |
| Ret | 21 | Hans Binder | Wolf-Williams-Ford | 49 | Wheel | 25 |
| Ret | 16 | Tom Pryce | Shadow-Ford | 46 | Engine | 14 |
| Ret | 9 | V.Brambilla | March-Ford | 38 | Electrical | 8 |
| Ret | 34 | H.J.Stuck | March-Ford | 37 | Electrical | 18 |
| Ret | 12 | Jochen Mass | McLaren-Ford | 35 | Accident | 12 |
| Ret | 28 | John Watson | Penske-Ford | 33 | Engine | 4 |
| Ret | 52 | K.Hoshino | Tyrrell-Ford | 27 | Tyre | 21 |
| Ret | 20 | Arturo Merzario | Wolf-Williams-Ford | 23 | Gearbox | 19 |
| Wth | 30 | Emerson Fittipaldi | Fittipaldi-Ford | 9 | Withdrew | 23 |
| Wth | 8 | Carlos Pace | Brabham-Alfa Romeo | 7 | Withdrew | 6 |
| Wth | 1 | Niki Lauda | Ferrari | 2 | Withdrew | 3 |
| Wth | 7 | Larry Perkins | Brabham-Alfa Romeo | 1 | Withdrew | 17 |
| Ret | 10 | Ronnie Peterson | March-Ford | 0 | Engine | 9 |
| DNQ | 54 | Tony Trimmer | Maki-Ford | | | |

Winning speed: 114.093mph Lap leaders: Hunt 1-61, Depailler 62-63, Andretti 64-73
Pole position: Andretti, 1m 12.770s, 133.995mph
Fastest lap: Hasemi, 1m 18.230s, 124.643mph

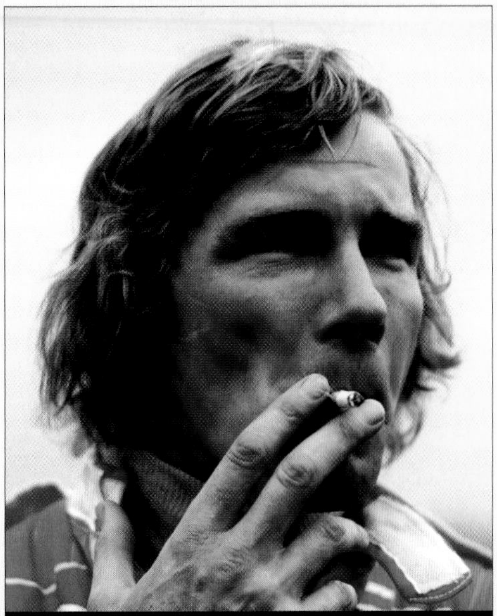
1976 world champion, James Hunt

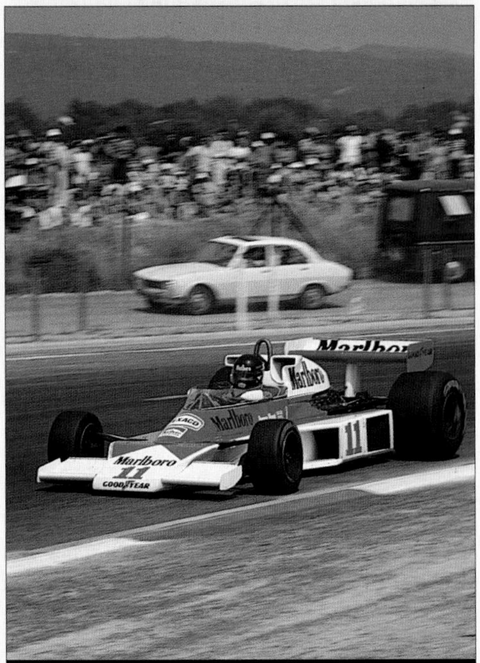

1976 world champion James Hunt in the M23 McLaren-Ford

# 1977

DRIVERS' CHAMPION: NIKI LAUDA
CONSTRUCTORS' CHAMPION: FERRARI

## DRIVERS' CHAMPIONSHIP

| POS | DRIVER | COUNTRY | CAR | POINTS |
|---|---|---|---|---|
| 1 | Niki Lauda | Austria | Ferrari | 72 |
| 2 | Jody Scheckter | South Africa | Wolf-Ford | 55 |
| 3 | Mario Andretti | USA | Lotus-Ford | 47 |
| 4 | Carlos Reutemann | Argentina | Ferrari | 42 |
| 5 | James Hunt | GB | McLaren-Ford | 40 |
| 6 | Jochen Mass | West Germany | McLaren-Ford | 25 |
| 7 | Alan Jones | Australia | Shadow-Ford | 22 |
| 8 | Gunnar Nilsson | Sweden | Lotus-Ford | 20 |
| = | Patrick Depailler | France | Tyrrell-Ford | 20 |
| 10 | Jacques Laffite | France | Ligier-Matra | 18 |
| 11 | Hans Stuck | West Germany | March-Ford, Brabham-Alfa Romeo | 12 |
| 12 | Emerson Fittipaldi | Brazil | Fittipaldi-Ford | 11 |
| 13 | John Watson | GB | Brabham-Alfa Romeo | 9 |
| 14 | Ronnie Peterson | Sweden | Tyrell-Ford | 7 |
| 15 | Carlos Pace | Brazil | Brabham-Alfa Romeo | 6 |
| = | Vittorio Brambilla | Italy | Surtees-Ford | 6 |
| 17 | Clay Regazzoni | Switzerland | Ensign-Ford | 5 |
| = | Patrick Tambay | France | Surtees-Ford, Ensign-Ford | 5 |
| 19 | Renzo Zorzi | Italy | Shadow-Ford | 1 |
| = | Jean-Pierre Jarier | France | Penske-Ford, Shadow-Ford, Ligier-Matra | 1 |
| = | Riccardo Patrese | Italy | Shadow-Ford | 1 |
| | Ian Scheckter | South Africa | March-Ford | |
| | Tom Pryce | GB | Shadow-Ford | |
| | Ingo Hoffman | Brazil | Fittipaldi-Ford | |
| | Hans Binder | Austria | Surtees-Ford, Penske-Ford | |
| | Larry Perkins | Australia | Stanley BRM, Surtees-Ford | |
| | Brett Lunger | USA | March-Ford, McLaren-Ford | |
| | Brian Henton | GB | March-Ford, Boro-Ensign-Ford | |
| | Patrick Neve | Belgium | March-Ford | |
| | Emilio de Villota | Spain | McLaren-Ford | |
| | Rupert Keegan | GB | Hesketh-Ford | |
| | Harald Ertl | Austria | Hesketh-Ford | |
| | Arturo Merzario | Italy | March-Ford, Shadow-Ford | |
| | Conny Andersson | Sweden | Stanley BRM | |
| | Jacky Ickx | Belgium | Ensign-Ford | |
| | David Purley | GB | Lec-Ford | |
| | Bernard de Dryver | Belgium | March-Ford | |
| | Jackie Oliver | GB | Shadow-Ford | |
| | Mikko Kozarowitsky | Finland | March-Ford | |
| | Gilles Villeneuve | Canada | McLaren-Ford | |
| | Vern Schuppan | Australia | Surtees-Ford | |
| | Jean-Pierre Jabouille | France | Renault | |
| | Brian McGuire | GB | McGuire-Ford | |
| | Guy Edwards | GB | Stanley BRM | |
| | Andy Sutcliffe | GB | March-Ford | |
| | Tony Trimmer | GB | Surtees-Ford | |
| | Hector Rebaque | Mexico | Hesketh-Ford | |
| | Hans Heyer | West Germany | Penske-Ford | |
| | Teddy Pilette | Belgium | Stanley BRM | |
| | Michael Bleekemolen | Netherland | March-Ford | |
| | Bruno Giacomelli | Italy | McLaren-Ford | |
| | Giorgio Francia | Italy | Brabham-Alfa Romeo | |
| | Loris Kessel | Switzerland | Williams-Ford | |
| | Ian Ashley | GB | Hesketh-Ford | |
| | Danny Ongais | USA | Penske-Ford | |
| | Kunimitsu Takahashi | Japan | Tyrrell-Ford | |
| | Kazuyoshi Hoshino | Japan | Kojima-Ford | |
| | Noritake Takahara | Japan | Kojima-Ford | |
| | Lamberto Leoni | Italy | Surtees-Ford | |
| | Hans Binder | Austria | Penske-Ford | |

Points for top six finishers (9, 6, 4, 3, 2, 1). Only the best eight scores from the first nine races and the best seven scores from the remaining eight races counted towards the championship.

## CONSTRUCTORS' CHAMPIONSHIP

| POS. | CONSTRUCTOR | POINTS |
|---|---|---|
| 1 | Ferrari | 95 |
| 2 | Lotus-Ford | 62 |
| 3 | McLaren-Ford | 60 |
| 4 | Wolf-Ford | 55 |
| 5 | Brabham-Alfa Romeo | 27 |
| 6 | Tyrrell-Ford | 27 |
| 7 | Shadow-Ford | 23 |
| 8 | Ligier-Matra | 18 |
| 9 | Fittipaldi-Ford | 11 |
| 10 | Ensign-Ford | 10 |
| 11 | Surtees-Ford | 6 |
| 12 | Penske-Ford | 1 |

Points for top six finishers (9, 6, 4, 3, 2, 1). Points only counted for top-placed car for each constructor. Only the best seven scores from the first eight races and the best seven scores from the remaining eight races counted towards the championship

## ARGENTINE GRAND PRIX: BUENOS AIRES *9 January Round: 1 Race: 281 53 x 3.708 miles*

| POS. | NO. | DRIVER | CAR-ENGINE | LAPS | TIME/RETIRED | GRID |
|---|---|---|---|---|---|---|
| 1 | 20 | Jody Scheckter | Wolf-Ford | 53 | 1:40'11.19 | 11 |
| 2 | 8 | Carlos Pace | Brabham-Alfa Romeo | 53 | +43.24 | 10 |
| 3 | 12 | Carlos Reutemann | Ferrari | 53 | +46.02 | 7 |
| 4 | 28 | Emerson Fittipaldi | Fittipaldi-Ford | 53 | +55.48 | 16 |
| 5 | 5 | Mario Andretti | Lotus-Ford | 51 | Wheel bearing | 8 |
| 6 | 22 | Clay Regazzoni | Ensign-Ford | 51 | +2 Laps | 12 |
| 7 | 19 | V.Brambilla | Surtees-Ford | 48 | Out of fuel | 13 |
| Ret | 10 | Ian Scheckter | March-Ford | 45 | Electrical | 17 |
| NC | 16 | Tom Pryce | Shadow-Ford | 45 | Not classified | 9 |
| Ret | 7 | John Watson | Brabham-Alfa Romeo | 41 | Suspension | 2 |
| Ret | 9 | Alex Ribeiro | March-Ford | 39 | Transmission | 20 |
| NC | 26 | Jacques Laffite | Ligier-Matra | 37 | Not classified | 15 |
| Ret | 4 | P.Depailler | Tyrrell-Ford | 32 | Overheating | 3 |
| Ret | 1 | James Hunt | McLaren-Ford | 31 | Suspension | 1 |
| Ret | 2 | Jochen Mass | McLaren-Ford | 28 | Spun off | 5 |
| Ret | 3 | Ronnie Peterson | Tyrrell-Ford | 28 | Spun off | 14 |
| Ret | 29 | Ingo Hoffman | Fittipaldi-Ford | 22 | Engine | 19 |
| Ret | 11 | Niki Lauda | Ferrari | 20 | Fuel system | 4 |
| Ret | 18 | Hans Binder | Surtees-Ford | 18 | Accident | 18 |
| Ret | 17 | Renzo Zorzi | Shadow-Ford | 2 | Gearbox | 21 |

Winning speed: 117.706mph
Lap leaders: Watson 1-10; Hunt 11-31; Pace 35-47; Scheckter 48-53
Pole position: Hunt, 1m48.680s, 122.838mph
Fastest lap: Hunt, 1m51.060s, 120.206mph

## BRAZILIAN GRAND PRIX: INTERLAGOS *23 January Round: 2 Race: 282 40 x 4.946 miles*

| POS. | NO. | DRIVER | CAR-ENGINE | LAPS | TIME/RETIRED | GRID |
|---|---|---|---|---|---|---|
| 1 | 12 | Carlos Reutemann | Ferrari | 40 | 1:45'07.72 | 2 |
| 2 | 1 | James Hunt | McLaren-Ford | 40 | +10.71 | 1 |
| 3 | 11 | Niki Lauda | Ferrari | 40 | +1'47.51 | 13 |
| 4 | 28 | Emerson Fittipaldi | Fittipaldi-Ford | 39 | +1 Lap | 16 |
| 5 | 6 | Gunnar Nilsson | Lotus-Ford | 39 | +1 Lap | 10 |
| 6 | 17 | Renzo Zorzi | Shadow-Ford | 39 | +1 Lap | 18 |
| 7 | 29 | Ingo Hoffman | Fittipaldi-Ford | 38 | +2 Laps | 19 |
| Ret | 8 | Carlos Pace | Brabham-Alfa Romeo | 33 | Accident | 12 |
| Ret | 16 | Tom Pryce | Shadow-Ford | 33 | Engine | 5 |
| Ret | 18 | Hans Binder | Surtees-Ford | 32 | Suspension | 20 |
| Ret | 7 | John Watson | Brabham-Alfa Romeo | 30 | Accident | 7 |
| Ret | 26 | Jacques Laffite | Ligier-Matra | 26 | Accident | 14 |
| Ret | 4 | P.Depailler | Tyrrell-Ford | 23 | Accident | 6 |
| Ret | 5 | Mario Andretti | Lotus-Ford | 19 | Ignition | 3 |
| Ret | 9 | Alex Ribeiro | March-Ford | 16 | Engine | 21 |
| Ret | 2 | Jochen Mass | McLaren-Ford | 12 | Accident | 4 |
| Ret | 3 | Ronnie Peterson | Tyrrell-Ford | 12 | Accident | 8 |
| Ret | 22 | Clay Regazzoni | Ensign-Ford | 12 | Accident | 9 |
| Ret | 19 | V.Brambilla | Surtees-Ford | 11 | Accident | 11 |
| Ret | 20 | Jody Scheckter | Wolf-Ford | 11 | Engine | 15 |
| Ret | 10 | Ian Scheckter | March-Ford | 1 | Transmission | 17 |
| Ret | 14 | Larry Perkins | BRM | 1 | Overheating | 22 |

Winning speed: 112.916mph Lap leaders: Pace 1-6; Hunt 7-22; Reutemann 23-40
Pole position: Hunt, 2m30.110s, 118.620mph
Fastest lap: Hunt, 2m34.550s, 115.212mph

## SOUTH AFRICAN GRAND PRIX: KYALAMI *5 March Round: 3 Race: 283 78 x 2.550miles*

| POS. | NO. | DRIVER | CAR-ENGINE | LAPS | TIME/RETIRED | GRID |
|---|---|---|---|---|---|---|
| 1 | 11 | Niki Lauda | Ferrari | 78 | 1:42'21.6 | 3 |
| 2 | 20 | Jody Scheckter | Wolf-Ford | 78 | +5.2 | 5 |
| 3 | 4 | P.Depailler | Tyrrell-Ford | 78 | +5.7 | 4 |
| 4 | 1 | James Hunt | McLaren-Ford | 78 | +9.5 | 1 |
| 5 | 2 | Jochen Mass | McLaren-Ford | 78 | +19.9 | 12 |
| 6 | 7 | John Watson | Brabham-Alfa Romeo | 78 | +20.2 | 11 |
| 7 | 19 | V.Brambilla | Surtees-Ford | 78 | +23.6 | 14 |
| 8 | 12 | Carlos Reutemann | Ferrari | 78 | +26.7 | 8 |
| 9 | 22 | Clay Regazzoni | Ensign-Ford | 78 | +46.2 | 16 |
| 10 | 28 | Emerson Fittipaldi | Fittipaldi-Ford | 78 | +1'11.7 | 9 |
| 11 | 18 | Hans Binder | Surtees-Ford | 77 | +1 Lap | 19 |
| 12 | 6 | Gunnar Nilsson | Lotus-Ford | 77 | +1 Lap | 10 |
| 13 | 8 | Carlos Pace | Brabham-Alfa Romeo | 76 | +2 Laps | 2 |
| 14 | 30 | Brett Lunger | March-Ford | 76 | +2 Laps | 23 |
| 15 | 14 | Larry Perkins | BRM | 73 | +5 Laps | 22 |
| Ret | 9 | Alex Ribeiro | March-Ford | 66 | Engine | 17 |
| Ret | 10 | H.J.Stuck | March-Ford | 55 | Engine | 18 |
| Ret | 5 | Mario Andretti | Lotus-Ford | 43 | Accident | 6 |
| Ret | 33 | Boy Hayje | March-Ford | 33 | Gearbox | 21 |
| Ret | 26 | Jacques Laffite | Ligier-Matra | 22 | Accident | 12 |
| Ret | 16 | Tom Pryce | Shadow-Ford | 22 | Fatal accident | 15 |
| Ret | 17 | Renzo Zorzi | Shadow-Ford | 21 | Fuel leak | 20 |
| Ret | 3 | Ronnie Peterson | Tyrrell-Ford | 5 | Fuel system | 7 |

Winning speed: 112.916mph Lap leaders: Hunt 1-6; Lauda 7-78
Pole position: Hunt, 1m15.960s, 120.858mph
Fastest lap: Watson, 1m17.630s, 118.258mph

## USA WEST GRAND PRIX: LONG BEACH *3 April Round: 4 Race: 284 80 x 2.020miles*

| POS. | NO. | DRIVER | CAR-ENGINE | LAPS | TIME/RETIRED | GRID |
|---|---|---|---|---|---|---|
| 1 | 5 | Mario Andretti | Lotus-Ford | 80 | 1:51'35.470 | 2 |
| 2 | 11 | Niki Lauda | Ferrari | 80 | +0.773 | 1 |
| 3 | 20 | Jody Scheckter | Wolf-Ford | 80 | +4.857 | 3 |
| 4 | 4 | P.Depailler | Tyrrell-Ford | 80 | +1'14.487 | 12 |
| 5 | 28 | Emerson Fittipaldi | Fittipaldi-Ford | 80 | +1'20.908 | 7 |
| 6 | 34 | Jean-Pierre Jarier | Penske-Ford | 79 | +1 Lap | 9 |
| 7 | 1 | James Hunt | McLaren-Ford | 79 | +1 Lap | 8 |
| 8 | 6 | Gunnar Nilsson | Lotus-Ford | 79 | +1 Lap | 16 |
| 9 | 26 | Jacques Laffite | Ligier-Matra | 78 | Electrical | 5 |
| 10 | 10 | Brian Henton | March-Ford | 77 | +3 Laps | 18 |
| 11 | 18 | Hans Binder | Surtees-Ford | 77 | +3 Laps | 19 |
| Ret | 3 | Ronnie Peterson | Tyrrell-Ford | 62 | Fuel system | 10 |
| Ret | 22 | Clay Regazzoni | Ensign-Ford | 57 | Gearbox | 13 |
| Ret | 8 | H.J.Stuck | Brabham-Alfa Romeo | 53 | Brakes | 17 |
| Ret | 17 | Alan Jones | Shadow-Ford | 40 | Gearbox | 14 |
| Ret | 2 | Jochen Mass | McLaren-Ford | 39 | Handling | 15 |
| DSQ | 7 | John Watson | Brabham-Alfa Romeo | 33 | Disqualified | 6 |
| Ret | 16 | Renzo Zorzi | Shadow-Ford | 27 | Gearbox | 20 |
| Ret | 9 | Alex Ribeiro | March-Ford | 15 | Gearbox | 22 |
| Ret | 12 | Carlos Reutemann | Ferrari | 5 | Accident | 4 |
| Ret | 30 | Brett Lunger | March-Ford | 4 | Accident | 21 |
| Ret | 19 | V.Brambilla | Surtees-Ford | 0 | Accident | 11 |

Winning speed: 86.889mph Lap leaders: Scheckter 1-76; Andretti 77-80
Pole position: Lauda, 1m21.650s, 89.063mph
Fastest lap: Lauda, 1m22.753s, 87.876mph

## SPANISH GRAND PRIX: JARAMA *8 May Round 5 Race 285 75 x 2.115miles*

| POS. | NO. | DRIVER | CAR-ENGINE | LAPS | TIME/RETIRED | GRID |
|---|---|---|---|---|---|---|
| 1 | 5 | Mario Andretti | Lotus-Ford | 75 | 1:42'52.22 | 1 |
| 2 | 12 | Carlos Reutemann | Ferrari | 75 | +15.85 | 4 |
| 3 | 20 | Jody Scheckter | Wolf-Ford | 75 | +24.51 | 5 |
| 4 | 2 | Jochen Mass | McLaren-Ford | 75 | +24.87 | 9 |
| 5 | 6 | Gunnar Nilsson | Lotus-Ford | 75 | +1'05.83 | 12 |
| 6 | 8 | H.J.Stuck | Brabham-Alfa Romeo | 74 | +1 Lap | 13 |
| 7 | 26 | Jacques Laffite | Ligier-Matra | 74 | +1 Lap | 2 |
| 8 | 3 | Ronnie Peterson | Tyrrell-Ford | 74 | +1 Lap | 15 |
| 9 | 18 | Hans Binder | Surtees-Ford | 73 | +2 Laps | 20 |
| 10 | 30 | Brett Lunger | March-Ford | 72 | +3 Laps | 25 |
| 11 | 10 | Ian Scheckter | March-Ford | 72 | +3 Laps | 17 |
| 12 | 27 | Patrick Neve | March-Ford | 71 | +4 Laps | 22 |
| 13 | 36 | E.de Villota | McLaren-Ford | 70 | +5 Laps | 23 |
| 14 | 28 | Emerson Fittipaldi | Fittipaldi-Ford | 70 | +5 Laps | 19 |
| Ret | 7 | John Watson | Brabham-Alfa Romeo | 64 | Fuel system | 6 |
| Ret | 17 | Alan Jones | Shadow-Ford | 56 | Accident | 14 |
| Ret | 24 | Rupert Keegan | Hesketh-Ford | 32 | Accident | 16 |
| Ret | 25 | Harald Ertl | Hesketh-Ford | 29 | Radiator | 18 |
| Ret | 16 | Renzo Zorzi | Shadow-Ford | 25 | Engine | 24 |
| Ret | 37 | Arturo Merzario | March-Ford | 16 | Suspension | 21 |
| Ret | 4 | P.Depailler | Tyrrell-Ford | 12 | Engine | 10 |
| Ret | 1 | James Hunt | McLaren-Ford | 10 | Engine | 7 |
| Ret | 22 | Clay Regazzoni | Ensign-Ford | 9 | Accident | 8 |
| Ret | 19 | V.Brambilla | Surtees-Ford | 9 | Accident | 11 |
| Ret | 11 | Niki Lauda | Ferrari | 0 | Injured | 3 |
| DNQ | 34 | Jean-Pierre Jarier | Penske-Ford | | | |
| DNQ | 9 | Alex Ribeiro | March-Ford | | | |
| DNQ | 33 | Boy Hayje | March-Ford | | | |
| DNQ | 38 | Brian Henton | March-Ford | | | |
| DNQ | 31 | David Purley | LEC-Ford | | | |
| DNQ | 35 | Conny Andersson | BRM | | | |

Winning speed: 92..526mph Lap leaders: Andretti 1-75
Pole position: Andretti, 1m18.700s, 96.754mph
Fastest lap: Laffite, 1m20.810s, 94.228mph

## MONACO GRAND PRIX: MONTE CARLO *22 May Round: 6 Race: 286 76 x 2.058 miles*

| POS. | NO. | DRIVER | CAR-ENGINE | LAPS | TIME/RETIRED | GRID |
|---|---|---|---|---|---|---|
| 1 | 20 | Jody Scheckter | Wolf-Ford | 76 | 1:57'52.77 | 2 |
| 2 | 11 | Niki Lauda | Ferrari | 76 | +0.89 | 6 |
| 3 | 12 | Carlos Reutemann | Ferrari | 76 | +32.80 | 3 |
| 4 | 2 | Jochen Mass | McLaren-Ford | 76 | +34.60 | 9 |
| 5 | 5 | Mario Andretti | Lotus-Ford | 76 | +35.55 | 10 |
| 6 | 17 | Alan Jones | Shadow-Ford | 76 | +36.61 | 11 |
| 7 | 26 | Jacques Laffite | Ligier-Matra | 76 | +1'04.44 | 16 |
| 8 | 19 | V.Brambilla | Surtees-Ford | 76 | +1'08.64 | 14 |
| 9 | 16 | Riccardo Patrese | Shadow-Ford | 75 | +1 Lap | 15 |
| 10 | 22 | Jacky Ickx | Ensign-Ford | 75 | +1 Lap | 17 |
| 11 | 34 | Jean-Pierre Jarier | Penske-Ford | 74 | +2 Laps | 12 |
| 12 | 24 | Rupert Keegan | Hesketh-Ford | 73 | +3 Laps | 20 |
| Ret | 6 | Gunnar Nilsson | Lotus-Ford | 51 | Gearbox | 13 |
| Ret | 7 | John Watson | Brabham-Alfa Romeo | 48 | Gearbox | 1 |
| Ret | 4 | P.Depailler | Tyrrell-Ford | 46 | Gearbox | 8 |
| Ret | 18 | Hans Binder | Surtees-Ford | 41 | Fuel system | 19 |
| Ret | 28 | Emerson Fittipaldi | Fittipaldi-Ford | 37 | Engine | 18 |
| Ret | 1 | James Hunt | McLaren-Ford | 25 | Engine | 7 |
| Ret | 8 | H.J.Stuck | Brabham-Alfa Romeo | 19 | Electrical | 5 |
| Ret | 3 | Ronnie Peterson | Tyrrell-Ford | 10 | Brakes | 4 |
| DNQ | 37 | Arturo Merzario | March-Ford | | | |
| DNQ | 33 | Boy Hayje | March-Ford | | | |
| DNQ | 25 | Harald Ertl | Hesketh-Ford | | | |
| DNQ | 22 | Clay Regazzoni | Ensign-Ford | | | |
| DNQ | 9 | Alex Ribeiro | March-Ford | | | |
| DNQ | 10 | Ian Scheckter | March-Ford | | | |

Winning speed: 79.610mph Lap leaders: Scheckter 1-76
Pole position: Watson, 1m 29.860s, 82.448mph
Fastest lap: Scheckter, 1m 31.070s, 81.352mph

# 1977 Season Statistics

**BELGIAN GRAND PRIX: ZOLDER** *5 June Round: 7 Race: 287 70 x 2.648 miles*

| POS. | NO. | DRIVER | CAR-ENGINE | LAPS | TIME/RETIRED | GRID |
|---|---|---|---|---|---|---|
| 1 | 6 | Gunnar Nilsson | Lotus-Ford | 70 | 1:55'05.71 | 3 |
| 2 | 11 | Niki Lauda | Ferrari | 70 | +14.19 | 11 |
| 3 | 3 | Ronnie Peterson | Tyrrell-Ford | 70 | +19.95 | 8 |
| 4 | 19 | V.Brambilla | Surtees-Ford | 70 | +24.98 | 12 |
| 5 | 17 | Alan Jones | Shadow-Ford | 70 | +1'15.47 | 17 |
| 6 | 8 | H.J.Stuck | Brabham-Alfa Romeo | 69 | +1 Lap | 18 |
| 7 | 1 | James Hunt | McLaren-Ford | 69 | +1 Lap | 9 |
| 8 | 4 | P.Depailler | Tyrrell-Ford | 69 | +1 Lap | 5 |
| 9 | 25 | Harald Ertl | Hesketh-Ford | 69 | +1 Lap | 25 |
| 10 | 27 | Patrick Neve | March-Ford | 68 | +2 Laps | 24 |
| 11 | 34 | Jean-Pierre Jarier | Penske-Ford | 68 | +2 Laps | 26 |
| 12 | 18 | Larry Perkins | Surtees-Ford | 67 | +3 Laps | 23 |
| 13 | 31 | David Purley | LEC-Ford | 67 | +3 Laps | 20 |
| 14 | 37 | Arturo Merzario | March-Ford | 65 | +5 Laps | 14 |
| NC | 33 | Boy Hayje | March-Ford | 63 | Not classified | 27 |
| Ret | 20 | Jody Scheckter | Wolf-Ford | 62 | Engine | 4 |
| Ret | 2 | Jochen Mass | McLaren-Ford | 39 | Accident | 6 |
| Ret | 26 | Jacques Laffite | Ligier-Matra | 32 | Engine | 10 |
| Ret | 22 | Clay Regazzoni | Ensign-Ford | 29 | Engine | 13 |
| Ret | 12 | Carlos Reutemann | Ferrari | 14 | Accident | 19 |
| Ret | 24 | Rupert Keegan | Hesketh-Ford | 14 | Accident | 7 |
| Ret | 16 | Riccardo Patrese | Shadow-Ford | 12 | Accident | 15 |
| Ret | 10 | Ian Scheckter | March-Ford | 8 | Accident | 21 |
| Ret | 28 | Emerson Fittipaldi | Fittipaldi-Ford | 2 | Electrical | 16 |
| Ret | 5 | Mario Andretti | Lotus-Ford | 0 | Accident | 1 |
| Ret | 7 | John Watson | Brabham-Alfa Romeo | 0 | Accident | 2 |
| DNQ | 36 | E.de Villota | McLaren-Ford | | | |
| DNQ | 9 | Alex Ribeiro | March-Ford | | | |
| DNQ | 35 | Conny Andersson | BRM | | | |
| DNQ | 38 | B.de Dryver | March-Ford | | | |
| DNQ | 39 | Hector Rebaque | Hesketh-Ford | | | |

Winning speed: 96.640mph Lap leaders: Scheckter 1-16; Mass 17-18; Lauda 23-49; Brambilla 19-22; Nilsson 50-70
Pole position: Adretti, 1m 24.640s, 112.640mph
Fastest lap: Nilsson, 1m 27.540s, 108.908mph

**SWEDISH GRAND PRIX: ANDERSTORP** *19 June Round: 8 Race: 238 72 x 2.497 miles*

| POS. | NO. | DRIVER | CAR-ENGINE | LAPS | TIME/RETIRED | GRID |
|---|---|---|---|---|---|---|
| 1 | 26 | Jacques Laffite | Ligier-Matra | 72 | 1:46'55.520 | 8 |
| 2 | 2 | Jochen Mass | McLaren-Ford | 72 | +8.449 | 9 |
| 3 | 12 | Carlos Reutemann | Ferrari | 72 | +14.369 | 12 |
| 4 | 4 | P.Depailler | Tyrrell-Ford | 72 | +16.308 | 6 |
| 5 | 7 | John Watson | Brabham-Alfa Romeo | 72 | +18.735 | 2 |
| 6 | 5 | Mario Andretti | Lotus-Ford | 72 | +25.277 | 1 |
| 7 | 22 | Clay Regazzoni | Ensign-Ford | 72 | +31.266 | 14 |
| 8 | 34 | Jean-Pierre Jarier | Penske-Ford | 72 | +1'04.567 | 17 |
| 9 | 16 | Jackie Oliver | Shadow-Ford | 72 | +1'22.479 | 16 |
| 10 | 8 | H.J.Stuck | Brabham-Alfa Romeo | 71 | +1 Lap | 5 |
| 11 | 30 | Brett Lunger | McLaren-Ford | 71 | +1 Lap | 22 |
| 12 | 1 | James Hunt | McLaren-Ford | 71 | +1 Lap | 3 |
| 13 | 24 | Rupert Keegan | Hesketh-Ford | 71 | +1 Lap | 24 |
| 14 | 31 | David Purley | LEC-Ford | 70 | +2 Laps | 19 |
| 15 | 27 | Patrick Neve | March-Ford | 69 | +3 Laps | 20 |
| 16 | 25 | Harald Ertl | Hesketh-Ford | 68 | +4 Laps | 23 |
| 17 | 17 | Alan Jones | Shadow-Ford | 67 | +5 Laps | 11 |
| 18 | 28 | Emerson Fittipaldi | Fittipaldi-Ford | 66 | +6 Laps | 18 |
| 19 | 6 | Gunnar Nilsson | Lotus-Ford | 64 | Wheel bearing | 7 |
| Ret | 10 | Ian Scheckter | March-Ford | 61 | Transmission | 21 |
| Ret | 19 | V.Brambilla | Surtees-Ford | 52 | Fuel pressure | 13 |
| Ret | 11 | Niki Lauda | Ferrari | 47 | Handling | 15 |
| Ret | 20 | Jody Scheckter | Wolf-Ford | 29 | Accident | 4 |
| Ret | 3 | Ronnie Peterson | Tyrrell-Ford | 7 | Ignition | 10 |
| DNQ | 9 | Alex Ribeiro | March-Ford | | | |
| DNQ | 36 | E.de Villota | McLaren-Ford | | | |
| DNQ | 18 | Larry Perkins | Surtees-Ford | | | |
| DNQ | 33 | Boy Hayje | March-Ford | | | |
| DNQ | 39 | Hector Rebaque | Hesketh-Ford | | | |
| DNQ | 35 | Conny Andersson | BRM | | | |
| DNQ | 32 | M.Kozarowitsky | March-Ford | | | |

Winning speed: 100.871mph Lap leaders: Watson 1; Andretti 2-69; Laffite 70-72
Pole position: Andretti, 1m 25.404s, 105.241mph
Fastest lap: Andretti, 1m 27.607s, 102.595mph

**FRENCH GRAND PRIX: DIJON-PRENOIS** *3 July Round: 9 Race: 289 80 x 2.361 miles*

| POS. | NO. | DRIVER | CAR-ENGINE | LAPS | TIME/RETIRED | GRID |
|---|---|---|---|---|---|---|
| 1 | 5 | Mario Andretti | Lotus-Ford | 80 | 1:39'40.13 | 1 |
| 2 | 7 | John Watson | Brabham-Alfa Romeo | 80 | +1.55 | 4 |
| 3 | 1 | James Hunt | McLaren-Ford | 80 | +33.87 | 2 |
| 4 | 6 | Gunnar Nilsson | Lotus-Ford | 80 | +1'11.08 | 3 |
| 5 | 11 | Niki Lauda | Ferrari | 80 | +1'14.15 | 9 |
| 6 | 12 | Carlos Reutemann | Ferrari | 79 | +1 Lap | 6 |
| 7 | 22 | Clay Regazzoni | Ensign-Ford | 79 | +1 Lap | 16 |
| 8 | 26 | Jacques Laffite | Ligier-Matra | 78 | +2 Laps | 5 |
| 9 | 2 | Jochen Mass | McLaren-Ford | 78 | +2 Laps | 7 |
| 10 | 24 | Rupert Keegan | Hesketh-Ford | 78 | +2 Laps | 14 |
| 11 | 28 | Emerson Fittipaldi | Fittipaldi-Ford | 77 | +3 Laps | 22 |
| 12 | 3 | Ronnie Peterson | Tyrrell-Ford | 77 | +3 Laps | 17 |
| 13 | 19 | V.Brambilla | Surtees-Ford | 77 | +3 Laps | 11 |
| NC | 10 | Ian Scheckter | March-Ford | 69 | Not classified | 20 |
| Ret | 20 | Jody Scheckter | Wolf-Ford | 66 | Accident | 8 |
| Ret | 8 | H.J.Stuck | Brabham-Alfa Romeo | 64 | Accident | 13 |
| Ret | 17 | Alan Jones | Shadow-Ford | 60 | Transmission | 10 |
| Ret | 37 | Arturo Merzario | March-Ford | 27 | Gearbox | 18 |
| Ret | 4 | P.Depailler | Tyrrell-Ford | 21 | Accident | 12 |
| Ret | 16 | Riccardo Patrese | Shadow-Ford | 6 | Engine | 15 |
| Ret | 31 | David Purley | LEC-Ford | 5 | Accident | 21 |
| Ret | 34 | Jean-Pierre Jarier | Penske-Ford | 4 | Accident | 19 |
| DNQ | 9 | Alex Ribeiro | March-Ford | | | |
| DNQ | 27 | Patrick Neve | March-Ford | | | |
| DNQ | 30 | Brett Lunger | McLaren-Ford | | | |
| DNQ | 25 | Harald Ertl | Hesketh-Ford | | | |
| DNQ | 18 | Larry Perkins | Surtees-Ford | | | |
| DNQ | 39 | Hector Rebaque | Hesketh-Ford | | | |
| DNQ | 18 | Patrick Tambay | Surtees-Ford | | | |
| DNQ | 35 | Conny Andersson | BRM | | | |

Winning speed: 113.715mph Lap leaders: Hunt 1-4; Watson 5-79; Andretti 80
Pole position: Andretti, 1m 12.210s, 117.717mph
Fastest lap: Andretti, 1m 13.750s, 115.259mph

**BRITISH GRAND PRIX: SILVERSTONE** *16 July Round:10 Race: 290 68 x 2.932 miles*

| POS. | NO. | DRIVER | CAR-ENGINE | LAPS | TIME/RETIRED | GRID |
|---|---|---|---|---|---|---|
| 1 | 1 | James Hunt | McLaren-Ford | 68 | 1:31'46.06 | 1 |
| 2 | 11 | Niki Lauda | Ferrari | 68 | +18.31 | 3 |
| 3 | 6 | Gunnar Nilsson | Lotus-Ford | 68 | +19.57 | 5 |
| 4 | 2 | Jochen Mass | McLaren-Ford | 68 | +47.76 | 11 |
| 5 | 8 | H.J.Stuck | Brabham-Alfa Romeo | 68 | +1'11.73 | 7 |
| 6 | 26 | Jacques Laffite | Ligier-Matra | 67 | +1 Lap | 15 |
| 7 | 17 | Alan Jones | Shadow-Ford | 67 | +1 Lap | 12 |
| 8 | 19 | V.Brambilla | Surtees-Ford | 67 | +1 Lap | 8 |
| 9 | 34 | Jean-Pierre Jarier | Penske-Ford | 67 | +1 Lap | 20 |
| 10 | 27 | Patrick Neve | March-Ford | 66 | +2 Laps | 26 |
| 11 | 40 | G.Villeneuve | McLaren-Ford | 66 | +2 Laps | 9 |
| 12 | 18 | Vern Schuppan | Surtees-Ford | 66 | +2 Laps | 23 |
| 13 | 30 | Brett Lunger | McLaren-Ford | 64 | +4 Laps | 19 |
| 14 | 5 | Mario Andretti | Lotus-Ford | 62 | Engine | 6 |
| 15 | 12 | Carlos Reutemann | Ferrari | 62 | +6 Laps | 14 |
| Ret | 7 | John Watson | Brabham-Alfa Romeo | 60 | Fuel system | 2 |
| Ret | 20 | Jody Scheckter | Wolf-Ford | 59 | Engine | 4 |
| Ret | 28 | Emerson Fittipaldi | Fittipaldi-Ford | 42 | Throttle | 22 |
| Ret | 37 | Arturo Merzario | March-Ford | 28 | Transmission | 17 |
| Ret | 16 | Riccardo Patrese | Shadow-Ford | 20 | Fuel pressure | 25 |
| Ret | 4 | P.Depailler | Tyrrell-Ford | 16 | Brakes | 18 |
| Ret | 15 | J.P.Jabouille | Renault | 16 | Turbo | 21 |
| Ret | 10 | Ian Scheckter | March-Ford | 6 | Accident | 24 |
| Ret | 3 | Ronnie Peterson | Tyrrell-Ford | 3 | Engine | 16 |
| Ret | 23 | Patrick Tambay | Ensign-Ford | 3 | Electrical | 10 |
| Ret | 24 | Rupert Keegan | Hesketh-Ford | 0 | Accident | 13 |
| DNQ | 9 | Alex Ribeiro | March-Ford | | | |
| DNQ | 22 | Clay Regazzoni | Ensign-Ford | | | |
| DNQ | 38 | Brian Henton | March-Ford | | | |
| DNQ | 36 | E.de Villota | McLaren-Ford | | | |
| DNPQ | 31 | David Purley | Lec-Ford | | | |
| DNPQ | 33 | Andy Sutcliff | March-Ford | | | |
| DNPQ | 35 | Guy Edwards | BRM | | | |
| DNPQ | 44 | Tony Trimmer | Surtees-Ford | | | |
| DNPQ | 45 | Brian McGuire | McGuire-Ford | | | |
| DNPQ | 32 | Mikko Kozarowitsky | March-Ford | | | |

Winning speed: 130.357mph Lap leaders: Watson 1-49; Hunt 50-68
Pole position: Hunt, 1m 18.490s, 134.478mph
Fastest lap: Hunt, 1m 19.600s, 132.603mph

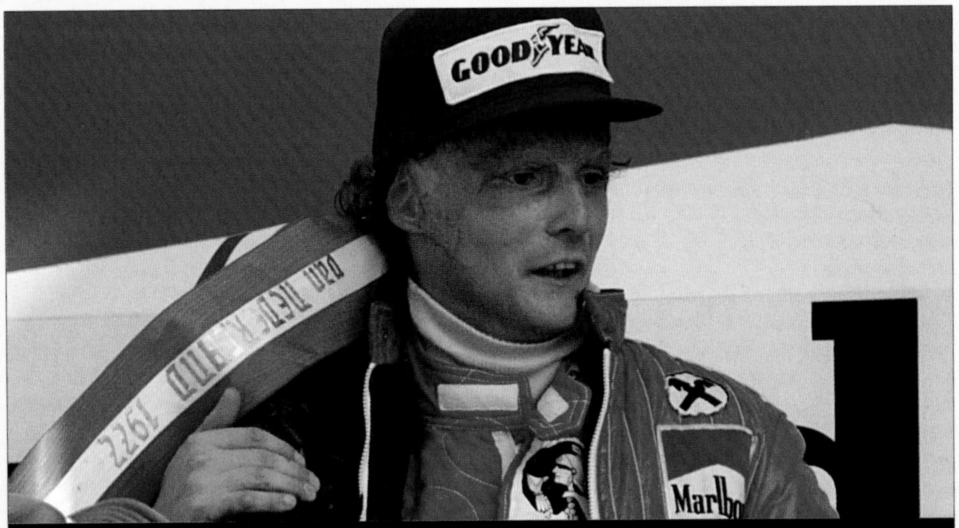

1977 world champion, Niki Lauda

**GERMAN GRAND PRIX: HOCKENHEIM** *31 July Round: 11 Race: 291 47 x 4.218 miles*

| POS. | NO. | DRIVER | CAR-ENGINE | LAPS | TIME/RETIRED | GRID |
|---|---|---|---|---|---|---|
| 1 | 11 | Niki Lauda | Ferrari | 47 | 1:31'48.62 | 3 |
| 2 | 20 | Jody Scheckter | Wolf-Ford | 47 | +14.33 | 1 |
| 3 | 8 | H.J.Stuck | Brabham-Alfa Romeo | 47 | +20.90 | 5 |
| 4 | 12 | Carlos Reutemann | Ferrari | 47 | +1'00.27 | 8 |
| 5 | 19 | V.Brambilla | Surtees-Ford | 47 | +1'27.37 | 10 |
| 6 | 23 | Patrick Tambay | Ensign-Ford | 47 | +1'29.81 | 11 |
| 7 | 18 | Vern Schuppan | Surtees-Ford | 46 | +1 Lap | 19 |
| 8 | 9 | Alex Ribeiro | March-Ford | 46 | +1 Lap | 20 |
| 9 | 3 | Ronnie Peterson | Tyrrell-Ford | 42 | Engine | 14 |
| 10 | 16 | Riccardo Patrese | Shadow-Ford | 42 | Wheel | 16 |
| Ret | 24 | Rupert Keegan | Hesketh-Ford | 40 | Accident | 23 |
| Ret | 5 | Mario Andretti | Lotus-Ford | 34 | Engine | 7 |
| Ret | 1 | James Hunt | McLaren-Ford | 32 | Fuel pump | 4 |
| Ret | 6 | Gunnar Nilsson | Lotus-Ford | 31 | Engine | 9 |
| Ret | 2 | Jochen Mass | McLaren-Ford | 26 | Gearbox | 13 |
| Ret | 4 | P.Depailler | Tyrrell-Ford | 22 | Engine | 15 |
| Ret | 26 | Jacques Laffite | Ligier-Matra | 21 | Engine | 6 |
| Ret | 25 | Hector Rebaque | Hesketh-Ford | 20 | Engine | 24 |
| Ret | 30 | Brett Lunger | McLaren-Ford | 14 | Accident | 21 |
| Ret | 10 | Ian Scheckter | March-Ford | 9 | Clutch | 18 |
| Ret | 35 | Hans Heyer | Penske-Ford | 9 | Transmission | 25 |
| Ret | 7 | John Watson | Brabham-Alfa Romeo | 8 | Engine | 2 |
| Ret | 34 | Jean-Pierre Jarier | Penske-Ford | 5 | Transmission | 12 |
| Ret | 17 | Alan Jones | Shadow-Ford | 0 | Accident | 17 |
| Ret | 22 | Clay Regazzoni | Ensign-Ford | 0 | Accident | 22 |
| DNQ | 27 | Patrick Neve | March-Ford | | | |
| DNQ | 36 | E.de Villota | McLaren-Ford | | | |
| DNQ | 28 | Emerson Fittipaldi | Fittipaldi-Ford | | | |
| DNQ | 37 | Arturo Merzario | March-Ford | | | |
| DNQ | 40 | Teddy Pilette | BRM | | | |

Winning speed: 129.573mph Lap leaders: Scheckter 1-12; Lauda 13-47
Pole position: Scheckter, 1m 53.070s, 134.311mph Fastest lap: Lauda, 1m 55.990s, 130.930mph

**AUSTRIAN GRAND RIX: OSTERREICHRING** *14 August Round: 12 Race: 292 54 x 3.692 miles*

| POS. | NO. | DRIVER | CAR-ENGINE | LAPS | TIME/RETIRED | GRID |
|---|---|---|---|---|---|---|
| 1 | 17 | Alan Jones | Shadow-Ford | 54 | 1:37'16.49 | 14 |
| 2 | 11 | Niki Lauda | Ferrari | 54 | +20.13 | 1 |
| 3 | 8 | H.J.Stuck | Brabham-Alfa Romeo | 54 | +34.50 | 4 |
| 4 | 12 | Carlos Reutemann | Ferrari | 54 | +34.75 | 5 |
| 5 | 3 | Ronnie Peterson | Tyrrell-Ford | 54 | +1'02.09 | 15 |
| 6 | 2 | Jochen Mass | McLaren-Ford | 53 | +1 Lap | 9 |
| 7 | 24 | Rupert Keegan | Hesketh-Ford | 53 | +1 Lap | 20 |
| 8 | 7 | John Watson | Brabham-Alfa Romeo | 53 | +1 Lap | 12 |
| 9 | 27 | Patrick Neve | March-Ford | 53 | +1 Lap | 22 |
| 10 | 30 | Brett Lunger | McLaren-Ford | 53 | +1 Lap | 17 |
| 11 | 28 | Emerson Fittipaldi | Fittipaldi-Ford | 53 | +1 Lap | 23 |
| 12 | 33 | Hans Binder | Penske-Ford | 53 | +1 Lap | 19 |
| 13 | 4 | P.Depailler | Tyrrell-Ford | 53 | +1 Lap | 10 |
| 14 | 34 | Jean-Pierre Jarier | Penske-Ford | 52 | +2 Laps | 18 |
| 15 | 19 | V.Brambilla | Surtees-Ford | 52 | +2 Laps | 13 |
| 16 | 18 | Vern Schuppan | Surtees-Ford | 52 | +2 Laps | 25 |
| 17 | 36 | E.de Villota | McLaren-Ford | 50 | Accident | 26 |
| Ret | 20 | Jody Scheckter | Wolf-Ford | 45 | Spun off | 8 |
| Ret | 1 | James Hunt | McLaren-Ford | 43 | Engine | 2 |
| Ret | 23 | Patrick Tambay | Ensign-Ford | 41 | Engine | 7 |
| Ret | 6 | Gunnar Nilsson | Lotus-Ford | 38 | Engine | 16 |
| Ret | 16 | Arturo Merzario | Shadow-Ford | 29 | Gearbox | 21 |
| Ret | 26 | Jacques Laffite | Ligier-Matra | 21 | Oil leak | 6 |
| Ret | 5 | Mario Andretti | Lotus-Ford | 11 | Engine | 3 |
| Ret | 10 | Ian Scheckter | March-Ford | 2 | Accident | 24 |
| Ret | 22 | Clay Regazzoni | Ensign-Ford | 0 | Accident | 11 |
| DNQ | 38 | Brian Henton | March-Ford | | | |
| DNQ | 39 | Ian Ashley | Hesketh-Ford | | | |
| DNQ | 25 | Hector Rebaque | Hesketh-Ford | | | |
| DNQ | 9 | Alex Ribeiro | March-Ford | | | |

Winning speed: 122.978mph Lap leaders: Andretti 1-11; Hunt 12-43; Jones 44-54
Pole position: Lauda, 1m 39.320s, 133.829mph Fastest lap: Watson, 1m 40.960s, 131.655mph

**DUTCH GRAND PRIX: ZANDVOORT** *28 August Round: 13 Race: 293 75 x 2.6626 miles*

| POS. | NO. | DRIVER | CAR-ENGINE | LAPS | TIME/RETIRED | GRID |
|---|---|---|---|---|---|---|
| 1 | 11 | Niki Lauda | Ferrari | 75 | 1:41'45.93 | 4 |
| 2 | 26 | Jacques Laffite | Ligier-Matra | 75 | +1.89 | 2 |
| 3 | 20 | Jody Scheckter | Wolf-Ford | 74 | +1 Lap | 15 |
| 4 | 28 | Emerson Fittipaldi | Fittipaldi-Ford | 74 | +1 Lap | 17 |
| 5 | 23 | Patrick Tambay | Ensign-Ford | 73 | Out of fuel | 12 |
| 6 | 12 | Carlos Reutemann | Ferrari | 73 | +2 Laps | 6 |
| 7 | 8 | H.J.Stuck | Brabham-Alfa Romeo | 73 | +2 Laps | 19 |
| 8 | 35 | Hans Binder | Penske-Ford | 73 | +2 Laps | 18 |
| 9 | 30 | Brett Lunger | McLaren-Ford | 73 | +2 Laps | 20 |
| 10 | 10 | Ian Scheckter | March-Ford | 73 | +2 Laps | 25 |
| 11 | 9 | Alex Ribeiro | March-Ford | 72 | +3 Laps | 24 |
| 12 | 19 | V.Brambilla | Surtees-Ford | 67 | Accident | 22 |
| 13 | 16 | Riccardo Patrese | Shadow-Ford | 67 | Engine | 16 |
| RDSQ | 38 | Brian Henton | Boro-Ford | 52 | Disqualified | 23 |
| Ret | 15 | J.P.Jabouille | Renault | 39 | Suspension | 10 |
| Ret | 6 | Gunnar Nilsson | Lotus-Ford | 34 | Accident | 5 |
| Ret | 17 | Alan Jones | Shadow-Ford | 32 | Engine | 13 |
| Ret | 4 | P.Depailler | Tyrrell-Ford | 31 | Engine | 11 |
| Ret | 3 | Ronnie Peterson | Tyrrell-Ford | 18 | Ignition | 7 |
| Ret | 22 | Clay Regazzoni | Ensign-Ford | 17 | Throttle | 9 |
| Ret | 5 | Mario Andretti | Lotus-Ford | 14 | Engine | 1 |
| Ret | 24 | Rupert Keegan | Hesketh-Ford | 8 | Accident | 26 |
| Ret | 1 | James Hunt | McLaren-Ford | 5 | Accident | 3 |
| Ret | 34 | Jean-Pierre Jarier | Penske-Ford | 4 | Ignition | 21 |
| Ret | 7 | John Watson | Brabham-Alfa Romeo | 2 | Oil leak | 8 |
| Ret | 2 | Jochen Mass | McLaren-Ford | 0 | Accident | 14 |
| DNQ | 27 | Patrick Neve | March-Ford | | | |
| DNQ | 37 | Arturo Merzario | March-Ford | | | |
| DNQ | 18 | Vern Schuppan | Surtees-Ford | | | |
| DNQ | 39 | Ian Ashley | Hesketh-Ford | | | |
| DNQ | 33 | Boy Hayje | March-Ford | | | |
| DNQ | 25 | Hector Rebaque | Hesketh-Ford | | | |
| DNQ | 29 | Teddy Pilette | BRM | | | |
| DNQ | 32 | M.Bleekemolen | March-Ford | | | |

Winning speed: 116.116mph Lap leaders: Hunt 1-5; Laffite 6-19; Lauda 20-75
Pole position: Andretti, 1m 18.650, 120.194mph Fastest lap: Lauda, 1m 19.990s, 118.181mph

## ITALIAN GRAND PRIX: MONZA 11 September Round: 14 Race: 294 52 x 3.604 miles

| POS. | NO. | DRIVER | CAR-ENGINE | LAPS | TIME/RETIRED | GRID |
|---|---|---|---|---|---|---|
| 1 | 5 | Mario Andretti | Lotus-Ford | 52 | 1:27'50.30 | 4 |
| 2 | 11 | Niki Lauda | Ferrari | 52 | +16.96 | 5 |
| 3 | 17 | Alan Jones | Shadow-Ford | 52 | +23.63 | 16 |
| 4 | 2 | Jochen Mass | McLaren-Ford | 52 | +28.48 | 9 |
| 5 | 22 | Clay Regazzoni | Ensign-Ford | 52 | +30.11 | 2 |
| 6 | 3 | Ronnie Peterson | Tyrrell-Ford | 52 | +1'19.22 | 12 |
| 7 | 27 | Patrick Neve | March-Ford | 50 | +2 Laps | 24 |
| 8 | 26 | Jacques Laffite | Ligier-Matra | 50 | +2 Laps | 8 |
| 9 | 24 | Rupert Keegan | Hesketh-Ford | 48 | +4 Laps | 23 |
| Ret | 10 | Ian Scheckter | March-Ford | 41 | Transmission | 17 |
| Ret | 12 | Carlos Reutemann | Ferrari | 39 | Spun off | 1 |
| Ret | 16 | Riccardo Patrese | Shadow-Ford | 39 | Spun off | 6 |
| Ret | 14 | Bruno Giacomelli | McLaren-Ford | 38 | Engine | 15 |
| Ret | 8 | H.J.Stuck | Brabham-Alfa Romeo | 31 | Engine | 11 |
| Ret | 1 | James Hunt | McLaren-Ford | 26 | Spun off | 1 |
| Ret | 4 | P.Depailler | Tyrrell-Ford | 24 | Engine | 13 |
| Ret | 20 | Jody Scheckter | Wolf-Ford | 23 | Engine | 3 |
| Ret | 15 | J.P.Jabouille | Renault | 23 | Engine | 20 |
| Ret | 34 | Jean-Pierre Jarier | Penske-Ford | 19 | Engine | 18 |
| Ret | 23 | Patrick Tambay | Ensign-Ford | 9 | Engine | 21 |
| Ret | 19 | V.Brambilla | Surtees-Ford | 5 | Accident | 10 |
| Ret | 6 | Gunnar Nilsson | Lotus-Ford | 4 | Suspension | 22 |
| Ret | 30 | Brett Lunger | McLaren-Ford | 4 | Engine | 19 |
| Ret | 7 | John Watson | Brabham-Alfa Romeo | 3 | Accident | 14 |
| DNQ | 9 | Alex Ribeiro | March-Ford | | | |
| DNQ | 28 | Emerson Fittipaldi | Fittipaldi-Ford | | | |
| DNQ | 18 | Lamberto Leoni | Surtees-Ford | | | |
| DNQ | 38 | Brian Henton | Boro-Ford | | | |
| DNQ | 36 | E.de Villota | McLaren-Ford | | | |
| DNQ | 25 | Ian Ashley | Hesketh-Ford | | | |
| DNQ | 29 | Teddy Pilette | BRM | | | |
| DNQ | 33 | Hans Binder | Penske-Ford | | | |
| DNQ | 41 | Loris Kessel | Williams-Ford | | | |
| DNQ | 21 | Giorgio Francia | Brabham-Alfa Romeo | | | |

Winning speed: 128.012mph  Lap leaders: Scheckter 1-9; Andretti 10-52
Pole position: Hunt, 1m 30.080s, 132.282mph
Fastest lap: Andretti, 1m 39.100s, 130.921mph

## USA EAST GRAND PRIX: WATKINS GLEN 2 October Round: 15 Race: 295 59 x 3.377 miles

| POS. | NO. | DRIVER | CAR-ENGINE | LAPS | TIME/RETIRED | GRID |
|---|---|---|---|---|---|---|
| 1 | 1 | James Hunt | McLaren-Ford | 59 | 1:58'23.267 | 1 |
| 2 | 5 | Mario Andretti | Lotus-Ford | 59 | +2.026 | 4 |
| 3 | 20 | Jody Scheckter | Wolf-Ford | 59 | +1'18.879 | 9 |
| 4 | 11 | Niki Lauda | Ferrari | 59 | +1'40.615 | 7 |
| 5 | 22 | Clay Regazzoni | Ensign-Ford | 59 | +1'48.138 | 19 |
| 6 | 12 | Carlos Reutemann | Ferrari | 58 | +1 Lap | 6 |
| 7 | 26 | Jacques Laffite | Ligier-Matra | 58 | +1 Lap | 10 |
| 8 | 24 | Rupert Keegan | Hesketh-Ford | 58 | +1 Lap | 20 |
| 9 | 16 | Jean-Pierre Jarier | Shadow-Ford | 58 | +1 Lap | 16 |
| 10 | 30 | Brett Lunger | McLaren-Ford | 57 | +2 Laps | 17 |
| 11 | 18 | Hans Binder | Surtees-Ford | 57 | +2 Laps | 25 |
| 12 | 7 | John Watson | Brabham-Alfa Romeo | 57 | +2 Laps | 3 |
| 13 | 28 | Emerson Fittipaldi | Fittipaldi-Ford | 57 | +2 Laps | 18 |
| 14 | 4 | P.Depailler | Tyrrell-Ford | 56 | +3 Laps | 8 |
| 15 | 9 | Alex Ribeiro | March-Ford | 56 | +3 Laps | 23 |
| 16 | 3 | Ronnie Peterson | Tyrrell-Ford | 56 | +3 Laps | 5 |
| 17 | 25 | Ian Ashley | Hesketh-Ford | 55 | +4 Laps | 22 |
| 18 | 27 | Patrick Neve | March-Ford | 55 | +4 Laps | 24 |
| 19 | 19 | V.Brambilla | Surtees-Ford | 54 | +5 Laps | 11 |
| Ret | 15 | J.P.Jabouille | Renault | 30 | Alternator | 14 |
| Ret | 6 | Gunnar Nilsson | Lotus-Ford | 17 | Accident | 12 |
| Ret | 8 | H.J.Stuck | Brabham-Alfa Romeo | 14 | Accident | 2 |
| Ret | 10 | Ian Scheckter | March-Ford | 10 | Accident | 21 |
| Ret | 2 | Jochen Mass | McLaren-Ford | 8 | Fuel pump | 15 |
| Ret | 14 | Danny Ongais | Penske-Ford | 6 | Accident | 26 |
| Ret | 17 | Alan Jones | Shadow-Ford | 3 | Accident | 13 |
| DNQ | 23 | Patrick Tambay | Ensign-Ford | | | |

Winning speed: 100.978mph  Lap leaders: Stuck 1-14; Hunt 15-59
Pole position: Hunt, 1m 40.863s, 120.532mph
Fastest lap: Peterson, 1m 51.854s, 108.688mph

## CANADIAN GRAND PRIX: MOSPORT PARK 9 October Round: 16 Race: 296 80 x 2.459

| POS. | NO. | DRIVER | CAR-ENGINE | LAPS | TIME/RETIRED | GRID |
|---|---|---|---|---|---|---|
| 1 | 20 | Jody Scheckter | Wolf-Ford | 80 | 1:40'00.00 | 9 |
| 2 | 4 | P.Depailler | Tyrrell-Ford | 80 | +6.77 | 6 |
| 3 | 2 | Jochen Mass | McLaren-Ford | 80 | +15.76 | 5 |
| 4 | 17 | Alan Jones | Shadow-Ford | 80 | +46.69 | 7 |
| 5 | 23 | Patrick Tambay | Ensign-Ford | 80 | +1'03.26 | 16 |
| 6 | 19 | V.Brambilla | Surtees-Ford | 78 | Accident | 15 |
| 7 | 14 | Danny Ongais | Penske-Ford | 78 | +2 Laps | 22 |
| 8 | 9 | Alex Ribeiro | March-Ford | 78 | +2 Laps | 23 |
| 9 | 5 | Mario Andretti | Lotus-Ford | 77 | Engine | 1 |
| 10 | 16 | Riccardo Patrese | Shadow-Ford | 76 | Spun off | 8 |
| 11 | 30 | Brett Lunger | McLaren-Ford | 76 | Engine | 20 |
| 12 | 21 | G.Villeneuve | Ferrari | 76 | Transmission | 17 |
| Ret | 1 | James Hunt | McLaren-Ford | 61 | Accident | 2 |
| Ret | 27 | Patrick Neve | March-Ford | 56 | Engine | 21 |
| Ret | 3 | Ronnie Peterson | Tyrrell-Ford | 34 | Fuel leak | 4 |
| Ret | 24 | Rupert Keegan | Hesketh-Ford | 32 | Accident | 25 |
| Ret | 18 | Hans Binder | Surtees-Ford | 31 | Accident | 24 |
| Ret | 10 | Ian Scheckter | March-Ford | 29 | Engine | 18 |
| Ret | 28 | Emerson Fittipaldi | Fittipaldi-Ford | 29 | Engine | 19 |
| Ret | 12 | Carlos Reutemann | Ferrari | 20 | Fuel system | 14 |
| Ret | 8 | H.J.Stuck | Brabham-Alfa Romeo | 19 | Engine | 13 |
| Ret | 6 | Gunnar Nilsson | Lotus-Ford | 17 | Accident | 4 |
| Ret | 26 | Jacques Laffite | Ligier-Matra | 12 | Transmission | 11 |
| Ret | 7 | John Watson | Brabham-Alfa Romeo | 1 | Suspension | 10 |
| Ret | 22 | Clay Regazzoni | Ensign-Ford | 0 | Accident | 14 |
| DNQ | 15 | J.P.Jabouille | Renault | | | |

Winning speed: 118.032mph  Lap leaders: Andretti 1-60, 62-78; Hunt 61; Scheckter 79-80
Pole position: Andretti, 1m 11.385s, 124.009mph
Fastest lap: Andretti, 1m 13.299s, 120.771mph

## JAPANESE GRAND PRIX: FUJI 23 October Round: 17 Race: 297 73 x 2.709 miles

| POS. | NO. | DRIVER | CAR-ENGINE | LAPS | TIME/RETIRED | GRID |
|---|---|---|---|---|---|---|
| 1 | 1 | James Hunt | McLaren-Ford | 73 | 1:31'51.68 | 2 |
| 2 | 12 | Carlos Reutemann | Ferrari | 73 | +1'02.45 | 7 |
| 3 | 4 | P.Depailler | Tyrrell-Ford | 73 | +1'06.39 | 15 |
| 4 | 17 | Alan Jones | Shadow-Ford | 73 | +1'06.61 | 12 |
| 5 | 26 | Jacques Laffite | Ligier-Matra | 72 | Out of fuel | 5 |
| 6 | 16 | Riccardo Patrese | Shadow-Ford | 72 | +1 Lap | 13 |
| 7 | 8 | H.J.Stuck | Brabham-Alfa Romeo | 72 | +1 Lap | 4 |
| 8 | 19 | V.Brambilla | Surtees-Ford | 71 | +2 Laps | 9 |
| 9 | 50 | K.Takahashi | Tyrrell-Ford | 71 | +2 Laps | 22 |
| 10 | 20 | Jody Scheckter | Wolf-Ford | 71 | +2 Laps | 6 |
| 11 | 52 | K.Hoshino | Kojima-Ford | 71 | +2 Laps | 11 |
| 12 | 9 | Alex Ribeiro | March-Ford | 69 | +4 Laps | 23 |
| Ret | 6 | Gunnar Nilsson | Lotus-Ford | 63 | Gearbox | 14 |
| Ret | 22 | Clay Regazzoni | Ensign-Ford | 43 | Gearbox | 10 |
| Ret | 7 | John Watson | Brabham-Alfa Romeo | 29 | Gearbox | 3 |
| Ret | 2 | Jochen Mass | McLaren-Ford | 28 | Engine | 8 |
| Ret | 23 | Patrick Tambay | Ensign-Ford | 14 | Engine | 16 |
| Ret | 3 | Ronnie Peterson | Tyrrell-Ford | 5 | Accident | 18 |
| Ret | 11 | G.Villeneuve | Ferrari | 5 | Accident | 20 |
| Ret | 27 | Jean-Pierre Jarier | Ligier-Matra | 3 | Engine | 17 |
| Ret | 5 | Mario Andretti | Lotus-Ford | 1 | Collision | 1 |
| Ret | 51 | N.Takahara | Kojima-Ford | 1 | Collision | 19 |
| Ret | 18 | Hans Binder | Surtees-Ford | 1 | Collision | 21 |

Winning speed: 129.146mph  Lap leaders: Hunt 1-73
Pole position: Andretti, 1m 12.230s, 134.997mph
Fastest lap: Scheckter, 1m 14.300s, 131.236mph

# 1978

**DRIVERS' CHAMPION: MARIO ANDRETTI
CONSTRUCTORS' CHAMPION: LOTUS FORD**

## DRIVERS' CHAMPIONSHIP

| POS | DRIVER | COUNTRY | CAR | POINTS |
|---|---|---|---|---|
| 1 | Mario Andretti | USA | Lotus-Ford | 64 |
| 2 | Ronnie Peterson | Sweden | Lotus-Ford | 51 |
| 3 | Carlos Reutemann | Argentina | Ferrari | 48 |
| 4 | Niki Lauda | Austria | Brabham-Alfa Romeo | 44 |
| 5 | Patrick Depailler | France | Tyrrell-Ford | 34 |
| 6 | John Watson | GB | Brabham-Alfa Romeo | 25 |
| 7 | Jody Scheckter | South Africa | Wolf-Ford | 24 |
| 8 | Jacques Laffite | France | Ligier-Matra | 19 |
| 9 | Emerson Fittipaldi | Brazil | Copersucar-Ford | 17 |
| = | Gilles Villeneuve | Canada | Ferrari | 17 |
| 11 | Riccardo Patrese | Italy | Arrows-Ford | 11 |
| = | Alan Jones | Australia | Williams-Ford | 11 |
| 13 | James Hunt | GB | McLaren-Ford | 8 |
| = | Patrick Tambay | France | McLaren-Ford | 8 |
| 15 | Didier Pironi | France | Tyrrell-Ford | 7 |
| 16 | Clay Regazzoni | Switzerland | Shadow-Ford | 4 |
| 17 | Jean-Pierre Jabouille | France | Renault | 3 |
| 18 | Hans-Joachim Stuck | West Germany | Shadow-Ford | 2 |
| 19 | Hector Rebaque | Mexico | Lotus-Ford | 1 |
| | Vittorio Brambilla | Italy | Surtees-Ford | 1 |
| | Derek Daly | Ireland | Hesketh-Ford | 1 |
| | Jochen Mass | West Germany | ATS-Ford | |
| | Brett Lunger | USA | McLaren-Ford, Ensign-Ford | |
| | Arturo Merzario | Italy | Merzario-Ford | |
| | Rupert Keegan | GB | Surtees-Ford | |
| | Jean-Pierre Jarier | France | ATS-Ford, Lotus-Ford | |
| | Danny Ongais | USA | Ensign-Ford, Shadow-Ford | |
| | Lamberto Leoni | Italy | Ensign-Ford | |
| | Eddie Cheever | USA | Theodore-Ford, Hesketh-Ford | |
| | Divina Galica | GB | Hesketh-Ford | |
| | Rolf Stommelen | West Germany | Arrows-Ford | |
| | Keke Rosberg | Finland | Theodore-Ford, ATS-Ford, Wolf-Ford | |
| | Rene Arnoux | France | Martini-Ford, Surtees-Ford | |
| | Jacky Ickx | Belgium | Ensign-Ford | |
| | Alberto Colombo | Italy | ATS-Ford, Merzario-Ford | |
| | Bruno Giacomelli | Italy | McLaren-Ford | |
| | Emilio de Villota | Spain | McLaren-Ford | |
| | Tony Trimmer | GB | McLaren-Ford | |
| | Geoff Lees | GB | Ensign-Ford | |
| | Nelson Piquet | Brazil | Ensign-Ford, McLaren-Ford, Brabham-Alfa Romeo | |
| | Harald Ertl | Austria | Ensign-Ford, ATS-Ford | |
| | Hans Binder | Austria | ATS-Ford | |
| | Carlo Franchi 'Gimax' | Italy | Surtees-Ford | |
| | Mike Bleekemolen | Netherlands | ATS-Ford | |
| | Bobby Rahal | USA | Wolf-Ford | |
| | Beppe Gabbiani | Italy | Surtees-Ford | |
| | Patrick Neve | Belgium | March-Ford | |
| | Bernard de Dryver | Belgium | Ensign-Ford | |

Points for top six finishers (9, 6, 4, 3, 2, 1). Only the best seven scores from the first eight races and the best seven scores from the remaining eight races counted towards the championship.

## CONSTRUCTORS' CHAMPIONSHIP

| POS. | CONSTRUCTOR | POINTS |
|---|---|---|
| 1 | Lotus-Ford | 86 |
| 2 | Ferrari | 58 |
| 3 | Brabham-Alfa Romeo | 53 |
| 4 | Tyrrell-Ford | 38 |
| 5 | Wolf-Ford | 24 |
| 6 | Ligier-Matra | 19 |
| 7 | Fittipaldi-Ford | 17 |
| 8 | McLaren-Ford | 15 |
| 9 | Williams-Ford | 11 |
| 10 | Arrows-Ford | 11 |
| 11 | Shadow-Ford | 6 |
| 12 | Renault | 3 |
| 13 | Surtees-Ford | 1 |
| 13 | Ensign-Ford | 1 |

Points for top six finishers (9, 6, 4, 3, 2, 1). Points only counted for top-placed car for each constructor. Only the best seven scores from the first eight races and the best seven scores from the remaining eight races counted towards the championship

*1977 world champion, Niki Lauda in the Ferrari 312/T2*

# 1978 Season Statistics

### ARGENTINE GRAND PRIX: BUENOS AIRES *NO.15 15 January Round: 1 Race: 298 52 x 3.708 miles*

| POS. | NO. | DRIVER | CAR-ENGINE | LAPS | TIME/RETIRED | GRID |
|---|---|---|---|---|---|---|
| 1 | 5 | Mario Andretti | Lotus-Ford | 52 | 1:37'04.47 | 1 |
| 2 | 1 | Niki Lauda | Brabham-Alfa Romeo | 52 | +13.21 | 5 |
| 3 | 4 | P.Depailler | Tyrrell-Ford | 52 | +13.64 | 10 |
| 4 | 7 | James Hunt | McLaren-Ford | 52 | +16.05 | 6 |
| 5 | 6 | Ronnie Peterson | Lotus-Ford | 52 | +1'14.85 | 3 |
| 6 | 8 | Patrick Tambay | McLaren-Ford | 52 | +1'19.90 | 9 |
| 7 | 11 | Carlos Reutemann | Ferrari | 52 | +1'22.60 | 2 |
| 8 | 12 | G.Villeneuve | Ferrari | 52 | +1'38.88 | 7 |
| 9 | 14 | Emerson Fittipaldi | Fittipaldi-Ford | 52 | +1'40.60 | 17 |
| 10 | 20 | Jody Scheckter | Wolf-Ford | 52 | +1'43.50 | 15 |
| 11 | 9 | Jochen Mass | ATS-Ford | 52 | +1'49.07 | 13 |
| 12 | 10 | Jean-Pierre Jarier | ATS-Ford | 51 | +1 Lap | 11 |
| 13 | 30 | Brett Lunger | McLaren-Ford | 51 | +1 Lap | 24 |
| 14 | 3 | Didier Pironi | Tyrrell-Ford | 51 | +1 Lap | 23 |
| 15 | 17 | Clay Regazzoni | Shadow-Ford | 51 | +1 Lap | 16 |
| 16 | 26 | Jacques Laffite | Ligier-Matra | 50 | Engine | 8 |
| 17 | 16 | H.J.Stuck | Shadow-Ford | 50 | +2 Laps | 18 |
| 18 | 19 | V.Brambilla | Surtees-Ford | 50 | +2 Laps | 12 |
| Ret | 2 | John Watson | Brabham-Alfa Romeo | 41 | Engine | 4 |
| Ret | 27 | Alan Jones | Williams-Ford | 36 | Fuel system | 14 |
| Ret | 22 | Danny Ongais | Ensign-Ford | 35 | Distributor | 21 |
| Ret | 23 | Lamberto Leoni | Ensign-Ford | 28 | Engine | 22 |
| Ret | 37 | Arturo Merzario | Merzario-Ford | 9 | Differential | 20 |
| Ret | 18 | Rupert Keegan | Surtees-Ford | 4 | Overheating | 19 |
| DNQ | 25 | Hector Rebaque | Lotus-Ford | | | |
| DNQ | 32 | Eddie Cheever | Theodore-Ford | | | |
| DNQ | 24 | Divina Galica | Hesketh-Ford | | | |

Winning speed: 119.187mph Lap leaders: Andretti 1-52
Pole position: Andretti, 1m 47.750s, 123.898mph
Fastest lap: Villeneuve, 1m 49.760s, 121.629mph

### BRAZILIAN GRAND PRIX: RIO DE JANEIRO *29 January Round: 2 Race: 299 63 x 3.126 miles*

| POS. | NO. | DRIVER | CAR-ENGINE | LAPS | TIME/RETIRED | GRID |
|---|---|---|---|---|---|---|
| 1 | 11 | Carlos Reutemann | Ferrari | 63 | 1:49'59.86 | 4 |
| 2 | 14 | Emerson Fittipaldi | Fittipaldi-Ford | 63 | +49.13 | 7 |
| 3 | 1 | Niki Lauda | Brabham-Alfa Romeo | 63 | +57.02 | 10 |
| 4 | 5 | Mario Andretti | Lotus-Ford | 63 | +1'33.12 | 3 |
| 5 | 17 | Clay Regazzoni | Shadow-Ford | 62 | +1 Lap | 15 |
| 6 | 3 | Didier Pironi | Tyrrell-Ford | 62 | +1 Lap | 19 |
| 7 | 9 | Jochen Mass | ATS-Ford | 62 | +1 Lap | 20 |
| 8 | 2 | John Watson | Brabham-Alfa Romeo | 61 | +2 Laps | 21 |
| 9 | 26 | Jacques Laffite | Ligier-Matra | 61 | +2 Laps | 14 |
| 10 | 36 | Riccardo Patrese | Arrows-Ford | 59 | +4 Laps | 18 |
| 11 | 27 | Alan Jones | Williams-Ford | 58 | +5 Laps | 8 |
| Ret | 25 | Hector Rebaque | Lotus-Ford | 40 | Physical | 22 |
| Ret | 12 | G.Villeneuve | Ferrari | 35 | Spun off | 6 |
| Ret | 8 | Patrick Tambay | McLaren-Ford | 34 | Spun off | 5 |
| Ret | 7 | James Hunt | McLaren-Ford | 25 | Spun off | 2 |
| Ret | 16 | H.J.Stuck | Shadow-Ford | 25 | Fuel system | 9 |
| Ret | 20 | Jody Scheckter | Wolf-Ford | 16 | Accident | 12 |
| Ret | 6 | Ronnie Peterson | Lotus-Ford | 15 | Collision | 1 |
| Ret | 22 | Danny Ongais | Ensign-Ford | 13 | Brakes | 23 |
| Ret | 30 | Brett Lunger | McLaren-Ford | 11 | Overheating | 13 |
| Ret | 4 | P.Depailler | Tyrrell-Ford | 8 | Accident | 11 |
| Ret | 18 | Rupert Keegan | Surtees-Ford | 5 | Accident | 24 |
| Ret | 23 | Lamberto Leoni | Ensign-Ford | 0 | Transmission | 17 |
| DNS | 10 | Jean-Pierre Jarier | ATS-Ford | 0 | Non starter | 16 |
| DNQ | 37 | Arturo Merzario | Merzario-Ford | | | |
| DNQ | 32 | Eddie Cheever | Theodore-Ford | | | |
| DNQ | 19 | V.Brambilla | Surtees-Ford | | | |
| DNQ | 24 | Divina Galica | Hesketh-Ford | | | |

Winning speed: 107.427mph Lap leaders: Reutemann 1-63
Pole position: Peterson, 1m 40.450, 112.036mph
Fastest lap: Reutemann, 1m 43.070s, 109.188mph

### SOUTH AFRICAN GRAND PRIX: KYALAMI *4 March Round: 3 Race: 300 78 x 2.550 miles*

| POS. | NO. | DRIVER | CAR-ENGINE | LAPS | TIME/RETIRED | GRID |
|---|---|---|---|---|---|---|
| 1 | 6 | Ronnie Peterson | Lotus-Ford | 78 | 1:42'15.767 | 12 |
| 2 | 4 | P.Depailler | Tyrrell-Ford | 78 | +0.466 | 11 |
| 3 | 2 | John Watson | Brabham-Alfa Romeo | 78 | +4.442 | 10 |
| 4 | 27 | Alan Jones | Williams-Ford | 78 | +38.986 | 18 |
| 5 | 26 | Jacques Laffite | Ligier-Matra | 78 | +1'09.218 | 13 |
| 6 | 3 | Didier Pironi | Tyrrell-Ford | 77 | +1 Lap | 14 |
| 7 | 5 | Mario Andretti | Lotus-Ford | 77 | +1 Lap | 2 |
| 8 | 10 | Jean-Pierre Jarier | ATS-Ford | 77 | +1 Lap | 17 |
| 9 | 36 | Rolf Stommelen | Arrows-Ford | 77 | +1 Lap | 22 |
| 10 | 25 | Hector Rebaque | Lotus-Ford | 77 | +1 Lap | 21 |
| 11 | 30 | Brett Lunger | McLaren-Ford | 76 | +2 Laps | 20 |
| 12 | 19 | V.Brambilla | Surtees-Ford | 76 | +2 Laps | 19 |
| Ret | 35 | Riccardo Patrese | Arrows-Ford | 63 | Engine | 7 |
| Ret | 20 | Jody Scheckter | Wolf-Ford | 59 | Spun off | 5 |
| Ret | 8 | Patrick Tambay | McLaren-Ford | 56 | Accident | 4 |
| Ret | 12 | G.Villeneuve | Ferrari | 55 | Oil leak | 8 |
| Ret | 11 | Carlos Reutemann | Ferrari | 55 | Spun off | 9 |
| Ret | 1 | Niki Lauda | Brabham-Alfa Romeo | 52 | Engine | 1 |
| Ret | 18 | Rupert Keegan | Surtees-Ford | 52 | Engine | 23 |
| Ret | 9 | Jochen Mass | ATS-Ford | 43 | Engine | 15 |
| Ret | 37 | Arturo Merzario | Merzario-Ford | 39 | Suspension | 26 |
| Ret | 15 | J.P.Jabouille | Renault | 38 | Engine | 6 |
| Ret | 32 | Keke Rosberg | Theodore-Ford | 15 | Clutch | 24 |
| Ret | 14 | Emerson Fittipaldi | Fittipaldi-Ford | 9 | Transmission | 16 |
| Ret | 24 | Eddie Cheever | Hesketh-Ford | 8 | Oil leak | 25 |
| Ret | 7 | James Hunt | McLaren-Ford | 5 | Engine | 3 |
| DNQ | 31 | Rene Arnoux | Martini-Ford | | | |
| DNQ | 17 | Clay Regazzoni | Shadow-Ford | | | |
| DNQ | 22 | Lamberto Leoni | Ensign-Ford | | | |
| DNQ | 16 | H.J.Stuck | Shadow-Ford | | | |

Winning speed: 116.704mph
Lap leaders: Andretti 1-20; Scheckter 21-26; Patrese 27-63; Depailler 64-77; Peterson 78
Pole position: Lauda, 1m 14.650s, 122.979mph
Fastest lap: Andretti, 1m 17.090s, 119.087mph

### USA WEST GRAND PRIX: LONG BEACH *2 April Round: 4 Race: 301 80.5 x 2.020 miles*

| POS. | NO. | DRIVER | CAR-ENGINE | LAPS | TIME/RETIRED | GRID |
|---|---|---|---|---|---|---|
| 1 | 11 | Carlos Reutemann | Ferrari | 80 | 1:52'01.301 | |
| 2 | 5 | Mario Andretti | Lotus-Ford | 80 | +11.061 | |
| 3 | 4 | P.Depailler | Tyrrell-Ford | 80 | +28.951 | |
| 4 | 6 | Ronnie Peterson | Lotus-Ford | 80 | +45.603 | |
| 5 | 26 | Jacques Laffite | Ligier-Matra | 80 | +1'22.884 | |
| 6 | 35 | Riccardo Patrese | Arrows-Ford | 79 | +1 Lap | |
| 7 | 27 | Alan Jones | Williams-Ford | 79 | +1 Lap | |
| 8 | 14 | Emerson Fittipaldi | Fittipaldi-Ford | 79 | +1 Lap | |
| 9 | 36 | Rolf Stommelen | Arrows-Ford | 79 | +1 Lap | |
| 10 | 17 | Clay Regazzoni | Shadow-Ford | 79 | +1 Lap | |
| 11 | 10 | Jean-Pierre Jarier | ATS-Ford | 75 | +5 Laps | |
| 12 | 8 | Patrick Tambay | McLaren-Ford | 74 | Accident | |
| Ret | 20 | Jody Scheckter | Wolf-Ford | 59 | Accident | |
| Ret | 19 | V.Brambilla | Surtees-Ford | 50 | Transmission | |
| Ret | 15 | J.P.Jabouille | Renault | 43 | Turbo | |
| Ret | 12 | G.Villeneuve | Ferrari | 38 | Accident | |
| Ret | 1 | Niki Lauda | Brabham-Alfa Romeo | 27 | Ignition | |
| Ret | 3 | Didier Pironi | Tyrrell-Ford | 25 | Gearbox | |
| Ret | 37 | Arturo Merzario | Merzario-Ford | 17 | Gearbox | |
| Ret | 9 | Jochen Mass | ATS-Ford | 11 | Brakes | |
| Ret | 2 | John Watson | Brabham-Alfa Romeo | 9 | Gearbox | |
| Ret | 7 | James Hunt | McLaren-Ford | 5 | Accident | |
| DNQ | 30 | Brett Lunger | McLaren-Ford | | | |
| DNQ | 22 | Lamberto Leoni | Ensign-Ford | | | |
| DNPQ | 32 | Keke Rosberg | Theodore-Ford | | | |
| DNPQ | 25 | Hector Rebaque | Lotus-Ford | | | |
| DNPQ | 39 | Danny Ongais | Shadow-Ford | | | |
| DNPQ | 24 | Derek Daly | Hesketh-Ford | | | |

Winning speed: 87.099mph lap Leaders: Villeneuve 1-38; Reutemann 39-80
Pole position: Reutemann, 1m 20.636s, 90.187mph
Fastest lap: Jones, 1m 22.215s, 88.454mph

### MONACO GRAND PRIX: MONTE CARLO *7 May Round: 5 Race: 302 75 x 2.058 miles*

| POS. | NO. | DRIVER | CAR-ENGINE | LAPS | TIME/RETIRED | GRID |
|---|---|---|---|---|---|---|
| 1 | 4 | P.Depailler | Tyrrell-Ford | 75 | 1:55'14.66 | 5 |
| 2 | 1 | Niki Lauda | Brabham-Alfa Romeo | 75 | +22.45 | 3 |
| 3 | 20 | Jody Scheckter | Wolf-Ford | 75 | +32.29 | 9 |
| 4 | 2 | John Watson | Brabham-Alfa Romeo | 75 | +33.53 | 2 |
| 5 | 3 | Didier Pironi | Tyrrell-Ford | 75 | +1'08.06 | 13 |
| 6 | 35 | Riccardo Patrese | Arrows-Ford | 75 | +1'08.77 | 14 |
| 7 | 8 | Patrick Tambay | McLaren-Ford | 74 | +1 Lap | 11 |
| 8 | 11 | Carlos Reutemann | Ferrari | 74 | +1 Lap | 1 |
| 9 | 14 | Emerson Fittipaldi | Fittipaldi-Ford | 74 | +1 Lap | 20 |
| 10 | 15 | J.P.Jabouille | Renault | 71 | +4 Laps | 12 |
| 11 | 5 | Mario Andretti | Lotus-Ford | 69 | +6 Laps | 4 |
| Ret | 12 | G.Villeneuve | Ferrari | 62 | Accident | 8 |
| Ret | 6 | Ronnie Peterson | Lotus-Ford | 56 | Gearbox | 7 |
| Ret | 7 | James Hunt | McLaren-Ford | 43 | Handling | 6 |
| Ret | 36 | Rolf Stommelen | Arrows-Ford | 38 | Driver unwell | 19 |
| Ret | 27 | Alan Jones | Williams-Ford | 29 | Oil leak | 10 |
| Ret | 22 | Jacky Ickx | Ensign-Ford | 27 | Brakes | 16 |
| Ret | 16 | H.J.Stuck | Shadow-Ford | 24 | Accident | 17 |
| Ret | 26 | Jacques Laffite | Ligier-Matra | 13 | Gearbox | 15 |
| Ret | 18 | Rupert Keegan | Surtees-Ford | 8 | Transmission | 18 |
| DNQ | 9 | Jochen Mass | ATS-Ford | | | |
| DNQ | 17 | Clay Regazzoni | Shadow-Ford | | | |
| DNQ | 10 | Jean-Pierre Jarier | ATS-Ford | | | |
| DNQ | 19 | V.Brambilla | Surtees-Ford | | | |
| DNPQ | 32 | Keke Rosberg | Theodore-Ford | | | |
| DNPQ | 24 | Derek Daly | Hesketh-Ford | | | |
| DNPQ | 31 | Rene Arnoux | Martini-Ford | | | |
| DNPQ | 25 | Hector Rebaque | Lotus-Ford | | | |
| DNPQ | 30 | Brett Lunger | McLaren-Ford | | | |
| DNPQ | 37 | Arturo Merzario | Merzario-Ford | | | |

Winning speed: 80.359mph Lap leaders: Watson 1-37; Depailler 38-75
Pole position: Reutemann, 1m 28.340s, 83.866mph
Fastest lap: Lauda, 1m 28.650s, 83.573mph

### BELGIAN GRAND PRIX: ZOLDER *21 May Round: 6 Race: 303 70 x 2.648 miles*

| POS. | NO. | DRIVER | CAR-ENGINE | LAPS | TIME/RETIRED | GRID |
|---|---|---|---|---|---|---|
| 1 | 5 | Mario Andretti | Lotus-Ford | 70 | 1:39'52.02 | 1 |
| 2 | 6 | Ronnie Peterson | Lotus-Ford | 70 | +9.90 | 7 |
| 3 | 11 | Carlos Reutemann | Ferrari | 70 | +24.34 | 2 |
| 4 | 12 | G.Villeneuve | Ferrari | 70 | +47.04 | 4 |
| 5 | 26 | Jacques Laffite | Ligier-Matra | 69 | Accident | 14 |
| 6 | 3 | Didier Pironi | Tyrrell-Ford | 69 | +1 Lap | 23 |
| 7 | 30 | Brett Lunger | McLaren-Ford | 69 | +1 Lap | 24 |
| 8 | 33 | Bruno Giacomelli | McLaren-Ford | 69 | +1 Lap | 21 |
| 9 | 31 | Rene Arnoux | Martini-Ford | 68 | +2 Laps | 19 |
| 10 | 27 | Alan Jones | Williams-Ford | 68 | +2 Laps | 11 |
| 11 | 9 | Jochen Mass | ATS-Ford | 68 | +2 Laps | 16 |
| 12 | 22 | Jacky Ickx | Ensign-Ford | 64 | +6 Laps | 22 |
| 13 | 19 | V.Brambilla | Surtees-Ford | 63 | Engine | 12 |
| NC | 15 | J.P.Jabouille | Renault | 56 | Not classified | 10 |
| Ret | 16 | H.J.Stuck | Shadow-Ford | 56 | Spun off | 10 |
| Ret | 20 | Jody Scheckter | Wolf-Ford | 53 | Spun off | 5 |
| Ret | 4 | P.Depailler | Tyrrell-Ford | 51 | Gearbox | 13 |
| Ret | 17 | Clay Regazzoni | Shadow-Ford | 40 | Transmission | 18 |
| Ret | 35 | Riccardo Patrese | Arrows-Ford | 31 | Suspension | 8 |
| Ret | 36 | Rolf Stommelen | Arrows-Ford | 26 | Spun off | 17 |
| Ret | 2 | John Watson | Brabham-Alfa Romeo | 18 | Accident | 9 |
| Ret | 1 | Niki Lauda | Brabham-Alfa Romeo | 0 | Accident | 3 |
| Ret | 7 | James Hunt | McLaren-Ford | 0 | Accident | 6 |
| Ret | 14 | Emerson Fittipaldi | Fittipaldi-Ford | 0 | Accident | 15 |
| DNQ | 18 | Rupert Keegan | Surtees-Ford | | | |
| DNQ | 24 | Derek Daly | Hesketh-Ford | | | |
| DNQ | 32 | Keke Rosberg | Theodore-Ford | | | |
| DNQ | 10 | Alberto Colombo | ATS-Ford | | | |
| DNPQ | 25 | Hector Rebaque | Lotus-Ford | | | |
| DNPQ | 37 | Arturo Merzario | Merzario-Ford | | | |

Winning speed: 111.376mph Lap leaders: Andretti 1-70
Pole position: Andretti, 1m 20.900s, 117.847mph
Fastest lap: Peterson, 1m 23.130s, 114.686mph

### SPANISH GRAND PRIX: JARAMA *4 June Round: 7 Race: 304 75 x 2.115 miles*

| POS. | NO. | DRIVER | CAR-ENGINE | LAPS | TIME/RETIRED | GRID |
|---|---|---|---|---|---|---|
| 1 | 5 | Mario Andretti | Lotus-Ford | 75 | 1:41'47.06 | 1 |
| 2 | 6 | Ronnie Peterson | Lotus-Ford | 75 | +19.56 | 2 |
| 3 | 26 | Jacques Laffite | Ligier-Matra | 75 | +37.24 | 10 |
| 4 | 20 | Jody Scheckter | Wolf-Ford | 75 | +1'00.06 | 9 |
| 5 | 2 | John Watson | Brabham-Alfa Romeo | 75 | +1'05.93 | 7 |
| 6 | 7 | James Hunt | McLaren-Ford | 74 | +1 Lap | 4 |
| 7 | 19 | V.Brambilla | Surtees-Ford | 74 | +1 Lap | 16 |
| 8 | 27 | Alan Jones | Williams-Ford | 74 | +1 Lap | 18 |
| 9 | 9 | Jochen Mass | ATS-Ford | 74 | +1 Lap | 17 |
| 10 | 12 | G.Villeneuve | Ferrari | 74 | +1 Lap | 5 |
| 11 | 18 | Rupert Keegan | Surtees-Ford | 73 | +2 Laps | 23 |
| 12 | 3 | Didier Pironi | Tyrrell-Ford | 71 | +4 Laps | 13 |
| 13 | 15 | J.P.Jabouille | Renault | 71 | +4 Laps | 11 |
| 14 | 36 | Rolf Stommelen | Arrows-Ford | 71 | +4 Laps | 19 |
| 15 | 17 | Clay Regazzoni | Shadow-Ford | 67 | Fuel pipe | 22 |
| Ret | 22 | Jacky Ickx | Ensign-Ford | 64 | Engine | 21 |
| Ret | 14 | Emerson Fittipaldi | Fittipaldi-Ford | 62 | Throttle | 15 |
| Ret | 11 | Carlos Reutemann | Ferrari | 57 | Accident | 3 |
| Ret | 1 | Niki Lauda | Brabham-Alfa Romeo | 56 | Engine | 6 |
| Ret | 4 | P.Depailler | Tyrrell-Ford | 51 | Engine | 12 |
| Ret | 16 | H.J.Stuck | Shadow-Ford | 45 | Suspension | 24 |
| Ret | 35 | Riccardo Patrese | Arrows-Ford | 21 | Engine | 8 |
| Ret | 25 | Hector Rebaque | Lotus-Ford | 21 | Exhaust | 20 |
| Ret | 8 | Patrick Tambay | McLaren-Ford | 16 | Spun off | 14 |
| DNQ | 37 | Arturo Merzario | Merzario-Ford | | | |
| DNQ | 30 | Brett Lunger | McLaren-Ford | | | |
| DNQ | 28 | E.de Villota | McLaren-Ford | | | |
| DNQ | 10 | Alberto Colombo | ATS-Ford | | | |
| DNPQ | 32 | Keke Rosberg | Theodore-Ford | | | |

Winning speed: 93.513mph Lap leaders: Hunt 1-5; Andretti 6-75
Pole position: Andretti, 1m 16.390s, 99.680mph
Fastest lap: Andretti, 1m 20.060s, 95.110mph

### SWEDISH GRAND PRIX: ANDERSTORP *17 June Round: 8 Race: 305 70 x 2.505 miles*

| POS. | NO. | DRIVER | CAR-ENGINE | LAPS | TIME/RETIRED | GRID |
|---|---|---|---|---|---|---|
| 1 | 1 | Niki Lauda | Brabham-Alfa Romeo | 70 | 1:41'00.606 | 3 |
| 2 | 35 | Riccardo Patrese | Arrows-Ford | 70 | +34.019 | 5 |
| 3 | 6 | Ronnie Peterson | Lotus-Ford | 70 | +34.105 | 4 |
| 4 | 8 | Patrick Tambay | McLaren-Ford | 69 | +1 Lap | 15 |
| 5 | 17 | Clay Regazzoni | Shadow-Ford | 69 | +1 Lap | 16 |
| 6 | 14 | Emerson Fittipaldi | Fittipaldi-Ford | 69 | +1 Lap | 13 |
| 7 | 26 | Jacques Laffite | Ligier-Matra | 69 | +1 Lap | 11 |
| 8 | 7 | James Hunt | McLaren-Ford | 69 | +1 Lap | 14 |
| 9 | 12 | G.Villeneuve | Ferrari | 69 | +1 Lap | 7 |
| 10 | 11 | Carlos Reutemann | Ferrari | 69 | +1 Lap | 8 |
| 11 | 16 | H.J.Stuck | Shadow-Ford | 68 | +2 Laps | 20 |
| 12 | 25 | Hector Rebaque | Lotus-Ford | 68 | +2 Laps | 21 |
| 13 | 9 | Jochen Mass | ATS-Ford | 68 | +2 Laps | 19 |
| 14 | 36 | Rolf Stommelen | Arrows-Ford | 67 | +3 Laps | 24 |
| 15 | 10 | Keke Rosberg | ATS-Ford | 63 | +7 Laps | 23 |
| Ret | 37 | Arturo Merzario | Merzario-Ford | 62 | Not classified | 22 |
| Ret | 5 | Mario Andretti | Lotus-Ford | 46 | Engine | 1 |
| Ret | 27 | Alan Jones | Williams-Ford | 46 | Wheel | 9 |
| Ret | 4 | P.Depailler | Tyrrell-Ford | 42 | Suspension | 12 |
| Ret | 15 | J.P.Jabouille | Renault | 28 | Engine | 10 |
| Ret | 2 | John Watson | Brabham-Alfa Romeo | 19 | Spun off | 2 |
| Ret | 20 | Jody Scheckter | Wolf-Ford | 16 | Overheating | 6 |
| Ret | 3 | Didier Pironi | Tyrrell-Ford | 8 | Accident | 17 |
| Ret | 19 | V.Brambilla | Surtees-Ford | 7 | Accident | 18 |
| DNQ | 18 | Rupert Keegan | Surtees-Ford | | | |
| DNQ | 30 | Brett Lunger | McLaren-Ford | | | |
| DNQ | 22 | Jacky Ickx | Ensign-Ford | | | |

Winning speed: 104.147mph Lap leaders: Andretti 1-38; Lauda 39-70
Pole position: Andretti, 1m 22.258s, 109.887mph
Fastest lap: Lauda, 1m 24.836s, 106.288mph

### FRENCH GRAND PRIX: PAUL RICARD *2 July Round: 9 Race: 306 54 x 3.610 miles*

| POS. | NO. | DRIVER | CAR-ENGINE | LAPS | TIME/RETIRED | GRID |
|---|---|---|---|---|---|---|
| 1 | 5 | Mario Andretti | Lotus-Ford | 54 | 1:38'51.92 | 2 |
| 2 | 6 | Ronnie Peterson | Lotus-Ford | 54 | +2.93 | 5 |
| 3 | 7 | James Hunt | McLaren-Ford | 54 | +19.80 | 4 |
| 4 | 2 | John Watson | Brabham-Alfa Romeo | 54 | +36.88 | 1 |
| 5 | 27 | Alan Jones | Williams-Ford | 54 | +41.81 | 14 |
| 6 | 20 | Jody Scheckter | Wolf-Ford | 54 | +54.53 | 7 |
| 7 | 26 | Jacques Laffite | Ligier-Matra | 54 | +54.74 | 10 |
| 8 | 35 | Riccardo Patrese | Arrows-Ford | 54 | +1'24.88 | 12 |
| 9 | 8 | Patrick Tambay | McLaren-Ford | 54 | +1'27.06 | 6 |
| 10 | 3 | Didier Pironi | Tyrrell-Ford | 54 | +1'29.98 | 16 |
| 11 | 16 | H.J.Stuck | Shadow-Ford | 53 | +1 Lap | 20 |
| 12 | 12 | G.Villeneuve | Ferrari | 53 | +1 Lap | 9 |
| 13 | 9 | Jochen Mass | ATS-Ford | 53 | +1 Lap | 25 |
| 14 | 31 | Rene Arnoux | Martini-Ford | 53 | +1 Lap | 18 |
| 15 | 36 | Rolf Stommelen | Arrows-Ford | 53 | +1 Lap | 21 |
| 16 | 10 | Keke Rosberg | ATS-Ford | 52 | +2 Laps | 26 |
| 17 | 19 | V.Brambilla | Surtees-Ford | 52 | +2 Laps | 19 |
| 18 | 11 | Carlos Reutemann | Ferrari | 49 | +5 Laps | 8 |
| Ret | 30 | Brett Lunger | McLaren-Ford | 45 | Engine | 24 |
| Ret | 14 | Emerson Fittipaldi | Fittipaldi-Ford | 43 | Suspension | 15 |
| Ret | 18 | Rupert Keegan | Surtees-Ford | 40 | Engine | 23 |
| Ret | 33 | Bruno Giacomelli | McLaren-Ford | 28 | Engine | 22 |
| Ret | 1 | Niki Lauda | Brabham-Alfa Romeo | 10 | Engine | 3 |
| Ret | 4 | P.Depailler | Tyrrell-Ford | 10 | Engine | 13 |
| Ret | 17 | Clay Regazzoni | Shadow-Ford | 4 | Electrical | 17 |
| Ret | 15 | J.P.Jabouille | Renault | 1 | Engine | 11 |
| DNQ | 37 | Arturo Merzario | Merzario-Ford | | | |
| DNQ | 22 | Derek Daly | Ensign-Ford | | | |
| DNQ | 25 | Hector Rebaque | Lotus-Ford | | | |

Winning speed: 118.312mph Lap leaders: Andretti 1-54
Pole position: Watson, 1m 44.420s, 124.477mph
Fastest lap: Reutemann, 1m 48.560s, 119.718mph

## BRITISH GRAND PRIX: BRANDS HATCH *16 July Round: 10 Race: 307 76 x 2.614 miles*

| POS. | NO. | DRIVER | CAR-ENGINE | LAPS | TIME/RETIRED | GRID |
|---|---|---|---|---|---|---|
| 1 | 11 | Carlos Reutemann | Ferrari | 76 | 1:42'12.39 | 8 |
| 2 | 1 | Niki Lauda | Brabham-Alfa Romeo | 76 | +1.23 | 4 |
| 3 | 2 | John Watson | Brabham-Alfa Romeo | 76 | +37.25 | 9 |
| 4 | 4 | P.Depailler | Tyrrell-Ford | 76 | +1'13.27 | 10 |
| 5 | 16 | H.J.Stuck | Shadow-Ford | 75 | +1 Lap | 18 |
| 6 | 8 | Patrick Tambay | McLaren-Ford | 75 | +1 Lap | 20 |
| 7 | 33 | Bruno Giacomelli | McLaren-Ford | 75 | +1 Lap | 16 |
| 8 | 30 | Brett Lunger | McLaren-Ford | 75 | +1 Lap | 24 |
| 9 | 19 | V.Brambilla | Surtees-Ford | 75 | +1 Lap | 25 |
| 10 | 26 | Jacques Laffite | Ligier-Matra | 73 | +3 Laps | 7 |
| NC | 9 | Jochen Mass | ATS-Ford | 66 | Not classified | 26 |
| Ret | 10 | Keke Rosberg | ATS-Ford | 59 | Suspension | 22 |
| Ret | 17 | Clay Regazzoni | Shadow-Ford | 49 | Gearbox | 17 |
| Ret | 15 | J.P.Jabouille | Renault | 46 | Turbo | 12 |
| Ret | 35 | Riccardo Patrese | Arrows-Ford | 40 | Suspension | 5 |
| Ret | 3 | Didier Pironi | Tyrrell-Ford | 40 | Gearbox | 19 |
| Ret | 20 | Jody Scheckter | Wolf-Ford | 36 | Gearbox | 3 |
| Ret | 14 | Emerson Fittipaldi | Fittipaldi-Ford | 32 | Engine | 11 |
| Ret | 37 | Arturo Merzario | Merzario-Ford | 32 | Fuel pump | 23 |
| Ret | 22 | Derek Daly | Ensign-Ford | 30 | Wheel | 15 |
| Ret | 5 | Mario Andretti | Lotus-Ford | 28 | Engine | 2 |
| Ret | 27 | Alan Jones | Williams-Ford | 26 | Transmission | 6 |
| Ret | 12 | G.Villeneuve | Ferrari | 19 | Transmission | 13 |
| Ret | 25 | Hector Rebaque | Lotus-Ford | 15 | Gearbox | 21 |
| Ret | 7 | James Hunt | McLaren-Ford | 8 | Accident | 14 |
| Ret | 6 | Ronnie Peterson | Lotus-Ford | 6 | Fuel system | 1 |
| DNQ | 18 | Rupert Keegan | Surtees-Ford | | | |
| DNQ | 36 | Rolf Stommelen | Arrows-Ford | | | |
| DNQ | 23 | Geoff Lees | Ensign-Ford | | | |
| DNQ | 40 | Tony Trimmer | McLaren-Ford | | | |

Winning speed: 116.625mph
Lap leaders: Andretti 1-23; Scheckter 24-33; Lauda 34-59; Reutemann 60-76
Pole position: Peterson, 1m 16.800s, 122.531mph
Fastest lap: Lauda, 1m 18.600s, 119.725mph

## GERMAN GRAND PRIX: HOCKENHEIM *30 July Round: 11 Race: 308 45 x 4.218 miles*

| POS. | NO. | DRIVER | CAR-ENGINE | LAPS | TIME/RETIRED | GRID |
|---|---|---|---|---|---|---|
| 1 | 5 | Mario Andretti | Lotus-Ford | 45 | 1:28'00.90 | 1 |
| 2 | 20 | Jody Scheckter | Wolf-Ford | 45 | +15.35 | 4 |
| 3 | 26 | Jacques Laffite | Ligier-Matra | 45 | +28.01 | 7 |
| 4 | 14 | Emerson Fittipaldi | Fittipaldi-Ford | 45 | +36.88 | 10 |
| 5 | 3 | Didier Pironi | Tyrrell-Ford | 45 | +57.26 | 16 |
| 6 | 25 | Hector Rebaque | Lotus-Ford | 45 | +1'37.86 | 18 |
| 7 | 2 | John Watson | Brabham-Alfa Romeo | 45 | +1'39.53 | 5 |
| 8 | 12 | G.Villeneuve | Ferrari | 45 | +1'56.87 | 15 |
| 9 | 35 | Riccardo Patrese | Arrows-Ford | 44 | +1 Lap | 14 |
| 10 | 32 | Keke Rosberg | Wolf-Ford | 42 | +3 Laps | 19 |
| 11 | 23 | Harald Ertl | Ensign-Ford | 41 | Engine | 17 |
| DSQ | 36 | Rolf Stommelen | Arrows-Ford | 42 | Disqualified | 23 |
| Ret | 6 | Ronnie Peterson | Lotus-Ford | 36 | Gearbox | 2 |
| Ret | 7 | James Hunt | McLaren-Ford | 34 | Disqualified | 8 |
| Ret | 27 | Alan Jones | Williams-Ford | 31 | Fuel system | 6 |
| Ret | 22 | Nelson Piquet | Ensign-Ford | 31 | Engine | 21 |
| Ret | 19 | V.Brambilla | Surtees-Ford | 24 | Fuel system | 20 |
| Ret | 8 | Patrick Tambay | McLaren-Ford | 16 | Accident | 11 |
| Ret | 11 | Carlos Reutemann | Ferrari | 14 | Fuel system | 12 |
| Ret | 1 | Niki Lauda | Brabham-Alfa Romeo | 11 | Engine | 3 |
| Ret | 15 | J.P.Jabouille | Renault | 5 | Engine | 9 |
| Ret | 9 | Jochen Mass | ATS-Ford | 1 | Accident | 22 |
| Ret | 16 | H.J.Stuck | Shadow-Ford | 1 | Accident | 24 |
| Ret | 4 | P.Depailler | Tyrrell-Ford | 0 | Accident | 13 |
| DNQ | 17 | Clay Regazzoni | Shadow-Ford | | | |
| DNQ | 10 | Jean-Pierre Jarier | ATS-Ford | | | |
| DNQ | 18 | Rupert Keegan | Surtees-Ford | | | |
| DNQ | 37 | Arturo Merzario | Merzario-Ford | | | |
| DNPQ | 31 | Rene Arnoux | Martini-Ford | | | |
| DNPQ | 30 | Brett Lunger | McLaren-Ford | | | |

Winning speed: 129.409mph Lap leaders: Peterson 1-4; Andretti 5-45
Pole position: Andretti, 1m 51.900s, 135.715mph
Fastest lap: Peterson, 1m 55.620s, 131.349mph

## AUSTRIAN GRAND PRIX: OSTERREICHRING *13 August Round: 12 Race: 309 54 x 3.692 miles*

| POS. | NO. | DRIVER | CAR-ENGINE | LAPS | TIME/RETIRED | GRID |
|---|---|---|---|---|---|---|
| 1 | 6 | Ronnie Peterson | Lotus-Ford | 54 | 1:41'21.57 | 1 |
| 2 | 4 | P.Depailler | Tyrrell-Ford | 54 | +47.44 | 14 |
| 3 | 12 | G.Villeneuve | Ferrari | 54 | +1'39.76 | 11 |
| 4 | 14 | Emerson Fittipaldi | Fittipaldi-Ford | 53 | +1 Lap | 6 |
| 5 | 26 | Jacques Laffite | Ligier-Matra | 53 | +1 Lap | 5 |
| 6 | 19 | V.Brambilla | Surtees-Ford | 53 | +1 Lap | 21 |
| 7 | 2 | John Watson | Brabham-Alfa Romeo | 53 | +1 Lap | 10 |
| 8 | 30 | Brett Lunger | McLaren-Ford | 52 | +2 Laps | 17 |
| 9 | 31 | Rene Arnoux | Martini-Ford | 52 | +2 Laps | 26 |
| NC | 17 | Clay Regazzoni | Shadow-Ford | 50 | Not classified | 22 |
| NC | 32 | Keke Rosberg | Wolf-Ford | 49 | Not classified | 25 |
| DSQ | 22 | Derek Daly | Ensign-Ford | 41 | Disqualified | 19 |
| Ret | 8 | Patrick Tambay | McLaren-Ford | 40 | Accident | 14 |
| Ret | 16 | H.J.Stuck | Shadow-Ford | 33 | Accident | 23 |
| Ret | 15 | J.P.Jabouille | Renault | 31 | Gearbox | 3 |
| DSQ | 11 | Carlos Reutemann | Ferrari | 28 | Disqualified | 12 |
| Ret | 1 | Niki Lauda | Brabham-Alfa Romeo | 27 | Accident | 4 |
| Ret | 3 | Didier Pironi | Tyrrell-Ford | 20 | Accident | 9 |
| Ret | 7 | James Hunt | McLaren-Ford | 7 | Accident | 8 |
| Ret | 27 | Alan Jones | Williams-Ford | 7 | Accident | 15 |
| Ret | 35 | Riccardo Patrese | Arrows-Ford | 7 | Accident | 16 |
| Ret | 23 | Harald Ertl | Ensign-Ford | 7 | Accident | 24 |
| Ret | 25 | Hector Rebaque | Lotus-Ford | 4 | Accident | 18 |
| Ret | 29 | Nelson Piquet | McLaren-Ford | 4 | Accident | 20 |
| Ret | 20 | Jody Scheckter | Wolf-Ford | 3 | Accident | 7 |
| Ret | 5 | Mario Andretti | Lotus-Ford | 0 | Accident | 2 |
| DNQ | 37 | Arturo Merzario | Merzario-Ford | | | |
| DNQ | 9 | Jochen Mass | ATS-Ford | | | |
| DNQ | 18 | Rupert Keegan | Surtees-Ford | | | |
| DNQ | 10 | Hans Binder | ATS-Ford | | | |
| DNPQ | 36 | Rolf Stommelen | Arrows-Ford | | | |

Winning speed: 118.022mph
Lap leaders: Peterson 1-18, 29-54; Reutemann 19-22; Villeneuve 23-28
Pole position: Peterson, 1m 37.710s, 136.034mph
Fastest lap: Peterson, 1m 43.120s, 128.897mph
Race stopped in the rain after the lap 7 accident; results were on aggregate. Lap leaders are given' on the road.'

## DUTCH GRAND PRIX: ZANDVOORT *27 August Round: 13 Race: 310 75 x 2.626 miles*

| POS. | NO. | DRIVER | CAR-ENGINE | LAPS | TIME/RETIRED | GRID |
|---|---|---|---|---|---|---|
| 1 | 5 | Mario Andretti | Lotus-Ford | 75 | 1:41'04.23 | 1 |
| 2 | 6 | Ronnie Peterson | Lotus-Ford | 75 | +0.32 | 2 |
| 3 | 1 | Niki Lauda | Brabham-Alfa Romeo | 75 | +12.21 | 3 |
| 4 | 2 | John Watson | Brabham-Alfa Romeo | 75 | +20.92 | 8 |
| 5 | 14 | Emerson Fittipaldi | Fittipaldi-Ford | 75 | +21.50 | 10 |
| 6 | 12 | G.Villeneuve | Ferrari | 75 | +45.95 | 5 |
| 7 | 11 | Carlos Reutemann | Ferrari | 75 | +1'00.52 | 4 |
| 8 | 26 | Jacques Laffite | Ligier-Matra | 74 | +1 Lap | 6 |
| 9 | 8 | Patrick Tambay | McLaren-Ford | 74 | +1 Lap | 14 |
| 10 | 7 | James Hunt | McLaren-Ford | 74 | +1 Lap | 7 |
| 11 | 25 | Hector Rebaque | Lotus-Ford | 74 | +1 Lap | 20 |
| 12 | 20 | Jody Scheckter | Wolf-Ford | 73 | +2 Laps | 15 |
| Ret | 33 | Bruno Giacomelli | McLaren-Ford | 60 | Spun off | 19 |
| Ret | 16 | H.J.Stuck | Shadow-Ford | 56 | Transmission | 18 |
| Ret | 31 | Rene Arnoux | Martini-Ford | 40 | Chassis | 23 |
| Ret | 37 | Arturo Merzario | Merzario-Ford | 40 | Engine | 27 |
| DSQ | 19 | V.Brambilla | Surtees-Ford | 37 | Disqualified | 22 |
| Ret | 15 | J.P.Jabouille | Renault | 35 | Engine | 9 |
| Ret | 30 | Brett Lunger | McLaren-Ford | 35 | Engine | 21 |
| Ret | 32 | Keke Rosberg | Wolf-Ford | 21 | Accident | 24 |
| Ret | 27 | Alan Jones | Williams-Ford | 17 | Throttle | 11 |
| Ret | 29 | Nelson Piquet | McLaren-Ford | 16 | Transmission | 26 |
| Ret | 4 | P.Depailler | Tyrrell-Ford | 13 | Engine | 12 |
| Ret | 22 | Derek Daly | Ensign-Ford | 10 | Transmission | 16 |
| Ret | 35 | Riccardo Patrese | Arrows-Ford | 0 | Accident | 13 |
| Ret | 3 | Didier Pironi | Tyrrell-Ford | 0 | Accident | 17 |
| DNQ | 17 | Clay Regazzoni | Shadow-Ford | | | |
| DNQ | 10 | M.Bleekemolen | ATS-Ford | | | |
| DNQ | 9 | Jochen Mass | ATS-Ford | | | |
| DNPQ | 23 | Harald Ertl | Ensign-Ford | | | |
| DNPQ | 39 | Danny Ongais | Shadow-Ford | | | |
| DNPQ | 36 | Rolf Stommelen | Arrows-Ford | | | |

Winning speed: 116.915mph Lap leaders: Andretti 1-75
Pole position: Andretti, 1m 16.360s, 123.799mph
Fastest lapSpeed: Lauda, 1m 19.570s, 118.805mph

## ITALIAN GRAND PRIX: MONZA *10 September Round: 14 Race: 311 40 x 3.604 miles*

| POS. | NO. | DRIVER | CAR-ENGINE | LAPS | TIME/RETIRED | GRID |
|---|---|---|---|---|---|---|
| 1 | 1 | Niki Lauda | Brabham-Alfa Romeo | 40 | 1:07'04.54 | 4 |
| 2 | 2 | John Watson | Brabham-Alfa Romeo | 40 | +1.48 | 7 |
| 3 | 11 | Carlos Reutemann | Ferrari | 40 | +20.47 | 11 |
| 4 | 26 | Jacques Laffite | Ligier-Matra | 40 | +37.53 | 8 |
| 5 | 8 | Patrick Tambay | McLaren-Ford | 40 | +40.39 | 19 |
| 6 | 5 | Mario Andretti | Lotus-Ford | 40 | + 46.33 | 1 |
| 7 | 12 | G.Villeneuve | Ferrari | 40 | +48.48 | 2 |
| 8 | 14 | Emerson Fittipaldi | Fittipaldi-Ford | 40 | +55.24 | 13 |
| 9 | 29 | Nelson Piquet | McLaren-Ford | 40 | +1'06.83 | 24 |
| 10 | 22 | Derek Daly | Ensign-Ford | 40 | +1'09.11 | 18 |
| 11 | 4 | P.Depailler | Tyrrell-Ford | 40 | +1'16.57 | 16 |
| 12 | 20 | Jody Scheckter | Wolf-Ford | 39 | +1 Lap | 9 |
| 13 | 27 | Alan Jones | Williams-Ford | 39 | +1 Lap | 6 |
| 14 | 33 | Bruno Giacomelli | McLaren-Ford | 39 | +1 Lap | 20 |
| Ret | 17 | Clay Regazzoni | Shadow-Ford | 33 | Not classified | 15 |
| Ret | 35 | Riccardo Patrese | Arrows-Ford | 28 | Engine | 12 |
| Ret | 7 | James Hunt | McLaren-Ford | 19 | Distributor | 10 |
| Ret | 37 | Arturo Merzario | Merzario-Ford | 14 | Engine | 22 |
| Ret | 15 | J.P.Jabouille | Renault | 6 | Engine | 3 |
| Ret | 6 | Ronnie Peterson | Lotus-Ford | 0 | Accident | 5 |
| Ret | 3 | Didier Pironi | Tyrrell-Ford | 0 | Accident | 14 |
| Ret | 16 | H.J.Stuck | Shadow-Ford | 0 | Accident | 17 |
| Ret | 30 | Brett Lunger | McLaren-Ford | 0 | Accident | 21 |
| Ret | 19 | V.Brambilla | Surtees-Ford | 0 | Accident | 23 |
| DNQ | 25 | Hector Rebaque | Lotus-Ford | | | |
| DNQ | 10 | Harald Ertl | ATS-Ford | | | |
| DNQ | 9 | M.Bleekemolen | ATS-Ford | | | |
| DNQ | 18 | Carlo Franchi | Surtees-Ford | | | |
| DNPQ | 23 | Harald Ertl | Ensign-Ford | | | |
| DNPQ | 32 | Keke Rosberg | Wolf-Ford | | | |
| DNPQ | 36 | Rolf Stommelen | Arrows-Ford | | | |
| DNPQ | 38 | Alberto Colombo | Merzario-Ford | | | |

Winning speed: 128.951mph Lap leaders: Villeneuve 1-34, Andretti 35-40
Pole position: Andretti, 1m 37.520s, 133.042mph
Fastest lap: Andretti, 1m 38.230s, 132.080mph
Race scheduled for 52 laps but stopped and shortened after the accident at the original start. Andretti and Villeneuve finished first and second but were pealised one minute after the race for jump starts.

## USA EAST GRAND PRIX: WATKINS GLEN *1 October Round: 15 Race: 312 59 x 3.377 miles*

| POS. | NO. | DRIVER | CAR-ENGINE | LAPS | TIME/RETIRED | GRID |
|---|---|---|---|---|---|---|
| 1 | 11 | Carlos Reutemann | Ferrari | 59 | 1:40'48.800 | 2 |
| 2 | 27 | Alan Jones | Williams-Ford | 59 | +19.739 | 3 |
| 3 | 20 | Jody Scheckter | Wolf-Ford | 59 | +45.701 | 11 |
| 4 | 15 | J.P.Jabouille | Renault | 59 | +1'25.007 | 9 |
| 5 | 14 | Emerson Fittipaldi | Fittipaldi-Ford | 59 | +1'28.089 | 13 |
| 6 | 8 | Patrick Tambay | McLaren-Ford | 59 | +1'50.210 | 18 |
| 7 | 7 | James Hunt | McLaren-Ford | 58 | +1 Lap | 6 |
| 8 | 22 | Derek Daly | Ensign-Ford | 58 | +1 Lap | 19 |
| 9 | 18 | Rene Arnoux | Surtees-Ford | 58 | +1 Lap | 21 |
| 10 | 3 | Didier Pironi | Tyrrell-Ford | 58 | +1 Lap | 16 |
| 11 | 26 | Jacques Laffite | Ligier-Matra | 58 | +1 Lap | 10 |
| 12 | 21 | Bobby Rahal | Wolf-Ford | 58 | +1 Lap | 20 |
| 13 | 23 | Brett Lunger | Ensign-Ford | 58 | +1 Lap | 24 |
| 14 | 17 | Clay Regazzoni | Shadow-Ford | 56 | +3 Laps | 17 |
| 15 | 55 | Jean-Pierre Jarier | Lotus-Ford | 55 | Out of fuel | 8 |
| 16 | 36 | Rolf Stommelen | Arrows-Ford | 54 | +5 Laps | 22 |
| Ret | 37 | Arturo Merzario | Merzario-Ford | 46 | Gearbox | 26 |
| Ret | 9 | M.Bleekemolen | ATS-Ford | 43 | Oil leak | 25 |
| Ret | 1 | Niki Lauda | Brabham-Alfa Romeo | 28 | Engine | 5 |
| Ret | 5 | Mario Andretti | Lotus-Ford | 27 | Engine | 1 |
| Ret | 2 | John Watson | Brabham-Alfa Romeo | 25 | Engine | 7 |
| Ret | 4 | P.Depailler | Tyrrell-Ford | 23 | Wheel | 12 |
| Ret | 12 | G.Villeneuve | Ferrari | 22 | Engine | 4 |
| Ret | 10 | Keke Rosberg | ATS-Ford | 21 | Transmission | 15 |
| Ret | 16 | H.J.Stuck | Shadow-Ford | 1 | Fuel system | 14 |
| Ret | 25 | Hector Rebaque | Lotus-Ford | 0 | Clutch | 23 |
| DNQ | 19 | Beppe Gabbiani | Surtees-Ford | | | |

Winning speed: 118.581mph Lap leaders: Andretti 1-2; Reutemann 3-59
Pole position: Andretti, 1m 38.114s, 123.909mph
Fastest lap: Jarier, 1m 39.557s, 122.113mph

## CANADIAN GRAND PRIX: MONTREAL *8 October Round: 16 Race: 313 70 x 2.796 miles*

| POS. | NO. | DRIVER | CAR-ENGINE | LAPS | TIME/RETIRED | GRID |
|---|---|---|---|---|---|---|
| 1 | 12 | G.Villeneuve | Ferrari | 70 | 1:57'49.196 | 3 |
| 2 | 20 | Jody Scheckter | Wolf-Ford | 70 | +13.372 | 2 |
| 3 | 11 | Carlos Reutemann | Ferrari | 70 | +19.408 | 11 |
| 4 | 35 | Riccardo Patrese | Arrows-Ford | 70 | +24.667 | 12 |
| 5 | 4 | P.Depailler | Tyrrell-Ford | 70 | +28.558 | 13 |
| 6 | 22 | Derek Daly | Ensign-Ford | 70 | +54.476 | 15 |
| 7 | 3 | Didier Pironi | Tyrrell-Ford | 70 | +1'21.250 | 18 |
| 8 | 8 | Patrick Tambay | McLaren-Ford | 70 | +1'26.560 | 17 |
| 9 | 27 | Alan Jones | Williams-Ford | 70 | +1'28.942 | 5 |
| 10 | 5 | Mario Andretti | Lotus-Ford | 69 | +1 Lap | 9 |
| 11 | 66 | Nelson Piquet | Brabham-Alfa Romeo | 69 | +1 Lap | 14 |
| 12 | 15 | J.P.Jabouille | Renault | 65 | +5 Laps | 22 |
| NC | 10 | Keke Rosberg | ATS-Ford | 58 | Not classified | 21 |
| Ret | 26 | Jacques Laffite | Ligier-Matra | 52 | Transmission | 10 |
| Ret | 7 | James Hunt | McLaren-Ford | 51 | Spun off | 19 |
| Ret | 55 | Jean-Pierre Jarier | Lotus-Ford | 49 | Oil leak | 1 |
| Ret | 18 | Rene Arnoux | Surtees-Ford | 37 | Engine | 16 |
| Ret | 21 | Bobby Rahal | Wolf-Ford | 16 | Fuel system | 20 |
| Ret | 2 | John Watson | Brabham-Alfa Romeo | 8 | Accident | 4 |
| Ret | 1 | Niki Lauda | Brabham-Alfa Romeo | 5 | Brakes | 7 |
| Ret | 16 | H.J.Stuck | Shadow-Ford | 1 | Accident | 8 |
| Ret | 14 | Emerson Fittipaldi | Fittipaldi-Ford | 0 | Accident | 6 |
| DNQ | 17 | Clay Regazzoni | Shadow-Ford | | | |
| DNQ | 19 | Beppe Gabbiani | Surtees-Ford | | | |
| DNQ | 37 | Arturo Merzario | Merzario-Ford | | | |
| DNQ | 25 | Hector Rebaque | Lotus-Ford | | | |
| DNQ | 36 | Rolf Stommelen | Arrows-Ford | | | |
| DNQ | 9 | M.Bleekemolen | ATS-Ford | | | |

Winning speed: 99.677mph Lap leaders: Jarier 1-49; Villeneuve 50-70
Pole position: Jarier, 1m 38.015s, 102.701mph Fastest lap: Jones, 1m 38.072s, 102.641mph

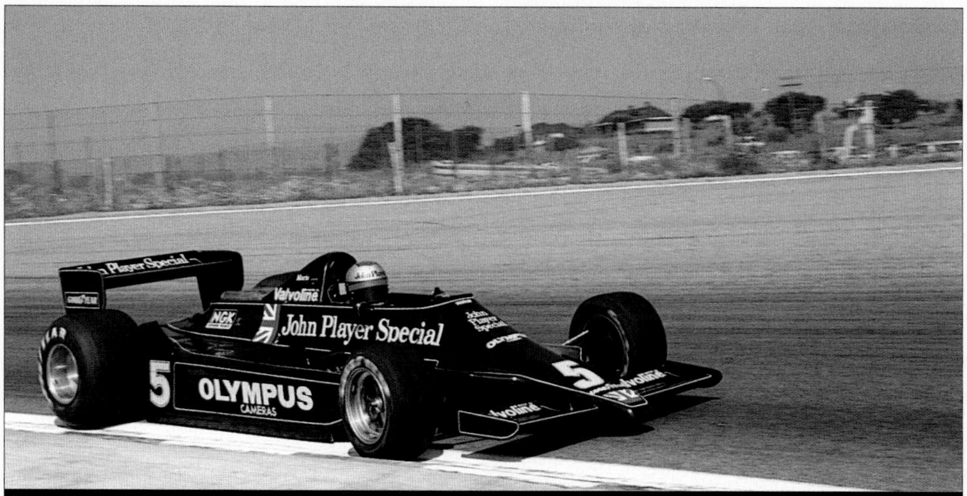


1978 world champion Mario Andretti in the Type 79 Lotus-Ford

# 1979

**DRIVERS' CHAMPION: JODY SCHECKTER**
**CONSTRUCTORS' CHAMPION: FERRARI**

## DRIVERS' CHAMPIONSHIP

| POS | DRIVER | COUNTRY | CAR | POINTS |
|---|---|---|---|---|
| 1 | Jody Scheckter | South Africa | Ferrari | 51(9) |
| 2 | Gilles Villeneuve | Canada | Ferrari | 47(6) |
| 3 | Alan Jones | Australia | Williams-Ford | 40(3) |
| 4 | Jacques Laffite | France | Ligier-Ford | 36 |
| 5 | Clay Regazzoni | Switzerland | Williams-Ford | 29(3) |
| 6 | Patrick Depailler | France | Ligier-Ford | 20(2) |
| = | Carlos Reutemann | Argentina | Lotus-Ford | 20(5) |
| 8 | Rene Arnoux | France | Renault | 17 |
| 9 | John Watson | GB | Mclaren-Ford | 15 |
| 10 | Jean-Pierre Jarier | France | Tyrrell-Ford | 14 |
| = | Mario Andretti | USA | Lotus-Ford | 14 |
| = | Didier Pironi | France | Tyrrell-Ford | 14 |
| 13 | Jean-Pierre Jabouille | France | Renault | 9 |
| 14 | Niki Lauda | Austria | Brabham-Alfa | 4 |
| 15 | Jochen Mass | West Germany | Arrows-Ford | 3 |
| = | Jacky Ickx | Belgium | Ligier-Ford | 3 |
| = | Nelson Piquet | Brazil | Brabham-Alfa, Brabham-Ford | 3 |
| = | Elio de Angelis | Italy | Shadow-Ford | 3 |
| 19 | Riccardo Patrese | Italy | Arrows-Ford | 2 |
| = | Hans Stuck | West Germany | ATS-Ford | 2 |
| 21 | Emerson Fittipaldi | Brazil | Copersucar-Ford | 1 |
| | Patrick Tambay | France | Mclaren-Ford | |
| | Jan Lammers | Netherlands | Shadow-Ford | |
| | Hector Rebaque | Mexico | Lotus-Ford, Rebaque-Ford | |
| | Arturo Merzario | Italy | Merzario-Ford | |
| | James Hunt | GB | Wolf-Ford | |
| | Derek Daly | Ireland | Ensign-Ford, Tyrrell-Ford | |
| | Bruno Giacomelli | Italy | Alfa-Romeo | |
| | Keke Rosberg | Finland | Wolf-Ford | |
| | Patrick Gaillard | France | Ensign-Ford | |
| | Geoff Lees | GB | Tyrrell-Ford | |
| | Vittorio Brambilla | Italy | Alfa Romeo | |
| | Marc Surer | Switzerland | Ensign-Ford | |
| | Ricardo Zunino | Argentina | Brabham-Ford | |
| | Gianfranco Brancatelli | Italy | Kauhsen-Ford, Merzario-Ford | |
| | Alex-Diaz Riberio | Brazil | Copersucur-Ford | |

Points for top six finishers (9, 6, 4, 3, 2, 1). Only the best four scores from the first seven races and the best four scores from the remaining eight races counted towards the championship.

## CONSTRUCTORS' CHAMPIONSHIP

| POS. | CONSTRUCTOR | POINTS |
|---|---|---|
| 1 | Ferrari | 113 |
| 2 | Williams-Ford | 75 |
| 3 | Ligier-Ford | 61 |
| 4 | Lotus-Ford | 39 |
| 5 | Tyrrell-Ford | 28 |
| 6 | Renault | 26 |
| 7 | McLaren-Ford | 15 |
| 8 | Brabham-Alfa Romeo | 7 |
| 9 | Arrows-Ford | 5 |
| 10 | Shadow-Ford | 3 |
| 11 | ATS-Ford | 2 |
| 12 | Fittipaldi-Ford | 1 |

Points for top six finishers (9, 6, 4, 3, 2, 1). Half points awarded for races stopped before half distance.

## ARGENTINE GRAND PRIX: BUENOS AIRES *21 January Round: 1 Race: 314 53 x 3.708 miles*

| POS. | NO. | DRIVER | CAR-ENGINE | LAPS | TIME/RETIRED | GRID |
|---|---|---|---|---|---|---|
| 1 | 26 | Jacques Laffite | Ligier-Ford | 53 | 1:36'03.21 | 1 |
| 2 | 2 | Carlos Reutemann | Lotus-Ford | 53 | +14.94 | 3 |
| 3 | 7 | John Watson | McLaren-Ford | 53 | +1'28.81 | 6 |
| 4 | 25 | P.Depailler | Ligier-Ford | 53 | +1'41.72 | 2 |
| 5 | 1 | Mario Andretti | Lotus-Ford | 52 | +1 Lap | 7 |
| 6 | 14 | Emerson Fittipaldi | Fittipaldi-Ford | 52 | +1 Lap | 11 |
| 7 | 18 | Elio de Angelis | Shadow-Ford | 52 | +1 Lap | 16 |
| 8 | 30 | Jochen Mass | Arrows-Ford | 51 | +2 Laps | 14 |
| 9 | 27 | Alan Jones | Williams-Ford | 51 | +2 Laps | 15 |
| 10 | 28 | Clay Regazzoni | Williams-Ford | 51 | +2 Laps | 17 |
| 11 | 22 | Derek Daly | Ensign-Ford | 51 | +2 Laps | 24 |
| Ret | 12 | G.Villeneuve | Ferrari | 48 | Engine | 10 |
| Ret | 31 | Hector Rebaque | Lotus-Ford | 46 | Suspension | 19 |
| Ret | 17 | Jan Lammers | Shadow-Ford | 42 | Transmission | 21 |
| Ret | 20 | James Hunt | Wolf-Ford | 41 | Electrical | 18 |
| Ret | 4 | Jean-Pierre Jarier | Tyrrell-Ford | 15 | Engine | 4 |
| Ret | 15 | J.P.Jabouille | Renault | 15 | Engine | 12 |
| Ret | 5 | Niki Lauda | Brabham-Alfa Romeo | 8 | Fuel system | 23 |
| Ret | 16 | Rene Arnoux | Renault | 6 | Engine | 25 |
| Ret | 11 | Jody Scheckter | Ferrari | 0 | Collision | 5 |
| Ret | 3 | Didier Pironi | Tyrrell-Ford | 0 | Collision | 8 |
| Ret | 8 | Patrick Tambay | McLaren-Ford | 0 | Collision | 9 |
| Ret | 6 | Nelson Piquet | Brabham-Alfa Romeo | 0 | Collision | 20 |
| Ret | 24 | Arturo Merzario | Merzario-Ford | 0 | Collision | 22 |
| DNS | 29 | Riccardo Patrese | Arrows-Ford | 0 | Non Starter | 13 |
| DNQ | 9 | H.J.Stuck | ATS-Ford | | | |

Winning speed: 122.770mph Lap leaders: Depailler 1-10; Laffite 11-53
Pole position: Laffite, 1m 44.200s, 128.119mph
Fastest lap: Laffite, 1m 46.910s, 124.872mph

## BRAZILIAN GRAND PRIX: INTERLAGOS *4 February Round: 2 Race: 315 40 x 4.893 miles*

| POS. | NO. | DRIVER | CAR-ENGINE | LAPS | TIME/RETIRED | GRID |
|---|---|---|---|---|---|---|
| 1 | 26 | Jacques Laffite | Ligier-Ford | 40 | 1:40'09.64 | 1 |
| 2 | 25 | P.Depailler | Ligier-Ford | 40 | +5.28 | 2 |
| 3 | 2 | Carlos Reutemann | Lotus-Ford | 40 | +44.14 | 3 |
| 4 | 3 | Didier Pironi | Tyrrell-Ford | 40 | +1'25.88 | 8 |
| 5 | 12 | G.Villeneuve | Ferrari | 39 | +1 Lap | 5 |
| 6 | 11 | Jody Scheckter | Ferrari | 39 | +1 Lap | 6 |
| 7 | 30 | Jochen Mass | Arrows-Ford | 39 | +1 Lap | 19 |
| 8 | 7 | John Watson | McLaren-Ford | 39 | +1 Lap | 14 |
| 9 | 29 | Riccardo Patrese | Arrows-Ford | 39 | +1 Lap | 16 |
| 10 | 15 | J.P.Jabouille | Renault | 39 | +1 Lap | 7 |
| 11 | 14 | Emerson Fittipaldi | Fittipaldi-Ford | 39 | +1 Lap | 9 |
| 12 | 18 | Elio de Angelis | Shadow-Ford | 39 | +1 Lap | 20 |
| 13 | 22 | Derek Daly | Ensign-Ford | 39 | +1 Lap | 23 |
| 14 | 17 | Jan Lammers | Shadow-Ford | 39 | +1 Lap | 21 |
| 15 | 28 | Clay Regazzoni | Williams-Ford | 38 | +2 Laps | 17 |
| Ret | 27 | Alan Jones | Williams-Ford | 33 | Fuel system | 13 |
| Ret | 9 | H.J.Stuck | ATS-Ford | 31 | Steering | 24 |
| Ret | 16 | Rene Arnoux | Renault | 28 | Spun off | 11 |
| Ret | 20 | James Hunt | Wolf-Ford | 7 | Steering | 10 |
| Ret | 8 | Patrick Tambay | McLaren-Ford | 7 | Collision | 18 |
| Ret | 5 | Niki Lauda | Brabham-Alfa Romeo | 5 | Gearbox | 12 |
| Ret | 6 | Nelson Piquet | Brabham-Alfa Romeo | 5 | Accident | 22 |
| Ret | 1 | Mario Andretti | Lotus-Ford | 2 | Fuel leak | 4 |
| Ret | 4 | Jean-Pierre Jarier | Tyrrell-Ford | 0 | Electrical | 15 |
| DNQ | 31 | Hector Rebaque | Lotus-Ford | | | |
| DNQ | 24 | Arturo Merzario | Merzario-Ford | | | |

Winning speed: 117.236mph Lap leaders: Laffite 1-40
Pole position: Laffite, 2m 23.070s, 123.112mph
Fasest Lap: Laffite, 2m 28.760s, 118.403mph

## SOUTH AFRICAN GRAND PRIX: KYALAMI *3 March Round: 3 Race: 316 78 x 2.550 miles*

| POS. | NO. | DRIVER | CAR-ENGINE | LAPS | TIME/RETIRED | GRID |
|---|---|---|---|---|---|---|
| 1 | 12 | G.Villeneuve | Ferrari | 78 | 1:41'49.96 | 3 |
| 2 | 11 | Jody Scheckter | Ferrari | 78 | +3.42 | 2 |
| 3 | 4 | Jean-Pierre Jarier | Tyrrell-Ford | 78 | +22.11 | 9 |
| 4 | 1 | Mario Andretti | Lotus-Ford | 78 | +27.88 | 8 |
| 5 | 2 | Carlos Reutemann | Lotus-Ford | 78 | +1'06.97 | 11 |
| 6 | 5 | Niki Lauda | Brabham-Alfa Romeo | 77 | +1 Lap | 4 |
| 7 | 6 | Nelson Piquet | Brabham-Alfa Romeo | 77 | +1 Lap | 12 |
| 8 | 20 | James Hunt | Wolf-Ford | 77 | +1 Lap | 13 |
| 9 | 28 | Clay Regazzoni | Williams-Ford | 76 | +2 Laps | 22 |
| 10 | 8 | Patrick Tambay | McLaren-Ford | 75 | +3 Laps | 17 |
| 11 | 29 | Riccardo Patrese | Arrows-Ford | 75 | +3 Laps | 16 |
| 12 | 30 | Jochen Mass | Arrows-Ford | 74 | +4 Laps | 20 |
| 13 | 14 | Emerson Fittipaldi | Fittipaldi-Ford | 74 | +4 Laps | 18 |
| Ret | 31 | Hector Rebaque | Lotus-Ford | 71 | Engine | 23 |
| Ret | 16 | Rene Arnoux | Renault | 67 | Tyre | 10 |
| Ret | 27 | Alan Jones | Williams-Ford | 63 | Suspension | 19 |
| Ret | 7 | John Watson | McLaren-Ford | 61 | Ignition | 14 |
| Ret | 9 | H.J.Stuck | ATS-Ford | 57 | Accident | 24 |
| Ret | 15 | J.P.Jabouille | Renault | 47 | Engine | 1 |
| Ret | 26 | Jacques Laffite | Ligier-Ford | 45 | Accident | 6 |
| Ret | 3 | Didier Pironi | Tyrrell-Ford | 25 | Throttle | 7 |
| Ret | 18 | Elio de Angelis | Shadow-Ford | 16 | Accident | 15 |
| Ret | 25 | P.Depailler | Ligier-Ford | 4 | Accident | 5 |
| Ret | 17 | Jan Lammers | Shadow-Ford | 2 | Accident | 21 |
| DNQ | 22 | Derek Daly | Ensign-Ford | | | |
| DNQ | 24 | Arturo Merzario | Merzario-Ford | | | |

Winning speed: 117.197mph
Lap leaders: Jabouille 1, Villeneuve 2-14, 53-78; Scheckter 15-52
Pole position: Jabouille, 1m 11.800s, 127.861mph
Fastest lap: Villeneuve, 1m 14.412s, 123.372mph
Race stopped after two laps because of rain and restarted on aggregate for the remaining 76 laps.

## USA WEST GRAND PRIX: LONG BEACH *8 April Round: 4 Race: 317 80.5 x 2.020*

| POS. | NO. | DRIVER | CAR-ENGINE | LAPS | TIME/RETIRED | GRID |
|---|---|---|---|---|---|---|
| 1 | 12 | G.Villeneuve | Ferrari | 80 | 1:50'25.40 | 1 |
| 2 | 11 | Jody Scheckter | Ferrari | 80 | +29.38 | 3 |
| 3 | 27 | Alan Jones | Williams-Ford | 80 | +59.69 | 10 |
| 4 | 1 | Mario Andretti | Lotus-Ford | 80 | +1'04.33 | 6 |
| 5 | 25 | P.Depailler | Ligier-Ford | 80 | +1'23.52 | 4 |
| 6 | 4 | Jean-Pierre Jarier | Tyrrell-Ford | 79 | +1 Lap | 7 |
| 7 | 18 | Elio de Angelis | Shadow-Ford | 78 | +2 Laps | 20 |
| 8 | 6 | Nelson Piquet | Brabham-Alfa Romeo | 78 | +2 Laps | 12 |
| 9 | 30 | Jochen Mass | Arrows-Ford | 78 | +2 Laps | 13 |
| DSQ | 3 | Didier Pironi | Tyrrell-Ford | 72 | Disqualified | 17 |
| Ret | 31 | Hector Rebaque | Lotus-Ford | 71 | Accident | 23 |
| Ret | 22 | Derek Daly | Ensign-Ford | 69 | Accident | 24 |
| Ret | 7 | John Watson | McLaren-Ford | 62 | Injection | 18 |
| DSQ | 9 | H.J.Stuck | ATS-Ford | 49 | Disqualified | 21 |
| Ret | 28 | Clay Regazzoni | Williams-Ford | 48 | Engine | 15 |
| Ret | 17 | Jan Lammers | Shadow-Ford | 47 | Suspension | 14 |
| Ret | 29 | Riccardo Patrese | Arrows-Ford | 40 | Brakes | 9 |
| Ret | 2 | Carlos Reutemann | Lotus-Ford | 21 | Transmission | 2 |
| Ret | 14 | Emerson Fittipaldi | Fittipaldi-Ford | 19 | Transmission | 16 |
| Ret | 24 | Arturo Merzario | Merzario-Ford | 13 | Engine | 22 |
| Ret | 26 | Jacques Laffite | Ligier-Ford | 8 | Brakes | 5 |
| Ret | 20 | James Hunt | Wolf-Ford | 0 | Transmission | 8 |
| Ret | 5 | Niki Lauda | Brabham-Alfa Romeo | 0 | Accident | 11 |
| Ret | 8 | Patrick Tambay | McLaren-Ford | 0 | Collision | 19 |

Winning speed: 87.808mph (based on time taken to complete 80 laps)
Lap leaders: Villeneuve 1-80
Pole position: Villeneuve, 1m 18.825s, 92.259mph
Fastest lap: Villeneuve, 1m 21.200s, 89.560mph
The start and finish lines were at a different position on the circuit.
The fraction of a lap is credited to the first lap leader.

## SPANISH GRAND PRIX: JARAMA *29 April Round: 5 Race: 318 75 x 2.115 miles*

| POS. | NO. | DRIVER | CAR-ENGINE | LAPS | TIME/RETIRED | GRID |
|---|---|---|---|---|---|---|
| 1 | 25 | P.Depailler | Ligier-Ford | 75 | 1:39'11.84 | 2 |
| 2 | 2 | Carlos Reutemann | Lotus-Ford | 75 | +20.94 | 8 |
| 3 | 1 | Mario Andretti | Lotus-Ford | 75 | +27.31 | 4 |
| 4 | 11 | Jody Scheckter | Ferrari | 75 | +28.68 | 5 |
| 5 | 4 | Jean-Pierre Jarier | Tyrrell-Ford | 75 | +30.39 | 12 |
| 6 | 3 | Didier Pironi | Tyrrell-Ford | 75 | +48.43 | 10 |
| 7 | 12 | G.Villeneuve | Ferrari | 75 | +52.31 | 3 |
| 8 | 30 | Jochen Mass | Arrows-Ford | 75 | +1'14.84 | 17 |
| 9 | 16 | Rene Arnoux | Renault | 74 | +1 Lap | 11 |
| 10 | 29 | Riccardo Patrese | Arrows-Ford | 74 | +1 Lap | 16 |
| 11 | 14 | Emerson Fittipaldi | Fittipaldi-Ford | 74 | +1 Lap | 19 |
| 12 | 17 | Jan Lammers | Shadow-Ford | 73 | +2 Laps | 24 |
| 13 | 8 | Patrick Tambay | McLaren-Ford | 72 | +3 Laps | 20 |
| 14 | 9 | H.J.Stuck | ATS-Ford | 69 | +6 Laps | 21 |
| Ret | 5 | Niki Lauda | Brabham-Alfa Romeo | 63 | Water leak | 6 |
| Ret | 31 | Hector Rebaque | Lotus-Ford | 58 | Engine | 23 |
| Ret | 27 | Alan Jones | Williams-Ford | 54 | Gearbox | 13 |
| Ret | 18 | Elio de Angelis | Shadow-Ford | 52 | Engine | 22 |
| Ret | 28 | Clay Regazzoni | Williams-Ford | 32 | Engine | 14 |
| Ret | 20 | James Hunt | Wolf-Ford | 26 | Brakes | 15 |
| Ret | 15 | J.P.Jabouille | Renault | 21 | Turbo | 9 |
| Ret | 7 | John Watson | McLaren-Ford | 21 | Engine | 18 |
| Ret | 26 | Jacques Laffite | Ligier-Ford | 15 | Engine | 1 |
| Ret | 6 | Nelson Piquet | Brabham-Alfa Romeo | 15 | Injection | 7 |
| DNQ | 22 | Derek Daly | Ensign-Ford | | | |
| DNQ | 24 | Arturo Merzario | Merzario-Ford | | | |
| DNQ | 36 | G.Brancatelli | Kauhsen-Ford | | | |

Winning speed: 95.952mph Lap leaders: Depailler 1-75
Pole position: Laffite, 1m 14.500s, 102.208mph
Fastest lap: Villeneuve, 1m 16.440s, 99.614mph

## BELGIAN GRAND PRIX: ZOLDER *13 May Round: 6 Race: 319 70 x 2.648 miles*

| POS. | NO. | DRIVER | CAR-ENGINE | LAPS | TIME/RETIRED | GRID |
|---|---|---|---|---|---|---|
| 1 | 11 | Jody Scheckter | Ferrari | 70 | 1:39'59.53 | 7 |
| 2 | 26 | Jacques Laffite | Ligier-Ford | 70 | +15.36 | 1 |
| 3 | 3 | Didier Pironi | Tyrrell-Ford | 70 | +35.17 | 12 |
| 4 | 2 | Carlos Reutemann | Lotus-Ford | 70 | +46.49 | 10 |
| 5 | 29 | Riccardo Patrese | Arrows-Ford | 70 | +1'04.31 | 16 |
| 6 | 7 | John Watson | McLaren-Ford | 70 | +1'05.85 | 19 |
| 7 | 12 | G.Villeneuve | Ferrari | 69 | +1 Lap | 6 |
| 8 | 9 | H.J.Stuck | ATS-Ford | 69 | +1 Lap | 20 |
| 9 | 14 | Emerson Fittipaldi | Fittipaldi-Ford | 68 | +2 Laps | 23 |
| 10 | 17 | Jan Lammers | Shadow-Ford | 68 | +2 Laps | 21 |
| 11 | 4 | Jean-Pierre Jarier | Tyrrell-Ford | 67 | +3 Laps | 11 |
| Ret | 25 | P.Depailler | Ligier-Ford | 46 | Accident | 2 |
| Ret | 20 | James Hunt | Wolf-Ford | 40 | Accident | 9 |
| Ret | 27 | Alan Jones | Williams-Ford | 39 | Electrical | 4 |
| Ret | 1 | Mario Andretti | Lotus-Ford | 27 | Brakes | 5 |
| Ret | 6 | Nelson Piquet | Brabham-Alfa Romeo | 23 | Engine | 3 |
| Ret | 5 | Niki Lauda | Brabham-Alfa Romeo | 23 | Engine | 13 |
| Ret | 16 | Rene Arnoux | Renault | 22 | Turbo | 18 |
| Ret | 35 | Bruno Giacomelli | Alfa Romeo | 21 | Accident | 14 |
| Ret | 18 | Elio de Angelis | Shadow-Ford | 21 | Accident | 24 |
| Ret | 30 | Jochen Mass | Arrows-Ford | 17 | Spun off | 22 |
| Ret | 31 | Hector Rebaque | Lotus-Ford | 13 | Transmission | 15 |
| Ret | 15 | J.P.Jabouille | Renault | 13 | Turbo | 17 |
| Ret | 28 | Clay Regazzoni | Williams-Ford | 1 | Accident | 8 |
| DNQ | 8 | Patrick Tambay | McLaren-Ford | | | |
| DNQ | 24 | Arturo Merzario | Merzario-Ford | | | |
| DNQ | 22 | Derek Daly | Ensign-Ford | | | |
| DNQ | 36 | G.Brancatelli | Kauhsen-Ford | | | |

Winning speed: 111.237mph
Lap leaders: Depailler 1-18, 40-46; Laffite 19-23, 47-53; Jones 24-39; Scheckter 54-70
Pole position: Laffite, 1m 21.130s, 117.513mph
Fastest lap: Villeneuve, 1m 23.090s, 114.741mph

## MONACO GRAND PRIX: MONTE CARLO *27 May Round: 7 Race: 320 76 x 2.058 miles*

| POS. | NO. | DRIVER | CAR-ENGINE | LAPS | TIME/RETIRED | GRID |
|---|---|---|---|---|---|---|
| 1 | 11 | Jody Scheckter | Ferrari | 76 | 1:55'22.48 | 1 |
| 2 | 28 | Clay Regazzoni | Williams-Ford | 76 | +0.44 | 16 |
| 3 | 2 | Carlos Reutemann | Lotus-Ford | 76 | +8.57 | 11 |
| 4 | 7 | John Watson | McLaren-Ford | 76 | +41.31 | 14 |
| 5 | 25 | P.Depailler | Ligier-Ford | 75 | Engine | 3 |
| 6 | 30 | Jochen Mass | Arrows-Ford | 69 | +7 Laps | 8 |
| Ret | 6 | Nelson Piquet | Brabham-Alfa Romeo | 68 | Transmission | 18 |
| NC | 15 | J.P.Jabouille | Renault | 68 | Not classified | 20 |
| Ret | 26 | Jacques Laffite | Ligier-Ford | 55 | Gearbox | 5 |
| Ret | 12 | G.Villeneuve | Ferrari | 54 | Transmission | 2 |
| Ret | 27 | Alan Jones | Williams-Ford | 43 | Steering | 9 |
| Ret | 4 | Jean-Pierre Jarier | Tyrrell-Ford | 34 | Suspension | 6 |
| Ret | 9 | H.J.Stuck | ATS-Ford | 30 | Wheel | 12 |
| Ret | 5 | Niki Lauda | Brabham-Alfa Romeo | 21 | Accident | 4 |
| Ret | 3 | Didier Pironi | Tyrrell-Ford | 21 | Accident | 7 |
| Ret | 1 | Mario Andretti | Lotus-Ford | 21 | Suspension | 13 |
| Ret | 14 | Emerson Fittipaldi | Fittipaldi-Ford | 17 | Engine | 17 |
| Ret | 16 | Rene Arnoux | Renault | 8 | Accident | 19 |
| Ret | 20 | James Hunt | Wolf-Ford | 4 | Transmission | 10 |
| Ret | 29 | Riccardo Patrese | Arrows-Ford | 4 | Suspension | 15 |
| DNQ | 18 | Elio de Angelis | Shadow-Ford | | | |
| DNQ | 8 | Patrick Tambay | McLaren-Ford | | | |
| DNQ | 17 | Jan Lammers | Shadow-Ford | | | |
| DNQ | 22 | Derek Daly | Ensign-Ford | | | |
| DNPQ | 24 | G.Brancatelli | Merzario-Ford | | | |

Winning speed: 81.338 mph Lap leaders: Scheckter 1-76
Pole position: Scheckter, 1m 26.450s, 85.700mph
Fastest lap: Depailler, 1m 28.820s, 83.413mph

**FRENCH GRAND PRIX: DIJON – PRENOIS** *1 July Round: 8 Race: 321 80 x 2.361 miles*

| POS. | NO. | DRIVER | CAR-ENGINE | LAPS | TIME/RETIRED | GRID |
|---|---|---|---|---|---|---|
| 1 | 15 | J.P.Jabouille | Renault | 80 | 1:35'20.42 | 1 |
| 2 | 12 | G.Villeneuve | Ferrari | 80 | +14.59 | 3 |
| 3 | 16 | Rene Arnoux | Renault | 80 | +14.83 | 2 |
| 4 | 27 | Alan Jones | Williams-Ford | 80 | +36.61 | 7 |
| 5 | 4 | Jean-Pierre Jarier | Tyrrell-Ford | 80 | +1'04.51 | 10 |
| 6 | 28 | Clay Regazzoni | Williams-Ford | 80 | +1'05.51 | 9 |
| 7 | 11 | Jody Scheckter | Ferrari | 79 | +1 Lap | 5 |
| 8 | 26 | Jacques Laffite | Ligier-Ford | 79 | +1 Lap | 8 |
| 9 | 20 | Keke Rosberg | Wolf-Ford | 79 | +1 Lap | 16 |
| 10 | 8 | Patrick Tambay | McLaren-Ford | 78 | +2 Laps | 20 |
| 11 | 7 | John Watson | McLaren-Ford | 78 | +2 Laps | 15 |
| 12 | 31 | Hector Rebaque | Lotus-Ford | 78 | +2 Laps | 23 |
| 13 | 2 | Carlos Reutemann | Lotus-Ford | 77 | +3 Laps | 13 |
| 14 | 29 | Riccardo Patrese | Arrows-Ford | 77 | +3 Laps | 19 |
| 15 | 30 | Jochen Mass | Arrows-Ford | 75 | +5 Laps | 22 |
| 16 | 18 | Elio de Angelis | Shadow-Ford | 75 | +5 Laps | 24 |
| 17 | 35 | Bruno Giacomelli | Alfa Romeo | 75 | +5 Laps | 17 |
| 18 | 17 | Jan Lammers | Shadow-Ford | 73 | +7 Laps | 21 |
| Ret | 3 | Didier Pironi | Tyrrell-Ford | 71 | Suspension | 11 |
| Ret | 14 | Emerson Fittipaldi | Fittipaldi-Ford | 53 | Engine | 18 |
| Ret | 6 | Nelson Piquet | Brabham-Alfa Romeo | 52 | Accident | 4 |
| Ret | 1 | Mario Andretti | Lotus-Ford | 51 | Brakes | 12 |
| Ret | 25 | Jacky Ickx | Ligier-Ford | 45 | Engine | 14 |
| Ret | 5 | Niki Lauda | Brabham-Alfa Romeo | 23 | Spun off | 6 |
| DNQ | 22 | Patrick Gaillard | Ensign-Ford | | | |
| DNQ | 24 | Arturo Merzario | Merzario-Ford | | | |

Winning speed: 118.877mph Lap leaders: Villeneuve 1-46; Jabouille 47-80
Pole position: Jabouille, 1m 7.190s, 126.512mph
Fastest lap: Arnoux, 1m 9.160s, 122.909mph

**BRITISH GRAND PRIX: SILVERSTONE** *14 July Round: 9 Race: 322 68 x 2.932 miles*

| POS. | NO. | DRIVER | CAR-ENGINE | LAPS | TIME/RETIRED | GRID |
|---|---|---|---|---|---|---|
| 1 | 28 | Clay Regazzoni | Williams-Ford | 68 | 1:26'11.17 | 4 |
| 2 | 16 | Rene Arnoux | Renault | 68 | +24.28 | 5 |
| 3 | 4 | Jean-Pierre Jarier | Tyrrell-Ford | 67 | +1 Lap | 16 |
| 4 | 7 | John Watson | McLaren-Ford | 67 | +1 Lap | 7 |
| 5 | 11 | Jody Scheckter | Ferrari | 67 | +1 Lap | 11 |
| 6 | 25 | Jacky Ickx | Ligier-Ford | 67 | +1 Lap | 17 |
| 7 | 8 | Patrick Tambay | McLaren-Ford | 66 | Out of fuel | 18 |
| 8 | 2 | Carlos Reutemann | Lotus-Ford | 66 | +2 Laps | 8 |
| 9 | 31 | Hector Rebaque | Lotus-Ford | 66 | +2 Laps | 24 |
| 10 | 3 | Didier Pironi | Tyrrell-Ford | 66 | +2 Laps | 15 |
| 11 | 17 | Jan Lammers | Shadow-Ford | 65 | +3 Laps | 21 |
| 12 | 18 | Elio de Angelis | Shadow-Ford | 65 | +3 Laps | 12 |
| 13 | 22 | Patrick Gaillard | Ensign-Ford | 65 | +3 Laps | 23 |
| 14 | 12 | G.Villeneuve | Ferrari | 63 | Fuel system | 13 |
| Ret | 29 | Riccardo Patrese | Arrows-Ford | 45 | Gearbox | 19 |
| Ret | 26 | Jacques Laffite | Ligier-Ford | 44 | Engine | 10 |
| Ret | 20 | Keke Rosberg | Wolf-Ford | 44 | Fuel system | 14 |
| Ret | 27 | Alan Jones | Williams-Ford | 38 | Water pump | 1 |
| Ret | 30 | Jochen Mass | Arrows-Ford | 37 | Gearbox | 20 |
| Ret | 14 | Emerson Fittipaldi | Fittipaldi-Ford | 25 | Engine | 22 |
| Ret | 15 | J.P.Jabouille | Renault | 21 | Turbo | 2 |
| Ret | 5 | Niki Lauda | Brabham-Alfa Romeo | 12 | Brakes | 6 |
| Ret | 1 | Mario Andretti | Lotus-Ford | 3 | Wheel | 9 |
| Ret | 6 | Nelson Piquet | Brabham-Alfa Romeo | 1 | Spun off | 3 |
| DNQ | 9 | H.J.Stuck | ATS-Ford | | | |
| DNQ | 24 | Arturo Merzario | Merzario-Ford | | | |

Winning speed: 138.799mph Lap leaders: Jones 1-38; Regazzoni 39-68
Pole position: Jones, 1m 11.880s, 146.845mph
Fastest lap: Regazzoni, 1m 14.400s, 141.871mph
E de Angelis penalised 1 minute for a jump start.

**GERMAN GRAND PRIX: HOCKENHEIM** *12 August Round: 11 Race: 323 45 x 4.218 miles*

| POS. | NO. | DRIVER | CAR-ENGINE | LAPS | TIME/RETIRED | GRID |
|---|---|---|---|---|---|---|
| 1 | 27 | Alan Jones | Williams-Ford | 45 | 1:24'48.83 | 2 |
| 2 | 28 | Clay Regazzoni | Williams-Ford | 45 | +2.91 | 6 |
| 3 | 26 | Jacques Laffite | Ligier-Ford | 45 | +18.39 | 3 |
| 4 | 11 | Jody Scheckter | Ferrari | 45 | +31.20 | 5 |
| 5 | 7 | John Watson | McLaren-Ford | 45 | +1'37.80 | 12 |
| 6 | 30 | Jochen Mass | Arrows-Ford | 44 | +1 Lap | 18 |
| 7 | 4 | Geoff Lees | Tyrrell-Ford | 44 | +1 Lap | 16 |
| 8 | 12 | G.Villeneuve | Ferrari | 44 | +1 Lap | 9 |
| 9 | 3 | Didier Pironi | Tyrrell-Ford | 44 | +1 Lap | 8 |
| 10 | 17 | Jan Lammers | Shadow-Ford | 44 | +1 Lap | 20 |
| 11 | 18 | Elio de Angelis | Shadow-Ford | 43 | +2 Laps | 21 |
| 12 | 6 | Nelson Piquet | Brabham-Alfa Romeo | 42 | Engine | 4 |
| Ret | 29 | Riccardo Patrese | Arrows-Ford | 34 | Tyre | 19 |
| Ret | 8 | Patrick Tambay | McLaren-Ford | 30 | Suspension | 15 |
| Ret | 20 | Keke Rosberg | Wolf-Ford | 29 | Engine | 17 |
| Ret | 5 | Niki Lauda | Brabham-Alfa Romeo | 27 | Engine | 7 |
| Ret | 25 | Jacky Ickx | Ligier-Ford | 24 | Tyre | 14 |
| Ret | 31 | Hector Rebaque | Lotus-Ford | 22 | Handling | 24 |
| Ret | 1 | Mario Andretti | Lotus-Ford | 16 | Transmission | 11 |
| Ret | 16 | Rene Arnoux | Renault | 9 | Tyre | 10 |
| Ret | 15 | J.P.Jabouille | Renault | 7 | Spun off | 1 |
| Ret | 14 | Emerson Fittipaldi | Fittipaldi-Ford | 4 | Electrical | 22 |
| Ret | 2 | Carlos Reutemann | Lotus-Ford | 1 | Accident | 13 |
| Ret | 9 | H.J.Stuck | ATS-Ford | 0 | Suspension | 23 |
| DNQ | 22 | Patrick Gaillard | Ensign-Ford | | | |
| DNQ | 24 | Arturo Merzario | Merzario-Ford | | | |

Winning speed: 134.293mph Lap leaders: Jones 1-45
Pole position: Jabouille, 1m 48.480s, 139.994mph
Fastest lap: Villeneuve, 1m 51.890s, 135.728mph

**AUSTRIAN GRAND PRIX: OSTERREICHRING** *12 August Round: 11 Race: 324 54 x 3.692 miles*

| POS. | NO. | DRIVER | CAR-ENGINE | LAPS | TIME/RETIRED | GRID |
|---|---|---|---|---|---|---|
| 1 | 27 | Alan Jones | Williams-Ford | 54 | 1:27'38.01 | 2 |
| 2 | 12 | G.Villeneuve | Ferrari | 54 | +36.05 | 5 |
| 3 | 26 | Jacques Laffite | Ligier-Ford | 54 | +46.77 | 8 |
| 4 | 11 | Jody Scheckter | Ferrari | 54 | +47.21 | 9 |
| 5 | 28 | Clay Regazzoni | Williams-Ford | 54 | +48.92 | 6 |
| 6 | 16 | Rene Arnoux | Renault | 53 | +1 Lap | 1 |
| 7 | 3 | Didier Pironi | Tyrrell-Ford | 53 | +1 Lap | 10 |
| 8 | 4 | Derek Daly | Tyrrell-Ford | 53 | +1 Lap | 11 |
| 9 | 7 | John Watson | McLaren-Ford | 53 | +1 Lap | 16 |
| 10 | 8 | Patrick Tambay | McLaren-Ford | 53 | +1 Lap | 14 |
| Ret | 5 | Niki Lauda | Brabham-Alfa Romeo | 45 | Engine | 4 |
| Ret | 22 | Patrick Gaillard | Ensign-Ford | 42 | Suspension | 24 |
| Ret | 29 | Riccardo Patrese | Arrows-Ford | 34 | Suspension | 13 |
| Ret | 18 | Elio de Angelis | Shadow-Ford | 34 | Engine | 22 |
| Ret | 6 | Nelson Piquet | Brabham-Alfa Romeo | 32 | Engine | 7 |
| Ret | 9 | H.J.Stuck | ATS-Ford | 28 | Engine | 18 |
| Ret | 25 | Jacky Ickx | Ligier-Ford | 26 | Engine | 21 |
| Ret | 2 | Carlos Reutemann | Lotus-Ford | 22 | Handling | 17 |
| Ret | 15 | J.P.Jabouille | Renault | 16 | Gearbox | 3 |
| Ret | 20 | Keke Rosberg | Wolf-Ford | 15 | Electrical | 19 |
| Ret | 14 | Emerson Fittipaldi | Fittipaldi-Ford | 15 | Brakes | 12 |
| Ret | 17 | Jan Lammers | Shadow-Ford | 3 | Accident | 23 |
| Ret | 30 | Jochen Mass | Arrows-Ford | 1 | Engine | 20 |
| Ret | 1 | Mario Andretti | Lotus-Ford | 0 | Clutch | 15 |
| DNQ | 31 | Hector Rebaque | Lotus-Ford | | | |
| DNQ | 24 | Arturo Merzario | Merzario-Ford | | | |

Winning speed: 136.508mph Lap leaders: Villeneuve 1-3; Jones 4-54
Pole position: Arnoux, 1m 34.070s, 141.298mph
Fastest lap: Arnoux; 1m 35.700s, 138.790mph

**DUTCH GRAND PRIX: ZANDVOORT** *26 August Round:12 Race: 325 75 x 2.626 miles*

| POS. | NO. | DRIVER | CAR-ENGINE | LAPS | TIME/RETIRED | GRID |
|---|---|---|---|---|---|---|
| 1 | 27 | Alan Jones | Williams-Ford | 75 | 1:41'19.775 | 2 |
| 2 | 11 | Jody Scheckter | Ferrari | 75 | +21.783 | 5 |
| 3 | 26 | Jacques Laffite | Ligier-Ford | 75 | +1'03.253 | 7 |
| 4 | 6 | Nelson Piquet | Brabham-Alfa Romeo | 74 | +1 Lap | 11 |
| 5 | 25 | Jacky Ickx | Ligier-Ford | 74 | +1 Lap | 20 |
| 6 | 30 | Jochen Mass | Arrows-Ford | 73 | +2 Laps | 18 |
| 7 | 31 | Hector Rebaque | Lotus-Ford | 73 | +2 Laps | 24 |
| Ret | 3 | Didier Pironi | Tyrrell-Ford | 51 | Suspension | 10 |
| Ret | 12 | G.Villeneuve | Ferrari | 49 | Tyre | 6 |
| Ret | 18 | Elio de Angelis | Shadow-Ford | 40 | Transmission | 22 |
| Ret | 20 | Keke Rosberg | Wolf-Ford | 33 | Engine | 8 |
| Ret | 15 | J.P.Jabouille | Renault | 26 | Clutch | 4 |
| Ret | 7 | John Watson | McLaren-Ford | 22 | Engine | 12 |
| Ret | 4 | Jean-Pierre Jarier | Tyrrell-Ford | 20 | Spun off | 16 |
| Ret | 9 | H.J.Stuck | ATS-Ford | 19 | Transmission | 15 |
| Ret | 17 | Jan Lammers | Shadow-Ford | 12 | Gearbox | 23 |
| Ret | 1 | Mario Andretti | Lotus-Ford | 9 | Suspension | 17 |
| Ret | 29 | Riccardo Patrese | Arrows-Ford | 7 | Brakes | 19 |
| Ret | 8 | Patrick Tambay | McLaren-Ford | 6 | Engin | 14e |
| Wth | 5 | Niki Lauda | Brabham-Alfa Romeo | 4 | Withdrew | 9 |
| Ret | 14 | Emerson Fittipaldi | Fittipaldi-Ford | 2 | Electrical | 21 |
| Ret | 2 | Carlos Reutemann | Lotus-Ford | 1 | Suspension | 13 |
| Ret | 16 | Rene Arnoux | Renault | 1 | Suspension | 1 |
| Ret | 28 | Clay Regazzoni | Williams-Ford | 0 | Accident | 3 |
| DNQ | 22 | Patrick Gaillard | Ensign-Ford | | | |
| DNQ | 24 | Arturo Merzario | Merzario-Ford | | | |

Winning speed: 116.616mph Lap Leaders: Jones 1-10, 47-75; Villeneuve 11-46
Pole position: Arnoux, 1m 15.461s, 125.274mph
Fastest lap: Villeneuve, 1m 19.438s, 119.001mph

**ITALIAN GRAND PRIX: MONZA** *9 September Round: 13 Race: 326 50 x 3.604 miles*

| POS. | NO. | DRIVER | CAR-ENGINE | LAPS | TIME/RETIRED | GRID |
|---|---|---|---|---|---|---|
| 1 | 11 | Jody Scheckter | Ferrari | 50 | 1:22'00.22 | 3 |
| 2 | 12 | G.Villeneuve | Ferrari | 50 | +0.46 | 5 |
| 3 | 28 | Clay Regazzoni | Williams-Ford | 50 | +4.78 | 6 |
| 4 | 5 | Niki Lauda | Brabham-Alfa Romeo | 50 | +54.40 | 9 |
| 5 | 1 | Mario Andretti | Lotus-Ford | 50 | +59.70 | 10 |
| 6 | 4 | Jean-Pierre Jarier | Tyrrell-Ford | 50 | +1'01.55 | 16 |
| 7 | 2 | Carlos Reutemann | Lotus-Ford | 50 | +1'24.14 | 13 |
| 8 | 14 | Emerson Fittipaldi | Fittipaldi-Ford | 49 | +1 Lap | 20 |
| 9 | 27 | Alan Jones | Williams-Ford | 49 | +1 Lap | 4 |
| 10 | 3 | Didier Pironi | Tyrrell-Ford | 49 | +1 Lap | 12 |
| 11 | 9 | H.J.Stuck | ATS-Ford | 49 | +1 Lap | 15 |
| 12 | 36 | V.Brambilla | Alfa Romeo | 49 | +1 Lap | 22 |
| 13 | 29 | Riccardo Patrese | Arrows-Ford | 47 | +3 Laps | 17 |
| 14 | 15 | J.P.Jabouille | Renault | 45 | Engine | 1 |
| Ret | 26 | Jacques Laffite | Ligier-Ford | 41 | Engine | 7 |
| Ret | 20 | Keke Rosberg | Wolf-Ford | 41 | Engine | 23 |
| Ret | 25 | Jacky Ickx | Ligier-Ford | 40 | Engine | 11 |
| Ret | 18 | Elio de Angelis | Shadow-Ford | 33 | Clutch | 24 |
| Ret | 35 | Bruno Giacomelli | Alfa Romeo | 28 | Spun off | 18 |
| Ret | 16 | Rene Arnoux | Renault | 13 | Engine | 2 |
| Ret | 7 | John Watson | McLaren-Ford | 13 | Accident | 19 |
| Ret | 8 | Patrick Tambay | McLaren-Ford | 3 | Engine | 14 |
| Ret | 30 | Jochen Mass | Arrows-Ford | 3 | Suspension | 21 |
| Ret | 6 | Nelson Piquet | Brabham-Alfa Romeo | 1 | Accident | 8 |
| DNQ | 17 | Jan Lammers | Shadow-Ford | | | |
| DNQ | 22 | Marc Surer | Ensign-Ford | | | |
| DNQ | 24 | Arturo Merzario | Merzario-Ford | | | |
| DNQ | 31 | Hector Rebaque | Rebaque-Ford | | | |

Winning speed: 131.846mph Lap leaders: Scheckter 1, 13-50; Arnoux 2-12
Pole position: Jabouille, 1m 34.580s, 137.177mph
Fastest lap: Regazzoni, 1m 35.600s, 135.714mph

**CANADIAN GRAND PRIX: MONTREAL** *30 September Round: 14 Race: 327 72 x 2.740 miles*

| POS. | NO. | DRIVER | CAR-ENGINE | LAPS | TIME/RETIRED | GRID |
|---|---|---|---|---|---|---|
| 1 | 27 | Alan Jones | Williams-Ford | 72 | 1:52'06.892 | 1 |
| 2 | 12 | G.Villeneuve | Ferrari | 72 | +1.080 | 2 |
| 3 | 28 | Clay Regazzoni | Williams-Ford | 72 | +1'13.656 | 3 |
| 4 | 11 | Jody Scheckter | Ferrari | 71 | +1 Lap | 9 |
| 5 | 3 | Didier Pironi | Tyrrell-Ford | 71 | +1 Lap | 6 |
| 6 | 7 | John Watson | McLaren-Ford | 70 | +2 Laps | 17 |
| 7 | 5 | Ricardo Zunino | Brabham-Ford | 68 | +4 Laps | 19 |
| 8 | 14 | Emerson Fittipaldi | Fittipaldi-Ford | 67 | +5 Laps | 15 |
| 9 | 17 | Jan Lammers | Shadow-Ford | 67 | +5 Laps | 21 |
| 10 | 1 | Mario Andretti | Lotus-Ford | 66 | Out of fuel | 10 |
| Ret | 6 | Nelson Piquet | Brabham-Ford | 61 | Gearbox | 4 |
| Ret | 36 | V.Brambilla | Alfa Romeo | 52 | Fuel system | 18 |
| Ret | 25 | Jacky Ickx | Ligier-Ford | 47 | Gearbox | 16 |
| Ret | 4 | Jean-Pierre Jarier | Tyrrell-Ford | 33 | Engine | 13 |
| Ret | 33 | Derek Daly | Tyrrell-Ford | 28 | Engine | 24 |
| Ret | 31 | Hector Rebaque | Rebaque-Ford | 26 | Chassis | 22 |
| Ret | 15 | J.P.Jabouille | Renault | 24 | Brakes | 7 |
| Ret | 18 | Elio de Angelis | Shadow-Ford | 24 | Ignition | 23 |
| Ret | 2 | Carlos Reutemann | Lotus-Ford | 23 | Suspension | 11 |
| Ret | 29 | Riccardo Patrese | Arrows-Ford | 20 | Spun off | 14 |
| Ret | 8 | Patrick Tambay | McLaren-Ford | 19 | Engine | 20 |
| Ret | 16 | Rene Arnoux | Renault | 14 | Accident | 8 |
| Ret | 9 | H.J.Stuck | ATS-Ford | 14 | Accident | 12 |
| Ret | 26 | Jacques Laffite | Ligier-Ford | 10 | Engine | 5 |
| DNQ | 30 | Jochen Mass | Arrows-Ford | | | |
| DNQ | 22 | Marc Surer | Ensign-Ford | | | |
| DNQ | 20 | Keke Rosberg | Wolf-Ford | | | |
| DNQ | 19 | Alex Ribeiro | Fittipaldi-Ford | | | |
| DNQ | 24 | Arturo Merzario | Merzario-Ford | | | |

Winning speed: 105.587mph Lap leaders: Villeneuve 1-50; Jones 51-72
Pole position: Jones, 1m 29.892s, 109.742mph
Fastest lap: Jones, 1m 31.272s, 108.082mph

**USA EAST GRAND PRIX: WATKINS GLEN** *7 October Round: 15 Race: 328 59 x 3.377 miles*

| POS. | NO. | DRIVER | CAR-ENGINE | LAPS | TIME/RETIRED | GRID |
|---|---|---|---|---|---|---|
| 1 | 12 | G.Villeneuve | Ferrari | 59 | 1:52'17.734 | 3 |
| 2 | 16 | Rene Arnoux | Renault | 59 | +48.787 | 7 |
| 3 | 3 | Didier Pironi | Tyrrell-Ford | 59 | +53.199 | 10 |
| 4 | 18 | Elio de Angelis | Shadow-Ford | 59 | +1'30.512 | 20 |
| 5 | 9 | H.J.Stuck | ATS-Ford | 59 | +1'41.259 | 14 |
| 6 | 7 | John Watson | McLaren-Ford | 58 | +1 Lap | 13 |
| 7 | 14 | Emerson Fittipaldi | Fittipaldi-Ford | 54 | +5 Laps | 23 |
| Ret | 6 | Nelson Piquet | Brabham-Ford | 53 | Transmission | 2 |
| Ret | 33 | Derek Daly | Tyrrell-Ford | 52 | Spun off | 15 |
| Ret | 11 | Jody Scheckter | Ferrari | 48 | Tyre | 16 |
| Ret | 29 | Riccardo Patrese | Arrows-Ford | 44 | Suspension | 19 |
| Ret | 27 | Alan Jones | Williams-Ford | 36 | Wheel | 1 |
| Ret | 22 | Marc Surer | Ensign-Ford | 32 | Engine | 21 |
| Ret | 28 | Clay Regazzoni | Williams-Ford | 29 | Accident | 5 |
| Ret | 5 | Ricardo Zunino | Brabham-Ford | 25 | Spun off | 9 |
| Ret | 15 | J.P.Jabouille | Renault | 24 | Engine | 8 |
| Ret | 20 | Keke Rosberg | Wolf-Ford | 20 | Accident | 12 |
| Ret | 8 | Patrick Tambay | McLaren-Ford | 20 | Engine | 22 |
| Ret | 4 | Jean-Pierre Jarier | Tyrrell-Ford | 18 | Accident | 11 |
| Ret | 1 | Mario Andretti | Lotus-Ford | 16 | Gearbox | 17 |
| Ret | 2 | Carlos Reutemann | Lotus-Ford | 6 | Spun off | 6 |
| Ret | 26 | Jacques Laffite | Ligier-Ford | 3 | Spun off | 4 |
| Ret | 25 | Jacky Ickx | Ligier-Ford | 2 | Spun off | 24 |
| Ret | 35 | Bruno Giacomelli | Alfa Romeo | 0 | Spun off | 18 |
| DNQ | 36 | V.Brambilla | Alfa Romeo | | | |
| DNQ | 30 | Jochen Mass | Arrows-Ford | | | |
| DNQ | 17 | Jan Lammers | Shadow-Ford | | | |
| DNQ | 31 | Hector Rebaque | Rebaque-Ford | | | |
| DNQ | 19 | Alex Ribeiro | Fittipaldi-Ford | | | |
| DNQ | 24 | Arturo Merzario | Merzario-Ford | | | |

Winning speed: 106.456mph Lap leaders: Villeneuve 1-31, 37-59; Jones 32-36
Pole position: Jones, 1m 35.615s, 127.147mph
Fastest lap: Piquet, 1m 40.054s, 127.147mph

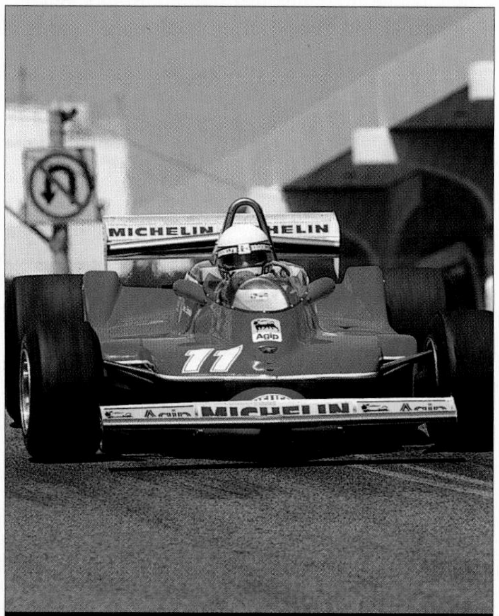

1979 world champion, Jody Scheckter in the Ferrari 312/T4

# 1980

## DRIVERS' CHAMPION: ALAN JONES
## CONSTRUCTORS' CHAMPION: WILLIAMS FORD

### DRIVERS' CHAMPIONSHIP

| POS. | DRIVER | NATIONALITY | CAR | POINTS |
|---|---|---|---|---|
| 1 | Alan Jones | Australia | Williams-Ford | 67 (4) |
| 2 | Nelson Piquet | Brazil | Brabham-Ford | 54 |
| 3 | Carlos Reutemann | Argentina | Williams-Ford | 42 (7) |
| 4 | Jacques Laffite | France | Ligier-Ford | 34 |
| 5 | Didier Pironi | France | Ligier-Ford | 32 |
| 6 | Rene Arnoux | France | Renault | 29 |
| 7 | Elio de Angelis | Italy | Lotus-Ford | 13 |
| 8 | Jean-Pierre Jabouille | France | Renault | 9 |
| 9 | Riccardo Patrese | Italy | Arrows-Ford | 7 |
| 10 | Keke Rosberg | Finland | Fittipaldi-Ford | 6 |
| 11 | Derek Daly | Ireland | Tyrrell-Ford | 6 |
| = | John Watson | GB | McLaren-Ford | 6 |
| = | Jean-Pierre Jarier | France | Tyrrell-Ford | 6 |
| = | Gilles Villeneuve | Canada | Ferrari | 6 |
| 15 | Emerson Fittipaldi | Brazil | Fittipaldi-Ford | 5 |
| = | Alain Prost | France | McLaren-Ford | 5 |
| 17 | Jochen Mass | West Germany | Arrows-Ford | 4 |
| = | Bruno Giacomelli | Italy | Alfa Romeo | 4 |
| 19 | Jody Scheckter | South Africa | Ferrari | 2 |
| 20 | Mario Andretti | USA | Lotus-Ford | 1 |
| = | Hector Rebaque | Mexico | Brabham-Ford | 1 |
| | Eddie Cheever | USA | Osella-Ford | |
| | Jan Lammers | Netherlands | ATS-Ford, Ensign-Ford | |
| | Marc Surer | Switzerland | ATS-Ford | |
| | Ricardo Zunino | Argentina | Brabham-Ford | |
| | Patrick Depallier | France | Alfa Romeo | |
| | David Kennedy | Ireland | Shadow-Ford | |
| | Clay Regazzoni | Switzerland | Ensign-Ford | |
| | Geoff Lees | GB | Shadow-Ford, Ensign-Ford, Williams-Ford | |
| | Tiff Needell | GB | Ensign-Ford | |
| | Rupert Keegan | GB | Williams-Ford | |
| | Nigel Mansell | GB | Lotus-Ford | |
| | Vittorio Brambilla | Italy | Alfa Romeo | |
| | Mike Thackwell | New Zealand | Tyrrell-Ford, Arrows-Ford | |
| | Andrea de Cesaris | Italy | Alfa Romeo | |
| | Stefan Johansson | Sweden | Shadow-Ford | |
| | Stephen South | GB | McLaren-Ford | |
| | Desire Wilson | South Africa | Williams-Ford | |
| | Harald Ertl | Austria | ATS-Ford | |
| | Manfred Winkelhock | West Germany | Arrows-Ford | |
| | Kevin Cogan | USA | Williams-Ford | |

Points for top six finishers (9, 6, 4, 3, 2, 1). Half points awarded for races stopped before half distance.

### CONSTRUCTORS' CHAMPIONSHIP

| POS. | CONSTRUCTOR | POINTS |
|---|---|---|
| 1 | Williams-Ford | 120 |
| 2 | Ligier-Ford | 66 |
| 3 | Brabham-Ford | 55 |
| 4 | Renault | 38 |
| 5 | Lotus-Ford | 14 |
| 6 | Tyrrell-Ford | 12 |
| 7 | Arrows-Ford | 11 |
| = | Fittipaldi-Ford | 11 |
| = | McLaren-Ford | 11 |
| 10 | Ferrari | 8 |
| 11 | Alfa Romeo | 4 |

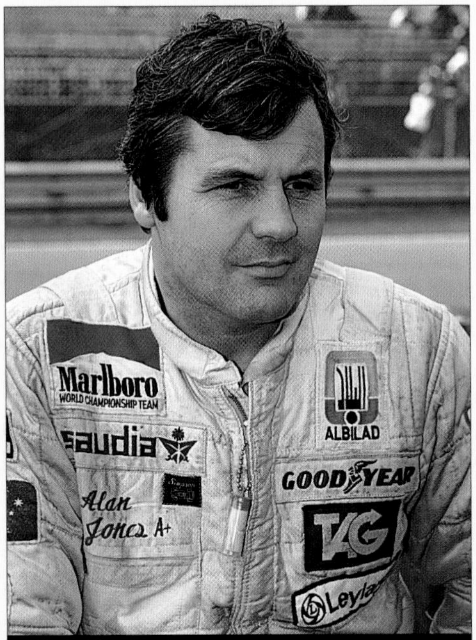


1980 world champion, Alan Jones

### ARGENTINE GRAND PRIX: BUENOS AIRES *13 January Round: 1 Race: 329 53 x 3.708 miles*

| POS. | NO. | DRIVER | CAR/ENGINE | LAPS | TIME/RETIRED | GRID |
|---|---|---|---|---|---|---|
| 1 | 27 | Alan Jones | Williams-Ford | 53 | 1:43'24.38 | 1 |
| 2 | 5 | Nelson Piquet | Brabham-Ford | 53 | +24.59 | 4 |
| 3 | 21 | Keke Rosberg | Fittipaldi-Ford | 53 | +1'18.64 | 13 |
| 4 | 4 | Derek Daly | Tyrrell-Ford | 53 | +1'23.48 | 22 |
| 5 | 23 | Bruno Giacomelli | Alfa Romeo | 52 | +1 Lap | 20 |
| 6 | 8 | Alain Prost | McLaren-Ford | 52 | +1 Lap | 12 |
| 7 | 6 | Ricardo Zunino | Brabham-Ford | 51 | +2 Laps | 16 |
| Ret | 22 | P.Depailler | Alfa Romeo | 46 | Engine | 23 |
| Ret | 1 | Jody Scheckter | Ferrari | 45 | Engine | 11 |
| NC | 14 | Clay Regazzoni | Ensign-Ford | 44 | Not classified | 15 |
| NC | 20 | E.Fittipaldi | Fittipaldi-Ford | 37 | Not classified | 24 |
| Ret | 2 | G.Villeneuve | Ferrari | 36 | Accident | 8 |
| Ret | 26 | Jacques Laffite | Ligier-Ford | 30 | Engine | 2 |
| Ret | 29 | Riccardo Patrese | Arrows-Ford | 27 | Engine | 7 |
| Ret | 9 | Marc Surer | ATS-Ford | 27 | Fire | 21 |
| Ret | 11 | Mario Andretti | Lotus-Ford | 20 | Fuel system | 6 |
| Ret | 30 | Jochen Mass | Arrows-Ford | 20 | Gearbox | 14 |
| Ret | 28 | Carlos Reutemann | Williams-Ford | 12 | Engine | 10 |
| Ret | 12 | Elio de Angelis | Lotus-Ford | 7 | Suspension | 5 |
| Ret | 7 | John Watson | McLaren-Ford | 5 | Gearbox | 17 |
| Ret | 15 | J.P.Jabouille | Renault | 3 | Gearbox | 9 |
| Ret | 16 | Rene Arnoux | Renault | 2 | Suspension | 19 |
| Ret | 25 | Didier Pironi | Ligier-Ford | 1 | Engine | 3 |
| Ret | 3 | J.P.Jarier | Tyrrell-Ford | 1 | Collision | 18 |
| DNQ | 18 | Dave Kennedy | Shadow-Ford | | | |
| DNQ | 17 | Stefan Johansson | Shadow-Ford | | | |
| DNQ | 10 | Jan Lammers | ATS-Ford | | | |
| DNQ | 31 | Eddie Cheever | Osella-Ford | | | |

Winning speed: 114.041mph Lap leaders: Jones 1-17, 30-53; Laffite 18-29
Pole position: Jones, 1m 44.170s, 128.156mph
Fastest lap: Jones, 1m 50.450s, 120.869mph

### BRAZILIAN GRAND PRIX: INTERLAGOS *27 January Round: 2 Race: 330 40 x 4.893 miles*

| POS. | NO. | DRIVER | CAR/ENGINE | LAPS | TIME/RETIRED | GRID |
|---|---|---|---|---|---|---|
| 1 | 16 | Rene Arnoux | Renault | 40 | 1:40'01.33 | 6 |
| 2 | 12 | Elio de Angelis | Lotus-Ford | 40 | +21.86 | 7 |
| 3 | 27 | Alan Jones | Williams-Ford | 40 | +1'06.11 | 10 |
| 4 | 25 | Didier Pironi | Ligier-Ford | 40 | +1'40.13 | 2 |
| 5 | 8 | Alain Prost | McLaren-Ford | 40 | +2'25.41 | 13 |
| 6 | 29 | Riccardo Patrese | Arrows-Ford | 39 | +1 Lap | 14 |
| 7 | 9 | Marc Surer | ATS-Ford | 39 | +1 Lap | 20 |
| 8 | 6 | Ricardo Zunino | Brabham-Ford | 39 | +1 Lap | 18 |
| 9 | 21 | Keke Rosberg | Fittipaldi-Ford | 39 | +1 Lap | 15 |
| 10 | 30 | Jochen Mass | Arrows-Ford | 39 | +1 Lap | 16 |
| 11 | 7 | John Watson | McLaren-Ford | 39 | +1 Lap | 23 |
| 12 | 3 | J.P.Jarier | Tyrrell-Ford | 39 | +1 Lap | 22 |
| 13 | 23 | Bruno Giacomelli | Alfa Romeo | 39 | +1 Lap | 17 |
| 14 | 4 | Derek Daly | Tyrrell-Ford | 38 | +2 Laps | 24 |
| 15 | 20 | E.Fittipaldi | Fittipaldi-Ford | 38 | +2 Laps | 19 |
| 16 | 2 | G.Villeneuve | Ferrari | 36 | Throttle | 3 |
| Ret | 22 | P.Depailler | Alfa Romeo | 33 | Electrical | 21 |
| Ret | 15 | J.P.Jabouille | Renault | 25 | Turbo | 1 |
| Ret | 5 | Nelson Piquet | Brabham-Ford | 14 | Suspension | 9 |
| Ret | 26 | Jacques Laffite | Ligier-Ford | 13 | Electrical | 5 |
| Ret | 14 | Clay Regazzoni | Ensign-Ford | 13 | Engine | 12 |
| Ret | 1 | Jody Scheckter | Ferrari | 10 | Engine | 8 |
| Ret | 11 | Mario Andretti | Lotus-Ford | 1 | Spun off | 4 |
| Ret | 28 | Carlos Reutemann | Williams-Ford | 1 | Halfshaft | 11 |
| DNQ | 10 | Jan Lammers | ATS-Ford | | | |
| DNQ | 18 | Dave Kennedy | Shadow-Ford | | | |
| DNQ | 17 | Stefan Johansson | Shadow-Ford | | | |
| DNQ | 31 | Eddie Cheever | Osella-Ford | | | |

Winning speed: 117.398mph Lap leaders: Villeneuve 1; jabouille 2-24; Arnoux 25-40
Pole position: Jabouille, 2m 21.400s, 124.566mph
Fastest lap: Arnoux, 2m 27.310s, 119.569mph

### SOUTH AFRICAN GRAND PRIX: KYALAMI *1 March Round: 3 Race: 331 78 x 2.550 miles*

| POS. | NO. | DRIVER | CAR/ENGINE | LAPS | TIME/RETIRED | GRID |
|---|---|---|---|---|---|---|
| 1 | 16 | Rene Arnoux | Renault | 78 | 1:36'52.54 | 2 |
| 2 | 26 | Jacques Laffite | Ligier-Ford | 78 | +34.07 | 4 |
| 3 | 25 | Didier Pironi | Ligier-Ford | 78 | +52.49 | 5 |
| 4 | 5 | Nelson Piquet | Brabham-Ford | 78 | +1'01.02 | 3 |
| 5 | 28 | Carlos Reutemann | Williams-Ford | 77 | +1 Lap | 6 |
| 6 | 30 | Jochen Mass | Arrows-Ford | 77 | +1 Lap | 19 |
| 7 | 3 | J.P.Jarier | Tyrrell-Ford | 77 | +1 Lap | 13 |
| 8 | 20 | E.Fittipaldi | Fittipaldi-Ford | 77 | +1 Lap | 18 |
| 9 | 14 | Clay Regazzoni | Ensign-Ford | 77 | +1 Lap | 20 |
| 10 | 6 | Ricardo Zunino | Brabham-Ford | 77 | +1 Lap | 17 |
| 11 | 7 | John Watson | McLaren-Ford | 76 | +2 Laps | 21 |
| 12 | 11 | Mario Andretti | Lotus-Ford | 76 | +2 Laps | 15 |
| 13 | 17 | Geoff Lees | Shadow-Ford | 70 | Suspension | 24 |
| Ret | 23 | Bruno Giacomelli | Alfa Romeo | 69 | Engine | 12 |
| Ret | 15 | J.P.Jabouille | Renault | 61 | Puncture | 1 |
| Ret | 4 | Derek Daly | Tyrrell-Ford | 61 | Puncture | 16 |
| Ret | 21 | Keke Rosberg | Fittipaldi-Ford | 58 | Accident | 23 |
| NC | 22 | P.Depailler | Alfa Romeo | 53 | Not classified | 7 |
| Ret | 27 | Alan Jones | Williams-Ford | 34 | Gearbox | 8 |
| Ret | 2 | G.Villeneuve | Ferrari | 31 | Transmission | 10 |
| Ret | 1 | Jody Scheckter | Ferrari | 14 | Engine | 9 |
| Ret | 29 | Riccardo Patrese | Arrows-Ford | 10 | Spun off | 11 |
| Ret | 31 | Eddie Cheever | Osella-Ford | 8 | Spun off | 22 |
| Ret | 12 | Elio de Angelis | Lotus-Ford | 1 | Spun off | 14 |
| DNS | 8 | Alain Prost | McLaren-Ford | | | |
| DNQ | 18 | Dave Kennedy | Shadow-Ford | | | |
| DNQ | 10 | Jan Lammers | ATS-Ford | | | |

Winning speed: 123.194mph Lap leaders: Jabouille 1-61; Arnoux 62-78
Pole position: Jabouille, 1m 10.000s, 131.148mph
Fastest lap: Arnoux, 1m 13.150s, 125.501mph

### USA WEST GRAND PRIX: LONG BEACH *30 March Round: 4 Race: 332 80.5 x 2.020 miles*

| POS. | NO. | DRIVER | CAR/ENGINE | LAPS | TIME/RETIRED | GRID |
|---|---|---|---|---|---|---|
| 1 | 5 | Nelson Piquet | Brabham-Ford | 80 | 1:50'18.550 | 1 |
| 2 | 29 | Riccardo Patrese | Arrows-Ford | 80 | +49.212 | 8 |
| 3 | 20 | E.Fittipaldi | Fittipaldi-Ford | 80 | +1'18.563 | 24 |
| 4 | 7 | John Watson | McLaren-Ford | 79 | +1 Lap | 21 |
| 5 | 1 | Jody Scheckter | Ferrari | 79 | +1 Lap | 16 |
| 6 | 25 | Didier Pironi | Ligier-Ford | 79 | +1 Lap | 9 |
| 7 | 30 | Jochen Mass | Arrows-Ford | 79 | +1 Lap | 17 |
| 8 | 4 | Derek Daly | Tyrrell-Ford | 79 | +1 Lap | 14 |
| 9 | 16 | Rene Arnoux | Renault | 78 | +2 Laps | 2 |
| 10 | 15 | J.P.Jabouille | Renault | 71 | +9 Laps | 11 |
| Ret | 21 | Keke Rosberg | Fittipaldi-Ford | 58 | Overheating | 22 |
| Ret | 14 | Clay Regazzoni | Ensign-Ford | 50 | Accident | 23 |
| Ret | 23 | Bruno Giacomelli | Alfa Romeo | 49 | Accident | 6 |
| Ret | 27 | Alan Jones | Williams-Ford | 47 | Accident | 5 |
| Ret | 2 | G.Villeneuve | Ferrari | 46 | Transmission | 10 |
| Ret | 22 | P.Depailler | Alfa Romeo | 40 | Suspension | 3 |
| Ret | 26 | Jacques Laffite | Ligier-Ford | 36 | Puncture | 13 |
| Ret | 31 | Eddie Cheever | Osella-Ford | 11 | Transmission | 19 |
| Ret | 28 | Carlos Reutemann | Williams-Ford | 3 | Transmission | 7 |
| Ret | 3 | J.P.Jarier | Tyrrell-Ford | 3 | Accident | 12 |
| Ret | 12 | Elio de Angelis | Lotus-Ford | 3 | Accident | 20 |
| Ret | 9 | Jan Lammers | ATS-Ford | 0 | Transmission | 15 |
| Ret | 11 | Mario Andretti | Lotus-Ford | 0 | Accident | 4 |
| DNQ | 18 | Dave Kennedy | Shadow-Ford | | | |
| DNQ | 17 | Geoff Lees | Shadow-Ford | | | |
| DNQ | 8 | Stephen South | McLaren-Ford | | | |

Winning speed: 88.451mph Fastest lap: Piquet 1-80
Pole position: Piquet, 1m 17.694s, 93.602mph
Fastest lap: Piquet, 1m 19.830s, 91.097mph

### BELGIAN GRAND PRIX: ZOLDER *4 May Round: 5 Race: 333 72 x 2.648 miles*

| POS. | NO. | DRIVER | CAR/ENGINE | LAPS | TIME/RETIRED | GRID |
|---|---|---|---|---|---|---|
| 1 | 25 | Didier Pironi | Ligier-Ford | 72 | 1:38'46.51 | 2 |
| 2 | 27 | Alan Jones | Williams-Ford | 72 | +47.37 | 1 |
| 3 | 28 | Carlos Reutemann | Williams-Ford | 72 | +1'24.12 | 4 |
| 4 | 16 | Rene Arnoux | Renault | 71 | +1 Lap | 6 |
| 5 | 3 | J.P.Jarier | Tyrrell-Ford | 71 | +1 Lap | 9 |
| 6 | 2 | G.Villeneuve | Ferrari | 71 | +1 Lap | 12 |
| 7 | 21 | Keke Rosberg | Fittipaldi-Ford | 71 | +1 Lap | 21 |
| 8 | 1 | Jody Scheckter | Ferrari | 70 | +2 Laps | 14 |
| 9 | 4 | Derek Daly | Tyrrell-Ford | 70 | +2 Laps | 11 |
| 10 | 12 | Elio de Angelis | Lotus-Ford | 69 | Spun off | 8 |
| 11 | 26 | Jacques Laffite | Ligier-Ford | 68 | +4 Laps | 3 |
| 12 | 9 | Jan Lammers | ATS-Ford | 64 | Engine | 15 |
| NC | 7 | John Watson | McLaren-Ford | 61 | Not classified | 20 |
| Ret | 29 | Riccardo Patrese | Arrows-Ford | 58 | Spun off | 16 |
| Ret | 11 | Mario Andretti | Lotus-Ford | 41 | Gearbox | 17 |
| Ret | 22 | P.Depailler | Alfa Romeo | 38 | Exhaust | 10 |
| Ret | 5 | Nelson Piquet | Brabham-Ford | 32 | Spun off | 7 |
| Ret | 8 | Alain Prost | McLaren-Ford | 29 | Transmission | 19 |
| Ret | 20 | E.Fittipaldi | Fittipaldi-Ford | 16 | Electrical | 24 |
| Ret | 14 | Tiff Needell | Ensign-Ford | 12 | Engine | 23 |
| Ret | 23 | Bruno Giacomelli | Alfa Romeo | 11 | Suspension | 18 |
| Ret | 6 | Ricardo Zunino | Brabham-Ford | 5 | Gearbox | 22 |
| Ret | 30 | Jochen Mass | Arrows-Ford | 1 | Spun off | 13 |
| Ret | 15 | J.P.Jabouille | Renault | 1 | Clutch | 5 |
| DNQ | 17 | Geoff Lees | Shadow-Ford | | | |
| DNQ | 18 | Dave Kennedy | Shadow-Ford | | | |
| DNQ | 31 | Eddie Cheever | Osella-Ford | | | |

Winning speed: 115.825mph Pironi 1-72
Pole position: Jones, 1m 19.120s, 120.498mph
Fastest lap: Laffite, m 20.880s, 117.876mph

### MONACO GRAND PRIX: MONTE CARLO *18 May Round: 6 Race: 334 76 x 2.058 miles*

| POS. | NO. | DRIVER | CAR/ENGINE | LAPS | TIME/RETIRED | GRID |
|---|---|---|---|---|---|---|
| 1 | 28 | Carlos Reutemann | Williams-Ford | 76 | 1:55'34.365 | 2 |
| 2 | 26 | Jacques Laffite | Ligier-Ford | 76 | +1'13.629 | 5 |
| 3 | 5 | Nelson Piquet | Brabham-Ford | 76 | +1'17.726 | 4 |
| 4 | 30 | Jochen Mass | Arrows-Ford | 75 | +1 Lap | 15 |
| 5 | 2 | G.Villeneuve | Ferrari | 75 | +1 Lap | 6 |
| 6 | 20 | E.Fittipaldi | Fittipaldi-Ford | 74 | +2 Laps | 18 |
| 7 | 11 | Mario Andretti | Lotus-Ford | 73 | +3 Laps | 19 |
| 8 | 29 | Riccardo Patrese | Arrows-Ford | 73 | +3 Laps | 11 |
| 9 | 12 | Elio de Angelis | Lotus-Ford | 68 | Accident | 14 |
| NC | 9 | Jan Lammers | ATS-Ford | 64 | Not classified | 13 |
| Ret | 25 | Didier Pironi | Ligier-Ford | 54 | Accident | 1 |
| Ret | 16 | Rene Arnoux | Renault | 53 | Accident | 20 |
| Ret | 22 | P.Depailler | Alfa Romeo | 50 | Engine | 7 |
| Ret | 1 | Jody Scheckter | Ferrari | 27 | Handling | 17 |
| Ret | 27 | Alan Jones | Williams-Ford | 25 | Differential | 3 |
| Ret | 15 | J.P.Jabouille | Renault | 25 | Gearbox | 16 |
| Ret | 23 | Bruno Giacomelli | Alfa Romeo | 0 | Accident | 8 |
| Ret | 3 | J.P.Jarier | Tyrrell-Ford | 0 | Accident | 9 |
| Ret | 8 | Alain Prost | McLaren-Ford | 0 | Accident | 10 |
| Ret | 4 | Derek Daly | Tyrrell-Ford | 0 | Accident | 12 |
| DNQ | 7 | John Watson | McLaren-Ford | | | |
| DNQ | 31 | Eddie Cheever | Osella-Ford | | | |
| DNQ | 17 | Geoff Lees | Shadow-Ford | | | |
| DNQ | 21 | Keke Rosberg | Fittipaldi-Ford | | | |
| DNQ | 6 | Ricardo Zunino | Brabham-Ford | | | |
| DNQ | 14 | Tiff Needell | Ensign-Ford | | | |
| DNQ | 18 | Dave Kennedy | Shadow-Ford | | | |

Winning speed: 81.199mph Lap leaders: Pironi 1-54; Reutemann 55-76
Pole position: Pironi, 1m 24.813s, 87.354mph
Fastest lap: Reutemann, 1m 27.418s, 84.751mph

### FRENCH GRAND PRIX: PAUL RICARD *29 June Round: 7 Race: 335 54 x 3.610 miles*

| POS. | NO. | DRIVER | CAR/ENGINE | LAPS | TIME/RETIRED | GRID |
|---|---|---|---|---|---|---|
| 1 | 27 | Alan Jones | Williams-Ford | 54 | 1:32'43.42 | 4 |
| 2 | 25 | Didier Pironi | Ligier-Ford | 54 | +4.52 | 3 |
| 3 | 26 | Jacques Laffite | Ligier-Ford | 54 | +30.26 | 1 |
| 4 | 5 | Nelson Piquet | Brabham-Ford | 54 | +1'14.88 | 8 |
| 5 | 16 | Rene Arnoux | Renault | 54 | +1'16.15 | 2 |
| 6 | 28 | Carlos Reutemann | Williams-Ford | 54 | +1'16.74 | 5 |
| 7 | 7 | John Watson | McLaren-Ford | 53 | +1 Lap | 13 |
| 8 | 2 | G.Villeneuve | Ferrari | 53 | +1 Lap | 17 |
| 9 | 29 | Riccardo Patrese | Arrows-Ford | 53 | +1 Lap | 18 |
| 10 | 30 | Jochen Mass | Arrows-Ford | 53 | +1 Lap | 15 |
| 11 | 4 | Derek Daly | Tyrrell-Ford | 52 | +2 Laps | 20 |
| 12 | 1 | Jody Scheckter | Ferrari | 52 | +2 Laps | 19 |
| 13 | 20 | E.Fittipaldi | Fittipaldi-Ford | 50 | Engine | 24 |
| 14 | 3 | J.P.Jarier | Tyrrell-Ford | 50 | +4 Laps | 16 |
| Ret | 31 | Eddie Cheever | Osella-Ford | 43 | Engine | 21 |
| Ret | 9 | Marc Surer | ATS-Ford | 26 | Gearbox | 11 |
| Ret | 22 | P.Depailler | Alfa Romeo | 25 | Handling | 10 |
| Ret | 11 | Mario Andretti | Lotus-Ford | 18 | Gearbox | 12 |
| Ret | 21 | Keke Rosberg | Fittipaldi-Ford | 8 | Spun off | 23 |
| Ret | 23 | Bruno Giacomelli | Alfa Romeo | 8 | Handling | 9 |
| Ret | 8 | Alain Prost | McLaren-Ford | 6 | Transmission | 7 |
| Ret | 12 | Elio de Angelis | Lotus-Ford | 3 | Clutch | 14 |
| Ret | 15 | J.P.Jabouille | Renault | 0 | Transmission | 6 |
| Ret | 6 | Ricardo Zunino | Brabham-Ford | 0 | Clutch | 22 |
| DNQ | 17 | Geoff Lees | Shadow-Ford | | | |
| DNQ | 14 | Jan Lammers | Ensign-Ford | | | |
| DNQ | 18 | Dave Kennedy | Shadow-Ford | | | |

Winning speed: 126.148mph Lap leaders: Laffite 1-34; Jones 35-54
Pole position: Laffite, 1m 38.880s, 131.438mph
Fastest lap: Jones, 1m 41.450s, 128.108mph

### BRITISH GRAND PRIX: BRANDS HATCH *13 July Round: 8 Race: 336 76 x 2.614 miles*

| POS. | NO. | DRIVER | CAR/ENGINE | LAPS | TIME/RETIRED | GRID |
|---|---|---|---|---|---|---|
| 1 | 27 | Alan Jones | Williams-Ford | 76 | 1:34'49.228 | 3 |
| 2 | 5 | Nelson Piquet | Brabham-Ford | 76 | +11.007 | 5 |
| 3 | 28 | Carlos Reutemann | Williams-Ford | 76 | +13.285 | 4 |
| 4 | 4 | Derek Daly | Tyrrell-Ford | 75 | +1 Lap | 10 |
| 5 | 3 | J.P.Jarier | Tyrrell-Ford | 75 | +1 Lap | 13 |
| 6 | 8 | Alain Prost | McLaren-Ford | 75 | +1 Lap | 7 |
| 7 | 6 | Hector Rebaque | Brabham-Ford | 74 | +2 Laps | 17 |
| 8 | 7 | John Watson | McLaren-Ford | 74 | Engine | 11 |
| 9 | 29 | Riccardo Patrese | Arrows-Ford | 73 | +3 Laps | 9 |
| 10 | 1 | Jody Scheckter | Ferrari | 73 | +3 Laps | 23 |
| 11 | 50 | Rupert Keegan | Williams-Ford | 73 | +3 Laps | 18 |
| 12 | 20 | E.Fittipaldi | Fittipaldi-Ford | 72 | +4 Laps | 21 |
| 13 | 30 | Jochen Mass | Arrows-Ford | 69 | +7 Laps | 22 |
| NC | 16 | Rene Arnoux | Renault | 67 | Not classified | 20 |
| Ret | 25 | Didier Pironi | Ligier-Ford | 63 | Tyre | 1 |
| Ret | 9 | Marc Surer | ATS-Ford | 59 | Engine | 14 |
| Ret | 11 | Mario Andretti | Lotus-Ford | 57 | Gearbox | 8 |
| Ret | 23 | Bruno Giacomelli | Alfa Romeo | 42 | Spun off | 6 |
| Ret | 2 | G.Villeneuve | Ferrari | 35 | Engine | 19 |
| Ret | 26 | Jacques Laffite | Ligier-Ford | 30 | Tyre | 2 |
| Ret | 22 | P.Depailler | Alfa Romeo | 27 | Engine | 12 |
| Ret | 31 | Eddie Cheever | Osella-Ford | 17 | Suspension | 24 |
| Ret | 12 | Elio de Angelis | Lotus-Ford | 16 | Suspension | 16 |
| Ret | 15 | J.P.Jabouille | Renault | 6 | Engine | 15 |
| DNQ | 14 | Jan Lammers | Ensign-Ford | | | |
| DNQ | 21 | Keke Rosberg | Fittipaldi-Ford | | | |
| DNQ | 43 | Desire Wilson | Williams-Ford | | | |

Winning speed: 125.710mph Lap leaders: Pironi 1-18; Laffite 19-30; Jones 31-76
Pole position: Pironi, 1m 11.004s, 132.533mph
Fastest lap: Pironi, 1m 12.368, 130.035mph

### GERMAN GRAND PRIX: HOCKENHEIM *10 August Round: 9 Race: 337 45 x 4.218 miles*

| POS. | NO. | DRIVER | CAR/ENGINE | LAPS | TIME/RETIRED | GRID |
|---|---|---|---|---|---|---|
| 1 | 26 | Jacques Laffite | Ligier-Ford | 45 | 1:22'59.73 | 5 |
| 2 | 28 | Carlos Reutemann | Williams-Ford | 45 | +3.19 | 4 |
| 3 | 27 | Alan Jones | Williams-Ford | 45 | +43.53 | 1 |
| 4 | 5 | Nelson Piquet | Brabham-Ford | 45 | +44.48 | 6 |
| 5 | 23 | Bruno Giacomelli | Alfa Romeo | 45 | +1'16.49 | 19 |
| 6 | 2 | G.Villeneuve | Ferrari | 45 | +1'28.72 | 16 |
| 7 | 11 | Mario Andretti | Lotus-Ford | 45 | +1'33.01 | 9 |
| 8 | 30 | Jochen Mass | Arrows-Ford | 45 | +1'47.75 | 17 |
| 9 | 29 | Riccardo Patrese | Arrows-Ford | 44 | +1 Lap | 10 |
| 10 | 4 | Derek Daly | Tyrrell-Ford | 44 | +1 Lap | 22 |
| 11 | 8 | Alain Prost | McLaren-Ford | 44 | +1 Lap | 14 |
| 12 | 9 | Marc Surer | ATS-Ford | 44 | +1 Lap | 13 |
| 13 | 1 | Jody Scheckter | Ferrari | 44 | +1 Lap | 21 |
| 14 | 14 | Jan Lammers | Ensign-Ford | 44 | +1 Lap | 24 |
| 15 | 3 | J.P.Jarier | Tyrrell-Ford | 44 | +1 Lap | 23 |
| 16 | 12 | Elio de Angelis | Lotus-Ford | 43 | Wheel bearing | 11 |
| Ret | 7 | John Watson | McLaren-Ford | 39 | Engine | 20 |
| Ret | 15 | J.P.Jabouille | Renault | 27 | Engine | 2 |
| Ret | 16 | Rene Arnoux | Renault | 26 | Engine | 3 |
| Ret | 31 | Eddie Cheever | Osella-Ford | 23 | Gearbox | 18 |
| Ret | 25 | Didier Pironi | Ligier-Ford | 18 | Transmission | 7 |
| Ret | 20 | E.Fittipaldi | Fittipaldi-Ford | 18 | Brakes | 12 |
| Ret | 21 | Keke Rosberg | Fittipaldi-Ford | 8 | Wheel bearing | 8 |
| Ret | 6 | Hector Rebaque | Brabham-Ford | 4 | Gearbox | 15 |
| DNQ | 50 | Rupert Keegan | Williams-Ford | | | |
| DNQ | 10 | Harald Ertl | ATS-Ford | | | |

Winning speed: 137.235mph Lap leaders: Jabouille 1-26; Jones 27-40; Laffite 41-45
Pole position: Jones, 1m 45.850s, 143.472 mph
Fastest lap: Jones, 1m 48.490s, 139.981mph

### AUSTRIAN GRAND PRIX: OSTERREICHRING *17 August Round: 10 Race: 338 54 x 3.692 miles*

| POS. | NO. | DRIVER | CAR/ENGINE | LAPS | TIME/RETIRED | GRID |
|---|---|---|---|---|---|---|
| 1 | 15 | J.P.Jabouille | Renault | 54 | 1:26'15.73 | 2 |
| 2 | 27 | Alan Jones | Williams-Ford | 54 | +0.82 | 3 |
| 3 | 28 | Carlos Reutemann | Williams-Ford | 54 | +19.36 | 4 |
| 4 | 26 | Jacques Laffite | Ligier-Ford | 54 | +42.02 | 5 |
| 5 | 5 | Nelson Piquet | Brabham-Ford | 54 | +1'02.81 | 7 |
| 6 | 12 | Elio de Angelis | Lotus-Ford | 54 | +1'14.97 | 9 |
| 7 | 8 | Alain Prost | McLaren-Ford | 54 | +1'33.41 | 12 |
| 8 | 2 | G.Villeneuve | Ferrari | 53 | +1 Lap | 15 |
| 9 | 16 | Rene Arnoux | Renault | 53 | +1 Lap | 1 |
| 10 | 6 | Hector Rebaque | Brabham-Ford | 53 | +1 Lap | 14 |
| 11 | 20 | E.Fittipaldi | Fittipaldi-Ford | 53 | +1 Lap | 23 |
| 12 | 9 | Marc Surer | ATS-Ford | 53 | +1 Lap | 16 |
| 13 | 1 | Jody Scheckter | Ferrari | 53 | +1 Lap | 22 |
| 14 | 29 | Riccardo Patrese | Arrows-Ford | 53 | +1 Lap | 18 |
| 15 | 50 | Rupert Keegan | Williams-Ford | 52 | +2 Laps | 20 |
| 16 | 21 | Keke Rosberg | Fittipaldi-Ford | 52 | +2 Laps | 11 |
| Ret | 43 | Nigel Mansell | Lotus-Ford | 40 | Engine | 24 |
| Ret | 7 | John Watson | McLaren-Ford | 34 | Engine | 21 |
| Ret | 23 | Bruno Giacomelli | Alfa Romeo | 28 | Wheel | 8 |
| Ret | 25 | Didier Pironi | Ligier-Ford | 25 | Handling | 13 |
| Ret | 3 | J.P.Jarier | Tyrrell-Ford | 25 | Electrical | 6 |
| Ret | 31 | Eddie Cheever | Osella-Ford | 23 | Wheel bearing | 19 |
| Ret | 4 | Derek Daly | Tyrrell-Ford | 12 | Brakes | 10 |
| Ret | 11 | Mario Andretti | Lotus-Ford | 6 | Engine | 17 |
| DNQ | 14 | Jan Lammers | Ensign-Ford | | | |
| DNQ | 30 | Jochen Mass | Arrows-Ford | | | |

Winning speed: 138.678mph Lap leaders: Jones 1-2; Arnoux 3-21; Jabouille 22-54
Pole position: Arnoux, 1m 30.270s, 147.246mph
Fastest lap: Arnoux, 1m 32.530s, 143.649mph

### DUTCH GRAND PRIX: ZANDVOORT *31 August Round: 11 Race: 339 72 x 2.642 miles*

| POS. | NO. | DRIVER | CAR/ENGINE | LAPS | TIME/RETIRED | GRID |
|---|---|---|---|---|---|---|
| 1 | 5 | Nelson Piquet | Brabham-Ford | 72 | 1:38'13.83 | |
| 2 | 16 | Rene Arnoux | Renault | 72 | +12.93 | |
| 3 | 26 | Jacques Laffite | Ligier-Ford | 72 | +13.43 | |
| 4 | 28 | Carlos Reutemann | Williams-Ford | 72 | +15.29 | |
| 5 | 3 | J.P.Jarier | Tyrrell-Ford | 72 | +1'00.02 | |
| 6 | 8 | Alain Prost | McLaren-Ford | 72 | +1'22.62 | |
| 7 | 2 | G.Villeneuve | Ferrari | 71 | +1 Lap | |
| 8 | 11 | Mario Andretti | Lotus-Ford | 70 | Out of fuel | |
| 9 | 1 | Jody Scheckter | Ferrari | 70 | +2 Laps | |
| 10 | 9 | Marc Surer | ATS-Ford | 69 | +3 Laps | |
| 11 | 27 | Alan Jones | Williams-Ford | 69 | +3 Laps | |
| Ret | 4 | Derek Daly | Tyrrell-Ford | 60 | Brakes | |
| Ret | 23 | Bruno Giacomelli | Alfa Romeo | 58 | Accident | |
| Ret | 31 | Eddie Cheever | Osella-Ford | 38 | Engine | |
| Ret | 29 | Riccardo Patrese | Arrows-Ford | 29 | Engine | |
| Ret | 15 | J.P.Jabouille | Renault | 23 | Handling | |
| Ret | 22 | V.Brambilla | Alfa Romeo | 21 | Accident | |
| Ret | 41 | Geoff Lees | Ensign-Ford | 21 | Accident | |
| Ret | 7 | John Watson | McLaren-Ford | 18 | Engine | |
| Ret | 20 | E.Fittipaldi | Fittipaldi-Ford | 16 | Brakes | |
| Ret | 43 | Nigel Mansell | Lotus-Ford | 15 | Brakes | |
| Ret | 12 | Elio de Angelis | Lotus-Ford | 2 | Accident | |
| Ret | 25 | Didier Pironi | Ligier-Ford | 2 | Accident | |
| Ret | 6 | Hector Rebaque | Brabham-Ford | 1 | Gearbox | |
| DNQ | 50 | Rupert Keegan | Williams-Ford | | | |
| DNQ | 14 | Jan Lammers | Ensign-Ford | | | |
| DNQ | 30 | Mike Thackwell | Arrows-Ford | | | |
| DNQ | 21 | Keke Rosberg | Fittipaldi-Ford | | | |

Winning speed: 116.193mph Lap leaders: Jones 1; Arnoux 2; Laffite 3-12, Piquet 13-72
Pole position: Arnoux, 1m 17.440s, 122.824mph
Fastest lap: Arnoux, 1m 19.350s, 119.867mph

### ITALIAN GRAND PRIX: IMOLA *14 September Round: 12 Race: 340 60 x 3.107 miles*

| POS. | NO. | DRIVER | CAR/ENGINE | LAPS | TIME/RETIRED | GRID |
|---|---|---|---|---|---|---|
| 1 | 5 | Nelson Piquet | Brabham-Ford | 60 | 1:38'07.52 | 5 |
| 2 | 27 | Alan Jones | Williams-Ford | 60 | +28.93 | 6 |
| 3 | 28 | Carlos Reutemann | Williams-Ford | 60 | +1'13.67 | 3 |
| 4 | 12 | Elio de Angelis | Lotus-Ford | 59 | +1 Lap | 18 |
| 5 | 21 | Keke Rosberg | Fittipaldi-Ford | 59 | +1 Lap | 11 |
| 6 | 25 | Didier Pironi | Ligier-Ford | 59 | +1 Lap | 13 |
| 7 | 8 | Alain Prost | McLaren-Ford | 59 | +1 Lap | 24 |
| 8 | 1 | Jody Scheckter | Ferrari | 59 | +1 Lap | 16 |
| 9 | 26 | Jacques Laffite | Ligier-Ford | 59 | +1 Lap | 20 |
| 10 | 16 | Rene Arnoux | Renault | 58 | +2 Laps | 1 |
| 11 | 50 | Rupert Keegan | Williams-Ford | 58 | +2 Laps | 21 |
| 12 | 31 | Eddie Cheever | Osella-Ford | 57 | +3 Laps | 17 |
| 13 | 3 | J.P.Jarier | Tyrrell-Ford | 54 | Brakes | 12 |
| Ret | 15 | J.P.Jabouille | Renault | 53 | Gearbox | 2 |
| Ret | 9 | Marc Surer | ATS-Ford | 45 | Engine | 23 |
| Ret | 11 | Mario Andretti | Lotus-Ford | 40 | Engine | 10 |
| Ret | 29 | Riccardo Patrese | Arrows-Ford | 38 | Engine | 7 |
| Ret | 4 | Derek Daly | Tyrrell-Ford | 33 | Accident | 22 |
| Ret | 7 | John Watson | McLaren-Ford | 20 | Wheel bearing | 14 |
| Ret | 6 | Hector Rebaque | Brabham-Ford | 18 | Suspension | 9 |
| Ret | 20 | E.Fittipaldi | Fittipaldi-Ford | 17 | Accident | 15 |
| Ret | 2 | G.Villeneuve | Ferrari | 5 | Puncture | 8 |
| Ret | 23 | Bruno Giacomelli | Alfa Romeo | 5 | Puncture | 4 |
| Ret | 22 | V.Brambilla | Alfa Romeo | 4 | Spun off | 19 |
| DNQ | 43 | Nigel Mansell | Lotus-Ford | | | |
| DNQ | 30 | M.Winkelhock | Arrows-Ford | | | |
| DNQ | 14 | Jan Lammers | Ensign-Ford | | | |
| DNQ | 41 | Geoff Lees | Ensign-Ford | | | |

Winning speed: 113.984mph Lap leaders: Arnoux 1-2; Jabouille 3; Piquet 4-60
Pole position: Arnoux, 1m 33.988s, 119.001mph
Fastest lap: Jones, 1m 36.089s, 116.399mph

### CANADIAN GRAND PRIX: MONTREAL *28 September Round: 13 Race 341 70 x 2.740 miles*

| POS. | NO. | DRIVER | CAR/ENGINE | LAPS | TIME/RETIRED | GRID |
|---|---|---|---|---|---|---|
| 1 | 27 | Alan Jones | Williams-Ford | 70 | 1:46'45.53 | 2 |
| 2 | 28 | Carlos Reutemann | Williams-Ford | 70 | +15.54 | 5 |
| 3 | 25 | Didier Pironi | Ligier-Ford | 70 | +19.07 | 3 |
| 4 | 7 | John Watson | McLaren-Ford | 70 | +30.98 | 7 |
| 5 | 2 | G.Villeneuve | Ferrari | 70 | +55.23 | 22 |
| 6 | 6 | Hector Rebaque | Brabham-Ford | 69 | +1 Lap | 10 |
| 7 | 3 | J.P.Jarier | Tyrrell-Ford | 69 | +1 Lap | 15 |
| 8 | 26 | Jacques Laffite | Ligier-Ford | 68 | Out of fuel | 9 |
| 9 | 21 | Keke Rosberg | Fittipaldi-Ford | 68 | +2 Laps | 6 |
| 10 | 12 | Elio de Angelis | Lotus-Ford | 68 | +2 Laps | 17 |
| 11 | 30 | Jochen Mass | Arrows-Ford | 67 | +3 Laps | 21 |
| 12 | 14 | Jan Lammers | Ensign-Ford | 66 | +4 Laps | 19 |
| Ret | 8 | Alain Prost | McLaren-Ford | 41 | Suspension | 12 |
| Ret | 16 | Rene Arnoux | Renault | 39 | Brakes | 23 |
| Ret | 15 | J.P.Jabouille | Renault | 25 | Suspension | 13 |
| Ret | 5 | Nelson Piquet | Brabham-Ford | 23 | Engine | 1 |
| Ret | 11 | Mario Andretti | Lotus-Ford | 11 | Engine | 18 |
| Ret | 22 | A.de Cesaris | Alfa Romeo | 8 | Engine | 8 |
| Ret | 31 | Eddie Cheever | Osella-Ford | 8 | Fuel system | 14 |
| Ret | 20 | E.Fittipaldi | Fittipaldi-Ford | 8 | Gearbox | 16 |
| Ret | 23 | Bruno Giacomelli | Alfa Romeo | 7 | Chassis | 4 |
| Ret | 29 | Riccardo Patrese | Arrows-Ford | 6 | Accident | 11 |
| Ret | 4 | Derek Daly | Tyrrell-Ford | 0 | Accident | 20 |
| Ret | 43 | Mike Thackwell | Tyrrell-Ford | 0 | Accident | 24 |
| DNQ | 9 | Marc Surer | ATS-Ford | | | |
| DNQ | 1 | Jody Scheckter | Ferrari | | | |
| DNQ | 50 | Rupert Keegan | Williams-Ford | | | |
| DNQ | 51 | Kevin Cogan | Williams-Ford | | | |

Winning speed: 107.804mph Lap leaders: Jones 1-2, 24-43; Piquet 3-23; Pironi 44-70
Pole position: Piquet, 1m 27.328s, 112.964mph
Fastest lap: Pironi, 28.769s, 111.130mph
Stopped after first lap pile-up and restarted for original distance. Pironi finished first but was deducted a minute for a jump start.

### USA EAST GRAND PRIX: WATKINS GLEN *5 October Round: 14 Race: 342 59 x 3.377 miles*

| POS. | NO. | DRIVER | CAR/ENGINE | LAPS | TIME/RETIRED | GRID |
|---|---|---|---|---|---|---|
| 1 | 27 | Alan Jones | Williams-Ford | 59 | 1:34'36.05 | 5 |
| 2 | 28 | Carlos Reutemann | Williams-Ford | 59 | +4.21 | 3 |
| 3 | 25 | Didier Pironi | Ligier-Ford | 59 | +12.57 | 7 |
| 4 | 12 | Elio de Angelis | Lotus-Ford | 59 | +29.69 | 4 |
| 5 | 26 | Jacques Laffite | Ligier-Ford | 58 | +1 Lap | 12 |
| 6 | 11 | Mario Andretti | Lotus-Ford | 58 | +1 Lap | 11 |
| 7 | 16 | Rene Arnoux | Renault | 58 | +1 Lap | 6 |
| 8 | 9 | Marc Surer | ATS-Ford | 57 | +2 Laps | 17 |
| 9 | 50 | Rupert Keegan | Williams-Ford | 57 | +2 Laps | 15 |
| 10 | 21 | Keke Rosberg | Fittipaldi-Ford | 57 | +2 Laps | 14 |
| 11 | 1 | Jody Scheckter | Ferrari | 56 | +3 Laps | 23 |
| NC | 7 | John Watson | McLaren-Ford | 50 | Not classified | 9 |
| Ret | 2 | G.Villeneuve | Ferrari | 49 | Accident | 18 |
| NC | 3 | J.P.Jarier | Tyrrell-Ford | 40 | Not classified | 22 |
| Ret | 30 | Jochen Mass | Arrows-Ford | 36 | Transmission | 24 |
| Ret | 23 | Bruno Giacomelli | Alfa Romeo | 31 | Electrical | 1 |
| Ret | 5 | Nelson Piquet | Brabham-Ford | 25 | Spun off | 2 |
| Ret | 6 | Hector Rebaque | Brabham-Ford | 20 | Engine | 8 |
| Ret | 31 | Eddie Cheever | Osella-Ford | 20 | Suspension | 16 |
| Ret | 29 | Riccardo Patrese | Arrows-Ford | 16 | Spun off | 20 |
| Ret | 14 | Jan Lammers | Ensign-Ford | 16 | Steering | 25 |
| Ret | 20 | E.Fittipaldi | Fittipaldi-Ford | 15 | Suspension | 19 |
| Ret | 4 | Derek Daly | Tyrrell-Ford | 3 | Spun off | 21 |
| Ret | 22 | A.de Cesaris | Alfa Romeo | 2 | Accident | 10 |
| DNS | 8 | Alain Prost | McLaren-Ford | 0 | Non starter | 13 |
| DNQ | 43 | Mike Thackwell | Tyrrell-Ford | | | |
| DNQ | 51 | Geoff Lees | Williams-Ford | | | |

Winning speed: 126.369mph Lap leaders: Giacomelli 1-31; Jones 32-59
Pole position: Giacomelli, 1m 33.291s, 130.315mph
Fastest lap: Jones, 1m 34.068s, 129.238mph

### Key to Abbreviations

| | | | |
|---|---|---|---|
| **DNPQ** | Did not pre-qualify | **NC** | Not classified |
| **DNQ** | Did not qualify | **Ret** | Retired |
| **DNS** | Did not start | **Wth** | Withdrawn |
| **DSQ** | Disqualified | | |

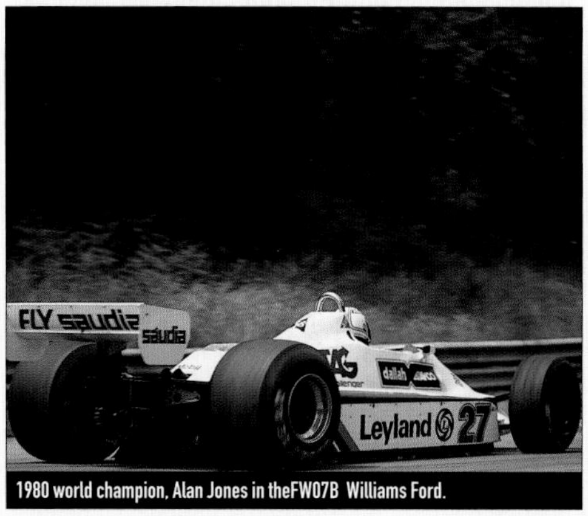

1980 world champion, Alan Jones in theFW07B Williams Ford.

# 1981

DRIVERS' CHAMPION: NELSON PIQUET
CONSTRUCTORS' CHAMPION: WILLIAMS FORD

## DRIVERS' CHAMPIONSHIP

| POS. | DRIVER | NATIONALITY | CAR | POINTS |
|---|---|---|---|---|
| 1 | Nelson Piquet | Brazil | Brabham-Ford | 50 |
| 2 | Carlos Reutemann | Argentina | Williams-Ford | 49 |
| 3 | Alan Jones | Australia | Williams-Ford | 46 |
| 4 | Jacques Laffite | France | Ligier-Ford | 44 |
| 5 | Alain Prost | France | Renault | 43 |
| 6 | John Watson | GB | McLaren-Ford | 27 |
| 7 | Gilles Villeneuve | Canada | Ferrari | 25 |
| 8 | Elio de Angelis | Italy | Lotus-Ford | 14 |
| 9 | Rene Arnoux | France | Renault | 11 |
| = | Hector Rebaque | Mexico | Brabham-Ford | 11 |
| 11 | Eddie Cheever | USA | Tyrell-Ford | 10 |
| = | Riccardo Patrese | Italy | Arrows-Ford | 10 |
| 13 | Didier Pironi | France | Ferrari | 9 |
| 14 | Nigel Mansell | GB | Lotus-Ford | 8 |
| 15 | Bruno Giacomelli | Italy | Alfa Romeo | 7 |
| 16 | Marc Surer | Switzerland | Ensign-Ford | 4 |
| 17 | Mario Andretti | USA | Alfa Romeo | 3 |
| 18 | Slim Borgudd | Sweden | ATS-Ford | 1 |
| = | Andrea de Cesaris | Italy | McLaren-Ford | 1 |
| = | Eliseo Salazar | Chile | Ensign-Ford | 1 |
| = | Patrick Tambay | France | Theodore-Ford | 1 |
| | | Talbot | Ligier-Matra | |
| | Slim Borgudd | Sweden | ATS-Ford | 1 |
| | Eliseo Salazar | Chile | March-Ford | 1 |
| | | | Ensign-Ford | |
| | Jean Pierre Jarier | France | Talbot Ligier-Matra | |
| | | | Osella-Ford | |
| | Keke Rosberg | Finland | Fittipaldi-Ford | |
| | Chico Serra | Brazil | Fittipaldi-Ford | |
| | Beppe Gabbiani | Italy | Osella-Ford | |
| | Siegfried Stohr | Italy | Arrows-Ford | |
| | Jan Lammers | Netherlands | ATS-Ford | |
| | Kevin Cogan | USA | Tyrrell-Ford | |
| | Ricardo Zunino | Argentina | Tyrrell-Ford | |
| | Derek Daly | Ireland | March-Ford | |
| | Jean Pierre Jabouille | France | Talbot Ligier-Matra | |
| | Michele Alboreto | Italy | Tyrrell-Ford | |
| | Miguel Angel Guerra | Argentina | Osella-Ford | |
| | Piercarlo Ghinzani | Italy | Osella-Ford | |
| | Brian Henton | GB | Toleman-Hart | |
| | Derek Warwick | GB | Toleman-Hart | |
| | Emilio de Villota | Italy | Williams-Ford | |
| | Giorgio Francia | Italy | Osella-Ford | |
| | Jacques Villeneuve Snr. | Canada | Arrows-Ford | |

Points for top six finishers (9, 6, 4, 3, 2, 1). Half points awarded for races stopped before half distance

## CONSTRUCTORS' CHAMPIONSHIP

| POS. | CONSTRUCTOR | POINTS |
|---|---|---|
| 1 | Williams-Ford | 95 |
| 2 | Brabham-Ford | 61 |
| 3 | Renault | 54 |
| 3 | Renault | 54 |
| 4 | Ligier-Matra | 44 |
| 5 | Ferrari | 34 |
| 6 | McLaren-Ford | 28 |
| 7 | Lotus-Ford | 22 |
| 8 | Arrows-Ford | 10 |
| 9 | Alfa Romeo | 10 |
| 10 | Tyrrell-Ford | 10 |
| 11 | Ensign-Ford | 5 |
| 12 | Theodore-Ford | 1 |
| 12 | ATS-Ford | 1 |

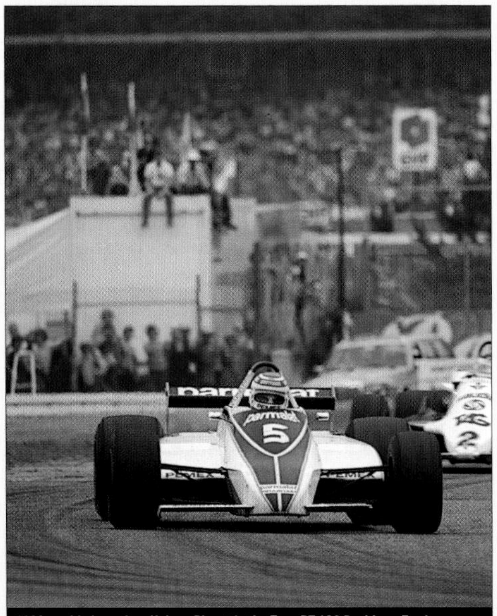

1981 world champion, Nelson Piquet in the Type BT 49C Brabham Ford.

## USA WEST GRAND PRIX: LONG BEACH *15 March Round: 1 Race: 343 80.5 x 2.020 miles*

| POS. | NO. | DRIVER | CAR/ENGINE | LAPS | TIME/RETIRED | GRID |
|---|---|---|---|---|---|---|
| 1 | 1 | Alan Jones | Williams-Ford | 80 | 1:50'41.33 | 2 |
| 2 | 2 | Carlos Reutemann | Williams-Ford | 80 | +9.19 | 3 |
| 3 | 5 | Nelson Piquet | Brabham-Ford | 80 | +34.92 | 4 |
| 4 | 22 | Mario Andretti | Alfa Romeo | 80 | +49.31 | 6 |
| 5 | 3 | Eddie Cheever | Tyrrell-Ford | 80 | +1'06.70 | 8 |
| 6 | 33 | Patrick Tambay | Theodore-Ford | 79 | +1 Lap | 17 |
| 7 | 21 | Chico Serra | Fittipaldi-Ford | 78 | +2 Laps | 18 |
| 8 | 16 | Rene Arnoux | Renault | 77 | +3 Laps | 20 |
| Ret | 14 | Marc Surer | Ensign-Ford | 70 | Fuel system | 19 |
| Ret | 28 | Didier Pironi | Ferrari | 67 | Fuel system | 11 |
| Ret | 25 | J.P.Jarier | Ligier-Matra | 64 | Fuel pump | 10 |
| Ret | 6 | Hector Rebaque | Brabham-Ford | 49 | Accident | 15 |
| Ret | 23 | Bruno Giacomelli | Alfa Romeo | 41 | Collision | 9 |
| Ret | 26 | Jacques Laffite | Ligier-Matra | 41 | Collision | 12 |
| Ret | 20 | Keke Rosberg | Fittipaldi-Ford | 41 | Engine | 16 |
| Ret | 9 | Jan Lammers | ATS-Ford | 41 | Collision | 21 |
| Ret | 29 | Riccardo Patrese | Arrows-Ford | 33 | Fuel system | 1 |
| Ret | 32 | Beppe Gabbiani | Osella-Ford | 26 | Accident | 24 |
| Ret | 12 | Nigel Mansell | Lotus-Ford | 25 | Accident | 7 |
| Ret | 27 | G.Villeneuve | Ferrari | 17 | Halfshaft | 5 |
| Ret | 7 | John Watson | McLaren-Ford | 16 | Brakes | 23 |
| Ret | 11 | Elio de Angelis | Lotus-Ford | 13 | Accident | 13 |
| Ret | 15 | Alain Prost | Renault | 0 | Collision | 14 |
| Ret | 8 | A.de Cesaris | McLaren-Ford | 0 | Collision | 22 |
| DNQ | 4 | Kevin Cogan | Tyrrell-Ford | | | |
| DNQ | 17 | Derek Daly | March-Ford | | | |
| DNQ | 31 | M.A.Guerra | Osella-Ford | | | |
| DNQ | 30 | Siegfried Stohr | Arrows-Ford | | | |
| DNQ | 18 | Eliseo Salazar | March-Ford | | | |

Winning speed: 87.597mph Lap leaders: Patrese 1-24; Reutemann 25-31; Jones 32-80
Pole position: Patrese, 1m 19.399s, 91.592mph
Fastest lap: Jones, 1m 20.901s, 89.891mph

## BRAZILIAN GRAND PRIX: RIO DE JANEIRO *29 March Round: 2 Race: 344 62 x 3.126 miles*

| POS. | NO. | DRIVER | CAR/ENGINE | LAPS | TIME/RETIRED | GRID |
|---|---|---|---|---|---|---|
| 1 | 2 | Carlos Reutemann | Williams-Ford | 62 | 2:00'23.66 | 2 |
| 2 | 1 | Alan Jones | Williams-Ford | 62 | +4.44 | 3 |
| 3 | 29 | Riccardo Patrese | Arrows-Ford | 62 | +1'03.08 | 4 |
| 4 | 14 | Marc Surer | Ensign-Ford | 62 | +1'17.03 | 18 |
| 5 | 11 | Elio de Angelis | Lotus-Ford | 62 | +1'26.42 | 10 |
| 6 | 26 | Jacques Laffite | Ligier-Matra | 62 | +1'26.83 | 16 |
| 7 | 25 | J.P.Jarier | Ligier-Matra | 62 | +1'30.25 | 23 |
| 8 | 7 | John Watson | McLaren-Ford | 61 | +1 Lap | 15 |
| 9 | 20 | Keke Rosberg | Fittipaldi-Ford | 61 | +1 Lap | 12 |
| 10 | 33 | Patrick Tambay | Theodore-Ford | 61 | +1 Lap | 19 |
| 11 | 12 | Nigel Mansell | Lotus-Ford | 61 | +1 Lap | 13 |
| 12 | 5 | Nelson Piquet | Brabham-Ford | 60 | +2 Laps | 1 |
| 13 | 4 | Ricardo Zunino | Tyrrell-Ford | 57 | +5 Laps | 24 |
| NC | 3 | Eddie Cheever | Tyrrell-Ford | 49 | Not classified | 14 |
| NC | 23 | Bruno Giacomelli | Alfa Romeo | 40 | Not classified | 6 |
| Ret | 27 | G.Villeneuve | Ferrari | 25 | Turbo | 7 |
| Ret | 6 | Hector Rebaque | Brabham-Ford | 22 | Spun off | 11 |
| Ret | 15 | Alain Prost | Renault | 20 | Collision | 5 |
| Ret | 30 | Siegfried Stohr | Arrows-Ford | 20 | Accident | 21 |
| Ret | 28 | Didier Pironi | Ferrari | 19 | Collision | 17 |
| Ret | 8 | A.de Cesaris | McLaren-Ford | 9 | Engine | 20 |
| Ret | 16 | Rene Arnoux | Renault | 0 | Collision | 8 |
| Ret | 22 | Mario Andretti | Alfa Romeo | 0 | Collision | 9 |
| Ret | 21 | Chico Serra | Fittipaldi-Ford | 0 | Collision | 22 |
| DNQ | 9 | Jan Lammers | ATS-Ford | | | |
| DNQ | 32 | Beppe Gabbiani | Osella-Ford | | | |
| DNQ | 31 | M.A.Guerra | Osella-Ford | | | |
| DNQ | 18 | Eliseo Salazar | March-Ford | | | |
| DNQ | 14 | Ricardo Londono | Ensign-Ford | | | |
| DNQ | 17 | Derek Daly | March-Ford | | | |

Winning speed: 96.592mph Lap leaders: Reutemann 1-62
Pole position: Piquet, 1m 35.079s, 118.365mph
Fastest lap: Surer, 54.302s, 98.459mph

## ARGENTINE GRAND PRIX: BUENOS AIRES *12 April Round: 3 Race: 345 53 x 3.708 miles*

| POS. | NO. | DRIVER | CAR/ENGINE | LAPS | TIME/RETIRED | GRID |
|---|---|---|---|---|---|---|
| 1 | 5 | Nelson Piquet | Brabham-Ford | 53 | 1:34'32.74 | 1 |
| 2 | 2 | Carlos Reutemann | Williams-Ford | 53 | +26.61 | 4 |
| 3 | 15 | Alain Prost | Renault | 53 | +49.98 | 2 |
| 4 | 1 | Alan Jones | Williams-Ford | 53 | +1'07.88 | 3 |
| 5 | 16 | Rene Arnoux | Renault | 53 | +1'31.85 | 5 |
| 6 | 11 | Elio de Angelis | Lotus-Ford | 52 | +1 Lap | 10 |
| 7 | 29 | Riccardo Patrese | Arrows-Ford | 52 | +1 Lap | 9 |
| 8 | 22 | Mario Andretti | Alfa Romeo | 52 | +1 Lap | 17 |
| 9 | 30 | Siegfried Stohr | Arrows-Ford | 52 | +1 Lap | 19 |
| 10 | 23 | Bruno Giacomelli | Alfa Romeo | 51 | Out of fuel | 22 |
| 11 | 8 | A.de Cesaris | McLaren-Ford | 51 | +2 Laps | 18 |
| 12 | 9 | Jan Lammers | ATS-Ford | 51 | +2 Laps | 23 |
| 13 | 4 | Ricardo Zunino | Tyrrell-Ford | 51 | +2 Laps | 24 |
| Ret | 27 | G.Villeneuve | Ferrari | 40 | Transmission | 7 |
| Ret | 33 | Patrick Tambay | Theodore-Ford | 36 | Oil leak | 14 |
| Ret | 7 | John Watson | McLaren-Ford | 36 | Transmission | 11 |
| Ret | 6 | Hector Rebaque | Brabham-Ford | 32 | Electrical | 6 |
| Ret | 21 | Chico Serra | Fittipaldi-Ford | 28 | Gearbox | 20 |
| Ret | 26 | Jacques Laffite | Ligier-Matra | 19 | Handling | 21 |
| Ret | 14 | Marc Surer | Ensign-Ford | 14 | Engine | 16 |
| Ret | 20 | Keke Rosberg | Fittipaldi-Ford | 4 | Fuel pump | 8 |
| Ret | 12 | Nigel Mansell | Lotus-Ford | 3 | Engine | 15 |
| Ret | 28 | Didier Pironi | Ferrari | 3 | Engine | 12 |
| Ret | 3 | Eddie Cheever | Tyrrell-Ford | 1 | Clutch | 13 |
| DNQ | 31 | M.A.Guerra | Osella-Ford | | | |
| DNQ | 32 | Beppe Gabbiani | Osella-Ford | | | |
| DNQ | 17 | Derek Daly | March-Ford | | | |
| DNQ | 25 | J.P.Jabouille | Ligier-Matra | | | |
| DNQ | 18 | Eliseo Salazar | March-Ford | | | |

Winning speed: 124.728mph Lap leaders: Piquet 1-53
Pole position: Piquet, 1m 42.665s, 130.035mph
Fastest lap: Piquet, 1m 45.287s, 126.797mph
Zunino penalised one lap for taking a short cut.

## SAN MARINO GRAND PRIX: IMOLA *3 May Round 4 Race: 346 60 x 3.132 miles*

| POS. | NO. | DRIVER | CAR/ENGINE | LAPS | TIME/RETIRED | GRID |
|---|---|---|---|---|---|---|
| 1 | 5 | Nelson Piquet | Brabham-Ford | 60 | 1:51'23.97 | 5 |
| 2 | 29 | Riccardo Patrese | Arrows-Ford | 60 | +4.58 | 9 |
| 3 | 2 | Carlos Reutemann | Williams-Ford | 60 | +6.34 | 2 |
| 4 | 6 | Hector Rebaque | Brabham-Ford | 60 | +22.89 | 13 |
| 5 | 28 | Didier Pironi | Ferrari | 60 | +25.87 | 6 |
| 6 | 8 | A.de Cesaris | McLaren-Ford | 60 | +1'06.61 | 14 |
| 7 | 27 | G.Villeneuve | Ferrari | 60 | +1'41.97 | 1 |
| 8 | 16 | Rene Arnoux | Renault | 59 | +1 Lap | 3 |
| 9 | 14 | Marc Surer | Ensign-Ford | 59 | +1 Lap | 21 |
| 10 | 7 | John Watson | McLaren-Ford | 58 | +2 Laps | 7 |
| 11 | 33 | Patrick Tambay | Theodore-Ford | 58 | +2 Laps | 16 |
| 12 | 1 | Alan Jones | Williams-Ford | 58 | +2 Laps | 8 |
| 13 | 10 | Slim Borgudd | ATS-Ford | 57 | +3 Laps | 24 |
| NC | 25 | J.P.Jabouille | Ligier-Matra | 45 | Not classified | 18 |
| Ret | 17 | Eliseo Salazar | March-Ford | 38 | Spun off | 23 |
| Ret | 4 | Michele Alboreto | Tyrrell-Ford | 31 | Collision | 17 |
| Ret | 32 | Beppe Gabbiani | Osella-Ford | 31 | Collision | 20 |
| Ret | 23 | Bruno Giacomelli | Alfa Romeo | 28 | Collision | 11 |
| Ret | 3 | Eddie Cheever | Tyrrell-Ford | 28 | Collision | 19 |
| Ret | 22 | Mario Andretti | Alfa Romeo | 26 | Gearbox | 12 |
| Ret | 20 | Keke Rosberg | Fittipaldi-Ford | 14 | Engine | 15 |
| Ret | 26 | Jacques Laffite | Ligier-Matra | 7 | Suspension | 10 |
| Ret | 15 | Alain Prost | Renault | 3 | Gearbox | 4 |
| Ret | 31 | M.A.Guerra | Osella-Ford | 0 | Accident | 22 |
| DNQ | 30 | Siegfried Stohr | Arrows-Ford | | | |
| DNQ | 18 | Derek Daly | March-Ford | | | |
| DNQ | 9 | Jan Lammers | ATS-Ford | | | |
| DNQ | 21 | Chico Serra | Fittipaldi-Ford | | | |
| DNQ | 36 | Derek Warwick | Toleman-Hart | | | |
| DNQ | 35 | Brian Henton | Toleman-Hart | | | |

Winning speed: 101.205mph Lap leaders: Villeneuve 1-14; Pironi 15-46; Piquet 47-60
Pole position: Villeneuve, 1m 34.523s, 119.274mph
Fastest lap: Villeneuve, 1m 48.064s, 104.329mph

## BELGIAN GRAND PRIX: ZOLDER *17 May Round: 5 Race:347 54 x 2.648 miles*

| POS. | NO. | DRIVER | CAR/ENGINE | LAPS | TIME/RETIRED | GRID |
|---|---|---|---|---|---|---|
| 1 | 2 | Carlos Reutemann | Williams-Ford | 54 | 1:16'31.61 | 1 |
| 2 | 26 | Jacques Laffite | Ligier-Matra | 54 | +36.06 | 9 |
| 3 | 12 | Nigel Mansell | Lotus-Ford | 54 | +43.69 | 10 |
| 4 | 27 | G.Villeneuve | Ferrari | 54 | +47.64 | 7 |
| 5 | 11 | Elio de Angelis | Lotus-Ford | 54 | +49.20 | 14 |
| 6 | 3 | Eddie Cheever | Tyrrell-Ford | 54 | +52.51 | 8 |
| 7 | 7 | John Watson | McLaren-Ford | 54 | +1'01.66 | 5 |
| 8 | 28 | Didier Pironi | Ferrari | 54 | +1'32.04 | 3 |
| 9 | 23 | Bruno Giacomelli | Alfa Romeo | 54 | +1'35.58 | 17 |
| 10 | 22 | Mario Andretti | Alfa Romeo | 53 | +1 Lap | 18 |
| 11 | 14 | Marc Surer | Ensign-Ford | 52 | +2 Laps | 15 |
| 12 | 4 | Michele Alboreto | Tyrrell-Ford | 52 | +2 Laps | 19 |
| 13 | 31 | P.Ghinzani | Osella-Ford | 50 | +4 Laps | 24 |
| Ret | 6 | Hector Rebaque | Brabham-Ford | 39 | Accident | 21 |
| Ret | 25 | J.P.Jabouille | Ligier-Matra | 35 | Transmission | 16 |
| Ret | 21 | Chico Serra | Fittipaldi-Ford | 29 | Engine | 20 |
| Ret | 32 | Beppe Gabbiani | Osella-Ford | 22 | Engine | 22 |
| Ret | 1 | Alan Jones | Williams-Ford | 19 | Accident | 6 |
| Ret | 8 | A.de Cesaris | McLaren-Ford | 11 | Gearbox | 23 |
| Ret | 5 | Nelson Piquet | Brabham-Ford | 10 | Accident | 2 |
| Ret | 20 | Keke Rosberg | Fittipaldi-Ford | 10 | Gearbox | 11 |
| Ret | 15 | Alain Prost | Renault | 2 | Clutch | 12 |
| Ret | 29 | Riccardo Patrese | Arrows-Ford | 0 | Collision | 4 |
| Ret | 30 | Siegfried Stohr | Arrows-Ford | 0 | Collision | 13 |
| DNQ | 18 | Derek Daly | March-Ford | | | |
| DNQ | 16 | Rene Arnoux | Renault | | | |
| DNQ | 17 | Eliseo Salazar | March-Ford | | | |
| DNQ | 9 | Slim Borgudd | ATS-Ford | | | |
| DNQ | 33 | Patrick Tambay | Theodore-Ford | | | |
| DNQ | 36 | Derek Warwick | Toleman-Hart | | | |
| DNQ | 35 | Brian Henton | Toleman-Hart | | | |

Winning speed: 112.123mph Lap leaders: Pironi 1-12; Jones 13-19; Reutemann 20-54
Pole position: Reutemann, 1m 22.280s, 115.870mph Fastest lap: Reutemann, 1m 23.300s, 114.452mph. Scheduled for 70 laps, but stopped early because of rain.

## MONACO GRAND PRIX: MONTE CARLO *31 May Round: 6 Race: 348 76 x 2.058 miles*

| POS. | NO. | DRIVER | CAR/ENGINE | LAPS | TIME/RETIRED | GRID |
|---|---|---|---|---|---|---|
| 1 | 27 | G.Villeneuve | Ferrari | 76 | 1:54'23.38 | 2 |
| 2 | 1 | Alan Jones | Williams-Ford | 76 | +39.91 | 7 |
| 3 | 26 | Jacques Laffite | Ligier-Matra | 76 | +1'29.24 | 8 |
| 4 | 28 | Didier Pironi | Ferrari | 75 | +1 Lap | 17 |
| 5 | 3 | Eddie Cheever | Tyrrell-Ford | 74 | +2 Laps | 15 |
| 6 | 14 | Marc Surer | Ensign-Ford | 74 | +2 Laps | 19 |
| 7 | 33 | Patrick Tambay | Theodore-Ford | 72 | +4 Laps | 16 |
| Ret | 5 | Nelson Piquet | Brabham-Ford | 53 | Spun off | 1 |
| Ret | 7 | John Watson | McLaren-Ford | 52 | Engine | 10 |
| Ret | 4 | Michele Alboreto | Tyrrell-Ford | 50 | Collision | 20 |
| Ret | 23 | Bruno Giacomelli | Alfa Romeo | 50 | Collision | 18 |
| Ret | 15 | Alain Prost | Renault | 45 | Engine | 9 |
| Ret | 2 | Carlos Reutemann | Williams-Ford | 33 | Gearbox | 4 |
| Ret | 11 | Elio de Angelis | Lotus-Ford | 32 | Engine | 6 |
| Ret | 16 | Rene Arnoux | Renault | 32 | Spun off | 13 |
| Ret | 29 | Riccardo Patrese | Arrows-Ford | 29 | Gearbox | 5 |
| Ret | 12 | Nigel Mansell | Lotus-Ford | 15 | Suspension | 3 |
| Ret | 30 | Siegfried Stohr | Arrows-Ford | 14 | Fuel system | 14 |
| Ret | 8 | A.de Cesaris | McLaren-Ford | 0 | Collision | 11 |
| Ret | 22 | Mario Andretti | Alfa Romeo | 0 | Collision | 12 |
| DNQ | 20 | Keke Rosberg | Fittipaldi-Ford | | | |
| DNQ | 25 | J.P.Jabouille | Ligier-Matra | | | |
| DNQ | 6 | Hector Rebaque | Brabham-Ford | | | |
| DNQ | 21 | Chico Serra | Fittipaldi-Ford | | | |
| DNQ | 32 | P.Ghinzani | Osella-Ford | | | |
| DNQ | 31 | Beppe Gabbiani | Osella-Ford | | | |
| DNPQ | 10 | Slim Borgudd | ATS-Ford | | | |
| DNPQ | 18 | Derek Daly | March-Ford | | | |
| DNPQ | 17 | Eliseo Salazar | March-Ford | | | |
| DNPQ | 35 | Brian Henton | Toleman-Hart | | | |
| DNPQ | 36 | Derek Warwick | Toleman-Hart | | | |

Winning speed: 82.039mph Lap leaders: Piquet 1-53, Jones 54-72; Villeneuve 73-76
Pole position: Piquet, 1m 25.710s, 86.440mph Fastest lap: Jones, 1m 27.470s, 84.700mph

## SPANISH GRAND PRIX: JARAMA *21 June Round: 7 Race: 349 80 x 2.058 miles*

| POS. | NO. | DRIVER | CAR/ENGINE | LAPS | TIME/RETIRED | GRID |
|---|---|---|---|---|---|---|
| 1 | 27 | G.Villeneuve | Ferrari | 80 | 1:46'35.01 | 7 |
| 2 | 26 | Jacques Laffite | Ligier-Matra | 80 | +0.22 | 1 |
| 3 | 7 | John Watson | McLaren-Ford | 80 | +0.58 | 4 |
| 4 | 2 | Carlos Reutemann | Williams-Ford | 80 | +1.01 | 3 |
| 5 | 11 | Elio de Angelis | Lotus-Ford | 80 | +1.24 | 10 |
| 6 | 12 | Nigel Mansell | Lotus-Ford | 80 | +28.58 | 11 |
| 7 | 1 | Alan Jones | Williams-Ford | 80 | +56.58 | 2 |
| 8 | 22 | Mario Andretti | Alfa Romeo | 80 | +1'00.80 | 8 |
| 9 | 16 | Rene Arnoux | Renault | 80 | +1'07.08 | 17 |
| 10 | 23 | Bruno Giacomelli | Alfa Romeo | 80 | +1'13.65 | 6 |
| 11 | 21 | Chico Serra | Fittipaldi-Ford | 79 | +1 Lap | 21 |
| 12 | 20 | Keke Rosberg | Fittipaldi-Ford | 78 | +2 Laps | 15 |
| 13 | 33 | Patrick Tambay | Theodore-Ford | 78 | +2 Laps | 16 |
| 14 | 14 | Eliseo Salazar | Ensign-Ford | 77 | +3 Laps | 24 |
| 15 | 28 | Didier Pironi | Ferrari | 76 | +4 Laps | 13 |
| 16 | 17 | Derek Daly | March-Ford | 75 | +5 Laps | 22 |
| NC | 3 | Eddie Cheever | Tyrrell-Ford | 62 | Not classified | 20 |
| Ret | 25 | J.P.Jabouille | Ligier-Matra | 51 | Brakes | 19 |
| Ret | 6 | Hector Rebaque | Brabham-Ford | 46 | Gearbox | 18 |
| Ret | 30 | Siegfried Stohr | Arrows-Ford | 43 | Ignition | 23 |
| Ret | 5 | Nelson Piquet | Brabham-Ford | 43 | Accident | 9 |
| Ret | 15 | Alain Prost | Renault | 28 | Spun off | 5 |
| Ret | 29 | Riccardo Patrese | Arrows-Ford | 21 | Brakes | 12 |
| Ret | 8 | A.de Cesaris | McLaren-Ford | 9 | Accident | 14 |
| DNQ | 4 | Michele Alboreto | Tyrrell-Ford | | | |
| DNQ | 31 | Beppe Gabbiani | Osella-Ford | | | |
| DNQ | 9 | Slim Borgudd | ATS-Ford | | | |
| DNQ | 35 | Brian Henton | Toleman-Hart | | | |
| DNQ | 36 | Derek Warwick | Toleman-Hart | | | |
| DNQ | 32 | Giorgio Francia | Osella-Ford | | | |

Winning speed: 92.681mph Lap leaders: Jones 1-13; Villeneuve 14-80
Pole position: Laffite, 1m 13.754s, 100.452mph
Fastest lap: Jones, 1m 17.818s, 95.206mph

## FRENCH GRAND PRIX: DIJON-PRENOIS *5 July Round: 8 Race: 350 80 x 2.361 miles*

| POS. | NO. | DRIVER | CAR/ENGINE | LAPS | TIME/RETIRED | GRID |
|---|---|---|---|---|---|---|
| 1 | 15 | Alain Prost | Renault | 80 | 1:35'48.13 | 3 |
| 2 | 7 | John Watson | McLaren-Ford | 80 | +2.29 | 2 |
| 3 | 5 | Nelson Piquet | Brabham-Ford | 80 | +24.22 | 4 |
| 4 | 16 | Rene Arnoux | Renault | 80 | +42.30 | 1 |
| 5 | 28 | Didier Pironi | Ferrari | 79 | +1 Lap | 14 |
| 6 | 11 | Elio de Angelis | Lotus-Ford | 79 | +1 Lap | 8 |
| 7 | 12 | Nigel Mansell | Lotus-Ford | 79 | +1 Lap | 13 |
| 8 | 22 | Mario Andretti | Alfa Romeo | 79 | +1 Lap | 10 |
| 9 | 6 | Hector Rebaque | Brabham-Ford | 78 | +2 Laps | 15 |
| 10 | 2 | Carlos Reutemann | Williams-Ford | 78 | +2 Laps | 7 |
| 11 | 8 | A.de Cesaris | McLaren-Ford | 78 | +2 Laps | 5 |
| 12 | 33 | Marc Surer | Theodore-Ford | 78 | +2 Laps | 21 |
| 13 | 3 | Eddie Cheever | Tyrrell-Ford | 77 | +3 Laps | 19 |
| 14 | 29 | Riccardo Patrese | Arrows-Ford | 77 | +3 Laps | 18 |
| 15 | 23 | Bruno Giacomelli | Alfa Romeo | 77 | +3 Laps | 12 |
| 16 | 4 | Michele Alboreto | Tyrrell-Ford | 77 | +3 Laps | 23 |
| 17 | 1 | Alan Jones | Williams-Ford | 76 | Collision | 9 |
| Ret | 26 | Jacques Laffite | Ligier-Matra | 57 | Suspension | 6 |
| Ret | 17 | Derek Daly | March-Ford | 55 | Engine | 20 |
| Ret | 27 | G.Villeneuve | Ferrari | 41 | Electrical | 11 |
| Ret | 25 | Patrick Tambay | Ligier-Matra | 30 | Wheel bearing | 16 |
| Ret | 20 | Keke Rosberg | Fittipaldi-Ford | 11 | Suspension | 17 |
| Ret | 14 | Eliseo Salazar | Ensign-Ford | 6 | Suspension | 22 |
| DNS | 21 | Chico Serra | Fittipaldi-Ford | 0 | Non starter | 24 |
| DNQ | 25 | Siegfried Stohr | Arrows-Ford | | | |
| DNQ | 35 | Brian Henton | Toleman-Hart | | | |
| DNQ | 9 | Slim Borgudd | ATS-Ford | | | |
| DNQ | 31 | Beppe Gabbiani | Osella-Ford | | | |
| DNQ | 36 | Derek Warwick | Toleman-Hart | | | |

Winning speed: 118.304mph Lap leaders: Piquet 1-58; Prost 59-80
Pole position: Arnoux, 1m 5.950s, 128.891mph Fastest lap: Prost, 1m 9.140s, 122.944mph
Stopped after 58 laps because of rain, then restarted for remaining distance; results were on aggregate.

## BRITISH GRAND PRIX: SILVERSTONE *18 July Round: 9 Race: 351 68 x 2.932 miles*

| POS. | NO. | DRIVER | CAR/ENGINE | LAPS | TIME/RETIRED | GRID |
|---|---|---|---|---|---|---|
| 1 | 7 | John Watson | McLaren-Ford | 68 | 1:26'54.80 | 5 |
| 2 | 2 | Carlos Reutemann | Williams-Ford | 68 | +40.65 | 9 |
| 3 | 26 | Jacques Laffite | Ligier-Matra | 67 | +1 Lap | 14 |
| 4 | 3 | Eddie Cheever | Tyrrell-Ford | 67 | +1 Lap | 23 |
| 5 | 6 | Hector Rebaque | Brabham-Ford | 67 | +1 Lap | 13 |
| 6 | 9 | Slim Borgudd | ATS-Ford | 67 | +1 Lap | 21 |
| 7 | 17 | Derek Daly | March-Ford | 66 | +2 Laps | 17 |
| 8 | 32 | J.P.Jarier | Osella-Ford | 65 | +3 Laps | 20 |
| 9 | 16 | Rene Arnoux | Renault | 64 | Distributor | 1 |
| 10 | 29 | Riccardo Patrese | Arrows-Ford | 64 | Engine | 10 |
| 11 | 33 | Marc Surer | Theodore-Ford | 61 | Out of fuel | 24 |
| Ret | 22 | Mario Andretti | Alfa Romeo | 59 | Throttle | 11 |
| Ret | 20 | Keke Rosberg | Fittipaldi-Ford | 56 | Suspension | 16 |
| DSQ | 11 | Elio de Angelis | Lotus-Ford | 25 | Disqualified | 22 |
| Ret | 15 | Alain Prost | Renault | 17 | Distributor | 2 |
| Ret | 25 | Patrick Tambay | Ligier-Matra | 15 | Clutch | 15 |
| Ret | 28 | Didier Pironi | Ferrari | 13 | Turbo | 4 |
| Ret | 5 | Nelson Piquet | Brabham-Ford | 11 | Tyre | 3 |
| Ret | 23 | Bruno Giacomelli | Alfa Romeo | 5 | Transmission | 12 |
| Ret | 27 | G.Villeneuve | Ferrari | 4 | Spun off | 8 |
| Ret | 1 | Alan Jones | Williams-Ford | 3 | Collision | 7 |
| Ret | 8 | A.de Cesaris | McLaren-Ford | 3 | Spun off | 6 |
| Ret | 4 | Michele Alboreto | Tyrrell-Ford | 1 | Clutch | 19 |
| Ret | 30 | Siegfried Stohr | Arrows-Ford | 0 | Spun of | 18 |
| DNQ | 21 | Chico Serra | Fittipaldi-Ford | | | |
| DNQ | 35 | Brian Henton | Toleman-Hart | | | |
| DNQ | 12 | Nigel Mansell | Lotus-Ford | | | |
| DNQ | 14 | Eliseo Salazar | Ensign-Ford | | | |
| DNQ | 36 | Derek Warwick | Toleman-Hart | | | |
| DNQ | 31 | Beppe Gabbiani | Osella-Ford | | | |

Winning speed: 137.638mph Lap leaders: Prost 1-16; Arnoux 17-60; Watson 61-68
Pole position: Arnoux, 1m 11.000s, 148.665mph
Fastest lap: Arnoux, 1m 15.067s, 140.610mph

## GERMAN GRAND PRIX: HOCKENHEIM *2 August Round: 10 Race: 352 45 x 4.218 miles*

| POS. | NO. | DRIVER | CAR/ENGINE | LAPS | TIME/RETIRED | GRID |
|---|---|---|---|---|---|---|
| 1 | 5 | Nelson Piquet | Brabham-Ford | 45 | 1:25'55.60 | 6 |
| 2 | 15 | Alain Prost | Renault | 45 | +11.52 | 1 |
| 3 | 26 | Jacques Laffite | Ligier-Matra | 45 | +1'04.60 | 7 |
| 4 | 6 | Hector Rebaque | Brabham-Ford | 45 | +1'39.69 | 16 |
| 5 | 3 | Eddie Cheever | Tyrrell-Ford | 45 | +1'50.52 | 18 |
| 6 | 7 | John Watson | McLaren-Ford | 44 | +1 Lap | 9 |
| 7 | 11 | Elio de Angelis | Lotus-Ford | 44 | +1 Lap | 14 |
| 8 | 32 | J.P.Jarier | Osella-Ford | 44 | +1 Lap | 17 |
| 9 | 22 | Mario Andretti | Alfa Romeo | 44 | +1 Lap | 12 |
| 10 | 27 | G.Villeneuve | Ferrari | 44 | +1 Lap | 8 |
| 11 | 1 | Alan Jones | Williams-Ford | 44 | +1 Lap | 4 |
| 12 | 30 | Siegfried Stohr | Arrows-Ford | 44 | +1 Lap | 24 |
| 13 | 16 | Rene Arnoux | Renault | 44 | +1 Lap | 2 |
| 14 | 33 | Marc Surer | Theodore-Ford | 43 | Suspension | 22 |
| 15 | 23 | Bruno Giacomelli | Alfa Romeo | 43 | +2 Laps | 19 |
| NC | 14 | Eliseo Salazar | Ensign-Ford | 39 | Not classified | 23 |
| Ret | 9 | Slim Borgudd | ATS-Ford | 35 | Engine | 20 |
| Ret | 2 | Carlos Reutemann | Williams-Ford | 27 | Engine | 3 |
| Ret | 29 | Riccardo Patrese | Arrows-Ford | 27 | Engine | 13 |
| Ret | 25 | Patrick Tambay | Ligier-Matra | 27 | Transmission | 11 |
| Ret | 17 | Derek Daly | March-Ford | 15 | Suspension | 21 |
| Ret | 12 | Nigel Mansell | Lotus-Ford | 13 | Fuel leak | 15 |
| Ret | 8 | A.de Cesaris | McLaren-Ford | 4 | Collision | 10 |
| Ret | 28 | Didier Pironi | Ferrari | 1 | Electrical | 5 |
| DNQ | 20 | Keke Rosberg | Fittipaldi-Ford | | | |
| DNQ | 35 | Brian Henton | Toleman-Hart | | | |
| DNQ | 31 | Beppe Gabbiani | Osella-Ford | | | |
| DNQ | 36 | Derek Warwick | Toleman-Hart | | | |
| DNQ | 4 | Michele Alboreto | Tyrrell-Ford | | | |
| DNQ | 21 | Chico Serra | Fittipaldi-Ford | | | |

Winning speed: 132.554mph Lap leaders: Prost 1-20; Jones 21-38; Piquet 39-45
Pole position: Prost, 1m 47.500s, 141.272mph
Fastest lap: Jones, 1m 52.420s, 135.088mph

## AUSTRIAN GRAND PRIX: OSTERREICHRING *16 August Round: 11 Race: 353 53 x 3.692 miles*

| POS. | NO. | DRIVER | CAR/ENGINE | LAPS | TIME/RETIRED | GRID |
|---|---|---|---|---|---|---|
| 1 | 26 | Jacques Laffite | Ligier-Matra | 53 | 1:27'36.47 | 4 |
| 2 | 16 | Rene Arnoux | Renault | 53 | +5.17 | 1 |
| 3 | 5 | Nelson Piquet | Brabham-Ford | 53 | +7.34 | 7 |
| 4 | 1 | Alan Jones | Williams-Ford | 53 | +12.04 | 6 |
| 5 | 2 | Carlos Reutemann | Williams-Ford | 53 | +31.85 | 5 |
| 6 | 7 | John Watson | McLaren-Ford | 53 | +1'31.14 | 12 |
| 7 | 11 | Elio de Angelis | Lotus-Ford | 52 | +1 Lap | 9 |
| 8 | 8 | A.de Cesaris | McLaren-Ford | 52 | +1 Lap | 18 |
| 9 | 28 | Didier Pironi | Ferrari | 52 | +1 Lap | 8 |
| 10 | 32 | J.P.Jarier | Osella-Ford | 51 | +2 Laps | 14 |
| 11 | 17 | Derek Daly | March-Ford | 47 | +6 Laps | 19 |
| Ret | 22 | Mario Andretti | Alfa Romeo | 46 | Engine | 13 |
| Ret | 9 | Slim Borgudd | ATS-Ford | 44 | Brakes | 21 |
| Ret | 29 | Riccardo Patrese | Arrows-Ford | 43 | Engine | 10 |
| Ret | 14 | Eliseo Salazar | Ensign-Ford | 43 | Oil pressure | 20 |
| Ret | 4 | Michele Alboreto | Tyrrell-Ford | 40 | Gearbox | 22 |
| Ret | 23 | Bruno Giacomelli | Alfa Romeo | 35 | Fire | 16 |
| Ret | 6 | Hector Rebaque | Brabham-Ford | 32 | Clutch | 15 |
| Ret | 30 | Siegfried Stohr | Arrows-Ford | 27 | Overheating | 24 |
| Ret | 15 | Alain Prost | Renault | 26 | Suspension | 2 |
| Ret | 25 | Patrick Tambay | Ligier-Matra | 26 | Engine | 17 |
| Ret | 12 | Nigel Mansell | Lotus-Ford | 23 | Engine | 11 |
| Ret | 27 | G.Villeneuve | Ferrari | 11 | Accident | 3 |
| Ret | 33 | Marc Surer | Theodore-Ford | 0 | Distributor | 23 |
| DNQ | 3 | Eddie Cheever | Tyrrell-Ford | | | |
| DNQ | 36 | Derek Warwick | Toleman-Hart | | | |
| DNQ | 35 | Brian Henton | Toleman-Hart | | | |
| DNQ | 31 | Beppe Gabbiani | Osella-Ford | | | |

Winning speed: 134.019mph
Lap leaders: Villeneuve 1; Prost 2-26; Arnoux 27-38; Laffite 39-53
Pole position: Arnoux, 1m 32.018s, 144.449mph
Fastest lap: Laffite, 1m 37.620s, 136.159mph

## DUTCH GRAND PRIX: ZANDVOORT *30 August Round: 12 Race: 354 72 x 2.642 miles*

| POS. | NO. | DRIVER | CAR/ENGINE | LAPS | TIME/RETIRED | GRID |
|---|---|---|---|---|---|---|
| 1 | 15 | Alain Prost | Renault | 72 | 1:40'22.43 | 1 |
| 2 | 5 | Nelson Piquet | Brabham-Ford | 72 | +8.24 | 3 |
| 3 | 1 | Alan Jones | Williams-Ford | 72 | +35.50 | 4 |
| 4 | 6 | Hector Rebaque | Brabham-Ford | 71 | +1 Lap | 15 |
| 5 | 11 | Elio de Angelis | Lotus-Ford | 71 | +1 Lap | 9 |
| 6 | 14 | Eliseo Salazar | Ensign-Ford | 70 | +2 Laps | 24 |
| 7 | 30 | Siegfried Stohr | Arrows-Ford | 69 | +3 Laps | 21 |
| 8 | 33 | Marc Surer | Theodore-Ford | 69 | +3 Laps | 20 |
| 9 | 4 | Michele Alboreto | Tyrrell-Ford | 68 | Engine | 25 |
| 10 | 9 | Slim Borgudd | ATS-Ford | 68 | +4 Laps | 23 |
| Ret | 22 | Mario Andretti | Alfa Romeo | 62 | Accident | 7 |
| Ret | 7 | John Watson | McLaren-Ford | 50 | Ignition | 8 |
| Ret | 3 | Eddie Cheever | Tyrrell-Ford | 46 | Suspension | 22 |
| Ret | 32 | J.P.Jarier | Osella-Ford | 29 | Transmission | 18 |
| Ret | 16 | Rene Arnoux | Renault | 21 | Engine | 2 |
| Ret | 23 | Bruno Giacomelli | Alfa Romeo | 19 | Tyre | 14 |
| Ret | 26 | Jacques Laffite | Ligier-Matra | 18 | Collision | 6 |
| Ret | 2 | Carlos Reutemann | Williams-Ford | 18 | Collision | 5 |
| Ret | 29 | Riccardo Patrese | Arrows-Ford | 16 | Suspension | 10 |
| Ret | 17 | Derek Daly | March-Ford | 5 | Suspension | 19 |
| Ret | 28 | Didier Pironi | Ferrari | 4 | Collision | 12 |
| Ret | 12 | Nigel Mansell | Lotus-Ford | 1 | Engine | 17 |
| Ret | 25 | Patrick Tambay | Ligier-Matra | 1 | Collision | 11 |
| Ret | 27 | G.Villeneuve | Ferrari | 0 | Collision | 16 |
| DNS | 8 | A.de Cesaris | McLaren-Ford | 0 | Non starter | |
| DNQ | 35 | Brian Henton | Toleman-Hart | | | |
| DNQ | 20 | Keke Rosberg | Fittipaldi-Ford | | | |
| DNQ | 21 | Chico Serra | Fittipaldi-Ford | | | |
| DNQ | 31 | Beppe Gabbiani | Osella-Ford | | | |
| DNQ | 36 | Derek Warwick | Toleman-Hart | | | |

Winning speed: 113.712mph Lap leaders: Prost 1-22, 24-72; Jones 23
Pole position: Prost, 1m 18.176s, 121.667mph
Fastest lap: Jones, 1m 21.830s, 116.234mph

## ITALIAN GRAND PRIX: MONZA *13 September Round: 13 Race: 355 52 x 3.604 miles*

| POS. | NO. | DRIVER | CAR/ENGINE | LAPS | TIME/RETIRED | GRID |
|---|---|---|---|---|---|---|
| 1 | 15 | Alain Prost | Renault | 52 | 1:26'33.897 | 3 |
| 2 | 1 | Alan Jones | Williams-Ford | 52 | +22.175 | 5 |
| 3 | 2 | Carlos Reutemann | Williams-Ford | 52 | +50.587 | 2 |
| 4 | 11 | Elio de Angelis | Lotus-Ford | 52 | +1'32.902 | 11 |
| 5 | 28 | Didier Pironi | Ferrari | 52 | +1'34.522 | 8 |
| 6 | 5 | Nelson Piquet | Brabham-Ford | 51 | Engine | 6 |
| 7 | 8 | A.de Cesaris | McLaren-Ford | 51 | Puncture | 16 |
| 8 | 23 | Bruno Giacomelli | Alfa Romeo | 50 | +2 Laps | 10 |
| 9 | 32 | J.P.Jarier | Osella-Ford | 50 | +2 Laps | 18 |
| 10 | 35 | Brian Henton | Toleman-Hart | 49 | +3 Laps | 23 |
| Ret | 22 | Mario Andretti | Alfa Romeo | 40 | Engine | 13 |
| Ret | 17 | Derek Daly | March-Ford | 36 | Gearbox | 19 |
| Ret | 25 | Patrick Tambay | Ligier-Matra | 22 | Puncture | 15 |
| Ret | 12 | Nigel Mansell | Lotus-Ford | 21 | Suspension | 12 |
| Ret | 7 | John Watson | McLaren-Ford | 19 | Accident | 7 |
| Ret | 29 | Riccardo Patrese | Arrows-Ford | 18 | Gearbox | 20 |
| Ret | 4 | Michele Alboreto | Tyrrell-Ford | 17 | Accident | 22 |
| Ret | 14 | Eliseo Salazar | Ensign-Ford | 13 | Spun off | 24 |
| Ret | 16 | Rene Arnoux | Renault | 12 | Spun off | 1 |
| Ret | 26 | Jacques Laffite | Ligier-Matra | 11 | Puncture | 4 |
| Ret | 3 | Eddie Cheever | Tyrrell-Ford | 11 | Spun off | 17 |
| Ret | 9 | Slim Borgudd | ATS-Ford | 10 | Spun off | 21 |
| Ret | 27 | G.Villeneuve | Ferrari | 5 | Engine | 9 |
| Ret | 6 | Hector Rebaque | Brabham-Ford | 1 | Electrical | 14 |
| DNQ | 33 | Marc Surer | Theodore-Ford | | | |
| DNQ | 31 | Beppe Gabbiani | Osella-Ford | | | |
| DNQ | 36 | Derek Warwick | Toleman-Hart | | | |
| DNQ | 30 | Siegfried Stohr | Arrows-Ford | | | |
| DNQ | 20 | Keke Rosberg | Fittipaldi-Ford | | | |
| DNQ | 21 | Chico Serra | Fittipaldi-Ford | | | |

Winning speed: 129.895mph Lap leaders: Prost 1-52
Pole position: Arnoux, 1m 33.467s, 138.811mph
Fastest lap: Reutemann, 1m 37.528s, 133.031mph

## CANADIAN GRAND PRIX: MONTREAL *27 September Round: 14 Race: 356 63 x 2.740 miles*

| POS. | NO. | DRIVER | CAR/ENGINE | LAPS | TIME/RETIRED | GRID |
|---|---|---|---|---|---|---|
| 1 | 26 | Jacques Laffite | Ligier-Matra | 63 | 2:01'25.20 | 10 |
| 2 | 7 | John Watson | McLaren-Ford | 63 | +6.23 | 9 |
| 3 | 27 | G.Villeneuve | Ferrari | 63 | +1'50.27 | 11 |
| 4 | 23 | Bruno Giacomelli | Alfa Romeo | 62 | +1 Lap | 15 |
| 5 | 5 | Nelson Piquet | Brabham-Ford | 62 | +1 Lap | 1 |
| 6 | 11 | Elio de Angelis | Lotus-Ford | 62 | +1 Lap | 7 |
| 7 | 22 | Mario Andretti | Alfa Romeo | 62 | +1 Lap | 16 |
| 8 | 17 | Derek Daly | March-Ford | 61 | +2 Laps | 20 |
| 9 | 33 | Marc Surer | Theodore-Ford | 61 | +2 Laps | 19 |
| 10 | 2 | Carlos Reutemann | Williams-Ford | 60 | +3 Laps | 2 |
| 11 | 4 | Michele Alboreto | Tyrrell-Ford | 59 | +4 Laps | 22 |
| 12 | 3 | Eddie Cheever | Tyrrell-Ford | 56 | Engine | 14 |
| Ret | 8 | A.de Cesaris | McLaren-Ford | 51 | Spun off | 13 |
| Ret | 15 | Alain Prost | Renault | 48 | Collision | 4 |
| Ret | 12 | Nigel Mansell | Lotus-Ford | 45 | Collision | 5 |
| Ret | 9 | Slim Borgudd | ATS-Ford | 40 | Spun off | 21 |
| Ret | 6 | Hector Rebaque | Brabham-Ford | 35 | Spun off | 6 |
| Ret | 32 | J.P.Jarier | Osella-Ford | 26 | Collision | 23 |
| Ret | 1 | Alan Jones | Williams-Ford | 24 | Handling | 3 |
| Ret | 28 | Didier Pironi | Ferrari | 24 | Ignition | 12 |
| Ret | 14 | Eliseo Salazar | Ensign-Ford | 8 | Spun off | 24 |
| Ret | 25 | Patrick Tambay | Ligier-Matra | 6 | Spun off | 17 |
| Ret | 29 | Riccardo Patrese | Arrows-Ford | 6 | Spun off | 18 |
| Ret | 16 | Rene Arnoux | Renault | 0 | Collision | 8 |
| DNQ | 20 | Keke Rosberg | Fittipaldi-Ford | | | |
| DNQ | 21 | Chico Serra | Fittipaldi-Ford | | | |
| DNQ | 35 | Brian Henton | Toleman-Hart | | | |
| DNQ | 30 | J.Villeneuve | Arrows-Ford | | | |
| DNQ | 36 | Derek Warwick | Toleman-Hart | | | |
| DNQ | 31 | Beppe Gabbiani | Osella-Ford | | | |

Winning speed: 85.308mph Lap leaders: Jones 1-6; Prost 7-12; Laffite 13-63
Pole position: Piquet, 1m 29.211s, 110.579mph
Fastest lap: Watson, 1m 49.475s, 90.111mph

## LAS VEGAS GRAND PRIX: CAESAR'S PALACE *17 October Round: 15 Race: 357 75 x 2.268 miles*

| POS. | NO. | DRIVER | CAR/ENGINE | LAPS | TIME/RETIRED | GRID |
|---|---|---|---|---|---|---|
| 1 | 1 | Alan Jones | Williams-Ford | 75 | 1:44'09.077 | 2 |
| 2 | 15 | Alain Prost | Renault | 75 | +20.048 | 5 |
| 3 | 23 | Bruno Giacomelli | Alfa Romeo | 75 | +20.428 | 8 |
| 4 | 12 | Nigel Mansell | Lotus-Ford | 75 | +47.473 | 9 |
| 5 | 5 | Nelson Piquet | Brabham-Ford | 75 | +1'16.438 | 4 |
| 6 | 26 | Jacques Laffite | Ligier-Matra | 75 | +1'18.175 | 12 |
| 7 | 7 | John Watson | McLaren-Ford | 75 | +1'18.497 | 6 |
| 8 | 2 | Carlos Reutemann | Williams-Ford | 74 | +1 Lap | 1 |
| 9 | 28 | Didier Pironi | Ferrari | 73 | +2 Laps | 18 |
| 10 | 20 | Keke Rosberg | Fittipaldi-Ford | 73 | +2 Laps | 20 |
| 11 | 29 | Riccardo Patrese | Arrows-Ford | 71 | +4 Laps | 11 |
| 12 | 8 | A.de Cesaris | McLaren-Ford | 69 | +6 Laps | 14 |
| 13 | 4 | Michele Alboreto | Tyrrell-Ford | 67 | Engine | 17 |
| NC | 14 | Eliseo Salazar | Ensign-Ford | 61 | Not classified | 24 |
| Ret | 36 | Derek Warwick | Toleman-Hart | 43 | Gearbox | 22 |
| Ret | 22 | Mario Andretti | Alfa Romeo | 29 | Suspension | 10 |
| DSQ | 27 | G.Villeneuve | Ferrari | 22 | Disqualified | 3 |
| Ret | 6 | Hector Rebaque | Brabham-Ford | 20 | Throttle | 16 |
| Ret | 33 | Marc Surer | Theodore-Ford | 19 | Suspension | 23 |
| Ret | 3 | Eddie Cheever | Tyrrell-Ford | 10 | Engine | 19 |
| Ret | 16 | Rene Arnoux | Renault | 10 | Electrical | 13 |
| Ret | 25 | Patrick Tambay | Ligier-Matra | 2 | Accident | 7 |
| Ret | 11 | Elio de Angelis | Lotus-Ford | 2 | Water leak | 15 |
| Ret | 32 | J.P.Jarier | Osella-Ford | 0 | Transmission | 21 |
| DNQ | 9 | Slim Borgudd | ATS-Ford | | | |
| DNQ | 21 | Chico Serra | Fittipaldi-Ford | | | |
| DNQ | 17 | Derek Daly | March-Ford | | | |
| DNQ | 30 | J.Villeneuve | Arrows-Ford | | | |
| DNQ | 35 | Brian Henton | Toleman-Hart | | | |
| DNQ | 31 | Beppe Gabbiani | Osella-Ford | | | |

Winning speed: 97.992mph Lap leaders: Jones 1-75
Pole position: Reutemann, 1m 17.821s, 104.918mph
Fastest lap: Pironi, 1m 20.156s, 101.861mph

# 1982

## DRIVERS' CHAMPION: KEKE ROSBERG
## CONSTRUCTORS' CHAMPION: FERRARI

### DRIVERS' CHAMPIONSHIP

| POS. | DRIVER | NATIONALITY | CAR | POINTS |
|---|---|---|---|---|
| 1 | Keke Rosberg | Finland | Williams-Ford | 44 |
| 2 | Didier Pironi | France | Ferrari | 39 |
| = | John Watson | GB | McLaren-Ford | 39 |
| 4 | Alain Prost | France | Renault | 34 |
| 5 | Niki Lauda | Austria | McLaren-Ford | 30 |
| 6 | Rene Arnoux | France | Renault | 28 |
| 7 | Patrick Tambay | France | Ferrari | 25 |
| = | Michele Alboreto | Italy | Tyrrell-Ford | 25 |
| 9 | Elio de Angelis | Italy | Lotus-Ford | 23 |
| 10 | Riccardo Patrese | Italy | Brabham-BMW | 21 |
| 11 | Nelson Piquet | Brazil | Brabham-BMW | 20 |
| 12 | Eddie Cheever | USA | Ligier-Matra | 15 |
| 13 | Derek Daly | Ireland | Theodore-Ford, Williams-Ford | 8 |
| 14 | Nigel Mansell | GB | Lotus-Ford | 7 |
| 15 | Carlos Reutemann | Argentina | Williams-Ford | 6 |
| = | Gilles Villeneuve | Canada | Ferrari | 6 |
| 17 | Andrea de Cesaris | Italy | Alfa Romeo | 5 |
| = | Jacques Lafitte | France | Ligier-Matra | 5 |
| 19 | Mario Andretti | USA | Williams-Ford, Ferrari | 4 |
| 20 | Jean-Pierre Jarier | France | Osella-Ford | 3 |
| = | Marc Surer | Switzerland | Arrows-Ford | 3 |
| 22 | Manfred Winkelhock | West Germany | ATS-Ford | 2 |
| = | Eliseo Salazar | Chile | ATS-Ford | 2 |
| = | Bruno Giacomelli | Italy | Alfa Romeo | 2 |
| = | Mauro Baldi | Italy | Arrows-Ford | 2 |
| 26 | Chico Serra | Brazil | Fittipaldi-Ford | 1 |
| | Jochen Mass | West Germany | March-Ford | |
| | Raul Boesel | Brazil | March-Ford | |
| | Slim Borgudd | Sweden | Tyrrell-Ford | |
| | Derek Warwick | GB | Toleman-Hart | |
| | Brian Henton | GB | Arrows-Ford, Tyrrell-Ford | |
| | Roberto Guerrero | Colombia | Ensign-Ford | |
| | Teo Fabi | Italy | Toleman-Hart | |
| | Riccardo Paletti | Italy | Osella-Ford | |
| | Geoff Lees | GB | Theodore-Ford, Lotus-Ford | |
| | Jan Lammers | Netherlands | Theodore-Ford | |
| | Emilio de Villota | Spain | March-Ford | |
| | Roberto Moreno | Brazil | Lotus-Ford | |
| | Tommy Byrne | Ireland | Theodore-Ford | |
| | Rupert Keegan | GB | March-Ford | |

Points for top six finishers (9, 6, 4, 3, 2, 1). Half points awarded for races stopped before half distance

### CONSTRUCTORS' CHAMPIONSHIP

| POS. | CONSTRUCTOR | POINTS |
|---|---|---|
| 1 | Ferrari | 74 |
| 2 | McLaren-Ford | 69 |
| 3 | Renault | 62 |
| 4 | Williams-Ford | 58 |
| 5 | Lotus-Ford | 30 |
| 6 | Tyrrell-Ford | 25 |
| 7 | Brabham-BMW | 22 |
| 8 | Ligier-Matra | 20 |
| 9 | Brabham-Ford | 19 |
| 10 | Alfa Romeo | 7 |
| 11 | Arrows-Ford | 5 |
| 12 | ATS-Ford | 4 |
| 13 | Osella-Ford | 3 |
| 14 | Fittipaldi-Ford | 1 |

Points for top six finishers (9, 6, 4, 3, 2, 1). Half points awarded for races stopped before half distance.

### SOUTH AFRICAN GRAND PRIX: KYALAMI *23 January Round: 1 Race: 358 77 x 2.550 miles*

| POS. | NO. | DRIVER | CAR/ENGINE | LAPS | TIME/RETIRED | GRID |
|---|---|---|---|---|---|---|
| 1 | 15 | Alain Prost | Renault | 77 | 1:32'08.401 | 5 |
| 2 | 5 | Carlos Reutemann | Williams-Ford | 77 | +14.946 | 8 |
| 3 | 16 | Rene Arnoux | Renault | 77 | +27.900 | 1 |
| 4 | 8 | Niki Lauda | McLaren-Ford | 77 | +32.113 | 13 |
| 5 | 6 | Keke Rosberg | Williams-Ford | 77 | +46.139 | 7 |
| 6 | 7 | John Watson | McLaren-Ford | 77 | +50.993 | 9 |
| 7 | 3 | Michele Alboreto | Tyrrell-Ford | 76 | +1 Lap | 10 |
| 8 | 11 | Elio de Angelis | Lotus-Ford | 76 | +1 Lap | 15 |
| 9 | 10 | Eliseo Salazar | ATS-Ford | 75 | +2 Laps | 12 |
| 10 | 9 | M.Winkelhock | ATS-Ford | 75 | +2 Laps | 20 |
| 11 | 23 | Bruno Giacomelli | Alfa Romeo | 74 | +3 Laps | 19 |
| 12 | 17 | Jochen Mass | March-Ford | 74 | +3 Laps | 22 |
| 13 | 22 | A.de Cesaris | Alfa Romeo | 73 | +4 Laps | 16 |
| 14 | 33 | Derek Daly | Theodore-Ford | 73 | +4 Laps | 24 |
| 15 | 18 | Raul Boesel | March-Ford | 72 | +5 Laps | 21 |
| 16 | 4 | Slim Borgudd | Tyrrell-Ford | 72 | +5 Laps | 23 |
| 17 | 20 | Chico Serra | Fittipaldi-Ford | 72 | +5 Laps | 25 |
| 18 | 28 | Didier Pironi | Ferrari | 71 | +6 Laps | 6 |
| Ret | 26 | Jacques Laffite | Ligier-Matra | 54 | Fuel system | 11 |
| Ret | 35 | Derek Warwick | Toleman-Hart | 43 | Accident | 14 |
| Ret | 2 | Riccardo Patrese | Brabham-BMW | 18 | Turbo | 4 |
| Ret | 25 | Eddie Cheever | Ligier-Matra | 11 | Fuel system | 17 |
| Ret | 27 | G.Villeneuve | Ferrari | 6 | Turbo | 3 |
| Ret | 1 | Nelson Piquet | Brabham-BMW | 3 | Spun off | 2 |
| Ret | 12 | Nigel Mansell | Lotus-Ford | 0 | Electrical | 18 |
| Ret | 31 | J.PJarier | Osella-Ford | 0 | Collision | 26 |
| DNQ | 30 | Mauro Baldi | Arrows-Ford | | | |
| DNQ | 32 | Riccardo Paletti | Osella-Ford | | | |
| DNQ | 29 | Brian Henton | Arrows-Ford | | | |
| DNQ | 14 | Roberto Guerrero | Ensign-Ford | | | |
| DNQ | 36 | Teo Fabi | Toleman-Hart | | | |

Winning speed: 127.865mph Lap leaders: Arnoux 1-13, 41-67; Prost 14-40, 68-77
Pole position: Arnoux, 1m 6.351s, 138.361mph
Fastest lap: Prost, 1m 8.278s, 134.456mph

### BRAZILIAN GRAND PRIX: RIO DE JANEIRO *21 March Round:2 Race: 359 63 x 3.126 miles*

| POS. | NO. | DRIVER | CAR/ENGINE | LAPS | TIME/RETIRED | GRID |
|---|---|---|---|---|---|---|
| 1 | 15 | Alain Prost | Renault | 63 | 1:44'33.134 | |
| 2 | 7 | John Watson | McLaren-Ford | 63 | +2.990 | |
| 3 | 12 | Nigel Mansell | Lotus-Ford | 63 | +36.859 | |
| 4 | 3 | Michele Alboreto | Tyrrell-Ford | 63 | +50.761 | |
| 5 | 9 | M.Winkelhock | ATS-Ford | 62 | +1 Lap | |
| 6 | 28 | Didier Pironi | Ferrari | 62 | +1 Lap | |
| 7 | 4 | Slim Borgudd | Tyrrell-Ford | 61 | +2 Laps | |
| 8 | 17 | Jochen Mass | March-Ford | 61 | +2 Laps | |
| 9 | 31 | J.PJarier | Osella-Ford | 60 | +3 Laps | |
| 10 | 30 | Mauro Baldi | Arrows-Ford | 57 | +6 Laps | |
| DSQ | 1 | Nelson Piquet | Brabham-Ford | 63 | Disqualified | |
| DSQ | 6 | Keke Rosberg | Williams-Ford | 63 | Disqualified | |
| Ret | 10 | Eliseo Salazar | ATS-Ford | 38 | Engine | |
| Ret | 20 | Chico Serra | Fittipaldi-Ford | 36 | Suspension | |
| Ret | 2 | Riccardo Patrese | Brabham-Ford | 34 | Physical | |
| Ret | 27 | G.Villeneuve | Ferrari | 29 | Spun off | |
| Ret | 8 | Niki Lauda | McLaren-Ford | 22 | Collision | |
| Ret | 16 | Rene Arnoux | Renault | 21 | Collision | |
| Ret | 5 | Carlos Reutemann | Williams-Ford | 21 | Collision | |
| Ret | 11 | Elio de Angelis | Lotus-Ford | 21 | Collision | |
| Ret | 25 | Eddie Cheever | Ligier-Matra | 19 | Water leak | |
| Ret | 23 | Bruno Giacomelli | Alfa Romeo | 16 | Clutch | |
| Ret | 26 | Jacques Laffite | Ligier-Matra | 15 | Chassis | |
| Ret | 22 | A.de Cesaris | Alfa Romeo | 14 | Chassis | |
| Ret | 33 | Derek Daly | Theodore-Ford | 12 | Spun off | |
| Ret | 18 | Raul Boesel | March-Ford | 11 | Spun off | |
| DNQ | 36 | Teo Fabi | Toleman-Hart | | | |
| DNQ | 29 | Brian Henton | Arrows-Ford | | | |
| DNQ | 35 | Derek Warwick | Toleman-Hart | | | |
| DNQ | 14 | Roberto Guerrero | Ensign-Ford | | | |
| DNPQ | 32 | Riccardo Paletti | Osella-Ford | | | |

Winning speed: 113.022mph Lap leaders: Villeneuve 1-29; Piquet 30-63
Pole position: Prost, 1m 28.808s, 126.723mph
Fastest lap Speed: Prost, 1m 37.016s, 116.002mph
Piquet and Rosberg finished first and second but were disqualified because their cars were underweight

### USA WEST GRAND PRIX: LONG BEACH *4 April Round: 3 Race: 360 75.5 x 2.130 miles*

| POS. | NO. | DRIVER | CAR/ENGINE | LAPS | TIME/RETIRED | GRID |
|---|---|---|---|---|---|---|
| 1 | 8 | Niki Lauda | McLaren-Ford | 75 | 1:58'25.318 | 2 |
| 2 | 6 | Keke Rosberg | Williams-Ford | 75 | +14.660 | 8 |
| 3 | 2 | Riccardo Patrese | Brabham-Ford | 75 | +1'19.143 | 18 |
| 4 | 3 | Michele Alboreto | Tyrrell-Ford | 75 | +1'20.947 | 12 |
| 5 | 11 | Elio de Angelis | Lotus-Ford | 74 | +1 Lap | 16 |
| 6 | 7 | John Watson | McLaren-Ford | 74 | +1 Lap | 11 |
| 7 | 12 | Nigel Mansell | Lotus-Ford | 73 | +2 Laps | 17 |
| 8 | 17 | Jochen Mass | March-Ford | 73 | +2 Laps | 21 |
| 9 | 18 | Raul Boesel | March-Ford | 70 | +5 Laps | 23 |
| 10 | 4 | Slim Borgudd | Tyrrell-Ford | 68 | +7 Laps | 24 |
| DSQ | 27 | G.Villeneuve | Ferrari | 75 | Disqualified | 7 |
| Ret | 25 | Eddie Cheever | Ligier-Matra | 59 | Gearbox | 13 |
| Ret | 22 | A.de Cesaris | Alfa Romeo | 33 | Spun off | 1 |
| Ret | 29 | Brian Henton | Arrows-Ford | 32 | Spun off | 20 |
| Ret | 14 | Roberto Guerrero | Ensign-Ford | 27 | Spun off | 19 |
| Ret | 26 | Jacques Laffite | Ligier-Matra | 26 | Spun off | 15 |
| Ret | 31 | J.PJarier | Osella-Ford | 26 | Transmission | 10 |
| Ret | 1 | Nelson Piquet | Brabham-Ford | 25 | Spun off | 6 |
| Ret | 33 | Derek Daly | Theodore-Ford | 23 | Spun off | 22 |
| Ret | 5 | Mario Andretti | Williams-Ford | 19 | Collision | 14 |
| Ret | 15 | Alain Prost | Renault | 10 | Spun off | 4 |
| Ret | 28 | Didier Pironi | Ferrari | 6 | Spun off | 9 |
| Ret | 16 | Rene Arnoux | Renault | 5 | Collision | 3 |
| Ret | 23 | Bruno Giacomelli | Alfa Romeo | 5 | Collision | 5 |
| Ret | 10 | Eliseo Salazar | ATS-Ford | 3 | Collision | 26 |
| Ret | 9 | M.Winkelhock | ATS-Ford | 1 | Collision | 25 |
| DNQ | 36 | Teo Fabi | Toleman-Hart | | | |
| DNQ | 32 | Riccardo Paletti | Osella-Ford | | | |
| DNQ | 20 | Chico Serra | Fittipaldi-Ford | | | |
| DNQ | 30 | Mauro Baldi | Arrows-Ford | | | |
| DNPQ | 35 | Derek Warwick | Toleman-Hart | | | |

Winning speed: 81.479mph Lap leaders: de Cesaris 1-14; Lauda 15-75
Pole position: de Cesaris, 1m 27.316s, 87.819mph
Fastest lap: Lauda, 1m 30.831s, 84.421mph
Villeneuve finished third but was disqualified for using an illegal front wing

### SAN MARINO GRAND PRIX: IMOLA *25 April Round:4 Race: 361 60 x 3.312 miles*

| POS. | NO. | DRIVER | CAR/ENGINE | LAPS | TIME/RETIRED | GRID |
|---|---|---|---|---|---|---|
| 1 | 28 | Didier Pironi | Ferrari | 60 | 1:36'38.887 | 4 |
| 2 | 27 | G.Villeneuve | Ferrari | 60 | +0.366 | 3 |
| 3 | 3 | Michele Alboreto | Tyrrell-Ford | 60 | +1'07.684 | 5 |
| 4 | 31 | J.PJarier | Osella-Ford | 59 | +1 Lap | 9 |
| 5 | 10 | Eliseo Salazar | ATS-Ford | 57 | Laps | 14 |
| DSQ | 9 | M.Winkelhock | ATS-Ford | 54 | Disqualified | 12 |
| NC | 36 | Teo Fabi | Toleman-Hart | 52 | Not classified | 10 |
| Ret | 16 | Rene Arnoux | Renault | 44 | Turbo | 1 |
| Ret | 23 | Bruno Giacomelli | Alfa Romeo | 24 | Engine | 6 |
| Ret | 32 | Riccardo Paletti | Osella-Ford | 7 | Suspension | 13 |
| Ret | 15 | Alain Prost | Renault | 6 | Engine | 2 |
| Ret | 22 | A.de Cesaris | Alfa Romeo | 4 | Electrical | 7 |
| Ret | 4 | Brian Henton | Tyrrell-Ford | 0 | Transmission | 11 |
| Ret | 35 | Derek Warwick | Toleman-Hart | 0 | Electrical | 8 |

Winning speed: 116.652mph
Lap leaders: Arnoux 1-26, 31-43; Villeneuve 27-30, 44-45,49-52,59; Pironi 46-48, 53-58,60
Pole position: Arnoux, 1m 29.765s, 125.596mph
Fastest lap: Pironi, 1m 35.036s, 118.630mph
The race was boycotted by FOCA teams following the disqualifications in Rio.
Winkelhock disqualified from sixth with an underweight car.

### BELGIAN GRAND PRIX: ZOLDER *9 May Round: 5 Race: 362 70 x 2.648 miles*

| POS. | NO. | DRIVER | CAR/ENGINE | LAPS | TIME/RETIRED | GRID |
|---|---|---|---|---|---|---|
| 1 | 7 | John Watson | McLaren-Ford | 70 | 1:35'41.995 | 10 |
| 2 | 6 | Keke Rosberg | Williams-Ford | 70 | +7.268 | 3 |
| 3 | 25 | Eddie Cheever | Ligier-Matra | 69 | +1 Lap | 14 |
| 4 | 11 | Elio de Angelis | Lotus-Ford | 68 | +2 Laps | 11 |
| 5 | 1 | Nelson Piquet | Brabham-BMW | 67 | +3 Laps | 8 |
| 6 | 20 | Chico Serra | Fittipaldi-Ford | 67 | +3 Laps | 23 |
| 7 | 29 | Marc Surer | Arrows-Ford | 66 | +4 Laps | 22 |
| 8 | 18 | Raul Boesel | March-Ford | 66 | +4 Laps | 24 |
| 9 | 26 | Jacques Laffite | Ligier-Matra | 66 | +4 Laps | 17 |
| DSQ | 8 | Niki Lauda | McLaren-Ford | 70 | Disqualified | 4 |
| Ret | 5 | Derek Daly | Williams-Ford | 60 | Spun off | 13 |
| Ret | 17 | Jochen Mass | March-Ford | 60 | Engine | 25 |
| Ret | 15 | Alain Prost | Renault | 59 | Spun off | 1 |
| Ret | 2 | Riccardo Patrese | Brabham-BMW | 52 | Spun off | 9 |
| Ret | 30 | Mauro Baldi | Arrows-Ford | 51 | Throttle | 26 |
| Ret | 31 | J.PJarier | Osella-Ford | 37 | Broken wing | 16 |
| Ret | 22 | A.de Cesaris | Alfa Romeo | 34 | Gearbox | 6 |
| Ret | 4 | Brian Henton | Tyrrell-Ford | 33 | Engine | 20 |
| Ret | 3 | Michele Alboreto | Tyrrell-Ford | 29 | Engine | 5 |
| Ret | 35 | Derek Warwick | Toleman-Hart | 29 | Transmission | 19 |
| Ret | 36 | Teo Fabi | Toleman-Hart | 13 | Brakes | 21 |
| Ret | 12 | Nigel Mansell | Lotus-Ford | 9 | Clutch | 7 |
| Ret | 16 | Rene Arnoux | Renault | 7 | Turbo | 2 |
| Ret | 9 | M.Winkelhock | ATS-Ford | 0 | Clutch | 12 |
| Ret | 23 | Bruno Giacomelli | Alfa Romeo | 0 | Collision | 15 |
| Ret | 10 | Eliseo Salazar | ATS-Ford | 0 | Collision | 18 |
| Wth | 28 | Didier Pironi | Ferrari | | | |
| DNS | 27 | Gilles Villeneuve | Ferrari | | Fatal accident | |
| DNQ | 14 | Roberto Guerrero | Ensign-Ford | | | |
| DNQ | 33 | Jan Lammers | Theodore-Ford | | | |
| DNPQ | 32 | Riccardo Paletti | Osella-Ford | | | |
| DNPQ | 19 | E.de Villota | March-Ford | | | |

Winning speed: 116.226mph Lap leaders: Arnoux 1-4; Rosberg 5-68; Watson 69-70
Pole position: Prost, 1m 15.701s, 125.941mph
Fastest lap: Watson, 1m 20.214, 118.855mph
Lauda disqualified from third for running an underweight car.

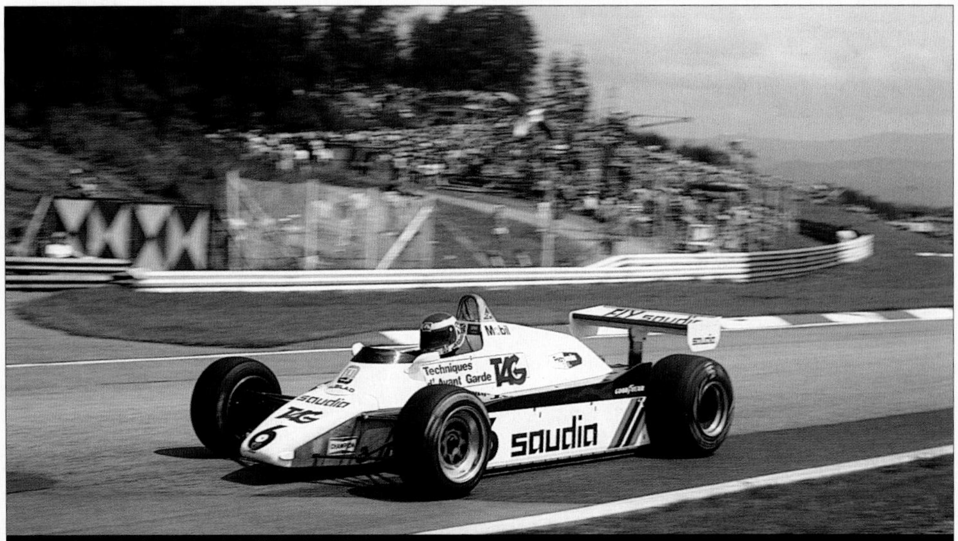

1982 world champion, Keke Rosberg in the Williams Ford FW08.

## MONACO GRAND PRIX: MONTE CARLO *23 May Round: 6 Race: 363 76 x 2.058 miles*

| POS. | NO. | DRIVER | CAR/ENGINE | LAPS | TIME/RETIRED | GRID |
|---|---|---|---|---|---|---|
| 1 | 2 | Riccardo Patrese | Brabham-Ford | 76 | 1:54'11.259 | 2 |
| 2 | 28 | Didier Pironi | Ferrari | 75 | Out of fuel | 5 |
| 3 | 22 | A.de Cesaris | Alfa Romeo | 75 | Out of fuel | 7 |
| 4 | 12 | Nigel Mansell | Lotus-Ford | 75 | +1 Lap | 11 |
| 5 | 11 | Elio de Angelis | Lotus-Ford | 75 | +Lap | 15 |
| 6 | 5 | Derek Daly | Williams-Ford | 74 | Accident | 8 |
| 7 | 15 | Alain Prost | Renault | 73 | Spun off | 4 |
| 8 | 4 | Brian Henton | Tyrrell-Ford | 72 | +4 Laps | 17 |
| 9 | 29 | Marc Surer | Arrows-Ford | 70 | +6 Laps | 19 |
| 10 | 3 | Michele Alboreto | Tyrrell-Ford | 69 | Suspension | 9 |
| Ret | 6 | Keke Rosberg | Williams-Ford | 64 | Collision | 6 |
| Ret | 8 | Niki Lauda | McLaren-Ford | 56 | Engine | 12 |
| Ret | 1 | Nelson Piquet | Brabham-BMW | 49 | Turbo | 13 |
| Ret | 7 | John Watson | McLaren-Ford | 35 | Electrical | 10 |
| Ret | 9 | M.Winkelhock | ATS-Ford | 31 | Differential | 14 |
| Ret | 26 | Jacques Laffite | Ligier-Matra | 29 | Handling | 18 |
| Ret | 25 | Eddie Cheever | Ligier-Matra | 27 | Oil leak | 16 |
| Ret | 10 | Eliseo Salazar | ATS-Ford | 22 | Mechanical | 20 |
| Ret | 16 | Rene Arnoux | Renault | 14 | Spun off | 1 |
| Ret | 23 | Bruno Giacomelli | Alfa Romeo | 4 | Halfshaft | 3 |
| DNQ | 30 | Mauro Baldi | Arrows-Ford | | | |
| DNQ | 33 | Jan Lammers | Theodore-Ford | | | |
| DNQ | 17 | Jochen Mass | March-Ford | | | |
| DNQ | 35 | Derek Warwick | Toleman-Hart | | | |
| DNQ | 31 | J.P.Jarier | Osella-Ford | | | |
| DNQ | 14 | Roberto Guerrero | Ensign-Ford | | | |
| DNPQ | 36 | Teo Fabi | Toleman-Hart | | | |
| DNPQ | 32 | Riccardo Paletti | Osella-Ford | | | |
| DNPQ | 18 | Raul Boesel | March-Ford | | | |
| DNPQ | 20 | Chico Serra | Fittipaldi-Ford | | | |
| DNPQ | 19 | E.de Villota | March-Ford | | | |

Winning speed: 82.184mph Lap leaders: Arnoux 1-14; Prost 15-73; Patrese 74, 76; Pironi 75
Pole position: Arnoux, 1m 23.281s, 88.961mph Fastest lap: Patrese, 1m 26.354s, 85.795mph

## USA EAST GRAND PRIX: DETROIT *6 June Round: 7 Race: 364 62x2.590 miles*

| POS. | NO. | DRIVER | CAR/ENGINE | LAPS | TIME/RETIRED | GRID |
|---|---|---|---|---|---|---|
| 1 | 7 | John Watson | McLaren-Ford | 62 | 1:58'41.043 | 17 |
| 2 | 25 | Eddie Cheever | Ligier-Matra | 62 | +15.726 | 9 |
| 3 | 28 | Didier Pironi | Ferrari | 62 | +28.077 | 4 |
| 4 | 6 | Keke Rosberg | Williams-Ford | 62 | +1'11.976 | 3 |
| 5 | 5 | Derek Daly | Williams-Ford | 62 | +1'23.757 | 12 |
| 6 | 26 | Jacques Laffite | Ligier-Matra | 61 | +1 Lap | 13 |
| 7 | 17 | Jochen Mass | March-Ford | 61 | +1 Lap | 18 |
| 8 | 29 | Marc Surer | Arrows-Ford | 61 | +1 Lap | 19 |
| 9 | 4 | Brian Henton | Tyrrell-Ford | 60 | +2 Laps | 20 |
| 10 | 16 | Rene Arnoux | Renault | 59 | +3 Laps | 15 |
| 11 | 20 | Chico Serra | Fittipaldi-Ford | 59 | +3 Laps | 26 |
| NC | 15 | Alain Prost | Renault | 54 | Not classified | 1 |
| Ret | 12 | Nigel Mansell | Lotus-Ford | 44 | Engine | 7 |
| Ret | 8 | Niki Lauda | McLaren-Ford | 40 | Collision | 10 |
| Ret | 3 | Michele Alboreto | Tyrrell-Ford | 40 | Spun off | 16 |
| Ret | 23 | Bruno Giacomelli | Alfa Romeo | 30 | Collision | 6 |
| Ret | 11 | Elio de Angelis | Lotus-Ford | 17 | Gearbox | 8 |
| Ret | 10 | Eliseo Salazar | ATS-Ford | 13 | Spun off | 25 |
| Ret | 14 | Roberto Guerrero | Ensign-Ford | 6 | Collision | 11 |
| Ret | 2 | Riccardo Patrese | Brabham-Ford | 6 | Collision | 14 |
| Ret | 22 | A.de Cesaris | Alfa Romeo | 2 | Transmission | 2 |
| Ret | 31 | J.P.Jarier | Osella-Ford | 2 | Ignition | 22 |
| Ret | 9 | M.Winkelhock | ATS-Ford | 1 | Spun off | 5 |
| Ret | 18 | Raul Boesel | March-Ford | 0 | Collision | 21 |
| Ret | 30 | Mauro Baldi | Arrows-Ford | 0 | Collision | 24 |
| Ret | 32 | Riccardo Paletti | Osella-Ford | 0 | Non starter | 23 |
| DNQ | 19 | E.de Villota | March-Ford | | | |
| DNQ | 1 | Nelson Piquet | Brabham-BMW | | | |
| DNQ | 33 | Jan Lammers | Theodore-Ford | | | |

Winning speed: 78.140mph
Lap leaders: Prost 1-22; Rosberg 23-36; Watson 37-62
Pole position: Prost, 1m 50.537s, 82.690mph Fastest lap: Prost, 1m 50.438s, 81.270mph
Race stopped after 6 laps because of an accident and restarted for 64 laps which were not completed as the race reached the two-hour mark.

## CANADIAN GRAND PRIX: MONTREAL *13 June Round: 8 Race: 365 70x2.740 miles*

| POS. | NO. | DRIVER | CAR/ENGINE | LAPS | TIME/RETIRED | GRID |
|---|---|---|---|---|---|---|
| 1 | 1 | Nelson Piquet | Brabham-BMW | 70 | 1:46'39.577 | 4 |
| 2 | 2 | Riccardo Patrese | Brabham-Ford | 70 | +13.799 | 8 |
| 3 | 7 | John Watson | McLaren-Ford | 70 | +1'01.836 | 6 |
| 4 | 11 | Elio de Angelis | Lotus-Ford | 69 | +1 Lap | 10 |
| 5 | 29 | Marc Surer | Arrows-Ford | 69 | +1 Lap | 16 |
| 6 | 22 | A.de Cesaris | Alfa Romeo | 68 | Out of fuel | 9 |
| 7 | 5 | Derek Daly | Williams-Ford | 68 | Out of fuel | 13 |
| 8 | 30 | Mauro Baldi | Arrows-Ford | 68 | +2 Laps | 17 |
| 9 | 28 | Didier Pironi | Ferrari | 67 | +3 Laps | 1 |
| 10 | 25 | Eddie Cheever | Ligier-Matra | 66 | Out of fuel | 12 |
| 11 | 17 | Jochen Mass | March-Ford | 66 | +4 Laps | 22 |
| NC | 4 | Brian Henton | Tyrrell-Ford | 59 | Not classified | 26 |
| Ret | 6 | Keke Rosberg | Williams-Ford | 52 | Gearbox | 7 |
| Ret | 18 | Raul Boesel | March-Ford | 47 | Engine | 21 |
| Ret | 3 | Michele Alboreto | Tyrrell-Ford | 41 | Engine | 15 |
| Ret | 15 | Alain Prost | Renault | 30 | Engine | 3 |
| Ret | 16 | Rene Arnoux | Renault | 28 | Spun off | 2 |
| Ret | 10 | Eliseo Salazar | ATS-Ford | 20 | Engine | 24 |
| Ret | 8 | Niki Lauda | McLaren-Ford | 17 | Clutch | 11 |
| Ret | 26 | Jacques Laffite | Ligier-Matra | 8 | Fuel system | 19 |
| Ret | 14 | Roberto Guerrero | Ensign-Ford | 2 | Clutch | 20 |
| Ret | 23 | Bruno Giacomelli | Alfa Romeo | 1 | Collision | 5 |
| Ret | 12 | Nigel Mansell | Lotus-Ford | 1 | Collision | 14 |
| Wth | 31 | J.P.Jarier | Osella-Ford | 0 | Withdrew | 18 |
| Ret | 32 | Riccardo Paletti | Osella-Ford | 0 | Fatal accident | 23 |
| Ret | 33 | Geoff Lees | Theodore-Ford | 0 | Collision | 25 |
| DNQ | 9 | M.Winkelhock | ATS-Ford | | | |
| DNQ | 19 | E.de Villota | March-Ford | | | |
| DNQ | 20 | Chico Serra | Fittipaldi-Ford | | | |

Winning speed: 107.904mph Lap leaders: Pironi 1; Arnoux 2-8; Piquet 9-70
Pole position: Pironi, 1m 27.509s, 112.730mph Fastest lap: Pironi, 1m 28.323s, 111.691mph
Race stopped after Paletti's accident and restarted for original distance.

## DUTCH GRAND PRIX: ZANDVOORT *3 July Round: 9 Race: 366 72 x 2.642 miles*

| POS. | NO. | DRIVER | CAR/ENGINE | LAPS | TIME/RETIRED | GRID |
|---|---|---|---|---|---|---|
| 1 | 28 | Didier Pironi | Ferrari | 72 | 1:38'03.254 | 4 |
| 2 | 1 | Nelson Piquet | Brabham-BMW | 72 | +21.649 | 3 |
| 3 | 6 | Keke Rosberg | Williams-Ford | 72 | +22.365 | 7 |
| 4 | 8 | Niki Lauda | McLaren-Ford | 72 | +1'23.720 | 5 |
| 5 | 5 | Derek Daly | Williams-Ford | 71 | +1 Lap | 12 |
| 6 | 30 | Mauro Baldi | Arrows-Ford | 71 | +1 Lap | 16 |
| 7 | 3 | Michele Alboreto | Tyrrell-Ford | 71 | +1 Lap | 14 |
| 8 | 27 | Patrick Tambay | Ferrari | 71 | +1 Lap | 6 |
| 9 | 7 | John Watson | McLaren-Ford | 71 | +1 Lap | 11 |
| 10 | 29 | Marc Surer | Arrows-Ford | 71 | +1 Lap | 17 |
| 11 | 23 | Bruno Giacomelli | Alfa Romeo | 70 | +2 Laps | 8 |
| 12 | 9 | M.Winkelhock | ATS-Ford | 70 | +2 Laps | 18 |
| 13 | 10 | Eliseo Salazar | ATS-Ford | 70 | +2 Laps | 25 |
| 14 | 31 | J.P.Jarier | Osella-Ford | 69 | +3 Laps | 23 |
| 15 | 2 | Riccardo Patrese | Brabham-BMW | 69 | +3 Laps | 10 |
| Ret | 17 | Jochen Mass | March-Ford | 60 | Engine | 24 |
| Ret | 33 | Jan Lammers | Theodore-Ford | 41 | Engine | 26 |
| Ret | 11 | Elio de Angelis | Lotus-Ford | 40 | Handling | 15 |
| Ret | 22 | A.de Cesaris | Alfa Romeo | 35 | Electrical | 9 |
| Ret | 15 | Alain Prost | Renault | 33 | Engine | 2 |
| Ret | 16 | Rene Arnoux | Renault | 21 | Spun off | 1 |
| Ret | 4 | Brian Henton | Tyrrell-Ford | 21 | Throttle | 20 |
| Ret | 18 | Raul Boesel | March-Ford | 21 | Engine | 22 |
| Ret | 20 | Chico Serra | Fittipaldi-Ford | 18 | Fuel system | 19 |
| Ret | 35 | Derek Warwick | Toleman-Hart | 15 | Oil leak | 13 |
| Ret | 26 | Jacques Laffite | Ligier-Matra | 4 | Handling | 21 |
| DNQ | 14 | Roberto Guerrero | Ensign-Ford | | | |
| DNQ | 36 | Teo Fabi | Toleman-Hart | | | |
| DNQ | 25 | Eddie Cheever | Ligier-Matra | | | |
| DNQ | 12 | Roberto Moreno | Lotus-Ford | | | |
| DNPQ | 19 | E.de Villota | March-Ford | | | |

Wining Speed: 116.402mph Lap leaders: Prost 1-4; Pironi 5-72
Pole position: Arnoux, 1m 14.233s, 128.130mph
Fastest lap: Warwick, 1m 19.780s, 119.221mph

## BRITISH GRAND PRIX: BRANDS HATCH *18 July Round: 10 Race: 367 76 x 2.414 miles*

| POS. | NO. | DRIVER | CAR/ENGINE | LAPS | TIME/RETIRED | GRID |
|---|---|---|---|---|---|---|
| 1 | 8 | Niki Lauda | McLaren-Ford | 76 | 1:35'33.812 | 5 |
| 2 | 28 | Didier Pironi | Ferrari | 76 | +25.726 | 4 |
| 3 | 27 | Patrick Tambay | Ferrari | 76 | +38.436 | 13 |
| 4 | 11 | Elio de Angelis | Lotus-Ford | 76 | +41.242 | 7 |
| 5 | 5 | Derek Daly | Williams-Ford | 76 | +41.430 | 10 |
| 6 | 15 | Alain Prost | Renault | 76 | +41.636 | 8 |
| 7 | 23 | Bruno Giacomelli | Alfa Romeo | 75 | +1 Lap | 14 |
| 8 | 4 | Brian Henton | Tyrrell-Ford | 75 | +1 Lap | 17 |
| 9 | 30 | Mauro Baldi | Arrows-Ford | 74 | +2 Laps | 26 |
| 10 | 17 | Jochen Mass | March-Ford | 73 | +3 Laps | 25 |
| Ret | 22 | A.de Cesaris | Alfa Romeo | 66 | Electrical | 11 |
| Ret | 25 | Eddie Cheever | Ligier-Matra | 60 | Engine | 24 |
| Ret | 29 | Marc Surer | Arrows-Ford | 59 | Engine | 22 |
| Ret | 6 | Keke Rosberg | Williams-Ford | 50 | Fuel system | 1 |
| Ret | 3 | Michele Alboreto | Tyrrell-Ford | 44 | Engine | 9 |
| Ret | 26 | Jacques Laffite | Ligier-Matra | 41 | Gearbox | 20 |
| Ret | 35 | Derek Warwick | Toleman-Hart | 40 | Halfshaft | 16 |
| Ret | 12 | Nigel Mansell | Lotus-Ford | 29 | Driver unwell | 23 |
| Ret | 1 | Nelson Piquet | Brabham-BMW | 9 | Fuel system | 3 |
| Ret | 14 | Roberto Guerrero | Ensign-Ford | 3 | Engine | 19 |
| Ret | 31 | J.P.Jarier | Osella-Ford | 2 | Collision | 18 |
| Ret | 20 | Chico Serra | Fittipaldi-Ford | 2 | Collision | 21 |
| Ret | 7 | John Watson | McLaren-Ford | 2 | Spun off | 12 |
| Ret | 2 | Riccardo Patrese | Brabham-BMW | 0 | Collision | 2 |
| Ret | 16 | Rene Arnoux | Renault | 0 | Collision | 6 |
| Ret | 36 | Teo Fabi | Toleman-Hart | 0 | Collision | 15 |
| DNQ | 9 | M.Winkelhock | ATS-Ford | | | |
| DNQ | 33 | Jan Lammers | Theodore-Ford | | | |
| DNQ | 10 | Eliseo Salazar | ATS-Ford | | | |
| DNQ | 18 | Raul Boesel | March-Ford | | | |

Winning speed: 124.732mph Lap leaders: Piquet 1-9; Lauda 10-76
Pole position: Rosberg, 1m 9.540s, 135.324mph
Fastest lap: Henton, 1m 13.028s, 128.860mph

## FRENCH GRAND PRIX: PAUL RICARD *25 July Round: 11 Race: 368 54 x 3.610 miles*

| POS. | NO. | DRIVER | CAR/ENGINE | LAPS | TIME/RETIRED | GRID |
|---|---|---|---|---|---|---|
| 1 | 16 | Rene Arnoux | Renault | 54 | 1:33'33.217 | 1 |
| 2 | 15 | Alain Prost | Renault | 54 | +17.308 | 2 |
| 3 | 28 | Didier Pironi | Ferrari | 54 | +42.128 | 3 |
| 4 | 27 | Patrick Tambay | Ferrari | 54 | +1'16.241 | 5 |
| 5 | 6 | Keke Rosberg | Williams-Ford | 54 | +1'30.994 | 10 |
| 6 | 3 | Michele Alboreto | Tyrrell-Ford | 54 | +1'32.339 | 15 |
| 7 | 5 | Derek Daly | Williams-Ford | 53 | +1 Lap | 11 |
| 8 | 8 | Niki Lauda | McLaren-Ford | 53 | +1 Lap | 9 |
| 9 | 23 | Bruno Giacomelli | Alfa Romeo | 53 | +1 Lap | 8 |
| 10 | 4 | Brian Henton | Tyrrell-Ford | 53 | +1 Lap | 23 |
| 11 | 9 | M.Winkelhock | ATS-Ford | 52 | +2 Laps | 18 |
| 12 | 12 | Geoff Lees | Lotus-Ford | 52 | +2 Laps | 24 |
| 13 | 29 | Marc Surer | Arrows-Ford | 52 | +2 Laps | 20 |
| 14 | 26 | Jacques Laffite | Ligier-Matra | 51 | +3 Laps | 16 |
| 15 | 35 | Derek Warwick | Toleman-Hart | 50 | +4 Laps | 14 |
| 16 | 25 | Eddie Cheever | Ligier-Matra | 49 | +5 Laps | 19 |
| Ret | 22 | A.de Cesaris | Alfa Romeo | 25 | Spun off | 7 |
| Ret | 1 | Nelson Piquet | Brabham-BMW | 23 | Engine | 6 |
| Ret | 11 | Elio de Angelis | Lotus-Ford | 17 | Fuel system | 13 |
| Ret | 7 | John Watson | McLaren-Ford | 13 | Electrical | 12 |
| Ret | 17 | Jochen Mass | March-Ford | 10 | Spun off | 26 |
| Ret | 30 | Mauro Baldi | Arrows-Ford | 10 | Collision | 25 |
| Ret | 2 | Riccardo Patrese | Brabham-BMW | 8 | Engine | 4 |
| Ret | 10 | Eliseo Salazar | ATS-Ford | 2 | Spun off | 22 |
| Ret | 31 | J.P.Jarier | Osella-Ford | 0 | Halfshaft | 17 |
| Ret | 36 | Teo Fabi | Toleman-Hart | 0 | Electrical | 21 |
| DNQ | 33 | Jan Lammers | Theodore-Ford | | | |
| DNQ | 14 | Roberto Guerrero | Ensign-Ford | | | |
| DNQ | 18 | Raul Boesel | March-Ford | | | |

Winning speed: 125.029mph Lap leaders: Arnoux 1-2, 24-54; Patrese 3-7; Piquet 8-23
Pole position: Arnoux, 1m 34.406s, 137.667mph
Fastest lap: Patrest, 1m 40.075s, 129.869mph

## GERMAN GRAND PRIX: HOCKENHEIM *8 August Round: 12 Race: 369 45 x 4.223 miles*

| POS. | NO. | DRIVER | CAR/ENGINE | LAPS | TIME/RETIRED | GRID |
|---|---|---|---|---|---|---|
| 1 | 27 | Patrick Tambay | Ferrari | 45 | 1:27'25.178 | 5 |
| 2 | 16 | Rene Arnoux | Renault | 45 | +16.379 | 3 |
| 3 | 6 | Keke Rosberg | Williams-Ford | 44 | +1 Lap | 9 |
| 4 | 3 | Michele Alboreto | Tyrrell-Ford | 44 | +1 Lap | 7 |
| 5 | 23 | Bruno Giacomelli | Alfa Romeo | 44 | +1 Lap | 11 |
| 6 | 29 | Marc Surer | Arrows-Ford | 44 | +1 Lap | 26 |
| 7 | 4 | Brian Henton | Tyrrell-Ford | 44 | +1 Lap | 17 |
| 8 | 14 | Roberto Guerrero | Ensign-Ford | 44 | +1 Lap | 21 |
| 9 | 12 | Nigel Mansell | Lotus-Ford | 43 | +2 Laps | 18 |
| 10 | 35 | Derek Warwick | Toleman-Hart | 43 | +2 Laps | 14 |
| 11 | 20 | Chico Serra | Fittipaldi-Ford | 43 | +2 Laps | 25 |
| Ret | 7 | John Watson | McLaren-Ford | 36 | Spun off | 10 |
| Ret | 26 | Jacques Laffite | Ligier-Matra | 36 | Handling | 15 |
| Ret | 5 | Derek Daly | Williams-Ford | 25 | Engine | 19 |
| Ret | 18 | Raul Boesel | March-Ford | 22 | Tyre | 24 |
| Ret | 11 | Elio de Angelis | Lotus-Ford | 21 | Handling | 13 |
| Ret | 1 | Nelson Piquet | Brabham-BMW | 18 | Collision | 4 |
| Ret | 10 | Eliseo Salazar | ATS-Ford | 17 | Collision | 22 |
| Ret | 15 | Alain Prost | Renault | 14 | Injection | 2 |
| Ret | 2 | Riccardo Patrese | Brabham-BMW | 13 | Engine | 6 |
| Ret | 22 | A.de Cesaris | Alfa Romeo | 9 | Gearbox | 8 |
| Ret | 25 | Eddie Cheever | Ligier-Matra | 8 | Fuel system | 12 |
| Ret | 30 | Mauro Baldi | Arrows-Ford | 6 | Fuel system | 23 |
| Ret | 31 | J.P.Jarier | Osella-Ford | 3 | Steering | 20 |
| Ret | 9 | M.Winkelhock | ATS-Ford | 3 | Clutch | 16 |
| DNS | 28 | Didier Pironi | Ferrari | 0 | Practice accident | 1 |
| DNQ | 33 | Tommy Byrne | Theodore-Ford | | | |
| DNQ | 17 | Rupert Keegan | March-Ford | | | |
| DNQ | 36 | Teo Fabi | Toleman-Hart | | | |

Winning speed: 130.444mph LapLeaders: Arnoux 1, Piquet 2-18, Tambay 19-45
Pole position: Pironi, 1m 47.947s, 140.851mph
Fastest lap: Piquet, 1m 54.035s, 133.331mph

## AUSTRIAN GRAND PRIX: OSTERREICHRING *15 August Round: 13 Race: 370 53 x 3.692 miles*

| POS. | NO. | DRIVER | CAR/ENGINE | LAPS | TIME/RETIRED | GRID |
|---|---|---|---|---|---|---|
| 1 | 11 | Elio de Angelis | Lotus-Ford | 53 | 1:25'02.212 | 7 |
| 2 | 6 | Keke Rosberg | Williams-Ford | 53 | +0.050 | 6 |
| 3 | 26 | Jacques Laffite | Ligier-Matra | 52 | +1 Lap | 14 |
| 4 | 27 | Patrick Tambay | Ferrari | 52 | +1 Lap | 4 |
| 5 | 8 | Niki Lauda | McLaren-Ford | 52 | +1 Lap | 10 |
| 6 | 30 | Mauro Baldi | Arrows-Ford | 52 | +1 Lap | 23 |
| 7 | 20 | Chico Serra | Fittipaldi-Ford | 51 | +2 Laps | 20 |
| 8 | 15 | Alain Prost | Renault | 48 | Injection | 3 |
| Ret | 7 | John Watson | McLaren-Ford | 44 | Engine | 18 |
| Ret | 4 | Brian Henton | Tyrrell-Ford | 32 | Engine | 19 |
| Ret | 1 | Nelson Piquet | Brabham-BMW | 31 | Electrical | 1 |
| Ret | 33 | Tommy Byrne | Theodore-Ford | 28 | Spun off | 26 |
| Ret | 29 | Marc Surer | Arrows-Ford | 28 | Engine | 21 |
| Ret | 2 | Riccardo Patrese | Brabham-BMW | 27 | Engine | 2 |
| Ret | 25 | Eddie Cheever | Ligier-Matra | 22 | Engine | 22 |
| Ret | 12 | Nigel Mansell | Lotus-Ford | 17 | Engine | 12 |
| Ret | 16 | Rene Arnoux | Renault | 16 | Injection | 5 |
| Ret | 9 | M.Winkelhock | ATS-Ford | 15 | Spun off | 25 |
| Ret | 35 | Derek Warwick | Toleman-Hart | 7 | Suspension | 15 |
| Ret | 36 | Teo Fabi | Toleman-Hart | 7 | Transmission | 17 |
| Ret | 14 | Roberto Guerrero | Ensign-Ford | 6 | Spun off | 16 |
| Ret | 3 | Michele Alboreto | Tyrrell-Ford | 1 | Spun off | 8 |
| Ret | 17 | Rupert Keegan | March-Ford | 1 | Steering | 24 |
| Ret | 5 | Derek Daly | Williams-Ford | 0 | Collision | 9 |
| Ret | 22 | A.de Cesaris | Alfa Romeo | 0 | Collision | 11 |
| Ret | 23 | Bruno Giacomelli | Alfa Romeo | 0 | Collision | 13 |
| DNQ | 18 | Raul Boesel | March-Ford | | | |
| DNQ | 31 | J.P.Jarier | Osella-Ford | | | |
| DNQ | 10 | Eliseo Salazar | ATS-Ford | | | |

Winning speed: 138.071mph Lap leaders: Piquet 1; Patrese 2-27; Prost 28-48; Angelis 49-53
Pole position : Piquet, 1m 27.612s, 151.713mph
Fastest lap: Piquet, 1m 33.699s, 141.857mph

## SWISS GRAND PRIX : DIJON-PRENOIS *29 August Round: 14 Race: 371 80 x 2.361 miles*

| POS. | NO. | DRIVER | CAR/ENGINE | LAPS | TIME/RETIRED | GRID |
|---|---|---|---|---|---|---|
| 1 | 6 | Keke Rosberg | Williams-Ford | 80 | 1:32'41.087 | 8 |
| 2 | 15 | Alain Prost | Renault | 80 | +4.442 | 1 |
| 3 | 8 | Niki Lauda | McLaren-Ford | 80 | +1'00.343 | 4 |
| 4 | 1 | Nelson Piquet | Brabham-BMW | 79 | +1 Lap | 6 |
| 5 | 2 | Riccardo Patrese | Brabham-BMW | 79 | +1 Lap | 3 |
| 6 | 11 | Elio de Angelis | Lotus-Ford | 79 | +1 Lap | 15 |
| 7 | 3 | Michele Alboreto | Tyrrell-Ford | 79 | +1 Lap | 12 |
| 8 | 12 | Nigel Mansell | Lotus-Ford | 79 | +1 Lap | 26 |
| 9 | 5 | Derek Daly | Williams-Ford | 79 | +1 Lap | 7 |
| 10 | 22 | A.de Cesaris | Alfa Romeo | 78 | +2 Laps | 5 |
| 11 | 4 | Brian Henton | Tyrrell-Ford | 78 | +2 Laps | 18 |
| 12 | 23 | Bruno Giacomelli | Alfa Romeo | 78 | +2 Laps | 9 |
| 13 | 7 | John Watson | McLaren-Ford | 77 | +3 Laps | 11 |
| 14 | 10 | Eliseo Salazar | ATS-Ford | 77 | +3 Laps | 25 |
| 15 | 29 | Marc Surer | Arrows-Ford | 76 | +4 Laps | 14 |
| 16 | 16 | Rene Arnoux | Renault | 75 | Injection | 2 |
| Ret | 25 | Eddie Cheever | Ligier-Matra | 70 | Handling | 16 |
| Ret | 9 | M.Winkelhock | ATS-Ford | 55 | Chassis | 20 |
| Ret | 31 | J.P.Jarier | Osella-Ford | 44 | Engine | 17 |
| Ret | 26 | Jacques Laffite | Ligier-Matra | 33 | Handling | 13 |
| Ret | 36 | Teo Fabi | Toleman-Hart | 31 | Engine | 23 |
| Ret | 18 | Raul Boesel | March-Ford | 31 | Water leak | 24 |
| Ret | 17 | Rupert Keegan | March-Ford | 25 | Spun off | 22 |
| Ret | 35 | Derek Warwick | Toleman-Hart | 24 | Engine | 21 |
| Ret | 14 | Roberto Guerrero | Ensign-Ford | 4 | Engine | 19 |
| Wth | 27 | Patrick Tambay | Ferrari | 0 | Injury | 10 |
| DNQ | 20 | Chico Serra | Fittipaldi-Ford | | | |
| DNQ | 33 | Tommy Byrne | Theodore-Ford | | | |
| DNQ | 30 | Mauro Baldi | Arrows-Ford | | | |

Winning speed: 122.283mph Lap leaders: Arnoux 1; Prost 2-78; Rosberg 79-80
Pole position: Prost, 1m 1.380s, 138.487mph
Fastest lap: Prost, 1m 7.477s, 125.974mph

### ITALIAN GRAND PRIX: MONZA *12 September Round: 15 Race: 372 52 x 3.604 miles*

| POS. | NO. | DRIVER | CAR/ENGINE | LAPS | TIME/RETIRED | GRID |
|---|---|---|---|---|---|---|
| 1 | 16 | Rene Arnoux | Renault | 52 | 1:22'25.734 | 6 |
| 2 | 27 | Patrick Tambay | Ferrari | 52 | +14.064 | 3 |
| 3 | 28 | Mario Andretti | Ferrari | 52 | +48.452 | 1 |
| 4 | 7 | John Watson | McLaren-Ford | 52 | +1'27.845 | 12 |
| 5 | 3 | Michele Alboreto | Tyrrell-Ford | 51 | +1 Lap | 11 |
| 6 | 25 | Eddie Cheever | Ligier-Matra | 51 | +1 Lap | 14 |
| 7 | 12 | Nigel Mansell | Lotus-Ford | 51 | +1 Lap | 23 |
| 8 | 6 | Keke Rosberg | Williams-Ford | 50 | +2 Laps | 7 |
| 9 | 10 | Eliseo Salazar | ATS-Ford | 50 | +2 Laps | 25 |
| 10 | 22 | A.de Cesaris | Alfa Romeo | 50 | +2 Laps | 9 |
| 11 | 20 | Chico Serra | Fittipaldi-Ford | 49 | +3 Laps | 26 |
| 12 | 30 | Mauro Baldi | Arrows-Ford | 49 | +3 Laps | 24 |
| NC | 14 | Roberto Guerrero | Ensign-Ford | 40 | Not classified | 18 |
| Ret | 11 | Elio de Angelis | Lotus-Ford | 33 | Throttle | 17 |
| Ret | 23 | Bruno Giacomelli | Alfa Romeo | 32 | Handling | 8 |
| Ret | 29 | Marc Surer | Arrows-Ford | 28 | Ignition | 19 |
| Ret | 15 | Alain Prost | Renault | 27 | Injection | 5 |
| Ret | 8 | Niki Lauda | McLaren-Ford | 21 | Brakes | 10 |
| Ret | 31 | J.P.Jarier | Osella-Ford | 10 | Wheel | 15 |
| Ret | 1 | Nelson Piquet | Brabham-BMW | 7 | Engine | 2 |
| Ret | 2 | Riccardo Patrese | Brabham-BMW | 6 | Clutch | 4 |
| Ret | 26 | Jacques Laffite | Ligier-Matra | 5 | Gearbox | 21 |
| Ret | 36 | Teo Fabi | Toleman-Hart | 2 | Engine | 22 |
| Ret | 5 | Derek Daly | Williams-Ford | 0 | Collision | 13 |
| Ret | 35 | Derek Warwick | Toleman-Hart | 0 | Collision | 16 |
| Ret | 4 | Brian Henton | Tyrrell-Ford | 0 | Collision | 20 |
| DNQ | 17 | Rupert Keegan | March-Ford | | | |
| DNQ | 9 | M.Winkelhock | ATS-Ford | | | |
| DNQ | 18 | Raul Boesel | March-Ford | | | |
| DNQ | 33 | Tommy Byrne | Theodore-Ford | | | |

Winning speed: 136.413mph Lap leaders: Arnoux 1-52
Pole position: Andretti, 1m 28.473s, 146.646mph
Fastest lap: Arnoux, 1m 33.619s, 138.585mph

### LAS VEGAS CAESARS PALACE: *25 September Round: 16 Race: 373 75 x 2.268 miles*

| POS. | NO. | DRIVER | CAR/ENGINE | LAPS | TIME/RETIRED | GRID |
|---|---|---|---|---|---|---|
| 1 | 3 | Michele Alboreto | Tyrrell-Ford | 75 | 1:41'56.888 | 3 |
| 2 | 7 | John Watson | McLaren-Ford | 75 | +27.292 | 9 |
| 3 | 25 | Eddie Cheever | Ligier-Matra | 75 | +56.450 | 4 |
| 4 | 15 | Alain Prost | Renault | 75 | +1'08.648 | 1 |
| 5 | 6 | Keke Rosberg | Williams-Ford | 75 | +1'11.375 | 6 |
| 6 | 5 | Derek Daly | Williams-Ford | 74 | +1 Lap | 14 |
| 7 | 29 | Marc Surer | Arrows-Ford | 74 | +1 Lap | 17 |
| 8 | 4 | Brian Henton | Tyrrell-Ford | 74 | +1 Lap | 19 |
| 9 | 22 | A.de Cesaris | Alfa Romeo | 73 | +2 Laps | 18 |
| 10 | 23 | Bruno Giacomelli | Alfa Romeo | 73 | +2 Laps | 16 |
| 11 | 30 | Mauro Baldi | Arrows-Ford | 73 | +2 Laps | 23 |
| 12 | 17 | Rupert Keegan | March-Ford | 73 | +2 Laps | 25 |
| 13 | 18 | Raul Boesel | March-Ford | 69 | +6 Laps | 24 |
| NC | 9 | M.Winkelhock | ATS-Ford | 62 | Not classified | 22 |
| Ret | 8 | Niki Lauda | McLaren-Ford | 53 | Engine | 13 |
| Ret | 33 | Tommy Byrne | Theodore-Ford | 39 | Spun off | 26 |
| Ret | 35 | Derek Warwick | Toleman-Hart | 32 | Ignition | 10 |
| Ret | 11 | Elio de Angelis | Lotus-Ford | 28 | Engine | 20 |
| Ret | 28 | Mario Andretti | Ferrari | 26 | Spun off | 7 |
| Ret | 1 | Nelson Piquet | Brabham-BMW | 26 | Engine | 12 |
| Ret | 16 | Rene Arnoux | Renault | 20 | Engine | 2 |
| Ret | 2 | Riccardo Patrese | Brabham-BMW | 17 | Clutch | 5 |
| Ret | 12 | Nigel Mansell | Lotus-Ford | 8 | Collision | 21 |
| Ret | 26 | Jacques Laffite | Ligier-Matra | 5 | Ignition | 11 |
| DNS | 27 | Patrick Tambay | Ferrari | 0 | Non starter | 8 |
| DNS | 14 | Roberto Guerrero | Ensign-Ford | 0 | Non starter | 15 |
| DNQ | 36 | Teo Fabi | Toleman-Hart | | | |
| DNQ | 10 | Eliseo Salazar | ATS-Ford | | | |
| DNQ | 20 | Chico Serra | Fittipaldi-Ford | | | |

Winning speed: 100.110mph Lap leaders: Prost 1, 15-51; Arnoux 2-14; Alboreto 52-75
Pole position: Prost, 1m 16.356s, 106.931mph
Fastest lap: Alboreto, 1m 19.639s, 102.523mph

# 1983

## DRIVERS' CHAMPION: NELSON PIQUET
## CONSTRUCTORS' CHAMPION: FERRARI

### DRIVERS' CHAMPIONSHIP

| POS. | DRIVER | NATIONALITY | CAR | POINTS |
|---|---|---|---|---|
| 1 | Nelson Piquet | Brazil | Brabham-BMW | 59 |
| 2 | Alain Prost | France | Renault | 57 |
| 3 | René Arnoux | France | Ferrari | 49 |
| 4 | Patrick Tambay | France | Ferrari | 40 |
| 5 | Keke Rosberg | Finland | Williams-Ford, Williams-Honda | 27 |
| 6 | John Watson | GB | McLaren-Ford, McLaren-TAG Porsche | 22 |
| = | Eddie Cheever | USA | Renault | 22 |
| 8 | Andrea de Cesaris | Italy | Alfa Romeo | 15 |
| 9 | Riccardo Patrese | Italy | Brabham-BMW | 13 |
| 10 | Niki Lauda | Austria | McLaren-Ford, McLaren-TAG Porsche | 12 |
| 11 | Jacques Laffite | France | Williams-Ford, Williams-Honda | 11 |
| 12 | Michele Alboreto | Italy | Tyrrell-Ford | 10 |
| = | Nigel Mansell | GB | Lotus-Ford, Lotus-Renault | 10 |
| 14 | Derek Warwick | GB | Toleman-Hart | 9 |
| 15 | Marc Surer | Switzerland | Arrows-Ford | 4 |
| 16 | Mauro Baldi | Italy | Alfa Romeo | 3 |
| 17 | Elio de Angelis | Italy | Lotus-Ford, Lotus-Renault | 2 |
| 18 | Danny Sullivan | USA | Tyrrell-Ford | 2 |
| 19 | Johnny Cecotto | Venezuela | Theodore-Ford | 1 |
| = | Bruno Giacomelli | Italy | Toleman-Hart | 1 |
| | Chico Serra | Brazil | Arrows-Ford | |
| | Eliseo Salazar | Chile | RAM-March-Ford | |
| | Manfred Winkelhock | West Germany | ATS-BMW | |
| | Roberto Guerrero | Colombia | Theodore-Ford | |
| | Raul Boesel | Brazil | Ligier-Ford | |
| | Jean-Pierre Jarier | France | Ligier-Ford | |
| | Corrado Fabi | Italy | Osella-Ford, Osella-Alfa Romeo | |
| | Piercarlo Ghinzani | Italy | Osella-Ford, Osella-Alfa Romeo | |
| | Alan Jones | Australia | Arrows-Ford | |
| | Jean-Louis Schlesser | France | RAM-March-Ford | |
| | Thierry Boutsen | Belgium | Arrows-Ford | |
| | Stefan Johansson | Sweden | Spirit-Honda | |
| | Jacques Villeneuve Snr. | Canada | RAM-March-Ford | |
| | Kenny Acheson | GB | RAM-March-Ford | |
| | Jonathan Palmer | GB | Williams-Ford | |

Points for top six finishers (9, 6, 4, 3, 2, 1). Half points awarded for races stopped before half distance.

### CONSTRUCTORS' CHAMPIONSHIP

| POS. | CONSTRUCTOR | POINTS |
|---|---|---|
| 1 | Ferrari | 89 |
| 2 | Renault | 79 |
| 3 | Brabham-BMW | 72 |
| 4 | Williams-Ford | 36 |
| 5 | McLaren-Ford | 34 |
| 6 | Alfa Romeo | 18 |
| 7 | Tyrrell-Ford | 12 |
| = | Lotus-Renault | 12 |
| 9 | Toleman-Hart | 10 |
| 10 | Arrows-Ford | 4 |
| 11 | Williams-Honda | 2 |
| 12 | Theodore | 1 |
| = | Lotus-Ford | 1 |

Points for top six finishers (9, 6, 4, 3, 2, 1). Half points awarded for races stopped before half distance.

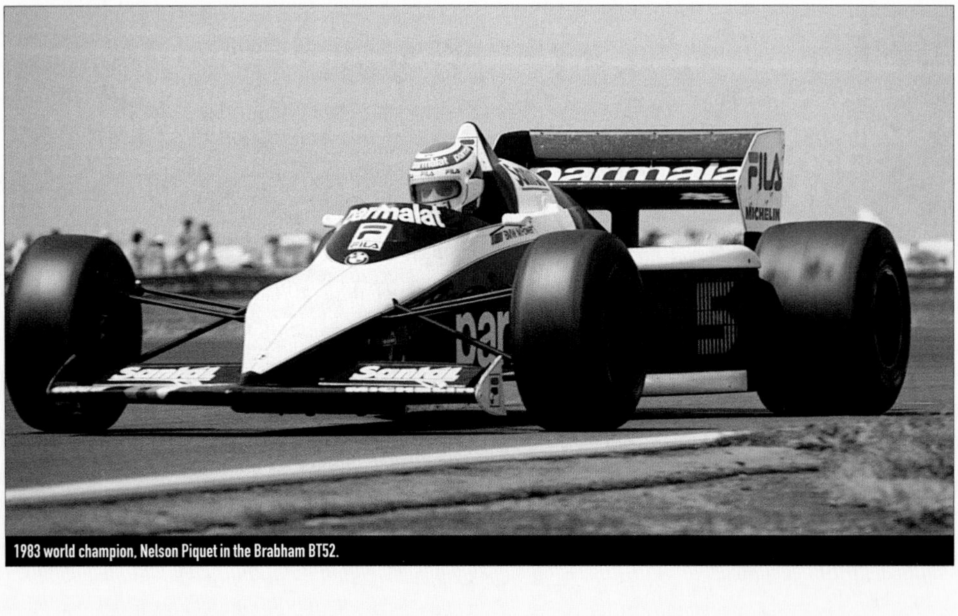
1983 world champion, Nelson Piquet in the Brabham BT52.

### BRAZILIAN GRAND PRIX: RIO DE JANEIRO *13 March Round:1 Race:374 63 x 3.126miles*

| POS. | NO. | DRIVER | CAR/ENGINE | LAPS | TIME/RETIRED | GRID |
|---|---|---|---|---|---|---|
| 1 | 5 | Nelson Piquet | Brabham-BMW | 63 | 1:48'27.731 | 4 |
| 3 | 8 | Niki Lauda | McLaren-Ford | 63 | +51.883 | 9 |
| 4 | 2 | Jacques Laffite | Williams-Ford | 63 | +1'13.951 | 18 |
| 5 | 27 | Patrick Tambay | Ferrari | 63 | +1'18.117 | 3 |
| 6 | 29 | Marc Surer | Arrows-Ford | 63 | +1'18.207 | 20 |
| 7 | 15 | Alain Prost | Renault | 62 | +1 Lap | 2 |
| 8 | 35 | Derek Warwick | Toleman-Hart | 62 | +1 Lap | 5 |
| 9 | 30 | Chico Serra | Arrows-Ford | 62 | +1 Lap | 23 |
| 10 | 28 | Rene Arnoux | Ferrari | 62 | +1 Lap | 6 |
| 11 | 4 | Danny Sullivan | Tyrrell-Ford | 62 | +1 Lap | 21 |
| 12 | 12 | Nigel Mansell | Lotus-Ford | 61 | +2 Laps | 22 |
| 13 | 34 | Johnny Cecotto | Theodore-Ford | 60 | +3 Laps | 19 |
| 14 | 17 | Eliseo Salazar | RAM-Ford | 59 | +4 Laps | 26 |
| 15 | 9 | M.Winkelhock | ATS-BMW | 59 | +4 Laps | 25 |
| DSQ | 1 | Keke Rosberg | Williams-Ford | 63 | Disqualified | 1 |
| DSQ | 11 | Elio de Angelis | Lotus-Renault/Ford | 60 | Disqualified | 13 |
| NC | 33 | Roberto Guerrero | Theodore-Ford | 53 | Not classified | 14 |
| Ret | 16 | Eddie Cheever | Renault | 41 | Brakes | 8 |
| Ret | 7 | John Watson | McLaren-Ford | 34 | Engine | 16 |
| Ret | 26 | Raul Boesel | Ligier-Ford | 25 | Engine | 17 |
| Ret | 23 | Mauro Baldi | Alfa Romeo | 23 | Collision | 10 |
| Ret | 25 | J.P.Jarier | Ligier-Ford | 22 | Suspension | 12 |
| Ret | 6 | Riccardo Patrese | Brabham-BMW | 19 | Exhaust | 7 |
| Ret | 31 | Corrado Fabi | Osella-Ford | 17 | Engine | 24 |
| Ret | 36 | Bruno Giacomelli | Toleman-Hart | 16 | Spun off | 15 |
| Ret | 3 | Michele Alboreto | Tyrrell-Ford | 7 | Engine | 11 |
| DNQ | 22 | A.de Cesaris | Alfa Romeo | | | |
| DNQ | 32 | P.Ghinzani | Osella-Ford | | | |

Winning speed: 108.948mph Lap leaders: Kosberg 1-6; Piquet 7-63
Pole position: Rosberg, 1m, 34.526s, 119.057mph
Fastest lap: Piquet, 1m 39.829s, 112.733mph
Rosberg finished second but was disqualified after being pushed after a pitstop.

### USA WEST GRAND PRIX: LONG BEACH *27 March Round:2 Race:375 75 x 2.035miles*

| POS. | NO. | DRIVER | CAR/ENGINE | LAPS | TIME/RETIRED | GRID |
|---|---|---|---|---|---|---|
| 1 | 7 | John Watson | McLaren-Ford | 75 | 1:53'34.889 | 22 |
| 2 | 8 | Niki Lauda | McLaren-Ford | 75 | +27.993 | 23 |
| 3 | 28 | Rene Arnoux | Ferrari | 75 | +1'13.638 | 2 |
| 4 | 2 | Jacques Laffite | Williams-Ford | 74 | +1 Lap | 4 |
| 5 | 29 | Marc Surer | Arrows-Ford | 74 | +1 Lap | 16 |
| 6 | 34 | Johnny Cecotto | Theodore-Ford | 74 | +1 Lap | 17 |
| 7 | 26 | Raul Boesel | Ligier-Ford | 73 | +2 Laps | 26 |
| 8 | 4 | Danny Sullivan | Tyrrell-Ford | 73 | +2 Laps | 9 |
| 9 | 3 | Michele Alboreto | Tyrrell-Ford | 73 | +2 Laps | 7 |
| 10 | 6 | Riccardo Patrese | Brabham-BMW | 72 | Distributor | 11 |
| 11 | 15 | Alain Prost | Renault | 72 | +3 Laps | 8 |
| 12 | 12 | Nigel Mansell | Lotus-Ford | 72 | +3 Laps | 13 |
| Ret | 16 | Eddie Cheever | Renault | 67 | Gearbox | 15 |
| Ret | 30 | Alan Jones | Arrows-Ford | 58 | Driver unwell | 12 |
| Ret | 5 | Nelson Piquet | Brabham-BMW | 51 | Throttle | 20 |
| Ret | 22 | A.de Cesaris | Alfa Romeo | 48 | Gearbox | 19 |
| Ret | 11 | Elio de Angelis | Lotus-Renault | 29 | Handling | 5 |
| Ret | 33 | Roberto Guerrero | Theodore-Ford | 27 | Gearbox | 18 |
| Ret | 25 | J.P.Jarier | Ligier-Ford | 26 | Collision | 10 |
| Ret | 36 | Bruno Giacomelli | Toleman-Hart | 26 | Battery | 14 |
| Ret | 23 | Mauro Baldi | Alfa Romeo | 26 | Spun off | 21 |
| Ret | 27 | Patrick Tambay | Ferrari | 25 | Collision | 1 |
| Ret | 1 | Keke Rosberg | Williams-Ford | 25 | Collision | 3 |
| Ret | 17 | Eliseo Salazar | RAM-Ford | 25 | Gearbox | 25 |
| Ret | 35 | Derek Warwick | Toleman-Hart | 11 | Spun off | 6 |
| Ret | 9 | M.Winkelhock | ATS-BMW | 3 | Spun off | 24 |
| DNQ | 31 | Corrado Fabi | Osella-Ford | | | |
| DNQ | 32 | P.Ghinzani | Osella-Ford | | | |

Winning speed: 80.625mph Lap leaders: Tambay 1-25; Laffite 26-44; Watson 45-75
Pole position: Tambay, 1m 26.117s, 85.070mph
Fastest lap: Lauda, 1m 28.330s, 82.939mph

### FRENCH GRAND PRIX: PAUL RICARD *17 April 1983 Round: 3 Race: 376 54 x 3.610miles*

| POS. | NO. | DRIVER | CAR/ENGINE | LAPS | TIME/RETIRED | GRID |
|---|---|---|---|---|---|---|
| 1 | 15 | Alain Prost | Renault | 54 | 1:34'13.913 | 1 |
| 2 | 5 | Nelson Piquet | Brabham-BMW | 54 | +29.720 | 6 |
| 3 | 16 | Eddie Cheever | Renault | 54 | +40.232 | 2 |
| 4 | 27 | Patrick Tambay | Ferrari | 54 | +1'06.880 | 11 |
| 5 | 1 | Keke Rosberg | Williams-Ford | 53 | +1 Lap | 16 |
| 6 | 2 | Jacques Laffite | Williams-Ford | 53 | +1 Lap | 19 |
| 7 | 28 | Rene Arnoux | Ferrari | 53 | +1 Lap | 4 |
| 8 | 3 | Michele Alboreto | Tyrrell-Ford | 53 | +1 Lap | 15 |
| 9 | 25 | J.P.Jarier | Ligier-Ford | 53 | +1 Lap | 20 |
| 10 | 29 | Marc Surer | Arrows-Ford | 53 | +1 Lap | 21 |
| 11 | 34 | Johnny Cecotto | Theodore-Ford | 52 | +2 Laps | 17 |
| 12 | 22 | A.de Cesaris | Alfa Romeo | 50 | +4 Laps | 7 |
| 13 | 36 | Bruno Giacomelli | Toleman-Hart | 49 | Gearbox | 13 |
| Ret | 26 | Raul Boesel | Ligier-Ford | 47 | Engine | 25 |
| Ret | 31 | Corrado Fabi | Osella-Ford | 36 | Engine | 23 |
| Ret | 9 | M.Winkelhock | ATS-BMW | 36 | Turbo | 10 |
| Ret | 8 | Niki Lauda | McLaren-Ford | 29 | Wheel bearing | 12 |
| Ret | 23 | Mauro Baldi | Alfa Romeo | 28 | Spun off | 8 |
| Ret | 30 | Chico Serra | Arrows-Ford | 26 | Gearbox | 26 |
| Ret | 33 | Roberto Guerrero | Theodore/Ford | 23 | Engine | 22 |
| Ret | 4 | Danny Sullivan | Tyrrell-Ford | 21 | Clutch | 24 |
| Ret | 11 | Elio de Angelis | Lotus-Renault | 20 | Electrical | 5 |
| Ret | 6 | Riccardo Patrese | Brabham-BMW | 19 | Water leak | 3 |
| Ret | 35 | Derek Warwick | Toleman-Hart | 14 | Engine | 9 |
| Ret | 12 | Nigel Mansell | Lotus-Ford | 6 | Physical | 18 |
| Ret | 7 | John Watson | McLaren-Ford | 3 | Engine | 14 |
| DNQ | 17 | Eliseo Salazar | RAM-Ford | | | |
| DNQ | 32 | P.Ghinzani | Osella-Ford | | | |
| DNQ | 18 | J.L.Schlesser | RAM-Ford | | | |

Winning speed: 124.129mph Lap leaders: Prost, 1-29, 33-54; Piquet 30-32
Pole position: Prost, 1 m 36.672s, 134.440mph
Fastest lap: Prost, 1m 42.695s, 126.555mph

## SAN MARINO GRAND PRIX: IMOLA *1 May Round:4 Race:377 60 x 3.132miles*

| POS. | NO. | DRIVER | CAR/ENGINE | LAPS | TIME/RETIRED | GRID |
|---|---|---|---|---|---|---|
| 1 | 27 | Patrick Tambay | Ferrari | 60 | 1:37'52.460 | 3 |
| 2 | 15 | Alain Prost | Renault | 60 | +48.781 | 4 |
| 3 | 28 | Rene Arnoux | Ferrari | 59 | +1 Lap | 1 |
| 4 | 1 | Keke Rosberg | Williams-Ford | 59 | +1 Lap | 11 |
| 5 | 7 | John Watson | McLaren-Ford | 59 | +1 Lap | 24 |
| 6 | 29 | Marc Surer | Arrows-Ford | 59 | +1 Lap | 12 |
| 7 | 2 | Jacques Laffite | Williams-Ford | 59 | +1 Lap | 16 |
| 8 | 30 | Chico Serra | Arrows-Ford | 58 | +2 Laps | 20 |
| 9 | 26 | Raul Boesel | Ligier-Ford | 58 | +2 Laps | 25 |
| 10 | 23 | Mauro Baldi | Alfa Romeo | 57 | Engine | 10 |
| 11 | 9 | M.Winkelhock | ATS-BMW | 57 | +3 Laps | 7 |
| 12 | 12 | Nigel Mansell | Lotus-Ford | 56 | Spun off | 15 |
| Ret | 6 | Riccardo Patrese | Brabham-BMW | 54 | Spun off | 5 |
| Ret | 22 | A.de Cesaris | Alfa Romeo | 45 | Ignition | 8 |
| Ret | 11 | Elio de Angelis | Lotus-Renault | 43 | Handling | 9 |
| Ret | 5 | Nelson Piquet | Brabham-BMW | 41 | Engine | 2 |
| Ret | 25 | J.P.Jarier | Ligier-Ford | 39 | Radiator | 19 |
| Ret | 4 | Danny Sullivan | Tyrrell-Ford | 37 | Collision | 22 |
| Ret | 35 | Derek Warwick | Toleman-Hart | 27 | Spun off | 14 |
| Ret | 31 | Corrado Fabi | Osella-Ford | 20 | Spun off | 26 |
| Ret | 36 | Bruno Giacomelli | Toleman-Hart | 20 | Suspension | 17 |
| Ret | 8 | Niki Lauda | McLaren-Ford | 11 | Spun off | 18 |
| Ret | 34 | Johnny Cecotto | Theodore-Ford | 11 | Spun off | 23 |
| Ret | 3 | Michele Alboreto | Tyrrell-Ford | 10 | Collision | 13 |
| Ret | 33 | Roberto Guerrero | Theodore-Ford | 3 | Spun off | 21 |
| Ret | 16 | Eddie Cheever | Renault | 1 | Turbo | 6 |
| DNQ | 17 | Eliseo Salazar | RAM-Ford | | | |
| DNQ | 32 | P.Ghinzani | Osella-Alfa Romeo | | | |

Winning speed: 115.190mph Lap leaders: Arnoux 1-5; Patrese 6-33; Tambay 34-60
Pole position: Arnoux, 1m 31.238s, 123.569mph
Fastest lap: Patrese, 1m 34.437s, 119.383mph

## MONACO GRAND PRIX: MONTE CARLO *22 May Roubd: 6 Race: 379 40x4.318 miles*

| POS. | NO. | DRIVER | CAR/ENGINE | LAPS | TIME/RETIRED | GRID |
|---|---|---|---|---|---|---|
| 1 | 1 | Keke Rosberg | Williams-Ford | 76 | 1:56'38.121 | 5 |
| 2 | 5 | Nelson Piquet | Brabham-BMW | 76 | +18.475 | 6 |
| 3 | 15 | Alain Prost | Renault | 76 | +31.366 | 1 |
| 4 | 27 | Patrick Tambay | Ferrari | 76 | +1'04.297 | 4 |
| 5 | 4 | Danny Sullivan | Tyrrell-Ford | 74 | +2 Laps | 20 |
| 6 | 23 | Mauro Baldi | Alfa Romeo | 74 | +2 Laps | 13 |
| 7 | 30 | Chico Serra | Arrows-Ford | 74 | +2 Laps | 15 |
| Ret | 6 | Riccardo Patrese | Brabham-BMW | 64 | Electrical | 17 |
| Ret | 2 | Jacques Laffite | Williams-Ford | 53 | Gearbox | 8 |
| Ret | 29 | Marc Surer | Arrows-Ford | 49 | Collision | 12 |
| Ret | 35 | Derek Warwick | Toleman-Hart | 49 | Collision | 10 |
| Ret | 11 | Elio de Angelis | Lotus-Renault | 49 | Halfshaft | 19 |
| Ret | 25 | J.P.Jarier | Ligier-Ford | 32 | Suspension | 9 |
| Ret | 16 | Eddie Cheever | Renault | 30 | Engine | 3 |
| Ret | 22 | A.de Cesaris | Alfa Romeo | 13 | Gearbox | 7 |
| Ret | 28 | Rene Arnoux | Ferrari | 6 | Suspension | 2 |
| Ret | 26 | Raul Boesel | Ligier-Ford | 3 | Collision | 18 |
| Ret | 9 | M.Winkelhock | ATS-BMW | 3 | Collision | 16 |
| Ret | 3 | Michele Alboreto | Tyrrell-Ford | 0 | Collision | 11 |
| Ret | 12 | Nigel Mansell | Lotus-Ford | 0 | Collision | 14 |
| DNQ | 36 | Bruno Giacomelli | Toleman-Hart | | | |
| DNQ | 8 | Niki Lauda | McLaren-Ford | | | |
| DNQ | 7 | John Watson | McLaren/Ford | | | |
| DNQ | 31 | Corrado Fabi | Osella-Ford | | | |
| DNQ | 17 | Eliseo Salazar | RAM-Ford | | | |
| DNQ | 32 | P.Ghinzani | Osella-Alfa Romeo | | | |
| DNPQ | 34 | Johnny Cecotto | Theodore-Ford | | | |
| DNPQ | 33 | Roberto Guerrero | Theodore-Ford | | | |

Winning speed: 80.459mph Lap leaders: Rosberg 1-76
Pole position: Prost, 1m 24.840s, 87.326mph
Fastest lap: Piquet, 1m 27.283s, 84.882mph

## BELGIAN GRAND PRIX: SPA-FRANCORCHAMPS

| POS. | NO. | DRIVER | CAR/ENGINE | LAPS | TIME/RETIRED | GRID |
|---|---|---|---|---|---|---|
| 1 | 15 | Alain Prost | Renault | 40 | 1:27'11.502 | 1 |
| 2 | 27 | Patrick Tambay | Ferrari | 40 | +23.182 | 2 |
| 3 | 16 | Eddie Cheever | Renault | 40 | +39.869 | 8 |
| 4 | 5 | Nelson Piquet | Brabham-BMW | 40 | +42.295 | 4 |
| 5 | 1 | Keke Rosberg | Williams-Ford | 40 | +50.480 | 9 |
| 6 | 2 | Jacques Laffite | Williams-Ford | 40 | +1'33.107 | 11 |
| 7 | 35 | Derek Warwick | Toleman-Hart | 40 | +1'58.539 | 22 |
| 8 | 36 | Bruno Giacomelli | Toleman-Hart | 40 | +2'38.273 | 16 |
| 9 | 11 | Elio de Angelis | Lotus-Renault | 39 | +1 Lap | 13 |
| 10 | 34 | Johnny Cecotto | Theodore-Ford | 39 | +1 Lap | 25 |
| 11 | 29 | Marc Surer | Arrows-Ford | 39 | +1 Lap | 10 |
| 12 | 4 | Danny Sullivan | Tyrrell-Ford | 39 | +1 Lap | 23 |
| 13 | 26 | Raul Boesel | Ligier-Ford | 39 | +1 Lap | 26 |
| 14 | 3 | Michele Alboreto | Tyrrell-Ford | 38 | +2 Laps | 17 |
| Ret | 8 | Niki Lauda | McLaren-Ford | 33 | Gearbox | 15 |
| Ret | 12 | Nigel Mansell | Lotus-Ford | 30 | Gearbox | 19 |
| Ret | 22 | A.de Cesaris | Alfa Romeo | 25 | Injection | 3 |
| Ret | 33 | Roberto Guerrero | Theodore-Ford | 23 | Engine | 14 |
| Ret | 28 | Rene Arnoux | Ferrari | 22 | Engine | 5 |
| Ret | 31 | Corrado Fabi | Osella-Ford | 19 | Wheel | 24 |
| Ret | 9 | M.Winkelhock | ATS-BMW | 18 | Spun off | 7 |
| Ret | 7 | John Watson | McLaren-Ford | 8 | Collision | 20 |
| Ret | 25 | J.P.Jarier | Ligier-Ford | 8 | Collision | 21 |
| Ret | 30 | Thierry Boutsen | Arrows-Ford | 4 | Suspension | 18 |
| Ret | 23 | Mauro Baldi | Alfa Romeo | 3 | Throttle | 12 |
| Ret | 6 | Riccardo Patrese | Brabham-BMW | 0 | Engine | 6 |
| DNQ | 32 | P.Ghinzani | Osella-Alfa Romeo | | | |
| DNQ | 17 | Eliseo Salazar | RAM-Ford | | | |

Winning speed: 119.135mph Lap leaders: de Cesaris 1-18; Prost 19-22, 24-40; Piquet 23
Pole position: Prost, 2m 4.615s, 124.740mph
Fastest lap: de Cesaris, 2m 7.493s, 121.924mph

## USA GRAND PRIX: DETROIT *5 June Round: 7 Race: 380 60 x 2.500 miles*

| POS. | NO. | DRIVER | CAR/ENGINE | LAPS | TIME/RETIRED | GRID |
|---|---|---|---|---|---|---|
| 1 | 3 | Michele Alboreto | Tyrrell-Ford | 60 | 1:50'53.669 | 6 |
| 2 | 1 | Keke Rosberg | Williams-Ford | 60 | +7.702 | 12 |
| 3 | 7 | John Watson | McLaren-Ford | 60 | +9.283 | 21 |
| 4 | 5 | Nelson Piquet | Brabham-BMW | 60 | +1'12.185 | 2 |
| 5 | 2 | Jacques Laffite | Williams-Ford | 60 | +1'32.603 | 20 |
| 6 | 12 | Nigel Mansell | Lotus-Ford | 59 | +1 Lap | 14 |
| 7 | 30 | Thierry Boutsen | Arrows-Ford | 59 | +1 Lap | 10 |
| 8 | 15 | Alain Prost | Renault | 59 | +1 Lap | 13 |
| 9 | 36 | Bruno Giacomelli | Toleman-Hart | 59 | +1 Lap | 17 |
| 10 | 26 | Raul Boesel | Ligier-Ford | 58 | +2 Laps | 23 |
| 11 | 29 | Marc Surer | Arrows-Ford | 58 | +2 Laps | 5 |
| 12 | 23 | Mauro Baldi | Alfa Romeo | 56 | +4 Laps | 25 |
| Ret | 8 | Niki Lauda | McLaren-Ford | 49 | Suspension | 18 |
| NC | 33 | Roberto Guerrero | Theodore-Ford | 38 | Not classified | 11 |
| Ret | 34 | Johnny Cecotto | Theodore-Ford | 34 | Gearbox | 26 |
| Ret | 22 | A.de Cesaris | Alfa Romeo | 33 | Turbo | 18 |
| Ret | 28 | Rene Arnoux | Ferrari | 31 | Electrical | 1 |
| Ret | 4 | Danny Sullivan | Tyrrell-Ford | 30 | Electrical | 16 |
| Ret | 25 | J.P.Jarier | Ligier/Ford | 29 | Wheel | 19 |
| Ret | 9 | M.Winkelhock | ATS-BMW | 26 | Collision | 22 |
| Ret | 35 | Derek Warwick | Toleman-Hart | 25 | Engine | 9 |
| Ret | 6 | Riccardo Patrese | Brabham-BMW | 24 | Brakes | 15 |
| Ret | 11 | Elio de Angelis | Lotus-Renault | 5 | Gearbox | 4 |
| Ret | 16 | Eddie Cheever | Renault | 4 | Distributor | 7 |
| Ret | 32 | P.Ghinzani | Osella-Alfa Romeo | 4 | Overheating | 24 |
| Ret | 27 | Patrick Tambay | Ferrari | 0 | Engine | 3 |
| DNQ | 31 | Corrado Fabi | Osella-Ford | | | |

Winning speed: 81.158mph Lap leaders: Piquet 1-9, 32-50; Arnoux 10-31; Alboreto 51-60
Pole position: Arnoux, 1m 44.734s, 85.932mph
Fastest lap: Watson, 1m 47.668s, 83.590mph

## CANADIAN GRAND PRIX: MONTREAL *12 June Round: 8 Race: 381 70 x 2.740 miles*

| POS. | NO. | DRIVER | CAR/ENGINE | LAPS | TIME/RETIRED | GRID |
|---|---|---|---|---|---|---|
| 1 | 28 | Rene Arnoux | Ferrari | 70 | 1:48'31.838 | 1 |
| 2 | 16 | Eddie Cheever | Renault | 70 | +42.029 | 6 |
| 3 | 27 | Patrick Tambay | Ferrari | 70 | +52.610 | 4 |
| 4 | 1 | Keke Rosberg | Williams-Ford | 70 | +1'17.048 | 9 |
| 5 | 15 | Alain Prost | Renault | 69 | +1 Lap | 2 |
| 6 | 7 | John Watson | McLaren-Ford | 69 | +1 Lap | 20 |
| 7 | 30 | Thierry Boutsen | Arrows-Ford | 69 | +1 Lap | 15 |
| 8 | 3 | Michele Alboreto | Tyrrell-Ford | 68 | +2 Laps | 17 |
| 9 | 9 | M.Winkelhock | ATS-BMW | 67 | +3 Laps | 7 |
| 10 | 23 | Danny Sullivan | Tyrell-Ford | 67 | +3 Laps | 22 |
| DSQ | 4 | Riccardo Patrese | Brabham-BMW | 56 | Gearbox | 5 |
| Ret | 6 | Riccardo Patrese | Brabham-BMW | 56 | Gearbox | 5 |
| Ret | 35 | Derek Warwick | Toleman-Hart | 47 | Turbo | 12 |
| Ret | 36 | Bruno Giacomelli | Toleman-Hart | 43 | Engine | 10 |
| Ret | 12 | Nigel Mansell | Lotus-Ford | 43 | Handling | 18 |
| Ret | 22 | A.de Cesaris | Alfa Romeo | 42 | Engine | 8 |
| Ret | 2 | Jacques Laffite | Williams-Ford | 37 | Gearbox | 13 |
| Ret | 26 | Raul Boesel | Ligier-Ford | 32 | Halfshaft | 24 |
| Ret | 33 | Roberto Guerrero | Theodore-Ford | 27 | Engine | 21 |
| Ret | 31 | Corrado Fabi | Osella-Ford | 26 | Engine | 25 |
| Ret | 34 | Johnny Cecotto | Theodore-Ford | 17 | Differential | 23 |
| Ret | 5 | Nelson Piquet | Brabham-BMW | 15 | Throttle | 3 |
| Ret | 8 | Niki Lauda | McLaren-Ford | 12 | Spun off | 19 |
| Ret | 11 | Elio de Angelis | Lotus-Renault | 1 | Throttle | 11 |
| Ret | 29 | Marc Surer | Arrows-Ford | 0 | Transmission | 14 |
| Ret | 25 | J.P.Jarier | Ligier-Ford | 0 | Gearbox | 16 |
| DNQ | 17 | J.Villeneuve | RAM-Ford | | | |
| DNQ | 32 | P.Ghinzani | Osella-Alfa Romeo | | | |

Winning speed: 106.044mph Lap leaders: Arnoux: 1-34, 39-70; Patrese 35-37; Tambay 38
Pole position: Arnoux: 1m 28.729s, 111.180mph
Fastest lap: Tambay, 1m 30.851s, 108.583mph

## BRITISH GRAND PRIX: SILVERSTONE *16 July Round: 9 Race: 382 67 x 2.932 miles*

| POS. | NO. | DRIVER | CAR/ENGINE | LAPS | TIME/RETIRED | GRID |
|---|---|---|---|---|---|---|
| 1 | 15 | Alain Prost | Renault | 67 | 1:24'39.780 | 3 |
| 2 | 5 | Nelson Piquet | Brabham-BMW | 67 | +19.161 | 6 |
| 3 | 27 | Patrick Tambay | Ferrari | 67 | +26.246 | 2 |
| 4 | 12 | Nigel Mansell | Lotus-Renault | 67 | +38.952 | 18 |
| 5 | 28 | Rene Arnoux | Ferrari | 67 | +58.874 | 1 |
| 6 | 8 | Niki Lauda | McLaren-Ford | 66 | +1 Lap | 15 |
| 7 | 23 | Mauro Baldi | Alfa Romeo | 66 | +1 Lap | 11 |
| 8 | 22 | A.de Cesaris | Alfa Romeo | 66 | +1 Lap | 9 |
| 9 | 7 | John Watson | McLaren-Ford | 66 | +1 Lap | 24 |
| 10 | 25 | J.P.Jarier | Ligier-Ford | 65 | +2 Laps | 25 |
| 11 | 1 | Keke Rosberg | Williams-Ford | 65 | +2 Laps | 13 |
| 12 | 2 | Jacques Laffite | Williams-Ford | 65 | +2 Laps | 20 |
| 13 | 3 | Michele Alboreto | Tyrrell-Ford | 65 | +2 Laps | 16 |
| 14 | 4 | Danny Sullivan | Tyrrell-Ford | 65 | +2 Laps | 23 |
| 15 | 30 | Thierry Boutsen | Arrows-Ford | 65 | +2 Laps | 17 |
| 16 | 33 | Roberto Guerrero | Theodore-Ford | 64 | +3 Laps | 21 |
| 17 | 29 | Marc Surer | Arrows-Ford | 64 | +3 Laps | 19 |
| Ret | 9 | M.Winkelhock | ATS-BMW | 49 | Engine | 8 |
| Ret | 26 | Raul Boesel | Ligier-Ford | 48 | Suspension | 22 |
| Ret | 32 | P.Ghinzani | Osella-Alfa Romeo | 46 | Fuel system | 26 |
| Ret | 35 | Derek Warwick | Toleman-Hart | 27 | Gearbox | 10 |
| Ret | 6 | Riccardo Patrese | Brabham-BMW | 9 | Turbo | 5 |
| Ret | 40 | Stefan Johansson | Spirit-Honda | 5 | Fuel pump | 15 |
| Ret | 16 | Eddie Cheever | Renault | 3 | Engine | 7 |
| Ret | 36 | Bruno Giacomelli | Toleman-Hart | 3 | Turbo | 12 |
| Ret | 11 | Elio de Angelis | Lotus-Renault | 1 | Turbo | 4 |
| DNQ | 34 | Johnny Cecotto | Theodore-Ford | | | |
| DNQ | 31 | Corrado Fabi | Osella-Alfa Romeo | | | |
| DNQ | 17 | Kenny Acheson | RAM-Ford | | | |

Winning speed: 139.218mph Lap leaders: Tambay 1-19; Prost 20-36, 42-67; Piquet 37-41
Pole position: Arnoux, 1m 9.462s, 151.956mph
Fastest lap: Prost, 1m 14.212s, 142.230mph

## GERMAN GRAND PRIX: HOCKENHEIM *7 August Round: 10 Race: 383 45 x 4.223 miles*

| POS. | NO. | DRIVER | CAR/ENGINE | LAPS | TIME/RETIRED | GRID |
|---|---|---|---|---|---|---|
| 1 | 28 | Rene Arnoux | Ferrari | 45 | 1:27'10.319 | 2 |
| 2 | 22 | A.de Cesaris | Alfa Romeo | 45 | +1'10.652 | 3 |
| 3 | 6 | Riccardo Patrese | Brabham-BMW | 45 | +1'44.093 | 8 |
| 4 | 15 | Alain Prost | Renault | 45 | +2'00.750 | 5 |
| 5 | 7 | John Watson | McLaren-Ford | 44 | +1 Lap | 23 |
| 6 | 2 | Jacques Laffite | Williams-Ford | 44 | +1 Lap | 15 |
| 7 | 29 | Marc Surer | Arrows-Ford | 44 | +1 Lap | 20 |
| 8 | 25 | J.P.Jarier | Ligier-Ford | 44 | +1 Lap | 19 |
| 9 | 30 | Thierry Boutsen | Arrows-Ford | 44 | +1 Lap | 14 |
| 10 | 1 | Keke Rosberg | Williams-Ford | 44 | +1 Lap | 12 |
| 11 | 34 | Johnny Cecotto | Theodore-Ford | 44 | +1 Lap | 22 |
| 12 | 4 | Danny Sullivan | Tyrrell-Ford | 43 | +2 Laps | 21 |
| 13 | 5 | Nelson Piquet | Brabham-BMW | 42 | Fire | 4 |
| D | 8 | Niki Lauda | McLaren-Ford | 44 | Disqualified | 18 |
| Ret | 16 | Eddie Cheever | Renault | 38 | Fuel system | 6 |
| Ret | 32 | P.Ghinzani | Osella-Alfa Romeo | 34 | Oil leak | 26 |
| Ret | 26 | Raul Boesel | Ligier-Ford | 27 | Engine | 25 |
| Ret | 23 | Mauro Baldi | Alfa Romeo | 24 | Turbo | 7 |
| Ret | 36 | Bruno Giacomelli | Toleman-Hart | 19 | Turbo | 10 |
| Ret | 35 | Derek Warwick | Toleman-Hart | 17 | Engine | 9 |
| Ret | 40 | Stefan Johansson | Spirit-Honda | 11 | Engine | 13 |
| Ret | 27 | Patrick Tambay | Ferrari | 11 | Engine | 1 |
| Ret | 11 | Elio de Angelis | Lotus-Renault | 10 | Engine | 11 |
| Ret | 3 | Michele Alboreto | Tyrrell-Ford | 4 | Fuel pump | 16 |
| Ret | 12 | Nigel Mansell | Lotus-Renault | 1 | Engine | 17 |
| Ret | 33 | Roberto Guerrero | Theodore-Ford | 0 | Engine | 24 |
| DNQ | 17 | Kenny Acheson | RAM-Ford | | | |
| DNQ | 31 | Corrado Fabi | Osella-Alfa Romeo | | | |
| DNQ | 9 | M.Winkelhock | ATS-BMW | | | |

Winning speed: 130.814mph Lap leaders: Tambay 1; Arnoux 2-23, 31-45; Piquet 24-30
Pole position: Tambay, 1m 49.328s, 139.072mph
Fastest lap: Arnoux, 1m 53.938s, 133.445mph
Lauda finished fith but was disqualified for being pushed after a pitstop

## AUSTRIAN GRAND PRIX: OSTERREICHRING *14 August Round: 11 Race: 384 53 x 3.692 miles*

| POS. | NO. | DRIVER | CAR/ENGINE | LAPS | TIME/RETIRED | GRID |
|---|---|---|---|---|---|---|
| 1 | 15 | Alain Prost | Renault | 53 | 1:24'32.745 | 5 |
| 2 | 28 | Rene Arnoux | Ferrari | 53 | +6.835 | 2 |
| 3 | 5 | Nelson Piquet | Brabham-BMW | 53 | +27.659 | 4 |
| 4 | 16 | Eddie Cheever | Renault | 53 | +28.395 | 8 |
| 5 | 12 | Nigel Mansell | Lotus-Renault | 52 | +1 Lap | 3 |
| 6 | 8 | Niki Lauda | McLaren-Ford | 51 | +2 Laps | 14 |
| 7 | 25 | J.P.Jarier | Ligier-Ford | 51 | +2 Laps | 20 |
| 8 | 1 | Keke Rosberg | Williams-Ford | 51 | +2 Laps | 15 |
| 9 | 7 | John Watson | McLaren-Ford | 51 | +2 Laps | 17 |
| 10 | 31 | Corrado Fabi | Osella-Alfa Romeo | 50 | +3 Laps | 26 |
| 11 | 32 | P.Ghinzani | Osella-Alfa Romeo | 49 | +4 Laps | 25 |
| 12 | 40 | Stefan Johansson | Spirit-Honda | 48 | +5 Laps | 16 |
| 13 | 30 | Thierry Boutsen | Arrows-Ford | 48 | +5 Laps | 19 |
| Ret | 9 | M.Winkelhock | ATS-BMW | 33 | Water leak | 13 |
| Ret | 22 | A.de Cesaris | Alfa Romeo | 31 | Out of fuel | 11 |
| Ret | 27 | Patrick Tambay | Ferrari | 30 | Ignition | 1 |
| Ret | 6 | Riccardo Patrese | Brabham-BMW | 29 | Engine | 6 |
| Ret | 33 | Roberto Guerrero | Theodore-Ford | 25 | Gearbox | 21 |
| Ret | 2 | Jacques Laffite | Williams-Ford | 21 | Vibrations | 24 |
| Ret | 23 | Mauro Baldi | Alfa Romeo | 13 | Oil leak | 9 |
| Ret | 3 | Michele Alboreto | Tyrrell-Ford | 8 | Collision | 18 |
| Ret | 35 | Derek Warwick | Toleman-Hart | 2 | Turbo | 10 |
| Ret | 36 | Bruno Giacomelli | Toleman-Hart | 1 | Radiator | 7 |
| Ret | 11 | Elio de Angelis | Lotus-Renault | 0 | Collision | 12 |
| Ret | 29 | Marc Surer | Arrows-Ford | 0 | Collision | 22 |
| Ret | 4 | Danny Sullivan | Tyrrell-Ford | 0 | Collision | 23 |
| DNQ | 26 | Raul Boesel | Ligier-Ford | | | |
| DNQ | 34 | Johnny Cecotto | Theodore-Ford | | | |
| DNQ | 17 | Kenny Acheson | RAM-Ford | | | |

Winning speed: 138.873mph
Lap leaders: Tambay 1-21; Arnoux 22-27, 38-47; Piquet 28-37; Prost 48-53
Pole position: Tambay, 1m 29.871s, 147.899mph
Fastest lap: Prost, 1m 33.961s, 141.462mph

## DUTCH GRAND PRIX: ZANDVOORT *28 August Round: 12 Race: 385 72 x 2.642 miles*

| POS. | NO. | DRIVER | CAR/ENGINE | LAPS | TIME/RETIRED | GRID |
|---|---|---|---|---|---|---|
| 1 | 28 | Rene Arnoux | Ferrari | 72 | 1:38'41.950 | 10 |
| 2 | 27 | Patrick Tambay | Ferrari | 72 | +20.839 | 2 |
| 3 | 7 | John Watson | McLaren-Ford | 72 | +43.741 | 15 |
| 4 | 35 | Derek Warwick | Toleman-Hart | 72 | +1'16.839 | 7 |
| 5 | 23 | Mauro Baldi | Alfa Romeo | 72 | +1'24.292 | 12 |
| 6 | 3 | Michele Alboreto | Tyrrell-Ford | 71 | +1 Lap | 18 |
| 7 | 40 | Stefan Johansson | Spirit-Honda | 70 | +2 Laps | 16 |
| 8 | 29 | Marc Surer | Arrows-Ford | 70 | +2 Laps | 14 |
| 9 | 6 | Riccardo Patrese | Brabham-BMW | 70 | +2 Laps | 6 |
| 10 | 26 | Raul Boesel | Ligier-Ford | 70 | +2 Laps | 24 |
| 11 | 31 | Corrado Fabi | Osella-Alfa Romeo | 68 | Engine | 25 |
| 12 | 33 | Roberto Guerrero | Theodore-Ford | 68 | +4 Laps | 20 |
| 13 | 36 | Bruno Giacomelli | Toleman-Hart | 68 | Spun off | 13 |
| 14 | 30 | Thierry Boutsen | Arrows/Ford | 65 | Engine | 21 |
| Ret | 1 | Keke Rosberg | Williams-Ford | 53 | Ignition | 23 |
| Ret | 9 | M.Winkelhock | ATS-BMW | 50 | Disqualified | 9 |
| Ret | 5 | Nelson Piquet | Brabham-BMW | 41 | Collision | 1 |
| Ret | 15 | Alain Prost | Renault | 41 | Spun off | 4 |
| Ret | 16 | Eddie Cheever | Renault | 39 | Electrical | 11 |
| Ret | 2 | Jacques Laffite | Williams/Ford | 37 | Handling | 17 |
| Ret | 12 | Nigel Mansell | Lotus-Renault | 26 | Spun off | 5 |
| Ret | 8 | Niki Lauda | McLaren-TAG | 25 | Brakes | 19 |
| Ret | 4 | Danny Sullivan | Tyrrell-Ford | 20 | Engine | 26 |
| Ret | 11 | Elio de Angelis | Lotus-Renault | 12 | Electrical | 3 |
| Ret | 22 | A.de Cesaris | Alfa Romeo | 5 | Engine | 8 |
| Ret | 25 | J.P.Jarier | Ligier/Ford | 3 | Suspension | 22 |
| DNQ | 32 | P.Ghinzani | Osella-Alfa Romeo | | | |
| DNQ | 34 | Johnny Cecotto | Theodore-Ford | | | |
| DNQ | 17 | Kenny Acheson | RAM-Ford | | | |

Winning speed: 115.642mph Lap leaders: Piquet 1-41; Arnoux 42-72
Pole position: Piquet, 1m 15.630s, 125.763mph
Fastest lap: Arnoux, 1m 19.863s, 119.097mph

## ITALIAN GRAND PRIX: MONZA *11 September Round: 13 Race: 386 52 x 3.604 miles*

| POS. | NO. | DRIVER | CAR/ENGINE | LAPS | TIME/RETIRED | GRID |
|---|---|---|---|---|---|---|
| 1 | 5 | Nelson Piquet | Brabham-BMW | 52 | 1:23'10.880 | 4 |
| 2 | 28 | Rene Arnoux | Ferrari | 52 | +10.212 | 3 |
| 3 | 16 | Eddie Cheever | Renault | 52 | +18.612 | 7 |
| 4 | 27 | Patrick Tambay | Ferrari | 52 | +29.023 | 2 |
| 5 | 11 | Elio de Angelis | Lotus-Renault | 52 | +53.680 | 8 |
| 6 | 35 | Derek Warwick | Toleman-Hart | 52 | +1'13.348 | 12 |
| 7 | 36 | Bruno Giacomelli | Toleman-Hart | 52 | +1'33.922 | 14 |
| 8 | 12 | Nigel Mansell | Lotus-Renault | 52 | +1'36.035 | 11 |
| 9 | 25 | J.P.Jarier | Ligier-Ford | 51 | +1 Lap | 19 |
| 10 | 29 | Marc Surer | Arrows-Ford | 51 | +1 Lap | 20 |
| 11 | 1 | Keke Rosberg | Williams-Ford | 51 | +1 Lap | 16 |
| 12 | 34 | Johnny Cecotto | Theodore-Ford | 50 | +2 Laps | 26 |
| 13 | 33 | Roberto Guerrero | Theodore-Ford | 50 | +2 Laps | 21 |
| Ret | 31 | Corrado Fabi | Osella-Alfa Romeo | 45 | Engine | 25 |
| Ret | 4 | Danny Sullivan | Tyrrell-Ford | 44 | Fuel pump | 22 |
| Ret | 30 | Thierry Boutsen | Arrows-Ford | 41 | Engine | 18 |
| Ret | 9 | M.Winkelhock | ATS-BMW | 35 | Exhaust | 9 |
| Ret | 3 | Michele Alboreto | Tyrrell-Ford | 28 | Clutch | 24 |
| Ret | 15 | Alain Prost | Renault | 26 | Turbo | 5 |
| Ret | 8 | Niki Lauda | McLaren-TAG | 24 | Electrical | 13 |
| Ret | 7 | John Watson | McLaren-TAG | 13 | Electrical | 15 |
| Ret | 32 | P.Ghinzani | Osella-Alfa Romeo | 10 | Gearbox | 23 |
| Ret | 23 | Mauro Baldi | Alfa Romeo | 4 | Turbo | 10 |
| Ret | 40 | Stefan Johansson | Spirit-Honda | 4 | Distributor | 17 |
| Ret | 6 | Riccardo Patrese | Brabham-BMW | 2 | Engine | 1 |
| Ret | 22 | A.de Cesaris | Alfa Romeo | 2 | Collision | 6 |
| DNQ | 26 | Raul Boesel | Ligier-Ford | | | |
| DNQ | 2 | Jacques Laffite | Williams-Ford | | | |
| DNQ | 17 | Kenny Acheson | RAM-Ford | | | |

Winning speed: 135.179 mph Lap leaders: Patrese 1-2; Piquet 3-52
Pole position: Patrese, 1m 29.122s, 145.578mph
Fastest lap: Piquet, 1m 34.431s, 137.394mph
Rosberg finished 9th, but penalised one minute for infringement at start.

## EUROPEAN GRAND PRIX: BRANDS HATCH *25 September Round: 14 Race: 387 76 x 2.614 miles*

| POS. | NO. | DRIVER | CAR/ENGINE | LAPS | TIME/RETIRED | GRID |
|---|---|---|---|---|---|---|
| 1 | 5 | Nelson Piquet | Brabham-BMW | 76 | 1:36'45.865 | 4 |
| 2 | 15 | Alain Prost | Renault | 76 | +6.571 | 8 |
| 3 | 12 | Nigel Mansell | Lotus-Renault | 76 | +30.315 | 3 |
| 4 | 22 | A.de Cesaris | Alfa Romeo | 76 | +34.396 | 14 |
| 5 | 35 | Derek Warwick | Toleman-Hart | 76 | +44.915 | 11 |
| 6 | 36 | Bruno Giacomelli | Toleman-Hart | 76 | +52.190 | 12 |
| 7 | 6 | Riccardo Patrese | Brabham-BMW | 76 | +1'12.684 | 2 |
| 8 | 9 | M.Winkelhock | ATS-BMW | 75 | +1 Lap | 9 |
| 9 | 28 | Rene Arnoux | Ferrari | 75 | +1 Lap | 5 |
| 10 | 16 | Eddie Cheever | Renault | 75 | +1 Lap | 7 |
| 11 | 30 | Thierry Boutsen | Arrows-Ford | 75 | +1 Lap | 18 |
| 12 | 33 | Roberto Guerrero | Theodore-Ford | 75 | +1 Lap | 21 |
| 13 | 42 | Jonathan Palmer | Williams-Ford | 74 | +2 Laps | 25 |
| 14 | 40 | Stefan Johansson | Spirit-Honda | 74 | +2 Laps | 19 |
| 15 | 26 | Raul Boesel | Ligier-Ford | 73 | +3 Laps | 23 |
| Ret | 27 | Patrick Tambay | Ferrari | 67 | Spun off | 6 |
| Ret | 3 | Michele Alboreto | Tyrrell-Ford | 64 | Engine | 26 |
| Ret | 32 | P.Ghinzani | Osella-Alfa Romeo | 63 | Throttle | 24 |
| Ret | 29 | Marc Surer | Arrows-Ford | 50 | Engine | 17 |
| Ret | 1 | Keke Rosberg | Williams-Ford | 43 | Engine | 16 |
| Ret | 23 | Mauro Baldi | Alfa Romeo | 39 | Clutch | 15 |
| Ret | 7 | John Watson | McLaren-TAG | 36 | Spun off | 10 |
| Ret | 4 | Danny Sullivan | Tyrrell-Ford | 27 | Oil leak | 20 |
| Ret | 8 | Niki Lauda | McLaren-TAG | 25 | Engine | 13 |
| Ret | 11 | Elio de Angelis | Lotus-Renault | 12 | Oil pump | 1 |
| Ret | 25 | J.P.Jarier | Ligier-Ford | 0 | Clutch | 22 |
| DNQ | 17 | Kenny Acheson | RAM-Ford | | | |
| DNQ | 31 | Corrado Fabi | Osella-Alfa Romeo | | | |
| DNQ | 2 | Jacques Laffite | Williams-Ford | | | |

Winning speed: 123.184mph Lap leaders: Patrese 1-10; Piquet 11-76
Pole position: de Angelis, 1m 12.092s, 130.533mph
Fastest lap: Mansell, 1m14.342s, 126.583mph

## SOUTH AFRICAN GRAND PRIX: KYALAMI *15 October Round: 15 Race: 388 77 x 2.550 miles*

| POS. | NO. | DRIVER | CAR/ENGINE | LAPS | TIME/RETIRED | GRID |
|---|---|---|---|---|---|---|
| 1 | 6 | Riccardo Patrese | Brabham-BMW | 77 | 1:33'25.708 | 3 |
| 2 | 22 | A.de Cesaris | Alfa Romeo | 77 | +9.319 | 9 |
| 3 | 5 | Nelson Piquet | Brabham-BMW | 77 | +21.969 | 2 |
| 4 | 35 | Derek Warwick | Toleman-Hart | 76 | +1 Lap | 13 |
| 5 | 1 | Keke Rosberg | Williams-Honda | 76 | +1 Lap | 6 |
| 6 | 16 | Eddie Cheever | Renault | 76 | +1 Lap | 14 |
| 7 | 4 | Danny Sullivan | Tyrrell-Ford | 75 | +2 Laps | 19 |
| 8 | 29 | Marc Surer | Arrows-Ford | 75 | +2 Laps | 22 |
| 9 | 30 | Thierry Boutsen | Arrows-Ford | 74 | +3 Laps | 20 |
| 10 | 25 | J.P.Jarier | Ligier-Ford | 73 | +4 Laps | 21 |
| 11 | 8 | Niki Lauda | McLaren-TAG | 71 | Electrical | 12 |
| 12 | 17 | Kenny Acheson | RAM-Ford | 71 | +6 Laps | 24 |
| NC | 12 | Nigel Mansell | Lotus-Renault | 68 | Not classified | 7 |
| NC | 26 | Raul Boesel | Ligier-Ford | 66 | Not classified | 23 |
| Ret | 3 | Michele Alboreto | Tyrrell-Ford | 60 | Engine | 18 |
| Ret | 27 | Patrick Tambay | Ferrari | 56 | Turbo | 1 |
| Ret | 36 | Bruno Giacomelli | Toleman-Hart | 56 | Turbo | 16 |
| Ret | 15 | Alain Prost | Renault | 35 | Turbo | 5 |
| Ret | 31 | Corrado Fabi | Osella-Alfa Romeo | 28 | Engine | 25 |
| Ret | 11 | Elio de Angelis | Lotus-Renault | 20 | Engine | 11 |
| DSQ | 7 | John Watson | McLaren-TAG | 18 | Disqualified | 15 |
| Ret | 28 | Rene Arnoux | Ferrari | 9 | Engine | 4 |
| Ret | 23 | Mauro Baldi | Alfa Romeo | 5 | Engine | 17 |
| Ret | 9 | M.Winkelhock | ATS-BMW | 1 | Engine | 8 |
| Ret | 2 | Jacques Laffite | Williams-Honda | 1 | Spun off | 10 |
| Ret | 32 | P.Ghinzani | Osella-Alfa Romeo | 1 | Engine | 26 |

Winning speed: 126.102mph Lap leaders: Piquet 1-59; Patrese 60-77
Pole position: Tambay, 1m 6.554s, 137.939mph
Fastest lap: Piquet, 1m 9.948s, 131.246mph

# 1984

## DRIVERS' CHAMPION: NIKI LAUDA
## CONSTRUCTORS' CHAMPION: McLAREN TAG PORSCHE

### DRIVERS' CHAMPIONSHIP

| POS. | DRIVER | NATIONALITY | CAR | POINTS |
|---|---|---|---|---|
| 1 | Niki Lauda | Austria | McLaren-TAG Porsche | 72 |
| 2 | Alain Prost | France | McLaren-TAG Porsche | 71.5 |
| 3 | Elio de Angelis | Italy | Lotus-Renault | 34 |
| 4 | Michele Alboreto | Italy | Ferrari | 30.5 |
| 5 | Nelson Piquet | Brazil | Brabham | 29 |
| 6 | René Arnoux | France | Ferrari | 27 |
| 7 | Derek Warwick | GB | Renault | 23 |
| 8 | Keke Rosberg | Finland | Williams-Honda | 20.5 |
| 9 | Ayrton Senna | Brazil | Toleman-Hart | 13 |
| = | Nigel Mansell | GB | Lotus-Renault | 13 |
| 11 | Patrick Tambay | France | Renault | 11 |
| 12 | Teo Fabi | Italy | Brabham-BMW | 9 |
| 13 | Riccardo Patrese | Italy | Alfa Romeo | 8 |
| 14 | Jacques Laffite | France | Williams-Honda | 5 |
| = | Thierry Boutsen | Belgium | Arrows-Ford, Arrows-BMW | 5 |
| 16 | Eddie Cheever | USA | Alfa Romeo | 3 |
| = | Stefan Johansson | Sweden | Tyrrell-Ford, Toleman-Hart | 3 |
| = | Andrea de Cesaris | Italy | Ligier-Renault | 3 |
| 19 | Piercarlo Ghinzani | Italy | Osella-Alfa Romeo | 2 |
| 20 | Marc Surer | Switzerland | Arrows-Ford, Arrows-BMW | 1 |
| | Jo Gartner | Austria | Osella-Alfa Romeo | |
| | Gerhard Berger | Austria | ATS-BMW | |
| | Martin Brundle | GB | Tyrrell-Ford | |
| | Jonathan Palmer | GB | RAM-Hart | |
| | Francois Hesnault | France | Ligier-Renault | |
| | Philippe Alliot | France | RAM-Hart | |
| | Johnny Cecotto | Venezuela | Toleman-Hart | |
| | Mauro Baldi | Italy | Spirit-Hart | |
| | Stefan Bellof | West Germany | Tyrrell-Ford | |
| | Manfred Winkelhock | West Germany | ATS-BMW, Brabham-BMW | |
| | Corrado Fabi | Italy | Brabham-BMW | |
| | Huub Rothengatter | Netherlands | Spirit-Hart, Spirit-Ford | |
| | Mike Thackwell | New Zealand | RAM-Hart, Tyrrell-Ford | |
| | Pierluigi Martini | Italy | Toleman-Hart | |
| | Philippe Streiff | France | Renault | |

Points for top six finishers (9, 6, 4, 3, 2, 1). Half points awarded for races stopped before half distance. Teams which entered only one car were ineligible for points for the second driver. This affected Osella and ATS in Monza. Points were not redistributed.

### CONSTRUCTORS' CHAMPIONSHIP

| POS. | CONSTRUCTOR | POINTS |
|---|---|---|
| 1 | McLaren-TAG | 143.5 |
| 2 | Ferrari | 57.5 |
| 3 | Lotus-Renault | 47 |
| 4 | Brabham-BMW | 38 |
| 5 | Renault | 34 |
| 6 | Williams-Honda | 25.5 |
| 7 | Toleman-Hart | 16 |
| 8 | Alfa Romeo | 11 |
| 9 | Arrows-Ford | 3 |
| 9 | Ligier-Renault | 3 |
| 9 | Arrows-BMW | 3 |
| 12 | Osella-Alfa Romeo | 2 |

Points for top six finishers (9, 6, 4, 3, 2, 1). Half points awarded for races stopped before half distance. Teams which entered only one car were ineligible for points for the second driver. This affected Osella and ATS in Monza. Points were not redistributed.

On 18 July, Tyrrell was disqualified from all the races so far that season, and banned from competing in remaining races, because the team had run illegal cars. They continued racing until 29th August, when the appeal was heard and rejected. The team would have scored points in Brazil (Brundle 5th), Belgium (Bellof 6th), San Marnio (Bellof 5th), Monaco (Bellof 3rd) and USA East (Brundle 2nd).

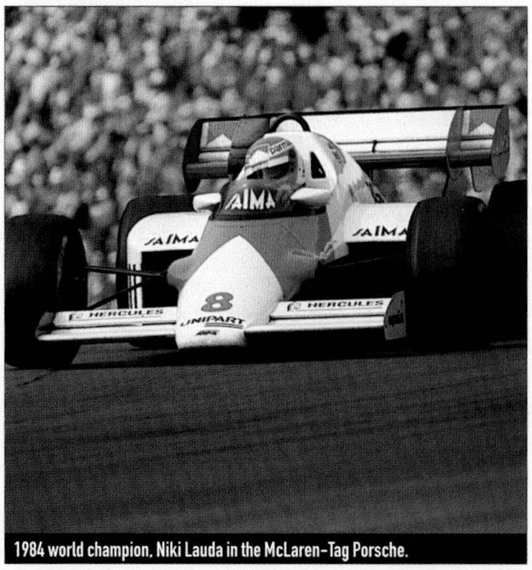

1984 world champion, Niki Lauda in the McLaren-Tag Porsche.

## BRAZILIAN GRAND PRIX: RIO DE JANEIRO *25 March Round: 1 Race: 389 61 x 3.126 miles*

| POS. | NO. | DRIVER | CAR/ENGINE | LAPS | TIME/RETIRED | GRID |
|---|---|---|---|---|---|---|
| 1 | 7 | Alain Prost | McLaren-TAG | 61 | 1:42'34.492 | 4 |
| 2 | 6 | Keke Rosberg | Williams-Honda | 61 | +40.514 | 9 |
| 3 | 11 | Elio de Angelis | Lotus/Renault | 61 | +59.128 | 1 |
| 4 | 23 | Eddie Cheever | Alfa Romeo | 60 | +1 Lap | 12 |
| 5 | 15 | Patrick Tambay | Renault | 59 | Out of fuel | 8 |
| 6 | 18 | Thierry Boutsen | Arrows-Ford | 59 | +2 Laps | 20 |
| 7 | 17 | Marc Surer | Arrows-Ford | 59 | +2 Laps | 24 |
| 8 | 10 | Jonathan Palmer | RAM-Hart | 58 | +3 Laps | 26 |
| DSQ | 3 | Martin Brundle | Tyrrell-Ford | 60 | Disqualified | 18 |
| Ret | 16 | Derek Warwick | Renault | 51 | Suspension | 3 |
| Ret | 26 | A.de Cesaris | Ligier-Renault | 42 | Gearbox | 14 |
| Ret | 22 | Riccardo Patrese | Alfa Romeo | 41 | Gearbox | 11 |
| Ret | 8 | Niki Lauda | McLaren-TAG | 38 | Electrical | 6 |
| Ret | 12 | Nigel Mansell | Lotus-Renault | 35 | Accident | 5 |
| Ret | 1 | Nelson Piquet | Brabham-BMW | 32 | Engine | 7 |
| Ret | 2 | Teo Fabi | Brabham-BMW | 32 | Turbo | 15 |
| Ret | 28 | Rene Arnoux | Ferrari | 30 | Battery | 10 |
| Ret | 24 | P.Ghinzani | Osella-Alfa Romeo | 28 | Gearbox | 21 |
| Ret | 25 | F.Hesnault | Ligier-Renault | 25 | Overheating | 19 |
| Ret | 9 | Philippe Alliot | RAM/Hart | 24 | Battery | 25 |
| Ret | 20 | Johnny Cecotto | Toleman-Hart | 18 | Turbo | 17 |
| Ret | 5 | Jacques Laffite | Williams-Honda | 15 | Electrical | 13 |
| Ret | 27 | Michele Alboreto | Ferrari | 14 | Brakes | 2 |
| Ret | 21 | Mauro Baldi | Spirit-Hart | 12 | Distributor | 23 |
| DSQ | 4 | Stefan Bellof | Tyrrell-Ford | 11 | Disqualified | 22 |
| Ret | 19 | Ayrton Senna | Toleman-Hart | 8 | Turbo | 16 |
| DSQ | 14 | M.Winkelhock | ATS-BMW | 0 | Disqualified | |

Winning speed: 111.544mph Lap leaders: Alboreto 1-11; Lauda 12-37; Prost 38,51-61; Warwick 39-50
Pole position: Angelis, 1m 28.392s, 127.320mph
Fastest lap: Prost, 1m 36.499s, 116.623mph

## SOUTH AFRICAN GRAND PRIX: KYALAMI *7 April Round: 2 Race: 390 75 x 2.550 miles*

| POS. | NO. | DRIVER | CAR/ENGINE | LAPS | TIME/RETIRED | GRID |
|---|---|---|---|---|---|---|
| 1 | 8 | Niki Lauda | McLaren-TAG | 75 | 1:29'23.430 | 8 |
| 2 | 7 | Alain Prost | McLaren-TAG | 75 | +1'05.950 | 5 |
| 3 | 16 | Derek Warwick | Renault | 74 | +1 Lap | 9 |
| 4 | 22 | Riccardo Patrese | Alfa Romeo | 73 | +2 Laps | 18 |
| 5 | 26 | A.de Cesaris | Ligier-Renault | 73 | +2 Laps | 14 |
| 6 | 19 | Ayrton Senna | Toleman-Hart | 72 | +3 Laps | 13 |
| 7 | 11 | Elio de Angelis | Lotus-Renault | 71 | +4 Laps | 7 |
| 8 | 21 | Mauro Baldi | Spirit/Hart | 71 | +4 Laps | 20 |
| 9 | 17 | Marc Surer | Arrows-Ford | 71 | +4 Laps | 23 |
| 10 | 25 | F.Hesnault | Ligier-Renault | 71 | +4 Laps | 17 |
| 11 | 27 | Michele Alboreto | Ferrari | 70 | Ignition | 10 |
| 12 | 18 | Thierry Boutsen | Arrows-Ford | 70 | +5 Laps | 26 |
| Ret | 3 | Martin Brundle | Tyrrell-Ford | 71 | Disqualified | 25 |
| Ret | 15 | Patrick Tambay | Renault | 66 | Out of fuel | 4 |
| Ret | 4 | Stefan Bellof | Tyrrell-Ford | 60 | Disqualified | 24 |
| Ret | 5 | Jacques Laffite | Williams-Honda | 60 | Transmission | 11 |
| Ret | 14 | M.Winkelhock | ATS-BMW | 53 | Engine | 12 |
| Ret | 6 | Keke Rosberg | Williams-Honda | 51 | Wheel | 2 |
| Ret | 12 | Nigel Mansell | Lotus-Renault | 51 | Turbo | 3 |
| Ret | 28 | Rene Arnoux | Ferrari | 40 | Injection | 15 |
| Ret | 1 | Nelson Piquet | Brabham-BMW | 29 | Turbo | 1 |
| Ret | 20 | Johnny Cecotto | Toleman-Hart | 26 | Tyre | 19 |
| Ret | 9 | Philippe Alliot | RAM-Hart | 24 | Engine | 22 |
| Ret | 10 | Jonathan Palmer | RAM-Hart | 22 | Gearbox | 21 |
| Ret | 2 | Teo Fabi | Brabham-BMW | 18 | Turbo | 6 |
| Ret | 23 | Eddie Cheever | Alfa Romeo | 4 | Radiator | 16 |
| Wth | 24 | P. Ghinzani | Osella-Alfa Romeo | 0 | Accident | 20 |

Winning speed: 128.375mph Lap leaders: Rosberg 1; Piquet 2-20; Lauda 21-75
Pole position: Piquet, 1m 4.871s, 141.518mph
Fastest lap: Tambay, 1m 8.877s, 133.287mph
Boutsen should have been placed 9th but a lap charting error cost him a lap. Protest by teams was too late to correct the error.

## BELGIAN GRAND PRIX: ZOLDER *29 April Round: 3 Race: 391 70 x 2.648 miles*

| POS. | NO. | DRIVER | CAR/ENGINE | LAPS | TIME/RETIRED | GRID |
|---|---|---|---|---|---|---|
| 1 | 27 | Michele Alboreto | Ferrari | 70 | 1:36'32.048 | 1 |
| 2 | 16 | Derek Warwick | Renault | 70 | +42.386 | 4 |
| 3 | 28 | Rene Arnoux | Ferrari | 70 | +1'09.803 | 2 |
| 4 | 6 | Keke Rosberg | Williams-Honda | 69 | Out of fuel | 3 |
| 5 | 11 | Elio de Angelis | Lotus-Renault | 69 | +1 Lap | 5 |
| 6 | 19 | Ayrton Senna | Toleman-Hart | 68 | +2 Laps | 19 |
| 7 | 15 | Patrick Tambay | Renault | 68 | +2 Laps | 12 |
| 8 | 17 | Marc Surer | Arrows-Ford | 68 | +2 Laps | 24 |
| 9 | 1 | Nelson Piquet | Brabham-BMW | 66 | Engine | 9 |
| 10 | 10 | Jonathan Palmer | RAM-Hart | 64 | +6 Laps | 26 |
| DSQ | 4 | Stefan Bellof | Tyrrell-Ford | 69 | Disqualified | 21 |
| Ret | 21 | Mauro Baldi | Spirit-Hart | 53 | Suspension | 25 |
| DSQ | 3 | Martin Brundle | Tyrrell-Ford | 51 | Disqualified | 22 |
| Ret | 26 | A.de Cesaris | Ligier-Renault | 42 | Accident | 13 |
| Ret | 2 | Teo Fabi | Brabham-BMW | 42 | Spun off | 18 |
| Ret | 14 | M.Winkelhock | ATS-BMW | 39 | Exhaust | 6 |
| Ret | 8 | Niki Lauda | McLaren-TAG | 35 | Water pump | 14 |
| Ret | 23 | Eddie Cheever | Alfa Romeo | 28 | Engine | 11 |
| Ret | 5 | Jacques Laffite | Williams-Honda | 15 | Electrical | 15 |
| Ret | 25 | F.Hesnault | Ligier-Renault | 15 | Radiator | 23 |
| Ret | 18 | Thierry Boutsen | Arrows-BMW | 15 | Engine | 17 |
| Ret | 24 | P.Ghinzani | Osella-Alfa Romeo | 14 | Transmission | 20 |
| Ret | 12 | Nigel Mansell | Lotus-Renault | 14 | Clutch | 10 |
| Ret | 7 | Alain Prost | McLaren-TAG | 5 | Distributor | 8 |
| Ret | 22 | Riccardo Patrese | Alfa Romeo | 2 | Ignition | 7 |
| Ret | 20 | Johnny Cecotto | Toleman-Hart | 1 | Clutch | 16 |
| DNQ | 9 | Philippe Alliot | RAM-Hart | | | |

Winning speed: 115.221mph Lap leaders: Alboreto 1-70
Pole position: Alboreto, 1m 14.846s, 127.379mph
Fastest lap: Arnoux, 1m 19.294s, 120.234mph

## SAN MARINO GRAND PRIX: IMOLA *6 May Round: 4 Race: 392 60 x 3.132 miles*

| POS. | NO. | DRIVER | CAR/ENGINE | LAPS | TIME/RETIRED | GRID |
|---|---|---|---|---|---|---|
| 1 | 7 | Alain Prost | McLaren-TAG | 60 | 1:36'53.679 | 2 |
| 2 | 28 | Rene Arnoux | Ferrari | 60 | +13.416 | 6 |
| 3 | 11 | Elio de Angelis | Lotus-Renault | 59 | Out of fuel | 11 |
| 4 | 16 | Derek Warwick | Renault | 59 | +1 Lap | 4 |
| 5 | 18 | Thierry Boutsen | Arrows-Ford | 59 | +1 Lap | 20 |
| 6 | 26 | A.de Cesaris | Ligier-Renault | 58 | Out of fuel | 12 |
| 7 | 23 | Eddie Cheever | Alfa Romeo | 58 | Out of fuel | 8 |
| 8 | 21 | Mauro Baldi | Spirit-Hart | 58 | +2 Laps | 24 |
| 9 | 10 | Jonathan Palmer | RAM-Hart | 57 | +3 Laps | 25 |
| DSQ | 4 | Stefan Bellof | Tyrrell-Ford | 59 | Disqualified | 21 |
| DSQ | 3 | Martin Brundle | Tyrrell-Ford | 55 | Disqualified | 22 |
| Ret | 9 | Philippe Alliot | RAM-Hart | 53 | Turbo | 23 |
| NC | 20 | Johnny Cecotto | Toleman-Hart | 52 | Not classified | 19 |
| Ret | 1 | Nelson Piquet | Brabham-BMW | 48 | Turbo | 1 |
| Ret | 2 | Teo Fabi | Brabham/BMW | 48 | Turbo | 9 |
| Ret | 30 | Jo Gartner | Osella-Alfa Romeo | 46 | Engine | 26 |
| Ret | 17 | Marc Surer | Arrows-BMW | 40 | Turbo | 16 |
| Ret | 14 | M.Winkelhock | ATS-BMW | 31 | Turbo | 7 |
| Ret | 27 | Michele Alboreto | Ferrari | 23 | Exhaust | 13 |
| Ret | 8 | Niki Lauda | McLaren-TAG | 15 | Engine | 5 |
| Ret | 5 | Jacques Laffite | Williams-Honda | 11 | Engine | 15 |
| Ret | 22 | Riccardo Patrese | Alfa Romeo | 6 | Electrical | 10 |
| Ret | 12 | Nigel Mansell | Lotus-Renault | 2 | Spun off | 18 |
| Ret | 6 | Keke Rosberg | Williams-Honda | 2 | Electrical | 3 |
| Ret | 15 | Patrick Tambay | Renault | 0 | Collision | 14 |
| Ret | 25 | F.Hesnault | Ligier-Renault | 0 | Collision | 17 |
| DNQ | 24 | P.Ghinzani | Osella-Alfa Romeo | | | |
| DNQ | 19 | Ayrton Senna | Toleman-Hart | | | |

Winning speed: 116.355mph Lap leaders: Prost 1-60
Pole position: Piquet, 1m 28.517s,127.367mph
Fastest lap: Piquet, 1m 33.275s, 120.870mph

## FRENCH GRAND PRIX: DIJON-PRENOIS *20 May Round: 5 Race: 393 79 x 2.415 miles*

| POS. | NO. | DRIVER | CAR/ENGINE | LAPS | TIME/RETIRED | GRID |
|---|---|---|---|---|---|---|
| 1 | 8 | Niki Lauda | McLaren-TAG | 79 | 1:31'11.951 | 9 |
| 2 | 15 | Patrick Tambay | Renault | 79 | +7.154 | 1 |
| 3 | 12 | Nigel Mansell | Lotus-Renault | 79 | +23.969 | 6 |
| 4 | 28 | Rene Arnoux | Ferrari | 79 | +43.706 | 11 |
| 5 | 11 | Elio de Angelis | Lotus-Renault | 79 | +1'06.125 | 2 |
| 6 | 6 | Keke Rosberg | Williams-Honda | 78 | +1 Lap | 4 |
| 7 | 7 | Alain Prost | McLaren-TAG | 78 | +1 Lap | 5 |
| 8 | 5 | Jacques Laffite | Williams-Honda | 78 | +1 Lap | 12 |
| 9 | 2 | Teo Fabi | Brabham-BMW | 78 | +1 Lap | 17 |
| 10 | 26 | A.de Cesaris | Ligier-Renault | 77 | +2 Laps | 26 |
| 11 | 18 | Thierry Boutsen | Arrows-BMW | 77 | +2 Laps | 14 |
| 12 | 24 | P.Ghinzani | Osella-Alfa Romeo | 74 | +5 Laps | 25 |
| 13 | 10 | Jonathan Palmer | RAM-Hart | 72 | +7 Laps | 21 |
| DSQ | 3 | Martin Brundle | Tyrrell-Ford | 76 | Disqualified | 23 |
| Ret | 21 | Mauro Baldi | Spirit-Hart | 61 | Engine | 24 |
| Ret | 16 | Derek Warwick | Renault | 53 | Accident | 7 |
| Ret | 17 | Marc Surer | Arrows-Ford | 51 | Accident | 19 |
| Ret | 23 | Eddie Cheever | Alfa Romeo | 51 | Engine | 16 |
| Ret | 19 | Ayrton Senna | Toleman-Hart | 35 | Turbo | 13 |
| Ret | 27 | Michele Alboreto | Ferrari | 33 | Engine | 10 |
| Ret | 20 | Johnny Cecotto | Toleman-Hart | 22 | Turbo | 18 |
| Ret | 22 | Riccardo Patrese | Alfa Romeo | 15 | Engine | 15 |
| Ret | 1 | Nelson Piquet | Brabham-BMW | 11 | Turbo | 3 |
| DSQ | 4 | Stefan Bellof | Tyrrell-Ford | 11 | Disqualified | 20 |
| Ret | 14 | M.Winkelhock | ATS-BMW | 5 | Clutch | 8 |
| Ret | 9 | Philippe Alliot | RAM-Hart | 4 | Electrical | 22 |

Winning speed: 125.532mph Lap leaders: Tambay 1-40, 54-62; Lauda 41-53, 63-79
Pole position: Tambay, 1m 2.200s, 139.791mph
Fastest lap: Prost, 1m 5.257s, 133.242mph

## MONACO GRAND PRIX: MONTE CARLO *3 June Round: 6 Race: 394 31 x 2.058 miles*

| POS. | NO. | DRIVER | CAR/ENGINE | LAPS | TIME/RETIRED | GRID |
|---|---|---|---|---|---|---|
| 1 | 7 | Alain Prost | McLaren-TAG | 31 | 1:01'07.740 | 1 |
| 2 | 19 | Ayrton Senna | Toleman-Hart | 31 | +7.446 | 13 |
| 3 | 28 | Rene Arnoux | Ferrari | 31 | +29.077 | 3 |
| 4 | 6 | Keke Rosberg | Williams-Honda | 31 | +35.246 | 10 |
| 5 | 11 | Elio de Angelis | Lotus-Renault | 31 | +44.439 | 11 |
| 6 | 27 | Michele Alboreto | Ferrari | 30 | +1 Lap | 4 |
| 7 | 24 | P.Ghinzani | Osella-Alfa Romeo | 30 | +1 Lap | 19 |
| 8 | 5 | Jacques Laffite | Williams-Honda | 30 | +1 Lap | 16 |
| DSQ | 4 | Stefan Bellof | Tyrrell-Ford | 31 | Disqualified | 20 |
| Ret | 22 | Riccardo Patrese | Alfa Romeo | 24 | Steering | 14 |
| Ret | 8 | Niki Lauda | McLaren-TAG | 23 | Spun off | 8 |
| Ret | 14 | M.Winkelhock | ATS-BMW | 22 | Spun off | 12 |
| Ret | 12 | Nigel Mansell | Lotus-Renault | 15 | Spun off | 2 |
| Ret | 1 | Nelson Piquet | Brabham-BMW | 14 | Electrical | 9 |
| Ret | 25 | F.Hesnault | Ligier-Renault | 12 | Electrical | 17 |
| Ret | 2 | Corrado Fabi | Brabham-BMW | 9 | Electrical | 15 |
| Ret | 20 | Johnny Cecotto | Toleman-Hart | 1 | Spun off | 18 |
| Ret | 16 | Derek Warwick | Renault | 0 | Collision | 5 |
| Ret | 15 | Patrick Tambay | Renault | 0 | Collision | 6 |
| Ret | 26 | A.de Cesaris | Ligier-Renault | 0 | Accident | 7 |
| DNQ | 17 | Marc Surer | Arrows-Ford | | | |
| DNQ | 3 | Martin Brundle | Tyrrell-Ford | | | |
| DNQ | 23 | Eddie Cheever | Alfa Romeo | | | |
| DNQ | 18 | Thierry Boutsen | Arrows-BMW | | | |
| DNQ | 10 | Jonathan Palmer | RAM-Hart | | | |
| DNQ | 21 | Mauro Baldi | Spirit-Hart | | | |
| DNQ | 9 | Philippe Alliot | RAM-Hart | | | |

Winning speed: 62.619mph Lap leaders: Prost 1-10, 16-31; Mansell 11-15
Pole position: Prost, 1m 22.661s, 89.628mph
Fastest lap: Senna, 1m 54.334s, 64.799mph
Race stopped before the scheduled 77 laps because of rain.

## CANADIAN GRAND PRIX: MONTREAL *17 June Round:7 Race:395 70 x 2.740miles*

| POS. | NO. | DRIVER | CAR/ENGINE | LAPS | TIME/RETIRED | GRID |
|---|---|---|---|---|---|---|
| 1 | 1 | Nelson Piquet | Brabham-BMW | 70 | 1:46'23.748 | 1 |
| 2 | 8 | Niki Lauda | McLaren-TAG | 70 | +2.612 | 8 |
| 3 | 7 | Alain Prost | McLaren-TAG | 70 | +1'28.032 | 2 |
| 4 | 11 | Elio de Angelis | Lotus-Renault | 69 | +1 Lap | 3 |
| 5 | 28 | Rene Arnoux | Ferrari | 68 | +2 Laps | 5 |
| 6 | 12 | Nigel Mansell | Lotus-Renault | 68 | +2 Laps | 7 |
| 7 | 19 | Ayrton Senna | Toleman-Hart | 68 | +2 Laps | 9 |
| 8 | 14 | M.Winkelhock | ATS-BMW | 68 | +2 Laps | 12 |
| 9 | 20 | Johnny Cecotto | Toleman-Hart | 68 | +2 Laps | 20 |
| 10 | 9 | Philippe Alliot | RAM-Hart | 65 | +5 Laps | 26 |
| 11 | 23 | Eddie Cheever | Alfa Romeo | 63 | Out of fuel | 11 |
| DSQ | 3 | Martin Brundle | Tyrrell-Ford | 68 | Disqualified | 21 |
| Ret | 17 | Marc Surer | Arrows-Ford | 59 | Engine | 23 |
| Ret | 16 | Derek Warwick | Renault | 57 | Chassis | 4 |
| NC | 21 | H.Rothengatter | Spirit-Hart | 56 | Not classified | 24 |
| DSQ | 4 | Stefan Bellof | Tyrrell-Ford | 52 | Disqualified | 22 |
| Ret | 26 | A.de Cesaris | Ligier-Renault | 40 | Brakes | 10 |
| Ret | 2 | Corrado Fabi | Brabham-BMW | 39 | Turbo | 16 |
| Ret | 18 | Thierry Boutsen | Arrows-BMW | 38 | Engine | 18 |
| Ret | 22 | Riccardo Patrese | Alfa Romeo | 37 | Accident | 14 |
| Ret | 6 | Keke Rosberg | Williams-Honda | 32 | Fuel system | 15 |
| Ret | 5 | Jacques Laffite | Williams-Honda | 31 | Turbo | 17 |
| Ret | 10 | Mike Thackwell | RAM-Hart | 29 | Turbo | 25 |
| Ret | 24 | P.Ghinzani | Osella-Alfa Romeo | 11 | Gearbox | 19 |
| Ret | 27 | Michele Alboreto | Ferrari | 10 | Engine | 6 |
| Ret | 25 | F.Hesnault | Ligier-Renault | 7 | Turbo | 13 |

Winning speed: 108.172mph Lap leaders: Piquet 1-70
Pole position: Piquet, 1m25.442s, 115.457mph
Fastest lap: Piquet, 1m 28.763s, 111.137mph

## USA EAST GRAND PRIX: DETROIT *24 June 1984 Round:8 Race:396 63 x 2.500miles*

| POS. | NO. | DRIVER | CAR/ENGINE | LAPS | TIME/RETIRED | GRID |
|---|---|---|---|---|---|---|
| 1 | 1 | Nelson Piquet | Brabham-BMW | 63 | 1:55'41.842 | 1 |
| 2 | 11 | Elio de Angelis | Lotus-Renault | 63 | +32.638 | 5 |
| 3 | 2 | Teo Fabi | Brabham-BMW | 63 | +1'26.528 | 23 |
| 4 | 7 | Alain Prost | McLaren/TAG | 63 | +1'55.258 | 2 |
| 5 | 5 | Jacques Laffite | Williams-Honda | 62 | +1 Lap | 19 |
| DSQ | 3 | Martin Brundle | Tyrrell-Ford | 63 | Disqualified | 11 |
| Ret | 27 | Michele Alboreto | Ferrari | 49 | Engine | 4 |
| Ret | 6 | Keke Rosberg | Williams-Honda | 47 | Turbo | 21 |
| Ret | 16 | Derek Warwick | Renault | 40 | Gearbox | 6 |
| DSQ | 4 | Stefan Bellof | Tyrrell-Ford | 33 | Accident | 16 |
| Ret | 15 | Patrick Tambay | Renault | 33 | Transmission | 9 |
| Ret | 9 | Philippe Alliot | RAM-Hart | 33 | Brakes | 20 |
| Ret | 8 | Niki Lauda | McLaren-TAG | 33 | Electrical | 10 |
| Ret | 12 | Nigel Mansell | Lotus-Renault | 27 | Gearbox | 3 |
| Ret | 18 | Thierry Boutsen | Arrows-BMW | 27 | Engine | 13 |
| Ret | 26 | A.de Cesaris | Ligier-Renault | 24 | Overheating | 12 |
| Ret | 20 | Johnny Cecotto | Toleman-Hart | 23 | Clutch | 17 |
| Ret | 23 | Eddie Cheever | Alfa Romeo | 21 | Engine | 8 |
| Ret | 19 | Ayrton Senna | Toleman-Hart | 21 | Accident | 7 |
| Ret | 22 | Riccardo Patrese | Alfa Romeo | 20 | Spun off | 25 |
| Ret | 25 | F.Hesnault | Ligier-Renault | 3 | Accident | 18 |
| Ret | 24 | P.Ghinzani | Osella-Alfa Romeo | 3 | Accident | 26 |
| Ret | 28 | Rene Arnoux | Ferrari | 2 | Accident | 15 |
| Ret | 10 | Jonathan Palmer | RAM/Hart | 2 | Tyre | 24 |
| Ret | 14 | M.Winkelhock | ATS-BMW | 0 | Engine | 14 |
| Ret | 17 | Marc Surer | Arrows-Ford | 0 | Accident | 22 |
| DNQ | 21 | H.Rothengatter | Spirit-Ford | | | |

Winning speed: 81.679mph Lap leaders: Piquet 1-63
Pole position: Piquet, 1m 40.980s, 89.127mph
Fastest lap: Warwick 1m 46.221s, 84.729mph
Stopped after forst lap accident. Restarted for total original distance.

## UBITED STATES GRAND PRIX: DALLAS *8 July Round:9 Race:397 67 x 2.424miles*

| POS. | NO. | DRIVER | CAR/ENGINE | LAPS | TIME/RETIRED | GRID |
|---|---|---|---|---|---|---|
| 1 | 6 | Keke Rosberg | Williams-Honda | 67 | 2:01'22.617 | 8 |
| 2 | 28 | Rene Arnoux | Ferrari | 67 | +22.464 | 4 |
| 3 | 11 | Elio de Angelis | Lotus-Renault | 66 | +1 Lap | 2 |
| 4 | 5 | Jacques Laffite | Williams-Honda | 65 | +2 Laps | 24 |
| 5 | 24 | P.Ghinzani | Osella-Alfa Romeo | 65 | +2 Laps | 18 |
| 6 | 12 | Nigel Mansell | Lotus-Renault | 64 | Gearbox | 1 |
| 7 | 2 | Corrado Fabi | Brabham-BMW | 64 | +3 Laps | 11 |
| 8 | 14 | M.Winkelhock | ATS-BMW | 64 | +3 Laps | 13 |
| Ret | 8 | Niki Lauda | McLaren-TAG | 60 | Spun off | 5 |
| Ret | 7 | Alain Prost | McLaren-TAG | 56 | Spun off | 7 |
| Ret | 18 | Thierry Boutsen | Arrows-BMW | 55 | Spun off | 20 |
| Ret | 27 | Michele Alboreto | Ferrari | 54 | Spun off | 9 |
| Ret | 17 | Marc Surer | Arrows-BMW | 54 | Spun off | 22 |
| Ret | 19 | Ayrton Senna | Toleman-Hart | 47 | Clutch | 6 |
| Ret | 10 | Jonathan Palmer | RAM-Hart | 46 | Electrical | 25 |
| Ret | 1 | Nelson Piquet | Brabham-BMW | 45 | Spun off | 12 |
| Ret | 15 | Patrick Tambay | Renault | 25 | Spun off | 10 |
| Ret | 20 | Johnny Cecotto | Toleman-Hart | 25 | Spun off | 15 |
| Ret | 26 | A.de Cesaris | Ligier-Renault | 15 | Spun off | 16 |
| Ret | 21 | H.Rothengatter | Spirit-Hart | 15 | Fuel leak | 23 |
| Ret | 22 | Riccardo Patrese | Alfa Romeo | 12 | Spun off | 21 |
| Ret | 16 | Derek Warwick | Renault | 10 | Spun off | 3 |
| Ret | 4 | Stefan Bellof | Tyrrell-Ford | 9 | Disqualified | 17 |
| Ret | 23 | Eddie Cheever | Alfa Romeo | 8 | Spun off | 14 |
| Ret | 25 | F.Hesnault | Ligier-Renault | 0 | Accident | 19 |
| DNQ | 3 | Martin Brundle | Tyrrell-Ford | | | |

Winning speed: 80.283mph Lap leaders: Mansell 1-35; Rosberg 36-48, 57-67; Prost 49-56
Pole position: Mansell, 1m 37.041s, 89.925mph
Fastest lap: Lauda, 1m 45.353s, 82.380mph

Scheduled for 78 laps, but stopped at 2 hours.

## BRITISH GRAND PRIX: BRANDS HATCH *22 July Round:10 Race: 398 71 x 2.614miles*

| POS. | NO. | DRIVER | CAR/ENGINE | LAPS | TIME/RETIRED | GRID |
|---|---|---|---|---|---|---|
| 1 | 8 | Niki Lauda | McLaren-TAG | 71 | 1:29'28.532 | 3 |
| 2 | 16 | Derek Warwick | Renault | 71 | +42.123 | 6 |
| 3 | 19 | Ayrton Senna | Toleman-Hart | 71 | +1'03.328 | 7 |
| 4 | 11 | Elio de Angelis | Lotus-Renault | 70 | +1 Lap | 4 |
| 5 | 27 | Michele Alboreto | Ferrari | 70 | +1 Lap | 9 |
| 6 | 28 | Rene Arnoux | Ferrari | 70 | +1 Lap | 13 |
| 7 | 1 | Nelson Piquet | Brabham-BMW | 70 | +1 Lap | 1 |
| 8 | 15 | Patrick Tambay | Renault | 69 | Turbo | 10 |
| 9 | 24 | P.Ghinzani | Osella-Alfa Romeo | 68 | +3 Laps | 21 |
| 10 | 26 | A.de Cesaris | Ligier-Renault | 68 | +3 Laps | 19 |
| 11 | 17 | Marc Surer | Arrows-BMW | 67 | +4 Laps | 15 |
| 12 | 22 | Riccardo Patrese | Alfa Romeo | 66 | +5 Laps | 17 |
| DSQ | 4 | Stefan Bellof | Tyrrell-Ford | 68 | Disqualified | 26 |
| NC | 21 | H.Rothengatter | Spirit-Hart | 62 | Not classified | 22 |
| Ret | 25 | F.Hesnault | Ligier-Renault | 43 | Electrical | 20 |
| Ret | 7 | Alain Prost | McLaren-TAG | 37 | Gearbox | 2 |
| Ret | 12 | Nigel Mansell | Lotus-Renault | 24 | Gearbox | 8 |
| Ret | 18 | Thierry Boutsen | Arrows-BMW | 24 | Electrical | 12 |
| Ret | 5 | Jacques Laffite | Williams-Honda | 14 | Water pump | 16 |
| Ret | 10 | Jonathan Palmer | RAM-Hart | 10 | Accident | 23 |
| Ret | 2 | Teo Fabi | Brabham-BMW | 9 | Electrical | 14 |
| Ret | 14 | M.Winkelhock | ATS-BMW | 8 | Spun off | 11 |
| Ret | 6 | Keke Rosberg | Williams-Honda | 5 | Engine | 5 |
| DSQ | 3 | Stefan Johansson | Tyrrell-Ford | 1 | Disqualified | 25 |
| Ret | 23 | Eddie Cheever | Alfa Romeo | 0 | Accident | 18 |
| Ret | 9 | Philippe Alliot | RAM-Hart | 0 | Accident | 24 |
| Ret | 30 | Jo Gartner | Osella-Alfa Romeo | 0 | Accident | 27 |
| DNQ | 20 | Johnny Cecotto | Toleman-Hart | | | |

Winning speed: 124.455mph Lap leaders: Piquet 1-11; Prost 12-37; Lauda 38-71
Pole position: Piquet 1m 10.869s, 132.786mph
Fastest lap: Lauda, 1m 13.191s, 128.573mph
Stopped after accident on lap 11. Race restarted for 60 laps, rather than remaining 64 laps.

## GERMAN GRAND PRIX: HOCKENHEIM *5 August Round:11 Race:399 44 x 4.223miles*

| POS. | NO. | DRIVER | CAR/ENGINE | LAPS | TIME/RETIRED | GRID |
|---|---|---|---|---|---|---|
| 1 | 7 | Alain Prost | McLaren-TAG | 44 | 1:24'43.210 | 1 |
| 2 | 8 | Niki Lauda | McLaren-TAG | 44 | +3.149 | 7 |
| 3 | 16 | Derek Warwick | Renault | 44 | +36.423 | 3 |
| 4 | 12 | Nigel Mansell | Lotus-Renault | 44 | +51.663 | 16 |
| 5 | 15 | Patrick Tambay | Renault | 44 | +1'11.949 | 4 |
| 6 | 28 | Rene Arnoux | Ferrari | 43 | +1 Lap | 10 |
| 7 | 26 | A.de Cesaris | Ligier-Renault | 43 | +1 Lap | 11 |
| 8 | 25 | F.Hesnault | Ligier-Renault | 43 | +1 Lap | 17 |
| 9 | 21 | H.Rothengatter | Spirit-Hart | 40 | +4 Laps | 24 |
| DSQ | 3 | Stefan Johansson | Tyrrell-Ford | 42 | Disqualified | 26 |
| Ret | 14 | M.Winkelhock | ATS-BMW | 31 | Gearbox | 13 |
| Ret | 23 | Eddie Cheever | Alfa Romeo | 29 | Engine | 18 |
| Ret | 2 | Teo Fabi | Brabham-BMW | 28 | Turbo | 8 |
| Ret | 1 | Nelson Piquet | Brabham-BMW | 23 | Gearbox | 5 |
| Ret | 22 | Riccardo Patrese | Alfa Romeo | 16 | Fuel system | 20 |
| Ret | 24 | P.Ghinzani | Osella-Alfa Romeo | 14 | Electrical | 21 |
| Ret | 30 | Jo Gartner | Osella-Alfa Romeo | 13 | Turbo | 23 |
| Ret | 27 | Michele Alboreto | Ferrari | 13 | Engine | 6 |
| Ret | 10 | Jonathan Palmer | RAM-Hart | 11 | Turbo | 25 |
| Ret | 6 | Keke Rosberg | Williams-Honda | 10 | Electrical | 19 |
| Ret | 5 | Jacques Laffite | Williams-Honda | 10 | Engine | 12 |
| Ret | 18 | Thierry Boutsen | Arrows-BMW | 8 | Engine | 15 |
| Ret | 11 | Elio de Angelis | Lotus-Renault | 8 | Turbo | 2 |
| Ret | 9 | Philippe Alliot | RAM-Hart | 7 | Overheating | 22 |
| Ret | 19 | Ayrton Senna | Toleman-Hart | 4 | Accident | 9 |
| Ret | 17 | Marc Surer | Arrows-BMW | 1 | Turbo | 14 |
| DNQ | 4 | Mike Thackwell | Tyrrell-Ford | | | |

Winning speed: 131.609 mph Lap leaders: de Angelis 1-7; Piquet 8-21; Prost 22-44
Pole position: Prost, 1m 47.012s, 142.082mph
Fastest lap: Prost, 1m 53.538s, 133.915mph

## AUSTRIAN GRAND PRIX: OSTERREICHRING *19 August Round:12 Race:400 51 x 3.692miles*

| POS. | NO. | DRIVER | CAR/ENGINE | LAPS | TIME/RETIRED | GRID |
|---|---|---|---|---|---|---|
| 1 | 8 | Niki Lauda | McLaren-TAG | 51 | 1:21'12.851 | 4 |
| 2 | 1 | Nelson Piquet | Brabham-BMW | 51 | +23.525 | 1 |
| 3 | 27 | Michele Alboreto | Ferrari | 51 | +48.998 | 12 |
| 4 | 2 | Teo Fabi | Brabham-BMW | 51 | +56.312 | 7 |
| 5 | 18 | Thierry Boutsen | Arrows-BMW | 50 | +1 Lap | 17 |
| 6 | 17 | Marc Surer | Arrows-BMW | 50 | +1 Lap | 19 |
| 7 | 28 | Rene Arnoux | Ferrari | 50 | +1 Lap | 15 |
| 8 | 25 | F.Hesnault | Ligier-Renault | 49 | +2 Laps | 21 |
| 9 | 10 | Jonathan Palmer | RAM-Hart | 49 | +2 Laps | 24 |
| 10 | 22 | Riccardo Patrese | Alfa Romeo | 48 | Out of fuel | 13 |
| 11 | 9 | Philippe Alliot | RAM-Hart | 48 | +3 Laps | 25 |
| 12 | 31 | Gerhard Berger | ATS-BMW | 48 | Gearbox | 20 |
| Ret | 15 | Patrick Tambay | Renault | 42 | Engine | 5 |
| Ret | 19 | Ayrton Senna | Toleman-Hart | 35 | Oil pressure | 10 |
| Ret | 12 | Nigel Mansell | Lotus-Renault | 32 | Engine | 8 |
| Ret | 7 | Alain Prost | McLaren-TAG | 28 | Spun off | 2 |
| Ret | 11 | Elio de Angelis | Lotus-Renault | 28 | Engine | 3 |
| NC | 21 | H.Rothengatter | Spirit-Hart | 23 | Not classified | 26 |
| Ret | 23 | Eddie Cheever | Alfa Romeo | 18 | Engine | 16 |
| Ret | 16 | Derek Warwick | Renault | 17 | Engine | 6 |
| Ret | 26 | A.de Cesaris | Ligier-Renault | 15 | Injection | 18 |
| Ret | 6 | Keke Rosberg | Williams-Honda | 15 | Handling | 9 |
| Ret | 5 | Jacques Laffite | Williams-Honda | 12 | Engine | 11 |
| Ret | 30 | Jo Gartner | Osella-Alfa Romeo | 6 | Engine | 22 |
| Ret | 24 | P.Ghinzani | Osella-Alfa Romeo | 4 | Gearbox | 23 |
| DSQ | 4 | Stefan Bellof | Tyrrell-Ford | 0 | Disqualified | |
| DNQ | 3 | Stefan Johansson | Tyrrell-Ford | | | |

Winning speed: 139.115mph Lap leaders: Piquet 1-39; Lauda 40-51
Pole position: Piquet, 1m 26.173s, 154.246mph
Fastest lap: Lauda, 1m 32.882s, 143.105mph
Race stopped on first lap and restarted for total original distance.

## DUTCH GRAND PRIX: ZANDVOORT 26 August Round:13 Race:401 71 x 2.642miles

| POS. | NO. | DRIVER | CAR/ENGINE | LAPS | TIME/RETIRED | GRID |
|---|---|---|---|---|---|---|
| 1 | 1 | Alain Prost | McLaren-TAG | 71 | 1:37'21.468 | 1 |
| 2 | 8 | Niki Lauda | McLaren-TAG | 71 | +10.283 | 6 |
| 3 | 12 | Nigel Mansell | Lotus-Renault | 71 | +1'19.544 | 12 |
| 4 | 11 | Elio de Angelis | Lotus-Renault | 70 | +1 Lap | 3 |
| 5 | 2 | Teo Fabi | Brabham-BMW | 70 | +1 Lap | 10 |
| 6 | 15 | Patrick Tambay | Renault | 70 | +1 Lap | 5 |
| 7 | 25 | F.Hesnault | Ligier-Renault | 69 | +2 Laps | 20 |
| 8 | 6 | Keke Rosberg | Williams-Honda | 68 | Out of fuel | 7 |
| 9 | 10 | Jonathan Palmer | RAM-Hart | 67 | +4 Laps | 22 |
| 10 | 9 | Philippe Alliot | RAM-Hart | 67 | +4 Laps | 26 |
| 11 | 28 | Rene Arnoux | Ferrari | 66 | Electrical | 15 |
| 12 | 30 | Jo Gartner | Osella-Alfa Romeo | 66 | +5 Laps | 23 |
| 13 | 23 | Eddie Cheever | Alfa Romeo | 65 | Out of fuel | 17 |
| DSQ | 4 | Stefan Bellof | Tyrrell/Ford | 69 | Disqualified | 24 |
| DSQ | 3 | Stefan Johansson | Tyrrell-Ford | 69 | Disqualified | 25 |
| Ret | 18 | Thierry Boutsen | Arrows-BMW | 59 | Accident | 11 |
| Ret | 21 | H.Rothengatter | Spirit-Hart | 53 | Throttle | 27 |
| Ret | 22 | Riccardo Patrese | Alfa Romeo | 51 | Engine | 18 |
| Ret | 26 | A.de Cesaris | Ligier-Renault | 31 | Engine | 14 |
| Ret | 5 | Jacques Laffite | Williams-Honda | 23 | Engine | 8 |
| Ret | 16 | Derek Warwick | Renault | 23 | Spun off | 4 |
| Ret | 14 | M.Winkelhock | ATS-BMW | 22 | Spun off | 16 |
| Ret | 19 | Ayrton Senna | Toleman-Hart | 19 | Engine | 13 |
| Ret | 17 | Marc Surer | Arrows-BMW | 17 | Wheel | 19 |
| Ret | 1 | Nelson Piquet | Brabham-BMW | 10 | Oil pressure | 2 |
| Ret | 24 | P.Ghinzani | Osella-Alfa Romeo | 8 | Fuel pump | 21 |
| Ret | 27 | Michele Alboreto | Ferrari | 7 | Engine | 9 |

Winning speed: 115.607mph  Lap leaders: Piquet 1-10; Prost 11-71
Pole position: Prost 1m 13.567s, 129.290mph
Fastest lap: Arnoux, 1m 19.465s, 119.694mph

## ITALIAN GRAND PRIX: MONZA 9 September Round:14 Race:402 51 x 3.604miles

| POS. | NO. | DRIVER | CAR/ENGINE | LAPS | TIME/RETIRED | GRID |
|---|---|---|---|---|---|---|
| 1 | 8 | Niki Lauda | McLaren-TAG | 51 | 1:20'29.065 | 4 |
| 2 | 27 | Michele Alboreto | Ferrari | 51 | +24.249 | 1 |
| 3 | 22 | Riccardo Patrese | Alfa Romeo | 50 | +1 Lap | 9 |
| 4 | 19 | Stefan Johansson | Toleman-Hart | 49 | +2 Laps | 17 |
| 5 | 30 | Jo Gartner | Osella-Alfa Romeo | 49 | +2 Laps | 24 |
| 6 | 31 | Gerhard Berger | ATS-BMW | 49 | +2 Laps | 20 |
| 7 | 24 | P.Ghinzani | Osella-Alfa Romeo | 48 | Out of fuel | 22 |
| 8 | 21 | H.Rothengatter | Spirit-Hart | 48 | +3 Laps | 25 |
| 9 | 23 | Eddie Cheever | Alfa Romeo | 45 | Out of fuel | 10 |
| 10 | 18 | Thierry Boutsen | Arrows-BMW | 45 | +6 Laps | 19 |
| Ret | 15 | Patrick Tambay | Renault | 43 | Throttle | 8 |
| Ret | 2 | Teo Fabi | Brabham-BMW | 43 | Engine | 5 |
| Ret | 17 | Marc Surer | Arrows-BMW | 43 | Engine | 15 |
| Ret | 16 | Derek Warwick | Renault | 31 | Oil pressure | 12 |
| Ret | 10 | Jonathan Palmer | RAM-Hart | 20 | Oil pressure | 26 |
| Ret | 1 | Nelson Piquet | Brabham-BMW | 15 | Engine | 1 |
| Ret | 11 | Elio de Angelis | Lotus-Renault | 14 | Gearbox | 3 |
| Ret | 12 | Nigel Mansell | Lotus-Renault | 13 | Spun off | 7 |
| Ret | 5 | Jacques Laffite | Williams-Honda | 10 | Turbo | 13 |
| Ret | 6 | Keke Rosberg | Williams-Honda | 8 | Turbo | 6 |
| Ret | 26 | A.de Cesaris | Ligier-Renault | 7 | Engine | 16 |
| Ret | 25 | F.Hesnault | Ligier-Renault | 7 | Spun off | 18 |
| Ret | 9 | Philippe Alliot | RAM-Hart | 6 | Electrical | 23 |
| Ret | 28 | Rene Arnoux | Ferrari | 5 | Gearbox | 14 |
| Ret | 7 | Alain Prost | McLaren-TAG | 3 | Engine | 2 |
| DNS | 14 | M.Winkelhock | ATS-BMW | 0 | Not started | 21 |
| DNQ | 20 | P.Martini | Toleman-Hart | | | |

Winning speed: 137.022mph  Lap leaders: Piquet 1-15; Tambay 16-42; Lauda 43-51
Pole position: Piquet, 1m 26.584s, 149.846mph
Fastest lap: Lauda, 1m 31.912s, 141.159mph

## EUROPEAN GRAND PRIX: NURBURGRING 7 October Round:15 Race:403 67 x 2.822miles

| POS. | NO. | DRIVER | CAR/ENGINE | LAPS | TIME/RETIRED | GRID |
|---|---|---|---|---|---|---|
| 1 | 7 | Alain Prost | McLaren-TAG | 67 | 1:35'13.284 | 2 |
| 2 | 27 | Michele Alboreto | Ferrari | 67 | +23.911 | 5 |
| 3 | 1 | Nelson Piquet | Brabham-BMW | 67 | +24.922 | 1 |
| 4 | 8 | Niki Lauda | McLaren-TAG | 67 | +43.086 | 15 |
| 5 | 28 | Rene Arnoux | Ferrari | 67 | +1'01.430 | 6 |
| 6 | 22 | Riccardo Patrese | Alfa Romeo | 66 | +1 Lap | 9 |
| 7 | 26 | A.de Cesaris | Ligier-Renault | 65 | +2 Laps | 17 |
| 8 | 21 | Mauro Baldi | Spirit-Hart | 65 | +2 Laps | 24 |
| 9 | 18 | Thierry Boutsen | Arrows-BMW | 64 | Ignition | 11 |
| 10 | 25 | F.Hesnault | Ligier-Renault | 64 | +3 Laps | 19 |
| 11 | 16 | Derek Warwick | Renault | 61 | Overheating | 7 |
| Ret | 30 | Jo Gartner | Osella-Alfa Romeo | 60 | Fuel system | 22 |
| Ret | 2 | Teo Fabi | Brabham-BMW | 57 | Gearbox | 10 |
| Ret | 12 | Nigel Mansell | Lotus-Renault | 51 | Engine | 8 |
| Ret | 15 | Patrick Tambay | Renault | 47 | Fuel system | 3 |
| Ret | 23 | Eddie Cheever | Alfa Romeo | 37 | Fuel pump | 13 |
| Ret | 9 | Philippe Alliot | RAM-Hart | 37 | Turbo | 25 |
| Ret | 10 | Jonathan Palmer | RAM-Hart | 35 | Turbo | 21 |
| Ret | 5 | Jacques Laffite | Williams-Honda | 27 | Engine | 14 |
| Ret | 11 | Elio de Angelis | Lotus-Renault | 25 | Turbo | 23 |
| Ret | 20 | Stefan Johansson | Toleman-Hart | 17 | Overheating | 26 |
| Ret | 6 | Keke Rosberg | Williams-Honda | 0 | Accident | 4 |
| Ret | 19 | Ayrton Senna | Toleman-Hart | 0 | Accident | 12 |
| Ret | 17 | Marc Surer | Arrows-BMW | 0 | Accident | 18 |
| Ret | 31 | Gerhard Berger | ATS-BMW | 0 | Accident | 16 |
| Ret | 24 | P.Ghinzani | Osella-Alfa Romeo | 0 | Accident | 20 |

Winning speed: 119.149mph  Lap leaders: Prost 1-67
Pole position: Piquet, 1m 18.871s, 128.820mph
Fastest lap: Alboreto/Piquet, 1m 23.146s, 122.197mph

## PORTUGUESE GRAND PRIX: ESTORIL 21 October Round:16 Race:404 70 x 2.703miles

| POS. | NO. | DRIVER | CAR/ENGINE | LAPS | TIME/RETIRED | GRID |
|---|---|---|---|---|---|---|
| 1 | 7 | Alain Prost | McLaren-TAG | 70 | 1:41'11.753 | 2 |
| 2 | 8 | Niki Lauda | McLaren-TAG | 70 | +13.425 | 11 |
| 3 | 19 | Ayrton Senna | Toleman-Hart | 70 | +20.042 | 3 |
| 4 | 27 | Michele Alboreto | Ferrari | 70 | +20.317 | 8 |
| 5 | 11 | Elio de Angelis | Lotus-Renault | 70 | +1'32.169 | 5 |
| 6 | 1 | Nelson Piquet | Brabham-BMW | 69 | +1 Lap | 1 |
| 7 | 15 | Patrick Tambay | Renault | 69 | +1 Lap | 7 |
| 8 | 22 | Riccardo Patrese | Alfa Romeo | 69 | +1 Lap | 12 |
| 9 | 28 | Rene Arnoux | Ferrari | 69 | +1 Lap | 17 |
| 10 | 2 | M.Winkelhock | Brabham-BMW | 69 | +1 Lap | 19 |
| 11 | 20 | Stefan Johansson | Toleman-Hart | 69 | +1 Lap | 10 |
| 12 | 26 | A.de Cesaris | Ligier-Renault | 69 | +1 Lap | 20 |
| 13 | 14 | Gerhard Berger | ATS-BMW | 68 | +2 Laps | 23 |
| 14 | 5 | Jacques Laffite | Williams-Honda | 67 | +3 Laps | 15 |
| 15 | 21 | Mauro Baldi | Spirit-Hart | 66 | +4 Laps | 25 |
| 16 | 30 | Jo Gartner | Osella-Alfa Romeo | 65 | Out of fuel | 24 |
| 17 | 23 | Eddie Cheever | Alfa Romeo | 64 | +6 Laps | 14 |
| Ret | 24 | P.Ghinzani | Osella-Alfa Romeo | 60 | Engine | 22 |
| Ret | 12 | Nigel Mansell | Lotus-Renault | 52 | Spun off | 4 |
| Ret | 16 | Derek Warwick | Renault | 51 | Gearbox | 9 |
| Ret | 33 | Philippe Streiff | Renault | 48 | Transmission | 13 |
| Ret | 6 | Keke Rosberg | Williams-Honda | 39 | Engine | 6 |
| Ret | 25 | F.Hesnault | Ligier-Renault | 31 | Electrical | 21 |
| Ret | 18 | Thierry Boutsen | Arrows-BMW | 24 | Transmission | 18 |
| Ret | 10 | Jonathan Palmer | RAM-Hart | 19 | Gearbox | 26 |
| Ret | 17 | Marc Surer | Arrows-BMW | 8 | Electrical | 16 |
| Ret | 9 | Philippe Alliot | RAM-Hart | 2 | Engine | 27 |

Winning speed: 112.183mph  Lap leaders: Rosberg 1-8; Prost 9-70
Pole position: Piquet, 1m 21.703s, 119.098mph
Fastest lap: Lauda, 1m 22.996s, 117.243mph

1984 world champion, Niki Lauda.

1985 world champion Alain Prost in the McLaren-TAG Porsche.

# 1985

DRIVERS' CHAMPION: ALAIN PROST
CONSTRUCTORS' CHAMPION: MCLAREN TAG PORSCHE

## DRIVERS' CHAMPIONSHIP

| POS. | DRIVER | NATIONALITY | CAR | POINTS |
|---|---|---|---|---|
| 1 | Alain Prost | France | McLaren-TAG Porsche | 73 (3) |
| 2 | Michele Alboreto | Italy | Ferrari | 53 |
| 3 | Keke Rosberg | Finland | Williams-Honda | 40 |
| 4 | Ayrton Senna | Brazil | Lotus-Renault | 38 |
| 5 | Elio de Angelis | Italy | Lotus-Renault | 33 |
| 6 | Nigel Mansell | GB | Williams-Honda | 31 |
| 7 | Stefan Johansson | Sweden | Tyrrell-Ford, Ferrari | 26 |
| 8 | Nelson Piquet | Brazil | Brabham-BMW | 21 |
| 9 | Jacques Laffite | France | Ligier-Renault | 16 |
| 10 | Niki Lauda | Austria | McLaren-TAG Porsche | 14 |
| 11 | Patrick Tambay | France | Renault | 11 |
| = | Thierry Boutsen | Brazil | Arrows-BMW | 11 |
| 13 | Marc Surer | Switzerland | Brabham-BMW | 5 |
| = | Derek Warwick | GB | Renault | 5 |
| 15 | Stefan Bellof | West Germany | Tyrrell-Ford | 4 |
| = | Philippe Streiff | France | Ligier-Renault, Tyrrell-Renault | 4 |
| 17 | René Arnoux | France | Ferrari | 3 |
| = | Andrea de Cesaris | Italy | Ligier-Renault | 3 |
| = | Gerhard Berger | Austria | Arrows-BMW | 3 |
| = | Ivan Capelli | Italy | Tyrrell-Renault | 3 |
| | Martin Brundle | GB | Tyrrell-Ford, Tyrrell-Renault | |
| | Philippe Alliot | France | RAM-Hart | |
| | Piercarlo Ghinzani | Italy | Osella-Alfa Romeo, Toleman-Hart | |
| | Manfred Winkelhock | West Germany | RAM-Hart | |
| | Eddie Cheever | USA | Alfa Romeo | |
| | Pierluigi Martini | Italy | Minardi-Ford, Minardi-Motori Moderni | |
| | Riccardo Patrese | Italy | Alfa Romeo | |
| | Francois Hesnault | France | Brabham-BMW | |
| | Mauro Baldi | Italy | Spirit-Hart | |
| | Jonathan Palmer | GB | Zakspeed | |
| | Teo Fabi | Italy | Toleman-Hart | |
| | Huub Rothengatter | Netherlands | Osella-Alfa Romeo | |
| | Kenny Acheson | GB | RAM-Hart | |
| | Alan Jones | Australia | Beatrice-Hart | |
| | Christian Danner | West Germany | Zakspeed | |
| | John Watson | GB | McLaren-TAG Porsche | |

Points for top six finishers (9, 6, 4, 3, 2, 1). Half points awarded for races stopped before half distance.

## CONSTRUCTORS' CHAMPIONSHIP

| POS. | CONSTRUCTOR | POINTS |
|---|---|---|
| 1 | McLaren-TAG | 90 |
| 2 | Ferrari | 82 |
| 3 | Williams-Honda | 71 |
| 4 | Lotus-Renault | 71 |
| 5 | Brabham-BMW | 26 |
| 6 | Ligier-Renault | 23 |
| 7 | Renault | 16 |
| 8 | Arrows-BMW | 14 |
| 9 | Tyrrell-Ford | 4 |
| 10 | Tyrrell-Renault | 3 |

Points for top six finishers (9, 6, 4, 3, 2, 1). Half points awarded for races stopped before half distance.

## BRAZILIAN GRAND PRIX: RIO DE JANEIRO *7 April Round:1 Race:405 61 x 3.126miles*

| POS. | NO. | DRIVER | CAR/ENGINE | LAPS | TIME/RETIRED | GRID |
|---|---|---|---|---|---|---|
| 1 | 2 | Alain Prost | McLaren-TAG | 61 | 1:41'26.115 | 6 |
| 2 | 27 | Michele Alboreto | Ferrari | 61 | +3.259 | 1 |
| 3 | 11 | Elio de Angelis | Lotus-Renault | 60 | +1 Lap | 3 |
| 4 | 28 | Rene Arnoux | Ferrari | 59 | +2 Laps | 7 |
| 5 | 15 | Patrick Tambay | Renault | 59 | +2 Laps | 11 |
| 6 | 26 | Jacques Laffite | Ligier-Renault | 59 | +2 Laps | 15 |
| 7 | 4 | Stefan Johansson | Tyrrell-Ford | 58 | +3 Laps | 23 |
| 8 | 3 | Martin Brundle | Tyrrell-Ford | 58 | +3 Laps | 21 |
| 9 | 10 | Philippe Alliot | RAM-Hart | 58 | +3 Laps | 20 |
| 10 | 16 | Derek Warwick | Renault | 57 | +4 Laps | 10 |
| 11 | 18 | Thierry Boutsen | Arrows-BMW | 57 | +4 Laps | 12 |
| 12 | 24 | P.Ghinzani | Osella-Alfa Romeo | 57 | +4 Laps | 22 |
| 13 | 9 | M.Winkelhock | RAM/Hart | 57 | +4 Laps | 16 |
| Ret | 17 | Gerhard Berger | Arrows-BMW | 51 | Suspension | 19 |
| Ret | 12 | Ayrton Senna | Lotus-Renault | 48 | Electrical | 4 |
| Ret | 23 | Eddie Cheever | Alfa Romeo | 42 | Engine | 18 |
| Ret | 29 | P.Martini | Minardi/Ford | 41 | Engine | 25 |
| Ret | 1 | Niki Lauda | McLaren-TAG | 27 | Fuel system | 9 |
| Ret | 25 | A.de Cesaris | Ligier-Renault | 26 | Accident | 13 |
| Ret | 22 | Riccardo Patrese | Alfa Romeo | 20 | Puncture | 14 |
| Ret | 6 | Keke Rosberg | Williams-Honda | 10 | Turbo | 2 |
| Ret | 8 | F.Hesnault | Brabham-BMW | 9 | Accident | 17 |
| Ret | 5 | Nigel Mansell | Williams-Honda | 8 | Exhaust | 5 |
| Ret | 21 | Mauro Baldi | Spirit-Hart | 7 | Turbo | 24 |
| Ret | 7 | Nelson Piquet | Brabham-BMW | 2 | Transmission | 8 |

Winning speed: 112.797mph Lap leaders: Rosberg 1-9; Alboreto 10-17; Prost 18-61
Pole position: Alboreto, 1m 27.768s, 128.225mph
Fastest lap: Prost, 1m 36.702s, 116.378mp

## PORTUGUESE GRAND PRIX: ESTORIL *21 April Round:2 Race: 406 67 x 2.703miles*

| POS. | NO. | DRIVER | CAR/ENGINE | LAPS | TIME/RETIRED | GRID |
|---|---|---|---|---|---|---|
| 1 | 12 | Ayrton Senna | Lotus-Renault | 67 | 2:00'28.006 | 1 |
| 2 | 27 | Michele Alboreto | Ferrari | 67 | +1'02.978 | 5 |
| 3 | 15 | Patrick Tambay | Renault | 66 | +1 Lap | 12 |
| 4 | 11 | Elio de Angelis | Lotus-Renault | 66 | +1 Lap | 4 |
| 5 | 5 | Nigel Mansell | Williams-Honda | 65 | +2 Laps | 9 |
| 6 | 4 | Stefan Bellof | Tyrrell-Ford | 65 | +2 Laps | 21 |
| 7 | 16 | Derek Warwick | Renault | 65 | +2 Laps | 6 |
| 8 | 28 | Stefan Johansson | Ferrari | 62 | +5 Laps | 11 |
| 9 | 24 | P.Ghinzani | Osella-Alfa Romeo | 61 | +6 Laps | 26 |
| NC | 9 | M.Winkelhock | RAM-Hart | 50 | Not classified | 15 |
| Ret | 1 | Niki Lauda | McLaren-TAG | 49 | Engine | 7 |
| Ret | 23 | Eddie Cheever | Alfa Romeo | 36 | Engine | 14 |
| Ret | 2 | Alain Prost | McLaren-TAG | 30 | Spun off | 2 |
| Ret | 25 | A.de Cesaris | Ligier-Renault | 29 | Tyre | 8 |
| Ret | 7 | Nelson Piquet | Brabham-BMW | 28 | Tyre | 16 |
| Ret | 18 | Thierry Boutsen | Arrows-BMW | 28 | Electrical | 10 |
| Ret | 3 | Martin Brundle | Tyrrell-Ford | 20 | Transmission | 22 |
| Ret | 21 | Mauro Baldi | Spirit-Hart | 19 | Spun off | 29 |
| Ret | 6 | Keke Rosberg | Williams-Honda | 16 | Spun off | 3 |
| Ret | 26 | Jacques Laffite | Ligier-Renault | 15 | Tyre | 18 |
| Ret | 17 | Gerhard Berger | Arrows-BMW | 12 | Spun off | 17 |
| Ret | 29 | P.Martini | Minardi-Ford | 12 | Spun off | 25 |
| Ret | 22 | Riccardo Patrese | Alfa Romeo | 4 | Spun off | 13 |
| Ret | 10 | Philippe Alliot | RAM-Hart | 3 | Spun off | 20 |
| Ret | 8 | F.Hesnault | Brabham-BMW | 3 | Electrical | 19 |
| Ret | 30 | Jonathan Palmer | Zakspeed | 2 | Suspension | 23 |

Winning speed: 90.198mph Lap leaders Senna 1-67
Pole position: Senna, 1m 21.007s, 120.121mph
Fastest lap: Senna, 1m 44.121s, 93.455mph
Scheduled for 69 laps but stopped after 2-hour mark.

## SAN MARINO GRAND PRIX: IMOLA *5 May Round:3 Race:407 60x3.132 miles*

| POS. | NO. | DRIVER | CAR/ENGINE | LAPS | TIME/RETIRED | GRID |
|---|---|---|---|---|---|---|
| 1 | 11 | Elio de Angelis | Lotus-Renault | 60 | 1:34'35.955 | 3 |
| 2 | 18 | Thierry Boutsen | Arrows-BMW | 59 | +1 Lap | 5 |
| 3 | 15 | Patrick Tambay | Renault | 59 | +1 Lap | 11 |
| 4 | 1 | Niki Lauda | McLaren-TAG | 59 | +1 Lap | 8 |
| 5 | 5 | Nigel Mansell | Williams-Honda | 58 | +2 Laps | 7 |
| 6 | 28 | Stefan Johansson | Ferrari | 57 | Out of fuel | 15 |
| 7 | 12 | Ayrton Senna | Lotus-Renault | 57 | Out of fuel | 1 |
| 8 | 7 | Nelson Piquet | Brabham-BMW | 57 | Out of fuel | 9 |
| 9 | 3 | Martin Brundle | Tyrrell-Ford | 56 | Out of fuel | 25 |
| 10 | 16 | Derek Warwick | Renault | 56 | Out of fuel | 14 |
| DSQ | 2 | Alain Prost | McLaren-TAG | 60 | Disqualified | 6 |
| Ret | 23 | Eddie Cheever | Alfa Romeo | 50 | Engine | 12 |
| NC | 24 | P.Ghinzani | Osella-Alfa Romeo | 46 | Not classified | 22 |
| Ret | 27 | Michele Alboreto | Ferrari | 29 | Electrical | 4 |
| Ret | 9 | M.Winkelhock | RAM-Hart | 27 | Engine | 23 |
| Ret | 10 | Philippe Alliot | RAM-Hart | 24 | Engine | 21 |
| Ret | 6 | Keke Rosberg | Williams-Honda | 23 | Brakes | 2 |
| Ret | 26 | Jacques Laffite | Ligier-Renault | 22 | Turbo | 16 |
| Ret | 29 | P.Martini | Minardi-Motori Moderni | 14 | Turbo | 19 |
| Ret | 25 | A.de Cesaris | Ligier-Renault | 11 | Spun off | 13 |
| Ret | 21 | Mauro Baldi | Spirit-Hart | 9 | Electrical | 26 |
| Ret | 8 | F.Hesnault | Brabham-BMW | 5 | Engine | 20 |
| Ret | 4 | Stefan Bellof | Tyrrell-Ford | 5 | Engine | 24 |
| Ret | 17 | Gerhard Berger | Arrows-BMW | 4 | Engine | 10 |
| Ret | 22 | Riccardo Patrese | Alfa Romeo | 4 | Engine | 18 |
| DNS | 30 | Jonathan Palmer | Zakspeed | 0 | Non starter | 17 |

Winning speed: 119.178 mph Lap leaders: Senna 1-56; Johansson 57; Prost 58-60
Pole position: Senna, 1m 27.327s, 129.103mph
Fastest lap: Alboreto, 1m 30.961s, 123.945mph
Prost was disqualified from first place for an underweight car.

## MONACO GRAND PRIX: MONTE CARLO *19 May Round:4 Race:408 78 x 2.058miles*

| POS. | NO. | DRIVER | CAR/ENGINE | LAPS | TIME/RETIRED | GRID |
|---|---|---|---|---|---|---|
| 1 | 2 | Alain Prost | McLaren-TAG | 78 | 1:51'58.034 | 5 |
| 2 | 27 | Michele Alboreto | Ferrari | 78 | +7.541 | 3 |
| 3 | 11 | Elio de Angelis | Lotus-Renault | 78 | +1'27.171 | 9 |
| 4 | 25 | A.de Cesaris | Ligier-Renault | 77 | +1 Lap | 8 |
| 5 | 16 | Derek Warwick | Renault | 77 | +1 Lap | 10 |
| 6 | 26 | Jacques Laffite | Ligier-Renault | 77 | +1 Lap | 16 |
| 7 | 5 | Nigel Mansell | Williams-Honda | 77 | +1 Lap | 2 |
| 8 | 6 | Keke Rosberg | Williams-Honda | 76 | +2 Laps | 7 |
| 9 | 18 | Thierry Boutsen | Arrows-BMW | 76 | +2 Laps | 6 |
| 10 | 3 | Martin Brundle | Tyrrell-Ford | 74 | +4 Laps | 18 |
| 11 | 30 | Jonathan Palmer | Zakspeed | 74 | +4 Laps | 19 |
| Ret | 1 | Niki Lauda | McLaren-TAG | 17 | Spun off | 14 |
| Ret | 22 | Riccardo Patrese | Alfa Romeo | 16 | Accident | 12 |
| Ret | 7 | Nelson Piquet | Brabham-BMW | 16 | Accident | 13 |
| Ret | 19 | Teo Fabi | Toleman-Hart | 16 | Turbo | 20 |
| Ret | 12 | Ayrton Senna | Lotus-Renault | 13 | Engine | 1 |
| Ret | 23 | Eddie Cheever | Alfa Romeo | 10 | Alternator | 4 |
| Ret | 28 | Stefan Johansson | Ferrari | 1 | Accident | 15 |
| Ret | 17 | Gerhard Berger | Arrows-BMW | 0 | Accident | 11 |
| Ret | 15 | Patrick Tambay | Renault | 0 | Accident | 17 |
| DNQ | 24 | P.Ghinzani | Osella-Alfa Romeo | | | |
| DNQ | 4 | Stefan Bellof | Tyrrell-Ford | | | |
| DNQ | 10 | Philippe Alliot | RAM-Hart | | | |
| DNQ | 9 | M.Winkelhock | RAM-Hart | | | |
| DNQ | 8 | F.Hesnault | Brabham-BMW | | | |
| DNQ | 29 | P.Martini | Minardi-Motori Moderni | | | |

Winning speed: 86.019mph Lap leaders: Senna 1-13; Alboreto 14-17, 24-31; Prost 18-23, 32-78
Pole position: Senna, 1m 20.450s, 92.091mph
Fastest lap: Alboreto, 1m 22.637s, 89.654mph

## CANADIAN GRAND PRIX: MONTREAL *16 June Round 5 Race 409 70 x 2.740 miles*

| POS. | NO. | DRIVER | CAR/ENGINE | LAPS | TIME/RETIRED | GRID |
|---|---|---|---|---|---|---|
| 1 | 27 | Michele Alboreto | Ferrari | 70 | 1:46'01.813 | 3 |
| 2 | 28 | Stefan Johansson | Ferrari | 70 | +1.957 | 4 |
| 3 | 2 | Alain Prost | McLaren-TAG | 70 | +4.341 | 5 |
| 4 | 6 | Keke Rosberg | Williams-Honda | 70 | + 27.821 | 8 |
| 5 | 11 | Elio de Angelis | Lotus-Renault | 70 | +43.349 | 1 |
| 6 | 5 | Nigel Mansell | Williams-Honda | 70 | +1'17.878 | 16 |
| 7 | 15 | Patrick Tambay | Renault | 69 | +1 Lap | 10 |
| 8 | 26 | Jacques Laffite | Ligier-Renault | 69 | +1 Lap | 19 |
| 9 | 18 | Thierry Boutsen | Arrows-BMW | 68 | +2 Laps | 7 |
| 10 | 22 | Riccardo Patrese | Alfa Romeo | 68 | +2 Laps | 13 |
| 11 | 4 | Stefan Bellof | Tyrrell-Ford | 68 | +2 Laps | 23 |
| 12 | 3 | Martin Brundle | Tyrrell-Ford | 68 | +2 Laps | 24 |
| 13 | 17 | Gerhard Berger | Arrows-BMW | 67 | +3 Laps | 12 |
| 14 | 25 | A.de Cesaris | Ligier-Renault | 67 | +3 Laps | 15 |
| 15 | 8 | Marc Surer | Brabham-BMW | 67 | +3 Laps | 20 |
| 16 | 12 | Ayrton Senna | Lotus-Renault | 65 | +5 Laps | 2 |
| 17 | 23 | Eddie Cheever | Alfa Romeo | 64 | +6 Laps | 11 |
| Ret | 29 | P.Martini | Minardi-Motori Moderni | 57 | Accident | 25 |
| Ret | 1 | Niki Lauda | McLaren-TAG | 37 | Engine | 17 |
| Ret | 24 | P.Ghinzani | Osella-Alfa Romeo | 35 | Engine | 22 |
| Ret | 10 | Philippe Alliot | RAM-Hart | 28 | Accident | 21 |
| Ret | 16 | Derek Warwick | Renault | 25 | Accident | 6 |
| Ret | 9 | M.Winkelhock | RAM-Hart | 5 | Accident | 14 |
| Ret | 19 | Teo Fabi | Toleman-Hart | 3 | Turbo | 18 |
| Ret | 7 | Nelson Piquet | Brabham-BMW | 0 | Transmission | 9 |

Winning speed: 108.686mph Lap leaders: de Angelis 1-15; Alboreto 16-70
Pole position: de Angelis, 1m24.567s, 116.652mph
Fastest lap: Senna, 1m27.445s, 112.812mph

## USA EAST GRAND PRIX: DETROIT *23 June Round 6 Race 410 63 x 2.500miles*

| POS. | NO. | DRIVER | CAR/ENGINE | LAPS | TIME/RETIRED | GRID |
|---|---|---|---|---|---|---|
| 1 | 6 | Keke Rosberg | Williams-Honda | 63 | 1:55'39.851 | 5 |
| 2 | 28 | Stefan Johansson | Ferrari | 63 | +57.549 | 9 |
| 3 | 27 | Michele Alboreto | Ferrari | 63 | +1'03.170 | 3 |
| 4 | 4 | Stefan Bellof | Tyrrell-Ford | 63 | +1'06.225 | 19 |
| 5 | 11 | Elio de Angelis | Lotus-Renault | 63 | +1'26.966 | 8 |
| 6 | 7 | Nelson Piquet | Brabham-BMW | 62 | +1 Lap | 10 |
| 7 | 18 | Thierry Boutsen | Arrows-BMW | 62 | +1 Lap | 21 |
| 8 | 8 | Marc Surer | Brabham-BMW | 62 | +1 Lap | 18 |
| 9 | 23 | Eddie Cheever | Alfa Romeo | 61 | +2 Laps | 7 |
| 10 | 25 | A.de Cesaris | Ligier-Renault | 61 | +2 Laps | 17 |
| 11 | 17 | Gerhard Berger | Arrows-BMW | 60 | +3 Laps | 24 |
| 12 | 26 | Jacques Laffite | Ligier-Renault | 58 | +5 Laps | 16 |
| Ret | 12 | Ayrton Senna | Lotus-Renault | 51 | Accident | 1 |
| Ret | 3 | Martin Brundle | Tyrrell-Ford | 30 | Accident | 18 |
| Ret | 10 | Philippe Alliot | RAM-Hart | 27 | Accident | 23 |
| Ret | 5 | Nigel Mansell | Williams-Honda | 26 | Accident | 2 |
| Ret | 2 | Alain Prost | McLaren-TAG | 19 | Brakes | 4 |
| Ret | 22 | Riccardo Patrese | Alfa Romeo | 19 | Electrical | 14 |
| Ret | 16 | Derek Warwick | Renault | 18 | Transmission | 6 |
| Ret | 15 | Patrick Tambay | Renault | 15 | Accident | 15 |
| Ret | 29 | P.Martini | Minardi-Motori Moderni | 11 | Engine | 25 |
| Ret | 1 | Niki Lauda | McLaren-TAG | 10 | Brakes | 12 |
| Ret | 19 | Teo Fabi | Toleman-Hart | 4 | Clutch | 13 |
| Ret | 9 | M.Winkelhock | RAM-Hart | 3 | Turbo | 20 |
| Ret | 24 | P.Ghinzani | Osella-Alfa Romeo | 0 | Accident | 22 |

Winning speed: 81.702mph Lap leaders: Senna 1-7; Rosberg 8-63
Pole position: Senna 1m42.051s, 88.191mph
Fastest lap: Senna 1m45.612s, 85.218mph

## FRENCH GRAND PRIX: PAUL RICARD *7 July Round 7 Race 411 53 x 3.610 miles*

| POS. | NO. | DRIVER | CAR/ENGINE | LAPS | TIME/RETIRED | GRID |
|---|---|---|---|---|---|---|
| 1 | 7 | Nelson Piquet | Brabham-BMW | 53 | 1:31'46.266 | 5 |
| 2 | 6 | Keke Rosberg | Williams-Honda | 53 | +6.660 | 1 |
| 3 | 2 | Alain Prost | McLaren-TAG | 53 | +9.285 | 4 |
| 4 | 28 | Stefan Johansson | Ferrari | 53 | +53.491 | 16 |
| 5 | 11 | Elio de Angelis | Lotus-Renault | 53 | +53.690 | 7 |
| 6 | 15 | Patrick Tambay | Renault | 53 | +1'15.167 | 10 |
| 7 | 16 | Derek Warwick | Renault | 53 | +1'44.212 | 11 |
| 8 | 8 | Marc Surer | Brabham-BMW | 52 | +1 Lap | 14 |
| 9 | 18 | Thierry Boutsen | Arrows-BMW | 52 | +1 Lap | 12 |
| 10 | 23 | Eddie Cheever | Alfa Romeo | 52 | +1 Lap | 18 |
| 11 | 22 | Riccardo Patrese | Alfa Romeo | 52 | +1 Lap | 17 |
| 12 | 9 | M.Winkelhock | RAM-Hart | 50 | +3 Laps | 20 |
| 13 | 4 | Stefan Bellof | Tyrrell-Ford | 50 | +3 Laps | 26 |
| 14 | 19 | Teo Fabi | Toleman-Hart | 49 | Fuel system | 19 |
| 15 | 24 | P.Ghinzani | Osella-Alfa Romeo | 49 | +4 Laps | 24 |
| Ret | 3 | Martin Brundle | Tyrrell-Renault | 32 | Gearbox | 21 |
| Ret | 1 | Niki Lauda | McLaren-TAG | 30 | Gearbox | 6 |
| Ret | 12 | Ayrton Senna | Lotus-Renault | 26 | Engine | 2 |
| Ret | 17 | Gerhard Berger | Arrows-BMW | 20 | Accident | 9 |
| Ret | 29 | P.Martini | Minardi-Motori Moderni | 19 | Accident | 25 |
| Ret | 10 | Philippe Alliot | RAM-Hart | 8 | Fuel system | 23 |
| Ret | 30 | Jonathan Palmer | Zakspeed | 6 | Engine | 22 |
| Ret | 27 | Michele Alboreto | Ferrari | 5 | Turbo | 3 |
| Ret | 25 | A.de Cesaris | Ligier-Renault | 4 | Steering | 13 |
| Ret | 26 | Jacques Laffite | Ligier-Renault | 2 | Turbo | 15 |
| DNS | 5 | Nigel Mansell | Williams-Honda | | Injured | 8 |

Winning speed: 125.097mph Lap leaders: Rosberg 1-10; Piquet 11-53
Pole position: Rosberg, 1m32.462s, 140.562mph
Fastest lap: Rosberg, 1m39.914s, 130.078mph

## BRITISH GRAND PRIX: SILVERSTONE *21 July Round 8 Race 412 65 x 2.932 miles*

| POS. | NO. | DRIVER | CAR/ENGINE | LAPS | TIME/RETIRED | GRID |
|---|---|---|---|---|---|---|
| 1 | 2 | Alain Prost | McLaren-TAG | 65 | 1:18'10.436 | 3 |
| 2 | 27 | Michele Alboreto | Ferrari | 64 | +1 Lap | 6 |
| 3 | 26 | Jacques Laffite | Ligier-Renault | 64 | +1 Lap | 16 |
| 4 | 7 | Nelson Piquet | Brabham-BMW | 64 | +1 Lap | 2 |
| 5 | 16 | Derek Warwick | Renault | 64 | +1 Lap | 12 |
| 6 | 8 | Marc Surer | Brabham-BMW | 63 | +2 Laps | 15 |
| 7 | 3 | Martin Brundle | Tyrrell-Renault | 63 | +2 Laps | 20 |
| 8 | 17 | Gerhard Berger | Arrows-BMW | 63 | +2 Laps | 17 |
| 9 | 22 | Riccardo Patrese | Alfa Romeo | 62 | +3 Laps | 14 |
| 10 | 12 | Ayrton Senna | Lotus-Renault | 60 | Injection | 4 |
| 11 | 4 | Stefan Bellof | Tyrrell-Ford | 59 | +6 Laps | 26 |
| Ret | 1 | Niki Lauda | McLaren-TAG | 57 | Electrical | 10 |
| Ret | 18 | Thierry Boutsen | Arrows-BMW | 57 | Spun off | 19 |
| Ret | 25 | A.de Cesaris | Ligier-Renault | 41 | Clutch | 7 |
| Ret | 29 | P.Martini | Minardi-Motori Moderni | 38 | Transmission | 23 |
| NC | 11 | Elio de Angelis | Lotus-Renault | 37 | Not classified | 8 |
| Ret | 9 | M.Winkelhock | RAM-Hart | 28 | Turbo | 18 |
| Ret | 6 | Keke Rosberg | Williams-Honda | 21 | Exhaust | 1 |
| Ret | 5 | Nigel Mansell | Williams-Honda | 17 | Clutch | 5 |
| Ret | 23 | Eddie Cheever | Alfa Romeo | 17 | Turbo | 22 |
| Ret | 30 | Jonathan Palmer | Zakspeed | 6 | Engine | 24 |
| Ret | 19 | Teo Fabi | Toleman-Hart | 4 | Transmission | 9 |
| Ret | 28 | Stefan Johansson | Ferrari | 1 | Accident | 11 |
| Ret | 15 | Patrick Tambay | Renault | 0 | Spun off | 13 |
| Ret | 10 | Philippe Alliot | RAM-Hart | 0 | Accident | 21 |
| Ret | 24 | P.Ghinzani | Osella-Alfa Romeo | 0 | Accident | 25 |

Winning speed: 146.274mph Lap leaders: Senna 1-57, 59; Prost 58, 60-65
Pole position: Rosberg, 1m5.591s, 160.925mph
Fastest lap: Prost, 1m9886s, 151.035mph
Scheduled for 66 laps, but stopped 1 lap early in error

## GERMAN GRAND PRIX: NURBURGRING *4 August Round 9 Race 413 67 x 2.822 miles*

| POS. | NO. | DRIVER | CAR/ENGINE | LAPS | TIME/RETIRED | GRID |
|---|---|---|---|---|---|---|
| 1 | 27 | Michele Alboreto | Ferrari | 67 | 1:35'31.337 | 8 |
| 2 | 2 | Alain Prost | McLaren-TAG | 67 | +11.661 | 3 |
| 3 | 26 | Jacques Laffite | Ligier-Renault | 67 | +51.154 | 13 |
| 4 | 18 | Thierry Boutsen | Arrows-BMW | 67 | +55.279 | 15 |
| 5 | 1 | Niki Lauda | McLaren-TAG | 67 | +1'13.972 | 12 |
| 6 | 5 | Nigel Mansell | Williams-Honda | 67 | +1'16.820 | 10 |
| 7 | 17 | Gerhard Berger | Arrows-BMW | 66 | +1 Lap | 17 |
| 8 | 3 | Stefan Bellof | Tyrrell-Renault | 66 | +1 Lap | 19 |
| 9 | 28 | Stefan Johansson | Ferrari | 66 | +1 Lap | 2 |
| 10 | 4 | Martin Brundle | Tyrrell-Ford | 63 | +4 Laps | 26 |
| 11 | 29 | P.Martini | Minardi-Motori Moderni | 62 | Engine | 27 |
| 12 | 6 | Keke Rosberg | Williams-Honda | 61 | Brakes | 4 |
| Ret | 23 | Eddie Cheever | Alfa Romeo | 45 | Turbo | 18 |
| Ret | 11 | Elio de Angelis | Lotus-Renault | 40 | Engine | 7 |
| Ret | 24 | H.Rothengatter | Osella-Alfa Romeo | 32 | Gearbox | 25 |
| Ret | 19 | Teo Fabi | Toleman-Hart | 29 | Clutch | 1 |
| Ret | 12 | Ayrton Senna | Lotus-Renault | 27 | Transmission | 5 |
| Ret | 16 | Derek Warwick | Renault | 25 | Ignition | 20 |
| Ret | 7 | Nelson Piquet | Brabham-BMW | 23 | Turbo | 6 |
| Ret | 15 | Patrick Tambay | Renault | 19 | Spun off | 16 |
| Ret | 8 | Marc Surer | Brabham-BMW | 15 | Engine | 11 |
| Ret | 9 | M.Winkelhock | RAM-Hart | 8 | Engine | 22 |
| Ret | 22 | Riccardo Patrese | Alfa Romeo | 8 | Gearbox | 9 |
| Ret | 14 | F.Hesnault | Renault | 8 | Clutch | 23 |
| Ret | 10 | Philippe Alliot | RAM-Hart | 8 | Oil pressure | 21 |
| Ret | 30 | Jonathan Palmer | Zakspeed | 7 | Alternator | 24 |
| Ret | 25 | A.de Cesaris | Ligier-Renault | 0 | Collision | 14 |

Winning speed: 118.774mph Lap leaders: Rosberg 1-15, 27-44; Senna 16-26; Alboreto 45-67
Pole position: Fabi, 1m17.429s, 131.219mph
Fastest lap: Lauda, 1m22.806s, 122.698mph

## AUSTRIAN GRAND PRIX: OSTERREICHRING *18 August Round 10 Race 414 52 x 3.692 miles*

| POS. | NO. | DRIVER | CAR/ENGINE | LAPS | TIME/RETIRED | GRID |
|---|---|---|---|---|---|---|
| 1 | 2 | Alain Prost | McLaren-TAG | 52 | 1:20'12.583 | 1 |
| 2 | 12 | Ayrton Senna | Lotus-Renault | 52 | +30.002 | 14 |
| 3 | 27 | Michele Alboreto | Ferrari | 52 | +34.356 | 9 |
| 4 | 28 | Stefan Johansson | Ferrari | 52 | +39.073 | 12 |
| 5 | 11 | Elio de Angelis | Lotus-Renault | 52 | +1'22.092 | 7 |
| 6 | 8 | Marc Surer | Brabham-BMW | 51 | +1 Lap | 11 |
| 7 | 3 | Stefan Bellof | Tyrrell-Renault | 49 | Out of fuel | 22 |
| 8 | 18 | Thierry Boutsen | Arrows-BMW | 49 | +3 Laps | 16 |
| 9 | 24 | H.Rothengatter | Osella-Alfa Romeo | 48 | +4 Laps | 24 |
| 10 | 15 | Patrick Tambay | Renault | 46 | Engine | 8 |
| Ret | 26 | Jacques Laffite | Ligier-Renault | 43 | Accident | 15 |
| Ret | 29 | P.Martini | Minardi-Motori Moderni | 40 | Suspension | 26 |
| Ret | 1 | Niki Lauda | McLaren-TAG | 39 | Engine | 3 |
| Ret | 17 | Gerhard Berger | Arrows-BMW | 33 | Turbo | 17 |
| Ret | 19 | Teo Fabi | Toleman-Hart | 31 | Electrical | 6 |
| Ret | 16 | Derek Warwick | Renault | 29 | Engine | 13 |
| Ret | 10 | Kenny Acheson | RAM-Hart | 28 | Engine | 23 |
| Ret | 7 | Nelson Piquet | Brabham-BMW | 26 | Exhaust | 5 |
| Ret | 5 | Nigel Mansell | Williams-Honda | 25 | Engine | 2 |
| Ret | 22 | Riccardo Patrese | Alfa Romeo | 25 | Engine | 10 |
| Ret | 30 | Jonathan Palmer | Zakspeed | 17 | Engine | 25 |
| Ret | 9 | Philippe Alliot | RAM-Hart | 16 | Turbo | 21 |
| Ret | 25 | A.de Cesaris | Ligier-Renault | 13 | Accident | 18 |
| Ret | 23 | Eddie Cheever | Alfa Romeo | 6 | Turbo | 20 |
| Ret | 6 | Keke Rosberg | Williams-Honda | 4 | Oil pressure | 4 |
| DNS | 20 | P.Ghinzani | Toleman-Hart | 0 | Non starter | 19 |
| DNQ | 4 | Martin Brundle | Tyrrel-Ford | | | |

Winning speed: 143.619mph Lap leaders: Prost 1-25, 40-52; Lauda 26-39
Pole position: Prost, 1m25.490s, 148.944mph
Fastest lap: Prost, 1m29.241s, 148.944mph
Restarted for total original distance after accident at first start.

## DUTCH GRAND PRIX: ZANDVOORT *25 August Round 11 Race 415 70 x 2.642 miles*

| POS. | NO. | DRIVER | CAR/ENGINE | LAPS | TIME/RETIRED | GRID |
|---|---|---|---|---|---|---|
| 1 | 1 | Niki Lauda | McLaren-TAG | 70 | 1:32'29.263 | 10 |
| 2 | 2 | Alain Prost | McLaren-TAG | 70 | +0.232 | 3 |
| 3 | 12 | Ayrton Senna | Lotus-Renault | 70 | +48.491 | 4 |
| 4 | 27 | Michele Alboreto | Ferrari | 70 | +48.837 | 16 |
| 5 | 11 | Elio de Angelis | Lotus-Renault | 69 | +1 Lap | 11 |
| 6 | 5 | Nigel Mansell | Williams-Honda | 69 | +1 Lap | 7 |
| 7 | 3 | Martin Brundle | Tyrrell-Renault | 69 | +1 Lap | 21 |
| 8 | 7 | Nelson Piquet | Brabham-BMW | 69 | +1 Lap | 1 |
| 9 | 17 | Gerhard Berger | Arrows-BMW | 68 | +2 Laps | 14 |
| 10 | 8 | Marc Surer | Brabham-BMW | 65 | Exhaust | 9 |
| NC | 24 | H.Rothengatter | Osella-Alfa Romeo | 56 | Not classified | 26 |
| Ret | 18 | Thierry Boutsen | Arrows-BMW | 54 | Suspension | 8 |
| Ret | 9 | Philippe Alliot | RAM-Hart | 52 | Engine | 25 |
| Ret | 4 | Stefan Bellof | Tyrrell-Renault | 39 | Engine | 22 |
| Ret | 16 | Derek Warwick | Renault | 27 | Gearbox | 12 |
| Ret | 25 | A.de Cesaris | Ligier-Renault | 25 | Turbo | 18 |
| Ret | 15 | Patrick Tambay | Renault | 22 | Transmission | 6 |
| Ret | 6 | Keke Rosberg | Williams-Honda | 20 | Engine | 2 |
| Ret | 19 | Teo Fabi | Toleman-Hart | 18 | Wheel bearing | 5 |
| Ret | 26 | Jacques Laffite | Ligier-Renault | 17 | Electrical | 13 |
| Ret | 30 | Jonathan Palmer | Zakspeed | 13 | Oil pressure | 23 |
| Ret | 20 | P.Ghinzani | Toleman-Hart | 12 | Engine | 15 |
| Ret | 28 | Stefan Johansson | Ferrari | 9 | Engine | 17 |
| Ret | 29 | P.Martini | Minardi/Motori Moderni | 1 | Accident | 24 |
| Ret | 23 | Eddie Cheever | Alfa Romeo | 1 | Turbo | 20 |
| Ret | 22 | Riccardo Patrese | Alfa Romeo | 1 | Turbo | 19 |
| DNQ | 10 | Kenny Acheson | RAM-Hart | | | |

Winning speed: 119.980mph Lap leaders: Rosberg 1-19; Prost 20-33; Lauda 34-70
Pole position: Piquet, 1m11.074s, 133.825mph
Fastest lap: Prost, 1m16.538s, 124.271mph

## ITALIAN GRAND PRIX: MONZA *8 September Round 12 Race 416 51 x 3.604 miles*

| POS. | NO. | DRIVER | CAR/ENGINE | LAPS | TIME/RETIRED | GRID |
|---|---|---|---|---|---|---|
| 1 | 2 | Alain Prost | McLaren-TAG | 51 | 1:17'59.451 | 5 |
| 2 | 7 | Nelson Piquet | Brabham-BMW | 51 | +51.635 | 4 |
| 3 | 12 | Ayrton Senna | Lotus-Renault | 51 | +1'00.390 | 1 |
| 4 | 8 | Marc Surer | Brabham-BMW | 51 | +1'00.609 | 9 |
| 5 | 28 | Stefan Johansson | Ferrari | 50 | +1 Lap | 10 |
| 6 | 11 | Elio de Angelis | Lotus-Renault | 50 | +1 Lap | 6 |
| 7 | 15 | Patrick Tambay | Renault | 50 | +1 Lap | 8 |
| 8 | 3 | Martin Brundle | Tyrrell-Renault | 50 | +1 Lap | 14 |
| 9 | 18 | Thierry Boutsen | Arrows-BMW | 50 | +1 Lap | 19 |
| 10 | 25 | Philippe Streiff | Ligier-Renault | 49 | +2 Laps | 3 |
| 11 | 5 | Nigel Mansell | Williams-Honda | 47 | Engine | 15 |
| 12 | 19 | Teo Fabi | Toleman-Hart | 47 | +4 Laps | 7 |
| 13 | 27 | Michele Alboreto | Ferrari | 45 | Engine | 2 |
| Ret | 6 | Keke Rosberg | Williams-Honda | 44 | Engine | 20 |
| Ret | 26 | Jacques Laffite | Ligier-Renault | 40 | Engine | 16 |
| Ret | 1 | Niki Lauda | McLaren-TAG | 33 | Transmission | 13 |
| Ret | 22 | Riccardo Patrese | Alfa Romeo | 31 | Exhaust | 22 |
| Ret | 24 | H.Rothengatter | Osella-Alfa Romeo | 26 | Engine | 26 |
| Ret | 9 | Philippe Alliot | RAM-Hart | 19 | Turbo | 11 |
| Ret | 17 | Gerhard Berger | Arrows-BMW | 13 | Engine | 12 |
| Ret | 16 | Derek Warwick | Renault | 9 | Transmission | 25 |
| Ret | 33 | Alan Jones | Lola-Hart | 6 | Engine | 17 |
| Ret | 23 | Eddie Cheever | Alfa Romeo | 3 | Engine | 24 |
| Ret | 10 | Kenny Acheson | RAM-Hart | 2 | Clutch | 23 |
| Ret | 29 | P.Martini | Minardi-Motori Moderni | 0 | Fuel pump | 21 |
| DNS | 20 | P.Ghinzani | Toleman-Hart | 0 | Non starter | |

Winning speed: 141.402mph Lap leaders: Rosberg 1-27, 40-44; Prost 28-39, 45-51
Pole position: Senna, 1m25.084s, 152.487mph
Fastest lap: Mansell, 1m28.283, 146.962mph

## BELGIAN GRAND PRIX: SPA-FRANCORCHAMPS *15 September Round 13 Race 417 43 x 4.312 miles*

| POS. | NO. | DRIVER | CAR/ENGINE | LAPS | TIME/RETIRED | GRID |
|---|---|---|---|---|---|---|
| 1 | 12 | Ayrton Senna | Lotus-Renault | 43 | 1:34'19.893 | |
| 2 | 5 | Nigel Mansell | Williams-Honda | 43 | +28.422 | |
| 3 | 2 | Alain Prost | McLaren-TAG | 43 | +55.109 | |
| 4 | 6 | Keke Rosberg | Williams-Honda | 43 | +1'15.290 | |
| 5 | 7 | Nelson Piquet | Brabham-BMW | 42 | +1 Lap | |
| 6 | 16 | Derek Warwick | Renault | 42 | +1 Lap | |
| 7 | 17 | Gerhard Berger | Arrows-BMW | 42 | +1 Lap | |
| 8 | 8 | Marc Surer | Brabham-BMW | 42 | +1 Lap | |
| 9 | 25 | Philippe Streiff | Ligier-Renault | 42 | +1 Lap | |
| 10 | 18 | Thierry Boutsen | Arrows-BMW | 40 | +3 Laps | |
| 11 | 26 | Jacques Laffite | Ligier-Renault | 38 | Accident | |
| 12 | 29 | P.Martini | Minardi-Motori Moderni | 38 | +5 Laps | |
| 13 | 3 | Martin Brundle | Tyrrell-Renault | 38 | +5 Laps | |
| NC | 24 | H.Rothengatter | Osella-Alfa Romeo | 37 | Not classified | |
| Ret | 22 | Riccardo Patrese | Alfa Romeo | 31 | Engine | |
| Ret | 23 | Eddie Cheever | Alfa Romeo | 26 | Gearbox | |
| Ret | 15 | Patrick Tambay | Renault | 24 | Gearbox | |
| Ret | 19 | Teo Fabi | Toleman-Hart | 23 | Throttle | |
| Ret | 11 | Elio de Angelis | Lotus-Renault | 17 | Turbo | |
| Ret | 30 | Christian Danner | Zakspeed | 16 | Gearbox | |
| Ret | 9 | Philippe Alliot | RAM-Hart | 10 | Accident | |
| Ret | 28 | Stefan Johansson | Ferrari | 7 | Spun off | |
| Ret | 20 | P.Ghinzani | Toleman-Hart | 7 | Accident | |
| Ret | 27 | Michele Alboreto | Ferrari | 3 | Clutch | |

Winning speed: 117.943mph Lap leaders: Senna 1-8, 10-43; de Angelis 9
Pole position: Prost, 1m55.306s, 134.636mph
Fastest lap: Prost, 2m1.730s, 127.531mph
Race postponed from 2nd June due to track conditions.

## EUROPEAN GRAND PRIX: BRANDS HATCH *6 October Round 14 Race 418 75 x 2.614 miles*

| POS. | NO. | DRIVER | CAR/ENGINE | LAPS | TIME/RETIRED | GRID |
|---|---|---|---|---|---|---|
| 1 | 5 | Nigel Mansell | Williams-Honda | 75 | 1:32'58.109 | |
| 2 | 12 | Ayrton Senna | Lotus-Renault | 75 | +21.396 | |
| 3 | 6 | Keke Rosberg | Williams-Honda | 75 | +58.533 | |
| 4 | 2 | Alain Prost | McLaren-TAG | 75 | +1'06.121 | |
| 5 | 11 | Elio de Angelis | Lotus-Renault | 74 | +1 Lap | |
| 6 | 18 | Thierry Boutsen | Arrows-BMW | 73 | +2 Laps | |
| 7 | 1 | John Watson | McLaren-TAG | 73 | +2 Laps | |
| 8 | 25 | Philippe Streiff | Ligier-Renault | 73 | +2 Laps | |
| 9 | 22 | Riccardo Patrese | Alfa Romeo | 73 | +2 Laps | |
| 10 | 17 | Gerhard Berger | Arrows-BMW | 73 | +2 Laps | |
| 11 | 23 | Eddie Cheever | Alfa Romeo | 73 | +2 Laps | |
| 12 | 15 | Patrick Tambay | Renault | 72 | +3 Laps | |
| Ret | 8 | Marc Surer | Brabham-BMW | 62 | Turbo | |
| Ret | 28 | Stefan Johansson | Ferrari | 59 | Electrical | |
| Ret | 26 | Jacques Laffite | Ligier-Renault | 58 | Engine | |
| Ret | 30 | Christian Danner | Zakspeed | 55 | Engine | |
| Ret | 4 | Ivan Capelli | Tyrrell-Renault | 44 | Accident | |
| Ret | 3 | Martin Brundle | Tyrrell-Renault | 40 | Water leak | |
| Ret | 19 | Teo Fabi | Toleman-Hart | 33 | Engine | |
| Ret | 9 | Philippe Alliot | RAM-Hart | 31 | Engine | |
| Ret | 20 | P.Ghinzani | Toleman-Hart | 16 | Engine | |
| Ret | 33 | Alan Jones | Lola-Hart | 13 | Radiator | |
| Ret | 27 | Michele Alboreto | Ferrari | 13 | Turbo | |
| Ret | 7 | Nelson Piquet | Brabham-BMW | 6 | Accident | |
| Ret | 16 | Derek Warwick | Renault | 4 | Injection | |
| Ret | 29 | P.Martini | Minardi-Motori Moderni | 3 | Accident | |
| DNQ | 24 | H.Rothengatter | Osella-Alfa Romeo | | | |

Winning speed: 126.527mph Lap leaders: Senna 1-8; Mansell 9-75
Pole position: Senna, 1m7.169s, 140.100mph
Fastest lap: Laffite, 1m11.526s, 131.566mph

## SOUTH AFRICAN GRAND PRIX: KYALAMI *19 October Round 15 Race 419 75 x 2.550 miles*

| POS. | NO. | DRIVER | CAR/ENGINE | LAPS | TIME/RETIRED | GRID |
|---|---|---|---|---|---|---|
| 1 | 5 | Nigel Mansell | Williams-Honda | 75 | 1:28'22.866 | 1 |
| 2 | 6 | Keke Rosberg | Williams-Honda | 75 | +7.572 | 3 |
| 3 | 2 | Alain Prost | McLaren-TAG | 74 | +1 Lap | 9 |
| 4 | 28 | Stefan Johansson | Ferrari | 74 | +1 Lap | 16 |
| 5 | 17 | Gerhard Berger | Arrows-BMW | 74 | +1 Lap | 11 |
| 6 | 18 | Thierry Boutsen | Arrows-BMW | 74 | +1 Lap | 10 |
| 7 | 3 | Martin Brundle | Tyrrell-Renault | 73 | +2 Laps | 17 |
| Ret | 11 | Elio de Angelis | Lotus-Renault | 52 | Engine | 6 |
| Ret | 29 | P.Martini | Minardi-Motori Moderni | 45 | Radiator | 20 |
| Ret | 1 | Niki Lauda | McLaren-TAG | 37 | Turbo | 8 |
| Ret | 4 | Philippe Streiff | Tyrrell-Renault | 16 | Accident | 19 |
| Ret | 12 | Ayrton Senna | Lotus-Renault | 8 | Engine | 4 |
| Ret | 27 | Michele Alboreto | Ferrari | 8 | Turbo | 15 |
| Ret | 7 | Nelson Piquet | Brabham-BMW | 6 | Engine | 2 |
| Ret | 20 | P.Ghinzani | Toleman-Hart | 4 | Engine | 13 |
| Ret | 19 | Teo Fabi | Toleman-Hart | 3 | Engine | 7 |
| Ret | 8 | Marc Surer | Brabham/BMW | 3 | Engine | 5 |
| Ret | 24 | H.Rothengatter | Osella-Alfa Romeo | 1 | Electrical | 21 |
| Ret | 22 | Riccardo Patrese | Alfa Romeo | 0 | Accident | 12 |
| Ret | 23 | Eddie Cheever | Alfa Romeo | 0 | Accident | 14 |
| DNS | | Alan Jones | Lola-Hart | 0 | Unwell | 18 |

Winning speed: 129.841mph Lap leaders: Mansell 1-7, 9-75; Rosberg 8
Pole position: Mansell, 1m02.366, 147.202mph
Fastest lap: Rosberg, 1m8.149s, 134.711mph
Prost's last lap was deducted because it was too slow.

## AUSTRALIAN GRAND PRIX: ADELAIDE *3 November Round 16 Race 420 82 x 2.348*

| POS. | NO. | DRIVER | CAR/ENGINE | LAPS | TIME/RETIRED | GRID |
|---|---|---|---|---|---|---|
| 1 | 6 | Keke Rosberg | Williams-Honda | 82 | 2:00'40.473 | 3 |
| 2 | 26 | Jacques Laffite | Ligier-Renault | 82 | +46.130 | 20 |
| 3 | 25 | Philippe Streiff | Ligier-Renault | 82 | +1'28.536 | 18 |
| 4 | 4 | Ivan Capelli | Tyrrell-Renault | 81 | +1 Lap | 22 |
| 5 | 28 | Stefan Johansson | Ferrari | 81 | +1 Lap | 15 |
| 6 | 17 | Gerhard Berger | Arrows-BMW | 81 | +1 Lap | 7 |
| 7 | 24 | H.Rothengatter | Osella-Alfa Romeo | 78 | +4 Laps | 25 |
| 8 | 29 | P.Martini | Minardi-Motori Moderni | 78 | +4 Laps | 23 |
| Ret | 12 | Ayrton Senna | Lotus-Renault | 62 | Engine | 1 |
| Ret | 27 | Michele Alboreto | Ferrari | 61 | Transmission | 5 |
| Ret | 1 | Niki Lauda | McLaren-TAG | 57 | Accident | 16 |
| Ret | 16 | Derek Warwick | Renault | 57 | Transmission | 12 |
| Ret | 3 | Martin Brundle | Tyrrell-Renault | 49 | Not classified | 17 |
| Ret | 8 | Marc Surer | Brabham-BMW | 42 | Engine | 6 |
| Ret | 22 | Riccardo Patrese | Alfa Romeo | 42 | Exhaust | 14 |
| Ret | 19 | Teo Fabi | Toleman-Hart | 40 | Engine | 24 |
| Ret | 18 | Thierry Boutsen | Arrows-BMW | 37 | Oil leak | 11 |
| Ret | 20 | P.Ghinzani | Toleman-Hart | 28 | Clutch | 21 |
| Ret | 2 | Alain Prost | McLaren-TAG | 26 | Engine | 4 |
| Ret | 15 | Patrick Tambay | Renault | 20 | Transmission | 8 |
| Ret | 33 | Alan Jones | Lola-Hart | 20 | Electrical | 19 |
| Ret | 11 | Elio de Angelis | Lotus-Renault | 18 | Disqualified | 10 |
| Ret | 7 | Nelson Piquet | Brabham-BMW | 14 | Fire | 9 |
| Ret | 23 | Eddie Cheever | Alfa Romeo | 5 | Engine | 13 |
| Ret | 5 | Nigel Mansell | Williams-Honda | 1 | Transmission | 2 |

Winning speed: 95.711mph Lap leaders: Rosberg 1-41, 44-52, 62-82; Senna 42-43, 53-55, 58-61, Lauda 56-57
Pole position: Senna, 1m19.843s, 105.847mph
Fastest lap: Rosberg, 1m23.758s, 100.900mph

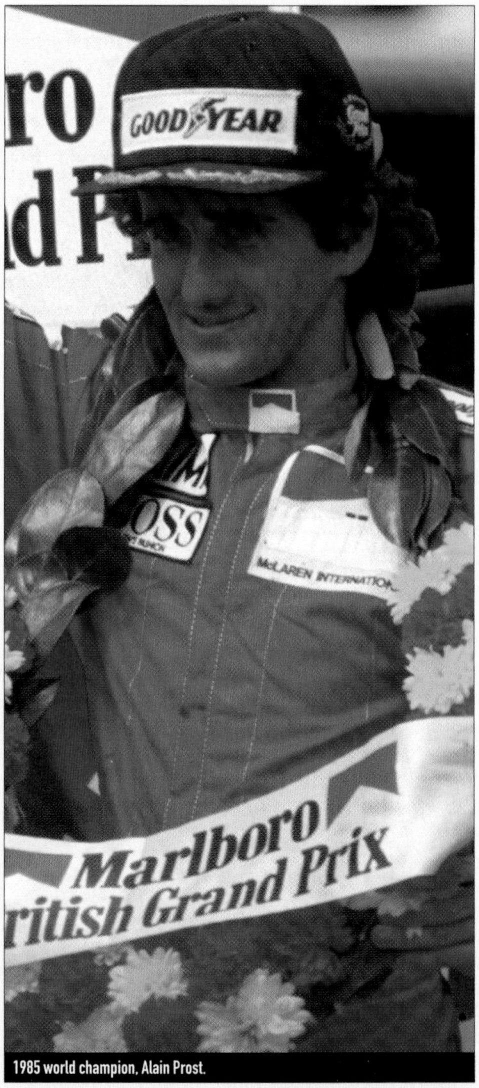

1985 world champion, Alain Prost.

 

# 1986

## DRIVERS' CHAMPION: ALAIN PROST
## CONSTRUCTORS' CHAMPION: WILLIAMS HONDA

### DRIVERS' CHAMPIONSHIP

| POS. | DRIVER | NATIONALITY | CAR | POINTS |
|---|---|---|---|---|
| 1 | Alain Prost | France | McLaren-TAG Porsche | 72(2) |
| 2 | Nigel Mansell | GB | Williams-Honda | 70(2) |
| 3 | Nelson Piquet | Brazil | Williams-Honda | 69 |
| 4 | Ayrton Senna | Brazil | Lotus-Renault | 55 |
| 5 | Stefan Johansson | Sweden | Ferrari | 23 |
| 6 | Keke Rosberg | Finland | McLaren-TAG Porsche | 22 |
| 7 | Gerhard Berger | Austria | Benetton-BMW | 17 |
| 8 | Jacques Laffite | France | Ligier-Renault | 14 |
| 9 | Michele Alboreto | Italy | Ferrari | 14 |
| = | René Arnoux | France | Ligier-Renault | 14 |
| 11 | Martin Brundle | GB | Tyrrell-Renault | 8 |
| 12 | Alan Jones | Australia | Beatrice-Hart | 4 |
| 13 | Johnny Dumfries | GB | Lotus-Renault | 3 |
| = | Philippe Streiff | France | Tyrrell-Renault | 3 |
| 15 | Teo Fabi | Italy | Benetton-BMW | 2 |
| = | Patrick Tambay | France | Beatrice-Hart | 2 |
| = | Riccardo Patrese | Italy | Brabham-BMW | 2 |
| 18 | Christian Danner | West Germany | Osella-Alfa Romeo, Arrows-BMW | 1 |
| = | Philippe Alliot | France | Ligier-Renault | 1 |
| | Elio de Angelis | Italy | Brabham-BMW | |
| | Jonathan Palmer | GB | Zakspeed | |
| | Thierry Boutsen | Belgium | Arrows-BMW | |
| | Marc Surer | Switzerland | Arrows-BMW | |
| | Piercarlo Ghinzani | Italy | Osella-Alfa Romeo | |
| | Andrea de Cesaris | Italy | Minardi-Motori Moderni | |
| | Alessandro Nannini | Italy | Minardi-Motori Moderni | |
| | Huub Rothengatter | Netherlands | Zakspeed | |
| | Derek Warwick | GB | Brabham-BMW | |
| | Eddie Cheever | USA | Beatrice-Ford | |
| | Alan Berg | Canada | Osella-Alfa Romeo | |
| | Ivan Capelli | Italy | AGS-Motori Moderni | |
| | Alex Caffi | Italy | Osella-Alfa Romeo | |

Points for top six finishers (9, 6, 4, 3, 2, 1). Half points awarded for races stopped before half distance.

### CONSTRUCTORS' CHAMPIONSHIP

| POS. | CONSTRUCTOR | POINTS |
|---|---|---|
| 1 | Williams-Honda | 141 |
| 2 | McLaren-TAG | 96 |
| 3 | Lotus-Renault | 58 |
| 4 | Ferrari | 37 |
| 5 | Ligier-Renault | 29 |
| 6 | Benetton-BMW | 19 |
| 7 | Tyrrell-Renault | 11 |
| 8 | Lola-Ford | 6 |
| 9 | Brabham-BMW | 2 |
| 10 | Arrows-BMW | 1 |

Points for top six finishers (9, 6, 4, 3, 2, 1). Half points awarded for races stopped before half distance.

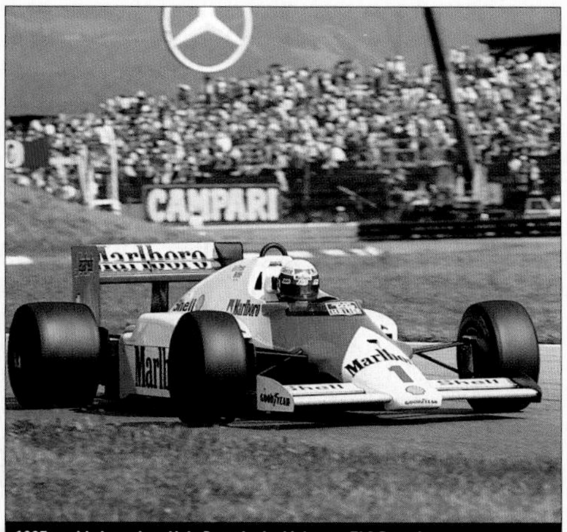


1985 world champion, Alain Prost in the McLaren-TAG Porsche.

### BRAZILIAN GRAND PRIX: RIO DE JANEIRO *23 March Round: 1 Race: 421 61 x 3.126 miles*

| POS. | NO. | DRIVER | CAR/ENGINE | LAPS | TIME/RETIRED | GRID |
|---|---|---|---|---|---|---|
| 1 | 6 | Nelson Piquet | Williams-Honda | 61 | 1:39'32.583 | 2 |
| 2 | 12 | Ayrton Senna | Lotus-Renault | 61 | +34.827 | 1 |
| 3 | 26 | Jacques Laffite | Ligier-Renault | 61 | +59.759 | 5 |
| 4 | 25 | Rene Arnoux | Ligier-Renault | 61 | +1'28.429 | 4 |
| 5 | 3 | Martin Brundle | Tyrrell-Renault | 60 | +1 Lap | 17 |
| 6 | 20 | Gerhard Berger | Benetton-BMW | 59 | +2 Laps | 16 |
| 7 | 4 | Philippe Streiff | Tyrrell-Renault | 59 | +2 Laps | 18 |
| 8 | 8 | Elio de Angelis | Brabham-BMW | 58 | +3 Laps | 14 |
| 9 | 11 | Johnny Dumfries | Lotus-Renault | 58 | +3 Laps | 11 |
| 10 | 19 | Teo Fabi | Benetton-BMW | 56 | +5 Laps | 12 |
| Ret | 18 | Thierry Boutsen | Arrows-BMW | 37 | Exhaust | 15 |
| Ret | 27 | Michele Alboreto | Ferrari | 35 | Fuel system | 6 |
| Ret | 1 | Alain Prost | McLaren-TAG | 30 | Engine | 9 |
| Ret | 22 | Christian Danner | Osella-Alfa Romeo | 29 | Engine | 24 |
| Ret | 28 | Stefan Johansson | Ferrari | 26 | Brakes | 8 |
| Ret | 16 | Patrick Tambay | Lola-Hart | 24 | Battery | 13 |
| Ret | 7 | Riccardo Patrese | Brabham-BMW | 21 | Water leak | 10 |
| Ret | 14 | Jonathan Palmer | Zakspeed | 20 | Engine | 21 |
| Ret | 17 | Marc Surer | Arrows-BMW | 19 | Engine | 20 |
| Ret | 24 | A.Nannini | Minardi-Motori Moderni | 18 | Clutch | 25 |
| Ret | 23 | A.de Cesaris | Minardi-Motori Moderni | 16 | Turbo | 22 |
| Ret | 21 | P.Ghinzani | Osella-Alfa Romeo | 16 | Engine | 23 |
| Ret | 2 | Keke Rosberg | McLaren-TAG | 6 | Engine | 7 |
| Ret | 15 | Alan Jones | Lola-Hart | 5 | Injection | 19 |
| Ret | 5 | Nigel Mansell | Williams-Honda | 0 | Spun of | 3 |

Winning speed: 114.941mph
Lap leaders: Senna 1-2, 19, 41; Piquet 3-18, 27-40, 42-61; Prost 20-26
Pole position: Senna, 1m25.501s, 131.625mph
Fastest lap: Piquet, 1m33.546s, 120.305mph

### SPANISH GRAND PRIX: JEREZ DE LA FRONTERA *13 April Round 2 Race 422 72 x 2.621 miles*

| POS. | NO. | DRIVER | CAR/ENGINE | LAPS | TIME/RETIRED | GRID |
|---|---|---|---|---|---|---|
| 1 | 12 | Ayrton Senna | Lotus-Renault | 72 | 1:48'47.735 | 1 |
| 2 | 5 | Nigel Mansell | Williams-Honda | 72 | +0.014 | 3 |
| 3 | 1 | Alain Prost | McLaren-TAG | 72 | +21.552 | 4 |
| 4 | 2 | Keke Rosberg | McLaren-TAG | 71 | +1 Lap | 5 |
| 5 | 19 | Teo Fabi | Benetton-BMW | 71 | +1 Lap | 9 |
| 6 | 20 | Gerhard Berger | Benetton-BMW | 71 | +1 Lap | 7 |
| 7 | 18 | Thierry Boutsen | Arrows-BMW | 68 | +4 Laps | 19 |
| 8 | 16 | Patrick Tambay | Lola-Hart | 66 | +6 Laps | 18 |
| Ret | 11 | Johnny Dumfries | Lotus-Renault | 52 | Gearbox | 10 |
| Ret | 3 | Martin Brundle | Tyrrell-Renault | 41 | Engine | 12 |
| Ret | 26 | Jacques Laffite | Ligier-Renault | 40 | Halfshaft | 8 |
| Ret | 17 | Marc Surer | Arrows-BMW | 39 | Fuel system | 22 |
| Ret | 6 | Nelson Piquet | Williams-Honda | 39 | Engine | 2 |
| Ret | 8 | Elio de Angelis | Brabham-BMW | 29 | Gearbox | 15 |
| Ret | 25 | Rene Arnoux | Ligier-Renault | 29 | Halfshaft | 6 |
| Ret | 27 | Michele Alboreto | Ferrari | 22 | Wheel bearing | 13 |
| Ret | 4 | Philippe Streiff | Tyrrell-Renault | 22 | Engine | 20 |
| Ret | 22 | Christian Danner | Osella-Alfa Romeo | 14 | Engine | 23 |
| Ret | 28 | Stefan Johansson | Ferrari | 11 | Brakes | 11 |
| Ret | 21 | P.Ghinzani | Osella-Alfa Romeo | 10 | Engine | 21 |
| Ret | 7 | Riccardo Patrese | Brabham-BMW | 8 | Gearbox | 14 |
| Ret | 23 | A.de Cesaris | Minardi-Motori Moderni | 1 | Differential | 24 |
| Ret | 14 | Jonathan Palmer | Zakspeed | 0 | Collision | 16 |
| Ret | 15 | Alan Jones | Lola-Hart | 0 | Collision | 17 |
| Ret | 24 | A.Nannini | Minardi-Motori Moderni | 0 | Differential | 25 |

Winning speed: 104.071mph Lap leaders: Senna 1-39, 63-72; Mansell 40-62
Pole position: Senna, 1m21.605s, 115.623mph
Fastest lap: Mansell 1m27.176s, 108.234mph

### SAN MARINO GRAND PRIX: IMOLA *27 April Round 3 Race 423 60 x 3.132 miles*

| POS. | NO. | DRIVER | CAR/ENGINE | LAPS | TIME/RETIRED | GRID |
|---|---|---|---|---|---|---|
| 1 | 1 | Alain Prost | McLaren-TAG | 60 | 1:32'28.408 | 4 |
| 2 | 6 | Nelson Piquet | Williams-Honda | 60 | +7.645 | 2 |
| 3 | 20 | Gerhard Berger | Benetton-BMW | 59 | +1 Lap | 9 |
| 4 | 28 | Stefan Johansson | Ferrari | 59 | +1 Lap | 7 |
| 5 | 2 | Keke Rosberg | McLaren-TAG | 58 | Out of fuel | 6 |
| 6 | 7 | Riccardo Patrese | Brabham-BMW | 58 | Out of fuel | 16 |
| 7 | 18 | Thierry Boutsen | Arrows-BMW | 58 | 2 Laps | 12 |
| 8 | 3 | Martin Brundle | Tyrrell-Renault | 58 | 2 Laps | 13 |
| 9 | 17 | Marc Surer | Arrows-BMW | 57 | 3 Laps | 15 |
| 10 | 27 | Michele Alboreto | Ferrari | 56 | Turbo | 5 |
| Ret | 21 | P.Ghinzani | Osella-Alfa Romeo | 52 | Out of fuel | 26 |
| Ret | 25 | Rene Arnoux | Ligier-Renault | 46 | Wheel | 8 |
| Ret | 4 | Philippe Streiff | Tyrrell-Renault | 41 | Transmission | 22 |
| Ret | 19 | Teo Fabi | Benetton-BMW | 39 | Engine | 10 |
| Ret | 14 | Jonathan Palmer | Zakspeed | 38 | Brakes | 20 |
| Ret | 22 | Christian Danner | Osella-Alfa Romeo | 31 | Electrical | 25 |
| Ret | 15 | Alan Jones | Lola-Ford | 28 | Overheating | 21 |
| Ret | 23 | A.de Cesaris | Minardi-Motori Moderni | 20 | Engine | 23 |
| Ret | 8 | Elio de Angelis | Brabham-BMW | 19 | Engine | 19 |
| Ret | 26 | Jacques Laffite | Ligier-Renault | 14 | Transmission | 14 |
| Ret | 12 | Ayrton Senna | Lotus-Renault | 11 | Wheel bearing | 1 |
| Ret | 5 | Nigel Mansell | Williams-Honda | 8 | Engine | 3 |
| Ret | 11 | Johnny Dumfries | Lotus-Renault | 8 | Wheel bearing | 17 |
| Ret | 29 | H.Rothengatter | Zakspeed | 7 | Turbo | 24 |
| Ret | 16 | Patrick Tambay | Lola-Hart | 5 | Engine | 11 |
| Ret | 24 | A.Nannini | Minardi-Motori Moderni | 0 | Accident | 18 |

Winning speed: 121.918mph Lap leaders: Piquet 1-28; Rosberg 29-32; Prost 33-60
Pole position: Senna, 1m25.050s, 132.559mph
Fastest lap: Piquet, 1m28.667, 127.152mph

### MONACO GRAND PRIX: MONTE CARLO *11 May Round 4 Race 424 78 x 2.068 miles*

| POS. | NO. | DRIVER | CAR/ENGINE | LAPS | TIME/RETIRED | GRID |
|---|---|---|---|---|---|---|
| 1 | 1 | Alain Prost | McLaren-TAG | 78 | 1:55'41.060 | 1 |
| 2 | 2 | Keke Rosberg | McLaren-TAG | 78 | +25.022 | 9 |
| 3 | 12 | Ayrton Senna | Lotus-Renault | 78 | +53.646 | 3 |
| 4 | 5 | Nigel Mansell | Williams-Honda | 78 | +1'11.402 | 2 |
| 5 | 25 | Rene Arnoux | Ligier-Renault | 77 | +1 Lap | 12 |
| 6 | 26 | Jacques Laffite | Ligier-Renault | 77 | +1 Lap | 7 |
| 7 | 6 | Nelson Piquet | Williams-Honda | 77 | +1 Lap | 11 |
| 8 | 18 | Thierry Boutsen | Arrows-BMW | 75 | +3 Laps | 14 |
| 9 | 17 | Marc Surer | Arrows-BMW | 75 | +3 Laps | 17 |
| 10 | 28 | Stefan Johansson | Ferrari | 75 | +3 Laps | 15 |
| 11 | 4 | Philippe Streiff | Tyrrell-Renault | 74 | +4 Laps | 13 |
| 12 | 14 | Jonathan Palmer | Zakspeed | 74 | +4 Laps | 19 |
| Ret | 3 | Martin Brundle | Tyrrell-Renault | 67 | Accident | 10 |
| Ret | 16 | Patrick Tambay | Lola-Ford | 67 | Accident | 8 |
| Ret | 20 | Gerhard Berger | Benetton-BMW | 42 | Steering | 5 |
| Ret | 7 | Riccardo Patrese | Brabham-BMW | 38 | Fuel pump | 6 |
| Ret | 27 | Michele Alboreto | Ferrari | 38 | Turbo | 4 |
| Ret | 8 | Elio de Angelis | Brabham-BMW | 31 | Engine | 20 |
| Ret | 19 | Teo Fabi | Benetton-BMW | 17 | Brakes | 16 |
| Ret | 15 | Alan Jones | Lola-Ford | 2 | Accident | 18 |
| DNQ | 21 | P.Ghinzani | Osella-Alfa Romeo | | | |
| DNQ | 11 | Johnny Dumfries | Lotus-Renault | | | |
| DNQ | 29 | H.Rothengatter | Zakspeed | | | |
| DNQ | 22 | Christian Danner | Osella-Alfa Romeo | | | |
| DNQ | 23 | A.de Cesaris | Minardi-Motori Moderni | | | |
| DNQ | 24 | A.Nannini | Minardi-Motori Moderni | | | |

Winning speed: 83.658mph Lap leaders: Prost 1-34, 42-78; Senna 35-41
Pole position: Prost, 1m26.607s, 90.098mph
Fastest lap: Prost, 1m26.607s, 85.958mph

### BELGIAN GRAND PRIX: SPA-FRANCORCHAMPS *25 May Round 5 Race 425 43 x 43 x 4.312 miles*

| POS. | NO. | DRIVER | CAR/ENGINE | LAPS | TIME/RETIRED | GRID |
|---|---|---|---|---|---|---|
| 1 | 5 | Nigel Mansell | Williams-Honda | 43 | 1:27'57.925 | 5 |
| 2 | 12 | Ayrton Senna | Lotus-Renault | 43 | +19.827 | 4 |
| 3 | 28 | Stefan Johansson | Ferrari | 43 | +26.592 | 11 |
| 4 | 27 | Michele Alboreto | Ferrari | 43 | +29.634 | 9 |
| 5 | 26 | Jacques Laffite | Ligier-Renault | 43 | +1'10.690 | 17 |
| 6 | 1 | Alain Prost | McLaren-TAG | 43 | +2'17.772 | 3 |
| 7 | 19 | Teo Fabi | Benetton-BMW | 42 | +1 Lap | 6 |
| 8 | 7 | Riccardo Patrese | Brabham-BMW | 42 | +1 Lap | 15 |
| 9 | 17 | Marc Surer | Arrows-BMW | 41 | +2 Laps | 21 |
| 10 | 20 | Gerhard Berger | Benetton-BMW | 41 | +2 Laps | 2 |
| 11 | 15 | Alan Jones | Lola-Ford | 40 | Out of fuel | 16 |
| 12 | 4 | Philippe Streiff | Tyrrell-Renault | 40 | +3 Laps | 18 |
| 13 | 14 | Jonathan Palmer | Zakspeed | 37 | +6 Laps | 20 |
| Ret | 23 | A.de Cesaris | Minardi-Motori Moderni | 35 | Out of fuel | 19 |
| Ret | 29 | H.Rothengatter | Zakspeed | 25 | Electrical | 23 |
| Ret | 3 | Martin Brundle | Tyrrell-Renault | 25 | Gearbox | 12 |
| Ret | 24 | A.Nannini | Minard-Motori Moderni | 24 | Gearbox | 22 |
| Ret | 25 | Rene Arnoux | Ligier-Renault | 23 | Engine | 7 |
| Ret | 6 | Nelson Piquet | Williams-Honda | 16 | Turbo | 1 |
| Ret | 18 | Thierry Boutsen | Arrows-BMW | 7 | Electrical | 14 |
| Ret | 11 | Johnny Dumfries | Lotus-Renault | 7 | Spun off | 13 |
| Ret | 2 | Keke Rosberg | McLaren-TAG | 6 | Engine | 8 |
| Ret | 21 | P.Ghinzani | Osella-Alfa Romeo | 3 | Engine | 24 |
| Ret | 22 | Christian Danner | Osella-Alfa Romeo | 2 | Engine | 25 |
| Ret | 16 | Patrick Tambay | Lola-Ford | 0 | Accident | 10 |

Winning speed: 126.479mph Lap leaders: Piquet 1-16; Senna 17-21; Johansson 22-23; Mansell 24-43
Pole position: Piquet 1m54.331, 135.784mph
Fastest lap: Prost, 1m59.282, 130.148mph

### CANADIAN GRAND PRIX: MONTREAL *15 June Round 6 Race 426 69 x 2.740 miles*

| POS. | NO. | DRIVER | CAR/ENGINE | LAPS | TIME/RETIRED | GRID |
|---|---|---|---|---|---|---|
| 1 | 5 | Nigel Mansell | Williams-Honda | 69 | 1:42'26.415 | 1 |
| 2 | 1 | Alain Prost | McLaren-TAG | 69 | +20.659 | 4 |
| 3 | 6 | Nelson Piquet | Williams-Honda | 69 | +36.262 | 3 |
| 4 | 2 | Keke Rosberg | McLaren-TAG | 69 | +1'35.673 | 6 |
| 5 | 12 | Ayrton Senna | Lotus-Renault | 68 | +1 Lap | 2 |
| 6 | 25 | Rene Arnoux | Ligier-Renault | 68 | +1 Lap | 5 |
| 7 | 26 | Jacques Laffite | Ligier-Renault | 68 | +1 Lap | 8 |
| 8 | 27 | Michele Alboreto | Ferrari | 68 | +1 Lap | 11 |
| 9 | 3 | Martin Brundle | Tyrrell-Renault | 67 | +2 Laps | 19 |
| 10 | 15 | Alan Jones | Lola-Ford | 66 | +3 Laps | 13 |
| 11 | 4 | Philippe Streiff | Tyrrell-Renault | 65 | +4 Laps | 17 |
| 12 | 29 | H.Rothengatter | Zakspeed | 63 | +6Laps | 24 |
| Ret | 7 | Riccardo Patrese | Brabham-BMW | 44 | Turbo | 9 |
| Ret | 21 | P.Ghinzani | Osella-Alfa Romeo | 43 | Gearbox | 23 |
| Ret | 23 | A.de Cesaris | Minardi-Motori Moderni | 40 | Gearbox | 21 |
| Ret | 18 | Thierry Boutsen | Arrows-BMW | 38 | Electrical | 12 |
| Ret | 20 | Gerhard Berger | Benetton-BMW | 34 | Turbo | 7 |
| Ret | 28 | Stefan Johansson | Ferrari | 29 | Accident | 18 |
| Ret | 11 | Johnny Dumfries | Lotus-Renault | 28 | Accident | 16 |
| Ret | 14 | Jonathan Palmer | Zakspeed | 24 | Engine | 22 |
| Ret | 8 | Derek Warwick | Brabham-BMW | 20 | Engine | 10 |
| Ret | 24 | A.Nannini | Minardi-Motori Moderni | 17 | Turbo | 20 |
| Ret | 19 | Teo Fabi | Benetton-BMW | 13 | Battery | 15 |
| Ret | 22 | Christian Danner | Osella-Alfa Romeo | 6 | Turbo | 25 |
| DNS | 16 | Patrick Tambay | Lola-Ford | 0 | Accident | 14 |

Winning speed: 110.744mph
Lap leaders: Mansell 1-16, 22-30, 32-69; Rosberg 17-21; Prost 31
Pole position: Mansell, 1m24.118s, 117.274mph
Fastest lap: Piquet, 1m25.443s, 115.456mph

### Key to Abbreviations

| | | | |
|---|---|---|---|
| **DNPQ** | Did not pre-qualify | **NC** | Not classified |
| **DNQ** | Did not qualify | **Ret** | Retired |
| **DNS** | Did not start | **Wth** | Withdrawn |
| **DSQ** | Disqualified | | |

1986 Season Statistics

## USA EAST GRAND PRIX: DETROIT *22 June Round 7 Race 427 63 x 2.500 miles*

| POS. | NO. | DRIVER | CAR/ENGINE | LAPS | TIME/RETIRED | GRID |
|---|---|---|---|---|---|---|
| 1 | 12 | Ayrton Senna | Lotus-Renault | 63 | 1:51'12.847 | 1 |
| 2 | 26 | Jacques Laffite | Ligier-Renault | 63 | +31.017 | 6 |
| 3 | 1 | Alain Prost | McLaren-TAG | 63 | +31.824 | 7 |
| 4 | 27 | Michele Alboreto | Ferrari | 63 | +1'30.936 | 11 |
| 5 | 5 | Nigel Mansell | Williams-Honda | 62 | +1 Lap | 2 |
| 6 | 7 | Riccardo Patrese | Brabham-BMW | 62 | +1 Lap | 8 |
| 7 | 11 | Johnny Dumfries | Lotus-Renault | 61 | +2 Laps | 14 |
| 8 | 14 | Jonathan Palmer | Zakspeed | 61 | +2 Laps | 20 |
| 9 | 4 | Philippe Streiff | Tyrrell-Renault | 61 | +2 Laps | 18 |
| 10 | 8 | Derek Warwick | Brabham-BMW | 60 | +3 Laps | 15 |
| Ret | 17 | Christian Danner | Arrows-BMW | 51 | Electrical | 19 |
| Ret | 25 | Rene Arnoux | Ligier-Renault | 46 | Accident | 4 |
| Ret | 18 | Thierry Boutsen | Arrows-BMW | 44 | Accident | 13 |
| Ret | 23 | A.de Cesaris | Minardi-Motori Moderni | 43 | Gearbox | 23 |
| Ret | 6 | Nelson Piquet | Williams-Honda | 41 | Accident | 3 |
| Ret | 28 | Stefan Johansson | Ferrari | 40 | Electrical | 5 |
| Ret | 19 | Teo Fabi | Benetton-BMW | 38 | Gearbox | 17 |
| Ret | 16 | Eddie Cheever | Lola-Ford | 37 | Steering | 10 |
| Ret | 15 | Alan Jones | Lola-Ford | 33 | Steering | 21 |
| Ret | 22 | Allen Berg | Osella-Alfa Romeo | 28 | Electrical | 25 |
| Ret | 3 | Martin Brundle | Tyrrell-Renault | 15 | Electrical | 16 |
| Ret | 21 | P.Ghinzani | Osella-Alfa Romeo | 14 | Turbo | 22 |
| Ret | 2 | Keke Rosberg | McLaren-TAG | 12 | Transmission | 9 |
| Ret | 20 | Gerhard Berger | Benetton-BMW | 8 | Engine | 12 |
| Ret | 24 | A.Nannini | Minardi-Motori Moderni | 3 | Turbo | 24 |
| Ret | 29 | H.Rothengatter | Zakspeed | 0 | Electrical | 26 |

Winning speed: 84.971mph
Lap leaders: Senna 1, 8-13, 39-63; Mansell 2-7; Arnoux 14-17; Laffite 18-30; Piquet 31-38
Pole position: Senna, 1m38.301s, 91.556mph
Fastest lap: Piquet, 1m41.233s, 88.904mph

## FRENCH GRAND PRIX: PAUL RICARD *6 July Round 8 Race 428 80 x 2.369 miles*

| POS. | NO. | DRIVER | CAR/ENGINE | LAPS | TIME/RETIRED | GRID |
|---|---|---|---|---|---|---|
| 1 | 5 | Nigel Mansell | Williams-Honda | 80 | 1:37'19.272 | 2 |
| 2 | 1 | Alain Prost | McLaren-TAG | 80 | +17.128 | 5 |
| 3 | 6 | Nelson Piquet | Williams-Honda | 80 | +37.545 | 3 |
| 4 | 2 | Keke Rosberg | McLaren-TAG | 80 | +48.703 | 7 |
| 5 | 25 | Rene Arnoux | Ligier-Renault | 79 | +1 Lap | 4 |
| 6 | 26 | Jacques Laffite | Ligier-Renault | 79 | +1 Lap | 11 |
| 7 | 7 | Riccardo Patrese | Brabham-BMW | 78 | +2 Laps | 16 |
| 8 | 27 | Michele Alboreto | Ferrari | 78 | +2 Laps | 6 |
| 9 | 8 | Derek Warwick | Brabham-BMW | 77 | +3 Laps | 14 |
| 10 | 3 | Martin Brundle | Tyrrell-Renault | 77 | +3 Laps | 15 |
| 11 | 17 | Christian Danner | Arrows-BMW | 76 | +4 Laps | 18 |
| NC | 18 | Thierry Boutsen | Arrows-BMW | 67 | Not classified | 21 |
| Ret | 16 | Patrick Tambay | Lola-Ford | 64 | Brakes | 13 |
| Ret | 11 | Johnny Dumfries | Lotus-Renault | 56 | Engine | 12 |
| Ret | 14 | Jonathan Palmer | Zakspeed | 46 | Engine | 22 |
| Ret | 4 | Philippe Streiff | Tyrrell-Renault | 43 | Fire | 17 |
| Ret | 29 | H.Rothengatter | Zakspeed | 32 | Accident | 24 |
| Ret | 22 | Allen Berg | Osella-Alfa Romeo | 25 | Turbo | 26 |
| Ret | 20 | Gerhard Berger | Benetton-BMW | 22 | Gearbox | 8 |
| Ret | 19 | Teo Fabi | Benetton-BMW | 7 | Engine | 9 |
| Ret | 28 | Stefan Johansson | Ferrari | 5 | Turbo | 10 |
| Ret | 12 | Ayrton Senna | Lotus-Renault | 3 | Accident | 1 |
| Ret | 21 | P.Ghinzani | Osella-Alfa Romeo | 3 | Accident | 25 |
| Ret | 24 | A.Nannini | Minardi-Motori Moderni | 3 | Accident | 19 |
| Ret | 23 | A.de Cesaris | Minardi-Motori Moderni | 3 | Turbo | 23 |
| Ret | 15 | Alan Jones | Lola-Ford | 2 | Accident | 20 |

Winning speed: 116.856mph Lap leaders: Mansell 1-25, 37-53, 59-80; Prost 26-36, 54-58
Pole position: Senna, 1m6.526s, 128.212mph
Fastest lap: Mansell, 1m9.993s, 121.861mph

## BRITISH GRAND PRIX: BRANDS HATCH *13 July Round 9 Race 429 75 x 2.614 miles*

| POS. | NO. | DRIVER | CAR/ENGINE | LAPS | TIME/RETIRED | GRID |
|---|---|---|---|---|---|---|
| 1 | 5 | Nigel Mansell | Williams-Honda | 75 | 1:30'38.471 | 2 |
| 2 | 6 | Nelson Piquet | Williams-Honda | 75 | +5.574 | 1 |
| 3 | 1 | Alain Prost | McLaren-TAG | 74 | +1 Lap | 6 |
| 4 | 25 | Rene Arnoux | Ligier-Renault | 73 | +2 Laps | 8 |
| 5 | 3 | Martin Brundle | Tyrrell-Renault | 72 | +3 Laps | 11 |
| 6 | 4 | Philippe Streiff | Tyrrell-Renault | 72 | +3 Laps | 16 |
| 7 | 11 | Johnny Dumfries | Lotus-Renault | 72 | +3 Laps | 10 |
| 8 | 8 | Derek Warwick | Brabham-BMW | 72 | +3 Laps | 9 |
| 9 | 14 | Jonathan Palmer | Zakspeed | 69 | +6 Laps | 22 |
| NC | 18 | Thierry Boutsen | Arrows-BMW | 62 | Not classified | 13 |
| Ret | 16 | Patrick Tambay | Lola-Ford | 60 | Gearbox | 17 |
| Ret | 27 | Michele Alboreto | Ferrari | 51 | Turbo | 12 |
| Ret | 24 | A.Nannini | Minardi-Motori Moderni | 50 | Steering | 20 |
| Ret | 19 | Teo Fabi | Benetton-BMW | 45 | Fuel system | 7 |
| Ret | 7 | Riccardo Patrese | Brabham-BMW | 39 | Engine | 15 |
| Ret | 12 | Ayrton Senna | Lotus-Renault | 27 | Gearbox | 3 |
| Ret | 29 | H.Rothengatter | Zakspeed | 24 | Engine | 25 |
| Ret | 23 | A.de Cesaris | Minardi-Motori Moderni | 23 | Electrical | 21 |
| Ret | 20 | Gerhard Berger | Benetton-BMW | 22 | Electrical | 4 |
| Ret | 15 | Alan Jones | Lola-Ford | 22 | Throttle | 14 |
| Ret | 28 | Stefan Johansson | Ferrari | 20 | Engine | 18 |
| Ret | 2 | Keke Rosberg | McLaren-TAG | 7 | Gearbox | 5 |
| Ret | 26 | Jacques Laffite | Ligier-Renault | 0 | Collision | 19 |
| Ret | 17 | Christian Danner | Arrows-BMW | 0 | Collision | 23 |
| Ret | 21 | P.Ghinzani | Osella-Alfa Romeo | 0 | Collision | 24 |
| Ret | 22 | Allen Berg | Osella-Alfa Romeo | 0 | Collision | 26 |

Winning speed: 129.775mph Lap leaders: Piquet 1-22; Mansell 23-75
Pole position: Piquet, 1m6.961s, 140.536mph
Fastest lap: Mansell, 1m9.593s, 135.220mph
Race stopped and restarted for total original distance after first lap pile-up.

## GERMAN GRAND PRIX: HOCKENHEIM *27 July Round 10 Race 430 44 x 4.223 miles*

| POS. | NO. | DRIVER | CAR/ENGINE | LAPS | TIME/RETIRED | GRID |
|---|---|---|---|---|---|---|
| 1 | 6 | Nelson Piquet | Williams-Honda | 44 | 1:22'08.263 | 5 |
| 2 | 12 | Ayrton Senna | Lotus-Renault | 44 | +15.437 | 3 |
| 3 | 5 | Nigel Mansell | Williams-Honda | 44 | +44.580 | 6 |
| 4 | 25 | Rene Arnoux | Ligier-Renault | 44 | +1'15.176 | 8 |
| 5 | 2 | Keke Rosberg | McLaren-TAG | 43 | Out of fuel | 1 |
| 6 | 1 | Alain Prost | McLaren-TAG | 43 | Out of fuel | 2 |
| 7 | 8 | Derek Warwick | Brabham-BMW | 43 | +1 Lap | 20 |
| 8 | 16 | Patrick Tambay | Lola-Ford | 43 | +1 Lap | 13 |
| 9 | 15 | Alan Jones | Lola-Ford | 42 | +2 Laps | 19 |
| 10 | 20 | Gerhard Berger | Benetton-BMW | 42 | +2 Laps | 4 |
| 11 | 28 | Stefan Johansson | Ferrari | 41 | Broken wing | 11 |
| 12 | 22 | Allen Berg | Osella-Alfa Romeo | 40 | +4 Laps | 26 |
| Ret | 17 | Christian Danner | Arrows-BMW | 38 | Turbo | 17 |
| Ret | 29 | H.Rothengatter | Zakspeed | 38 | Gearbox | 24 |
| Ret | 14 | Jonathan Palmer | Zakspeed | 37 | Engine | 16 |
| Ret | 3 | Martin Brundle | Tyrrell-Renault | 34 | Electrical | 15 |
| Ret | 7 | Riccardo Patrese | Brabham/BMW | 22 | Turbo | 7 |
| Ret | 23 | A.de Cesaris | Minardi-Motori Moderni | 20 | Gearbox | 23 |
| Ret | 24 | A.Nannini | Minardi-Motori Moderni | 19 | Overheating | 22 |
| Ret | 11 | Johnny Dumfries | Lotus-Renault | 17 | Radiator | 12 |
| Ret | 18 | Thierry Boutsen | Arrows-BMW | 13 | Turbo | 21 |
| Ret | 26 | Philippe Alliot | Ligier-Renault | 11 | Engine | 14 |
| Ret | 21 | P.Ghinzani | Osella-Alfa Romeo | 10 | Clutch | 25 |
| Ret | 4 | Philippe Streiff | Tyrrell-Renault | 7 | Engine | 18 |
| Ret | 27 | Michele Alboreto | Ferrari | 6 | Transmission | 10 |
| Ret | 19 | Teo Fabi | Benetton-BMW | 0 | Accident | 9 |

Winning speed: 135.747mph
Lap leaders: Senna 1; Rosberg 2-5; 15-19; 27-38; Piquet 6-14, 21-26, 39-44; Prost 20
Pole position: Rosberg, 1m42.013s, 149.044mph
Fastest lap: Berger, 1m46.604s, 142.626mph

## HUNGARIAN GRAND PRIX: HUNGARORING *10 August Round 11 Race 431 76 x 2.494 miles*

| POS. | NO. | DRIVER | CAR/ENGINE | LAPS | TIME/RETIRED | GRID |
|---|---|---|---|---|---|---|
| 1 | 6 | Nelson Piquet | Williams-Honda | 76 | 2:00'34.508 | 2 |
| 2 | 12 | Ayrton Senna | Lotus-Renault | 76 | 17.673 | 1 |
| 3 | 5 | Nigel Mansell | Williams-Honda | 75 | +1 Lap | 4 |
| 4 | 28 | Stefan Johansson | Ferrari | 75 | +1 Lap | 7 |
| 5 | 11 | Johnny Dumfries | Lotus-Renault | 74 | +2 Laps | 8 |
| 6 | 3 | Martin Brundle | Tyrrell-Renault | 74 | +2 Laps | 16 |
| 7 | 16 | Patrick Tambay | Lola-Ford | 74 | +2 Laps | 6 |
| 8 | 4 | Philippe Streiff | Tyrrell-Renault | 74 | +2 Laps | 18 |
| 9 | 26 | Philippe Alliot | Ligier-Renault | 73 | +3 Laps | 12 |
| 10 | 14 | Jonathan Palmer | Zakspeed | 70 | +6 Laps | 24 |
| Ret | 25 | Rene Arnoux | Ligier-Renault | 48 | Engine | 9 |
| Ret | 15 | Alan Jones | Lola-Ford | 46 | Differential | 10 |
| Ret | 20 | Gerhard Berger | Benetton-BMW | 44 | Transmission | 11 |
| Ret | 18 | Thierry Boutsen | Arrows-BMW | 40 | Electrical | 22 |
| Ret | 2 | Keke Rosberg | McLaren-TAG | 34 | Suspension | 5 |
| Ret | 19 | Teo Fabi | Benetton-BMW | 32 | Transmission | 13 |
| Ret | 24 | A.Nannini | Minardi-Motori Moderni | 30 | Engine | 17 |
| Ret | 27 | Michele Alboreto | Ferrari | 29 | Accident | 15 |
| Ret | 8 | Derek Warwick | Brabham-BMW | 28 | Accident | 19 |
| Ret | 1 | Alain Prost | McLaren-TAG | 23 | Accident | 3 |
| Ret | 21 | P.Ghinzani | Osella-Alfa Romeo | 15 | Suspension | 23 |
| Ret | 17 | Christian Danner | Arrows-BMW | 7 | Suspension | 21 |
| Ret | 7 | Riccardo Patrese | Brabham-BMW | 5 | Gearbox | 14 |
| Ret | 23 | A.de Cesaris | Minardi-Motori Moderni | 5 | Engine | 20 |
| Ret | 29 | H.Rothengatter | Zakspeed | 2 | Radiator | 25 |
| Ret | 22 | Allen Berg | Osella-Alfa Romeo | 1 | Turbo | 26 |

Winning speed: 94.327mph Lap leaders: Senna 1-11, 36-56; Piquet 12-35, 57-76
Pole position: Senna, 1m29.450s, 100.381mph
Fastest lap: Piquet, 1m31.001s, 98.670mph

## AUSTRIAN GRAND PRIX: OSTERREICHRING *17 August Round 12 Race 432 52 x 3.692 miles*

| POS. | NO. | DRIVER | CAR/ENGINE | LAPS | TIME/RETIRED | GRID |
|---|---|---|---|---|---|---|
| 1 | 1 | Alain Prost | McLaren-TAG | 52 | 1:21'22.531 | 5 |
| 2 | 27 | Michele Alboreto | Ferrari | 51 | +1 Lap | 9 |
| 3 | 28 | Stefan Johansson | Ferrari | 50 | +2 Laps | 14 |
| 4 | 15 | Alan Jones | Lola-Ford | 50 | +2 Laps | 16 |
| 5 | 16 | Patrick Tambay | Lola-Ford | 50 | +2 Laps | 13 |
| 6 | 17 | Christian Danner | Arrows-BMW | 49 | +3 Laps | 22 |
| 7 | 20 | Gerhard Berger | Benetton/BMW | 49 | +3 Laps | 2 |
| 8 | 29 | H.Rothengatter | Zakspeed | 48 | +4 Laps | 24 |
| 9 | 2 | Keke Rosberg | McLaren-TAG | 47 | Electrical | 3 |
| 10 | 25 | Rene Arnoux | Ligier-Renault | 47 | +5 Laps | 12 |
| 11 | 21 | P.Ghinzani | Osella-Alfa Romeo | 46 | +6 Laps | 25 |
| Ret | 5 | Nigel Mansell | Williams-Honda | 32 | Halfshaft | 6 |
| Ret | 6 | Nelson Piquet | Williams-Honda | 29 | Engine | 7 |
| Ret | 18 | Thierry Boutsen | Arrows-BMW | 25 | Turbo | 18 |
| Ret | 19 | Teo Fabi | Benetton-BMW | 17 | Engine | 1 |
| Ret | 26 | Philippe Alliot | Ligier-Renault | 16 | Engine | 11 |
| Ret | 24 | A.Nannini | Minardi-Motori Moderni | 13 | Suspension | 19 |
| Ret | 23 | A.de Cesaris | Minardi-Motori Moderni | 13 | Clutch | 23 |
| Ret | 12 | Ayrton Senna | Lotus-Renault | 13 | Engine | 8 |
| Ret | 3 | Martin Brundle | Tyrrell-Renault | 12 | Turbo | 17 |
| Ret | 4 | Philippe Streiff | Tyrrell/Renault | 10 | Engine | 20 |
| Ret | 11 | Johnny Dumfries | Lotus-Renault | 9 | Engine | 15 |
| Ret | 14 | Jonathan Palmer | Zakspeed | 8 | Engine | 21 |
| Ret | 22 | Allen Berg | Osella-Alfa Romeo | 6 | Electrical | 26 |
| Ret | 7 | Riccardo Patrese | Brabham-BMW | 2 | Engine | 4 |
| DNS | 8 | Derek Warwick | Brabham-BMW | 0 | Non starter | 10 |

Winning speed: 141.561mph Lap leaders: Berger 1-25; Mansell 26-28; Prost 29-52
Pole position: Fabi, 1m23.549s, 159.091mph
Fastest lap: Berger, 1m29.444, 148.606mph

## ITALIAN GRAND PRIX: MONZA *7 September Round 13 Race 433 51 x 3.604 miles*

| POS. | NO. | DRIVER | CAR/ENGINE | LAPS | TIME/RETIRED | GRID |
|---|---|---|---|---|---|---|
| 1 | 6 | Nelson Piquet | Williams-Honda | 51 | 1:17'42.889 | 6 |
| 2 | 5 | Nigel Mansell | Williams-Honda | 51 | +9.828 | 3 |
| 3 | 28 | Stefan Johansson | Ferrari | 51 | +22.915 | 12 |
| 4 | 2 | Keke Rosberg | McLaren-TAG | 51 | +53.809 | 8 |
| 5 | 20 | Gerhard Berger | Benetton-BMW | 50 | +1 Lap | 4 |
| 6 | 15 | Alan Jones | Lola-Ford | 49 | +2 Laps | 18 |
| 7 | 18 | Thierry Boutsen | Arrows-BMW | 49 | +2 Laps | 13 |
| 8 | 17 | Christian Danner | Arrows-BMW | 49 | +2 Laps | 16 |
| 9 | 4 | Philippe Streiff | Tyrrell-Renault | 49 | +2 Laps | 23 |
| 10 | 3 | Martin Brundle | Tyrrell-Renault | 49 | +2 Laps | 20 |
| NC | 22 | Alex Caffi | Osella-Alfa Romeo | 45 | Not classified | 27 |
| Ret | 19 | Teo Fabi | Benetton-BMW | 44 | Puncture | 1 |
| Ret | 27 | Michele Alboreto | Ferrari | 33 | Engine | 9 |
| Ret | 23 | A.de Cesaris | Minardi-Motori Moderni | 33 | Engine | 21 |
| Ret | 31 | Ivan Capelli | AGS/Motori Moderni | 31 | Puncture | 25 |
| Ret | 25 | Rene Arnoux | Ligier-Renault | 30 | Gearbox | 11 |
| Ret | 14 | Jonathan Palmer | Zakspeed | 27 | Engine | 22 |
| DSQ | 1 | Alain Prost | McLaren-TAG | 27 | Disqualified | 2 |
| Ret | 26 | Philippe Alliot | Ligier-Renault | 22 | Engine | 14 |
| Ret | 11 | Johnny Dumfries | Lotus-Renault | 18 | Gearbox | 17 |
| Ret | 8 | Derek Warwick | Brabham-BMW | 16 | Spun off | 7 |
| Ret | 24 | A.Nannini | Minardi-Motori Moderni | 15 | Electrical | 19 |
| Ret | 21 | P.Ghinzani | Osella-Alfa Romeo | 12 | Suspension | 26 |
| Ret | 16 | Patrick Tambay | Lola-Ford | 2 | Accident | 15 |
| Ret | 7 | Riccardo Patrese | Brabham-BMW | 2 | Accident | 10 |
| Ret | 29 | H.Rothengatter | Zakspeed | 1 | Engine | 24 |
| Ret | 12 | Ayrton Senna | Lotus-Renault | 0 | Transmission | 5 |

Winning speed: 141.905mph
Lap leaders: Berger 1-6, 25-26; Mansell 7-24, 27-37; Piquet 38-51
Pole position: Fabi, 1m24.078s, 154.312mph
Fastest lap: Fabi, 1m28.099, 147.269mph

## PORTUGUESE GRAND PRIX: ESTORIL *21 September Round 14 Race 434 70 x 2.703 miles*

| POS. | NO. | DRIVER | CAR/ENGINE | LAPS | TIME/RETIRED | GRID |
|---|---|---|---|---|---|---|
| 1 | 5 | Nigel Mansell | Williams-Honda | 70 | 1:37'21.900 | 2 |
| 2 | 1 | Alain Prost | McLaren-TAG | 70 | +18.7722 | 3 |
| 3 | 6 | Nelson Piquet | Williams-Honda | 70 | +49.274 | 6 |
| 4 | 12 | Ayrton Senna | Lotus-Renault | 69 | Out of fuel | 1 |
| 5 | 27 | Michele Alboreto | Ferrari | 69 | +1 Lap | 13 |
| 6 | 28 | Stefan Johansson | Ferrari | 69 | +1 Lap | 8 |
| 7 | 25 | Rene Arnoux | Ligier-Renault | 69 | +1 Lap | 10 |
| 8 | 19 | Teo Fabi | Benetton-BMW | 68 | +2 Laps | 5 |
| 9 | 11 | Johnny Dumfries | Lotus/Renault | 68 | +2 Laps | 15 |
| 10 | 18 | Thierry Boutsen | Arrows-BMW | 67 | +3 Laps | 21 |
| 11 | 17 | Christian Danner | Arrows-BMW | 67 | +3 Laps | 22 |
| 12 | 14 | Jonathan Palmer | Zakspeed | 67 | +3 Laps | 20 |
| 13 | 22 | Allen Berg | Osella-Alfa Romeo | 63 | +7 Laps | 27 |
| Ret | 7 | Riccardo Patrese | Brabham/BMW | 62 | Engine | 9 |
| NC | 16 | Patrick Tambay | Lola/Ford | 62 | Not classified | 14 |
| NC | 24 | A.Nannini | Minardi-Motori Moderni | 60 | Not classified | 18 |
| Ret | 20 | Gerhard Berger | Benetton/BMW | 44 | Spun off | 4 |
| Ret | 23 | A.de Cesaris | Minardi-Motori Moderni | 43 | Spun off | 16 |
| Ret | 2 | Keke Rosberg | McLaren-TAG | 41 | Electrical | 7 |
| Ret | 8 | Derek Warwick | Brabham-BMW | 41 | Electrical | 12 |
| Ret | 26 | Philippe Alliot | Ligier-Renault | 39 | Engine | 11 |
| Ret | 4 | Philippe Streiff | Tyrrell-Renault | 28 | Engine | 23 |
| Ret | 3 | Martin Brundle | Tyrrell-Renault | 18 | Engine | 19 |
| Ret | 15 | Alan Jones | Lola-Ford | 10 | Spun off | 17 |
| Ret | 29 | H.Rothengatter | Zakspeed | 9 | Transmission | 26 |
| Ret | 21 | P.Ghinzani | Osella-Alfa Romeo | 8 | Engine | 24 |
| Ret | 31 | Ivan Capelli | AGS-Motori Moderni | 6 | Transmission | 25 |

Winning speed: 116.597mph Lap leaders: Mansell 1-70
Pole position: Senna, 1m16.673s, 126.911mph
Fastest lap: Mansell, 1m20.943s, 120.216mph

## MEXICAN GRAND PRIX: MEXICO CITY *12 October Round: 15 Race: 435 68 x 2.747 miles*

| POS. | NO. | DRIVER | CAR/ENGINE | LAPS | TIME/RETIRED | GRID |
|---|---|---|---|---|---|---|
| 1 | 20 | Gerhard Berger | Benetton-BMW | 68 | 1:33'18.700 | 4 |
| 2 | 1 | Alain Prost | McLaren-TAG | 68 | +25.438 | 6 |
| 3 | 12 | Ayrton Senna | Lotus-Renault | 68 | +52.513 | 1 |
| 4 | 6 | Nelson Piquet | Williams-Honda | 67 | +1 Lap | 2 |
| 5 | 5 | Nigel Mansell | Williams-Honda | 67 | +1 Lap | 3 |
| 6 | 26 | Philippe Alliot | Ligier-Renault | 67 | +1 Lap | 10 |
| 7 | 18 | Thierry Boutsen | Arrows-BMW | 66 | +2 Laps | 21 |
| 8 | 23 | A.de Cesaris | Minardi-Motori Moderni | 66 | +2 Laps | 22 |
| 9 | 17 | Christian Danner | Arrows-BMW | 66 | +2 Laps | 20 |
| 10 | 14 | Jonathan Palmer | Zakspeed | 65 | Out of fuel | 18 |
| 11 | 3 | Martin Brundle | Tyrrell-Renault | 65 | +3 Laps | 16 |
| 12 | 28 | Stefan Johansson | Ferrari | 64 | Turbo | 14 |
| 13 | 7 | Riccardo Patrese | Brabham-BMW | 64 | Spun off | 5 |
| 14 | 24 | A.Nannini | Minardi-Motori Moderni | 64 | +4 Laps | 24 |
| 15 | 25 | Rene Arnoux | Ligier-Renault | 63 | Engine | 13 |
| 16 | 22 | Allen Berg | Osella-Alfa Romeo | 61 | +7 Laps | 26 |
| Ret | 11 | Johnny Dumfries | Lotus-Renault | 53 | Electrical | 17 |
| Ret | 8 | Derek Warwick | Brabham-BMW | 37 | Engine | 7 |
| Ret | 15 | Alan Jones | Lola-Ford | 35 | Tyre | 15 |
| Ret | 2 | Keke Rosberg | McLaren-TAG | 32 | Puncture | 11 |
| Ret | 27 | Michele Alboreto | Ferrari | 10 | Turbo | 12 |
| Ret | 21 | P.Ghinzani | Osella-Alfa Romeo | 8 | Turbo | 25 |
| Ret | 4 | Philippe Streiff | Tyrrell-Renault | 8 | Turbo | 19 |
| Ret | 19 | Teo Fabi | Benetton-BMW | 4 | Engine | 9 |
| Ret | 16 | Patrick Tambay | Lola-Ford | 0 | Accident | 8 |
| DNS | 29 | Huub Rothengatter | Zakspeed | 0 | Accident | 23 |

Winning speed: 120.115mph Lap leaders: Piquet 1-31; Senna 32-35; Berger 36-68
Pole position: Senna, 1m 16.990s, 128.452mph
Fastest lap: Piquet, 1m 19.360s, 124.616mph

AUSTRALIAN GRAND PRIX: ADELAIDE *26 October Round: 16 Race: 436 82 x 2.348 miles*

| POS. | NO. | DRIVER | CAR/ENGINE | LAPS | TIME/RETIRED | GRID |
|---|---|---|---|---|---|---|
| 1 | 1 | Alain Prost | McLaren-TAG | 82 | 1:54'20.388 | 4 |
| 2 | 6 | Nelson Piquet | Williams-Honda | 82 | +4.205 | 2 |
| 3 | 28 | Stefan Johansson | Ferrari | 81 | +1 Lap | 12 |
| 4 | 3 | Martin Brundle | Tyrrell-Renault | 81 | +1 Lap | 16 |
| 5 | 4 | Philippe Streiff | Tyrrell-Renault | 80 | Out of fuel | 10 |
| 6 | 11 | Johnny Dumfries | Lotus-Renault | 80 | +2 Laps | 14 |
| 7 | 25 | Rene Arnoux | Ligier-Renault | 79 | +3 Laps | 5 |
| 8 | 26 | Philippe Alliot | Ligier-Renault | 79 | +3 Laps | 8 |
| 9 | 14 | Jonathan Palmer | Zakspeed | 77 | +5 Laps | 21 |
| 10 | 19 | Teo Fabi | Benetton-BMW | 77 | +5 Laps | 13 |
| NC | 16 | Patrick Tambay | Lola-Ford | 70 | Not classified | 17 |
| Ret | 5 | Nigel Mansell | Williams-Honda | 63 | Tyre | 1 |
| Ret | 7 | Riccardo Patrese | Brabham-BMW | 63 | Electrical | 19 |
| Ret | 2 | Keke Rosberg | McLaren-TAG | 62 | Tyre | 7 |
| NC | 22 | Allen Berg | Osella-Alfa Romeo | 61 | Not classified | 26 |
| Ret | 8 | Derek Warwick | Brabham-BMW | 57 | Brakes | 20 |
| Ret | 17 | Christian Danner | Arrows-BMW | 52 | Engine | 24 |
| Ret | 18 | Thierry Boutsen | Arrows-BMW | 50 | Engine | 22 |
| Ret | 12 | Ayrton Senna | Lotus-Renault | 43 | Engine | 3 |
| Ret | 23 | A.de Cesaris | Minardi-Motori Moderni | 40 | Mechanical | 11 |
| Ret | 20 | Gerhard Berger | Benetton-BMW | 40 | Engine | 6 |
| Ret | 29 | H.Rothengatter | Zakspeed | 29 | Suspension | 23 |
| Ret | 15 | Alan Jones | Lola-Ford | 16 | Engine | 15 |
| Ret | 24 | A.Nannini | Minardi-Motori Moderni | 10 | Accident | 18 |
| Ret | 21 | P.Ghinzani | Osella-Alfa Romeo | 2 | Transmission | 25 |
| Ret | 27 | Michele Alboreto | Ferrari | 0 | Accident | 9 |

Winning speed: 101.041mph Lap leaders: Piquet 1-6, 63-64; Rosberg 7-62; Prost 65-82
Pole position: Mansell, 1m 18.403s, 107.820mph
Fastest lap: Piquet, 20.787s, 104.638mph

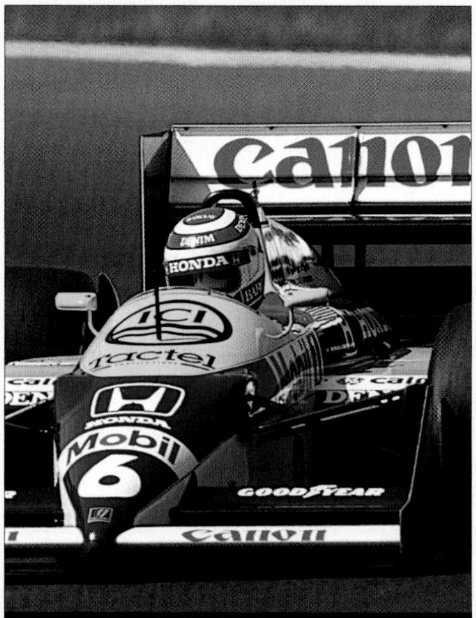


1987 world champion, Nelson Piquet in the Williams Honda.

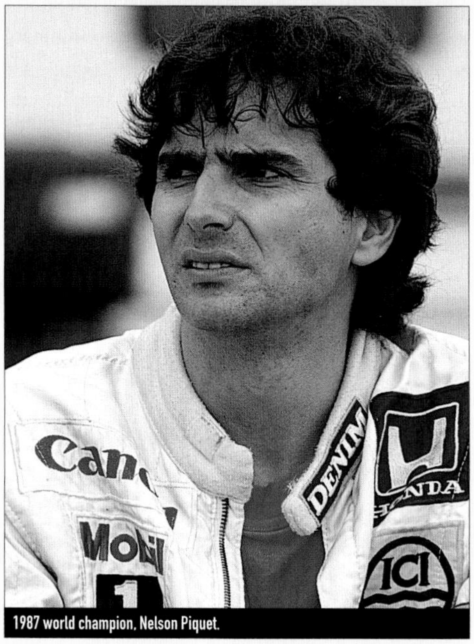

1987 world champion, Nelson Piquet.

# 1987

## DRIVERS' CHAMPION: NELSON PIQUET
## CONSTRUCTORS' CHAMPION: WILLIAMS-HONDA

### DRIVERS' CHAMPIONSHIP

| POS. | DRIVER | NATIONALITY | CAR | POINTS |
|---|---|---|---|---|
| 1 | Nelson Piquet | Brazil | Williams-Honda | 73 (3) |
| 2 | Nigel Mansell | GB | Williams-Honda | 61 |
| 3 | Ayrton Senna | Brazil | Lotus-Honda | 57 |
| 4 | Alain Prost | France | McLaren-TAG Porsche | 46 |
| 5 | Gerhard Berger | Austria | Ferrari | 36 |
| 6 | Stefan Johansson | Sweden | McLaren-TAG Porsche | 30 |
| 7 | Michele Alboreto | Italy | Ferrari | 17 |
| 8 | Thierry Boutsen | Belgium | Benetton-Ford | 16 |
| 9 | Teo Fabi | Italy | Benetton-Ford | 12 |
| 10 | Eddie Cheever | USA | Arrows-Megatron BMW | 8 |
| 11 | Jonathan Palmer | GB | Tyrrell-Ford | 7 |
| = | Saturo Nakajima | Japan | Lotus-Honda | 7 |
| 13 | Riccardo Patrese | Italy | Brabham-BMW, Williams-Honda | 6 |
| 14 | Andrea de Cesaris | Italy | Brabham-BMW | 4 |
| = | Philippe Streiff | France | Tyrrell-Ford | 4 |
| 16 | Derek Warwick | GB | Arrows-Megatron BMW, | 3 |
| 17 | Philippe Alliot | France | Lola-Ford | 3 |
| 18 | Martin Brundle | GB | Zakspeed | 2 |
| 19 | Rene Arnoux | France | Ligier-Megatron BMW | 1 |
| = | Ivan Capelli | Italy | March-Ford | 1 |
| = | Roberto Moreno | Brazil | AGS-Ford | 1 |
| | Yannick Dalmas | France | Lola-Ford | |
| | Piercarlo Ghinzani | Italy | Ligier-Megatron BMW | |
| | Alessandro Nannini | Italy | Minardi-Motori Moderni | |
| | Adrian Campos | Spain | Minardi-Motori Moderni | |
| | Christian Danner | West Germany | Zakspeed | |
| | Alex Caffi | Italy | Osella-Alfa Romeo | |
| | Pascal Fabre | France | AGS-Ford - | |
| | Gabriele Tarquini | Italy | Osella-Alfa Romeo | |
| | Nicola Larini | Italy | Coloni-Ford | |
| | Franco Forini | Italy | Osella-Alfa Romeo | |
| | Stefano Modena | Italy | Brabham-BMW | |

Points for top six finishers (9, 6, 4, 3, 2, 1). Only the best eleven scores counted towards the championship. Drivers not valid for points if the constructor had entered only one car. Half points awarded for races stopped before half distance. Teams which entered only one car, such as Lola, did not score points for their second round.

### CONSTRUCTORS' CHAMPIONSHIP

| POS. | CONSTRUCTOR | POINTS |
|---|---|---|
| 1 | Williams-Honda | 137 |
| 2 | McLaren-TAG Porsche | 76 |
| 3 | Lotus-Honda | 64 |
| 4 | Ferrari | 53 |
| 5 | Benetton-Ford | 28 |
| 6 | Tyrrell-Ford | 11 |
| 7 | Arrows-Megatron | 11 |
| 8 | Brabham-BMW | 10 |
| 9 | Lola-Ford | 3 |
| 10 | Zakspeed | 2 |
| 11 | Ligier-Megatron | 1 |
| 11 | March-Ford | 1 |
| 11 | AGS-Ford | 1 |

Points for top six finishers (9, 6, 4, 3, 2, 1). Half points awarded for races stopped before half distance.
Teams which entered only one car, such as Lola, did not score points for their second round.

BRAZILIAN GRAND PRIX: RIO DE JANEIRO *12 April Round: 1 Race: 437 61 x 3.126 miles*

| POS. | NO. | DRIVER | CAR/ENGINE | LAPS | TIME/RETIRED | GRID |
|---|---|---|---|---|---|---|
| 1 | 1 | Alain Prost | McLaren-TAG | 61 | 1:39'45.141 | 5 |
| 2 | 6 | Nelson Piquet | Williams-Honda | 61 | +40.547 | 2 |
| 3 | 2 | Stefan Johansson | McLaren-TAG | 61 | +56.758 | 10 |
| 4 | 28 | Gerhard Berger | Ferrari | 61 | +1'39.235 | 7 |
| 5 | 20 | Thierry Boutsen | Benetton-Ford | 60 | +1 Lap | 6 |
| 6 | 5 | Nigel Mansell | Williams-Honda | 60 | +1 Lap | 1 |
| 7 | 11 | Satoru Nakajima | Lotus-Honda | 59 | +2 Laps | 12 |
| 8 | 27 | Michele Alboreto | Ferrari | 58 | Spun off | 9 |
| 9 | 10 | Christian Danner | Zakspeed | 58 | +3 Laps | 17 |
| 10 | 3 | Jonathan Palmer | Tyrrell-Ford | 58 | +3 Laps | 18 |
| 11 | 4 | Philippe Streiff | Tyrrell-Ford | 57 | +4 Laps | 20 |
| 12 | 14 | Pascal Fabre | AGS-Ford | 55 | +6 Laps | 22 |
| Ret | 18 | Eddie Cheever | Arrows-Megatron | 52 | Overheating | 14 |
| Ret | 12 | Ayrton Senna | Lotus-Honda | 50 | Engine | 3 |
| Ret | 7 | Riccardo Patrese | Brabham-BMW | 48 | Electrical | 11 |
| Ret | 8 | A.de Cesaris | Brabham-BMW | 21 | Differential | 13 |
| Ret | 17 | Derek Warwick | Arrows-Megatron | 20 | Engine | 8 |
| Wth | 21 | Alex Caffi | Osella-Alfa Romeo | 20 | Withdrew | 21 |
| Ret | 24 | A.Nannini | Minardi-Motori Moderni | 17 | Suspension | 15 |
| Ret | 9 | Martin Brundle | Zakspeed | 15 | Turbo | 19 |
| Ret | 19 | Teo Fabi | Benetton-Ford | 9 | Turbo | 4 |
| DSQ | 23 | Adrian Campos | Minardi-Motori Moderni | 3 | Disqualified | 16 |
| DNS | 16 | Ivan Capelli | March-Ford | 0 | Non starter | 23 |

Winning speed: 114.700mph
Lap leaders: Piquet 1-7, 17-20; Senna 8-12; Prost 13-16, 21-61
Pole position: Mansell, 1m 26.128s, 130.666mph
Fastest lap: Piquet, 1m 33.861s, 119.901mph

SAN MARINO GRAND PRIX: IMOLA *3 May Round: 2 Race: 438 59 x 3.132 miles*

| POS. | NO. | DRIVER | CAR/ENGINE | LAPS | TIME/RETIRED | GRID |
|---|---|---|---|---|---|---|
| 1 | 1 | Alain Prost | McLaren-TAG | 61 | 1:39'45.141 | 14 |
| 1 | 5 | Nigel Mansell | Williams-Honda | 59 | +1:31'24.076 | 2 |
| 2 | 12 | Ayrton Senna | Lotus-Honda | 59 | +27.5453 | 1 |
| 3 | 27 | Michele Alboreto | Ferrari | 59 | +39.144 | 7 |
| 4 | 2 | Stefan Johansson | McLaren-TAG | 59 | +1'00.588 | 9 |
| 5 | 9 | Martin Brundle | Zakspeed | 57 | +2 Laps | 16 |
| 6 | 11 | Satoru Nakajima | Lotus-Honda | 57 | Out of fuel | 13 |
| 7 | 10 | Christian Danner | Zakspeed | 57 | +2 Laps | 19 |
| 8 | 4 | Philippe Streiff | Tyrrell-Ford | 57 | +2 Laps | 22 |
| 9 | 7 | Riccardo Patrese | Brabham-BMW | 57 | +2 Laps | 8 |
| 10 | 30 | Philippe Alliot | Lola-Ford | 56 | +3 Laps | 23 |
| 11 | 17 | Derek Warwick | Arrows-Megatron | 55 | Out of fuel | 11 |
| 12 | 21 | Alex Caffi | Osella-Alfa Romeo | 54 | Out of fuel | 21 |
| 13 | 14 | Pascal Fabre | AGS-Ford | 53 | +6 Laps | 26 |
| Ret | 19 | Teo Fabi | Benetton-Ford | 51 | Turbo | 5 |
| Ret | 20 | Thierry Boutsen | Benetton-Ford | 48 | Engine | 12 |
| Ret | 18 | Eddie Cheever | Arrows-Megatron | 48 | Clutch | 10 |
| Ret | 3 | Jonathan Palmer | Tyrrell-Ford | 48 | Clutch | 25 |
| Ret | 8 | A.de Cesaris | Brabham-BMW | 39 | Spun off | 15 |
| Ret | 23 | Adrian Campos | Minardi-Motori Moderni | 30 | Gearbox | 18 |
| Ret | 22 | G.Tarquini | Osella-Alfa Romeo | 26 | Gearbox | 27 |
| Ret | 24 | A.Nannini | Minardi-Motori Moderni | 25 | Turbo | 17 |
| Ret | 16 | Ivan Capelli | March-Ford | 18 | Engine | 24 |
| Ret | 28 | Gerhard Berger | Ferrari | 16 | Electrical | 6 |
| Ret | 1 | Alain Prost | McLaren-TAG | 14 | Electrical | 4 |
| Ret | 26 | P.Ghinzani | Ligier-Megatron | 7 | Handling | 20 |
| DNS | 6 | Nelson Piquet | Williams-Honda | 0 | Injury | |
| DNS | 25 | Rene Arnoux | Ligier-Megatron | 0 | Suspension | |

Winning speed: 121.292 Lap leaders: Senna 1, 25-26; Mansell 2-21, 27-59; Alboreto 22-24
Pole position: Senna, 1m 25.826s, 131.361mph
Fastest lap: Fabi, 1m 29.246s, 126.327mph

BELGIAN GRAND PRIX: SPA-FRANCORCHAMPS *17 May Round: 3 Race: 439 43 x 4.312 miles*

| POS. | NO. | DRIVER | CAR/ENGINE | LAPS | TIME/RETIRED | GRID |
|---|---|---|---|---|---|---|
| 1 | 1 | Alain Prost | McLaren-TAG | 43 | 1:27'03.217 | 6 |
| 2 | 2 | Stefan Johansson | McLaren-TAG | 43 | +24.764 | 10 |
| 3 | 8 | A.de Cesaris | Brabham-BMW | 42 | +1 Lap | 13 |
| 4 | 18 | Eddie Cheever | Arrows-Megatron | 42 | +1 Lap | 11 |
| 5 | 11 | Satoru Nakajima | Lotus-Honda | 42 | +1 Lap | 15 |
| 6 | 25 | Rene Arnoux | Ligier-Megatron | 41 | +2 Laps | 16 |
| 7 | 26 | P.Ghinzani | Ligier-Megatron | 40 | +3 Laps | 17 |
| 8 | 30 | Philippe Alliot | Lola-Ford | 40 | +3 Laps | 22 |
| 9 | 4 | Philippe Streiff | Tyrrell-Ford | 39 | +4 Laps | 23 |
| 10 | 14 | Pascal Fabre | AGS-Ford | 38 | +5 Laps | 25 |
| Ret | 19 | Teo Fabi | Benetton-Ford | 34 | Engine | 9 |
| Ret | 9 | Martin Brundle | Zakspeed | 19 | Overheating | 18 |
| Ret | 20 | Thierry Boutsen | Benetton-Ford | 18 | Wheel bearing | 7 |
| Ret | 5 | Nigel Mansell | Williams-Honda | 17 | Accident | 1 |
| Ret | 16 | Ivan Capelli | March-Ford | 14 | Engine | 21 |
| Ret | 6 | Nelson Piquet | Williams-Honda | 11 | Exhaust | 2 |
| Ret | 21 | Alex Caffi | Osella-Alfa Romeo | 11 | Fuel leak | 26 |
| Ret | 27 | Michele Alboreto | Ferrari | 9 | Transmission | 5 |
| Ret | 10 | Christian Danner | Zakspeed | 9 | Brakes | 20 |
| Ret | 17 | Derek Warwick | Arrows-Megatron | 8 | Radiator | 12 |
| Ret | 7 | Riccardo Patrese | Brabham-BMW | 5 | Clutch | 8 |
| Ret | 28 | Gerhard Berger | Ferrari | 2 | Engine | 4 |
| Ret | 24 | A.Nannini | Minardi-Motori Moderni | 1 | Turbo | 14 |
| Ret | 12 | Ayrton Senna | Lotus-Honda | 0 | Accident | 3 |
| Ret | 23 | Adrian Campos | Minardi-Motori Moderni | 0 | Gearbox | 19 |
| Ret | 3 | Jonathan Palmer | Tyrrell-Ford | 0 | Accident | 24 |

Winning speed: 127.804 Lap leaders: Piquet 1-9; Prost 10-43
Pole position: Mansell, 1m 52.026s, 138.578mph
Fastest lap: Prost, 1m 57.153s, 132.513mph
Race stopped after accident on lap 2 and restarted for total original distance.

MONACO GRAND PRIX: MONTE CARLO *31 May Round: 4 Race: 440 78 x 2.068 miles*

| POS. | NO. | DRIVER | CAR/ENGINE | LAPS | TIME/RETIRED | GRID |
|---|---|---|---|---|---|---|
| 1 | 12 | Ayrton Senna | Lotus-Honda | 78 | 1:57'54.085 | 2 |
| 2 | 6 | Nelson Piquet | Williams-Honda | 78 | +33.212 | 3 |
| 3 | 27 | Michele Alboreto | Ferrari | 78 | +1'12.839 | 5 |
| 4 | 28 | Gerhard Berger | Ferrari | 77 | +1 Lap | 8 |
| 5 | 3 | Jonathan Palmer | Tyrrell-Ford | 76 | +2 Laps | 15 |
| 6 | 16 | Ivan Capelli | March-Ford | 76 | +2 Laps | 19 |
| 7 | 9 | Martin Brundle | Zakspeed | 76 | +2 Laps | 14 |
| 8 | 19 | Teo Fabi | Benetton-Ford | 76 | +2 Laps | 12 |
| 9 | 1 | Alain Prost | McLaren-TAG | 75 | Engine | 4 |
| 10 | 11 | Satoru Nakajima | Lotus-Honda | 75 | +3 Laps | 17 |
| 11 | 25 | Rene Arnoux | Ligier-Megatron | 74 | +4 Laps | 22 |
| 12 | 26 | P.Ghinzani | Ligier-Megatron | 74 | +4 Laps | 20 |
| 13 | 14 | Pascal Fabre | AGS-Ford | 71 | +7 Laps | 24 |
| Ret | 18 | Eddie Cheever | Arrows-Megatron | 59 | Overheating | 6 |
| Ret | 17 | Derek Warwick | Arrows-Megatron | 58 | Gearbox | 11 |
| Ret | 2 | Stefan Johansson | McLaren-TAG | 57 | Engine | 7 |
| Ret | 30 | Philippe Alliot | Lola-Ford | 42 | Engine | 18 |
| Ret | 7 | Riccardo Patrese | Brabham-BMW | 41 | Electrical | 10 |
| Ret | 21 | Alex Caffi | Osella-Alfa Romeo | 39 | Electrical | 16 |
| Ret | 8 | A.de Cesaris | Brabham-BMW | 38 | Suspension | 21 |
| Ret | 5 | Nigel Mansell | Williams-Honda | 29 | Turbo | 1 |
| Ret | 24 | A.Nannini | Minardi-Motori Moderni | 21 | Electrical | 13 |
| Ret | 4 | Philippe Streiff | Tyrrell-Ford | 9 | Accident | 23 |
| Ret | 20 | Thierry Boutsen | Benetton-Ford | 5 | Transmission | 9 |
| DSQ | 10 | Christian Danner | Zakspeed | 0 | Excluded | |
| DNS | 23 | Adrian Campos | Minardi-Motori Moderni | 0 | Non starter | |

Winning speed: 82.085mph Lap leaders: Mansell 1-29; Senna 30-78
Pole position: Mansell, 1m 23.039s, 89.651mph
Fastest lap: Senna, 27.685s, 84.901mph

 

1987 Season Statistics

## UNITED STATES GRAND PRIX: DETROIT *21 June Round: 5 Race: 441 63 x 2.500 miles*

| POS. | NO. | DRIVER | CAR/ENGINE | LAPS | TIME/RETIRED | GRID |
|---|---|---|---|---|---|---|
| 1 | 12 | Ayrton Senna | Lotus-Honda | 63 | 1:50'16.358 | 2 |
| 2 | 6 | Nelson Piquet | Williams-Honda | 63 | +33.819 | 3 |
| 3 | 1 | Alain Prost | McLaren-TAG | 63 | +45.327 | 5 |
| 4 | 28 | Gerhard Berger | Ferrari | 63 | +1'02.601 | 12 |
| 5 | 5 | Nigel Mansell | Williams-Honda | 62 | +1 Lap | 1 |
| 6 | 18 | Eddie Cheever | Arrows-Megatron | 60 | +3 Laps | 6 |
| 7 | 2 | Stefan Johansson | McLaren-TAG | 60 | +3 Laps | 11 |
| 8 | 10 | Christian Danner | Zakspeed | 60 | +3 Laps | 16 |
| 9 | 7 | Riccardo Patrese | Brabham-BMW | 60 | +3 Laps | 9 |
| 10 | 25 | Rene Arnoux | Ligier-Megatron | 60 | +3 Laps | 21 |
| 11 | 3 | Jonathan Palmer | Tyrrell-Ford | 60 | +3 Laps | 13 |
| 12 | 14 | Pascal Fabre | AGS-Ford | 58 | +5 Laps | 26 |
| Ret | 20 | Thierry Boutsen | Benetton-Ford | 52 | Brakes | 4 |
| Ret | 26 | P.Ghinzani | Ligier-Megatron | 51 | Clutch | 23 |
| Ret | 4 | Philippe Streiff | Tyrrell-Ford | 44 | Wheel | 14 |
| Ret | 30 | Philippe Alliot | Lola-Ford | 38 | Accident | 20 |
| Ret | 27 | Michele Alboreto | Ferrari | 25 | Gearbox | 7 |
| Ret | 24 | A.Nannini | Minardi-Motori Moderni | 22 | Gearbox | 18 |
| Ret | 9 | Martin Brundle | Zakspeed | 16 | Turbo | 15 |
| Ret | 17 | Derek Warwick | Arrows-Megatron | 12 | Accident | 10 |
| Ret | 16 | Ivan Capelli | March-Ford | 9 | Electrical | 22 |
| Ret | 19 | Teo Fabi | Benetton-Ford | 6 | Accident | 8 |
| Ret | 21 | Alex Caffi | Osella-Alfa Romeo | 3 | Transmission | 19 |
| Ret | 8 | A.de Cesaris | Brabham-BMW | 2 | Gearbox | 17 |
| Ret | 23 | Adrian Campos | Minardi-Motori Moderni | 1 | Accident | 25 |
| Ret | 11 | Satoru Nakajima | Lotus-Honda | 0 | Accident | 24 |

Winning speed: 85.697 Lap leaders: Mansell 1-33; Senna 34-63
Pole position: Mansell, 1m 39.264s, 90.340mph
Fastest lap: Senna, 1m 40.464s, 90.667mph

## FRENCH GRAND PRIX: PAUL RICARD *5 July Round:6 Race: 442 80 x 2.369 miles*

| POS. | NO. | DRIVER | CAR/ENGINE | LAPS | TIME/RETIRED | GRID |
|---|---|---|---|---|---|---|
| 1 | 5 | Nigel Mansell | Williams-Honda | 80 | 1:37'03.839 | 1 |
| 2 | 6 | Nelson Piquet | Williams-Honda | 80 | +7.711 | 4 |
| 3 | 1 | Alain Prost | McLaren-TAG | 80 | +55.255 | 2 |
| 4 | 12 | Ayrton Senna | Lotus-Honda | 79 | +1 Lap | 3 |
| 5 | 19 | Teo Fabi | Benetton/Ford | 77 | +3 Laps | 7 |
| 6 | 4 | Philippe Streiff | Tyrrell-Ford | 76 | +4 Laps | 25 |
| 7 | 3 | Jonathan Palmer | Tyrrell-Ford | 76 | +4 Laps | 24 |
| 8 | 2 | Stefan Johansson | McLaren-TAG | 74 | +6 Laps | 9 |
| 9 | 14 | Pascal Fabre | AGS/Ford | 74 | +6 Laps | 26 |
| Ret | 28 | Gerhard Berger | Ferrari | 71 | Suspension | 6 |
| NC | 11 | Satoru Nakajima | Lotus-Honda | 71 | Not classified | 16 |
| Ret | 27 | Michele Alboreto | Ferrari | 64 | Engine | 8 |
| Ret | 17 | Derek Warwick | Arrows-Megatron | 62 | Turbo | 10 |
| Ret | 30 | Philippe Alliot | Lola-Ford | 57 | Gearbox | 23 |
| Ret | 16 | Ivan Capelli | March-Ford | 52 | Engine | 22 |
| Ret | 23 | Adrian Campos | Minardi-Motori Moderni | 52 | Turbo | 21 |
| Ret | 25 | Rene Arnoux | Ligier-Megatron | 33 | Exhaust | 13 |
| Ret | 20 | Thierry Boutsen | Benetton-Ford | 31 | Engine | 5 |
| Ret | 10 | Christian Danner | Zakspeed | 26 | Overheating | 19 |
| Ret | 26 | P.Ghinzani | Ligier-Megatron | 24 | Engine | 17 |
| Ret | 24 | A.Nannini | Minardi-Motori Moderni | 23 | Turbo | 15 |
| Ret | 7 | Riccardo Patrese | Brabham-BMW | 19 | Differential | 12 |
| Ret | 9 | Martin Brundle | Zakspeed | 18 | Wheel | 18 |
| Ret | 21 | Alex Caffi | Osella-Alfa Romeo | 11 | Engine | 20 |
| Ret | 8 | A.de Cesaris | Brabham-BMW | 2 | Turbo | 11 |
| Ret | 18 | Eddie Cheever | Arrows-Megatron | 0 | Electrical | 14 |

Winning speed: 117.166mph Lap leaders: Mansell 1-35,46-80; Piquet, 36-45
Pole position: Mansell, 1m 6.454s, 128.351mph
Fastest lap: Piquet, 1m 9.548s, 122.641mph

## BRITISH GRAND PRIX: SILVERSTONE *12 July Round: 7 Race: 443 65 x 2.969 miles*

| POS. | NO. | DRIVER | CAR/ENGINE | LAPS | TIME/RETIRED | GRID |
|---|---|---|---|---|---|---|
| 1 | 5 | Nigel Mansell | Williams-Honda | 65 | 1:19'11.780 | 2 |
| 2 | 6 | Nelson Piquet | Williams-Honda | 65 | +1.918 | 1 |
| 3 | 12 | Ayrton Senna | Lotus-Honda | 64 | +1 Lap | 3 |
| 4 | 11 | Satoru Nakajima | Lotus-Honda | 63 | +2 Laps | 12 |
| 5 | 17 | Derek Warwick | Arrows-Megatron | 63 | +2 Laps | 13 |
| 6 | 19 | Teo Fabi | Benetton-Ford | 63 | +2 Laps | 6 |
| 7 | 20 | Thierry Boutsen | Benetton-Ford | 62 | +3 Laps | 5 |
| 8 | 3 | Jonathan Palmer | Tyrrell-Ford | 60 | +5 Laps | 23 |
| 9 | 14 | Pascal Fabre | AGS-Ford | 59 | +6 Laps | 25 |
| Ret | 4 | Philippe Streiff | Tyrrell-Ford | 57 | Engine | 22 |
| NC | 9 | Martin Brundle | Zakspeed | 54 | Not classified | 17 |
| Ret | 1 | Alain Prost | McLaren-TAG | 53 | Engine | 4 |
| Ret | 27 | Michele Alboreto | Ferrari | 52 | Suspension | 7 |
| Ret | 18 | Eddie Cheever | Arrows-Megatron | 45 | Engine | 14 |
| Ret | 23 | Adrian Campos | Minardi-Motori Moderni | 34 | Fuel system | 19 |
| Ret | 21 | Alex Caffi | Osella-Alfa Romeo | 32 | Engine | 20 |
| Ret | 10 | Christian Danner | Zakspeed | 32 | Gearbox | 18 |
| Ret | 7 | Riccardo Patrese | Brabham-BMW | 28 | Turbo | 11 |
| Ret | 2 | Stefan Johansson | McLaren-TAG | 18 | Engine | 10 |
| Ret | 24 | A.Nannini | Minardi-Motori Moderni | 10 | Engine | 15 |
| Ret | 8 | A.de Cesaris | Brabham-BMW | 8 | Turbo | 9 |
| Ret | 28 | Gerhard Berger | Ferrari | 7 | Accident | 8 |
| Ret | 30 | Philippe Alliot | Lola-Ford | 7 | Gearbox | 21 |
| Ret | 25 | Rene Arnoux | Ligier-Megatron | 3 | Electrical | 16 |
| Ret | 16 | Ivan Capelli | March-Ford | 3 | Accident | 24 |
| DSQ | 26 | P.Ghinzani | Ligier-Megatron | 0 | Excluded | 19 |

Winning speed: 146.208 Lap leaders: Piquet 1-62; Mansell 63-65
Pole position: Piquet, 1m 7.110s, 159.267mph
Fastest lap: Mansell 1m 9.832s, 153.059mph

## GERMAN GRAND PRIX: HOCKENHEIM *26 July Round: 8 Race: 444 44 x 4.223 miles*

| POS. | NO. | DRIVER | CAR/ENGINE | LAPS | TIME/RETIRED | GRID |
|---|---|---|---|---|---|---|
| 1 | 6 | Nelson Piquet | Williams-Honda | 44 | 1:21'25.091 | 4 |
| 2 | 2 | Stefan Johansson | McLaren-TAG | 44 | +1'39.591 | 8 |
| 3 | 12 | Ayrton Senna | Lotus-Honda | 43 | +1 Lap | 2 |
| 4 | 4 | Philippe Streiff | Tyrrell-Ford | 43 | +1 Lap | 22 |
| 5 | 3 | Jonathan Palmer | Tyrrell-Ford | 43 | +1 Lap | 23 |
| 6 | 30 | Philippe Alliot | Lola-Ford | 42 | +2 Laps | 21 |
| 7 | 1 | Alain Prost | McLaren-TAG | 39 | Electrical | 3 |
| NC | 9 | Martin Brundle | Zakspeed | 34 | Not classified | 19 |
| Ret | 26 | P.Ghinzani | Ligier-Megatron | 32 | Engine | 17 |
| Ret | 23 | Adrian Campos | Minardi-Motori Moderni | 28 | Engine | 18 |
| Ret | 20 | Thierry Boutsen | Benetton-Ford | 26 | Engine | 6 |
| Ret | 5 | Nigel Mansell | Williams-Honda | 25 | Engine | 1 |
| Ret | 24 | A.Nannini | Minardi-Motori Moderni | 25 | Engine | 16 |
| Ret | 17 | Derek Warwick | Arrows-Megatron | 23 | Turbo | 13 |
| Ret | 10 | Christian Danner | Zakspeed | 21 | Halfshaft | 20 |
| Ret | 28 | Gerhard Berger | Ferrari | 19 | Turbo | 10 |
| Ret | 19 | Teo Fabi | Benetton-Ford | 18 | Engine | 9 |
| Ret | 21 | Alex Caffi | Osella-Alfa Romeo | 17 | Engine | 26 |
| Ret | 8 | A.de Cesaris | Brabham-BMW | 12 | Engine | 7 |
| Ret | 27 | Michele Alboreto | Ferrari | 10 | Turbo | 5 |
| Ret | 14 | Pascal Fabre | AGS-Ford | 10 | Engine | 25 |
| Ret | 18 | Eddie Cheever | Arrows-Megatron | 9 | Throttle | 15 |
| Ret | 11 | Satoru Nakajima | Lotus-Honda | 9 | Suspension | 14 |
| Ret | 16 | Ivan Capelli | March-Ford | 7 | Engine | 24 |
| Ret | 25 | Rene Arnoux | Ligier-Megatron | 6 | Ignition | 12 |
| Ret | 7 | Riccardo Patrese | Brabham-BMW | 5 | Ignition | 11 |

Winning speed: 136.946mph
Lap leaders: Senna 1; Mansell 2-7, 19-22; Prost 8-18, 23-39; Piquet 40-44
Pole position: Mansell, 1m 42.166s, 148.168mph
Fastest lap: Mansell, 1m 45.716s, 143.824mph

## HUNGARIAN GRAND PRIX: HUNGARORING *9 August Round: 9 Race: 445 76 x 2.494 miles*

| POS. | NO. | DRIVER | CAR/ENGINE | LAPS | TIME/RETIRED | GRID |
|---|---|---|---|---|---|---|
| 1 | 6 | Nelson Piquet | Williams-Honda | 76 | 1:59'26.793 | 3 |
| 2 | 12 | Ayrton Senna | Lotus-Honda | 76 | +37.727 | 6 |
| 3 | 1 | Alain Prost | McLaren-TAG | 76 | +1'27.456 | 4 |
| 4 | 20 | Thierry Boutsen | Benetton-Ford | 75 | +1 Lap | 7 |
| 5 | 7 | Riccardo Patrese | Brabham-BMW | 75 | +1 Lap | 10 |
| 6 | 17 | Derek Warwick | Arrows-Megatron | 74 | +2 Laps | 9 |
| 7 | 3 | Jonathan Palmer | Tyrrell-Ford | 74 | +2 Laps | 16 |
| 8 | 18 | Eddie Cheever | Arrows-Megatron | 74 | +2 Laps | 11 |
| 9 | 4 | Philippe Streiff | Tyrrell-Ford | 74 | +2 Laps | 14 |
| 10 | 16 | Ivan Capelli | March-Ford | 74 | +2 Laps | 18 |
| 11 | 24 | A.Nannini | Minardi-Motori Moderni | 73 | +3 Laps | 20 |
| 12 | 26 | P.Ghinzani | Ligier-Megatron | 73 | +3 Laps | 25 |
| 13 | 14 | Pascal Fabre | AGS-Ford | 71 | +5 Laps | 26 |
| 14 | 5 | Nigel Mansell | Williams-Honda | 70 | Wheel | 1 |
| Ret | 21 | Alex Caffi | Osella-Alfa Romeo | 64 | Fuel system | 21 |
| Ret | 25 | Rene Arnoux | Ligier-Megatron | 57 | Electrical | 19 |
| Ret | 30 | Philippe Alliot | Lola-Ford | 48 | Accident | 15 |
| Ret | 9 | Martin Brundle | Zakspeed | 45 | Turbo | 22 |
| Ret | 27 | Michele Alboreto | Ferrari | 43 | Engine | 5 |
| Ret | 8 | A.de Cesaris | Brabham-BMW | 43 | Gearbox | 13 |
| Ret | 2 | Stefan Johansson | McLaren-TAG | 14 | Gearbox | 8 |
| Ret | 19 | Teo Fabi | Benetton-Ford | 14 | Gearbox | 12 |
| Ret | 23 | Adrian Campos | Minardi-Motori Moderni | 14 | Spun off | 24 |
| Ret | 28 | Gerhard Berger | Ferrari | 13 | Differential | 2 |
| Ret | 10 | Christian Danner | Zakspeed | 3 | Engine | 23 |
| Ret | 11 | Satoru Nakajima | Lotus-Honda | 1 | Gearbox | 17 |

Winning speed: 95.218mph Lap leaders: Mansell 1-70; Piquet 71-76
Pole position: Mansell, 1m 28.047s, 101.980mph
Fastest lap: Piquet, 1m 30.149s, 99.602mph

## AUSTRIAN GRAND PRIX: OSTERREICHRING *16 August Round: 10 Race: 446 52 x 3.692 miles*

| POS. | NO. | DRIVER | CAR/ENGINE | LAPS | TIME/RETIRED | GRID |
|---|---|---|---|---|---|---|
| 1 | 5 | Nigel Mansell | Williams-Honda | 52 | 1:18'44.898 | 2 |
| 2 | 6 | Nelson Piquet | Williams-Honda | 52 | +55.704 | 1 |
| 3 | 19 | Teo Fabi | Benetton-Ford | 51 | +1 Lap | 5 |
| 4 | 20 | Thierry Boutsen | Benetton-Ford | 51 | +1 Lap | 4 |
| 5 | 12 | Ayrton Senna | Lotus-Honda | 50 | +2 Laps | 7 |
| 6 | 1 | Alain Prost | McLaren-TAG | 50 | +2 Laps | 9 |
| 7 | 2 | Stefan Johansson | McLaren-TAG | 50 | +2 Laps | 14 |
| 8 | 26 | P.Ghinzani | Ligier-Megatron | 50 | +2 Laps | 18 |
| 9 | 10 | Christian Danner | Zakspeed | 49 | +3 Laps | 20 |
| 10 | 25 | Rene Arnoux | Ligier-Megatron | 49 | +3 Laps | 16 |
| 11 | 16 | Ivan Capelli | March-Ford | 49 | +3 Laps | 23 |
| 12 | 30 | Philippe Alliot | Lola-Ford | 49 | +3 Laps | 22 |
| 13 | 11 | Satoru Nakajima | Lotus-Honda | 49 | +3 Laps | 13 |
| 14 | 3 | Jonathan Palmer | Tyrrell-Ford | 47 | +5 Laps | 24 |
| DSQ | 9 | Martin Brundle | Zakspeed | 48 | Disqualified | 17 |
| NC | 14 | Pascal Fabre | AGS-Ford | 45 | Not classified | 26 |
| Ret | 7 | Riccardo Patrese | Brabham-BMW | 43 | Engine | 8 |
| Ret | 27 | Michele Alboreto | Ferrari | 42 | Turbo | 6 |
| Ret | 8 | A.de Cesaris | Brabham-BMW | 35 | Engine | 10 |
| Ret | 17 | Derek Warwick | Arrows-Megatron | 35 | Engine | 11 |
| Ret | 18 | Eddie Cheever | Arrows-Megatron | 31 | Tyre | 12 |
| Ret | 28 | Gerhard Berger | Ferrari | 5 | Turbo | 3 |
| Ret | 23 | Adrian Campos | Minardi-Motori Moderni | 3 | Electrical | 19 |
| Ret | 24 | A.Nannini | Minardi-Motori Moderni | 1 | Engine | 15 |
| Ret | 21 | Alex Caffi | Osella-Alfa Romeo | 0 | Electrical | 21 |
| Ret | 4 | Philippe Streiff | Tyrrell-Ford | 0 | Accident | 25 |

Winning speed: 146.284mph Lap leaders: Piquet 1-20; Mansell 21-52
Pole position: Piquet, 1m 23.357s, 159.457mph
Fastest lap: Mansell, 1m 28.318s, 150.500mph
Race stopped twice due to first lap accidents. Eventually restarted for total original distance.

## ITALIAN GRAND PRIX: MONZA *6 September Round: 11 Race: 447 50 x 3.604 miles*

| POS. | NO. | DRIVER | CAR/ENGINE | LAPS | TIME/RETIRED | GRID |
|---|---|---|---|---|---|---|
| 1 | 6 | Nelson Piquet | Williams-Honda | 50 | 1:14'47.707 | 1 |
| 2 | 12 | Ayrton Senna | Lotus-Honda | 50 | +1.806 | 4 |
| 3 | 5 | Nigel Mansell | Williams-Honda | 50 | +49.036 | 2 |
| 4 | 28 | Gerhard Berger | Ferrari | 50 | +57.979 | 3 |
| 5 | 20 | Thierry Boutsen | Benetton-Ford | 50 | +1'21.319 | 6 |
| 6 | 2 | Stefan Johansson | McLaren-TAG | 50 | +1'28.787 | 11 |
| 7 | 19 | Teo Fabi | Benetton-Ford | 49 | +1 Lap | 7 |
| 8 | 26 | P.Ghinzani | Ligier-Megatron | 48 | +2 Laps | 19 |
| 9 | 10 | Christian Danner | Zakspeed | 48 | +2 Laps | 16 |
| 10 | 25 | Rene Arnoux | Ligier-Megatron | 48 | +2 Laps | 15 |
| 11 | 11 | Satoru Nakajima | Lotus-Honda | 47 | +3 Laps | 14 |
| 12 | 4 | Philippe Streiff | Tyrrell-Ford | 47 | +3 Laps | 24 |
| 13 | 16 | Ivan Capelli | March-Ford | 47 | +3 Laps | 25 |
| 14 | 3 | Jonathan Palmer | Tyrrell/Ford | 47 | +3 Laps | 22 |
| 15 | 1 | Alain Prost | McLaren-TAG | 46 | +4 Laps | 5 |
| 16 | 24 | A.Nannini | Minardi-Motori Moderni | 45 | +5 Laps | 18 |
| Ret | 9 | Martin Brundle | Zakspeed | 43 | Gearbox | 17 |
| Ret | 30 | Philippe Alliot | Lola-Ford | 37 | Spun off | 23 |
| Ret | 23 | Adrian Campos | Minardi-Motori Moderni | 34 | Engine | 20 |
| Ret | 18 | Eddie Cheever | Arrows-Megatron | 27 | Halfshaft | 13 |
| Ret | 22 | Franco Forini | Osella-Alfa Romeo | 27 | Turbo | 26 |
| Ret | 21 | Alex Caffi | Osella/Alfa Romeo | 16 | Suspension | 21 |
| Ret | 27 | Michele Alboreto | Ferrari | 13 | Turbo | 8 |
| Ret | 17 | Derek Warwick | Arrows-Megatron | 9 | Electrical | 12 |
| Ret | 8 | A.de Cesaris | Brabham-BMW | 7 | Suspension | 10 |
| Ret | 7 | Riccardo Patrese | Brabham-BMW | 5 | Engine | 9 |
| DNQ | 32 | Nicola Larini | Coloni-Ford | | | |
| DNQ | 14 | Pascal Fabre | AGS-Ford | | | |

Winning speed: 144.553mph Lap leaders: Piquet 1-23, 43-50; Senna 24-42
Pole position: Piquet, 1m 23.460s, 155.454mph
Fastest lap: Senna, 1m 26.796s, 149.480mph

## PORTUGUESE GRAND PRIX: ESTORIL *20 September Round: 12 Race: 448 70 x 2.703 miles*

| POS. | NO. | DRIVER | CAR/ENGINE | LAPS | TIME/RETIRED | GRID |
|---|---|---|---|---|---|---|
| 1 | 1 | Alain Prost | McLaren-TAG | 70 | 1:37'03.906 | 3 |
| 2 | 28 | Gerhard Berger | Ferrari | 70 | +20.493 | 1 |
| 3 | 6 | Nelson Piquet | Williams-Honda | 70 | +1'03.295 | 4 |
| 4 | 19 | Teo Fabi | Benetton-Ford | 69 | Out of fuel | 10 |
| 5 | 2 | Stefan Johansson | McLaren-TAG | 69 | +1 Lap | 8 |
| 6 | 18 | Eddie Cheever | Arrows-Megatron | 68 | +2 Laps | 11 |
| 7 | 12 | Ayrton Senna | Lotus-Honda | 68 | +2 Laps | 5 |
| 8 | 11 | Satoru Nakajima | Lotus-Honda | 68 | +2 Laps | 15 |
| 9 | 16 | Ivan Capelli | March-Ford | 67 | +3 Laps | 22 |
| 10 | 3 | Jonathan Palmer | Tyrrell-Ford | 67 | +3 Laps | 24 |
| 11 | 24 | A.Nannini | Minardi-Motori Moderni | 66 | Out of fuel | 14 |
| 12 | 4 | Philippe Streiff | Tyrrell-Ford | 66 | +4 Laps | 21 |
| 13 | 17 | Derek Warwick | Arrows-Megatron | 66 | +4 Laps | 12 |
| 14 | 20 | Thierry Boutsen | Benetton-Ford | 64 | +6 Laps | 9 |
| Ret | 8 | A.de Cesaris | Brabham-BMW | 54 | Injection | 13 |
| Ret | 27 | Michele Alboreto | Ferrari | 38 | Gearbox | 6 |
| Ret | 9 | Martin Brundle | Zakspeed | 35 | Gearbox | 17 |
| Ret | 22 | Franco Forini | Osella-Alfa Romeo | 32 | Suspension | 26 |
| Ret | 30 | Philippe Alliot | Lola-Ford | 31 | Engine | 19 |
| Ret | 25 | Rene Arnoux | Ligier-Megatron | 29 | Radiator | 18 |
| Ret | 21 | Alex Caffi | Osella-Alfa Romeo | 27 | Turbo | 25 |
| Ret | 26 | P.Ghinzani | Ligier-Megatron | 24 | Ignition | 23 |
| Ret | 23 | Adrian Campos | Minardi-Motori Moderni | 24 | Accident | 20 |
| Ret | 5 | Nigel Mansell | Williams-Honda | 13 | Electrical | 2 |
| Ret | 7 | Riccardo Patrese | Brabham-BMW | 13 | Engine | 7 |
| DNS | 10 | Christian Danner | Zakspeed | 0 | Accident | 16 |
| DNQ | 14 | Pascal Fabre | AGS-Ford | | | |

Winning speed: 116.957mph
Lap leaders: Mansell 1; Berger 2-33, 36-67; Alboreto 34-35; Prost 68-70
Pole position: Berger, 1m 17.620s, 125.363mph
Fastest lap: Berger, 1m 19.282s, 122.735mph
Race stopped after accident on second lap and restarted for total original distance.

## SPANISH GRAND PRIX: JEREZ DE LA FRONTERA *27 September Round: 13 Race: 449 72 x 2.621 miles*

| POS. | NO. | DRIVER | CAR/ENGINE | LAPS | TIME/RETIRED | GRID |
|---|---|---|---|---|---|---|
| 1 | 5 | Nigel Mansell | Williams-Honda | 72 | 1:49'12.692 | 2 |
| 2 | 1 | Alain Prost | McLaren-TAG | 72 | +22.225 | 7 |
| 3 | 2 | Stefan Johansson | McLaren-TAG | 72 | +30.818 | 11 |
| 4 | 6 | Nelson Piquet | Williams-Honda | 72 | +31.450 | 1 |
| 5 | 12 | Ayrton Senna | Lotus-Honda | 72 | +1'13.507 | 5 |
| 6 | 30 | Philippe Alliot | Lola-Ford | 71 | +1 Lap | 17 |
| 7 | 4 | Philippe Streiff | Tyrrell-Ford | 71 | +1 Lap | 15 |
| 8 | 18 | Eddie Cheever | Arrows-Megatron | 70 | Out of fuel | 13 |
| 9 | 11 | Satoru Nakajima | Lotus-Honda | 70 | +2 Laps | 18 |
| 10 | 17 | Derek Warwick | Arrows-Megatron | 70 | +2 Laps | 12 |
| 11 | 9 | Martin Brundle | Zakspeed | 70 | +2 Laps | 20 |
| 12 | 16 | Ivan Capelli | March-Ford | 70 | +2 Laps | 19 |
| 13 | 7 | Riccardo Patrese | Brabham-BMW | 68 | +4 Laps | 9 |
| 14 | 23 | Adrian Campos | Minardi-Motori Moderni | 68 | +4 Laps | 24 |
| 15 | 27 | Michele Alboreto | Ferrari | 67 | Engine | 4 |
| 16 | 20 | Thierry Boutsen | Benetton-Ford | 66 | Accident | 8 |
| Ret | 28 | Gerhard Berger | Ferrari | 62 | Engine | 3 |
| Ret | 3 | Jonathan Palmer | Tyrrell-Ford | 55 | Collision | 16 |
| Ret | 25 | Rene Arnoux | Ligier-Megatron | 55 | Collision | 14 |
| Ret | 10 | Christian Danner | Zakspeed | 50 | Transmission | 22 |
| Ret | 24 | A.Nannini | Minardi-Motori Moderni | 45 | Turbo | 21 |
| Ret | 19 | Teo Fabi | Benetton-Ford | 40 | Brakes | 6 |
| Ret | 8 | A.de Cesaris | Brabham-BMW | 26 | Gearbox | 10 |
| Ret | 26 | P.Ghinzani | Ligier-Megatron | 24 | Ignition | 23 |
| Ret | 14 | Pascal Fabre | AGS-Ford | 10 | Clutch | 25 |
| Ret | 32 | Nicola Larini | Coloni-Ford | 8 | Suspension | 26 |
| DNQ | 21 | Alex Caffi | Osella-Alfa Romeo | | | |
| DNQ | 22 | Franco Forini | Osella-Alfa Romeo | | | |

Winning speed: 103.675mph Lap leaders: Mansell 1-72
Pole position: Piquet, 1m 22.461s, 114.423mph
Fastest lap: Berger, 1m 26.986s, 108.470mph

**MEXICAN GRAND PRIX: MEXICO CITY** *18 October Round: 14 Race: 450 63 x 2.747 miles*

| POS. | NO. | DRIVER | CAR/ENGINE | LAPS | TIME/RETIRED | GRID |
|---|---|---|---|---|---|---|
| 1 | 5 | Nigel Mansell | Williams-Honda | 63 | 1:26'24.207 | 1 |
| 2 | 6 | Nelson Piquet | Williams-Honda | 63 | +26.176 | 3 |
| 3 | 7 | Riccardo Patrese | Brabham-BMW | 63 | +1'26.879 | 8 |
| 4 | 18 | Eddie Cheever | Arrows-Megatron | 63 | +1'41.352 | 12 |
| 5 | 19 | Teo Fabi | Benetton-Ford | 61 | +2 Laps | 6 |
| 6 | 30 | Philippe Alliot | Lola-Ford | 60 | +3 Laps | 24 |
| 7 | 3 | Jonathan Palmer | Tyrrell-Ford | 60 | +3 Laps | 22 |
| 8 | 4 | Philippe Streiff | Tyrrell-Ford | 60 | +3 Laps | 25 |
| 9 | 29 | Yannick Dalmas | Lola-Ford | 59 | +4 Laps | 23 |
| Ret | 12 | Ayrton Senna | Lotus-Honda | 54 | Spun off | 7 |
| Ret | 16 | Ivan Capelli | March-Ford | 51 | Water leak | 20 |
| Ret | 21 | Alex Caffi | Osella-Alfa Romeo | 50 | Engine | 26 |
| Ret | 26 | P.Ghinzani | Ligier-Megatron | 43 | Water leak | 21 |
| Ret | 23 | Adrian Campos | Minardi-Motori Moderni | 32 | Transmission | 19 |
| Ret | 25 | Rene Arnoux | Ligier-Megatron | 29 | Overheating | 18 |
| Ret | 17 | Derek Warwick | Arrows-Megatron | 26 | Accident | 11 |
| Ret | 8 | A.de Cesaris | Brabham-BMW | 22 | Accident | 10 |
| Ret | 28 | Gerhard Berger | Ferrari | 20 | Turbo | 2 |
| Ret | 20 | Thierry Boutsen | Benetton-Ford | 15 | Electrical | 4 |
| Ret | 24 | A.Nannini | Minardi-Motori Moderni | 13 | Turbo | 14 |
| Ret | 27 | Michele Alboreto | Ferrari | 12 | Engine | 9 |
| Ret | 9 | Martin Brundle | Zakspeed | 3 | Turbo | 13 |
| Ret | 2 | Stefan Johansson | McLaren-TAG | 1 | Accident | 15 |
| Ret | 11 | Satoru Nakajima | Lotus-Honda | 1 | Accident | 16 |
| Ret | 10 | Christian Danner | Zakspeed | 1 | Accident | 17 |
| Ret | 1 | Alain Prost | McLaren-TAG | 0 | Collision | 5 |
| DNQ | 14 | Pascal Fabre | AGS-Ford | | | |

Winning speed: 120.180mph Lap leaders: Berger 1, 15-20; Boutsen 2-14; Mansell 21-30; Piquet 31-63
Pole position: Mansell, 1m 18.383s, 126.169mph
Fastest lap: Piquet, 19.132s, 124.975mph
Race stopped after 30 laps due to Warwick accident and restarted on aggregate for 33, rather than the remaining 36, laps. Mansell, therefore, did not lead the last lap despite winning the race.

**JAPANESE GRAND PRIX: SUZUKA** *1 November Round: 15 Race: 451 51 x 3.641 miles*

| POS. | NO. | DRIVER | CAR/ENGINE | LAPS | TIME/RETIRED | GRID |
|---|---|---|---|---|---|---|
| 1 | 28 | Gerhard Berger | Ferrari | 51 | 1:32'58.072 | 1 |
| 2 | 12 | Ayrton Senna | Lotus-Honda | 51 | +17.384 | 7 |
| 3 | 2 | Stefan Johansson | McLaren-TAG | 51 | +17.694 | 9 |
| 4 | 27 | Michele Alboreto | Ferrari | 51 | +1'20.441 | 4 |
| 5 | 20 | Thierry Boutsen | Benetton-Ford | 51 | +1'25.576 | 3 |
| 6 | 11 | Satoru Nakajima | Lotus-Honda | 51 | +1'36.479 | 11 |
| 7 | 1 | Alain Prost | McLaren-TAG | 50 | +1 Lap | 2 |
| 8 | 3 | Jonathan Palmer | Tyrrell-Ford | 50 | +1 Lap | 19 |
| 9 | 18 | Eddie Cheever | Arrows-Megatron | 50 | Out of fuel | 12 |
| 10 | 17 | Derek Warwick | Arrows-Megatron | 50 | +1 Lap | 13 |
| 11 | 7 | Riccardo Patrese | Brabham-BMW | 49 | +2 Laps | 8 |
| 12 | 4 | Philippe Streiff | Tyrrell-Ford | 49 | +2 Laps | 25 |
| 13 | 26 | P.Ghinzani | Ligier-Megatron | 48 | +3 Laps | 24 |
| 14 | 29 | Yannick Dalmas | Lola-Ford | 47 | +4 Laps | 22 |
| 15 | 6 | Nelson Piquet | Williams-Honda | 46 | Engine | 5 |
| Ret | 25 | Rene Arnoux | Ligier-Megatron | 44 | Out of fuel | 17 |
| Ret | 21 | Alex Caffi | Osella-Alfa Romeo | 43 | Out of fuel | 23 |
| Ret | 14 | Roberto Moreno | AGS-Ford | 38 | Electrical | 26 |
| Ret | 24 | A.Nannini | Minardi-Motori Moderni | 35 | Engine | 14 |
| Ret | 9 | Martin Brundle | Zakspeed | 32 | Engine | 15 |
| Ret | 8 | A.de Cesaris | Brabham-BMW | 26 | Engine | 10 |
| Ret | 19 | Teo Fabi | Benetton-Ford | 16 | Engine | 6 |
| Ret | 10 | Christian Danner | Zakspeed | 13 | Engine | 16 |
| Ret | 16 | Ivan Capelli | March-Ford | 13 | Accident | 20 |
| Ret | 23 | Adrian Campos | Minardi-Motori Moderni | 2 | Engine | 21 |
| Ret | 30 | Philippe Alliot | Lola-Ford | 0 | Accident | 18 |
| DNS | 5 | Nigel Mansell | Williams-Honda | 0 | Accident | |

Winning speed: 119.829mph Lap leaders: Berger 1-24, 26-51; Senna 25
Pole position: Berger, 1m 40.042s, 131.007mph
Fastest lap: Prost, 1m 43.844s, 126.211mph

**AUSTRALIAN GRAND PRIX: ADELAIDE** *15 November Round: 16 Race: 452 82 x 2.348 miles*

| POS. | NO. | DRIVER | CAR/ENGINE | LAPS | TIME/RETIRED | GRID |
|---|---|---|---|---|---|---|
| 1 | 28 | Gerhard Berger | Ferrari | 82 | 1:52'56.144 | 1 |
| 2 | 27 | Michele Alboreto | Ferrari | 82 | +1'07.884 | 6 |
| 3 | 20 | Thierry Boutsen | Benetton-Ford | 81 | +1 Lap | 5 |
| 4 | 3 | Jonathan Palmer | Tyrrell-Ford | 80 | +2 Laps | 19 |
| 5 | 29 | Yannick Dalmas | Lola-Ford | 79 | +3 Laps | 21 |
| 6 | 14 | Roberto Moreno | AGS-Ford | 79 | +3 Laps | 25 |
| 7 | 10 | Christian Danner | Zakspeed | 79 | +3 Laps | 24 |
| 8 | 8 | A.de Cesaris | Brabham-BMW | 78 | Spun off | 10 |
| 9 | 5 | Riccardo Patrese | Williams-Honda | 76 | Oil leak | 7 |
| DSQ | 12 | Ayrton Senna | Lotus-Honda | 82 | Disqualified | 4 |
| Ret | 6 | Nelson Piquet | Williams-Honda | 58 | Brakes | 3 |
| Ret | 16 | Ivan Capelli | March-Ford | 58 | Spun off | 23 |
| Ret | 1 | Alain Prost | McLaren-TAG | 53 | Brakes | 2 |
| Ret | 18 | Eddie Cheever | Arrows-Megatron | 53 | Overheating | 11 |
| Ret | 2 | Stefan Johansson | McLaren-TAG | 48 | Brakes | 8 |
| Ret | 19 | Teo Fabi | Benetton-Ford | 46 | Brakes | 9 |
| Ret | 23 | Adrian Campos | Minardi-Motori Moderni | 46 | Transmission | 26 |
| Ret | 30 | Philippe Alliot | Lola-Ford | 45 | Electrical | 17 |
| Ret | 25 | Rene Arnoux | Ligier-Megatron | 41 | Ignition | 20 |
| Ret | 7 | Stefano Modena | Brabham-BMW | 31 | Physical | 15 |
| Ret | 26 | P.Ghinzani | Ligier-Megatron | 26 | Ignition | 22 |
| Ret | 11 | Satoru Nakajima | Lotus-Honda | 22 | Suspension | 14 |
| Ret | 17 | Derek Warwick | Arrows-Megatron | 19 | Transmission | 12 |
| Ret | 9 | Martin Brundle | Zakspeed | 18 | Engine | 16 |
| Ret | 4 | Philippe Streiff | Tyrrell-Ford | 6 | Spun off | 18 |
| Ret | 24 | A.Nannini | Minardi-Motori Moderni | 0 | Accident | 13 |
| DNQ | 21 | Alex Caffi | Osella-Alfa Romeo | | | |

Winning speed: 102.297mph Lap leaders: Berger 1-82
Pole position: Berger, 1m 17.267s, 109.405mph
Fastest lap: Berger, 1m 20.416s, 105.121mph
Senna finished in second but was disqualified because of irregular brake ducts.

# 1988

## DRIVERS' CHAMPION: AYRTON SENNA
## CONSTRUCTORS' CHAMPION: McLAREN HONDA

**DRIVERS' CHAMPIONSHIP**

| POS. | DRIVER | NATIONALITY | CAR | POINTS |
|---|---|---|---|---|
| 1 | Ayrton Senna | Brazil | McLaren-Honda | 90(4) |
| 2 | Alain Prost | France | McLaren-Honda | 87(18) |
| 3 | Gerhard Berger | Austria | Ferrari | 41 |
| 4 | Thierry Boutsen | Belgium | Benetton-Ford | 27 |
| 5 | Michele Alboreto | Italy | Ferrari | 24 |
| 6 | Nelson Piquet | Brazil | Lotus-Honda | 22 |
| 7 | Ivan Capelli | Italy | March-Judd | 17 |
| = | Derek Warwick | GB | Arrows-Megatron BMW | 17 |
| 9 | Nigel Mansell | GB | Williams-Judd | 12 |
| 10 | Alessandro Nannini | Italy | Benetton-Ford | 12 |
| 11 | Riccardo Patrese | Italy | Williams-Judd | 8 |
| 12 | Eddie Cheever | USA | Arrows-Megatron BMW | 6 |
| 13 | Mauricio Gugelmin | Brazil | March-Judd | 5 |
| = | Jonathan Palmer | GB | Tyrrell-Ford | 5 |
| 15 | Andrea de Cesaris | Italy | Rial-Ford | 3 |
| 16 | Saturo Nakajima | Japan | Lotus-Honda | 1 |
| = | Pierluigi Martini | Italy | Minardi-Ford | 1 |
| | Julian Bailey | GB | Tyrrell-Ford | |
| | Piercarlo Ghinzani | Italy | Zakspeed | |
| | Bernd Schneider | West Germany | Zakspeed | |
| | Philippe Streiff | France | AGS-Ford | |
| | Nicola Larini | Italy | Osella-Alfa Romeo | |
| | Luis Perez Sala | Spain | Minardi-Ford | |
| | Rene Arnoux | France | Ligier-Judd | |
| | Stefan Johansson | Sweden | Ligier-Judd | |
| | Philipe Alliot | France | Lola-Ford | |
| | Yannick Dalmas | France | Lola-Ford | |
| | Gabriele Tarquini | Italy | Coloni-Ford | |
| | Oscar Larrauri | Argentina | EuroBrun-Ford | |
| | Stefano Modena | Italy | EuroBrun-Ford | |
| | Alex Caffi | Italy | Dallara-Ford | |
| | Adrian Campos | Spain | Minardi-Ford | |
| | Martin Brundle | GB | Williams-Judd | |
| | Jean-Louis Schlesser | France | Williams-Judd | |
| | Aguri Suzuki | Japan | Lola-Ford | |
| | Pierre-Henri Raphanel | France | Lola-Ford | |

Points for top six finishers (9, 6, 4, 3, 2, 1). Only the best eleven scores counted towards the championship. Drivers not valid for points if the constructor had entered only one car. Half points awarded for races stopped before half distance.

**CONSTRUCTORS' CHAMPIONSHIP**

| POS. | CONSTRUCTOR | POINTS |
|---|---|---|
| 1 | McLaren-Honda | 199 |
| 2 | Ferrari | 65 |
| 3 | Benetton-Ford | 39 |
| 4 | Lotus-Honda | 23 |
| 5 | Arrows-Megatron | 23 |
| 6 | March-Judd | 22 |
| 7 | Williams-Judd | 20 |
| 8 | Tyrrell-Ford | 5 |
| 9 | Rial-Ford | 3 |
| 10 | Minardi-Ford | 1 |

Points for top six finishers (9, 6, 4, 3, 2, 1). Half points awarded for races stopped before half distance.

**BRAZILIAN GRAND PRIX: RIO DE JANEIRO** *3 April Round: 1 Race: 453 60 x 3.126 miles*

| POS. | NO. | DRIVER | CAR/ENGINE | LAPS | TIME/RETIRED | GRID |
|---|---|---|---|---|---|---|
| 1 | 11 | Alain Prost | McLaren-Honda | 60 | 1:36'06.857 | 3 |
| 2 | 28 | Gerhard Berger | Ferrari | 60 | +9.873 | 4 |
| 3 | 1 | Nelson Piquet | Lotus-Honda | 60 | +1'08.581 | 5 |
| 4 | 17 | Derek Warwick | Arrows-Megatron | 60 | +1'13.348 | 11 |
| 5 | 27 | Michele Alboreto | Ferrari | 60 | +1'14.556 | 6 |
| 6 | 2 | Satoru Nakajima | Lotus-Honda | 59 | +1 Lap | 10 |
| 7 | 20 | Thierry Boutsen | Benetton-Ford | 59 | +1 Lap | 7 |
| 8 | 18 | Eddie Cheever | Arrows-Megatron | 59 | +1 Lap | 15 |
| 9 | 26 | Stefan Johansson | Ligier-Judd | 57 | +3 Laps | 21 |
| Ret | 22 | A.de Cesaris | Rial-Ford | 53 | Engine | 14 |
| Ret | 3 | Jonathan Palmer | Tyrrell-Ford | 47 | Transmission | 22 |
| Ret | 24 | Luis Perez-Sala | Minardi-Ford | 46 | Chassis | 20 |
| Ret | 30 | Philippe Alliot | Lola-Ford | 40 | Suspension | 16 |
| Ret | 31 | G.Tarquini | Coloni-Ford | 35 | Suspension | 25 |
| Ret | 14 | Philippe Streiff | AGS-Ford | 35 | Brakes | 19 |
| Ret | 29 | Yannick Dalmas | Lola-Ford | 32 | Engine | 17 |
| DSQ | 12 | Ayrton Senna | McLaren-Honda | 31 | Disqualified | 1 |
| Ret | 25 | Rene Arnoux | Ligier-Judd | 23 | Clutch | 18 |
| Ret | 33 | Stefano Modena | EuroBrun-Ford | 20 | Engine | 24 |
| Ret | 5 | Nigel Mansell | Williams-Judd | 18 | Engine | 2 |
| Ret | 19 | A.Nannini | Benetton-Ford | 7 | Engine | 12 |
| Ret | 6 | Riccardo Patrese | Williams-Judd | 6 | Engine | 8 |
| Ret | 16 | Ivan Capelli | March-Judd | 6 | Engine | 9 |
| Ret | 23 | Adrian Campos | Minardi-Ford | 5 | Chassis | 23 |
| Ret | 15 | M.Gugelmin | March-Judd | 0 | Gearbox | 13 |
| Ret | 32 | Oscar Larrauri | EuroBrun-Ford | 0 | Electrical | 26 |
| DNQ | 4 | Julian Bailey | Tyrrell-Ford | | | |
| DNQ | 9 | P.Ghinzani | Zakspeed | | | |
| DNQ | 21 | Nicola Larini | Osella-Alfa Romeo | | | |
| DNQ | 10 | Bernd Schneider | Zakspeed | | | |
| DNPQ | 36 | Alex Caffi | Dallara-Ford | | | |

Winning speed: 117.090mph Lap leaders: Prost 1-60
Pole position: Senna, 1m 28.096s, 127.747mph Fastest lap: Berger, 1m 32.943s, 121.085mph

**SAN MARINO GRAND PRIX: IMOLA** *1 May Round: 2 Race: 454 60 x 3.132 miles*

| POS. | NO. | DRIVER | CAR/ENGINE | LAPS | TIME/RETIRED | GRID |
|---|---|---|---|---|---|---|
| 1 | 12 | Ayrton Senna | McLaren-Honda | 60 | 1:32'41.264 | 1 |
| 2 | 11 | Alain Prost | McLaren-Honda | 60 | +2.334 | 2 |
| 3 | 1 | Nelson Piquet | Lotus-Honda | 59 | +1 Lap | 3 |
| 4 | 20 | Thierry Boutsen | Benetton-Ford | 59 | +1 Lap | 8 |
| 5 | 28 | Gerhard Berger | Ferrari | 59 | +1 Lap | 5 |
| 6 | 19 | A.Nannini | Benetton-Ford | 59 | +1 Lap | 4 |
| 7 | 18 | Eddie Cheever | Arrows-Megatron | 59 | +1 Lap | 7 |
| 8 | 2 | Satoru Nakajima | Lotus-Honda | 59 | +1 Lap | 12 |
| 9 | 17 | Derek Warwick | Arrows-Megatron | 58 | +2 Laps | 14 |
| 10 | 14 | Philippe Streiff | AGS-Ford | 58 | +2 Laps | 13 |
| 11 | 24 | Luis Perez-Sala | Minardi-Ford | 58 | +2 Laps | 18 |
| 12 | 29 | Yannick Dalmas | Lola-Ford | 58 | +2 Laps | 19 |
| 13 | 6 | Riccardo Patrese | Williams-Judd | 58 | +2 Laps | 6 |
| 14 | 3 | Jonathan Palmer | Tyrrell-Ford | 58 | +2 Laps | 23 |
| 15 | 15 | M.Gugelmin | March-Judd | 58 | +2 Laps | 20 |
| 16 | 23 | Adrian Campos | Minardi-Ford | 57 | +3 Laps | 22 |
| 17 | 30 | Philippe Alliot | Lola-Ford | 57 | +3 Laps | 15 |
| 18 | 27 | Michele Alboreto | Ferrari | 54 | Engine | 10 |
| NC | 33 | Stefano Modena | EuroBrun-Ford | 52 | Not classified | 26 |
| Ret | 4 | Julian Bailey | Tyrrell-Ford | 48 | Gearbox | 21 |
| Ret | 5 | Nigel Mansell | Williams-Judd | 42 | Engine | 11 |
| Ret | 31 | G.Tarquini | Coloni-Ford | 40 | Fuel system | 17 |
| Ret | 36 | Alex Caffi | Dallara-Ford | 18 | Gearbox | 24 |
| Ret | 9 | P.Ghinzani | Zakspeed | 16 | Gearbox | 25 |
| Ret | 16 | Ivan Capelli | March-Judd | 2 | Gearbox | 9 |
| Ret | 22 | A.de Cesaris | Rial-Ford | 0 | Suspension | 16 |
| DSQ | 21 | Nicola Larini | Osella-Alfa Romeo | 0 | Excluded | |
| DNQ | 32 | Oscar Larrauri | EuroBrun-Ford | | | |
| DNQ | 26 | Stefan Johansson | Ligier-Judd | | | |
| DNQ | 25 | Rene Arnoux | Ligier-Judd | | | |
| DNQ | 10 | Bernd Schneider | Zakspeed | | | |

Winning speed: 121.636mph Lap leaders: Senna 1-60
Pole position: Senna, 1m 27.148s, 129.368mph Fastest lap: Prost, 1m 29.685s, 125.708mph

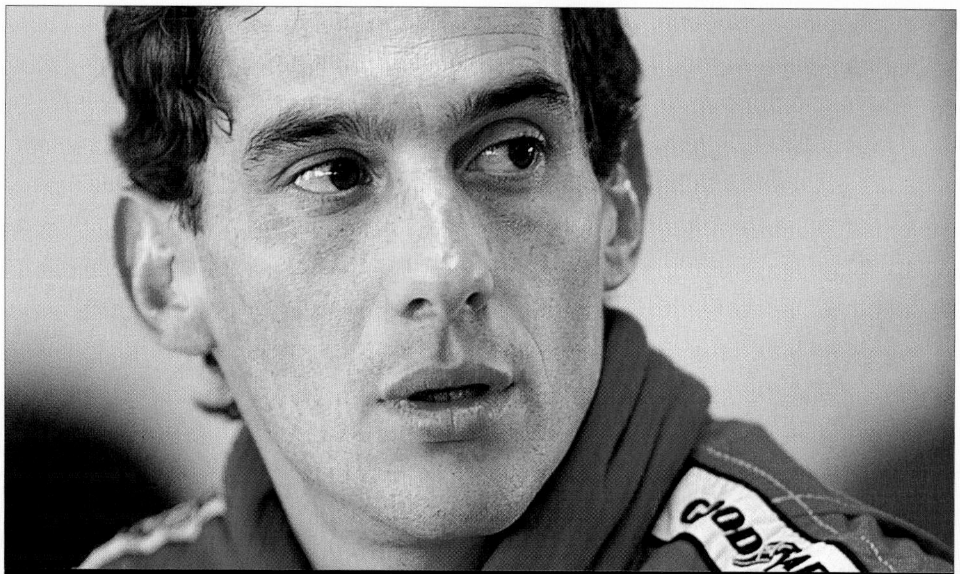
1988 world champion Ayrton Senna.

**MONACO GRAND PRIX: MONTE CARLO** *15 May Round: 3 Race: 455 78 x 2.068 miles*

| POS. | NO. | DRIVER | CAR/ENGINE | LAPS | TIME/RETIRED | GRID |
|---|---|---|---|---|---|---|
| 1 | 11 | Alain Prost | McLaren-Honda | 78 | 1:57'17.077 | 2 |
| 2 | 28 | Gerhard Berger | Ferrari | 78 | +20.453 | 3 |
| 3 | 27 | Michele Alboreto | Ferrari | 78 | +41.229 | 4 |
| 4 | 17 | Derek Warwick | Arrows-Megatron | 77 | +1 Lap | 7 |
| 5 | 3 | Jonathan Palmer | Tyrrell-Ford | 77 | +1 Lap | 10 |
| 6 | 6 | Riccardo Patrese | Williams-Judd | 77 | +1 Lap | 8 |
| 7 | 29 | Yannick Dalmas | Lola-Ford | 77 | +1 Lap | 21 |
| 8 | 20 | Thierry Boutsen | Benetton-Ford | 76 | +2 Laps | 16 |
| 9 | 21 | Nicola Larini | Osella | 75 | +3 Laps | 25 |
| 10 | 16 | Ivan Capelli | March-Judd | 72 | +6 Laps | 22 |
| Ret | 12 | Ayrton Senna | McLaren-Honda | 66 | Spun off | 1 |
| Ret | 30 | Philippe Alliot | Lola-Ford | 50 | Collision | 13 |
| Ret | 15 | M.Gugelmin | March-Judd | 45 | Fuel pump | 14 |
| Ret | 9 | P.Ghinzani | Zakspeed | 43 | Gearbox | 23 |
| Ret | 19 | A.Nannini | Benetton-Ford | 38 | Gearbox | 6 |
| Ret | 24 | Luis Perez-Sala | Minardi-Ford | 36 | Halfshaft | 15 |
| Ret | 5 | Nigel Mansell | Williams-Judd | 32 | Collision | 5 |
| Ret | 22 | A.de Cesaris | Rial-Ford | 28 | Engine | 19 |
| Ret | 25 | Rene Arnoux | Ligier-Judd | 17 | Engine | 20 |
| Ret | 32 | Oscar Larrauri | EuroBrun-Ford | 14 | Brakes | 18 |
| Ret | 18 | Eddie Cheever | Arrows-Megatron | 8 | Engine | 9 |
| Ret | 26 | Stefan Johansson | Ligier-Judd | 6 | Engine | 26 |
| Ret | 31 | G.Tarquini | Coloni-Ford | 5 | Suspension | 24 |
| Ret | 1 | Nelson Piquet | Lotus-Honda | 0 | Collision | 11 |
| Ret | 36 | Alex Caffi | Dallara-Ford | 0 | Spun off | 17 |
| Ret | 14 | Philippe Streiff | AGS-Ford | 0 | Throttle | 12 |
| DSQ | 33 | Stefano Modena | EuroBrun-Ford | 0 | Excluded | |
| DNQ | 2 | Satoru Nakajima | Lotus-Honda | | | |
| DNQ | 10 | Bernd Schneider | Zakspeed | | | |
| DNQ | 23 | Adrian Campos | Minardi-Ford | | | |
| DNQ | 4 | Julian Bailey | Tyrrell-Ford | | | |

Winning speed: 82.516mph Lap leaders: Senna 1-66; Prost 67-78
Pole position: Senna, 1m 23.998s, 88.627mph
Fastest lap: Senna, 1m 26.321s, 86.242mph

**CANADIAN GRAND PRIX: MONTREAL** *12 June Round: 5 Race: 457 69 x 2.728 miles*

| POS. | NO. | DRIVER | CAR/ENGINE | LAPS | TIME/RETIRED | GRID |
|---|---|---|---|---|---|---|
| 1 | 12 | Ayrton Senna | McLaren-Honda | 69 | 1:39'46.618 | 1 |
| 2 | 11 | Alain Prost | McLaren-Honda | 69 | +5.934 | 2 |
| 3 | 20 | Thierry Boutsen | Benetton-Ford | 69 | +51.409 | 7 |
| 4 | 1 | Nelson Piquet | Lotus-Honda | 68 | +1 Lap | 6 |
| 5 | 16 | Ivan Capelli | March-Judd | 68 | +1 Lap | 14 |
| 6 | 3 | Jonathan Palmer | Tyrrell-Ford | 67 | +2 Laps | 19 |
| 7 | 17 | Derek Warwick | Arrows-Megatron | 67 | +2 Laps | 16 |
| 8 | 31 | G.Tarquini | Coloni-Ford | 67 | +2 Laps | 26 |
| 9 | 22 | A.de Cesaris | Rial-Ford | 66 | Out of fuel | 12 |
| 10 | 30 | Philippe Alliot | Lola-Ford | 66 | Electrical | 17 |
| 11 | 2 | Satoru Nakajima | Lotus-Honda | 66 | +3 Laps | 13 |
| 12 | 33 | Stefano Modena | EuroBrun-Ford | 66 | +3 Laps | 15 |
| 13 | 24 | Luis Perez-Sala | Minardi-Ford | 64 | +5 Laps | 21 |
| 14 | 9 | P.Ghinzani | Zakspeed | 63 | Engine | 22 |
| Ret | 15 | M.Gugelmin | March-Judd | 54 | Gearbox | 18 |
| Ret | 14 | Philippe Streiff | AGS-Ford | 41 | Suspension | 10 |
| Ret | 25 | Rene Arnoux | Ligier-Judd | 36 | Transmission | 20 |
| Ret | 27 | Michele Alboreto | Ferrari | 33 | Engine | 4 |
| Ret | 6 | Riccardo Patrese | Williams-Judd | 32 | Engine | 11 |
| Ret | 18 | Eddie Cheever | Arrows-Megatron | 31 | Throttle | 8 |
| Ret | 5 | Nigel Mansell | Williams-Judd | 28 | Engine | 9 |
| Ret | 26 | Stefan Johansson | Ligier-Judd | 24 | Engine | 25 |
| Ret | 28 | Gerhard Berger | Ferrari | 22 | Electrical | 3 |
| Ret | 19 | A.Nannini | Benetton-Ford | 15 | Ignition | 5 |
| Ret | 32 | Oscar Larrauri | EuroBrun-Ford | 8 | Chassis | 24 |
| Ret | 4 | Julian Bailey | Tyrrell-Ford | 0 | Collision | 23 |
| DNQ | 23 | Adrian Campos | Minardi-Ford | | | |
| DNQ | 21 | Nicola Larini | Osella | | | |
| DNQ | 29 | Yannick Dalmas | Lola-Ford | | | |
| DNQ | 10 | Bernd Schneider | Zakspeed | | | |
| DNPQ | 36 | Alex Caffi | Dallara-Ford | | | |

Winning speed: 113.184mph Lap leaders: Prost 1-18; Senna 19-69
Pole position: Senna, 1m 21.681s, 120.226mph
Fastest lap: Senna, 1m 24.973s, 115.568mph

**FRENCH GRAND PRIX: PAUL RICARD** *3 July Round: 7 Race: 459 80 x 2.369 miles*

| POS. | NO. | DRIVER | CAR/ENGINE | LAPS | TIME/RETIRED | GRID |
|---|---|---|---|---|---|---|
| 1 | 11 | Alain Prost | McLaren-Honda | 80 | 1:37'37.328 | 1 |
| 2 | 12 | Ayrton Senna | McLaren-Honda | 80 | +31.752 | 2 |
| 3 | 27 | Michele Alboreto | Ferrari | 80 | +1'06.505 | 4 |
| 4 | 28 | Gerhard Berger | Ferrari | 79 | +1 Lap | 3 |
| 5 | 1 | Nelson Piquet | Lotus-Honda | 79 | +1 Lap | 7 |
| 6 | 19 | A.Nannini | Benetton-Ford | 79 | +1 Lap | 6 |
| 7 | 2 | Satoru Nakajima | Lotus-Honda | 79 | +1 Lap | 8 |
| 8 | 15 | M.Gugelmin | March-Judd | 79 | +1 Lap | 16 |
| 9 | 16 | Ivan Capelli | March-Judd | 79 | +1 Lap | 10 |
| 10 | 22 | A.de Cesaris | Rial-Ford | 78 | +2 Laps | 12 |
| 11 | 18 | Eddie Cheever | Arrows-Megatron | 78 | +2 Laps | 13 |
| 12 | 36 | Alex Caffi | Dallara-Ford | 78 | +2 Laps | 14 |
| 13 | 29 | Yannick Dalmas | Lola-Ford | 78 | +2 Laps | 19 |
| 14 | 33 | Stefano Modena | EuroBrun-Ford | 77 | +3 Laps | 20 |
| 15 | 23 | P.Martini | Minardi-Ford | 77 | +3 Laps | 22 |
| NC | 24 | Luis Perez-Sala | Minardi-Ford | 70 | Not classified | 25 |
| Ret | 32 | Oscar Larrauri | EuroBrun-Ford | 64 | Clutch | 26 |
| Ret | 21 | Nicola Larini | Osella | 56 | Halfshaft | 24 |
| Ret | 10 | Bernd Schneider | Zakspeed | 55 | Gearbox | 21 |
| Ret | 5 | Nigel Mansell | Williams-Judd | 48 | Suspension | 9 |
| Ret | 30 | Philippe Alliot | Lola-Ford | 46 | Electrical | 18 |
| Ret | 3 | Jonathan Palmer | Tyrrell-Ford | 40 | Engine | 23 |
| Ret | 6 | Riccardo Patrese | Williams-Judd | 35 | Brakes | 15 |
| Ret | 20 | Thierry Boutsen | Benetton-Ford | 28 | Engine | 5 |
| Ret | 14 | Philippe Streiff | AGS-Ford | 20 | Fuel leak | 17 |
| Ret | 17 | Derek Warwick | Arrows-Megatron | 11 | Spun off | 11 |
| DSQ | 9 | P.Ghinzani | Zakspeed | 0 | Excluded | |
| DNQ | 25 | Rene Arnoux | Ligier-Judd | | | |
| DNQ | 4 | Julian Bailey | Tyrrell-Ford | | | |
| DNQ | 26 | Stefan Johansson | Ligier-Judd | | | |
| DNPQ | 31 | G.Tarquini | Coloni-Ford | | | |

Winning speed: 116.496mph Lap leaders: Prost 1-36, 61-80; Senna 37-60
Pole position: Prost, 1m 7.589s, 126.196mph
Fastest lap: Prost, 1m 11.737s, 118.899mph

**MEXICAN GRAND PRIX: MEXICO CITY** *29 May Round: 4 Race: 456 67 x 2.747 miles*

| POS. | NO. | DRIVER | CAR/ENGINE | LAPS | TIME/RETIRED | GRID |
|---|---|---|---|---|---|---|
| 1 | 11 | Alain Prost | McLaren-Honda | 67 | 1:30'15.737 | 2 |
| 2 | 12 | Ayrton Senna | McLaren/Honda | 67 | +7.104 | 1 |
| 3 | 28 | Gerhard Berger | Ferrari | 67 | +57.314 | 3 |
| 4 | 27 | Michele Alboreto | Ferrari | 66 | +1 Lap | 5 |
| 5 | 17 | Derek Warwick | Arrows-Megatron | 66 | +1 Lap | 9 |
| 6 | 18 | Eddie Cheever | Arrows-Megatron | 66 | +1 Lap | 7 |
| 7 | 19 | A.Nannini | Benetton-Ford | 65 | +2 Laps | 8 |
| 8 | 20 | Thierry Boutsen | Benetton-Ford | 64 | +3 Laps | 11 |
| 9 | 29 | Yannick Dalmas | Lola-Ford | 64 | +3 Laps | 22 |
| 10 | 26 | Stefan Johansson | Ligier-Judd | 63 | +4 Laps | 24 |
| 11 | 24 | Luis Perez-Sala | Minardi-Ford | 63 | +4 Laps | 25 |
| 12 | 14 | Philippe Streiff | AGS-Ford | 63 | +4 Laps | 19 |
| 13 | 32 | Oscar Larrauri | EuroBrun-Ford | 63 | +4 Laps | 26 |
| 14 | 31 | G.Tarquini | Coloni-Ford | 62 | +5 Laps | 21 |
| 15 | 9 | P.Ghinzani | Zakspeed | 61 | +6 Laps | 18 |
| 16 | 16 | Ivan Capelli | March-Judd | 61 | +6 Laps | 10 |
| Ret | 1 | Nelson Piquet | Lotus-Honda | 58 | Engine | 4 |
| Ret | 22 | A.de Cesaris | Rial-Ford | 52 | Gearbox | 12 |
| Ret | 2 | Satoru Nakajima | Lotus-Honda | 27 | Engine | 6 |
| Ret | 5 | Nigel Mansell | Williams-Judd | 20 | Engine | 14 |
| Ret | 10 | Bernd Schneider | Zakspeed | 16 | Engine | 15 |
| Ret | 6 | Riccardo Patrese | Williams-Judd | 16 | Engine | 17 |
| Ret | 25 | Rene Arnoux | Ligier-Judd | 13 | Collision | 20 |
| Ret | 36 | Alex Caffi | Dallara-Ford | 13 | Brakes | 23 |
| Ret | 15 | M.Gugelmin | March/Judd | 10 | Electrical | 16 |
| Ret | 30 | Philippe Alliot | Lola-Ford | 0 | Suspension | 13 |
| DSQ | 33 | Stefano Modena | EuroBrun-Ford | 0 | Excluded | |
| DNQ | 3 | Jonathan Palmer | Tyrrell-Ford | | | |
| DNQ | 21 | Nicola Larini | Osella | | | |
| DNQ | 4 | Julian Bailey | Tyrrell-Ford | | | |
| DNQ | 23 | Adrian Campos | Minardi-Ford | | | |

Winning speed: 122.346mph Lap leaders: Prost 1-67
Pole position: Senna, 1m 17.468s, 127.659mph
Fastest lap: Prost, 1m 18.608s, 125.808mph

**UNITED STATES GRAND PRIX: DETROIT** *19 June Round: 6 Race: 458 63 x 2.500 miles*

| POS. | NO. | DRIVER | CAR/ENGINE | LAPS | TIME/RETIRED | GRID |
|---|---|---|---|---|---|---|
| 1 | 12 | Ayrton Senna | McLaren-Honda | 63 | 1:54'56.035 | 1 |
| 2 | 11 | Alain Prost | McLaren-Honda | 63 | +38.713 | 4 |
| 3 | 20 | Thierry Boutsen | Benetton-Ford | 62 | +1 Lap | 5 |
| 4 | 22 | A.de Cesaris | Rial-Ford | 62 | +1 Lap | 12 |
| 5 | 3 | Jonathan Palmer | Tyrrell-Ford | 62 | +1 Lap | 17 |
| 6 | 23 | P.Martini | Minardi-Ford | 62 | +1 Lap | 16 |
| 7 | 29 | Yannick Dalmas | Lola-Ford | 61 | +2 Laps | 24 |
| 8 | 36 | Alex Caffi | Dallara-Ford | 61 | +2 Laps | 21 |
| 9 | 4 | Julian Bailey | Tyrrell-Ford | 59 | Spun off | 22 |
| Ret | 24 | Luis Perez-Sala | Minardi-Ford | 54 | Gearbox | 25 |
| Ret | 30 | Philippe Alliot | Lola-Ford | 46 | Halfshaft | 14 |
| Ret | 33 | Stefano Modena | EuroBrun-Ford | 46 | Spun off | 19 |
| Ret | 27 | Michele Alboreto | Ferrari | 45 | Collision | 3 |
| Ret | 25 | Rene Arnoux | Ligier-Judd | 45 | Overheating | 20 |
| Ret | 15 | M.Gugelmin | March-Judd | 34 | Engine | 13 |
| Ret | 6 | Riccardo Patrese | Williams-Judd | 26 | Engine | 10 |
| Ret | 1 | Nelson Piquet | Lotus-Honda | 26 | Spun off | 8 |
| Ret | 32 | Oscar Larrauri | EuroBrun-Ford | 26 | Gearbox | 23 |
| Ret | 17 | Derek Warwick | Arrows-Megatron | 24 | Spun off | 9 |
| Ret | 5 | Nigel Mansell | Williams-Judd | 18 | Engine | 6 |
| Ret | 14 | Philippe Streiff | AGS-Ford | 15 | Suspension | 11 |
| Ret | 19 | A.Nannini | Benetton-Ford | 14 | Suspension | 7 |
| Ret | 18 | Eddie Cheever | Arrows-Megatron | 14 | Electrical | 15 |
| Ret | 21 | Nicola Larini | Osella | 7 | Engine | 26 |
| Ret | 28 | Gerhard Berger | Ferrari | 6 | Puncture | 2 |
| Ret | 26 | Stefan Johansson | Ligier-Judd | 2 | Overheating | 18 |
| DNS | 16 | Ivan Capelli | March-Judd | 0 | Accident | |
| DNQ | 2 | Satoru Nakajima | Lotus-Honda | | | |
| DNQ | 10 | Bernd Schneider | Zakspeed | | | |
| DNQ | 9 | P.Ghinzani | Zakspeed | | | |
| DNPQ | 31 | G.Tarquini | Coloni-Ford | | | |

Winning speed: 82.221mph Lap leaders: Senna 1-63
Pole position: Senna, 1m 40.606s, 89.458mph
Fastest lap: Prost, 1m 44.836s, 85.848mph

**BRITISH GRAND PRIX: SILVERSTONE** *10 July Round: 8 Race: 460 65 x 2.969 miles*

| POS. | NO. | DRIVER | CAR/ENGINE | LAPS | TIME/RETIRED | GRID |
|---|---|---|---|---|---|---|
| 1 | 12 | Ayrton Senna | McLaren-Honda | 65 | 1:33'16.367 | 3 |
| 2 | 5 | Nigel Mansell | Williams-Judd | 65 | +23.344 | 11 |
| 3 | 19 | A.Nannini | Benetton-Ford | 65 | +51.214 | 8 |
| 4 | 15 | M.Gugelmin | March-Judd | 65 | +1'11.378 | 5 |
| 5 | 1 | Nelson Piquet | Lotus-Honda | 65 | +1'20.835 | 7 |
| 6 | 17 | Derek Warwick | Arrows-Megatron | 64 | +1 Lap | 9 |
| 7 | 18 | Eddie Cheever | Arrows-Megatron | 64 | +1 Lap | 13 |
| 8 | 6 | Riccardo Patrese | Williams-Judd | 64 | +1 Lap | 15 |
| 9 | 28 | Gerhard Berger | Ferrari | 64 | +1 Lap | 1 |
| 10 | 2 | Satoru Nakajima | Lotus-Honda | 64 | +1 Lap | 10 |
| 11 | 36 | Alex Caffi | Dallara-Ford | 64 | +1 Lap | 21 |
| 12 | 33 | Stefano Modena | EuroBrun-Ford | 64 | +1 Lap | 20 |
| 13 | 29 | Yannick Dalmas | Lola-Ford | 63 | +2 Laps | 23 |
| 14 | 30 | Philippe Alliot | Lola-Ford | 63 | +2 Laps | 22 |
| 15 | 23 | P.Martini | Minardi-Ford | 63 | +2 Laps | 19 |
| 16 | 4 | Julian Bailey | Tyrrell-Ford | 63 | +2 Laps | 24 |
| 17 | 27 | Michele Alboreto | Ferrari | 62 | Out of fuel | 2 |
| 18 | 25 | Rene Arnoux | Ligier-Judd | 62 | +3 Laps | 25 |
| 19 | 21 | Nicola Larini | Osella | 60 | Out of fuel | 26 |
| Ret | 20 | Thierry Boutsen | Benetton-Ford | 38 | Transmission | 12 |
| Ret | 16 | Ivan Capelli | March-Judd | 34 | Alternator | 6 |
| Ret | 11 | Alain Prost | McLaren-Honda | 24 | Handling | 4 |
| Ret | 3 | Jonathan Palmer | Tyrrell-Ford | 14 | Engine | 17 |
| Ret | 22 | A.de Cesaris | Rial-Ford | 9 | Clutch | 14 |
| Ret | 14 | Philippe Streiff | AGS-Ford | 8 | Broken wing | 16 |
| Ret | 24 | Luis Perez-Sala | Minardi-Ford | 0 | Suspension | 18 |
| DNQ | 32 | Oscar Larrauri | EuroBrun-Ford | | | |
| DNQ | 9 | P.Ghinzani | Zakspeed | | | |
| DNQ | 26 | Stefan Johansson | Ligier-Judd | | | |
| DNQ | 10 | Bernd Schneider | Zakspeed | | | |
| DNPQ | 31 | G.Tarquini | Coloni/Ford | | | |

Winning speed: 124.142mph Lap leaders: Berger 1-13; Senna 14-65
Pole position: Berger, 1m 10.133s, 152.402mph
Fastest lap: Mansell, 1m 23.308s, 128.300mph

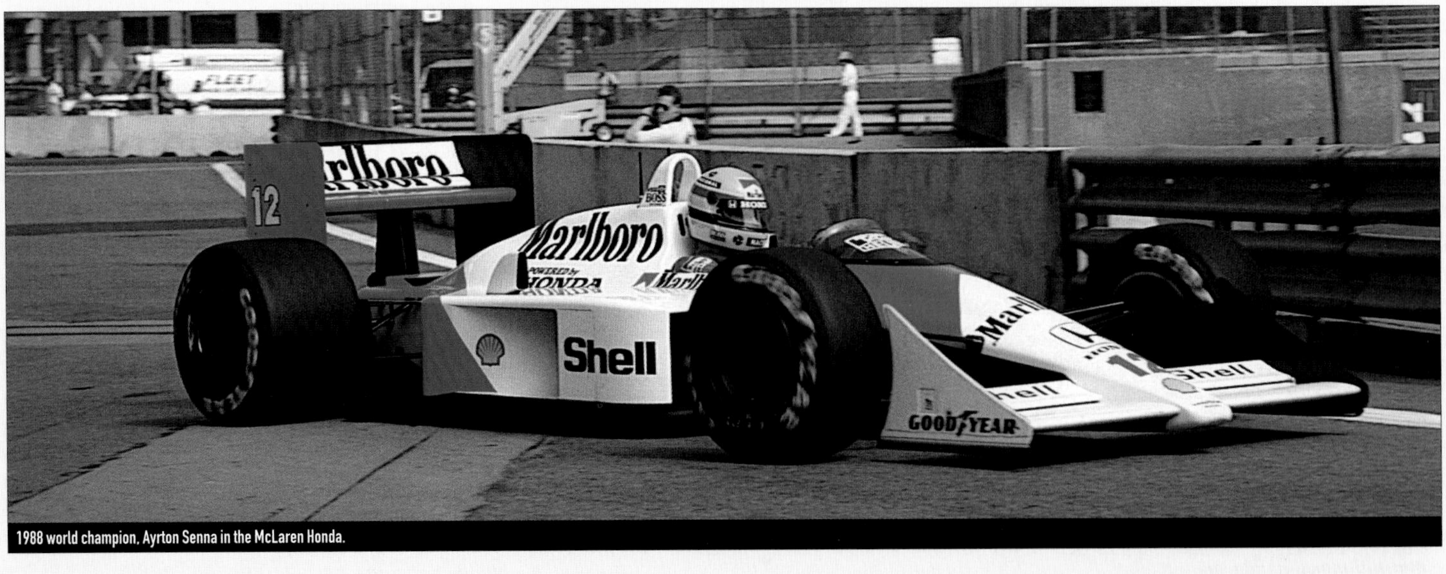


1988 world champion, Ayrton Senna in the McLaren Honda.

## GERMAN GRAND PRIX: HOCKENHEIM *24 July Round: 9 Race: 461 44 x 4.223 miles*

| POS. | NO. | DRIVER | CAR/ENGINE | LAPS | TIME/RETIRED | GRID |
|---|---|---|---|---|---|---|
| 1 | 12 | Ayrton Senna | McLaren-Honda | 44 | 1:32'54.188 | 1 |
| 2 | 11 | Alain Prost | McLaren-Honda | 44 | +13.609 | 2 |
| 3 | 28 | Gerhard Berger | Ferrari | 44 | +52.095 | 3 |
| 4 | 27 | Michele Alboreto | Ferrari | 44 | +1'40.912 | 4 |
| 5 | 16 | Ivan Capelli | March-Judd | 44 | +1'49.606 | 7 |
| 6 | 20 | Thierry Boutsen | Benetton-Ford | 43 | +1 Lap | 9 |
| 7 | 17 | Derek Warwick | Arrows-Megatron | 43 | +1 Lap | 12 |
| 8 | 15 | M.Gugelmin | March-Judd | 43 | +1 Lap | 10 |
| 9 | 2 | Satoru Nakajima | Lotus-Honda | 43 | +1 Lap | 8 |
| 10 | 18 | Eddie Cheever | Arrows-Megatron | 43 | +1 Lap | 15 |
| 11 | 3 | Jonathan Palmer | Tyrrell-Ford | 43 | +1 Lap | 24 |
| 12 | 10 | Bernd Schneider | Zakspeed | 43 | +1 Lap | 22 |
| 13 | 22 | A.de Cesaris | Rial-Ford | 42 | +2 Laps | 14 |
| 14 | 9 | P.Ghinzani | Zakspeed | 42 | +2 Laps | 23 |
| 15 | 36 | Alex Caffi | Dallara-Ford | 42 | +2 Laps | 19 |
| 16 | 32 | Oscar Larrauri | EuroBrun-Ford | 42 | +2 Laps | 26 |
| 17 | 25 | Rene Arnoux | Ligier-Judd | 41 | +3 Laps | 17 |
| 18 | 19 | A.Nannini | Benetton-Ford | 40 | +4 Laps | 6 |
| 19 | 29 | Yannick Dalmas | Lola-Ford | 39 | Clutch | 21 |
| Ret | 14 | Philippe Streiff | AGS-Ford | 38 | Throttle | 16 |
| Ret | 6 | Riccardo Patrese | Williams-Judd | 34 | Spun off | 13 |
| Ret | 21 | Nicola Larini | Osella | 27 | Engine | 18 |
| Ret | 5 | Nigel Mansell | Williams-Judd | 16 | Spun off | 11 |
| Ret | 33 | Stefano Modena | EuroBrun-Ford | 15 | Engine | 25 |
| Ret | 30 | Philippe Alliot | Lola-Ford | 8 | Spun off | 20 |
| Ret | 1 | Nelson Piquet | Lotus-Honda | 1 | Spun off | 5 |
| DNQ | 24 | Luis Perez-Sala | Minardi-Ford | | | |
| DNQ | 26 | Stefan Johansson | Ligier-Judd | | | |
| DNQ | 4 | Julian Bailey | Tyrrell-Ford | | | |
| DNQ | 23 | P.Martini | Minardi-Ford | | | |
| DNPQ | 31 | G.Tarquini | Coloni-Ford | | | |

Winning speed: 120.017mph Lap leaders: Senna 1-44 Pole position: Senna, 1m 44.596s, 145.364mph. Fastest lap: Nannini, 2m 3.032s, 123.581mph

## HUNGARY GRAND PRIX: HUNGARORING *7 August Round: 10 Race: 462 76 x 2.494 miles*

| POS. | NO. | DRIVER | CAR/ENGINE | LAPS | TIME/RETIRED | GRID |
|---|---|---|---|---|---|---|
| 1 | 12 | Ayrton Senna | McLaren-Honda | 76 | 1:57'47.081 | 1 |
| 2 | 11 | Alain Prost | McLaren-Honda | 76 | +0.529 | 7 |
| 3 | 20 | Thierry Boutsen | Benetton-Ford | 76 | +31.410 | 3 |
| 4 | 28 | Gerhard Berger | Ferrari | 76 | +1'28.670 | 9 |
| 5 | 15 | M.Gugelmin | March-Judd | 75 | +1 Lap | 8 |
| 6 | 6 | Riccardo Patrese | Williams-Judd | 75 | +1 Lap | 6 |
| 7 | 2 | Satoru Nakajima | Lotus-Honda | 73 | +3 Laps | 19 |
| 8 | 1 | Nelson Piquet | Lotus-Honda | 73 | +3 Laps | 13 |
| 9 | 29 | Yannick Dalmas | Lola-Ford | 73 | +3 Laps | 17 |
| 10 | 24 | Luis Perez-Sala | Minardi-Ford | 72 | +4 Laps | 11 |
| 11 | 33 | Stefano Modena | EuroBrun-Ford | 72 | +4 Laps | 26 |
| 12 | 30 | Philippe Alliot | Lola-Ford | 72 | +4 Laps | 20 |
| 13 | 31 | G.Tarquini | Coloni-Ford | 71 | +5 Laps | 22 |
| Ret | 17 | Derek Warwick | Arrows-Megatron | 65 | Brakes | 12 |
| Ret | 5 | Nigel Mansell | Williams-Judd | 60 | Driver unwell | 2 |
| Ret | 18 | Eddie Cheever | Arrows-Megatron | 55 | Brakes | 14 |
| Ret | 27 | Michele Alboreto | Ferrari | 40 | Electrical | 15 |
| Ret | 25 | Rene Arnoux | Ligier-Judd | 32 | Engine | 25 |
| Ret | 22 | A.de Cesaris | Rial-Ford | 28 | Halfshaft | 18 |
| Ret | 19 | A.Nannini | Benetton-Ford | 24 | Overheating | 5 |
| Ret | 36 | Alex Caffi | Dallara-Ford | 22 | Engine | 10 |
| Ret | 26 | Stefan Johansson | Ligier-Judd | 19 | Throttle | 24 |
| Ret | 23 | P.Martini | Minardi-Ford | 8 | Collision | 16 |
| Ret | 14 | Philippe Streiff | AGS-Ford | 8 | Collision | 23 |
| Ret | 16 | Ivan Capelli | March-Judd | 5 | Engine | 4 |
| Ret | 3 | Jonathan Palmer | Tyrrell-Ford | 3 | Engine | 21 |
| DNQ | 32 | Oscar Larrauri | EuroBrun-Ford | | | |
| DNQ | 10 | Bernd Schneider | Zakspeed | | | |
| DNQ | 4 | Julian Bailey | Tyrrell-Ford | | | |
| DNQ | 9 | P.Ghinzani | Zakspeed | | | |
| DNPQ | 21 | Nicola Larini | Osella | | | |

Winning speed: 96.562mph Lap leaders: Senna 1-76
Pole position: Senna, 1m 27.635s, 102.460mph. Fastest lap: Prost, 1m 30.639s, 99.064mph

## BELGIAN GRAND PRIX: SPA-FRANCORCHAMPS *28 August Round: 11 Race: 463 43 x 4.312 miles*

| POS. | NO. | DRIVER | CAR/ENGINE | LAPS | TIME/RETIRED | GRID |
|---|---|---|---|---|---|---|
| 1 | 12 | Ayrton Senna | McLaren-Honda | 43 | 1:28'00.549 | 1 |
| 2 | 11 | Alain Prost | McLaren-Honda | 43 | +30.470 | 2 |
| 3 | 16 | Ivan Capelli | March-Judd | 43 | +1'15.768 | 14 |
| 4 | 1 | Nelson Piquet | Lotus-Honda | 43 | +1'23.628 | 9 |
| 5 | 17 | Derek Warwick | Arrows-Megatron | 43 | +1'25.355 | 10 |
| 6 | 18 | Eddie Cheever | Arrows-Megatron | 42 | +1 Lap | 11 |
| 7 | 5 | Martin Brundle | Williams-Judd | 42 | +1 Lap | 12 |
| 8 | 36 | Alex Caffi | Dallara-Ford | 42 | +1 Lap | 15 |
| 9 | 30 | Philippe Alliot | Lola-Ford | 42 | +1 Lap | 16 |
| 10 | 14 | Philippe Streiff | AGS-Ford | 42 | +1 Lap | 18 |
| 11 | 26 | Stefan Johansson | Ligier-Judd | 39 | Engine | 20 |
| 12 | 3 | Jonathan Palmer | Tyrrell-Ford | 39 | Throttle | 21 |
| 13 | 10 | Bernd Schneider | Zakspeed | 38 | Gearbox | 25 |
| DSQ | 20 | Thierry Boutsen | Benetton-Ford | 43 | Disqualified | 6 |
| DSQ | 19 | A.Nannini | Benetton-Ford | 43 | Disqualified | 7 |
| Ret | 31 | G.Tarquini | Coloni-Ford | 36 | Steering | 22 |
| Ret | 27 | Michele Alboreto | Ferrari | 35 | Engine | 4 |
| Ret | 6 | Riccardo Patrese | Williams-Judd | 30 | Engine | 5 |
| Ret | 15 | M.Gugelmin | March-Judd | 29 | Spun off | 13 |
| Ret | 9 | P.Ghinzani | Zakspeed | 25 | Oil leak | 24 |
| Ret | 2 | Satoru Nakajima | Lotus-Honda | 22 | Engine | 8 |
| Ret | 21 | Nicola Larini | Osella | 14 | Fuel system | 26 |
| Ret | 28 | Gerhard Berger | Ferrari | 11 | Injection | 3 |
| Ret | 29 | Yannick Dalmas | Lola-Ford | 9 | Engine | 23 |
| Ret | 22 | A.de Cesaris | Rial-Ford | 2 | Collision | 19 |
| Ret | 25 | Rene Arnoux | Ligier-Judd | 2 | Collision | 17 |
| DNQ | 24 | Luis Perez-Sala | Minardi-Ford | | | |
| DNQ | 23 | P.Martini | Minardi-Ford | | | |
| DNQ | 33 | Stefano Modena | EuroBrun-Ford | | | |
| DNQ | 4 | Julian Bailey | Tyrrell/Ford | | | |
| DNPQ | 32 | Oscar Larrauri | EuroBrun-Ford | | | |

Winning speed: 126.416mph Lap leaders: Senna 1-43. Pole position: Senna, 1m 53.718s, 136.516mph. Fastest lap: Berger, 2m 0.772s, 128.543mph. Boutsen and Nannini finished third and fourth but were disqualified because of fuel irregularities.

## ITALIAN GRAND PRIX: MONZA *11 September Round: 12 Race: 464 51 x 3.604 miles*

| POS. | NO. | DRIVER | CAR/ENGINE | LAPS | TIME/RETIRED | GRID |
|---|---|---|---|---|---|---|
| 1 | 28 | Gerhard Berger | Ferrari | 51 | 1:17'39.744 | 3 |
| 2 | 27 | Michele Alboreto | Ferrari | 51 | +0.502 | 4 |
| 3 | 18 | Eddie Cheever | Arrows-Megatron | 51 | +35.532 | 5 |
| 4 | 17 | Derek Warwick | Arrows-Megatron | 51 | +36.114 | 6 |
| 5 | 16 | Ivan Capelli | March-Judd | 51 | +52.522 | 11 |
| 6 | 20 | Thierry Boutsen | Benetton-Ford | 51 | +59.878 | 8 |
| 7 | 6 | Riccardo Patrese | Williams-Judd | 51 | +1'14.743 | 10 |
| 8 | 15 | M.Gugelmin | March-Judd | 51 | +1'32.566 | 13 |
| 9 | 19 | A.Nannini | Benetton-Ford | 50 | +1 Lap | 9 |
| 10 | 12 | Ayrton Senna | McLaren-Honda | 49 | Collision | 1 |
| 11 | 5 | J.L.Schlesser | Williams-Judd | 49 | +2 Laps | 22 |
| 12 | 4 | Julian Bailey | Tyrrell-Ford | 49 | +2 Laps | 26 |
| 13 | 25 | Rene Arnoux | Ligier-Judd | 49 | +2 Laps | 24 |
| Ret | 11 | Alain Prost | McLaren-Honda | 34 | Engine | 2 |
| Ret | 30 | Philippe Alliot | Lola-Ford | 33 | Engine | 20 |
| Ret | 14 | Philippe Streiff | AGS-Ford | 31 | Clutch | 23 |
| Ret | 10 | Bernd Schneider | Zakspeed | 28 | Engine | 15 |
| Ret | 22 | A.de Cesaris | Rial-Ford | 27 | Chassis | 18 |
| Ret | 9 | P.Ghinzani | Zakspeed | 25 | Engine | 16 |
| Ret | 36 | Alex Caffi | Dallara-Ford | 24 | Engine | 21 |
| Ret | 29 | Yannick Dalmas | Lola-Ford | 17 | Radiator | 25 |
| Ret | 23 | P.Martini | Minardi-Ford | 15 | Engine | 14 |
| Ret | 2 | Satoru Nakajima | Lotus-Honda | 14 | Engine | 12 |
| Ret | 24 | Luis Perez-Sala | Minardi-Ford | 12 | Gearbox | 19 |
| Ret | 1 | Nelson Piquet | Lotus-Honda | 11 | Clutch | 7 |
| Ret | 21 | Nicola Larini | Osella | 2 | Engine | 17 |
| DNQ | 3 | Jonathan Palmer | Tyrrell-Ford | | | |
| DNQ | 26 | Stefan Johansson | Ligier-Judd | | | |
| DNQ | 31 | G.Tarquini | Coloni-Ford | | | |
| DNQ | 33 | Stefano Modena | EuroBrun-Ford | | | |
| DNPQ | 32 | Oscar Larrauri | EuroBrun-Ford | | | |

Winning speed: 142.000mph Lap leaders: Senna 1-49; Berger 50-51
Pole position: Senna, 1m 25.974s, 150.909mph Fastest lap: Alboreto, 1m 29.070s, 145.663mph

## PORTUGUESE GRAND PRIX: ESTORIL *25 September Round: 13 Race: 465 70 x 2.703 miles*

| POS. | NO. | DRIVER | CAR/ENGINE | LAPS | TIME/RETIRED | GRID |
|---|---|---|---|---|---|---|
| 1 | 11 | Alain Prost | McLaren-Honda | 70 | 1:37'40.958 | 1 |
| 2 | 16 | Ivan Capelli | March-Judd | 70 | +9.553 | 3 |
| 3 | 20 | Thierry Boutsen | Benetton-Ford | 70 | +44.619 | 13 |
| 4 | 17 | Derek Warwick | Arrows-Megatron | 70 | +1'07.419 | 10 |
| 5 | 27 | Michele Alboreto | Ferrari | 70 | +1'11.884 | 7 |
| 6 | 12 | Ayrton Senna | McLaren-Honda | 70 | +1'18.269 | 2 |
| 7 | 36 | Alex Caffi | Dallara-Ford | 69 | +1 Lap | 17 |
| 8 | 24 | Luis Perez-Sala | Minardi-Ford | 68 | +2 Laps | 19 |
| 9 | 14 | Philippe Streiff | AGS-Ford | 68 | +2 Laps | 21 |
| 10 | 25 | Rene Arnoux | Ligier-Judd | 68 | +2 Laps | 23 |
| 11 | 31 | G.Tarquini | Coloni-Ford | 65 | +5 Laps | 26 |
| 12 | 21 | Nicola Larini | Osella | 63 | +7 Laps | 25 |
| Ret | 15 | M.Gugelmin | March-Judd | 59 | Engine | 5 |
| Ret | 5 | Nigel Mansell | Williams-Judd | 54 | Spun off | 6 |
| Ret | 3 | Jonathan Palmer | Tyrrell-Ford | 53 | Overheating | 22 |
| Ret | 19 | A.Nannini | Benetton-Ford | 52 | Handling | 9 |
| Ret | 28 | Gerhard Berger | Ferrari | 35 | Spun off | 4 |
| Ret | 1 | Nelson Piquet | Lotus-Honda | 34 | Clutch | 8 |
| Ret | 6 | Riccardo Patrese | Williams-Judd | 29 | Radiator | 11 |
| Ret | 23 | P.Martini | Minardi-Ford | 27 | Engine | 14 |
| Ret | 29 | Yannick Dalmas | Lola-Ford | 20 | Alternator | 15 |
| Ret | 2 | Satoru Nakajima | Lotus-Honda | 16 | Spun off | 16 |
| Ret | 22 | A.de Cesaris | Rial-Ford | 11 | Halfshaft | 12 |
| Ret | 18 | Eddie Cheever | Arrows-Megatron | 10 | Turbo | 18 |
| Ret | 30 | Philippe Alliot | Lola-Ford | 7 | Engine | 20 |
| Ret | 26 | Stefan Johansson | Ligier-Judd | 4 | Engine | 24 |
| DNQ | 4 | Julian Bailey | Tyrrell-Ford | | | |
| DNQ | 9 | P.Ghinzani | Zakspeed | | | |
| DNQ | 33 | Stefano Modena | EuroBrun-Ford | | | |
| DNQ | 10 | Bernd Schneider | Zakspeed | | | |
| DNPQ | 32 | Oscar Larrauri | EuroBrun-Ford | | | |

Winning speed: 116.218 mph Lap leaders: Senna 1; Prost 2-70
Pole position: Prost, 1m 17.411s, 125.701mph Fastest lap: Berger, 1m 21.961s, 118.723mph

## SPANISH GRAND PRIX: JEREZ DE LA FRONTERA *2 October Round: 14 Race: 466 72 x 2.621 miles*

| POS. | NO. | DRIVER | CAR/ENGINE | LAPS | TIME/RETIRED | GRID |
|---|---|---|---|---|---|---|
| 1 | 11 | Alain Prost | McLaren-Honda | 72 | 1:48'43.851 | 2 |
| 2 | 5 | Nigel Mansell | Williams-Judd | 72 | +26.232 | 3 |
| 3 | 19 | A.Nannini | Benetton-Ford | 72 | +35.446 | 5 |
| 4 | 12 | Ayrton Senna | McLaren-Honda | 72 | +46.710 | 1 |
| 5 | 6 | Riccardo Patrese | Williams-Judd | 72 | +47.430 | 7 |
| 6 | 28 | Gerhard Berger | Ferrari | 72 | +51.813 | 8 |
| 7 | 15 | M.Gugelmin | March-Judd | 72 | +1'15.964 | 11 |
| 8 | 1 | Nelson Piquet | Lotus-Honda | 72 | +1'17.309 | 9 |
| 9 | 20 | Thierry Boutsen | Benetton-Ford | 72 | +1'17.655 | 4 |
| 10 | 36 | Alex Caffi | Dallara-Ford | 71 | +1 Lap | 18 |
| 11 | 29 | Yannick Dalmas | Lola-Ford | 71 | +1 Lap | 16 |
| 12 | 24 | Luis Perez-Sala | Minardi-Ford | 70 | +2 Laps | 24 |
| 13 | 33 | Stefano Modena | EuroBrun-Ford | 70 | +2 Laps | 26 |
| 14 | 30 | Philippe Alliot | Lola-Ford | 69 | +3 Laps | 12 |
| Ret | 26 | Stefan Johansson | Ligier-Judd | 62 | Wheel | 21 |
| Ret | 18 | Eddie Cheever | Arrows-Megatron | 60 | Chassis | 25 |
| Ret | 16 | Ivan Capelli | March-Judd | 45 | Engine | 6 |
| Ret | 17 | Derek Warwick | Arrows-Megatron | 41 | Chassis | 17 |
| Ret | 22 | A.de Cesaris | Rial-Ford | 37 | Engine | 23 |
| Ret | 14 | Philippe Streiff | AGS-Ford | 16 | Engine | 13 |
| Ret | 27 | Michele Alboreto | Ferrari | 15 | Engine | 10 |
| Ret | 23 | P.Martini | Minardi-Ford | 15 | Gearbox | 20 |
| Ret | 2 | Satoru Nakajima | Lotus-Honda | 14 | Spun off | 15 |
| Ret | 21 | Nicola Larini | Osella | 9 | Suspension | 14 |
| Ret | 3 | Jonathan Palmer | Tyrrell-Ford | 4 | Chassis | 22 |
| Ret | 25 | Rene Arnoux | Ligier-Judd | 0 | Throttle | 19 |
| DNQ | 10 | Bernd Schneider | Zakspeed | | | |
| DNQ | 32 | Oscar Larrauri | EuroBrun-Ford | | | |
| DNQ | 4 | Julian Bailey | Tyrrell-Ford | | | |
| DNQ | 9 | P.Ghinzani | Zakspeed | | | |
| DNPQ | 31 | G.Tarquini | Coloni-Ford | | | |

Winning speed: 104.133mph Lap leaders: Prost 1-72
Pole position: Senna, 1m 24.067s, 112.237mph Fastest lap: Prost, 1m 27.845s, 107.410mph

## JAPANESE GRAND PRIX: SUZUKA *30 October Round: 15 Race: 467 51 x 3.641 miles*

| POS. | NO. | DRIVER | CAR/ENGINE | LAPS | TIME/RETIRED | GRID |
|---|---|---|---|---|---|---|
| 1 | 12 | Ayrton Senna | McLaren-Honda | 51 | 1:33'26.173 | 1 |
| 2 | 11 | Alain Prost | McLaren-Honda | 51 | +13.363 | 2 |
| 3 | 20 | Thierry Boutsen | Benetton-Ford | 51 | +36.109 | 10 |
| 4 | 28 | Gerhard Berger | Ferrari | 51 | +1'26.714 | 3 |
| 5 | 19 | A.Nannini | Benetton-Ford | 51 | +1'30.603 | 12 |
| 6 | 6 | Riccardo Patrese | Williams-Judd | 51 | +1'37.615 | 11 |
| 7 | 2 | Satoru Nakajima | Lotus-Honda | 50 | +1 Lap | 6 |
| 8 | 14 | Philippe Streiff | AGS-Ford | 50 | +1 Lap | 18 |
| 9 | 30 | Philippe Alliot | Lola-Ford | 50 | +1 Lap | 19 |
| 10 | 15 | M.Gugelmin | March-Judd | 50 | +1 Lap | 13 |
| 11 | 27 | Michele Alboreto | Ferrari | 50 | +1 Lap | 9 |
| 12 | 3 | Jonathan Palmer | Tyrrell-Ford | 50 | +1 Lap | 16 |
| 13 | 23 | P.Martini | Minardi-Ford | 49 | +2 Laps | 17 |
| 14 | 4 | Julian Bailey | Tyrrell-Ford | 49 | +2 Laps | 26 |
| 15 | 24 | Luis Perez-Sala | Minardi-Ford | 49 | +2 Laps | 22 |
| 16 | 29 | Aguri Suzuki | Lola-Ford | 48 | +3 Laps | 20 |
| 17 | 25 | Rene Arnoux | Ligier-Judd | 48 | +3 Laps | 23 |
| Ret | 22 | A.de Cesaris | Rial-Ford | 36 | Overheating | 14 |
| Ret | 18 | Eddie Cheever | Arrows-Megatron | 35 | Ignition | 15 |
| Ret | 21 | Nicola Larini | Osella | 34 | Brakes | 24 |
| Ret | 1 | Nelson Piquet | Lotus-Honda | 34 | Physical | 5 |
| Ret | 5 | Nigel Mansell | Williams-Judd | 24 | Collision | 8 |
| Ret | 36 | Alex Caffi | Dallara-Ford | 22 | Spun off | 21 |
| Ret | 16 | Ivan Capelli | March-Judd | 19 | Electrical | 4 |
| Ret | 17 | Derek Warwick | Arrows-Megatron | 16 | Spun off | 7 |
| Ret | 10 | Bernd Schneider | Zakspeed | 14 | Physical | 25 |
| DNQ | 26 | Stefan Johansson | Ligier-Judd | | | |
| DNQ | 32 | Oscar Larrauri | EuroBrun-Ford | | | |
| DNQ | 9 | P.Ghinzani | Zakspeed | | | |
| DNQ | 33 | Stefano Modena | EuroBrun-Ford | | | |
| DNPQ | 31 | G.Tarquini | Coloni-Ford | | | |

Winning speed: 119.229mph Lap leaders: Prost 1-15, 17-27; Capelli 16; Senna 28-51
Pole position: Senna, 1m 41.853s, 128.678mph. Fastest lap: Senna, 1m 46.326s, 123.264mph

## AUSTRALIAN GRAND PRIX: ADELAIDE *13 November Round: 16 Race: 468 82 x 2.349 miles*

| POS. | NO. | DRIVER | CAR/ENGINE | LAPS | TIME/RETIRED | GRID |
|---|---|---|---|---|---|---|
| 1 | 11 | Alain Prost | McLaren-Honda | 82 | 1:53'14.676 | 2 |
| 2 | 12 | Ayrton Senna | McLaren-Honda | 82 | +36.787 | 1 |
| 3 | 1 | Nelson Piquet | Lotus-Honda | 82 | +47.546 | 5 |
| 4 | 6 | Riccardo Patrese | Williams-Judd | 82 | +1'20.088 | 6 |
| 5 | 20 | Thierry Boutsen | Benetton-Ford | 81 | +1 Lap | 10 |
| 6 | 16 | Ivan Capelli | March-Judd | 81 | +1 Lap | 9 |
| 7 | 23 | P.Martini | Minardi-Ford | 80 | +2 Laps | 14 |
| 8 | 22 | A.de Cesaris | Rial-Ford | 77 | Out of fuel | 15 |
| 9 | 26 | Stefan Johansson | Ligier-Judd | 76 | Out of fuel | 22 |
| 10 | 30 | Philippe Alliot | Lola-Ford | 75 | Out of fuel | 24 |
| 11 | 14 | Philippe Streiff | AGS-Ford | 73 | Electrical | 16 |
| Ret | 9 | P.Ghinzani | Zakspeed | 69 | Fuel system | 26 |
| Ret | 5 | Nigel Mansell | Williams-Judd | 65 | Spun off | 3 |
| Ret | 19 | A.Nannini | Benetton-Ford | 63 | Spun off | 8 |
| Ret | 33 | Stefano Modena | EuroBrun-Ford | 63 | Halfshaft | 20 |
| Ret | 17 | Derek Warwick | Arrows-Megatron | 52 | Engine | 7 |
| Ret | 18 | Eddie Cheever | Arrows-Megatron | 51 | Engine | 18 |
| Ret | 15 | M.Gugelmin | March-Judd | 46 | Collision | 19 |
| Ret | 2 | Satoru Nakajima | Lotus-Honda | 45 | Collision | 13 |
| Ret | 24 | Luis Perez-Sala | Minardi-Ford | 41 | Engine | 21 |
| Ret | 36 | Alex Caffi | Dallara-Ford | 32 | Clutch | 11 |
| Ret | 28 | Gerhard Berger | Ferrari | 25 | Collision | 4 |
| Ret | 25 | Rene Arnoux | Ligier-Judd | 24 | Collision | 23 |
| Ret | 3 | Jonathan Palmer | Tyrrell-Ford | 16 | Transmission | 17 |
| Ret | 32 | Oscar Larrauri | EuroBrun-Ford | 12 | Halfshaft | 25 |
| Ret | 27 | Michele Alboreto | Ferrari | 0 | Collision | 12 |
| DNQ | 31 | G.Tarquini | Coloni-Ford | | | |
| DNQ | 4 | Julian Bailey | Tyrrell-Ford | | | |
| DNQ | 29 | P.H.Raphanel | Lola-Ford | | | |
| DNQ | 10 | Bernd Schneider | Zakspeed | | | |
| DNPQ | 21 | Nicola Larini | Osella | | | |

Winning speed: 102.045mph Lap leaders: Prost 1-13, 26-82; Berger 14-25
Pole position: Senna, 1m 17.748s, 108.757mph. Fastest lap: Prost, 21.216s, 104.113mph

# 1989

## DRIVERS' CHAMPION: ALAIN PROST
## CONSTRUCTORS' CHAMPION: McLAREN HONDA

### DRIVERS' CHAMPIONSHIP

| POS. | DRIVER | NATIONALITY | CAR | POINTS |
|---|---|---|---|---|
| 1 | Alain Prost | France | McLaren-Honda | 76(5) |
| 2 | Ayrton Senna | Brazil | Mclaren-Honda | 60 |
| 3 | Riccardo Patrese | Italy | Williams-Renault | 40 |
| 4 | Nigel Mansell | GB | Ferrari | 38 |
| 5 | Thierry Boutsen | Belgium | Williams-Renault | 37 |
| 6 | Alessandro Nannini | Italy | Benetton-Ford | 32 |
| 7 | Gerhard Berger | Austria | Ferrari | 21 |
| 8 | Nelson Piquet | Brazil | Lotus-Judd | 12 |
| 9 | Jean Alesi | France | Tyrrell-Ford | 8 |
| 10 | Derek Warwick | GB | Arrows-Judd | 7 |
| 11 | Michele Alboreto | Italy | Tyrrell-Ford, Lola-Lamborghini | 6 |
| = | Eddie Cheever | USA | Arrows-Judd | 6 |
| = | Stefan Johansson | Sweden | Onyx-Ford | 6 |
| 14 | Johnny Herbert | GB | Benetton-Ford, Tyrrell-Ford | 5 |
| 15 | Pierluigi Martini | Italy | Minardi-Ford | 5 |
| 16 | Mauricio Gugelmin | Brazil | March-Judd | 4 |
| = | Stefano Modena | Italy | Brabham-Judd | 4 |
| = | Andrea de Cesaris | Italy | Dallara-Ford | 4 |
| 19 | Alex Caffi | Italy | Dallara-Ford | 4 |
| 20 | Martin Brundle | GB | Brabham-Judd | 4 |
| 21 | Christian Danner | Germany | Rial-Ford | 3 |
| = | Saturo Nakajima | Japan | Lotus-Judd | 3 |
| 23 | Rene Arnoux | France | Ligier-Ford | 2 |
| = | Emanuele Pirro | Italy | Benetton-Ford | 2 |
| 25 | Jonathan Palmer | GB | Tyrrell-Ford | 2 |
| 26 | Gabriele Tarquini | Italy | AGS-Ford | 1 |
| = | Olivier Grouillard | France | Ligier-Ford | 1 |
| = | Luis Perez Sala | Spain | Minardi-Ford | 1 |
| = | Phillipe Alliot | France | Lola-Lamborghini | 1 |
| | Ivan Capelli | Italy | March-Judd | |
| | Nicola Larini | Italy | Osella-Ford | |
| | Roberto Moreno | Brazil | Coloni-Ford | |
| | Bertrand Gachot | Belgium | Onyx-Ford, Rial-Ford | |
| | Piercarlo Ghinzani | Italy | Osella-Ford | |
| | Bernd Schneider | Germany | Zakspeed-Yamaha | |
| | Gregor Foitek | Switzerland | EuroBrun-Judd, Rial-Ford | |
| | Aguri Suzuki | Japan | Zakspeed-Yamaha | |
| | Volker Weidler | Germany | Rial-Ford | |
| | Pierre-Henri Raphanel | France | Coloni-Ford, Rial-Ford | |
| | Joachim Winkelhock | Germany | AGS-Ford | |
| | Yannick Dalmas | France | Lola-Lamborghini, AGS-Ford | |
| | Martin Donnelly | GB | Arrows-Ford | |
| | Eric Bernard | France | Lola-Lamborghini | |
| | Enrico Bertaggia | Italy | Coloni-Ford | |
| | Oscar Larrauri | Argentina | EuroBrun-Judd | |
| | JJ Lehto | Finland | Onyx-Ford | |
| | Paolo Barilla | Italy | Minardi-Ford | |

Points for top six finishers (9, 6, 4, 3, 2, 1). Only the best eleven scores counted towards the championship. Drivers not valid for points if the constructor had entered only one car. Half points awarded for races stopped before half distance.

### CONSTRUCTORS' CHAMPIONSHIP

| POS. | CONSTRUCTOR | POINTS |
|---|---|---|
| 1 | McLaren-Honda | 141 |
| 2 | Williams-Renault | 77 |
| 3 | Ferrari | 59 |
| 4 | Benetton-Ford | 39 |
| 5 | Tyrrell-Ford | 16 |
| 6 | Lotus-Judd | 15 |
| 7 | Arrows-Ford | 13 |
| 8 | Dallara-Ford | 8 |
| 9 | Brabham-Judd | 8 |
| 10 | Onyx-Ford | 6 |
| 11 | Minardi-Ford | 6 |
| 12 | March-Judd | 4 |
| 13 | Rial-Ford | 3 |
| 14 | Ligier-Ford | 3 |
| 15 | AGS-Ford | 1 |
| 15 | Lola-Lamborghini | 1 |

Points for top six finishers (9, 6, 4, 3, 2, 1). Half points awarded for races stopped before half distance.

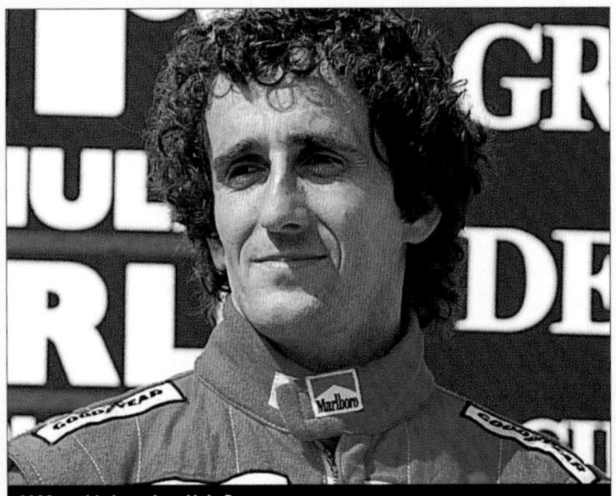

1989 world champion, Alain Prost.

### BRAZILIAN GRAND PRIX: RIO DE JANEIRO *26 March Round: 1 Race: 469 61 x 3.126 miles*

| POS. | NO. | DRIVER | CAR/ENGINE | LAPS | TIME/RETIRED | GRID |
|---|---|---|---|---|---|---|
| 1 | 27 | Nigel Mansell | Ferrari | 61 | 1:38'58.744 | 6 |
| 2 | 2 | Alain Prost | McLaren-Honda | 61 | +7.809 | 5 |
| 3 | 15 | M.Gugelmin | March-Judd | 61 | +9.370 | 12 |
| 4 | 20 | Johnny Herbert | Benetton-Ford | 61 | +10.493 | 10 |
| 5 | 9 | Derek Warwick | Arrows-Ford | 61 | +17.866 | 8 |
| 6 | 19 | A.Nannini | Benetton-Ford | 61 | +18.241 | 11 |
| 7 | 3 | Jonathan Palmer | Tyrrell-Ford | 60 | +1 Lap | 18 |
| 8 | 12 | Satoru Nakajima | Lotus-Judd | 60 | +1 Lap | 21 |
| 9 | 26 | O.Grouillard | Ligier-Ford | 60 | +1 Lap | 22 |
| 10 | 4 | Michele Alboreto | Tyrrell-Ford | 59 | +2 Laps | 20 |
| 11 | 1 | Ayrton Senna | McLaren-Honda | 59 | +2 Laps | 1 |
| 12 | 30 | Philippe Alliot | Lola-Lamborghini | 58 | +3 Laps | 26 |
| 13 | 22 | A.de Cesaris | Dallara-Ford | 57 | +4 Laps | 15 |
| 14 | 38 | Christian Danner | Rial-Ford | 56 | +5 Laps | 17 |
| Ret | 6 | Riccardo Patrese | Williams-Renault | 51 | Alternator | 2 |
| Ret | 10 | Eddie Cheever | Arrows-Ford | 37 | Collision | 24 |
| Ret | 34 | Bernd Schneider | Zakspeed-Yamaha | 36 | Collision | 25 |
| Ret | 7 | Martin Brundle | Brabham-Judd | 27 | Halfshaft | 13 |
| Ret | 16 | Ivan Capelli | March-Judd | 22 | Suspension | 7 |
| Ret | 11 | Nelson Piquet | Lotus-Judd | 10 | Fuel system | 9 |
| DSQ | 17 | Nicola Larini | Osella-Ford | 10 | Disqualified | 19 |
| Ret | 8 | Stefano Modena | Brabham-Judd | 9 | Halfshaft | 14 |
| Ret | 5 | Thierry Boutsen | Williams-Renault | 3 | Engine | 4 |
| Ret | 23 | P.Martini | Minardi-Ford | 2 | Chassis | 16 |
| Ret | 28 | Gerhard Berger | Ferrari | 0 | Collision | 3 |
| Ret | 24 | Luis Perez-Sala | Minardi-Ford | 0 | Collision | 23 |
| DNQ | 29 | Yannick Dalmas | Lola-Lamborghini | | | |
| DNQ | 25 | Rene Arnoux | Ligier-Ford | | | |
| DNQ | 33 | Gregor Foitek | EuroBrun-Judd | | | |
| DNQ | 31 | Roberto Moreno | Coloni-Ford | | | |
| DNPQ | 21 | Alex Caffi | Dallara-Ford | | | |
| DNPQ | 18 | P.Ghinzani | Osella-Ford | | | |
| DNPQ | 39 | Volker Weidler | Rial-Ford | | | |
| DNPQ | 32 | P.H.Raphanel | Coloni-Ford | | | |
| DNPQ | 41 | J.Winkelhock | AGS-Ford | | | |
| DNPQ | 35 | Aguri Suzuki | Zakspeed-Yamaha | | | |
| DNPQ | 36 | Stefan Johansson | Onyx-Ford | | | |
| DNPQ | 37 | Bertrand Gachot | Onyx-Ford | | | |

Winning speed: 115.596mph
Lap leaders: Patrese 1-15, 21-22; Mansell 16-20, 28-44, 47-61; Prost 23-27, 45-46
Pole position: Senna, 1m 25.302s, 131.932mph
Fastest lap: Patrese, 1m 32.507s, 121.656mph

### SAN MARINO GRAND PRIX: IMOLA *23 April Round: 2 Race: 470 58 x 3.132 miles*

| POS. | NO. | DRIVER | CAR/ENGINE | LAPS | TIME/RETIRED | GRID |
|---|---|---|---|---|---|---|
| 1 | 1 | Ayrton Senna | McLaren-Honda | 58 | 1:26'51.245 | 1 |
| 2 | 2 | Alain Prost | McLaren-Honda | 58 | +40.225 | 2 |
| 3 | 19 | A.Nannini | Benetton-Ford | 57 | +1 Lap | 7 |
| 4 | 5 | Thierry Boutsen | Williams-Renault | 57 | +1 Lap | 6 |
| 5 | 9 | Derek Warwick | Arrows-Ford | 57 | +1 Lap | 12 |
| 6 | 3 | Jonathan Palmer | Tyrrell-Ford | 57 | +1 Lap | 25 |
| 7 | 21 | Alex Caffi | Dallara-Ford | 57 | +1 Lap | 9 |
| 8 | 40 | G.Tarquini | AGS-Ford | 57 | +1 Lap | 18 |
| 9 | 10 | Eddie Cheever | Arrows-Ford | 56 | +2 Laps | 21 |
| 10 | 22 | A.de Cesaris | Dallara-Ford | 56 | +2 Laps | 16 |
| 11 | 20 | Johnny Herbert | Benetton-Ford | 56 | +2 Laps | 23 |
| 12 | 17 | Nicola Larini | Osella-Ford | 52 | Spun off | 14 |
| Ret | 7 | Martin Brundle | Brabham-Judd | 51 | Fuel system | 22 |
| NC | 12 | Satoru Nakajima | Lotus-Judd | 46 | Not classified | 24 |
| Ret | 24 | Luis Perez-Sala | Minardi-Ford | 43 | Spun off | 15 |
| Ret | 15 | M.Gugelmin | March-Judd | 39 | Transmission | 19 |
| Ret | 11 | Nelson Piquet | Lotus-Judd | 29 | Engine | 8 |
| Ret | 27 | Nigel Mansell | Ferrari | 23 | Gearbox | 3 |
| Ret | 6 | Riccardo Patrese | Williams-Renault | 21 | Engine | 4 |
| Ret | 8 | Stefano Modena | Brabham-Judd | 19 | Spun off | 17 |
| Ret | 23 | P.Martini | Minardi-Ford | 6 | Gearbox | 11 |
| DSQ | 26 | O.Grouillard | Ligier-Ford | 4 | Disqualified | 10 |
| Ret | 28 | Gerhard Berger | Ferrari | 3 | Accident | 5 |
| Ret | 16 | Ivan Capelli | March-Judd | 1 | Spun off | 11 |
| Ret | 30 | Philippe Alliot | Lola-Lamborghini | 0 | Electrical | 20 |
| Ret | 29 | Yannick Dalmas | Lola-Lamborghini | 0 | Electrical | 26 |
| DNQ | 4 | Michele Alboreto | Tyrrell-Ford | | | |
| DNQ | 25 | Rene Arnoux | Ligier-Ford | | | |
| DNQ | 38 | Christian Danner | Rial-Ford | | | |
| DNQ | 31 | Roberto Moreno | Coloni-Ford | | | |
| DNPQ | 37 | Bertrand Gachot | Onyx-Ford | | | |
| DNPQ | 33 | Gregor Foitek | EuroBrun-Judd | | | |
| DNPQ | 18 | P.Ghinzani | Osella-Ford | | | |
| DNPQ | 36 | Stefan Johansson | Onyx-Ford | | | |
| DNPQ | 41 | J.Winkelhock | AGS-Ford | | | |
| DNPQ | 32 | P.H.Raphanel | Coloni-Ford | | | |
| DNPQ | 35 | Aguri Suzuki | Zakspeed-Yamaha | | | |
| DNPQ | 34 | Bernd Schneider | Zakspeed-Yamaha | | | |
| DNPQ | 39 | Volker Weidler | Rial-Ford | | | |

Winning speed: 125.479mph Lap leaders: Senna 1-58
Pole position: Senna, 1m 26.010s, 131.080mph
Fastest lap: Prost, 1m 26.795s, 129.894mph
Stopped after 3 laps because of Berger's accident and resumed on aggregate for another 55 laps, rather than the remaining 58 laps.

### MONACO GRAND PRIX: MONTE CARLO *7 May Round: 3 Race: 471 77 x 2.068 miles*

| POS. | NO. | DRIVER | CAR/ENGINE | LAPS | TIME/RETIRED | GRID |
|---|---|---|---|---|---|---|
| 1 | 1 | Ayrton Senna | McLaren-Honda | 77 | 1:53'33.251 | 1 |
| 2 | 2 | Alain Prost | McLaren-Honda | 77 | +52.529 | 2 |
| 3 | 8 | Stefano Modena | Brabham-Judd | 76 | +1 Lap | 8 |
| 4 | 21 | Alex Caffi | Dallara-Ford | 75 | +2 Laps | 9 |
| 5 | 4 | Michele Alboreto | Tyrrell-Ford | 75 | +2 Laps | 12 |
| 6 | 7 | Martin Brundle | Brabham-Judd | 75 | +2 Laps | 4 |
| 7 | 10 | Eddie Cheever | Arrows-Ford | 75 | +2 Laps | 20 |
| 8 | 19 | A.Nannini | Benetton-Ford | 74 | +3 Laps | 15 |
| 9 | 3 | Jonathan Palmer | Tyrrell-Ford | 74 | +3 Laps | 23 |
| 10 | 5 | Thierry Boutsen | Williams-Renault | 74 | +3 Laps | 3 |
| 11 | 16 | Ivan Capelli | March-Judd | 73 | +4 Laps | 22 |
| 12 | 25 | Rene Arnoux | Ligier-Ford | 73 | +4 Laps | 21 |
| 13 | 22 | A.de Cesaris | Dallara-Ford | 73 | +4 Laps | 10 |
| 14 | 20 | Johnny Herbert | Benetton-Ford | 73 | +4 Laps | 24 |
| 15 | 6 | Riccardo Patrese | Williams-Renault | 73 | +4 Laps | 7 |
| Ret | 24 | Luis Perez-Sala | Minardi-Ford | 48 | Overheating | 26 |
| Ret | 40 | G.Tarquini | AGS-Ford | 46 | Electrical | 13 |
| Ret | 31 | Roberto Moreno | Coloni-Ford | 44 | Gearbox | 25 |
| Ret | 30 | Philippe Alliot | Lola-Lamborghini | 38 | Engine | 17 |
| Ret | 15 | M.Gugelmin | March-Judd | 36 | Engine | 14 |
| Ret | 11 | Nelson Piquet | Lotus-Judd | 32 | Collision | 19 |
| Ret | 27 | Nigel Mansell | Ferrari | 30 | Gearbox | 5 |
| Ret | 32 | P.H.Raphanel | Coloni-Ford | 19 | Gearbox | 18 |
| Ret | 26 | O.Grouillard | Ligier-Ford | 4 | Gearbox | 16 |
| Ret | 23 | P.Martini | Minardi-Ford | 3 | Clutch | 11 |
| Ret | 9 | Derek Warwick | Arrows-Ford | 2 | Electrical | 6 |
| DNQ | 38 | Christian Danner | Rial-Ford | | | |
| DNQ | 29 | Yannick Dalmas | Lola-Lamborghini | | | |
| DNQ | 12 | Satoru Nakajima | Lotus-Judd | | | |
| DNPQ | 18 | P.Ghinzani | Osella-Ford | | | |
| DNPQ | 36 | Stefan Johansson | Onyx-Ford | | | |
| DNPQ | 17 | Nicola Larini | Osella-Ford | | | |
| DNPQ | 34 | Bernd Schneider | Zakspeed-Yamaha | | | |
| DNPQ | 37 | Bertrand Gachot | Onyx-Ford | | | |
| DNPQ | 33 | Gregor Foitek | EuroBrun-Judd | | | |
| DNPQ | 39 | Volker Weidler | Rial-Ford | | | |
| DNPQ | 35 | Aguri Suzuki | Zakspeed-Yamaha | | | |
| DNPQ | 41 | J.Winkelhock | AGS-Ford | | | |

Winning speed: 84.134mph Lap leaders: Senna 1-77
Pole position: Senna, 1m 22.308s, 90.447mph
Fastest lap: Prost, 25.501s, 87.069mph

### MEXICO GRAND PRIX: MEXICO CITY *28 May Round: 4 Race: 472 69 x 2.747 miles*

| POS. | NO. | DRIVER | CAR/ENGINE | LAPS | TIME/RETIRED | GRID |
|---|---|---|---|---|---|---|
| 1 | 1 | Ayrton Senna | McLaren-Honda | 69 | 1:35'21.431 | 1 |
| 2 | 6 | Riccardo Patrese | Williams-Renault | 69 | +15.560 | 5 |
| 3 | 4 | Michele Alboreto | Tyrrell-Ford | 69 | +31.254 | 7 |
| 4 | 19 | A.Nannini | Benetton-Ford | 69 | +45.495 | 13 |
| 5 | 2 | Alain Prost | McLaren-Honda | 69 | +56.113 | 2 |
| 6 | 40 | G.Tarquini | AGS-Ford | 68 | +1 Lap | 17 |
| 7 | 10 | Eddie Cheever | Arrows-Ford | 68 | +1 Lap | 24 |
| 8 | 26 | O.Grouillard | Ligier-Ford | 68 | +1 Lap | 11 |
| 9 | 7 | Martin Brundle | Brabham-Judd | 68 | +1 Lap | 20 |
| 10 | 8 | Stefano Modena | Brabham-Judd | 68 | +1 Lap | 9 |
| 11 | 11 | Nelson Piquet | Lotus-Judd | 68 | +1 Lap | 26 |
| 12 | 38 | Christian Danner | Rial-Ford | 67 | +2 Laps | 23 |
| 13 | 21 | Alex Caffi | Dallara-Ford | 67 | +2 Laps | 19 |
| 14 | 25 | Rene Arnoux | Ligier-Ford | 66 | +3 Laps | 25 |
| 15 | 20 | Johnny Herbert | Benetton-Ford | 66 | +3 Laps | 18 |
| Ret | 23 | P.Martini | Minardi-Ford | 53 | Engine | 22 |
| Ret | 27 | Nigel Mansell | Ferrari | 43 | Gearbox | 3 |
| Ret | 9 | Derek Warwick | Arrows-Ford | 35 | Electrical | 10 |
| Ret | 12 | Satoru Nakajima | Lotus-Judd | 35 | Spun off | 15 |
| Ret | 30 | Philippe Alliot | Lola-Lamborghini | 28 | Not classified | 16 |
| Ret | 22 | A.de Cesaris | Dallara-Ford | 20 | Suspension | 12 |
| Ret | 28 | Gerhard Berger | Ferrari | 16 | Gearbox | 6 |
| Ret | 36 | Stefan Johansson | Onyx-Ford | 16 | Transmission | 21 |
| Ret | 5 | Thierry Boutsen | Williams-Renault | 15 | Electrical | 8 |
| Ret | 3 | Jonathan Palmer | Tyrrell-Ford | 9 | Throttle | 14 |
| Ret | 16 | Ivan Capelli | March-Judd | 1 | Transmission | 4 |
| DNQ | 24 | Luis Perez-Sala | Minardi-Ford | | | |
| DNQ | 15 | M.Gugelmin | March-Judd | | | |
| DNQ | 29 | Yannick Dalmas | Lola-Lamborghini | | | |
| DNQ | 31 | Roberto Moreno | Coloni-Ford | | | |
| DNPQ | 37 | Bertrand Gachot | Onyx-Ford | | | |
| DNPQ | 33 | Gregor Foitek | EuroBrun-Judd | | | |
| DNPQ | 17 | Nicola Larini | Osella-Ford | | | |
| DNPQ | 39 | Volker Weidler | Rial-Ford | | | |
| DNPQ | 34 | Bernd Schneider | Zakspeed-Yamaha | | | |
| DNPQ | 35 | Aguri Suzuki | Zakspeed-Yamaha | | | |
| DNPQ | 18 | P.Ghinzani | Osella-Ford | | | |
| DNPQ | 41 | J.Winkelhock | AGS-Ford | | | |
| DNPQ | 32 | P.H.Raphanel | Coloni-Ford | | | |

Winning speed: 119.267mph Lap leaders: Senna 1-69
Pole position: Senna, 1m 17.876s, 126.990mph
Fastest lap: Mansell, 1m 20.420s, 122.973mph
Stopped after two laps because of an accident and restarted for original distance.

### UNITED STATES GRAND PRIX: PHOENIX *4 June Round: 5 Race: 473 75 x 2.360 miles*

| POS. | NO. | DRIVER | CAR/ENGINE | LAPS | TIME/RETIRED | GRID |
|---|---|---|---|---|---|---|
| 1 | 2 | Alain Prost | McLaren-Honda | 75 | 2:01'33.133 | 2 |
| 2 | 6 | Riccardo Patrese | Williams-Renault | 75 | +39.696 | 14 |
| 3 | 10 | Eddie Cheever | Arrows-Ford | 75 | +43.210 | 17 |
| 4 | 38 | Christian Danner | Rial-Ford | 74 | +1 Lap | 26 |
| 5 | 20 | Johnny Herbert | Benetton-Ford | 74 | +1 Lap | 25 |
| 6 | 5 | Thierry Boutsen | Williams-Renault | 74 | +1 Lap | 16 |
| 7 | 40 | G.Tarquini | AGS-Ford | 73 | Engine | 24 |
| 8 | 22 | A.de Cesaris | Dallara-Ford | 70 | +5 Laps | 13 |
| 9 | 3 | Jonathan Palmer | Tyrrell-Ford | 69 | Fuel system | 21 |
| Ret | 28 | Gerhard Berger | Ferrari | 61 | Alternator | 8 |
| Ret | 21 | Alex Caffi | Dallara-Ford | 52 | Collision | 6 |
| Ret | 11 | Nelson Piquet | Lotus-Judd | 52 | Spun off | 22 |
| Ret | 36 | Stefan Johansson | Onyx-Ford | 50 | Suspension | 19 |
| Ret | 24 | Luis Perez-Sala | Minardi-Ford | 46 | Engine | 20 |
| Ret | 1 | Ayrton Senna | McLaren-Honda | 44 | Electrical | 1 |
| Ret | 7 | Martin Brundle | Brabham-Judd | 43 | Brakes | 5 |
| Ret | 8 | Stefano Modena | Brabham-Judd | 37 | Brakes | 7 |
| Ret | 27 | Nigel Mansell | Ferrari | 31 | Alternator | 4 |
| Ret | 23 | P.Martini | Minardi-Ford | 26 | Engine | 15 |
| Ret | 12 | Satoru Nakajima | Lotus-Judd | 24 | Throttle | 23 |
| Ret | 16 | Ivan Capelli | March-Judd | 22 | Transmission | 11 |
| Ret | 15 | M.Gugelmin | March-Judd | 20 | Brakes | 18 |
| Ret | 4 | Michele Alboreto | Tyrrell-Ford | 17 | Gearbox | 9 |
| Ret | 19 | A.Nannini | Benetton-Ford | 10 | Physical | 3 |
| Ret | 9 | Derek Warwick | Arrows-Ford | 7 | Collision | 10 |
| Ret | 30 | Philippe Alliot | Lola-Lamborghini | 3 | Spun off | 12 |
| DNQ | 26 | O.Grouillard | Ligier-Ford | | | |
| DNQ | 31 | Roberto Moreno | Coloni-Ford | | | |
| DNQ | 25 | Rene Arnoux | Ligier-Ford | | | |
| DNQ | 29 | Yannick Dalmas | Lola-Lamborghini | | | |
| DNPQ | 18 | P.Ghinzani | Osella-Ford | | | |
| DNPQ | 32 | P.H.Raphanel | Coloni-Ford | | | |
| DNPQ | 33 | Gregor Foitek | EuroBrun-Judd | | | |
| DNPQ | 17 | Nicola Larini | Osella-Ford | | | |
| DNPQ | 41 | J.Winkelhock | AGS-Ford | | | |
| DNPQ | 39 | Volker Weidler | Rial-Ford | | | |
| DNPQ | 35 | Aguri Suzuki | Zakspeed-Yamaha | | | |
| DNPQ | 34 | Bernd Schneider | Zakspeed-Yamaha | | | |
| DNPQ | 37 | Bertrand Gachot | Onyx-Ford | | | |

Winning speed: 87.370mph Lap leaders: Senna 1-33; Prost 34-75
Pole position: Senna, 1m 30.108s, 94.287mph
Fastest lap: Senna, 1m 33.969s, 90.413mph
Race scheduled for 81 lapsbut stopped after two-hour mark.

### CANADIAN GRAND PRIX: MONTREAL *18 June Round: 6 Race: 474 69 x 2.728 miles*

| POS. | NO. | DRIVER | CAR/ENGINE | LAPS | TIME/RETIRED | GRID |
|---|---|---|---|---|---|---|
| 1 | 5 | Thierry Boutsen | Williams-Renault | 69 | 2:01'24.073 | 6 |
| 2 | 6 | Riccardo Patrese | Williams-Renault | 69 | +30.007 | 3 |
| 3 | 22 | A.de Cesaris | Dallara-Ford | 69 | +1'36.649 | 9 |
| 4 | 11 | Nelson Piquet | Lotus-Judd | 69 | +1'41.484 | 19 |
| 5 | 25 | Rene Arnoux | Ligier-Ford | 68 | +1 Lap | 22 |
| 6 | 21 | Alex Caffi | Dallara-Ford | 67 | +2 Laps | 8 |
| 7 | 1 | Ayrton Senna | McLaren-Honda | 66 | Engine | 2 |
| 8 | 38 | Christian Danner | Rial-Ford | 66 | +3 Laps | 23 |
| Ret | 31 | Roberto Moreno | Coloni-Ford | 57 | Differential | 26 |
| Ret | 9 | Derek Warwick | Arrows-Ford | 40 | Engine | 12 |
| Ret | 3 | Jonathan Palmer | Tyrrell-Ford | 35 | Spun off | 14 |
| Ret | 17 | Nicola Larini | Osella-Ford | 33 | Electrical | 15 |
| Ret | 16 | Ivan Capelli | March-Judd | 28 | Spun off | 21 |
| Ret | 30 | Philippe Alliot | Lola-Lamborghini | 26 | Spun off | 10 |
| DSQ | 36 | Stefan Johansson | Onyx-Ford | 13 | Disqualified | 18 |
| Ret | 24 | Luis Perez-Sala | Minardi-Ford | 11 | Spun off | 24 |
| Ret | 15 | M.Gugelmin | March-Judd | 11 | Electrical | 17 |
| Ret | 28 | Gerhard Berger | Ferrari | 6 | Gearbox | 4 |
| Ret | 40 | G.Tarquini | AGS-Ford | 6 | Spun off | 25 |
| Ret | 10 | Eddie Cheever | Arrows-Ford | 3 | Spun off | 16 |
| Ret | 2 | Alain Prost | McLaren-Honda | 2 | Suspension | 1 |
| DSQ | 27 | Nigel Mansell | Ferrari | 0 | Disqualified | 5 |
| Ret | 8 | Stefano Modena | Brabham-Judd | 0 | Collision | 7 |
| Ret | 23 | P.Martini | Minardi-Ford | 0 | Collision | 11 |
| DSQ | 19 | A.Nannini | Benetton-Ford | 0 | Disqualified | 13 |
| Ret | 4 | Michele Alboreto | Tyrrell-Ford | 0 | Electrical | 20 |
| DNQ | 12 | Satoru Nakajima | Lotus-Judd | | | |
| DNQ | 29 | Yannick Dalmas | Lola-Lamborghini | | | |
| DNQ | 20 | Johnny Herbert | Benetton-Ford | | | |
| DNQ | 26 | O.Grouillard | Ligier-Ford | | | |
| DNPQ | 7 | Martin Brundle | Brabham-Judd | | | |
| DNPQ | 37 | Bertrand Gachot | Onyx-Ford | | | |
| DNPQ | 33 | Gregor Foitek | EuroBrun-Judd | | | |
| DNPQ | 18 | P.Ghinzani | Osella-Ford | | | |
| DNPQ | 34 | Bernd Schneider | Zakspeed-Yamaha | | | |
| DNPQ | 41 | J.Winkelhock | AGS-Ford | | | |
| DNPQ | 39 | Volker Weidler | Rial-Ford | | | |
| DNPQ | 35 | Aguri Suzuki | Zakspeed-Yamaha | | | |
| DNPQ | 32 | P.H.Raphanel | Coloni-Ford | | | |

Winning speed: 93.024mph
Lap leaders: Prost 1; Senna 2-3, 39-66; Patrese 4-34; Warwick 35-38; Boutsen 67-69
Pole position: Prost, 1m 20.973s, 121.277mph
Fastest lap: Palmer, 1m 31.925s, 106.828mph

### FRENCH GRAND PRIX: PAUL RICARD *9 July Round: 7 Race: 475 80 x 2.369 miles*

| POS. | NO. | DRIVER | CAR/ENGINE | LAPS | TIME/RETIRED | GRID |
|---|---|---|---|---|---|---|
| 1 | 2 | Alain Prost | McLaren-Honda | 80 | 1:38'29.411 | 1 |
| 2 | 27 | Nigel Mansell | Ferrari | 80 | +44.017 | 3 |
| 3 | 6 | Riccardo Patrese | Williams-Renault | 80 | +1'06.921 | 8 |
| 4 | 4 | Jean Alesi | Tyrrell-Ford | 80 | +1'13.232 | 16 |
| 5 | 36 | Stefan Johansson | Onyx-Ford | 79 | +1 Lap | 13 |
| 6 | 26 | O.Grouillard | Ligier-Ford | 79 | +1 Lap | 17 |
| 7 | 10 | Eddie Cheever | Arrows-Ford | 79 | +1 Lap | 25 |
| 8 | 11 | Nelson Piquet | Lotus-Judd | 78 | +2 Laps | 20 |
| 9 | 20 | Emanuele Pirro | Benetton-Ford | 78 | +2 Laps | 24 |
| 10 | 3 | Jonathan Palmer | Tyrrell-Ford | 78 | +2 Laps | 9 |
| 11 | 29 | Eric Bernard | Lola-Lamborghini | 77 | +3 Laps | 15 |
| 12 | 9 | Martin Donnelly | Arrows-Ford | 77 | +3 Laps | 14 |
| 13 | 37 | Bertrand Gachot | Onyx-Ford | 76 | Engine | 11 |
| Ret | 15 | M.Gugelmin | March-Judd | 71 | Not classified | 10 |
| Ret | 8 | Stefano Modena | Brabham-Judd | 67 | Engine | 22 |
| Ret | 5 | Thierry Boutsen | Williams-Renault | 50 | Gearbox | 5 |
| Ret | 12 | Satoru Nakajima | Lotus-Judd | 49 | Engine | 19 |
| Ret | 16 | Ivan Capelli | March-Judd | 43 | Engine | 12 |
| Ret | 19 | A.Nannini | Benetton-Ford | 40 | Suspension | 4 |
| Ret | 23 | P.Martini | Minardi-Ford | 31 | Engine | 23 |
| Ret | 30 | Philippe Alliot | Lola-Lamborghini | 30 | Engine | 7 |
| Ret | 40 | G.Tarquini | AGS-Ford | 30 | Engine | 21 |
| Ret | 28 | Gerhard Berger | Ferrari | 29 | Clutch | 6 |
| Ret | 21 | Alex Caffi | Dallara-Ford | 27 | Clutch | 26 |
| Ret | 25 | Rene Arnoux | Ligier-Ford | 14 | Gearbox | 18 |
| Ret | 1 | Ayrton Senna | McLaren-Honda | 0 | Differential | 2 |
| DNQ | 22 | A.de Cesaris | Dallara-Ford | | | |
| DNQ | 24 | Luis Perez-Sala | Minardi-Ford | | | |
| DNQ | 38 | Christian Danner | Rial-Ford | | | |
| DNQ | 31 | Roberto Moreno | Coloni-Ford | | | |
| DNPQ | 17 | Nicola Larini | Osella-Ford | | | |
| DNPQ | 7 | Martin Brundle | Brabham-Judd | | | |
| DNPQ | 39 | Volker Weidler | Rial-Ford | | | |
| DNPQ | 34 | Bernd Schneider | Zakspeed-Yamaha | | | |
| DNPQ | 18 | P.Ghinzani | Osella-Ford | | | |
| DNPQ | 32 | P.H.Raphanel | Coloni-Ford | | | |
| DNPQ | 35 | Aguri Suzuki | Zakspeed-Yamaha | | | |
| DNPQ | 33 | Gregor Foitek | EuroBrun-Judd | | | |
| DNPQ | 41 | J.Winkelhock | AGS-Ford | | | |

Winning speed: 115.469mph Lap leaders: Prost 1-80
Pole position: Prost, 1m 7.203s, 126.920mph
Fastest lap: Gugelmin, 1m 12.090s, 118.317mph
Race stopped after first lap accident and restarted for total original distance.

### BRITISH GRAND PRIX: SILVERSTONE *16 July Round: 8 Race: 476 64 x 2.970 miles*

| POS. | NO. | DRIVER | CAR/ENGINE | LAPS | TIME/RETIRED | GRID |
|---|---|---|---|---|---|---|
| 1 | 2 | Alain Prost | McLaren-Honda | 64 | 1:19'22.131 | 2 |
| 2 | 27 | Nigel Mansell | Ferrari | 64 | +19.369 | 3 |
| 3 | 19 | A.Nannini | Benetton-Ford | 64 | +48.019 | 9 |
| 4 | 11 | Nelson Piquet | Lotus-Judd | 64 | +1'06.735 | 10 |
| 5 | 23 | P.Martini | Minardi-Ford | 63 | +1 Lap | 11 |
| 6 | 24 | Luis Perez-Sala | Minardi-Ford | 63 | +1 Lap | 15 |
| 7 | 26 | O.Grouillard | Ligier-Ford | 63 | +1 Lap | 24 |
| 8 | 12 | Satoru Nakajima | Lotus-Judd | 63 | +1 Lap | 16 |
| 9 | 9 | Derek Warwick | Arrows-Ford | 62 | +2 Laps | 19 |
| 10 | 5 | Thierry Boutsen | Williams-Renault | 62 | +2 Laps | 7 |
| 11 | 20 | Emanuele Pirro | Benetton-Ford | 62 | +2 Laps | 26 |
| 12 | 37 | Bertrand Gachot | Onyx-Ford | 62 | +2 Laps | 21 |
| Ret | 15 | M.Gugelmin | March-Judd | 54 | Gearbox | 6 |
| Ret | 7 | Martin Brundle | Brabham-Judd | 49 | Engine | 20 |
| Ret | 28 | Gerhard Berger | Ferrari | 49 | Gearbox | 4 |
| Ret | 29 | Eric Bernard | Lola-Lamborghini | 46 | Engine | 13 |
| Ret | 30 | Philippe Alliot | Lola-Lamborghini | 39 | Engine | 12 |
| Ret | 3 | Jonathan Palmer | Tyrrell-Ford | 32 | Spun off | 18 |
| Ret | 8 | Stefano Modena | Brabham-Judd | 31 | Engine | 14 |
| Ret | 4 | Jean Alesi | Tyrrell-Ford | 28 | Spun off | 22 |
| Ret | 17 | Nicola Larini | Osella-Ford | 23 | Handling | 17 |
| Ret | 6 | Riccardo Patrese | Williams-Renault | 19 | Spun off | 5 |
| Ret | 16 | Ivan Capelli | March-Judd | 15 | Transmission | 8 |
| Ret | 22 | A.de Cesaris | Dallara-Ford | 14 | Engine | 25 |
| Ret | 1 | Ayrton Senna | McLaren-Honda | 11 | Spun off | 1 |
| Ret | 31 | Roberto Moreno | Coloni-Ford | 2 | Gearbox | 23 |
| DNQ | 25 | Rene Arnoux | Ligier-Ford | | | |
| DNQ | 10 | Eddie Cheever | Arrows-Ford | | | |
| DNQ | 40 | G.Tarquini | AGS-Ford | | | |
| DNQ | 38 | Christian Danner | Rial-Ford | | | |
| DNPQ | 36 | Stefan Johansson | Onyx-Ford | | | |
| DNPQ | 21 | Alex Caffi | Dallara-Ford | | | |
| DNPQ | 33 | Gregor Foitek | EuroBrun-Judd | | | |
| DNPQ | 18 | P.Ghinzani | Osella-Ford | | | |
| DNPQ | 41 | Yannick Dalmas | AGS-Ford | | | |
| DNPQ | 34 | Bernd Schneider | Zakspeed-Yamaha | | | |
| DNPQ | 32 | P.H.Raphanel | Coloni-Ford | | | |
| DNPQ | 35 | Aguri Suzuki | Zakspeed-Yamaha | | | |
| DNPQ | 39 | Volker Weidler | Rial-Ford | | | |

Winning speed: 143.694mph Lap leaders: Senna 1-11; Prost 10-64
Pole position: Senna, 1m 9.099s, 154.735mph
Fastest lap: Mansell, 1m 12.017s, 148.465mph

### GERMAN GRAND PRIX: HOCKENHEIM *30 July Round: 9 Race: 477 45 x 4.223 miles*

| POS. | NO. | DRIVER | CAR/ENGINE | LAPS | TIME/RETIRED | GRID |
|---|---|---|---|---|---|---|
| 1 | 1 | Ayrton Senna | McLaren-Honda | 45 | 1:21'43.302 | 1 |
| 2 | 2 | Alain Prost | McLaren-Honda | 45 | +18.151 | 2 |
| 3 | 27 | Nigel Mansell | Ferrari | 45 | +1'23.254 | 3 |
| 4 | 6 | Riccardo Patrese | Williams-Renault | 44 | +1 Lap | 5 |
| 5 | 11 | Nelson Piquet | Lotus-Judd | 44 | +1 Lap | 8 |
| 6 | 9 | Derek Warwick | Arrows-Ford | 44 | +1 Lap | 17 |
| 7 | 22 | A.de Cesaris | Dallara-Ford | 44 | +1 Lap | 21 |
| 8 | 7 | Martin Brundle | Brabham-Judd | 44 | +1 Lap | 12 |
| 9 | 23 | P.Martini | Minardi-Ford | 44 | +1 Lap | 13 |
| 10 | 4 | Jean Alesi | Tyrrell-Ford | 43 | +2 Laps | 10 |
| 11 | 25 | Rene Arnoux | Ligier-Ford | 42 | +3 Laps | 23 |
| 12 | 10 | Eddie Cheever | Arrows-Ford | 40 | Fuel system | 25 |
| Ret | 8 | Stefano Modena | Brabham-Judd | 37 | Engine | 16 |
| Ret | 12 | Satoru Nakajima | Lotus-Judd | 36 | Spun off | 18 |
| Ret | 16 | Ivan Capelli | March-Judd | 32 | Electrical | 22 |
| Ret | 15 | M.Gugelmin | March-Judd | 28 | Gearbox | 14 |
| Ret | 20 | Emanuele Pirro | Benetton-Ford | 26 | Spun off | 9 |
| Ret | 30 | Philippe Alliot | Lola-Lamborghini | 20 | Oil leak | 15 |
| Ret | 3 | Jonathan Palmer | Tyrrell-Ford | 16 | Engine | 19 |
| Ret | 28 | Gerhard Berger | Ferrari | 13 | Spun off | 4 |
| Ret | 36 | Stefan Johansson | Onyx-Ford | 8 | Overheating | 24 |
| Ret | 19 | A.Nannini | Benetton-Ford | 6 | Electrical | 7 |
| Ret | 5 | Thierry Boutsen | Williams-Renault | 4 | Collision | 6 |
| Ret | 21 | Alex Caffi | Dallara-Ford | 2 | Engine | 20 |
| Ret | 29 | Michele Alboreto | Lola-Lamborghini | 1 | Electrical | 26 |
| Ret | 26 | O.Grouillard | Ligier-Ford | 0 | Gearbox | 11 |
| DNQ | 24 | Luis Perez-Sala | Minardi-Ford | | | |
| DNQ | 37 | Bertrand Gachot | Onyx-Ford | | | |
| DNQ | 38 | Christian Danner | Rial-Ford | | | |
| DSQ | 39 | Volker Weidler | Rial-Ford | | | |
| DNPQ | 41 | Yannick Dalmas | AGS-Ford | | | |
| DNPQ | 17 | Nicola Larini | Osella-Ford | | | |
| DNPQ | 40 | G.Tarquini | AGS-Ford | | | |
| DNPQ | 18 | P.Ghinzani | Osella-Ford | | | |
| DNPQ | 31 | Roberto Moreno | Coloni-Ford | | | |
| DNPQ | 32 | P.H.Raphanel | Coloni-Ford | | | |
| DNPQ | 33 | Gregor Foitek | EuroBrun-Judd | | | |
| DNPQ | 35 | Aguri Suzuki | Zakspeed-Yamaha | | | |
| DNPQ | 34 | Bernd Schneider | Zakspeed-Yamaha | | | |

Winning speed: 139.539mph Lap leaders: Senna 1-19, 43-45; Prost 20-42
Pole position: Senna, 1m 42.300s, 148.626mph
Fastest lap: Senna, 1m 45.884s, 143.595mph

### HUNGARIAN GRAND PRIX: HUNGARORING *13 August Round: 10 Race: 478 77 x 2.466 miles*

| POS. | NO. | DRIVER | CAR/ENGINE | LAPS | TIME/RETIRED | GRID |
|---|---|---|---|---|---|---|
| 1 | 27 | Nigel Mansell | Ferrari | 77 | 1:49'38.650 | 12 |
| 2 | 1 | Ayrton Senna | McLaren-Honda | 77 | +25.967 | 2 |
| 3 | 5 | Thierry Boutsen | Williams-Renault | 77 | +38.354 | 4 |
| 4 | 2 | Alain Prost | McLaren-Honda | 77 | +44.177 | 5 |
| 5 | 10 | Eddie Cheever | Arrows-Ford | 77 | +45.106 | 16 |
| 6 | 11 | Nelson Piquet | Lotus-Judd | 77 | +1'12.039 | 17 |
| 7 | 21 | Alex Caffi | Dallara-Ford | 77 | +1'24.225 | 3 |
| 8 | 20 | Emanuele Pirro | Benetton-Ford | 76 | +1 Lap | 25 |
| 9 | 4 | Jean Alesi | Tyrrell-Ford | 76 | +1 Lap | 11 |
| 10 | 9 | Derek Warwick | Arrows-Ford | 76 | +1 Lap | 9 |
| 11 | 8 | Stefano Modena | Brabham-Judd | 76 | +1 Lap | 8 |
| 12 | 7 | Martin Brundle | Brabham-Judd | 75 | +2 Laps | 15 |
| 13 | 3 | Jonathan Palmer | Tyrrell-Ford | 73 | +4 Laps | 19 |
| Ret | 24 | Luis Perez-Sala | Minardi-Ford | 57 | Collision | 23 |
| Ret | 28 | Gerhard Berger | Ferrari | 56 | Gearbox | 6 |
| Ret | 6 | Riccardo Patrese | Williams-Renault | 54 | Water leak | 1 |
| Ret | 36 | Stefan Johansson | Onyx-Ford | 48 | Gearbox | 24 |
| Ret | 19 | A.Nannini | Benetton-Ford | 46 | Gearbox | 7 |
| Ret | 37 | Bertrand Gachot | Onyx-Ford | 38 | Gearbox | 21 |
| Ret | 12 | Satoru Nakajima | Lotus-Judd | 33 | Accident | 20 |
| Ret | 15 | M.Gugelmin | March-Judd | 27 | Electrical | 13 |
| Ret | 16 | Ivan Capelli | March-Judd | 26 | Wheel | 14 |
| Ret | 29 | Michele Alboreto | Lola-Lamborghini | 26 | Engine | 26 |
| Ret | 18 | P.Ghinzani | Osella-Ford | 20 | Electrical | 22 |
| Ret | 23 | P.Martini | Minardi-Ford | 19 | Wheel | 10 |
| Ret | 22 | A.de Cesaris | Dallara-Ford | 0 | Clutch | 18 |
| DNQ | 25 | Rene Arnoux | Ligier-Ford | | | |
| DNQ | 26 | O.Grouillard | Ligier-Ford | | | |
| DNQ | 38 | Christian Danner | Rial-Ford | | | |
| DNQ | 39 | Volker Weidler | Rial-Ford | | | |
| DNPQ | 17 | Nicola Larini | Osella-Ford | | | |
| DNPQ | 30 | Philippe Alliot | Lola-Lamborghini | | | |
| DNPQ | 41 | Yannick Dalmas | AGS-Ford | | | |
| DNPQ | 34 | Bernd Schneider | Zakspeed-Yamaha | | | |
| DNPQ | 40 | G.Tarquini | AGS-Ford | | | |
| DNPQ | 31 | Roberto Moreno | Coloni-Ford | | | |
| DNPQ | 33 | Gregor Foitek | EuroBrun-Judd | | | |
| DNPQ | 35 | Aguri Suzuki | Zakspeed-Yamaha | | | |
| DNPQ | 32 | P.H.Raphanel | Coloni-Ford | | | |

Winning speed: 103.891mph Lap leaders: Patrese 1-52; Senna 53-57; Mansell 58-77
Pole position: Patrese, 1m 19.726s, 111.333mph
Fastest lap: Mansell, 1m 22.637s, 107.411mph

## BELGIAN GRAND PRIX: SPA-FRANCORCHAMPS *27 August Round: 11 Race: 479 44 x 4.132 miles*

| POS. | NO. | DRIVER | CAR/ENGINE | LAPS | TIME/RETIRED | GRID |
|---|---|---|---|---|---|---|
| 1 | 1 | Ayrton Senna | McLaren-Honda | 44 | 1:40'54.196 | 1 |
| 2 | 2 | Alain Prost | McLaren-Honda | 44 | +1.304 | 2 |
| 3 | 27 | Nigel Mansell | Ferrari | 44 | +1.824 | 6 |
| 4 | 5 | Thierry Boutsen | Williams-Renault | 44 | +54.418 | 4 |
| 5 | 19 | A.Nannini | Benetton-Ford | 44 | +1'08.805 | 7 |
| 6 | 9 | Derek Warwick | Arrows-Ford | 44 | +1'18.316 | 10 |
| 7 | 15 | M.Gugelmin | March-Judd | 43 | +1 Lap | 9 |
| 8 | 36 | Stefan Johansson | Onyx-Ford | 43 | +1 Lap | 15 |
| 9 | 23 | P.Martini | Minardi-Ford | 43 | +1 Lap | 14 |
| 10 | 20 | Emanuele Pirro | Benetton-Ford | 43 | +1 Lap | 13 |
| 11 | 22 | A.de Cesaris | Dallara-Ford | 43 | +1 Lap | 18 |
| 12 | 16 | Ivan Capelli | March-Judd | 43 | +1 Lap | 19 |
| 13 | 26 | O.Grouillard | Ligier-Ford | 43 | +1 Lap | 26 |
| 14 | 3 | Jonathan Palmer | Tyrrell-Ford | 42 | +2 Laps | 21 |
| 15 | 24 | Luis Perez-Sala | Minardi-Ford | 41 | +3 Laps | 25 |
| 16 | 30 | Philippe Alliot | Lola-Lamborghini | 39 | Engine | 11 |
| Ret | 10 | Eddie Cheever | Arrows-Ford | 38 | Wheel | 24 |
| Ret | 37 | Bertrand Gachot | Onyx-Ford | 21 | Spun off | 23 |
| Ret | 6 | Riccardo Patrese | Williams-Renault | 20 | Collision | 5 |
| Ret | 29 | Michele Alboreto | Lola-Lamborghini | 19 | Collision | 22 |
| Ret | 21 | Alex Caffi | Dallara-Ford | 13 | Spun off | 12 |
| Ret | 7 | Martin Brundle | Brabham-Judd | 12 | Brakes | 20 |
| Ret | 28 | Gerhard Berger | Ferrari | 9 | Spun off | 3 |
| Ret | 8 | Stefano Modena | Brabham-Judd | 9 | Handling | 8 |
| Ret | 25 | Rene Arnoux | Ligier-Ford | 4 | Collision | 17 |
| Ret | 4 | Johnny Herbert | Tyrrell-Ford | 3 | Spun off | 16 |
| DNQ | 12 | Satoru Nakajima | Lotus-Judd | | | |
| DNQ | 11 | Nelson Piquet | Lotus-Judd | | | |
| DNQ | 38 | Christian Danner | Rial-Ford | | | |
| DNQ | 39 | P.H.Raphanel | Rial-Ford | | | |
| DNPQ | 17 | Nicola Larini | Osella-Ford | | | |
| DNPQ | 18 | P.Ghinzani | Osella-Ford | | | |
| DNPQ | 31 | Roberto Moreno | Coloni-Ford | | | |
| DNPQ | 40 | G.Tarquini | AGS-Ford | | | |
| DNPQ | 34 | Bernd Schneider | Zakspeed-Yamaha | | | |
| DNPQ | 35 | Aguri Suzuki | Zakspeed-Yamaha | | | |
| DNPQ | 41 | Yannick Dalmas | AGS-Ford | | | |
| DNPQ | 33 | Gregor Foitek | EuroBrun-Judd | | | |
| DNPQ | 32 | Enrico Bertaggia | Coloni-Ford | | | |

Winning speed: 112.826mph Lap leaders: Senna 1-44
Pole position: Senna, 1m 50.867s, 140.027mph Fastest lap: Prost, 2m 11.571s, 117.992mph

## ITALIAN GRAND PRIX: MONZA *10 September Round: 12 Race: 480 53 x 3.604 miles*

| POS. | NO. | DRIVER | CAR/ENGINE | LAPS | TIME/RETIRED | GRID |
|---|---|---|---|---|---|---|
| 1 | 2 | Alain Prost | McLaren-Honda | 53 | 1:19'27.550 | 4 |
| 2 | 28 | Gerhard Berger | Ferrari | 53 | +7.326 | 2 |
| 3 | 5 | Thierry Boutsen | Williams-Renault | 53 | +14.975 | 6 |
| 4 | 6 | Riccardo Patrese | Williams-Renault | 53 | +38.722 | 5 |
| 5 | 4 | Jean Alesi | Tyrrell-Ford | 52 | +1 Lap | 10 |
| 6 | 7 | Martin Brundle | Brabham-Judd | 52 | +1 Lap | 12 |
| 7 | 23 | P.Martini | Minardi-Ford | 52 | +1 Lap | 15 |
| 8 | 24 | Luis Perez-Sala | Minardi-Ford | 51 | +2 Laps | 26 |
| 9 | 25 | Rene Arnoux | Ligier-Ford | 51 | +2 Laps | 23 |
| 10 | 12 | Satoru Nakajima | Lotus-Judd | 51 | Suspension | 19 |
| 11 | 21 | Alex Caffi | Dallara-Ford | 47 | Engine | 20 |
| Ret | 22 | A.de Cesaris | Dallara-Ford | 45 | Engine | 17 |
| Ret | 1 | Ayrton Senna | McLaren-Honda | 44 | Engine | 1 |
| Ret | 27 | Nigel Mansell | Ferrari | 41 | Gearbox | 3 |
| Ret | 37 | Bertrand Gachot | Onyx-Ford | 38 | Radiator | 22 |
| Ret | 19 | A.Nannini | Benetton-Ford | 33 | Brakes | 8 |
| Ret | 16 | Ivan Capelli | March-Judd | 30 | Engine | 18 |
| Ret | 26 | O.Grouillard | Ligier-Ford | 30 | Exhaust | 21 |
| Ret | 11 | Nelson Piquet | Lotus-Judd | 23 | Spun off | 11 |
| Ret | 3 | Jonathan Palmer | Tyrrell-Ford | 18 | Engine | 14 |
| Ret | 9 | Derek Warwick | Arrows-Ford | 18 | Fuel system | 16 |
| Ret | 17 | Nicola Larini | Osella-Ford | 16 | Gearbox | 24 |
| Ret | 29 | Michele Alboreto | Lola-Lamborghini | 14 | Electrical | 13 |
| Ret | 15 | M.Gugelmin | March-Judd | 14 | Throttle | 25 |
| Ret | 30 | Philippe Alliot | Lola-Lamborghini | 1 | Spun off | 7 |
| Ret | 20 | Emanuele Pirro | Benetton-Ford | 0 | Transmission | 9 |
| DNQ | 8 | Stefano Modena | Brabham-Judd | | | |
| DNQ | 10 | Eddie Cheever | Arrows-Ford | | | |
| DNQ | 38 | Christian Danner | Rial-Ford | | | |
| DNQ | 39 | P.H.Raphanel | Rial-Ford | | | |
| DNPQ | 36 | Stefan Johansson | Onyx-Ford | | | |
| DNPQ | 40 | G.Tarquini | AGS-Ford | | | |
| DSQ | 31 | Roberto Moreno | Coloni-Ford | | | |
| DNPQ | 18 | P.Ghinzani | Osella-Ford | | | |
| DNPQ | 34 | Bernd Schneider | Zakspeed-Yamaha | | | |
| DNPQ | 35 | Aguri Suzuki | Zakspeed-Yamaha | | | |
| DNPQ | 33 | Oscar Larrauri | EuroBrun-Judd | | | |
| DNPQ | 41 | Yannick Dalmas | AGS-Ford | | | |
| DNPQ | 32 | Enrico Bertaggia | Coloni-Ford | | | |

Winning speed: 144.232mph Lap leaders: Senna 1-44; Prost 45-53
Pole position: Senna, 1m 23.720s, 154.972mph Fastest lap: Prost, 1m 28.107s, 147.255mph

## PORTUGUESE GRAND PRIX: ESTORIL *24 September Round: 13 Race: 481 71 x 2.703 miles*

| POS. | NO. | DRIVER | CAR/ENGINE | LAPS | TIME/RETIRED | GRID |
|---|---|---|---|---|---|---|
| 1 | 28 | Gerhard Berger | Ferrari | 71 | 1:36'48.546 | 2 |
| 2 | 2 | Alain Prost | McLaren-Honda | 71 | +32.637 | 4 |
| 3 | 36 | Stefan Johansson | Onyx-Ford | 71 | +55.325 | 12 |
| 4 | 19 | A.Nannini | Benetton-Ford | 71 | +1'22.369 | 13 |
| 5 | 23 | P.Martini | Minardi-Ford | 70 | +1 Lap | 5 |
| 6 | 3 | Jonathan Palmer | Tyrrell-Ford | 70 | +1 Lap | 18 |
| 7 | 12 | Satoru Nakajima | Lotus-Judd | 70 | +1 Lap | 25 |
| 8 | 7 | Martin Brundle | Brabham-Judd | 70 | +1 Lap | 10 |
| 9 | 30 | Philippe Alliot | Lola-Lamborghini | 70 | +1 Lap | 17 |
| 10 | 15 | M.Gugelmin | March-Judd | 69 | +2 Laps | 14 |
| 11 | 29 | Michele Alboreto | Lola-Lamborghini | 69 | +2 Laps | 21 |
| 12 | 24 | Luis Perez-Sala | Minardi-Ford | 69 | +2 Laps | 9 |
| 13 | 25 | Rene Arnoux | Ligier-Ford | 69 | +2 Laps | 23 |
| 14 | 8 | Stefano Modena | Brabham-Judd | 69 | +2 Laps | 11 |
| Ret | 6 | Riccardo Patrese | Williams-Renault | 60 | Overheating | 6 |
| Ret | 5 | Thierry Boutsen | Williams-Renault | 60 | Overheating | 8 |
| Ret | 1 | Ayrton Senna | McLaren-Honda | 48 | Collision | 1 |
| DSQ | 27 | Nigel Mansell | Ferrari | 48 | Disqualified | 3 |
| Ret | 9 | Derek Warwick | Arrows-Ford | 37 | Accident | 22 |
| Ret | 11 | Nelson Piquet | Lotus-Judd | 33 | Collision | 20 |
| Ret | 21 | Alex Caffi | Dallara-Ford | 33 | Collision | 7 |
| Ret | 20 | Emanuele Pirro | Benetton-Ford | 29 | Suspension | 16 |
| Ret | 16 | Ivan Capelli | March-Judd | 25 | Engine | 24 |
| Ret | 10 | Eddie Cheever | Arrows-Ford | 24 | Spun off | 26 |
| Ret | 22 | A.de Cesaris | Dallara-Ford | 17 | Electrical | 19 |
| Ret | 31 | Roberto Moreno | Coloni-Ford | 11 | Electrical | 15 |
| DNQ | 4 | Johnny Herbert | Tyrrell-Ford | | | |
| DNQ | 26 | O.Grouillard | Ligier-Ford | | | |
| DNQ | 39 | P.H.Raphanel | Rial-Ford | | | |
| DSQ | 38 | Christian Danner | Rial-Ford | | | |
| DNPQ | 41 | Yannick Dalmas | AGS-Ford | | | |
| DNPQ | 37 | J J Lehto | Onyx-Ford | | | |
| DNPQ | 18 | P.Ghinzani | Osella-Ford | | | |
| DNPQ | 33 | Oscar Larrauri | EuroBrun-Judd | | | |
| DNPQ | 40 | G.Tarquini | AGS-Ford | | | |
| DSQ | 17 | Nicola Larini | Osella-Ford | | | |
| DNPQ | 35 | Aguri Suzuki | Zakspeed-Yamaha | | | |
| DNPQ | 34 | Bernd Schneider | Zakspeed-Yamaha | | | |
| DNPQ | 32 | Enrico Bertaggia | Coloni-Ford | | | |

Winning speed: 118.942mph Lap leaders: Berger 1-23, 41-71; Mansell 24-39; Martini 40
Pole position; Senna, 1m 15.468s, 128.938mph Fastest lap: Berger, 1m 18.986s, 123.195mph

## SPANISH GRAND PRIX: JEREZ DE LA FRONTERA *1 October Round: 14 Race: 482 73 x 2.621 miles*

| POS. | NO. | DRIVER | CAR/ENGINE | LAPS | TIME/RETIRED | GRID |
|---|---|---|---|---|---|---|
| 1 | 1 | Ayrton Senna | McLaren-Honda | 73 | 1:47'48.264 | 1 |
| 2 | 28 | Gerhard Berger | Ferrari | 73 | +27.051 | 2 |
| 3 | 2 | Alain Prost | McLaren-Honda | 73 | +53.788 | 3 |
| 4 | 4 | Jean Alesi | Tyrrell-Ford | 72 | +1 Lap | 9 |
| 5 | 6 | Riccardo Patrese | Williams-Renault | 72 | +1 Lap | 6 |
| 6 | 30 | Philippe Alliot | Lola-Lamborghini | 72 | +1 Lap | 5 |
| 7 | 22 | A.de Cesaris | Dallara-Ford | 72 | +1 Lap | 15 |
| 8 | 11 | Nelson Piquet | Lotus-Judd | 71 | +2 Laps | 7 |
| 9 | 9 | Derek Warwick | Arrows-Ford | 71 | +2 Laps | 16 |
| 10 | 3 | Jonathan Palmer | Tyrrell-Ford | 71 | +2 Laps | 13 |
| Ret | 10 | Eddie Cheever | Arrows-Ford | 61 | Engine | 22 |
| Ret | 20 | Emanuele Pirro | Benetton-Ford | 59 | Spun off | 10 |
| Ret | 21 | Alex Caffi | Dallara-Ford | 55 | Engine | 23 |
| Ret | 7 | Martin Brundle | Brabham-Judd | 51 | Spun off | 8 |
| Ret | 15 | M.Gugelmin | March-Judd | 47 | Collision | 26 |
| Ret | 24 | Luis Perez-Sala | Minardi-Ford | 47 | Spun off | 20 |
| Ret | 5 | Thierry Boutsen | Williams-Renault | 40 | Fuel pump | 21 |
| Ret | 26 | O.Grouillard | Ligier-Ford | 34 | Engine | 24 |
| Ret | 23 | P.Martini | Minardi-Ford | 27 | Spun off | 4 |
| Ret | 16 | Ivan Capelli | March-Judd | 23 | Transmission | 19 |
| Ret | 37 | J J Lehto | Onyx-Ford | 20 | Gearbox | 17 |
| Ret | 18 | P.Ghinzani | Osella-Ford | 17 | Gearbox | 25 |
| Ret | 19 | A.Nannini | Benetton-Ford | 14 | Spun off | 14 |
| Ret | 8 | Stefano Modena | Brabham-Judd | 11 | Electrical | 12 |
| Ret | 17 | Nicola Larini | Osella-Ford | 6 | Suspension | 11 |
| Ret | 12 | Satoru Nakajima | Lotus-Judd | 0 | Collision | 18 |
| DNQ | 25 | Rene Arnoux | Ligier-Ford | | | |
| DNQ | 39 | P.H.Raphanel | Rial-Ford | | | |
| DNQ | 38 | Gregor Foitek | Rial-Ford | | | |
| DNPQ | 40 | G.Tarquini | AGS-Ford | | | |
| DNPQ | 36 | Stefan Johansson | Onyx-Ford | | | |
| DNPQ | 31 | Roberto Moreno | Coloni-Ford | | | |
| DNPQ | 29 | Michele Alboreto | Lola-Lamborghini | | | |
| DNPQ | 35 | Aguri Suzuki | Zakspeed-Yamaha | | | |
| DNPQ | 41 | Yannick Dalmas | AGS-Ford | | | |
| DNPQ | 34 | Bernd Schneider | Zakspeed-Yamaha | | | |
| DNPQ | 33 | Oscar Larrauri | EuroBrun-Judd | | | |
| DNPQ | 32 | Enrico Bertaggia | Coloni-Ford | | | |

Winning speed: 106.487mph Lap leaders: Senna 1-73
Pole position: Senna, 1m 20.291s, 117.515mph
Fastest lap: Senna, 1m 25.779s, 109.997mph

## JAPANESE GRAND PRIX: SUZUKA *22 October Round: 15 Race: 483 53 x 3.641 miles*

| POS. | NO. | DRIVER | CAR/ENGINE | LAPS | TIME/RETIRED | GRID |
|---|---|---|---|---|---|---|
| 1 | 19 | A.Nannini | Benetton-Ford | 53 | 1:35'06.277 | 6 |
| 2 | 6 | Riccardo Patrese | Williams-Renault | 53 | +11.904 | 5 |
| 3 | 5 | Thierry Boutsen | Williams-Renault | 53 | +13.446 | 7 |
| 4 | 11 | Nelson Piquet | Lotus-Judd | 53 | +1'44.225 | 11 |
| 5 | 7 | Martin Brundle | Brabham-Judd | 52 | +1 Lap | 13 |
| 6 | 9 | Derek Warwick | Arrows-Ford | 52 | +1 Lap | 25 |
| 7 | 15 | M.Gugelmin | March-Judd | 52 | +1 Lap | 20 |
| 8 | 10 | Eddie Cheever | Arrows-Ford | 52 | +1 Lap | 24 |
| 9 | 21 | Alex Caffi | Dallara-Ford | 52 | +1 Lap | 15 |
| 10 | 22 | A.de Cesaris | Dallara-Ford | 51 | +2 Laps | 16 |
| DSQ | 1 | Ayrton Senna | McLaren-Honda | 53 | Disqualified | 1 |
| Ret | 2 | Alain Prost | McLaren-Honda | 46 | Collision | 2 |
| Ret | 8 | Stefano Modena | Brabham-Judd | 46 | Engine | 9 |
| Ret | 27 | Nigel Mansell | Ferrari | 43 | Engine | 4 |
| Ret | 12 | Satoru Nakajima | Lotus-Judd | 41 | Engine | 12 |
| Ret | 4 | Jean Alesi | Tyrrell-Ford | 37 | Gearbox | 18 |
| Ret | 30 | Philippe Alliot | Lola-Lamborghini | 36 | Engine | 8 |
| Ret | 28 | Gerhard Berger | Ferrari | 34 | Gearbox | 3 |
| Ret | 20 | Emanuele Pirro | Benetton-Ford | 33 | Collision | 22 |
| Ret | 26 | O.Grouillard | Ligier-Ford | 31 | Engine | 23 |
| Ret | 16 | Ivan Capelli | March-Judd | 27 | Suspension | 17 |
| Ret | 17 | Nicola Larini | Osella-Ford | 21 | Brakes | 10 |
| Ret | 3 | Jonathan Palmer | Tyrrell-Ford | 20 | Fuel leak | 26 |
| Ret | 34 | Bernd Schneider | Zakspeed-Yamaha | 1 | Gearbox | 21 |
| Ret | 24 | Luis Perez-Sala | Minardi-Ford | 0 | Collision | 14 |
| Ret | 23 | Paolo Barilla | Minardi-Ford | 0 | Clutch | 19 |
| DNQ | 25 | Rene Arnoux | Ligier-Ford | | | |
| DNQ | 29 | Michele Alboreto | Lola-Lamborghini | | | |
| DNQ | 38 | P.H.Raphanel | Rial-Ford | | | |
| DNQ | 39 | Bertrand Gachot | Rial-Ford | | | |
| DNPQ | 18 | P.Ghinzani | Osella-Ford | | | |
| DNPQ | 31 | Roberto Moreno | Coloni-Ford | | | |
| DNPQ | 36 | Stefan Johansson | Onyx-Ford | | | |
| DNPQ | 35 | Aguri Suzuki | Zakspeed-Yamaha | | | |
| DNPQ | 33 | Oscar Larrauri | EuroBrun-Judd | | | |
| DNPQ | 37 | J J Lehto | Onyx-Ford | | | |
| DNPQ | 40 | G.Tarquini | AGS-Ford | | | |
| DNPQ | 41 | Yannick Dalmas | AGS-Ford | | | |
| DNPQ | 32 | Enrico Bertaggia | Coloni-Ford | | | |

Winning speed: 121.731mph
Lap leaders: Prost 1-20, 24-46; Senna 21-23, 47-48, 51-53; Nannini 49-50
Pole position: Senna, 1m 38.041s, 133.681mph
Fastest lap: Prost, 1m 43.506s, 126.623mph
Senna finished first but was disqualified for reckless driving; he also recorded the fastest lap of 1m 43.025s.

## AUSTRALIAN GRAND PRIX: ADELAIDE *5 November Round: 16 Race: 484 70 x 2.349 miles*

| POS. | NO. | DRIVER | CAR/ENGINE | LAPS | TIME/RETIRED | GRID |
|---|---|---|---|---|---|---|
| 1 | 5 | Thierry Boutsen | Williams-Renault | 70 | 2:00'17.421 | 5 |
| 2 | 19 | A.Nannini | Benetton-Ford | 70 | +28.658 | 4 |
| 3 | 6 | Riccardo Patrese | Williams-Renault | 70 | +37.683 | 6 |
| 4 | 12 | Satoru Nakajima | Lotus-Judd | 70 | +42.331 | 23 |
| 5 | 20 | Emanuele Pirro | Benetton-Ford | 68 | +2 Laps | 13 |
| 6 | 23 | P.Martini | Minardi-Ford | 67 | +3 Laps | 3 |
| 7 | 15 | M.Gugelmin | March-Judd | 66 | +4 Laps | 25 |
| 8 | 8 | Stefano Modena | Brabham-Judd | 64 | +6 Laps | 8 |
| Ret | 10 | Eddie Cheever | Arrows-Ford | 42 | Spun off | 22 |
| Ret | 37 | J J Lehto | Onyx-Ford | 27 | Electrical | 17 |
| Ret | 26 | O.Grouillard | Ligier-Ford | 22 | Spun off | 24 |
| Ret | 11 | Nelson Piquet | Lotus-Judd | 19 | Collision | 18 |
| Ret | 18 | P.Ghinzani | Osella-Ford | 18 | Collision | 21 |
| Ret | 27 | Nigel Mansell | Ferrari | 17 | Spun off | 7 |
| Ret | 1 | Ayrton Senna | McLaren-Honda | 13 | Collision | 1 |
| Ret | 21 | Alex Caffi | Dallara-Ford | 13 | Spun off | 10 |
| Ret | 16 | Ivan Capelli | March-Judd | 13 | Radiator | 16 |
| Ret | 22 | A.de Cesaris | Dallara-Ford | 12 | Spun off | 9 |
| Ret | 7 | Martin Brundle | Brabham-Judd | 12 | Collision | 12 |
| Ret | 9 | Derek Warwick | Arrows-Ford | 7 | Spun off | 20 |
| Ret | 30 | Philippe Alliot | Lola-Lamborghini | 6 | Collision | 19 |
| Ret | 28 | Gerhard Berger | Ferrari | 6 | Collision | 14 |
| Ret | 4 | Jean Alesi | Tyrrell-Ford | 5 | Electrical | 15 |
| Ret | 25 | Rene Arnoux | Ligier-Ford | 4 | Collision | 26 |
| Wth | 2 | Alain Prost | McLaren-Honda | 0 | Withdrew | 2 |
| Ret | 17 | Nicola Larini | Osella-Ford | 0 | Electrical | 11 |
| DNQ | 3 | Jonathan Palmer | Tyrrell-Ford | | | |
| DNQ | 24 | Luis Perez-Sala | Minardi-Ford | | | |
| DNQ | 39 | Bertrand Gachot | Rial-Ford | | | |
| DNQ | 38 | P.H.Raphanel | Rial-Ford | | | |
| DNPQ | 36 | Stefan Johansson | Onyx-Ford | | | |
| DNPQ | 29 | Michele Alboreto | Lola-Lamborghini | | | |
| DNPQ | 34 | Bernd Schneider | Zakspeed-Yamaha | | | |
| DNPQ | 31 | Roberto Moreno | Coloni-Ford | | | |
| DNPQ | 33 | Oscar Larrauri | EuroBrun-Judd | | | |
| DNPQ | 35 | Aguri Suzuki | Zakspeed-Yamaha | | | |
| DNPQ | 41 | Yannick Dalmas | AGS-Ford | | | |
| DNPQ | 40 | G.Tarquini | AGS-Ford | | | |
| DNPQ | 32 | Enrico Bertaggia | Coloni-Ford | | | |

Winning speed: 82.009mph Lap leaders: Senna 1-13; Boutsen 14-70
Pole position; Senna, 1m 16.665s, 110.293mph
Fastest lap: Nakajima, 1m 38.480s, 85.861mph
Race stopped after first lap accident and restarted for total original distance. However, the racewas stopped before the full 81 laps when it passed the two-hour mark.

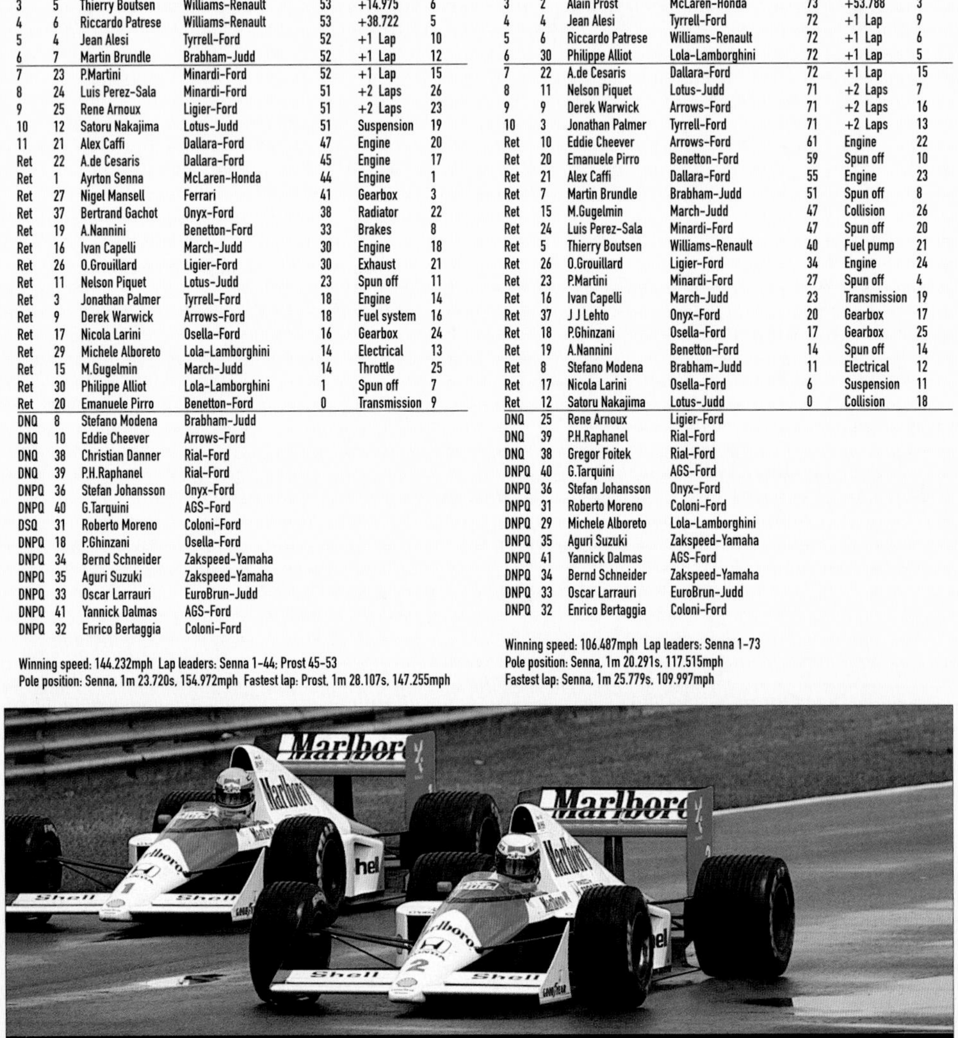

1988 world champion, Ayrton Senna and 1989 world champion Alain Prost.

# 1990

## DRIVERS' CHAMPION: AYRTON SENNA
## CONSTRUCTORS' CHAMPION: McLAREN HONDA

### DRIVERS' CHAMPIONSHIP

| POS. | DRIVER | NATIONALITY | CAR | POINTS |
|---|---|---|---|---|
| 1 | Ayrton Senna | Brazil | McLaren-Honda | 78 |
| 2 | Alain Prost | France | Ferrari | 71(2) |
| 3 | Nelson Piquet | Brazil | Benetton-Ford | 43(1) |
| = | Gerhard Berger | Austria | McLaren-Honda | 43 |
| 5 | Nigel Mansell | GB | Ferrari | 37 |
| 6 | Thierry Boutsen | Belgium | Williams-Renault | 34 |
| 7 | Riccardo Patrese | Italy | Williams-Renault | 23 |
| 8 | Alessandro Nannini | Italy | Benetton-Ford | 21 |
| 9 | Jean Alesi | France | Tyrrell-Ford | 13 |
| 10 | Ivan Capelli | Italy | Leyton House-Judd | 6 |
| = | Roberto Moreno | Brazil | EuroBrun-Judd | 6 |
| = | Aguri Suzuki | Japan | Lola-Lamborghini | 6 |
| 13 | Eric Bernard | France | Lola-Lamborghini | 5 |
| 14 | Derek Warwick | GB | Lotus-Lamborghini | 3 |
| = | Saturo Nakajima | Japan | Tyrrell-Ford | 3 |
| 16 | Stefano Modena | Italy | Brabham-Judd | 2 |
| = | Alex Caffi | Italy | Arrows-Ford | 2 |
| 18 | Mauricio Gugelmin | Brazil | Leyton House-Judd | 1 |
| | Nicola Larini | Italy | Ligier-Ford | |
| | Pierluigi Martini | Italy | Minardi-Ford | |
| | Andrea de Cesaris | Italy | Dallara-Ford | |
| | Philippe Alliot | France | Ligier-Ford | |
| | Michele Alboreto | Italy | Arrows-Ford | |
| | Olivier Grouillard | France | Osella-Ford | |
| | Gabriele Tarquini | Italy | AGS-Ford | |
| | Yannick Dalmas | France | AGS-Ford | |
| | Paolo Barilla | Italy | Minardi-Ford, Minardi-Ford | |
| | Bertrand Gachot | Belgium | Coloni-Subaru, Coloni-Ford | |
| | Claudio Langes | Italy | EuroBrun | |
| | JJ Lehto | Finland | Onyx-Ford, Monteverdi-Ford | |
| | Gregor Foitek | Switzerland | Brabham-Judd, Onyx-Ford, Monteverdi-Ford | |
| | Bernd Schneider | Germany | Arrows-Ford | |
| | Gianni Morbidelli | Italy | Dallara-Ford, Minardi-Ford | |
| | Stefan Johansson | Sweden | Onyx-Ford | |
| | Gary Brabham | Australia | Life | |
| | Martin Donnelly | GB | Lotus-Lamborghini | |
| | Emanuele Pirro | Italy | Dallara-Ford | |
| | David Brabham | Australia | Brabham-Judd | |
| | Bruno Giacomelli | Italy | Life, Life-Judd | |
| | Johnny Herbert | GB | Lotus-Lamborghini | |

**Points for top six finishers (9, 6, 4, 3, 2, 1). Only the best eleven scores counted towards the championship. Drivers not valid for points if the constructor had entered only one car. Half points awarded for races stopped before half distance.**

### CONSTRUCTORS' CHAMPIONSHIP

| POS. | CONSTRUCTOR | POINTS |
|---|---|---|
| 1 | McLaren-Honda | 121 |
| 2 | Ferrari | 110 |
| 3 | Benetton-Ford | 71 |
| 4 | Williams-Renault | 57 |
| 5 | Tyrrell-Ford | 16 |
| 6 | Lola-Lamborghini | 11 |
| 7 | Leyton House-Judd | 7 |
| 8 | Lotus-Lamborghini | 3 |
| 9 | Brabham-Judd | 2 |
| 9 | Arrows-Ford | 2 |

**Points for top six finishers (9, 6, 4, 3, 2, 1). Half points awarded for races stopped before half distance.**

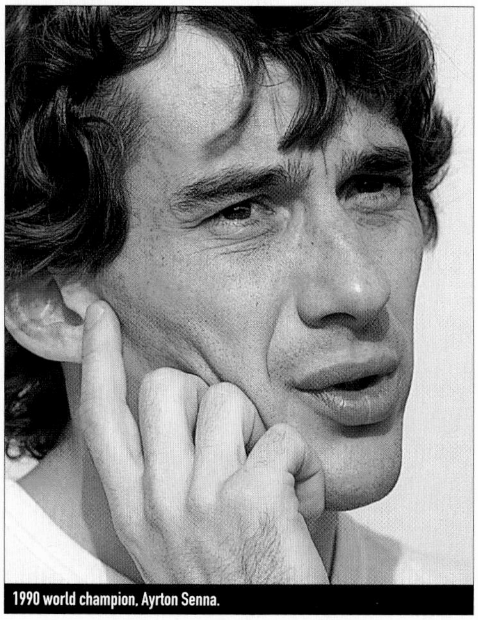

1990 world champion, Ayrton Senna.

### UNITED STATES GRAND PRIX: PHOENIX *11 March Round: 1 Race: 485 72 x 2.360 miles*

| POS. | NO. | DRIVER | CAR/ENGINE | LAPS | TIME/RETIRED | GRID |
|---|---|---|---|---|---|---|
| 1 | 27 | Ayrton Senna | McLaren-Honda | 72 | 1:52'32.829 | 5 |
| 2 | 4 | Jean Alesi | Tyrrell-Ford | 72 | +8.685 | 4 |
| 3 | 5 | Thierry Boutsen | Williams-Renault | 72 | +54.080 | 9 |
| 4 | 20 | Nelson Piquet | Benetton-Ford | 72 | +1'08.358 | 6 |
| 5 | 8 | Stefano Modena | Brabham-Judd | 72 | +1'09.503 | 10 |
| 6 | 3 | Satoru Nakajima | Tyrrell-Ford | 71 | +1 Lap | 11 |
| 7 | 23 | P.Martini | Minardi-Ford | 71 | +1 Lap | 2 |
| 8 | 29 | Eric Bernard | Lola-Lamborghini | 71 | +1 Lap | 15 |
| 9 | 6 | Riccardo Patrese | Williams-Renault | 71 | +1 Lap | 12 |
| 10 | 9 | Michele Alboreto | Arrows-Ford | 70 | +2 Laps | 21 |
| 11 | 19 | A.Nannini | Benetton-Ford | 70 | +2 Laps | 22 |
| 12 | 10 | Bernd Schneider | Arrows-Ford | 70 | +2 Laps | 20 |
| 13 | 33 | Roberto Moreno | EuroBrun-Judd | 67 | +5 Laps | 16 |
| 14 | 15 | M.Gugelmin | Leyton House-Judd | 66 | +6 Laps | 25 |
| Ret | 24 | Paolo Barilla | Minardi-Ford | 54 | Physical | 14 |
| Ret | 30 | Aguri Suzuki | Lola-Lamborghini | 53 | Brakes | 18 |
| Ret | 2 | Nigel Mansell | Ferrari | 49 | Engine | 17 |
| Ret | 28 | Gerhard Berger | McLaren-Honda | 44 | Clutch | 1 |
| Ret | 7 | Gregor Foitek | Brabham-Judd | 39 | Accident | 23 |
| Ret | 14 | O.Grouillard | Osella-Ford | 39 | Collision | 8 |
| Ret | 22 | A.de Cesaris | Dallara-Ford | 25 | Engine | 3 |
| Ret | 1 | Alain Prost | Ferrari | 21 | Oil leak | 7 |
| Ret | 16 | Ivan Capelli | Leyton House-Judd | 20 | Electrical | 26 |
| Ret | 11 | Derek Warwick | Lotus-Lamborghini | 6 | Gearbox | 24 |
| Ret | 25 | Nicola Larini | Ligier-Ford | 4 | Throttle | 13 |
| DNS | 12 | Martin Donnelly | Lotus-Lamborghini | 0 | Gearbox | 19 |
| DSQ | 26 | Philippe Alliot | Ligier-Ford | | | |
| DNQ | 35 | Stefan Johansson | Onyx-Ford | | | |
| DNQ | 21 | G.Morbidelli | Dallara-Ford | | | |
| DNQ | 36 | J J Lehto | Onyx-Ford | | | |
| DNPQ | 17 | G.Tarquini | AGS-Ford | | | |
| DNPQ | 18 | Yannick Dalmas | AGS-Ford | | | |
| DNPQ | 34 | Claudio Langes | EuroBrun-Judd | | | |
| DNPQ | 39 | Gary Brabham | Life | | | |
| DNPQ | 31 | Bertrand Gachot | Coloni-Subaru | | | |

Winning speed: 90.586mph Lap leaders: Alesi 1-34; Senna 35-72
Pole position: Berger, 1m 28.664s, 95.822mph
Fastest lap: Berger, 1m 31.050s, 93.311mph

### BRAZILIAN GRAND PRIX: INTERLAGOS *25 March Round: 2 Race: 486 71 x 2.687 miles*

| POS. | NO. | DRIVER | CAR/ENGINE | LAPS | TIME/RETIRED | GRID |
|---|---|---|---|---|---|---|
| 1 | 1 | Alain Prost | Ferrari | 71 | 1:37'21.258 | 6 |
| 2 | 28 | Gerhard Berger | McLaren-Honda | 71 | +13.564 | 2 |
| 3 | 27 | Ayrton Senna | McLaren-Honda | 71 | +37.722 | 1 |
| 4 | 2 | Nigel Mansell | Ferrari | 71 | +47.266 | 5 |
| 5 | 5 | Thierry Boutsen | Williams-Renault | 70 | +1 Lap | 3 |
| 6 | 20 | Nelson Piquet | Benetton-Ford | 70 | +1 Lap | 13 |
| 7 | 4 | Jean Alesi | Tyrrell-Ford | 70 | +1 Lap | 7 |
| 8 | 3 | Satoru Nakajima | Tyrrell-Ford | 70 | +1 Lap | 19 |
| 9 | 23 | P.Martini | Minardi-Ford | 69 | +2 Laps | 8 |
| 10 | 19 | A.Nannini | Benetton-Ford | 68 | Puncture | 15 |
| 11 | 25 | Nicola Larini | Ligier-Ford | 68 | +3 Laps | 20 |
| 12 | 26 | Philippe Alliot | Ligier-Ford | 68 | +3 Laps | 10 |
| 13 | 6 | Riccardo Patrese | Williams-Renault | 65 | Oil pressure | 4 |
| 14 | 21 | G.Morbidelli | Dallara-Ford | 64 | +7 Laps | 16 |
| Ret | 10 | Alex Caffi | Arrows-Ford | 49 | Clutch | 25 |
| Ret | 12 | Martin Donnelly | Lotus-Lamborghini | 43 | Spun off | 14 |
| Ret | 8 | Stefano Modena | Brabham-Judd | 39 | Spun off | 12 |
| Ret | 24 | Paolo Barilla | Minardi-Ford | 38 | Engine | 17 |
| Ret | 18 | Yannick Dalmas | AGS-Ford | 28 | Suspension | 26 |
| Ret | 11 | Derek Warwick | Lotus-Lamborghini | 25 | Electrical | 24 |
| Ret | 30 | Aguri Suzuki | Lola-Lamborghini | 24 | Suspension | 18 |
| Ret | 9 | Michele Alboreto | Arrows-Ford | 24 | Suspension | 23 |
| Ret | 7 | Gregor Foitek | Brabham-Judd | 14 | Transmission | 22 |
| Ret | 29 | Eric Bernard | Lola-Lamborghini | 13 | Gearbox | 11 |
| Ret | 14 | O.Grouillard | Osella-Ford | 8 | Collision | 21 |
| Ret | 22 | A.de Cesaris | Dallara-Ford | 0 | Collision | 9 |
| DNQ | 35 | Stefan Johansson | Onyx-Ford | | | |
| DNQ | 36 | J J Lehto | Onyx-Ford | | | |
| DNQ | 16 | Ivan Capelli | Leyton House-Judd | | | |
| DNQ | 15 | M.Gugelmin | Leyton House-Judd | | | |
| DNPQ | 17 | G.Tarquini | AGS-Ford | | | |
| DNPQ | 33 | Roberto Moreno | EuroBrun-Judd | | | |
| DNPQ | 31 | Bertrand Gachot | Coloni-Subaru | | | |
| DNPQ | 34 | Claudio Langes | EuroBrun-Judd | | | |
| DNPQ | 39 | Gary Brabham | Life | | | |

Winning speed: 117.596mph Lap leaders: Senna 1-32, 35-40; Berger 33-34; Prost 41-71
Pole position: Senna, 1m 17.277s, 125.196mph
Fastest lap: Berger, 1m 19.899s, 121.087mph

### SAN MARINO GRAND PRIX: IMOLA *13 May Round: 3 Race: 487 61 x 3.132 miles*

| POS. | NO. | DRIVER | CAR/ENGINE | LAPS | TIME/RETIRED | GRID |
|---|---|---|---|---|---|---|
| 1 | 6 | Riccardo Patrese | Williams-Renault | 61 | 1:30'55.478 | 3 |
| 2 | 28 | Gerhard Berger | McLaren-Honda | 61 | +5.117 | 2 |
| 3 | 19 | A.Nannini | Benetton-Ford | 61 | +6.240 | 9 |
| 4 | 1 | Alain Prost | Ferrari | 61 | +6.843 | 6 |
| 5 | 20 | Nelson Piquet | Benetton-Ford | 61 | +53.112 | 8 |
| 6 | 4 | Jean Alesi | Tyrrell-Ford | 60 | +1 Lap | 7 |
| 7 | 11 | Derek Warwick | Lotus-Lamborghini | 60 | +1 Lap | 10 |
| 8 | 12 | Martin Donnelly | Lotus-Lamborghini | 60 | +1 Lap | 11 |
| 9 | 26 | Philippe Alliot | Ligier-Ford | 60 | +1 Lap | 16 |
| 10 | 25 | Nicola Larini | Ligier-Ford | 59 | +2 Laps | 20 |
| 11 | 24 | Paolo Barilla | Minardi-Ford | 59 | +2 Laps | 26 |
| 12 | 36 | J J Lehto | Onyx-Ford | 59 | +2 Laps | 25 |
| 13 | 29 | Eric Bernard | Lola-Lamborghini | 56 | Clutch | 13 |
| Ret | 14 | O.Grouillard | Osella-Ford | 52 | Wheel | 32 |
| Ret | 2 | Nigel Mansell | Ferrari | 38 | Engine | 5 |
| Ret | 35 | Gregor Foitek | Onyx-Ford | 35 | Engine | 23 |
| Ret | 8 | Stefano Modena | Brabham-Judd | 31 | Brakes | 14 |
| Ret | 22 | A.de Cesaris | Dallara-Ford | 29 | Wheel | 17 |
| Ret | 15 | M.Gugelmin | Leyton House-Judd | 24 | Electrical | 12 |
| Ret | 5 | Thierry Boutsen | Williams-Renault | 17 | Engine | 4 |
| Ret | 30 | Aguri Suzuki | Lola-Lamborghini | 17 | Clutch | 15 |
| Ret | 27 | Ayrton Senna | McLaren-Honda | 3 | Wheel | 1 |
| Ret | 21 | Emanuele Pirro | Dallara-Ford | 2 | Spun off | 21 |
| Ret | 16 | Ivan Capelli | Leyton House-Judd | 0 | Collision | 18 |
| Ret | 3 | Satoru Nakajima | Tyrrell-Ford | 0 | Collision | 19 |
| Ret | 33 | Roberto Moreno | EuroBrun-Judd | 0 | Throttle | 24 |
| DNS | 23 | Pierluigi Martini | Minardi-Ford | 0 | Accident | |
| DNQ | 10 | Alex Caffi | Arrows-Ford | | | |
| DNQ | 9 | Michele Alboreto | Arrows-Ford | | | |
| DNQ | 7 | David Brabham | Brabham-Judd | | | |
| DNPQ | 31 | Bertrand Gachot | Coloni-Subaru | | | |
| DNPQ | 34 | Claudio Langes | EuroBrun-Judd | | | |
| DNPQ | 39 | Bruno Giacomelli | Life | | | |
| DNPQ | 17 | G.Tarquini | AGS-Ford | | | |

Winning speed: 126.061mph
Lap leaders: Senna 1-3; Boutsen 4-17; Berger 18-50; Patrese 51-61
Pole position: Senna, 1m 23.220s, 135.474mph
Fastest lap: Nannini, 1m 27.156s, 129.356mph

### MONACO GRAND PRIX: MONTE CARLO *27 May Round: 4 Race: 488 78 x 3.326 miles*

| POS. | NO. | DRIVER | CAR/ENGINE | LAPS | TIME/RETIRED | GRID |
|---|---|---|---|---|---|---|
| 1 | 27 | Ayrton Senna | McLaren-Honda | 78 | 1:52'46.982 | 1 |
| 2 | 4 | Jean Alesi | Tyrrell-Ford | 78 | +1.087 | 3 |
| 3 | 28 | Gerhard Berger | McLaren-Honda | 78 | +2.073 | 5 |
| 4 | 5 | Thierry Boutsen | Williams-Renault | 77 | +1 Lap | 6 |
| 5 | 10 | Alex Caffi | Arrows-Ford | 76 | +2 Laps | 22 |
| 6 | 29 | Eric Bernard | Lola-Lamborghini | 76 | +2 Laps | 24 |
| 7 | 35 | Gregor Foitek | Onyx-Ford | 72 | Collisio | 20 |
| Ret | 11 | Derek Warwick | Lotus-Lamborghini | 66 | Spun off | 13 |
| Ret | 2 | Nigel Mansell | Ferrari | 63 | Battery | 7 |
| Ret | 24 | Paolo Barilla | Minardi-Ford | 52 | Gearbox | 19 |
| Ret | 36 | J J Lehto | Onyx-Ford | 52 | Gearbox | 26 |
| Ret | 26 | Philippe Alliot | Ligier-Ford | 47 | Gearbox | 18 |
| Ret | 6 | Riccardo Patrese | Williams-Renault | 41 | Distributor | 4 |
| Ret | 22 | A.de Cesaris | Dallara-Ford | 38 | Engine | 12 |
| Ret | 3 | Satoru Nakajima | Tyrrell-Ford | 36 | Spun off | 21 |
| Ret | 1 | Alain Prost | Ferrari | 30 | Battery | 2 |
| Ret | 19 | A.Nannini | Benetton-Ford | 20 | Gearbox | 16 |
| Ret | 7 | David Brabham | Brabham-Judd | 16 | Transmission | 25 |
| Ret | 16 | Ivan Capelli | Leyton House-Judd | 13 | Brakes | 23 |
| Ret | 25 | Nicola Larini | Ligier-Ford | 12 | Differential | 17 |
| Ret | 30 | Aguri Suzuki | Lola-Lamborghini | 11 | Steering | 15 |
| Ret | 23 | P.Martini | Minardi-Ford | 7 | Electrical | 8 |
| Ret | 12 | Martin Donnelly | Lotus-Lamborghini | 6 | Gearbox | 11 |
| Ret | 8 | Stefano Modena | Brabham-Judd | 3 | Transmission | 14 |
| Ret | 21 | Emanuele Pirro | Dallara-Ford | 0 | Engine | 9 |
| DSQ | 20 | Nelson Piquet | Benetton-Ford | 0 | Disqualified | 10 |
| DNQ | 9 | Michele Alboreto | Arrows-Ford | | | |
| DNQ | 14 | O.Grouillard | Osella-Ford | | | |
| DNQ | 15 | M.Gugelmin | Leyton House-Judd | | | |
| DNQ | 33 | Roberto Moreno | EuroBrun-Judd | | | |
| DNPQ | 17 | G.Tarquini | AGS-Ford | | | |
| DNPQ | 18 | Yannick Dalmas | AGS-Ford | | | |
| DNPQ | 34 | Claudio Langes | EuroBrun-Judd | | | |
| DNPQ | 31 | Bertrand Gachot | Coloni-Subaru | | | |
| DNPQ | 39 | Bruno Giacomelli | Life | | | |

Winning speed: 85.810mph Lap leaders: Senna 1-78
Pole position: Senna, 1m 21.314s, 91.553mph
Fastest lap: Senna, 1m 24.468s, 88.134mph
Race stpped after first lap accident and restared for original distance.

## CANADIAN GRAND PRIX: MONTRÉAL *10 June Round: 5 Race: 489 70 X 2.728 miles*

| POS. | NO. | DRIVER | CAR/ENGINE | LAPS | TIME/RETIRED | GRID |
|---|---|---|---|---|---|---|
| 1 | 27 | Ayrton Senna | McLaren-Honda | 70 | 1:42'56.400 | 1 |
| 2 | 20 | Nelson Piquet | Benetton-Ford | 70 | +10.497 | 5 |
| 3 | 2 | Nigel Mansell | Ferrari | 70 | +13.385 | 7 |
| 4 | 28 | Gerhard Berger | McLaren-Honda | 70 | +14.854 | 2 |
| 5 | 1 | Alain Prost | Ferrari | 70 | +15.820 | 3 |
| 6 | 11 | Derek Warwick | Lotus-Lamborghini | 68 | +2 Laps | 11 |
| 7 | 8 | Stefano Modena | Brabham-Judd | 68 | +2 Laps | 10 |
| 8 | 10 | Alex Caffi | Arrows-Ford | 68 | +2 Laps | 26 |
| 9 | 29 | Eric Bernard | Lola-Lamborghini | 67 | +3 Laps | 23 |
| 10 | 16 | Ivan Capelli | Leyton House-Judd | 67 | +3 Laps | 24 |
| 11 | 3 | Satoru Nakajima | Tyrrell-Ford | 67 | +3 Laps | 13 |
| 12 | 30 | Aguri Suzuki | Lola-Lamborghini | 66 | +4 Laps | 18 |
| 13 | 14 | O.Grouillard | Osella-Ford | 65 | +5 Laps | 15 |
| Ret | 12 | Martin Donnelly | Lotus-Lamborghini | 57 | Engine | 12 |
| Ret | 35 | Gregor Foitek | Onyx-Ford | 53 | Engine | 21 |
| Ret | 22 | A.de Cesaris | Dallara-Ford | 50 | Gearbox | 25 |
| Ret | 36 | J J Lehto | Onyx-Ford | 46 | Engine | 22 |
| Ret | 6 | Riccardo Patrese | Williams-Renault | 44 | Brakes | 9 |
| Ret | 26 | Philippe Alliot | Ligier-Ford | 34 | Engine | 17 |
| Ret | 4 | Jean Alesi | Tyrrell-Ford | 26 | Spun off | 8 |
| Ret | 19 | A.Nannini | Benetton-Ford | 21 | Spun off | 4 |
| Ret | 5 | Thierry Boutsen | Williams-Renault | 19 | Collision | 6 |
| Ret | 25 | Nicola Larini | Ligier-Ford | 18 | Collision | 20 |
| Ret | 21 | Emanuele Pirro | Dallara-Ford | 11 | Collision | 19 |
| Ret | 9 | Michele Alboreto | Arrows-Ford | 11 | Collision | 14 |
| Ret | 23 | P.Martini | Minardi-Ford | 0 | Spun off | 16 |
| DNQ | 33 | Roberto Moreno | EuroBrun-Judd | | | |
| DNQ | 15 | M.Gugelmin | Leyton House-Judd | | | |
| DNQ | 24 | Paolo Barilla | Minardi-Ford | | | |
| DNQ | 7 | David Brabham | Brabham-Judd | | | |
| DNPQ | 17 | G.Tarquini | AGS-Ford | | | |
| DNPQ | 18 | Yannick Dalmas | AGS-Ford | | | |
| DNPQ | 31 | Bertrand Gachot | Coloni-Subaru | | | |
| DNPQ | 34 | Claudio Langes | EuroBrun-Judd | | | |
| DNPQ | 39 | Bruno Giacomelli | Life | | | |

Winning speed: 111.296mph Lap leaders: Senna 1-11; Nannini 12-14; Berger 15-70
Pole position: Senna, 1m 20.339s, 122.143mph
Fastest lap: Berger, 1m 22.077s, 119.646mph
Berger finished first but was penalised one minute for a jump start.

## MEXICAN GRAND PRIX: MEXICO CITY *24 June Round: 6 Race: 490 69 x 2.747 miles*

| POS. | NO. | DRIVER | CAR/ENGINE | LAPS | TIME/RETIRED | GRID |
|---|---|---|---|---|---|---|
| 1 | 1 | Alain Prost | Ferrari | 69 | 1:32'35.783 | 13 |
| 2 | 2 | Nigel Mansell | Ferrari | 69 | +25.351 | 4 |
| 3 | 28 | Gerhard Berger | McLaren-Honda | 69 | +25.530 | 1 |
| 4 | 19 | A.Nannini | Benetton-Ford | 69 | +41.099 | 14 |
| 5 | 5 | Thierry Boutsen | Williams-Renault | 69 | +46.669 | 5 |
| 6 | 20 | Nelson Piquet | Benetton-Ford | 69 | +46.943 | 8 |
| 7 | 4 | Jean Alesi | Tyrrell-Ford | 69 | +49.077 | 6 |
| 8 | 12 | Martin Donnelly | Lotus-Lamborghini | 69 | +1'06.142 | 12 |
| 9 | 6 | Riccardo Patrese | Williams-Renault | 69 | +1'09.918 | 2 |
| 10 | 11 | Derek Warwick | Lotus-Lamborghini | 68 | +1 Lap | 11 |
| 11 | 8 | Stefano Modena | Brabham-Judd | 68 | +1 Lap | 10 |
| 12 | 23 | P.Martini | Minardi-Ford | 68 | +1 Lap | 7 |
| 13 | 22 | A.de Cesaris | Dallara-Ford | 68 | +1 Lap | 15 |
| 14 | 24 | Paolo Barilla | Minardi-Ford | 67 | +2 Laps | 16 |
| 15 | 35 | Gregor Foitek | Onyx-Ford | 67 | +2 Laps | 23 |
| 16 | 25 | Nicola Larini | Ligier-Ford | 67 | +2 Laps | 24 |
| 17 | 9 | Michele Alboreto | Arrows-Ford | 66 | +3 Laps | 17 |
| 18 | 26 | Philippe Alliot | Ligier-Ford | 66 | +3 Laps | 22 |
| 19 | 14 | O.Grouillard | Osella-Ford | 65 | +4 Laps | 20 |
| 20 | 27 | Ayrton Senna | McLaren-Honda | 63 | Tyre | 3 |
| Ret | 36 | J J Lehto | Onyx-Ford | 26 | Engine | 26 |
| Ret | 29 | Eric Bernard | Lola-Lamborghini | 12 | Brakes | 25 |
| Ret | 30 | Aguri Suzuki | Lola-Lamborghini | 11 | Collision | 19 |
| Ret | 3 | Satoru Nakajima | Tyrrell-Ford | 11 | Collision | 9 |
| Ret | 7 | David Brabham | Brabham-Judd | 11 | Electrical | 21 |
| Ret | 21 | Emanuele Pirro | Dallara-Ford | 10 | Engine | 18 |
| DSQ | 33 | Roberto Moreno | EuroBrun-Judd | | | |
| DNQ | 16 | Ivan Capelli | Leyton House-Judd | | | |
| DNQ | 15 | M.Gugelmin | Leyton House-Judd | | | |
| DNQ | 10 | Alex Caffi | Arrows-Ford | | | |
| DNPQ | 18 | Yannick Dalmas | AGS-Ford | | | |
| DNPQ | 17 | G.Tarquini | AGS-Ford | | | |
| DNPQ | 31 | Bertrand Gachot | Coloni-Subaru | | | |
| DNPQ | 34 | Claudio Langes | EuroBrun-Judd | | | |
| DNPQ | 39 | Bruno Giacomelli | Life | | | |

Winning speed: 122.823mph Lap leaders: Senna 1-60; Prost 61-69
Pole position: Berger, 1m 17.227s, 128.057mph
Fastest lap: Prost, 1m 17.958s, 126.857mph

## FRENCH GRAND PRIX: PAUL RICARD *8 July Round: 7 Race: 491 80 x 2.369 miles*

| POS. | NO. | DRIVER | CAR/ENGINE | LAPS | TIME/RETIRED | GRID |
|---|---|---|---|---|---|---|
| 1 | 1 | Alain Prost | Ferrari | 80 | 1:33'29.606 | 4 |
| 2 | 16 | Ivan Capelli | Leyton House-Judd | 80 | +8.626 | 7 |
| 3 | 27 | Ayrton Senna | McLaren-Honda | 80 | +11.606 | 3 |
| 4 | 20 | Nelson Piquet | Benetton-Ford | 80 | +41.207 | 9 |
| 5 | 28 | Gerhard Berger | McLaren-Honda | 80 | +42.219 | 2 |
| 6 | 6 | Riccardo Patrese | Williams-Renault | 80 | +1'09.351 | 6 |
| 7 | 30 | Aguri Suzuki | Lola-Lamborghini | 79 | +1 Lap | 14 |
| 8 | 29 | Eric Bernard | Lola-Lamborghini | 79 | +1 Lap | 11 |
| 9 | 26 | Philippe Alliot | Ligier-Ford | 79 | +1 Lap | 12 |
| 10 | 9 | Michele Alboreto | Arrows-Ford | 79 | +1 Lap | 18 |
| 11 | 11 | Derek Warwick | Lotus-Lamborghini | 79 | +1 Lap | 16 |
| 12 | 12 | Martin Donnelly | Lotus-Lamborghini | 79 | +1 Lap | 17 |
| 13 | 8 | Stefano Modena | Brabham-Judd | 78 | +2 Laps | 20 |
| 14 | 25 | Nicola Larini | Ligier-Ford | 78 | +2 Laps | 19 |
| 15 | 7 | David Brabham | Brabham-Judd | 77 | +3 Laps | 25 |
| 16 | 19 | A.Nannini | Benetton-Ford | 75 | Electrical | 5 |
| 17 | 18 | Yannick Dalmas | AGS-Ford | 75 | 5 Laps | 26 |
| 18 | 2 | Nigel Mansell | Ferrari | 72 | Engine | 1 |
| DSQ | 22 | A.de Cesaris | Dallara-Ford | 78 | Disqualified | 21 |
| Ret | 3 | Satoru Nakajima | Tyrrell-Ford | 63 | Gearbox | 15 |
| Ret | 15 | M.Gugelmin | Leyton House-Judd | 58 | Engine | 10 |
| Ret | 23 | P.Martini | Minardi-Ford | 40 | Electrical | 23 |
| Ret | 4 | Jean Alesi | Tyrrell-Ford | 23 | Differential | 13 |
| Ret | 10 | Alex Caffi | Arrows-Ford | 22 | Suspension | 22 |
| Ret | 5 | Thierry Boutsen | Williams-Renault | 8 | Engine | 8 |
| Ret | 21 | Emanuele Pirro | Dallara/Ford | 7 | Brakes | 24 |
| DNQ | 24 | Paolo Barilla | Minardi-Ford | | | |
| DNQ | 17 | G.Tarquini | AGS-Ford | | | |
| DNQ | 35 | Gregor Foitek | Onyx-Ford | | | |
| DNQ | 36 | J J Lehto | Onyx-Ford | | | |
| DNPQ | 14 | O.Grouillard | Osella-Ford | | | |
| DNPQ | 33 | Roberto Moreno | EuroBrun-Judd | | | |
| DNPQ | 34 | Claudio Langes | EuroBrun-Judd | | | |
| DNPQ | 31 | Bertrand Gachot | Coloni-Subaru | | | |
| DNPQ | 39 | Bruno Giacomelli | Life | | | |

Winning speed: 121.640mph Lap leaders: Berger 1-27; Senna 28-29; Mansell 30-31; Patrese 32; Capelli 33-77; Prost 78-80
Pole position: Mansell, 1m 4.402s, 132.441mph
Fastest lap: Mansell, 1m 8.012s, 125.411mph

## BRITISH GRAND PRIX: SILVERSTONE *15 July Round:8 Race: 492 64 x 2.970 miles*

| POS. | NO. | DRIVER | CAR/ENGINE | LAPS | TIME/RETIRED | GRID |
|---|---|---|---|---|---|---|
| 1 | 1 | Alain Prost | Ferrari | 64 | 1:18'30.999 | 5 |
| 2 | 5 | Thierry Boutsen | Williams-Renault | 64 | +39.092 | 4 |
| 3 | 27 | Ayrton Senna | McLaren-Honda | 64 | +43.088 | 2 |
| 4 | 29 | Eric Bernard | Lola-Lamborghini | 64 | +1'15.302 | 8 |
| 5 | 20 | Nelson Piquet | Benetton-Ford | 64 | +1'24.003 | 11 |
| 6 | 30 | Aguri Suzuki | Lola-Lamborghini | 63 | +1 Lap | 9 |
| 7 | 10 | Alex Caffi | Arrows-Ford | 63 | +1 Lap | 17 |
| 8 | 4 | Jean Alesi | Tyrrell-Ford | 63 | +1 Lap | 6 |
| 9 | 8 | Stefano Modena | Brabham-Judd | 62 | +2 Laps | 20 |
| 10 | 25 | Nicola Larini | Ligier-Ford | 62 | +2 Laps | 21 |
| 11 | 21 | Emanuele Pirro | Dallara-Ford | 62 | +2 Laps | 19 |
| 12 | 24 | Paolo Barilla | Minardi-Ford | 62 | +2 Laps | 24 |
| 13 | 26 | Philippe Alliot | Ligier-Ford | 61 | +3 Laps | 22 |
| 14 | 28 | Gerhard Berger | McLaren-Honda | 60 | Throttle | 3 |
| Ret | 2 | Nigel Mansell | Ferrari | 55 | Gearbox | 1 |
| Ret | 16 | Ivan Capelli | Leyton House-Judd | 48 | Fuel leak | 10 |
| Ret | 12 | Martin Donnelly | Lotus-Lamborghini | 48 | Engine | 14 |
| Ret | 11 | Derek Warwick | Lotus-Lamborghini | 46 | Engine | 16 |
| Ret | 17 | G.Tarquini | AGS-Ford | 41 | Engine | 26 |
| Ret | 9 | Michele Alboreto | Arrows-Ford | 37 | Engine | 25 |
| Ret | 6 | Riccardo Patrese | Williams-Renault | 26 | Chassis | 7 |
| Ret | 3 | Satoru Nakajima | Tyrrell-Ford | 20 | Electrical | 12 |
| Ret | 19 | A.Nannini | Benetton-Ford | 15 | Collision | 13 |
| Ret | 22 | A.de Cesaris | Dallara-Ford | 12 | Fuel system | 23 |
| Ret | 23 | P.Martini | Minardi-Ford | 3 | Alternator | 18 |
| DNS | 15 | M.Gugelmin | Leyton House-Judd | | Fuel pump | 8 |
| DNQ | 14 | O.Grouillard | Osella-Ford | | | |
| DNQ | 7 | David Brabham | Brabham-Judd | | | |
| DNQ | 36 | J J Lehto | Onyx-Ford | | | |
| DNQ | 35 | Gregor Foitek | Onyx-Ford | | | |
| DNPQ | 33 | Roberto Moreno | EuroBrun-Judd | | | |
| DNPQ | 18 | Yannick Dalmas | AGS-Ford | | | |
| DNPQ | 34 | Claudio Langes | EuroBrun-Judd | | | |
| DNPQ | 31 | Bertrand Gachot | Coloni-Subaru | | | |
| DNPQ | 39 | Bruno Giacomelli | Life | | | |

Winning speed: 145.253mph
Lap leaders: Senna 1-11; Mansell 12-21, 28-42; Berger 22-27; Prost 43-64
Pole position: Mansell, 1m 7.428s, 158.569mph
Fastest lap: Mansell, 1m 11.291s, 149.977mph

## GERMAN GRAND PRIX: HOCKENHEIM *29 July Round: 9 Race: 493 45 x 4.227 miles*

| POS. | NO. | DRIVER | CAR/ENGINE | LAPS | TIME/RETIRED | GRID |
|---|---|---|---|---|---|---|
| 1 | 27 | Ayrton Senna | McLaren-Honda | 45 | 1:20'47.164 | 1 |
| 2 | 19 | A.Nannini | Benetton-Ford | 45 | +6.520 | 9 |
| 3 | 28 | Gerhard Berger | McLaren-Honda | 45 | +8.553 | 2 |
| 4 | 1 | Alain Prost | Ferrari | 45 | +45.270 | 3 |
| 5 | 6 | Riccardo Patrese | Williams-Renault | 45 | +48.028 | 5 |
| 6 | 5 | Thierry Boutsen | Williams-Renault | 45 | +1'21.491 | 6 |
| 7 | 16 | Ivan Capelli | Leyton House-Judd | 44 | +1 Lap | 10 |
| 8 | 11 | Derek Warwick | Lotus-Lamborghini | 44 | +1 Lap | 16 |
| 9 | 10 | Alex Caffi | Arrows-Ford | 44 | +1 Lap | 18 |
| 10 | 25 | Nicola Larini | Ligier/Ford | 43 | +2 Laps | 22 |
| 11 | 4 | Jean Alesi | Tyrrell-Ford | 40 | Transmission | 8 |
| NC | 36 | J J Lehto | Onyx-Ford | 39 | Not classified | 25 |
| Ret | 29 | Eric Bernard | Lola-Lamborghini | 35 | Fuel pump | 12 |
| Ret | 30 | Aguri Suzuki | Lola-Lamborghini | 33 | Clutch | 11 |
| Ret | 3 | Satoru Nakajima | Tyrrell-Ford | 24 | Engine | 13 |
| Ret | 20 | Nelson Piquet | Benetton-Ford | 23 | Engine | 7 |
| Ret | 23 | P.Martini | Minardi-Ford | 20 | Engine | 15 |
| Ret | 35 | Gregor Foitek | Onyx-Ford | 19 | Spun off | 26 |
| Ret | 2 | Nigel Mansell | Ferrari | 15 | Broken wing | 4 |
| Ret | 15 | M.Gugelmin | Leyton House-Judd | 12 | Engine | 14 |
| Ret | 7 | David Brabham | Brabham-Judd | 12 | Engine | 21 |
| Ret | 9 | Michele Alboreto | Arrows-Ford | 10 | Engine | 19 |
| Ret | 12 | Martin Donnelly | Lotus-Lamborghini | 1 | Clutch | 20 |
| Ret | 8 | Stefano Modena | Brabham-Judd | 0 | Clutch | 17 |
| Ret | 21 | Emanuele Pirro | Dallara-Ford | 0 | Collision | 23 |
| DSQ | 26 | Philippe Alliot | Ligier-Ford | 0 | Disqualified | 24 |
| DNQ | 14 | O.Grouillard | Osella-Ford | | | |
| DNQ | 24 | Paolo Barilla | Minardi-Ford | | | |
| DNQ | 18 | Yannick Dalmas | AGS-Ford | | | |
| DNQ | 22 | A.de Cesaris | Dallara-Ford | | | |
| DNPQ | 17 | G.Tarquini | AGS-Ford | | | |
| DNPQ | 33 | Roberto Moreno | EuroBrun-Judd | | | |
| DNPQ | 31 | Bertrand Gachot | Coloni-Ford | | | |
| DNPQ | 34 | Claudio Langes | EuroBrun-Judd | | | |
| DNPQ | 39 | Bruno Giacomelli | Life | | | |

Winning speed: 141.259mph Lap leaders: Senna 1-17, 34-45; Nannini 18-33
Pole position: Senna, 40.198s, 151.856mph
Fastest lap: Boutsen, 1m 45.602s, 144.085mph

## HUNGARIAN GRAND PRIX: HUNGARORING *12 August Round: 10 Race: 494 77 x 2.466 miles*

| POS. | NO. | DRIVER | CAR/ENGINE | LAPS | TIME/RETIRED | GRID |
|---|---|---|---|---|---|---|
| 1 | 5 | Thierry Boutsen | Williams-Renault | 77 | 1:49'30.597 | 1 |
| 2 | 27 | Ayrton Senna | McLaren-Honda | 77 | +0.288 | 4 |
| 3 | 20 | Nelson Piquet | Benetton-Ford | 77 | +27.893 | 9 |
| 4 | 6 | Riccardo Patrese | Williams-Renault | 77 | +31.833 | 2 |
| 5 | 11 | Derek Warwick | Lotus-Lamborghini | 77 | +1'14.244 | 11 |
| 6 | 29 | Eric Bernard | Lola-Lamborghini | 77 | +1'24.308 | 12 |
| 7 | 12 | Martin Donnelly | Lotus-Lamborghini | 76 | +1 Lap | 18 |
| 8 | 15 | M.Gugelmin | Leyton House-Judd | 76 | +1 Lap | 17 |
| 9 | 10 | Alex Caffi | Arrows-Ford | 76 | +1 Lap | 26 |
| 10 | 21 | Emanuele Pirro | Dallara-Ford | 76 | +1 Lap | 13 |
| 11 | 25 | Nicola Larini | Ligier-Ford | 76 | +1 Lap | 25 |
| 12 | 9 | Michele Alboreto | Arrows-Ford | 75 | +2 Laps | 22 |
| 13 | 17 | G.Tarquini | AGS-Ford | 74 | +3 Laps | 24 |
| 14 | 26 | Philippe Alliot | Ligier-Ford | 74 | +3 Laps | 21 |
| 15 | 24 | Paolo Barilla | Minardi-Ford | 74 | +3 Laps | 23 |
| 16 | 28 | Gerhard Berger | McLaren-Honda | 72 | Collision | 3 |
| 17 | 2 | Nigel Mansell | Ferrari | 71 | Collision | 5 |
| Ret | 19 | A.Nannini | Benetton-Ford | 64 | Collision | 7 |
| Ret | 16 | Ivan Capelli | Leyton House-Judd | 56 | Gearbox | 16 |
| Ret | 30 | Aguri Suzuki | Lola-Lamborghini | 37 | Engine | 19 |
| Ret | 1 | Alain Prost | Ferrari | 36 | Gearbox | 8 |
| Ret | 4 | Jean Alesi | Tyrrell-Ford | 36 | Collision | 6 |
| Ret | 8 | Stefano Modena | Brabham-Judd | 35 | Engine | 20 |
| Ret | 23 | P.Martini | Minardi-Ford | 35 | Collision | 14 |
| Ret | 22 | A.de Cesaris | Dallara-Ford | 22 | Engine | 10 |
| Ret | 3 | Satoru Nakajima | Tyrrell-Ford | 9 | Brakes | 15 |
| DNQ | 18 | Yannick Dalmas | AGS-Ford | | | |
| DNQ | 7 | David Brabham | Brabham-Judd | | | |
| DNQ | 36 | J J Lehto | Onyx-Ford | | | |
| DNQ | 35 | Gregor Foitek | Onyx-Ford | | | |
| DNPQ | 14 | O.Grouillard | Osella-Ford | | | |
| DNPQ | 31 | Bertrand Gachot | Coloni-Ford | | | |
| DNPQ | 33 | Roberto Moreno | EuroBrun-Judd | | | |
| DNPQ | 34 | Claudio Langes | EuroBrun-Judd | | | |
| DNPQ | 39 | Bruno Giacomelli | Life | | | |

Winning speed: 104.019mph Lap leaders: Boutsen 1-77
Pole position: Boutsen, 1m 17.919s, 113.915mph
Fastest lap: Patrese, 1m 22.058s, 108.169mph

## BELGIAN GRAND PRIX: SPA-FRANCORCHAMPS *26 August Round: 11 Race: 495 44 x 4.312 miles*

| POS. | NO. | DRIVER | CAR/ENGINE | LAPS | TIME/RETIRED | GRID |
|---|---|---|---|---|---|---|
| 1 | 27 | Ayrton Senna | McLaren-Honda | 44 | 1:26'31.997 | 1 |
| 2 | 1 | Alain Prost | Ferrari | 44 | +3.550 | 3 |
| 3 | 28 | Gerhard Berger | McLaren-Honda | 44 | +28.462 | 2 |
| 4 | 19 | A.Nannini | Benetton-Ford | 44 | +49.337 | 6 |
| 5 | 20 | Nelson Piquet | Benetton-Ford | 44 | +1'29.650 | 8 |
| 6 | 15 | M.Gugelmin | Leyton House-Judd | 44 | +1'48.851 | 14 |
| 7 | 16 | Ivan Capelli | Leyton House-Judd | 43 | +1 Lap | 12 |
| 8 | 4 | Jean Alesi | Tyrrell-Ford | 43 | +1 Lap | 9 |
| 9 | 29 | Eric Bernard | Lola-Lamborghini | 43 | +1 Lap | 15 |
| 10 | 10 | Alex Caffi | Arrows-Ford | 43 | +1 Lap | 19 |
| 11 | 11 | Derek Warwick | Lotus-Lamborghini | 43 | +1 Lap | 18 |
| 12 | 12 | Martin Donnelly | Lotus-Lamborghini | 43 | +1 Lap | 22 |
| 13 | 9 | Michele Alboreto | Arrows-Ford | 43 | +1 Lap | 26 |
| 14 | 25 | Nicola Larini | Ligier-Ford | 42 | +2 Laps | 21 |
| 15 | 23 | P.Martini | Minardi-Ford | 42 | +2 Laps | 16 |
| 16 | 14 | O.Grouillard | Osella-Ford | 42 | +2 Laps | 23 |
| 17 | 8 | Stefano Modena | Brabham-Judd | 39 | Engine | 13 |
| Ret | 7 | David Brabham | Brabham-Judd | 36 | Electrical | 24 |
| Ret | 22 | A.de Cesaris | Dallara-Ford | 27 | Engine | 20 |
| Ret | 5 | Thierry Boutsen | Williams-Renault | 21 | Transmission | 4 |
| Ret | 2 | Nigel Mansell | Ferrari | 19 | Handling | 5 |
| Ret | 6 | Riccardo Patrese | Williams-Renault | 18 | Gearbox | 7 |
| Ret | 21 | Emanuele Pirro | Dallara-Ford | 5 | Water leak | 17 |
| Ret | 3 | Satoru Nakajima | Tyrrell-Ford | 4 | Engine | 10 |
| Ret | 30 | Aguri Suzuki | Lola-Lamborghini | 0 | Accident | 11 |
| Ret | 24 | Paolo Barilla | Minardi-Ford | 0 | Accident | 25 |
| DNQ | 26 | Philippe Alliot | Ligier-Ford | | | |
| DNQ | 17 | G.Tarquini | AGS-Ford | | | |
| DNQ | 18 | Yannick Dalmas | AGS-Ford | | | |
| DNQ | 31 | Bertrand Gachot | Coloni-Ford | | | |
| DNPQ | 33 | Roberto Moreno | EuroBrun-Judd | | | |
| DNPQ | 34 | Claudio Langes | EuroBrun-Judd | | | |
| DNPQ | 39 | Bruno Giacomelli | Life | | | |

Winning speed: 131.562mph Lap leaders: Senna 1-44
Pole position: Senna, 1m 50.365s, 140.664mph Fastest Speed: Prost, 1m 55.087s, 134.892mph
Race stopped twice because of the Barilla and Suzuki accidents, but run for total original distance.

## ITALIAN GRAND PRIX: MONZA *9 September Round: 12 Race: 496 53 x 3.604 miles*

| POS. | NO. | DRIVER | CAR/ENGINE | LAPS | TIME/RETIRED | GRID |
|---|---|---|---|---|---|---|
| 1 | 27 | Ayrton Senna | McLaren-Honda | 53 | 1:17'57.878 | 1 |
| 2 | 1 | Alain Prost | Ferrari | 53 | +6.054 | 2 |
| 3 | 28 | Gerhard Berger | McLaren-Honda | 53 | +7.404 | 3 |
| 4 | 2 | Nigel Mansell | Ferrari | 53 | +56.219 | 4 |
| 5 | 6 | Riccardo Patrese | Williams-Renault | 53 | +1'25.274 | 7 |
| 6 | 3 | Satoru Nakajima | Tyrrell-Ford | 52 | +1 Lap | 14 |
| 7 | 20 | Nelson Piquet | Benetton-Ford | 52 | +1 Lap | 9 |
| 8 | 19 | A.Nannini | Benetton-Ford | 52 | +1 Lap | 8 |
| 9 | 10 | Alex Caffi | Arrows-Ford | 51 | +2 Laps | 21 |
| 10 | 22 | A.de Cesaris | Dallara-Ford | 51 | +2 Laps | 25 |
| 11 | 25 | Nicola Larini | Ligier-Ford | 51 | +2 Laps | 26 |
| 12 | 9 | Michele Alboreto | Arrows-Ford | 50 | Spun off | 22 |
| 13 | 26 | Philippe Alliot | Ligier-Ford | 50 | +3 Laps | 20 |
| Ret | 18 | Yannick Dalmas | AGS-Ford | 45 | Not classified | 24 |
| Ret | 16 | Ivan Capelli | Leyton House-Judd | 36 | Engine | 16 |
| Ret | 30 | Aguri Suzuki | Lola-Lamborghini | 36 | Electrical | 18 |
| Ret | 14 | O.Grouillard | Osella-Ford | 27 | Wheel bearing | 23 |
| Ret | 15 | M.Gugelmin | Leyton House-Judd | 24 | Engine | 10 |
| Ret | 8 | Stefano Modena | Brabham-Judd | 21 | Engine | 17 |
| Ret | 5 | Thierry Boutsen | Williams-Renault | 18 | Suspension | 6 |
| Ret | 11 | Derek Warwick | Lotus-Lamborghini | 15 | Clutch | 12 |
| Ret | 21 | Emanuele Pirro | Dallara-Ford | 14 | Spun off | 19 |
| Ret | 12 | Martin Donnelly | Lotus-Lamborghini | 13 | Engine | 11 |
| Ret | 29 | Eric Bernard | Lola-Lamborghini | 10 | Clutch | 13 |
| Ret | 23 | P.Martini | Minardi-Ford | 7 | Suspension | 15 |
| Ret | 4 | Jean Alesi | Tyrrell-Ford | 4 | Spun off | 5 |
| DNQ | 17 | G.Tarquini | AGS-Ford | | | |
| DNQ | 24 | Paolo Barilla | Minardi-Ford | | | |
| DNQ | 7 | David Brabham | Brabham-Judd | | | |
| DNQ | 31 | Bertrand Gachot | Coloni-Ford | | | |
| DNPQ | 33 | Roberto Moreno | EuroBrun-Judd | | | |
| DNPQ | 34 | Claudio Langes | EuroBrun-Judd | | | |
| DNPQ | 39 | Bruno Giacomelli | Life | | | |

Winning speed: 146.997mph Lap leaders: Senna 1-53
Pole position: Senna, 1m 22.533s, 157.201mph Fastest lap: Senna, 1m 26.254s, 150.419mph
Race stopped after first lap accident and restarted for total original distance.

## PURTUGUESE GRAND PRIX: ESTORIL *23 September Round: 13 Race: 497 61 x 2.703 miles*

| POS. | NO. | DRIVER | CAR/ENGINE | LAPS | TIME/RETIRED | GRID |
|---|---|---|---|---|---|---|
| 1 | 2 | Nigel Mansell | Ferrari | 61 | 1:22'11.014 | 1 |
| 2 | 27 | Ayrton Senna | McLaren-Honda | 61 | +2.808 | 3 |
| 3 | 1 | Alain Prost | Ferrari | 61 | +4.189 | 2 |
| 4 | 28 | Gerhard Berger | McLaren-Honda | 61 | +5.896 | 4 |
| 5 | 20 | Nelson Piquet | Benetton-Ford | 61 | +57.418 | 6 |
| 6 | 19 | A.Nannini | Benetton-Ford | 61 | +58.249 | 9 |
| 7 | 6 | Riccardo Patrese | Williams-Renault | 60 | +1 Lap | 5 |
| 8 | 4 | Jean Alesi | Tyrrell-Ford | 60 | +1 Lap | 8 |
| 9 | 9 | Michele Alboreto | Arrows-Ford | 60 | +1 Lap | 19 |
| 10 | 25 | Nicola Larini | Ligier-Ford | 59 | +2 Laps | 22 |
| 11 | 23 | P.Martini | Minardi-Ford | 59 | +2 Laps | 16 |
| 12 | 15 | M.Gugelmin | Leyton House-Judd | 59 | +2 Laps | 14 |
| 13 | 10 | Alex Caffi | Arrows-Ford | 58 | Accident | 17 |
| 14 | 30 | Aguri Suzuki | Lola-Lamborghini | 58 | Accident | 11 |
| 15 | 21 | Emanuele Pirro | Dallara-Ford | 58 | +3 Laps | 13 |
| Ret | 26 | Philippe Alliot | Ligier-Ford | 52 | Accident | 20 |
| Ret | 7 | David Brabham | Brabham-Judd | 52 | Gearbox | 25 |
| Ret | 16 | Ivan Capelli | Leyton House-Judd | 51 | Engine | 12 |
| Ret | 5 | Thierry Boutsen | Williams-Renault | 30 | Engine | 7 |
| Ret | 29 | Eric Bernard | Lola-Lamborghini | 24 | Gearbox | 10 |
| Ret | 8 | Stefano Modena | Brabham-Judd | 21 | Gearbox | 23 |
| Ret | 12 | Martin Donnelly | Lotus-Lamborghini | 14 | Alternator | 15 |
| Ret | 11 | Derek Warwick | Lotus-Lamborghini | 5 | Throttle | 21 |
| Ret | 18 | Yannick Dalmas | AGS-Ford | 3 | Halfshaft | 24 |
| Ret | 22 | A.de Cesaris | Dallara-Ford | 0 | Spun off | 18 |
| DNS | 22 | Satoru Nakajima | Tyrrell-Ford | 0 | Accident | |
| DNQ | 14 | O.Grouillard | Osella-Ford | | | |
| DNQ | 24 | Paolo Barilla | Minardi-Ford | | | |
| DNQ | 17 | G.Tarquini | AGS-Ford | | | |
| DNQ | 31 | Bertrand Gachot | Coloni-Ford | | | |
| DNPQ | 33 | Roberto Moreno | EuroBrun-Judd | | | |
| DNPQ | 34 | Claudio Langes | EuroBrun-Judd | | | |
| DNPQ | 39 | Bruno Giacomelli | Life-Judd | | | |

Winning speed: 120.375mph Lap leaders: Senna 1-28, 32-49; Berger 29-31; Mansell 50-61
Pole position: Mansell, 1m 13.557s, 132.288mph
Fastest lap: Patrese, 1m 18.306s, 124.265mph
Scheduled for 71 laps, but stopped early because of the Suzuki-Caffi collision.

## SPANISH GRAND PRIX: JEREZ DE LA FRONTERA *30 September Round: 14 Race: 498 73 x 2.621 miles*

| POS. | NO. | DRIVER | CAR/ENGINE | LAPS | TIME/RETIRED | GRID |
|---|---|---|---|---|---|---|
| 1 | 1 | Alain Prost | Ferrari | 73 | 1:48'01.461 | 2 |
| 2 | 2 | Nigel Mansell | Ferrari | 73 | +22.064 | 3 |
| 3 | 19 | A.Nannini | Benetton-Ford | 73 | +34.874 | 9 |
| 4 | 5 | Thierry Boutsen | Williams-Renault | 73 | +43.296 | 7 |
| 5 | 6 | Riccardo Patrese | Williams-Renault | 73 | +57.530 | 6 |
| 6 | 30 | Aguri Suzuki | Lola-Lamborghini | 73 | +1'03.728 | 15 |
| 7 | 25 | Nicola Larini | Ligier-Ford | 72 | +1 Lap | 20 |
| 8 | 15 | M.Gugelmin | Leyton House-Judd | 72 | +1 Lap | 12 |
| 9 | 18 | Yannick Dalmas | AGS-Ford | 72 | +1 Lap | 23 |
| 10 | 9 | Michele Alboreto | Arrows-Ford | 71 | +2 Laps | 25 |
| Ret | 11 | Derek Warwick | Lotus-Lamborghini | 63 | Gearbox | 10 |
| Ret | 16 | Ivan Capelli | Leyton House-Judd | 59 | Physical | 19 |
| Ret | 28 | Gerhard Berger | McLaren-Honda | 56 | Collision | 5 |
| Ret | 27 | Ayrton Senna | McLaren-Honda | 53 | Radiator | 1 |
| Ret | 20 | Nelson Piquet | Benetton-Ford | 47 | Battery | 8 |
| Ret | 22 | A.de Cesaris | Dallara-Ford | 47 | Engine | 17 |
| Ret | 14 | O.Grouillard | Osella-Ford | 45 | Wheel bearing | 21 |
| Ret | 23 | P.Martini | Minardi-Ford | 41 | Spun off | 11 |
| Ret | 26 | Philippe Alliot | Ligier/Ford | 22 | Spun off | 13 |
| Ret | 29 | Eric Bernard | Lola-Lamborghini | 20 | Gearbox | 18 |
| Ret | 3 | Satoru Nakajima | Tyrrell-Ford | 13 | Spun off | 14 |
| Ret | 17 | G.Tarquini | AGS-Ford | 5 | Engine | 22 |
| Ret | 8 | Stefano Modena | Brabham-Judd | 5 | Collision | 24 |
| Ret | 4 | Jean Alesi | Tyrrell-Ford | 0 | Spun off | 4 |
| Ret | 21 | Emanuele Pirro | Dallara-Ford | 0 | Throttle | 16 |
| DNS | 12 | Martin Donnelly | Lotus-Lamborghini | 0 | Injured | |
| DNQ | 7 | David Brabham | Brabham-Judd | | | |
| DNQ | 24 | Paolo Barilla | Minardi-Ford | | | |
| DNQ | 10 | Bernd Schneider | Arrows-Ford | | | |
| DNQ | 31 | Bertrand Gachot | Coloni-Ford | | | |
| DNPQ | 33 | Roberto Moreno | EuroBrun-Judd | | | |
| DNPQ | 34 | Claudio Langes | EuroBrun-Judd | | | |
| DNPQ | 39 | Bruno Giacomelli | Life-Judd | | | |

Winning speed: 106.270mph Lap leaders: Senna 1-26; Piquet 27-28; Prost 29-73
Pole position: Senna, 1m18,387s, 120.369mph
Fastest lap: Patrese, 1m 24.513s, 111.644mph

## JAPANESE GRAND PRIX SUZUKA *21 October Round: 15 Race: 499 53 x 3.641 miles*

| POS. | NO. | DRIVER | CAR/ENGINE | LAPS | TIME/RETIRED | GRID |
|---|---|---|---|---|---|---|
| 1 | 20 | Nelson Piquet | Benetton-Ford | 53 | 1:34'36.824 | 6 |
| 2 | 19 | Roberto Moreno | Benetton-Ford | 53 | +7.223 | 8 |
| 3 | 30 | Aguri Suzuki | Lola-Lamborghini | 53 | +22.469 | 9 |
| 4 | 6 | Riccardo Patrese | Williams-Renault | 53 | +36.258 | 7 |
| 5 | 5 | Thierry Boutsen | Williams-Renault | 53 | +46.884 | 5 |
| 6 | 3 | Satoru Nakajima | Tyrrell-Ford | 53 | +1'12.350 | 13 |
| 7 | 25 | Nicola Larini | Ligier-Ford | 52 | +1 Lap | 17 |
| 8 | 23 | P.Martini | Minardi-Ford | 52 | +1 Lap | 10 |
| 9 | 10 | Alex Caffi | Arrows-Ford | 52 | +1 Lap | 23 |
| 10 | 26 | Philippe Alliot | Ligier-Ford | 52 | +1 Lap | 20 |
| Ret | 11 | Derek Warwick | Lotus-Lamborghini | 38 | Gearbox | 11 |
| Ret | 12 | Johnny Herbert | Lotus-Lamborghini | 31 | Engine | 14 |
| Ret | 9 | Michele Alboreto | Arrows-Ford | 28 | Engine | 24 |
| Ret | 2 | Nigel Mansell | Ferrari | 26 | Transmission | 3 |
| Ret | 21 | Emanuele Pirro | Dallara-Ford | 24 | Alternator | 18 |
| Ret | 29 | Eric Bernard | Lola-Lamborghini | 24 | Engine | 16 |
| Ret | 24 | G.Morbidelli | Minardi-Ford | 18 | Spun off | 19 |
| Ret | 16 | Ivan Capelli | Leyton House-Judd | 16 | Ignition | 12 |
| Ret | 22 | A.de Cesaris | Dallara-Ford | 13 | Spun off | 25 |
| Ret | 15 | M.Gugelmin | Leyton House-Judd | 5 | Engine | 15 |
| Ret | 7 | David Brabham | Brabham-Judd | 2 | Clutch | 22 |
| Ret | 28 | Gerhard Berger | McLaren-Honda | 1 | Spun off | 4 |
| Ret | 27 | Ayrton Senna | McLaren-Honda | 0 | Collision | 1 |
| Ret | 1 | Alain Prost | Ferrari | 0 | Collision | 2 |
| Ret | 8 | Stefano Modena | Brabham-Judd | 0 | Collision | 21 |
| DNS | 4 | Jean Alesi | Tyrrell-Ford | 0 | Driver unwell | |
| DNQ | 14 | O.Grouillard | Osella-Ford | | | |
| DNQ | 17 | G.Tarquini | AGS-Ford | | | |
| DNQ | 18 | Yannick Dalmas | AGS-Ford | | | |
| DNQ | 31 | Bertrand Gachot | Coloni-Ford | | | |

Winning speed 122.362mph Lap leaders: Berger 1; Mansell 2-26; Piquet 27-53
Pole position: Senna 1m36.996s, 135.121mph
Fastest lap; Patrese, 1m44.233s, 125.740mph

## AUSTRALIAN GRAND PRIX ADELAIDE *4 November Round 16 Race 500 81 x 2.349 miles*

| POS. | NO. | DRIVER | CAR/ENGINE | LAPS | TIME/RETIRED | GRID |
|---|---|---|---|---|---|---|
| 1 | 20 | Nelson Piquet | Benetton-Ford | 81 | 1:49'44.570 | 7 |
| 2 | 2 | Nigel Mansell | Ferrari | 81 | +3.129 | 3 |
| 3 | 1 | Alain Prost | Ferrari | 81 | +37.259 | 4 |
| 4 | 28 | Gerhard Berger | McLaren-Honda | 81 | +46.862 | 2 |
| 5 | 5 | Thierry Boutsen | Williams-Renault | 81 | +1'51.160 | 9 |
| 6 | 6 | Riccardo Patrese | Williams-Renault | 80 | +1 Lap | 6 |
| 7 | 19 | Roberto Moreno | Benetton-Ford | 80 | +1 Lap | 8 |
| 8 | 4 | Jean Alesi | Tyrrell-Ford | 80 | +1 Lap | 5 |
| 9 | 23 | P.Martini | Minardi-Ford | 79 | +2 Laps | 10 |
| 10 | 25 | Nicola Larini | Ligier-Ford | 79 | +2 Laps | 12 |
| 11 | 26 | Philippe Alliot | Ligier-Ford | 78 | +3 Laps | 19 |
| 12 | 8 | Stefano Modena | Brabham-Judd | 77 | +4 Laps | 17 |
| 13 | 14 | O.Grouillard | Osella-Ford | 74 | +7 Laps | 22 |
| Ret | 21 | Emanuele Pirro | Dallara-Ford | 68 | Engine | 21 |
| Ret | 27 | Ayrton Senna | McLaren-Honda | 61 | Spun off | 1 |
| Ret | 17 | G.Tarquini | AGS-Ford | 58 | Engine | 26 |
| Ret | 12 | Johnny Herbert | Lotus-Lamborghini | 57 | Clutch | 18 |
| Ret | 3 | Satoru Nakajima | Tyrrell-Ford | 53 | Spun off | 13 |
| Ret | 16 | Ivan Capelli | Leyton House-Judd | 46 | Throttle | 14 |
| Ret | 11 | Derek Warwick | Lotus-Lamborghini | 43 | Gearbox | 11 |
| Ret | 15 | M.Gugelmin | Leyton House-Judd | 27 | Brakes | 16 |
| Ret | 22 | A.de Cesaris | Dallara-Ford | 23 | Electrical | 15 |
| Ret | 29 | Eric Bernard | Lola-Lamborghini | 21 | Gearbox | 23 |
| Ret | 24 | G.Morbidelli | Minardi-Ford | 20 | Gearbox | 20 |
| Ret | 7 | David Brabham | Brabham-Judd | 18 | Spun off | 25 |
| Ret | 30 | Aguri Suzuki | Lola-Lamborghini | 6 | Transmission | 24 |
| DNQ | 9 | Michele Alboreto | Arrows-Ford | | | |
| DNQ | 18 | Yannick Dalmas | AGS-Ford | | | |
| DNQ | 10 | Alex Caffi | Arrows-Ford | | | |
| DNQ | 31 | Bertrand Gachot | Coloni-Ford | | | |

Winning speed: 104.017mph Lap leaders: Senna 1-61; Piquet 62-81
Pole position: Senna 1m15.671s, 111.742mph
Fastest lap: Mansell 1m18.203s, 108.124mph

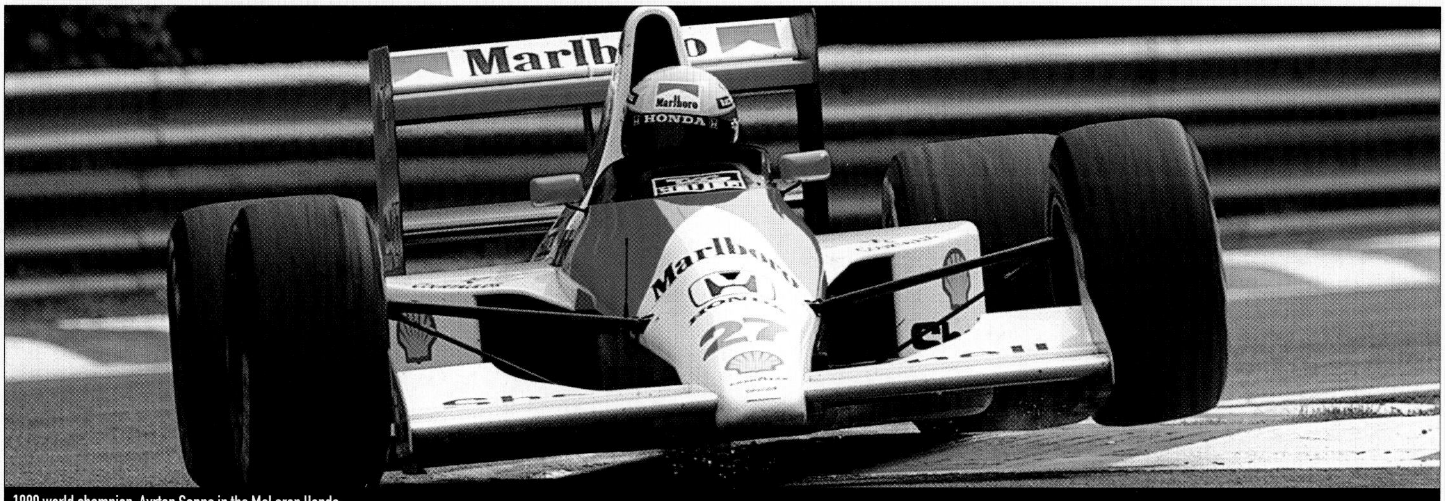

1990 world champion, Ayrton Senna in the McLaren Honda.

# 1991

## DRIVERS' CHAMPION: AYRTON SENNA
## CONSTRUCTORS' CHAMPION: McLAREN HONDA

### DRIVERS' CHAMPIONSHIP

| POS. | DRIVER | NATIONALITY | CAR | POINTS |
|---|---|---|---|---|
| 1 | Ayrton Senna | Brazil | McLaren-Honda | 96 |
| 2 | Nigel Mansell | GB | Williams-Renault | 72 |
| 3 | Riccardo Patrese | Italy | Williams-Renault | 53 |
| 4 | Gerhard Berger | Austria | McLaren-Honda | 43 |
| 5 | Alain Prost | France | Ferrari | 34 |
| 6 | Nelson Piquet | Brazil | Benetton-Ford | 26.5 |
| 7 | Jean Alesi | France | Ferrari | 21 |
| 8 | Stefano Modena | Italy | Tyrrell-Honda | 10 |
| 9 | Andrea de Cesaris | Italy | Jordan-Ford | 9 |
| 10 | Roberto Moreno | Brazil | Benetton-Ford, Jordan-Ford, Minardi-Ferrari | 8 |
| 11 | Pierluigi Martini | Italy | Minardi-Ferrari | 6 |
| 12 | J.J. Lehto | Finland | Dallara-Judd | 4 |
| = | Bertrand Gachot | Belgium | Jordan-Ford, Lola-Ford | 4 |
| = | Michael Schumacher | Germany | Jordan-Ford, Benetton-Ford | 4 |
| 15 | Saturo Nakajima | Japan | Tyrrell-Honda | 2 |
| = | Mika Häkkinen | Finland | Lotus-Judd | 2 |
| = | Martin Brundle | GB | Brabham-Yamaha | 2 |
| 18 | Aguri Suzuki | Japan | Lola-Ford | 1 |
| = | Julian Bailey | GB | Lotus-Ford | 1 |
| = | Emmanuele Pirro | Italy | Dallara-Judd | 1 |
| = | Eric Bernard | France | Lola-Ford | 1 |
| = | Ivan Capelli | Italy | Leyton House-Ilmor | 1 |
| = | Mark Blundell | GB | Brabham-Yamaha | 1 |
| 24 | Gianni Morbidelli | Italy | Minardi-Ferrari, Ferrari | 0.5 |
| | Mauricio Gugelmin | Brazil | Leyton House-Ilmor | |
| | Thierry Boutsen | Belgium | Ligier-Lamborghini | |
| | Gabriele Tarquini | Italy | AGS-Ford, Fondmetal-Ford | |
| | Nicola Larini | Italy | Lamborghini | |
| | Michele Alboreto | Italy | Footwork-Porsche, Footwork-Ford | |
| | Alex Caffi | Italy | Footwork-Porsche, Footwork-Ford | |
| | Olivier Grouillard | France | Fondmetal-Ford, AGS-Ford | |
| | Erik Comas | France | Ligier-Lamborghini, Ligier-Lamborghini | |
| | Pedro Chaves | Portugal | Coloni-Ford | |
| | Eric Van de Poele | Belgium | Lamborghini | |
| | Stephen Johansson | Sweden | AGS-Ford, Footwork-Porsche, Footwork-Ford | |
| | Fabrio Barbazza | Italy | AGS-Ford | |
| | Johnny Herbert | GB | Lotus-Judd | |
| | Michael Bartels | Germany | Lotus-Judd | |
| | Alessandro Zanardi | Italy | Jordan-Ford | |
| | Karl Wendlinger | Austria | Leyton House-Ilmor | |
| | Naoki Hattori | Japan | Coloni-Ford | |

Points for top six finishers (9, 6, 4, 3, 2, 1). Half points awarded for races stopped before half distance.

### CONSTRUCTORS' CHAMPIONSHIP

| POS. | CONSTRUCTOR | POINTS |
|---|---|---|
| 1 | McLaren-Honda | 139 |
| 2 | Williams-Renault | 125 |
| 3 | Ferrari | 55.5 |
| 4 | Benetton-Ford | 38.5 |
| 5 | Jordan-Ford | 13 |
| 6 | Tyrrell-Honda | 12 |
| 7 | Minardi-Ferrari | 6 |
| 8 | Dallara-Judd | 5 |
| 9 | Lotus-Judd | 3 |
| 9 | Brabham-Yamaha | 3 |
| 11 | Lola-Ford | 2 |
| 12 | Leyton House-Ilmor | 1 |

Points for top six finishers (9, 6, 4, 3, 2, 1). Half points awarded for races stopped before half distance.

### UNITED STATES GRAND PRIX: PHOENIX *10 March Round: 1 Race: 501 81 x 2.312 miles*

| POS. | NO. | DRIVER | CAR/ENGINE | LAPS | TIME/RETIRED | GRID |
|---|---|---|---|---|---|---|
| 1 | 1 | Ayrton Senna | McLaren-Honda | 81 | 2:00'47.828 | 1 |
| 2 | 27 | Alain Prost | Ferrari | 81 | +16.322 | 2 |
| 3 | 20 | Nelson Piquet | Benetton-Ford | 81 | +17.376 | 5 |
| 4 | 4 | Stefano Modena | Tyrrell-Honda | 81 | +25.409 | 11 |
| 5 | 3 | Satoru Nakajima | Tyrrell-Honda | 80 | +1 Lap | 16 |
| 6 | 30 | Aguri Suzuki | Lola-Ford | 79 | +2 Laps | 21 |
| 7 | 34 | Nicola Larini | Lamborghini | 78 | +3 Laps | 17 |
| 8 | 17 | G.Tarquini | AGS-Ford | 77 | +4 Laps | 22 |
| 9 | 23 | P.Martini | Minardi-Ferrari | 75 | Engine | 15 |
| 10 | 32 | Bertrand Gachot | Jordan-Ford | 75 | Engine | 14 |
| 11 | 7 | Martin Brundle | Brabham-Yamaha | 73 | +8 Laps | 12 |
| 12 | 28 | Jean Alesi | Ferrari | 72 | Gearbox | 6 |
| Ret | 11 | Mika Hakkinen | Lotus-Judd | 59 | Engine | 13 |
| Ret | 6 | Riccardo Patrese | Williams-Renault | 49 | Gearbox | 3 |
| Ret | 19 | Roberto Moreno | Benetton-Ford | 49 | Collision | 8 |
| Ret | 9 | Michele Alboreto | Footwork-Porsche | 41 | Engine | 25 |
| Ret | 16 | Ivan Capelli | Leyton House-Ilmor | 40 | Gearbox | 18 |
| Ret | 25 | Thierry Boutsen | Ligier-Lamborghini | 40 | Engine | 20 |
| Ret | 2 | Gerhard Berger | McLaren-Honda | 36 | Fuel pump | 7 |
| Ret | 5 | Nigel Mansell | Williams-Renault | 35 | Gearbox | 4 |
| Ret | 15 | M.Gugelmin | Leyton House-Ilmor | 34 | Gearbox | 23 |
| Ret | 8 | Mark Blundell | Brabham-Yamaha | 32 | Spun off | 24 |
| Ret | 21 | Emanuele Pirro | Dallara-Judd | 16 | Gearbox | 9 |
| Ret | 24 | G.Morbidelli | Minardi-Ferrari | 15 | Gearbox | 26 |
| Ret | 22 | J J Lehto | Dallara-Judd | 12 | Gearbox | 10 |
| Ret | 29 | Eric Bernard | Lola-Ford | 4 | Engine | 19 |
| DNQ | 10 | Alex Caffi | Footwork-Porsche | | | |
| DNQ | 18 | Stefan Johansson | AGS-Ford | | | |
| DNQ | 26 | Erik Comas | Ligier-Lamborghini | | | |
| DNQ | 12 | Julian Bailey | Lotus-Judd | | | |
| DNPQ | 33 | A.de Cesaris | Jordan-Ford | | | |
| DNPQ | 31 | P.M.Chaves | Coloni-Ford | | | |
| DNPQ | 14 | O.Grouillard | Fondmetal-Ford | | | |
| DNPQ | 35 | E.van de Poele | Lamborghini | | | |

Winning speed: 93.018mph Lap leaders: Senna 1-81
Pole position: Senna, 1m 21.434s, 102.208mph
Fastest lap: Alesi, 1m 26.758s, 95.936mph
Scheduled for 82 laps but stopped after two-hour mark.

### BRAZILIAN GRAND PRIX: INTERLAGOS *24 March Round: 2 Race: 502 71 x 2.687 miles*

| POS. | NO. | DRIVER | CAR/ENGINE | LAPS | TIME/RETIRED | GRID |
|---|---|---|---|---|---|---|
| 1 | 1 | Ayrton Senna | McLaren-Honda | 71 | 1:38'28.128 | 1 |
| 2 | 6 | Riccardo Patrese | Williams-Renault | 71 | +2.991 | 2 |
| 3 | 2 | Gerhard Berger | McLaren-Honda | 71 | +5.416 | 4 |
| 4 | 27 | Alain Prost | Ferrari | 71 | +19.369 | 6 |
| 5 | 20 | Nelson Piquet | Benetton-Ford | 71 | +21.960 | 7 |
| 6 | 28 | Jean Alesi | Ferrari | 71 | +23.641 | 5 |
| 7 | 19 | Roberto Moreno | Benetton-Ford | 70 | +1 Lap | 14 |
| 8 | 24 | G.Morbidelli | Minardi-Ferrari | 69 | +2 Laps | 21 |
| 9 | 11 | Mika Hakkinen | Lotus-Judd | 68 | +3 Laps | 22 |
| 10 | 25 | Thierry Boutsen | Ligier-Lamborghini | 68 | +3 Laps | 18 |
| 11 | 21 | Emanuele Pirro | Dallara-Judd | 68 | +3 Laps | 12 |
| 12 | 7 | Martin Brundle | Brabham-Yamaha | 67 | +4 Laps | 26 |
| 13 | 32 | Bertrand Gachot | Jordan-Ford | 63 | Fuel system | 10 |
| Ret | 5 | Nigel Mansell | Williams-Renault | 59 | Gearbox | 3 |
| Ret | 26 | Erik Comas | Ligier-Lamborghini | 50 | Engine | 23 |
| Ret | 23 | P.Martini | Minardi-Ferrari | 47 | Spun off | 20 |
| Ret | 8 | Mark Blundell | Brabham-Yamaha | 34 | Engine | 25 |
| Ret | 29 | Eric Bernard | Lola-Ford | 33 | Radiator | 11 |
| Ret | 22 | J J Lehto | Dallara-Judd | 22 | Electrical | 19 |
| Ret | 33 | A.de Cesaris | Jordan-Ford | 20 | Engine | 13 |
| Ret | 4 | Stefano Modena | Tyrrell-Honda | 19 | Gearbox | 9 |
| Ret | 16 | Ivan Capelli | Leyton House-Ilmor | 16 | Transmission | 15 |
| Ret | 3 | Satoru Nakajima | Tyrrell-Honda | 12 | Spun off | 16 |
| Ret | 15 | M.Gugelmin | Leyton House-Ilmor | 9 | Physical | 8 |
| Ret | 17 | G.Tarquini | AGS-Ford | 0 | Suspension | 24 |
| Ret | 30 | Aguri Suzuki | Lola-Ford | 0 | Fuel pump | 17 |
| DNQ | 10 | Alex Caffi | Footwork-Porsche | | | |
| DNQ | 18 | Stefan Johansson | AGS-Ford | | | |
| DNQ | 9 | Michele Alboreto | Footwork-Porsche | | | |
| DNQ | 12 | Julian Bailey | Lotus-Judd | | | |
| DNPQ | 35 | E.van de Poele | Lamborghini | | | |
| DNPQ | 34 | Nicola Larini | Lamborghini | | | |
| DNPQ | 31 | P.M.Chaves | Coloni-Ford | | | |
| DNPQ | 14 | O.Grouillard | Fondmetal-Ford | | | |

Winning speed: 116.265mph Lap leaders: Senna 1-71
Pole position: Senna, 1m 16.392s, 126.646mph
Fastest lap: Mansell, 1m 20.436s, 120.279mph

### SAN MARINO GRAND PRIX: IMOLA *28 April Round: 3 Race: 503 61 x 3.132 miles*

| POS. | NO. | DRIVER | CAR/ENGINE | LAPS | TIME/RETIRED | GRID |
|---|---|---|---|---|---|---|
| 1 | 1 | Ayrton Senna | McLaren-Honda | 61 | 1:35'14.750 | 1 |
| 2 | 2 | Gerhard Berger | McLaren-Honda | 61 | +1.675 | 5 |
| 3 | 22 | J J Lehto | Dallara-Judd | 60 | +1 Lap | 16 |
| 4 | 23 | P.Martini | Minardi-Ferrari | 59 | +2 Laps | 9 |
| 5 | 11 | Mika Hakkinen | Lotus-Judd | 58 | +3 Laps | 25 |
| 6 | 12 | Julian Bailey | Lotus-Judd | 58 | +3 Laps | 26 |
| 7 | 25 | Thierry Boutsen | Ligier-Lamborghini | 58 | +3 Laps | 24 |
| 8 | 8 | Mark Blundell | Brabham-Yamaha | 58 | +3 Laps | 23 |
| 9 | 35 | E.van de Poele | Lamborghini | 57 | Out of fuel | 21 |
| 10 | 26 | Erik Comas | Ligier-Lamborghini | 57 | +4 Laps | 19 |
| 11 | 7 | Martin Brundle | Brabham-Yamaha | 57 | +4 Laps | 18 |
| 12 | 15 | M.Gugelmin | Leyton House-Ilmor | 55 | Engine | 15 |
| 13 | 19 | Roberto Moreno | Benetton-Ford | 54 | Engine | 13 |
| Ret | 4 | Stefano Modena | Tyrrell-Honda | 41 | Transmission | 6 |
| Ret | 33 | A.de Cesaris | Jordan-Ford | 37 | Gearbox | 11 |
| Ret | 32 | Bertrand Gachot | Jordan-Ford | 37 | Suspension | 12 |
| Ret | 16 | Ivan Capelli | Leyton House-Ilmor | 24 | Spun off | 22 |
| Ret | 29 | Eric Bernard | Lola-Ford | 17 | Engine | 17 |
| Ret | 6 | Riccardo Patrese | Williams-Renault | 17 | Electrical | 2 |
| Ret | 3 | Satoru Nakajima | Tyrrell-Honda | 15 | Transmission | 10 |
| Ret | 24 | G.Morbidelli | Minardi-Ferrari | 10 | Gearbox | 8 |
| Ret | 28 | Jean Alesi | Ferrari | 2 | Spun off | 7 |
| Ret | 30 | Aguri Suzuki | Lola-Ford | 2 | Spun off | 20 |
| Ret | 20 | Nelson Piquet | Benetton-Ford | 1 | Spun off | 14 |
| Ret | 5 | Nigel Mansell | Williams-Renault | 0 | Collision | 4 |
| Ret | 27 | Alain Prost | Ferrari | 0 | Spun off | 3 |
| DNQ | 17 | G.Tarquini | AGS-Ford | | | |
| DNQ | 18 | F.Barbazza | AGS-Ford | | | |
| DNQ | 10 | Alex Caffi | Footwork-Porsche | | | |
| DNQ | 9 | Michele Alboreto | Footwork-Porsche | | | |
| DNPQ | 21 | Emanuele Pirro | Dallara-Judd | | | |
| DNPQ | 14 | O.Grouillard | Fondmetal-Ford | | | |
| DNPQ | 34 | Nicola Larini | Lamborghini | | | |
| DNPQ | 31 | P.M.Chaves | Coloni-Ford | | | |

Winning speed: 120.342mph Lap leaders: Patrese 1-9; Senna 10-61
Pole position: Senna, 1m 21.877s, 137.696mph
Fastest lap: Berger, 1m 26.531s, 130.290mph

### MONACO GRAND PRIX: MONTE CARLO *12 May Round: 4 Race: 504 78 x 2.068 miles*

| POS. | NO. | DRIVER | CAR/ENGINE | LAPS | TIME/RETIRED | GRID |
|---|---|---|---|---|---|---|
| 1 | 1 | Ayrton Senna | McLaren-Honda | 78 | 1:53'02.334 | 1 |
| 2 | 5 | Nigel Mansell | Williams-Renault | 78 | +18.348 | 5 |
| 3 | 28 | Jean Alesi | Ferrari | 78 | +47.455 | 9 |
| 4 | 19 | Roberto Moreno | Benetton-Ford | 77 | +1 Lap | 8 |
| 5 | 27 | Alain Prost | Ferrari | 77 | +1 Lap | 7 |
| 6 | 21 | Emanuele Pirro | Dallara-Judd | 77 | +1 Lap | 12 |
| 7 | 25 | Thierry Boutsen | Ligier-Lamborghini | 76 | +2 Laps | 16 |
| 8 | 32 | Bertrand Gachot | Jordan-Ford | 76 | +2 Laps | 24 |
| 9 | 29 | Eric Bernard | Lola-Ford | 76 | +2 Laps | 21 |
| 10 | 26 | Erik Comas | Ligier-Lamborghini | 76 | +2 Laps | 23 |
| 11 | 22 | J J Lehto | Dallara-Judd | 75 | +3 Laps | 13 |
| 12 | 23 | P.Martini | Minardi-Ferrari | 72 | +6 Laps | 14 |
| Ret | 11 | Mika Hakkinen | Lotus-Judd | 64 | Oil leak | 26 |
| Ret | 24 | G.Morbidelli | Minardi-Ferrari | 49 | Gearbox | 17 |
| Ret | 15 | M.Gugelmin | Leyton House-Ilmor | 43 | Throttle | 15 |
| Ret | 4 | Stefano Modena | Tyrrell-Honda | 42 | Engine | 2 |
| Ret | 6 | Riccardo Patrese | Williams-Renault | 42 | Spun off | 3 |
| Ret | 8 | Mark Blundell | Brabham-Yamaha | 41 | Spun off | 22 |
| Ret | 9 | Michele Alboreto | Footwork-Porsche | 39 | Engine | 25 |
| Ret | 3 | Satoru Nakajima | Tyrrell-Honda | 35 | Spun off | 11 |
| Ret | 30 | Aguri Suzuki | Lola-Ford | 24 | Spun off | 19 |
| Ret | 33 | A.de Cesaris | Jordan-Ford | 21 | Throttle | 10 |
| Ret | 16 | Ivan Capelli | Leyton House-Ilmor | 12 | Brakes | 18 |
| Ret | 17 | G.Tarquini | AGS-Ford | 9 | Gearbox | 20 |
| Ret | 2 | Gerhard Berger | McLaren-Honda | 9 | Spun off | 6 |
| Ret | 20 | Nelson Piquet | Benetton-Ford | 0 | Suspension | 4 |
| DNQ | 12 | Julian Bailey | Lotus-Judd | | | |
| DNQ | 18 | F.Barbazza | AGS-Ford | | | |
| DNQ | 10 | Alex Caffi | Footwork-Porsche | | | |
| DNQ | 7 | Martin Brundle | Brabham-Yamaha | | | |
| DNPQ | 34 | Nicola Larini | Lamborghini | | | |
| DNPQ | 35 | E.van de Poele | Lamborghini | | | |
| DNPQ | 31 | P.M.Chaves | Coloni-Ford | | | |
| DNPQ | 14 | O.Grouillard | Fondmetal-Ford | | | |

Winning speed: 85.615mph Lap leaders: Senna 1-78
Pole position: Senna, 1m 20.344s, 92.658mph
Fastest lap: Prost, 1m 24.368s, 88.239mph

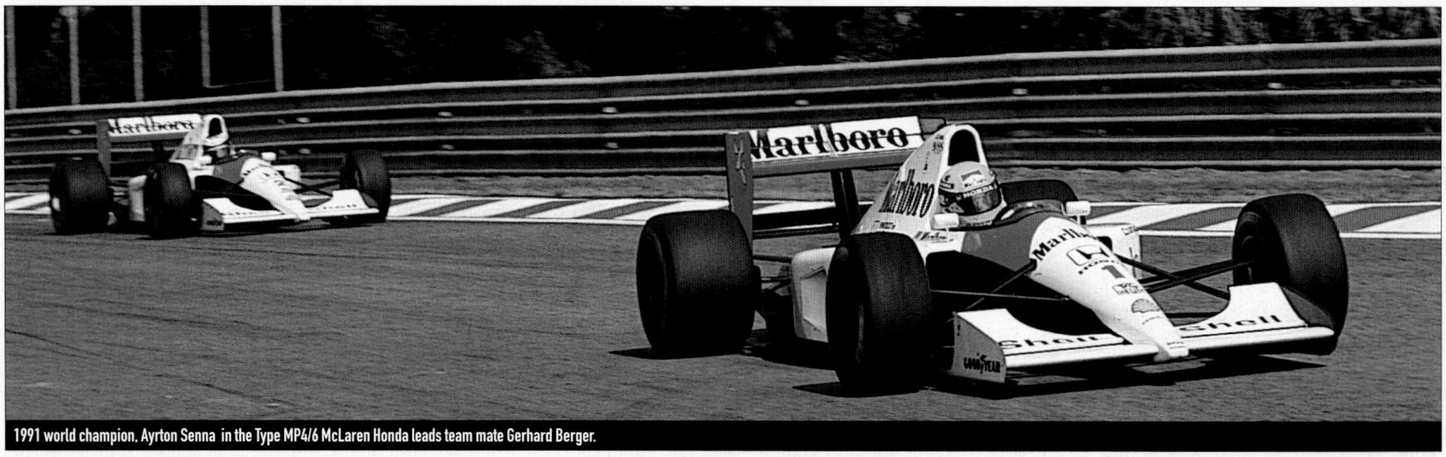


1991 world champion, Ayrton Senna in the Type MP4/6 McLaren Honda leads team mate Gerhard Berger.

## CANADIAN GRAND PRIX: MONTREAL *2 June Round:5 Race: 505 69 x 2.753 miles*

| POS. | NO. | DRIVER | CAR/ENGINE | LAPS | TIME/RETIRED | GRID |
|---|---|---|---|---|---|---|
| 1 | 20 | Nelson Piquet | Benetton-Ford | 69 | 1:38'51.490 | 8 |
| 2 | 4 | Stefano Modena | Tyrrell-Honda | 69 | +31.832 | 9 |
| 3 | 6 | Riccardo Patrese | Williams-Renault | 69 | +42.217 | 1 |
| 4 | 33 | A.de Cesaris | Jordan-Ford | 69 | +1'20.210 | 11 |
| 5 | 32 | Bertrand Gachot | Jordan-Ford | 69 | +1'22.351 | 14 |
| 6 | 5 | Nigel Mansell | Williams-Renault | 68 | Electrical | 2 |
| 7 | 23 | P.Martini | Minardi-Ferrari | 68 | +1 Lap | 18 |
| 8 | 26 | Erik Comas | Ligier-Lamborghini | 68 | +1 Lap | 26 |
| 9 | 21 | Emanuele Pirro | Dallara-Judd | 68 | +1 Lap | 10 |
| 10 | 3 | Satoru Nakajima | Tyrrell-Honda | 67 | +2 Laps | 12 |
| Ret | 15 | M.Gugelmin | Leyton House-Ilmor | 61 | Engine | 23 |
| Ret | 22 | J J Lehto | Dallara-Judd | 50 | Engine | 17 |
| Ret | 10 | Stefan Johansson | Footwork-Porsche | 48 | Throttle | 25 |
| Ret | 16 | Ivan Capelli | Leyton House-Ilmor | 42 | Engine | 13 |
| Ret | 28 | Jean Alesi | Ferrari | 34 | Engine | 7 |
| Ret | 29 | Eric Bernard | Lola-Ford | 29 | Gearbox | 19 |
| Ret | 27 | Alain Prost | Ferrari | 27 | Gearbox | 4 |
| Ret | 25 | Thierry Boutsen | Ligier-Lamborghini | 27 | Engine | 16 |
| Ret | 1 | Ayrton Senna | McLaren-Honda | 25 | Alternator | 3 |
| Ret | 11 | Mika Hakkinen | Lotus-Judd | 21 | Spun off | 24 |
| Ret | 7 | Martin Brundle | Brabham-Yamaha | 21 | Engine | 20 |
| Ret | 24 | G.Morbidelli | Minardi-Ferrari | 20 | Spun off | 15 |
| Ret | 19 | Roberto Moreno | Benetton-Ford | 10 | Suspension | 5 |
| Ret | 2 | Gerhard Berger | McLaren-Honda | 4 | Injection | 6 |
| Ret | 30 | Aguri Suzuki | Lola-Ford | 3 | Fuel leak | 22 |
| Ret | 9 | Michele Alboreto | Footwork-Porsche | 2 | Throttle | 21 |
| DNQ | 18 | F.Barbazza | AGS-Ford | | | |
| DNQ | 17 | G.Tarquini | AGS-Ford | | | |
| DNQ | 8 | Mark Blundell | Brabham-Yamaha | | | |
| DNQ | 12 | Johnny Herbert | Lotus-Judd | | | |
| DNPQ | 14 | O.Grouillard | Fondmetal-Ford | | | |
| DNPQ | 34 | Nicola Larini | Lamborghini | | | |
| DNPQ | 35 | E.van de Poele | Lamborghini | | | |
| DNPQ | 31 | P.M.Chaves | Coloni-Ford | | | |

Winning speed: 115.277mph Lap leaders: Mansell 1-68; Piquet 69
Pole position: Patrese, 1m 19.837s, 124.123mph
Fastest lap: Mansell, 1m 22.385s, 120.284mph

## FRENCH GRAND PRIX: MAGNY-COURS *7 July Round: 7 Race: 507 72 x 2.654 miles*

| POS. | NO. | DRIVER | CAR/ENGINE | LAPS | TIME/RETIRED | GRID |
|---|---|---|---|---|---|---|
| 1 | 5 | Nigel Mansell | Williams-Renault | 72 | 1:38'00.056 | 4 |
| 2 | 27 | Alain Prost | Ferrari | 72 | +5.003 | 2 |
| 3 | 1 | Ayrton Senna | McLaren-Honda | 72 | +34.934 | 3 |
| 4 | 28 | Jean Alesi | Ferrari | 72 | +35.920 | 6 |
| 5 | 6 | Riccardo Patrese | Williams-Renault | 71 | +1 Lap | 1 |
| 6 | 33 | A.de Cesaris | Jordan-Ford | 71 | +1 Lap | 13 |
| 7 | 15 | M.Gugelmin | Leyton House-Ilmor | 70 | +2 Laps | 9 |
| 8 | 20 | Nelson Piquet | Benetton-Ford | 70 | +2 Laps | 7 |
| 9 | 23 | P.Martini | Minardi-Ferrari | 70 | +2 Laps | 12 |
| 10 | 12 | Johnny Herbert | Lotus-Judd | 70 | +2 Laps | 20 |
| 11 | 26 | Erik Comas | Ligier-Lamborghini | 70 | +2 Laps | 14 |
| 12 | 25 | Thierry Boutsen | Ligier/Lamborghini | 69 | +3 Laps | 16 |
| Ret | 19 | Roberto Moreno | Benetton-Ford | 63 | Physical | 8 |
| Ret | 4 | Stefano Modena | Tyrrell-Honda | 57 | Gearbox | 11 |
| Ret | 14 | O.Grouillard | Fondmetal-Ford | 47 | Oil leak | 21 |
| Ret | 29 | Eric Bernard | Lola-Ford | 43 | Transmission | 23 |
| Ret | 22 | J J Lehto | Dallara-Judd | 39 | Tyre | 26 |
| Ret | 8 | Mark Blundell | Brabham-Yamaha | 36 | Spun off | 17 |
| Ret | 30 | Aguri Suzuki | Lola-Ford | 32 | Transmission | 22 |
| Ret | 9 | Michele Alboreto | Footwork-Ford | 31 | Gearbox | 25 |
| Ret | 7 | Martin Brundle | Brabham-Yamaha | 21 | Gearbox | 24 |
| Ret | 3 | Satoru Nakajima | Tyrrell-Honda | 12 | Spun off | 18 |
| Ret | 24 | G.Morbidelli | Minardi-Ferrari | 8 | Collision | 10 |
| Ret | 16 | Ivan Capelli | Leyton House-Ilmor | 7 | Spun off | 15 |
| Ret | 2 | Gerhard Berger | McLaren-Honda | 6 | Engine | 5 |
| Ret | 32 | Bertrand Gachot | Jordan-Ford | 0 | Spun off | 19 |
| DNQ | 11 | Mika Hakkinen | Lotus-Judd | | | |
| DNQ | 18 | F.Barbazza | AGS-Ford | | | |
| DNQ | 17 | G.Tarquini | AGS-Ford | | | |
| DNQ | 10 | Stefan Johansson | Footwork-Ford | | | |
| DNPQ | 21 | Emanuele Pirro | Dallara-Judd | | | |
| DNPQ | 34 | Nicola Larini | Lamborghini | | | |
| DNPQ | 35 | E.van de Poele | Lamborghini | | | |
| DNPQ | 31 | P.M.Chaves | Coloni-Ford | | | |

Winning speed: 116.986mph Lap leaders: Prost 1-21, 32-54; Mansell 22-31, 55-72
Pole position: Patrese, 1m 14.559s, 128.140mph
Fastest lap: Mansell, 1m 19.168s, 120.680mph

## GERMAN GRAND PRIX: HOCKENHEIM *28 July Round: 9 Race: 509 45 x 4.227 miles*

| POS. | NO. | DRIVER | CAR/ENGINE | LAPS | TIME/RETIRED | GRID |
|---|---|---|---|---|---|---|
| 1 | 5 | Nigel Mansell | Williams-Renault | 45 | 1:19'29.661 | 1 |
| 2 | 6 | Riccardo Patrese | Williams-Renault | 45 | +13.779 | 4 |
| 3 | 28 | Jean Alesi | Ferrari | 45 | +17.618 | 6 |
| 4 | 2 | Gerhard Berger | McLaren-Honda | 45 | +32.651 | 3 |
| 5 | 33 | A.de Cesaris | Jordan-Ford | 45 | +1'17.537 | 7 |
| 6 | 32 | Bertrand Gachot | Jordan-Ford | 45 | +1'40.605 | 11 |
| 7 | 1 | Ayrton Senna | McLaren-Honda | 44 | Out of fuel | 2 |
| 8 | 19 | Roberto Moreno | Benetton-Ford | 44 | +1 Lap | 9 |
| 9 | 25 | Thierry Boutsen | Ligier-Lamborghini | 44 | +1 Lap | 17 |
| 10 | 21 | Emanuele Pirro | Dallara-Judd | 44 | +1 Lap | 18 |
| 11 | 7 | Martin Brundle | Brabham-Yamaha | 43 | +2 Laps | 15 |
| 12 | 8 | Mark Blundell | Brabham-Yamaha | 43 | +2 Laps | 21 |
| 13 | 4 | Stefano Modena | Tyrrell-Honda | 41 | +4 Laps | 14 |
| Ret | 27 | Alain Prost | Ferrari | 37 | Spun off | 5 |
| Ret | 16 | Ivan Capelli | Leyton House-Ilmor | 36 | Engine | 12 |
| Ret | 22 | J J Lehto | Dallara-Judd | 35 | Engine | 20 |
| Ret | 20 | Nelson Piquet | Benetton-Ford | 27 | Engine | 8 |
| Ret | 3 | Satoru Nakajima | Tyrrell-Honda | 26 | Gearbox | 13 |
| Ret | 26 | Erik Comas | Ligier-Lamborghini | 22 | Engine | 26 |
| Ret | 15 | M.Gugelmin | Leyton House-Ilmor | 21 | Gearbox | 16 |
| Ret | 11 | Mika Hakkinen | Lotus-Judd | 19 | Engine | 23 |
| Ret | 30 | Aguri Suzuki | Lola-Ford | 15 | Engine | 22 |
| Ret | 24 | G.Morbidelli | Minardi-Ferrari | 14 | Differential | 19 |
| Ret | 23 | P.Martini | Minardi-Ferrari | 11 | Differential | 10 |
| Ret | 29 | Eric Bernard | Lola-Ford | 9 | Transmission | 25 |
| Ret | 34 | Nicola Larini | Lamborghini | 0 | Spun of | 24 |
| DNQ | 9 | Michele Alboreto | Footwork-Ford | | | |
| DNQ | 12 | Michael Bartels | Lotus-Judd | | | |
| DNQ | 17 | G.Tarquini | AGS-Ford | | | |
| DNQ | 35 | E.van de Poele | Lamborghini | | | |
| DNPQ | 14 | O.Grouillard | Fondmetal-Ford | | | |
| DNPQ | 10 | Alex Caffi | Footwork-Ford | | | |
| DNPQ | 18 | F.Barbazza | AGS-Ford | | | |
| DNPQ | 31 | P.M.Chaves | Coloni-Ford | | | |

Winning speed: 143.554mph Lap leaders: Mansell 1-18, 21-45; Alesi 19-20
Pole position: Mansell, 1m 37.087s, 156.722mph
Fastest lap: Patrese, 1m 43.569s, 146.913mph

## MEXICAN GRAND PRIX: MEXICO CITY *16 June Round:6 Race: 506 67 x 2.747 miles*

| POS. | NO. | DRIVER | CAR/ENGINE | LAPS | TIME/RETIRED | GRID |
|---|---|---|---|---|---|---|
| 1 | 6 | Riccardo Patrese | Williams-Renault | 67 | 1:29'52.205 | 1 |
| 2 | 5 | Nigel Mansell | Williams-Renault | 67 | +1.336 | 2 |
| 3 | 1 | Ayrton Senna | McLaren-Honda | 67 | +57.356 | 3 |
| 4 | 33 | A.de Cesaris | Jordan-Ford | 66 | +1 Lap | 11 |
| 5 | 19 | Roberto Moreno | Benetton-Ford | 66 | +1 Lap | 9 |
| 6 | 29 | Eric Bernard | Lola-Ford | 66 | +1 Lap | 18 |
| 7 | 24 | G.Morbidelli | Minardi-Ferrari | 66 | +1 Lap | 23 |
| 8 | 25 | Thierry Boutsen | Ligier-Lamborghini | 65 | +2 Laps | 14 |
| 9 | 11 | Mika Hakkinen | Lotus-Judd | 65 | +2 Laps | 24 |
| 10 | 12 | Johnny Herbert | Lotus-Judd | 65 | +2 Laps | 25 |
| 11 | 4 | Stefano Modena | Tyrrell-Honda | 65 | +2 Laps | 8 |
| 12 | 3 | Satoru Nakajima | Tyrrell-Honda | 64 | +3 Laps | 13 |
| Ret | 8 | Mark Blundell | Brabham-Yamaha | 54 | Engine | 12 |
| Ret | 32 | Bertrand Gachot | Jordan-Ford | 51 | Spun off | 20 |
| Ret | 30 | Aguri Suzuki | Lola-Ford | 48 | Gearbox | 19 |
| Ret | 20 | Nelson Piquet | Benetton-Ford | 44 | Wheel bearing | 6 |
| Ret | 28 | Jean Alesi | Ferrari | 42 | Clutch | 4 |
| Ret | 22 | J J Lehto | Dallara-Judd | 30 | Engine | 16 |
| Ret | 9 | Michele Alboreto | Footwork-Porsche | 24 | Engine | 26 |
| Ret | 7 | Martin Brundle | Brabham-Yamaha | 20 | Wheel | 17 |
| Ret | 16 | Ivan Capelli | Leyton House-Ilmor | 19 | Engine | 22 |
| Ret | 27 | Alain Prost | Ferrari | 16 | Alternator | 7 |
| Ret | 15 | M.Gugelmin | Leyton House-Ilmor | 15 | Engine | 21 |
| Ret | 14 | O.Grouillard | Fondmetal-Ford | 13 | Engine | 10 |
| Ret | 2 | Gerhard Berger | McLaren-Honda | 5 | Engine | 5 |
| Ret | 23 | P.Martini | Minardi-Ferrari | 4 | Spun off | 15 |
| DNQ | 26 | Erik Comas | Ligier-Lamborghini | | | |
| DNQ | 17 | G.Tarquini | AGS-Ford | | | |
| DNQ | 10 | Stefan Johansson | Footwork-Porsche | | | |
| DNQ | 18 | F.Barbazza | AGS-Ford | | | |
| DNPQ | 34 | Nicola Larini | Lamborghini | | | |
| DNPQ | 35 | E.van de Poele | Lamborghini | | | |
| DNPQ | 31 | P.M.Chaves | Coloni-Ford | | | |
| DNPQ | 21 | Emanuele Pirro | Dallara-Judd | | | |

Winning speed: 122.880mph Lap leaders: Mansell 1-14; Patrese 15-67
Pole position: Patrese, 1m 16.696s, 128.944mph
Fastest lap: Mansell, 1m 16.788s, 128.790mph

## BRITISH GRAND PRIX: SILVERSTONE *14 July Round: 8 Race: 507 59 x 3.247 miles*

| POS. | NO. | DRIVER | CAR/ENGINE | LAPS | TIME/RETIRED | GRID |
|---|---|---|---|---|---|---|
| 1 | 5 | Nigel Mansell | Williams-Renault | 59 | 1:27'35.479 | 1 |
| 2 | 2 | Gerhard Berger | McLaren-Honda | 59 | +42.293 | 4 |
| 3 | 27 | Alain Prost | Ferrari | 59 | +1'00.150 | 5 |
| 4 | 1 | Ayrton Senna | McLaren-Honda | 58 | Out of fuel | 2 |
| 5 | 20 | Nelson Piquet | Benetton-Ford | 58 | +1 Lap | 8 |
| 6 | 32 | Bertrand Gachot | Jordan-Ford | 58 | +1 Lap | 17 |
| 7 | 4 | Stefano Modena | Tyrrell-Honda | 58 | +1 Lap | 10 |
| 8 | 3 | Satoru Nakajima | Tyrrell-Honda | 58 | +1 Lap | 15 |
| 9 | 23 | P.Martini | Minardi-Ferrari | 58 | +1 Lap | 23 |
| 10 | 21 | Emanuele Pirro | Dallara-Judd | 57 | +2 Laps | 18 |
| 11 | 24 | G.Morbidelli | Minardi-Ferrari | 57 | +2 Laps | 20 |
| 12 | 11 | Mika Hakkinen | Lotus-Judd | 57 | +2 Laps | 25 |
| 13 | 22 | J J Lehto | Dallara-Judd | 56 | +3 Laps | 11 |
| 14 | 12 | Johnny Herbert | Lotus-Judd | 55 | Oil pressure | 24 |
| Ret | 8 | Mark Blundell | Brabham-Yamaha | 52 | Engine | 12 |
| Ret | 33 | A.de Cesaris | Jordan-Ford | 41 | Spun off | 13 |
| Ret | 28 | Jean Alesi | Ferrari | 31 | Collision | 6 |
| Ret | 30 | Aguri Suzuki | Lola-Ford | 29 | Collision | 22 |
| Ret | 25 | Thierry Boutsen | Ligier-Lamborghini | 29 | Engine | 19 |
| Ret | 7 | Martin Brundle | Brabham-Yamaha | 28 | Throttle | 14 |
| Ret | 9 | Michele Alboreto | Footwork-Ford | 25 | Transmission | 26 |
| Ret | 15 | M.Gugelmin | Leyton House-Ilmor | 24 | Chassis | 9 |
| Ret | 19 | Roberto Moreno | Benetton-Ford | 21 | Gearbox | 7 |
| Ret | 29 | Eric Bernard | Lola-Ford | 21 | Transmission | 21 |
| Ret | 16 | Ivan Capelli | Leyton House-Ilmor | 16 | Spun off | 16 |
| Ret | 6 | Riccardo Patrese | Williams-Renault | 1 | Collision | 3 |
| DNQ | 26 | Erik Comas | Ligier-Lamborghini | | | |
| DNQ | 10 | Stefan Johansson | Footwork-Ford | | | |
| DNQ | 18 | F.Barbazza | AGS-Ford | | | |
| DNQ | 17 | G.Tarquini | AGS-Ford | | | |
| DNPQ | 14 | O.Grouillard | Fondmetal-Ford | | | |
| DNPQ | 34 | Nicola Larini | Lamborghini | | | |
| DNPQ | 35 | E.van de Poele | Lamborghini | | | |
| DNPQ | 31 | P.M.Chaves | Coloni-Ford | | | |

Winning speed: 131.239mph Lap leaders: Mansell 1-59
Pole position: Mansell, 1m 20.939s, 144.422mph
Fastest lap: Mansell, 1m26.379s, 135.336mph

## HUNGARIAN GRAND PRIX: HUNGARORING *11 August Round: 10 Race: 510 77 x 2.466 miles*

| POS. | NO. | DRIVER | CAR/ENGINE | LAPS | TIME/RETIRED | GRID |
|---|---|---|---|---|---|---|
| 1 | 1 | Ayrton Senna | McLaren-Honda | 77 | 1:49'12.796 | 1 |
| 2 | 5 | Nigel Mansell | Williams-Renault | 77 | +4.599 | 3 |
| 3 | 6 | Riccardo Patrese | Williams-Renault | 77 | +15.594 | 2 |
| 4 | 2 | Gerhard Berger | McLaren-Honda | 77 | +21.856 | 5 |
| 5 | 28 | Jean Alesi | Ferrari | 77 | +31.389 | 6 |
| 6 | 16 | Ivan Capelli | Leyton House-Ilmor | 76 | +1 Lap | 9 |
| 7 | 33 | A.de Cesaris | Jordan-Ford | 76 | +1 Lap | 17 |
| 8 | 19 | Roberto Moreno | Benetton-Ford | 76 | +1 Lap | 15 |
| 9 | 32 | Bertrand Gachot | Jordan-Ford | 76 | +1 Lap | 16 |
| 10 | 26 | Erik Comas | Ligier-Lamborghini | 75 | +2 Laps | 25 |
| 11 | 15 | M.Gugelmin | Leyton House-Ilmor | 75 | +2 Laps | 13 |
| 12 | 4 | Stefano Modena | Tyrrell-Honda | 75 | +2 Laps | 8 |
| 13 | 24 | G.Morbidelli | Minardi-Ferrari | 75 | +2 Laps | 23 |
| 14 | 11 | Mika Hakkinen | Lotus-Judd | 74 | +3 Laps | 26 |
| 15 | 3 | Satoru Nakajima | Tyrrell-Honda | 74 | +3 Laps | 14 |
| 16 | 34 | Nicola Larini | Lamborghini | 74 | +3 Laps | 24 |
| 17 | 25 | Thierry Boutsen | Ligier-Lamborghini | 71 | Engine | 19 |
| Ret | 23 | P.Martini | Minardi-Ferrari | 65 | Engine | 18 |
| Ret | 8 | Mark Blundell | Brabham-Yamaha | 62 | Tyre | 20 |
| Ret | 7 | Martin Brundle | Brabham-Yamaha | 59 | Physical | 10 |
| Ret | 22 | J J Lehto | Dallara-Judd | 49 | Engine | 12 |
| Ret | 20 | Nelson Piquet | Benetton-Ford | 38 | Gearbox | 11 |
| Ret | 29 | Eric Bernard | Lola-Ford | 38 | Engine | 21 |
| Ret | 30 | Aguri Suzuki | Lola-Ford | 38 | Engine | 22 |
| Ret | 21 | Emanuele Pirro | Dallara-Judd | 37 | Engine | 7 |
| Ret | 27 | Alain Prost | Ferrari | 28 | Engine | 4 |
| DNQ | 14 | O.Grouillard | Fondmetal-Ford | | | |
| DNQ | 9 | Michele Alboreto | Footwork-Ford | | | |
| DNQ | 35 | E.van de Poele | Lamborghini | | | |
| DNQ | 12 | Michael Bartels | Lotus-Judd | | | |
| DNPQ | 17 | G.Tarquini | AGS-Ford | | | |
| DNPQ | 10 | Alex Caffi | Footwork-Ford | | | |
| DNPQ | 18 | F.Barbazza | AGS-Ford | | | |
| DNPQ | 31 | P.M.Chaves | Coloni-Ford | | | |

Winning speed: 104.301mph Lap leaders: Senna 1-77
Pole position: Senna, 1m 16.147s, 116.566mph
Fastest lap: Gachot, 1m 21.547s, 108.847mph

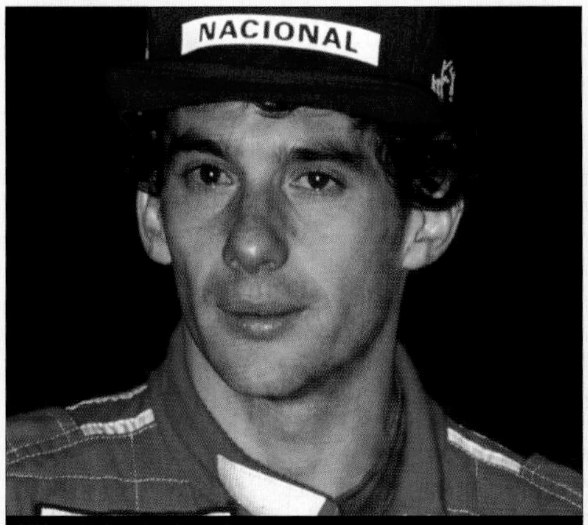

1991 world champion, Ayrton Senna.

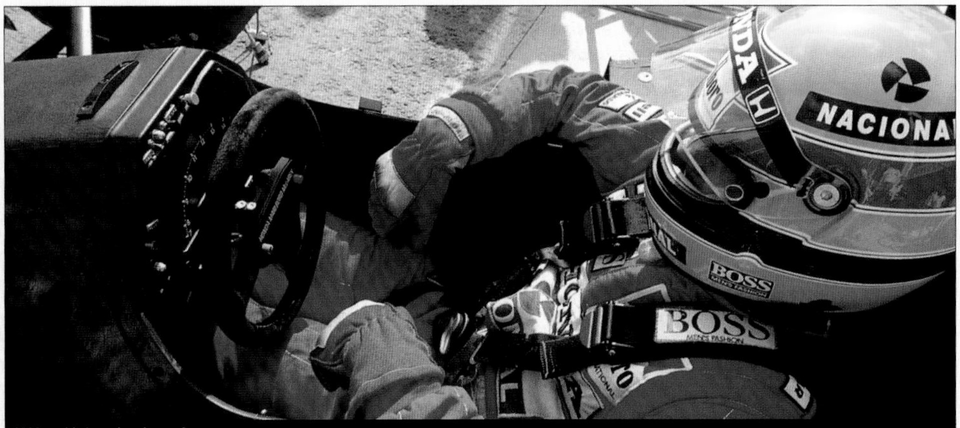

1991 world champion, Ayrton Senna.

### BELGIAN GRAND PRIX: SPA-FRANCORCHAMPS *25 August Round: 11 Race: 511 44 x 4.312 miles*

| POS. | NO. | DRIVER | CAR/ENGINE | LAPS | TIME/RETIRED | GRID |
|---|---|---|---|---|---|---|
| 1 | 1 | Ayrton Senna | McLaren-Honda | 44 | 1:27'17.669 | 1 |
| 2 | 2 | Gerhard Berger | McLaren-Honda | 44 | +1.901 | 4 |
| 3 | 20 | Nelson Piquet | Benetton-Ford | 44 | +32.176 | 6 |
| 4 | 19 | Roberto Moreno | Benetton-Ford | 44 | +37.310 | 8 |
| 5 | 6 | Riccardo Patrese | Williams-Renault | 44 | +57.187 | 17 |
| 6 | 8 | Mark Blundell | Brabham-Yamaha | 44 | +1'40.035 | 13 |
| 7 | 12 | Johnny Herbert | Lotus-Judd | 44 | +1'44.599 | 21 |
| 8 | 21 | Emanuele Pirro | Dallara-Judd | 43 | +1 Lap | 25 |
| 9 | 7 | Martin Brundle | Brabham-Yamaha | 43 | +1 Lap | 16 |
| 10 | 14 | O.Grouillard | Fondmetal-Ford | 43 | +1 Lap | 23 |
| 11 | 25 | Thierry Boutsen | Ligier-Lamborghini | 43 | +1 Lap | 18 |
| 12 | 23 | P.Martini | Minardi-Ferrari | 42 | Gearbox | 9 |
| 13 | 33 | A.de Cesaris | Jordan-Ford | 41 | Engine | 11 |
| Ret | 4 | Stefano Modena | Tyrrell-Honda | 33 | Oil leak | 10 |
| Ret | 22 | J J Lehto | Dallara-Judd | 33 | Oil pressure | 14 |
| Ret | 28 | Jean Alesi | Ferrari | 30 | Engine | 5 |
| Ret | 24 | G.Morbidelli | Minardi-Ferrari | 29 | Gearbox | 19 |
| Ret | 11 | Mika Hakkinen | Lotus-Judd | 25 | Engine | 24 |
| Ret | 26 | Erik Comas | Ligier-Lamborghini | 25 | Engine | 26 |
| Ret | 5 | Nigel Mansell | Williams-Renault | 22 | Electrical | 3 |
| Ret | 29 | Eric Bernard | Lola-Ford | 21 | Gearbox | 20 |
| Ret | 16 | Ivan Capelli | Leyton House-Ilmor | 13 | Engine | 12 |
| Ret | 3 | Satoru Nakajima | Tyrrell-Honda | 7 | Spun off | 22 |
| Ret | 27 | Alain Prost | Ferrari | 2 | Fuel leak | 2 |
| Ret | 15 | M.Gugelmin | Leyton House-Ilmor | 1 | Engine | 15 |
| Ret | 32 | M.Schumacher | Jordan-Ford | 0 | Clutch | 7 |
| DNQ | 30 | Aguri Suzuki | Lola-Ford | | | |
| DNQ | 34 | Nicola Larini | Lamborghini | | | |
| DNQ | 10 | Alex Caffi | Footwork-Ford | | | |
| DNQ | 35 | E.van de Poele | Lamborghini | | | |
| DNPQ | 9 | Michele Alboreto | Footwork-Ford | | | |
| DNPQ | 17 | G.Tarquini | AGS-Ford | | | |
| DNPQ | 31 | P.M.Chaves | Coloni-Ford | | | |
| DNPQ | 18 | F.Barbazza | AGS-Ford | | | |

Winning speed: 130.415mph
Lap leaders: Senna 1-14, 31-44; Mansell 15-16, 18-21; Piquet 17; Alesi 22-30
Pole position: Senna, 1m 47.811s, 143.996mph
Fastest lap: Moreno, 1m 55.161s, 134.806mph

### ITALIAN GRAND PRIX: MONZA *8 September Round: 12 Race: 512 53 x 3.604 miles*

| POS. | NO. | DRIVER | CAR/ENGINE | LAPS | TIME/RETIRED | GRID |
|---|---|---|---|---|---|---|
| 1 | 5 | Nigel Mansell | Williams-Renault | 53 | 1:17'54.319 | 2 |
| 2 | 1 | Ayrton Senna | McLaren-Honda | 53 | +16.262 | 1 |
| 3 | 27 | Alain Prost | Ferrari | 53 | +16.829 | 5 |
| 4 | 2 | Gerhard Berger | McLaren-Honda | 53 | +27.719 | 3 |
| 5 | 19 | M.Schumacher | Benetton-Ford | 53 | +34.463 | 7 |
| 6 | 20 | Nelson Piquet | Benetton-Ford | 53 | +45.600 | 8 |
| 7 | 33 | A.de Cesaris | Jordan-Ford | 53 | +51.136 | 14 |
| 8 | 16 | Ivan Capelli | Leyton House-Ilmor | 53 | +1'15.019 | 12 |
| 9 | 24 | G.Morbidelli | Minardi-Ferrari | 52 | +1 Lap | 17 |
| 10 | 21 | Emanuele Pirro | Dallara-Judd | 52 | +1 Lap | 16 |
| 11 | 26 | Erik Comas | Ligier-Lamborghini | 52 | +1 Lap | 22 |
| 12 | 8 | Mark Blundell | Brabham-Yamaha | 52 | +1 Lap | 11 |
| 13 | 7 | Martin Brundle | Brabham-Yamaha | 52 | +1 Lap | 19 |
| 14 | 11 | Mika Hakkinen | Lotus-Judd | 49 | +4 Laps | 25 |
| 15 | 15 | M.Gugelmin | Leyton House-Ilmor | 49 | +4 Laps | 18 |
| 16 | 34 | Nicola Larini | Lamborghini | 48 | +5 Laps | 23 |
| Ret | 14 | O.Grouillard | Fondmetal-Ford | 46 | Engine | 26 |
| Ret | 22 | J J Lehto | Dallara-Judd | 35 | Overheating | 20 |
| Ret | 4 | Stefano Modena | Tyrrell-Honda | 32 | Engine | 13 |
| Ret | 28 | Jean Alesi | Ferrari | 29 | Engine | 6 |
| Ret | 6 | Riccardo Patrese | Williams-Renault | 27 | Gearbox | 4 |
| Ret | 3 | Satoru Nakajima | Tyrrell-Honda | 24 | Throttle | 15 |
| Ret | 29 | Eric Bernard | Lola-Ford | 21 | Engine | 24 |
| Ret | 23 | P.Martini | Minardi-Ferrari | 8 | Spun off | 10 |
| Ret | 32 | Roberto Moreno | Jordan-Ford | 2 | Spun off | 9 |
| Ret | 25 | Thierry Boutsen | Ligier-Lamborghini | 1 | Spun off | 21 |
| DNQ | 9 | Michele Alboreto | Footwork-Ford | | | |
| DNQ | 12 | Michael Bartels | Lotus-Judd | | | |
| DNQ | 35 | E.van de Poele | Lamborghini | | | |
| DNQ | 30 | Aguri Suzuki | Lola-Ford | | | |
| DNPQ | 18 | F.Barbazza | AGS-Ford | | | |
| DNPQ | 17 | G.Tarquini | AGS-Ford | | | |
| DNPQ | 10 | Alex Caffi | Footwork-Ford | | | |
| DNPQ | 31 | P.M.Chaves | Coloni-Ford | | | |

Winning speed: 147.109mph Lap leaders: Senna 1-25, 27-33; Patrese 26; Mansell 34-53
Pole position: Senna, 1m 21.114s, 159.951mph
Fastest lap: Senna, 1m 26.061s, 150.756mph

### PORTUGUESE GRAND PRIX: ESTORIL *22 September Round: 13 Race: 513 71 x 2.703 miles*

| POS. | NO. | DRIVER | CAR/ENGINE | LAPS | TIME/RETIRED | GRID |
|---|---|---|---|---|---|---|
| 1 | 6 | Riccardo Patrese | Williams-Renault | 71 | 1:35'42.304 | 1 |
| 2 | 1 | Ayrton Senna | McLaren-Honda | 71 | +20.941 | 3 |
| 3 | 28 | Jean Alesi | Ferrari | 71 | +53.554 | 6 |
| 4 | 23 | P.Martini | Minardi-Ferrari | 71 | +1'03.498 | 8 |
| 5 | 20 | Nelson Piquet | Benetton-Ford | 71 | +1'10.033 | 11 |
| 6 | 19 | M.Schumacher | Benetton-Ford | 71 | +1'16.582 | 10 |
| 7 | 15 | M.Gugelmin | Leyton House-Ilmor | 70 | +1 Lap | 7 |
| 8 | 33 | A.de Cesaris | Jordan-Ford | 70 | +1 Lap | 14 |
| 9 | 24 | G.Morbidelli | Minardi-Ferrari | 70 | +1 Lap | 13 |
| 10 | 32 | Roberto Moreno | Jordan-Ford | 70 | +1 Lap | 16 |
| 11 | 26 | Erik Comas | Ligier-Lamborghini | 70 | +1 Lap | 23 |
| 12 | 7 | Martin Brundle | Brabham-Yamaha | 69 | +2 Laps | 19 |
| 13 | 3 | Satoru Nakajima | Tyrrell-Honda | 68 | +3 Laps | 21 |
| 14 | 11 | Mika Hakkinen | Lotus-Judd | 68 | +3 Laps | 26 |
| 15 | 9 | Michele Alboreto | Footwork-Ford | 68 | +3 Laps | 24 |
| 16 | 25 | Thierry Boutsen | Ligier-Lamborghini | 68 | +3 Laps | 20 |
| 17 | 16 | Ivan Capelli | Leyton House-Ilmor | 64 | Spun off | 9 |
| Ret | 4 | Stefano Modena | Tyrrell-Honda | 56 | Engine | 12 |
| DSQ | 5 | Nigel Mansell | Williams-Renault | 51 | Disqualified | 4 |
| Ret | 30 | Aguri Suzuki | Lola-Ford | 40 | Transmission | 25 |
| Ret | 27 | Alain Prost | Ferrari | 39 | Engine | 5 |
| Ret | 2 | Gerhard Berger | McLaren-Honda | 37 | Engine | 2 |
| Ret | 21 | Emanuele Pirro | Dallara-Judd | 18 | Engine | 17 |
| Ret | 22 | J J Lehto | Dallara-Judd | 14 | Gearbox | 18 |
| Ret | 8 | Mark Blundell | Brabham-Yamaha | 12 | Suspension | 15 |
| Ret | 12 | Johnny Herbert | Lotus-Judd | 1 | Engine | 22 |
| DNQ | 29 | Eric Bernard | Lola-Ford | | | |
| DNQ | 17 | G.Tarquini | AGS-Ford | | | |
| DNQ | 34 | Nicola Larini | Lamborghini | | | |
| DNQ | 35 | E.van de Poele | Lamborghini | | | |
| DNPQ | 18 | F.Barbazza | AGS-Ford | | | |
| DNPQ | 14 | O.Grouillard | Fondmetal-Ford | | | |
| DNPQ | 10 | Alex Caffi | Footwork-Ford | | | |
| DNPQ | 31 | P.M.Chaves | Coloni-Ford | | | |

Winning speed: 120.314mph Lap leaders: Patrese 1-17, 30-71; Mansell 18-29
Pole position: Patrese, 1m 13.001s, 133.295mph
Fastest lap: Mansell, 1m 18.179s, 124.467mph
Dispite his disqualification, Mansell's fastest lap was not discounted.

### SPANISH GRAND PRIX: MONTMELO *29 September Round: 14 Race 514 65 x 2.950*

| POS. | NO. | DRIVER | CAR/ENGINE | LAPS | TIME/RETIRED | GRID |
|---|---|---|---|---|---|---|
| 1 | 5 | Nigel Mansell | Williams-Renault | 65 | 1:38'41.541 | 2 |
| 2 | 27 | Alain Prost | Ferrari | 65 | +11.331 | 6 |
| 3 | 6 | Riccardo Patrese | Williams-Renault | 65 | +15.909 | 4 |
| 4 | 28 | Jean Alesi | Ferrari | 65 | +22.772 | 7 |
| 5 | 1 | Ayrton Senna | McLaren-Honda | 65 | +1'02.402 | 3 |
| 6 | 19 | M.Schumacher | Benetton-Ford | 65 | +1'19.468 | 5 |
| 7 | 15 | M.Gugelmin | Leyton House-Ilmor | 64 | +1 Lap | 13 |
| 8 | 22 | J J Lehto | Dallara-Judd | 64 | +1 Lap | 15 |
| 9 | 32 | A.Zanardi | Jordan-Ford | 64 | +1 Lap | 20 |
| 10 | 7 | Martin Brundle | Brabham-Yamaha | 63 | +2 Laps | 11 |
| 11 | 20 | Nelson Piquet | Benetton-Ford | 63 | +2 Laps | 10 |
| 12 | 14 | G.Tarquini | Fondmetal-Ford | 63 | +2 Laps | 22 |
| 13 | 23 | P.Martini | Minardi-Ferrari | 63 | +2 Laps | 19 |
| 14 | 24 | G.Morbidelli | Minardi-Ferrari | 62 | Collision | 16 |
| 15 | 21 | Emanuele Pirro | Dallara-Judd | 62 | +3 Laps | 9 |
| 16 | 4 | Stefano Modena | Tyrrell-Honda | 62 | +3 Laps | 14 |
| 17 | 3 | Satoru Nakajima | Tyrrell-Honda | 62 | +3 Laps | 18 |
| Ret | 8 | Mark Blundell | Brabham-Yamaha | 49 | Engine | 12 |
| Ret | 26 | Erik Comas | Ligier-Lamborghini | 36 | Electrical | 25 |
| Ret | 2 | Gerhard Berger | McLaren-Honda | 33 | Electrical | 1 |
| Ret | 9 | Michele Alboreto | Footwork-Ford | 23 | Engine | 24 |
| Ret | 33 | A.de Cesaris | Jordan-Ford | 22 | Electrical | 17 |
| Ret | 11 | Mika Hakkinen | Lotus-Judd | 5 | Spun off | 21 |
| Ret | 16 | Ivan Capelli | Leyton House-Ilmor | 1 | Collision | 8 |
| Ret | 29 | Eric Bernard | Lola-Ford | 0 | Collision | 23 |
| Ret | 25 | Thierry Boutsen | Ligier-Lamborghini | 0 | Collision | 26 |
| DNQ | 30 | Aguri Suzuki | Lola-Ford | | | |
| DNQ | 34 | Nicola Larini | Lamborghini | | | |
| DNQ | 12 | Michael Bartels | Lotus-Judd | | | |
| DNQ | 35 | E.van de Poele | Lamborghini | | | |
| DNPQ | 10 | Alex Caffi | Footwork-Ford | | | |
| DNPQ | 18 | F.Barbazza | AGS-Ford | | | |
| DNPQ | 17 | O.Grouillard | AGS-Ford | | | |

Winning speed: 116.561mph
Lap leaders: Berger 1-8, 12-20; Mansell 9, 21-65; Patrese 10; Senna 11
Pole position: Berger, 1m 18.751s, 134.839mph
Fastest lap: Patrese, 1m 22.837s, 128.188mph

### JAPANESE GRAND PRIX: SUZUKA *20 October Round: 15 Race: 515 53 x 3.644 miles*

| POS. | NO. | DRIVER | CAR/ENGINE | LAPS | TIME/RETIRED | GRID |
|---|---|---|---|---|---|---|
| 1 | 2 | Gerhard Berger | McLaren-Honda | 53 | 1:32'10.695 | 1 |
| 2 | 1 | Ayrton Senna | McLaren-Honda | 53 | +0.344 | 2 |
| 3 | 6 | Riccardo Patrese | Williams-Renault | 53 | +56.731 | 5 |
| 4 | 27 | Alain Prost | Ferrari | 53 | +1'20.761 | 4 |
| 5 | 7 | Martin Brundle | Brabham-Yamaha | 52 | +1 Lap | 19 |
| 6 | 4 | Stefano Modena | Tyrrell-Honda | 52 | +1 Lap | 14 |
| 7 | 20 | Nelson Piquet | Benetton-Ford | 52 | +1 Lap | 10 |
| 8 | 15 | M.Gugelmin | Leyton House-Ilmor | 52 | +1 Lap | 18 |
| 9 | 25 | Thierry Boutsen | Ligier-Lamborghini | 52 | +1 Lap | 17 |
| 10 | 10 | Alex Caffi | Footwork-Ford | 51 | +2 Laps | 26 |
| 11 | 14 | G.Tarquini | Fondmetal-Ford | 50 | + 3 Laps | 24 |
| Ret | 26 | Erik Comas | Ligier-Lamborghini | 41 | Alternator | 20 |
| Ret | 23 | P.Martini | Minardi-Ferrari | 39 | Electrical | 7 |
| Ret | 19 | M.Schumacher | Benetton-Ford | 34 | Engine | 9 |
| Ret | 12 | Johnny Herbert | Lotus-Judd | 31 | Engine | 23 |
| Ret | 3 | Satoru Nakajima | Tyrrell-Honda | 30 | Spun off | 15 |
| Ret | 30 | Aguri Suzuki | Lola-Ford | 26 | Engine | 25 |
| Ret | 24 | G.Morbidelli | Minardi-Ferrari | 15 | Wheel | 8 |
| Ret | 5 | Nigel Mansell | Williams-Renault | 9 | Spun off | 3 |
| Ret | 32 | A.Zanardi | Jordan-Ford | 7 | Gearbox | 13 |
| Ret | 11 | Mika Hakkinen | Lotus-Judd | 4 | Engine | 21 |
| Ret | 33 | A.de Cesaris | Jordan-Ford | 1 | Collision | 11 |
| Ret | 22 | J J Lehto | Dallara-Judd | 1 | Collision | 12 |
| Ret | 21 | Emanuele Pirro | Dallara-Judd | 1 | Collision | 16 |
| Ret | 16 | Karl Wendlinger | Leyton House-Ilmor | 1 | Collision | 22 |
| Ret | 28 | Jean Alesi | Ferrari | 0 | Engine | 6 |
| DNQ | 9 | Michele Alboreto | Footwork-Ford | | | |
| DNQ | 34 | Nicola Larini | Lamborghini | | | |
| DNQ | 35 | E. van de Poele | Lamborghini | | | |
| DNQ | 29 | Eric Bernard | Lola-Ford | | | |
| DNPQ | 8 | Mark Blundell | Brabham-Yamaha | | | |
| DNPQ | 31 | Naoki Hattori | Coloni-Ford | | | |

Winning speed: 125.702mph
Lap leaders: Berger 1-17, 53; Senna 18-21, 24-52; Patrese 22-23
Pole position: Berger, 1m 34.700s, 138.515mph
Fastest lap: Senna, 1m 41.532s, 129.195mph

### AUSTRALIAN GRAND PRIX: ADELAIDE *3 November Round: 16 Race: 516 14 x 2.349 miles*

| POS. | NO. | DRIVER | CAR/ENGINE | LAPS | TIME/RETIRED | GRID |
|---|---|---|---|---|---|---|
| 1 | 1 | Ayrton Senna | McLaren-Honda | 14 | 24'34.899 | 1 |
| 2 | 5 | Nigel Mansell | Williams-Renault | 14 | +1.259 | 3 |
| 3 | 2 | Gerhard Berger | McLaren-Honda | 14 | +5.120 | 2 |
| 4 | 20 | Nelson Piquet | Benetton-Ford | 14 | +30.103 | 5 |
| 5 | 6 | Riccardo Patrese | Williams-Renault | 14 | +50.537 | 4 |
| 6 | 27 | G.Morbidelli | Ferrari | 14 | +51.069 | 8 |
| 7 | 21 | Emanuele Pirro | Dallara-Judd | 14 | +52.361 | 13 |
| 8 | 33 | A.de Cesaris | Jordan-Ford | 14 | +1'00.431 | 12 |
| 9 | 32 | A.Zanardi | Jordan-Ford | 14 | +1'15.567 | 16 |
| 10 | 4 | Stefano Modena | Tyrrell-Honda | 14 | +1'20.370 | 9 |
| 11 | 12 | Johnny Herbert | Lotus-Judd | 14 | +1'22.073 | 21 |
| 12 | 22 | J J Lehto | Dallara-Judd | 14 | +1'38.519 | 11 |
| 13 | 9 | Michele Alboreto | Footwork-Ford | 14 | +1'39.303 | 15 |
| 14 | 15 | M.Gugelmin | Leyton House-Ilmor | 13 | +1 Lap | 14 |
| 15 | 10 | Alex Caffi | Footwork-Ford | 13 | +1 Lap | 23 |
| 16 | 24 | Roberto Moreno | Minardi-Ferrari | 13 | +1 Lap | 18 |
| 17 | 8 | Mark Blundell | Brabham-Yamaha | 13 | +1 Lap | 17 |
| 18 | 26 | Erik Comas | Ligier-Lamborghini | 13 | +1 Lap | 22 |
| 19 | 11 | Mika Hakkinen | Lotus-Judd | 13 | +1 Lap | 25 |
| 20 | 16 | Karl Wendlinger | Leyton House-Ilmor | 12 | +2 Laps | 26 |
| Ret | 23 | P.Martini | Minardi-Ferrari | 8 | Spun off | 10 |
| Ret | 19 | M.Schumacher | Benetton-Ford | 5 | Collision | 6 |
| Ret | 28 | Jean Alesi | Ferrari | 5 | Collision | 7 |
| Ret | 34 | Nicola Larini | Lamborghini | 5 | Spun off | 19 |
| Ret | 25 | Thierry Boutsen | Ligier-Lamborghini | 5 | Collision | 20 |
| Ret | 3 | Satoru Nakajima | Tyrrell-Honda | 4 | Spun off | 24 |
| DNQ | 30 | Aguri Suzuki | Lola-Ford | | | |
| DNQ | 7 | Martin Brundle | Brabham-Yamaha | | | |
| DNQ | 35 | E.van de Poele | Lamborghini | | | |
| DNQ | 29 | Bertrand Gachot | Lola-Ford | | | |
| DNPQ | 14 | G.Tarquini | Fondmetal-Ford | | | |
| DNPQ | 31 | Naoki Hattori | Coloni-Ford | | | |

Winning speed: 80.262mph Lap leaders: Senna 1-14
Pole position: Senna, 1m 14.041s, 114.202mph
Fastest lap: Berger, 1m 41.141s, 83.602mph
Scheduled for 81 laps, but stopped early because of rain. Half points awarded.

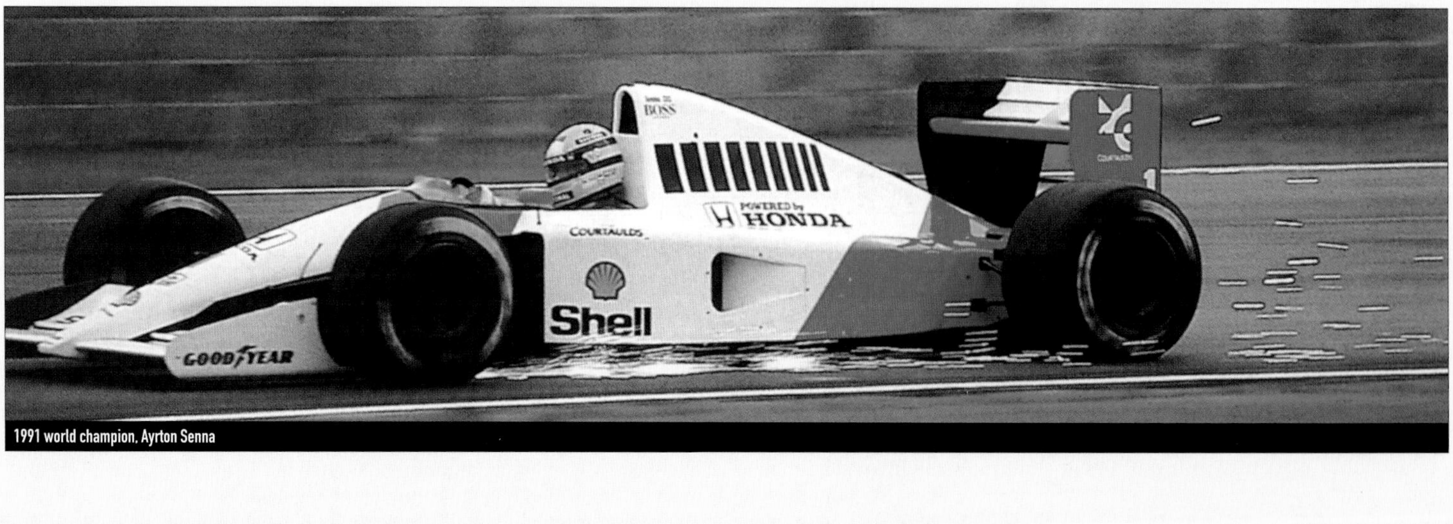

1991 world champion, Ayrton Senna

# 1992

## DRIVERS' CHAMPION: NIGEL MANSELL
## CONSTRUCTORS' CHAMPION: WILLIAMS RENAULT

### DRIVERS' CHAMPIONSHIP

| POS. | DRIVER | NATIONALITY | CAR | POINTS |
|---|---|---|---|---|
| 1 | Nigel Mansell | GB | Williams-Renault | 108 |
| 2 | Riccardo Patrese | Italy | Williams-Renault | 56 |
| 3 | Michael Schumacher | Germany | Benetton-Ford | 53 |
| 4 | Ayrton Senna | Brazil | McLaren-Honda | 50 |
| 5 | Gerhard Berger | Austria | McLaren-Honda | 49 |
| 6 | Martin Brundle | GB | Benetton-Ford | 38 |
| 7 | Jean Alesi | France | Ferrari | 18 |
| 8 | Miki Häkkinen | Finland | Lotus-Ford | 11 |
| 9 | Andrea de Cesaris | Italy | Tyrrell-Ilmor | 8 |
| 10 | Michele Alboreto | Italy | Footwork-Mugen | 6 |
| 11 | Erik Comas | France | Ligier-Renault | 4 |
| 12 | Karl Wendlinger | Austria | March-Ilmor | 3 |
| = | Ivan Capelli | Italy | Ferrari | 3 |
| 14 | Thierry Boutsen | Belgium | Ligier-Renault | 2 |
| = | Pierluigi Martini | Italy | Dallara-Ferrari | 2 |
| = | Johnny Herbert | GB | Lotus-Ford | 2 |
| 17 | Bertrand Gachot | Belgium | Larrousse-Lamborghini | 1 |
| = | Christian Fittipaldi | Brazil | Minardi-Lamborghini | 1 |
| = | Stefano Modena | Italy | Jordan-Yamaha | 1 |
| | Mauricio Gugelmin | Brazil | Jordan-Yamaha | |
| | Olivier Grouillard | France | Tyrrell-Ilmor | |
| | Gabriele Tarquini | Italy | Fondmetal-Ford | |
| | J.J. Lehto | Finland | Dallara-Ferrari | |
| | Gianni Morbidelli | Italy | Minardi-Lamborghini | |
| | Ukyo Katayama | Japan | Larrousse-Lamborghini | |
| | Aguri Suzuki | Japan | Footwork-Mugen | |
| | Eric van de Poele | Belgium | Brabham-Judd, Fondmetal-Ford | |
| | Andrea Chiesa | Switzerland | Fondmetal-Ford | |
| | Paul Belmondo | France | March-Ilmor | |
| | Giovanna Amati | Italy | Brabham-Judd | |
| | Enrico Bertaggia | Italy | Coloni-Judd, Andrea Moda-Judd | |
| | Alex Caffi | Italy | Coloni-Judd, Andrea Moda-Judd | |
| | Perry McCarthy | GB | Andrea Moda-Judd | |
| | Roberto Moreno | Brazil | Andrea Moda-Judd | |
| | Damon Hill | GB | Brabham-Judd | |
| | Alessandro Zanardi | Italy | Minardi-Lamborghini | |
| | Emanuele Naspetti | Italy | March-Ilmor | |
| | Nicola Larini | Italy | Ferrari | |
| | Jan Lammers | Netherlands | March-Ilmor | |

Points for top six finishers (10, 6, 4, 3, 2, 1). Half points awarded for races stopped before half distance.

### CONSTRUCTORS' CHAMPIONSHIP

| POS. | CONSTRUCTOR | POINTS |
|---|---|---|
| 1 | Williams-Renault | 164 |
| 2 | McLaren-Honda | 99 |
| 3 | Benetton-Ford | 91 |
| 4 | Ferrari | 21 |
| 5 | Lotus-Ford | 13 |
| 6 | Tyrrell-Ilmor | 8 |
| 7 | Footwork-Mugen-Honda | 6 |
| 7 | Ligier-Renault | 6 |
| 9 | March-Ilmor | 3 |
| 10 | Dallara-Ferrari | 2 |
| 11 | Venturi-Lamborghini | 1 |
| 11 | Minardi-Lamborghini | 1 |
| 11 | Jordan-Yamaha | 1 |

Points for top six finishers (10, 6, 4, 3, 2, 1). Half points awarded for races stopped before half distance.

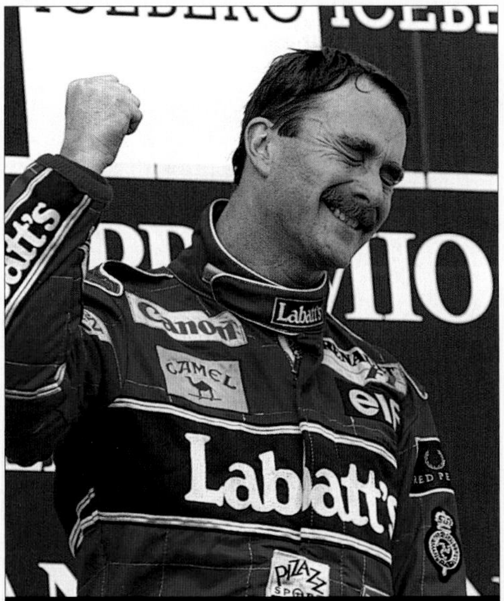

1992 world champion Nigel Mansell

### SOUTH AFRICAN GRAND PRIX: KYALAMI *1 March Round: 1 Race: 517 72 x 2.648 miles*

| POS. | NO. | DRIVER | CAR/ENGINE | LAPS | TIME/RETIRED | GRID |
|---|---|---|---|---|---|---|
| 1 | 5 | Nigel Mansell | Williams-Renault | 72 | 1:36'45.320 | 1 |
| 2 | 6 | Riccardo Patrese | Williams-Renault | 72 | +24.360 | 4 |
| 3 | 1 | Ayrton Senna | McLaren-Honda | 72 | +34.675 | 2 |
| 4 | 19 | M.Schumacher | Benetton-Ford | 72 | +47.863 | 6 |
| 5 | 2 | Gerhard Berger | McLaren-Honda | 72 | +1'13.634 | 3 |
| 6 | 12 | Johnny Herbert | Lotus-Ford | 71 | +1 Lap | 11 |
| 7 | 26 | Erik Comas | Ligier-Renault | 71 | +1 Lap | 13 |
| 8 | 10 | Aguri Suzuki | Footwork-Mugen-Honda | 70 | +2 Laps | 16 |
| 9 | 11 | Mika Hakkinen | Lotus-Ford | 70 | +2 Laps | 21 |
| 10 | 9 | Michele Alboreto | Footwork-Mugen-Honda | 70 | +2 Laps | 17 |
| 11 | 33 | M.Gugelmin | Jordan-Yamaha | 70 | +2 Laps | 23 |
| 12 | 30 | Ukyo Katayama | Venturi-Lamborghini | 68 | +4 Laps | 18 |
| 13 | 7 | E.van de Poele | Brabham-Judd | 68 | +4 Laps | 26 |
| Ret | 3 | O.Grouillard | Tyrrell-Ilmor | 62 | Engine | 12 |
| Ret | 25 | Thierry Boutsen | Ligier-Renault | 60 | Fuel system | 14 |
| Ret | 22 | P.Martini | Dallara-Ferrari | 56 | Clutch | 25 |
| Ret | 24 | G.Morbidelli | Minardi-Lamborghini | 55 | Engine | 19 |
| Ret | 21 | J J Lehto | Dallara-Ferrari | 46 | Gearbox | 24 |
| Ret | 23 | C.Fittipaldi | Minardi-Lamborghini | 43 | Alternator | 20 |
| Ret | 4 | A.de Cesaris | Tyrrell-Ilmor | 41 | Engine | 10 |
| Ret | 27 | Jean Alesi | Ferrari | 40 | Engine | 5 |
| Ret | 28 | Ivan Capelli | Ferrari | 28 | Engine | 9 |
| Ret | 15 | G.Tarquini | Fondmetal-Ford | 23 | Engine | 15 |
| Ret | 16 | Karl Wendlinger | March-Ilmor | 13 | Overheating | 7 |
| Ret | 29 | Bertrand Gachot | Venturi-Lamborghini | 8 | Steering | 22 |
| Ret | 20 | Martin Brundle | Benetton-Ford | 1 | Clutch | 8 |
| DNQ | 17 | Paul Belmondo | March-Ilmor | | | |
| DNQ | 14 | Andrea Chiesa | Fondmetal-Ford | | | |
| DNQ | 32 | Stefano Modena | Jordan-Yamaha | | | |
| DNQ | 8 | Giovanna Amati | Brabham-Judd | | | |

Winning Position: 118.215mph Lap leaders: Mansell 1-72
Pole position: Mansell, 1m 15.486s, 126.270mph
Fastest lap: Mansell, 1m 17.578s, 122.865mph

### MEXICAN GRAND PRIX: MEXICO CITY *22 March Round: 2 Race: 518 69 x 2.747 miles*

| POS. | NO. | DRIVER | CAR/ENGINE | LAPS | TIME/RETIRED | GRID |
|---|---|---|---|---|---|---|
| 1 | 5 | Nigel Mansell | Williams-Renault | 69 | 1:31'53.587 | 1 |
| 2 | 6 | Riccardo Patrese | Williams-Renault | 69 | +12.971 | 2 |
| 3 | 19 | M.Schumacher | Benetton-Ford | 69 | +21.429 | 3 |
| 4 | 2 | Gerhard Berger | McLaren-Honda | 69 | +33.347 | 5 |
| 5 | 4 | A.de Cesaris | Tyrrell-Ilmor | 68 | +1 Lap | 11 |
| 6 | 11 | Mika Hakkinen | Lotus-Ford | 68 | +1 Lap | 18 |
| 7 | 12 | Johnny Herbert | Lotus-Ford | 68 | +1 Lap | 12 |
| 8 | 21 | J J Lehto | Dallara-Ferrari | 68 | +1 Lap | 7 |
| 9 | 26 | Erik Comas | Ligier-Renault | 67 | +2 Laps | 26 |
| 10 | 25 | Thierry Boutsen | Ligier-Renault | 67 | +2 Laps | 22 |
| 11 | 29 | Bertrand Gachot | Venturi-Lamborghini | 66 | +3 Laps | 13 |
| 12 | 30 | Ukyo Katayama | Venturi-Lamborghini | 66 | +3 Laps | 24 |
| 13 | 9 | Michele Alboreto | Footwork-Mugen-Honda | 65 | +4 Laps | 25 |
| Ret | 20 | Martin Brundle | Benetton-Ford | 47 | Engine | 4 |
| Ret | 15 | G.Tarquini | Fondmetal-Ford | 45 | Clutch | 14 |
| Ret | 14 | Andrea Chiesa | Fondmetal-Ford | 37 | Spun off | 23 |
| Ret | 22 | P.Martini | Dallara-Ferrari | 36 | Handling | 9 |
| Ret | 27 | Jean Alesi | Ferrari | 31 | Engine | 10 |
| Ret | 24 | G.Morbidelli | Minardi-Lamborghini | 29 | Spun off | 21 |
| Ret | 32 | Stefano Modena | Jordan-Yamaha | 17 | Gearbox | 15 |
| Ret | 3 | O.Grouillard | Tyrrell-Ilmor | 12 | Engine | 16 |
| Ret | 1 | Ayrton Senna | McLaren-Honda | 11 | Transmission | 6 |
| Ret | 23 | C.Fittipaldi | Minardi-Lamborghini | 2 | Spun off | 17 |
| Ret | 33 | M.Gugelmin | Jordan-Yamaha | 0 | Engine | 8 |
| Ret | 16 | Karl Wendlinger | March-Ilmor | 0 | Collision | 19 |
| Ret | 28 | Ivan Capelli | Ferrari | 0 | Collision | 20 |
| DNQ | 10 | Aguri Suzuki | Footwork-Mugen-Honda | | | |
| DNQ | 17 | Paul Belmondo | March-Ilmor | | | |
| DNQ | 7 | E.van de Poele | Brabham-Judd | | | |
| DNQ | 8 | Giovanna Amati | Brabham-Judd | | | |

Winning speed: 123.762mph Lap leaders: Mansell 1-69
Pole position: Mansell, 1m 16.346s, 129.535mph
Fastest lap: Berger: 1m 17.711s, 127.260mph

### BRAZILIAN GRAND PRIX: INTERLAGOS *5 April Round: 3 Race: 519 71 x 2.687 miles*

| POS. | NO. | DRIVER | CAR/ENGINE | LAPS | TIME/RETIRED | GRID |
|---|---|---|---|---|---|---|
| 1 | 5 | Nigel Mansell | Williams-Renault | 71 | 1:36'51.85 | 1 |
| 2 | 6 | Riccardo Patrese | Williams-Renault | 71 | +29.330 | 2 |
| 3 | 19 | M.Schumacher | Benetton-Ford | 70 | +1 Lap | 5 |
| 4 | 27 | Jean Alesi | Ferrari | 70 | +1 Lap | 6 |
| 5 | 28 | Ivan Capelli | Ferrari | 70 | +1 Lap | 11 |
| 6 | 9 | Michele Alboreto | Footwork-Mugen-Honda | 70 | +1 Lap | 14 |
| 7 | 24 | G.Morbidelli | Minardi-Lamborghini | 69 | +2 Laps | 23 |
| 8 | 21 | J J Lehto | Dallara-Ferrari | 69 | +2 Laps | 16 |
| 9 | 30 | Ukyo Katayama | Venturi-Lamborghini | 68 | +3 Laps | 25 |
| 10 | 11 | Mika Hakkinen | Lotus-Ford | 67 | +4 Laps | 24 |
| Ret | 15 | G.Tarquini | Fondmetal-Ford | 62 | Engine | 19 |
| Ret | 16 | Karl Wendlinger | March-Ilmor | 55 | Clutch | 9 |
| Ret | 23 | C.Fittipaldi | Minardi-Lamborghini | 54 | Gearbox | 20 |
| Ret | 3 | O.Grouillard | Tyrrell-Ilmor | 52 | Engine | 17 |
| Ret | 26 | Erik Comas | Ligier-Renault | 42 | Gearbox | 15 |
| Ret | 12 | Johnny Herbert | Lotus-Ford | 36 | Spun off | 26 |
| Ret | 25 | Thierry Boutsen | Ligier-Renault | 36 | Collision | 10 |
| Ret | 33 | M.Gugelmin | Jordan-Yamaha | 36 | Gearbox | 21 |
| Ret | 20 | Martin Brundle | Benetton-Ford | 30 | Collision | 7 |
| Ret | 22 | P.Martini | Dallara-Ferrari | 24 | Clutch | 8 |
| Ret | 29 | Bertrand Gachot | Venturi-Lamborghini | 23 | Suspension | 18 |
| Ret | 4 | A.de Cesaris | Tyrrell-Ilmor | 21 | Engine | 13 |
| Ret | 1 | Ayrton Senna | McLaren-Honda | 17 | Engine | 3 |
| Ret | 2 | Gerhard Berger | McLaren-Honda | 4 | Electrical | 4 |
| Ret | 10 | Aguri Suzuki | Footwork-Mugen-Honda | 2 | Engine | 22 |
| Ret | 32 | Stefano Modena | Jordan-Yamaha | 1 | Gearbox | 12 |
| DNQ | 14 | Andrea Chiesa | Fondmetal-Ford | | | |
| DNQ | 17 | Paul Belmondo | March-Ilmor | | | |
| DNQ | 7 | E.van de Poele | Brabham-Judd | | | |
| DNQ | 8 | Giovanna Amati | Brabham-Judd | | | |
| DNPQ | 34 | Roberto Moreno | Moda-Judd | | | |

Winning speed: 118.191mph Lap leaders: Patrese 1-31; Mansell 32-71
Pole position: Mansell, 1m 15.703s, 127.799mph
Fastest lap: Patrese, 1m 19.490s, 121.710mph

### SPANISH GRAND PRIX: MONTMELÓ *3 May Round: 4 Race: 520 65 x 2.950 miles*

| POS. | NO. | DRIVER | CAR/ENGINE | LAPS | TIME/RETIRED | GRID |
|---|---|---|---|---|---|---|
| 1 | 5 | Nigel Mansell | Williams-Renault | 65 | 1:56'10.674 | 1 |
| 2 | 19 | M.Schumacher | Benetton-Ford | 65 | +23.914 | 2 |
| 3 | 27 | Jean Alesi | Ferrari | 65 | +26.462 | 8 |
| 4 | 2 | Gerhard Berger | McLaren-Honda | 65 | +1'20.647 | 7 |
| 5 | 9 | Michele Alboreto | Footwork-Mugen-Honda | 64 | +1 Lap | 16 |
| 6 | 22 | P.Martini | Dallara-Ferrari | 63 | +2 Laps | 13 |
| 7 | 10 | Aguri Suzuki | Footwork-Mugen-Honda | 63 | +2 Laps | 19 |
| 8 | 16 | Karl Wendlinger | March-Ilmor | 63 | +2 Laps | 9 |
| 9 | 1 | Ayrton Senna | McLaren-Honda | 62 | Spun off | 3 |
| 10 | 28 | Ivan Capelli | Ferrari | 62 | Spun off | 5 |
| 11 | 23 | C.Fittipaldi | Minardi-Lamborghini | 61 | +4 Laps | 22 |
| 12 | 17 | Paul Belmondo | March-Ilmor | 61 | +4 Laps | 23 |
| Ret | 21 | J J Lehto | Dallara-Ferrari | 56 | Spun off | 12 |
| Ret | 15 | G.Tarquini | Fondmetal-Ford | 56 | Spun off | 18 |
| Ret | 11 | Mika Hakkinen | Lotus-Ford | 56 | Spun off | 21 |
| Ret | 26 | Erik Comas | Ligier-Renault | 55 | Spun off | 10 |
| Ret | 29 | Bertrand Gachot | Venturi-Lamborghini | 35 | Engine | 24 |
| Ret | 3 | O.Grouillard | Tyrrell-Ilmor | 30 | Spun off | 15 |
| Ret | 24 | G.Morbidelli | Minardi-Lamborghini | 26 | Handling | 25 |
| Ret | 33 | M.Gugelmin | Jordan-Yamaha | 24 | Spun off | 17 |
| Ret | 14 | Andrea Chiesa | Fondmetal-Ford | 22 | Spun off | 20 |
| Ret | 6 | Riccardo Patrese | Williams-Renault | 19 | Spun off | 4 |
| Ret | 12 | Johnny Herbert | Lotus-Ford | 13 | Spun off | 26 |
| Ret | 25 | Thierry Boutsen | Ligier-Renault | 11 | Engine | 14 |
| Ret | 20 | Martin Brundle | Benetton-Ford | 4 | Spun off | 6 |
| Ret | 4 | A.de Cesaris | Tyrrell-Ilmor | 2 | Engine | 11 |
| DNQ | 30 | Ukyo Katayama | Venturi-Lamborghini | | | |
| DNQ | 7 | E.van de Poele | Brabham-Judd | | | |
| DNQ | 32 | Stefano Modena | Jordan-Yamaha | | | |
| DNQ | 8 | Damon Hill | Brabham-Judd | | | |
| DNPQ | 34 | Roberto Moreno | Moda-Judd | | | |
| DNPQ | 35 | Perry McCarthy | Moda-Judd | | | |

Winning speed: 99.017mph Lap leaders: Mansell 1-65
Pole position: Mansell, 1m 20.190s, 132.420mph
Fastest lap: Mansell, 1m 42.503s, 103.594mph

### SAN MARINO GRAND PRIX: IMOLA *17 May Round: 5 Race: 521 60 x 3.132 miles*

| POS. | NO. | DRIVER | CAR/ENGINE | LAPS | TIME/RETIRED | GRID |
|---|---|---|---|---|---|---|
| 1 | 5 | Nigel Mansell | Williams-Renault | 60 | 1:28'40.927 | 1 |
| 2 | 6 | Riccardo Patrese | Williams-Renault | 60 | +9.451 | 2 |
| 3 | 1 | Ayrton Senna | McLaren-Honda | 60 | +48.984 | 3 |
| 4 | 20 | Martin Brundle | Benetton-Ford | 60 | +53.007 | 6 |
| 5 | 9 | Michele Alboreto | Footwork-Mugen-Honda | 59 | +1 Lap | 9 |
| 6 | 22 | P.Martini | Dallara-Ferrari | 59 | +1 Lap | 15 |
| 7 | 33 | M.Gugelmin | Jordan-Yamaha | 58 | +2 Laps | 18 |
| 8 | 3 | O.Grouillard | Tyrrell-Ilmor | 58 | +2 Laps | 20 |
| 9 | 26 | Erik Comas | Ligier-Renault | 58 | +2 Laps | 13 |
| 10 | 10 | Aguri Suzuki | Footwork-Mugen-Honda | 58 | +2 Laps | 11 |
| 11 | 21 | J J Lehto | Dallara-Ferrari | 57 | Engine | 16 |
| 12 | 16 | Karl Wendlinger | March-Ilmor | 57 | +3 Laps | 12 |
| 13 | 17 | Paul Belmondo | March-Ilmor | 57 | +3 Laps | 24 |
| 14 | 4 | A.de Cesaris | Tyrrell-Ilmor | 55 | Fuel system | 14 |
| Ret | 30 | Ukyo Katayama | Venturi-Lamborghini | 40 | Spun off | 17 |
| Ret | 27 | Jean Alesi | Ferrari | 39 | Collision | 7 |
| Ret | 2 | Gerhard Berger | McLaren-Honda | 39 | Collision | 4 |
| Ret | 29 | Bertrand Gachot | Venturi-Lamborghini | 32 | Spun off | 19 |
| Ret | 25 | Thierry Boutsen | Ligier-Renault | 29 | Engine | 10 |
| Ret | 32 | Stefano Modena | Jordan-Yamaha | 25 | Gearbox | 23 |
| Ret | 24 | G.Morbidelli | Minardi-Lamborghini | 24 | Engine | 21 |
| Ret | 15 | G.Tarquini | Fondmetal-Ford | 24 | Engine | 22 |
| Ret | 19 | M.Schumacher | Benetton-Ford | 20 | Spun off | 5 |
| Ret | 28 | Ivan Capelli | Ferrari | 11 | Spun off | 8 |
| Ret | 23 | C.Fittipaldi | Minardi-Lamborghini | 8 | Gearbox | 25 |
| Ret | 12 | Johnny Herbert | Lotus-Ford | 8 | Gearbox | 26 |
| DNQ | 11 | Mika Hakkinen | Lotus-Ford | | | |
| DNQ | 14 | Andrea Chiesa | Fondmetal-Ford | | | |
| DNQ | 8 | Damon Hill | Brabham-Judd | | | |
| DNQ | 7 | E.van de Poele | Brabham-Judd | | | |
| DNPQ | 34 | Roberto Moreno | Moda-Judd | | | |
| DNPQ | 35 | Perry McCarthy | Moda-Judd | | | |

Winning speed: 127.130mph Lap leaders: Mansell 1-60
Pole position: Mansell, 1m 21.842sec, 137.755mph
Fastest lap: Patrese, 1m 26.100s, 130.943mph

### Key to Abbreviations

| | | | |
|---|---|---|---|
| DNPQ | Did not pre-qualify | NC | Not classified |
| DNQ | Did not qualify | Ret | Retired |
| DNS | Did not start | Wth | Withdrawn |
| DSQ | Disqualified | | |

MONACO GRAND PRIX: MONTE CARLO *31 May Round: 6 Race: 522 78 x 2.068 miles*

| POS. | NO. | DRIVER | CAR/ENGINE | LAPS | TIME/RETIRED | GRID |
|---|---|---|---|---|---|---|
| 1 | 1 | Ayrton Senna | McLaren-Honda | 78 | 1:50'59.372 | 3 |
| 2 | 5 | Nigel Mansell | Williams-Renault | 78 | +0.215 | 1 |
| 3 | 6 | Riccardo Patrese | Williams-Renault | 78 | +31.843 | 2 |
| 4 | 19 | M.Schumacher | Benetton-Ford | 78 | +39.294 | 6 |
| 5 | 20 | Martin Brundle | Benetton-Ford | 78 | +1'21.347 | 7 |
| 6 | 29 | Bertrand Gachot | Venturi-Lamborghini | 77 | +1 Lap | 15 |
| 7 | 9 | Michele Alboreto | Footwork-Mugen-Honda | 77 | +1 Lap | 11 |
| 8 | 23 | C.Fittipaldi | Minardi-Lamborghini | 77 | +1 Lap | 17 |
| 9 | 21 | J J Lehto | Dallara-Ferrari | 76 | +2 Laps | 20 |
| 10 | 26 | Erik Comas | Ligier-Renault | 76 | +2 Laps | 23 |
| 11 | 10 | Aguri Suzuki | Footwork-Mugen-Honda | 76 | +2 Laps | 19 |
| 12 | 25 | Thierry Boutsen | Ligier-Renault | 75 | +3 Laps | 22 |
| Ret | 28 | Ivan Capelli | Ferrari | 60 | Spun off | 8 |
| Ret | 2 | Gerhard Berger | McLaren-Honda | 32 | Gearbox | 5 |
| Ret | 11 | Mika Hakkinen | Lotus-Ford | 30 | Gearbox | 14 |
| Ret | 27 | Jean Alesi | Ferrari | 28 | Gearbox | 4 |
| Ret | 33 | M.Gugelmin | Jordan-Yamaha | 18 | Gearbox | 13 |
| Ret | 12 | Johnny Herbert | Lotus-Ford | 17 | Spun off | 9 |
| Ret | 34 | Roberto Moreno | Moda-Judd | 11 | Engine | 26 |
| Ret | 4 | A.de Cesaris | Tyrrell-Ilmor | 9 | Gearbox | 10 |
| Ret | 15 | G.Tarquini | Fondmetal-Ford | 9 | Engine | 25 |
| Ret | 32 | Stefano Modena | Jordan-Yamaha | 6 | Spun off | 21 |
| Ret | 3 | O.Grouillard | Tyrrell-Ilmor | 4 | Transmission | 24 |
| Ret | 16 | Karl Wendlinger | March-Ilmor | 1 | Gearbox | 16 |
| Ret | 24 | G.Morbidelli | Minardi-Lamborghini | 1 | Gearbox | 12 |
| Ret | 22 | P.Martini | Dallara-Ferrari | 0 | Spun off | 18 |
| DNQ | 7 | E.van de Poele | Brabham-Judd | | | |
| DNQ | 8 | Damon Hill | Brabham-Judd | | | |
| DNQ | 14 | Andrea Chiesa | Fondmetal-Ford | | | |
| DNQ | 17 | Paul Belmondo | March-Ilmor | | | |
| DNPQ | 30 | Ukyo Katayama | Venturi-Lamborghini | | | |
| DNPQ | 35 | Perry McCarthy | Moda-Judd | | | |

Winning speed: 87.196mph Lap leaders: Mansell 1-70; Senna 71-78
Pole position: Mansell, 1m 19.495s, 93.648mph
Fastest lap: Mansell, 1m 21.598s, 91.234mph

CANADIAN GRAND PRIX: MONTRÉAL *14 June Round: 7 Race: 523 69 x 2.753 miles*

| POS. | NO. | DRIVER | CAR/ENGINE | LAPS | TIME-RETIRED | GRID |
|---|---|---|---|---|---|---|
| 1 | 2 | Gerhard Berger | McLaren-Honda | 69 | 1:37'08.299 | 4 |
| 2 | 19 | M.Schumacher | Benetton-Ford | 69 | +12.401 | 5 |
| 3 | 27 | Jean Alesi | Ferrari | 69 | +1'07.327 | 8 |
| 4 | 16 | Karl Wendlinger | March-Ilmor | 68 | +1 Lap | 12 |
| 5 | 4 | A.de Cesaris | Tyrrell-Ilmor | 68 | +1 Lap | 14 |
| 6 | 26 | Erik Comas | Ligier-Renault | 68 | +1 Lap | 22 |
| 7 | 9 | Michele Alboreto | Footwork-Mugen-Honda | 68 | +1 Lap | 16 |
| 8 | 22 | P.Martini | Dallara-Ferrari | 68 | +1 Lap | 15 |
| 9 | 21 | J J Lehto | Dallara-Ferrari | 68 | +1 Lap | 23 |
| 10 | 25 | Thierry Boutsen | Ligier-Renault | 67 | +2 Laps | 21 |
| 11 | 24 | G.Morbidelli | Minardi-Lamborghini | 67 | +2 Laps | 13 |
| 12 | 3 | O.Grouillard | Tyrrell-Ilmor | 67 | +2 Laps | 26 |
| 13 | 23 | C.Fittipaldi | Minardi-Lamborghini | 65 | +4 Laps | 25 |
| 14 | 17 | Paul Belmondo | March-Ilmor | 64 | +5 Laps | 20 |
| Ret | 30 | Ukyo Katayama | Venturi-Lamborghini | 61 | Engine | 11 |
| Ret | 20 | Martin Brundle | Benetton-Ford | 45 | Transmission | 7 |
| Ret | 6 | Riccardo Patrese | Williams-Renault | 43 | Gearbox | 2 |
| Ret | 1 | Ayrton Senna | McLaren-Honda | 37 | Electrical | 1 |
| Ret | 32 | Stefano Modena | Jordan-Yamaha | 36 | Transmission | 17 |
| Ret | 11 | Mika Hakkinen | Lotus-Ford | 35 | Gearbox | 10 |
| Ret | 12 | Johnny Herbert | Lotus-Ford | 34 | Clutch | 6 |
| Ret | 28 | Ivan Capelli | Ferrari | 18 | Spun off | 9 |
| Ret | 5 | Nigel Mansell | Williams-Renault | 14 | Spun off | 3 |
| Ret | 33 | M.Gugelmin | Jordan-Yamaha | 14 | Transmission | 24 |
| DSQ | 29 | Bertrand Gachot | Venturi-Lamborghini | 14 | Disqualified | 19 |
| Ret | 15 | G.Tarquini | Fondmetal-Ford | 0 | Transmission | 18 |
| DNQ | 10 | Aguri Suzuki | Footwork-Mugen-Honda | | | |
| DNQ | 7 | E.van de Poele | Brabham-Judd | | | |
| DNQ | 14 | Andrea Chiesa | Fondmetal-Ford | | | |
| DNQ | 8 | Damon Hill | Brabham-Judd | | | |
| DNPQ | 34 | Roberto Moreno | Moda-Judd | | | |

Winning speed: 117.318mph Lap leaders: Senna 1-37; Berger 38-69
Pole position: Senna, 1m 19.775s, 124.220mph
Fastest lap: Berger: 1m 22.325s, 120.372mph

FRENCH GRAND PRIX: MAGNY-COURS *5 July Round: 8 Race: 524 69 x 2.641 miles*

| POS. | NO. | DRIVER | CAR/ENGINE | LAPS | TIME/RETIRED | GRID |
|---|---|---|---|---|---|---|
| 1 | 5 | Nigel Mansell | Williams-Renault | 69 | 1:38'08.459 | 1 |
| 2 | 6 | Riccardo Patrese | Williams-Renault | 69 | +46.447 | 2 |
| 3 | 20 | Martin Brundle | Benetton-Ford | 69 | +1'12.579 | 7 |
| 4 | 11 | Mika Hakkinen | Lotus-Ford | 68 | +1 Lap | 11 |
| 5 | 26 | Erik Comas | Ligier-Renault | 68 | +1 Lap | 10 |
| 6 | 12 | Johnny Herbert | Lotus-Ford | 68 | +1 Lap | 12 |
| 7 | 9 | Michele Alboreto | Footwork-Mugen-Honda | 68 | +1 Lap | 14 |
| 8 | 24 | G.Morbidelli | Minardi-Lamborghini | 68 | +1 Lap | 16 |
| 9 | 21 | J J Lehto | Dallara-Ferrari | 67 | +2 Laps | 17 |
| 10 | 22 | P.Martini | Dallara-Ferrari | 67 | +2 Laps | 25 |
| 11 | 3 | O.Grouillard | Tyrrell-Ilmor | 66 | +3 Laps | 22 |
| Ret | 27 | Jean Alesi | Ferrari | 61 | Engine | 6 |
| Ret | 4 | A.de Cesaris | Tyrrell-Ilmor | 51 | Spun off | 19 |
| Ret | 30 | Ukyo Katayama | Venturi-Lamborghini | 49 | Engine | 18 |
| Ret | 25 | Thierry Boutsen | Ligier-Renault | 46 | Spun off | 9 |
| Ret | 28 | Ivan Capelli | Ferrari | 38 | Engine | 8 |
| Ret | 16 | Karl Wendlinger | March-Ilmor | 33 | Gearbox | 21 |
| Ret | 32 | Stefano Modena | Jordan-Yamaha | 25 | Engine | 20 |
| Ret | 10 | Aguri Suzuki | Footwork-Mugen-Honda | 20 | Collision | 15 |
| Ret | 19 | M.Schumacher | Benetton-Ford | 17 | Collision | 5 |
| Ret | 2 | Gerhard Berger | McLaren-Honda | 10 | Engine | 4 |
| Ret | 15 | G.Tarquini | Fondmetal-Ford | 6 | Throttle | 23 |
| Ret | 1 | Ayrton Senna | McLaren-Honda | 0 | Collision | 3 |
| Ret | 29 | Bertrand Gachot | Venturi-Lamborghini | 0 | Collision | 13 |
| Ret | 33 | M.Gugelmin | Jordan-Yamaha | 0 | Collision | 24 |
| Ret | 14 | Andrea Chiesa | Fondmetal-Ford | 0 | Collision | 26 |
| DNQ | 17 | Paul Belmondo | March-Ilmor | | | |
| DNQ | 23 | C.Fittipaldi | Minardi-Lamborghini | | | |
| DNQ | 7 | E.van de Poele | Brabham-Judd | | | |
| DNQ | 8 | Damon Hill | Brabham-Judd | | | |

Winning speed: 111.401mph Lap leaders: Patrese 1-18; Mansell 19-69
Pole position: Mansell, 1m 13.864s, 128.709mph
Fastest lap: Mansell, 1m 17.070s, 123.355mph
Race stopped for rain after 18 laps. Restarted on aggregate for 51 laps, rather than the remaining 54 laps.

BRITISH GRAND PRIX: SILVERSTONE *12 July Round: 9 Race: 525 59 x 3.247 miles*

| POS. | NO. | DRIVER | CAR/ENGINE | LAPS | TIME/RETIRED | GRID |
|---|---|---|---|---|---|---|
| 1 | 5 | Nigel Mansell | Williams-Renault | 59 | 1:25'42.991 | 1 |
| 2 | 6 | Riccardo Patrese | Williams-Renault | 59 | +39.094 | 2 |
| 3 | 20 | Martin Brundle | Benetton-Ford | 59 | +48.395 | 6 |
| 4 | 19 | M.Schumacher | Benetton-Ford | 59 | +53.267 | 4 |
| 5 | 2 | Gerhard Berger | McLaren-Honda | 59 | +55.795 | 5 |
| 6 | 11 | Mika Hakkinen | Lotus-Ford | 59 | +1'20.138 | 9 |
| 7 | 9 | Michele Alboreto | Footwork-Mugen-Honda | 58 | +1 Lap | 12 |
| 8 | 26 | Erik Comas | Ligier-Renault | 58 | +1 Lap | 10 |
| 9 | 28 | Ivan Capelli | Ferrari | 58 | +1 Lap | 14 |
| 10 | 25 | Thierry Boutsen | Ligier-Renault | 57 | +2 Laps | 13 |
| 11 | 3 | O.Grouillard | Tyrrell-Ilmor | 57 | +2 Laps | 20 |
| 12 | 10 | Aguri Suzuki | Footwork-Mugen-Honda | 57 | +2 Laps | 17 |
| 13 | 21 | J J Lehto | Dallara-Ferrari | 57 | +2 Laps | 19 |
| 14 | 15 | G.Tarquini | Fondmetal-Ford | 57 | +2 Laps | 15 |
| 15 | 22 | P.Martini | Dallara-Ferrari | 56 | +3 Laps | 22 |
| 16 | 8 | Damon Hill | Brabham-Judd | 55 | +4 Laps | 26 |
| 17 | 24 | G.Morbidelli | Minardi-Lamborghini | 53 | Engine | 25 |
| Ret | 1 | Ayrton Senna | McLaren-Honda | 52 | Transmission | 3 |
| Ret | 4 | A.de Cesaris | Tyrrell-Ilmor | 46 | Spun off | 18 |
| Ret | 27 | Jean Alesi | Ferrari | 43 | Mechanical | 8 |
| Ret | 32 | Stefano Modena | Jordan-Yamaha | 43 | Engine | 23 |
| Ret | 33 | M.Gugelmin | Jordan-Yamaha | 37 | Engine | 24 |
| Ret | 29 | Bertrand Gachot | Venturi-Lamborghini | 32 | Wheel | 11 |
| Ret | 12 | Johnny Herbert | Lotus-Ford | 31 | Transmission | 7 |
| Ret | 16 | Karl Wendlinger | March-Ilmor | 27 | Gearbox | 21 |
| Ret | 30 | Ukyo Katayama | Venturi-Lamborghini | 27 | Transmission | 16 |
| DNQ | 23 | A.Zanardi | Minardi-Lamborghini | | | |
| DNQ | 17 | Paul Belmondo | March-Ilmor | | | |
| DNQ | 14 | Andrea Chiesa | Fondmetal-Ford | | | |
| DNQ | 7 | E.van de Poele | Brabham-Judd | | | |
| DNPQ | 34 | Roberto Moreno | Moda-Judd | | | |
| DNPQ | 35 | Perry McCarthy | Moda-Judd | | | |

Winning speed: 134.109mph Lap leaders: Mansell 1-59
Pole position: Mansell, 1m 18.965s, 148.043mph Fastest lap: Mansell, 1m 22.539s, 141.633mph

GERMAN GRAND PRIX: HOCKENHEIM *26 July Round: 10 Race: 526 45 x 4.235 miles*

| POS. | NO. | DRIVER | CAR/ENGINE | LAPS | TIME/RETIRED | GRID |
|---|---|---|---|---|---|---|
| 1 | 5 | Nigel Mansell | Williams-Renault | 45 | 1:18'22.032 | 1 |
| 2 | 1 | Ayrton Senna | McLaren-Honda | 45 | +4.500 | 3 |
| 3 | 19 | M.Schumacher | Benetton-Ford | 45 | +34.462 | 6 |
| 4 | 20 | Martin Brundle | Benetton-Ford | 45 | +36.959 | 9 |
| 5 | 27 | Jean Alesi | Ferrari | 45 | +1'12.607 | 5 |
| 6 | 26 | Erik Comas | Ligier-Renault | 45 | +1'36.498 | 7 |
| 7 | 25 | Thierry Boutsen | Ligier-Renault | 45 | +1'37.180 | 8 |
| 8 | 6 | Riccardo Patrese | Williams-Renault | 44 | Spun off | 2 |
| 9 | 9 | Michele Alboreto | Footwork-Mugen-Honda | 44 | +1 Lap | 17 |
| 10 | 21 | J J Lehto | Dallara-Ferrari | 44 | +1 Lap | 21 |
| 11 | 22 | P.Martini | Dallara-Ferrari | 44 | +1 Lap | 18 |
| 12 | 24 | G.Morbidelli | Minardi-Lamborghini | 44 | +1 Lap | 26 |
| 13 | 17 | Paul Belmondo | March-Ilmor | 44 | +1 Lap | 22 |
| 14 | 29 | Bertrand Gachot | Venturi-Lamborghini | 44 | +1 Lap | 25 |
| 15 | 33 | M.Gugelmin | Jordan-Yamaha | 43 | +2 Laps | 23 |
| 16 | 16 | Karl Wendlinger | March-Ilmor | 42 | +3 Laps | 10 |
| Ret | 15 | G.Tarquini | Fondmetal-Ford | 33 | Engine | 19 |
| Ret | 4 | A.de Cesaris | Tyrrell-Ilmor | 25 | Engine | 20 |
| Ret | 12 | Johnny Herbert | Lotus-Ford | 23 | Engine | 11 |
| Ret | 28 | Ivan Capelli | Ferrari | 21 | Engine | 12 |
| Ret | 11 | Mika Hakkinen | Lotus-Ford | 21 | Engine | 13 |
| Ret | 2 | Gerhard Berger | McLaren-Honda | 16 | Electrical | 4 |
| Ret | 3 | O.Grouillard | Tyrrell-Ilmor | 8 | Engine | 14 |
| Ret | 30 | Ukyo Katayama | Venturi-Lamborghini | 8 | Spun off | 16 |
| Ret | 10 | Aguri Suzuki | Footwork-Mugen-Honda | 1 | Spun off | 15 |
| Ret | 23 | A.Zanardi | Minardi-Lamborghini | 1 | Gearbox | 24 |
| DNQ | 32 | Stefano Modena | Jordan-Yamaha | | | |
| DNQ | 7 | E.van de Poele | Brabham-Judd | | | |
| DNQ | 14 | Andrea Chiesa | Fondmetal-Ford | | | |
| DNQ | 8 | Damon Hill | Brabham-Judd | | | |
| DNPQ | 34 | Roberto Moreno | Moda-Judd | | | |
| DNPQ | 35 | Perry McCarthy | Moda-Judd | | | |

Winning speed: 145.897mph Lap leaders: Mansell 1-14, 20-45; Patrese 15-19
Pole position: Mansell, 1m 37.960s, 155.622mph
Fastest lap: Patrese, 1m 41.591s, 150.060mph

HUNGARIAN GRAND PRIX: HUNGARORING *16 August Round: 11 Race: 527 77 x 2.466 miles*

| POS. | NO. | DRIVER | CAR/ENGINE | LAPS | TIME/RETIRED | GRID |
|---|---|---|---|---|---|---|
| 1 | 1 | Ayrton Senna | McLaren-Honda | 77 | 1:46'19.216 | 3 |
| 2 | 5 | Nigel Mansell | Williams-Renault | 77 | +40.139 | 2 |
| 3 | 2 | Gerhard Berger | McLaren-Honda | 77 | +50.782 | 5 |
| 4 | 11 | Mika Hakkinen | Lotus-Ford | 77 | +54.313 | 16 |
| 5 | 20 | Martin Brundle | Benetton-Ford | 77 | +57.498 | 6 |
| 6 | 28 | Ivan Capelli | Ferrari | 76 | +1 Lap | 10 |
| 7 | 9 | Michele Alboreto | Footwork-Mugen-Honda | 75 | +2 Laps | 7 |
| 8 | 4 | A.de Cesaris | Tyrrell-Ilmor | 75 | +2 Laps | 19 |
| 9 | 17 | Paul Belmondo | March-Ilmor | 74 | +3 Laps | 17 |
| 10 | 33 | M.Gugelmin | Jordan-Yamaha | 73 | +4 Laps | 21 |
| 11 | 8 | Damon Hill | Brabham-Judd | 73 | +4 Laps | 25 |
| Ret | 19 | M.Schumacher | Benetton-Ford | 63 | Broken wing | 4 |
| Ret | 6 | Riccardo Patrese | Williams-Renault | 55 | Engine | 1 |
| Ret | 22 | P.Martini | Dallara-Ferrari | 40 | Gearbox | 26 |
| Ret | 30 | Ukyo Katayama | Venturi-Lamborghini | 35 | Engine | 20 |
| Ret | 27 | Jean Alesi | Ferrari | 14 | Halfshaft | 9 |
| Ret | 29 | Bertrand Gachot | Venturi-Lamborghini | 13 | Broken wing | 15 |
| Ret | 10 | Aguri Suzuki | Footwork-Mugen-Honda | 13 | Collision | 14 |
| Ret | 3 | O.Grouillard | Tyrrell-Ilmor | 13 | Collision | 22 |
| Ret | 16 | Karl Wendlinger | March-Ilmor | 13 | Collision | 23 |
| Ret | 32 | Stefano Modena | Jordan-Yamaha | 13 | Collision | 24 |
| Ret | 14 | E.van de Poele | Fondmetal-Ford | 2 | Spun off | 18 |
| Ret | 25 | Thierry Boutsen | Ligier-Renault | 0 | Collision | 8 |
| Ret | 26 | Erik Comas | Ligier-Renault | 0 | Collision | 11 |
| Ret | 15 | G.Tarquini | Fondmetal-Ford | 0 | Collision | 12 |
| Ret | 12 | Johnny Herbert | Lotus-Ford | 0 | Collision | 13 |
| DNQ | 24 | G.Morbidelli | Minardi-Lamborghini | | | |
| DNQ | 21 | J J Lehto | Dallara-Ferrari | | | |
| DNQ | 23 | A.Zanardi | Minardi-Lamborghini | | | |
| DNQ | 34 | Roberto Moreno | Moda-Judd | | | |
| DNPQ | 35 | Perry McCarthy | Moda-Judd | | | |

Winning speed: 107.139mph Lap leaders: Patrese 1-38; Senna 39-77
Pole position: Patrese, 1m 15.476s, 117.602mph
Fastest lap: Mansell, 1m 18.308s, 113.349mph

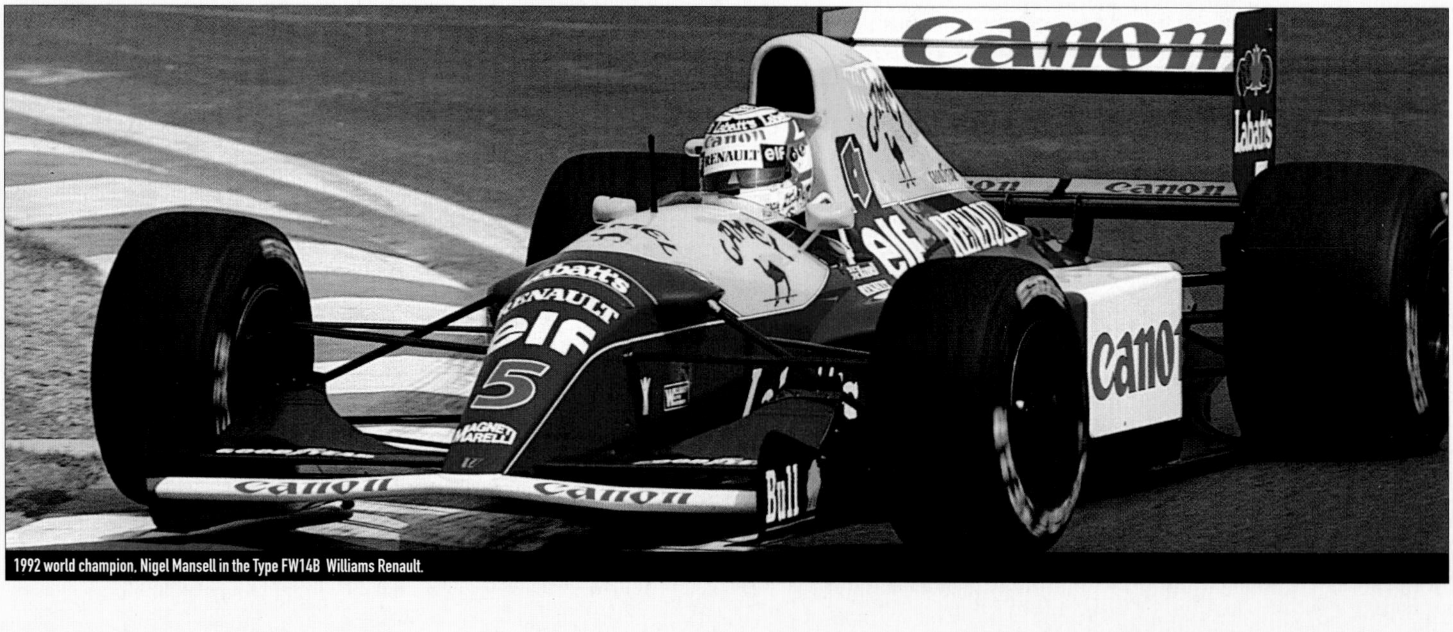

1992 world champion, Nigel Mansell in the Type FW14B Williams Renault.

BELGIAN GRAND PRIX: SPA-FRANCORCHAMPS *30 August Round: 12 Race: 528 44 x 4.333 miles*

| POS. | NO. | DRIVER | CAR/ENGINE | LAPS | TIME/RETIRED | GRID |
|---|---|---|---|---|---|---|
| 1 | 19 | M.Schumacher | Benetton-Ford | 44 | 1:36'10.721 | 3 |
| 2 | 5 | Nigel Mansell | Williams-Renault | 44 | +36.595 | 1 |
| 3 | 6 | Riccardo Patrese | Williams-Renault | 44 | +43.897 | 4 |
| 4 | 20 | Martin Brundle | Benetton-Ford | 44 | +46.059 | 9 |
| 5 | 1 | Ayrton Senna | McLaren-Honda | 44 | +1'08.369 | 2 |
| 6 | 11 | Mika Hakkinen | Lotus-Ford | 44 | +1'10.030 | 8 |
| 7 | 21 | J J Lehto | Dallara-Ferrari | 44 | +1'38.237 | 16 |
| 8 | 4 | A.de Cesaris | Tyrrell-Ilmor | 43 | +1 Lap | 13 |
| 9 | 10 | Aguri Suzuki | Footwork-Mugen-Honda | 43 | +1 Lap | 25 |
| 10 | 14 | E.van de Poele | Fondmetal-Ford | 43 | +1 Lap | 15 |
| 11 | 16 | Karl Wendlinger | March-Ilmor | 43 | +1 Lap | 18 |
| 12 | 17 | E.Naspetti | March-Ilmor | 43 | +1 Lap | 21 |
| 13 | 12 | Johnny Herbert | Lotus-Ford | 42 | Engine | 10 |
| 14 | 33 | M.Gugelmin | Jordan-Yamaha | 42 | +2 Laps | 24 |
| 15 | 32 | Stefano Modena | Jordan-Yamaha | 42 | +2 Laps | 17 |
| 16 | 24 | G.Morbidelli | Minardi-Lamborghini | 42 | +2 Laps | 23 |
| 17 | 30 | Ukyo Katayama | Venturi-Lamborghini | 42 | +2 Laps | 26 |
| 18 | 29 | Bertrand Gachot | Venturi-Lamborghini | 40 | Spun off | 20 |
| Ret | 25 | Thierry Boutsen | Ligier-Renault | 27 | Spun off | 7 |
| Ret | 28 | Ivan Capelli | Ferrari | 25 | Engine | 12 |
| Ret | 15 | G.Tarquini | Fondmetal-Ford | 25 | Engine | 11 |
| Ret | 9 | Michele Alboreto | Footwork-Mugen-Honda | 20 | Gearbox | 14 |
| Ret | 27 | Jean Alesi | Ferrari | 7 | Puncture | 5 |
| Ret | 3 | O.Grouillard | Tyrrell-Ilmor | 1 | Collision | 22 |
| Ret | 2 | Gerhard Berger | McLaren-Honda | 0 | Transmission | 6 |
| Ret | 22 | P.Martini | Dallara-Ferrari | 0 | Spun off | 19 |
| DNQ | 23 | C.Fittipaldi | Minardi-Lamborghini | | | |
| DNQ | 34 | Roberto Moreno | Moda-Judd | | | |
| DNQ | 35 | Perry McCarthy | Moda-Judd | | | |
| DNQ | 26 | Erik Comas | Ligier-Renault | | | |

Winning speed: 118.948mph Lap leaders: Senna 1, 7-10; Mansell 2-3, 11-33, Patrese 4-6; Schumacher 34-44
Pole position: Mansell, 1m 50.545s, 141.123mph
Fastest lap: Schumacher, 1m 53.791s, 137.097mph

ITALIAN GRAND PRIX: MONZA *13 September Round: 13 Race: 529 53 x 3.604 miles*

| POS. | NO. | DRIVER | CAR/ENGINE | LAPS | TIME/RETIRED | GRID |
|---|---|---|---|---|---|---|
| 1 | 1 | Ayrton Senna | McLaren-Honda | 53 | 1:18'15.349 | 2 |
| 2 | 20 | Martin Brundle | Benetton-Ford | 53 | +17.050 | 9 |
| 3 | 19 | M.Schumacher | Benetton-Ford | 53 | +24.373 | 6 |
| 4 | 2 | Gerhard Berger | McLaren-Honda | 53 | +1'25.490 | 5 |
| 5 | 6 | Riccardo Patrese | Williams-Renault | 53 | +1'33.158 | 4 |
| 6 | 4 | A.de Cesaris | Tyrrell-Ilmor | 52 | +1 Lap | 21 |
| 7 | 9 | Michele Alboreto | Footwork-Mugen-Honda | 52 | +1 Lap | 16 |
| 8 | 22 | P.Martini | Dallara-Ferrari | 52 | +1 Lap | 22 |
| 9 | 30 | Ukyo Katayama | Venturi-Lamborghini | 50 | Transmission | 23 |
| 10 | 16 | Karl Wendlinger | March-Ilmor | 50 | +3 Laps | 17 |
| 11 | 21 | J J Lehto | Dallara-Ferrari | 47 | Engine | 14 |
| Ret | 33 | M.Gugelmin | Jordan-Yamaha | 46 | Transmission | 26 |
| Ret | 5 | Nigel Mansell | Williams-Renault | 41 | Electrical | 1 |
| Ret | 25 | Thierry Boutsen | Ligier-Renault | 41 | Throttle | 8 |
| Ret | 26 | Erik Comas | Ligier-Renault | 35 | Spun off | 15 |
| Ret | 15 | G.Tarquini | Fondmetal-Ford | 30 | Gearbox | 20 |
| Ret | 3 | O.Grouillard | Tyrrell-Ilmor | 26 | Engine | 18 |
| Ret | 12 | Johnny Herbert | Lotus-Ford | 18 | Engine | 13 |
| Ret | 17 | E.Naspetti | March-Ilmor | 17 | Spun off | 24 |
| Ret | 27 | Jean Alesi | Ferrari | 12 | Fuel system | 3 |
| Ret | 28 | Ivan Capelli | Ferrari | 12 | Spun off | 7 |
| Ret | 24 | G.Morbidelli | Minardi-Lamborghini | 12 | Engine | 12 |
| Ret | 29 | Bertrand Gachot | Venturi-Lamborghini | 11 | Engine | 10 |
| Ret | 11 | Mika Hakkinen | Lotus-Ford | 5 | Engine | 11 |
| Ret | 10 | Aguri Suzuki | Footwork-Mugen-Honda | 2 | Suspension | 19 |
| Ret | 14 | E.van de Poele | Fondmetal-Ford | 0 | Clutch | 25 |
| DNQ | 23 | C.Fittipaldi | Minardi-Lamborghini | | | |
| DNQ | 32 | Stefano Modena | Jordan-Yamaha | | | |

Winning speed: 146.450mph Lap leaders: Mansell 1-19; Patrese 20-47; Senna 48-53
Pole position: Mansell, 1m 22.221s, 157.797mph
Fastest lap: Mansell, 1m 26.119s, 150.655mph

PORTUGUESE GRAND PRIX: ESTORIL *27 September Round: 14 Race: 530 71 x 2.703 miles*

| POS. | NO. | DRIVER | CAR/ENGINE | LAPS | TIME/RETIRED | GRID |
|---|---|---|---|---|---|---|
| 1 | 5 | Nigel Mansell | Williams-Renault | 71 | 1:34'46.659 | 1 |
| 2 | 2 | Gerhard Berger | McLaren-Honda | 71 | +37.533 | 4 |
| 3 | 1 | Ayrton Senna | McLaren-Honda | 70 | +1 Lap | 3 |
| 4 | 20 | Martin Brundle | Benetton-Ford | 70 | +1 Lap | 6 |
| 5 | 11 | Mika Hakkinen | Lotus-Ford | 70 | +1 Lap | 7 |
| 6 | 9 | Michele Alboreto | Footwork-Mugen-Honda | 70 | +1 Lap | 8 |
| 7 | 19 | M.Schumacher | Benetton-Ford | 69 | +2 Laps | 5 |
| 8 | 25 | Thierry Boutsen | Ligier-Renault | 69 | +2 Laps | 11 |
| 9 | 4 | A.de Cesaris | Tyrrell-Ilmor | 69 | +2 Laps | 12 |
| 10 | 10 | Aguri Suzuki | Footwork-Mugen-Honda | 68 | +3 Laps | 17 |
| 11 | 17 | E.Naspetti | March-Ilmor | 68 | +3 Laps | 23 |
| 12 | 23 | C.Fittipaldi | Minardi-Lamborghini | 68 | +3 Laps | 26 |
| 13 | 32 | Stefano Modena | Jordan-Yamaha | 68 | +3 Laps | 24 |
| 14 | 24 | G.Morbidelli | Minardi-Lamborghini | 68 | +3 Laps | 18 |
| Ret | 21 | J J Lehto | Dallara-Ferrari | 51 | Physical | 19 |
| Ret | 16 | Karl Wendlinger | March-Ilmor | 48 | Gearbox | 22 |
| Ret | 26 | Erik Comas | Ligier-Renault | 47 | Engine | 14 |
| Ret | 30 | Ukyo Katayama | Venturi-Lamborghini | 46 | Spun off | 25 |
| Ret | 22 | P.Martini | Dallara-Ferrari | 44 | Puncture | 21 |
| Ret | 6 | Riccardo Patrese | Williams-Renault | 43 | Collision | 2 |
| Ret | 28 | Ivan Capelli | Ferrari | 34 | Engine | 16 |
| Ret | 3 | O.Grouillard | Tyrrell-Ilmor | 27 | Gearbox | 15 |
| Ret | 29 | Bertrand Gachot | Venturi-Lamborghini | 25 | Engine | 13 |
| Ret | 33 | M.Gugelmin | Jordan-Yamaha | 19 | Electrical | 20 |
| Ret | 27 | Jean Alesi | Ferrari | 12 | Spun off | 10 |
| Ret | 12 | Johnny Herbert | Lotus-Ford | 2 | Collision | 9 |

Winning speed: 121.491mph Lap leaders: Mansell 1-71
Pole position: Mansell, 1m 13.041s, 133.222mph
Fastest lap: Senna, 1m 16.272s, 127.579mph

JAPANESE GRAND PRIX: SUZUKA *25 October Round: 15 Race: 531 53 x 3.644 miles*

| POS. | NO. | DRIVER | CAR/ENGINE | LAPS | TIME/RETIRED | GRID |
|---|---|---|---|---|---|---|
| 1 | 6 | Riccardo Patrese | Williams-Renault | 53 | 1:33'09.553 | 2 |
| 2 | 2 | Gerhard Berger | McLaren-Honda | 53 | +13.729 | 4 |
| 3 | 20 | Martin Brundle | Benetton-Ford | 53 | +1'15.503 | 13 |
| 4 | 4 | A.de Cesaris | Tyrrell-Ilmor | 52 | +1 Lap | 9 |
| 5 | 27 | Jean Alesi | Ferrari | 52 | +1 Lap | 15 |
| 6 | 23 | C.Fittipaldi | Minardi-Lamborghini | 52 | +1 Lap | 12 |
| 7 | 32 | Stefano Modena | Jordan-Yamaha | 52 | +1 Lap | 17 |
| 8 | 10 | Aguri Suzuki | Footwork-Mugen-Honda | 52 | +1 Lap | 16 |
| 9 | 21 | J J Lehto | Dallara-Ferrari | 52 | +1 Lap | 22 |
| 10 | 22 | P.Martini | Dallara-Ferrari | 52 | +1 Lap | 19 |
| 11 | 30 | Ukyo Katayama | Venturi-Lamborghini | 52 | +1 Lap | 20 |
| 12 | 28 | Nicola Larini | Ferrari | 52 | +1 Lap | 11 |
| 13 | 17 | E.Naspetti | March-Ilmor | 51 | +2 Laps | 26 |
| 14 | 24 | G.Morbidelli | Minardi-Lamborghini | 51 | +2 Laps | 14 |
| 15 | 9 | Michele Alboreto | Footwork-Mugen-Honda | 51 | +2 Laps | 24 |
| Ret | 5 | Nigel Mansell | Williams-Renault | 44 | Engine | 1 |
| Ret | 11 | Mika Hakkinen | Lotus-Ford | 44 | Engine | 7 |
| Ret | 29 | Bertrand Gachot | Venturi-Lamborghini | 39 | Collision | 18 |
| Ret | 26 | Erik Comas | Ligier-Renault | 36 | Engine | 8 |
| Ret | 16 | Jan Lammers | March-Ilmor | 27 | Clutch | 23 |
| Ret | 33 | M.Gugelmin | Jordan-Yamaha | 22 | Spun off | 25 |
| Ret | 12 | Johnny Herbert | Lotus-Ford | 15 | Gearbox | 6 |
| Ret | 19 | M.Schumacher | Benetton-Ford | 13 | Gearbox | 5 |
| Ret | 3 | O.Grouillard | Tyrrell-Ilmor | 6 | Spun off | 21 |
| Ret | 25 | Thierry Boutsen | Ligier-Renault | 3 | Gearbox | 10 |
| Ret | 1 | Ayrton Senna | McLaren-Honda | 2 | Engine | 3 |

Winning speed: 124.379mph Lap leaders: Mansell 1-35; Patrese 36-53
Pole position: Mansell, 1m 37.360s, 134.731mph
Fastest lap: Mansell, 1m 40.646s, 130.332mph

AUSTRALIAN GRAND PRIX: ADELAIDE *8 November Round: 16 Race: 532 81 x 2.349 miles*

| POS. | NO. | DRIVER | CAR/ENGINE | LAPS | TIME/RETIRED | GRID |
|---|---|---|---|---|---|---|
| 1 | 2 | Gerhard Berger | McLaren-Honda | 81 | 1:46'54.786 | 4 |
| 2 | 19 | M.Schumacher | Benetton-Ford | 81 | +0.741 | 5 |
| 3 | 20 | Martin Brundle | Benetton-Ford | 81 | +54.156 | 8 |
| 4 | 27 | Jean Alesi | Ferrari | 80 | +1 Lap | 6 |
| 5 | 25 | Thierry Boutsen | Ligier-Renault | 80 | +1 Lap | 22 |
| 6 | 32 | Stefano Modena | Jordan-Yamaha | 80 | +1 Lap | 15 |
| 7 | 11 | Mika Hakkinen | Lotus-Ford | 80 | +1 Lap | 10 |
| 8 | 10 | Aguri Suzuki | Footwork-Mugen-Honda | 79 | +2 Laps | 18 |
| 9 | 23 | C.Fittipaldi | Minardi-Lamborghini | 79 | +2 Laps | 17 |
| 10 | 24 | G.Morbidelli | Minardi-Lamborghini | 79 | +2 Laps | 16 |
| 11 | 28 | Nicola Larini | Ferrari | 79 | +2 Laps | 19 |
| 12 | 16 | Jan Lammers | March-Ilmor | 78 | +3 Laps | 25 |
| 13 | 12 | Johnny Herbert | Lotus-Ford | 77 | +4 Laps | 12 |
| Ret | 21 | J J Lehto | Dallara-Ferrari | 70 | Gearbox | 24 |
| Ret | 17 | E.Naspetti | March-Ilmor | 55 | Gearbox | 23 |
| Ret | 29 | Bertrand Gachot | Venturi-Lamborghini | 51 | Fuel system | 21 |
| Ret | 6 | Riccardo Patrese | Williams-Renault | 50 | Engine | 3 |
| Ret | 30 | Ukyo Katayama | Venturi-Lamborghini | 35 | Differential | 26 |
| Ret | 4 | A.de Cesaris | Tyrrell-Ilmor | 29 | Engine | 7 |
| Ret | 5 | Nigel Mansell | Williams-Renault | 18 | Collision | 1 |
| Ret | 1 | Ayrton Senna | McLaren-Honda | 18 | Collision | 2 |
| Ret | 33 | M.Gugelmin | Jordan-Yamaha | 7 | Spun off | 20 |
| Ret | 26 | Erik Comas | Ligier-Renault | 4 | Engine | 9 |
| Ret | 9 | Michele Alboreto | Footwork-Mugen-Honda | 0 | Spun off | 11 |
| Ret | 3 | O.Grouillard | Tyrrell-Ilmor | 0 | Collision | 13 |
| Ret | 22 | P.Martini | Dallara-Ferrari | 0 | Collision | 14 |

Winning speed: 106.770mph Lap leaders: Mansell 1-18; Patrese 19-50; Berger 51-81
Pole position: Mansell, 1m13.372s, 114.680mph
Fastest lap: Schumacher, 1m 16.078s, 111.144mph

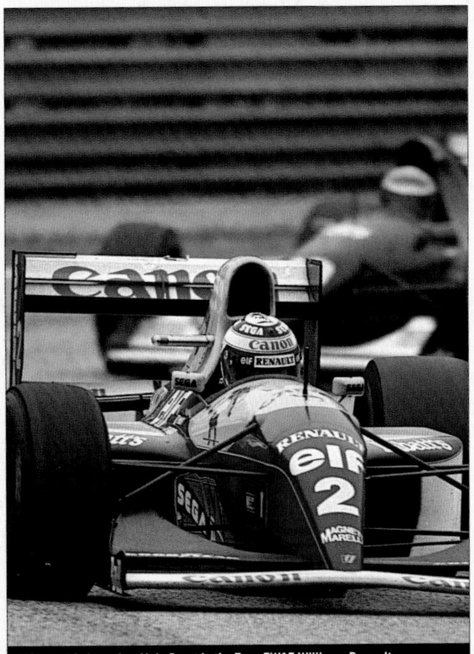
1993 world champion Alain Prost in the Type FW15 Williams Renault.

# 1993

DRIVERS' CHAMPION: ALAIN PROST
CONSTRUCTORS' CHAMPION: WILLIAMS RENAULT

DRIVERS' CHAMPIONSHIP

| POS. | DRIVER | NATIONALITY | CAR | POINTS |
|---|---|---|---|---|
| 1 | Alain Prost | France | Williams-Renault | 99 |
| 2 | Ayrton Senna | Brazil | McLaren-Ford | 73 |
| 3 | Damon Hill | GB | Williams-Renault | 69 |
| 4 | Michael Schumacher | Germany | Benetton-Ford | 52 |
| 5 | Riccardo Patrese | Italy | Benetton-Ford | 20 |
| 6 | Jean Alesi | France | Ferrari | 16 |
| 7 | Martin Brundle | GB | Ligier-Renault | 13 |
| 8 | Gerhard Berger | Austria | Ferrari | 12 |
| 9 | Johnny Herbert | GB | Lotus-Ford | 11 |
| 10 | Mark Blundell | GB | Ligier-Renault | 10 |
| 11 | Michael Andretti | USA | McLaren-Ford | 7 |
| = | Karl Wendlinger | Austria | Sauber-Ilmor | 7 |
| 13 | J.J. Lehto | Finland | Sauber-Ilmor | 5 |
| = | Christian Fittipaldi | Brazil | Minardi-Ford | 5 |
| 15 | Mika Hakkinen | Finland | McLaren-Ford | 4 |
| = | Derek Warwick | GB | Footwork-Mugen | 4 |
| 17 | Philippe Alliot | France | Larrousse-Lamborghini | 2 |
| = | Rubens Barrichello | Brazil | Jordan-Hart | 2 |
| = | Fabrizio Barbazza | Italy | Minardi-Ford | 2 |
| 20 | Alessandro Zanardi | Italy | Lotus-Ford | 1 |
| = | Erik Comas | France | Larrouse-Lamborghini | 1 |
| = | Eddie Irvine | GB | Jordan-Hart | 1 |
| | Michele Alboreto | Italy | Lola BMS-Ferrari | |
| | Aguri Suzuki | Japan | Footwork-Mugen | |
| | Luca Badoer | Italy | Lola BMS-Ferrari | |
| | Ivan Capelli | Italy | Jordan-Hart | |
| | Ukyo Katayama | Japan | Tyrrell-Yamaha | |
| | Andrea de Cesaris | Italy | Tyrrell-Yamaha | |
| | Thierry Boutsen | Belgium | Jordan-Hart | |
| | Pierluigi Martini | Italy | Minardi-Ford | |
| | Marco Apicella | Italy | Jordan-Hart | |
| | Pedro Lamy | Portugal | Lotus-Ford | |
| | Emanuele Naspetti | Italy | Jordan-Hart | |
| | Jean-Marc Gounon | France | Minardi-Ford | |
| | Toshio Suzuki | Japan | Larrousse-Lamborghini | |

Points for top six finishers (10, 6, 4, 3, 2, 1). Half points awarded for races stopped before half distance.

CONSTRUCTORS' CHAMPIONSHIP

| POS. | CONSTRUCTOR | POINTS |
|---|---|---|
| 1 | Williams-Renault | 168 |
| 2 | McLaren-Ford | 84 |
| 3 | Benetton-Ford | 72 |
| 4 | Ferrari | 28 |
| 5 | Ligier-Renault | 23 |
| 6 | Lotus-Ford | 12 |
| 7 | Sauber | 12 |
| 8 | Minardi-Ford | 7 |
| 9 | Footwork-Mugen-Honda | 4 |
| 10 | Larrousse-Lamborghini | 3 |
| 10 | Jordan-Hart | 3 |

Points for top six finishers (10, 6, 4, 3, 2, 1). Half points awarded for races stopped before half distance.

SOUTH AFRICAN GRAND PRIX: KYALAMI *14 March Round: 1 Race: 533 72 x 2.648 miles*

| POS. | NO. | DRIVER | CAR/ENGINE | LAPS | TIME/RETIRED | GRID |
|---|---|---|---|---|---|---|
| 1 | 2 | Alain Prost | Williams-Renault | 72 | 1:38'45.082 | 1 |
| 2 | 8 | Ayrton Senna | McLaren-Ford | 72 | +1'19.824 | 2 |
| 3 | 26 | Mark Blundell | Ligier-Renault | 71 | +1 Lap | 8 |
| 4 | 23 | C.Fittipaldi | Minardi-Ford | 71 | +1 Lap | 13 |
| 5 | 30 | J J Lehto | Sauber | 70 | +2 Laps | 6 |
| 6 | 28 | Gerhard Berger | Ferrari | 69 | Engine | 15 |
| 7 | 9 | Derek Warwick | Footwork-Mugen-Honda | 69 | Spun off | 22 |
| Ret | 25 | Martin Brundle | Ligier-Renault | 57 | Spun off | 12 |
| Ret | 21 | Michele Alboreto | Lola-Ferrari | 55 | Overheating | 25 |
| Ret | 20 | Erik Comas | Larrousse-Lamborghini | 51 | Engine | 19 |
| Ret | 6 | Riccardo Patrese | Benetton-Ford | 46 | Spun off | 7 |
| Ret | 5 | M.Schumacher | Benetton-Ford | 39 | Spun off | 3 |
| Ret | 12 | Johnny Herbert | Lotus-Ford | 38 | Fuel system | 17 |
| Ret | 29 | Karl Wendlinger | Sauber | 33 | Engine | 10 |
| Ret | 14 | R.Barrichello | Jordan-Hart | 31 | Gearbox | 14 |
| Ret | 27 | Jean Alesi | Ferrari | 30 | Suspension | 5 |
| Ret | 19 | Philippe Alliot | Larrousse-Lamborghini | 27 | Spun off | 11 |
| Ret | 24 | F.Barbazza | Minardi-Ford | 21 | Collision | 24 |
| Ret | 10 | Aguri Suzuki | Footwork-Mugen-Honda | 21 | Collision | 20 |
| Ret | 22 | Luca Badoer | Lola-Ferrari | 20 | Gearbox | 26 |
| Ret | 0 | Damon Hill | Williams-Renault | 16 | Collision | 4 |
| Ret | 11 | A.Zanardi | Lotus-Ford | 16 | Collision | 16 |
| Ret | 7 | Michael Andretti | McLaren-Ford | 4 | Collision | 9 |
| Ret | 15 | Ivan Capelli | Jordan-Hart | 2 | Spun off | 18 |
| Ret | 3 | Ukyo Katayama | Tyrrell-Yamaha | 1 | Transmission | 21 |
| Ret | 4 | A.de Cesaris | Tyrrell-Yamaha | 0 | Transmission | 23 |

Winning speed: 115.825mph Lap leaders: Senna 1-23; Prost 24-72
Pole position: Prost, 1m 15.696s, 125.919mph
Fastest lap: Prost, 19.492s, 119.906mph

## BRAZILIAN GRAND PRIX: INTERLAGOS *28 March Round: 2 Race: 534 71 x 2.687 miles*

| POS. | NO. | DRIVER | CAR/ENGINE | LAPS | TIME/RETIRED | GRID |
|---|---|---|---|---|---|---|
| 1 | 8 | Ayrton Senna | McLaren-Ford | 71 | 1:51'15.485 | 3 |
| 2 | 0 | Damon Hill | Williams-Renault | 71 | +16.625 | 2 |
| 3 | 5 | M.Schumacher | Benetton-Ford | 71 | +45.436 | 4 |
| 4 | 12 | Johnny Herbert | Lotus-Ford | 71 | +46.557 | 12 |
| 5 | 26 | Mark Blundell | Ligier-Renault | 71 | +52.127 | 10 |
| 6 | 11 | A.Zanardi | Lotus-Ford | 70 | +1 Lap | 15 |
| 7 | 19 | Philippe Alliot | Larrousse-Lamborghini | 70 | +1 Lap | 11 |
| 8 | 27 | Jean Alesi | Ferrari | 70 | +1 Lap | 9 |
| 9 | 9 | Derek Warwick | Footwork-Mugen-Honda | 69 | +2 Laps | 18 |
| 10 | 20 | Erik Comas | Larrousse-Lamborghini | 69 | +2 Laps | 27 |
| 11 | 21 | Michele Alboreto | Lola-Ferrari | 68 | +3 Laps | 25 |
| 12 | 22 | Luca Badoer | Lola-Ferrari | 68 | +3 Laps | 21 |
| Ret | 29 | Karl Wendlinger | Sauber | 61 | Engine | 8 |
| Ret | 30 | J J Lehto | Sauber | 52 | Electrical | 7 |
| Ret | 4 | A.de Cesaris | Tyrrell-Yamaha | 48 | Fuel system | 23 |
| Ret | 2 | Alain Prost | Williams-Renault | 29 | Collision | 1 |
| Ret | 23 | C.Fittipaldi | Minardi-Ford | 28 | Collision | 20 |
| Ret | 10 | Aguri Suzuki | Footwork-Mugen-Honda | 27 | Spun off | 19 |
| Ret | 3 | Ukyo Katayama | Tyrrell-Yamaha | 26 | Spun off | 22 |
| Ret | 14 | R.Barrichello | Jordan-Hart | 13 | Gearbox | 14 |
| Ret | 6 | Riccardo Patrese | Benetton-Ford | 3 | Suspension | 6 |
| Ret | 7 | Michael Andretti | McLaren-Ford | 0 | Collision | 5 |
| Ret | 28 | Gerhard Berger | Ferrari | 0 | Collision | 13 |
| Ret | 25 | Martin Brundle | Ligier-Renault | 0 | Collision | 16 |
| Ret | 24 | F.Barbazza | Minardi-Ford | 0 | Collision | 24 |
| DNQ | 15 | Ivan Capelli | Jordan-Hart | | | |

Winning speed: 102.900mph Lap leaders: Prost 1-29; Hill 30-41; Senna 42-71
Pole position: Prost, 1m 15.866s, 127.524mph
Fastest lap: Schumacher, 1m 20.024s, 120.898mph

## EUROPEAN GRAND PRIX: DONINGTON PARK *11 April Round: 3 Race: 535 76x2.500 miles*

| POS. | NO. | DRIVER | CAR/ENGINE | LAPS | TIME/RETIRED | GRID |
|---|---|---|---|---|---|---|
| 1 | 8 | Ayrton Senna | McLaren-Ford | 76 | 1:50'46.570 | 4 |
| 2 | 0 | Damon Hill | Williams-Renault | 76 | +1'23.199 | 2 |
| 3 | 2 | Alain Prost | Williams-Renault | 75 | +1 Lap | 1 |
| 4 | 12 | Johnny Herbert | Lotus-Ford | 75 | +1 Lap | 11 |
| 5 | 6 | Riccardo Patrese | Benetton-Ford | 74 | +2 Laps | 10 |
| 6 | 24 | F.Barbazza | Minardi-Ford | 74 | +2 Laps | 20 |
| 7 | 23 | C.Fittipaldi | Minardi-Ford | 73 | +3 Laps | 16 |
| 8 | 11 | A.Zanardi | Lotus-Ford | 72 | +4 Laps | 13 |
| 9 | 20 | Erik Comas | Larrousse-Lamborghini | 72 | +4 Laps | 17 |
| 10 | 14 | R.Barrichello | Jordan-Hart | 70 | Fuel system | 12 |
| 11 | 21 | Michele Alboreto | Lola-Ferrari | 70 | +6 Laps | 24 |
| Ret | 9 | Derek Warwick | Footwork-Mugen-Honda | 66 | Gearbox | 14 |
| Ret | 15 | Thierry Boutsen | Jordan-Hart | 61 | Throttle | 19 |
| Ret | 4 | A.de Cesaris | Tyrrell-Yamaha | 55 | Gearbox | 25 |
| Ret | 27 | Jean Alesi | Ferrari | 36 | Gearbox | 9 |
| Ret | 10 | Aguri Suzuki | Footwork-Mugen-Honda | 29 | Gearbox | 23 |
| Ret | 19 | Philippe Alliot | Larrousse-Lamborghini | 27 | Collision | 15 |
| Ret | 5 | M.Schumacher | Benetton-Ford | 22 | Spun off | 3 |
| Ret | 26 | Mark Blundell | Ligier-Renault | 20 | Spun off | 21 |
| Ret | 28 | Gerhard Berger | Ferrari | 19 | Suspension | 8 |
| Ret | 30 | J J Lehto | Sauber | 13 | Handling | 7 |
| Ret | 3 | Ukyo Katayama | Tyrrell-Yamaha | 11 | Clutch | 18 |
| Ret | 25 | Martin Brundle | Ligier-Renault | 7 | Spun off | 22 |
| Ret | 29 | Karl Wendlinger | Sauber | 0 | Collision | 5 |
| Ret | 7 | Michael Andretti | McLaren-Ford | 0 | Collision | 6 |
| DNQ | 22 | Luca Badoer | Lola-Ferrari | | | |

Winning speed: 102.901mph
Lap leaders: Senna 1-18, 20-34, 39-76; Prost 19, 35-38
Pole position: Prost, 1m 10.458s, 127.724mph
Fastest lap: Senna, 1m 18.029s, 115.331mph

## SAN MARINO GRAND PRIX: IMOLA *25 April Round: 4 Race: 536 61 x 3.132 miles*

| POS. | NO. | DRIVER | CAR/ENGINE | LAPS | TIME/RETIRED | GRID |
|---|---|---|---|---|---|---|
| 1 | 2 | Alain Prost | Williams-Renault | 61 | 1:33'20.413 | 1 |
| 2 | 5 | M.Schumacher | Benetton-Ford | 61 | +32.410 | 3 |
| 3 | 25 | Martin Brundle | Ligier-Renault | 60 | +1 Lap | 10 |
| 4 | 30 | J J Lehto | Sauber | 59 | Engine | 16 |
| 5 | 19 | Philippe Alliot | Larrousse-Lamborghini | 59 | +2 Laps | 14 |
| 6 | 24 | F.Barbazza | Minardi-Ford | 59 | +2 Laps | 25 |
| 7 | 22 | Luca Badoer | Lola-Ferrari | 58 | +3 Laps | 24 |
| 8 | 12 | Johnny Herbert | Lotus-Ford | 57 | Engine | 12 |
| 9 | 10 | Aguri Suzuki | Footwork-Mugen-Honda | 54 | +7 Laps | 21 |
| Ret | 11 | A.Zanardi | Lotus-Ford | 53 | Spun off | 20 |
| Ret | 29 | Karl Wendlinger | Sauber | 48 | Engine | 9 |
| Ret | 8 | Ayrton Senna | McLaren-Ford | 42 | Hydraulics | 4 |
| Ret | 27 | Jean Alesi | Ferrari | 40 | Clutch | 9 |
| Ret | 23 | C.Fittipaldi | Minardi-Ford | 36 | Steering | 23 |
| Ret | 7 | Michael Andretti | McLaren-Ford | 32 | Spun off | 6 |
| Ret | 9 | Derek Warwick | Footwork-Mugen-Honda | 29 | Spun off | 15 |
| Ret | 3 | Ukyo Katayama | Tyrrell-Yamaha | 22 | Engine | 22 |
| Ret | 0 | Damon Hill | Williams-Renault | 20 | Brakes | 2 |
| Ret | 20 | Erik Comas | Larrousse-Lamborghini | 18 | Engine | 17 |
| Ret | 4 | A.de Cesaris | Tyrrell-Yamaha | 18 | Gearbox | 18 |
| Ret | 14 | R.Barrichello | Jordan-Hart | 17 | Spun off | 13 |
| Ret | 28 | Gerhard Berger | Ferrari | 8 | Gearbox | 8 |
| Ret | 15 | Thierry Boutsen | Jordan-Hart | 1 | Gearbox | 19 |
| Ret | 26 | Mark Blundell | Ligier-Renault | 0 | Spun off | 7 |
| Ret | 6 | Riccardo Patrese | Benetton-Ford | 0 | Spun off | 11 |
| DNQ | 21 | Michele Alboreto | Lola-Ferrari | | | |

Winning speed: 122.799mph Lap leaders: Hill 1-11; Prost 12-61
Pole position: Prost, 1m 22.070s, 137.372mph
Fastest lap: Prost, 26.128s, 130.900mph

## SPANISH GRAND PRIX: MONTMELO *9 May Round: 5 Race: 537 65 x 2.950 miles*

| POS. | NO. | DRIVER | CAR/ENGINE | LAPS | TIME/RETIRED | GRID |
|---|---|---|---|---|---|---|
| 1 | 2 | Alain Prost | Williams-Renault | 65 | 1:32'27.685 | 1 |
| 2 | 8 | Ayrton Senna | McLaren-Ford | 65 | +16.873 | 3 |
| 3 | 5 | M.Schumacher | Benetton-Ford | 65 | +27.125 | 4 |
| 4 | 6 | Riccardo Patrese | Benetton-Ford | 64 | +1 Lap | 5 |
| 5 | 7 | Michael Andretti | McLaren-Ford | 64 | +1 Lap | 7 |
| 6 | 28 | Gerhard Berger | Ferrari | 63 | +2 Laps | 11 |
| 7 | 26 | Mark Blundell | Ligier-Renault | 63 | +2 Laps | 12 |
| 8 | 23 | C.Fittipaldi | Minardi-Ford | 63 | +2 Laps | 20 |
| 9 | 20 | Erik Comas | Larrousse-Lamborghini | 63 | +2 Laps | 14 |
| 10 | 10 | Aguri Suzuki | Footwork-Mugen-Honda | 63 | +2 Laps | 19 |
| 11 | 15 | Thierry Boutsen | Jordan-Hart | 62 | +3 Laps | 21 |
| 12 | 14 | R.Barrichello | Jordan-Hart | 62 | +3 Laps | 17 |
| 13 | 9 | Derek Warwick | Footwork-Mugen-Honda | 62 | +3 Laps | 16 |
| 14 | 11 | A.Zanardi | Lotus-Ford | 60 | Engine | 15 |
| Ret | 30 | J J Lehto | Sauber | 53 | Engine | 9 |
| Ret | 22 | Luca Badoer | Lola-Ferrari | 43 | Overheating | 22 |
| Ret | 29 | Karl Wendlinger | Sauber | 42 | Fuel system | 6 |
| Ret | 4 | A.de Cesaris | Tyrrell-Yamaha | 42 | Disqualified | 24 |
| Ret | 0 | Damon Hill | Williams-Renault | 41 | Engine | 2 |
| Ret | 27 | Jean Alesi | Ferrari | 40 | Engine | 8 |
| Ret | 24 | F.Barbazza | Minardi-Ford | 37 | Spun off | 25 |
| Ret | 19 | Philippe Alliot | Larrousse-Lamborghini | 26 | Transmission | 13 |
| Ret | 25 | Martin Brundle | Ligier-Renault | 11 | Spun off | 18 |
| Ret | 3 | Ukyo Katayama | Tyrrell-Yamaha | 11 | Spun off | 23 |
| Ret | 12 | Johnny Herbert | Lotus-Ford | 2 | Suspension | 10 |
| DNQ | 21 | Michele Alboreto | Lola-Ferrari | | | |

Winning speed: 124.415mph Lap leaders: Hill 1-10; Prost 11-65
Pole position: Prost, 1m 17.809s, 136.472mph
Fastest lap: Schumacher, 1m 20.989s, 131.113mph

## MONACO GRAND PRIX: MONTE CARLO *23 May Round: 6 Race: 538 78 x 2.068 miles*

| POS. | NO. | DRIVER | CAR/ENGINE | LAPS | TIME/RETIRED | GRID |
|---|---|---|---|---|---|---|
| 1 | 8 | Ayrton Senna | McLaren-Ford | 78 | 1:52'10.947 | 3 |
| 2 | 0 | Damon Hill | Williams-Renault | 78 | +52.118 | 4 |
| 3 | 27 | Jean Alesi | Ferrari | 78 | +1'03.362 | 5 |
| 4 | 2 | Alain Prost | Williams-Renault | 77 | +1 Lap | 1 |
| 5 | 23 | C.Fittipaldi | Minardi-Ford | 76 | +2 Laps | 17 |
| 6 | 25 | Martin Brundle | Ligier-Renault | 76 | +2 Laps | 13 |
| 7 | 11 | A.Zanardi | Lotus-Ford | 76 | +2 Laps | 20 |
| 8 | 7 | Michael Andretti | McLaren-Ford | 76 | +2 Laps | 9 |
| 9 | 14 | R.Barrichello | Jordan-Hart | 76 | +2 Laps | 16 |
| 10 | 4 | A.de Cesaris | Tyrrell-Yamaha | 76 | +2 Laps | 19 |
| 11 | 24 | F.Barbazza | Minardi-Ford | 75 | +3 Laps | 25 |
| 12 | 19 | Philippe Alliot | Larrousse-Lamborghini | 75 | +3 Laps | 15 |
| 13 | 29 | Karl Wendlinger | Sauber | 74 | +4 Laps | 8 |
| 14 | 28 | Gerhard Berger | Ferrari | 70 | Collision | 7 |
| Ret | 12 | Johnny Herbert | Lotus-Ford | 61 | Gearbox | 14 |
| Ret | 6 | Riccardo Patrese | Benetton-Ford | 53 | Engine | 6 |
| Ret | 20 | Erik Comas | Larrousse-Lamborghini | 51 | Collision | 10 |
| Ret | 10 | Aguri Suzuki | Footwork-Mugen-Honda | 46 | Spun off | 18 |
| Ret | 9 | Derek Warwick | Footwork-Mugen-Honda | 43 | Throttle | 12 |
| Ret | 5 | M.Schumacher | Benetton-Ford | 32 | Hydraulics | 2 |
| Ret | 3 | Ukyo Katayama | Tyrrell-Yamaha | 31 | Engine | 22 |
| Ret | 21 | Michele Alboreto | Lola-Ferrari | 28 | Gearbox | 24 |
| Ret | 30 | J J Lehto | Sauber | 23 | Collision | 11 |
| Ret | 15 | Thierry Boutsen | Jordan-Hart | 12 | Suspension | 23 |
| Ret | 26 | Mark Blundell | Ligier-Renault | 3 | Spun off | 21 |
| DNQ | 22 | Luca Badoer | Lola-Ferrari | | | |

Winning speed: 86.269mph Lap leaders: Prost 1-11; Schumacher 12-32; Senna 33-78
Pole position: Prost, 1m 20.557s, 92.413mph
Fastest lap: Prost, 1m 23.604s, 89.045mph

## CANADIAN GRAND PRIX: MONTREAL *13 June 69 x 2.753 miles Round: 7 Race: 539 69 x 2.753 miles*

| POS. | NO. | DRIVER | CAR/ENGINE | LAPS | TIME/RETIRED | GRID |
|---|---|---|---|---|---|---|
| 1 | 2 | Alain Prost | Williams-Renault | 69 | 1:36'41.822 | 1 |
| 2 | 5 | M.Schumacher | Benetton-Ford | 69 | +14.527 | 3 |
| 3 | 0 | Damon Hill | Williams-Renault | 69 | +52.685 | 2 |
| 4 | 28 | Gerhard Berger | Ferrari | 68 | +1 Lap | 5 |
| 5 | 25 | Martin Brundle | Ligier-Renault | 68 | +1 Lap | 7 |
| 6 | 29 | Karl Wendlinger | Sauber | 68 | +1 Lap | 9 |
| 7 | 30 | J J Lehto | Sauber | 68 | +1 Lap | 11 |
| 8 | 20 | Erik Comas | Larrousse-Lamborghini | 68 | +1 Lap | 13 |
| 9 | 23 | C.Fittipaldi | Minardi-Ford | 67 | +2 Laps | 17 |
| 10 | 12 | Johnny Herbert | Lotus-Ford | 67 | +2 Laps | 20 |
| 11 | 11 | A.Zanardi | Lotus-Ford | 67 | +2 Laps | 21 |
| 12 | 15 | Thierry Boutsen | Jordan-Hart | 67 | +2 Laps | 24 |
| 13 | 10 | Aguri Suzuki | Footwork-Mugen-Honda | 66 | +3 Laps | 16 |
| 14 | 7 | Michael Andretti | McLaren-Ford | 66 | +3 Laps | 12 |
| 15 | 22 | Luca Badoer | Lola-Ferrari | 65 | +4 Laps | 25 |
| 16 | 9 | Derek Warwick | Footwork-Mugen-Honda | 65 | +4 Laps | 18 |
| 17 | 3 | Ukyo Katayama | Tyrrell-Yamaha | 64 | +5 Laps | 22 |
| 18 | 8 | Ayrton Senna | McLaren-Ford | 62 | Electrical | 8 |
| Ret | 6 | Riccardo Patrese | Benetton-Ford | 52 | Physical | 4 |
| Ret | 4 | A.de Cesaris | Tyrrell-Yamaha | 45 | Spun off | 19 |
| Ret | 24 | F.Barbazza | Minardi-Ford | 33 | Gearbox | 23 |
| Ret | 27 | Jean Alesi | Ferrari | 23 | Engine | 6 |
| Ret | 26 | Mark Blundell | Ligier-Renault | 13 | Spun off | 10 |
| Ret | 14 | R.Barrichello | Jordan-Hart | 10 | Electrical | 14 |
| Ret | 19 | Philippe Alliot | Larrousse-Lamborghini | 8 | Engine | 15 |
| DNQ | 21 | Michele Alboreto | Lola-Ferrari | | | |

Winning speed: 117.853mph Lap leaders: Hill 1-5; Prost 6-69
Pole position: Prost, 1m 18.987s, 125.459mph
Fastest lap: Schumacher, 1m 21.500s, 121.591mph

## FRENCH GRAND PRIX: MAGNY-COURS *4 July Round: 8 Race: 540 72 x 2.641 miles*

| POS. | NO. | DRIVER | CAR/ENGINE | LAPS | TIME/RETIRED | GRID |
|---|---|---|---|---|---|---|
| 1 | 2 | Alain Prost | Williams-Renault | 72 | 1:38'35.241 | 2 |
| 2 | 0 | Damon Hill | Williams-Renault | 72 | +0.342 | 1 |
| 3 | 5 | M.Schumacher | Benetton-Ford | 72 | +21.209 | 7 |
| 4 | 8 | Ayrton Senna | McLaren-Ford | 72 | +32.405 | 5 |
| 5 | 25 | Martin Brundle | Ligier-Renault | 72 | +33.795 | 3 |
| 6 | 7 | Michael Andretti | McLaren-Ford | 71 | +1 Lap | 16 |
| 7 | 14 | R.Barrichello | Jordan-Hart | 71 | +1 Lap | 8 |
| 8 | 23 | C.Fittipaldi | Minardi-Ford | 71 | +1 Lap | 23 |
| 9 | 19 | Philippe Alliot | Larrousse-Lamborghini | 70 | +2 Laps | 10 |
| 10 | 6 | Riccardo Patrese | Benetton-Ford | 70 | +2 Laps | 12 |
| 11 | 15 | Thierry Boutsen | Jordan-Hart | 70 | +2 Laps | 20 |
| 12 | 10 | Aguri Suzuki | Footwork-Mugen-Honda | 70 | +2 Laps | 13 |
| 13 | 9 | Derek Warwick | Footwork-Mugen-Honda | 70 | +2 Laps | 15 |
| 14 | 28 | Gerhard Berger | Ferrari | 70 | +2 Laps | 14 |
| 15 | 4 | A.de Cesaris | Tyrrell-Yamaha | 68 | +4 Laps | 25 |
| 16 | 20 | Erik Comas | Larrousse-Lamborghini | 66 | Gearbox | 9 |
| Ret | 27 | Jean Alesi | Ferrari | 47 | Engine | 6 |
| Ret | 22 | Luca Badoer | Lola-Ferrari | 28 | Suspension | 22 |
| Ret | 29 | Karl Wendlinger | Sauber | 25 | Gearbox | 11 |
| Ret | 30 | J J Lehto | Sauber | 22 | Gearbox | 18 |
| Ret | 26 | Mark Blundell | Ligier-Renault | 20 | Spun off | 4 |
| Ret | 12 | Johnny Herbert | Lotus-Ford | 16 | Spun off | 19 |
| Ret | 24 | F.Barbazza | Minardi-Ford | 16 | Gearbox | 24 |
| Ret | 3 | Ukyo Katayama | Tyrrell-Yamaha | 9 | Engine | 21 |
| Ret | 11 | A.Zanardi | Lotus-Ford | 3 | Suspension | 17 |
| DNQ | 21 | Michele Alboreto | Lola-Ferrari | | | |

Winning speed: 115.718mph Pole position: Hill 1-26; Prost 27-72
Pole position: Hill, 1m 14.382s, 127.813mph
Fastest lap: Schumacher, 1m 19.256, 119.953mph

## BRITISH GRAND PRIX: SILVERSTONE *11 July Round: 9 Race: 541 11 July 59 x 3.247 miles*

| POS. | NO. | DRIVER | CAR/ENGINE | LAPS | TIME/RETIRED | GRID |
|---|---|---|---|---|---|---|
| 1 | 2 | Alain Prost | Williams-Renault | 59 | 1:25'38.189 | 1 |
| 2 | 5 | M.Schumacher | Benetton-Ford | 59 | +7.660 | 3 |
| 3 | 6 | Riccardo Patrese | Benetton-Ford | 59 | +1'17.482 | 5 |
| 4 | 12 | Johnny Herbert | Lotus-Ford | 59 | +1'18.407 | 7 |
| 5 | 8 | Ayrton Senna | McLaren-Ford | 58 | Out of fuel | 4 |
| 6 | 9 | Derek Warwick | Footwork-Mugen-Honda | 58 | +1 Lap | 8 |
| 7 | 26 | Mark Blundell | Ligier-Renault | 58 | +1 Lap | 9 |
| 8 | 30 | J J Lehto | Sauber | 58 | +1 Lap | 16 |
| 9 | 27 | Jean Alesi | Ferrari | 58 | +1 Lap | 12 |
| 10 | 14 | R.Barrichello | Jordan-Hart | 58 | +1 Lap | 15 |
| 11 | 19 | Philippe Alliot | Larrousse-Lamborghini | 57 | +2 Laps | 24 |
| 12 | 23 | C.Fittipaldi | Minardi-Ford | 56 | Gearbox | 19 |
| 13 | 3 | Ukyo Katayama | Tyrrell-Yamaha | 55 | +4 Laps | 22 |
| 14 | 25 | Martin Brundle | Ligier-Renault | 53 | Gearbox | 6 |
| NC | 4 | A.de Cesaris | Tyrrell-Yamaha | 43 | Not classified | 21 |
| Ret | 0 | Damon Hill | Williams-Renault | 41 | Engine | 2 |
| Ret | 11 | A.Zanardi | Lotus-Ford | 41 | Suspension | 14 |
| Ret | 15 | Thierry Boutsen | Jordan-Hart | 41 | Wheel bearing | 23 |
| Ret | 22 | Luca Badoer | Lola-Ferrari | 32 | Electrical | 25 |
| Ret | 24 | P.Martini | Minardi-Ford | 31 | Physical | 20 |
| Ret | 29 | Karl Wendlinger | Sauber | 24 | Spun off | 18 |
| Ret | 28 | Gerhard Berger | Ferrari | 10 | Suspension | 13 |
| Ret | 10 | Aguri Suzuki | Footwork-Mugen-Honda | 8 | Spun off | 10 |
| Ret | 7 | Michael Andretti | McLaren-Ford | 0 | Spun off | 11 |
| Ret | 20 | Erik Comas | Larrousse-Lamborghini | 0 | Halfshaft | 17 |
| DNQ | 21 | Michele Alboreto | Lola-Ferrari | | | |

Winning speed: 134.235mph Lap leaders: Hill 1-41; Prost 42-59
Pole position: Prost, 1m 19.006s, 147.966mph
Fastest lap: Hill, 22.515s, 141.674mph

## GERMAN GRAND PRIX: HOCKENHEIM *25 July Round: 10 Race: 542 45 x 4.235 miles*

| POS. | NO. | DRIVER | CAR/ENGINE | LAPS | TIME/RETIRED | GRID |
|---|---|---|---|---|---|---|
| 1 | 2 | Alain Prost | Williams-Renault | 45 | 1:18'40.885 | 1 |
| 2 | 5 | M.Schumacher | Benetton-Ford | 45 | +16.664 | 3 |
| 3 | 26 | Mark Blundell | Ligier-Renault | 45 | +59.349 | 5 |
| 4 | 8 | Ayrton Senna | McLaren-Ford | 45 | +1'08.229 | 4 |
| 5 | 6 | Riccardo Patrese | Benetton-Ford | 45 | +1'31.516 | 7 |
| 6 | 28 | Gerhard Berger | Ferrari | 45 | +1'34.754 | 9 |
| 7 | 27 | Jean Alesi | Ferrari | 45 | +1'35.841 | 10 |
| 8 | 25 | Martin Brundle | Ligier-Renault | 44 | +1 Lap | 6 |
| 9 | 29 | Karl Wendlinger | Sauber | 44 | +1 Lap | 14 |
| 10 | 12 | Johnny Herbert | Lotus-Ford | 44 | +1 Lap | 13 |
| 11 | 23 | C.Fittipaldi | Minardi-Ford | 44 | +1 Lap | 20 |
| 12 | 19 | Philippe Alliot | Larrousse-Lamborghini | 44 | +1 Lap | 23 |
| 13 | 15 | Thierry Boutsen | Jordan-Hart | 44 | +1 Lap | 24 |
| 14 | 24 | P.Martini | Minardi-Ford | 44 | +1 Lap | 22 |
| 15 | 0 | Damon Hill | Williams-Renault | 43 | Tyre | 2 |
| 16 | 21 | Michele Alboreto | Lola-Ferrari | 43 | +2 Laps | 26 |
| 17 | 9 | Derek Warwick | Footwork-Mugen-Honda | 42 | +3 Laps | 11 |
| Ret | 14 | R.Barrichello | Jordan-Hart | 34 | Wheel bearing | 17 |
| Ret | 3 | Ukyo Katayama | Tyrrell-Yamaha | 28 | Halfshaft | 21 |
| Ret | 30 | J J Lehto | Sauber | 22 | Spun off | 18 |
| Ret | 11 | A.Zanardi | Lotus-Ford | 19 | Spun off | 15 |
| Ret | 10 | Aguri Suzuki | Footwork-Mugen-Honda | 9 | Collision | 8 |
| Ret | 7 | Michael Andretti | McLaren-Ford | 4 | Collision | 12 |
| Ret | 22 | Luca Badoer | Lola-Ferrari | 4 | Suspension | 25 |
| Ret | 4 | A.de Cesaris | Tyrrell-Yamaha | 1 | Gearbox | 19 |
| Ret | 20 | Erik Comas | Larrousse-Lamborghini | 0 | Gearbox | 16 |

Winning speed: 145.314mph Lap leaders: Hill 1-7, 10-43; Prost 8-9, 44-45
Pole position: Prost, 1m 38.748s, 154.380mph
Fastest lap: Schumacher, 1m 41.859s, 149.665mph

HUNGARIAN GRAND PRIX: HUNGARORING *15 August Round: 11 Race: 542 45 x 4.235 miles*

| POS. | NO. | DRIVER | CAR/ENGINE | LAPS | TIME/RETIRED | GRID |
|---|---|---|---|---|---|---|
| 1 | 0 | Damon Hill | Williams-Renault | 77 | 1:47'39.09 | 2 |
| 2 | 6 | Riccardo Patrese | Benetton-Ford | 77 | +1'11.915 | 5 |
| 3 | 28 | Gerhard Berger | Ferrari | 77 | +1'18.042 | 6 |
| 4 | 9 | Derek Warwick | Footwork-Mugen-Honda | 76 | +1 Lap | 9 |
| 5 | 25 | Martin Brundle | Ligier-Renault | 76 | +1 Lap | 13 |
| 6 | 29 | Karl Wendlinger | Sauber | 76 | +1 Lap | 17 |
| 7 | 26 | Mark Blundell | Ligier-Renault | 76 | +1 Lap | 12 |
| 8 | 19 | Philippe Alliot | Larrousse-Lamborghini | 75 | +2 Laps | 19 |
| 9 | 15 | Thierry Boutsen | Jordan-Hart | 75 | +2 Laps | 24 |
| 10 | 3 | Ukyo Katayama | Tyrrell-Yamaha | 73 | +4 Laps | 23 |
| 11 | 4 | A.de Cesaris | Tyrrell-Yamaha | 72 | +5 Laps | 22 |
| 12 | 2 | Alain Prost | Williams-Renault | 70 | +7 Laps | 1 |
| Ret | 24 | P.Martini | Minardi-Ford | 59 | Spun off | 7 |
| Ret | 20 | Erik Comas | Larrousse-Lamborghini | 54 | Engine | 18 |
| Ret | 11 | A.Zanardi | Lotus-Ford | 45 | Gearbox | 21 |
| Ret | 10 | Aguri Suzuki | Footwork-Mugen-Honda | 41 | Spun off | 10 |
| Ret | 21 | Michele Alboreto | Lola-Ferrari | 39 | Overheating | 25 |
| Ret | 12 | Johnny Herbert | Lotus-Ford | 38 | Spun off | 20 |
| Ret | 22 | Luca Badoer | Lola-Ferrari | 37 | Spun off | 26 |
| Ret | 5 | M.Schumacher | Benetton-Ford | 26 | Fuel pump | 3 |
| Ret | 23 | C.Fittipaldi | Minardi-Ford | 22 | Suspension | 14 |
| Ret | 27 | Jean Alesi | Ferrari | 22 | Spun off | 8 |
| Ret | 30 | J J Lehto | Sauber | 18 | Engine | 15 |
| Ret | 8 | Ayrton Senna | McLaren-Ford | 17 | Throttle | 4 |
| Ret | 7 | Michael Andretti | McLaren-Ford | 15 | Throttle | 11 |
| Ret | 14 | R.Barrichello | Jordan-Hart | 0 | Collision | 16 |

Winning speed: 105.814mph Lap leaders: Hill 1-77
Pole position: Prost, 14.631s, 118.934mph
Fastest lap: Prost, 1m 19.633s, 111.463mph

BELGIAN GRAND PRIX: SPA-FRANCORCHAMPS *29 August Round: 12 Race: 544 44 x 4.333 miles*

| POS. | NO. | DRIVER | CAR/ENGINE | LAPS | TIME/RETIRED | GRID |
|---|---|---|---|---|---|---|
| 1 | 0 | Damon Hill | Williams-Renault | 44 | 1:24'32.124 | 2 |
| 2 | 5 | M.Schumacher | Benetton-Ford | 44 | +3.668 | 3 |
| 3 | 2 | Alain Prost | Williams-Renault | 44 | +14.988 | 1 |
| 4 | 8 | Ayrton Senna | McLaren-Ford | 44 | +1'39.763 | 5 |
| 5 | 12 | Johnny Herbert | Lotus-Ford | 43 | +1 Lap | 10 |
| 6 | 6 | Riccardo Patrese | Benetton-Ford | 43 | +1 Lap | 8 |
| 7 | 25 | Martin Brundle | Ligier-Renault | 43 | +1 Lap | 11 |
| 8 | 7 | Michael Andretti | McLaren-Ford | 43 | +1 Lap | 14 |
| 9 | 30 | J J Lehto | Sauber | 43 | +1 Lap | 9 |
| 10 | 28 | Gerhard Berger | Ferrari | 42 | Collision | 16 |
| 11 | 26 | Mark Blundell | Ligier-Renault | 42 | Collision | 15 |
| 12 | 19 | Philippe Alliot | Larrousse-Lamborghini | 42 | +2 Laps | 18 |
| 13 | 22 | Luca Badoer | Lola-Ferrari | 42 | +2 Laps | 24 |
| 14 | 21 | Michele Alboreto | Lola-Ferrari | 41 | +3 Laps | 25 |
| 15 | 3 | Ukyo Katayama | Tyrrell-Yamaha | 40 | +4 Laps | 23 |
| Ret | 20 | Erik Comas | Larrousse-Lamborghini | 37 | Fuel pump | 19 |
| Ret | 9 | Derek Warwick | Footwork-Mugen-Honda | 28 | Engine | 7 |
| Ret | 29 | Karl Wendlinger | Sauber | 27 | Engine | 12 |
| Ret | 4 | A.de Cesaris | Tyrrell-Yamaha | 24 | Engine | 17 |
| Ret | 23 | C.Fittipaldi | Minardi-Ford | 15 | Spun off | 22 |
| Ret | 24 | P.Martini | Minardi-Ford | 15 | Spun off | 21 |
| Ret | 10 | Aguri Suzuki | Footwork-Mugen-Honda | 14 | Gearbox | 6 |
| Ret | 14 | R.Barrichello | Jordan-Hart | 11 | Wheel bearing | 13 |
| Ret | 27 | Jean Alesi | Ferrari | 4 | Suspension | 4 |
| Ret | 15 | Thierry Boutsen | Jordan-Hart | 0 | Gearbox | 20 |
| DNQ | 11 | A. Zanardi | Lotus-Ford | 0 | Accident | |

Winning speed: 135.331mph Lap leaders: Prost 1-30; Hill 31-44
Pole position: Prost, 1m 47.571s, 145.024mph Fastest lap: Prost, 1m 51.095s, 140.424mph

ITALIAN GRAND PRIX: MONZA *12 September Round: 13 Race: 545 53 x 3.604 miles*

| POS. | NO. | DRIVER | CAR/ENGINE | LAPS | TIME/RETIRED | GRID |
|---|---|---|---|---|---|---|
| 1 | 0 | Damon Hill | Williams-Renault | 53 | 1:17'07.509 | 2 |
| 2 | 27 | Jean Alesi | Ferrari | 53 | +40.012 | 3 |
| 3 | 7 | Michael Andretti | McLaren-Ford | 52 | +1 Lap | 9 |
| 4 | 29 | Karl Wendlinger | Sauber | 52 | +1 Lap | 15 |
| 5 | 6 | Riccardo Patrese | Benetton-Ford | 52 | +1 Lap | 10 |
| 6 | 20 | Erik Comas | Larrousse-Lamborghini | 51 | +2 Laps | 20 |
| 7 | 24 | P.Martini | Minardi-Ford | 51 | +2 Laps | 22 |
| 8 | 23 | C.Fittipaldi | Minardi-Ford | 51 | +2 Laps | 24 |
| 9 | 19 | Philippe Alliot | Larrousse-Lamborghini | 51 | +2 Laps | 16 |
| 10 | 22 | Luca Badoer | Lola-Ferrari | 51 | +2 Laps | 25 |
| 11 | 11 | Pedro Lamy | Lotus-Ford | 49 | Electrical | 26 |
| 12 | 2 | Alain Prost | Williams-Renault | 48 | Engine | 1 |
| 13 | 4 | A.de Cesaris | Tyrrell-Yamaha | 47 | Oil pressure | 18 |
| 14 | 3 | Ukyo Katayama | Tyrrell-Yamaha | 47 | +6 Laps | 17 |
| Ret | 21 | Michele Alboreto | Lola-Ferrari | 23 | Suspension | 23 |
| Ret | 5 | M.Schumacher | Benetton-Ford | 21 | Engine | 5 |
| Ret | 26 | Mark Blundell | Ligier-Renault | 20 | Spun off | 14 |
| Ret | 28 | Gerhard Berger | Ferrari | 15 | Suspension | 6 |
| Ret | 12 | Johnny Herbert | Lotus-Ford | 14 | Spun off | 7 |
| Ret | 25 | Martin Brundle | Ligier-Renault | 8 | Collision | 12 |
| Ret | 8 | Ayrton Senna | McLaren-Ford | 8 | Collision | 4 |
| Ret | 10 | Aguri Suzuki | Footwork-Mugen-Honda | 0 | Collision | 8 |
| Ret | 9 | Derek Warwick | Footwork-Mugen-Honda | 0 | Collision | 11 |
| Ret | 30 | J J Lehto | Sauber | 0 | Collision | 13 |
| Ret | 14 | R.Barrichello | Jordan-Hart | 0 | Collision | 19 |
| Ret | 15 | Marco Apicella | Jordan-Hart | 0 | Collision | 23 |

Winning speed: 148.597mph Lap leaders: Prost 1-48; Hill 49-53
Pole position: Prost, 1m 21.179s, 159.822mphFastest lap: Hill, 1m 23.575s, 155.241mph

PORTUGUESE GRAND PRIX: ESTORIL *26 September Round: 14 Race: 546 71 x 2.703 miles*

| POS. | NO. | DRIVER | CAR/ENGINE | LAPS | TIME/RETIRED | GRID |
|---|---|---|---|---|---|---|
| 1 | 5 | M.Schumacher | Benetton-Ford | 71 | 1:32'46.309 | 6 |
| 2 | 2 | Alain Prost | Williams-Renault | 71 | +0.982 | 2 |
| 3 | 0 | Damon Hill | Williams-Renault | 71 | +8.206 | 1 |
| 4 | 27 | Jean Alesi | Ferrari | 71 | +1'07.605 | 5 |
| 5 | 29 | Karl Wendlinger | Sauber | 70 | +1 Lap | 13 |
| 6 | 25 | Martin Brundle | Ligier-Renault | 70 | +1 Lap | 11 |
| 7 | 30 | J J Lehto | Sauber | 69 | +2 Laps | 12 |
| 8 | 24 | P.Martini | Minardi-Ford | 69 | +2 Laps | 19 |
| 9 | 23 | C.Fittipaldi | Minardi-Ford | 69 | +2 Laps | 24 |
| 10 | 19 | Philippe Alliot | Larrousse-Lamborghini | 69 | +2 Laps | 20 |
| 11 | 20 | Erik Comas | Larrousse-Lamborghini | 68 | +3 Laps | 22 |
| 12 | 4 | A.de Cesaris | Tyrrell-Yamaha | 68 | +3 Laps | 17 |
| 13 | 14 | R.Barrichello | Jordan-Hart | 68 | +3 Laps | 15 |
| 14 | 22 | Luca Badoer | Lola-Ferrari | 68 | +3 Laps | 26 |
| 15 | 9 | Derek Warwick | Footwork-Mugen-Honda | 63 | Collision | 9 |
| 16 | 6 | Riccardo Patrese | Benetton-Ford | 63 | Collision | 7 |
| Ret | 11 | Pedro Lamy | Lotus-Ford | 61 | Spun off | 18 |
| Ret | 12 | Johnny Herbert | Lotus-Ford | 60 | Spun off | 14 |
| Ret | 26 | Mark Blundell | Ligier-Renault | 51 | Collision | 10 |
| Ret | 21 | Michele Alboreto | Lola-Ferrari | 38 | Gearbox | 25 |
| Ret | 28 | Gerhard Berger | Ferrari | 35 | Spun off | 8 |
| Ret | 7 | Mika Hakkinen | McLaren-Ford | 32 | Spun off | 3 |
| Ret | 10 | Aguri Suzuki | Footwork-Mugen-Honda | 27 | Gearbox | 16 |
| Ret | 8 | Ayrton Senna | McLaren-Ford | 19 | Engine | 4 |
| Ret | 3 | Ukyo Katayama | Tyrrell-Yamaha | 12 | Spun off | 21 |
| Ret | 15 | E.Naspetti | Jordan-Hart | 8 | Engine | 23 |

Winning speed: 124.118mph Lap leaders: Alesi 1-19; Prost 20-29; Schumacher 30-71
Pole position: Hill, 1m 11.494s, 136.105mph Fastest lap: Hill, 1m 14.859s, 129.987mph

JAPANESE GRAND PRIX: SUZUKA *24 October Round: 15 Race: 547 53 x 3.644 miles*

| POS. | NO. | DRIVER | CAR/ENGINE | LAPS | TIME/RETIRED | GRID |
|---|---|---|---|---|---|---|
| 1 | 8 | Ayrton Senna | McLaren-Ford | 53 | 1:40'27.912 | 2 |
| 2 | 2 | Alain Prost | Williams-Renault | 53 | +11.435 | 1 |
| 3 | 7 | Mika Hakkinen | McLaren-Ford | 53 | +26.129 | 3 |
| 4 | 0 | Damon Hill | Williams-Renault | 53 | +1'23.538 | 6 |
| 5 | 14 | R.Barrichello | Jordan-Hart | 53 | +1'35.101 | 12 |
| 6 | 15 | Eddie Irvine | Jordan-Hart | 53 | +1'46.421 | 8 |
| 7 | 26 | Mark Blundell | Ligier-Renault | 52 | +1 Lap | 17 |
| 8 | 30 | J J Lehto | Sauber | 52 | +1 Lap | 11 |
| 9 | 25 | Martin Brundle | Ligier-Renault | 51 | +2 Laps | 15 |
| 10 | 24 | P.Martini | Minardi-Ford | 51 | +2 Laps | 22 |
| 11 | 12 | Johnny Herbert | Lotus-Ford | 51 | +2 Laps | 19 |
| 12 | 19 | Toshio Suzuki | Larrousse-Lamborghini | 51 | +2 Laps | 23 |
| 13 | 11 | Pedro Lamy | Lotus-Ford | 49 | Spun off | 20 |
| 14 | 9 | Derek Warwick | Footwork-Mugen-Honda | 48 | Collision | 7 |
| Ret | 6 | Riccardo Patrese | Benetton-Ford | 45 | Spun off | 10 |
| Ret | 28 | Gerhard Berger | Ferrari | 40 | Engine | 5 |
| Ret | 10 | Aguri Suzuki | Footwork-Mugen-Honda | 28 | Spun off | 9 |
| Wth | 23 | Jean-Marc Gounon | Minardi-Ford | 26 | Withdrew | 13 |
| Ret | 3 | Ukyo Katayama | Tyrrell-Yamaha | 26 | Engine | 24 |
| Ret | 29 | Karl Wendlinger | Sauber | 25 | Engine | 16 |
| Ret | 20 | Erik Comas | Larrousse-Lamborghini | 17 | Engine | 21 |
| Ret | 5 | M.Schumacher | Benetton-Ford | 10 | Collision | 4 |
| Ret | 27 | Jean Alesi | Ferrari | 7 | Engine | 14 |
| Ret | 4 | A.de Cesaris | Tyrrell-Yamaha | 0 | Collision | 18 |

Winning speed: 115.334mph Lap leaders: Senna 1-13, 21-53; Prost 14-20
Pole position: Prost, 1m 37.154s, 135.017mph Fastest lap: Prost, 1m 41.176s, 129.649mph

AUSTRALIAN GRAND PRIX: ADELAIDE *7 November Round: 16 Race: 548 79 x 2.349 miles*

| POS. | NO. | DRIVER | CAR/ENGINE | LAPS | TIME/RETIRED | GRID |
|---|---|---|---|---|---|---|
| 1 | 8 | Ayrton Senna | McLaren-Ford | 79 | 1:43'27.476 | 1 |
| 2 | 2 | Alain Prost | Williams-Renault | 79 | + 9.259 | 2 |
| 3 | 0 | Damon Hill | Williams-Renault | 79 | +33.902 | 3 |
| 4 | 27 | Jean Alesi | Ferrari | 78 | +1 Lap | 7 |
| 5 | 28 | Gerhard Berger | Ferrari | 78 | +1 Lap | 6 |
| 6 | 25 | Martin Brundle | Ligier-Renault | 78 | +1 Lap | 8 |
| 7 | 10 | Aguri Suzuki | Footwork-Mugen-Honda | 78 | +1 Lap | 10 |
| 8 | 6 | Riccardo Patrese | Benetton-Ford | 77 | Fuel system | 9 |
| 9 | 26 | Mark Blundell | Ligier-Renault | 77 | +2 Laps | 14 |
| 10 | 9 | Derek Warwick | Footwork-Mugen-Honda | 77 | +2 Laps | 17 |
| 11 | 14 | R.Barrichello | Jordan-Hart | 76 | +3 Laps | 13 |
| 12 | 20 | Erik Comas | Larrousse-Lamborghini | 76 | +3 Laps | 21 |
| 13 | 4 | A.de Cesaris | Tyrrell-Yamaha | 75 | +4 Laps | 15 |
| 14 | 19 | Toshio Suzuki | Larrousse-Lamborghini | 74 | +5 Laps | 24 |
| 15 | 29 | Karl Wendlinger | Sauber | 73 | Brakes | 11 |
| Ret | 30 | J J Lehto | Sauber | 56 | Spun off | 12 |
| Ret | 23 | Jean-Marc Gounon | Minardi-Ford | 34 | Spun off | 22 |
| Ret | 7 | Mika Hakkinen | McLaren-Ford | 28 | Brakes | 5 |
| Ret | 5 | M.Schumacher | Benetton-Ford | 19 | Engine | 4 |
| Ret | 3 | Ukyo Katayama | Tyrrell-Yamaha | 11 | Spun off | 18 |
| Ret | 15 | Eddie Irvine | Jordan-Hart | 10 | Spun off | 19 |
| Ret | 12 | Johnny Herbert | Lotus-Ford | 9 | Suspension | 20 |
| Ret | 24 | P.Martini | Minardi-Ford | 5 | Gearbox | 16 |
| Ret | 11 | Pedro Lamy | Lotus-Ford | 0 | Collision | 23 |

Winning speed: 107.611mph Lap leaders: Senna 1-23, 29-79; Prost 24-28
Pole position: Senna, 1m 13.371s, 115.245mph Fastest lap: Hill, 1m 15.381s, 112.172mph

# 1994

## DRIVERS' CHAMPION: MICHAEL SCHUMACHER
## CONSTRUCTORS' CHAMPION: WILLIAMS RENAULT

### DRIVERS' CHAMPIONSHIP

| POS. | DRIVER | NATIONALITY | CAR | POINTS |
|---|---|---|---|---|
| 1 | Michael Schumacher | Germany | Benetton-Ford | 92 |
| 2 | Damon Hill | GB | Williams-Renault | 91 |
| 3 | Gerhard Berger | Austria | Ferrari | 41 |
| 4 | Mika Hakkinen | Finland | McLaren-Peugeot | 26 |
| 5 | Jean Alesi | France | Ferrari | 24 |
| 6 | Rubens Barrichello | Brazil | Jordan-Hart | 19 |
| 7 | Martin Brundle | GB | McLaren-Peugeot | 16 |
| 8 | David Coulthard | GB | Williams-Renault | 14 |
| 9 | Nigel Mansell | GB | Williams-Renault | 13 |
| 10 | Jos Verstappen | Netherlands | Benetton-Ford | 10 |
| 11 | Olivier Panis | France | Ligier-Renault | 9 |
| 12 | Mark Blundell | GB | Tyrrell-Yamaha | 8 |
| 13 | Heinz-Harald Frentzen | Germany | Sauber-Mercedes | 7 |
| 14 | Nicola Larini | Italy | Ferrari | 6 |
| 15 | Christian Fittipaldi | Brazil | Footwork-Ford | 6 |
| 16 | Eddie Irvine | GB | Jordan-Hart | 6 |
| 17 | Ukyo Katayama | Japan | Tyrrell-Yamaha | 5 |
| 18 | Eric Bernard | France | Ligier-Renault, Lotus-Mugen Honda | 4 |
| 19 | Karl Wendlinger | Austria | Sauber-Mercedes | 4 |
| = | Andrea de Cesaris | Italy | Jordan-Hart, Sauber-Mercedes | 4 |
| 21 | Pierluigi Martini | Italy | Minardi-Ford | 4 |
| 22 | Gianni Morbidelli | Italy | Footwork-Ford | 3 |
| 23 | Erik Comas | France | Larrousse-Ford | 2 |
| 24 | Michele Alboreto | Italy | Minardi-Ford | 1 |
| = | JJ Lehto | Finland | Benetton-Ford, Sauber-Mercedes | 1 |
| | Johnny Herbert | GB | Lotus-Mugen Honda, Ligier-Renault, Benetton-Ford | |
| | Pedro Lamy | Portugal | Lotus-Mugen Honda | |
| | David Brabham | Australia | Simtek-Ford | |
| | Ayrton Senna | Brazil | Williams-Renault | |
| | Olivier Beretta | Italy | Larrousse-Ford | |
| | Bertrand Gachot | Belgium | Pacific-Ilmor | |
| | Jean-Paul Belmondo | France | Pacific-Ilmor | |
| | Roland Ratzenberger | Austria | Simtek-Ford | |
| | Aguri Suzuki | Japan | Jordan-Hart | |
| | Alessandro Zanardi | Italy | Lotus-Mugen Honda | |
| | Jean-Marc Gounon | France | Simtek-Ford | |
| | Phillipe Alliot | France | McLaren-Peugeot, Larrousse-Ford | |
| | Phillipe Adams | Belgium | Lotus-Mugen Honda | |
| | Mika Salo | Finland | Lotus-Mugen Honda | |
| | Yannick Dalmas | France | Larrousse-Ford | |
| | Domenico Schiattarella | Italy | Simtek-Ford | |
| | Hideki Noda | Japan | Larrousse-Ford | |
| | Franck Lagorce | France | Ligier-Renault | |
| | Taki Inoue | Japan | Simtek-Ford | |
| | Jean-Denis Deletraz | Switzerland | Larrousse-Ford | |
| | Andrea Montermini | Italy | Simtek-Ford | |

Points for top six finishers (10, 6, 4, 3, 2, 1). Half points awarded for races stopped before half distance.

### CONSTUCTORS' CHAMPIONSHIP

| POS. | CONSTRUCTOR | POINTS |
|---|---|---|
| 1 | Williams-Renault | 118 |
| 2 | Benetton-Ford | 103 |
| 3 | Ferrari | 71 |
| 4 | McLaren-Peugeot | 42 |
| 5 | Jordan-Hart | 28 |
| 6 | Ligier-Renault | 13 |
| 7 | Tyrrell-Yamaha | 13 |
| 8 | Sauber-Mercedes | 12 |
| 9 | Footwork-Ford | 9 |
| 10 | Minardi-Ford | 5 |
| 11 | Larrousse-Ford | 2 |

Points for top six finishers (10, 6, 4, 3, 2, 1). Half points awarded for races stopped before half distance.

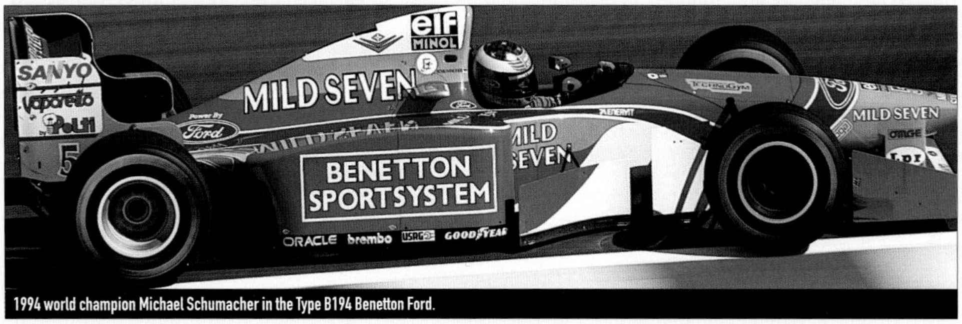

1994 world champion Michael Schumacher in the Type B194 Benetton Ford.

### BRAZILIAN GRAND PRIX: INTERLAGOS *27 March Round: 1 Race: 549 71 x 2.687 miles*

| POS. | NO. | DRIVER | CAR/ENGINE | LAPS | TIME/RETIRED | GRID |
|---|---|---|---|---|---|---|
| 1 | 5 | M.Schumacher | Benetton-Ford | 71 | 1:35'38.759 | 2 |
| 2 | 0 | Damon Hill | Williams-Renault | 70 | +1 Lap | 4 |
| 3 | 27 | Jean Alesi | Ferrari | 70 | +1 Lap | 3 |
| 4 | 14 | R.Barrichello | Jordan-Hart | 70 | +1 Lap | 14 |
| 5 | 3 | Ukyo Katayama | Tyrrell-Yamaha | 69 | +2 Laps | 10 |
| 6 | 29 | Karl Wendlinger | Sauber-Mercedes | 69 | +2 Laps | 7 |
| 7 | 12 | Johnny Herbert | Lotus-Mugen-Honda | 69 | +2 Laps | 21 |
| 8 | 23 | P.Martini | Minardi-Ford | 69 | +2 Laps | 15 |
| 9 | 20 | Erik Comas | Larrousse-Ford | 68 | +3 Laps | 13 |
| 10 | 11 | Pedro Lamy | Lotus-Mugen-Honda | 68 | +3 Laps | 24 |
| 11 | 26 | Olivier Panis | Ligier-Renault | 68 | +3 Laps | 19 |
| 12 | 31 | David Brabham | Simtek-Ford | 67 | +4 Laps | 26 |
| Ret | 2 | Ayrton Senna | Williams-Renault | 55 | Spun off | 1 |
| Ret | 8 | Martin Brundle | McLaren-Peugeot | 34 | Collision | 18 |
| Ret | 15 | Eddie Irvine | Jordan-Hart | 34 | Collision | 16 |
| Ret | 6 | Jos Verstappen | Benetton-Ford | 34 | Collision | 9 |
| Ret | 25 | Eric Bernard | Ligier-Renault | 33 | Collision | 20 |
| Ret | 4 | Mark Blundell | Tyrrell-Yamaha | 21 | Spun off | 12 |
| Ret | 9 | C.Fittipaldi | Footwork-Ford | 21 | Gearbox | 11 |
| Ret | 30 | H-H.Frentzen | Sauber-Mercedes | 15 | Spun off | 5 |
| Ret | 7 | Mika Hakkinen | McLaren-Peugeot | 13 | Engine | 8 |
| Ret | 24 | Michele Alboreto | Minardi-Ford | 7 | Engine | 22 |
| Ret | 10 | G.Morbidelli | Footwork-Ford | 5 | Gearbox | 6 |
| Ret | 28 | Gerhard Berger | Ferrari | 5 | Engine | 17 |
| Ret | 19 | Olivier Beretta | Larrousse-Ford | 2 | Collision | 23 |
| Ret | 34 | Bertrand Gachot | Pacific-Ilmor | 1 | Collision | 25 |
| DNQ | 32 | R.Ratzenberger | Simtek-Ford | | | |
| DNQ | 33 | Paul Belmondo | Pacific-Ilmor | | | |

Winning speed: 119.696mph Lap leaders: Senna 1-21; Schumacher 22-71
Pole position: Senna, 1m 15.962s, 127.363mph
Fastest lap: Schumacher, 1m 18.455s, 123.316mph

### PACIFIC GRAND PRIX: AIDA *17 April Round: 2 Race: 550 83 x 2.301 miles*

| POS. | NO. | DRIVER | CAR/ENGINE | LAPS | TIME/RETIRED | GRID |
|---|---|---|---|---|---|---|
| 1 | 5 | M.Schumacher | Benetton-Ford | 83 | 1:46'01.6932 | |
| 2 | 28 | Gerhard Berger | Ferrari | 83 | +1'15.300 | 5 |
| 3 | 14 | R.Barrichello | Jordan-Hart | 82 | +1 Lap | 8 |
| 4 | 9 | C.Fittipaldi | Footwork-Ford | 82 | +1 Lap | 9 |
| 5 | 30 | H-H.Frentzen | Sauber-Mercedes | 82 | +1 Lap | 11 |
| 6 | 20 | Erik Comas | Larrousse-Ford | 80 | +3 Laps | 16 |
| 7 | 12 | Johnny Herbert | Lotus-Mugen-Honda | 80 | +3 Laps | 23 |
| 8 | 11 | Pedro Lamy | Lotus-Mugen-Honda | 79 | +4 Laps | 24 |
| 9 | 26 | Olivier Panis | Ligier-Renault | 78 | +5 Laps | 22 |
| 10 | 25 | Eric Bernard | Ligier-Renault | 78 | +5 Laps | 18 |
| 11 | 32 | R.Ratzenberger | Simtek-Ford | 78 | +5 Laps | 26 |
| Ret | 10 | G.Morbidelli | Footwork-Ford | 69 | Engine | 13 |
| Ret | 29 | Karl Wendlinger | Sauber-Mercedes | 69 | Collision | 19 |
| Ret | 24 | Michele Alboreto | Minardi-Ford | 69 | Collision | 15 |
| Ret | 8 | Martin Brundle | McLaren-Peugeot | 67 | Overheating | 6 |
| Ret | 23 | P.Martini | Minardi-Ford | 63 | Spun off | 17 |
| Ret | 6 | Jos Verstappen | Benetton-Ford | 54 | Spun off | 10 |
| Ret | 0 | Damon Hill | Williams-Renault | 49 | Transmission | 3 |
| Ret | 15 | Aguri Suzuki | Jordan-Hart | 44 | Steering | 20 |
| Ret | 3 | Ukyo Katayama | Tyrrell-Yamaha | 42 | Engine | 14 |
| Ret | 7 | Mika Hakkinen | McLaren-Peugeot | 19 | Gearbox | 4 |
| Ret | 19 | Olivier Beretta | Larrousse-Ford | 14 | Electrical | 21 |
| Ret | 31 | David Brabham | Simtek-Ford | 2 | Electrical | 25 |
| Ret | 2 | Ayrton Senna | Williams-Renault | 0 | Collision | 1 |
| Ret | 27 | Nicola Larini | Ferrari | 0 | Collision | 7 |
| Ret | 4 | Mark Blundell | Tyrrell-Yamaha | 0 | Collision | 12 |
| DNQ | 34 | Bertrand Gachot | Pacific-Ilmor | | | |
| DNQ | 33 | Paul Belmondo | Pacific-Ilmor | | | |

Winning speed: 108.072mph Lap leaders: Schumacher 1-83
Pole position: Senna, 1m 10.218s, 117.967mph
Fastest lap: Schumacher, 1m 14.023s, 111.903mph

### SAN MARINO GRAND PRIX: IMOLA *1 May Round: 3 Race: 551 58 x 3.132 miles*

| POS. | NO. | DRIVER | CAR/ENGINE | LAPS | TIME/RETIRED | GRID |
|---|---|---|---|---|---|---|
| 1 | 5 | M.Schumacher | Benetton-Ford | 58 | 1:28'28.642 | 2 |
| 2 | 27 | Nicola Larini | Ferrari | 58 | +54.942 | 6 |
| 3 | 7 | Mika Hakkinen | McLaren-Peugeot | 58 | +1'10.679 | 8 |
| 4 | 29 | Karl Wendlinger | Sauber-Mercedes | 58 | +1'13.658 | 10 |
| 5 | 3 | Ukyo Katayama | Tyrrell-Yamaha | 57 | +1 Lap | 9 |
| 6 | 0 | Damon Hill | Williams-Renault | 57 | +1 Lap | 4 |
| 7 | 30 | H-H.Frentzen | Sauber-Mercedes | 57 | +1 Lap | 7 |
| 8 | 8 | Martin Brundle | McLaren-Peugeot | 57 | +1 Lap | 13 |
| 9 | 4 | Mark Blundell | Tyrrell-Yamaha | 56 | +2 Laps | 12 |
| 10 | 12 | Johnny Herbert | Lotus-Mugen-Honda | 56 | +2 Laps | 20 |
| 11 | 26 | Olivier Panis | Ligier-Renault | 56 | +2 Laps | 19 |
| 12 | 25 | Eric Bernard | Ligier-Renault | 55 | +3 Laps | 17 |
| 13 | 9 | C.Fittipaldi | Footwork-Ford | 54 | Spun off | 16 |
| Ret | 15 | A.de Cesaris | Jordan-Hart | 49 | Spun off | 21 |
| Ret | 24 | Michele Alboreto | Minardi-Ford | 44 | Wheel | 15 |
| Ret | 10 | G.Morbidelli | Footwork-Ford | 40 | Engine | 11 |
| Ret | 23 | P.Martini | Minardi-Ford | 37 | Spun off | 14 |
| Ret | 31 | David Brabham | Simtek-Ford | 27 | Spun off | 24 |
| Ret | 34 | Bertrand Gachot | Pacific-Ilmor | 23 | Engine | 25 |
| Ret | 19 | Olivier Beretta | Larrousse-Ford | 17 | Engine | 23 |
| Ret | 28 | Gerhard Berger | Ferrari | 16 | Suspension | 3 |
| Ret | 2 | Ayrton Senna | Williams-Renault | 5 | Fatal Accident | 1 |
| Ret | 20 | Erik Comas | Larrousse-Ford | 5 | Vibrations | 18 |
| Ret | 6 | J J Lehto | Benetton-Ford | 0 | Collision | 5 |
| Ret | 11 | Pedro Lamy | Lotus-Mugen-Honda | 0 | Collision | 22 |
| DNS | 32 | R. Ratzenberger | Simtek-Ford | | Fatal accident | 26 |
| DNQ | 33 | Paul Belmondo | Pacific-Ilmor | | | |
| DNQ | 14 | R.Barrichello | Jordan-Hart | | | |

Winning speed: 123.177mph Lap leaders: Senna 1-5; Berger 6-14; Häkkinen 15-18; Larini 19-23; Schumacher 24-58
Pole position: Senna, 1m 21.548s, 138.252mph
Fastest lap: Hill, 1m 24.335s, 133.683mph
Race stopped after seven laps because of Senna's accident. Restarted on aggregate for a further 51 laps.

### MONACO GRAND PRIX: MONTE CARLO *15 May Round: 4 Race: 552 78 x 2.068 miles*

| POS. | NO. | DRIVER | CAR/ENGINE | LAPS | TIME/RETIRED | GRID |
|---|---|---|---|---|---|---|
| 1 | 5 | M.Schumacher | Benetton-Ford | 78 | 1:49'55.372 | 1 |
| 2 | 8 | Martin Brundle | McLaren-Peugeot | 78 | +37.278 | 8 |
| 3 | 28 | Gerhard Berger | Ferrari | 78 | +1'16.824 | 3 |
| 4 | 15 | A.de Cesaris | Jordan-Hart | 77 | +1 Lap | 14 |
| 5 | 27 | Jean Alesi | Ferrari | 77 | +1 Lap | 5 |
| 6 | 24 | Michele Alboreto | Minardi-Ford | 77 | +1 Lap | 12 |
| 7 | 6 | J J Lehto | Benetton-Ford | 77 | +1 Lap | 17 |
| 8 | 19 | Olivier Beretta | Larrousse-Ford | 76 | +2 Laps | 18 |
| 9 | 26 | Olivier Panis | Ligier-Renault | 76 | +2 Laps | 20 |
| 10 | 20 | Erik Comas | Larrousse-Ford | 75 | +3 Laps | 13 |
| 11 | 11 | Pedro Lamy | Lotus-Mugen-Honda | 73 | +5 Laps | 19 |
| Ret | 12 | Johnny Herbert | Lotus-Mugen-Honda | 68 | Gearbox | 16 |
| Ret | 33 | Paul Belmondo | Pacific-Ilmor | 53 | Physical | 24 |
| Ret | 34 | Bertrand Gachot | Pacific-Ilmor | 49 | Gearbox | 23 |
| Ret | 9 | C.Fittipaldi | Footwork-Ford | 47 | Gearbox | 6 |
| Ret | 31 | David Brabham | Simtek-Ford | 45 | Collision | 22 |
| Ret | 4 | Mark Blundell | Tyrrell-Yamaha | 40 | Engine | 10 |
| Ret | 3 | Ukyo Katayama | Tyrrell-Yamaha | 38 | Gearbox | 11 |
| Ret | 25 | Eric Bernard | Ligier-Renault | 34 | Spun off | 21 |
| Ret | 14 | R.Barrichello | Jordan-Hart | 27 | Electrical | 15 |
| Ret | 7 | Mika Hakkinen | McLaren-Peugeot | 0 | Collision | 2 |
| Ret | 0 | Damon Hill | Williams-Renault | 0 | Collision | 4 |
| Ret | 10 | G.Morbidelli | Footwork-Ford | 0 | Collision | 7 |
| Ret | 23 | P.Martini | Minardi-Ford | 0 | Collision | 9 |
| Wth | 30 | H-H.Frentzen | Sauber-Mercedes | | | |
| DNQ | 29 | Karl Wendlinger | Sauber-Mercedes | | Accident | |

Winning speed: 88.042mph Lap leaders: Schumacher 1-78
Pole position: Schumacher, 1m 18.560s, 94.762mph
Fastest lap: Schumacher, 1m 21.076s, 91.822mph

### SPANISH GRAND PRIX: MONTMELÓ *29 May Round: 5 Race: 553 65 x 2.950 miles*

| POS. | NO. | DRIVER | CAR/ENGINE | LAPS | TIME/RETIRED | GRID |
|---|---|---|---|---|---|---|
| 1 | 0 | Damon Hill | Williams-Renault | 65 | 1:36'14.374 | 2 |
| 2 | 5 | M.Schumacher | Benetton-Ford | 65 | +24.166 | 1 |
| 3 | 4 | Mark Blundell | Tyrrell-Yamaha | 65 | +1'26.969 | 11 |
| 4 | 27 | Jean Alesi | Ferrari | 64 | +1 Lap | 6 |
| 5 | 23 | P.Martini | Minardi-Ford | 64 | +1 Lap | 18 |
| 6 | 15 | Eddie Irvine | Jordan-Hart | 64 | +1 Lap | 13 |
| 7 | 26 | Olivier Panis | Ligier-Renault | 63 | +2 Laps | 19 |
| 8 | 25 | Eric Bernard | Ligier-Renault | 62 | +3 Laps | 20 |
| 9 | 11 | A.Zanardi | Lotus-Mugen-Honda | 62 | +3 Laps | 23 |
| 10 | 31 | David Brabham | Simtek-Ford | 61 | +4 Laps | 24 |
| 11 | 8 | Martin Brundle | McLaren-Peugeot | 59 | Transmission | 8 |
| Ret | 6 | J J Lehto | Benetton-Ford | 53 | Engine | 4 |
| Ret | 7 | Mika Hakkinen | McLaren-Peugeot | 48 | Engine | 3 |
| Ret | 12 | Johnny Herbert | Lotus-Mugen-Honda | 41 | Spun off | 22 |
| Ret | 14 | R.Barrichello | Jordan-Hart | 39 | Spun off | 5 |
| Ret | 9 | C.Fittipaldi | Footwork-Ford | 35 | Engine | 21 |
| Ret | 2 | David Coulthard | Williams-Renault | 32 | Electrical | 9 |
| Ret | 34 | Bertrand Gachot | Pacific-Ilmor | 32 | Broken wing | 25 |
| Ret | 28 | Gerhard Berger | Ferrari | 27 | Gearbox | 7 |
| Ret | 10 | G.Morbidelli | Footwork-Ford | 24 | Fuel system | 15 |
| Ret | 30 | H-H.Frentzen | Sauber-Mercedes | 21 | Gearbox | 12 |
| Ret | 20 | Erik Comas | Larrousse-Ford | 19 | Radiator | 16 |
| Ret | 3 | Ukyo Katayama | Tyrrell-Yamaha | 16 | Engine | 10 |
| Ret | 24 | Michele Alboreto | Minardi-Ford | 4 | Engine | 14 |
| Ret | 33 | Paul Belmondo | Pacific-Ilmor | 2 | Spun off | 26 |
| Ret | 19 | Olivier Beretta | Larrousse-Ford | 0 | Engine | 17 |
| DNQ | 32 | A.Montermini | Simtek-Ford | | | |

Winning speed: 119.531mph
Lap leaders: Schumacher 1-22, 41-45; Häkkinen 23-30; Hill 31-40, 46-65
Pole position: Schumacher, 1m 21.908s, 129.642mph
Fastest lap: Schumacher, 1m 25.155s, 124.699mph

### CANADIAN GRAND PRIX: MONTRÉAL *12 June Round: 6 Race: 554 69 x 2.765 miles*

| POS. | NO. | DRIVER | CAR/ENGINE | LAPS | TIME/RETIRED | GRID |
|---|---|---|---|---|---|---|
| 1 | 5 | M.Schumacher | Benetton-Ford | 69 | 1:44'31.887 | 1 |
| 2 | 0 | Damon Hill | Williams-Renault | 69 | +39.660 | 4 |
| 3 | 27 | Jean Alesi | Ferrari | 69 | +1'13.388 | 2 |
| 4 | 28 | Gerhard Berger | Ferrari | 69 | +1'15.609 | 3 |
| 5 | 2 | David Coulthard | Williams-Renault | 68 | +1 Lap | 5 |
| 6 | 6 | J J Lehto | Benetton-Ford | 68 | +1 Lap | 20 |
| 7 | 14 | R.Barrichello | Jordan-Hart | 68 | +1 Lap | 6 |
| 8 | 12 | Johnny Herbert | Lotus-Mugen-Honda | 68 | +1 Lap | 17 |
| 9 | 23 | P.Martini | Minardi-Ford | 68 | +1 Lap | 15 |
| 10 | 4 | Mark Blundell | Tyrrell-Yamaha | 67 | Spun off | 13 |
| 11 | 24 | Michele Alboreto | Minardi-Ford | 67 | +2 Laps | 18 |
| 12 | 26 | Olivier Panis | Ligier-Renault | 67 | +2 Laps | 19 |
| 13 | 25 | Eric Bernard | Ligier-Renault | 66 | +3 Laps | 24 |
| 14 | 31 | David Brabham | Simtek-Ford | 65 | +4 Laps | 25 |
| 15 | 11 | A.Zanardi | Lotus-Mugen-Honda | 62 | +7 Laps | 23 |
| DSQ | 9 | C.Fittipaldi | Footwork-Ford | 68 | Disqualified | 16 |
| Ret | 7 | Mika Hakkinen | McLaren-Peugeot | 61 | Engine | 7 |
| Ret | 19 | Olivier Beretta | Larrousse-Ford | 57 | Engine | 22 |
| Ret | 10 | G.Morbidelli | Footwork-Ford | 50 | Transmission | 11 |
| Ret | 34 | Bertrand Gachot | Pacific-Ilmor | 47 | Oil pressure | 26 |
| Ret | 20 | Erik Comas | Larrousse-Ford | 45 | Clutch | 21 |
| Ret | 3 | Ukyo Katayama | Tyrrell-Yamaha | 44 | Collision | 9 |
| Ret | 15 | Eddie Irvine | Jordan-Hart | 40 | Spun off | 8 |
| Ret | 29 | A.de Cesaris | Sauber-Mercedes | 24 | Oil pressure | 14 |
| Ret | 30 | H-H.Frentzen | Sauber-Mercedes | 5 | Spun off | 10 |
| Ret | 8 | Martin Brundle | McLaren-Peugeot | 3 | Electrical | 12 |
| DNQ | 33 | Paul Belmondo | Pacific-Ilmor | | | |

Winning speed: 109.513mph Lap leaders: Schumacher 1-69
Pole position: Schumacher, 1m 26.178s, 115.509mph
Fastest lap: Schumacher, 1m 28.927s, 111.939mph
Fittipaldi disqualified from sixth place due to an underweight car.

### FRENCH GRAND PRIX: MAGNY COURS *3 July Round: 7 Race: 555 72 x 2.641 miles*

| POS. | NO. | DRIVER | CAR/ENGINE | LAPS | TIME/RETIRED | GRID |
|---|---|---|---|---|---|---|
| 1 | 5 | M.Schumacher | Benetton-Ford | 72 | 1:38'35.704 | 3 |
| 2 | 0 | Damon Hill | Williams-Renault | 72 | +12.642 | 1 |
| 3 | 28 | Gerhard Berger | Ferrari | 72 | +52.765 | 5 |
| 4 | 30 | H-H.Frentzen | Sauber-Mercedes | 71 | +1 Lap | 10 |
| 5 | 23 | P.Martini | Minardi-Ford | 70 | +2 Laps | 16 |
| 6 | 29 | A.de Cesaris | Sauber-Mercedes | 70 | +2 Laps | 11 |
| 7 | 12 | Johnny Herbert | Lotus-Mugen-Honda | 70 | +2 Laps | 19 |
| 8 | 9 | C.Fittipaldi | Footwork-Ford | 70 | +2 Laps | 18 |
| 9 | 32 | Jean-Marc Gounon | Simtek-Ford | 68 | +4 Laps | 26 |
| 10 | 4 | Mark Blundell | Tyrrell-Yamaha | 67 | +5 Laps | 17 |
| 11 | 20 | Erik Comas | Larrousse-Ford | 66 | Engine | 20 |
| Ret | 3 | Ukyo Katayama | Tyrrell-Yamaha | 53 | Spun off | 14 |
| Ret | 7 | Mika Hakkinen | McLaren-Peugeot | 48 | Engine | 9 |
| Ret | 2 | Nigel Mansell | Williams-Renault | 45 | Gearbox | 2 |
| Ret | 27 | Jean Alesi | Ferrari | 41 | Collision | 4 |
| Ret | 14 | R.Barrichello | Jordan-Hart | 41 | Collision | 7 |
| Ret | 25 | Eric Bernard | Ligier-Renault | 40 | Gearbox | 15 |
| Ret | 19 | Olivier Beretta | Larrousse-Ford | 36 | Engine | 25 |
| Ret | 8 | Martin Brundle | McLaren-Peugeot | 29 | Engine | 12 |
| Ret | 10 | G.Morbidelli | Footwork-Ford | 28 | Collision | 22 |
| Ret | 26 | Olivier Panis | Ligier-Renault | 28 | Collision | 13 |
| Ret | 31 | David Brabham | Simtek-Ford | 28 | Transmission | 24 |
| Ret | 6 | Jos Verstappen | Benetton-Ford | 25 | Spun off | 8 |
| Ret | 15 | Eddie Irvine | Jordan-Hart | 24 | Gearbox | 6 |
| Ret | 24 | Michele Alboreto | Minardi-Ford | 21 | Engine | 21 |
| Ret | 11 | A.Zanardi | Lotus-Mugen-Honda | 20 | Engine | 23 |
| DNQ | 34 | Bertrand Gachot | Pacific-Ilmor | | | |
| DNQ | 33 | Paul Belmondo | Pacific-Ilmor | | | |

Winning speed: 115.709mph Lap leaders: Schumacher 1-37,45-72; Hill 38-44
Pole position: Hill, 1m 16.282s, 124.629mph
Fastest lap: Hill, 1m 19.678s, 119.317mph

### BRITISH GRAND PRIX: SILVERSTONE ROUND: *8 Race: 556 60 x 3.142 miles*

| POS. | NO. | DRIVER | CAR/ENGINE | LAPS | TIME/RETIRED | GRID |
|---|---|---|---|---|---|---|
| 1 | 0 | Damon Hill | Williams-Renault | 60 | 1:30'03.640 | 1 |
| 2 | 27 | Jean Alesi | Ferrari | 60 | +1'08.128 | 4 |
| 3 | 7 | Mika Hakkinen | McLaren-Peugeot | 60 | +1'40.659 | 5 |
| 4 | 14 | R.Barrichello | Jordan-Hart | 60 | +1'41.751 | 6 |
| 5 | 2 | David Coulthard | Williams-Renault | 59 | +1 Lap | 7 |
| 6 | 3 | Ukyo Katayama | Tyrrell-Yamaha | 59 | +1 Lap | 8 |
| 7 | 30 | H-H.Frentzen | Sauber-Mercedes | 59 | +1 Lap | 13 |
| 8 | 6 | Jos Verstappen | Benetton-Ford | 59 | +1 Lap | 10 |
| 9 | 9 | C.Fittipaldi | Footwork-Ford | 58 | +2 Laps | 20 |
| 10 | 23 | P.Martini | Minardi-Ford | 58 | +2 Laps | 14 |
| 11 | 12 | Johnny Herbert | Lotus-Mugen-Honda | 58 | +2 Laps | 21 |
| 12 | 26 | Olivier Panis | Ligier-Renault | 58 | +2 Laps | 15 |
| 13 | 25 | Eric Bernard | Ligier-Renault | 58 | +2 Laps | 23 |
| 14 | 19 | Olivier Beretta | Larrousse-Ford | 58 | +2 Laps | 24 |
| 15 | 31 | David Brabham | Simtek-Ford | 57 | +3 Laps | 25 |
| 16 | 32 | Jean-Marc Gounon | Simtek-Ford | 57 | +3 Laps | 26 |
| DSQ | 5 | M.Schumacher | Benetton-Ford | 60 | Disqualified | 2 |
| Ret | 24 | Michele Alboreto | Minardi-Ford | 48 | Engine | 17 |
| Ret | 28 | Gerhard Berger | Ferrari | 32 | Engine | 3 |
| Ret | 4 | Mark Blundell | Tyrrell-Yamaha | 20 | Gearbox | 11 |
| Ret | 20 | Erik Comas | Larrousse-Ford | 12 | Engine | 22 |
| Ret | 29 | A.de Cesaris | Sauber-Mercedes | 11 | Engine | 18 |
| Ret | 10 | G.Morbidelli | Footwork-Ford | 5 | Engine | 16 |
| Ret | 11 | A.Zanardi | Lotus-Mugen-Honda | 4 | Engine | 19 |
| Ret | 8 | Martin Brundle | McLaren-Peugeot | 0 | Engine | 9 |
| Ret | 15 | Eddie Irvine | Jordan-Hart | 0 | Engine | 12 |
| DNQ | 34 | Bertrand Gachot | Pacific-Ilmor | | | |
| DNQ | 33 | Paul Belmondo | Pacific-Ilmor | | | |

Winning speed: 125.606mph
Lap leaders: Hill 1-14, 27-60; Schumacher 15-17, 22-26; Berger 18-21
Pole position: Hill, 1m 24.960s, 133.147mph
Fastest lap: Hill, 1m 27.100s, 129.876mph
Scumacher disqualified from second for overtaking on the formation lap.

### GERMAN GRAND PRIX: HOCKENHEIM *31 July Round: 9 Race: 557 45 x 4.240 miles*

| POS. | NO. | DRIVER | CAR/ENGINE | LAPS | TIME/RETIRED | GRID |
|---|---|---|---|---|---|---|
| 1 | 28 | Gerhard Berger | Ferrari | 45 | 1:22'37.272 | 1 |
| 2 | 26 | Olivier Panis | Ligier-Renault | 45 | +54.779 | 12 |
| 3 | 25 | Eric Bernard | Ligier-Renault | 45 | +1'05.0421 | 14 |
| 4 | 9 | C.Fittipaldi | Footwork-Ford | 45 | +1'21.609 | 17 |
| 5 | 10 | G.Morbidelli | Footwork-Ford | 45 | +1'30.544 | 16 |
| 6 | 20 | Erik Comas | Larrousse-Ford | 45 | +1'45.445 | 22 |
| 7 | 19 | Olivier Beretta | Larrousse-Ford | 44 | +1 Lap | 24 |
| 8 | 0 | Damon Hill | Williams-Renault | 44 | +1 Lap | 3 |
| Ret | 32 | Jean-Marc Gounon | Simtek-Ford | 39 | Engine | 26 |
| Ret | 31 | David Brabham | Simtek-Ford | 37 | Clutch | 25 |
| Ret | 5 | M.Schumacher | Benetton-Ford | 20 | Engine | 4 |
| Ret | 8 | Martin Brundle | McLaren-Peugeot | 19 | Engine | 13 |
| Ret | 2 | David Coulthard | Williams-Renault | 17 | Electrical | 6 |
| Ret | 6 | Jos Verstappen | Benetton-Ford | 15 | Fire | 19 |
| Ret | 3 | Ukyo Katayama | Tyrrell-Yamaha | 6 | Throttle | 5 |
| Ret | 27 | Jean Alesi | Ferrari | 0 | Engine | 2 |
| Ret | 4 | Mark Blundell | Tyrrell-Yamaha | 0 | Collision | 7 |
| Ret | 7 | Mika Hakkinen | McLaren-Peugeot | 0 | Collision | 8 |
| Ret | 30 | H-H.Frentzen | Sauber-Mercedes | 0 | Collision | 9 |
| Ret | 15 | Eddie Irvine | Jordan-Hart | 0 | Collision | 10 |
| Ret | 14 | R.Barrichello | Jordan-Hart | 0 | Collision | 11 |
| Ret | 12 | Johnny Herbert | Lotus-Mugen-Honda | 0 | Collision | 15 |
| Ret | 29 | A.de Cesaris | Sauber-Mercedes | 0 | Collision | 18 |
| Ret | 23 | P.Martini | Minardi-Ford | 0 | Collision | 20 |
| Ret | 11 | A.Zanardi | Lotus-Mugen-Honda | 0 | Collision | 21 |
| Ret | 24 | Michele Alboreto | Minardi-Ford | 0 | Collision | 23 |
| DNQ | 33 | Paul Belmondo | Pacific-Ilmor | | | |
| DNQ | 34 | Bertrand Gachot | Pacific-Ilmor | | | |

Winning speed: 138.548mph Lap leaders: Berger 1-45
Pole position: Berger, 1m 43.582s, 147.348mph
Fastest lap: Coulthard, 1m 46.211s, 143.701mph

**HUNGARIAN GRAND PRIX: HUNGARORING** *14 August Round: 10 Race: 558 77 x 2.466 miles*

| POS. | NO. | DRIVER | CAR/ENGINE | LAPS | TIME/RETIRED | GRID |
|---|---|---|---|---|---|---|
| 1 | 5 | M.Schumacher | Benetton-Ford | 77 | 1:48'00.185 | 1 |
| 2 | 0 | Damon Hill | Williams-Renault | 77 | +20.827 | 2 |
| 3 | 6 | Jos Verstappen | Benetton-Ford | 77 | +1'10.329 | 12 |
| 4 | 8 | Martin Brundle | McLaren-Peugeot | 76 | Electrical | 6 |
| 5 | 4 | Mark Blundell | Tyrrell-Yamaha | 76 | +1 Lap | 11 |
| 6 | 26 | Olivier Panis | Ligier-Renault | 76 | +1 Lap | 9 |
| 7 | 24 | Michele Alboreto | Minardi-Ford | 75 | +2 Laps | 20 |
| 8 | 20 | Erik Comas | Larrousse-Ford | 75 | +2 Laps | 21 |
| 9 | 19 | Olivier Beretta | Larrousse-Ford | 75 | +2 Laps | 25 |
| 10 | 25 | Eric Bernard | Ligier-Renault | 75 | +2 Laps | 18 |
| 11 | 31 | David Brabham | Simtek-Ford | 74 | +3 Laps | 23 |
| 12 | 28 | Gerhard Berger | Ferrari | 72 | Engine | 4 |
| 13 | 11 | A.Zanardi | Lotus-Mugen-Honda | 72 | +5 Laps | 22 |
| 14 | 9 | C.Fittipaldi | Footwork-Ford | 69 | Transmission | 16 |
| Ret | 2 | David Coulthard | Williams-Renault | 59 | Spun off | 3 |
| Ret | 27 | Jean Alesi | Ferrari | 58 | Gearbox | 13 |
| Ret | 23 | P.Martini | Minardi-Ford | 58 | Spun off | 15 |
| Ret | 30 | H-H.Frentzen | Sauber-Mercedes | 39 | Gearbox | 8 |
| Ret | 12 | Johnny Herbert | Lotus-Mugen-Honda | 34 | Electrical | 24 |
| Ret | 29 | A.de Cesaris | Sauber-Mercedes | 30 | Collision | 17 |
| Ret | 10 | G.Morbidelli | Footwork-Ford | 30 | Collision | 19 |
| Ret | 7 | Philippe Alliot | McLaren-Peugeot | 21 | Water leak | 14 |
| Ret | 32 | Jean-Marc Gounon | Simtek-Ford | 9 | Handling | 26 |
| Ret | 3 | Ukyo Katayama | Tyrrell-Yamaha | 0 | Collision | 5 |
| Ret | 15 | Eddie Irvine | Jordan-Hart | 0 | Collision | 7 |
| Ret | 14 | R.Barrichello | Jordan-Hart | 0 | Collision | 10 |
| DNQ | 34 | Bertrand Gachot | Pacific-Ilmor | | | |
| DNQ | 33 | Paul Belmondo | Pacific-Ilmor | | | |

Winning speed: 105.470mph Lap leaders: Schmacher 1-16, 26-77; Hill 17-25
Pole position: Schumacher, 1m 18.258s, 113.422mph
Fastest lap: Schumacher, 1m 20.881s, 109.743mph

**BELGIAN GRAND PRIX: SPA-FRANCORCHAMPS** *28 August Round: 11 Race: 559 44 x 4.350 miles*

| POS. | NO. | DRIVER | CAR/ENGINE | LAPS | TIME/RETIRED | GRID |
|---|---|---|---|---|---|---|
| 1 | 0 | Damon Hill | Williams-Renault | 44 | 1:28'47.170 | 3 |
| 2 | 7 | Mika Hakkinen | McLaren-Peugeot | 44 | +51.381 | 8 |
| 3 | 6 | Jos Verstappen | Benetton-Ford | 44 | +1'10.453 | 6 |
| 4 | 2 | David Coulthard | Williams-Renault | 44 | +1'45.787 | 7 |
| 5 | 4 | Mark Blundell | Tyrrell-Yamaha | 43 | +1 Lap | 12 |
| 6 | 10 | G.Morbidelli | Footwork-Ford | 43 | +1 Lap | 14 |
| 7 | 26 | Olivier Panis | Ligier-Renault | 43 | +1 Lap | 17 |
| 8 | 23 | P.Martini | Minardi-Ford | 43 | +1 Lap | 10 |
| 9 | 24 | Michele Alboreto | Minardi-Ford | 43 | +1 Lap | 18 |
| 10 | 25 | Eric Bernard | Ligier-Renault | 42 | +2 Laps | 16 |
| 11 | 32 | Jean-Marc Gounon | Simtek-Ford | 42 | +2 Laps | 25 |
| 12 | 12 | Johnny Herbert | Lotus-Mugen-Honda | 41 | +3 Laps | 20 |
| 13 | 15 | Eddie Irvine | Jordan-Hart | 40 | Alternator | 4 |
| DSQ | 5 | M.Schumacher | Benetton-Ford | 44 | Disqualified | 2 |
| Ret | 9 | C.Fittipaldi | Footwork-Ford | 33 | Engine | 24 |
| Ret | 31 | David Brabham | Simtek-Ford | 29 | Wheel | 21 |
| Ret | 29 | A.de Cesaris | Sauber-Mercedes | 27 | Throttle | 15 |
| Ret | 8 | Martin Brundle | McLaren-Peugeot | 24 | Spun off | 13 |
| Ret | 14 | R.Barrichello | Jordan-Hart | 19 | Spun off | 1 |
| Ret | 3 | Ukyo Katayama | Tyrrell-Yamaha | 18 | Engine | 23 |
| Ret | 11 | Philippe Adams | Lotus-Mugen-Honda | 15 | Spun off | 26 |
| Ret | 28 | Gerhard Berger | Ferrari | 11 | Engine | 11 |
| Ret | 19 | Philippe Alliot | Larrousse-Ford | 11 | Engine | 19 |
| Ret | 30 | H-H.Frentzen | Sauber-Mercedes | 10 | Halfshaft | 9 |
| Ret | 20 | Erik Comas | Larrousse-Ford | 3 | Engine | 22 |
| Ret | 27 | Jean Alesi | Ferrari | 2 | Engine | 5 |
| DNQ | 34 | Bertrand Gachot | Pacific-Ilmor | | | |
| DNQ | 33 | Paul Belmondo | Pacific-Ilmor | | | |

Winning speed: 129.351mph Lap leaders: Schumacher 1-28, 30-44; Coulthard 29
Pole position: Barrichello, 2m 21.163s, 110.941mph
Fastest lap: Hill, 1m 57.117s, 133.719mph
Scumacher disqualified from first place and banned for two further races due to an illegal plank

**ITALIAN GRAND PRIX: MONZA** *11 September Round: 12 Race: 560 53 x 3.604 miles*

| POS. | NO. | DRIVER | CAR/ENGINE | LAPS | TIME/RETIRED | GRID |
|---|---|---|---|---|---|---|
| 1 | 0 | Damon Hill | Williams-Renault | 53 | 1:18'02.754 | 3 |
| 2 | 28 | Gerhard Berger | Ferrari | 53 | +4.930 | 2 |
| 3 | 7 | Mika Hakkinen | McLaren-Peugeot | 53 | +25.640 | 7 |
| 4 | 14 | R.Barrichello | Jordan-Hart | 53 | +50.634 | 16 |
| 5 | 8 | Martin Brundle | McLaren-Peugeot | 53 | +1'25.575 | 15 |
| 6 | 2 | David Coulthard | Williams-Renault | 52 | Out of fuel | 5 |
| 7 | 25 | Eric Bernard | Ligier-Renault | 52 | +1 Lap | 12 |
| 8 | 20 | Erik Comas | Larrousse-Ford | 52 | +1 Lap | 24 |
| 9 | 5 | J J Lehto | Benetton-Ford | 52 | +1 Lap | 20 |
| 10 | 26 | Olivier Panis | Ligier-Renault | 51 | +2 Laps | 6 |
| Ret | 31 | David Brabham | Simtek-Ford | 46 | Puncture | 26 |
| Ret | 3 | Ukyo Katayama | Tyrrell-Yamaha | 45 | Spun off | 14 |
| Ret | 9 | C.Fittipaldi | Footwork-Ford | 43 | Engine | 19 |
| Ret | 15 | Eddie Irvine | Jordan-Hart | 41 | Engine | 9 |
| Ret | 4 | Mark Blundell | Tyrrell-Yamaha | 39 | Spun off | 21 |
| Ret | 23 | P.Martini | Minardi-Ford | 30 | Spun off | 18 |
| Ret | 24 | Michele Alboreto | Minardi-Ford | 28 | Gearbox | 22 |
| Ret | 30 | H-H.Frentzen | Sauber-Mercedes | 22 | Engine | 11 |
| Ret | 29 | A.de Cesaris | Sauber-Mercedes | 20 | Engine | 8 |
| Ret | 32 | Jean-Marc Gounon | Simtek-Ford | 20 | Gearbox | 25 |
| Ret | 19 | Yannick Dalmas | Larrousse-Ford | 18 | Spun off | 23 |
| Ret | 27 | Jean Alesi | Ferrari | 14 | Gearbox | 1 |
| Ret | 12 | Johnny Herbert | Lotus-Mugen-Honda | 13 | Alternator | 4 |
| Ret | 6 | Jos Verstappen | Benetton-Ford | 0 | Collision | 10 |
| Ret | 11 | A.Zanardi | Lotus-Mugen-Honda | 0 | Collision | 13 |
| Ret | 10 | G.Morbidelli | Footwork-Ford | 0 | Collision | 17 |
| DNQ | 34 | Bertrand Gachot | Pacific-Ilmor | | | |
| DNQ | 33 | Paul Belmondo | Pacific-Ilmor | | | |

Winning speed: 146.844mph
Lap leaders: Alesi 1-14; Brger 15-23; Hill 24, 29-53; Coulthard 25, 27-28; Häkkinen 26
Pole position: Alesi, 1m 23.844s, 154.743mph
Fastest lap: Hill, 1m 25.930s, 150.986mph
Race stopped after first lap pile-up and restarted for total original distance.

**PURTUGESE GRAND PRIX: ESTORILL** *25 September Round: 13 Race: 561 71 x 2.709 miles*

| POS. | NO. | DRIVER | CAR/ENGINE | LAPS | TIME/RETIRED | GRID |
|---|---|---|---|---|---|---|
| 1 | 0 | Damon Hill | Williams-Renault | 71 | 1:41'10.165 | 2 |
| 2 | 2 | David Coulthard | Williams-Renault | 71 | +0.603 | 3 |
| 3 | 7 | Mika Hakkinen | McLaren-Peugeot | 71 | +20.193 | 4 |
| 4 | 14 | R.Barrichello | Jordan-Hart | 71 | +28.003 | 8 |
| 5 | 6 | Jos Verstappen | Benetton-Ford | 71 | +29.385 | 10 |
| 6 | 8 | Martin Brundle | McLaren-Peugeot | 71 | +52.702 | 7 |
| 7 | 15 | Eddie Irvine | Jordan-Hart | 70 | +1 Lap | 13 |
| 8 | 9 | C.Fittipaldi | Footwork-Ford | 70 | +1 Lap | 11 |
| 9 | 10 | G.Morbidelli | Footwork-Ford | 70 | +1 Lap | 16 |
| 10 | 25 | Eric Bernard | Ligier-Renault | 70 | +1 Lap | 21 |
| 11 | 12 | Johnny Herbert | Lotus-Mugen-Honda | 70 | +1 Lap | 20 |
| 12 | 23 | P.Martini | Minardi-Ford | 69 | +2 Laps | 18 |
| 13 | 24 | Michele Alboreto | Minardi-Ford | 69 | +2 Laps | 19 |
| 14 | 19 | Yannick Dalmas | Larrousse-Ford | 69 | +2 Laps | 23 |
| 15 | 32 | Jean-Marc Gounon | Simtek-Ford | 67 | +4 Laps | 26 |
| 16 | 11 | Philippe Adams | Lotus-Mugen-Honda | 67 | +4 Laps | 25 |
| Ret | 26 | Olivier Panis | Ligier-Renault | 70 | Disqualified | 15 |
| Ret | 4 | Mark Blundell | Tyrrell-Yamaha | 61 | Engine | 12 |
| Ret | 5 | J J Lehto | Benetton-Ford | 60 | Spun off | 14 |
| Ret | 29 | A.de Cesaris | Sauber-Mercedes | 54 | Spun off | 17 |
| Ret | 27 | Jean Alesi | Ferrari | 38 | Collision | 5 |
| Ret | 31 | David Brabham | Simtek-Ford | 36 | Collision | 24 |
| Ret | 30 | H-H.Frentzen | Sauber-Mercedes | 31 | Differential | 9 |
| Ret | 20 | Erik Comas | Larrousse-Ford | 27 | Suspension | 22 |
| Ret | 3 | Ukyo Katayama | Tyrrell-Yamaha | 26 | Gearbox | 6 |
| Ret | 28 | Gerhard Berger | Ferrari | 7 | Gearbox | 1 |
| DNQ | 34 | Bertrand Gachot | Pacific-Ilmor | | | |
| DNQ | 33 | Paul Belmondo | Pacific-Ilmor | | | |

Winning speed: 114.077mph Lap leaders: Berger 1-7; Coulthard 8-17, 26-27; Hill 18, 28-71; Alesi 19-22; Barrichello 23-25
Pole position: Berger, 1m 20.608s, 120.993mph
Fastest lap: Coulthard, 1m 22.446s, 118.296mph

**EUROPEAN GRAND PRIX: JEREZ DE LA FRONTERA** *16 October Round: 14 Race: 562 69 x 2.751 miles*

| POS. | NO. | DRIVER | CAR/ENGINE | LAPS | TIME/RETIRED | GRID |
|---|---|---|---|---|---|---|
| 1 | 5 | M.Schumacher | Benetton-Ford | 69 | 1:40'26.689 | 1 |
| 2 | 0 | Damon Hill | Williams-Renault | 69 | +24.689 | 2 |
| 3 | 7 | Mika Hakkinen | McLaren-Peugeot | 69 | +1'09.648 | 9 |
| 4 | 15 | Eddie Irvine | Jordan-Hart | 69 | +1'18.446 | 10 |
| 5 | 28 | Gerhard Berger | Ferrari | 68 | +1 Lap | 6 |
| 6 | 30 | H-H.Frentzen | Sauber-Mercedes | 68 | +1 Lap | 4 |
| 7 | 3 | Ukyo Katayama | Tyrrell-Yamaha | 68 | +1 Lap | 13 |
| 8 | 25 | Johnny Herbert | Ligier-Renault | 68 | +1 Lap | 7 |
| 9 | 26 | Olivier Panis | Ligier-Renault | 68 | +1 Lap | 11 |
| 10 | 27 | Jean Alesi | Ferrari | 68 | +1 Lap | 16 |
| 11 | 10 | G.Morbidelli | Footwork-Ford | 68 | +1 Lap | 8 |
| 12 | 14 | R.Barrichello | Jordan-Hart | 68 | +1 Lap | 5 |
| 13 | 4 | Mark Blundell | Tyrrell-Yamaha | 68 | +1 Lap | 14 |
| 14 | 24 | Michele Alboreto | Minardi-Ford | 67 | +2 Laps | 20 |
| 15 | 23 | P.Martini | Minardi-Ford | 67 | +2 Laps | 17 |
| 16 | 12 | A.Zanardi | Lotus-Mugen-Honda | 67 | +2 Laps | 21 |
| 17 | 9 | C.Fittipaldi | Footwork-Ford | 66 | +3 Laps | 19 |
| 18 | 11 | Eric Bernard | Lotus-Mugen-Honda | 66 | +3 Laps | 22 |
| 19 | 32 | D.Schiattarella | Simtek-Ford | 64 | +5 Laps | 26 |
| Ret | 2 | Nigel Mansell | Williams-Renault | 47 | Spun off | 3 |
| Ret | 31 | David Brabham | Simtek-Ford | 42 | Engine | 25 |
| Ret | 29 | A.de Cesaris | Sauber-Mercedes | 37 | Throttle | 18 |
| Ret | 20 | Erik Comas | Larrousse-Ford | 37 | Alternator | 23 |
| Ret | 6 | Jos Verstappen | Benetton-Ford | 15 | Spun off | 12 |
| Ret | 19 | Hideki Noda | Larrousse-Ford | 10 | Gearbox | 24 |
| Ret | 8 | Martin Brundle | McLaren-Peugeot | 8 | Engine | 15 |
| DNQ | 34 | Bertrand Gachot | Pacific-Ilmor | | | |
| DNQ | 33 | Paul Belmondo | Pacific-Ilmor | | | |

Winning speed: 113.405mph Lap leaders: Hill 1-17, 33-34; Schumacher 18-32, 35-69
Pole position: Schumacher, 1m 22.762s, 119.682mph
Fastest lap: Schumacher, 1m 25.040s, 116.476mph

**JAPANESE GRAND PRIX: SUZUKA** *6 November Round: 15 Race: 563 50 x 3.644 miles*

| POS. | NO. | DRIVER | CAR/ENGINE | LAPS | TIME/RETIRED | GRID |
|---|---|---|---|---|---|---|
| 1 | 0 | Damon Hill | Williams-Renault | 50 | 1:55'53.532 | 2 |
| 2 | 5 | M.Schumacher | Benetton-Ford | 50 | +3.365 | 1 |
| 3 | 27 | Jean Alesi | Ferrari | 50 | +52.045 | 7 |
| 4 | 2 | Nigel Mansell | Williams-Renault | 50 | +56.074 | 4 |
| 5 | 15 | Eddie Irvine | Jordan-Hart | 50 | +1'42.107 | 6 |
| 6 | 30 | H-H.Frentzen | Sauber-Mercedes | 50 | +1'59.863 | 3 |
| 7 | 7 | Mika Hakkinen | McLaren-Peugeot | 50 | +2'02.985 | 8 |
| 8 | 9 | C.Fittipaldi | Footwork-Ford | 49 | +1 Lap | 18 |
| 9 | 20 | Erik Comas | Larrousse-Ford | 49 | +1 Lap | 22 |
| 10 | 11 | Mika Salo | Lotus-Mugen-Honda | 49 | +1 Lap | 25 |
| 11 | 26 | Olivier Panis | Ligier-Renault | 49 | +1 Lap | 19 |
| 12 | 31 | David Brabham | Simtek-Ford | 48 | +2 Laps | 24 |
| 13 | 12 | A.Zanardi | Lotus-Mugen-Honda | 48 | +2 Laps | 17 |
| Ret | 4 | Mark Blundell | Tyrrell-Yamaha | 26 | Engine | 13 |
| Ret | 14 | R.Barrichello | Jordan-Hart | 16 | Gearbox | 10 |
| Ret | 8 | Martin Brundle | McLaren-Peugeot | 13 | Spun off | 9 |
| Ret | 10 | G.Morbidelli | Footwork-Ford | 13 | Spun off | 12 |
| Ret | 28 | Gerhard Berger | Ferrari | 10 | Ignition | 11 |
| Ret | 25 | Franck Lagorce | Ligier-Renault | 10 | Collision | 20 |
| Ret | 23 | P.Martini | Minardi-Ford | 10 | Collision | 16 |
| Ret | 24 | Michele Alboreto | Minardi-Ford | 10 | Spun off | 21 |
| Ret | 6 | Johnny Herbert | Benetton-Ford | 3 | Spun off | 5 |
| Ret | 3 | Ukyo Katayama | Tyrrell-Yamaha | 3 | Spun off | 14 |
| Ret | 32 | Taki Inoue | Simtek-Ford | 3 | Spun off | 26 |
| Ret | 29 | J J Lehto | Sauber-Mercedes | 0 | Engine | 15 |
| Ret | 19 | Hideki Noda | Larrousse-Ford | 0 | Spun off | 23 |
| DNQ | 34 | Bertrand Gachot | Pacific-Ilmor | | | |
| DNQ | 33 | Paul Belmondo | Pacific-Ilmor | | | |

Winning speed: 94.322mph Lap leaders: Schumacher 1-18; Hill 19-50
Pole position: Schumacher, 1m 37.209s, 134.940mph
Fastest lap: Hill, 1m 56.597s, 112.502mph
Race stopped after 13 laps due to rain and restarted on aggregate for 37 laps, rather than the scheduled remaining 40 laps.

**AUSTRALIAN GRAND PRIX: ADELAIDE** *13 November Round: 16 Race: 564 81 x 2.349 miles*

| POS. | NO. | DRIVER | CAR/ENGINE | LAPS | TIME/RETIRED | GRID |
|---|---|---|---|---|---|---|
| 1 | 2 | Nigel Mansell | Williams-Renault | 81 | 1:47'51.480 | 1 |
| 2 | 28 | Gerhard Berger | Ferrari | 81 | +2.511 | 11 |
| 3 | 8 | Martin Brundle | McLaren-Peugeot | 81 | +52.487 | 9 |
| 4 | 14 | R.Barrichello | Jordan-Hart | 81 | +1'10.530 | 5 |
| 5 | 26 | Olivier Panis | Ligier-Renault | 80 | +1 Lap | 12 |
| 6 | 27 | Jean Alesi | Ferrari | 80 | +1 Lap | 8 |
| 7 | 30 | H-H.Frentzen | Sauber-Mercedes | 80 | +1 Lap | 10 |
| 8 | 9 | C.Fittipaldi | Footwork-Ford | 80 | +1 Lap | 19 |
| 9 | 23 | P.Martini | Minardi-Ford | 79 | +2 Laps | 18 |
| 10 | 29 | J J Lehto | Sauber-Mercedes | 79 | +2 Laps | 17 |
| 11 | 25 | Franck Lagorce | Ligier-Renault | 79 | +2 Laps | 20 |
| 12 | 7 | Mika Hakkinen | McLaren-Peugeot | 76 | Spun off | 4 |
| Ret | 24 | Michele Alboreto | Minardi-Ford | 69 | Suspension | 16 |
| Ret | 4 | Mark Blundell | Tyrrell-Yamaha | 66 | Collision | 13 |
| Ret | 20 | J-D.Deletraz | Larrousse-Ford | 56 | Gearbox | 25 |
| Ret | 11 | Mika Salo | Lotus-Mugen-Honda | 49 | Electrical | 22 |
| Ret | 31 | David Brabham | Simtek-Ford | 49 | Engine | 24 |
| Ret | 12 | A.Zanardi | Lotus-Mugen-Honda | 40 | Throttle | 14 |
| Ret | 5 | M.Schumacher | Benetton-Ford | 35 | Collision | 2 |
| Ret | 0 | Damon Hill | Williams-Renault | 35 | Collision | 3 |
| Ret | 32 | D.Schiattarella | Simtek-Ford | 21 | Gearbox | 26 |
| Ret | 3 | Ukyo Katayama | Tyrrell-Yamaha | 19 | Spun off | 15 |
| Ret | 19 | Hideki Noda | Larrousse-Ford | 18 | Oil leak | 23 |
| Ret | 10 | G.Morbidelli | Footwork-Ford | 17 | Oil leak | 21 |
| Ret | 15 | Eddie Irvine | Jordan-Hart | 15 | Spun off | 6 |
| Ret | 6 | Johnny Herbert | Benetton-Ford | 13 | Gearbox | 7 |
| DNQ | 33 | Paul Belmondo | Pacific-Ilmor | | | |
| DNQ | 34 | Bertrand Gachot | Pacific-Ilmor | | | |

Winning speed: 105.834mph
Lap leaders: Schumacher 1-35, Mansell 36-53, 64-81; Berger 54-63
Pole position: Mansell, 1m 16.179s, 110.997mph
Fastest lap: Schumacher, 1m 17.140s, 109.614mph

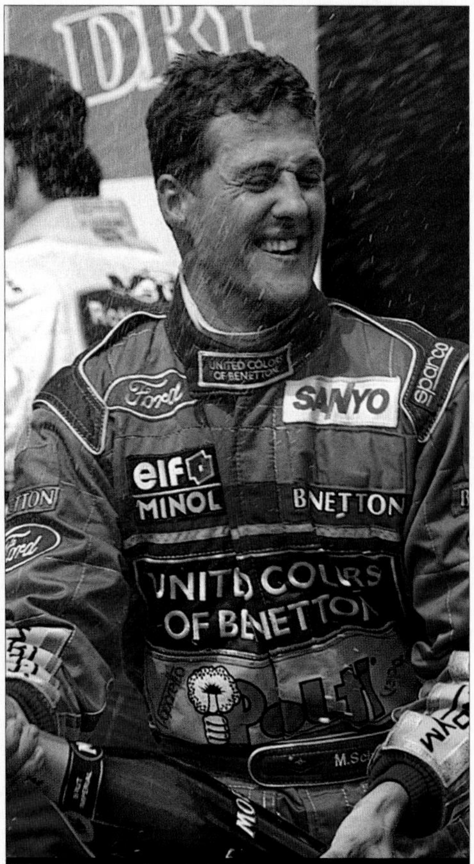


1994 world champion, Michael Schumacher.

# 1995

## DRIVERS' CHAMPION: MICHAEL SCHUMACHER
## CONSTRUCTORS' CHAMPION: BENETTON RENAULT

### DRIVERS' CHAMPIONSHIP

| POS. | DRIVER | NATIONALITY | CAR | POINTS |
|---|---|---|---|---|
| 1 | Michael Schumacher | Germany | Benetton-Renault | 102 |
| 2 | Damon Hill | GB | Williams-Renault | 69 |
| 3 | David Coulthard | GB | Williams-Renault | 49 |
| 4 | Johnny Herbert | GB | Benetton-Renault | 45 |
| 5 | Jean Alesi | France | Ferrari | 42 |
| 6 | Gerhard Berger | Austria | Ferrari | 31 |
| 7 | Mika Hakkinen | Finland | McLaren-Mercedes | 17 |
| 8 | Olivier Panis | France | Ligier-Mugen Honda | 16 |
| 9 | Heinz-Harald Frentzen | Germany | Sauber-Ford | 15 |
| 10 | Mark Blundell | GB | McLaren-Mercedes | 13 |
| 11 | Rubens Barrichello | Brazil | Jordan-Peugeot | 11 |
| 12 | Eddie Irvine | GB | Jordan-Peugeot | 10 |
| 13 | Martin Brundle | GB | Ligier-Mugen Honda | 7 |
| 14 | Mika Salo | Finland | Tyrrell-Yamaha | 5 |
| = | Gianni Morbidelli | Italy | Arrows-Hart | 5 |
| 16 | Jean-Christophe Boullion | France | Sauber-Ford | 3 |
| 17 | Aguri Suzuki | Japan | Ligier-Mugen Honda | 1 |
| = | Pedro Lamy | Portugal | Minardi-Ford | 1 |
| | Giovanni Lavaggi | Italy | Pacific-Ford | |
| | Ukyo Katayama | Japan | Tyrrell-Yamaha | |
| | Pierluigi Martini | Italy | Minardi-Ford | |
| | Luca Badoer | Italy | Minardi-Ford | |
| | Karl Wendlinger | Austria | Sauber-Ford | |
| | Bertrand Gachot | Belgium | Pacific-Ford | |
| | Taki Inoue | Japan | Arrows-Hart | |
| | Andrea Montermini | Italy | Pacific-Ford | |
| | Roberto Moreno | Italy | Forti-Ford | |
| | Jos Verstappen | Netherland | Simtek-Ford | |
| | Pedro Diniz | Belgium | Forti-Ford | |
| | Domenico Schiattarella | Italy | Simtek-Ford | |
| | Nigel Mansell | GB | McLaren-Mercedes | |
| | Massimiliano Papis | Italy | Arrows-Hart | |
| | Gabriele Tarquini | Italy | Tyrrell-Yamaha | |
| | Jean-Denis Deletraz | Switzerland | Pacific-Ford | |
| | Jan Magnussen | Denmark | McLaren-Mercedes | |

Points for top six finishers (10, 6, 4, 3, 2, 1). Half points awarded for races stopped before half distance.

### CONSTRUCTORS' CHAMPIONSHIP

| POS. | CONSTRUCTOR | POINTS |
|---|---|---|
| 1 | Benetton-Renault | 137 |
| 2 | Williams-Renault | 112 |
| 3 | Ferrari | 73 |
| 4 | McLaren-Mercedes | 30 |
| 5 | Ligier-Mugen-Honda | 24 |
| 6 | Jordan-Peugeot | 21 |
| 7 | Sauber-Ford | 18 |
| 8 | Footwork-Hart | 5 |
| 9 | Tyrrell-Yamaha | 5 |
| 10 | Minardi-Ford | 1 |

Points for top six finishers (10, 6, 4, 3, 2, 1). Half points awarded for races stopped before half distance. Benetton and Williams did not score constructors' points in Brazil due to fuel irregularities.

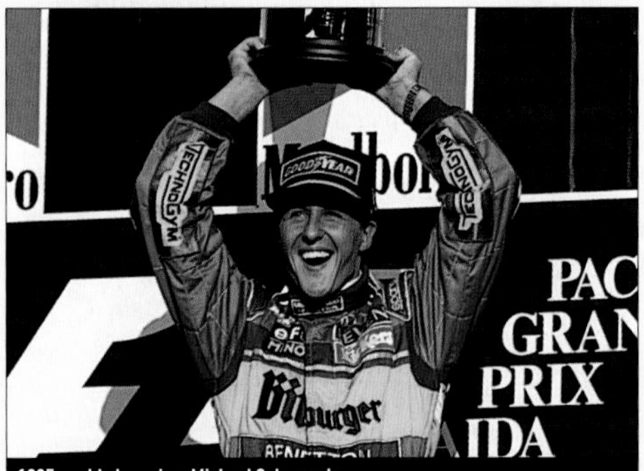
1995 world champion, Michael Schumacher.

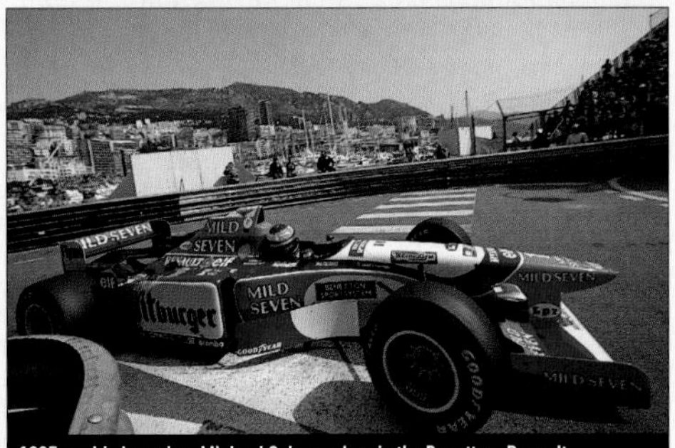
1995 world champion, Michael Schumacher in the Benetton-Renault.

### BRAZILIAN GRAND PRIX: INTERLAGOS *26 March Round: 1 Race:565 71 x 2.687 miles*

| POS. | NO. | DRIVER | CAR/ENGINE | LAPS | TIME/RETIRED | GRID |
|---|---|---|---|---|---|---|
| 1 | 1 | M.Schumacher | Benetton-Renault | 71 | 1:38'34.154 | 2 |
| 2 | 6 | David Coulthard | Williams-Renault | 71 | +8.060 | 3 |
| 3 | 28 | Gerhard Berger | Ferrari | 70 | +1 Lap | 5 |
| 4 | 8 | Mika Hakkinen | McLaren-Mercedes | 70 | +1 Lap | 7 |
| 5 | 27 | Jean Alesi | Ferrari | 70 | +1 Lap | 6 |
| 6 | 7 | Mark Blundell | McLaren-Mercedes | 70 | +1 Lap | 9 |
| 7 | 4 | Mika Salo | Tyrrell-Yamaha | 69 | +2 Laps | 12 |
| 8 | 25 | Aguri Suzuki | Ligier-Mugen-Honda | 69 | +2 Laps | 15 |
| 9 | 17 | A.Montermini | Pacific-Ford | 65 | +6 Laps | 22 |
| 10 | 21 | Pedro Diniz | Forti-Ford | 64 | +7 Laps | 25 |
| Ret | 9 | G.Morbidelli | Footwork-Hart | 62 | Engine | 13 |
| Ret | 10 | Taki Inoue | Footwork-Hart | 48 | Engine | 21 |
| Ret | 24 | Luca Badoer | Minardi-Ford | 47 | Gearbox | 18 |
| Ret | 22 | Roberto Moreno | Forti-Ford | 47 | Spun off | 23 |
| Ret | 29 | Karl Wendlinger | Sauber-Ford | 41 | Electrical | 19 |
| Ret | 5 | Damon Hill | Williams-Renault | 30 | Gearbox | 1 |
| Ret | 2 | Johnny Herbert | Benetton-Renault | 30 | Collision | 4 |
| Ret | 16 | Bertrand Gachot | Pacific-Ford | 23 | Gearbox | 20 |
| Ret | 14 | R.Barrichello | Jordan-Peugeot | 16 | Gearbox | 16 |
| Ret | 12 | Jos Verstappen | Simtek-Ford | 16 | Gearbox | 24 |
| Ret | 3 | Ukyo Katayama | Tyrrell-Yamaha | 15 | Spun off | 11 |
| Ret | 15 | Eddie Irvine | Jordan-Peugeot | 15 | Clutch | 8 |
| Ret | 11 | D.Schiattarella | Simtek-Ford | 12 | Steering | 26 |
| Ret | 30 | H-H.Frentzen | Sauber-Ford | 10 | Electrical | 14 |
| Ret | 26 | Olivier Panis | Ligier-Mugen-Honda | 0 | Collision | 10 |
| Ret | 23 | P.Martini | Minardi-Ford | 0 | Gearbox | 17 |

Winning speed: 116.146mph
Lap leaders: Schumacher: 1-17, 31-35, 47-71; Hill 18-21, 23-30; Coulthard 22, 36-46
Pole position: Hill, 1m 20.081s, 120.812mph
Fastest lap: Schumacher, 1m 20.921s, 119.558mph

### ARGENTINE GRAND PRIX: BUENOS AIRES *9 April Round: 2 Race: 566 72 x 2.646 miles*

| POS. | NO. | DRIVER | CAR/ENGINE | LAPS | TIME/RETIRED | GRID |
|---|---|---|---|---|---|---|
| 1 | 5 | Damon Hill | Williams-Renault | 72 | 1:53'14.532 | 2 |
| 2 | 27 | Jean Alesi | Ferrari | 72 | +6.407 | 6 |
| 3 | 1 | M.Schumacher | Benetton-Renault | 72 | +33.376 | 3 |
| 4 | 2 | Johnny Herbert | Benetton-Renault | 71 | +1 Lap | 11 |
| 5 | 30 | H-H.Frentzen | Sauber-Ford | 70 | +2 Laps | 9 |
| 6 | 28 | Gerhard Berger | Ferrari | 70 | +2 Laps | 8 |
| 7 | 26 | Olivier Panis | Ligier-Mugen-Honda | 70 | +2 Laps | 18 |
| 8 | 3 | Ukyo Katayama | Tyrrell-Yamaha | 69 | +3 Laps | 15 |
| 9 | 11 | D.Schiattarella | Simtek-Ford | 68 | +4 Laps | 20 |
| NC | 21 | Pedro Diniz | Forti-Ford | 63 | Not classified | 25 |
| NC | 22 | Roberto Moreno | Forti-Ford | 63 | Not classified | 24 |
| Ret | 4 | Mika Salo | Tyrrell-Yamaha | 48 | Collision | 7 |
| Ret | 25 | Aguri Suzuki | Ligier-Mugen-Honda | 47 | Collision | 19 |
| Ret | 23 | P.Martini | Minardi-Ford | 44 | Spun off | 16 |
| Ret | 9 | G.Morbidelli | Footwork-Hart | 43 | Electrical | 12 |
| Ret | 10 | Taki Inoue | Footwork-Hart | 40 | Spun off | 26 |
| Ret | 14 | R.Barrichello | Jordan-Peugeot | 33 | Oil pressure | 10 |
| Ret | 12 | Jos Verstappen | Simtek-Ford | 23 | Gearbox | 14 |
| Ret | 6 | David Coulthard | Williams-Renault | 16 | Electrical | 1 |
| Ret | 7 | Mark Blundell | McLaren-Mercedes | 9 | Oil leak | 17 |
| Ret | 15 | Eddie Irvine | Jordan-Peugeot | 6 | Engine | 4 |
| Ret | 17 | A.Montermini | Pacific-Ford | 1 | Collision | 22 |
| Ret | 8 | Mika Hakkinen | McLaren-Mercedes | 0 | Collision | 5 |
| Ret | 29 | Karl Wendlinger | Sauber-Ford | 0 | Collision | 21 |
| Ret | 16 | Bertrand Gachot | Pacific-Ford | 0 | Collision | 23 |
| DNS | 24 | Luca Badoer | Minardi-Ford | 0 | Not started | 13 |

Winning speed: 100.902mph
Lap leaders: Coulthard 1-5; Schumacher 6-10,17; Hill 11-16, 26-72; Alesi 18-25
Pole position: Coulthard, 1m53.241s, 105.246mph
Fastest lap: Schumacher, 1m30.522s, 105.246mph
Race stopped after two pile-ups on the first lap and restarted for total original distance.

### SAN MARINO GRAND PRIX: IMOLA *30 April Round: 3 Race: 567 63 x 3.042 miles*

| POS. | NO. | DRIVER | CAR/ENGINE | LAPS | TIME/RETIRED | GRID |
|---|---|---|---|---|---|---|
| 1 | 5 | Damon Hill | Williams-Renault | 63 | 1:41'42.552 | 4 |
| 2 | 27 | Jean Alesi | Ferrari | 63 | +18.510 | 5 |
| 3 | 28 | Gerhard Berger | Ferrari | 63 | +43.116 | 2 |
| 4 | 6 | David Coulthard | Williams-Renault | 63 | +51.890 | 3 |
| 5 | 8 | Mika Hakkinen | McLaren-Mercedes | 62 | +1 Lap | 6 |
| 6 | 30 | H-H.Frentzen | Sauber-Ford | 62 | +1 Lap | 14 |
| 7 | 2 | Johnny Herbert | Benetton-Renault | 61 | +2 Laps | 8 |
| 8 | 15 | Eddie Irvine | Jordan-Peugeot | 61 | +2 Laps | 7 |
| 9 | 26 | Olivier Panis | Ligier-Mugen-Honda | 61 | +2 Laps | 12 |
| 10 | 7 | Nigel Mansell | McLaren-Mercedes | 61 | +2 Laps | 9 |
| 11 | 25 | Aguri Suzuki | Ligier-Mugen-Honda | 60 | +3 Laps | 16 |
| 12 | 23 | P.Martini | Minardi-Ford | 59 | +4 Laps | 18 |
| 13 | 9 | G.Morbidelli | Footwork-Hart | 59 | +4 Laps | 11 |
| 14 | 24 | Luca Badoer | Minardi-Ford | 59 | +4 Laps | 20 |
| 15 | 21 | Pedro Diniz | Forti-Ford | 56 | +7 Laps | 26 |
| 16 | 22 | Roberto Moreno | Forti-Ford | 56 | +7 Laps | 25 |
| Ret | 29 | Karl Wendlinger | Sauber-Ford | 43 | Wheel | 21 |
| Ret | 16 | Bertrand Gachot | Pacific-Ford | 36 | Gearbox | 22 |
| Ret | 11 | D.Schiattarella | Simtek-Ford | 35 | Suspension | 23 |
| Ret | 14 | R.Barrichello | Jordan-Peugeot | 31 | Transmission | 10 |
| Ret | 3 | Ukyo Katayama | Tyrrell-Yamaha | 23 | Spun off | 15 |
| Ret | 4 | Mika Salo | Tyrrell-Yamaha | 19 | Engine | 13 |
| Ret | 17 | A.Montermini | Pacific-Ford | 15 | Gearbox | 24 |
| Ret | 12 | Jos Verstappen | Simtek-Ford | 14 | Gearbox | 17 |
| Ret | 10 | Taki Inoue | Footwork-Hart | 12 | Spun off | 19 |
| Ret | 1 | M.Schumacher | Benetton-Renault | 10 | Spun off | 1 |

Winning speed: 113.041mph
Lap leaders: Schumacher 1-9; Coulthard 10; Berger 11-21; Hill 22-63
Pole position: Schumacher, 1m27.274s, 125.465mph
Fastest lap: Berger, 1m29.568s, 122.251mph

### SPANISH GRAND PRIX: MONTMELÓ *14 May Round: 4 Race: 568 65 x 2.937 miles*

| POS. | NO. | DRIVER | CAR/ENGINE | LAPS | TIME/RETIRED | GRID |
|---|---|---|---|---|---|---|
| 1 | 1 | M.Schumacher | Benetton-Renault | 65 | 1:34'20.507 | 1 |
| 2 | 2 | Johnny Herbert | Benetton-Renault | 65 | +51.988 | 7 |
| 3 | 28 | Gerhard Berger | Ferrari | 65 | +1'05.237 | 3 |
| 4 | 5 | Damon Hill | Williams-Renault | 65 | +2'01.749 | 5 |
| 5 | 15 | Eddie Irvine | Jordan-Peugeot | 64 | +1 Lap | 6 |
| 6 | 26 | Olivier Panis | Ligier-Mugen-Honda | 64 | +1 Lap | 15 |
| 7 | 14 | R.Barrichello | Jordan-Peugeot | 64 | +1 Lap | 8 |
| 8 | 30 | H-H.Frentzen | Sauber-Ford | 64 | +1 Lap | 12 |
| 9 | 25 | Martin Brundle | Ligier-Mugen-Honda | 64 | +1 Lap | 11 |
| 10 | 4 | Mika Salo | Tyrrell-Yamaha | 64 | +1 Lap | 13 |
| 11 | 9 | G.Morbidelli | Footwork-Hart | 63 | +2 Laps | 14 |
| 12 | 12 | Jos Verstappen | Simtek-Ford | 63 | +2 Laps | 16 |
| 13 | 29 | Karl Wendlinger | Sauber-Ford | 63 | +2 Laps | 20 |
| 14 | 23 | P.Martini | Minardi-Ford | 62 | +3 Laps | 19 |
| 15 | 11 | D.Schiattarella | Simtek-Ford | 61 | +4 Laps | 22 |
| Ret | 3 | Ukyo Katayama | Tyrrell-Yamaha | 56 | Engine | 17 |
| Ret | 6 | David Coulthard | Williams-Renault | 54 | Gearbox | 4 |
| Ret | 8 | Mika Hakkinen | McLaren-Mercedes | 53 | Fuel system | 9 |
| Ret | 10 | Taki Inoue | Footwork-Hart | 43 | Transmission | 18 |
| Ret | 16 | Bertrand Gachot | Pacific-Ford | 43 | Fire | 24 |
| Ret | 22 | Roberto Moreno | Forti-Ford | 39 | Overheating | 25 |
| Ret | 27 | Jean Alesi | Ferrari | 25 | Engine | 2 |
| Ret | 24 | Luca Badoer | Minardi-Ford | 21 | Gearbox | 21 |
| Ret | 7 | Nigel Mansell | McLaren-Mercedes | 18 | Handling | 10 |
| Ret | 21 | Pedro Diniz | Forti-Ford | 17 | Gearbox | 26 |
| DNS | 17 | A.Montermini | Pacific-Ford | 0 | Not started | 23 |

Winning speed: 121.367mph Lap leaders: Schumacher 1-65
Pole position: Schumacher, 1m 21.452s, 129.819mph
Fastest lap: Hill, 1m 24.531s, 125.090mph

### MONACO GRAND PRIX: MONTE CARLO *28 May Round: 5 Race 569 78 x 2.068 miles*

| POS. | NO. | DRIVER | CAR/ENGINE | LAPS | TIME/RETIRED | GRID |
|---|---|---|---|---|---|---|
| 1 | 1 | M.Schumacher | Benetton-Renault | 78 | 1:53'11.258 | 2 |
| 2 | 5 | Damon Hill | Williams-Renault | 78 | +34.817 | 1 |
| 3 | 28 | Gerhard Berger | Ferrari | 78 | +1'11.447 | 4 |
| 4 | 2 | Johnny Herbert | Benetton-Renault | 77 | +1 Lap | 7 |
| 5 | 7 | Mark Blundell | McLaren-Mercedes | 77 | +1 Lap | 10 |
| 6 | 30 | H-H.Frentzen | Sauber-Ford | 76 | +2 Laps | 14 |
| 7 | 23 | P.Martini | Minardi-Ford | 76 | +2 Laps | 18 |
| 8 | 29 | J-C.Boullion | Sauber-Ford | 74 | +4 Laps | 19 |
| 9 | 9 | G.Morbidelli | Footwork-Hart | 74 | +4 Laps | 13 |
| 10 | 21 | Pedro Diniz | Forti-Ford | 72 | +6 Laps | 22 |
| Ret | 24 | Luca Badoer | Minardi-Ford | 68 | Suspension | 16 |
| Ret | 26 | Olivier Panis | Ligier-Mugen-Honda | 65 | Spun off | 12 |
| Ret | 4 | Mika Salo | Tyrrell-Yamaha | 63 | Gearbox | 17 |
| Ret | 14 | R.Barrichello | Jordan-Peugeot | 60 | Throttle | 11 |
| Ret | 16 | Bertrand Gachot | Pacific-Ford | 42 | Gearbox | 21 |
| Ret | 27 | Jean Alesi | Ferrari | 41 | Spun off | 5 |
| Ret | 25 | Martin Brundle | Ligier-Mugen-Honda | 40 | Spun off | 8 |
| Ret | 10 | Taki Inoue | Footwork-Hart | 27 | Gearbox | 26 |
| Ret | 3 | Ukyo Katayama | Tyrrell-Yamaha | 26 | Spun off | 15 |
| DSQ | 17 | A.Montermini | Pacific-Ford | 23 | Disqualified | 25 |
| Ret | 15 | Eddie Irvine | Jordan-Peugeot | 22 | Spun off | 9 |
| Ret | 6 | David Coulthard | Williams-Renault | 16 | Gearbox | 3 |
| Ret | 22 | Roberto Moreno | Forti-Ford | 9 | Brakes | 24 |
| Ret | 8 | Mika Hakkinen | McLaren-Mercedes | 8 | Engine | 6 |
| DSQ | 11 | D.Schiattarella | Simtek-Ford | 0 | Not started | 20 |
| Ret | 12 | Jos Verstappen | Simtek-Ford | 0 | Gearbox | 23 |

Winning speed: 85.530mph Lap leaders: Hill 1-23; Schumacher 24-35, 37-78; Alesi 36
Pole position: Hill, 1m 21.952s, 90.840mph
Fastest lap: Alesi, 1m 24.621s, 87.975
Stopped after first lap accident and restarted for total original distance.

### CANADIAN GRAND PRIX: MONTRÉAL *11 June Round: 6 Race:570 68 x 2.753 miles*

| POS. | NO. | DRIVER | CAR/NGINE | LAPS | TIME/RETIRED | GRID |
|---|---|---|---|---|---|---|
| 1 | 27 | Jean Alesi | Ferrari | 68 | 1:44'54.171 | 5 |
| 2 | 14 | R.Barrichello | Jordan-Peugeot | 68 | +31.477 | 9 |
| 3 | 15 | Eddie Irvine | Jordan-Peugeot | 68 | +35.980 | 8 |
| 4 | 26 | Olivier Panis | Ligier-Mugen-Honda | 68 | +41.314 | 11 |
| 5 | 1 | M.Schumacher | Benetton-Renault | 68 | +44.676 | 1 |
| 6 | 9 | G.Morbidelli | Footwork-Hart | 67 | +1 Lap | 13 |
| 7 | 4 | Mika Salo | Tyrrell-Yamaha | 67 | +1 Lap | 15 |
| 8 | 24 | Luca Badoer | Minardi-Ford | 67 | +1 Lap | 19 |
| 9 | 10 | Taki Inoue | Footwork-Hart | 66 | +2 Laps | 22 |
| 10 | 25 | Martin Brundle | Ligier-Mugen-Honda | 61 | Collision | 14 |
| 11 | 28 | Gerhard Berger | Ferrari | 61 | Collision | 4 |
| Ret | 23 | P.Martini | Minardi-Ford | 60 | Throttle | 17 |
| Ret | 22 | Roberto Moreno | Forti-Ford | 54 | Fuel system | 23 |
| Ret | 5 | Damon Hill | Williams-Renault | 50 | Gearbox | 2 |
| Ret | 7 | Mark Blundell | McLaren-Mercedes | 47 | Engine | 10 |
| Ret | 3 | Ukyo Katayama | Tyrrell-Yamaha | 42 | Engine | 16 |
| Ret | 16 | Bertrand Gachot | Pacific-Ford | 36 | Battery | 20 |
| Ret | 30 | H-H.Frentzen | Sauber-Ford | 26 | Engine | 12 |
| Ret | 21 | Pedro Diniz | Forti-Ford | 26 | Gearbox | 24 |
| Ret | 29 | J-C.Boullion | Sauber-Ford | 19 | Spun off | 18 |
| Ret | 17 | A.Montermini | Pacific-Ford | 5 | Gearbox | 21 |
| Ret | 6 | David Coulthard | Williams-Renault | 1 | Spun off | 3 |
| Ret | 2 | Johnny Herbert | Benetton-Renault | 0 | Collision | 6 |
| Ret | 8 | Mika Hakkinen | McLaren-Mercedes | 0 | Collision | 7 |

Winning speed: 107.060mph Lap leaders: Schumacher 1-57; Alesi 58-68
Pole position: Schumacher, 1m 27.661s, 113.045mph
Fastest lap: Schumacher, 1m 29.174s, 111.127mph
Scheduled for 69 laps but stopped early due to a track invasion.

### FRENCH GRAND PRIX: MAGNY-COURS *2 July Round: 7 Race: 571 72 x 2.641 miles*

| POS. | NO. | DRIVER | CAR/ENGINE | LAPS | TIME/RETIRED | GRID |
|---|---|---|---|---|---|---|
| 1 | 1 | M.Schumacher | Benetton-Renault | 72 | 1:38'28.429 | 2 |
| 2 | 5 | Damon Hill | Williams-Renault | 72 | +31.309 | 1 |
| 3 | 6 | David Coulthard | Williams-Renault | 72 | +1'02.826 | 3 |
| 4 | 25 | Martin Brundle | Ligier-Mugen-Honda | 72 | +1'03.293 | 9 |
| 5 | 27 | Jean Alesi | Ferrari | 72 | +1'17.869 | 4 |
| 6 | 14 | R.Barrichello | Jordan-Peugeot | 71 | +1 Lap | 5 |
| 7 | 8 | Mika Hakkinen | McLaren-Mercedes | 71 | +1 Lap | 8 |
| 8 | 26 | Olivier Panis | Ligier-Mugen-Honda | 71 | +1 Lap | 6 |
| 9 | 15 | Eddie Irvine | Jordan-Peugeot | 71 | +1 Lap | 11 |
| 10 | 30 | H-H.Frentzen | Sauber-Ford | 71 | +1 Lap | 12 |
| 11 | 7 | Mark Blundell | McLaren-Mercedes | 70 | +2 Laps | 13 |
| 12 | 28 | Gerhard Berger | Ferrari | 70 | +2 Laps | 7 |
| 13 | 24 | Luca Badoer | Minardi-Ford | 69 | +3 Laps | 17 |
| 14 | 9 | G.Morbidelli | Footwork-Hart | 69 | +3 Laps | 16 |
| 15 | 4 | Mika Salo | Tyrrell-Yamaha | 69 | +3 Laps | 14 |
| 16 | 22 | Roberto Moreno | Forti-Ford | 66 | +6 Laps | 24 |
| NC | 17 | A.Montermini | Pacific-Ford | 62 | Not classified | 21 |
| Ret | 29 | J-C.Boullion | Sauber-Ford | 48 | Gearbox | 15 |
| Ret | 16 | Bertrand Gachot | Pacific-Ford | 24 | Gearbox | 22 |
| Ret | 23 | P.Martini | Minardi-Ford | 23 | Gearbox | 20 |
| Ret | 2 | Johnny Herbert | Benetton-Renault | 2 | Spun off | 10 |
| Ret | 10 | Taki Inoue | Footwork-Hart | 0 | Collision | 18 |
| Ret | 3 | Ukyo Katayama | Tyrrell-Yamaha | 0 | Collision | 19 |
| Ret | 21 | Pedro Diniz | Forti-Ford | 0 | Spun off | 23 |

Winning speed: 115.781mph Lap leaders: Hill 1-21; Schumacher 22-72
Pole position: Hill, 1m17.225s, 123.108mph
Fastest lap: Schumacher, 1m20.218s, 118.514mph

### BRITISH GRAND PRIX: SILVERSTONE *16 July Round: 8 Race: 572 61 x 3.142 miles*

| POS. | NO. | DRIVER | CAR/ENGINE | LAPS | TIME/RETIRED | GRID |
|---|---|---|---|---|---|---|
| 1 | 2 | Johnny Herbert | Benetton-Renault | 61 | 1:34'35.093 | 5 |
| 2 | 27 | Jean Alesi | Ferrari | 61 | +16.479 | 6 |
| 3 | 6 | David Coulthard | Williams-Renault | 61 | +23.888 | 3 |
| 4 | 26 | Olivier Panis | Ligier-Mugen-Honda | 61 | +1'33.168 | 13 |
| 5 | 7 | Mark Blundell | McLaren-Mercedes | 61 | +1'48.172 | 10 |
| 6 | 30 | H-H.Frentzen | Sauber-Ford | 60 | +1 Lap | 12 |
| 7 | 23 | P.Martini | Minardi-Ford | 60 | +1 Lap | 15 |
| 8 | 4 | Mika Salo | Tyrrell-Yamaha | 60 | +1 Lap | 23 |
| 9 | 29 | J-C.Boullion | Sauber-Ford | 60 | +1 Lap | 16 |
| 10 | 24 | Luca Badoer | Minardi-Ford | 60 | +1 Lap | 18 |
| 11 | 14 | R.Barrichello | Jordan-Peugeot | 59 | Collision | 9 |
| 12 | 16 | Bertrand Gachot | Pacific-Ford | 58 | +3 Laps | 21 |
| Ret | 22 | Roberto Moreno | Forti-Ford | 48 | Engine | 22 |
| Ret | 1 | M.Schumacher | Benetton-Renault | 45 | Collision | 2 |
| Ret | 5 | Damon Hill | Williams-Renault | 45 | Collision | 1 |
| Ret | 9 | M.Papis | Footwork-Hart | 28 | Spun off | 17 |
| Ret | 3 | Ukyo Katayama | Tyrrell-Yamaha | 22 | Out of fuel | 14 |
| Ret | 17 | A.Montermini | Pacific-Ford | 21 | Spun off | 24 |
| Ret | 8 | Mika Hakkinen | McLaren-Mercedes | 20 | Electrical | 8 |
| Ret | 28 | Gerhard Berger | Ferrari | 20 | Wheel | 4 |
| Ret | 25 | Martin Brundle | Ligier-Mugen-Honda | 16 | Spun off | 11 |
| Ret | 10 | Taki Inoue | Footwork-Hart | 16 | Spun off | 19 |
| Ret | 21 | Pedro Diniz | Forti-Ford | 13 | Gearbox | 20 |
| Ret | 15 | Eddie Irvine | Jordan-Peugeot | 2 | Electrical | 0 |

Winning speed: 121.592mph Lap leaders: Hill 1-22, 32-41; Schumacher 23-31, 42-45; Herbert 46-48, 51-61; Coulthard 49-50
Pole position: Hill, 1m 28.124s, 128.367mph
Fastest lap: Hill, 1m 29.752s, 126.038mph

### GERMAN GRAND PRIX: HOCKENHEIM *30 July Round 9 Race 573 45 x 4.240 miles*

| POS. | NO. | DRIVER | CAR/ENGINE | LAPS | TIME/RETIRED | GRID |
|---|---|---|---|---|---|---|
| 1 | 1 | M.Schumacher | Benetton-Renault | 45 | 1:22'56.043 | 2 |
| 2 | 6 | David Coulthard | Williams-Renault | 45 | +5.988 | 3 |
| 3 | 28 | Gerhard Berger | Ferrari | 45 | +1'08.097 | 4 |
| 4 | 2 | Johnny Herbert | Benetton-Renault | 45 | +1'23.436 | 9 |
| 5 | 29 | J-C.Boullion | Sauber-Ford | 44 | +1 Lap | 14 |
| 6 | 25 | Aguri Suzuki | Ligier-Mugen-Honda | 44 | +1 Lap | 18 |
| 7 | 3 | Ukyo Katayama | Tyrrell-Yamaha | 44 | +1 Lap | 17 |
| 8 | 17 | A.Montermini | Pacific-Ford | 42 | +3 Laps | 23 |
| 9 | 15 | Eddie Irvine | Jordan-Peugeot | 41 | +4 Laps | 6 |
| Ret | 8 | Mika Hakkinen | McLaren-Mercedes | 33 | Engine | 7 |
| Ret | 30 | H-H.Frentzen | Sauber-Ford | 32 | Engine | 11 |
| Ret | 24 | Luca Badoer | Minardi-Ford | 28 | Oil leak | 16 |
| Ret | 16 | Giovanni Lavaggi | Pacific-Ford | 27 | Gearbox | 24 |
| Ret | 22 | Roberto Moreno | Forti-Ford | 27 | Halfshaft | 22 |
| Ret | 14 | R.Barrichello | Jordan-Peugeot | 20 | Engine | 5 |
| Ret | 7 | Mark Blundell | McLaren-Mercedes | 17 | Engine | 8 |
| Ret | 26 | Olivier Panis | Ligier-Mugen-Honda | 13 | Water leak | 12 |
| Ret | 27 | Jean Alesi | Ferrari | 12 | Engine | 10 |
| Ret | 23 | P.Martini | Minardi-Ford | 11 | Engine | 20 |
| Ret | 10 | Taki Inoue | Footwork-Hart | 9 | Gearbox | 19 |
| Ret | 21 | Pedro Diniz | Forti-Ford | 8 | Brakes | 21 |
| Ret | 5 | Damon Hill | Williams-Renault | 1 | Spun off | 1 |
| Ret | 4 | Mika Salo | Tyrrell-Yamaha | 0 | Clutch | 13 |
| Ret | 9 | M.Papis | Footwork-Hart | 0 | Gearbox | 15 |

Winning Speed: 138.019 mph Lap leaders: Hill 1; Schumacher 2-19, 24-45; Coulthard 20-23
Pole position: Hill, 1m 44.385s, 146.215mph
Fastest lap: Schumacher, 1m 48.824s, 140.250mph

### HUNGARIAN GRAND PRIX: HUNGARORING *13 August Round: 10 Race: 574 77 x 2.466 miles*

| POS. | NO. | DRIVER | CAR/ENGINE | LAPS | TIME/RETIRED | GRID |
|---|---|---|---|---|---|---|
| 1 | 5 | Damon Hill | Williams-Renault | 77 | 1:46'25.721 | 1 |
| 2 | 6 | David Coulthard | Williams-Renault | 77 | +33.398 | 2 |
| 3 | 28 | Gerhard Berger | Ferrari | 76 | +1 Lap | 4 |
| 4 | 2 | Johnny Herbert | Benetton-Renault | 76 | +1 Lap | 9 |
| 5 | 30 | H-H.Frentzen | Sauber-Ford | 76 | +1 Lap | 11 |
| 6 | 26 | Olivier Panis | Ligier-Mugen-Honda | 76 | +1 Lap | 10 |
| 7 | 14 | R.Barrichello | Jordan-Peugeot | 76 | +1 Lap | 14 |
| 8 | 24 | Luca Badoer | Minardi-Ford | 75 | +2 Laps | 12 |
| 9 | 23 | Pedro Lamy | Minardi-Ford | 74 | +3 Laps | 15 |
| 10 | 29 | J-C.Boullion | Sauber-Ford | 74 | +3 Laps | 19 |
| 11 | 1 | M.Schumacher | Benetton-Renault | 73 | Engine | 3 |
| 12 | 17 | A.Montermini | Pacific-Ford | 73 | +4 Laps | 22 |
| 13 | 15 | Eddie Irvine | Jordan-Peugeot | 70 | Clutch | 7 |
| Ret | 25 | Martin Brundle | Ligier-Mugen-Honda | 67 | Engine | 8 |
| Ret | 4 | Mika Salo | Tyrrell-Yamaha | 58 | Throttle | 16 |
| Ret | 7 | Mark Blundell | McLaren-Mercedes | 54 | Fuel leak | 13 |
| Ret | 3 | Ukyo Katayama | Tyrrell-Yamaha | 46 | Spun off | 17 |
| Ret | 9 | M.Papis | Footwork/Hart | 45 | Brakes | 20 |
| Ret | 27 | Jean Alesi | Ferrari | 42 | Engine | 6 |
| Ret | 21 | Pedro Diniz | Forti-Ford | 32 | Engine | 23 |
| Ret | 10 | Taki Inoue | Footwork-Hart | 13 | Engine | 18 |
| Ret | 22 | Roberto Moreno | Forti-Ford | 8 | Gearbox | 21 |
| Ret | 16 | Giovanni Lavaggi | Pacific-Ford | 5 | Spun off | 24 |
| Ret | 8 | Mika Hakkinen | McLaren-Mercedes | 3 | Engine | 5 |

Winning speed: 107.030mph Lap leaders: Hill 1-77
Pole position: Hill, 1m 16.982s, 115.302mph
Fastest lap: Hill, 1m 20.247s, 110.611mph

### BELGIAN GRAND PRIX: SPA-FRANCORCHAMPS *27 August Round: 11 Race: 575 44 x 4.333 miles*

| POS. | NO. | DRIVER | CAR/ENGINE | LAPS | TIME/RETIRED | GRID |
|---|---|---|---|---|---|---|
| 1 | 1 | M.Schumacher | Benetton-Renault | 44 | 1:36'47.875 | 16 |
| 2 | 5 | Damon Hill | Williams-Renault | 44 | +19.493 | 8 |
| 3 | 25 | Martin Brundle | Ligier-Mugen-Honda | 44 | +24.998 | 13 |
| 4 | 30 | H-H.Frentzen | Sauber-Ford | 44 | +26.972 | 10 |
| 5 | 7 | Mark Blundell | McLaren-Mercedes | 44 | +33.772 | 6 |
| 6 | 14 | R.Barrichello | Jordan-Peugeot | 44 | +39.674 | 12 |
| 7 | 2 | Johnny Herbert | Benetton-Renault | 44 | +54.048 | 4 |
| 8 | 4 | Mika Salo | Tyrrell-Yamaha | 44 | +54.548 | 11 |
| 9 | 26 | Olivier Panis | Ligier-Mugen-Honda | 44 | +1'06.170 | 9 |
| 10 | 23 | Pedro Lamy | Minardi-Ford | 44 | +1'19.789 | 17 |
| 11 | 29 | J-C.Boullion | Sauber-Ford | 43 | +1 Lap | 14 |
| 12 | 10 | Taki Inoue | Footwork-Hart | 43 | +1 Lap | 18 |
| 13 | 21 | Pedro Diniz | Forti-Ford | 42 | +2 Laps | 24 |
| 14 | 22 | Roberto Moreno | Forti-Ford | 42 | +2 Laps | 22 |
| Ret | 3 | Ukyo Katayama | Tyrrell-Yamaha | 28 | Spun off | 15 |
| Ret | 16 | Giovanni Lavaggi | Pacific-Ford | 27 | Gearbox | 23 |
| Ret | 24 | Luca Badoer | Minardi-Ford | 23 | Spun off | 19 |
| Ret | 28 | Gerhard Berger | Ferrari | 22 | Electrical | 1 |
| Ret | 15 | Eddie Irvine | Jordan-Peugeot | 21 | Fire | 7 |
| Ret | 9 | M.Papis | Footwork-Hart | 20 | Spun off | 20 |
| Ret | 17 | A.Montermini | Pacific-Ford | 18 | Out of fuel | 21 |
| Ret | 6 | David Coulthard | Williams-Renault | 13 | Gearbox | 5 |
| Ret | 27 | Jean Alesi | Ferrari | 4 | Suspension | 2 |
| Ret | 8 | Mika Hakkinen | McLaren-Mercedes | 1 | Spun off | 3 |

Winning speed: 118.187mph Lap leaders: Herbert 1, 4-5; Alesi 2-3; Coulthard 6-13; Hill 14-15, 19-21, 24; Schumacher 16-18, 22-23, 25-44
Pole position: Berger, 1m 54.392s, 136.377mph
Fastest lap: Coulthard, 1m 53.412s, 137.555mph

### ITALIAN GRAND PRIX: MONZA *10 September Round: 12 Race: 576 53 x 3.585 miles*

| POS. | NO. | DRIVER | CAR/ENGINE | LAPS | TIME/RETIRED | GRID |
|---|---|---|---|---|---|---|
| 1 | 2 | Johnny Herbert | Benetton-Renault | 53 | 1:18'27.916 | 8 |
| 2 | 8 | Mika Hakkinen | McLaren-Mercedes | 53 | +17.779 | 7 |
| 3 | 30 | H-H.Frentzen | Sauber-Ford | 53 | +24.321 | 10 |
| 4 | 7 | Mark Blundell | McLaren-Mercedes | 53 | +28.223 | 9 |
| 5 | 4 | Mika Salo | Tyrrell-Yamaha | 52 | +1 Lap | 16 |
| 6 | 29 | J-C.Boullion | Sauber-Ford | 52 | +1 Lap | 14 |
| 7 | 9 | M.Papis | Footwork-Hart | 52 | +1 Lap | 15 |
| 8 | 10 | Taki Inoue | Footwork-Hart | 52 | +1 Lap | 20 |
| 9 | 21 | Pedro Diniz | Forti-Ford | 50 | +3 Laps | 23 |
| 10 | 3 | Ukyo Katayama | Tyrrell-Yamaha | 47 | +6 Laps | 17 |
| Ret | 27 | Jean Alesi | Ferrari | 45 | Wheel bearing | 5 |
| Ret | 14 | R.Barrichello | Jordan-Peugeot | 43 | Clutch | 6 |
| Ret | 15 | Eddie Irvine | Jordan-Peugeot | 40 | Engine | 12 |
| Ret | 28 | Gerhard Berger | Ferrari | 32 | Suspension | 3 |
| Ret | 24 | Luca Badoer | Minardi-Ford | 26 | Spun off | 18 |
| Ret | 1 | M.Schumacher | Benetton-Renault | 23 | Collision | 2 |
| Ret | 5 | Damon Hill | Williams-Renault | 23 | Collision | 4 |
| Ret | 26 | Olivier Panis | Ligier-Mugen-Honda | 20 | Spun off | 13 |
| Ret | 6 | David Coulthard | Williams-Renault | 13 | Spun off | 1 |
| Ret | 25 | Martin Brundle | Ligier-Mugen-Honda | 10 | Puncture | 11 |
| Ret | 16 | Giovanni Lavaggi | Pacific-Ford | 6 | Spun off | 24 |
| Ret | 23 | Pedro Lamy | Minardi-Ford | 0 | Transmission | 19 |
| Ret | 17 | A.Montermini | Pacific-Ford | 0 | Accident | 21 |
| Ret | 22 | Roberto Moreno | Forti-Ford | 0 | Accident | 22 |

Winning speed: 145.285mph Lap leaders: Coulthard: 1-13; Berger 14-24; Alesi 25, 30-45; Barichello 26; Häkkinen 27; Herbert 28-29, 46-53
Pole position: Coulthard, 1m 24.462s, 152.816mph
Fastest lap: Berger, 1m: 26.419s, 149.355mph
Stopped after first lap accident and restarted for total original distance.

### PORTUGUESE GRAND PRIX: ESTORIL *24 September Round: 13 Race: 577 71 x 2.709 miles*

| POS. | NO. | DRIVER | CAR/ENGINE | LAPS | TIME/RETIRED | GRID |
|---|---|---|---|---|---|---|
| 1 | 6 | David Coulthard | Williams-Renault | 71 | 1:41'52.145 | 1 |
| 2 | 1 | M.Schumacher | Benetton-Renault | 71 | +7.248 | 3 |
| 3 | 5 | Damon Hill | Williams-Renault | 71 | +22.121 | 2 |
| 4 | 28 | Gerhard Berger | Ferrari | 71 | +1'24.879 | 4 |
| 5 | 27 | Jean Alesi | Ferrari | 71 | +1'25.429 | 7 |
| 6 | 30 | H-H.Frentzen | Sauber-Ford | 70 | +1 Lap | 5 |
| 7 | 2 | Johnny Herbert | Benetton-Renault | 70 | +1 Lap | 6 |
| 8 | 25 | Martin Brundle | Ligier-Mugen-Honda | 70 | +1 Lap | 9 |
| 9 | 7 | Mark Blundell | McLaren-Mercedes | 70 | +1 Lap | 12 |
| 10 | 15 | Eddie Irvine | Jordan-Peugeot | 70 | +1 Lap | 10 |
| 11 | 14 | R.Barrichello | Jordan-Peugeot | 70 | +1 Lap | 8 |
| 12 | 29 | J-C.Boullion | Sauber-Ford | 70 | +1 Lap | 14 |
| 13 | 4 | Mika Salo | Tyrrell-Yamaha | 69 | +2 Laps | 15 |
| 14 | 24 | Luca Badoer | Minardi-Ford | 68 | +3 Laps | 18 |
| 15 | 10 | Taki Inoue | Footwork-Hart | 68 | +3 Laps | 19 |
| 16 | 21 | Pedro Diniz | Forti-Ford | 66 | +5 Laps | 22 |
| 17 | 22 | Roberto Moreno | Forti-Ford | 64 | +7 Laps | 23 |
| Ret | 17 | A.Montermini | Pacific-Ford | 53 | Gearbox | 21 |
| Ret | 8 | Mika Hakkinen | McLaren-Mercedes | 44 | Engine | 13 |
| Ret | 16 | J-D.Deletraz | Pacific-Ford | 14 | Physical | 24 |
| Ret | 26 | Olivier Panis | Ligier-Mugen-Honda | 10 | Spun off | 11 |
| Ret | 23 | Pedro Lamy | Minardi-Ford | 7 | Gearbox | 17 |
| Ret | 3 | Ukyo Katayama | Tyrrell-Yamaha | 0 | Collision | 16 |
| Ret | 9 | M.Papis | Footwork-Hart | 0 | Gearbox | 20 |

Winning speed: 113.288mph Lap leaders: Coulthard 1-38, 44-71; Hill 39-43
Pole position: Coulthard, 1m 20.537s, 121.100mph
Fastest lap: Coulthard, 1m 23.220s, 117.196mph
Stopped after first lap accident and restarted for total original distance.

### EUROPEAN GRAND PRIX: NURBURGRING *1 October Round 14 Race 578 67 x 2.831 miles*

| POS. | NO. | DRIVER | CAR/ENGINE | LAPS | TIME/RETIRED | GRID |
|---|---|---|---|---|---|---|
| 1 | 1 | M.Schumacher | Benetton-Renault | 67 | 1:39'59.044 | 3 |
| 2 | 27 | Jean Alesi | Ferrari | 67 | +2.684 | 6 |
| 3 | 6 | David Coulthard | Williams-Renault | 67 | +35.382 | 1 |
| 4 | 14 | R.Barrichello | Jordan-Peugeot | 66 | +1 Lap | 11 |
| 5 | 2 | Johnny Herbert | Benetton-Renault | 66 | +1 Lap | 7 |
| 6 | 15 | Eddie Irvine | Jordan-Peugeot | 66 | +1 Lap | 5 |
| 7 | 25 | Martin Brundle | Ligier-Mugen-Honda | 66 | +1 Lap | 12 |
| 8 | 8 | Mika Hakkinen | McLaren-Mercedes | 65 | +2 Laps | 9 |
| 9 | 23 | Pedro Lamy | Minardi-Ford | 64 | +3 Laps | 16 |
| 10 | 4 | Mika Salo | Tyrrell-Yamaha | 64 | +3 Laps | 15 |
| 11 | 24 | Luca Badoer | Minardi-Ford | 64 | +3 Laps | 18 |
| 12 | 9 | M.Papis | Footwork-Hart | 64 | +3 Laps | 17 |
| 13 | 21 | Pedro Diniz | Forti-Ford | 62 | +5 Laps | 22 |
| 14 | 3 | G.Tarquini | Tyrrell-Yamaha | 61 | +6 Laps | 19 |
| 15 | 16 | J-D.Deletraz | Pacific-Ford | 60 | +7 Laps | 24 |
| Ret | 5 | Damon Hill | Williams-Renault | 58 | Spun off | 2 |
| Ret | 17 | A.Montermini | Pacific-Ford | 45 | Out of fuel | 20 |
| Ret | 29 | J-C.Boullion | Sauber/Ford | 44 | Collision | 13 |
| Ret | 28 | Gerhard Berger | Ferrari | 40 | Electrical | 4 |
| Ret | 22 | Roberto Moreno | Forti-Ford | 22 | Halfshaft | 23 |
| Ret | 30 | H-H.Frentzen | Sauber-Ford | 17 | Spun off | 8 |
| Ret | 26 | Olivier Panis | Ligier-Mugen-Honda | 14 | Spun off | 14 |
| Ret | 7 | Mark Blundell | McLaren-Mercedes | 14 | Accident | 10 |
| Ret | 10 | Taki Inoue | Footwork-Hart | 0 | Electrical | 21 |

Winning speed: 113.823mph Lap leaders: Coulthard 1-12; Alesi 13-64; Schumacher 65-67
Pole position: Coulthard, 1m 18.738s, 129.435mph
Fastest lap: Schumacher, 1m 21.180s, 125.542mph

### PACIFIC GRAND PRIX: AIDA *22 October Round: 15 Race: 579 83 x 2.301 miles*

| POS. | NO. | DRIVER | CAR/ENGINE | LAPS | TIME/RETIRED | GRID |
|---|---|---|---|---|---|---|
| 1 | 1 | M.Schumacher | Benetton-Renault | 83 | 1:48'49.972 | 3 |
| 2 | 6 | David Coulthard | Williams-Renault | 83 | +14.920 | 1 |
| 3 | 5 | Damon Hill | Williams-Renault | 83 | +48.333 | 2 |
| 4 | 28 | Gerhard Berger | Ferrari | 82 | +1 Lap | 5 |
| 5 | 27 | Jean Alesi | Ferrari | 82 | +1 Lap | 4 |
| 6 | 2 | Johnny Herbert | Benetton-Renault | 82 | +1 Lap | 7 |
| 7 | 30 | H-H.Frentzen | Sauber-Ford | 82 | +1 Lap | 8 |
| 8 | 26 | Olivier Panis | Ligier-Mugen-Honda | 81 | +2 Laps | 9 |
| 9 | 7 | Mark Blundell | McLaren-Mercedes | 81 | +2 Laps | 10 |
| 10 | 8 | Jan Magnussen | McLaren-Mercedes | 81 | +2 Laps | 12 |
| 11 | 15 | Eddie Irvine | Jordan-Peugeot | 81 | +2 Laps | 6 |
| 12 | 4 | Mika Salo | Tyrrell-Yamaha | 80 | +3 Laps | 18 |
| 13 | 23 | Pedro Lamy | Minardi-Ford | 80 | +3 Laps | 14 |
| 14 | 3 | Ukyo Katayama | Tyrrell-Yamaha | 80 | +3 Laps | 17 |
| 15 | 24 | Luca Badoer | Minardi-Ford | 80 | +3 Laps | 16 |
| 16 | 22 | Roberto Moreno | Forti-Ford | 78 | +5 Laps | 22 |
| 17 | 21 | Pedro Diniz | Forti-Ford | 77 | +6 Laps | 21 |
| Ret | 14 | R.Barrichello | Jordan-Peugeot | 67 | Electrical | 11 |
| Ret | 9 | G.Morbidelli | Footwork-Hart | 53 | Engine | 19 |
| Ret | 10 | Taki Inoue | Footwork-Hart | 38 | Electrical | 20 |
| Ret | 17 | A.Montermini | Pacific-Ford | 14 | Gearbox | 23 |
| Ret | 25 | Aguri Suzuki | Ligier-Mugen-Honda | 10 | Spun off | 13 |
| Ret | 29 | J-C.Boullion | Sauber-Ford | 7 | Spun off | 15 |
| Ret | 16 | Bertrand Gachot | Pacific-Ford | 2 | Gearbox | 24 |

Winning speed: 105.287mph Lap leaders: Coulthard 1-49; Schumacher 50-83
Pole position: Coulthard, 1m 14.013s, 111.918mph
Fastest lap: Schumacher, 1m 16.374s, 108.458mph

### JAPANESE GRAND PRIX: SUZUKA *29 October Round: 16 Race: 580 53 x 3.644 miles*

| POS. | NO. | DRIVER | CAR/ENGINE | LAPS | TIME/RETIRED | GRID |
|---|---|---|---|---|---|---|
| 1 | 1 | M.Schumacher | Benetton-Renault | 53 | 1:36'52.930 | 1 |
| 2 | 8 | Mika Hakkinen | McLaren-Mercedes | 53 | +19.337 | 3 |
| 3 | 2 | Johnny Herbert | Benetton-Renault | 53 | +1'23.804 | 9 |
| 4 | 15 | Eddie Irvine | Jordan-Peugeot | 53 | +1'42.136 | 7 |
| 5 | 26 | Olivier Panis | Ligier-Mugen-Honda | 52 | +1 Lap | 11 |
| 6 | 4 | Mika Salo | Tyrrell-Yamaha | 52 | +1 Lap | 12 |
| 7 | 7 | Mark Blundell | McLaren-Mercedes | 52 | +1 Lap | 23 |
| 8 | 30 | H-H.Frentzen | Sauber-Ford | 52 | +1 Lap | 8 |
| 9 | 24 | Luca Badoer | Minardi-Ford | 51 | +2 Laps | 17 |
| 10 | 29 | Karl Wendlinger | Sauber-Ford | 51 | +2 Laps | 15 |
| 11 | 23 | Pedro Lamy | Minardi-Ford | 51 | +2 Laps | 16 |
| 12 | 10 | Taki Inoue | Footwork-Hart | 51 | +2 Laps | 18 |
| Ret | 5 | Damon Hill | Williams-Renault | 40 | Spun off | 4 |
| Ret | 6 | David Coulthard | Williams-Renault | 39 | Spun off | 6 |
| Ret | 21 | Pedro Diniz | Forti-Ford | 32 | Spun off | 20 |
| Ret | 27 | Jean Alesi | Ferrari | 24 | Transmission | 2 |
| Ret | 17 | A.Montermini | Pacific-Ford | 23 | Spun off | 19 |
| Ret | 28 | Gerhard Berger | Ferrari | 16 | Electrical | 5 |
| Ret | 14 | R.Barrichello | Jordan-Peugeot | 15 | Spun off | 10 |
| Ret | 3 | Ukyo Katayama | Tyrrell-Yamaha | 12 | Spun off | 13 |
| Ret | 16 | Bertrand Gachot | Pacific/Ford | 6 | Halfshaft | 22 |
| Ret | 22 | Roberto Moreno | Forti-Ford | 1 | Gearbox | 21 |
| Ret | 9 | G.Morbidelli | Footwork-Hart | 0 | Spun off | 14 |
| DNS | 25 | Aguri Suzuki | Ligier-Mugen-Honda | 0 | Accident | |

Winning speed: 119.521mph
Lap leaders: Schumacher 1-10, 12-31, 36-53; Häkkinen 11; Hill 32-35
Pole position: Schumacher, 1m 38.023s, 133.820mph
Fastest lap: Schumacher, 1m 42.976s, 127.383mph

### AUSTRALIAN GRAND PRIX: ADELAIDE *12 November Round: 17 Race: 581 81 x 2.349 miles*

| POS. | NO. | DRIVER | CAR/ENGINE | LAPS | TIME/RETIRED | GRID |
|---|---|---|---|---|---|---|
| 1 | 5 | Damon Hill | Williams-Renault | 81 | 1:49'15.946 | 1 |
| 2 | 26 | Olivier Panis | Ligier-Mugen-Honda | 79 | +2 Laps | 12 |
| 3 | 9 | G.Morbidelli | Footwork-Hart | 79 | +2 Laps | 13 |
| 4 | 7 | Mark Blundell | McLaren-Mercedes | 79 | +2 Laps | 10 |
| 5 | 4 | Mika Salo | Tyrrell-Yamaha | 78 | +3 Laps | 14 |
| 6 | 23 | Pedro Lamy | Minardi-Ford | 78 | +3 Laps | 17 |
| 7 | 21 | Pedro Diniz | Forti-Ford | 77 | +4 Laps | 21 |
| 8 | 16 | Bertrand Gachot | Pacific-Ford | 76 | +5 Laps | 23 |
| Ret | 3 | Ukyo Katayama | Tyrrell-Yamaha | 70 | Engine | 16 |
| Ret | 2 | Johnny Herbert | Benetton-Renault | 69 | Transmission | 8 |
| Ret | 15 | Eddie Irvine | Jordan-Peugeot | 62 | Engine | 9 |
| Ret | 30 | H-H.Frentzen | Sauber-Ford | 39 | Gearbox | 6 |
| Ret | 28 | Gerhard Berger | Ferrari | 34 | Engine | 4 |
| Ret | 25 | Martin Brundle | Ligier/Mugen-Honda | 29 | Spun off | 11 |
| Ret | 1 | M.Schumacher | Benetton-Renault | 25 | Collision | 3 |
| Ret | 27 | Jean Alesi | Ferrari | 23 | Collision | 5 |
| Ret | 22 | Roberto Moreno | Forti-Ford | 21 | Spun off | 20 |
| Ret | 14 | R.Barrichello | Jordan-Peugeot | 20 | Spun off | 7 |
| Ret | 6 | David Coulthard | Williams/Renault | 19 | Spun off | 2 |
| Ret | 10 | Taki Inoue | Footwork-Hart | 15 | Spun off | 19 |
| Ret | 29 | Karl Wendlinger | Sauber-Ford | 8 | Physical | 18 |
| Ret | 17 | A.Montermini | Pacific-Ford | 2 | Gearbox | 22 |
| Ret | 24 | Luca Badoer | Minardi-Ford | 0 | Electrical | 15 |
| DNS | 8 | Mika Hakkinen | McLaren-Mercedes | 0 | Accident | |

Winning speed: 104.471mph Lap leaders: Coulthard 1-19; Schumacher 20-21; Hill 22-81
Pole position: Hill, 1m 15.505s, 111.988mph
Fastest lap: Hill, 1m 17.943s, 108.485mph

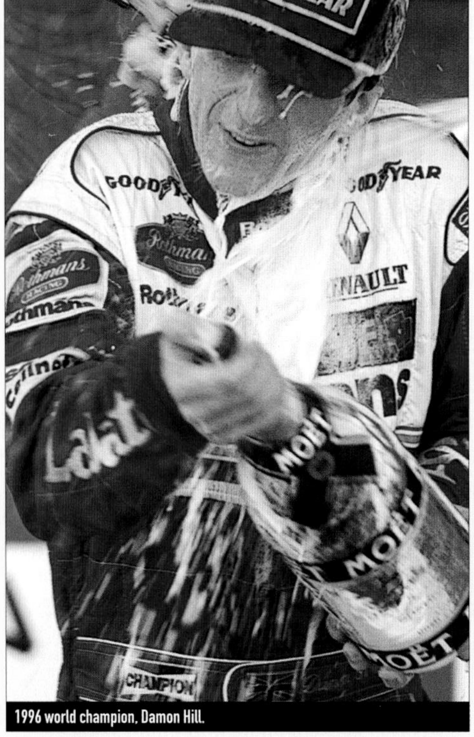

1996 world champion, Damon Hill.

# 1996

## DRIVERS' CHAMPION: DAMON HILL
## CONSTRUCTORS' CHAMPION: WILLIAMS RENAULT

### DRIVERS' CHAMPIONSHIP

| POS. | DRIVER | NATIONALITY | CAR | POINTS |
|---|---|---|---|---|
| 1 | Damon Hill | GB | Williams-Renault | 97 |
| 2 | Jacques Villeneuve | Canada | Williams-Renault | 78 |
| 3 | Michael Schumacher | Germany | Ferrari | 59 |
| 4 | Jean Alesi | France | Benetton-Renault | 47 |
| 5 | Mika Häkkinen | Finland | McLaren-Mercedes | 31 |
| 6 | Gerhard Berger | Austria | Benetton-Renault | 21 |
| 7 | David Coulthard | GB | McLaren-Mercedes | 18 |
| 8 | Rubens Barrichello | Brazil | Jordan-Peugeot | 14 |
| 9 | Olivier Panis | France | Ligier-Mugen Honda | 13 |
| 10 | Eddie Irvine | GB | Ferrari | 11 |
| 11 | Martin Brundle | GB | Jordan-Peugeot | 8 |
| 12 | Heinz-Harald Frentzen | Germany | Sauber-Ford | 7 |
| 13 | Mika Salo | Finland | Tyrrell-Yamaha | 5 |
| 14 | Johnny Herbert | GB | Sauber-Ford | 4 |
| 15 | Pedro Diniz | Brazil | Ligier-Mugen Honda | 2 |
| 16 | Jos Verstappen | Netherlands | Footwork-Hart | 1 |
| | Ukyo Katayama | Japan | Tyrrell-Yamaha | |
| | Pedro Lamy | Portugal | Minardi-Ford | |
| | Giancarlo Fisichella | Italy | Minardi-Ford | |
| | Ricardo Rosset | Brazil | Footwork-Hart | |
| | Andrea Montermini | Italy | Forti-Ford | |
| | Luca Badoer | Italy | Forti-Ford | |
| | Tarso Marques | Brazil | Minardi-Ford | |
| | Giovanni Lavaggi | Italy | Minardi-Ford | |

Points for top six finishers (10, 6, 4, 3, 2, 1). Half points awarded for races stopped before half distance.

### CONSTRUCTORS' CHAMPIONSHIP

| POS. | CONSTRUCTOR | POINTS |
|---|---|---|
| 1 | Williams-Renault | 175 |
| 2 | Ferrari | 70 |
| 3 | Benetton-Renault | 68 |
| 4 | McLaren-Mercedes | 49 |
| 5 | Jordan-Peugeot | 22 |
| 6 | Ligier-Mugen-Honda | 15 |
| 7 | Sauber-Ford | 11 |
| 8 | Tyrrell-Yamaha | 5 |
| 9 | Footwork-Hart | 1 |

Points for top six finishers (10, 6, 4, 3, 2, 1). Half points awarded for races stopped before half distance.

### AUSTRALIAN GRAND PRIX: MELBOURNE *10 March Round: 1 Race: 582 58 x 3.295 miles*

| POS. | NO. | DRIVER | CAR/ENGINE | LAPS | TIME/RETIRED | GRID |
|---|---|---|---|---|---|---|
| 1 | 5 | Damon Hill | Williams-Renault | 58 | 1:32'50.491 | 2 |
| 2 | 6 | J.Villeneuve | Williams-Renault | 58 | +38.020 | 1 |
| 3 | 2 | Eddie Irvine | Ferrari | 58 | +1'02.571 | 3 |
| 4 | 4 | Gerhard Berger | Benetton-Renault | 58 | +1'17.037 | 7 |
| 5 | 7 | Mika Hakkinen | McLaren-Mercedes | 58 | +1'35.071 | 5 |
| 6 | 19 | Mika Salo | Tyrrell-Yamaha | 57 | +1 Lap | 10 |
| 7 | 9 | Olivier Panis | Ligier-Mugen-Honda | 57 | +1 Lap | 11 |
| 8 | 15 | H-H.Frentzen | Sauber-Ford | 57 | +1 Lap | 9 |
| 9 | 16 | Ricardo Rosset | Footwork-Hart | 56 | +2 Laps | 18 |
| 10 | 10 | Pedro Diniz | Ligier-Mugen-Honda | 56 | +2 Laps | 20 |
| 11 | 18 | Ukyo Katayama | Tyrrell-Yamaha | 55 | +3 Laps | 15 |
| Ret | 20 | Pedro Lamy | Minardi-Ford | 42 | Safety belt | 17 |
| Ret | 1 | M.Schumacher | Ferrari | 32 | Brakes | 4 |
| Ret | 21 | G.Fisichella | Minardi-Ford | 32 | Clutch | 16 |
| Ret | 11 | R.Barrichello | Jordan-Peugeot | 29 | Engine | 8 |
| Ret | 8 | David Coulthard | McLaren-Mercedes | 24 | Throttle | 13 |
| Ret | 17 | Jos Verstappen | Footwork-Hart | 15 | Engine | 12 |
| Ret | 3 | Jean Alesi | Benetton-Renault | 9 | Collision | 6 |
| Ret | 12 | Martin Brundle | Jordan-Peugeot | 1 | Spun off | 19 |
| DNS | 14 | Johnny Herbert | Sauber-Ford | 0 | Not started | 14 |
| DNQ | 22 | Luca Badoer | Forti-Ford | | | |
| DNQ | 23 | A.Montermini | Forti-Ford | | | |

Winning speed: 123.489mph Lap leaders: Villeneuve 1-29, 33-53; Hill 30-32, 54-58
Pole position: Villeneuve, 1m 32.371s, 128.398mph
Fastest lap: Villeneuve, 1m 33.421s, 126.955mph
Race stopped after first lap because of Brundle's barrel roll and restarted for total original distance.

### BRAZILIAN GRAND PRIX: INTERLAGOS *31 March Round: 2 Race: 583 71 x 2.687 miles*

| POS. | NO. | DRIVER | CAR/ENGINE | LAPS | TIME/RETIRED | GRID |
|---|---|---|---|---|---|---|
| 1 | 5 | Damon Hill | Williams-Renault | 71 | 1:49'52.976 | 1 |
| 2 | 3 | Jean Alesi | Benetton-Renault | 71 | +17.982 | 5 |
| 3 | 1 | M.Schumacher | Ferrari | 70 | +1 Lap | 4 |
| 4 | 7 | Mika Hakkinen | McLaren-Mercedes | 70 | +1 Lap | 7 |
| 5 | 19 | Mika Salo | Tyrrell-Yamaha | 70 | +1 Lap | 11 |
| 6 | 9 | Olivier Panis | Ligier-Mugen-Honda | 70 | +1 Lap | 15 |
| 7 | 2 | Eddie Irvine | Ferrari | 70 | +1 Lap | 10 |
| 8 | 10 | Pedro Diniz | Ligier-Mugen-Honda | 69 | +2 Laps | 22 |
| 9 | 18 | Ukyo Katayama | Tyrrell-Yamaha | 69 | +2 Laps | 16 |
| 10 | 20 | Pedro Lamy | Minardi-Ford | 68 | +3 Laps | 18 |
| 11 | 22 | Luca Badoer | Forti-Ford | 67 | +4 Laps | 19 |
| 12 | 12 | Martin Brundle | Jordan-Peugeot | 64 | Spun off | 6 |
| Ret | 11 | R.Barrichello | Jordan-Peugeot | 59 | Spun off | 2 |
| Ret | 15 | H-H.Frentzen | Sauber-Ford | 36 | Engine | 9 |
| Ret | 8 | David Coulthard | McLaren-Mercedes | 29 | Spun off | 14 |
| Ret | 14 | Johnny Herbert | Sauber-Ford | 28 | Engine | 12 |
| Ret | 6 | J.Villeneuve | Williams-Renault | 26 | Spun off | 3 |
| Ret | 4 | Gerhard Berger | Benetton-Renault | 26 | Hydraulics | 8 |
| Ret | 23 | A.Montermini | Forti-Ford | 26 | Spun off | 20 |
| Ret | 16 | Ricardo Rosset | Footwork-Hart | 24 | Spun off | 17 |
| Ret | 17 | Jos Verstappen | Footwork-Hart | 19 | Engine | 13 |
| Ret | 21 | Tarso Marques | Minardi-Ford | 0 | Spun off | 21 |

Winning speed: 104.188mph Lap leaders: Hill 1-39, 43-71; Alesi 40-42
Pole position: Hill, 1m 18.111s, 123.859mph
Fastest lap: Hill, 1m 21.547s, 118.640mph

### ARGENTINIAN GRAND PRIX: BUENOS AIRES *7 April Round: 3 Race: 584 72 x 2.646 miles*

| POS. | NO. | DRIVER | CAR/ENGINE | LAPS | TIME/RETIRED | GRID |
|---|---|---|---|---|---|---|
| 1 | 5 | Damon Hill | Williams-Renault | 72 | 1:54'55.322 | 1 |
| 2 | 6 | J.Villeneuve | Williams-Renault | 72 | +12.167 | 3 |
| 3 | 3 | Jean Alesi | Benetton-Renault | 72 | +14.754 | 4 |
| 4 | 11 | R.Barrichello | Jordan-Peugeot | 72 | +55.131 | 6 |
| 5 | 2 | Eddie Irvine | Ferrari | 72 | +1'04.991 | 10 |
| 6 | 17 | Jos Verstappen | Footwork-Hart | 72 | +1'08.913 | 7 |
| 7 | 8 | David Coulthard | McLaren-Mercedes | 72 | +1'13.400 | 9 |
| 8 | 9 | Olivier Panis | Ligier-Mugen-Honda | 72 | +1'14.295 | 12 |
| 9 | 14 | Johnny Herbert | Sauber-Ford | 71 | +1 Lap | 17 |
| 10 | 23 | A.Montermini | Forti-Ford | 69 | +3 Laps | 22 |
| Ret | 4 | Gerhard Berger | Benetton-Renault | 56 | Suspension | 5 |
| Ret | 1 | M.Schumacher | Ferrari | 46 | Broken wing | 2 |
| Ret | 20 | Pedro Lamy | Minardi-Ford | 39 | Transmission | 19 |
| Ret | 19 | Mika Salo | Tyrrell-Yamaha | 36 | Throttle | 16 |
| Ret | 12 | Martin Brundle | Jordan-Peugeot | 34 | Collision | 15 |
| Ret | 21 | Tarso Marques | Minardi-Ford | 33 | Collision | 14 |
| Ret | 15 | H-H.Frentzen | Sauber-Ford | 32 | Spun off | 11 |
| Ret | 10 | Pedro Diniz | Ligier-Mugen-Honda | 29 | Fire | 18 |
| Ret | 18 | Ukyo Katayama | Tyrrell-Yamaha | 28 | Transmission | 13 |
| Ret | 16 | Ricardo Rosset | Footwork-Hart | 24 | Oil pump | 20 |
| Ret | 22 | Luca Badoer | Forti-Ford | 24 | Collision | 21 |
| Ret | 7 | Mika Hakkinen | McLaren-Mercedes | 19 | Throttle | 8 |

Winning speed: 99.428mph Lap leaders: Hill 1-72
Pole position: Hill, 1m 30.346s, 105.451mph
Fastest lap: Alesi, 1m 29.413s, 106.552mph

### EUROPEAN GRAND PRIX: NÜRBURGRING *28 April Round: 4 Race: 585 67 x 2.831 miles*

| POS. | NO. | DRIVER | CAR/ENGINE | LAPS | TIME/RETIRED | GRID |
|---|---|---|---|---|---|---|
| 1 | 6 | J.Villeneuve | Williams-Renault | 67 | 1:33'26.473 | 2 |
| 2 | 1 | M.Schumacher | Ferrari | 67 | +0.762 | 3 |
| 3 | 8 | David Coulthard | McLaren-Mercedes | 67 | +32.834 | 6 |
| 4 | 5 | Damon Hill | Williams-Renault | 67 | +33.511 | 1 |
| 5 | 11 | R.Barrichello | Jordan-Peugeot | 67 | +33.713 | 5 |
| 6 | 12 | Martin Brundle | Jordan-Peugeot | 67 | +55.567 | 11 |
| 7 | 14 | Johnny Herbert | Sauber-Ford | 67 | +1'18.027 | 12 |
| 8 | 7 | Mika Hakkinen | McLaren-Mercedes | 67 | +1'18.438 | 9 |
| 9 | 4 | Gerhard Berger | Benetton-Renault | 67 | +1'21.061 | 8 |
| 10 | 10 | Pedro Diniz | Ligier-Mugen-Honda | 66 | +1 Lap | 17 |
| 11 | 16 | Ricardo Rosset | Footwork-Hart | 65 | +2 Laps | 20 |
| 12 | 20 | Pedro Lamy | Minardi-Ford | 65 | +2 Laps | 19 |
| 13 | 21 | G.Fisichella | Minardi-Ford | 65 | +2 Laps | 18 |
| Ret | 19 | Mika Salo | Tyrrell-Yamaha | 66 | Disqualified | 14 |
| Ret | 18 | Ukyo Katayama | Tyrrell-Yamaha | 65 | Disqualified | 16 |
| Ret | 15 | H-H.Frentzen | Sauber-Ford | 59 | Brakes | 10 |
| Ret | 17 | Jos Verstappen | Footwork-Hart | 38 | Engine | 13 |
| Ret | 9 | Olivier Panis | Ligier-Mugen-Honda | 6 | Collision | 15 |
| Ret | 2 | Eddie Irvine | Ferrari | 6 | Electrical | 7 |
| Ret | 3 | Jean Alesi | Benetton-Renault | 1 | Collision | 4 |
| DNQ | 23 | A.Montermini | Forti-Ford | | | |
| DNQ | 22 | Luca Badoer | Forti-Ford | | | |

Winning speed: 121.793mph Lap leaders: Villeneuve 1-67
Pole position: Hill, 1m 18.941s,129.103mph
Fastest lap: Hill, 1m 21.363s, 125.259mph

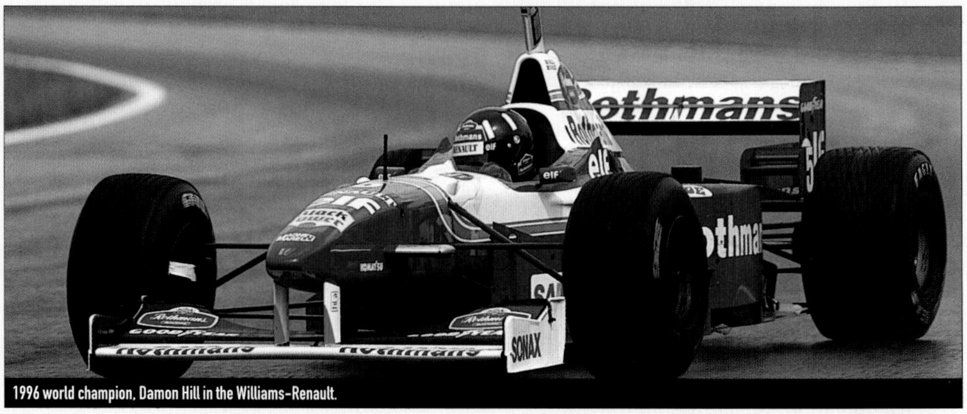

1996 world champion, Damon Hill in the Williams-Renault.

## SAN MARINO GRAND PRIX: IMOLA *5 May Round: 5 Race: 586 63 x 3.040 miles*

| POS. | NO. | DRIVER | CAR/ENGINE | LAPS | TIME/RETIRED | GRID |
|---|---|---|---|---|---|---|
| 1 | 5 | Damon Hill | Williams-Renault | 63 | 1:35'26.156 | 2 |
| 2 | 1 | M.Schumacher | Ferrari | 63 | +16.460 | 1 |
| 3 | 4 | Gerhard Berger | Benetton-Renault | 63 | +46.891 | 7 |
| 4 | 2 | Eddie Irvine | Ferrari | 63 | +1'01.583 | 6 |
| 5 | 11 | R.Barrichello | Jordan-Peugeot | 63 | +1'18.490 | 9 |
| 6 | 3 | Jean Alesi | Benetton-Renault | 62 | +1 Lap | 5 |
| 7 | 10 | Pedro Diniz | Ligier-Mugen-Honda | 62 | +1 Lap | 17 |
| 8 | 7 | Mika Hakkinen | McLaren-Mercedes | 61 | Engine | 11 |
| 9 | 20 | Pedro Lamy | Minardi-Ford | 61 | +2 Laps | 18 |
| 10 | 22 | Luca Badoer | Forti-Ford | 59 | +4 Laps | 21 |
| 11 | 6 | J.Villeneuve | Williams-Renault | 57 | Suspension | 3 |
| Ret | 9 | Olivier Panis | Ligier-Mugen-Honda | 54 | Engine | 13 |
| Ret | 18 | Ukyo Katayama | Tyrrell-Yamaha | 45 | Spun off | 16 |
| Ret | 8 | David Coulthard | McLaren-Mercedes | 44 | Hydraulics | 4 |
| Ret | 16 | Ricardo Rosset | Footwork-Hart | 40 | Engine | 20 |
| Ret | 17 | Jos Verstappen | Footwork-Hart | 38 | Hydraulics | 14 |
| Ret | 12 | Martin Brundle | Jordan-Peugeot | 36 | Spun off | 12 |
| Ret | 15 | H-H.Frentzen | Sauber-Ford | 32 | Brakes | 10 |
| Ret | 21 | G.Fisichella | Minardi-Ford | 30 | Engine | 19 |
| Ret | 14 | Johnny Herbert | Sauber-Ford | 25 | Electrical | 15 |
| Ret | 19 | Mika Salo | Tyrrell-Yamaha | 23 | Engine | 8 |
| DNQ | 23 | A.Montermini | Forti-Ford | | | |

Winning speed: 120.397mph Lap leaders: Coulthard 1-19; Schumacher 20; Hill 21-63
Pole position: Schumacher, 1m 26.890s, 125.942mph
Fastest lap: Hill, 1m 28.931s, 123.051mph

## MONACO GRAND PRIX: MONTE CARLO *19 May Round: 6 Race: 587 75 x 2.068 miles*

| POS. | NO. | DRIVER | CAR/ENGINE | LAPS | TIME/RETIRED | GRID |
|---|---|---|---|---|---|---|
| 1 | 9 | Olivier Panis | Ligier-Mugen-Honda | 75 | 2:00'45.629 | 14 |
| 2 | 8 | David Coulthard | McLaren-Mercedes | 75 | +4.828 | 5 |
| 3 | 14 | Johnny Herbert | Sauber-Ford | 75 | +37.503 | 13 |
| 4 | 15 | H-H.Frentzen | Sauber-Ford | 74 | +1 Lap | 9 |
| 5 | 19 | Mika Salo | Tyrrell-Yamaha | 70 | Collision | 11 |
| 6 | 7 | Mika Hakkinen | McLaren-Mercedes | 70 | Collision | 8 |
| 7 | 2 | Eddie Irvine | Ferrari | 68 | Collision | 7 |
| Ret | 6 | J.Villeneuve | Williams-Renault | 66 | Collision | 10 |
| Ret | 3 | Jean Alesi | Benetton-Renault | 60 | Suspension | 3 |
| Ret | 22 | Luca Badoer | Forti-Ford | 60 | Collision | 21 |
| Ret | 5 | Damon Hill | Williams-Renault | 40 | Engine | 2 |
| Ret | 12 | Martin Brundle | Jordan-Peugeot | 30 | Spun off | 16 |
| Ret | 4 | Gerhard Berger | Benetton-Renault | 9 | Gearbox | 4 |
| Ret | 10 | Pedro Diniz | Ligier-Mugen-Honda | 5 | Transmission | 17 |
| Ret | 16 | Ricardo Rosset | Footwork-Hart | 3 | Spun off | 20 |
| Ret | 18 | Ukyo Katayama | Tyrrell-Yamaha | 2 | Spun off | 15 |
| Ret | 1 | M.Schumacher | Ferrari | 0 | Spun off | 1 |
| Ret | 11 | R.Barrichello | Jordan-Peugeot | 0 | Spun off | 6 |
| Ret | 17 | Jos Verstappen | Footwork-Hart | 0 | Spun off | 12 |
| Ret | 21 | G.Fisichella | Minardi-Ford | 0 | Collision | 18 |
| Ret | 20 | Pedro Lamy | Minardi-Ford | 0 | Collision | 19 |
| DNS | 23 | A. Montermini | Forti-Ford | 0 | Collision | 19 |

Winning speed: 77.059mph Lap leaders: Hill 1-27, 30-40; Alesi 28-29, 41-59; Panis 60-75
Pole position: Schumacher, 1m 20.356s, 92.644mph
Fastest lap: Alesi, 1m 25.205s, 87.372mph

## SPANISH GRAND PRIX: MONTMELÓ *2 June Round: 7 Race: 588 65 x 2.937 miles*

| POS. | NO. | DRIVER | CAR/ENGINE | LAPS | TIME/RETIRED | GRID |
|---|---|---|---|---|---|---|
| 1 | 1 | M.Schumacher | Ferrari | 65 | 1:59'49.307 | 3 |
| 2 | 3 | Jean Alesi | Benetton-Renault | 65 | +45.302 | 4 |
| 3 | 6 | J.Villeneuve | Williams-Renault | 65 | +48.388 | 2 |
| 4 | 15 | H-H.Frentzen | Sauber-Ford | 64 | +1 Lap | 11 |
| 5 | 7 | Mika Hakkinen | McLaren-Mercedes | 64 | +1 Lap | 10 |
| 6 | 10 | Pedro Diniz | Ligier-Mugen-Honda | 63 | +2 Laps | 17 |
| Ret | 17 | Jos Verstappen | Footwork-Hart | 47 | Spun off | 13 |
| Ret | 11 | R.Barrichello | Jordan-Peugeot | 45 | Differential | 7 |
| Ret | 4 | Gerhard Berger | Benetton-Renault | 44 | Spun off | 5 |
| Ret | 14 | Johnny Herbert | Sauber-Ford | 20 | Spun off | 14 |
| Ret | 12 | Martin Brundle | Jordan-Peugeot | 17 | Differential | 15 |
| DSQ | 19 | Mika Salo | Tyrrell-Yamaha | 16 | Disqualified | 12 |
| Ret | 5 | Damon Hill | Williams-Renault | 10 | Spun off | 1 |
| Ret | 18 | Ukyo Katayama | Tyrrell-Yamaha | 8 | Electrical | 16 |
| Ret | 2 | Eddie Irvine | Ferrari | 1 | Spun off | 6 |
| Ret | 9 | Olivier Panis | Ligier-Mugen-Honda | 1 | Collision | 8 |
| Ret | 21 | G.Fisichella | Minardi-Ford | 1 | Collision | 19 |
| Ret | 8 | David Coulthard | McLaren-Mercedes | 0 | Collision | 14 |
| Ret | 20 | Pedro Lamy | Minardi-Ford | 0 | Collision | 18 |
| Ret | 16 | Ricardo Rosset | Footwork-Hart | 0 | Collision | 20 |
| DNQ | 22 | Luca Badoer | Forti-Ford | | | |
| DNQ | 23 | A.Montermini | Forti-Ford | | | |

Winning speed: 95.558mph Lap leaders: Villeneuve 1-11; Schumacher 12-65
Pole position: Hill, 1m 20.650s, 131.110mph
Fastest lap: Schumacher, 1m 45.517s, 100.211mph

## CANADIAN GRAND PRIX: MONTRÉAL *16 June Round: 69 Race: 589 69x2.747 miles*

| POS. | NO. | DRIVER | CAR/ENGINE | LAPS | TIME/RETIRED | GRID |
|---|---|---|---|---|---|---|
| 1 | 5 | Damon Hill | Williams-Renault | 69 | 1:36'03.465 | 1 |
| 2 | 6 | J.Villeneuve | Williams-Renault | 69 | +4.183 | 2 |
| 3 | 3 | Jean Alesi | Benetton-Renault | 69 | +54.656 | 4 |
| 4 | 8 | David Coulthard | McLaren-Mercedes | 69 | +1'03.673 | 10 |
| 5 | 7 | Mika Hakkinen | McLaren-Mercedes | 68 | +1 Lap | 6 |
| 6 | 12 | Martin Brundle | Jordan-Peugeot | 68 | +1 Lap | 9 |
| 7 | 14 | Johnny Herbert | Sauber-Ford | 68 | +1 Lap | 15 |
| 8 | 21 | G.Fisichella | Minardi-Ford | 67 | +2 Laps | 16 |
| Ret | 20 | Pedro Lamy | Minardi-Ford | 44 | Collision | 19 |
| Ret | 22 | Luca Badoer | Forti-Ford | 44 | Gearbox | 20 |
| Ret | 4 | Gerhard Berger | Benetton-Renault | 42 | Spun off | 7 |
| Ret | 1 | M.Schumacher | Ferrari | 41 | Halfshaft | 3 |
| Ret | 9 | Olivier Panis | Ligier-Mugen-Honda | 39 | Engine | 11 |
| Ret | 19 | Mika Salo | Tyrrell-Yamaha | 39 | Engine | 14 |
| Ret | 10 | Pedro Diniz | Ligier-Mugen-Honda | 38 | Engine | 18 |
| Ret | 11 | R.Barrichello | Jordan-Peugeot | 22 | Clutch | 8 |
| Ret | 23 | A.Montermini | Forti-Ford | 22 | Electrical | 22 |
| Ret | 15 | H-H.Frentzen | Sauber-Ford | 19 | Gearbox | 12 |
| Ret | 17 | Jos Verstappen | Footwork-Hart | 10 | Engine | 13 |
| Ret | 16 | Ricardo Rosset | Footwork-Hart | 6 | Collision | 21 |
| Ret | 18 | Ukyo Katayama | Tyrrell-Yamaha | 6 | Collision | 17 |
| Ret | 2 | Eddie Irvine | Ferrari | 1 | Suspension | 5 |

Winning speed: 118.397 Lap leaders: Hill 1-27,36-39; Villeneuve 28-35
Pole position: Hill, 1m 21.059s, 122.004mph
Fastest lap: Villeneuve, 1m 21.916s, 120.727mph

## FRENCH GRAND PRIX: MAGNY-COURS *30 June Round: 9 Race: 590 72 x 2.641 miles*

| POS. | NO. | DRIVER | CAR/ENGINE | LAPS | TIME/RETIRED | GRID |
|---|---|---|---|---|---|---|
| 1 | 5 | Damon Hill | Williams-Renault | 72 | 1:36'28.795 | 2 |
| 2 | 6 | J.Villeneuve | Williams-Renault | 72 | +8.127 | 6 |
| 3 | 3 | Jean Alesi | Benetton-Renault | 72 | +46.442 | 3 |
| 4 | 4 | Gerhard Berger | Benetton-Renault | 72 | +46.859 | 4 |
| 5 | 7 | Mika Hakkinen | McLaren-Mercedes | 72 | +1'02.774 | 5 |
| 6 | 8 | David Coulthard | McLaren-Mercedes | 71 | +1 Lap | 7 |
| 7 | 9 | Olivier Panis | Ligier-Mugen-Honda | 71 | +1 Lap | 9 |
| 8 | 12 | Martin Brundle | Jordan-Peugeot | 71 | +1 Lap | 8 |
| 9 | 11 | R.Barrichello | Jordan-Peugeot | 71 | +1 Lap | 10 |
| 10 | 19 | Mika Salo | Tyrrell-Yamaha | 70 | +2 Laps | 13 |
| 11 | 16 | Ricardo Rosset | Footwork-Hart | 69 | +3 Laps | 19 |
| 12 | 20 | Pedro Lamy | Minardi-Ford | 69 | +3 Laps | 18 |
| DSQ | 14 | Johnny Herbert | Sauber-Ford | 70 | Disqualified | 16 |
| Ret | 15 | H-H.Frentzen | Sauber-Ford | 56 | Throttle | 12 |
| Ret | 18 | Ukyo Katayama | Tyrrell-Yamaha | 33 | Engine | 14 |
| Ret | 22 | Luca Badoer | Forti-Ford | 29 | Fuel system | 20 |
| Ret | 10 | Pedro Diniz | Ligier-Mugen-Honda | 28 | Engine | 11 |
| Ret | 17 | Jos Verstappen | Footwork-Hart | 10 | Steering | 15 |
| Ret | 2 | Eddie Irvine | Ferrari | 5 | Gearbox | 22 |
| Ret | 21 | G.Fisichella | Minardi-Ford | 2 | Fuel pump | 17 |
| Ret | 23 | A.Montermini | Forti-Ford | 2 | Electrical | 21 |
| Ret | 1 | M.Schumacher | Ferrari | 0 | Engine | 1 |

Winning speed: 118.174mph Lap leaders: Hill 1-27, 31-72; Villeneuve 28-30
Pole position: Schumacher, 1m 15.989, 125.110mph
Fastest lap: Villeneuve: 1m 18.610s, 120.939mph

## BRITISH GRAND PRIX: SILVERSTONE *14 July Round: 10 Race: 591 61 x 3.152 miles*

| POS. | NO. | DRIVER | CAR/ENGINE | LAPS | TIME/RETIRED | GRID |
|---|---|---|---|---|---|---|
| 1 | 6 | J.Villeneuve | Williams-Renault | 61 | 1:33'00.874 | 2 |
| 2 | 4 | Gerhard Berger | Benetton-Renault | 61 | +19.026 | 7 |
| 3 | 7 | Mika Hakkinen | McLaren-Mercedes | 61 | +50.830 | 4 |
| 4 | 11 | R.Barrichello | Jordan-Peugeot | 61 | +1'06.716 | 6 |
| 5 | 8 | David Coulthard | McLaren-Mercedes | 61 | +1'22.507 | 9 |
| 6 | 12 | Martin Brundle | Jordan-Peugeot | 60 | +1 Lap | 8 |
| 7 | 19 | Mika Salo | Tyrrell-Yamaha | 60 | +1 Lap | 14 |
| 8 | 15 | H-H.Frentzen | Sauber-Ford | 60 | +1 Lap | 11 |
| 9 | 14 | Johnny Herbert | Sauber-Ford | 60 | +1 Lap | 13 |
| 10 | 17 | Jos Verstappen | Footwork-Hart | 60 | +1 Lap | 15 |
| 11 | 21 | G.Fisichella | Minardi-Ford | 59 | +2 Laps | 18 |
| Ret | 3 | Jean Alesi | Benetton-Renault | 44 | Brakes | 5 |
| Ret | 9 | Olivier Panis | Ligier-Mugen-Honda | 40 | Handling | 16 |
| Ret | 10 | Pedro Diniz | Ligier-Mugen-Honda | 38 | Engine | 17 |
| Ret | 5 | Damon Hill | Williams-Renault | 26 | Wheel | 1 |
| Ret | 20 | Pedro Lamy | Minardi-Ford | 21 | Gearbox | 19 |
| Ret | 16 | Ricardo Rosset | Footwork-Hart | 13 | Electrical | 20 |
| Ret | 18 | Ukyo Katayama | Tyrrell-Yamaha | 12 | Engine | 12 |
| Ret | 2 | Eddie Irvine | Ferrari | 5 | Differential | 10 |
| Ret | 1 | M.Schumacher | Ferrari | 3 | Hydraulics | 3 |
| DNQ | 23 | A.Montermini | Forti-Ford | | | |
| DNQ | 22 | Luca Badoer | Forti-Ford | | | |

Winning speed: 124.011mph Lap leaders: Villeneuve 1-23, 31-61; Alesi 24-30
Pole position: Hill, 1m 26.875s, 130.598mph
Fastest lap: Villeneuve, 1m 29.288s, 127.069mph

## GERMAN GRAND PRIX: HOCKENHEIM *28 July Round: 1 Race: 592 45 x 4.240 miles*

| POS. | NO. | DRIVER | CAR/ENGINE | LAPS | TIME/RETIRED | GRID |
|---|---|---|---|---|---|---|
| 1 | 5 | Damon Hill | Williams-Renault | 45 | 1:21'43.417 | 1 |
| 2 | 3 | Jean Alesi | Benetton-Renault | 45 | +11.452 | 5 |
| 3 | 6 | J.Villeneuve | Williams-Renault | 45 | +33.926Q | 6 |
| 4 | 1 | M.Schumacher | Ferrari | 45 | +41.517 | 3 |
| 5 | 8 | David Coulthard | McLaren-Mercedes | 45 | +42.196 | 7 |
| 6 | 11 | R.Barrichello | Jordan-Peugeot | 45 | +1'42.099 | 9 |
| 7 | 9 | Olivier Panis | Ligier-Mugen-Honda | 45 | +1'43.912 | 12 |
| 8 | 15 | H-H.Frentzen | Sauber-Ford | 44 | +1 Lap | 13 |
| 9 | 19 | Mika Salo | Tyrrell-Yamaha | 44 | +1 Lap | 15 |
| 10 | 12 | Martin Brundle | Jordan-Peugeot | 44 | +1 Lap | 10 |
| 11 | 16 | Ricardo Rosset | Footwork-Hart | 44 | +1 Lap | 19 |
| 12 | 20 | Pedro Lamy | Minardi-Ford | 43 | +2 Laps | 18 |
| 13 | 4 | Gerhard Berger | Benetton-Renault | 42 | Engine | 2 |
| Ret | 2 | Eddie Irvine | Ferrari | 34 | Engine | 8 |
| Ret | 14 | Johnny Herbert | Sauber-Ford | 25 | Vibrations | 14 |
| Ret | 10 | Pedro Diniz | Ligier-Mugen-Honda | 19 | Engine | 11 |
| Ret | 18 | Ukyo Katayama | Tyrrell-Yamaha | 19 | Spun off | 16 |
| Ret | 7 | Mika Hakkinen | McLaren-Mercedes | 13 | Gearbox | 4 |
| Ret | 17 | Jos Verstappen | Footwork-Hart | 0 | Collision | 17 |
| DNQ | 21 | Giovanni Lavaggi | Minardi-Ford | | | |

Winning speed: 140.063mph Lap leaders: Berger 1-23, 35-42; Hill 24-34, 43-45
Pole position: Hill, 1m 43.912s, 146.880mph
Fastest lap: Hill, 1m 46.504s, 143.306mph

## HUNGARIAN GRAND PRIX: HUNGARORING *11 August Round: 12 Race: 593 77 x 2.466 miles*

| POS. | NO. | DRIVER | CAR/ENGINE | LAPS | TIME/RETIRED | GRID |
|---|---|---|---|---|---|---|
| 1 | 6 | J.Villeneuve | Williams-Renault | 77 | 1:46'21.134 | 3 |
| 2 | 5 | Damon Hill | Williams-Renault | 77 | +0.771 | 2 |
| 3 | 3 | Jean Alesi | Benetton-Renault | 77 | +1'24.212 | 5 |
| 4 | 7 | Mika Hakkinen | McLaren-Mercedes | 76 | +1 Lap | 7 |
| 5 | 9 | Olivier Panis | Ligier-Mugen-Honda | 76 | +1 Lap | 11 |
| 6 | 11 | R.Barrichello | Jordan-Peugeot | 75 | +2 Laps | 13 |
| 7 | 18 | Ukyo Katayama | Tyrrell-Yamaha | 74 | +3 Laps | 14 |
| 8 | 16 | Ricardo Rosset | Footwork-Hart | 74 | +3 Laps | 18 |
| 9 | 1 | M.Schumacher | Ferrari | 70 | Throttle | 1 |
| 10 | 21 | Giovanni Lavaggi | Minardi-Ford | 69 | Spun off | 20 |
| Ret | 4 | Gerhard Berger | Benetton-Renault | 64 | Engine | 6 |
| Ret | 15 | H-H.Frentzen | Sauber-Ford | 50 | Electrical | 10 |
| Ret | 14 | Johnny Herbert | Sauber-Ford | 35 | Engine | 8 |
| Ret | 2 | Eddie Irvine | Ferrari | 31 | Gearbox | 4 |
| Ret | 20 | Pedro Lamy | Minardi-Ford | 24 | Suspension | 19 |
| Ret | 8 | David Coulthard | McLaren-Mercedes | 23 | Engine | 9 |
| Ret | 17 | Jos Verstappen | Footwork-Hart | 10 | Spun off | 17 |
| Ret | 12 | Martin Brundle | Jordan-Peugeot | 5 | Spun off | 12 |
| Ret | 10 | Pedro Diniz | Ligier-Mugen-Honda | 1 | Collision | 15 |
| Ret | 19 | Mika Salo | Tyrrell-Yamaha | 0 | Collision | 16 |

Winning speed: 107.107mph
Lap leaders: Schumacher 1-18; Villeneuve 19-21, 25-58, 64-77; Hill 22-24, 59-63
Pole position: Schumacher, 1m 17.129s, 115.082mph
Fastest lap: Hill, 1m 20.093s, 110.823mph

## BELGIAN GRAND PRIX: SPA-FRANCORCHAMPS *25 August Round: 13 Race: 594 44 x 4.330 miles*

| POS. | NO. | DRIVER | CAR/ENGINE | LAPS | TIME/RETIRED | GRID |
|---|---|---|---|---|---|---|
| 1 | 1 | M.Schumacher | Ferrari | 44 | 1:28'15.125 | 3 |
| 2 | 6 | J.Villeneuve | Williams-Renault | 44 | +5.602 | 1 |
| 3 | 7 | Mika Hakkinen | McLaren-Mercedes | 44 | +15.710 | 6 |
| 4 | 3 | Jean Alesi | Benetton-Renault | 44 | +19.125 | 7 |
| 5 | 5 | Damon Hill | Williams-Renault | 44 | +29.179 | 2 |
| 6 | 4 | Gerhard Berger | Benetton-Renault | 44 | +29.896 | 5 |
| 7 | 19 | Mika Salo | Tyrrell-Yamaha | 44 | +1'00.754 | 13 |
| 8 | 18 | Ukyo Katayama | Tyrrell-Yamaha | 44 | +1'40.227 | 17 |
| 9 | 16 | Ricardo Rosset | Footwork-Hart | 43 | +1 Lap | 18 |
| 10 | 20 | Pedro Lamy | Minardi-Ford | 43 | +1 Lap | 19 |
| Ret | 8 | David Coulthard | McLaren-Mercedes | 37 | Spun off | 4 |
| Ret | 12 | Martin Brundle | Jordan-Peugeot | 34 | Engine | 8 |
| Ret | 2 | Eddie Irvine | Ferrari | 29 | Gearbox | 9 |
| Ret | 11 | R.Barrichello | Jordan-Peugeot | 29 | Suspension | 10 |
| Ret | 10 | Pedro Diniz | Ligier-Mugen-Honda | 22 | Electrical | 15 |
| Ret | 17 | Jos Verstappen | Footwork-Hart | 11 | Accident | 16 |
| Ret | 15 | H-H.Frentzen | Sauber-Ford | 0 | Collision | 11 |
| Ret | 14 | Johnny Herbert | Sauber-Ford | 0 | Collision | 12 |
| Ret | 9 | Olivier Panis | Ligier-Mugen-Honda | 0 | Collision | 14 |
| DNQ | 21 | Giovanni Lavaggi | Minardi-Ford | | | |

Winning speed: 129.520mph Lap leaders: Villeneuve 1-14, 30-32;
Coulthard 15-21; Häkkinen 22-23; Schumacher 24-29, 33-44
Pole position: Villeneuve, 1m 50.574s, 140.964mph
Fastest lap: Berger, 1m 53.067s, 137.856mph

## ITALIAN GRAND PRIX: MONZA *8 September Round: 14 Race: 595 53 x 3.585 miles*

| POS. | NO. | DRIVER | CAR/ENGINE | LAPS | TIME/RETIRED | GRID |
|---|---|---|---|---|---|---|
| 1 | 1 | M.Schumacher | Ferrari | 53 | 1:17'43.632 | 3 |
| 2 | 3 | Jean Alesi | Benetton-Renault | 53 | +18.265 | 6 |
| 3 | 7 | Mika Hakkinen | McLaren-Mercedes | 53 | +1'06.635 | 4 |
| 4 | 12 | Martin Brundle | Jordan-Peugeot | 53 | +1'25.217 | 9 |
| 5 | 11 | R.Barrichello | Jordan-Peugeot | 53 | +1'25.475 | 10 |
| 6 | 10 | Pedro Diniz | Ligier-Mugen-Honda | 52 | +1 Lap | 14 |
| 7 | 6 | J.Villeneuve | Williams-Renault | 52 | +1 Lap | 2 |
| 8 | 17 | Jos Verstappen | Footwork-Hart | 52 | +1 Lap | 15 |
| 9 | 14 | Johnny Herbert | Sauber-Ford | 51 | Engine | 12 |
| 10 | 18 | Ukyo Katayama | Tyrrell-Yamaha | 51 | +2 Laps | 16 |
| Ret | 16 | Ricardo Rosset | Footwork-Hart | 36 | Spun off | 19 |
| Ret | 2 | Eddie Irvine | Ferrari | 23 | Spun off | 7 |
| Ret | 20 | Pedro Lamy | Minardi-Ford | 12 | Engine | 18 |
| Ret | 19 | Mika Salo | Tyrrell-Yamaha | 9 | Engine | 17 |
| Ret | 15 | H-H.Frentzen | Sauber-Ford | 7 | Spun off | 13 |
| Ret | 5 | Damon Hill | Williams-Renault | 5 | Spun off | 1 |
| Ret | 21 | Giovanni Lavaggi | Minardi-Ford | 5 | Engine | 20 |
| Ret | 4 | Gerhard Berger | Benetton-Renault | 4 | Hydraulics | 8 |
| Ret | 9 | Olivier Panis | Ligier-Mugen-Honda | 2 | Spun off | 11 |
| Ret | 8 | David Coulthard | McLaren-Mercedes | 1 | Spun off | 5 |

Winning speed: 146.665mph Lap leaders: Hill 1-5; Alesi 6-30; Schumacher 31-53
Pole position: Hill, 1m 24.204s, 153.284mph
Fastest lap: Schumacher, 1m 26.110s, 149.891mph

## PUTUGESE GRAND PRIX: ESTORIL *22 September Round: 15 Race: 596 70 x 2.709 miles*

| POS. | NO. | DRIVER | CAR/ENGINE | LAPS | TIME/RETIRED | GRID |
|---|---|---|---|---|---|---|
| 1 | 6 | J.Villeneuve | Williams-Renault | 70 | 1:40'22.915 | 2 |
| 2 | 5 | Damon Hill | Williams-Renault | 70 | +19.966 | 1 |
| 3 | 1 | M.Schumacher | Ferrari | 70 | +53.765 | 4 |
| 4 | 3 | Jean Alesi | Benetton-Renault | 70 | +55.109 | 3 |
| 5 | 2 | Eddie Irvine | Ferrari | 70 | +1'27.389 | 6 |
| 6 | 4 | Gerhard Berger | Benetton-Renault | 70 | +1'33.141 | 5 |
| 7 | 15 | H-H.Frentzen | Sauber-Ford | 69 | +1 Lap | 11 |
| 8 | 14 | Johnny Herbert | Sauber-Ford | 69 | +1 Lap | 12 |
| 9 | 12 | Martin Brundle | Jordan-Peugeot | 69 | +1 Lap | 10 |
| 10 | 9 | Olivier Panis | Ligier-Mugen-Honda | 69 | +1 Lap | 15 |
| 11 | 19 | Mika Salo | Tyrrell-Yamaha | 69 | +1 Lap | 13 |
| 12 | 18 | Ukyo Katayama | Tyrrell-Yamaha | 68 | +2 Laps | 14 |
| 13 | 8 | David Coulthard | McLaren-Mercedes | 68 | +2 Laps | 8 |
| 14 | 16 | Ricardo Rosset | Footwork-Hart | 67 | +3 Laps | 17 |
| 15 | 21 | Giovanni Lavaggi | Minardi-Ford | 65 | +5 Laps | 20 |
| 16 | 20 | Pedro Lamy | Minardi-Ford | 65 | +5 Laps | 19 |
| Ret | 7 | Mika Hakkinen | McLaren-Mercedes | 52 | Collision | 7 |
| Ret | 17 | Jos Verstappen | Footwork-Hart | 47 | Engine | 16 |
| Ret | 10 | Pedro Diniz | Ligier-Mugen-Honda | 46 | Collision | 18 |
| Ret | 11 | R.Barrichello | Jordan-Peugeot | 41 | Spun off | 9 |

Winning speed: 113.353mph
Lap leaders: Hill 1-17, 22-33, 36-48; Alesi 18-21; Villeneuve 34-35, 49-70
Pole position: Hill, 1m 20.330s, 121.412mph
Fastest lap: Villeneuve, 1m 22.873s, 117.687mph

## JAPANESE GRAND PRIX: SUZUKA *13 October Round: 16 Race: 597 52 x 3.644 miles*

| POS. | NO. | DRIVER | CAR/ENGINE | LAPS | TIME/RETIRED | GRID |
|---|---|---|---|---|---|---|
| 1 | 5 | Damon Hill | Williams-Renault | 52 | 1:32'33.791 | 2 |
| 2 | 1 | M.Schumacher | Ferrari | 52 | +1.883 | 3 |
| 3 | 7 | Mika Hakkinen | McLaren-Mercedes | 52 | +3.212 | 5 |
| 4 | 4 | Gerhard Berger | Benetton-Renault | 52 | +26.526 | 4 |
| 5 | 12 | Martin Brundle | Jordan-Peugeot | 52 | +1'07.120 | 10 |
| 6 | 15 | H-H.Frentzen | Sauber-Ford | 52 | +1'21.186 | 7 |
| 7 | 9 | Olivier Panis | Ligier-Mugen-Honda | 52 | +1'24.510 | 12 |
| 8 | 8 | David Coulthard | McLaren-Mercedes | 52 | +1'25.233 | 8 |
| 9 | 11 | R.Barrichello | Jordan-Peugeot | 52 | +1'41.065 | 11 |
| 10 | 14 | Johnny Herbert | Sauber-Ford | 52 | +1'41.799 | 13 |
| 11 | 17 | Jos Verstappen | Footwork-Hart | 51 | +1 Lap | 17 |
| 12 | 20 | Pedro Lamy | Minardi-Ford | 50 | +2 Laps | 18 |
| 13 | 16 | Ricardo Rosset | Footwork-Hart | 50 | +2 Laps | 19 |
| Ret | 2 | Eddie Irvine | Ferrari | 39 | Collision | 6 |
| Ret | 18 | Ukyo Katayama | Tyrrell-Yamaha | 37 | Engine | 14 |
| Ret | 6 | J.Villeneuve | Williams-Renault | 36 | Wheel | 1 |
| Ret | 19 | Mika Salo | Tyrrell-Yamaha | 20 | Engine | 15 |
| Ret | 10 | Pedro Diniz | Ligier-Mugen-Honda | 13 | Spun off | 16 |
| Ret | 3 | Jean Alesi | Benetton-Renault | 0 | Spun off | 9 |
| DNQ | 21 | Giovanni Lavaggi | Minardi-Ford | | | |

Winning speed: 122.733mph Lap leaders: Hill 1-52
Pole position: Villeneuve, 1m 38.909s, 132.621mph
Fastest lap: Villeneuve, 1m 44.043s,126.077mph

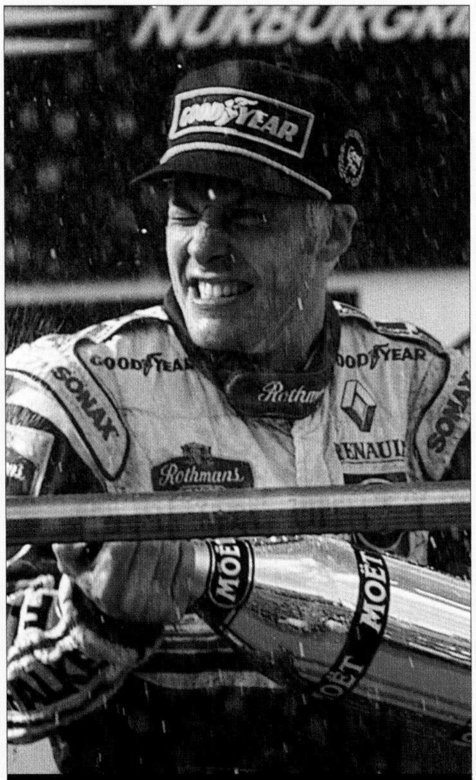


1997 world champion, Jacques Villeneuve

# 1997

## DRIVERS' CHAMPION: JACQUES VILLENEUVE
## CONSTRUCTORS' CHAMPION: WILLIAMS RENAULT

### DRIVERS' CHAMPIONSHIP

| POS. | DRIVER | NATIONALITY | CAR | POINTS |
|---|---|---|---|---|
| 1 | Jacques Villeneuve | Canada | Williams-Renault | 81 |
| - | Michael Schumacher | Germany | Ferrari | 78 |
| 2 | Heinz-Harald Frentzen | Germany | Williams-Renault | 42 |
| 3 | Jean Alesi | France | Benetton-Renault | 36 |
| 4 | David Coulthard | GB | McLaren-Mercedes | 36 |
| 5 | Gerhard Berger | Austria | Benetton-Renault | 27 |
| 6 | Mika Häkkinen | Finland | McLaren-Mercedes | 27 |
| 7 | Eddie Irvine | GB | Ferrari | 24 |
| 8 | Giancarlo Fisichella | Italy | Jordan-Peugeot | 20 |
| 9 | Olivier Panis | France | Prost-Mugen Honda | 16 |
| 10 | Johnny Herbert | GB | Sauber-Petronas | 15 |
| 11 | Ralf Schumacher | Germany | Jordan-Peugeot | 13 |
| 12 | Damon Hill | GB | Arrows-Yamaha | 7 |
| 13 | Rubens Barrichello | Brazil | Stewart-Ford | 6 |
| 14 | Alexander Wurz | Austria | Benetton-Renault | 4 |
| 15 | Jarno Trulli | Italy | Minardi-Hart, Prost-Mugen Honda | 3 |
| 16 | Mika Salo | Finland | Tyrrell-Ford | 2 |
| = | Shinji Nakano | Japan | Prost-Mugen Honda | 2 |
| = | Pedro Diniz | GB | Arrows-Yamaha | 2 |
| 19 | Nicola Larini | Italy | Sauber-Petronas | 1 |
| | Jos Verstappen | Netherlands | Tyrrell-Ford | |
| | Ukyo Katayama | Japan | Minardi-Hart | |
| | Jan Magnussen | Denmark | Stewart-Ford | |
| | Ricardo Rosset | Brazil | Lola-Ford | |
| | Vincenzo Sospiri | Italy | Lola-Ford | |
| | Gianni Morbidelli | Italy | Sauber-Petronas | |
| | Norberto Fontana | Argentina | Sauber-Petronas | |
| | Tarso Marques | Brazil | Minardi-Hart | |

Points for top six finishers (10, 6, 4, 3, 2, 1). Half points awarded for races stopped before half distance. Michael Schumacher's second place in the championship was taken away after he tried to take out Jacques Villeneuve at the European Grand Prix.

### CONSTRUCTORS' CHAMPIONSHIP

| POS. | CONSTRUCTOR | POINTS |
|---|---|---|
| 1 | Williams-Renault | 123 |
| 2 | Ferrari | 102 |
| 3 | Benetton-Renault | 67 |
| 4 | McLaren-Mercedes | 63 |
| 5 | Jordan-Peugeot | 33 |
| 6 | Prost-Mugen-Honda | 21 |
| 7 | Sauber-Petronas | 16 |
| 8 | Arrows-Yamaha | 9 |
| 9 | Stewart-Ford | 6 |
| 10 | Tyrrell-Ford | 2 |

Points for top six finishers (10, 6, 4, 3, 2, 1). Half points awarded for races stopped before half distance.

## AUSTRALIAN GRAND PRIX: MELBOURNE *9 March Round: 1 Race: 598 58 x 3.295 miles*

| POS. | NO. | DRIVER | CAR/ENGINE | LAPS | TIME/RETIRED | GRID |
|---|---|---|---|---|---|---|
| 1 | 10 | David Coulthard | McLaren-Mercedes | 58 | 1:30'28.718 | 4 |
| 2 | 5 | M.Schumacher | Ferrari | 58 | +20.046 | 3 |
| 3 | 9 | Mika Hakkinen | McLaren-Mercedes | 58 | +22.177 | 6 |
| 4 | 8 | Gerhard Berger | Benetton-Renault | 58 | +22.841 | 10 |
| 5 | 14 | Olivier Panis | Prost-Mugen-Honda | 58 | +1'00.308 | 9 |
| 6 | 17 | Nicola Larini | Sauber-Petronas | 58 | +1'36.040 | 13 |
| 7 | 15 | Shinji Nakano | Prost-Mugen-Honda | 56 | +2 Laps | 16 |
| 8 | 4 | H-H.Frentzen | Williams-Renault | 55 | Brakes | 2 |
| 9 | 21 | Jarno Trulli | Minardi-Hart | 55 | +3 Laps | 17 |
| 10 | 2 | Pedro Diniz | Arrows-Yamaha | 54 | +4 Laps | 22 |
| Ret | 22 | R.Barrichello | Stewart-Ford | 49 | Engine | 11 |
| Ret | 19 | Mika Salo | Tyrrell-Ford | 42 | Engine | 18 |
| Ret | 23 | Jan Magnussen | Stewart-Ford | 36 | Suspension | 19 |
| Ret | 7 | Jean Alesi | Benetton-Renault | 34 | Out of fuel | 8 |
| Ret | 20 | Ukyo Katayama | Minardi-Hart | 32 | Electrical | 15 |
| Ret | 12 | G.Fisichella | Jordan-Peugeot | 14 | Spun off | 14 |
| Ret | 18 | Jos Verstappen | Tyrrell-Ford | 2 | Spun off | 21 |
| Ret | 11 | Ralf Schumacher | Jordan-Peugeot | 1 | Gearbox | 12 |
| Ret | 3 | J.Villeneuve | Williams-Renault | 0 | Collision | 1 |
| Ret | 6 | Eddie Irvine | Ferrari | 0 | Collision | 5 |
| Ret | 16 | Johnny Herbert | Sauber-Petronas | 0 | Collision | 7 |
| DNS | 1 | Damon Hill | Arrows-Yamaha | 0 | Throttle | 20 |
| DNQ | 24 | Vincenzo Sospiri | Lola-Ford | | | |
| DNQ | 25 | Ricardo Rosset | Lola-Ford | | | |

Winning speed: 126.710mph Lap leaders: Frentzen 1-17, 33-39; Coulthard 18-32, 40-58;
Pole position: Villeneuve, 1m 29.369s, 132.690mph
Fastest lap: Frentzen, 1m 30.585s, 130.930mph

## BRAZILIAN GRAND PRIX: INTERLAGOS *30 March Round: 2 Race: 599 72 x 2.667 miles*

| POS. | NO. | DRIVER | CAR/ENGINE | LAPS | TIME/RETIRED | GRID |
|---|---|---|---|---|---|---|
| 1 | 3 | J.Villeneuve | Williams-Renault | 72 | 1:36'06.990 | 1 |
| 2 | 8 | Gerhard Berger | Benetton-Renault | 72 | +4.190 | 3 |
| 3 | 14 | Olivier Panis | Prost-Mugen-Honda | 72 | +15.870 | 5 |
| 4 | 9 | Mika Hakkinen | McLaren-Mercedes | 72 | +33.033 | 4 |
| 5 | 5 | M.Schumacher | Ferrari | 72 | +33.731 | 2 |
| 6 | 7 | Jean Alesi | Benetton-Renault | 72 | +34.020 | 6 |
| 7 | 16 | Johnny Herbert | Sauber-Petronas | 72 | +50.912 | 13 |
| 8 | 12 | G.Fisichella | Jordan-Peugeot | 72 | +1'00.639 | 7 |
| 9 | 4 | H-H.Frentzen | Williams-Renault | 72 | +1'15.402 | 8 |
| 10 | 10 | David Coulthard | McLaren-Mercedes | 71 | +1 Lap | 12 |
| 11 | 17 | Nicola Larini | Sauber-Petronas | 71 | +1 Lap | 19 |
| 12 | 21 | Jarno Trulli | Minardi-Hart | 71 | +1 Lap | 17 |
| 13 | 19 | Mika Salo | Tyrrell-Ford | 71 | +1 Lap | 22 |
| 14 | 15 | Shinji Nakano | Prost-Mugen-Honda | 71 | +1 Lap | 15 |
| 15 | 18 | Jos Verstappen | Tyrrell-Ford | 70 | +2 Laps | 21 |
| 16 | 6 | Eddie Irvine | Ferrari | 70 | +2 Laps | 14 |
| 17 | 1 | Damon Hill | Arrows-Yamaha | 68 | Engine | 9 |
| 18 | 20 | Ukyo Katayama | Minardi-Hart | 67 | +5 Laps | 18 |
| Ret | 11 | Ralf Schumacher | Jordan-Peugeot | 52 | Electrical | 10 |
| Ret | 22 | R.Barrichello | Stewart-Ford | 16 | Suspension | 11 |
| Ret | 2 | Pedro Diniz | Arrows-Yamaha | 15 | Suspension | 16 |
| Ret | 23 | Jan Magnussen | Stewart-Ford | 0 | Accident | 20 |

Winning speed: 119.870mph Lap leaders: Villeneuve 1-45, 49-72; Berger 46-48
Pole position: Villeneuve, 1m 16.004s, 126.320mph
Fastest lap: Villeneuve, 1m 18.397s, 122.470mph
Race stopped after first lap accident and restarted for total original distance.

## ARGENTINE GRAND PRIX: BUENOS AIRES *13 April Round: 3 Race: 600 72 x 2.646 miles*

| POS. | NO. | DRIVER | CAR/ENGINE | LAPS | TIME/RETIRED | GRID |
|---|---|---|---|---|---|---|
| 1 | 3 | J.Villeneuve | Williams-Renault | 72 | 1:52'01.715 | 1 |
| 2 | 6 | Eddie Irvine | Ferrari | 72 | +0.979 | 7 |
| 3 | 11 | Ralf Schumacher | Jordan-Peugeot | 72 | +12.089 | 6 |
| 4 | 16 | Johnny Herbert | Sauber-Petronas | 72 | +29.919 | 8 |
| 5 | 9 | Mika Hakkinen | McLaren-Mercedes | 72 | +30.351 | 17 |
| 6 | 8 | Gerhard Berger | Benetton-Renault | 72 | +31.393 | 12 |
| 7 | 7 | Jean Alesi | Benetton-Renault | 72 | +46.359 | 11 |
| 8 | 19 | Mika Salo | Tyrrell-Ford | 71 | +1 Lap | 19 |
| 9 | 21 | Jarno Trulli | Minardi-Hart | 71 | +1 Lap | 18 |
| 10 | 23 | Jan Magnussen | Stewart-Ford | 66 | Engine | 15 |
| Ret | 17 | Nicola Larini | Sauber-Petronas | 63 | Spun off | 14 |
| Ret | 2 | Pedro Diniz | Arrows-Yamaha | 50 | Engine | 22 |
| Ret | 15 | Shinji Nakano | Prost-Mugen-Honda | 49 | Engine | 20 |
| Ret | 18 | Jos Verstappen | Tyrrell-Ford | 43 | Engine | 16 |
| Ret | 20 | Ukyo Katayama | Minardi-Hart | 37 | Spun off | 21 |
| Ret | 1 | Damon Hill | Arrows-Yamaha | 33 | Engine | 13 |
| Ret | 12 | G.Fisichella | Jordan-Peugeot | 24 | Collision | 9 |
| Ret | 22 | R.Barrichello | Stewart-Ford | 24 | Hydraulics | 5 |
| Ret | 14 | Olivier Panis | Prost-Mugen-Honda | 18 | Electrical | 3 |
| Ret | 4 | H-H.Frentzen | Williams-Renault | 5 | Clutch | 2 |
| Ret | 5 | M.Schumacher | Ferrari | 0 | Collision | 4 |
| Ret | 10 | David Coulthard | McLaren-Mercedes | 0 | Collision | 10 |

Winning speed: 102.000mph Lap leaders: Villeneuve 1-38, 45-72; Irivine 39-44
Pole position: Villeneuve, 1m 24.473s, 112.770mph
Fastest lap: Berger, 1m 27.981s, 108.290mph

## SAN MARINO GRAND PRIX: IMOLA *27 April Round: 4 Race: 601 62 x 3.063 miles*

| POS. | NO. | DRIVER | CAR/ENGINE | LAPS | TIME/RETIRED | GRID |
|---|---|---|---|---|---|---|
| 1 | 4 | H-H.Frentzen | Williams-Renault | 62 | 1:31'00.673 | 2 |
| 2 | 5 | M.Schumacher | Ferrari | 62 | +1.237 | 3 |
| 3 | 6 | Eddie Irvine | Ferrari | 62 | +1'18.343 | 9 |
| 4 | 12 | G.Fisichella | Jordan-Peugeot | 62 | +1'23.388 | 6 |
| 5 | 7 | Jean Alesi | Benetton-Renault | 61 | +1 Lap | 14 |
| 6 | 9 | Mika Hakkinen | McLaren-Mercedes | 61 | +1 Lap | 8 |
| 7 | 17 | Nicola Larini | Sauber-Petronas | 61 | +1 Lap | 12 |
| 8 | 14 | Olivier Panis | Prost-Mugen-Honda | 61 | +1 Lap | 4 |
| 9 | 19 | Mika Salo | Tyrrell-Ford | 60 | +2 Laps | 19 |
| 10 | 18 | Jos Verstappen | Tyrrell-Ford | 60 | +2 Laps | 21 |
| 11 | 20 | Ukyo Katayama | Minardi-Hart | 59 | +3 Laps | 22 |
| Ret | 2 | Pedro Diniz | Arrows-Yamaha | 53 | Gearbox | 17 |
| Ret | 3 | J.Villeneuve | Williams-Renault | 40 | Gearbox | 1 |
| Ret | 10 | David Coulthard | McLaren-Mercedes | 38 | Engine | 10 |
| Ret | 22 | R.Barrichello | Stewart-Ford | 32 | Engine | 13 |
| Ret | 16 | Johnny Herbert | Sauber-Petronas | 18 | Electrical | 7 |
| Ret | 11 | Ralf Schumacher | Jordan-Peugeot | 17 | Transmission | 5 |
| Ret | 15 | Shinji Nakano | Prost-Mugen-Honda | 11 | Collision | 18 |
| Ret | 1 | Damon Hill | Arrows-Yamaha | 11 | Collision | 15 |
| Ret | 8 | Gerhard Berger | Benetton-Renault | 4 | Spun off | 11 |
| Ret | 23 | Jan Magnussen | Stewart-Ford | 2 | Spun off | 16 |
| DNS | 21 | Jarno Trulli | Minardi-Hart | 0 | Gearbox | 20 |

Winning speed: 125.210mph Lap leaders: Villeneuve 1-25; Frentzen 26-43, 45-62; M Schumacher 44
Pole position: Villeneuve, 1m 23.303s, 132.370mph
Fastest lap: Frentzen, 1m 25.531s, 128.940mph

### MONACO GRAND PRIX: MONTE CARLO *11 May Round: 5 Race: 602 62 x 2.092 miles*

| POS. | NO. | DRIVER | CAR/ENGINE | LAPS | TIME/RETIRED | GRID |
|---|---|---|---|---|---|---|
| 1 | 5 | M.Schumacher | Ferrari | 62 | 2:00'05.654 | 2 |
| 2 | 22 | R.Barrichello | Stewart-Ford | 62 | +53.306 | 10 |
| 3 | 6 | Eddie Irvine | Ferrari | 62 | +1'22.108 | 15 |
| 4 | 14 | Olivier Panis | Prost-Mugen-Honda | 62 | +1'44.402 | 12 |
| 5 | 19 | Mika Salo | Tyrrell-Ford | 61 | +1 Lap | 14 |
| 6 | 12 | G.Fisichella | Jordan-Peugeot | 61 | +1 Lap | 4 |
| 7 | 23 | Jan Magnussen | Stewart-Ford | 61 | +1 Lap | 19 |
| 8 | 18 | Jos Verstappen | Tyrrell-Ford | 60 | +2 Laps | 22 |
| 9 | 8 | Gerhard Berger | Benetton-Renault | 60 | +2 Laps | 17 |
| 10 | 20 | Ukyo Katayama | Minardi-Hart | 60 | +2 Laps | 20 |
| Ret | 4 | H-H.Frentzen | Williams-Renault | 39 | Spun off | 1 |
| Ret | 15 | Shinji Nakano | Prost-Mugen-Honda | 36 | Spun off | 21 |
| Ret | 17 | Nicola Larini | Sauber-Petronas | 24 | Spun off | 11 |
| Ret | 7 | Jean Alesi | Benetton-Renault | 16 | Spun off | 9 |
| Ret | 3 | J.Villeneuve | Williams-Renault | 16 | Spun off | 3 |
| Ret | 11 | Ralf Schumacher | Jordan-Peugeot | 10 | Spun off | 6 |
| Ret | 16 | Johnny Herbert | Sauber-Petronas | 9 | Spun off | 7 |
| Ret | 21 | Jarno Trulli | Minardi-Hart | 7 | Spun off | 18 |
| Ret | 10 | David Coulthard | McLaren-Mercedes | 1 | Spun off | 5 |
| Ret | 9 | Mika Hakkinen | McLaren-Mercedes | 1 | Collision | 8 |
| Ret | 1 | Damon Hill | Arrows-Yamaha | 1 | Spun off | 13 |
| Ret | 2 | Pedro Diniz | Arrows-Yamaha | 0 | Spun off | 16 |

Winning speed: 64.790mph Lap leaders: M Schumacher 1-62
Pole position: Frentzen, 1m 18.216s, 96.290mph
Fastest lap: M Schumacher, 1m 53.315s, 66.450mph
Scheduled for 78 laps but stopped after two-hour mark.

### SPANISH GRAND PRIX: MONTMELO *25 May Round: 6 Race: 603 64 x 2.937 miles*

| POS. | NO. | DRIVER | CAR/ENGINE | LAPS | TIME/RETIRED | GRID |
|---|---|---|---|---|---|---|
| 1 | 3 | J.Villeneuve | Williams-Renault | 64 | 1:30'35.896 | 1 |
| 2 | 14 | Olivier Panis | Prost-Mugen-Honda | 64 | +5.804 | 12 |
| 3 | 7 | Jean Alesi | Benetton-Renault | 64 | +12.534 | 4 |
| 4 | 5 | M.Schumacher | Ferrari | 64 | +17.979 | 7 |
| 5 | 16 | Johnny Herbert | Sauber-Petronas | 64 | +27.986 | 10 |
| 6 | 10 | David Coulthard | McLaren-Mercedes | 64 | +29.744 | 3 |
| 7 | 9 | Mika Hakkinen | McLaren-Mercedes | 64 | +48.785 | 5 |
| 8 | 4 | H-H.Frentzen | Williams-Renault | 64 | +1'04.139 | 2 |
| 9 | 12 | G.Fisichella | Jordan-Peugeot | 64 | +1'04.767 | 8 |
| 10 | 8 | Gerhard Berger | Benetton-Renault | 64 | +1'05.670 | 6 |
| 11 | 18 | Jos Verstappen | Tyrrell-Ford | 63 | +1 Lap | 19 |
| 12 | 6 | Eddie Irvine | Ferrari | 63 | +1 Lap | 11 |
| 13 | 23 | Jan Magnussen | Stewart-Ford | 63 | +1 Lap | 22 |
| 14 | 17 | G.Morbidelli | Sauber-Petronas | 62 | +2 Laps | 13 |
| 15 | 21 | Jarno Trulli | Minardi-Hart | 62 | +2 Laps | 18 |
| Ret | 2 | Pedro Diniz | Arrows-Yamaha | 53 | Engine | 21 |
| Ret | 11 | Ralf Schumacher | Jordan-Peugeot | 50 | Engine | 9 |
| Ret | 22 | R.Barrichello | Stewart-Ford | 37 | Engine | 17 |
| Ret | 19 | Mika Salo | Tyrrell-Ford | 35 | Puncture | 14 |
| Ret | 15 | Shinji Nakano | Prost-Mugen-Honda | 34 | Gearbox | 16 |
| Ret | 1 | Damon Hill | Arrows-Yamaha | 17 | Engine | 15 |
| Ret | 20 | Ukyo Katayama | Minardi-Hart | 11 | Gearbox | 20 |

Winning speed: 124.780mph Lap leaders: Villeneuve 1-20, 22-45, 47-64; Alesi 21; M Schumacher 46
Pole position: Villeneuve, 1m 16.525s, 138.210mph
Fastest lap: Fisichella, 1m 22.242s, 128.920mph

### CANADIAN GRAND PRIX: MONTREAL *15 June Round: 7 Race: 604 54 x 2.747 miles*

| POS. | NO. | DRIVER | CAR/ENGINE | LAPS | TIME/RETIRED | GRID |
|---|---|---|---|---|---|---|
| 1 | 5 | M.Schumacher | Ferrari | 54 | 1:17'40.646 | 1 |
| 2 | 7 | Jean Alesi | Benetton/Renault | 54 | +2.565 | 8 |
| 3 | 12 | G.Fisichella | Jordan-Peugeot | 54 | +3.219 | 6 |
| 4 | 4 | H-H.Frentzen | Williams-Renault | 54 | +3.768 | 4 |
| 5 | 16 | Johnny Herbert | Sauber-Petronas | 54 | +4.716 | 13 |
| 6 | 15 | Shinji Nakano | Prost-Mugen-Honda | 54 | +36.701 | 19 |
| 7 | 10 | David Coulthard | McLaren-Mercedes | 54 | +37.753 | 5 |
| 8 | 2 | Pedro Diniz | Arrows-Yamaha | 53 | +1 Lap | 16 |
| 9 | 1 | Damon Hill | Arrows-Yamaha | 53 | +1 Lap | 15 |
| 10 | 17 | G.Morbidelli | Sauber-Petronas | 53 | +1 Lap | 18 |
| 11 | 14 | Olivier Panis | Prost-Mugen-Honda | 51 | Spun off | 10 |
| Ret | 19 | Mika Salo | Tyrrell-Ford | 46 | Engine | 17 |
| Ret | 18 | Jos Verstappen | Tyrrell-Ford | 42 | Gearbox | 14 |
| Ret | 8 | Alexander Wurz | Benetton-Renault | 35 | Transmission | 11 |
| Ret | 22 | R.Barrichello | Stewart-Ford | 33 | Gearbox | 3 |
| Ret | 21 | Jarno Trulli | Minardi-Hart | 32 | Engine | 20 |
| Ret | 11 | Ralf Schumacher | Jordan-Peugeot | 14 | Spun off | 7 |
| Ret | 20 | Ukyo Katayama | Minardi-Hart | 5 | Spun off | 22 |
| Ret | 3 | J.Villeneuve | Williams-Renault | 1 | Spun off | 2 |
| Ret | 9 | Mika Hakkinen | McLaren-Mercedes | 0 | Collision | 9 |
| Ret | 6 | Eddie Irvine | Ferrari | 0 | Collision | 12 |
| Ret | 23 | Jan Magnussen | Stewart-Ford | 0 | Spun off | 21 |

Winning speed: 114.580mph Lap leaders: M Schumacher 1-27, 40-43, 52-54; Coulthard 28-39, 44-51;
Pole position: M Schumacher, 1m 18.095s, 126.630mph Fastest lap: Coulthard, 1m 19.635s, 124.190mph. Race stopped before the scheduled 69 laps because of Panis's accident.

### FRENCH GRAND PRIX: MAGNY-COURS *29 June Round: 8 Race: 605 72 x 2.641 miles*

| POS. | NO. | DRIVER | CAR/ENGINE | LAPS | TIME/RETIRED | GRID |
|---|---|---|---|---|---|---|
| 1 | 5 | M.Schumacher | Ferrari | 72 | 1:38'50.492 | 1 |
| 2 | 4 | H-H.Frentzen | Williams/Renault | 72 | +23.537 | 2 |
| 3 | 6 | Eddie Irvine | Ferrari | 72 | +1'14.801 | 5 |
| 4 | 3 | J.Villeneuve | Williams-Renault | 72 | +1'21.784 | 4 |
| 5 | 7 | Jean Alesi | Benetton-Renault | 72 | +1'22.735 | 8 |
| 6 | 11 | Ralf Schumacher | Jordan-Peugeot | 72 | +1'29.871 | 3 |
| 7 | 10 | David Coulthard | McLaren-Mercedes | 71 | Collision | 9 |
| 8 | 16 | Johnny Herbert | Sauber-Petronas | 71 | +1 Lap | 14 |
| 9 | 12 | G.Fisichella | Jordan-Peugeot | 71 | +1 Lap | 11 |
| 10 | 14 | Jarno Trulli | Prost-Mugen-Honda | 70 | +2 Laps | 6 |
| 11 | 20 | Ukyo Katayama | Minardi-Hart | 70 | +2 Laps | 21 |
| 12 | 1 | Damon Hill | Arrows-Yamaha | 69 | +3 Laps | 17 |
| Ret | 19 | Mika Salo | Tyrrell-Ford | 61 | Electrical | 19 |
| Ret | 8 | Alexander Wurz | Benetton-Renault | 60 | Spun off | 7 |
| Ret | 2 | Pedro Diniz | Arrows-Yamaha | 58 | Spun off | 16 |
| Ret | 17 | Norberto Fontana | Sauber-Petronas | 40 | Spun off | 20 |
| Ret | 22 | R.Barrichello | Stewart-Ford | 36 | Engine | 13 |
| Ret | 23 | Jan Magnussen | Stewart-Ford | 33 | Brakes | 15 |
| Ret | 9 | Mika Hakkinen | McLaren-Mercedes | 18 | Engine | 10 |
| Ret | 18 | Jos Verstappen | Tyrrell-Ford | 15 | Spun off | 18 |
| Ret | 15 | Shinji Nakano | Prost-Mugen-Honda | 7 | Spun off | 12 |
| Ret | 21 | Tarso Marques | Minardi-Hart | 5 | Engine | 22 |

Winning speed: 115.350mph Lap leaders: M Schumacher 1-22, 24-46, 48-72; Frentzen 23, 47
Pole position: M Schumacher, 1m 14.4548s, 127.440mph
Fastest lap: M Schumacher, 1m 17.910s, 122.030mph

### BRITISH GRAND PRIX: SILVERSTONE *13 July Round: 9 Race: 606 59 x 3.194 miles*

| POS. | NO. | DRIVER | CAR/ENGINE | LAPS | TIME/RETIRED | GRID |
|---|---|---|---|---|---|---|
| 1 | 3 | J.Villeneuve | Williams-Renault | 59 | 1:28'01.665 | 1 |
| 2 | 7 | Jean Alesi | Benetton-Renault | 59 | +10.205 | 11 |
| 3 | 8 | Alexander Wurz | Benetton-Renault | 59 | +11.296 | 8 |
| 4 | 10 | David Coulthard | McLaren-Mercedes | 59 | +31.229 | 6 |
| 5 | 11 | Ralf Schumacher | Jordan-Peugeot | 59 | +31.880 | 5 |
| 6 | 1 | Damon Hill | Arrows-Yamaha | 59 | +1'13.552 | 12 |
| 7 | 12 | G.Fisichella | Jordan-Peugeot | 58 | +1 Lap | 10 |
| 8 | 14 | Jarno Trulli | Prost-Mugen-Honda | 58 | +1 Lap | 13 |
| 9 | 17 | Norberto Fontana | Sauber-Petronas | 58 | +1 Lap | 14 |
| 10 | 21 | Tarso Marques | Minardi-Hart | 58 | +1 Lap | 21 |
| 11 | 15 | Shinji Nakano | Prost-Mugen-Honda | 57 | Engine | 15 |
| Ret | 9 | Mika Hakkinen | McLaren-Mercedes | 52 | Engine | 3 |
| Ret | 23 | Jan Magnussen | Stewart-Ford | 50 | Engine | 16 |
| Ret | 18 | Jos Verstappen | Tyrrell-Ford | 45 | Engine | 20 |
| Ret | 6 | Eddie Irvine | Ferrari | 44 | Halfshaft | 7 |
| Ret | 19 | Mika Salo | Tyrrell-Ford | 44 | Engine | 18 |
| Ret | 16 | Johnny Herbert | Sauber-Petronas | 42 | Electrical | 9 |
| Ret | 5 | M.Schumacher | Ferrari | 38 | Wheel bearing | 4 |
| Ret | 22 | R.Barrichello | Stewart-Ford | 37 | Engine | 22 |
| Ret | 2 | Pedro Diniz | Arrows-Yamaha | 29 | Engine | 17 |
| Ret | 4 | H-H.Frentzen | Williams-Renault | 0 | Collision | 2 |
| Ret | 20 | Ukyo Katayama | Minardi-Hart | 0 | Spun off | 19 |

Winning speed: 128.440mph Lap leaders: Villeneuve 1-22, 38-44, 53-59; M Schumacher 23-37; Hakkinen 45-52
Pole position: Villeneuve, 1m 21.598s, 140.920mph
Fastest lap: M Schumacher, 1m 24.475s, 136.110mph

### GERMAN GRAND PRIX: HOCKENHEIM *27 July Round: 10 Race: 607 45 x 4.240 miles*

| POS. | NO. | DRIVER | CAR/ENGINE | LAPS | TIME/RETIRED | GRID |
|---|---|---|---|---|---|---|
| 1 | 8 | Gerhard Berger | Benetton-Renault | 45 | 1:20'59.046 | 1 |
| 2 | 5 | M.Schumacher | Ferrari | 45 | +17.527 | 4 |
| 3 | 9 | Mika Hakkinen | McLaren-Mercedes | 45 | +24.770 | 3 |
| 4 | 14 | Jarno Trulli | Prost-Mugen-Honda | 45 | +27.165 | 11 |
| 5 | 11 | Ralf Schumacher | Jordan-Peugeot | 45 | +29.995 | 7 |
| 6 | 7 | Jean Alesi | Benetton-Renault | 45 | +34.717 | 6 |
| 7 | 15 | Shinji Nakano | Prost-Mugen-Honda | 45 | +1'19.722 | 17 |
| 8 | 1 | Damon Hill | Arrows-Yamaha | 44 | +1 Lap | 13 |
| 9 | 17 | Norberto Fontana | Sauber-Petronas | 44 | +1 Lap | 18 |
| 10 | 18 | Jos Verstappen | Tyrrell-Ford | 44 | +1 Lap | 20 |
| 11 | 12 | G.Fisichella | Jordan-Peugeot | 40 | +5 Laps | 2 |
| Ret | 22 | R.Barrichello | Stewart-Ford | 33 | Engine | 12 |
| Ret | 19 | Mika Salo | Tyrrell-Ford | 33 | Clutch | 19 |
| Ret | 3 | J.Villeneuve | Williams-Renault | 33 | Spun off | 9 |
| Ret | 23 | Jan Magnussen | Stewart-Ford | 27 | Engine | 15 |
| Ret | 20 | Ukyo Katayama | Minardi-Hart | 23 | Out of fuel | 22 |
| Ret | 16 | Johnny Herbert | Sauber-Petronas | 8 | Accident | 14 |
| Ret | 2 | Pedro Diniz | Arrows-Yamaha | 8 | Accident | 16 |
| Ret | 10 | David Coulthard | McLaren-Mercedes | 1 | Transmission | 8 |
| Ret | 4 | H-H.Frentzen | Williams-Renault | 1 | Collision | 5 |
| Ret | 6 | Eddie Irvine | Ferrari | 1 | Collision | 10 |
| Ret | 21 | Tarso Marques | Minardi-Hart | 0 | Gearbox | 21 |

Winning speed: 141.350mph Lap leaders: Berger 1-17, 25-45; Fisichella 18-24
Pole position: Berger, 1m 41.873s, 149.830mph
Fastest lap: Berger, 1m 45.747s, 144.330mph

### HUNGARIAN GRAND PRIX: HUNGARORING *10 August Round: 11 Race: 608 77 x 2.465 miles*

| POS. | NO. | DRIVER | CAR/NGINE | LAPS | TIME/RETIRED | GRID |
|---|---|---|---|---|---|---|
| 1 | 3 | J.Villeneuve | Williams-Renault | 77 | 1:45'47.149 | 2 |
| 2 | 1 | Damon Hill | Arrows-Yamaha | 77 | +9.079' | 3 |
| 3 | 16 | Johnny Herbert | Sauber-Petronas | 77 | +20.445 | 10 |
| 4 | 5 | M.Schumacher | Ferrari | 77 | +30.501 | 1 |
| 5 | 11 | Ralf Schumacher | Jordan-Peugeot | 77 | +30.715 | 14 |
| 6 | 15 | Shinji Nakano | Prost-Mugen-Honda | 77 | +41.512 | 16 |
| 7 | 14 | Jarno Trulli | Prost-Mugen-Honda | 77 | +1'15.552 | 12 |
| 8 | 8 | Gerhard Berger | Benetton-Renault | 77 | +1'16.409 | 7 |
| 9 | 6 | Eddie Irvine | Ferrari | 76 | +1 Lap | 5 |
| 10 | 20 | Ukyo Katayama | Minardi-Hart | 76 | +1 Lap | 20 |
| 11 | 7 | Jean Alesi | Benetton-Renault | 76 | +1 Lap | 9 |
| 12 | 21 | Tarso Marques | Minardi-Hart | 75 | +2 Laps | 22 |
| 13 | 19 | Mika Salo | Tyrrell-Ford | 75 | +2 Laps | 21 |
| Ret | 10 | David Coulthard | McLaren-Mercedes | 65 | Electrical | 8 |
| Ret | 18 | Jos Verstappen | Tyrrell-Ford | 61 | Gearbox | 18 |
| Ret | 2 | Pedro Diniz | Arrows-Yamaha | 53 | Electrical | 19 |
| Ret | 12 | G.Fisichella | Jordan-Peugeot | 42 | Spun off | 13 |
| Ret | 4 | H-H.Frentzen | Williams-Renault | 29 | Fuel leak | 6 |
| Ret | 22 | R.Barrichello | Stewart-Ford | 29 | Engine | 11 |
| Ret | 9 | Mika Hakkinen | McLaren-Mercedes | 12 | Hydraulics | 4 |
| Ret | 17 | G.Morbidelli | Sauber-Petronas | 7 | Engine | 15 |
| Ret | 23 | Jan Magnussen | Stewart-Ford | 5 | Accident | 17 |

Winning speed: 107.680mph Lap leaders: M Schumacher 1-10; Hill 11-25, 30-76; Frentzen 26-29; Villeneuve 77
Pole position: M Schumacher, 1m 14.672s, 118.890mph
Fastest lap: Frentzen, 1m 18.372s, 113.260mph

### BELGIAN GRAND PRIX: SPA-FRANCORCHAMPS *24 August Round: 12 Race: 609 44 x 4.330 miles*

| POS. | NO. | DRIVER | CAR/ENGINE | LAPS | TIME/RETIRED | GRID |
|---|---|---|---|---|---|---|
| 1 | 5 | M.Schumacher | Ferrari | 44 | 1:33'46.717 | 3 |
| 2 | 12 | G.Fisichella | Jordan-Peugeot | 44 | +26.753 | 4 |
| 3 | 4 | H-H.Frentzen | Williams-Renault | 44 | +32.147 | 7 |
| 4 | 16 | Johnny Herbert | Sauber-Petronas | 44 | +39.025 | 11 |
| 5 | 3 | J.Villeneuve | Williams-Renault | 44 | +42.103 | 1 |
| 6 | 8 | Gerhard Berger | Benetton-Renault | 44 | +1'03.741 | 15 |
| 7 | 2 | Pedro Diniz | Arrows-Yamaha | 44 | +1'25.931 | 8 |
| 8 | 7 | Jean Alesi | Benetton-Renault | 44 | +1'42.008 | 2 |
| 9 | 17 | G.Morbidelli | Sauber-Petronas | 44 | +1'42.582 | 13 |
| 10 | 6 | Eddie Irvine | Ferrari | 43 | +1 Lap | 17 |
| 11 | 19 | Mika Salo | Tyrrell-Ford | 43 | +1 Lap | 19 |
| 12 | 23 | Jan Magnussen | Stewart-Ford | 43 | +1 Lap | 18 |
| 13 | 1 | Damon Hill | Arrows-Yamaha | 42 | +2 Laps | 9 |
| 14 | 20 | Ukyo Katayama | Minardi-Hart | 42 | +2 Laps | 20 |
| 15 | 14 | Jarno Trulli | Prost-Mugen-Honda | 42 | +2 Laps | 14 |
| DNS | 9 | Mika Hakkinen | McLaren-Mercedes | 44 | Disqualified | 5 |
| Ret | 18 | Jos Verstappen | Tyrrell-Ford | 25 | Spun off | 21 |
| Ret | 11 | Ralf Schumacher | Jordan-Peugeot | 21 | Spun off | 6 |
| Ret | 10 | David Coulthard | McLaren-Mercedes | 19 | Spun off | 10 |
| Ret | 21 | Tarso Marques | Minardi-Hart | 18 | Spun off | 22 |
| Ret | 22 | R.Barrichello | Stewart-Ford | 8 | Steering | 12 |
| Ret | 15 | Shinji Nakano | Prost-Mugen-Honda | 5 | Electrical | 16 |

Winning speed: 121.880mph Lap leaders: Villeneuve 1-4; M Schumacher 5-44
Pole position: Villeneuve, 1m 49.450s, 142.390mph
Fastest lap: Villeneuve, 1m 52.692s, 138.310mph
Häkkinen disqualified from third place after racing under appeal against a fuel irregularity.

### ITALIAN GRAND PRIX: MONZA *7 September Round: 13 Race: 610 53 x 3.585 miles*

| POS. | NO. | DRIVER | CAR/ENGINE | LAPS | TIME/RETIRED | GRID |
|---|---|---|---|---|---|---|
| 1 | 10 | David Coulthard | McLaren-Mercedes | 53 | 1:17'04.609 | 6 |
| 2 | 7 | Jean Alesi | Benetton-Renault | 53 | +1.937 | 1 |
| 3 | 4 | H-H.Frentzen | Williams-Renault | 53 | +4.343 | 2 |
| 4 | 12 | G.Fisichella | Jordan-Peugeot | 53 | +5.871 | 3 |
| 5 | 3 | J.Villeneuve | Williams-Renault | 53 | +6.416 | 4 |
| 6 | 5 | M.Schumacher | Ferrari | 53 | +11.481 | 9 |
| 7 | 8 | Gerhard Berger | Benetton-Renault | 53 | +12.471 | 7 |
| 8 | 6 | Eddie Irvine | Ferrari | 53 | +17.639 | 10 |
| 9 | 9 | Mika Hakkinen | McLaren-Mercedes | 53 | +49.373 | 5 |
| 10 | 14 | Jarno Trulli | Prost-Mugen-Honda | 53 | +1'02.706 | 16 |
| 11 | 15 | Shinji Nakano | Prost-Mugen-Honda | 53 | +1'03.327 | 15 |
| 12 | 17 | G.Morbidelli | Sauber-Petronas | 52 | +1 Lap | 18 |
| 13 | 22 | R.Barrichello | Stewart-Ford | 52 | +1 Lap | 11 |
| 14 | 21 | Tarso Marques | Minardi-Hart | 50 | +3 Laps | 22 |
| Ret | 1 | Damon Hill | Arrows-Yamaha | 46 | Engine | 14 |
| Ret | 11 | Ralf Schumacher | Jordan-Peugeot | 39 | Collision | 8 |
| Ret | 16 | Johnny Herbert | Sauber-Petronas | 38 | Collision | 12 |
| Ret | 19 | Mika Salo | Tyrrell-Ford | 33 | Engine | 19 |
| Ret | 23 | Jan Magnussen | Stewart-Ford | 31 | Transmission | 13 |
| Ret | 18 | Jos Verstappen | Tyrrell-Ford | 12 | Gearbox | 20 |
| Ret | 20 | Ukyo Katayama | Minardi-Hart | 8 | Spun off | 21 |
| Ret | 2 | Pedro Diniz | Arrows-Yamaha | 4 | Suspension | 17 |

Winning speed: 147.910mph Lap leaders: Alesi 1-31; Hakkinen 32-33; M Schumacher 34; Coulthard 35-53
Pole position: Alesi, 1m 22.990s, 155.510mph
Fastest lap: Hakkinen, 1m 24.808s, 152.190mph

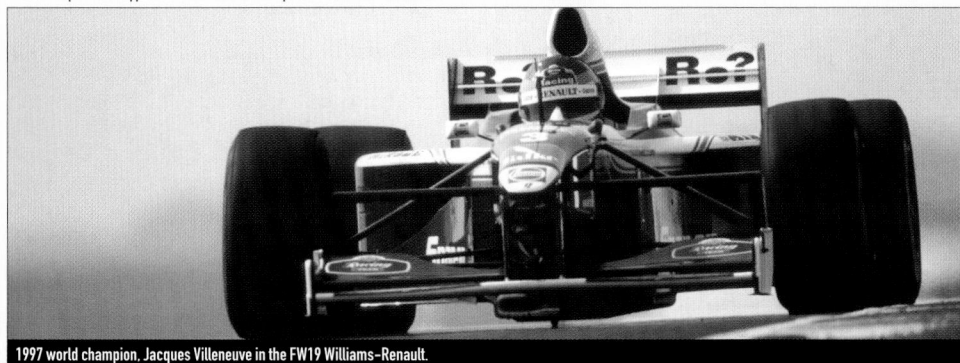

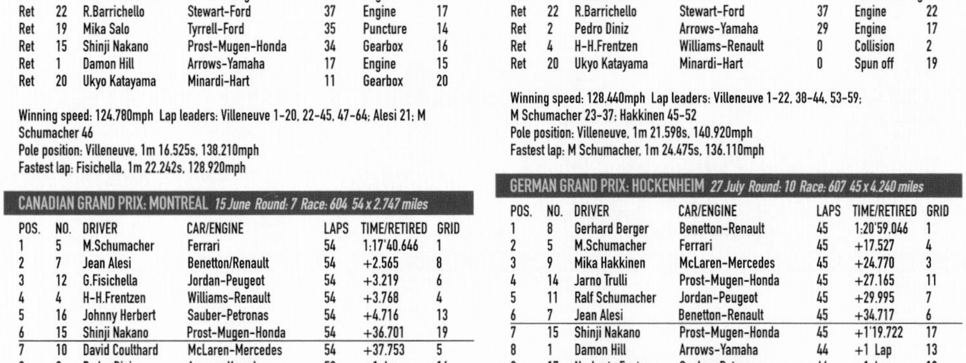
1997 world champion, Jacques Villeneuve in the FW19 Williams-Renault.

## AUSTRIAN GRAND PRIX: A1-RING *21 September Round: 14 Race: 611 71 x 2.686 miles*

| POS. | NO. | DRIVER | CAR/ENGINE | LAPS | TIME/RETIRED | GRID |
|---|---|---|---|---|---|---|
| 1 | 3 | J.Villeneuve | Williams-Renault | 71 | 1:27'35.999 | 1 |
| 2 | 10 | David Coulthard | McLaren-Mercedes | 71 | +2.909 | 10 |
| 3 | 4 | H.-H.Frentzen | Williams-Renault | 71 | +3.962 | 4 |
| 4 | 12 | G.Fisichella | Jordan-Peugeot | 71 | +12.127 | 14 |
| 5 | 11 | Ralf Schumacher | Jordan-Peugeot | 71 | +31.859 | 11 |
| 6 | 5 | M.Schumacher | Ferrari | 71 | +33.410 | 9 |
| 7 | 1 | Damon Hill | Arrows-Yamaha | 71 | +37.207 | 7 |
| 8 | 16 | Johnny Herbert | Sauber-Petronas | 71 | +49.057 | 12 |
| 9 | 17 | G.Morbidelli | Sauber-Petronas | 71 | +1'06.455 | 13 |
| 10 | 8 | Gerhard Berger | Benetton-Renault | 70 | +1 Lap | 18 |
| 11 | 20 | Ukyo Katayama | Minardi-Hart | 69 | +2 Laps | 19 |
| 12 | 18 | Jos Verstappen | Tyrrell-Ford | 69 | +2 Laps | 20 |
| 13 | 2 | Pedro Diniz | Arrows-Yamaha | 67 | +4 Laps | 17 |
| 14 | 22 | R.Barrichello | Stewart-Ford | 64 | Spun off | 5 |
| Ret | 14 | Jarno Trulli | Prost-Mugen-Honda | 58 | Engine | 13 |
| Ret | 23 | Jan Magnussen | Stewart-Ford | 58 | Engine | 6 |
| Ret | 15 | Shinji Nakano | Prost-Mugen-Honda | 57 | Engine | 16 |
| Ret | 19 | Mika Salo | Tyrrell-Ford | 48 | Gearbox | 21 |
| Ret | 6 | Eddie Irvine | Ferrari | 38 | Collision | 8 |
| Ret | 7 | Jean Alesi | Benetton-Renault | 37 | Collision | 15 |
| Ret | 9 | Mika Hakkinen | McLaren-Mercedes | 1 | Engine | 2 |

Winning speed: 130.630mph
Lap leaders: Trulli 1-37; Villeneuve 38-40, 44-71; M Schumacher 41-42; Coulthard 43
Pole position: Villeneuve, 1m 10.304s, 137.540mph
Fastest lap: Villeneuve, 1m 11.814s, 134.660mph

## LUXEMBOURG GRAND PRIX: NURBURGRING *28 September Round: 15 Race: 612 67 x 2.831 miles*

| POS. | NO. | DRIVER | CAR/ENGINE | LAPS | TIME/RETIRED | GRID |
|---|---|---|---|---|---|---|
| 1 | 3 | J.Villeneuve | Williams-Renault | 67 | 1:31'27.843 | 2 |
| 2 | 7 | Jean Alesi | Benetton-Renault | 67 | +11.770 | 10 |
| 3 | 4 | H.-H.Frentzen | Williams-Renault | 67 | +13.480 | 3 |
| 4 | 8 | Gerhard Berger | Benetton-Renault | 67 | +16.416 | 7 |
| 5 | 2 | Pedro Diniz | Arrows-Yamaha | 67 | +43.147 | 15 |
| 6 | 14 | Olivier Panis | Prost-Mugen-Honda | 67 | +43.750 | 11 |
| 7 | 16 | Johnny Herbert | Sauber-Petronas | 67 | +44.354 | 16 |
| 8 | 1 | Damon Hill | Arrows-Yamaha | 67 | +44.777 | 13 |
| 9 | 17 | G.Morbidelli | Sauber-Petronas | 66 | +1 Lap | 19 |
| 10 | 19 | Mika Salo | Tyrrell-Ford | 66 | +1 Lap | 20 |
| Ret | 18 | Jos Verstappen | Tyrrell-Ford | 50 | Spun off | 21 |
| Ret | 9 | Mika Hakkinen | McLaren-Mercedes | 43 | Engine | 1 |
| Ret | 22 | R.Barrichello | Stewart-Ford | 43 | Gearbox | 9 |
| Ret | 10 | David Coulthard | McLaren-Mercedes | 42 | Engine | 6 |
| Ret | 23 | Jan Magnussen | Stewart-Ford | 40 | Halfshaft | 12 |
| Ret | 6 | Eddie Irvine | Ferrari | 22 | Engine | 14 |
| Ret | 15 | Shinji Nakano | Prost-Mugen-Honda | 16 | Engine | 17 |
| Ret | 5 | M.Schumacher | Ferrari | 2 | Suspension | 5 |
| Ret | 21 | Tarso Marques | Minardi-Hart | 1 | Engine | 18 |
| Ret | 20 | Ukyo Katayama | Minardi-Hart | 1 | Collision | 22 |
| Ret | 12 | G.Fisichella | Jordan-Peugeot | 0 | Collision | 4 |
| Ret | 11 | Ralf Schumacher | Jordan-Peugeot | 0 | Collision | 8 |

Winning speed: 124.420mph
Lap leaders: Hakkinen 1-28, 32-43; Coulthard 2-30; Villeneuve 44-67
Pole position: Hakkinen, 1m 16.602s, 133.050mph
Fastest lap: Frentzen, 1m 18.802s, 129.320mph

## JAPANESE GRAND PRIX: SUZUKA *12 October Round: 16 Race: 613 53 x 3.644 miles*

| POS. | NO. | DRIVER | CAR/ENGINE | LAPS | TIME/RETIRED | GRID |
|---|---|---|---|---|---|---|
| 1 | 5 | M.Schumacher | Ferrari | 53 | 1:29'48.446 | 2 |
| 2 | 4 | H.-H.Frentzen | Williams-Renault | 53 | +1.378 | 6 |
| 3 | 6 | Eddie Irvine | Ferrari | 53 | +26.384 | 3 |
| 4 | 9 | Mika Hakkinen | McLaren-Mercedes | 53 | +27.129 | 4 |
| 5 | 7 | Jean Alesi | Benetton-Renault | 53 | +40.403 | 7 |
| 6 | 16 | Johnny Herbert | Sauber-Petronas | 53 | +41.630 | 8 |
| 7 | 12 | G.Fisichella | Jordan-Peugeot | 53 | +56.825 | 9 |
| 8 | 8 | Gerhard Berger | Benetton-Renault | 53 | +1'00.429 | 5 |
| 9 | 11 | Ralf Schumacher | Jordan-Peugeot | 53 | +1'22.036 | 13 |
| 10 | 10 | David Coulthard | McLaren-Mercedes | 52 | Engine | 11 |
| 11 | 1 | Damon Hill | Arrows-Yamaha | 52 | +1 Lap | 17 |
| 12 | 2 | Pedro Diniz | Arrows-Yamaha | 52 | +1 Lap | 16 |
| 13 | 18 | Jos Verstappen | Tyrrell-Ford | 52 | +1 Lap | 21 |
| DSQ | 3 | J.Villeneuve | Williams-Renault | 53 | Disqualified | 1 |
| Ret | 21 | Tarso Marques | Minardi-Hart | 46 | Gearbox | 20 |
| Ret | 19 | Mika Salo | Tyrrell-Ford | 46 | Engine | 22 |
| Ret | 14 | Olivier Panis | Prost-Mugen-Honda | 36 | Engine | 10 |
| Ret | 15 | Shinji Nakano | Prost-Mugen-Honda | 22 | Wheel bearing | 10 |
| Ret | 20 | Ukyo Katayama | Minardi-Hart | 8 | Engine | 19 |
| Ret | 22 | R.Barrichello | Stewart-Ford | 6 | Spun off | 12 |
| Ret | 23 | Jan Magnussen | Stewart-Ford | 3 | Spun off | 14 |
| DNS | 17 | G. Morbidelli | Sauber-Petronas | 0 | Accident | |

Winning speed: 128.940mph
Lap leaders: Villeneuve 1-2, 17-20; Irvine 3-16, 22-24; Frentzen 21, 34-37;
M Schumacher 25-33, 38-53
Pole position: Villeneuve, 1m 36.071s, 136.440mph
Fastest lap: Frentzen, 1m 38.942s, 132.580mph
Villeneuve finished fifth but raced under appeal and was disqualified for
ignoring a yellow flag in practice.

## EUROPEAN GRAND PRIX: JEREZ *26 October Round: 17 Race: 614 69 x 2.751 miles*

| POS. | NO. | DRIVER | CAR/ENGINE | LAPS | TIME/RETIRED | GRID |
|---|---|---|---|---|---|---|
| 1 | 9 | Mika Hakkinen | McLaren-Mercedes | 69 | 1:38'57.771 | 5 |
| 2 | 10 | David Coulthard | McLaren-Mercedes | 69 | +1.654 | 6 |
| 3 | 3 | J.Villeneuve | Williams-Renault | 69 | +1.803 | 1 |
| 4 | 8 | Gerhard Berger | Benetton-Renault | 69 | +1.919 | 8 |
| 5 | 6 | Eddie Irvine | Ferrari | 69 | +3.789 | 7 |
| 6 | 4 | H.-H.Frentzen | Williams-Renault | 69 | +4.537 | 3 |
| 7 | 14 | Olivier Panis | Prost-Mugen-Honda | 69 | +1'07.145 | 9 |
| 8 | 16 | Johnny Herbert | Sauber-Petronas | 69 | +1'12.961 | 14 |
| 9 | 23 | Jan Magnussen | Stewart-Ford | 69 | +1'17.487 | 11 |
| 10 | 15 | Shinji Nakano | Prost-Mugen-Honda | 69 | +1'18.215 | 15 |
| 11 | 12 | G.Fisichella | Jordan-Peugeot | 69 | +1 Lap | 17 |
| 12 | 19 | Mika Salo | Tyrrell-Ford | 68 | +1 Lap | 21 |
| 13 | 7 | Jean Alesi | Benetton-Renault | 68 | +1 Lap | 10 |
| 14 | 17 | Norberto Fontana | Sauber-Petronas | 68 | +1 Lap | 18 |
| 15 | 21 | Tarso Marques | Minardi-Hart | 68 | +1 Lap | 20 |
| 16 | 18 | Jos Verstappen | Tyrrell-Ford | 68 | +1 Lap | 22 |
| 17 | 20 | Ukyo Katayama | Minardi-Hart | 68 | +1 Lap | 19 |
| Ret | 5 | M.Schumacher | Ferrari | 47 | Collision | 2 |
| Ret | 1 | Damon Hill | Arrows-Yamaha | 47 | Gearbox | 4 |
| Ret | 11 | Ralf Schumacher | Jordan-Peugeot | 44 | Water leak | 16 |
| Ret | 22 | R.Barrichello | Stewart-Ford | 30 | Gearbox | 12 |
| Ret | 2 | Pedro Diniz | Arrows-Yamaha | 11 | Spun off | 13 |

Winning speed: 115.100mph
Lap leaders: M Schumacher 1-21, 28-42, 45-47;
Villeneuve 22, 43-44, 48-68; Frentzen 23-27; Hakkinen 69
Pole position: Villeneuve, 1m 21.072s, 122.160mph
Fastest lap: Frentzen, 1m 23.135s, 119.150mph
Villeneuve, M Schumacher and Frentzen each set the same time in qualifying;
starting order was decided by who recorded the time first.

1998 and 1999 world champion, Mika Häkkinen.

# 1998

DRIVERS' CHAMPION: MIKA HÄKKINEN
CONSTRUCTORS' CHAMPION: McLAREN MERCEDES

### DRIVERS' CHAMPIONSHIP

| POS. | DRIVER | NATIONALITY | CAR | POINTS |
|---|---|---|---|---|
| 1 | Mika Hakkinen | Finland | McLaren-Mercedes | 100 |
| 2 | Michael Schumacher | Germany | Ferrari | 86 |
| 3 | David Coulthard | GB | McLaren-Mercedes | 56 |
| 4 | Eddie Irvine | GB | Ferrari | 47 |
| 5 | Damon Hill | GB | Jordan-Mugen-Honda | 20 |
| 6 | acques Villeneuve | Canada | Williams-Mecachrome | 19 |
| 7 | Alexander Wurz | Austria | Benetton-Playlife | 17 |
| 8 | Heinz-Harald Frentzen | Germany | Williams-Mecachrome | 17 |
| 9 | Giancarlo Fisichella | Italy | Benetton-Playlife | 16 |
| 10 | Ralf Schumacher | Germany | Jordan-Mugen-Honda | 14 |
| 11 | Jean Alesi | France | Sauber-Petronas | 9 |
| 12 | Rubens Barrichello | Brazil | Stewart-Ford | 4 |
| 13 | Mika Salo | Finland | Arrows | 3 |
| = | Pedro Diniz | Brazil | Arrows | 3 |
| 15 | Johnny Herbert | GB | Sauber-Petronas | 1 |
| = | Jan Magnussen | Denmark | Stewart-Ford | 1 |
| = | Jarno Trulli | Italy | Prost-Peugeot | 1 |
| | Oliver Panis | France | Prost-Peugeot | |
| | Shinji Nakano | Japan | Minardi-Ford | |
| | Esteban Tuero | Argentina | Minardi-Ford | |
| | Toranosuke Takagi | Japan | Tyrell-Ford | |
| | Ricardo Rosset | Brazil | Tyrrell-Ford | |
| | Jos Verstappen | Netherlands | Stewart-Ford | |

Points for top six finishers (10, 6, 4, 3, 2, 1). Half points awarded for races
stopped before half distance.

### CONSTRUCTORS' CHAMPIONSHIP

| POS. | CONSTRUCTOR | POINTS |
|---|---|---|
| 1 | McLaren-Mercedes | 156 |
| 2 | Ferrari | 133 |
| 3 | Williams-Mecachrome | 38 |
| 4 | Jordan-Mugen-Honda | 34 |
| 5 | Benetton-Playlife | 33 |
| 6 | Sauber-Petronas | 10 |
| 7 | Arrows | 6 |
| 8 | Stewart-Ford | 5 |
| 9 | Prost-Peugeot | 1 |

Points for top six finishers (10, 6, 4, 3, 2, 1). Half points awarded for races
stopped before half distance.

## AUSTRALIAN GRAND PRIX: MELBOURNE *8 March Round: 1 Race: 615 58 x 3.295 miles*

| POS. | NO. | DRIVER | CAR/ENGINE | LAPS | TIME/RETIRED | GRID |
|---|---|---|---|---|---|---|
| 1 | 8 | Mika Hakkinen | McLaren-Mercedes | 58 | 1:31'45.996 | 1 |
| 2 | 7 | David Coulthard | McLaren-Mercedes | 58 | +0.702 | 2 |
| 3 | 2 | H.-H.Frentzen | Williams-Mecachrome | 57 | +1 Lap | 6 |
| 4 | 4 | Eddie Irvine | Ferrari | 57 | +1 Lap | 8 |
| 5 | 1 | J.Villeneuve | Williams-Mecachrome | 57 | +1 Lap | 4 |
| 6 | 15 | Johnny Herbert | Sauber-Petronas | 57 | +1 Lap | 5 |
| 7 | 6 | Alexander Wurz | Benetton-Playlife | 57 | +1 Lap | 11 |
| 8 | 9 | Damon Hill | Jordan-Mugen-Honda | 57 | +1 Lap | 10 |
| 9 | 11 | Olivier Panis | Prost-Peugeot | 57 | +1 Lap | 12 |
| Ret | 5 | G.Fisichella | Benetton-Playlife | 43 | Broken wing | 7 |
| Ret | 14 | Jean Alesi | Sauber-Petronas | 41 | Engine | 9 |
| Ret | 12 | Jarno Trulli | Prost-Peugeot | 26 | Gearbox | 11 |
| Ret | 20 | Ricardo Rosset | Tyrrell-Ford | 25 | Gearbox | 19 |
| Ret | 17 | Mika Salo | Arrows | 23 | Gearbox | 16 |
| Ret | 23 | Esteban Tuero | Minardi-Ford | 22 | Engine | 17 |
| Ret | 22 | Shinji Nakano | Minardi-Ford | 8 | Halfshaft | 22 |
| Ret | 3 | M.Schumacher | Ferrari | 5 | Engine | 3 |
| Ret | 16 | Pedro Diniz | Arrows | 2 | Gearbox | 20 |
| Ret | 10 | Ralf Schumacher | Jordan-Mugen-Honda | 1 | Collision | 9 |
| Ret | 19 | Jan Magnussen | Stewart-Ford | 1 | Collision | 18 |
| Ret | 21 | T.Takagi | Tyrrell-Ford | 1 | Spun off | 13 |
| Ret | 18 | R.Barrichello | Stewart-Ford | 0 | Gearbox | 14 |

Winning speed: 124.960mph  Lap leaders: Hakkinen 1-23, 25-35, 56-58; Coulthard 24, 36-55
Pole position: Hakkinen, 1m 30.010s, 131.790mph
Fastest lap: Hakkinen, 1m 31.649s, 129.430mph

**BRAZILIAN GRAND PRIX: INTERLAGOS** *29 March Round: 2 Race: 616 72 x 2.667 miles*

| POS. | NO. | DRIVER | CAR/ENGINE | LAPS | TIME/RETIRED | GRID |
|---|---|---|---|---|---|---|
| 1 | 8 | Mika Hakkinen | McLaren-Mercedes | 72 | 1:37'11.74 | 17 |
| 2 | 7 | David Coulthard | McLaren-Mercedes | 72 | +1.102 | 2 |
| 3 | 3 | M.Schumacher | Ferrari | 72 | +1'00.550 | 4 |
| 4 | 6 | Alexander Wurz | Benetton-Playlife | 72 | +1'07.453 | 5 |
| 5 | 2 | H-H.Frentzen | Williams-Mecachrome | 71 | +1 Lap | 3 |
| 6 | 5 | G.Fisichella | Benetton-Playlife | 71 | +1 Lap | 7 |
| 7 | 1 | J.Villeneuve | Williams-Mecachrome | 71 | +1 Lap | 10 |
| 8 | 4 | Eddie Irvine | Ferrari | 71 | +1 Lap | 6 |
| 9 | 14 | Jean Alesi | Sauber-Petronas | 71 | +1 Lap | 15 |
| 10 | 19 | Jan Magnussen | Stewart-Ford | 70 | +2 Laps | 16 |
| 11 | 15 | Johnny Herbert | Sauber-Petronas | 67 | Physical | 14 |
| DSQ | 9 | Damon Hill | Jordan-Mugen-Honda | 70 | Disqualified | 11 |
| Ret | 11 | Olivier Panis | Prost-Peugeot | 63 | Engine | 9 |
| Ret | 18 | R.Barrichello | Stewart-Ford | 56 | Gearbox | 13 |
| Ret | 20 | Ricardo Rosset | Tyrrell-Ford | 52 | Gearbox | 21 |
| Ret | 23 | Esteban Tuero | Minardi-Ford | 44 | Throttle | 19 |
| Ret | 16 | Pedro Diniz | Arrows | 26 | Gearbox | 22 |
| Ret | 21 | T.Takagi | Tyrrell-Ford | 19 | Engine | 17 |
| Ret | 17 | Mika Salo | Arrows | 18 | Engine | 20 |
| Ret | 12 | Jarno Trulli | Prost-Peugeot | 17 | Fuel pump | 12 |
| Ret | 22 | Shinji Nakano | Minardi-Ford | 3 | Spun off | 18 |
| Ret | 10 | Ralf Schumacher | Jordan-Mugen-Honda | 0 | Spun off | 8 |

Winning speed: 118.530mph Lap leaders: Hakkinen 1-72
Pole position: Hakkinen, 1m 17.092s, 142.540mph
Fastest lap: Hakkinen, 1m 19.337s, 121.010mph

**ARGENTINE GRAND PRIX: BUENOS AIRES** *12 April Round: 3 Race: 617 72 x 2.646 miles*

| POS. | NO. | DRIVER | CAR/ENGINE | LAPS | TIME/RETIRED | GRID |
|---|---|---|---|---|---|---|
| 1 | 3 | M.Schumacher | Ferrari | 72 | 1:48'36.17 | 25 |
| 2 | 8 | Mika Hakkinen | McLaren-Mercedes | 72 | +22.898 | 3 |
| 3 | 4 | Eddie Irvine | Ferrari | 72 | +57.745 | 4 |
| 4 | 6 | Alexander Wurz | Benetton-Playlife | 72 | +1'08.134 | 8 |
| 5 | 14 | Jean Alesi | Sauber-Petronas | 72 | +1'18.286 | 11 |
| 6 | 7 | David Coulthard | McLaren-Mercedes | 72 | +1'19.751 | 1 |
| 7 | 5 | G.Fisichella | Benetton-Playlife | 72 | +1'28.437 | 10 |
| 8 | 9 | Damon Hill | Jordan-Mugen-Honda | 71 | +1 Lap | 9 |
| 9 | 2 | H-H.Frentzen | Williams-Mecachrome | 71 | +1 Lap | 6 |
| 10 | 18 | R.Barrichello | Stewart-Ford | 70 | +2 Laps | 14 |
| 11 | 12 | Jarno Trulli | Prost-Peugeot | 70 | +2 Laps | 16 |
| 12 | 21 | T.Takagi | Tyrrell-Ford | 70 | +2 Laps | 13 |
| 13 | 22 | Shinji Nakano | Minardi-Ford | 69 | +3 Laps | 19 |
| 14 | 20 | Ricardo Rosset | Tyrrell-Ford | 68 | +4 Laps | 21 |
| 15 | 11 | Olivier Panis | Prost-Peugeot | 65 | Engine | 15 |
| Ret | 23 | Esteban Tuero | Minardi-Ford | 63 | Spun off | 20 |
| Ret | 1 | J.Villeneuve | Williams-Mecachrome | 52 | Collision | 7 |
| Ret | 15 | Johnny Herbert | Sauber-Petronas | 46 | Collision | 12 |
| Ret | 10 | Ralf Schumacher | Jordan-Mugen-Honda | 22 | Suspension | 5 |
| Ret | 17 | Mika Salo | Arrows | 18 | Gearbox | 17 |
| Ret | 19 | Jan Magnussen | Stewart-Ford | 17 | Transmission | 22 |
| Ret | 16 | Pedro Diniz | Arrows | 13 | Gearbox | 18 |

Winning speed: 105.200mph
Lap leaders: Coulthard 1-4; M Schumacher 5-28, 43-72; Hakkinen 29-42
Pole position: Coulthard, 1m 25.852s, 110.910mph
Fastest lap: Wurz, 1m 28.179s, 108.040mph

**SAN MARINO GRAND PRIX: IMOLA** *26 April Round: 4 Race: 618 62 x 3.063 miles*

| POS. | NO. | DRIVER | CAR/ENGINE | LAPS | TIME/RETIRED | GRID |
|---|---|---|---|---|---|---|
| 1 | 7 | David Coulthard | McLaren-Mercedes | 62 | 1:34'24.59 | 1 |
| 2 | 3 | M.Schumacher | Ferrari | 62 | +4.554 | 3 |
| 3 | 4 | Eddie Irvine | Ferrari | 62 | +51.775 | 4 |
| 4 | 1 | J.Villeneuve | Williams-Mecachrome | 62 | +54.590 | 6 |
| 5 | 2 | H-H.Frentzen | Williams-Mecachrome | 62 | +1'17.476 | 8 |
| 6 | 14 | Jean Alesi | Sauber-Petronas | 61 | +1 Lap | 12 |
| 7 | 10 | Ralf Schumacher | Jordan-Mugen-Honda | 60 | +2 Laps | 9 |
| 8 | 23 | Esteban Tuero | Minardi-Ford | 60 | +2 Laps | 19 |
| 9 | 17 | Mika Salo | Arrows | 60 | +2 Laps | 14 |
| 10 | 9 | Damon Hill | Jordan-Mugen-Honda | 57 | Hydraulics | 7 |
| 11 | 11 | Olivier Panis | Prost-Peugeot | 56 | +6 Laps | 13 |
| Ret | 20 | Ricardo Rosset | Tyrrell-Ford | 48 | Engine | 22 |
| Ret | 21 | T.Takagi | Tyrrell-Ford | 40 | Engine | 15 |
| Ret | 12 | Jarno Trulli | Prost-Peugeot | 34 | Throttle | 16 |
| Ret | 22 | Shinji Nakano | Minardi-Ford | 27 | Engine | 21 |
| Ret | 16 | Pedro Diniz | Arrows | 18 | Engine | 18 |
| Ret | 8 | Mika Hakkinen | McLaren-Mercedes | 17 | Gearbox | 2 |
| Ret | 5 | G.Fisichella | Benetton-Playlife | 17 | Spun off | 10 |
| Ret | 6 | Alexander Wurz | Benetton-Playlife | 17 | Engine | 5 |
| Ret | 15 | Johnny Herbert | Sauber-Petronas | 12 | Puncture | 11 |
| Ret | 19 | Jan Magnussen | Stewart-Ford | 8 | Transmission | 20 |
| Ret | 18 | R.Barrichello | Stewart-Ford | 0 | Spun off | 17 |

Winning speed: 120.620mph Lap leaders: Coulthard 1-62
Pole position: Coulthard, 1m 25.973s, 128.180mph
Fastest lap: M Schumacher, 1m 29.345s, 123.430mph

**SPANISH GRAND PRIX: CATALUNYA** *10 May Round: 5 Race: 619 65 x 2.937 miles*

| POS. | NO. | DRIVER | CAR/ENGINE | LAPS | TIME/RETIRED | GRID |
|---|---|---|---|---|---|---|
| 1 | 8 | Mika Hakkinen | McLaren-Mercedes | 65 | 1:33'37.621 | 1 |
| 2 | 7 | David Coulthard | McLaren-Mercedes | 65 | +9.439 | 2 |
| 3 | 3 | M.Schumacher | Ferrari | 65 | +47.095 | 3 |
| 4 | 6 | Alexander Wurz | Benetton-Playlife | 65 | +1'02.538 | 5 |
| 5 | 18 | R.Barrichello | Stewart-Ford | 64 | +1 Lap | 9 |
| 6 | 1 | J.Villeneuve | Williams-Mecachrome | 64 | +1 Lap | 10 |
| 7 | 15 | Johnny Herbert | Sauber-Petronas | 64 | +1 Lap | 7 |
| 8 | 2 | H-H.Frentzen | Williams-Mecachrome | 63 | +2 Laps | 13 |
| 9 | 12 | Jarno Trulli | Prost-Peugeot | 63 | +2 Laps | 16 |
| 10 | 14 | Jean Alesi | Sauber-Petronas | 63 | +2 Laps | 14 |
| 11 | 10 | Ralf Schumacher | Jordan-Mugen-Honda | 63 | +2 Laps | 11 |
| 12 | 19 | Jan Magnussen | Stewart-Ford | 63 | +2 Laps | 18 |
| 13 | 21 | T.Takagi | Tyrrell-Ford | 63 | +2 Laps | 21 |
| 14 | 22 | Shinji Nakano | Minardi-Ford | 63 | +2 Laps | 20 |
| 15 | 23 | Esteban Tuero | Minardi-Ford | 63 | +2 Laps | 19 |
| 16 | 11 | Olivier Panis | Prost-Peugeot | 60 | +5 Laps | 12 |
| Ret | 9 | Damon Hill | Jordan-Mugen-Honda | 46 | Engine | 8 |
| Ret | 4 | Eddie Irvine | Ferrari | 28 | Collision | 6 |
| Ret | 5 | G.Fisichella | Benetton-Playlife | 28 | Collision | 4 |
| Ret | 17 | Mika Salo | Arrows | 21 | Engine | 17 |
| Ret | 16 | Pedro Diniz | Arrows | 20 | Engine | 15 |
| DNQ | 20 | Ricardo Rosset | Tyrrell-Ford | | | |

Winning speed: 122.330mph Lap leaders: Hakkinen 1-26, 28-45, 47-65; Coulthard 27, 46
Pole position: Hakkinen, 1m 20.262s, 131.730mph Fastest lap: Hakkinen, 1m 24.275s, 125.500mph

**MONACO GRAND PRIX: MONTE CARLO** *24 May Round: 6 Race: 620 78 x 2.092 miles*

| POS. | NO. | DRIVER | CAR/ENGINE | LAPS | TIME/RETIRED | GRID |
|---|---|---|---|---|---|---|
| 1 | 8 | Mika Hakkinen | McLaren-Mercedes | 78 | 1:51'23.595 | 1 |
| 2 | 5 | G.Fisichella | Benetton-Playlife | 78 | +11.475 | 3 |
| 3 | 4 | Eddie Irvine | Ferrari | 78 | +41.378 | 7 |
| 4 | 17 | Mika Salo | Arrows | 78 | +1'00.363 | 8 |
| 5 | 1 | J.Villeneuve | Williams-Mecachrome | 77 | +1 Lap | 13 |
| 6 | 16 | Pedro Diniz | Arrows | 77 | +1 Lap | 12 |
| 7 | 15 | Johnny Herbert | Sauber-Petronas | 77 | +1 Lap | 9 |
| 8 | 9 | Damon Hill | Jordan-Mugen-Honda | 76 | +2 Laps | 15 |
| 9 | 22 | Shinji Nakano | Minardi-Ford | 76 | +2 Laps | 19 |
| 10 | 3 | M.Schumacher | Ferrari | 76 | +2 Laps | 4 |
| 11 | 21 | T.Takagi | Tyrrell-Ford | 76 | +2 Laps | 20 |
| 12 | 14 | Jean Alesi | Sauber-Petronas | 72 | Gearbox | 11 |
| Ret | 12 | Jarno Trulli | Prost-Peugeot | 56 | Gearbox | 10 |
| Ret | 11 | Olivier Panis | Prost-Peugeot | 49 | Wheel | 18 |
| Ret | 10 | Ralf Schumacher | Jordan-Mugen-Honda | 44 | Suspension | 16 |
| Ret | 6 | Alexander Wurz | Benetton-Playlife | 42 | Spun off | 6 |
| Ret | 19 | Jan Magnussen | Stewart-Ford | 30 | Suspension | 17 |
| Ret | 7 | David Coulthard | McLaren-Mercedes | 17 | Engine | 2 |
| Ret | 18 | R.Barrichello | Stewart-Ford | 11 | Suspension | 14 |
| Ret | 2 | H-H.Frentzen | Williams-Mecachrome | 9 | Collision | 5 |
| Ret | 23 | Esteban Tuero | Minardi-Ford | 0 | Spun off | 21 |
| DNQ | 20 | Ricardo Rosset | Tyrrell-Ford | | | |

Winning speed: 87.900mph Lap leaders: Hakkinen 1-78
Pole position: Hakkinen, 1m 19.798s, 94.380mph Fastest lap: Hakkinen, 1m 22.948s, 90.800mph

**CANADIAN GRAND PRIX: MONTREAL** *7 June Round: 7 Race: 621 69 x 2.747 miles*

| POS. | NO. | DRIVER | CAR/ENGINE | LAPS | TIME/RETIRED | GRID |
|---|---|---|---|---|---|---|
| 1 | 3 | M.Schumacher | Ferrari | 69 | 1:40'57.355 | 3 |
| 2 | 5 | G.Fisichella | Benetton-Playlife | 69 | +16.662 | 4 |
| 3 | 4 | Eddie Irvine | Ferrari | 69 | +1'00.059 | 8 |
| 4 | 6 | Alexander Wurz | Benetton-Playlife | 69 | +1'03.232 | 11 |
| 5 | 18 | R.Barrichello | Stewart-Ford | 69 | +1'21.513 | 13 |
| 6 | 19 | Jan Magnussen | Stewart-Ford | 68 | +1 Lap | 20 |
| 7 | 22 | Shinji Nakano | Minardi-Ford | 68 | +1 Lap | 18 |
| 8 | 20 | Ricardo Rosset | Tyrrell-Ford | 68 | +1 Lap | 22 |
| 9 | 16 | Pedro Diniz | Arrows | 68 | +1 Lap | 19 |
| 10 | 1 | J.Villeneuve | Williams-Mecachrome | 63 | +6 Laps | 6 |
| Ret | 23 | Esteban Tuero | Minardi-Ford | 53 | Electrical | 21 |
| Ret | 9 | Damon Hill | Jordan-Mugen-Honda | 42 | Electrical | 10 |
| Ret | 11 | Olivier Panis | Prost-Peugeot | 39 | Spun off | 15 |
| Ret | 2 | H-H.Frentzen | Williams-Mecachrome | 20 | Spun off | 7 |
| Ret | 7 | David Coulthard | McLaren-Mercedes | 18 | Throttle | 1 |
| Ret | 15 | Johnny Herbert | Sauber-Petronas | 18 | Spun off | 12 |
| Ret | 17 | Mika Salo | Arrows | 18 | Spun off | 17 |
| Ret | 8 | Mika Hakkinen | McLaren-Mercedes | 0 | Gearbox | 2 |
| Ret | 10 | Ralf Schumacher | Jordan-Mugen-Honda | 0 | Gearbox | 5 |
| Ret | 14 | Jean Alesi | Sauber-Petronas | 0 | Collision | 9 |
| Ret | 12 | Jarno Trulli | Prost-Peugeot | 0 | Collision | 14 |
| Ret | 21 | T.Takagi | Tyrrell-Ford | 0 | Transmission | 16 |

Winning speed: 112.650mph
Lap leaders: Coulthard 1-18; M Schumacher 19, 44-69; Fisichella 20-43
Pole position: Coulthard, 1m 18.213s, 126.440mph
Fastest lap: M Schumacher, 1m 19.379s, 124.590mph
Race stopped after first lap accident and restarted for total original distance.

**FRENCH GRAND PRIX: MAGNY-COURS** *28 June Round: 8 Race: 622 71 x 2.641 miles*

| POS. | NO. | DRIVER | CAR/ENGINE | LAPS | TIME/RETIRED | GRID |
|---|---|---|---|---|---|---|
| 1 | 3 | M.Schumacher | Ferrari | 71 | 1:34'45.026 | 2 |
| 2 | 4 | Eddie Irvine | Ferrari | 71 | +19.575 | 4 |
| 3 | 8 | Mika Hakkinen | McLaren-Mercedes | 71 | +19.747 | 1 |
| 4 | 1 | J.Villeneuve | Williams-Mecachrome | 71 | +1'06.965 | 5 |
| 5 | 6 | Alexander Wurz | Benetton-Playlife | 70 | +1 Lap | 10 |
| 6 | 7 | David Coulthard | McLaren-Mercedes | 70 | +1 Lap | 3 |
| 7 | 14 | Jean Alesi | Sauber-Petronas | 70 | +1 Lap | 11 |
| 8 | 15 | Johnny Herbert | Sauber-Petronas | 70 | +1 Lap | 13 |
| 9 | 5 | G.Fisichella | Benetton-Playlife | 70 | +1 Lap | 9 |
| 10 | 18 | R.Barrichello | Stewart-Ford | 69 | +2 Laps | 14 |
| 11 | 11 | Olivier Panis | Prost-Peugeot | 69 | +2 Laps | 16 |
| 12 | 19 | Jos Verstappen | Stewart-Ford | 69 | +2 Laps | 15 |
| 13 | 17 | Mika Salo | Arrows | 69 | +2 Laps | 19 |
| 14 | 16 | Pedro Diniz | Arrows | 69 | +2 Laps | 17 |
| 15 | 2 | H-H.Frentzen | Williams-Mecachrome | 68 | Suspension | 8 |
| 16 | 10 | Ralf Schumacher | Jordan-Mugen-Honda | 68 | +3 Laps | 6 |
| 17 | 22 | Shinji Nakano | Minardi-Ford | 65 | Engine | 21 |
| Ret | 21 | T.Takagi | Tyrrell-Ford | 60 | Engine | 20 |
| Ret | 12 | Jarno Trulli | Prost-Peugeot | 55 | Spun off | 12 |
| Ret | 23 | Esteban Tuero | Minardi-Ford | 41 | Gearbox | 22 |
| Ret | 9 | Damon Hill | Jordan-Mugen-Honda | 19 | Hydraulics | 7 |
| Ret | 20 | Ricardo Rosset | Tyrrell-Ford | 16 | Hydraulics | 18 |

Winning speed: 118.660mph Lap leaders: M Schumacher 1-22, 24-71; Irvine 23
Pole position: Hakkinen, 1m 14.929s, 126.790mph Fastest lap: Coulthard, 1m 17.523s, 122.630mph

**BRITISH GRAND PRIX: SILVERSTONE** *12 July Round: 9 Race: 623 60 x 3.194 miles*

| POS. | NO. | DRIVER | CAR/ENGINE | LAPS | TIME/RETIRED | GRID |
|---|---|---|---|---|---|---|
| 1 | 3 | M.Schumacher | Ferrari | 60 | 1:47'02.450 | 2 |
| 2 | 8 | Mika Hakkinen | McLaren-Mercedes | 60 | +22.465 | 1 |
| 3 | 4 | Eddie Irvine | Ferrari | 60 | +29.199 | 5 |
| 4 | 6 | Alexander Wurz | Benetton-Playlife | 59 | +1 Lap | 11 |
| 5 | 5 | G.Fisichella | Benetton-Playlife | 59 | +1 Lap | 10 |
| 6 | 10 | Ralf Schumacher | Jordan-Mugen-Honda | 59 | +1 Lap | 21 |
| 7 | 1 | J.Villeneuve | Williams-Mecachrome | 59 | +1 Lap | 3 |
| 8 | 22 | Shinji Nakano | Minardi-Ford | 58 | +2 Laps | 19 |
| 9 | 21 | T.Takagi | Tyrrell-Ford | 56 | +4 Laps | 17 |
| Ret | 14 | Jean Alesi | Sauber-Petronas | 53 | Electrical | 8 |
| Ret | 16 | Pedro Diniz | Arrows | 45 | Spun off | 12 |
| Ret | 11 | Olivier Panis | Prost-Peugeot | 40 | Spun off | 22 |
| Ret | 18 | R.Barrichello | Stewart-Ford | 39 | Spun off | 16 |
| Ret | 19 | Jos Verstappen | Stewart-Ford | 38 | Engine | 15 |
| Ret | 7 | David Coulthard | McLaren-Mercedes | 37 | Spun off | 4 |
| Ret | 12 | Jarno Trulli | Prost-Peugeot | 37 | Spun off | 14 |
| Ret | 20 | Ricardo Rosset | Tyrrell-Ford | 29 | Spun off | 20 |
| Ret | 23 | Esteban Tuero | Minardi-Ford | 29 | Spun off | 18 |
| Ret | 15 | Johnny Herbert | Sauber-Petronas | 27 | Spun off | 9 |
| Ret | 17 | Mika Salo | Arrows | 27 | Throttle | 13 |
| Ret | 2 | H-H.Frentzen | Williams-Mecachrome | 15 | Spun off | 6 |
| Ret | 9 | Damon Hill | Jordan-Mugen-Honda | 13 | Spun off | 7 |

Winning speed: 107.380mph Lap leaders: Hakkinen 1-50; Schumacher 51-60
Pole position: Hakkinen, 1m 23.271s, 138.040mph Fastest lap: M Schumacher, 1m 24.475s, 136.110mph
M Schumacher took victory in the pitlane.

**AUSTRIAN GRAND PRIX: A1-RING** *26 July Round: 10 Race: 624 71 x 2.684 miles*

| POS. | NO. | DRIVER | CAR/ENGINE | LAPS | TIME/RETIRED | GRID |
|---|---|---|---|---|---|---|
| 1 | 8 | Mika Hakkinen | McLaren-Mercedes | 71 | 1:30'44.086 | 3 |
| 2 | 7 | David Coulthard | McLaren-Mercedes | 71 | +5.289 | 14 |
| 3 | 3 | M.Schumacher | Ferrari | 71 | +39.092 | 4 |
| 4 | 4 | Eddie Irvine | Ferrari | 71 | +43.976 | 8 |
| 5 | 10 | Ralf Schumacher | Jordan-Mugen-Honda | 71 | +50.654 | 9 |
| 6 | 1 | J.Villeneuve | Williams-Mecachrome | 71 | +53.202 | 11 |
| 7 | 9 | Damon Hill | Jordan-Mugen-Honda | 71 | +1'13.624 | 15 |
| 8 | 15 | Johnny Herbert | Sauber-Petronas | 70 | +1 Lap | 18 |
| 9 | 6 | Alexander Wurz | Benetton-Playlife | 70 | +1 Lap | 17 |
| 10 | 12 | Jarno Trulli | Prost-Peugeot | 70 | +1 Lap | 16 |
| 11 | 22 | Shinji Nakano | Minardi-Ford | 70 | +1 Lap | 21 |
| 12 | 20 | Ricardo Rosset | Tyrrell-Ford | 69 | +2 Laps | 22 |
| Ret | 19 | Jos Verstappen | Stewart-Ford | 51 | Engine | 12 |
| Ret | 23 | Esteban Tuero | Minardi-Ford | 30 | Spun off | 19 |
| Ret | 5 | G.Fisichella | Benetton-Playlife | 21 | Collision | 1 |
| Ret | 14 | Jean Alesi | Sauber-Petronas | 21 | Collision | 2 |
| Ret | 2 | H-H.Frentzen | Williams-Mecachrome | 16 | Engine | 7 |
| Ret | 18 | R.Barrichello | Stewart-Ford | 8 | Brakes | 5 |
| Ret | 16 | Pedro Diniz | Arrows | 3 | Collision | 13 |
| Ret | 17 | Mika Salo | Arrows | 1 | Collision | 6 |
| Ret | 11 | Olivier Panis | Prost-Peugeot | 0 | Clutch | 10 |
| Ret | 21 | T.Takagi | Tyrrell-Ford | 0 | Collision | 20 |

Winning speed: 126.000mph Lap leaders: Hakkinen 1-34, 37-71; Coulthard 35-36
Pole position: Fisichella, 1m 29.598s, 107.840mph
Fastest lap: Coulthard, 1m 12.878s, 132.570mph

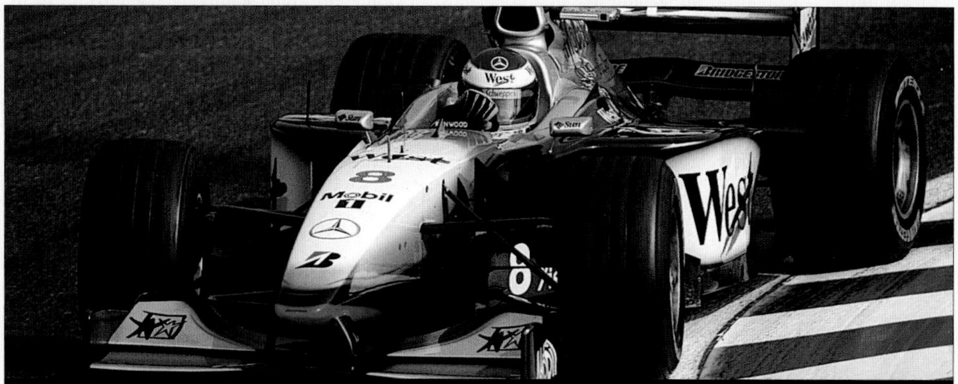

1998 and 1999 world champion, Mika Hakkinen in the McLaren Mercedes.

**GERMAN GRAND PRIX: HOCKENHEIM** *2 August Round: 11 Race: 625 45 x 4.240 miles*

| POS. | NO. | DRIVER | CAR/ENGINE | LAPS | TIME/RETIRED | GRID |
|---|---|---|---|---|---|---|
| 1 | 8 | Mika Hakkinen | McLaren-Mercedes | 45 | 1:20'47.984 | 1 |
| 2 | 7 | David Coulthard | McLaren-Mercedes | 45 | +0.426 | 2 |
| 3 | 1 | J.Villeneuve | Williams-Mecachrome | 45 | +2.577 | 3 |
| 4 | 9 | Damon Hill | Jordan-Mugen-Honda | 45 | +7.185 | 5 |
| 5 | 3 | M.Schumacher | Ferrari | 45 | +12.613 | 9 |
| 6 | 10 | Ralf Schumacher | Jordan-Mugen-Honda | 45 | +29.738 | 4 |
| 7 | 5 | G.Fisichella | Benetton-Playlife | 45 | +31.026 | 8 |
| 8 | 4 | Eddie Irvine | Ferrari | 45 | +31.649 | 6 |
| 9 | 2 | H-H.Frentzen | Williams-Mecachrome | 45 | +32.784 | 10 |
| 10 | 14 | Jean Alesi | Sauber-Petronas | 45 | +48.371 | 11 |
| 11 | 6 | Alexander Wurz | Benetton-Playlife | 45 | +57.994 | 7 |
| 12 | 12 | Jarno Trulli | Prost-Peugeot | 44 | +1 Lap | 14 |
| 13 | 21 | T.Takagi | Tyrrell-Ford | 44 | +1 Lap | 15 |
| 14 | 17 | Mika Salo | Arrows | 44 | +1 Lap | 17 |
| 15 | 11 | Olivier Panis | Prost-Peugeot | 44 | +1 Lap | 16 |
| 16 | 23 | Esteban Tuero | Minardi/Ford | 43 | +2 Laps | 21 |
| Ret | 15 | Johnny Herbert | Sauber-Petronas | 37 | Gearbox | 12 |
| Ret | 22 | Shinji Nakano | Minardi-Ford | 36 | Gearbox | 20 |
| Ret | 18 | R.Barrichello | Stewart-Ford | 27 | Gearbox | 13 |
| Ret | 19 | Jos Verstappen | Stewart-Ford | 24 | Gearbox | 19 |
| Ret | 16 | Pedro Diniz | Arrows | 2 | Throttle | 18 |
| DNQ | 20 | Ricardo Rosset | Tyrrell-Ford | | | |

Winning speed: 141.670mph Lap leaders: Hakkinen 1-25, 28-45; Coulthard 26-27
Pole position: Hakkinen, 1m 41.838s, 149.890mph
Fastest lap: Coulthard, 1m 46.116s, 143.830mph

**HUNGARIAN GRAND PRIX: HUNGARORING** *16 August Round: 12 Race: 626 77 x 2.468 miles*

| POS. | NO. | DRIVER | CAR/ENGINE | LAPS | TIME/RETIRED | GRID |
|---|---|---|---|---|---|---|
| 1 | 3 | M.Schumacher | Ferrari | 77 | 1:45'25.550 | 3 |
| 2 | 7 | David Coulthard | McLaren-Mercedes | 77 | +9.433 | 2 |
| 3 | 1 | J.Villeneuve | Williams-Mecachrome | 77 | +44.444 | 6 |
| 4 | 9 | Damon Hill | Jordan-Mugen-Honda | 77 | +55.076 | 4 |
| 5 | 2 | H-H.Frentzen | Williams-Mecachrome | 77 | +56.510 | 7 |
| 6 | 8 | Mika Hakkinen | McLaren-Mercedes | 76 | +1 Lap | 1 |
| 7 | 14 | Jean Alesi | Sauber-Petronas | 76 | +1 Lap | 11 |
| 8 | 5 | G.Fisichella | Benetton-Playlife | 76 | +1 Lap | 8 |
| 9 | 10 | Ralf Schumacher | Jordan-Mugen-Honda | 76 | +1 Lap | 10 |
| 10 | 15 | Johnny Herbert | Sauber-Petronas | 76 | +1 Lap | 15 |
| 11 | 16 | Pedro Diniz | Arrows | 74 | +3 Laps | 12 |
| 12 | 11 | Olivier Panis | Prost-Peugeot | 74 | +3 Laps | 20 |
| 13 | 19 | Jos Verstappen | Stewart-Ford | 74 | +3 Laps | 17 |
| 14 | 21 | T.Takagi | Tyrrell-Ford | 74 | +3 Laps | 18 |
| 15 | 22 | Shinji Nakano | Minardi-Ford | 74 | +3 Laps | 19 |
| 16 | 6 | Alexander Wurz | Benetton-Playlife | 69 | Gearbox | 9 |
| Ret | 18 | R.Barrichello | Stewart-Ford | 54 | Gearbox | 14 |
| Ret | 12 | Jarno Trulli | Prost-Peugeot | 28 | Engine | 16 |
| Ret | 17 | Mika Salo | Arrows | 18 | Gearbox | 13 |
| Ret | 4 | Eddie Irvine | Ferrari | 13 | Gearbox | 5 |
| Ret | 23 | Esteban Tuero | Minardi-Ford | 13 | Engine | 21 |
| DNQ | 20 | Ricardo Rosset | Tyrrell-Ford | | | |

Winning speed: 108.160mph Lap leaders: Hakkinen 1-46; M Schumacher 47-77
Pole position: Hakkinen, 1m 16.973s, 115.430mph
Fastest lap: M Schumacher, 1m 19.286s, 112.060mph

**BELGIAN GRAND PRIX: SPA-FRANCORCHAMPS** *30 August Round: 13 Race: 627 44 x 4.330 miles*

| POS. | NO. | DRIVER | CAR/ENGINE | LAPS | TIME/RETIRED | GRID |
|---|---|---|---|---|---|---|
| 1 | 9 | Damon Hill | Jordan-Mugen-Honda | 44 | 1:43'47.407 | 3 |
| 2 | 10 | Ralf Schumacher | Jordan-Mugen-Honda | 44 | +0.932 | 8 |
| 3 | 14 | Jean Alesi | Sauber-Petronas | 44 | +7.240 | 10 |
| 4 | 2 | H-H.Frentzen | Williams-Mecachrome | 44 | +32.243 | 9 |
| 5 | 16 | Pedro Diniz | Arrows | 44 | +51.682 | 16 |
| 6 | 12 | Jarno Trulli | Prost-Peugeot | 42 | +2 Laps | 13 |
| 7 | 7 | David Coulthard | McLaren-Mercedes | 39 | +5 Laps | 2 |
| 8 | 22 | Shinji Nakano | Minardi-Ford | 39 | +5 Laps | 21 |
| Ret | 5 | G.Fisichella | Benetton-Playlife | 26 | Collision | 7 |
| Ret | 3 | M.Schumacher | Ferrari | 25 | Collision | 4 |
| Ret | 4 | Eddie Irvine | Ferrari | 25 | Spun off | 5 |
| Ret | 23 | Esteban Tuero | Minardi-Ford | 17 | Gearbox | 22 |
| Ret | 1 | J.Villeneuve | Williams-Mecachrome | 16 | Spun off | 6 |
| Ret | 21 | T.Takagi | Tyrrell-Ford | 10 | Spun off | 19 |
| Ret | 19 | Jos Verstappen | Stewart-Ford | 8 | Engine | 17 |
| Ret | 8 | Mika Hakkinen | McLaren-Mercedes | 0 | Collision | 1 |
| Ret | 6 | Alexander Wurz | Benetton-Playlife | 0 | Collision | 11 |
| Ret | 15 | Johnny Herbert | Sauber-Petronas | 0 | Collision | 12 |
| DNS | 18 | R.Barrichello | Stewart-Ford | 0 | Collision | 15 |
| DNS | 11 | Olivier Panis | Prost-Peugeot | 0 | Collision | 14 |
| DNS | 17 | Mika Salo | Arrows | 0 | Collision | 18 |
| DNS | 20 | Ricardo Rosset | Tyrrell-Ford | 0 | Collision | 20 |

Winning speed: 110.130mph Lap leaders: Hill 1-7, 26-44; M Schumacher 8-25
Pole position: Hakkinen, 1m 48.682s, 143.390mph
Fastest lap: M Schumacher, 2m 03.766s, 125.940mph
Race stopped after the first lap because of a pile up. New start for the original total distance.

**ITALIAN GRAND PRIX: MONZA** *13 September Round: 14 Race: 628 53 x 3.585 miles*

| POS. | NO. | DRIVER | CAR/ENGINE | LAPS | TIME/RETIRED | GRID |
|---|---|---|---|---|---|---|
| 1 | 3 | M.Schumacher | Ferrari | 53 | 1:17'09.672 | 1 |
| 2 | 4 | Eddie Irvine | Ferrari | 53 | +37.977 | 5 |
| 3 | 10 | Ralf Schumacher | Jordan-Mugen-Honda | 53 | +41.152 | 6 |
| 4 | 8 | Mika Hakkinen | McLaren-Mercedes | 53 | +55.671 | 3 |
| 5 | 14 | Jean Alesi | Sauber-Petronas | 53 | +1'01.872 | 8 |
| 6 | 9 | Damon Hill | Jordan-Mugen-Honda | 53 | +1'06.688 | 14 |
| 7 | 2 | H-H.Frentzen | Williams-Mecachrome | 52 | +1 Lap | 12 |
| 8 | 5 | G.Fisichella | Benetton-Playlife | 52 | +1 Lap | 11 |
| 9 | 21 | T.Takagi | Tyrrell-Ford | 52 | +1 Lap | 19 |
| 10 | 18 | R.Barrichello | Stewart-Ford | 52 | +1 Lap | 13 |
| 11 | 23 | Esteban Tuero | Minardi-Ford | 51 | +2 Laps | 22 |
| 12 | 20 | Ricardo Rosset | Tyrrell-Ford | 51 | +2 Laps | 18 |
| 13 | 12 | Jarno Trulli | Prost-Peugeot | 50 | +3 Laps | 10 |
| Ret | 19 | Jos Verstappen | Stewart-Ford | 39 | Gearbox | 17 |
| Ret | 1 | J.Villeneuve | Williams-Mecachrome | 37 | Spun off | 2 |
| Ret | 17 | Mika Salo | Arrows | 32 | Throttle | 16 |
| Ret | 6 | Alexander Wurz | Benetton-Playlife | 24 | Gearbox | 7 |
| Ret | 7 | David Coulthard | McLaren-Mercedes | 16 | Engine | 4 |
| Ret | 11 | Olivier Panis | Prost-Peugeot | 15 | Vibrations | 9 |
| Ret | 22 | Shinji Nakano | Minardi-Ford | 13 | Engine | 21 |
| Ret | 15 | Johnny Herbert | Sauber-Petronas | 12 | Spun off | 15 |
| Ret | 16 | Pedro Diniz | Arrows | 10 | Spun off | 20 |

Winning speed: 147.630mph
Lap leaders: Hakkinen 1-7, 32-34; Coulthard 8-16, M Schumacher 17-31, 35-53
Pole position: M Schumacher, 1m 25.289s, 151.320mph
Fastest lap: Hakkinen, 1m 25.139s, 151.560mph

**LUXEMBOURG GRAND PRIX: NURBURGRING** *27 September Round: 15 Race: 628 67 x 2.831 miles*

| POS. | NO. | DRIVER | CAR/ENGINE | LAPS | TIME/RETIRED | GRID |
|---|---|---|---|---|---|---|
| 1 | 8 | Mika Hakkinen | McLaren-Mercedes | 67 | 1:32'14.789 | 3 |
| 2 | 3 | M.Schumacher | Ferrari | 67 | +2.211 | 1 |
| 3 | 7 | David Coulthard | McLaren-Mercedes | 67 | +34.163 | 5 |
| 4 | 4 | Eddie Irvine | Ferrari | 67 | +58.182 | 2 |
| 5 | 2 | H-H.Frentzen | Williams-Mecachrome | 67 | +1'00.247 | 7 |
| 6 | 5 | G.Fisichella | Benetton-Playlife | 67 | +1'01.359 | 4 |
| 7 | 6 | Alexander Wurz | Benetton-Playlife | 67 | +1'04.789 | 8 |
| 8 | 1 | J.Villeneuve | Williams-Mecachrome | 66 | +1 Lap | 9 |
| 9 | 9 | Damon Hill | Jordan-Mugen-Honda | 66 | +1 Lap | 10 |
| 10 | 14 | Jean Alesi | Sauber-Petronas | 66 | +1 Lap | 11 |
| 11 | 18 | R.Barrichello | Stewart-Ford | 65 | +2 Laps | 12 |
| 12 | 11 | Olivier Panis | Prost-Peugeot | 65 | +2 Laps | 15 |
| 13 | 19 | Jos Verstappen | Stewart-Ford | 65 | +2 Laps | 18 |
| 14 | 17 | Mika Salo | Arrows | 65 | +2 Laps | 16 |
| 15 | 22 | Shinji Nakano | Minardi-Ford | 65 | +2 Laps | 20 |
| 16 | 21 | T.Takagi | Tyrrell-Ford | 65 | +2 Laps | 19 |
| Ret | 23 | Esteban Tuero | Minardi-Ford | 56 | Engine | 21 |
| Ret | 10 | Ralf Schumacher | Jordan-Mugen-Honda | 53 | Brakes | 6 |
| Ret | 15 | Johnny Herbert | Sauber-Petronas | 37 | Engine | 13 |
| Ret | 20 | Ricardo Rosset | Tyrrell-Ford | 36 | Engine | 22 |
| Ret | 12 | Jarno Trulli | Prost-Peugeot | 6 | Transmission | 14 |
| Ret | 16 | Pedro Diniz | Arrows | 6 | Hydraulics | 17 |

Winning speed: 123.360mph Lap leaders: M Schumacher 1-24; Hakkinen 25-67
Pole position: M Schumacher, 1m 18.561s, 129.730mph
Fastest lap: Hakkinen, 1m 20.450s, 126.680mph

**JAPANESE GRAND PRIX: SUZUKA** *1 November Round: 16 Race: 629 51 x 3.644 miles*

| POS. | NO. | DRIVER | CAR/ENGINE | LAPS | TIME/RETIRED | GRID |
|---|---|---|---|---|---|---|
| 1 | 8 | Mika Hakkinen | McLaren-Mercedes | 51 | 1:27'22.535 | 2 |
| 2 | 4 | Eddie Irvine | Ferrari | 51 | +6.491 | 4 |
| 3 | 7 | David Coulthard | McLaren-Mercedes | 51 | +27.662 | 3 |
| 4 | 9 | Damon Hill | Jordan-Mugen-Honda | 51 | +1'13.491 | 8 |
| 5 | 2 | H-H.Frentzen | Williams-Mecachrome | 51 | +1'13.857 | 5 |
| 6 | 1 | J.Villeneuve | Williams-Mecachrome | 51 | +1'15.867 | 6 |
| 7 | 14 | Jean Alesi | Sauber-Petronas | 51 | +1'36.053 | 12 |
| 8 | 5 | G.Fisichella | Benetton-Playlife | 51 | +1'41.302 | 10 |
| 9 | 6 | Alexander Wurz | Benetton-Playlife | 50 | +1 Lap | 9 |
| 10 | 15 | Johnny Herbert | Sauber-Petronas | 50 | +1 Lap | 11 |
| 11 | 11 | Olivier Panis | Prost-Peugeot | 50 | +1 Lap | 13 |
| 12 | 12 | Jarno Trulli | Prost-Peugeot | 48 | +3 Laps | 14 |
| Ret | 22 | Shinji Nakano | Minardi-Ford | 40 | Throttle | 20 |
| Ret | 3 | M.Schumacher | Ferrari | 31 | Tyre | 1 |
| Ret | 21 | T.Takagi | Tyrrell-Ford | 28 | Collision | 17 |
| Ret | 23 | Esteban Tuero | Minardi-Ford | 28 | Collision | 21 |
| Ret | 18 | R.Barrichello | Stewart-Ford | 25 | Hydraulics | 16 |
| Ret | 19 | Jos Verstappen | Stewart-Ford | 21 | Gearbox | 19 |
| Ret | 17 | Mika Salo | Arrows | 14 | Hydraulics | 15 |
| Ret | 10 | Ralf Schumacher | Jordan-Mugen-Honda | 13 | Engine | 7 |
| Ret | 16 | Pedro Diniz | Arrows | 2 | Spun off | 18 |
| DNQ | 20 | Ricardo Rosset | Tyrrell-Ford | | | |

Winning speed: 127.540mph Lap leaders: Hakkinen 1-51
Pole position: M Schumacher, 1m 36.293s, 136.120mph
Fastest lap: M Schumacher, 1m 40.190s, 130.930mph
Race stopped and restarted twice due to Trulli and then M Schumacher starting on the grid.
Race distance reduced by a lap each time to 51 laps.

# 1999

## DRIVERS' CHAMPION: MIKA HÄKKINEN
## CONSTRUCTORS' CHAMPION: FERRARI

**DRIVERS' CHAMPIONSHIP**

| POS. | DRIVER | NATIONALITY | CAR | POINTS |
|---|---|---|---|---|
| 1 | Mika Häkkinen | Finland | McLaren-Mercedes | 76 |
| 2 | Eddie Irvine | GB | Ferrari | 74 |
| 3 | Heinz-Harald Frentzen | Germany | Jordan-Mugan Honda | 54 |
| 4 | David Coulthard | GB | McLaren-Mercedes | 48 |
| 5 | Michael Schumacher | Germany | Ferrari | 44 |
| 6 | Ralf Schumacher | Germany | Williams-Supertec | 35 |
| 7 | Rubens Barrichello | Brazil | Stewart-Ford | 21 |
| 8 | Johnny Herbert | GB | Stewart-Ford | 15 |
| 9 | Giancarlo Fisichella | Italy | Benetton-PlayLife | 13 |
| 10 | Mika Salo | Finland | BAR-Supertec, Ferrari | 10 |
| 11 | Jarno Trulli | Italy | Prost-Peugeot | 7 |
| 12 | Damon Hill | GB | Jordan-Mugan Honda | 6 |
| 13 | Alexander Wurz | Austria | Benetton-PlayLife | 3 |
| = | Pedro Diniz | Brazil | Sauber-Petronas | 3 |
| 15 | Oliver Panis | France | Prost-Peugeot | 2 |
| = | Jean Alesi | France | Sauber-Petronas | 2 |
| 17 | Pedro de la Rosa | Spain | Arrows | 1 |
| = | Marc Gene | Spain | Minardi-Ford | 1 |
| | Alessandro Zanardi | Italy | Williams-Supertec | |
| | Jacques Villeneuve | Canada | BAR-Supertec | |
| | Ricardo Zonta | Brazil | BAR-Supertec | |
| | Toranosuke Takagi | Japan | Arrows | |
| | Luca Badoer | Italy | Minardi-Ford | |
| | Stephane Sarrazin | France | Minardi-Ford | |

Points for top six finishers (10, 6, 4, 3, 2, 1). Half points awarded for races stopped before half distance. Michael Schumacher's second place in the championship was taken away after he tried to take out Jacques Villeneuve at the European Grand Prix.

**CONSTRUCTORS' CHAMPIONSHIP**

| POS. | CONSTRUCTOR | POINTS |
|---|---|---|
| 1 | Ferrari | 128 |
| 2 | McLaren-Mercedes | 124 |
| 3 | Jordan-Mugen-Honda | 61 |
| 4 | Stewart-Ford | 36 |
| 5 | Williams-Supertec | 35 |
| 6 | Benetton-Playlife | 16 |
| 7 | Prost-Peugeot | 9 |
| 8 | Sauber-Petronas | 5 |
| 9 | Arrows | 1 |
| 10 | Minardi-Ford | 1 |

Points for top six finishers (10, 6, 4, 3, 2, 1). Half points awarded for races stopped before half distance.

**AUSTRALIAN GRAND PRIX: MELBOURNE** *7 March Round: 1 Race: 630 57 x 3.295 miles*

| POS. | NO. | DRIVER | CAR/ENGINE | LAPS | TIME/RETIRED | GRID |
|---|---|---|---|---|---|---|
| 1 | 4 | Eddie Irvine | Ferrari | 57 | 1:35'01.659 | 6 |
| 2 | 8 | H-H.Frentzen | Jordan-Mugen-Honda | 57 | +1.027 | 5 |
| 3 | 6 | Ralf Schumacher | Williams-Supertec | 57 | +7.012 | 8 |
| 4 | 9 | G.Fisichella | Benetton-Playlife | 57 | +33.418 | 7 |
| 5 | 16 | R.Barrichello | Stewart-Ford | 57 | +54.698 | 4 |
| 6 | 14 | Pedro de la Rosa | Arrows | 57 | +1'24.317 | 18 |
| 7 | 15 | T.Takagi | Arrows | 57 | +1'26.288 | 17 |
| 8 | 3 | M.Schumacher | Ferrari | 56 | +1 Lap | 3 |
| DNS | 17 | Johnny Herbert | Stewart-Ford | 0 | Fire | 13 |
| Ret | 23 | Ricardo Zonta | BAR-Supertec | 48 | Gearbox | 19 |
| Ret | 20 | Luca Badoer | Minardi-Ford | 42 | Gearbox | 21 |
| Ret | 10 | Alexander Wurz | Benetton-Playlife | 28 | Suspension | 10 |
| Ret | 12 | Pedro Diniz | Sauber-Petronas | 27 | Transmission | 14 |
| Ret | 21 | Marc Gene | Minardi-Ford | 25 | Collision | 22 |
| Ret | 19 | Jarno Trulli | Prost-Peugeot | 25 | Collision | 12 |
| Ret | 18 | Olivier Panis | Prost-Peugeot | 23 | Wheel | 20 |
| Ret | 1 | Mika Hakkinen | McLaren-Mercedes | 21 | Throttle | 1 |
| Ret | 5 | A.Zanardi | Williams/Supertec | 20 | Spun off | 15 |
| Ret | 2 | David Coulthard | McLaren-Mercedes | 13 | Hydraulics | 2 |
| Ret | 22 | J.Villeneuve | BAR-Supertec | 13 | Broken wing | 11 |
| Ret | 7 | Damon Hill | Jordan-Mugen-Honda | 0 | Collision | 9 |
| Ret | 11 | Jean Alesi | Sauber-Petronas | 0 | Gearbox | 16 |

Winning speed: 118.590mph Lap leaders: Hakkinen 1-17; Irvine 18-57
Pole position: Hakkinen, 1m 30.462s, 131.130mph
Fastest lap: M Schumacher, 1m 32.112s, 128.780mph

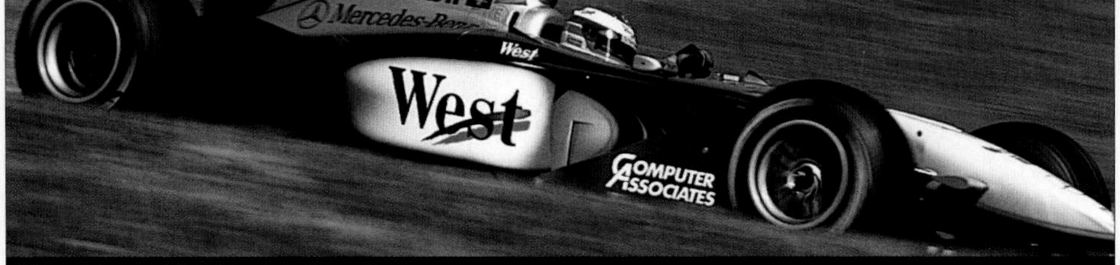


1999 world champion, Mika Hakkinen in the McLaren Mercedes.

**BRAZILIAN GRAND PRIX: INTERLAGOS** *11 April Round: 2 Race: 631 72 x 2.667 miles*

| POS. | NO. | DRIVER | CAR/ENGINE | LAPS | TIME/RETIRED | GRID |
|---|---|---|---|---|---|---|
| 1 | 1 | Mika Hakkinen | McLaren-Mercedes | 72 | 1:36'03.785 | 1 |
| 2 | 3 | M.Schumacher | Ferrari | 72 | +4.925 | 4 |
| 3 | 8 | H-H.Frentzen | Jordan-Mugen-Honda | 71 | +1 Lap | 8 |
| 4 | 6 | Ralf Schumacher | Williams-Supertec | 71 | +1 Lap | 11 |
| 5 | 4 | Eddie Irvine | Ferrari | 71 | +1 Lap | 6 |
| 6 | 18 | Olivier Panis | Prost-Peugeot | 71 | +1 Lap | 12 |
| 7 | 10 | Alexander Wurz | Benetton-Playlife | 70 | +2 Laps | 9 |
| 8 | 15 | T.Takagi | Arrows | 69 | +3 Laps | 19 |
| 9 | 21 | Marc Gene | Minardi-Ford | 69 | +3 Laps | 20 |
| Ret | 14 | Pedro de la Rosa | Arrows | 52 | Hydraulics | 17 |
| Ret | 22 | J.Villeneuve | BAR-Supertec | 49 | Hydraulics | 21 |
| Ret | 5 | A.Zanardi | Williams-Supertec | 43 | Gearbox | 16 |
| Ret | 16 | R.Barrichello | Stewart-Ford | 42 | Engine | 3 |
| Ret | 12 | Pedro Diniz | Sauber-Petronas | 42 | Collision | 15 |
| Ret | 9 | G.Fisichella | Benetton-Playlife | 38 | Clutch | 5 |
| Ret | 20 | S.Sarrazin | Minardi-Ford | 31 | Spun off | 18 |
| Ret | 11 | Jean Alesi | Sauber-Petronas | 27 | Gearbox | 14 |
| Ret | 2 | David Coulthard | McLaren-Mercedes | 22 | Gearbox | 2 |
| Ret | 19 | Jarno Trulli | Prost/Peugeot | 21 | Gearbox | 13 |
| Ret | 17 | Johnny Herbert | Stewart-Ford | 15 | Hydraulics | 10 |
| Ret | 7 | Damon Hill | Jordan-Mugen-Honda | 10 | Collision | 7 |
| DNQ | 23 | Ricardo Zonta | Bar-Supertec | | Accident | |

Winning speed: 119.921mph Lap leaders: Hakkinen 1-3, 38-72; Barrichello 4-26; M Schumacher 27-37
Pole position: Hakkinen, 1m 16.568s, 125.394mph
Fastest lap: Hakkinen, 1m 18.448s, 123.629mph

**SAN MARINO GRAND PRIX: IMOLA** *2 May Round: 3 Race: 632 62 x 3.063 miles*

| POS. | NO. | DRIVER | CAR/ENGINE | LAPS | TIME/RETIRED | GRID |
|---|---|---|---|---|---|---|
| 1 | 3 | M.Schumacher | Ferrari | 62 | 1:33'44.792 | 3 |
| 2 | 2 | David Coulthard | McLaren-Mercedes | 62 | +4.265 | 2 |
| 3 | 16 | R.Barrichello | Stewart-Ford | 61 | +1 Lap | 6 |
| 4 | 7 | Damon Hill | Jordan-Mugen-Honda | 61 | +1 Lap | 8 |
| 5 | 9 | G.Fisichella | Benetton-Playlife | 61 | +1 Lap | 16 |
| 6 | 11 | Jean Alesi | Sauber-Petronas | 61 | +1 Lap | 13 |
| 7 | 23 | Mika Salo | BAR-Supertec | 59 | +3 Laps | 19 |
| 8 | 20 | Luca Badoer | Minardi-Ford | 59 | +3 Laps | 22 |
| 9 | 21 | Marc Gene | Minardi-Ford | 59 | +3 Laps | 21 |
| 10 | 17 | Johnny Herbert | Stewart-Ford | 58 | Engine | 12 |
| 11 | 5 | A.Zanardi | Williams-Supertec | 58 | Spun off | 10 |
| Ret | 12 | Pedro Diniz | Sauber-Petronas | 49 | Spun off | 15 |
| Ret | 18 | Olivier Panis | Prost-Peugeot | 48 | Throttle | 11 |
| Ret | 4 | Eddie Irvine | Ferrari | 46 | Engine | 4 |
| Ret | 8 | H-H.Frentzen | Jordan-Mugen-Honda | 46 | Spun off | 7 |
| Ret | 15 | T.Takagi | Arrows | 29 | Fuel pressure | 20 |
| Ret | 6 | Ralf Schumacher | Williams-Supertec | 28 | Throttle | 9 |
| Ret | 1 | Mika Hakkinen | McLaren-Mercedes | 17 | Spun off | 1 |
| Ret | 14 | Pedro de la Rosa | Arrows | 5 | Spun off | 18 |
| Ret | 10 | Alexander Wurz | Benetton-Playlife | 5 | Spun off | 17 |
| Ret | 22 | J.Villeneuve | BAR-Supertec | 0 | Gearbox | 14 |
| Ret | 19 | Jarno Trulli | Prost-Peugeot | 0 | Spun off | 5 |

Winning speed: 119.921mph Lap leaders: Hakkinen 1-3, 38-72; Barrichello 4-26; M Schumacher 27-37
Pole position: Hakkinen, 1m 16.568s, 125.394mph
Fastest lap: Hakkinen, 1m 18.448s, 123.629mph

**MONACO GRAND PRIX: MONTE CARLO** *16 May Round: 4 Race: 633 78 x 2.092 miles*

| POS. | NO. | DRIVER | CAR/ENGINE | LAPS | TIME/RETIRED | GRID |
|---|---|---|---|---|---|---|
| 1 | 3 | M.Schumacher | Ferrari | 78 | 1:49'31.812 | 2 |
| 2 | 4 | Eddie Irvine | Ferrari | 78 | +30.476 | 4 |
| 3 | 1 | Mika Hakkinen | McLaren-Mercedes | 78 | +37.483 | 1 |
| 4 | 8 | H-H.Frentzen | Jordan-Mugen-Honda | 78 | +54.009 | 6 |
| 5 | 9 | G.Fisichella | Benetton-Playlife | 77 | +1 Lap | 9 |
| 6 | 10 | Alexander Wurz | Benetton-Playlife | 77 | +1 Lap | 10 |
| 7 | 19 | Jarno Trulli | Prost-Peugeot | 77 | +1 Lap | 7 |
| 8 | 5 | A.Zanardi | Williams-Supertec | 76 | +2 Laps | 11 |
| 9 | 16 | R.Barrichello | Stewart-Ford | 71 | Spun off | 5 |
| Ret | 6 | Ralf Schumacher | Williams-Supertec | 54 | Spun off | 16 |
| Ret | 11 | Jean Alesi | Sauber-Petronas | 50 | Suspension | 14 |
| Ret | 12 | Pedro Diniz | Sauber-Petronas | 49 | Suspension | 15 |
| Ret | 18 | Olivier Panis | Prost-Peugeot | 40 | Engine | 18 |
| Ret | 2 | David Coulthard | McLaren-Mercedes | 36 | Gearbox | 3 |
| Ret | 23 | Mika Salo | BAR-Supertec | 36 | Brakes | 12 |
| Ret | 15 | T.Takagi | Arrows | 36 | Engine | 19 |
| Ret | 22 | J.Villeneuve | BAR-Supertec | 32 | Oil leak | 8 |
| Ret | 17 | Johnny Herbert | Stewart-Ford | 32 | Suspension | 13 |
| Ret | 14 | Pedro de la Rosa | Arrows | 30 | Gearbox | 21 |
| Ret | 21 | Marc Gene | Minardi-Ford | 24 | Spun off | 22 |
| Ret | 20 | Luca Badoer | Minardi-Ford | 10 | Gearbox | 20 |
| Ret | 7 | Damon Hill | Jordan-Mugen-Honda | 3 | Collision | 17 |

Winning speed: 89.390mph Lap leaders: M Schumacher 1-78
Pole position: Hakkinen 1m 20.547s, 93.500mph
Fastest lap: Hakkinen, 1m 22.259s, 91.560mph

**SPANISH GRAND PRIX: CATALUNYA** *30 May Round: 5 Race: 634 65 x 2.938 miles*

| POS. | NO. | DRIVER | CAR/ENGINE | LAPS | TIME/RETIRED | GRID |
|---|---|---|---|---|---|---|
| 1 | 1 | Mika Hakkinen | McLaren-Mercedes | 65 | 1:34'13.665 | 1 |
| 2 | 2 | David Coulthard | McLaren-Mercedes | 65 | +6.238 | 3 |
| 3 | 3 | M.Schumacher | Ferrari | 65 | +10.845 | 4 |
| 4 | 4 | Eddie Irvine | Ferrari | 65 | +30.182 | 2 |
| 5 | 6 | Ralf Schumacher | Williams-Supertec | 65 | +1'27.208 | 10 |
| 6 | 19 | Jarno Trulli | Prost-Peugeot | 64 | +1 Lap | 9 |
| 7 | 7 | Damon Hill | Jordan-Mugen-Honda | 64 | +1 Lap | 11 |
| 8 | 23 | Mika Salo | BAR-Supertec | 64 | +1 Lap | 16 |
| 9 | 9 | G.Fisichella | Benetton-Playlife | 64 | +1 Lap | 13 |
| 10 | 10 | Alexander Wurz | Benetton-Playlife | 64 | +1 Lap | 18 |
| 11 | 14 | Pedro de la Rosa | Arrows | 63 | +2 Laps | 19 |
| 12 | 15 | T.Takagi | Arrows | 62 | +3 Laps | 20 |
| Ret | 16 | R.Barrichello | Stewart-Ford | 64 | Disqualified | 7 |
| Ret | 20 | Luca Badoer | Minardi-Ford | 50 | Spun off | 22 |
| Ret | 22 | J.Villeneuve | BAR-Supertec | 40 | Gearbox | 6 |
| Ret | 12 | Pedro Diniz | Sauber-Petronas | 40 | Transmission | 12 |
| Ret | 17 | Johnny Herbert | Stewart-Ford | 40 | Transmission | 14 |
| Ret | 8 | H-H.Frentzen | Jordan-Mugen-Honda | 35 | Halfshaft | 8 |
| Ret | 11 | Jean Alesi | Sauber-Petronas | 27 | Transmission | 5 |
| Ret | 5 | A.Zanardi | Williams-Supertec | 24 | Gearbox | 17 |
| Ret | 18 | Olivier Panis | Prost-Peugeot | 24 | Gearbox | 15 |
| Ret | 21 | Marc Gene | Minardi-Ford | 0 | Gearbox | 21 |

Winning speed: 121.550mph Lap leaders: Hakkinen 1-23, 27-44, 46-65; Coulthard 24-26, 45
Pole position: Hakkinen, 1m 22.088s, 128.850mph
Fastest lap: M Schumacher, 1m 24.982s, 124.450mph

**CANADIAN GRAND PRIX: MONTREAL** *13 June Round: 6 Race: 635 69 x 2.747 miles*

| POS. | NO. | DRIVER | CAR/ENGINE | LAPS | TIME/RETIRED | GRID |
|---|---|---|---|---|---|---|
| 1 | 1 | Mika Hakkinen | McLaren-Mercedes | 69 | 1:41'35.727 | 2 |
| 2 | 9 | G.Fisichella | Benetton-Playlife | 69 | +0.782 | 7 |
| 3 | 4 | Eddie Irvine | Ferrari | 69 | +1.797 | 3 |
| 4 | 6 | Ralf Schumacher | Williams-Supertec | 69 | +2.392 | 13 |
| 5 | 17 | Johnny Herbert | Stewart-Ford | 69 | +2.805 | 10 |
| 6 | 12 | Pedro Diniz | Sauber-Petronas | 69 | +3.711 | 18 |
| 7 | 2 | David Coulthard | McLaren-Mercedes | 69 | +5.004 | 4 |
| 8 | 21 | Marc Gene | Minardi-Ford | 68 | +1 Lap | 22 |
| 9 | 18 | Olivier Panis | Prost-Peugeot | 68 | +1 Lap | 15 |
| 10 | 20 | Luca Badoer | Minardi-Ford | 67 | +2 Laps | 21 |
| 11 | 8 | H-H.Frentzen | Jordan-Mugen-Honda | 65 | Brakes | 6 |
| Ret | 5 | A.Zanardi | Williams-Supertec | 50 | Brakes | 12 |
| Ret | 15 | T.Takagi | Arrows | 41 | Transmission | 19 |
| Ret | 22 | J.Villeneuve | BAR-Supertec | 34 | Spun off | 16 |
| Ret | 3 | M.Schumacher | Ferrari | 29 | Spun off | 1 |
| Ret | 14 | Pedro de la Rosa | Arrows | 22 | Transmission | 20 |
| Ret | 7 | Damon Hill | Jordan-Mugen-Honda | 14 | Spun off | 14 |
| Ret | 16 | R.Barrichello | Stewart-Ford | 14 | Steering | 5 |
| Ret | 23 | Ricardo Zonta | BAR-Supertec | 2 | Spun off | 17 |
| Ret | 11 | Jean Alesi | Sauber-Petronas | 0 | Collision | 8 |
| Ret | 19 | Jarno Trulli | Prost-Peugeot | 0 | Collision | 9 |
| Ret | 10 | Alexander Wurz | Benetton-Playlife | 0 | Transmission | 11 |

Winning speed: 111.940mph Lap leaders: M Schumacher 1-29; Hakkinen 30-69
Pole position: M Schumacher, 1m 19.298s, 124.710mph
Fastest lap: Irvine, 1m 20.382s, 123.030mph

**FRENCH GRAND PRIX: MAGNY-COURS** *27 June Round: 7 Race: 636 72 x 2.641 miles*

| POS. | NO. | DRIVER | CAR/ENGINE | LAPS | TIME/RETIRED | GRID |
|---|---|---|---|---|---|---|
| 1 | 8 | H-H.Frentzen | Jordan-Mugen-Honda | 72 | 1:58'24.343 | 5 |
| 2 | 1 | Mika Hakkinen | McLaren-Mercedes | 72 | +11.092 | 14 |
| 3 | 16 | R.Barrichello | Stewart-Ford | 72 | +43.432 | 1 |
| 4 | 6 | Ralf Schumacher | Williams-Supertec | 72 | +45.475 | 16 |
| 5 | 3 | M.Schumacher | Ferrari | 72 | +47.881 | 6 |
| 6 | 4 | Eddie Irvine | Ferrari | 72 | +48.901 | 17 |
| 7 | 19 | Jarno Trulli | Prost-Peugeot | 72 | +57.771 | 8 |
| 8 | 18 | Olivier Panis | Prost-Peugeot | 72 | +58.531 | 3 |
| 9 | 23 | Ricardo Zonta | BAR-Supertec | 72 | +1'28.764 | 10 |
| 10 | 20 | Luca Badoer | Minardi-Ford | 71 | +1 Lap | 20 |
| 11 | 14 | Pedro de la Rosa | Arrows | 71 | +1 Lap | 21 |
| DSQ | 15 | T.Takagi | Arrows | 71 | Disqualified | 22 |
| Ret | 9 | G.Fisichella | Benetton-Playlife | 42 | Spun off | 7 |
| Ret | 7 | Damon Hill | Jordan-Mugen-Honda | 31 | Electrical | 18 |
| Ret | 5 | A.Zanardi | Williams-Supertec | 26 | Engine | 15 |
| Ret | 22 | J.Villeneuve | BAR-Supertec | 25 | Spun off | 12 |
| Ret | 10 | Alexander Wurz | Benetton-Playlife | 25 | Spun off | 13 |
| Ret | 21 | Marc Gene | Minardi-Ford | 25 | Spun off | 19 |
| Ret | 11 | Jean Alesi | Sauber-Petronas | 24 | Spun off | 2 |
| Ret | 2 | David Coulthard | McLaren-Mercedes | 9 | Electrical | 4 |
| Ret | 12 | Pedro Diniz | Sauber-Petronas | 6 | Transmission | 11 |
| Ret | 17 | Johnny Herbert | Stewart-Ford | 4 | Gearbox | 9 |

Winning speed: 96.303mph Lap leaders: Barrichello 1-5, 10-43, 55-59; Coulthard 6-9; M Schumacher 44-54; Hakkinen 60-65; Frentzen 66-72
Pole position: Barrichello, 1m 38.441s, 96.580mph
Fastest lap: Coulthard, 1m 19.227s, 120.000mph

**BRITISH GRAND PRIX: SILVERSTONE** *11 July Round: 8 Race: 637 60 x 3.194 miles*

| POS. | NO. | DRIVER | CAR/ENGINE | LAPS | TIME/RETIRED | GRID |
|---|---|---|---|---|---|---|
| 1 | 2 | David Coulthard | McLaren-Mercedes | 60 | 1:32'30.144 | 3 |
| 2 | 4 | Eddie Irvine | Ferrari | 60 | +1.829 | 4 |
| 3 | 6 | Ralf Schumacher | Williams-Supertec | 60 | +27.411 | 8 |
| 4 | 8 | H-H.Frentzen | Jordan-Mugen-Honda | 60 | +27.789 | 5 |
| 5 | 7 | Damon Hill | Jordan-Mugen-Honda | 60 | +38.606 | 6 |
| 6 | 12 | Pedro Diniz | Sauber-Petronas | 60 | + 53.643 | 12 |
| 7 | 9 | G.Fisichella | Benetton-Playlife | 60 | +54.614 | 17 |
| 8 | 16 | R.Barrichello | Stewart-Ford | 60 | +1'08.590 | 7 |
| 9 | 19 | Jarno Trulli | Prost-Peugeot | 60 | +1'12.045 | 14 |
| 10 | 10 | Alexander Wurz | Benetton-Playlife | 60 | +1'12.123 | 18 |
| 11 | 5 | A.Zanardi | Williams-Supertec | 60 | +1'17.124 | 13 |
| 12 | 17 | Johnny Herbert | Stewart-Ford | 60 | +1'17.709 | 11 |
| 13 | 18 | Olivier Panis | Prost-Peugeot | 60 | +1'20.492 | 15 |
| 14 | 11 | Jean Alesi | Sauber-Petronas | 59 | +1 Lap | 10 |
| 15 | 21 | Marc Gene | Minardi-Ford | 58 | +2 Laps | 22 |
| 16 | 15 | T.Takagi | Arrows | 58 | +2 Laps | 19 |
| Ret | 23 | Ricardo Zonta | BAR-Supertec | 41 | Suspension | 16 |
| Ret | 1 | Mika Hakkinen | McLaren-Mercedes | 35 | Wheel | 1 |
| Ret | 22 | J.Villeneuve | BAR-Supertec | 29 | Halfshaft | 9 |
| Ret | 20 | Luca Badoer | Minardi-Ford | 6 | Gearbox | 21 |
| Ret | 14 | Pedro de la Rosa | Arrows | 0 | Gearbox | 20 |
| DNS | 3 | M.Schumacher | Ferrari | 0 | Spun off | 2 |

Winning speed: 124.261mph Lap leaders: Hakkinen 1-24; Irvine 25-26; Coulthard 27-42, 46-60; Frentzen 43-44; Hill 45
Pole position: Hakkinen, 1m 24.804s, 135.588mph
Fastest lap: Hakkinen, 1m 28.309s, 130.206mph
Race stopped after Villeneuve and Zanardi were stranded on the grid. M Schumacher's accident accured after the red flags were out. New start for total original distance.

**AUSTRIAN GRAND PRIX: A1-RING** *25 July Round: 9 Race: 638 71 x 2.684 miles*

| POS. | NO. | DRIVER | CAR/ENGINE | LAPS | TIME/RETIRED | GRID |
|---|---|---|---|---|---|---|
| 1 | 4 | Eddie Irvine | Ferrari | 71 | 1:28'12.438 | 3 |
| 2 | 2 | David Coulthard | McLaren-Mercedes | 71 | +0.313 | 2 |
| 3 | 1 | Mika Hakkinen | McLaren-Mercedes | 71 | +22.282 | 1 |
| 4 | 8 | H-H.Frentzen | Jordan-Mugen-Honda | 71 | +52.803 | 4 |
| 5 | 10 | Alexander Wurz | Benetton-Playlife | 71 | +1'06.358 | 10 |
| 6 | 12 | Pedro Diniz | Sauber-Petronas | 71 | +1'10.933 | 16 |
| 7 | 19 | Jarno Trulli | Prost-Peugeot | 70 | +1 Lap | 13 |
| 8 | 7 | Damon Hill | Jordan-Mugen-Honda | 70 | +1 Lap | 11 |
| 9 | 3 | Mika Salo | Ferrari | 70 | +1 Lap | 7 |
| 10 | 18 | Olivier Panis | Prost-Peugeot | 70 | +1 Lap | 18 |
| 11 | 21 | Marc Gene | Minardi-Ford | 70 | +1 Lap | 22 |
| 12 | 9 | G.Fischella | Benetton-Playlife | 68 | Engine | 12 |
| 13 | 20 | Luca Badoer | Minardi-Ford | 68 | +3 Laps | 19 |
| 14 | 17 | Johnny Herbert | Stewart-Ford | 67 | +4 Laps | 6 |
| 15 | 23 | Ricardo Zonta | BAR-Supertec | 63 | Clutch | 15 |
| Ret | 16 | R.Barrichello | Stewart-Ford | 55 | Engine | 5 |
| Ret | 11 | Jean Alesi | Sauber-Petronas | 49 | Out of fuel | 17 |
| Ret | 14 | Pedro de la Rosa | Arrows | 38 | Spun off | 21 |
| Ret | 5 | A.Zanardi | Williams-Supertec | 35 | Out of fuel | 14 |
| Ret | 22 | J.Villeneuve | BAR-Supertec | 34 | Halfshaft | 9 |
| Ret | 15 | T.Takagi | Arrows | 25 | Engine | 20 |
| Ret | 6 | Ralf Schumacher | Williams-Supertec | 8 | Spun off | 8 |

Winning speed: 129.616mph Lap leaders: Coulthard 1-39; Irvine 40-71
Pole position: Hakkinen, 1m 10.954s, 136.169mph
Fastest lap: Hakkinen, 1m 12.107s, 133.992mph

**GERMAN GRAND PRIX: HOCKENHEIM** *1 August Round: 10 Race: 639 45 x 4.240 miles*

| POS. | NO. | DRIVER | CAR/ENGINE | LAPS | TIME/RETIRED | GRID |
|---|---|---|---|---|---|---|
| 1 | 4 | Eddie Irvine | Ferrari | 45 | 1:21'58.594 | 5 |
| 2 | 3 | Mika Salo | Ferrari | 45 | +1.007 | 4 |
| 3 | 8 | H-H.Frentzen | Jordan-Mugen-Honda | 45 | +5.195 | 2 |
| 4 | 6 | Ralf Schumacher | Williams-Supertec | 45 | +12.809 | 11 |
| 5 | 2 | David Coulthard | McLaren-Mercedes | 45 | +16.823 | 3 |
| 6 | 18 | Olivier Panis | Prost-Peugeot | 45 | +29.879 | 7 |
| 7 | 10 | Alexander Wurz | Benetton-Playlife | 45 | +33.333 | 13 |
| 8 | 11 | Jean Alesi | Sauber-Petronas | 45 | +1'11.291 | 21 |
| 9 | 21 | Marc Gene | Minardi-Ford | 45 | +1'48.318 | 15 |
| 10 | 20 | Luca Badoer | Minardi-Ford | 44 | +1 Lap | 19 |
| 11 | 17 | Johnny Herbert | Stewart-Ford | 40 | Gearbox | 17 |
| Ret | 14 | Pedro de la Rosa | Arrows | 37 | Spun off | 20 |
| Ret | 1 | Mika Hakkinen | McLaren-Mercedes | 25 | Tyre | 1 |
| Ret | 5 | A.Zanardi | Williams-Supertec | 21 | Differential | 14 |
| Ret | 23 | Ricardo Zonta | BAR-Supertec | 20 | Engine | 18 |
| Ret | 15 | T.Takagi | Arrows | 15 | Engine | 22 |
| Ret | 7 | Damon Hill | Jordan-Mugen-Honda | 13 | Brakes | 8 |
| Ret | 19 | Jarno Trulli | Prost-Peugeot | 10 | Engine | 9 |
| Ret | 9 | G.Fisichella | Benetton-Playlife | 7 | Suspension | 10 |
| Ret | 16 | R.Barrichello | Stewart-Ford | 6 | Hydraulics | 6 |
| Ret | 22 | J.Villeneuve | BAR-Supertec | 0 | Collision | 12 |
| Ret | 12 | Pedro Diniz | Sauber-Petronas | 0 | Collision | 16 |

Winning speed: 139.636mph Lap leaders: Hakkinen 1-24; Salo 25; Irvine 26-45
Pole position: Hakkinen, 1m 42.950s, 148.266mph
Fastest lap: Coulthard, 1m 45.270s, 144.985mph

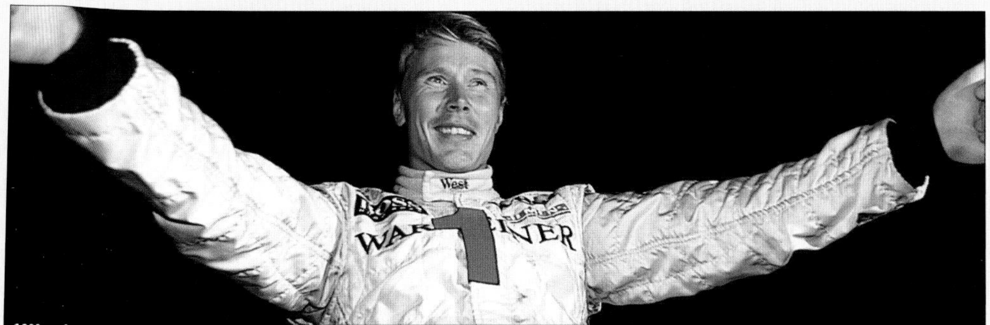


1999 world champion, Mika Hakkinen

## HUNGARIAN GRAND PRIX: HUNGARORING *15 August Round: 11 Race: 640 77 x 2.469 miles*

| POS. | NO. | DRIVER | CAR/ENGINE | LAPS | TIME/RETIRED | GRID |
|---|---|---|---|---|---|---|
| 1 | 1 | Mika Hakkinen | McLaren-Mercedes | 77 | 1:46'23.536 | 1 |
| 2 | 2 | David Coulthard | McLaren-Mercedes | 77 | +9.706 | 3 |
| 3 | 4 | Eddie Irvine | Ferrari | 77 | +27.228 | 2 |
| 4 | 8 | H-H.Frentzen | Jordan-Mugen-Honda | 77 | +31.815 | 5 |
| 5 | 16 | R.Barrichello | Stewart-Ford | 77 | +43.808 | 8 |
| 6 | 7 | Damon Hill | Jordan-Mugen-Honda | 77 | +55.726 | 6 |
| 7 | 10 | Alexander Wurz | Benetton-Playlife | 77 | +1'01.012 | 7 |
| 8 | 19 | Jarno Trulli | Prost-Peugeot | 76 | +1 Lap | 13 |
| 9 | 6 | Ralf Schumacher | Williams-Supertec | 76 | +1 Lap | 16 |
| 10 | 18 | Olivier Panis | Prost-Peugeot | 76 | +1 Lap | 14 |
| 11 | 17 | Johnny Herbert | Stewart-Ford | 76 | +1 Lap | 10 |
| 12 | 3 | Mika Salo | Ferrari | 75 | +2 Laps | 18 |
| 13 | 23 | Ricardo Zonta | BAR-Supertec | 75 | +2 Laps | 17 |
| 14 | 20 | Luca Badoer | Minardi-Ford | 75 | +2 Laps | 19 |
| 15 | 14 | Pedro de la Rosa | Arrows | 75 | +2 Laps | 20 |
| 16 | 11 | Jean Alesi | Sauber-Petronas | 74 | Fuel pressure | 11 |
| 17 | 21 | Marc Gene | Minardi-Ford | 74 | +3 Laps | 22 |
| Ret | 22 | J.Villeneuve | BAR-Supertec | 60 | Clutch | 9 |
| Ret | 9 | G.Fisichella | Benetton-Playlife | 52 | Engine | 4 |
| Ret | 15 | T.Takagi | Arrows | 26 | Transmission | 21 |
| Ret | 12 | Pedro Diniz | Sauber-Petronas | 19 | Spun off | 12 |
| Ret | 5 | A.Zanardi | Williams-Supertec | 10 | Differential | 15 |

Winning speed: 107.206mph Lap leaders: Hakkinen 1-77
Pole position: Hakkinen, 1m 18.156s, 113.718mph
Fastest lap: Coulthard, 1m 20.699s, 110.134mph

## BELGIAN GRAND PRIX: SPA-FRANCORCHAMPS *9 August Round: 12 Race: 641 77 x 2.469 miles*

| POS. | NO. | DRIVER | CAR/ENGINE | LAPS | TIME/RETIRED | GRID |
|---|---|---|---|---|---|---|
| 1 | 2 | David Coulthard | McLaren-Mercedes | 44 | 1:25'43.057 | 2 |
| 2 | 1 | Mika Hakkinen | McLaren-Mercedes | 44 | +10.469 | 1 |
| 3 | 8 | H-H.Frentzen | Jordan-Mugen-Honda | 44 | +33.433 | 3 |
| 4 | 4 | Eddie Irvine | Ferrari | 44 | +44.948 | 6 |
| 5 | 6 | Ralf Schumacher | Williams-Supertec | 44 | +48.067 | 5 |
| 6 | 7 | Damon Hill | Jordan-Mugen-Honda | 44 | +54.916 | 4 |
| 7 | 3 | Mika Salo | Ferrari | 44 | +56.249 | 9 |
| 8 | 5 | A.Zanardi | Williams-Supertec | 44 | +1'07.022 | 8 |
| 9 | 11 | Jean Alesi | Sauber-Petronas | 44 | +1'13.848 | 16 |
| 10 | 16 | R.Barrichello | Stewart-Ford | 44 | +1'20.742 | 7 |
| 11 | 9 | G.Fisichella | Benetton-Playlife | 44 | +1'32.195 | 13 |
| 12 | 19 | Jarno Trulli | Prost-Peugeot | 44 | +1'36.154 | 12 |
| 13 | 18 | Olivier Panis | Prost-Peugeot | 44 | +1'41.543 | 17 |
| 14 | 10 | Alexander Wurz | Benetton-Playlife | 44 | +1'57.745 | 15 |
| 15 | 22 | J.Villeneuve | BAR-Supertec | 43 | +1 Lap | 11 |
| 16 | 21 | Marc Gene | Minardi-Ford | 43 | +1 Lap | 21 |
| Ret | 14 | Pedro de la Rosa | Arrows | 35 | Transmission | 22 |
| Ret | 20 | Luca Badoer | Minardi-Ford | 33 | Suspension | 20 |
| Ret | 23 | Ricardo Zonta | BAR-Supertec | 33 | Gearbox | 14 |
| Ret | 17 | Johnny Herbert | Stewart-Ford | 27 | Brakes | 10 |
| Ret | 12 | Pedro Diniz | Sauber-Petronas | 19 | Spun off | 18 |
| Ret | 15 | T.Takagi | Arrows | 0 | Clutch | 19 |

Winning speed: 133.349mph Lap leaders: Coulthard 1-44
Pole position: Hakkinen, 1m 50.329s, 141.296mph
Fastest lap: Hakkinen, 1m 53.955s, 136.788mph

## ITALIAN GRAND PRIX: MONZA *12 September Round: 13 Race: 642 53 x 3.585 miles*

| POS. | NO. | DRIVER | CAR/ENGINE | LAPS | TIME/RETIRED | GRID |
|---|---|---|---|---|---|---|
| 1 | 8 | H-H.Frentzen | Jordan-Mugen-Honda | 53 | 1:17'02.923 | 2 |
| 2 | 6 | Ralf Schumacher | Williams-Supertec | 53 | +3.272 | 5 |
| 3 | 3 | Mika Salo | Ferrari | 53 | +11.932 | 6 |
| 4 | 16 | R.Barrichello | Stewart-Ford | 53 | +17.630 | 7 |
| 5 | 2 | David Coulthard | McLaren-Mercedes | 53 | +18.142 | 3 |
| 6 | 4 | Eddie Irvine | Ferrari | 53 | +27.402 | 8 |
| 7 | 5 | A.Zanardi | Williams-Supertec | 53 | +28.047 | 4 |
| 8 | 22 | J.Villeneuve | BAR-Supertec | 53 | +41.797 | 11 |
| 9 | 11 | Jean Alesi | Sauber-Petronas | 53 | +42.198 | 13 |
| 10 | 7 | Damon Hill | Jordan-Mugen-Honda | 53 | +56.259 | 9 |
| 11 | 18 | Olivier Panis | Prost-Peugeot | 52 | Engine | 10 |
| Ret | 17 | Johnny Herbert | Stewart-Ford | 40 | Clutch | 15 |
| Ret | 15 | T.Takagi | Arrows | 35 | Spun off | 22 |
| Ret | 14 | Pedro de la Rosa | Arrows | 35 | Withdrew | 21 |
| Ret | 1 | Mika Hakkinen | McLaren-Mercedes | 29 | Spun off | 1 |
| Ret | 19 | Jarno Trulli | Prost-Peugeot | 29 | Overheating | 12 |
| Ret | 23 | Ricardo Zonta | BAR-Supertec | 25 | Wheel bearing | 18 |
| Ret | 20 | Luca Badoer | Minardi-Ford | 23 | Collision | 19 |
| Ret | 10 | Alexander Wurz | Benetton-Playlife | 11 | Electrical | 14 |
| Ret | 12 | Pedro Diniz | Sauber-Petronas | 1 | Spun off | 16 |
| Ret | 9 | G.Fisichella | Benetton-Playlife | 1 | Spun off | 17 |
| Ret | 21 | Marc Gene | Minardi-Ford | 0 | Collision | 20 |

Winning speed: 147.855mph Lap leaders: Hakkinen 1-29; Frentzen 30-35, 37-53; Salo 36
Pole position: Hakkinen, 1m 22.432s, 156.586mph
Fastest lap: R Schumacher, 1m 25.579s, 150.832mph

## EUROPEAN GRAND PRIX: NURBURGRING *26 September Round: 14 Race: 643 66 x 2.831 miles*

| POS. | NO. | DRIVER | CAR/ENGINE | LAPS | TIME/RETIRED | GRID |
|---|---|---|---|---|---|---|
| 1 | 17 | Johnny Herbert | Stewart-Ford | 66 | 1:41'54.314 | 14 |
| 2 | 19 | Jarno Trulli | Prost-Peugeot | 66 | +22.619 | 10 |
| 3 | 16 | R.Barrichello | Stewart-Ford | 66 | +22.866 | 15 |
| 4 | 6 | Ralf Schumacher | Williams-Supertec | 66 | +39.508 | 4 |
| 5 | 1 | Mika Hakkinen | McLaren-Mercedes | 66 | +1'02.950 | 3 |
| 6 | 21 | Marc Gene | Minardi-Ford | 66 | +1'05.154 | 20 |
| 7 | 4 | Eddie Irvine | Ferrari | 66 | +1'06.683 | 9 |
| 8 | 23 | Ricardo Zonta | BAR-Supertec | 65 | +1 Lap | 17 |
| 9 | 18 | Olivier Panis | Prost-Peugeot | 65 | +1 Lap | 5 |
| 10 | 22 | J.Villeneuve | BAR-Supertec | 61 | Clutch | 8 |
| Ret | 20 | Luca Badoer | Minardi-Ford | 53 | Gearbox | 19 |
| Ret | 14 | Pedro de la Rosa | Arrows | 52 | Gearbox | 22 |
| Ret | 9 | G.Fisichella | Benetton-Playlife | 48 | Spun off | 6 |
| Ret | 3 | Mika Salo | Ferrari | 44 | Brakes | 12 |
| Ret | 15 | T.Takagi | Arrows | 42 | Spun off | 21 |
| Ret | 2 | David Coulthard | McLaren-Mercedes | 37 | Spun off | 2 |
| Ret | 11 | Jean Alesi | Sauber-Petronas | 35 | Halfshaft | 16 |
| Ret | 8 | H-H.Frentzen | Jordan-Mugen-Honda | 32 | Electrical | 1 |
| Ret | 5 | A.Zanardi | Williams-Supertec | 10 | Collision | 18 |
| Ret | 7 | Damon Hill | Jordan-Mugen-Honda | 0 | Electrical | 7 |
| Ret | 10 | Alexander Wurz | Benetton-Playlife | 0 | Collision | 11 |
| Ret | 12 | Pedro Diniz | Sauber-Petronas | 0 | Collision | 13 |

Winning speed: 110.004mph Lap leaders: Frentzen 1-32; Coulthard 33-37; R Schumacher 38-44, 49; Fisichella 45-48; Herbert 50-66
Pole position: Frentzen, 1m 19.910s, 127.538mph
Fastest lap: Hakkinen, 1m 21.282s, 125.384mph

## MALAYSIAN GRAND PRIX: SEPANG *17 October Round: 15 Race: 644 56 x 3.444 miles*

| POS. | NO. | DRIVER | CAR/ENGINE | LAPS | TIME/RETIRED | GRID |
|---|---|---|---|---|---|---|
| 1 | 4 | Eddie Irvine | Ferrari | 56 | 1:36'38.494 | 2 |
| 2 | 3 | M.Schumacher | Ferrari | 56 | +1.040 | 1 |
| 3 | 1 | Mika Hakkinen | McLaren-Mercedes | 56 | +9.743 | 4 |
| 4 | 17 | Johnny Herbert | Stewart-Ford | 56 | +17.538 | 5 |
| 5 | 16 | R.Barrichello | Stewart-Ford | 56 | +32.296 | 6 |
| 6 | 8 | H-H.Frentzen | Jordan-Mugen-Honda | 56 | +34.884 | 14 |
| 7 | 11 | Jean Alesi | Sauber-Petronas | 56 | +54.408 | 15 |
| 8 | 10 | Alexander Wurz | Benetton-Playlife | 56 | +1'00.934 | 7 |
| 9 | 21 | Marc Gene | Minardi-Ford | 55 | +1 Lap | 19 |
| 10 | 5 | A.Zanardi | Williams-Supertec | 55 | +1 Lap | 16 |
| 11 | 9 | G.Fisichella | Benetton-Playlife | 52 | +4 Laps | 11 |
| Ret | 22 | J.Villeneuve | BAR-Supertec | 48 | Hydraulics | 10 |
| Ret | 12 | Pedro Diniz | Sauber-Petronas | 44 | Spun off | 17 |
| Ret | 14 | Pedro de la Rosa | Arrows | 30 | Engine | 20 |
| Ret | 20 | Luca Badoer | Minardi-Ford | 15 | Spun off | 21 |
| Ret | 2 | David Coulthard | McLaren-Mercedes | 14 | Fuel pressure | 3 |
| Ret | 6 | Ralf Schumacher | Williams-Supertec | 7 | Spun off | 8 |
| Ret | 15 | T.Takagi | Arrows | 7 | Transmission | 22 |
| Ret | 23 | Ricardo Zonta | BAR-Supertec | 6 | Engine | 13 |
| Ret | 18 | Olivier Panis | Prost-Peugeot | 5 | Engine | 12 |
| Ret | | Damon Hill | Jordan-Mugen-Honda | 0 | Collision | 9 |
| Ret | 19 | Jarno Trulli | Prost-Peugeot | 0 | Engine | 18 |

Winning speed: 119.526mph Lap leaders: M Schumacher 1-3, 26-28, 42-52; Irvine 4-25, 29-41, 53-56
Pole position: M Schumacher, 1m 39.688s, 124.372mph
Fastest lap: M Schumacher, 1m 40.267s, 123.654mph
Irvine and M Schumacher were originally disqualified from first and second places because of illegal bodywork, but reinstated after appeal.

## JAPANESE GRAND PRIX: SUZUKA *31 October Round: 16 Race: 645 53 x 3.644 miles*

| POS. | NO. | DRIVER | CAR/ENGINE | LAPS | TIME/RETIRED | GRI |
|---|---|---|---|---|---|---|
| 1 | 1 | Mika Hakkinen | McLaren-Mercedes | 53 | 1:31'18.785 | 2 |
| 2 | 3 | M.Schumacher | Ferrari | 53 | +5.015 | 1 |
| 3 | 4 | Eddie Irvine | Ferrari | 53 | +1'35.688 | 5 |
| 4 | 8 | H-H.Frentzen | Jordan-Mugen-Honda | 53 | +1'38.635 | 4 |
| 5 | 6 | Ralf Schumacher | Williams-Supertec | 53 | +1'39.494 | 9 |
| 6 | 11 | Jean Alesi | Sauber-Petronas | 52 | +1 Lap | 10 |
| 7 | 17 | Johnny Herbert | Stewart-Ford | 52 | +1 Lap | 8 |
| 8 | 16 | R.Barrichello | Stewart-Ford | 52 | +1 Lap | 13 |
| 9 | 22 | J.Villeneuve | BAR-Supertec | 52 | +1 Lap | 11 |
| 10 | 10 | Alexander Wurz | Benetton-Playlife | 52 | +1 Lap | 15 |
| 11 | 12 | Pedro Diniz | Sauber-Petronas | 52 | +1 Lap | 17 |
| 12 | 23 | Ricardo Zonta | BAR-Supertec | 52 | +1 Lap | 18 |
| 13 | 14 | Pedro de la Rosa | Arrows | 51 | +2 Laps | 20 |
| 14 | 9 | G.Fisichella | Benetton-Playlife | 47 | Engine | 14 |
| Ret | 15 | T.Takagi | Arrows | 43 | Gearbox | 19 |
| Ret | 20 | Luca Badoer | Minardi-Ford | 43 | Engine | 22 |
| Ret | 2 | David Coulthard | McLaren-Mercedes | 39 | Hydraulics | 3 |
| Ret | 21 | Marc Gene | Minardi-Ford | 31 | Gearbox | 20 |
| Wth | 7 | Damon Hill | Jordan-Mugen-Honda | 21 | Withdrew | 12 |
| Ret | 18 | Olivier Panis | Prost-Peugeot | 19 | Alternator | 6 |
| Ret | 19 | Jarno Trulli | Prost-Peugeot | 3 | Engine | 7 |
| Ret | 5 | A.Zanardi | Williams-Supertec | 0 | Electrical | 8 |

Winning speed: 126.813mph Lap leaders: Hakkinen 1-19, 23-53; M Schumacher 20-22
Pole position: M Schumacher, 1m 37.470s, 134.585mph
Fastest lap: M Schumacher, 1m 41.319s, 129.466mph

# 2000

## DRIVERS' CHAMPION: MICHAEL SCHUMACHER
## CONSTRUCTORS' CHAMPION: FERRARI

### DRIVERS' CHAMPIONSHIP

| POS. | DRIVER | NATIONALITY | CAR | POINTS |
|---|---|---|---|---|
| 1 | Michael Schumacher | Germany | Ferrari | 108 |
| 2 | Mika Häkkinen | Finland | McLaren-Mercedes | 89 |
| 3 | David Coulthard | GB | McLaren-Mercedes | 73 |
| 4 | Rubens Barrichello | Brazil | Ferrari | 62 |
| 5 | Ralf Schumacher | Germany | Williams-BMW | 24 |
| 6 | Giancarlo Fisichella | Italy | Benetton-PlayLife | 18 |
| 7 | Jacques Villeneuve | Canada | BAR-Honda | 17 |
| 8 | Jenson Button | GB | Williams-BMW | 12 |
| 9 | Heinz-Harald Frentzen | Germany | Jordan-Honda | 11 |
| 10 | Jarno Trulli | Italy | Jordan-Honda | 6 |
| 11 | Mika Salo | Finland | Sauber-Petronas | 6 |
| 12 | Jos Verstappen | Netherlands | Arrows-Supertec | 5 |
| 13 | Eddie Irvine | GB | Jaguar-Ford | 4 |
| 14 | Ricardo Zonta | Brazil | BAR-Honda | 3 |
| 15 | Pedro de la Rosa | Spain | Arrows-Supertec | 2 |
| 16 | Alexander Wurz | Austria | Benetton-PlayLife | 2 |
| | Pedro Diniz | Brazil | Sauber-Petronas | |
| | Johnny Herbert | GB | Jaguar-Ford | |
| | Jean Alesi | France | Prost-Peugeot | |
| | Nick Heidfeld | Germany | Prost-Peugeot | |
| | Marc Gene | Spain | Minardi-Fondmetal | |
| | Gaston Mazzacane | Argentina | Minardi-Fondmetal | |
| | Luciano Burti | Brazil | Jaguar-Ford | |

Points for top six finishers (10, 6, 4, 3, 2, 1). Only the best eleven scores counted towards the championship. Drivers not valid for points if the constructor had entered only one car. Half points awarded for races stopped before half distance.

### CONSTRUCTORS' CHAMPIONSHIP

| POS. | CONSTRUCTOR | POINTS |
|---|---|---|
| 1 | Ferrari | 170 |
| 2 | McLaren-Mercedes | 152 |
| 3 | Williams-BMW | 36 |
| 4 | Benetton-Playlife | 20 |
| 5 | BAR-Honda | 20 |
| 6 | Jordan-Mugen-Honda | 17 |
| 7 | Arrows-Supertec | 7 |
| 8 | Sauber-Petronas | 6 |
| 9 | Jaguar-Cosworth | 4 |

Points for top six finishers (10, 6, 4, 3, 2, 1). Half points awarded for races stopped before half distance. McLaren did not score constructors' points for Häkkinen in Austria due to a missing seal.

## AUSTRALIAN GRAND PRIX: MELBOURNE *12 March Round: 1 Race: 647 58 x 3.295 miles*

| POS. | NO. | DRIVER | CAR/ENGINE | LAPS | TIME/RETIRED | GRI |
|---|---|---|---|---|---|---|
| 1 | 3 | M.Schumacher | Ferrari | 58 | 1:34'01.987 | 3 |
| 2 | 4 | R.Barrichello | Ferrari | 58 | +11.415 | 4 |
| 3 | 9 | Ralf Schumacher | Williams-BMW | 58 | +20.009 | 11 |
| 4 | 22 | J.Villeneuve | BAR-Honda | 58 | +44.447 | 8 |
| 5 | 11 | G.Fisichella | Benetton-Playlife | 58 | +45.165 | 9 |
| 6 | 23 | Ricardo Zonta | BAR-Honda | 58 | +46.468 | 16 |
| 7 | 12 | Alexander Wurz | Benetton-Playlife | 58 | +46.915 | 14 |
| 8 | 20 | Marc Gene | Minardi-Fondmetal | 57 | +1 Lap | 18 |
| 9 | 15 | Nick Heidfeld | Prost-Peugeot | 56 | +2 Laps | 15 |
| DSQ | 17 | Mika Salo | Sauber-Petronas | 58 | Disqualified | 10 |
| Ret | 10 | Jenson Button | Williams-BMW | 46 | Engine | 21 |
| Ret | 16 | Pedro Diniz | Sauber-Petronas | 41 | Transmission | 19 |
| Ret | 21 | Gaston Mazzacane | Minardi-Fondmetal | 40 | Gearbox | 22 |
| Ret | 5 | H-H.Frentzen | Jordan-Mugen-Honda | 39 | Hydraulics | 8 |
| Ret | 6 | Jarno Trulli | Jordan-Mugen-Honda | 35 | Engine | 6 |
| Ret | 14 | Jean Alesi | Prost-Peugeot | 27 | Hydraulics | 17 |
| Ret | 1 | Mika Hakkinen | McLaren-Mercedes | 18 | Engine | 1 |
| Ret | 19 | Jos Verstappen | Arrows-Supertec | 16 | Suspension | 13 |
| Ret | 2 | David Coulthard | McLaren-Mercedes | 11 | Engine | 2 |
| Ret | 18 | Pedro de la Rosa | Arrows-Supertec | 6 | Suspension | 12 |
| Ret | 7 | Eddie Irvine | Jaguar-Cosworth | 6 | Spun off | 7 |
| Ret | 8 | Johnny Herbert | Jaguar-Cosworth | 1 | Clutch | 20 |

Winning speed: 121.947mph Lap leaders: Häkkinen 1-18; M Schumacher 19-29, 36-44, 46-58; Frentzen 30-35; Barrichello 45.
Pole position: Häkkinen, 1m 30.556s, 130.996mph
Fastest lap: Barrichello, 1m 31.481s, 129.671mph
Salo disqualified from sixth place.

**BRAZILIAN GRAND PRIX: INTERLAGOS** *26 April Round: 2 Race: 648 71 x 2.677 miles*

| POS. | NO. | DRIVER | CAR/ENGINE | LAPS | TIME/RETIRED | GRID |
|---|---|---|---|---|---|---|
| 1 | 3 | M.Schumacher | Ferrari | 71 | 1:31'35.271 | 3 |
| 2 | 11 | G.Fisichella | Benetton-Playlife | 71 | +39.898 | 5 |
| 3 | 5 | H-H.Frentzen | Jordan-Mugen-Honda | 71 | +42.268 | 7 |
| 4 | 6 | Jarno Trulli | Jordan-Mugen-Honda | 71 | +1'12.780 | 12 |
| 5 | 9 | Ralf Schumacher | Williams-BMW | 70 | +1 Lap | 11 |
| 6 | 10 | Jenson Button | Williams-BMW | 70 | +1 Lap | 9 |
| 7 | 19 | Jos Verstappen | Arrows-Supertec | 70 | +1 Lap | 14 |
| 8 | 18 | Pedro de la Rosa | Arrows-Supertec | 70 | +1 Lap | 16 |
| 9 | 23 | Ricardo Zonta | BAR-Honda | 69 | +2 Laps | 8 |
| 10 | 21 | Gaston Mazzacane | Minardi-Fondmetal | 69 | +2 Laps | 20 |
| DSQ | 2 | David Coulthard | McLaren-Mercedes | 71 | Disqualified | 2 |
| Ret | 8 | Johnny Herbert | Jaguar-Cosworth | 51 | Gearbox | 17 |
| Ret | 20 | Marc Gene | Minardi-Fondmetal | 31 | Engine | 18 |
| Ret | 1 | Mika Hakkinen | McLaren-Mercedes | 30 | Oil pressure | 1 |
| Ret | 4 | R.Barrichello | Ferrari | 27 | Hydraulics | 4 |
| Ret | 7 | Eddie Irvine | Jaguar-Cosworth | 20 | Spun off | 6 |
| Ret | 22 | J.Villeneuve | BAR-Honda | 16 | Gearbox | 10 |
| Ret | 14 | Jean Alesi | Prost-Peugeot | 11 | Electrical | 15 |
| Ret | 15 | Nick Heidfeld | Prost-Peugeot | 9 | Engine | 19 |
| Ret | 12 | Alexander Wurz | Benetton-Playlife | 6 | Engine | 13 |
| Wth | 16 | Pedro Diniz | Sauber-Petronas | | Safety concerns | |
| Wth | 17 | Mika Salo | Sauber-Petronas | | Safety concerns | |

Winning speed: 124.525mph Lap leaders: Häkkinen 1, 23-29; M Schumacher 2-20, 30-71; Barrichello 21-22
Pole position: Häkkinen, 1m 14.111s, 130.061mph
Fastest lap: M Schumacher, 1m 14.755s, 128.940mph

**SAN MARINO GRAND PRIX: IMOLA** *9 April Round: 3 Race: 649 62 x 3.065 miles*

| POS. | NO. | DRIVER | CAR/ENGINE | LAPS | TIME/RETIRED | GRID |
|---|---|---|---|---|---|---|
| 1 | 3 | M.Schumacher | Ferrari | 62 | 1:31'39.776 | 2 |
| 2 | 1 | Mika Hakkinen | McLaren-Mercedes | 62 | +1.168 | 1 |
| 3 | 2 | David Coulthard | McLaren-Mercedes | 62 | +51.008 | 3 |
| 4 | 4 | R.Barrichello | Ferrari | 62 | +1'29.276 | 4 |
| 5 | 22 | J.Villeneuve | BAR-Honda | 61 | +1 Lap | 9 |
| 6 | 17 | Mika Salo | Sauber-Petronas | 61 | +1 Lap | 12 |
| 7 | 7 | Eddie Irvine | Jaguar-Cosworth | 61 | +1 Lap | 7 |
| 8 | 16 | Pedro Diniz | Sauber-Petronas | 61 | +1 Lap | 10 |
| 9 | 12 | Alexander Wurz | Benetton-Playlife | 61 | +1 Lap | 11 |
| 10 | 8 | Johnny Herbert | Jaguar-Cosworth | 61 | +1 Lap | 17 |
| 11 | 11 | G.Fisichella | Benetton-Playlife | 61 | +1 Lap | 19 |
| 12 | 23 | Ricardo Zonta | BAR-Honda | 61 | +1 Lap | 14 |
| 13 | 21 | Gaston Mazzacane | Minardi-Fondmetal | 60 | +2 Laps | 20 |
| 14 | 19 | Jos Verstappen | Arrows-Supertec | 59 | +3 Laps | 16 |
| 15 | 6 | Jarno Trulli | Jordan-Mugen-Honda | 58 | Gearbox | 8 |
| Ret | 18 | Pedro de la Rosa | Arrows-Supertec | 49 | Spun off | 13 |
| Ret | 9 | Ralf Schumacher | Williams-BMW | 45 | Fuel system | 5 |
| Ret | 14 | Jean Alesi | Prost-Peugeot | 25 | Hydraulics | 15 |
| Ret | 15 | Nick Heidfeld | Prost-Peugeot | 22 | Hydraulics | 22 |
| Ret | 10 | Jenson Button | Williams-BMW | 5 | Engine | 18 |
| Ret | 20 | Marc Gene | Minardi-Fondmetal | 5 | Spun off | 21 |
| Ret | 5 | H-H.Frentzen | Jordan-Mugen-Honda | 4 | Gearbox | 6 |

Winning speed: 124.301mph Lap leaders: Häkkinen 1-44, M Schumacher 45-62
Pole position: Häkkinen, 1m 24.714s, 130.259mph
Fastest lap: Häkkinen, 1m 26.523s, 127.536mph

**BRITISH GRAND PRIX: SILVERSTONE** *23 April Round: 4 Race: 650 60 x 3.194 miles*

| POS. | NO. | DRIVER | CAR/ENGINE | LAPS | TIME/RETIRED | GRID |
|---|---|---|---|---|---|---|
| 1 | 2 | David Coulthard | McLaren-Mercedes | 60 | 1:28'50.108 | 4 |
| 2 | 1 | Mika Hakkinen | McLaren-Mercedes | 60 | +1.477 | 3 |
| 3 | 3 | M.Schumacher | Ferrari | 60 | +19.917 | 5 |
| 4 | 9 | Ralf Schumacher | Williams-BMW | 60 | +41.312 | 7 |
| 5 | 10 | Jenson Button | Williams-BMW | 60 | +57.759 | 6 |
| 6 | 6 | Jarno Trulli | Jordan-Mugen-Honda | 60 | +1'19.273 | 11 |
| 7 | 11 | G.Fisichella | Benetton-Playlife | 59 | +1 Lap | 12 |
| 8 | 17 | Mika Salo | Sauber-Petronas | 59 | +1 Lap | 18 |
| 9 | 12 | Alexander Wurz | Benetton-Playlife | 59 | +1 Lap | 20 |
| 10 | 14 | Jean Alesi | Prost-Peugeot | 59 | +1 Lap | 15 |
| 11 | 16 | Pedro Diniz | Sauber-Petronas | 59 | +1 Lap | 13 |
| 12 | 8 | Johnny Herbert | Jaguar-Cosworth | 59 | +1 Lap | 14 |
| 13 | 7 | Eddie Irvine | Jaguar-Cosworth | 59 | +1 Lap | 9 |
| 14 | 20 | Marc Gene | Minardi-Fondmetal | 59 | +1 Lap | 21 |
| 15 | 21 | Gaston Mazzacane | Minardi-Fondmetal | 59 | +1 Lap | 22 |
| 16 | 22 | J.Villeneuve | BAR-Honda | 56 | Gearbox | 10 |
| 17 | 5 | H-H.Frentzen | Jordan-Mugen-Honda | 54 | Gearbox | 2 |
| Ret | 15 | Nick Heidfeld | Prost-Peugeot | 51 | Engine | 17 |
| Ret | 23 | Ricardo Zonta | BAR-Honda | 36 | Spun off | 16 |
| Ret | 4 | R.Barrichello | Ferrari | 35 | Hydraulics | 1 |
| Ret | 18 | Pedro de la Rosa | Arrows-Supertec | 26 | Electrical | 19 |
| Ret | 19 | Jos Verstappen | Arrows-Supertec | 20 | Electrical | 8 |

Winning speed: 129.410mph Lap leaders: Barrichello 1-30, 33-35; Coulthard 31-32, 42-60; M Schumacher 36-38; Frentzen 39-41
Pole position: Barrichello, 1m 25.703s, 134.185mph
Fastest lap: Häkkinen, 1m 26.217s, 133.386mph

**SPANISH GRAND PRIX: MONTMELO** *7 May Round: 5 Race: 651 65 x 2.939 miles*

| POS. | NO. | DRIVER | CAR/ENGINE | LAPS | TIME/RETIRED | GRID |
|---|---|---|---|---|---|---|
| 1 | 1 | Mika Hakkinen | McLaren-Mercedes | 65 | 1:33'55.390 | 2 |
| 2 | 2 | David Coulthard | McLaren-Mercedes | 65 | +16.066 | 4 |
| 3 | 4 | R.Barrichello | Ferrari | 65 | +29.112 | 3 |
| 4 | 9 | Ralf Schumacher | Williams-BMW | 65 | +37.311 | 5 |
| 5 | 3 | M.Schumacher | Ferrari | 65 | +47.983 | 1 |
| 6 | 5 | H-H.Frentzen | Jordan-Mugen-Honda | 65 | +1'21.925 | 8 |
| 7 | 17 | Mika Salo | Sauber-Petronas | 64 | +1 Lap | 12 |
| 8 | 23 | Ricardo Zonta | BAR-Honda | 64 | +1 Lap | 16 |
| 9 | 11 | G.Fisichella | Benetton-Playlife | 64 | +1 Lap | 13 |
| 10 | 12 | Alexander Wurz | Benetton-Playlife | 64 | +1 Lap | 18 |
| 11 | 7 | Eddie Irvine | Jaguar-Cosworth | 64 | +1 Lap | 9 |
| 12 | 6 | Jarno Trulli | Jordan-Mugen-Honda | 64 | +1 Lap | 7 |
| 13 | 8 | Johnny Herbert | Jaguar-Cosworth | 64 | +1 Lap | 14 |
| 14 | 20 | Marc Gene | Minardi-Fondmetal | 63 | +2 Laps | 20 |
| 15 | 21 | Gaston Mazzacane | Minardi-Fondmetal | 63 | +2 Laps | 21 |
| 16 | 15 | Nick Heidfeld | Prost-Peugeot | 62 | +3 Laps | 19 |
| 17 | 10 | Jenson Button | Williams-BMW | 61 | Engine | 10 |
| Ret | 19 | Jos Verstappen | Arrows-Supertec | 25 | Gearbox | 11 |
| Ret | 22 | J.Villeneuve | BAR-Honda | 21 | Hydraulics | 6 |
| Ret | 14 | Jean Alesi | Prost-Peugeot | 1 | Collision | 17 |
| Ret | 18 | Pedro de la Rosa | Arrows-Supertec | 1 | Collision | 22 |
| Ret | 16 | Pedro Diniz | Sauber-Petronas | 0 | Spun off | 15 |

Winning speed: 121.990mph Lap leaders: M Schumacher 1-23, 27-41; Häkkinen 24-26, 42-65
Pole position: M Schumacher, 1m 20.974s, 130.668mph
Fastest lap: Häkkinen, 1m 24.470s, 125.260mph

**EUROPEAN GRAND PRIX: NÜRBURGRING** *21 May Round: 6 Race: 652 67 x 2.831 miles*

| POS. | NO. | DRIVER | CAR/ENGINE | LAPS | TIME/RETIRED | GRID |
|---|---|---|---|---|---|---|
| 1 | 3 | M.Schumacher | Ferrari | 67 | 1:42'00.307 | 2 |
| 2 | 1 | Mika Hakkinen | McLaren-Mercedes | 67 | +13.822 | 3 |
| 3 | 2 | David Coulthard | McLaren-Mercedes | 66 | +1 Lap | 1 |
| 4 | 4 | R.Barrichello | Ferrari | 66 | +1 Lap | 4 |
| 5 | 11 | G.Fisichella | Benetton-Playlife | 66 | +1 Lap | 7 |
| 6 | 18 | Pedro de la Rosa | Arrows-Supertec | 66 | +1 Lap | 12 |
| 7 | 16 | Pedro Diniz | Sauber-Petronas | 65 | +2 Laps | 15 |
| 8 | 21 | Gaston Mazzacane | Minardi-Fondmetal | 65 | +2 Laps | 21 |
| 9 | 14 | Jean Alesi | Prost-Peugeot | 65 | +2 Laps | 17 |
| 10 | 10 | Jenson Button | Williams-BMW | 62 | Electrical | 5 |
| 11 | 8 | Johnny Herbert | Jaguar-Cosworth | 61 | Collision | 16 |
| 12 | 12 | Alexander Wurz | Benetton-Playlife | 61 | Collision | 14 |
| Ret | 23 | Ricardo Zonta | BAR-Honda | 51 | Spun off | 18 |
| Ret | 20 | Marc Gene | Minardi-Fondmetal | 47 | Throttle | 20 |
| Ret | 22 | J.Villeneuve | BAR-Honda | 46 | Engine | 9 |
| Ret | 7 | Eddie Irvine | Jaguar-Cosworth | 29 | Collision | 8 |
| Ret | 19 | Jos Verstappen | Arrows-Supertec | 29 | Spun off | 13 |
| Ret | 9 | Ralf Schumacher | Williams-BMW | 29 | Collision | 5 |
| Ret | 17 | Mika Salo | Sauber-Petronas | 27 | Halfshaft | 19 |
| Ret | 5 | H-H.Frentzen | Jordan-Mugen-Honda | 2 | Engine | 10 |
| Ret | 6 | Jarno Trulli | Jordan-Mugen-Honda | 0 | Collision | 6 |
| DSQ | 15 | Nick Heidfeld | Prost-Peugeot | 0 | Disqualified | |

Winning speed: 111.561mph Lap leaders: Häkkinen 1-10, 36-45; M Schumacher 11-15, 17-35, 46-67; Barrichello 16
Pole position: Coulthard, 1m 17.529s, 131.454mph
Fastest lap: M Schumacher, 1m 22.269s, 123.880mph

**MONACO GRAND PRIX: MONTE CARLO** *4 June Round: 7 Race: 653 78 x 2.094 miles*

| POS. | NO. | DRIVER | CAR/ENGINE | LAPS | TIME/RETIRED | GRID |
|---|---|---|---|---|---|---|
| 1 | 2 | David Coulthard | McLaren-Mercedes | 78 | 1:49'28.213 | 3 |
| 2 | 4 | R.Barrichello | Ferrari | 78 | +15.889 | 6 |
| 3 | 11 | G.Fisichella | Benetton-Playlife | 78 | +18.522 | 8 |
| 4 | 7 | Eddie Irvine | Jaguar-Cosworth | 78 | +1'05.924 | 10 |
| 5 | 17 | Mika Salo | Sauber-Petronas | 78 | +1'20.775 | 13 |
| 6 | 1 | Mika Hakkinen | McLaren-Mercedes | 77 | +1 Lap | 5 |
| 7 | 22 | J.Villeneuve | BAR-Honda | 77 | +1 Lap | 17 |
| 8 | 15 | Nick Heidfeld | Prost-Peugeot | 77 | +1 Lap | 18 |
| 9 | 8 | Johnny Herbert | Jaguar-Cosworth | 76 | +2 Laps | 4 |
| 10 | 5 | H-H.Frentzen | Jordan-Mugen-Honda | 70 | Spun off | 14 |
| Ret | 19 | Jos Verstappen | Arrows-Supertec | 60 | Spun off | 15 |
| Ret | 3 | M.Schumacher | Ferrari | 55 | Suspension | 1 |
| Ret | 23 | Ricardo Zonta | BAR-Honda | 48 | Spun off | 20 |
| Ret | 9 | Ralf Schumacher | Williams-BMW | 37 | Spun off | 9 |
| Ret | 6 | Jarno Trulli | Jordan-Mugen-Honda | 36 | Gearbox | 2 |
| Ret | 16 | Pedro Diniz | Sauber-Petronas | 30 | Spun off | 19 |
| Ret | 14 | Jean Alesi | Prost-Peugeot | 29 | Transmission | 7 |
| Ret | 21 | Gaston Mazzacane | Minardi-Fondmetal | 22 | Spun off | 22 |
| Ret | 20 | Marc Gene | Minardi-Fondmetal | 21 | Gearbox | 21 |
| Ret | 12 | Alexander Wurz | Benetton-Playlife | 18 | Spun off | 12 |
| Ret | 10 | Jenson Button | Williams-BMW | 16 | Engine | 14 |
| DNS | 18 | Pedro de la Rosa | Arrows-Supertec | 0 | | 16 |

Winning speed: 89.522mph Lap leaders: M Schumacher 1-55; Coulthard 56-78
Pole position: M Schumacher 1m 19.475s, 94.853mph
Fastest lap: Häkkinen, 1m 21.571s, 92.416mph
Race stopped by mistake after one lap. Restarted for total original distance.

**CANADIAN GRAND PRIX: MONTREAL** *18 June Round: 8 Race: 654 69 x 2.747 miles*

| POS. | NO. | DRIVER | CAR/ENGINE | LAPS | TIME/RETIRED | GRID |
|---|---|---|---|---|---|---|
| 1 | 3 | M.Schumacher | Ferrari | 69 | 1:41'12.313 | 1 |
| 2 | 4 | R.Barrichello | Ferrari | 69 | +0.174 | 3 |
| 3 | 11 | G.Fisichella | Benetton-Playlife | 69 | +15.365 | 10 |
| 4 | 1 | Mika Hakkinen | McLaren-Mercedes | 69 | +18.561 | 4 |
| 5 | 19 | Jos Verstappen | Arrows-Supertec | 69 | +52.208 | 13 |
| 6 | 6 | Jarno Trulli | Jordan-Mugen-Honda | 69 | +1'01.687 | 7 |
| 7 | 2 | David Coulthard | McLaren-Mercedes | 69 | +1'02.216 | 2 |
| 8 | 23 | Ricardo Zonta | BAR-Honda | 69 | +1'10.455 | 8 |
| 9 | 12 | Alexander Wurz | Benetton-Playlife | 69 | +1'19.899 | 14 |
| 10 | 16 | Pedro Diniz | Sauber-Petronas | 69 | +1'54.544 | 19 |
| 11 | 10 | Jenson Button | Williams-BMW | 68 | +1 Lap | 18 |
| 12 | 21 | Gaston Mazzacane | Minardi-Fondmetal | 68 | +1 Lap | 22 |
| 13 | 7 | Eddie Irvine | Jaguar-Cosworth | 66 | +3 Laps | 16 |
| 14 | 9 | Ralf Schumacher | Williams-BMW | 64 | Collision | 12 |
| 15 | 22 | J.Villeneuve | BAR-Honda | 64 | Collision | 6 |
| 16 | 20 | Marc Gene | Minardi-Fondmetal | 64 | Spun off | 20 |
| Ret | 18 | Pedro de la Rosa | Arrows-Supertec | 48 | Collision | 9 |
| Ret | 17 | Mika Salo | Sauber-Petronas | 42 | Electrical | 15 |
| Ret | 14 | Jean Alesi | Prost-Peugeot | 38 | Electrical | 17 |
| Ret | 15 | Nick Heidfeld | Prost-Peugeot | 34 | Engine | 21 |
| Ret | 5 | H-H.Frentzen | Jordan-Mugen-Honda | 32 | Brakes | 5 |
| Ret | 8 | Johnny Herbert | Jaguar-Cosworth | 14 | Gearbox | 11 |

Winning speed: 112.374mph Lap leaders: M Schumacher 1-34, 43-69; Barrichello 35-42
Pole position: M Schumacher, 1m 18.439s, 126.079mph
Fastest lap: Häkkinen, 1m 19.049s, 125.106mph

**FRENCH GRAND PRIX: MAGNY-COURS** *2 July Round: 9 Race: 655 72 x 2.641 miles*

| POS. | NO. | DRIVER | CAR/ENGINE | LAPS | TIME/RETIRED | GRID |
|---|---|---|---|---|---|---|
| 1 | 2 | David Coulthard | McLaren-Mercedes | 72 | 1:38'05.538 | 1 |
| 2 | 1 | Mika Hakkinen | McLaren-Mercedes | 72 | +14.748 | 4 |
| 3 | 4 | R.Barrichello | Ferrari | 72 | +32.409 | 3 |
| 4 | 22 | J.Villeneuve | BAR-Honda | 72 | +1'01.322 | 7 |
| 5 | 9 | Ralf Schumacher | Williams-BMW | 72 | +1'03.981 | 5 |
| 6 | 6 | Jarno Trulli | Jordan-Mugen-Honda | 72 | +1'15.605 | 9 |
| 7 | 5 | H-H.Frentzen | Jordan-Mugen-Honda | 71 | +1 Lap | 8 |
| 8 | 10 | Jenson Button | Williams-BMW | 71 | +1 Lap | 10 |
| 9 | 11 | G.Fisichella | Benetton-Playlife | 71 | +1 Lap | 14 |
| 10 | 17 | Mika Salo | Sauber-Petronas | 71 | +1 Lap | 12 |
| 11 | 16 | Pedro Diniz | Sauber-Petronas | 71 | +1 Lap | 15 |
| 12 | 15 | Nick Heidfeld | Prost-Peugeot | 71 | +1 Lap | 16 |
| 13 | 7 | Eddie Irvine | Jaguar-Cosworth | 70 | +2 Laps | 6 |
| 14 | 14 | Jean Alesi | Prost-Peugeot | 70 | +2 Laps | 18 |
| 15 | 20 | Marc Gene | Minardi-Fondmetal | 70 | +2 Laps | 21 |
| Ret | 3 | M.Schumacher | Ferrari | 58 | Engine | 1 |
| Ret | 18 | Pedro de la Rosa | Arrows-Supertec | 45 | Transmission | 13 |
| Ret | 12 | Alexander Wurz | Benetton-Playlife | 34 | Spun off | 17 |
| Ret | 21 | Gaston Mazzacane | Minardi-Fondmetal | 31 | Spun off | 22 |
| Ret | 19 | Jos Verstappen | Arrows-Supertec | 25 | Transmission | 20 |
| Ret | 8 | Johnny Herbert | Jaguar-Cosworth | 20 | Gearbox | 11 |
| Ret | 23 | Ricardo Zonta | BAR-Honda | 16 | Spun off | 19 |

Winning speed: 116.259mph Lap leaders: M Schumacher 1-24, 26-39; Coulthard 25, 40-72
Pole position: M Schumacher, 1m 15.632s, 125.729mph
Fastest lap: Coulthard, 1m 19.479s, 119.644mph

**AUSTRIAN GRAND PRIX: A1 RING** *16 August Round: 10 Race: 656 71 x 2.688 miles*

| POS. | NO. | DRIVER | CAR/ENGINE | LAPS | TIME/RETIRED | GRID |
|---|---|---|---|---|---|---|
| 1 | 1 | Mika Hakkinen | McLaren-Mercedes | 71 | 1:28'15.818 | 1 |
| 2 | 2 | David Coulthard | McLaren-Mercedes | 71 | +12.535 | 2 |
| 3 | 4 | R.Barrichello | Ferrari | 71 | +30.795 | 3 |
| 4 | 22 | J.Villeneuve | BAR-Honda | 70 | +1 Lap | 7 |
| 5 | 10 | Jenson Button | Williams-BMW | 70 | +1 Lap | 18 |
| 6 | 17 | Mika Salo | Sauber-Petronas | 70 | +1 Lap | 9 |
| 7 | 8 | Johnny Herbert | Jaguar-Cosworth | 70 | +1 Lap | 16 |
| 8 | 20 | Marc Gene | Minardi-Fondmetal | 70 | +1 Lap | 20 |
| 9 | 16 | Pedro Diniz | Sauber-Petronas | 70 | +1 Lap | 11 |
| 10 | 12 | Alexander Wurz | Benetton-Playlife | 70 | +1 Lap | 14 |
| 11 | 7 | Luciano Burti | Jaguar-Cosworth | 69 | +2 Laps | 21 |
| 12 | 21 | Gaston Mazzacane | Minardi-Fondmetal | 68 | +3 Laps | 22 |
| Ret | 23 | Ricardo Zonta | BAR-Honda | 58 | Engine | 6 |
| Ret | 9 | Ralf Schumacher | Williams-BMW | 52 | Brakes | 19 |
| Ret | 15 | Nick Heidfeld | Prost-Peugeot | 41 | Collision | 13 |
| Ret | 14 | Jean Alesi | Prost-Peugeot | 41 | Collision | 17 |
| Ret | 18 | Pedro de la Rosa | Arrows-Supertec | 32 | Gearbox | 12 |
| Ret | 19 | Jos Verstappen | Arrows-Supertec | 14 | Engine | 10 |
| Ret | 5 | H-H.Frentzen | Jordan-Mugen-Honda | 4 | Oil leak | 15 |
| Ret | 3 | M.Schumacher | Ferrari | 0 | Collision | 4 |
| Ret | 6 | Jarno Trulli | Jordan-Mugen-Honda | 0 | Collision | 5 |
| Ret | 11 | G.Fisichella | Benetton-Playlife | 0 | Collision | 8 |

Winning speed: 129.737mph Lap leaders: Häkkinen 1-38, 39-42; Coulthard 43-71
Pole position: Häkkinen, 1m 10.410s, 137.437mph
Fastest lap: Coulthard, 1m 11.783s, 134.808mph

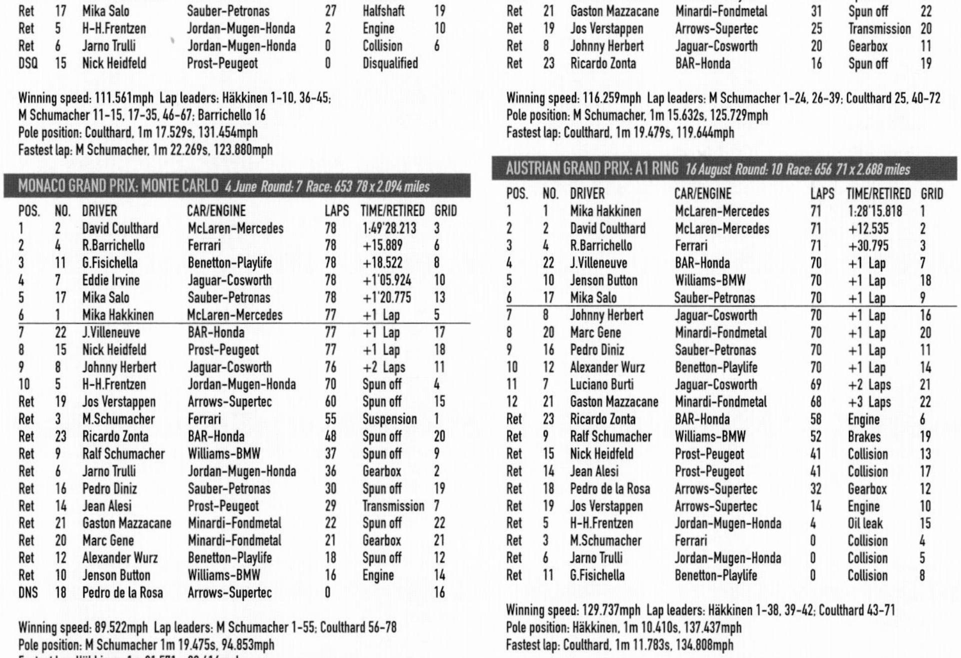

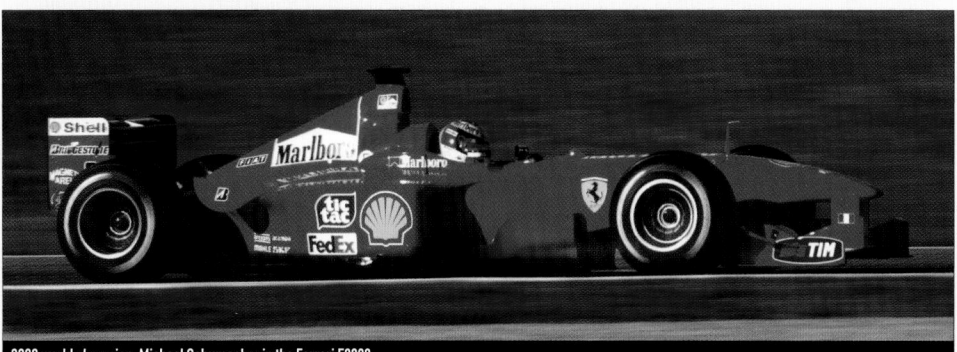

2000 world champion, Michael Schumacher in the Ferrari F2000.

2000 Season Statistics

### GERMAN GRAND PRIX: HOCKENHEIM *30 July Round: 11 Race: 657 45 x 4.241 miles*

| POS. | NO. | DRIVER | CAR/ENGINE | LAPS | TIME/RETIRED | GRID |
|---|---|---|---|---|---|---|
| 1 | 4 | R.Barrichello | Ferrari | 45 | 1:25'34.418 | 18 |
| 2 | 1 | Mika Hakkinen | McLaren-Mercedes | 45 | +7.452 | 4 |
| 3 | 2 | David Coulthard | McLaren-Mercedes | 45 | +21.168 | 1 |
| 4 | 10 | Jenson Button | Williams-BMW | 45 | +22.685 | 16 |
| 5 | 17 | Mika Salo | Sauber-Petronas | 45 | +27.112 | 15 |
| 6 | 18 | Pedro de la Rosa | Arrows-Supertec | 45 | +29.080 | 5 |
| 7 | 9 | Ralf Schumacher | Williams-BMW | 45 | +30.898 | 14 |
| 8 | 22 | J.Villeneuve | BAR-Honda | 45 | +47.537 | 9 |
| 9 | 6 | Jarno Trulli | Jordan-Mugen-Honda | 45 | +50.901 | 6 |
| 10 | 7 | Eddie Irvine | Jaguar-Cosworth | 45 | +1'19.664 | 10 |
| 11 | 21 | Gaston Mazzacane | Minardi-Fondmetal | 45 | +1'29.504 | 21 |
| 12 | 15 | Nick Heidfeld | Prost-Peugeot | 40 | Alternator | 13 |
| Ret | 5 | H-H.Frentzen | Jordan-Mugen-Honda | 39 | Gearbox | 17 |
| Ret | 19 | Jos Verstappen | Arrows-Supertec | 39 | Spun off | 11 |
| Ret | 23 | Ricardo Zonta | BAR-Honda | 37 | Spun off | 12 |
| Ret | 20 | Marc Gene | Minardi-Fondmetal | 33 | Engine | 22 |
| Ret | 12 | Alexander Wurz | Benetton-Playlife | 31 | Electrical | 7 |
| Ret | 16 | Pedro Diniz | Sauber-Petronas | 29 | Collision | 19 |
| Ret | 14 | Jean Alesi | Prost-Peugeot | 29 | Collision | 20 |
| Ret | 8 | Johnny Herbert | Jaguar-Cosworth | 12 | Gearbox | 8 |
| Ret | 3 | M.Schumacher | Ferrari | 0 | Collision | 2 |
| Ret | 11 | G.Fisichella | Benetton-Playlife | 0 | Collision | 3 |

Winning speed: 133.806mph Lap leaders: Häkkinen 1-25, 28-35; Coulthard 26-27; Barrichello 36-45
Pole position: Coulthard, 1m 45.697s, 144.441mph
Fastest lap: Barrichello, 1m 44.300s, 146.376mph

### HUNGARIAN GRAND PRIX: HUNGARORING *13 August Round: 12 Race: 658 77 x 2.470 miles*

| POS. | NO. | DRIVER | CAR/ENGINE | LAPS | TIME/RETIRED | GRID |
|---|---|---|---|---|---|---|
| 1 | 1 | Mika Hakkinen | McLaren-Mercedes | 77 | 1:45'33.869 | 3 |
| 2 | 3 | M.Schumacher | Ferrari | 77 | +7.917 | 1 |
| 3 | 2 | David Coulthard | McLaren-Mercedes | 77 | +8.455 | 2 |
| 4 | 4 | R.Barrichello | Ferrari | 77 | +44.157 | 5 |
| 5 | 9 | Ralf Schumacher | Williams-BMW | 77 | +50.437 | 4 |
| 6 | 5 | H-H.Frentzen | Jordan-Mugen-Honda | 77 | +1'08.099 | 6 |
| 7 | 6 | Jarno Trulli | Jordan-Mugen-Honda | 76 | +1 Lap | 12 |
| 8 | 7 | Eddie Irvine | Jaguar-Cosworth | 76 | +1 Lap | 10 |
| 9 | 10 | Jenson Button | Williams-BMW | 76 | +1 Lap | 8 |
| 10 | 17 | Mika Salo | Sauber-Petronas | 76 | +1 Lap | 9 |
| 11 | 12 | Alexander Wurz | Benetton-Playlife | 76 | +1 Lap | 11 |
| 12 | 22 | J.Villeneuve | BAR-Honda | 75 | +2 Laps | 16 |
| 13 | 19 | Jos Verstappen | Arrows-Supertec | 75 | +2 Laps | 20 |
| 14 | 23 | Ricardo Zonta | BAR-Honda | 75 | +2 Laps | 18 |
| 15 | 20 | Marc Gene | Minardi-Fondmetal | 74 | +3 Laps | 21 |
| 16 | 18 | Pedro de la Rosa | Arrows-Supertec | 73 | +4 Laps | 15 |
| Ret | 21 | Gaston Mazzacane | Minardi-Fondmetal | 68 | Engine | 22 |
| Ret | 8 | Johnny Herbert | Jaguar-Cosworth | 67 | Gearbox | 17 |
| Ret | 16 | Pedro Diniz | Sauber-Petronas | 62 | Transmission | 13 |
| Ret | 11 | G.Fisichella | Benetton-Playlife | 31 | Brakes | 7 |
| Ret | 15 | Nick Heidfeld | Prost-Peugeot | 22 | Electrical | 19 |
| Ret | 14 | Jean Alesi | Prost-Peugeot | 11 | Suspension | 14 |

Winning speed: 108.096mph Lap leaders: Häkkinen 1-31, 33-77; Coulthard 32
Pole position: M Schumacher, 1m 17.514s, 114.712mph
Fastest lap: Häkkinen, 1m 20.028s, 111.109mph

### BELGIAN GRAND PRIX: SPA-FRANCORCHAMPS *27 August Round: 13 Race: 659 44 x 4.330 miles*

| POS. | NO. | DRIVER | CAR/ENGINE | LAPS | TIME/RETIRED | GRID |
|---|---|---|---|---|---|---|
| 1 | 1 | Mika Hakkinen | McLaren-Mercedes | 44 | 1:28'14.494 | 1 |
| 2 | 3 | M.Schumacher | Ferrari | 44 | +1.104 | 2 |
| 3 | 9 | Ralf Schumacher | Williams-BMW | 44 | +38.096 | 6 |
| 4 | 2 | David Coulthard | McLaren-Mercedes | 44 | +43.281 | 5 |
| 5 | 10 | Jenson Button | Williams-BMW | 44 | +49.914 | 3 |
| 6 | 5 | H-H.Frentzen | Jordan-Mugen-Honda | 44 | +55.984 | 8 |
| 7 | 22 | J.Villeneuve | BAR-Honda | 44 | +1'12.380 | 7 |
| 8 | 8 | Johnny Herbert | Jaguar-Cosworth | 44 | +1'27.808 | 9 |
| 9 | 17 | Mika Salo | Sauber-Petronas | 44 | +1'28.670 | 18 |
| 10 | 7 | Eddie Irvine | Jaguar-Cosworth | 44 | +1'31.555 | 12 |
| 11 | 16 | Pedro Diniz | Sauber-Petronas | 44 | +1'34.123 | 15 |
| 12 | 23 | Ricardo Zonta | BAR-Honda | 43 | +1 Lap | 13 |
| 13 | 12 | Alexander Wurz | Benetton-Playlife | 43 | +1 Lap | 19 |
| 14 | 20 | Marc Gene | Minardi-Fondmetal | 43 | +1 Lap | 21 |
| 15 | 19 | Jos Verstappen | Arrows-Supertec | 43 | +1 Lap | 20 |
| 16 | 18 | Pedro de la Rosa | Arrows-Supertec | 42 | +2 Laps | 16 |
| 17 | 21 | Gaston Mazzacane | Minardi-Fondmetal | 42 | +2 Laps | 22 |
| Ret | 4 | R.Barrichello | Ferrari | 32 | Fuel pressure | 10 |
| Ret | 14 | Jean Alesi | Prost-Peugeot | 32 | Fuel pressure | 17 |
| Ret | 15 | Nick Heidfeld | Prost-Peugeot | 12 | Engine | 14 |
| Ret | 11 | G.Fisichella | Benetton-Playlife | 8 | Electrical | 11 |
| Ret | 6 | Jarno Trulli | Jordan-Mugen-Honda | 4 | Collision | 2 |

Winning speed: 129.535mph Lap leaders: Häkkinen 1-12, 23-27, 41-44; M Schumacher 13-22, 28-40
Pole position: Häkkinen, 1m 50.646s, 140.872mph
Fastest lap: Barrichello, 1m 53.803s, 136.964mph

### ITALIAN GRAND PRIX: MONZA *10 September Round: 14 Race: 660 53 x 3.600 miles*

| POS. | NO. | DRIVER | CAR/ENGINE | LAPS | TIME/RETIRED | GRID |
|---|---|---|---|---|---|---|
| 1 | 3 | M.Schumacher | Ferrari | 53 | 1:27'31.638 | 1 |
| 2 | 1 | Mika Hakkinen | McLaren-Mercedes | 53 | +3.810 | 3 |
| 3 | 9 | Ralf Schumacher | Williams-BMW | 53 | +52.432 | 7 |
| 4 | 19 | Jos Verstappen | Arrows-Supertec | 53 | +59.938 | 11 |
| 5 | 12 | Alexander Wurz | Benetton-Playlife | 53 | +1'07.426 | 13 |
| 6 | 23 | Ricardo Zonta | BAR-Honda | 53 | +1'09.293 | 17 |
| 7 | 17 | Mika Salo | Sauber-Petronas | 52 | +1 Lap | 15 |
| 8 | 16 | Pedro Diniz | Sauber-Petronas | 52 | +1 Lap | 16 |
| 9 | 20 | Marc Gene | Minardi-Fondmetal | 52 | +1 Lap | 21 |
| 10 | 21 | Gaston Mazzacane | Minardi-Fondmetal | 52 | +1 Lap | 22 |
| 11 | 11 | G.Fisichella | Benetton-Playlife | 52 | +1 Lap | 9 |
| 12 | 14 | Jean Alesi | Prost-Peugeot | 51 | +2 Laps | 19 |
| Ret | 15 | Nick Heidfeld | Prost-Peugeot | 15 | Spun off | 20 |
| Ret | 22 | J.Villeneuve | BAR-Honda | 14 | Electrical | 4 |
| Ret | 10 | Jenson Button | Williams-BMW | 10 | Spun off | 12 |
| Ret | 8 | Johnny Herbert | Jaguar-Cosworth | 1 | Spun off | 18 |
| Ret | 4 | R.Barrichello | Ferrari | 0 | Collision | 2 |
| Ret | 2 | David Coulthard | McLaren-Mercedes | 0 | Collision | 5 |
| Ret | 6 | Jarno Trulli | Jordan-Mugen-Honda | 0 | Collision | 6 |
| Ret | 5 | H-H.Frentzen | Jordan-Mugen-Honda | 0 | Collision | 8 |
| Ret | 18 | Pedro de la Rosa | Arrows-Supertec | 0 | Collision | 10 |
| Ret | 7 | Eddie Irvine | Jaguar-Cosworth | 0 | Spun off | 14 |

Winning speed: 130.666mph Lap leaders: M Schumacher 1-39, 43-53; Häkkinen 40-42
Pole position: M Schumacher, 1m 23.770s, 154.692mph
Fastest lap: Häkkinen, 1m 25.595s, 151.394mph

### UNITED STATES GRAND PRIX: INDIANAPOLIS *24 September Round: 15 Race: 661 73 x 2.605 miles*

| POS. | NO. | DRIVER | CAR/ENGINE | LAPS | TIME/RETIRED | GRID |
|---|---|---|---|---|---|---|
| 1 | 3 | M.Schumacher | Ferrari | 73 | 1:36'30.883 | 1 |
| 2 | 4 | R.Barrichello | Ferrari | 73 | +12.118 | 4 |
| 3 | 5 | H-H.Frentzen | Jordan-Mugen-Honda | 73 | +17.368 | 7 |
| 4 | 22 | J.Villeneuve | BAR-Honda | 73 | +17.936 | 8 |
| 5 | 2 | David Coulthard | McLaren-Mercedes | 73 | +28.813 | 2 |
| 6 | 23 | Ricardo Zonta | BAR-Honda | 73 | +51.694 | 12 |
| 7 | 7 | Eddie Irvine | Jaguar-Cosworth | 73 | +1'11.115 | 17 |
| 8 | 16 | Pedro Diniz | Sauber-Petronas | 72 | +1 Lap | 9 |
| 9 | 15 | Nick Heidfeld | Prost-Peugeot | 72 | +1 Lap | 16 |
| 10 | 12 | Alexander Wurz | Benetton-Playlife | 72 | +1 Lap | 11 |
| 11 | 8 | Johnny Herbert | Jaguar-Cosworth | 72 | +1 Lap | 19 |
| 12 | 20 | Marc Gene | Minardi-Fondmetal | 72 | +1 Lap | 22 |
| Ret | 14 | Jean Alesi | Prost-Peugeot | 64 | Engine | 20 |
| Ret | 21 | Gaston Mazzacane | Minardi-Fondmetal | 59 | Engine | 21 |
| Ret | 9 | Ralf Schumacher | Williams-BMW | 58 | Engine | 10 |
| Ret | 18 | Pedro de la Rosa | Arrows-Supertec | 45 | Gearbox | 18 |
| Ret | 11 | G.Fisichella | Benetton-Playlife | 44 | Engine | 15 |
| Ret | 19 | Jos Verstappen | Arrows-Supertec | 34 | Brakes | 13 |
| Ret | 1 | Mika Hakkinen | McLaren-Mercedes | 25 | Engine | 3 |
| Ret | 17 | Mika Salo | Sauber-Petronas | 18 | Spun off | 14 |
| Ret | 10 | Jenson Button | Williams-BMW | 14 | Engine | 6 |
| Ret | 6 | Jarno Trulli | Jordan-Mugen-Honda | 12 | Collision | 5 |

Winning speed: 118.203mph Lap leaders: Coulthard 1-6; M Schumacher 7-73
Pole position: M Schumacher, 1m 14.266s, 126.265mph
Fastest lap: Coulthard, 1m 14.711s, 125.513mph

### JAPANESE GRAND PRIX: SUZUKA *8 October Round: 16 Race: 662 53 x 3.644 miles*

| POS. | NO. | DRIVER | CAR/ENGINE | LAPS | TIME/RETIRED | GRID |
|---|---|---|---|---|---|---|
| 1 | 3 | M.Schumacher | Ferrari | 53 | 1:29'53.435 | 1 |
| 2 | 1 | Mika Hakkinen | McLaren-Mercedes | 53 | +1.837 | 2 |
| 3 | 2 | David Coulthard | McLaren-Mercedes | 53 | +1'09.914 | 3 |
| 4 | 4 | R.Barrichello | Ferrari | 53 | +1'19.191 | 4 |
| 5 | 10 | Jenson Button | Williams-BMW | 53 | +1'25.694 | 5 |
| 6 | 22 | J.Villeneuve | BAR-Honda | 52 | +1 Lap | 9 |
| 7 | 8 | Johnny Herbert | Jaguar-Cosworth | 52 | +1 Lap | 10 |
| 8 | 7 | Eddie Irvine | Jaguar-Cosworth | 52 | +1 Lap | 7 |
| 9 | 23 | Ricardo Zonta | BAR-Honda | 52 | +1 Lap | 18 |
| 10 | 17 | Mika Salo | Sauber-Petronas | 52 | +1 Lap | 19 |
| 11 | 16 | Pedro Diniz | Sauber-Petronas | 52 | +1 Lap | 20 |
| 12 | 18 | Pedro de la Rosa | Arrows-Supertec | 52 | +1 Lap | 13 |
| 13 | 6 | Jarno Trulli | Jordan-Mugen-Honda | 52 | +1 Lap | 15 |
| 14 | 11 | G.Fisichella | Benetton-Playlife | 52 | +1 Lap | 12 |
| 15 | 21 | Gaston Mazzacane | Minardi-Fondmetal | 51 | +2 Laps | 22 |
| Ret | 20 | Marc Gene | Minardi-Fondmetal | 46 | Engine | 21 |
| Ret | 9 | Ralf Schumacher | Williams-BMW | 41 | Spun off | 6 |
| Ret | 15 | Nick Heidfeld | Prost-Peugeot | 41 | Suspension | 16 |
| Ret | 12 | Alexander Wurz | Benetton-Playlife | 37 | Spun off | 11 |
| Ret | 5 | H-H.Frentzen | Jordan-Mugen-Honda | 29 | Hydraulics | 8 |
| Ret | 14 | Jean Alesi | Prost-Peugeot | 19 | Engine | 17 |
| Ret | 19 | Jos Verstappen | Arrows-Supertec | 9 | Electrical | 14 |

Winning speed: 128.820mph
Lap leaders: Häkkinen 1-21, 25-36; M Schumacher 22-23, 37-53; Coulthard 24
Pole position: M Schumacher, 1m 35.825s, 136.889mph
Fastest lap: Häkkinen, 1m 39.189s, 132.246mph

### MALAYSIAN GRAND PRIX: SEPANG *22 October Round: 17 Race: 663 56 x 3.444 miles*

| POS. | NO. | DRIVER | CAR/ENGINE | LAPS | TIME/RETIRED | GRID |
|---|---|---|---|---|---|---|
| 1 | 3 | M.Schumacher | Ferrari | 56 | 1:35'54.235 | 1 |
| 2 | 2 | David Coulthard | McLaren-Mercedes | 56 | +0.732 | 3 |
| 3 | 4 | R.Barrichello | Ferrari | 56 | +18.444 | 4 |
| 4 | 1 | Mika Hakkinen | McLaren-Mercedes | 56 | +35.269 | 2 |
| 5 | 22 | J.Villeneuve | BAR-Honda | 56 | +1'10.692 | 6 |
| 6 | 7 | Eddie Irvine | Jaguar-Cosworth | 56 | +1'12.568 | 7 |
| 7 | 12 | Alexander Wurz | Benetton-Playlife | 56 | +1'29.314 | 5 |
| 8 | 17 | Mika Salo | Sauber-Petronas | 55 | +1 Lap | 17 |
| 9 | 11 | G.Fisichella | Benetton-Playlife | 55 | +1 Lap | 13 |
| 10 | 19 | Jos Verstappen | Arrows-Supertec | 55 | +1 Lap | 15 |
| 11 | 14 | Jean Alesi | Prost-Peugeot | 55 | +1 Lap | 18 |
| 12 | 6 | Jarno Trulli | Jordan-Mugen-Honda | 55 | +1 Lap | 9 |
| 13 | 21 | Gaston Mazzacane | Minardi-Fondmetal | 50 | Engine | 22 |
| Ret | 8 | Johnny Herbert | Jaguar-Cosworth | 48 | Suspension | 12 |
| Ret | 23 | Ricardo Zonta | BAR-Honda | 46 | Engine | 11 |
| Ret | 9 | Ralf Schumacher | Williams-BMW | 43 | Engine | 8 |
| Ret | 20 | Marc Gene | Minardi-Fondmetal | 36 | Wheel | 21 |
| Ret | 10 | Jenson Button | Williams-BMW | 18 | Engine | 16 |
| Ret | 5 | H-H.Frentzen | Jordan-Mugen-Honda | 7 | Electrical | 10 |
| Ret | 18 | Pedro de la Rosa | Arrows-Supertec | 0 | Collision | 14 |
| Ret | 15 | Nick Heidfeld | Prost-Peugeot | 0 | Collision | 19 |
| Ret | 16 | Pedro Diniz | Sauber-Petronas | 0 | Collision | 20 |

Winning speed: 120.670mph Lap leaders: Häkkinen 1-2; Coulthard 3-17; M Schumacher 18-24, 26-39, 42-56; Barrichello 25, 40-41
Pole position: M Schumacher, 1m 37.397s, 127.307mph
Fastest lap: Häkkinen, 1m 38.543s, 125.826mph

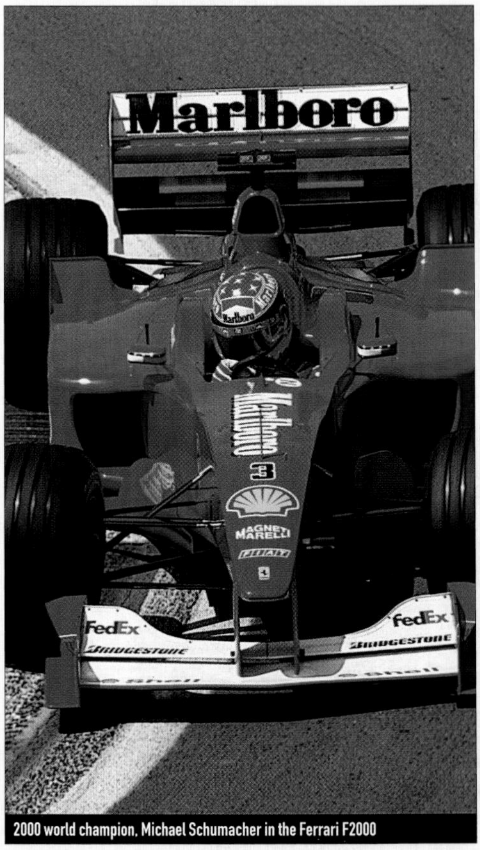

2000 world champion, Michael Schumacher in the Ferrari F2000

## A

ACEA 16
Acer 313
Adbelnour, Simone 42, 130
Adecco 313
Agusta 569
Ainsley-Cowlishaw, Mike 351
Albers, Christijan 370
Alboreto, Michele 16, 17, 78, 110
Alesi, Jean 15, 20, 26, 28, 33, 34, 63, 64, 74, 76,
    78, 89, 119, 167, 171, 174, 180, 184, 186, 191,
    192, 198, 200, 205, 216, 222, 223, 224, 225,
    226, 252, 264, 271, 273, 278, 290, 291, 300,
    301, 304, 309, 314, 315, 316, 317, 318, 319,
    320, 321, 322, 323, 324, 325, 326, 328, 329,
    337, 340, 344, 349, 350, 354, 392, 396, 400,
    408, 412, 416, 424, 432, 437, 440, 448, 456,
    461, 464, 472, 477, 480, 485, 488, 493, 496,
    501, 504, 508, 512, 516, 520, 531, 538, 540,
    544, 555, 559, 567
Alesi, Jose 79
Alesi, Kumiko 517
Ali, Muhammed 56
Allen, James 28, 452
Allsport 17
Alonso, Fernando 12, 15, 33, 91, 92, 106, 132,
    266, 272, 273, 297, 326, 340, 341, 346, 352,
    361, 366, 367, 368, 369, 370, 371, 372, 373,
    374, 375, 376, 377, 378, 379, 380, 381, 382,
    392, 396, 400, 408, 416, 424, 432, 440, 444,
    448, 456, 464, 467, 469, 472, 476, 480, 484,
    488, 496, 501, 504, 509, 512, 520, 534, 541,
    556
Al Waleed, Prince Khaled 24, 28, 313
Anderson, Gary 12, 13, 283,
Andersson, Ove 15, 24
Andretti, Michael 52, 56
AP 530
Arisco 46
Arnault, Bernard 313
Arnoux, René 76
Asiatech 18, 26, 335, 340, 342, 343, 345, 346,
    348, 349, 350, 351, 352, 353, 354, 355, 379,
    382, 504
Astromega 93
Audi 16, 17
Automobile Club de France 26
Auto Sport Racing 93

## B

B3 Technologies 309
Badoer, Luca 14, 111, 115, 116, 562, 564
Baldisserri, Luca 405
Balestre, Jean-Marie 524
BAR Honda 12, 13, 14, 15, 17, 18, 20, 28, 60, 76,
    84, 86, 89, 90, 92, 107, 158, 165, 179, 186, 187,
    188, 189, 192, 193, 194, 197, 198, 199, 200,
    205, 210, 211, 212, 213, 214, 215, 216, 217,
    218, 219, 221, 222, 223, 224, 225, 226, 231,
    236, 237, 238, 239, 240, 241, 242, 243, 244,
    245, 246, 247, 248, 249, 250, 251, 252, 275,
    276, 277, 293, 296, 303, 316, 344, 345, 347,
    350, 388, 392, 396, 400, 408, 412, 416, 424,
    427, 432, 464, 468, 480, 484, 488, 501, 504,
    508, 530, 533, 535, 536, 538, 540, 543, 545,
    547, 549, 554, 559, 561, 563, 565, 567
Barnard, John 309, 524
Barrichello, Eduardo 45
Barrichello, Rubens 14, 17, 18, 24, 32, 36, 41, 44,
    66, 64, 70, 85, 86, 102, 106, 107, 108, 109, 110,
    111, 112, 113, 114, 115, 116, 117, 118, 119,
    120, 121, 122, 132, 137, 140, 141, 143, 144,
    147, 148, 158, 159, 160, 162, 165, 168, 172,
    173, 174, 183, 184, 188, 191, 197, 208, 210,
    211, 212, 213, 214, 216, 217, 218, 219, 223,
    275, 303, 341, 342, 344, 347, 366, 388, 392,
    395, 396, 400, 404, 408, 412, 416, 421, 424,
    428, 432, 436, 440, 444, 448, 453, 456, 461,
    464, 472, 477, 480, 483, 484, 488, 492, 496,
    500, 504, 508, 512, 516, 520, 540, 543, 544,
    548, 555, 561, 562, 564, 566
Barrichello, Sylvana 45, 404
Bauer, Jo 542
Beaumont, Trevor 338
Bell 15
Benetton, Luciano 14, 15
Benetton Renault 12, 14, 15, 16, 18, 24, 34, 41,
    45, 64, 68, 78, 82, 84, 117, 119, 136, 142, 145,
    164, 165, 179, 188, 192, 205, 221, 223, 225,
    226, 245, 252, 262, 263, 264, 265, 266, 267,
    268, 269, 270, 271, 272, 273, 274, 275, 276,
    277, 278, 283, 289, 290, 302, 303, 304, 312,
    315, 316, 318, 319, 323, 325, 335, 340, 341,
    344, 349, 350, 351, 361, 364, 368, 369, 370,
    371, 372, 374, 380, 400, 408, 413, 416, 424,
    432, 436, 440, 448, 464, 468, 476, 477, 480,
    493, 496, 500, 504, 508, 512, 520, 530, 533,
    535, 536, 538, 541, 543, 545, 546, 549, 554,
    558, 561, 563, 565, 566
Benson & Hedges 209, 500
Berger, Christina 162
Berger, Gerhard 34, 48, 79, 84, 155, 161, 162, 164,
    171, 268, 413
Berlusconi, Silvio 17
Bernoldi, Enrique 12, 15, 33, 40, 84, 86, 90, 138,
    146, 183, 217, 267, 269, 273, 293, 325, 330,
    335, 340, 341, 342, 343, 344, 345, 346, 347,
    348, 349, 350, 351, 352, 353, 354, 355, 356,
    367, 375, 376, 392, 400, 408, 424, 432, 437,
    440, 448, 456, 464, 472, 476, 480, 484, 488,
    496, 501, 504, 509, 512, 520, 533, 538, 565
Bertelsmann 18, 313
BMW 12, 13, 16, 20, 24, 48, 61, 79, 77, 94, 101,
    113, 136, 143, 158, 159, 161, 162, 164, 165,
    167, 169, 170, 171, 172, 174, 208, 244, 411,
    416, 445, 452, 456, 472, 476, 512, 544, 554
BMW Williams 12, 13, 14, 15, 16, 17, 18, 26, 28,
    38, 41, 48, 52, 56, 63, 61, 66, 68, 74, 77, 79, 81,
    82, 109, 111, 113, 114, 117, 119, 120, 121, 122,
    127, 132, 135, 140, 142, 143, 146, 147, 148,
    158, 159, 160, 161, 162, 163, 164, 165, 166,
    167, 168, 169, 170, 171, 172, 173, 174, 188,
    194, 199, 205, 211, 212, 214, 223, 236, 240,
    243, 244, 250, 257, 264, 272, 275, 289, 291,
    294, 296, 301, 303, 304, 316, 319, 323, 342,
    344, 353, 388, 396, 400, 404, 408, 412, 416,
    420, 424, 428, 432, 437, 440, 443, 444, 448,
    452, 456, 460, 464, 468, 472, 475, 476, 480,
    484, 488, 492, 496, 499, 500, 504, 508, 512,
    516, 520, 525, 530, 533, 535, 536, 538, 540,
    542, 546, 548, 554, 558, 560, 562, 564, 566,
    568
Brabham 24, 524
Bracks, Steve 366
Bradshaw, Ann 484
Brambilla, Vittorio 18
Brawn, Ross 38, 101, 107, 108, 109,110, 111, 112,
    114, 115, 116, 117, 119, 120, 121, 122, 220,
    404, 452, 484, 525
BRDC 13
Brembo 109, 530, 533, 535, 536, 538, 540, 544,
    546, 549, 554, 561, 562, 564, 566
Briatore, Flavio 12, 18, 24, 26, 64, 68, 79, 83, 84,
    91, 92, 120, 257, 262, 264, 265, 266, 268, 269,
    270, 273, 274, 275, 276, 277, 316, 361, 413,
    436, 500, 504
Bridgestone 13, 16, 18, 28, 79, 109, 110, 111, 113,
    115, 116, 119, 122, 135, 138, 143, 146, 147,
    158, 160, 165, 170, 174, 184, 185, 187, 188,
    189, 190, 191, 192, 193, 194, 195, 196, 197,
    199, 200, 210, 213, 214, 215, 216, 217, 219,
    220, 224, 225, 226, 239, 244, 245, 269, 272,
    343, 344, 345, 346, 347, 348, 349, 350, 352,
    353, 354, 355, 408, 412, 429, 444, 459, 460,
    516, 562
Brinkmann, Cora 28, 48, 420
British Airways 445
British American Tobacco 17, 28
Brown, David 63, 211, 214, 226
Brundle, Martin 26, 84, 405
Brunner, Gustav 15, 17, 93, 361, 366, 371, 372,
    377, 530, 539, 541, 544, 569
Burti, Luciano 16, 17, 20, 24, 33, 72, 80, 86, 88,
    90, 93, 94, 117, 119, 169, 184, 197, 283, 288,
    289, 290, 291, 292, 301, 309, 318, 319, 320,
    321, 322, 323, 324, 325, 326, 327, 328, 329,
    342, 343, 346, 347, 348, 351, 352, 366, 377,
    378, 379, 388, 392, 400, 408, 416, 420, 424,
    432, 440, 448, 456, 464, 472, 475, 476, 480,
    484, 488, 492, 531, 533, 538, 540, 567
Button, Jenson 33, 35, 50, 62, 64, 68, 82, 146, 164,
    184, 198, 200, 223, 224, 225, 257, 262, 263,
    264, 265, 266, 267, 268, 269, 270, 271, 272,
    273, 274, 275, 276, 277, 278, 290, 301, 302,
    304, 316, 319, 323, 326, 328, 329, 340, 346,
    347, 350, 351, 352, 355, 370, 372, 380, 392,
    400, 408, 413, 416, 420, 424, 432, 436, 440,
    448, 456, 464, 468, 472, 480, 484, 488, 492,
    496, 500, 504, 508, 512, 520, 535, 540, 546,
    549, 555, 561
Button, John 82
Button, Simone 82
Byrne, Rory 38, 101, 118

## C

Camel 78
Campbell, Naomi 436
Cantarella, Paolo 16
Cantoni, Carlo 46
Carbon Industries 531, 539, 540, 542, 546, 554,
    559, 562, 564
Castro-Neves, Helio 90
Cevert, François 76
Champman, Colin 525

Charouz, Antonin 94
Chello 338
Clarke, Kenneth 15
Clark, Jim 477, 554
Clear, Jock 238, 248, 250
Coca-Cola 94, 328
Collins, Peter 52, 64, 67
Collis, Andrew 157
Coombs, Sean 'Puff Daddy' 436
Cooper, John 13
Cosworth 14, 15, 18, 20, 101, 128, 208, 267, 284,
    288, 290, 291, 292, 293, 335, 348, 350, 351,
    352, 353, 354, 355, 361, 366, 567
Coton, Didier 76
Coughlan, Mike 335, 340, 341, 342, 343, 344,
    345, 346, 348, 532
Coulthard, David 13, 14, 15, 16, 17, 18, 20, 24, 26,
    32, 34, 40, 44, 52, 63, 64, 70, 76, 84, 90, 106,
    107, 108, 110, 111, 112, 115, 116, 117, 118,
    119, 121, 127, 132, 133, 134, 135, 136, 137,
    138, 139, 140, 141, 142, 143, 144, 145, 146,
    147, 148, 158, 160, 161, 165, 166, 168, 183,
    188, 189, 192, 194, 195, 199, 210, 211, 212,
    213, 214, 216, 217, 220, 222, 237, 265, 275,
    294, 320, 321, 322, 326, 337, 341, 344, 345,
    346, 347, 350, 354, 366, 372, 388, 392, 396,
    400, 404, 408, 412, 416, 420, 424, 429, 432,
    436, 440, 444, 448, 452, 456, 460, 464, 468,
    472, 476, 480, 484, 488, 493, 496, 501, 504,
    508, 512, 516, 520, 533, 534, 536, 539, 541,
    543, 544, 546, 548, 564
Credit Suisse 14, 183
Crisp, Trevor 284, 350

D
D'Agostino, Pino 101
DaimlerChrysler 16
de Cortanze, André 17
Davidson, Antony 232
Decorzent, René 63
de Ferran, Gil 56
de la Rosa, Pedro 12, 15, 17, 33, 72, 79, 80, 85,
    88, 90, 92, 93, 113, 119, 127, 171, 182, 190,
    195, 197, 198, 208, 214, 221, 222, 224, 250,
    251, 271, 274, 284, 290, 291, 292, 293, 294,
    295, 296, 297, 298, 299, 300, 301, 302, 303,
    304, 309, 321, 324, 326, 330, 335, 340, 346,
    347, 349, 352, 354, 355, 372, 375, 376, 381,
    420, 424, 432, 440, 448, 456, 461, 464, 472,
    477, 480, 484, 488, 493, 496, 501, 504, 509,
    512, 520
Dennis, Evelyn 18, 140
Dennis, Ron 15, 16, 17, 18, 24, 26, 28, 40, 52, 62,
    66, 70, 77, 84, 90, 106, 132, 136, 137, 138, 139,
    140, 141, 142, 143, 144, 145, 147, 183, 283,
    310, 315, 338, 404, 420, 436, 461, 485, 500,
    517
Deutsche Bank 338
Deutsche Post 209
di Montezemolo, Luca 17, 36, 72, 112, 118
Diniz, Abilio 309
Diniz, Pedro 12, 13, 15, 18, 89, 93, 182, 309, 323,
    527
Dobringer, Daniel 48
Douglas, Michael 420

Duchess of York 436
Dupasquier, Pierre 12, 13, 170, 304, 413, 477
Durand, Henri 12, 309, 314, 315, 316, 317
Duran, Raimon 12

E
Ecclestone, Bernie 12, 13, 14, 16, 17, 18, 24, 26,
    28, 70, 243, 313, 500, 508, 524
Eeckelaert, Jacky 187, 196, 200
Elf 94
Ellis, Mark 17, 72, 285, 292, 297
EM.TV 13, 14, 24
Enge, Bretislav 94
Enge, Tomas 33, 94, 199, 304, 309, 328, 329, 330,
    356, 381, 382, 501, 504, 512, 520
Eurobet 338
EuroBusiness 105
European Aviation 361,
European Minardi 12, 13, 14, 15, 17, 18, 20, 26,
    28, 64, 68, 79, 82, 88, 91, 92, 93, 95, 132, 189,
    257, 263, 264, 266, 267, 269, 274, 275, 277,
    290, 297, 316, 321, 330, 335, 341, 344, 351,
    353, 366, 367, 368, 369, 370, 371, 372, 373,
    374, 375, 376, 377, 378, 379, 380, 381, 382,
    408, 412, 424, 440, 452, 456, 467, 469, 472,
    476, 480, 485, 501, 504, 512, 530, 533, 534,
    537, 538, 540, 543, 545, 546, 549, 554, 559,
    561, 563, 565, 567, 568

F
Fangio, Juan Manuel 24, 34, 38, 118
Faure, Patrick 14, 271, 275
Ferrari 12, 13, 14, 15, 16, 17, 18, 20, 24, 26, 28,
    34, 40, 44, 56, 63, 66, 70, 75, 78, 81, 84, 88, 95,
    101, 106, 107, 108, 109, 110, 111, 112, 113,
    114, 115, 116, 117, 118, 119, 120, 121, 122,
    127, 132, 133, 134, 135, 136, 137, 138, 139,
    140, 142, 143, 144, 146, 147, 148, 158, 159,
    161, 162, 163, 164, 165, 166, 167, 168, 169,
    172, 173, 174, 179, 184, 187, 188, 189, 192,
    194, 196, 197, 199, 208, 210, 211, 213, 214,
    216, 220, 237, 244, 260, 263, 275, 286, 292,
    296, 309, 314, 316, 317, 319, 322, 324, 325,
    328, 329, 344, 345, 346, 351, 364, 370, 387,
    388, 392, 395, 396, 400, 404, 408, 412, 419,
    429, 432, 437, 440, 443, 444, 448, 452, 456,
    460, 464, 468, 472, 475, 476, 480, 483, 484,
    488, 491, 493, 496, 500, 504, 508, 512, 515,
    520, 525, 530, 533, 534, 536, 538, 540, 543,
    544, 546, 548, 555, 558, 561, 562, 564, 566,
    568
Ferrari, Enzo 524
FIA 13, 14, 16, 17, 24, 26, 67, 72, 85, 101, 113,
    141, 184, 185, 188, 217, 240, 252, 346, 362,
    366, 373, 376, 378, 379, 388, 453, 456, 476,
    500, 524, 540, 542, 566
Fiat 16, 404
Firestone 294
Firman, Ralph 64
Fisher, Gavin 153, 169
Fisichella, Giancarlo 24, 33, 45, 68, 76, 82, 91,
    119, 136, 145, 184, 197, 198, 209, 211, 216,
    257, 262, 263, 264, 265, 266, 267, 268, 269,
    270, 271, 272, 273, 274, 275, 276, 277, 278,
    304, 316, 320, 323, 325, 326, 330, 340, 348,

349, 350, 352, 354, 368, 376, 392, 396, 400,
    408, 412, 416, 424, 432, 440, 444, 448, 456,
    464, 468, 472, 480, 485, 488, 492, 496, 501,
    504, 508, 512, 520, 536, 538, 540, 546, 549,
    555
Fittipaldi, Emerson 56
Fondmetal 18, 361,
Footwork Arrows 84
Ford Motor Company 13, 16, 38, 88, 294, 303,
    350, 377
Forghieri, Mauro 555
Formula One Commission 12, 13
Formula One Constructors Association 524
Formula One Contracts Reocognition Board 52
Formula One Management 15, 16, 28
Formula One Technical Working Group 12
Foster, Trevor 209, 210, 211, 213, 215, 223, 224
Franchitti, Dario 18, 56
Frentzen, Harald 75
Frentzen, Heinz-Harald 14, 16, 18, 20, 24, 28, 33,
    34, 58, 62, 64, 74, 85, 86, 106, 119, 132, 158,
    160, 162, 184, 186, 187, 190, 192, 193, 194,
    205, 210, 211, 212, 213, 214, 215, 216, 217,
    218, 219, 220, 221, 224, 225, 226, 236, 237,
    292, 293, 294, 296, 297, 301, 309, 320, 326,
    327, 328, 329, 330, 336, 341, 344, 352, 353,
    378, 388, 392, 396, 400, 408, 416, 420, 424,
    429, 432, 440, 453, 456, 459, 464, 468, 472,
    485, 488, 492, 496, 501, 504, 512, 520, 535,
    539, 541, 544, 545, 549, 559, 561, 567
Freydel, Connie 56, 421
Fungeling, Heribert 37

G
Ganassi, Chip 56
Gascoyne, Mike 14, 18, 205, 257, 262, 263, 264,
    265, 266, 268, 269, 270, 271, 274, 275, 276,
    541
Gené, Marc 372, 381, 565, 566
George, Tony 508
Gericom 366
Ghislimberti, Paolo 504
Gillard, Tim 66
Giovanardi, Fabrizio 116
Gloucester Rugby Football Club 350
Goodman, Louise 159, 312
Goodyear 17
Gorne, Rick 14, 89
Goschel, Burkhard 452
GP Racing 93
Grace, David 26
Grand Prix Drivers' Association 72
Green, Ellie 28, 61
Griffiths, Louise 82
Gurdjian, Philippe 20
Gurney, Dan 28

H
Haberfeld, Mario 90
Haffa, Florian 24
Haffa, Thomas 24
Häkkinen, Erja 52, 130, 412, 420, 517
Häkkinen, Hugo 52, 130, 412, 420
Häkkinen, Mika 13, 16, 17, 18, 20, 24, 26, 28, 32,
    40, 42, 52, 60, 63, 66, 76, 84, 93, 106, 110, 112,

113, 116, 117, 121, 122, 127, 132, 133, 134, 135, 136, 137, 138, 139, 140, 141, 142, 143, 144, 145, 146, 147, 148, 158, 159, 160, 162, 164, 168, 169, 170, 183, 184, 187, 188, 189, 190, 191, 197, 208, 210, 211, 212, 213, 214, 217, 218, 222, 245, 271, 275, 277, 278, 294, 316, 328, 336, 341, 346, 349, 388, 392, 397, 400, 405, 408, 412, 416, 420, 424, 429, 432, 436, 440, 444, 448, 452, 456, 460, 464, 468, 472, 477, 480, 484, 488, 493, 496, 500, 504, 507, 508, 512, 516, 520, 533, 536, 538, 541, 543, 544, 546, 548, 555, 562, 564

Hallam, Steve 148

Hamashima, Hirohide 103

Hamidy, Eghbal 14, 205, 335

Handford, Mark 283, 299, 304

HANS 16

Haug, Norbert 12, 13, 77, 90, 139, 143, 146

Hayes, Walter 13

Head, Patrick 17, 18, 49, 56, 153, 158, 159, 160, 163, 164, 165, 166, 168, 169, 171, 173, 405, 412, 428, 445, 460, 525, 538

Heidfeld, Nick 26, 32, 62, 94, 136, 171, 179, 184, 185, 186, 187, 188, 189, 190, 191, 192, 193, 194, 195, 196, 197, 198, 199, 200, 209, 210, 212, 220, 221, 222, 225, 226, 236, 276, 294, 295, 299, 301, 303, 304, 309, 319, 322, 340, 346, 354, 382, 392, 400, 405, 408, 416, 424, 429, 432, 436, 440, 444, 448, 453, 456, 461, 464, 468, 472, 477, 480, 485, 488, 492, 496, 501, 504, 509, 512, 520, 567

Heidfeld, Wolfgang 62

Herbert, Johnny 15, 45, 64, 84, 336, 340

Hervey, Lady Victoria 42

Hill, Damon 34, 41, 58, 74, 336, 429

His, Jean-Jacques 262, 272

Hitco 530, 535, 536, 539, 540, 546, 549, 554, 559

Holloway, Tim 205

Honda 14, 72, 77, 205, 210, 211, 212, 213, 214, 215, 216, 217, 218, 219, 221, 223, 236, 237, 238, 239, 240, 241, 242, 244, 245, 247, 248, 249, 252, 392, 459, 472, 501, 515, 530, 538, 541

Honda Racing Development 244

Hosaki, Takefumi 232,

HSBC 20

Hubbert, Jurgen 12, 28

Hucknall, Mick 420

Hugenholtz, John 566

Hugo Boss 412

Hunt, David 28

Hunt, James 28, 57, 524

Hunter, Rachel 436

I

Illien, Mario 28, 127,

Ilmor Engineering 17, 18, 28, 142, 169

Infineon 209

Intertechnic 304

Irvine, Eddie 14, 20, 26, 33, 36, 45, 70, 79, 80, 84, 88, 158, 164, 180, 187, 188, 189, 191, 192, 195, 198, 199, 216, 218, 219, 221, 241, 242, 278, 283, 288, 289, 290, 291, 292, 293, 294, 295, 296, 297, 298, 299, 300, 301, 302, 303, 304, 312, 314, 317, 319, 323, 327, 329, 340, 345, 350, 353, 354, 355, 379, 388, 392, 400, 408, 412, 416, 424, 432, 435, 436, 440, 448, 451, 456, 464, 468, 472, 480, 484, 488, 492, 496, 504, 509, 512, 520, 530, 537, 547, 548

Irvine, Edmund 70

Irvine, Kathleen 70

ITV 13, 26, 312, 452

Iveco 404

J

Jackson, Michael 34

Jaguar Cars 15, 301

Jaguar Racing 12, 13, 14, 15, 16, 17, 18, 20, 24, 26, 38, 54, 56, 68, 70, 79, 80, 88, 92, 93, 94, 139, 158, 164, 179, 184, 188, 189, 191, 192, 195, 198, 214, 218, 219, 222, 224, 241, 242, 245, 257, 269, 272, 273, 274, 275, 276, 283, 288, 289, 290, 291, 292, 293, 294, 295, 296, 297, 298, 299, 300, 301, 302, 303, 304, 312, 317, 318, 319, 323, 324, 327, 335, 342, 343, 344, 345, 348, 350, 352, 354, 355, 366, 372, 381, 388, 408, 413, 420, 424, 432, 435, 436, 440, 451, 456, 464, 468, 477, 484, 492, 496, 501, 504, 509, 520, 530, 533, 535, 537, 538, 540, 543, 545, 547, 549, 554, 559, 561, 563, 565

Jannace, Maria 28

Jones, Alan 58, 106, 428

Jordan, Eddie 18, 20, 24, 26, 28, 70, 74, 78, 80, 205, 211, 212, 213, 215, 217, 218, 219, 220, 221, 222, 223, 225, 226, 299, 330, 453, 493

Jordan Honda 13, 14, 16, 18, 20, 24, 26, 28, 46, 48, 64, 68, 70, 74, 76, 79, 81, 84, 86, 92, 116, 132, 135, 142, 144, 171, 179, 188, 189, 191, 192, 193, 194, 196, 197, 198, 199, 200, 205, 210, 211, 212, 213, 214, 215, 216, 217, 218, 219, 220, 221, 222, 223, 224, 225, 226, 231, 236, 237, 238, 239, 240, 241, 242, 244, 247, 248, 249, 251, 252, 273, 274, 275, 276, 278, 294, 296, 312, 321, 326, 327, 328, 335, 344, 346, 371, 381, 397, 403, 408, 413, 416, 420, 424, 429, 440, 448, 453, 456, 459, 460, 464, 468, 476, 485, 488, 493, 496, 500, 504, 508, 512, 517, 530, 533, 535, 536, 538, 540, 542, 544, 546, 549, 554, 559, 561, 563, 565, 567, 568

Jordan Mugen-Honda 94

K

Kanaan, Tony 90

Kane, Johnny 336

Karno, Fred 445

Karthikeyan, Narain 209

Katayama, Ukyo 64

Kingdom Holdings 329

King Juan Carlos of Spain 266, 420

Kirch Gruppe 13, 14, 16, 28

Kirch, Leo 26

Kirch Media 28

Klatten, Werner 24

Klum, Heidi 42

Kristensen, Tom 93

Kulpinski, Jules 239

L

LaBelle, Patti 508

Lauda Air 12

Lauda, Niki 12, 14, 15, 17, 18, 20, 24, 54, 63, 72, 81, 88, 283, 288, 291, 292, 295, 296, 298, 299, 300, 301, 302, 303, 350, 352

Lavaggi, Giovanni 93

Leberer, Josef 67

Lees, Tony 368

Lehto, JJ 84

Leinders, Bas 429

Lemarie, Patrick 232, 244

Ligier 64, 76, 236, 248

Lloyd, David 239, 241

Lotterer, Andre 302

Lotus 26, 28, 52, 67, 187, 525

Lucent 28

Lucky Strike 86, 232

LVMH 313

M

Madonna 34

Magnum Corporation Berhad 20, 95, 364, 379

Magnussen, Jan 84

Manning, Darren 232

Mansell, Nigel 18, 28, 41, 52, 57, 62, 64, 78, 122, 336, 428, 460, 516

Marconi 28

Marlboro 34, 52, 78, 105

Marques, Tarso 20, 33, 56, 86, 91, 92, 93, 134, 213, 266, 316, 321, 326, 341, 346, 361, 366, 367, 368, 370, 371, 369, 372, 373, 374, 375, 376, 377, 378, 379, 392, 397, 380, 400, 408, 412, 424, 432, 440, 448, 452, 456, 464, 480, 485, 488, 496, 537, 545, 559

Martinelli, Paolo 101, 109, 110, 118

Massa, Felipe 26, 183

Mastercard 209, 559

Mateschitz, Dietrich 12, 15, 20, 24, 28, 179, 338, 356

Mazzacane, Gaston 12, 16, 17, 33, 80, 89, 93, 309, 314, 315, 316, 317, 341, 366, 392, 400, 412, 416, 530, 534

McLaren 127, 139, 153, 283, 524

McLaren Honda 78

McLaren Mercedes 12, 13, 14, 15, 16, 17, 18, 20, 24, 26, 28, 40, 52, 62, 66, 68, 71, 75, 76, 81, 84, 90, 93, 94, 106, 109, 112, 116, 117, 121, 122, 132, 133, 134, 135, 136, 137, 138, 139, 140, 141, 142, 143, 144, 145, 146, 147, 148, 158, 161, 162, 164, 165, 166, 167, 170, 171, 173, 179, 188, 189, 194, 195, 196, 198, 199, 210, 211, 212, 217, 218, 222, 244, 245, 275, 289, 294, 295, 310, 316, 326, 337, 341, 344, 345, 371, 388, 392, 397, 400, 405, 408, 412, 416, 420, 424, 428, 436, 440, 444, 448, 453, 456, 460, 464, 468, 472, 480, 484, 488, 492, 496, 500, 504, 507, 508, 516, 520, 530, 533, 534, 536, 538, 540, 543, 544, 546, 548, 554, 558, 561, 562, 564, 566

McNally, Patrick 17

McNish, Allan 16

Mercedes 12, 13, 17, 28, 45, 52, 62, 86, 94, 110, 113, 127, 132, 134, 136, 138, 139, 143, 169,

208, 244, 257, 445, 544
MGPE 338
Michael, Sam 14, 48, 153, 159, 160, 167, 168, 169, 205
Michelin 12, 13, 15, 16, 48, 88, 113, 122, 143, 153, 158, 159, 160, 161, 162, 163, 165, 166, 167, 168, 169, 170, 172, 174, 211, 262, 265, 268, 269, 270, 272, 273, 276, 277, 289, 290, 291, 292, 293, 298, 299, 302, 303, 304, 312, 316, 317, 318, 319, 320, 321, 322, 323, 324, 325, 326, 327, 328, 330, 370, 371, 411, 412, 416, 429, 444, 448, 452, 456, 460, 476, 504, 554, 562
Mild Seven 64
Minardi, Giancarlo 91, 378
Minassian, Nicolas 90
Minogue, Dannii 61
Minogue, Kylie 468
Monti, Mario 14
Montoya, Juan Pablo 12, 13, 18, 20, 26, 32, 50, 52, 56, 60, 62, 69, 82, 84, 108, 109, 111, 113, 116, 120, 121, 122, 134, 135, 137, 140, 141, 142, 147, 158, 159, 160, 161, 162, 163, 164, 165, 166, 167, 168, 169, 170, 171, 172, 173, 174, 189, 190, 194, 196, 212, 213, 214, 216, 219, 220, 222, 224, 226, 234, 236, 240, 243, 288, 293, 294, 295, 301, 314, 327, 337, 342, 345, 346, 355, 364, 379, 380, 388, 392, 396, 400, 404, 408, 412, 416, 420, 424, 428, 432, 436, 440, 444, 448, 452, 456, 460, 464, 468, 472, 476, 480, 485, 488, 492, 496, 499, 500, 504, 508, 512, 516, 520, 534, 544, 546, 548, 560, 562, 564
Morbidelli, Gianni 15
Morgan Grenfell Private Equity 20, 28, 356
Morgan, Paul 17, 18, 127, 140
Mosley, Max 14, 16, 26, 524
Motor Club of Argentina 381
Mower, Derek 94
Mugen-Honda 64, 206
Mumm 461

N

Nakano, Shinji 91
Naseem, Prince 56
Nasser, Jacques 20, 38, 294, 350
Nelson, Rod 260
Newey, Adrian 18, 24, 40, 77, 127, 133, 134, 135, 136, 138, 139, 140, 142, 144, 283, 294, 295, 534, 541
Nichols, Steve 13, 283, 290, 304
Nishizawa, Katzutoshi 244
Nordic Racing 94
Nortel 28

O

Oastler, Malcolm 12, 231, 238, 240, 244, 246, 249
Octagon 13, 16, 20
Olvey, Steve 26
Orange Arrows Asiatech 12, 14, 15, 17, 18, 20, 26, 28, 40, 80, 82, 84, 90, 91, 92, 112, 138, 146, 179, 191, 217, 221, 263, 267, 271, 274, 275, 277, 293, 299, 304, 312, 320, 325, 335, 340, 341, 342, 343, 344, 345, 346, 347, 348, 349,

350, 351, 352, 353, 354, 355, 356, 367, 372, 374, 375, 376, 377, 378, 381, 392, 397, 400, 408, 424, 432, 437, 440, 448, 453, 456, 464, 476, 480, 484, 488, 492, 496, 501, 508, 517, 530, 531, 535, 537, 539, 540, 542, 544, 546, 549, 554, 559, 561, 563, 565, 567

P

Panis, Olivier 13, 14, 33, 64, 76, 90, 91, 107, 141, 161, 163, 184, 185, 186, 187, 188, 189, 190, 210, 212, 213, 215, 217, 219, 221, 222, 223, 233, 236, 237, 238, 239, 240, 241, 242, 243, 244, 245, 246, 247, 248, 249, 250, 252, 293, 297, 316, 323, 325, 329, 330, 337, 346, 347, 348, 351, 353, 354, 382, 392, 396, 400, 408, 412, 416, 424, 427, 432, 440, 448, 456, 464, 468, 472, 476, 480, 485, 488, 496, 501, 504, 512, 520, 533, 538, 541, 547, 554, 563
Paragon 131
Paul Stewart Racing 14, 41, 45, 81, 84
Pelé 436
Penske, Roger 28
Petronas 179, 185
Peugeot 52, 63, 309, 335, 341
Philip Morris 18, 70
Phillips, Ian 207
Pi Electronics 15, 287
Piaggio 452
Piccinini, Marco 524
Piquet, Nelson 58, 90
Pirelli 78
Pironi, Didier 76
Pischetsrieder, Bernd 16
Pizzonia, Antonio 565
Poelie-Zeewald, Peter 76
Pollock, Barbara 86
Pollock, Craig 12, 14, 15, 17, 18, 20, 26, 28, 60, 77, 86, 120, 231, 238, 239, 240, 243, 244, 245, 246, 248, 225, 421, 436, 508
Porsche 525
Postlethwaite, Harvey 72
Premier Automotive Group 15
Premier Performance Division 15, 88
Prince Albert of Monaco 436
Prince Khaled Al Waleed 328
Prince Rainier 158
Promatecme 90
Prost 12, 13, 14, 15, 16, 17, 18, 20, 24, 26, 28, 62, 64, 66, 72, 74, 79, 76, 80, 88, 91, 93, 94, 117,157, 167, 179, 184, 199, 222, 243, 244, 260, 263, 264, 272, 274, 275, 277, 290, 292, 301, 304, 309, 314, 315, 316, 318, 319, 320, 321, 322, 323, 324, 325, 326, 327, 328, 329, 330, 336, 341, 344, 351, 366, 368, 372, 378, 382, 408, 432, 440, 448, 456, 464, 475, 476, 484, 488, 492, 496, 501, 520, 530, 531, 534, 536, 539, 541, 544, 546, 549, 554, 559, 561, 563, 565, 568
Prost, Alain 12, 13, 15, 17, 18, 24, 28, 37, 54, 58, 62, 66, 78, 76, 89, 115, 118, 119, 122, 292, 301, 309, 314, 315, 316, 318, 319, 320, 321, 322, 323, 325, 327, 328, 329, 330, 428, 485, 488, 496, 516
PSN 12, 14, 93, 309, 317, 318
Putt, John 207

R

Rafanelli, Gabriele 94
Rahal, Bobby 13, 14, 15, 17, 18, 20, 24, 56, 72, 81, 88, 283, 288, 289, 291, 292, 293, 295, 296, 297, 299, 300, 301
Rahal, Debi 300
Räikkönen, Kimi 12, 13, 24, 26, 28, 32, 42, 52, 63, 66, 90, 92, 168, 179, 184, 185, 186, 187, 188, 189, 190, 191, 192, 193, 194, 195, 196, 197, 198, 199, 200, 206, 213, 217, 219, 220, 222, 226, 252, 270, 278, 290, 293, 294, 296, 301, 303, 304, 321, 322, 329, 341, 347, 349, 354, 355, 364, 381, 382, 392, 408, 416, 424, 432, 437, 440, 444, 448, 456, 464, 468, 472, 480, 485, 488, 492, 496, 501, 504, 508, 512, 517, 520, 561, 563
Ramirez, Jo 142
Rampf, Willy 179, 188, 197, 198
Ratzenberger, Roland 525
Red Bull 12, 15, 24, 28, 62, 90, 183, 193, 338, 356
Red Bull Junior Team 90
Reitzle, Wolfgang 15, 283, 301
Renault 12, 13, 14, 16, 24, 64, 68, 78, 83, 90, 92, 208, 257, 262, 263, 264, 265, 267, 269, 270, 271, 274, 303, 335, 350, 382, 392, 485, 504
Renault Sport 271, 272
Repsol 85
Ress, Leo 179
Ressler, Neil 283,291
Reynard 89
Reynard, Adrian 12, 14, 15, 18, 240, 246
Rice, Katheryn 484
Rinland, Sergio 179, 338, 347, 354, 355, 539, 567, 568
Rivaldo 420
Roberts, Julia 436
Robertson, David 67
Robertson, Steve 66
Rodriguez, Geraldo 86
Rodriguez, Gonzalo 93
Rorvik, Hogie 82
Rosberg, Keke 12, 52, 58, 76
Rosenthal, Jim 452
Rosset, Ricardo 84
Rubython, Tom 18
Rumi, Gabriele 14, 17, 18, 361, 372
Russell, John 283, 539

S

Salo, Mika 12, 84, 182
Sami, Ekrem 157
Sassen, Frank 13
Sato, Takuma 13, 26, 28, 79, 209, 232, 244
Sauber, Peter 12, 14, 15, 24, 66, 79, 179, 184, 186, 187, 188, 189, 191, 192, 194, 195, 196, 199, 200, 325, 338
Sauber Petronas 12, 13, 16, 26, 62, 66, 74, 79, 90, 92, 109, 136, 162, 179, 184, 185, 186, 187, 188, 189, 190, 191, 192, 193, 194, 195, 196, 197, 198, 199, 200, 205, 219, 220, 222, 225, 226, 231, 236, 244, 248, 249, 273, 276, 294, 295, 301, 310, 316, 319, 322, 325, 338, 344, 346, 347, 371, 381, 405, 416, 424, 429, 432, 436, 444, 453, 456, 461, 472, 480, 485, 488, 492,

501, 508, 512, 517, 520, 527, 530, 531, 534,
536, 538, 540, 544, 546, 549, 554, 559, 561,
563, 565, 568
Scheckter, Tomas 94
Schubert 15
Schumacher, Corinna 34, 48, 118
Schumacher, Elisabeth 37, 461
Schumacher, Gina Maria 36, 48
Schumacher, Michael 12, 13, 14, 15, 16, 17, 18,
20, 24, 26, 28, 32, 34, 40, 44, 48, 52, 56, 60, 66,
70, 74, 78, 84, 88, 95, 101, 106, 107, 108, 109,
110, 111, 112, 113, 114, 115, 116, 117, 118,
119, 120, 121, 122, 131, 132, 133, 134, 136,
137, 138, 139, 140, 141, 142, 143, 144, 147,
148, 153, 158, 160, 161, 162, 163, 165, 166,
167, 168, 171, 172, 173, 174, 181, 184, 189,
194, 197, 209, 210, 211, 212, 219, 220, 224,
232, 250, 266, 275, 276, 277, 278, 292, 301,
312, 316, 325, 336, 341, 345, 351, 382, 387,
388, 392, 396, 400, 404, 408, 412, 416, 419,
420, 424, 428, 432, 436, 440, 443, 444, 448,
452, 456, 460, 464, 468, 472, 475, 476, 480,
483, 484, 488, 491, 492, 496, 500, 504, 508,
512, 515, 520, 534, 539, 541, 543, 544, 548,
555, 560, 562, 564, 566, 568
Schumacher, Mick 37, 48
Schumacher, Ralf 12, 15, 16, 18, 20, 28, 32, 36,
48, 56, 69, 79, 77, 82, 85, 92, 107, 108, 109,
110, 113, 114, 115, 119, 120, 122, 132, 133,
135, 140, 144, 148, 158, 159, 160, 161, 162,
163, 164, 165, 166, 167, 168, 169, 170, 171,
173, 174, 184, 190, 194, 195, 208, 211, 212,
213, 214, 223, 232, 236, 242, 259, 261, 271,
293, 294, 336, 340, 341, 342, 345, 346, 355,
388, 392, 396, 400, 405, 408, 411, 412, 416,
420, 424, 428, 432, 436, 440, 443, 444, 448,
452, 456, 460, 464, 468, 472, 475, 476, 480,
484, 488, 492, 496, 500, 504, 508, 512, 516,
520, 549, 561, 562, 564, 567
Schumacher, Rolf 48, 461
Scuderia 78, 183
Sears, David 56
Senna, Ayrton 34, 41, 45, 52, 56, 66, 72, 74, 78,
90, 118, 157, 428, 436, 517, 525
Shell 18, 107, 110, 119
Silman, Roger 17, 338
Simtek 84
Skoda 94
SLEC 12, 13, 15, 18, 26, 28
Sonique 420
Spanish Automobile Federation 81
Spires, Di 36
Spires, Stuart 36
Stallone, Sylvester 17
Stanford, Dickie 168
Stansfield, Lisa 292
Stepney, Nigel 14, 36, 102, 106
Stevens, John 64
Stewart Ford 64
Stewart, Jackie 14, 20, 41, 89, 283, 288, 289, 292,
445, 468
Stewart, Paul 12, 13, 41
Stoddart, Paul 14, 15, 17, 26, 28, 91, 95, 361, 366,
367, 368, 370, 371, 372, 373, 374, 375, 376,
377, 378, 379, 380, 381, 382

Suganuma, Hisao 113
Sultan of Brunei 364, 370
Supernova Racing 94
Symonds, Pat 257, 262, 263, 264, 266, 267, 269,
270, 271, 272, 275, 277

T
Tag McLaren 28
Takagi, Tora 93
Takahashi, Tadasu 237
Taylor, Ruth 42
Team ShionogiNova 80
Telefónica 92, 93
Teoh, Arianna 95
Theissen, Mario 12, 13, 155, 554, 560
Todt, Jean 12, 24, 34, 44, 70, 101, 109, 111, 112,
113, 114, 115, 116, 118, 119, 120, 404, 432,
452, 483, 485
Toet, Willem 531
Tombazis, Nic 118
Toyota 13, 15, 16, 17, 20, 24, 371, 372, 377, 379,
539, 544
Toyota Motorsport 15
Tracy, Paul 56
Tredozi, Gabriele 371, 547
Trulli, Jarno 24, 32, 64, 68, 75, 79, 76, 83, 91,
110, 133, 135, 142, 144, 146, 158, 160, 161,
162, 168, 182, 186, 188, 191, 192, 194, 196,
198, 199, 200, 205, 210, 211, 212, 213, 214,
215, 216, 217, 218, 219, 220, 221, 222, 223,
224, 225, 226, 236, 237, 240, 247, 251, 252,
260, 273, 274, 276, 277, 296, 301, 302, 303,
304, 320, 321, 325, 328, 346, 347, 350, 353,
392, 397, 400, 403, 408, 412, 416, 424, 429,
432, 440, 444, 448, 452, 456, 460, 464, 468,
472, 480, 485, 488, 493, 496, 500, 504, 508,
512, 520, 535, 538, 541, 544, 545, 547, 548,
554, 565, 567
Tuero, Esteban 91
Tyrrell 24, 78, 84, 366, 531
Tyrrell, Ken 15, 24, 84

U
UFA Sports 18, 313, 325
University Hospital 327
Unser, Al 56

V
Verstappen, Jos 33, 56, 84, 90, 111, 134, 153, 159,
160, 163, 171, 184, 190, 191, 193, 198, 242,
211, 221, 224, 262, 271, 273, 287, 289, 290,
293, 295, 301, 314, 320, 321, 323, 324, 326,
329, 330, 335, 340, 341, 342, 343, 344, 345,
346, 347, 348, 349, 350, 351, 352, 353, 354,
355, 356, 372, 392, 396, 400, 405, 408, 412,
416, 424, 432, 437, 440, 448, 453, 456, 464,
472, 476, 480, 485, 488, 492, 496, 501, 504,
512, 520, 535, 537, 539, 541, 542, 544, 545,
547, 563, 565
Villadelprat, Joan 12, 309, 316, 324, 329
Villeneuve, Gilles 60, 78
Villeneuve, Jacques 13, 14, 15, 16, 18, 26, 28, 32,
34, 56, 60, 74, 76, 86, 92, 120, 153, 158, 159,
160, 162, 165, 184, 186, 188, 189, 193, 194,

196, 198, 200, 213, 214, 215, 216, 221, 222,
223, 224, 226, 231, 236, 237, 238, 239, 240,
241, 242, 243, 244, 245, 246, 247, 248, 249,
250, 251, 252, 262, 271, 293, 294, 296, 301,
303, 304, 312, 316, 320, 324, 325, 336, 340,
342, 345, 347, 349, 350, 353, 354, 381, 388,
392, 396, 400, 408, 413, 416, 421, 424, 427,
428, 432, 436, 440, 444, 448, 456, 464, 468,
472, 475, 477, 480, 485, 488, 492, 496, 500,
504, 508, 512, 517, 520, 533, 538, 541, 556
Villeneuve, Joann 60
Vodafone 18, 112
Volkswagen 16

W
Walker, Murray 13, 26, 28, 82, 512
Walkinshaw, Tom 12, 14, 15, 17, 20, 28, 85, 90,
138, 299, 335, 344, 347, 348, 350, 351, 352,
353, 355, 356, 375, 445
Walton, John 320, 324, 326
Warsteiner 452
Watkins, Sid 20, 52
Watson, John 64, 72
Webber, Mark 12, 260
Weber, Willi 48
Wendlinger, Karl 74
West Surrey Racing 41, 81
Whiting, Charlie 18, 24, 60, 72, 154, 243, 452,
477, 480, 524, 538
Whitmarsh, Martin 15, 77
Wichlinski, Heidi 42, 130
Williams 153, 162, 170, 411, 476
Williams, Frank 13, 52, 56, 77, 159, 162, 212,
243, 248, 376, 405, 412
Williams Renault 78, 330
Willis, Geoff 153, 169
Wilson, Justin 26, 94, 209, 429
Windsor, Lady Helen 20
World Racing Team 94
World Trade Centre 120
Wright, Derek 18
Wright, Jim 157
Wright, Peter 17
Wurz, Alex 13, 24, 64, 76

Y
Yoong, Alex 20, 28, 33, 91, 92, 94, 95, 329, 330,
361, 378, 379, 380, 381, 382, 501, 504, 508,
512, 520
Yoong, Hanifah 95
Yoong, Joanna 95
Yoong, Philipa 95

Z
Zanardi, Alex 13, 26, 50, 504
Zanarini, Enrico 288, 290
Zeta Jones, Catherine 420
Zonta, Joanir 86
Zonta, Ricardo 20, 33, 64, 75, 76, 86, 191, 206,
217, 221, 321, 347, 351, 448, 464, 476, 480